The Thomas Guide®

M000302210

San Diego County
street guide

TELL US WHAT YOU THINK — comment card on last page

Contents

Introduction

Maps

Lists and Indexes

PageFinder™ Map U.S. Patent No. 5,419,586
Canadian Patent No. 2,116,425
Patente Mexicana No. 188186

RAND McNALLY

Rand McNally Consumer Affairs
P.O. Box 7600
Chicago IL 60680-9915

randmcnally.com

For comments or suggestions, please call
(800) 777-MAPS (6277)
or email us at:
consumeraffairs@randmcnally.com

Legend

- Freeway
- Interchange/ramp
- Highway
- Primary road
- Secondary road
- Minor road
- Restricted road
- Alley
- Unpaved road
- Tunnel
- Toll road
- High occupancy vehicle lane
- Stacked multiple roadways
- Proposed road
- Proposed freeway
- Freeway under construction
- One-way road
- Two-way road
- Trail, walkway
- Stairs
- Railroad
- Rapid transit
- Rapid transit, underground
- Ferry
- City boundary
- County boundary
- State boundary
- International boundary
- Military base, Indian reservation
- Township, range, rancho
- River, creek, shoreline
- 98607 ZIP code boundary, ZIP code
- 5 Interstate
- 5 Interstate (Business)
- 3 U.S. highway
- 1 4 8 9 State highways
- Carpool lane
- A Street list marker
- Street name continuation
- Street name change
- Station (train, bus)
- Building (see List of Abbreviations page)
- Building footprint
- Public elementary school
- Public high school
- Private elementary school
- Private high school
- Shopping center
- Fire station
- Library
- Mission
- Winery
- Campground
- H Hospital
- Mountain
- Section corner
- Boat launch
- Gate, locks, barricades
- Lighthouse
- Dry lake, beach
- Dam
- Intermittent lake, marsh
- 29 Exit number
- Coaster, Metrolink Station
- Regional Bus
- Trolley

we've got you COVERED

Rand McNally's broad selection of products is perfect for your every need. Whether you're looking for the convenience of write-on wipe-off laminated maps, extra maps for every car, or a Road Atlas to plan your next vacation or to use as a reference, Rand McNally has you covered.

Street Guides

- Los Angeles & Orange Counties
- Los Angeles & San Bernardino Counties
- Los Angeles & Ventura Counties
- Los Angeles County
- Orange County
- Orange County - Easy to Read
- Riverside & Orange Counties
- Riverside & San Diego Counties
- Riverside County
- San Bernardino & Riverside Counties
- San Bernardino County
- San Diego & Orange Counties
- San Diego County
- Ventura County
- Oceanside/ Escondido
- Ontario/ Pomona
- Orange County, Central
- Orange County, Northern
- Orange County, Southern
- Palm Springs/ Desert Cities
- River Cities
- Riverside
- San Bernardino/ Fontana
- San Diego
- San Fernando Valley
- San Gabriel Valley/ Pasadena
- Santa Clarita Valley
- Southern California Freeways
- Temecula/ Murrieta
- Thousand Oaks/ Simi Valley
- Ventura/ Oxnard
- Victorville/ Barstow

Folded Maps

EasyFinder® Laminated Maps

- Glendale/ Burbank
- Long Beach
- Los Angeles & Vicinity
- Los Angeles to San Diego Regional
- Los Angeles/ Hollywood
- Palm Springs
- Pasadena/ San Gabriel
- Riverside
- San Diego
- San Diego & Vicinity
- San Fernando Valley
- Santa Ana/ Costa Mesa
- The South Bay/ Torrance/ Beach Cities
- Southern California
- West LA/ Santa Monica

Paper Maps

- Hemet/ Perris
- Lancaster/ Palmdale
- Long Beach/ Carson/ Torrance
- Los Angeles
- Los Angeles & Vicinity
- Moreno Valley/ Banning
- North San Diego/ Encinitas

Wall Maps

- Southern California Arterial

Road Atlases

- California Road Atlas
- Road Atlas
- Road Atlas & Travel Guide
- Large Scale Road Atlas
- Midsize Road Atlas
- Deluxe Midsize Road Atlas
- Pocket Road Atlas

Wherever Rand McNally products are sold or at
www.randmcnally.com

San Diego International Airport (SAN)

San Diego International Airport (Lindbergh Field) is owned and operated by the San Diego County Regional Airport Authority.

Each terminal has been assigned a color which corresponds to all access and driving signs: Terminal 1 is blue, Terminal 2 is purple and the Commuter Terminal is orange.

Check the internet at **www.san.org** for current airline terminal locations.

REFER TO MAP PAGE AND GRID 1288 F1

Road signs are color coded to match the terminal colors

Terminal 2 West

- America West
- Continental
- Delta
- Hawaiian
- JetBlue
- Sun Country
- US Airways
- WestJet

Terminal 2 East

- AeroMexico
- Aloha
- American
- Northwest

Terminal 1

- AirCanada
- Alaska
- Frontier
- Midwest
- Southwest
- United

Commuter Terminal

- Alaska Commuter
- American Eagle
- Continental Express
- Delta Connection
- Northwest Airlink
- Skywest
- United Express

WEST Terminal 2 EAST

Terminal 1

Parking

Parking

AIR LN

Air Cargo

STILLWATER RD

Commuter Terminal

WINSHIP LN

Parking

N HARBOR

Parking

N

MAP NOT TO SCALE

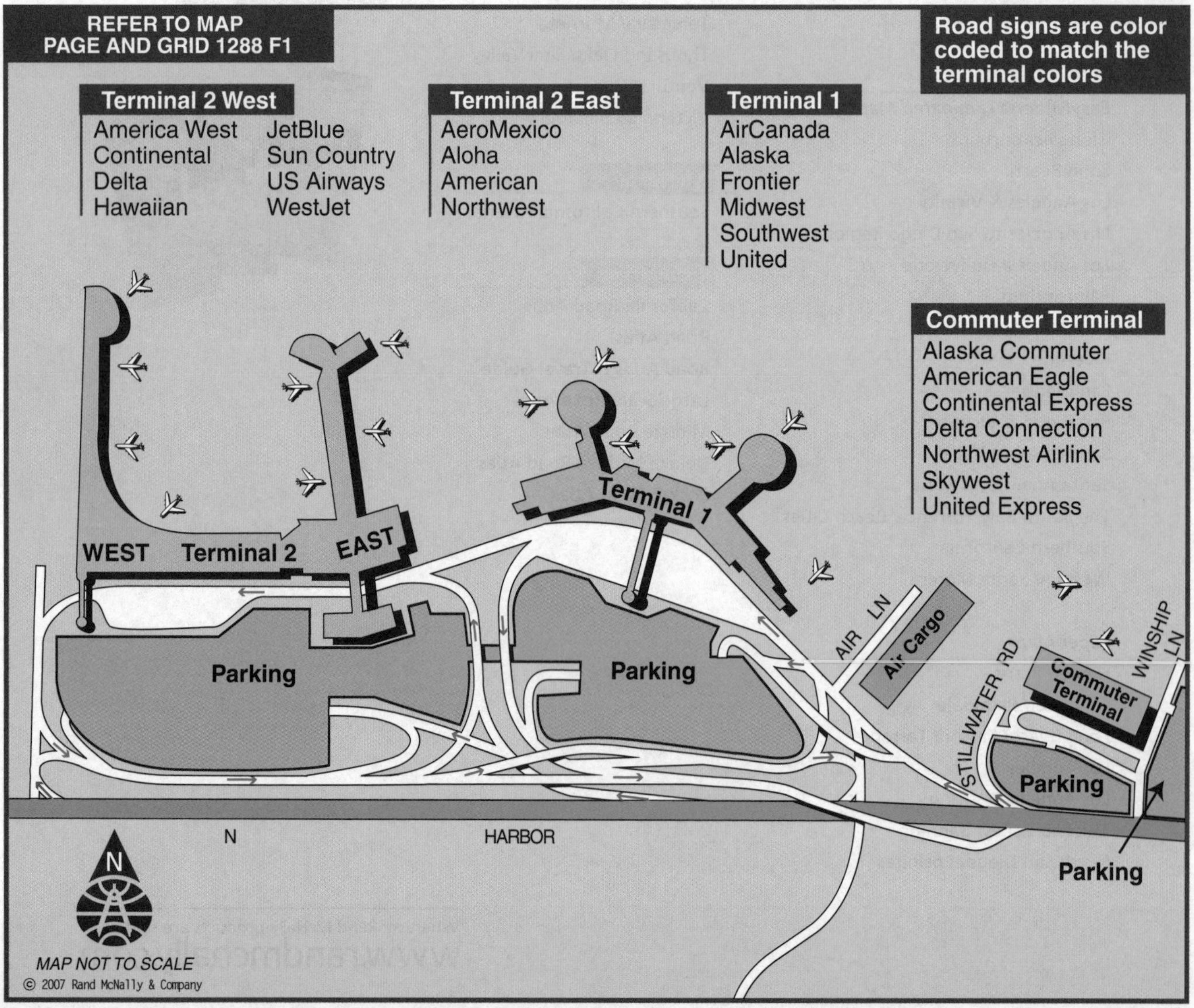

SAN DIEGO COUNTY REGIONAL BUS, TROLLEY, TRAIN, FERRY, AND TAXI INFORMATION

MAJOR BUS, TROLLEY, AND TRAIN STATION LOCATIONS
For the location of major bus, trolley, and train stations, see the "Transportation" heading in the Points of Interest Index of this Guide.

MAJOR PARK AND RIDE LOTS
For the location of major park and ride lots, see the "Park and Ride" heading in the Points of Interest Index of this Guide.

INFORMATION AND TRIP PLANNING
Website - Log on to **www.sdcommute.com**, or **www.transitosandiego.com** for information in Spanish.

Regional Transit Map (RTM) - The RTM shows all of San Diego County's public transportation routes. For your copy, call 619-233-3004, or send your name, address, and $1.00 to the Metropolitan Transit System (MTS) at 1255 Imperial Ave, Suite 1000, San Diego, CA 92101-7490. You can also download an RTM and other maps from our website at www.sdcommute.com under Rider Information.

The Transit Store - Located in downtown San Diego at 102 Broadway, purchase passes, tokens, and souvenirs. Open: Monday - Friday, 9:00 a.m. to 5:00 p.m.; closed on weekends and major holidays.

eStore - Visit the eStore at www.sdcommute.com to purchase MTS monthly passes and Day Trippers on-line.

Regional Telephone Information - Transit information specialists are on duty from 5:30 a.m. to 8:30 p.m. Monday - Friday, and weekends from 7:00 a.m. to 7:00 p.m. to answer questions about public transit routes, schedules, and the nearest pass/ticket sales outlets. Call 511 (formerly 1-800-COMMUTE). TTY/TDD for persons with hearing impairments: 619-234-5005 or toll-free 1-888-722-4889. Please have the following information: your departure point, destination point, day and time of travel.

SAN DIEGO BUS AND TROLLEY SYSTEM
Metropolitan Transit System (MTS) Trolley - Bright red trolleys provide service on Blue, Orange, Green Lines throughout the metropolitan area including: downtown San Diego, Mission Valley, San Diego State University (SDSU), Old Town, South Bay, U.S. Border, and East County. Trolleys operate seven days a week, early in the morning to late night, with base 15-minute service most of the day.

Buses - MTS and North County Transit District (NCTD) buses serve the metropolitan area including: San Diego Zoo, Balboa Park, the International Airport, Mission Beach, Pacific Beach, La Jolla, area colleges and universities, and regional shopping, medical, and employment centers. Frequency and hours of operation vary; consult individual route timetables or visit www.sdcommute.com for schedule information.

FARES AND TRANSFERS
MTS Trolley - Trolley cash tickets are priced according to the number of stations traveled. One-way tickets, good for two hours, and round-trip tickets, good for a return trip any time on date purchased, are available from self-serve ticket machines at each stop. Senior/disabled riders pay discounted fare. Exact fare in coins is recommended; some machines accept $1, $5, $10, and $20 bills. Multi-day passes are also available from most trolley ticket machines. For current fare information, call 511 or visit www.sdcommute.com

Buses - For current fare information for MTS and NCTD BREEZE buses, call 511 or visit www.sdcommute.com

Transfers - Transfers between buses and/or trolleys are free or require an upgrade if the second fare is higher.

Day Tripper Passes - The Day Tripper pass provides unlimited rides on the Trolley and most MTS and Breeze regional buses. Day Trippers are available for one, two, three, or four days and may be purchased from most trolley ticket machines, TheTransit Store, eStore at www.sdcommute.com, and many outlets throughout the region. Purchase 100 Day Tripper passes or more and receive a group discount, call 619-231-1466 for details or visit www.sdcommute.com/groupsales.

Monthly Passes and Tokens - Monthly passes and tokens are economic alternatives to the cash fare for adult riders who ride MTS and NCTD bus and rail systems. All types of fare media are available at the The Transit Store, via the eStore, and by mail (send your check or money order payable to SANDAG to: SANDAG Pass Sales, 401 B Street, Suite 800, San Diego, CA 92101). All Vons, Ralphs and Longs stores and other outlets sell monthly passes and other select types of fare media.

ACCESSIBLE SERVICE
The MTS and NCTD bus and rail operators have 100 percent wheelchair accessible service. Call 619-234-3004 for more information. In compliance with the Americans with Disabilities Act (ADA), those customers who cannot reach or ride regular bus and rail routes due to a mobility impairment can use MTS ACCESS or ADA Suburban Paratransit. Eligible customers must be certified through MTS by calling 1-877-232-7433. To schedule a trip, call MTS ACCESS at 1-888-517-9627 or ADA Suburban Paratransit at 1-800-921-9664. For NCTD Lift: call 1-760-726-1111.

QUALCOMM STADIUM
MTS Trolley Green Line provides regular service to Qualcomm Stadium. MTS and NCTD also offer special express bus service to and from Qualcomm Stadium for select major sporting events. For information on regular bus routes and express buses, call 1-800-COMMUTE, or visit www.sdcommute.com.

PETCO PARK
MTS Trolley Blue and Orange Lines provide service to PETCO Park, which is located next to the 12th & Imperial Transfer Station. For most games, special event trolley service will also operate from Mission Valley to the ballpark via the Convention Center and Gaslamp Quarter. Many MTS Bus routes operate within walking distance of ballpark. For detailed information, call 1-800-COMMUTE, or visit www.sdcommute.com.

BAY FERRY
The San Diego Bay Ferry operates between Coronado and San Diego, seven days a week from 9:00 a.m. to 9:00 p.m. (until 10:00 p.m. on Friday and Saturday), leaving San Diego on the hour and Coronado on the half-hour. A one-way fare is $3.00; bicycles are $0.50. For more information, call 619-234-4111.

AMTRAK, COASTAL EXPRESS RAIL "COASTER", METROLINK
AMTRAK - Currently, eleven AMTRAK trains operate between San Diego and Los Angeles. Trains stop at three San Diego County Stations: Santa Fe Depot in Centre City San Diego, Solana Beach, and the Oceanside Transit Center. On weekends, select trains stop at the Old Town Transit Center. For Amtrak information, call 1-800-USA-RAIL (1-800-872-7245) or visit www.amtrak.com.
COASTER - Trains operate between the Oceanside Transit Center and San Diego's Santa Fe Depot, with six intermediate stations from Old Town Transit Center to Carlsbad Village. Coaster provides 11 round-trip trains throughout the day, Monday - Thursday with additional late-night trains on Friday. Coasters also operate late night service Monday–Thursday from Santa Fe Depot for Padres baseball games at Petco Park. On Saturday, Coaster runs four round-trip trains, there is no Sunday service available. There are monthly pass discounts for seniors (60 and older), youth (6-18 years), and persons with disabilities (proof of age or disability required). For information, visit www.gonctd.com or call 1-800-COASTER.

METROLINK - Weekday morning and afternoon rush-hour, high-speed rail service connecting Oceanside Transit Center with 54 stations throughout Orange, Los Angeles, San Bernardino, Riverside, and Ventura Counties. For information, call 1-800-371-LINK, or go to www.metrolinktrains.com.

TAXIS
Taxicab stands are located at most major employment, recreation, and shopping centers. Your fare will be displayed on the meter and will include a flat "flag drop" charge plus a per-mile and/or per-hour charge. All cabs leaving the International Airport charge a uniform rate of fare. Fares for all other cab trips vary from company to company, but cannot exceed a fixed amount set by MTS. The Taxicab Administration welcomes taxicab service comments. Call 619-235-2650.

This information is provided by Metropolitan Transit System (MTS), North County Transit District (NCTD), and SANDAG.

MTS SANDAG NCTD

EXISTING HIGH-OCCUPANCY VEHICLE (HOV) LANES SUMMARY

ROUTE DESCRIPTION	DIRECTION	MILES	OCCUPANCY	DAYS & HOURS OF OPERATION
I-15: SR 56/Ted Williams Parkway to SR 163	Southbound	8	2+	(M-F) 5:45 a.m. - 11:00 a.m.
I-15: SR 163 to SR 56/Ted Williams Parkway	Northbound	8	2+	(M-F) 11:30 a.m. - 7:00 p.m.
				(F-M) 7:00 p.m. - 4:30 a.m.
SR 54: Briarwood Rd to I-805	Westbound	3	2+	PART-TIME
SR 54: I-805 to Briarwood Rd	Eastbound	3	2+	PART-TIME
I-5: I-805 to Via De La Valle	Northbound	5	2+	FULL-TIME
I-805: at I-5/I-805 Interchange	Northbound	1/2	2+	FULL-TIME

Downtown San Diego

Points of Interest

1	Aerospace Museum (Balboa Park)	D3
2	Amtrak Station	B5
3	Best Western Bayside Inn	B5
4	Botanical Building (Balboa Park)	E2
5	Broadway Pier	A5
6	Cabot, Cabot & Forbes Building	B5
7	Carousel (Balboa Park)	E2
8	Casa de Balboa Building (Balboa Park)	E3
9	Casa del Prado (Balboa Park)	E2
10	Childrens Museum of San Diego	C6
11	City Administration Building (City Hall)	C5
12	Civic Center	C5
13	Clarion Hotel Bay View	D6
14	Copley Symphony Hall	D5
15	County Administration Center	B4
16	Courtyard Downtown	D5
17	Embarcadero Marina Park (North & South)	C7
18	Embassy Suites San Diego Bay	B6
19	Emerald Plaza	C5
20	Fashion Institute of Design & Merchandising	C5
21	Federal Jail	C6
22	Federal Office Building & Courthouse	C5
23	Firehouse Museum	B4
24	First National Bank Building	B5
25	Gaslamp Quarter	D6
26	Greater San Diego Chamber of Commerce	B5
27	Hall of Champions Sports Museum (Balboa Park)	E3
28	Historical Museum & Research Archives	E3
29	Holiday Inn Harbor View	C4
30	Holiday Inn on the Bay	B5
31	Horton Grand Hotel	C6
32	Horton Plaza	C6
33	House of Hospitality (Balboa Park)	E3
34	House of Pacific Relations (Balboa Park)	D3
35	International Visitors Information Center	C5
36	Japanese Friendship Garden (Balboa Park)	E3
37	Manchester Grand Hyatt	B6
38	Maritime Museum (San Diego Bay)	B5
39	Marriott Downtown	D5
40	Marriott San Diego Marina	C7
41	Marston House (Balboa Park)	D1
42	Mingei International Museum (Balboa Park)	E3
43	Museum of Contemporary Art San Diego	B5
44	Museum of Man (Balboa Park)	E3
45	Museum of Photographic Arts (Balboa Park)	E3
46	Natural History Museum (Balboa Park)	E2
47	Naval Medical Center	F3
48	Old Globe Theater (Balboa Park)	E3
49	Omni San Diego Hotel	D7
50	Petco Park	D7
51	Plaza de Panama (Balboa Park)	E3
52	Police Headquarters	E5
53	Radisson Harbor View	C4
54	Reuben H. Fleet Space Theater & Science Center	E3
55	San Diego Automotive Museum (Balboa Park)	D3
56	San Diego Central Library	D5
57	San Diego City College	E5
58	San Diego City Operations Building	C5
59	San Diego Concourse & Civic Theater	C5
60	San Diego Convention Center	C7
61	San Diego Coronado Ferry (Broadway Pier)	A5
62	San Diego County Court House	C5
63	San Diego Cruise Ship Terminal	A5
64	San Diego Fire Department Headquarters	D5
65	San Diego Model Railroad Museum (Balboa Park)	E3
66	San Diego Museum of Art (Balboa Park)	E2
67	San Diego Repertory Theatre	C6
68	San Diego Unified Port District	A2
69	San Diego Visitors & Convention Center	C5
70	Seaport Village (Shopping Area)	B6
71	Sempra Energy Building	C5
72	Spanish Village Art Center (Balboa Park)	E2
73	Starlight Bowl (Balboa Park)	D3
74	State Office Building	C5
75	Sushi Performance & Visual Art	D6
76	Timken Museum of Art (Balboa Park)	E2
77	Union Bank of California Building	C5
78	US Grant Hotel	C5
79	USS Midway	A6
80	Veterans Museum & Memorial Center	E3
81	Veterans War Memorial (Balboa Park)	E1
82	Villa Montezuma Museum	F6
83	Westgate Hotel	C5
84	Westin Hotel Horton Plaza	C5
85	Westminster Manor	C4
86	William Heath Davis House Museum	C6
87	Wyndham Emerald Plaza Hotel	C5

Map Scale

0 .125 .25 .375 .50 Miles

0 .25 .50 Kilometers

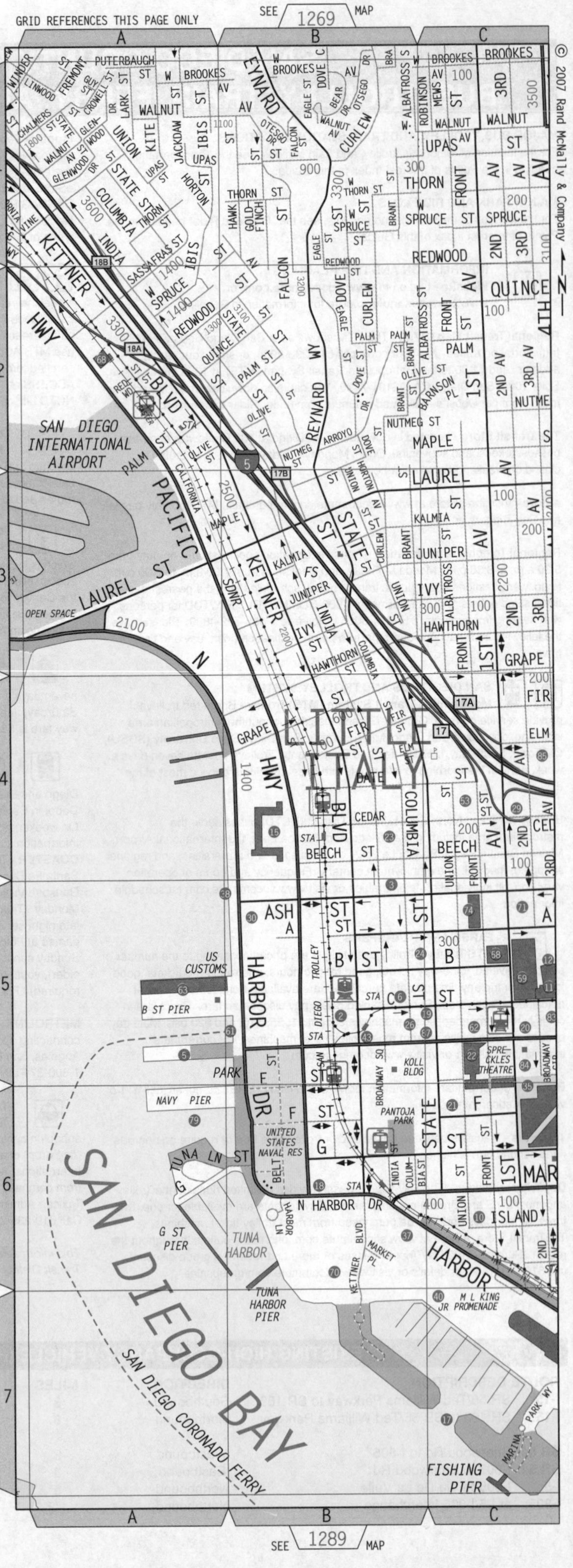

SEE 1269 MAP

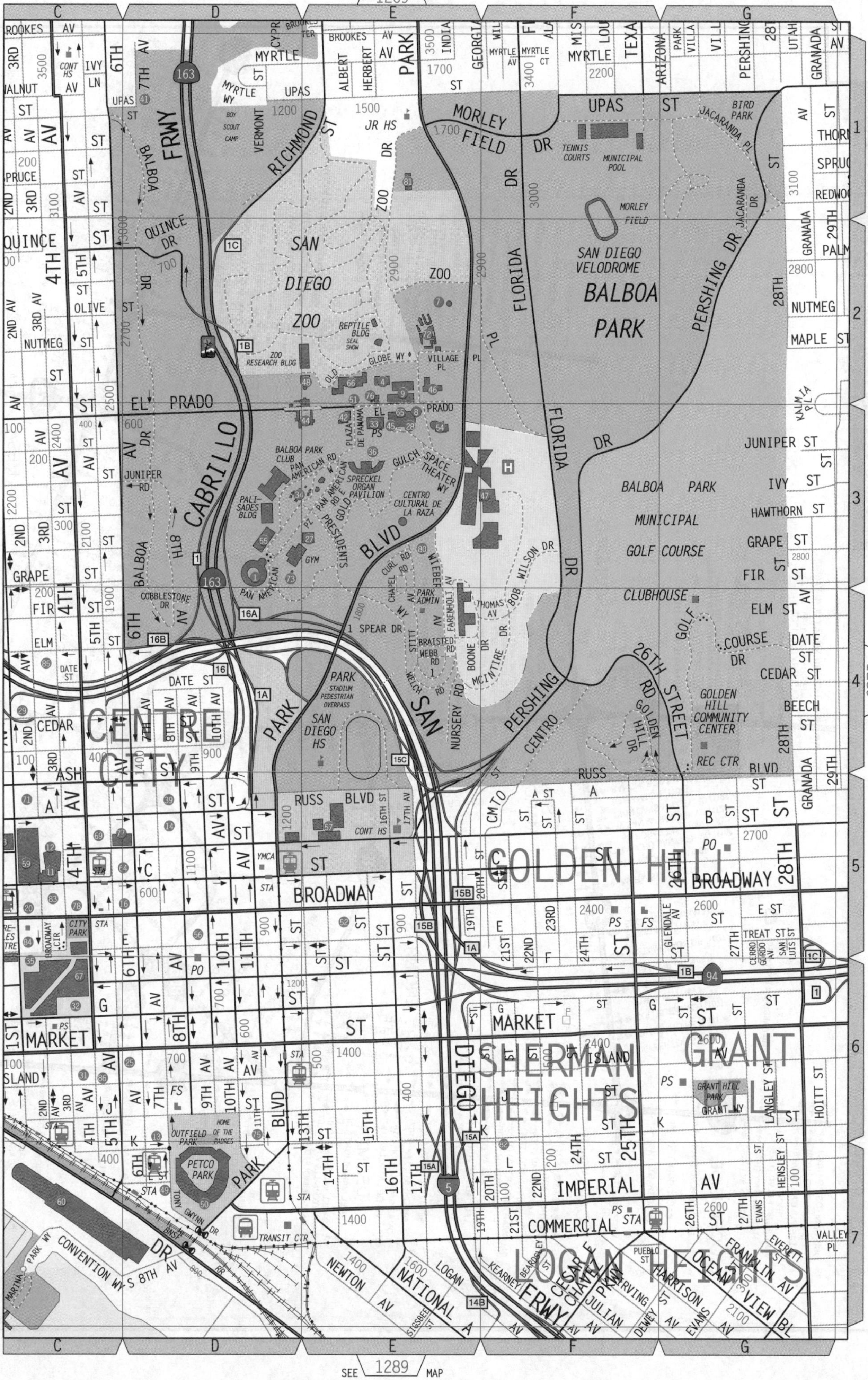

SEE 1289 MAP

SEE 1289 MAP

SAN DIEGO COUNTY FREEWAY ACCESS MAP

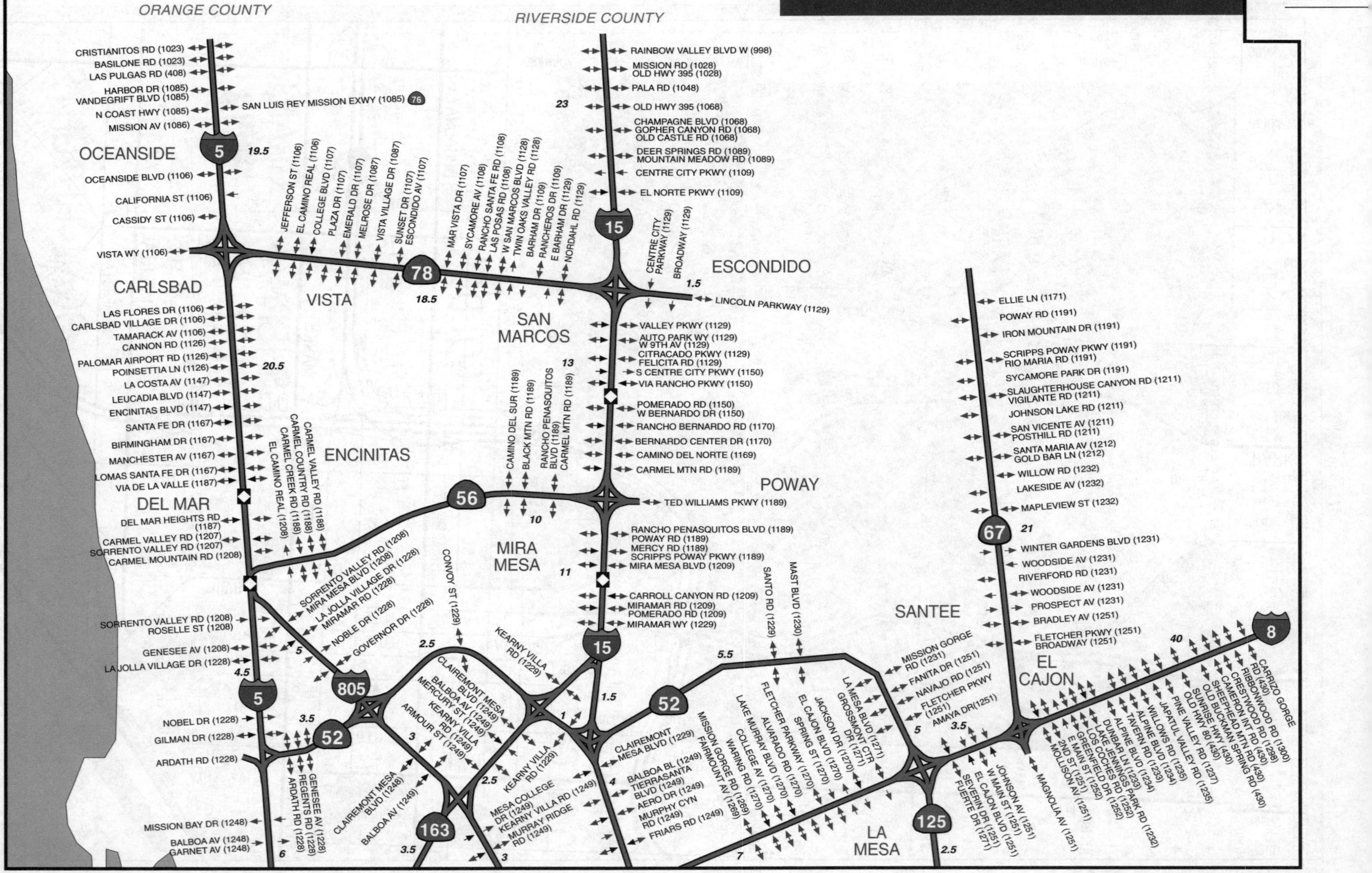

LEGEND
ON RAMP
OFF RAMP
ON/OFF RAMP
ON RAMP WITH CARPOOL RAMP
CARPOOL RAMP ONLY
TOLL ROAD
FREEWAY WITH CARPOOL LANE
5 SAN DIEGO FRWY
8 ROUTE 8 FRWY MISSION VALLEY FRWY OCEAN BEACH FRWY
15 ESCONDIDO FRWY
15 ROUTE 15 FRWY
52 ROUTE 52 FRWY
54 SOUTH BAY FRWY
56 TED WILLIAMS FRWY
67 ROUTE 67 FRWY
78 ROUTE 78 FRWY
94 MARTIN LUTHER KING JR FRWY ROUTE 94 FRWY
163 CABRILLO FRWY
805 JACOB DEKEMA FRWY
905 ROUTE 905 FRWY
125 ROUTE 125 FRWY
4.5 ITALICIZED NUMBERS ALONG THE FREEWAY INDICATE THE DISTANCE (IN MILES) BETWEEN FREEWAY INTERCHANGES.
(712) THE NUMBER IN PARENTHESES FOLLOWING EACH STREETNAME REFERS TO THE ATLAS PAGE ON WHICH IT APPEARS.
NOT TO SCALE
© 2007 Rand McNally & Company
N
LEMON GROVE
NATIONAL CITY
CHULA VISTA
IMPERIAL BEACH
CORONADO
PACIFIC OCEAN
U.S.A.
MEXICO
GROSSMONT BLVD (1271)
LEMON AV (1271)
BROADWAY (1270)
SPRING ST (1271)
CAMPO RD (1271)
AVOCADO BLVD (1271)
CALAVO DR (1271)
CAMPO RD (1271)
SWEETWATER SPRINGS BLVD (1271)
KENWOOD DR (1271)
BANCROFT DR (1271)
JAMACHA BLVD (1291)
TROY ST (1270)
E JAMACHA RD (1290)
PARADISE VALLEY RD (1291)
SAN MIGUEL RD (1291)
SAN MIGUEL RANCH RD (1311)
E H ST (1311)
OTAY LAKES RD (1311)
OLYMPIC PKWY (1311)
BIRCH RD (1331)
BRIARWOOD RD (1290)
WOODMAN ST (1310)
REO DR (1310)
PLAZA BONITA CTR WY (1310)
BROADWAY (1271)
SPRING ST (1270)
GROVE ST (1270)
LEMON GROVE AV (1270)
WAITE DR (1270)
MASSACHUSETTS AV (1270)
COLLEGE AV (1270)
BROADWAY (1270)
COLLEGE GROVE WY (1270)
FEDERAL BLVD (1290)
BAYVIEW HTS WY (1290)
KELTON RD (1290)
EUCLID AV (1290)
49TH ST (1290)
47TH ST (1289)
HOME AV (1289)
MARKET ST (1289)
IMPERIAL AV (1289)
47TH ST (1289)
43RD ST (1289)
PALM AV (1289)
PLAZA BLVD (1310)
SWEETWATER RD (1310)
BONITA RD (1310)
H ST (1310)
TELEGRAPH CANYON RD (1310)
ORANGE AV (1330)
MAIN ST (1330)
PALM AV (1330)
OTAY MESA RD (1351)
SAN YSIDRO BLVD (1350)
PICADOR BL (1350)
SMYTHE AV (1350)
BEYER BLVD (1350)
VIA DE SAN YSIDRO (1350)
SAN YSIDRO BLVD (1350)
DAIRY MART RD (1350)
TOCAYO AV (1350)
CORONADO AV (1350)
PALM AV (1330)
MAIN ST (1330)
PALOMAR ST (1330)
INDUSTRIAL BL (1330)
L ST (1330)
J ST (1330)
H ST (1329)
E ST (1309)
HIGHLAND AV (1310)
4TH AV (1310)
NATIONAL CITY BLVD (1309)
BROADWAY (1309)
ADAMS AV (1269)
EL CAJON BLVD (1269)
UNIVERSITY AV (1269)
HOME AV (1289)
HOME AV (1289)
HOME AV (1289)
MARKET ST (1289)
IMPERIAL AV (1289)
OCEANVIEW BLVD (1289)
NORTH PARK WY (1269)
UNIVERSITY AV (1269)
BOUNDARY ST (1269)
EL CAJON BLVD (1269)
MADISON AV (1269)
MESA COLLEGE DR (1249)
GENESEE AV (1249)
FRIARS RD (1269)
TEXAS ST (1269)
QUALCOMM WY (1269)
CAMINO DEL RIO N (1269)
MISSION CENTER RD (1269)
BROADWAY (1289)
32ND ST (1289)
28TH ST (1289)
25TH ST (1289)
19TH ST (1289)
MARINA WY (1309)
24TH ST (1309)
HARBOR DR (1309)
CIVIC CENTER DR (1309)
PLAZA BLVD (1309)
8TH ST (1309)
DIVISION ST (1309)
MAIN ST (1289)
WABASH BLVD (1289)
BOSTON AV (1289)
28TH AV (1289)
6TH AV (1269)
WASHINGTON ST (1269)
UNIVERSITY AV (1269)
ROBINSON AV (1269)
RICHMOND ST (1269)
QUINCE DR (1269)
PARK BLVD (1289)
CROSBY ST (1289)
LOGAN AV (1289)
IMPERIAL AV (1289)
17TH ST (1289)
J ST (1289)
G ST (1289)
F ST (1289)
E ST (1289)
C ST (1289)
B ST (1289)
PERSHING DR (1289)
PARK BLVD (1289)
A ST (1289)
ASH ST (1289)
HOTEL CIR (1268)
TAYLOR ST (1268)
LINDA VISTA RD (1268)
MORENA BL (1268)
CM DL RIO W (1268)
INDIA ST (1268)
PACIFIC HWY (1268)
GRAPE ST (1289)
STATE ST (1289)
HAWTHORN ST (1289) (AIRPORT)
BRANT ST (1289)
FRONT ST (1289)
1ST AV (1289)
5TH AV (1289)
6TH AV (1289)
CM DL RIO W (1268)
MOORE ST (1268)
OLD TOWN AV (1268)
WASHINGTON ST (1268)
SASSAFRAS ST (1268) (AIRPORT)
MISSION BAY DR (1248)
CLAIREMONT DR (1248)
TECOLOTE RD (1268)
SEA WORLD DR (1268)
ROSECRANS ST (1268)
MIDWAY DR (1268)
W MISSION BAY DR (1268)
SUNSET CLIFFS BLVD (1268)
NIMITZ BLVD (1268)
5
8
15
54
75
94
125
163
805
905
1
1.5
2
2.5
3
3.5
4
5
6
6.5
7

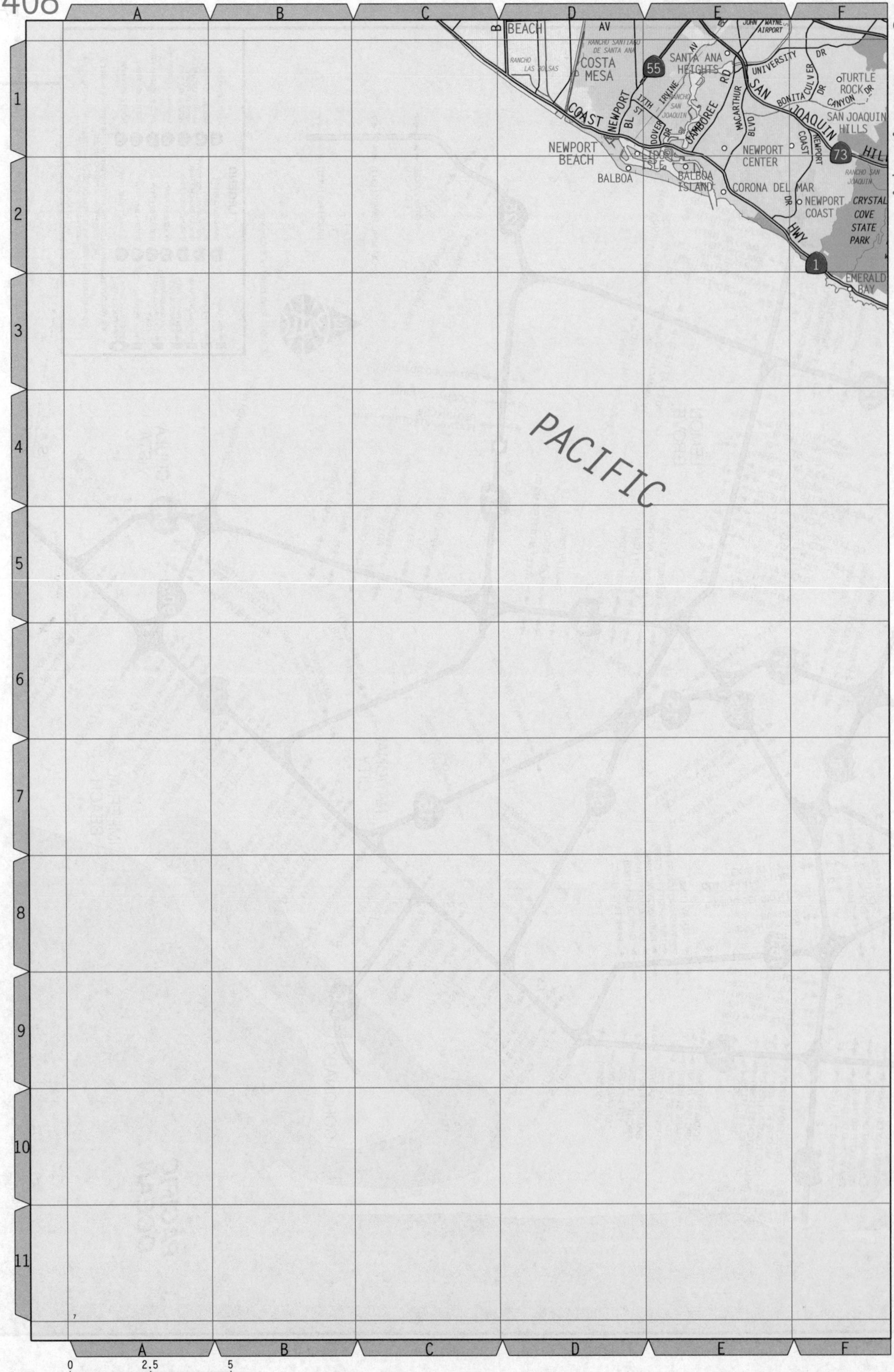
SAN DIEGO CO.
BEACH
AV
COSTA MESA
SANTA ANA HEIGHTS
JOHN WAYNE AIRPORT
UNIVERSITY
DR
TURTLE ROCK
CANYON
SAN JOAQUIN HILLS
COAST
NEWPORT
BL
17TH
ST
IRVINE
AV
DOVER
DR
JAMBOREE
RD
MACARTHUR
BLVD
SAN JOAQUIN
BONITA
CULVER
DR
HILLS
NEWPORT BEACH
BALBOA
LIDO ISLE
BALBOA ISLAND
NEWPORT CENTER
CORONA DEL MAR
NEWPORT COAST
CRYSTAL COVE STATE PARK
HWY
EMERALD BAY
55
73
1
PACIFIC
A
B
C
D
E
F
1
2
3
4
5
6
7
8
9
10
11
0
2.5
5
miles 1 in. = 4 mi.

ORANGE CO
RIVERSIDE CO
SAN DIEGO CO
CLEVELAND NATIONAL FOREST
CALIFORNIA COASTAL NATIONAL MONUMENT
OCEAN
PACIFIC
LAKE FOREST
RANCHO SANTA MARGARITA
LAGUNA WOODS
LAGUNA HILLS
MISSION VIEJO
ALISO VIEJO
LAGUNA BEACH
LAGUNA NIGUEL
SAN JUAN CAPISTRANO
DANA POINT
CAPISTRANO BEACH
SAN CLEMENTE
COTO DE CAZA
DOVE CANYON
LAS FLORES
LADERA RANCH
TALEGA
SAN JUAN HOT SPRINGS
EL CARISO
SAN ONOFRE
SAN ONOFRE STATE BEACH
MARINE CORPS BASE
CAMP JOSEPH H PENDLETON
CAMP PENDLETON
SOUTH OCEANSIDE
92028
92055
1023
1085
1105
SEE 409 MAP
0 2.5 5 miles 1 in. = 4 mi.

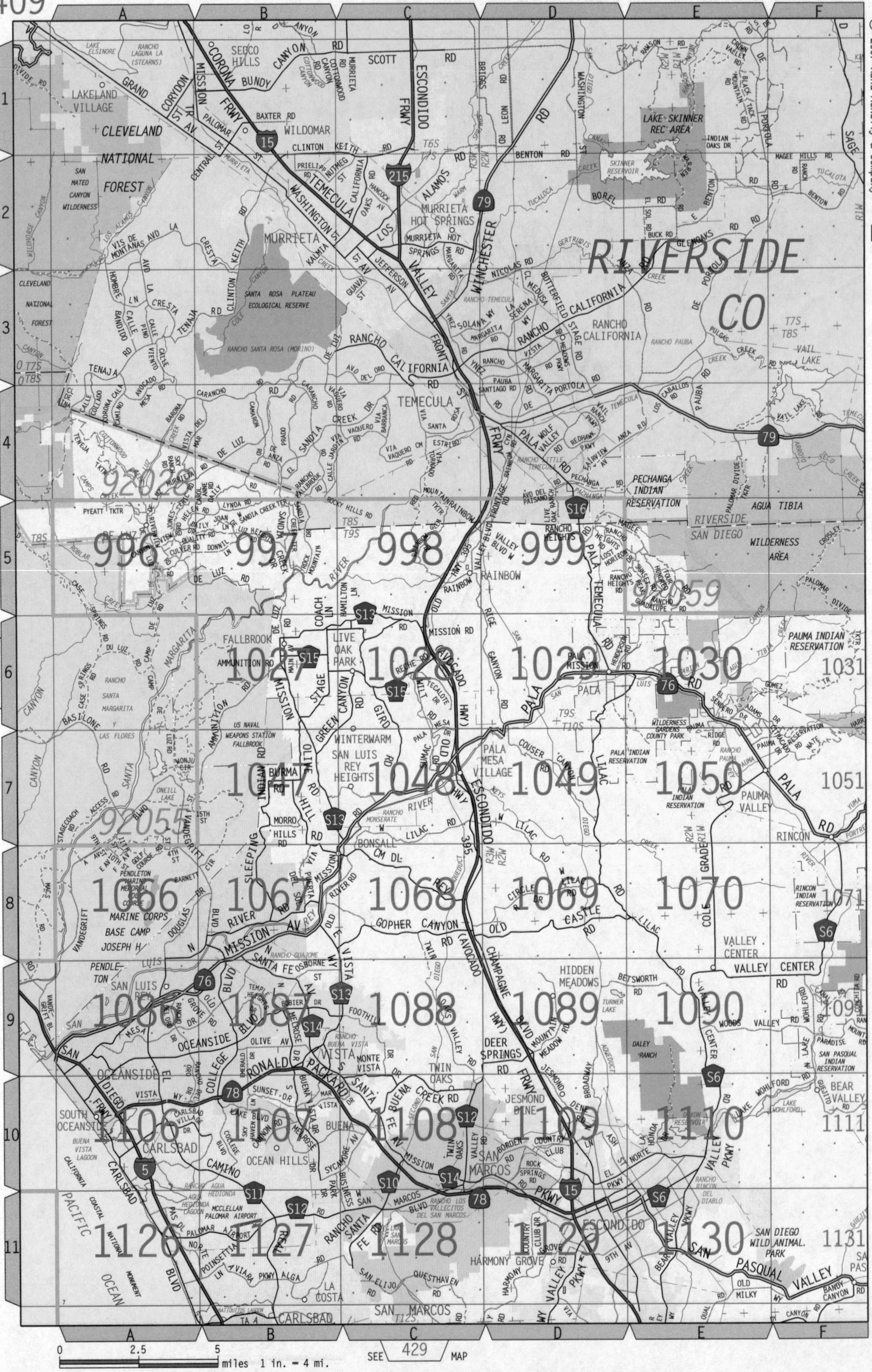

A B C D E F
1 2 3 4 5 6 7 8 9 10 11
LAKE ELSINORE
LAKELAND VILLAGE
CLEVELAND NATIONAL FOREST
SAN MATEO CANYON WILDERNESS
SEDCO HILLS
WILDOMAR
MURRIETA
MURRIETA HOT SPRINGS
SANTA ROSA PLATEAU ECOLOGICAL RESERVE
LAKE SKINNER REC AREA
SKINNER RESERVOIR
RIVERSIDE CO
RANCHO CALIFORNIA
TEMECULA
VAIL LAKE
PECHANGA INDIAN RESERVATION
AGUA TIBIA WILDERNESS AREA
RIVERSIDE
SAN DIEGO
92028
996 997 998 999
DE LUZ
RAINBOW
RANCHO HEIGHTS
92059
FALLBROOK
LIVE OAK PARK
1027 1028 1029 1030 1031
PALA MISSION
PALA
PAUMA INDIAN RESERVATION
US NAVAL WEAPONS STATION FALLBROOK
WINTERWARM
SAN LUIS REY HEIGHTS
PALA MESA VILLAGE
WILDERNESS GARDENS COUNTY PARK
PALA INDIAN RESERVATION
1047 1048 1049 1050 1051
PAUMA VALLEY
MORRO HILLS
BONSALL
RINCON
92055
1066 1067 1068 1069 1070 1071
PENDLETON MARINE MEMORIAL GOLF COURSE
MARINE CORPS BASE CAMP JOSEPH H
RINCON INDIAN RESERVATION
VALLEY CENTER
PENDLETON
SAN LUIS REY
HIDDEN MEADOWS
1086 1087 1088 1089 1090 1091
DEER SPRINGS
TWIN OAKS
DALEY RANCH
MONTE VISTA
VISTA
OCEANSIDE
SAN PASQUAL INDIAN RESERVATION
BEAR VALLEY
SOUTH OCEANSIDE
CARLSBAD VILLAGE
1106 1107 1108 1109 1110 1111
CARLSBAD
OCEAN HILLS
BUENA
JESMOND DENE
BUENA VISTA LAGOON
SAN MARCOS
ESCONDIDO
PACIFIC OCEAN
AGUA HEDIONDA LAGOON
MCCLELLAN PALOMAR AIRPORT
1126 1127 1128 1129 1130 1131
HARMONY GROVE
SAN DIEGO WILD ANIMAL PARK
LA COSTA
SAN MARCOS
CARLSBAD
15 215 79 76 78 5 395 S16 S13 S15 S14 S12 S11 S10 S6
SEE 408 MAP
SEE 429 MAP
0 2.5 5
miles 1 in. = 4 mi.
N

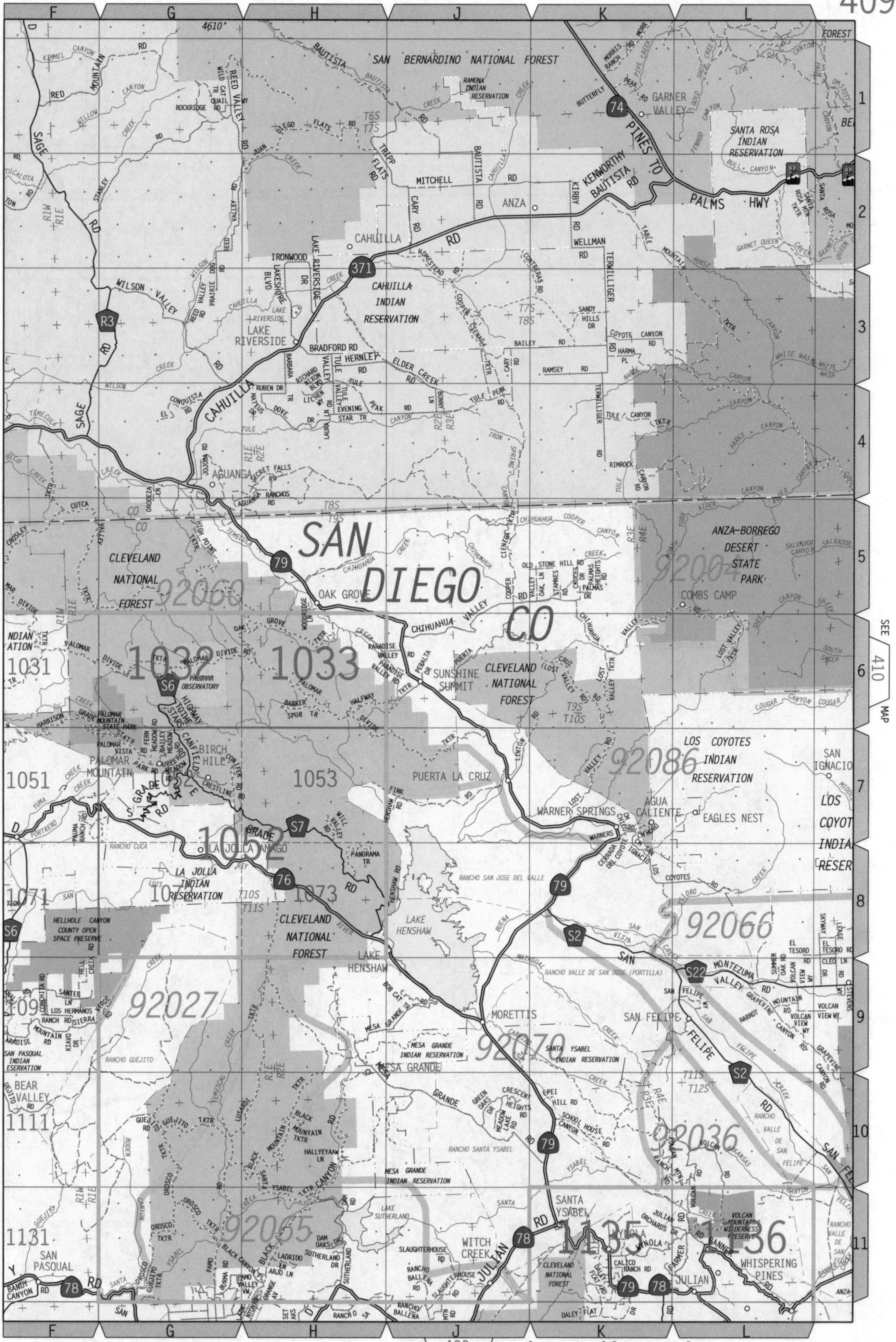
F
G
H
J
K
L
1
2
3
4
5
6
7
8
9
10
11
SAN BERNARDINO NATIONAL FOREST
RAMONA INDIAN RESERVATION
GARNER VALLEY
SANTA ROSA INDIAN RESERVATION
PINES TO PALMS HWY
KENWORTHY BAUTISTA RD
ANZA
CAHUILLA
CAHUILLA INDIAN RESERVATION
LAKE RIVERSIDE
WILSON VALLEY
SAGE RD
AGUANGA
SAN DIEGO CO
CLEVELAND NATIONAL FOREST
OAK GROVE
ANZA-BORREGO DESERT STATE PARK
COMBS CAMP
92060
92004
1031
1032
1033
PALOMAR OBSERVATORY
SUNSHINE SUMMIT
CHIHUAHUA VALLEY
PALOMAR MOUNTAIN STATE PARK
PALOMAR MOUNTAIN
BIRCH HILL
1051
1053
PUERTA LA CRUZ
LOS COYOTES INDIAN RESERVATION
92086
SAN IGNACIO
WARNER SPRINGS
AGUA CALIENTE
EAGLES NEST
1052
LA JOLLA AMAGO
LA JOLLA INDIAN RESERVATION
1071
1073
RANCHO SAN JOSE DEL VALLE
HELLHOLE CANYON COUNTY OPEN SPACE PRESERVE
LAKE HENSHAW
92066
MONTEZUMA VALLEY
92027
MORETTIS
SAN FELIPE
MESA GRANDE INDIAN RESERVATION
MESA GRANDE
SANTA YSABEL INDIAN RESERVATION
92070
SAN PASQUAL INDIAN RESERVATION
BEAR VALLEY
1111
92036
RANCHO SANTA YSABEL
SANTA YSABEL
1131
LAKE SUTHERLAND
92065
WITCH CREEK
1135
1136
VOLCAN MOUNTAIN WILDERNESS PRESERVE
JULIAN
WHISPERING PINES
SAN PASQUAL
SEE 410 MAP
SEE 429 MAP
0
2.5
5
miles 1 in. = 4 mi.

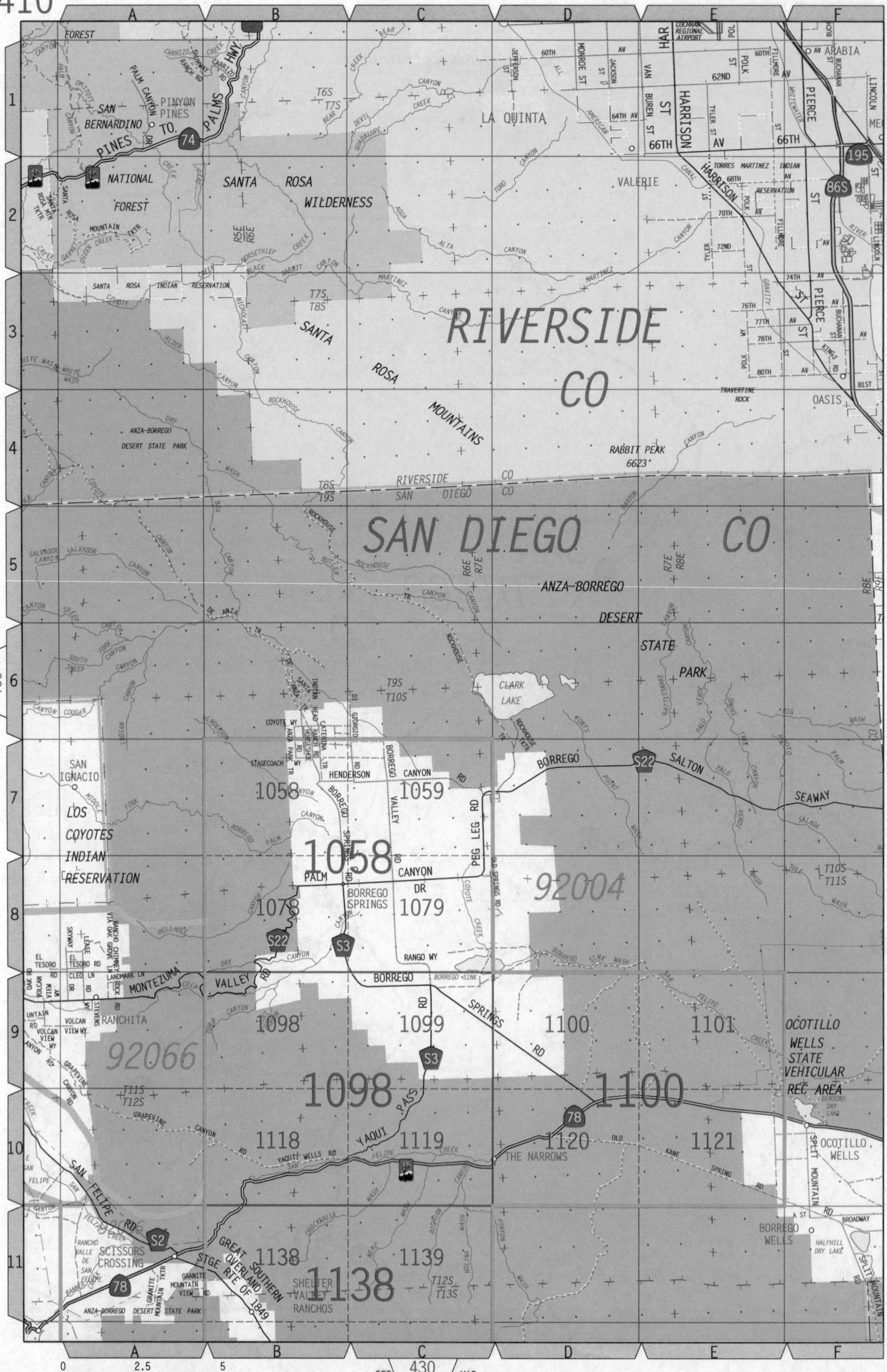
RIVERSIDE CO
SAN DIEGO CO
SANTA ROSA MOUNTAINS
SANTA ROSA WILDERNESS
SAN BERNARDINO NATIONAL FOREST
PINYON PINES
PINES TO PALMS HWY
LA QUINTA
VALERIE
ARABIA
OASIS
TRAVERTINE ROCK
RABBIT PEAK 6623'
SANTA ROSA INDIAN RESERVATION
ANZA-BORREGO DESERT STATE PARK
CLARK LAKE
LOS COYOTES INDIAN RESERVATION
SAN IGNACIO
BORREGO SPRINGS
92004
92066
RANCHITA
OCOTILLO WELLS STATE VEHICULAR REC AREA
OCOTILLO WELLS
BORREGO WELLS
THE NARROWS
SCISSORS CROSSING
SHELTER VALLEY RANCHOS
GREAT SOUTHERN OVERLAND STGE RTE OF 1849
1058
1059
1078
1079
1098
1099
1100
1101
1118
1119
1120
1121
1138
1139
SEE 409 MAP
SEE 430 MAP
0 2.5 5 miles 1 in. = 4 mi.

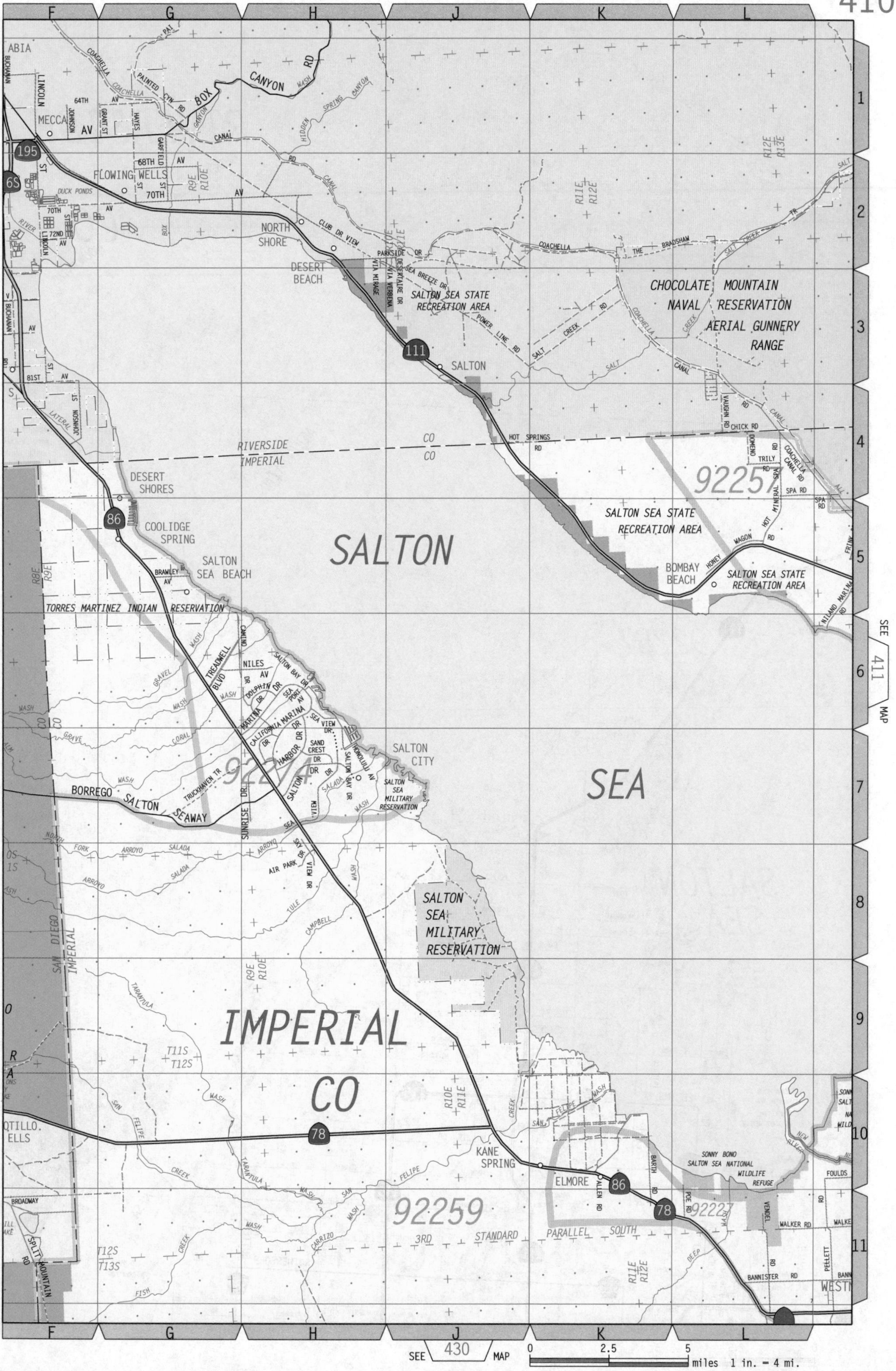
F
G
H
J
K
L
1
2
3
4
5
6
7
8
9
10
11
SALTON
SEA
IMPERIAL
CO
RIVERSIDE
IMPERIAL
CO
CO
MECCA
ABIA
LINCOLN
BUCHANAN
64TH
AV
JOHNSON
GRANT ST
HAYES
COACHELLA
PAINTED CYN RD
BOX CANYON RD
PAI
CANAL
GARFIELD
68TH
70TH
72ND
DUCK PONDS
FLOWING WELLS
R9E R10E
HIDDEN SPRING CANYON
NORTH SHORE
CLUB DR VIEW
DESERT BEACH
PARKSIDE DR
VIA MIRAGE
VIA VERBENA
DESERTAIRE DR
SEA BREEZE DR
SALTON SEA STATE RECREATION AREA
POWER LINE RD
SALT CREEK RD
COACHELLA
THE BRADSHAW
SALT CREEK
CHOCOLATE MOUNTAIN NAVAL RESERVATION AERIAL GUNNERY RANGE
R11E R12E
R12E R13E
SALTON
CANAL
VAUGHN RD
CHICK RD
DOMENO
TRILY RD
COACHELLA CANAL RD
HOT SPRINGS RD
81ST
LATERAL
DESERT SHORES
COOLIDGE SPRING
SALTON SEA BEACH
BRAWLEY AV
TORRES MARTINEZ INDIAN RESERVATION
92257
SPA RD
HOT MINERAL SPA
WAGON
HONEY
BOMBAY BEACH
SALTON SEA STATE RECREATION AREA
NILAND MARINA RD
SEE 411 MAP
R8E R9E
CAMINO
TREADWELL BLVD
NILES AV
SALTON BAY DR
DOLPHIN DR
SEA PORT AV
MARINA DR
CALIFORNIA MARINA DR
SEA VIEW DR
HARBOR DR
SAND CREST DR
SALTON BAY DR
HONOLULU AV
SALTON CITY
SALTON SEA MILITARY RESERVATION
92274
TRUCKHAVEN TR
BORREGO SALTON SEAWAY
SUNRISE DR
AIR PARK DR
VIEW DR
ARROYO SALADA
NORTH FORK
GRAVEL WASH
CORAL WASH
TULE WASH
CAMPBELL
SALTON SEA MILITARY RESERVATION
SAN DIEGO
IMPERIAL
R9E R10E
TARANTULA
T11S T12S
SAN FELIPE
R10E R11E
CREEK
WASH
KANE SPRING
ELMORE
ALLEN RD
BARTH RD
POE RD
92227
SONNY BONO SALTON SEA NATIONAL WILDLIFE REFUGE
VENDEL
FOULDS
WALKER RD
NEW RIVER
92259
3RD STANDARD PARALLEL SOUTH
R11E R12E
DEEP
BANNISTER RD
PELLETT
WESTM
FELIPE
CARRIZO WASH
FISH
SPLIT MOUNTAIN RD
T12S T13S
BROADWAY
OCOTILLO WELLS
195
6S
111
86
78
SEE 430 MAP
0 2.5 5 miles 1 in. = 4 mi.

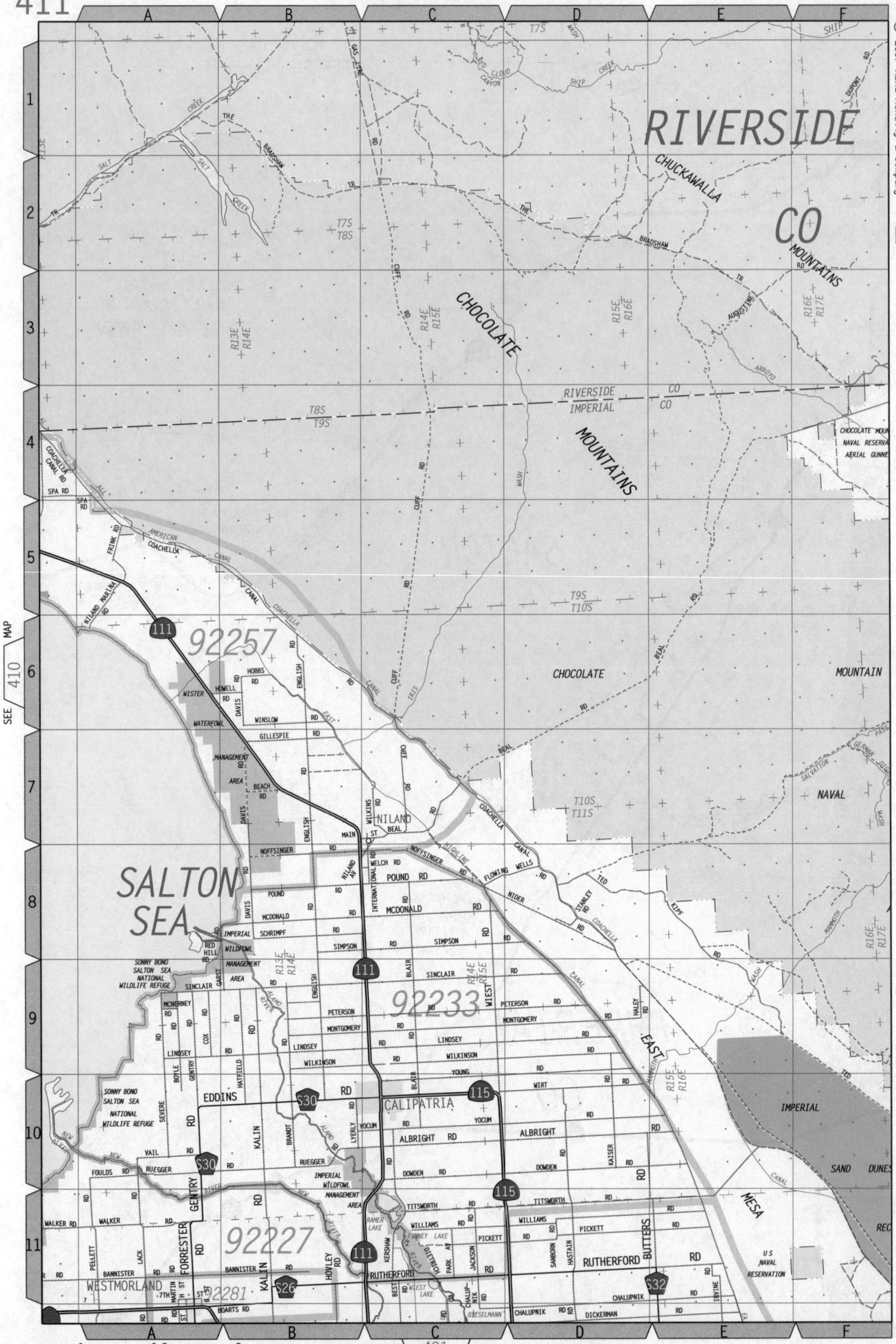

A
B
C
D
E
F
1
2
3
4
5
6
7
8
9
10
11
RIVERSIDE
CO
CHUCKAWALLA
MOUNTAINS
CHOCOLATE
MOUNTAINS
RIVERSIDE CO
IMPERIAL CO
T7S
T8S
T9S
T10S
T11S
R13E R14E
R14E R15E
R15E R16E
R16E R17E
BRADSHAW
THE
TR
SALT CREEK
RED CLOUD CANYON
SHIP CREEK
GAS LINE RD
CUFF RD
AUGUSTINE
ARROYO
WASH
CHOCOLATE MOUNTAIN NAVAL RESERVATION AERIAL GUNNERY
COACHELLA CANAL RD
SPA RD
FRINK RD
NILAND MARINA RD
AMERICAN CANAL
COACHELLA CANAL
111
92257
CHOCOLATE
MOUNTAIN
NAVAL
BEAL RD
IRIS
SALVATION
GERMAN DIGGINGS
HOBBS RD
HOWELL
WINSLOW
GILLESPIE
DAVIS
ENGLISH
WISTER WATERFOWL MANAGEMENT AREA
BEACH RD
NILAND
WILKINS
MAIN ST
NOFFSINGER
HIGHLINE
FLOWING WELLS
NIDER
STANLEY RD
TED
KIPF
MAMMOTH
SALTON SEA
POUND RD
MCDONALD
SIMPSON
SCHRIMPF
IMPERIAL WILDFOWL MANAGEMENT AREA
RED HILL RD
SONNY BONO SALTON SEA NATIONAL WILDLIFE REFUGE
SINCLAIR
BLAIR
WIEST
INTERNATIONAL
NILAND AV
WELCH RD
92233
PETERSON
MONTGOMERY
LINDSEY
WILKINSON
YOUNG
WIRT
MCNERNEY RD
BOYLE
GENTRY
COX
HATFIELD
ALAMO RIVER
EDDINS
S30
CALIPATRIA
115
YOCUM
ALBRIGHT RD
DOWDEN
RUEGGER
VAIL
FOULDS
NEW RIVER
SEVERE
KALIN
BRANDT
LYERLY
TITSWORTH
WILLIAMS
PICKETT
RAMER LAKE
FINNEY LAKE
KERSHAW
DIETRICH
PARK AV
JACKSON
SANBORN
HASTAIN
RUTHERFORD
BUTTERS
S32
EAST MESA
IMPERIAL SAND DUNES
US NAVAL RESERVATION
WALKER RD
PELLETT
LACK
FORRESTER RD
92227
BANNISTER
HOWLEY
S26
WESTMORLAND
92281
BOARTS RD
MARTIN ST
H ST
B ST
7TH
BEST
WIEST LAKE
CHALUPNIK
GIESELMANN
DICKERMAN
IRVINE
SEE 410 MAP
SEE 431 MAP
0
2.5
5
miles 1 in. = 4 mi.
N

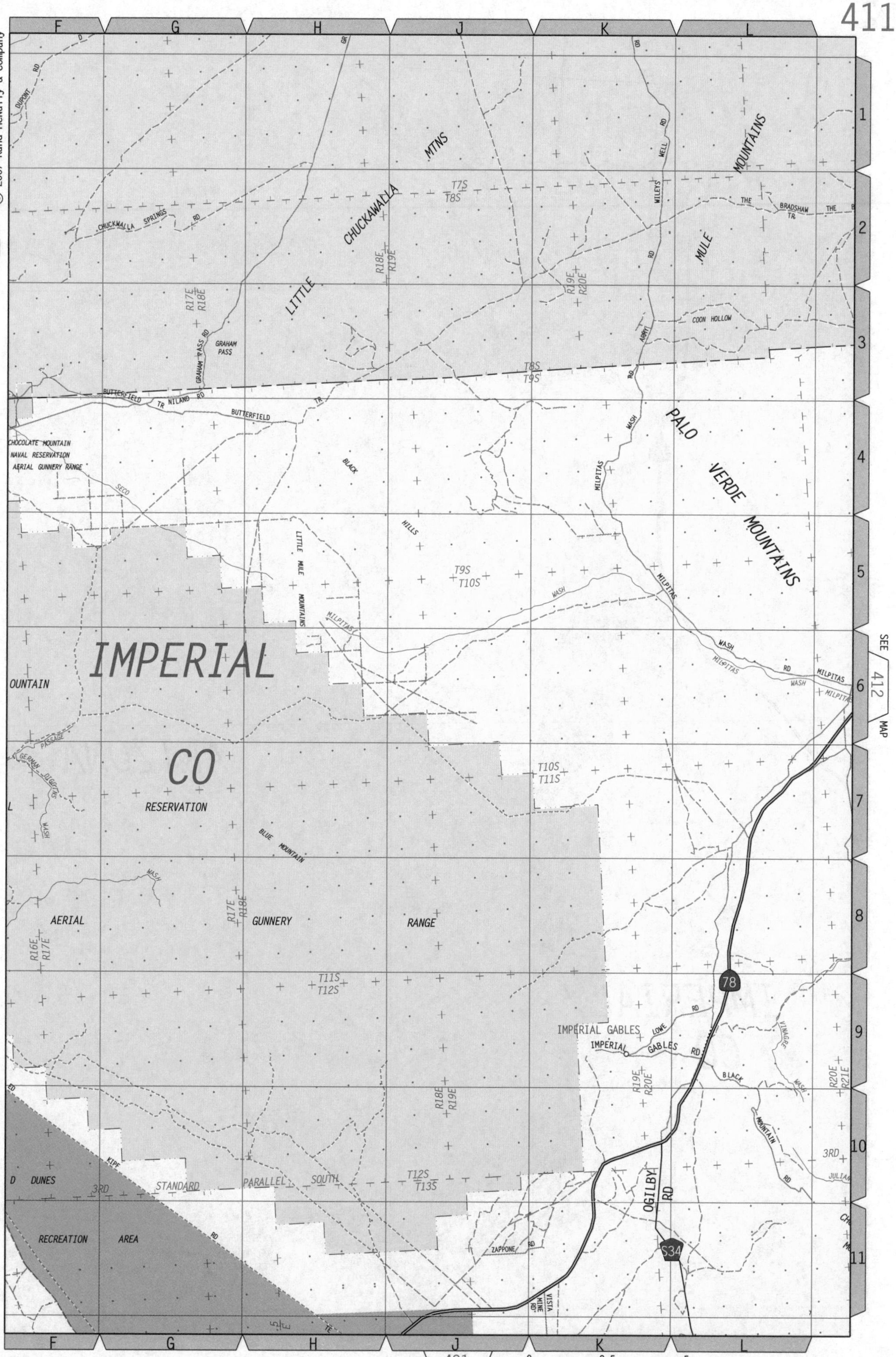

F
G
H
J
K
L
1
2
3
4
5
6
7
8
9
10
11
DUPONT RD
LITTLE CHUCKAWALLA MTNS
CHUCKWALLA SPRINGS RD
T7S
T8S
R17E R18E
R18E R19E
R19E R20E
GRAHAM PASS RD
GRAHAM PASS
WILEYS WELL RD
MULE MOUNTAINS
THE BRADSHAW TR
COON HOLLOW
ARMY RD
T8S
T9S
BUTTERFIELD TR
NILAND RD
BUTTERFIELD
CHOCOLATE MOUNTAIN NAVAL RESERVATION AERIAL GUNNERY RANGE
SECO
BLACK HILLS
PALO VERDE MOUNTAINS
MILPITAS WASH
LITTLE MULE MOUNTAINS
T9S
T10S
MILPITAS WASH RD
SEE 412 MAP
IMPERIAL
CO
OUNTAIN
PASSAGE
GERMAN DIGGINGS WASH
T10S
T11S
RESERVATION
BLUE MOUNTAIN
WASH
AERIAL
GUNNERY
RANGE
R17E R18E
R16E R17E
78
T11S
T12S
IMPERIAL GABLES
IMPERIAL
LOWE RD
GABLES RD
BLACK MOUNTAIN WASH
VINAGRE WASH
R19E R20E
R20E R21E
R18E R19E
KIPPE
D DUNES
3RD STANDARD PARALLEL SOUTH
T12S
T13S
OGILBY RD
3RD
JULIAN
RECREATION AREA
RD
ZAPPONE RD
S34
MINE RD
VISTA
SEE 431 MAP
0
2.5
5
miles 1 in. = 4 mi.

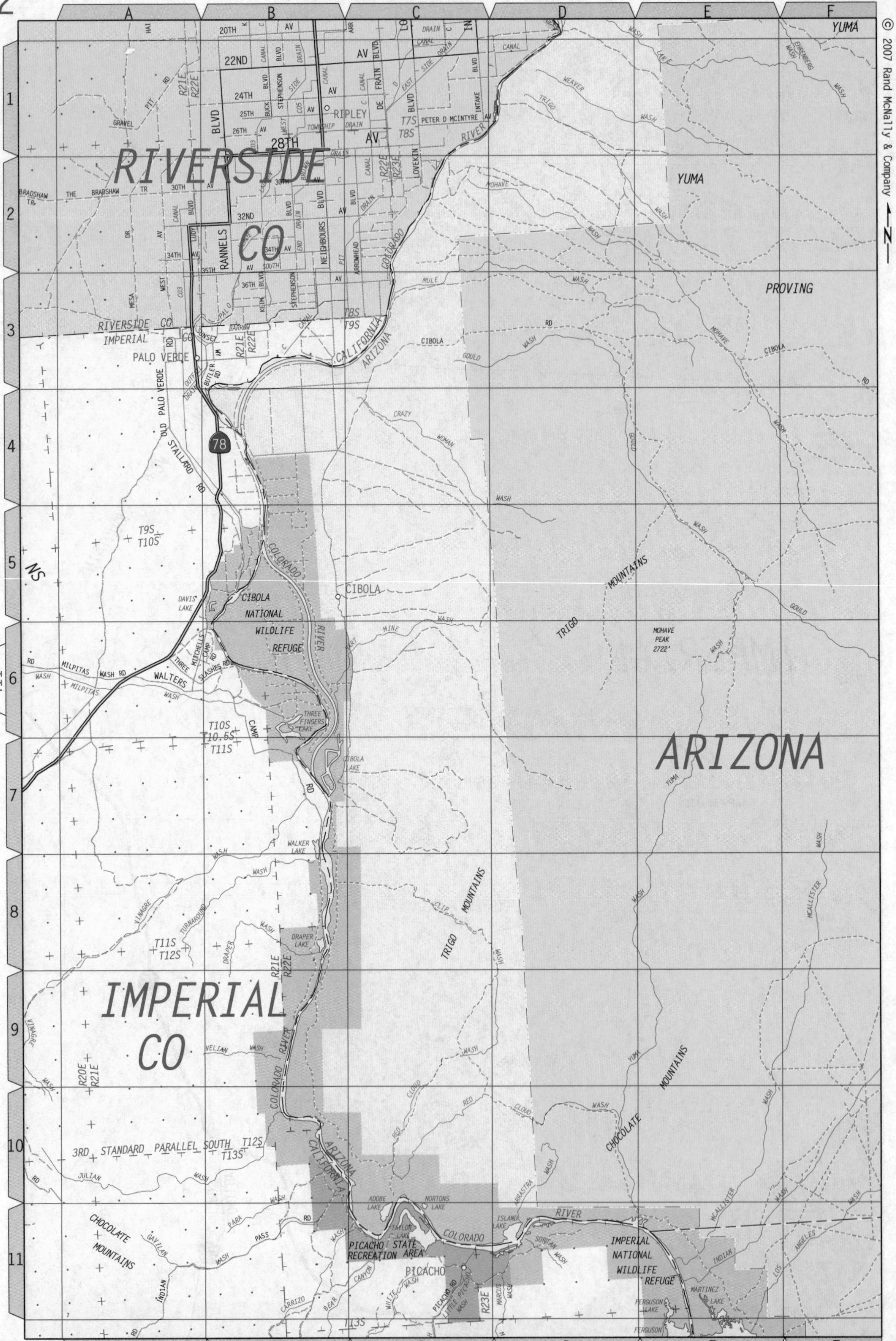
RIVERSIDE CO
IMPERIAL CO
ARIZONA
RIPLEY
PALO VERDE
CIBOLA
WALTERS
PICACHO
CIBOLA NATIONAL WILDLIFE REFUGE
IMPERIAL NATIONAL WILDLIFE REFUGE
PICACHO STATE RECREATION AREA
TRIGO MOUNTAINS
CHOCOLATE MOUNTAINS
MOHAVE PEAK 2722'
YUMA
PROVING
COLORADO RIVER
3RD STANDARD PARALLEL SOUTH
SEE 411 MAP
SEE 432 MAP
0 2.5 5 miles 1 in. = 4 mi.

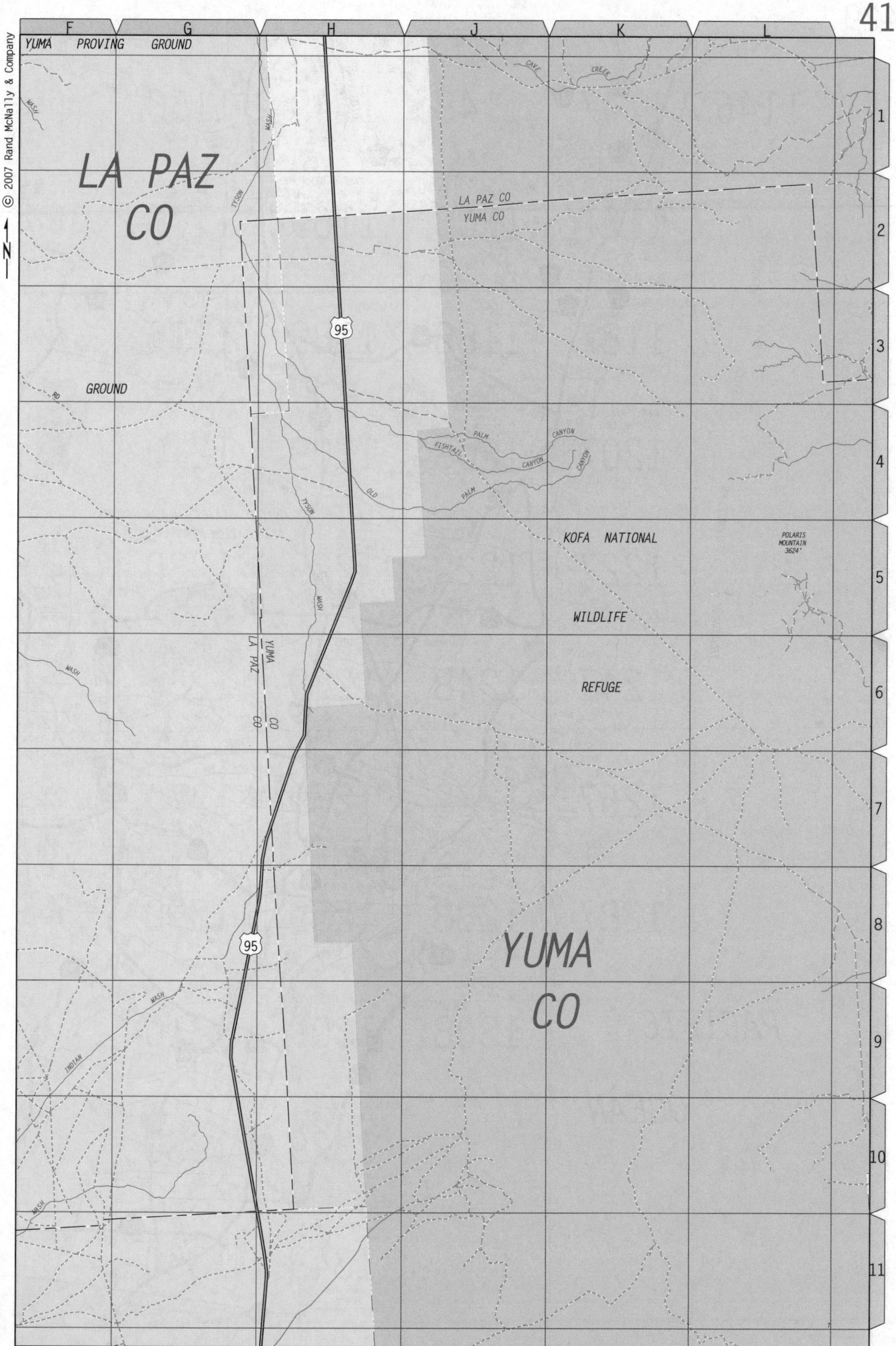
F
G
H
J
K
L
1
2
3
4
5
6
7
8
9
10
11
YUMA PROVING GROUND
LA PAZ CO
WASH
TYSON
CAVE CREEK
LA PAZ CO
YUMA CO
95
GROUND
RD
PALM CANYON
FISHTAIL CANYON
CANYON
OLD PALM
KOFA NATIONAL
WILDLIFE
REFUGE
POLARIS MOUNTAIN 3624'
YUMA
LA PAZ CO
CO
YUMA CO
INDIAN WASH
SAN DIEGO CO.
0
2.5
5
miles 1 in. = 4 mi.

SEE 432 MAP

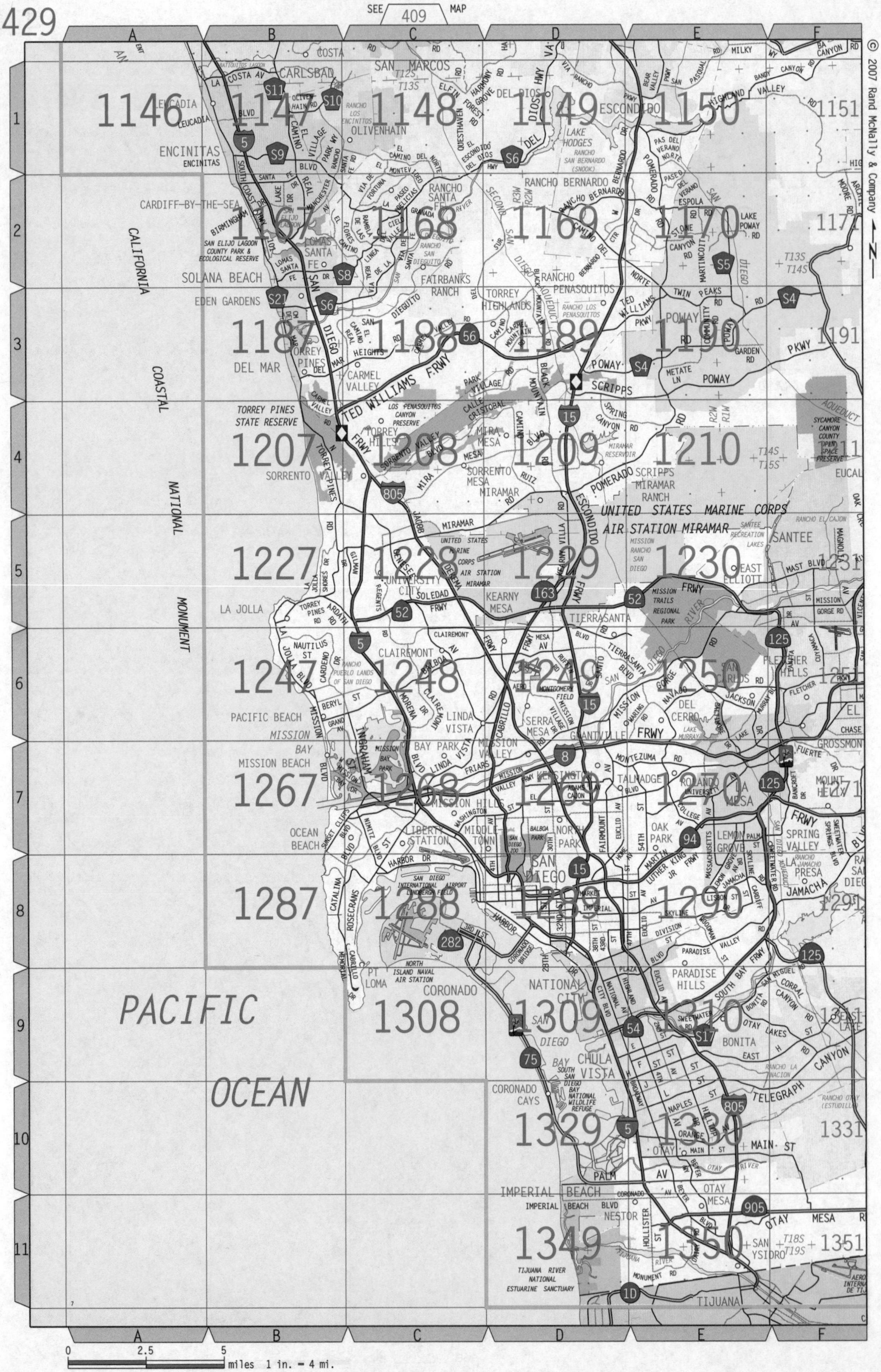
SEE 409 MAP
A
B
C
D
E
F
1
2
3
4
5
6
7
8
9
10
11
1146
1147
1148
1149
1150
1151
1167
1168
1169
1170
1171
1187
1188
1189
1190
1191
1207
1208
1209
1210
1227
1228
1229
1230
1247
1248
1249
1250
1267
1268
1269
1270
1287
1288
1289
1290
1308
1309
1310
1329
1330
1331
1349
1350
1351
CARLSBAD
SAN MARCOS
LEUCADIA
ENCINITAS
OLIVENHAIN
ESCONDIDO
LAKE HODGES
RANCHO BERNARDO
CARDIFF-BY-THE-SEA
RANCHO SANTA FE
LAKE POWAY
SAN ELIJO LAGOON COUNTY PARK & ECOLOGICAL RESERVE
SOLANA BEACH
EDEN GARDENS
FAIRBANKS RANCH
TORREY HIGHLANDS
RANCHO PENASQUITOS
POWAY
DEL MAR
TORREY PINES
CARMEL VALLEY
TED WILLIAMS FRWY
SCRIPPS
TORREY PINES STATE RESERVE
LOS PENASQUITOS CANYON PRESERVE
TORREY HILLS
SORRENTO VALLEY
MIRA MESA
SORRENTO MESA
MIRAMAR
MIRAMAR RESERVOIR
SCRIPPS MIRAMAR RANCH
SYCAMORE CANYON COUNTY OPEN SPACE PRESERVE
UNITED STATES MARINE CORPS AIR STATION MIRAMAR
SANTEE
CALIFORNIA COASTAL NATIONAL MONUMENT
UNIVERSITY CITY
KEARNY MESA
LA JOLLA
TIERRASANTA
MISSION TRAILS REGIONAL PARK
CLAIREMONT
FLETCHER HILLS
PACIFIC BEACH
MISSION BAY
LINDA VISTA
SERRA MESA
SAN CARLOS
DEL CERRO
GRANTVILLE
MISSION BEACH
BAY PARK
MISSION VALLEY
GROSSMONT
MISSION HILLS
KENSINGTON
TALMADGE
ROLANDO
LA MESA
MOUNT HELIX
OCEAN BEACH
LIBERTY STATION
MIDDLETOWN
NORTH PARK
OAK PARK
LEMON GROVE
SPRING VALLEY
LA PRESA
JAMACHA
SAN DIEGO
SAN DIEGO INTERNATIONAL AIRPORT LINDBERGH FIELD
NORTH ISLAND NAVAL AIR STATION
PT LOMA
CORONADO
NATIONAL CITY
PARADISE HILLS
PACIFIC OCEAN
SAN DIEGO BAY
CHULA VISTA
BONITA
CORONADO CAYS
OTAY
OTAY MESA
IMPERIAL BEACH
NESTOR
SAN YSIDRO
TIJUANA RIVER NATIONAL ESTUARINE SANCTUARY
TIJUANA
© 2007 Rand McNally & Company
0
2.5
5
miles 1 in. = 4 mi.

SAN DIEGO CO.

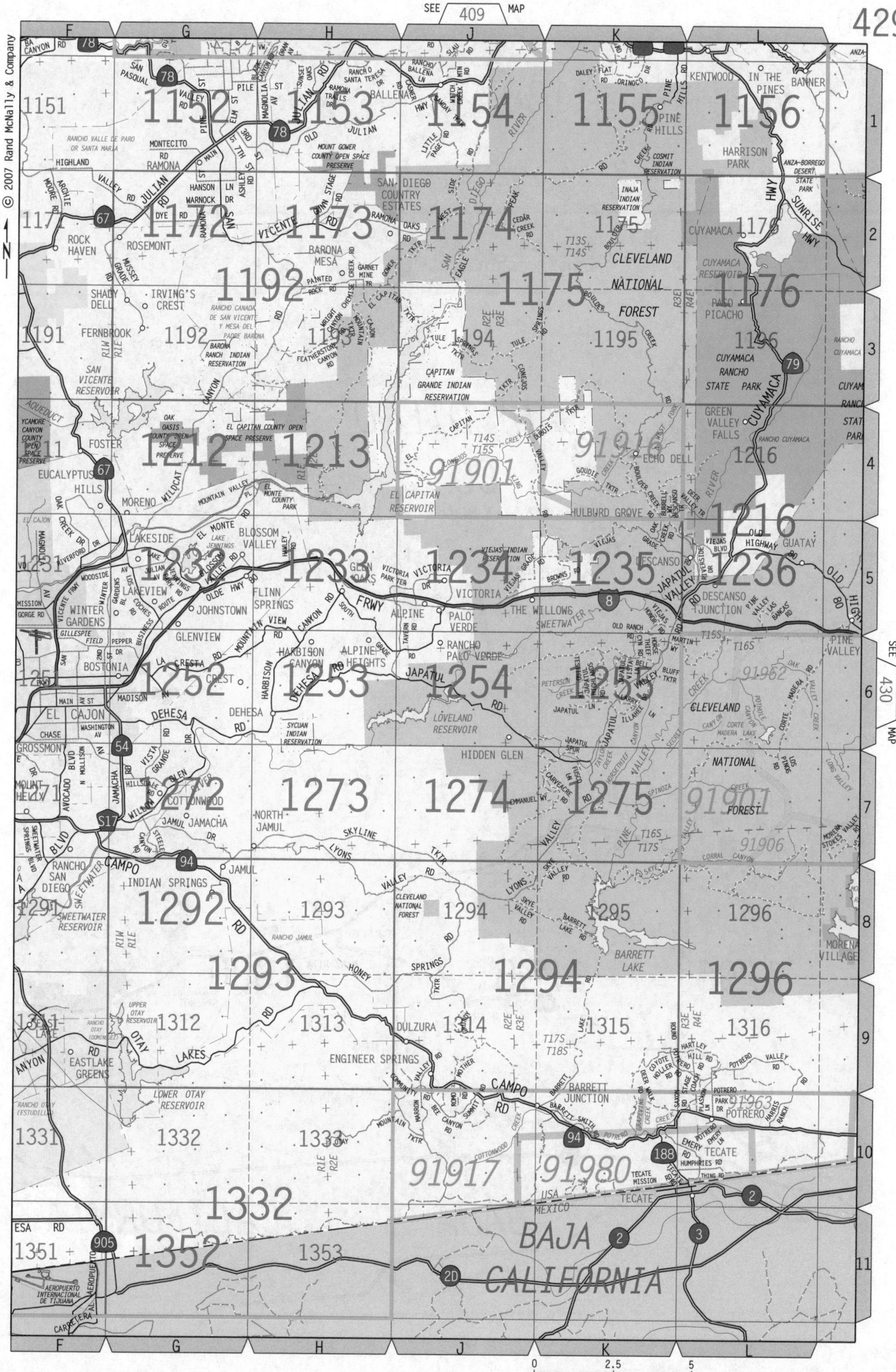
SEE 409 MAP
F
G
H
J
K
L
1
2
3
4
5
6
7
8
9
10
11
1151
1152
1153
1154
1155
1156
1171
1172
1173
1174
1175
1176
1191
1192
1193
1194
1195
1196
1211
1212
1213
1216
1231
1232
1233
1234
1235
1236
1251
1252
1253
1254
1255
1271
1272
1273
1274
1275
1291
1292
1293
1294
1295
1296
1311
1312
1313
1314
1315
1316
1331
1332
1333
1351
1352
1353
SAN PASQUAL
RAMONA
JULIAN
BALLENA
PINE HILLS
KENTWOOD IN THE PINES
BANNER
HARRISON PARK
ANZA-BORREGO DESERT STATE PARK
MOUNT GOWER COUNTY OPEN SPACE PRESERVE
SAN DIEGO COUNTRY ESTATES
INAJA INDIAN RESERVATION
COSMIT INDIAN RESERVATION
ROCK HAVEN
ROSEMONT
BARONA MESA
CUYAMACA
CUYAMACA RESERVOIR
CLEVELAND NATIONAL FOREST
SHADY DELL
IRVING'S CREST
BARONA RANCH INDIAN RESERVATION
FERNBROOK
SAN VICENTE RESERVOIR
PASO PICACHO
CUYAMACA RANCHO STATE PARK
CAPITAN GRANDE INDIAN RESERVATION
EL CAPITAN COUNTY OPEN SPACE PRESERVE
OAK OASIS COUNTY OPEN SPACE PRESERVE
SYCAMORE CANYON COUNTY OPEN SPACE PRESERVE
FOSTER
EUCALYPTUS HILLS
MORENO
EL MONTE COUNTY PARK
EL CAPITAN RESERVOIR
GREEN VALLEY FALLS
ECHO DELL
HULBURD GROVE
91916
91901
LAKESIDE
BLOSSOM VALLEY
GLEN OAKS
VIEJAS INDIAN RESERVATION
DESCANSO
GUATAY
LAKEVIEW
WINTER GARDENS
JOHNSTOWN
FLINN SPRINGS
ALPINE
VICTORIA
THE WILLOWS
DESCANSO JUNCTION
PINE VALLEY
GILLESPIE FIELD
GLENVIEW
BOSTONIA
HARBISON CANYON
ALPINE HEIGHTS
PALO VERDE
RANCHO PALO VERDE
CREST
EL CAJON
DEHESA
LOVELAND RESERVOIR
SYCUAN INDIAN RESERVATION
HIDDEN GLEN
GROSSMONT
MOUNT HELIX
COTTONWOOD
JAMACHA
NORTH JAMUL
91906
RANCHO SAN DIEGO
INDIAN SPRINGS
JAMUL
SWEETWATER RESERVOIR
CLEVELAND NATIONAL FOREST
BARRETT LAKE
MORENA VILLAGE
UPPER OTAY RESERVOIR
DULZURA
ENGINEER SPRINGS
EASTLAKE GREENS
LOWER OTAY RESERVOIR
BARRETT JUNCTION
POTRERO
91963
TECATE
91917
91980
TECATE MISSION
USA
MEXICO
BAJA CALIFORNIA
AEROPUERTO INTERNACIONAL DE TIJUANA
SEE 430 MAP
0
2.5
5
miles 1 in. = 4 mi.

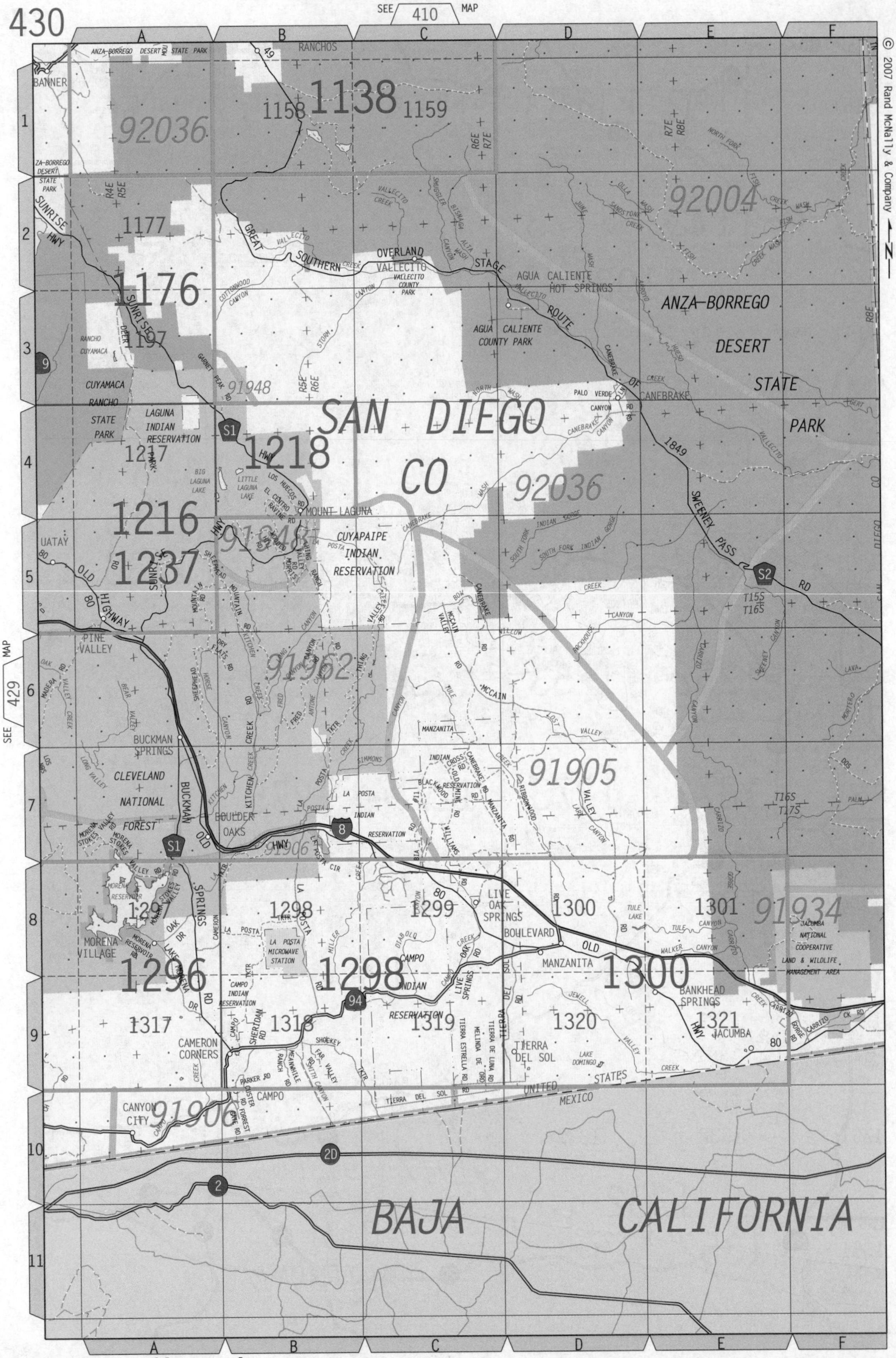
SEE 410 MAP
SEE 429 MAP
A
B
C
D
E
F
1
2
3
4
5
6
7
8
9
10
11
SAN DIEGO CO
ANZA-BORREGO DESERT STATE PARK
CUYAMACA RANCHO STATE PARK
LAGUNA INDIAN RESERVATION
CUYAPAIPE INDIAN RESERVATION
CAMPO INDIAN RESERVATION
CLEVELAND NATIONAL FOREST
AGUA CALIENTE COUNTY PARK
VALLECITO COUNTY PARK
JACUMBA NATIONAL COOPERATIVE LAND & WILDLIFE MANAGEMENT AREA
LA POSTA MICROWAVE STATION
BANNER
RANCHOS
OVERLAND
VALLECITO
AGUA CALIENTE HOT SPRINGS
PALO VERDE
MOUNT LAGUNA
UATAY
PINE VALLEY
BUCKMAN SPRINGS
BOULDER OAKS
LA POSTA
MORENA VILLAGE
LIVE OAK SPRINGS
BOULEVARD
MANZANITA
CAMPO
CAMERON CORNERS
TIERRA DEL SOL
BANKHEAD SPRINGS
JACUMBA
CANYON CITY
UNITED STATES
MEXICO
BAJA CALIFORNIA
92036
92004
91948
91962
91905
91906
91934
1138
1158
1159
1176
1177
1197
1216
1217
1218
1237
1296
1297
1298
1299
1300
1301
1317
1318
1319
1320
1321
GREAT SOUTHERN OVERLAND STAGE ROUTE OF 1849
SWEENEY PASS RD
SUNRISE HWY
OLD HIGHWAY 80
BUCKMAN SPRINGS RD
OLD HWY 80
LA POSTA RD
INDIAN RESERVATION RD
CANEBRAKE
0
2.5
5
miles 1 in. = 4 mi.

SEE 410 MAP

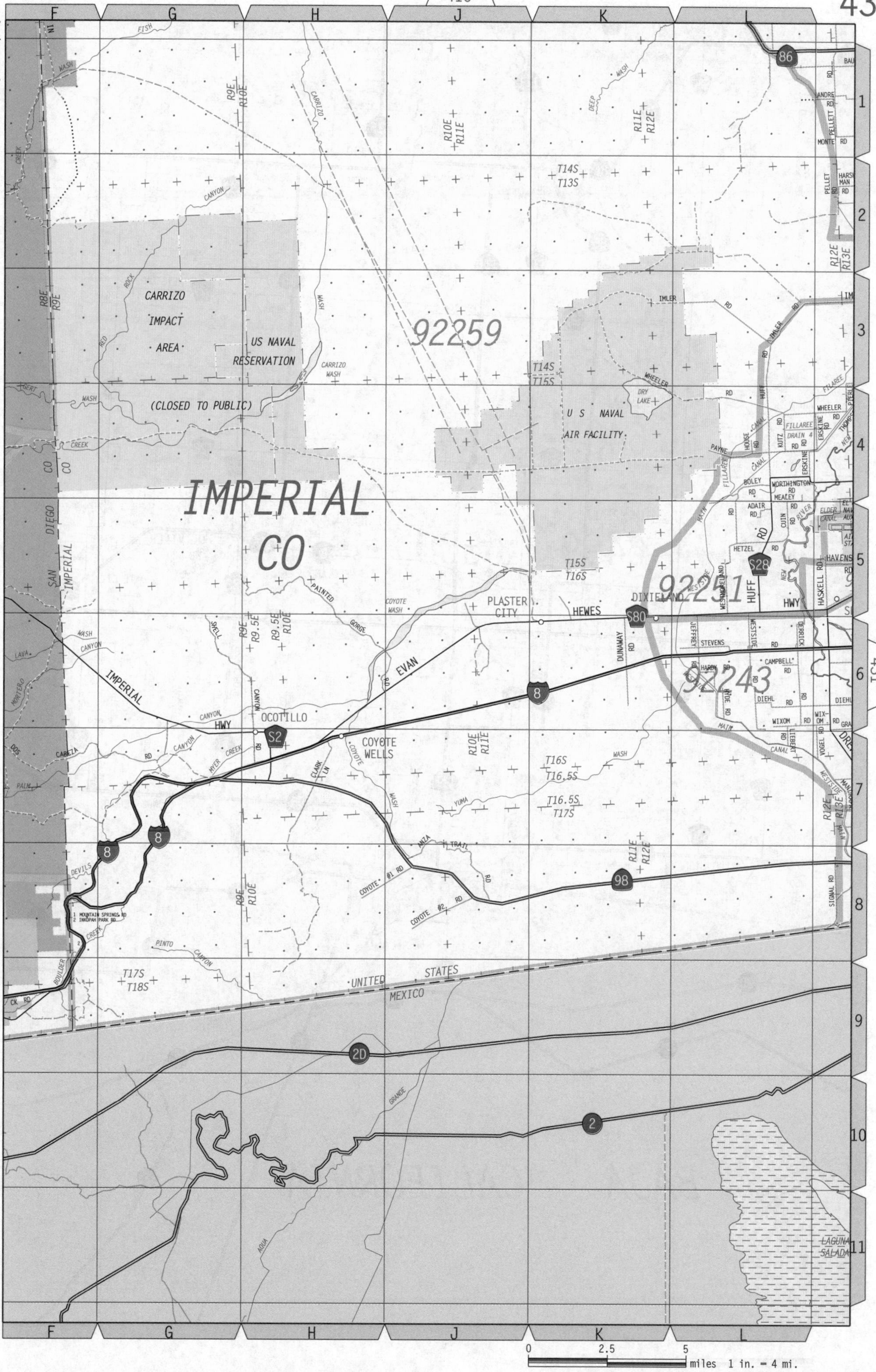

SEE 431 MAP

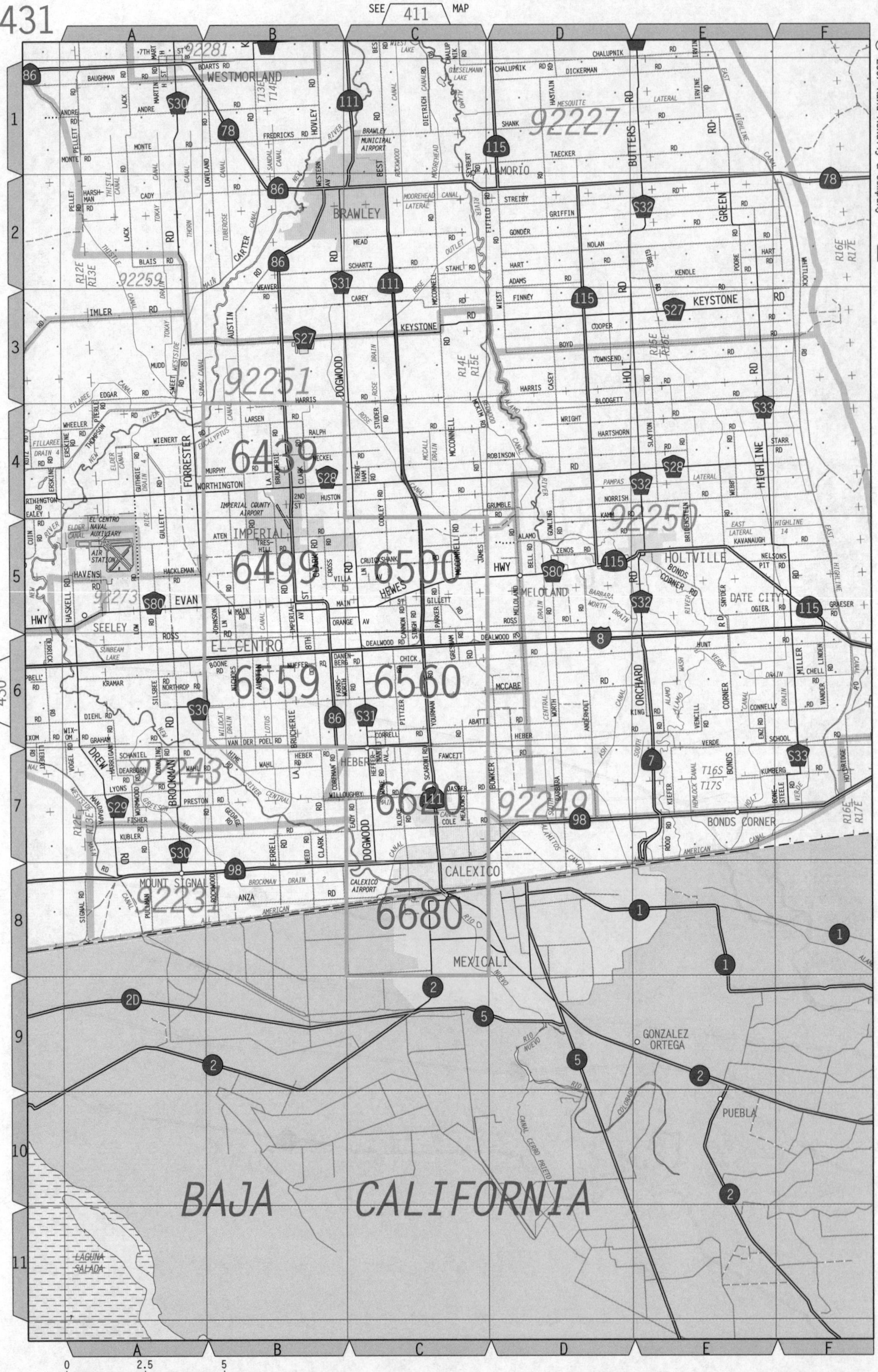

SEE 411 MAP
SEE 430 MAP
A B C D E F
1 2 3 4 5 6 7 8 9 10 11
WESTMORLAND
BRAWLEY
BRAWLEY MUNICIPAL AIRPORT
ALAMORIO
92281
92227
92259
92251
92273
92243
92231
92249
92250
6439
6499
6500
6559
6560
6620
6680
IMPERIAL
IMPERIAL COUNTY AIRPORT
EL CENTRO
EL CENTRO NAVAL AUXILIARY AIR STATION
SEELEY
HEBER
HOLTVILLE
DATE CITY
MELOLAND
BONDS CORNER
MOUNT SIGNAL
CALEXICO
CALEXICO AIRPORT
MEXICALI
GONZALEZ ORTEGA
PUEBLA
LAGUNA SALADA
BAJA CALIFORNIA
KEYSTONE
HEWES
EVAN HEWES HWY
DOGWOOD
FORRESTER
HIGHLINE
ORCHARD
BUTTERS RD
NEW RIVER
ALAMO RIVER
R12E R13E
R14E R15E
R15E R16E
R16E R17E
T13E T14E
T16S T17S
0 2.5 5
miles 1 in. = 4 mi.

SEE 411 MAP

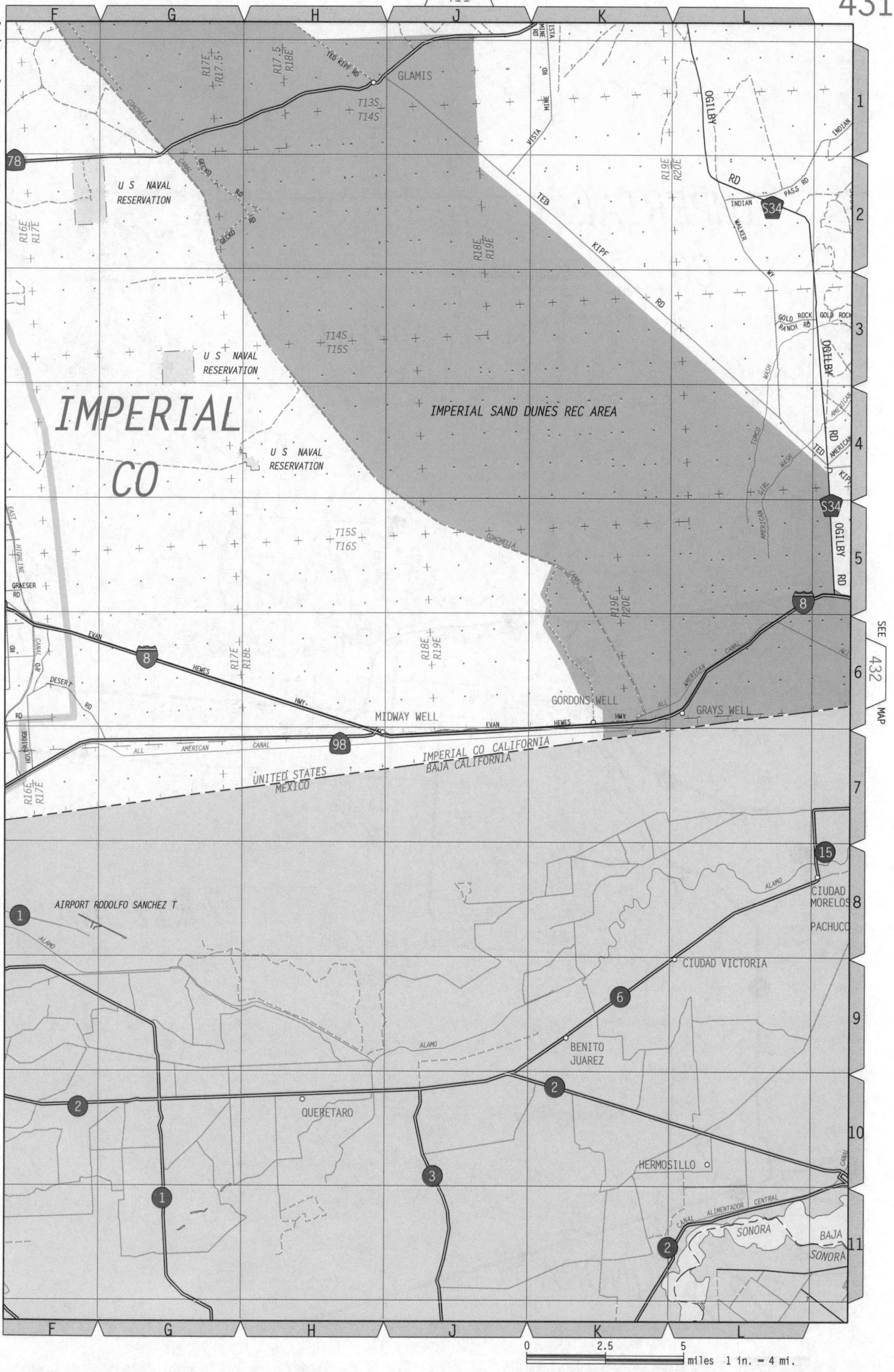

F G H J K L
1 2 3 4 5 6 7 8 9 10 11
© 2007 Rand McNally & Company
SAN DIEGO CO.
IMPERIAL CO
IMPERIAL SAND DUNES REC AREA
U S NAVAL RESERVATION
GLAMIS
TED KIPF RD
OGILBY RD
INDIAN PASS RD
GOLD ROCK RANCH RD
MIDWAY WELL
GORDONS WELL
GRAYS WELL
EVAN HEWES HWY
ALL AMERICAN CANAL
COACHELLA CANAL
IMPERIAL CO CALIFORNIA
BAJA CALIFORNIA
UNITED STATES
MEXICO
AIRPORT RODOLFO SANCHEZ T
CIUDAD MORELOS
PACHUCO
CIUDAD VICTORIA
BENITO JUAREZ
QUERETARO
HERMOSILLO
CANAL ALIMENTADOR CENTRAL
SONORA
BAJA SONORA
ALAMO
SEE 432 MAP
0 2.5 5 miles 1 in. = 4 mi.

SEE 412 MAP
SEE 431 MAP
A
B
C
D
E
F
1
2
3
4
5
6
7
8
9
10
11
IMPERIAL CO
92283
ARIZONA
BAJA CALIFORNIA NORTE
SONORA
FISHERS
IMPERIAL NATIONAL WILDLIFE REFUGE
IMPERIAL RESERVOIR
MITTRY LAKE WILDLIFE AREA
MITTRY LAKE
SENATOR WASH RES
SQUAW LAKE
MARTINEZ LAKE
FERGUSON LAKE
FERGUSON
COLORADO RIVER
YUMA CO
IMPERIAL CO
GILA RIVER
GRAVITY CANAL
GRAVITY MAIN CANAL
IMPERIAL DAM
DAM
PICACHO RD
PICACHO WASH
OGILBY RD
OGILBY
FELICITY
CENTER OF THE WORLD DR
IMPERIAL SAND DUNES REC AREA
ANDRADE
AMERICAN CANAL
ALL AMERICAN CANAL
FORT YUMA INDIAN RESERVATION
SIDEWINDER RD
BARNEY OLDFIELD RD
INDIAN PASS RD
GOLD ROCK RANCH RD
TUMCO WASH
KIPF RD
TED
AMERICAN GIRL MINE RD
BARD
WINTERHAVEN
MEHRING
COLBY RD
YORK RD
FLOOD RD
FISHER RD
COCOPAH RD
ROSS
INDIAN ROCK RD
ARNOLD RD
QUICK RD
HORNE RD
PASCUAL RD
PICACHO RD
HAUGHTELIN LAKE
BARD LAKE
WILKINS RD
PEREZ RD
UNITED STATES
MEXICO
VICENTE GUERRERO
YUMA
YUMA INTERNATIONAL AIRPORT
AVENUE A
THACKER LATERAL
CENTRAL CANAL
EAST DRAIN
B MAIN LATERAL
A CANAL
B CANAL
VALLEY MAIN CANAL
SOUTH GILA CANAL
NORTH GILA MAIN CANAL
OUTLET DRAIN
SOMERTON
GADSDEN
CUMMINGS LATERAL
MAIN CANAL
WEST MAIN CANAL
ALAMO
ALIMENTADOR CENTRAL CANAL
CIUDAD MORELOS
PACHUCO
SAN LUIS
SAN LUIS RIO COLORADO
BAJA CALIF
SONORA
T13S
T14S
T13.5S
T14.5S
T15S
T16S
R20E
R21E
R22E
R23E
R24E
8
186
95
S24
S34
2
15
40
41
0
2.5
5
miles 1 in. = 4 mi.

SEE 412 MAP
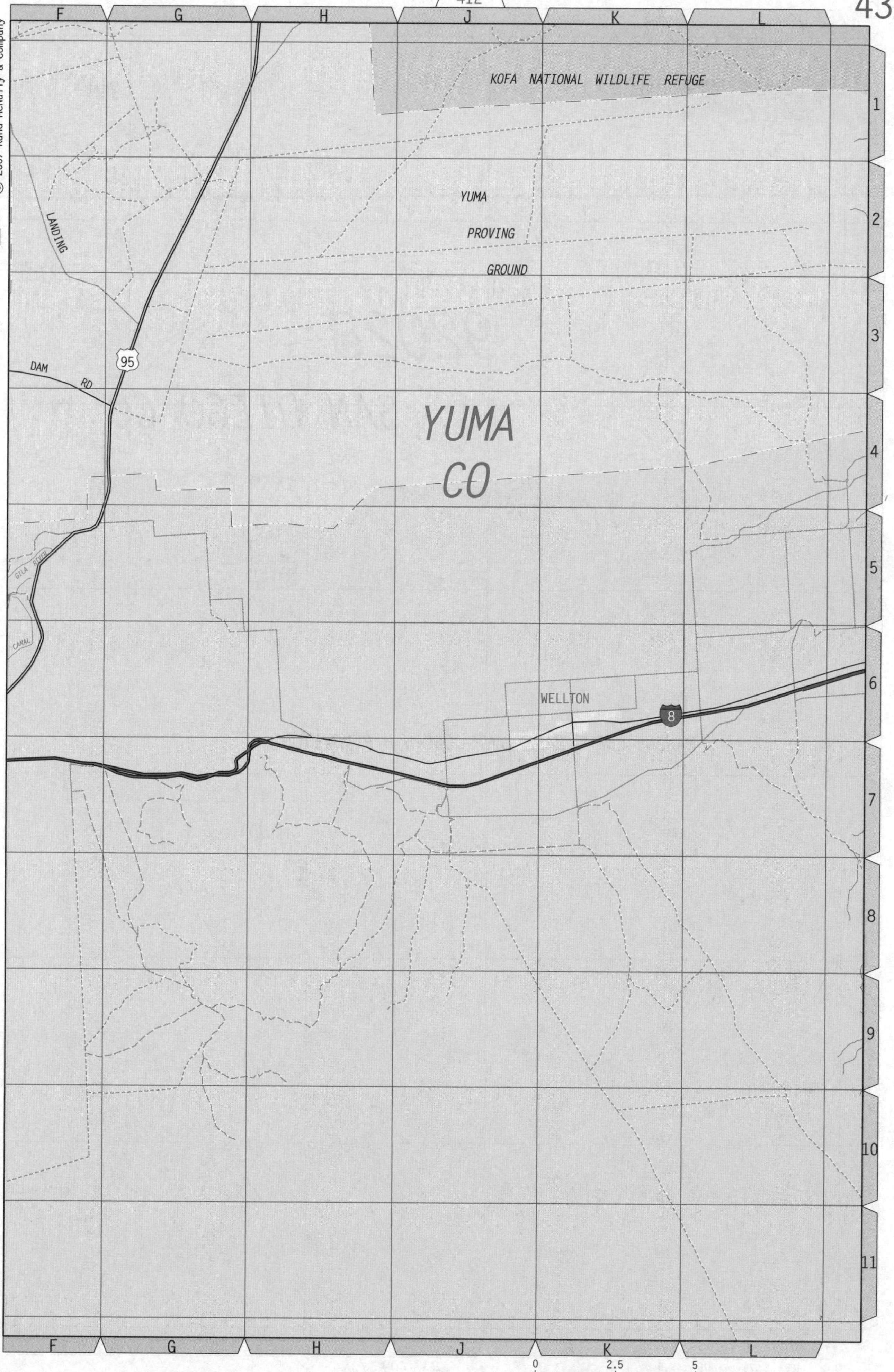
F G H J K L
1 2 3 4 5 6 7 8 9 10 11
KOFA NATIONAL WILDLIFE REFUGE
YUMA
PROVING
GROUND
LANDING
DAM RD
95
YUMA
CO
GILA RIVER
CANAL
WELLTON
8
0 2.5 5 miles 1 in. = 4 mi.

SEE RIV 976 MAP
A
B
C
D
E
1
2
3
4
5
6
7
26
CLEVELAND NATIONAL FOREST
25
CAMPS CREEK
30
PYEATT
TKT
R5W
R4W
36
35
31
CREEK
FERN
92028
SAN DIEGO CO
T8S
T9S
ROBLAR
R5W
R4W
CREEK
6
2
1
SEE 408 MAP
MARINE CORPS BASE CAMP JOSEPH H PENDLETON
RD
RANCHO
SANTA
MARGARITA
Y
LAS
FLORES
CASE
SPRINGS
RD
11
MONTIJO
12
7
ROBLAR
CREEK
18
13
LAS PULGAS CANYON
SEE 409 MAP
0 .125 .25 .375 .5
miles 1 in. = 1900 ft.

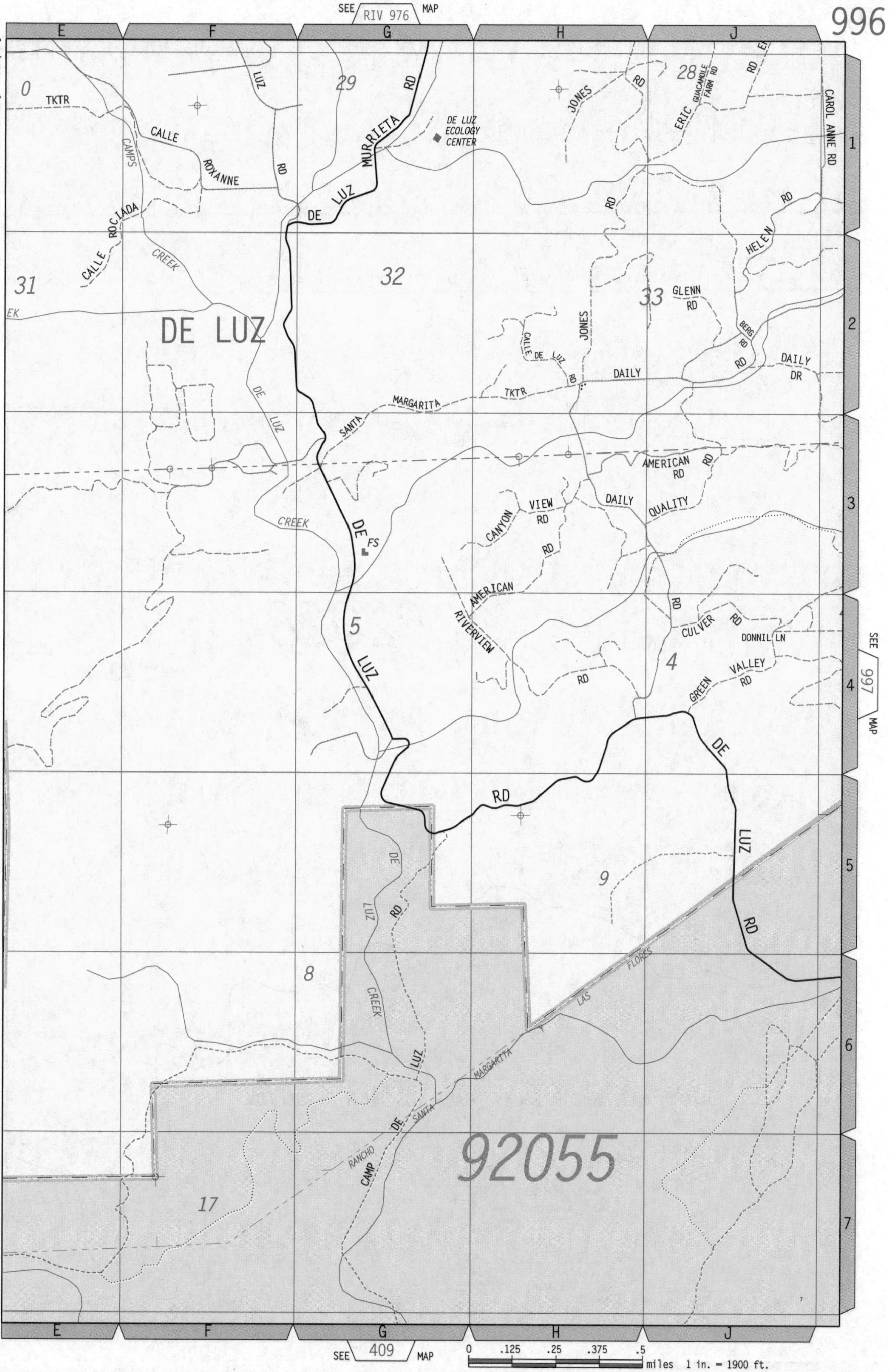
SEE RIV 976 MAP
E
F
G
H
J
1
2
3
4
5
6
7
TKTR
CALLE
ROXANNE
CAMPS
ROCIADA
CALLE
CREEK
LUZ
RD
29
MURRIETA
RD
DE
LUZ
DE LUZ ECOLOGY CENTER
JONES
RD
28
ERIC
GUACAMOLE FARM RD
RD
CAROL ANNE RD
RD
HELEN
31
32
DE LUZ
33
GLENN RD
JONES
CALLE DE LUZ RD
BERG RD
RD
DAILY DR
DAILY
SANTA
MARGARITA
TKTR
DE
LUZ
AMERICAN RD
RD
CANYON
VIEW RD
DAILY
QUALITY
CREEK
DE
FS
RD
AMERICAN
RIVERVIEW
RD
CULVER
RD
DONNIL LN
5
LUZ
4
RD
GREEN
VALLEY RD
SEE 997 MAP
DE
RD
LUZ
9
DE
LUZ
RD
RD
8
CREEK
LAS FLORES
LUZ
MARGARITA
SANTA
DE
RANCHO
CAMP
92055
17
SEE 409 MAP
0 .125 .25 .375 .5
miles 1 in. = 1900 ft.

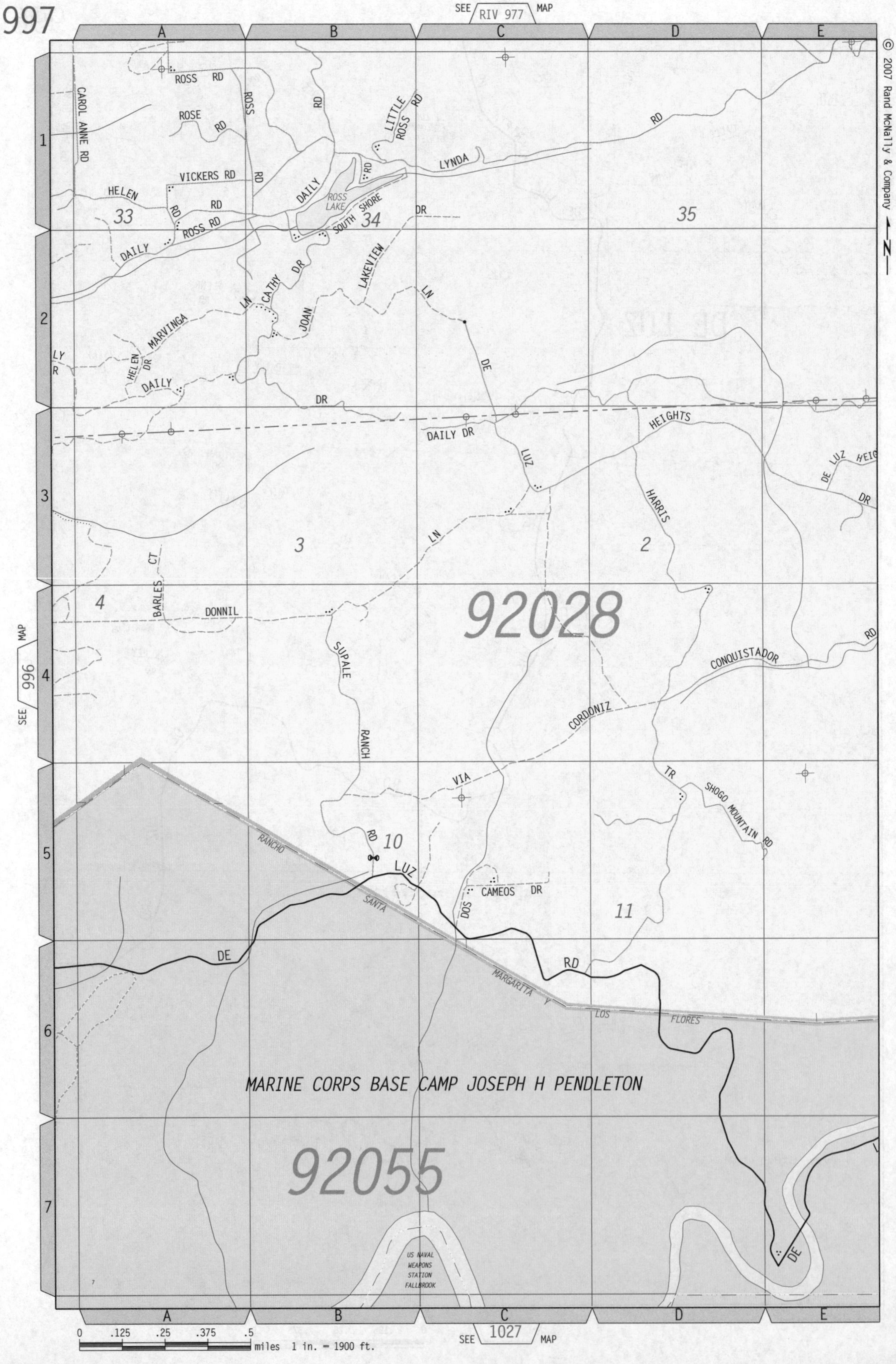
SEE RIV 977 MAP
SAN DIEGO CO.
A B C D E
1 2 3 4 5 6 7
ROSS RD
CAROL ANNE RD
ROSE RD
ROSS RD
RD
LITTLE ROSS RD
RD
LYNDA
VICKERS RD
HELEN RD
DAILY
ROSS LAKE
RD
33
RD
ROSS RD
SOUTH SHORE
34
DR
35
DAILY
CATHY DR
LAKEVIEW
LN
LN
JOAN
MARVINGA
HELEN DR
DE
DAILY
DR
DAILY DR
HEIGHTS
LUZ
DE LUZ HEIG
DR
HARRIS
3
LN
2
CT
4
BARLES
DONNIL
92028
RD
SUPALE
CONQUISTADOR
SEE 996 MAP
CORDONIZ
RANCH
TR
VIA
SHOGO MOUNTAIN RD
RANCHO
RD
10
LUZ
SANTA
CAMEOS DR
DOS
11
DE
RD
MARGARITA Y
LOS
FLORES
MARINE CORPS BASE CAMP JOSEPH H PENDLETON
92055
US NAVAL WEAPONS STATION FALLBROOK
DE
0 .125 .25 .375 .5 miles 1 in. = 1900 ft.
SEE 1027 MAP

SEE RIV 977 MAP

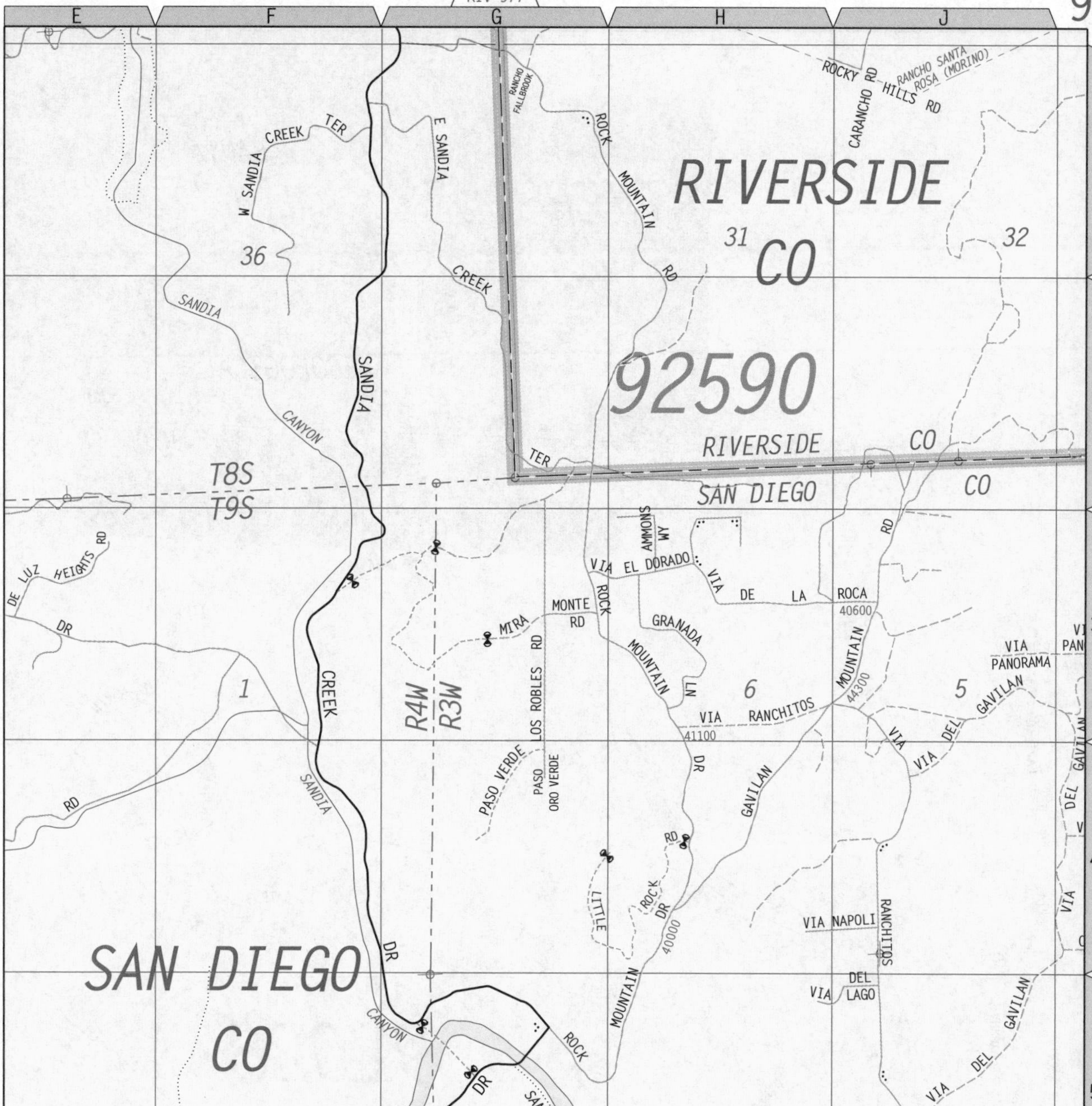

SEE 998 MAP

SEE 1027 MAP

0 .125 .25 .375 .5 miles 1 in. = 1900 ft.

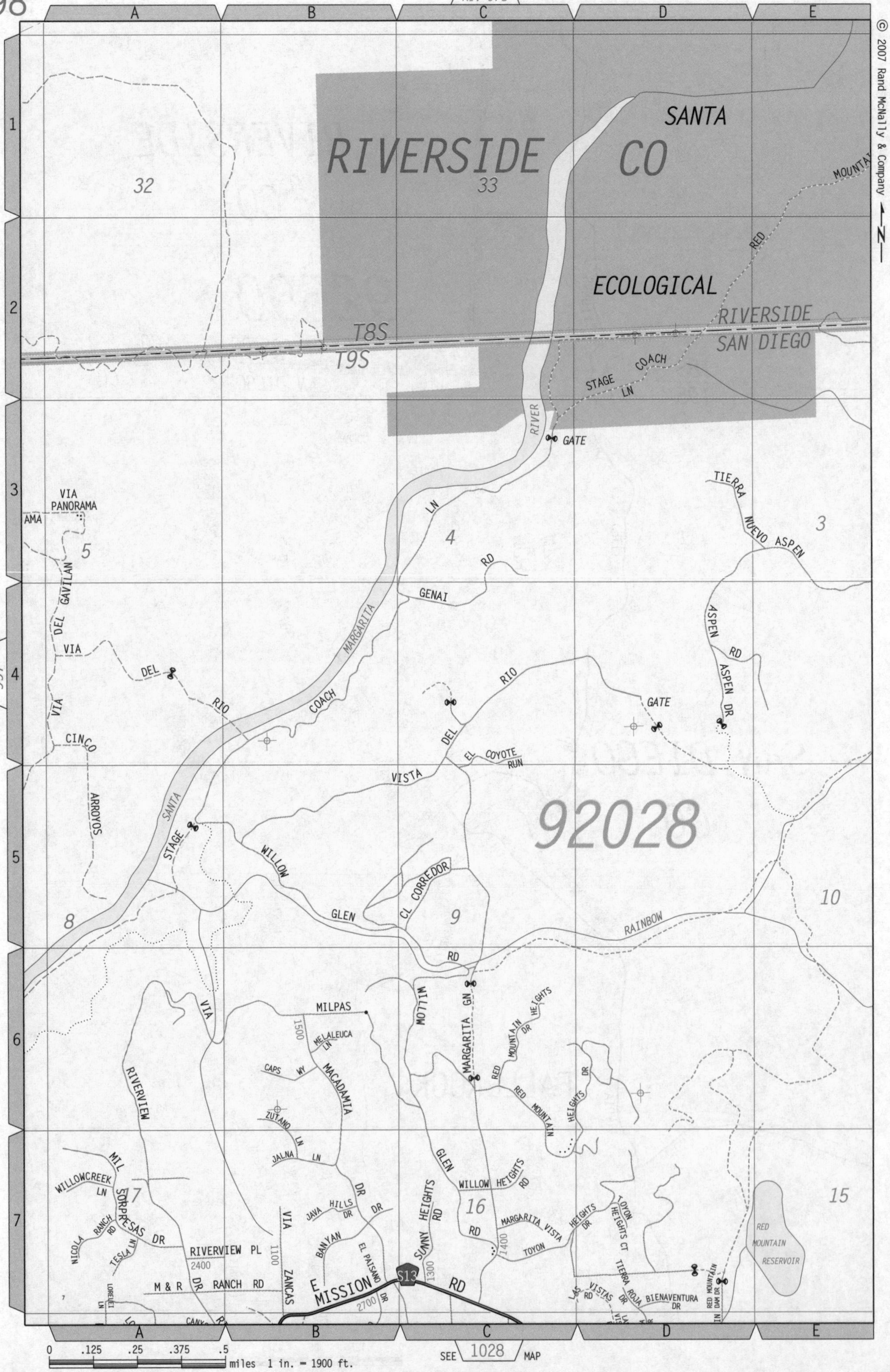
SEE RIV 978 MAP
SEE 997 MAP
SEE 1028 MAP
SAN DIEGO CO.
RIVERSIDE CO
SANTA
ECOLOGICAL
RIVERSIDE
SAN DIEGO
T8S
T9S
92028
STAGE COACH LN
GATE
RIVER
SANTA MARGARITA
VIA PANORAMA
VIA DEL GAVILAN
VIA DEL RIO
CINCO ARROYOS
GENAI RD
DEL RIO VISTA
EL COYOTE RUN
WILLOW GLEN RD
CL CORREDOR
RAINBOW
TIERRA NUEVO ASPEN
ASPEN RD
ASPEN DR
RED MOUNTAIN
MILPAS
MELALEUCA LN
CAPS WY
MACADAMIA DR
ZUTANO LN
JALNA LN
RIVERVIEW
MARGARITA GN
RED MOUNTAIN HEIGHTS DR
WILLOW HEIGHTS RD
MARGARITA VISTA RD
TOYON HEIGHTS DR
TOYON HEIGHTS CT
SUNNY HEIGHTS RD
JAVA HILLS DR
BANYAN DR
EL PAISANO DR
VIA ZANCAS
E MISSION RD
S13
RIVERVIEW PL
M & R RANCH RD
WILLOWCREEK LN
MIL SORPRESAS DR
NICOLA RANCH RD
TESLA LN
LAS VISTAS RD
TIERRA ROJA DR
BIENAVENTURA DR
RED MOUNTAIN DAM DR
RED MOUNTAIN RESERVOIR
32
33
3
4
5
8
9
10
15
16
17
1500
2400
1100
2700
1300
1400
A
B
C
D
E
1
2
3
4
5
6
7
0 .125 .25 .375 .5
miles 1 in. = 1900 ft.

SEE RIV 978 MAP

SEE 999 MAP

SEE 1028 MAP

0 .125 .25 .375 .5 miles 1 in. = 1900 ft.

SEE RIV 979 MAP

SEE 998 MAP

SEE 1029 MAP

0 .125 .25 .375 .5 miles 1 in. = 1900 ft.

SEE RIV 979 MAP

E F G H J

AVD DEL PAISANO
GARDNER DR
RANCHO VIEW DR
SHADY OAKS LN
PARK PL
DR
PINE CREST LN
HOMESTEAD LN
LOS ENCINOS DR
CAROL ANN LN
PALA RD
47000
LIVE OAK RANCH RD
47300
PINECREST ST
OAKS
33
S16
34
PECHANGA INDIAN RESERVATION
PALA CREEK
RAINBOW
47800
T8S
T9S
RIVERSIDE CO
SAN DIEGO CO
RAINBOW HEIGHTS DR
MAGEE RD
35900
11900
11700
MAGEE HEIGHTS RD
RANCHO HEIGHTS RD
RAINBOW RD
10235
CO
4
37100
11400
PALA
3
2
12400
TEMEPA RD
92028
38683
OAK HILLS LN
CREEK
TEMECULA RD
HIDDEN OAKS RD
LOST HORIZON DR
RANCHO HEIGHTS RD
9
10
11
S16
PALA
RD
41800
FARRA ST
16
ARUBA
92059
15
14
ARUBA RD

1 2 3 4 5 6 7

SEE 409 MAP

SEE 1029 MAP

0 .125 .25 .375 .5 miles 1 in. = 1900 ft.

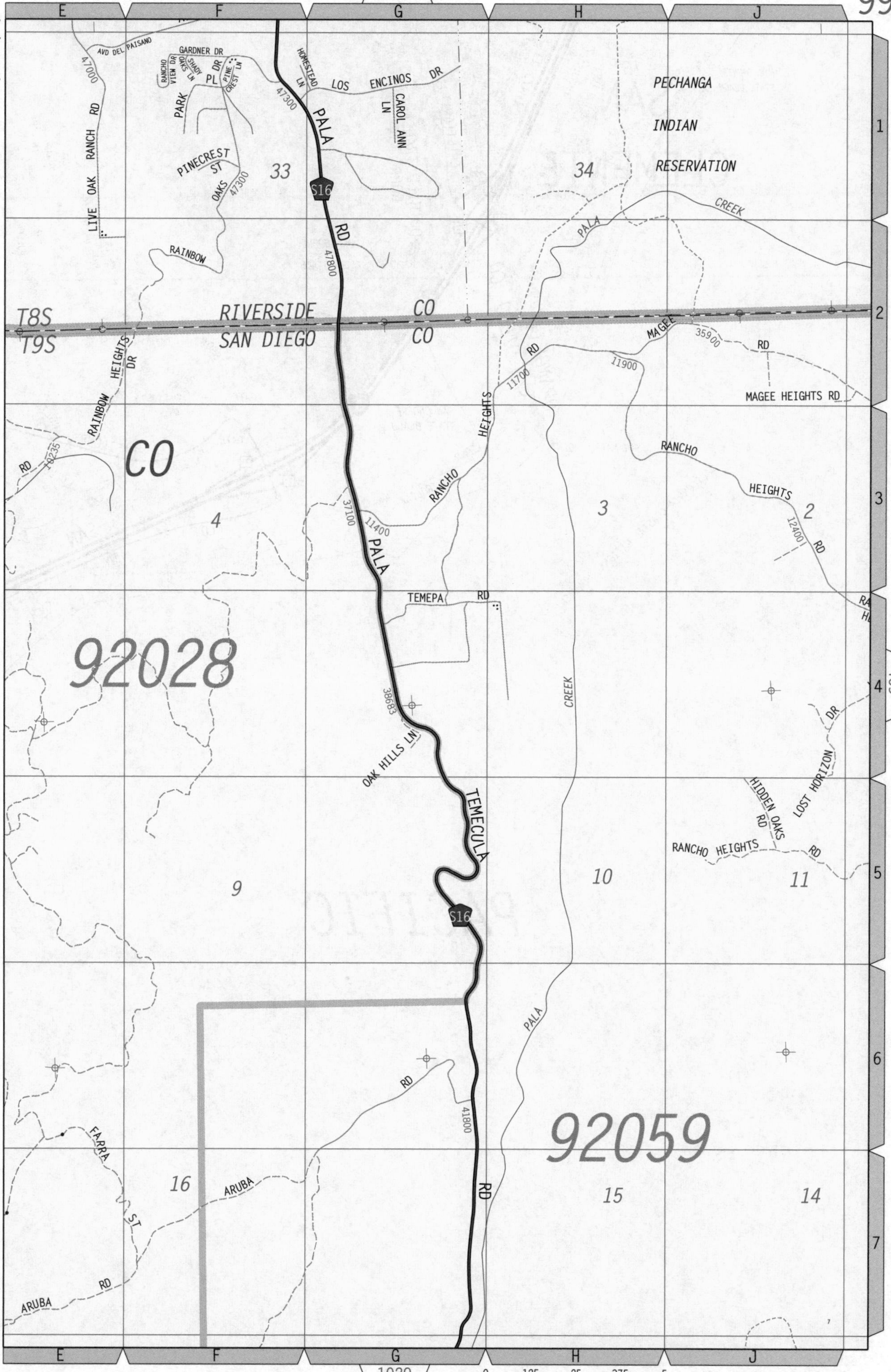

SEE ORG 993 MAP

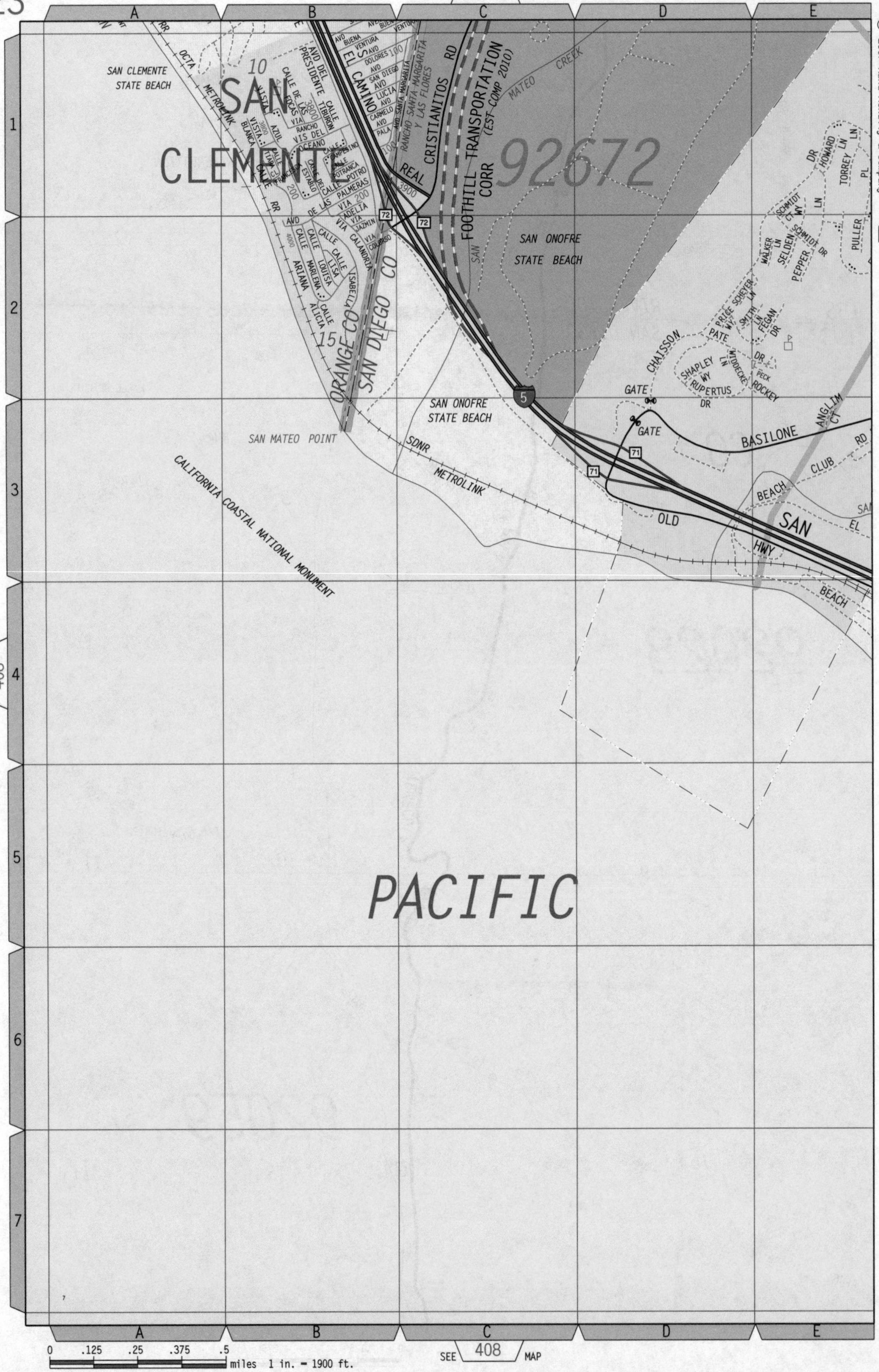

SEE 408 MAP

SEE 408 MAP

SEE ORG 993 MAP

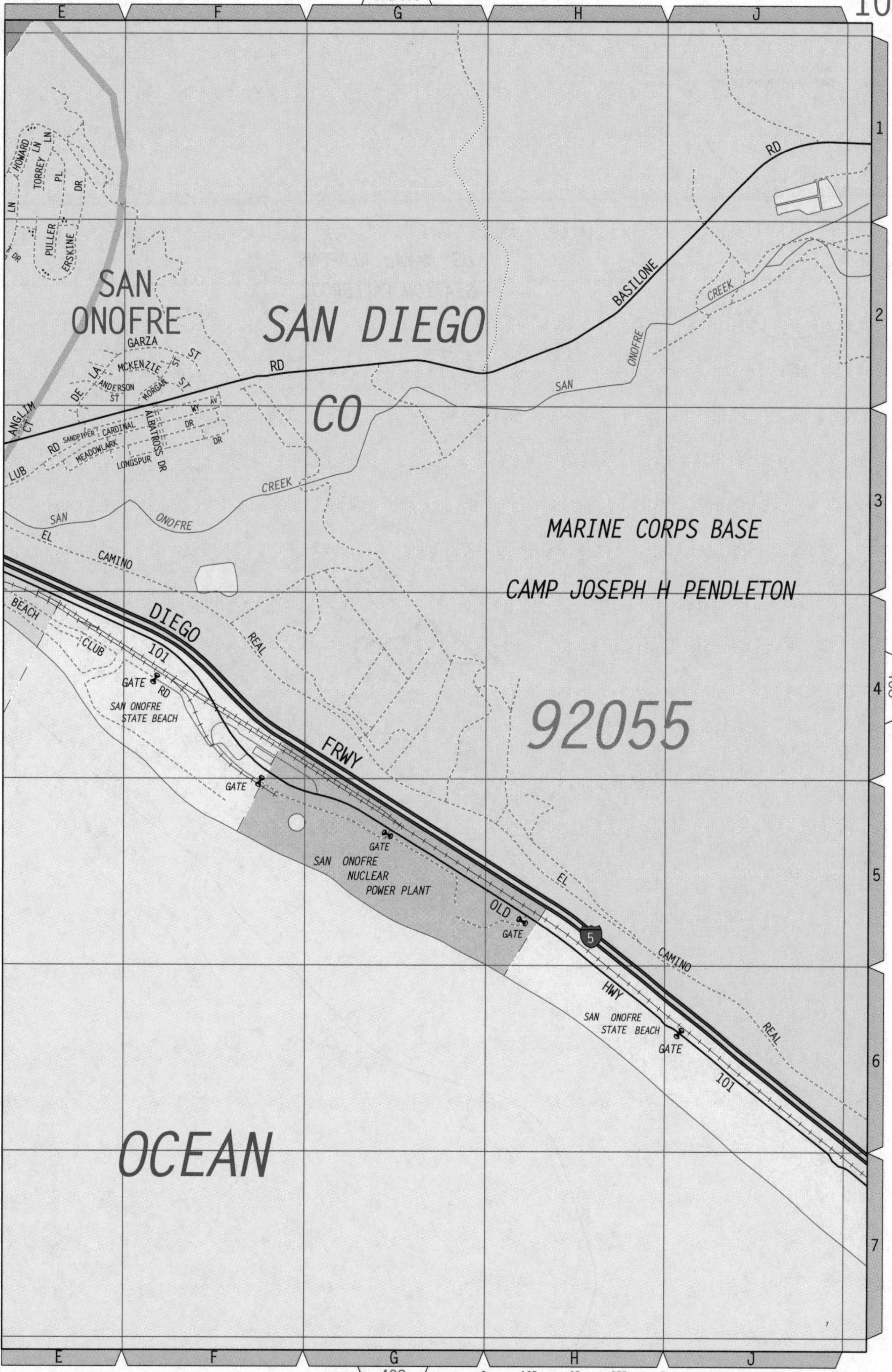

SAN DIEGO CO.

SEE 408 MAP

SEE 408 MAP

0 .125 .25 .375 .5 miles 1 in. = 1900 ft.

SEE 997 MAP

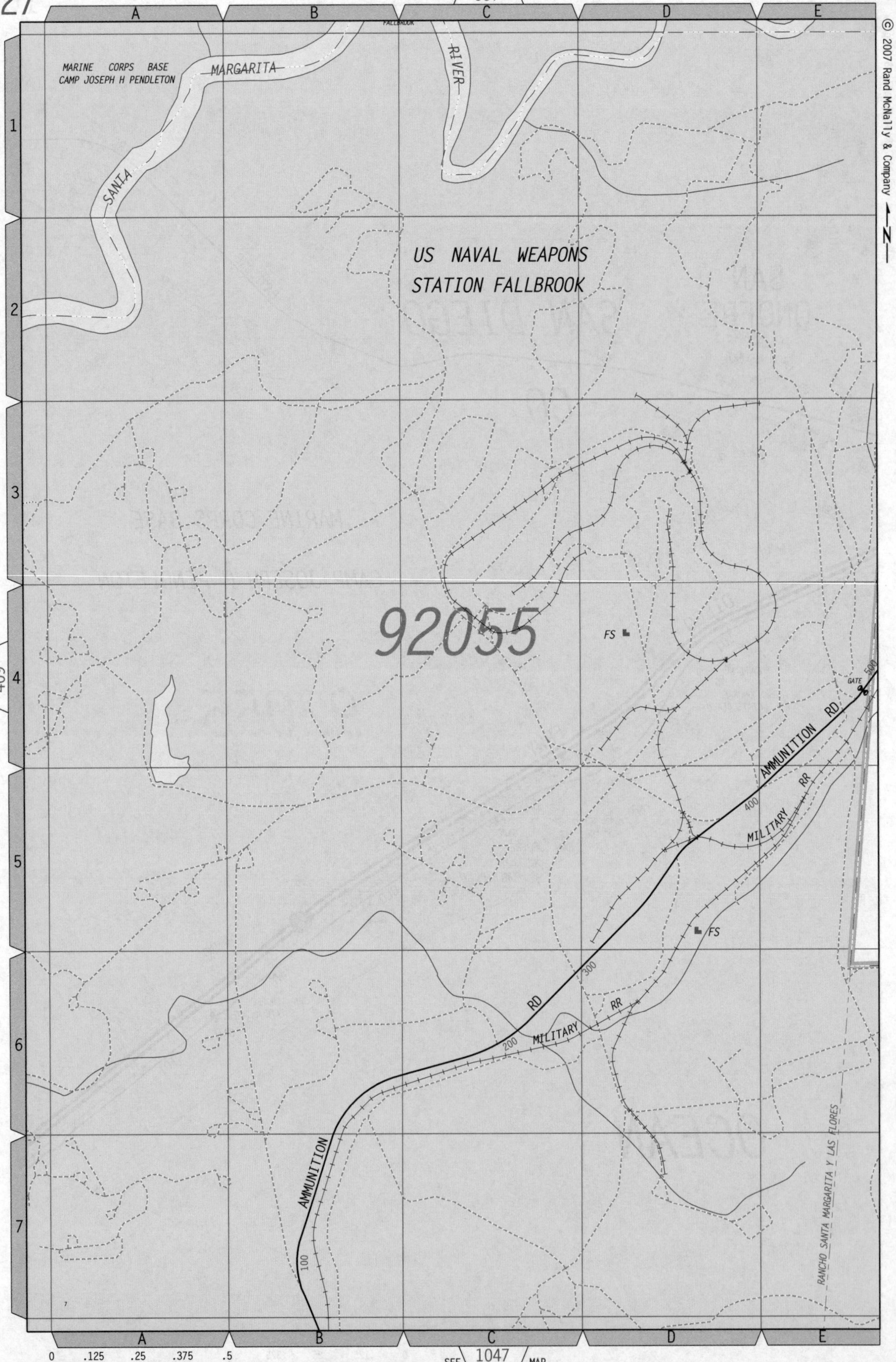

SEE 409 MAP

SEE 1047 MAP

0 .125 .25 .375 .5 miles 1 in. = 1900 ft.

SAN DIEGO CO.

SEE 997 MAP

SEE 1047 MAP

0 .125 .25 .375 .5 miles 1 in. = 1900 ft.

SAN DIEGO CO.

SEE 998 MAP

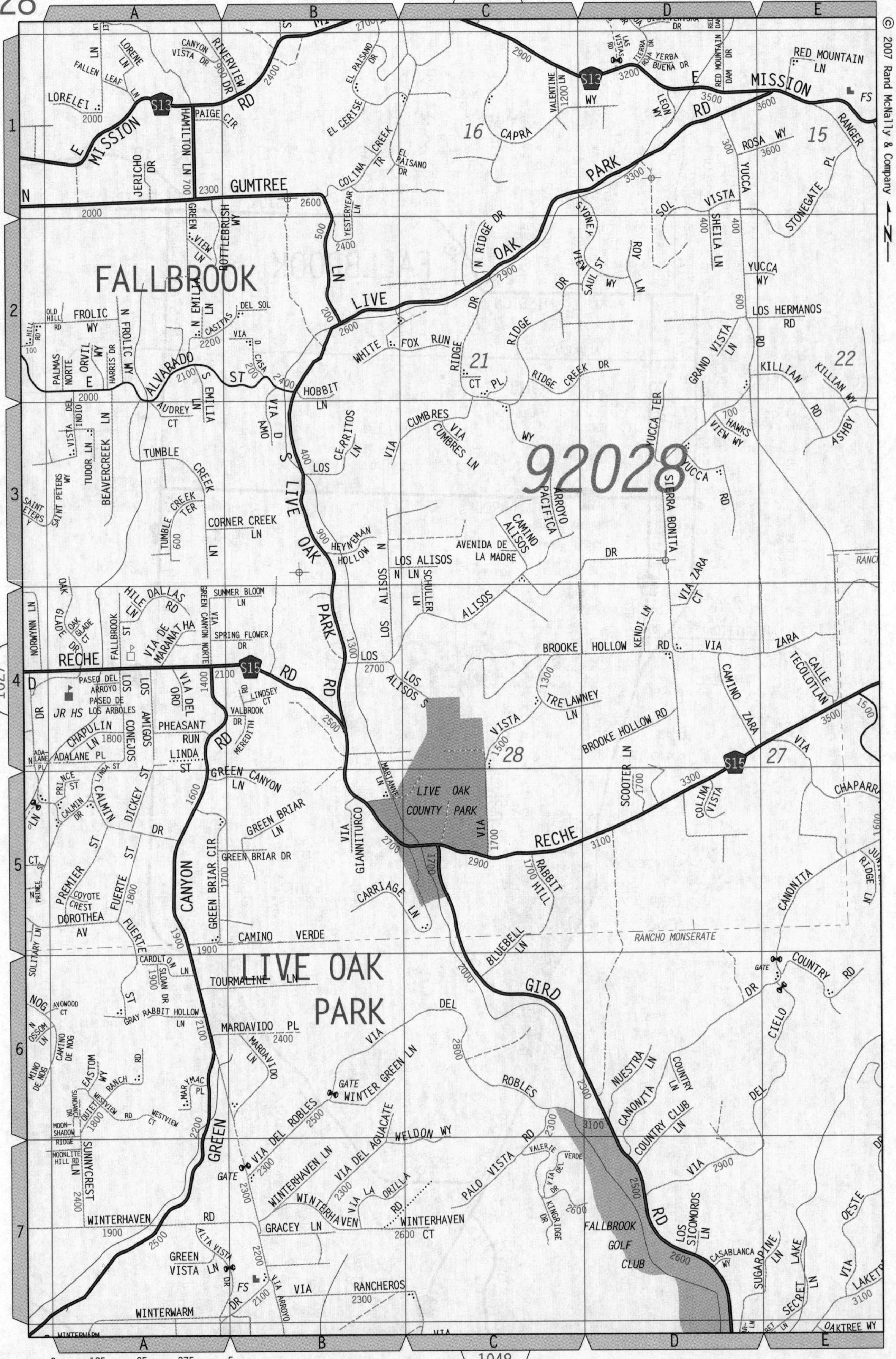

SEE 1027 MAP

SEE 1048 MAP

0 .125 .25 .375 .5 miles 1 in. = 1900 ft.

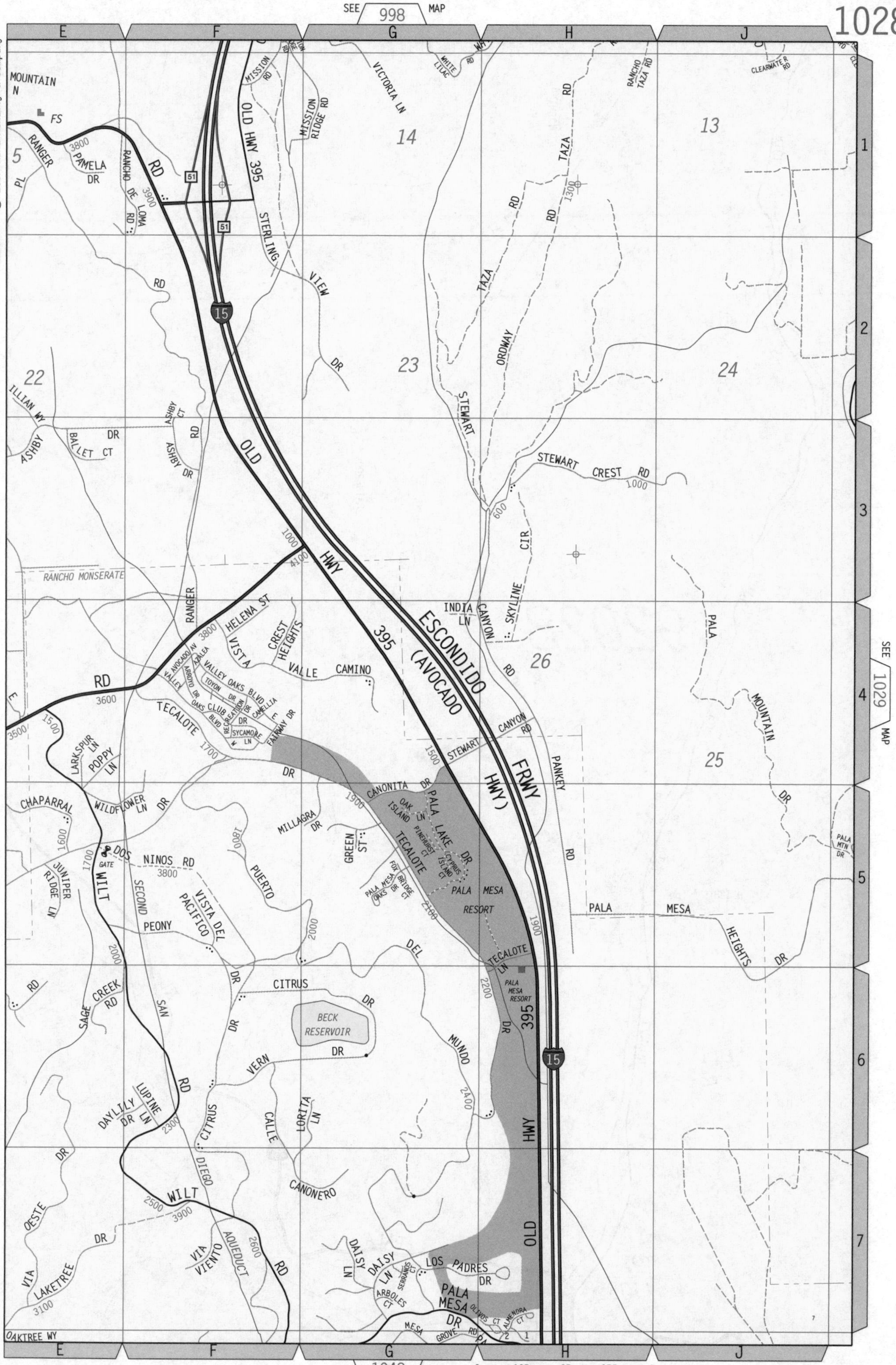
SEE 998 MAP
SEE 1029 MAP
SEE 1048 MAP
E
F
G
H
J
1
2
3
4
5
6
7
MOUNTAIN
FS
RANGER
PL
PAMELA
DR
RD
RANCHO DE LOMA RD
MISSION RD
OLD HWY 395
MISSION RIDGE RD
VICTORIA LN
WHITE LILAC RD
RANCHO TAZA RD
TAZA RD
CLEARWATER RD
STERLING VIEW DR
ORDWAY RD
STEWART
STEWART CREST RD
CIR
SKYLINE
INDIA LN
CANYON RD
ILLIAN WY
ASHBY
BALLET CT
ASHBY CT
ASHBY DR
OLD HWY
RANCHO MONSERATE
ESCONDIDO FRWY
(AVOCADO HWY)
HELENA ST
VISTA
CREST HEIGHTS
VALLE CAMINO
RANGER RD
AVOCADO AV
AZALEA
ARROYO DR
VALLEY OAKS BLVD
TOYON DR
CLUB
OAKS BLVD
RECREATION DR
CAMELLIA
SYCAMORE LN
FAIRWAY DR
TECALOTE DR
STEWART CANYON RD
PANKEY RD
PALA MOUNTAIN DR
PALA MTN DR
LARKSPUR LN
POPPY LN
CHAPARRAL
WILDFLOWER LN
DR
CANONITA DR
OAK ISLAND LN
PALA LAKE DR
PINEHURST CT
CYPRESS ISLAND CT
MILLAGRA DR
GREEN ST
TECALOTE
FOX BRIDGE CT
PALA MESA OAKS DR
PALA MESA RESORT
DOS NINOS RD
GATE
WILT
SECOND
JUNIPER RIDGE LN
PUERTO
VISTA DEL PACIFICO
PEONY
PALA MESA HEIGHTS DR
TECALOTE LN
DEL MUNDO DR
SAGE CREEK RD
CITRUS DR
BECK RESERVOIR
VERN DR
SAN DIEGO RD
LUPINE LN
DAYLILY DR
CALLE LORITA LN
CANONERO
WILT RD
OESTE DR
LAKETREE DR
VIA VIENTO
AQUEDUCT RD
DAISY LN
SERRANOS CT
ARBOLES CT
LOS PADRES DR
PALA MESA DR
OLIVOS CT
ALMENDRA CT
MESA GROVE RD
OAKTREE WY
VIA
14
13
22
23
24
26
25
5
51
15
395
3800
3900
1300
1000
600
1500
1700
3600
3500
1900
1800
1600
2000
2100
2200
2300
2400
2500
2600
3100
0 .125 .25 .375 .5
miles 1 in. = 1900 ft.

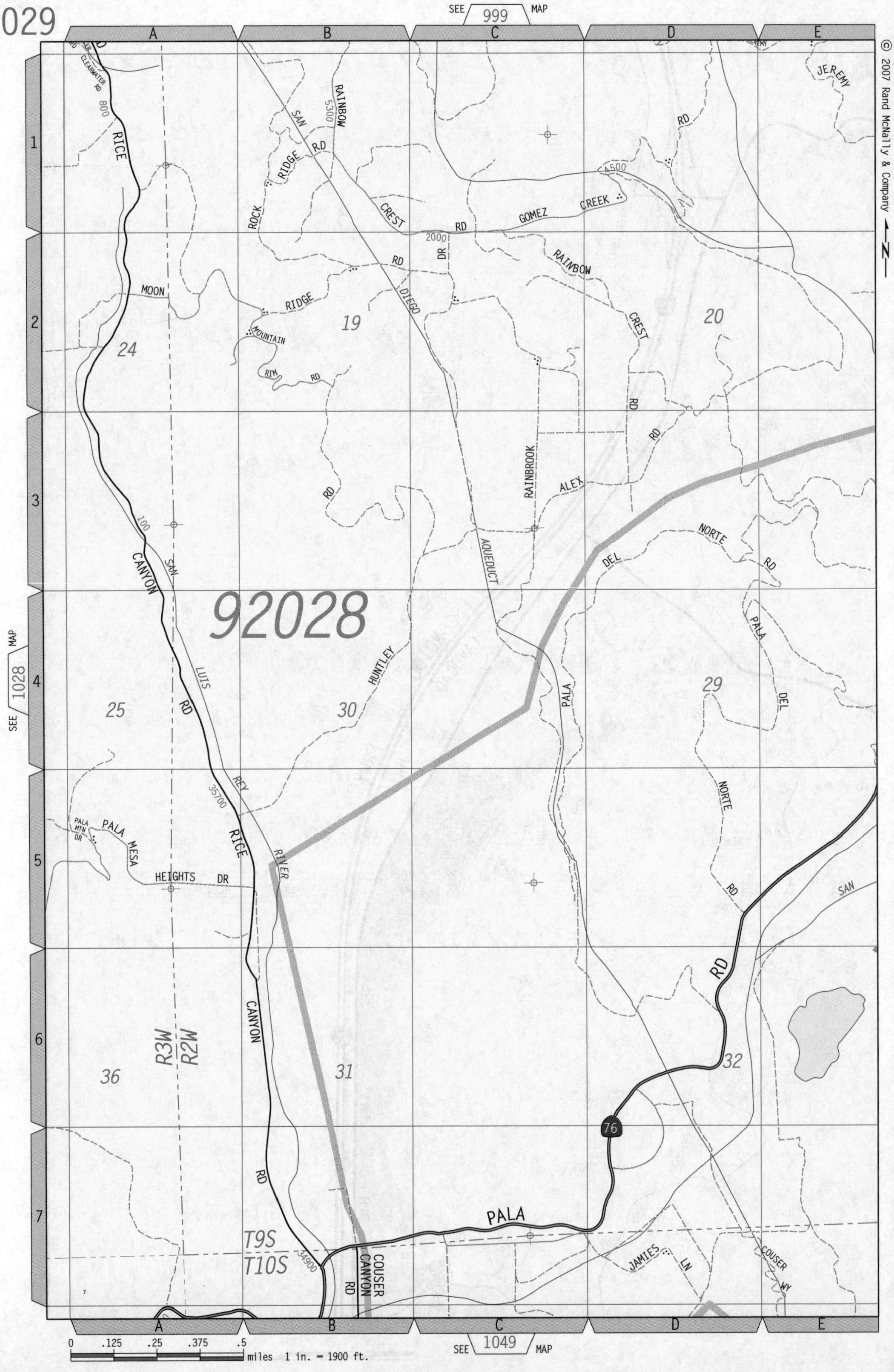
SEE 999 MAP
SEE 1028 MAP
SEE 1049 MAP
SAN DIEGO CO.
A
B
C
D
E
1
2
3
4
5
6
7
92028
CLEARWATER RD
RICE CANYON RD
SAN LUIS REY RIVER
RAINBOW CREST RD
ROCK RIDGE RD
MOON RIDGE RD
MOUNTAIN RIM RD
GOMEZ CREEK RD
DR
SAN DIEGO AQUEDUCT
RAINBROOK RD
ALEX RD
DEL NORTE RD
PALA DEL NORTE RD
PALA RD
HUNTLEY RD
PALA MESA HEIGHTS DR
PALA MTN DR
JEREMY
JAMIES LN
COUSER CANYON RD
COUSER WY
SAN
76
R3W
R2W
T9S
T10S
19
20
24
25
29
30
31
32
36
800
100
5300
4500
2000
35700
34900
0
.125
.25
.375
.5
miles 1 in. = 1900 ft.

SEE 999 MAP

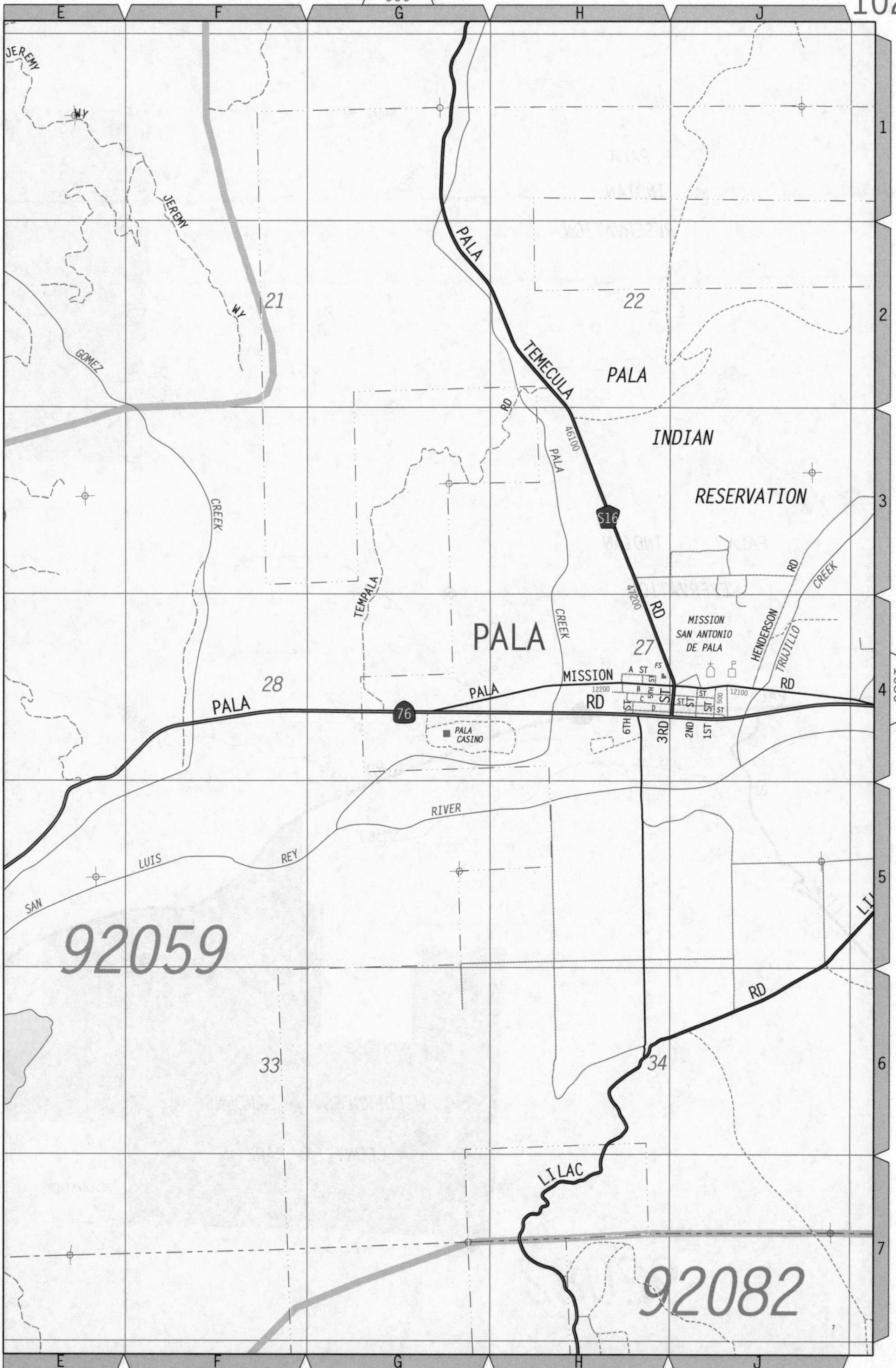

SEE 1030 MAP

SEE 1049 MAP

0 .125 .25 .375 .5 miles 1 in. = 1900 ft.

N

SEE 409 MAP

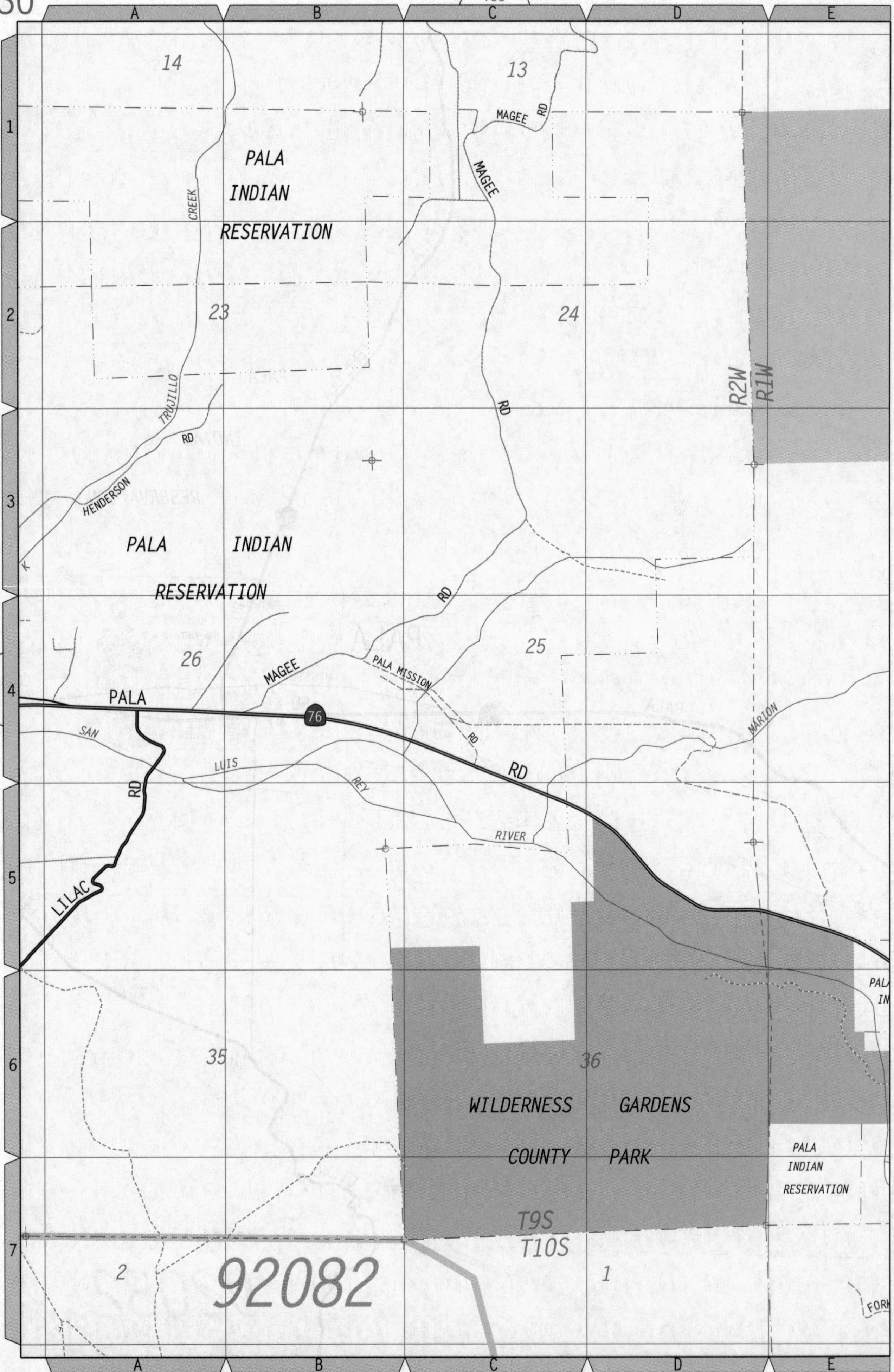

SEE 1029 MAP

SEE 1050 MAP

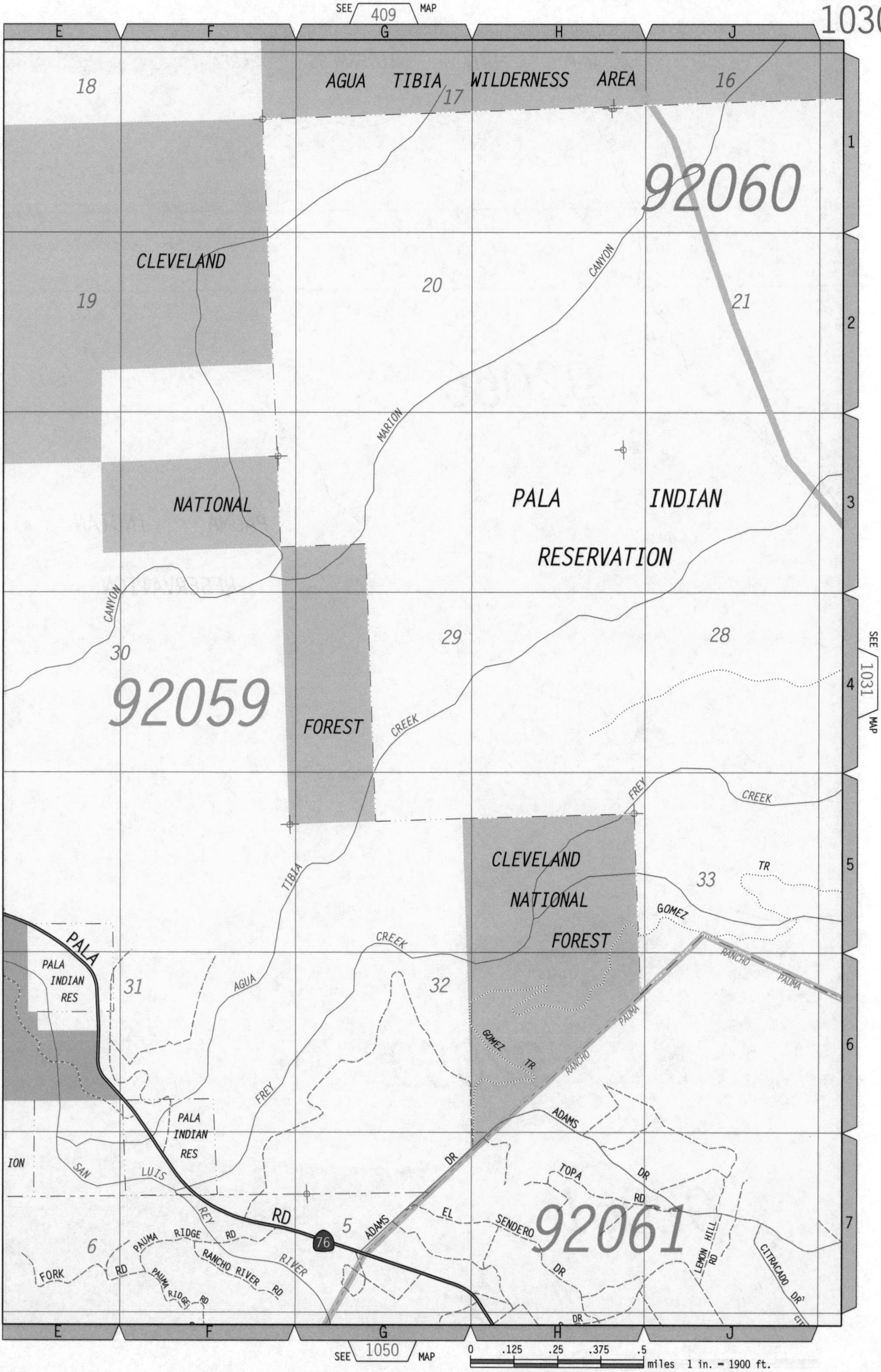
SEE 409 MAP
SEE 1031 MAP
SEE 1050 MAP
AGUA TIBIA WILDERNESS AREA
92060
92059
92061
CLEVELAND NATIONAL FOREST
PALA INDIAN RESERVATION
CLEVELAND NATIONAL FOREST
PALA INDIAN RES
PALA INDIAN RES
MARION CANYON
AGUA TIBIA CREEK
FREY CREEK
GOMEZ TR
GOMEZ CREEK
RANCHO PAUMA
PALA RD
SAN LUIS REY RIVER
76
ADAMS DR
EL SENDERO DR
TOPA DR
LEMON HILL RD
CITRACADO DR
PAUMA RIDGE RD
RANCHO RIVER RD
FORK RD
0 .125 .25 .375 .5 miles 1 in. = 1900 ft.

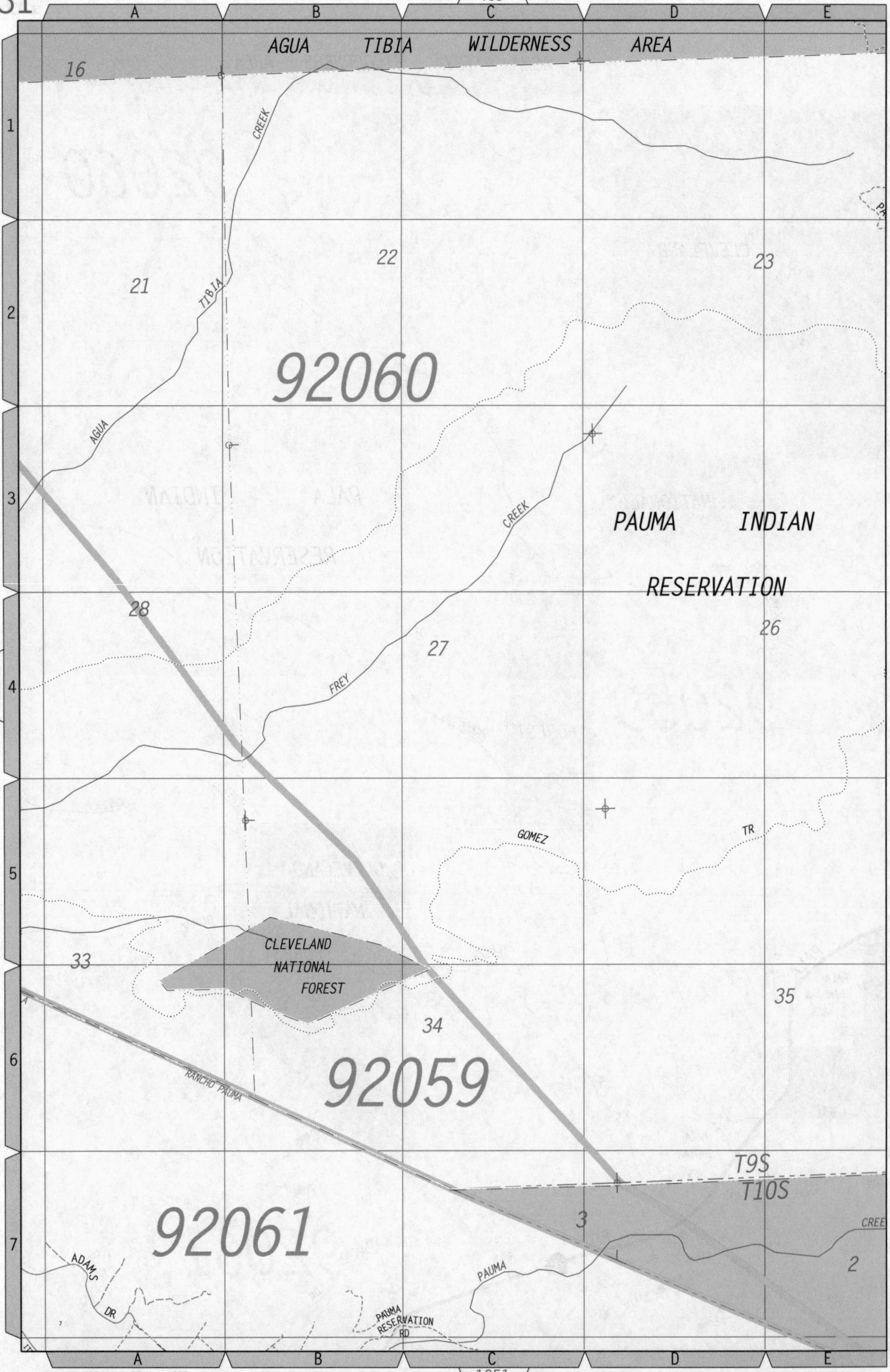
SEE 409 MAP
A
B
C
D
E
AGUA TIBIA WILDERNESS AREA
16
1
CREEK
TIBIA
AGUA
21
22
23
2
92060
3
CREEK
PAUMA INDIAN
RESERVATION
28
26
27
FREY
4
SEE 1030 MAP
GOMEZ
TR
5
CLEVELAND
NATIONAL
FOREST
33
34
35
6
RANCHO PAUMA
92059
T9S
T10S
3
92061
CREE
2
7
ADAMS
DR
PAUMA
PAUMA
RESERVATION
RD
SEE 1051 MAP
0 .125 .25 .375 .5 miles 1 in. = 1900 ft.

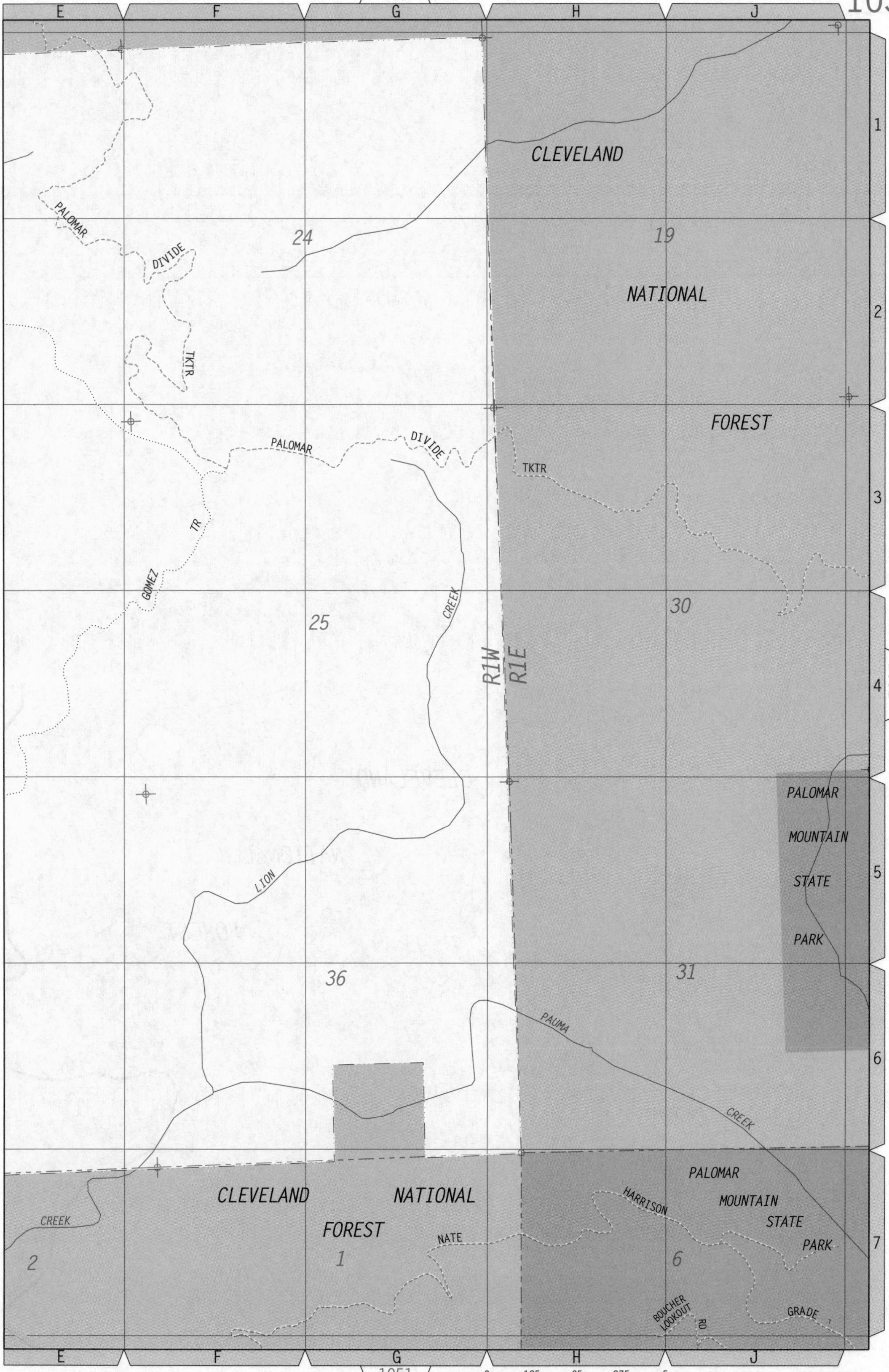
SEE 409 MAP
E
F
G
H
J
1
2
3
4
5
6
7
CLEVELAND
NATIONAL
FOREST
19
24
PALOMAR
DIVIDE
TKTR
PALOMAR
DIVIDE
TKTR
GOMEZ
TR
CREEK
25
30
R1W
R1E
SEE 1032 MAP
PALOMAR
MOUNTAIN
STATE
PARK
LION
36
31
PAUMA
CREEK
CLEVELAND
NATIONAL
FOREST
CREEK
2
1
NATE
HARRISON
PALOMAR
MOUNTAIN
STATE
PARK
6
BOUCHER
LOOKOUT
RD
GRADE
SEE 1051 MAP
0
.125
.25
.375
.5
miles 1 in. = 1900 ft.

SEE 409 MAP

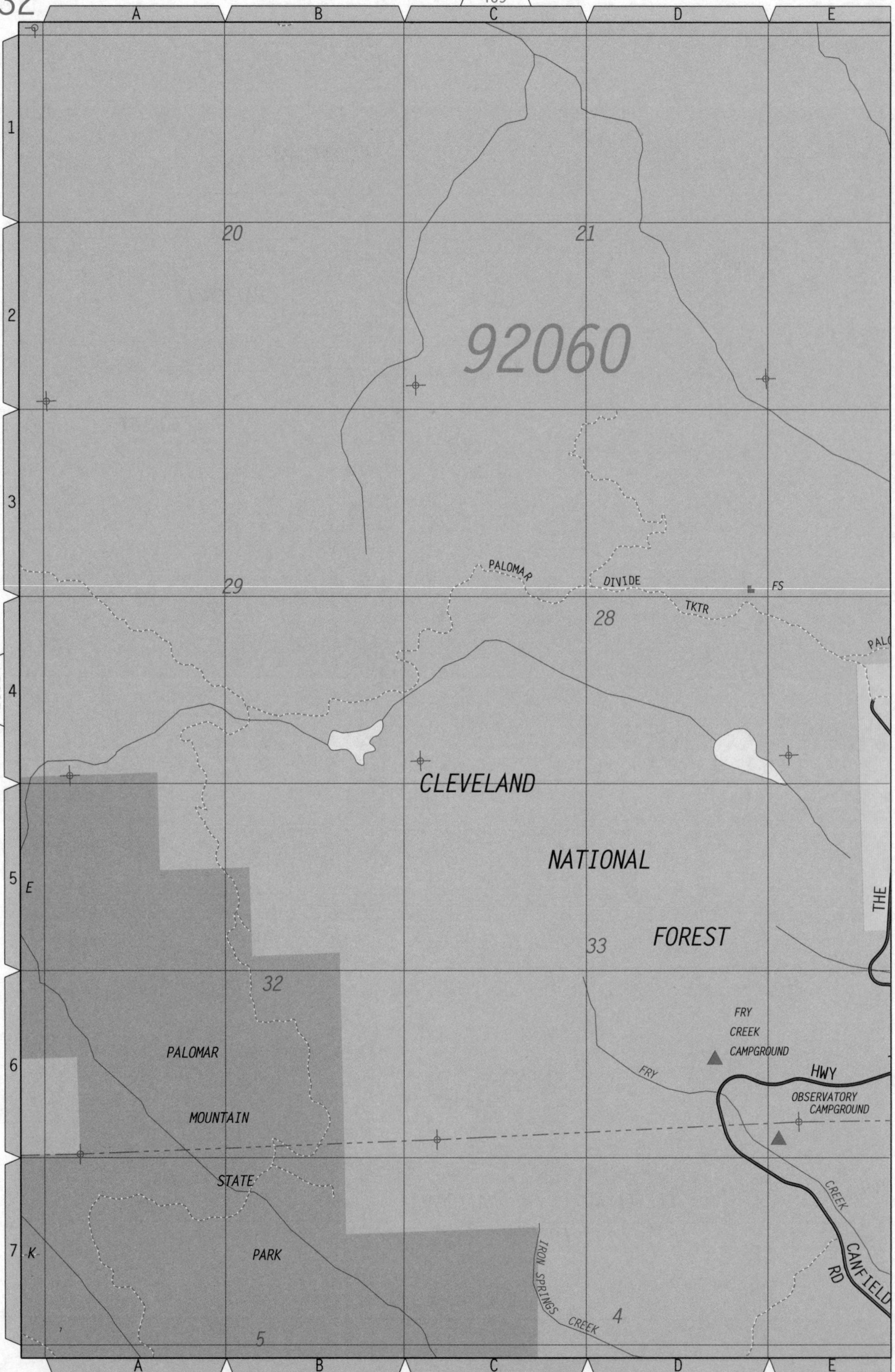

SEE 1031 MAP

SEE 1052 MAP

0 .125 .25 .375 .5 miles 1 in. = 1900 ft.

SEE 409 MAP

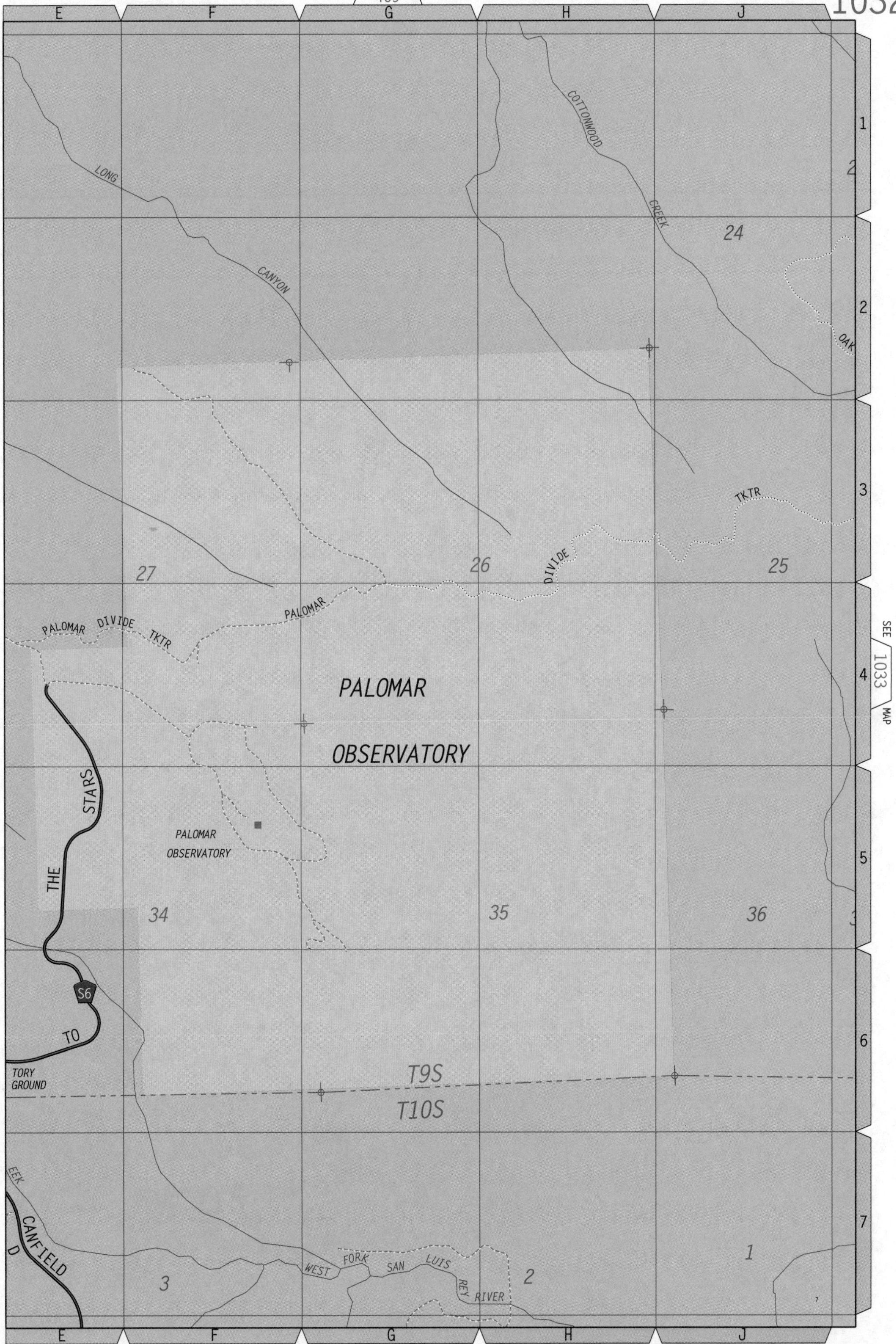

SEE 1033 MAP

SEE 1052 MAP

0 .125 .25 .375 .5 miles 1 in. = 1900 ft.

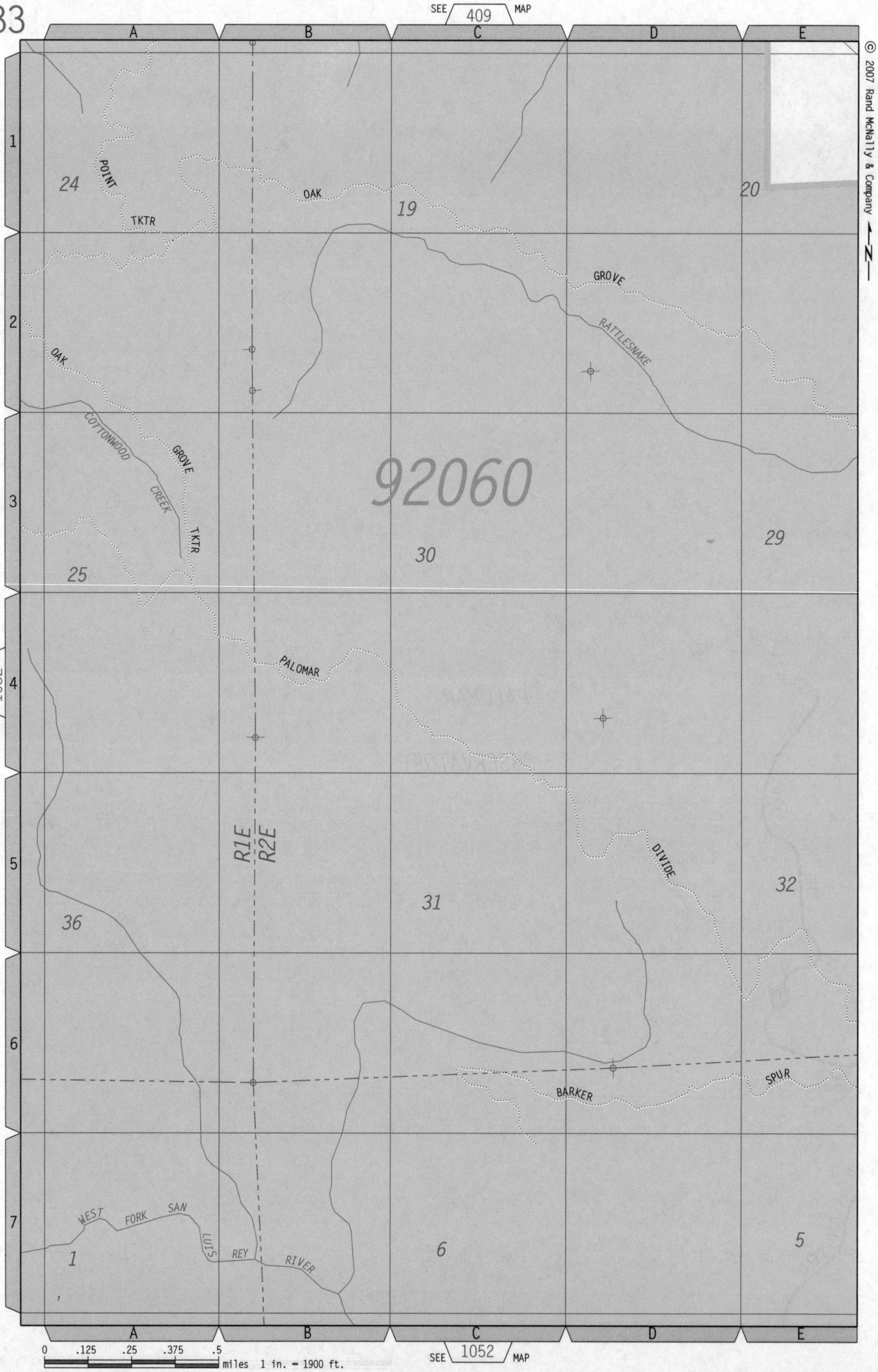
SEE 409 MAP
A
B
C
D
E
1
2
3
4
5
6
7
SAN DIEGO CO.
© 2007 Rand McNally & Company
N
SEE 1032 MAP
POINT
TKTR
OAK
GROVE
RATTLESNAKE
COTTONWOOD
CREEK
PALOMAR
DIVIDE
BARKER
SPUR
WEST FORK SAN LUIS REY RIVER
92060
24
19
20
25
30
29
36
31
32
1
6
5
R1E
R2E
0 .125 .25 .375 .5 miles 1 in. = 1900 ft.
SEE 1052 MAP

SEE 409 MAP

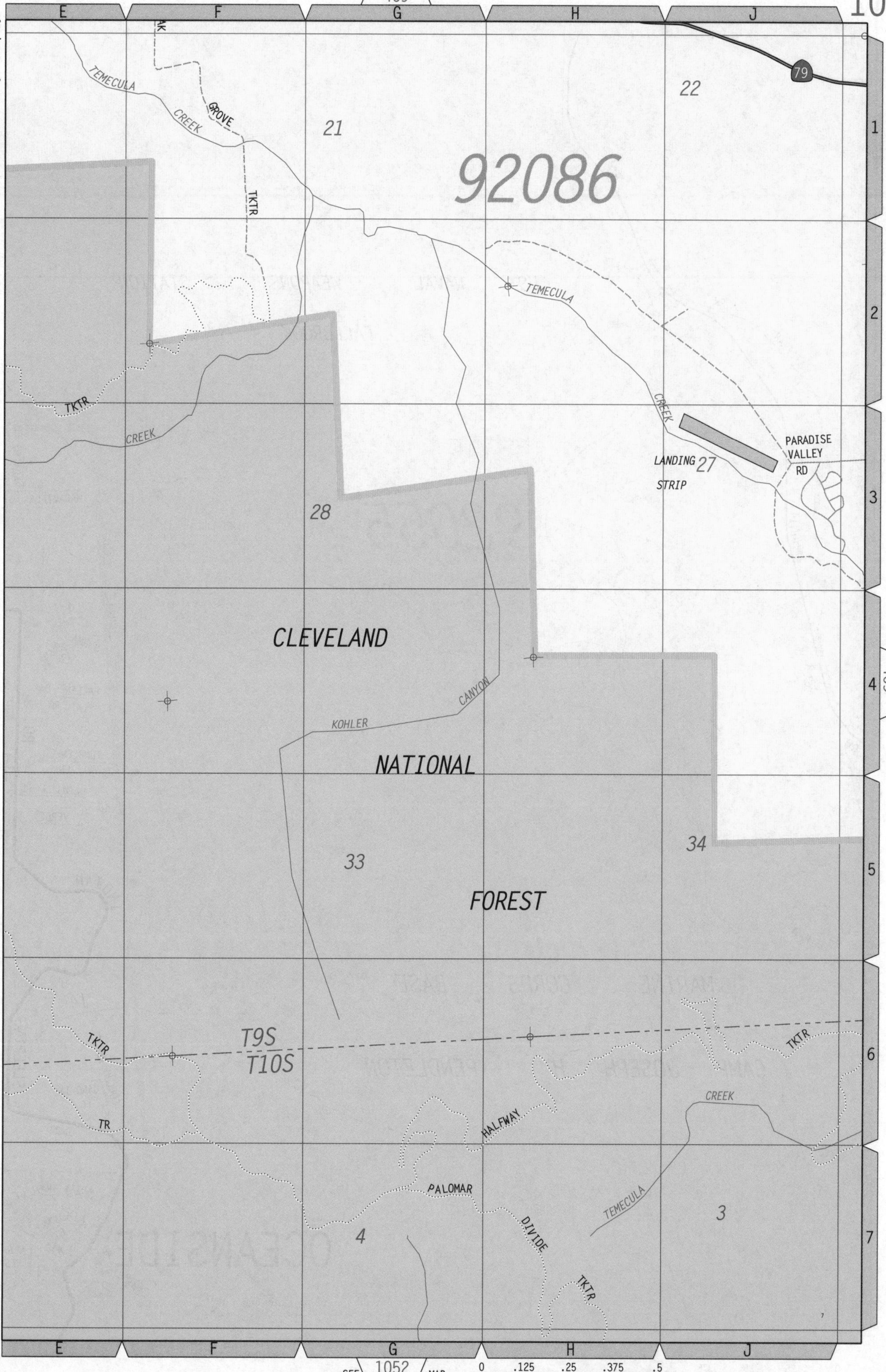

SEE 409 MAP

SEE 1052 MAP

0 .125 .25 .375 .5 miles 1 in. = 1900 ft.

SEE 1027 MAP

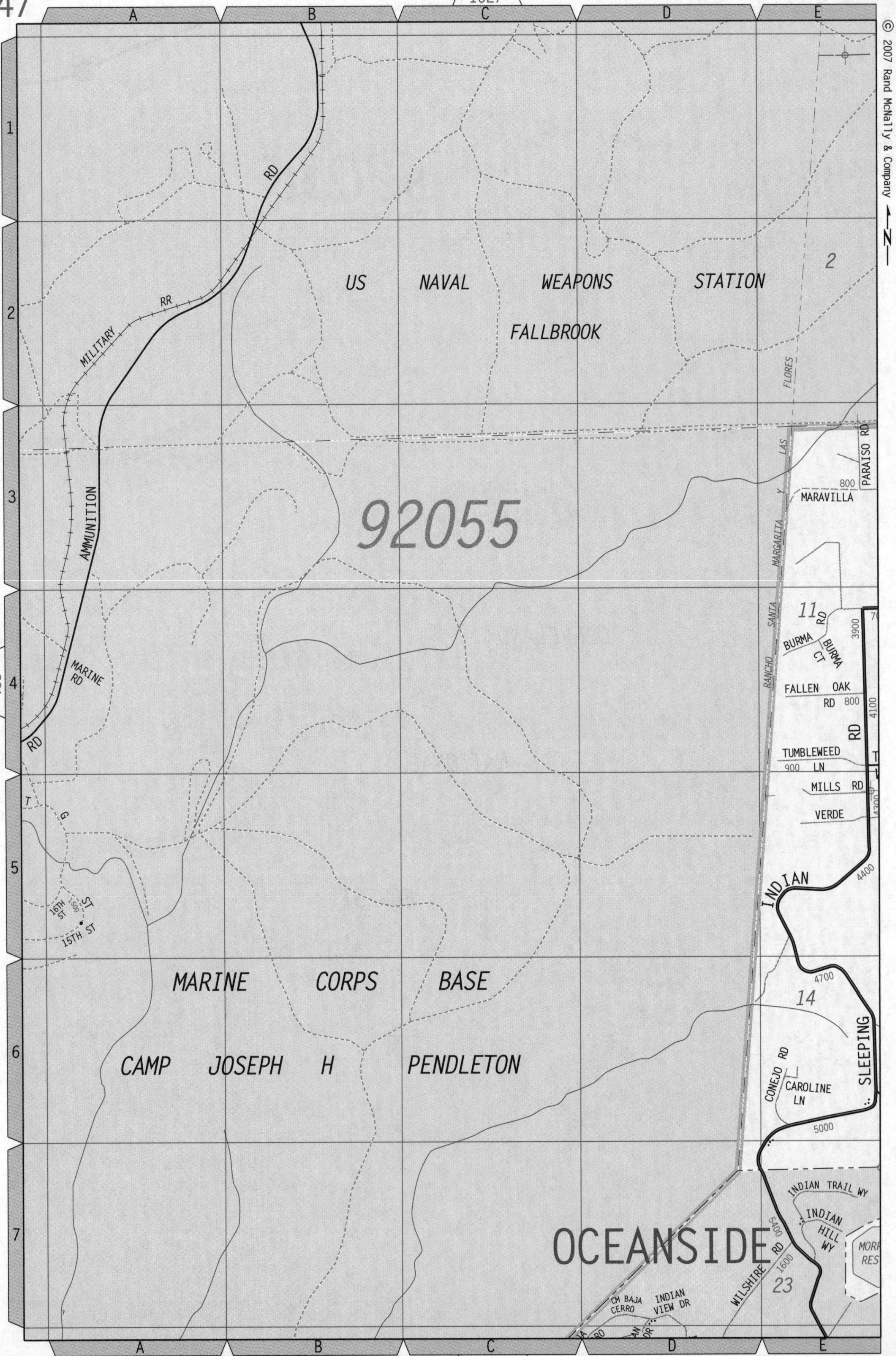

SEE 409 MAP

SEE 1067 MAP

0 .125 .25 .375 .5 miles 1 in. = 1900 ft.

SEE 1027 MAP

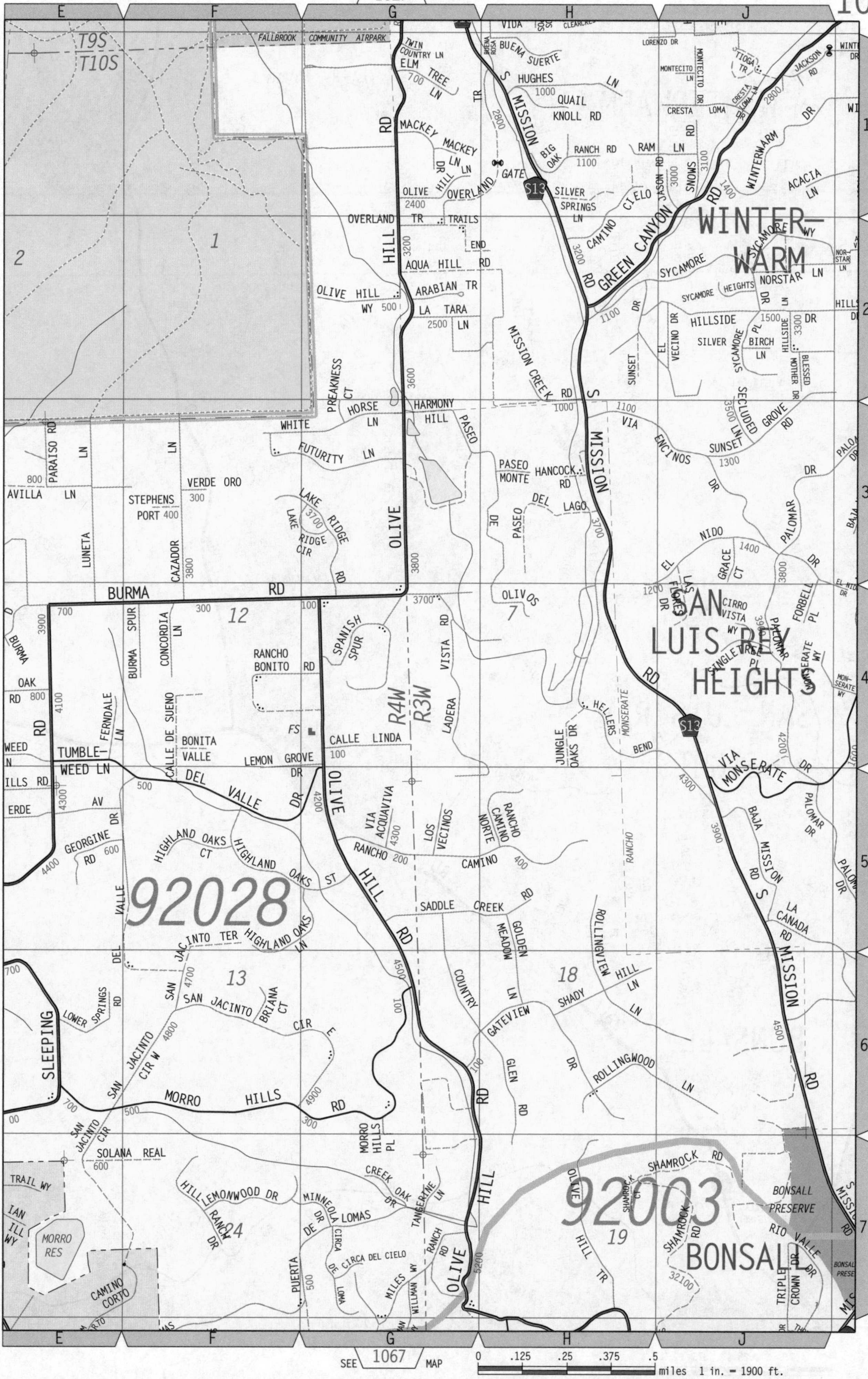

SEE 1048 MAP

SEE 1067 MAP

SEE 1028 MAP

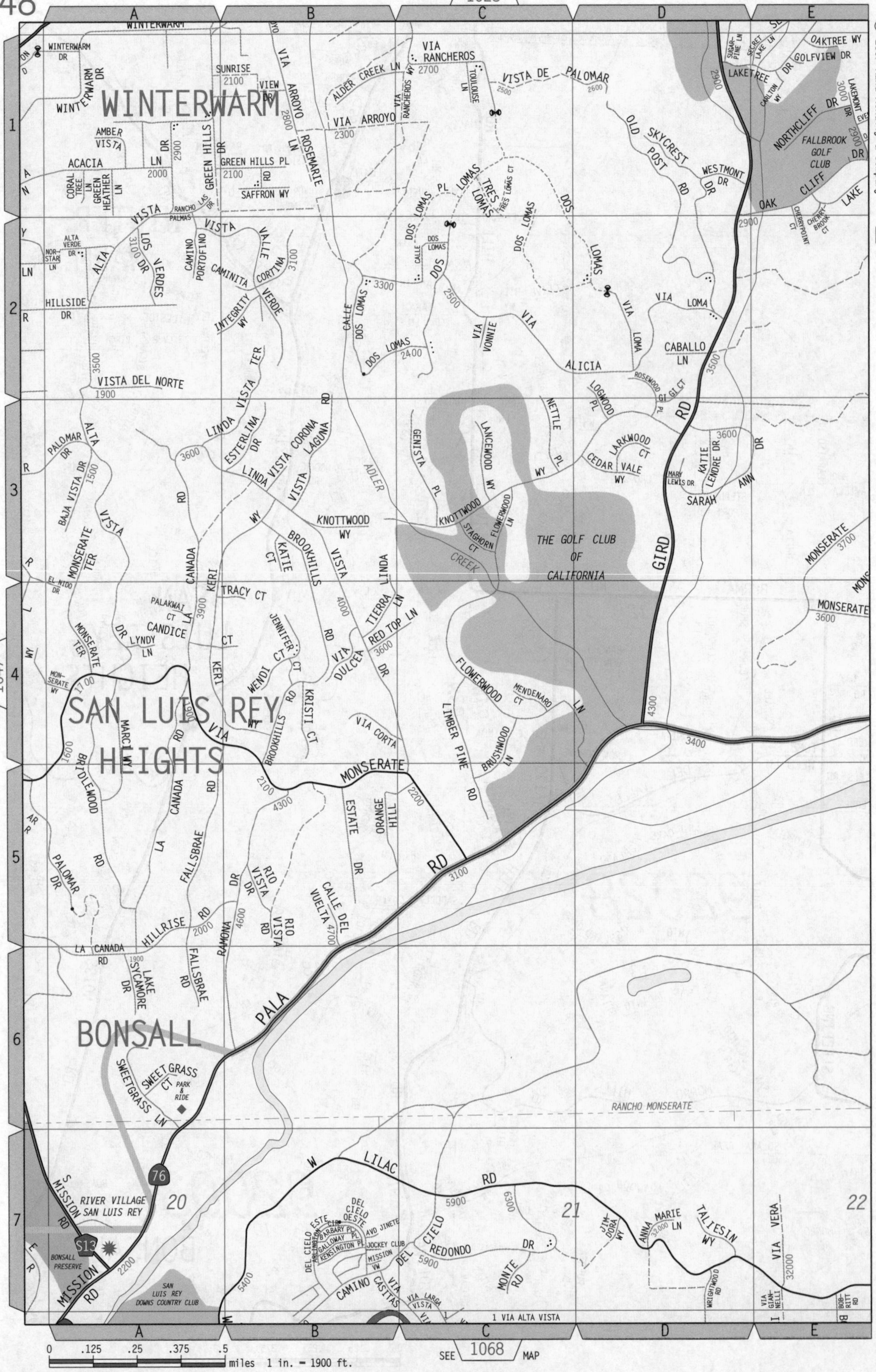

SEE 1047 MAP

SEE 1068 MAP

0 .125 .25 .375 .5 miles 1 in. = 1900 ft.

SEE 1028 MAP

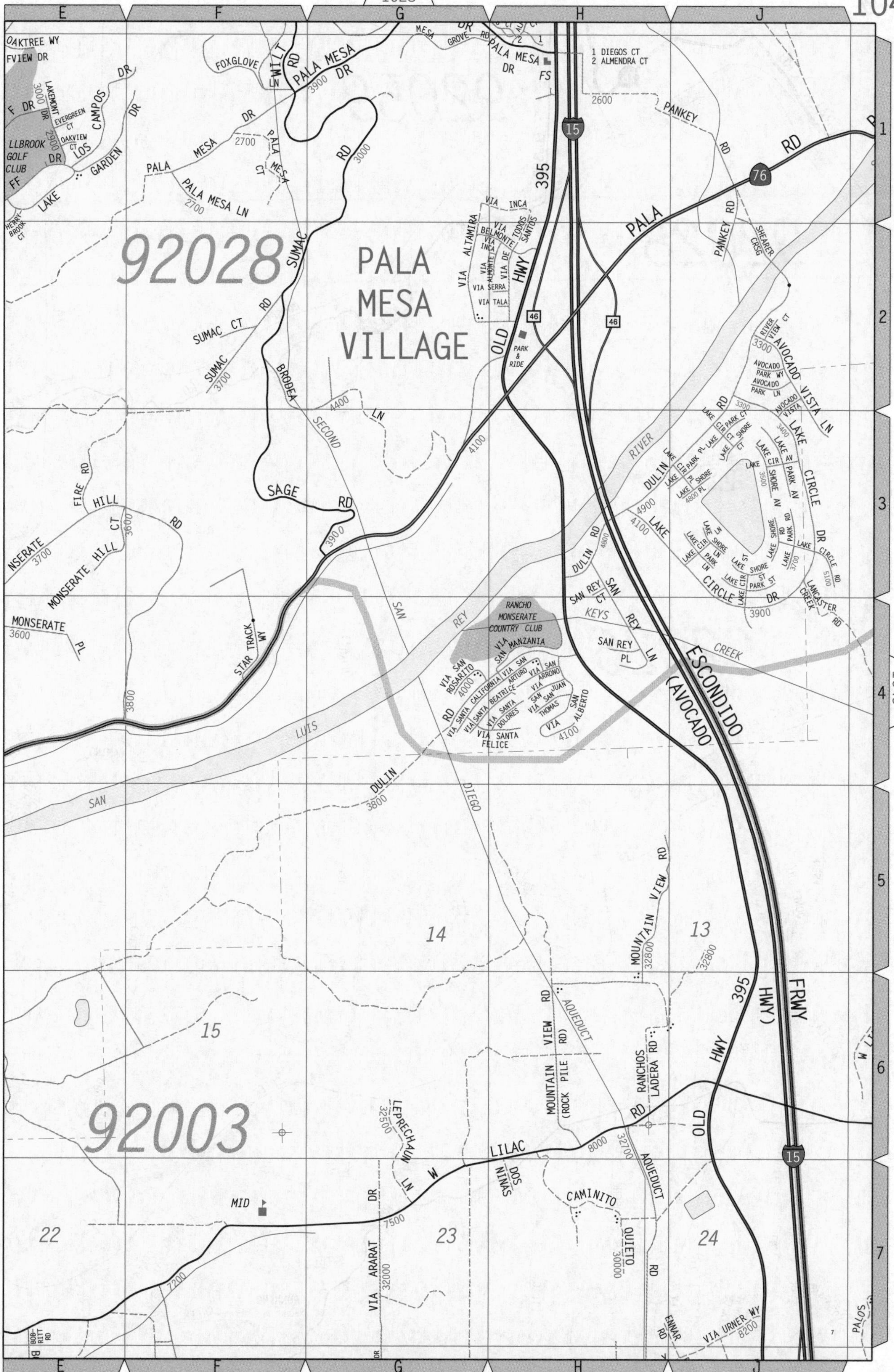

SEE 1068 MAP

0 .125 .25 .375 .5 miles 1 in. = 1900 ft.

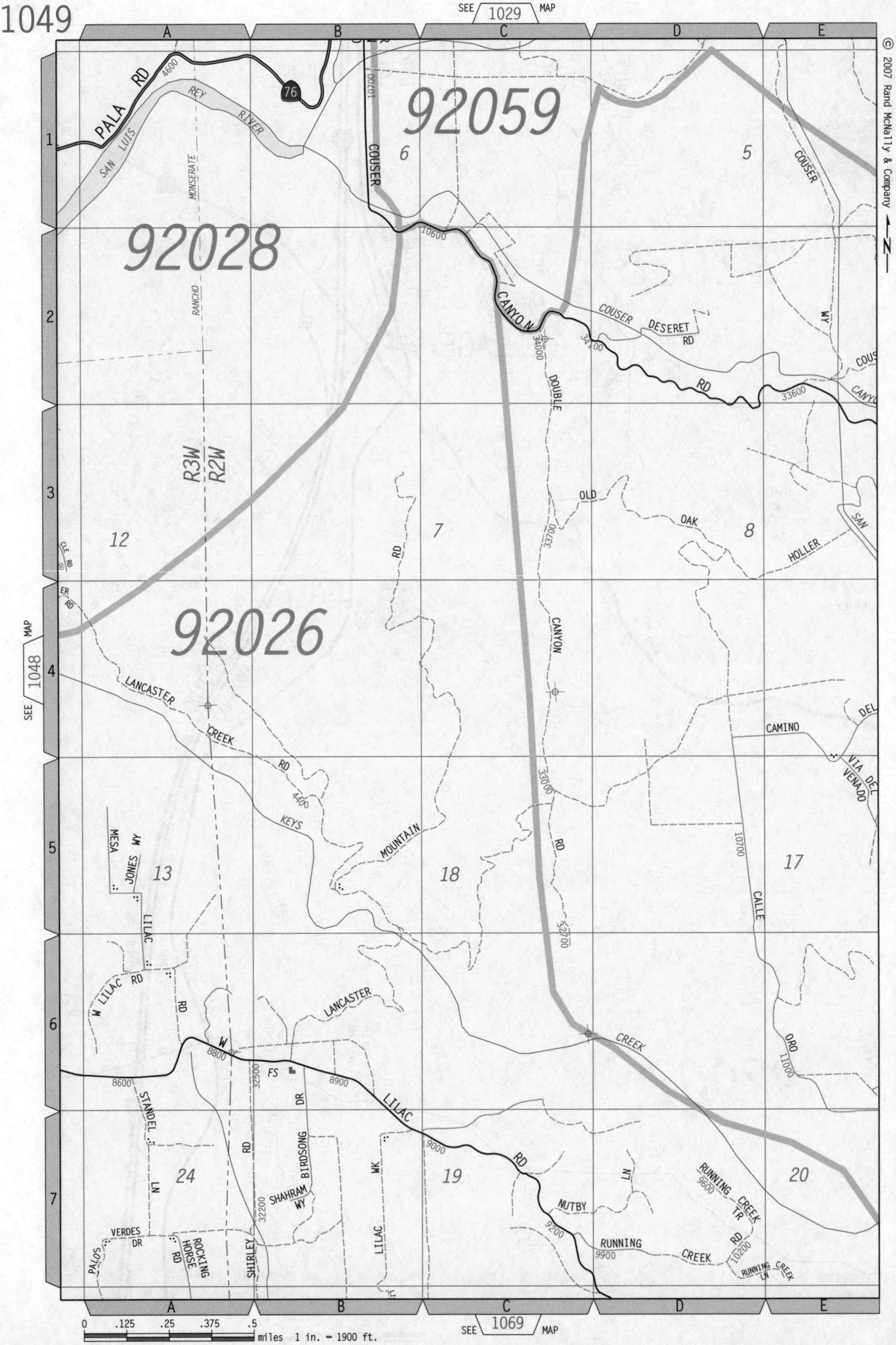
SEE 1029 MAP
A
B
C
D
E
PALA RD
4600
76
SAN LUIS REY RIVER
10700
92059
92028
COUSER
6
5
COUSER WY
MONSERATE
10600
RANCHO
CANYON N
COUSER
DESERET RD
34000
34100
DOUBLE
RD
33600
COUS
CANYO
R3W
R2W
12
7
OLD
OAK
8
HOLLER
SAN
33700
92026
CANYON
SEE 1048 MAP
LANCASTER
CREEK
RD
4400
KEYS
33000
CAMINO
DEL
VIA DEL VENADO
MOUNTAIN
RD
MESA
JONES WY
13
18
10700
17
LILAC
CALLE
32700
W LILAC RD
RD
LANCASTER
CREEK
ORO
11000
W
8800
8600
32500
FS
8900
STANDEL
DR
LILAC
BIRDSONG
RD
9000
RD
WK
19
20
24
LN
SHAHRAM WY
32200
RUNNING CREEK TR
9600
LN
NUTBY
9200
VERDES DR
ROCKING HORSE RD
PALOS
SHIRLEY
LILAC
RUNNING
9900
CREEK
RD
10200
RUNNING CREEK LN
1
2
3
4
5
6
7
SEE 1069 MAP
0 .125 .25 .375 .5 miles 1 in. = 1900 ft.

SAN DIEGO CO.

SEE 1029 MAP

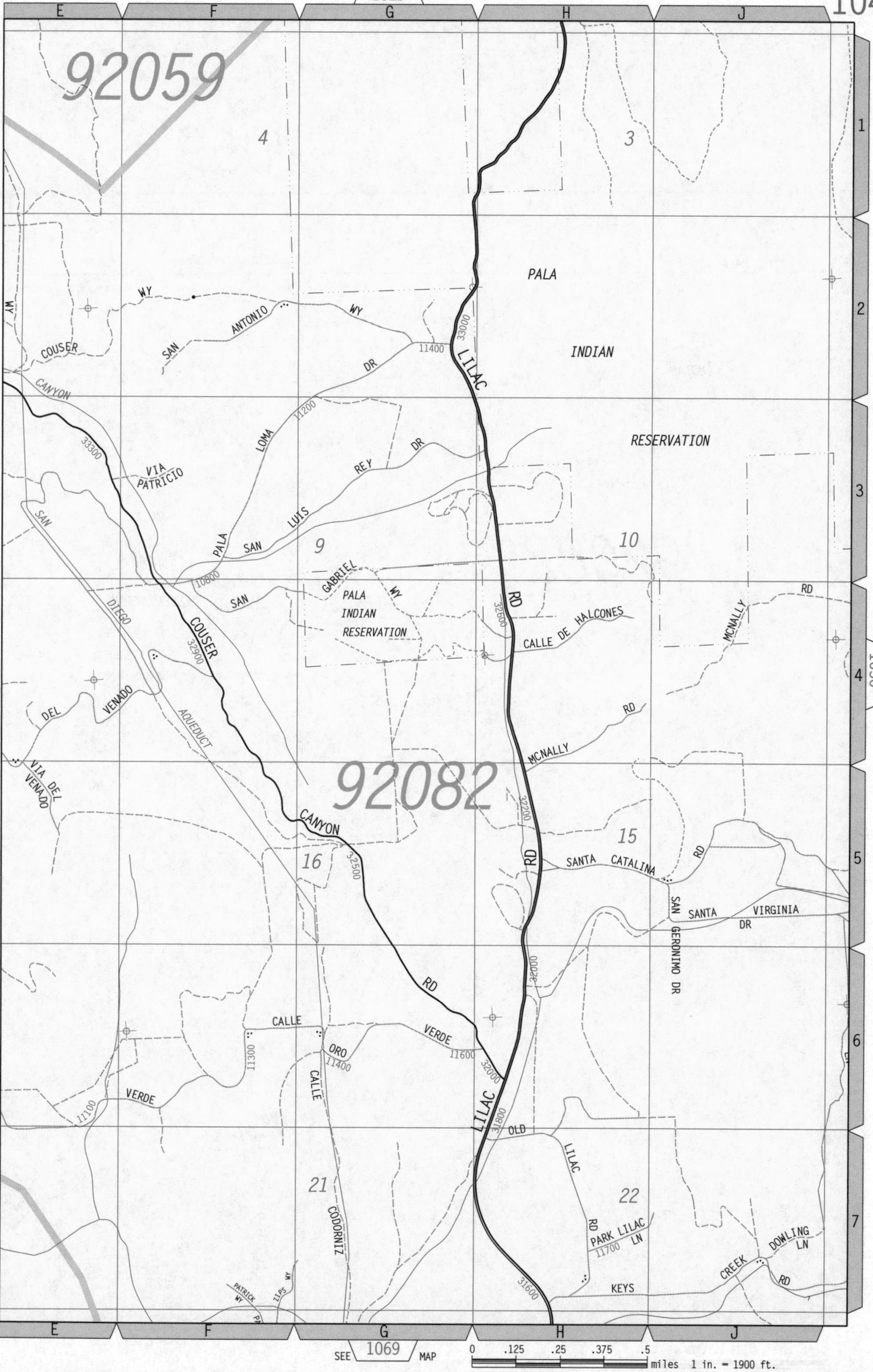

SEE 1050 MAP

SAN DIEGO CO.

SEE 1069 MAP

0 .125 .25 .375 .5 miles 1 in. = 1900 ft.

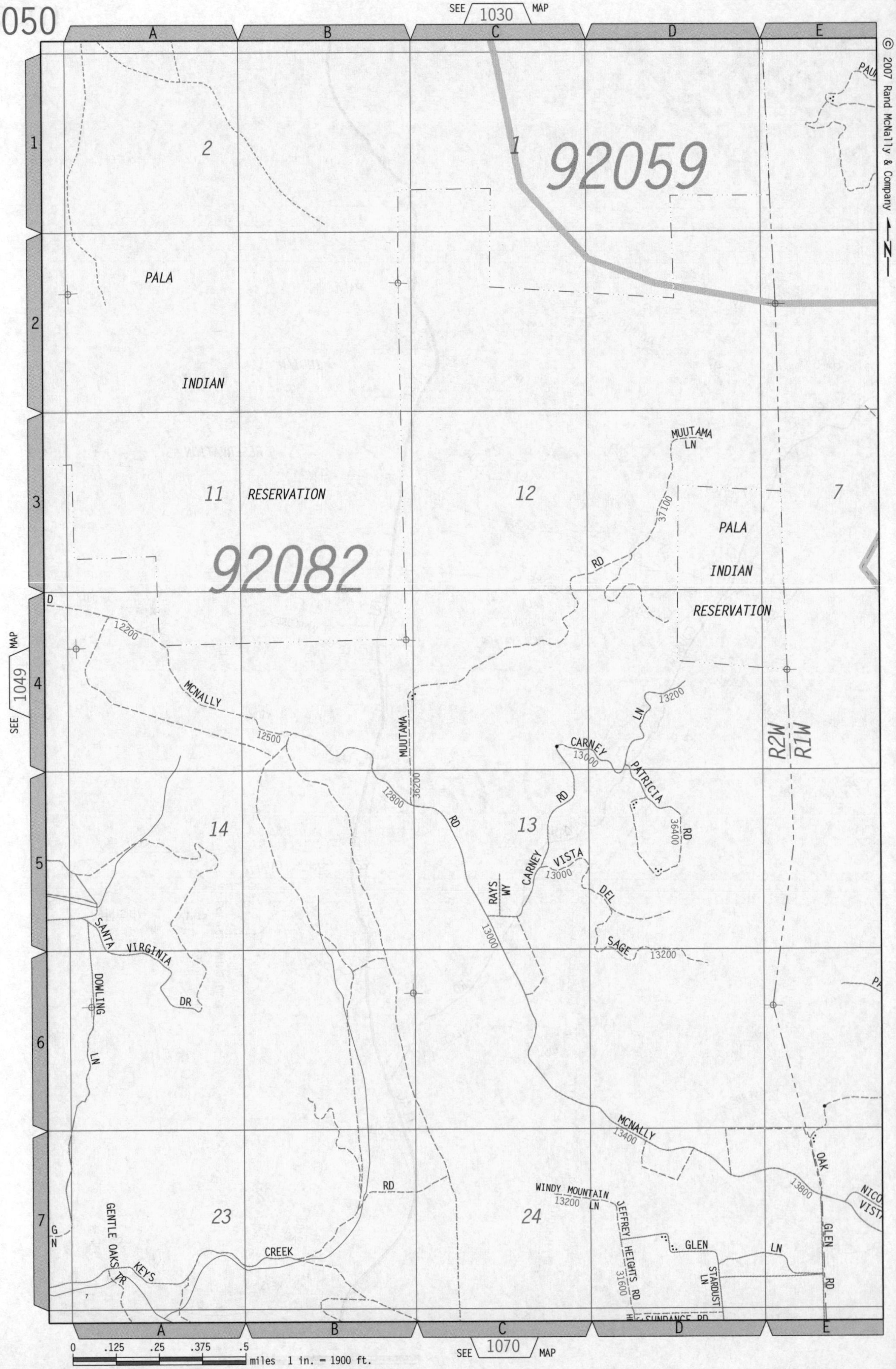
SEE 1030 MAP
SEE 1049 MAP
SEE 1070 MAP
A
B
C
D
E
1
2
3
4
5
6
7
92059
92082
PALA
INDIAN
RESERVATION
PALA
INDIAN
RESERVATION
2
1
11
12
7
14
13
23
24
MUUTAMA LN
37100
RD
MCNALLY
12200
12500
MUUTAMA
36200
12800
RD
13200
LN
CARNEY
13000
RD
PATRICIA
36400
RD
R2W
R1W
CARNEY
VISTA
13000
DEL
SAGE
13200
RAYS WY
13000
SANTA
VIRGINIA
DR
DOWLING
LN
MCNALLY
13400
OAK
13800
RD
WINDY MOUNTAIN
13200
LN
JEFFREY
HEIGHTS
31600
RD
GLEN
LN
GLEN
RD
STARDUST
LN
SUNDANCE RD
GENTLE OAKS
TR
KEYS
CREEK
0
.125
.25
.375
.5
miles 1 in. = 1900 ft.

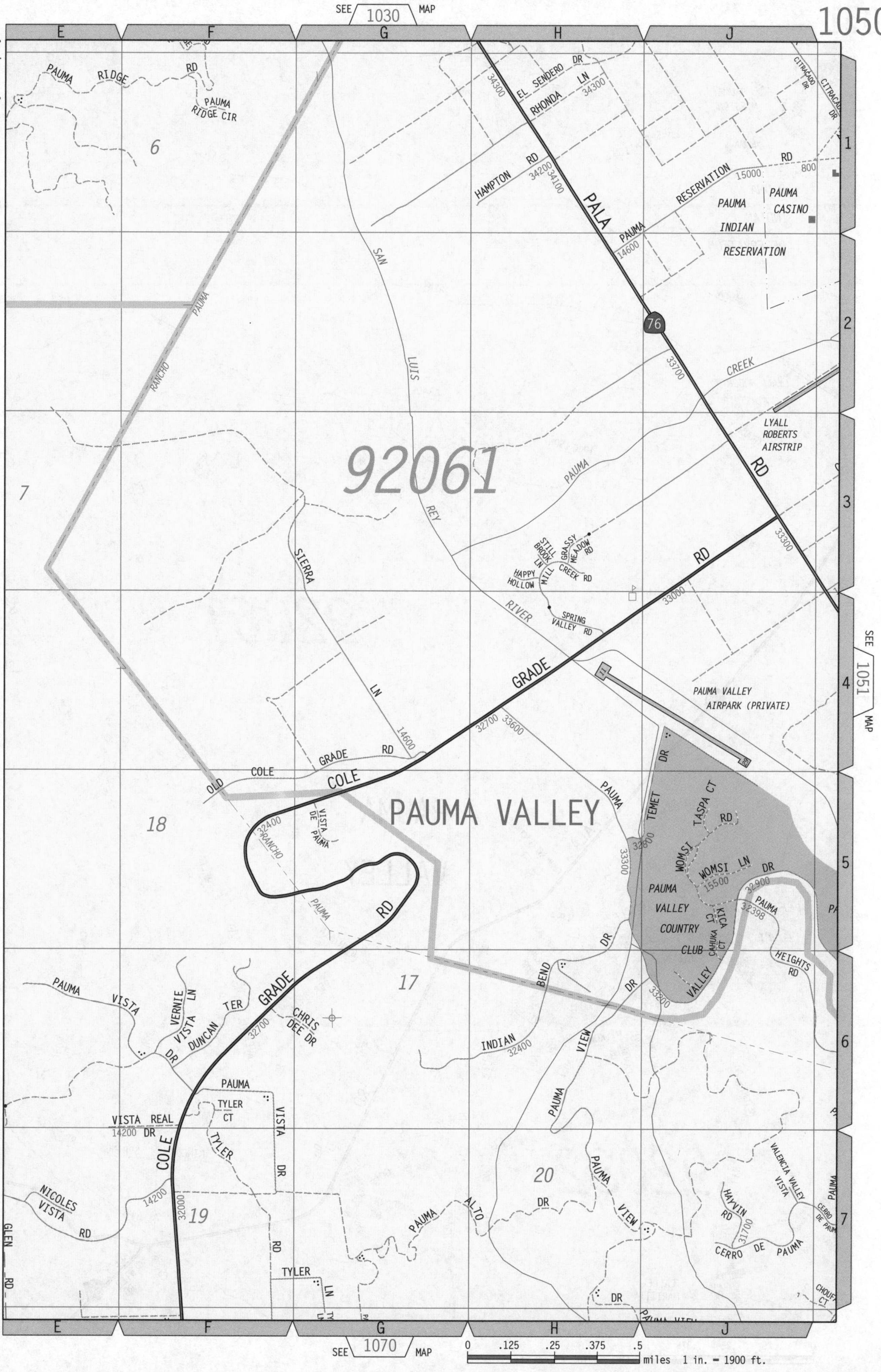
SEE 1030 MAP
SEE 1051 MAP
SEE 1070 MAP
E
F
G
H
J
1
2
3
4
5
6
7
92061
PAUMA VALLEY
PAUMA RIDGE RD
PAUMA RIDGE CIR
EL SENDERO DR
RHONDA LN
HAMPTON RD
PALA RD
PAUMA RESERVATION RD
PAUMA INDIAN RESERVATION
PAUMA CASINO
CITRACADO DR
76
CREEK
LYALL ROBERTS AIRSTRIP
PAUMA
SAN LUIS REY RIVER
RANCHO PAUMA
SIERRA LN
STILL BROOK LN
GRASSY MEADOW RD
HAPPY HOLLOW
MILL CREEK RD
SPRING VALLEY RD
COLE GRADE RD
OLD COLE GRADE RD
PAUMA VALLEY AIRPARK (PRIVATE)
TEMET DR
TASPA CT
WOMSI LN
WOMSI RD
PAUMA VALLEY COUNTRY CLUB
KICA CT
CAHUKA CT
PAUMA VALLEY DR
PAUMA HEIGHTS RD
VISTA DE PAUMA
BEND DR
INDIAN VIEW DR
PAUMA VISTA
VERNIE LN
VISTA DR
DUNCAN TER
CHRIS DEE DR
PAUMA VISTA DR
TYLER CT
VISTA REAL DR
TYLER RD
NICOLES VISTA RD
GLEN RD
TYLER LN
PAUMA ALTO DR
PAUMA VIEW DR
HAYVIN RD
CERRO DE PAUMA
VALENCIA VALLEY VISTA
CHOUFA CT
6
7
17
18
19
20
34300
34200
34100
15000
800
14600
33700
33300
33000
32700
33600
14600
32400
32800
33300
15500
32900
32398
33200
32700
32400
14200
14200
32000
31700
0 .125 .25 .375 .5
miles 1 in. = 1900 ft.

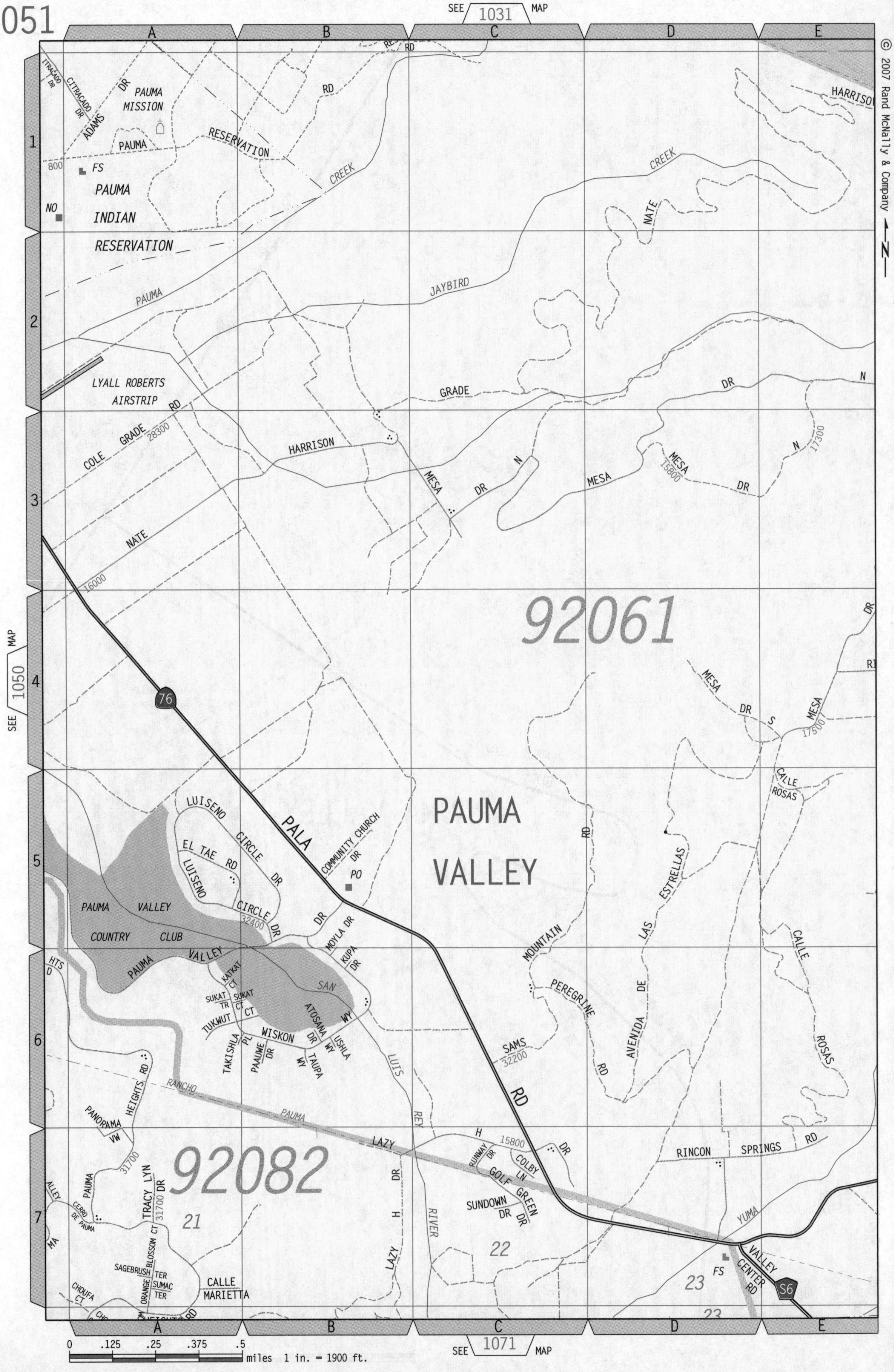
SEE 1031 MAP
SEE 1050 MAP
SEE 1071 MAP
A
B
C
D
E
1
2
3
4
5
6
7
PAUMA MISSION
PAUMA INDIAN RESERVATION
CITRACADO DR
ADAMS DR
PAUMA
RESERVATION
RD
CREEK
FS
NO
800
PAUMA
JAYBIRD
HARRISON
NATE
CREEK
LYALL ROBERTS AIRSTRIP
COLE GRADE RD
28300
GRADE
HARRISON
MESA DR
N
MESA
15800
DR
MESA
N
17300
DR
NATE
16000
92061
76
MESA DR
S
MESA
17500
CALLE ROSAS
PAUMA VALLEY
LUISENO CIRCLE DR
EL TAE RD
LUISENO CIRCLE DR
32400
PALA
COMMUNITY CHURCH DR
PO
DR
MOYLA DR
KUPA DR
PAUMA VALLEY COUNTRY CLUB
PAUMA VALLEY
MOUNTAIN RD
LAS ESTRELLAS
AVENIDA DE
PEREGRINE RD
CALLE ROSAS
SAMS
32200
KATKAT CT
SUKAT TR
SUKAT CT
TUKWUT CT
TAKISHLA PL
WISKON DR
PAAUWE DR
ATOSANA DR
TAUPA WY
USHLA WY
SAN
WY
LUIS
REY
RIVER
HTS D
HEIGHTS RD
RANCHO
PAUMA
PANORAMA VW
31700
PAUMA
CERRO DE PAUMA
ALLEY
MA
TRACY LYN DR
31700
92082
21
LAZY H DR
LAZY H
H
15800
RUNWAY DR
COLBY LN
GOLF GREEN DR
SUNDOWN DR
DR
RD
22
RINCON SPRINGS RD
YUMA
VALLEY CENTER RD
FS
23
23
S6
BLOSSOM CT
SAGEBRUSH TER
ORANGE
SUMAC TER
CHOUFA CT
CALLE MARIETTA
HEIGHTS RD
0 .125 .25 .375 .5 miles 1 in. = 1900 ft.

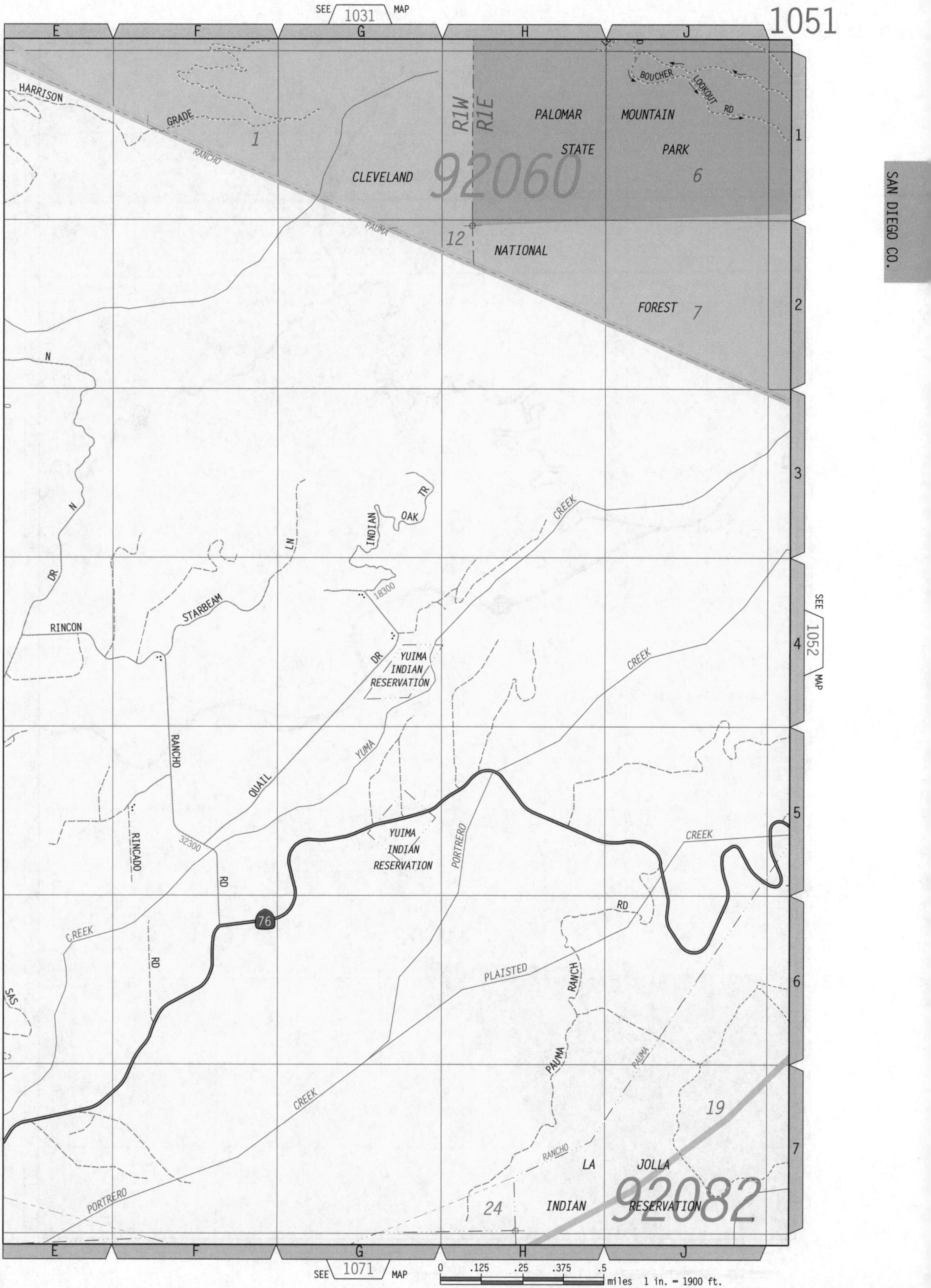
SEE 1031 MAP
E
F
G
H
J
HARRISON
GRADE
RANCHO
1
R1W
R1E
PALOMAR
MOUNTAIN
STATE
PARK
BOUCHER
LOOKOUT
RD
CLEVELAND
92060
6
PAUMA
12
NATIONAL
FOREST
7
N
N
DR
INDIAN
OAK
TR
LN
CREEK
18300
RINCON
STARBEAM
DR
YUIMA
INDIAN
RESERVATION
CREEK
RANCHO
YUMA
QUAIL
RINCADO
32300
RD
YUIMA
INDIAN
RESERVATION
PORTRERO
CREEK
76
RD
CREEK
RD
PLAISTED
RANCH
SAS
PAUMA
PAUMA
CREEK
19
RANCHO
LA
JOLLA
PORTRERO
24
INDIAN
RESERVATION
92082
1
2
3
4
5
6
7
SEE 1052 MAP
SEE 1071 MAP
0 .125 .25 .375 .5
miles 1 in. = 1900 ft.
SAN DIEGO CO.

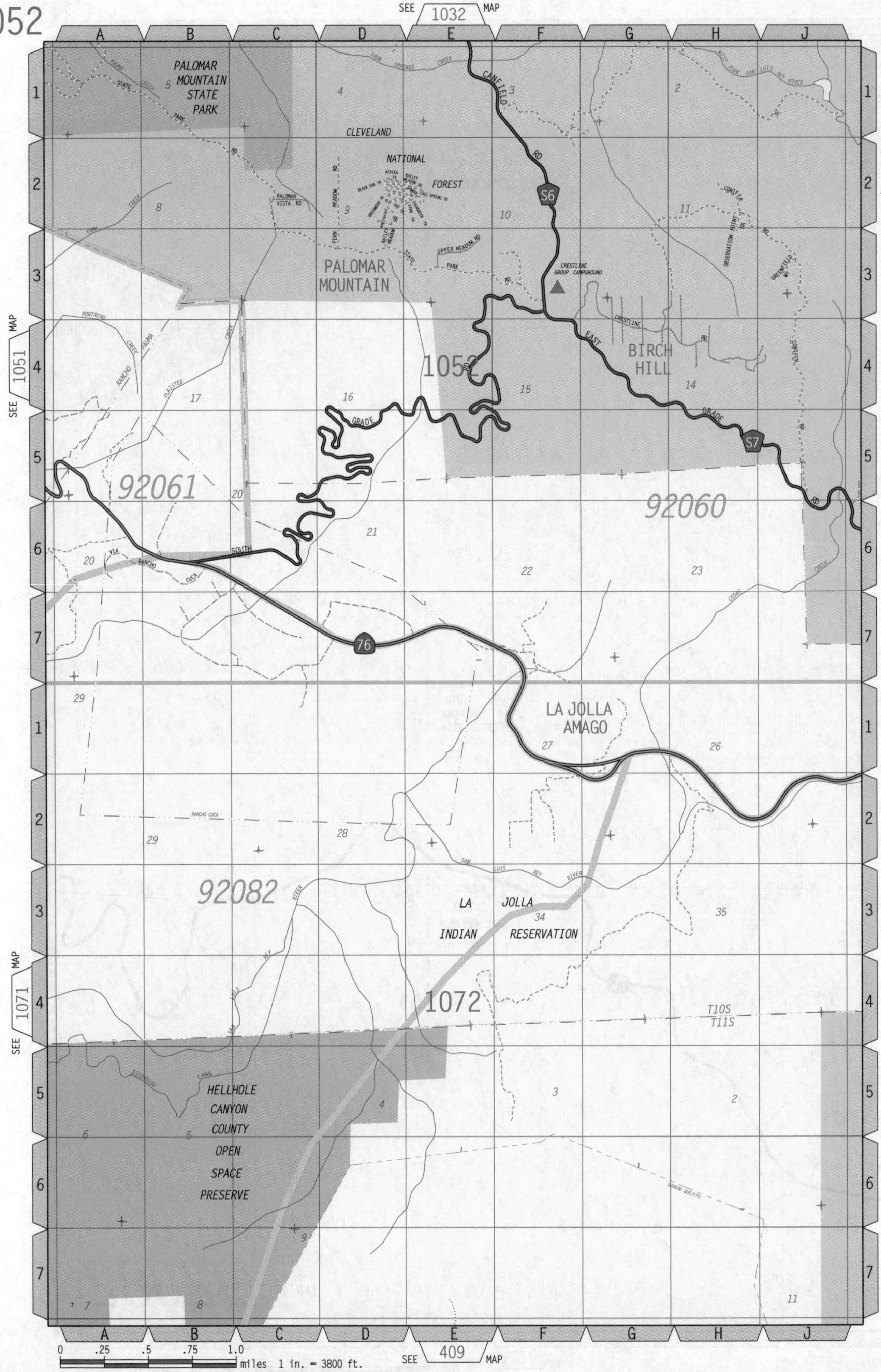
SEE 1032 MAP
SEE MAP 1051
SEE MAP 1071
SEE 409 MAP
PALOMAR MOUNTAIN STATE PARK
CLEVELAND NATIONAL FOREST
PALOMAR MOUNTAIN
BIRCH HILL
CRESTLINE GROUP CAMPGROUND
CANFIELD RD
EAST GRADE RD
SOUTH GRADE RD
STATE PARK RD
PALOMAR VISTA RD
UPPER MEADOW RD
CRESTLINE RD
OBSERVATION POINT DR
CONIFER RD
GREENFIELD WY
RANCHO CUCA
VIA RANCHO
PLAISTED CREEK
RANCHO PALMA CREEK
PORTRERO
IRON SPRINGS CREEK
WEST FORK SAN LUIS REY RIVER
SAN LUIS REY RIVER
CEDAR CREEK
ESCONDIDO CANAL
RANCHO GUEJITO
92061
92060
92082
1052
1072
LA JOLLA AMAGO
LA JOLLA INDIAN RESERVATION
HELLHOLE CANYON COUNTY OPEN SPACE PRESERVE
T10S
T11S
S6
S7
76
miles 1 in. = 3800 ft.
0 .25 .5 .75 1.0

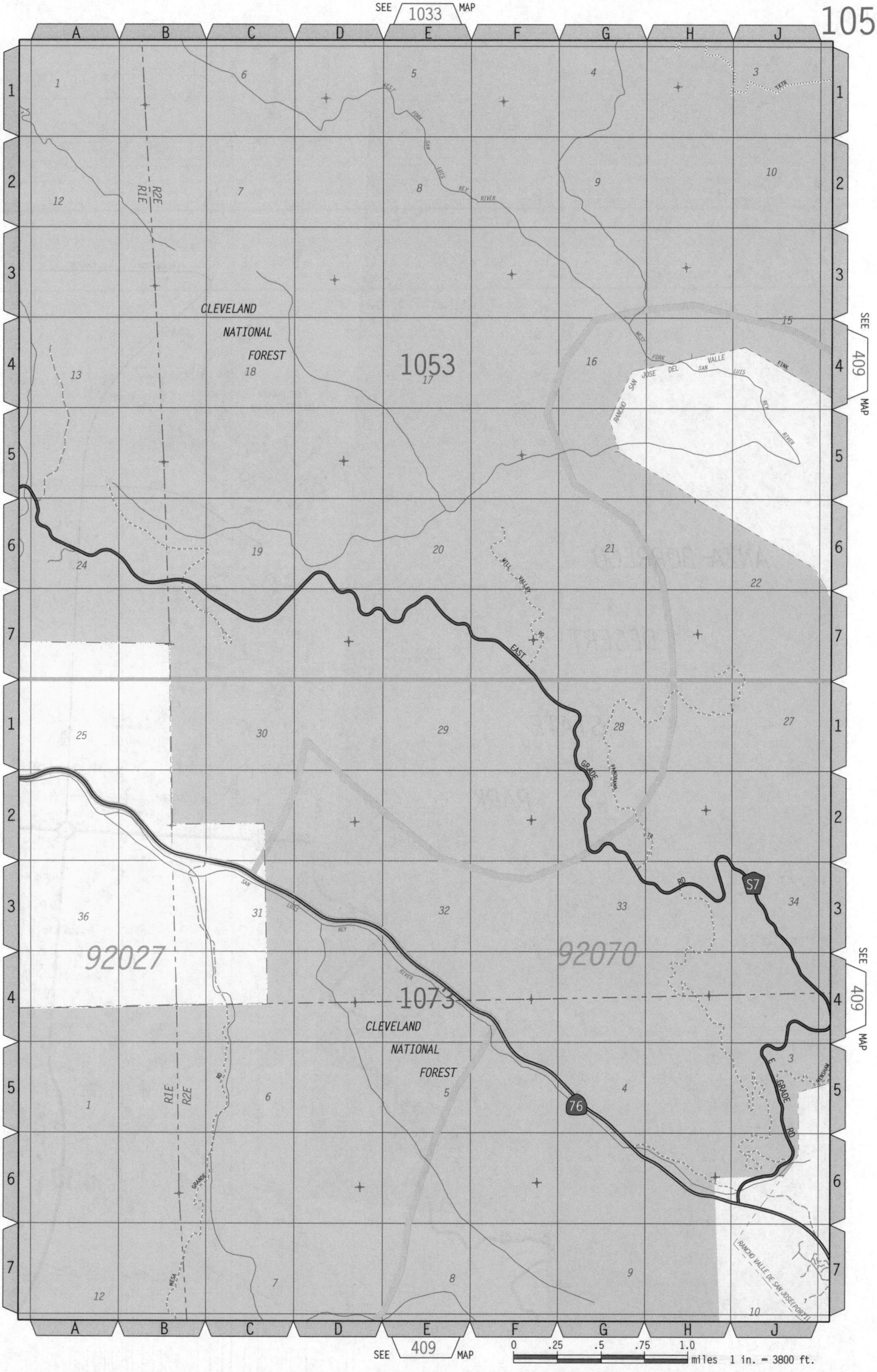
SEE 1033 MAP
SEE 409 MAP
SEE 409 MAP
SEE 409 MAP
CLEVELAND NATIONAL FOREST
1053
1073
92027
92070
R2E R1E
R1E R2E
WEST FORK SAN LUIS REY RIVER
RANCHO SAN JOSE DEL VALLE
SAN LUIS REY RIVER
EAST GRADE RD
WILL VALLEY RD
PANORAMA TR
S7
76
MESA GRANDE RD
E GRADE RD
RANCHO VALLE DE SAN JOSE(PORT)
0 .25 .5 .75 1.0 miles 1 in. = 3800 ft.

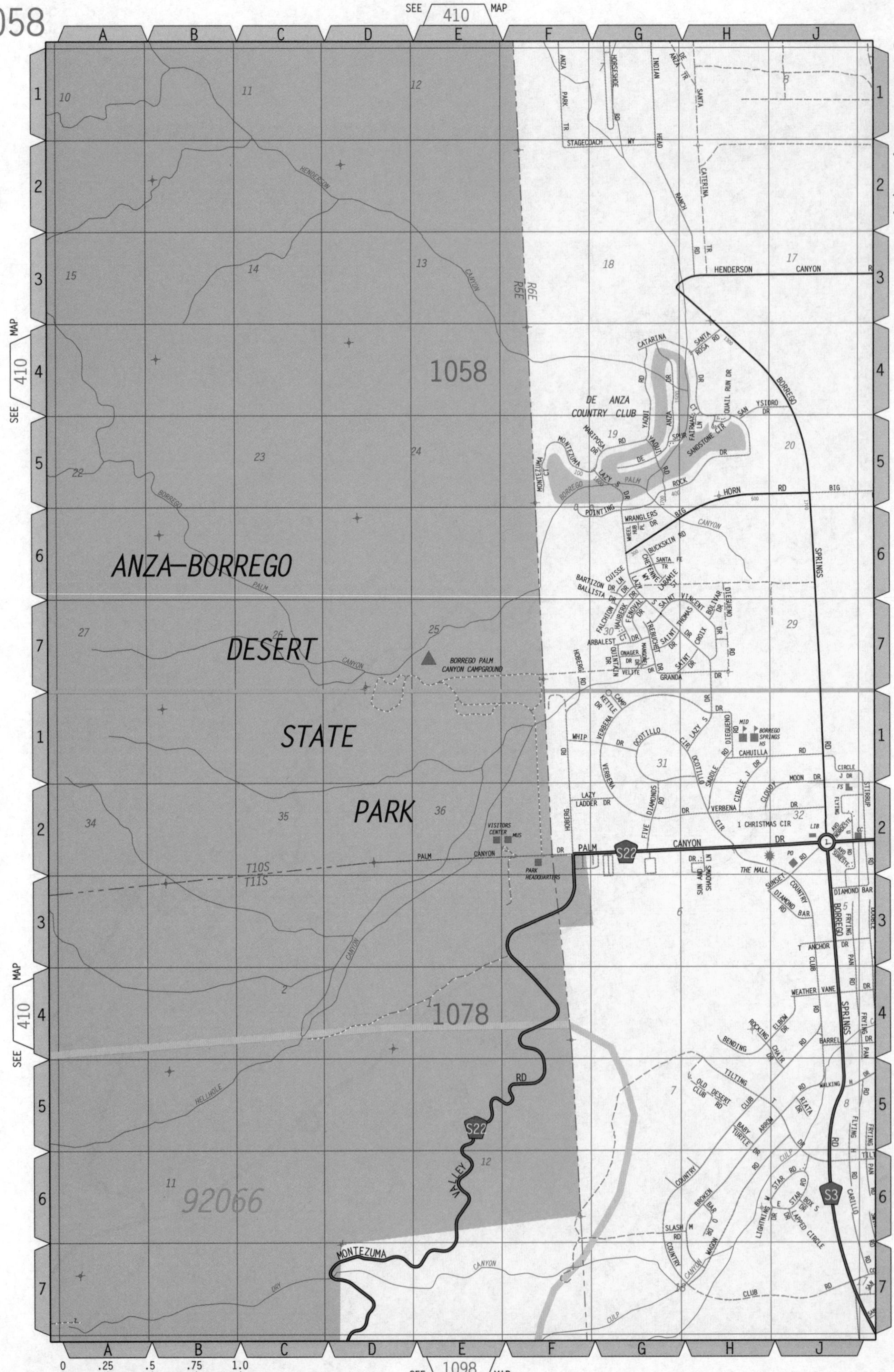

SEE 410 MAP
SEE 410 MAP
SEE 410 MAP
SEE 1098 MAP
A B C D E F G H J
1 2 3 4 5 6 7
ANZA-BORREGO
DESERT
STATE
PARK
1058
1078
92066
DE ANZA COUNTRY CLUB
BORREGO PALM CANYON CAMPGROUND
VISITORS CENTER
MUS
PARK HEADQUARTERS
HENDERSON CANYON
BORREGO SPRINGS RD
PALM CANYON DR
S22
S3
MONTEZUMA VALLEY RD
HELLHOLE CANYON
DRY CANYON
CULP CANYON
BIG HORN RD
STAGECOACH WY
HORSESHOE RD
INDIAN HEAD RANCH RD
DE ANZA TR
SANTA CATERINA TR
CATARINA
SANTA ROSA RD
QUAIL RUN DR
SAN YSIDRO DR
YAQUI RD
SANDSTONE CIR
MARIPOSA RD
MONTEZUMA DR
LAZY S DR
POINTING ROCK DR
WRANGLERS DR
BUCKSKIN RD
SANTA FE TR
CHEYENNE WY
LARAMIE ST
SAINT VINCENT DR
SAINT THOMAS DR
DIEGUENO RD
HOBERG RD
VERBENA DR
WHIP RD
KETTLE CAMP DR
OCOTILLO CIR
FIVE DIAMONDS RD
LAZY LADDER RD
CAHUILLA RD
MOON DR
CIRCLE J DR
CHRISTMAS CIR
STIRRUP
THE MALL
SUN AND SHADOWS LN
SUNSET DIAMOND RD
COUNTRY BAR
DIAMOND BAR
FRYING PAN RD
T ANCHOR DR
CLUB CIR
WEATHER VANE DR
ROCKING CHAIR RD
ELBOW DR
BENDING
BARREL
WALKING H DR
RIATA DR
TILTING T
OLD DESERT CLUB RD
BABY TURTLE DR
ARROW
COUNTRY CLUB RD
BROKEN BAR O
SLASH M RD
STAR RD
BOX S DR
LAPPED CIRCLE
LIGHTNING W
CARILLO
WAGON
CANYON
MID
BORREGO SPRINGS HS
LIB
PO
FS
R6E
R5E
T10S
T11S
0 .25 .5 .75 1.0 miles 1 in. = 3800 ft.

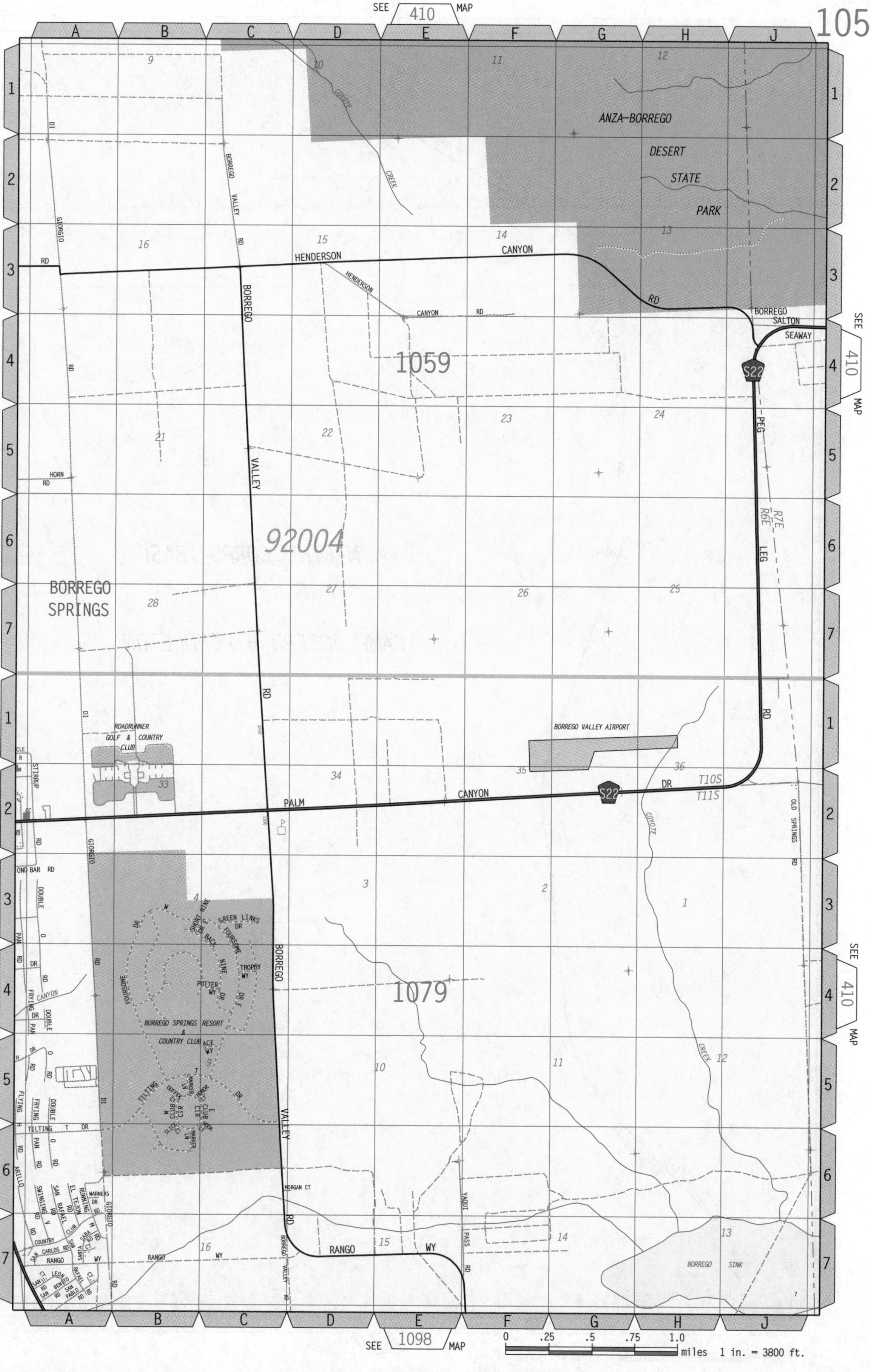
SEE 410 MAP
SEE 1098 MAP
ANZA–BORREGO DESERT STATE PARK
BORREGO SPRINGS
92004
1059
1079
HENDERSON CANYON RD
BORREGO VALLEY RD
BORREGO SALTON SEAWAY
PEG LEG RD
PALM CANYON DR
S22
COYOTE CREEK
BORREGO VALLEY AIRPORT
ROADRUNNER GOLF & COUNTRY CLUB
BORREGO SPRINGS RESORT & COUNTRY CLUB
GIORGIO RD
HORN RD
RANGO WY
YAQUI PASS RD
MORGAN CT
OLD SPRINGS RD
BORREGO SINK
T10S
T11S
R6E
R7E
0 .25 .5 .75 1.0 miles 1 in. = 3800 ft.

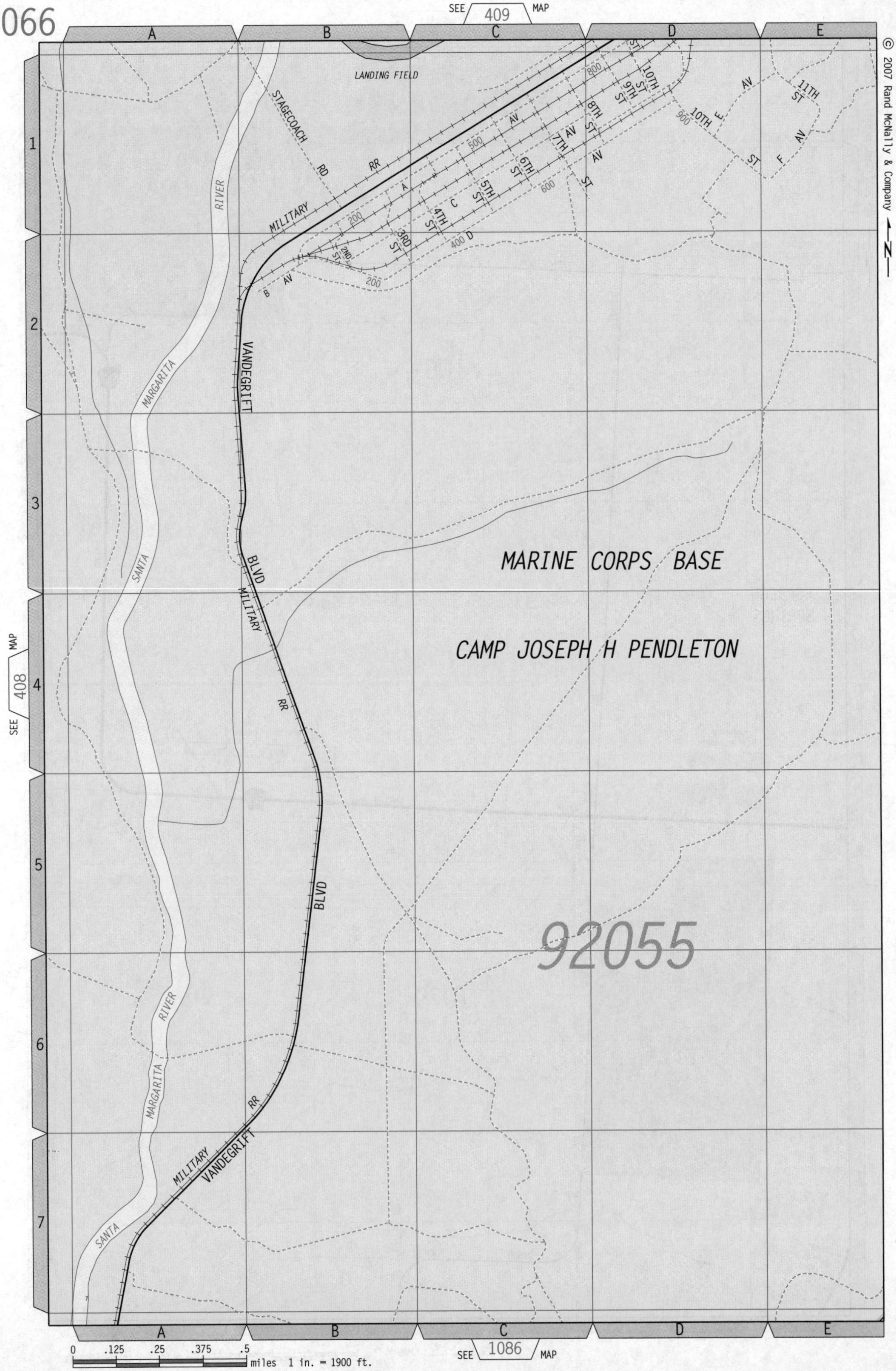
SEE 409 MAP
SEE 408 MAP
SEE 1086 MAP
A
B
C
D
E
1
2
3
4
5
6
7
LANDING FIELD
STAGECOACH RD
MILITARY RR
VANDEGRIFT BLVD
MILITARY RR
SANTA MARGARITA RIVER
A AV
B AV
C AV
D AV
E AV
F AV
2ND ST
3RD ST
4TH ST
5TH ST
6TH ST
7TH ST
8TH ST
9TH ST
10TH ST
11TH ST
200
400
500
600
800
900
MARINE CORPS BASE
CAMP JOSEPH H PENDLETON
92055
0 .125 .25 .375 .5 miles 1 in. = 1900 ft.
N

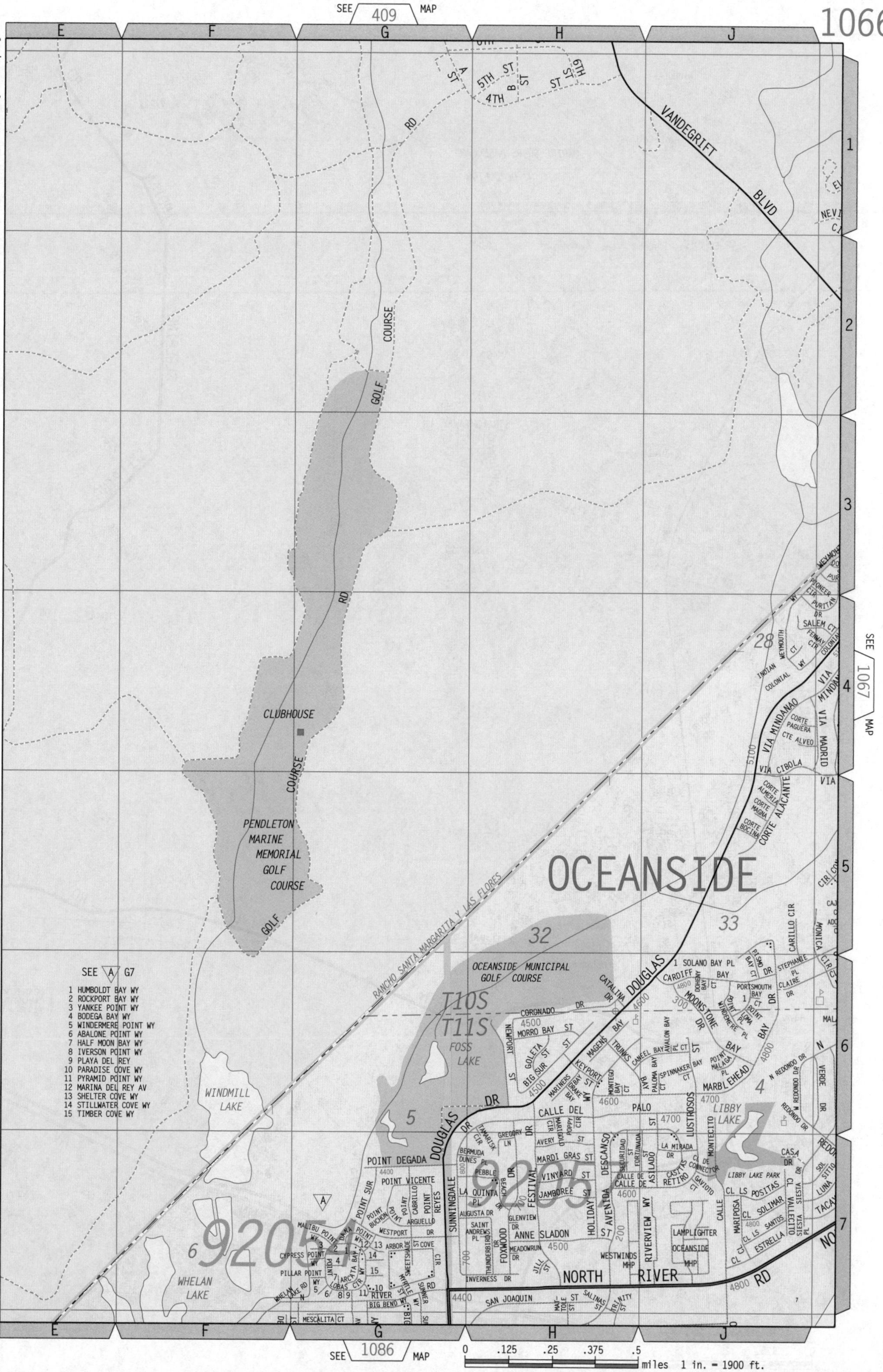
SEE 409 MAP
SEE 1067 MAP
SEE 1086 MAP
VANDEGRIFT BLVD
GOLF COURSE RD
CLUBHOUSE
PENDLETON MARINE MEMORIAL GOLF COURSE
WINDMILL LAKE
WHELAN LAKE
RANCHO SANTA MARGARITA Y LAS FLORES
OCEANSIDE
OCEANSIDE MUNICIPAL GOLF COURSE
FOSS LAKE
LIBBY LAKE
LIBBY LAKE PARK
T10S
T11S
92054
DOUGLAS DR
NORTH RIVER RD
SAN JOAQUIN
CORONADO DR
MORRO BAY ST
CALLE DEL PALO
MARDI GRAS ST
VINYARD ST
JAMBOREE ST
ANNE SLADON
RIVERVIEW WY
LAMPLIGHTER
OCEANSIDE MHP
WESTWINDS MHP
MOONSTONE DR
MARBLEHEAD BAY DR
PORTSMOUTH BAY CT
CARDIFF BAY
SOLANO BAY PL
VIA MINDANAO
VIA CIBOLA
VIA MADRID
CORTE ALACANTE
POINT DEGADA
POINT VICENTE
SUNNINGDALE
INVERNESS DR
MESCALITA CT
BIG BEND WY
SEE A G7
1 HUMBOLDT BAY WY
2 ROCKPORT BAY WY
3 YANKEE POINT WY
4 BODEGA BAY WY
5 WINDERMERE POINT WY
6 ABALONE POINT WY
7 HALF MOON BAY WY
8 IVERSON POINT WY
9 PLAYA DEL REY
10 PARADISE COVE WY
11 PYRAMID POINT WY
12 MARINA DEL REY AV
13 SHELTER COVE WY
14 STILLWATER COVE WY
15 TIMBER COVE WY
0 .125 .25 .375 .5 miles 1 in. = 1900 ft.

SEE 1047 MAP

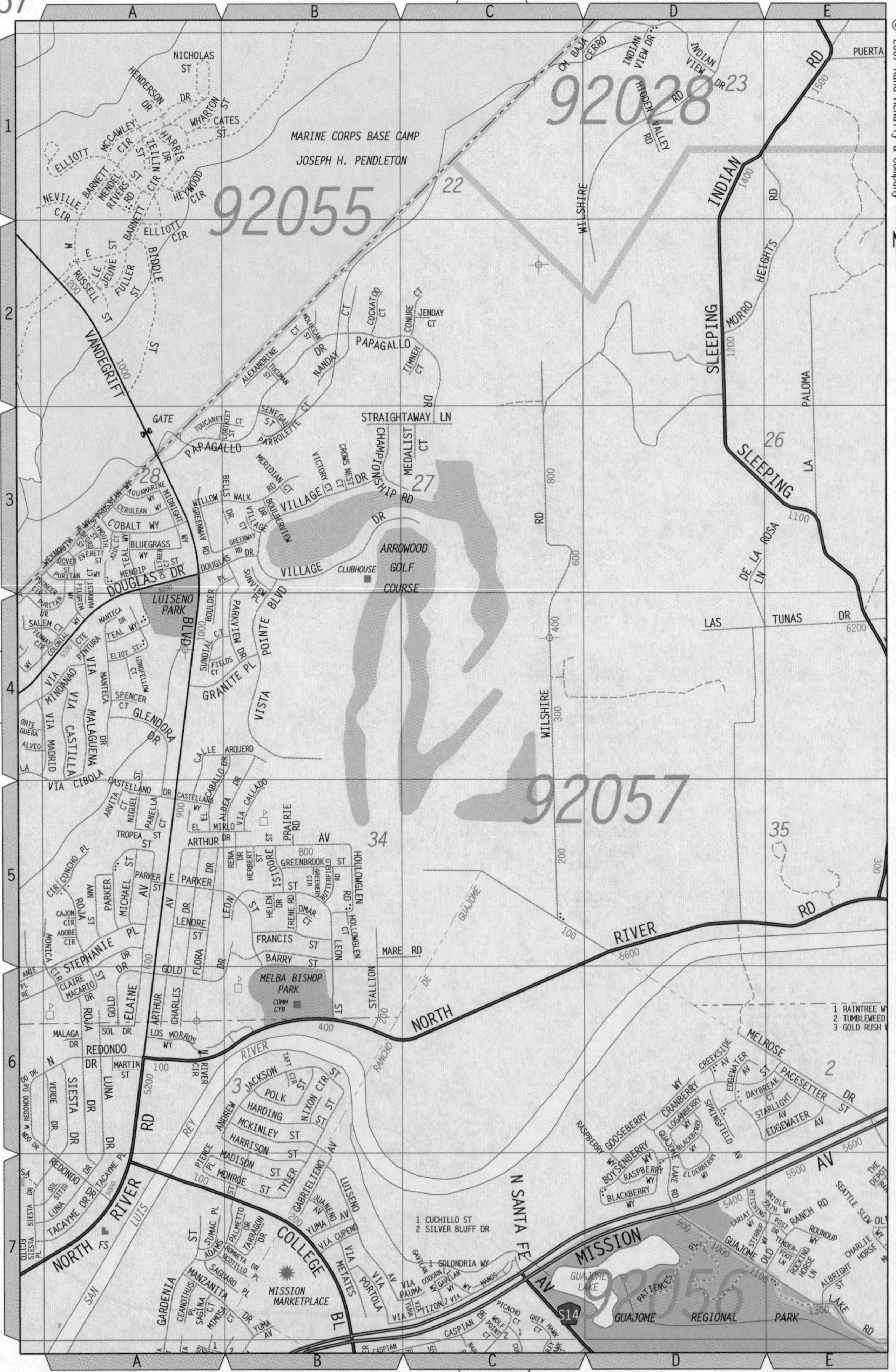

SEE 1066 MAP

SEE 1087 MAP

0 .125 .25 .375 .5 miles 1 in. = 1900 ft.

SEE 1047 MAP

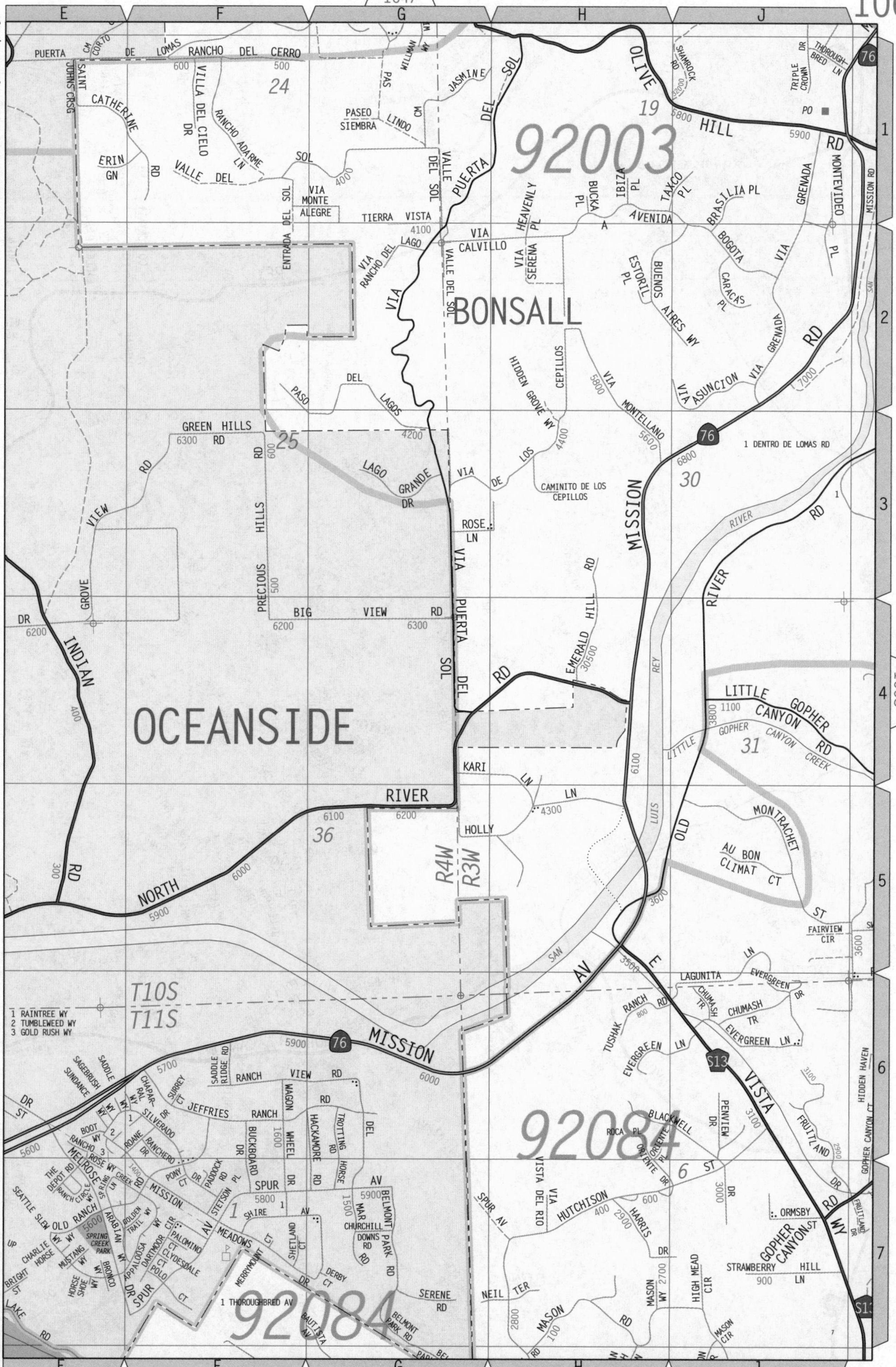

SEE 1068 MAP

SEE 1087 MAP

0 .125 .25 .375 .5 miles 1 in. = 1900 ft.

SEE 1048 MAP

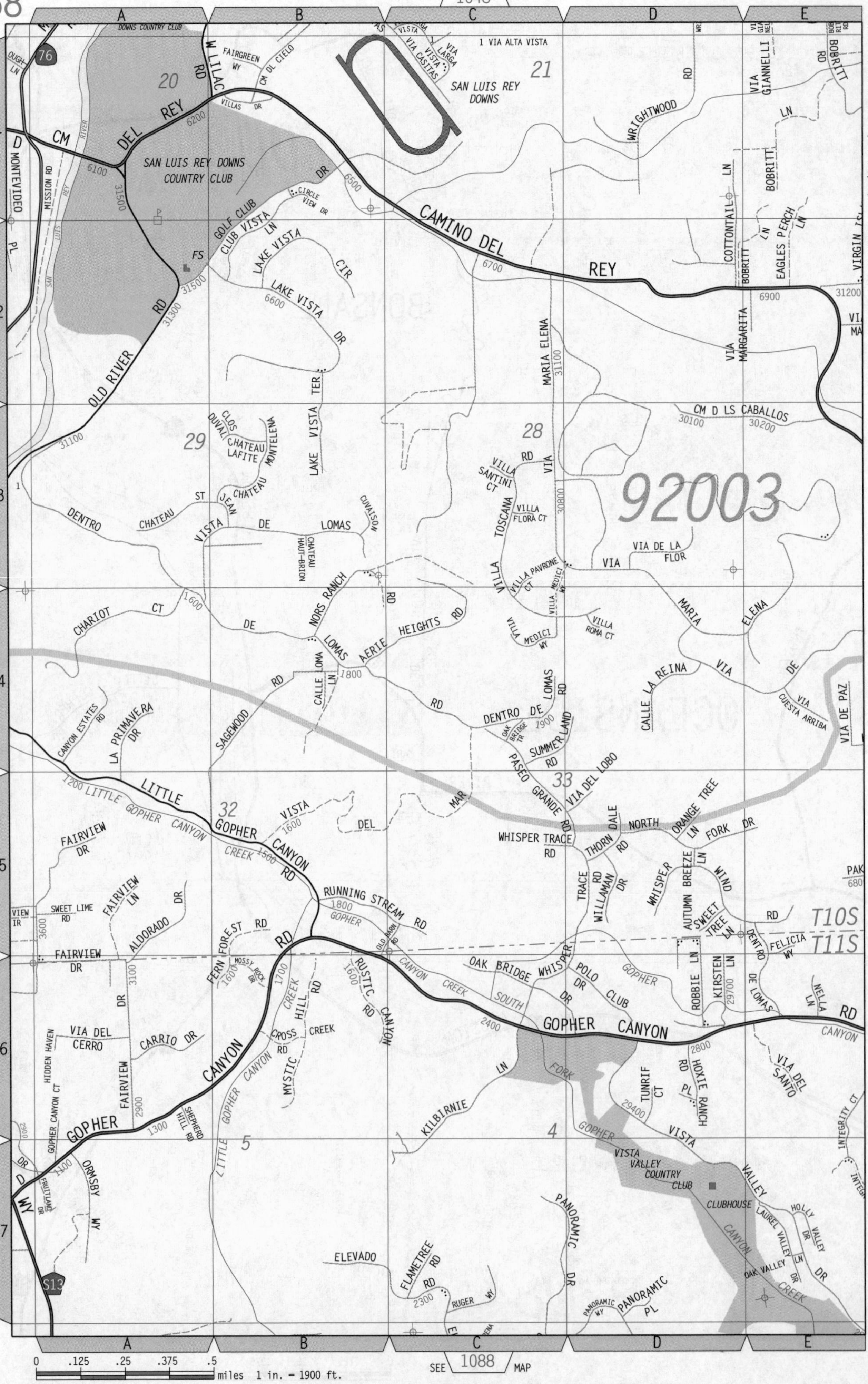

0 .125 .25 .375 .5 miles 1 in. = 1900 ft.

SEE 1067 MAP

SEE 1088 MAP

SEE 1048 MAP

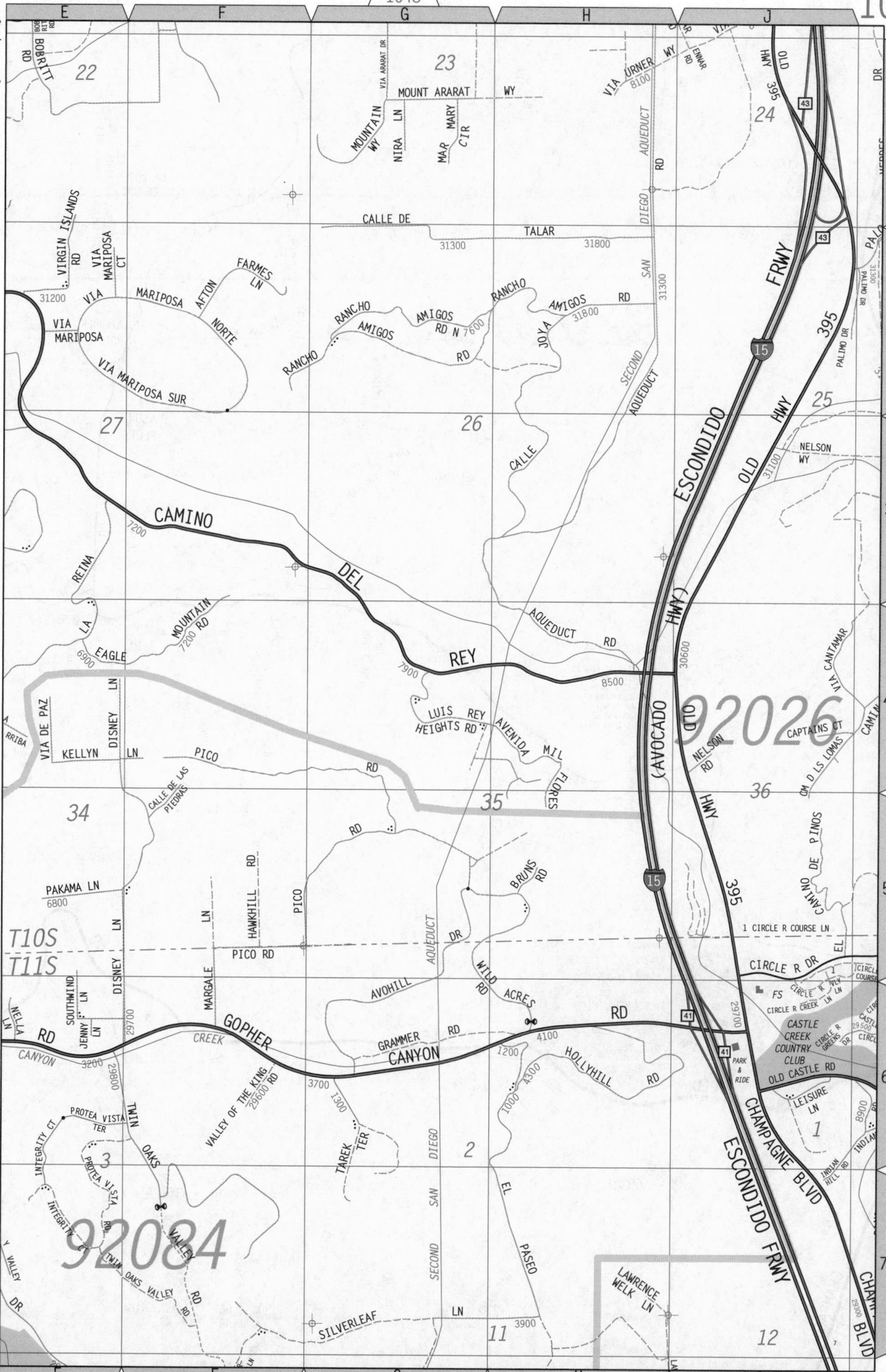

E F G H J
1 2 3 4 5 6 7

SAN DIEGO CO.

SEE 1069 MAP

SEE 1088 MAP

0 .125 .25 .375 .5 miles 1 in. = 1900 ft.

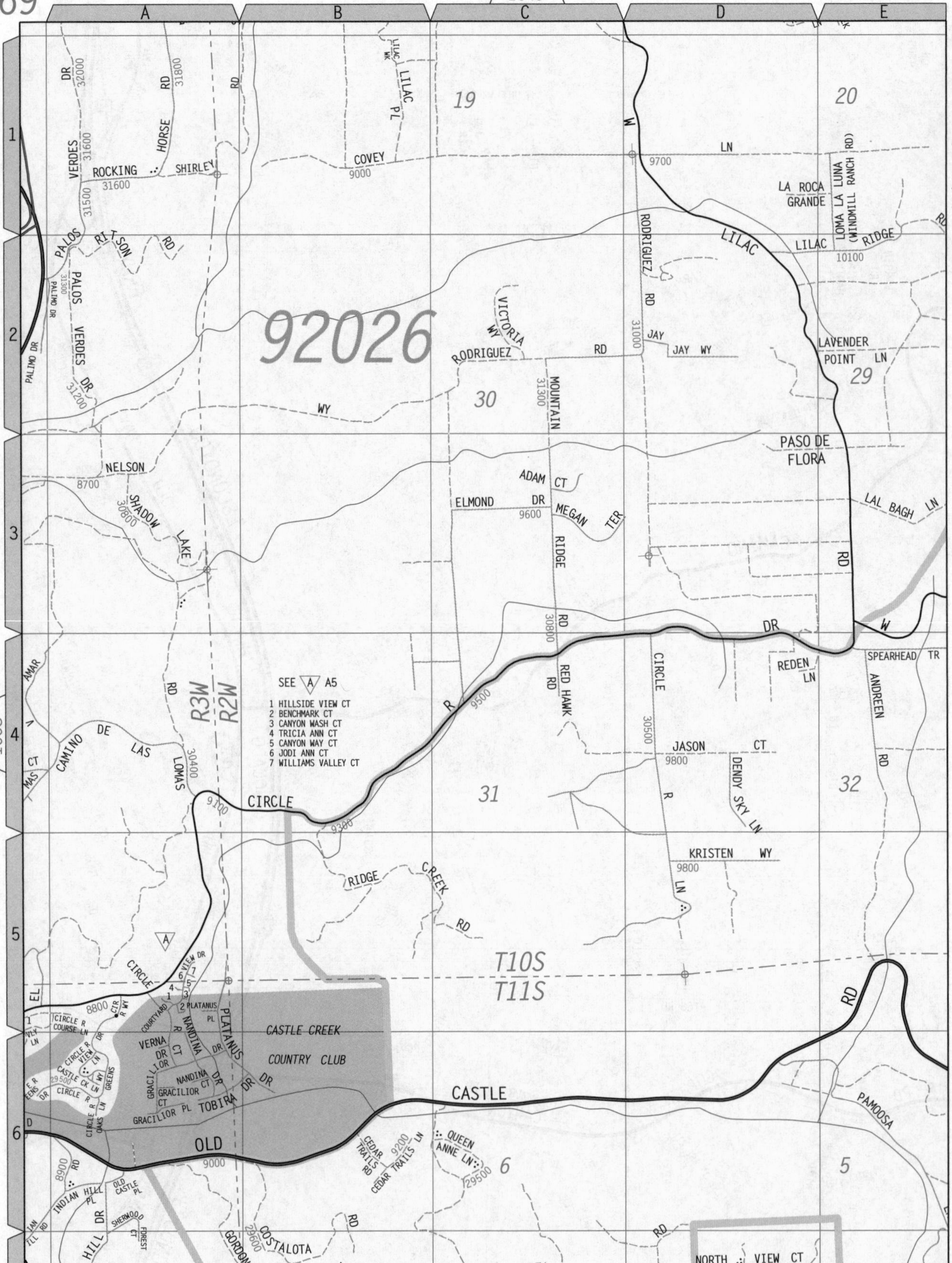
SEE 1049 MAP
SEE 1089 MAP
SEE 1068 MAP
SAN DIEGO CO.
© 2007 Rand McNally & Company
92026
ROCKING HORSE RD
SHIRLEY
PALOS VERDES DR
RITSON RD
COVEY LN
LILAC RD
LILAC PL
W LILAC RD
RODRIGUEZ RD
LA ROCA GRANDE
LOMA LA LUNA (WINDMILL RANCH RD)
LILAC RIDGE
VICTORIA WY
RODRIGUEZ WY
JAY RD
JAY WY
MOUNTAIN RIDGE RD
LAVENDER POINT LN
PASO DE FLORA
NELSON
SHADOW LAKE RD
ADAM CT
ELMOND DR
MEGAN TER
LAL BAGH LN
W CIRCLE R DR
SPEARHEAD TR
REDEN LN
ANDREEN RD
RED HAWK RD
CIRCLE R LN
JASON CT
DENDY SKY LN
KRISTEN WY
CAMINO DE LAS LOMAS
AMAR
R3W
R2W
SEE A A5
1 HILLSIDE VIEW CT
2 BENCHMARK CT
3 CANYON WASH CT
4 TRICIA ANN CT
5 CANYON WAY CT
6 JODI ANN CT
7 WILLIAMS VALLEY CT
CIRCLE
RIDGE CREEK RD
T10S
T11S
CASTLE CREEK COUNTRY CLUB
PLATANUS DR
NANDINA CT
VERNA DR
GRACILIOR PL
TOBIRA DR
OLD CASTLE RD
PAMOOSA
CEDAR TRAILS RD
QUEEN ANNE LN
INDIAN HILL RD
SANDY HILL DR
SHERWOOD FOREST CT
GORDON HILL RD
COSTALOTA
VISTA ALETA
NORTH VIEW CT
NORTH VIEW LN
WELK HIGHLAND DR
WELK VIEW DR
CALLE DE LA REINA
CASTLE VIEW DR
KIWI MEADOW LN
CHAMPAGNE BLVD
DEER PARK ESCONDIDO
0 .125 .25 .375 .5 miles 1 in. = 1900 ft.

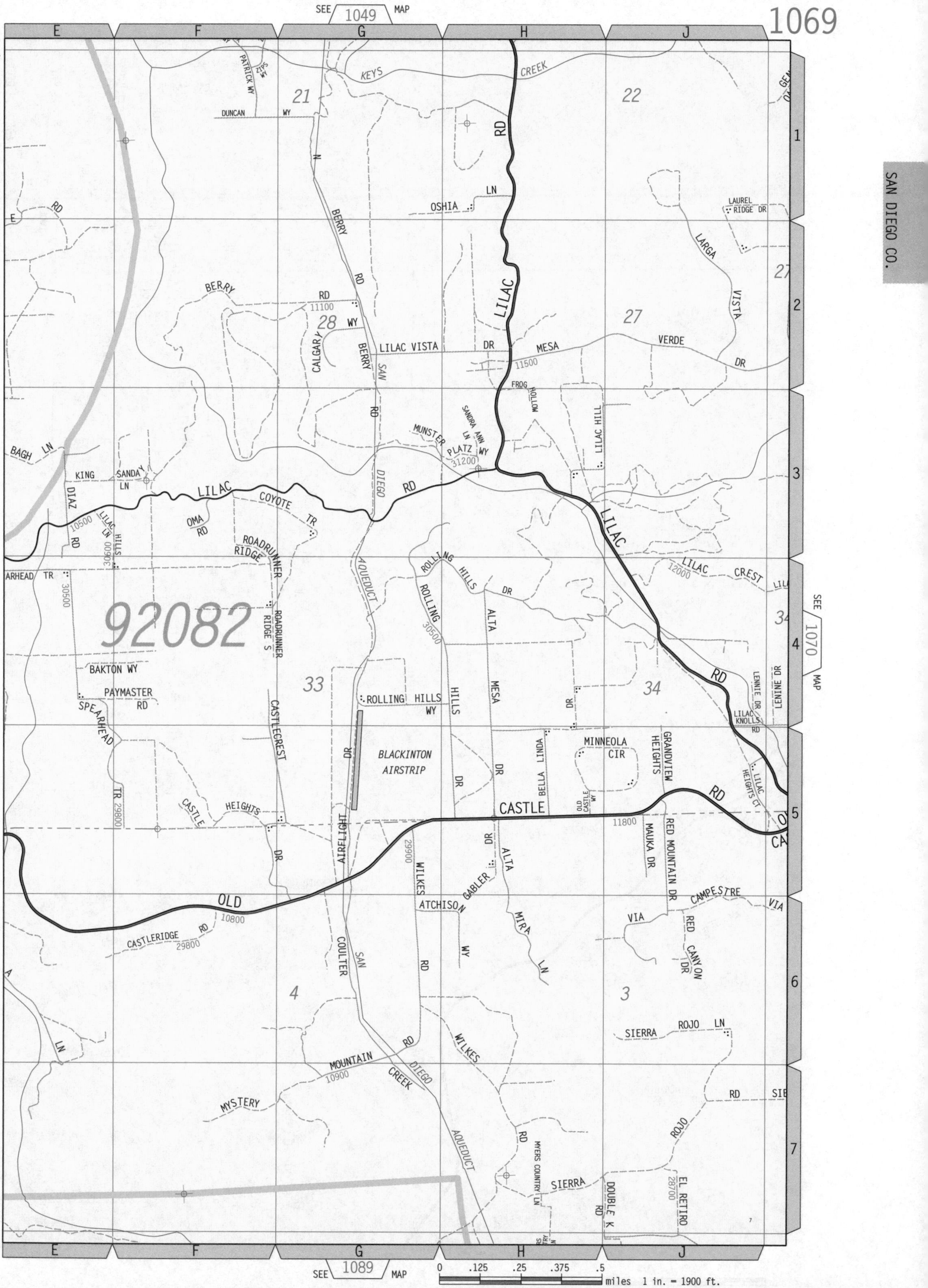
SEE 1049 MAP
E
F
G
H
J
1
2
3
4
5
6
7
SAN DIEGO CO.
SEE 1070 MAP
SEE 1089 MAP
92082
21
22
27
28
33
34
4
3
KEYS CREEK
PATRICK WY
ZIPS WY
DUNCAN WY
LILAC RD
OSHIA LN
N BERRY RD
BERRY RD
11100
CALGARY WY
LILAC VISTA DR
MESA VERDE DR
11500
FROG HOLLOW
LAUREL RIDGE DR
LARGA VISTA
SAN DIEGO RD
MUNSTER PLATZ WY
SANDRA ANN LN
31200
LILAC HILL
BAGH LN
KING LN
SANDAY
DIAZ RD
10500
LILAC HILLS
LILAC RD
COYOTE TR
OMA RD
ROADRUNNER RIDGE
30600
ARHEAD TR
30500
ROLLING HILLS DR
LILAC CREST
12000
ALTA MESA DR
ROADRUNNER RIDGE S
ROLLING HILLS
30500
AQUEDUCT
BAKTON WY
PAYMASTER RD
SPEARHEAD TR
ROLLING HILLS WY
LENIE DR
LENINE DR
LILAC KNOLLS RD
CASTLECREST
BLACKINTON AIRSTRIP
AIRFLIGHT DR
BELLA LINDA
MINNEOLA CIR
GRANDVIEW HEIGHTS
LILAC HEIGHTS CT
CASTLE HEIGHTS DR
29800
OLD CASTLE WY
CASTLE RD
11800
29900
ALTA DR
GABLER
MAUKA DR
RED MOUNTAIN DR
WILKES RD
ATCHISON WY
CAMPESTRE VIA
VIA
RED CANYON DR
OLD
10800
CASTLERIDGE RD
29800
MIRA LN
COULTER
SAN DIEGO
SIERRA ROJO LN
MOUNTAIN CREEK RD
10900
WILKES
LN
MYSTERY
RD
AQUEDUCT
MYERS COUNTRY LN
SIERRA
DOUBLE K RD
28700
EL RETIRO
ROJO
0 .125 .25 .375 .5 miles 1 in. = 1900 ft.

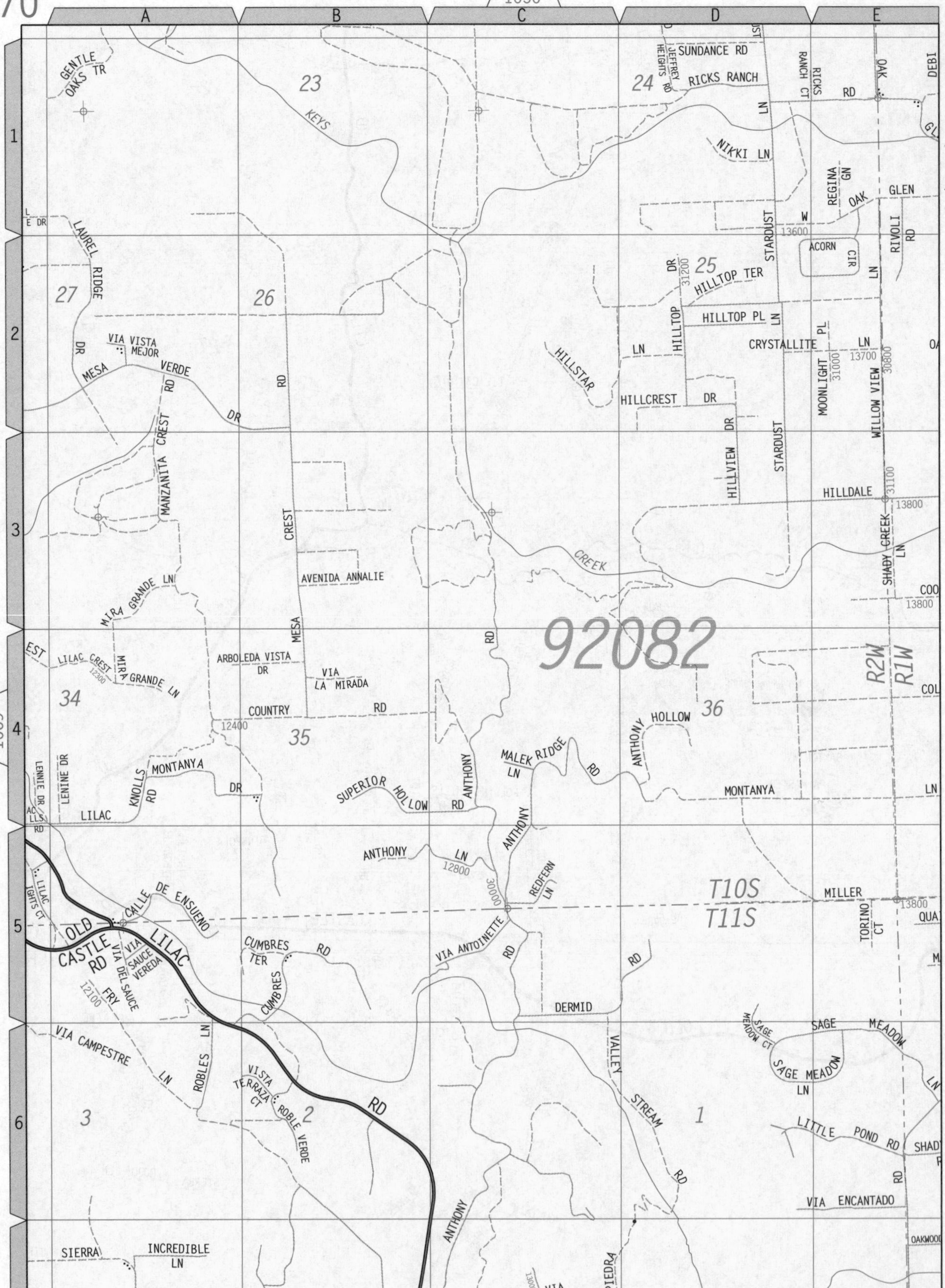
SEE 1050 MAP
SEE 1069 MAP
SEE 1090 MAP
92082
T10S
T11S
R2W
R1W
GENTLE OAKS TR
KEYS CREEK
SUNDANCE RD
JEFFREY HEIGHTS RD
RICKS RANCH LN
RICKS RANCH CT
OAK RD
NIKKI LN
REGINA GN
OAK GLEN
STARDUST W
ACORN CIR
RIVOLI RD
LAUREL RIDGE DR
HILLTOP DR
HILLTOP TER
HILLTOP PL
HILLTOP LN
CRYSTALLITE LN
MOONLIGHT PL
WILLOW VIEW LN
HILLSTAR LN
HILLCREST DR
HILLVIEW DR
STARDUST
VIA VISTA MEJOR
MESA VERDE DR
MESA CREST RD
MANZANITA CREST RD
HILLDALE
SHADY CREEK LN
MIRA GRANDE LN
AVENIDA ANNALIE
ANTHONY RD
LILAC CREST
ARBOLEDA VISTA DR
VIA LA MIRADA
COUNTRY RD
ANTHONY HOLLOW
MALEK RIDGE LN
MALEK RIDGE RD
LENINE DR
LILAC HGTS RD
KNOLLS RD
MONTANYA DR
SUPERIOR HOLLOW RD
MONTANYA LN
ANTHONY LN
REDFERN LN
MILLER
TORINO CT
CALLE DE ENSUENO
OLD CASTLE RD
LILAC RD
VIA DEL SAUCE
VIA VEREDA
CUMBRES TER
CUMBRES RD
VIA ANTOINETTE RD
DERMID
VALLEY STREAM RD
SAGE MEADOW CT
SAGE MEADOW LN
VIA CAMPESTRE LN
FRY
ROBLES LN
VISTA TERRAZA CT
ROBLE VERDE
LITTLE POND RD
VIA ENCANTADO
SIERRA
INCREDIBLE LN
ROJO
VIA SUENA
VIA PIEDRA
MISTY
MILLER RD
VIA DE LUNA
LITTLE CREEK LN
BLUE SAGE LN
WILMINGTON AV
STONEGATE DR
PALOS TIERRA RD
OAKWOOD
0 .125 .25 .375 .5 miles 1 in. = 1900 ft.

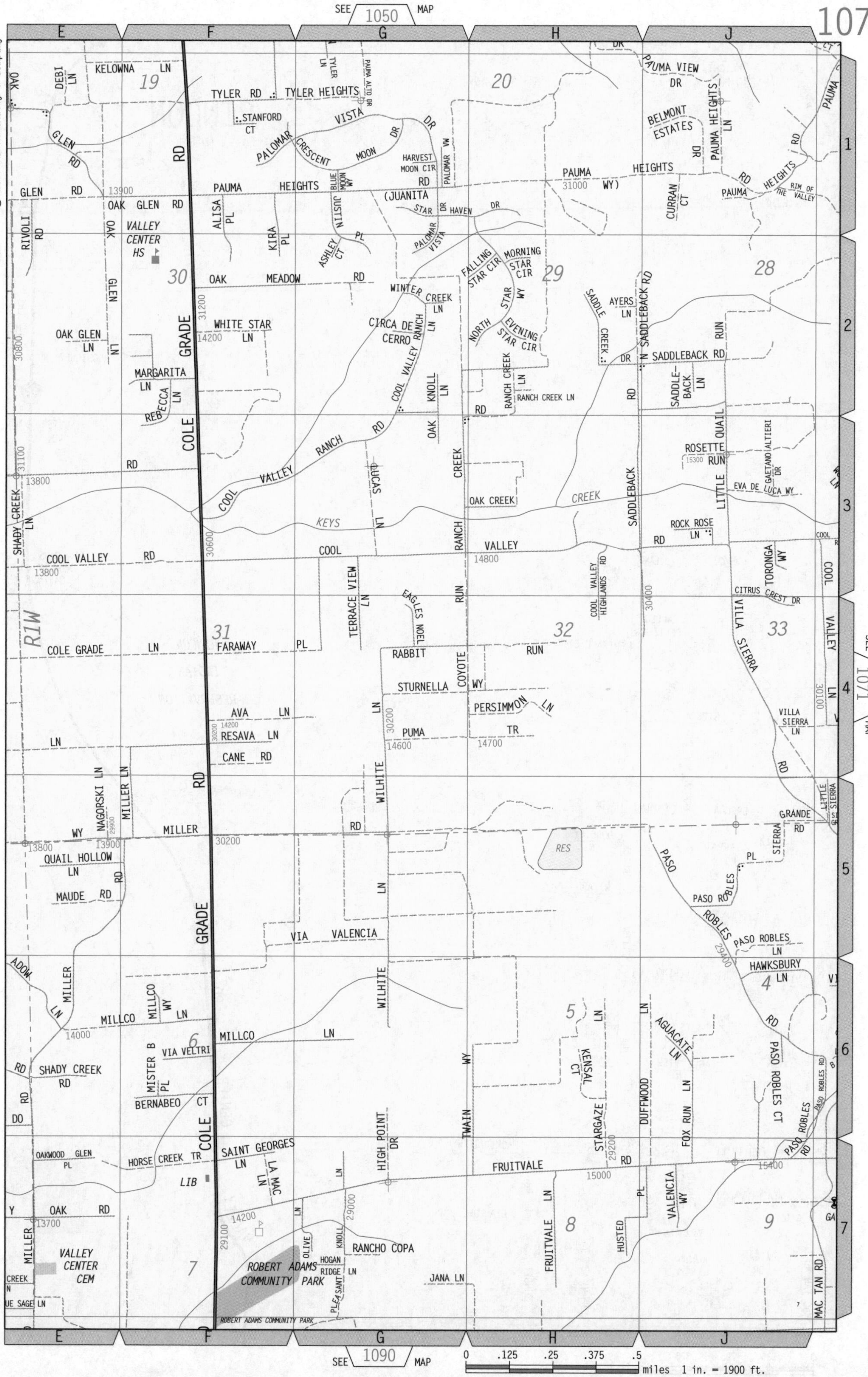
SEE 1050 MAP
E
F
G
H
J
KELOWNA LN
DEBI LN
OAK
TYLER RD
TYLER HEIGHTS
TYLER LN
PAUMA ALTO DR
STANFORD CT
PALOMAR
CRESCENT
VISTA
MOON DR
DR
HARVEST MOON CIR
PALOMAR VW
BLUE MOON WY
PAUMA VIEW DR
BELMONT ESTATES DR
PAUMA HEIGHTS LN
PAUMA
RD
GLEN RD
GLEN RD
PAUMA HEIGHTS
PAUMA 31000 WY)
HEIGHTS
(JUANITA
STAR HAVEN DR
PAUMA HEIGHTS RD
RIM OF THE VALLEY
CURRAN CT
13900
OAK GLEN RD
RIVOLI RD
VALLEY CENTER HS
OAK GLEN LN
ALISA PL
KIRA PL
JUSTIN PL
ASHLEY CT
PALOMAR VISTA
FALLING STAR CIR
MORNING STAR CIR
NORTH STAR WY
EVENING STAR CIR
OAK MEADOW RD
WINTER CREEK LN
CIRCA DE CERRO
RANCH
COOL VALLEY
SADDLE CREEK DR
AYERS LN
SADDLEBACK RD
N SADDLEBACK RD
RUN
OAK GLEN LN
WHITE STAR LN
14200
31200
30800
MARGARITA LN
REBECCA LN
COLE GRADE RD
KNOLL LN
OAK
RANCH CREEK LN
RANCH CREEK LN
RD
SADDLE-BACK LN
ROSETTE RUN
15300
GAETANO DR
ALTIERI
LITTLE QUAIL
EVA DE LUCA WY
RD
31100
13800
COOL VALLEY RANCH RD
LUCAS LN
CREEK
OAK CREEK
CREEK
SADDLEBACK
KEYS
ROCK ROSE LN
RD
SHADY CREEK LN
COOL VALLEY RD
30600
COOL
VALLEY
14800
RANCH
COOL VALLEY HIGHLANDS RD
30400
TORONGA WY
COOL
13800
TERRACE VIEW LN
EAGLES NOEL
RUN
CITRUS CREST DR
VILLA SIERRA RD
COOL VALLEY LN
R1W
31
32
33
COLE GRADE LN
FARAWAY PL
RABBIT
RUN
COYOTE
STURNELLA WY
PERSIMMON LN
30100
VILLA SIERRA LN
AVA LN
14200
30200
RESAVA LN
LN
30200
PUMA TR
14600
14700
LN
CANE RD
NAGORSKI LN
MILLER LN
WILHITE
RD
MILLER
WY
29900
13800
13900
30200
RES
GRANDE RD
LITTLE SIERRA
QUAIL HOLLOW LN
RD
MAUDE RD
LN
PASO
PASO ROBLES
PL
SIERRA
VIA VALENCIA
ROBLES
PASO ROBLES LN
29400
HAWKSBURY LN
MEADOW
MILLER LN
MILLCO WY
MILLCO LN
14000
WILHITE
MILLCO LN
5
6
4
AGUACATE LN
RD
PASO ROBLES CT
PASO ROBLES RD
VIA VELTRI
SHADY CREEK RD
MISTER B PL
KENSAL CT
DUFFWOOD
FOX RUN LN
BERNABEO CT
TWAIN WY
HIGH POINT DR
STARGAZE LN
29200
PASO ROBLES RD
DO
COLE
OAKWOOD GLEN PL
HORSE CREEK TR
SAINT GEORGES LN
LA MAC LN
FRUITVALE
RD
15000
15400
LIB
LN
VALENCIA WY
PL
OAK RD
13700
14200
29100
29000
LN
FRUITVALE LN
8
9
7
MILLER
VALLEY CENTER CEM
ROBERT ADAMS COMMUNITY PARK
OLIVE
KNOLL
HOGAN RIDGE LN
RANCHO COPA
HUSTED
CREEK
PLEASANT
JANA LN
MAC TAN RD
ROBERT ADAMS COMMUNITY PARK
19
20
28
29
30
1
2
3
4
5
6
7
SEE 1071 MAP
SEE 1090 MAP
0 .125 .25 .375 .5 miles 1 in. = 1900 ft.

SAN DIEGO CO.

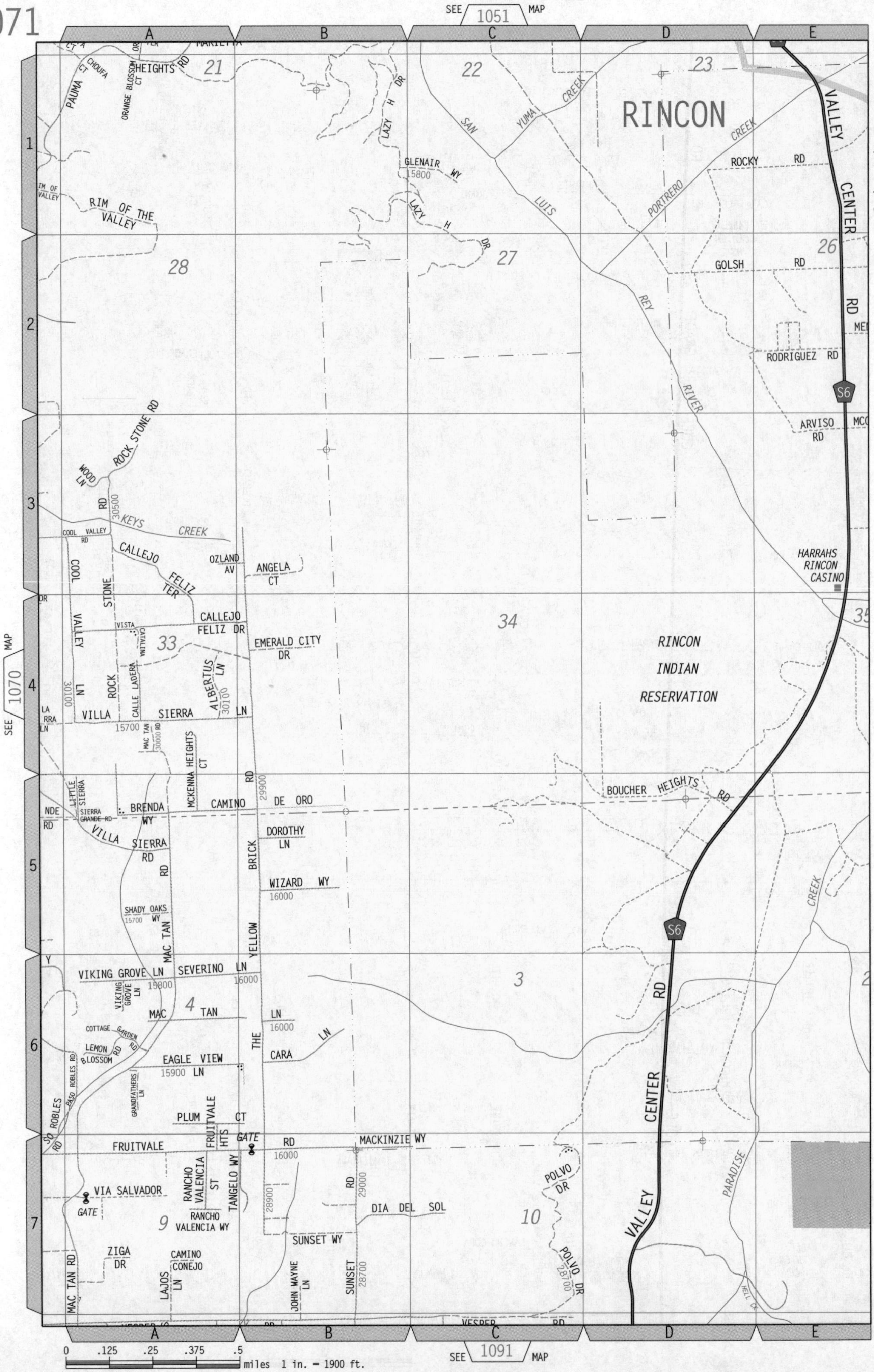
SEE 1051 MAP
A
B
C
D
E
1
2
3
4
5
6
7
RINCON
RINCON INDIAN RESERVATION
HARRAHS RINCON CASINO
21
22
23
26
27
28
33
34
35
3
4
9
10
MARIETTA
HEIGHTS RD
PAUMA CT
CHOUFA CT
ORANGE BLOSSOM CT
RIM OF THE VALLEY
IM OF VALLEY
LAZY H DR
GLENAIR WY
15800
SAN LUIS REY RIVER
YUMA CREEK
PORTRERO CREEK
ROCKY RD
GOLSH RD
RODRIGUEZ RD
ARVISO RD
VALLEY CENTER RD
S6
ROCK STONE RD
WOOD LN
30500
KEYS CREEK
COOL VALLEY RD
COOL VALLEY LN
CALLEJO FELIZ TER
CALLEJO FELIZ DR
OZLAND AV
ANGELA CT
EMERALD CITY DR
STONE
VISTA CATALINA
ROCK
CALLE LADERA
ALBERTUS LN
30100
VILLA SIERRA LN
15700
MAC TAN RD
30000
MCKENNA HEIGHTS CT
LITTLE SIERRA
SIERRA GRANDE RD
BRENDA WY
CAMINO DE ORO
29900
BRICK
BOUCHER HEIGHTS RD
VILLA SIERRA RD
DOROTHY LN
WIZARD WY
16000
SHADY OAKS WY
MAC TAN RD
YELLOW
VIKING GROVE LN
VIKING GROVE LN
SEVERINO LN
15800
MAC TAN LN
THE
CARA LN
COTTAGE GARDEN RD
LEMON BLOSSOM RD
EAGLE VIEW LN
15900
PASO ROBLES RD
SO ROBLES RD
GRANDFATHERS LN
PLUM CT
FRUITVALE HTS
FRUITVALE RD
GATE
MACKINZIE WY
RANCHO VALENCIA ST
RANCHO VALENCIA WY
TANGELO WY
28900
29000
VIA SALVADOR
POLVO DR
28700
DIA DEL SOL
SUNSET WY
SUNSET RD
JOHN WAYNE LN
ZIGA DR
CAMINO CONEJO
LAJOS LN
MAC TAN RD
VESPER RD
PARADISE CREEK
CREEK
SEE 1070 MAP
0 .125 .25 .375 .5 miles 1 in. = 1900 ft.
SEE 1091 MAP

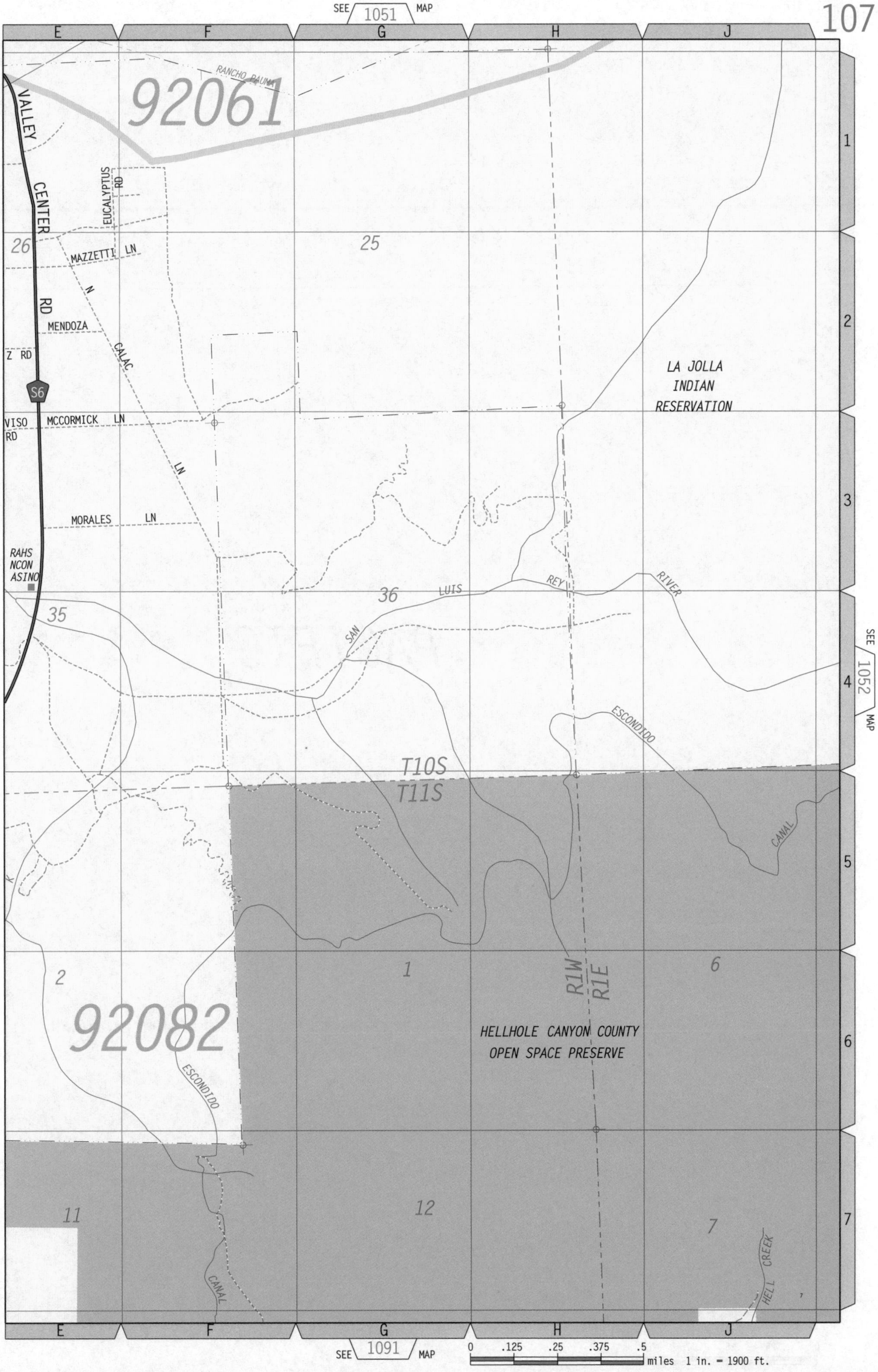
SEE 1051 MAP
E
F
G
H
J
92061
RANCHO PAUMA
VALLEY
CENTER
RD
EUCALYPTUS
RD
MAZZETTI LN
N
CALAC
LN
MENDOZA
Z RD
S6
VISO
RD
MCCORMICK LN
MORALES LN
RAHS
NCON
ASINO
26
25
35
36
SAN
LUIS
REY
RIVER
LA JOLLA
INDIAN
RESERVATION
ESCONDIDO
T10S
T11S
CANAL
2
1
6
92082
R1W
R1E
HELLHOLE CANYON COUNTY
OPEN SPACE PRESERVE
ESCONDIDO
11
12
7
CANAL
HELL
CREEK
1
2
3
4
5
6
7
SEE 1052 MAP
SEE 1091 MAP
0 .125 .25 .375 .5
miles 1 in. = 1900 ft.

SEE 408 MAP

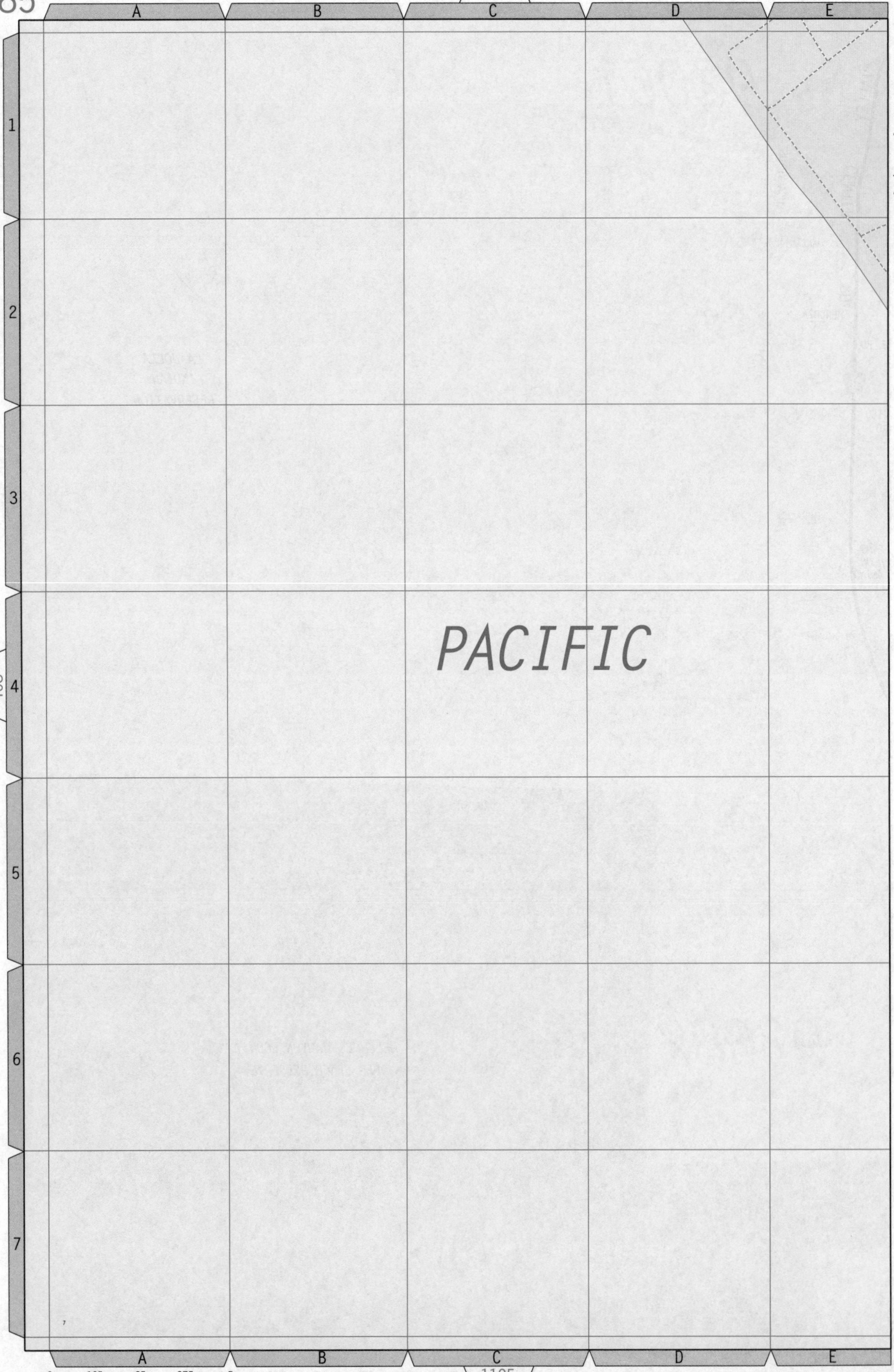

SEE 408 MAP

SEE 1105 MAP

0 .125 .25 .375 .5 miles 1 in. = 1900 ft.

N

SEE 408 MAP

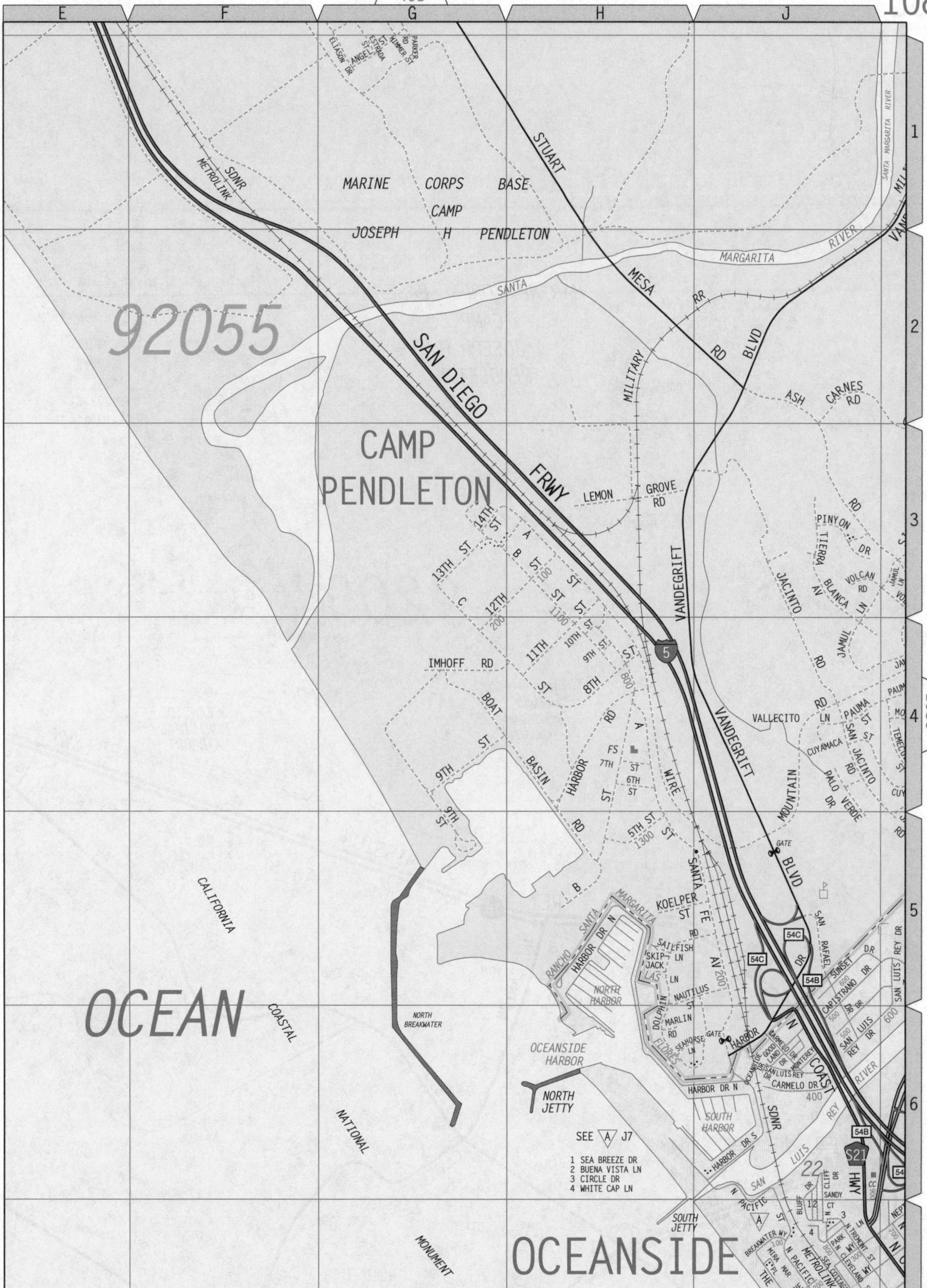

SEE 1086 MAP

SEE 1105 MAP

0 .125 .25 .375 .5 miles 1 in. = 1900 ft.

SEE 1066 MAP

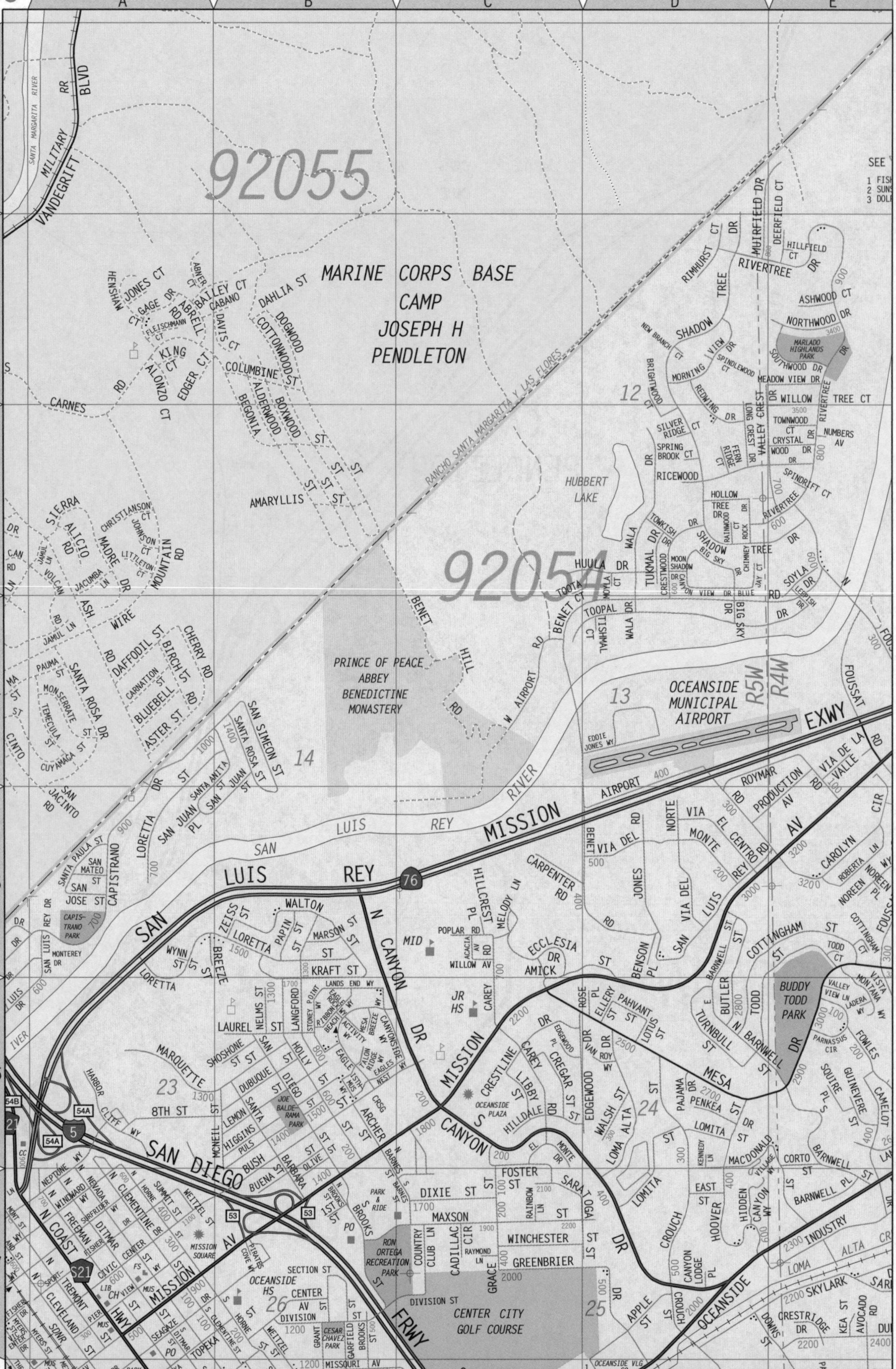

SEE 1085 MAP

SEE 1106 MAP

0 .125 .25 .375 .5 miles 1 in. = 1900 ft.

SEE 1066 MAP
E
F
G
H
J
1
2
3
4
5
6
7
SEE 1087 MAP
SEE 1106 MAP
0 .125 .25 .375 .5 miles 1 in. = 1900 ft.
SAN LUIS REY
OCEANSIDE
92057
92056
WHELAN LAKE
WHELAN LAKE RD
BRISAS ST
SAN LUIS REY RIVER
CALLE JOVEN
CALLE MONTECITO
DESCANSO
OLD RIVER ST
N DOUGLAS DR
PALA VISTA
VIA RIO
N OLD GROVE RD
PALA FRAZEE
ALLENDE AV
MISSION AV
76
EL CAMINO REAL
MISSION SAN LUIS REY DE FRANCIA
HERITAGE PARK
ALL SAINTS CEMETERY
IVEY RANCH PARK
MISSION DOUGLAS PLAZA
MISSION PLAZA REAL
OLD GROVE MARKETPLACE
OCEANSIDE CENTER
FIRESIDE PARK
LANCER AV
APRICOT TREE WY
PARKSIDE DR
LOS ARBOLITOS BL
RANCHO DEL ORO DR
SAN RAMON DR
STAGE COACH RD
VISTA BELLA
VISTA CAMPANA
EL CAMINO HS
MARTIN LUTHER KING JR PARK
MESA DR
FOUSSAT RD
FLAMINGO DR
PARK & RIDE
COPPERWOOD CENTER
TROPICANA DR
LAS VEGAS DR
MERCADO DE OCEANA
EMERALD ISLE GOLF COURSE
DEARBORN ST
OCEAN RANCH BLVD
SEE A J2
1 CAROB WY
2 HAZEL WY
3 JUNIPER WY
4 HYACINTH WY
5 AZALEA WY
6 CHESTNUT WY
7 CURRANT WY
8 CARDINAL WY
9 BLACKBIRD WY
10 LARK WY
SEE C H3
1 ALICIA WY
2 ADELIA WY
3 RAMONA WY
4 BORROMEO CT
5 MARIANA WY
6 CECILIA WY
7 ARABELLA WY
SEE D G2
1 FISHERMAN LN
2 SUNSET WY
3 DOLPHIN LN
SEE B J7
1 CROWN VIEW TER
OCEANSIDE BLVD
ALTA LOMA
TERRACE GARDENS MHP
OCEAN SHORES HS
SPRINTER (UNDER CONST)
SDNR
ALTA CREEK
HENIE HILLS DR
AVENIDA DE LOYOLA
CALLE BUENA VENTURA
SAN HELENA DR
SEA CLIFF WY
SAN TOMAS
PALISADES PARK
ETERNAL HILLS CEMETERY
EL CAMINO COUNTRY CLUB
SKYLINE DR
OCEANVIEW RD
GOLFCREST DR
DUNSTAN ST
SARBONNE DR
FIRE MTN PARK
JOSEPH CARRASCO PARK
CASERAS DR
COLUMBIA

SEE 1067 MAP

SEE 1086 MAP

0 .125 .25 .375 .5 miles 1 in. = 1900 ft.

SEE 1107 MAP

SEE 1067 MAP

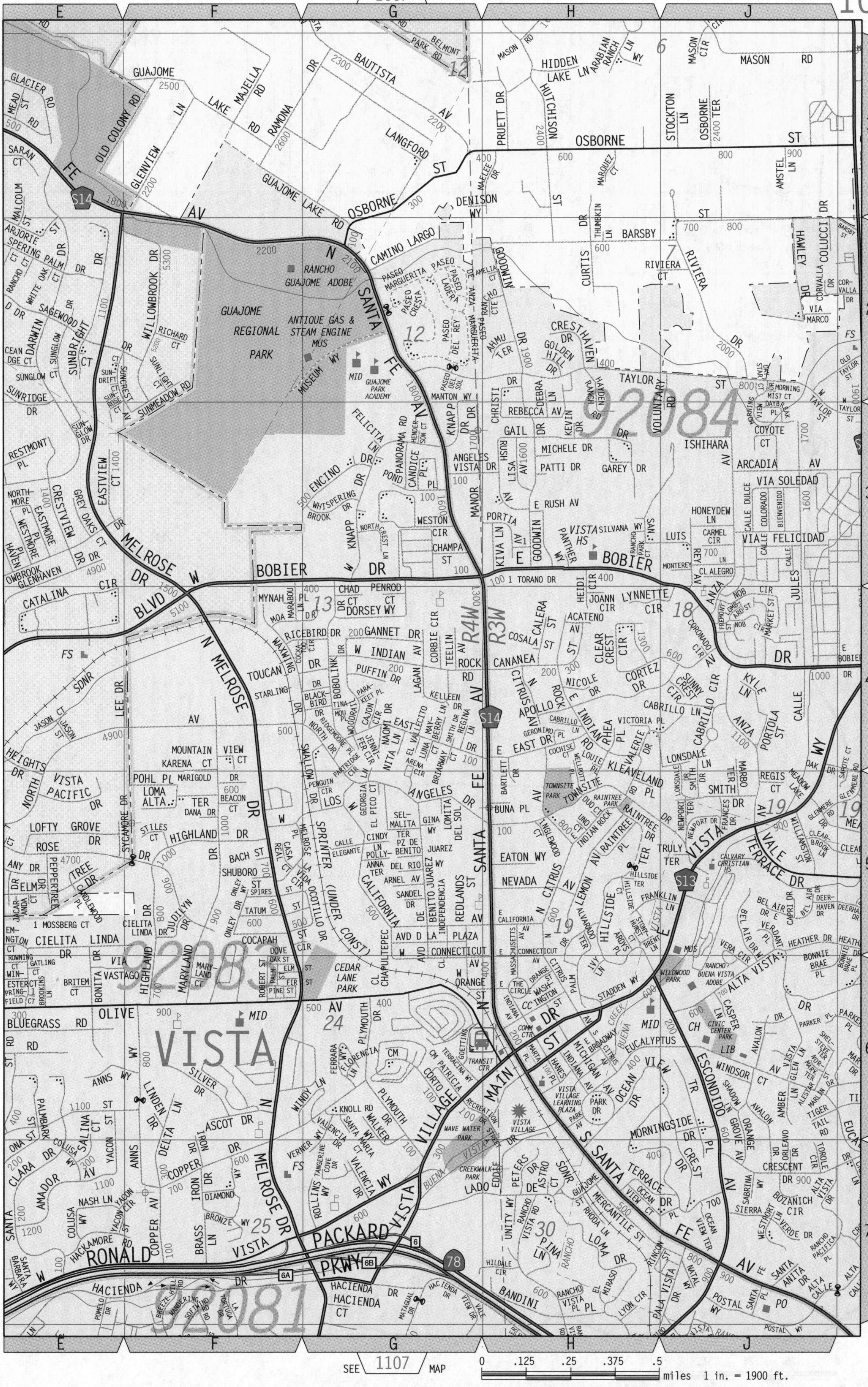

SEE 1088 MAP

SEE 1107 MAP

0 .125 .25 .375 .5 miles 1 in. = 1900 ft.

SEE 1068 MAP

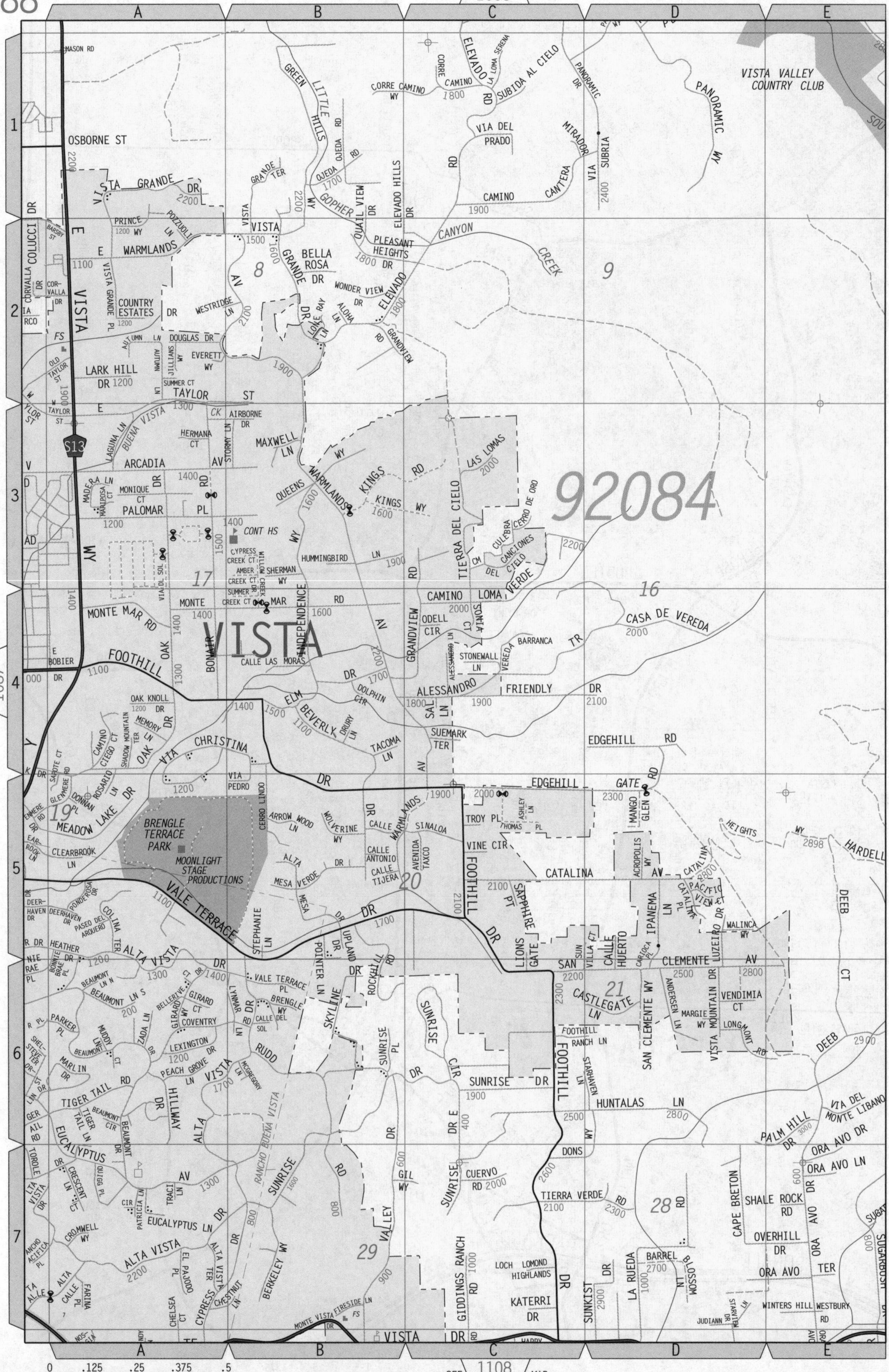

SEE 1087 MAP

SEE 1108 MAP

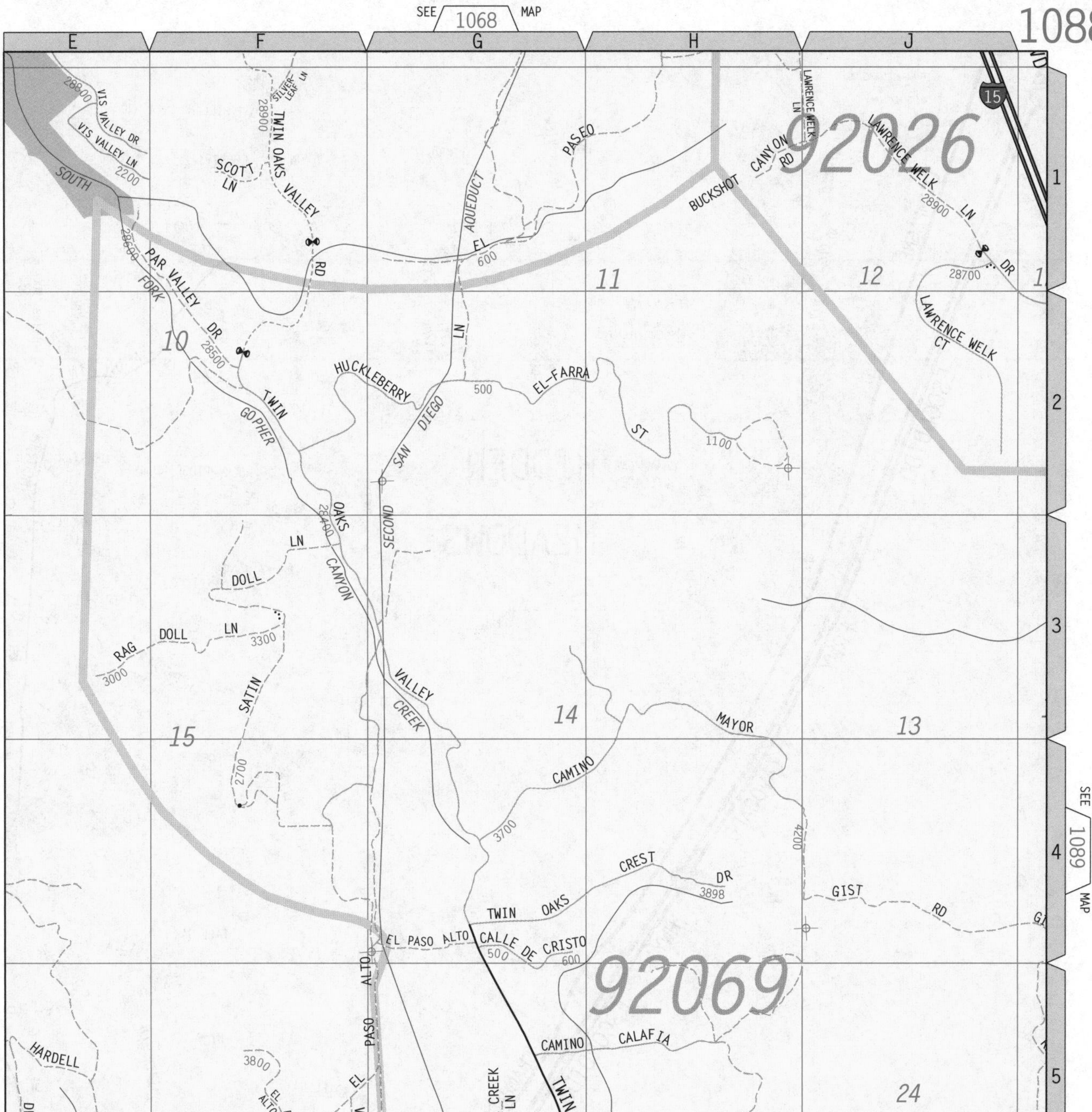

0 .125 .25 .375 .5 miles 1 in. = 1900 ft.

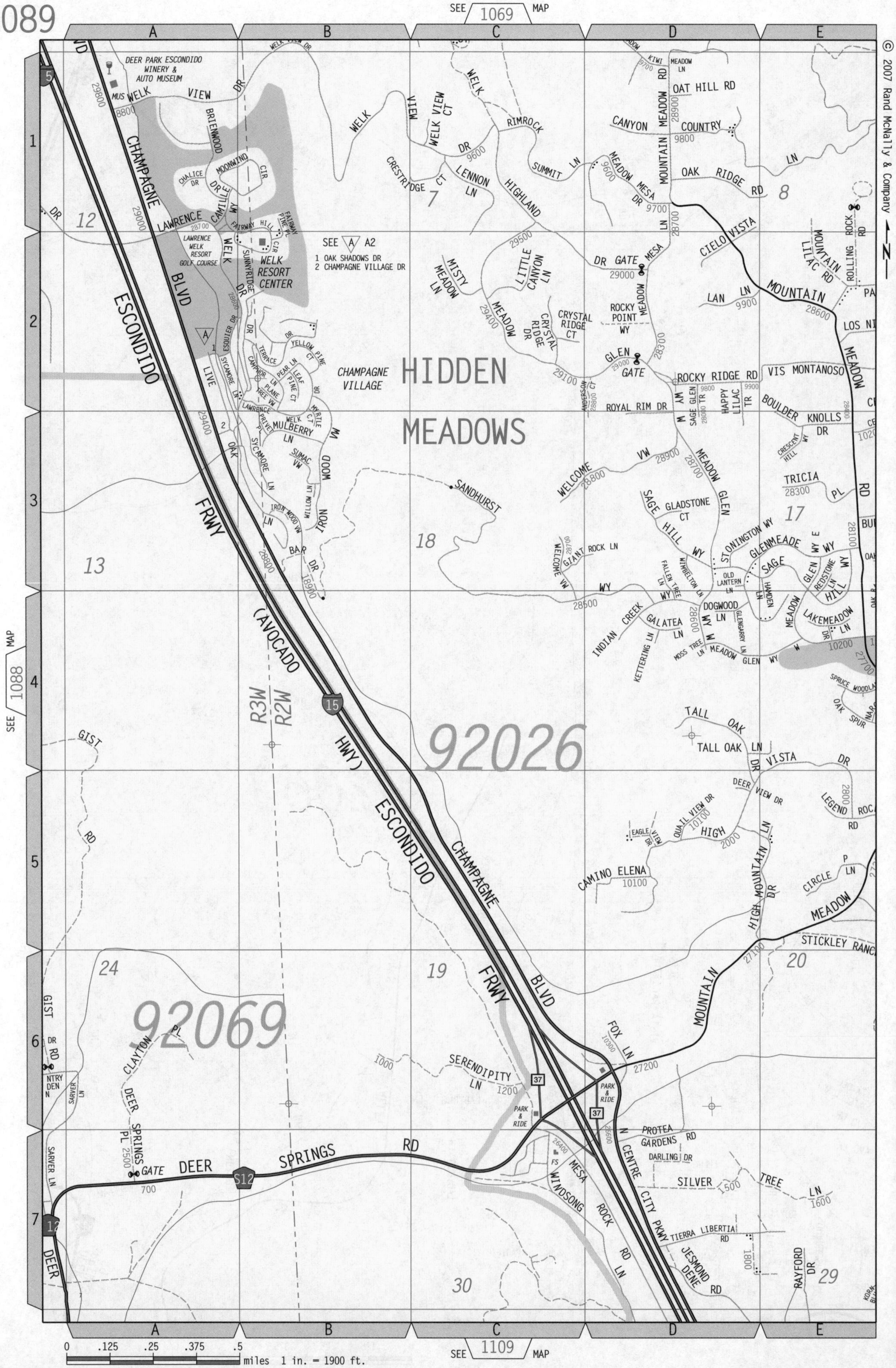

SEE 1069 MAP
SEE 1088 MAP
SEE 1109 MAP
A
B
C
D
E
1
2
3
4
5
6
7
DEER PARK ESCONDIDO WINERY & AUTO MUSEUM
MUS
WELK VIEW DR
BRIENWOOD
MOONWIND
CHALICE DR
CIR
CAMILLE WY
LAWRENCE
FAIRWAY HILL CIR
FAIRWAY PINE PL
LAWRENCE WELK RESORT GOLF COURSE
WELK RESORT CENTER
SUNNYRIDGE DR
SEE A A2
1 OAK SHADOWS DR
2 CHAMPAGNE VILLAGE DR
CHAMPAGNE BLVD
ESCONDIDO FRWY
(AVOCADO HWY)
CHAMPAGNE VILLAGE
HIDDEN MEADOWS
MULBERRY LN
SUMAC VW
WOOD WY
IRON WOOD VW
BAR DR
SANDHURST
WELK VIEW CT
RIMROCK
CRESTRIDGE CT
LENNON LN
HIGHLAND
SUMMIT LN
MEADOW MESA DR
MOUNTAIN MEADOW RD
KIWI
MEADOW LN
OAT HILL RD
CANYON COUNTRY
OAK RIDGE RD
CIELO VISTA
MOUNTAIN
MOUNTAIN LILAC RD
ROLLING ROCK RD
MISTY MEADOW LN
LITTLE CANYON LN
MEADOW DR
CRYSTAL RIDGE DR
CRYSTAL RIDGE CT
DR GATE MESA
ROCKY POINT WY
MEADOW
GLEN GATE
ROCKY RIDGE RD
VIS MONTANOSO
ROYAL RIM DR
SAGE GLEN TR
HAPPY LILAC TR
BOULDER KNOLLS DR
CRESCENT HILL WY
WELCOME VW
MEADOW GLEN
SAGE HILL WY
GLADSTONE CT
TRICIA PL
STONINGTON WY
GLENMEADE WY E
GIANT ROCK LN
OLD LANTERN LN
SAGE GLEN WY
REDSTONE WY
HILL
DOGWOOD LN
INDIAN CREEK
GALATEA
KETTERING LN
MOSS TREE LN
MEADOW GLEN WY
LAKEMEADOW LN
SPRUCE WOODLAND
OAK SPUR
TALL OAK
TALL OAK LN
VISTA DR
DEER VIEW DR
QUAIL VIEW DR
EAGLE VIEW DR
HIGH
HIGH MOUNTAIN DR
LN
LEGEND ROCK RD
CAMINO ELENA
CIRCLE P LN
MEADOW
STICKLEY RANCH
MOUNTAIN
FOX LN
SERENDIPITY LN
PARK & RIDE
PROTEA GARDENS RD
DARLING DR
SILVER TREE LN
CENTRE CITY PKWY
MESA ROCK RD
WINDSONG LN
TIERRA LIBERTIA RD
JESMOND DENE RD
RAYFORD DR
DEER SPRINGS RD
DEER SPRINGS PL
GATE
CLAYTON PL
GIST RD
SARVER LN
R3W
R2W
92026
92069
12
13
7
8
17
18
19
20
24
29
30
15
37
S12
12
0
.125
.25
.375
.5
miles 1 in. = 1900 ft.

SEE 1069 MAP

SEE 1090 MAP

0 .125 .25 .375 .5 miles 1 in. = 1900 ft.

SEE 1070 MAP

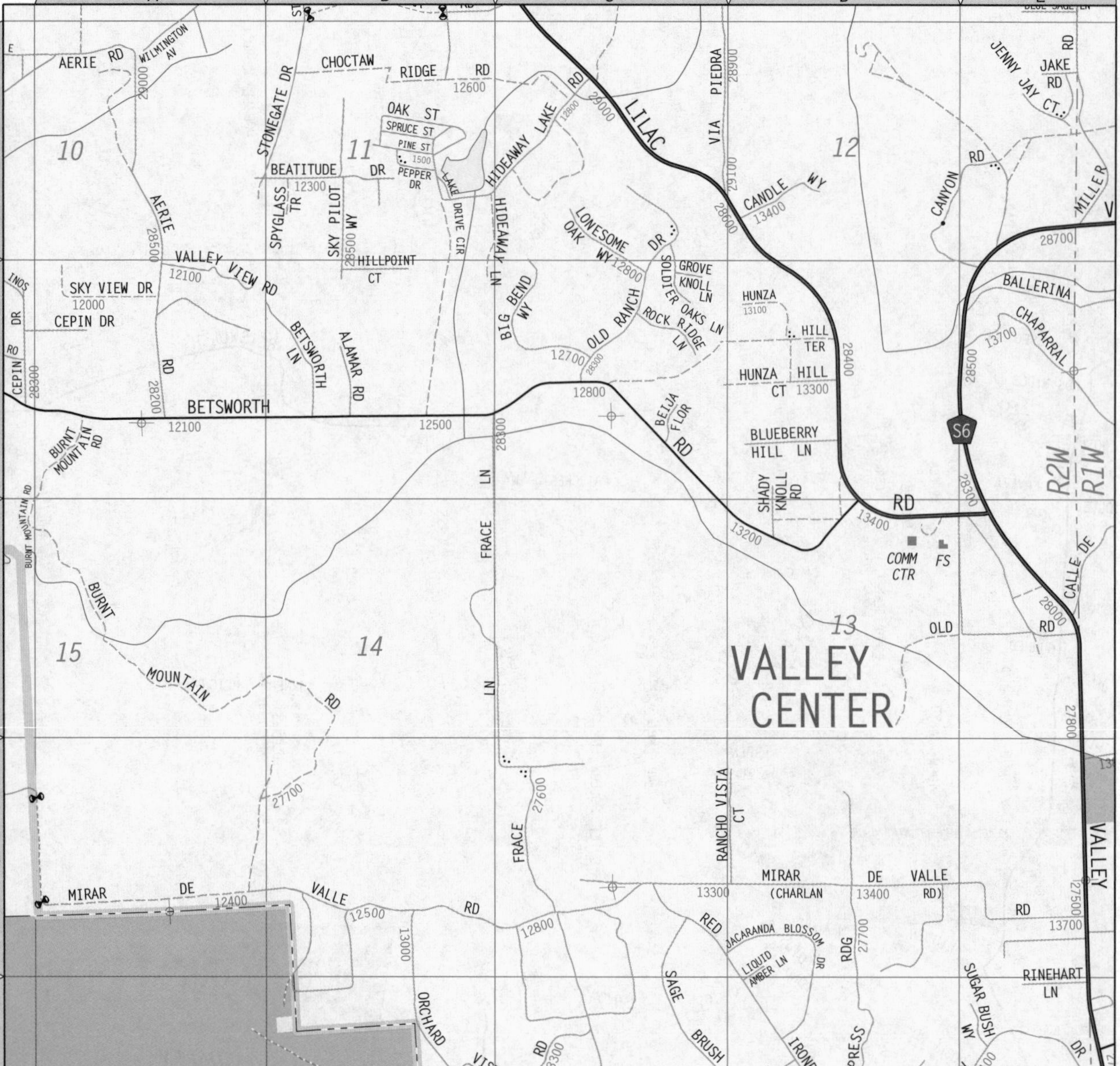

SEE 1110 MAP

0 .125 .25 .375 .5 miles 1 in. = 1900 ft.

SEE 1070 MAP
E
F
G
H
J
ROBERT ADAMS COMMUNITY PARK
VALLEY CENTER SCHOOL RD
COLE GRADE RD
SCHOOL
BUS LN
FS
PO
JAKE RD
CT.
MILLER
VALLEY
VESPER
RD
JANA LN
ALMONA WY
VESPER RD
TAN RD
MAC RD
CENTER RD
S6
JUBA RD
LIZARD ROCKS RD
GRADE RD
RINA LN
INDIAN CREEK RD
ARRAL
COLE
TURTLE ROCK RD
IRISH OAKS RD
ROCK HILL RANCH RD
ROUND TREE RD
GLEN TREE RD
QUEENSBRIDGE
ROUND TREE
EAGLEHILL RD
SERENITY PTH
ORANGE TER
TER
R2W
R1W
VISTA
CALLE DE VISTA
CALLE DE
RD
92082
SUNDAY DR
COOL WATER RANCH
QUIET PL
(CL DE VISTA)
RD
COOL
COBB LN
SEE 1091 MAP
WINGED FOOT CIR
SAINT ANDREWS
WOODS VALLEY GOLF CLUB
CLUBHOUSE
MERION CIR
MUIRFIELD AV
AUGUSTA
SUNNINGDALE WY
SAINT ANDREWS
INTERLACHEN TER
INVERNESS AV
LN
COEUR D ALENE CT
PEBBLE BEACH WY
MEDINAH WY
SAWGRASS CIR
RIVIERA WY
CYPRESS POINT TER
SUNNINGDALE WY
DR
VALLEY VISTA DR
KARIBU LN
HAZELTINE RD
CHARLAN RD
NEHART LN
WOODS
VALLEY RD
WOODS VALLEY CT
COUNTRY OAKS LN
RIDGE RANCH CT
CENTER
TOYON RIDGE TR
OAKMONT
RIDGE
CANYON RD
RIDGE
RIDGE RANCH RD
SHADOWOOD LN
WOODSTOCK PL
R
RANCH
RD
RIDGE OAK LN
ENGELMANN
92027
RD
1
2
3
4
5
6
7
7
8
9
16
17
18
19
20
21
28
29
30
SAN DIEGO CO.
SEE 1110 MAP
0 .125 .25 .375 .5 miles 1 in. = 1900 ft.

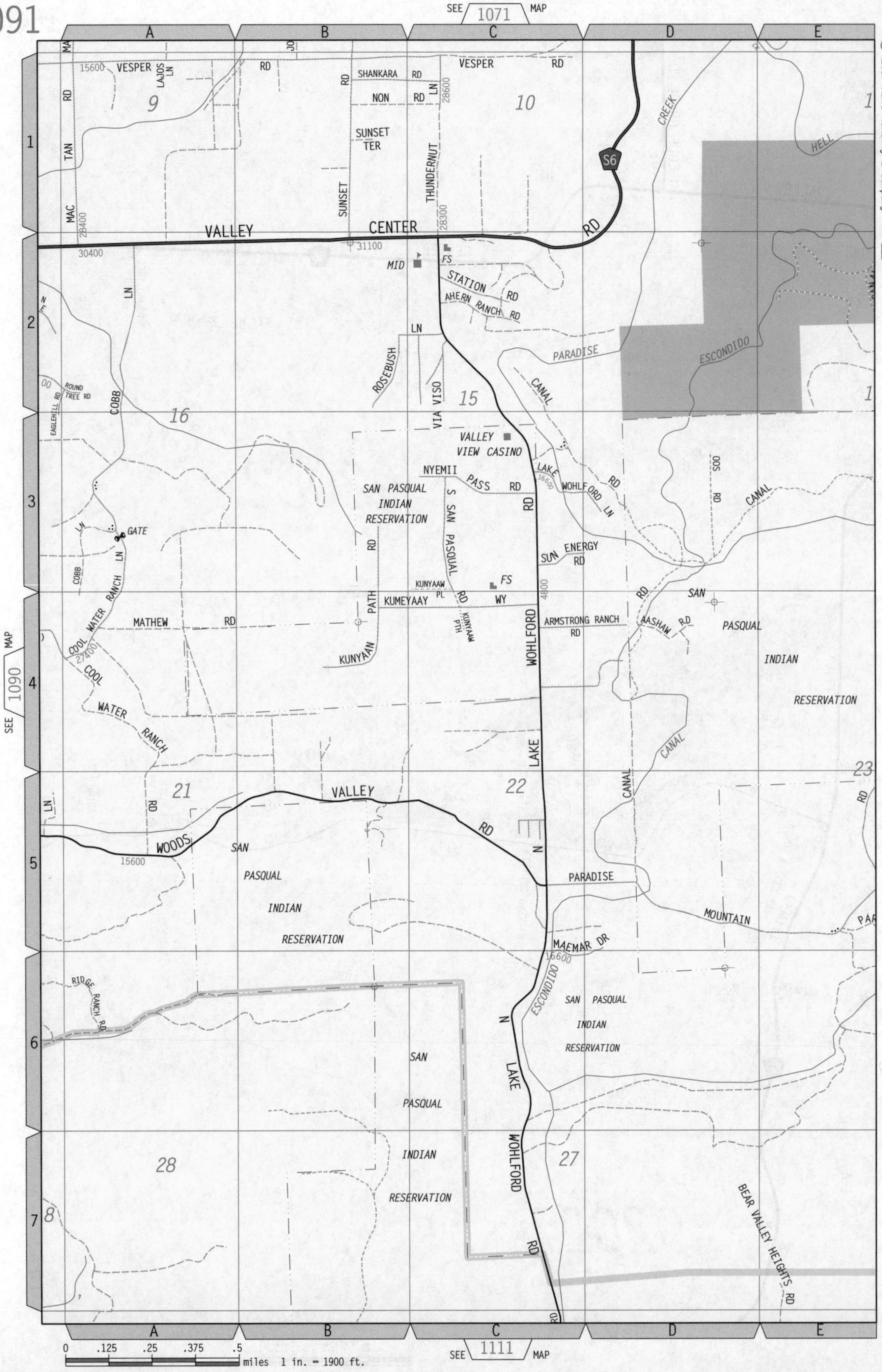
SEE 1071 MAP
A
B
C
D
E
1
2
3
4
5
6
7
VESPER RD
15600
LAJOS LN
TAN RD
MAC
28400
SHANKARA RD
NON RD
SUNSET TER
SUNSET
THUNDERNUT LN
28600
28300
VESPER RD
9
10
S6
CREEK
HELL
VALLEY CENTER RD
30400
31100
MID
FS
STATION RD
AHERN RANCH RD
LN
ROSEBUSH
VIA VISO
PARADISE
ESCONDIDO
CANAL
COBB LN
ROUND TREE RD
EAGLEHILL RD
16
15
VALLEY VIEW CASINO
NYEMII PASS RD
SAN PASQUAL INDIAN RESERVATION
S SAN PASQUAL RD
LAKE WOHLFORD RD
1660
WOHLFORD LN
OOS RD
CANAL
GATE
COBB LN
SUN ENERGY RD
KUNYAAW PL
FS
KUMEYAAY WY
KUNYAAW PTH
4800
PATH RD
MATHEW RD
COOL WATER RANCH
27400
KUNYAAN
ARMSTRONG RANCH RD
AASHAW RD
RD
SAN PASQUAL INDIAN RESERVATION
SEE 1090 MAP
COOL WATER RANCH
WOHLFORD LAKE
CANAL
CANAL
21
22
23
LN
RD
VALLEY WOODS RD
15600
SAN PASQUAL INDIAN RESERVATION
N
PARADISE
MOUNTAIN
PAR
MAEMAR DR
15600
ESCONDIDO
RIDGE RANCH RD
N LAKE WOHLFORD RD
SAN PASQUAL INDIAN RESERVATION
SAN PASQUAL INDIAN RESERVATION
28
27
8
BEAR VALLEY HEIGHTS RD
RD
SEE 1111 MAP
0 .125 .25 .375 .5
miles 1 in. = 1900 ft.

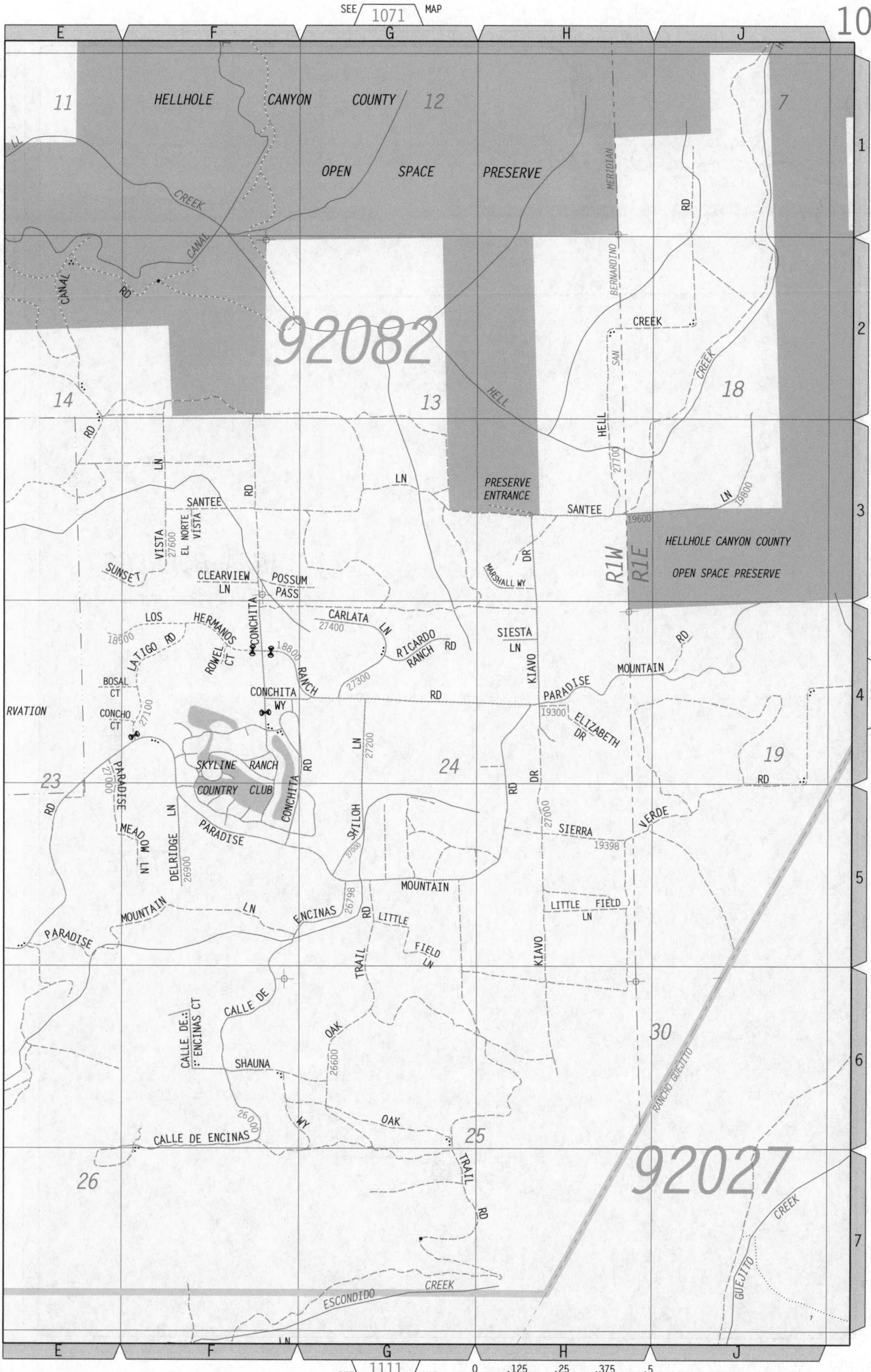
SEE 1071 MAP
E
F
G
H
J
1
2
3
4
5
6
7
HELLHOLE CANYON COUNTY OPEN SPACE PRESERVE
11
12
7
13
14
18
19
23
24
25
26
30
92082
92027
CREEK
CANAL
RD
MERIDIAN
BERNARDINO
SAN
CREEK
HELL
HELL
CREEK
27700
LN
SANTEE
PRESERVE ENTRANCE
SANTEE
19600
19800
HELLHOLE CANYON COUNTY OPEN SPACE PRESERVE
R1W
R1E
VISTA
27600
EL NORTE VISTA
SUNSET
CLEARVIEW LN
POSSUM PASS
CONCHITA
CARLATA LN
27400
MARSHALL WY
DR
LOS HERMANOS
18500
LATIGO RD
ROWEL CT
18800
RICARDO RANCH RD
SIESTA LN
KIAVO
MOUNTAIN RD
PARADISE
BOSAL CT
CONCHO CT
27100
CONCHITA WY
RANCH
27300
RD
19300
ELIZABETH DR
SEE 409 MAP
RVATION
SKYLINE RANCH COUNTRY CLUB
CONCHITA RD
LN
27200
PARADISE
27000
MEAD
NT MO
LN
DELRIDGE
26900
PARADISE
SHILOH
27000
RD
DR
27000
SIERRA
19398
VERDE
MOUNTAIN
LITTLE FIELD LN
MOUNTAIN
LN
ENCINAS
26798
RD
LITTLE
FIELD LN
PARADISE
TRAIL
KIAVO
CALLE DE
CALLE DE ENCINAS CT
SHAUNA
OAK
26600
RANCHO GUEJITO
26000
WY
OAK
CALLE DE ENCINAS
TRAIL
RD
CREEK
GUEJITO
ESCONDIDO
CREEK
LN
E
F
G
H
J
SEE 1111 MAP
0 .125 .25 .375 .5
miles 1 in. = 1900 ft.

SAN DIEGO CO.

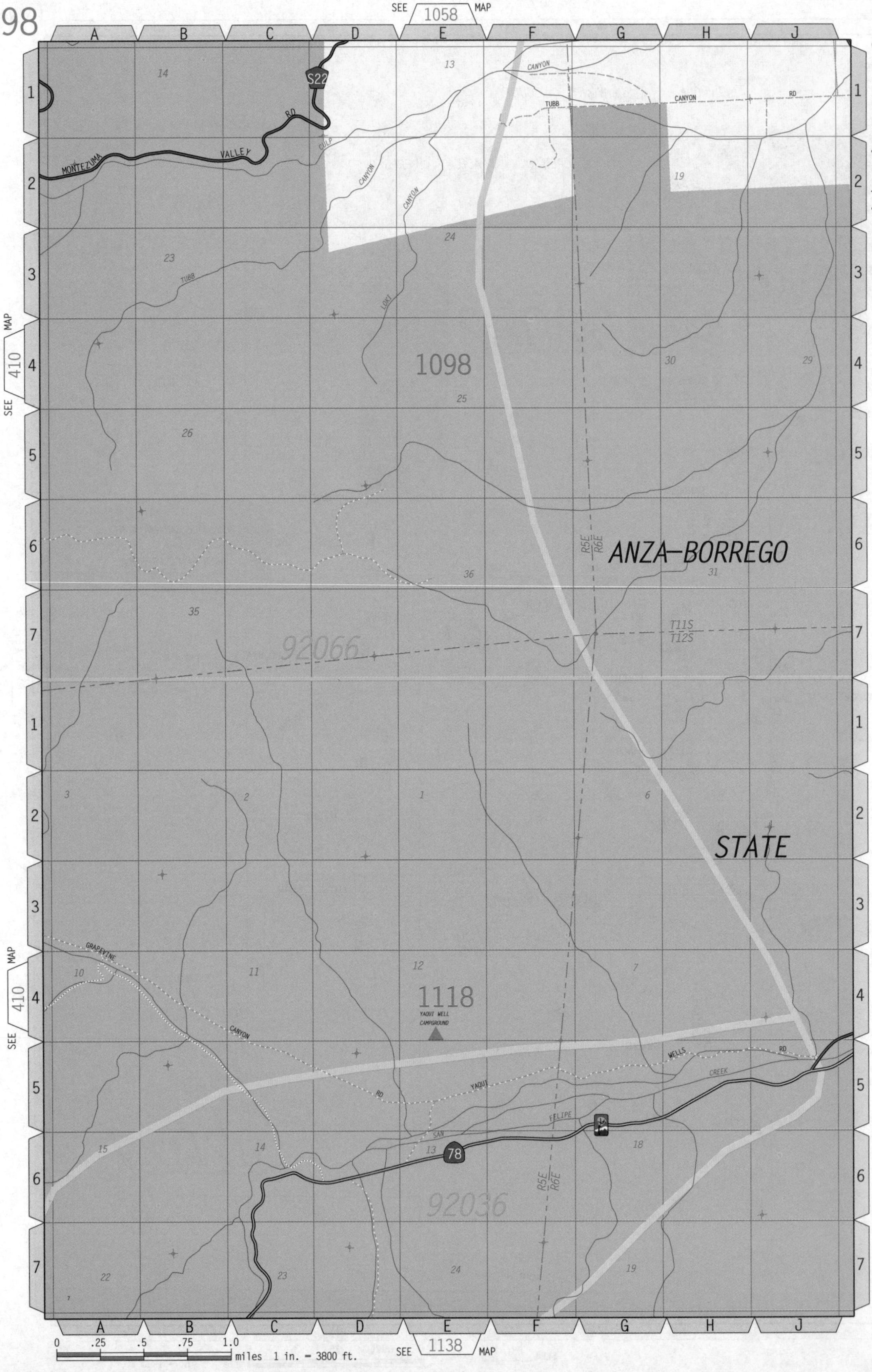
SEE 1058 MAP
SEE 410 MAP
SEE 410 MAP
SEE 1138 MAP
1098
1118
ANZA-BORREGO
STATE
MONTEZUMA VALLEY RD
S22
CULP CANYON
CANYON
TUBB CANYON RD
TUBB
LOKI
CANYON
R5E R6E
T11S T12S
92066
92036
GRAPEVINE CANYON
YAQUI WELL CAMPGROUND
YAQUI WELLS RD
SAN FELIPE CREEK
78
0 .25 .5 .75 1.0 miles 1 in. = 3800 ft.

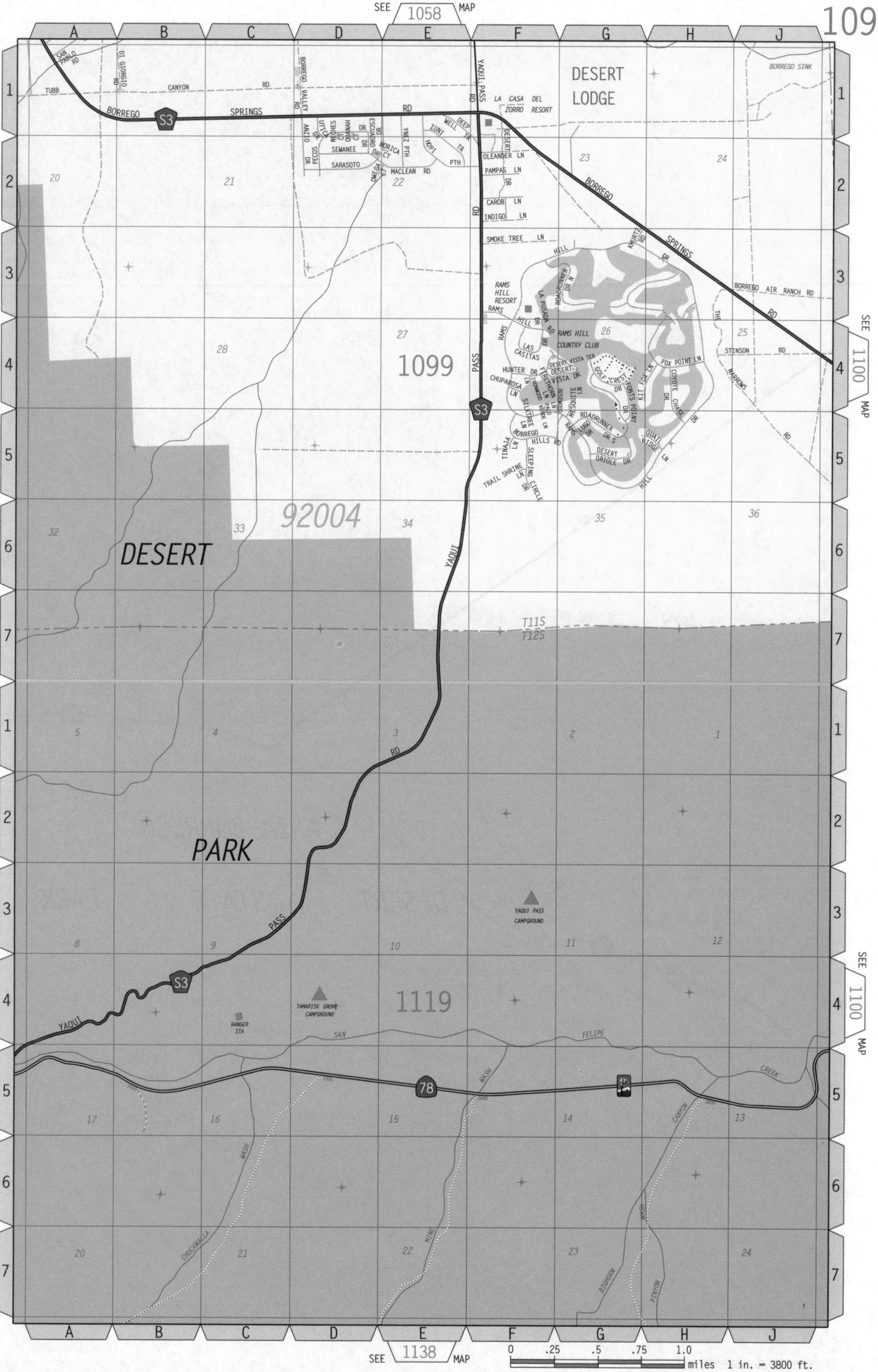
SEE 1058 MAP
DESERT LODGE
LA CASA DEL ZORRO RESORT
BORREGO SPRINGS RD
S3
TUBB CANYON RD
DI GIORGIO RD
SAN PABLO RD
BORREGO VALLEY RD
YAQUI PASS RD
RAMS HILL RESORT
RAMS HILL COUNTRY CLUB
1099
92004
DESERT
PARK
BORREGO AIR RANCH RD
STINSON RD
SEE 1100 MAP
YAQUI PASS CAMPGROUND
TAMARISK GROVE CAMPGROUND
RANGER STA
1119
SAN FELIPE CREEK
78
T11S
T12S
SEE 1138 MAP
miles 1 in. = 3800 ft.

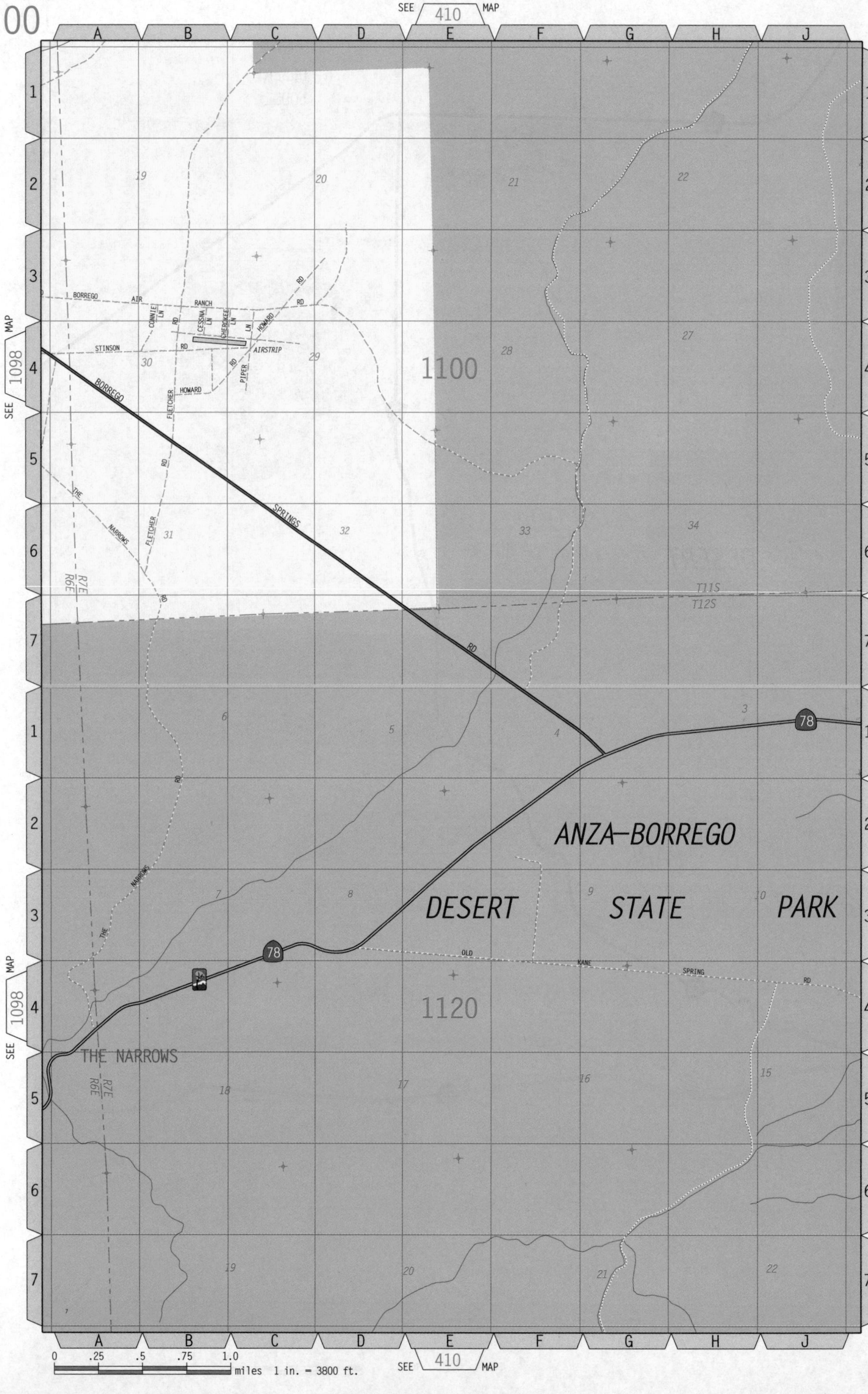
SEE MAP 410
SEE MAP 1098
1100
1120
BORREGO AIR RANCH RD
STINSON RD
HOWARD
CONNIE LN
CESSNA LN
CHEROKEE LN
HOWARD LN
PIPER RD
AIRSTRIP
FLETCHER RD
BORREGO SPRINGS RD
THE NARROWS
T11S
T12S
R7E
R6E
78
ANZA-BORREGO DESERT STATE PARK
OLD KANE SPRING RD
0 .25 .5 .75 1.0
miles 1 in. = 3800 ft.

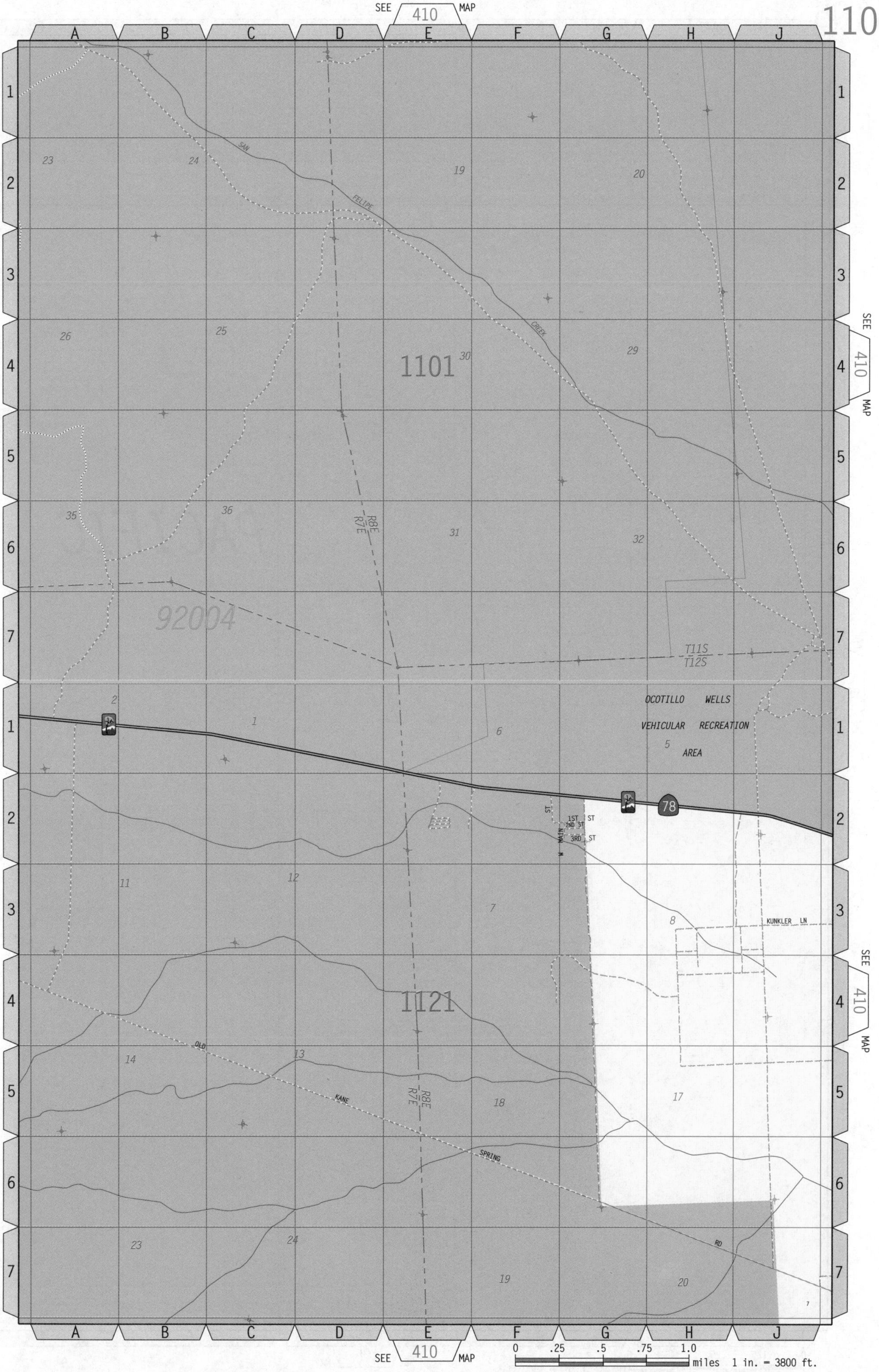
SEE 410 MAP
A B C D E F G H J
1 2 3 4 5 6 7
1101
1121
92004
SAN FELIPE CREEK
R8E R7E
T11S T12S
OCOTILLO WELLS VEHICULAR RECREATION AREA
78
1ST ST
2ND ST
3RD ST
W MAIN ST
KUNKLER LN
OLD KANE SPRING RD
23 24 19 20 26 25 30 29 35 36 31 32
2 1 6 5 11 12 7 8 14 13 18 17 23 24 19 20
0 .25 .5 .75 1.0 miles 1 in. = 3800 ft.

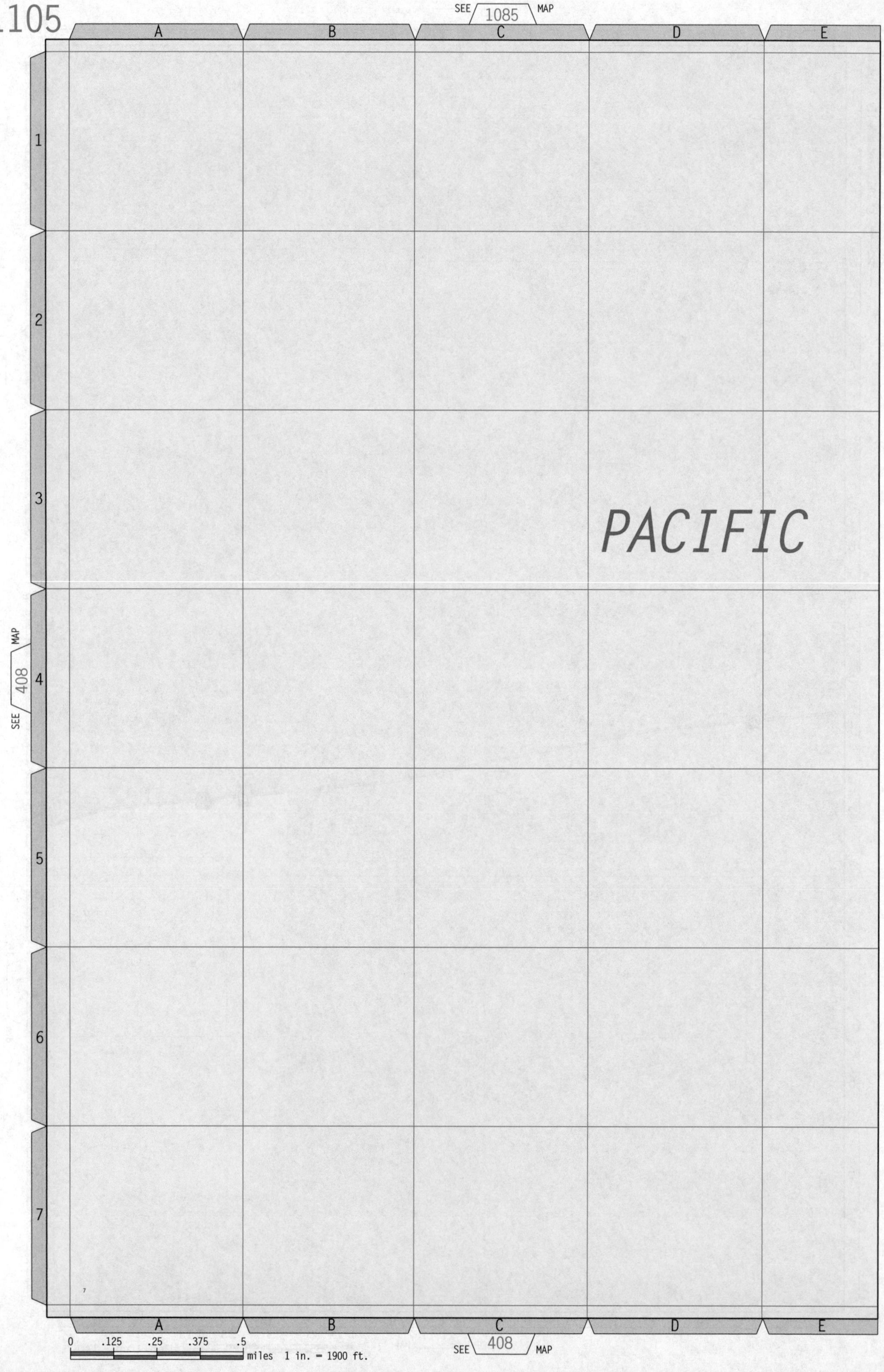
SEE 1085 MAP
A
B
C
D
E
1
2
3
4
5
6
7
PACIFIC
SEE 408 MAP
SEE 408 MAP
0 .125 .25 .375 .5 miles 1 in. = 1900 ft.

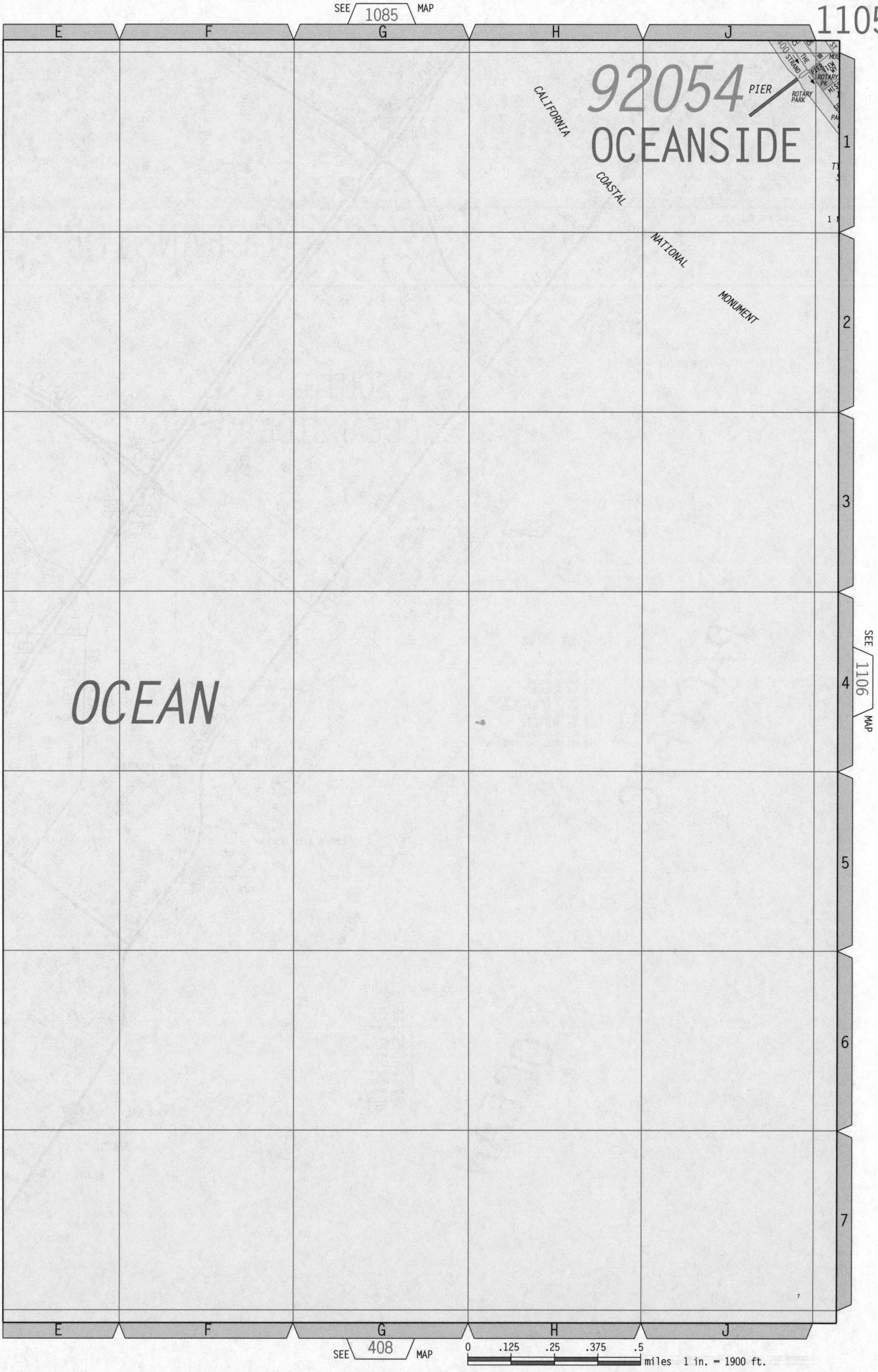
SEE 1085 MAP
E
F
G
H
J
92054
OCEANSIDE
PIER
ROTARY PARK
THE STRAND
CALIFORNIA
COASTAL
NATIONAL
MONUMENT
1
2
3
4
5
6
7
SEE 1106 MAP
OCEAN
SEE 408 MAP
0
.125
.25
.375
.5
miles 1 in. = 1900 ft.

SEE 1086 MAP

SEE 1105 MAP

SEE 1126 MAP

SEE 1086 MAP

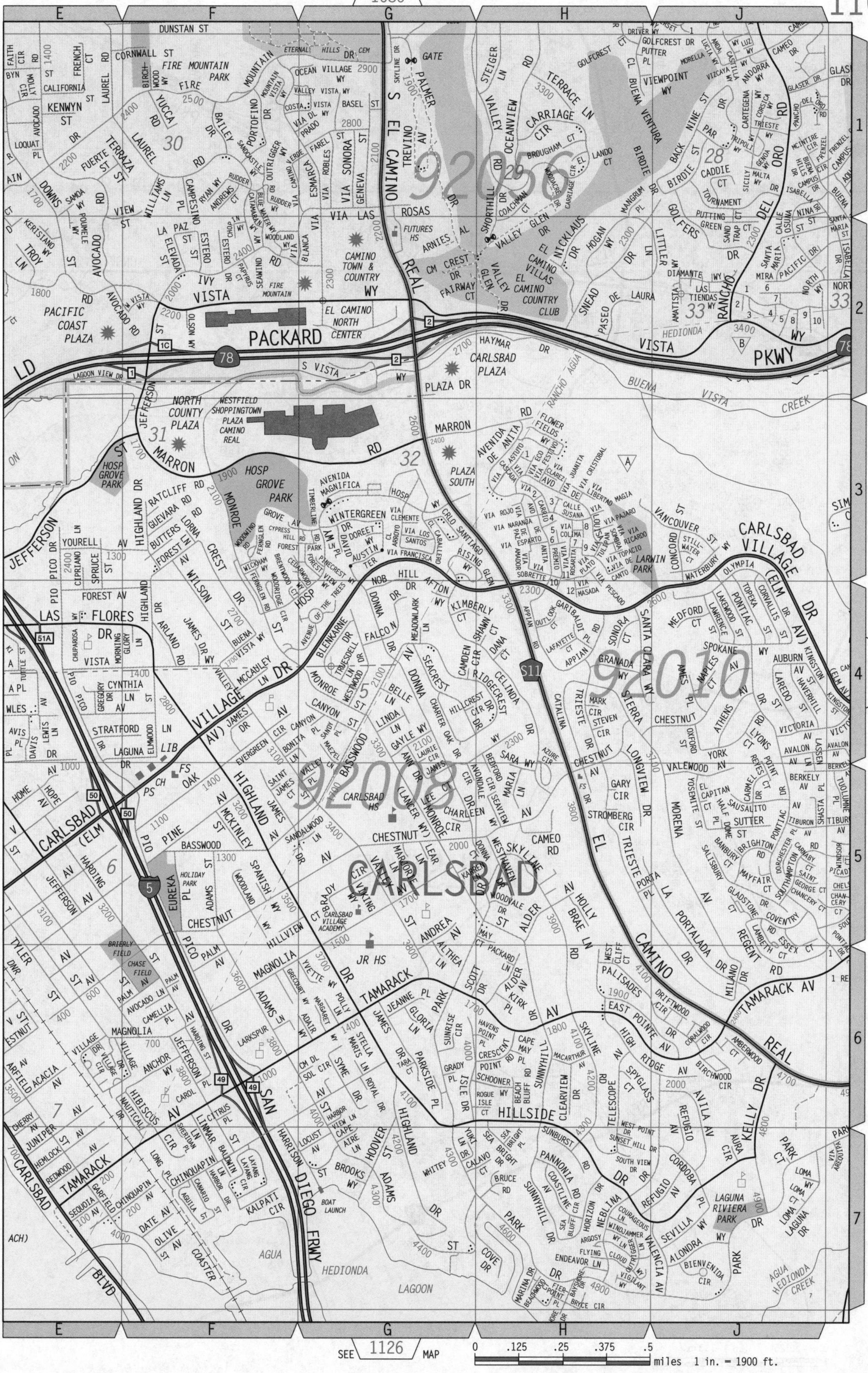

SEE 1107 MAP

SEE 1126 MAP

0 .125 .25 .375 .5 miles 1 in. = 1900 ft.

SAN DIEGO CO.

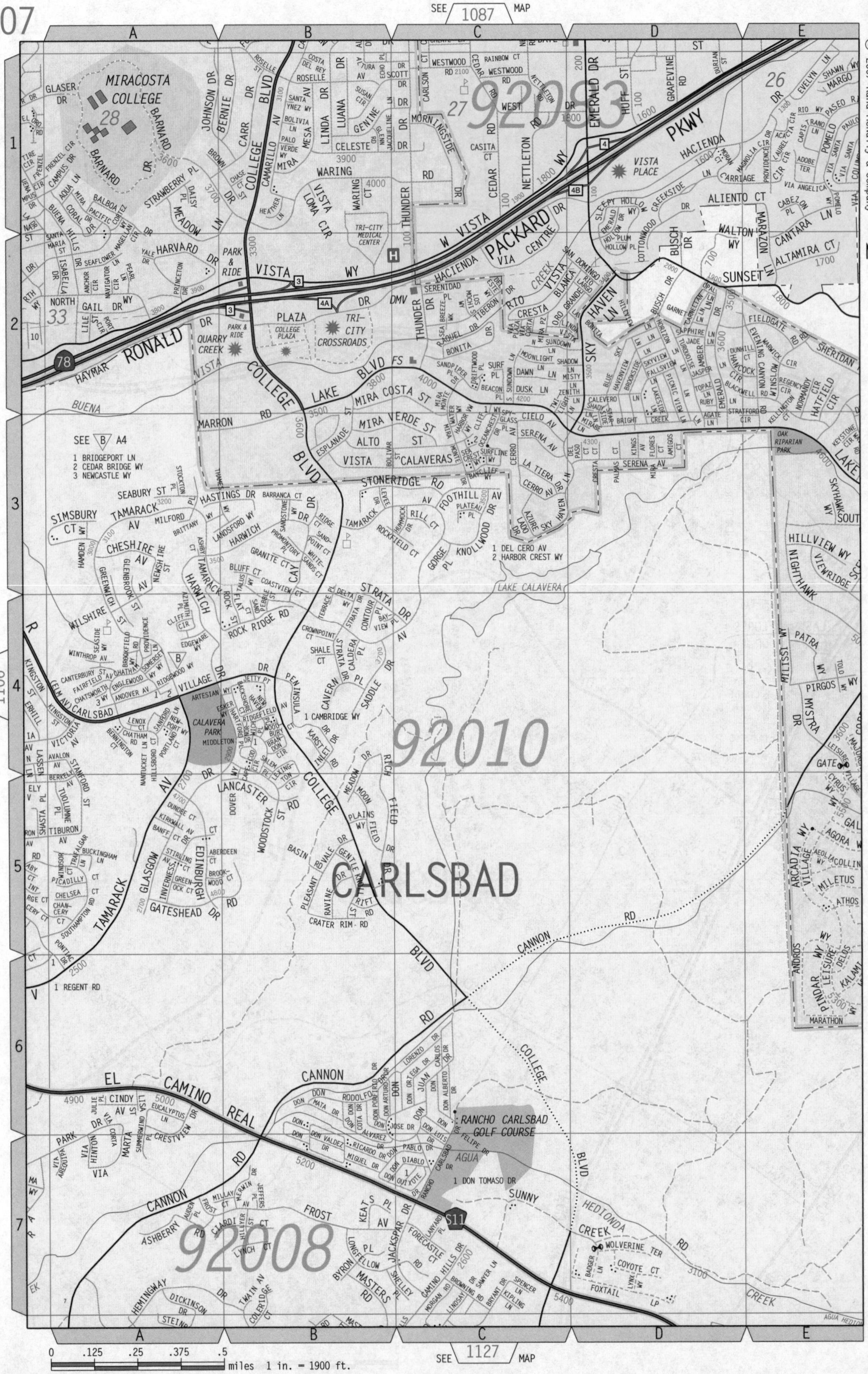

0 .125 .25 .375 .5 miles 1 in. = 1900 ft.

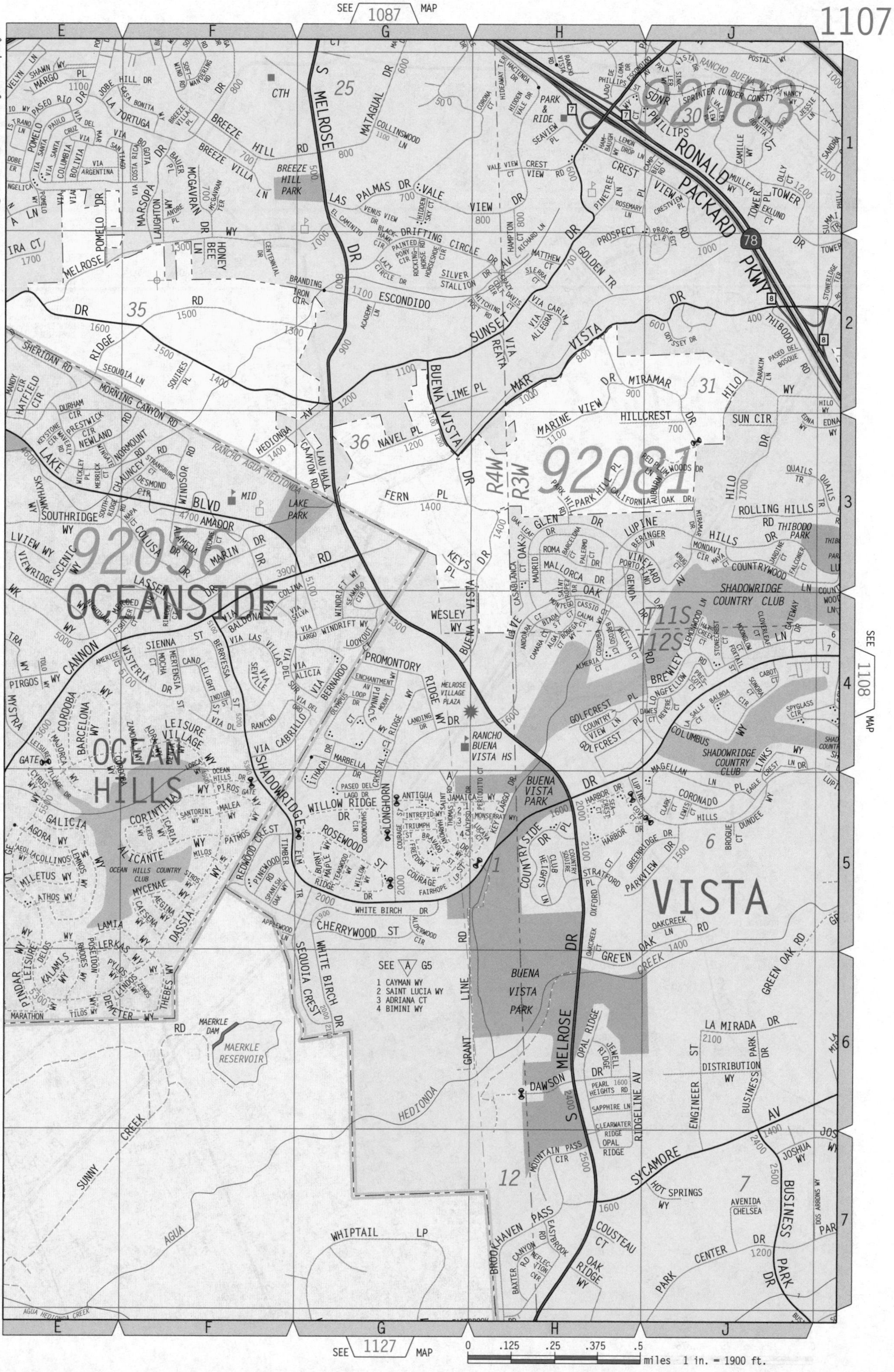

SEE 1087 MAP
SEE 1108 MAP
SEE 1127 MAP
E
F
G
H
J
1
2
3
4
5
6
7
92083
92081
92056
OCEANSIDE
OCEAN HILLS
VISTA
R4W
R3W
T11S
T12S
S MELROSE DR
MELROSE DR
RONALD PACKARD PKWY
78
SUNSET DR
MAR VISTA DR
BUENA VISTA DR
ESCONDIDO AV
LAKE BLVD
CANNON RD
COLLEGE BLVD
SHADOWRIDGE DR
SHADOWRIDGE COUNTRY CLUB
BREEZE HILL RD
BREEZE HILL PARK
LAKE PARK
BUENA VISTA PARK
RANCHO BUENA VISTA HS
MELROSE VILLAGE PLAZA
THIBODO PARK
MAERKLE DAM
MAERKLE RESERVOIR
OCEAN HILLS COUNTRY CLUB
RANCHO AGUA HEDIONDA
SUNNY CREEK
AGUA HEDIONDA CREEK
SYCAMORE AV
BUSINESS PARK DR
WHIPTAIL LP
GREEN OAK RD
LA MIRADA DR
DISTRIBUTION WY
ENGINEER ST
WHITE BIRCH DR
SEQUOIA CREST
CHERRYWOOD ST
ROSEWOOD ST
WILLOW RIDGE DR
PROMONTORY RIDGE WY
HILO DR
MIRAMAR DR
HILLCREST DR
ROLLING HILLS RD
SEE A G5
1 CAYMAN WY
2 SAINT LUCIA WY
3 ADRIANA CT
4 BIMINI WY
0 .125 .25 .375 .5
miles 1 in. = 1900 ft.

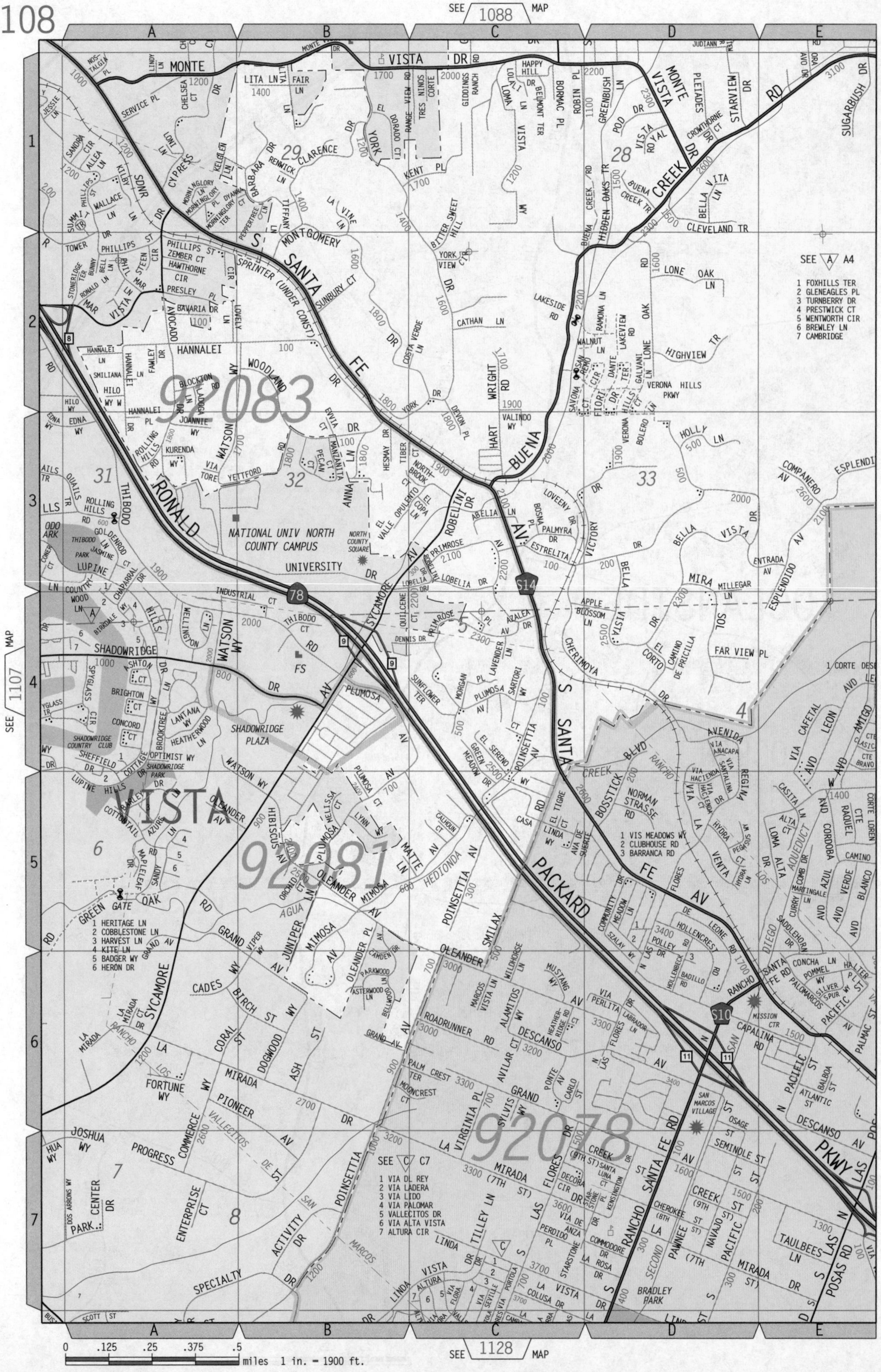

SEE 1088 MAP
SEE 1107 MAP
SEE 1128 MAP
A
B
C
D
E
1
2
3
4
5
6
7
92083
92081
92078
VISTA
MONTE VISTA DR
S SANTA FE AV
BUENA CREEK RD
MONTE VISTA DR
RONALD PACKARD PKWY
UNIVERSITY DR
SHADOWRIDGE DR
SYCAMORE AV
HANNALEI DR
LA MIRADA DR
OLEANDER AV
POINSETTIA AV
SMILAX RD
GRAND AV
DESCANSO AV
LAS POSAS RD
RANCHO SANTA FE RD
CLEVELAND TR
LONE OAK LN
HIGHVIEW TR
ROBELINI DR
CHERIMOYA DR
BOSSTICK BLVD
MIRA VISTA DR
NATIONAL UNIV NORTH COUNTY CAMPUS
NORTH COUNTY SQUARE
SHADOWRIDGE PLAZA
SHADOWRIDGE COUNTRY CLUB
SAN MARCOS VILLAGE
MISSION CTR
BRADLEY PARK
SPRINTER (UNDER CONST)
FS
SEE A A4
1 FOXHILLS TER
2 GLENEAGLES PL
3 TURNBERRY DR
4 PRESTWICK CT
5 WENTWORTH CIR
6 BREWLEY LN
7 CAMBRIDGE
1 HERITAGE LN
2 COBBLESTONE LN
3 HARVEST LN
4 KITE LN
5 BADGER WY
6 HERON DR
1 VIS MEADOWS WY
2 CLUBHOUSE RD
3 BARRANCA RD
SEE C C7
1 VIA DL REY
2 VIA LADERA
3 VIA LIDO
4 VIA PALOMAR
5 VALLECITOS DR
6 VIA ALTA VISTA
7 ALTURA CIR
0 .125 .25 .375 .5
miles 1 in. = 1900 ft.

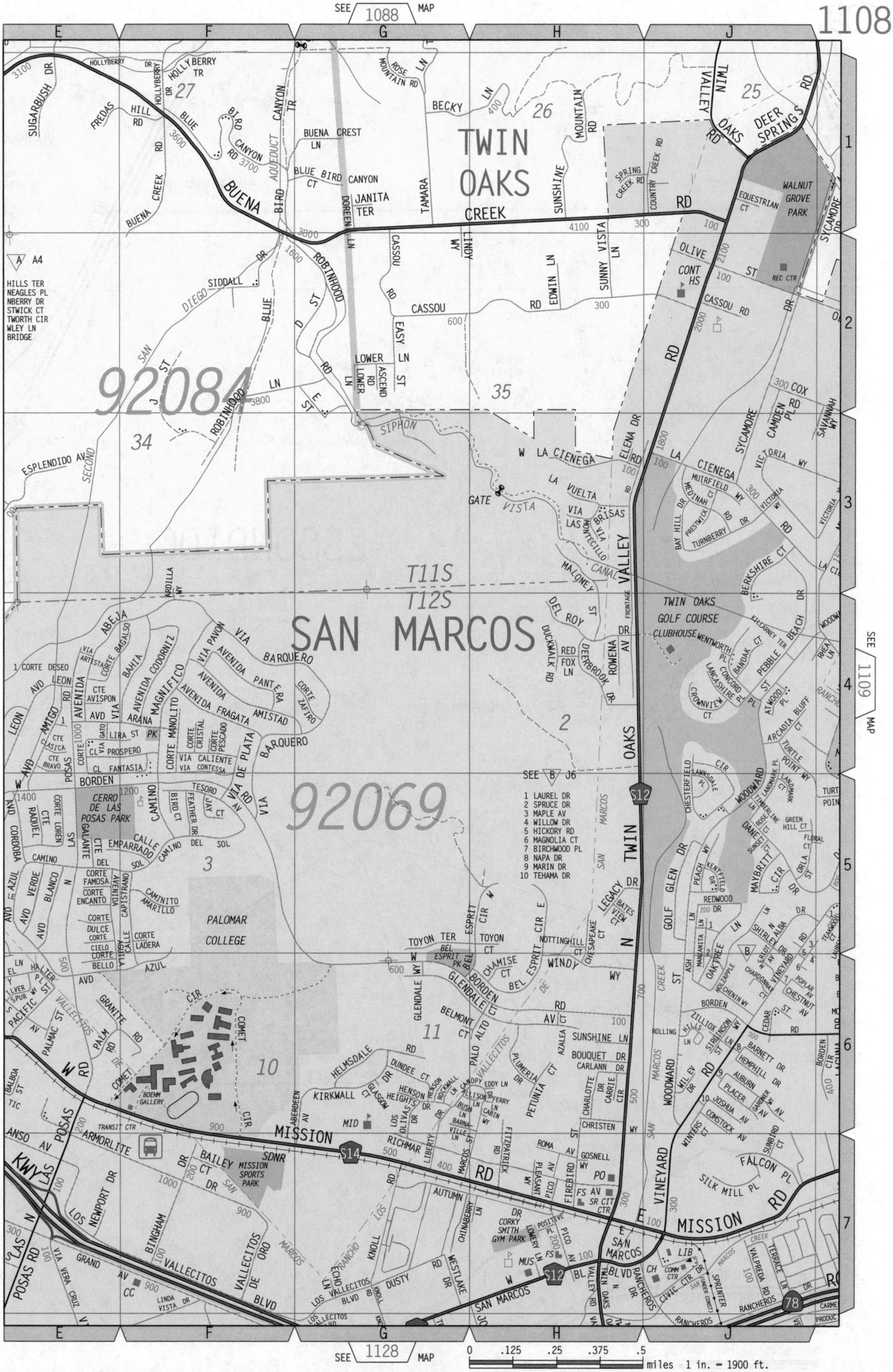

SEE 1088 MAP
E
F
G
H
J
1
2
3
4
5
6
7
TWIN OAKS
SAN MARCOS
92084
92069
T11S
T12S
BUENA CREEK RD
TWIN OAKS VALLEY RD
DEER SPRINGS RD
WALNUT GROVE PARK
SYCAMORE DR
OLIVE ST
CONT HS
CASSOU RD
COX RD
LA CIENEGA
W LA CIENEGA
SAN DIEGO AQUEDUCT
SIPHON
ROBINHOOD RD
SIDDALL DR
BLUE BIRD CANYON RD
ESPLENDIDO AV
TWIN OAKS GOLF COURSE
CLUBHOUSE
PALOMAR COLLEGE
CERRO DE LAS POSAS PARK
BOEHM GALLERY
SDNR MISSION SPORTS PARK
CORKY SMITH GYM PARK
BEL ESPRIT PK
BORDEN RD
MISSION RD
E MISSION RD
W SAN MARCOS BLVD
LAS POSAS RD
VALLECITOS
ARMORLITE DR
GRAND AV
RANCHEROS DR
CIVIC CTR DR
VINEYARD RD
WOODWARD ST
SEE B J6
1 LAUREL DR
2 SPRUCE DR
3 MAPLE AV
4 WILLOW DR
5 HICKORY RD
6 MAGNOLIA CT
7 BIRCHWOOD PL
8 NAPA DR
9 MARIN DR
10 TEHAMA DR
A A4
HILLS TER
NEAGLES PL
NBERRY DR
STWICK CT
TWORTH CIR
WLEY LN
BRIDGE
S12
S14
78
SEE 1109 MAP
SEE 1128 MAP
0 .125 .25 .375 .5
miles 1 in. = 1900 ft.

SEE 1089 MAP

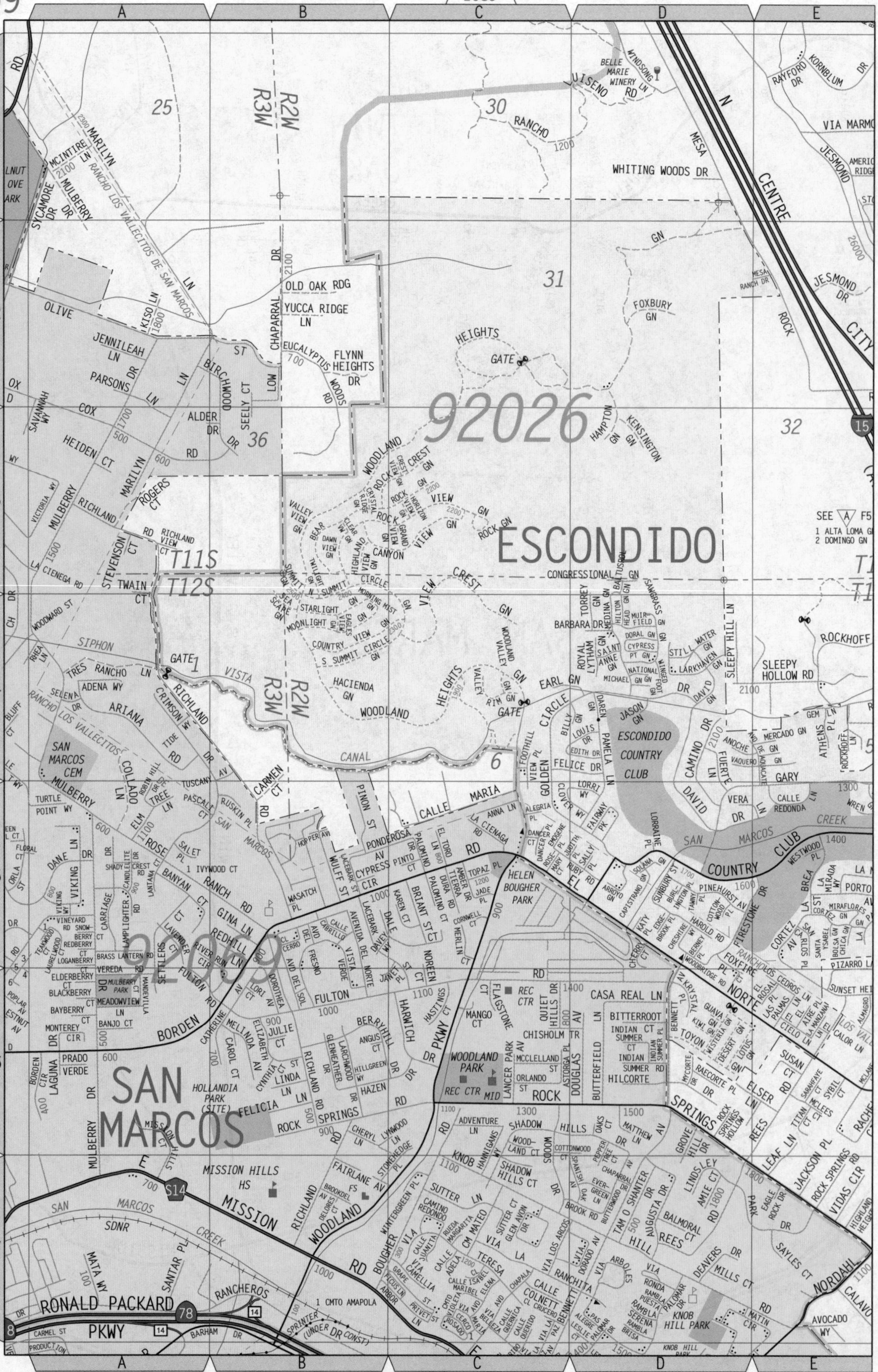

SEE 1108 MAP

SEE 1129 MAP

0 .125 .25 .375 .5 miles 1 in. = 1900 ft.

SEE 1089 MAP

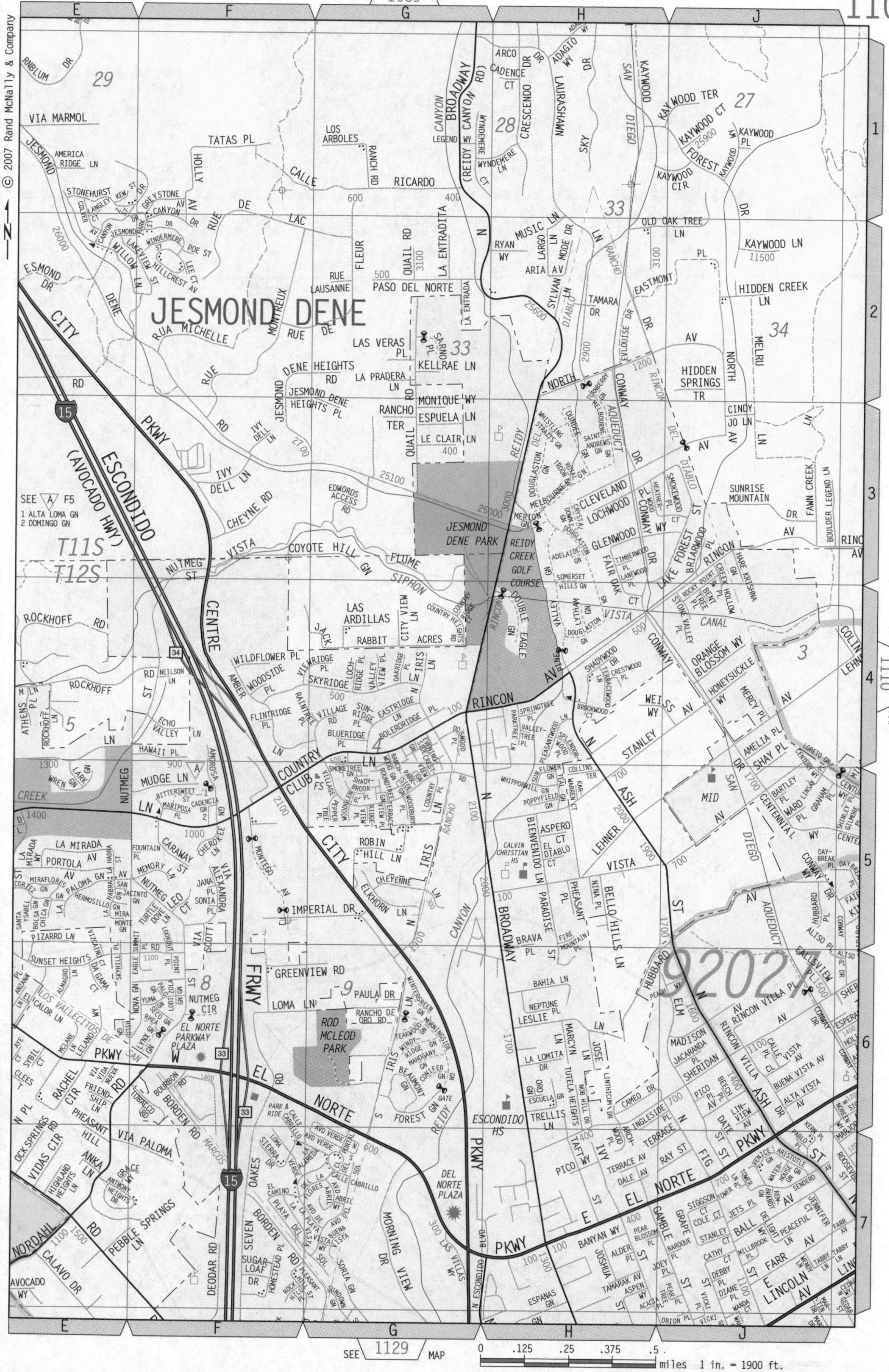

SEE 1129 MAP

0 .125 .25 .375 .5 miles 1 in. = 1900 ft.

SEE 1090 MAP

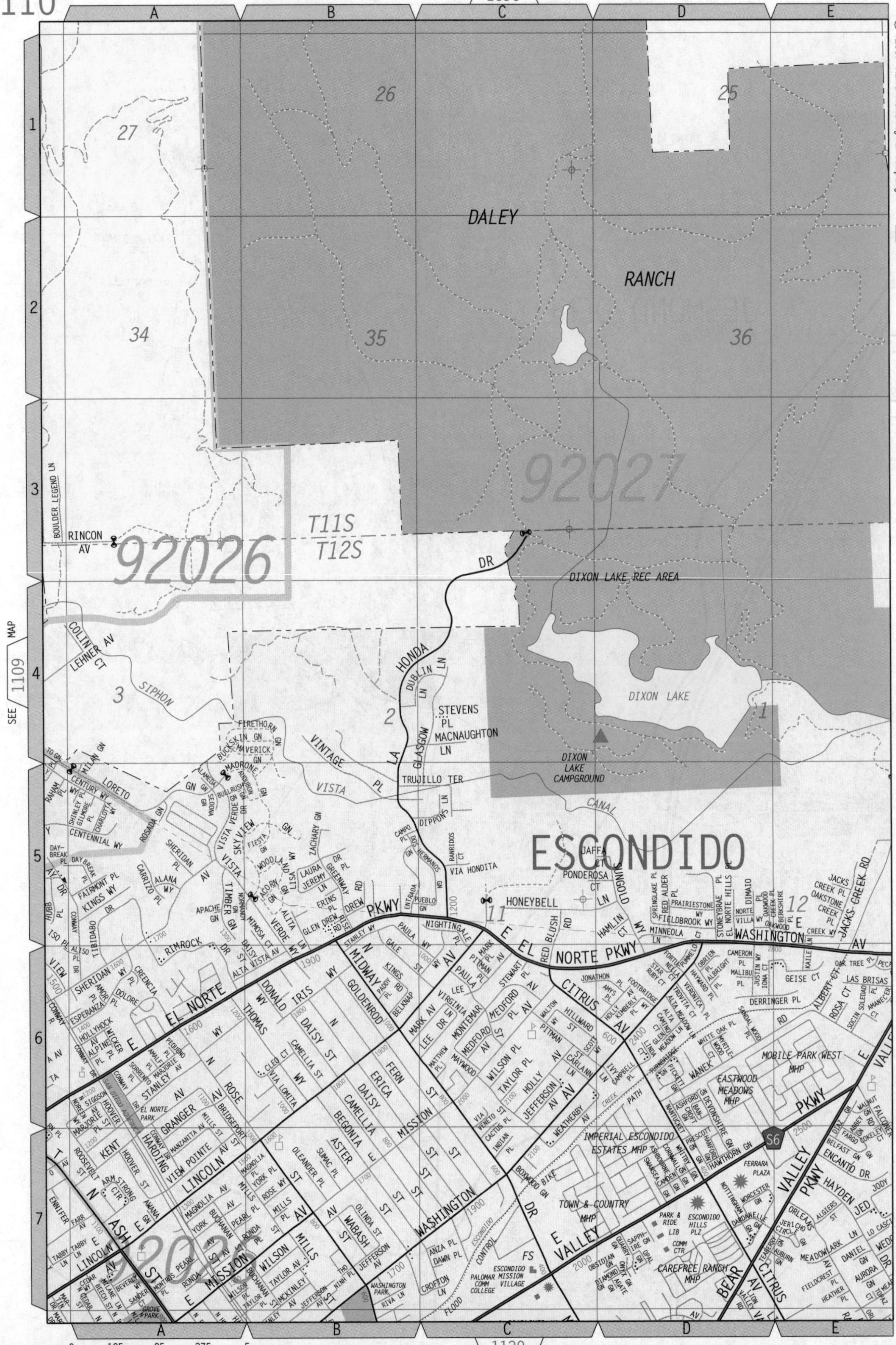

SEE 1109 MAP

SEE 1130 MAP

SEE 1090 MAP

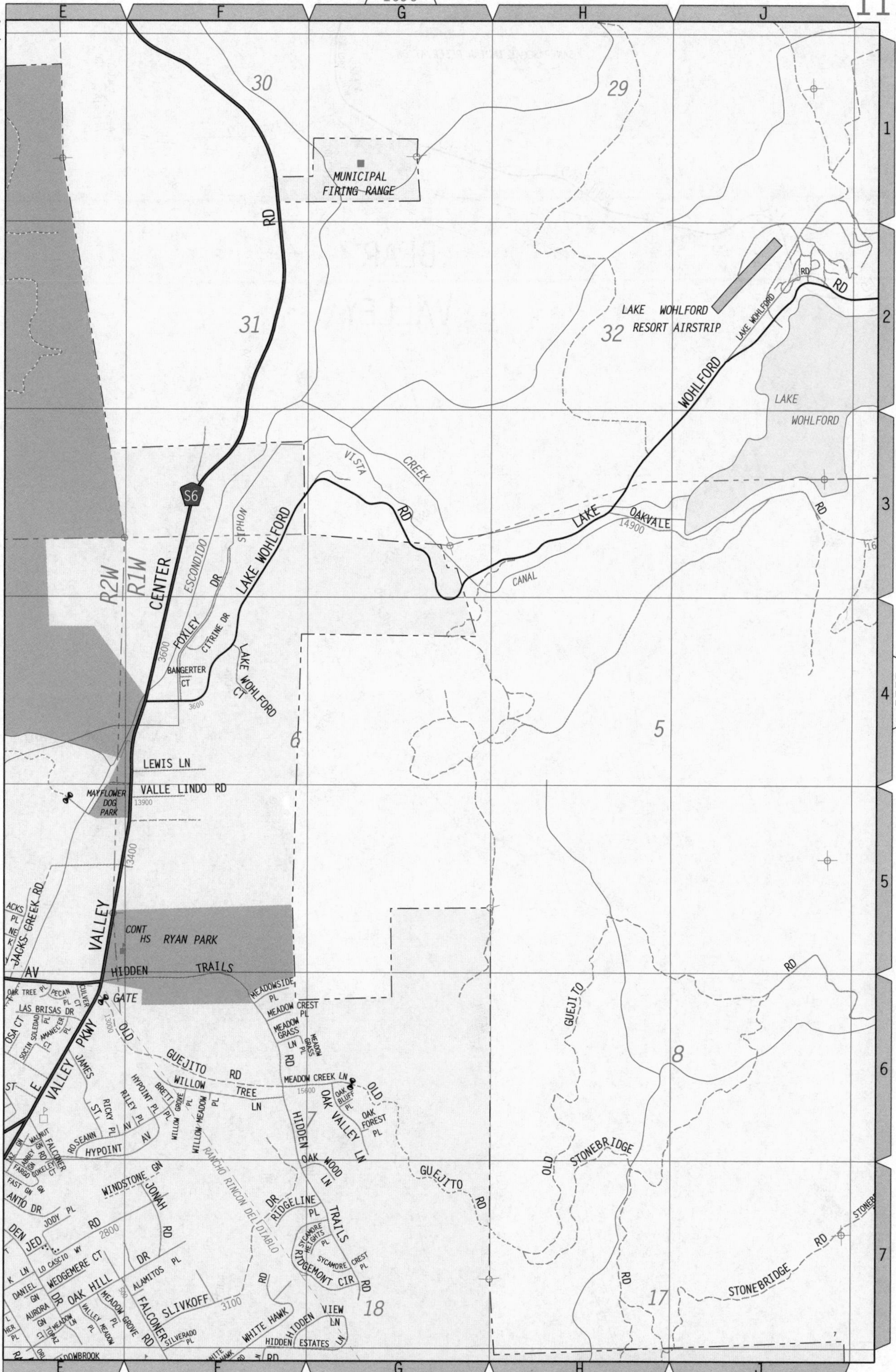

SEE 1111 MAP

SEE 1130 MAP

0 .125 .25 .375 .5 miles 1 in. = 1900 ft.

SEE 1091 MAP

SEE 1110 MAP

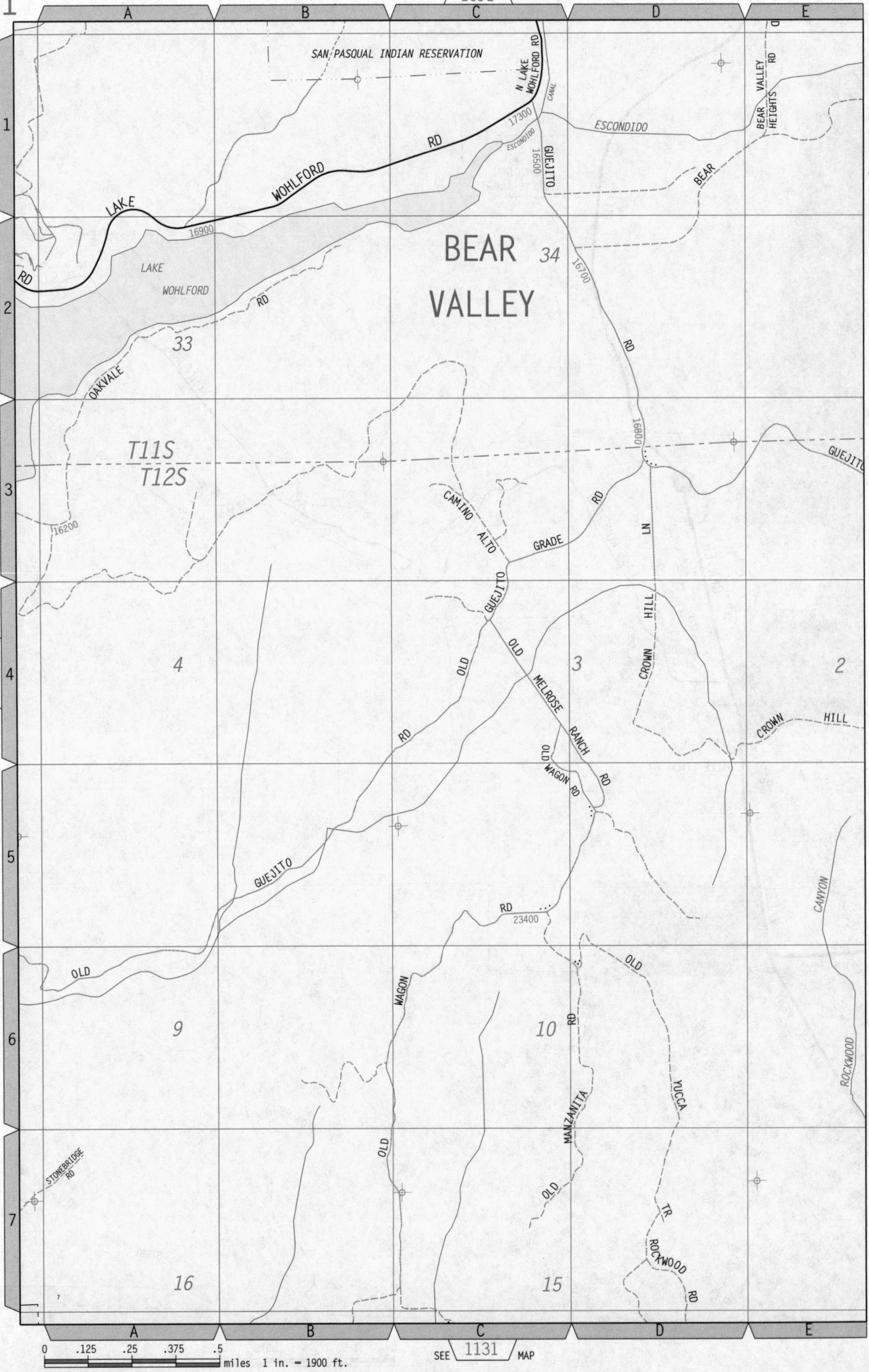

SEE 1131 MAP

0 .125 .25 .375 .5 miles 1 in. = 1900 ft.

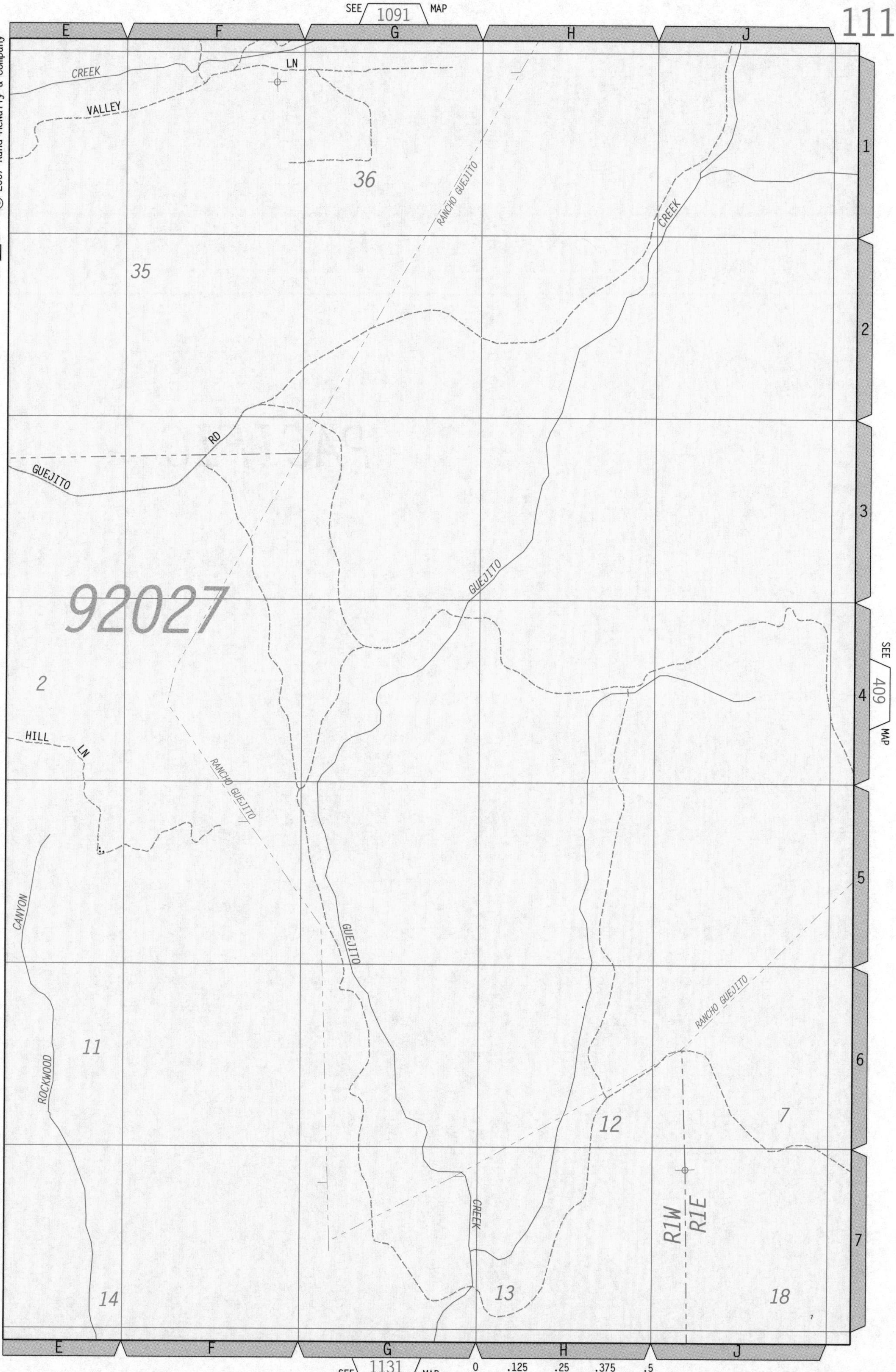
SEE 1091 MAP
E
F
G
H
J
CREEK
VALLEY
LN
36
RANCHO GUEJITO
CREEK
35
RD
GUEJITO
92027
GUEJITO
2
HILL
LN
RANCHO GUEJITO
CANYON
GUEJITO
11
ROCKWOOD
RANCHO GUEJITO
12
7
CREEK
R1W
R1E
13
14
18
1
2
3
4
5
6
7
SEE 409 MAP
SEE 1131 MAP
0
.125
.25
.375
.5
miles 1 in. = 1900 ft.

SEE 1106 MAP
A
B
C
D
E
1
2
3
4
5
6
7
PACIFIC
SEE 408 MAP
SEE 1146 MAP
0 .125 .25 .375 .5 miles 1 in. = 1900 ft.
N

SEE 1106 MAP

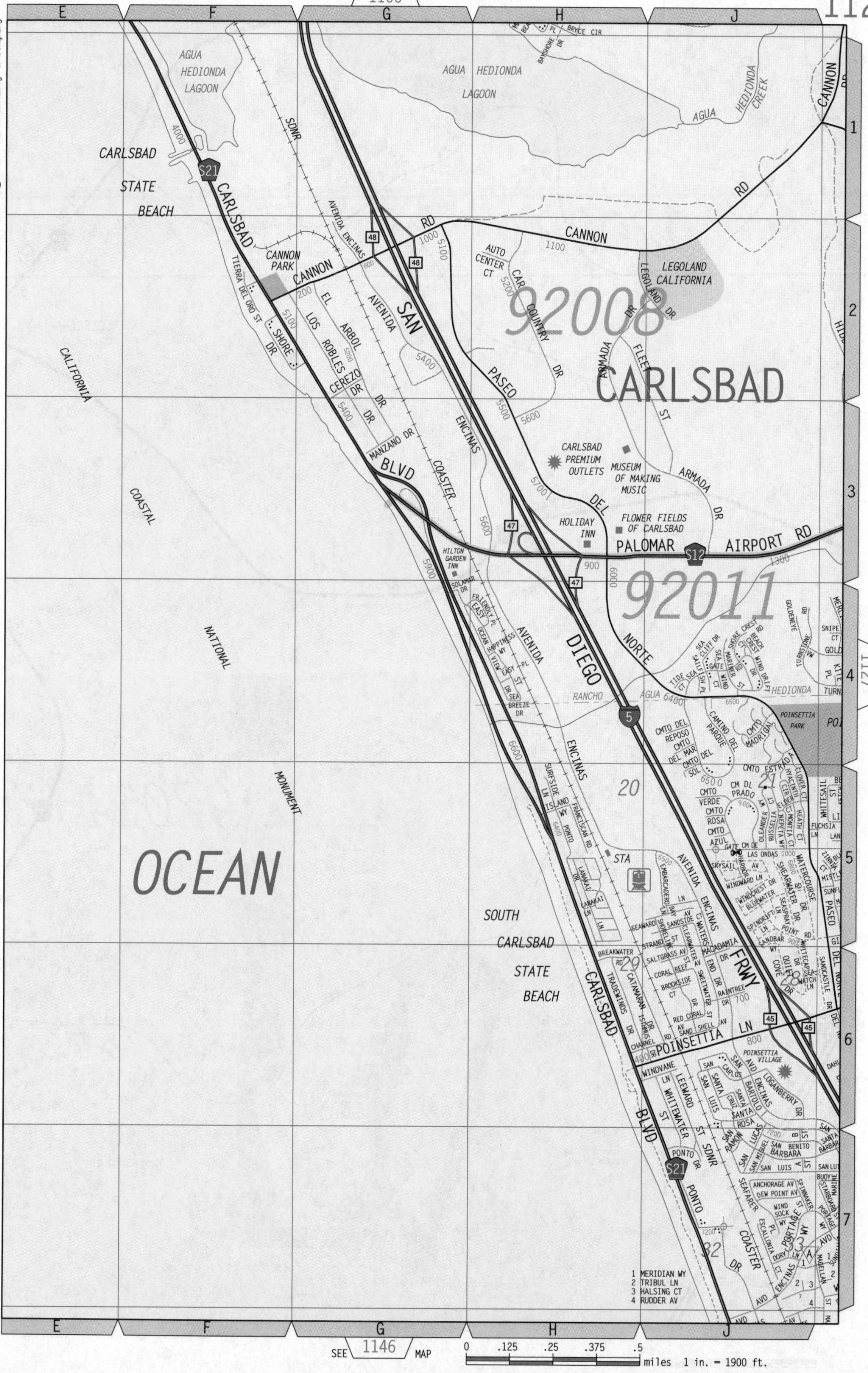

SEE 1127 MAP

SEE 1146 MAP

SEE 1107 MAP

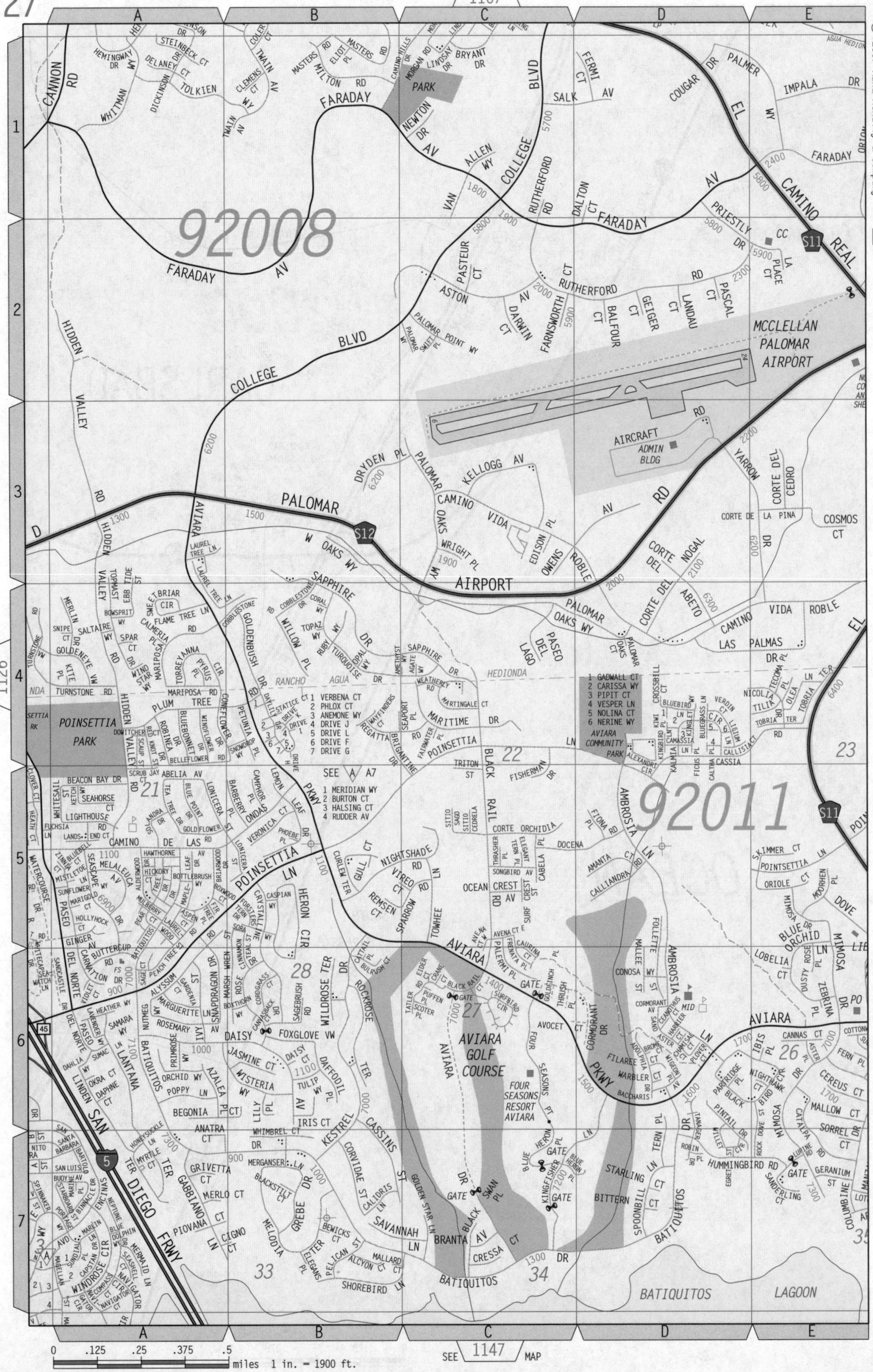

SEE 1126 MAP

SEE 1147 MAP

0 .125 .25 .375 .5 miles 1 in. = 1900 ft.

SEE 1107 MAP

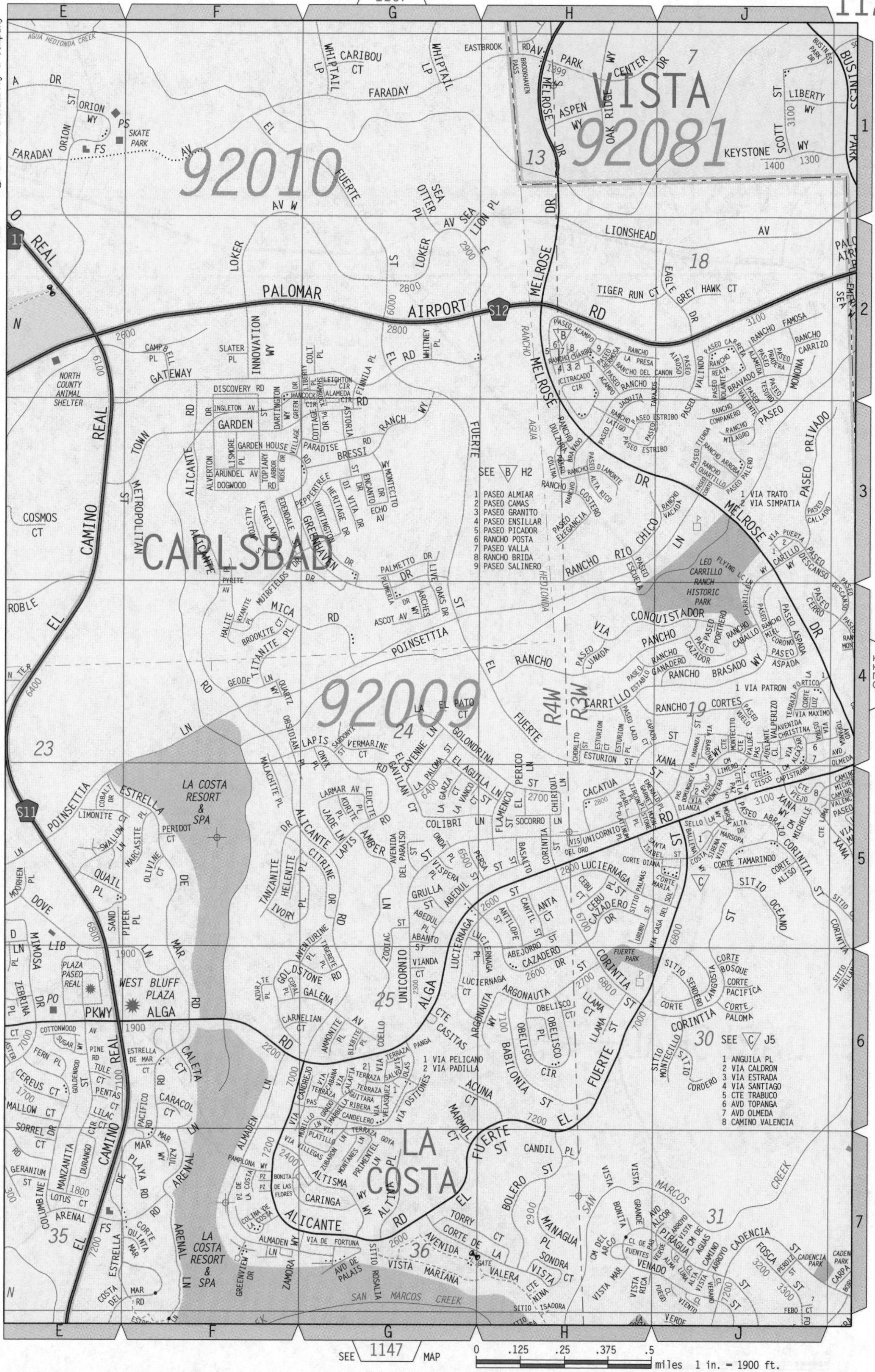

SEE 1128 MAP

SEE 1147 MAP

0 .125 .25 .375 .5 miles 1 in. = 1900 ft.

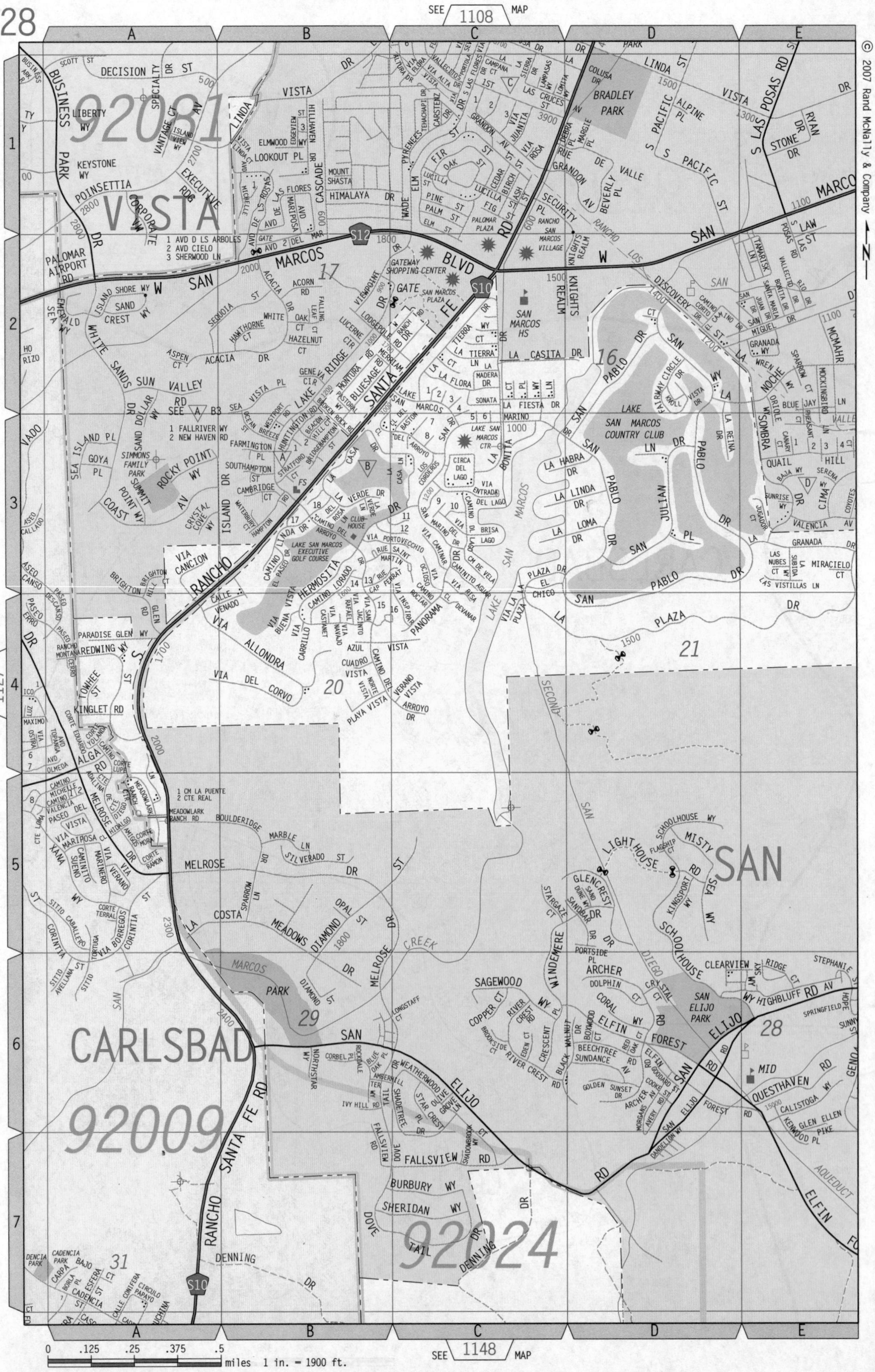
SEE 1108 MAP
SEE 1127 MAP
SEE 1148 MAP
SAN DIEGO CO.
92081
VISTA
92009
CARLSBAD
92024
SAN
LAKE SAN MARCOS COUNTRY CLUB
LAKE SAN MARCOS EXECUTIVE GOLF COURSE
SAN MARCOS HS
BRADLEY PARK
SAN ELIJO PARK
SIMMONS FAMILY PARK
ROCKY POINT
GATEWAY SHOPPING CENTER
PALOMAR AIRPORT RD
W SAN MARCOS BLVD
RANCHO SANTA FE RD
SAN ELIJO RD
MELROSE DR
BUSINESS PARK DR
S LAS POSAS RD
LA COSTA MEADOWS DR
SAN MARCOS CREEK
AQUEDUCT
0 .125 .25 .375 .5 miles 1 in. = 1900 ft.

SEE 1108 MAP

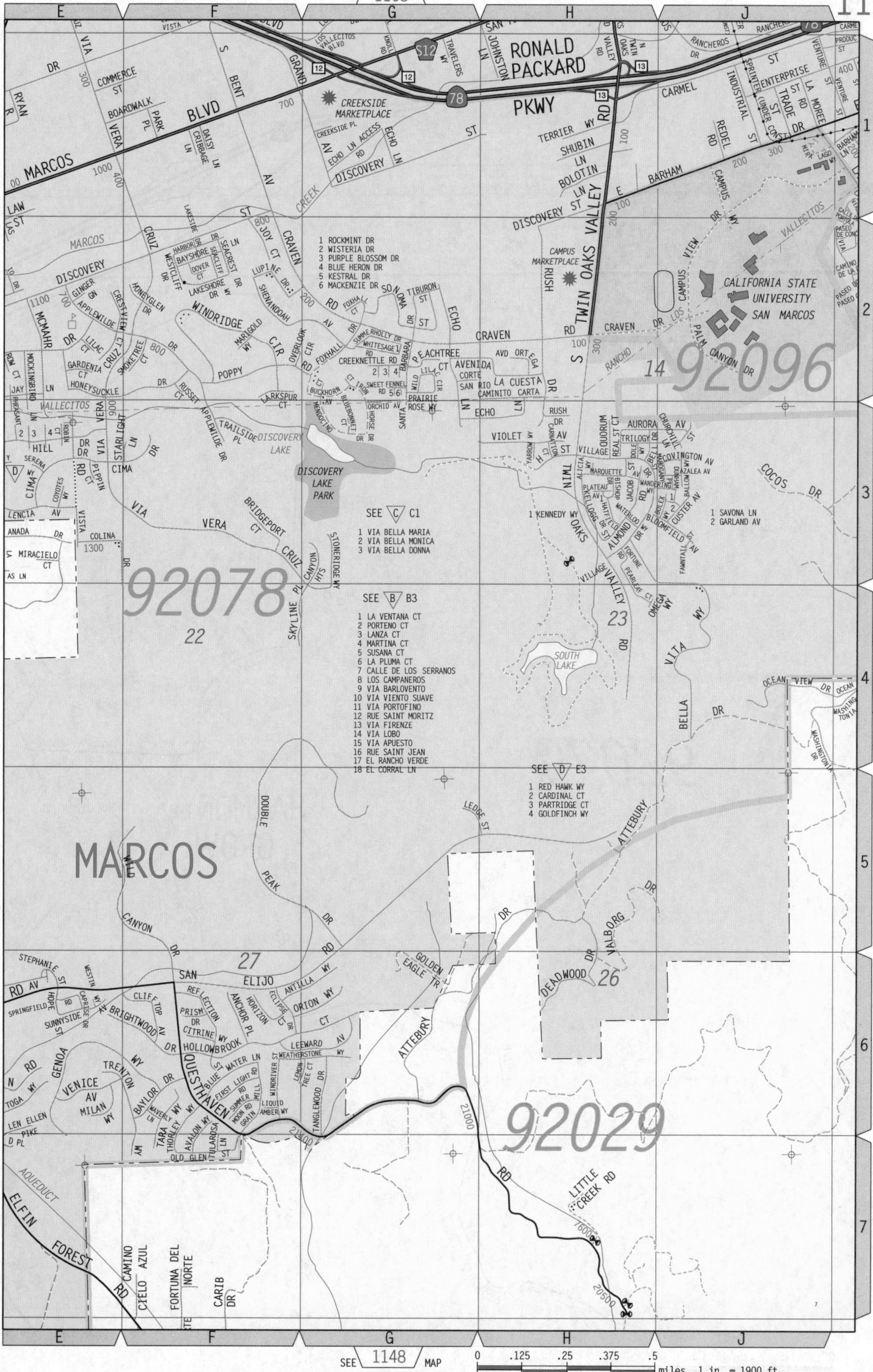

SEE 1148 MAP

0 .125 .25 .375 .5 miles 1 in. = 1900 ft.

SEE 1109 MAP

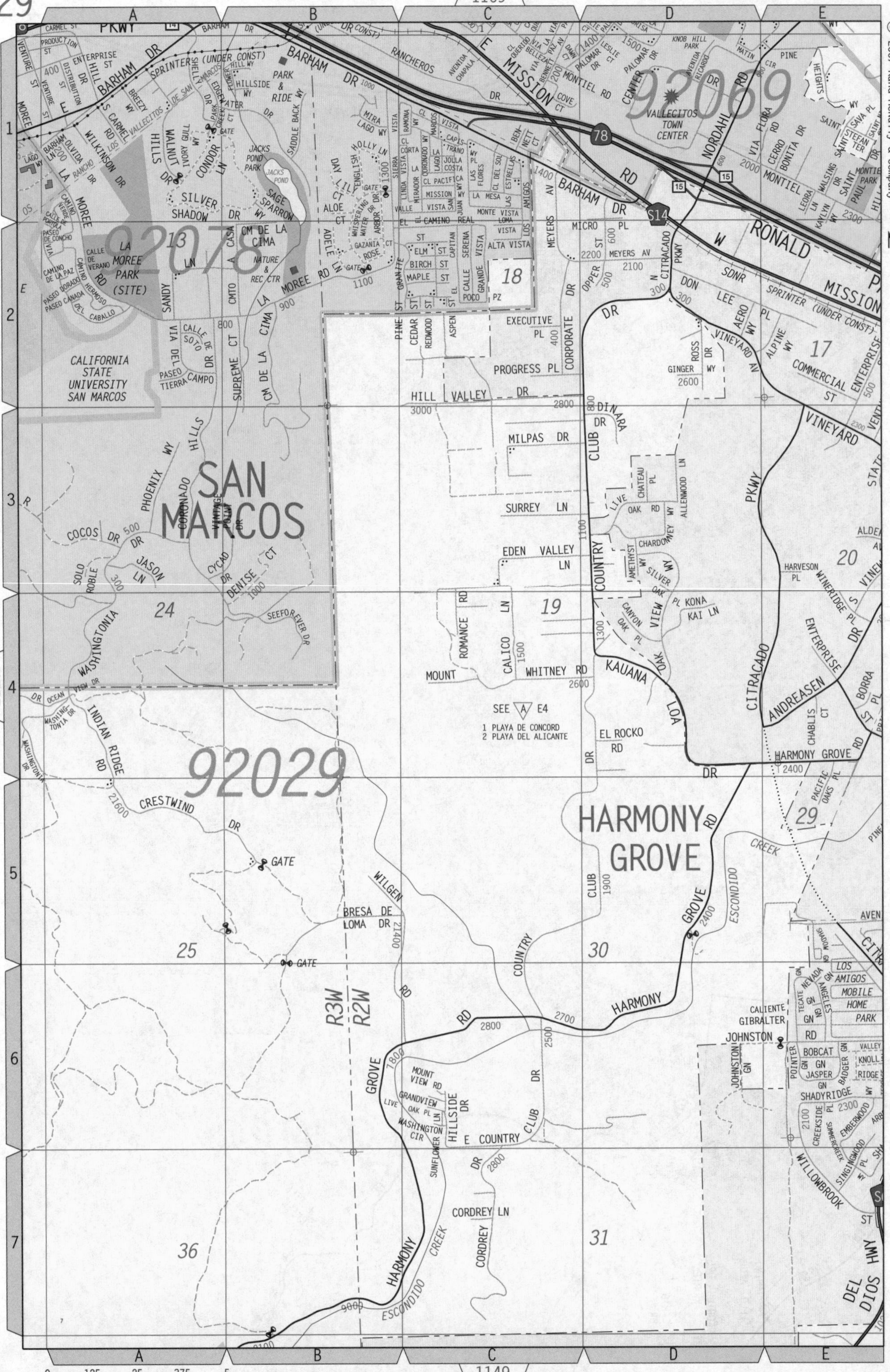

SEE 1128 MAP

SEE 1149 MAP

0 .125 .25 .375 .5 miles 1 in. = 1900 ft.

SEE 1109 MAP

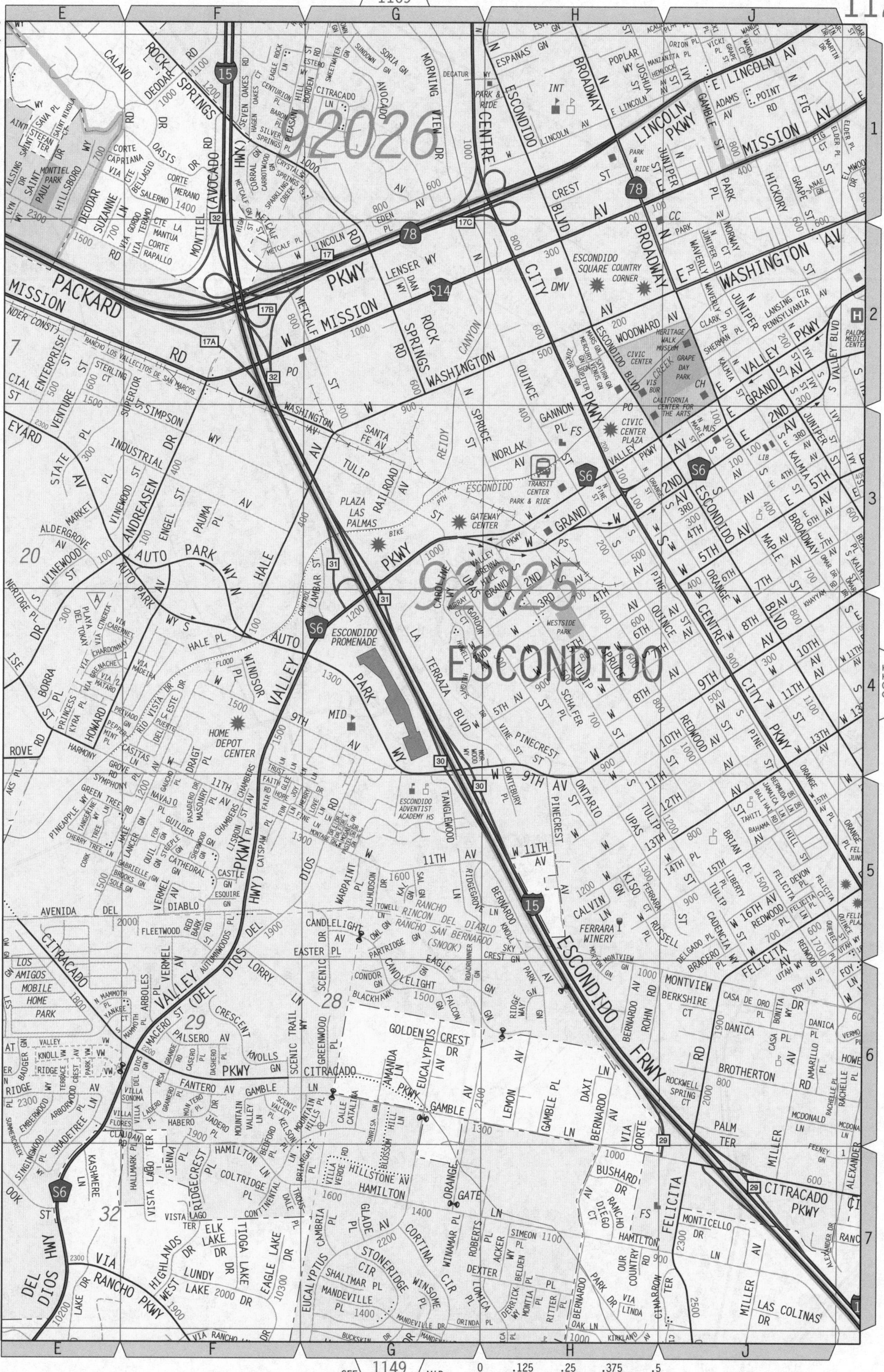

SEE 1130 MAP

SEE 1149 MAP

0 .125 .25 .375 .5 miles 1 in. = 1900 ft.

SEE 1110 MAP

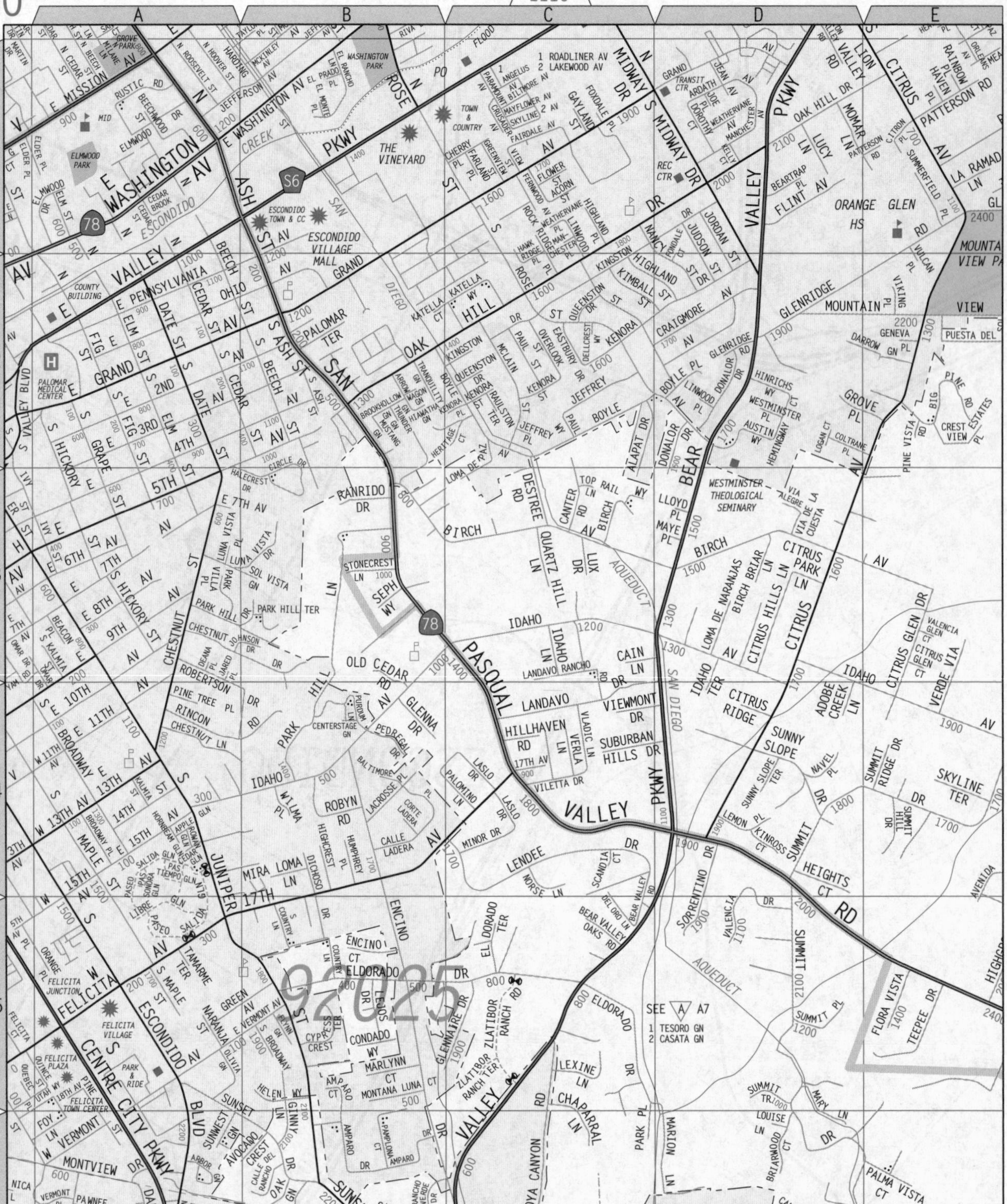

SEE 1129 MAP

0 .125 .25 .375 .5 miles 1 in. = 1900 ft.

SEE 1150 MAP

SEE 1110 MAP
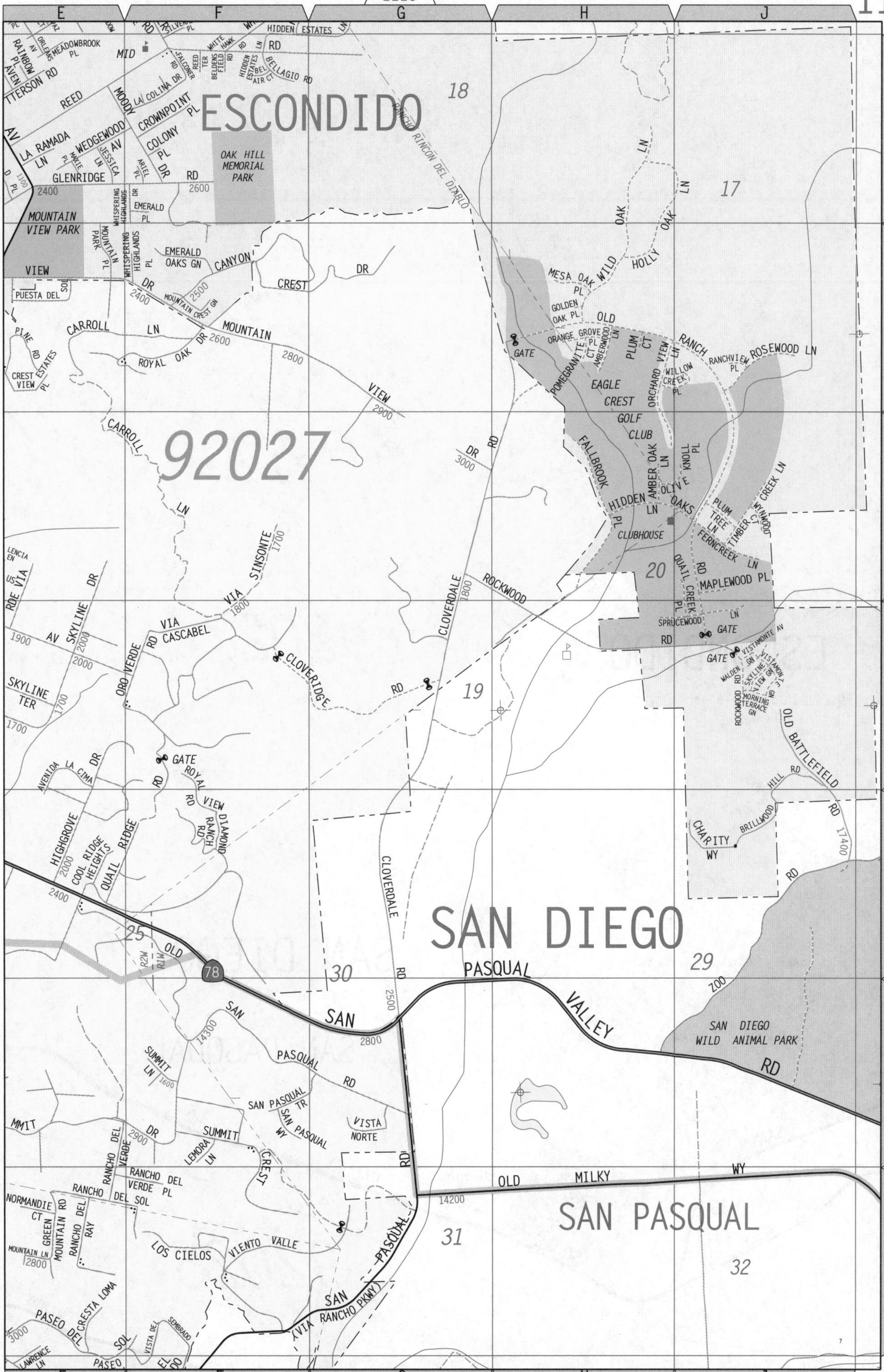

SEE 1131 MAP
SEE 1150 MAP
0 .125 .25 .375 .5 miles 1 in. = 1900 ft.

SEE 1111 MAP
A
B
C
D
E
1
2
3
4
5
6
7
SAN DIEGO CO.
SEE 1130 MAP
16
15
21
22
28
27
33
34
OLD WAGON RD
24300
RD
ROCKWOOD
16200
BARELIA RD
ESCONDIDO
RD
16600
92027
ROCKWOOD
17400
SAN DIEGO
WILD ANIMAL PARK
SAN DIEGO
SAN PASQUAL
ROCKWOOD
SAN
SAN PASQUAL BATTLEFIELD STATE HISTORIC PARK
SAN DIEGO ARCHAEOLOGICAL CENTER
VALLEY
RD
CREEK
OLD MILKY WY
PASQUAL
YSABEL
92025
SANTA
YSABEL CREEK RD
BANDY
YSABEL
0 .125 .25 .375 .5
miles 1 in. = 1900 ft.
SEE 1151 MAP

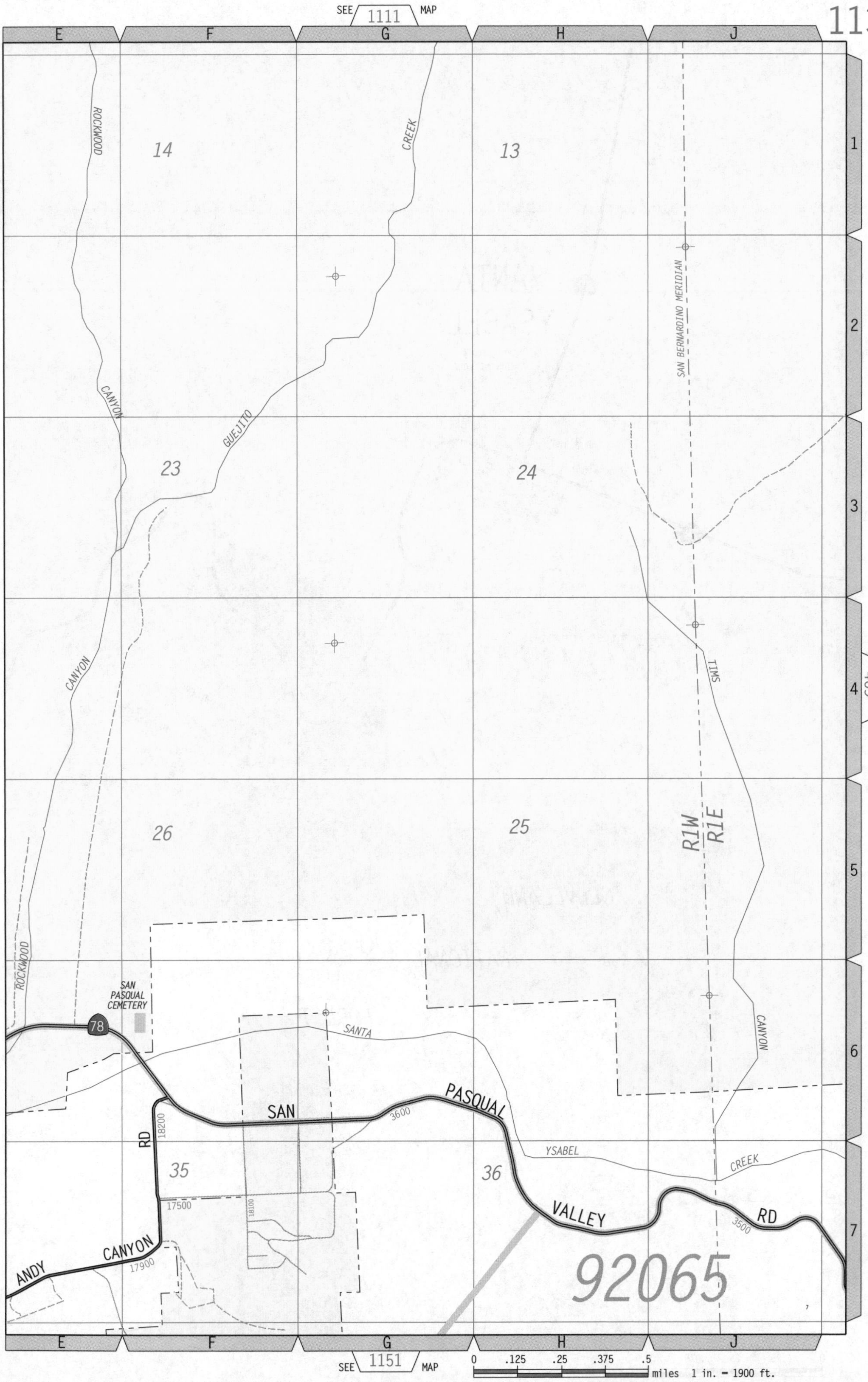
SEE 1111 MAP
E
F
G
H
J
1
2
3
4
5
6
7
14
13
23
24
26
25
35
36
ROCKWOOD
CANYON
CREEK
GUEJITO
SAN BERNARDINO MERIDIAN
R1W
R1E
TIMS
CANYON
SEE 409 MAP
SAN PASQUAL CEMETERY
78
SANTA
YSABEL
CREEK
SAN
PASQUAL
VALLEY
RD
3600
3500
18200
17500
18100
17900
ANDY
CANYON
RD
92065
SEE 1151 MAP
0
.125
.25
.375
.5
miles 1 in. = 1900 ft.

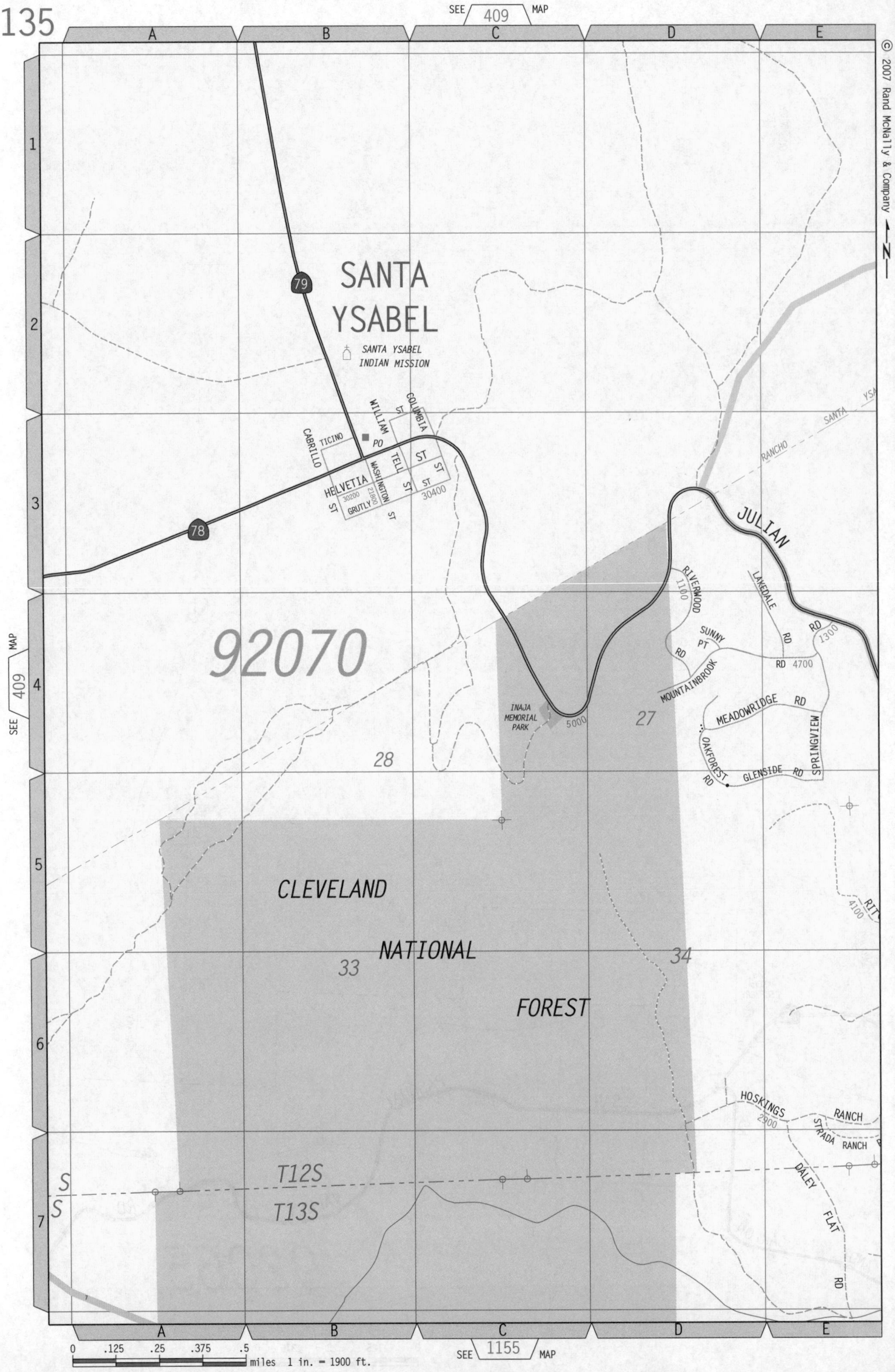
SEE 409 MAP
SEE 409 MAP
SEE 1155 MAP
A
B
C
D
E
1
2
3
4
5
6
7
SANTA YSABEL
SANTA YSABEL INDIAN MISSION
79
78
COLUMBIA
ST
WILLIAM
PO
TICINO
CABRILLO
HELVETIA
ST
30200
GRUTLY
21800
WASHINGTON
ST
TELL
ST
ST
ST
ST
30400
92070
RANCHO SANTA YSA
JULIAN
RIVERWOOD
1100
LAKEDALE
RD
SUNNY PT
RD
RD
1300
RD 4700
MOUNTAINBROOK
MEADOWRIDGE RD
OAKFOREST RD
GLENSIDE RD
SPRINGVIEW
INAJA MEMORIAL PARK
5000
27
28
CLEVELAND
NATIONAL
FOREST
33
34
4100
HOSKINGS RANCH
2900
STRADA RANCH
DALEY FLAT RD
T12S
T13S
0 .125 .25 .375 .5 miles 1 in. = 1900 ft.

SEE 409 MAP

SEE 1136 MAP
SEE 1155 MAP

0 .125 .25 .375 .5 miles 1 in. = 1900 ft.

SEE 409 MAP

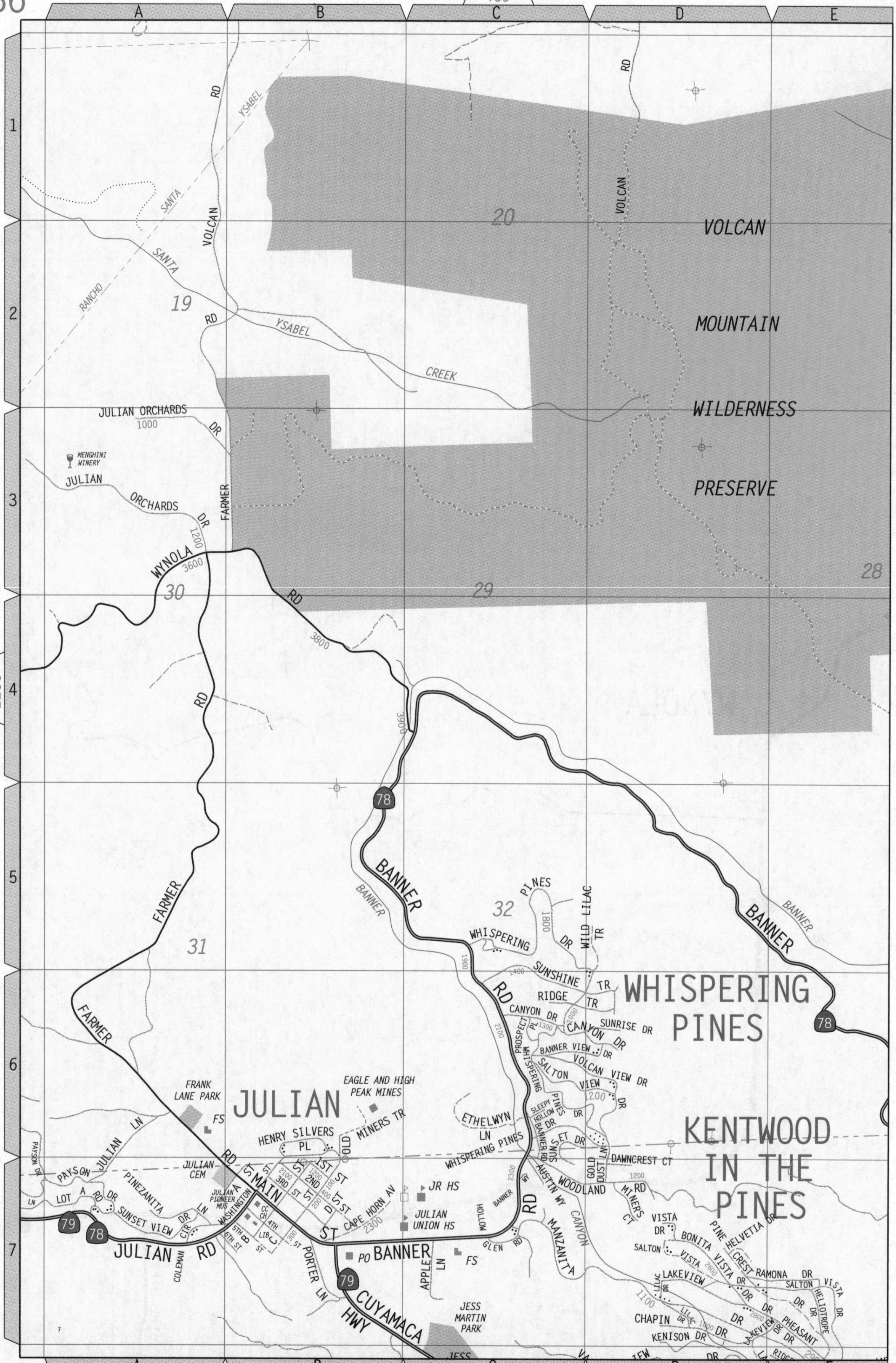

SEE 1135 MAP

SEE 1156 MAP

0 .125 .25 .375 .5 miles 1 in. = 1900 ft.

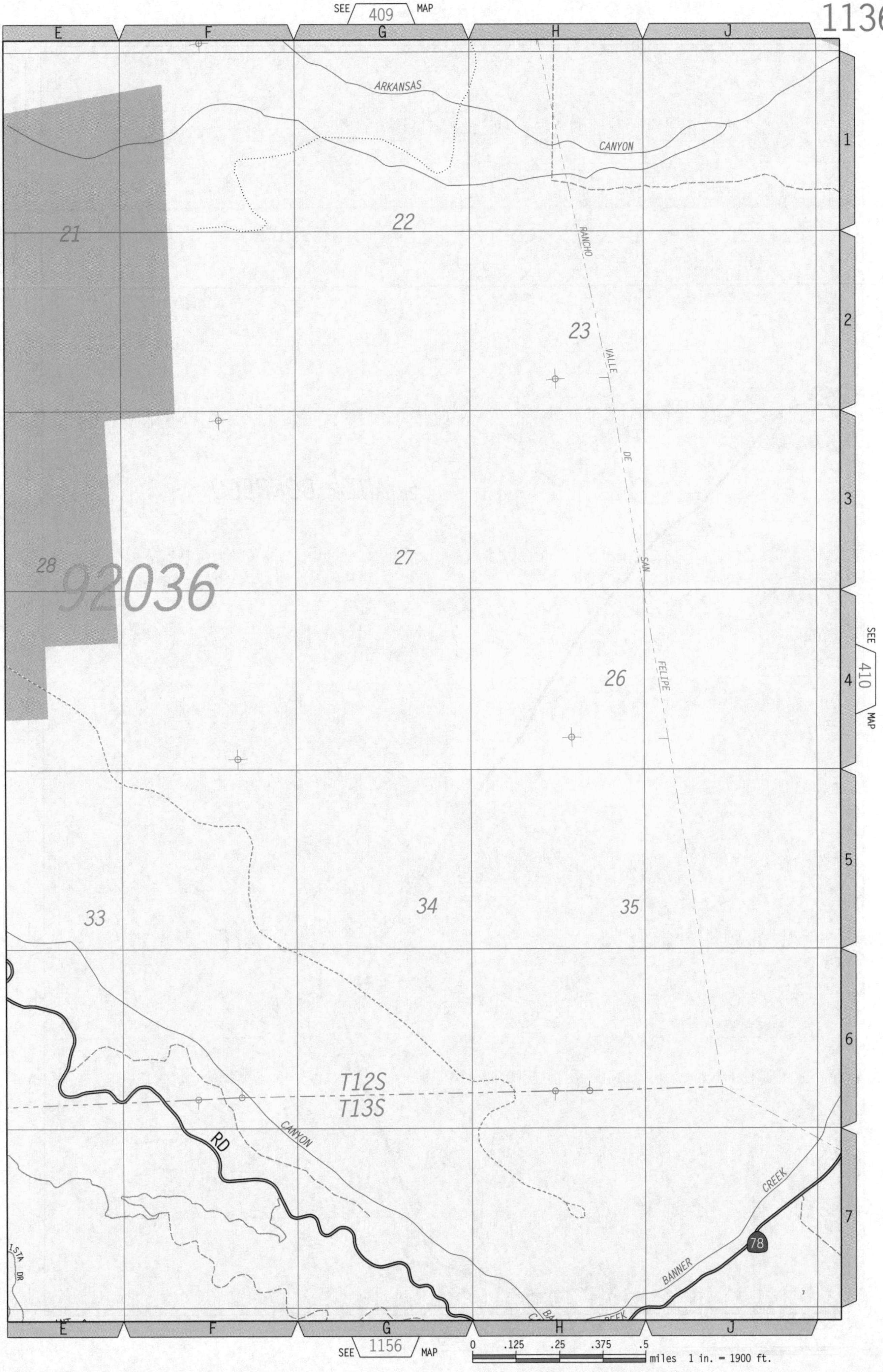
SEE 409 MAP
E
F
G
H
J
ARKANSAS
CANYON
21
22
RANCHO
23
VALLE
DE
SAN
FELIPE
27
28
92036
26
SEE 410 MAP
33
34
35
T12S
T13S
RD
CANYON
CREEK
78
BANNER
1
2
3
4
5
6
7
SEE 1156 MAP
0 .125 .25 .375 .5
miles 1 in. = 1900 ft.

SEE 1098 MAP

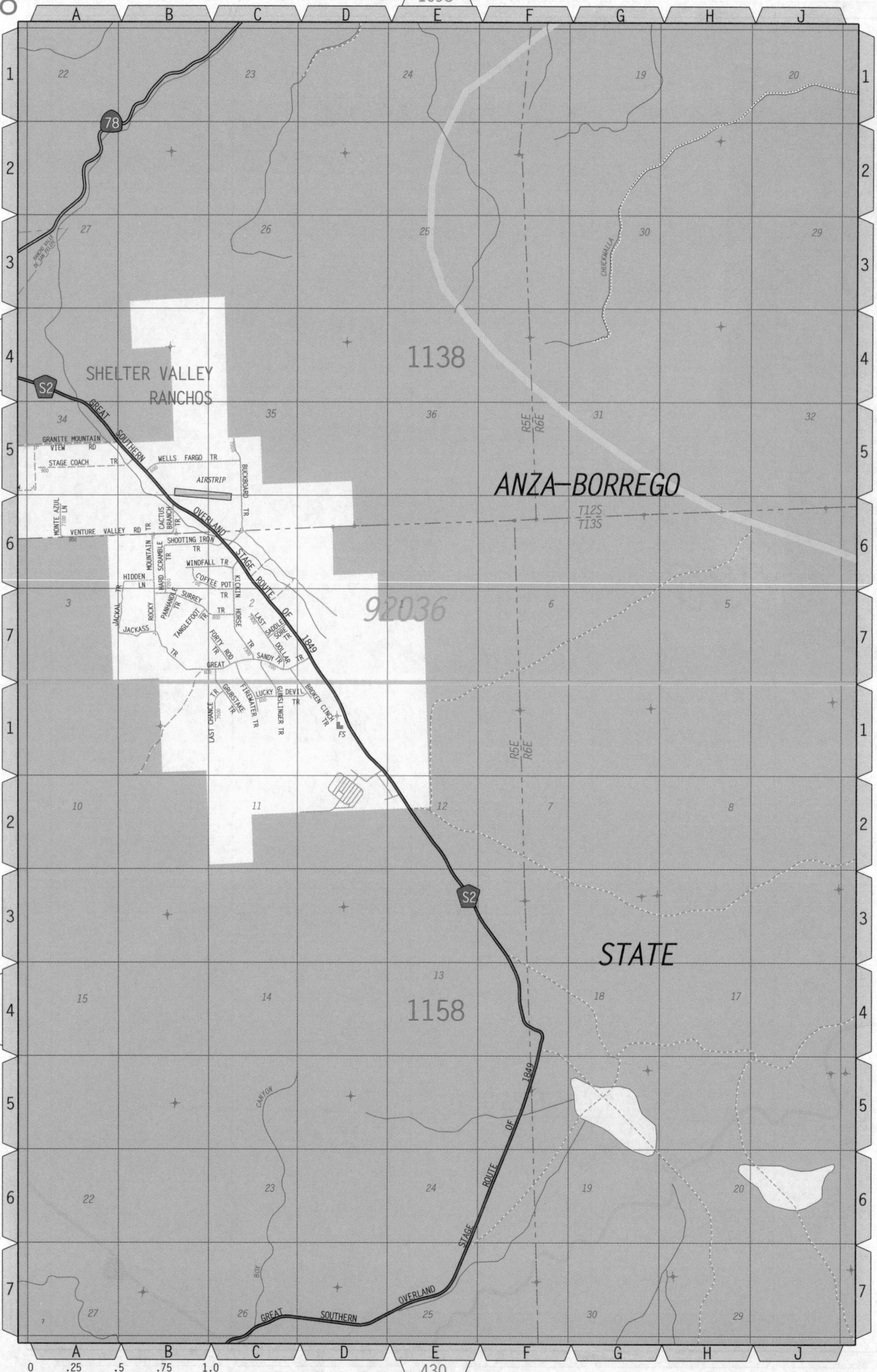

SEE 410 MAP

SEE 430 MAP

SEE 430 MAP

0 .25 .5 .75 1.0 miles 1 in. = 3800 ft.

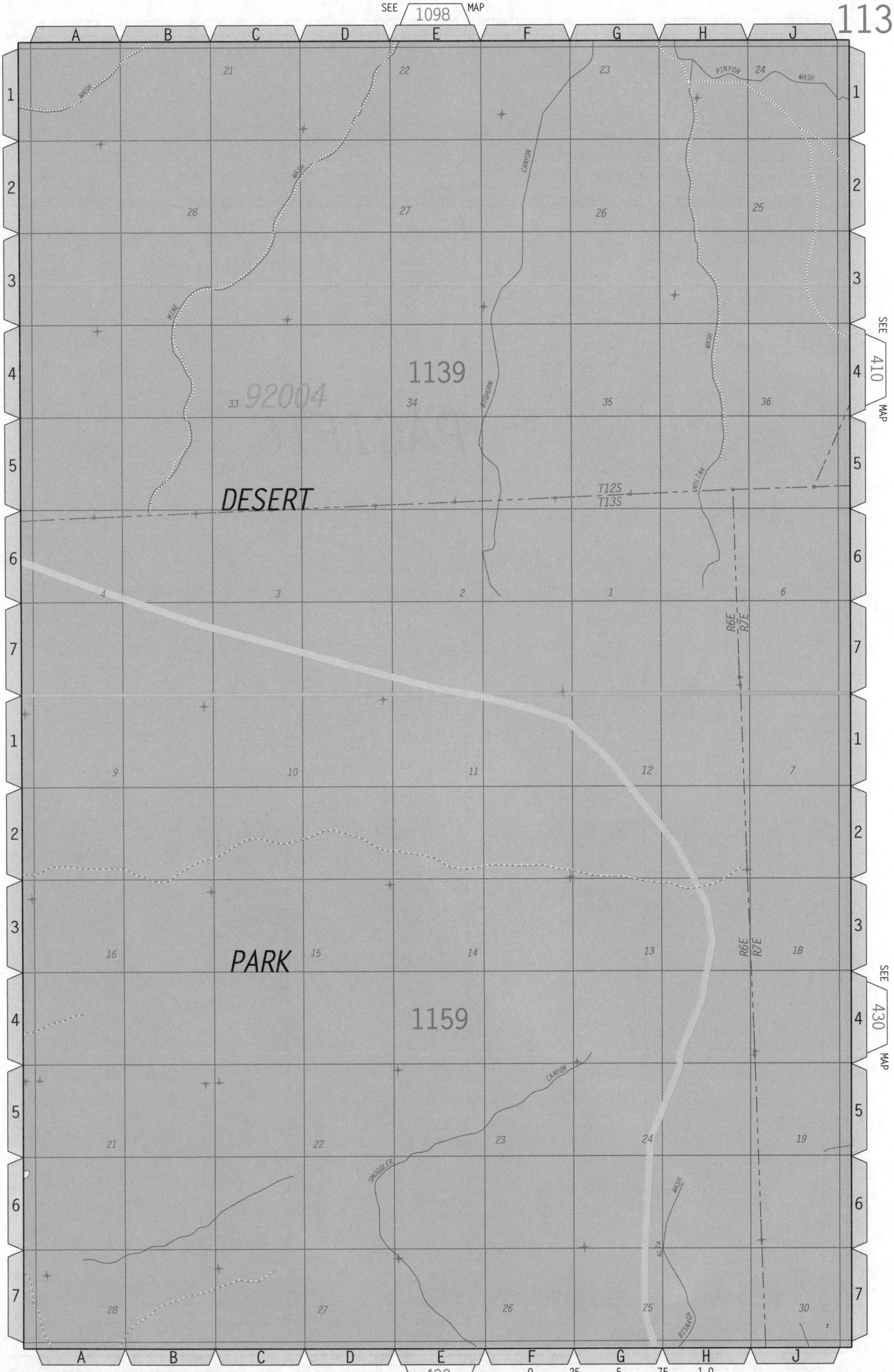
SEE 1098 MAP
SEE 410 MAP
SEE 430 MAP
SEE 430 MAP
1139
1159
92004
DESERT
PARK
WASH
MINE
WASH
CANYON
BIGHORN
PINYON
WASH
WASH
VADLINA
T12S
T13S
R6E
R7E
R6E
R7E
CANYON
SMUGGLER
WASH
ALTA
BISNAGA
0 .25 .5 .75 1.0
miles 1 in. = 3800 ft.

SEE 1126 MAP

SEE 429 MAP

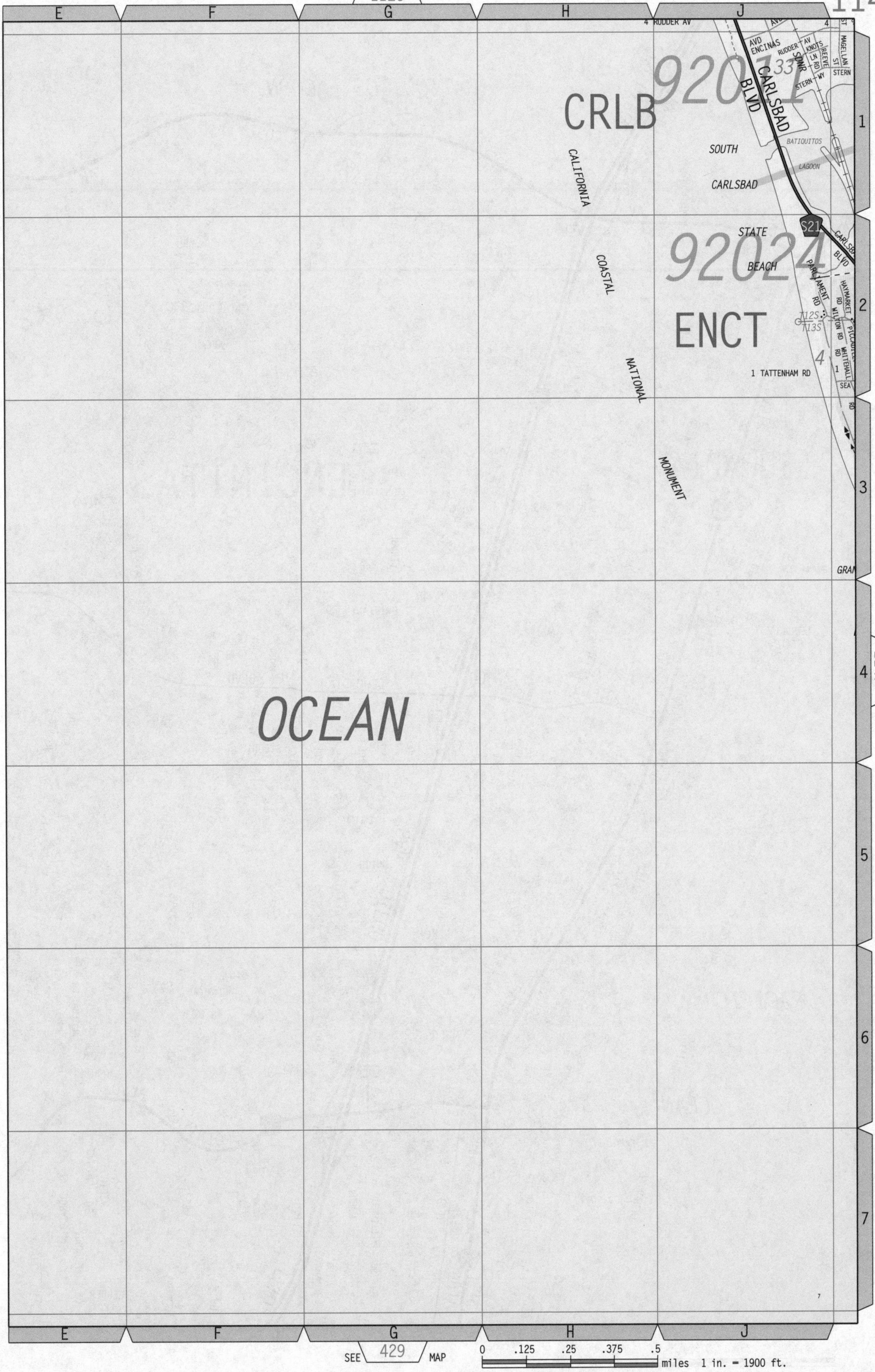
SEE 1126 MAP
CRLB
92011
92024
ENCT
CARLSBAD BLVD
SOUTH CARLSBAD STATE BEACH
CALIFORNIA COASTAL NATIONAL MONUMENT
BATIQUITOS LAGOON
AVD ENCINAS
RUDDER AV
KNOTS LN
REEVE ST
MAGELLAN ST
STERN WY
STERN
PARLIAMENT RD
HAYMARKET RD
WILTON RD
PICCADILLY
WHITEHALL
1 TATTENHAM RD
4 RUDDER AV
S21
OCEAN
SEE 1147 MAP
SEE 429 MAP
0 .125 .25 .375 .5 miles 1 in. = 1900 ft.
E F G H J
1 2 3 4 5 6 7

SEE 1127 MAP

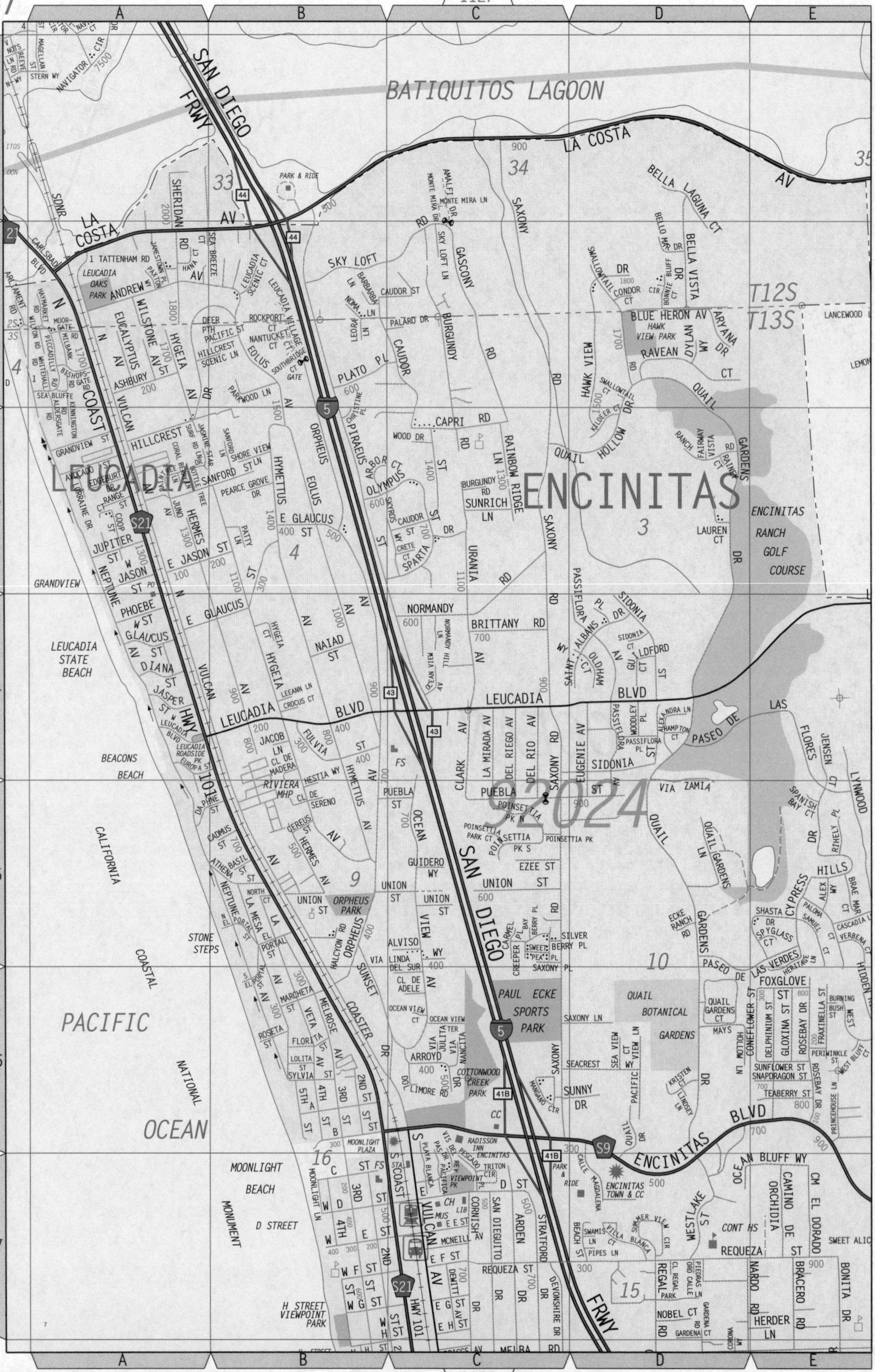

0 .125 .25 .375 .5 miles 1 in. = 1900 ft.

SEE 1167 MAP

SEE 1127 MAP

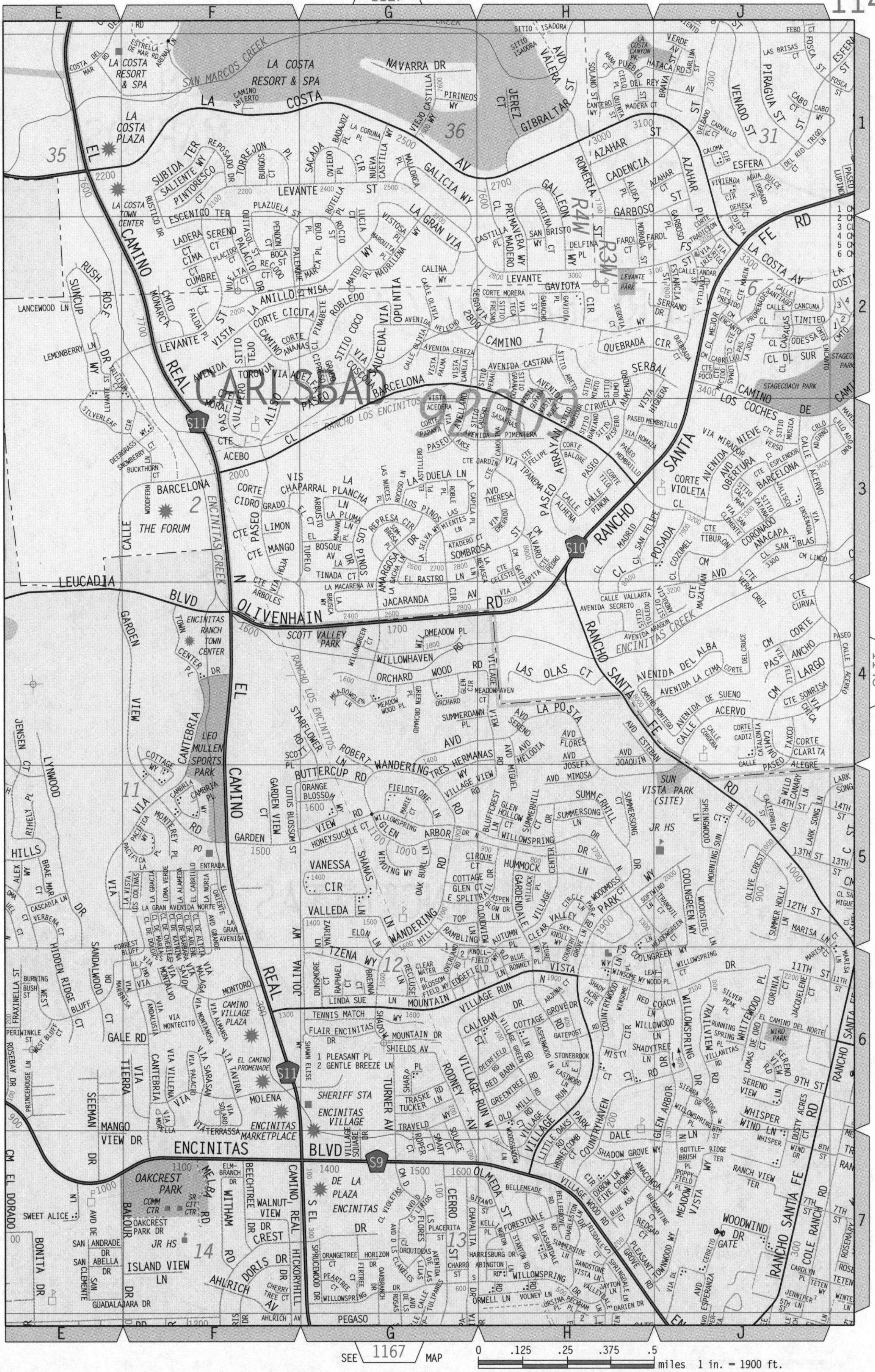

SEE 1148 MAP

SEE 1167 MAP

0 .125 .25 .375 .5 miles 1 in. = 1900 ft.

SEE 1128 MAP

SEE 1147 MAP

SEE 1168 MAP

0 .125 .25 .375 .5 miles 1 in. = 1900 ft.

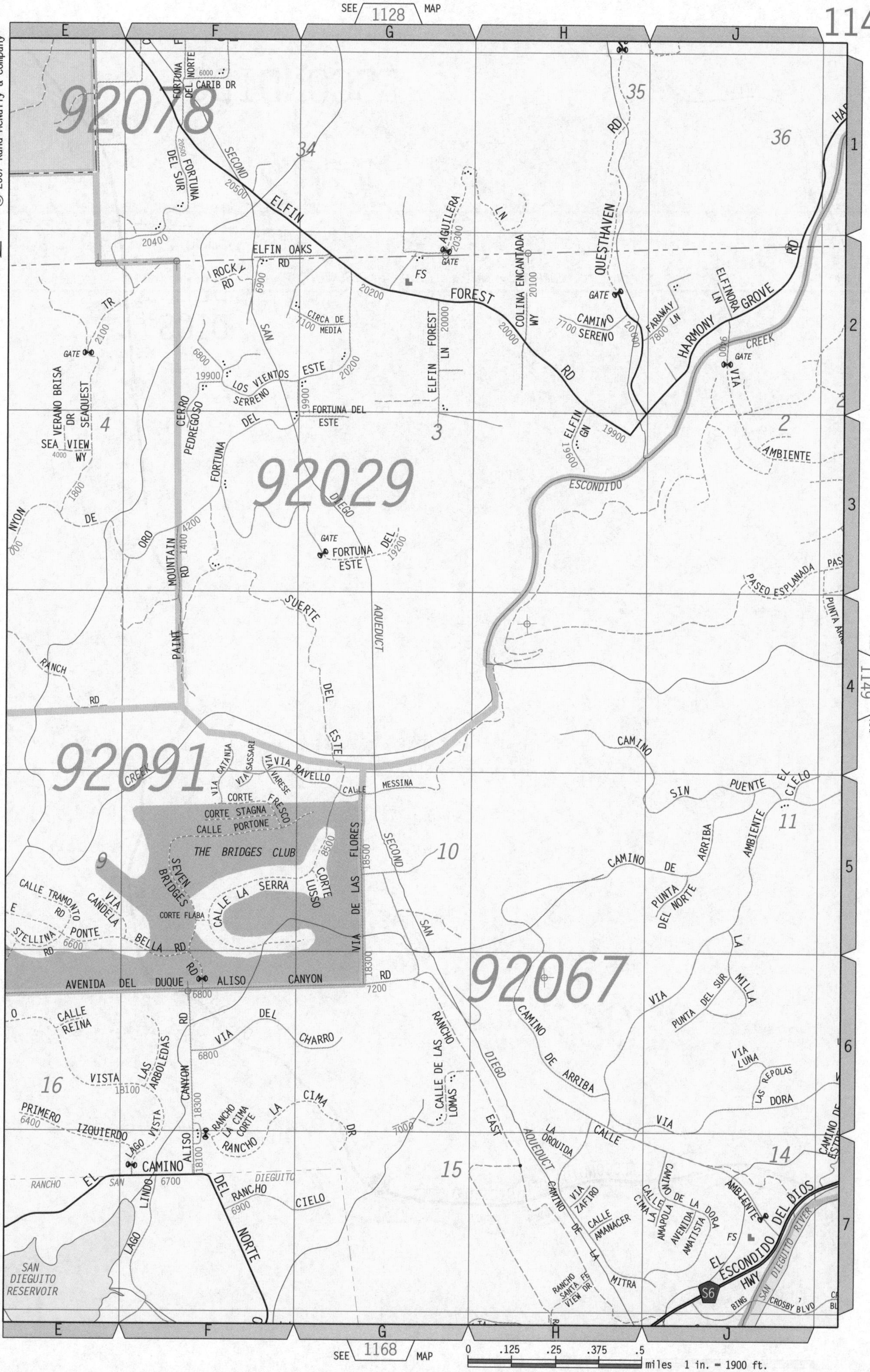
SEE 1128 MAP
SEE 1149 MAP
SEE 1168 MAP
92078
92029
92091
92067
ELFIN FOREST RD
HARMONY GROVE RD
ESCONDIDO CREEK
SAN DIEGO AQUEDUCT
SECOND SAN DIEGO AQUEDUCT
CERRO PEDREGOSO
PAINT MOUNTAIN RD
FORTUNA DEL NORTE
FORTUNA DEL SUR
FORTUNA DEL ESTE
CARIB DR
ELFIN OAKS RD
ROCKY RD
CIRCA DE MEDIA
LOS VIENTOS
SERRENO
AGUILERA
COLINA ENCANTADA WY
QUESTHAVEN RD
CAMINO SERENO
FARAWAY LN
ELFINORA LN
ELFIN GN
ELFIN FOREST LN
SUERTE DEL ESTE
SEAQUEST DR
VERANO BRISA
SEA VIEW WY
ORO
RANCH RD
VIA CATANIA
VIA SASSARI
VIA VARESE
VIA RAVELLO
CALLE MESSINA
CORTE FRESCO
CORTE STAGNA
CALLE PORTONE
THE BRIDGES CLUB
SEVEN BRIDGES
CALLE LA SERRA
CORTE LUSSO
CORTE FLABA
VIA DE LAS FLORES
CALLE TRAMONTO
VIA CANDELA
PONTE BELLA RD
STELLINA RD
AVENIDA DEL DUQUE
ALISO CANYON RD
CALLE REINA
VIA DEL CHARRO
LAS ARBOLEDAS
VISTA
PRIMERO
IZQUIERDO
LAGO VISTA
RANCHO LA CIMA
CORTE RANCHO
LA CIMA DR
CAMINO DEL NORTE
RANCHO CIELO
LAGO LINDO
SAN DIEGUITO RESERVOIR
CALLE DE LAS LOMAS
RANCHO
CAMINO SIN PUENTE
EL CIELO
AMBIENTE
CAMINO DE ARRIBA
PUNTA DEL NORTE
VIA LA MILLA
PUNTA DEL SUR
VIA LUNA
LAS REPOLAS
DORA
CAMINO DE ESTRELLA
PASEO ESPLANADA
PUNTA ARRIBA
CALLE VIA
LA ORQUIDA
VIA ZAFIRO
CALLE AMANACER
CALLE CIMA LA
AMAPOLA
CAMINO DE LA DORA
AVENIDA AMATISTA
CAMINO DE LA MITRA
RANCHO SANTA FE VIEW DR
EL ESCONDIDO DEL DIOS HWY
S6
SAN DIEGUITO RIVER
BING CROSBY BLVD
GATE
FS
0 .125 .25 .375 .5 miles 1 in. = 1900 ft.

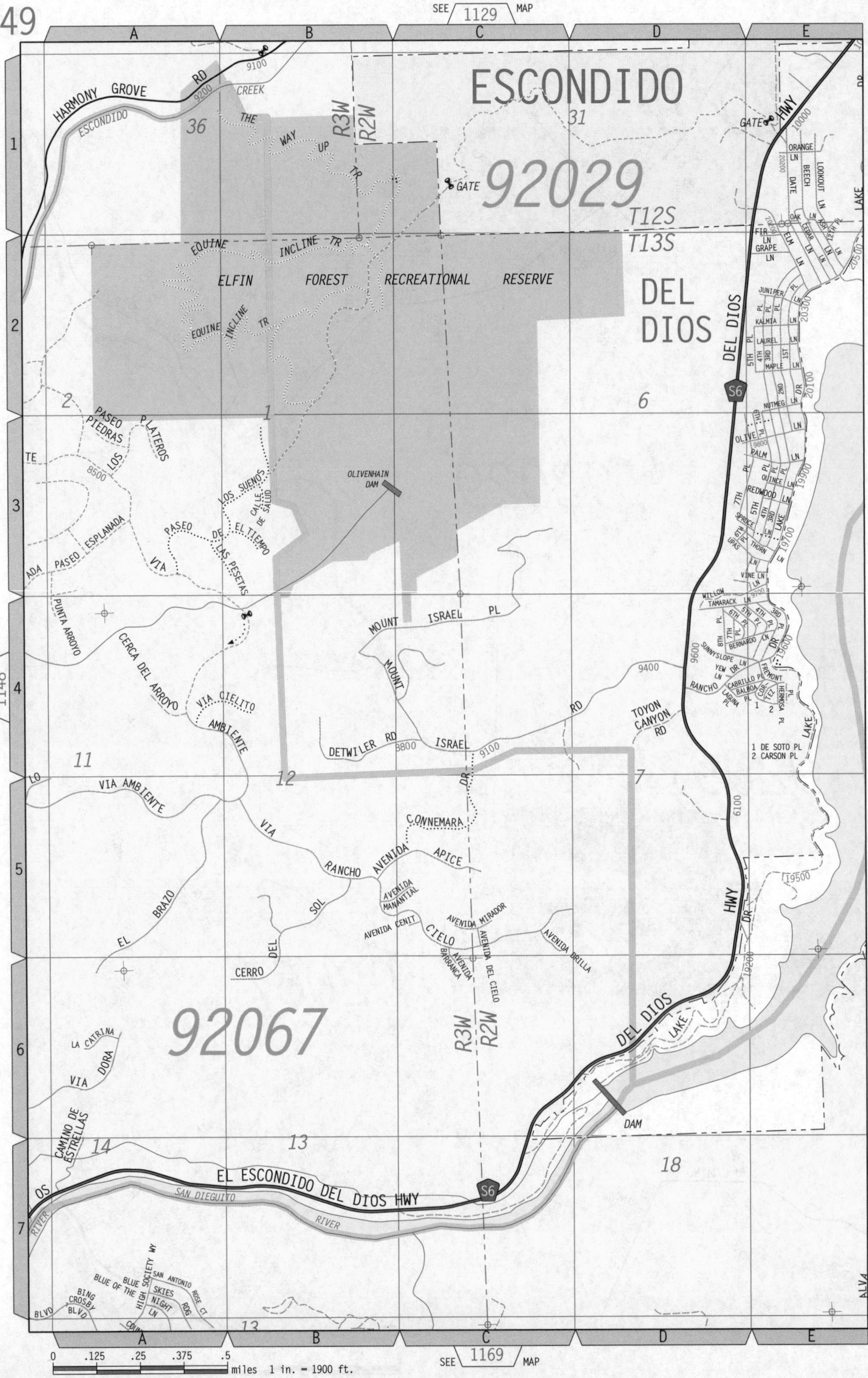

SEE 1129 MAP
ESCONDIDO
92029
T12S
T13S
R3W
R2W
DEL DIOS
ELFIN FOREST RECREATIONAL RESERVE
HARMONY GROVE RD
ESCONDIDO CREEK
THE WAY UP TR
EQUINE INCLINE TR
GATE
OLIVENHAIN DAM
MOUNT ISRAEL RD
DETWILER RD
TOYON CANYON RD
DEL DIOS HWY
VIA AMBIENTE
VIA RANCHO
AVENIDA APICE
CONNEMARA
CERCA DEL ARROYO
VIA CIELITO
PUNTA ARROYO
PASEO ESPLANADA
PASEO PIEDRAS
LOS PLATEROS
EL BRAZO
CERRO DEL SOL
CIELO
LA CATRINA
VIA DORA
CAMINO DE ESTRELLAS
EL ESCONDIDO DEL DIOS HWY
SAN DIEGUITO RIVER
LAKE
DAM
92067
1 DE SOTO PL
2 CARSON PL
SEE 1148 MAP
SEE 1169 MAP
SAN DIEGO CO.
0 .125 .25 .375 .5 miles 1 in. = 1900 ft.

SEE 1129 MAP

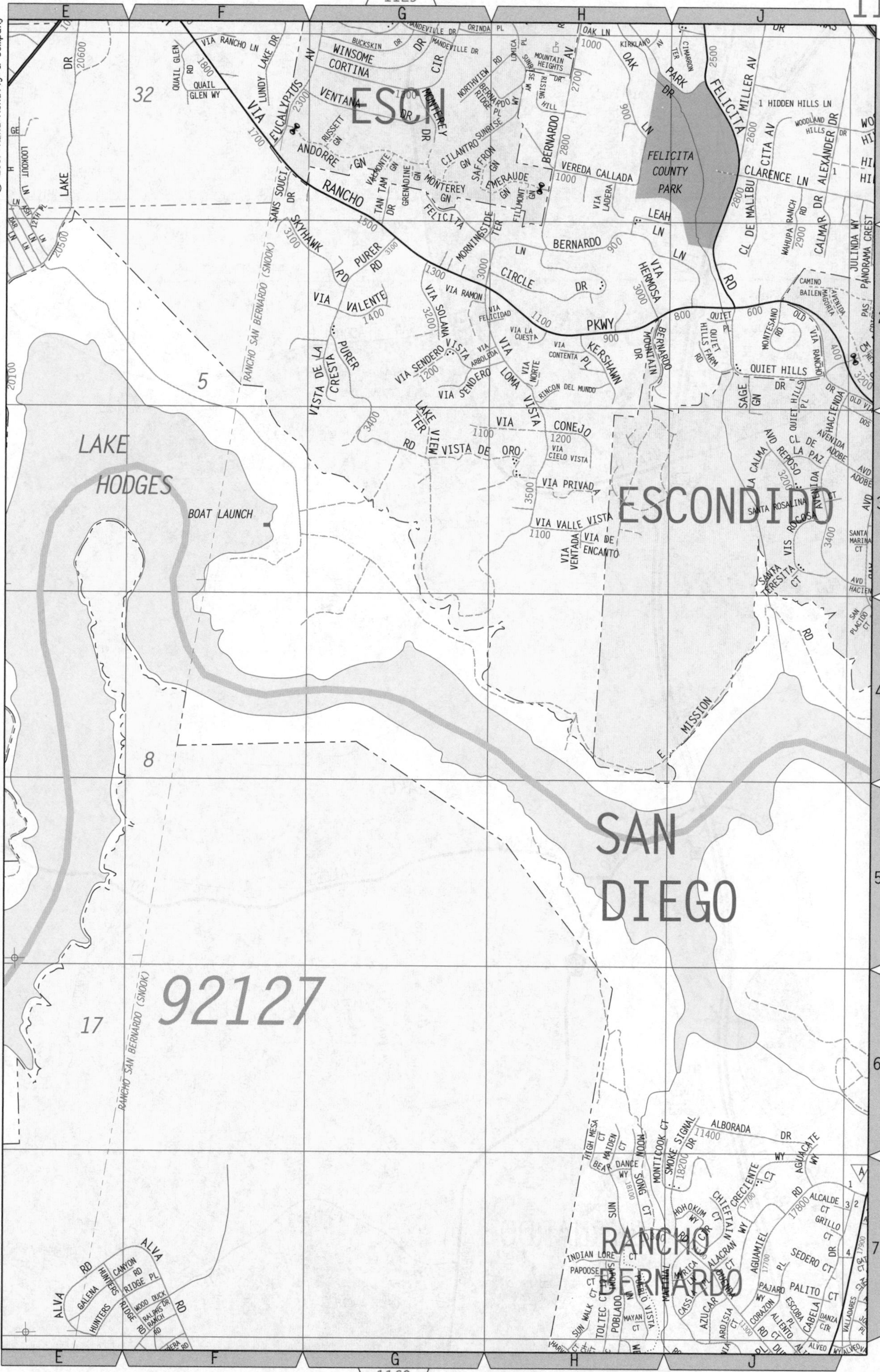

SEE 1150 MAP

SEE 1169 MAP

0 .125 .25 .375 .5 miles 1 in. = 1900 ft.

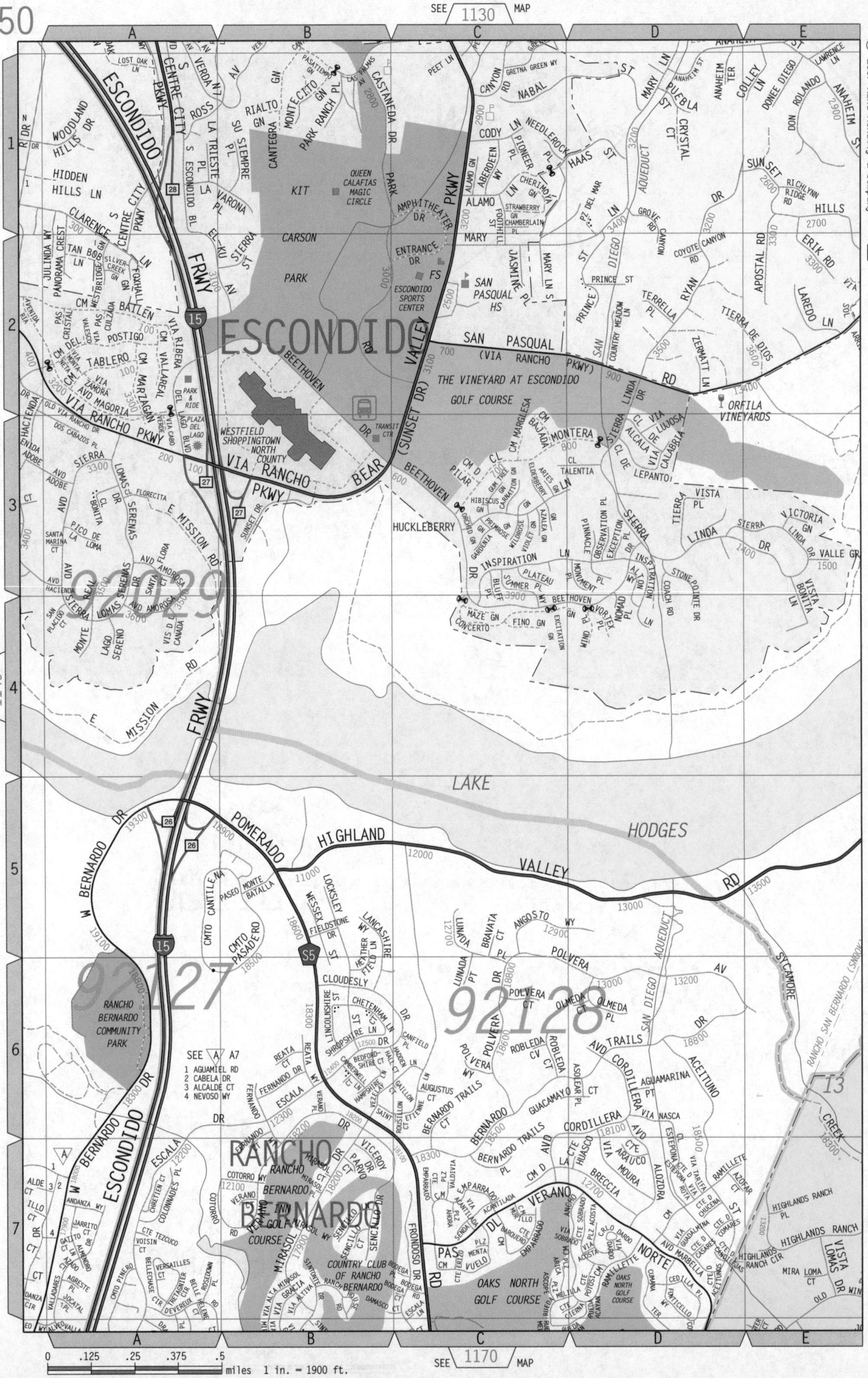
SEE 1130 MAP
SEE 1149 MAP
SEE 1170 MAP
A
B
C
D
E
1
2
3
4
5
6
7
ESCONDIDO
ESCONDIDO FRWY
15
CENTRE CITY PKWY
KIT CARSON PARK
QUEEN CALAFIAS MAGIC CIRCLE
AMPHITHEATER DR
ENTRANCE DR
ESCONDIDO SPORTS CENTER
SAN PASQUAL HS
VALLEY PKWY
SAN PASQUAL (VIA RANCHO PKWY) RD
THE VINEYARD AT ESCONDIDO GOLF COURSE
ORFILA VINEYARDS
WESTFIELD SHOPPINGTOWN NORTH COUNTY
PARK & RIDE
TRANSIT CTR
BEAR VALLEY (SUNSET DR) PKWY
VIA RANCHO PKWY
BEETHOVEN
HUCKLEBERRY
E MISSION RD
92029
92027
LAKE HODGES
HIGHLAND VALLEY RD
POMERADO RD
W BERNARDO DR
S5
92127
92128
RANCHO BERNARDO COMMUNITY PARK
SEE A7
1 AGUAMIEL RD
2 CABELA DR
3 ALCALDE CT
4 NEVOSO WY
RANCHO BERNARDO
RANCHO BERNARDO INN GOLF COURSE
COUNTRY CLUB OF RANCHO BERNARDO
OAKS NORTH GOLF COURSE
BERNARDO TRAILS DR
CORDILLERA
SAN DIEGO AQUEDUCT
SYCAMORE CREEK
HIGHLANDS RANCH RD
0 .125 .25 .375 .5
miles 1 in. = 1900 ft.

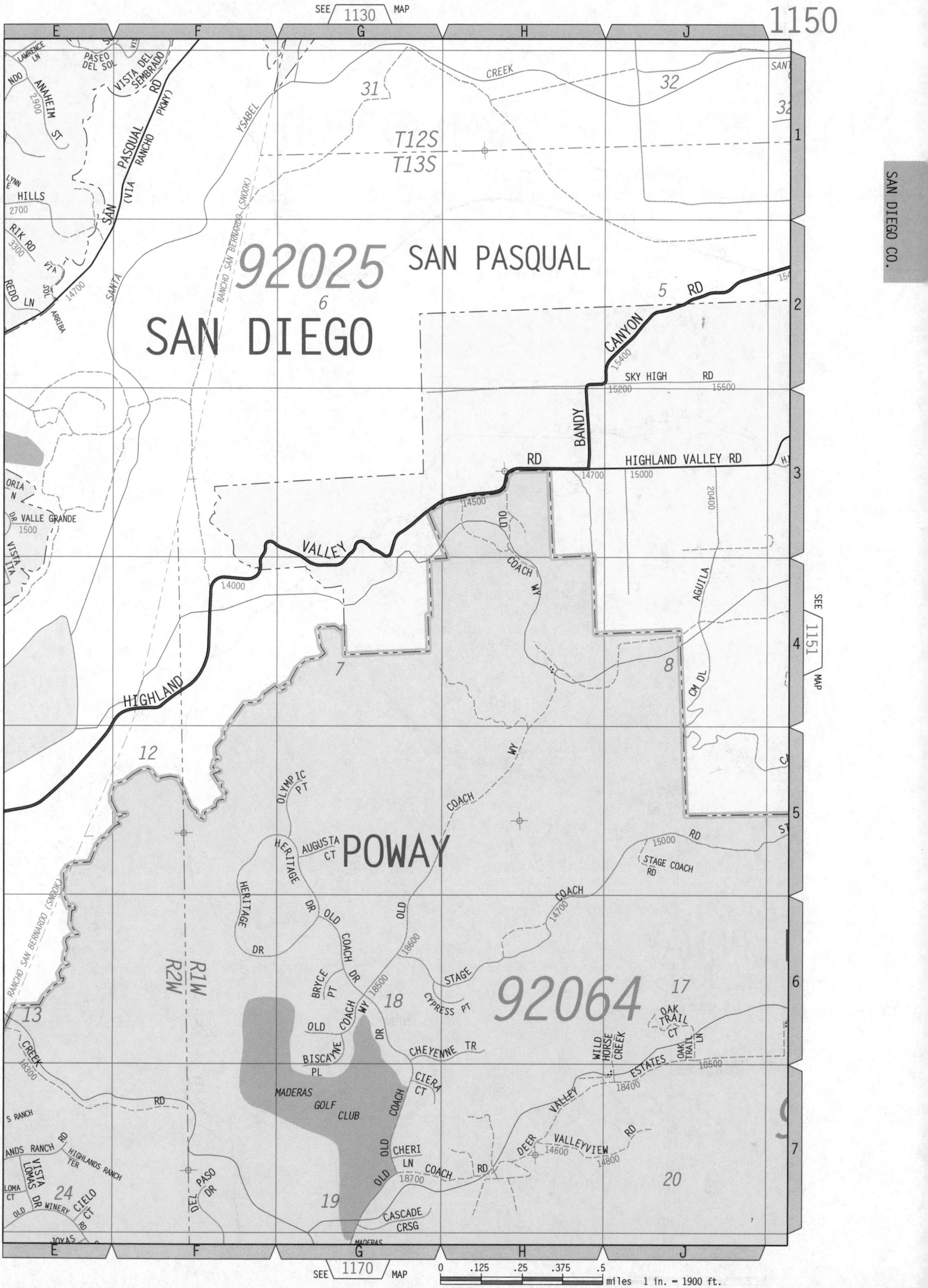

0 .125 .25 .375 .5 miles 1 in. = 1900 ft.

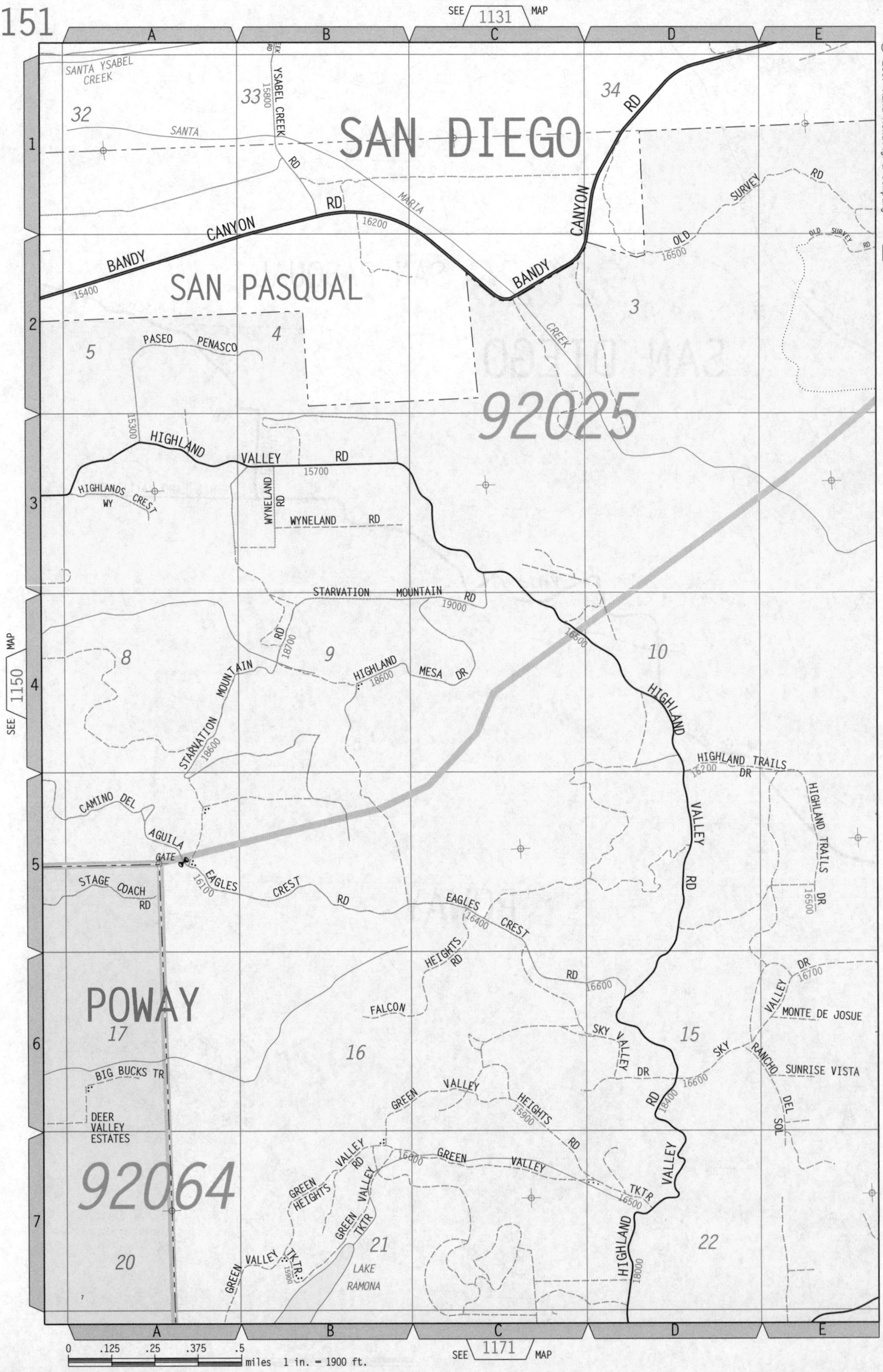

SEE 1131 MAP
SEE 1150 MAP
SEE 1171 MAP
SAN DIEGO
SAN PASQUAL
POWAY
92025
92064
SANTA YSABEL CREEK
YSABEL CREEK RD
15800
SANTA MARIA CREEK
BANDY CANYON RD
15400
16200
OLD SURVEY RD
16500
PASEO PENASCO
HIGHLAND VALLEY RD
15300
15700
16500
16200
18400
18000
HIGHLANDS CREST WY
WYNELAND RD
STARVATION MOUNTAIN RD
19000
18700
18600
HIGHLAND MESA DR
HIGHLAND TRAILS DR
16500
CAMINO DEL AGUILA
GATE
EAGLES CREST RD
16100
16400
STAGE COACH RD
HEIGHTS RD
16600
FALCON
SKY VALLEY DR
16700
MONTE DE JOSUE
SKY RANCHO DEL SOL
SUNRISE VISTA
BIG BUCKS TR
DEER VALLEY ESTATES
GREEN VALLEY HEIGHTS RD
15900
GREEN VALLEY TKTR
16000
GREEN HEIGHTS
GREEN VALLEY TKTR.
15900
LAKE RAMONA
32
33
34
3
4
5
8
9
10
15
16
17
20
21
22
0 .125 .25 .375 .5 miles 1 in. = 1900 ft.

SEE 1131 MAP

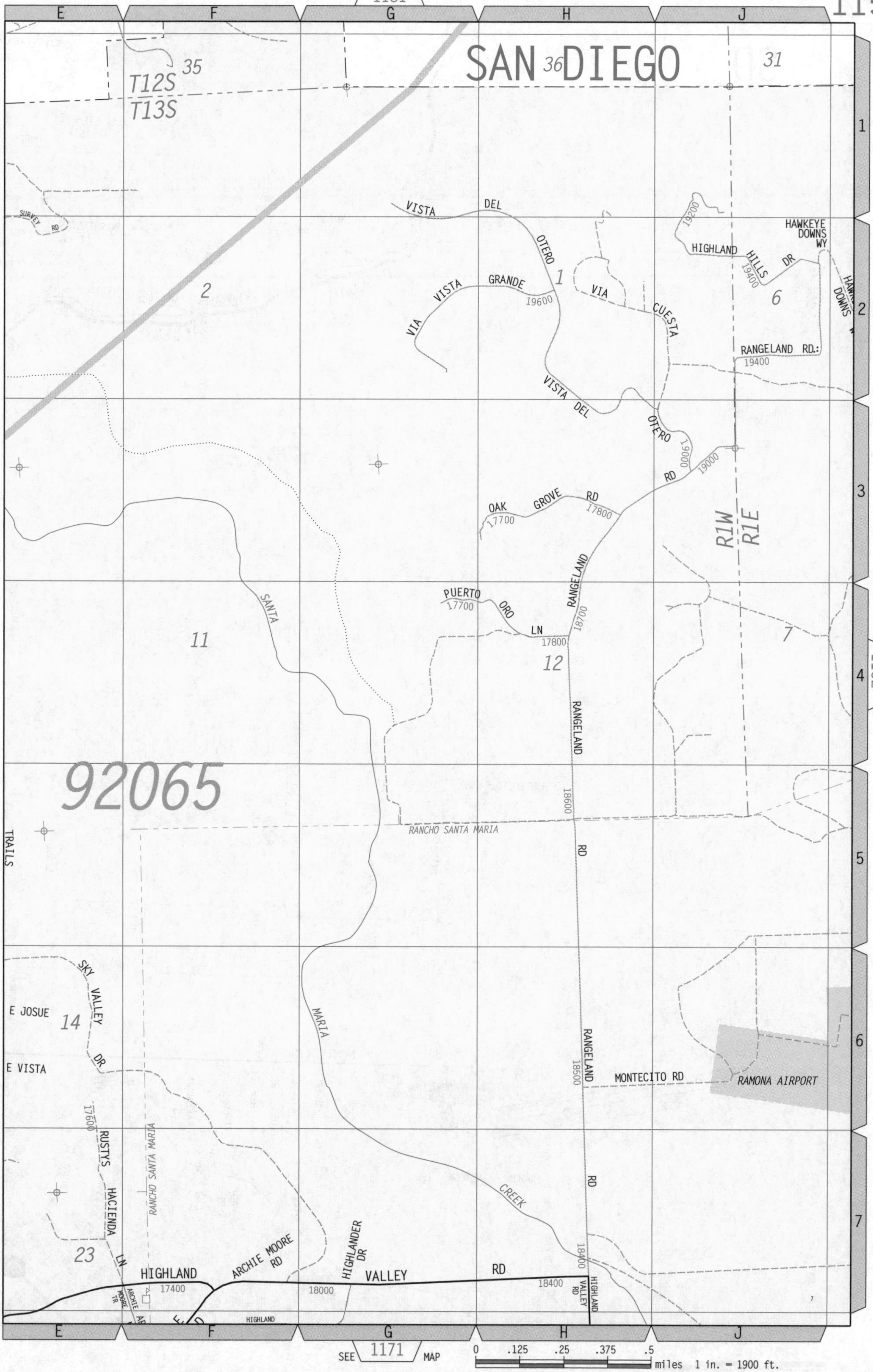

SEE 1152 MAP

SEE 1171 MAP

0 .125 .25 .375 .5 miles 1 in. = 1900 ft.

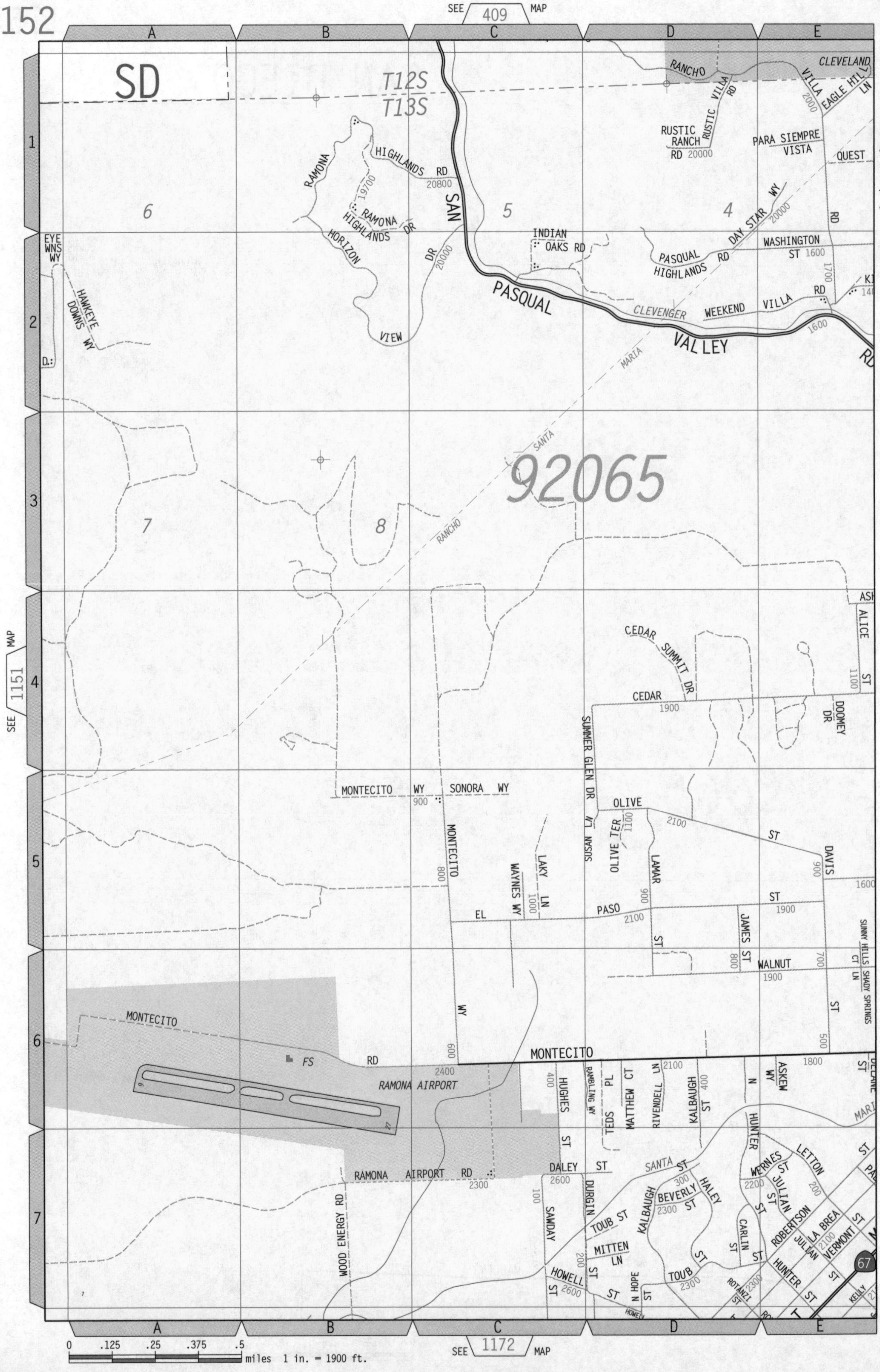
SEE 409 MAP
SEE 1151 MAP
SEE 1172 MAP
A
B
C
D
E
1
2
3
4
5
6
7
SD
T12S
T13S
92065
RAMONA HIGHLANDS RD
20800
19700
RAMONA HIGHLANDS DR
HORIZON VIEW DR
20000
SAN PASQUAL VALLEY RD
INDIAN OAKS RD
RANCHO
RUSTIC VILLA RD
RUSTIC RANCH RD
20000
CLEVELAND
VILLA
EAGLE HILL LN
2000
PARA SIEMPRE VISTA
QUEST
RD
DAY STAR WY
20000
WASHINGTON ST
1600
1700
PASQUAL HIGHLANDS RD
CLEVENGER
WEEKEND VILLA RD
1600
EYE WNS WY
HAWKEYE DOWNS WY
D
SANTA MARIA
RANCHO
ASH
ALICE ST
1100
CEDAR SUMMIT DR
CEDAR
1900
DOOMEY DR
SUMMER GLEN DR
MONTECITO WY
900
SONORA WY
MONTECITO WY
800
600
OLIVE ST
2100
OLIVE TER
1100
SAXON LN
LAKY LN
1000
WAYNES WY
LAMAR ST
900
DAVIS ST
900
700
500
1600
EL PASO ST
2100
1900
JAMES ST
800
WALNUT
1900
SUNNY HILLS CT
SHADY SPRINGS LN
MONTECITO RD
FS
2400
RAMONA AIRPORT
MONTECITO
1800
ST
DECANTE
HUGHES ST
400
RAMBLING WY
TEDS PL
MATTHEW CT
RIVENDELL LN
2100
KALBAUGH ST
400
N HUNTER
ASKEW WY
MARIA
LETTON
WERNES ST
JULIAN ST
2200
200
DALEY ST
RAMONA AIRPORT RD
2300
2600
SANTA ST
300
BEVERLY ST
2300
HALEY
KALBAUGH
WOOD ENERGY RD
SAMDAY
100
DURGIN
TOUB ST
MITTEN LN
CARLIN ST
ROBERTSON
LA BREA
2100
JULIAN
VERMONT ST
ST
HOWELL ST
2600
200
ST
N HOPE ST
TOUB ST
2300
ROTANZI
2300
HUNTER ST
67
KELLY
HOWELL
0 .125 .25 .375 .5
miles 1 in. = 1900 ft.

SEE 409 MAP

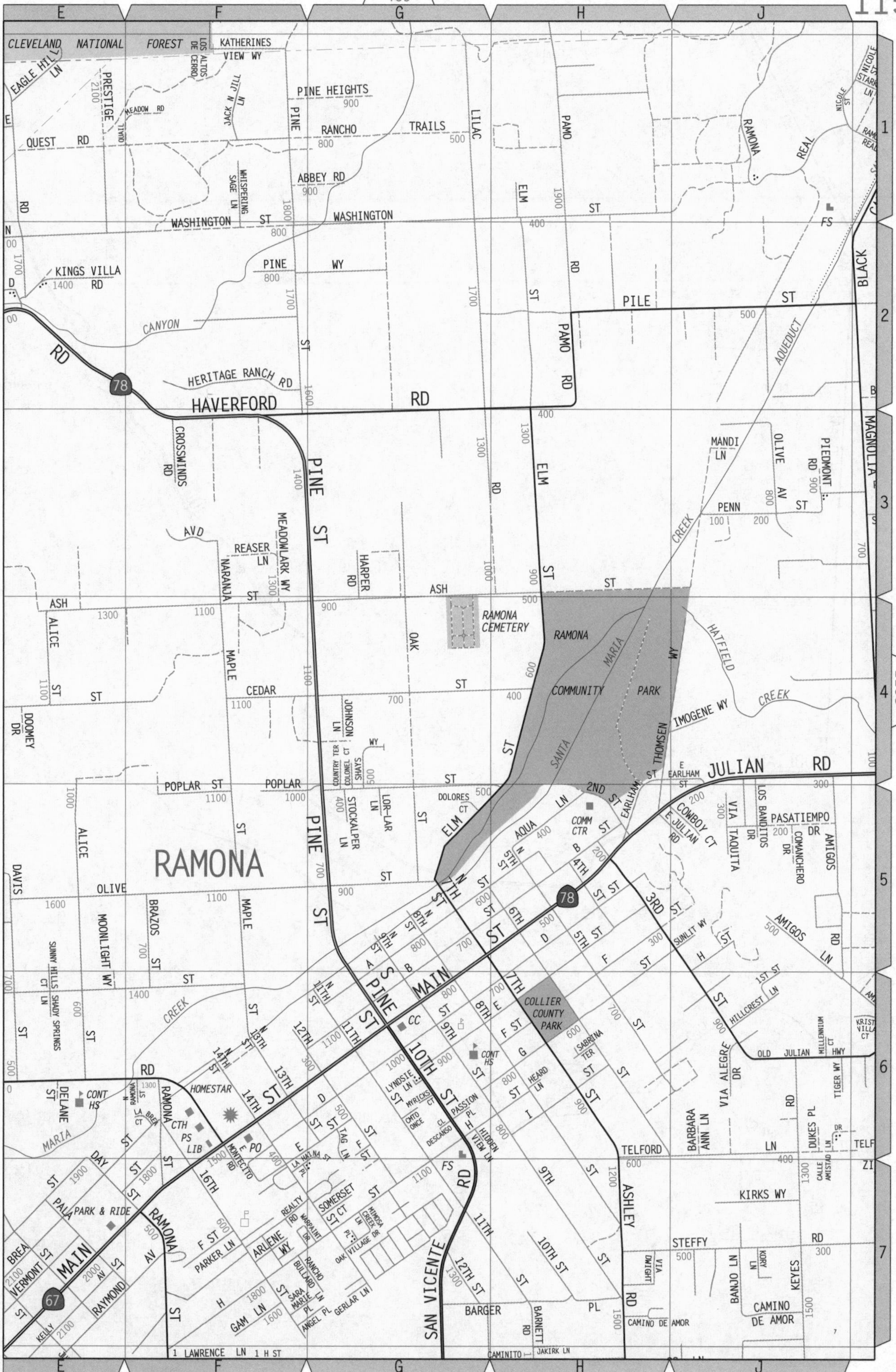

SEE 1153 MAP

SEE 1172 MAP

0 .125 .25 .375 .5 miles 1 in. = 1900 ft.

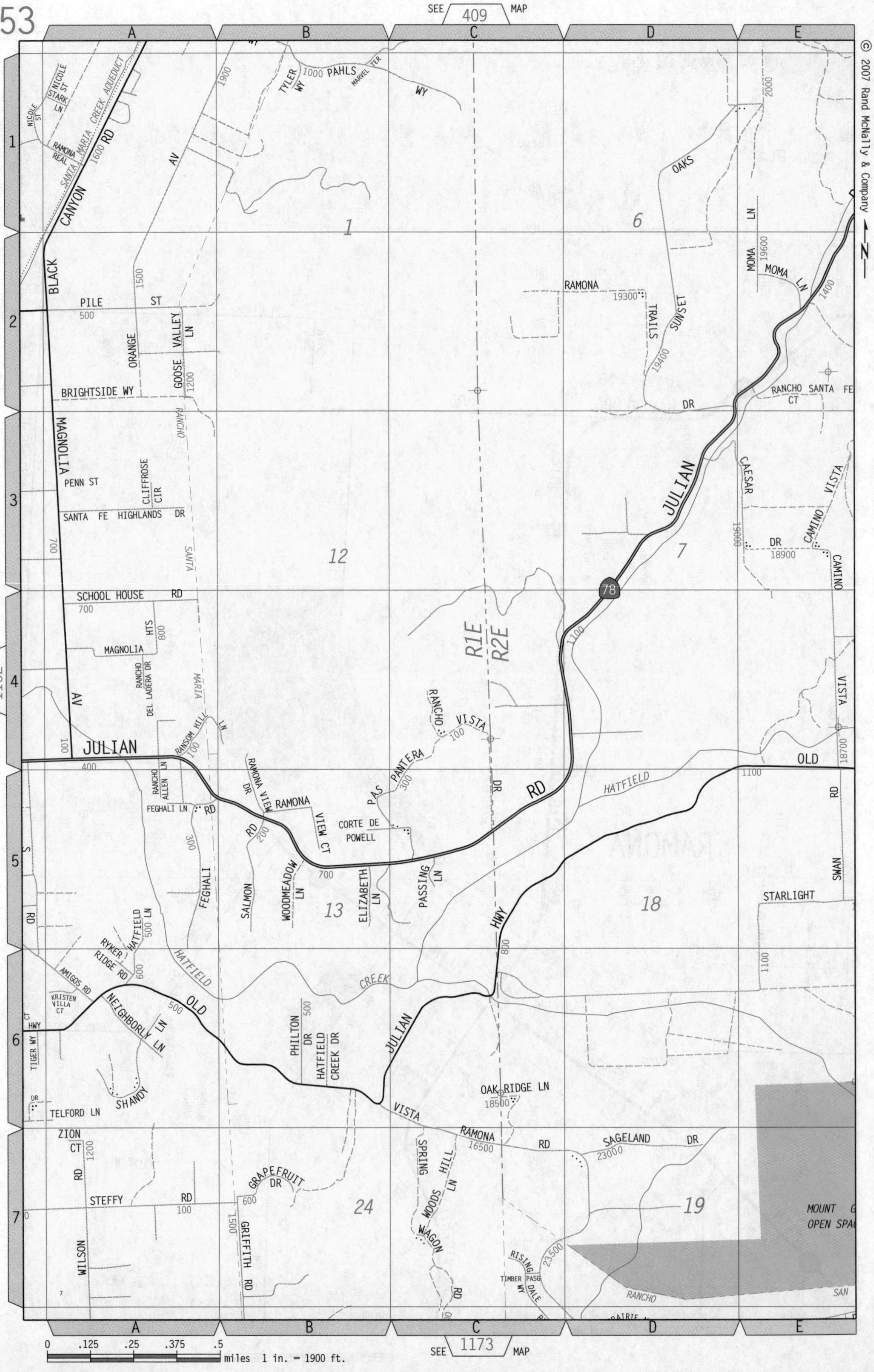
SEE 409 MAP
SEE 1152 MAP
SEE 1173 MAP
A
B
C
D
E
1
2
3
4
5
6
7
BLACK CANYON RD
SANTA MARIA CREEK AQUEDUCT
NICOLE ST
STARK LN
RAMONA REAL
TYLER WY
PAHLS WY
MARVEL TER
PILE ST
ORANGE AV
GOOSE VALLEY LN
BRIGHTSIDE WY
MAGNOLIA AV
PENN ST
CLIFFROSE CIR
SANTA FE HIGHLANDS DR
SCHOOL HOUSE RD
MAGNOLIA HTS
RANCHO DEL LADERA DR
RANCHO SANTA MARIA
RANSOM HILL LN
JULIAN RD
RANCHO ALLEN LN
FEGHALI LN
RAMONA VIEW DR
RAMONA VIEW CT
CORTE DE POWELL
PAS PANTERA
RANCHO VISTA DR
R1E
R2E
RAMONA
TRAILS
SUNSET OAKS DR
MOMA LN
RANCHO SANTA FE CT
CAESAR DR
CAMINO VISTA
78
HATFIELD
OLD JULIAN HWY
FEGHALI
SALMON RD
WOODMEADOW LN
ELIZABETH LN
PASSING LN
STARLIGHT
SWAN RD
RYKER RIDGE RD
HATFIELD LN
AMIGOS RD
KRISTEN VILLA CT
NEIGHBORLY LN
HATFIELD CREEK
PHILTON DR
HATFIELD CREEK DR
TIGER WY
SHANDY DR
TELFORD LN
OAK RIDGE LN
VISTA RAMONA RD
SAGELAND DR
ZION CT
STEFFY RD
GRAPEFRUIT DR
GRIFFITH RD
SPRING WOODS HILL LN
WAGON RD
RISING DALE
TIMBER PASG WY
RANCHO SAN
MOUNT G
OPEN SPA
WILSON RD
1
6
7
12
13
18
19
24
0 .125 .25 .375 .5 miles 1 in. = 1900 ft.

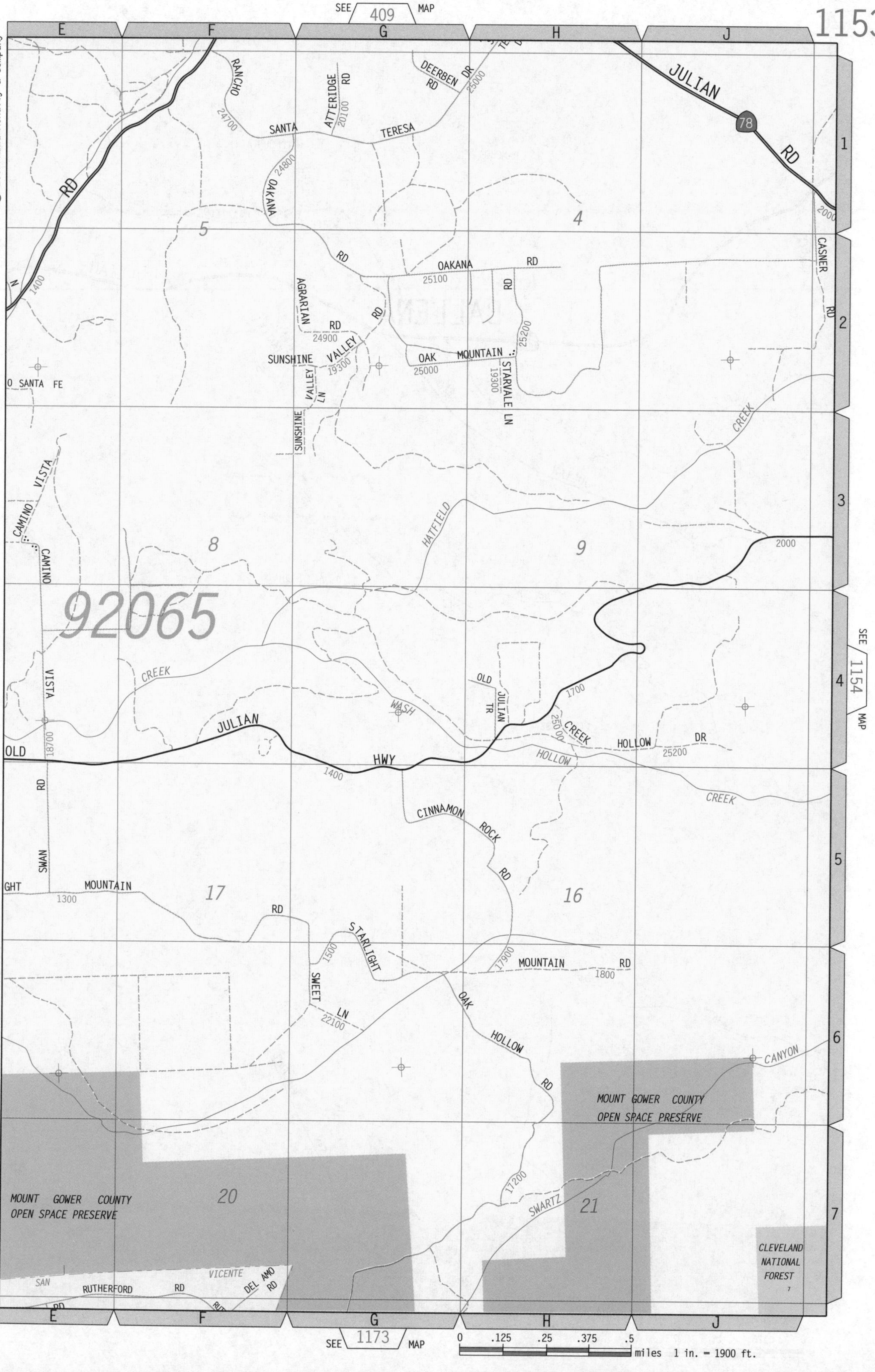
SEE 409 MAP
E
F
G
H
J
1
2
3
4
5
6
7
JULIAN RD
78
RD
N 1400
RANCHO 24700
SANTA
ATTERIDGE RD 20100
TERESA
DEERBEN DR RD 25000
OAKANA 24800
RD
5
4
2000
CASNER RD
OAKANA RD 25100
AGRARIAN RD 24900
RD
25200
SUNSHINE VALLEY 19300
OAK MOUNTAIN 25000
STARVALE LN 19300
VALLEY LN
SUNSHINE
O SANTA FE
CREEK
CAMINO VISTA
CAMINO
HATFIELD
8
9
2000
92065
CREEK
OLD JULIAN TR
1700
VISTA
WASH
25000
CREEK HOLLOW DR 25200
18700
OLD
JULIAN
HWY
1400
HOLLOW
CREEK
SEE 1154 MAP
RD
CINNAMON ROCK RD
SWAN
GHT MOUNTAIN 1300
17
16
RD
STARLIGHT 1500
17900
MOUNTAIN RD 1800
SWEET LN 22100
OAK HOLLOW RD
CANYON
MOUNT GOWER COUNTY OPEN SPACE PRESERVE
20
17200
SWARTZ
21
MOUNT GOWER COUNTY OPEN SPACE PRESERVE
CLEVELAND NATIONAL FOREST
SAN
VICENTE
RUTHERFORD RD
DEL AMO RD
E
F
G
H
J
SEE 1173 MAP
0 .125 .25 .375 .5 miles 1 in. = 1900 ft.

SEE 409 MAP

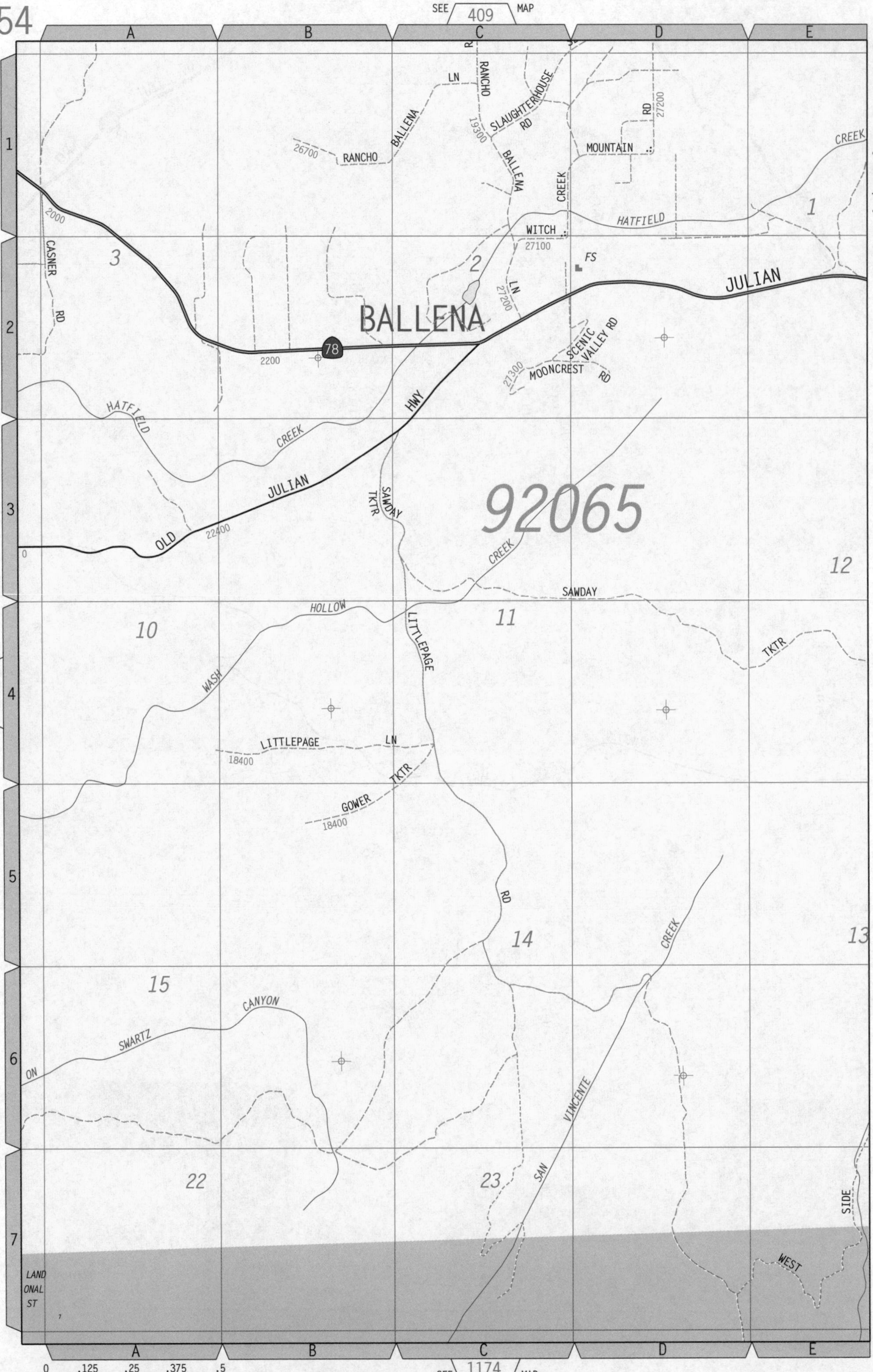

SEE 1153 MAP

SEE 1174 MAP

SEE 409 MAP

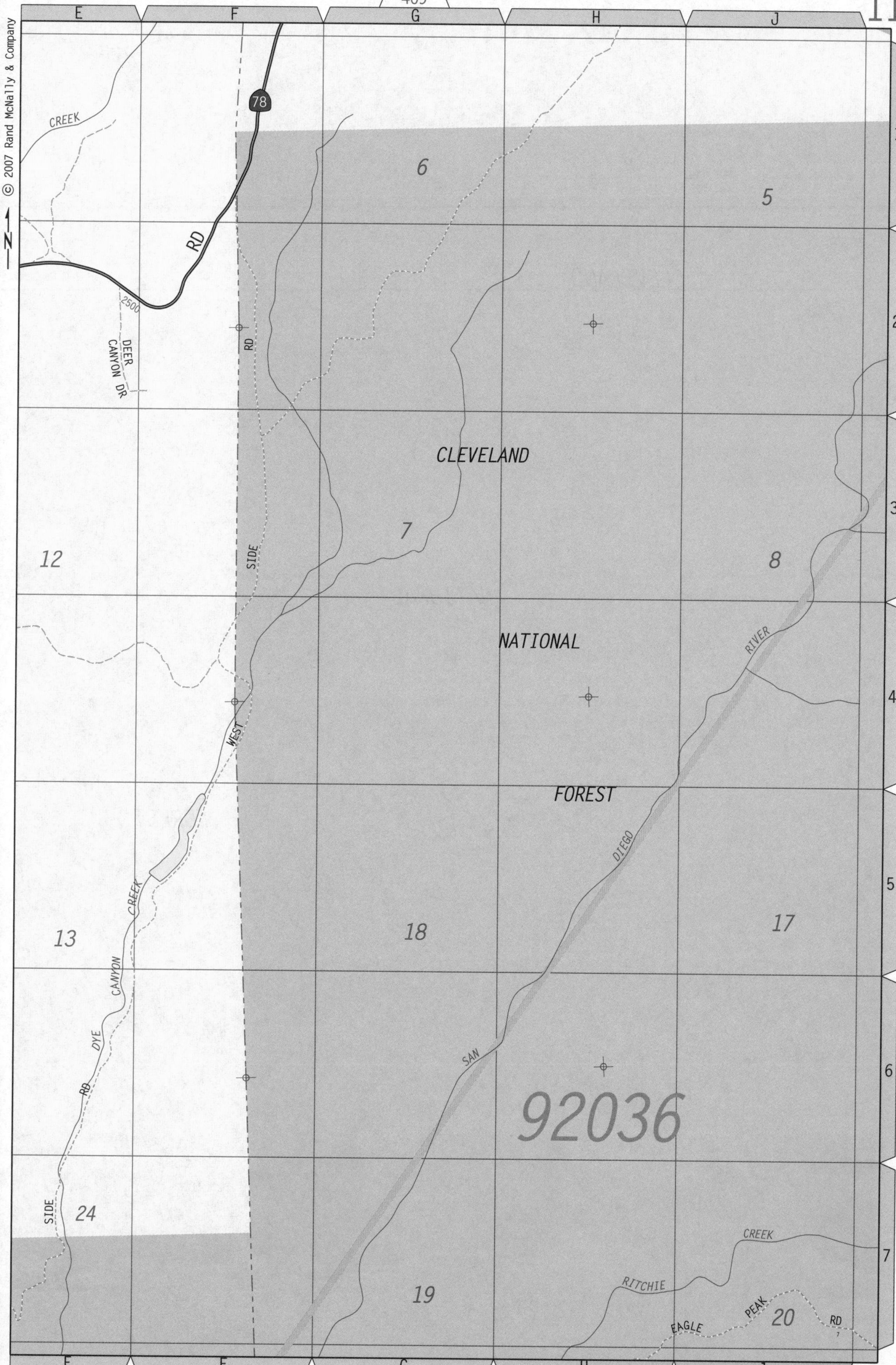

SEE 1155 MAP

SEE 1174 MAP

SAN DIEGO CO.

SEE 1135 MAP

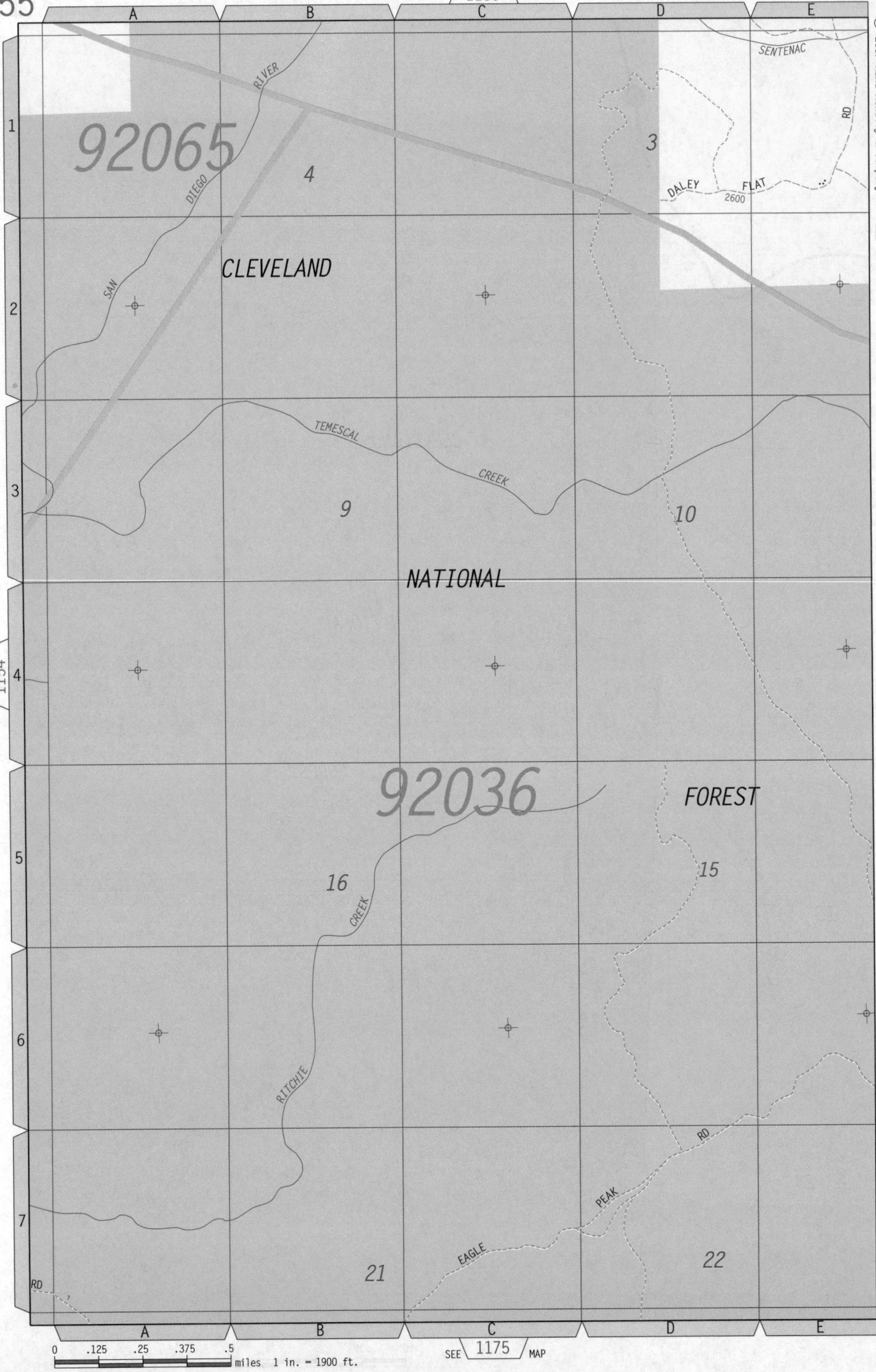

SEE 1154 MAP

SEE 1175 MAP

0 .125 .25 .375 .5 miles 1 in. = 1900 ft.

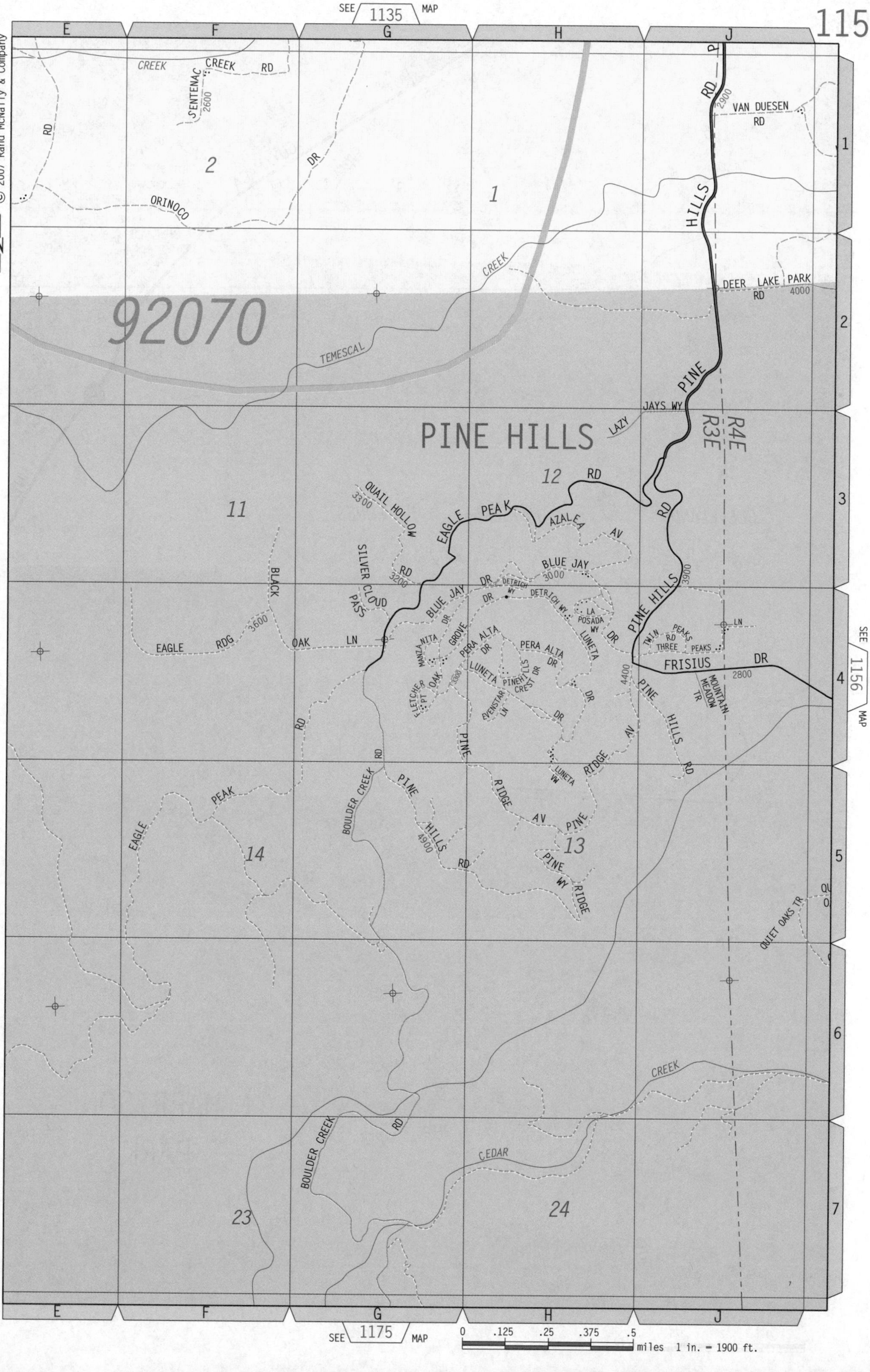
SEE 1135 MAP
SEE 1156 MAP
SEE 1175 MAP
E F G H J
1 2 3 4 5 6 7
92070
PINE HILLS
CREEK
CREEK RD
SENTENAC
2600
RD
DR
ORINOCO
VAN DUESEN RD
2900
PINE HILLS RD
DEER LAKE PARK RD
4000
CREEK
TEMESCAL
JAYS WY
LAZY
R4E
R3E
12
RD
11
QUAIL HOLLOW
3300
EAGLE PEAK
AZALEA AV
SILVER CLOUD PASS
RD
3200
BLUE JAY
3000
BLACK
DR
DETRICH WY
BLUE JAY DR
LA POSADA WY
PINE HILLS
3900
LN
3600
EAGLE RDG
OAK LN
MANZANITA
GROVE
PERA ALTA DR
LUNETA DR
TWIN PEAKS RD
THREE PEAKS
FRISIUS DR
2800
4400
MOUNTAIN MEADOW TR
FLETCHER PT
OAK
3300
LUNETA
PINEHILLS CREST DR
EVENSTAR LN
DR
PINE HILLS RD
RD
BOULDER CREEK
PINE
RIDGE
AV
LUNETA VW
PINE RIDGE AV
EAGLE
PEAK
14
4900
PINE HILLS RD
13
PINE WY
RIDGE
QUIET OAKS TR
CREEK
BOULDER CREEK RD
CEDAR
23
24
0 .125 .25 .375 .5
miles 1 in. = 1900 ft.

SAN DIEGO CO.

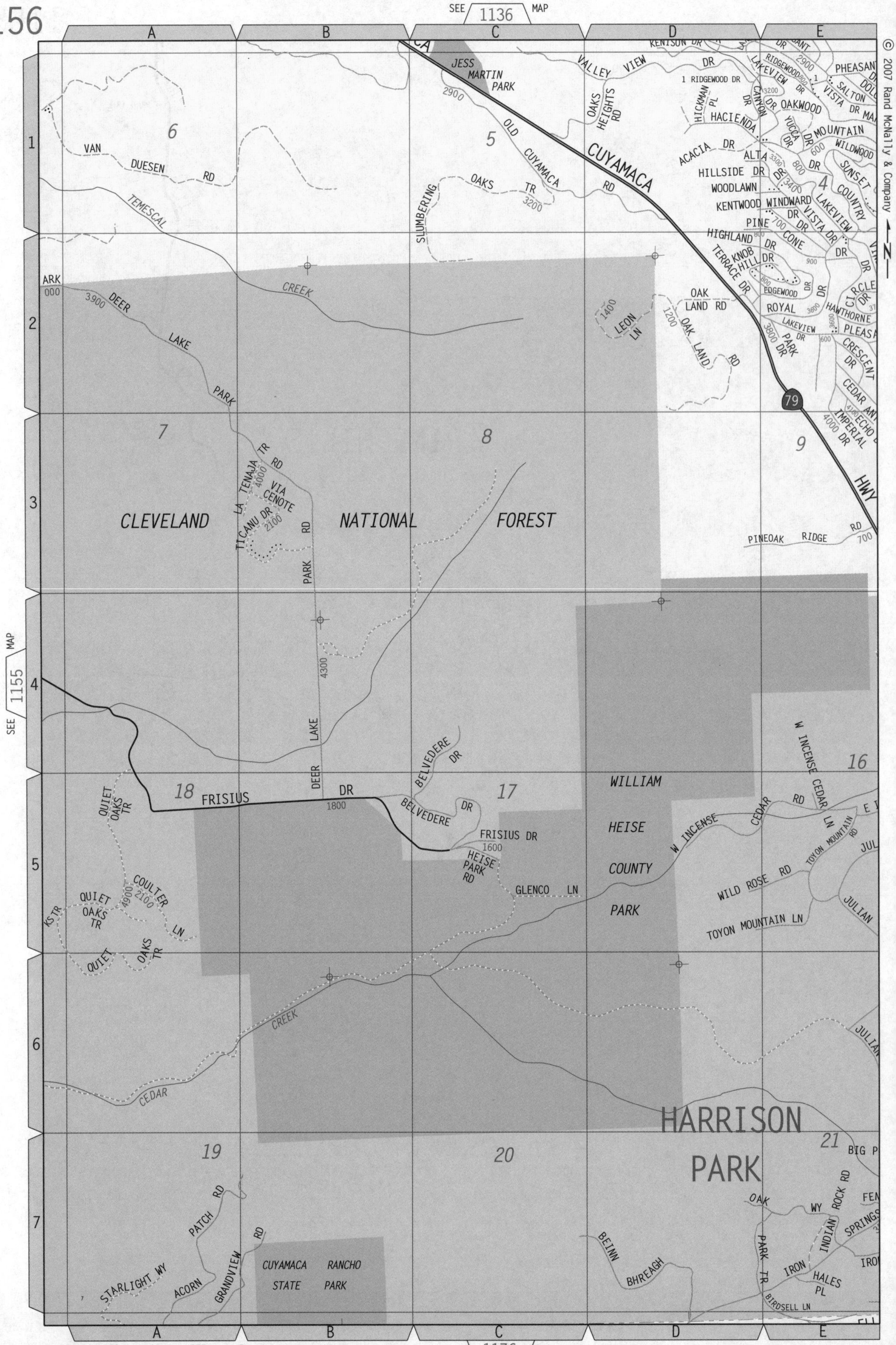
SEE 1136 MAP
SEE 1155 MAP
SEE 1176 MAP
A
B
C
D
E
1
2
3
4
5
6
7
CLEVELAND NATIONAL FOREST
WILLIAM HEISE COUNTY PARK
HARRISON PARK
JESS MARTIN PARK
CUYAMACA RANCHO STATE PARK
CUYAMACA HWY
79
VAN DUESEN RD
TEMESCAL CREEK
DEER LAKE PARK RD
OLD CUYAMACA RD
OAKS TR
SLUMBERING
VALLEY VIEW DR
OAKS HEIGHTS RD
LA TENAJA TR
VIA CENOTE
TICANU DR
FRISIUS DR
BELVEDERE DR
HEISE PARK RD
GLENCO LN
W INCENSE CEDAR RD
WILD ROSE RD
TOYON MOUNTAIN LN
TOYON MOUNTAIN RD
QUIET OAKS TR
COULTER LN
CEDAR CREEK
LEON LN
OAK LAND RD
PINEOAK RIDGE RD
HICKMAN PL
HACIENDA DR
CANYON DR
OAKWOOD
MOUNTAIN
ACACIA DR
ALTA
HILLSIDE DR
WOODLAWN
KENTWOOD
WINDWARD DR
VISTA DR
LAKEVIEW
PINE CONE
HIGHLAND DR
KNOB HILL DR
TERRACE DR
EDGEWOOD
ROYAL
PARK DR
CRESCENT DR
HAWTHORNE
IMPERIAL
ECHO
CEDAR
RIDGEWOOD DR
PHEASANT
SALTON
SUNSET
COUNTRY
JULIAN
PATCH RD
STARLIGHT WY
ACORN
GRANDVIEW RD
BEINN BHREAGH
OAK WY
PARK TR
INDIAN ROCK RD
IRON
HALES PL
BIRDSELL LN
BIG P
SPRINGS
.125
.25
.375
.5
miles 1 in. = 1900 ft.
© 2007 Rand McNally & Company

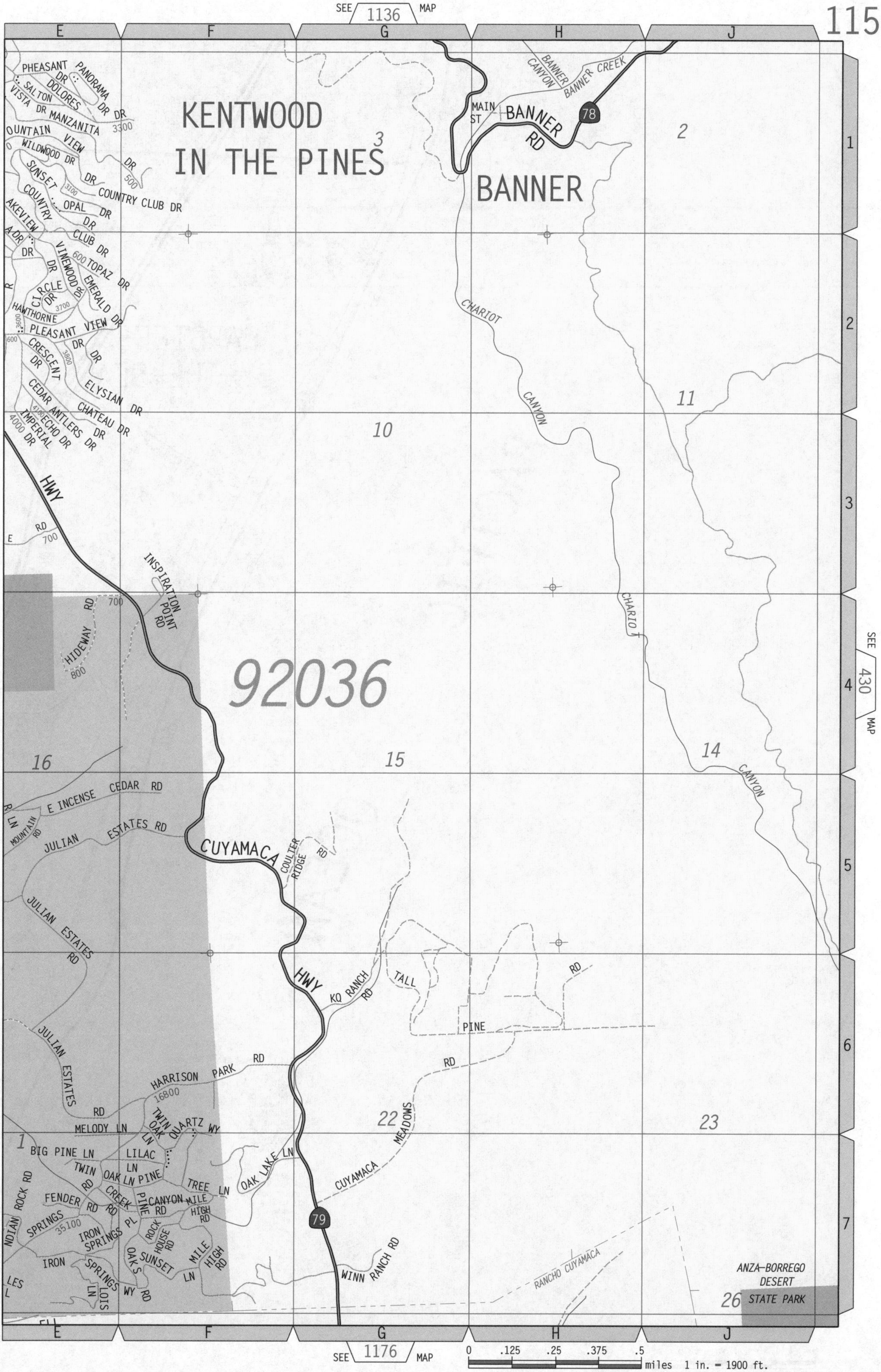
SEE 1136 MAP
E
F
G
H
J
1
2
3
4
5
6
7
SEE 430 MAP
SEE 1176 MAP
KENTWOOD
IN THE PINES
BANNER
92036
PHEASANT DR
PANORAMA DR
DOLORES
SALTON
VISTA DR
MANZANITA DR
3300
MOUNTAIN VIEW
WILDWOOD DR
DR
500
SUNSET DR
3100
COUNTRY CLUB DR
OPAL DR
COUNTRY CLUB DR
LAKEVIEW DR
A DR
VINEWOOD DR
600
TOPAZ DR
EMERALD DR
CIRCLE DR
3700
HAWTHORNE
3600
PLEASANT VIEW DR
600
CRESCENT DR
3800
DR
ELYSIAN DR
CEDAR ANTLERS DR
CHATEAU DR
4000
ECHO DR
IMPERIAL DR
4000
HWY
RD
700
INSPIRATION POINT RD
RD
700
HIDEWAY
800
MAIN ST
BANNER RD
78
BANNER CANYON
BANNER CREEK
CHARIOT
CANYON
CHARIO
CANYON
3
2
10
11
14
15
16
22
23
1
26
E INCENSE CEDAR RD
MOUNTAIN RD
JULIAN ESTATES RD
CUYAMACA
COULTER RIDGE RD
JULIAN ESTATES RD
HWY
KQ RANCH RD
TALL
RD
PINE
RD
JULIAN ESTATES RD
HARRISON PARK RD
16800
MELODY LN
TWIN OAK LN
QUARTZ WY
MEADOWS
BIG PINE LN
LILAC LN
TWIN OAK LN
PINE
OAK LAKE LN
TREE LN
CREEK RD
PINE
CANYON RD
MILE HIGH RD
CUYAMACA
FENDER RD
ROCK RD
SPRINGS
35100
IRON SPRINGS PL
ROCK HOUSE RD
79
IRON
SPRINGS WY RD
OAKS
SUNSET
MILE HIGH RD
LN
LOIS LN
WINN RANCH RD
RANCHO CUYAMACA
ANZA-BORREGO DESERT STATE PARK
0
.125
.25
.375
.5
miles 1 in. = 1900 ft.

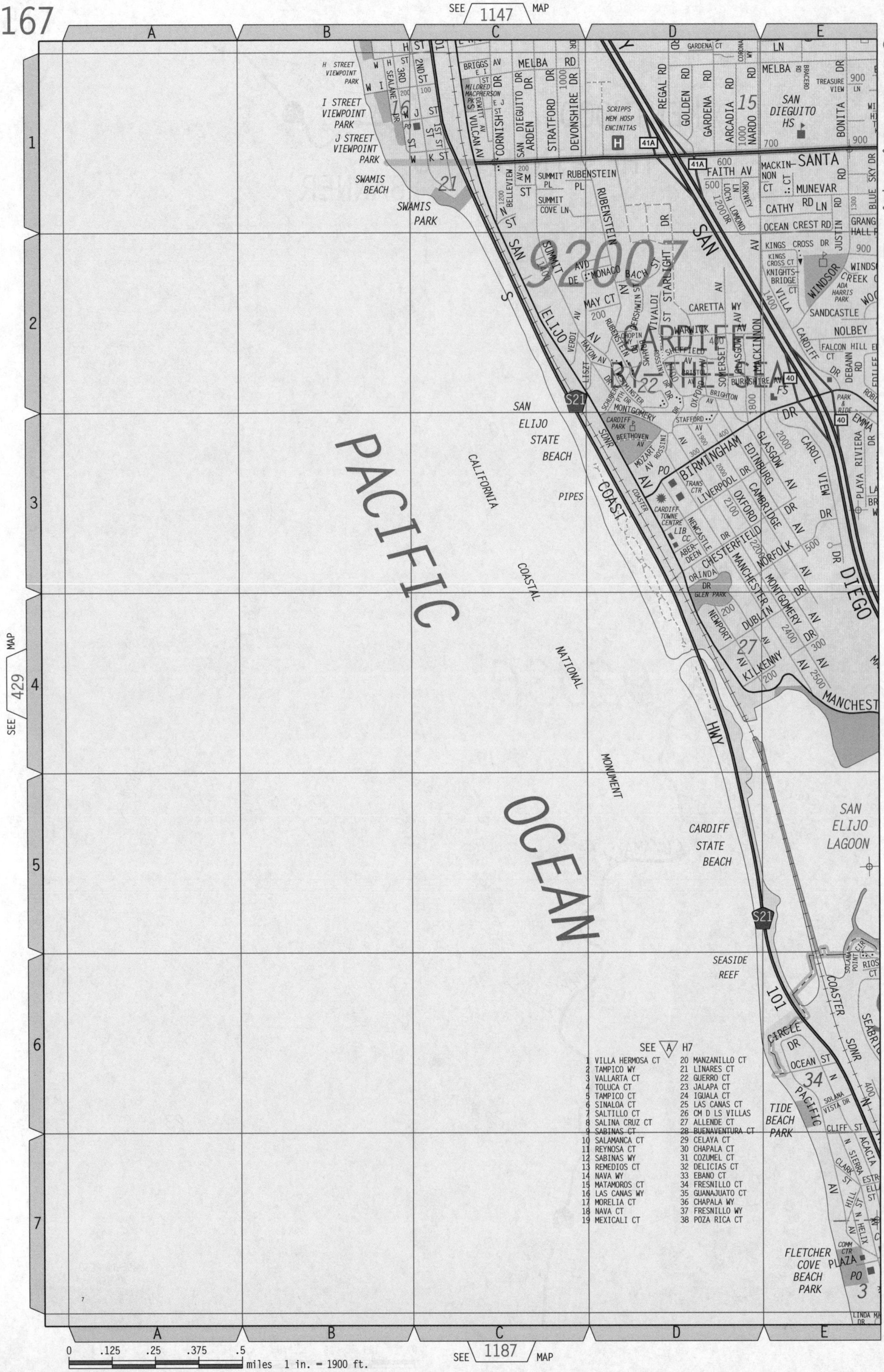
SEE 1147 MAP
SEE 429 MAP
SEE 1187 MAP
A
B
C
D
E
1
2
3
4
5
6
7
PACIFIC
OCEAN
92007
CARDIFF BY-THE-SEA
SAN ELIJO STATE BEACH
CALIFORNIA COASTAL NATIONAL MONUMENT
PIPES
CARDIFF STATE BEACH
SEASIDE REEF
SAN ELIJO LAGOON
SWAMIS BEACH
SWAMIS PARK
H STREET VIEWPOINT PARK
I STREET VIEWPOINT PARK
J STREET VIEWPOINT PARK
SCRIPPS MEM HOSP ENCINITAS
SAN DIEGUITO HS
CARDIFF PARK
GLEN PARK
ADA HARRIS PARK
TIDE BEACH PARK
FLETCHER COVE BEACH PARK
CARDIFF TOWNE CENTRE
SAN ELIJO AV
COAST HWY
S21
101
SAN DIEGO FWY
SANTA FE DR
BIRMINGHAM DR
MANCHESTER AV
SEE A H7
1 VILLA HERMOSA CT
2 TAMPICO WY
3 VALLARTA CT
4 TOLUCA CT
5 TAMPICO CT
6 SINALOA CT
7 SALTILLO CT
8 SALINA CRUZ CT
9 SABINAS CT
10 SALAMANCA CT
11 REYNOSA CT
12 SABINAS WY
13 REMEDIOS CT
14 NAVA WY
15 MATAMOROS CT
16 LAS CANAS WY
17 MORELIA CT
18 NAVA CT
19 MEXICALI CT
20 MANZANILLO CT
21 LINARES CT
22 GUERRO CT
23 JALAPA CT
24 IGUALA CT
25 LAS CANAS CT
26 CM D LS VILLAS
27 ALLENDE CT
28 BUENAVENTURA CT
29 CELAYA CT
30 CHAPALA CT
31 COZUMEL CT
32 DELICIAS CT
33 EBANO CT
34 FRESNILLO CT
35 GUANAJUATO CT
36 CHAPALA WY
37 FRESNILLO WY
38 POZA RICA CT
0 .125 .25 .375 .5 miles 1 in. = 1900 ft.

SEE 1147 MAP

SAN DIEGO CO.

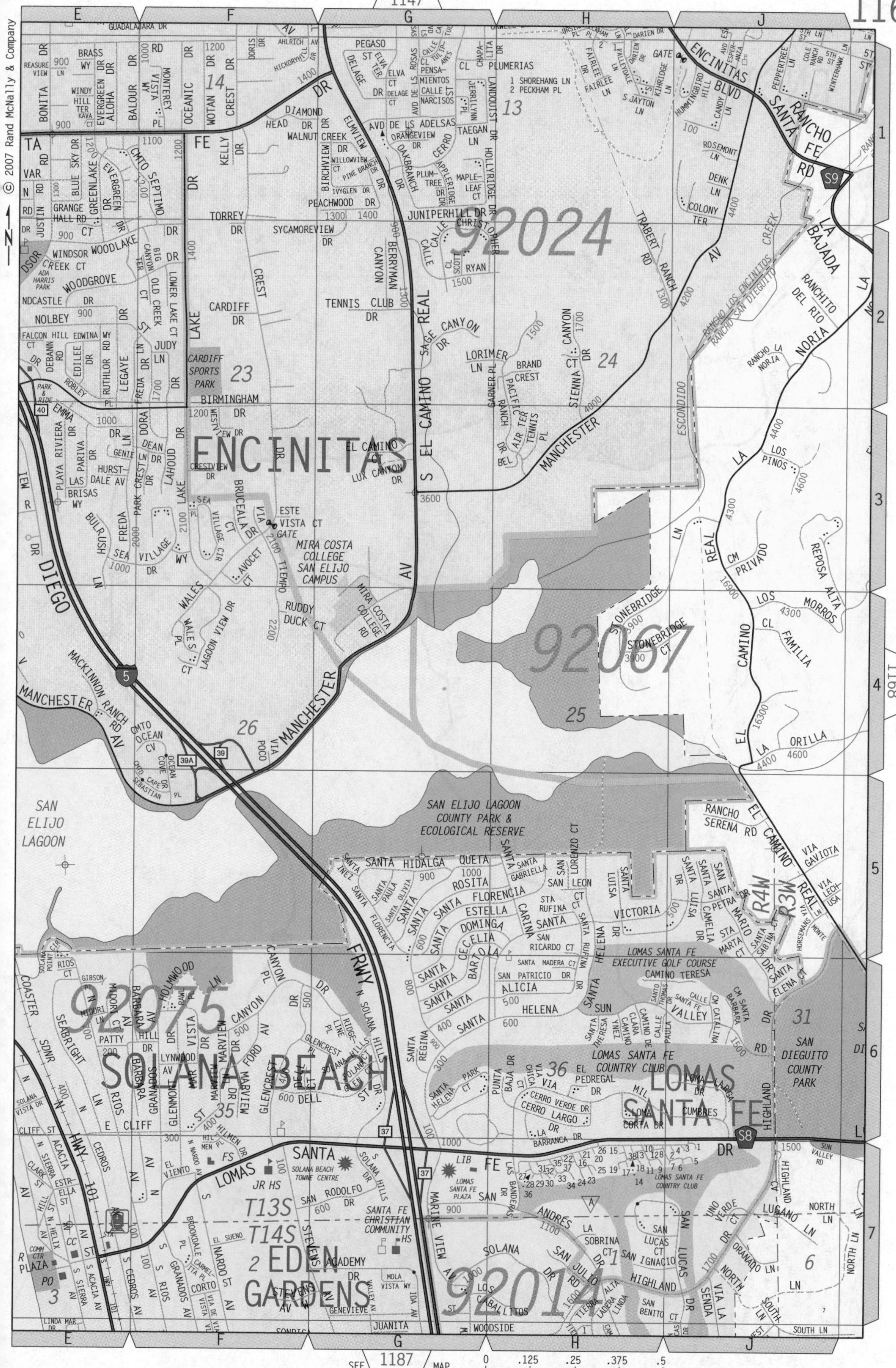

SEE 1168 MAP

SEE 1187 MAP

0 .125 .25 .375 .5 miles 1 in. = 1900 ft.

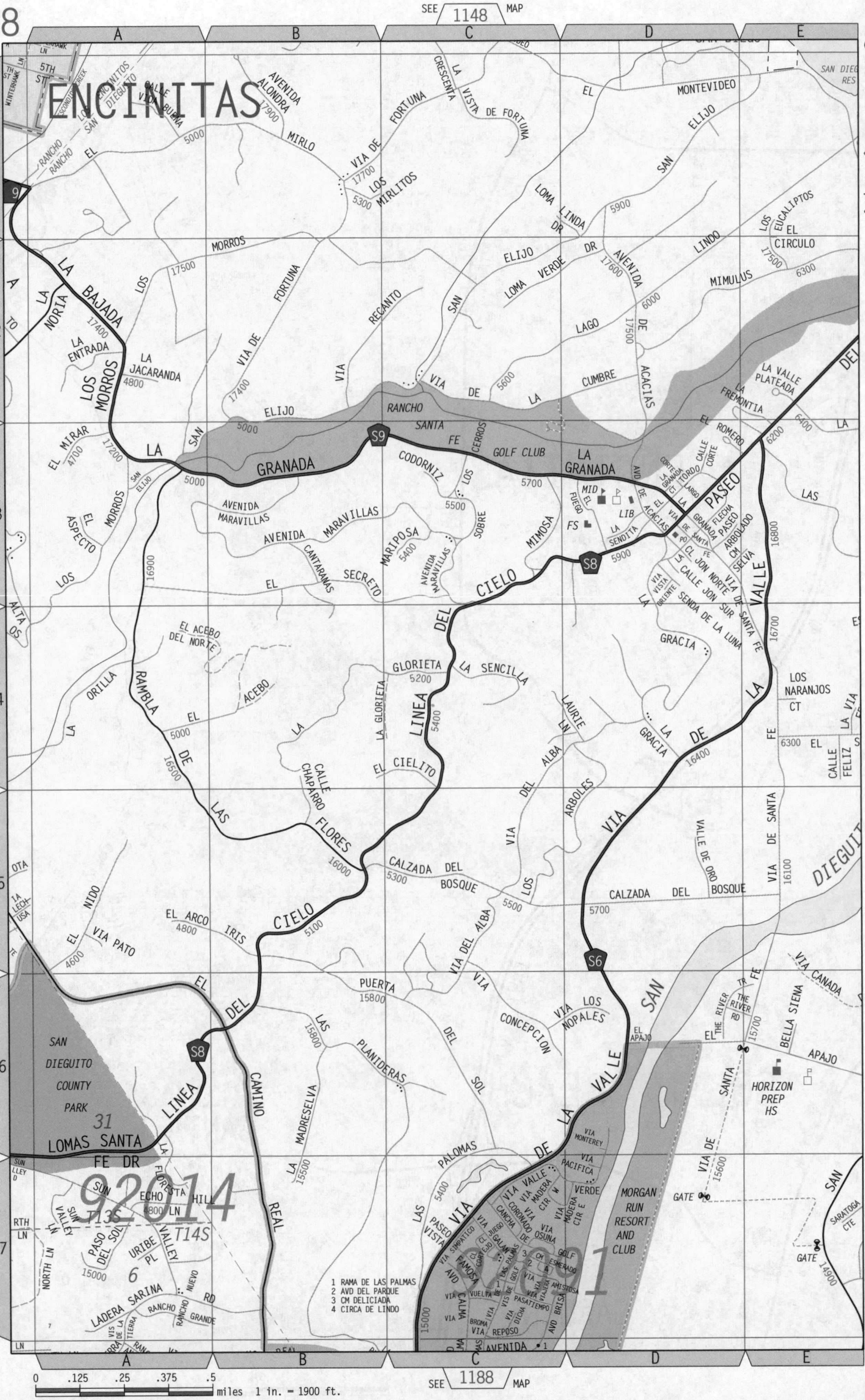
SEE 1148 MAP
SEE 1167 MAP
SEE 1188 MAP
ENCINITAS
SAN DIEGUITO COUNTY PARK
MORGAN RUN RESORT AND CLUB
HORIZON PREP HS
RANCHO SANTA FE GOLF CLUB
92014
92091
LA GRANADA
LOS MORROS
LA BAJADA
LINEA DEL CIELO
VIA DE LA VALLE
PASEO DELICIAS
EL CAMINO REAL
LOMAS SANTA FE DR
RAMBLA DE LAS FLORES
CALZADA DEL BOSQUE
AVENIDA DE ACACIAS
VIA DE SANTA FE
SAN ELIJO
VIA DE FORTUNA
LA VISTA DE FORTUNA
MONTEVIDEO
LOMA LINDA DR
LOMA VERDE DR
MIMULUS
LAGO LINDO
VIA DE LA CUMBRE
EL MIRAR
EL ASPECTO
LOS MORROS
LA ORILLA
EL NIDO
VIA PATO
EL ARCO IRIS
PUERTA
LAS PLANIDERAS
MADRESELVA
CONCEPCION
VIA LOS NOPALES
VIA DEL ALBA
VIA DE LOS ARBOLES
LA GRACIA
LOS NARANJOS CT
EL FEIZ
BELLA SIENA
VIA CANADA
EL APAJO
THE RIVER RD
SAN DIEGUITO
S6
S8
S9
9
GATE
1 RAMA DE LAS PALMAS
2 AVD DEL PARQUE
3 CM DELICIADA
4 CIRCA DE LINDO
0 .125 .25 .375 .5 miles 1 in. = 1900 ft.

SEE 1148 MAP

SEE 1169 MAP

SEE 1188 MAP

0 .125 .25 .375 .5 miles 1 in. = 1900 ft.

SAN DIEGO CO.

SEE 1149 MAP

SEE 1168 MAP

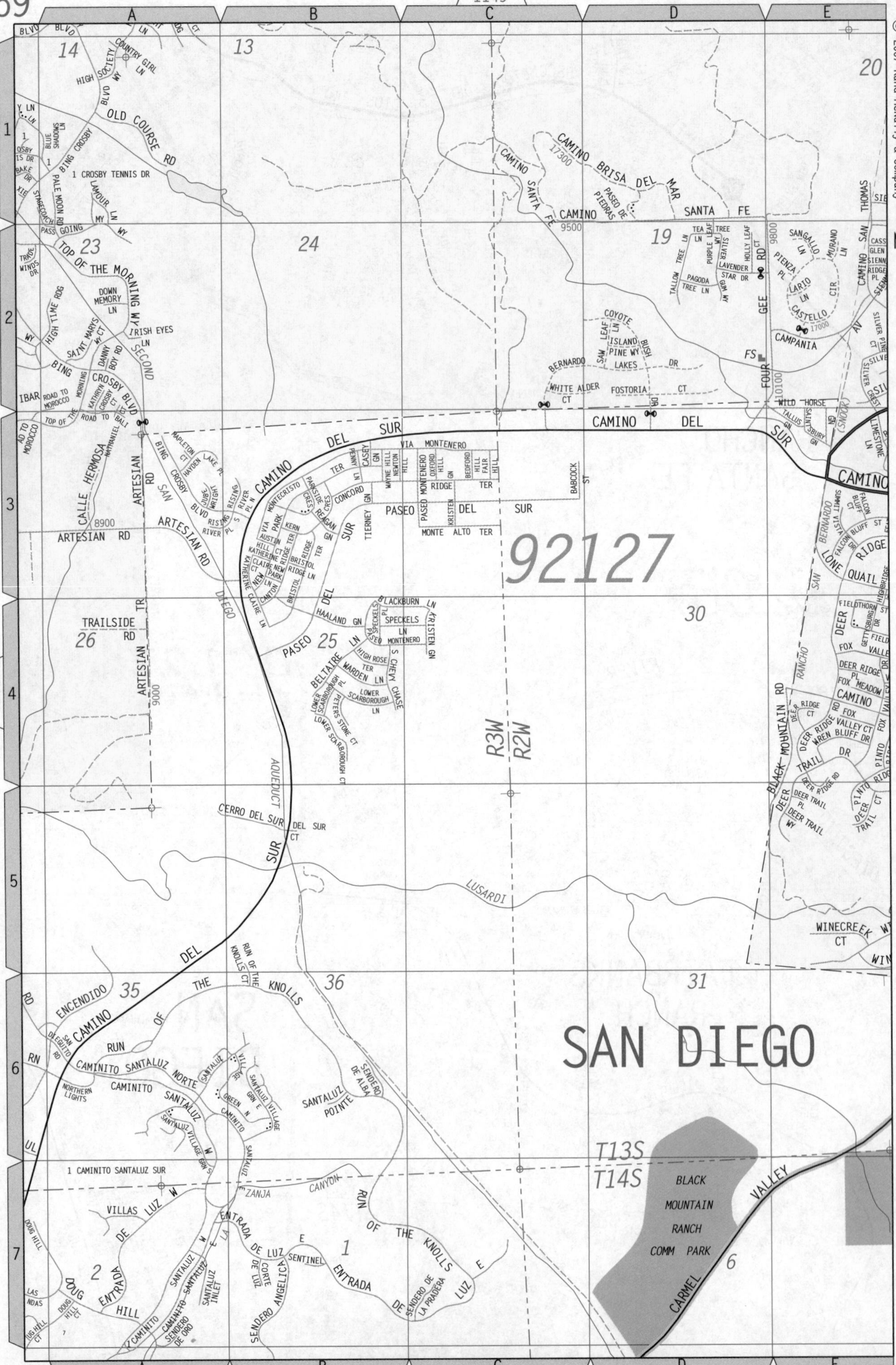

SEE 1189 MAP

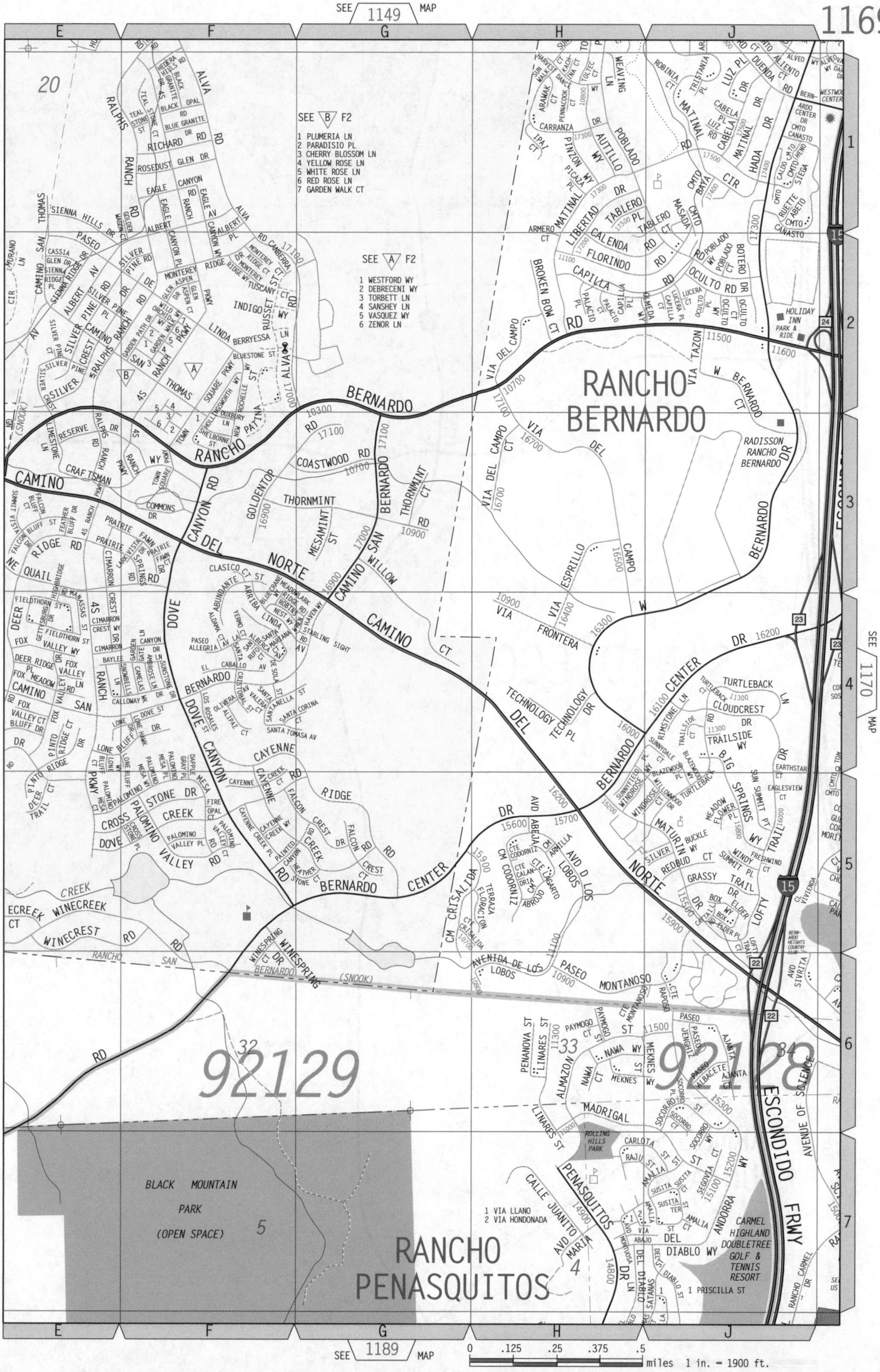
SEE 1149 MAP
SEE 1189 MAP
SEE 1170 MAP
SAN DIEGO CO.
E
F
G
H
J
1
2
3
4
5
6
7
RANCHO BERNARDO
RANCHO PENASQUITOS
92129
92128
BLACK MOUNTAIN PARK (OPEN SPACE)
SEE B F2
1 PLUMERIA LN
2 PARADISIO PL
3 CHERRY BLOSSOM LN
4 YELLOW ROSE LN
5 WHITE ROSE LN
6 RED ROSE LN
7 GARDEN WALK CT
SEE A F2
1 WESTFORD WY
2 DEBRECENI WY
3 TORBETT LN
4 SANSHEY LN
5 VASQUEZ WY
6 ZENOR LN
1 VIA LLANO
2 VIA HONDONADA
1 PRISCILLA ST
RANCHO BERNARDO RD
CAMINO DEL NORTE
BERNARDO CENTER DR
DOVE CANYON RD
ESCONDIDO FRWY
AVENUE OF SCIENCE
W BERNARDO DR
VIA DEL CAMPO
TECHNOLOGY DR
PASEO MONTANOSO
AVENIDA DE LOS LOBOS
PENASQUITOS DR
CALLE JUANITO
AVD MARIA
MADRIGAL
HOLIDAY INN
PARK & RIDE
RADISSON RANCHO BERNARDO
ROLLING HILLS PARK
CARMEL HIGHLAND DOUBLETREE GOLF & TENNIS RESORT
BERNARDO HEIGHTS COUNTRY CLUB
WINECREEK
WINECREST RD
CREEK
(SNOOK)
0 .125 .25 .375 .5
miles 1 in. = 1900 ft.

SEE 1150 MAP

SAN DIEGO CO.

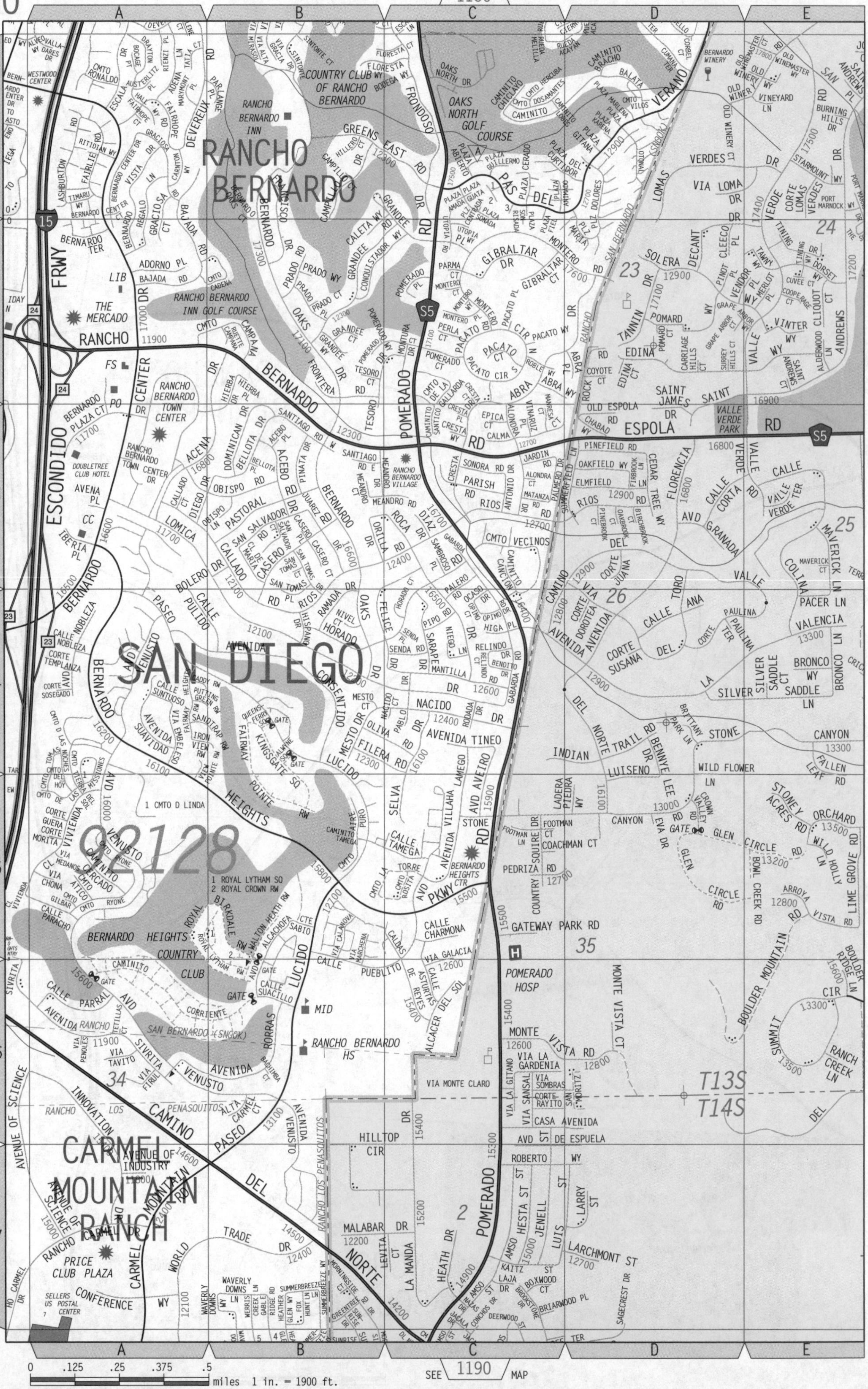

SEE 1169 MAP

SEE 1190 MAP

0 .125 .25 .375 .5 miles 1 in. = 1900 ft.

SEE 1150 MAP

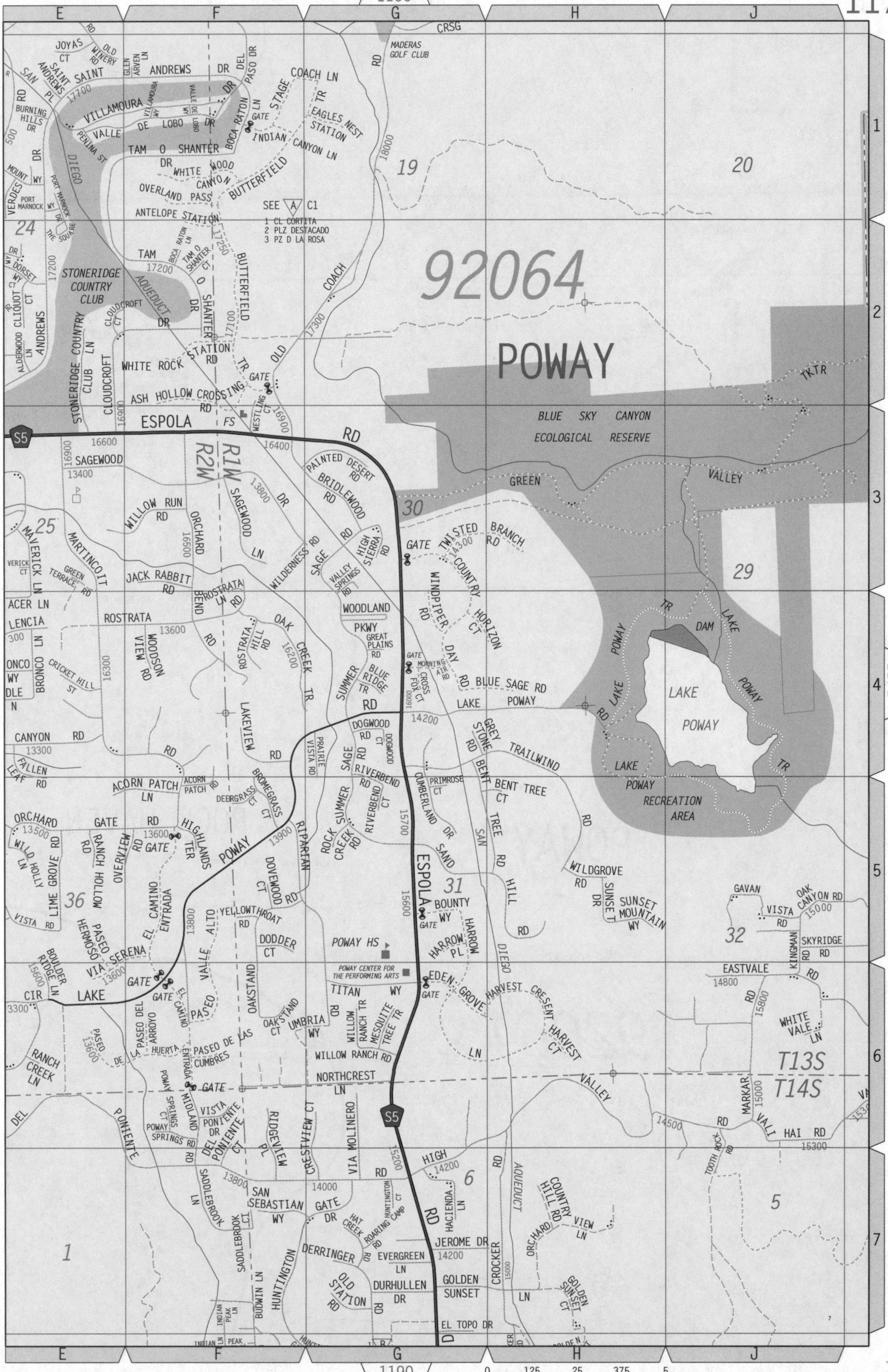

SEE 1171 MAP

SEE 1190 MAP

0 .125 .25 .375 .5 miles 1 in. = 1900 ft.

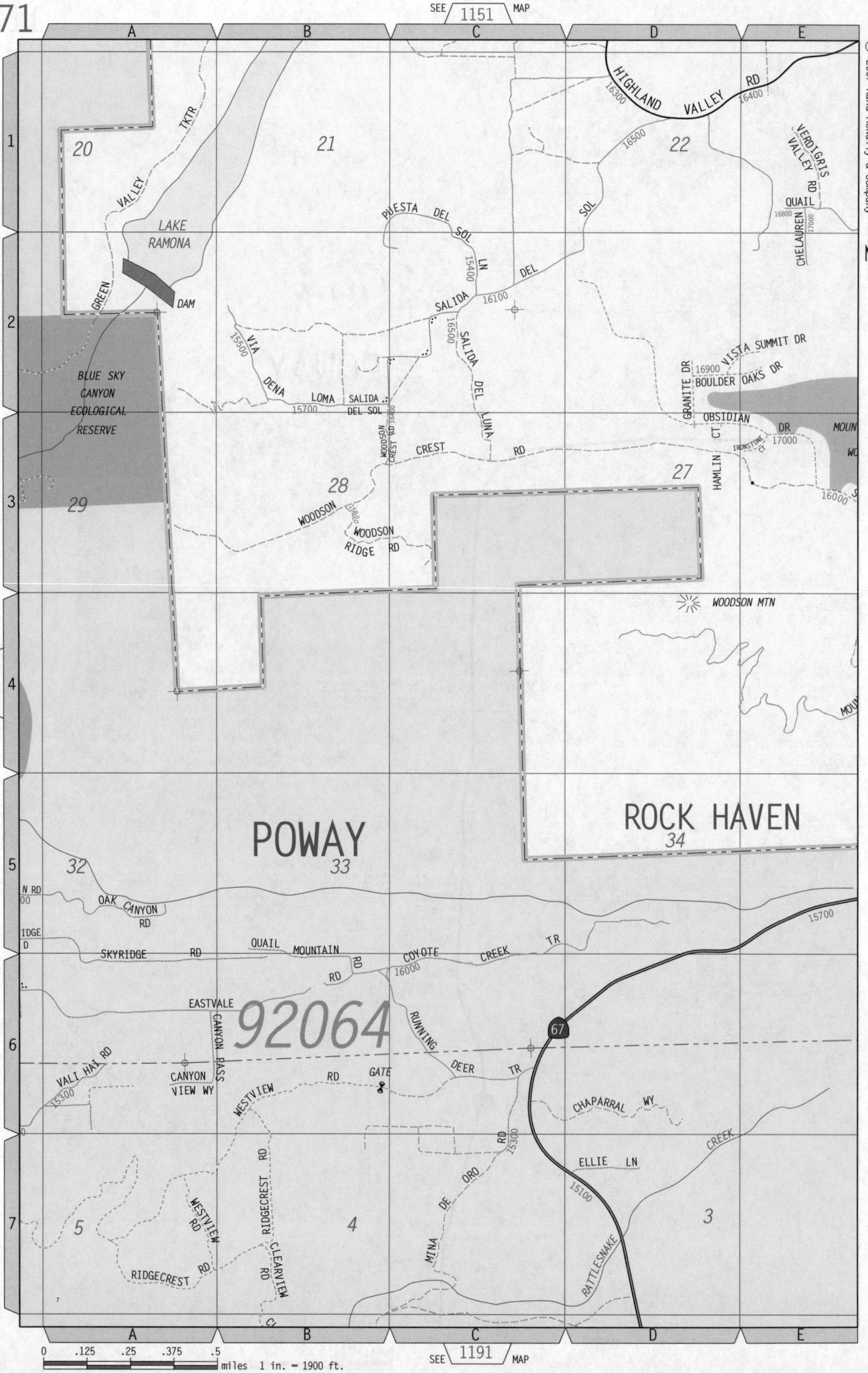
SEE 1151 MAP
SEE 1170 MAP
SEE 1191 MAP
SAN DIEGO CO.
HIGHLAND VALLEY RD
VERDIGRIS VALLEY RD
QUAIL
CHELAUREN
VALLEY
TKTR
GREEN
LAKE RAMONA
DAM
PUESTA DEL SOL LN
SALIDA DEL SOL
VIA DENA
LOMA
SALIDA DEL SOL
SALIDA DEL LUNA
WOODSON CREST RD
CREST RD
VISTA SUMMIT DR
BOULDER OAKS DR
GRANITE DR
OBSIDIAN DR
HAMLIN CT
IRONSTONE CT
BLUE SKY CANYON ECOLOGICAL RESERVE
WOODSON
WOODSON RIDGE RD
WOODSON MTN
POWAY
ROCK HAVEN
92064
OAK CANYON RD
SKYRIDGE RD
QUAIL MOUNTAIN RD
COYOTE CREEK TR
EASTVALE
CANYON PASS
RUNNING DEER TR
67
VALI HAI RD
CANYON VIEW WY
WESTVIEW RD
GATE
CHAPARRAL WY
MINA DE ORO RD
ELLIE LN
CREEK
RIDGECREST RD
CLEARVIEW RD
RATTLESNAKE
miles 1 in. = 1900 ft.

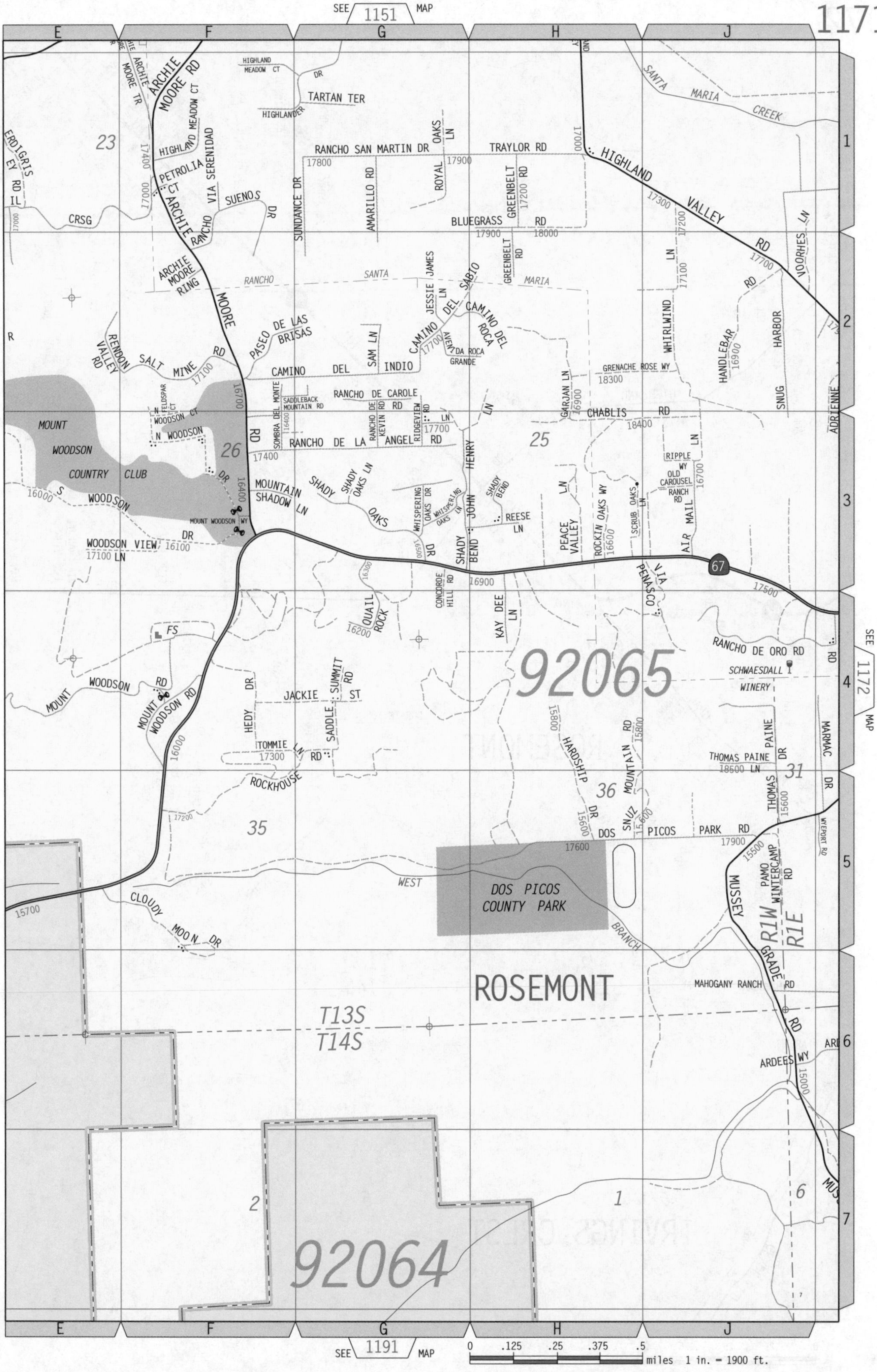
SEE 1151 MAP
SEE 1172 MAP
SEE 1191 MAP
E
F
G
H
J
1
2
3
4
5
6
7
ARCHIE MOORE RD
ARCHIE MOORE TR
HIGHLAND MEADOW CT
TARTAN TER
HIGHLANDER
HIGHLAND MEADOW CT
PETROLIA CT
VIA SERENIDAD
SUENOS DR
RANCHO SAN MARTIN DR
TRAYLOR RD
OAKS LN
ROYAL
AMARILLO RD
SUNDANCE DR
GREENBELT RD
BLUEGRASS RD
HIGHLAND VALLEY RD
SANTA MARIA CREEK
VOORHES LN
CRSG
RANCHO SANTA MARIA
ARCHIE MOORE RING
MOORE RD
JESSIE JAMES LN
CAMINO DEL SABIO
CAMINO DEL ROCA
AVENIDA ROCA GRANDE
PASEO DE LAS BRISAS
RENDON VALLEY RD
SALT MINE RD
CAMINO DEL INDIO
SAM LN
WHIRLWIND LN
HANDLEBAR
HARBOR
SNUG
ADRIENNE
GRENACHE ROSE WY
GARJAN LN
CHABLIS RD
RANCHO DE CAROLE
SADDLEBACK MOUNTAIN RD
SOMBRA DEL MONTE
RANCHO DE KEVIN RD
RIDGEVIEW
RANCHO DE LA ANGEL RD
HENRY LN
RIPPLE WY
OLD CAROUSEL RANCH RD
MOUNT WOODSON COUNTRY CLUB
FELDSPAR CT
WOODSON CT
N WOODSON
S WOODSON
MOUNTAIN SHADOW LN
SHADY OAKS LN
WHISPERING OAKS DR
JOHN
SHADY BEND
REESE LN
PEACE VALLEY LN
ROCKIN OAKS WY
SCRUB OAKS LN
AIR MAIL LN
MOUNT WOODSON WY
WOODSON VIEW DR
67
VIA PENASCO
CONCORDE HILL RD
QUAIL ROCK
KAY DEE LN
RANCHO DE ORO RD
FS
92065
SCHWAESDALL WINERY
MOUNT WOODSON RD
HEDY DR
JACKIE ST
SUMMIT RD
SADDLE
TOMMIE LN
ROCKHOUSE
HARDSHIP DR
MOUNTAIN RD
THOMAS PAINE LN
PAINE DR
MARMAC DR
SNUZ
DOS PICOS PARK RD
WEST BRANCH
DOS PICOS COUNTY PARK
CLOUDY MOON DR
MUSSEY GRADE RD
PAMO WINTERCAMP RD
R1W
R1E
ROSEMONT
MAHOGANY RANCH RD
T13S
T14S
ARDEES WY
92064
23
26
25
35
36
31
2
1
6
0 .125 .25 .375 .5
miles 1 in. = 1900 ft.

SEE 1152 MAP

SEE 1171 MAP

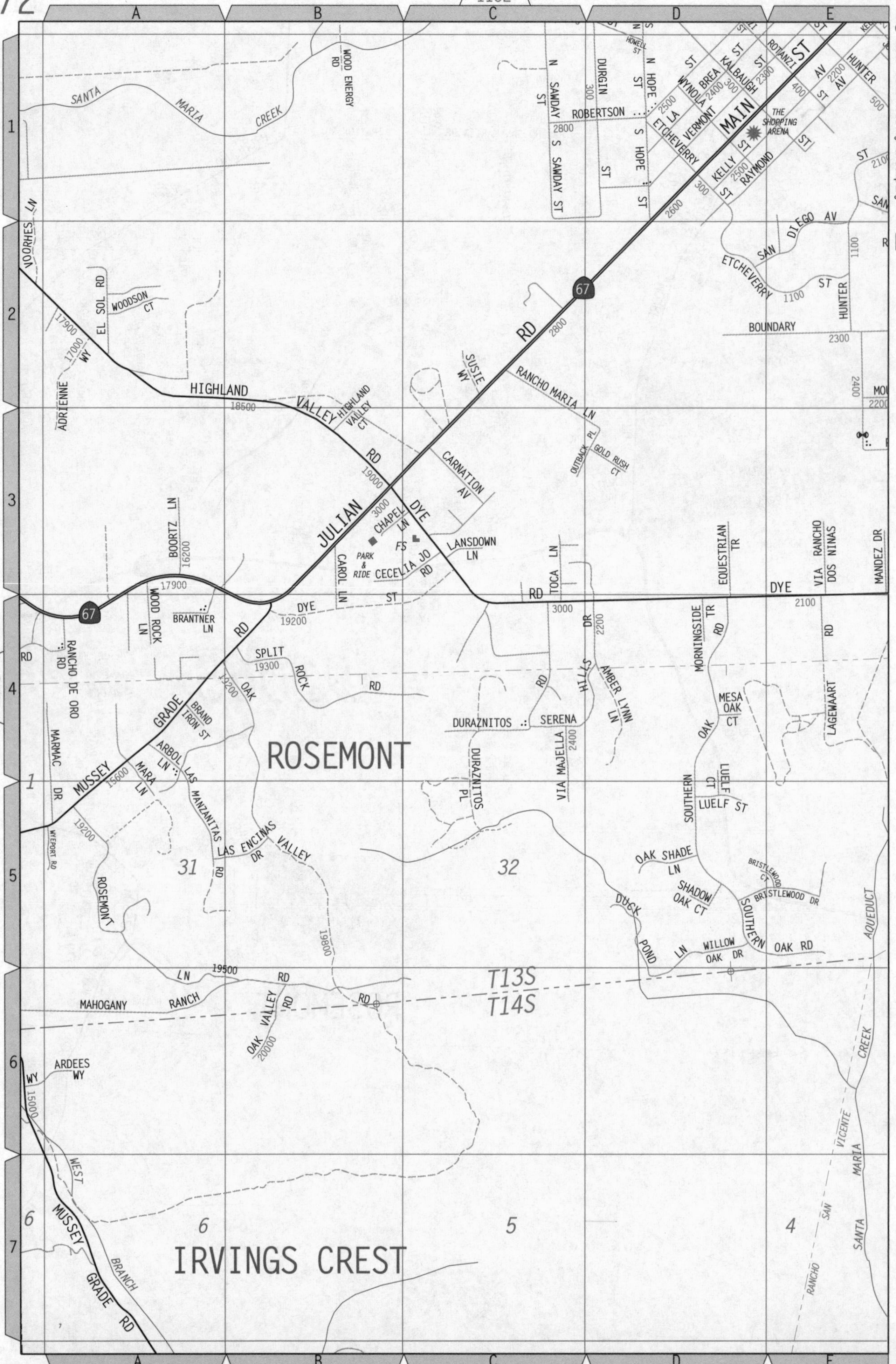

SEE 1192 MAP

0 .125 .25 .375 .5 miles 1 in. = 1900 ft.

SEE 1152 MAP

SEE 1192 MAP

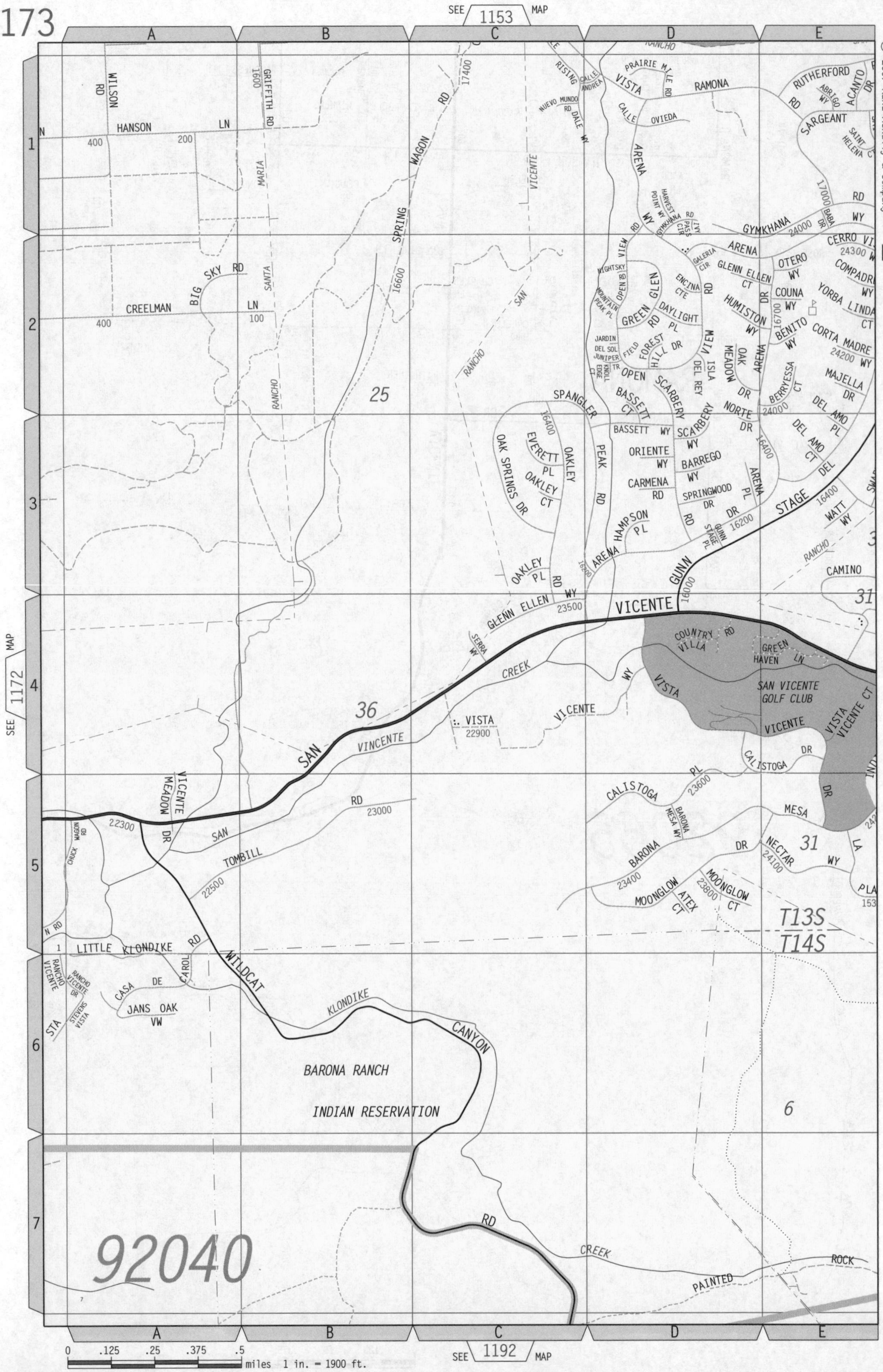

SEE 1153 MAP
SEE 1172 MAP
SEE 1192 MAP
A
B
C
D
E
1
2
3
4
5
6
7
WILSON RD
HANSON LN
400
200
GRIFFITH RD
1600
SANTA MARIA
SPRING WAGON RD
17400
16600
BIG SKY RD
CREELMAN LN
100
RANCHO
RANCHO SAN VICENTE
25
36
31
6
RANCHO
RISING
CALLE ANDREA
NUEVO MUNDO RD
DALE WY
VISTA
PRAIRIE MILE RD
RAMONA
CALLE OVIEDA
ARENA WY
HARVEST POINT WY
GYMKHANA PASS CIR
IVY RD
RUTHERFORD RD
ABRIGO WY
ACANTO
SARGEANT
SAINT HELENA CT
17000
BABA DR
GYMKHANA RD
24000
ARENA WY
CERRO VISTA WY
24300
GALERIA CIR
GLENN ELLEN CT
OTERO WY
COMPADRE WY
NIGHTSKY
OPEN RD
VIEW RD
MOUNTAIN PEAK PL
GREEN GLEN RD
ENCINA CTE
DAYLIGHT PL
HUMISTON WY
COUNA WY
16700
YORBA LINDA CT
JARDIN DEL SOL
JUNIPER TR
FIELD
FOREST HILL DR
VIEW
KNOLL EDGE CT
OPEN
ISLA DEL REY
OAK MEADOW DR
ARENA
BENITO WY
CORTA MADRE WY
24200
MAJELLA DR
SPANGLER PEAK RD
16400
BASSETT CT
SCARBERY WY
BERRYESSA CT
NORTE DR
24000
DEL AMO PL
DEL AMO CT
BASSETT WY
ORIENTE WY
BARREGO WY
EVERETT PL
OAKLEY CT
OAKLEY
OAK SPRINGS DR
CARMENA RD
SPRINGWOOD DR
ARENA PL
DEL
HAMPSON PL
GUNN STAGE PL
16200
STAGE
WATT WY
16400
OAKLEY PL RD
16200
ARENA
GUNN
16000
CAMINO
GLENN ELLEN WY
23500
VICENTE
SERRA WY
COUNTRY VILLA RD
GREEN HAVEN LN
CREEK
WY
VISTA
SAN VICENTE GOLF CLUB
VICENTE
VISTA VICENTE CT
VISTA
22900
VICENTE
SAN VICENTE
CALISTOGA DR
CALISTOGA PL
23600
BARONA MESA WY
MESA
DR
VICENTE MEADOW DR
RD
23000
22300
CHUCK WAGON RD
SAN
TOMBILL
22500
BARONA DR
23400
NECTAR WY
24100
LA
PLA
153
MOONGLOW CT
ATEX CT
MOONGLOW CT
23800
T13S
T14S
N RD
LITTLE KLONDIKE RD
RANCHO VICENTE
RANCHO VICENTE DR
CAROL
CASA DE
JANS OAK VW
STA
STEVENS VISTA
WILDCAT
KLONDIKE
CANYON
BARONA RANCH
INDIAN RESERVATION
RD
CREEK
ROCK
PAINTED
92040
0
.125
.25
.375
.5
miles 1 in. = 1900 ft.

SEE 1153 MAP

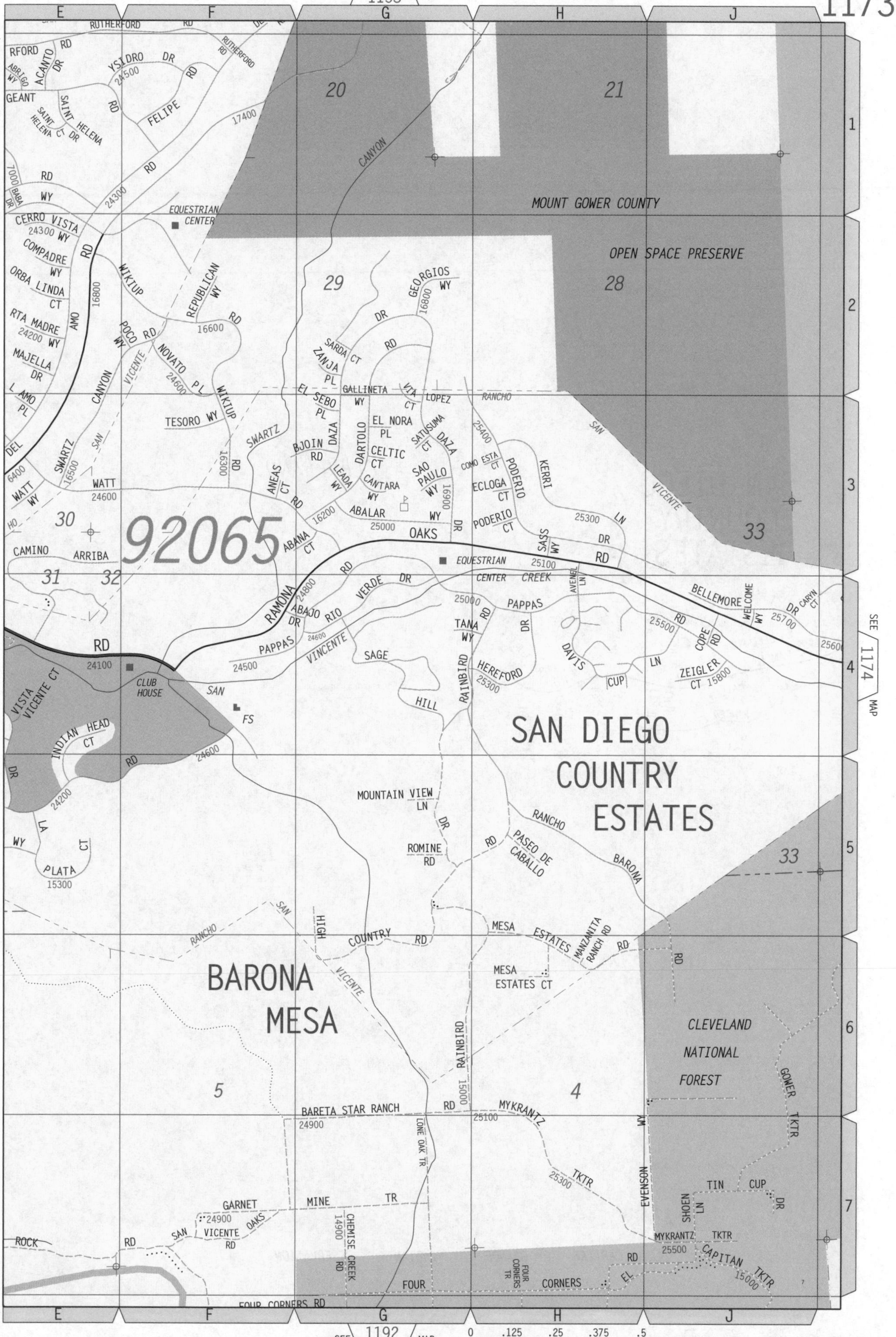

SEE 1192 MAP

SEE 1154 MAP

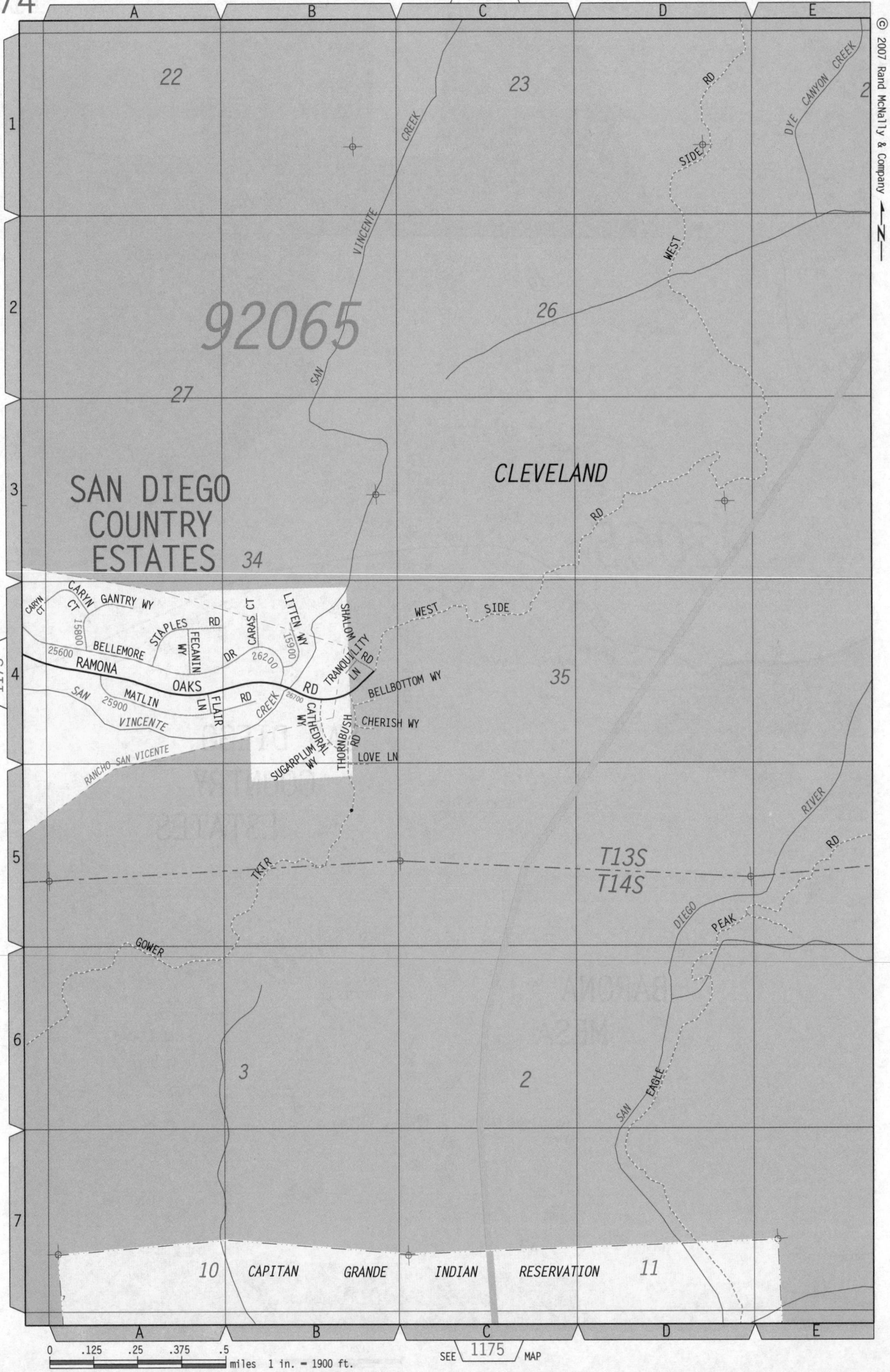

SEE 1173 MAP

SEE 1175 MAP

SEE 1154 MAP

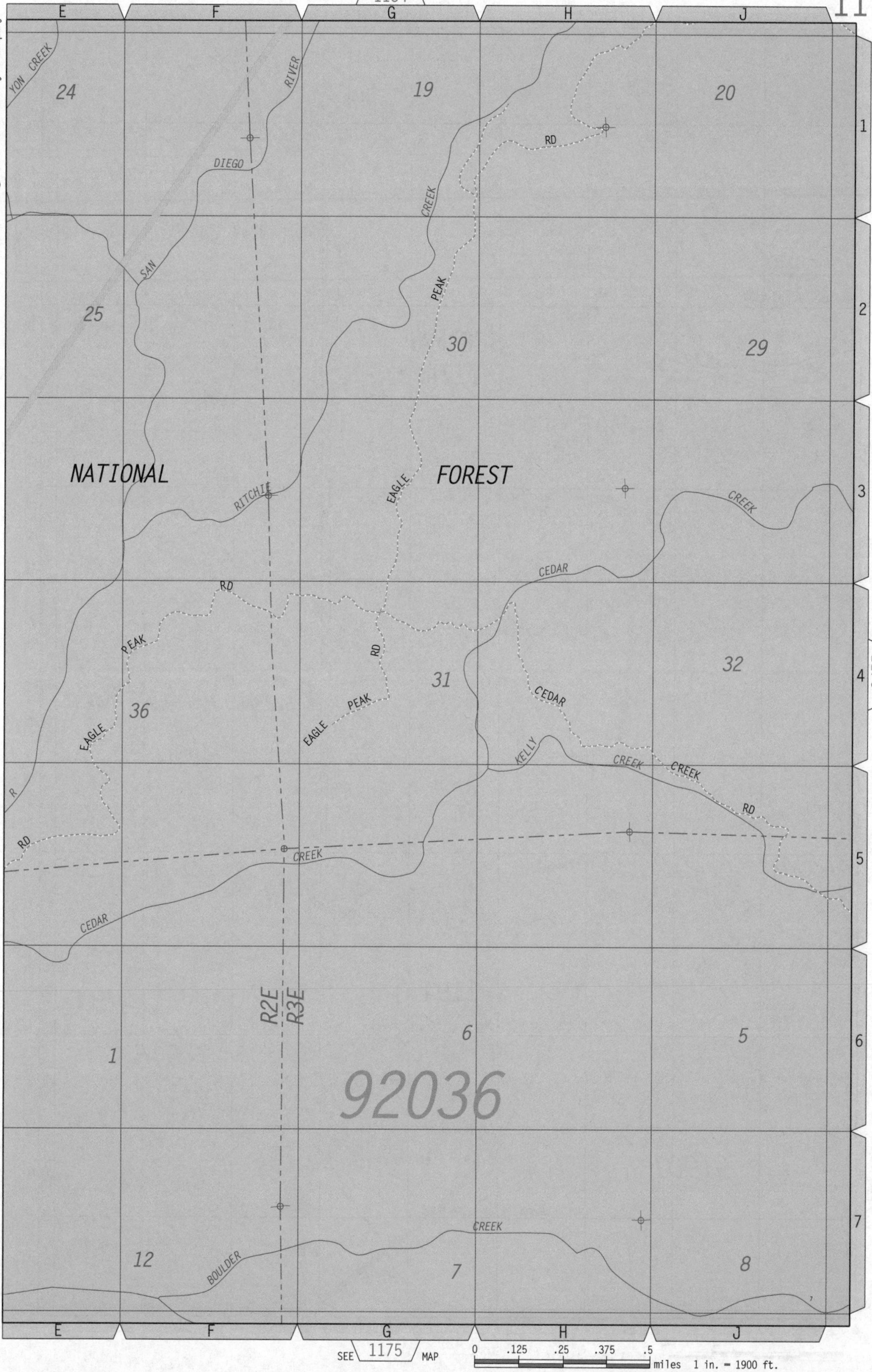

SEE 1175 MAP

SEE 1175 MAP

0 .125 .25 .375 .5 miles 1 in. = 1900 ft.

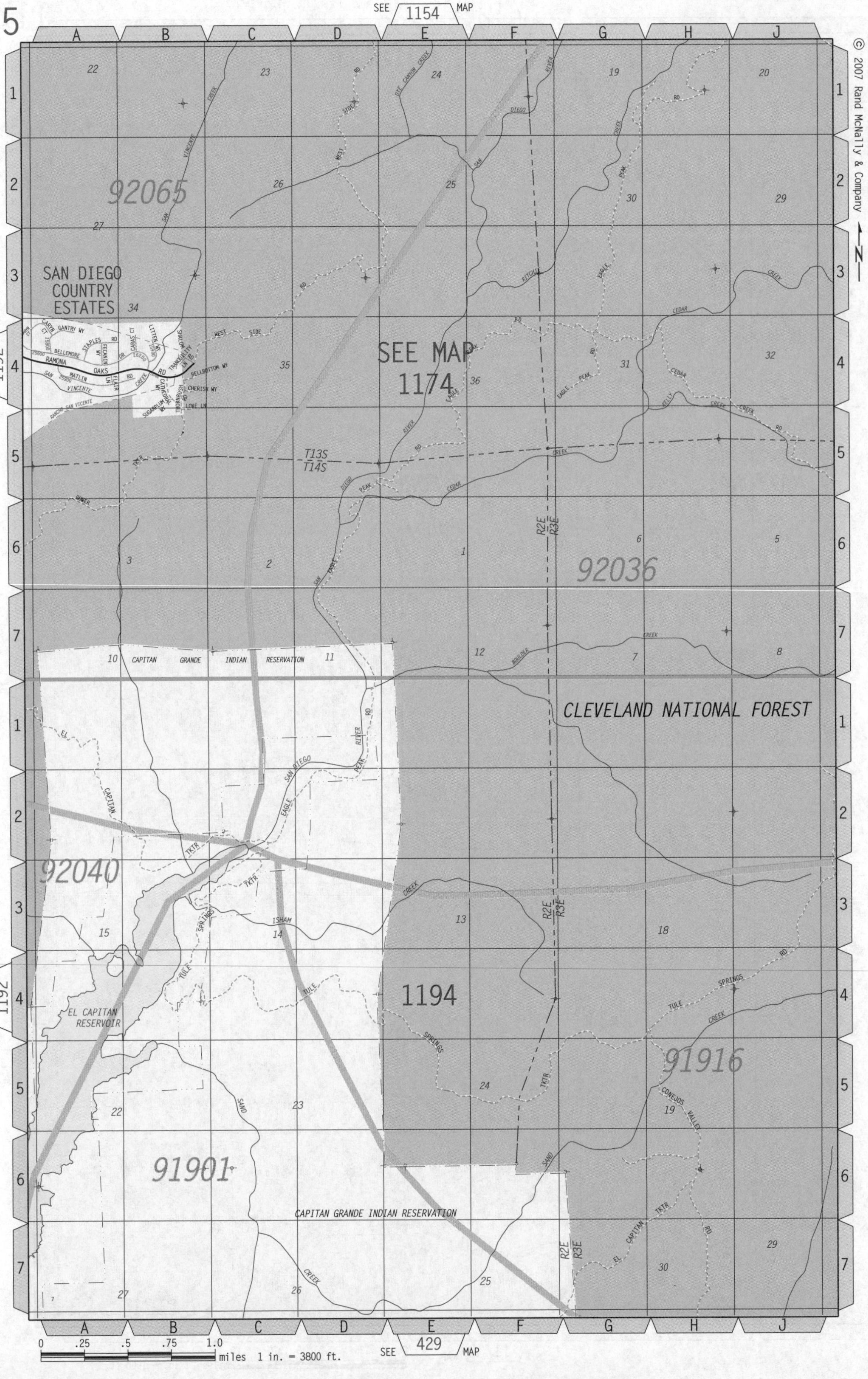
SEE 1154 MAP
SAN DIEGO CO.
92065
SAN DIEGO COUNTRY ESTATES
SEE 1192 MAP
SEE MAP 1174
T13S
T14S
R2E
R3E
92036
CAPITAN GRANDE INDIAN RESERVATION
CLEVELAND NATIONAL FOREST
92040
EL CAPITAN RESERVOIR
1194
91916
91901
CAPITAN GRANDE INDIAN RESERVATION
SEE 429 MAP
0 .25 .5 .75 1.0 miles 1 in. = 3800 ft.

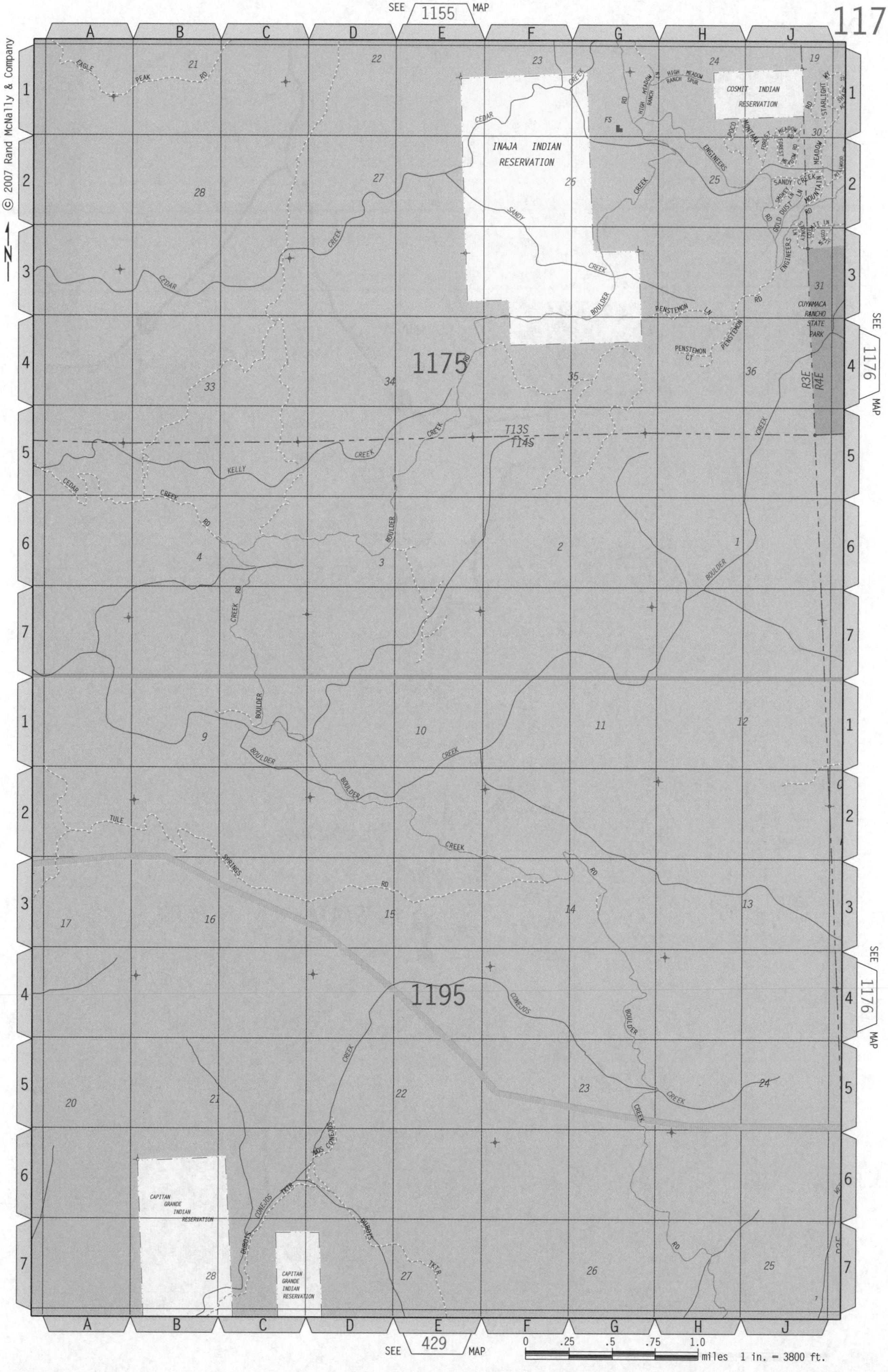

SEE 1155 MAP
SEE 1176 MAP
SEE 429 MAP
A B C D E F G H J
1 2 3 4 5 6 7
1175
1195
EAGLE PEAK RD
INAJA INDIAN RESERVATION
COSMIT INDIAN RESERVATION
CUYAMACA RANCHO STATE PARK
CAPITAN GRANDE INDIAN RESERVATION
CEDAR CREEK
SANDY CREEK
BOULDER CREEK
KELLY CREEK
CEDAR CREEK RD
BOULDER CREEK RD
TULE SPRINGS RD
CONEJOS CREEK
DOS CONEJOS
HIGH MEADOW RD
HIGH MEADOW RANCH SPUR
ENGINEERS RD
PENSTEMON LN
PENSTEMON CT
PENSTEMON
POCO MONTANA
FOREST MEADOW RD
SANDY CREEK
SMOKEY LN
GOLD DUST LN
MOUNTAIN MEADOW
STARLIGHT WY
FS
T13S
T14S
R3E
R4E
0 .25 .5 .75 1.0 miles 1 in. = 3800 ft.

SEE 1156 MAP

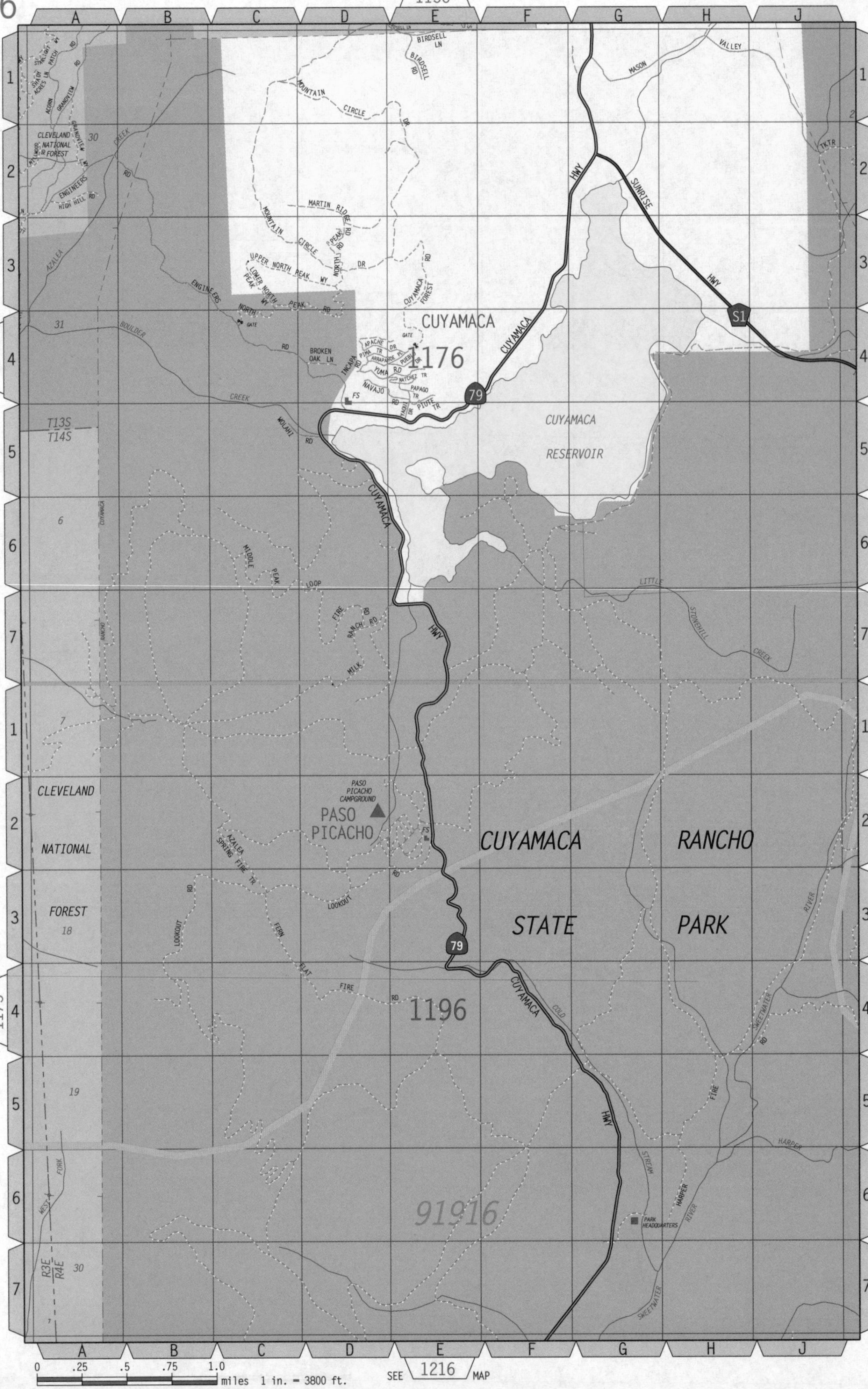

SEE 1175 MAP

SEE 1216 MAP

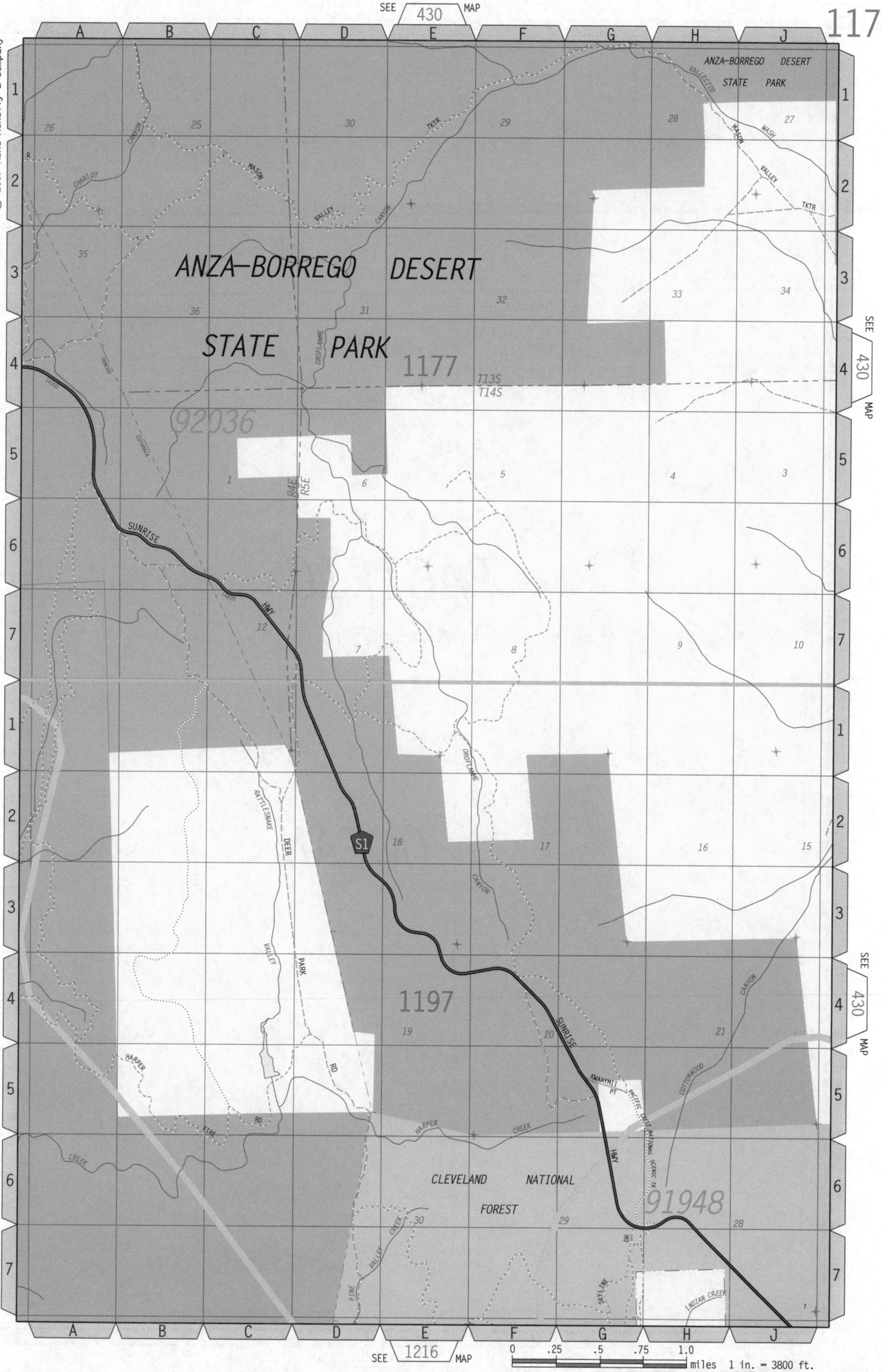
SEE 430 MAP
ANZA-BORREGO DESERT STATE PARK
ANZA-BORREGO DESERT STATE PARK
1177
T13S
T14S
R4E
R5E
92036
SUNRISE HWY
S1
1197
CLEVELAND NATIONAL FOREST
91948
RATTLESNAKE
DEER PARK RD
VALLEY
HARPER CREEK
HARPER FIRE RD
OROFLAMME CANYON
CHARIOT CANYON
MASON VALLEY
VALLECITO WASH
COTTONWOOD CANYON
PACIFIC CREST NATIONAL SCENIC TR
KWAAYMII PT
PINE VALLEY CREEK
SKYLINE DR
INDIAN CREEK
SEE 1216 MAP
0 .25 .5 .75 1.0 miles 1 in. = 3800 ft.

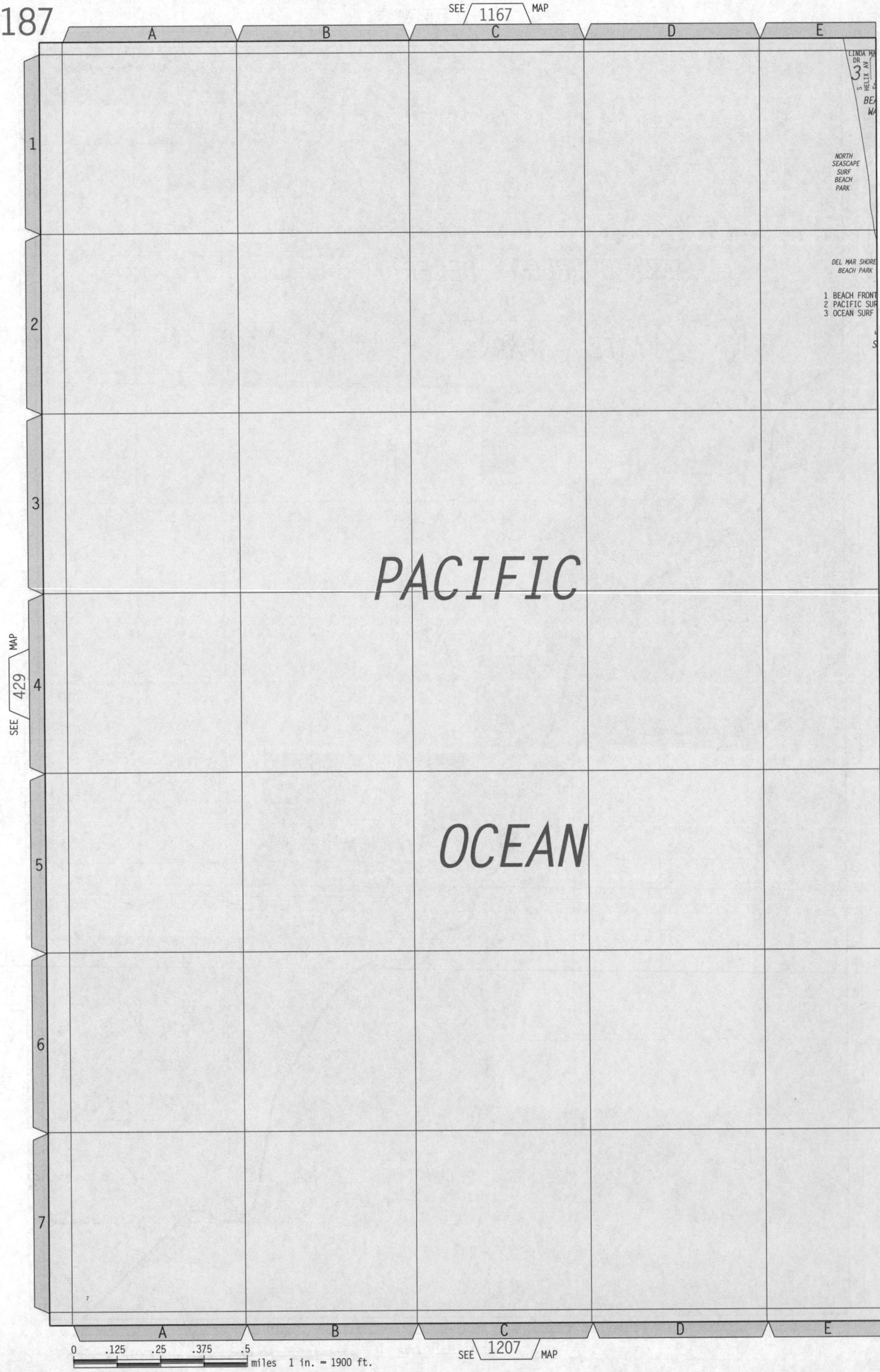
SEE 1167 MAP
A
B
C
D
E
1
2
3
4
5
6
7
SEE 429 MAP
LINDA MA
DR
3
S HELIX AV
NORTH SEASCAPE SURF BEACH PARK
DEL MAR SHORE BEACH PARK
1 BEACH FRONT
2 PACIFIC SUR
3 OCEAN SURF
PACIFIC
OCEAN
SEE 1207 MAP
0 .125 .25 .375 .5
miles 1 in. = 1900 ft.

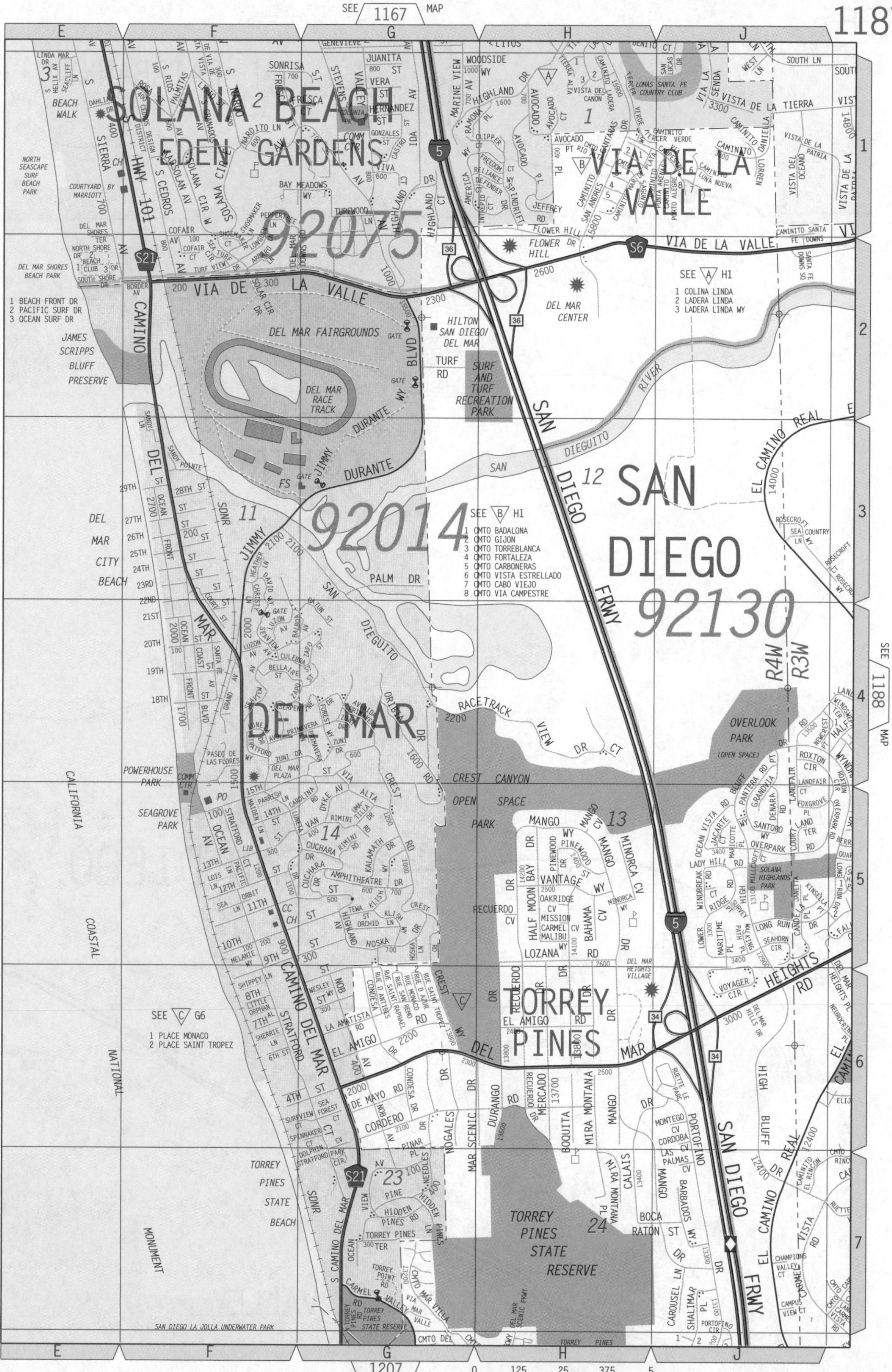
SEE 1167 MAP
SEE 1188 MAP
SEE 1207 MAP
SOLANA BEACH
EDEN GARDENS
92075
VIA DE LA VALLE
DEL MAR FAIRGROUNDS
DEL MAR RACE TRACK
SURF AND TURF RECREATION PARK
HILTON SAN DIEGO/ DEL MAR
DEL MAR CENTER
FLOWER HILL
92014
SAN DIEGO
92130
DEL MAR
TORREY PINES
TORREY PINES STATE RESERVE
TORREY PINES STATE BEACH
CREST CANYON OPEN SPACE PARK
OVERLOOK PARK (OPEN SPACE)
SOLANA HIGHLANDS PARK
POWERHOUSE PARK
SEAGROVE PARK
JAMES SCRIPPS BLUFF PRESERVE
DEL MAR CITY BEACH
DEL MAR SHORES BEACH PARK
NORTH SEASCAPE SURF BEACH PARK
CALIFORNIA COASTAL NATIONAL MONUMENT
SAN DIEGO LA JOLLA UNDERWATER PARK
SAN DIEGO FRWY
CAMINO DEL MAR
EL CAMINO REAL
DEL MAR HEIGHTS RD
SAN DIEGUITO RIVER
SEE A H1
1 COLINA LINDA
2 LADERA LINDA
3 LADERA LINDA WY
SEE B H1
1 CMTO BADALONA
2 CMTO GIJON
3 CMTO TORREBLANCA
4 CMTO FORTALEZA
5 CMTO CARBONERAS
6 CMTO VISTA ESTRELLADO
7 CMTO CABO VIEJO
8 CMTO VIA CAMPESTRE
SEE C G6
1 PLACE MONACO
2 PLACE SAINT TROPEZ
1 BEACH FRONT DR
2 PACIFIC SURF DR
3 OCEAN SURF DR
R4W R3W
0 .125 .25 .375 .5 miles 1 in. = 1900 ft.

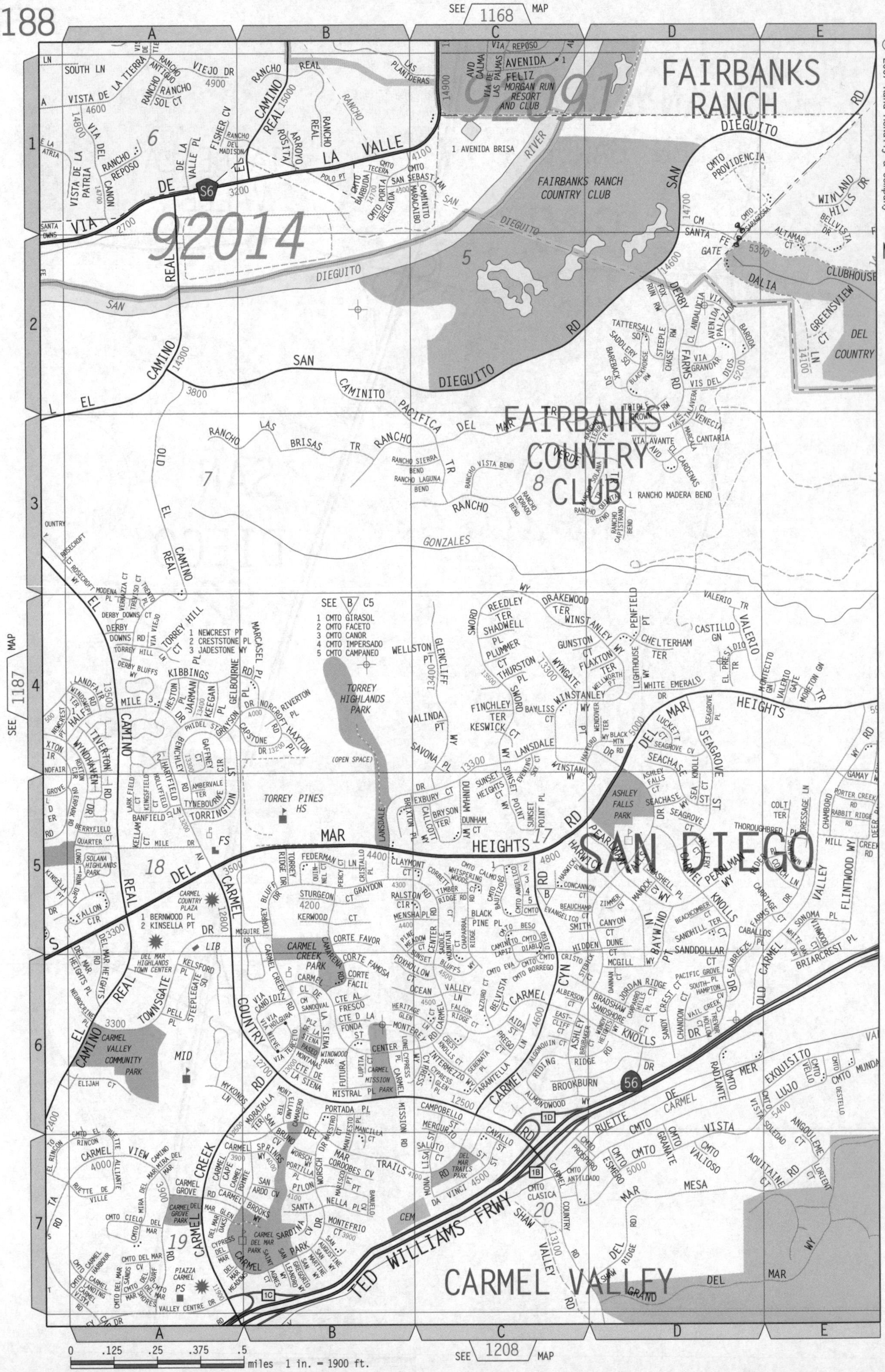
SEE 1168 MAP
SEE 1187 MAP
SEE 1208 MAP
FAIRBANKS RANCH
92091
92014
FAIRBANKS RANCH COUNTRY CLUB
FAIRBANKS COUNTRY CLUB
MORGAN RUN RESORT AND CLUB
SAN DIEGO
CARMEL VALLEY
TORREY HIGHLANDS PARK
(OPEN SPACE)
TORREY PINES HS
ASHLEY FALLS PARK
SOLANA HIGHLANDS PARK
CARMEL COUNTRY PLAZA
DEL MAR HIGHLANDS TOWN CENTER
CARMEL CREEK PARK
CARMEL VALLEY COMMUNITY PARK
CARMEL MISSION PARK
CARMEL GROVE PARK
CARMEL DEL MAR PARK
PIAZZA CARMEL
DEL MAR TRAILS PARK
CEM
MID
LIB
FS
PS
TED WILLIAMS FRWY
SAN DIEGUITO RD
DEL MAR HEIGHTS RD
EL CAMINO REAL
CARMEL COUNTRY RD
CARMEL VALLEY RD
CARMEL CREEK RD
VIA DE LA VALLE
S6
56
SEE B C5
1 CMTO GIRASOL
2 CMTO FACETO
3 CMTO CANOR
4 CMTO IMPERSADO
5 CMTO CAMPANEO
1 NEWCREST PT
2 CRESTSTONE PL
3 JADESTONE WY
1 BERNWOOD PL
2 KINSELLA PT
1 AVENIDA BRISA
1 RANCHO MADERA BEND
0 .125 .25 .375 .5 miles 1 in. = 1900 ft.

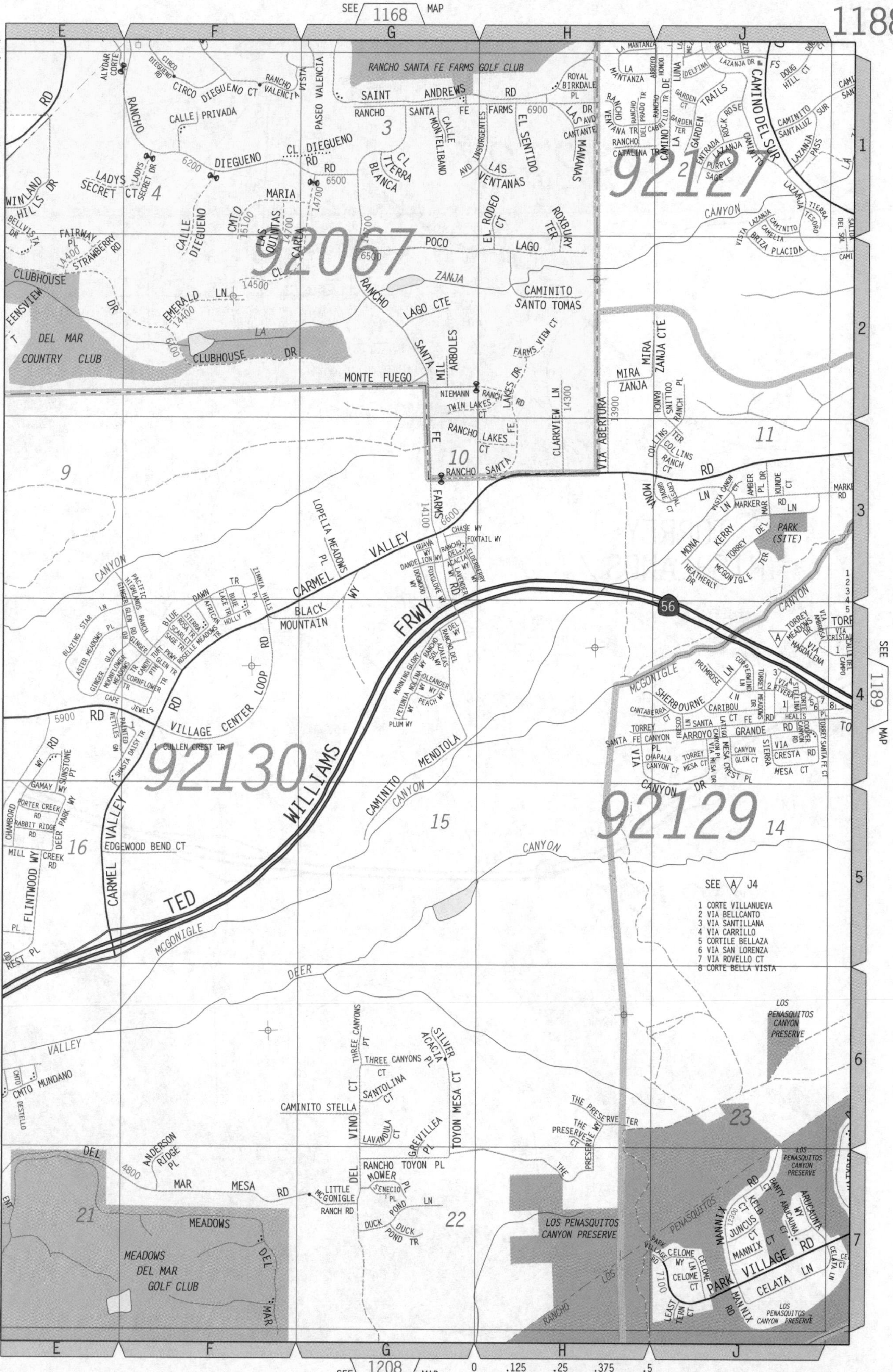

SEE 1168 MAP
SEE 1208 MAP
SEE 1189 MAP
SAN DIEGO CO.
E
F
G
H
J
1
2
3
4
5
6
7
92067
92127
92130
92129
RANCHO SANTA FE FARMS GOLF CLUB
SAINT ANDREWS RD
RANCHO SANTA FE FARMS RD
CIRCO DIEGUENO CT
CALLE PRIVADA
CL DIEGUENO RD
DIEGUENO
PASEO VALENCIA
RANCHO VALENCIA
ROYAL BIRKDALE PL
EL SENTIDO
LAS MANANAS
CALLE MONTELIBANO
CL TIERRA BLANCA
AVD INSURGENTES
LAS VENTANAS
LADYS SECRET CT
LADYS SECRET DR
WINLAND HILLS DR
MARIA
CALLE DIEGUENO
CMTO LAS QUINTAS
CARLA
EL RODEO CT
ROXBURY TER
POCO LAGO
FAIRWAY PL
STRAWBERRY RD
CLUBHOUSE DR
ZANJA
CAMINITO SANTO TOMAS
EMERALD LN
RANCHO LAGO CTE
DEL MAR COUNTRY CLUB
LA CLUBHOUSE DR
SANTA MIL ARBOLES
FARMS VIEW CT
MONTE FUEGO
LAKES DR
NIEMANN RANCH
TWIN LAKES CT
RANCHO LAKES CT
CLARKVIEW LN
VIA ABERTURA
MIRA ZANJA
ZANJA CTE
COLLINS RANCH PL
COLLINS RANCH TER
COLLINS RANCH CT
LA MANTANZA
CAMINO DE LUNA
DELFINA
LAZANJA DR
CAMINO DEL SUR
DOUG HILL CT
GARDEN TRAILS
ROCK ROSE
ENTRADA
PURPLE SAGE
CAMINITO SANTALUZ SUR
LAZANJA PASS
TIERRA TESORO
CAMINITO BRIZA PLACIDA
CANYON
CARMEL VALLEY RD
LOPELIA MEADOWS PL
BLACK MOUNTAIN WY
MONA LN
MARKER RD
KUNDE CT
AMBER PL
PARK (SITE)
KERRY
TORREY DEL MAR
HEATHERLY DR
MCGONIGLE TER
TED WILLIAMS FRWY
56
MCGONIGLE CANYON
PRIMROSE LN
SHERBOURNE
CARIBOU
TORREY MEADOWS
VIA MAGDALENA
SANTA FE CANYON
ARROYO GRANDE RD
VIA CRESTA
MESA CT
SIERRA
CANYON DR
VILLAGE CENTER LOOP
CULLEN CREST TR
EDGEWOOD BEND CT
CARMEL VALLEY
FLINTWOOD WY
PORTER CREEK RD
RABBIT RIDGE RD
MILL CREEK RD
DEER PARK WY
CAMINITO MENDIOLA
CANYON
DEER
VALLEY
CMTO MUNDANO
THREE CANYONS PT
THREE CANYONS CT
SILVER ACACIA PL
SANTOLINA CT
CAMINITO STELLA
TOYON MESA CT
VINO DEL CT
GREVILLEA PL
LAVANDULA CT
RANCHO TOYON PL
MOWER PL
LITTLE MCGONIGLE RANCH RD
DUCK POND LN
DUCK POND TR
THE PRESERVE TER
THE PRESERVE CT
THE PRESERVE WY
LOS PENASQUITOS CANYON PRESERVE
ANDERSON RIDGE PL
DEL MAR MESA RD
MEADOWS DEL MAR
MEADOWS DEL MAR GOLF CLUB
PARK VILLAGE RD
MANNIX RD
MANNIX CT
JUNCUS CT
KELD
BANTY
ARUCAUNA WY
CELOME WY
CELOME CT
CELATA LN
LEAST TERN CT
RANCHO LOS PENASQUITOS
SEE A J4
1 CORTE VILLANUEVA
2 VIA BELLCANTO
3 VIA SANTILLANA
4 VIA CARRILLO
5 CORTILE BELLAZA
6 VIA SAN LORENZA
7 VIA ROVELLO CT
8 CORTE BELLA VISTA
0 .125 .25 .375 .5 miles 1 in. = 1900 ft.

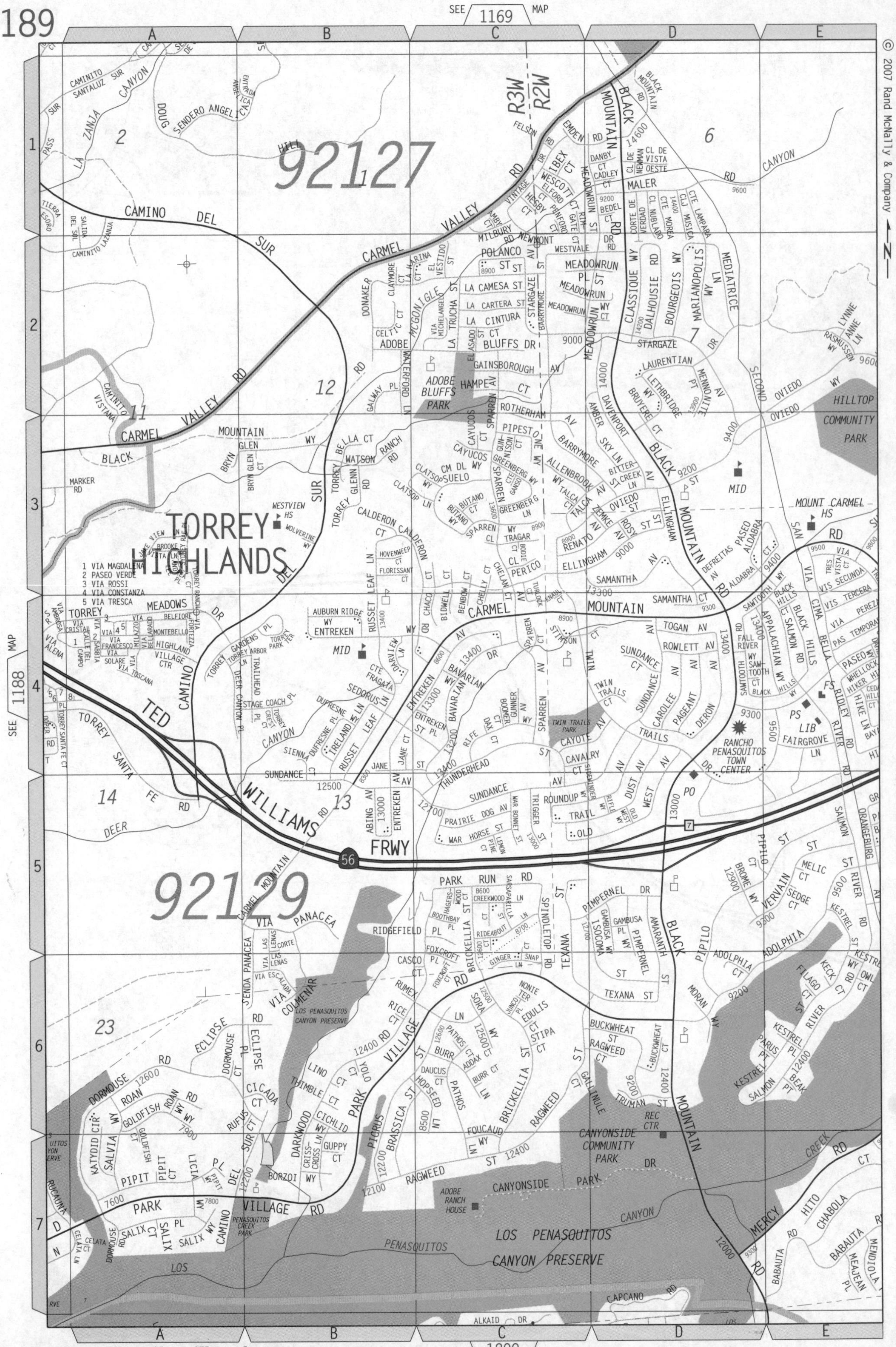
SEE 1169 MAP
SEE 1209 MAP
SEE 1188 MAP
A
B
C
D
E
1
2
3
4
5
6
7
R3W
R2W
92127
92129
TORREY HIGHLANDS
1 VIA MAGDALENA
2 PASEO VERDE
3 VIA ROSSI
4 VIA CONSTANZA
5 VIA TRESCA
CAMINO DEL SUR
CARMEL VALLEY RD
CARMEL MOUNTAIN RD
BLACK MOUNTAIN RD
TED WILLIAMS FRWY
56
7
ADOBE BLUFFS PARK
HILLTOP COMMUNITY PARK
TWIN TRAILS PARK
WESTVIEW HS
MOUNT CARMEL HS
RANCHO PENASQUITOS TOWN CENTER
CANYONSIDE COMMUNITY PARK
ADOBE RANCH HOUSE
REC CTR
LOS PENASQUITOS CANYON PRESERVE
PENASQUITOS CREEK PARK
MID
PO
PS
FS
LIB
0 .125 .25 .375 .5
miles 1 in. = 1900 ft.

SEE 1169 MAP

SEE 1209 MAP

0 .125 .25 .375 .5 miles 1 in. = 1900 ft.

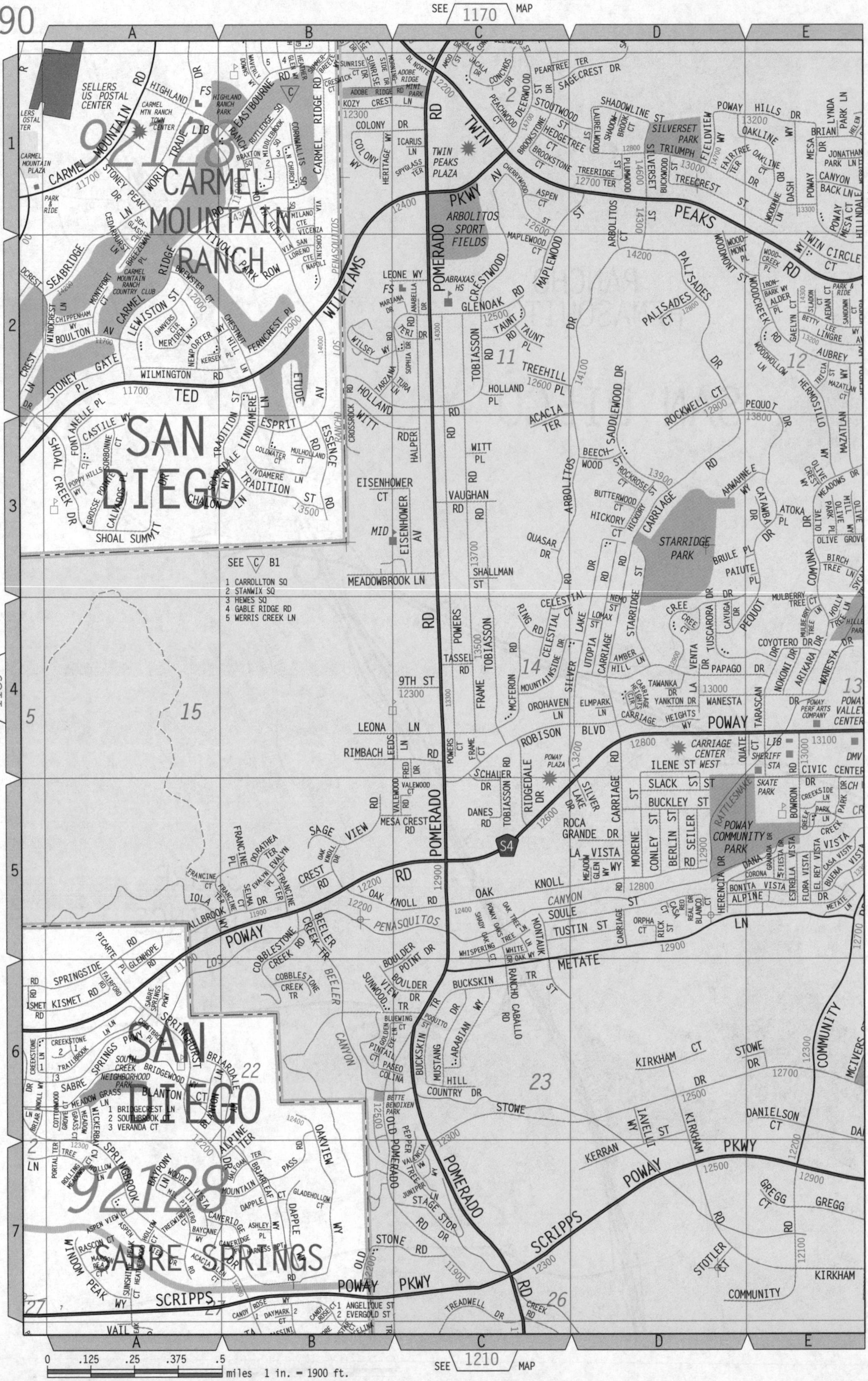
SEE 1170 MAP
SEE 1210 MAP
SEE 1189 MAP
A
B
C
D
E
1
2
3
4
5
6
7
92128
CARMEL MOUNTAIN RANCH
SAN DIEGO
SABRE SPRINGS
SELLERS US POSTAL CENTER
CARMEL MOUNTAIN PLAZA
TWIN PEAKS PLAZA
ARBOLITOS SPORT FIELDS
SILVERSET PARK
STARRIDGE PARK
CARRIAGE CENTER
POWAY PLAZA
POWAY COMMUNITY PARK
SKATE PARK
POWAY PERF ARTS COMPANY
POWAY VALLEY CENTER
CIVIC CENTER
DMV
CARMEL MOUNTAIN RANCH COUNTRY CLUB
HIGHLAND RANCH PARK
SOUTH CREEK NEIGHBORHOOD PARK
BETTE BENDIXEN PARK
ABRAXAS HS
CARMEL MOUNTAIN RD
TED WILLIAMS PKWY
TWIN PEAKS RD
POMERADO RD
POWAY RD
SCRIPPS POWAY PKWY
ESPOLA RD
OAK KNOLL RD
METATE LN
ROBISON BLVD
COMMUNITY RD
PENASQUITOS CANYON
LOS PENASQUITOS CANYON
SEE C B1
1 CARROLLTON SQ
2 STANWIX SQ
3 HEWES SQ
4 GABLE RIDGE RD
5 WERRIS CREEK LN
1 BRIDGECREST LN
2 SOUTHBROOK CT
3 VERANDA CT
1 ANGELIQUE ST
2 EVERGOLD ST
S4
11
12
13
14
15
22
23
26
27
5
0 .125 .25 .375 .5
miles 1 in. = 1900 ft.

SEE 1170 MAP

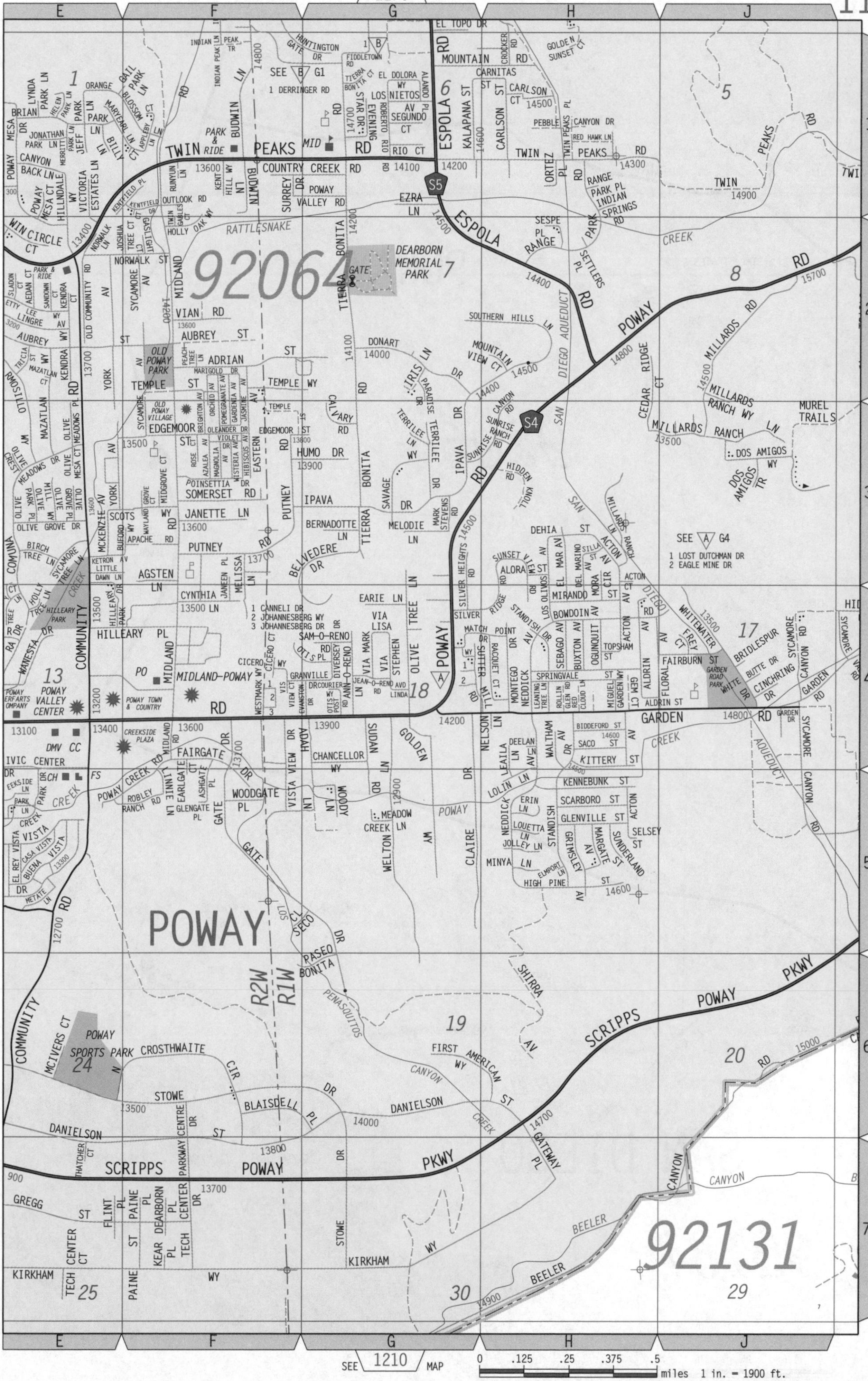

SEE 1191 MAP

SEE 1210 MAP

0 .125 .25 .375 .5
miles 1 in. = 1900 ft.

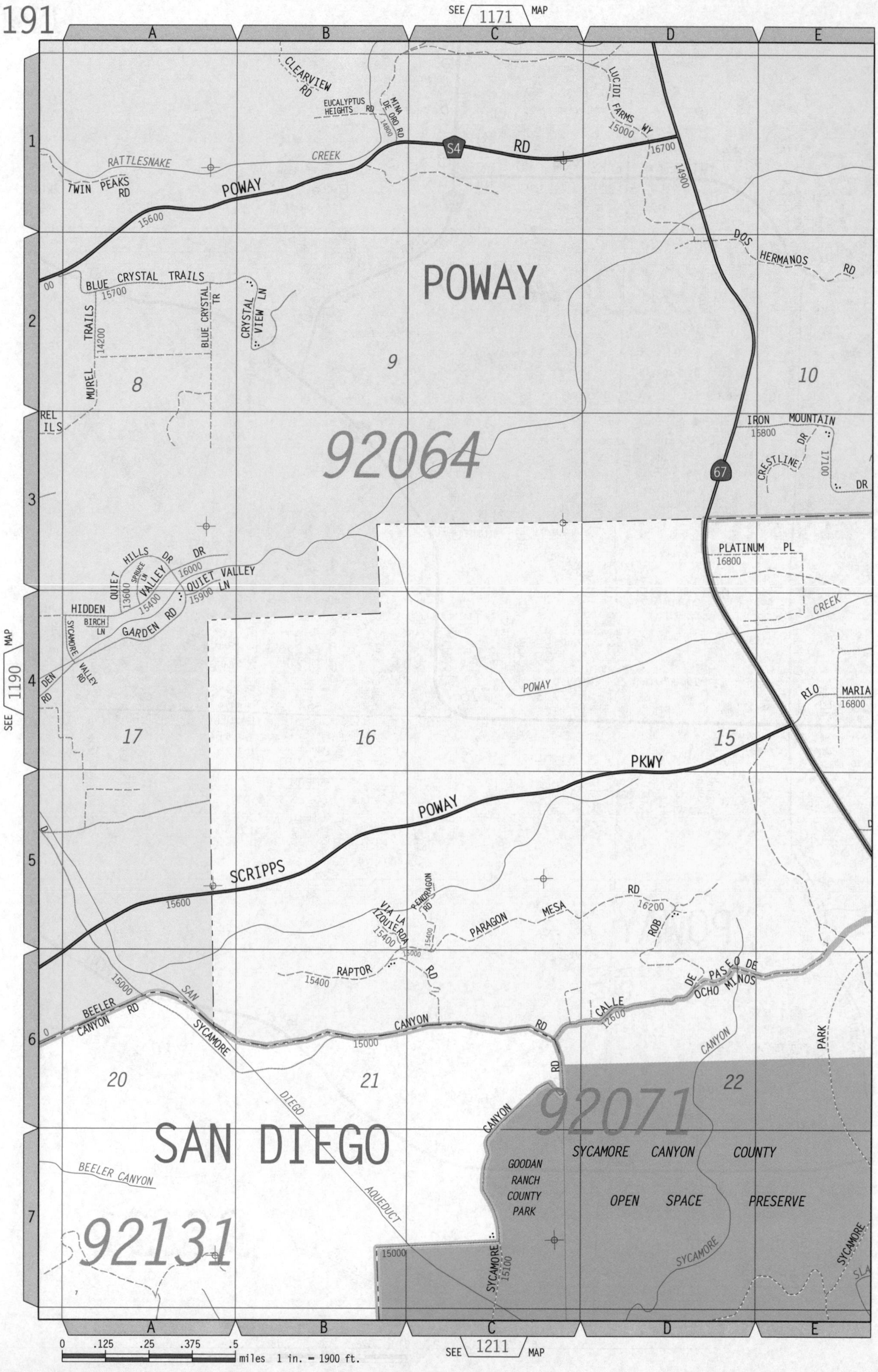
SEE 1171 MAP
SEE 1190 MAP
SEE 1211 MAP
POWAY
92064
92071
92131
SAN DIEGO
POWAY RD
S4
67
RATTLESNAKE CREEK
TWIN PEAKS RD
CLEARVIEW RD
EUCALYPTUS HEIGHTS RD
MINA DE ORO RD
LUCIDI FARMS WY
DOS HERMANOS RD
BLUE CRYSTAL TRAILS
BLUE CRYSTAL TR
CRYSTAL VIEW LN
MUREL TRAILS
IRON MOUNTAIN DR
CRESTLINE DR
PLATINUM PL
QUIET HILLS DR
SPRUCE LN
VALLEY
QUIET VALLEY LN
HIDDEN GARDEN RD
BIRCH LN
SYCAMORE VALLEY RD
POWAY CREEK
RIO MARIA
POWAY PKWY
SCRIPPS
PARAGON MESA RD
VIA LA IZQUIERDA
RENDRAGON RD
ROB
RAPTOR RD
PASEO DE OCHO MINOS
CALLE DE
BEELER CANYON RD
SYCAMORE CANYON RD
SAN DIEGO AQUEDUCT
BEELER CANYON
GOODAN RANCH COUNTY PARK
SYCAMORE CANYON COUNTY OPEN SPACE PRESERVE
PARK
SYCAMORE
8
9
10
15
16
17
20
21
22
0 .125 .25 .375 .5 miles 1 in. = 1900 ft.

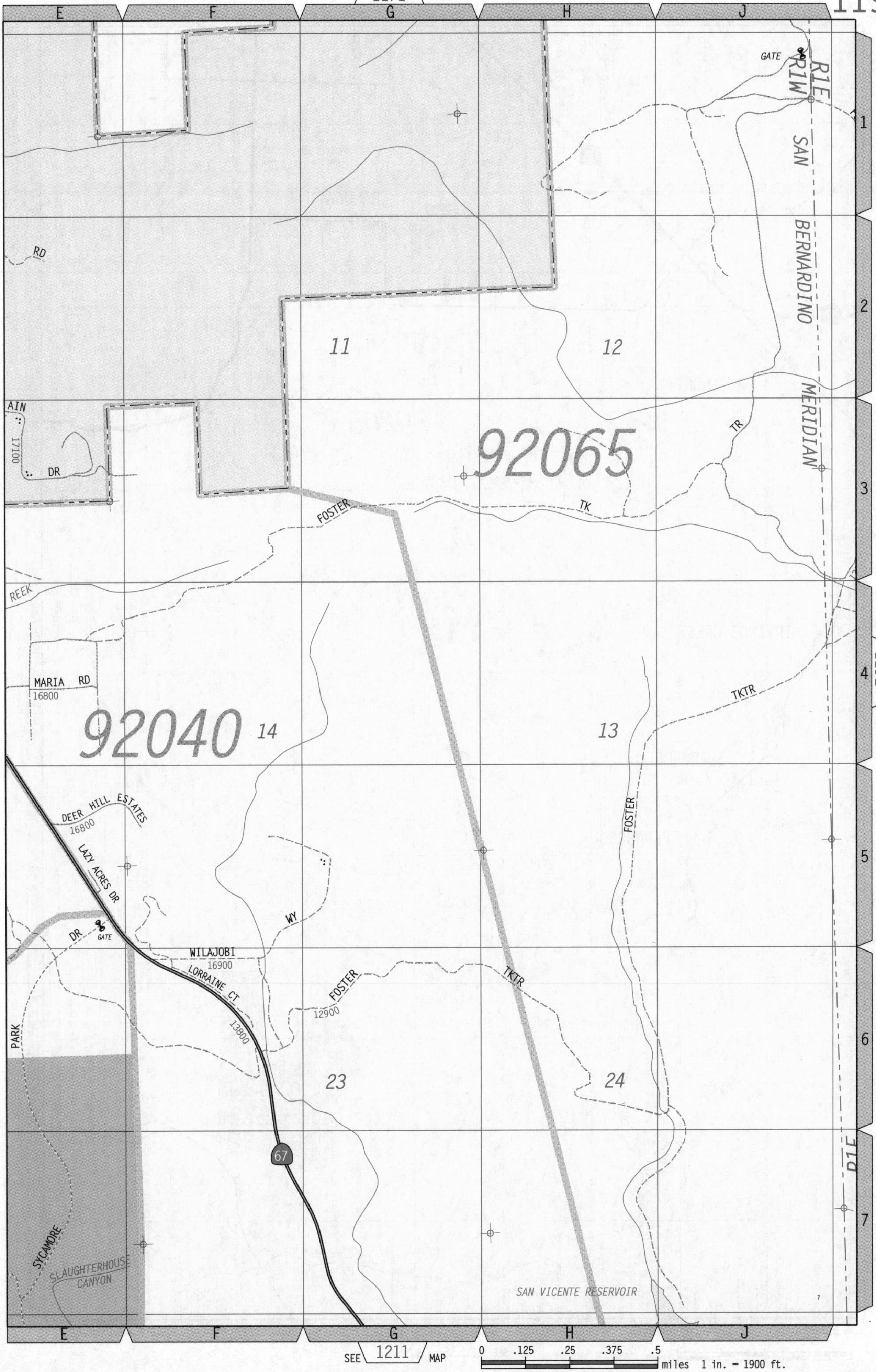

SEE 1171 MAP
E F G H J
GATE
R1E R1W
SAN BERNARDINO MERIDIAN
SAN DIEGO CO.
RD
AIN
17100
DR
11
12
92065
TR
TK
FOSTER
REEK
MARIA RD
16800
92040
14
13
TKTR
SEE 1192 MAP
DEER HILL ESTATES
16800
LAZY ACRES DR
FOSTER
WY
DR
GATE
WILAJOBI
16900
LORRAINE CT
13800
FOSTER
12900
TKTR
PARK
23
24
67
SYCAMORE
SLAUGHTERHOUSE CANYON
SAN VICENTE RESERVOIR
R1E
1 2 3 4 5 6 7
SEE 1211 MAP
0 .125 .25 .375 .5 miles 1 in. = 1900 ft.

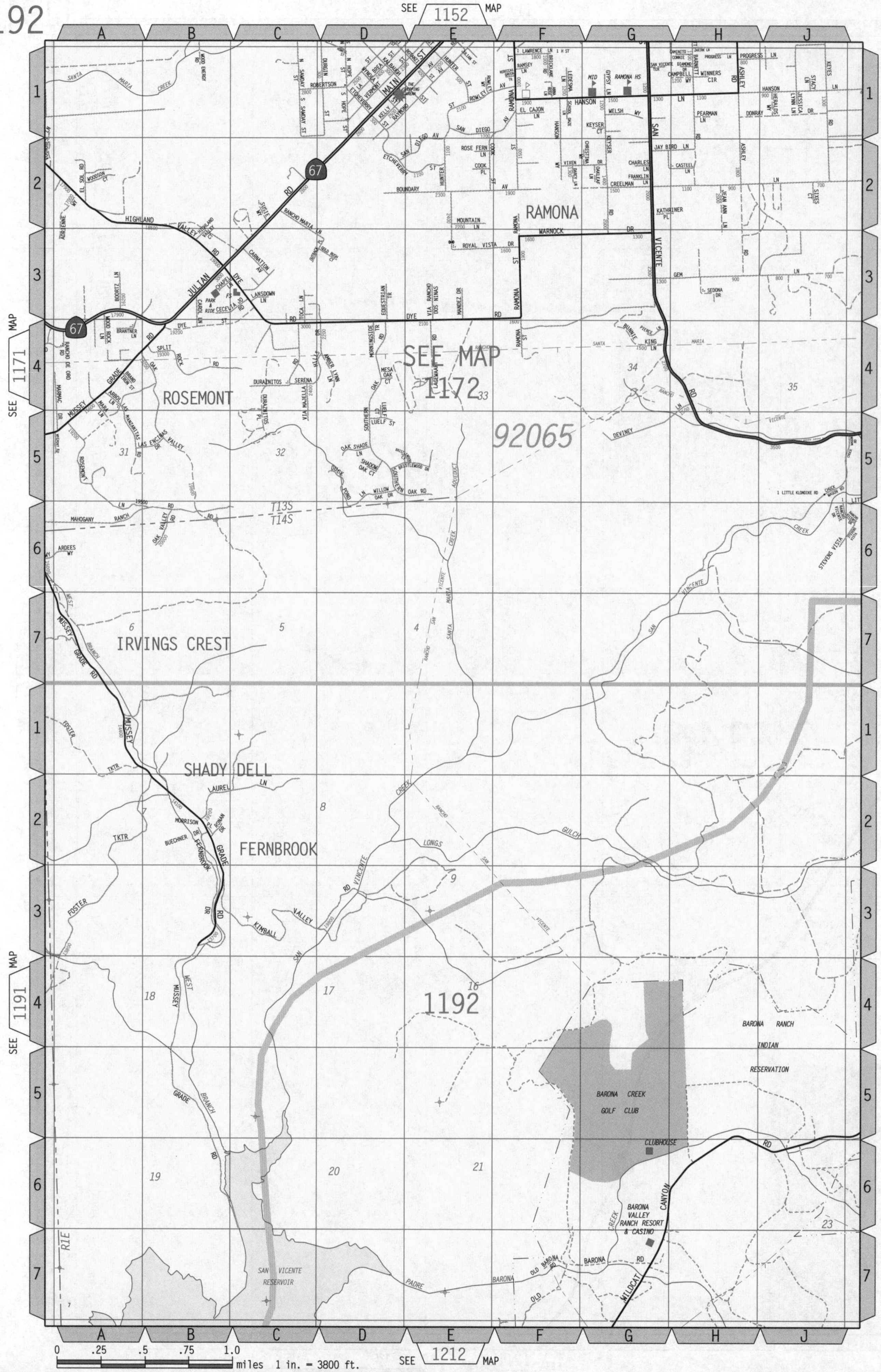
SEE 1152 MAP
SEE MAP 1171
SEE MAP 1191
SEE 1212 MAP
SEE MAP 1172
RAMONA
ROSEMONT
IRVINGS CREST
SHADY DELL
FERNBROOK
92065
1192
67
MAIN ST
SAN VICENTE RD
DYE RD
JULIAN RD
HIGHLAND VALLEY RD
MUSSEY GRADE RD
WEST MUSSEY GRADE RD
SAN DIEGO AV
BOUNDARY AV
WARNOCK DR
MONTECITO RD
SANTA MARIA CREEK
KIMBALL VALLEY
BARONA RANCH INDIAN RESERVATION
BARONA CREEK GOLF CLUB
CLUBHOUSE
BARONA VALLEY RANCH RESORT & CASINO
WILDCAT CANYON RD
SAN VICENTE RESERVOIR
T13S
T14S
MID
RAMONA HS
0 .25 .5 .75 1.0
miles 1 in. = 3800 ft.

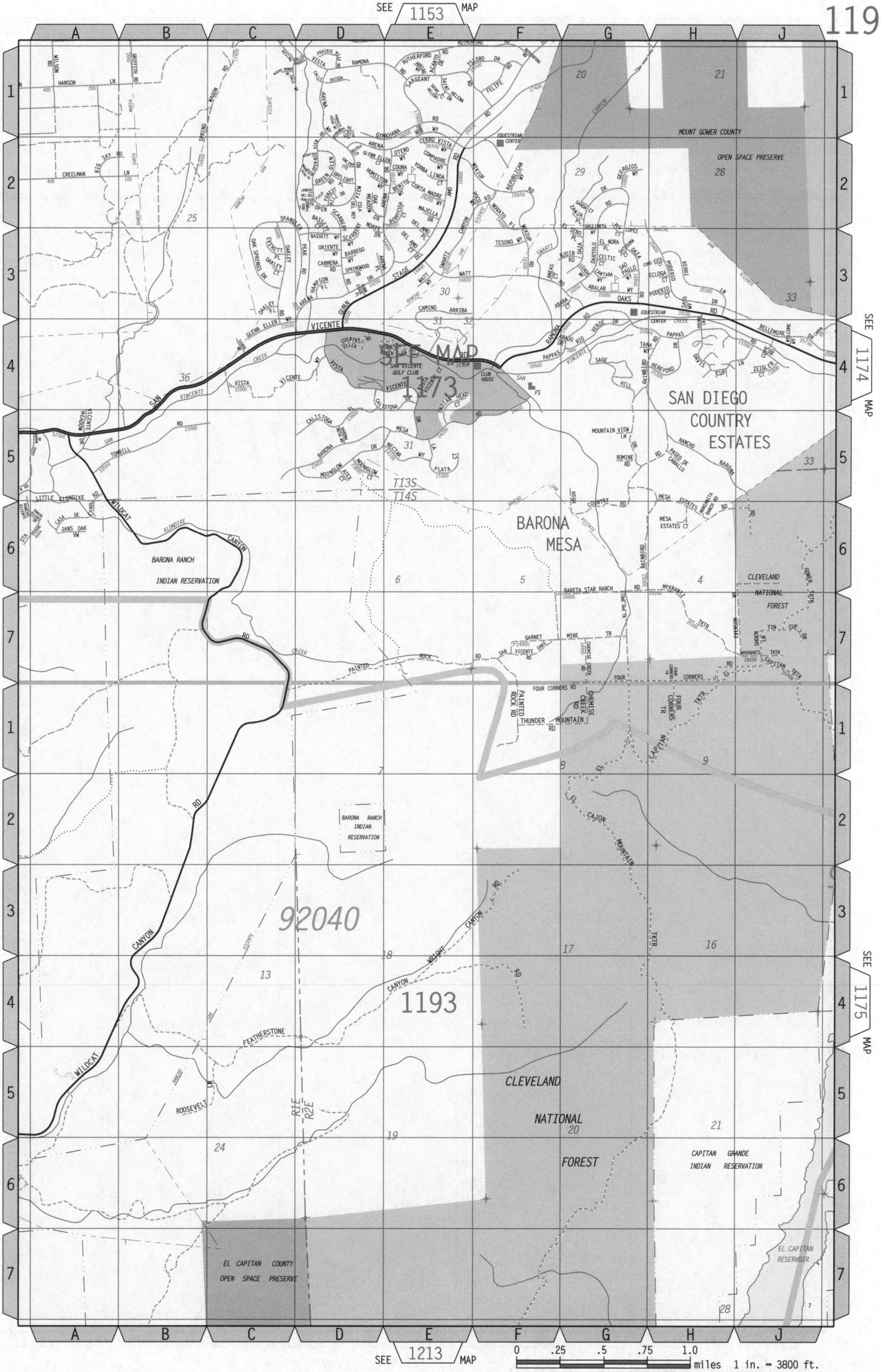
SEE 1153 MAP
SEE 1174 MAP
SEE 1175 MAP
SEE 1213 MAP
SEE MAP 1173
SAN DIEGO COUNTRY ESTATES
BARONA MESA
BARONA RANCH INDIAN RESERVATION
MOUNT GOWER COUNTY OPEN SPACE PRESERVE
CLEVELAND NATIONAL FOREST
CAPITAN GRANDE INDIAN RESERVATION
EL CAPITAN COUNTY OPEN SPACE PRESERVE
EL CAPITAN RESERVOIR
SAN VICENTE GOLF CLUB
92040
1193
T13S
T14S
R1E
R2E
WILDCAT CANYON RD
SAN VICENTE RD
EL CAJON MOUNTAIN TKTR
FOUR CORNERS RD
PAINTED ROCK RD
THUNDER MOUNTAIN RD
MOUNTAIN VIEW LN
WRIGHT CANYON RD
FEATHERSTONE
ROOSEVELT
0 .25 .5 .75 1.0 miles 1 in. = 3800 ft.

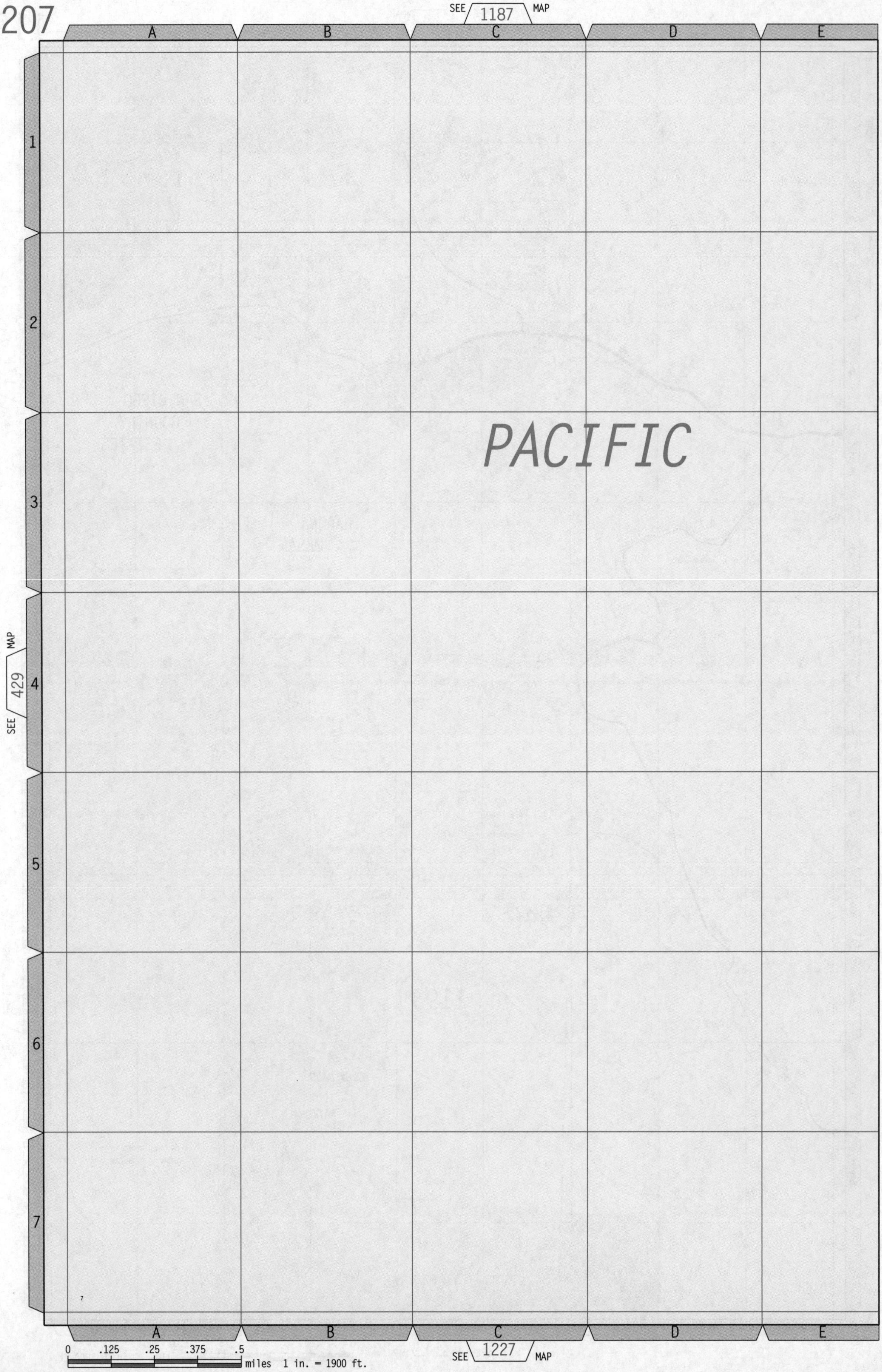

SEE 1187 MAP
A
B
C
D
E
1
2
3
4
5
6
7
SEE 429 MAP
PACIFIC
SEE 1227 MAP
0 .125 .25 .375 .5
miles 1 in. = 1900 ft.

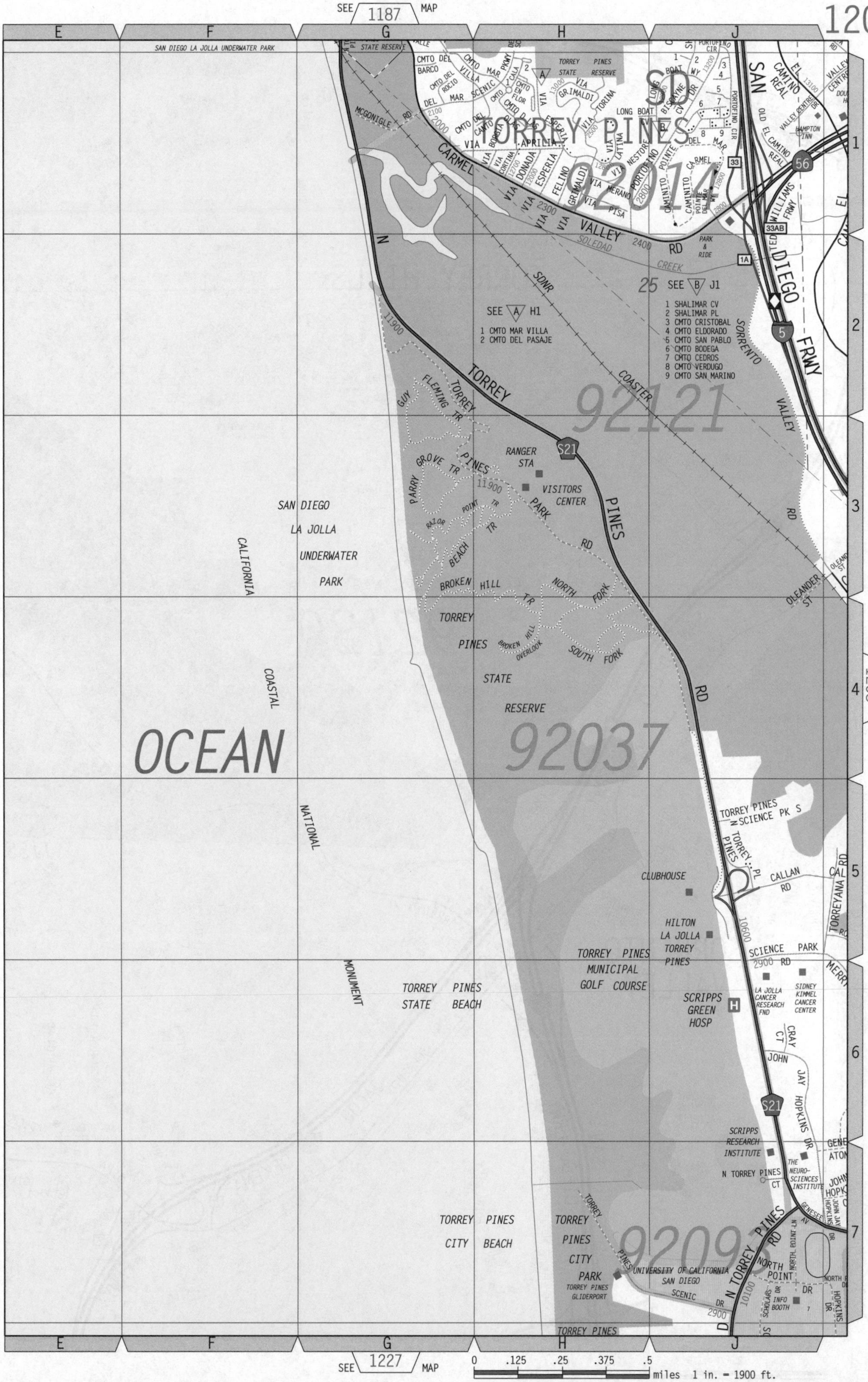
SEE 1187 MAP
SEE 1208 MAP
SEE 1227 MAP
E
F
G
H
J
1
2
3
4
5
6
7
SAN DIEGO LA JOLLA UNDERWATER PARK
STATE RESERVE
TORREY PINES STATE RESERVE
SD
TORREY PINES
92014
92121
92037
92093
CARMEL VALLEY RD
SOLEDAD CREEK
SDNR
COASTER
PARK & RIDE
SEE A H1
1 CMTO MAR VILLA
2 CMTO DEL PASAJE
SEE B J1
1 SHALIMAR CV
2 SHALIMAR PL
3 CMTO CRISTOBAL
4 CMTO ELDORADO
5 CMTO SAN PABLO
6 CMTO BODEGA
7 CMTO CEDROS
8 CMTO VERDUGO
9 CMTO SAN MARINO
SAN DIEGO FRWY
EL CAMINO REAL
OLD EL CAMINO REAL
HAMPTON INN
WILLIAMS FRWY
SORRENTO VALLEY RD
OLEANDER ST
N TORREY PINES RD
MCGONIGLE RD
GUY FLEMING TR
TORREY PINES TR
PARRY GROVE TR
RAZOR POINT TR
BEACH TR
BROKEN HILL TR
NORTH FORK
SOUTH FORK
BROKEN HILL OVERLOOK
RANGER STA
VISITORS CENTER
PARK RD
TORREY PINES STATE RESERVE
SAN DIEGO LA JOLLA UNDERWATER PARK
CALIFORNIA COASTAL NATIONAL MONUMENT
OCEAN
TORREY PINES N SCIENCE PK S
TORREY PINES PL
CALLAN RD
TORREYANA RD
CLUBHOUSE
HILTON LA JOLLA TORREY PINES
TORREY PINES MUNICIPAL GOLF COURSE
SCIENCE PARK RD
LA JOLLA CANCER RESEARCH FND
SIDNEY KIMMEL CANCER CENTER
SCRIPPS GREEN HOSP
CRAY CT
JOHN JAY HOPKINS DR
SCRIPPS RESEARCH INSTITUTE
N TORREY PINES CT
THE NEURO-SCIENCES INSTITUTE
GENESEE AV
TORREY PINES STATE BEACH
TORREY PINES CITY BEACH
TORREY PINES CITY PARK
TORREY PINES GLIDERPORT
UNIVERSITY OF CALIFORNIA SAN DIEGO
SCENIC DR
NORTH POINT DR
INFO BOOTH
SCHOLARS DR
TORREY PINES
0 .125 .25 .375 .5 miles 1 in. = 1900 ft.

SEE 1188 MAP

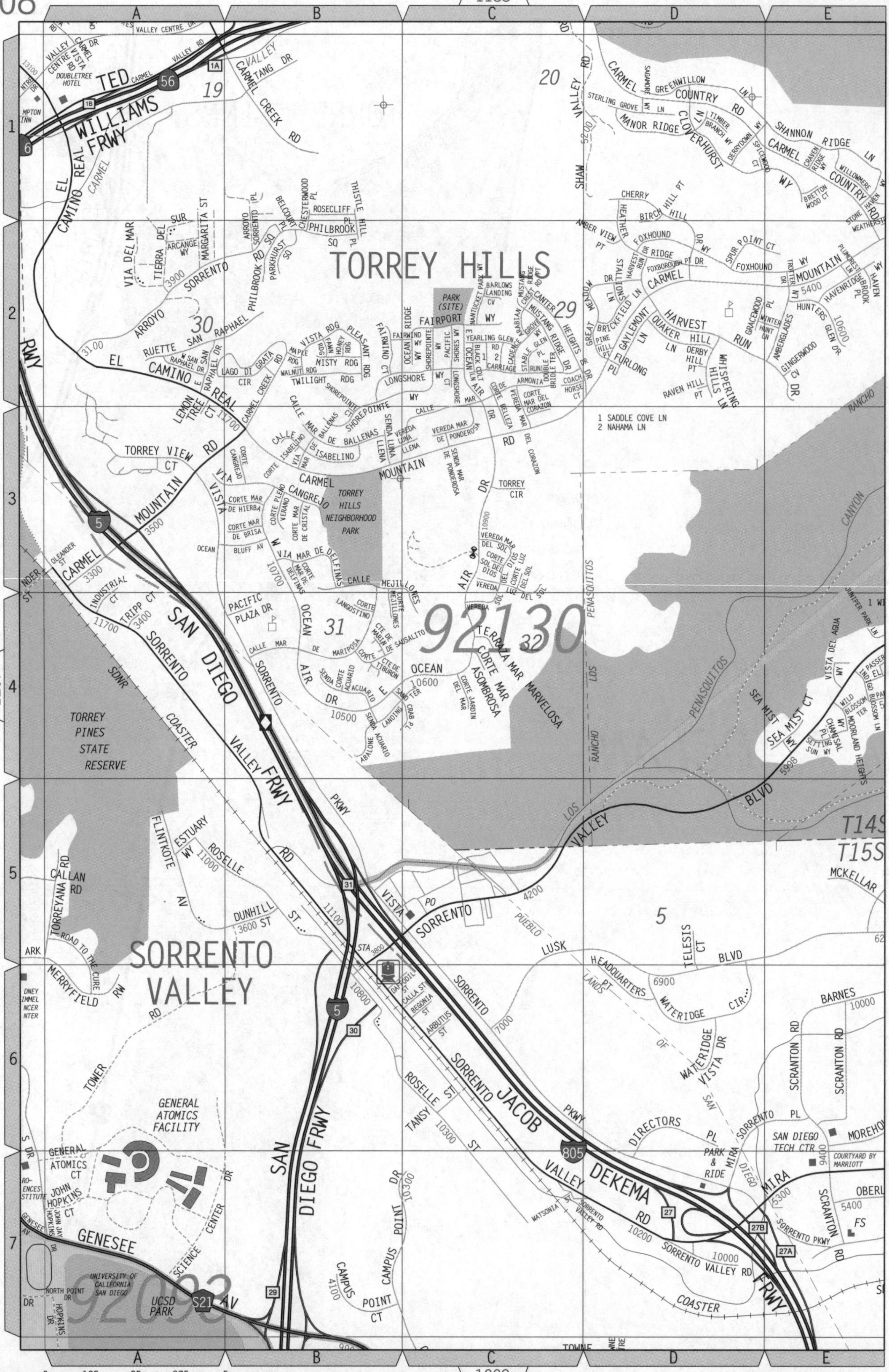

SEE 1207 MAP

SEE 1228 MAP

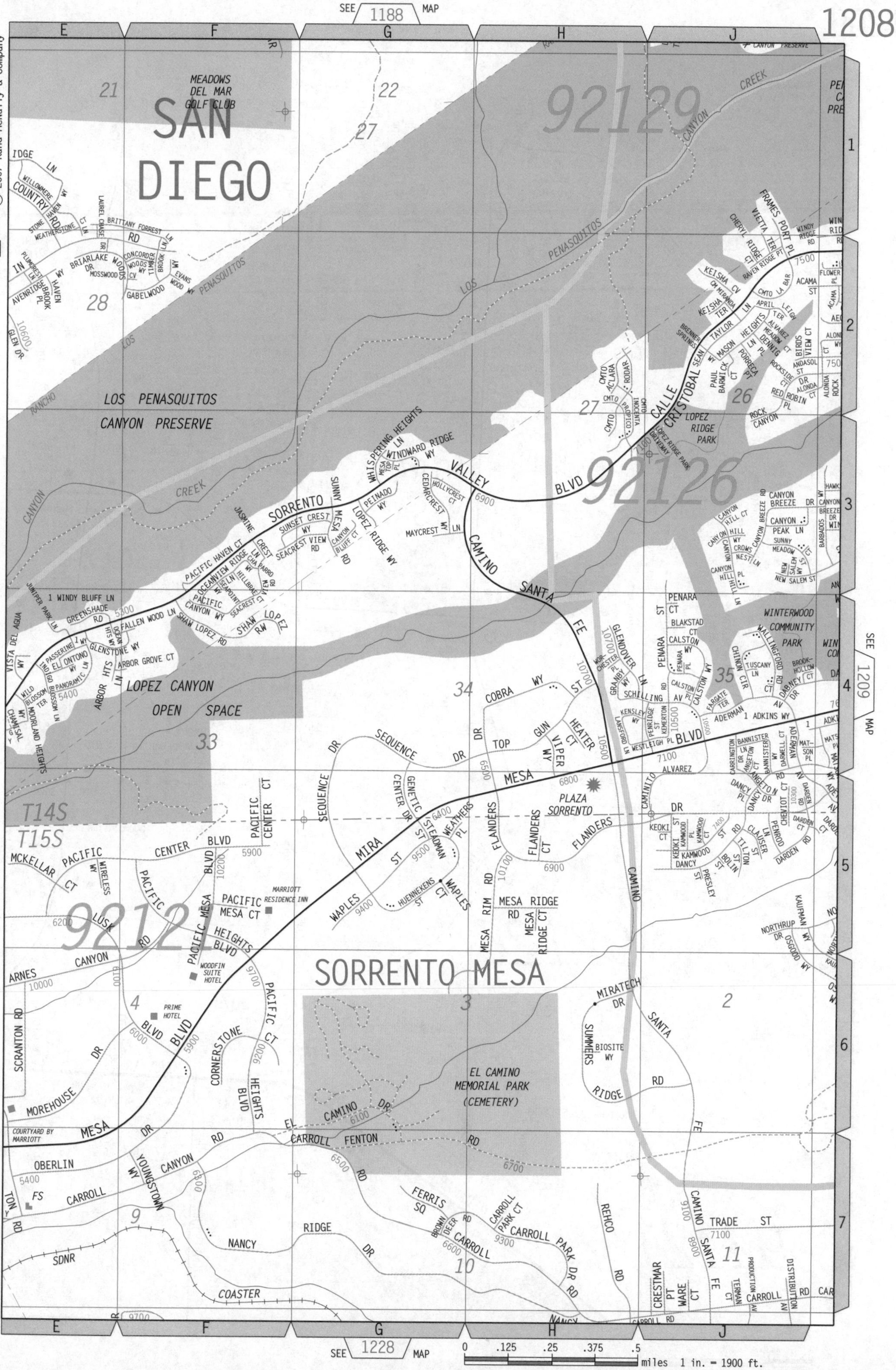
SEE 1188 MAP
SEE 1228 MAP
SEE 1209 MAP
SAN DIEGO
92129
92126
92121
MEADOWS DEL MAR GOLF CLUB
LOS PENASQUITOS CANYON PRESERVE
LOPEZ CANYON OPEN SPACE
LOPEZ RIDGE PARK
WINTERWOOD COMMUNITY PARK
SORRENTO MESA
PLAZA SORRENTO
EL CAMINO MEMORIAL PARK (CEMETERY)
MARRIOTT RESIDENCE INN
WOODFIN SUITE HOTEL
PRIME HOTEL
COURTYARD BY MARRIOTT
SORRENTO VALLEY BLVD
CAMINO SANTA FE
CALLE CRISTOBAL
MIRA MESA BLVD
PACIFIC HEIGHTS BLVD
PACIFIC CENTER BLVD
LUSK BLVD
CARROLL CANYON RD
CARROLL RD
FLANDERS DR
SEQUENCE DR
TOP GUN ST
LOS PENASQUITOS CANYON CREEK
T14S
T15S
SDNR
COASTER
0 .125 .25 .375 .5 miles 1 in. = 1900 ft.

SEE 1189 MAP

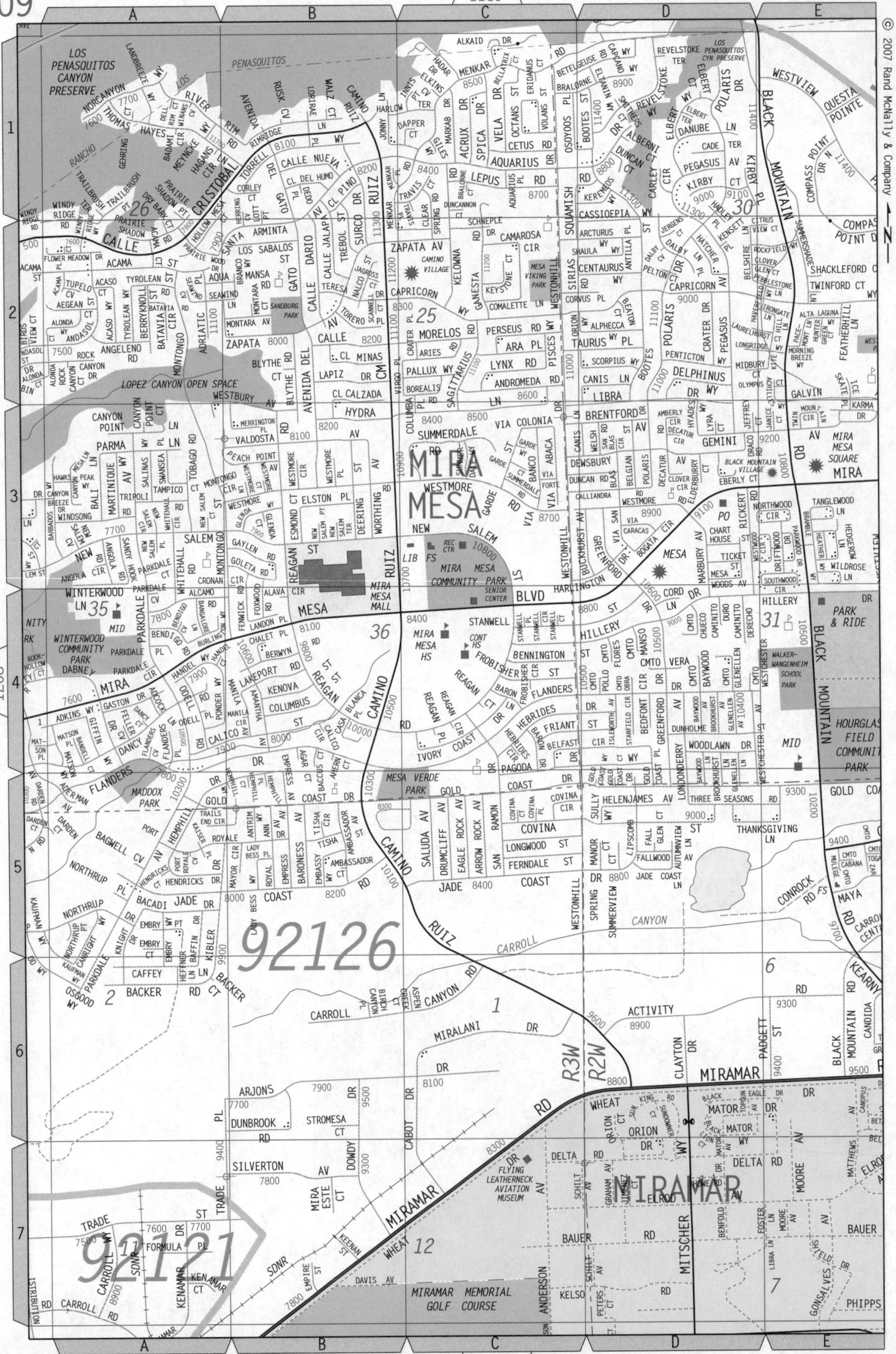

SEE 1208 MAP

0 .125 .25 .375 .5 miles 1 in. = 1900 ft.

SEE 1229 MAP

SEE 1189 MAP

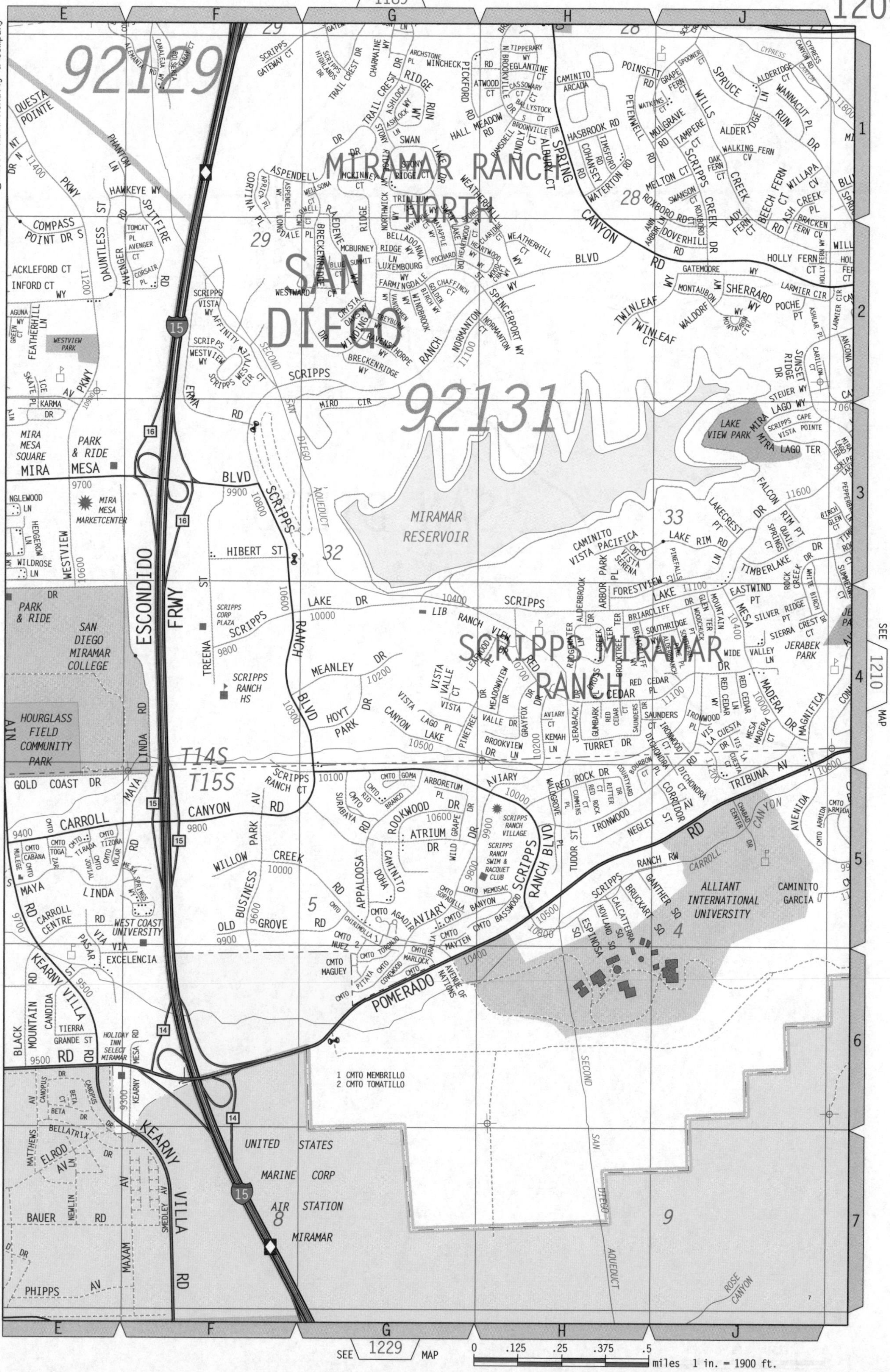

SEE 1210 MAP

SEE 1229 MAP

0 .125 .25 .375 .5 miles 1 in. = 1900 ft.

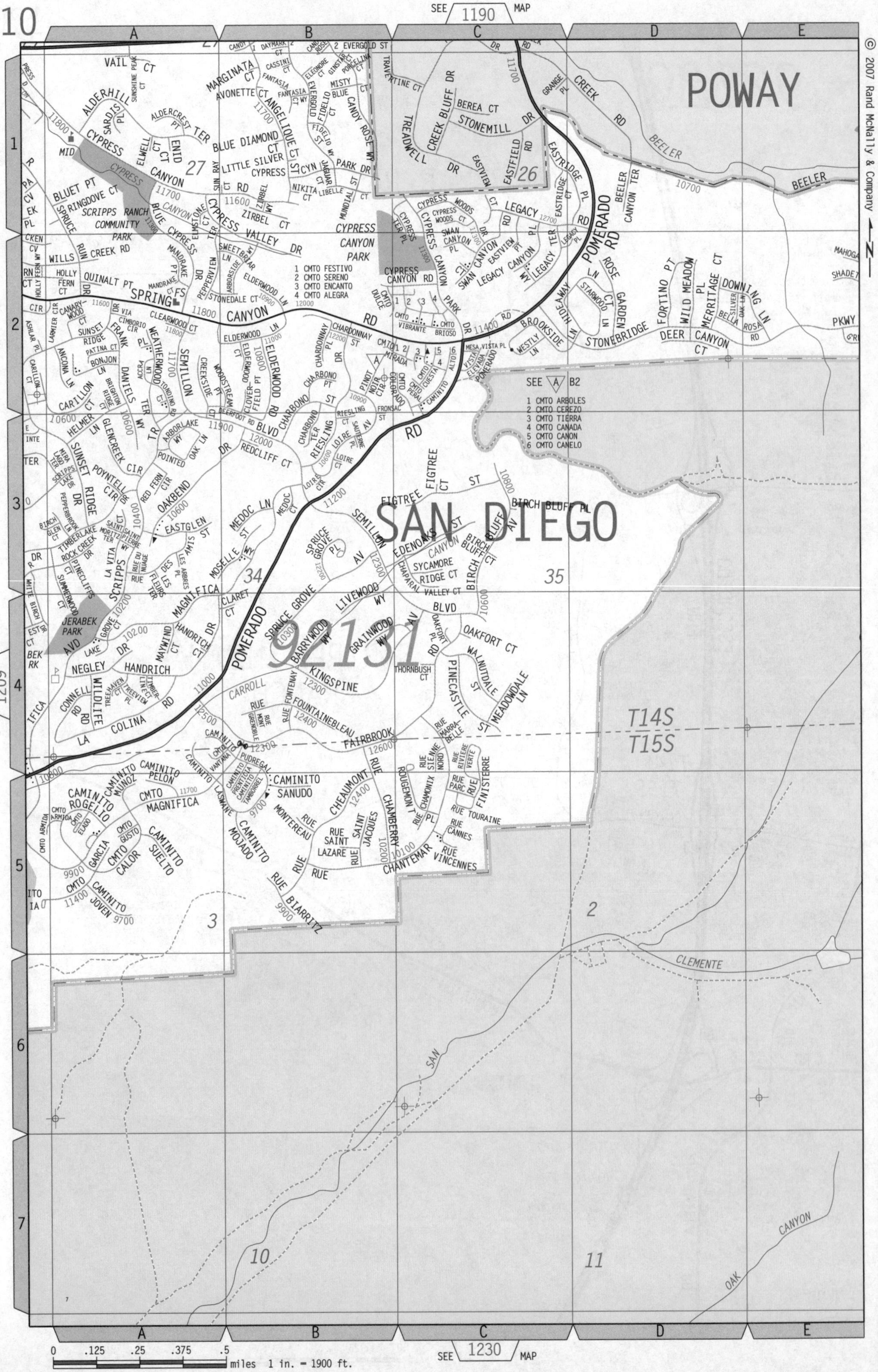
SEE 1190 MAP
SEE 1230 MAP
SEE 1209 MAP
POWAY
SAN DIEGO
92131
T14S
T15S
POMERADO RD
SPRING CANYON RD
CYPRESS CANYON PARK
SCRIPPS RANCH COMMUNITY PARK
JERABEK PARK
BEELER CANYON TER
STONEBRIDGE PKWY
SEMILLON BLVD
CARROLL CANYON
CLEMENTE
OAK CANYON
SAN
SEE A B2
1 CMTO ARBOLES
2 CMTO CEREZO
3 CMTO TIERRA
4 CMTO CANADA
5 CMTO CANON
6 CMTO CANELO
1 CMTO FESTIVO
2 CMTO SERENO
3 CMTO ENCANTO
4 CMTO ALEGRA
0 .125 .25 .375 .5
miles 1 in. = 1900 ft.

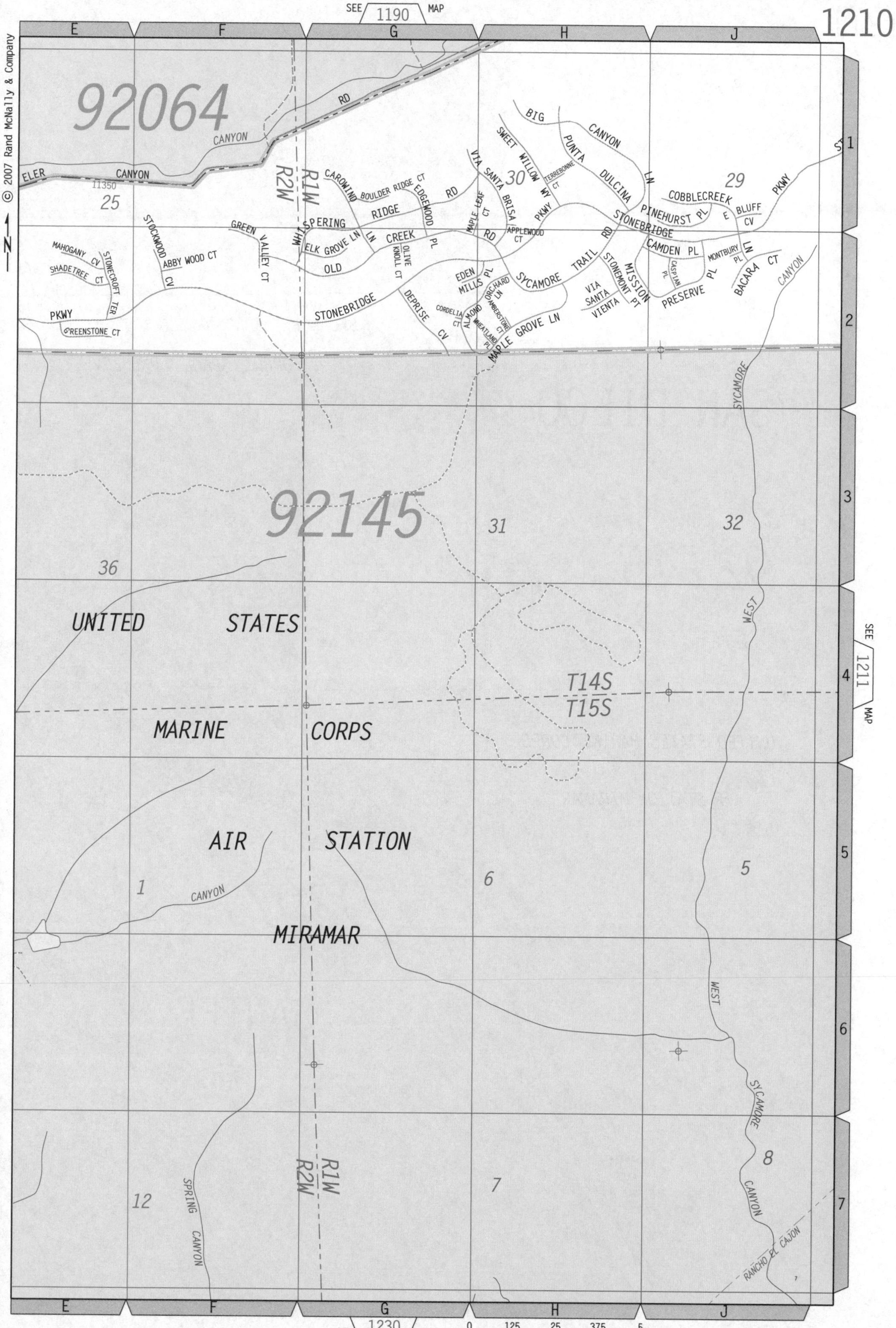
SEE 1190 MAP
E
F
G
H
J
92064
RD
CANYON
ELER
CANYON
11350
25
R1W
R2W
BIG
CANYON
SWEET WILLOW WY
PUNTA DULCINA LN
TERREBONNE CT
VIA SANTA BRISA
30
29
CAROWIND
BOULDER RIDGE CT
EDGEWOOD
RD
RIDGE
WHISPERING
MAPLE LEAF CT
COBBLECREEK
PINEHURST PL
E
BLUFF CV
PKWY
ST
STONEBRIDGE
PKWY
APPLEWOOD CT
RD
STOCKWOOD CV
GREEN VALLEY CT
ELK GROVE LN
CREEK
OLD
OLIVE KNOLL CT
PL
MAHOGANY CV
SHADETREE CT
STONECROFT TER
ABBY WOOD CT
EDEN MILLS PL
SYCAMORE TRAIL RD
CAMDEN PL
CASPIAN PL
MONTBURY PL
LN
BACARA CT
CANYON
STONEMONT PT
MISSION
VIA SANTA VIENTA
PRESERVE PL
PKWY
GREENSTONE CT
STONEBRIDGE
DEPRISE CV
CORDELIA CT
ALMOND CT
ORCHARD LN
AMBERSTONE CT
WHEATLAND PL
MAPLE GROVE LN
SYCAMORE
92145
31
32
36
UNITED STATES
MARINE CORPS
AIR STATION
MIRAMAR
WEST
T14S
T15S
1
CANYON
6
5
WEST
SYCAMORE
8
CANYON
12
SPRING CANYON
R1W
R2W
7
RANCHO EL CAJON
1
2
3
4
5
6
7
SEE 1211 MAP
SAN DIEGO CO.
SEE 1230 MAP
0 .125 .25 .375 .5
miles 1 in. = 1900 ft.

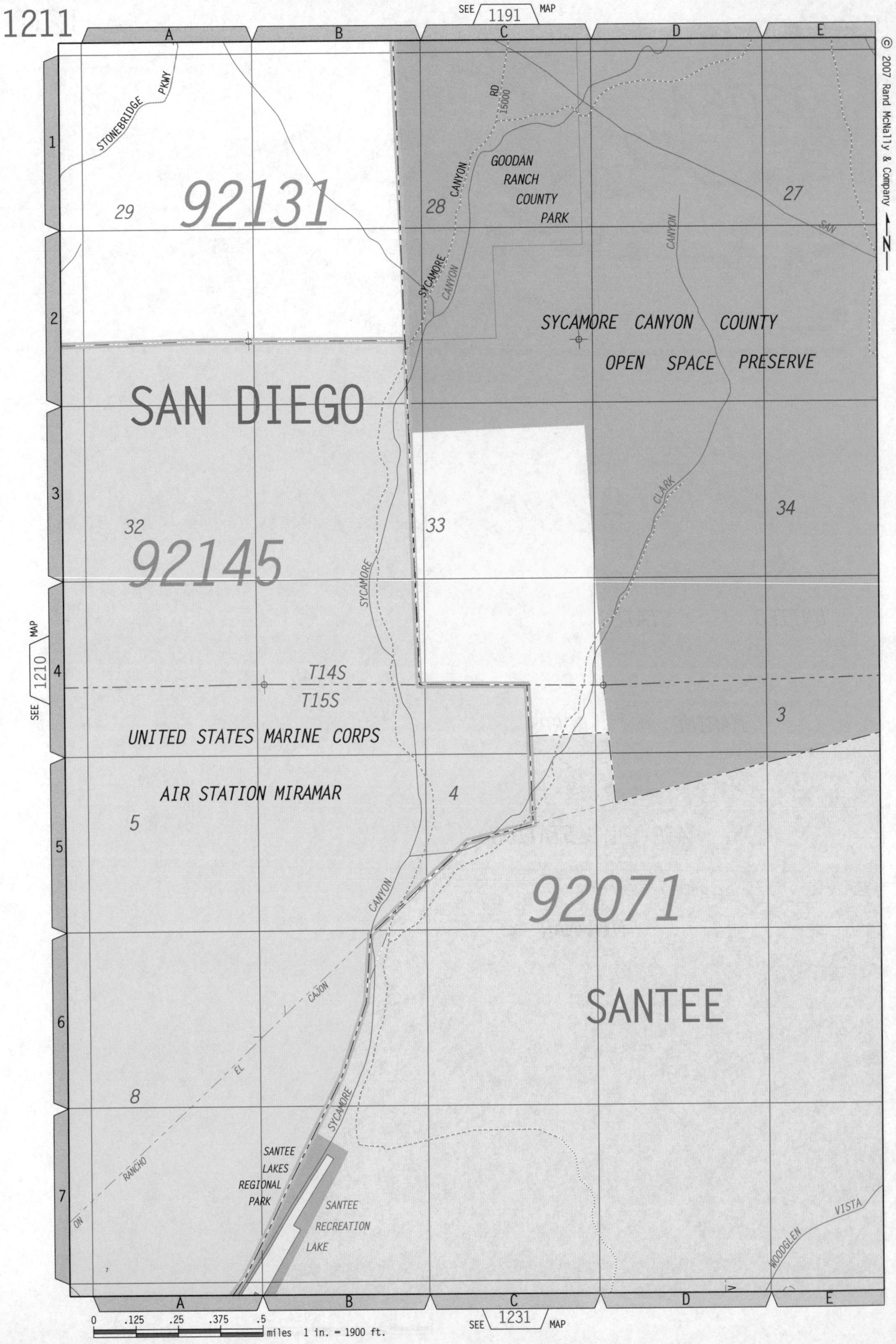

SEE 1191 MAP
SAN DIEGO CO.
STONEBRIDGE PKWY
92131
29
28
27
GOODAN RANCH COUNTY PARK
RD 15000
CANYON
SYCAMORE
CANYON
SYCAMORE CANYON COUNTY OPEN SPACE PRESERVE
SAN
SAN DIEGO
CLARK
32
33
34
92145
SYCAMORE
T14S
T15S
3
UNITED STATES MARINE CORPS
AIR STATION MIRAMAR
4
5
CANYON
92071
CAJON
EL
SANTEE
8
SYCAMORE
RANCHO
ON
SANTEE LAKES REGIONAL PARK
SANTEE RECREATION LAKE
WOODGLEN VISTA
SEE 1210 MAP
SEE 1231 MAP
0 .125 .25 .375 .5 miles 1 in. = 1900 ft.

SEE 1191 MAP

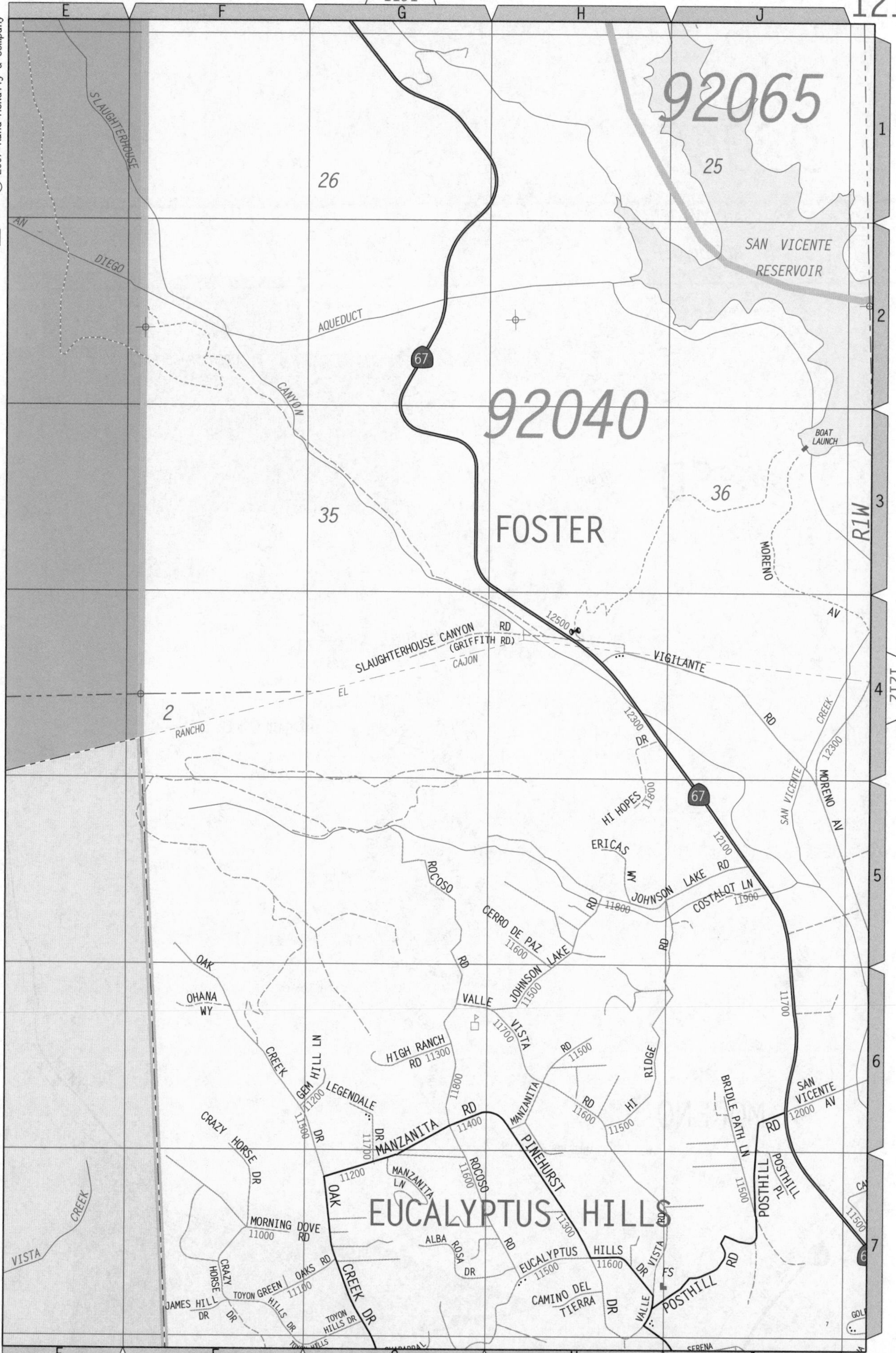

SEE 1212 MAP

SEE 1231 MAP

0 .125 .25 .375 .5 miles 1 in. = 1900 ft.

SEE 1192 MAP

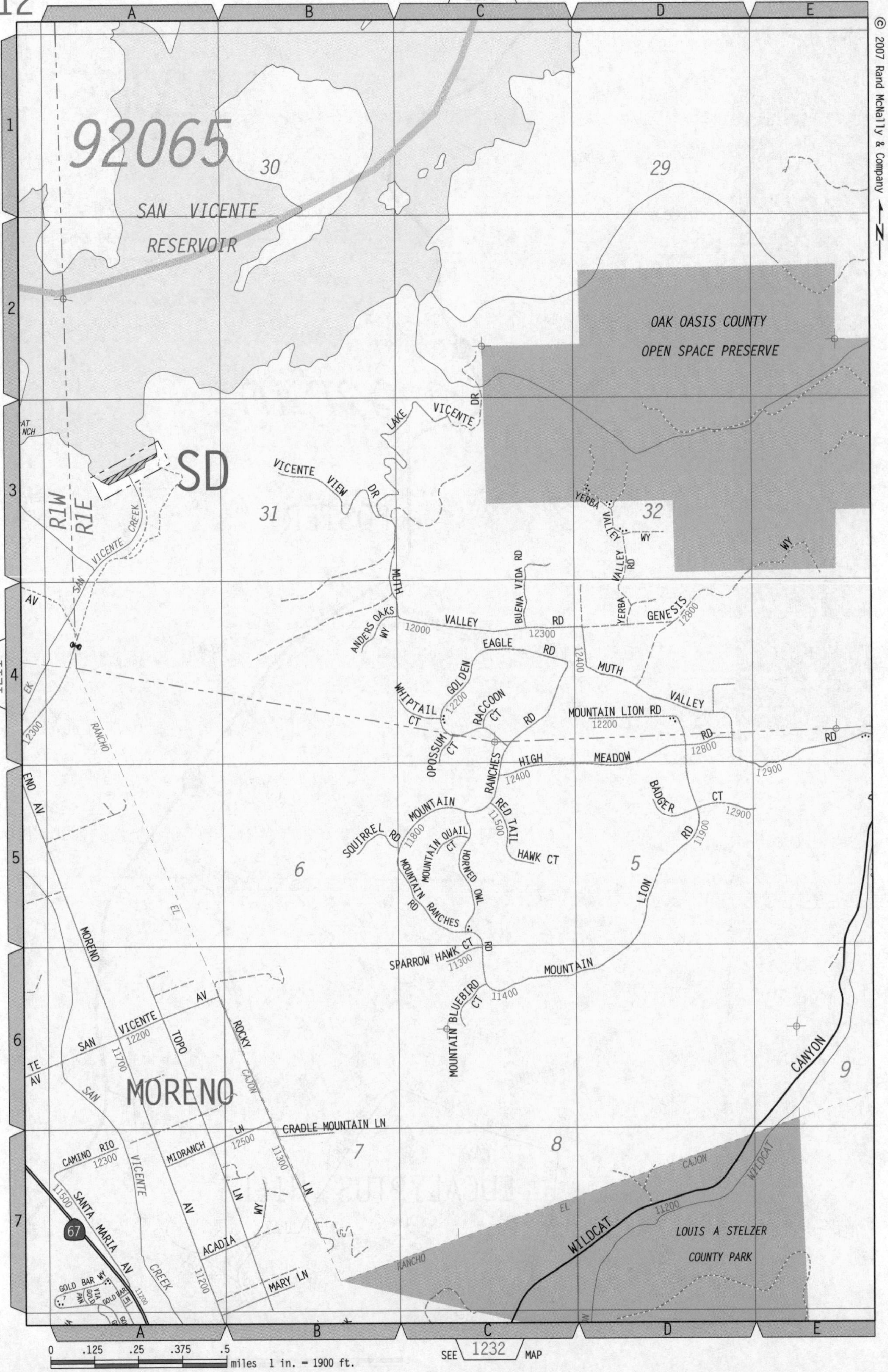

SEE 1232 MAP

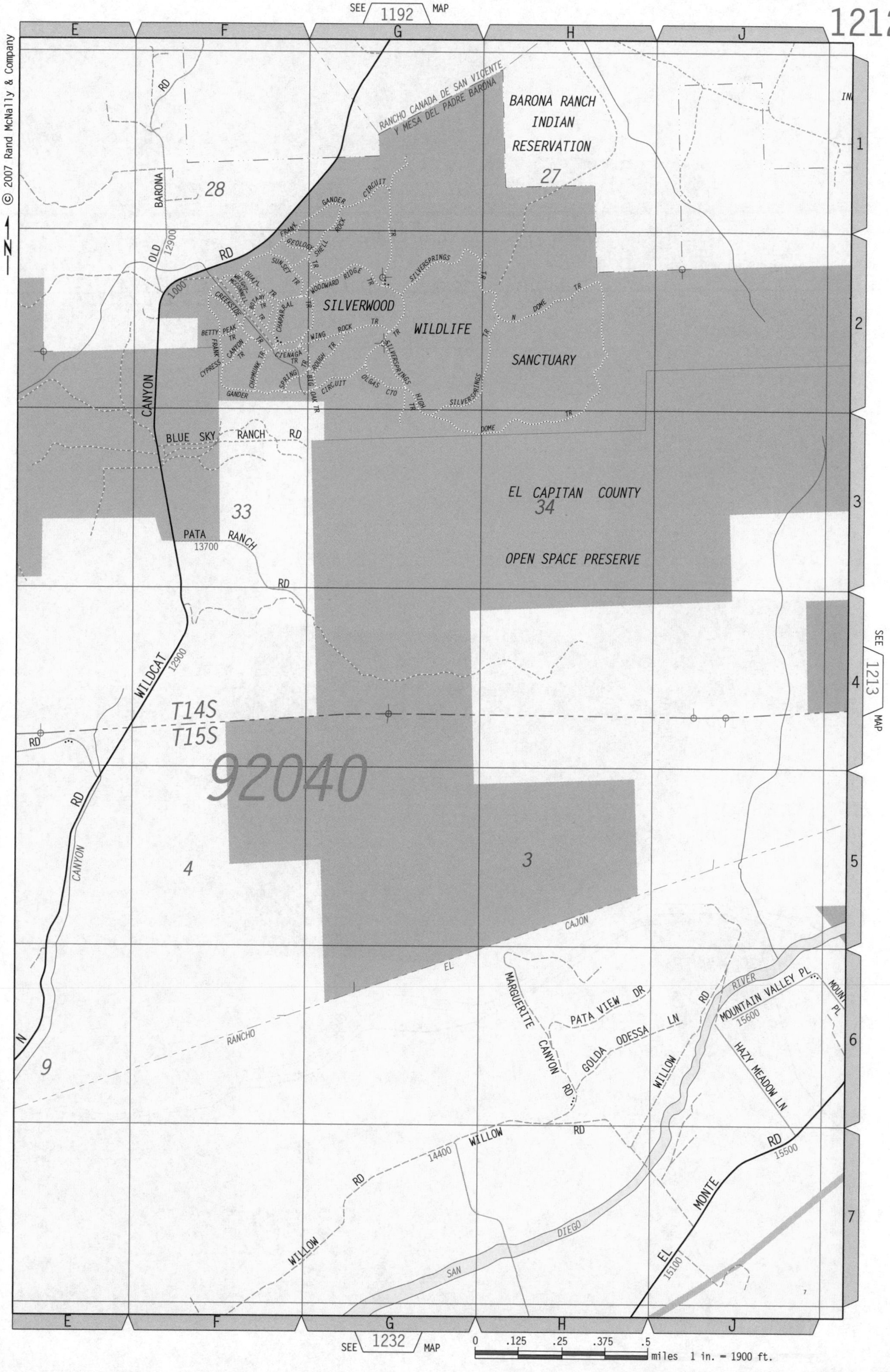
SEE 1192 MAP
E
F
G
H
J
1
2
3
4
5
6
7
BARONA RANCH INDIAN RESERVATION
RANCHO CANADA DE SAN VICENTE Y MESA DEL PADRE BARONA
27
28
BARONA
OLD
12900
RD
1000
SILVERWOOD
WILDLIFE
SANCTUARY
GANDER
CIRCUIT
FRANK
GEOLOGY
SHELL
ROCK
TR
SUNSET
QUAIL
CREEKSIDE
BOTANY
WOODWARD RIDGE
SILVERSPRINGS
N DOME TR
BETTY PEAK TR
CHAPARRAL
CIENAGA
WING ROCK TR
CANYON
CYPRESS
CHIPMUNK TR
SPRING TR
ROUGH TR
BIG OAK TR
OLGAS CTO
HIGH TR
DOME
CANYON
BLUE SKY RANCH RD
EL CAPITAN COUNTY
34
OPEN SPACE PRESERVE
33
PATA RANCH RD
13700
WILDCAT
12900
T14S
T15S
92040
RD
CANYON
4
3
SEE 1213 MAP
CAJON
EL
RANCHO
9
N
MARGUERITE CANYON RD
PATA VIEW DR
GOLDA ODESSA LN
WILLOW RD
RIVER
MOUNTAIN VALLEY PL
15600
HAZY MEADOW LN
WILLOW RD
14400
RD
15500
EL MONTE
15100
SAN DIEGO
WILLOW
SEE 1232 MAP
0 .125 .25 .375 .5
miles 1 in. = 1900 ft.

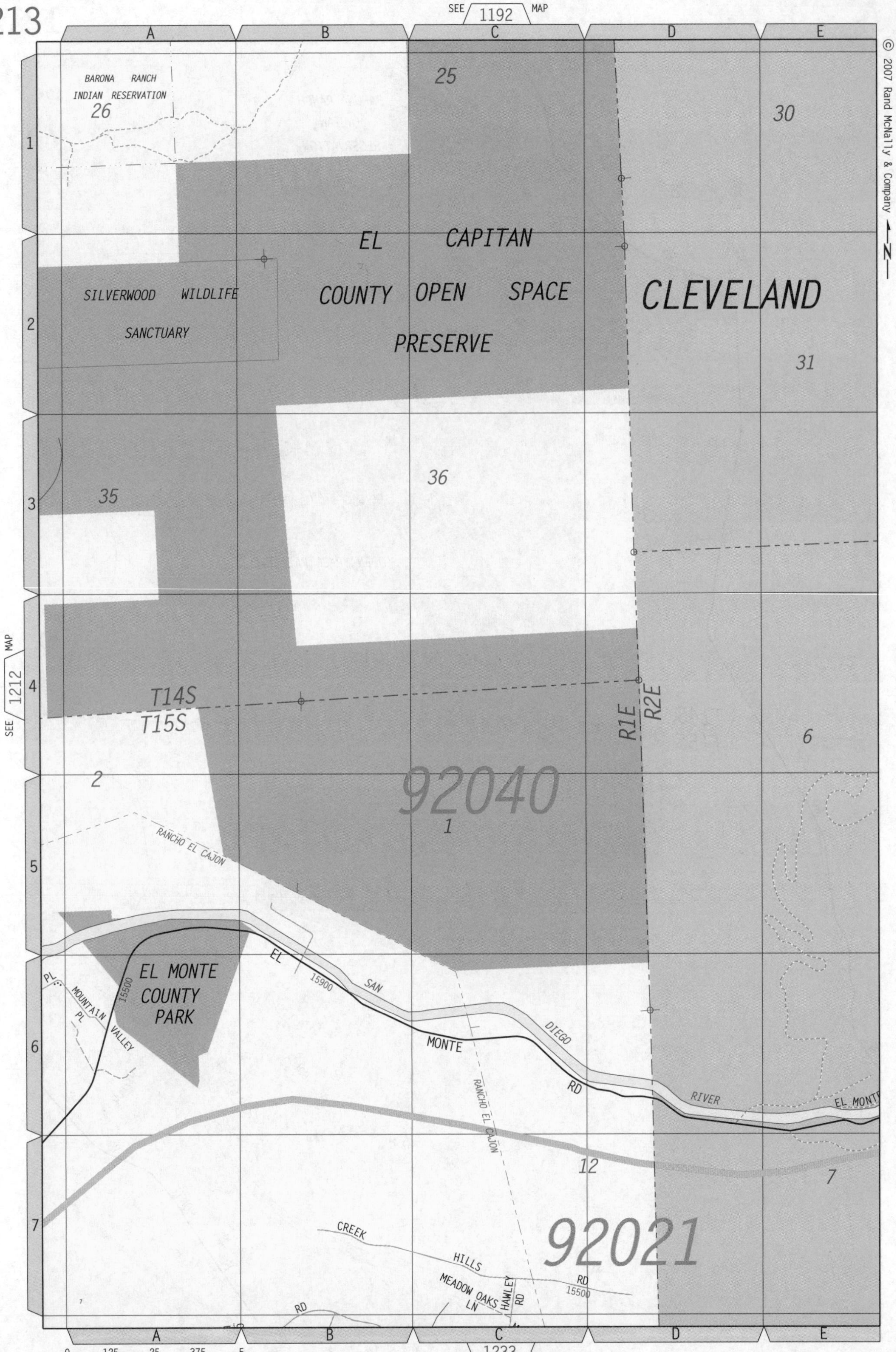
SEE 1192 MAP
A
B
C
D
E
1
2
3
4
5
6
7
SEE 1212 MAP
SEE 1233 MAP
BARONA RANCH
INDIAN RESERVATION
26
25
30
EL CAPITAN
COUNTY OPEN SPACE
PRESERVE
SILVERWOOD WILDLIFE
SANCTUARY
CLEVELAND
31
36
35
T14S
T15S
R1E
R2E
6
2
92040
1
RANCHO EL CAJON
EL MONTE
COUNTY
PARK
15500
PL
MOUNTAIN
PL
VALLEY
EL
15900
SAN
MONTE
DIEGO
RD
RIVER
EL MONTE
RANCHO EL CAJON
12
7
92021
CREEK
HILLS
RD
15500
MEADOW OAKS
LN
HAWLEY
RD
RD
0 .125 .25 .375 .5
miles 1 in. = 1900 ft.

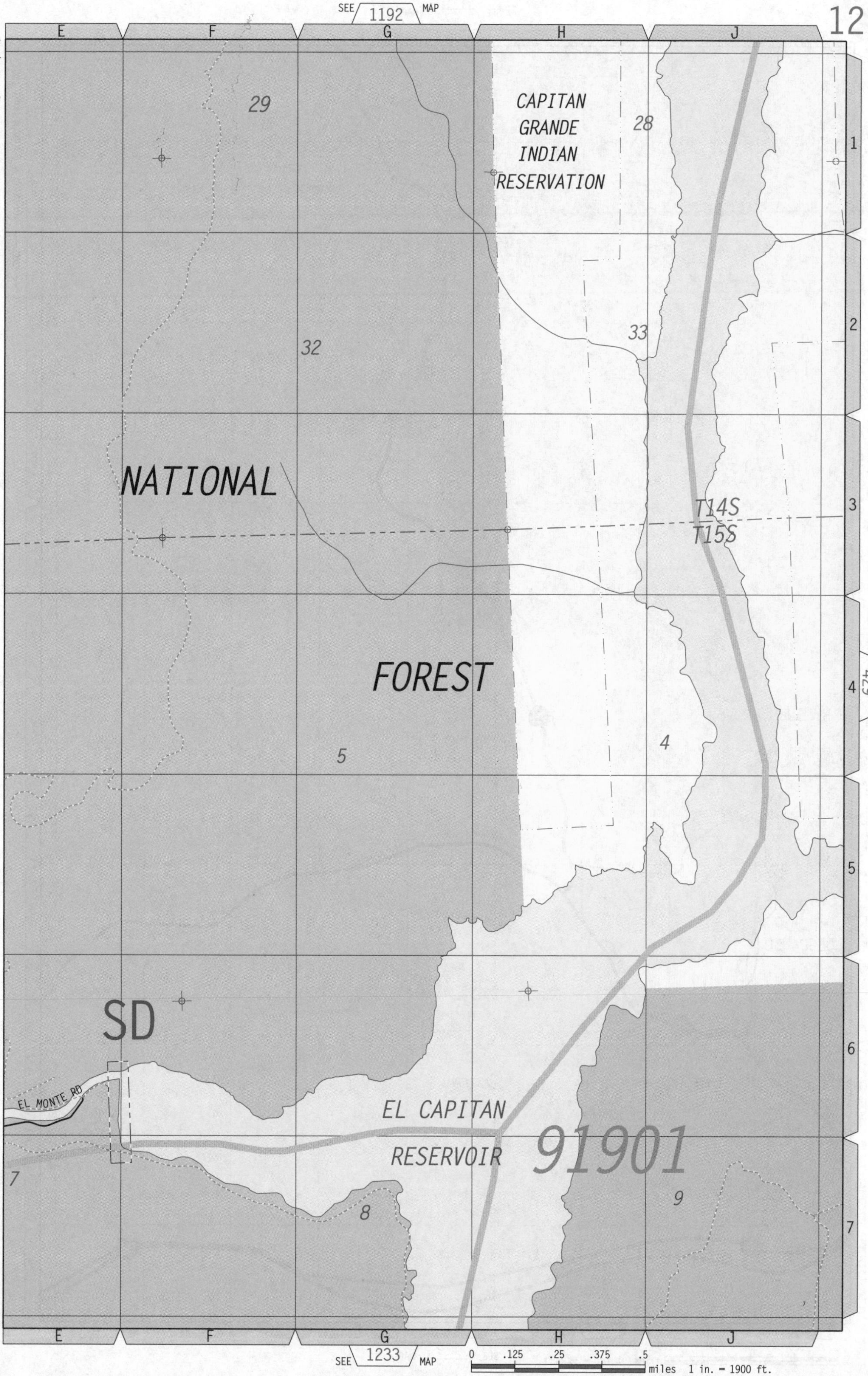
SEE 1192 MAP
E
F
G
H
J
1
2
3
4
5
6
7
SAN DIEGO CO.
29
28
CAPITAN
GRANDE
INDIAN
RESERVATION
33
32
NATIONAL
T14S
T15S
SEE 429 MAP
FOREST
5
4
SD
EL MONTE RD
EL CAPITAN
RESERVOIR
91901
7
8
9
SEE 1233 MAP
0
.125
.25
.375
.5
miles 1 in. = 1900 ft.

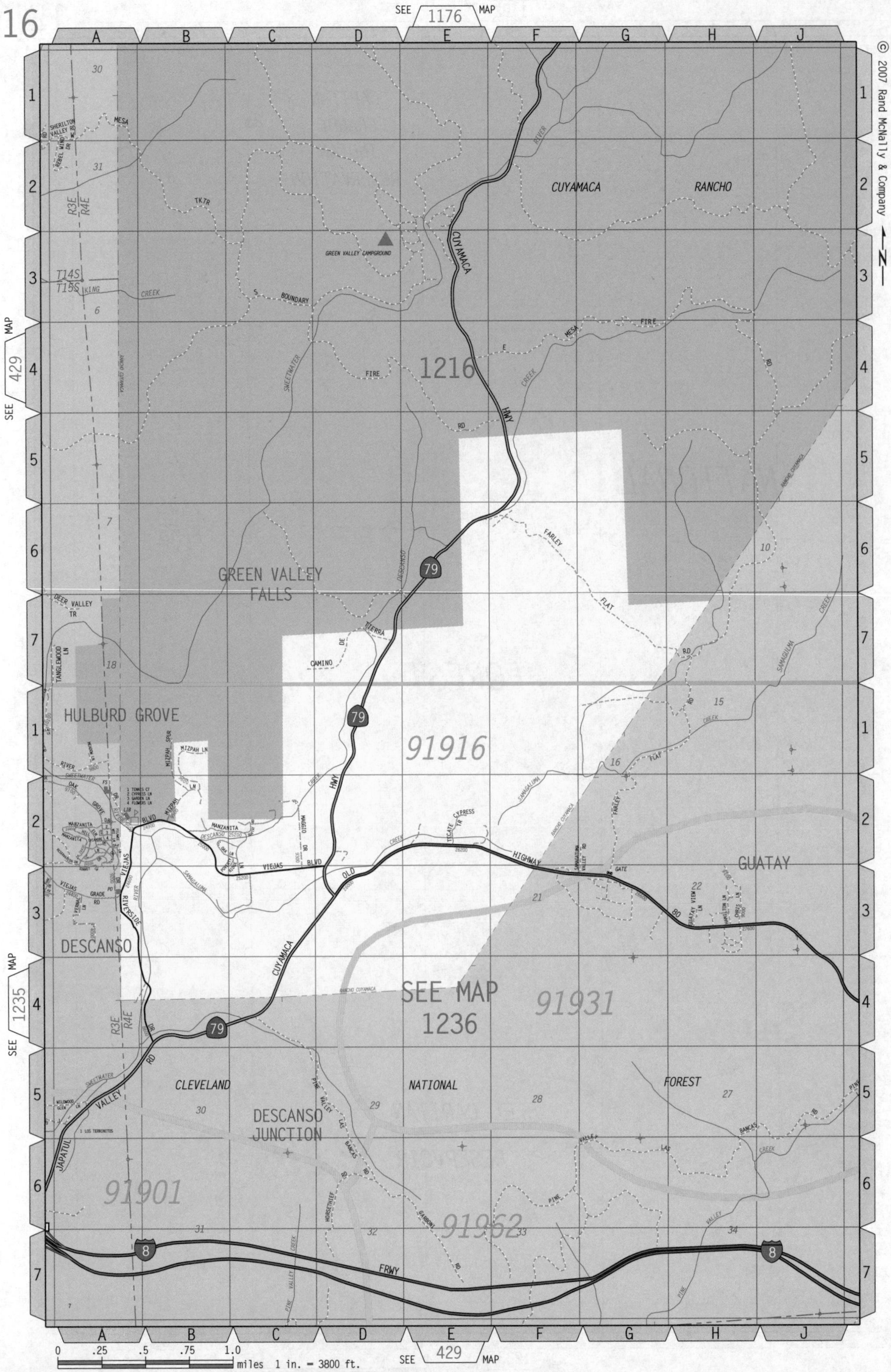
SEE 1176 MAP
SEE 429 MAP
SEE 1235 MAP
SEE 429 MAP
A B C D E F G H J
1 2 3 4 5 6 7
1216
CUYAMACA RANCHO
GREEN VALLEY CAMPGROUND
GREEN VALLEY FALLS
HULBURD GROVE
DESCANSO
GUATAY
DESCANSO JUNCTION
CLEVELAND NATIONAL FOREST
SEE MAP 1236
91916
91931
91901
91962
CUYAMACA HWY
79
8
FRWY
VIEJAS BLVD
OLD HIGHWAY 80
RIVERSIDE DR
JAPATUL VALLEY RD
FARLEY FLAT RD
MESA FIRE RD
BOUNDARY
SWEETWATER RIVER
KING CREEK
SAMAGATUMA CREEK
PINE VALLEY CREEK
LAS BANCAS RD
HORSETHIEF RD
DEER VALLEY TR
TANGLEWOOD LN
MIZPAH LN
MANZANITA
CAMINO DE TIERRA
RANCHO CUYAMACA
TECATE CYPRESS TR
OAK GROVE
VIEJAS GRADE RD
R3E R4E
T14S T15S
0 .25 .5 .75 1.0
miles 1 in. = 3800 ft.

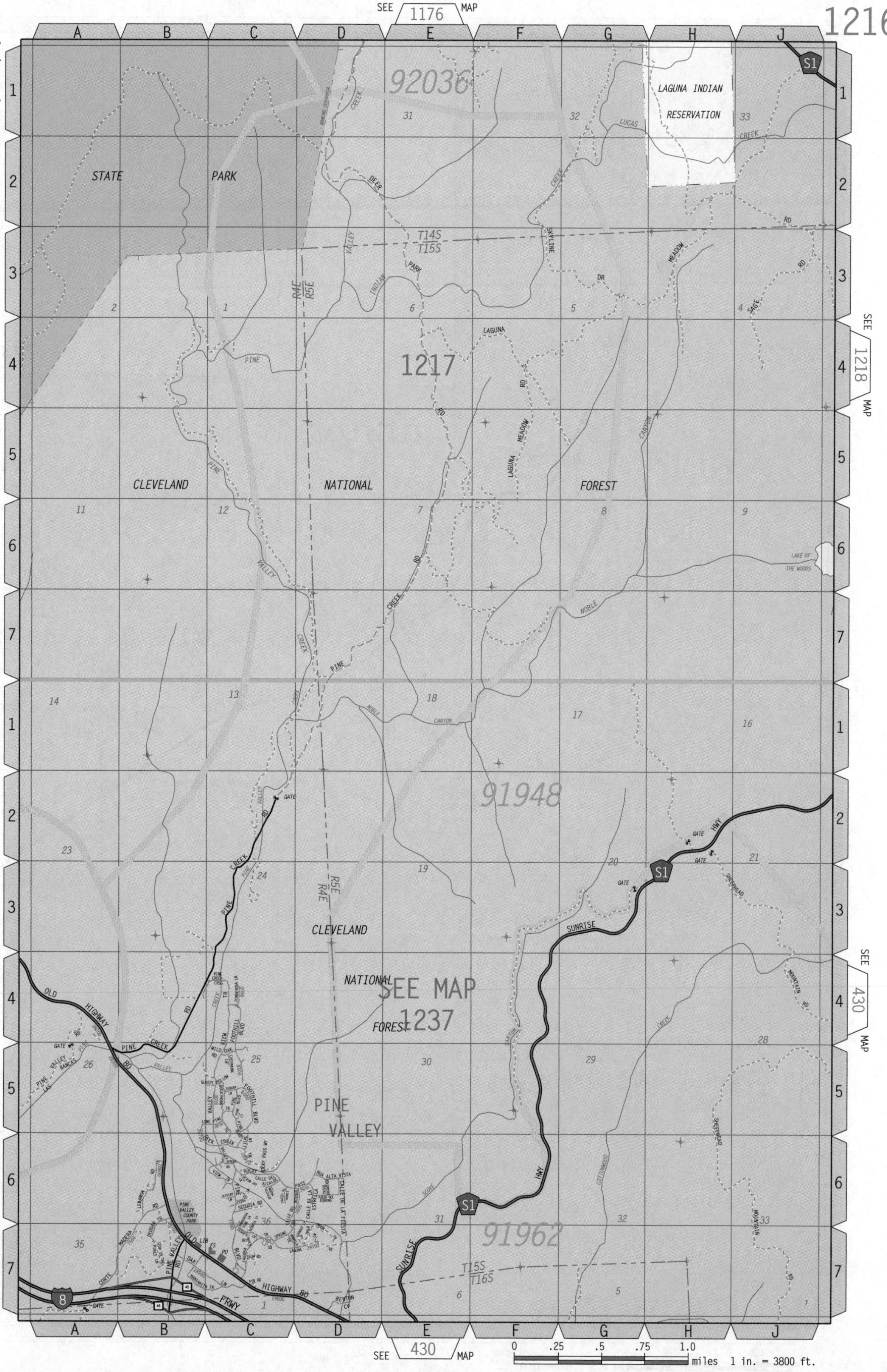
SEE 1176 MAP
SEE 1218 MAP
SEE 430 MAP
SEE 430 MAP
SAN DIEGO CO.
92036
LAGUNA INDIAN RESERVATION
STATE PARK
1217
CLEVELAND NATIONAL FOREST
LAKE OF THE WOODS
91948
CLEVELAND NATIONAL FOREST
SEE MAP 1237
PINE VALLEY
PINE VALLEY COUNTY PARK
91962
T14S T15S
R4E R5E
T15S T16S
OLD HIGHWAY 80
SUNRISE HWY
FRWY
0 .25 .5 .75 1.0 miles 1 in. = 3800 ft.

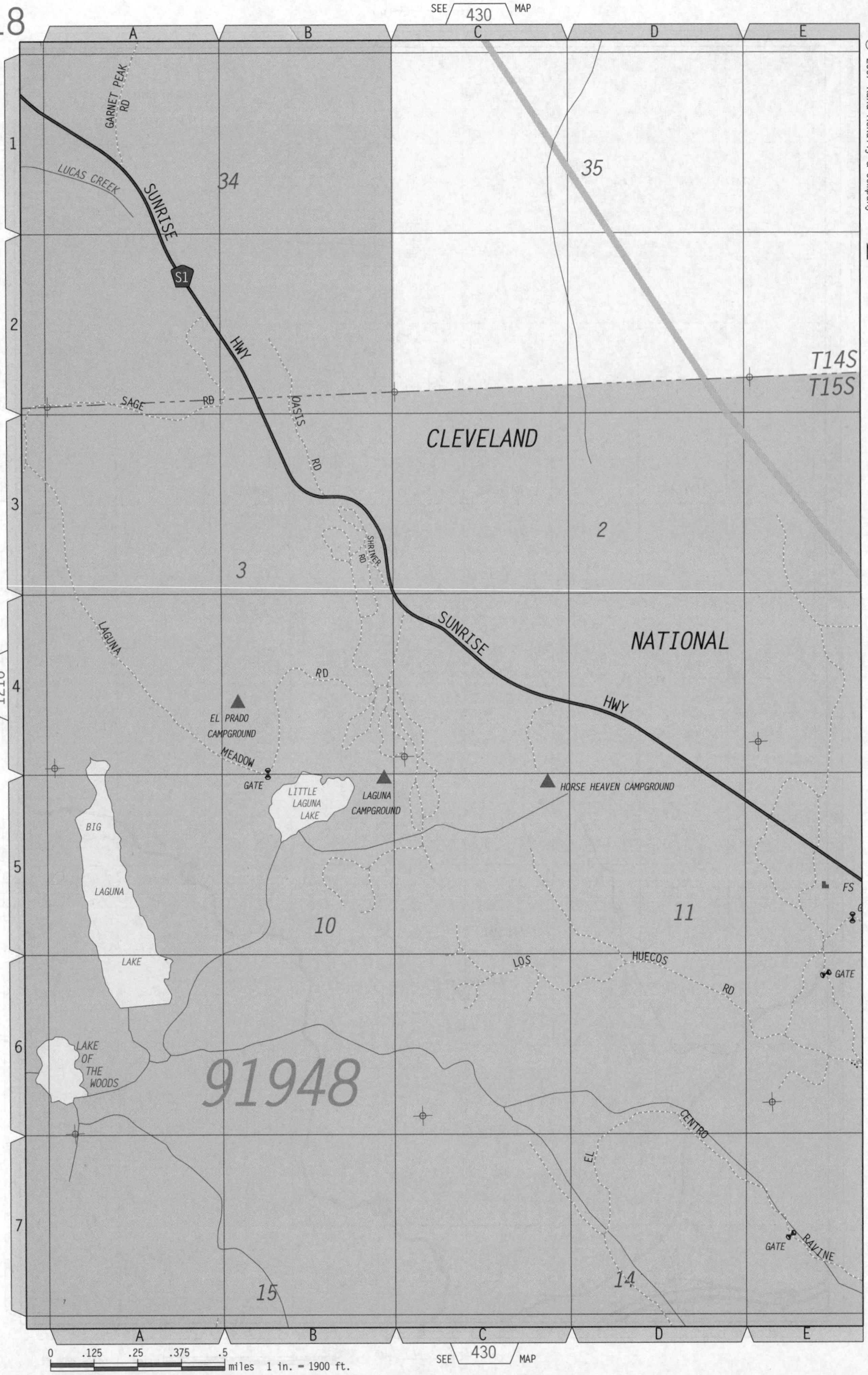
SEE 430 MAP
A
B
C
D
E
1
2
3
4
5
6
7
SAN DIEGO CO.
GARNET PEAK RD
LUCAS CREEK
SUNRISE
S1
HWY
34
35
T14S
T15S
SAGE RD
OASIS RD
CLEVELAND
2
3
SHRINER RD
SUNRISE
NATIONAL
HWY
LAGUNA
RD
SEE 1216 MAP
EL PRADO CAMPGROUND
MEADOW
GATE
LITTLE LAGUNA LAKE
LAGUNA CAMPGROUND
HORSE HEAVEN CAMPGROUND
BIG LAGUNA LAKE
FS
10
11
LOS HUECOS RD
GATE
LAKE OF THE WOODS
91948
EL CENTRO
RAVINE
GATE
15
14
A
B
C
D
E
0 .125 .25 .375 .5 miles 1 in. = 1900 ft.
SEE 430 MAP

SEE 430 MAP
E
F
G
H
J
36
31
32
92036
T14S
T15S
1
6
5
R6E
R5E
MONUMENT
PEAK
RD
FOREST
PIEDRA TRACT
FS
GATE
12
7
FAA
RADAR
STATION
SUNRISE
HWY
BOILING SPRINGS RD
MOUNT
LAGUNA
PICNIC GROUNDS
LOS
HUECOS
RD
EL CENTRO
TER
S1
PO
13
AVINE
RD
91962
18
CUYAPAIPE INDIAN RESERVATION
1
2
3
4
5
6
7
SAN DIEGO CO.
0 .125 .25 .375 .5
miles 1 in. = 1900 ft.

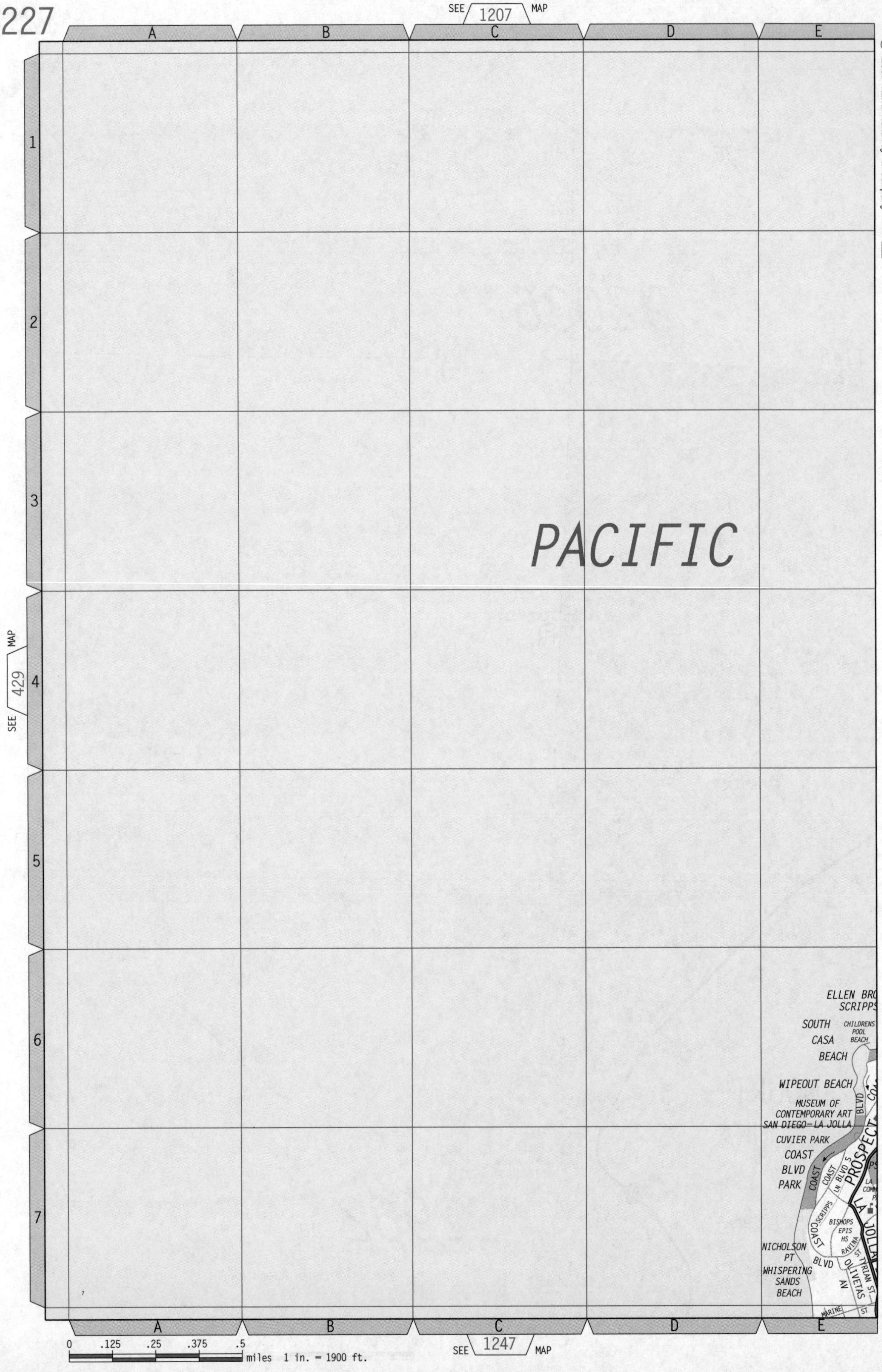
SEE 1207 MAP
A
B
C
D
E
1
2
3
4
5
6
7
SEE 429 MAP
PACIFIC
ELLEN BR
SCRIPPS
SOUTH
CASA
BEACH
CHILDRENS
POOL
BEACH
WIPEOUT BEACH
MUSEUM OF
CONTEMPORARY ART
SAN DIEGO-LA JOLLA
CUVIER PARK
COAST
BLVD
PARK
COAST
BLVD
COAST
LN
BLVD S
PROSPECT
LA
JOLLA
SCRIPPS
COAST
BLVD
BISHOPS
EPIS
HS
RAVINA
ST
TYRIAN ST
OLIVETAS
AV
NICHOLSON
PT
WHISPERING
SANDS
BEACH
MARINE
ST
0
.125
.25
.375
.5
miles 1 in. = 1900 ft.
SEE 1247 MAP

SEE 1207 MAP

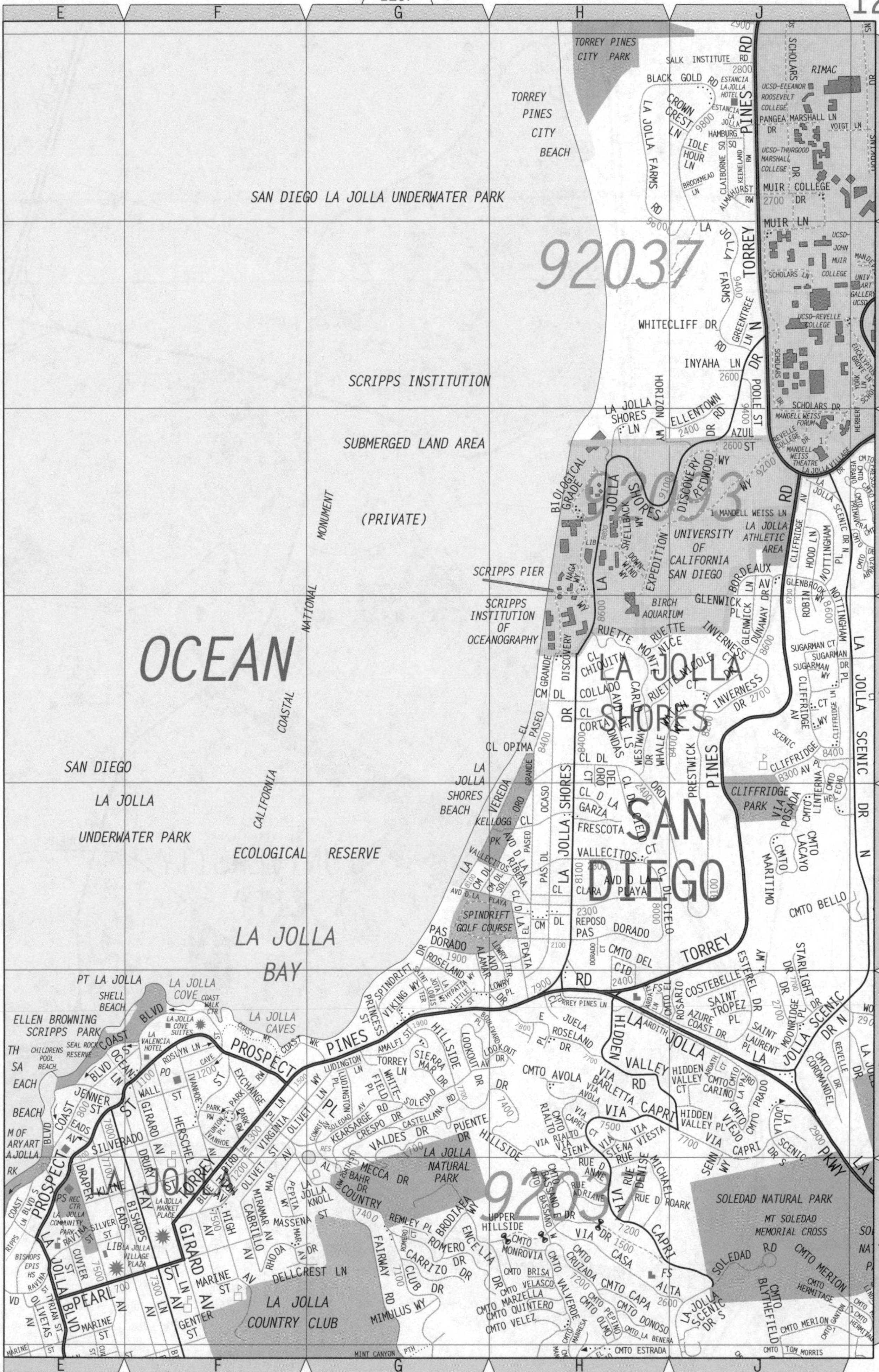

SEE 1228 MAP

SEE 1247 MAP

0 .125 .25 .375 .5 miles 1 in. = 1900 ft.

SAN DIEGO CO.

SEE 1208 MAP

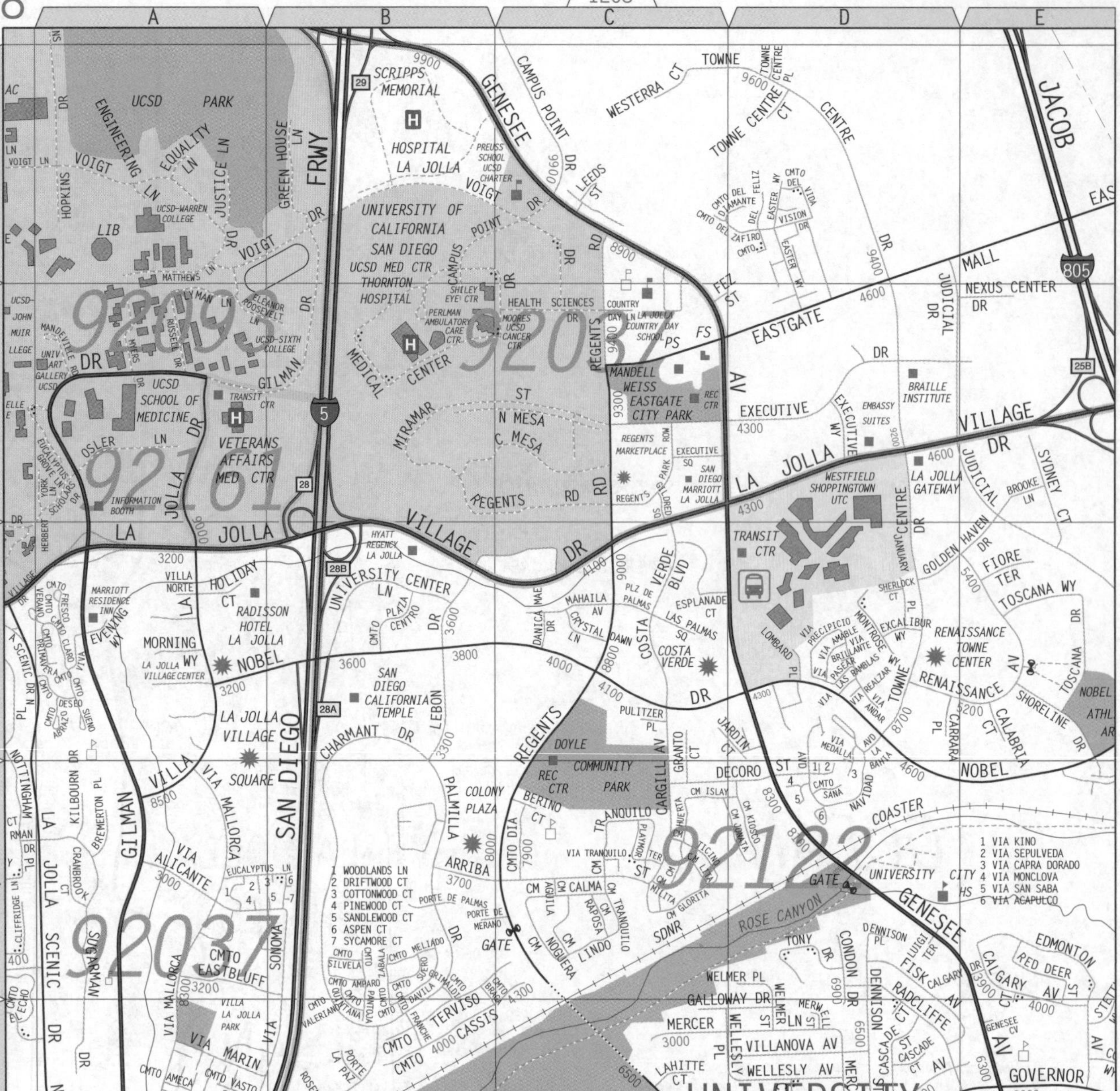

SEE 1227 MAP

SEE 1248 MAP

0 .125 .25 .375 .5 miles 1 in. = 1900 ft.

SEE 1208 MAP

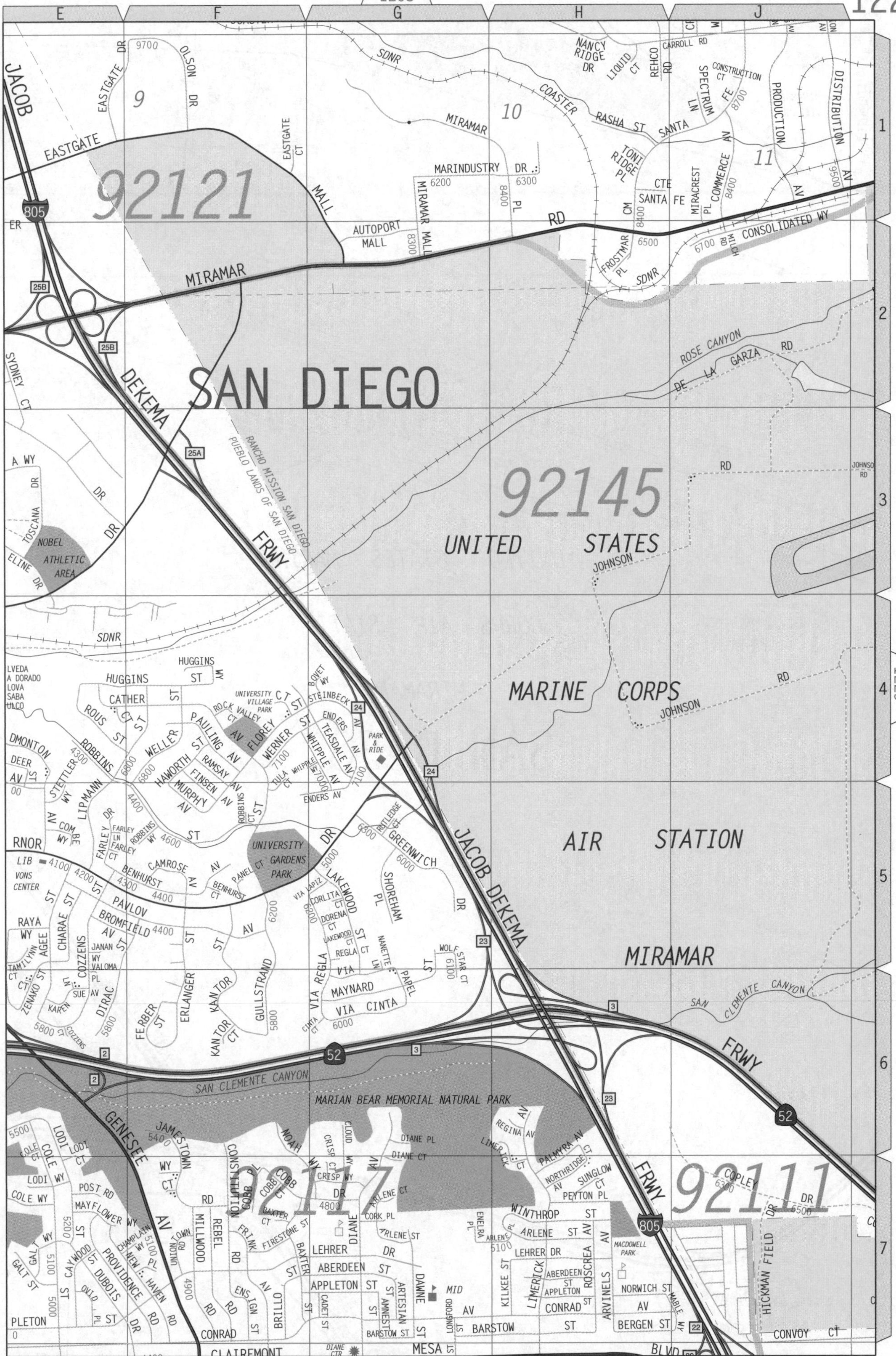

SEE 1229 MAP

SEE 1248 MAP

0 .125 .25 .375 .5 miles 1 in. = 1900 ft.

SEE 1209 MAP

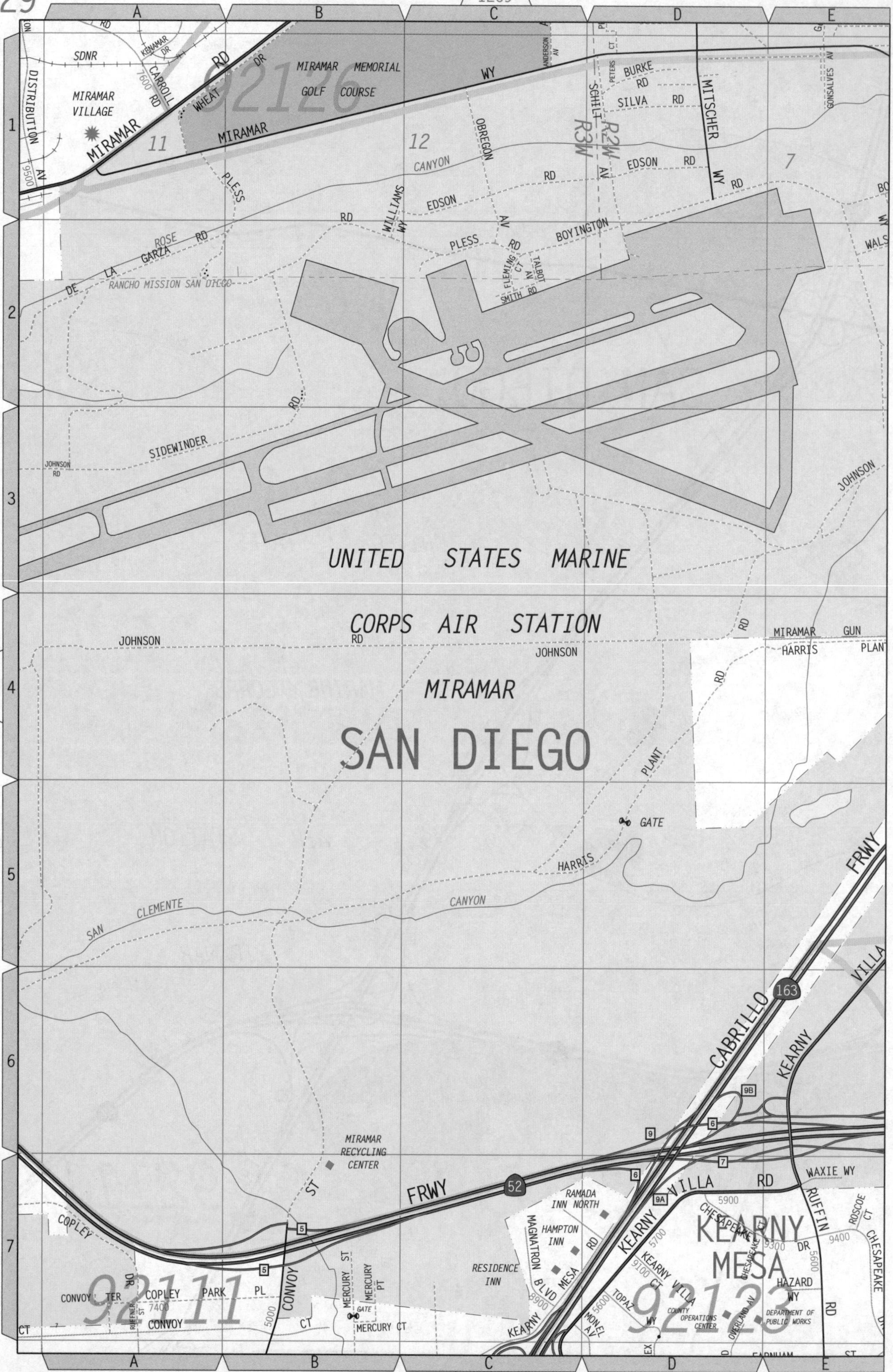

SEE 1228 MAP

SEE 1249 MAP

0 .125 .25 .375 .5 miles 1 in. = 1900 ft.

SEE 1209 MAP

SEE 1230 MAP
SEE 1249 MAP

0 .125 .25 .375 .5 miles 1 in. = 1900 ft.

SAN DIEGO CO.

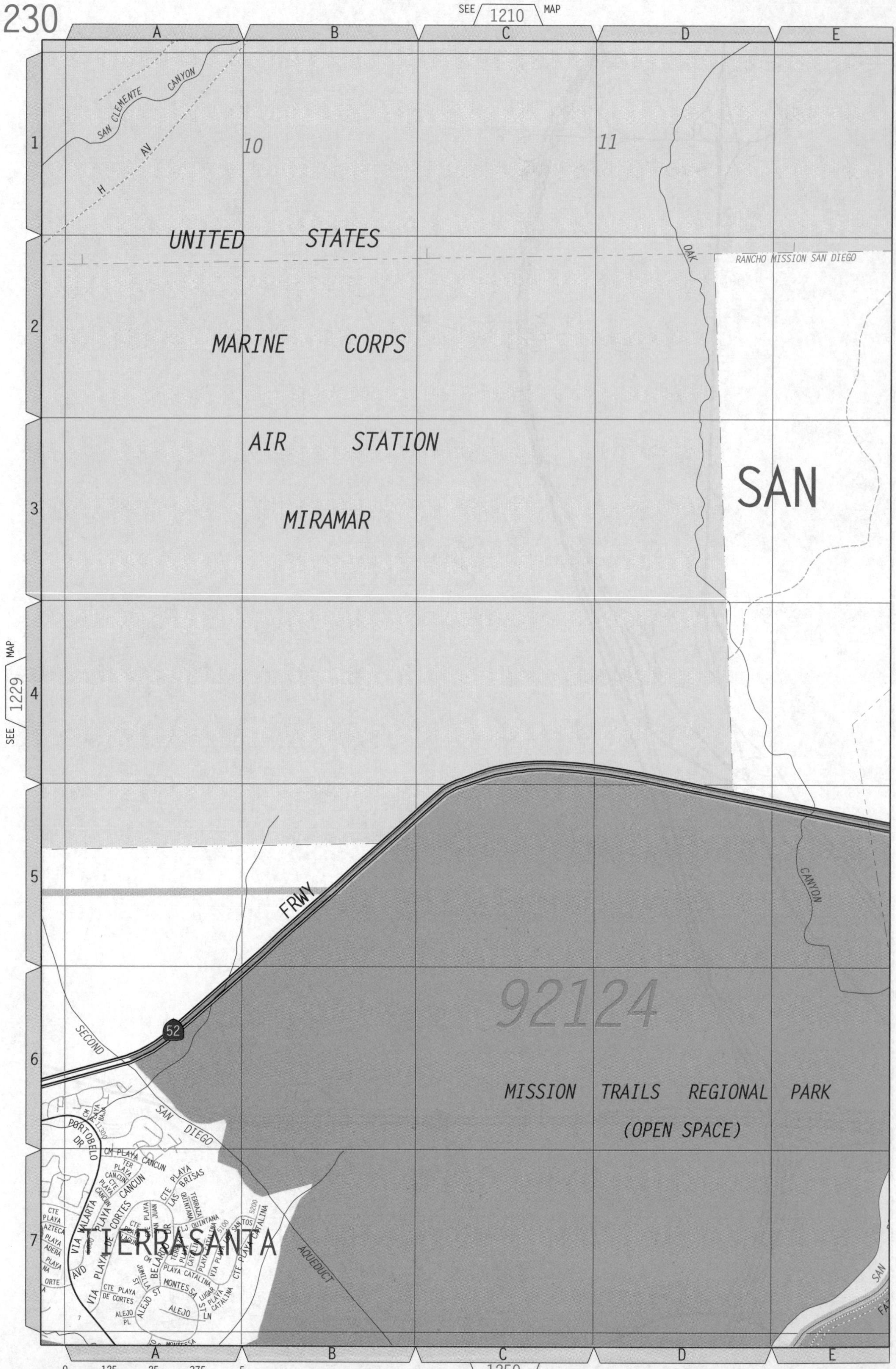
SEE 1210 MAP
A
B
C
D
E
1
2
3
4
5
6
7
SEE 1229 MAP
SAN CLEMENTE CANYON
H AV
10
11
UNITED STATES
MARINE CORPS
AIR STATION
MIRAMAR
OAK
RANCHO MISSION SAN DIEGO
SAN
FRWY
CANYON
92124
52
SECOND
SAN DIEGO
MISSION TRAILS REGIONAL PARK
(OPEN SPACE)
PORTOBELO DR
CM PLAYA CANCUN
CTE PLAYA CANCUN
CTE PLAYA LAS BRISAS
VIA VALARTA
PLAYA CORTES
TIERRASANTA
AQUEDUCT
VIA PLAYA DE CORTES
CTE PLAYA DE CORTES
PLAYA CATALINA
CTE PLAYA CATALINA
MONTESSA ST
ALEJO ST
ALEJO PL
ALEJO
BELARDO DR
LUGAR PLAYA CATALINA
AVD
SEE 1250 MAP
0 .125 .25 .375 .5
miles 1 in. = 1900 ft.

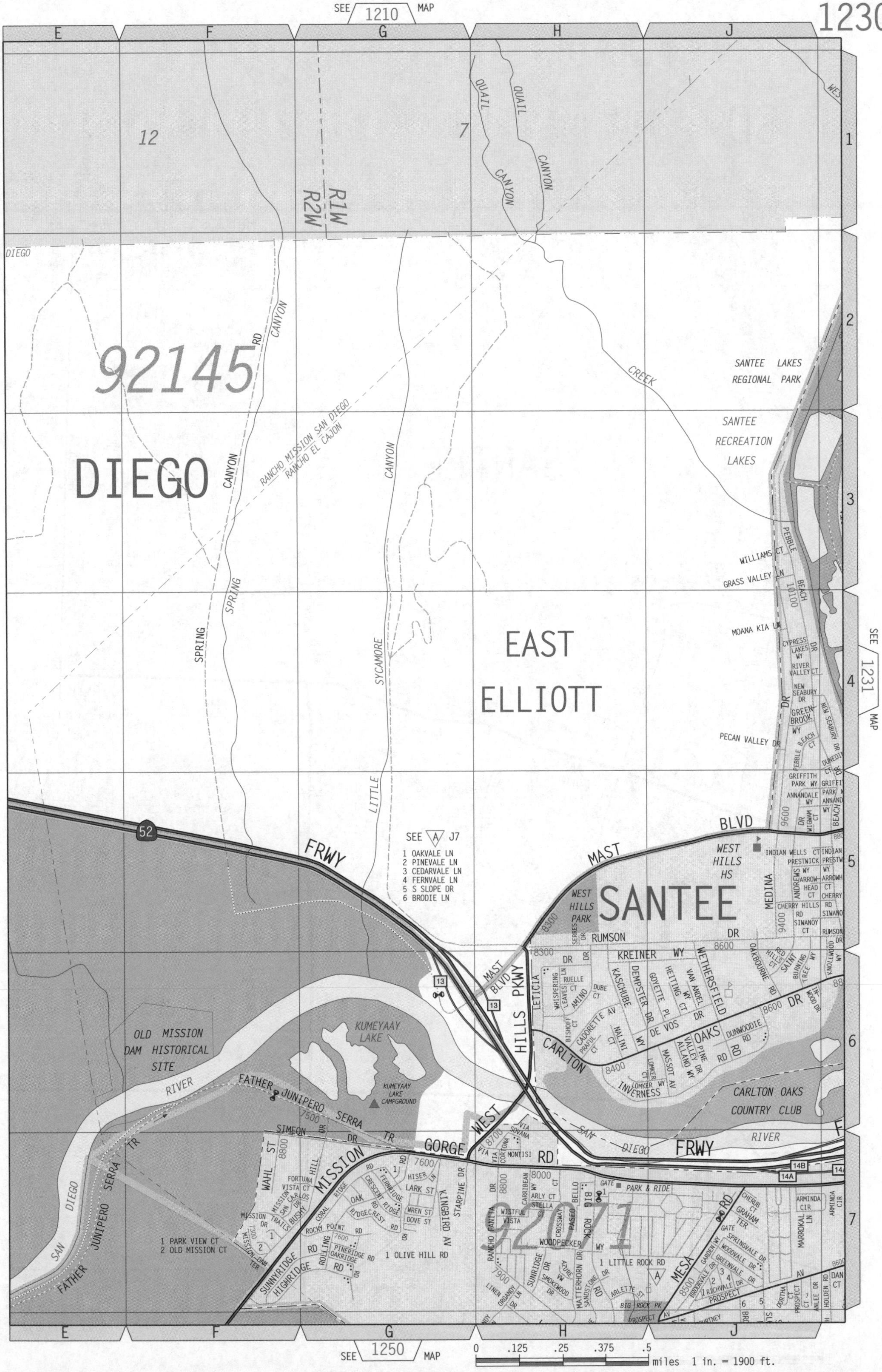
SEE 1210 MAP
SEE 1231 MAP
SEE 1250 MAP
E
F
G
H
J
1
2
3
4
5
6
7
12
7
R1W
R2W
QUAIL CANYON
QUAIL CANYON
92145
DIEGO
EAST ELLIOTT
SANTEE
92071
SPRING CANYON RD
SPRING CANYON
SYCAMORE CANYON
LITTLE SYCAMORE CANYON
RANCHO MISSION SAN DIEGO
RANCHO EL CAJON
CREEK
SANTEE LAKES REGIONAL PARK
SANTEE RECREATION LAKES
WILLIAMS CT
GRASS VALLEY LN
PEBBLE BEACH DR
MOANA KIA LN
PECAN VALLEY DR
52
FRWY
MAST BLVD
WEST HILLS HS
WEST HILLS PARK
SEE A J7
1 OAKVALE LN
2 PINEVALE LN
3 CEDARVALE LN
4 FERNVALE LN
5 S SLOPE DR
6 BRODIE LN
RUMSON DR
KREINER WY
WETHERSFIELD
MEDINA
CARLTON OAKS DR
CARLTON OAKS COUNTRY CLUB
WEST HILLS PKWY
INVERNESS
KUMEYAAY LAKE
KUMEYAAY LAKE CAMPGROUND
OLD MISSION DAM HISTORICAL SITE
SAN DIEGO RIVER
SAN DIEGO FRWY
FATHER JUNIPERO SERRA TR
MISSION GORGE RD
SIMEON DR
1 PARK VIEW CT
2 OLD MISSION CT
1 OLIVE HILL RD
PARK & RIDE
WOODPECKER WY
1 LITTLE ROCK RD
MESA RD
BIG ROCK RD
PROSPECT AV
14A
14B
0 .125 .25 .375 .5
miles 1 in. = 1900 ft.

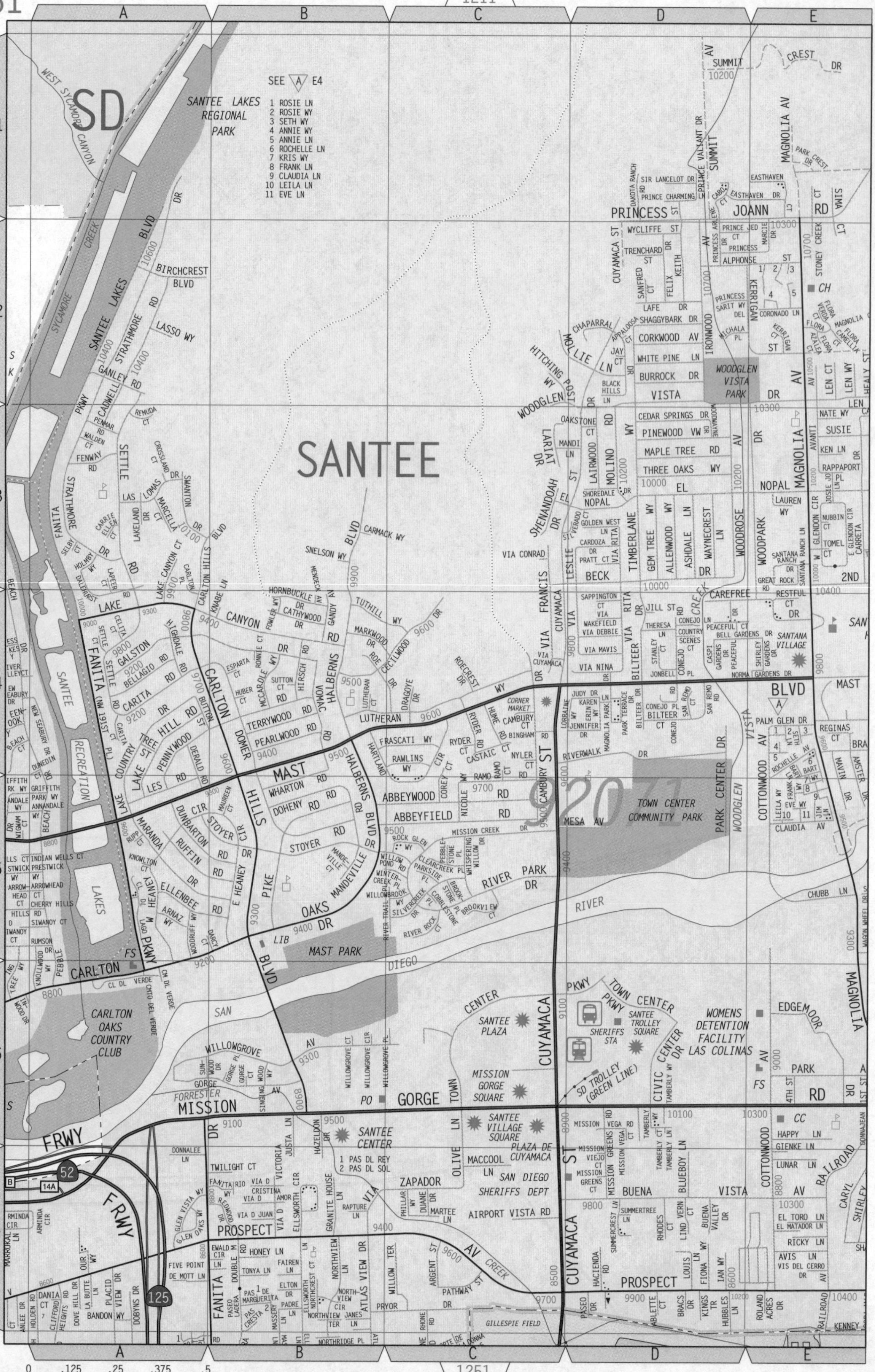
SEE 1211 MAP
SEE 1251 MAP
SEE 1230 MAP
SANTEE
SD
92071
SANTEE LAKES REGIONAL PARK
SEE A E4
1 ROSIE LN
2 ROSIE WY
3 SETH WY
4 ANNIE WY
5 ANNIE LN
6 ROCHELLE LN
7 KRIS WY
8 FRANK LN
9 CLAUDIA LN
10 LEILA LN
11 EVE LN
WOODGLEN VISTA PARK
TOWN CENTER COMMUNITY PARK
MAST PARK
CARLTON OAKS COUNTRY CLUB
SANTEE PLAZA
MISSION GORGE SQUARE
SANTEE VILLAGE SQUARE
PLAZA DE CUYAMACA
SANTEE CENTER
SANTEE TROLLEY SQUARE
SHERIFFS STA
SAN DIEGO SHERIFFS DEPT
WOMENS DETENTION FACILITY LAS COLINAS
SANTANA VILLAGE
CORNER MARKET
SD TROLLEY (GREEN LINE)
GILLESPIE FIELD
SAN DIEGO RIVER
MISSION GORGE RD
MAST BLVD
CUYAMACA ST
MAGNOLIA AV
CARLTON OAKS DR
PROSPECT AV
WOODSIDE AV
SANTEE LAKES BLVD
FANITA PKWY
CARLTON HILLS BLVD
PRINCESS JOANN RD
WOODGLEN VISTA DR
FRWY
52
125
0 .125 .25 .375 .5 miles 1 in. = 1900 ft.

SEE 1211 MAP

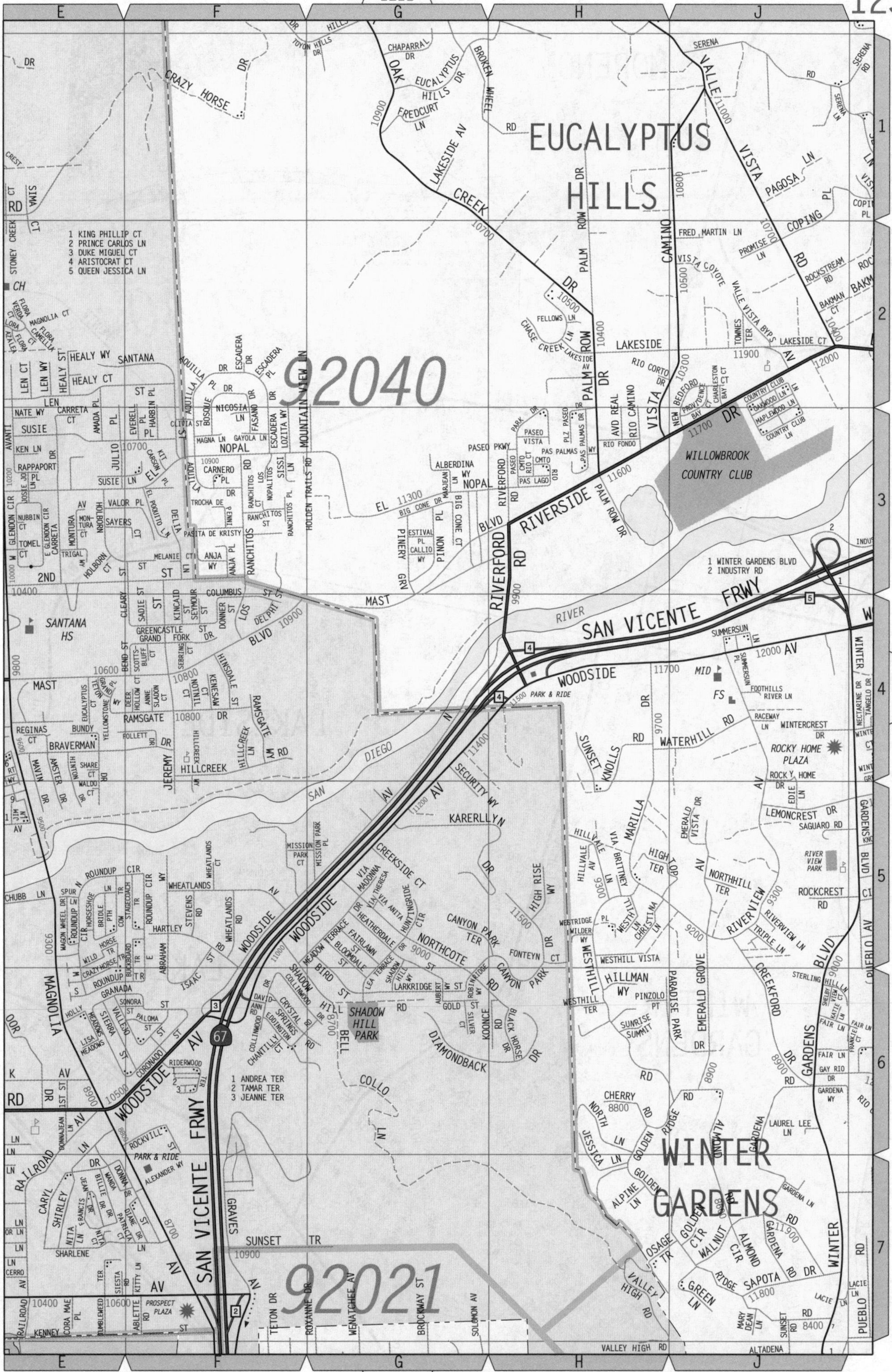

SEE 1232 MAP

SEE 1251 MAP

0 .125 .25 .375 .5 miles 1 in. = 1900 ft.

SEE 1212 MAP

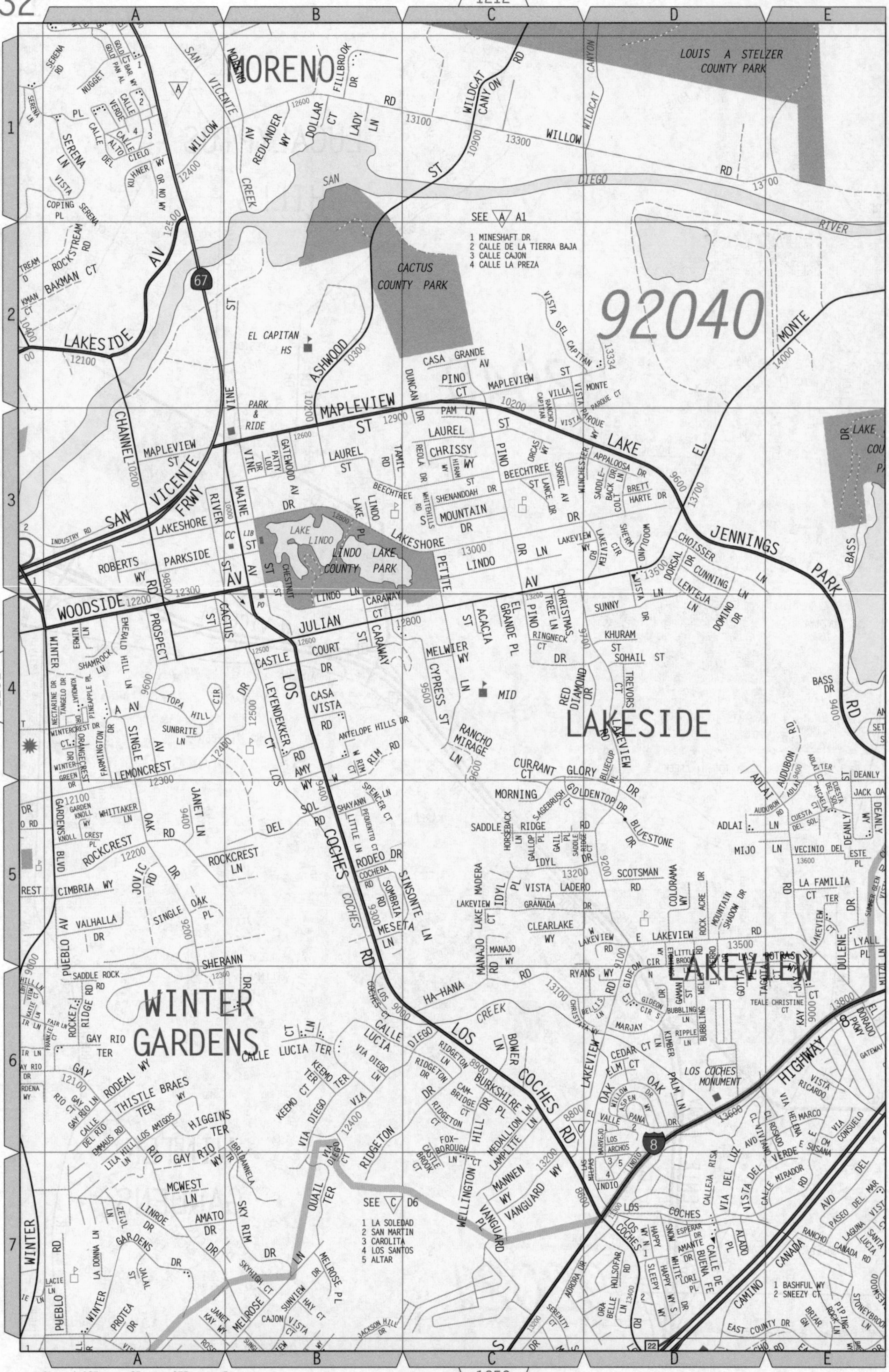

SEE 1231 MAP

SEE 1252 MAP

0 .125 .25 .375 .5 miles 1 in. = 1900 ft.

SEE 1212 MAP

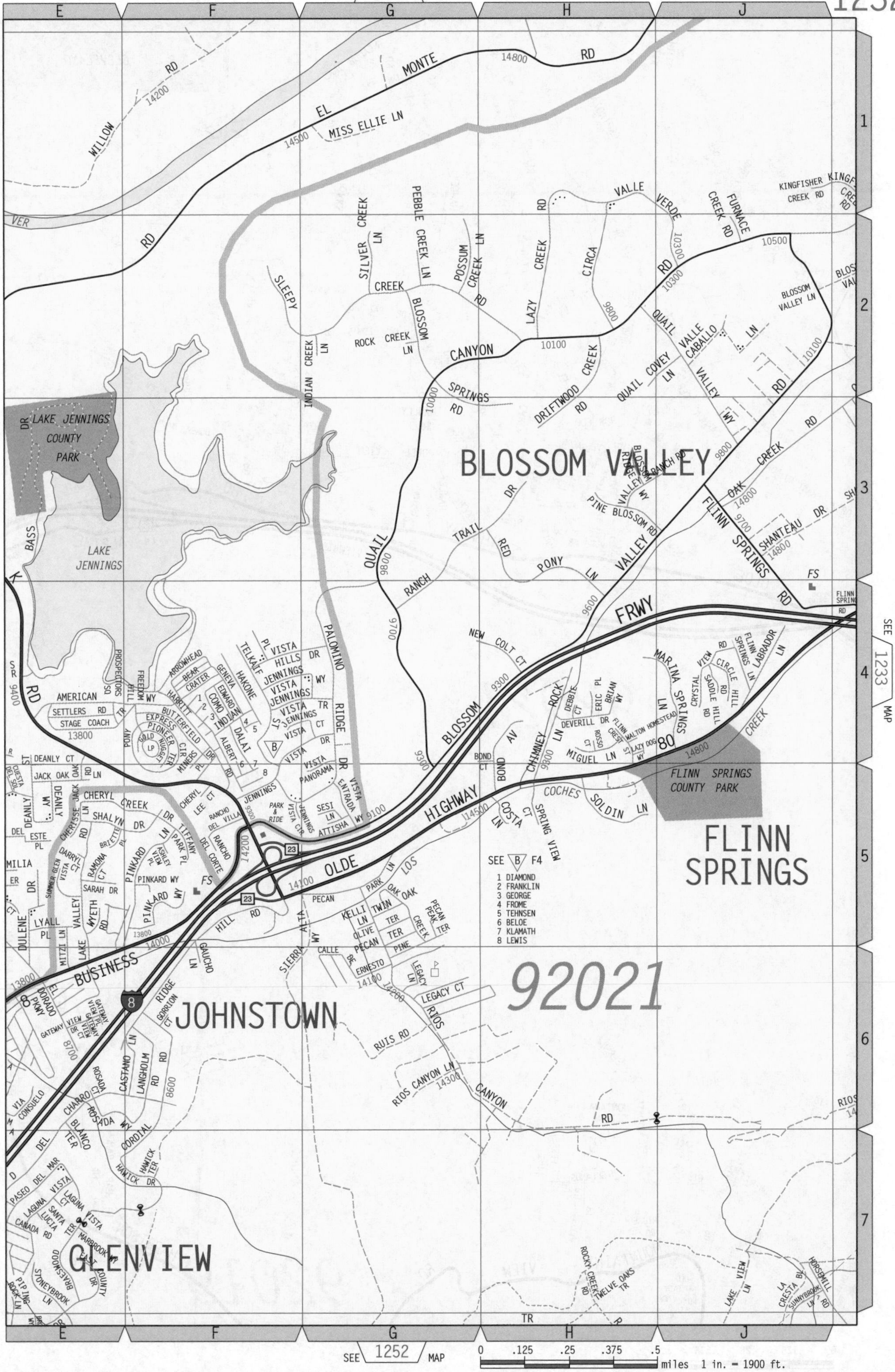

SEE 1252 MAP

0 .125 .25 .375 .5 miles 1 in. = 1900 ft.

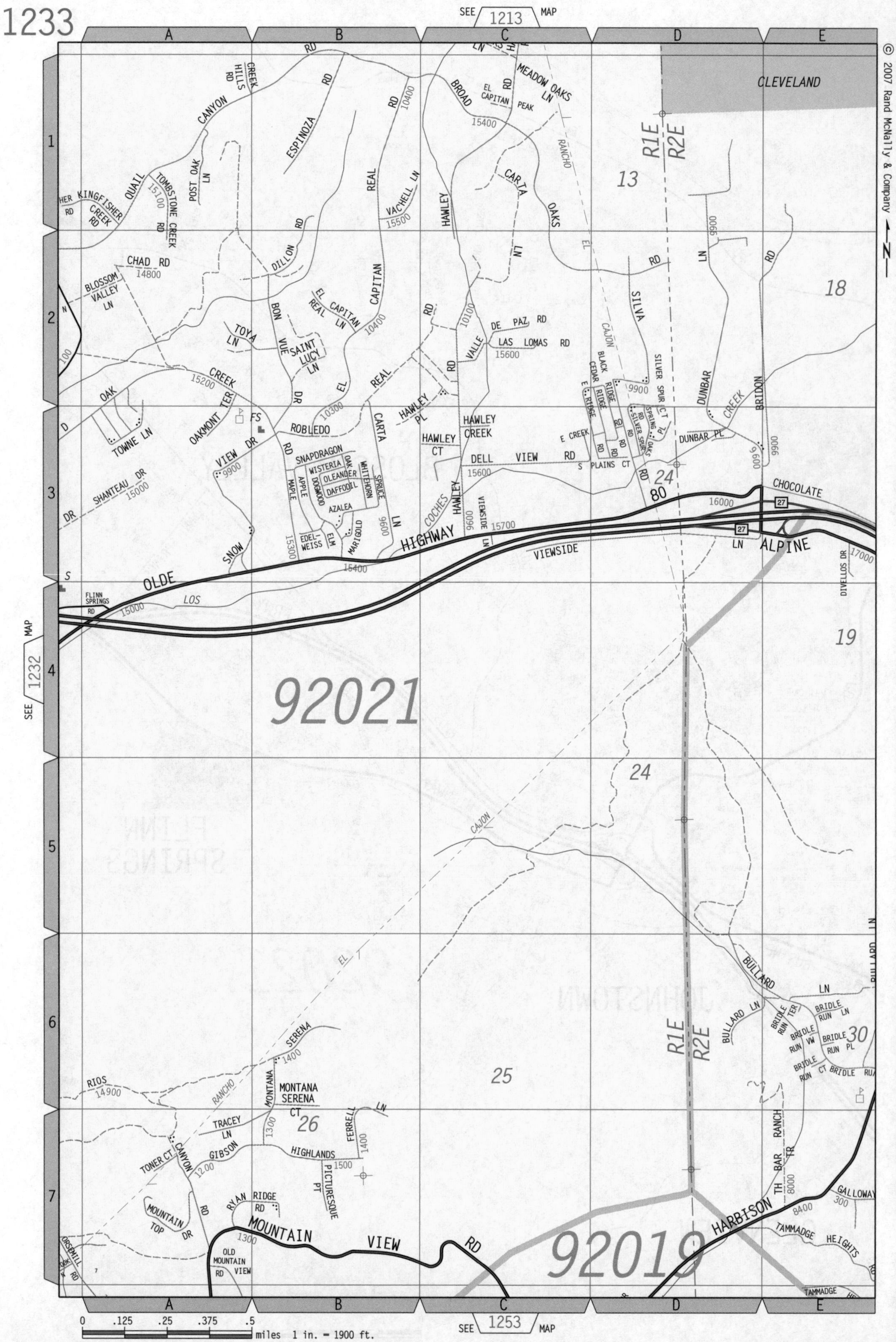
SEE 1213 MAP
SEE 1232 MAP
SEE 1253 MAP
SAN DIEGO CO.
© 2007 Rand McNally & Company
CLEVELAND
R1E R2E
92021
92019
FLINN SPRINGS
JOHNSTOWN
OLDE HIGHWAY 80
ALPINE
CHOCOLATE
MOUNTAIN VIEW RD
HARBISON
CANYON
ESPINOZA RD
EL CAPITAN REAL RD
HAWLEY CREEK
DELL VIEW RD
LAS LOMAS RD
DE PAZ RD
SILVA RD
DUNBAR LN
BRIDON RD
BULLARD LN
BRIDLE RUN LN
GALLOWAY
TAMMADGE HEIGHTS
MONTANA SERENA CT
GIBSON HIGHLANDS
PICTURESQUE PT
RYAN RIDGE RD
MOUNTAIN TOP DR
TONER CT
TRACEY LN
FERRELL LN
ROBLEDO
SNAPDRAGON
WISTERIA
OLEANDER
DAFFODIL
AZALEA
MARIGOLD
SPRUCE LN
CHAD RD
BLOSSOM VALLEY LN
KINGFISHER CREEK RD
QUAIL CANYON RD
TOMBSTONE CREEK RD
POST OAK LN
DILLON RD
VACHELL LN
MEADOW OAKS LN
BROAD RD
OAKMONT TER
TOWNE LN
SHANTEAU DR
VIEWSIDE
miles 1 in. = 1900 ft.

SEE 1213 MAP

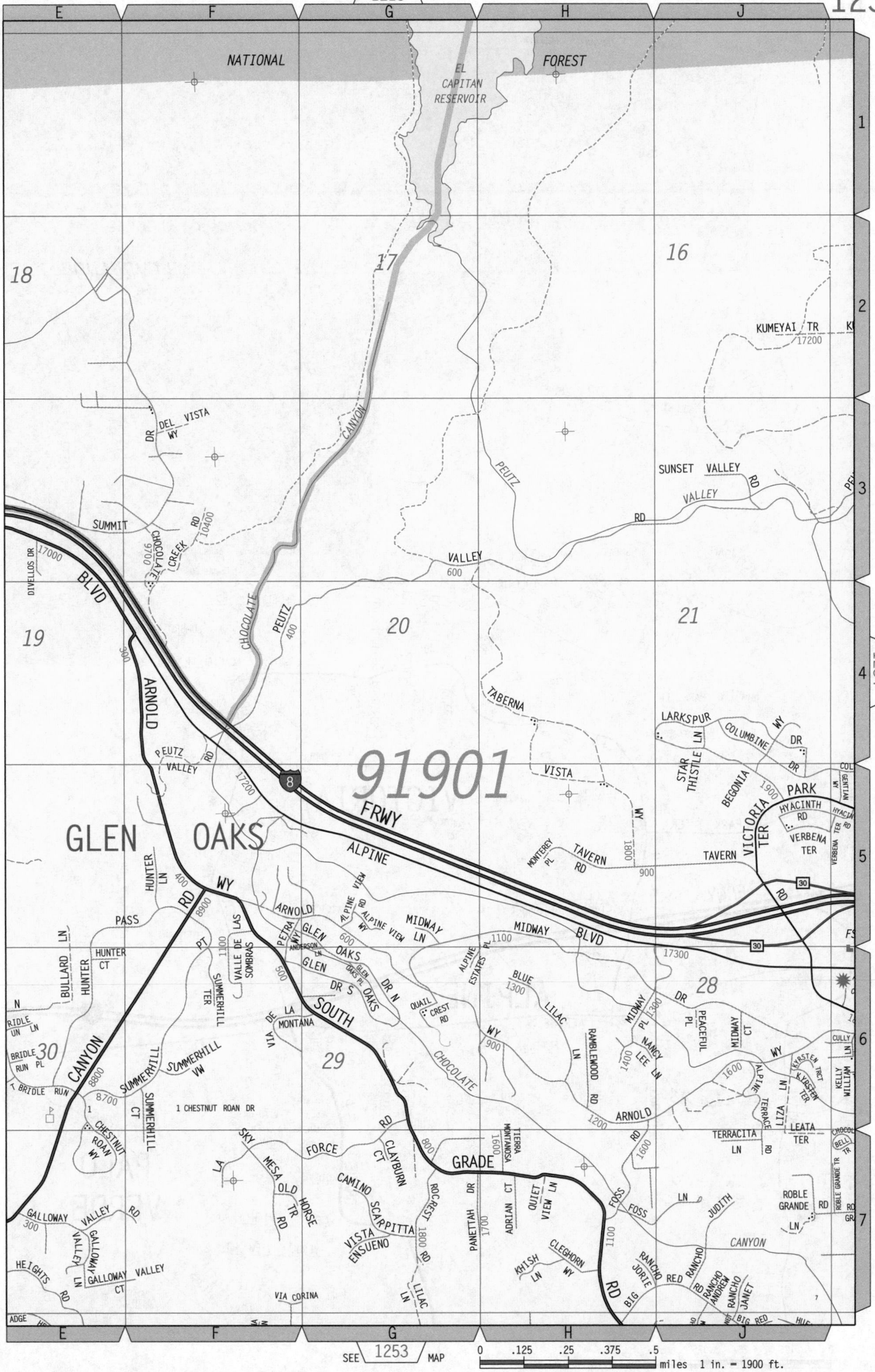

SEE 1234 MAP

SEE 1253 MAP

0 .125 .25 .375 .5 miles 1 in. = 1900 ft.

SEE 429 MAP

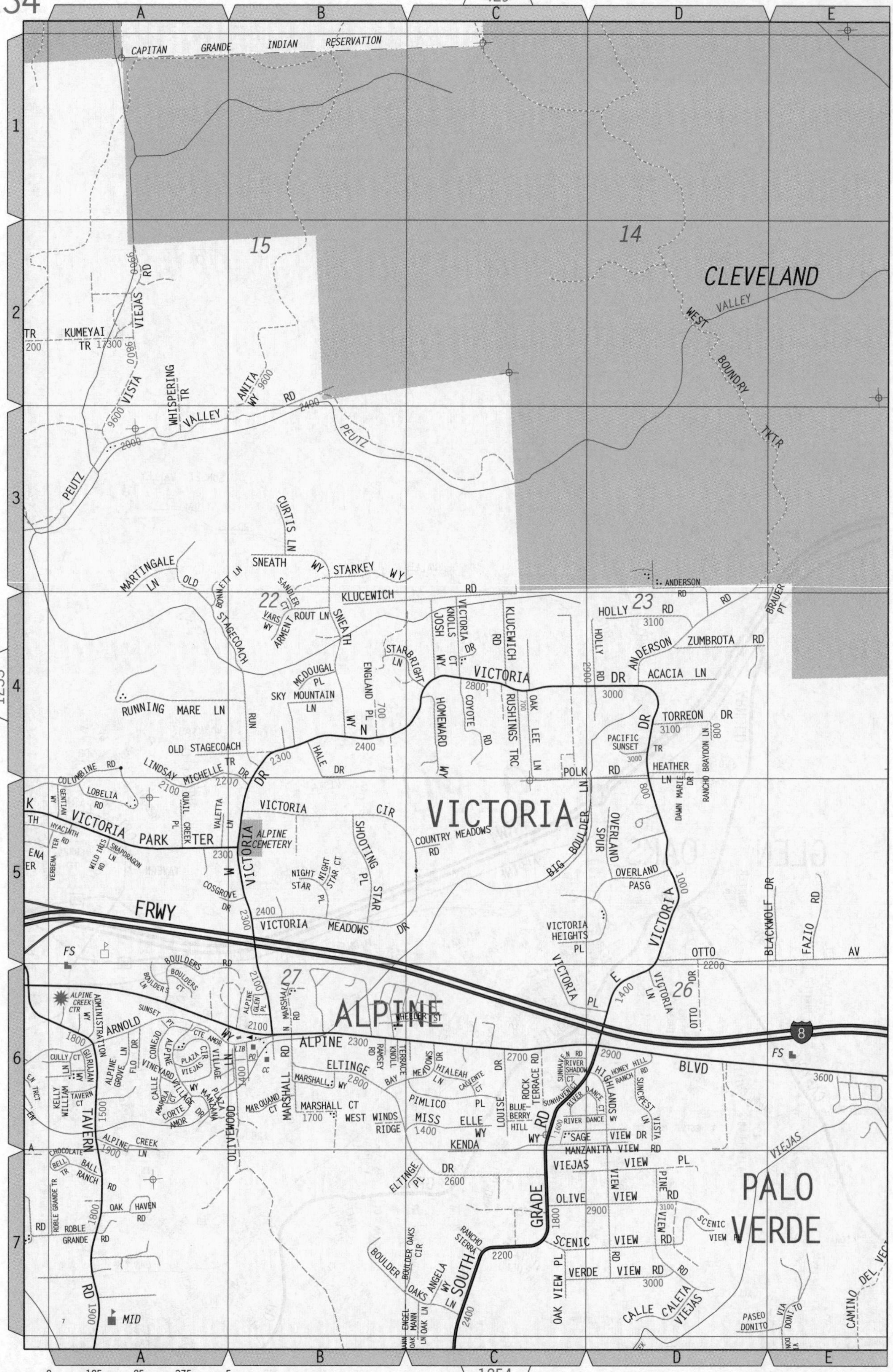

SEE 1233 MAP

SEE 1254 MAP

SAN DIEGO CO.

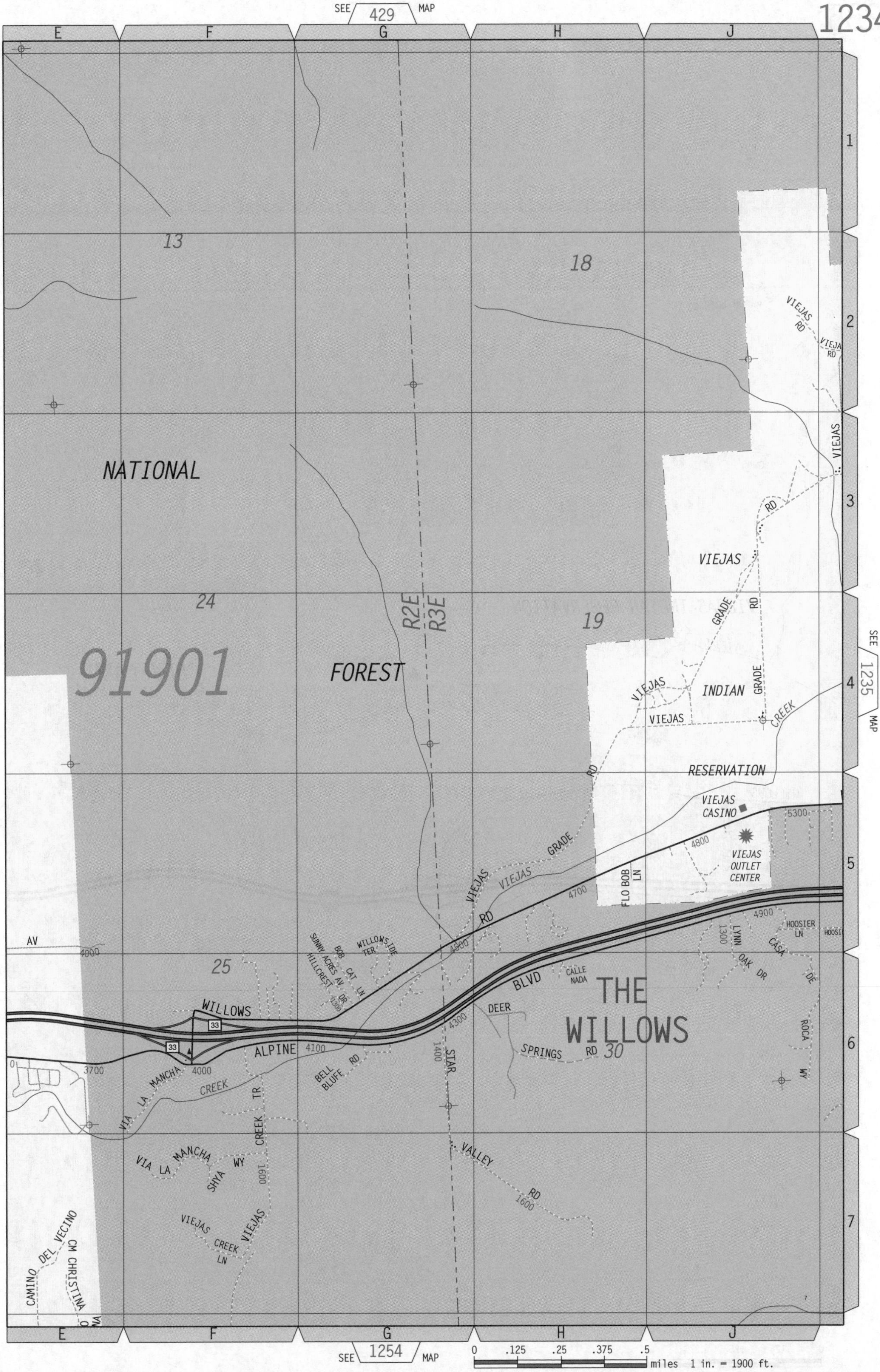

SEE 429 MAP
E
F
G
H
J
1
2
3
4
5
6
7
13
18
19
24
25
30
NATIONAL
FOREST
91901
R2E
R3E
VIEJAS
INDIAN
RESERVATION
VIEJAS RD
VIEJAS GRADE RD
VIEJAS CREEK
VIEJAS CASINO
VIEJAS OUTLET CENTER
FLO BOB LN
THE WILLOWS
WILLOWS RD
ALPINE BLVD
33
DEER
SPRINGS RD
STAR
VALLEY RD
BELL BLUFF RD
CREEK
VIA LA MANCHA
VIA LA MANCHA WY
SHYA
CREEK TR
VIEJAS CREEK LN
CAMINO DEL VECINO
CM CHRISTINA
WILLOWSIDE TER
BOB CAT LN
SUNNY ACRES AV
HILLCREST DR
CALLE NADA
LYNN OAK DR
CASA DE ROCA WY
HOOSIER LN
AV
3700
4000
4100
4300
4700
4800
4900
5300
1300
1400
1600
SEE 1235 MAP
SEE 1254 MAP
0 .125 .25 .375 .5
miles 1 in. = 1900 ft.

SEE 429 MAP

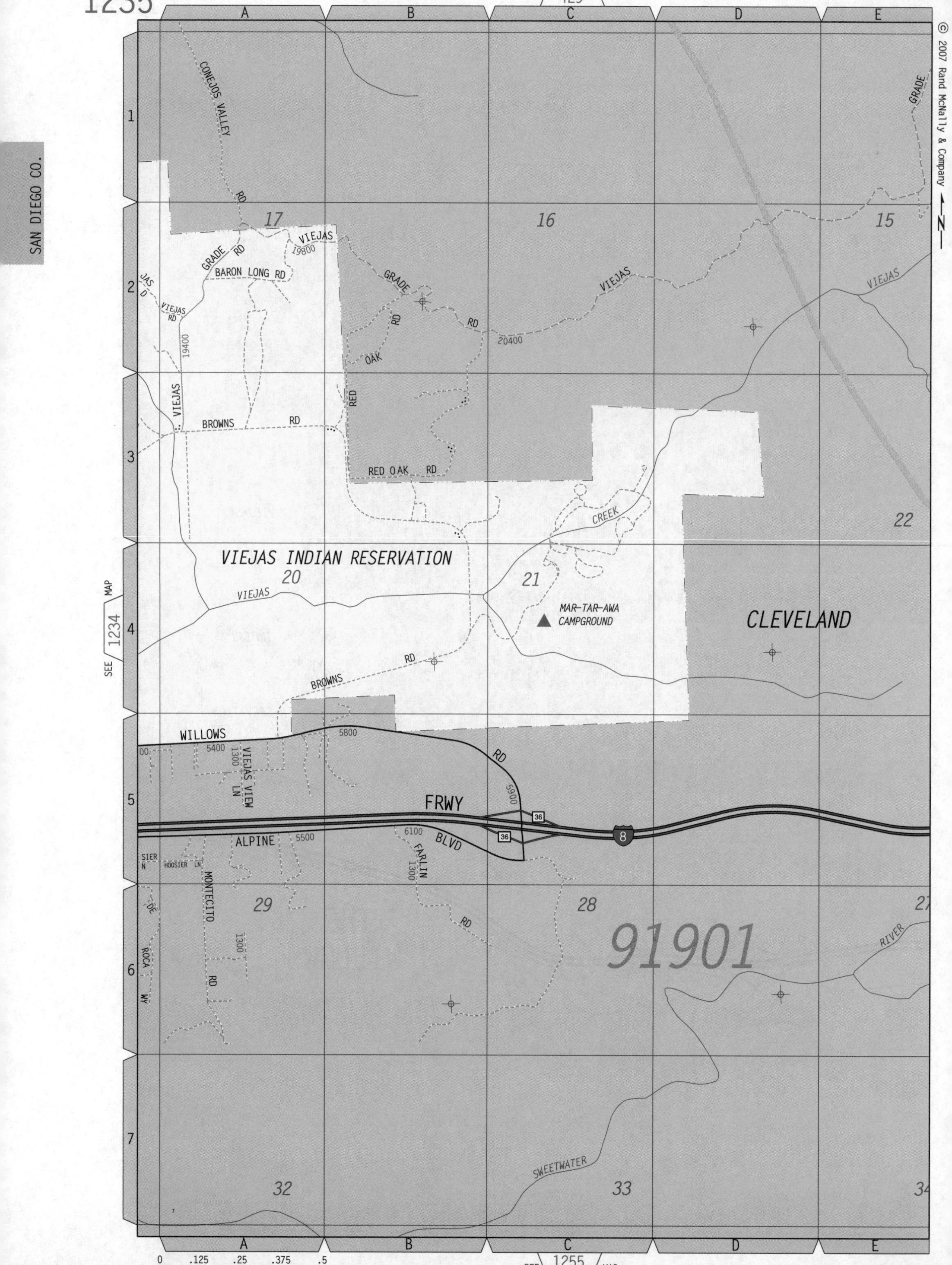

SEE 1234 MAP

SEE 1255 MAP

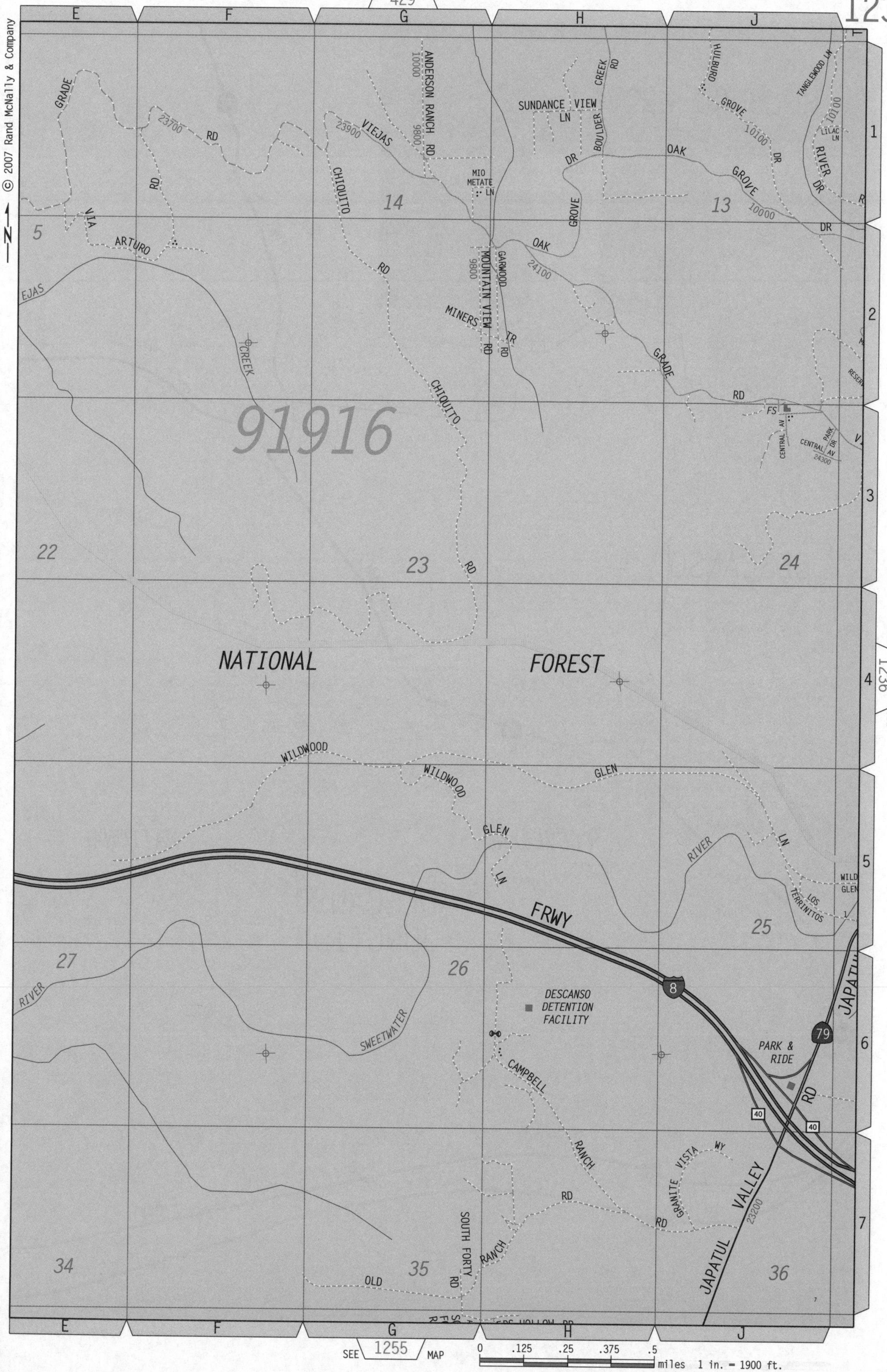
SEE 429 MAP
SEE 1236 MAP
SEE 1255 MAP
SAN DIEGO CO.
91916
NATIONAL
FOREST
ANDERSON RANCH RD
VIEJAS
CHIQUITO
MIO METATE LN
SUNDANCE VIEW LN
BOULDER CREEK RD
HULBURD
GROVE
OAK GROVE DR
TANGLEWOOD LN
LILAC LN
RIVER DR
VIA ARTURO
OAK GROVE
GARWOOD
MOUNTAIN VIEW RD
MINERS TR
CHIQUITO RD
GRADE RD
CENTRAL AV
PARK DR
FS
CREEK
WILDWOOD GLEN LN
RIVER
LOS TERRINITOS
FRWY
SWEETWATER RIVER
DESCANSO DETENTION FACILITY
CAMPBELL RANCH RD
PARK & RIDE
GRANITE VISTA WY
JAPATUL VALLEY RD
SOUTH FORTY RD
RANCH
OLD
miles 1 in. = 1900 ft.
0 .125 .25 .375 .5

SEE 1216 MAP

SEE 1235 MAP

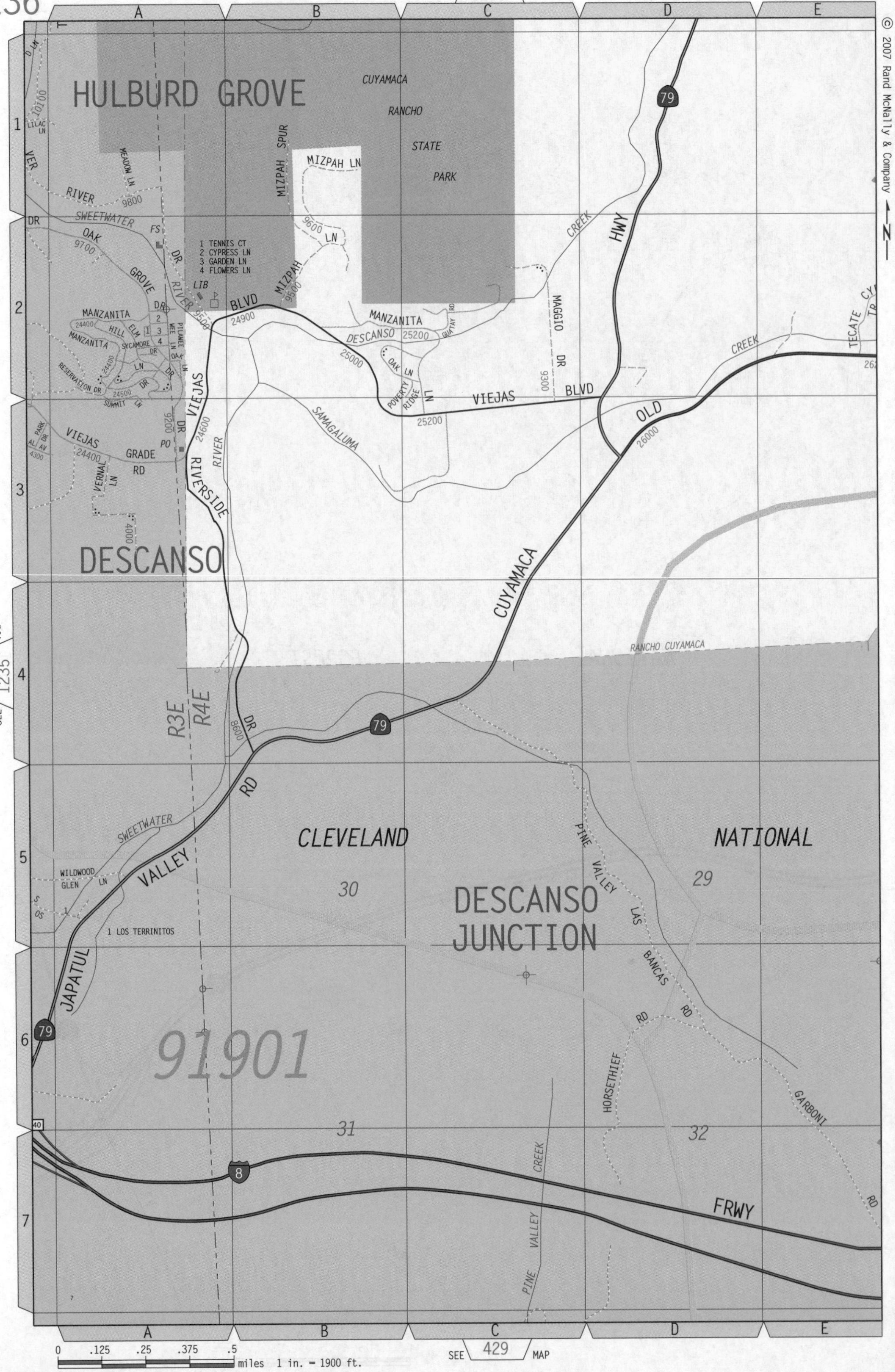

SEE 429 MAP

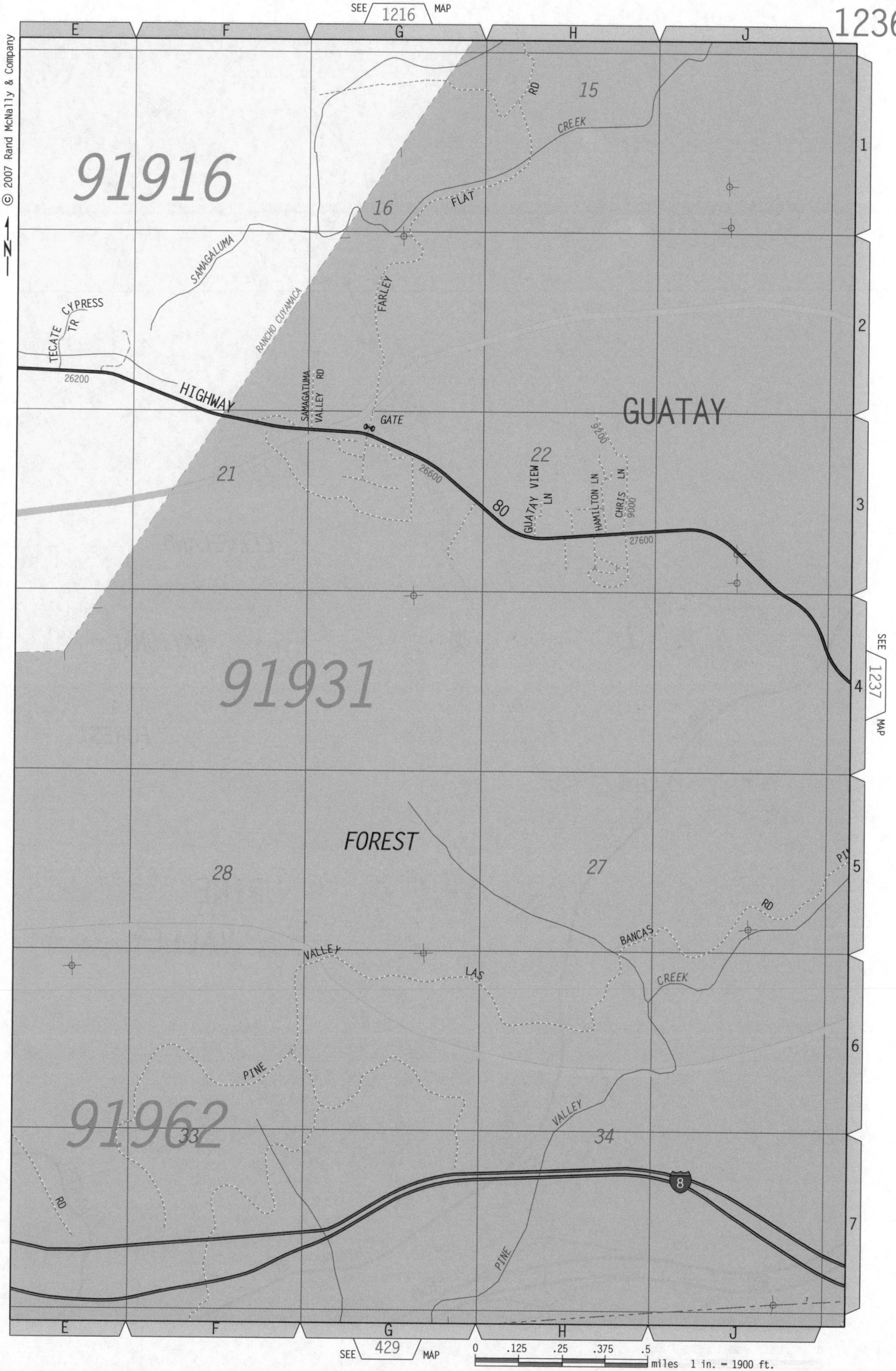
SEE 1216 MAP
SEE 1237 MAP
SEE 429 MAP
E
F
G
H
J
1
2
3
4
5
6
7
N
91916
91931
91962
GUATAY
FOREST
15
16
21
22
27
28
33
34
FLAT CREEK RD
FARLEY
SAMAGALUMA
RANCHO CUYAMACA
TECATE CYPRESS TR
26200
HIGHWAY 80
SAMAGATUMA VALLEY RD
GATE
26600
GUATAY VIEW LN
HAMILTON LN
CHRIS LN
9200
9000
27600
LAS BANCAS CREEK
PINE VALLEY
RD
8
0 .125 .25 .375 .5
miles 1 in. = 1900 ft.

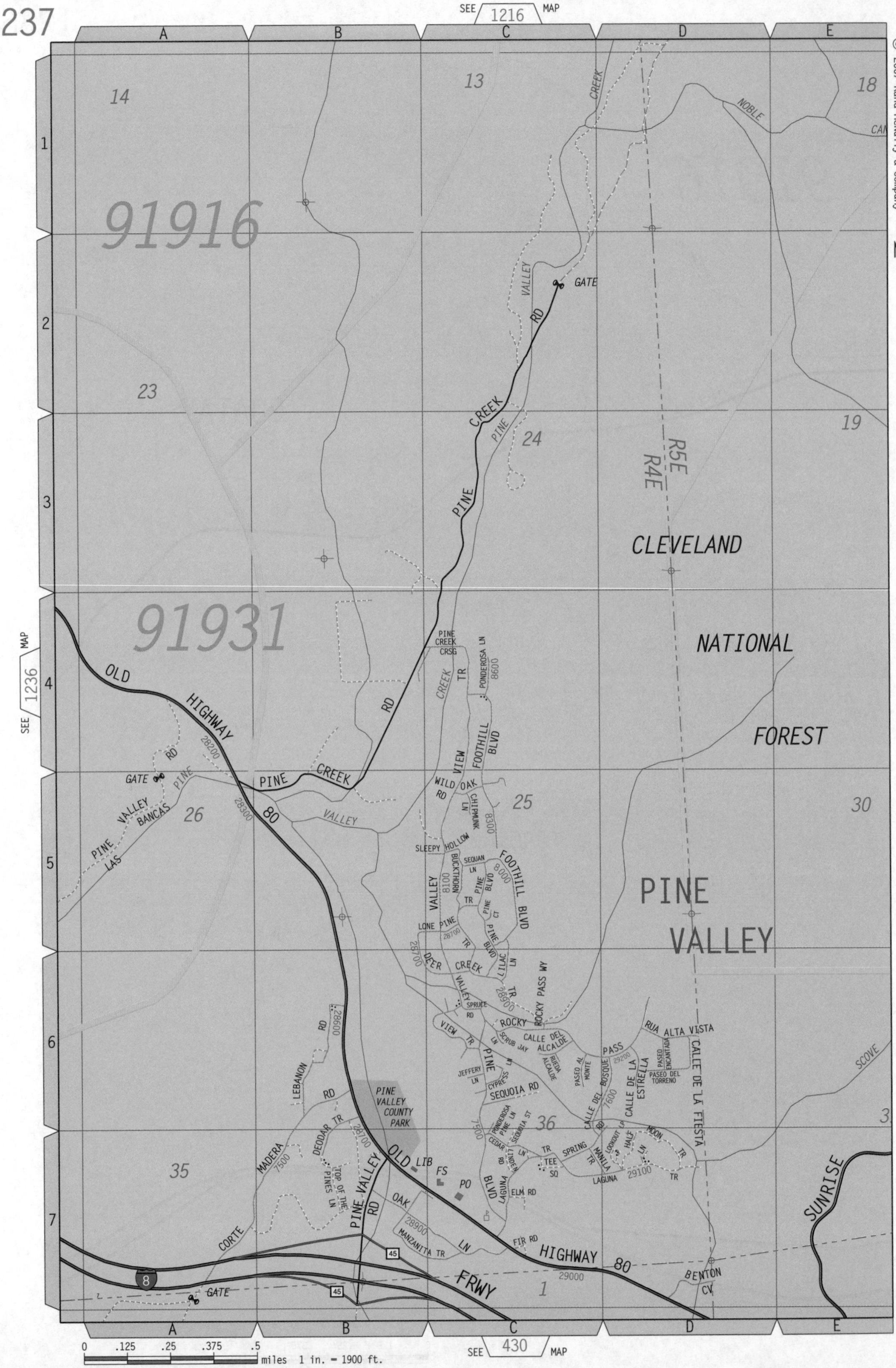
SEE 1216 MAP
SEE 1236 MAP
SEE 430 MAP
A
B
C
D
E
1
2
3
4
5
6
7
14
13
18
23
24
19
26
25
30
35
36
1
91916
91931
CLEVELAND
NATIONAL
FOREST
PINE
VALLEY
R5E
R4E
CREEK
NOBLE
VALLEY
GATE
RD
PINE
CREEK
PINE
RD
OLD
HIGHWAY
80
28200
28300
GATE
PINE
VALLEY
BANCAS
LAS
PINE
CREEK
VALLEY
PINE CREEK CRSG
PONDEROSA LN
8600
CREEK
TR
FOOTHILL BLVD
VIEW
WILD OAK RD
CHIPMUNK LN
8300
SLEEPY HOLLOW
SEQUAN LN
BUCKTHORN
8100
VALLEY
FOOTHILL BLVD
8000
PINE BLVD
TR
PINE CT
LONE PINE
28700
TR
PINE BLVD
LILAC LN
DEER CREEK
VALLEY
28900
TR
ROCKY PASS WY
SPRUCE RD
ROCKY
VIEW TR
LN
SCRUB JAY
CALLE DEL ALCALDE
RUEDA ALCALDE
PASEO AL MONTE
PASS
29200
RUA ALTA VISTA
PASEO ENCANTADA
PASEO DEL TORRENO
CALLE DE LA FIESTA
CALLE DE LA ESTRELLA
CALLE DEL BOSQUE
7600
JEFFERY LN
PINE
CYPRESS LN
SEQUOIA RD
PONDEROSA PINE LN
SEQUOIA ST
CEDAR RD
LINDEN LN
TR
SPRING
TEE SO
TR
MANILA
LOOKOUT LP
HALF MOON TR
LN
LAGUNA
29100
TR
LAGUNA
BLVD
ELM RD
28600
RD
LEBANON
RD
PINE VALLEY COUNTY PARK
DEODAR TR
28700
MADERA
7500
TOP OF THE PINES LN
OLD
LIB
FS
PO
PINE VALLEY RD
OAK
28900
MANZANITA TR
LN
FIR RD
HIGHWAY
80
29000
CORTE
45
8
FRWY
GATE
45
BENTON CV
SUNRISE
SCOVE
0 .125 .25 .375 .5
miles 1 in. = 1900 ft.

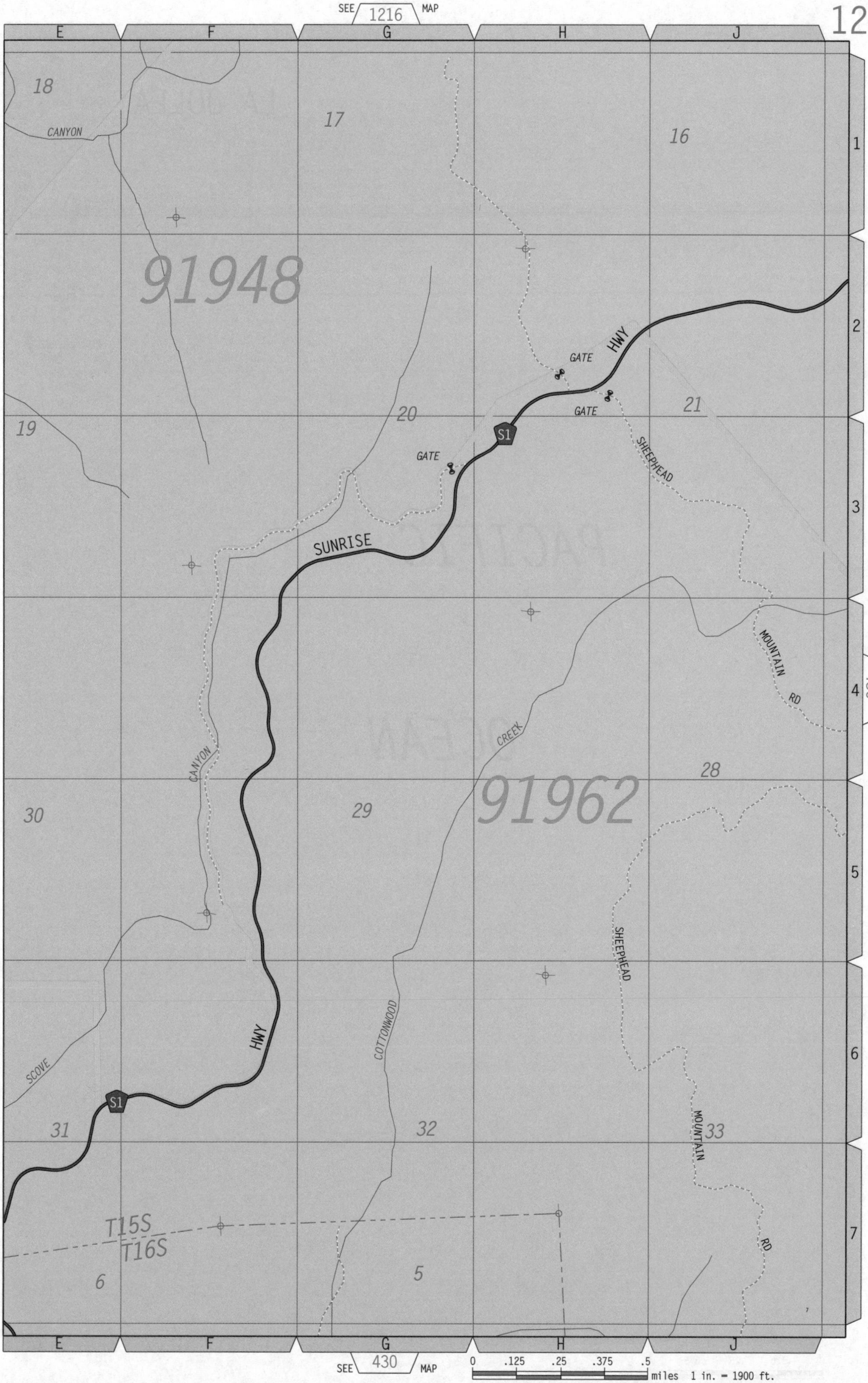
SEE 1216 MAP
E
F
G
H
J
1
2
3
4
5
6
7
18
CANYON
17
16
91948
GATE
HWY
GATE
21
19
20
S1
GATE
SHEEPHEAD
SUNRISE
MOUNTAIN
RD
SEE 430 MAP
CREEK
CANYON
28
30
29
91962
SHEEPHEAD
COTTONWOOD
HWY
SCOVE
S1
31
32
MOUNTAIN
33
T15S
T16S
RD
6
5
SEE 430 MAP
0 .125 .25 .375 .5
miles 1 in. = 1900 ft.

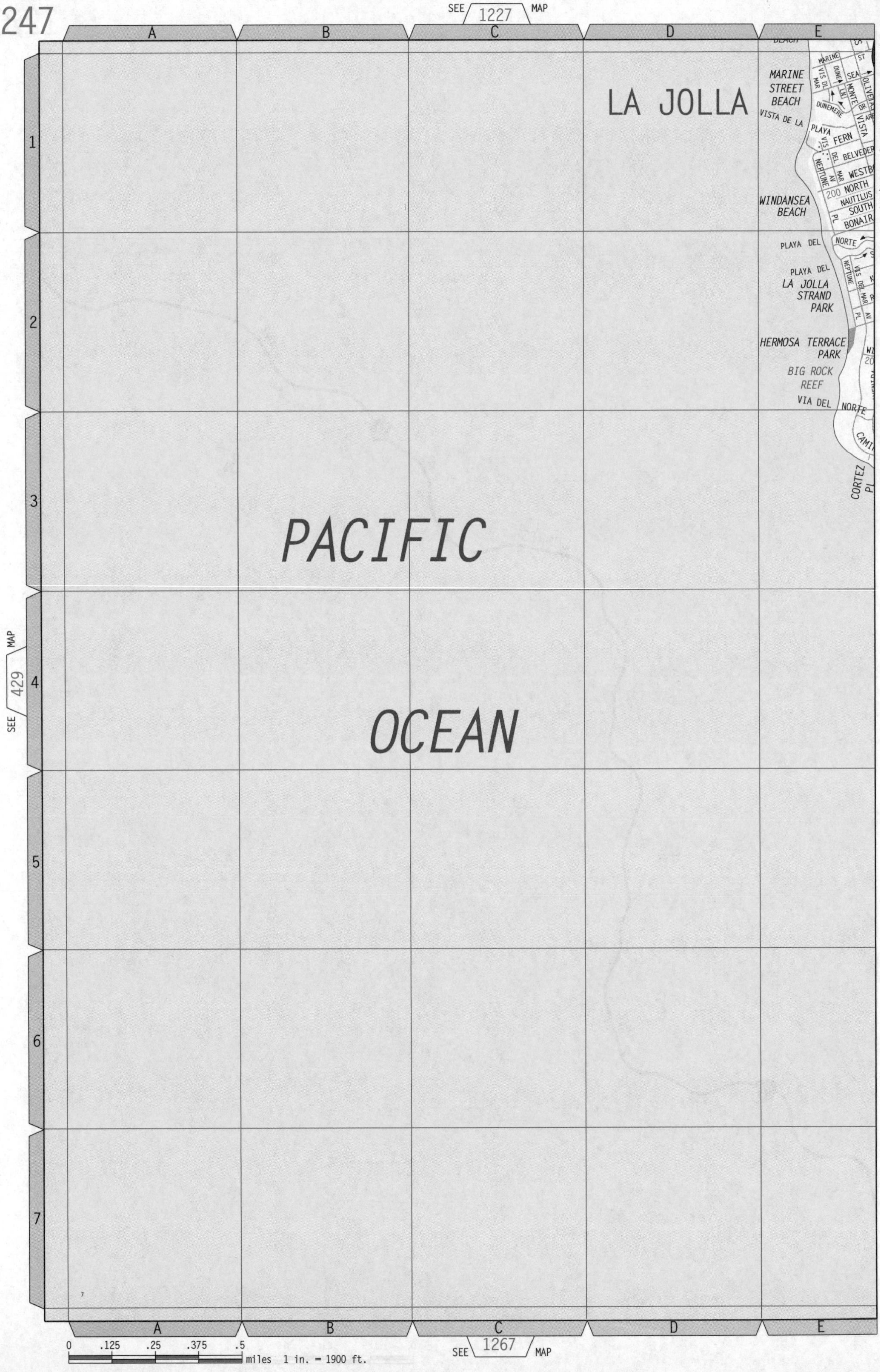
SEE 1227 MAP
A
B
C
D
E
1
2
3
4
5
6
7
LA JOLLA
MARINE STREET BEACH
VISTA DE LA
MARINE
ST
SEA
DUNEMERE
PLAYA
FERN
BELVEDERE
NEPTUNE
WESTB
200
NORTH
NAUTILUS
SOUTH
BONAIR
WINDANSEA BEACH
PLAYA DEL
NORTE
PLAYA DEL
LA JOLLA STRAND PARK
HERMOSA TERRACE PARK
BIG ROCK REEF
VIA DEL
NORTE
CORTEZ PL
PACIFIC
OCEAN
SEE 429 MAP
SEE 1267 MAP
0 .125 .25 .375 .5
miles 1 in. = 1900 ft.

SEE 1227 MAP

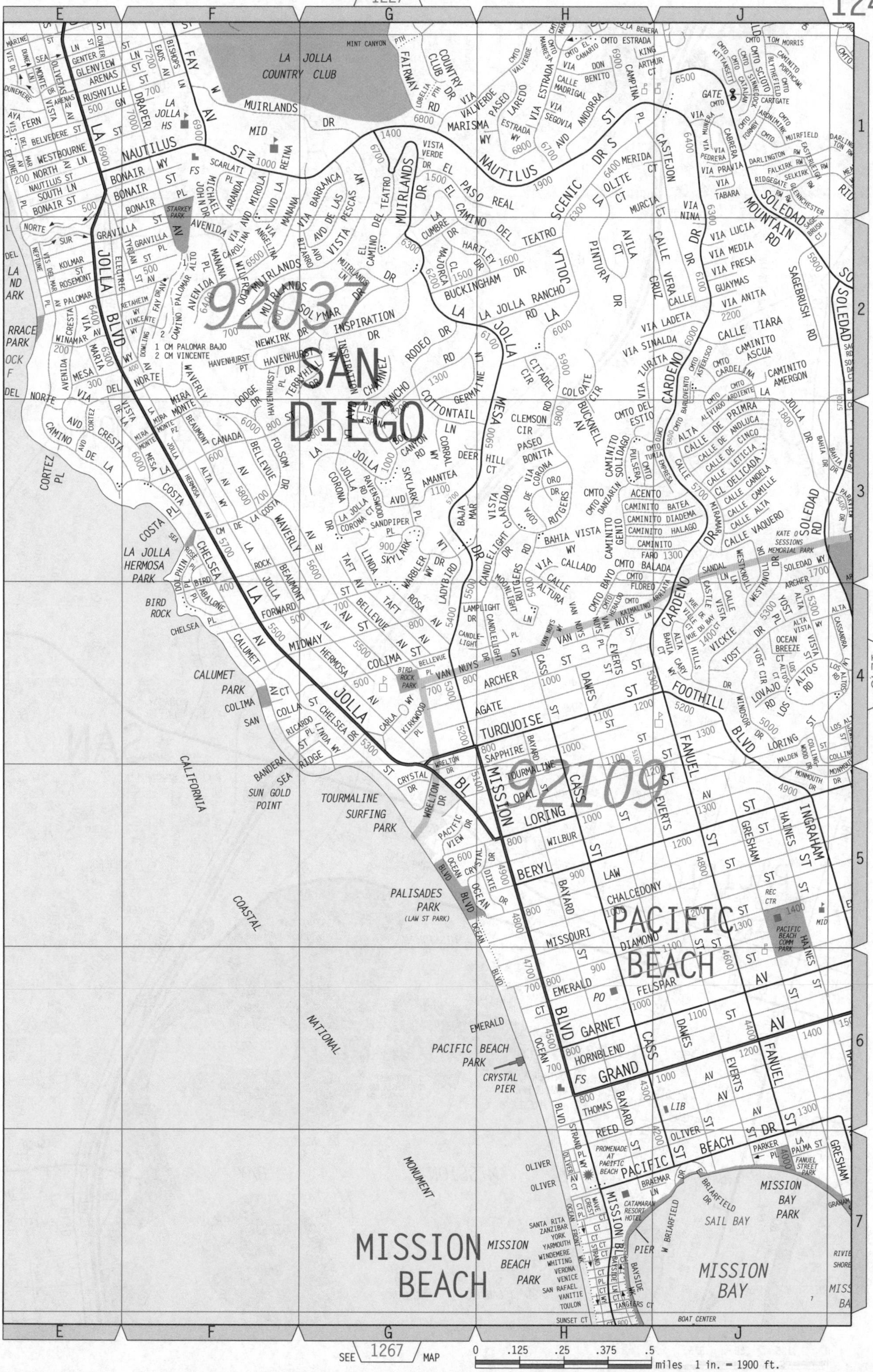

SEE 1248 MAP

SEE 1267 MAP

0 .125 .25 .375 .5 miles 1 in. = 1900 ft.

SEE 1228 MAP

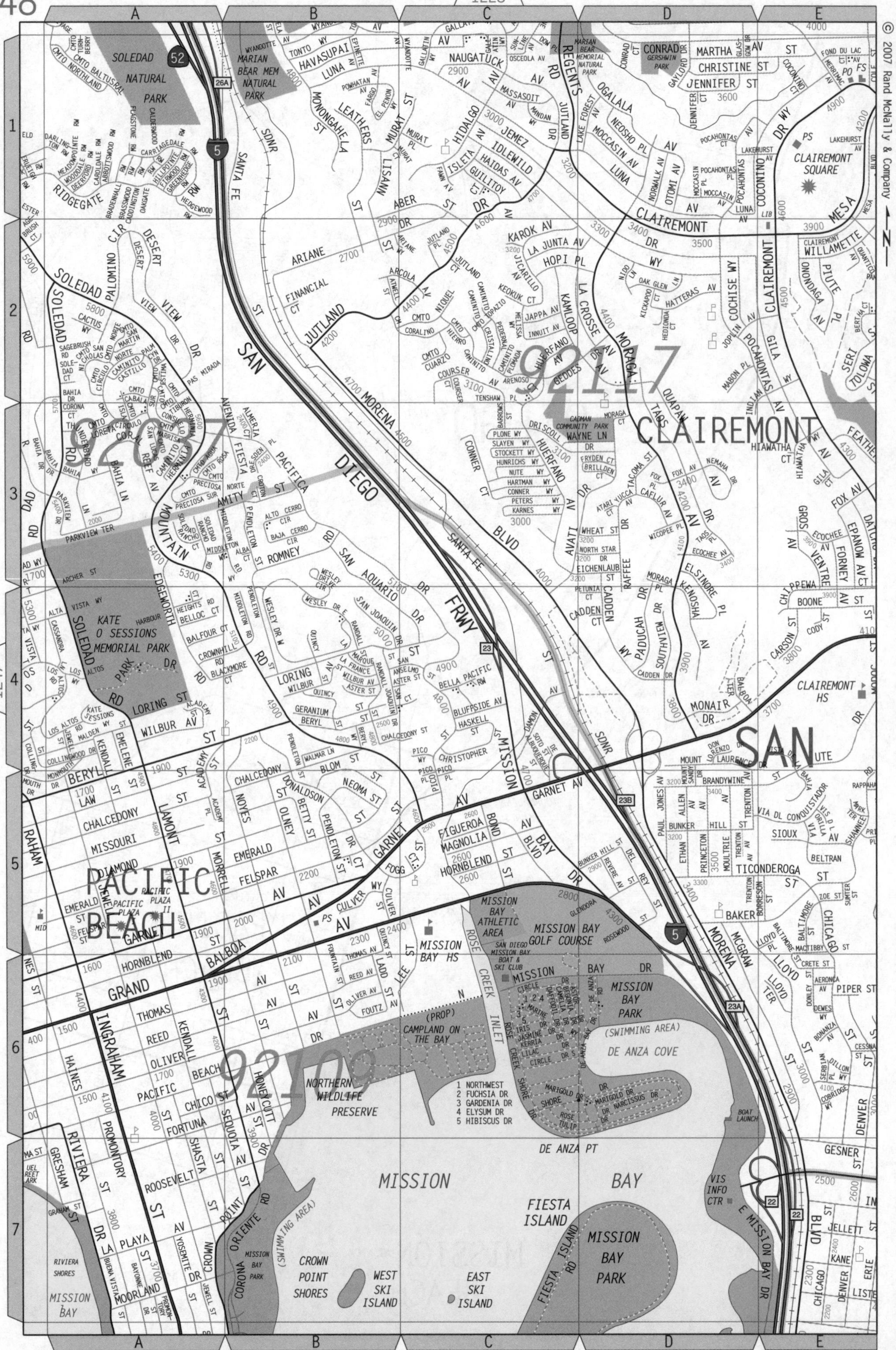

SEE 1247 MAP

0 .125 .25 .375 .5 miles 1 in. = 1900 ft.

SEE 1268 MAP

SEE 1228 MAP

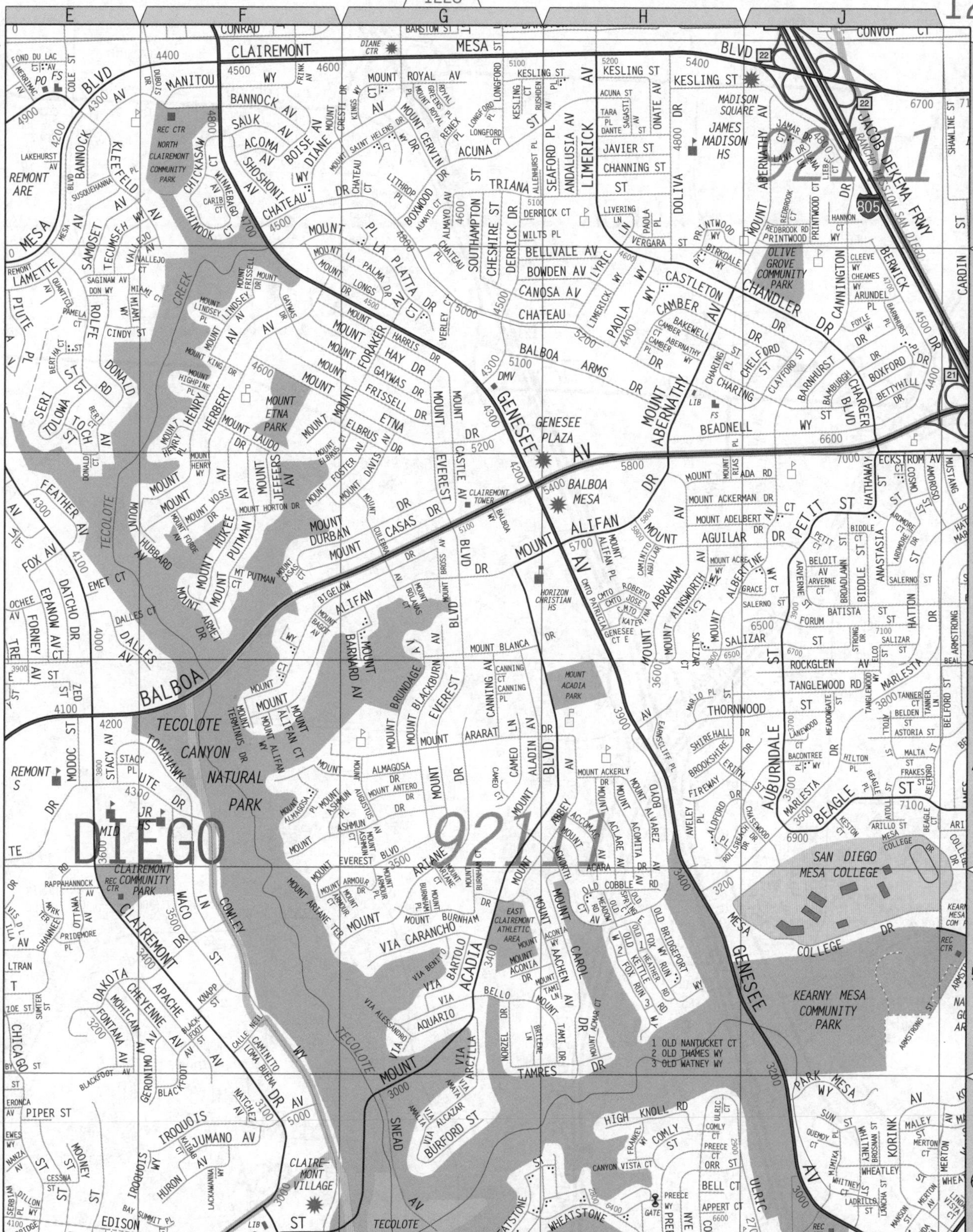

SEE 1268 MAP

0 .125 .25 .375 .5 miles 1 in. = 1900 ft.

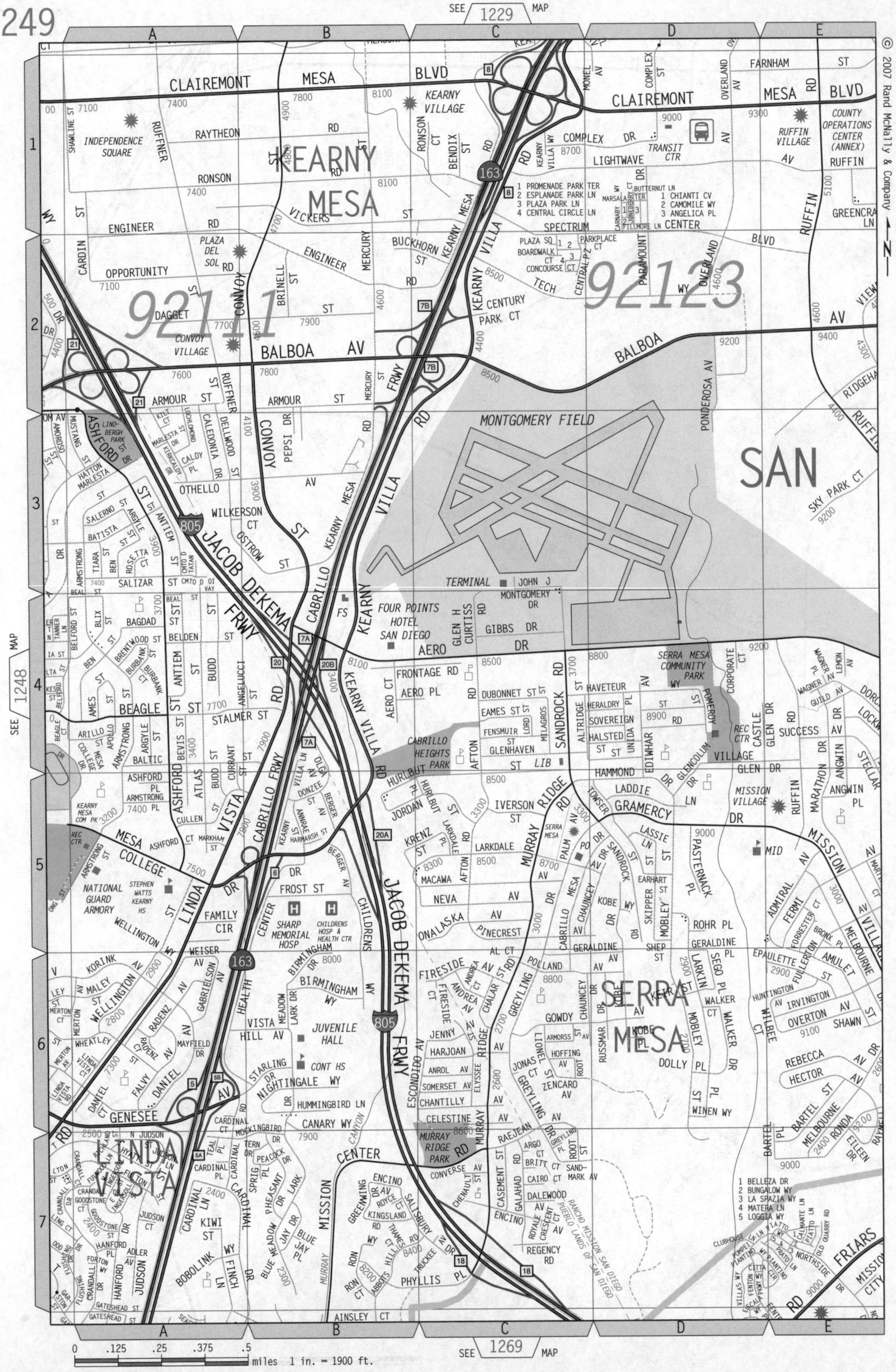
SEE 1229 MAP
SEE 1248 MAP
SEE 1269 MAP
© 2007 Rand McNally & Company
KEARNY MESA
92111
92123
SAN
SERRA MESA
LINDA VISTA
CLAIREMONT MESA BLVD
BALBOA AV
AERO DR
MONTGOMERY FIELD
TERMINAL JOHN J MONTGOMERY DR
JACOB DEKEMA FRWY
CABRILLO FRWY
KEARNY VILLA RD
CONVOY ST
RUFFNER ST
ARMOUR ST
ENGINEER RD
OPPORTUNITY RD
DAGGET ST
RONSON RD
RAYTHEON RD
INDEPENDENCE SQUARE
KEARNY VILLAGE
PLAZA DEL SOL
CONVOY VILLAGE
RUFFIN VILLAGE
COUNTY OPERATIONS CENTER (ANNEX)
TRANSIT CTR
SPECTRUM CENTER
LIGHTWAVE AV
COMPLEX DR
CENTURY PARK CT
PONDEROSA AV
SKY PARK CT
LINDBERGH PARK
FOUR POINTS HOTEL SAN DIEGO
CABRILLO HEIGHTS PARK
SERRA MESA COMMUNITY PARK
MISSION VILLAGE
REC CTR
KEARNY MESA COM PK
NATIONAL GUARD ARMORY
STEPHEN WATTS KEARNY HS
SHARP MEMORIAL HOSP
CHILDRENS HOSP & HEALTH CTR
JUVENILE HALL
CONT HS
MURRAY RIDGE PARK
MESA COLLEGE DR
LINDA VISTA RD
GENESEE AV
MISSION CENTER RD
MURRAY RIDGE RD
SANDROCK RD
GRAMERCY DR
MISSION GORGE
FRIARS RD
HAMMOND DR
GLEN DR
BEAGLE ST
MISSION VILLAGE DR
1 PROMENADE PARK TER
2 ESPLANADE PARK LN
3 PLAZA PARK LN
4 CENTRAL CIRCLE LN
1 CHIANTI CV
2 CAMOMILE WY
3 ANGELICA PL
1 BELLEZA DR
2 BUNGALOW WY
3 LA SPAZIA WY
4 MATERA LN
5 LOGGIA WY
RANCHO MISSION SAN DIEGO PUEBLO LANDS OF SAN DIEGO
0 .125 .25 .375 .5 miles 1 in. = 1900 ft.

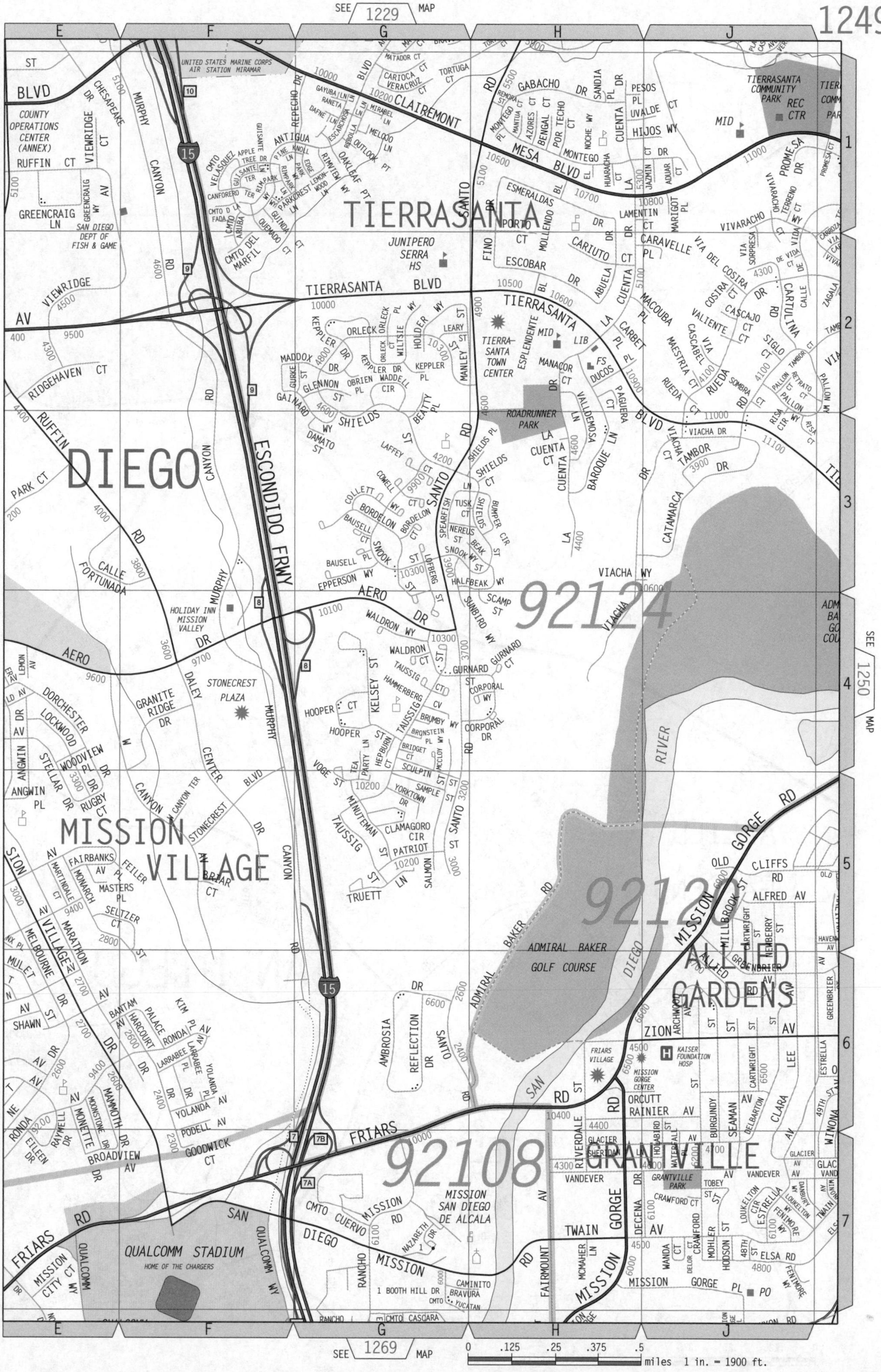

SEE 1229 MAP
SEE 1250 MAP
SEE 1269 MAP
TIERRASANTA
DIEGO
MISSION VILLAGE
ALLIED GARDENS
GRANTVILLE
92124
92120
92108
ESCONDIDO FRWY
15
UNITED STATES MARINE CORPS AIR STATION MIRAMAR
COUNTY OPERATIONS CENTER (ANNEX)
SAN DIEGO DEPT OF FISH & GAME
TIERRASANTA COMMUNITY PARK
REC CTR
JUNIPERO SERRA HS
TIERRASANTA TOWN CENTER
ROADRUNNER PARK
HOLIDAY INN MISSION VALLEY
STONECREST PLAZA
ADMIRAL BAKER GOLF COURSE
FRIARS VILLAGE
MISSION GORGE CENTER
KAISER FOUNDATION HOSP
GRANTVILLE PARK
MISSION SAN DIEGO DE ALCALA
QUALCOMM STADIUM
HOME OF THE CHARGERS
CLAIREMONT MESA BLVD
TIERRASANTA BLVD
AERO DR
FRIARS RD
MISSION GORGE RD
SAN DIEGO MISSION RD
SANTO RD
MURPHY CANYON RD
SAN DIEGO RIVER
0 .125 .25 .375 .5 miles 1 in. = 1900 ft.

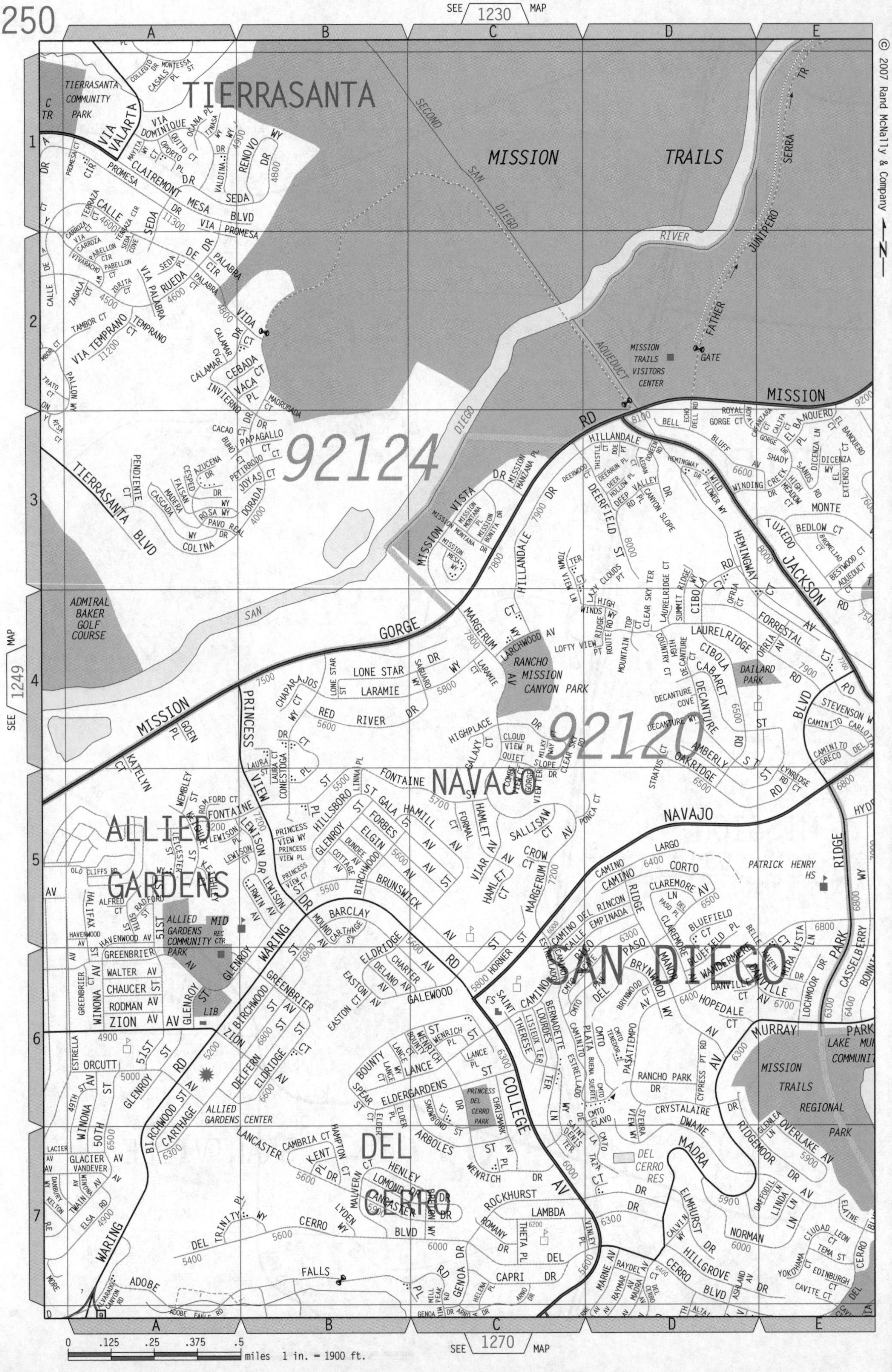
SEE 1230 MAP
SEE 1249 MAP
SEE 1270 MAP
TIERRASANTA
TIERRASANTA COMMUNITY PARK
MISSION TRAILS
SAN DIEGO RIVER
SECOND SAN DIEGO AQUEDUCT
MISSION TRAILS VISITORS CENTER
92124
92120
ADMIRAL BAKER GOLF COURSE
MISSION GORGE RD
TIERRASANTA BLVD
CLAIREMONT MESA BLVD
RANCHO MISSION CANYON PARK
DAILARD PARK
NAVAJO
NAVAJO RD
ALLIED GARDENS
ALLIED GARDENS COMMUNITY PARK
ALLIED GARDENS CENTER
SAN DIEGO
PATRICK HENRY HS
JACKSON DR
COLLEGE AV
WARING RD
DEL CERRO
DEL CERRO BLVD
DEL CERRO RES
PRINCESS DEL CERRO PARK
LAKE MURRAY COMMUNITY
MISSION TRAILS REGIONAL PARK
0 .125 .25 .375 .5 miles 1 in. = 1900 ft.

SEE 1230 MAP

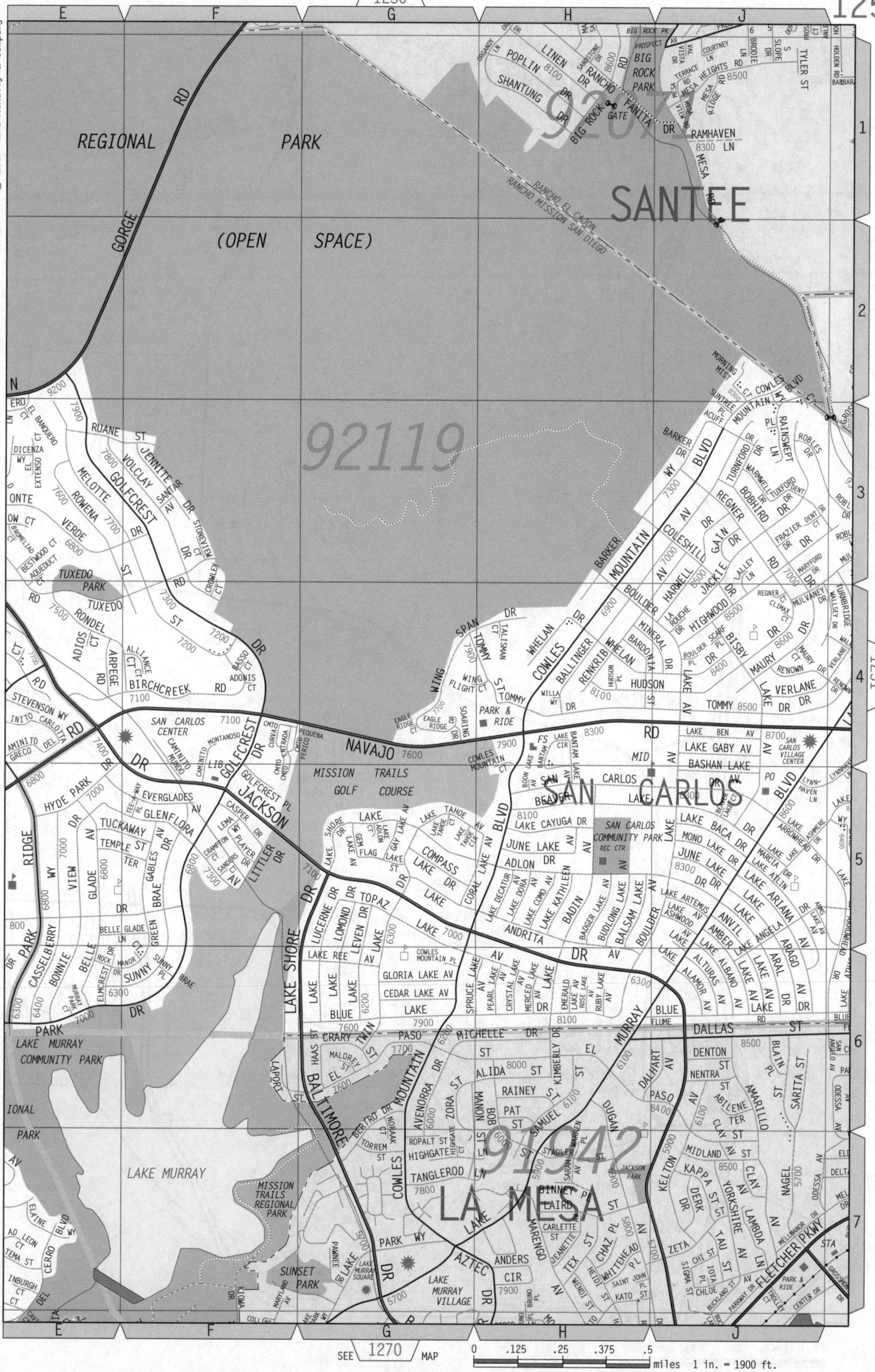

SEE 1270 MAP

0 .125 .25 .375 .5 miles 1 in. = 1900 ft.

SEE 1231 MAP

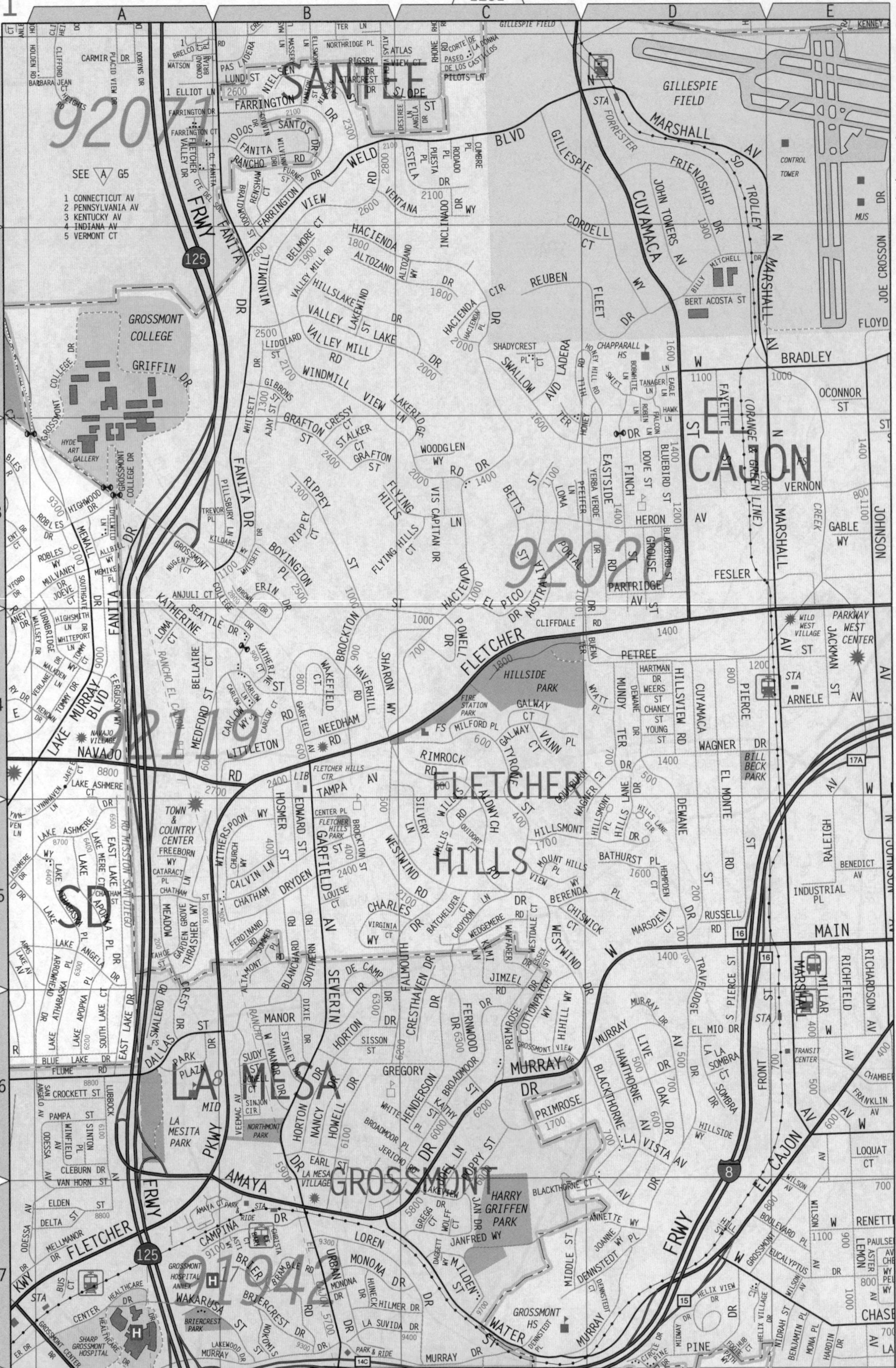

0 .125 .25 .375 .5 miles 1 in. = 1900 ft.

SEE 1271 MAP

SEE 1250 MAP

SEE 1231 MAP

SEE 1252 MAP

SEE 1271 MAP

0 .125 .25 .375 .5 miles 1 in. = 1900 ft.

SEE 1232 MAP

SEE 1251 MAP

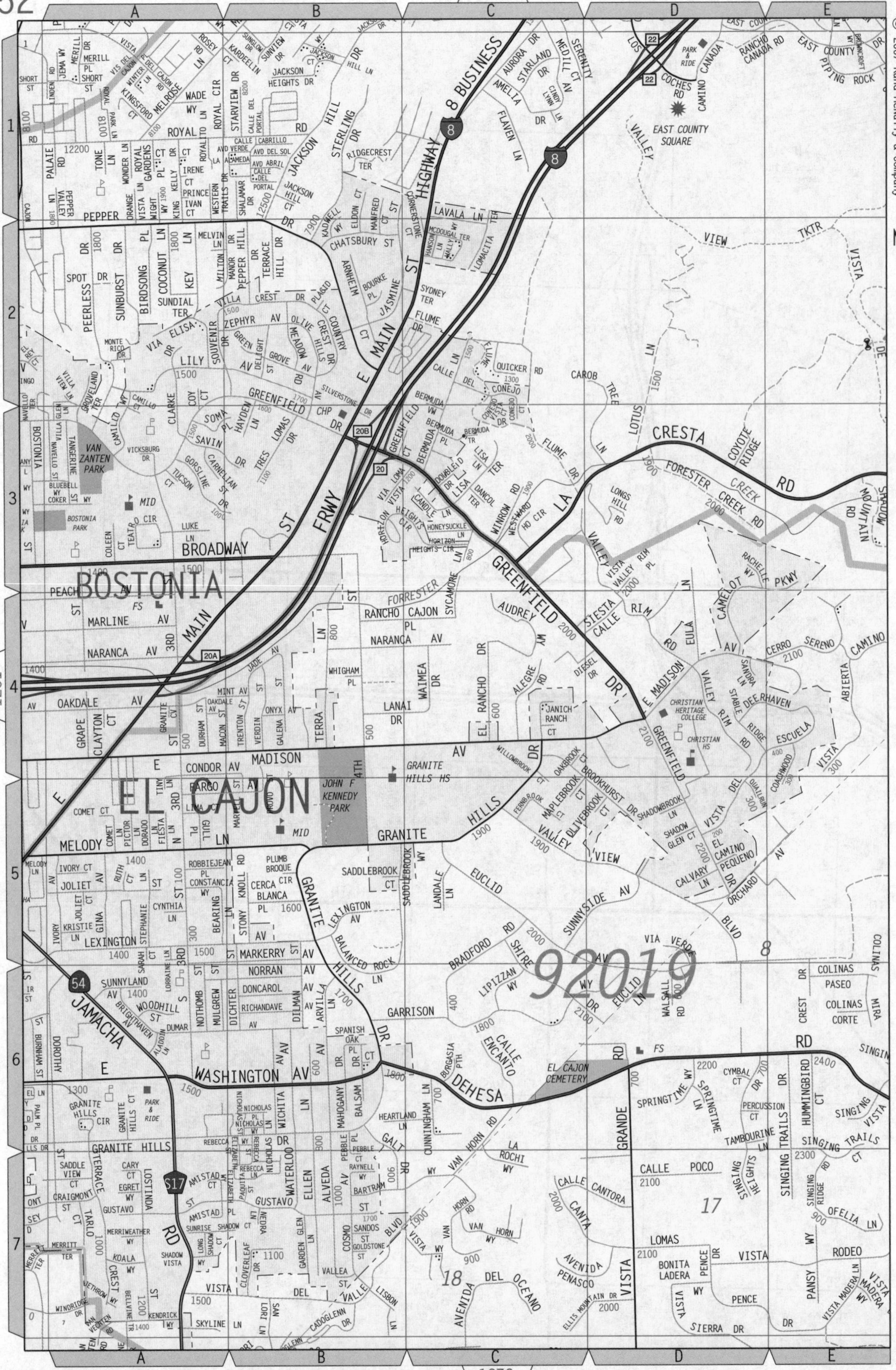

SEE 1272 MAP

0 .125 .25 .375 .5 miles 1 in. = 1900 ft.

SEE 1232 MAP

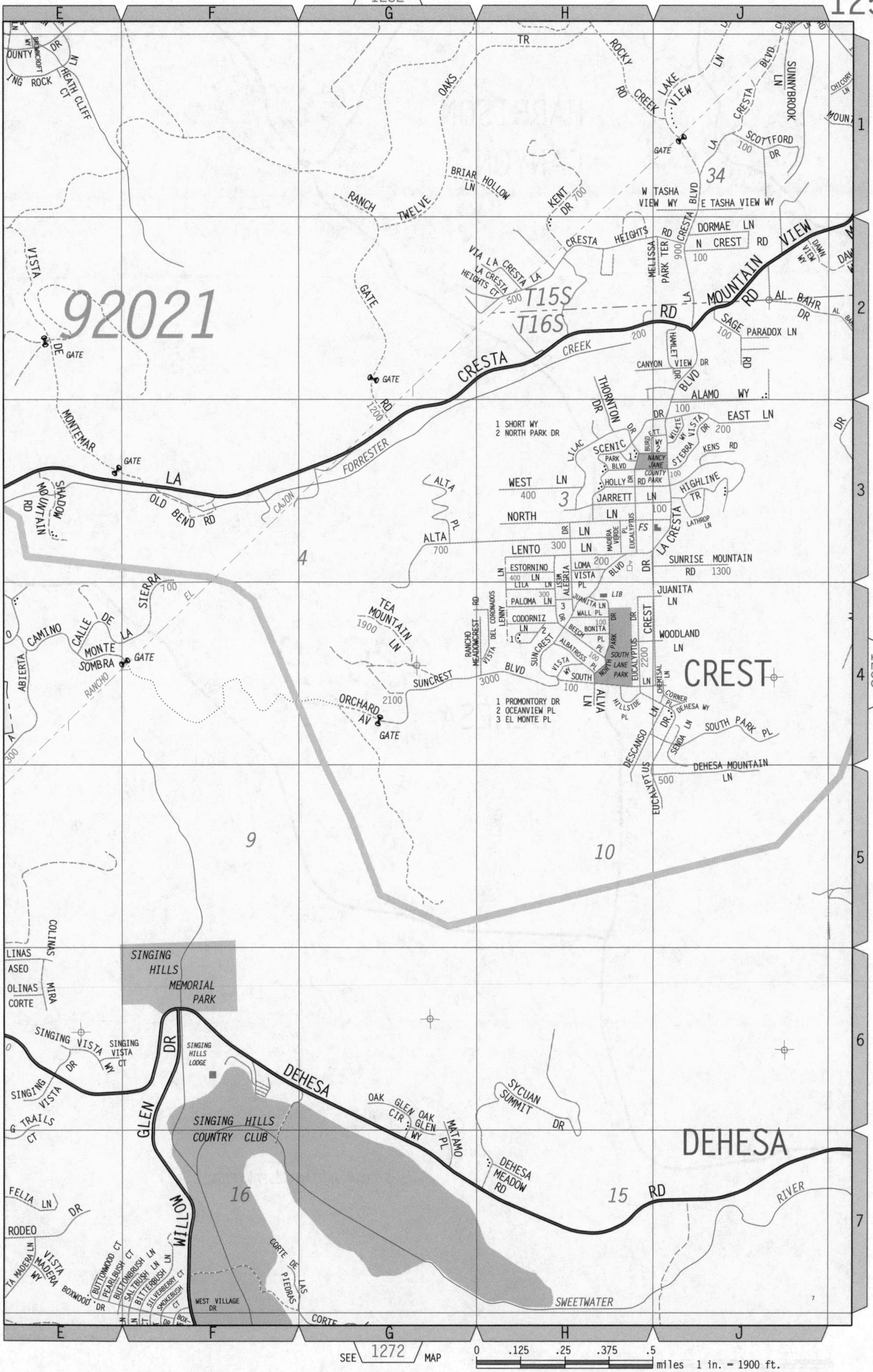

SEE 1253 MAP

SEE 1272 MAP

0 .125 .25 .375 .5 miles 1 in. = 1900 ft.

SEE 1233 MAP
SEE 1252 MAP
SEE 1273 MAP
SAN DIEGO CO.
A
B
C
D
E
1
2
3
4
5
6
7
92021
92019
HARBISON CANYON
DEHESA
MOUNTAIN VIEW RD
HORSEMILL RD
OLD MOUNTAIN VIEW RD
ALONZO DR
CHICORY LN
MOUNTAIN VIEW PL
STONERIDGE RD
DAWN VIEW WY
DAWN EW
FRANCES DR
W NOAKES ST
EDITHA DR
ALMYRA WY
MILDRED WY
NOAKES ST
E NOAKES
HUDSON LN
RIDGE LN
PATRICK DR
OLD IRONSIDES COUNTY PARK
KRISHEN HEIGHTS RD
LA CRESTA TR
GLADIOLA LN
SUMMIT LN
PATRICK
CROWS NEST LN
KELLY DR
NORMANDY WY
POST TR
LINGEL
ROSALIE DR
SAINT GEORGE
SNOWDEN PL
WARFIELD WY
COCHRAN TR
SAINT GEORGE DR
PLACER TR
RIDGE TR
ETHEL TR
SILVERBROOK
COLLIER
RENFRO WY
LOOKOUT TR
TAYLOR WY
HARBISON CANYON RD
CANYON RIM DR
AL BAHR DR
TAMMADGE HEIGHTS
T15S
T16S
R1E
R2E
WILLSON
RED GUM RD
RIVER
MOOREFIELD DR
TRAFALGAR RD
CALLE DE NICOLE
VISTA DE LA MONTANA
STALLION
RIGGS RD
OAKS
STALLION RD
OAKS LN
SWEETWATER RD
DEHESA
QUAIL HAVEN LN
FS
SYCUAN
SYCUAN CASINO
SYCUAN FORK
NORTH
DEHESA
SLOANE CANYON RD
SWEETWATER RIVER
SYCUAN INDIAN RESERVATION
35
36
31
2
1
11
12
14
13
0
.125
.25
.375
.5
miles 1 in. = 1900 ft.

SEE 1233 MAP

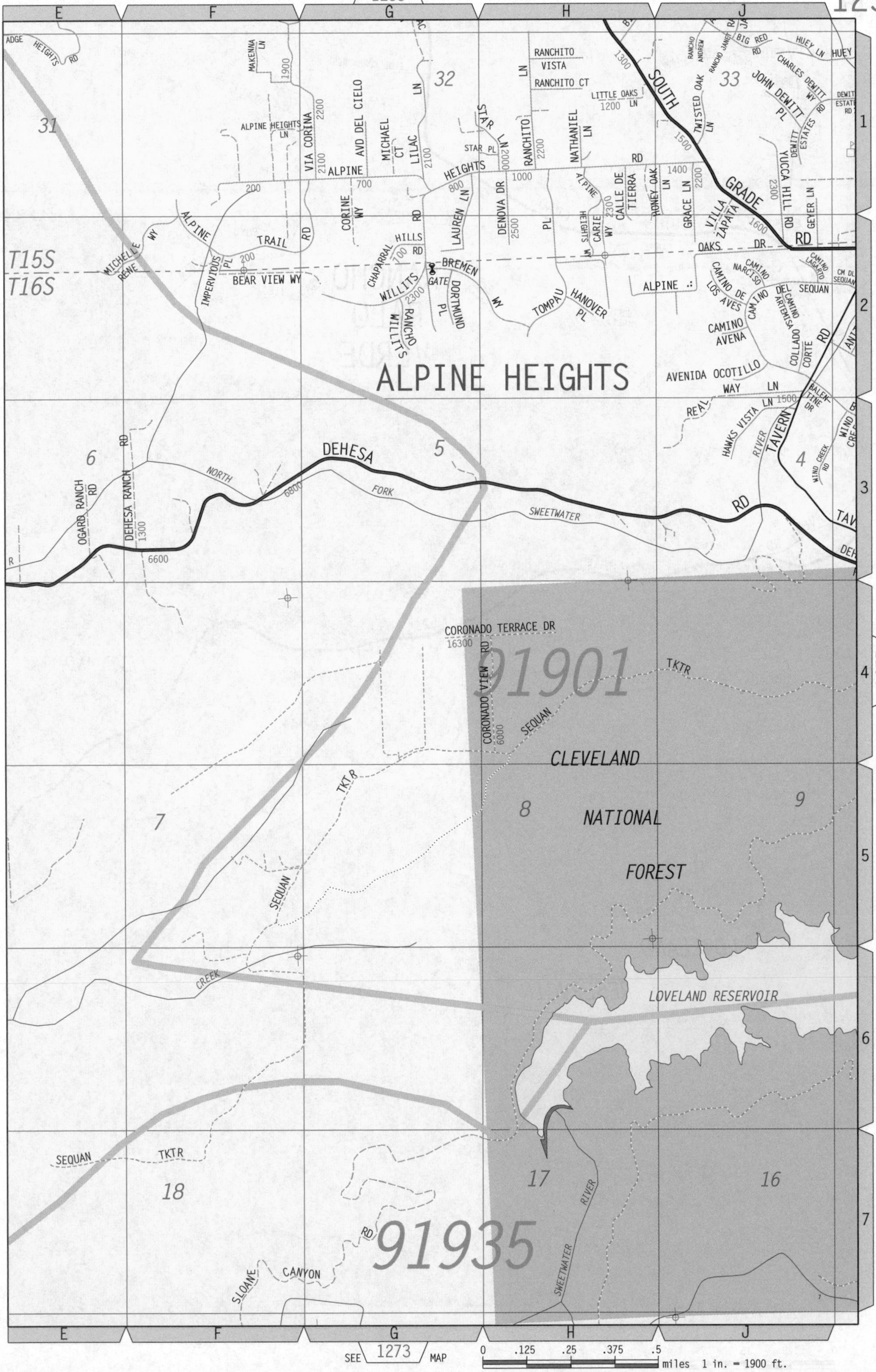

SEE 1254 MAP

SEE 1273 MAP

0 .125 .25 .375 .5 miles 1 in. = 1900 ft.

SEE 1234 MAP

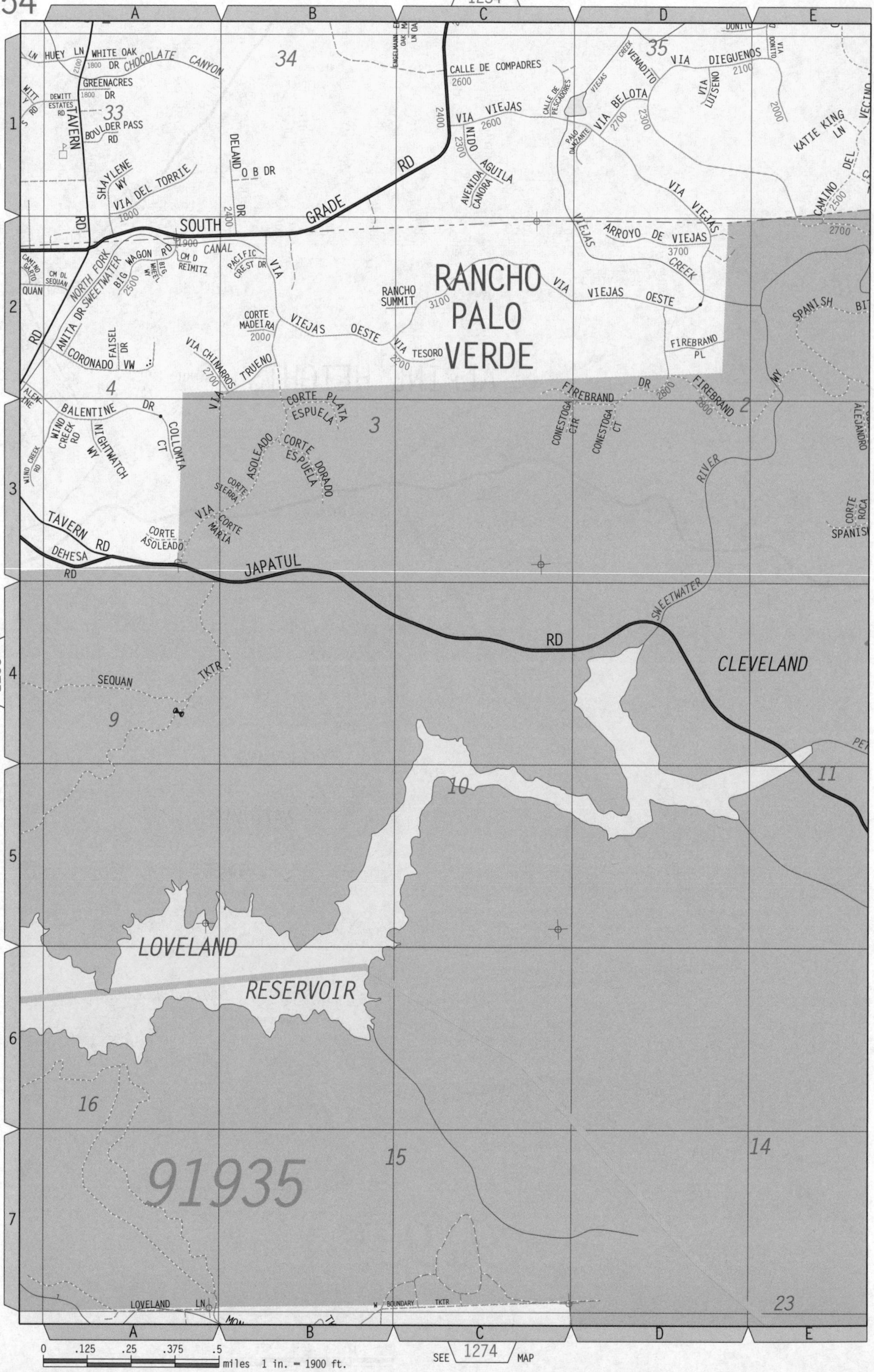

SEE 1253 MAP

SEE 1274 MAP

0 .125 .25 .375 .5 miles 1 in. = 1900 ft.

SAN DIEGO CO.

SEE 1234 MAP

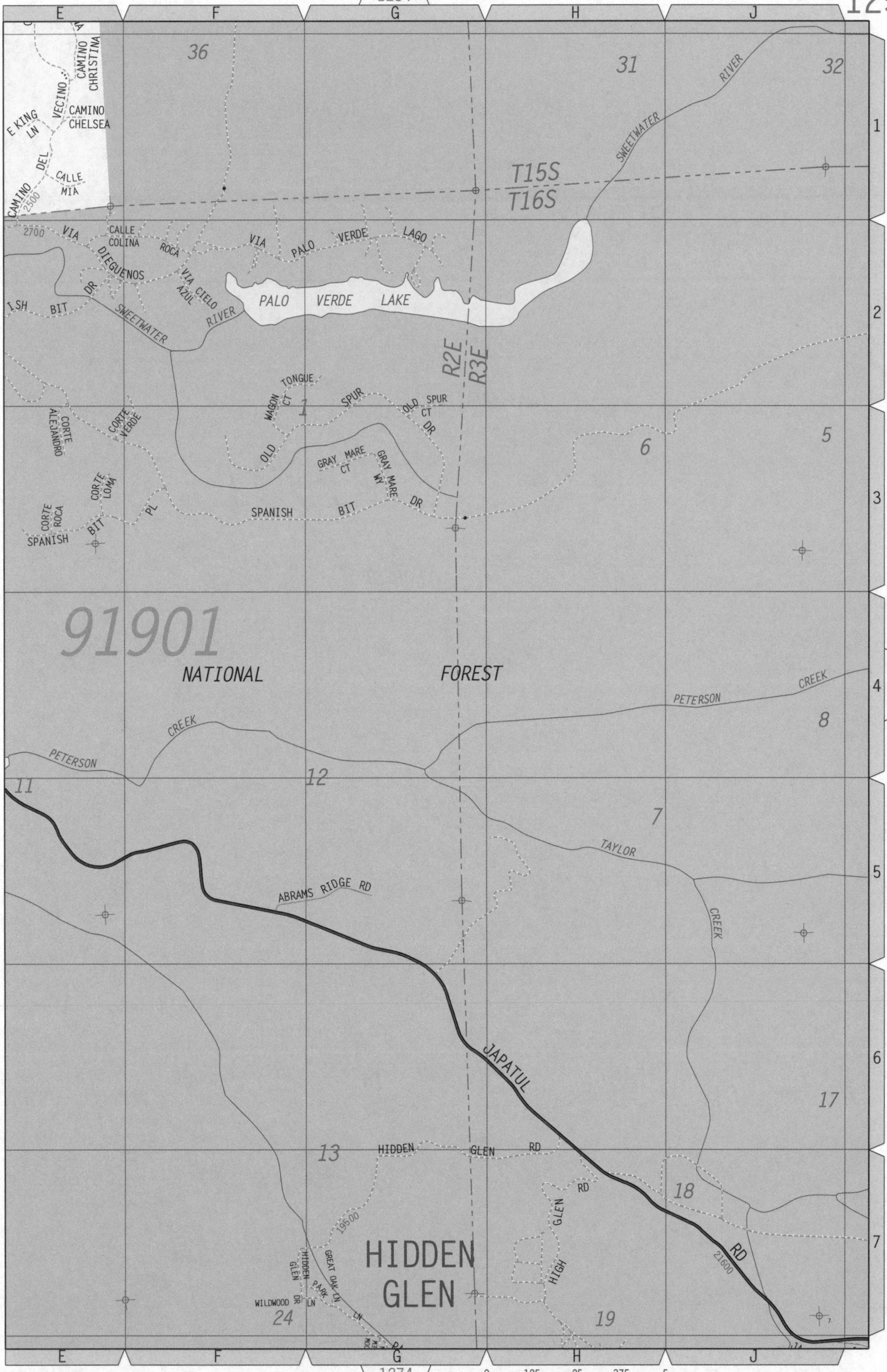

SEE 1255 MAP

SEE 1274 MAP

0 .125 .25 .375 .5 miles 1 in. = 1900 ft.

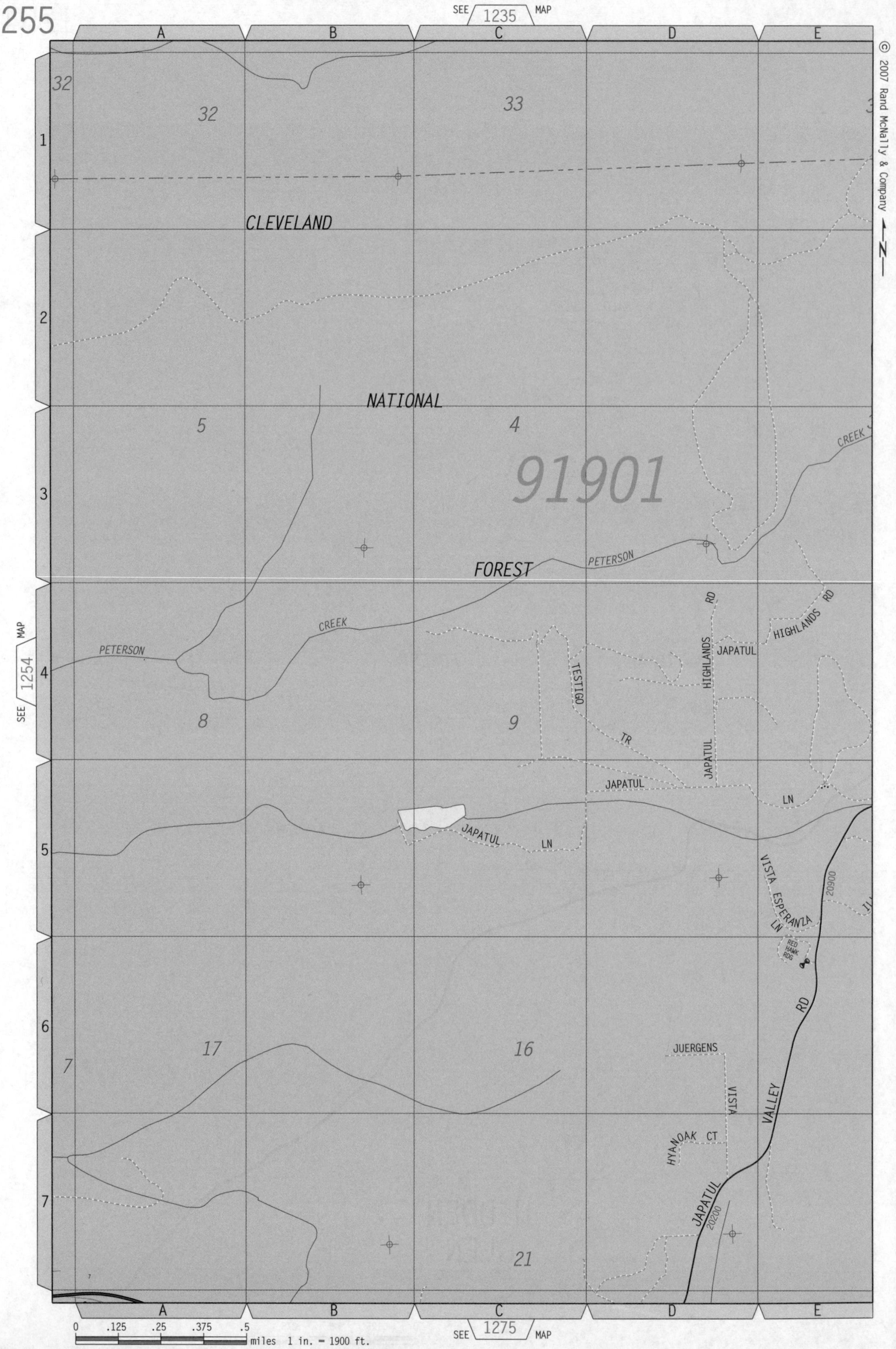
SEE 1235 MAP
SEE 1254 MAP
SEE 1275 MAP
SAN DIEGO CO.
© 2007 Rand McNally & Company
CLEVELAND
NATIONAL
FOREST
91901
PETERSON
CREEK
PETERSON
CREEK
HIGHLANDS RD
HIGHLANDS RD
JAPATUL
TESTIGO TR
JAPATUL
JAPATUL LN
JAPATUL LN
VISTA ESPERANZA LN
RED HAWK RDG
JAPATUL VALLEY RD
20900
20200
JUERGENS
VISTA
HYANOAK CT
32
33
5
4
8
9
17
16
7
21
0 .125 .25 .375 .5 miles 1 in. = 1900 ft.

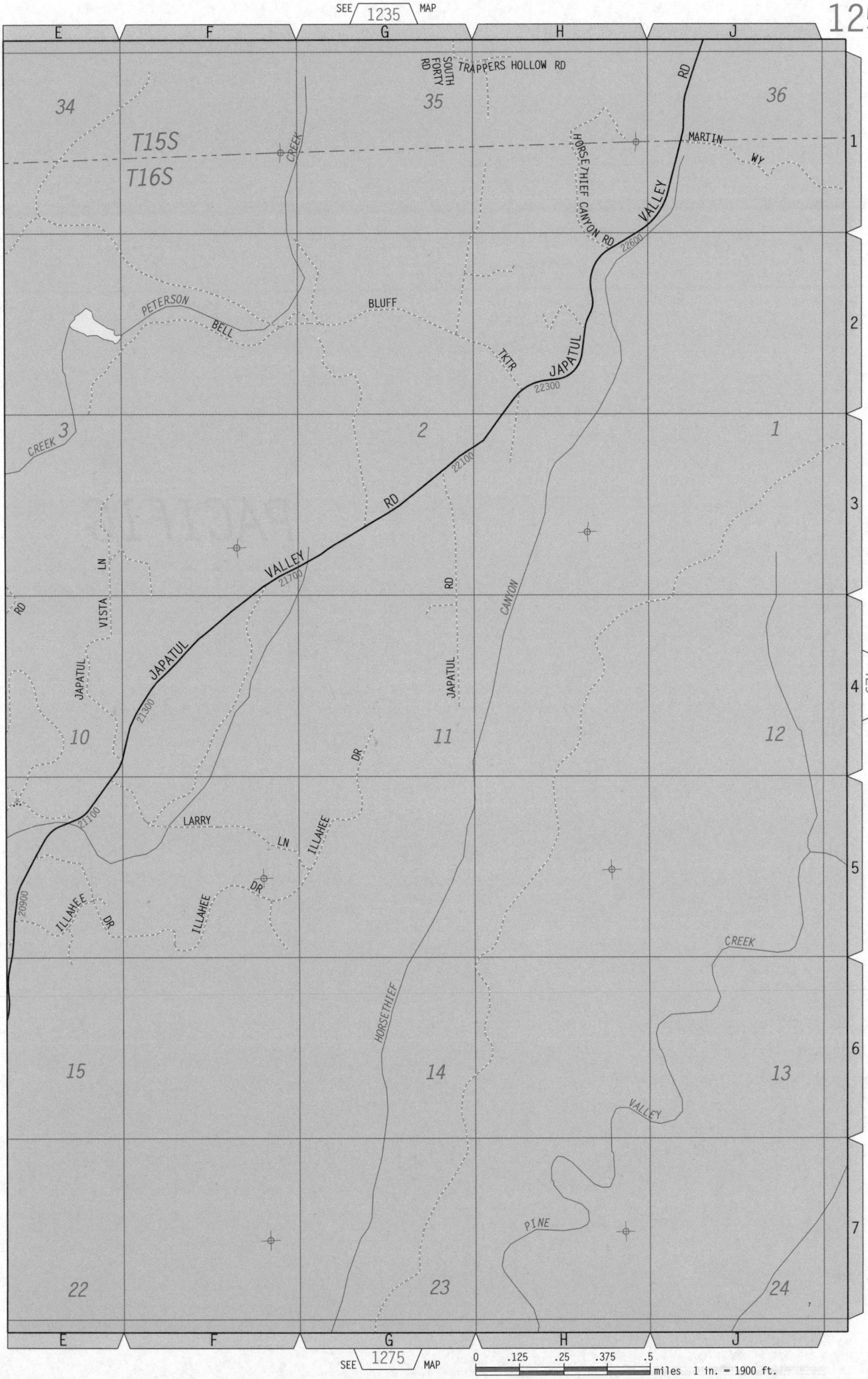
SEE 1235 MAP
E
F
G
H
J
SOUTH FORTY RD
TRAPPERS HOLLOW RD
34
35
36
T15S
T16S
CREEK
MARTIN
WY
HORSETHIEF CANYON RD
VALLEY
RD
22600
PETERSON
BELL
BLUFF
TKTR
JAPATUL
22300
CREEK
3
2
1
RD
22100
VALLEY
21700
VISTA
LN
JAPATUL
RD
CANYON
JAPATUL
JAPATUL
21300
10
11
12
DR
LARRY
LN
ILLAHEE
21100
DR
ILLAHEE
ILLAHEE
DR
20900
CREEK
HORSETHIEF
15
14
13
VALLEY
PINE
22
23
24
1
2
3
4
5
6
7
SEE 429 MAP
SEE 1275 MAP
0
.125
.25
.375
.5
miles 1 in. = 1900 ft.

SEE 1247 MAP
A
B
C
D
E
1
2
3
4
5
6
7
SEE 429 MAP
PACIFIC
SEE 1287 MAP
0 .125 .25 .375 .5
miles 1 in. = 1900 ft.
N

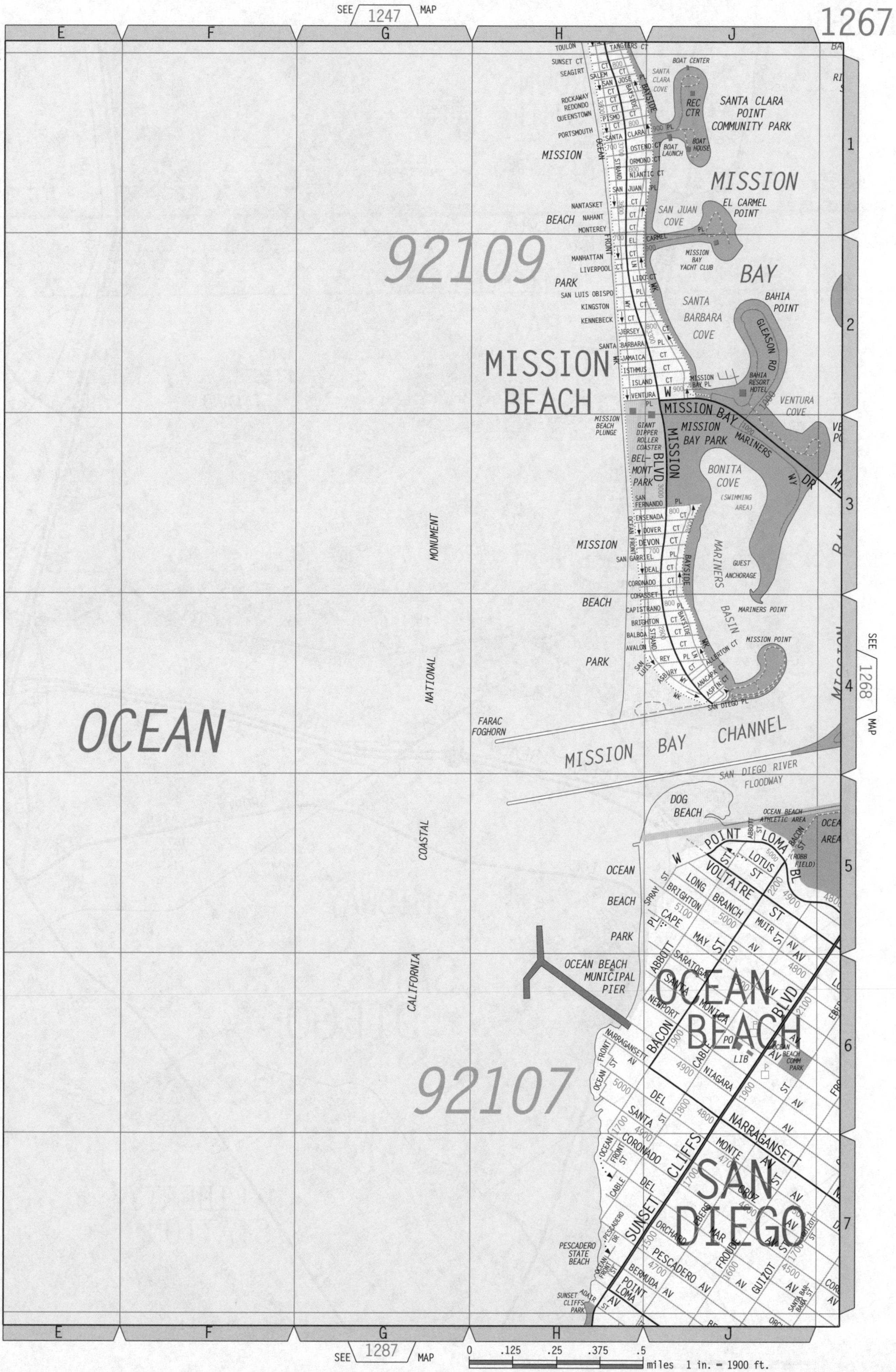
SEE 1247 MAP
E
F
G
H
J
1
2
3
4
5
6
7
92109
92107
OCEAN
MISSION BEACH
MISSION BEACH PARK
MISSION BAY
SANTA CLARA POINT COMMUNITY PARK
BOAT CENTER
REC CTR
BOAT LAUNCH
BOAT HOUSE
SANTA CLARA COVE
SAN JUAN COVE
EL CARMEL POINT
MISSION BAY YACHT CLUB
SANTA BARBARA COVE
BAHIA POINT
GLEASON RD
BAHIA RESORT HOTEL
VENTURA COVE
MISSION BAY PARK
MISSION BEACH PLUNGE
GIANT DIPPER ROLLER COASTER
BELMONT PARK
MISSION BLVD
MISSION BAY DR
MARINERS WY
BONITA COVE
(SWIMMING AREA)
MARINERS BASIN
GUEST ANCHORAGE
MARINERS POINT
MISSION POINT
CALIFORNIA COASTAL NATIONAL MONUMENT
FARAC FOGHORN
MISSION BAY CHANNEL
SAN DIEGO RIVER FLOODWAY
DOG BEACH
OCEAN BEACH ATHLETIC AREA
(ROBB FIELD)
OCEAN BEACH PARK
OCEAN BEACH MUNICIPAL PIER
OCEAN BEACH
W POINT LOMA BL
VOLTAIRE ST
NARRAGANSETT AV
SUNSET CLIFFS BLVD
SAN DIEGO
LIB
PO
OCEAN BEACH COMM PARK
PESCADERO STATE BEACH
SUNSET CLIFFS PARK
POINT LOMA AV
SEE 1268 MAP
SEE 1287 MAP
0 .125 .25 .375 .5
miles 1 in. = 1900 ft.

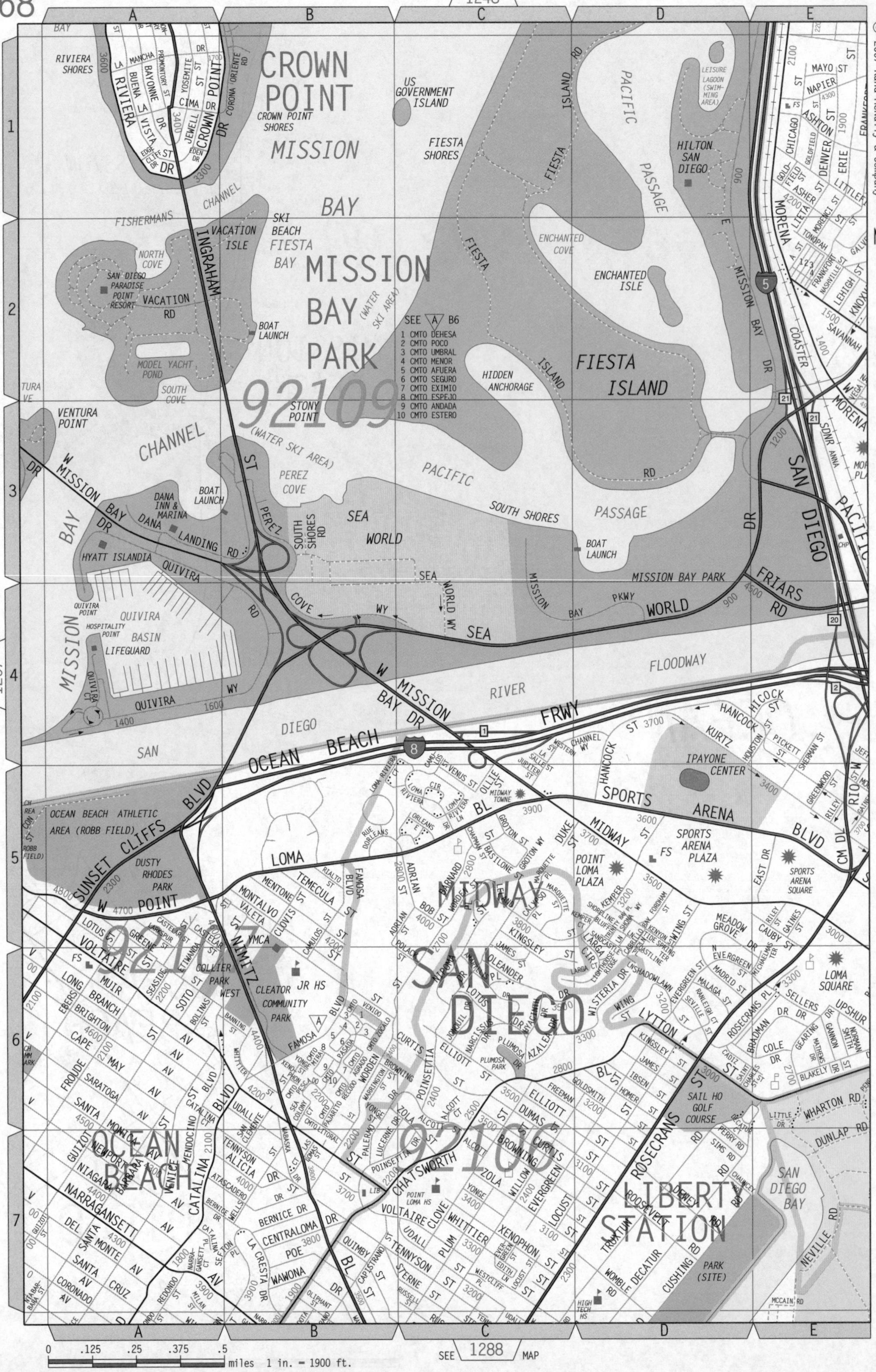

SEE 1248 MAP
CROWN POINT
MISSION BAY
MISSION BAY PARK
92109
FIESTA ISLAND
PACIFIC PASSAGE
SEA WORLD
SAN DIEGO RIVER
FLOODWAY
OCEAN BEACH FRWY
SPORTS ARENA BLVD
MIDWAY
SAN DIEGO
92107
92106
OCEAN BEACH
LIBERTY STATION
SAN DIEGO BAY
SEE 1267 MAP
SEE 1288 MAP
SAN DIEGO CO.
miles 1 in. = 1900 ft.

SEE 1248 MAP

SEE 1269 MAP

SEE 1288 MAP

0 .125 .25 .375 .5 miles 1 in. = 1900 ft.

SEE 1249 MAP

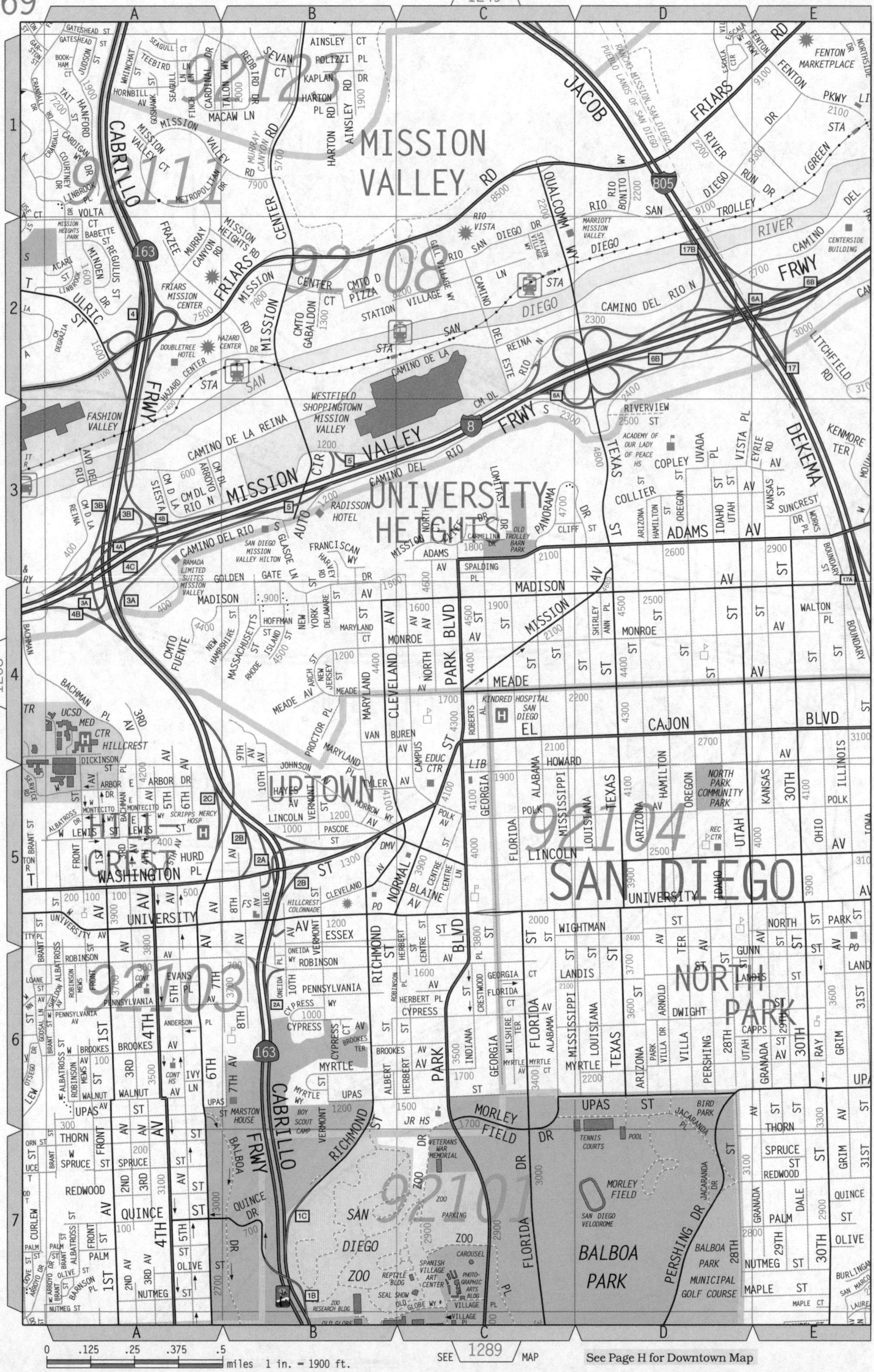

SEE 1268 MAP
SEE 1289 MAP
See Page H for Downtown Map

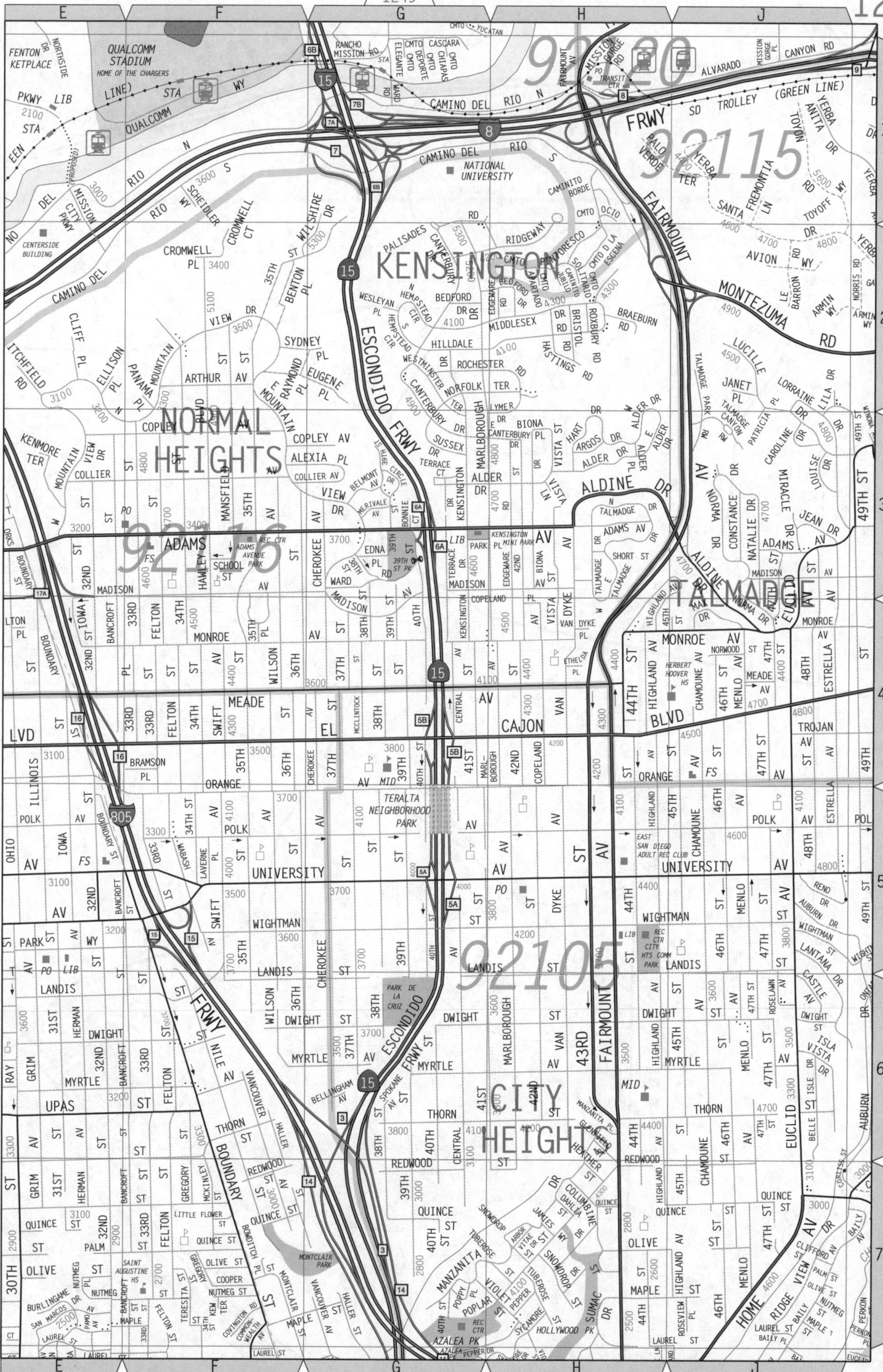

SEE 1270 MAP

0 .125 .25 .375 .5 miles 1 in. = 1900 ft.

SEE 1250 MAP
SEE 1269 MAP
SEE 1290 MAP
A
B
C
D
E
1
2
3
4
5
6
7
© 2007 Rand McNally & Company
SAN DIEGO
92120
92182
92115
92105
92114
ROLANDO
OAK PARK
FRWY
SAN DIEGO STATE UNIVERSITY
ALVARADO HOSPITAL MED CTR
MISSION TRAILS REGIONAL PARK
COX ARENA
OPEN AIR THEATER
TRANSIT CTR
MONTEZUMA
COLLEGE
EL CAJON BLVD
UNIVERSITY AV
COLLEGE AV
54TH ST
COLLWOOD BLVD
49TH ST
WINONA
CHOLLAS PKWY
STREAMVIEW DR
MONTEZUMA PARK
THE COLLEGE CENTER
CLAY PARK
CAMPUS PLAZA
ROLANDO CENTER
ROLANDO PARK
COLINA PARK GOLF COURSE
COLINA DEL SOL COMMUNITY PARK
REC CTR
CONT HS
MID
WILL C CRAWFORD HS
UNIVERSITY COMMUNITY MEDICAL CENTER
UNIVERSITY SQUARE
CHOLLAS COMMUNITY PARK
CHOLLAS HEIGHTS RESERVOIR
MARKETPLACE AT THE GROVE
PARK & RIDE
MARTIN LUTHER KING BLVD
OAK PARK
0 .125 .25 .375 .5 miles 1 in. = 1900 ft.

SEE 1250 MAP

SEE 1271 MAP

SEE 1290 MAP

0 .125 .25 .375 .5 miles 1 in. = 1900 ft.

SAN DIEGO CO.

SEE 1251 MAP

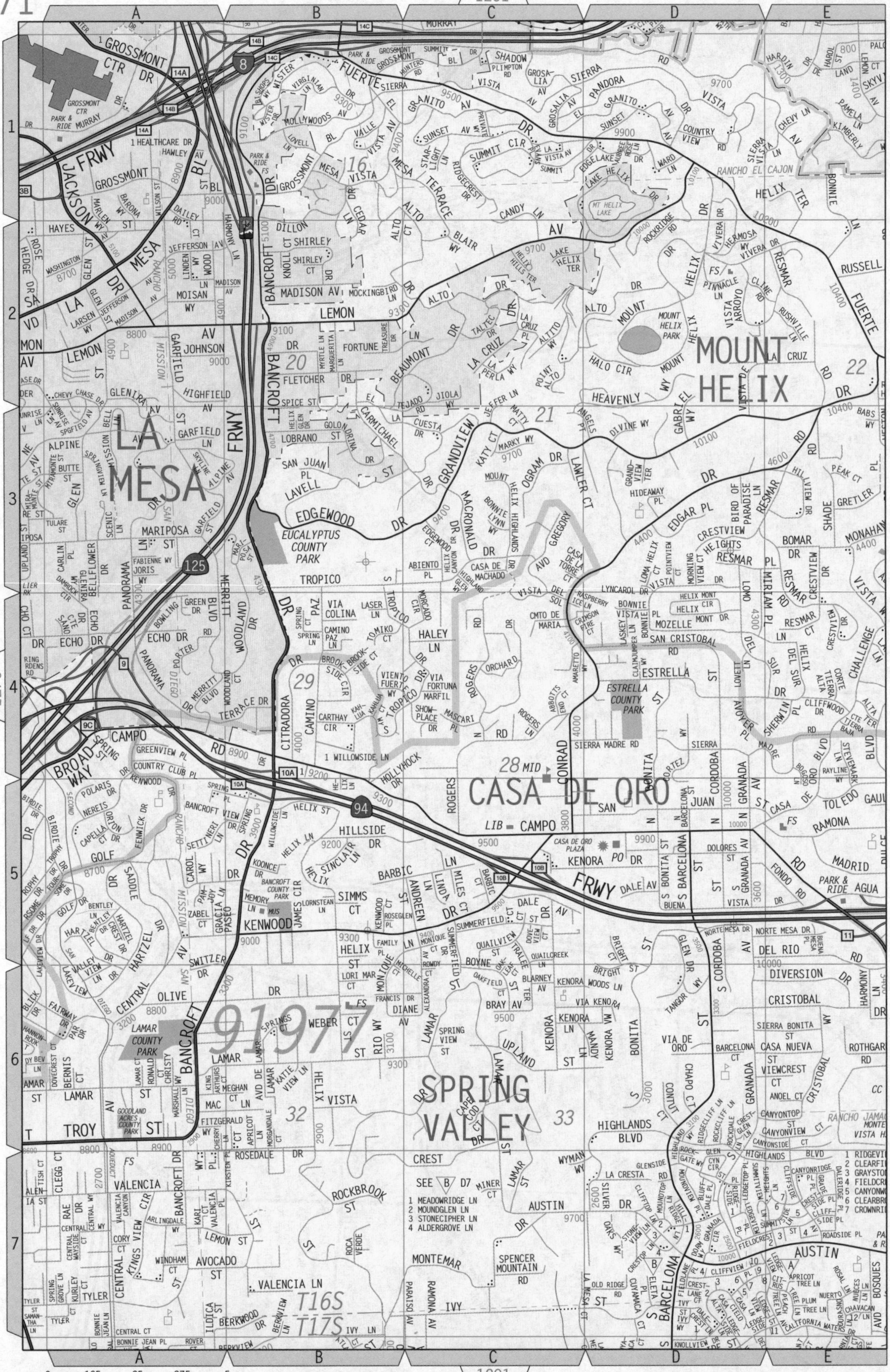

SEE 1270 MAP

SEE 1291 MAP

0 .125 .25 .375 .5 miles 1 in. = 1900 ft.

SEE 1251 MAP

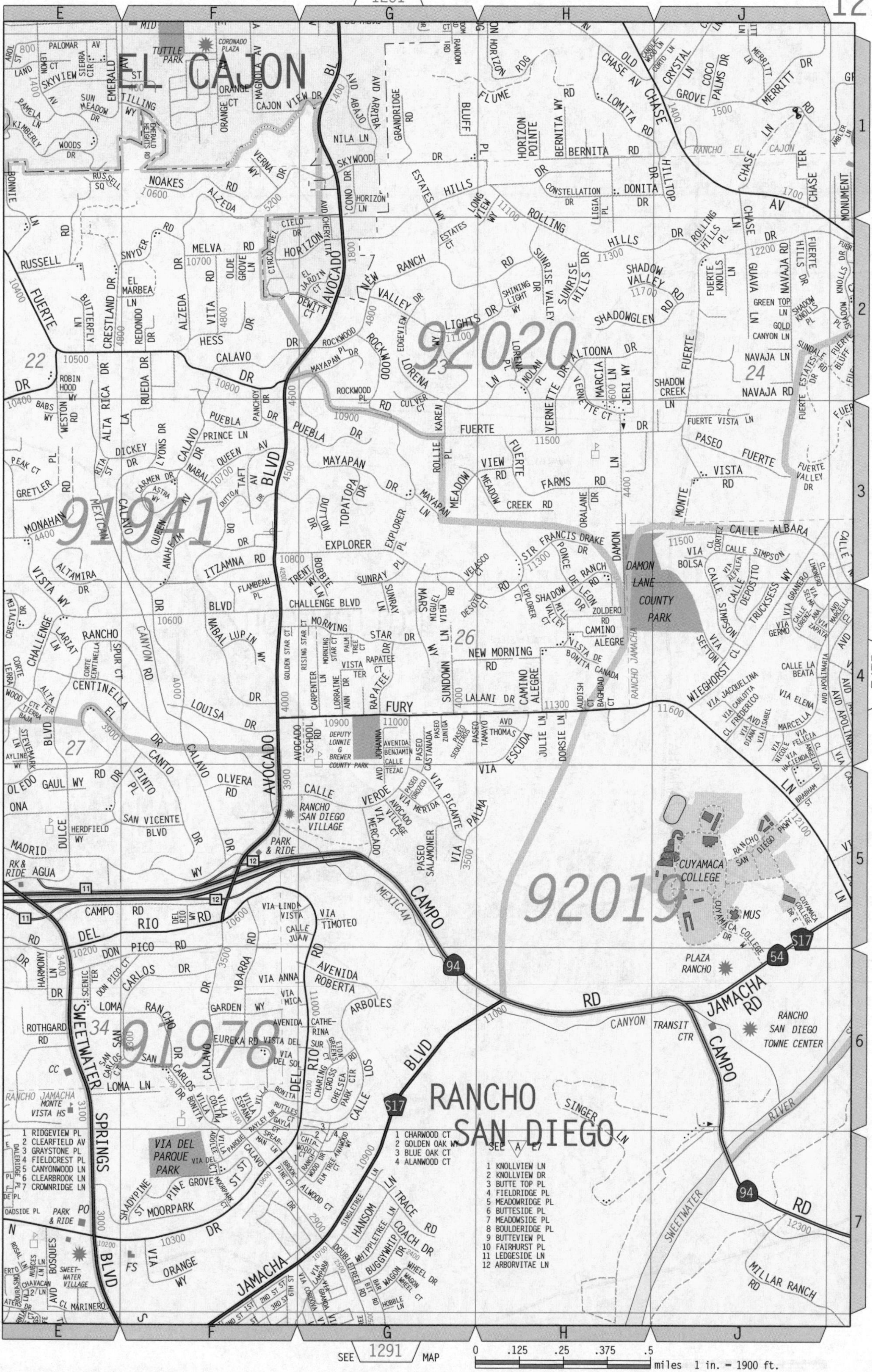

SEE 1272 MAP

SEE 1291 MAP

SAN DIEGO CO.

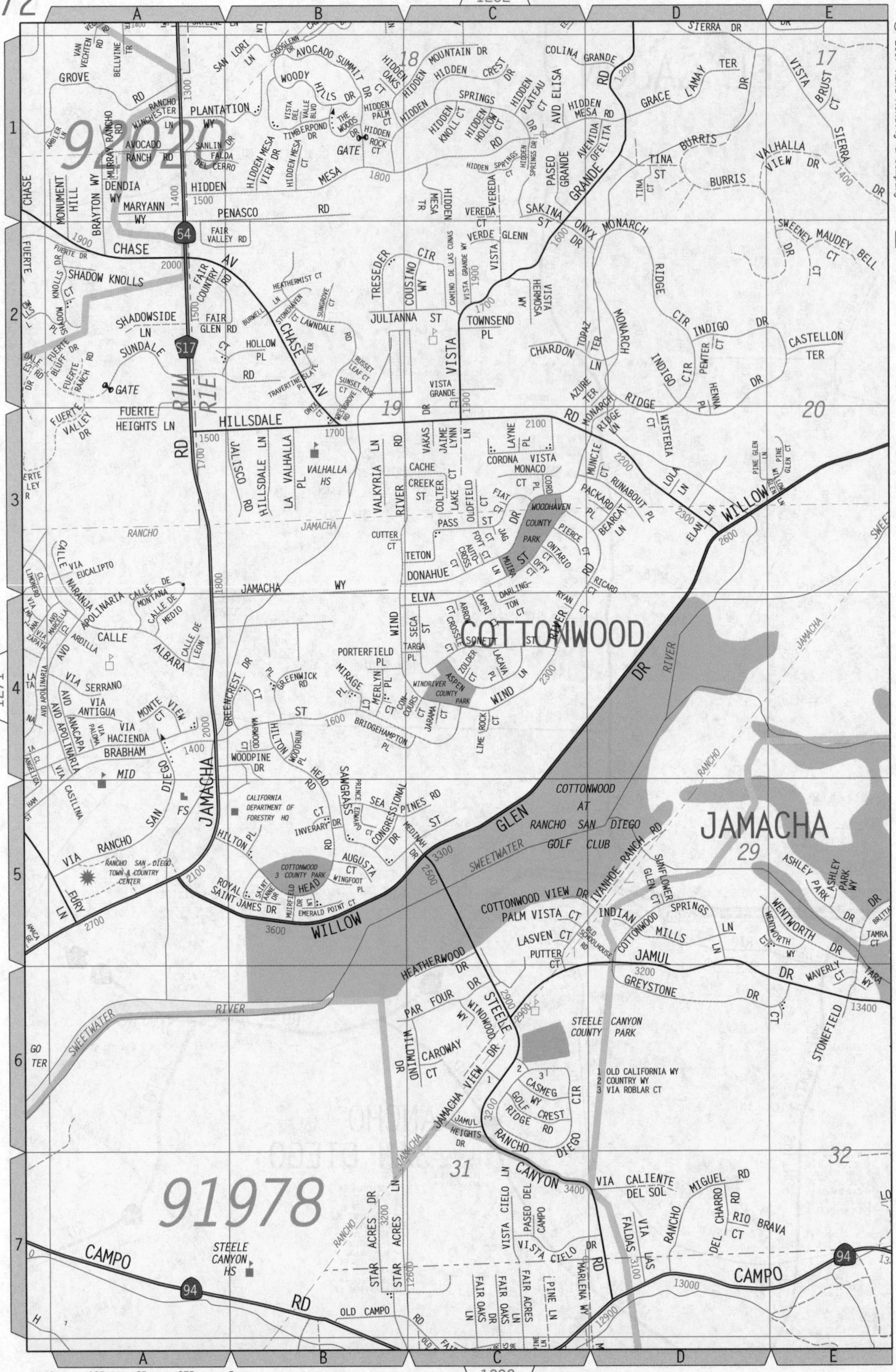
SEE 1252 MAP
A
B
C
D
E
1
2
3
4
5
6
7
92020
91978
COTTONWOOD
JAMACHA
18
17
19
20
29
31
32
54
S17
94
CHASE
CHASE AV
GROVE
PLANTATION WY
AVOCADO RANCH RD
MONUMENT HILL
BRAYTON WY
DENDIA WY
MARYANN WY
PENASCO RD
HIDDEN MESA RD
AVOCADO SUMMIT DR
HIDDEN MOUNTAIN DR
HIDDEN SPRINGS RD
COLINA GRANDE
GRACE LAMAY TER
SIERRA DR
VISTA BRUST CT
TINA ST
BURRIS
VALHALLA VIEW DR
MONARCH RIDGE CIR
INDIGO DR
CASTELLON TER
AVD ELISA
PASEO GRANDE
AVENIDA GRANDE
OFELITA
SAKINA ST
ONYX DR
VISTA GRANDE RD
JULIANNA ST
TOWNSEND PL
CHARDON LN
TOPAZ TER
AZURE TER
SHADOW KNOLLS
SHADOWSIDE LN
SUNDALE RD
FAIR GLEN RD
HOLLOW PL
FUERTE HEIGHTS LN
FUERTE VALLEY DR
HILLSDALE RD
VALHALLA HS
JALISCO RD
HILLSDALE LN
LA VALHALLA PL
VALKYRIA LN
CACHE CREEK ST
CORONA VISTA
MONACO CT
WOODHAVEN COUNTY PARK
RUNABOUT PL
PACKARD PL
BEARCAT LN
WILLOW RD
JAMACHA WY
JAMACHA RD
RIVER WIND DR
ELVA
DONAHUE CT
TETON
COTTONWOOD
SONETT ST
ASPEN COUNTY PARK
WIND LN
PORTERFIELD PL
BRIDGEHAMPTON PL
CALLE ALBARA
VIA SERRANO
VIA ANTIGUA
MONTE VIEW CT
VIA HACIENDA
BRABHAM
MID
VIA RANCHO SAN DIEGO
RANCHO SAN DIEGO TOWN & COUNTRY CENTER
FURY LN
CALIFORNIA DEPARTMENT OF FORESTRY HQ
COTTONWOOD COUNTY PARK
AUGUSTA CT
SEA PINES RD
COTTONWOOD AT RANCHO SAN DIEGO GOLF CLUB
SWEETWATER RIVER
GLEN DR
IVANHOE RANCH RD
COTTONWOOD VIEW DR
PALM VISTA CT
LASVEN CT
INDIAN SPRINGS
MILLS LN
JAMUL DR
GREYSTONE DR
WENTWORTH DR
ASHLEY PARK WY
HEATHERWOOD DR
PAR FOUR DR
WINDWOOD WY
STEELE CANYON RD
STEELE CANYON COUNTY PARK
1 OLD CALIFORNIA WY
2 COUNTRY WY
3 VIA ROBLAR CT
CASMEG WY
GOLF CREST RD
RANCHO DIEGO CIR
JAMACHA VIEW DR
JAMUL HEIGHTS DR
CARAWAY CT
WILDWIND DR
CANYON RD
VIA CALIENTE DEL SOL
RANCHO MIGUEL RD
DEL CHARRO RD
RIO BRAVA CT
VIA LAS FALDAS
STAR ACRES DR
STAR ACRES LN
STEELE CANYON HS
CAMPO RD
OLD CAMPO RD
FAIR OAKS LN
FAIR ACRES LN
PINE LN
MARLENA WY
VISTA CIELO DR
STONEFIELD CT
SEE 1271 MAP
SEE 1292 MAP
0 .125 .25 .375 .5 miles 1 in. = 1900 ft.

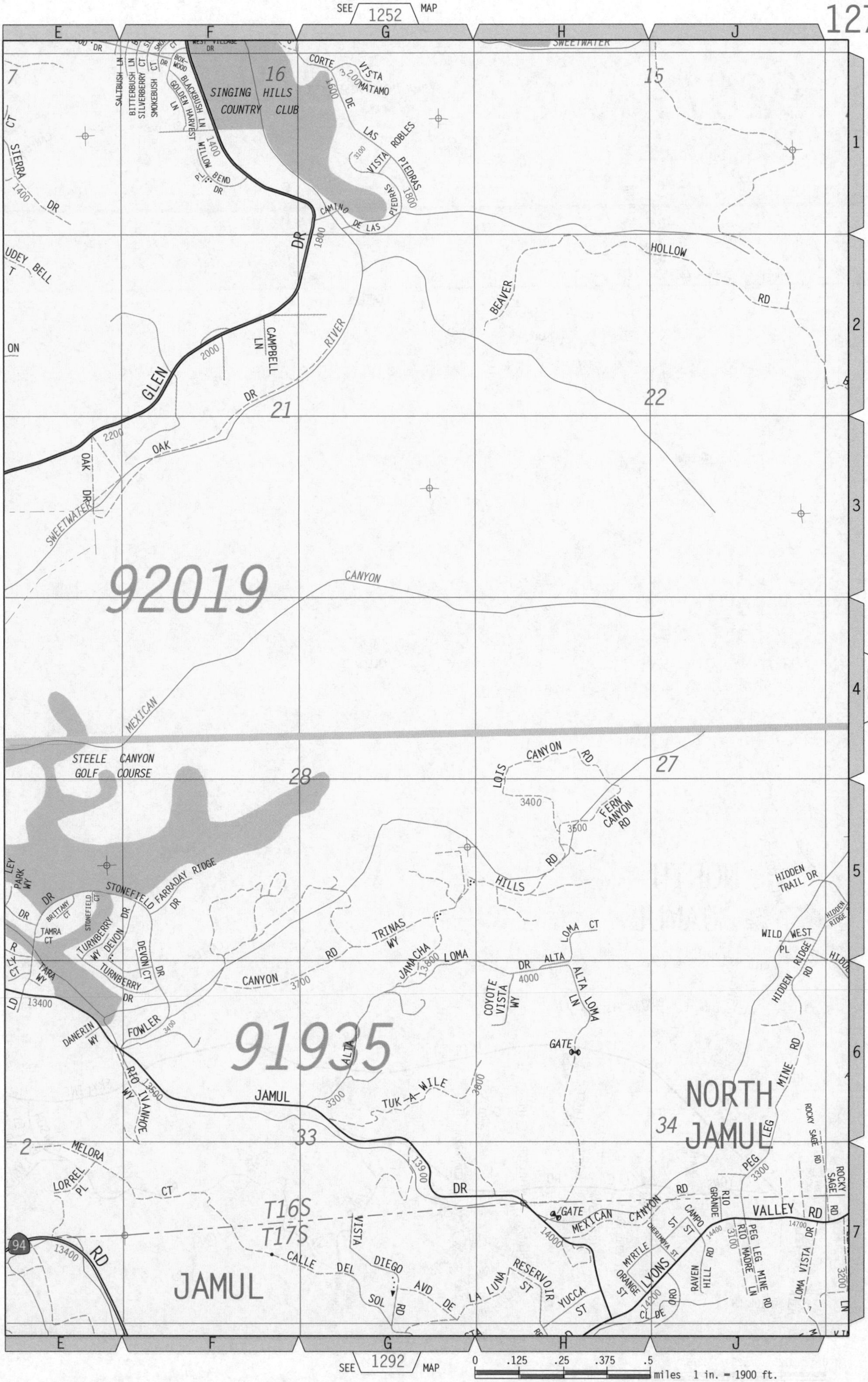
SEE 1252 MAP
SEE 1273 MAP
SEE 1292 MAP
SINGING HILLS COUNTRY CLUB
STEELE CANYON GOLF COURSE
92019
91935
NORTH JAMUL
JAMUL
T16S
T17S
GLEN OAK DR
SWEETWATER RIVER DR
MEXICAN CANYON RD
JAMUL DR
HOLLOW RD
BEAVER
CAMPBELL LN
CORTE VISTA MATAMO
DE LAS ROBLES
VISTA PIEDRAS
CAMINO DE LAS PIEDRAS
LOIS CANYON RD
FERN CANYON RD
HILLS RD
TRINAS WY
CANYON RD
JAMACHA LOMA DR
ALTA LOMA CT
ALTA LOMA LN
COYOTE VISTA WY
TUK-A-WILE
STONEFIELD CT
FARRADAY RIDGE DR
TURNBERRY DR
DEVON CT
FOWLER
DANERIN WY
RIO IVANHOE WY
MELORA
LORREL PL
VISTA DIEGO
CALLE DEL SOL RD
AVD DE LA LUNA
RESERVOIR ST
YUCCA ST
LYONS VALLEY RD
MYRTLE ST
ORANGE ST
CL DE ORO
CAMPO ST
RIO GRANDE RD
RIO MADRE LN
PEG LEG MINE RD
RAVEN HILL RD
LOMA VISTA DR
ROCKY SAGE RD
HIDDEN TRAIL DR
HIDDEN RIDGE RD
WILD WEST PL
GATE
0 .125 .25 .375 .5 miles 1 in. = 1900 ft.

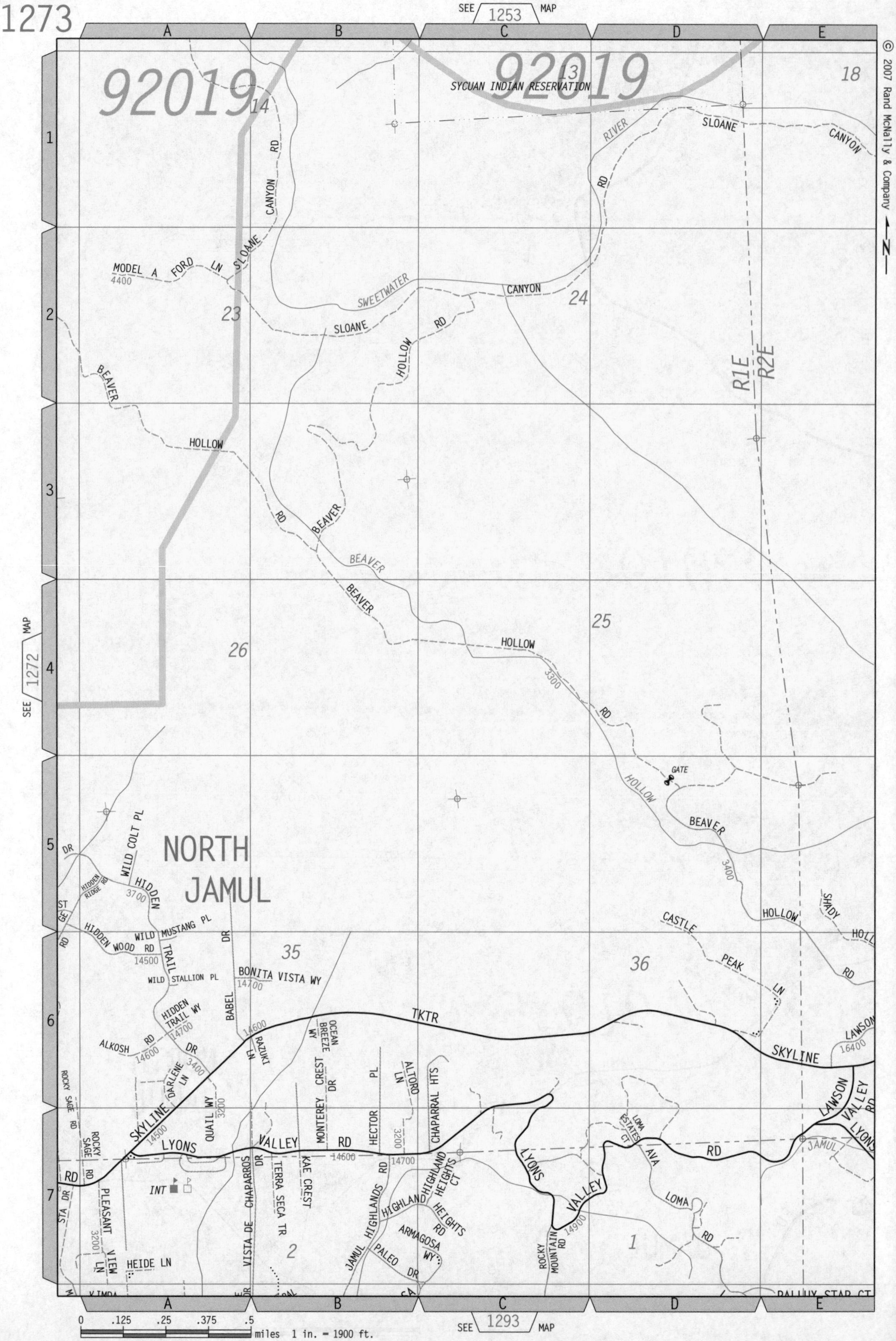
SEE 1253 MAP
SEE 1293 MAP
SEE 1272 MAP
SAN DIEGO CO.
© 2007 Rand McNally & Company
92019
92019
SYCUAN INDIAN RESERVATION
NORTH JAMUL
SLOANE CANYON RD
MODEL A FORD LN
SWEETWATER RIVER
CANYON
BEAVER HOLLOW RD
BEAVER
R1E
R2E
GATE
CASTLE PEAK LN
SHADY HOLLOW RD
WILD COLT PL
HIDDEN RIDGE RD
HIDDEN DR
WILD MUSTANG PL
HIDDEN WOOD RD
TRAIL DR
WILD STALLION PL
HIDDEN TRAIL WY
BONITA VISTA WY
BABEL DR
ALKOSH RD
DARLENE LN
SKYLINE TKTR
LAWSON VALLEY RD
RAZUKI LN
OCEAN BREEZE WY
MONTEREY CREST DR
HECTOR PL
ALTORO LN
CHAPARRAL HTS
QUAIL WY
LYONS VALLEY RD
ROCKY SAGE RD
PLEASANT VIEW LN
HEIDE LN
INT
VISTA DE CHAPARROS DR
TERRA SECA TR
KAE CREST
JAMUL HIGHLANDS RD
HIGHLAND HEIGHTS CT
HIGHLAND HEIGHTS RD
ARMAGOSA WY
PALEO DR
ROCKY MOUNTAIN RD
LOMA ESTATES CT
AVA
LOMA RD
JAMUL
RALLY STAR CT
KIMDA
STA DR
0 .125 .25 .375 .5 miles 1 in. = 1900 ft.

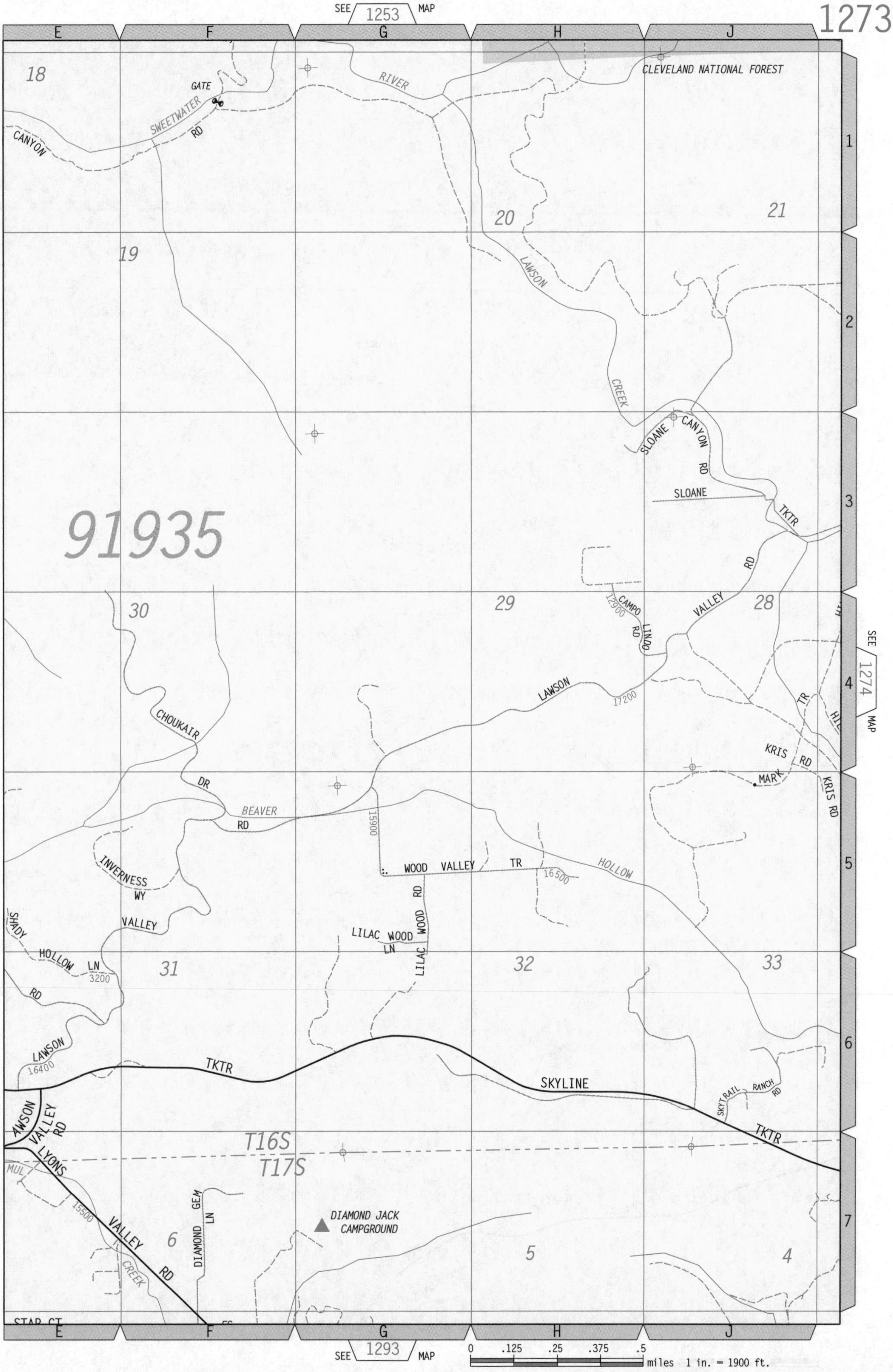
SEE 1253 MAP
E
F
G
H
J
1
2
3
4
5
6
7
SAN DIEGO CO.
18
GATE
SWEETWATER
RIVER
RD
CANYON
CLEVELAND NATIONAL FOREST
20
21
19
LAWSON
CREEK
SLOANE
CANYON
RD
SLOANE
TKTR
91935
RD
VALLEY
CAMPO
12900
RD
LINDO
30
29
28
SEE 1274 MAP
LAWSON
17200
TR
CHOUKAIR
DR
KRIS
RD
MARK
KRIS RD
BEAVER
RD
15900
INVERNESS
WY
WOOD
VALLEY
TR
16500
HOLLOW
RD
SHADY
VALLEY
LILAC
WOOD
LN
WOOD
LILAC
HOLLOW
LN
3200
31
32
33
RD
LAWSON
16400
TKTR
SKYLINE
SKYRAIL
RANCH
RD
AWSON
VALLEY
RD
TKTR
LYONS
T16S
T17S
MUL
15500
DIAMOND JACK
CAMPGROUND
VALLEY
GEM
LN
DIAMOND
6
5
4
CREEK
RD
STAR CT
FS
SEE 1293 MAP
0
.125
.25
.375
.5
miles 1 in. = 1900 ft.

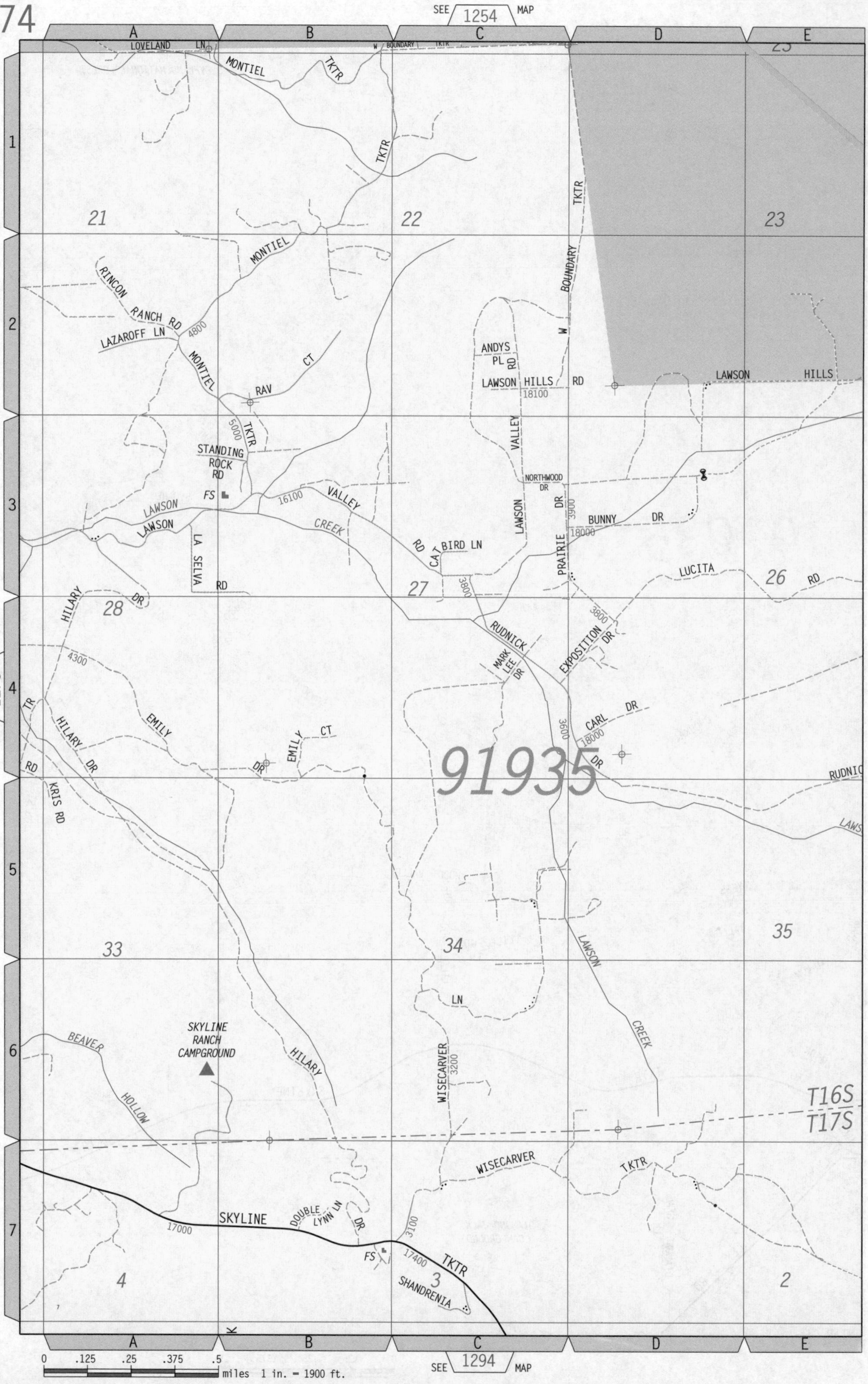
SEE 1254 MAP
SAN DIEGO CO.
SEE 1273 MAP
SEE 1294 MAP
LOVELAND LN
MONTIEL
TKTR
W BOUNDARY TKTR
21
22
23
RINCON RANCH RD
LAZAROFF LN
4800
MONTIEL
CT
RAV
5000
TKTR
STANDING ROCK RD
FS
16100
VALLEY
LAWSON
CREEK
RD
CAT BIRD LN
LA SELVA RD
HILARY DR
28
27
3800
ANDYS PL
RD
LAWSON HILLS RD
18100
VALLEY
LAWSON
NORTHWOOD DR
DR
3900
PRAIRIE
BUNNY DR
18000
LUCITA
26
RD
RUDNICK
3800
EXPOSITION DR
MARK LEE DR
4300
EMILY
HILARY DR
TR
RD
KRIS RD
EMILY CT
DR
CARL DR
18000
3600
DR
91935
RUDNIC
LAWS
33
34
35
LAWSON CREEK
LN
SKYLINE RANCH CAMPGROUND
BEAVER HOLLOW
HILARY
WISECARVER
3200
T16S
T17S
WISECARVER
TKTR
SKYLINE
17000
DOUBLE LYNN LN
DR
3100
FS
17400
TKTR
SHANDRENIA
4
3
2
0 .125 .25 .375 .5
miles 1 in. = 1900 ft.

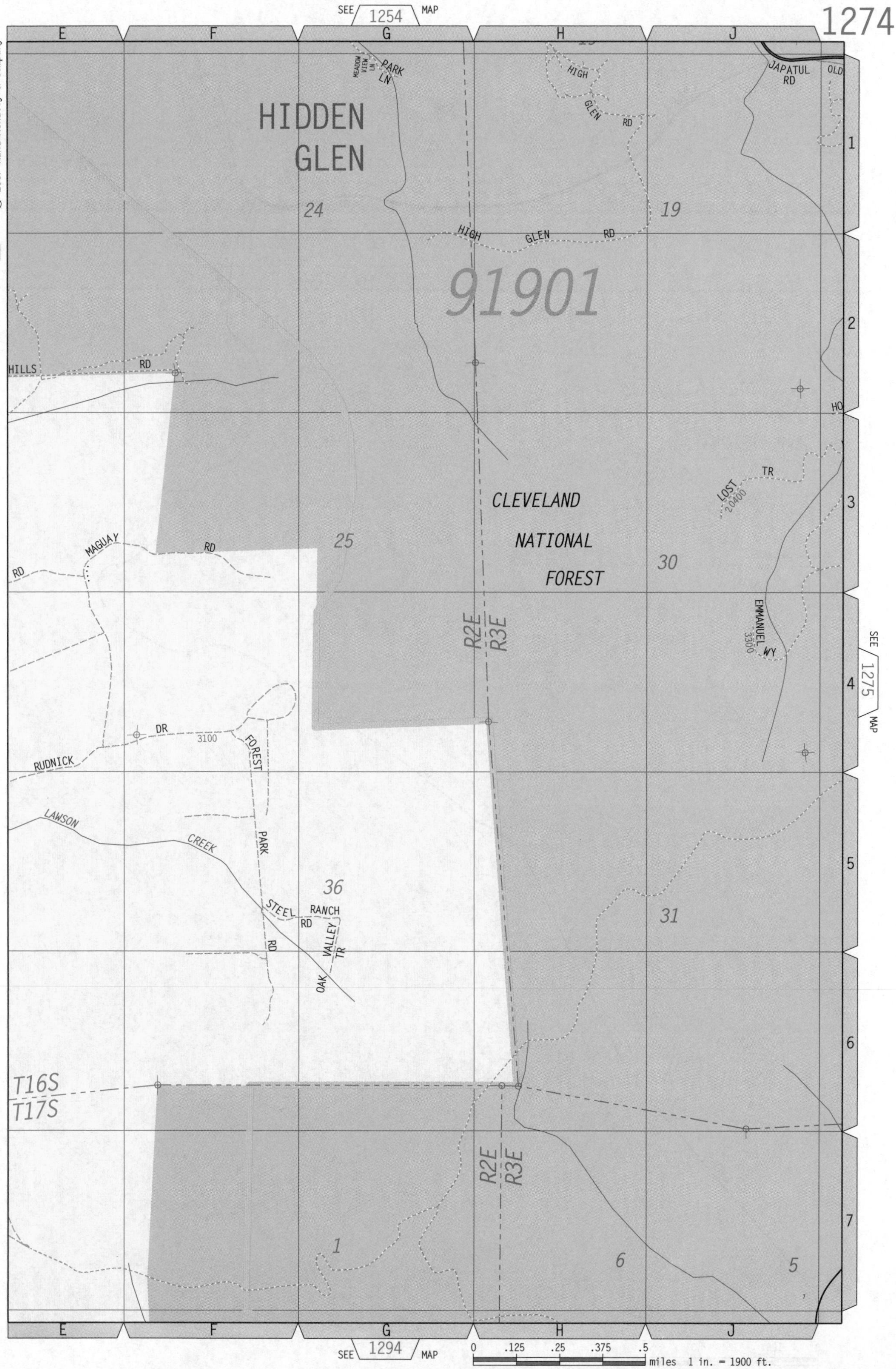
SEE 1254 MAP
E
F
G
H
J
HIDDEN
GLEN
MEADOW VIEW LN
PARK LN
HIGH
GLEN
RD
JAPATUL RD
OLD
24
19
HIGH GLEN RD
91901
HILLS
RD
HO
LOST TR
20400
CLEVELAND
NATIONAL
FOREST
MAGUAY RD
RD
25
30
EMMANUEL WY
3300
R2E
R3E
RUDNICK
DR
3100
FOREST PARK RD
LAWSON CREEK
36
STEEL RANCH RD
OAK VALLEY TR
31
T16S
T17S
1
6
5
1
2
3
4
5
6
7
SEE 1275 MAP
SAN DIEGO CO.
SEE 1294 MAP
0
.125
.25
.375
.5
miles 1 in. = 1900 ft.

SEE 1255 MAP

SEE 1274 MAP

SEE 1294 MAP

0 .125 .25 .375 .5 miles 1 in. = 1900 ft.

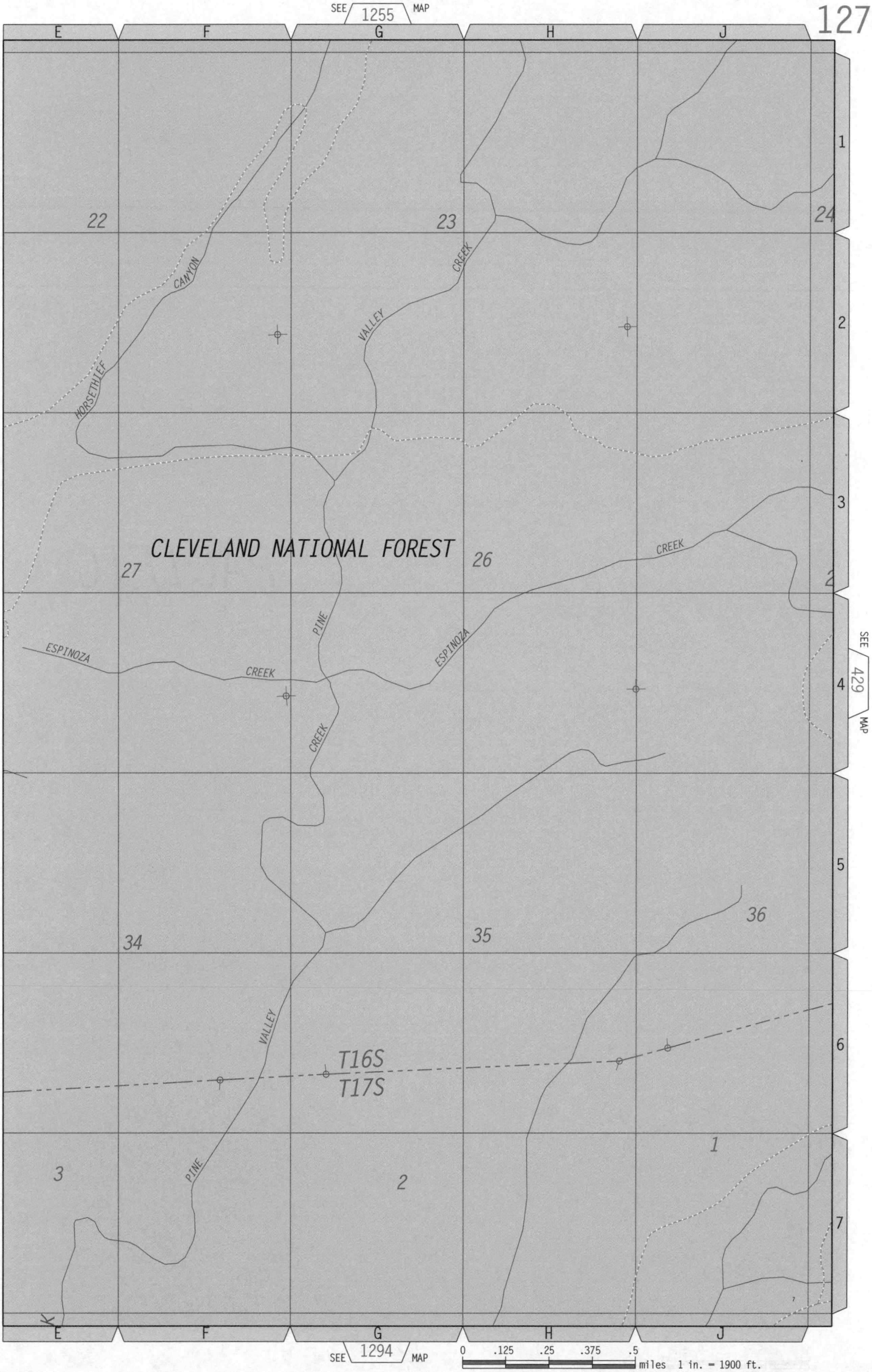
SEE 1255 MAP
E
F
G
H
J
1
2
3
4
5
6
7
22
23
24
CANYON
CREEK
VALLEY
HORSETHIEF
CLEVELAND NATIONAL FOREST
27
26
CREEK
PINE
ESPINOZA
CREEK
ESPINOZA
CREEK
SEE 429 MAP
36
34
35
VALLEY
T16S
T17S
1
3
PINE
2
SEE 1294 MAP
0 .125 .25 .375 .5
miles 1 in. = 1900 ft.

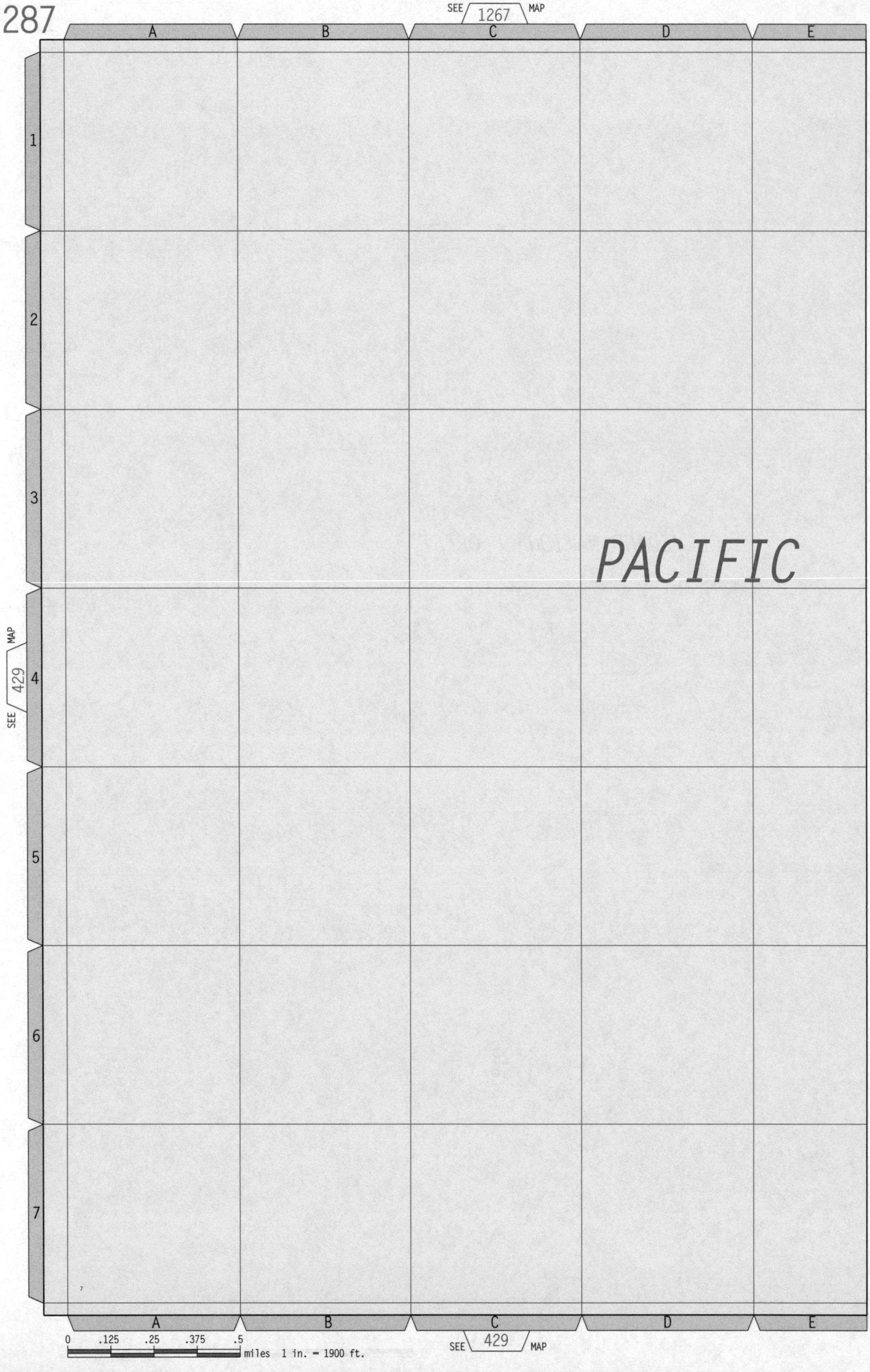
SEE 1267 MAP
A
B
C
D
E
1
2
3
4
5
6
7
PACIFIC
SEE 429 MAP
SEE 429 MAP
0 .125 .25 .375 .5
miles 1 in. = 1900 ft.

SEE 1267 MAP

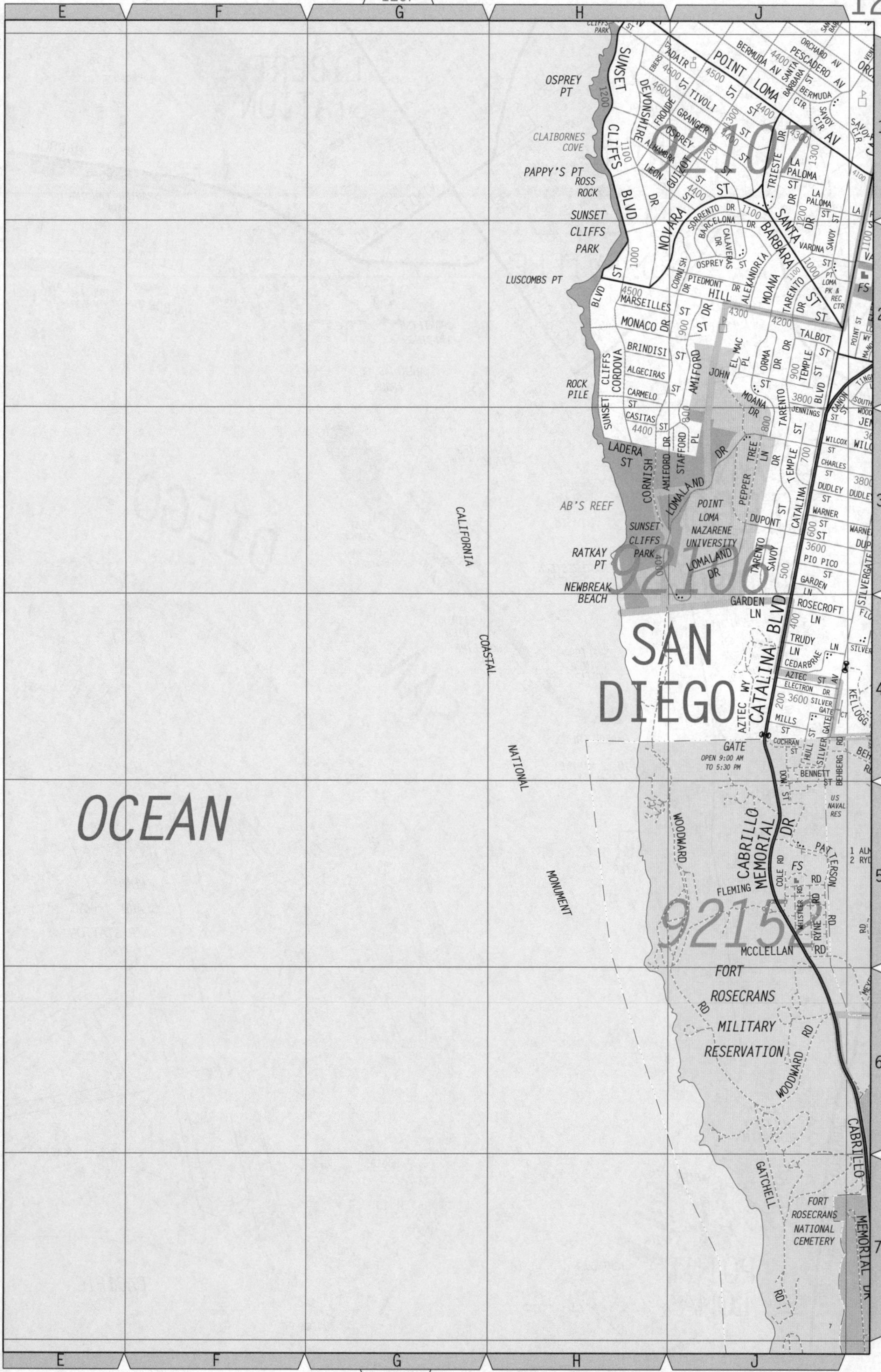

SEE 1288 MAP

SEE 429 MAP

0 .125 .25 .375 .5 miles 1 in. = 1900 ft.

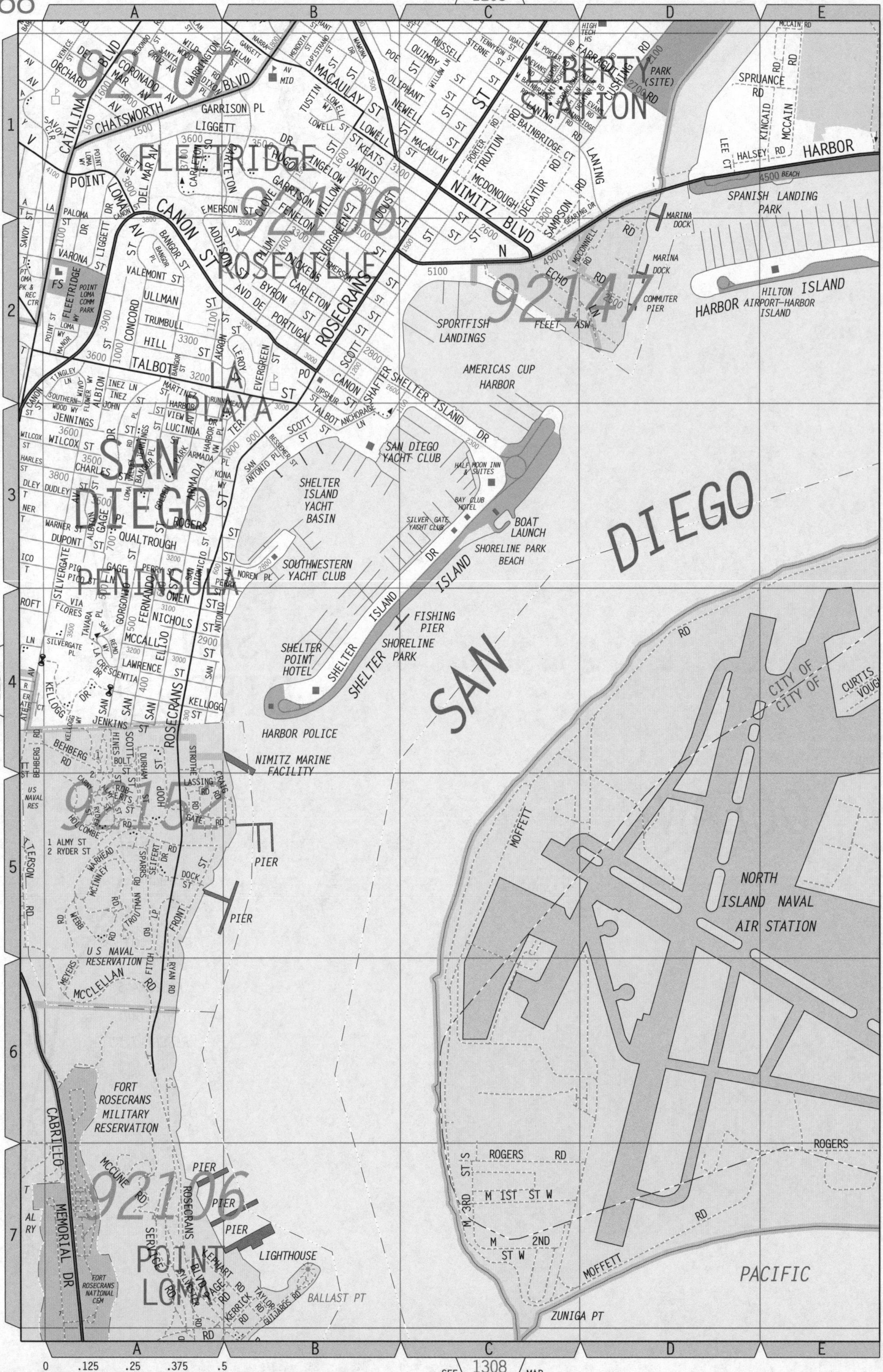

SEE 1268 MAP
SAN DIEGO CO.
92107
92106
92147
92152
LIBERTY STATION
FLEETRIDGE
ROSEVILLE
LA PLAYA
SAN DIEGO PENINSULA
POINT LOMA
SAN DIEGO
SPANISH LANDING PARK
HARBOR ISLAND
HILTON AIRPORT-HARBOR ISLAND
SPORTFISH LANDINGS
AMERICAS CUP HARBOR
SAN DIEGO YACHT CLUB
SHELTER ISLAND YACHT BASIN
SOUTHWESTERN YACHT CLUB
HALF MOON INN & SUITES
BAY CLUB HOTEL
SILVER GATE YACHT CLUB
BOAT LAUNCH
SHORELINE PARK BEACH
FISHING PIER
SHELTER POINT HOTEL
SHORELINE PARK
HARBOR POLICE
NIMITZ MARINE FACILITY
PIER
US NAVAL RES
U S NAVAL RESERVATION
FORT ROSECRANS MILITARY RESERVATION
FORT ROSECRANS NATIONAL CEM
LIGHTHOUSE
BALLAST PT
ZUNIGA PT
NORTH ISLAND NAVAL AIR STATION
PACIFIC
ROSECRANS ST
CANON ST
TALBOT ST
NIMITZ BLVD
HARBOR DR
SHELTER ISLAND DR
CATALINA BLVD
CABRILLO MEMORIAL DR
CHATSWORTH BLVD
POINT LOMA AV
SEE 1287 MAP
0 .125 .25 .375 .5 miles 1 in. = 1900 ft.
SEE 1308 MAP

SEE 1268 MAP
SAN DIEGO INTERNATIONAL AIRPORT
TERMINAL 2
TERMINAL 1
COMMUTER TERMINAL
AIR FREIGHT BUILDING
GODDARD WY
STILLWATER RD
WINSHIP LN
AIR LN
HARBOR DR
LINDBERGH FIELD
OPEN SPACE
LAUREL ST
PACIFIC HWY
U S COAST GUARD STATION
92101
SHERATON SAN DIEGO HOTEL & MARINA EAST
HARBOR ISLAND DR
SHERATON SAN DIEGO HOTEL & MARINA WEST
HARBOR ISLAND DR PARK
LITTLE ITALY
KETTNER BLVD
INDIA ST
STATE ST
COLUMBIA ST
COUNTY ADMINISTRATION CENTER
SAN DIEGO MARITIME MUSEUM
ASH ST
HOLIDAY INN ON THE BAY
US CUSTOMS
SAN DIEGO CRUISE SHIP TERMINAL
B ST PIER
BROADWAY
BROADWAY PIER
NAVY PIER
USS MIDWAY
UNITED STATES NAVAL RES
BAY
SAN DIEGO LIMITS
SAN CORONADO
CURTIS VOUGHT
PIER
G ST PIER
TUNA HARBOR
EMBASSY SUITES SAN DIEGO BAY
MANCHESTER GRAND HYATT
SEAPORT VILLAGE
TUNA HARBOR PIER
SEE 1289 MAP
EMBARCADERO MARINA PARK NORTH
SAN DIEGO CORONADO FERRY
SEE A J6
1 SOLEDAD PL
2 GLORIETTA PL
QUENTIN ROOSEVELT BLVD
92135
NORTH ISLAND NAVAL AIR STATION
MCCAIN BLVD
BAYVIEW PARK
HARBORVIEW PARK
CENTENNIAL PARK
CORONADO FERRY & FISHING PIER
FERRY LANDING MARKETPLACE
CORONADO
SEA N AIR GOLF COURSE
92118
ALAMEDA BLVD
ORANGE AV
GLORIETTA BLVD
POMONA AV
SPRECKELS PARK
OCEAN BLVD
SUNSET PARK
CORONADO MUNICIPAL BEACH
NORTH BEACH
CENTRAL BEACH
LIFEGUARD FACILITY
STAR PARK
CORONADO GOLF COURSE
CALIFORNIA COASTAL NATIONAL MONUMENT
OCEAN
SEE 1308 MAP
0 .125 .25 .375 .5 miles 1 in. = 1900 ft.

SEE 1269 MAP

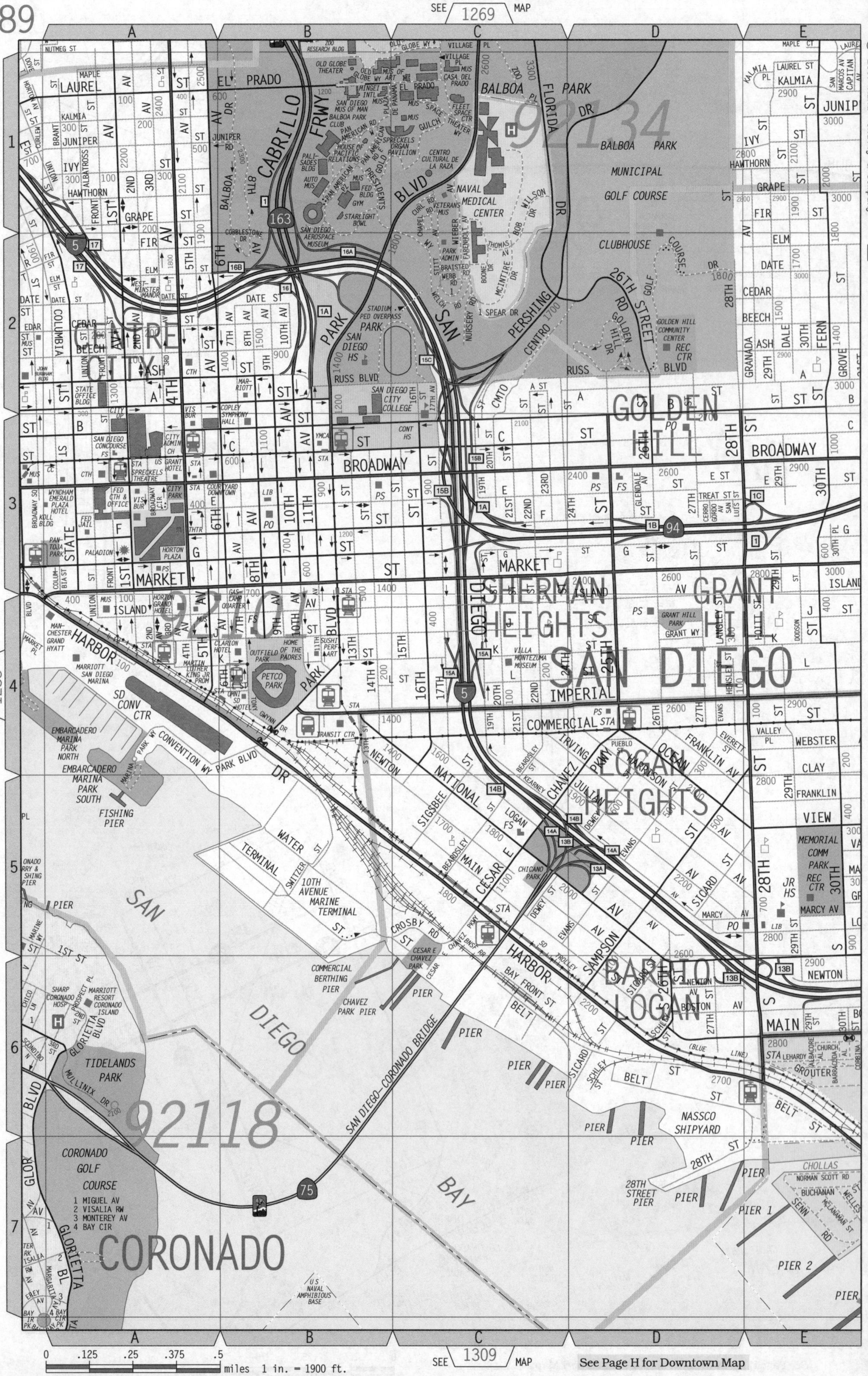

0 .125 .25 .375 .5 miles 1 in. = 1900 ft.

SEE 1309 MAP

See Page H for Downtown Map

SEE 1269 MAP

SAN DIEGO CO.

SEE 1290 MAP

SEE 1309 MAP

0 .125 .25 .375 .5 miles 1 in. = 1900 ft.

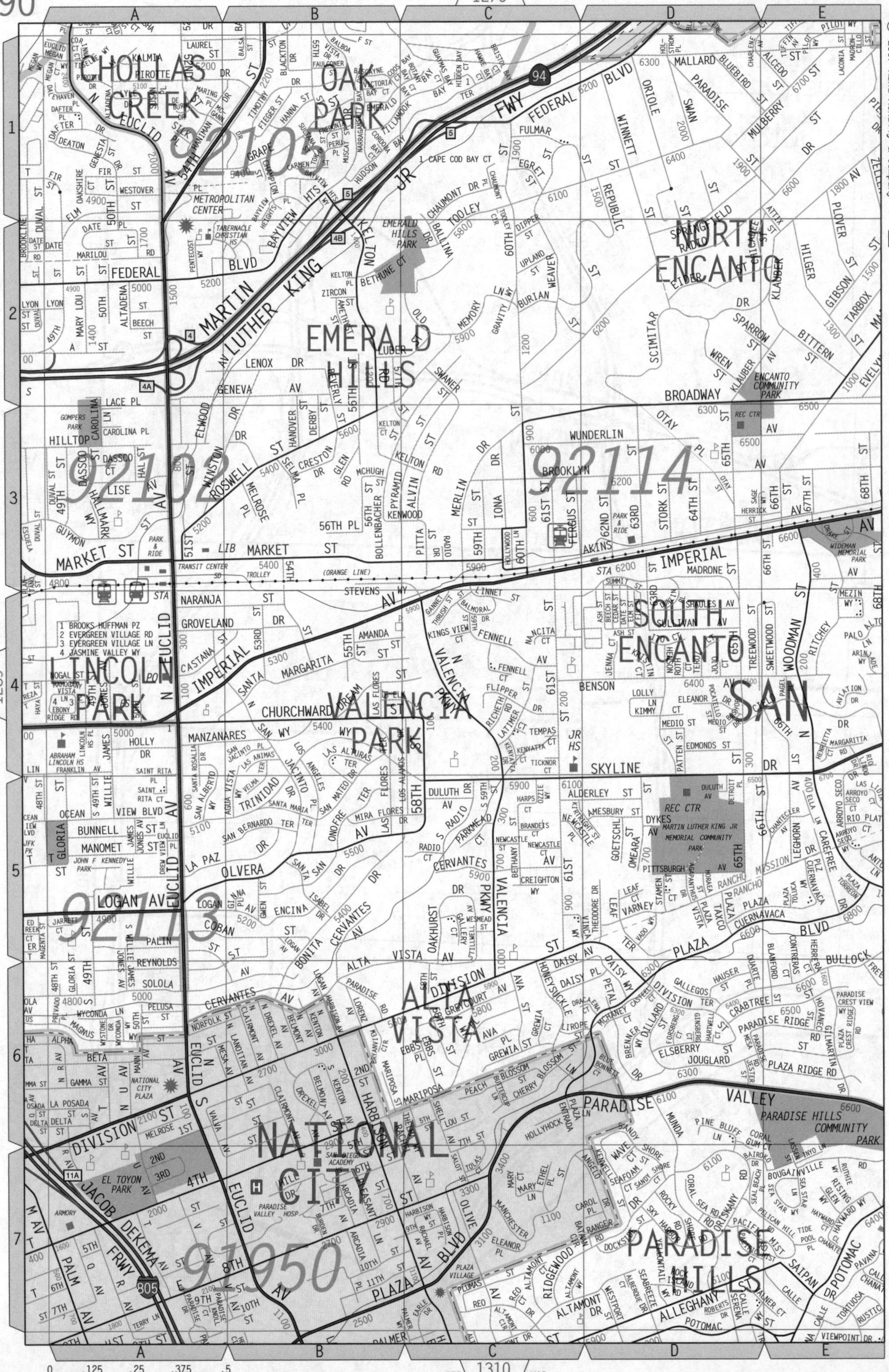
SEE 1270 MAP
A
B
C
D
E
1
2
3
4
5
6
7
CHOLLAS CREEK
OAK PARK
92105
EMERALD HILLS
NORTH ENCANTO
92114
92102
LINCOLN PARK
VALENCIA PARK
SOUTH ENCANTO
SAN
92113
ALTA VISTA
NATIONAL CITY
91950
PARADISE HILLS
MARTIN LUTHER KING JR FWY
94
805
METROPOLITAN CENTER
EMERALD HILLS PARK
ENCANTO COMMUNITY PARK
GOMPERS PARK
WIDEMAN MEMORIAL PARK
JOHN F KENNEDY PARK
MARTIN LUTHER KING JR MEMORIAL COMMUNITY PARK
PARADISE HILLS COMMUNITY PARK
EL TOYON PARK
NATIONAL CITY PLAZA
PARADISE VALLEY HOSP
ABRAHAM LINCOLN HS
1 BROOKS HUFFMAN PZ
2 EVERGREEN VILLAGE RD
3 EVERGREEN VILLAGE LN
4 JASMINE VALLEY WY
1 CAPE COD BAY CT
SEE 1289 MAP
SEE 1310 MAP
0 .125 .25 .375 .5
miles 1 in. = 1900 ft.

SEE 1270 MAP

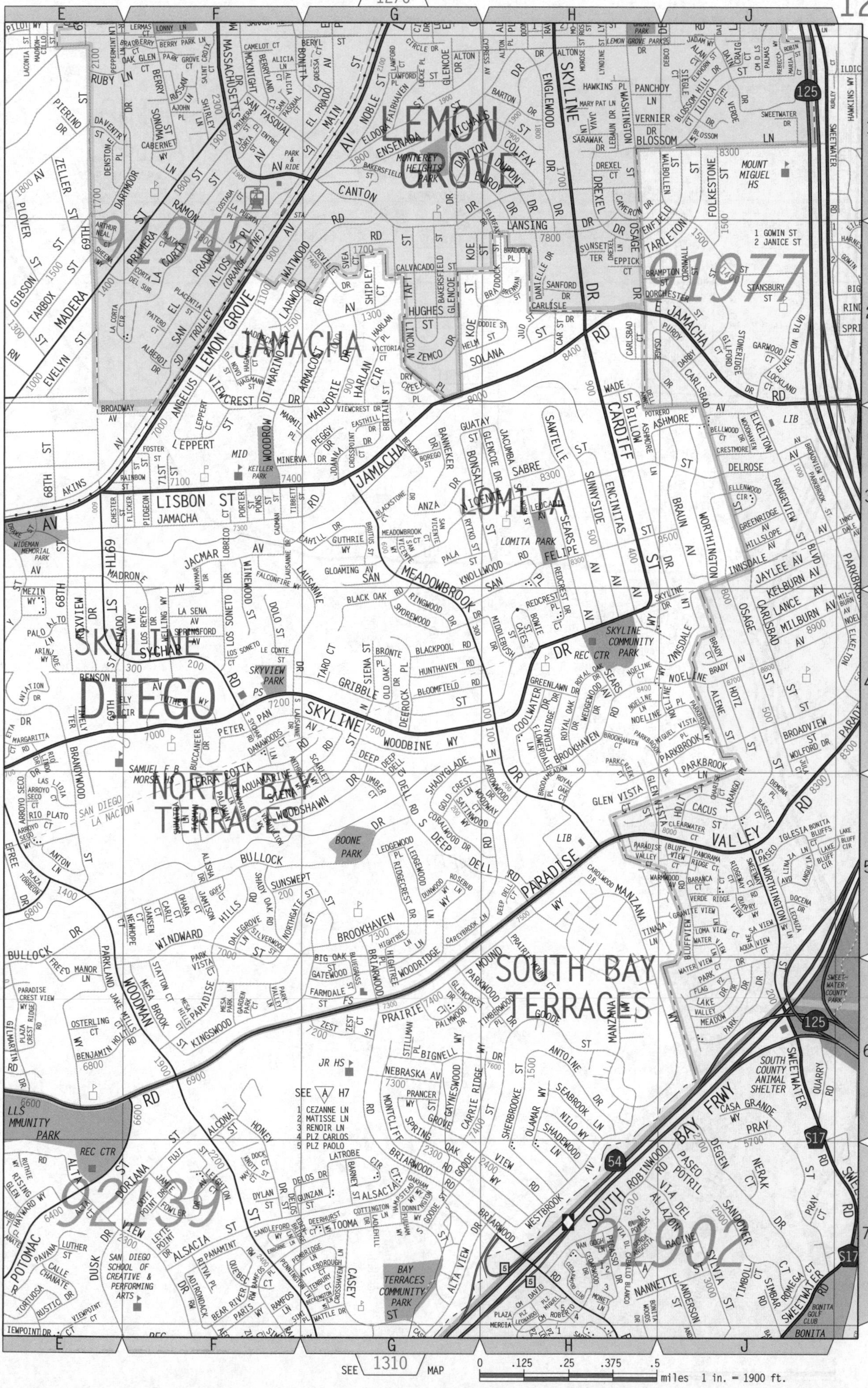

SEE 1291 MAP
SEE 1310 MAP

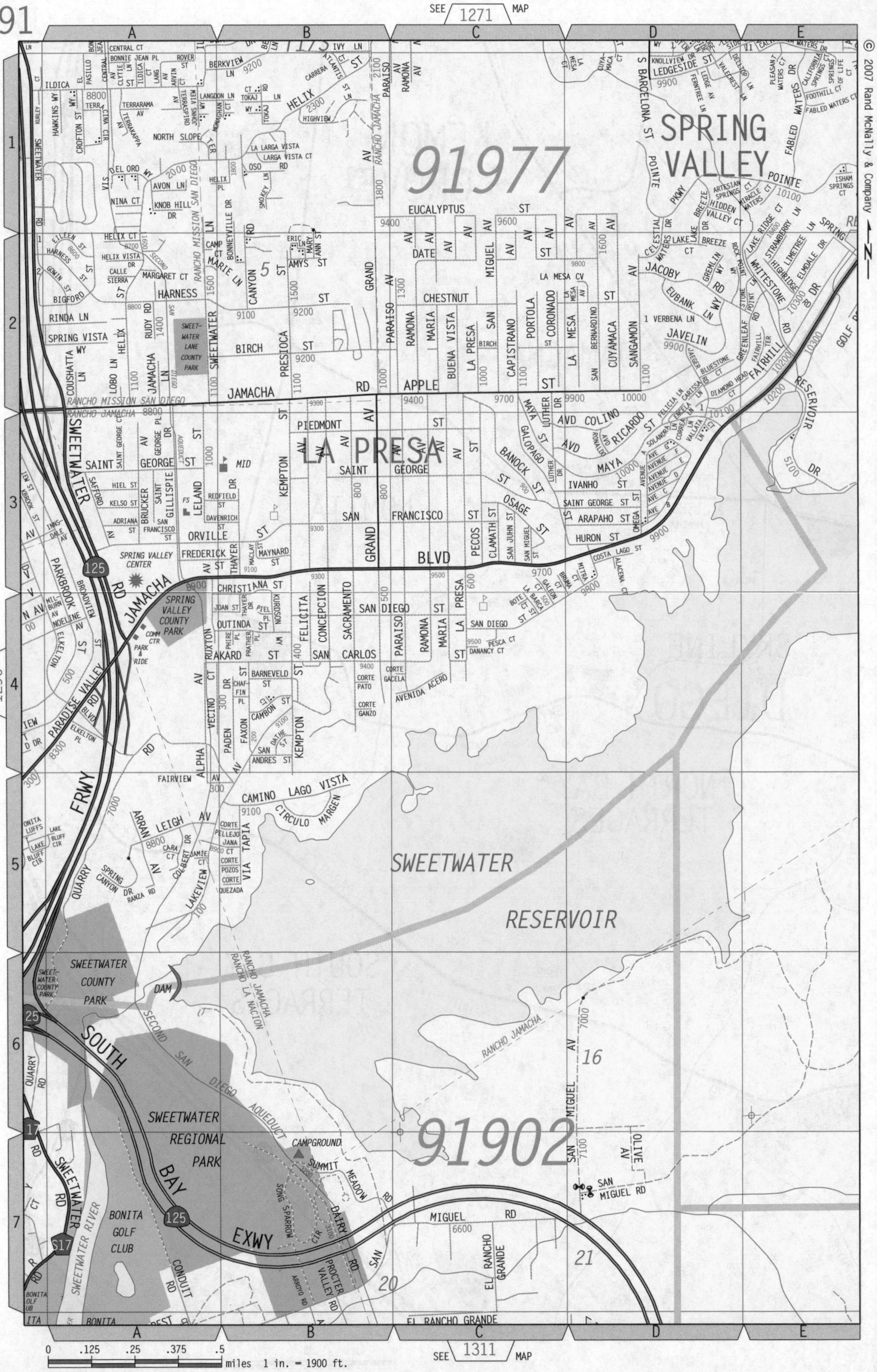
SEE 1271 MAP
SEE 1290 MAP
SEE 1311 MAP
A
B
C
D
E
1
2
3
4
5
6
7
91977
SPRING VALLEY
LA PRESA
91902
SWEETWATER
RESERVOIR
SWEETWATER LANE COUNTY PARK
SPRING VALLEY COUNTY PARK
SPRING VALLEY CENTER
SWEETWATER COUNTY PARK
SWEETWATER REGIONAL PARK
BONITA GOLF CLUB
SWEETWATER RIVER
DAM
CAMPGROUND
SWEETWATER FRWY
SOUTH BAY EXWY
JAMACHA RD
JAMACHA BLVD
SAN DIEGO ST
SAN MIGUEL AV
SAN MIGUEL RD
MIGUEL RD
EL RANCHO GRANDE
RANCHO MISSION SAN DIEGO
RANCHO JAMACHA
RANCHO LA NACION
SECOND SAN DIEGO AQUEDUCT
CAMINO LAGO VISTA
CIRCULO MARGEN
CHESTNUT ST
BIRCH ST
APPLE ST
EUCALYPTUS ST
SAINT GEORGE ST
SAN FRANCISCO ST
SAN CARLOS ST
HELIX ST
GRAND AV
PARAISO AV
RAMONA AV
MARIA AV
LA PRESA AV
KEMPTON ST
SWEETWATER ST
PRESIOCA ST
ORVILLE ST
FREDERICK ST
CHRISTIANA ST
AKARD ST
PARADISE VALLEY RD
QUARRY RD
FAIRVIEW AV
LEIGH AV
ALPHA AV
VIA TAPIA
LAKEVIEW AV
HARNESS ST
RINDA LN
SPRING VISTA WY
BIGFORD ST
RESERVOIR DR
FAIRHILL DR
JAVELIN
JACOBY
RICARDO ST
MAYA ST
AVD COLINO
IVANHO ST
ARAPAHO ST
HURON ST
PECOS ST
CLAMATH ST
OSAGE ST
BANOCK ST
SAN JUAN ST
COSTA LAGO ST
PIEDMONT ST
FELICITA
CONCEPCION
SACRAMENTO
AVENIDA ACERO
CONDUIT RD
PROCTER VALLEY RD
SUMMIT
MEADOW RD
DAIRY RD
SONG SPARROW
OLIVE AV
EL RANCHO GRANDE
16
20
21
5
125
25
17
S17
0 .125 .25 .375 .5
miles 1 in. = 1900 ft.

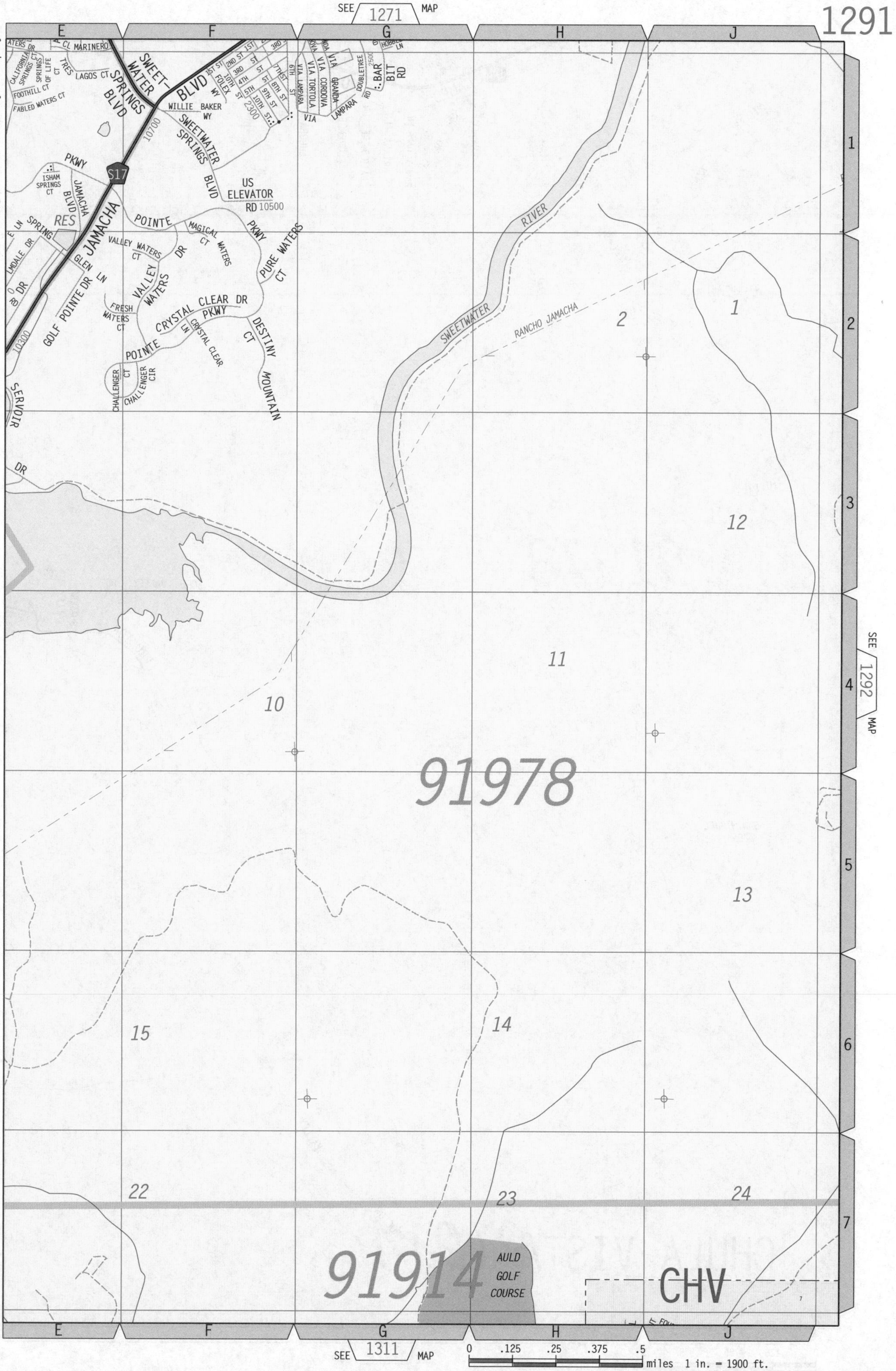
SEE 1271 MAP
SEE 1292 MAP
SEE 1311 MAP
SAN DIEGO CO.
E
F
G
H
J
1
2
3
4
5
6
7
SWEETWATER SPRINGS BLVD
SWEETWATER BLVD
SWEETWATER SPRINGS BLVD
WILLIE BAKER WY
CL MARINERO
LAGOS CT
TRES
FOOTHILL CT
FABLED WATERS CT
S17
10700
10300
10500
US ELEVATOR RD
ISHAM SPRINGS CT
PKWY
JAMACHA BLVD
JAMACHA
RES
SPRING
GLEN LN
GOLF POINTE DR
POINTE
MAGICAL CT
WATERS
PKWY
PURE WATERS CT
VALLEY WATERS CT
VALLEY WATERS DR
FRESH WATERS CT
CRYSTAL CLEAR DR
CRYSTAL CLEAR LN
PKWY
DESTINY CT
MOUNTAIN
POINTE
CHALLENGER CT
CHALLENGER CIR
SERVOIR
DR
1ST ST
2ND ST
3RD
4TH
5TH
6TH
7TH
8TH ST
9TH ST
10TH ST
FOLEX WY
2300
VIA TORTOLA
VIA CORDOVA
VIA GRANDA
VIA LAMPARA
LAMPARA
DOUBLETREE RD
2500
BAR BIT RD
HOBBLE LN
SWEETWATER RIVER
RANCHO JAMACHA
1
2
10
11
12
13
14
15
22
23
24
91978
91914
AULD GOLF COURSE
CHV
0
.125
.25
.375
.5
miles 1 in. = 1900 ft.

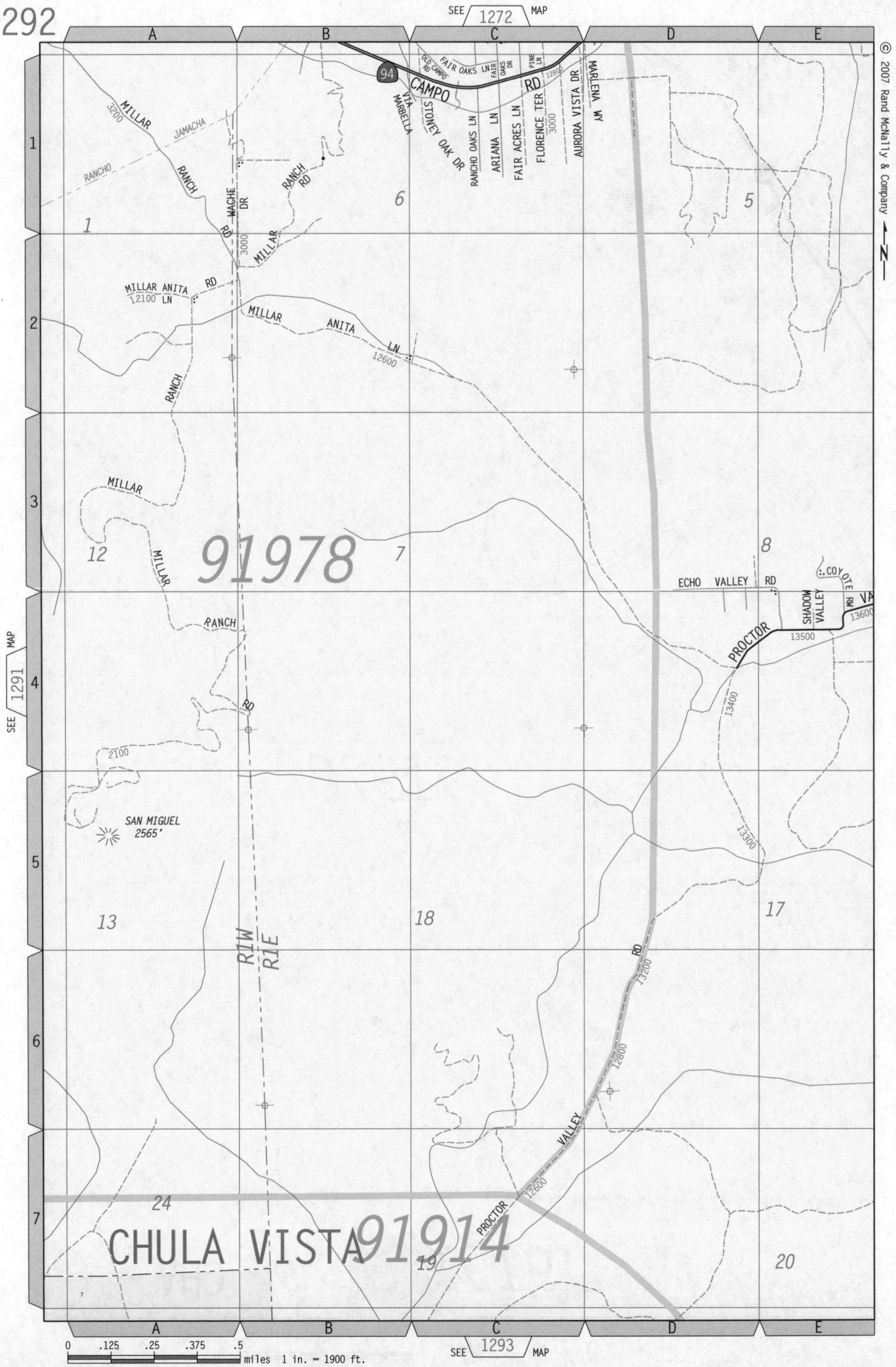
SEE 1272 MAP
SAN DIEGO CO.
© 2007 Rand McNally & Company
A
B
C
D
E
1
2
3
4
5
6
7
94
CAMPO RD
OLD CAMPO RD
FAIR OAKS LN
FAIR OAKS DR
PINE LN
12800
MARLENA WY
AURORA VISTA DR
3000
FLORENCE TER
FAIR ACRES LN
ARIANA LN
RANCHO OAKS LN
STONEY OAK DR
VIA MARBELLA
3200
MILLAR RANCH RD
JAMACHA
RANCHO
WACHE DR
3000
MILLAR RANCH RD
MILLAR ANITA RD
MILLAR ANITA LN
12100
12600
1
5
6
7
8
12
91978
ECHO VALLEY RD
COYOTE
SHADOW VALLEY
RW
VA
13600
13500
PROCTOR
13400
2100
SAN MIGUEL
2565'
13300
13
17
18
R1W
R1E
RD
13200
12800
VALLEY
12600
PROCTOR
24
CHULA VISTA
91914
19
20
SEE 1291 MAP
SEE 1293 MAP
0 .125 .25 .375 .5 miles 1 in. = 1900 ft.

SEE 1272 MAP

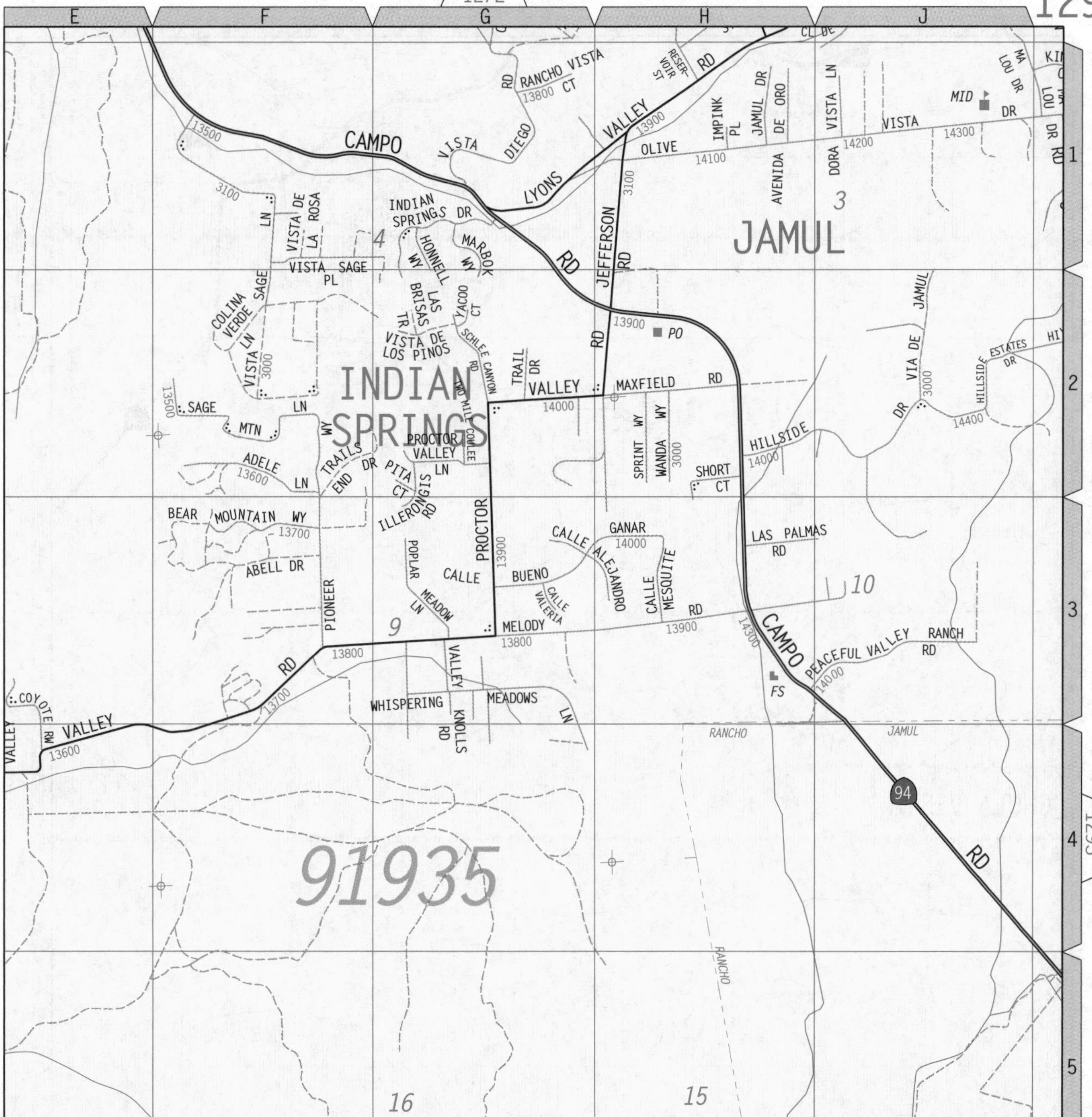

SEE 1293 MAP

0 .125 .25 .375 .5 miles 1 in. = 1900 ft.

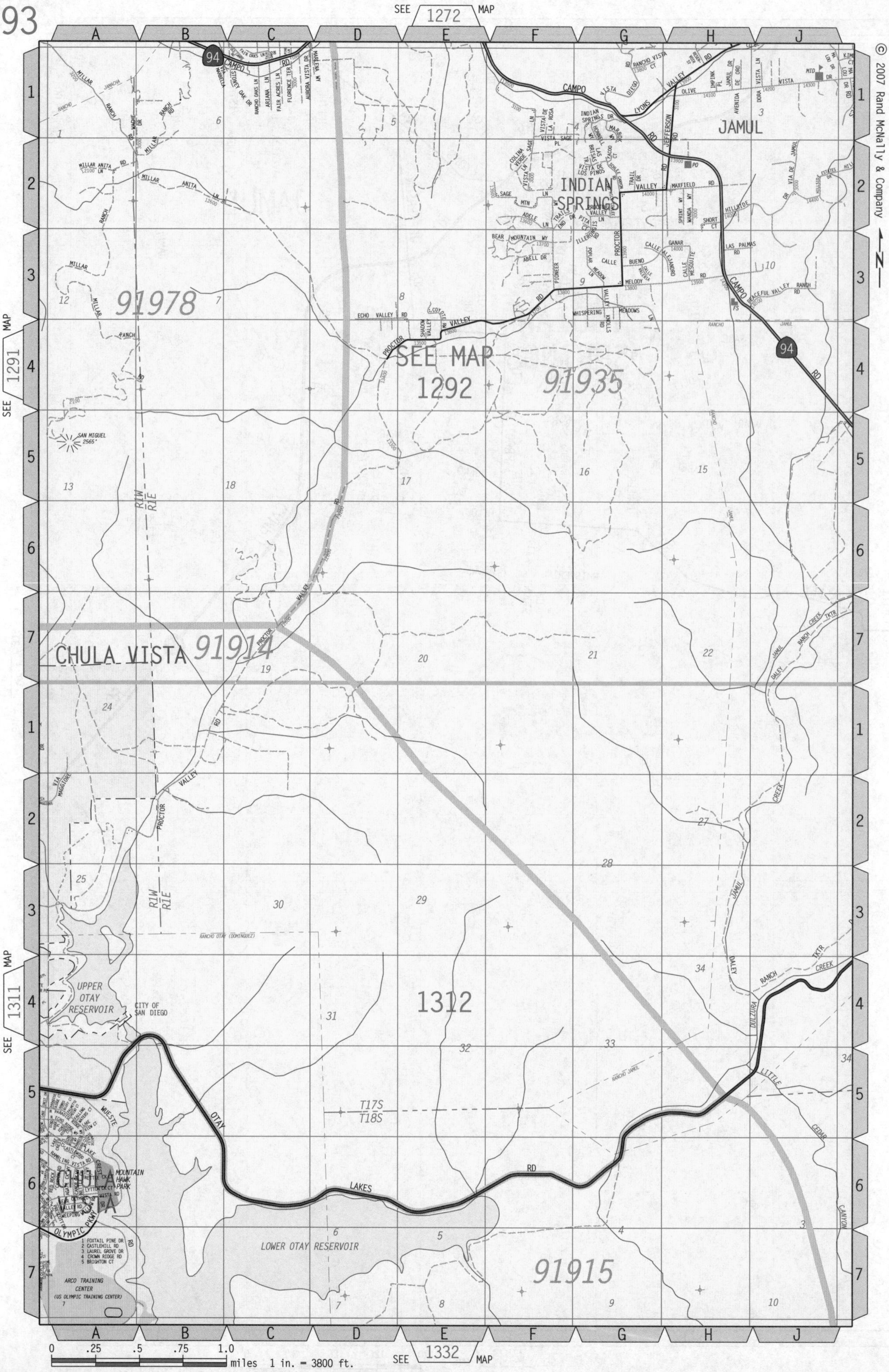
SEE 1272 MAP
SEE 1291 MAP
SEE 1311 MAP
SEE 1332 MAP
SEE MAP 1292
1312
JAMUL
INDIAN SPRINGS
CHULA VISTA
91978
91935
91914
91915
SAN MIGUEL 2565'
UPPER OTAY RESERVOIR
CITY OF SAN DIEGO
LOWER OTAY RESERVOIR
MOUNTAIN HAWK PARK
ARCO TRAINING CENTER (US OLYMPIC TRAINING CENTER)
1 FOXTAIL PINE DR
2 CASTLEHILL RD
3 LAUREL GROVE DR
4 CROWN RIDGE RD
5 BRIGHTON CT
CAMPO RD
LYONS VALLEY RD
JEFFERSON RD
PROCTOR VALLEY RD
OTAY LAKES RD
DULZURA RANCH
JAMUL DALEY RANCH
RANCHO OTAY (DOMINGUEZ)
RANCHO JAMUL
R1W R1E
T17S T18S
0 .25 .5 .75 1.0 miles 1 in. = 3800 ft.

SEE 1273 MAP

SAN DIEGO CO.

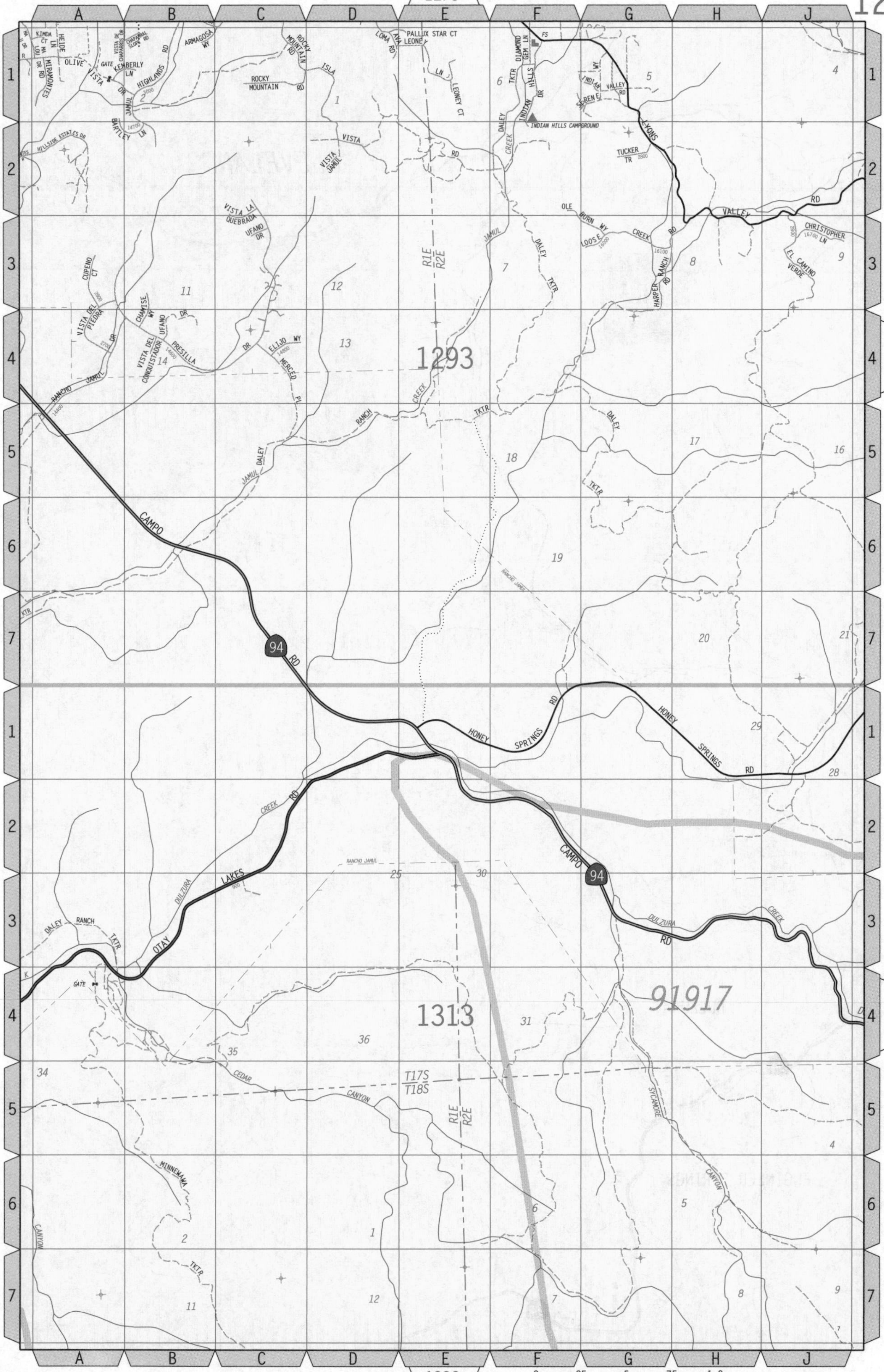

SEE 1294 MAP

SEE 1294 MAP

SEE 1332 MAP

0 .25 .5 .75 1.0 miles 1 in. = 3800 ft.

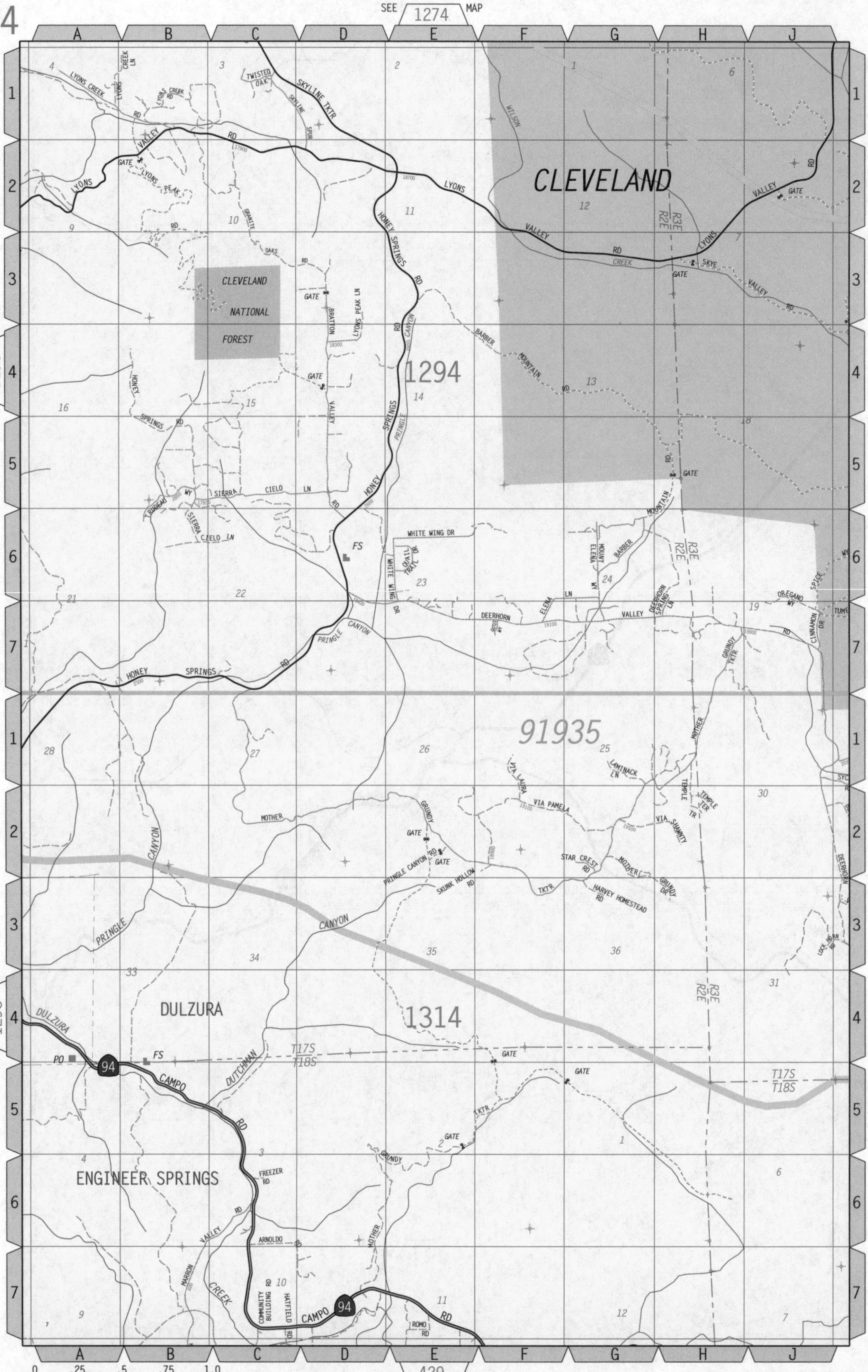
SEE 1274 MAP
SEE 1293 MAP
SEE 429 MAP
CLEVELAND
CLEVELAND NATIONAL FOREST
1294
91935
1314
DULZURA
ENGINEER SPRINGS
LYONS VALLEY RD
LYONS CREEK
LYONS PEAK
SKYLINE TKTR
TWISTED OAK
HONEY SPRINGS RD
PRINGLE CANYON
GRANITE OAKS RD
BRATTON
LYONS PEAK LN
BARBER MOUNTAIN RD
SIERRA CIELO LN
WHITE WING DR
QUAIL TRAIL DR
DEERHORN VALLEY RD
DEERHORN SPRINGS LN
MOUNT ELENA WY
ELENA LN
OREGANO WY
CINNAMON DR
SPICE WY
GRUNDY TKTR
SKYE VALLEY RD
MOTHER GRUNDY TKTR
LAMINACK LN
VIA LAURA
VIA PAMELA
VIA SHAMMY
TEMPLE TR
STAR CREST RD
HARVEY HOMESTEAD RD
SKUNK HOLLOW RD
MOTHER GRUNDY DR
DULZURA
CAMPO RD
DUTCHMAN
FREEZER RD
ARNOLDO RD
MARRON VALLEY RD
COMMUNITY BUILDING RD
HATFIELD RD
ROMO
PO
FS
GATE
94
R3E R2E
T17S T18S
0 .25 .5 .75 1.0 miles 1 in. = 3800 ft.

SEE 1275 MAP

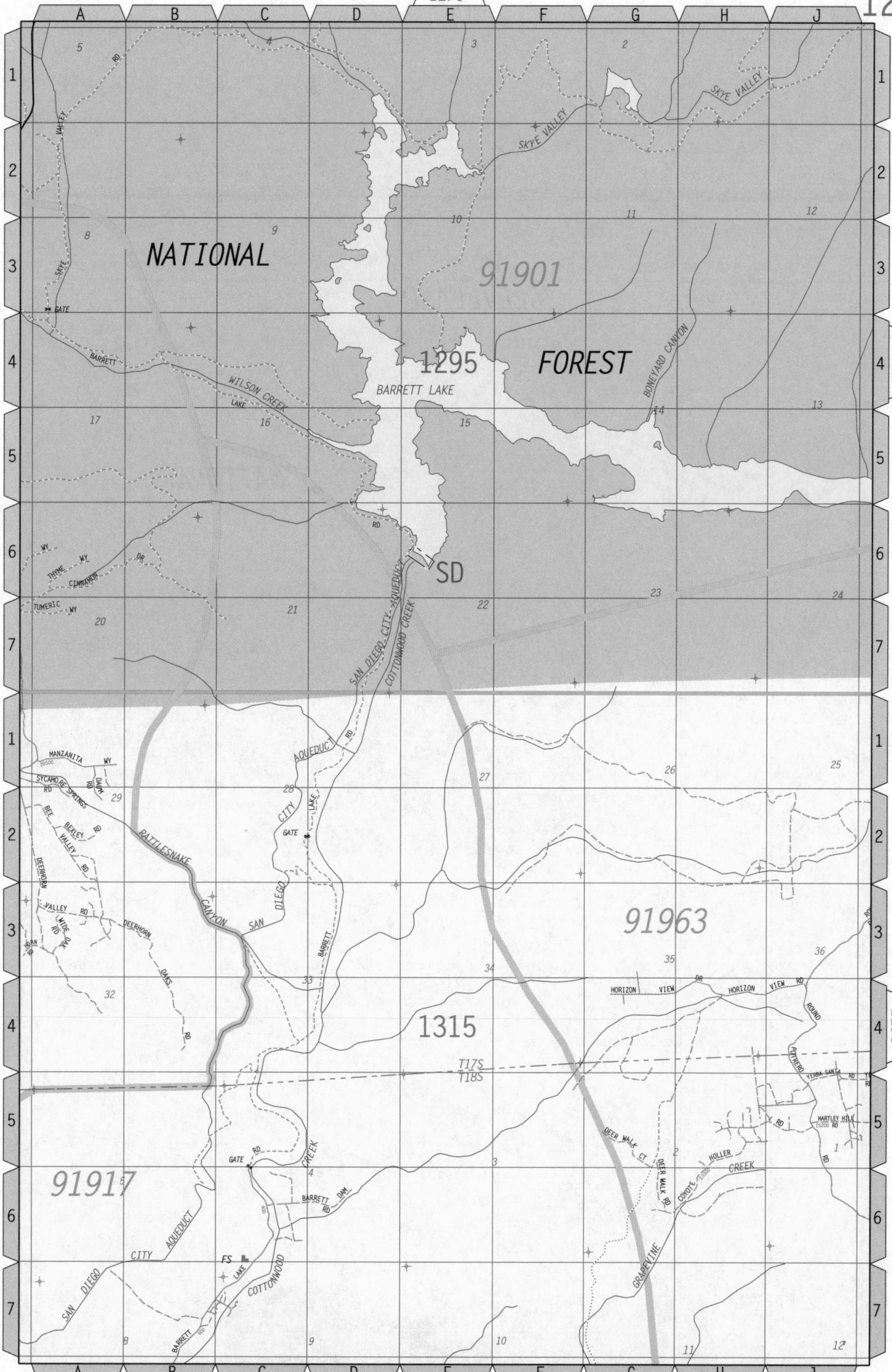

SEE 1296 MAP

SEE 1296 MAP

SEE 429 MAP

0 .25 .5 .75 1.0 miles 1 in. = 3800 ft.

SAN DIEGO CO.

SEE 429 MAP

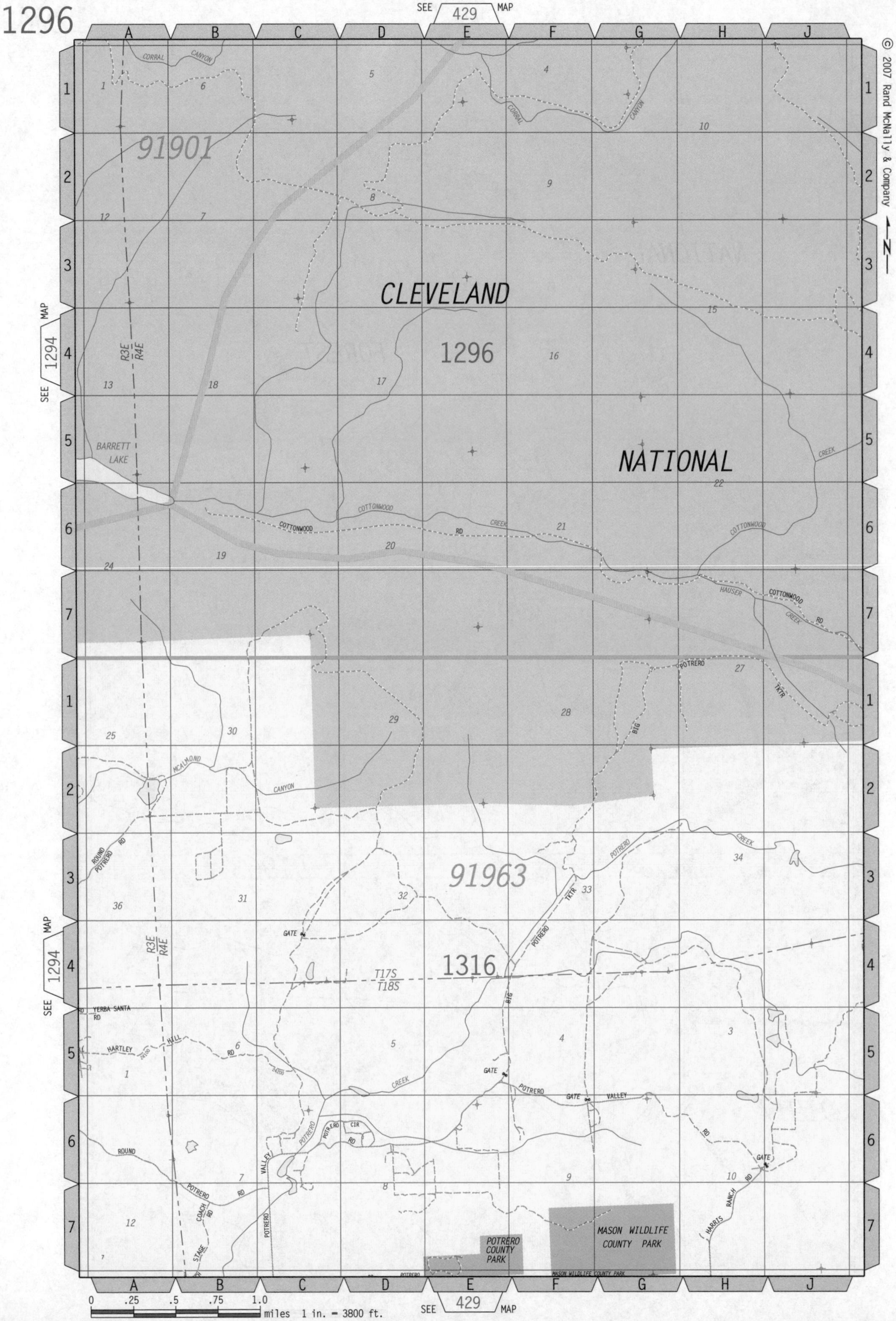

SEE 429 MAP

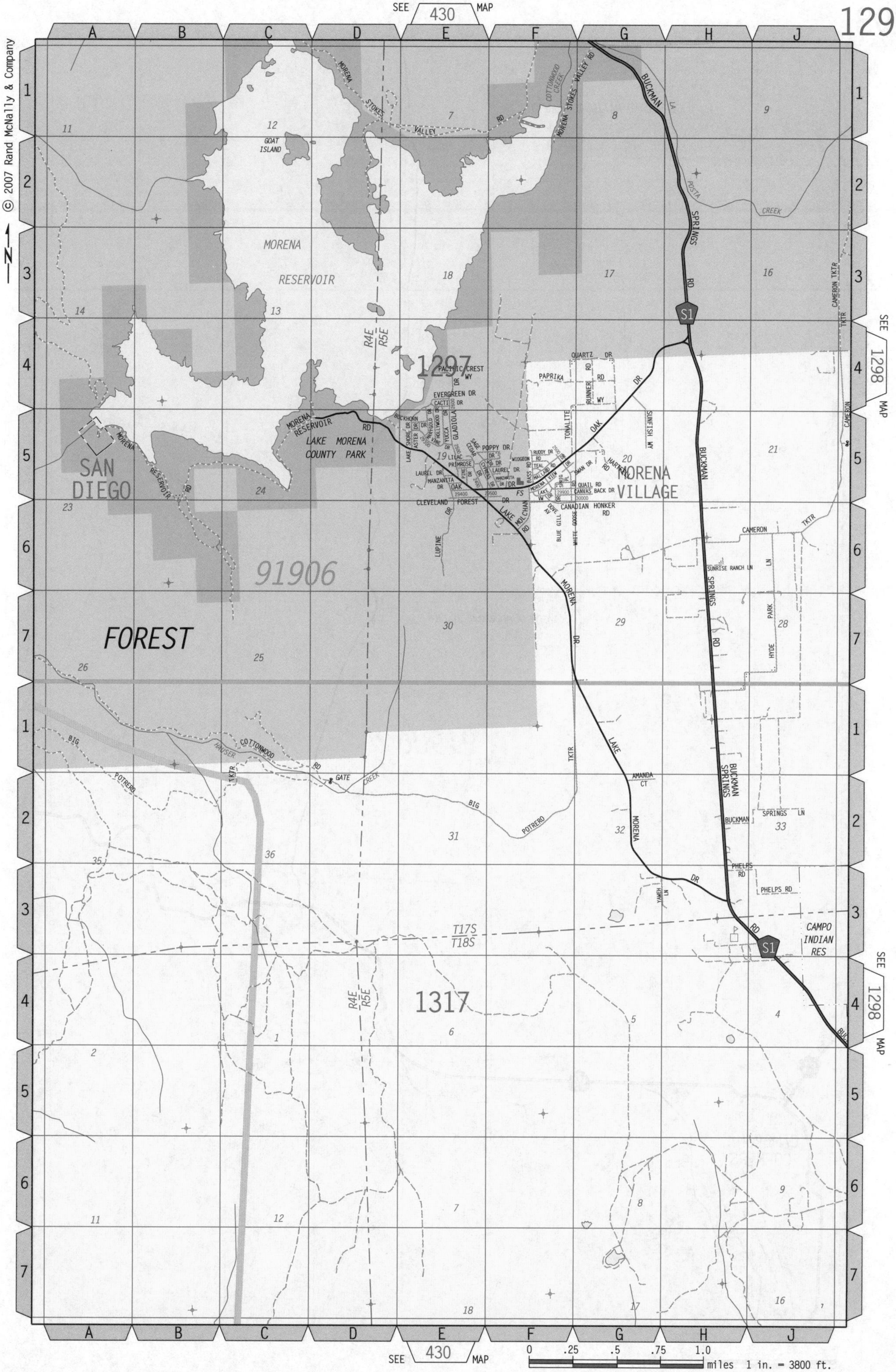

0 .25 .5 .75 1.0 miles 1 in. = 3800 ft.

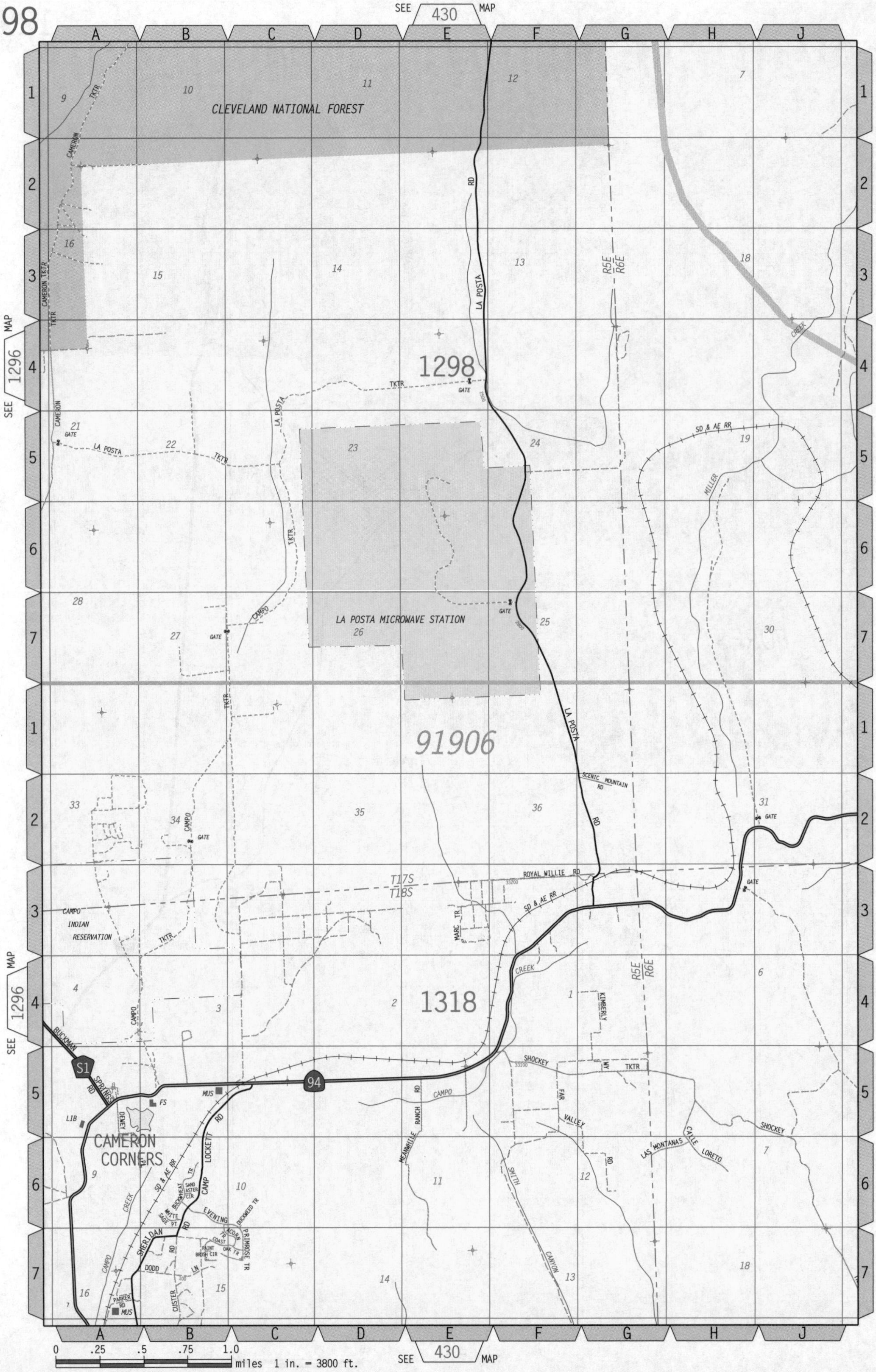
SEE 430 MAP
A
B
C
D
E
F
G
H
J
1
2
3
4
5
6
7
CLEVELAND NATIONAL FOREST
CAMERON TKTR
TKTR
LA POSTA RD
R5E
R6E
SEE 1296 MAP
1298
GATE
LA POSTA
CAMERON
SD & AE RR
MILLER
CREEK
LA POSTA MICROWAVE STATION
CAMPO
91906
SCENIC MOUNTAIN RD
ROYAL WILLIE RD
T17S
T18S
CAMPO INDIAN RESERVATION
MARC TR
1318
KIMBERLY
BUCKMAN SPRINGS RD
S1
94
FS
MUS
LIB
DEWEY
CAMERON CORNERS
LOCKETT RD
CAMP RD
SHOCKEY
FAR VALLEY RD
MEANWHILE RANCH RD
SMITH CANYON
LAS MONTANAS
CALLE LORETO
SHERIDAN
EVENING
DUCKWEED TR
PRIMROSE TR
DODD
CUSTER LN
PARKER RD
SAND ASTER CIR
BUCKWHEAT TR
WHITE SAGE PT
ACORN TR
COAST OAK TR
PAINT BRUSH CIR
0 .25 .5 .75 1.0 miles 1 in. = 3800 ft.
SEE 430 MAP

SEE 430 MAP

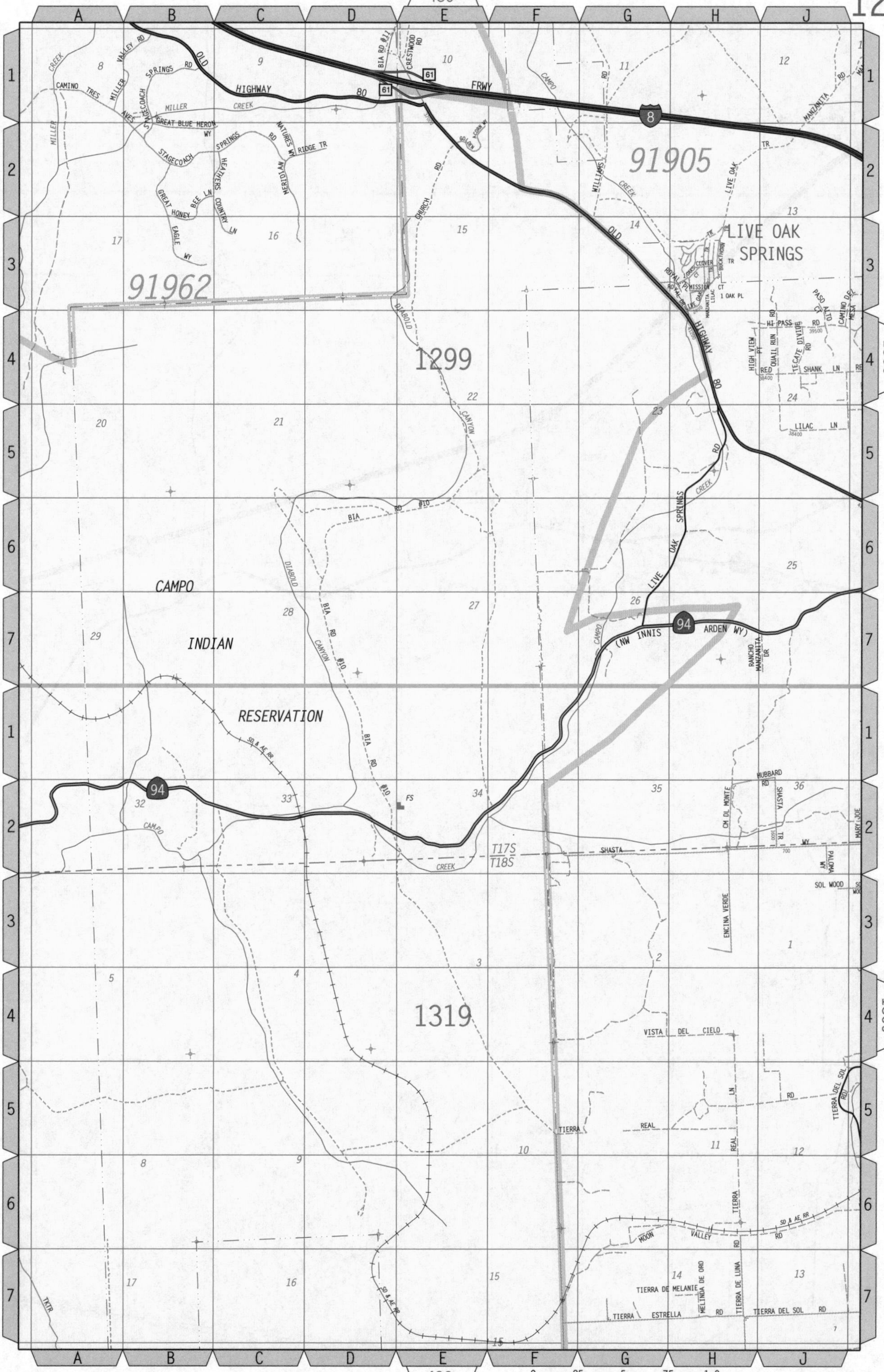

SEE 1300 MAP
SEE 1300 MAP
SEE 430 MAP

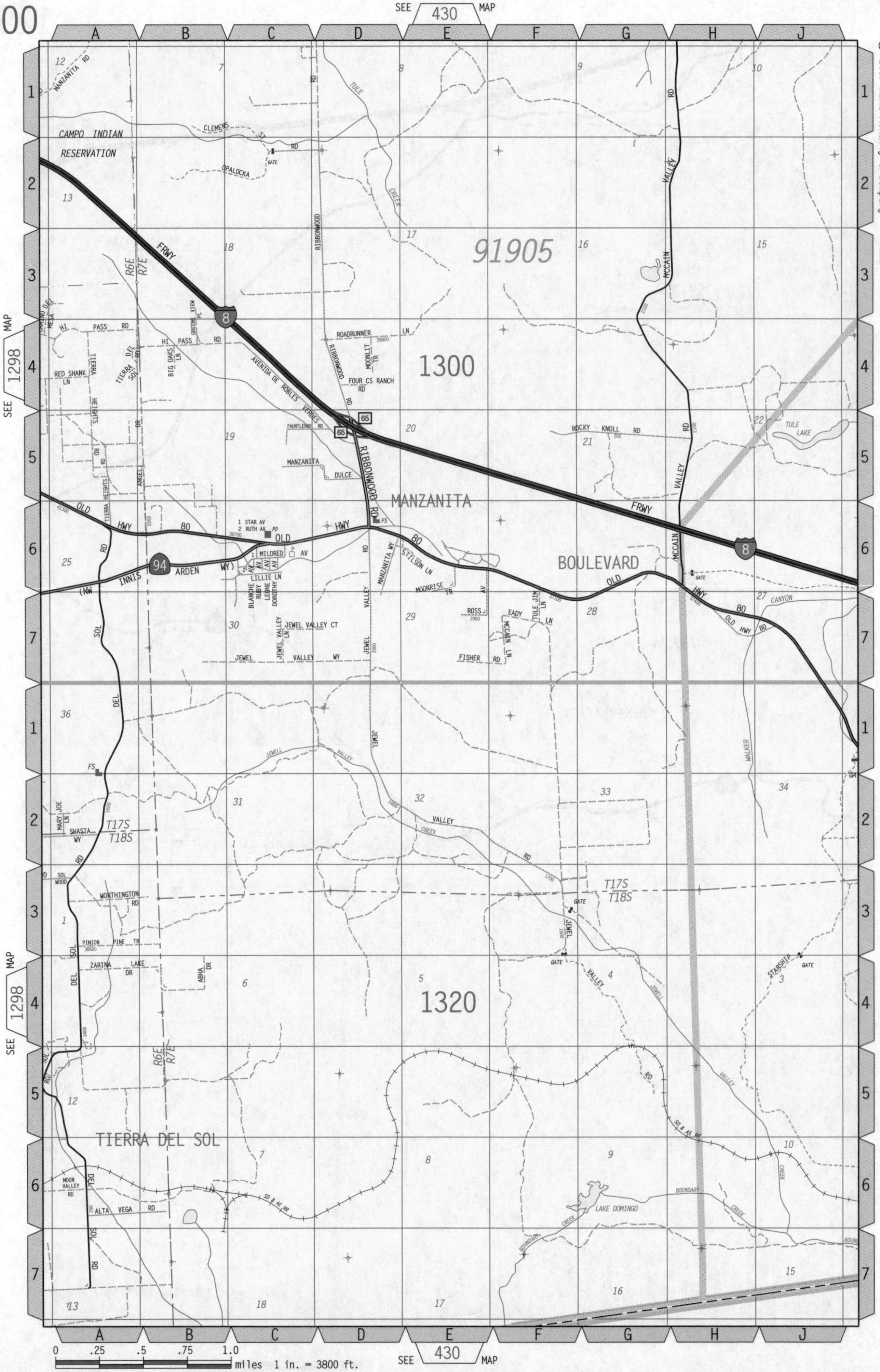
SEE 430 MAP
SEE 1298 MAP
SEE 1298 MAP
SEE 430 MAP
CAMPO INDIAN
RESERVATION
MANZANITA RD
CLEMENS ST
OPALOCKA
RD
GATE
TULE
CREEK
RIBBONWOOD
FRWY
8
91905
1300
R6E
R7E
HI PASS RD
GREENE VIEW PL
TIERRA DEL SOL RD
BIG OAKS LN
RED SHANK LN
TIERRA HEIGHTS RD
ANGEL DR
AVENIDA DE ROBLES VERDES
ROADRUNNER LN
MOONLIT TR
FOUR CS RANCH RD
FAUNTLEROY RD
65
MANZANITA
DULCE
RIBBONWOOD RD
MANZANITA
OLD HWY 80
1 STAR AV
2 RUTH AV
PO
FS
94
(NW INNIS ARDEN WY)
MILDRED AV
LILLIE LN
BLANCHE
RUBY
LEONE
DOROTHY
JEWEL VALLEY CT
JEWEL VALLEY WY
JEWEL VALLEY LN
MANZANITA WY
STILSON LN
MOONRISE TR
ROSS
EADY
TULE JIM LN
MCCAIN LN
FISHER RD
BOULEVARD
MCCAIN VALLEY RD
ROCKY KNOLL RD
TULE LAKE
CANYON
OLD HWY 80
SOL
DEL
T17S
T18S
MARY JOE LN
SHASTA WY
WOOD
WORTHINGTON RD
PINION PINE TR
ZARINA LAKE DR
ABHA DR
JEWEL VALLEY CREEK
VALLEY RD
WALKER
STARSHIP
1320
SD & AE RR
TIERRA DEL SOL
MOON VALLEY RD
ALTA VEGA RD
LAKE DOMINGO
BOUNDARY CREEK
0 .25 .5 .75 1.0 miles 1 in. = 3800 ft.

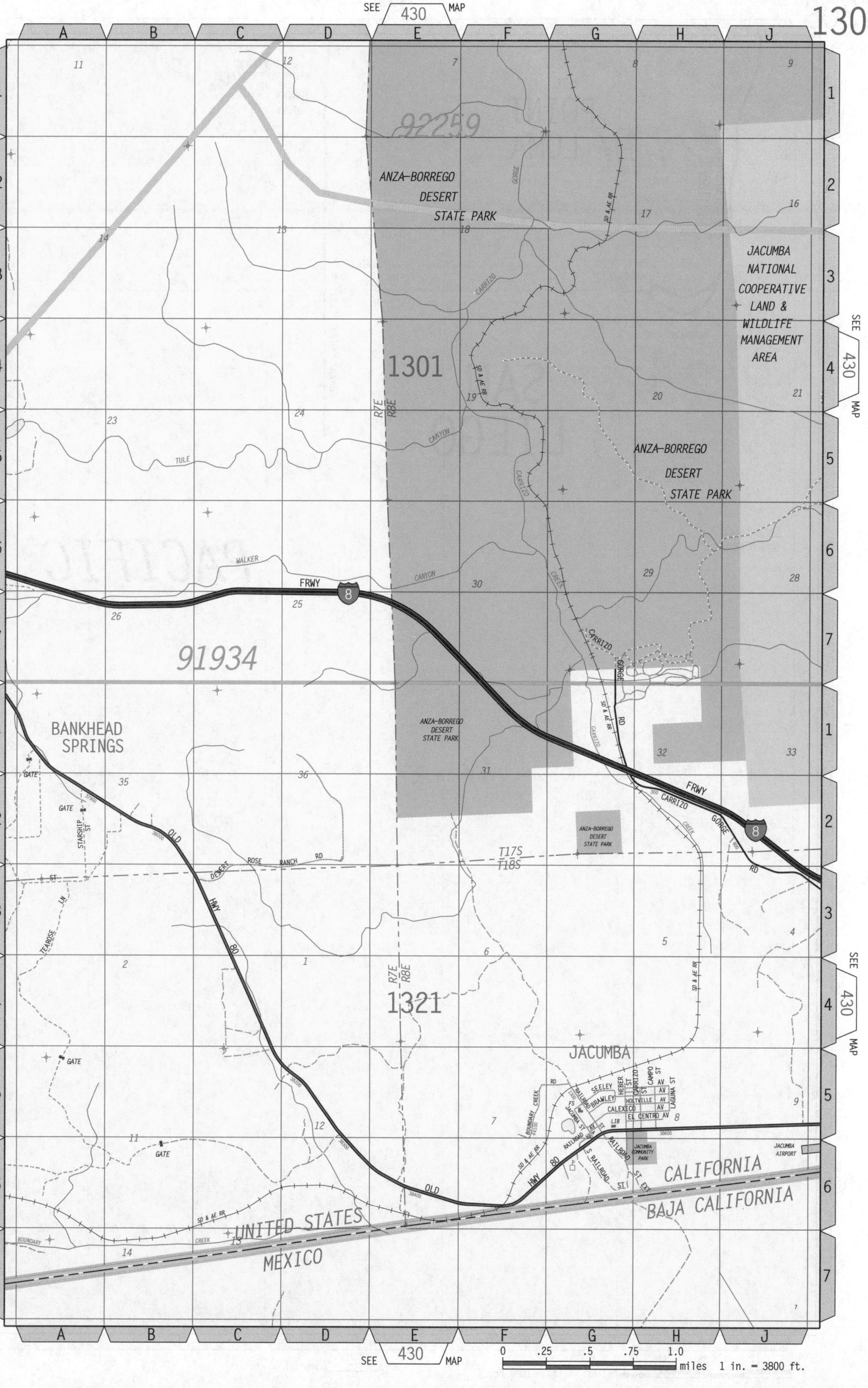
SEE 430 MAP
92259
ANZA-BORREGO DESERT STATE PARK
JACUMBA NATIONAL COOPERATIVE LAND & WILDLIFE MANAGEMENT AREA
1301
R7E R8E
SD & AE RR
CARRIZO
GORGE
CANYON
TULE
WALKER
CREEK
FRWY
8
91934
BANKHEAD SPRINGS
GATE
STARSHIP ST
OLD DESERT ROSE RANCH RD
T17S
T18S
TEAROSE LN
OLD HWY 80
CARRIZO GORGE RD
1321
JACUMBA
SEELEY
HEBER ST
CARRIZO ST
CAMPO ST
BRAWLEY
HOLTVILLE AV
LAGUNA ST
CALEXICO AV
EL CENTRO AV
BOUNDARY CREEK RD
RAILROAD ST
JACUMBA ST
S RAILROAD ST EXT
LIB
JACUMBA COMMUNITY PARK
JACUMBA AIRPORT
CALIFORNIA
BAJA CALIFORNIA
UNITED STATES
MEXICO
BOUNDARY CREEK
0 .25 .5 .75 1.0
miles 1 in. = 3800 ft.

SEE 1288 MAP

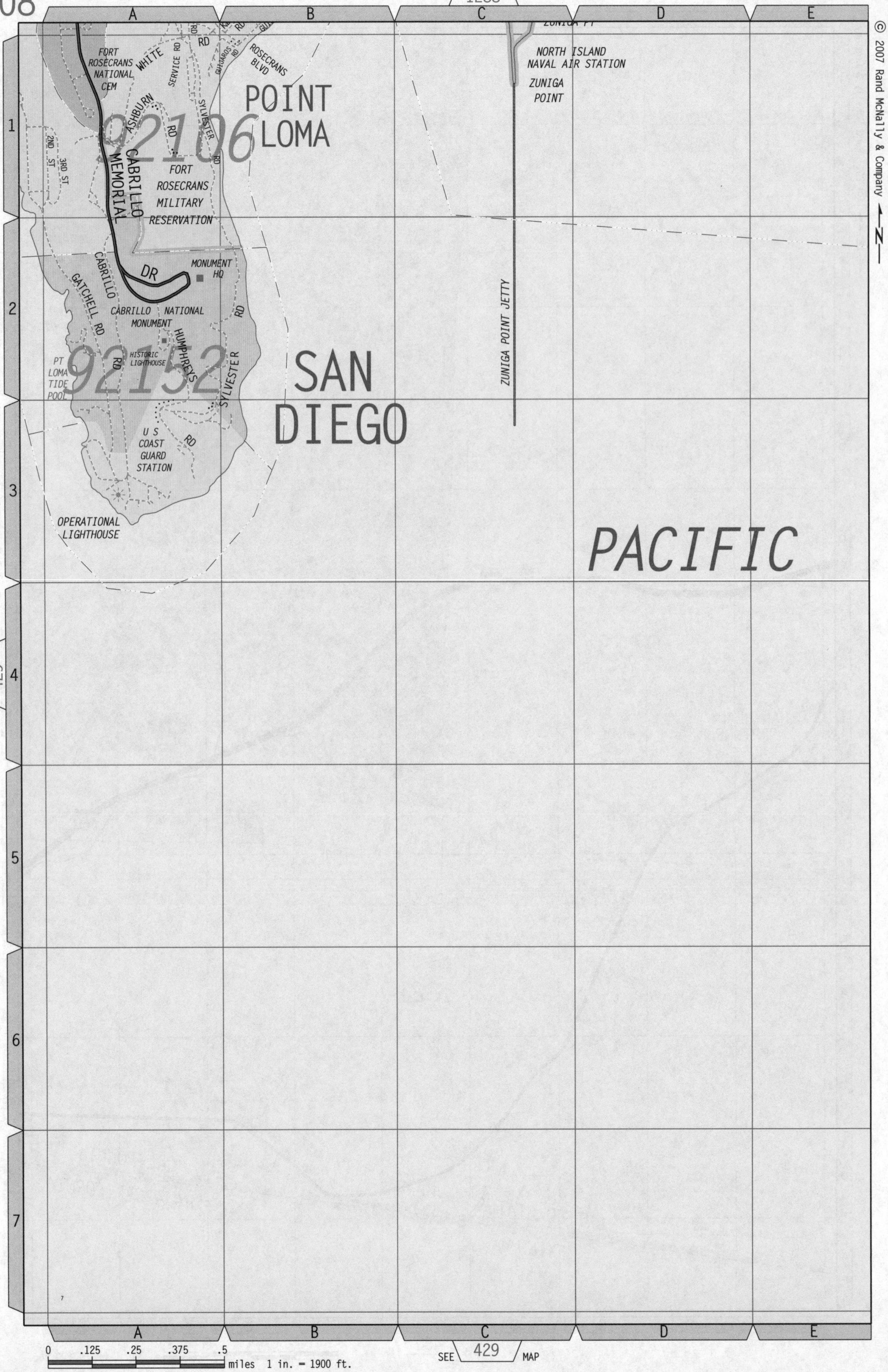

SEE 429 MAP

SEE 429 MAP

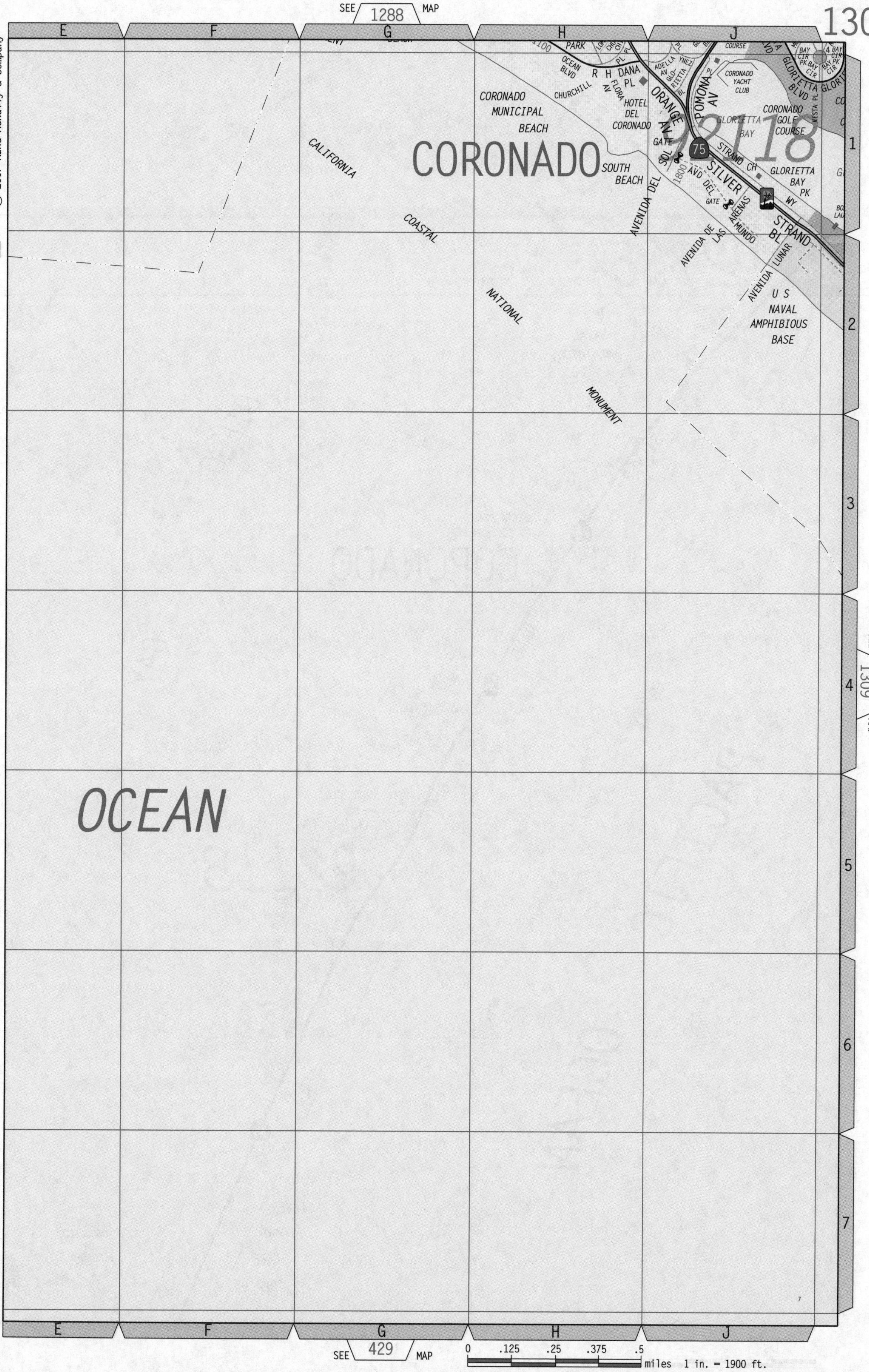
SEE 1288 MAP
E
F
G
H
J
1
2
3
4
5
6
7
SEE 1309 MAP
CORONADO
92118
CORONADO MUNICIPAL BEACH
HOTEL DEL CORONADO
CORONADO YACHT CLUB
CORONADO GOLF COURSE
GLORIETTA BAY
GLORIETTA BAY PK
SOUTH BEACH
OCEAN BLVD
R H DANA PL
CHURCHILL
FLORA AV
ORANGE AV
POMONA AV
ADELLA AV
GLORIETTA BL
GLORIETTA BLVD
STRAND CH
STRAND BL
SILVER STRAND BL
AVENIDA DEL SOL
AVD DEL ARENAS
AVENIDA DE LAS ARENAS
MUNDO
AVENIDA LUNAR
GATE
75
1800
PARK
U S NAVAL AMPHIBIOUS BASE
CALIFORNIA
COASTAL
NATIONAL
MONUMENT
OCEAN
SEE 429 MAP
0 .125 .25 .375 .5
miles 1 in. = 1900 ft.

SEE 1289 MAP
SEE 1308 MAP
SEE 1329 MAP
A
B
C
D
E
1
2
3
4
5
6
7
CORONADO GOLF COURSE
GLORIETTA BLVD
VISTA PL
GLORIETTA BAY
BOAT LAUNCH
GLORIETTA BAY PARK
PIER 3
SAN DIEGO BAY
CITY
92155
92118
INCHON RD
ENIWETOK RD
KWAJALEIN RD
ROI WY
ROI RD
MAKIN RD
GUADALCANAL RD
BOUGAINVILLE RD
TULAGI
ATTU RD
MUNDA RD
LAE
TARAWA
ADMIRALTY
RENDOVA RD
STRAND
VELLA
LAVELLA RD
RENDOVA WY
RENDOVA CIR
US NAVAL AMPHIBIOUS BASE
SILVER STRAND BLVD
75
DELTA BEACH (US GOVERNMENT)
CORONADO
PACIFIC OCEAN
CALIFORNIA COASTAL NATIONAL MONUMENT
NAVY YACHT CLUB
PALAU
OKINAWA RD
LEYTE RD
1100
PALAU CIR
SAIPAN RD
1300
WAKE RD
1400
LEYTE
ATTU AV
INCHON CT
DA NANG DR
SILVER STRAND STATE BEACH
LOEWS CORONADO BAY RESORT
CORONADO BAY RD
CROW ISL
0 .125 .25 .375 .5 miles 1 in. = 1900 ft.

SEE 1289 MAP

SEE 1310 MAP
SEE 1329 MAP

0 .125 .25 .375 .5 miles 1 in. = 1900 ft.

SEE 1290 MAP

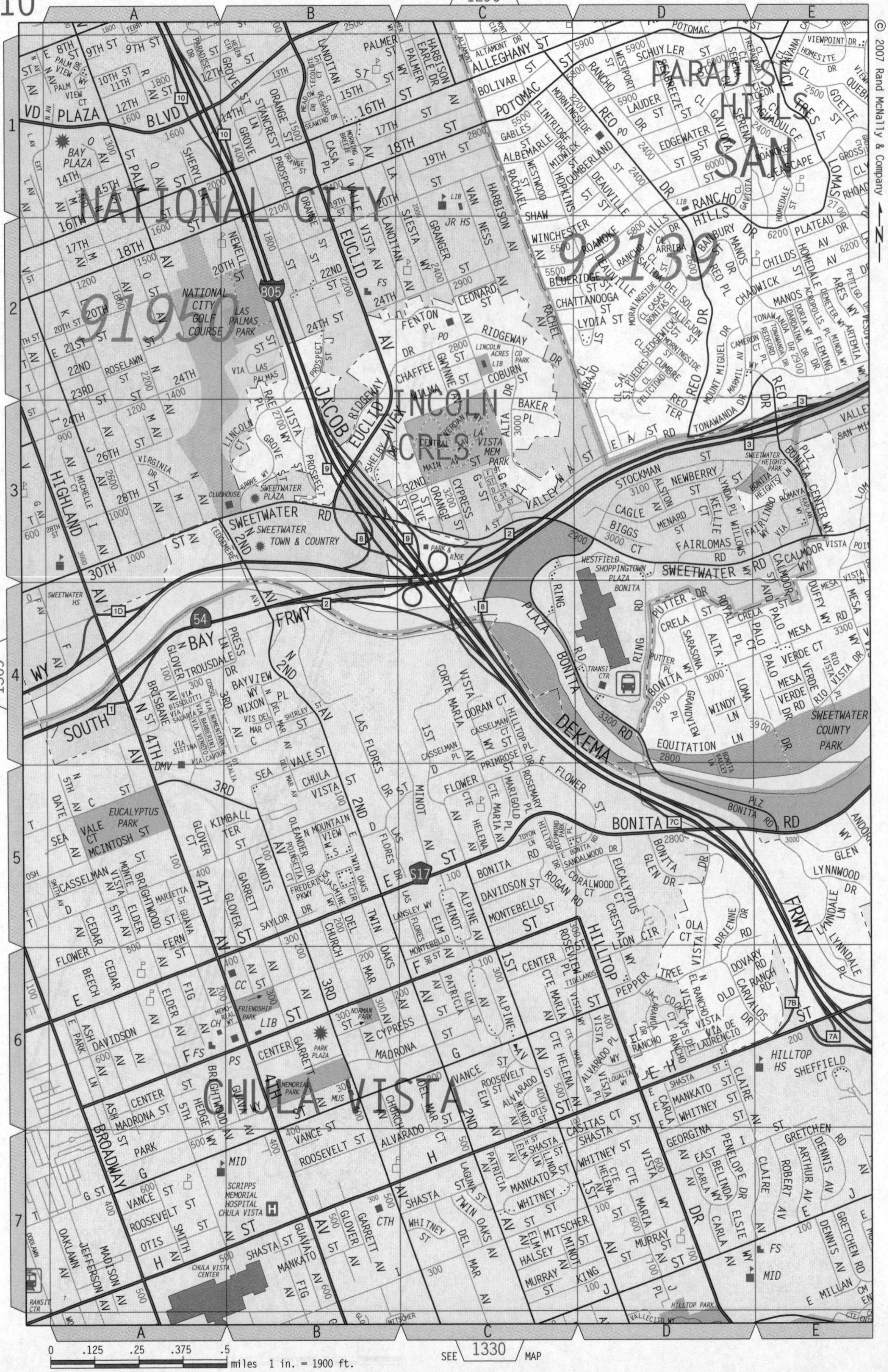

SEE 1330 MAP

0 .125 .25 .375 .5 miles 1 in. = 1900 ft.

SEE 1290 MAP

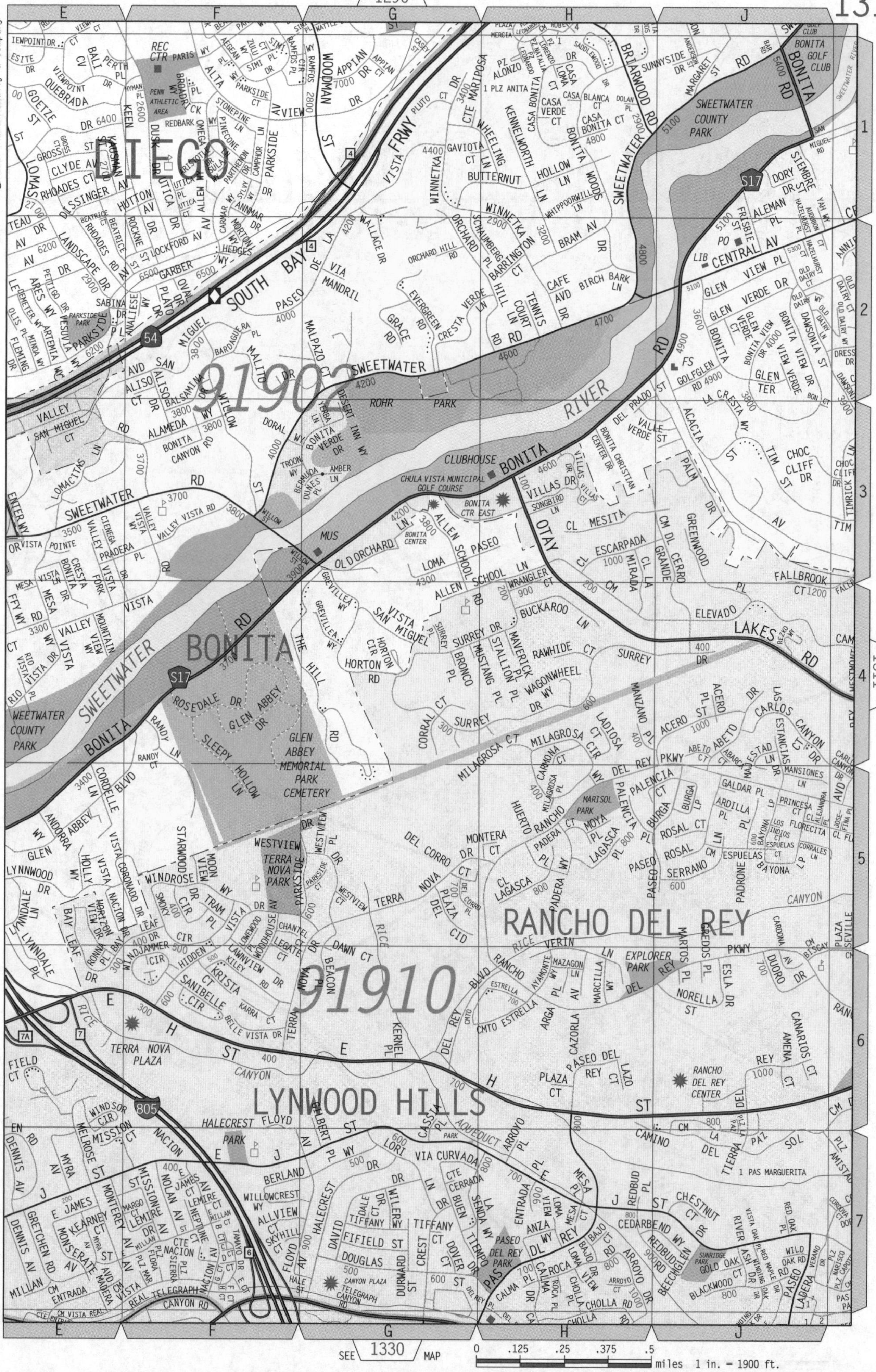

SEE 1311 MAP

SEE 1330 MAP

0 .125 .25 .375 .5 miles 1 in. = 1900 ft.

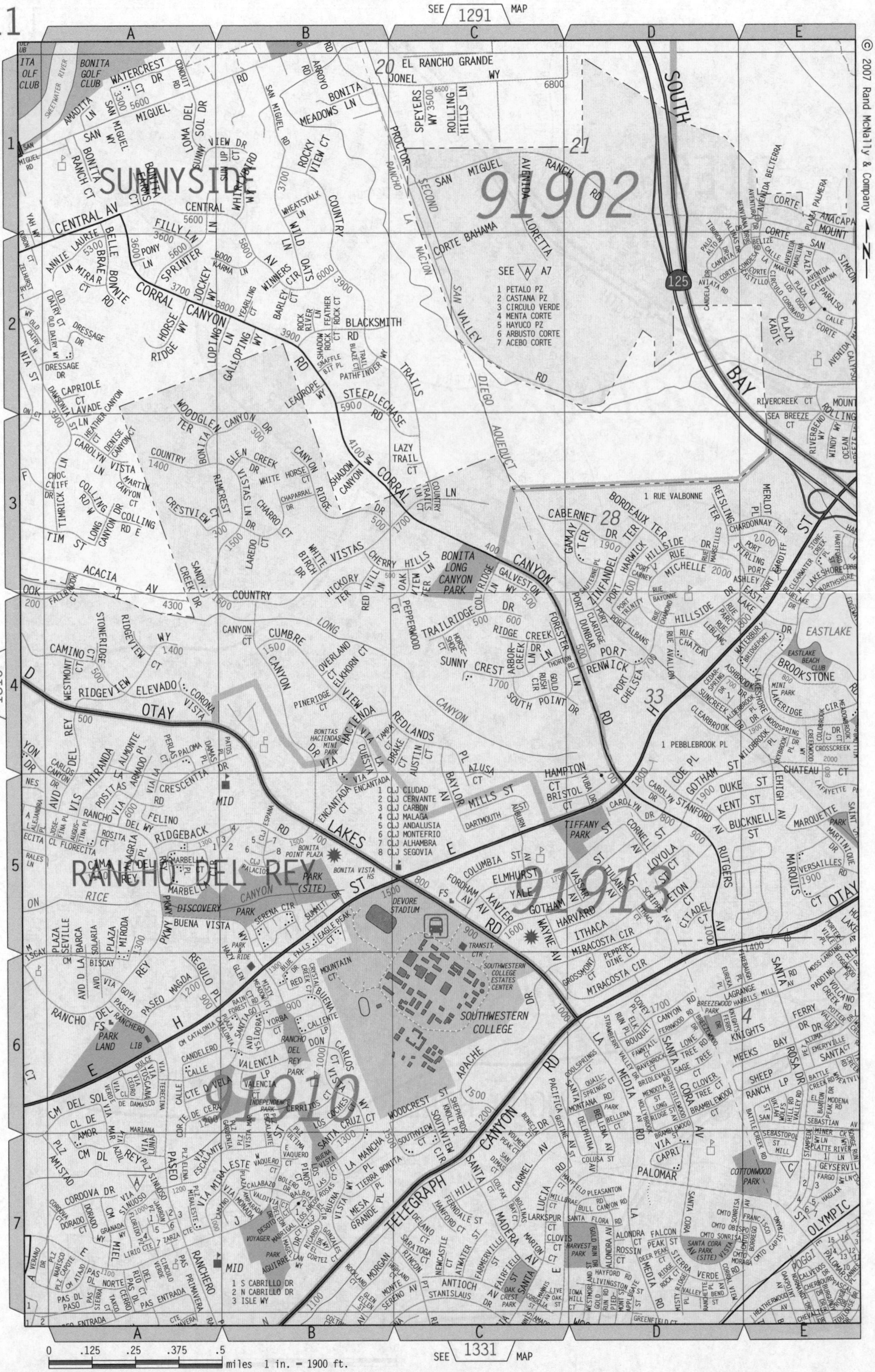
SEE 1291 MAP
A
B
C
D
E
1
2
3
4
5
6
7
SUNNYSIDE
91902
91913
91910
RANCHO DEL REY
EASTLAKE
BONITA GOLF CLUB
CENTRAL AV
CORRAL CANYON RD
PROCTOR VALLEY RD
SAN MIGUEL RANCH RD
SOUTH BAY
125
SAN DIEGO AQUEDUCT
BONITA LONG CANYON PARK
OTAY LAKES RD
EAST H ST
TELEGRAPH CANYON RD
SOUTHWESTERN COLLEGE
DEVORE STADIUM
RUTGERS AV
PASEO RANCHERO
OLYMPIC
TIFFANY PARK
COTTONWOOD PARK
HARVEST PARK
VOYAGER PARK
AGUIRRE PARK
SEE A A7
1 PETALO PZ
2 CASTANA PZ
3 CIRCULO VERDE
4 MENTA CORTE
5 HAYUCO PZ
6 ARBUSTO CORTE
7 ACEBO CORTE
1 CLJ CIUDAD
2 CLJ CERVANTE
3 CLJ CARBON
4 CLJ MALAGA
5 CLJ ANDALUSIA
6 CLJ MONTEFRIO
7 CLJ ALHAMBRA
8 CLJ SEGOVIA
1 S CABRILLO DR
2 N CABRILLO DR
3 ISLE WY
1 RUE VALBONNE
1 PEBBLEBROOK PL
SEE 1310 MAP
SEE 1331 MAP
0 .125 .25 .375 .5
miles 1 in. = 1900 ft.

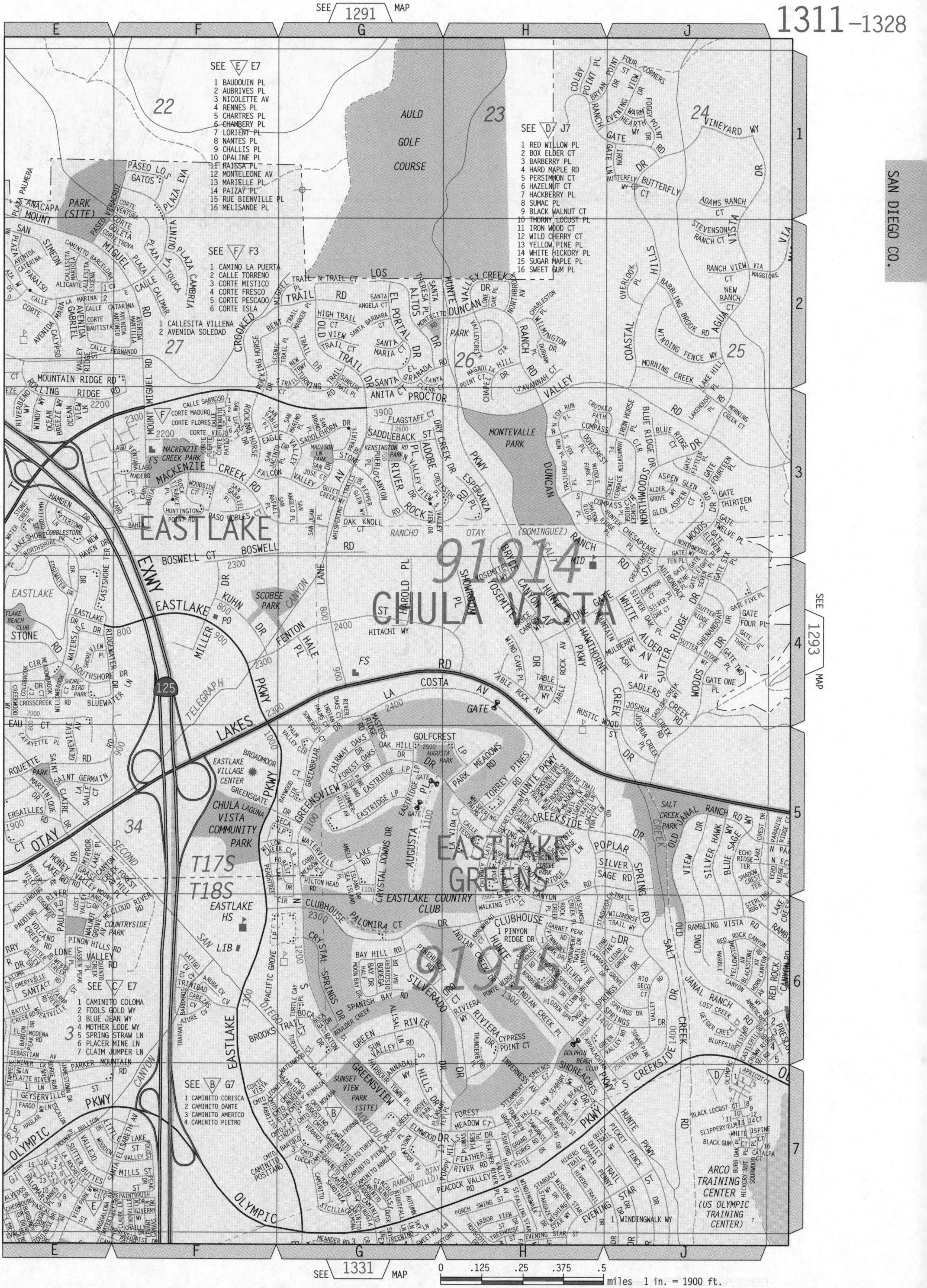
SEE 1291 MAP
SEE 1293 MAP
SEE 1331 MAP
SAN DIEGO CO.
© 2007 Rand McNally & Company
E F G H J
1 2 3 4 5 6 7
SEE E E7
1 BAUDOUIN PL
2 AUBRIVES PL
3 NICOLETTE AV
4 RENNES PL
5 CHARTRES PL
6 CHAMBERY PL
7 LORIENT PL
8 NANTES PL
9 CHALLIS PL
10 OPALINE PL
11 RAISSA PL
12 MONTELEONE AV
13 MARIELLE PL
14 PAIZAY PL
15 RUE BIENVILLE PL
16 MELISANDE PL
SEE D J7
1 RED WILLOW PL
2 BOX ELDER CT
3 BARBERRY PL
4 HARD MAPLE RD
5 PERSIMMON CT
6 HAZELNUT CT
7 HACKBERRY PL
8 SUMAC PL
9 BLACK WALNUT CT
10 THORNY LOCUST PL
11 IRON WOOD CT
12 WILD CHERRY CT
13 YELLOW PINE PL
14 WHITE HICKORY PL
15 SUGAR MAPLE PL
16 SWEET GUM PL
SEE F F3
1 CAMINO LA PUERTA
2 CALLE TORRENO
3 CORTE MISTICO
4 CORTE FRESCO
5 CORTE PESCADO
6 CORTE ISLA
1 CALLESITA VILLENA
2 AVENIDA SOLEDAD
SEE C E7
1 CAMINITO COLOMA
2 FOOLS GOLD WY
3 BLUE JEAN WY
4 MOTHER LODE WY
5 SPRING STRAW LN
6 PLACER MINE LN
7 CLAIM JUMPER LN
SEE B G7
1 CAMINITO CORISCA
2 CAMINITO DANTE
3 CAMINITO AMERICO
4 CAMINITO PIETRO
AULD GOLF COURSE
MONTEVALLE PARK
MACKENZIE CREEK PARK
SCOBEE PARK
EASTLAKE
CHULA VISTA
91914
91915
EASTLAKE GREENS
EASTLAKE COUNTRY CLUB
EASTLAKE VILLAGE CENTER
CHULA VISTA COMMUNITY PARK
EASTLAKE HS
SALT CREEK PARK
SUNSET VIEW PARK (SITE)
DOLPHIN BEACH CLUB
ARCO TRAINING CENTER (US OLYMPIC TRAINING CENTER)
OTAY LAKES RD
EASTLAKE PKWY
OLYMPIC PKWY
PROCTOR VALLEY RD
HUNTE PKWY
125
T17S
T18S
0 .125 .25 .375 .5
miles 1 in. = 1900 ft.

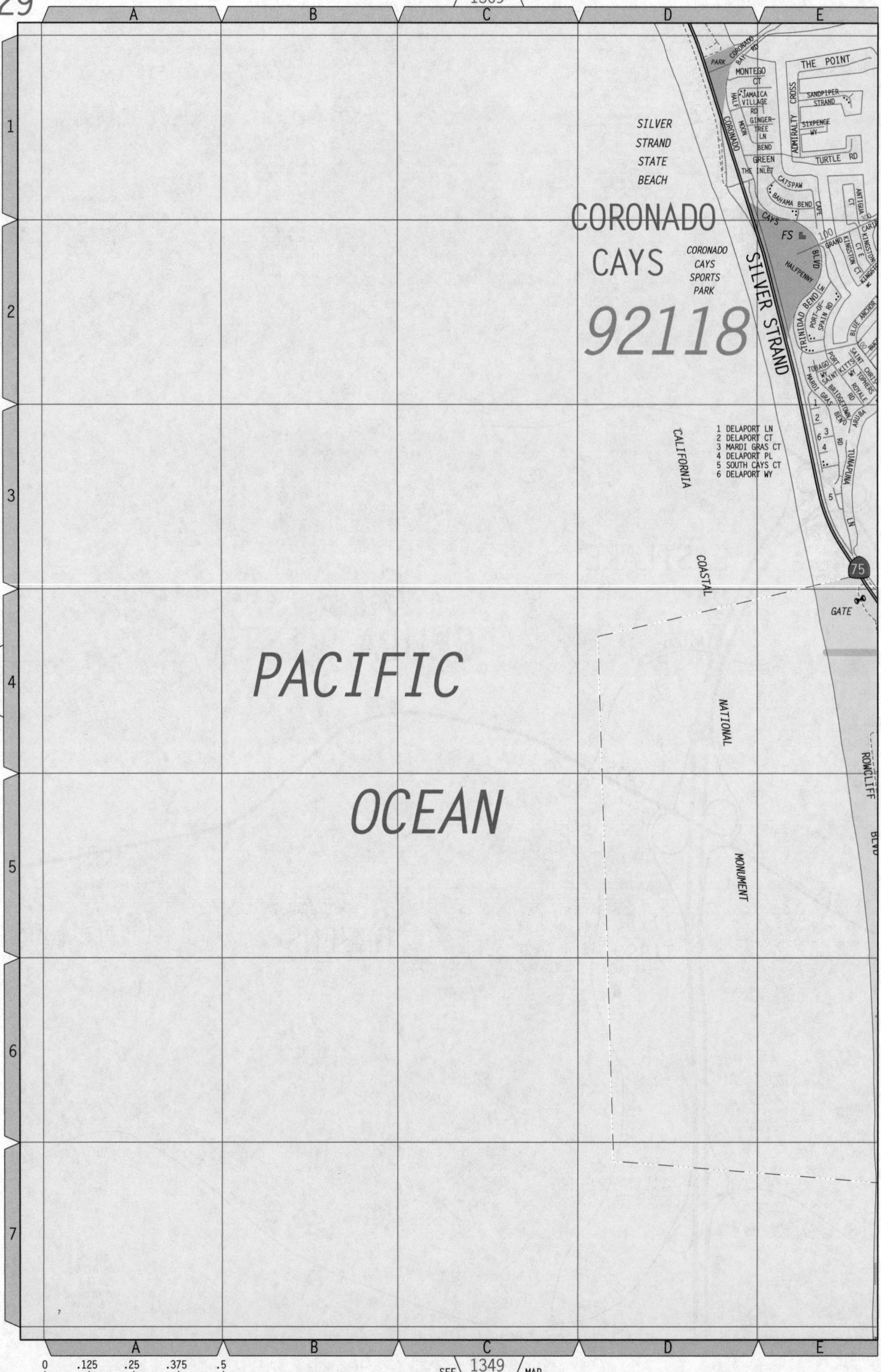
SEE 1309 MAP
SAN DIEGO CO.
SILVER STRAND STATE BEACH
CORONADO CAYS
CORONADO CAYS SPORTS PARK
92118
SILVER STRAND
CORONADO BAY RD
PARK
MONTEGO CT
JAMAICA VILLAGE RD
GINGER-TREE LN
HALF MOON BEND
GREEN
THE INLET
CORONADO
THE POINT
SANDPIPER STRAND
ADMIRALTY CROSS
SIXPENGE WY
TURTLE RD
CATSPAW
BAHAMA BEND
CAPE
ANTIGUA CT
CAYS
FS
GRAND
KINGSTON CT
HALFPENNY
BLVD
TRINIDAD BEND
PORT-OF-SPAIN RD
BLUE ANCHOR
TOBAGO WY
PORT SAINT KITTS
SAINT CHRISTOPHERS
ROYALE RD
MARDI GRAS
BRIDGETOWN BEND
ARUBA
TUNAPUNA LN
1 DELAPORT LN
2 DELAPORT CT
3 MARDI GRAS CT
4 DELAPORT PL
5 SOUTH CAYS CT
6 DELAPORT WY
CALIFORNIA COASTAL NATIONAL MONUMENT
75
GATE
ROWCLIFF BLVD
PACIFIC OCEAN
SEE 429 MAP
SEE 1349 MAP
0 .125 .25 .375 .5 miles 1 in. = 1900 ft.

SEE 1309 MAP

SEE 1330 MAP

SEE 1349 MAP

0 .125 .25 .375 .5 miles 1 in. = 1900 ft.

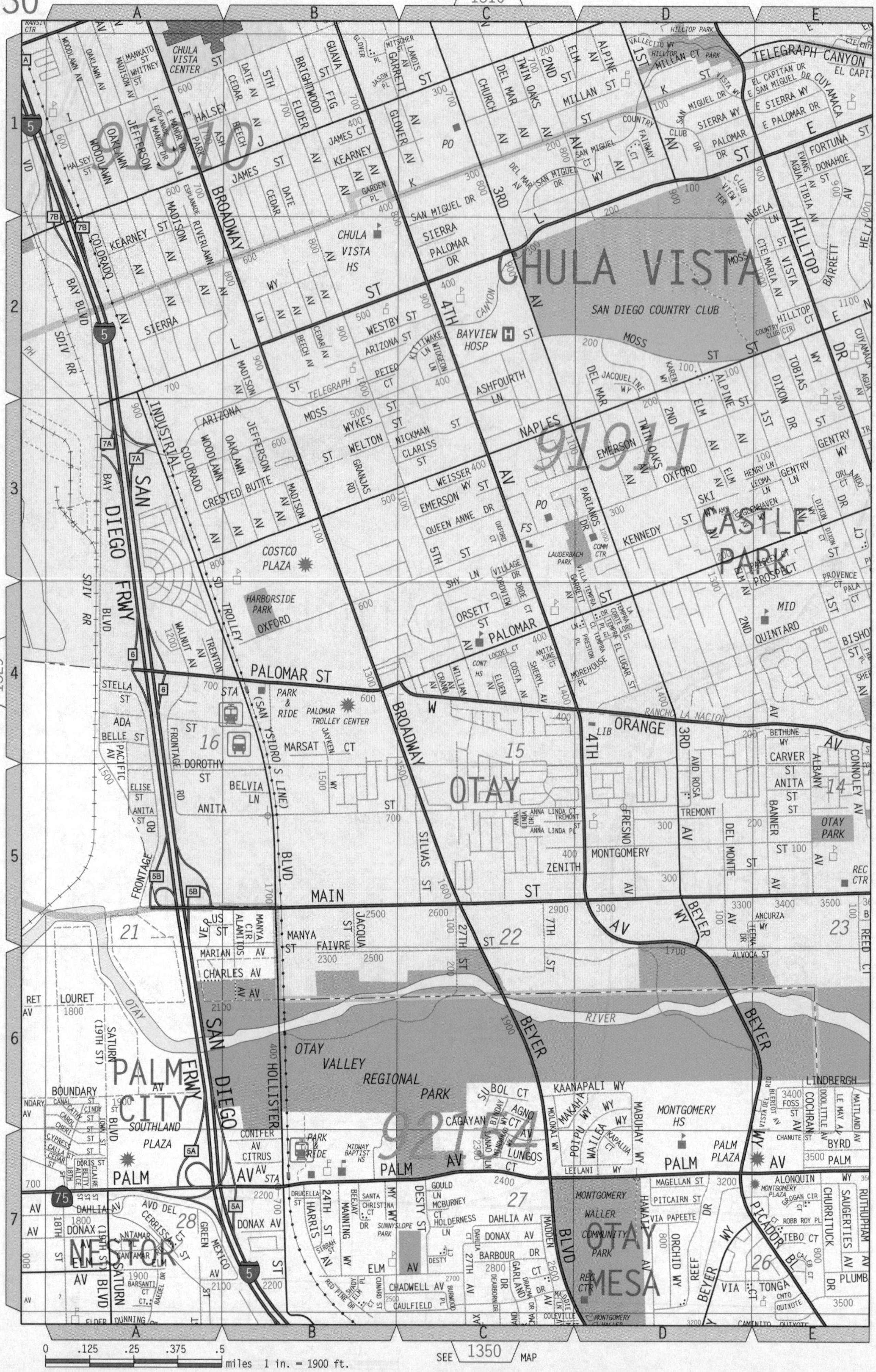

SEE 1310 MAP
SEE 1329 MAP
SEE 1350 MAP
A
B
C
D
E
1
2
3
4
5
6
7
CHULA VISTA
91910
91911
92154
CASTLE PARK
OTAY
PALM CITY
NESTOR
OTAY MESA
SAN DIEGO COUNTRY CLUB
CHULA VISTA CENTER
CHULA VISTA HS
BAYVIEW HOSP
COSTCO PLAZA
HARBORSIDE PARK
PALOMAR TROLLEY CENTER
PARK & RIDE
OTAY VALLEY REGIONAL PARK
OTAY RIVER
SOUTHLAND PLAZA
MONTGOMERY HS
MONTGOMERY WALLER COMMUNITY PARK
PALM PLAZA
OTAY PARK
SAN DIEGO FRWY
BROADWAY
TELEGRAPH CANYON RD
PALOMAR ST
MAIN ST
PALM AV
ORANGE AV
BEYER BLVD
HOLLISTER ST
INDUSTRIAL BLVD
0 .125 .25 .375 .5
miles 1 in. = 1900 ft.

SEE 1310 MAP

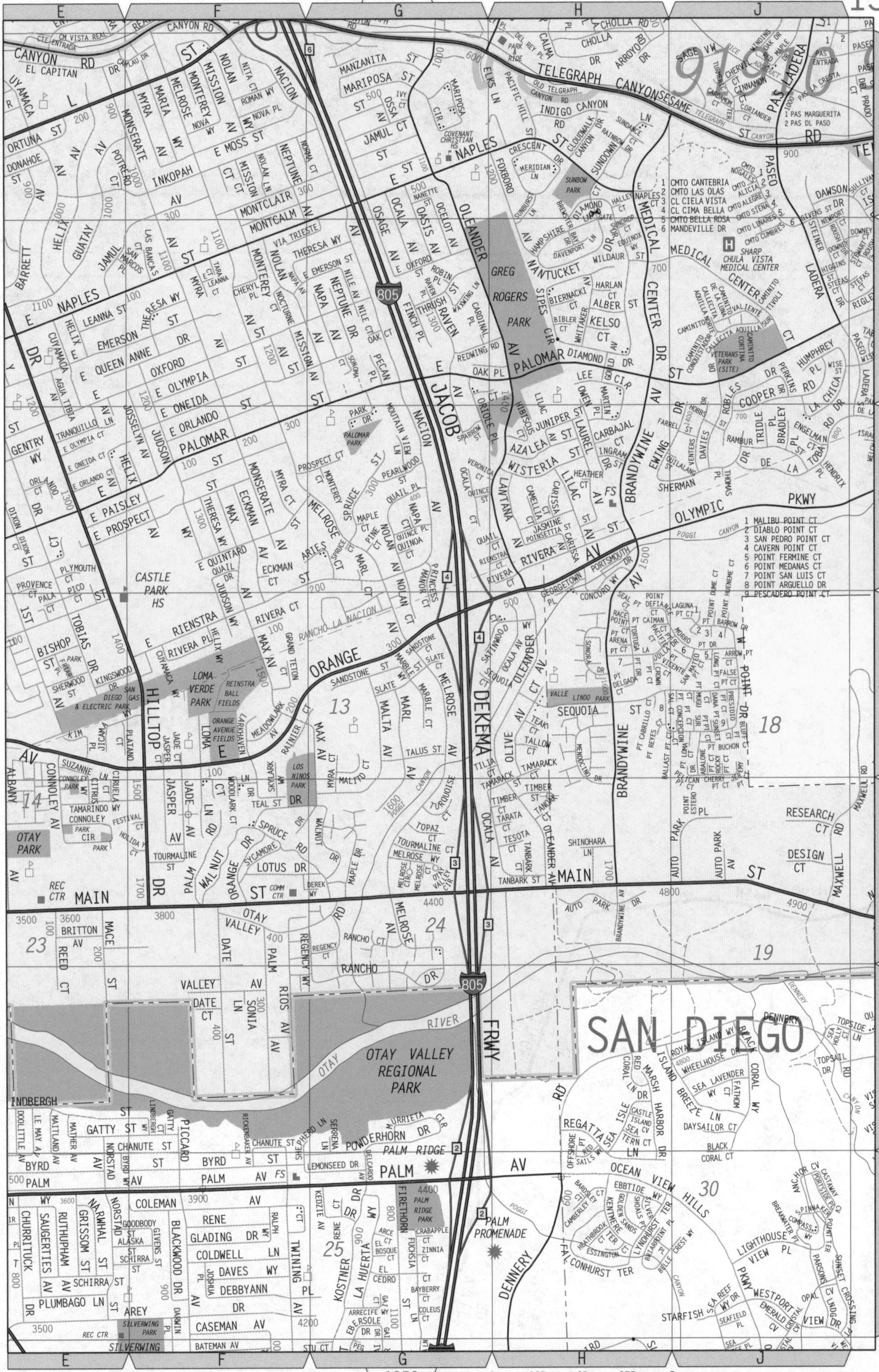

SEE 1331 MAP

SEE 1350 MAP

0 .125 .25 .375 .5 miles 1 in. = 1900 ft.

SEE 1311 MAP

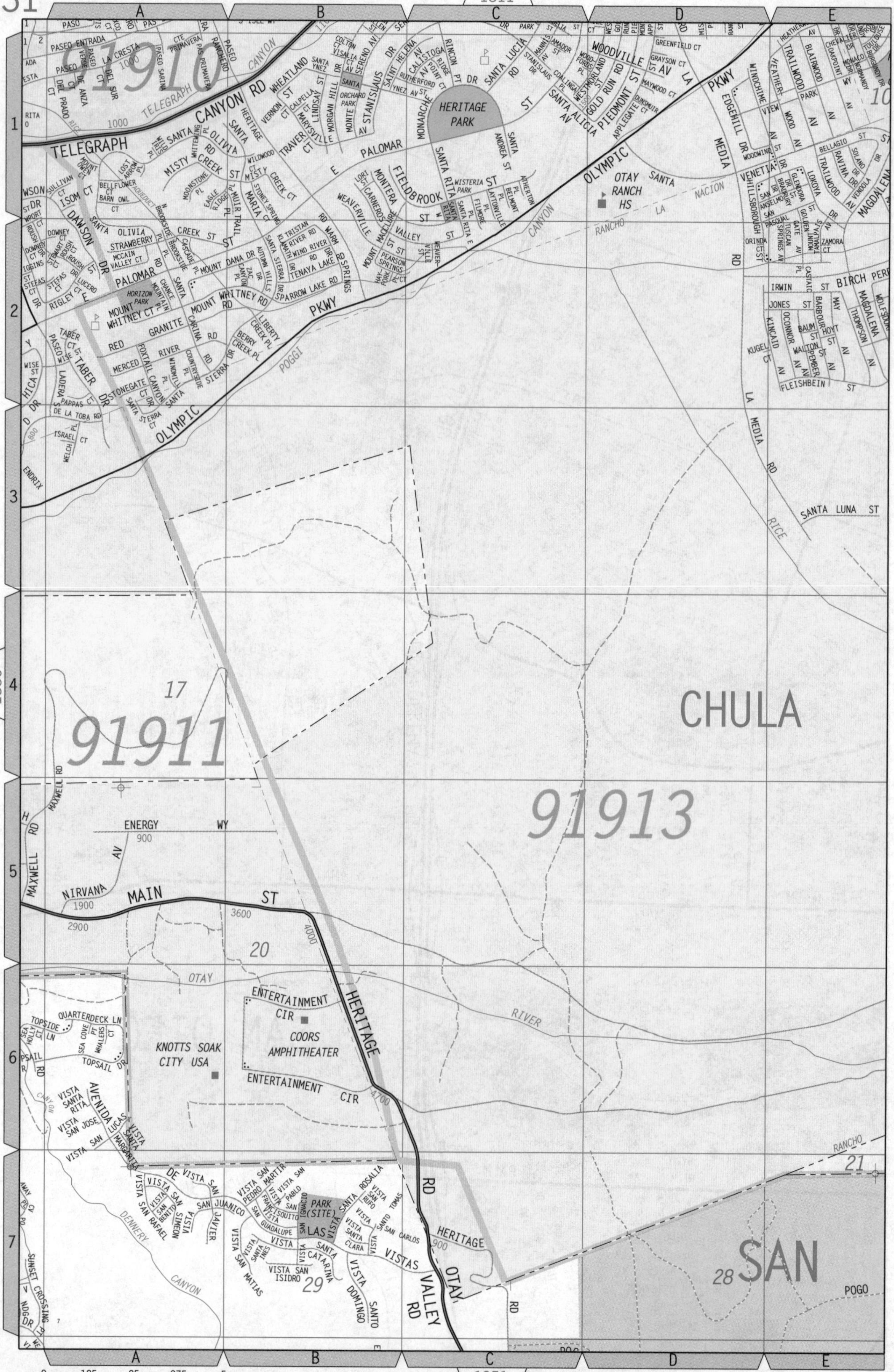

SEE 1330 MAP

SEE 1351 MAP

0 .125 .25 .375 .5 miles 1 in. = 1900 ft.

SEE 1311 MAP

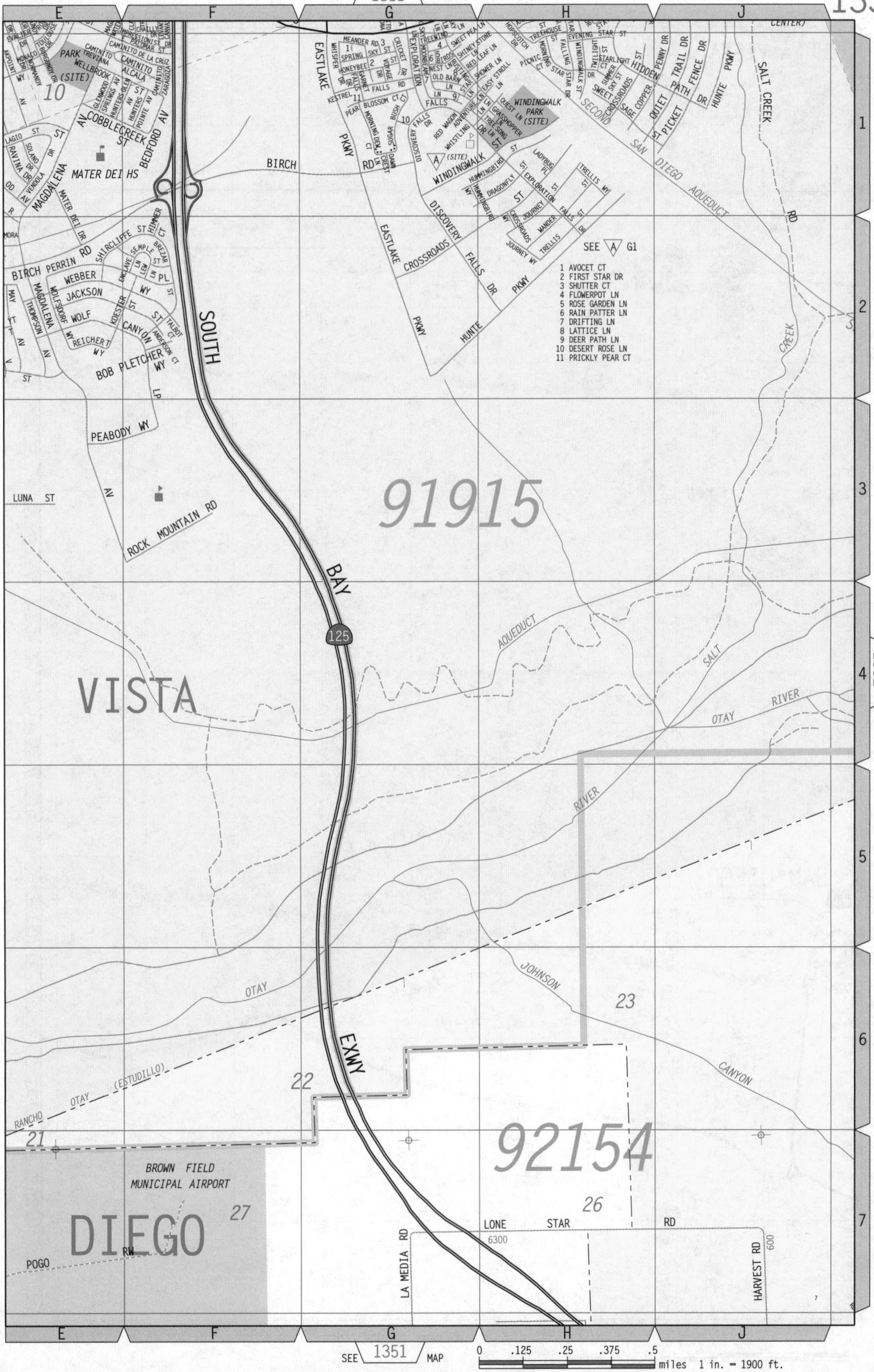

SEE 1351 MAP

0 .125 .25 .375 .5 miles 1 in. = 1900 ft.

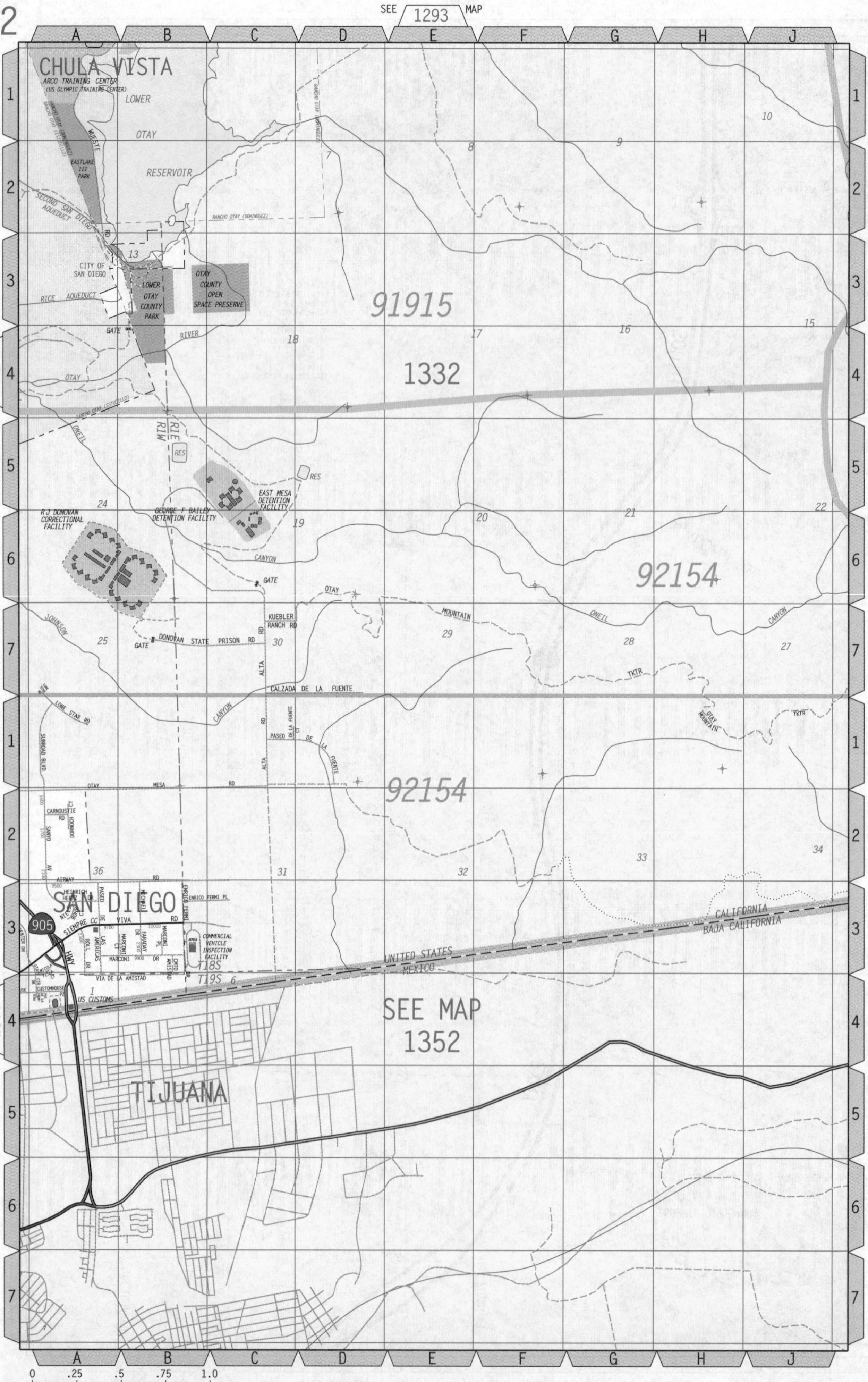
SEE 1293 MAP
SEE MAP 1331
SEE MAP 1351
CHULA VISTA
ARCO TRAINING CENTER
(US OLYMPIC TRAINING CENTER)
LOWER
OTAY
RESERVOIR
WUESTE
EASTLAKE III PARK
SECOND SAN DIEGO AQUEDUCT
RANCHO OTAY (DOMINGUEZ)
CITY OF SAN DIEGO
RICE AQUEDUCT
LOWER OTAY COUNTY PARK
OTAY COUNTY OPEN SPACE PRESERVE
GATE
RIVER
OTAY
91915
1332
ONEIL
R1E
R1W
RES
EAST MESA DETENTION FACILITY
GEORGE F BAILEY DETENTION FACILITY
RJ DONOVAN CORRECTIONAL FACILITY
CANYON
OTAY
MOUNTAIN
ONEIL
CANYON
92154
JOHNSON
KUEBLER RANCH RD
DONOVAN STATE PRISON RD
ALTA
CALZADA DE LA FUENTE
TKTR
LONE STAR RD
CANYON
PASEO DE LA FUENTE
OTAY MESA RD
92154
SANYO
AIRWAY
RD
SAN DIEGO
ENRICO FERMI PL
SIEMPRE VIVA
905
CARNOUSTIE
HEINRICH HERTZ
LAS AMERICAS
MARCONI
FARADAY
COMMERCIAL VEHICLE INSPECTION FACILITY
HWY
VIA DE LA AMISTAD
T18S
T19S
US CUSTOMS
CUSTOMHOUSE
UNITED STATES
MEXICO
CALIFORNIA
BAJA CALIFORNIA
SEE MAP 1352
TIJUANA
0 .25 .5 .75 1.0
miles 1 in. = 3800 ft.

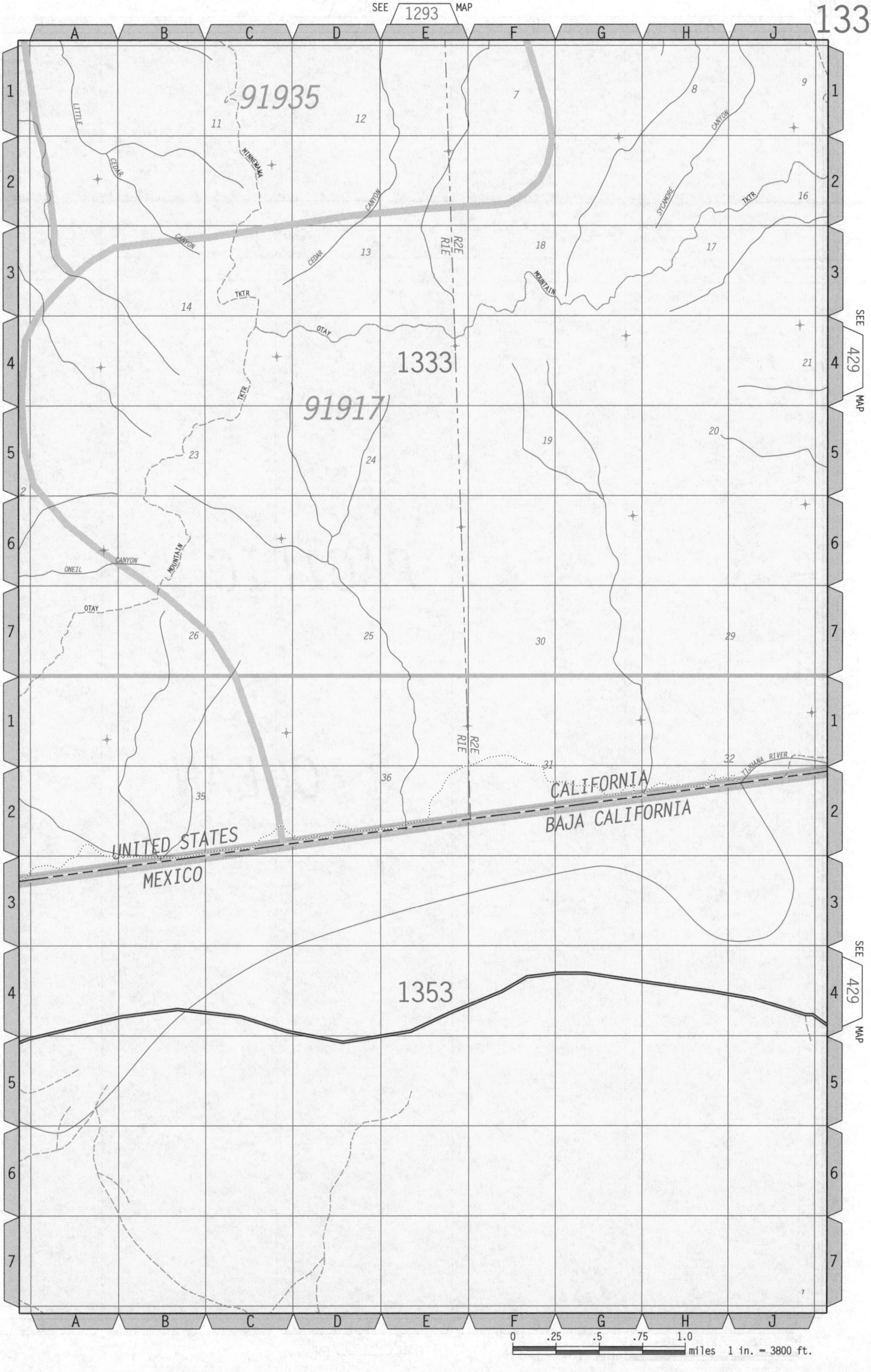
SEE 1293 MAP
91935
91917
1333
1353
LITTLE CEDAR
MINNEWAWA
CANYON
CEDAR
CANYON
TKTR
OTAY
MOUNTAIN
SYCAMORE
CANYON
R2E R1E
ONEIL CANYON
MOUNTAIN
OTAY
TIJUANA RIVER
CALIFORNIA
BAJA CALIFORNIA
UNITED STATES
MEXICO
SEE 429 MAP
SAN DIEGO CO.
0 .25 .5 .75 1.0 miles 1 in. = 3800 ft.

SEE 1329 MAP

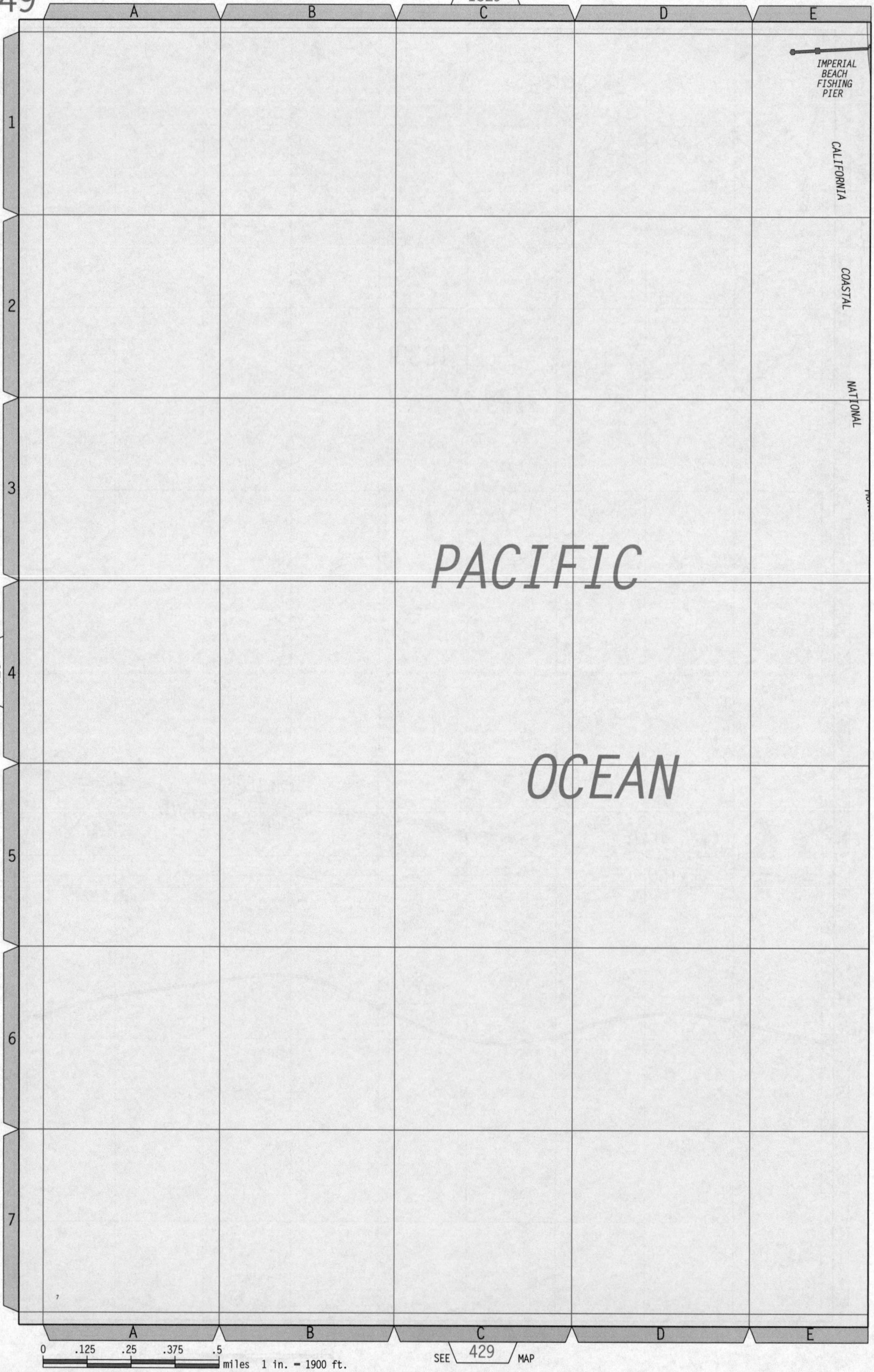

SEE 429 MAP

SEE 429 MAP

SEE 1329 MAP

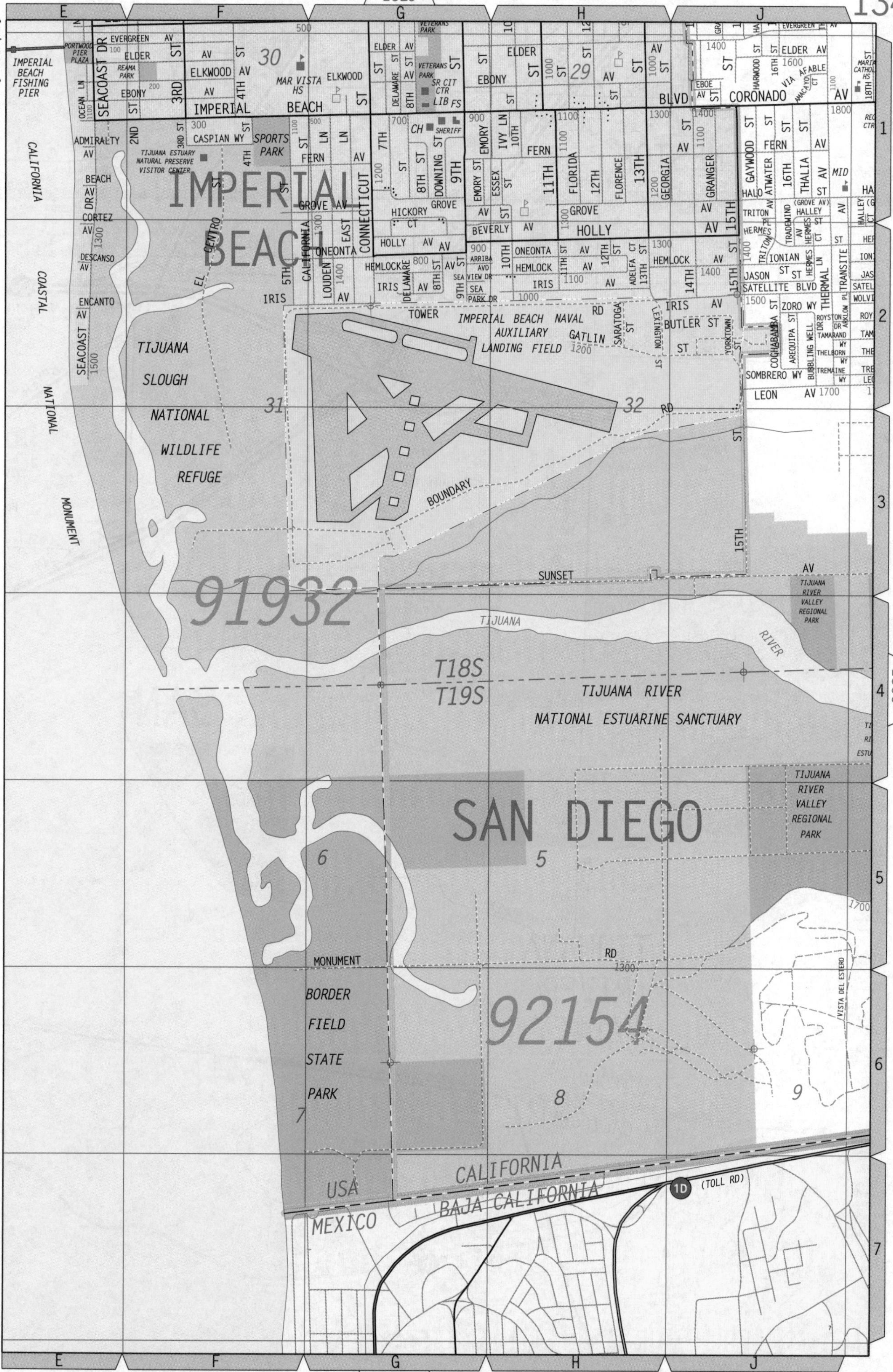

SEE 1350 MAP

SEE 429 MAP

0 .125 .25 .375 .5 miles 1 in. = 1900 ft.

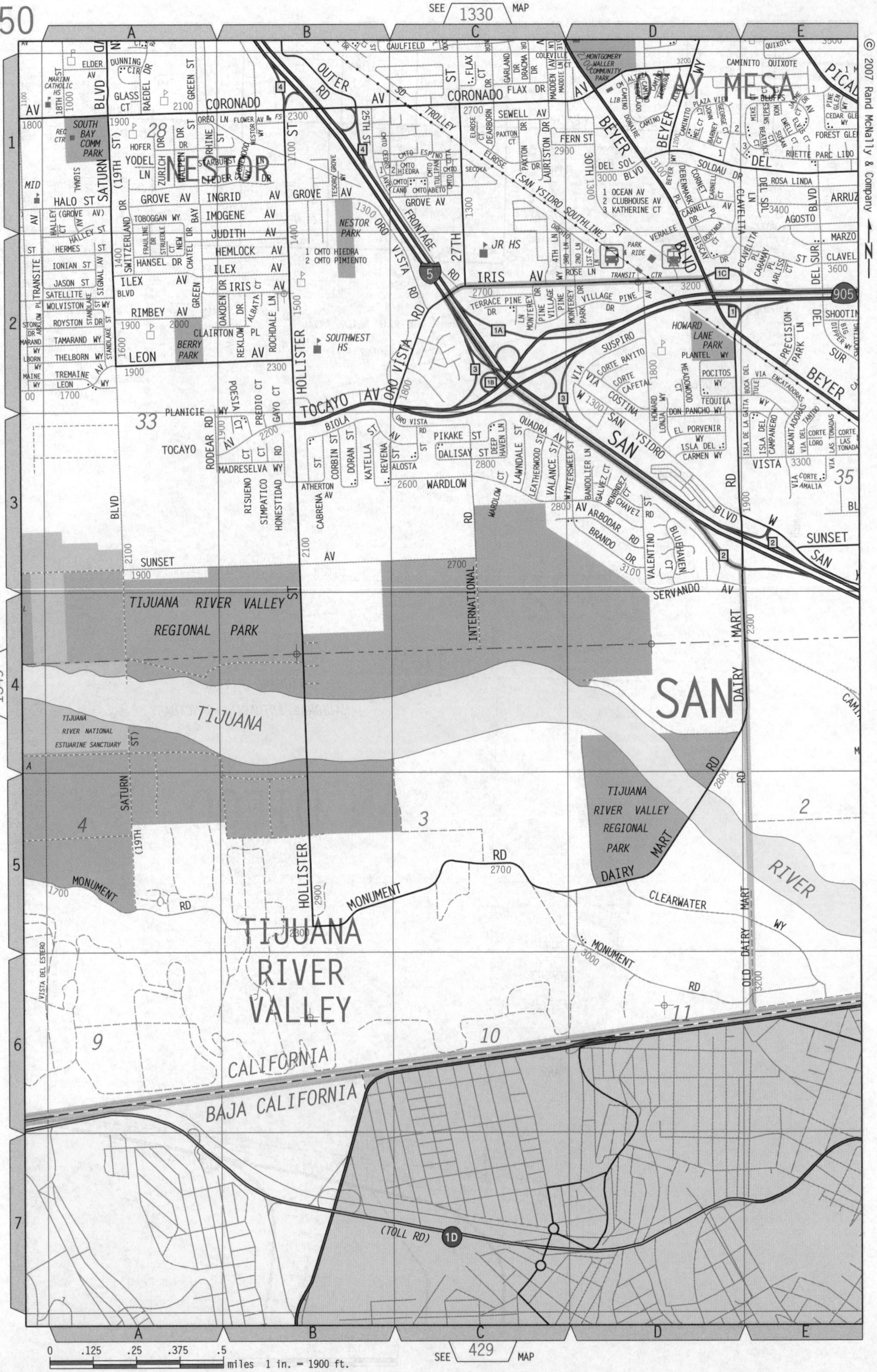

SEE 1330 MAP
SEE 1349 MAP
SEE 429 MAP
NESTOR
NESTOR PARK
BERRY PARK
SOUTH BAY COMM PARK
SOUTHWEST HS
JR HS
MONTGOMERY WALLER COMMUNITY PARK
HOWARD LANE PARK
TIJUANA RIVER VALLEY REGIONAL PARK
TIJUANA RIVER NATIONAL ESTUARINE SANCTUARY
TIJUANA
TIJUANA RIVER VALLEY
SAN
RIVER
CALIFORNIA
BAJA CALIFORNIA
CORONADO AV
GROVE AV
IRIS AV
TOCAYO AV
HOLLISTER ST
SATURN BLVD
SUNSET AV
MONUMENT RD
DAIRY MART RD
OLD DAIRY MART RD
CLEARWATER WY
SAN YSIDRO BLVD
BEYER BLVD
INTERNATIONAL RD
WARDLOW RD
ORO VISTA RD
FRONTAGE RD
SERVANDO AV
(TOLL RD)
miles 1 in. = 1900 ft.
0 .125 .25 .375 .5

SEE 1330 MAP

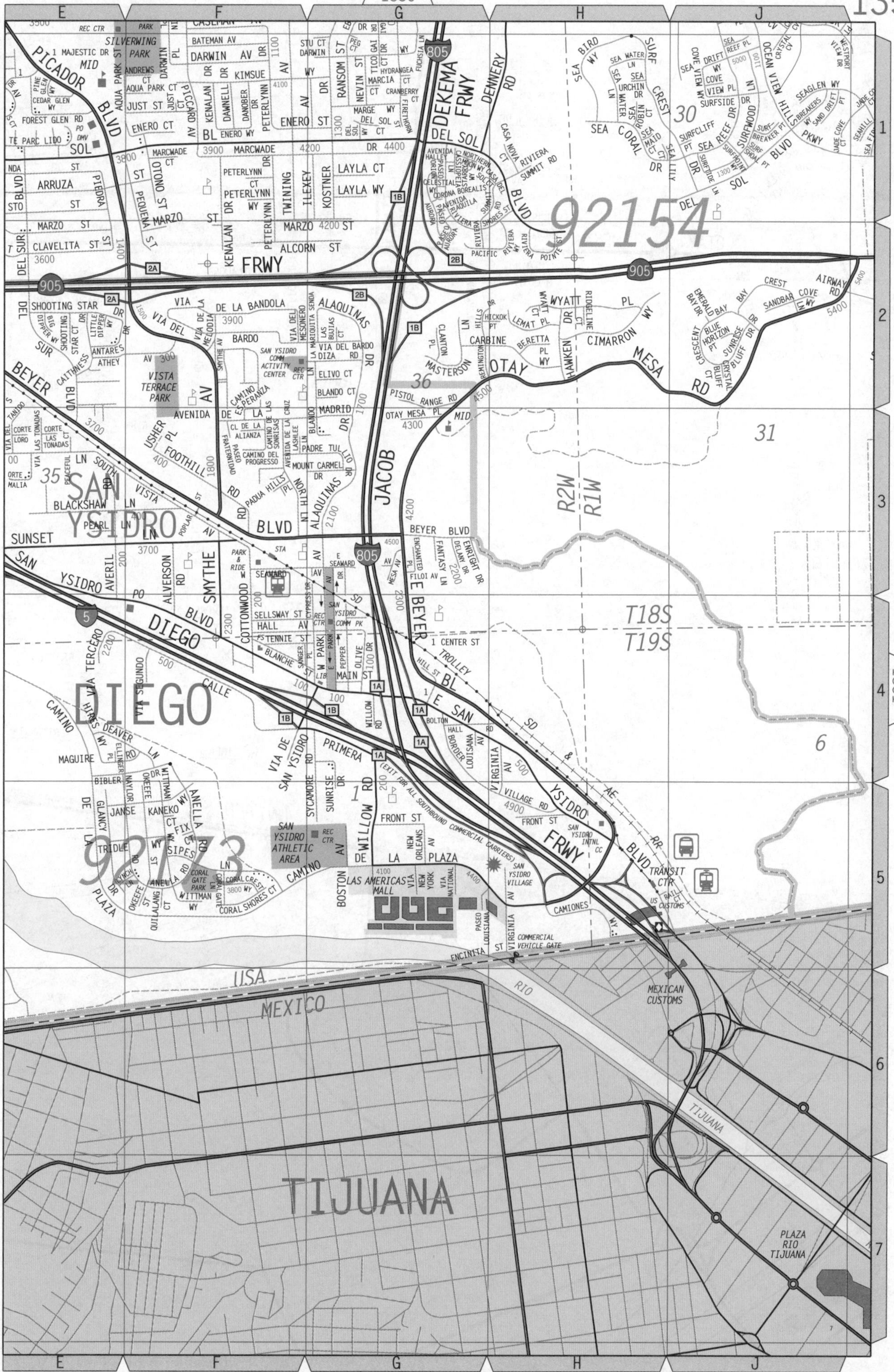

SEE 1351 MAP

SEE 429 MAP

0 .125 .25 .375 .5 miles 1 in. = 1900 ft.

SEE 1331 MAP

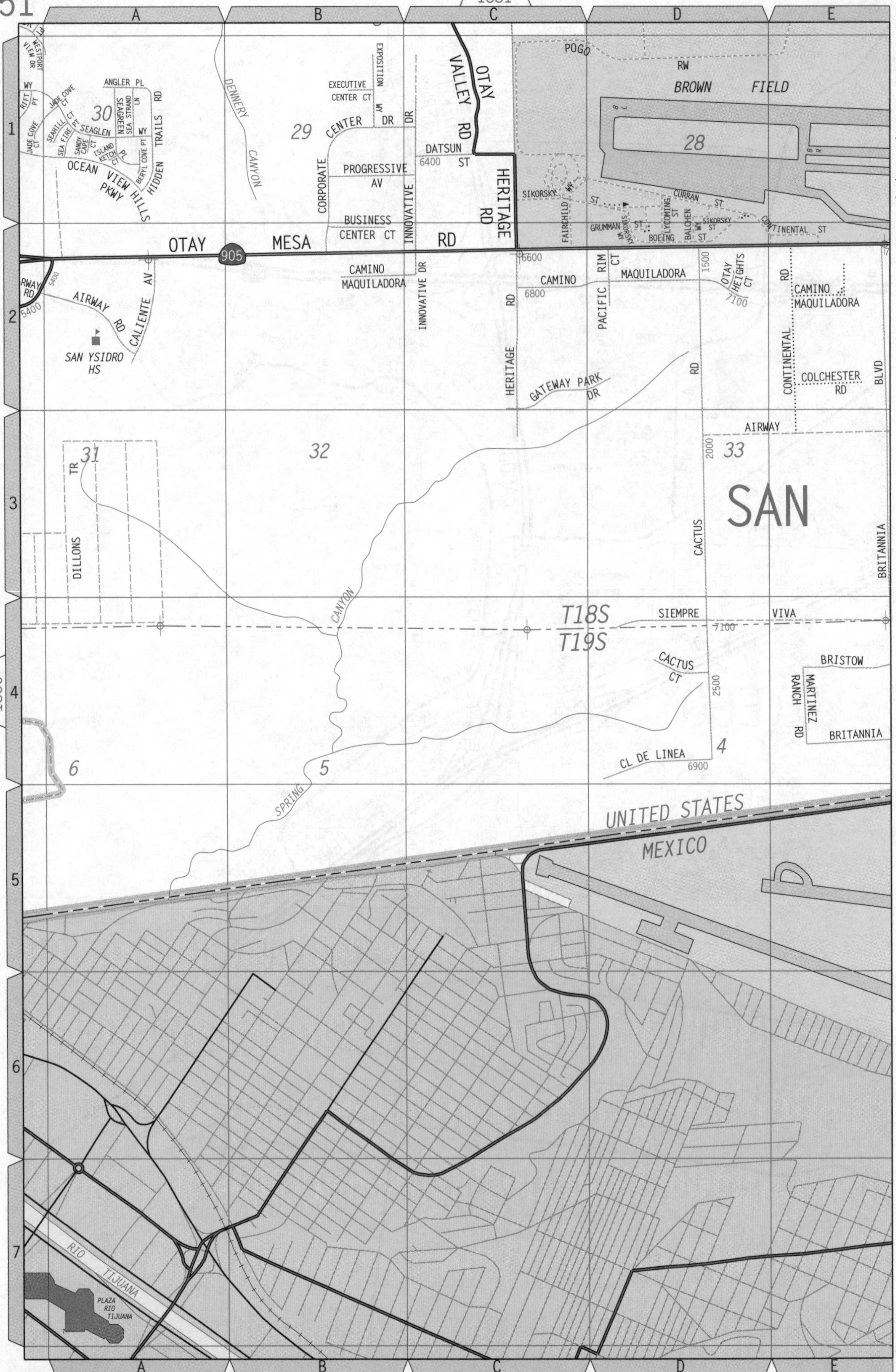

SEE 429 MAP

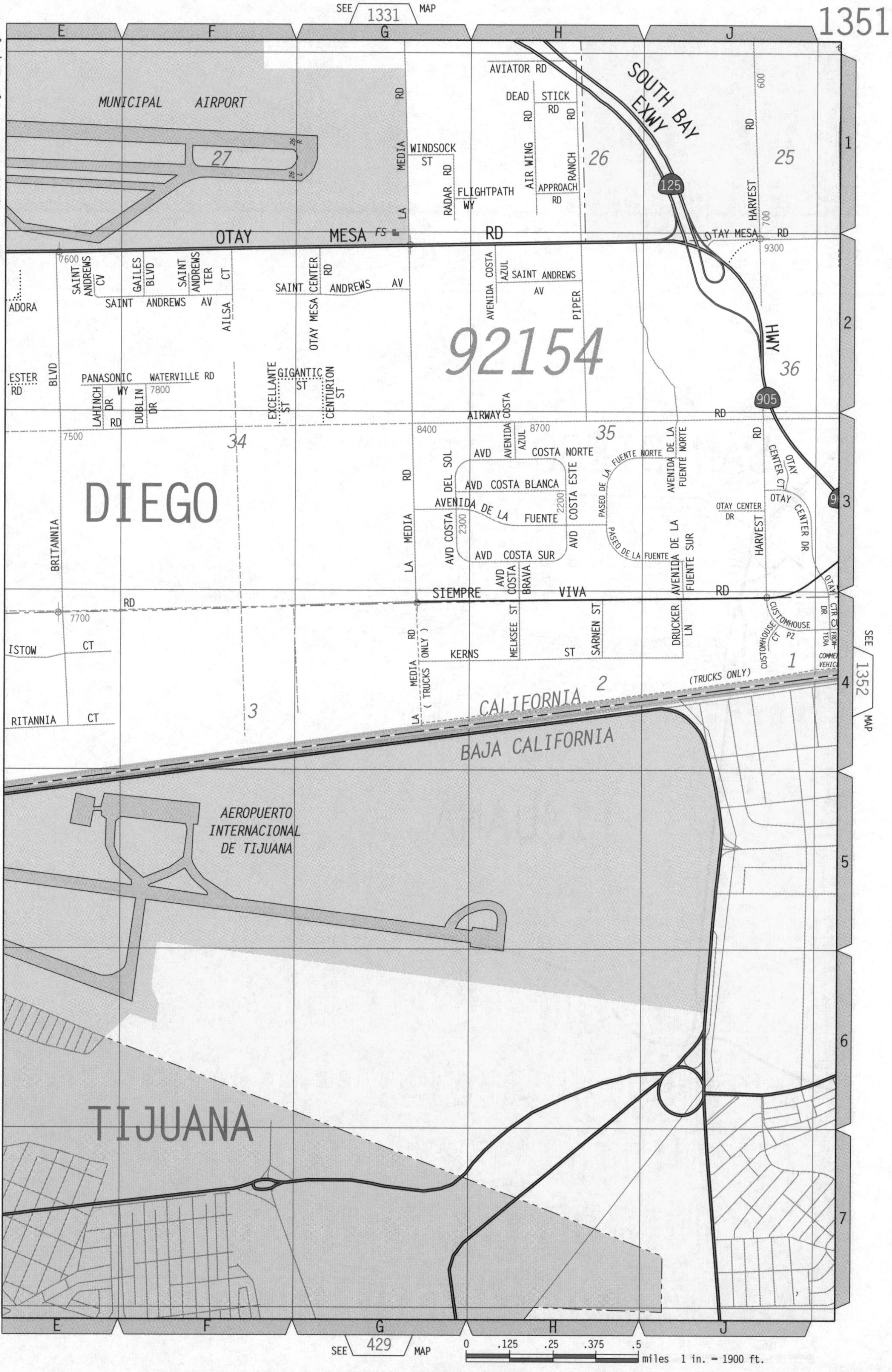
SEE 1331 MAP
E
F
G
H
J
MUNICIPAL AIRPORT
27
AVIATOR RD
DEAD STICK RD
SOUTH BAY EXWY
WINDSOCK ST
AIR WING RD
RANCH RD
26
25
125
RADAR RD
FLIGHTPATH WY
APPROACH RD
HARVEST RD
LA MEDIA RD
OTAY MESA RD
OTAY MESA RD
7600
9300
SAINT ANDREWS CV
GAILES BLVD
SAINT ANDREWS TER
CT
SAINT ANDREWS AV
AILSA
SAINT ANDREWS AV
OTAY MESA CENTER RD
AVENIDA COSTA AZUL
SAINT ANDREWS AV
PIPER
ADORA
92154
HWY
36
905
ESTER RD
BLVD
PANASONIC WY
WATERVILLE RD
7800
LAHINCH DR
DUBLIN DR
RD
GIGANTIC ST
EXCELLANTE ST
CENTURION ST
AIRWAY
COSTA
RD
7500
8400
8700
34
35
DIEGO
AVD
AVENIDA AZUL
COSTA NORTE
PASEO DE LA FUENTE NORTE
AVENIDA DE LA FUENTE NORTE
OTAY CENTER CT
DEL SOL
AVD COSTA BLANCA
AVENIDA DE LA FUENTE
2200
COSTA ESTE
OTAY CENTER DR
OTAY CENTER DR
AVD COSTA
2300
AVD COSTA SUR
AVD
PASEO DE LA FUENTE
AVENIDA DE LA FUENTE SUR
HARVEST
BRITANNIA
AVD COSTA BRAVA
SIEMPRE VIVA RD
RD
7700
CUSTOMHOUSE PZ
CUSTOMHOUSE CT
MELKSEE ST
SARNEN ST
DRUCKER LN
ISTOW CT
KERNS ST
LA MEDIA RD (TRUCKS ONLY)
(TRUCKS ONLY)
1
2
3
CALIFORNIA
BAJA CALIFORNIA
RITANNIA CT
SEE 1352 MAP
AEROPUERTO INTERNACIONAL DE TIJUANA
TIJUANA
1
2
3
4
5
6
7
SEE 429 MAP
0 .125 .25 .375 .5 miles 1 in. = 1900 ft.

SEE 1332 MAP
A
B
C
D
E
1
2
3
4
5
6
7
CALZADA DE LA FUENTE
LONE STAR RD
CANYON
SUNROAD BLVD
PASEO DE LA FUENTE
DE LA FUENTE CT
ALTA RD
OTAY MESA RD
1600
CARNOUSTIE RD
DORNOCH CT
1700
SANYO AV
2100
36
31
AIRWAY RD
9500
HEINRICH HERTZ DR
PASEO DE LAS AMERICAS
MICHAEL
ENRICO FERMI DR
ENRICO FERMI PL
SAN DIEGO
NIELS BOHR CT
905
SIEMPRE VIVA RD
9700
10000
CENTER DR
CC
2300
ROLL DR
MARCONI CT
FARADAY DR
MARCONI PL
OTAY MESA INSPECTION FACILITY
HWY
MARCONI DR
9900
CMTO AMISTAD
T18S
T19S
6
UNITED STATES
MEXICO
NICOLA TESLA CT
OTAY CTR DR
VIA DE LA AMISTAD
CUSTOMHOUSE PZ
PAS DE LA FRONTERA
1
US CUSTOMS
COMMERCIAL VEHICLE GATE
SEE 1351 MAP
TIJUANA
SEE 429 MAP
0
.125
.25
.375
.5
miles 1 in. = 1900 ft.

SEE 1332 MAP

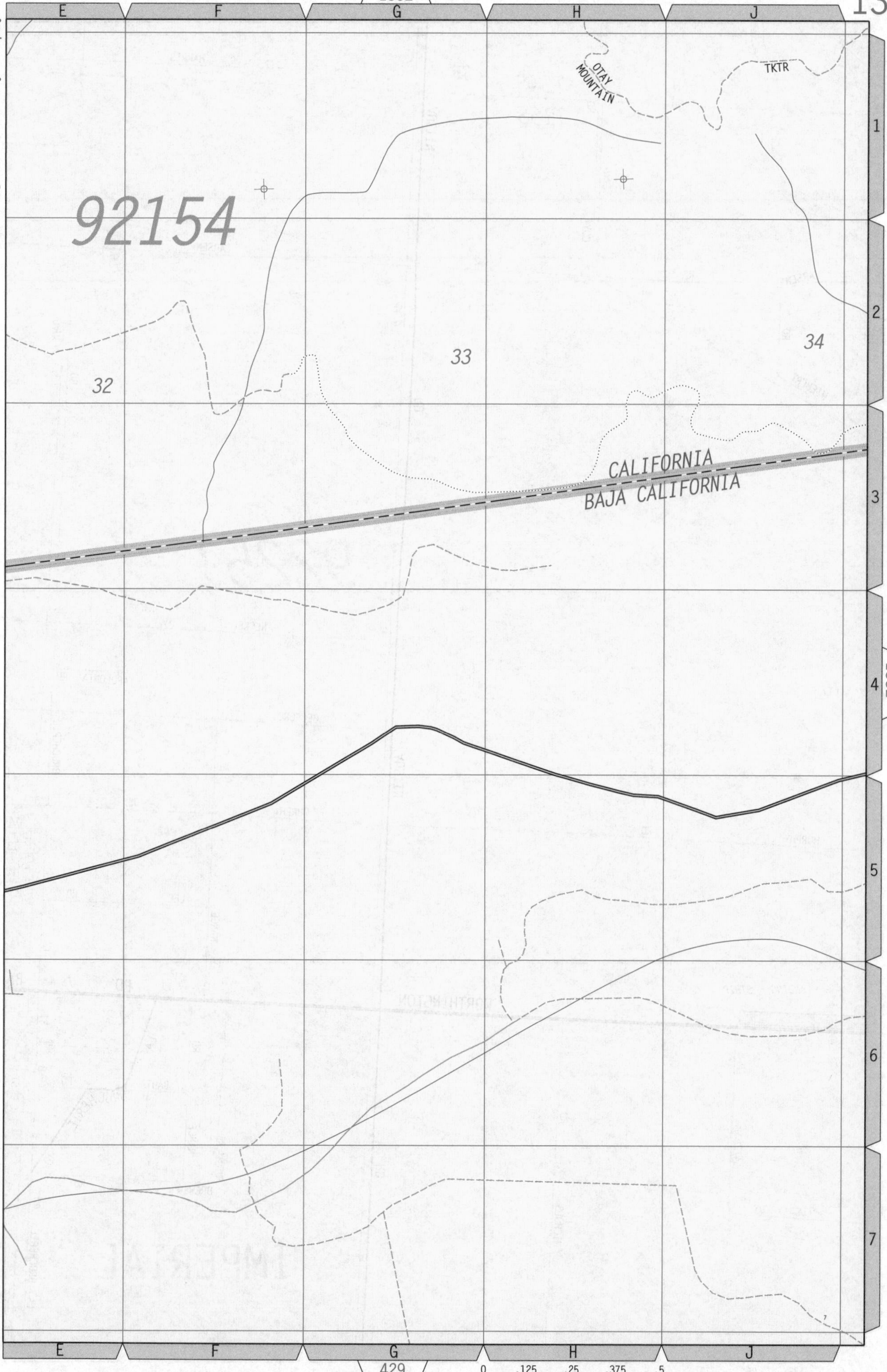

SEE 1332 MAP

SEE 429 MAP

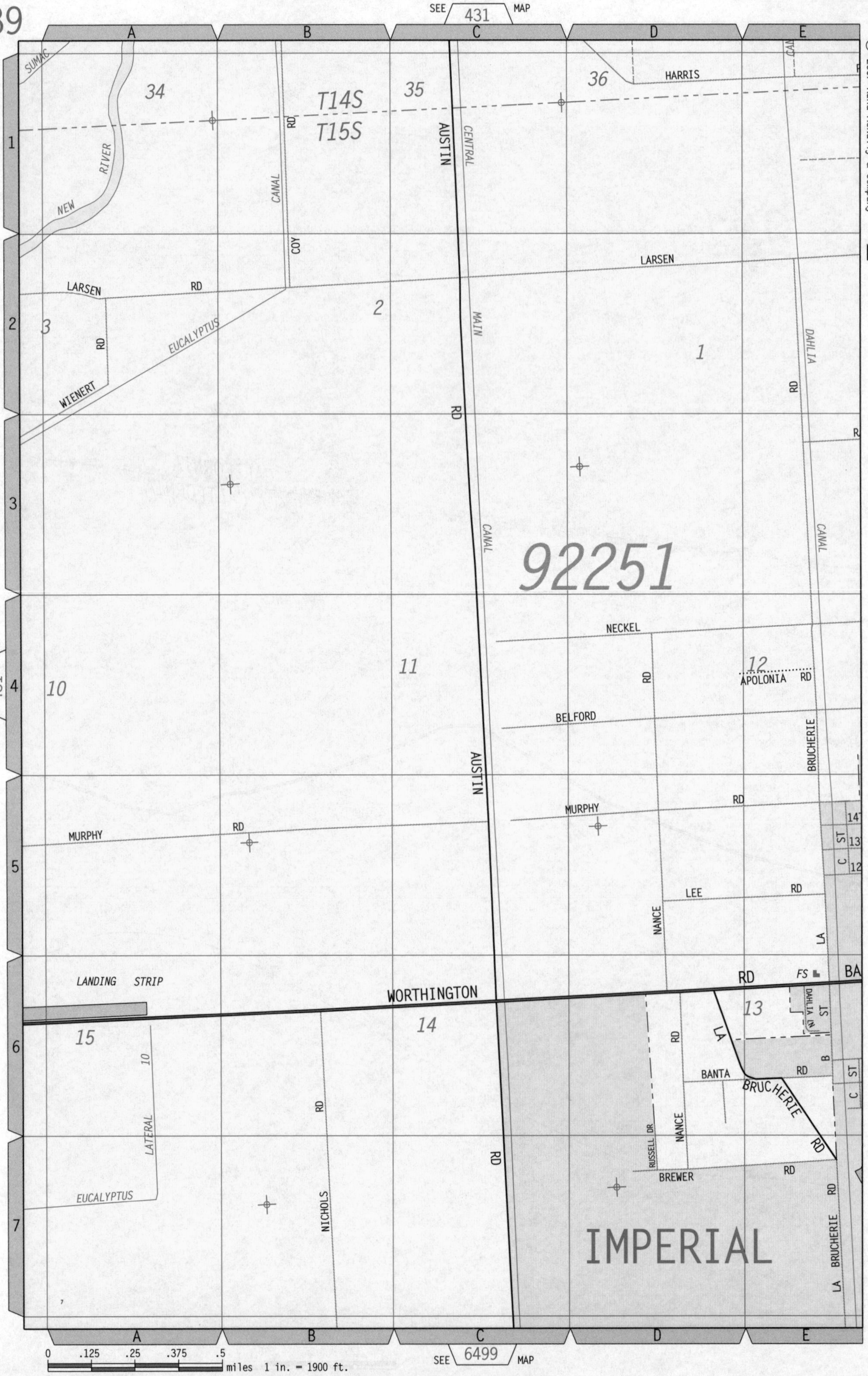
SEE 431 MAP
A
B
C
D
E
1
2
3
4
5
6
7
SAN DIEGO CO.
SUMAC
34
35
36
T14S
T15S
HARRIS
NEW RIVER
CANAL
COY RD
AUSTIN RD
CENTRAL MAIN CANAL
LARSEN RD
LARSEN
EUCALYPTUS
WIENERT RD
3
2
1
DAHLIA CANAL RD
92251
NECKEL
NANCE RD
12
APOLONIA RD
BELFORD
BRUCHERIE
10
11
SEE 431 MAP
AUSTIN
MURPHY RD
MURPHY
RD
LEE RD
LA
C ST
14
13
12
LANDING STRIP
WORTHINGTON RD
FS
BA
15
14
13
10 LATERAL
NICHOLS RD
DAHLIA LN
ST
LA BRUCHERIE RD
B
BANTA RD
RUSSELL DR
NANCE
BREWER RD
EUCALYPTUS
IMPERIAL
LA BRUCHERIE RD
SEE 6499 MAP
0 .125 .25 .375 .5 miles 1 in. = 1900 ft.

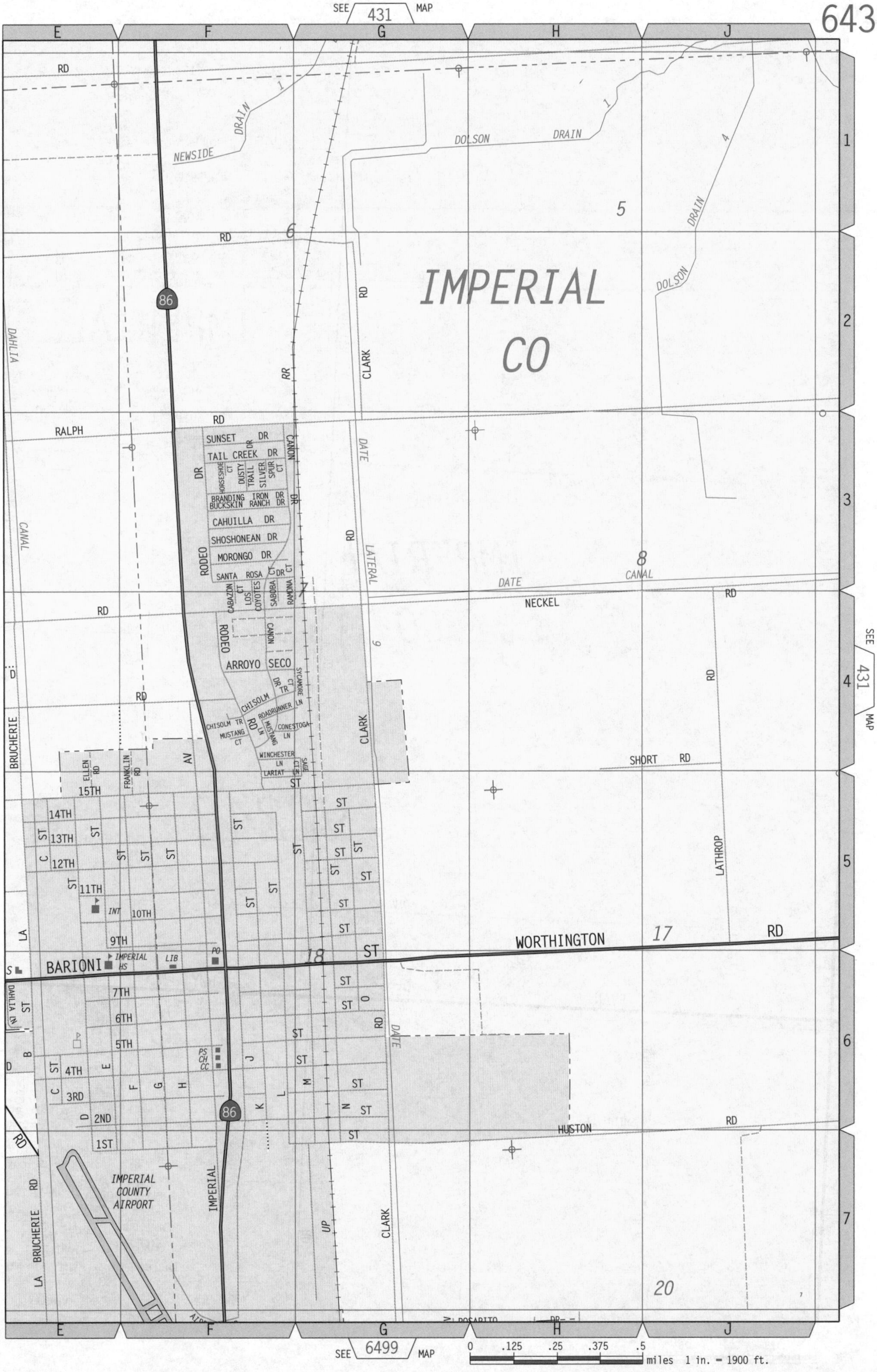

SEE 6499 MAP

0 .125 .25 .375 .5 miles 1 in. = 1900 ft.

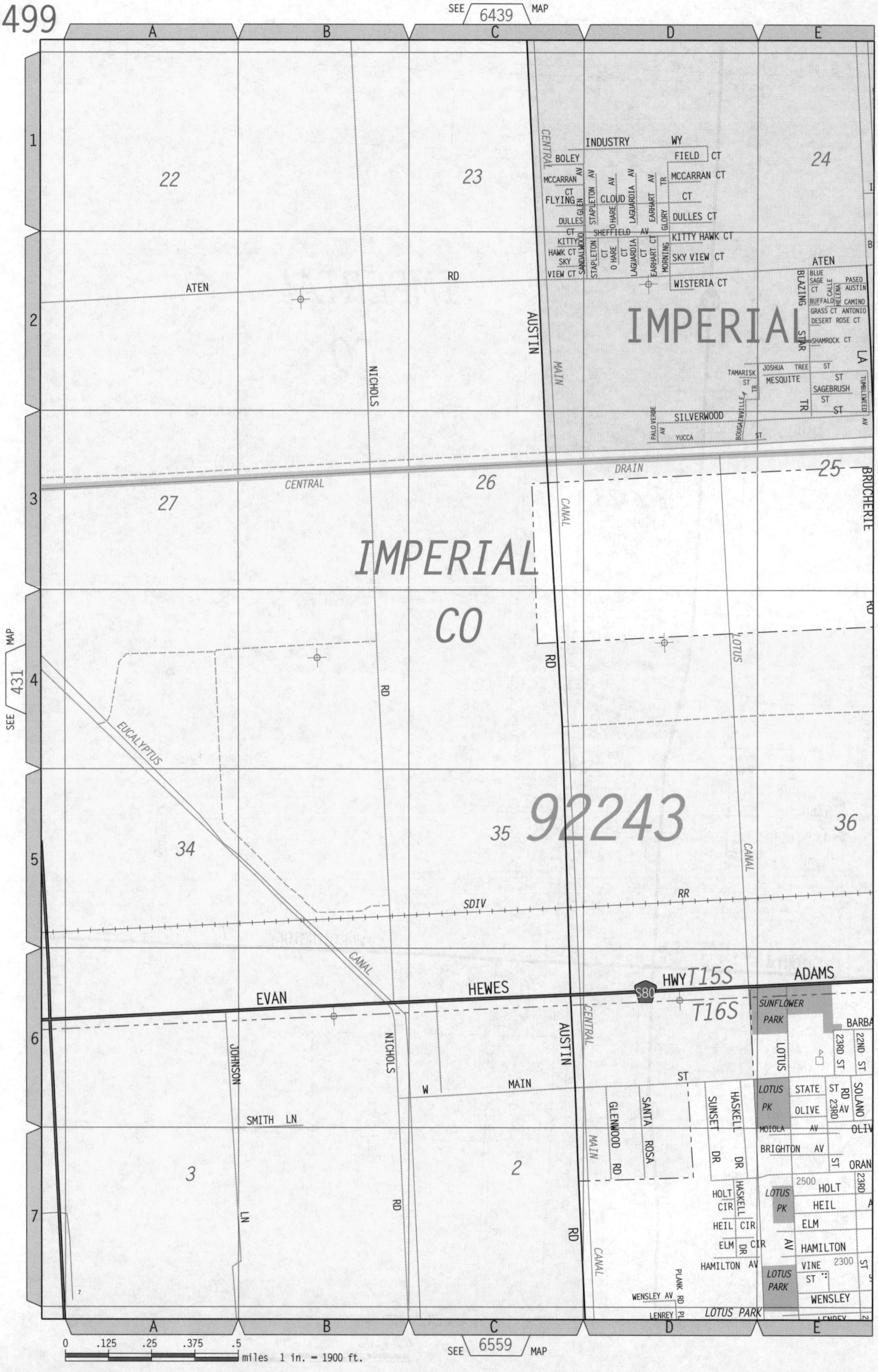

SEE 6439 MAP
SEE 431 MAP
SEE 6559 MAP
A
B
C
D
E
1
2
3
4
5
6
7
22
23
24
27
26
25
34
35
36
3
2
IMPERIAL
IMPERIAL
CO
92243
ATEN
RD
ATEN
NICHOLS
RD
AUSTIN
RD
CENTRAL
MAIN
CANAL
CENTRAL
DRAIN
BRUCHERIE
RD
LOTUS
CANAL
EUCALYPTUS
CANAL
SDIV
RR
EVAN
HEWES
HWY
S80
T15S
T16S
ADAMS
JOHNSON
LN
SMITH LN
NICHOLS
RD
W
MAIN
ST
AUSTIN
RD
CENTRAL
MAIN
CANAL
GLENWOOD
RD
SANTA
ROSA
SUNSET
DR
HASKELL
DR
INDUSTRY
WY
BOLEY
FIELD CT
MCCARRAN CT
FLYING
CLOUD
CT
DULLES CT
KITTY HAWK CT
SKY VIEW CT
WISTERIA CT
SHEFFIELD AV
STAPLETON
O HARE
LAGUARDIA
EARHART
MORNING
GLORY
SANDALWOOD
GLEN
BLAZING
STAR
BLUE SAGE CT
BUFFALO
GRASS CT
DESERT ROSE CT
CALLE HELENA
PASEO AUSTIN
CAMINO ANTONIO
SHAMROCK CT
JOSHUA TREE ST
TAMARISK ST
MESQUITE
SAGEBRUSH ST
TR
ST
TUMBLEWEED AV
SILVERWOOD
PALO VERDE AV
YUCCA
ST
BOUGAINVILLE
LA
SUNFLOWER PARK
BARBA
23RD ST
22ND ST
LOTUS
LOTUS PK
STATE
OLIVE
23RD RD
AV
SOLANO
OLIV
MOIOLA AV
BRIGHTON AV
ST
ORAN
2500
23RD
HOLT
LOTUS PK
HEIL
ELM
HAMILTON
HOLT CIR
HASKELL
HEIL CIR
ELM DR CIR
HAMILTON AV
AV
VINE ST
2300
LOTUS PARK
WENSLEY
LENREY
WENSLEY AV
PLANK RD
LENREY PL
LOTUS PARK
0 .125 .25 .375 .5 miles 1 in. = 1900 ft.

SEE 6439 MAP

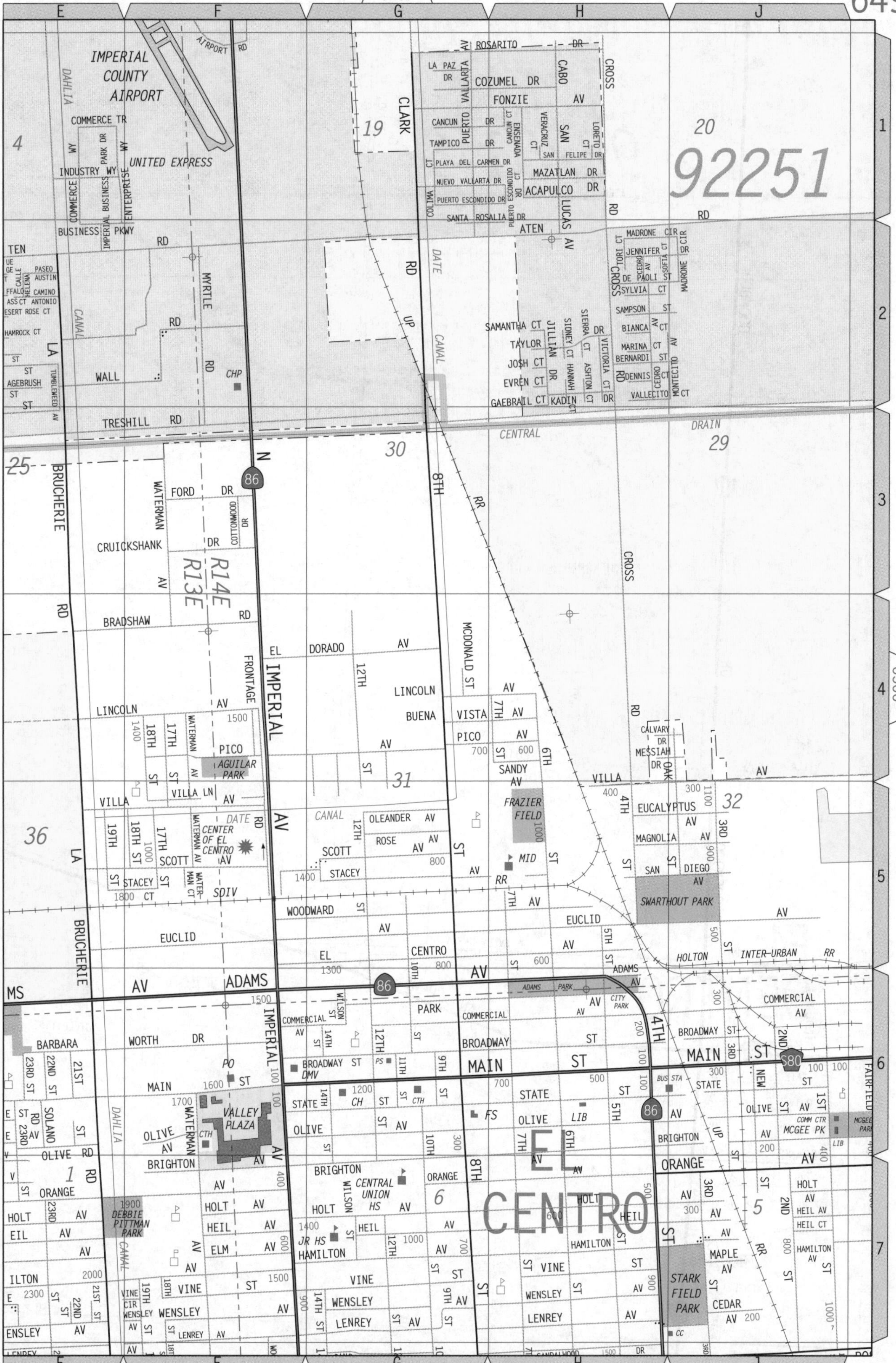

SEE 6500 MAP

SEE 6559 MAP

0 .125 .25 .375 .5 miles 1 in. = 1900 ft.

SAN DIEGO CO.

SAN DIEGO CO.

SEE 431 MAP

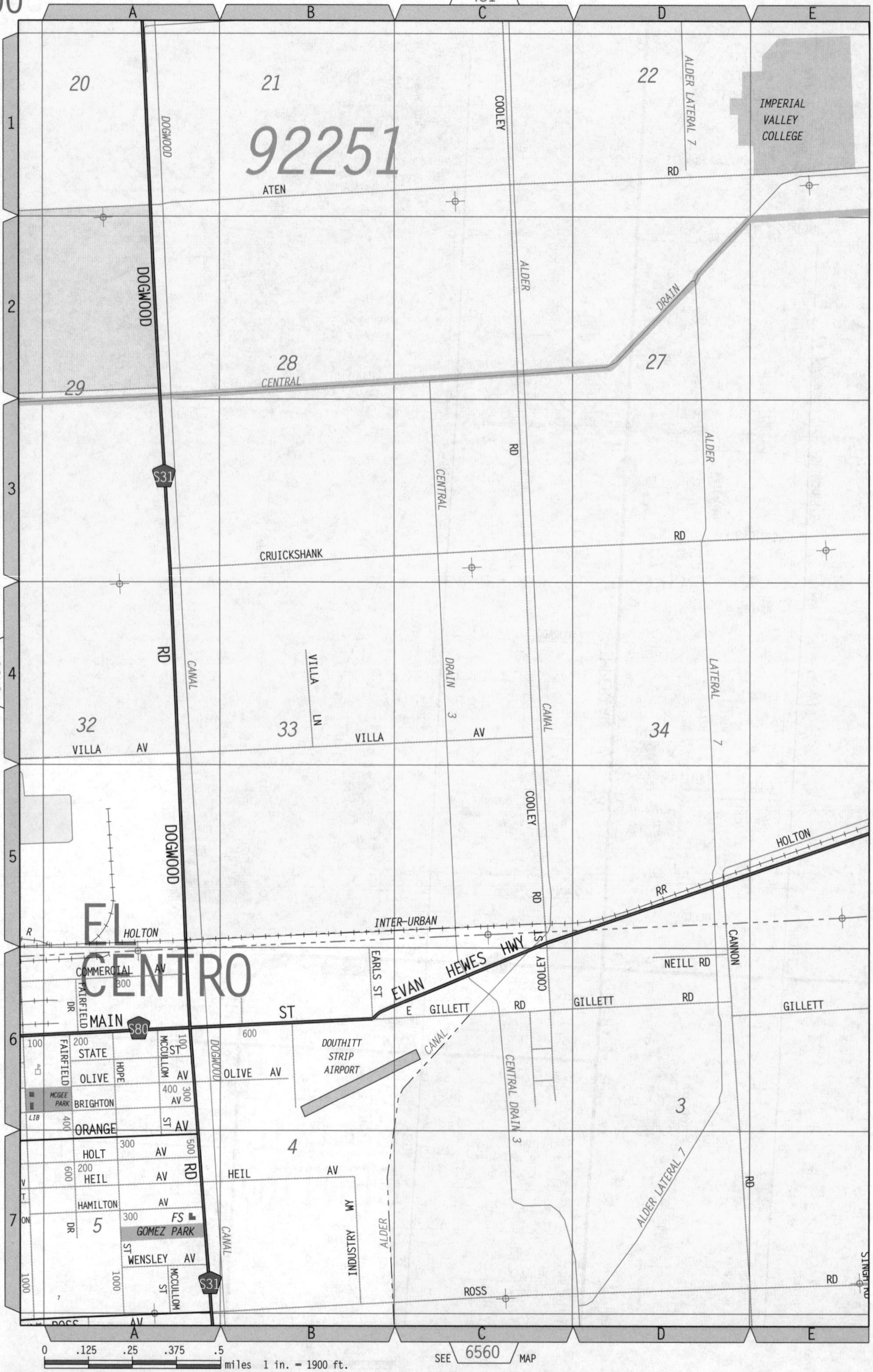

SEE 6499 MAP

SEE 6560 MAP

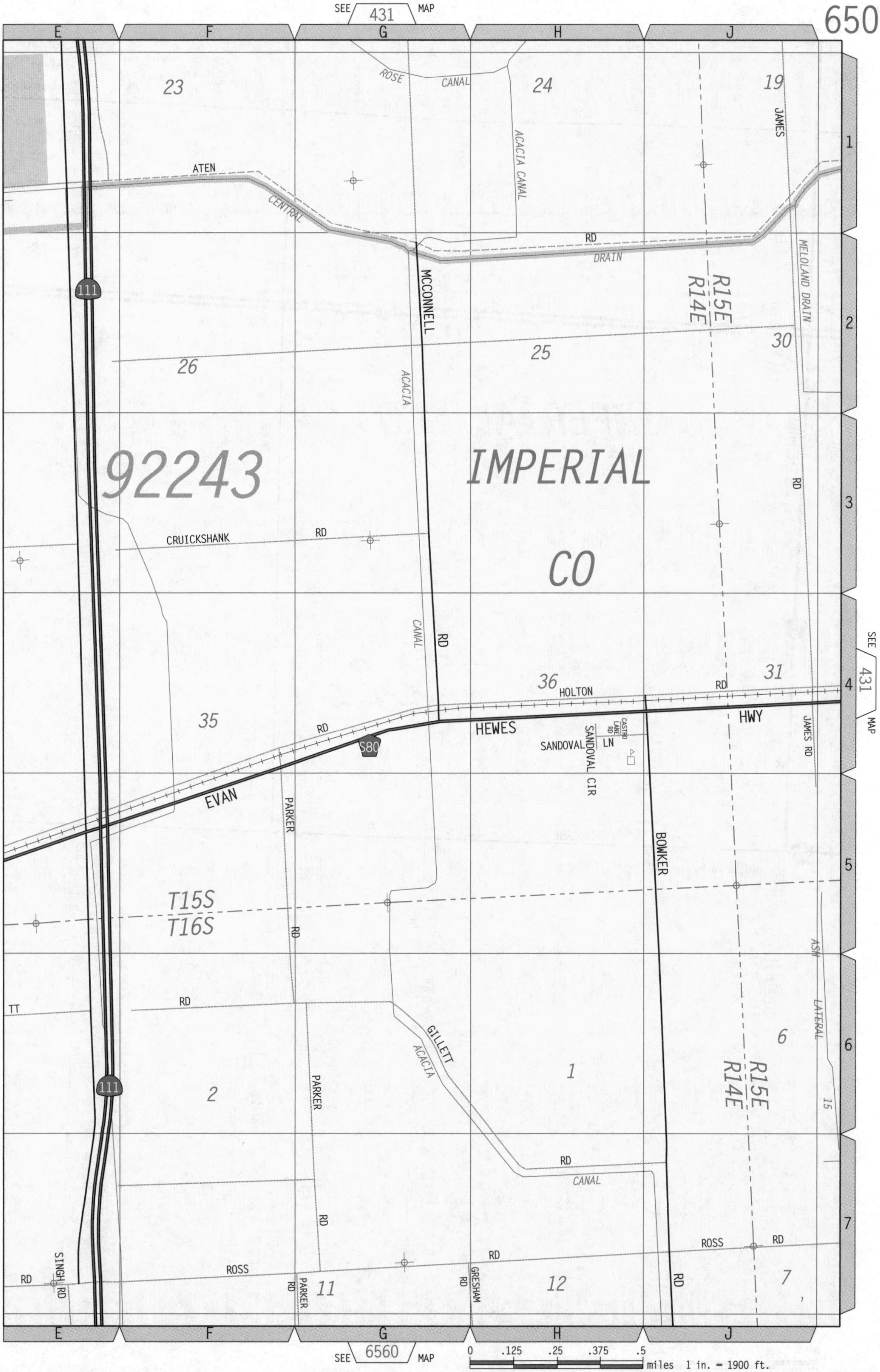
SEE 431 MAP
E
F
G
H
J
23
ROSE
CANAL
24
19
JAMES
ACACIA CANAL
1
ATEN
CENTRAL
RD
DRAIN
MELOLAND DRAIN
MCCONNELL
111
R15E
R14E
2
30
25
26
ACACIA
92243
IMPERIAL
RD
3
CRUICKSHANK
RD
CO
CANAL
RD
SEE 431 MAP
36
HOLTON
RD
31
4
35
RD
HEWES
HWY
CASTRO LANE RD
JAMES RD
SANDOVAL
LN
SANDOVAL CIR
S80
EVAN
PARKER
BOWKER
5
T15S
T16S
RD
ASH
TT
RD
GILLETT
LATERAL
6
ACACIA
6
1
R15E
R14E
111
2
PARKER
15
RD
CANAL
7
RD
ROSS
RD
SINGH RD
RD
ROSS
RD
GRESHAM
RD
RD
PARKER
11
12
RD
7
SEE 6560 MAP
0 .125 .25 .375 .5
miles 1 in. = 1900 ft.
N

SAN DIEGO CO.

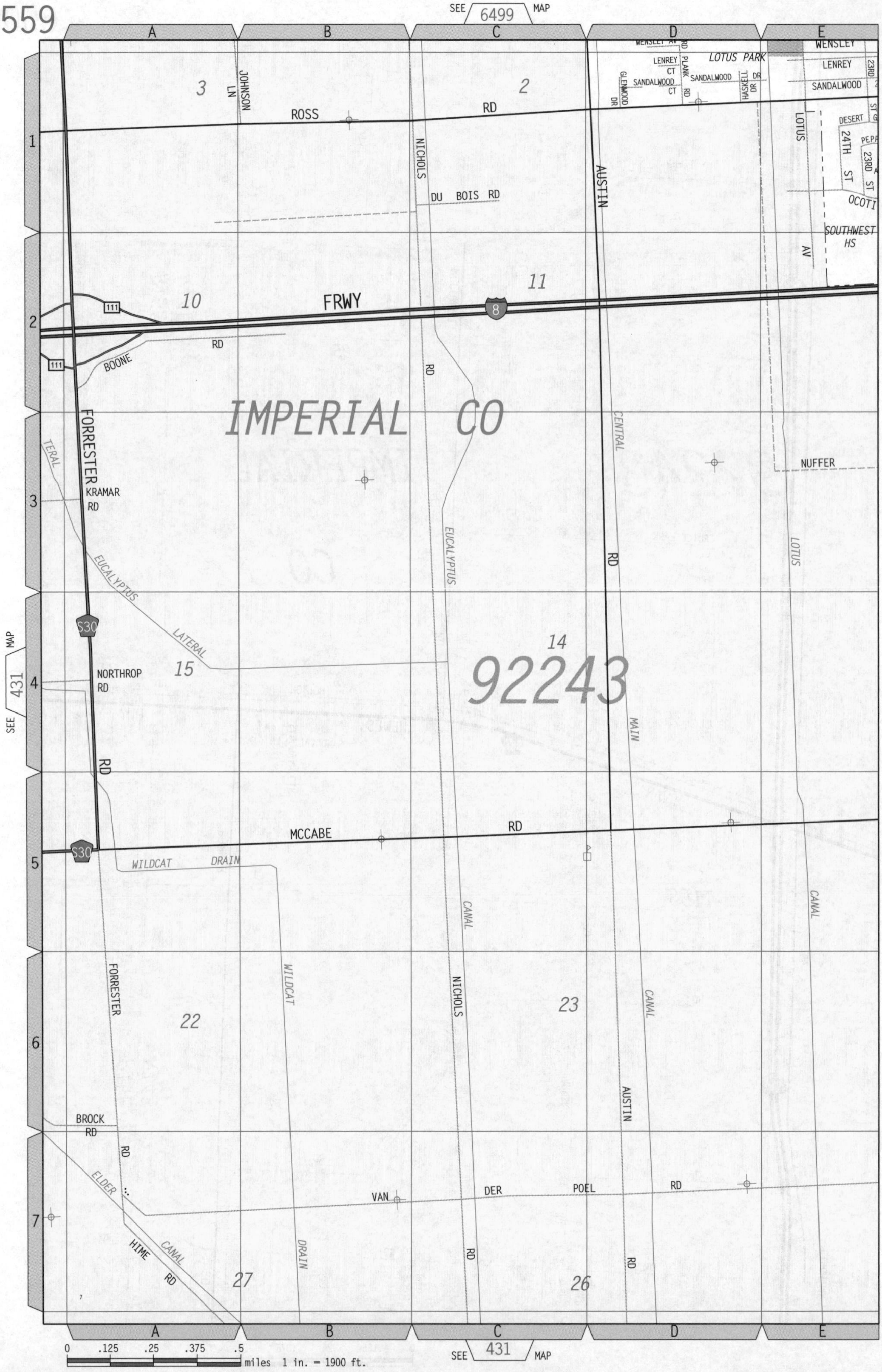
SEE 6499 MAP
A
B
C
D
E
1
2
3
4
5
6
7
SAN DIEGO CO.
SEE 431 MAP
JOHNSON LN
ROSS RD
WENSLEY AV
LENREY CT
PLANK RD
LOTUS PARK
SANDALWOOD CT
GLENWOOD DR
SANDALWOOD
HASKELL DR
WENSLEY
LENREY
SANDALWOOD
23RD
LOTUS
DESERT
24TH ST
23RD ST
OCOTI
SOUTHWEST HS
AV
NICHOLS
DU BOIS RD
AUSTIN
FRWY
8
111
BOONE
RD
IMPERIAL CO
CENTRAL
TERAL
FORRESTER
KRAMAR RD
NUFFER
EUCALYPTUS
EUCALYPTUS
LOTUS
S30
LATERAL
NORTHROP RD
92243
MAIN
RD
MCCABE
WILDCAT
DRAIN
CANAL
CANAL
WILDCAT
NICHOLS
CANAL
AUSTIN
BROCK RD
ELDER
HIME RD
CANAL
VAN
DER
POEL
DRAIN
3
2
10
11
14
15
22
23
27
26
0
.125
.25
.375
.5
miles 1 in. = 1900 ft.
SEE 431 MAP

SEE 6499 MAP

SEE 431 MAP

0 .125 .25 .375 .5 miles 1 in. = 1900 ft.

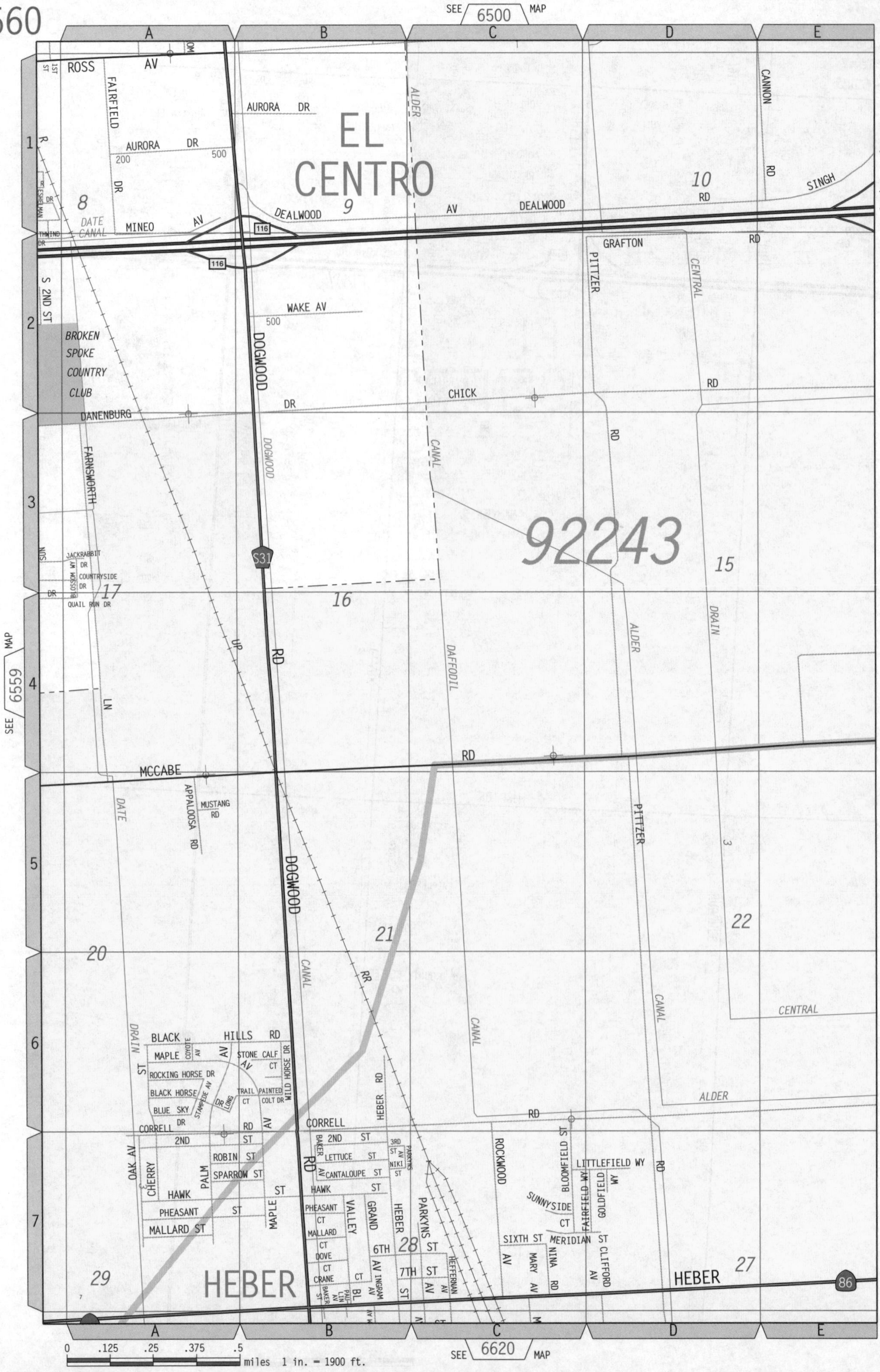
SEE 6500 MAP
SEE 6559 MAP
SEE 6620 MAP
A
B
C
D
E
1
2
3
4
5
6
7
EL CENTRO
92243
HEBER
ROSS AV
FAIRFIELD DR
AURORA DR
ALDER
CANNON RD
SINGH RD
DEALWOOD AV
MINEO AV
DATE CANAL
116
S 2ND ST
WAKE AV
GRAFTON RD
PITZZER RD
CENTRAL DRAIN
BROKEN SPOKE COUNTRY CLUB
DANENBURG DR
CHICK RD
DOGWOOD RD
ALDER CANAL
FARNSWORTH LN
JACKRABBIT DR
COUNTRYSIDE DR
QUAIL RUN DR
S31
UP
DAFFODIL
MCCABE RD
APPALOOSA RD
MUSTANG RD
DATE DRAIN
CANAL
RR
CENTRAL
ALDER
BLACK HILLS RD
MAPLE AV
STONE CALF AV
ROCKING HORSE DR
BLACK HORSE DR
BLUE SKY DR
WILD HORSE DR
CORRELL RD
2ND ST
ROBIN ST
SPARROW ST
HAWK ST
PHEASANT ST
MALLARD ST
OAK AV
CHERRY ST
PALM AV
MAPLE ST
LETTUCE ST
CANTALOUPE ST
VALLEY
GRAND AV
HEBER AV
PARKYNS ST
HEFFERMAN AV
6TH ST
7TH ST
ROCKWOOD AV
BLOOMFIELD ST
LITTLEFIELD WY
FAIRFIELD WY
GOLDFIELD WY
SUNNYSIDE CT
MERIDIAN ST
SIXTH ST
MARY AV
NINA RD
CLIFFORD AV
HEBER RD
86
8
9
10
15
16
17
20
21
22
27
28
29
0
.125
.25
.375
.5
miles 1 in. = 1900 ft.

SEE 6500 MAP

SEE 431 MAP

SEE 6620 MAP

SEE 6560 MAP
A
B
C
D
E
1
2
3
4
5
6
7
86
HEBER RD
9TH
10TH
11TH
14TH ST
INGRAM AV
PARKYNS AV
HEFFERNAN
HEBER ST
ST
AV
MARY AV
CLIFFORD AV
28
29
27
DATE DRAIN
DOGWOOD
DOGWOOD RD
FAWCETT
S31
PITZER RD
DAFFODIL CANAL
UP RR
WARE RD
32
33
34
CANAL
JASPER RD
JASPER
CENTRAL MAIN CANAL
WILLOUGHBY RD
CENTRAL
SEE 431 MAP
EADY RD
BEECH
4
3
2
KLOKE RD
COLE RD
COLE
NEW RIVER
MADDOX RD
PRUETT RD
UP
9231
9
10
11
ALL
KLOKE RD
EADY AV
M. KNECHEL
GARCIA AV
CANAL
SEE 6680 MAP
0 .125 .25 .375 .5 miles 1 in. = 1900 ft.

SEE 6560 MAP

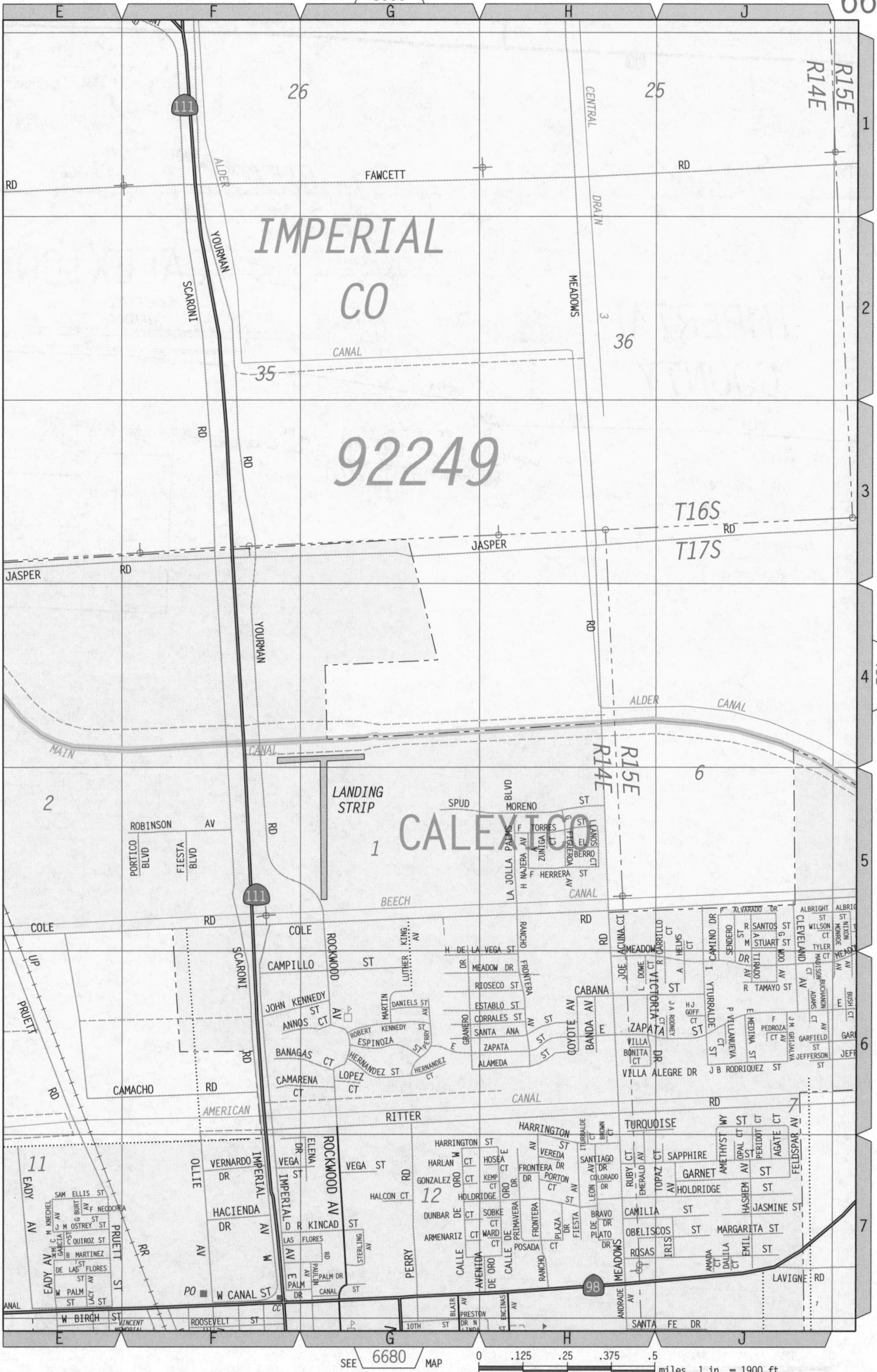

SEE 431 MAP

SEE 6680 MAP

0 .125 .25 .375 .5 miles 1 in. = 1900 ft.

SAN DIEGO CO.

SEE 6620 MAP

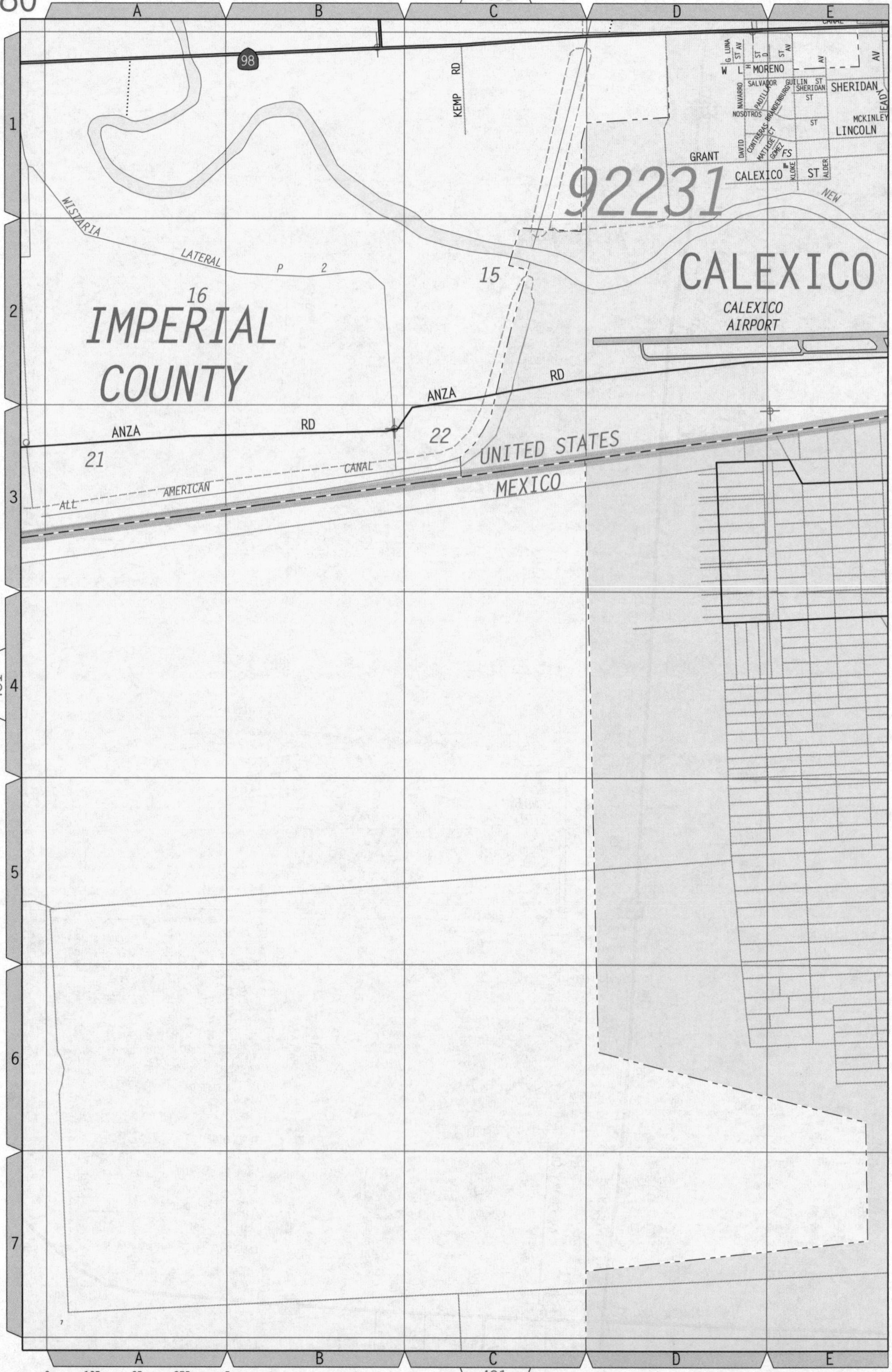

SEE 431 MAP

SEE 431 MAP

0 .125 .25 .375 .5 miles 1 in. = 1900 ft.

SEE 6620 MAP
MEXICALI
CALIFORNIA
BAJA CALIFORNIA
CALEXICO HS
JR HS
CRUMMERT PARK
EMERSON PARK
LEGION PARK
VINCENT MEMORIAL HS
AURORA HS
CAMP SALVATION
ROCKWOOD PLAZA
CALEXICO MISSION HS
US CUSTOMS
LIB
PS
FS
CH
CTH
111
RIVER
RIO NUEVO
UP RR
CO
SAN DIEGO CO.
SEE 431 MAP
SEE 431 MAP
0 .125 .25 .375 .5 miles 1 in. = 1900 ft.

Cities and Communities

Community Name	Abbr.	County	ZIP Code	Map Page
Agua Caliente		SDCo	92086	409
Agua Caliente Hot Spgs		SDCo	92036	430
Alamorio		ImCo	92227	431
Allied Gardens		SDCo	92120	1250
Alpine		SDCo	91901	1234
Alpine Heights		SDCo	91901	1253
Alta Vista		SDCo	92114	1290
Andrade		ImCo		432
Ballena		SDCo	92065	1154
Bankhead Springs		SDCo	91934	1321
Banner		SDCo	92036	1156
Bard		ImCo	92283	432
Barona Mesa		SDCo	92065	1173
Barrett Junction		SDCo	91917	429
Barrio Logan		SDCo	92113	1289
Bay Park		SDCo	92110	1268
Bear Valley		SDCo	92027	1111
Birch Hill		SDCo	92060	1052
Blossom Valley		SDCo	92021	1232
Bombay Beach		ImCo		410
Bonds Corner		ImCo	92250	431
Bonita		SDCo	91902	1310
Bonsall		SDCo	92003	1048
Borrego Springs		SDCo	92004	1059
Borrego Wells		SDCo	92004	410
Bostonia		SDCo	92021	1252
Boulder Oaks		SDCo	91962	430
Boulevard		SDCo	91905	1300
* Brawley	BRW	ImCo	92227	431
Broadway Heights		SDCo	92114	1270
Buckman Springs		SDCo	91962	430
* Calexico	CALX	ImCo	92231	6620
* Calipatria	CLPT	ImCo	92233	411
Cameron Corners		SDCo	91906	1318
Camp Pendleton		SDCo	92055	1085
Campo		SDCo	91906	1318
Canebrake		SDCo	92036	430
Canyon City		SDCo	91906	430
* Carlsbad	CRLB	SDCo	92008	1106
Carmel Mtn Ranch		SDCo	92128	1190
Carmel Valley		SDCo	92130	1188
Casa De Oro		SDCo	91977	1271
Castle Park		SDCo	91911	1330
Centre City		SDCo	92101	1289
Chollas Creek		SDCo	92105	1290
Chollas View		SDCo	92102	1289
* Chula Vista	CHV	SDCo	91910	1310
City Heights		SDCo	92105	1269
Clairemont		SDCo	92117	1248
Combs Camp		SDCo	92004	409
Coolidge Spring		ImCo	92274	410
* Coronado	CORD	SDCo	92118	1288
Coronado Cays		SDCo	92118	1329
Cottonwood		SDCo	92019	1272
Coyote Wells		ImCo	92259	430
Crest		SDCo	92021	1252
Crown Point		SDCo	92109	1268
Cuyamaca		SDCo	92036	1176
Date City		ImCo	92250	431
De Luz		SDCo	92028	996
Dehesa		SDCo	92019	1253
Del Cerro		SDCo	92120	1250
Del Dios		SDCo	92029	1149
* Del Mar	DLMR	SDCo	92014	1187
Descanso		SDCo	91916	1236
Descanso Junction		SDCo	91916	1236
Desert Lodge		SDCo	92004	1099
Desert Shores		ImCo	92274	410
Dixieland		ImCo	92251	430
Dulzura		SDCo	91917	1314
Eagles Nest		SDCo	92086	409
East Elliott		SDCo	92145	1230
Eastlake		SDCo	91913	1311
Eastlake Greens		SDCo	91915	1311
Echo Dell		SDCo	91916	429
Eden Gardens		SDCo	92075	1187
* El Cajon	ELCJ	SDCo	92020	1251
* El Centro	ELCN	ImCo	92243	6559
Elmore		ImCo	92227	410
Emerald Hills		SDCo	92114	1290
* Encinitas	ENCT	SDCo	92024	1147
Engineer Springs		SDCo	91917	1314
* Escondido	ESCN	SDCo	92025	1129
Eucalyptus Hills		SDCo	92040	1211
Fairbanks Country Club		SDCo	92130	1188
Fairbanks Ranch		SDCo	92067	1168
Fallbrook		SDCo	92028	1027
Felicity		ImCo		432
Fernbrook		SDCo	92065	1192
Fleetridge		SDCo	92106	1288
Fletcher Hills		SDCo	92020	1251
Flinn Springs		SDCo	92021	1232
Foster		SDCo	92040	1211
Glamis		ImCo		431
Glen Oaks		SDCo	91901	1233
Glenview		SDCo	92021	1232
Golden Hill		SDCo	92102	1289
Gordons Well		ImCo		431
Grant Hill		SDCo	92102	1289
Grantville		SDCo	92120	1249
Grays Well		ImCo		431
Green Valley Falls		SDCo	92916	1216
Grossmont		SDCo	91942	1251
Guatay		SDCo	91931	1236
Harbison Canyon		SDCo	92019	1253
Harmony Grove		SDCo	92029	1129
Harrison Park		SDCo	92036	1156
Heber		ImCo	92249	6560
Hidden Glen		SDCo	91901	1254
Hidden Meadows		SDCo	92026	1089
Hillcrest		SDCo	92103	1269
* Holtville	HOLT	ImCo	92250	431
Hulburd Grove		SDCo	91916	1236
* Imperial	IMP	ImCo	92251	6499
* Imperial Beach	IMPB	SDCo	91932	1349
-- Imperial County	ImCo	ImCo		
Imperial Gables		ImCo		411
Indian Springs		SDCo	91935	1292
Irving's Crest		SDCo	92065	1172
Jacumba		SDCo	91934	1321
Jamacha (SD)		SDCo	92114	1290
Jamacha (SDCO)		SDCo	91935	1272
Jamul		SDCo	91935	1292
Jesmond Dene		SDCo	92026	1109
Johnstown		SDCo	92021	1232
Julian		SDCo	92036	1136
Kane Spring		ImCo	92259	410
Kearny Mesa		SDCo	92111	1249
Kensington		SDCo	92116	1269
Kentwood In The Pines		SDCo	92036	1156
La Costa		SDCo	92009	1127
La Jolla		SDCo	92037	1227
La Jolla Amago		SDCo	92060	1052
La Jolla Shores		SDCo	92037	1227
* La Mesa	LMSA	SDCo	91941	1270
La Playa		SDCo	92106	1288
La Presa		SDCo	91977	1291
Lake Henshaw		SDCo	92070	409
Lakeside		SDCo	92040	1232
Lakeview		SDCo	92040	1232
* Lemon Grove	LMGR	SDCo	91945	1270
Leucadia		SDCo	92024	1147
Liberty Station		SDCo	92106	1268
Lincoln Acres		SDCo	91950	1310
Lincoln Park		SDCo	92102	1290
Linda Vista		SDCo	92111	1249
Little Italy		SDCo	92101	1288
Live Oak Park		SDCo	92028	1028
Live Oak Springs		SDCo	91905	1299
Logan Heights		SDCo	92113	1289
Loma Portal		SDCo	92110	1268

*Indicates incorporated city

Cities and Communities

Community Name	Abbr.	County	ZIP Code	Map Page
Lomas Santa Fe		SDCo	92075	1167
Lomita		SDCo	92114	1290
Lynwood Hills		SDCo	91910	1310
Manzanita		SDCo	91905	1300
Meloland		ImCo	92243	431
Memorial		SDCo	92113	1289
Mesa Grande		SDCo	92070	409
Middletown		SDCo	92103	1268
Midway		SDCo	92106	1268
Midway Well		ImCo		431
Mira Mesa		SDCo	92126	1209
Miramar		SDCo	92126	1209
Miramar Ranch N		SDCo	92131	1209
Mission Bay Park		SDCo	92109	1268
Mission Beach		SDCo	92109	1267
Mission Hills		SDCo	92103	1268
Mission Valley		SDCo	92108	1269
Mission Village		SDCo	92123	1249
Morena Village		SDCo	91906	1297
Moreno		SDCo	92040	1212
Morettis		SDCo	92070	409
Mount Helix		SDCo	91941	1271
Mount Hope		SDCo	92102	1289
Mount Laguna		SDCo	91948	1218
Mount Signal		ImCo	92231	431
Mountain View		SDCo	92113	1289
* National City	NATC	SDCo	91950	1309
Navajo		SDCo	92120	1250
Naval Amp Base		SDCo	92155	1309
Nestor		SDCo	92154	1350
Niland		ImCo	92257	411
Normal Heights		SDCo	92116	1269
North Bay Terraces		SDCo	92114	1290
North Encanto		SDCo	92114	1290
North Island NAS		SDCo	92135	1288
North Jamul		SDCo	91935	1272
North Park		SDCo	92104	1269
Oak Grove		SDCo	92086	409
Oak Park		SDCo	92105	1270
Ocean Beach		SDCo	92107	1267
Ocean Hills		SDCo	92056	1107
* Oceanside	OCN	SDCo	92054	1086
Ocotillo		ImCo	92259	430
Ocotillo Wells		SDCo	92004	410
Ogilby		ImCo		432
Old Town		SDCo	92110	1268
Olivenhain		SDCo	92024	1148
Otay		SDCo	91911	1330
Otay Mesa		SDCo	92154	1350
Pacific Beach		SDCo	92109	1247
Pala		SDCo	92059	1029
Pala Mesa Village		SDCo	92028	1048
Palm City		SDCo	92154	1330
Palo Verde		ImCo		412
Palo Verde		SDCo	91901	1234
Palomar Mountain		SDCo	92060	1052
Paradise Hills		SDCo	92139	1290
Paso Picacho		SDCo	92036	1196
Pauma Valley		SDCo	92061	1050
Peninsula		SDCo	92106	1288
Picacho		ImCo		412
Pine Hills		SDCo	92036	1155
Pine Valley		SDCo	91962	1237
Plaster City		ImCo	92259	430
Point Loma		SDCo	92106	1308
Potrero		SDCo	91963	429
* Poway	PWY	SDCo	92064	1190
Puerta La Cruz		SDCo	92086	409
Rainbow		SDCo	92028	998
Ramona		SDCo	92065	1152
Ranchita		SDCo	92066	410
Rancho Bernardo		SDCo	92128	1170
Rancho Del Rey		SDCo	91910	1311
Rancho Palo Verde		SDCo	91901	1254
Rancho Penasquitos		SDCo	92129	1189
Rancho San Diego		SDCo	91978	1271
Rancho Santa Fe		SDCo	92067	1168
Rincon		SDCo	92082	1071
Rock Haven		SDCo	92065	1171
Rolando		SDCo	92115	1270
Rosemont		SDCo	92065	1172
Roseville		SDCo	92106	1288
Sabre Springs		SDCo	92128	1189
Salton City		ImCo	92274	410
Salton Sea Beach		ImCo	92274	410
San Carlos		SDCo	92119	1250
* San Clemente	SCLE	OrCo	92672	1023
* San Diego	SD	SDCo	92101	1289
San Diego Country Ests		SDCo	92065	1173
-- San Diego County	SDCo	SDCo		
San Felipe		SDCo	92086	409
San Ignacio		SDCo	92086	410
San Luis Rey		SDCo	92054	1086
San Luis Rey Heights		SDCo	92028	1048
* San Marcos	SMCS	SDCo	92069	1108
San Onofre		SDCo	92672	1023
San Pasqual		SDCo	92025	1131
San Ysidro		SDCo	92173	1350
Santa Ysabel		SDCo	92070	1135
* Santee	SNTE	SDCo	92071	1231
Scissors Crossing		SDCo	92036	410
Scripps Miramar Ranch		SDCo	92131	1209
Seeley		ImCo	92273	431
Serra Mesa		SDCo	92123	1249
Shady Dell		SDCo	92065	1192
Shelltown		SDCo	92113	1289
Shelter Valley Ranchos		SDCo	92036	1138
Sherman Heights		SDCo	92102	1289
Skyline		SDCo	92114	1290
* Solana Beach	SOLB	SDCo	92075	1167
Sorrento Mesa		SDCo	92121	1208
Sorrento Valley		SDCo	92121	1208
South Bay Terraces		SDCo	92139	1290
South Encanto		SDCo	92114	1290
South Oceanside		SDCo	92054	1106
South Park		SDCo	92102	1289
Southcrest		SDCo	92113	1289
Spring Valley		SDCo	91977	1271
Stockton		SDCo	92102	1289
Sunnyside		SDCo	91902	1311
Sunshine Summit		SDCo	92086	409
Talmadge		SDCo	92115	1269
Tecate		SDCo	91980	429
The Narrows		SDCo	92004	1120
The Willows		SDCo	91901	1234
Tierra Del Sol		SDCo	91905	1320
Tierrasanta		SDCo	92124	1229
Tijuana River Valley		SDCo	92154	1350
Torrey Highlands		SDCo	92129	1189
Torrey Hills		SDCo	92130	1208
Torrey Pines		SDCo	92014	1187
Twin Oaks		SDCo	92069	1108
University City		SDCo	92122	1228
University Heights		SDCo	92116	1269
Uptown		SDCo	92103	1269
Valencia Park		SDCo	92114	1290
Vallecito		SDCo	92036	430
Valley Center		SDCo	92082	1090
Via De La Valle		SDCo	92014	1187
Victoria		SDCo	91901	1234
* Vista	VSTA	SDCo	92083	1087
Warner Springs		SDCo	92086	409
* Westmorland	WEST	ImCo	92281	411
Whispering Pines		SDCo	92036	1136
Winter Gardens		SDCo	92040	1232
Winterhaven		ImCo	92283	432
Winterwarm		SDCo	92028	1048
Witch Creek		SDCo	92065	409
Wynola		SDCo	92036	1135

*Indicates incorporated city

List of Abbreviations

PREFIXES AND SUFFIXES

AL	ALLEY
ARC	ARCADE
AV, AVE	AVENUE
AVCT	AVENUE COURT
AVD	AVENIDA
AVD D LA	AVENIDA DE LA
AVD D LOS	AVENIDA DE LOS
AVD DE	AVENIDA DE
AVD DE LAS	AVENIDA DE LAS
AVD DEL	AVENIDA DEL
AVDR	AVENUE DRIVE
AVEX	AVENUE EXTENSION
AV OF	AVENUE OF
AV OF THE	AVENUE OF THE
AVPL	AVENUE PLACE
BAY	BAY
BEND	BEND
BL, BLVD	BOULEVARD
BLCT	BOULEVARD COURT
BLEX	BOULEVARD EXTENSION
BRCH	BRANCH
BRDG	BRIDGE
BYPS	BYPASS
BYWY	BYWAY
CIDR	CIRCLE DRIVE
CIR	CIRCLE
CL	CALLE
CL DE	CALLE DE
CL DL	CALLE DEL
CL D LA	CALLE DE LA
CL D LAS	CALLE DE LAS
CL D LOS	CALLE DE LOS
CL EL	CALLE EL
CLJ	CALLEJON
CL LA	CALLE LA
CL LAS	CALLE LAS
CL LOS	CALLE LOS
CLTR	CLUSTER
CM	CAMINO
CM DE	CAMINO DE
CM DL	CAMINO DEL
CM D LA	CAMINO DE LA
CM D LAS	CAMINO DE LAS
CM D LOS	CAMINO DE LOS
CMTO	CAMINITO
CMTO DEL	CAMINITO DEL
CMTO D LA	CAMINITO DE LA
CMTO D LAS	CAMINITO DE LAS
CMTO D LOS	CAMINITO DE LOS
CNDR	CENTER DRIVE
COM	COMMON
COMS	COMMONS
CORR	CORRIDOR
CRES	CRESCENT
CRLO	CIRCULO
CRSG	CROSSING
CST	CIRCLE STREET
CSWY	CAUSEWAY
CT	COURT
CTAV	COURT AVENUE
CTE	CORTE
CTE D	CORTE DE
CTE DEL	CORTE DEL
CTE D LAS	CORTE DE LAS
CTO	CUT OFF
CTR	CENTER
CTST	COURT STREET
CUR	CURVE
CV	COVE
DE	DE
DIAG	DIAGONAL
DR	DRIVE
DRAV	DRIVE AVENUE
DRCT	DRIVE COURT
DRLP	DRIVE LOOP
DVDR	DIVISION DR
EXAV	EXTENSION AVENUE
EXBL	EXTENSION BOULEVARD
EXRD	EXTENSION ROAD
EXST	EXTENSION STREET
EXT	EXTENSION
EXWY	EXPRESSWAY
FOREST RT	FOREST ROUTE
FRWY	FREEWAY
FRY	FERRY
GDNS	GARDENS
GN, GLN	GLEN
GRN	GREEN
GRV	GROVE
HTS	HEIGHTS
HWY	HIGHWAY
ISL	ISLE
JCT	JUNCTION
LN	LANE
LNCR	LANE CIRCLE
LNDG	LANDING
LNDR	LAND DRIVE
LNLP	LANE LOOP
LP	LOOP
MNR	MANOR
MT	MOUNT
MTWY	MOTORWAY
MWCR	MEWS COURT
MWLN	MEWS LANE
NFD	NAT'L FOREST DEV
NK	NOOK
OH	OUTER HIGHWAY
OVL	OVAL
OVLK	OVERLOOK
OVPS	OVERPASS
PAS	PASEO
PAS DE	PASEO DE
PAS DE LA	PASEO DE LA
PAS DE LAS	PASEO DE LAS
PAS DE LOS	PASEO DE LOS
PAS DL	PASEO DEL
PASG	PASSAGE
PAS LA	PASEO LA
PAS LOS	PASEO LOS
PASS	PASS
PIKE	PIKE
PK	PARK
PKDR	PARK DRIVE
PKWY, PKY	PARKWAY
PL	PLACE
PLWY	PLACE WAY
PLZ, PZ	PLAZA
PT	POINT
PTAV	POINT AVENUE
PTH	PATH
PZ DE	PLAZA DE
PZ DEL	PLAZA DEL
PZ D LA	PLAZA DE LA
PZ D LAS	PLAZA DE LAS
PZWY	PLAZA WAY
RAMP	RAMP
RD	ROAD
RDAV	ROAD AVENUE
RDBP	ROAD BYPASS
RDCT	ROAD COURT
RDEX	ROAD EXTENSION
RDG	RIDGE
RDSP	ROAD SPUR
RDWY	ROAD WAY
RR	RAILROAD
RUE	RUE
RUE D	RUE D
RW	ROW
RY	RAILWAY
SKWY	SKYWAY
SQ	SQUARE
ST	STREET
STAV	STREET AVENUE
STCT	STREET COURT
STDR	STREET DRIVE
STEX	STREET EXTENSION
STLN	STREET LANE
STLP	STREET LOOP
ST OF	STREET OF
ST OF THE	STREET OF THE
STOV	STREET OVERPASS
STPL	STREET PLACE
STPM	STREET PROMENADE
STWY	STREET WAY
STXP	STREET EXPRESSWAY
TER	TERRACE
TFWY	TRAFFICWAY
THWY	THROUGHWAY
TKTR	TRUCK TRAIL
TPKE	TURNPIKE
TRC	TRACE
TRCT	TERRACE COURT
TR, TRL	TRAIL
TRWY	TRAIL WAY
TTSP	TRUCK TRAIL SPUR
TUN	TUNNEL
UNPS	UNDERPASS
VIA D	VIA DE
VIA DL	VIA DEL
VIA D LA	VIA DE LA
VIA D LAS	VIA DE LAS
VIA D LOS	VIA DE LOS
VIA LA	VIA LA
VW	VIEW
VWY	VIEW WAY
VIS	VISTA
VIS D	VISTA DE
VIS D L	VISTA DE LA
VIS D LAS	VISTA DE LAS
VIS DEL	VISTA DEL
WK	WALK
WY	WAY
WYCR	WAY CIRCLE
WYDR	WAY DRIVE
WYLN	WAY LANE
WYPL	WAY PLACE

DIRECTIONS

E	EAST
KPN	KEY PENINSULA NORTH
KPS	KEY PENINSULA SOUTH
N	NORTH
NE	NORTHEAST
NW	NORTHWEST
S	SOUTH
SE	SOUTHEAST
SW	SOUTHWEST
W	WEST

BUILDINGS

CC	CHAMBER OF COMMERCE
CH	CITY HALL
CHP	CALIFORNIA HIGHWAY PATROL
COMM CTR	COMMUNITY CENTER
CON CTR	CONVENTION CENTER
CONT HS	CONTINUATION HIGH SCHOOL
CTH	COURT HOUSE
DMV	DEPT OF MOTOR VEHICLES
FAA	FEDERAL AVIATION ADMIN
FS	FIRE STATION
HOSP	HOSPITAL
HS	HIGH SCHOOL
INT	INTERMEDIATE SCHOOL
JR HS	JUNIOR HIGH SCHOOL
LIB	LIBRARY
MID	MIDDLE SCHOOL
MUS	MUSEUM
PO	POST OFFICE
PS	POLICE STATION
SR CIT CTR	SENIOR CITIZENS CENTER
STA	STATION
THTR	THEATER
VIS BUR	VISITORS BUREAU

OTHER ABBREVIATIONS

BCH	BEACH
BLDG	BUILDING
CEM	CEMETERY
CK	CREEK
CO	COUNTY
COMM	COMMUNITY
CTR	CENTER
EST	ESTATE
HIST	HISTORIC
HTS	HEIGHTS
LK	LAKE
MDW	MEADOW
MED	MEDICAL
MEM	MEMORIAL
MHP	MOBILE HOME PARK
MT	MOUNT
MTN	MOUNTAIN
NATL	NATIONAL
PKG	PARKING
PLGD	PLAYGROUND
RCH	RANCH
RCHO	RANCHO
REC	RECREATION
RES	RESERVOIR
RIV	RIVER
RR	RAILROAD
SPG	SPRING
STA	SANTA
VLG	VILLAGE
VLY	VALLEY
VW	VIEW

STREET Block City ZIP Pg-Grid

A

A AV
100 CORD 92118 1288-J6
200 SDCo 92055 1066-B1
200 NATC 91950 1289-H7
200 NATC 91950 1309-H1
12200 SDCo 92040 1232-A4
A AVD
5500 SDCo 92003 1067-H2
A ST
- NATC 91950 1310-C3
- SDCo 92055 409-A7
- SDCo 92055 1066-G1
- SDCo 91934 (1321-G5 See Page 1300)
- CHV 91910 1309-J6
100 ENCT 92024 1147-B6
100 SD 92101 1289-A2
400 SDCo 92055 1085-H3
500 SDCo 92065 1152-G5
500 SD 92101 1288-J2
1000 IMPB 91932 1329-F7
1300 SD 92110 1268-E2
2200 SD 92102 1289-C2
2600 SDCo 92036 1136-B7
4900 SD 92102 1290-A2
6200 SDCo 92004 410-F11
7300 CRLB 92011 1126-J7
11800 SDCo 92059 1029-H4
E A ST
3000 SD 92139 1310-D3
W A ST
2900 NATC 91950 1310-D3
AARON CT
2500 SD 92105 1270-A7
AARON WY
8200 SDCo 92040 1251-J1
AASHAW RD
- SDCo 92082 1091-D4
ABAJO DR
15900 SDCo 92065 1173-G4
ABALAR WY
24800 SDCo 92065 1173-G3
ABALONE PL
5600 SD 92037 1247-F4
ABALONE LANDING TER
- SD 92130 1208-B4
ABALONE POINT CT
1600 CHV 91911 1330-J4
ABALONE POINT WY
700 OCN 92054 1066-E6
ABANA CT
16000 SDCo 92065 1173-F3
ABANTO ST
6700 CRLB 92009 1127-G5
ABARCA CT
1000 CHV 91910 1310-J4
ABATTI RD
- ImCo 92249 431-D6
- ImCo 92249 6560-F6
ABBE ST
1900 SD 92111 1268-J1
ABBEY GN
2700 ESCN 92027 1110-E7
ABBEY RD
800 SDCo 92065 1152-F1
ABBEYFIELD RD
9500 SNTE 92071 1231-C5
ABBEYWOOD RD
9600 SNTE 92071 1231-C5
ABBOTS HILL RD
8200 SD 92123 1249-B7
ABBOTT ST
1900 SD 92107 1267-J5
ABBOTTS END CT
- SDCo 91977 1271-C4
ABBOTTSWOOD RW
6000 SD 92037 1248-A1
ABBY WOOD CT
- SD 92131 1210-F2
ABBYWOOD DR
700 OCN 92057 1087-C1
ABEDUL PL
6700 CRLB 92009 1127-G5
ABEDUL ST
2500 CRLB 92009 1127-G5
ABEJORRO ST
2700 CRLB 92009 1127-H6
ABELIA AV
- CRLB 92011 1127-A5
ABELIA LN
1900 SDCo 92083 1108-C3
2100 SDCo 92084 1108-C3
ABELL DR
13700 SDCo 91935 1292-F3
ABER ST
2900 SD 92117 1248-C1
ABERDEEN AV
- SMCS 92069 1108-G6
ABERDEEN CT
- CRLB 92010 1107-A5
ABERDEEN DR
100 ENCT 92007 1167-D3
ABERDEEN ST
4700 SD 92117 1228-G7
ABERDEEN WY
3100 ESCN 92025 1150-C1
ABERNATHY WY
5700 SD 92117 1248-H2
ABETO CT
1000 CHV 91910 1310-J4
ABETO DR
400 CHV 91910 1310-J4
ABHA DR
- SDCo 91905 (1320-B4 See Page 1300)
ABIENTO PL
9400 SDCo 91941 1271-C3
ABILENE TER
8400 LMSA 91942 1250-J6
ABING AV
13000 SD 92129 1189-B5
ABINGTON LN
1600 ENCT 92024 1147-H7
ABINGTON RD
300 ENCT 92024 1147-H7
ABLETTE CT
8500 SNTE 92071 1231-D7
ABLETTE RD
8500 ELCJ 92020 1231-F7
8500 SNTE 92071 1231-F7
ABNER CT
- SDCo 92055 1086-A2
ABRA DR
12600 SD 92128 1170-C2
ABRA PL
12800 SD 92128 1170-D2
ABRA WY
17000 SD 92128 1170-C2
ABRAHAM WY
9200 SNTE 92071 1231-F6
ABRAMS RIDGE RD
- SDCo 91901 1254-F5
ABRELL RD
- SDCo 92055 1086-A2
ABRIGO WY
17300 SDCo 92065 1173-E1
ABRIL WY
- ESCN 92026 1109-G7
ABUELA DR
5000 SD 92124 1249-H2
ABUNDANTE ST
- SDCo 92127 1169-F4
ACACIA AV
100 CRLB 92008 1106-E6
800 OCN 92054 1086-C5
3700 SDCo 91902 1310-J3
4000 SDCo 91902 1311-A3
4300 LMSA 91941 1270-H3
N ACACIA AV
200 SOLB 92075 1167-E7
S ACACIA AV
100 SOLB 92075 1167-E7
ACACIA CIR
- VSTA 92081 1107-E1
ACACIA CT
- SD 92113 1289-F6
ACACIA DR
- SD 92102 1289-G4
1900 SMCS 92078 1128-A2
3300 SDCo 92036 1156-D1
ACACIA LN
- ESCN 92025 1130-A6
1500 SDCo 92028 1047-J1
1600 SDCo 92028 1048-A1
3100 SDCo 91901 1234-D4
ACACIA PL
300 ESCN 92026 1109-H7
ACACIA ST
3200 LMGR 91945 1270-H6
3400 SD 92113 1289-F6
9600 SDCo 92040 1232-C4
ACACIA TER
12600 PWY 92064 1190-C3
ACACIA WY
- ELCJ 92019 1251-J6
100 CORD 92118 1288-G7
ACACIA GLEN CT
11900 SD 92128 1190-A7
ACACIA GROVE WY
- SD 92113 1289-G6
ACADEMY DR
700 SOLB 92075 1167-G7
ACADEMY LN
1100 VSTA 92081 1107-G2
ACADEMY PL
4700 SD 92109 1248-A5
ACADEMY RD
300 OCN 92057 1086-H2
ACADEMY ST
4800 SD 92109 1248-A4
ACADIA WY
12500 SDCo 92040 1212-A7
ACAMA CT
11300 SD 92126 1209-A2
ACAMA PL
7600 SD 92126 1209-A2
ACAMA ST
7400 SD 92126 1208-J2
7400 SD 92126 1209-A2
ACANTO DR
17300 SDCo 92065 1173-E1
ACAPULCO DR
- ImCo 92251 6499-H1
- IMP 92251 6499-H1
ACARI ST
7200 SD 92111 1269-A2
ACASO CT
7600 SD 92126 1209-A2
ACASO WY
11100 SD 92126 1209-A2
ACATENO AV
300 VSTA 92084 1087-H4
ACCESS RD
- SDCo 92055 409-A7
ACCOMAC AV
3400 SD 92111 1248-H4
ACCRA LN
11100 SD 92131 1210-A2
ACE ST
3400 SD 92105 1270-B6
ACE WY
1100 SDCo 92004 (1079-C5 See Page 1058)
ACEBO CTE
1100 CHV 91910 1311-C2
ACEBO DR
16700 SD 92128 1170-B3
ACEBO PL
12100 SD 92128 1170-B3
ACEITUNO ST
18200 SD 92128 1150-D6
ACENA DR
16700 SD 92128 1170-A3
ACERO PL
400 CHV 91910 1310-J4
ACERO ST
1000 CHV 91910 1310-J4
ACHESON ST
1400 SD 92111 1268-J2
ACHILLES WY
- SD 92126 1209-E2
ACKER WY
2000 ESCN 92029 1129-H7
ACOMA AV
4500 SD 92117 1248-F1
ACORN CIR
- SDCo 92082 1070-D2
ACORN GN
1900 ESCN 92027 1110-B5
ACORN RD
1900 SMCS 92078 1128-B2
ACORN ST
1700 ESCN 92027 1130-C1
6100 SD 92115 1270-C3
ACORN TR
- SDCo 91906 (1318-C7 See Page 1298)
ACORN PATCH LN
13600 PWY 92064 1170-E5
ACORN PATCH RD
- SDCo 92036 1156-A7
- SDCo 92036 1176-A1
13700 PWY 92064 1170-F5
ACROPOLIS PL
2900 SD 92139 1310-E2
ACROPOLIS WY
- VSTA 92084 1088-D5
ACRUX DR
11300 SD 92126 1209-C1
ACTIVITY DR
1200 VSTA 92081 1108-B7
ACTIVITY RD
9000 SD 92126 1209-D6
ACTIVITY WY
400 OCN 92054 1086-B6
ACTON AV
13000 PWY 92064 1190-H3
13000 PWY 92064 1190-H5
13400 PWY 92064 1190-H4
ACTON CT
14600 PWY 92064 1190-H3
ACUFF DR
8400 SD 92119 1250-J3
ACUNA CT
2600 CRLB 92009 1127-G6
ACUNA ST
4900 SD 92117 1248-G1
ACWORTH AV
3100 SD 92111 1248-H4
ADA ST
200 SD 92113 1289-G4
700 CHV 91911 1330-A4
ADAGIO WY
11200 SDCo 92026 1089-H7
11200 SDCo 92026 1109-H1
ADAH LN
12800 PWY 92064 1190-F4
ADAIR RD
- ImCo 92251 430-L5
ADAIR ST
4400 SD 92107 1287-H1
4700 SD 92107 1267-H7
ADAIR WY
3800 CRLB 92008 1106-G6
ADALANE PL
1600 SDCo 92028 1027-J4
1600 SDCo 92028 1028-A4
ADAM CT
9700 SDCo 92026 1069-C3
ADAMS AV
400 ELCN 92243 6499-H6
400 ESCN 92026 1129-J1
1600 SD 92116 1269-C3
4700 SD 92115 1269-J3
4800 SD 92115 1270-A3
6800 LMSA 91941 1270-E3
ADAMS AV Rt#-S80
600 ELCN 92243 6499-E6
600 ImCo 92243 6499-E6
ADAMS AV Rt#-86
400 ELCN 92243 6499-F6
ADAMS CT
- CALX 92231 6620-J6
ADAMS DR
14900 SDCo 92059 1030-G7
15200 SDCo 92061 1030-H6
15200 SDCo 92061 1031-A7
15400 SDCo 92061 1051-A1
15600 SDCo 92061 1050-J1
ADAMS RD
- ImCo 92227 431-D2
ADAMS RUN
- ENCT 92024 1148-D4
ADAMS ST
3400 CRLB 92008 1106-F5
4700 OCN 92057 1067-A7
8200 LMGR 91945 1270-H6
ADAMS RANCH CT
- CHV 91914 1311-J1
ADCOCK LN
10600 SD 92126 1209-A4
ADDAX CT
12400 SD 92129 1189-C6
ADDISON ST
3300 SD 92106 1288-A2
ADELAIDE AV
5500 SD 92115 1270-B4
ADELAIDE GN
- ESCN 92026 1109-H3
ADELANTE AV
6700 SD 92120 1270-E1
6700 LMSA 91942 1270-E1
ADELE LN
1100 SMCS 92078 1129-B2
13700 SDCo 91935 1292-F2
ADELE ST
800 ELCJ 92021 1251-G2
ADELFA CT
1400 IMPB 91932 1349-H2
ADELIA WY
100 OCN 92057 1086-G6
ADELLA AV
700 CORD 92118 1288-J7
1100 CORD 92118 1308-J1
ADELLA LN
400 CORD 92118 1288-J7
ADELPHI PL
4700 SD 92115 1270-A3
ADENA LN
17500 SD 92128 1150-A7
17500 SD 92128 1170-A1
ADENA WY
- SMCS 92069 1109-A4
ADERMAN AV
10300 SD 92126 1209-A5
10400 SD 92126 1208-J4
ADIOS CT
7300 SD 92119 1250-E4
ADIRONDACK PL
900 CHV 91914 1311-J4
ADIRONDACK RW
2400 SD 92139 1290-F7
2400 SD 92139 1310-F1
ADKINS WY
7600 SD 92126 1208-J4
7600 SD 92126 1209-A4
ADLAI CT
- SDCo 92040 1232-E4
ADLAI LN
13500 SDCo 92040 1232-D5
ADLAI RD
9200 SDCo 92040 1232-D5
ADLAI TER
- SDCo 92040 1232-E5
ADLER AV
7400 SD 92111 1249-A7
ADLER WY
4700 OCN 92057 1087-A1
ADMINISTRATION WY
1300 SDCo 91901 1234-A6
ADMIRAL AV
2900 SD 92123 1249-E5
ADMIRAL BAKER RD
2400 SD 92124 1249-H6
2400 SD 92120 1249-H6
ADMIRALTY AV
- IMPB 91932 1349-E1
ADMIRALTY RD
2200 CORD 92155 1309-A2
ADMIRALTY CROSS
- CORD 92118 1329-E1
ADOBE CIR
600 OCN 92057 1067-A5
ADOBE DR
6200 SD 92115 1270-C2
ADOBE LN
11200 SDCo 92021 1251-J2
ADOBE PL
700 CHV 91914 1311-G3
ADOBE TER
1200 VSTA 92081 1107-E1
ADOBE BLUFFS DR
8700 SD 92129 1189-B2
ADOBE CREEK LN
1900 SDCo 92027 1130-D4
ADOBE FALLS PL
5600 SD 92120 1250-C7
ADOBE FALLS RD
5200 SD 92120 1250-A7
5500 SD 92120 1270-A1
ADOBE NORTE AV
1100 SDCo 92026 1027-H4
ADOBE RIDGE RD
12200 PWY 92064 1190-B1
ADOLPHIA CT
12700 SD 92129 1189-D6
ADOLPHIA DR
6800 CRLB 92011 1127-D6
ADOLPHIA ST
9200 SD 92129 1189-E6
ADONIS CT
7300 SD 92119 1250-F4
ADORNO PL
11900 SD 92128 1170-A2
ADRA WY
4700 OCN 92056 1107-F4
ADRIAN CT
1700 SDCo 91901 1233-H7
ADRIAN ST
2800 SD 92110 1268-B5
13600 PWY 92064 1190-F2
ADRIANA CT
1800 VSTA 92081 1107-G6
ADRIANA ST
8700 SDCo 91977 1291-A3
ADRIATIC PL
11100 SD 92126 1209-A2
ADRIENNE DR
4300 SDCo 91910 1310-D5
ADRIENNE WY
16600 SDCo 92065 1172-A3
ADUAR CT
5300 SD 92124 1249-J1
ADVENTURE LN
- CHV 91915 1331-G1
1200 SMCS 92069 1109-C6
AEDAN CT
8100 SD 92120 1250-D3
14300 PWY 92064 1190-E2
AEGEAN CT
7500 SD 92126 1209-A2
AEGEAN DR
2500 SD 92139 1310-F1
AEGEAN PL
6700 SD 92139 1310-F1
AEGEAN WY
6700 SD 92139 1310-F1
AEGINA WY
5000 OCN 92056 1107-F5
AEOLIA WY
4000 OCN 92056 1107-E5
AERIE RD
28200 SDCo 92082 1090-A1
29100 SDCo 92082 1089-J1
AERIE HEIGHTS RD
1300 SDCo 92003 1068-B4
AERO CT
3500 SD 92123 1249-B4
AERO DR
7900 SD 92111 1249-C4
7900 SD 92123 1249-C4
9900 SD 92124 1249-G4
AERO PL
8200 SD 92123 1249-B4
AERO WY
600 ESCN 92029 1129-D2
AERONCA AV
4100 SD 92117 1248-E6
AFFINITY CT
- SD 92131 1209-F2
AFRICAN HOLLY TR
- SD 92130 1188-F4
AFTON RD
3000 SD 92123 1249-C4
AFTON WY
2200 CRLB 92008 1106-G4
AFTON FARMES LN
31200 SDCo 92003 1068-F2
AGAPANTHUS DR
1300 SD 92114 1290-D5
AGAR CT
10300 SD 92126 1209-B4
AGATE CT
- CALX 92231 6620-J6
AGATE GN
- ESCN 92027 1110-D7
AGATE LN
4400 OCN 92056 1107-D3
AGATE ST
700 SD 92109 1247-H4
AGATE WY
- CRLB 92011 1127-C4
AGATE CREEK WY
1400 CHV 91915 (1312-A6 See Page 1293)
AGAVE FLATS LN
2500 CHV 91915 1311-H5
AGEE ST
5800 SD 92122 1228-E5
AGNO CT
2700 SD 92154 1330-C6
AGORA WY
4700 OCN 92056 1107-E5
AGOSTO ST
3400 SD 92154 1350-E1
AGRARIAN RD
25000 SDCo 92065 1153-G2
AGRESTE PL
11600 SD 92127 1150-A7
AGSTEN LN
13600 PWY 92064 1190-F3
AGUACATE LN
15200 SDCo 92082 1070-J6
AGUACATE WY
17800 SD 92127 1149-J7
AGUA DULCE BLVD
3900 SDCo 91941 1271-E5
4700 SDCo 91977 1271-E5
AGUA DULCE CT
7500 CRLB 92009 1147-J1
AGUAMARINA PT
13000 SD 92128 1150-D6
AGUAMIEL RD
17700 SD 92127 1149-J7
17900 SD 92127 1150-A6
AGUA TIBIA AV
900 CHV 91911 1330-E1
AGUA VISTA DR
- CHV 91914 1311-J2
AGUA VISTA WY
300 SD 92114 1290-B5
AGUILA ST
4000 CRLB 92008 1106-F7
AGUILERA LN
20300 SDCo 92029 1148-G2
AGUIRRE DR
1200 CHV 91910 1311-B7
A HELMS CT
- CALX 92231 6620-J6
AHERN CT
10300 SD 92126 1209-B5
AHERN RANCH RD
28100 SDCo 92082 1091-C2
AHLRICH AV
1200 ENCT 92024 1147-F7
1300 ENCT 92024 1167-F1
AHMU TER
200 VSTA 92084 1087-H2
AHWAHNEE WY
13600 PWY 92064 1190-D3
AIDA ST
12600 SD 92130 1188-C6
AILSA CT
1600 SD 92154 1351-F2
AINSLEY CT
8200 SD 92123 1269-B1
AINSLEY RD
1900 SD 92123 1269-B1
2000 SD 92123 1249-B7
AIR LN
2300 SD 92101 1288-F1
AIR WY
4600 SD 92102 1289-J2
AIRBORNE DR
1200 VSTA 92084 1088-B3
AIRCRAFT RD
2000 CRLB 92008 1127-D3
AIRFLIGHT DR
30000 SDCo 92082 1069-G5
AIR MAIL LN
16600 SDCo 92065 1171-J3
AIROSO AV
6400 SD 92120 1270-D1
6900 LMSA 91942 1270-E1
AIR PARK DR
- ImCo 92259 410-H8
AIR PARK RD
1700 SDCo 92028 1027-G6
AIRPORT DR
10500 ELCJ 92020 1251-E1
10500 SDCo 92020 1251-E1
AIRPORT RD
- IMP 92251 6439-F7
- IMP 92251 6499-F1
100 OCN 92054 1086-D5
W AIRPORT RD
- OCN 92054 1086-C4
AIRPORT VISTA RD
9700 SNTE 92071 1231-C7
AIRWAY RD
- SD 92154 1350-J2
7100 SD 92154 1351-A2
9200 SD 92154 1352-A3
9400 SDCo 92154 1352-A3
AIR WING RD
1200 SD 92154 1351-H1
AJANTA CT
11300 SD 92129 1169-J6
AJAY ST
1500 ELCJ 92020 1251-B3
AJOHN PL
- LMGR 91945 1290-F1
AKARD ST
9000 SDCo 91977 1291-B4
AKINS AV
5900 SD 92114 1290-D3
AKITA LN
- ENCT 92024 1148-D4
AKRON ST
1100 SD 92106 1288-B2
AL CT
8600 SD 92123 1249-C6
ALABAMA ST
600 IMPB 91932 1329-F7
2200 SD 92101 1269-C6
2400 SD 92104 1269-C5
4300 SD 92116 1269-C5
ALABAR WY
4100 OCN 92056 1087-C6
ALACENA CT
500 SDCo 91977 1291-D3
ALACRAN CT
17700 SD 92127 1149-J7
ALADDIN LN
600 ELCJ 92019 1252-A6
ALADO PL
8400 SDCo 92021 1232-D7
ALAGRIA PL
600 CHV 91910 1311-A5
ALAMAR RD
28300 SDCo 92082 1090-B2
ALAMEDA BLVD
- CORD 92118 1288-G7
- CORD 92135 1288-G7
ALAMEDA BLVD Rt#-282
300 CORD 92135 1288-G6
300 CORD 92118 1288-G6
ALAMEDA CIR
- CRLB 92009 1127-G2
ALAMEDA DR
3900 SD 92103 1268-G5
4900 OCN 92056 1107-F3
ALAMEDA GN
1500 ESCN 92027 1110-A5
ALAMEDA PL
3700 SD 92103 1268-G6
3700 SD 92110 1268-G6
ALAMEDA ST
- CALX 92231 6620-G6
ALAMEDA TER
1900 SD 92103 1268-G5
ALAMEDA WY
3700 SDCo 91902 1310-F3
ALAMITOS AV
100 SD 92154 1330-B5
ALAMITOS PL
2900 ESCN 92027 1110-F7
ALAMITOS WY
500 SMCS 92078 1108-C6
ALAMO CT
4500 LMSA 91941 1270-E4
ALAMO DR
4300 SD 92115 1270-D3
ALAMO GN
3200 ESCN 92025 1150-C1
ALAMO LN
700 ESCN 92025 1150-C1
700 SDCo 92025 1150-C1
ALAMO RD
1000 ImCo 92250 431-D5
ALAMO WY
- OCN 92057 1086-J2
100 SDCo 92021 1252-J2
4400 LMSA 91941 1270-E3
ALAMO WY
4400 SD 92115 1270-E3
ALAMOSA PARK DR
5100 OCN 92057 1087-C1
ALAN CT
2100 LMGR 91945 1290-J1
ALANA CIR
4100 OCN 92056 1087-C7
ALANA WY
1500 ESCN 92027 1110-A5
ALANDO PL
14700 PWY 92064 1190-G1
ALANWOOD CT
2900 SDCo 91978 1271-G7
ALAPAT DR
1600 ESCN 92027 1130-C2
ALAQUINAS DR
1600 SD 92173 1350-G2
ALASKA ST
3700 SD 92154 1330-E7
ALAVA CIR
8000 SD 92126 1209-B4
ALBA CT
2200 SD 92109 1248-B3
ALBACORE AL
- SD 92136 1289-E6
AL BAHR DR
300 SDCo 92021 1252-J2
300 SDCo 92021 1253-A2
1400 SD 92037 1227-G7
ALBANY AV
1400 CHV 91911 1330-E4
ALBA ROSA DR
11500 SDCo 92040 1211-G7
ALBATA CT
1500 SD 92154 1350-B2
ALBATROSS DR
- SDCo 92055 1023-F3
4100 SD 92103 1269-A5
ALBATROSS PL
100 SDCo 92021 1252-H4
ALBATROSS ST
2000 SD 92101 1289-A1
2900 SD 92103 1269-A6
ALBATROSS WY
1000 OCN 92057 1087-A3
ALBEMARLE ST
5500 SD 92139 1310-C1
ALBER ST
- CHV 91911 1330-H2
ALBERDI DR
7300 LMGR 91945 1290-F2
ALBERDINA WY
11400 SDCo 92040 1231-G3
ALBERNI CT
11300 SD 92126 1209-D1
ALBERQUE CT
2000 SD 92139 1290-D7
ALBERSON CT
4800 SD 92130 1188-C6
ALBERT
9200 SDCo 92040 1232-F4
ALBERT AV
- SDCo 92127 1169-E2
ALBERT CT
- ESCN 92027 1110-E6
ALBERT PL
- SDCo 92127 1169-F2
ALBERT ST
3400 SD 92103 1269-B6
ALBERTA AV
800 OCN 92054 1106-B1
ALBERTA CT
- NATC 91950 1289-H7
- SD 92113 1289-H7
ALBERTA PL
1000 SD 92103 1268-J6
ALBERTUS LN
30100 SDCo 92082 1071-A4
ALBION ST
500 SD 92106 1288-A2
ALBORADA DR
11500 SD 92127 1149-J6
ALBRIGHT PL
2600 ESCN 92027 1110-D6
4500 SD 92115 1270-B3
ALBRIGHT RD
- ImCo 92233 411-C10
ALBRIGHT ST
- CALX 92231 6620-J5
5400 OCN 92057 1067-E7
ALBUQUERQUE ST
4600 SD 92109 1248-C4
ALBURY CT
11600 SD 92131 1209-H1
ALCACER DEL SOL
12500 SD 92128 1170-C6
ALCALA CT
1500 SD 92111 1268-H2
ALCALA DR
3600 OCN 92054 1086-F2
ALCALA PL
1500 SD 92111 1268-H2
ALCALA KNOLLS DR
6500 SD 92111 1268-H2
ALCALDE CT
11400 SD 92127 1149-J7
11400 SD 92127 1150-A6
ALCAMO RD
7700 SD 92126 1209-A4
ALCARAS CT
400 OCN 92057 1086-J4
ALCEDO ST
2100 SD 92114 1290-E1
ALCONA ST
6900 SD 92139 1290-F6
ALCORN PL
5200 SD 92115 1270-A3
ALCORN ST
4000 SD 92154 1350-F2
ALCOTT CT
2400 SD 92106 1268-C6
ALCOTT ST
3000 SD 92106 1268-C6
ALCYON CT
- CRLB 92011 1127-B7
N ALDA DR
600 SMCS 92069 1108-J5
700 SMCS 92069 1109-A5
ALDABRA CT
9300 SD 92129 1189-D3
ALDAMA CT
16500 SDCo 92127 1169-F4
ALDEA DR
700 OCN 92057 1067-B5
ALDEA PL
7600 CRLB 92009 1147-H1
ALDEN WY
800 OCN 92057 1087-C2
ALDER AV
900 CALX 92231 6680-E1
1000 ImCo 92231 6680-E1
3800 CRLB 92008 1106-H5
ALDER DR
600 SMCS 92069 1109-A3
4000 SD 92116 1269-G3
E ALDER DR
4800 SD 92116 1269-H3
W ALDER DR
4800 SD 92116 1269-H3
ALDER PL
300 ESCN 92026 1109-H7
4800 SD 92116 1269-H3
13200 PWY 92064 1190-E2
ALDER ST
- CORD 92118 1288-G7
ALDERBRANCH PT
10400 SD 92131 1209-J4
ALDERBROOK DR
10400 SD 92131 1209-H4
ALDERBROOK PL
1900 CHV 91913 1311-D4
ALDER CREEK LN
2300 SDCo 92028 1048-B1
ALDERCREST PT
11600 SD 92131 1210-A1
ALDERGROVE AV
2000 ESCN 92029 1129-E3
ALDERGROVE LN
9800 SDCo 91977 1271-C7
ALDER GROVE WY
2800 CHV 91914 1311-J3
ALDERHILL TER
11500 SD 92131 1210-A1
ALDERIDGE CT
11300 SD 92131 1209-J1
ALDERIDGE LN
11600 SD 92131 1209-J1
ALDERLEY ST
6100 SD 92114 1290-C5
ALDERNEY CT
1200 OCN 92054 1106-D2
ALDERSGATE RD
1700 ENCT 92024 1147-A2
ALDERSON ST
300 ELCJ 92019 1251-J6
ALDERWOOD CIR
1900 VSTA 92081 1107-G5
ALDERWOOD DR
6800 CRLB 92011 1127-A5
ALDERWOOD LN
17000 PWY 92064 1170-E2
ALDERWOOD ST
- SDCo 92055 1086-B2
ALDFORD DR
3400 SD 92111 1248-H4
ALDFORD PL
6200 SD 92111 1248-H4
ALDINE DR
4300 SD 92115 1269-J3
4300 SD 92116 1269-H3
ALDORADO DR
1400 SDCo 92084 1068-A5
ALDRIN AV
13300 PWY 92064 1190-H4
ALDRIN ST
14600 PWY 92064 1190-H4
ALDWYCH RD
300 ELCJ 92020 1251-C5
ALEGRE RD
700 SDCo 92019 1252-C4
ALEGRIA DR
1800 SDCo 92021 1252-H4
ALEGRIA PL
2000 ESCN 92026 1109-C5
ALEJANDRA PL
600 CHV 91910 1310-J5
ALEJO LN
11200 SD 92124 1230-A7
ALEJO PL
11100 SD 92124 1230-A7
ALEJO ST
4900 SD 92124 1230-A7
4900 SD 92124 1250-A1
ALEMAN PL
5200 SDCo 91902 1310-J1
ALEMANIA RD
11800 SD 92129 1189-E7
11800 SD 92129 1209-F1
ALENE ST
500 SDCo 91977 1290-J4
ALESSANDRO LN
1200 VSTA 92084 1088-C4
ALESSANDRO TR
1800 VSTA 92084 1088-C4
1800 SDCo 92084 1088-C4
ALESTAR ST
200 VSTA 92084 1087-J6
ALEX RD
10100 SDCo 92028 1029-C3
ALEX WY
- ENCT 92024 1147-E5
ALEXANDER DR
1900 ESCN 92025 1130-A7
2100 SDCo 92025 1130-A7
2200 SDCo 92025 1129-J7
2400 SDCo 92029 1149-J1
2400 SDCo 92029 1150-A1
ALEXANDER WY
10500 SNTE 92071 1231-F7
ALEXANDRA AV
3300 SDCo 91977 1271-C6
ALEXANDRA LN
900 ENCT 92024 1147-D4
ALEXANDRI CIR
6300 CRLB 92011 1127-D4
ALEXANDRIA DR
- ELCJ 92021 1251-H5
1000 SD 92107 1287-J2
ALEXANDRINE CT
- OCN 92057 1067-B2
ALEXIA PL
- SD 92116 1269-F3
ALFORD ST
3200 LMGR 91945 1270-F6
ALFRED AV
4600 SD 92120 1249-J5
4800 SD 92120 1250-A5
ALFRED CT
4900 SD 92120 1250-A5
ALGA CT
1400 VSTA 92081 1107-H4
ALGA RD
1900 CRLB 92009 1127-F6
2000 CRLB 92009 1128-A4
ALGECIRAS ST
4400 SD 92107 1287-H2
ALGIERS ST
2500 ESCN 92027 1110-E7
ALGONQUIN CT
- SD 92130 1188-C6
ALHAMBRA ST
4400 SD 92107 1287-H1
ALHUDSON DR
1700 ESCN 92029 1129-G5
ALI WY
400 SDCo 92028 1027-E5

STREET
Block City ZIP Pg-Grid

ALICANTE CV
2200 CHV 91914 1311-E2
ALICANTE RD
2500 CRLB 92009 1127-F3
ALICANTE WY
4900 OCN 92056 1107-F5
ALICE ST
400 SDCo 92065 1152-E4
600 SD 92154 1330-A7
3200 SD 92105 1270-C6
4500 SD 92115 1270-C3
ALICIA CT
2000 LMGR 91945 1290-F1
ALICIA DR
3900 SD 92107 1268-B7
ALICIA LN
7300 LMGR 91945 1290-F1
ALICIA WY
- SMCS 92078 1128-H3
100 OCN 92057 1086-F6
ALICIO RD
- SDCo 92055 1086-A3
ALIDA ST
7800 LMSA 91942 1250-H6
ALIENTO CT
600 VSTA 92081 1107-D1
11400 SD 92127 1149-J7
11400 SD 92127 1169-J1
ALIENTO WY
- OCN 92057 1086-G2
ALIPAZ CT
3900 OCN 92054 1086-G2
16300 SDCo 92127 1169-F4
ALISA PL
31300 SDCo 92082 1070-F1
ALISAL LN
- CHV 91915 1311-G6
ALISHA DR
1400 SD 92114 1290-F5
ALISO CT
3700 SDCo 91902 1310-F2
ALISO DR
3400 SDCo 91902 1310-F2
ALISO PL
1400 ESCN 92027 1109-J5
1400 ESCN 92027 1110-A6
ALISO WY
- OCN 92057 1087-A2
ALISO CANYON RD
6800 SDCo 92091 1148-F6
6800 SDCo 92067 1148-F6
N ALISO CANYON RD
18100 SDCo 92067 1148-F7
ALITA LN
1300 ESCN 92027 1110-B5
ALKAID DR
11500 SD 92126 1209-C1
ALKOSH RD
14500 SDCo 91935 1273-A6
ALLANO WY
9200 SNTE 92071 1230-J6
ALLBILL WY
8900 SD 92119 1251-A3
ALLBROOK DR
11800 PWY 92064 1190-A5
ALLEA LN
1200 VSTA 92083 1108-A1
ALLEGHANY ST
5500 SD 92139 1310-C1
5800 SD 92139 1290-D7
ALLEGRO LN
- SD 92127 1168-J7
ALLEN DR
2100 ELCN 92243 6559-F2
ALLEN RD
- ImCo 92227 410-K10
4300 SD 92103 1268-H4
ALLENBROOK WY
8900 SD 92129 1189-C3
ALLENDE AV
4500 OCN 92057 1086-J1
4500 OCN 92057 1087-A1
ALLENDE CT
100 SOLB 92075 1167-D6
ALLENHURST PL
4700 SD 92117 1248-G1
ALLEN SCHOOL LN
4200 CHV 91902 1310-G4
4200 SDCo 91902 1310-G4
ALLEN SCHOOL RD
3800 CHV 91902 1310-G3
3800 SDCo 91902 1310-G3
ALLENWOOD LN
500 ESCN 92029 1129-D3
ALLENWOOD WY
10000 SNTE 92071 1231-D3
ALLERTON CT
800 SD 92109 1267-J4
ALLEW WY
2800 SD 92139 1310-F1
ALLIANCE CT
7200 SD 92119 1250-F4
ALLIED RD
4700 SD 92120 1249-J6
ALLISON AV
8000 LMSA 91941 1270-J2
ALLISON LN
- SMCS 92069 1108-G6
3600 LMGR 91945 1270-G6
ALLSPICE
500 OCN 92057 1086-H4
ALLSTON ST
- CRLB 92009 1127-F3
ALLVIEW CT
400 CHV 91910 1310-F7
ALMA PL
4600 SD 92115 1270-B3
ALMADEN LN
7000 CRLB 92009 1127-F7
ALMAGRO LN
- SDCo 92026 1109-E6
ALMAHURST RW
3100 SD 92037 1227-J1
ALMAYO AV
4600 SD 92117 1248-G1
ALMAYO CT
4900 SD 92117 1248-G1
ALMAZON ST
11100 SD 92129 1169-H6
ALMENDRA CT
2700 SDCo 92028 1028-H7
2700 SDCo 92028 1048-H1
ALMENDRO LN
17900 SD 92127 1150-A7
ALMERIA CT
1000 VSTA 92081 1107-H4
2300 SD 92037 1248-B3
ALMONA WY
- SDCo 92082 1090-H1
ALMOND CIR
8500 SDCo 92040 1231-J7
ALMOND RD
- SMCS 92078 1128-H3
8600 SDCo 92040 1231-J6

ALMOND ST
100 SDCo 92028 1027-F4
ALMOND ORCHARD LN
- SD 92131 1210-G2
- SD 92145 1210-G2
ALMONDWOOD WY
4800 SD 92130 1188-C6
ALMONTE PL
500 CHV 91910 1311-A4
ALMY ST
- SD 92152 1288-A5
ALMYRA RD
100 SDCo 92019 1253-C1
ALOE CT
1100 SMCS 92078 1129-B1
ALOHA DR
1000 ENCT 92024 1167-E1
ALOHA LN
2000 SDCo 92084 1088-B2
ALOHA PL
4200 SD 92103 1268-G5
ALONDA CT
11000 SD 92126 1208-J2
11000 SD 92126 1209-A2
ALONDA WY
7500 SD 92126 1209-A2
ALONDRA AV
1200 CHV 91913 1311-D7
ALONDRA CT
1600 CHV 91913 1311-D7
12700 SD 92128 1170-C3
ALONDRA DR
16700 SD 92128 1170-C3
ALONDRA WY
4800 CRLB 92008 1106-J7
ALONQUIN WY
3400 SD 92154 1330-E7
ALONZO CT
- SDCo 92055 1086-A2
ALONZO DR
1300 SDCo 92021 1253-A1
ALORA ST
14400 PWY 92064 1190-H3
ALOSTA ST
2400 SD 92154 1350-C3
ALPHA AV
200 SDCo 91977 1291-A4
ALPHA ST
1600 NATC 91950 1289-J6
1600 NATC 91950 1290-A6
1600 SD 92113 1289-G6
ALPHECCA WY
8800 SD 92126 1209-D2
ALPHONSE ST
10200 SNTE 92071 1231-D2
ALPINE AV
200 CHV 91910 1310-C5
700 CHV 91910 1330-D1
1000 CHV 91911 1330-D2
8500 LMSA 91941 1270-J3
8500 LMSA 91941 1271-A3
ALPINE BLVD
800 SDCo 91901 1233-G5
1700 SDCo 91901 1234-B6
5800 SDCo 91901 1235-A5
16000 SDCo 92021 1233-E3
ALPINE DR
13000 PWY 92064 1190-D5
ALPINE LN
300 OCN 92054 1106-C2
11500 SDCo 92040 1231-H7
ALPINE PL
1400 ESCN 92027 1110-A6
1400 SMCS 92078 1128-D1
ALPINE TER
11900 SD 92128 1190-B7
ALPINE WY
600 ESCN 92029 1129-E2
ALPINE CREEK LN
1900 SDCo 91901 1234-A6
ALPINE ESTATES PL
1200 SDCo 91901 1233-G6
ALPINE GLEN PL
2100 SDCo 91901 1234-B6
ALPINE GROVE LN
1400 SDCo 91901 1234-A6
ALPINE HEIGHTS LN
500 SDCo 91901 1253-F1
ALPINE HEIGHTS RD
200 SDCo 91901 1253-G1
ALPINE HEIGHTS WY
2200 SDCo 91901 1253-H1
ALPINE OAKS DR
1000 SDCo 91901 1253-H2
ALPINE TERRACE RD
1500 SDCo 91901 1233-J6
ALPINE TRAIL RD
300 SDCo 91901 1253-F2
ALPINE VIEW RD
600 SDCo 91901 1233-G5
ALPINE VIEW WY
600 SDCo 91901 1233-G5
ALPINE VILLAGE DR
- SDCo 91901 1234-A6
ALPS LN
11500 SDCo 92026 1089-H4
ALPS TER
- SDCo 92026 1089-H4
ALPS WY
11400 SDCo 92026 1089-H4
11600 SDCo 92082 1089-H4
ALSACIA CT
2200 SD 92139 1290-G7
ALSACIA ST
6700 SD 92139 1290-F7
ALSTON AV
3600 NATC 91950 1310-D3
ALTA CT
- SMCS 92069 1108-E5
6600 SD 92139 1290-E7
ALTA DR
2800 SDCo 91950 1310-C3
ALTA LN
200 SDCo 92021 1252-G3
4500 LMSA 91941 1270-H3
ALTA PL
1800 SDCo 92021 1252-G3
ALTA RD
500 SDCo 92154 1332-C7
500 SDCo 92154 1352-C1
ALTA TER
10200 SDCo 91941 1271-E4
ALTA WY
- SD 92037 1247-F3
ALTA BAHIA CT
5300 SD 92109 1247-J4
ALTA CALLE
1000 VSTA 92084 1088-A7
1000 VSTA 92084 1087-J7
ALTA CAMINO CT
2300 ESCN 92027 1110-D6
ALTA CARMEL CT
12000 SD 92128 1170-B6

ALTADENA AV
2200 SD 92105 1290-A1
3000 SD 92105 1270-A5
4200 SD 92115 1270-A5
ALTADENA RD
11800 SDCo 92040 1251-J1
ALTADENA ST
1400 SD 92102 1290-A2
ALTAIR CT
6500 SD 92120 1270-D1
ALTA LAGUNA WY
9300 SD 92126 1209-E2
ALTA LA JOLLA DR
1500 SD 92037 1247-J3
1700 SD 92037 1248-A3
ALTA LOMA CT
3800 SDCo 91935 1272-H6
ALTA LOMA DR
3300 SDCo 91935 1272-G6
3600 SDCo 91902 1310-D4
ALTA LOMA GN
800 ESCN 92026 1109-E3
ALTA LOMA LN
3900 SDCo 91935 1272-H6
ALTAMAR CT
14400 SDCo 92067 1188-E2
ALTA MEADOW LN
500 ESCN 92027 1110-D6
ALTA MESA DR
100 VSTA 92084 1088-B5
30400 SDCo 92082 1069-H4
ALTA MESA WY
5900 SD 92115 1270-C4
ALTAMIRA CT
1700 VSTA 92081 1107-E2
ALTAMIRA DR
4200 SDCo 91941 1271-E3
ALTA MIRA LN
30000 SDCo 92082 1069-H5
ALTAMIRA PL
1800 SD 92103 1268-H4
ALTAMIRANO WY
4300 SD 92103 1268-F4
ALTAMONT CIR
1900 SD 92139 1290-C7
1900 SD 92139 1310-C1
ALTAMONT CT
1800 SD 92139 1290-C7
ALTAMONT DR
5700 SD 92139 1310-C1
5700 SD 92139 1290-C7
ALTAMONT PL
1900 SD 92139 1310-C1
ALTAMONT RD
9100 LMSA 91942 1251-B5
ALTAMONT WY
1900 SD 92139 1290-C7
ALTAR
- SDCo 92040 1232-B7
ALTA RICA DR
4600 SDCo 91941 1271-E3
ALTA VEGA RD
- SDCo 91905 (1320-A6 See Page 1300)
ALTA VERDE DR
1600 SDCo 92028 1048-A2
ALTA VIEW DR
1800 SD 92139 1290-E7
2400 SD 92139 1310-F1
ALTA VISTA
- SMCS 92078 1129-C2
7300 CRLB 92009 1127-J7
ALTA VISTA AV
1100 ESCN 92027 1109-J6
1700 ESCN 92027 1110-A6
5600 SD 92114 1290-B6
ALTA VISTA CT
- OCN 92057 1086-J3
ALTA VISTA DR
600 VSTA 92084 1087-J6
1000 VSTA 92084 1088-A5
2500 SDCo 92028 1028-A7
2600 SDCo 92028 1048-A2
3300 SDCo 92036 1156-D1
ALTA VISTA ST
5100 SD 92109 1247-J4
ALTA VISTA TER
900 VSTA 92084 1088-A7
ALTA VISTA WY
1700 SD 92109 1247-J4
1700 SD 92109 1248-A4
ALTHEA LN
3800 CRLB 92008 1106-G6
ALTISMA WY
2200 CRLB 92009 1127-G7
ALTITO WY
4800 SDCo 91941 1271-C2
ALTIVA PL
7300 CRLB 92009 1127-G7
ALTO CT
9300 SDCo 91941 1271-B2
ALTO DR
9300 SDCo 91941 1271-C1
9500 LMSA 91941 1271-C2
ALTO ST
4000 OCN 92056 1107-B3
ALTO TER
900 SDCo 92028 1027-G1
ALTO CERRO CIR
2400 SD 92109 1248-B3
ALTON DR
7700 LMGR 91945 1290-G1
ALTON PL
2200 LMGR 91945 1270-H7
2200 LMGR 91945 1290-H1
ALTON WY
4000 ESCN 92025 1150-D3
ALTOONA DR
11600 SDCo 92020 1271-H2
ALTORO LN
3200 SDCo 91935 1273-B6
ALTOZANO DR
1800 ELCJ 92020 1251-B2
ALTOZANO WY
1700 ELCJ 92020 1251-C2
ALTRIDGE ST
3400 SD 92123 1249-C4
ALTURA CIR
1700 SMCS 92078 1108-B7
ALTURA DR
700 SMCS 92078 1108-C7
800 SMCS 92078 1128-C1
2900 OCN 92056 1087-B7
2900 OCN 92056 1107-B1
ALTURA PL
1800 SD 92103 1268-H5
ALTURAS LN
600 SDCo 92028 1027-E4
ALTURAS RD
400 SDCo 92028 1027-E3
ALUMNI PL
5000 SD 92115 1270-D2
ALVA LN
100 SDCo 92028 1027-J2

ALVA LN
2300 SDCo 92021 1252-H4
ALVA RD
- SD 92127 1149-E7
17100 SD 92127 1169-F1
ALVARADO CT
100 SDCo 92028 1027-H2
6300 SD 92120 1270-D1
ALVARADO PL
200 CHV 91910 1310-D6
ALVARADO RD
6100 SD 92120 1270-C1
6700 LMSA 91941 1270-E2
6700 SD 92115 1270-E2
ALVARADO ST
100 CHV 91910 1310-C6
1500 OCN 92054 1106-C3
E ALVARADO ST
100 SDCo 92028 1027-F2
1800 SDCo 92028 1028-A2
W ALVARADO ST
100 SDCo 92028 1027-E2
500 SDCo 92055 1027-E2
ALVARADO TER
400 VSTA 92084 1087-H5
ALVARADO CANYON RD
- SD 92120 1250-A7
- SD 92120 1270-A1
4300 SD 92120 1269-J1
ALVAREZ MEADOW CT
11300 SD 92126 1208-J2
ALVEDA AV
600 ELCJ 92019 1252-B7
600 SDCo 92019 1252-B7
ALVEO WY
11600 SD 92127 1169-J1
11600 SD 92127 1170-A1
ALVERSON RD
1000 SD 92173 1350-F4
ALVERTON DR
- CRLB 92009 1127-F3
ALVIN ST
600 SD 92114 1290-C3
ALVISO WY
300 ENCT 92024 1147-C5
ALVOCA ST
1300 CHV 91911 1330-D6
ALWOOD CT
2900 SDCo 91978 1271-G7
ALWYNE SQ
16100 SD 92128 1170-B4
ALYDAR CTE
5800 SDCo 92067 1168-E7
5800 SDCo 92067 1188-E1
ALYSSUM RD
900 CRLB 92011 1127-A6
ALYSSUM WY
400 OCN 92057 1086-J4
ALZEDA DR
5200 ELCJ 92020 1271-F1
5200 SDCo 91941 1271-F1
5200 SDCo 92020 1271-F1
AMACAYO CT
1000 SD 92154 1349-J1
AMADA CT
- CALX 92231 6620-J7
AMADA PL
10300 SNTE 92071 1231-E3
AMADITA LN
5500 SDCo 91902 1311-A1
AMADOR AV
1100 VSTA 92083 1087-E7
AMADOR DR
4900 OCN 92056 1107-F3
AMADOR ST
1500 CHV 91913 1331-C1
AMALFI DR
1800 ENCT 92024 1147-C1
AMALFI PL
1200 ESCN 92027 1110-A6
AMALFI ST
1700 SD 92037 1227-G6
AMALIA CT
11100 SD 92129 1169-J7
AMALIA ST
15100 SD 92129 1169-J7
AMANDA CT
- SDCo 91906 (1317-G2 See Page 1296)
AMANDA LN
2100 SDCo 92029 1129-G6
2100 ESCN 92029 1129-G6
AMANDA ST
5600 SD 92114 1290-B4
AMANECER PL
3000 ESCN 92027 1110-E6
AMANTA CT
1600 CRLB 92011 1127-D5
AMANTE DR
13400 SDCo 92021 1232-D7
AMANTHA AV
10400 SD 92126 1209-B4
AMAPOLA CT
- SDCo 91901 1234-A6
AMARANTH ST
12700 SD 92129 1189-D5
AMARETTO WY
4100 SDCo 91977 1271-C4
AMARGOSA DR
1300 ENCT 92024 1147-G4
7900 CRLB 92009 1147-G4
AMARILLO AV
5700 LMSA 91942 1250-J6
AMARILLO PL
1900 ESCN 92025 1129-J6
AMARILLO RD
17200 SDCo 92065 1171-G1
AMARO CT
10300 SD 92124 1229-G7
AMARO DR
5600 SD 92124 1229-G7
AMARYLLIS DR
3600 SD 92106 1268-C6
AMARYLLIS ST
- SDCo 92055 1086-B3
AMATISTA WY
- OCN 92056 1106-J2
AMATO DR
8500 SDCo 92040 1232-A7
AMAYA CT
5500 LMSA 91942 1251-A7
AMAYA DR
5600 LMSA 91942 1251-B7
AMBASSADOR AV
10100 SD 92126 1209-B5
AMBASSADOR CT
8100 SD 92126 1209-B5
AMBER DR
900 SMCS 92069 1109-C5
AMBER LN
- CRLB 92009 1127-G5
300 VSTA 92084 1087-J6
2200 ESCN 92026 1109-F4
3400 OCN 92056 1107-D2

AMBER LN
4000 CHV 91902 1310-G3
AMBER PL
- SD 92130 1188-J3
6800 LMGR 91945 1270-E7
AMBER CREEK CT
- VSTA 92084 1088-B3
AMBERCREST DR
- CHV 91915 1311-J6
AMBER CREST PL
- SD 92128 1189-J3
AMBERGLADES LN
10600 SD 92130 1208-E2
AMBER HILL LN
12800 PWY 92064 1190-D4
AMBERHILL TER
- SMCS 92078 1128-B6
AMBER LAKE AV
6200 SD 92119 1250-J5
AMBERLY CIR
9000 SD 92126 1209-D3
AMBERLY ST
6400 SD 92120 1250-D4
AMBER LYNN LN
2300 SDCo 92065 1172-D4
AMBER OAK LN
- ESCN 92027 1130-H3
AMBER SKY LN
13900 SD 92129 1189-D2
AMBERSTONE CT
- SD 92131 1210-H2
AMBERVALE TER
3900 SD 92130 1188-A5
AMBER VIEW PT
- SD 92130 1208-C2
AMBER VISTA
2800 SDCo 92028 1048-A1
AMBERWOOD CT
4700 CRLB 92008 1106-J6
AMBERWOOD DR
2700 OCN 92056 1087-E5
AMBERWOOD LN
- ESCN 92027 1130-H2
AMBLER LN
1200 SDCo 92020 1271-J1
1200 SDCo 92020 1272-A1
AMBROSE LN
- SD 92127 1169-F4
AMBROSIA DR
6400 SD 92124 1249-G6
AMBROSIA LN
6900 CRLB 92011 1127-D5
AMBY CT
14400 SD 92129 1189-C1
AMELIA CT
- VSTA 92084 1087-G2
AMELIA DR
8100 SDCo 92021 1252-C1
AMELIA PL
- ESCN 92026 1109-J4
AMELIA ISLAND DR
2300 CHV 91915 1311-G5
AMENA CT
800 CHV 91910 1310-J6
AMERICA WY
800 SOLB 92014 1187-G1
AMERICAN AV
3800 LMSA 91941 1270-J5
AMERICAN RD
2200 SDCo 92028 996-J3
AMERICAN WY
13800 SDCo 92040 1232-E4
AMERICAN GIRL MINE RD
- ImCo - 432-A4
AMERICA RIDGE LN
- SDCo 92026 1109-E1
AMERICE CT
3900 OCN 92056 1107-E4
AMES PL
3500 CRLB 92010 1106-J4
AMES ST
3500 CRLB 92010 1106-J4
AMESBURY ST
3500 SD 92111 1249-A4
AMETHYST CT
800 OCN 92057 1087-B2
AMETHYST ST
1300 SD 92114 1290-B2
AMETHYST WY
- CALX 92231 6620-J7
- CRLB 92011 1127-B4
900 ESCN 92029 1129-D3
AMHERST ST
6600 SD 92115 1270-D2
AMICK ST
2300 OCN 92054 1086-C5
AMIE CT
1800 SMCS 92069 1109-D7
AMIFORD DR
700 SD 92107 1287-J2
AMIGOS CT
3600 OCN 92056 1107-D3
AMIGOS LN
500 SDCo 92065 1152-J5
AMIGOS RD
100 SDCo 92065 1152-J5
600 SDCo 92065 1153-A6
AMIGOS WY
100 SDCo 92028 1027-H2
AMINO DR
8300 SNTE 92071 1230-H6
AMISTAD CT
900 ELCJ 92019 1252-A7
AMISTAD PL
900 ELCJ 92019 1252-A7
AMITY ST
2300 SD 92109 1248-B3
AMMONITE PL
- CRLB 92009 1127-G6
AMMONS WY
40700 SDCo 92028 997-H3
AMMUNITION RD
- SDCo 92055 1047-A3
100 SDCo 92028 1027-E4
100 SDCo 92055 1027-E5
AMNEST ST
4900 SD 92117 1228-G7
AMOR PL
1400 ESCN 92027 1110-A6
AMOROSA GN
2100 ESCN 92026 1109-F4
AMOROSO ST
4100 SD 92111 1248-J3
4100 SD 92111 1249-A3
AMPARO CT
- ESCN 92025 1130-B5
AMPARO DR
- ESCN 92025 1130-B6
- SDCo 92025 1130-B6
AMPHITHEATER DR
- ESCN 92025 1150-C1
AMPHITHEATRE DR
500 DLMR 92014 1187-G5

AMPUDIA ST
3800 SD 92110 1268-F5
4200 SD 92103 1268-G5
4400 SD 92108 1268-G5
AMSO ST
14900 PWY 92064 1170-C7
14900 PWY 92064 1190-C1
AMSTEL LN
2300 SDCo 92084 1087-J1
AMSTER DR
9500 SNTE 92071 1231-E4
AMULET ST
2700 SD 92123 1249-E6
AMY ST
100 CHV 91911 1330-D3
AMY WY
12500 SDCo 92040 1232-B4
AMYS PL
600 ESCN 92027 1110-D6
AMYS ST
9200 SDCo 91977 1291-B2
ANABELLA DR
14200 PWY 92064 1190-C2
ANACAPA CT
800 SD 92109 1267-J4
ANACONDA LN
2000 ENCT 92024 1147-H7
ANAHEIM DR
10500 SDCo 91941 1271-F3
ANAHEIM ST
2600 SDCo 92025 1130-D7
2600 SDCo 92025 1150-D1
ANAHEIM TER
3000 SDCo 92025 1130-D7
3000 SDCo 92025 1150-D1
ANALIESE WY
3000 SD 92139 1310-F2
ANASTASIA ST
3900 SD 92111 1248-J3
ANATRA CT
900 CRLB 92011 1127-A7
ANAWOOD WY
2900 SDCo 91978 1271-G7
ANCHOR CIR
3200 OCN 92056 1107-A2
ANCHOR CV
- SD 92154 1330-J7
ANCHOR PL
- SMCS 92078 1128-F6
ANCHOR WY
500 CRLB 92008 1106-F6
ANCHORAGE AV
- CRLB 92011 1126-J7
ANCHORAGE LN
1000 SD 92106 1288-B3
ANCONA LN
10700 SD 92131 1210-A2
ANCURZA WY
3300 CHV 91911 1330-E5
ANDA LUCIA WY
2100 OCN 92056 1106-J1
2100 OCN 92056 1086-J7
ANDALUSIA AV
4700 SD 92117 1248-H1
ANDANZA WY
11600 SD 92127 1150-A7
ANDASOL ST
7400 SD 92126 1208-J2
7400 SD 92126 1209-A2
ANDERHOLT RD
1100 ImCo 92250 431-D6
ANDERS CIR
7900 LMSA 91942 1250-H7
ANDERSEN LN
- VSTA 92084 1088-D6
ANDERS OAKS WY
- SDCo 92040 1212-B4
ANDERSON AV
- SD 92126 1209-C7
- SD 92126 1229-C1
ANDERSON CT
- CHV 91913 1331-F2
- SDCo 92026 1089-D2
ANDERSON LN
1700 SDCo 91901 1233-F6
ANDERSON PL
500 SD 92103 1269-A6
ANDERSON RD
500 SDCo 91901 1234-D3
5600 SDCo 92028 999-C3
ANDERSON ST
- SDCo 92055 1023-E2
3000 SDCo 91902 1290-J7
3000 SDCo 91902 1310-J1
ANDERSON RANCH RD
9800 SDCo 91916 1235-G1
ANDERSON RIDGE PL
- SD 92130 1188-F7
ANDES RD
300 SDCo 92021 1251-F1
ANDORRA CT
1400 VSTA 92081 1107-H4
ANDORRA WY
3000 OCN 92056 1106-J1
4200 SDCo 91910 1310-E5
15000 SD 92129 1169-J7
ANDORRE GN
1400 ESCN 92029 1149-F1
ANDOVER AV
2800 CRLB 92010 1107-A4
ANDOVER RD
1200 ELCJ 92019 1251-J6
ANDRADE AV
900 CALX 92231 6680-H2
900 CALX 92231 6620-H7
ANDRE PL
1300 VSTA 92081 1107-F1
ANDRE RD
1200 ImCo 92227 431-A1
ANDREA AV
1700 CRLB 92008 1106-G5
2800 SD 92123 1249-C6
ANDREA CT
8500 SD 92123 1249-C6
ANDREA TER
10700 SNTE 92071 1231-F6
ANDREA LEE PL
- SD 92129 1189-A3
ANDREASEN DR
700 ESCN 92029 1129-F3
ANDREEN RD
30500 SDCo 92082 1069-E4
ANDREEN ST
3700 SDCo 91977 1271-C5
ANDREW AV
100 ENCT 92024 1147-A2
ANDREW JACKSON ST
5000 OCN 92057 1067-A6
ANDREWS CT
1900 OCN 92054 1106-F1
3700 SD 92154 1350-F1
ANDREWS ST
3400 SD 92103 1268-H6

ANDROMEDA RD
8500 SD 92126 1209-C2
ANDROS CT
5800 SD 92115 1270-C5
ANDROS PL
5700 SD 92115 1270-B5
ANDROS WY
4100 OCN 92056 1107-E6
ANDY LN
1800 OCN 92054 1106-D2
ANDYS PL
- SDCo 91935 1274-C2
ANEAS CT
16200 SDCo 92065 1173-F3
ANELLA RD
3200 SD 92173 1350-F5
ANEMONE WY
- CRLB 92011 1127-B4
ANGEL DR
2200 SDCo 91905 1300-B5
ANGEL PL
1500 SDCo 92065 1152-G7
ANGEL ST
- SDCo 92055 1085-G1
ANGELA CT
16000 SDCo 92082 1071-B3
ANGELA LN
- CHV 91911 1330-D2
ANGELA WY
2600 SDCo 91901 1234-C7
ANGELENO RD
7600 SD 92126 1209-A2
ANGELES GN
1800 ESCN 92029 1129-E6
ANGELES VISTA DR
100 VSTA 92084 1087-G3
ANGELICA PL
- SD 92123 1249-D1
ANGELINA RD
5200 OCN 92056 1087-D3
ANGELIQUE ST
11500 SD 92131 1210-B1
11800 SD 92131 1190-B7
ANGELL AV
2500 SD 92122 1228-B6
ANGELL PL
6200 SD 92122 1228-B5
ANGELO DR
800 NATC 91950 1290-D7
1000 SD 92139 1290-D7
ANGELS PT
4700 SDCo 91941 1271-C3
ANGELUCCI ST
3500 SD 92111 1249-B4
ANGELUS AV
- ESCN 92027 1130-C1
800 SD 92114 1290-F3
900 LMGR 91945 1290-F3
900 LMGR 92114 1290-F3
ANGETON CT
7500 SD 92126 1208-J4
ANGETON DR
7500 SD 92126 1208-J5
ANGILA DR
8400 ELCJ 92020 1251-C1
8400 SNTE 92071 1251-C1
ANGLER PL
- SD 92154 1351-A1
ANGLIM CT
- SDCo 92055 1023-E3
- SDCo 92672 1023-E3
ANGOLA CIR
7500 SD 92126 1209-A3
ANGOLA RD
10800 SD 92126 1209-A3
ANGOSTO WY
12900 SD 92128 1150-C5
ANGOULEME CT
- SD 92130 1188-E6
ANGUILA PL
- CRLB 92009 1127-J6
ANGUS CT
1000 SMCS 92069 1109-B6
ANGWIN DR
3400 SD 92123 1249-E5
ANGWIN PL
9300 SD 92123 1249-E5
ANILLO WY
7700 CRLB 92009 1147-F2
ANITA DR
2700 SDCo 91901 1254-A2
ANITA ST
100 CHV 91911 1330-A5
ANITA WY
9600 SDCo 91901 1234-B2
ANITA JUNE CT
400 CHV 91911 1330-C4
ANJA PL
10000 SDCo 92040 1231-F3
ANJA WY
10900 SDCo 92040 1231-F3
ANJULI CT
- ELCJ 92020 1251-A3
ANKA LN
1600 SDCo 92026 1109-E7
ANLEE DR
8500 SNTE 92071 1230-J7
ANN DR
3400 CRLB 92008 1106-G4
ANN ST
500 ELCJ 92021 1251-H4
600 OCN 92057 1067-A5
ANNA AV
2700 SD 92110 1268-E3
ANNA LN
1100 SMCS 92069 1109-C5
1800 SDCo 92083 1108-B3
ANNADALE WY
- CHV 91915 1311-G7
ANNA LINDA CT
400 CHV 91911 1330-C5
ANNA LINDA DR
1600 CHV 91911 1330-C5
ANNA LINDA PL
400 CHV 91911 1330-C5
ANNA MARIE LN
5200 SDCo 92003 1048-D7
ANNANDALE WY
8800 SNTE 92071 1230-J5
8800 SNTE 92071 1231-A5
ANNAPOLIS AV
7200 LMSA 91941 1270-F4
ANN ARBOR LN
11400 SD 92131 1209-H2
ANNA ROSE LN
1200 SDCo 92065 1172-F1
ANNE SLADON CT
9700 SNTE 92071 1231-F4
ANNE SLADON ST
4400 OCN 92057 1066-H7
ANNETTE ST
2800 OCN 92056 1087-C7
ANNETTE WY
1500 ELCJ 92020 1251-D7

STREET / Block City ZIP Pg-Grid

ANNIE LN
10300 SNTE 92071 1231-B1
ANNIE WY
9600 SNTE 92071 1231-B1
ANNIE LAURIE LN
5400 SDCo 91902 1311-A2
ANNMAR DR
6700 SD 92139 1310-F1
ANN-O-RENO LN
13200 PWY 92064 1190-G4
ANNOS CT
100 CALX 92231 6620-F6
ANNRAE ST
3100 SD 92123 1249-B5
ANNS WY
200 VSTA 92083 1087-E6
ANOCHE GN
1400 ESCN 92026 1109-D4
ANOEL CT
10000 SDCo 91977 1271-E6
ANROL AV
8600 SD 92123 1249-C6
ANTA CT
2700 CRLB 92009 1127-H5
ANTARES DR
1600 SD 92173 1350-E2
ANTELOPE HILLS DR
12600 SDCo 92040 1232-B4
ANTELOPE STATION
13600 PWY 92064 1170-F1
ANTHONY DR
2100 SD 92113 1289-H7
ANTHONY LN
12700 SDCo 92082 1070-B5
ANTHONY RD
29200 SDCo 92082 1070-C4
ANTHONY HEIGHTS DR
1400 SDCo 92026 1109-E7
ANTHONY HOLLOW
30200 SDCo 92082 1070-D4
ANTHONY RIDGE RD
13200 SDCo 92082 1070-C5
ANTHRACITE WY
100 SD 92114 1290-F4
ANTIBODY WY
- OCN 92056 1087-A5
ANTIEM ST
SD 92111 1249-A3
ANTIGUA BLVD
5200 SD 92124 1249-F1
5500 SD 92124 1229-G7
6500 SD 92124 1230-A7
ANTIGUA CT
- CORD 92118 1329-E1
ANTIGUA DR
1800 VSTA 92081 1107-G5
ANTILLA PL
11200 SD 92126 1209-D2
ANTILLA WY
- SMCS 92078 1128-F6
ANTILOPE ST
6700 CRLB 92009 1127-H5
ANTIOCH AV
1400 CHV 91913 1311-C7
ANTIOCH PL
4600 SD 92115 1270-A3
ANTLERS DR
4000 SDCo 92036 1156-E3
ANTOINE DR
1300 SD 92139 1290-H6
ANTON LN
6700 SD 92114 1290-E5
ANTONIO DR
16700 SD 92128 1170-C3
ANTRIM WY
10200 SD 92126 1209-B5
ANVIL LAKE AV
6200 SD 92119 1250-J5
ANZA AV
900 VSTA 92084 1087-J4
ANZA CT
- ELCJ 92020 1251-H6
ANZA DR
7900 SD 92114 1290-G3
ANZA PL
1700 ESCN 92027 1110-C7
ANZA RD
- ImCo 92231 431-B8
- ImCo 92231 6680-C2
- CALX 92231 6680-J2
N ANZA ST
900 ELCJ 92021 1251-H3
900 SDCo 92021 1251-H3
S ANZA ST
100 ELCJ 92020 1251-H6
ANZA WY
700 CHV 91910 1310-H7
ANZA PARK TR
500 SDCo 92004 410-B6
500 SDCo 92004 1058-F1
ANZA TRAIL RD
- ImCo 92259 430-J8
ANZIO DR
3800 SDCo 92004 (1099-D1 See Page 1098)
APACHE AV
3200 SD 92117 1248-F5
APACHE DR
1500 CHV 91910 1311-C6
34600 SDCo 92036 1176-D4
APACHE GN
1800 ESCN 92027 1110-A5
APACHE RD
13500 PWY 92064 1190-F3
APACHE ST
4200 OCN 92056 1087-C5
APOLLO DR
200 VSTA 92084 1087-H4
APOLLO ST
3400 SD 92111 1249-A4
APORE ST
3900 LMSA 91941 1270-G5
APOSTAL RD
2800 SDCo 92025 1150-E2
APPALACHIAN PL
1400 CHV 91915 1311-H6
APPALACHIAN WY
13400 SD 92129 1189-E4
APPALOOSA CT
- SNTE 92071 1231-D2
APPALOOSA DR
13300 SDCo 92040 1232-D3
APPALOOSA RD
- ImCo 92243 6560-A5
9700 SD 92131 1209-G5
APPALOOSA WY
1700 OCN 92057 1067-F7
APPERT CT
6600 SD 92111 1248-H6
APPIAN CT
- SD 92139 1310-G1
APPIAN DR
2900 SD 92139 1310-G1

APPIAN RD
2300 CRLB 92010 1106-H4
APPLE
9600 SDCo 92021 1233-B3
APPLE GN
- ESCN 92025 1130-A4
APPLE ST
1900 OCN 92054 1086-D7
9400 SDCo 91977 1291-C2
APPLE BLOSSOM LN
100 SDCo 92084 1108-D4
APPLE BLOSSOM WY
3500 OCN 92054 1086-F2
APPLEBY CT
14600 PWY 92064 1190-F1
APPLEBY LN
14600 PWY 92064 1190-F1
APPLEGATE ST
- CHV 91913 1311-D7
- CHV 91913 1331-D1
APPLERIDGE DR
700 ENCT 92024 1167-G1
APPLESTILL RD
- ImCo 92243 6559-G5
APPLETON CT
800 OCN 92057 1087-C2
APPLETON ST
4000 SD 92117 1228-E7
APPLE TREE DR
9700 SD 92124 1249-F1
APPLEWILDE DR
700 SMCS 92078 1128-E2
APPLEWOOD CT
- SD 92131 1210-H2
APPLEWOOD DR
700 ELCJ 92021 1251-G4
APPLEWOOD LN
2000 VSTA 92081 1107-F5
APPROACH RD
8700 SD 92154 1351-H1
APRICA PL
- SD 92131 1209-F1
APRICOT CT
- CHV 91915 1311-J7
APRICOT LN
2900 SDCo 91977 1271-B6
APRICOT TREE LN
2300 SDCo 91977 1271-E7
APRICOT TREE WY
3400 OCN 92054 1086-E3
APRIL CT
3800 SD 92122 1228-E5
APRIL LEIGH TER
11300 SD 92126 1208-J2
AQUA LN
200 SDCo 92065 1152-H5
3600 OCN 92056 1107-A1
AQUA AZUL WY
- SDCo 92027 1090-D7
- SDCo 92082 1090-D7
AQUA HILL RD
2400 SDCo 92028 1047-G2
AQUA MANSA RD
7900 SD 92126 1209-A2
AQUAMARINE RD
7300 SD 92114 1290-F5
AQUAMARINE WY
- OCN 92057 1067-A3
AQUA PARK CT
3700 SD 92154 1350-F1
AQUA PARK ST
1100 SD 92154 1350-E1
AQUARIUS DR
8300 SD 92126 1209-C1
AQUARIUS PL
11200 SD 92126 1209-C1
AQUARIUS RD
- SD 92126 1209-F7
AQUA VIEW CT
8300 SDCo 91977 1290-J5
AQUEDUCT CT
6700 SD 92119 1250-E3
AQUEDUCT RD
31700 SDCo 92003 1068-H2
32200 SDCo 92003 1048-H7
AQUILLA DR
10100 SDCo 92040 1231-F3
AQUILLA PL
10300 SDCo 92040 1231-F2
AQUITAINE CT
- SD 92130 1188-D7
ARA PL
8500 SD 92126 1209-C2
ARABELLA WY
200 OCN 92057 1086-G6
ARABIAN TR
2400 SDCo 92028 1047-G2
ARABIAN WY
1600 OCN 92057 1067-E7
12500 PWY 92064 1190-C6
ARABIAN CREST RD
- SD 92130 1208-C2
ARABIAN RANCH LN
2600 SDCo 92084 1087-H1
2600 SDCo 92084 1067-H7
ARABIAN RANCH WY
500 SDCo 92084 1087-H1
ARAGON DR
3600 SD 92115 1270-D3
ARAGON WY
4300 SD 92115 1270-D4
ARANDA AV
6600 SD 92037 1247-F1
ARAPAHO ST
9700 SDCo 91977 1291-D3
ARAWAK CT
17700 SD 92127 1169-H1
ARBALEST DR
300 SDCo 92004 1058-G7
ARBODAR RD
2800 SD 92154 1350-D3
ARBOL LN
15700 SDCo 92065 1172-A4
ARBOLEDA RD
800 SDCo 92021 1251-G1
ARBOLEDA VISTA DR
12500 SDCo 92082 1070-A4
ARBOLES CT
4100 SDCo 92028 1028-G7
ARBOLES PL
2000 ESCN 92029 1129-F6
ARBOLES ST
5800 SD 92120 1250-C7
ARBOLITA LN
- SDCo 92028 1027-H6
ARBOLITOS CT
14200 PWY 92064 1190-D2
ARBOLITOS DR
14000 PWY 92064 1190-D3
ARBOR CT
1400 ENCT 92024 1147-B3
ARBOR DR
700 SD 92103 1268-H5

E ARBOR DR
100 SD 92103 1269-A5
W ARBOR DR
100 SD 92103 1269-A5
ARBOR GN
- ESCN 92025 1130-A6
ARBOR LN
100 SMCS 92069 1109-B7
ARBOR COVE CIR
4300 OCN 92054 1066-G7
ARBORCREEK LN
600 CHV 91902 1311-C4
ARBORETUM PL
10600 SD 92131 1209-G5
ARBOR GLEN WY
- OCN 92057 1087-A1
ARBOR GROVE CT
5600 SD 92121 1208-F4
ARBOR HEIGHTS LN
10600 SD 92121 1208-E4
ARBORLAKE WY
11800 SD 92131 1210-A3
ARBOR PARK PL
10500 SD 92131 1209-H4
ARBOR ROSE DR
- CRLB 92009 1127-F3
ARBORSIDE WY
11200 SD 92131 1210-B2
ARBOR VIEW ST
2300 CHV 91915 1311-H7
ARBOR VITAE DR
4100 SD 92105 1269-H7
ARBORVITAE LN
2200 SDCo 91977 1271-H7
ARBORWOOD PL
2000 ESCN 92029 1129-E6
ARBUCKLE PL
700 CRLB 92008 1106-E5
ARBUSTO CT
7900 CRLB 92009 1147-G3
ARBUSTO CTE
1100 CHV 91910 1311-C2
ARBUTUS ST
3800 SD 92121 1208-C6
ARCADIA AV
600 NATC 91950 1290-B7
800 VSTA 92084 1087-J3
1000 VSTA 92084 1088-A3
2400 LMGR 91945 1270-G7
ARCADIA DR
4300 SD 92103 1268-J4
ARCADIA PL
800 NATC 91950 1290-B7
ARCADIA RD
1000 ENCT 92024 1167-D1
ARCADIA WY
5300 OCN 92056 1107-E5
ARCADIA BLUFF CT
- SMCS 92069 1108-J4
ARCANGE WY
- SD 92130 1208-A2
ARCARO LN
300 SOLB 92075 1187-F2
ARCATA BAY WY
4200 OCN 92054 1066-G7
ARCE CT
4300 SD 92154 1330-G7
ARCH ST
4400 SD 92116 1269-B4
ARCHER RD
- SMCS 92078 1128-D6
ARCHER ST
200 OCN 92054 1086-B6
700 SD 92109 1247-H4
1700 SD 92109 1248-A3
ARCHES WY
- CRLB 92009 1127-G4
ARCHIE MOORE RD
16400 SDCo 92065 1171-F1
17400 SDCo 92065 1151-F7
ARCHIE MOORE TR
17400 SDCo 92065 1151-F7
17400 SDCo 92065 1171-F1
ARCHIE MOORE RING
- SDCo 92065 1171-F2
ARCHSTONE PL
- SD 92131 1209-G1
ARCHWOOD AV
6600 SD 92120 1249-J6
ARCHWOOD PL
1400 ESCN 92026 1109-H7
ARCO DR
3600 SDCo 92026 1109-H1
ARCOLA AV
2700 SD 92117 1248-B2
ARCTURUS WY
8700 SD 92126 1209-D2
ARDATH AV
2000 ESCN 92027 1130-D1
ARDATH CT
2500 SD 92037 1227-J6
ARDATH LN
7800 SD 92037 1227-H6
ARDEES WY
- SDCo 92065 1171-J6
- SDCo 92065 1172-A6
ARDEN DR
400 ENCT 92024 1147-C7
600 ENCT 92024 1167-C1
ARDEN WY
1400 SDCo 92028 1027-J4
4100 SD 92103 1268-G5
ARDILLA PL
1000 CHV 91910 1310-J5
ARDILLA WY
- SMCS 92069 1108-F3
ARDISIA CT
17800 SD 92127 1149-J7
17800 SD 92127 1169-J1
ARDITH RD
2500 SD 92037 1227-H6
ARDMORE CT
7000 SD 92111 1248-J3
ARDMORE DR
3900 SD 92111 1248-J3
ARDYS PL
200 VSTA 92084 1087-H5
ARENA CIR
1000 VSTA 92083 1087-G4
ARENA DR
15900 SDCo 92065 1173-E2
ARENA PL
16200 SDCo 92065 1173-D3
ARENA WY
23700 SDCo 92065 1173-D1
ARENAL LN
7100 CRLB 92009 1127-F7
7200 CRLB 92009 1147-F1
ARENAL RD
1800 CRLB 92011 1127-E7
1900 CRLB 92009 1127-E7
ARENAS AV
400 SD 92037 1247-E1

ARENAS ST
500 SD 92037 1247-E1
ARENDO DR
4400 SD 92115 1270-D4
AREQUIPA ST
1500 SD 92154 1349-J2
ARES WY
2900 SD 92139 1310-E2
AREY DR
3400 SD 92154 1330-F7
ARGA PL
600 CHV 91910 1310-H6
ARGENT ST
8600 SNTE 92071 1231-C7
ARGO CT
8700 SD 92123 1249-C7
ARGONAUTA ST
2600 CRLB 92009 1127-H6
ARGONAUTA WY
7100 CRLB 92009 1127-H6
ARGONNE CT
5000 SD 92117 1228-D7
ARGONNE ST
- SD 92140 1268-F6
3400 SD 92117 1228-D7
ARGOS DR
4300 SD 92116 1269-H3
ARGOSY LN
4700 CRLB 92008 1106-H7
ARGUELLO ST
4200 SD 92103 1268-G5
ARGUS WY
200 OCN 92057 1087-A1
ARGYLE ST
3400 SD 92111 1249-A3
ARIA AV
500 SDCo 92026 1109-H2
ARIANA LN
3100 SDCo 91978 1292-C1
ARIANA RD
- SMCS 92069 1109-A4
ARIANE DR
2700 SD 92117 1248-B2
ARIANE WY
4500 SD 92117 1248-C2
ARIEL PL
- ESCN 92027 1130-F1
ARIES CT
1400 CHV 91911 1330-G3
ARIES GN
3700 ESCN 92025 1150-C3
ARIES RD
8300 SD 92126 1209-C2
ARIKARA DR
13300 PWY 92064 1190-E4
ARILLO ST
7000 SD 92111 1248-J4
7200 SD 92111 1249-A4
ARINJADE WY
- SD 92114 1290-E4
ARIRANG LN
11300 SDCo 92026 1089-H7
ARISTA CT
2400 SD 92103 1268-G4
ARISTA DR
4300 SD 92103 1268-G4
ARISTA ST
3800 SD 92110 1268-F5
4100 SD 92103 1268-G4
4400 SD 92108 1268-G4
ARISTA WY
3900 OCN 92054 1086-G1
ARISTOCRAT CT
10600 SNTE 92071 1231-E2
ARISTOTLE DR
2700 SD 92139 1310-F1
ARISTOTLE GN
1200 ESCN 92026 1109-J7
ARIZONA AV
5300 LMSA 91942 1270-E1
ARIZONA ST
4000 CHV 91911 1330-B2
3400 SD 92104 1269-D5
4300 SD 92116 1269-D3
ARJO LN
23000 SDCo 92065 409-H11
ARJONS DR
7900 SD 92126 1209-B6
ARJUNA CT
300 ENCT 92024 1147-H6
ARKLOW PL
1500 SD 92154 1349-J2
ARLAND RD
2700 CRLB 92008 1106-F4
ARLENE CT
5100 SD 92117 1228-G7
ARLENE PL
5100 SD 92117 1228-G7
ARLENE ST
4800 SD 92117 1228-G7
ARLENE WY
1500 SDCo 92065 1152-F7
ARLETTE ST
8100 SNTE 92071 1230-H7
ARLINGDALE WY
8900 SDCo 91977 1271-A7
ARLINGTON CIR
- SDCo 92003 1048-B7
ARLINGTON DR
300 OCN 92057 1086-J4
ARLINGTON PL
1300 ELCJ 92021 1251-J2
ARLINGTON ST
3600 SD 92117 1228-D7
ARLISS CT
- SD 92154 1350-E2
ARLY CT
7900 SNTE 92071 1230-H7
ARMACOST RD
900 SD 92114 1290-G2
ARMADA DR
5300 CRLB 92008 1126-H2
ARMADA PL
700 SD 92106 1288-A3
ARMADA TER
700 SD 92106 1288-A3
ARMADALE RD
1700 SDCo 92028 1027-H6
ARMAGOSA WY
3200 SDCo 91935 1293-B1
3300 SDCo 91935 1273-B7
ARMENARIZ CT
700 CALX 92231 6620-G7
ARMENTROUT LN
2400 SDCo 91901 1234-B4
ARMERO CT
11000 SD 92127 1169-H1
ARMIN WY
4900 SD 92115 1269-J2
4900 SD 92115 1270-A2
ARMINDA CIR
8600 SNTE 92071 1230-J7
8600 SNTE 92071 1231-A7

ARMITAGE ST
3600 SD 92117 1228-D7
ARMORLITE DR
900 SMCS 92069 1108-E7
ARMORSS ST
8800 SD 92123 1249-C6
ARMOUR ST
7600 SD 92111 1249-A2
ARMS LAKE AV
6300 SD 92119 1250-J5
6300 SD 92119 1251-A5
ARMSTRONG CIR
1200 ESCN 92026 1110-A7
1200 ESCN 92027 1110-A7
ARMSTRONG PL
7400 SD 92111 1249-A5
ARMSTRONG ST
2900 SD 92111 1248-J5
2900 SD 92111 1249-A3
ARMSTRONG RANCH RD
- SDCo 92082 1091-C4
ARNAZ WY
9200 SNTE 92071 1231-A5
ARNEL AV
300 VSTA 92083 1087-G5
ARNELE AV
700 ELCJ 92020 1251-E4
ARNHEIM CT
1500 ELCJ 92021 1252-B2
ARNIES AL
3000 OCN 92056 1106-G2
ARNO DR
6100 SD 92120 1270-C1
6100 SD 92120 1250-C7
ARNOLD AV
3300 SD 92101 1269-D6
3400 SD 92104 1269-D6
ARNOLD RD
- ImCo 92283 432-C5
ARNOLD WY
100 SDCo 91901 1233-F4
1700 SDCo 91901 1234-A6
ARNOLDO RD
1400 SDCo 91917 (1314-C6 See Page 1294)
ARNOLDSON AV
2600 SD 92122 1228-B5
ARNOLDSON CT
6100 SD 92122 1228-B6
ARNOLDSON PL
6100 SD 92122 1228-B5
ARNOTT ST
2500 SD 92110 1248-F7
AROSA ST
6000 SD 92115 1270-C3
ARPEGE RD
7200 SD 92119 1250-E4
ARRAN AV
100 SDCo 91977 1291-A5
ARRAPAHOE PL
34600 SDCo 92036 1176-D4
ARRECIFE WY
4300 SD 92154 1330-G7
ARRIBA AVD
900 IMPB 91932 1349-G2
ARRIBA ST
3700 SD 92122 1228-B4
ARRIBA LINDA AV
- SDCo 92127 1169-F3
E ARRIETA CIR
4100 LMSA 91941 1270-J4
W ARRIETA CIR
4100 LMSA 91941 1270-H4
ARROW CT
2000 SDCo 92019 1272-C4
ARROW GN
500 ESCN 92027 1130-B2
ARROWGRASS WY
3200 SD 92115 1270-D6
ARROWHEAD
14100 SDCo 92040 1232-F4
ARROWHEAD CT
2400 CHV 91915 1311-H6
4600 OCN 92056 1087-C3
8800 SNTE 92071 1230-J5
8800 SNTE 92071 1231-A5
ARROW PT CT
600 CHV 91911 1330-J4
ARROW ROCK AV
10200 SD 92126 1209-C5
ARROWWOOD DR
100 SD 92114 1290-H4
ARROW WOOD LN
1500 VSTA 92084 1088-B5
ARROYA VISTA RD
13200 PWY 92064 1170-E5
ARROYO AV
- CALX 92231 6680-H2
1900 OCN 92056 1087-C5
ARROYO CT
700 CHV 91910 1310-H7
ARROYO DR
300 ENCT 92024 1147-C6
600 SD 92103 1288-J1
900 CHV 91910 1310-H7
1000 CHV 91910 1330-H1
1600 SDCo 92028 1028-F4
3000 SD 92103 1268-J7
3000 SD 92103 1269-A7
ARROYO GN
1700 ESCN 92026 1109-D5
ARROYO PL
800 CHV 91910 1310-H7
ARROYO RD
3400 SDCo 91902 1291-B7
3400 SDCo 91902 1311-B1
ARROYO CANYON RD
2500 SDCo 92025 1130-D7
ARROYO DE VIEJAS
3800 SDCo 91901 1254-D2
ARROYO GRANDE RD
- SD 92129 1188-J4
ARROYO HONDO
- SD 92127 1168-H7
- SD 92127 1188-H1
ARROYO LINDO AV
4900 SD 92117 1228-C7
ARROYO PACIFICA
700 SDCo 92028 1028-C3
ARROYO ROSITA
14800 SDCo 92014 1188-B1
14800 SDCo 92014 1188-B1
ARROYO SECO
300 IMP 92251 6439-F4
ARROYO SECO CT
6700 SD 92114 1290-E5
ARROYO SECO DR
400 SD 92114 1290-E5
ARROYO SECO WY
6700 SD 92114 1290-E5
ARROYO SORRENTO PL
3800 SD 92130 1208-B2
ARROYO SORRENTO RD
3100 SD 92130 1208-A2

ARROYO VISTA
500 SDCo 92028 1027-H3
3100 CRLB 92009 1127-J7
ARROYO VISTA WY
4200 OCN 92057 1086-J3
ARRUZA ST
3400 SD 92154 1350-E1
ART ST
4700 SD 92115 1270-D2
ARTEMIA WY
3000 SD 92139 1310-E2
ARTESIAN RD
6100 SDCo 92067 1168-G3
6100 SDCo 92127 1168-G3
7900 SD 92127 1169-A3
7900 SDCo 92127 1169-A3
ARTESIAN ST
5000 SD 92117 1228-G7
ARTESIAN TR
9000 SD 92127 1169-A4
9000 SDCo 92127 1169-A4
ARTESIAN WY
- CRLB 92010 1107-A4
ARTESIAN SPRINGS CT
10400 SDCo 91977 1291-D1
ARTHUR AV
500 OCN 92057 1067-A5
600 CHV 91910 1310-E7
3300 SD 92116 1269-F2
ARTHUR NEAL CT
1400 LMGR 91945 1290-E2
1400 LMGR 92114 1290-E2
ARUBA BEND
- CORD 92118 1329-E3
ARUBA CV
1200 CHV 91915 1311-F6
ARUBA RD
- SDCo 92059 999-F7
6400 SDCo 92028 999-C6
ARUCAUNA CT
7400 SD 92129 1188-J7
ARUCAUNA WY
12100 SD 92129 1188-J7
12100 SD 92129 1189-A7
ARUNDEL AV
- CRLB 92009 1127-F3
ARUNDEL PL
6500 SD 92117 1248-J2
ARVERNE CT
6800 SD 92111 1248-J3
ARVERNE ST
3800 SD 92111 1248-J3
ARVILLA LN
1700 SDCo 92019 1252-B6
1700 ELCJ 92019 1252-B6
ARVIN CT
2100 SDCo 91977 1291-A1
ARVINELS AV
4900 SD 92117 1228-H7
ARVISO RD
- SDCo 92082 1071-E3
ARVITA CT
- OCN 92057 1067-A5
ARYANA DR
1700 ENCT 92024 1147-D2
ASBURY CT
700 SD 92109 1267-J4
ASCEND RD
1700 SDCo 92069 1108-G2
ASCOT AV
- CRLB 92009 1127-G4
ASCOT DR
600 VSTA 92083 1087-F6
ASCOT ST
5800 SD 92115 1270-C5
ASH AV
200 CHV 91910 1310-A6
600 CHV 91910 1330-A1
800 CHV 91911 1330-A1
ASH LN
800 SMCS 92069 1108-J6
20200 SDCo 92029 1149-E1
ASH RD
- SDCo 92055 1085-J2
- SDCo 92055 1086-A4
ASH ST
100 SD 92101 1289-A2
100 SDCo 92028 1027-F3
100 SDCo 92065 1152-G3
100 OCN 92054 1106-A1
300 CHV 91910 1310-A6
500 SD 92101 1288-J2
500 SMCS 92078 1128-C1
2400 VSTA 92081 1108-B6
2800 SD 92102 1289-E2
3600 SD 92105 1289-G2
6200 SD 92114 1290-D4
N ASH ST
500 ESCN 92027 1130-A1
500 ESCN 92025 1130-A1
800 ESCN 92027 1110-A7
900 ESCN 92026 1110-A7
1100 ESCN 92027 1109-J6
1200 ESCN 92026 1109-H5
1700 SDCo 92026 1109-H5
N ASH ST Rt#-78
100 ESCN 92025 1130-A1
500 ESCN 92027 1130-A1
S ASH ST
300 ESCN 92025 1130-B2
S ASH ST Rt#-78
100 ESCN 92027 1130-B2
100 ESCN 92025 1130-B2
ASHBERRY RD
- CRLB 92008 1107-A7
ASHBOURNE GN
- ESCN 92027 1110-D7
ASHBROOK DR
700 CHV 91913 1311-D4
ASHBURN RD
3000 SD 92106 1308-A1
ASHBURTON RD
17500 SD 92128 1170-A1
ASHBURY ST
100 ENCT 92024 1147-A2
ASHBY CT
- SDCo 92028 1028-F3
3600 CRLB 92010 1107-A3
ASHBY DR
- SDCo 92028 1028-E3
ASHBY ST
4600 SD 92115 1270-B3
ASH CREEK PL
11400 SD 92131 1209-J1
ASHDALE LN
10000 SNTE 92071 1231-D3
ASHER ST
4100 SD 92110 1268-E1
ASHFORD CT
7500 SD 92111 1249-A5
ASHFORD GN
2400 ESCN 92027 1110-D6
ASHFORD PL
7400 SD 92111 1249-A5

ASHFORD ST
3200 SD 92111 1249-A3
ASHFORD CASTLE DR
1300 CHV 91915 1311-H7
ASHFOURTH LN
300 CHV 91911 1330-C2
ASHGATE PL
13000 PWY 92064 1190-F5
ASH HOLLOW CROSSING RD
13100 PWY 92064 1170-F2
ASHLAND AV
5600 SD 92120 1270-D1
5600 SD 92120 1250-D7
ASHLAR PL
10800 SD 92131 1209-J2
ASHLEY CT
30900 SDCo 92082 1070-G2
ASHLEY LN
- VSTA 92084 1088-C5
ASHLEY PL
11900 SD 92128 1190-B7
ASHLEY RD
1100 SDCo 92065 1152-H7
1300 SDCo 92065 1172-H1
ASHLEY FALLS CT
5000 SD 92130 1188-D5
ASHLEY FALLS DR
12600 SD 92130 1188-C6
ASHLEY PARK DR
3300 SDCo 91935 1272-E5
ASHLEY PARK WY
3100 SDCo 91935 1272-E5
ASHLEY VIEW PL
- SDCo 92021 1232-F5
ASHLOCK LN
- SD 92131 1209-G1
ASHLOCK WY
- SD 92131 1209-G1
ASHMORE AV
8600 SD 92114 1290-H3
8800 SDCo 91977 1290-H3
ASHMORE LN
700 SD 92114 1290-H3
ASHTON CT
- IMP 92251 6499-H2
900 VSTA 92081 1108-A4
ASHTON ST
4100 SD 92110 1268-E1
ASHWOOD CT
3400 OCN 92054 1086-E2
ASHWOOD ST
10100 SDCo 92040 1232-B2
ASILADO ST
200 OCN 92057 1066-J7
ASKEW WY
400 SDCo 92065 1152-E6
ASOLEAR PL
18600 SD 92128 1150-D6
ASPEN CT
2000 SMCS 92078 1128-A2
3300 SD 92037 1228-B4
6800 CRLB 92011 1127-A5
12700 PWY 92064 1190-C1
ASPEN DR
3400 SDCo 92028 998-D4
ASPEN GN
- SDCo 92026 1089-F4
ASPEN LN
1900 SDCo 92019 1272-C4
ASPEN RD
3400 SDCo 92028 998-E3
ASPEN ST
- SMCS 92078 1129-C2
3400 OCN 92054 1086-E2
ASPEN WY
- SDCo 92040 1232-D6
300 ESCN 92026 1109-H7
1300 VSTA 92081 1127-H1
ASPEN CREEK CT
- SD 92126 1209-C6
ASPEN CREEK WY
- OCN 92057 1086-J2
ASPENDELL DR
- SD 92131 1209-F1
ASPENDELL WY
- SD 92131 1209-F1
ASPEN GLEN CT
2800 CHV 91914 1311-J3
ASPEN GLEN RD
800 CHV 91914 1311-J3
ASPEN GLOW DR
1700 ENCT 92024 1147-H5
ASPEN VIEW CT
- SD 92128 1190-A7
ASPEN VIEW DR
- SD 92128 1190-A7
ASPENWOOD LN
200 ENCT 92024 1147-H6
ASPERO CT
- ESCN 92026 1109-H5
ASPIN CT
800 SD 92109 1267-J4
ASTER AV
800 ELCJ 92020 1251-E7
ASTER DR
2500 SDCo 91906 (1297-E5 See Page 1296)
ASTER PL
7000 CRLB 92011 1127-E6
ASTER ST
- SDCo 92055 1086-A4
2400 SD 92109 1248-B4
N ASTER ST
500 ESCN 92027 1110-B7
ASTER MEADOWS PL
- SD 92130 1188-E4
ASTERWOOD LN
- SDCo 92081 1108-B6
- VSTA 92081 1108-B6
ASTI WY
5800 LMSA 91942 1251-B7
ASTON AV
1800 CRLB 92008 1127-C2
ASTOR DR
- SD 92109 1248-C6
ASTORGA PL
600 SMCS 92069 1109-C6
ASTORIA ST
- CRLB 92009 1127-G3
7000 SD 92111 1248-J4
7100 SD 92111 1249-A4
ASTRA WY
4400 SDCo 91941 1271-F3
ASTRO CT
200 VSTA 92083 1087-H7
ATADERO CT
2800 CRLB 92009 1147-G3
ATARI CT
3200 SD 92117 1248-D3
ATASCADERO DR
3800 SD 92107 1268-A7
ATCHISON WY
- SDCo 92082 1069-G6

STREET
Block City ZIP Pg-Grid

ATEN RD
- ImCo 92251 6500-B1
100 ImCo 92251 6499-A2
100 IMP 92251 6499-E2
100 IMP 92251 6500-B1
800 ImCo 92251 431-A5
ATEX CT
23600 SDCo 92065 1173-D5
ATHENA ST
100 ENCT 92024 1147-B5
ATHENS AV
2700 CRLB 92010 1106-J4
ATHENS PL
1300 ESCN 92026 1109-E4
ATHENS ST
4300 SD 92115 1270-C4
ATHERTON AV
1900 SD 92154 1350-B3
ATHERTON PL
1400 CHV 91913 1331-C1
ATHEY AV
300 SD 92173 1350-E2
ATHOS WY
4700 OCN 92056 1107-E5
A TIRADO AV
- CALX 92231 6620-J5
ATLANTA DR
4700 SD 92115 1270-A3
ATLANTIC ST
1400 SMCS 92069 1108-E6
ATLANTIS ST
9100 SDCo 91977 1271-B7
9100 SDCo 91977 1291-B1
ATLAS ST
3100 SD 92111 1249-A5
ATLAS VIEW CT
9400 SNTE 92071 1251-C1
ATLAS VIEW DR
8500 SNTE 92071 1251-B1
8500 SNTE 92071 1231-B7
ATOKA PL
13600 PWY 92064 1190-E3
ATOLL ST
3400 SD 92111 1248-J4
ATOSANA DR
32100 SDCo 92061 1051-B6
ATRIUM DR
10400 SD 92131 1209-G5
ATTEBURY DR
300 SDCo 92078 1128-G6
300 SMCS 92078 1128-H5
400 SMCS 92029 1128-H5
700 SDCo 92029 1128-H5
21800 SDCo 92029 1129-A4
ATTERIDGE RD
20100 SDCo 92065 1153-G1
ATTISHA WY
14200 SDCo 92040 1232-G5
ATTIX ST
1700 SD 92114 1290-E1
ATTLEBOROUGH CT
7000 SD 92139 1290-G7
ATTU AV
- CORD 92118 1309-D6
ATTU RD
3300 CORD 92155 1309-A2
ATWATER ST
1100 SD 92154 1349-J1
1200 CHV 91913 1311-C7
ATWELL ST
4400 SD 92117 1248-B2
ATWOOD CT
10600 SD 92131 1209-G1
ATWOOD PL
- SMCS 92069 1108-J4
AUBERGINE CT
- OCN 92056 1087-D2
AUBERT WY
9000 SNTE 92071 1231-G6
AU BON CLIMAT CT
- SDCo 92003 1067-J5
AUBREE ROSE LN
5200 SDCo 91941 1271-D1
AUBREY ST
13200 PWY 92064 1190-E2
AUBRIVES PL
- CHV 91913 1311-F1
AUBURN AV
400 SMCS 92069 1108-J6
700 CHV 91913 1311-C5
2700 CRLB 92010 1106-J4
4100 OCN 92056 1087-C5
AUBURN DR
4700 SD 92105 1269-J5
4700 SD 92105 1270-A6
AUBURN GN
100 ESCN 92027 1110-E7
AUBURNDALE ST
3500 SD 92111 1248-J4
AUBURN RIDGE WY
- SD 92129 1189-B4
AUBURN WOODS DR
- SDCo 92081 1107-J3
AUDEN PL
- CRLB 92008 1107-A7
AUDISH CT
- SDCo 91941 1271-H4
- SDCo 92019 1271-H4
AUDREY CT
- SDCo 92028 1028-A3
AUDREY LN
3400 SD 92115 1270-C5
AUDREY WY
800 SDCo 92019 1252-C4
AUDUBON CT
3600 SDCo 91902 1310-J1
AUDUBON GN
2000 ESCN 92027 1110-A5
AUDUBON RD
9400 SDCo 92040 1232-D5
AUGUST CT
2200 SD 92110 1268-G1
AUGUST ST
5000 SD 92110 1268-G1
AUGUSTA CT
- PWY 92064 1150-G5
1700 SDCo 92019 1272-B5
AUGUSTA DR
- SDCo 92082 1090-G4
500 SMCS 92069 1109-D7
4400 OCN 92057 1066-G7
AUGUSTA PL
1000 CHV 91915 1311-G5
AUGUSTANA PL
5200 SD 92115 1270-A3
AUGUSTINA PL
600 CHV 91910 1311-A5
AUGUSTUS CT
- SD 92128 1150-C6
AUKLET WY
4300 OCN 92057 1086-J3
4300 OCN 92057 1087-A3
AURA CIR
2000 CRLB 92008 1106-J7

AURALIE DR
2600 SDCo 92025 1130-B7
AURORA AV
- SMCS 92078 1128-H3
AURORA CT
- ELCN 92243 6559-E1
AURORA DR
200 ELCN 92243 6560-A1
200 ELCN 92243 6559-F1
13000 SDCo 92021 1252-C1
13100 SDCo 92021 1232-C7
AURORA GN
2600 ESCN 92027 1110-E7
AURORA ST
400 SD 92102 1289-J3
AURORA VISTA DR
3100 SDCo 91978 1272-C7
3100 SDCo 91978 1292-C1
AUSTERLITZ PL
11900 SD 92128 1170-A1
AUSTIN AV
- SD 92145 1229-F2
AUSTIN CT
1300 VSTA 92083 1087-E7
1500 CHV 91902 1311-C4
AUSTIN DR
4700 SD 92115 1270-A3
9700 SDCo 91977 1271-C7
10200 SDCo 91978 1271-E7
AUSTIN RD
- ImCo 92251 6439-C1
- IMP 92251 6439-C4
1100 ImCo 92243 6559-D1
1800 ImCo 92243 6499-C6
1800 ELCN 92243 6499-C2
1800 ELCN 92243 6559-D1
2100 ImCo 92251 6499-C2
2300 IMP 92251 6499-C2
3600 ImCo 92227 431-B3
AUSTIN TER
- CRLB 92008 1106-G3
AUSTIN WY
- SDCo 92036 1136-C7
1400 ESCN 92027 1130-D2
AUSTIN HILL CT
- SD 92127 1169-B3
AUSTRALIA ST
1100 ELCJ 92020 1251-C4
AUTILLO WY
10800 SD 92127 1169-H1
AUTO CIR
4900 SD 92108 1269-B3
AUTO CENTER CT
1000 CRLB 92008 1126-H2
AUTOCROSS CT
1900 SDCo 92019 1272-C3
AUTO PARK AV
1700 CHV 91911 1330-J5
AUTO PARK DR
500 CHV 91911 1330-H5
AUTO PARK PL
1700 CHV 91911 1330-J5
AUTO PARK WY
1100 ESCN 92029 1129-F4
AUTO PARK WY N
1500 ESCN 92029 1129-F3
AUTO PARK WY S
1500 ESCN 92029 1129-E3
AUTOPORT MALL
5700 SD 92121 1228-G2
AUTUMN DR
200 SMCS 92069 1108-G7
2200 OCN 92056 1087-D5
AUTUMN LN
- VSTA 92084 1088-A2
AUTUMN PL
1800 ENCT 92024 1147-H5
AUTUMN BREEZE LN
- SDCo 92084 1068-D5
AUTUMN HILLS DR
1400 CHV 91913 1331-B2
AUTUMN LEAF DR
900 SDCo 92028 1027-G4
AUTUMN SKY LN
- CHV 91915 1311-G7
- CHV 91915 1331-G1
AUTUMNVIEW LN
10100 SD 92126 1209-D5
AUTUMNWOODS PL
1400 ESCN 92029 1129-F6
AVA LN
14200 SDCo 92082 1070-F4
AVA PL
5800 SD 92114 1290-C6
AVA ST
1300 SD 92114 1290-C6
AVA LOMA RD
3100 SDCo 91935 1293-D1
3100 SDCo 91935 1273-D7
AVALON AV
2700 CRLB 92010 1106-J4
2700 CRLB 92010 1107-A4
AVALON CT
700 SD 92109 1267-H4
AVALON DR
100 VSTA 92084 1087-J6
4300 SD 92103 1268-J4
AVALON WY
- SMCS 92078 1128-F7
AVALON BAY PL
300 OCN 92057 1066-J6
AVANTI AV
10200 SNTE 92071 1231-E2
AVATI DR
4000 SD 92117 1248-C3
AVELEY PL
3400 SD 92111 1248-H4
AVENA CT E
- CRLB 92011 1127-C5
AVENA CT W
- CRLB 92011 1127-C5
AVENA PL
11600 SD 92128 1170-A3
AVENEL LN
15900 SDCo 92065 1173-H4
AVENGER CT
9800 SD 92126 1209-F2
AVENGER RD
11300 SD 92126 1209-F2
AVENIDA ABAJO
400 ELCJ 92020 1271-G1
AVENIDA ABEJA
- SD 92127 1169-H5
400 SMCS 92069 1108-E4
AVENIDA ABRIL
- ESCN 92026 1109-G7
12400 SDCo 92021 1252-B1
AVENIDA ACERO
9400 SDCo 91977 1291-C4
AVENIDA ADOBE
400 ESCN 92029 1149-J3
400 ESCN 92029 1150-A3
AVENIDA AGUILA
500 SMCS 92069 1108-E5

AVENIDA ALAMAR
7900 SD 92037 1227-G5
AVENIDA ALCACHOFA
15400 SD 92128 1170-B5
AVENIDA ALCOR
3100 CRLB 92009 1127-J7
AVENIDA ALMADA
1600 OCN 92056 1087-C3
AVENIDA ALONDRA
17900 SDCo 92067 1168-B1
AVENIDA ALOZDRA
17800 SD 92128 1150-D7
AVENIDA ALTA MIRA
1700 OCN 92056 1087-C4
AVENIDA ALTERAS
6000 SDCo 92067 1168-H5
AVENIDA AMANTEA
1000 SD 92037 1247-G3
AVENIDA AMAPOLA
- CRLB 92009 1148-B2
AVENIDA AMATISTA
17800 SDCo 92067 1148-J7
AVENIDA AMIGO
700 SMCS 92069 1108-E4
AVENIDA AMISTAD
- SMCS 92069 1108-F4
AVENIDA AMOROSA
3500 ESCN 92029 1150-A3
AVENIDA ANACAPA
3200 CRLB 92009 1147-J3
11600 SDCo 92019 1272-A4
AVENIDA ANDANTE
1500 OCN 92056 1087-C4
AVENIDA ANDORRA
1500 OCN 92056 1087-C4
6600 SD 92037 1247-H1
AVENIDA ANGULIA
8400 SDCo 91977 1290-J5
AVENIDA ANNALIE
12600 SDCo 92082 1070-B3
AVENIDA ANTONIO
- CHV 91914 1311-F2
AVENIDA APICE
- SDCo 92067 1149-C5
AVENIDA APOLINARIA
11500 SDCo 92019 1272-A4
11500 SDCo 92019 1271-J4
AVENIDA AQUILA
- SD 92154 1350-G1
AVENIDA ARAGON
- CRLB 92009 1147-H4
1800 OCN 92056 1087-B5
AVENIDA ARANA
400 SMCS 92069 1108-F4
AVENIDA ARRIBA
1400 ELCJ 92020 1271-G1
AVENIDA ARROYO PASAJERO
16700 SDCo 92067 1168-F5
AVENIDA AVEIRO
16000 SD 92128 1170-C5
AVENIDA AZUL
1300 SMCS 92069 1108-E5
AVENIDA BARRANCA
- SDCo 92067 1149-C5
AVENIDA BELTERRA
- CHV 91914 1311-E1
AVENIDA BENJAMIN
10900 SDCo 91941 1271-G4
AVENIDA BIZARRO
6600 SD 92037 1247-F2
AVENIDA BLANCO
500 SMCS 92069 1108-E5
AVENIDA BOSQUES
2100 SDCo 91977 1271-E7
AVENIDA BRISA
3800 SDCo 92091 1168-C7
3800 SDCo 92091 1188-C1
AVENIDA BUENA VENTURA
100 SCLE 92672 1023-B1
AVENIDA CALAFIA
4500 OCN 92057 1087-A2
AVENIDA CALMA
15900 SDCo 92091 1168-C7
15900 SDCo 92091 1188-C1
AVENIDA CAMPANA
900 SDCo 92028 1027-G3
AVENIDA CANORA
400 OCN 92057 1087-A4
2400 SDCo 91901 1254-C1
AVENIDA CANTANTE
6900 SDCo 92067 1188-H1
AVENIDA CANTARIA
5100 SD 92130 1188-D3
AVENIDA CARMELO
100 SCLE 92672 1023-B1
AVENIDA CASTANA
2800 CRLB 92009 1147-H2
AVENIDA CATERINA
- CHV 91914 1311-E2
AVENIDA CATHERINA
10700 SDCo 91978 1271-G6
AVENIDA CENIT
- SDCo 92067 1149-B5
AVENIDA CEREZA
2800 CRLB 92009 1147-G2
AVENIDA CHAMNEZ
5900 SD 92037 1247-G2
AVENIDA CHAPALA
100 SMCS 92069 1109-C7
100 SMCS 92069 1129-C1
AVENIDA CHELSEA
2400 VSTA 92081 1107-J7
AVENIDA CHERYLITA
1700 ELCJ 92020 1271-G2
AVENIDA CHRISTINA
3100 CRLB 92009 1127-J4
AVENIDA CIELO
600 SMCS 92078 1128-A2
AVENIDA CIRCO
5700 SD 92124 1229-G7
AVENIDA CIRUELA
2900 CRLB 92009 1147-H3
AVENIDA CODORNIZ
- SMCS 92069 1108-F4
AVENIDA COLINO
9700 SDCo 91977 1291-D3
AVENIDA CONSENTIDO
11900 SD 92128 1170-B4
AVENIDA CORDILLERA
17800 SD 92128 1150-D6
AVENIDA CORDOBA
700 SMCS 92069 1108-E5
AVENIDA CORTEZ
200 SD 92037 1247-E3
AVENIDA COSTA AZUL
2000 SD 92154 1351-H2
AVENIDA COSTA BLANCA
8600 SD 92154 1351-H3
AVENIDA COSTA BRAVA
2300 SD 92154 1351-H3

AVENIDA COSTA DEL SOL
2200 SD 92154 1351-G3
AVENIDA COSTA ESTE
2200 SD 92154 1351-H3
AVENIDA COSTA NORTE
8500 SD 92154 1351-H3
AVENIDA COSTA SUR
8500 SD 92154 1351-H3
AVENIDA CRESTA
6000 SD 92037 1247-E2
AVENIDA CUATRO VIENTOS
6000 SDCo 92067 1168-H4
AVENIDA CUESTA DEL SOL
16400 SDCo 92067 1168-F6
AVENIDA CUESTA LOS OSOS
6000 SDCo 92067 1168-E6
AVENIDA DE ACACIAS
16900 SDCo 92067 1168-D2
AVENIDA DE ANITA
2700 CRLB 92010 1106-H3
AVENIDA DE AQUACATE
2000 ESCN 92026 1109-E4
AVENIDA DE BENITO JUAREZ
500 VSTA 92083 1087-G5
AVENIDA DE CONTENTA
17500 SDCo 92067 1168-J1
AVENIDA DE ESPUELA
12600 PWY 92064 1170-C6
AVENIDA DE LA BARCA
700 CHV 91910 1311-A5
AVENIDA DE LA CANTINA
10200 SD 92129 1189-G4
AVENIDA DE LA CRUZ
1800 SD 92173 1350-F3
AVENIDA DE LA FUENTE
8400 SD 92154 1351-H3
AVENIDA DE LA FUENTE NORTE
1500 SD 92154 1351-J3
AVENIDA DE LA FUENTE SUR
2300 SD 92154 1351-J3
AVENIDA DEL ALBA
- CRLB 92009 1147-J4
AVENIDA DE LA LUNA
13800 SDCo 91935 1272-H7
AVENIDA DE LA MADRE
2900 SDCo 92028 1028-C3
AVENIDA DE LA MADRID
100 SD 92173 1350-G3
AVENIDA DE LAMAR
3000 SDCo 91977 1271-B6
AVENIDA DE LA PLATA
4000 OCN 92056 1087-C4
4900 OCN 92057 1087-C2
AVENIDA DE LA PLAYA
- ESCN 92026 1109-G7
2000 SD 92037 1227-H5
AVENIDA DE LA PLAZA
200 VSTA 92083 1087-G5
AVENIDA DE LA RIBERA
2100 SD 92037 1227-H5
AVENIDA DE LA RONDA
6800 SDCo 92067 1168-F7
AVENIDA DE LAS ADELSAS
1400 ENCT 92024 1167-G1
AVENIDA DE LAS ARENAS
1800 CORD 92118 1308-J2
AVENIDA DE LAS ESTRELLAS
32300 SDCo 92061 1051-D5
AVENIDA DE LAS FLORES
3300 SMCS 92078 1128-B1
AVENIDA DE LAS LILAS
200 ENCT 92024 1147-G7
AVENIDA DE LAS ONDAS
8400 SD 92037 1227-H4
AVENIDA DE LAS PALMERAS
200 SCLE 92672 1023-B1
AVENIDA DE LAS PESCAS
6600 SD 92037 1247-G1
AVENIDA DE LAS ROSAS
300 ENCT 92024 1147-G7
300 ENCT 92024 1167-G1
500 SMCS 92078 1128-B1
AVENIDA DE LAS TIENDAS
- SD 92108 1268-J3
AVENIDA DE LAS VISTAS
- SD 92154 1331-B7
AVENIDA DEL CHARRO
13500 SDCo 92021 1232-E6
AVENIDA DEL CIELO
- SDCo 92067 1149-C6
2100 SDCo 91901 1253-G1
AVENIDA DEL DIABLO
1800 ESCN 92029 1129-F5
2300 SDCo 92029 1129-F5
AVENIDA DEL DUQUE
6200 SDCo 92067 1148-E6
6200 SDCo 92091 1148-E6
AVENIDA DEL FRESNO
800 SMCS 92069 1109-B5
AVENIDA DEL GADO
100 OCN 92057 1087-A2
AVENIDA DEL GATO
8200 SD 92126 1209-B1
AVENIDA DEL GENERAL
12900 SD 92129 1189-G5
AVENIDA DEL MAR
3300 SMCS 92078 1128-B2
AVENIDA DEL MEXICO
1900 SD 92154 1330-A7
AVENIDA DEL MUNDO
1700 CORD 92118 1308-J1
AVENIDA DEL NORTE
700 SMCS 92069 1109-B6
AVENIDA DEL OCEANO
- SDCo 92019 1252-C7
- SDCo 92019 1272-C1
AVENIDA DEL ORO
1800 OCN 92056 1087-B5
AVENIDA DE LOS ARBOLES
3300 SMCS 92078 1128-A2

AVENIDA DE LOS CLAVELES
200 ENCT 92024 1147-G7
AVENIDA DE LOS LIRIOS
100 ENCT 92024 1147-G7
AVENIDA DE LOS LOBOS
10800 SD 92127 1169-H5
AVENIDA DE LOS OLIVOS
16300 SDCo 92067 1168-F6
AVENIDA DE LOUISA
2800 CRLB 92010 1106-H3
AVENIDA DE LOYOLA
3300 OCN 92056 1086-H7
AVENIDA DEL PAISANO
32100 RivC 92592 999-E1
AVENIDA DEL PARAISO ST
6500 CRLB 92009 1127-G5
AVENIDA DEL PARQUE
3800 SDCo 92091 1168-B7
AVENIDA DEL PRESIDENTE
2900 SCLE 92672 1023-B1
3900 SDCo 92672 1023-B1
AVENIDA DEL REY
500 CHV 91910 1311-A4
AVENIDA DEL RIO
- SD 92108 1269-A3
AVENIDA DEL SOL
- ESCN 92026 1109-G7
700 SMCS 92069 1109-B5
1300 CORD 92118 1308-J1
1500 SDCo 92021 1251-G2
12400 SDCo 92021 1252-B1
AVENIDA DE MONACO
100 ENCT 92007 1167-D2
AVENIDA DE NOG
1500 SDCo 92028 1027-J6
AVENIDA DE ORO
1100 CALX 92231 6620-H7
3000 SDCo 91935 1292-H1
AVENIDA DE PALAIS
2400 CRLB 92009 1127-G7
AVENIDA DE POMPEII
16600 SDCo 92127 1168-H3
AVENIDA DE PORTUGAL
2800 SD 92106 1288-B2
AVENIDA DE ROBLES VERDES
- SDCo 91905 1300-C4
AVENIDA DE SAN CLEMENTE
500 ENCT 92024 1147-E7
AVENIDA DESCANSO
- OCN 92057 1086-H1
- OCN 92057 1066-H7
AVENIDA DE SUENO
- CRLB 92009 1147-J4
AVENIDA DE SUENOS
1700 OCN 92056 1087-C4
AVENIDA DE SUERTE
200 SMCS 92069 1108-D5
AVENIDA DIESTRO
7900 CRLB 92009 1148-A2
AVENIDA DOLORES
100 SCLE 92672 1023-B1
AVENIDA DRILLA
- SDCo 92067 1149-C6
AVENIDA ELENA
100 SMCS 92069 1109-C7
AVENIDA ELISA
1200 SDCo 92019 1272-C1
AVENIDA EMPRESA
4500 OCN 92056 1087-C3
AVENIDA ENCINAS
- CRLB 92011 1146-J1
5000 CRLB 92008 1126-G2
5700 CRLB 92011 1126-H4
7100 CRLB 92011 1127-A7
AVENIDA ESPERANZA
100 ENCT 92024 1147-J7
100 ENCT 92024 1167-J1
AVENIDA ESTEBAN
1100 ENCT 92024 1147-H4
AVENIDA FELIZ
3700 SDCo 92091 1188-C1
AVENIDA FIESTA
5400 SD 92037 1248-B3
AVENIDA FLORENCIA
16200 PWY 92064 1170-D3
AVENIDA FLORES
1800 ENCT 92024 1147-H4
AVENIDA FLORESTA
6200 SDCo 92067 1168-F5
AVENIDA FRAGATA
- SMCS 92069 1108-F4
AVENIDA FRONTERA
1100 OCN 92057 1087-A4
AVENIDA GABRIEL
- CHV 91914 1311-E2
AVENIDA GRANADA
13000 PWY 92064 1170-D3
AVENIDA GRANDE
500 ENCT 92024 1147-F5
13000 SD 92129 1189-G5
AVENIDA GREGORY
4200 SDCo 91977 1271-C3
AVENIDA GUILLERMO
1500 OCN 92056 1087-C4
AVENIDA HACIENDA
3100 ESCN 92029 1149-J3
3100 ESCN 92029 1150-A3
AVENIDA HALLEY
- SD 92154 1350-G1
AVENIDA HELECHO
2800 CRLB 92009 1147-G2
AVENIDA INSURGENTES
14700 SDCo 92067 1188-H1
AVENIDA JINETE
32000 SDCo 92003 1048-B7
AVENIDA JOAQUIN
1900 ENCT 92024 1147-H5
AVENIDA JOHANNA
3700 SDCo 91941 1271-G4
AVENIDA JOSEFA
1800 ENCT 92024 1147-H5
AVENIDA KIRJAH
7800 SD 92037 1228-A6
AVENIDA LA BAHIA
8600 SD 92122 1228-D3
AVENIDA LA CIMA
- CRLB 92009 1147-J4
- ENCT 92024 1147-J4
2300 SDCo 92027 1130-E4
AVENIDA LA CUESTA
- SMCS 92078 1128-H2
AVENIDA LADERA
1500 ELCJ 92020 1251-C2
AVENIDA LAMEGO
15900 SD 92128 1170-C5

AVENIDA LA POSTA
1400 ENCT 92024 1147-H4
AVENIDA LA REINA
6600 SD 92037 1247-F1
AVENIDA LAS BRISAS
100 OCN 92057 1086-J2
AVENIDA LAS PERLAS
16400 SDCo 92067 1168-F7
AVENIDA LA VALENCIA
12700 PWY 92064 1170-D4
12700 SD 92128 1170-D4
AVENIDA LEON
900 SMCS 92069 1108-E4
AVENIDA LINDA
14000 PWY 92064 1190-G4
AVENIDA LOMA DE ORO
6200 SDCo 92067 1168-F5
AVENIDA LORENZO
4300 OCN 92057 1086-J2
AVENIDA LORETTA
- CHV 91902 1311-C1
AVENIDA LUCIA
100 SCLE 92672 1023-B1
AVENIDA LUIS
16900 SDCo 92067 1168-F3
AVENIDA LUNAR
1200 CORD 92118 1308-J2
AVENIDA MADERA
800 CHV 91910 1310-E7
800 CHV 91910 1330-E1
AVENIDA MAGNIFICA
2200 CRLB 92008 1106-G3
9900 SD 92131 1209-J4
9900 SD 92131 1210-A4
AVENIDA MAGORIA
3000 ESCN 92029 1149-J2
3000 ESCN 92029 1150-A2
AVENIDA MANANA
6400 SD 92037 1247-F2
AVENIDA MANANTIAL
- SDCo 92067 1149-B5
AVENIDA MANESSA
4500 OCN 92057 1087-A4
AVENIDA MANTILLA
- CHV 91914 1311-F2
1500 OCN 92056 1087-B3
AVENIDA MARA
2200 CHV 91914 1311-E2
AVENIDA MARAVILLA
- CRLB 92009 1148-A1
AVENIDA MARAVILLAS
4700 SDCo 92067 1168-B3
AVENIDA MARBELLA
12900 SD 92128 1150-D7
AVENIDA MARCELLA
11500 SDCo 92019 1271-J4
11900 SDCo 92019 1272-A4
AVENIDA MARCO
8600 SDCo 92021 1232-E6
AVENIDA MARGUARITA
200 OCN 92057 1087-A2
AVENIDA MARIA
11000 SD 92129 1169-H7
AVENIDA MARIPOSA
600 SMCS 92078 1128-B1
AVENIDA MARLINA
- CHV 91914 1311-E2
AVENIDA MELODIA
1600 ENCT 92024 1147-H4
AVENIDA MICHELLE
500 SMCS 92078 1128-B1
AVENIDA MIGUEL
1200 ENCT 92024 1147-H5
AVENIDA MILAGRO
- SDCo 92082 1089-J2
AVENIDA MIL FLORES
7900 SDCo 92003 1068-H4
AVENIDA MIMOSA
1800 ENCT 92024 1147-H5
AVENIDA MIRADOR
- SDCo 92067 1149-C5
AVENIDA MIRA VISTA
1700 OCN 92056 1087-C4
AVENIDA MIROLA
6600 SD 92037 1247-F1
AVENIDA MOLINO VIEJO
16600 SDCo 92067 1168-G7
AVENIDA MONTUOSA
14900 SD 92129 1169-H7
AVENIDA NARANJA
- SDCo 92065 1152-F3
AVENIDA NAVIDAD
7600 SD 92122 1228-D4
AVENIDA NIEVE
3300 CRLB 92009 1147-J3
AVENIDA NOBLEZA
16200 SD 92128 1170-A4
AVENIDA NORDESTE
- SDCo 92004 (1078-J2 See Page 1058)
AVENIDA OBERTURA
3300 CRLB 92009 1147-J3
AVENIDA OCEANO
1500 OCN 92056 1087-C4
AVENIDA OCOTILLO
2500 SDCo 91901 1253-J2
AVENIDA OFELITA
1300 SDCo 92019 1272-D1
AVENIDA OLMEDA
3100 CRLB 92009 1127-J6
3100 CRLB 92009 1128-A4
AVENIDA ORTEGA
- SMCS 92078 1128-H2
AVENIDA PALA
100 SCLE 92672 1023-B1
AVENIDA PALIZADA
14300 SD 92130 1188-D2
AVENIDA PALO VERDE
3700 SDCo 91902 1310-E4
AVENIDA PANTERA
- CRLB 92009 1148-A4
- SMCS 92069 1108-F4
AVENIDA PENASCO
2000 SDCo 92019 1252-C7
AVENIDA PEREGRINA
17300 SDCo 92067 1168-H1
AVENIDA PICACHO
6100 SDCo 92067 1168-G4
AVENIDA PIMENTERA
2900 CRLB 92009 1147-H3
AVENIDA PLAYA CANCUN
5000 SD 92124 1230-A7
AVENIDA PLAYA VERACRUZ
10700 SD 92124 1229-J7
10700 SD 92124 1249-J1
AVENIDA PRIMAVERA
400 DLMR 92014 1187-F4
AVENIDA PRIVADO
4500 OCN 92057 1087-A3
AVENIDA REAL
10200 SDCo 92040 1231-H3

AVENIDA REGINA
- SMCS 92069 1108-D4
AVENIDA REPOSO
3200 ESCN 92029 1149-J3
AVENIDA RICARDO
800 SMCS 92069 1129-D1
9700 SDCo 91977 1291-D3
AVENIDA ROBERTA
10700 SDCo 91978 1271-G6
AVENIDA ROCA GRANDE
- SDCo 92065 1171-H2
AVENIDA RONALDO
800 SDCo 91977 1291-D3
AVENIDA RORRAS
15100 SD 92128 1170-B6
AVENIDA ROSA
1400 CHV 91911 1330-D4
AVENIDA SANCHEZ
5700 SD 92124 1229-H7
AVENIDA SAN DIEGO
100 SCLE 92672 1023-B1
AVENIDA SAN FERNANDO
100 SCLE 92672 1023-B1
AVENIDA SAN MIGUEL
3700 NATC 91902 1310-F2
3700 SDCo 91902 1310-F2
AVENIDA SANTA MARGARITA
100 SCLE 92672 1023-C1
AVENIDA SECRETO
- CRLB 92009 1147-H4
AVENIDA SEGOVIA
1700 OCN 92056 1087-C5
AVENIDA SERENO
1300 ENCT 92024 1147-H4
AVENIDA SEVILLA
1700 OCN 92056 1087-C4
AVENIDA SIERRA
3300 ESCN 92029 1150-A3
AVENIDA SIVRITA
11500 SD 92128 1169-J6
11500 SD 92128 1170-A6
AVENIDA SOBRINA
1100 OCN 92057 1087-A3
AVENIDA SOLARIA
700 CHV 91910 1311-A5
AVENIDA SOLEDAD
- CHV 91914 1311-F2
4300 OCN 92057 1086-J2
AVENIDA SUAVIDAD
16200 SD 92128 1170-A4
AVENIDA SURESTE
700 SDCo 92004 (1078-J2 See Page 1058)
AVENIDA TAXCO
800 VSTA 92084 1088-C5
AVENIDA THERESA
2900 CRLB 92009 1147-H3
AVENIDA THOMAS
11200 SDCo 91941 1271-H4
AVENIDA TINEO
12500 SD 92128 1170-C4
AVENIDA TOPANGA
3100 CRLB 92009 1127-J6
3100 CRLB 92009 1128-A4
AVENIDA TORONJA
- CRLB 92009 1147-F2
AVENIDA VALERA
2700 CRLB 92009 1127-H7
2800 CRLB 92009 1147-H1
AVENIDA VENUSTO
15000 SD 92128 1170-A4
AVENIDA VERDE
- SDCo 92021 1252-B1
500 SMCS 92069 1108-E5
1500 SDCo 92021 1251-G2
AVENIDA VERDE N
- ESCN 92026 1109-G7
AVENIDA VERDE S
- ESCN 92026 1109-G7
AVENIDA VILLAHA
15700 SD 92128 1170-C5
AVENIDA VISTA LABERA
1700 OCN 92056 1087-C4
AVENIDA WILFREDO
6400 SD 92037 1247-F2
AVENIDA YSIDORA
800 CHV 91910 1311-B6
AVENORRA DR
6100 LMSA 91942 1250-G6
AVENTURA DR
- CHV 91914 1311-E1
AVENTURINE PL
- CRLB 92009 1127-G6
A ZUNIGA CT
- CALX 92231 6620-H5
AVENUE A
10000 SDCo 91977 1291-D3
AVENUE B
9900 SDCo 91977 1291-D3
AVENUE C
9900 SDCo 91977 1291-D3
AVENUE D
9900 SDCo 91977 1291-D3
AVENUE E
9900 SDCo 91977 1291-D3
AVENUE F
9900 SDCo 91977 1291-D3
AVENUE G
9900 SDCo 91977 1291-D3
AVENUE OF ARTS
- SD 92182 1270-B1
AVENUE OF INDUSTRY
11800 SD 92128 1170-A7
AVENUE OF NATIONS
- SD 92131 1209-G6
AVENUE OF SCIENCE
15000 SD 92128 1169-J6
15000 SD 92128 1170-A7
AVENUE OF THE TREES
2000 CRLB 92008 1106-G4
AVERIL RD
100 SD 92173 1350-E3
AVERY RD
- SMCS 92078 1128-D6
AVERY ST
4600 OCN 92057 1066-H7
AVES LN
200 SDCo 92028 1027-H3
AVIARA DR
7000 CRLB 92011 1127-C6
AVIARA PKWY
1100 CRLB 92011 1127-A3
1800 CRLB 92009 1127-E6
AVIARY CT
10800 SD 92131 1209-H4
AVIARY DR
9700 SD 92131 1209-G5
AVIATA RD
- CHV 91914 1311-D2
AVIATION DR
6600 SD 92114 1290-E4

STREET
Block City ZIP Pg-Grid

AVIATION RD
200 SDCo 92028 1027-E4
E AVIATION RD
100 SDCo 92028 1027-F3
AVIATOR RD
8600 SD 92154 1351-H1
AVILA AV
4900 CRLB 92008 1106-J6
AVILA CT
2000 SD 92037 1247-H2
AVILAR CT
600 SMCS 92078 1108-C6
AVION WY
4700 SD 92115 1269-J2
AVIS LN
10300 SNTE 92071 1231-E7
AVOCADO AV
300 ELCJ 92020 1251-G6
1000 ESCN 92026 1129-G1
3500 SDCo 92028 1028-F4
AVOCADO BLVD
1100 ELCJ 92020 1251-G7
1100 ELCJ 92020 1271-G2
1400 SDCo 92020 1271-G2
3500 SDCo 91978 1271-F5
3500 SDCo 91941 1271-G2
3500 SDCo 91977 1271-F5
AVOCADO CT
700 SOLB 92014 1187-H1
AVOCADO DR
1500 SDCo 92083 1108-A2
1500 VSTA 92083 1108-A2
AVOCADO HWY I-15
- ESCN - 1109-E3
- ESCN - 1129-F1
- RivC - 998-H3
- RivC - 999-A2
- SDCo - 998-H3
- SDCo - 1028-G4
- SDCo - 1048-H4
- SDCo - 1068-H4
- SDCo - 1088-J1
- SDCo - 1089-B4
- SDCo - 1109-E3
- SDCo - 1129-F1
AVOCADO LN
700 CRLB 92008 1106-F6
AVOCADO PL
800 SOLB 92014 1187-H1
900 SD 92014 1187-H1
AVOCADO PT
2700 SD 92014 1187-H1
2700 SOLB 92014 1187-H1
AVOCADO RD
1300 OCN 92054 1086-E7
1400 OCN 92054 1106-E1
AVOCADO ST
100 ENCT 92024 1147-A3
9200 SDCo 91977 1271-A7
AVOCADO WY
1500 SDCo 92026 1109-E7
1500 SMCS 92069 1109-E7
AVOCADO CREST
100 SDCo 92025 1130-A6
AVOCADO KNOLL LN
- SDCo 92028 1027-H6
AVOCADO PARK LN
5000 SDCo 92028 1048-J2
AVOCADO PARK WY
5000 SDCo 92028 1048-J2
AVOCADO RANCH RD
1800 SDCo 92019 1272-A1
1800 SDCo 92020 1272-A1
AVOCADO SCHOOL RD
3800 SDCo 91941 1271-G4
AVOCADO SUMMIT DR
1100 SDCo 92019 1272-B1
AVOCADO VILLAGE CT
3600 SDCo 91941 1271-G5
AVOCADO VISTA
5000 SDCo 92028 1048-J2
AVOCADO VISTA LN
3300 SDCo 92028 1048-J2
AVOCET CT
- CHV 91915 1331-H2
1200 ENCT 92007 1167-F3
1500 CRLB 92011 1127-C6
AVOCET WY
4400 OCN 92057 1087-A3
AVOHILL DR
29700 SDCo 92084 1068-G6
AVON DR
4200 LMSA 91941 1270-H4
AVON LN
1900 SDCo 91977 1291-A1
AVONDALE CIR
3500 CRLB 92008 1106-G5
AVONDALE ST
3600 SD 92117 1228-D7
AVONETTE CT
12000 SD 92131 1210-B1
AVOWOOD CT
- SDCo 92028 1027-J6
- SDCo 92028 1028-A6
AVOYER PL
4100 SDCo 91941 1271-D4
AWANA GN
1000 ESCN 92027 1110-A7
AWARD RW
3000 SD 92122 1228-C6
AYAMONTE WY
600 CHV 91910 1310-H6
AYERS LN
- SDCo 92082 1070-H2
AZADO CT
11600 SD 92127 1150-A7
AZAHAR CT
3000 CRLB 92009 1147-J1
AZAHAR PL
3200 CRLB 92009 1147-J1
AZAHAR ST
3000 CRLB 92009 1147-H1
AZALEA
3500 SDCo 92028 1028-F4
15300 SDCo 92021 1233-B3
AZALEA AV
- SDCo 92036 1155-H3
- SMCS 92078 1128-J3
13900 PWY 92064 1190-F3
AZALEA CT
- SMCS 92069 1108-H6
AZALEA DR
100 SDCo 92083 1108-C4
100 SDCo 92084 1108-C4
2700 SD 92106 1268-C6
AZALEA GN
3800 ESCN 92025 1150-C3
AZALEA PL
7100 CRLB 92011 1127-A6
AZALEA ST
500 CHV 91911 1330-H3
AZALEA TR
- SDCo 92060 1052-D2

AZALEA WY
200 OCN 92057 1086-J5
AZALEA SPRING FIRE TR
- SDCo 92036 (1196-C2 See Page 1176)
AZIMUTH PL
- CRLB 92010 1107-A4
AZOFAR CT
18400 SD 92128 1150-D7
AZORES CT
5400 SD 92124 1249-H1
AZTEC DR
5400 LMSA 91942 1270-H1
5500 LMSA 91942 1250-G7
AZTEC ST
3600 SD 92152 1287-J4
4100 OCN 92056 1087-C5
AZTEC WK
5400 SD 92182 1270-B2
5500 SD 92115 1270-B2
AZTEC WY
3500 SD 92152 1287-J4
AZTEC CIRCLE DR
5500 SD 92182 1270-B1
5900 SD 92115 1270-B1
AZUAGA ST
9900 SD 92129 1189-F4
AZUCAR WY
17600 SD 92127 1149-J7
17600 SD 92127 1169-J1
AZUCENA DR
11400 SD 92124 1250-A3
AZUL CT
- OCN 92057 1067-A3
AZUL ST
2700 SD 92037 1227-J3
2700 SD 92093 1227-J3
AZUL WY
- OCN 92057 1087-A2
AZUL VISTA
- SDCo 92078 1128-B4
AZURE CIR
3600 CRLB 92008 1106-H4
AZURE CV
2000 CHV 91915 1311-F6
AZURE LN
2300 VSTA 92081 1108-A5
AZURE TER
1900 SDCo 92019 1272-C2
AZURE VW
8000 SNTE 92071 1230-H7
AZURE WY
1900 ENCT 92024 1147-H5
AZURE COAST DR
2400 SD 92037 1227-J6
AZURE LADO DR
3600 OCN 92056 1107-C3
AZURITE PL
- CRLB 92009 1127-F6
AZUSA CT
1600 CHV 91902 1311-C4
AZUSA ST
1100 SD 92110 1268-F3
AZZURO CT
12700 SD 92130 1188-C6

B

B AV
- SDCo 92055 1066-B2
100 CORD 92118 1288-J7
100 NATC 91950 1289-H7
200 NATC 91950 1309-H1
B CT
800 CHV 91910 1310-F7
B RD E
- CORD 92135 1288-F5
B ST
- SDCo 92059 1029-H4
- CHV 91910 1309-J6
100 SDCo 92036 1136-B7
100 ENCT 92024 1147-B6
100 IMP 92251 6439-E6
200 SDCo 92065 1152-G5
300 SD 92101 1289-A3
400 SDCo 92055 1066-H1
400 SDCo 92055 1085-H3
500 SD 92101 1288-J3
1300 SD 92110 1268-F2
1400 SD 92102 1289-D2
2500 NATC 91950 1310-C3
2700 ImCo 92251 6439-E6
7200 CRLB 92011 1126-J7
BABA DR
16900 SDCo 92065 1173-E1
BABAUTA RD
9300 SD 92129 1189-E7
BABBLING BROOK RD
- CHV 91914 1311-J2
BABCOCK ST
- SD 92127 1169-C3
BABEL DR
3500 SDCo 91935 1273-A6
BABETTE ST
7300 SD 92111 1269-A2
BABILONIA ST
7100 CRLB 92009 1127-H6
BABS WY
10400 SDCo 91941 1271-E3
BABY TURTLE DR
500 SDCo 92004 (1078-H5 See Page 1058)
BACADI DR
7700 SD 92126 1209-A5
BACARA CT
- SD 92131 1210-J2
BACCHARIS AV
6800 CRLB 92011 1127-D6
BACCUS CT
10300 SD 92126 1209-B5
BACH ST
- ENCT 92007 1167-D2
600 VSTA 92083 1087-F5
BACHELOR LN
11000 SDCo 92026 1089-G6
BACHIMBA CT
12300 SD 92128 1170-B6
BACHMAN PL
4100 SD 92103 1269-A4
4200 SD 92103 1268-J4
4200 SD 92108 1268-J4
BACKER CT
9900 SD 92126 1209-A6
BACKER RD
7600 SD 92126 1209-A6
BACK NINE DR
2800 SDCo 92004 (1079-C3 See Page 1058)
BACK NINE ST
2300 OCN 92056 1106-J1
BACKSHORE CT
- CRLB 92010 1107-B4

BACON ST
1600 SD 92107 1267-J5
BACONTREE PL
3500 SD 92111 1248-J4
BACONTREE WY
6900 SD 92111 1248-J4
BADAJOZ PL
2400 CRLB 92009 1147-G1
BADAMI CIR
7900 SD 92126 1209-A1
BADGER CT
12800 SDCo 92040 1212-D5
BADGER GN
2000 ESCN 92029 1129-E6
BADGER LN
- CRLB 92010 1107-D7
BADGER WY
1000 VSTA 92081 1108-A6
BADGER LAKE AV
6300 SD 92119 1250-H5
BADILLO RD
3500 SMCS 92069 1108-D6
BAFFIN DR
10000 SD 92126 1209-A6
BAFLE ST
- SDCo 92028 1027-G5
BAGDAD ST
7400 SD 92111 1249-A4
BAGHDAD CT
- SDCo 92019 1271-H4
BAGLEY DR
3300 SD 92110 1268-E6
BAGWELL CV
7600 SD 92126 1209-A5
BAHAMA BEND
- CORD 92118 1329-E1
BAHAMA CV
14100 SD 92014 1187-H5
BAHAMA DR
- ESCN 92025 1129-J5
BAHIA DR
2300 SD 92037 1247-J3
2300 SD 92037 1248-A2
BAHIA LN
- OCN 92054 1086-G3
100 ESCN 92026 1109-H6
5400 SD 92037 1248-A3
BAHIA WY
1900 SD 92037 1248-A3
BAHIA VISTA WY
1600 SD 92037 1247-H3
BAILEY CT
- SDCo 92055 1086-A2
900 SMCS 92069 1108-F7
BAILEY DR
1800 OCN 92054 1106-F1
BAILEY MEADOW RD
- SDCo 92060 1052-E2
BAILY AV
2200 SD 92105 1289-J1
2400 SD 92105 1269-J7
2600 SD 92105 1270-A7
BAILY PL
4700 SD 92105 1269-J7
4700 SD 92105 1289-J1
BAINBRIDGE CT
2600 SD 92106 1288-C1
E BAINBRIDGE RD
- SD 92106 1288-C1
W BAINBRIDGE RD
- SD 92106 1288-C1
BAINBRIDGE ST
3100 SD 92136 1309-F1
BAIROKO DR
1900 SD 92139 1290-D7
BAJA CT
4900 SD 92115 1270-B3
BAJA DR
5400 SD 92115 1270-B3
BAJA WY
1100 SMCS 92078 1128-E3
BAJA CERRO CIR
2400 SD 92109 1248-B3
BAJADA RD
11900 SD 92128 1170-A1
BAJA MAR
5700 SD 92037 1247-G3
BAJA MISSION RD
4300 SDCo 92028 1047-J5
BAJA VISTA DR
3700 SDCo 92028 1048-A3
3900 OCN 92054 1086-G1
BAJER ST
6200 SD 92122 1228-B6
BAJO CT
700 CHV 91910 1310-H7
3300 CRLB 92009 1128-A7
BAJO DR
900 CHV 91910 1310-H7
BAJO TER
900 SDCo 92028 1027-G1
BAKER AV
- ImCo 92249 6560-B7
BAKER PL
2900 SDCo 91950 1310-C3
BAKER ST
- ImCo 92249 6560-B7
- ImCo 92249 6620-B1
3300 SD 92117 1248-D5
BAKER WY
- OCN 92054 1066-G7
500 OCN 92054 1086-G1
BAKERSFIELD ST
1300 LMGR 91945 1290-G1
1400 LMGR 91945 1290-G2
BAKEWELL ST
5700 SD 92117 1248-H2
BAKMAN CT
12100 SDCo 92040 1231-J2
12100 SDCo 92040 1232-A2
BAKTON WY
10200 SDCo 92082 1069-E4
BALANCED ROCK LN
1700 SDCo 92019 1252-B5
BALBOA AV
1900 SD 92109 1248-A6
1900 DLMR 92014 1187-F4
3000 SD 92117 1248-F4
4200 SD 92111 1248-F4
6000 CORD 92118 1288-G6
7000 SD 92117 1249-B2
7000 SD 92111 1249-B2
8100 SD 92123 1249-D2
BALBOA AV Rt#-274
9800 SD 92123 1249-F2
BALBOA CIR
1200 CHV 91910 1311-B7
2000 VSTA 92081 1107-J4
BALBOA CT
700 SD 92109 1267-H4
BALBOA DR
1800 SD 92101 1289-B1
2500 SD 92103 1269-B7
2500 SD 92103 1289-B1

BALBOA DR
3700 OCN 92056 1107-A1
BALBOA PL
9700 SDCo 92029 1149-D4
BALBOA ST
100 SMCS 92069 1108-E6
BALBOA TER
3700 SD 92117 1248-D4
BALBOA WY
4100 SD 92111 1248-G3
BALBOA ARMS DR
5100 SD 92117 1248-G2
BALBOA VISTA DR
2300 SD 92105 1270-B7
2300 SD 92105 1290-B1
BALCHEN WY
- SD 92154 1351-D2
BALDRICH ST
7100 LMSA 91942 1270-F1
BALDWIN LN
4000 CRLB 92008 1106-F7
BALDWIN ST
8100 LMGR 91945 1270-H6
BALENTINE DR
- SDCo 91901 1253-J2
- SDCo 91901 1254-A3
BALFOUR CT
2100 SD 92109 1248-A4
5900 CRLB 92008 1127-D2
BALI CV
2400 SD 92139 1310-E1
BALI LN
10900 SD 92126 1209-A3
BALI WY
- OCN 92057 1087-A1
BALI HAI RD
- ESCN 92025 1129-J5
BALKIS LN
7200 LMGR 91945 1270-F7
BALL AV
700 ESCN 92026 1109-J7
1000 ESCN 92027 1109-J7
BALLANTYNE ST
100 ELCJ 92020 1251-G4
600 ELCJ 92021 1251-G4
900 SDCo 92021 1251-G3
BALLARD ST
100 ELCJ 92019 1251-J6
BALLAST POINT CT
1600 CHV 91911 1330-H4
BALLATA CT
1100 VSTA 92081 1107-H4
BALLENA WY
6900 CRLB 92009 1127-J5
BALLERINA LN
13700 SDCo 92082 1090-E2
BALLET CT
- SDCo 92028 1028-E3
BALLINA DR
1800 SD 92114 1290-C2
BALLINGER AV
6600 SD 92119 1250-H4
BALLISTA DR
300 SDCo 92004 1058-F6
BALLOW WY
- SMCS 92078 1128-J3
BALL RANCH RD
1700 SDCo 91901 1234-A7
BALLYBUNION SQ
11400 SD 92128 1189-J2
BALLYSTOCK CT
10700 SD 92131 1209-H1
BALMORAL CT
1400 SMCS 92069 1109-D7
BALMORAL DR
5800 SD 92114 1290-C4
BALOUR DR
500 ENCT 92024 1147-F7
900 ENCT 92024 1167-E1
BALSA ST
2300 SD 92105 1290-B1
2400 SD 92105 1270-B7
BALSAM CT
600 ELCJ 92019 1252-B6
BALSAM DR
- NATC 91950 1289-H7
- SD 92113 1289-H7
600 ELCJ 92019 1252-B6
BALSAMINA DR
3800 SDCo 91902 1310-F3
BALSAM LAKE AV
6300 SD 92119 1250-H5
BALTIC ST
7400 SD 92111 1249-A4
BALTIMORE DR
4900 LMSA 91941 1270-G1
5100 LMSA 91942 1270-G1
5500 LMSA 91942 1250-G6
5900 SD 91942 1250-G6
6100 SD 92119 1250-G6
BALTIMORE PL
1500 ESCN 92025 1130-B4
BALTIMORE ST
3300 SD 92117 1248-E5
BALTUSROL GN
2100 ESCN 92026 1109-D3
BAMBOO LN
100 SDCo 92028 1027-H2
BAMBURGH DR
6500 SD 92117 1248-J2
BAMBURGH PL
4500 SD 92117 1248-J2
BANAGAS CT
100 CALX 92231 6620-F6
BANBURY CT
2600 CRLB 92010 1106-J5
BANBURY DR
26900 SDCo 92082 1090-D6
BANBURY ST
6000 SD 92139 1310-D2
BANCROFT DR
2600 SDCo 91977 1271-A6
3900 LMSA 91941 1271-B2
3900 LMSA 91977 1271-B2
4900 SDCo 91941 1271-B2
BANCROFT GN
400 ESCN 92027 1110-D6
BANCROFT ST
400 SD 92102 1289-F2
2100 SD 92104 1289-E1
2500 SD 92104 1269-E5
4400 SD 92116 1269-E4
S BANCROFT ST
400 SD 92113 1289-F5
BANCROFT VIEW DR
8900 SDCo 91977 1271-A5
BANDA AV
- CALX 92231 6620-H6
BANDAK CT
- SMCS 92069 1108-J4
BANDELL CT
10500 SD 92126 1209-A4
BANDERA ST
300 SD 92037 1247-F5

BANDINI PL
300 VSTA 92083 1087-H7
BANDINI ST
3400 SD 92140 1268-G6
3600 SD 92110 1268-G5
3900 SD 92103 1268-G5
BANDOLIER LN
1900 SD 92154 1350-D3
BANDON WY
8800 SNTE 92071 1231-A7
BANDY CANYON RD
15200 SDCo 92025 1150-H3
15300 SD 92025 1150-H3
15300 SD 92025 1151-A2
17000 SD 92025 1131-E7
17700 SDCo 92025 1131-E7
BANFF CT
2700 CRLB 92010 1107-A5
BANFIELD LN
- SD 92130 1188-A5
BANGALORE LN
10700 SD 92126 1209-A4
BANGERTER CT
3600 ESCN 92027 1110-F4
BANGOR PL
3400 SD 92106 1288-A2
BANGOR ST
700 SD 92106 1288-A2
BANJO CT
600 SMCS 92069 1109-A6
BANJO LN
1400 SDCo 92065 1152-J7
BANKS ST
5300 SD 92110 1268-F3
BANNEKER DR
800 SD 92114 1290-G3
BANNER AV
1200 CHV 91911 1330-E5
BANNER RD
1300 SDCo 92036 1136-C6
BANNER RD Rt#-78
1200 SDCo 92036 1136-B5
36100 SDCo 92036 1156-H1
BANNER WY
2300 SDCo 92036 1136-C7
BANNER VIEW DR
1200 SDCo 92036 1136-C6
BANNING ST
4300 SD 92107 1268-B6
BANNISTER LN
10500 SD 92126 1208-J4
BANNISTER RD
- ImCo 92227 410-L11
- ImCo 92227 411-A11
- ImCo 92281 411-B11
BANNISTER WY
10500 SD 92126 1208-J4
BANNOCK AV
4200 SD 92117 1248-E1
BANOCK ST
800 SDCo 91977 1291-C3
BANTA RD
- IMP 92251 6439-D6
500 ImCo 92251 6439-D6
BANTAM AV
9400 SD 92123 1249-E6
BANTAM LAKE AV
6500 SD 92119 1250-H4
BANTAM LAKE CIR
6500 SD 92119 1250-H4
BANTY CT
12200 SD 92129 1188-J7
BANUELO CV
12300 SD 92130 1188-B7
BANYAN CT
- SMCS 92069 1109-A5
BANYAN DR
1300 SDCo 92028 998-B7
BANYAN WY
300 ESCN 92026 1109-H7
BANYONWOOD DR
700 OCN 92057 1087-C1
BAR DR
28500 SDCo 92026 1089-B3
BARANCA CT
8300 SDCo 91977 1290-J5
BARBADOS CIR
300 SDCo 92028 1027-F5
BARBADOS CV
2000 CHV 91915 1311-F6
BARBADOS WY
10800 SD 92126 1209-A3
13300 SD 92014 1187-J7
BARBARA AV
200 SOLB 92075 1167-E6
BARBARA DR
1100 SDCo 92084 1108-B1
2000 ESCN 92026 1109-C4
BARBARA LN
2700 OCN 92056 1087-B6
BARBARA WY
- ELCN 92243 6559-F2
BARBARA ANN LN
1100 SDCo 92065 1152-J6
BARBARA ANN PL
5100 SD 92115 1270-E2
BARBARA JEAN CT
- SNTE 92071 1251-A1
BARBARA WORTH DR
1800 ELCN 92243 6499-E6
BARBARA WORTH RD
- ImCo 92249 431-D7
BARBARBA LN
1700 ENCT 92024 1147-B2
BARBAROSSA CT
5800 SD 92115 1270-B3
BARBAROSSA DR
4700 SD 92115 1270-C3
BARBAROSSA PL
4800 SD 92115 1270-C3
BARBARY PL
5700 SDCo 92003 1048-B7
BARBER MOUNTAIN RD
2300 SDCo 91935 1294-F4
BARBERRY PL
- CHV 91915 1311-H1
- CRLB 92011 1127-B5
BARBIC CT
3700 SDCo 91977 1271-C5
BARBIC LN
9300 SDCo 91977 1271-B5
BAR BIT RD
2300 SDCo 91978 1271-G7
2300 SDCo 91978 1291-G1
BARBOUR AV
- CHV 91913 1331-E2
BARBOUR DR
2700 SD 92154 1330-C7
BARBY PL
3000 SD 92117 1228-C7
BARCELONA CT
1900 VSTA 92081 1107-H3
3200 SDCo 91977 1271-D6

BARCELONA DR
1000 SD 92107 1287-J2
N BARCELONA ST
3900 SDCo 91977 1271-D5
S BARCELONA ST
2000 SDCo 91977 1291-D1
2200 SDCo 91977 1271-D5
BARCELONA WY
4700 OCN 92056 1107-E4
BARCLAY AV
5400 SD 92120 1250-B5
BARD RD Rt#-S24
1100 ImCo 92283 432-D5
BARDAGUERA PL
3900 SDCo 91902 1310-F2
BARDONIA ST
6600 SD 92119 1250-H4
BARDSLEY CT
- SD 92154 1330-H7
BAREBACK SQ
5100 SD 92130 1188-D2
BARELIA RD
1600 SDCo 92027 1131-C3
BARETA STAR RANCH RD
24900 SDCo 92065 1173-G7
BARGER PL
900 SDCo 92065 1152-G7
BARHAM DR
600 SMCS 92078 1109-A7
600 SMCS 92078 1129-B1
1500 ESCN 92029 1129-C1
E BARHAM DR
100 SMCS 92078 1128-H1
100 SMCS 92096 1128-H1
300 SMCS 92078 1129-A1
BARHAM LN
100 SMCS 92078 1129-A1
BARHAVEN LN
100 SDCo 92028 1027-H3
N BARHAVEN LN
100 SDCo 92028 1027-H2
BARI CT
5800 LMSA 91942 1251-B7
BARIN ST
- CORD 92135 1288-F4
BARIONI ST Rt#-S28
100 IMP 92251 431-B4
100 IMP 92251 6439-E6
BARK ST
5900 SD 92105 1270-C6
BARKEATH DR
7300 LMGR 91945 1270-F6
BARKER DR
8400 SD 92119 1250-J3
BARKER WY
6800 SD 92119 1250-H3
BARKLA ST
5400 SD 92122 1228-A7
BARLES CT
38800 SDCo 92028 997-A4
BARLEY CT
5700 SDCo 91902 1311-B2
BARLEY DR
2300 VSTA 92081 1108-A5
BARLOWS LANDING CV
- SD 92130 1208-C2
BARNARD DR
3500 OCN 92056 1107-A1
BARNARD ST
2800 SD 92110 1268-C5
BARNAVILLE LN
500 SMCS 92069 1108-G6
N BARNES ST
100 OCN 92054 1086-B6
S BARNES ST
100 OCN 92054 1086-B7
BARNES CANYON RD
9900 SD 92121 1208-E6
BARNETT AV
3000 SD 92110 1268-E6
3000 SD 92140 1268-E6
E BARNETT CIR
- SDCo 92055 1067-A2
W BARNETT CIR
- SDCo 92055 1067-A1
BARNETT DR
500 SMCS 92069 1108-J6
BARNETT RD
1200 SDCo 92065 1152-H7
1200 SDCo 92065 1172-H1
BARNEVELD ST
9100 SDCo 91977 1291-B4
BARNEY CT
1100 SD 92154 1350-D1
BARNEY ST
2200 SD 92139 1290-G7
BARNEY OLDFIELD RD
- ImCo - 432-B3
- ImCo 92283 432-B3
BARNHURST DR
6500 SD 92117 1248-J2
BARNHURST PL
4500 SD 92117 1248-J2
BARN OWL CT
- CHV 91913 1331-A1
BARNSON PL
2700 SD 92103 1269-A7
BARNWELL PL
500 OCN 92054 1086-E7
E BARNWELL ST
400 OCN 92054 1086-D6
N BARNWELL ST
100 OCN 92054 1086-D6
S BARNWELL ST
100 OCN 92054 1086-E6
BAR O DR
3300 SDCo 92004 (1078-H6 See Page 1058)
BARON DR
10300 SD 92126 1209-C4
BARON LN
10500 SD 92126 1209-C4
BARON PL
900 ESCN 92026 1129-F1
BARONA WY
5100 LMSA 91941 1271-A1
BARONA MESA RD
23300 SDCo 92065 1173-D5
BARONA MESA WY
15400 SDCo 92065 1173-D5
BARONESS AV
10100 SD 92126 1209-B5
BARON LONG RD
- SDCo 91901 1235-A2
BAROQUE LN
10800 SD 92124 1249-H3
BAROQUE PL
500 ESCN 92026 1109-J7
BAROQUE TER
4800 OCN 92057 1087-B2
BARR AV
800 SD 92103 1268-J4

BARRACUDA AL
- SD 92136 1289-E6
BARRANCA CT
3600 CRLB 92010 1107-B3
BARRANCA RD
3500 SMCS 92069 1108-D5
BARREGO WY
23600 SDCo 92065 1173-D3
BARREL DR
600 SDCo 92004 (1078-J4 See Page 1058)
700 SDCo 92004 (1079-A4 See Page 1058)
BARREL BLOSSOM LN
2700 SDCo 92084 1088-D7
BARRET
- ELCN 92243 6559-J1
BARRETT AV
900 CHV 91911 1330-E2
BARRETT DAM RD
- SDCo 91917 (1315-C6 See Page 1294)
BARRETT LAKE RD
- SD 91901 (1295-A4 See Page 1294)
- SDCo 91901 (1295-A4 See Page 1294)
- SDCo 91917 (1295-A4 See Page 1294)
- SDCo 91935 (1295-A4 See Page 1294)
- SDCo 91917 (1315-D3 See Page 1294)
1300 SDCo 91917 429-K10
BARRETT SMITH RD
- SDCo 91917 429-K10
BARRETT VIEW RD
3400 SDCo 91901 1275-B4
BARRINGTON CT
4600 SDCo 91902 1310-H2
BARROWS ST
4300 SD 92117 1248-C3
BARRY ST
5000 OCN 92057 1067-B5
BARRYMORE ST
13800 SD 92129 1189-C2
BARRYWOOD WY
10300 SD 92131 1210-B4
BARSANTI CT
1900 SD 92154 1330-A7
BARSBY ST
300 SDCo 92084 1087-H2
900 VSTA 92084 1087-H2
1000 VSTA 92084 1088-A2
BARSKY LN
1000 SDCo 92028 1027-H4
BARSTOW ST
4800 SD 92117 1228-G7
BART LN
9600 SNTE 92071 1231-E4
BART WY
10300 SNTE 92071 1231-E4
BARTEL PL
2400 SD 92123 1249-E7
BARTEL ST
2500 SD 92123 1249-E7
BARTH RD
6100 ImCo 92227 410-K10
BARTIZON DR
300 SDCo 92004 1058-F6
BARTLETT AV
3500 OCN 92057 1086-F5
BARTLETT DR
1000 VSTA 92084 1087-H5
BARTLEY LN
14700 SDCo 91935 1293-A2
BARTLEY PL
1200 ESCN 92026 1109-J5
BARTOLA RD
- SDCo 92028 998-G7
BARTON DR
7800 LMGR 91945 1290-H1
BARTON PEAK DR
1100 CHV 91913 1311-E6
BARTRAM WY
1600 ELCJ 92019 1252-B7
1600 SDCo 92019 1252-B7
BASALTO ST
6500 CRLB 92009 1127-H5
BASCOMB PL
3600 SD 92117 1228-D7
BASEL ST
2900 OCN 92054 1106-G1
BASHAN LAKE AV
8300 SD 92119 1250-J5
BASHFUL WY
8500 SDCo 92021 1232-E7
BASIL ST
100 ENCT 92024 1147-B5
BASILICA ST
100 OCN 92057 1086-H3
BASILICA WY
100 OCN 92057 1086-H3
BASILONE RD
- SDCo 92055 408-K6
- SDCo 92055 409-A6
- SDCo 92672 1023-D3
200 SDCo 92055 1023-H2
BASILONE ST
3800 SD 92110 1268-C5
BASIN RD
- CRLB 92010 1107-B5
BASS DR
10100 SDCo 92040 1232-E3
BASS LN
3700 OCN 92054 1086-G2
BASS RD
2400 SDCo 91906 (1297-F5 See Page 1296)
BASS ST
3800 LMSA 91941 1270-F5
BASSETT CT
100 SDCo 91977 1290-J5
16300 SDCo 92065 1173-D2
BASSETT WY
23500 SDCo 92065 1173-D3
BASSMORE DR
13700 SD 92129 1189-F3
BASSO CT
7300 SD 92119 1250-F4
BASSWOOD AV
700 IMPB 91932 1329-G6
1200 CRLB 92008 1106-F5
BATAAN CIR
5900 SD 92139 1290-C7
BATAVIA CIR
11100 SD 92126 1209-A2
BATAVIA RD
7700 SD 92126 1209-A2
BATCHELDER CT
2000 ELCJ 92020 1251-C5
BATEMAN AV
4000 SD 92154 1350-F1

STREET Block	City	ZIP	Pg-Grid
BATES LN			
1200	SDCo	92021	1251-G1
BATES ST			
5700	SD	92115	1270-B5
BATES VIEW CT			
-	SMCS	92069	1108-H5
BATHURST PL			
1300	ELCJ	92020	1251-D5
BATIQUITOS DR			
1300	CRLB	92011	1127-A6
E BATIQUITOS DR			
900	CRLB	92011	1127-C7
BATISTA ST			
6900	SD	92111	1248-J3
7300	SD	92111	1249-A3
BATTLE CREEK RD			
1100	CHV	91913	1311-E6
BAUDOUIN PL			
-	CHV	91913	1311-F1
BAUER PL			
600	VSTA	92081	1107-F1
BAUER RD			
-	SD	92126	1209-C7
BAUGHMAN RD			
1300	ImCo	92227	431-A1
BAUM ST			
-	CHV	91913	1331-E2
BAUSELL CT			
10100	SD	92124	1249-G3
BAUSELL PL			
10100	SD	92124	1249-G3
BAUTISTA AV			
2300	SDCo	92084	1087-G1
2500	SDCo	92084	1067-F7
BAUTISTA CT			
100	OCN	92057	1086-H3
BAVARIA DR			
100	SDCo	92083	1108-A2
100	VSTA	92083	1108-A2
BAVARIAN DR			
13100	SD	92129	1189-C4
BAVARIAN WY			
8400	SD	92129	1189-C4
BAXTER CT			
4600	SD	92117	1228-F7
BAXTER ST			
5000	SD	92117	1228-F7
BAXTER CANYON RD			
2200	VSTA	92081	1107-H7
BAY BLVD			
200	CHV	91910	1309-H6
300	CHV	91910	1329-J1
600	CHV	91910	1330-A2
600	CHV	91911	1330-A3
1200	SD	91911	1330-A3
BAY CIR			
900	CORD	92118	1288-J7
900	CORD	92118	1289-A7
900	CORD	92118	1308-J1
900	CORD	92118	1309-A1
BAY LN			
-	CRLB	92011	1126-J5
BAYAMON RD			
9500	SD	92129	1189-E4
BAYARD ST			
4000	SD	92109	1247-H4
BAYBERRY CT			
800	SMCS	92069	1109-A6
4300	SD	92154	1330-G7
BAYBERRY DR			
1800	OCN	92054	1106-E2
BAY BERRY PL			
-	ENCT	92024	1147-C5
BAYCANE WY			
11800	SD	92128	1190-A7
BAY CANYON CT			
2700	SD	92117	1248-E7
BAYCLIFF WY			
4100	OCN	92056	1107-C3
BAY CREST LN			
-	SD	92154	1350-J2
BAY FRONT ST			
1900	SD	92113	1289-C6
BAY HILL DR			
1600	SMCS	92069	1108-J3
BAY HILL RD			
2300	CHV	91915	1311-G6
BAY LEAF DR			
300	CHV	91910	1310-E5
BAY LEAF WY			
3700	OCN	92057	1086-H4
BAYLEE LN			
-	SDCo	92127	1169-E4
BAYLISS CT			
4900	SD	92130	1188-C4
BAYLOR AV			
700	CHV	91902	1311-C5
700	CHV	91913	1311-C5
BAYLOR DR			
-	SMCS	92078	1128-F6
4700	SD	92115	1270-A3
BAY MARINA DR			
700	NATC	91950	1309-G4
BAY MEADOWS DR			
1400	SDCo	91901	1234-B6
BAY MEADOWS WY			
400	SOLB	92075	1187-F1
BAYONA LP			
500	CHV	91910	1310-J5
BAYONET TER			
13400	SD	92128	1189-H4
BAYONNE DR			
3400	SD	92109	1268-A1
3600	SD	92109	1248-A7
BAYPONY LN			
11800	SD	92128	1190-A7
BAYSHORE DR			
4700	CRLB	92008	1106-H7
4700	CRLB	92008	1126-H1
BAYSHORE LN			
800	SMCS	92078	1128-F2
BAYSIDE LN			
800	SD	92109	1267-H1
3800	SD	92109	1247-H7
BAYSIDE PKWY			
900	CHV	91910	1329-H1
BAYSIDE WK			
2600	SD	92109	1267-H1
3800	SD	92109	1247-H7
BAY SUMMIT PL			
4600	SD	92117	1248-E6
BAY VIEW CT			
4000	SD	92103	1268-H5
BAYVIEW PL			
3600	CRLB	92010	1107-B4
BAYVIEW WY			
200	CHV	91910	1310-B4
BAYVIEW HEIGHTS DR			
1600	SD	92105	1290-B2
BAYVIEW HEIGHTS PL			
5400	SD	92105	1290-B1
BAYVIEW HEIGHTS WY			
1800	SD	92114	1290-B1
1800	SD	92105	1290-B1
BAYWIND PT			
12800	SD	92130	1188-D6
BAYWOOD AV			
10400	SD	92126	1209-D4
BAYWOOD CIR			
1000	CHV	91915	1311-G5
5100	OCN	92056	1087-D2
BAYWOOD LN			
10300	SD	92126	1209-D5
BEACH AV			
-	IMPB	91932	1349-E1
200	CALX	92231	6680-H2
BEACH RD			
-	ImCo	92257	411-B7
BEACH ST			
-	ENCT	92024	1147-D7
BEACH BLUFF RD			
4100	CRLB	92008	1106-H6
BEACH CLUB DR			
100	SOLB	92075	1187-E2
BEACH CLUB RD			
-	SDCo	92055	1023-E4
-	SDCo	92672	1023-E3
BEACHCOMBER CT			
5200	SD	92130	1188-D5
BEACH CREST CT			
900	CRLB	92011	1126-J4
BEACH FRONT DR			
700	SOLB	92075	1187-E2
BEACHWOOD CT			
-	CRLB	92008	1106-H7
BEACHWOOD WY			
1100	OCN	92057	1087-B2
BEACON CT			
600	VSTA	92083	1087-F5
BEACON DR			
700	SD	92114	1290-G3
BEACON PL			
500	CHV	91910	1310-G6
700	ESCN	92025	1130-A3
4100	OCN	92056	1107-C2
BEACON BAY DR			
1000	CRLB	92011	1127-A5
BEACON HILL CT			
1100	SMCS	92078	1128-B3
BEADNELL WY			
6500	SD	92117	1248-H2
BEAGLE CT			
3400	SD	92111	1248-J4
3400	SD	92111	1249-A4
BEAGLE PL			
3400	SD	92111	1248-J4
BEAGLE ST			
6900	SD	92111	1248-J4
7200	SD	92111	1249-A4
BEAK PT			
9300	SD	92129	1189-E6
BEAK WY			
3900	SD	92124	1249-H3
BEAL RD			
-	ImCo	-	411-E6
400	ImCo	92257	411-C7
BEAL ST			
7300	SD	92111	1249-A4
BEAMAN LN			
1200	SDCo	92028	1027-G4
BEAN ST			
3200	SD	92101	1268-H7
BEANIE LN			
1200	SDCo	92021	1251-J3
BEAR			
14100	SDCo	92040	1232-F4
BEAR DR			
3500	SD	92103	1268-J6
BEARCAT LN			
1800	SDCo	92019	1272-D3
BEAR CREEK PL			
2300	CHV	91915	1311-G7
BEAR DANCE WY			
11100	SD	92127	1149-H7
BEARDSLEY ST			
600	SD	92113	1289-C4
BEARING LN			
100	ELCJ	92019	1252-A5
BEAR MOUNTAIN WY			
13600	SDCo	91935	1292-F3
BEAR RIVER RW			
6800	SD	92139	1290-F7
6800	SD	92139	1310-F1
BEAR ROCK GN			
2200	ESCN	92026	1109-B3
BEARTRAP PL			
2100	ESCN	92027	1130-D1
BEAR VALLEY LN			
16500	SDCo	92027	1111-D1
BEAR VALLEY PKWY			
300	ESCN	92025	1130-C7
300	ESCN	92025	1150-B3
300	SDCo	92025	1130-C7
1100	SDCo	92027	1130-D3
1700	ESCN	92027	1130-D3
2400	ESCN	92027	1110-D7
BEAR VALLEY RD			
-	CHV	91915	(1312-A6 See Page 1293)
900	SDCo	92025	1130-C5
BEAR VALLEY HEIGHTS RD			
25700	SDCo	92027	1111-E1
26000	SDCo	92027	1091-D7
BEAR VALLEY OAKS RD			
1900	SDCo	92025	1130-C5
BEAR VIEW WY			
400	SDCo	91901	1253-F2
BEATITUDE DR			
12300	SDCo	92082	1090-B1
BEATON CT			
11100	SD	92126	1209-D2
BEATRICE CT			
1100	SD	92154	1350-E1
6300	SD	92139	1310-E2
BEATRICE ST			
2700	SD	92139	1310-E2
BEATTY PL			
4600	SD	92124	1249-G3
BEAUCHAMP CT			
4900	SD	92130	1188-C5
BEAUMONT AV			
5300	SD	92037	1247-F3
BEAUMONT CIR			
1000	VSTA	92084	1088-A6
BEAUMONT CT			
300	VSTA	92084	1088-A6
BEAUMONT DR			
100	VSTA	92084	1088-A6
4700	SDCo	91941	1271-B2
4700	LMSA	91941	1271-B2
BEAUMONT GN			
400	ESCN	92026	1109-G6
BEAUMONT LN N			
100	VSTA	92084	1088-A6
BEAUMONT LN S			
100	VSTA	92084	1088-A6
BEAVERCREEK LN			
200	SDCo	92028	1028-A3
BEAVER HOLLOW RD			
3100	SDCo	91935	1273-B3
3400	SDCo	92019	1272-H2
3400	SDCo	92019	1273-A2
BEAVER LAKE CT			
6400	SD	92119	1250-J5
BEAVER LAKE DR			
7900	SD	92119	1250-H5
BECK DR			
9900	SNTE	92071	1231-D3
BECKINGTON LN			
7000	SD	92139	1290-G7
BECKINGTON WY			
2600	SD	92139	1290-G7
BECKY LN			
600	SDCo	92069	1108-G1
BECKY PL			
2100	SD	92104	1289-G1
BEDEL CT			
9100	SD	92129	1189-D1
BEDFONT CIR			
10400	SD	92126	1209-D4
BEDFORD AV			
-	CHV	91913	1331-F1
3900	OCN	92056	1087-B7
BEDFORD CIR			
3500	CRLB	92008	1106-H4
BEDFORD DR			
4100	SD	92116	1269-G2
BEDFORD PL			
1900	ESCN	92029	1129-F7
BEDFORD HILL			
-	SD	92127	1169-C3
BEDFORDSHIRE CT			
12600	SD	92128	1150-B6
BEDLOW CT			
6700	SD	92119	1250-E3
BEE CANYON RD			
18000	SDCo	91917	429-J10
BEECH AV			
100	CRLB	92008	1106-D5
200	CHV	91910	1310-A6
600	CHV	91910	1330-B1
800	CHV	91911	1330-B2
BEECH LN			
20100	SDCo	92029	1149-E1
BEECH PL			
100	SDCo	92021	1252-H4
1400	ESCN	92026	1109-J6
BEECH ST			
100	SD	92101	1289-A2
100	SDCo	92028	1027-E3
200	ELCJ	92020	1251-F4
300	SD	92114	1290-D4
500	SD	92101	1288-J2
2800	SD	92102	1289-E2
3800	SD	92105	1289-G2
5000	SD	92102	1290-A2
N BEECH ST			
100	ESCN	92025	1130-A1
900	ESCN	92026	1110-A7
900	ESCN	92026	1130-A1
S BEECH ST			
100	ESCN	92025	1130-B2
BEECH FERN CT			
11400	SD	92131	1209-J1
BEECHGLEN DR			
1000	CHV	91910	1310-J7
BEECHTREE DR			
100	ENCT	92024	1147-F7
BEECHTREE RD			
-	SMCS	92078	1128-D6
BEECHTREE ST			
12800	SDCo	92040	1232-B3
BEECHWOOD CT			
8000	LMGR	91945	1270-J7
BEECHWOOD LN			
100	OCN	92054	1106-C2
BEECHWOOD ST			
600	ESCN	92025	1130-A1
12600	PWY	92064	1190-D3
BEEJAY DR			
700	SD	92154	1330-B7
BEELER CANYON RD			
11100	PWY	92064	1210-E1
11100	SD	92131	1210-E1
14900	PWY	92064	1190-H7
14900	PWY	92064	1191-A6
14900	SD	92131	1190-H7
BEELER CANYON TER			
11400	SD	92131	1210-D1
BEELER CREEK TR			
12700	PWY	92064	1190-B5
BEETHOVEN AV			
100	ENCT	92007	1167-D3
BEETHOVEN DR			
600	ESCN	92025	1150-B2
BEE VALLEY RD			
20600	SDCo	91935	(1314-J2 See Page 1294)
20600	SDCo	91935	(1315-A2 See Page 1294)
BEGONIA CT			
900	CRLB	92011	1127-A6
BEGONIA DR			
-	SD	92109	1248-C6
BEGONIA ST			
-	SDCo	92055	1086-B2
3800	SD	92121	1208-C6
N BEGONIA ST			
500	ESCN	92027	1110-B6
BEGONIA WY			
2400	SDCo	91901	1233-J5
BEHBERG RD			
-	SD	92106	1287-J4
-	SD	92152	1287-J4
-	SD	92152	1288-A4
BEIJA FLOR			
-	SDCo	92082	1090-C2
BEINN BHREAGH			
-	SDCo	92036	1156-D7
-	SDCo	92036	1176-D1
BEL AIR CT			
-	ESCN	92027	1130-F1
BEL AIR DR			
700	VSTA	92084	1087-J5
BELAIR DR			
1100	SDCo	92028	1027-H2
BEL AIR DR E			
900	VSTA	92084	1087-J5
BEL AIR DR W			
100	VSTA	92084	1087-J5
BEL AIR TER			
1800	ENCT	92024	1167-H3
BELARDO DR			
5200	SD	92124	1230-A7
BELA VISTA AV			
-	ELCJ	92021	1251-J5
E BELCHER ST			
-	CALX	92231	6680-H1
BELCOURT PL			
-	SD	92130	1208-B1
BELDEN PL			
2100	ESCN	92029	1129-H7
BELDEN ST			
7000	SD	92111	1248-J4
7200	SD	92111	1249-A4
BELDENS FIELD RD			
900	ESCN	92027	1130-F1
BEL ESPRIT CIR E			
800	SMCS	92069	1108-H6
BEL ESPRIT CIR W			
800	SMCS	92069	1108-H6
BELFAST CIR			
8600	SD	92126	1209-C4
BELFAST GN			
100	ESCN	92027	1110-E7
BELFORA WY			
100	OCN	92057	1087-A4
BELFORD RD			
-	IMP	92251	6439-C4
400	ImCo	92251	6439-C4
BELFORD ST			
3500	SD	92111	1248-J4
3600	SD	92111	1249-A4
BELGIAN ST			
10900	SD	92126	1209-D3
BELINDA WY			
600	CHV	91910	1310-D7
BELIO LN			
2900	LMGR	91945	1270-E7
BELIZE RD			
-	CHV	91914	1311-E2
BELIZE WY			
-	OCN	92057	1087-A2
BELKNAP WY			
2000	ESCN	92027	1110-B6
BELL CT			
6600	SD	92111	1248-H6
BELL DR			
-	SMCS	92078	1128-H3
BELL RD			
-	ImCo	92250	431-D5
BELLA COLLINA			
-	ENCT	92024	1148-C5
BELLA COLLINA ST			
4900	OCN	92056	1087-C3
BELLADONNA WY			
-	SD	92131	1209-G2
BELLAGIO RD			
-	ESCN	92027	1130-F1
9200	SNTE	92071	1231-A4
BELLAGIO ST			
-	CHV	91913	1331-E1
BELLAIRE CT			
800	ELCJ	92020	1251-A4
BELLAIRE ST			
300	DLMR	92014	1187-F4
BELLAKAREN PL			
7800	SD	92037	1228-A6
BELLA LAGUNA CT			
-	ENCT	92024	1147-D1
BELLA LINDA DR			
-	SDCo	92082	1069-H5
BELLA PACIFIC RW			
2700	SD	92109	1248-C4
BELLA ROSA DR			
1600	SDCo	92084	1088-B2
BELLA ROSA RD			
-	SD	92131	1210-D2
BELLA SIENA			
15800	SDCo	92067	1168-E6
BELLATRIX CT			
11400	SD	92126	1209-C1
BELLATRIX DR			
-	SD	92126	1209-E7
BELLA VISTA DR			
1500	ENCT	92024	1147-D2
1900	SDCo	92084	1108-D3
BELLA VITA LN			
-	SDCo	92084	1108-D1
BELLA VITA WY			
-	SMCS	92078	1128-J4
BELL BLUFF AV			
6400	SD	92119	1250-D3
BELL BLUFF RD			
1400	SDCo	91901	1234-G6
BELL BLUFF TKTR			
-	SDCo	91901	1255-F2
BELLBOTTOM WY			
-	SDCo	92065	1174-B4
BELL COLLO LN			
8700	SNTE	92071	1231-G6
BELLE LN			
3300	CRLB	92008	1106-G4
BELLE ST			
-	SD	91911	1330-A4
800	CHV	91911	1330-A4
BELLEAIRE ST			
1400	OCN	92054	1106-D2
BELLEAU WOOD			
-	SD	92101	1268-G7
-	SD	92140	1268-F6
BELLE BONNIE BRAE RD			
3600	SDCo	91902	1311-A2
BELLECHASE CIR			
17700	SD	92128	1150-A7
BELLE CREST WY			
-	SD	92154	1330-H7
BELLE FLEUR WY			
-	SD	92128	1189-G6
BELLEFLOWER RD			
1300	CRLB	92011	1127-A4
BELLE GLADE AV			
6400	SD	92119	1250-E6
BELLE GLADE LN			
7000	SD	92119	1250-E5
BELLEGROVE RD			
1800	ENCT	92024	1147-H7
BELLE HAVEN DR			
6600	SD	92120	1250-D5
BELLE HELENE CT			
17600	SD	92128	1150-A7
17600	SD	92128	1170-A1
BELLE ISLE DR			
3100	SD	92105	1269-J6
BELLEMEADE RD			
1600	ENCT	92024	1147-H7
BELLEMORE DR			
25500	SDCo	92065	1173-J4
25700	SDCo	92065	1174-A4
BELLENA AV			
1100	CHV	91913	1311-D6
BELLENA CT			
1600	CHV	91913	1311-D6
BELLERIVE CT			
100	VSTA	92084	1088-A6
BELLERIVE DR			
100	VSTA	92084	1088-A6
BELLEVIEW AV			
1300	ENCT	92007	1167-C1
BELLE VISTA DR			
400	CHV	91910	1310-F6
BELLEVUE AV			
5300	SD	92037	1247-F3
BELLEVUE PL			
700	SD	92037	1247-G4
BELLEZA DR			
-	SD	92108	1249-D7
BELLFLOWER CT			
-	CHV	91913	1331-A1
BELLFLOWER DR			
4300	LMSA	91941	1271-A3
BELL GARDENS DR			
10200	SNTE	92071	1231-D4
BELLINGHAM AV			
3600	SD	92105	1269-G6
BELLINGTON LN			
1700	SDCo	92028	1027-J3
BELLIS LN			
9000	SDCo	92040	1232-D6
BELLOC CT			
2100	SD	92109	1248-A4
BELLO HILLS LN			
1800	SDCo	92026	1109-H5
1800	ESCN	92026	1109-H5
BELLO MAR DR			
1300	ENCT	92024	1147-D1
BELLOTA DR			
16800	SD	92128	1170-B3
BELLOTA PL			
12100	SD	92128	1170-B3
BELLS DR			
-	OCN	92057	1067-B3
BELLVALE AV			
5100	SD	92117	1248-G2
BELLVER CIR			
1200	SDCo	92028	1027-H3
BELLVINE TR			
1100	SDCo	92019	1252-A7
1100	SDCo	92019	1272-A1
1100	SDCo	92020	1272-A1
BELLVISTA DR			
14400	SDCo	92067	1188-E1
BELLWOOD CT			
8800	SDCo	91977	1290-J3
BELLWOOD LN			
-	SDCo	92081	1108-B6
-	VSTA	92081	1108-B6
BELMONT AV			
100	NATC	91950	1290-B6
3800	SD	92116	1269-G3
N BELMONT AV			
100	NATC	91950	1290-B6
100	SD	92114	1290-B6
BELMONT CT			
300	SMCS	92069	1108-G6
BELMONT PL			
1400	CHV	91913	1331-C1
BELMONT TER			
1100	SDCo	92084	1108-C1
BELMONT ESTATES DR			
-	SDCo	92082	1070-J1
BELMONT PARK RD			
1400	OCN	92057	1067-G7
1400	OCN	92057	1087-G1
BELMORE CT			
1900	ELCJ	92020	1251-B2
BELOE			
9200	SDCo	92040	1232-H5
BELOIT AV			
6800	SD	92111	1248-J3
BELSHIRE LN			
11300	SD	92126	1209-D2
BELT ST			
600	SD	92101	1288-J3
2000	SD	92113	1289-C6
2700	SD	92136	1289-E6
BELTAIRE LN			
-	SD	92127	1169-B4
BELVEDERE DR			
4700	SDCo	92036	1156-B5
13900	PWY	92064	1190-F3
BELVEDERE ST			
200	SD	92037	1247-E1
BELVIA LN			
700	CHV	91911	1330-B5
BELVISTA CT			
4600	SD	92130	1188-C6
BELVUE DR			
3700	LMSA	91941	1270-J5
BEN ST			
3500	SD	92111	1249-A3
BENAVENTE PL			
9700	SD	92129	1189-F5
BENAVENTE ST			
9600	SD	92129	1189-F6
BENAVENTE WY			
12600	SD	92129	1189-F6
BENBOW CT			
13400	SD	92129	1189-C4
BENCHLEY RD			
13200	SD	92130	1188-A4
BENCHMARK CT			
-	SDCo	92026	1069-B4
BEND ST			
9800	SNTE	92071	1231-F4
BENDIGO CV			
10700	SD	92126	1209-A4
BENDIGO RD			
7700	SD	92126	1209-A4
BENDING ELBOW DR			
2800	SDCo	92004	(1078-H4 See Page 1058)
BENDITO DR			
12600	SD	92128	1170-C4
BENDIX ST			
4800	SD	92111	1249-C1
BENECIA CT			
1100	CHV	91913	1311-C6
BENEDICT AV			
700	ELCJ	92020	1251-E5
BENET RD			
200	OCN	92054	1086-C4
BENET HILL RD			
-	OCN	92054	1086-C4
BENEVENTE DR			
200	OCN	92057	1086-J4
BENFIELD CT			
4400	SD	92113	1289-J5
BENFOLD DR			
-	SD	92126	1209-D7
BENGAL CT			
5400	SD	92124	1249-H1
BENHURST AV			
4200	SD	92122	1228-F5
BENHURST CT			
6300	SD	92122	1228-F5
BENICIA ST			
1100	SD	92110	1268-F2
BENICIA WY			
100	OCN	92057	1086-H3
BENITO WY			
23900	SDCo	92065	1173-E2
BENJAMIN PL			
1100	ELCJ	92020	1251-E7
BENJAMIN HOLT RD			
6800	SD	92114	1290-E6
BENNETT AV			
100	SMCS	92069	1129-C1
200	SMCS	92069	1109-D6
500	SDCo	92026	1109-D6
800	ESCN	92026	1109-D6
BENNETT CT			
100	SMCS	92078	1129-C1
BENNETT ST			
-	SD	92152	1287-J4
BENNINGTON CT			
3700	CRLB	92010	1107-A4
BENNINGTON ST			
8600	SD	92126	1209-C4
BENNY WY			
800	ELCJ	92019	1251-J7
BENNYE LEE DR			
16100	PWY	92064	1170-D4
BENSON AV			
6100	SD	92114	1290-D4
BENSON PL			
100	OCN	92054	1086-D5
S BENT AV			
100	SMCS	92078	1108-F7
100	SMCS	92078	1128-F1
BENTLEY DR			
3500	SDCo	91977	1271-A5
BENTLEY LN			
3500	SDCo	91977	1271-A5
BENTON CV			
6800	SDCo	91962	1237-D7
BENTON PL			
600	ELCJ	92020	1251-H6
5100	SD	92116	1269-F2
BENTON WY			
4800	LMSA	91941	1270-F2
4800	SD	92115	1270-F2
BENT TRAIL DR			
-	CHV	91914	1311-F2
BENT TREE CT			
14300	PWY	92064	1170-H5
BENT TREE PL			
2200	ESCN	92026	1109-J4
BENT TREE RD			
15200	PWY	92064	1170-G4
BENTWOOD DR			
600	SDCo	92021	1251-G1
BENVIANA DR			
-	CHV	91914	1311-D1
BEREA CT			
-	PWY	92064	1210-C1
BERENDA PL			
1400	ELCJ	92020	1251-C5
BERETTA PL			
-	SD	92154	1350-H2
BERG RD			
39600	SDCo	92028	996-J2
BERGEN ST			
5500	SD	92117	1228-H7
BERGER AV			
3100	SD	92123	1249-B5
BERGMAN ST			
3700	SD	92105	1270-B5
BERINGER LN			
1300	VSTA	92081	1107-H3
BERINO CT			
3900	SD	92122	1228-C4
BERKELEY DR			
7200	LMSA	91941	1270-F4
BERKELEY WY			
700	VSTA	92084	1088-B7
BERKELY AV			
2700	CRLB	92010	1106-J5
2700	CRLB	92010	1107-A5
BERKSHIRE CT			
900	ESCN	92025	1129-J6
1500	SMCS	92069	1108-J3
BERKSHIRE PL			
-	ESCN	92027	1110-E5
BERKVIEW LN			
9000	SDCo	91977	1271-B7
9000	SDCo	91977	1291-A1
BERKWOOD DR			
9000	SDCo	91977	1271-A7
BERLAND WY			
400	CHV	91910	1310-F7
BERLIN ST			
12900	PWY	92064	1190-D5
BERMUDA AV			
4400	SD	92107	1287-J1
4600	SD	92107	1267-H7
BERMUDA CIR			
4300	SD	92107	1287-J1
BERMUDA LN			
-	ESCN	92025	1129-J5
1200	ELCJ	92021	1252-C3
BERMUDA PL			
1200	ELCJ	92021	1252-C3
BERMUDA TR			
1200	ELCJ	92021	1252-C3
1200	SDCo	92021	1252-C3
BERMUDA VW			
-	ELCJ	92021	1252-C2
BERMUDA DUNES PL			
4000	CHV	91902	1310-F3
4400	OCN	92057	1066-G7
BERNABE CT			
14200	SD	92129	1189-H2
BERNABE DR			
10500	SD	92129	1189-G2
BERNABEO CT			
-	SDCo	92082	1070-F6
BERNADETTE LN			
5900	SD	92120	1250-C6
BERNADINE PL			
4200	SD	92115	1270-B4
BERNADOTTE LN			
13900	PWY	92064	1190-G3
BERNARDI ST			
-	IMP	92251	6499-H2
BERNARDINO LN			
3400	SDCo	92084	1088-F7
BERNARDO AV			
900	SDCo	92029	1129-H6
900	SDCo	92029	1149-H1
1100	ESCN	92029	1129-H5
1900	ESCN	92025	1129-H6
W BERNARDO CT			
11500	SD	92127	1169-J2
W BERNARDO DR			
16100	SD	92127	1169-J3
17700	SD	92127	1149-J7
17700	SD	92127	1150-A5
BERNARDO LN			
3000	SDCo	92029	1149-H2
BERNARDO TER			
11800	SD	92128	1170-A2
BERNARDO CENTER CT			
11900	SD	92128	1170-A1
BERNARDO CENTER DR			
-	SDCo	92127	1169-G5
11600	SD	92127	1169-J1
11600	SD	92127	1170-A1
16400	SD	92128	1170-A1
BERNARDO HEIGHTS PKWY			
15700	PWY	92064	1170-A4
15700	SD	92128	1170-A4
BERNARDO LAKES DR			
-	SD	92127	1169-C2
9300	SDCo	92127	1169-C2
BERNARDO MOUNTAIN DR			
3100	ESCN	92029	1149-H2
3100	SDCo	92029	1149-H2
BERNARDO OAKS CT			
12100	SD	92128	1170-B1
BERNARDO OAKS DR			
16300	SD	92128	1170-B1
BERNARDO PLAZA CT			
11700	SD	92128	1170-A3
BERNARDO PLAZA DR			
11900	SD	92128	1170-A3
BERNARDO RIDGE PL			
-	ESCN	92029	1149-G1
BERNARDO TRAILS CT			
18300	SD	92128	1150-C6
BERNARDO TRAILS DR			
18300	SD	92128	1150-C7
BERNARDO TRAILS PL			
17900	SD	92128	1150-C7
BERNARDO VISTA DR			
17300	SD	92128	1170-A2
BERNEY PL			
1700	ESCN	92026	1109-D5
BERNICE DR			
3800	SD	92107	1268-A7
BERNIE DR			
3000	OCN	92056	1087-B7
3000	OCN	92056	1107-B1
BERNIS CT			
3100	SDCo	91977	1271-A6
BERNITA RD			
900	SDCo	92020	1271-H1
BERNITA WY			
1400	SDCo	92020	1271-H1
BERNWOOD PL			
3600	SD	92130	1188-A5
BERRY RD			
11100	SDCo	92082	1069-F2
N BERRY RD			
-	SDCo	92082	1069-G1
BERRY ST			
1900	LMGR	91945	1290-F1
2200	LMGR	91945	1270-F7
BERRY CREEK PL			
1400	CHV	91913	1331-B2
BERRYDALE ST			
1700	ELCJ	92021	1251-G2
1700	SDCo	92021	1251-G2
BERRYESSA CT			
23900	SDCo	92065	1173-E2
BERRYESSA LN			
10600	SDCo	92127	1169-F2
BERRYESSA ST			
5100	OCN	92056	1107-F4
BERRYFIELD CT			
-	SD	92130	1188-A5
BERRYHILL DR			
500	SMCS	92069	1109-B6
BERRYKNOLL ST			
11100	SD	92126	1209-A2
BERRYLAND CT			
2000	LMGR	91945	1290-F1
BERRYMAN CANYON			
-	ENCT	92024	1167-G2
BERRY PARK LN			
-	LMGR	91945	1270-F7
7000	LMGR	91945	1290-F1
BERT CT			
4200	SD	92117	1248-E2
BERT LN			
100	OCN	92054	1086-G2
BERT ACOSTA ST			
10000	ELCJ	92020	1251-D2
BERTHA CT			
4400	SD	92117	1248-E2
BERTHA ST			
4400	SD	92117	1248-E2
BERTING ST			
4400	SD	92115	1270-B4
BERTRO DR			
5800	LMSA	91942	1250-G7
BERVY ST			
1500	SD	92110	1268-E2
BERWICK DR			
4300	SD	92117	1248-J2
BERWICK WOODS			
2100	SDCo	92028	1027-G6
BERWYN RD			
7900	SD	92126	1209-B4
BERYL ST			
700	SD	92109	1247-H5
1600	SD	92109	1248-B4
7300	LMGR	91945	1290-F1
7400	LMGR	91945	1270-G7
BERYL WY			
4800	SD	92109	1248-B4
BERYL COVE PT			
-	SD	92154	1351-A1
BESSEMER ST			
2800	SD	92106	1288-B3
BEST RD			
4600	BRW	92227	431-C1
4600	ImCo	92227	431-C1
5000	ImCo	92227	411-C11
BESTVIEW DR			
700	SDCo	92021	1251-G2
BESTWOOD CT			
6700	SD	92119	1250-E3
BETA CT			
-	SD	92126	1209-E6
BETA DR			
-	SD	92126	1209-E6
BETA ST			
100	NATC	91950	1290-A6
1400	SD	92113	1289-G6
1700	NATC	91950	1289-J6
BETELGEUSE WY			
8700	SD	92126	1209-C1
BETH PL			
2400	LMGR	91945	1270-F7
BETHANY PL			
-	ELCJ	92021	1251-J3
BETHANY ST			
400	SD	92114	1290-C5
BETHUNE CT			
5600	SD	92114	1290-B2
BETHUNE WY			
100	CHV	91911	1330-E4
BETSWORTH LN			
28300	SDCo	92082	1090-B2
BETSWORTH RD			
11200	SDCo	92082	1089-J2
11800	SDCo	92082	1090-A2
BETSY CT			
2500	SD	92110	1248-F7

STREET
Block City ZIP Pg-Grid

BETTS ST
1100 ELCJ 92020 1251-C3
BETTY ST
600 SD 92154 1330-A7
4600 SD 92109 1248-B5
BETTYHILL DR
6900 SD 92117 1248-J2
BETTY JO MCNEECE LP
- ImCo 92243 6559-G5
BETTY LEE WY
13200 PWY 92064 1190-E2
BEVERLY AV
900 IMPB 91932 1349-G2
BEVERLY DR
700 VSTA 92084 1088-B4
4300 LMSA 91941 1270-H3
BEVERLY LN
1500 ELCN 92243 6559-J3
BEVERLY PL
500 SMCS 92078 1128-D1
BEVERLY ST
1000 SD 92114 1290-B2
2300 SDCo 92065 1152-D7
BEVERLY WY
1100 ESCN 92026 1110-A7
BEVERLY GLEN DR
4500 OCN 92056 1087-D5
BEVIS ST
3300 SD 92111 1249-A4
BEVNER CT
5100 SD 92105 1270-A7
BEWICKS CT
- CRLB 92011 1127-B7
BEXLEY RD
20500 SDCo 91935 (1315-A2 See Page 1294)
BEYER BLVD
2300 CHV 91911 1330-C6
2300 SD 92154 1330-C6
2700 SD 92154 1350-D1
3200 SD 92173 1350-E2
E BEYER BLVD
2200 SD 92173 1350-G4
BEYER WY
100 CHV 91911 1330-D5
100 SD 92154 1330-D6
700 SD 92154 1350-D1
BIADA ST
1300 VSTA 92081 1107-H4
BIANCA CT
- IMP 92251 6499-H2
BIANCA ST
5000 SD 92110 1268-F2
BIA RD #10
- SDCo 91906 (1299-D6 See Page 1298)
- SDCo 91906 (1319-D1 See Page 1298)
BIA RD #11
- SDCo 91905 430-C7
- SDCo 91962 430-C7
- SDCo 91962 (1299-D1 See Page 1298)
BIBLER CT
- CHV 91911 1330-H2
BIBLER DR
- SD 92173 1350-E5
BIDDEFORD ST
14500 PWY 92064 1190-H4
BIDDLE CT
6900 SD 92111 1248-J3
BIDDLE ST
- SDCo 92055 1067-A2
3800 SD 92111 1248-J3
BIDWELL CT
13400 SD 92129 1189-C4
BIENAVENTURA DR
- SDCo 92028 998-D7
BIENVENIDA CIR
1800 CRLB 92008 1106-J7
BIENVENIDO LN
1900 ESCN 92026 1109-H5
BIERNACKI CT
- CHV 91911 1330-H2
BIG BEND WY
- OCN 92054 1066-G7
500 OCN 92054 1086-G1
12600 SDCo 92082 1090-C2
BIG BOULDER LN
3400 SDCo 91901 1234-C5
BIG BUCKS TR
- PWY 92064 1151-A6
BIG CANYON LN
- SD 92131 1210-H1
BIG CANYON TER
1400 ENCT 92007 1167-F2
BIG CAT TR
3500 SDCo 91901 1275-B3
BIG CONE CT
- SDCo 92040 1231-G3
BIG CONE DR
- SDCo 92040 1231-G3
BIG DIPPER WY
1600 SD 92173 1350-E2
BIGFORD ST
8600 SDCo 91977 1290-J2
8600 SDCo 91977 1291-A2
BIGGS CT
3000 NATC 91950 1310-D3
BIG HORN CT
600 ELCJ 92019 1251-H6
BIG HORN RD
300 SDCo 92004 1058-J5
700 SDCo 92004 (1059-A5 See Page 1058)
BIGNELL DR
7300 SD 92139 1290-G6
BIG OAK ST
7200 SD 92114 1290-G6
BIG OAK RANCH RD
1000 SDCo 92028 1047-H1
BIG OAKS LN
- SDCo 91905 1300-B4
BIG PINE LN
35000 SDCo 92036 1156-E7
BIG PINE RD
2200 ESCN 92027 1130-E2
2200 SDCo 92027 1130-E2
BIG POTRERO TKTR
- SDCo 91963 1296-H7
- SDCo 91906 (1317-E2 See Page 1296)
- SDCo 91963 (1316-G1 See Page 1296)
- SDCo 91963 (1317-A1 See Page 1296)
2200 SDCo 91906 (1297-F7 See Page 1296)
BIG RED RD
1200 SDCo 91901 1233-H7
1200 SDCo 91901 1253-J1
BIG ROCK RD
8300 SNTE 92071 1250-H1
8500 SNTE 92071 1230-H7
BIG SKY DR
- OCN 92054 1086-D3
BIG SKY RD
- SDCo 92065 1173-A2
BIG SPRINGS WY
15800 SD 92127 1169-J4
BIG SUR ST
4500 OCN 92057 1066-H6
BIG VIEW RD
500 OCN 92057 1067-F4
BIG WAGON RD
2500 SDCo 91901 1254-A2
BIG WHEEL WY
2600 SDCo 91901 1254-A2
BILLIE DR
8700 SNTE 92071 1231-E7
BILLINGS ST
900 ELCJ 92020 1251-G7
BILLMAN ST
3600 SD 92115 1270-D5
BILLOW DR
300 SD 92114 1290-H3
BILLY GN
2000 ESCN 92026 1109-C4
BILLY LN
14600 PWY 92064 1190-E1
BILLY MITCHELL DR
1100 ELCJ 92020 1251-D2
BILOXI ST
2500 SD 92105 1270-B7
BILTEER CT
10000 SNTE 92071 1231-D4
BILTEER DR
9800 SNTE 92071 1231-D4
BILTMORE AV
- ESCN 92027 1130-C1
BILTMORE ST
5000 SD 92117 1228-E7
BIMINI WY
1800 VSTA 92081 1107-G6
BINDAY WY
2200 SD 92154 1330-C6
BING ST
6500 SD 92115 1270-D5
BING CROSBY BLVD
- SD 92127 1169-A3
- SDCo 92067 1148-J7
- SDCo 92067 1168-J2
- SDCo 92127 1148-J7
- SDCo 92127 1149-A7
- SDCo 92127 1168-J2
- SDCo 92127 1169-A1
BINGHAM DR
100 SMCS 92069 1108-F7
BINGHAM RD
9700 SNTE 92071 1231-C4
BINNACLE DR
- CRLB 92011 1127-A7
BINNACLE WY
3500 OCN 92054 1086-E6
BINNEY PL
8000 LMSA 91942 1250-H7
BIOLA AV
2300 SD 92154 1350-B3
BIOLOGICAL GRADE
8700 SD 92093 1227-H3
BIONA DR
4600 SD 92116 1269-H3
BIONA PL
4200 SD 92116 1269-H3
BIOSITE WY
- SD 92121 1208-H6
BIRCH AV
800 ESCN 92027 1130-C3
800 SDCo 92027 1130-C3
BIRCH LN
13000 PWY 92064 1191-A4
BIRCH RD
- CHV 91913 1331-E2
- CHV 91915 1331-F1
- SDCo 92055 1086-A4
BIRCH ST
- SMCS 92078 1129-C2
500 SMCS 92078 1128-C1
1000 SDCo 91977 1291-B2
2400 VSTA 92081 1108-A6
3600 SD 92113 1289-G6
W BIRCH ST
- CALX 92231 6680-E1
BIRCH WY
1200 SDCo 92027 1130-C3
BIRCH BARK LN
3400 SDCo 91902 1310-H2
BIRCH BLUFF AV
10600 SD 92131 1210-C3
BIRCH BLUFF CT
12500 SD 92131 1210-C3
BIRCH BLUFF PL
12500 SD 92131 1210-C3
BIRCH BRIAR LN
1500 SDCo 92027 1130-D3
BIRCHBROOK CT
12600 PWY 92064 1170-D3
BIRCH CANYON PL
- SD 92126 1209-B6
BIRCHCREEK RD
6900 SD 92119 1250-F4
BIRCHCREST BLVD
9100 SNTE 92071 1231-A2
BIRCH GLEN CT
11700 SD 92131 1209-J3
11700 SD 92131 1210-A3
BIRCH HILL PT
- SD 92130 1208-D1
BIRCHLEY
700 OCN 92054 1106-C1
BIRCH TREE LN
13200 PWY 92064 1190-E3
BIRCHVIEW DR
700 ENCT 92024 1167-G1
BIRCHWOOD CIR
4700 CRLB 92008 1106-J6
BIRCHWOOD DR
1700 SMCS 92069 1109-A2
BIRCHWOOD PL
200 SMCS 92069 1108-H5
BIRCHWOOD ST
6300 SD 92120 1250-B5
BIRCHWOOD WY
2400 OCN 92054 1106-F1
BIRD CT
- SMCS 92069 1108-F5
BIRD ST
9200 SNTE 92071 1231-G6
BIRD HAVEN LN
- SDCo 92028 1027-H4
BIRDIE DR
2300 OCN 92056 1106-H1
3500 SDCo 91941 1271-A5
3500 SDCo 91977 1271-A5
3600 SDCo 91941 1270-J5
BIRDIE ST
2300 OCN 92056 1106-J1
BIRD OF PARADISE LN
4500 SDCo 91941 1271-D3
BIRD ROCK AV
100 SD 92037 1247-F4
BIRDSELL LN
17100 SDCo 92036 1156-E7
17100 SDCo 92036 1176-E1
BIRDSELL RD
17100 SDCo 92036 1176-E1
BIRDS NEST LN
- CHV 91915 1331-G1
BIRDSONG DR
32400 SDCo 92026 1049-B7
BIRDSONG PL
1600 SDCo 92021 1252-A2
BIRDS VIEW CT
11100 SD 92126 1208-J2
BIRKDALE PL
5500 SD 92117 1248-H2
BIRKDALE WY
1800 VSTA 92081 1108-A4
5500 SD 92117 1248-H2
BIRMINGHAM DR
100 ENCT 92007 1167-D3
1200 ENCT 92024 1167-F3
7900 SD 92123 1249-B6
BIRMINGHAM WY
7900 SD 92123 1249-B6
BISBY LAKE AV
6400 SD 92119 1250-J4
BISCAY DR
3200 SD 92154 1350-D2
BISCAYNE BAY
5700 SD 92105 1290-B1
BISCAYNE CV
12900 SD 92014 1207-J1
BISCAYNE PL
18500 PWY 92064 1150-G6
BISHOFF CT
8300 SNTE 92071 1230-H6
BISHOP DR
- SMCS 92078 1128-H3
6400 SD 92114 1290-D4
BISHOP ST
- CHV 91911 1330-E4
BISHOPS LN
7100 SD 92037 1247-F1
7300 SD 92037 1227-F7
BISHOPS WY
5400 LMSA 91941 1271-B1
5400 SDCo 91941 1271-B1
BISHOPSGATE RD
100 ENCT 92024 1147-A2
BISON CT
600 ELCJ 92019 1251-H6
BITTERBUSH LN
1200 SDCo 92019 1252-F7
1300 SDCo 92019 1272-F1
BITTERCREEK LN
9100 SD 92129 1189-D3
BITTERN CT
1800 CRLB 92011 1127-D7
BITTERN ST
1200 SD 92114 1290-E2
BITTERROOT CT
1500 ESCN 92026 1109-D6
1500 SMCS 92069 1109-D6
BITTERSWEET ST
900 ESCN 92026 1109-F5
BITTER SWEET HILL
1700 SDCo 92084 1108-C2
BIXBITE PL
- CRLB 92009 1127-G6
BIXEL DR
5100 SD 92115 1270-A1
BJOIN RD
24700 SDCo 92065 1173-G3
BLACKBERRY CT
800 SMCS 92069 1109-A6
BLACKBERRY WY
5400 OCN 92057 1067-D6
BLACK BIRD CIR
1700 CRLB 92011 1127-D6
BLACKBIRD DR
500 VSTA 92083 1087-G4
BLACKBIRD ST
1000 ELCJ 92020 1251-D3
BLACKBIRD WY
200 OCN 92057 1086-J6
BLACKBURN LN
- SD 92127 1169-B4
BLACKBUSH LN
2700 SDCo 92019 1272-F1
BLACK CANYON PL
- SDCo 92065 409-G11
BLACK CANYON RD
1400 SDCo 92065 1153-A2
21000 SDCo 92065 409-H11
23500 SDCo 92070 409-H11
BLACK CANYON WY
- OCN 92057 1086-J2
BLACK COLT LN
- SD 92130 1208-C2
BLACK CORAL CT
4800 SD 92154 1330-J6
BLACK CORAL WY
400 SD 92154 1330-J6
BLACK DUCK WY
4200 OCN 92057 1086-J3
4200 OCN 92057 1087-A3
BLACK EAGLE DR
- SD 92126 1209-D6
BLACKFOOT AV
4200 SD 92117 1248-F6
BLACKFOOT ST
4700 SD 92117 1248-F5
BLACK GOLD RD
9600 SD 92037 1227-H1
BLACK GRANITE DR
- SDCo 92127 1169-F1
BLACK GUM CT
- CHV 91915 1311-J7
BLACKHAWK AV
1800 OCN 92056 1087-D5
BLACKHAWK CIR
700 VSTA 92081 1107-G1
BLACKHAWK GN
1300 ESCN 92029 1129-G6
BLACK HILLS CT
9400 SD 92129 1189-E4
BLACK HILLS LN
- SNTE 92071 1231-D2
BLACK HILLS RD
- ImCo 92243 6560-A6
13400 SD 92129 1189-E4
BLACK HILLS WY
9300 SD 92129 1189-D4
BLACK HORSE DR
- ImCo 92243 6560-A6
- SNTE 92071 1231-H6
BLACKHORSE RW
14000 SD 92130 1188-D2
BLACK LION CT
- SD 92126 1209-D6
BLACK LOCUST CT
- CHV 91915 1311-J7
BLACKMORE CT
2100 SD 92109 1248-A4
BLACK MOUNTAIN RD
- ImCo - 411-L9
- SD 92130 1189-A3
4100 LMSA 91941 1270-J4
4700 SD 92130 1188-D4
9400 SD 92126 1209-E1
11100 SD 92126 1189-D5
11100 SD 92129 1189-D1
15600 SDCo 92127 1169-E5
15900 SD 92127 1169-E5
BLACK MOUNTAIN TKTR
19500 SDCo 92065 409-H10
BLACK MOUNTAIN WY
6400 SD 92130 1188-G4
BLACK OAK LN
- SDCo 92036 1155-F3
BLACK OAK RD
7400 SD 92114 1290-G4
BLACK OAK TR
- SDCo 92060 1052-D2
BLACK OPAL RD
- SDCo 92127 1169-F1
BLACK PINE PL
4600 SD 92130 1188-C5
BLACKPOOL RD
7800 SD 92114 1290-G4
BLACK RAIL CT
- CRLB 92011 1127-C6
BLACK RAIL RD
- CRLB 92011 1127-C4
BLACK RIDGE RD
9700 SDCo 92021 1233-D2
BLACKSHAW LN
400 SD 92173 1350-E3
BLACKSMITH RD
5800 SDCo 91902 1311-B2
BLACKSTILT CT
900 CRLB 92011 1127-B7
BLACKSTONE AV
1400 CHV 91915 1311-J6
BLACKSTONE CT
7600 SD 92114 1290-G3
BLACK SWAN PL
7300 CRLB 92011 1127-C7
BLACKTHORNE AV
400 ELCJ 92020 1251-D6
BLACKTHORNE CT
1600 ELCJ 92020 1251-C7
BLACKTON DR
2400 SD 92105 1270-B7
2400 SD 92105 1290-B1
4100 LMSA 91941 1270-F4
BLACK WALNUT CT
- CHV 91915 1311-H1
BLACK WALNUT DR
- SMCS 92078 1128-C6
BLACKWELL DR
2700 SDCo 92084 1067-H6
BLACKWELL RD
- ImCo 92283 432-D5
4500 OCN 92056 1107-D2
BLACKWOLF DR
- SDCo 91901 1234-E5
BLACKWOOD DR
700 SD 92154 1330-F7
BLACKWOOD RD
- SDCo 91905 430-C7
800 CHV 91910 1310-J7
BLAIN PL
6100 LMSA 91942 1250-J6
BLAINE AV
1500 SD 92103 1269-C5
BLAIR AV
100 CALX 92231 6680-G2
1000 CALX 92231 6620-G7
BLAIR CT
900 SD 92113 1289-H5
BLAIR RD
- ImCo 92233 411-C9
BLAIR WY
9500 SDCo 91941 1271-C2
BLAIRWOOD AV
- CHV 91913 1311-E7
- CHV 91913 1331-E1
BLAIS RD
- ImCo 92259 431-A2
BLAISDELL PL
13700 PWY 92064 1190-F6
BLAKELY DR
3000 SD 92110 1268-E6
BLAKSTAD CT
7100 SD 92126 1208-J4
BLANCHARD RD
100 ELCJ 92020 1251-B5
100 LMSA 91942 1251-B5
BLANCHE AV
- SDCo 91905 1300-C7
BLANCHE ST
3000 SD 92173 1350-F4
BLANCO CT
12800 PWY 92064 1190-D5
BLANCO TER
8500 SDCo 92021 1232-E6
BLANDO CT
100 SD 92173 1350-G2
BLANDO LN
1700 SD 92173 1350-G3
BLANFORD ST
1500 SD 92114 1290-E5
BLANTON CT
11800 SD 92128 1190-A6
BLANTON LN
12200 SD 92128 1190-A6
BLARNEY AV
9600 SDCo 91977 1271-C6
BLAXTON DR
1500 ELCN 92243 6559-J1
BLAZEWOOD PL
16000 SD 92127 1169-J5
BLAZEWOOD WY
16000 SD 92127 1169-J4
BLAZING STAR LN
- SD 92130 1188-E4
BLAZING STAR TR
- IMP 92251 6499-E2
BLENKARNE DR
3000 CRLB 92008 1106-G4
BLERIOT AV
500 SD 92154 1330-E6
BLESSED MOTHER DR
3400 SDCo 92028 1047-J2
BLISS CIR
- OCN 92056 1087-D5
BLIX ST
7300 SD 92111 1249-A4
BLOCH ST
5100 SD 92122 1228-A7
BLOCKTON RD
200 SDCo 92083 1108-A2
BLODGETT RD
1300 ImCo 92250 431-D4
BLOM ST
2300 SD 92109 1248-B5
BLOOMDALE ST
9200 SNTE 92071 1231-G5
BLOOMFIELD AV
- SMCS 92078 1128-H3
BLOOMFIELD RD
7700 SD 92114 1290-G4
BLOOMFIELD ST
- ImCo 92249 6560-C7
BLOSSOM LN
7900 LMGR 91945 1290-H1
8400 SDCo 91977 1290-H1
BLOSSOM WY
- ELCN 92243 6560-A4
200 OCN 92054 1086-F3
8200 LMGR 91945 1290-J1
BLOSSOM FIELD WY
1600 ENCT 92024 1147-G6
BLOSSOM HILL CT
8200 LMGR 91945 1290-J1
BLOSSOM HILL DR
8300 LMGR 91945 1290-J1
BLOSSOM HILL LN
1700 ESCN 92029 1129-G7
BLOSSOM RIDGE WY
- SDCo 92021 1232-H3
BLOSSOM SPRINGS RD
9800 SDCo 92021 1232-G2
BLOSSOM VALLEY LN
15000 SDCo 92021 1233-A2
15000 SDCo 92021 1232-J2
BLOSSOM VALLEY RD
9000 SDCo 92040 1232-G4
9000 SDCo 92021 1232-G4
BLUE ANCHOR CAY RD
- CORD 92118 1329-E2
BLUE ASH CT
100 ENCT 92024 1147-H7
BLUE ASH DR
- LMGR 91945 1270-D7
- SD 92114 1270-D7
BLUEBELL CT
800 CRLB 92011 1127-A5
BLUEBELL LN
1900 SDCo 92028 1028-C6
BLUEBELL ST
- SDCo 92055 1086-A4
BLUEBELL WY
1300 ELCJ 92021 1251-J3
1300 ELCJ 92021 1252-A3
BLUEBERRY CIR
400 OCN 92054 1086-G2
BLUEBERRY HILL
- SDCo 92028 998-G5
1400 SDCo 91901 1234-C6
BLUEBERRY HILL LN
13200 SDCo 92082 1090-D2
BLUE BIRD LN
900 SD 92037 1227-F7
BLUEBIRD LN
- CRLB 92011 1127-D4
200 OCN 92057 1086-H2
BLUEBIRD ST
1300 ELCJ 92020 1251-D3
2100 SD 92114 1290-D1
BLUE BIRD CANYON CT
3700 SDCo 92084 1108-G1
BLUE BIRD CANYON RD
1800 SDCo 92084 1108-F1
BLUE BIRD CANYON TR
900 SDCo 92084 1088-G7
1000 SDCo 92084 1108-F2
BLUEBIRD PARK RD
100 SDCo 92028 1027-F1
BLUEBONNET CT
900 SMCS 92078 1128-G3
BLUEBONNET DR
6400 CRLB 92011 1127-A4
BLUE BONNET PL
1800 ENCT 92024 1147-H6
BLUE BONNETT CT
500 NATC 91950 1290-D6
BLUEBOY LN
8800 SNTE 92071 1231-D7
BLUE CRANE WY
- SDCo 92127 1169-F4
BLUE CRYSTAL TR
15500 PWY 92064 1191-A2
BLUE CRYSTAL TRAILS
15300 PWY 92064 1190-J2
15300 PWY 92064 1191-A2
BLUECUP PL
9300 SDCo 92040 1232-D4
BLUE CYPRESS DR
11200 SD 92131 1210-A1
BLUE DAWN TR
- SD 92130 1188-F4
BLUE DIAMOND CT
12000 SD 92131 1210-B1
BLUE DOLPHIN WY
- CRLB 92011 1127-A7
BLUE FALLS DR
1300 CHV 91910 1311-B6
BLUEFIELD CT
6600 SD 92120 1250-D5
BLUEFIELD PL
6400 SD 92120 1250-D6
BLUE GILL DR
2400 SDCo 91906 (1297-F6 See Page 1296)
BLUEGILL LN
600 OCN 92054 1086-G2
BLUE GRANITE DR
- SDCo 92127 1169-F1
BLUEGRASS LN
- CRLB 92011 1127-D4
BLUEGRASS RD
1000 VSTA 92083 1087-E6
17900 SDCo 92065 1171-G1
BLUEGRASS ST
400 SD 92114 1290-G6
BLUEGRASS WY
- OCN 92057 1067-A3
BLUEHAVEN CT
1800 SD 92154 1350-D3
BLUE HERON AV
1300 ENCT 92024 1147-D2
BLUE HERON DR
300 SMCS 92078 1128-G2
BLUE HERON PL
7200 CRLB 92011 1127-C7
BLUE HORIZON PT
- SD 92154 1350-J2
BLUE JAY CT
- OCN 92054 1086-D4
BLUE JAY DR
2400 SD 92123 1249-B7
3000 SDCo 92036 1155-H3
BLUE JAY LN
1000 SMCS 92078 1128-E2
BLUE JAY PL
7900 SD 92123 1249-B7
BLUE JEAN WY
1200 CHV 91913 1311-E6
BLUE LACE TR
- SD 92130 1188-F3
BLUE LAKE CT
6900 LMGR 91945 1270-E7
BLUE LAKE DR
7500 SD 92119 1250-G6
8600 SD 92119 1251-A6
BLUELAKE DR
1100 OCN 92054 1086-C1
BLUE LILAC LN
1300 SDCo 91901 1233-H6
BLUE MOON WY
3400 SDCo 92082 1070-G1
BLUE OAK CT
3000 SDCo 91978 1271-G7
BLUE OAK PL
- SMCS 92078 1128-B6
BLUE OF THE NIGHT LN
- SDCo 92127 1149-A7
- SDCo 92127 1169-A1
BLUE ORCHID LN
6900 CRLB 92011 1127-E5
BLUE POINT DR
- CRLB 92011 1127-A5
BLUE RIDGE CT
2800 CHV 91914 1311-J3
BLUE RIDGE DR
700 CHV 91914 1311-J3
BLUERIDGE PL
400 ESCN 92026 1109-G4
BLUERIDGE ST
1800 OCN 92056 1087-C5
5500 SD 92139 1310-C2
BLUE RIDGE TR
14000 PWY 92064 1170-G4
BLUE SAGE CT
- IMP 92251 6499-E2
BLUESAGE DR
900 SDCo 92078 1128-B2
BLUE SAGE LN
13800 SDCo 92082 1070-E7
BLUE SAGE RD
14300 PWY 92064 1170-G4
BLUE SAGE WY
400 OCN 92057 1086-J4
1200 CHV 91915 1311-J5
BLUE SHADOWS LN
- SDCo 92127 1168-J1
- SDCo 92127 1169-A1
BLUE SKIES RDG
- SDCo 92127 1149-A7
- SDCo 92127 1169-A1
BLUE SKY DR
- ImCo 92243 6560-A6
1200 ENCT 92007 1167-E1
BLUE SKY LN
- OCN 92056 1107-D2
BLUE SKY RANCH RD
- SDCo 92040 1212-F3
BLUESPRINGS LN
200 OCN 92054 1106-C2
BLUESTONE CT
10100 SDCo 91977 1291-D2
BLUESTONE DR
13300 SDCo 92040 1232-D5
BLUESTONE ST
10500 SDCo 92127 1169-F2
BLUE SUMMIT CT
- SD 92131 1209-G2
BLUET PT
- SD 92131 1210-A1
BLUE WATER LN
- SMCS 92078 1128-F6
BLUEWATER LN
2100 CHV 91913 1311-E4
BLUEWATER RD
800 CRLB 92011 1126-J5
BLUE WATER WY
1900 OCN 92054 1106-F1
BLUEWING CT
12300 PWY 92064 1190-B6
BLUFF CT
3500 CRLB 92010 1107-B3
E BLUFF CV
- SD 92131 1210-J1
BLUFF DR
200 OCN 92054 1085-J7
BLUFF PL
3900 ESCN 92025 1150-C3
5000 SDCo 92020 1271-G1
BLUFF WY
200 OCN 92054 1086-F6
BLUFFCREST LN
800 ENCT 92024 1147-H5
BLUFFDALE PL
2700 SDCo 91977 1271-D7
BLUFF POINT RD
100 SDCo 92028 1027-F1
BLUFF PT CT
1600 CHV 91911 1330-J4
BLUFFS AV
1100 SD 92154 1350-E1
BLUFFSIDE AV
2600 SD 92109 1248-C4
BLUFFSIDE DR
- CHV 91915 1311-J6
- CHV 91915 (1312-A6 See Page 1293)
BLUFFVIEW CT
8200 SDCo 91977 1290-J5
BLUFFVIEW RD
400 SDCo 91977 1290-J5
BLY ST
3400 SD 92115 1270-D6
BLYTHE CT
8100 SD 92126 1209-B2
BLYTHE RD
11000 SD 92126 1209-B2
BOARDWALK
900 SMCS 92078 1128-E1
BOARDWALK CT
- SD 92123 1249-C2
BOARTS RD Rt#-S26
400 ImCo 92281 411-B11
400 ImCo 92281 431-B1
BOAT BASIN RD
400 SDCo 92055 1085-G4
BOB LN
- OCN 92054 1086-G3
BOB ST
3900 SD 92110 1268-C5
5900 LMSA 91942 1250-H6
BOBBIE LN
4200 SDCo 91941 1271-G3
BOBCAT GN
2400 ESCN 92029 1129-E6
BOB CAT LN
1200 SDCo 91901 1234-G5
BOB CAT TR
27100 SDCo 92070 409-H9
BOBHIRD DR
6900 SD 92119 1250-J3
E BOBIER DR
100 VSTA 92084 1087-H3
100 VSTA 92084 1088-A4
W BOBIER DR
100 VSTA 92083 1087-F3
500 OCN 92056 1087-F3
BOBOLINK DR
1100 VSTA 92083 1087-G4
BOBOLINK WY
7600 SD 92123 1249-A7
BOB PLETCHER WY
- CHV 91913 1331-E2
BOBRITT LN
31500 SDCo 92003 1068-E1
BOBRITT RD
31900 SDCo 92003 1068-E1
31900 SDCo 92003 1048-E7
BOBWHITE LN
1500 ELCJ 92020 1251-D2
BOB WILSON DR
2100 SD 92134 1289-C1
BOCA ST
2200 CRLB 92009 1147-F2
BOCA DEL TULE
1700 SD 92173 1350-E2
BOCAGE PT
17500 SD 92128 1170-A1
BOCA RATON DR
1200 CHV 91915 1311-G6
BOCA RATON LN
17200 PWY 92064 1170-F1
17200 PWY 92064 1170-F2
BOCA RATON ST
1200 CHV 91915 1311-G6
2600 SD 92014 1187-H7
BOCAW PL
5100 SD 92115 1270-E1
BODEGA CT
12400 SD 92128 1150-B7
BODEGA PL
12400 SD 92128 1150-B7
BODEGA RD
12400 SD 92128 1150-C7
BODEGA WY
1300 VSTA 92081 1107-H4
12400 SD 92128 1170-B1
BODEGA BAY DR
1200 CHV 91915 1311-G6
BODEGA BAY WY
4200 OCN 92054 1066-E6
BODIE CT
13600 SD 92129 1189-C3
BOEING ST
- SD 92154 1351-D2
BOGATA CIR
8900 SD 92126 1209-D3
BOGOSO LN
3900 SDCo 91977 1271-E4
BOGOTA
- SDCo 92003 1067-J2
BOILING SPRINGS RD
- SDCo 91948 1218-F6
BOISE AV
4700 SD 92117 1248-F1
BOLERO DR
- CHV 91910 1311-B7
12000 SD 92128 1170-A4
BOLERO LN
2100 SDCo 92084 1108-D3
BOLERO ST
7300 CRLB 92009 1127-H7
BOLERORIDGE PL
100 ESCN 92026 1109-G4
BOLEX WY
- SMCS 92078 1128-J3
BOLEY RD
2100 ImCo 92251 430-L4
BOLEY FIELD CT
- IMP 92251 6499-C1
BOLIN ST
10100 SD 92126 1208-J5
BOLINAS ST
2200 SD 92107 1268-A6
BOLINAS BAY CT
1200 CHV 91913 1311-C7
BOLIVAR DR
1900 SDCo 92004 1058-H7
BOLIVAR ST
3600 OCN 92056 1107-B3
5500 SD 92139 1310-C1
BOLIVIA LN
3700 OCN 92056 1107-B1
BOLLENBACHER ST
600 SD 92114 1290-B3
BOLO PL
7700 CRLB 92009 1147-G2
BOLOTIN LN
100 SMCS 92078 1128-H1
BOLSA CHICA GN
2000 ESCN 92026 1109-E5
BOLSERIA LN
9500 SD 92129 1189-F7
9500 SD 92129 1209-F1
BOLT ST
- SD 92152 1288-A4
BOLTON HALL RD
300 SD 92173 1350-G4
BOMAR DR
4400 SDCo 91941 1271-E3
BON CT
3800 SDCo 91902 1310-J2
BONAIR PL
500 SD 92037 1247-F1
BONAIR RD
1300 VSTA 92084 1088-A4
BONAIR ST
500 SD 92037 1247-E1
BONAIR WY
500 SD 92037 1247-E1
BONANZA AV
4100 SD 92117 1248-E6
BOND AV
9300 SDCo 92021 1232-H5
BOND CT
14400 SDCo 92021 1232-G4
BOND ST
4400 SD 92109 1248-C5
BONDS CORNER RD
- HOLT 92250 431-E5
900 ImCo 92250 431-E5
BONESTEELE RD Rt#-S33
700 ImCo 92250 431-F7
BONILLO DR
4100 SD 92115 1270-D4
BONITA DR
- SMCS 92078 1128-E2
700 ENCT 92024 1167-E7
700 VSTA 92083 1087-E6
800 ENCT 92024 1167-E1

SAN DIEGO CO.

STREET
Block City ZIP Pg-Grid

BONITA DR
4100 OCN 92056 1107-C2
5200 SD 92114 1290-B6
BONITA LN
1700 CRLB 92008 1106-F4
BONITA PL
100 SDCo 92021 1252-H4
7200 LMSA 91941 1270-F3
BONITA RD Rt#-S17
- CHV 91910 1310-D5
2800 SDCo 91910 1310-E4
3000 SDCo 91902 1310-J1
3600 CHV 91902 1310-H3
E BONITA RD
- CHV 91910 1310-C5
W BONITA RD
- CHV 91910 1310-C5
BONITA ST
2000 LMGR 91945 1290-F1
2200 LMGR 91945 1270-F7
N BONITA ST
4100 SDCo 91977 1271-D5
S BONITA ST
3000 SDCo 91977 1271-D5
BONITA WY
1100 SDCo 92019 1251-J7
BONITA BLUFFS CT
8500 SDCo 91977 1290-J5
BONITA CANYON DR
200 CHV 91902 1311-A3
BONITA CANYON RD
3500 SDCo 91902 1310-F3
BONITA CHRISTIAN CENTER DR
- SDCo 91902 1310-H3
BONITA FARMS CT
- SDCo 91902 1311-A1
BONITA GLEN DR
200 CHV 91910 1310-D5
200 SDCo 91910 1310-D5
BONITA GLEN TER
3600 SDCo 91902 1310-J2
BONITA HEIGHTS LN
3300 NATC 91950 1310-E3
3300 SDCo 91950 1310-E3
BONITA LADERA WY
2100 SDCo 92019 1252-D7
BONITA MEADOWS LN
6000 SDCo 91902 1311-B1
BONITA MESA RD
2900 SDCo 91902 1310-D4
BONITA RANCH CT
- SDCo 91902 1311-A1
BONITA VALLE
400 SDCo 92028 1047-F4
BONITA VALLEY LN
- SDCo 91902 1310-D4
BONITA VERDE DR
3600 CHV 91902 1310-G3
BONITA VIEW DR
3600 SDCo 91902 1310-J2
BONITA VISTA
13000 PWY 92064 1190-D5
BONITA VISTA DR
2500 SDCo 92036 1136-D7
BONITA VISTA WY
14700 SDCo 91935 1273-A6
BONITA WOODS DR
3000 SDCo 91902 1290-H7
3000 SDCo 91902 1310-H1
BONITO AV
300 IMPB 91932 1329-F7
BONJON LN
10800 SD 92131 1210-A2
BONNETT LN
- SDCo 91901 1234-A4
BONNEYVILLE DR
1700 SDCo 91977 1291-B2
BONNIE CT
4700 SD 92116 1269-G3
BONNIE LN
10300 SDCo 91941 1271-E1
BONNIE BLUFF CIR
1300 ENCT 92024 1147-D2
BONNIE BLUFF CT
1500 ENCT 92024 1147-D2
BONNIE BRAE PL
1000 VSTA 92084 1087-J6
1000 VSTA 92084 1088-A6
BONNIE JEAN LN
8700 SDCo 91977 1271-A7
8700 SDCo 91977 1291-A1
BONNIE JEAN PL
8800 SDCo 91977 1291-A1
BONNIE LYNN WY
9500 SDCo 91941 1271-C3
BONNIE VIEW DR
6400 SD 92119 1250-E6
BONNIE VISTA DR
9800 SDCo 91941 1271-D4
BONNIE VISTA PL
9800 SDCo 91941 1271-D4
BONSALL ST
500 SD 92114 1290-G3
BONUS DR
1800 SD 92110 1268-F2
BON VUE DR
9800 SDCo 92021 1233-B2
BOOKHAM CT
7400 SD 92111 1269-A1
BOOMER CT
13200 SD 92129 1189-C4
BOOMVANG CT
300 OCN 92054 1086-E5
BOONE DR
- SD 92134 1289-C2
BOONE RD
- ImCo 92243 6559-A2
BOONE ST
3800 SD 92117 1248-E4
BOON LAKE AV
6500 SD 92119 1250-H5
BOORTZ LN
16200 SDCo 92065 1172-A3
BOOT WY
5600 OCN 92057 1067-E6
BOOTES ST
11000 SD 92126 1209-D1
BOOTHBAY PL
8500 SD 92129 1189-C5
BOOTH HILL DR
10800 SD 92108 1249-G7
BOQUITA DR
13600 SD 92014 1187-H6
BORANA ST
1500 SD 92111 1268-H2
BORDEAUX AV
2700 SD 92037 1227-J3
BORDEAUX TER
1900 CHV 91913 1311-D3
BORDELON CT
3700 SD 92124 1249-G3
BORDELON ST
10000 SD 92124 1249-G3

BORDEN CIR
400 SMCS 92069 1109-A6
BORDEN RD
200 SMCS 92069 1108-J6
500 SMCS 92069 1109-A6
1000 ESCN 92026 1129-G1
1200 ESCN 92026 1109-F6
W BORDEN RD
100 SMCS 92069 1108-E5
BORDER AV
100 DLMR 92014 1187-F2
BORDER VILLAGE RD
4500 SD 92173 1350-G4
BOREALIS RD
8300 SD 92126 1209-C2
BOREGO ST
7700 SD 92114 1290-G3
BOREN ST
3600 SD 92115 1270-D5
BORICA CT
1500 SDCo 92004 (1099-E2 See Page 1098)
BORLA PL
7300 CRLB 92009 1128-A7
7300 CRLB 92009 1148-A1
BORMAC PL
1100 SDCo 92084 1108-C1
BORNE CT
11800 SD 92129 1189-E7
BORNER ST
4500 SD 92102 1289-J4
BORRA CT
4200 OCN 92056 1087-C6
4200 VSTA 92083 1087-C6
BORRA PL
900 ESCN 92029 1129-E4
BORREGO CT
200 OCN 92057 1086-J4
BORREGO AIR RANCH RD
- SDCo 92004 (1099-J3 See Page 1098)
2600 SDCo 92004 1100-A3
BORREGO HILLS RD
2000 SDCo 92004 (1099-F5 See Page 1098)
BORREGO SALTON SEAWAY
- SDCo 92004 (1059-J3 See Page 1058)
BORREGO SALTON SEAWAY Rt#-S22
- ImCo 92004 410-F7
- ImCo 92259 410-F7
- ImCo 92274 410-F7
- SDCo 92004 410-D7
- SDCo 92004 (1059-J4 See Page 1058)
BORREGO SPRINGS RD
- SDCo 92004 (1120-F1 See Page 1100)
1200 SDCo 92004 1058-J4
1300 CHV 91915 1311-H6
1900 SDCo 92004 (1078-J1 See Page 1058)
4500 SDCo 92004 (1099-G2 See Page 1098)
5500 SDCo 92004 1100-A4
BORREGO SPRINGS RD Rt#-S3
2500 SDCo 92004 (1078-J3 See Page 1058)
3500 SDCo 92004 (1079-A7 See Page 1058)
3500 SDCo 92004 (1099-A1 See Page 1098)
BORREGO VALLEY RD
3200 SDCo 92004 (1059-C2 See Page 1058)
3200 SDCo 92004 (1079-C4 See Page 1058)
3300 SDCo 92004 (1099-D1 See Page 1098)
BORRESON ST
3400 SD 92117 1248-E5
BORROMEO CT
- OCN 92057 1086-G6
BORZOI WY
8100 SD 92129 1189-B7
BOSAL CT
18200 SDCo 92082 1091-E4
BOSCOVICH RD
- ImCo 92283 432-D5
BOSNA PL
2200 SDCo 92084 1108-C3
BOSQUE DR
10300 SDCo 92040 1231-F3
BOSSTICK BLVD
100 SMCS 92069 1108-D5
BOSTON AV
- SD 92173 1350-G5
2600 SD 92113 1289-D6
BOSTON CT
- LMSA 91941 1270-G5
BOSTONIA ST
1100 ELCJ 92021 1251-J3
BOSWELL CT
2300 CHV 91914 1311-F4
BOSWELL RD
2300 CHV 91914 1311-F3
BOSWORTH CT
500 ELCJ 92019 1251-J6
BOSWORTH ST
1200 ELCJ 92019 1251-J6
1300 ELCJ 92019 1252-A6
BOTANY BAY CT
2100 SD 92105 1290-C1
BOTE CT
9600 SDCo 91977 1291-C4
BOTELLA PL
2300 CRLB 92009 1147-G1
BOTERO DR
17000 SD 92127 1169-J2
BOTHE AV
5000 SD 92122 1228-B7
BOTTLEBRUSH CT
700 OCN 92054 1086-F1
BOTTLEBRUSH PL
2100 ENCT 92024 1147-J7
BOTTLEBRUSH WY
200 SDCo 92028 1028-B2
1200 CRLB 92011 1127-A5
BOTTLE TREE LN
- ENCT 92024 1147-A3
BOUCHER HEIGHTS RD
- SDCo 92082 1071-D5
BOUCHER LOOKOUT RD
- SDCo 92060 1031-H7
- SDCo 92060 1051-J1
- SDCo 92060 1052-A1
BOUGAINVILLE RD
3000 CORD 92155 1309-B2
6300 SD 92139 1290-E7

BOUGAINVILLEA TR
- IMP 92251 6499-D3
BOUGHER RD
200 SMCS 92069 1109-B7
BOULDER DR
8500 LMSA 91941 1270-J2
BOULDER PASS
11100 SDCo 92026 1089-G4
BOULDER PL
- OCN 92057 1067-A4
4700 LMSA 91941 1270-J3
8400 SD 92119 1250-J4
BOULDER CREEK RD
1500 OCN 92056 1087-D4
3000 SDCo 92036 1155-G5
4700 SDCo 92036 1175-G3
10000 SDCo 91916 429-K4
10000 SDCo 91916 (1195-G4 See Page 1175)
10000 SDCo 91916 1235-H1
10000 SDCo 92036 (1195-C1 See Page 1175)
BOULDER CREEK ST
2200 CHV 91915 1311-G6
BOULDERIDGE DR
- SMCS 92078 1128-A5
BOULDERIDGE PL
2300 SDCo 91977 1271-H7
BOULDER KNOLLS DR
10000 SDCo 92026 1089-E2
BOULDER LAKE AV
6200 SD 92119 1250-H4
BOULDER LEGEND LN
2400 SDCo 92026 1109-J3
BOULDER MOUNTAIN RD
15600 PWY 92064 1170-E6
BOULDER OAKS CIR
- SDCo 91901 1234-C7
BOULDER OAKS DR
16900 SDCo 92065 1171-D2
BOULDER OAKS LN
2400 SDCo 91901 1234-B7
BOULDER PASS RD
- SDCo 91901 1254-A1
BOULDER PT DR
12200 PWY 92064 1190-B6
BOULDER RIDGE CT
- SD 92131 1210-G1
BOULDER RIDGE LN
15600 PWY 92064 1170-E5
BOULDERS CT
- SDCo 91901 1234-A6
BOULDERS LN
- SDCo 91901 1234-A6
BOULDERS RD
- SDCo 91901 1234-A6
BOULDER VIEW DR
12100 PWY 92064 1190-C6
BOULDERVIEW DR
- OCN 92057 1067-B3
BOULEVARD AV
700 IMPB 91932 1329-G6
BOULEVARD DR
6900 LMSA 91941 1270-E4
6900 SD 92115 1270-E4
BOULEVARD PL
1100 ELCJ 92020 1251-D7
7800 SD 92037 1227-G6
BOULTON AV
11600 SD 92128 1190-A2
BOUNDARY AV
1700 SD 92154 1329-H6
1700 SD 92154 1330-A6
1900 SDCo 92065 1172-D2
BOUNDARY RD
400 IMPB 91932 1349-G3
BOUNDARY ST
400 SD 92113 1289-H5
1900 SD 92104 1289-F1
2500 SD 92104 1269-E5
4300 SD 92116 1269-E3
N BOUNDARY ST
600 SD 92102 1289-G3
W BOUNDARY TKTR
4800 SDCo 91935 1254-B7
18100 SDCo 91935 1274-D2
BOUNDARY CREEK RD
44100 SDCo 91934 (1321-F5 See Page 1300)
S BOUNDARY FIRE RD
- SDCo 91916 1216-C3
BOUNTY CT
6400 SD 92120 1250-B6
BOUNTY ST
5600 SD 92120 1250-B6
BOUNTY WY
14200 PWY 92064 1170-G5
BOUQUET DR
100 SMCS 92069 1108-H6
BOUQUET CANYON RD
1700 CHV 91913 1311-D6
BOURBON CT
9900 SD 92131 1209-H5
BOURBON RD
1200 ESCN 92026 1109-F6
BOURGEOIS WY
14200 SD 92129 1189-D2
BOURKE PL
1700 ELCJ 92020 1252-B2
BOUSSACK LN
3500 OCN 92057 1086-F5
BOVET WY
7400 SD 92122 1228-G4
BOWDEN AV
5100 SD 92117 1248-G2
BOWDITCH PL
2800 SD 92104 1269-F7
BOWDOIN RD
14400 PWY 92064 1190-H4
BOWEN RD
8300 LMGR 91945 1270-J7
BOWER LN
8900 SDCo 92040 1232-C6
BOWIE ST
300 SD 92114 1290-H4
BOWKER RD
800 ImCo 92249 431-D7
1600 ImCo 92243 6560-J2
1700 ImCo 92243 6500-J5
BOWL CREEK RD
15800 PWY 92064 1170-E5
BOWLING GREEN DR
8800 LMSA 91941 1271-A4
BOWRON RD
12800 PWY 92064 1190-E5
BOWSPRIT DR
3500 OCN 92054 1086-F6
BOWSPRIT WY
- CRLB 92011 1127-A4
BOW WILLOW TRAIL WY
1100 CHV 91915 1311-H5
BOX CANYON RD
- SDCo 92028 1027-G1
5800 SD 92037 1247-G3

BOX ELDER CT
- CHV 91915 1311-H1
BOX ELDER PL
11400 SD 92127 1169-J5
BOX ELDER WY
11500 SD 92127 1169-J5
BOXFORD DR
6800 SD 92117 1248-J2
BOX S DR
3300 SDCo 92004 (1078-J6 See Page 1058)
BOXTHORN WY
- CRLB 92011 1127-B6
BOXWOOD CT
- SMCS 92078 1128-D6
900 CRLB 92011 1127-A5
12700 PWY 92064 1170-C7
BOXWOOD DR
2500 SDCo 92019 1252-E7
2600 SDCo 92019 1272-F1
4600 SD 92117 1248-G1
BOXWOOD GN
500 ESCN 92027 1110-C7
BOXWOOD ST
- SDCo 92055 1086-B3
BOXWOOD WY
- OCN 92054 1106-E2
BOYCE LN
3300 SD 92105 1270-A6
BOYD AV
3200 SD 92111 1248-H4
BOYD RD
- ImCo 92227 431-D3
- ImCo 92250 431-D3
BOYINGTON PL
2400 ELCJ 92020 1251-B3
BOYINGTON RD
- SD 92145 1229-E1
BOYLE AV
600 ESCN 92027 1130-B2
1100 SDCo 92027 1130-C2
BOYLE PL
1700 ESCN 92027 1130-D2
BOYLE RD
- ImCo 92233 411-A10
BOYLSTON ST
4500 SD 92102 1289-J3
BOYNE ST
3400 SDCo 91977 1271-C6
BOYSENBERRY WY
500 OCN 92057 1067-D7
BOZANICH CIR
600 VSTA 92084 1087-J7
BRABHAM ST
1700 SDCo 92019 1272-A4
1700 SDCo 92019 1271-J5
BRACERO PL
800 ESCN 92025 1129-J6
BRACERO RD
700 ENCT 92024 1147-E7
800 ENCT 92024 1167-E1
BRACKEN FERN CV
11400 SD 92131 1209-J2
11400 SD 92131 1210-A2
BRACS DR
8500 SNTE 92071 1231-D7
BRADBERRY CT
7000 LMGR 91945 1290-E1
BRADDOCK PL
8100 SD 92114 1290-H2
BRADDOCK ST
1200 SD 92114 1290-H2
1400 LMGR 91945 1290-H2
BRADDON WY
1600 SDCo 92021 1251-J2
BRADENHALL RW
6000 SD 92037 1248-A1
BRADFORD RD
600 SDCo 92019 1252-C6
BRADFORD ST
6000 SD 92115 1270-D3
BRADLEY AV
100 SDCo 92020 1251-G2
100 SDCo 92021 1251-G2
800 ELCJ 92021 1251-G2
W BRADLEY AV
100 SDCo 92020 1251-E2
100 ELCJ 92020 1251-E2
BRADLEY CT
- SDCo 92021 1251-H2
BRADLEY PL
1400 CHV 91911 1330-J3
BRADLEY ST
2400 OCN 92056 1087-C6
BRADMAN DR
3200 SD 92110 1268-E6
BRADRURY DR
- CHV 91913 1331-E1
BRADSHAW CT
4800 SD 92130 1188-D6
BRADSHAW RD
- ELCN 92243 6499-E4
BRADY AV
8700 SDCo 91977 1290-J4
BRADY CIR
- CRLB 92008 1106-G5
BRADY CT
600 SDCo 91977 1290-J4
BRAEBURN RD
4400 SD 92116 1269-H2
BRAE MAR CT
- ENCT 92024 1147-E5
BRAEMAR LN
900 SD 92109 1247-H7
BRAEMAR TER
- SDCo 92028 1027-G6
BRAESWOOD TER
13600 SDCo 92021 1232-E7
BRAGG ST
5300 SD 92122 1228-B7
BRAHMS RD
1600 ENCT 92007 1167-D2
BRAIDWOOD ST
2000 ELCJ 92020 1251-B1
BRAISTED RD
1700 SD 92101 1289-C2
BRALORNE CT
11200 SD 92126 1209-C1
BRALORNE WY
8700 SD 92126 1209-C1
BRAM AV
4700 SDCo 91902 1310-H2
BRAMBLE RD
9200 LMSA 91942 1251-B7
BRAMBLE WY
10600 SD 92126 1209-E3
BRAMBLEWOOD CT
1700 CHV 91913 1311-D6
BRAMBLEWOOD ST
1700 CHV 91913 1311-D7
BRAMPTON ST
8100 SDCo 91977 1290-H2
BRAMSON PL
3200 SD 92104 1269-F4

BRANCH CT
3600 OCN 92054 1086-F1
BRANCO WY
11200 SD 92126 1209-B2
BRAND CREST
3700 ENCT 92024 1167-H2
BRANDEE WY
- SDCo 92028 1027-G2
BRANDEIS CT
6000 SD 92114 1290-C5
BRANDEIS DR
2800 OCN 92056 1087-A7
BRANDENBURG
900 CALX 92231 6680-E1
BRANDENBURG LN
100 SDCo 92028 1027-G2
BRANDING IRON CIR
1200 VSTA 92081 1107-F2
BRANDING IRON DR
- IMP 92251 6439-F3
BRAND IRON ST
15700 SDCo 92065 1172-A4
BRANDO DR
2800 SD 92154 1350-D3
BRANDON CIR
2900 CRLB 92010 1107-B4
N BRANDON RD
100 SDCo 92028 1027-G2
S BRANDON RD
100 SDCo 92028 1027-G2
BRANDT RD
- ImCo 92233 411-B10
BRANDYWINE AV
1400 CHV 91911 1330-H3
BRANDYWINE ST
3100 SD 92117 1248-D5
3600 OCN 92057 1086-G5
BRANDYWOOD ST
100 SD 92114 1290-E4
BRANFORD RD
10000 SD 92129 1189-F3
BRANICOLE LN
12100 SD 92129 1189-F7
BRANMAN DR
- SD 92102 1289-G4
BRANNICK PL
2800 SD 92122 1228-B5
BRANT ST
300 SD 92103 1269-A6
2100 SD 92101 1289-A1
3800 SD 92103 1268-J5
BRANTA AV
1400 CRLB 92011 1127-C7
BRANT CANYON LN
1800 SDCo 92028 1027-J3
BRANTING ST
6100 SD 92122 1228-C5
BRANTNER LN
15900 SDCo 92065 1172-A4
BRASILIA PL
- SDCo 92003 1067-J2
BRASS LN
100 VSTA 92083 1087-F7
BRASS WY
900 ENCT 92024 1167-E1
BRASSICA ST
12200 SD 92129 1189-B7
BRASS LANTERN RD
700 SMCS 92069 1109-A5
BRASSWOOD RW
6300 SD 92037 1248-A1
BRATTON VALLEY RD
2600 SDCo 91935 1294-D3
BRAUER PT
500 SDCo 91901 1234-E4
BRAUN AV
300 SD 92114 1290-J3
BRAVA PL
100 ESCN 92026 1109-H5
BRAVA ST
7400 CRLB 92009 1147-J1
BRAVADO ST
2000 VSTA 92081 1107-G5
BRAVATA CT
18800 SD 92128 1150-C5
BRAVERMAN DR
10400 SNTE 92071 1231-E4
BRAVO CT
5500 SD 92124 1229-G7
BRAVO DR
- CALX 92231 6620-H7
BRAWLEY AV
- SDCo 91934 (1321-G5 See Page 1300)
- ImCo 92274 410-G5
BRAXTON SQ
12100 SD 92128 1190-B1
BRAY AV
9500 SDCo 91977 1271-C6
BRAYTON WY
1400 SDCo 92020 1272-A2
BRAZOS ST
600 SDCo 92065 1152-F5
BREAKERS WY
- SD 92154 1350-J1
BREAKWATER PT
- SD 92154 1330-J7
BREAKWATER RD
100 CRLB 92011 1126-H6
BREAKWATER WY
100 OCN 92054 1085-J7
BRECKENRIDGE DR
- SD 92131 1209-G2
BRECKENRIDGE WY
- SD 92131 1209-G2
BREEZE ST
1300 OCN 92054 1086-A5
BREEZE HILL RD
700 VSTA 92081 1107-F1
900 VSTA 92081 1087-F7
BREEZE VILLA LN
700 VSTA 92081 1107-F1
BREEZE VILLA PL
1000 VSTA 92081 1107-F1
BREEZEWAY PL
14200 SD 92128 1190-A2
BREEZEWOOD DR
1000 CHV 91913 1311-D6
BREEZY WY
200 SMCS 92078 1129-A1
BRELCO RD
- SNTE 92071 1251-A1
BREMEN WY
800 SDCo 91901 1253-G2
BREMERTON PL
3100 SD 92037 1228-A4
BREMS ST
3700 SD 92115 1270-D5
BRENDA WY
- SDCo 92082 1071-A5
BRENGLE WY
1500 VSTA 92084 1088-B6
BRENNA CT
400 ENCT 92024 1147-G6

BRENNA HILL PL
- ESCN 92025 1129-G3
BRENNAN ST
8100 SD 92114 1290-H2
BRENNER WY
1600 SD 92114 1290-D6
BRENNER SPRINGS WY
11300 SD 92126 1208-J2
BRENT LN
100 VSTA 92084 1087-H5
BRENTFORD AV
8700 SD 92126 1209-D3
BRENTWOOD CT
2800 CRLB 92008 1106-F3
BRENTWOOD ST
7400 SD 92111 1249-A4
BRESA DE LOMA DR
21300 SDCo 92029 1129-B5
BRESSI RANCH WY
- CRLB 92009 1127-G3
BRETON WY
5700 SD 92120 1250-C7
BRETT PL
100 ESCN 92027 1110-F6
BRETT HARTE DR
13500 SDCo 92040 1232-D3
BRETTON WOOD CT
5500 SD 92130 1208-E1
BREWER RD
500 IMP 92251 6439-D7
500 ImCo 92251 6439-D7
BREWLEY LN
1000 VSTA 92081 1107-J4
1000 VSTA 92081 1108-E2
BREWSTER CT
11900 SD 92128 1190-A2
BREWSTER BAY DR
1200 CHV 91911 1330-H1
BREZAR ST
- CHV 91913 1331-F2
BRIAN PL
- SNTE 92071 1231-A7
- SNTE 92071 1251-A1
1500 ESCN 92025 1129-J5
BRIAN WY
9400 SDCo 92021 1232-H4
BRIANA CT
4700 SDCo 92028 1047-F6
BRIAND AV
2900 SD 92122 1228-C5
BRIAN PARK LN
13300 PWY 92064 1190-E1
BRIANT ST
900 SMCS 92069 1109-C5
BRIAR CT
- SD 92123 1249-F5
BRIAR GN
8400 SDCo 92021 1232-E7
8400 SDCo 92021 1252-E1
BRIARCLIFF DR
11000 SD 92131 1209-H4
BRIARCLIFF WY
10400 SD 92131 1209-H4
BRIARCREST PL
- SD 92130 1188-E6
BRIARDALE WY
12200 SD 92128 1190-A6
E BRIARFIELD DR
1000 SD 92109 1247-J7
W BRIARFIELD DR
1000 SD 92109 1247-J7
BRIARGATE PL
1900 ESCN 92029 1129-G7
BRIAR HOLLOW LN
800 SDCo 92021 1252-G1
BRIAR KNOLL WY
- SD 92128 1189-J6
BRIARLAKE WOODS DR
- SD 92130 1208-E2
BRIARLEAF WY
11900 SD 92128 1190-B7
BRIARPOINT PL
- SD 92154 1330-H7
BRIAR RIDGE RD
4600 OCN 92056 1087-D3
BRIARWAY CT
1000 VSTA 92083 1087-G5
BRIARWOOD CT
2400 SDCo 92025 1130-D6
BRIARWOOD DR
6800 CRLB 92011 1127-A5
BRIARWOOD PL
900 OCN 92056 1087-D2
2300 ESCN 92026 1109-J3
12700 PWY 92064 1170-C7
BRIARWOOD RD
400 SD 92114 1290-G5
500 SD 92139 1290-G5
600 SDCo 92139 1290-H7
1300 SDCo 91902 1290-H7
2900 SDCo 91902 1310-H1
BRICKELLIA ST
12100 SD 92129 1189-C6
BRICKFIELD LN
- SD 92130 1208-D2
BRICKLANE RD
900 SDCo 92065 1172-F1
BRIDANNELA TR
8700 SDCo 92040 1232-B6
BRIDENSTINE RD
2300 ImCo 92250 431-E4
BRIDGECREST LN
12400 SD 92128 1190-A6
BRIDGEHAMPTON PL
1700 SDCo 92019 1272-B4
BRIDGEHAMPTON ST
1100 SMCS 92078 1128-B3
BRIDGEPORT
2000 CHV 91913 1311-E4
BRIDGEPORT CT
- SMCS 92078 1128-F3
BRIDGEPORT LN
3500 CRLB 92010 1107-A3
N BRIDGEPORT ST
1000 ESCN 92027 1110-A6
BRIDGET CT
10200 SD 92124 1249-G4
BRIDGETOWN BEND
1700 CORD 92118 1329-E2
BRIDGEVIEW DR
1500 SD 92105 1289-G2
BRIDGEWOOD WY
11700 SD 92128 1190-A6
BRIDLE PTH
9300 SNTE 92071 1231-E5
BRIDLE RUN
8800 SDCo 91901 1233-E6
BRIDLE CREEK LN
3100 SDCo 92069 1088-G5
BRIDLE PATH LN
11400 SDCo 92040 1211-J6
BRIDLE PATH WY
1000 OCN 92057 1067-E7

BRIDLE RUN CT
200 SDCo 91901 1233-E6
BRIDLE RUN LN
300 SDCo 91901 1233-E6
BRIDLE RUN PL
300 SDCo 91901 1233-E6
BRIDLE RUN TER
200 SDCo 91901 1233-E6
BRIDLE RUN VW
200 SDCo 91901 1233-E6
BRIDLESPUR
14900 PWY 92064 1190-J4
BRIDLEVALE RD
1700 CHV 91913 1311-D6
BRIDLEWOOD LN
- SDCo 92082 1090-D6
BRIDLEWOOD RD
- SDCo 92028 1048-A4
16400 PWY 92064 1170-G3
BRIDON RD
9800 SDCo 92021 1233-E2
BRIDOON TER
3800 ENCT 92024 1148-C2
BRIENWOOD DR
28800 SDCo 92026 1089-A1
BRIER RD
9100 LMSA 91942 1251-B7
BRIERCREST DR
9200 LMSA 91942 1251-B7
BRIETTE PL
- SDCo 92021 1232-E5
BRIGANTINE CT
2100 ENCT 92024 1147-H7
BRIGANTINE DR
6500 CRLB 92011 1127-B4
BRIGGS AV
- ENCT 92024 1167-C1
BRIGHT CT
3400 SDCo 91977 1271-D5
BRIGHT ST
9800 SDCo 91977 1271-D6
BRIGHT CREEK LN
100 OCN 92056 1107-D3
BRIGHTHAVEN AV
500 ELCJ 92019 1252-A6
BRIGHTON AV
100 ELCN 92243 6499-H6
100 ELCN 92243 6500-A6
300 ENCT 92007 1167-D2
4400 SD 92107 1268-A6
4700 SD 92107 1267-J5
14000 PWY 92064 1190-F3
BRIGHTON CT
- CHV 91915 1311-J6
- CHV 91915 (1312-A7 See Page 1293)
700 SD 92109 1267-H4
900 VSTA 92081 1108-A4
BRIGHTON DR
- OCN 92056 1087-D1
BRIGHTON RD
2600 CRLB 92010 1106-J5
BRIGHTON GLEN RD
- SMCS 92078 1128-A3
BRIGHTON HILL CT
- SMCS 92078 1128-A3
BRIGHTON RIDGE CT
10700 SD 92131 1210-A2
BRIGHTSIDE WY
800 SDCo 92065 1153-A2
BRIGHTWOOD AV
100 CHV 91910 1310-A5
600 CHV 91910 1330-B1
BRIGHTWOOD CT
3200 OCN 92054 1086-D2
BRIGHTWOOD DR
- SMCS 92078 1128-E6
BRILENE LN
3100 SD 92111 1248-G5
BRILLDEN CT
3100 SD 92117 1248-D3
BRILLO ST
5000 SD 92117 1228-F7
BRILLWOOD HILL RD
15100 ESCN 92027 1130-J5
15100 SD 92027 1130-J5
BRINDISI ST
4400 SD 92107 1287-H2
BRINELL ST
4600 SD 92111 1249-B2
BRINSER ST
2200 SD 92136 1289-E7
3400 SD 92136 1309-F1
BRIOSO CT
1100 VSTA 92081 1107-H4
BRISAS CT
200 OCN 92054 1086-G1
BRISAS ST
100 OCN 92054 1086-G1
BRISBANE ST
- CHV 91910 1310-A4
BRISBANE WY
- OCN 92054 1086-G1
- OCN 92057 1086-J3
BRISTLECONE CT
4600 OCN 92056 1087-D4
BRISTLEWOOD CT
- SDCo 92065 1172-D5
BRISTLEWOOD DR
- SDCo 92065 1172-D5
BRISTOL AV
400 ENCT 92007 1167-D2
BRISTOL CT
1700 CHV 91902 1311-C5
BRISTOL RD
5000 SD 92116 1269-H2
BRISTOL BAY CT
2000 SD 92105 1290-C1
BRISTOL RIDGE LN
- SD 92127 1169-B3
BRISTOL RIDGE TER
- SD 92127 1169-B4
BRISTOW CT
7400 SD 92154 1351-E4
BRITAIN ST
800 SD 92114 1290-G3
BRITANNIA BLVD
1500 SD 92154 1351-E3
BRITANNIA CT
7400 SD 92154 1351-E4
BRITEM CT
- VSTA 92083 1087-E6
BRITT CT
8700 SD 92123 1249-C7
BRITTANY CT
3500 SDCo 91935 1272-E5
BRITTANY RD
800 ENCT 92024 1147-C4
BRITTANY WY
3500 CRLB 92010 1107-A3
BRITTANY FORREST LN
- SD 92130 1208-E1
BRITTANY PARK LN
16100 PWY 92064 1170-D4

STREET
Block City ZIP Pg-Grid

BRITTON AV
3600 CHV 91911 1330-E5
BRIXTON PL
13000 SD 92130 1188-B5
BRIZA PLACIDA
- SD 92127 1188-J2
BROAD AV
3300 SD 92113 1289-F5
BROADLAWN ST
3900 SD 92111 1248-J3
BROADMOOR CT
1000 CHV 91915 1311-F5
BROADMOOR DR
5900 LMSA 91942 1251-C6
BROADMOOR PL
9400 LMSA 91942 1251-B6
BROAD OAKS RD
15300 SDCo 92021 1233-C1
BROADRICK PL
6500 SD 92139 1310-F1
BROADRICK WY
2600 SD 92139 1310-F1
BROADVIEW AV
9300 SD 92123 1249-E7
BROADVIEW ST
400 SDCo 91977 1290-J3
400 SDCo 91977 1291-A3
BROADWAY
- SDCo 92004 410-F11
- CHV 91910 1309-J5
- NATC 91950 1309-J5
100 ELCJ 92021 1251-G3
100 SD 92101 1289-B3
100 CHV 91910 1310-A7
400 CHV 91910 1330-A1
500 SD 92101 1288-J3
800 CHV 91911 1330-B4
1300 ELCJ 92021 1252-A3
1500 ELCJ 92019 1252-A3
1600 OCN 92054 1106-C3
1600 SDCo 92019 1252-A3
1700 SD 92102 1289-E3
6200 SD 92114 1290-D2
7100 LMGR 91945 1270-J5
8300 SDCo 91941 1270-J5
8300 SDCo 91945 1270-J5
8500 SDCo 91941 1271-A4
E BROADWAY
100 VSTA 92084 1087-H6
N BROADWAY
100 ESCN 92025 1129-H1
800 ESCN 92026 1129-H1
1100 ESCN 92026 1109-H5
2900 SDCo 92026 1109-G1
17900 SDCo 92026 1089-H5
N BROADWAY Rt#-78
600 ESCN 92025 1129-H2
S BROADWAY
100 ESCN 92025 1129-J3
900 ESCN 92025 1130-A4
BROADWAY AV
6900 LMGR 92114 1290-E3
6900 SD 92114 1290-E3
BROADWAY CIR
900 SD 92101 1289-A3
BROADWAY LN
3600 LMGR 91945 1270-J5
BROADWAY PL
1300 ESCN 92025 1130-A4
BROADWAY SQ
- SD 92101 1288-J3
BROADWAY ST
700 ELCN 92243 6499-F6
BROADWAY WEST CHANNEL
- ELCJ 92020 1251-F2
BROCK CT
8100 LMGR 91945 1270-H7
BROCK RD
- ImCo 92243 6559-A6
BROCKBANK PL
5100 SD 92115 1270-C1
BROCKMAN RD Rt#-S30
500 ImCo 92231 431-A7
600 ImCo 92243 431-A7
BROCKTON ST
400 ELCJ 92020 1251-B4
400 ELCJ 92020 1251-B5
500 ELCJ 92020 1251-B4
BROCKWAY ST
11200 SDCo 92021 1231-G7
11200 SDCo 92021 1251-G1
BROCKWOOD DR
500 ELCJ 92021 1251-G4
BRODEA LN
4000 SDCo 92028 1048-F2
BRODIAEA WY
7300 SD 92037 1227-G7
BRODIE LN
8500 SNTE 92071 1230-G5
8500 SNTE 92071 1250-J1
BROGUE CT
1500 VSTA 92081 1107-J5
BROKEN ARROW LN
1400 SDCo 92028 1027-J4
BROKEN ARROW RD
2800 SDCo 92004 (1078-H6 See Page 1058)
BROKEN BOW CT
17000 SD 92127 1169-H2
BROKEN CINCH TR
7500 SDCo 92036 1138-C7
7500 SDCo 92036 (1158-D1 See Page 1138)
BROKEN HITCH RD
1300 OCN 92056 1087-D3
BROKEN OAK LN
34200 SDCo 92036 1176-D4
BROKEN ROCK RD
1700 SDCo 92078 1128-B2
1700 SMCS 92078 1128-B2
BROKEN WHEEL RD
10800 SDCo 92040 1231-G1
BROME CT
1600 CRLB 92011 1127-D6
BROME WY
12900 SD 92129 1189-D5
BROMEGRASS CT
15800 PWY 92064 1170-F4
BROMELIAD CT
7600 SD 92119 1250-E3
BROMFIELD AV
4300 SD 92122 1228-E5
BROMLEY WY
5600 SD 92120 1270-D1
BRONCO LN
16400 PWY 92064 1170-E4
BRONCO PL
300 CHV 91902 1310-G4
BRONCO WY
1600 OCN 92057 1067-E7
13300 PWY 92064 1170-E4
BRONSTEIN PL
10200 SD 92124 1249-G4
BRONTE PL
7500 SD 92114 1290-G4
BRONX PL
2800 SD 92123 1249-E5
BRONZE WY
600 VSTA 92083 1087-F7
BROOK RD
1400 SMCS 92069 1109-C7
BROOKBURN DR
4800 SD 92130 1188-C6
BROOK CANYON RD
2400 ESCN 92025 1130-C7
2400 SDCo 92025 1130-C7
BROOKDALE PL
100 SOLB 92075 1167-F7
BROOKDEL AV
- SMCS 92069 1109-B7
BROOKE CT
- LMSA 91941 1270-H5
BROOKE GN
1300 SDCo 92028 1027-J6
BROOKE LN
- SD 92122 1228-E2
BROOKE RD
1800 SDCo 92028 1027-J6
BROOKE CREST LN
1300 SDCo 92028 1027-H6
BROOKE HOLLOW RD
1200 SDCo 92028 1028-C4
BROOKES AV
500 SD 92103 1269-B6
W BROOKES AV
100 SD 92103 1268-J6
200 SD 92103 1269-A6
BROOKES TER
1200 SD 92103 1269-B6
BROOKE VISTA LN
- SD 92129 1189-A3
BROOKFIELD WY
3500 CRLB 92010 1107-A4
BROOKHAVEN CT
8100 SD 92114 1290-H4
BROOKHAVEN PASS
2200 VSTA 92081 1107-H7
2200 VSTA 92081 1127-H1
BROOKHAVEN RD
7000 SD 92114 1290-H4
BROOKHILLS RD
3700 SDCo 92028 1048-B3
BROOKHOLLOW CT
10600 SD 92126 1208-J4
BROOKHOLLOW GN
600 ESCN 92027 1130-B2
BROOKHURST AV
10400 SD 92126 1209-D4
BROOKHURST DR
1900 ELCJ 92019 1252-C4
BROOKHURST LN
2600 SDCo 92025 1130-B7
10300 SD 92126 1209-D5
BROOKINS LN
700 VSTA 92083 1087-E6
BROOKITE CT
- CRLB 92009 1127-F4
BROOKLINE ST
1600 SD 92102 1289-J2
BROOKLYN AV
5800 SD 92114 1290-C3
BROOKMEAD LN
2600 SD 92037 1227-J1
BROOKMEADOW PL
7900 SD 92114 1290-H5
BROOKPINE CT
3000 SDCo 91978 1271-F7
BROOKS GN
1900 ESCN 92029 1129-E5
BROOKS ST
300 OCN 92054 1086-B7
400 OCN 92054 1106-B1
N BROOKS ST
100 OCN 92054 1086-B7
S BROOKS ST
300 OCN 92054 1086-B7
BROOKS WY
4200 CRLB 92008 1106-G7
BROOKSHIRE ST
3500 SD 92111 1248-H4
BROOKS HUFFMAN PZ
- SD 92102 1290-A4
- SD 92114 1290-A4
BROOKSIDE CIR
9200 SDCo 91977 1271-B4
BROOKSIDE CT
- CRLB 92011 1126-J6
- SMCS 92078 1128-E4
9200 SDCo 91977 1271-B4
BROOKSIDE LN
- SD 92131 1210-C2
- OCN 92056 1107-D2
3100 ENCT 92024 1148-B5
N BROOKSIDE PL
- CHV 91913 1331-A1
S BROOKSIDE PL
- CHV 91913 1331-A2
BROOKSTONE CT
12600 PWY 92064 1190-C1
BROOKSTONE DR
14600 PWY 92064 1190-C1
14900 PWY 92064 1170-C7
BROOKSTONE PL
300 SNTE 92071 1231-C5
BROOKSTONE RD
700 CHV 91913 1311-E4
BROOKS TRAIL CT
2200 CHV 91915 1311-F6
BROOKTREE LN
800 VSTA 92081 1108-A4
BROOKTREE TER
10400 SD 92131 1209-H4
BROOKVALE DR
8500 SNTE 92071 1230-J7
BROOKVIEW CT
200 SNTE 92071 1231-C5
BROOKVIEW LN
10700 SD 92131 1209-H4
N BROOKVILLE DR
10600 SD 92131 1209-H1
11800 SD 92131 1189-H7
S BROOKVILLE DR
10600 SD 92131 1209-H1
BROOKWOOD CT
2200 ESCN 92026 1109-H4
4700 CRLB 92010 1107-A5
BROOKWOOD PL
900 OCN 92056 1087-D1
BROSNAN ST
2800 SD 92111 1248-J6
BROTHERTON RD
300 ESCN 92025 1130-A6
600 ESCN 92025 1129-J6
BROUGHAM CT
3100 OCN 92056 1106-H1
BROWN CT
- CALX 92231 6620-H7
BROWN DR
2500 ELCJ 92020 1251-B3
BROWN ST
3900 OCN 92056 1107-A1
BROWNCROFT WY
8500 SDCo 92021 1252-E1
BROWN DEER RD
9100 SD 92121 1208-G7
BROWNELL ST
5100 SD 92110 1268-F2
BROWNING CT
1200 VSTA 92083 1087-E6
BROWNING RD
5100 CRLB 92008 1107-C7
BROWNING ST
3000 SD 92106 1268-C7
3800 SD 92107 1268-B6
BROWNS RD
- SDCo 91901 1235-A3
BRUBAKER CT
12600 SD 92130 1188-C6
BRUCE CT
6900 LMSA 91941 1270-E3
BRUCE RD
1700 CRLB 92008 1106-H7
BRUCEALA CT
2000 ENCT 92007 1167-F3
BRUCKART SQ
9900 SD 92131 1209-H5
BRUCKER AV
700 SDCo 91977 1291-A3
BRULE PL
13000 PWY 92064 1190-D3
BRUMA CT
500 SDCo 91977 1291-C3
BRUMBY WY
10200 SD 92124 1249-G4
BRUNEI CT
7400 LMGR 91945 1270-G7
BRUNNER ST
1200 SD 92110 1268-G2
BRUNO PL
5600 LMSA 91942 1250-H7
5600 LMSA 91942 1270-H1
BRUNS RD
1700 SDCo 92084 1068-H5
BRUNSWICK AV
5400 SD 92120 1250-B5
BRUSHWOOD LN
- SDCo 92028 1048-C5
BRUST CT
2500 SDCo 92019 1272-E1
BRUTUS ST
500 SD 92114 1290-G3
BRUYERE CT
13800 SD 92129 1189-D2
BRYAN CT
7800 LMGR 91945 1270-H6
BRYAN ST
4100 OCN 92056 1087-C6
BRYAN POINT DR
- CHV 91914 1311-H1
BRYANT DR
2200 CRLB 92008 1107-C7
2200 CRLB 92008 1127-C1
BRYANT ST
1200 SD 92113 1289-F6
BRYANVIEW CIR
1300 SD 92114 1290-B6
BRYCE CIR
4700 CRLB 92008 1106-H7
BRYCE LN
100 SDCo 92028 1027-H2
BRYCE PT
- PWY 92064 1150-G6
BRYCE CANYON AV
800 CHV 91914 1311-H3
BRYCE CANYON WY
2600 CHV 91914 1311-H4
BRYN GLEN CT
- SD 92129 1189-B3
BRYN GLEN WY
- SD 92129 1189-A3
BRYNWOOD CT
6200 SD 92120 1250-D6
BRYNWOOD WY
6400 SD 92120 1250-D6
BRYSON TER
4600 SD 92130 1188-C5
BUBBLING LN
13400 SDCo 92040 1232-D6
BUBBLING WELL DR
1500 SD 92154 1349-J2
BUBBLING WELLS RD
9000 SDCo 92040 1232-D6
BUCCANEER DR
100 SD 92114 1290-F4
BUCCANEER WY
- CORD 92118 1329-E2
BUCHANAN ST
600 ESCN 92027 1110-B7
2800 SD 92136 1289-E7
N BUCHANAN ST
800 ESCN 92027 1110-A7
BUCHANON AV
- CALX 92231 6620-J6
BUCKA PL
- SDCo 92003 1067-H1
BUCKAROO LN
900 CHV 91902 1310-H4
BUCKBOARD DR
1500 OCN 92057 1067-F6
BUCKBOARD LN
1400 SDCo 92028 1027-J4
BUCKBOARD TR
7100 SDCo 92036 1138-C5
9200 SNTE 92071 1231-F6
BUCKEYE CT
900 ELCJ 92021 1251-H2
BUCKEYE DR
1300 SDCo 92021 1251-H3
1300 ELCJ 92021 1251-H2
BUCKHORN AV
700 SMCS 92078 1128-G2
BUCKHORN DR
29300 SDCo 91906 (1297-D5 See Page 1296)
BUCKHORN ST
8300 SD 92111 1249-B2
BUCKHURST AV
10800 SD 92126 1209-D3
BUCKINGHAM DR
1400 SD 92037 1247-G2
BUCKINGHAM LN
4500 CRLB 92010 1107-A5
BUCKLAND ST
8400 LMSA 91942 1250-J7
8400 LMSA 91942 1270-J1
BUCKLEY ST
12800 PWY 92064 1190-D5
BUCKMAN SPRINGS LN
2200 SDCo 91906 (1317-H2 See Page 1296)
BUCKMAN SPRINGS RD Rt#-S1
1300 SDCo 91906 (1318-A4 See Page 1298)
1300 SDCo 91906 (1317-H1 See Page 1296)
2100 SDCo 91906 (1297-G1 See Page 1296)
2600 SDCo 91906 430-A7
2600 SDCo 91962 430-A7
BUCKNELL AV
5800 SD 92037 1247-H3
BUCKNELL ST
1900 CHV 91913 1311-D5
BUCKSHOT CANYON RD
29100 SDCo 92026 1088-H1
BUCKSKIN DR
1400 ESCN 92029 1129-G7
1400 ESCN 92029 1149-G1
BUCKSKIN GN
1800 ESCN 92027 1110-A4
BUCKSKIN RD
400 SDCo 92004 1058-G6
1100 ELCJ 92019 1251-H6
BUCKSKIN TR
12200 PWY 92064 1190-C6
BUCKSKIN RANCH DR
- IMP 92251 6439-F3
BUCKTHORN CT
- CRLB 92024 1147-F3
BUCKTHORN TR
2400 SDCo 91905 (1299-H3 See Page 1298)
8000 SDCo 91962 1237-C5
BUCKWHEAT CT
12600 SD 92129 1189-D6
BUCKWHEAT ST
9000 SD 92129 1189-D6
BUCKWHEAT TR
1200 SDCo 91906 (1318-B6 See Page 1298)
BUCKWOOD ST
14600 PWY 92064 1190-D1
BUCKY LN
800 NATC 91950 1289-H6
BUDD ST
3300 SD 92111 1249-A4
BUDLONG LAKE AV
6300 SD 92119 1250-H5
BUDMUIR PL
4300 SD 92105 1289-H1
BUDWIN LN
14500 PWY 92064 1190-F1
14800 PWY 92064 1170-F7
BUECHNER DR
14100 SDCo 92065 1192-B2
BUENA PL
900 CRLB 92008 1106-E4
BUENA ST
1300 OCN 92054 1086-B7
BUENA TER
800 ELCJ 92020 1251-D4
BUENA CAPRI
900 SDCo 92028 1027-H7
BUENA CREEK RD
- SDCo 92069 1088-H7
100 SMCS 92069 1108-F1
200 SDCo 92069 1108-F1
1500 SDCo 92084 1108-F1
BUENA CREEK TR
1500 SDCo 92084 1108-D1
BUENA CREST LN
3700 SDCo 92069 1108-G1
3700 SDCo 92084 1108-G1
BUENA FLORES
2500 SDCo 92028 1027-H7
BUENA HILLS DR
3000 OCN 92056 1106-J1
3100 OCN 92056 1107-A1
BUENA MESA PL
10100 SDCo 91977 1271-E5
BUENA ROSA
2500 SDCo 92028 1027-H7
2600 SDCo 92028 1047-H1
BUENA ROSA CT
900 SDCo 92028 1027-H7
BUENA SUERTE
900 SDCo 92028 1047-H1
BUENA TIERRA WY
700 OCN 92057 1086-J3
BUENA VALLEY DR
8700 SNTE 92071 1231-D7
BUENAVENTURA CT
100 SOLB 92075 1167-D7
BUENA VIDA RD
12300 SDCo 92040 1212-C4
BUENA VISTA
- ESCN 92026 1109-G7
13200 PWY 92064 1190-E5
BUENA VISTA AV
600 ELCN 92243 6499-G4
1100 ESCN 92027 1109-J6
1200 SDCo 91977 1291-C2
2400 LMGR 91945 1270-G7
9800 SNTE 92071 1231-D7
BUENA VISTA CIR
2300 CRLB 92008 1106-D4
BUENA VISTA CT
1000 CHV 91910 1311-B7
BUENA VISTA DR
1000 VSTA 92081 1107-G2
1200 SDCo 92081 1107-G2
9900 SDCo 91977 1271-D5
BUENA VISTA LN
1000 OCN 92054 1085-H6
BUENA VISTA ST
3300 SD 92109 1268-A1
3600 SD 92109 1248-A7
BUENA VISTA WY
800 CHV 91910 1311-A5
1000 CRLB 92008 1106-E4
BUENOS AV
1000 SD 92110 1268-E3
BUENOS AIRES WY
31200 SDCo 92003 1067-H2
BUENOS TIEMPOS
900 SDCo 92028 1027-H7
BUEN TIEMPO DR
800 CHV 91910 1310-G7
BUFFALO GRASS CT
- IMP 92251 6499-E2
BUFFUM DR
3500 OCN 92057 1086-F5
BUFORD WY
13700 PWY 92064 1190-F3
BUGGYWHIP DR
10800 SDCo 91978 1271-G7
BUHO CT
4000 SD 92124 1250-A3
BUISSON ST
6200 SD 92122 1228-C5
BULLARD LN
100 SDCo 91901 1233-D6
BULL CANYON RD
1600 CHV 91913 1311-D7
BULLOCK DR
6400 SD 92114 1290-F5
BULLRUSH GN
2000 ESCN 92027 1110-A5
BULRUSH CT
- CRLB 92011 1127-B6
BULRUSH LN
2000 ENCT 92007 1167-E3
BUMANN RD
3300 ENCT 92024 1148-C4
BUMPER CIR
4000 SD 92124 1249-H3
BUNA PL
100 VSTA 92084 1087-H5
BUNCHE AV
3100 SD 92122 1228-C5
BUNCHE TER
6300 SD 92122 1228-C5
BUNCHE WY
6300 SD 92122 1228-C5
BUNDY DR
9500 SNTE 92071 1231-E4
BUNGALOW WY
- SD 92108 1249-D7
BUNKER HILL ST
2900 SD 92109 1248-D5
3200 SD 92109 1248-D5
BUNKER VIEW WY
2100 OCN 92056 1086-J7
BUNNELL ST
4800 SD 92113 1290-A5
BUNNIE KING LN
1300 SDCo 92065 1172-G4
BUNNY DR
18000 SDCo 91935 1274-D3
BUNNY BELL LN
1400 VSTA 92083 1108-A2
BUOY AV
- CRLB 92011 1127-A7
BURBANK CT
3500 SD 92111 1249-A4
BURBANK ST
7400 SD 92111 1249-A4
BURBURY WY
- SMCS 92024 1128-B7
BURDEN DR
700 NATC 91950 1290-B7
BURDETT WY
100 SDCo 92021 1252-H3
BURFORD ST
5300 SD 92111 1248-G6
BURGA LP
500 CHV 91910 1310-J5
BURGASIA PTH
500 SDCo 92019 1252-C6
BURGENER BLVD
2100 SD 92110 1268-G1
2300 SD 92110 1248-F6
BURGOS CT
2400 CRLB 92009 1147-F1
BURGUNDY DR
1300 CHV 91913 1311-E7
1400 CHV 91913 1331-E1
BURGUNDY RD
1400 ENCT 92024 1147-C2
BURGUNDY ST
6300 SD 92120 1249-J7
BURIAN ST
6000 SD 92114 1290-C2
BURKE RD
- SD 92145 1229-D1
800 VSTA 92083 1087-E6
BURKSHIRE AV
600 ENCT 92007 1167-D2
BURKSHIRE PL
8800 SDCo 92040 1232-C6
BURLINGAME DR
3000 SD 92104 1269-E7
BURLINGTON PL
1800 ESCN 92026 1109-D5
BURLINGTON WY
7800 SD 92126 1209-A4
BURMA CT
- SDCo 92028 1047-E4
BURMA RD
100 SDCo 92028 1047-E4
400 SDCo 92065 409-G11
BURMA SPUR
3900 SDCo 92028 1047-F4
BURNABY ST
1100 ELCJ 92020 1251-G7
BURNED OAK LN
10200 SDCo 92026 1089-E3
BURNED OAK TER
28200 SDCo 92026 1089-F3
BURNELL AV
7600 LMGR 91945 1270-G6
BURNET ST
1700 ELCJ 92021 1251-G2
BURNHAM ST
600 ELCJ 92019 1251-J6
BURNING BUSH ST
800 ENCT 92024 1147-E6
BURNING HILLS DR
13300 PWY 92064 1170-E1
BURNING TREE WY
9300 SNTE 92071 1230-J6
BURNS CT
900 SD 92113 1289-G5
BURNT MAPLE WY
1800 VSTA 92081 1107-G5
BURNT MOUNTAIN RD
27700 SDCo 92082 1090-A2
27900 SDCo 92082 1089-J3
BURR CT
12400 SD 92129 1189-C6
BURR LN
8400 SD 92129 1189-C6
BURRIS DR
1200 SDCo 92019 1272-D1
BURR OAK PL
- CHV 91915 1311-J7
BURROCK DR
10000 SNTE 92071 1231-D2
BURROUGHS ST
1400 OCN 92054 1106-C2
1900 SD 92111 1268-J1
2100 SD 92111 1248-J7
BURTON CT
- CRLB 92011 1127-B5
BURTON ST
1400 SD 92111 1268-J2
BURWELL LN
- SDCo 92019 1272-B2
BURWOOD PL
900 SD 92154 1330-C7
BUS CT
5700 LMSA 91942 1251-A7
BUSCH DR
800 SDCo 92081 1107-D2
800 VSTA 92081 1107-D2
3400 OCN 92056 1107-D2
BUSH LN
- SMCS 92069 1108-G6
BUSH ST
400 OCN 92054 1086-B7
600 SD 92103 1268-J6
BUSHARD DR
1000 SDCo 92029 1129-H7
BUSHWOOD CT
7800 LMGR 91945 1270-H7
BUSHY HILL DR
8700 SD 92071 1230-F7
8700 SNTE 92071 1230-F7
BUSINESS PKWY
- IMP 92251 6499-E2
BUSINESS CENTER CT
- SD 92154 1351-B2
BUSINESS PARK AV
9600 SD 92131 1209-F5
BUSINESS PARK DR
2000 VSTA 92081 1107-J6
2500 VSTA 92081 1128-A1
2500 VSTA 92081 1127-J1
2800 SMCS 92078 1128-A1
BUTANO CT
8700 SD 92129 1189-C3
BUTANO WY
13700 SD 92129 1189-C3
BUTLER PL
6400 SD 92115 1270-D5
BUTLER RD
- ImCo - 412-B3
BUTLER ST
1300 IMPB 91932 1349-J2
2800 OCN 92054 1086-D6
BUTTE ST
8500 LMSA 91941 1270-J3
8500 LMSA 91941 1271-A3
BUTTERCUP LN
600 NATC 91950 1290-C6
BUTTERCUP RD
800 CRLB 92011 1127-A6
1600 ENCT 92024 1147-G5
BUTTERFIELD DR
- SDCo 92040 1232-F4
BUTTERFIELD LN
700 SMCS 92069 1109-D6
BUTTERFIELD RD
700 OCN 92057 1067-B5
BUTTERFIELD TR
- ImCo - 411-G4
17000 PWY 92064 1170-F1
BUTTERFLY CT
- CHV 91914 1311-J1
BUTTERFLY LN
4800 SDCo 91941 1271-E2
BUTTERFLY WY
- CHV 91914 1311-J1
BUTTERNUT LN
- SD 92123 1249-D1
BUTTERNUT HOLLOW LN
4700 SDCo 91902 1310-G1
BUTTERS RD
1700 CRLB 92008 1106-F3
5500 ImCo 92227 411-E11
BUTTERS RD Rt#-S32
4300 ImCo 92227 431-E1
5300 ImCo 92227 411-E11
BUTTERWOOD AV
500 SMCS 92069 1109-D7
BUTTERWOOD CT
12600 PWY 92064 1190-D3
BUTTESIDE PL
2400 SDCo 91977 1271-H7
BUTTE TOP PL
2400 SDCo 91977 1271-H7
BUTTEVIEW PL
2400 SDCo 91977 1271-H7
BUTTON ST
9700 SNTE 92071 1231-A4
BUTTONBRUSH LN
1200 SDCo 92019 1252-E7
1300 SDCo 92019 1272-E1
BUTTONWOOD CT
1200 SDCo 92019 1252-E7
BUXTON AV
13400 PWY 92064 1190-H4
BYRD ST
3500 SD 92154 1330-E7
BYRD WY
600 SD 92154 1330-E7
BYRON PL
2300 CRLB 92008 1107-B7
BYRON ST
3000 SD 92106 1288-B2

C

C AV
100 CORD 92118 1288-J7
200 SDCo 92055 1066-C1
500 NATC 91950 1309-H1
C CT
200 CHV 91910 1310-F7
C ST
- SDCo 92036 1136-B7
- CHV 91910 1310-B4
100 SDCo 92059 1029-H4
100 ENCT 92024 1147-B7
100 SD 92101 1289-B3
100 CHV 91910 1309-J5
500 IMP 92251 6439-E5
500 SD 92101 1288-J3
700 IMPB 91932 1329-F7
700 SDCo 92055 1085-G3
1000 ENCT 92024 1148-A5
1300 SD 92110 1268-F2
1300 SD 92102 1289-H2
1500 NATC 91950 1309-J2
2500 NATC 91950 1310-C3
CABALLERO CANYON RD
26800 SDCo 92026 1089-G6
CABALLO LN
3400 SDCo 92028 1048-D2
CABALLOS PL
- SD 92130 1188-D5
CABANA ST
- CALX 92231 6620-H6
CABANA WY
- OCN 92057 1087-A2
CABANO
- SDCo 92055 1086-B2
CABARET ST
6100 SD 92120 1250-D4
CABAZON CT
- IMP 92251 6439-F4
CABELA DR
17400 SD 92127 1169-J1
17800 SD 92127 1149-J7
18000 SD 92127 1150-A6
CABELA PL
6500 CRLB 92011 1127-C5
11400 SD 92127 1169-J1
CABERNET DR
1800 CHV 91913 1311-C3
CABERNET WY
7100 LMGR 91945 1290-F1
CABEZAS CV
1200 CHV 91915 1311-F6
CABEZON PL
700 VSTA 92081 1107-E1
12500 SD 92129 1189-F6
CABIN WY
- SMCS 92069 1108-H6
CABLE CT
600 OCN 92054 1086-F2
CABLE ST
1500 SD 92107 1267-J6
CABO CT
400 OCN 92054 1086-G2
3300 CRLB 92009 1147-J1
10900 SNTE 92071 1231-D1
CABO WY
3300 CRLB 92009 1147-J1
3300 CRLB 92009 1148-A1
CABO BAHIA
2100 CHV 91914 1311-E3
CABO SAN LUCAS AV
- ImCo 92251 6499-H1
- IMP 92251 6499-H1
CABOT CT
1100 VSTA 92081 1107-J4
CABOT DR
9300 SD 92126 1209-C7
CABRENA ST
1800 SD 92154 1350-B3
CABRILLO AV
600 CORD 92118 1288-G6
7300 SD 92037 1227-F7
CABRILLO CIR
1100 VSTA 92084 1087-J4
N CABRILLO DR
1100 CHV 91910 1311-B7
S CABRILLO DR
1100 CHV 91910 1311-B7
CABRILLO FRWY Rt#-163
- SD - 1229-D6
- SD - 1249-B4
- SD - 1269-A1
- SD - 1269-B6
- SD - 1289-B1
CABRILLO LN
200 VSTA 92084 1087-H4
CABRILLO PL
2600 CRLB 92008 1106-E4
9700 SDCo 92029 1149-D4
CABRILLO RD
- SD 92152 1308-A2
CABRILLO ST
21800 SDCo 92070 1135-B3
CABRILLO BAY LN
- SD 92110 1268-D6
CABRILLO MEMORIAL DR
- SD 92106 1287-J5
- SD 92106 1288-A6
- SD 92106 1308-A1
- SD 92152 1288-A6
- SD 92152 1308-A1
1800 SD 92152 1287-J5
CABRILLO MESA DR
2900 SD 92123 1249-C5
CACAO CT
11600 SD 92124 1250-A3
CACATUA ST
2800 CRLB 92009 1127-H5
CACHE CREEK ST
1700 SDCo 92019 1272-C3
CACHO CT
11400 SDCo 92021 1251-H1
CACTI DR
29400 SDCo 91906 (1297-E4 See Page 1296)
CACTUS CT
6900 SD 92154 1351-D4
CACTUS PL
2000 ESCN 92027 1110-C7
CACTUS RD
1500 SD 92154 1351-D3
CACTUS ST
9700 SDCo 92040 1232-A4
CACTUS WY
5800 SD 92037 1248-A2
CACTUS BRANCH TR
7100 SDCo 92036 1138-B6
CACTUSRIDGE CT
3600 SD 92105 1289-G2
CACTUSRIDGE ST
1400 SD 92105 1289-G2
CACTUS TRAIL LN
2600 CHV 91915 1311-H5
CACTUSVIEW DR
3600 SD 92105 1289-G2
CACUS ST
8100 SDCo 91977 1290-J5
CADDEN CT
3200 SD 92117 1248-C4
CADDEN DR
3300 SD 92117 1248-D4
CADDEN WY
3800 SD 92117 1248-D4
CADDIE CT
2300 OCN 92056 1106-J1
CADDINGTON RW
6000 SD 92037 1248-A2
CADDY RW
12100 SD 92128 1170-A4
CADE TER
9000 SD 92126 1209-D1
CADENA DR
3900 OCN 92054 1086-G2
CADENCE CT
11000 SDCo 92026 1109-H1
CADENCE GROVE WY
- SD 92130 1208-C2
CADENCIA GN
800 ESCN 92026 1109-F5
CADENCIA ST
3000 CRLB 92009 1147-H1
3100 CRLB 92009 1127-J7
3200 CRLB 92009 1128-A7
3300 CRLB 92009 1148-A1
CADENCIA WY
1600 ESCN 92025 1129-J5
CADES WY
2400 VSTA 92081 1108-A6
CADET ST
5000 SD 92117 1228-G7
CADILLAC CIR
300 OCN 92054 1086-C7
CADIZ ST
2700 SD 92110 1268-D6
CADLEY CT
9100 SD 92129 1189-D1
CADMAN ST
500 SD 92114 1290-F3
CADMUS ST
100 ENCT 92024 1147-B5

SAN DIEGO CO.

STREET Block City ZIP Pg-Grid

CADOGLENN DR
1200 SDCo 92019 1252-B7
1300 SDCo 92019 1272-B1
CADORETTE AV
9300 SNTE 92071 1230-H6
CADO VIEW CT
- SDCo 92027 1090-D7
- SDCo 92082 1090-D7
CADWELL RD
10300 SNTE 92071 1231-A3
CADY RD
- ImCo 92227 431-A2
CAESAR DR
18900 SDCo 92065 1153-E3
CAESENA WY
5000 OCN 92056 1107-F5
CAFANZARA CT
8200 SD 92119 1250-E3
CAFE AVD
8500 SDCo 91902 1310-H2
CAFFEY LN
7600 SD 92126 1209-A6
CAFLUR AV
4100 SD 92117 1248-D3
CAGAYAN AV
2600 SD 92154 1330-C6
CAGLE ST
3000 NATC 91950 1310-D3
CAHILL DR
7400 SD 92114 1290-G3
CAHUILLA DR
- IMP 92251 6439-F3
CAHUILLA RD
500 SDCo 92004 (1078-H1 See Page 1058)
CAHUKA CT
32300 SDCo 92061 1050-J6
CAIN LN
1200 SDCo 92027 1130-C3
CAIRO CT
8700 SD 92123 1249-C7
CAITHNESS DR
1600 SD 92173 1350-E2
CAJON CIR
600 OCN 92057 1067-A5
1100 VSTA 92083 1087-G4
CAJON PL
1600 CORD 92118 1288-J7
CAJON RD
7900 SDCo 92021 1251-J1
CAJON WY
4600 SD 92115 1270-B3
CAJON GREENS DR
1000 ELCJ 92021 1251-H2
CAJON GREENS PL
1500 ELCJ 92021 1251-H2
CAJON VIEW DR
300 ELCJ 92020 1271-F1
300 ELCJ 91941 1271-F1
300 SDCo 91941 1271-F1
300 SDCo 92020 1271-F1
CAJON VISTA CT
12500 SDCo 92021 1232-B7
CALABRIA CT
7100 SD 92122 1228-E3
N CALAC LN
31000 SDCo 92082 1071-E2
CALAIS DR
13400 SD 92014 1187-H7
CALAMAR CT
11600 SD 92124 1250-B2
CALAMAR CV
11600 SD 92124 1250-A2
CALAMAR DR
11600 SD 92124 1250-A2
CALAVERAS DR
1000 SD 92107 1287-J2
CALAVO CT
1700 CRLB 92008 1106-G7
CALAVO DR
1000 SDCo 92026 1109-E7
1000 SDCo 92026 1129-E1
2600 SDCo 91978 1271-F6
3600 SDCo 91977 1271-F4
3700 SDCo 91941 1271-F2
6500 SDCo 92020 1271-F2
CALAVO RD
1400 SDCo 92028 1027-H5
CALCATTERRA SQ
9900 SD 92131 1209-H5
CALDAS DE REYES
15400 SD 92128 1170-C5
CALDERA PL
3700 CRLB 92010 1107-B4
CALDERON CT
8400 SD 92129 1189-B3
CALDERON RD
- SD 92129 1189-B3
CALDERWOOD RW
2900 SD 92037 1248-A1
CALDY PL
7600 SD 92111 1249-A3
CALEB CT
900 SD 92154 1330-E7
CALEDONIA DR
4100 SD 92111 1249-A3
CALENDA RD
11200 SD 92127 1169-H2
CALERA ST
1300 VSTA 92084 1087-H4
CALETA CT
2000 CRLB 92009 1127-F6
CALETA WY
12400 SD 92128 1170-B2
CALEVERO LN
100 OCN 92056 1107-D2
CALEXICO AV
- SDCo 91934 (1321-G5 See Page 1300)
CALEXICO ST
800 CALX 92231 6680-D1
CALGARY AV
3900 SD 92122 1228-E4
CALGARY CT
1400 VSTA 92083 1087-D7
6500 SD 92122 1228-E5
CALGARY DR
6500 SD 92122 1228-D4
CALGARY WY
11100 SDCo 92082 1069-G2
CALHOUN CT
2500 SDCo 92081 1108-C5
CALHOUN ST
2600 SD 92110 1268-F4
CALIBAN CT
200 ENCT 92024 1147-G6
CALIBAN DR
200 ENCT 92024 1147-G6
CALICO CIR
10400 SD 92126 1209-B4
CALICO LN
1400 SDCo 92029 1129-C4
CALICO ST
7800 SD 92126 1209-A4
CALICO RANCH RD
3600 SDCo 92036 1135-F5
CALICO RANCH GATE
3600 SDCo 92036 1135-F5
CALIDRIS LN
7200 CRLB 92011 1127-B7
CALIENTE AV
- SD 92154 1351-A2
CALIENTE CT
1400 SDCo 91901 1234-C6
CALIENTE GN
2200 ESCN 92029 1129-D6
CALIENTE LP
1300 CHV 91910 1311-B6
CALIFA CT
8100 SD 92119 1250-E3
E CALIFORNIA AV
100 VSTA 92084 1087-H5
W CALIFORNIA AV
100 VSTA 92083 1087-G5
CALIFORNIA DR
- ImCo 92274 410-H7
CALIFORNIA ST
700 SD 92101 1288-J1
700 OCN 92054 1106-D1
1000 ENCT 92024 1147-J5
1100 IMPB 91932 1349-G2
2100 SD 92110 1268-G6
2800 SD 92101 1268-H7
CALIFORNIA OAK DR
- SDCo 92081 1107-H3
- VSTA 92081 1107-H3
CALIFORNIA SPRINGS CT
- SDCo 91977 1271-E7
- SDCo 91977 1291-E1
CALIFORNIA WATERS DR
- SDCo 91977 1271-E7
- SDCo 91977 1291-E1
CALINA WY
7700 CRLB 92009 1147-G2
CALISTOGA AV
1200 CHV 91913 1331-C1
CALISTOGA DR
15500 SDCo 92065 1173-D4
CALISTOGA PL
23500 SDCo 92065 1173-D5
CALISTOGA WY
- SMCS 92078 1128-E6
CALLA AV
100 IMPB 91932 1329-E7
CALLA ST
1700 SD 92154 1329-J7
1700 SD 92154 1330-A7
3800 SD 92121 1208-C6
CALLADO CT
16700 SD 92128 1170-A3
CALLADO RD
11900 SD 92128 1170-B3
CALLAN RD
2800 SD 92121 1207-J5
2800 SD 92037 1207-J5
2900 SD 92121 1208-A5
CALLCOTT WY
13000 SD 92130 1188-C5
CALLE PL
1400 ESCN 92027 1109-J6
CALLE ABAJO
3000 NATC 91950 1310-D2
3000 SD 92139 1310-D2
CALLE ABUELITO
12900 SD 92129 1189-G5
CALLE ACERVO
1500 CRLB 92009 1147-J3
1500 ENCT 92024 1147-J4
7200 CRLB 92009 1148-A4
CALLE ADELA
300 SMCS 92069 1109-C7
CALLE AGUADULCE
2400 SD 92139 1310-E1
CALLE ALBARA
11500 SDCo 92019 1271-J3
11700 SDCo 92019 1272-A4
CALLE ALEGRO
700 VSTA 92084 1087-J3
CALLE ALEJANDRO
3000 SDCo 91935 1292-H3
CALLE ALHENA
3000 CRLB 92009 1147-H3
CALLE ALICIA
400 SCLE 92672 1023-B2
CALLE ALMA
7300 CRLB 92009 1127-J7
CALLE ALTA
1500 SD 92037 1247-J3
CALLE ALTO
- SDCo 92040 1232-A1
CALLE ALTURA
1400 SD 92037 1247-H4
CALLE AMANACER
7700 SDCo 92067 1148-H7
CALLE AMBIENTE
7600 SDCo 92067 1148-J7
CALLE AMISTAD DR
300 SDCo 92065 1152-J6
300 SDCo 92065 1153-A6
CALLE AMISTAD LN
1200 SDCo 92065 1152-J7
CALLE ANA
16400 PWY 92064 1170-D4
CALLE ANACAPA
1000 ENCT 92024 1148-A5
CALLE ANDALUCIA
14300 SD 92130 1188-D2
CALLE ANDAR
- CRLB 92009 1147-J2
CALLE ANDREA
- SDCo 92065 1173-D1
CALLE ANGELICA
11600 SDCo 92019 1271-J4
CALLE ANTONIO
1800 VSTA 92084 1088-B5
CALLE ARDILLA
12000 SDCo 92019 1272-A4
CALLE ARIANA
3800 SCLE 92672 1023-B2
CALLE ARQUERO
4900 OCN 92057 1067-B4
CALLE ARRIBA
5800 SD 92139 1310-D2
CALLE ARROYO
2700 CRLB 92008 1106-G3
CALLE ASTURTAS
15500 SD 92128 1170-C6
CALLE BARCELONA
1200 CRLB 92024 1147-F3
1200 ENCT 92024 1147-F3
2000 CRLB 92009 1147-G2
CALLE BENDITO
- CHV 91914 1311-F3
CALLE BIENVENIDO
1300 VSTA 92084 1087-J3
CALLE BOLERO
200 OCN 92057 1087-A1
CALLE BONITA
300 ESCN 92029 1150-A3
CALLE BUENA VENTURA
1900 OCN 92056 1086-H7
2000 OCN 92056 1106-H1
CALLE BUENO GANAR
13900 SDCo 91935 1292-G3
CALLE CABALLERO
2700 CRLB 92008 1106-G3
CALLE CABALLEROS
13000 SD 92129 1189-G5
CALLE CABRILLO
- ESCN 92026 1109-F6
800 SMCS 92069 1109-B5
1500 SDCo 92021 1251-G2
12500 SDCo 92021 1252-B1
CALLE CAJON
- SDCo 92040 1232-C2
CALLE CALETA VIEJAS
2900 SDCo 91901 1234-D7
CALLE CALZADA
8200 SD 92126 1209-B2
CALLE CAMILLE
1600 SD 92037 1247-J3
CALLE CAMPESINO
200 SCLE 92672 1023-B1
CALLE CAMPOSECO
6100 SDCo 92067 1168-F4
CALLE CANCUNA
3300 CRLB 92009 1147-J2
CALLE CANDELA
1600 SD 92037 1247-J3
CALLE CANDELERO
1200 CHV 91910 1311-A6
CALLE CANONERO
3900 SDCo 92028 1028-F7
CALLE CANTORA
2000 SDCo 92019 1252-D7
CALLE CAPISTRANO
500 SMCS 92069 1108-F5
CALLE CARACAS
3300 CRLB 92009 1147-J2
CALLE CARDENAS
13900 SD 92130 1188-D3
CALLE CARLA
14500 SDCo 92067 1188-G2
CALLE CASAS BONITAS
5700 SD 92139 1310-D2
CALLE CATALINA
1700 ESCN 92029 1129-G6
CALLE CATALONIA
- CRLB 92009 1147-J4
CALLE CATARINA
- CHV 91914 1311-E2
CALLE CERRO
900 SMCS 92069 1109-B5
CALLE CHANATE
2200 SD 92139 1290-E7
CALLE CHAPARRO
5400 SDCo 92067 1168-B4
CALLE CHAPULTEPEC
500 VSTA 92083 1087-G6
CALLE CHARMONA
12600 SD 92128 1170-C5
CALLE CHIQUITA
2300 SD 92037 1227-H4
CALLE CHRISTOPHER
1300 ENCT 92024 1167-G2
CALLE CIELA VISTA
800 CHV 91911 1330-J1
CALLE CIMA
7800 SDCo 92067 1148-H7
CALLE CIMA BELLA
800 CHV 91911 1330-J1
CALLECITA WY
2300 OCN 92056 1087-D5
CALLECITA AQUILLA NORTE
1300 CHV 91911 1330-J2
CALLECITA AQUILLA SUR
700 CHV 91911 1330-J2
CALLE CLARA
2200 SD 92037 1227-H5
CALLE CODORNIZ
11100 SDCo 92082 1049-G7
13300 SDCo 92082 1069-G1
CALLE COLINA
13200 PWY 92064 1170-E3
CALLE COLINA ROCA
- SDCo 91901 1254-E2
CALLE COLNETT
1200 SMCS 92069 1109-C7
CALLE COLORADO
1600 VSTA 92084 1087-J3
CALLE CONEJO
- SDCo 91901 1234-A6
CALLE CONIFERA
- CRLB 92009 1128-A7
- CRLB 92009 1148-A1
CALLE CONTENTA
200 SDCo 92028 1027-H3
CALLE CORAZON
400 OCN 92057 1087-A4
CALLE CORDOBA
- CRLB 92009 1147-J4
CALLE CORREDOR
2100 SDCo 92028 998-C5
CALLE CORTA
- SMCS 92078 1129-C1
2300 SD 92037 1227-H4
16700 PWY 92064 1170-D4
CALLE CORTE
17100 SDCo 92067 1168-D3
CALLE CORTEJO
16000 SDCo 92091 1168-C7
CALLE CORTEZ
4300 SDCo 92019 1271-J3
CALLE CORTITA
12500 SD 92128 1170-F2
CALLE COZUMEL
7900 CRLB 92009 1147-J3
CALLE CRISTOBAL
7200 SD 92126 1209-A1
7300 SD 92126 1208-J3
CALLE CRUCERO
1300 SMCS 92069 1109-C7
CALLE CUMBRE
2900 SD 92139 1310-D2
CALLE DARIO
11100 SD 92126 1209-B2
CALLE DE ADELE
300 ENCT 92024 1147-C6
CALLE DE ALCALA
900 ESCN 92025 1150-D3
CALLE DE ALICIA
500 ENCT 92024 1147-F5
CALLE DE AMOR
- CHV 91910 1311-A7
CALLE DE ANDLUCA
1600 SD 92037 1247-J3
CALLE DE ARLENE
500 ENCT 92024 1147-F5
CALLE DE BARBARA
500 ENCT 92024 1147-F5
CALLE DE BUENA FE
8500 SDCo 92021 1232-D7
CALLE DE CASITAS
4600 OCN 92057 1066-J7
CALLE DE CHERIE
500 ENCT 92024 1147-F5
CALLE DE CINCO
1600 SD 92037 1247-J3
CALLE DE COMPADRES
2600 SDCo 91901 1254-C1
CALLE DE CONNECTOR
4600 OCN 92057 1066-J7
CALLE DE CRISTO
3000 SDCo 92069 1088-G4
CALLE DE DAMASCO
- CHV 91910 1311-A6
CALLE DE DE LUZ RD
- SDCo 92028 996-H2
CALLE DE DOLORES RD
500 ENCT 92024 1147-F5
CALLE DE ENCINAS
26000 SDCo 92082 1091-G5
CALLE DE ENCINAS CT
27000 SDCo 92082 1091-F6
CALLE DE ENSUENO
12300 SDCo 92082 1070-A5
CALLE DE ERNESTO
14100 SDCo 92021 1232-G6
CALLE DE FUENTES
7300 CRLB 92009 1127-H7
CALLE DE HALCONES
12300 SDCo 92082 1049-H4
CALLE DE KATRINA
500 ENCT 92024 1147-F5
CALLE DE LA ALIANZA
200 SD 92173 1350-F3
CALLE DE LA ESTRELLA
7700 SDCo 91962 1237-D6
CALLE DE LA FIESTA
7700 SDCo 91962 1237-D6
CALLE DE LA GARZA
2300 SD 92037 1227-H5
CALLE DEL ALCALDE
7700 SDCo 91962 1237-C6
CALLE DEL ALCAZAR
7700 SDCo 92067 1168-G5
CALLE DE LA PALOMA
300 SDCo 92028 1027-H3
CALLE DE LA PAZ
500 ESCN 92029 1149-J3
CALLE DE LA PLATA
7900 SD 92037 1227-H5
CALLE DEL ARCO
1400 SDCo 92028 998-J7
CALLE DE LA REINA
9700 SDCo 92026 1069-D7
9700 SDCo 92082 1069-D7
CALLE DEL ARROYO
1500 SDCo 92078 1128-C3
CALLE DE LAS FOCAS
3800 SCLE 92672 1023-B1
CALLE DE LA SIENA
12600 SD 92130 1188-B6
CALLE DE LA SIERRA
500 SDCo 92019 1252-F4
CALLE DE LAS LOMAS
7000 SDCo 92067 1148-G6
CALLE DE LAS PIEDRAS
3300 SDCo 92084 1068-F5
CALLE DE LAS ROSAS
12700 SD 92129 1189-F5
CALLE DE LA TIERRA BAJA
- SDCo 92040 1232-C2
CALLE DEL BASTON
1000 SDCo 92078 1128-C3
CALLE DEL BOSQUE
7600 SDCo 91962 1237-D6
CALLE DEL CAMPANARIO
16200 SDCo 92067 1168-F6
CALLE DEL CAMPO
- SD 92129 1189-A4
CALLE DEL CIELO
- SDCo 92040 1232-A1
8000 SD 92037 1227-H5
CALLE DEL CONEJO
1800 ELCJ 92021 1252-C2
CALLE DEL CRUCE
6600 SDCo 92067 1168-H5
CALLE DE LEON
12000 SDCo 92019 1272-A4
CALLE DE LEPANTO
900 ESCN 92025 1150-D3
CALLE DEL ESTABLO
3800 SCLE 92672 1023-B1
CALLE DELGADO
1400 NATC 91950 1310-B1
CALLE DEL GRECO
4600 OCN 92056 1087-B3
CALLE DEL HUMO
8100 SD 92126 1209-B1
CALLE DELICADA
1600 SD 92037 1247-J3
CALLE DE LIMAR
1000 SDCo 92028 1027-H6
CALLE DE LINEA
6900 SD 92154 1351-D4
CALLE DEL LAGO
9400 SNTE 92071 1231-A5
CALLE DEL NIDO
16200 SDCo 92067 1168-E6
CALLE DEL ORO
2300 SD 92037 1227-H5
CALLE DE LOS NINOS
13100 SD 92129 1189-G5
CALLE DE LOS POTROS
5100 SDCo 91902 1290-H7
CALLE DE LOS SERRANOS
1100 SDCo 92078 1128-G4
CALLE DEL PALO
4500 OCN 92057 1066-H6
CALLE DEL PORTAL
- ESCN 92026 1109-G7
7900 SDCo 92021 1252-B1
CALLE DEL RANCHO
100 SDCo 92025 1130-B6
CALLE DEL RIO
12000 SDCo 92040 1232-A6
CALLE DEL SOL
- SMCS 92078 1129-C1
1400 VSTA 92084 1088-B6
13700 SDCo 91935 1272-G7
13700 SDCo 91935 1292-G1
CALLE DEL SUR
3300 CRLB 92009 1147-J2
CALLE DEL VERDE
8900 SNTE 92071 1231-A6
CALLE DEL VUELTA
4700 SDCo 92028 1048-B5
CALLE DE MADERA
200 ENCT 92024 1147-B4
CALLE DE MALIBU
2800 SDCo 92029 1149-J2
CALLE DE MARIA
500 ENCT 92024 1147-F5
12000 SD 92128 1170-B3
CALLE DE MEDIO
12000 SDCo 92019 1272-A4
CALLE DE MONTANA
12000 SDCo 92019 1272-A4
CALLE DE NEWMAN
14500 SD 92129 1189-D1
CALLE DE NICOLE
- SDCo 92019 1253-C4
CALLE DE ORO
3100 SDCo 91935 1272-J7
3100 SDCo 91935 1292-J1
CALLE DE ORO E
1200 CALX 92231 6620-H7
CALLE DE ORO W
1200 CALX 92231 6620-G7
CALLE DE PESCADORES
2400 SDCo 91901 1254-C1
CALLE DE PORTOLA
- SMCS 92078 1129-A1
CALLE DEPOSITO
11800 SDCo 92019 1271-J4
CALLE DE PRIMRA
1600 SD 92037 1247-J3
CALLE DE RETIRO
4600 OCN 92057 1066-J7
CALLE DE ROB
12600 SDCo 92064 1191-D5
12600 SDCo 92071 1191-D5
CALLE DE SALUD
- SDCo 92067 1149-B3
CALLE DESCANSO
- SDCo 92065 1152-G6
CALLE DE SERENO
200 ENCT 92024 1147-B5
CALLE DE SOTO
- SMCS 92078 1129-A2
CALLE DE SUENO
4100 SDCo 92028 1047-F4
CALLE DE TALAR
31300 SDCo 92003 1068-H2
CALLE DE TIERRA
2200 SDCo 91901 1253-H1
CALLE DEVANAR
1500 SDCo 92078 1128-C4
CALLE DE VERANO
- SMCS 92078 1129-A2
CALLE DE VIDA
4200 SD 92124 1249-J2
4400 SD 92124 1250-B2
CALLE DE VISTA
13800 SDCo 92082 1090-E3
27300 SDCo 92082 1091-A4
CALLE DE VISTA OESTE
9200 SD 92129 1189-D1
CALLE DIEGUENO
15100 SDCo 92067 1188-F2
CALLE DIEGUENO RD
6700 SDCo 92067 1188-G1
CALLE DOS LAGOS
7600 SDCo 92067 1168-J2
CALLE DOS LOMAS
2200 SDCo 92028 1048-B2
CALLE DULCE
- CHV 91910 1311-A6
1600 VSTA 92084 1087-J3
CALLE ELEGANTE
- VSTA 92083 1087-G5
CALLE EMPARRADO
500 SMCS 92069 1108-E5
CALLE EMPINADA
6100 SD 92120 1250-D5
CALLE ENCANTO
500 SDCo 92019 1252-C6
CALLE ENTRE
1900 LMGR 91945 1290-F1
CALLE ESCARPADA
1000 CHV 91902 1310-H3
CALLE ESTEPONA
18000 SD 92128 1150-D6
CALLE ESTRELLA
4700 OCN 92057 1066-J7
CALLE FAMILIA
4300 SDCo 92067 1167-J4
CALLE FANITA
8000 SNTE 92071 1251-A1
CALLE FANTASIA
1100 SMCS 92069 1108-E4
CALLE FELICIDAD
900 ESCN 92025 1150-D3
CALLE FELIZ
16400 SDCo 92067 1168-E4
CALLE FERNANDO
- CHV 91914 1311-F2
CALLE FLORECITA
200 ESCN 92029 1150-A3
1100 CHV 91910 1310-J5
1100 CHV 91910 1311-A5
CALLE FORTUNADA
3800 SD 92123 1249-E3
CALLE FRANCESCA
3800 SCLE 92672 1023-B1
CALLE FREDERICO
11600 SDCo 92019 1271-J4
CALLE FRESCOTA
2100 SD 92037 1227-H5
CALLE FUEGO
3100 CRLB 92009 1127-J7
CALLE GAVANZO
3500 CRLB 92009 1148-A2
CALLE GAVIOTA
2400 SD 92139 1310-D1
CALLE GOYA
1300 OCN 92056 1087-B3
CALLE GUAYMAS
2100 SD 92037 1247-J2
CALLE GUERNICA
100 SMCS 92069 1109-C7
CALLE HACIENDA
2700 CRLB 92010 1106-C6
CALLE HELENA
- IMP 92251 6499-E2
CALLE HERMOSA
16700 SDCo 92127 1169-A3
CALLE HIDALGO
- CRLB 92009 1128-A5
CALLE HUERTO
100 VSTA 92084 1088-D6
CALLE INDEPENDENCIA
500 VSTA 92083 1087-G5
CALLE ISABEL
100 SMCS 92069 1109-C7
CALLE ISABELINO
- SD 92130 1208-B3
CALLE ISABELLA
4000 SCLE 92672 1023-B2
CALLE JALAPA
11200 SD 92126 1209-B2
CALLE JALISCO
7800 CRLB 92009 1147-J3
CALLEJA RISA
8400 SDCo 92021 1232-D7
CALLEJO FELIZ DR
15900 SDCo 92082 1071-A4
CALLEJO FELIZ TER
30400 SDCo 92082 1071-A3
CALLEJON ST
2800 SD 92139 1310-D2
CALLEJON ALHAMBRA
1300 CHV 91910 1311-B5
CALLEJON ANDALUSIA
1300 CHV 91910 1311-B5
CALLEJON CARBON
1300 CHV 91910 1311-C5
CALLEJON CERVANTE
1300 CHV 91910 1311-B5
CALLEJON CIUDAD
700 CHV 91910 1311-B5
CALLEJON ESPANA
600 CHV 91910 1311-B5
CALLEJON MALAGA
600 CHV 91910 1311-B5
CALLEJON MONTEFRIO
1300 CHV 91910 1311-C5
CALLEJON MUSICA
14400 SD 92129 1189-D1
CALLE JON NORTE
16900 SDCo 92067 1168-D3
CALLEJON PALACIOS
1300 CHV 91910 1311-B5
CALLEJON QUINTANA
11500 SD 92124 1230-A7
CALLEJON SEGOVIA
1300 CHV 91910 1311-B5
CALLE JON SUR
16900 SDCo 92067 1168-D3
CALLE JOVEN
4600 OCN 92057 1086-J1
CALLE JOYA
31200 SDCo 92003 1068-H2
CALLE JUAN
10700 SDCo 91978 1271-F5
CALLE JUANITA
300 SMCS 92069 1109-C7
CALLE JUANITO
15000 SD 92129 1169-H7
CALLE JUEGO
16000 SDCo 92091 1168-C7
CALLE JUELA
7800 SD 92037 1227-H6
CALLE JULES
1200 VSTA 92084 1087-J4
CALLE LA BEATA
11600 SDCo 92019 1271-J4
CALLE LADERA
600 ESCN 92025 1130-B4
30100 SDCo 92082 1071-A4
CALLE LAGASCA
800 CHV 91910 1310-H5
CALLE LA MARINA E
- CHV 91914 1311-E2
CALLE LA MARINA W
- CHV 91914 1311-E2
CALLE LA MIRADA
200 CHV 91902 1310-H3
CALLE LA PREZA
- SDCo 92040 1232-C2
CALLE LA QUINTA
300 CHV 91914 1311-F2
CALLE LA REINA
30300 SDCo 92003 1068-D4
CALLE LAS CASAS
1600 OCN 92056 1087-C4
CALLE LA SERRA
8500 SDCo 92091 1148-F5
CALLE LAS MORAS
1500 VSTA 92084 1088-B4
CALLE LAS PALMAS
- ELCJ 92021 1251-H5
1800 OCN 92056 1087-C4
CALLE LAS POSITAS
4700 OCN 92057 1066-J7
CALLE LETICIA
1600 SD 92037 1247-J3
CALLE LIMONERO
11900 SDCo 92019 1271-J3
11900 SDCo 92019 1272-A4
CALLE LINDA
100 SDCo 92028 1047-G4
CALLE LISA
4000 SCLE 92672 1023-B2
CALLE LOMA LN
30400 SDCo 92003 1068-B4
CALLE LOMAS
- CRLB 92009 1147-J2
CALLE LOMEDA
1400 SDCo 92028 997-H7
CALLE LORENZANA
11900 SDCo 92019 1271-J4
11900 SDCo 92019 1272-A4
CALLE LORETO
- SDCo 91906 (1318-H6 See Page 1298)
CALLE LOS ARBOLES
3000 SDCo 91978 1271-G6
CALLE LOS SANTOS
4700 OCN 92057 1066-J7
CALLE LOUISA
4000 SCLE 92672 1023-B2
CALLE LUCIA
9000 SDCo 92040 1232-B6
CALLE LUCIA CT
9000 SDCo 92040 1232-B6
CALLE LUCIA LN
9000 SDCo 92040 1232-B6
CALLE LUCIA TER
12400 SDCo 92040 1232-B6
CALLE LUNA
7300 CRLB 92009 1127-J7
CALLE MADERO
7600 CRLB 92009 1147-H2
CALLE MADRID
7900 CRLB 92009 1147-H3
CALLE MADRIGAL
1900 SD 92037 1247-H1
CALLE MAGDALENA
100 ENCT 92024 1147-D7
CALLE MAJORCA
6200 SD 92037 1247-G2
CALLE MARBELLA
1400 OCN 92056 1087-C3
CALLE MAR DE ARMONIA
4400 SD 92130 1208-C2
CALLE MAR DE BALLENAS
- SD 92130 1208-B3
CALLE MAR DE MARIPOSA
- SD 92130 1208-B4
CALLE MARGARITA
3300 ENCT 92024 1148-B4
CALLE MARIA
1100 SDCo 92069 1109-C5
1200 SMCS 92069 1109-C5
CALLE MARIBEL
100 SMCS 92069 1109-C7
CALLE MARIETTA
- SDCo 92082 1051-A7
CALLE MARINERO
10100 SDCo 91977 1271-E7
10100 SDCo 91977 1291-E1
CALLE MARIPOSA
300 OCN 92057 1066-J7
CALLE MARISELDA
6100 SD 92124 1229-H7
CALLE MARLENA
4000 SCLE 92672 1023-B2
CALLE MAYOR
17200 SDCo 92067 1168-H5
CALLE MEJILLONES
4200 SD 92130 1208-B3
CALLE MEJOR
- CRLB 92009 1147-J2
CALLE MESITA
1000 CHV 91902 1310-H3
CALLE MESQUITE
3000 SDCo 91935 1292-H3
CALLE MESSINA
- SDCo 92067 1148-G5
- SDCo 92091 1148-G5
CALLE MIA
3400 SDCo 91901 1254-E1
CALLE MINAS
8200 SD 92126 1209-B2
CALLE MIRADOR
8600 SDCo 92021 1232-E7
CALLE MIRAMAR
5500 SD 92037 1247-J3
CALLE MONTECITO
200 OCN 92057 1066-J7
200 OCN 92057 1086-J1
CALLE MONTELIBANO
14800 SDCo 92067 1188-G1
CALLE MONTERA
700 ESCN 92025 1150-C3
CALLE MORELOS
8100 SD 92126 1209-C2
CALLE NADA
1400 SDCo 91901 1234-H6
CALLE NARANJA
11900 SDCo 92019 1272-A3
CALLE NARCISOS
1500 ENCT 92024 1167-G1
CALLE NEIL
4800 SD 92117 1248-F5
4800 SD 92111 1248-F5
CALLE NIQUEL
1800 OCN 92056 1087-B5
CALLE NOBLEZA
11700 SD 92128 1170-A4
CALLE NORTE
8500 LMGR 91945 1270-J7
CALLE NUBLADO
14400 SD 92129 1189-D1
CALLE NUEVA
8200 SD 92126 1209-B1
CALLE ODESSA
3300 CRLB 92009 1147-J2
CALLE OLIVIA
7800 CRLB 92009 1147-G2
CALLE OPIMA
1900 SD 92037 1227-H4
CALLE ORO VERDE
10700 SDCo 92082 1049-E6
CALLE ORQUIDEAS
1500 ENCT 92024 1147-G7
CALLE OSUNA
3100 OCN 92056 1106-J2
3100 OCN 92056 1107-A1
CALLE OVIEDA
- SDCo 92065 1173-D1
CALLE PACIFICA
- SMCS 92078 1129-C1
CALLE PALMITO
- CRLB 92009 1148-A2
CALLE PARACHO
11500 SD 92128 1170-A5
11500 SD 92128 1169-J5
CALLE PARRAL
11800 SD 92128 1170-A6
CALLE PAULA
600 SOLB 92075 1167-J6
CALLE PAVANA
6200 SD 92139 1290-E7
6200 SD 92139 1310-E1
CALLE PENSAMIENTOS
1500 ENCT 92024 1167-G1
CALLE PEQUENA
6600 SDCo 92067 1168-H5
CALLE PERICO
8800 SD 92129 1189-C3
CALLE PINABETE
- CRLB 92009 1147-G2
CALLE PINO
8200 SD 92126 1209-B1
CALLE PINON
8000 CRLB 92009 1147-H3
CALLE PLATICO
1700 OCN 92056 1087-C4
CALLE PLATINO
4000 OCN 92056 1087-B6
CALLE PLUMERIAS
1600 ENCT 92024 1167-G1
CALLE POCO
2100 SDCo 92019 1252-D7
CALLE PONTE BELLA RD
6500 SDCo 92091 1148-E5
CALLE PORTONE
6800 SDCo 92091 1148-F5
CALLE POSADA
7900 CRLB 92009 1147-J3
CALLE POTRANCA
200 SCLE 92672 1023-B1
CALLE POTRO
200 SCLE 92672 1023-B1
CALLE PRIMERA
200 SD 92173 1350-G4
CALLE PRIVADA
14800 SDCo 92067 1188-F1
CALLE PROSPERO
1100 SMCS 92069 1108-E4
CALLE PUEBLITO
15300 SD 92128 1170-B6
CALLE PULIDO
16400 SD 92128 1170-A4

SAN DIEGO CO. STREET INDEX

STREET
Block City ZIP Pg-Grid

CALLE QUEBRADA
2400 SD 92139 1310-E1
CALLE QUERIDO
100 SMCS 92069 1109-C7
100 SMCS 92069 1129-C1
CALLE RANCHO VISTA
2600 ENCT 92024 1148-A5
CALLE REDONDA LN
1400 ESCN 92026 1109-E5
CALLE REGAL
700 ENCT 92024 1147-D7
CALLE REINA
6500 SDCo 92067 1148-E6
CALLE RICARDO
400 SDCo 92026 1109-G1
CALLE ROCIADA
1900 SDCo 92028 996-E1
CALLE ROSADO
8700 SDCo 92021 1232-E6
CALLE ROSAS
32000 SDCo 92061 1051-E5
CALLE ROXANNE
40000 SDCo 92028 996-F1
CALLE RYAN
1400 ENCT 92024 1167-G2
CALLE SABROSO
- CHV 91914 1311-F3
CALLE SALIDA DEL SOL
2800 SD 92139 1310-D2
CALLE SAL SI PUEDES
5600 SD 92139 1310-D2
CALLE SAN BLAS
3300 CRLB 92009 1147-J3
CALLE SAN CLEMENTE
2400 ENCT 92024 1148-A5
CALLE SAN FELIPE
7900 CRLB 92009 1147-H3
CALLE SAN MIGUEL
2400 ENCT 92024 1148-A5
CALLE SANTA CATALINA
2600 ENCT 92024 1148-A5
CALLE SANTA CRUZ
800 ENCT 92024 1148-A6
CALLE SANTA FE
600 SOLB 92075 1167-J6
CALLE SANTANDER
4000 OCN 92056 1087-B3
CALLE SANTIAGO
900 CHV 91910 1311-B6
7700 CRLB 92009 1147-J2
CALLE SCOTT
1300 ENCT 92024 1167-G2
CALLE SECO
13700 PWY 92064 1190-G5
CALLE SERENA
- SMCS 92078 1129-C2
2100 SD 92139 1290-D7
2100 SD 92139 1310-D1
17200 SDCo 92067 1168-H6
CALLE SIERRA
8700 SDCo 91977 1291-A2
CALLE SIMPSON
11500 SDCo 92019 1271-J3
CALLE SINALOA
1800 VSTA 92084 1088-C5
CALLESITA ESCENA
300 CHV 91914 1311-E2
CALLESITA MARIOLA
300 CHV 91914 1311-E2
CALLESITA VILLENA
300 CHV 91914 1311-F2
CALLE SOBRADO
4900 OCN 92056 1087-C3
CALLE SOLIMAR
4700 OCN 92057 1066-J7
CALLE SONIA
1200 SDCo 92028 1027-H4
CALLE STELLINA RD
18300 SDCo 92091 1148-E5
CALLE SUACILLO
12100 SD 92128 1170-B6
CALLE SUNTUOSO
11900 SD 92128 1170-A4
CALLE SUR
8500 LMGR 91945 1270-J7
CALLE SUSANA
2600 CRLB 92010 1106-H3
CALLE TALENTIA
800 ESCN 92025 1150-C3
CALLE TAMEGA
12500 SD 92128 1170-C5
CALLE TECOLOTLAN
1300 SDCo 92028 1028-E4
CALLE TEMPRA
1300 CHV 91911 1330-D4
CALLE TESORO
1000 CHV 91915 1311-H5
CALLE TEZAC
10900 SDCo 91941 1271-G5
CALLE TIARA
2200 SD 92037 1247-J2
3800 SCLE 92672 1023-B1
CALLE TIBURON
3800 SCLE 92672 1023-B1
CALLE TIERRA BLANCA
6500 SDCo 92067 1188-G1
CALLE TIJERA
1800 VSTA 92084 1088-B5
CALLE TIMITEO
3300 CRLB 92009 1147-J2
3400 CRLB 92009 1148-A2
CALLE TOCON
6100 SD 92139 1310-E1
CALLE TORRENO
- CHV 91914 1311-F2
CALLE TORTUOSA
2100 SD 92139 1290-E7
CALLE TRAGAR
8800 SD 92129 1189-C3
CALLE TRAMONTO RD
18300 SDCo 92091 1148-E5
CALLE TREPADORA
5800 SD 92139 1290-D7
5800 SD 92139 1310-D1
CALLE TRES LOMAS
2200 SD 92139 1310-E1
CALLE TRES VISTAS
- ENCT 92024 1148-B4
CALLE TRUCKSESS
11700 SDCo 92019 1271-J4
CALLE TULIPANES
1500 ENCT 92024 1147-G7
1500 ENCT 92024 1167-G1
CALLE ULTIMO
1200 OCN 92056 1087-B4
CALLE VALENCIA
6100 SDCo 92067 1168-G7
CALLE VALERIA
3000 SDCo 91935 1292-G3
CALLE VALLARTA
3200 CRLB 92009 1147-H4

STREET
Block City ZIP Pg-Grid

CALLE VALLECITO
300 OCN 92057 1066-J7
CALLE VALPERIZO
3000 CRLB 92009 1127-J4
CALLE VAQUERO
1400 SD 92037 1247-J3
CALLE VENADO
1600 SDCo 92078 1128-B4
CALLE VENECIA
14000 SD 92130 1188-D3
CALLE VERA CRUZ
6200 SD 92037 1247-J2
CALLE VERANO
7300 CRLB 92009 1127-J7
CALLE VERDE
- SDCo 92040 1232-A1
10800 SDCo 91941 1271-G5
CALLE VIDA BUENA
17900 SDCo 92067 1168-A1
CALLE VIENTO
3100 CRLB 92009 1127-J7
CALLE VIOLETAS
1500 ENCT 92024 1147-G7
CALLE VISTA
1100 SMCS 92078 1129-C1
5300 SD 92109 1247-J4
CALLE VISTA AV
1100 ESCN 92027 1109-J6
CALLE VIVIANO
8600 SDCo 92021 1232-D6
CALLE VIVIENDA
11700 SD 92128 1169-J5
11700 SD 92128 1170-A5
CALLIANDRA RD
- CRLB 92011 1127-D5
8800 SD 92126 1209-D3
CALLIGRAPHY CT
4700 OCN 92057 1087-B2
CALLIO WY
- SDCo 92040 1231-G3
CALLISIA CT
- CRLB 92011 1127-D4
CALLOWAY DR
- SDCo 92127 1169-E4
CALMA CT
1200 VSTA 92081 1107-H4
12600 SD 92128 1170-C3
CALMA DR
900 CHV 91910 1310-H7
900 CHV 91910 1330-H1
CALMA PL
600 CHV 91910 1310-H7
CALMANTE LN
- SD 92108 1249-E7
CALMAR DR
2800 SDCo 92029 1149-J2
CALMERIA PL
6400 CRLB 92011 1127-A4
CALMIN DR
1100 SDCo 92028 1027-J4
1700 SDCo 92028 1028-A5
CALMIN WY
1600 SDCo 92028 1027-J4
CALMOOR ST
4000 NATC 91950 1310-E3
CALMOOR WY
3700 NATC 91950 1310-E3
CALOMA CIR
7500 CRLB 92009 1147-J1
CALPELLA CT
- CHV 91913 1331-B1
CALSTON PL
7100 SD 92126 1208-J4
CALSTON WY
10600 SD 92126 1208-J4
CALTHA PL
- CRLB 92011 1127-D5
CALUMET AV
5300 SD 92037 1247-F4
CALVACADO ST
7500 LMGR 91945 1290-G2
CALVADOS PL
- SD 92128 1190-A3
CALVARY DR
300 ELCN 92243 6499-H4
CALVARY LN
100 ELCJ 92019 1252-D5
CALVARY RD
13900 PWY 92064 1190-G3
CALVEDOS DR
1800 CHV 91913 1311-E7
CALVIN LN
1200 ESCN 92025 1129-H5
2500 ELCJ 92020 1251-B5
CALVIN WY
5700 SD 92120 1250-D7
CALYPSO DR
1800 VSTA 92081 1107-H5
CALYPSO PL
3000 SD 92106 1268-C5
CALZADA DE LA FUENTE
- SDCo 92154 1332-C7
CALZADA DEL BOSQUE
5300 SDCo 92067 1168-C5
CAMACHO RD
300 CALX 92231 6620-E6
300 ImCo 92231 6620-E6
CAMARA CT
1400 VSTA 92081 1107-H4
CAMARENA CT
100 CALX 92231 6620-F6
CAMARENA RD
12700 SD 92130 1188-B5
CAMARERO CT
12500 SD 92130 1188-B6
CAMARGO CT
14300 SD 92129 1189-H2
CAMARILLO AV
3000 OCN 92056 1087-B7
3000 OCN 92056 1107-B1
CAMAROSA CIR
11200 SD 92126 1209-C2
CAMASSIA LN
- CRLB 92011 1127-D4
CAMBER CT
5600 SD 92117 1248-H2
CAMBER DR
5500 SD 92117 1248-H2
CAMBER PL
5700 SD 92117 1248-H2
CAMBERLEY CT
- SD 92154 1330-H7
CAMBERWELL CT
12600 SD 92128 1150-B6
CAMBERWELL LN
18300 SD 92128 1150-B6
CAMBON CT
9100 SDCo 91977 1291-B4
CAMBON ST
9100 SDCo 91977 1291-B4
CAMBRIA CT
5500 SD 92120 1250-B7

STREET
Block City ZIP Pg-Grid

CAMBRIA PL
- ENCT 92024 1147-F5
1600 ESCN 92029 1129-G7
CAMBRIA WY
- ENCT 92024 1147-F5
CAMBRIDGE
1900 VSTA 92081 1108-E2
CAMBRIDGE AV
1900 ENCT 92007 1167-D3
CAMBRIDGE CT
1100 SMCS 92078 1128-B3
3800 OCN 92056 1087-A7
8800 SDCo 92040 1232-C6
CAMBRIDGE WY
4500 CRLB 92010 1107-B4
CAMBURY CT
9700 SNTE 92071 1231-C4
CAMBURY DR
9400 SNTE 92071 1231-C5
E CAMDEN AV
100 ELCJ 92020 1251-G6
W CAMDEN AV
100 ELCJ 92020 1251-F6
CAMDEN CIR
3400 CRLB 92008 1106-G4
CAMDEN DR
- VSTA 92081 1108-B6
CAMDEN GN
- ESCN 92027 1110-D7
CAMDEN PL
- SD 92131 1210-J2
- SMCS 92069 1108-J3
CAMELAS WK
- SDCo 92127 1169-F4
CAMELIA DR
- SD 92109 1248-C6
CAMELIA ST
1100 OCN 92054 1106-C2
CAMELLIA
3500 SDCo 92028 1028-F4
CAMELLIA CT
1400 CHV 91911 1330-H3
CAMELLIA DR
7100 LMSA 91941 1270-F3
CAMELLIA PL
700 CRLB 92008 1106-F6
N CAMELLIA ST
600 ESCN 92027 1110-B6
CAMELOT CT
7200 LMGR 91945 1290-F1
CAMELOT DR
300 OCN 92054 1086-E6
CAMELOT PKWY
- ELCJ 92019 1252-D4
CAMEO CT
3700 SD 92111 1248-G4
CAMEO DR
500 ESCN 92026 1109-H6
1700 VSTA 92083 1087-D6
3400 OCN 92056 1086-J7
3400 OCN 92056 1106-J1
3500 OCN 92056 1087-A7
CAMEO LN
3600 SD 92111 1248-G4
CAMEO RD
2200 CRLB 92008 1106-H5
CAMERO ST
5400 SD 92105 1270-B5
CAMERON CT
6000 SD 92139 1310-D2
CAMERON DR
1600 LMGR 91945 1290-H1
8100 SDCo 91977 1290-H1
CAMERON PL
2700 ESCN 92027 1110-D6
CAMERON TKTR
2200 SDCo 91906 (1297-J3 See Page 1296)
2300 SDCo 91906 1298-A2
2400 SDCo 91906 430-B7
CAMILIA ST
- CALX 92231 6620-H7
CAMILLE WY
200 VSTA 92083 1107-J1
8900 SDCo 92026 1089-A1
CAMILLO CT
1400 ELCJ 92021 1252-A2
CAMILLO WY
1200 ELCJ 92021 1252-A3
CAMINATA BREVE
13900 SD 92129 1189-H3
CAMINATA DELUZ
10700 SD 92129 1189-H3
CAMINATA DOURO
11000 SD 92129 1189-H2
CAMINATA EBRO
10700 SD 92129 1189-H2
CAMINATA SOLEADO
14300 SD 92129 1189-H2
CAMINATA TAUGUS
14300 SD 92129 1189-H2
CAMINITA AMADOR
14000 SD 92129 1189-H2
CAMINITA CORTINA
3100 SDCo 92028 1048-A2
CAMINITO ABETO
2600 SD 92154 1350-C1
CAMINITO ABRAZO
8700 SD 92037 1228-A3
CAMINITO ABRUZZO
- CHV 91915 1311-G7
CAMINITO A CASA
400 SMCS 92078 1129-B2
CAMINITO ACENTO
1300 SD 92037 1247-H3
CAMINITO ACLARA
11200 SD 92126 1208-H2
CAMINITO AFUERA
2300 SD 92107 1268-C2
CAMINITO AGADIR
10200 SD 92131 1209-G5
CAMINITO AGRADO
2300 SD 92107 1268-B6
CAMINITO AGUA
5400 SD 92037 1248-A3
CAMINITO AGUAR
1500 SDCo 92078 1128-C3
CAMINITO AGUILAR
3800 SD 92111 1248-H3
CAMINITO AIRE PURO
15800 SD 92128 1170-B5
CAMINITO ALCALA
- CHV 91913 1331-F1
CAMINITO ALEGRA
11000 SD 92131 1210-B2
CAMINITO ALEGRE
800 CHV 91911 1330-J1
CAMINITO ALICIA
800 CHV 91911 1330-J1
CAMINITO ALIVIADO
1600 SD 92037 1247-J3
CAMINITO ALMONTE
14000 SD 92129 1189-H3

STREET
Block City ZIP Pg-Grid

CAMINITO ALTO
10800 SD 92131 1210-C2
CAMINITO ALVAREZ
11100 SD 92126 1208-J4
CAMINITO AMAPOLA
100 SMCS 92069 1109-B7
CAMINITO AMARILLO
1100 SMCS 92069 1108-F5
CAMINITO AMECA
3100 SD 92037 1228-A5
CAMINITO AMERGON
1800 SD 92037 1247-J2
CAMINITO AMERIGO
- CHV 91915 1311-G7
CAMINITO AMISTAD
2400 SD 92154 1352-B3
CAMINITO AMPARO
3900 SD 92122 1228-B4
CAMINITO ANDADA
2300 SD 92107 1268-C3
CAMINITO ANDRETA
6200 SD 92111 1268-H2
CAMINITO ANGELICO
12900 SD 92130 1188-C5
CAMINITO ANTILDADO
4800 SD 92130 1188-C7
CAMINITO ANZIO
10500 SD 92129 1189-H3
CAMINITO APARTADO
5200 SD 92108 1269-H2
CAMINITO ARALIA
10300 SD 92131 1209-G6
CAMINITO ARAYA
6200 SD 92122 1228-E5
CAMINITO ARBOLES
10900 SD 92131 1210-C2
CAMINITO ARCADA
10800 SD 92131 1209-H1
CAMINITO ARDIENTE
1700 SD 92037 1247-J2
CAMINITO ARENOSO
3000 SD 92117 1248-C2
CAMINITO ARMIDA
11400 SD 92131 1209-J5
11400 SD 92131 1210-A5
CAMINITO ARONIMINK
2500 SD 92037 1247-J1
CAMINITO ARRIATA
1300 SD 92037 1247-J4
CAMINITO ARUBA
5200 SD 92124 1249-F2
CAMINITO ASCUA
1800 SD 92037 1247-J2
CAMINITO ASTERISCO
1600 SD 92037 1247-J2
CAMINITO ATICO
15700 SD 92128 1170-A5
CAMINITO AUGOSTINO
- CHV 91915 1311-G7
CAMINITO AVELLANO
2500 SD 92154 1350-B1
CAMINITO AVOLA
7600 SD 92037 1227-H6
CAMINITO AZUL
800 CRLB 92011 1126-J5
CAMINITO BADALONA
3000 SD 92014 1187-H3
CAMINITO BAEZA
6100 SD 92122 1228-E6
CAMINITO BALADA
1300 SD 92037 1247-H3
CAMINITO BALATA
17500 SD 92128 1170-D1
CAMINITO BALTUSRAL
6400 SD 92037 1248-A1
CAMINITO BANYON
10300 SD 92131 1209-H5
CAMINITO BARBUDA
14700 SD 92014 1188-B1
CAMINITO BARCELONA
300 CHV 91914 1311-E2
CAMINITO BARLOVENTO
1600 SD 92037 1247-J3
CAMINITO BARTOLO
- CHV 91915 1311-G7
CAMINITO BASILIO
6200 SD 92111 1268-G3
CAMINITO BASSANO E
7300 SD 92037 1227-H7
CAMINITO BASSANO W
7300 SD 92037 1227-H7
CAMINITO BASSWOOD
10500 SD 92131 1209-H5
CAMINITO BATEA
1300 SD 92037 1247-J3
CAMINITO BAUTIZO
12900 SD 92130 1188-C5
CAMINITO BAYA
17400 SD 92127 1169-J1
CAMINITO BAYO
5400 SD 92037 1247-H4
CAMINITO BAYWOOD
10500 SD 92126 1209-D4
CAMINITO BELLA ROSA
800 CHV 91911 1330-J2
CAMINITO BELLO
2900 SD 92037 1227-J5
2900 SD 92037 1228-A5
CAMINITO BESO
12800 SD 92130 1188-C5
CAMINITO BLYTHEFIELD
6400 SD 92037 1247-J1
6600 SD 92037 1227-J7
CAMINITO BODEGA
12900 SD 92014 1207-J2
CAMINITO BOLSA
9700 SD 92129 1189-F4
CAMINITO BONANZA
7700 CRLB 92009 1148-A1
CAMINITO BORDE
5400 SD 92108 1269-H1
CAMINITO BORREGO
- CHV 91913 1311-E7
4700 SD 92130 1188-C6
CAMINITO BRACHO
13000 SD 92128 1170-D1
CAMINITO BRAGA
7000 SD 92122 1228-B4
CAMINITO BRAVURA
10700 SD 92108 1249-G7
CAMINITO BRIOSO
12400 SD 92131 1210-C2
CAMINITO BRISA
1800 SD 92037 1227-H7
CAMINITO BUENA SUERTE
6200 SD 92120 1250-D6
CAMINITO CABALA
2200 SD 92037 1248-A2
CAMINITO CABANA
9400 SD 92126 1209-E5
CAMINITO CABO VIEJO
3300 SD 92014 1187-H3

STREET
Block City ZIP Pg-Grid

CAMINITO CACHORRO
5000 SD 92105 1270-A7
CAMINITO CADENA
12000 SD 92128 1170-B2
CAMINITO CALA
2300 SD 92014 1207-H1
CAMINITO CALDO
- SD 92127 1169-J1
CAMINITO CALMOSO
4700 SD 92130 1188-C5
CAMINITO CALOR
9700 SD 92131 1210-A5
CAMINITO CAMELIA
- SD 92127 1188-J1
CAMINITO CAMPANA
11900 SD 92128 1170-B2
CAMINITO CAMPANEO
4700 SD 92130 1188-B4
CAMINITO CANADA
10900 SD 92131 1210-C3
CAMINITO CANASTO
17200 SD 92127 1169-J1
CAMINITO CANCION
12700 SD 92128 1170-C3
CAMINITO CANELO
12400 SD 92131 1210-C3
CAMINITO CANON
12400 SD 92131 1210-C3
CAMINITO CANOR
4700 SD 92130 1188-B4
CAMINITO CANTARAS
15800 SD 92014 1187-H1
CAMINITO CANTEBRIA
800 CHV 91911 1330-J1
CAMINITO CANTILENA
18600 SD 92128 1150-A5
CAMINITO CAPA
2000 SD 92037 1227-H7
CAMINITO CAPE SEBASTIAN
2900 ENCT 92007 1167-F5
CAMINITO CAPISTRANO
- CHV 91913 1311-E7
CAMINITO CARBONERAS
3000 SD 92014 1187-H3
CAMINITO CARDELINA
5800 SD 92037 1247-J2
CAMINITO CARINO
2600 SD 92037 1227-J6
CAMINITO CARLOTTA
7200 SD 92120 1250-E4
CAMINITO CARMEL
13300 SD 92014 1207-J1
CAMINITO CARMEL LNDG
3500 SD 92130 1188-A7
CAMINITO CARMEL HARBOUR
12100 SD 92130 1188-A7
CAMINITO CAROLINA
1200 ENCT 92024 1148-B5
CAMINITO CARRENA
6200 SD 92122 1228-E5
CAMINITO CARTA
- SMCS 92078 1128-H2
CAMINITO CARTGATE
2400 SD 92037 1247-J1
CAMINITO CASCARA
10500 SD 92108 1269-G1
CAMINITO CASSIS
3900 SD 92122 1228-B5
CAMINITO CASTILLO
2200 SD 92037 1248-A2
CAMINITO CATALAN
6400 SD 92037 1247-J1
CAMINITO CEDRO
1200 SD 92154 1350-B1
CAMINITO CEDROS
2700 SD 92014 1207-J2
CAMINITO CENTRO
1300 SD 92102 1289-C2
1400 SD 92101 1289-C2
CAMINITO CERCADO
15700 SD 92128 1170-A5
CAMINITO CEREZO
10900 SD 92131 1210-C3
CAMINITO CHIAPAS
5900 SD 92108 1269-G1
CAMINITO CHICLAYO
17600 SD 92128 1170-C1
CAMINITO CHIRIMOLLA
9900 SD 92131 1209-G5
CAMINITO CHOLLAS
2700 SD 92105 1270-C7
CAMINITO CHUECO
10600 SD 92126 1209-D4
CAMINITO CIELO DEL MAR
3600 SD 92130 1188-A7
CAMINITO CIERA
13300 SD 92129 1189-G4
CAMINITO CINZIA
- CHV 91915 1311-G7
CAMINITO CIRCULO NORTE
2000 SD 92037 1248-A2
CAMINITO CIRCULO SUR
2000 SD 92037 1248-A3
CAMINITO CITA
1200 SD 92154 1350-C1
CAMINITO CLARO
8800 SD 92037 1228-A3
CAMINITO CLASICA
4800 SD 92130 1188-C7
CAMINITO CLAVO
6100 SD 92120 1250-D7
CAMINITO COLOMA
1200 CHV 91913 1311-E6
CAMINITO COLORADO
10800 SD 92131 1210-B2
CAMINITO CONNIE
- SDCo 92065 1172-H1
CAMINITO CONQUISTADOR
1300 CHV 91911 1330-J2
CAMINITO CONSUELO
5500 SD 92037 1248-A3
CAMINITO COROMANDEL
7500 SD 92037 1227-J6
CAMINITO CORRIENTE
11800 SD 92128 1170-A6
CAMINITO CORSICA
- CHV 91915 1311-G7
CAMINITO CORTINA
1300 CHV 91911 1330-J2
CAMINITO COVEWOOD
10200 SD 92131 1209-G6
CAMINITO CREMONA
- CHV 91915 1311-G7
CAMINITO CRISTALINO
4400 SD 92117 1248-C2
CAMINITO CRISTO
4700 SD 92130 1188-C6

STREET
Block City ZIP Pg-Grid

CAMINITO CRISTOBAL
13000 SD 92014 1207-J2
CAMINITO CRUZADA
7100 SD 92037 1227-H7
CAMINITO CUADRO
9800 SD 92129 1189-F4
CAMINITO CUARZO
4400 SD 92117 1248-C2
CAMINITO CUERVO
10200 SD 92108 1249-G7
CAMINITO CUESTA
10800 SD 92131 1210-C2
CAMINITO CUMBRES
800 CHV 91911 1330-J2
CAMINITO CURVA
6900 SD 92119 1250-F4
CAMINITO DANIELLA
3400 SD 92014 1187-J1
3400 SOLB 92014 1187-J1
CAMINITO DANTE
- CHV 91915 1311-F7
CAMINITO DANZARIN
5600 SD 92037 1247-H3
CAMINITO DAVILA
3900 SD 92122 1228-B5
CAMINITO DE CONEJOS
- SDCo 92067 1168-F1
CAMINITO DEHESA
3900 SD 92107 1268-C2
CAMINITO DE LA CRUZ
- CHV 91913 1331-F1
CAMINITO DE LA ESCENA
4300 SD 92108 1269-H2
CAMINITO DE LA FADA
9700 SD 92124 1249-F1
CAMINITO DE LA GALLARDA
12500 SD 92128 1170-C3
CAMINITO DE LA LUNA
1300 CHV 91911 1330-J2
CAMINITO DE LAS MISSIONES
11700 SD 92128 1170-A5
CAMINITO DE LAS NOCHES
16000 SD 92128 1170-A4
CAMINITO DE LAS OLAS
12800 SD 92014 1207-H1
CAMINITO DE LAS PALMAS
16700 SDCo 92127 1168-J3
CAMINITO DE LA TAZA
5900 SD 92120 1250-D7
CAMINITO DEL BARCO
2100 SD 92014 1207-G1
CAMINITO DEL CANTO
12900 SD 92014 1207-H1
CAMINITO DEL CERVATO
6300 SD 92111 1268-H1
CAMINITO DEL CID
7900 SD 92037 1227-H6
CAMINITO DEL DIAMANTE
4300 SD 92121 1228-D1
CAMINITO DEL ESTIO
5800 SD 92037 1247-H3
CAMINITO DEL FELIZ
9500 SD 92121 1228-D1
CAMINITO DEL GRECO
6700 SD 92120 1250-E4
CAMINITO DEL HOY
11700 SD 92128 1170-A5
CAMINITO DE LINDA
16000 SD 92128 1170-A5
CAMINITO DEL MAR
800 CRLB 92011 1126-J4
CAMINITO DEL MAR CV
3900 SD 92130 1188-A7
CAMINITO DEL MARFIL
9700 SD 92124 1249-F2
CAMINITO DEL MAR SANDS
12200 SD 92130 1188-A7
CAMINITO DEL MAR SHORES
12100 SD 92130 1188-A7
CAMINITO DEL MAR SURF
3900 SD 92130 1188-A7
CAMINITO DEL OESTE
6100 SD 92111 1268-H1
CAMINITO DE LOS CEPILLOS
- SDCo 92003 1067-H3
CAMINITO DE LOS ESCOSES
17500 SDCo 92067 1168-J1
CAMINITO DEL PASAJE
12900 SD 92014 1207-H2
CAMINITO DEL PASTEL
6300 SD 92111 1268-H1
CAMINITO DEL REPOSO
800 CRLB 92011 1126-J4
CAMINITO DEL ROCIO
13000 SD 92014 1207-G1
CAMINITO DEL SOL
800 CRLB 92011 1126-J5
CAMINITO DEL VERDE
9200 SNTE 92071 1231-A6
CAMINITO DEL VIDA
9600 SD 92121 1228-D1
CAMINITO DEL VIENTECITO
16700 SDCo 92127 1168-J3
CAMINITO DEL ZAFIRO
4300 SD 92121 1228-D1
CAMINITO DE MARIA
4200 SDCo 91977 1271-C4
CAMINITO DE OI VAY
7500 SD 92111 1249-A3
CAMINITO DE PIZZA
8000 SD 92108 1269-B2
CAMINITO DEPORTE
5900 SD 92108 1269-G1
CAMINITO DERECHO
10600 SD 92126 1209-D4
CAMINITO DESEO
2900 SD 92037 1228-A3
CAMINITO DESTELLO
12600 SD 92130 1188-E6
CAMINITO DE TATAN
3800 SD 92111 1249-A3
CAMINITO DIA
7900 SD 92122 1228-C4
CAMINITO DIABLO
4700 SD 92130 1188-C5
CAMINITO DIADEMA
1300 SD 92037 1247-J3
CAMINITO DIEGO
12700 SD 92130 1188-C5

STREET
Block City ZIP Pg-Grid

CAMINITO DOHA
9700 SD 92131 1209-G5
CAMINITO DONOSO
7000 SD 92037 1227-H7
CAMINITO DOSAMANTES
12900 SD 92128 1170-C1
CAMINITO DULCE
11000 SD 92131 1210-B2
CAMINITO DURO
10600 SD 92126 1209-D4
CAMINITO EASTBLUFF
3300 SD 92037 1228-A4
CAMINITO ELADO
11400 SD 92131 1210-A5
CAMINITO EL CANARIO
2000 SD 92037 1227-H7
2000 SD 92037 1247-H1
CAMINITO ELDA
- CHV 91915 1311-G7
CAMINITO ELDORADO
2700 SD 92014 1207-J2
CAMINITO ELEGANTE
5900 SD 92108 1269-G1
CAMINITO EL RINCON
3500 SD 92130 1187-J7
3500 SD 92130 1188-A6
CAMINITO EL ROSARIO
7800 SD 92037 1227-J6
CAMINITO EMPRESA
5700 SD 92037 1247-J3
CAMINITO ENCANTO
7700 CRLB 92009 1147-J2
11000 SD 92131 1210-B2
CAMINITO EN FLOR
12800 SD 92014 1207-H1
CAMINITO ENTRADA
6900 SD 92119 1250-F4
CAMINITO ESMERO
12300 SD 92130 1188-D7
CAMINITO ESPEJO
4000 SD 92107 1268-C3
CAMINITO ESPINO
2500 SD 92154 1350-C1
CAMINITO ESTERO
2300 SD 92107 1268-C3
CAMINITO ESTIMA
5600 SD 92037 1248-A2
CAMINITO ESTRADA
900 CRLB 92011 1126-J5
7000 SD 92037 1227-H7
7000 SD 92037 1247-H1
CAMINITO ESTRELLA
700 CHV 91910 1310-H6
CAMINITO ESTRELLADO
6100 SD 92120 1250-C6
CAMINITO EVA
4700 SD 92130 1188-C6
CAMINITO EVANGELICO
4700 SD 92130 1188-C5
CAMINITO EXIMIO
2300 SD 92107 1268-C2
CAMINITO EXQUISITO
4800 SD 92130 1188-E6
CAMINITO FABRIZIO
- CHV 91915 1311-F7
CAMINITO FACETO
4700 SD 92130 1188-B4
CAMINITO FARO
1300 SD 92037 1247-H3
CAMINITO FESTIVO
12300 SD 92131 1210-B2
CAMINITO FLECHA
6300 SD 92111 1268-H3
CAMINITO FLOREO
1300 SD 92037 1247-H4
CAMINITO FLORES
10500 SD 92126 1209-D4
CAMINITO FORMBY
6400 SD 92037 1247-J1
CAMINITO FORTALEZA
3000 SD 92014 1187-H3
CAMINITO FRANCHE
7000 SD 92122 1228-B5
CAMINITO FRANCISCO
- CHV 91913 1311-E7
CAMINITO FRESCO
8900 SD 92037 1228-A3
CAMINITO FUENTE
4400 SD 92116 1269-A4
CAMINITO GABALDON
1300 SD 92108 1269-B2
CAMINITO GANDARA
3200 SD 92037 1228-A5
CAMINITO GANTON
2800 SD 92037 1227-J7
2800 SD 92037 1228-A7
CAMINITO GARCIA
11400 SD 92131 1209-J5
11400 SD 92131 1210-A5
CAMINITO GARIBAY
- CHV 91915 1311-G7
CAMINITO GENIO
5500 SD 92037 1247-H3
CAMINITO GIANNA
8000 SD 92037 1228-A5
CAMINITO GIJON
3000 SD 92014 1187-H3
CAMINITO GILBAR
15700 SD 92128 1170-A5
CAMINITO GIRASOL
4700 SD 92130 1188-B4
CAMINITO GLENELLEN
10500 SD 92126 1209-D4
CAMINITO GOMA
10300 SD 92131 1209-G5
CAMINITO GRACIELA
1200 ENCT 92024 1148-B5
CAMINITO GRANATE
12300 SD 92130 1188-D7
CAMINITO GRIMALDI
7000 SD 92122 1228-B4
CAMINITO GUSTO
11500 SD 92131 1210-A5
CAMINITO HALAGO
1300 SD 92037 1247-J3
CAMINITO HELECHO
8300 SD 92037 1227-J5
CAMINITO HENO
17500 SD 92127 1169-J1
CAMINITO HERALDO
5400 SD 92037 1247-H4
CAMINITO HERCUBA
17600 SD 92128 1170-C1
CAMINITO HERMINIA
5400 SD 92037 1248-A3
CAMINITO HERMITAGE
6600 SD 92037 1227-J7
6600 SD 92037 1228-A7
CAMINITO HIEDRA
2500 SD 92154 1350-C1
CAMINITO HIERRO
4400 SD 92117 1248-C2
CAMINITO IMPERSADO
4700 SD 92130 1188-B4

SAN DIEGO CO.

STREET
Block City ZIP Pg-Grid

CAMINITO INOCENTA
11100 SD 92126 1208-H2
CAMINITO ISLA
5600 SD 92037 1248-A3
CAMINITO JOSE
5500 SD 92111 1248-H3
CAMINITO JOVEN
9700 SD 92131 1210-A5
CAMINITO JOVIAL
10100 SD 92126 1209-E5
CAMINITO JUANICO
6200 SD 92111 1268-G3
CAMINITO JUBILO
5200 SD 92108 1269-H2
CAMINITO KATERINA
5500 SD 92111 1248-H3
CAMINITO KITTANSETT
6500 SD 92037 1247-J1
CAMINITO LA BAR
11500 SD 92126 1208-J2
CAMINITO LA BENERA
7000 SD 92037 1227-H7
CAMINITO LACAYO
8200 SD 92037 1227-J5
CAMINITO LADERA
14900 SOLB 92014 1187-H1
CAMINITO LA PAZ
2500 SD 92037 1227-J6
CAMINITO LAPIZ
4700 SD 92130 1188-C6
CAMINITO LAS OLAS
800 CHV 91911 1330-J1
CAMINITO LASWANE
9700 SD 92131 1210-A5
CAMINITO LA TORRE
15600 SD 92128 1170-C5
CAMINITO LAURA
1300 ENCT 92024 1148-B5
CAMINITO LAZANJA
- SD 92127 1168-J7
- SD 92127 1188-J1
- SD 92127 1189-A2
CAMINITO LAZARO
6300 SD 92111 1268-H3
CAMINITO LEON
7700 CRLB 92009 1148-A2
CAMINITO LEONZIO
- CHV 91915 1311-F7
CAMINITO LINARES
800 CHV 91911 1330-J2
CAMINITO LINDRICK
6600 SD 92037 1228-A7
CAMINITO LINTERNA
8300 SD 92037 1227-J5
CAMINITO LISTO
6400 SD 92111 1268-H1
CAMINITO LITORAL
3800 SD 92107 1268-B7
CAMINITO LIVORNO
- CHV 91915 1311-G7
CAMINITO LOBES
13000 SD 92128 1170-C1
CAMINITO LOMA BUENA
3100 SD 92117 1248-F5
CAMINITO LORETA
1900 SD 92037 1248-A3
CAMINITO LORREN
14700 SD 92014 1187-J1
CAMINITO LUCCA
- CHV 91915 1311-G7
CAMINITO LUISITO
6200 SD 92111 1268-H2
CAMINITO LUNA NUEVA
3300 SD 92014 1187-J1
CAMINITO MADRIGAL
900 CRLB 92011 1126-J4
CAMINITO MAGNIFICA
11400 SD 92131 1210-A5
CAMINITO MAGUEY
10200 SD 92131 1209-G6
CAMINITO MALAGA
7700 CRLB 92009 1148-A2
CAMINITO MALLORCA
8000 SD 92037 1228-A5
CAMINITO MANRESA
7000 SD 92037 1227-H7
7000 SD 92037 1247-H1
CAMINITO MANSO
10600 SD 92126 1209-D4
CAMINITO MARACAIBO
14700 SD 92014 1188-C1
CAMINITO MARCIAL
6200 SD 92111 1268-H2
CAMINITO MAR DE PLATA
14700 SD 92014 1187-H1
CAMINITO MARIA
15100 SDCo 92067 1188-F1
CAMINITO MARITIMO
8200 SD 92037 1227-J5
CAMINITO MARLOCK
9800 SD 92131 1209-G6
CAMINITO MARRISA
2100 SD 92037 1248-A3
CAMINITO MAR VILLA
2200 SD 92014 1207-H1
13100 SD 92014 1187-G7
CAMINITO MARZELLA
1800 SD 92037 1227-H7
CAMINITO MASADA
17300 SD 92127 1169-J1
CAMINITO MAYTEN
10400 SD 92131 1209-G6
CAMINITO MELIADO
4000 SD 92122 1228-B4
CAMINITO MEMBRILLO
9900 SD 92131 1209-G6
CAMINITO MEMOSAC
10500 SD 92131 1209-H5
CAMINITO MENDIOLA
- SD 92130 1188-G4
CAMINITO MENOR
4000 SD 92107 1268-C2
CAMINITO MERION
2700 SD 92037 1227-J7
2700 SD 92037 1228-A7
CAMINITO MINDY
5200 SD 92105 1270-A7
CAMINITO MIRA
2300 SD 92107 1268-B6
CAMINITO MIRADA
12300 SD 92131 1210-B2
CAMINITO MIRA DEL MAR
12100 SD 92130 1188-A7
CAMINITO MODENA
8200 SD 92037 1228-A5
CAMINITO MOJADO
9700 SD 92131 1210-B5
CAMINITO MONARCA
7700 CRLB 92009 1147-F2
CAMINITO MONROVIA
1800 SD 92037 1227-H7
CAMINITO MONTANOSO
6800 SD 92119 1250-F4
CAMINITO MONTAROSA
- CHV 91915 1311-G7
CAMINITO MONTEROSA
- CHV 91915 1311-G7
CAMINITO MORAGA
- CHV 91913 1311-D7
CAMINITO MUIRFIELD
2400 SD 92037 1247-J1
CAMINITO MULEGE
10100 SD 92126 1209-E5
CAMINITO MUNDANO
5500 SD 92130 1188-E6
CAMINITO MUNDO
6800 SD 92119 1250-F4
CAMINITO MUNOZ
9700 SD 92131 1210-A5
CAMINITO NAZARIO
- CHV 91915 1311-G7
CAMINITO NIQUEL
2900 SD 92117 1248-C2
CAMINITO NOGALES
800 CHV 91911 1330-J1
CAMINITO NORINA
- CHV 91915 1311-G7
CAMINITO NORTE
5700 SD 92037 1248-A2
CAMINITO NORTHLAND
6400 SD 92037 1248-A1
6400 SD 92037 1228-A7
CAMINITO NOVARA
- CHV 91915 1311-G7
CAMINITO NUEZ
10100 SD 92131 1209-G6
CAMINITO OBISPO
- CHV 91913 1311-D7
CAMINITO OBRA
10500 SD 92126 1209-D4
CAMINITO OCEAN CV
2400 ENCT 92007 1167-F4
CAMINITO OCIO
4400 SD 92108 1269-H1
CAMINITO OLMO
7100 SD 92037 1227-H7
CAMINITO ONCE
- SDCo 92065 1152-G6
CAMINITO ORENSE ESTE
14600 SD 92129 1189-J1
CAMINITO ORENSE OESTE
14700 SD 92129 1189-J1
CAMINITO PACIFICA TR
- SD 92130 1188-B2
CAMINITO PADOVA
- CHV 91915 1311-G7
CAMINITO PAJARITO
2200 SD 92107 1268-B6
CAMINITO PAN
6000 SD 92120 1250-D6
CAMINITO PANTOJA
7100 SD 92122 1228-B4
CAMINITO PARTIDA
6300 SD 92111 1268-H3
CAMINITO PASADA
2200 SD 92107 1268-B6
CAMINITO PASADERO
18500 SD 92128 1150-B6
CAMINITO PATRICIA
3900 SD 92111 1248-H3
CAMINITO PEDERNAL
4400 SD 92117 1248-C2
CAMINITO PELON
9800 SD 92131 1210-A5
CAMINITO PEPINO
7100 SD 92037 1227-H7
CAMINITO PEQUENA
7300 SD 92119 1250-G4
CAMINITO PERAL
12300 SD 92131 1210-C2
CAMINITO PERICO
6900 SD 92119 1250-G4
CAMINITO PERUGIA
- CHV 91915 1311-G7
CAMINITO PESCADO
2200 SD 92107 1268-B6
CAMINITO PIENZA
- CHV 91915 1311-G7
CAMINITO PIETRO
- CHV 91915 1311-F7
CAMINITO PIMIENTO
1200 SD 92154 1350-B2
CAMINITO PINERO
17800 SD 92128 1150-A7
CAMINITO PINTORESCO
4200 SD 92108 1269-H2
CAMINITO PITAYA
10200 SD 92131 1209-G6
CAMINITO PLATA
6100 SD 92120 1250-C6
CAMINITO PLAZA VW
1100 SD 92154 1350-D1
CAMINITO PLAZA CENTRO
8800 SD 92122 1228-B3
CAMINITO PLOMADA
4400 SD 92117 1248-C2
CAMINITO POCO
2400 SD 92107 1268-C2
CAMINITO POINTE DEL MAR
12800 SD 92014 1207-J1
CAMINITO POLLO
10500 SD 92126 1209-D4
CAMINITO PORTA DELGADA
14700 SD 92014 1188-B1
14700 SDCo 92014 1188-B1
CAMINITO PORTHCAWL
2500 SD 92037 1247-J1
CAMINITO PORTO ALEGRE
14700 SD 92014 1187-J1
CAMINITO POSITANO
- CHV 91915 1311-F7
CAMINITO PRADO
2700 SD 92037 1227-J6
CAMINITO PRECIOSA NORTE
2200 SD 92037 1248-A3
CAMINITO PRECIOSA SUR
2200 SD 92037 1248-A3
CAMINITO PRENTICIA
11700 SD 92131 1210-B5
CAMINITO PRIMAVERA
8800 SD 92037 1228-A3
CAMINITO PROPICO
6900 SD 92126 1208-H2
CAMINITO PROSPERO
12400 SD 92130 1188-C7
CAMINITO PROVIDENCIA
5300 SD 92067 1188-D1
CAMINITO PUDREGAL
9700 SD 92131 1210-B4
CAMINITO PUERTO
7700 CRLB 92009 1148-A2
CAMINITO PULSERA
5700 SD 92037 1247-H3
CAMINITO PUNTA ARENAS
14700 SD 92014 1187-J1
CAMINITO QUEVEDO
14100 SD 92129 1189-H3
CAMINITO QUIETO
32000 SDCo 92003 1048-H7
CAMINITO QUINTANA
7100 SD 92122 1228-B4
CAMINITO QUINTERO
1800 SD 92037 1227-H7
CAMINITO QUIXOTE
3100 SD 92154 1330-E7
3100 SD 92154 1350-E1
CAMINITO RADIANTE
12500 SD 92130 1188-D6
CAMINITO RECODO
2300 SD 92107 1268-B6
CAMINITO RIALTO
7400 SD 92037 1227-H6
CAMINITO RICARDO
3100 ENCT 92024 1148-B5
CAMINITO RIMINI
10400 SD 92129 1189-G3
CAMINITO RINALDO
- CHV 91915 1311-G7
CAMINITO RIO
11500 SDCo 92040 1231-H3
CAMINITO RIO CT
10200 SDCo 92040 1231-H3
CAMINITO RIO ALTA
2900 SD 92014 1187-H1
CAMINITO RIO BRANCO
10200 SD 92131 1209-G5
CAMINITO ROBERTO
5600 SD 92111 1248-H3
CAMINITO RODAR
11100 SD 92126 1208-H2
CAMINITO ROGELIO
9800 SD 92131 1210-A5
CAMINITO RONALDO
11800 SD 92128 1170-A1
CAMINITO ROSA
800 CRLB 92011 1126-J5
5400 SD 92037 1248-A3
CAMINITO ROSITA
12500 SD 92128 1170-C5
CAMINITO RYONE
11800 SD 92128 1170-A5
CAMINITO SACATE
6100 SD 92120 1250-C6
CAMINITO SAGUNTO
3000 SD 92014 1187-H1
CAMINITO SALADO
6200 SD 92111 1268-H2
CAMINITO SANA
4400 SD 92122 1228-D4
CAMINITO SAN LUCAS
5400 SD 92037 1248-A3
CAMINITO SAN MARINO
2700 SD 92014 1207-J2
CAMINITO SAN MARTIN
2100 SD 92037 1248-A2
CAMINITO SAN NICHOLAS
2000 SD 92037 1248-A2
CAMINITO SAN PABLO
2700 SD 92014 1207-J2
CAMINITO SAN SEBASTIAN
4500 SD 92014 1188-B1
CAMINITO SANTA FE DOWNS
2600 SD 92014 1187-J1
CAMINITO SANTALUZ E
- SD 92127 1169-B6
- SD 92127 1189-A1
CAMINITO SANTALUZ W
- SD 92127 1169-A6
- SD 92127 1189-A1
CAMINITO SANTALUZ NORTE
- SD 92127 1169-A6
CAMINITO SANTALUZ SUR
- SD 92127 1169-A7
- SD 92127 1188-J1
- SD 92127 1189-A1
CAMINITO SANTICO
16900 SD 92128 1170-C3
CAMINITO SANTO TOMAS
14500 SDCo 92067 1188-H2
CAMINITO SANUDO
11800 SD 92131 1210-B5
CAMINITO SARAGOSSA
14400 SD 92067 1188-D1
CAMINITO SARDINIA
- CHV 91915 1311-G7
CAMINITO SCIOTO
6500 SD 92037 1247-J1
CAMINITO SECOYA
2600 SD 92154 1350-C1
CAMINITO SEGURO
2300 SD 92107 1268-C2
CAMINITO SEPTIMO
1200 ENCT 92007 1167-F1
CAMINITO SERENO
12300 SD 92131 1210-B2
CAMINITO SICILIA
- CHV 91915 1311-G7
CAMINITO SIEGA
17300 SD 92127 1169-J1
CAMINITO SIENA
800 CHV 91911 1330-J1
CAMINITO SIERRA
3400 CRLB 92009 1147-J2
3500 CRLB 92009 1148-A2
CAMINITO SILVELA
3900 SD 92122 1228-B4
CAMINITO SINNECOCK
6400 SD 92037 1247-J1
CAMINITO SOLIDAGO
1400 SD 92037 1247-H3
CAMINITO SOLITARIO
5200 SD 92108 1269-H2
CAMINITO SONOMA
7900 SD 92037 1228-A5
CAMINITO SONRISA
- CHV 91913 1311-D7
CAMINITO SOPADILLA
10500 SD 92131 1209-G5
CAMINITO STELLA
- SD 92130 1188-G6
CAMINITO SUELTO
9700 SD 92131 1210-A5
CAMINITO SUENO
6800 CRLB 92009 1128-A5
8700 SD 92037 1228-A3
CAMINITO SUERO
4000 SD 92122 1228-B4
CAMINITO SULMONA
10400 SD 92129 1189-G3
CAMINITO SURABAYA
10200 SD 92131 1209-G5
CAMINITO TAMBORREL
11700 SD 92131 1210-B5
CAMINITO TAMEGA
12500 SD 92128 1170-B5
CAMINITO TECERA
4400 SD 92014 1188-B1
CAMINITO TELMO
6200 SD 92111 1268-H2
CAMINITO TENEDOR
6200 SD 92120 1250-D6
CAMINITO TERCER VERDE
3000 SD 92014 1187-H1
CAMINITO TERVISO
3900 SD 92122 1228-B5
CAMINITO TIBURON
2100 SD 92037 1248-A3
CAMINITO TIERRA
10900 SD 92131 1210-C3
CAMINITO TIERRA DEL SOL
16100 SD 92128 1170-A5
CAMINITO TINGO
7700 CRLB 92009 1148-A2
CAMINITO TIRADA
9500 SD 92126 1209-E5
CAMINITO TIVOLI
700 CHV 91911 1330-J2
CAMINITO TIZONA
9600 SD 92126 1209-E5
CAMINITO TOGA
9500 SD 92126 1209-E5
CAMINITO TOMAS
16000 SD 92128 1170-A4
CAMINITO TOMATILLO
9900 SD 92131 1209-G6
CAMINITO TOM MORRIS
2600 SD 92037 1247-J1
CAMINITO TOPAZIO
3000 SD 92117 1248-C2
CAMINITO TORONJO
10200 SD 92131 1209-G6
CAMINITO TORREBLANCA
3000 SD 92014 1187-H3
CAMINITO TREVIANA
- CHV 91913 1331-E1
CAMINITO TULIPAN
1200 SD 92154 1350-C1
CAMINITO TURIA
1600 SD 92037 1247-H3
CAMINITO TURIN
- CHV 91915 1311-G7
CAMINITO TURNBERRY
6400 SD 92037 1248-A1
CAMINITO UMBRAL
4000 SD 92107 1268-C2
CAMINITO VALERIANO
3800 SD 92122 1228-B5
CAMINITO VALIENTE
700 CHV 91911 1330-J2
CAMINITO VALIOSO
12400 SD 92130 1188-D7
CAMINITO VALVERDE
7000 SD 92037 1227-H7
7000 SD 92037 1247-H1
CAMINITO VANTANA
11700 SD 92131 1210-A4
CAMINITO VASTO
3200 SD 92037 1228-A5
CAMINITO VECINOS
16400 SD 92128 1170-C3
CAMINITO VELASCO
1800 SD 92037 1227-H7
CAMINITO VELASQUEZ
5300 SD 92124 1249-F1
CAMINITO VELEZ
1800 SD 92037 1227-H7
CAMINITO VELLO
5500 SD 92130 1188-E6
CAMINITO VENIDO
2400 SD 92107 1268-B6
2400 SD 92110 1268-B6
CAMINITO VERA
8900 SD 92126 1209-D4
CAMINITO VERANO
8900 SD 92037 1228-A3
8900 SD 92037 1227-J3
CAMINITO VERANZA
- CHV 91915 1311-G7
CAMINITO VERDE
800 CRLB 92011 1126-J5
CAMINITO VERDUGO
2700 SD 92014 1207-J2
CAMINITO VIA CAMPESTRE
3100 SD 92014 1187-H3
CAMINITO VIBRANTE
12300 SD 92131 1210-C2
CAMINITO VIEJO
2500 SD 92037 1227-J6
CAMINITO VILOS
13000 SD 92128 1170-D1
CAMINITO VIOLETA
100 SMCS 92069 1109-C7
CAMINITO VISTA ESTRELLADO
14700 SD 92014 1187-H3
CAMINITO VISTA LUJO
4900 SD 92130 1188-D7
CAMINITO VISTANA
- SD 92130 1189-A2
CAMINITO VISTA PACIFICA
11000 SD 92131 1209-H3
CAMINITO VISTA SERENA
11100 SD 92131 1209-H3
CAMINITO VISTA SOLEDAD
12500 SD 92130 1188-D6
CAMINITO VIVA
8800 SD 92037 1228-A3
CAMINITO VIZZINI
10400 SD 92129 1189-G3
CAMINITO VOLAR
10100 SD 92126 1209-E5
CAMINITO WESTCHESTER
10500 SD 92126 1209-E4
CAMINITO YUCATAN
5900 SD 92108 1249-G7
5900 SD 92108 1269-G1
CAMINITO ZABALA
7100 SD 92122 1228-B4
CAMINITO ZAR
10100 SD 92126 1209-E5
CAMINITO ZARAGOZA
- CHV 91913 1331-F1
CAMINITO ZOCALO
2400 SD 92107 1268-B6
2400 SD 92110 1268-B6
CAMINITO ZOPILOTE
2600 SD 92105 1270-A7
CAMINO DR
- CALX 92231 6620-J6
- ImCo 92274 410-G6
2000 ESCN 92026 1109-D4
CAMINO ABIERTO
- CRLB 92009 1147-F1
CAMINO ABROJO
10900 SD 92127 1169-H5
CAMINO ACAMPO
17100 SDCo 92067 1168-G5
CAMINO AGUILA
7800 SD 92122 1228-C4
CAMINO ALEGRE
3400 CRLB 92009 1147-J5
4000 SDCo 91941 1271-H4
CAMINO ALETA
3000 SD 92154 1350-D1
CAMINO ALISOS
3100 SDCo 92028 1028-C3
CAMINO ALTEZA
3000 SD 92154 1350-D1
CAMINO ALTO
- SDCo 92027 1111-C3
CAMINO ALVARO
1200 CRLB 92009 1147-H3
CAMINO AMERO
6900 SD 92111 1268-J2
CAMINO ANCHO
17500 SD 92128 1150-D7
CAMINO ANTONIO
- IMP 92251 6499-E2
CAMINO ARENA
3500 CRLB 92009 1148-A3
CAMINO ARMILLA
15800 SD 92127 1169-H5
CAMINO ARRIBA
15900 SDCo 92065 1173-E3
CAMINO ARROYO
3100 CRLB 92009 1127-J7
CAMINO ARTEMISA
2600 SDCo 91901 1253-J2
CAMINO ATAJO
900 CHV 91910 1310-J7
900 CHV 91910 1311-A7
CAMINO AVENA
2500 SDCo 91901 1253-J2
CAMINO BAILEN
100 ESCN 92029 1150-A2
300 ESCN 92029 1149-J2
CAMINO BAJA CERRO
1200 OCN 92028 1047-D7
1200 OCN 92028 1067-C1
CAMINO BAJADA
3600 ESCN 92025 1150-C3
CAMINO BERDECIO
6800 SD 92111 1268-J2
CAMINO BISCAY
1100 CHV 91910 1310-J6
1100 CHV 91910 1311-A6
CAMINO BRISA DEL MAR
17300 SDCo 92127 1169-D1
CAMINO CABRILLO
- CRLB 92009 1147-J2
CAMINO CALABAZO
1000 CHV 91910 1311-B7
CAMINO CALAFIA
200 SDCo 92069 1088-H5
CAMINO CALMA
3900 SD 92122 1228-C4
CAMINO CANADA
13200 SDCo 92021 1252-D1
13500 SDCo 92021 1232-E7
CAMINO CANTERA
2000 SDCo 92084 1088-C1
CAMINO CAPISTRANO
6500 CRLB 92009 1127-J5
CAMINO CATALINA
700 SOLB 92075 1167-J6
CAMINO CATALONIA
1200 CHV 91910 1311-A6
CAMINO CEREZA
- CRLB 92009 1148-A1
CAMINO CHELSEA
- SDCo 91901 1254-E1
CAMINO CHICO
31300 SDCo 92086 409-K7
CAMINO CHRISTINA
- SDCo 91901 1234-E7
- SDCo 91901 1254-E1
CAMINO CIEGO CT
1000 VSTA 92084 1088-A4
CAMINO CIELO
800 SDCo 92028 1047-H1
CAMINO CIELO AZUL
20700 SDCo 92029 1128-F7
20700 SDCo 92029 1148-F1
CAMINO CODORNIZ
10800 SD 92127 1169-H5
CAMINO CONEJO
15800 SDCo 92082 1071-A7
CAMINO COPETE
1100 SD 92111 1268-H2
CAMINO CORALINO
2900 SD 92117 1248-C2
CAMINO CORONADO
3200 CRLB 92009 1147-J3
CAMINO CORTE
3400 CRLB 92009 1147-J4
CAMINO CORTO
100 VSTA 92083 1087-G6
1500 OCN 92028 1047-E7
1500 OCN 92028 1067-E1
6200 SD 92120 1250-D5
CAMINO CORTO DR
- SMCS 92078 1128-D2
CAMINO COSTANERO
6300 SD 92111 1268-H3
CAMINO CREST DR
3000 OCN 92056 1106-G2
CAMINO CRISALIDA
15700 SD 92127 1169-G5
CAMINO CULEBRA
1900 VSTA 92084 1088-C3
1900 SDCo 92084 1088-C3
CAMINO DAVID
4800 SDCo 91902 1290-H7
4900 SDCo 91902 1310-H1
CAMINO DE AGUAS
3100 CRLB 92009 1127-J7
CAMINO DE AMIGOS
1800 CRLB 92009 1128-A5
CAMINO DE AMOR
500 SDCo 92065 1152-H7
CAMINO DE ARRIBA
7400 SDCo 92067 1148-J5
CAMINO DE CLARA
600 SOLB 92075 1167-H6
CAMINO DE ESTRELLAS
18000 SDCo 92067 1149-A7
CAMINO DEGRAZIA
6900 SD 92111 1268-J2
6900 SD 92111 1269-A2
CAMINO DE LA BRECCIA
12700 SD 92128 1150-D7
CAMINO DE LA CIMA
300 SMCS 92078 1129-B2
CAMINO DE LA COSTA
700 SD 92037 1247-F3
CAMINO DE LA DORA
7700 SDCo 92067 1148-J7
CAMINO DEL AGUILA
19300 SDCo 92025 1150-J4
20200 SDCo 92025 1151-A5
20300 SDCo 92065 1151-A5
CAMINO DE LA LUNA
- SD 92127 1168-J7
- SD 92127 1188-J1
CAMINO DE LA MITRA
7700 SDCo 92067 1148-H7
CAMINO DE LA PAZ
- SMCS 92078 1129-A2
CAMINO DE LA PLAZA
2200 SD 92173 1350-E5
CAMINO DEL ARCO
3100 CRLB 92009 1127-H7
CAMINO DE LA REINA
100 SD 92108 1268-J4
100 SD 92108 1269-C2
CAMINO DE LA ROSA
- SD 92127 1168-J7
CAMINO DEL ARROYO
5000 SD 92108 1269-A3
CAMINO DEL ARROYO DR
1400 SDCo 92078 1128-B3
1500 SMCS 92078 1128-B3
CAMINO DE LAS CUNAS
1900 SDCo 92019 1272-C2
CAMINO DE LAS FLORES
100 ENCT 92024 1147-G7
CAMINO DE LA SIESTA
5000 SD 92108 1269-A3
CAMINO DE LAS LOMAS
3500 SDCo 92084 1088-F6
30400 SDCo 92026 1069-A4
30500 SDCo 92026 1068-J4
CAMINO DE LAS ONDAS
900 CRLB 92011 1126-J5
1000 CRLB 92011 1127-B5
CAMINO DE LAS PALMAS
2200 LMGR 91945 1270-J7
2200 LMGR 91945 1290-J1
CAMINO DE LAS PIEDRAS
2900 SDCo 92019 1272-G1
CAMINO DE LAS SONRISAS
1800 SD 92173 1350-F3
CAMINO DE LAS VILLAS
1100 SOLB 92075 1167-D6
CAMINO DEL CERRO GRANDE
100 CHV 91902 1310-J3
CAMINO DEL CIELO
5500 SDCo 92003 1068-B1
5600 SDCo 92003 1048-C7
CAMINO DEL COLLADO
2100 SD 92037 1227-H4
CAMINO DEL ESTE
5000 SD 92108 1269-C2
CAMINO DELICIADA
16000 SDCo 92091 1168-B7
CAMINO DEL INDIO
16700 SDCo 92065 1171-G2
CAMINO DEL LAGO
1200 SDCo 92078 1128-C3
CAMINO DEL MAR Rt#-S21
400 DLMR 92014 1187-F4
S CAMINO DEL MAR Rt#-S21
100 DLMR 92014 1187-G7
CAMINO DEL MESA
- SDCo 91905 (1299-J3 See Page 1298)
- SDCo 91905 1300-A4
CAMINO DEL MONTE
- SDCo 91905 (1319-H2 See Page 1298)
CAMINO DEL NORTE
14200 PWY 92064 1170-B7
14200 PWY 92064 1190-C1
14200 SD 92128 1170-B7
14600 SD 92128 1169-H5
15100 SD 92127 1169-H5
16200 SDCo 92127 1169-F3
CAMINO DEL ORO
8100 SD 92037 1227-H5
CAMINO DE LOS AVES
2500 SDCo 91901 1253-J2
CAMINO DE LOS CABALLOS
30100 SDCo 92003 1068-D3
CAMINO DE LOS COCHES
3400 CRLB 92009 1147-J3
3400 CRLB 92009 1148-A2
CAMINO DEL PAJARO
6200 SDCo 92067 1168-F6
CAMINO DEL PARQUE
6400 CRLB 92011 1126-J4
CAMINO DEL POSTIGO
100 ESCN 92029 1150-A2
400 ESCN 92029 1149-J2
CAMINO DEL PRADO
800 CRLB 92011 1126-J5
CAMINO DEL PROGRESSO
200 SD 92173 1350-F3
CAMINO DEL RANCHO
2300 ENCT 92024 1148-A5
2400 ENCT 92024 1148-A5
CAMINO DEL REPOSO
2100 SD 92037 1227-H5
CAMINO DEL REY
- CHV 91910 1311-A7
5400 SDCo 92003 1068-A1
5900 SDCo 92003 1067-J1
8500 SDCo 92026 1068-G4
CAMINO DEL RINCON
6000 SD 92120 1250-D5
CAMINO DEL RIO
- CALX 92231 6680-J2
CAMINO DEL RIO N
- SD 92120 1269-H1
500 SD 92108 1269-F1
CAMINO DEL RIO S
400 SD 92108 1269-F1
CAMINO DEL RIO W
3600 SD 92110 1268-E5
CAMINO DEL ROCA
17800 SDCo 92065 1171-H2
CAMINO DEL SABIO
17100 SDCo 92065 1171-G2
CAMINO DEL SEQUAN
1200 SDCo 91901 1253-J2
1300 SDCo 91901 1254-A2
CAMINO DEL SOL
100 SD 92037 1227-H5
500 SMCS 92069 1108-F5
1000 CHV 91910 1310-J7
1000 CHV 91910 1311-A6
CAMINO DEL SOL CIR
1100 CRLB 92008 1106-G6
CAMINO DEL SUELO
13700 SD 92129 1189-C3
CAMINO DEL SUR
- SD 92127 1168-J7
- SD 92127 1188-J1
- SD 92127 1189-B2
- SDCo 92127 1169-E3
12100 SD 92129 1189-B3
16100 SD 92127 1169-B3
CAMINO DEL TIERRA
11600 SDCo 92040 1211-H7
CAMINO DEL VALLE
12800 PWY 92064 1170-D3
CAMINO DEL VECINO
- SDCo 91901 1234-E7
2500 SDCo 91901 1254-E1
CAMINO DEL VENADO
10400 SDCo 92082 1049-E4
CAMINO DEL VERDE
9200 SNTE 92071 1231-A6
CAMINO DE MONTECILLO
17100 SDCo 92067 1168-H6
CAMINO DE NOG
1500 SDCo 92028 1027-J6
1600 SDCo 92028 1028-A6
CAMINO DE ORCHIDIA
500 ENCT 92024 1147-E7
CAMINO DE ORO
15900 SDCo 92082 1071-B5
CAMINO DE PAIS
1500 SDCo 92028 1027-J6
CAMINO DE PALMAS
1300 SDCo 92028 1027-J7
CAMINO DE PILAR
3600 ESCN 92025 1150-C3
CAMINO DE PRICILLA
- SDCo 92084 1108-D4
CAMINO DE REIMITZ
- SDCo 91901 1254-A2
CAMINO DE TIERRA
- SDCo 91916 1216-D7
CAMINO DE VELA
1400 SDCo 92078 1128-C3
CAMINO DONAIRE
1100 SD 92154 1350-D1
CAMINO EL DORADO
500 ENCT 92024 1147-E7
CAMINO ELENA
10100 SDCo 92026 1089-D5
CAMINO ELEVADO
200 CHV 91902 1310-J4
200 SDCo 91902 1310-J4
400 CHV 91902 1311-A4
CAMINO EMPARRADO
12500 SD 92128 1150-C7
CAMINO ENCANTO
- CRLB 92009 1147-J2
CAMINO ENTRADA
100 CHV 91910 1330-E1
100 CHV 91910 1310-E7
CAMINO ESMERADO
3800 SDCo 92091 1168-C7
CAMINO ESPERANZA
1800 SD 92173 1350-F3
CAMINO ESPUELAS
1000 CHV 91910 1310-J5
CAMINO ESTRELLADO
6700 SD 92120 1250-C5
CAMINO GATO
7900 CRLB 92009 1147-H3
CAMINO GLORITA
7700 SD 92122 1228-C4
CAMINO HERMOSO
- SMCS 92078 1129-A2
CAMINO HILLS DR
2300 CRLB 92008 1107-C7
2300 CRLB 92008 1127-C1
CAMINO HUERTA
7800 SD 92122 1228-C4
CAMINO ISLAY
4100 SD 92122 1228-C4
CAMINO JASMINE
5300 SDCo 92003 1067-G1
CAMINO JONATA
7800 SD 92122 1228-D4
CAMINO JUNIPERO
- CRLB 92009 1148-A1
CAMINO KIOSCO
7900 SD 92122 1228-D4
CAMINO LAGARTO
2500 SDCo 91901 1253-J2
CAMINO LAGO DE CRISTAL
16800 SDCo 92067 1168-G6
CAMINO LAGO VISTA
8900 SDCo 91977 1291-B5
CAMINO LA PAZ
- CHV 91910 1310-J7
CAMINO LA PUENTE
6600 CRLB 92009 1128-A5
CAMINO LA PUERTA
- CHV 91914 1311-F2
CAMINO LARGO
100 SDCo 92084 1087-G2
100 VSTA 92084 1087-G2
3400 CRLB 92009 1147-J4
6000 SD 92120 1250-D5
CAMINO LIMERO
6500 CRLB 92009 1127-J5
CAMINO LINDA DR
1300 SDCo 92078 1128-B3
CAMINO LINDO
- CRLB 92009 1147-J3
- CRLB 92009 1148-A3
3800 SD 92122 1228-C4
CAMINO LITA
4200 SD 92122 1228-C4
CAMINO LOMA VERDE
1900 VSTA 92084 1088-C4
2000 SDCo 92084 1088-C4

STREET Block City ZIP Pg-Grid

CAMINO LORADO
1600 SDCo 92078 1128-B3
CAMINO LUJAN
6700 SD 92111 1268-J2
CAMINO MAGNIFICO
800 SMCS 92069 1108-F4
CAMINO MANGANA
1400 SD 92111 1268-J2
CAMINO MAQUILADORA
6800 SD 92154 1351-B2
CAMINO MARGLESA
3600 ESCN 92025 1150-C3
CAMINO MARZAGAN
3200 ESCN 92029 1150-A2
CAMINO MATEO
300 SMCS 92069 1109-C7
CAMINO MAYOR
3700 SDCo 92069 1088-H3
CAMINO MICHELLE
3400 CRLB 92009 1127-J5
3400 CRLB 92009 1128-A5
CAMINO MIEL
1000 CHV 91910 1311-A7
CAMINO MILITA
4100 SD 92122 1228-C4
CAMINO MIRA DEL MAR
12600 SD 92130 1188-A7
CAMINO MIRANDA
11100 SD 92126 1208-J2
CAMINO MONTEGO
8000 CRLB 92009 1147-J4
CAMINO MONTE SOMBRA
2400 SDCo 92019 1252-E4
CAMINO MORO
- SDCo 92086 409-K7
CAMINO MURILLO
17700 SD 92128 1150-C7
CAMINO NARCISO
2500 SDCo 91901 1253-J2
CAMINO NOGUERA
7700 SD 92122 1228-C4
CAMINO PACHECO
1400 SD 92111 1268-J2
CAMINO PALOMAR ALTO
6500 SD 92037 1247-F2
CAMINO PALOMAR BAJO
700 SD 92037 1247-F2
CAMINO PARQUE
300 OCN 92057 1086-H3
CAMINO PATRICIA
100 VSTA 92083 1087-G6
CAMINO PAZ
4000 SDCo 91977 1271-B4
4200 SDCo 91941 1271-B4
CAMINO PAZ LN
9200 SDCo 91941 1271-B4
CAMINO PLAYA ACAPULCO
5000 SD 92124 1229-J7
CAMINO PLAYA AZUL
5200 SD 92124 1229-J7
CAMINO PLAYA BAJA
5000 SD 92124 1230-A6
CAMINO PLAYA CANCUN
11300 SD 92124 1230-A7
CAMINO PLAYA CARMEL
10900 SD 92124 1229-J7
CAMINO PLAYA CATALINA
11500 SD 92124 1230-A7
CAMINO PLAYA DE ORO
5000 SD 92124 1229-J7
CAMINO PLAYA MALAGA
5000 SD 92124 1229-J7
CAMINO PLAYA NORTE
5300 SD 92124 1229-J7
5300 SD 92124 1230-A7
CAMINO PLAYA PORTOFINO
5000 SD 92124 1229-H7
CAMINO PORTOFINO
3000 SDCo 92028 1048-A2
CAMINO PRIVADO
4300 SDCo 92067 1167-J3
CAMINO RAINBOW
1900 SDCo 92028 998-J6
CAMINO RAMILLETTE
12800 SD 92128 1150-D7
CAMINO RAPOSA
7800 SD 92122 1228-C4
CAMINO REDONDO
300 SMCS 92069 1109-C7
CAMINO REGALADO
1100 SD 92154 1350-D1
CAMINO REVUELTOS
6900 SD 92111 1268-J2
CAMINO RICO
6000 SD 92120 1250-C6
CAMINO RIO
12100 SDCo 92040 1212-A7
CAMINO ROBERTO
4800 SDCo 91902 1310-H1
4800 SDCo 91902 1290-H7
CAMINO ROBLEDO
- CRLB 92009 1147-G2
CAMINO ROCIAR
1600 SDCo 92078 1128-C4
CAMINO RUIZ
9400 SD 92126 1209-B1
CAMINO SAN BERNARDO
- SD 92127 1169-E4
16900 SDCo 92127 1169-G3
CAMINO SANDOVAL
4200 SD 92130 1188-B6
CAMINO SAN IGNACIO
32200 SDCo 92086 409-K8
CAMINO SANTA BARBARA
700 SOLB 92075 1167-J6
CAMINO SANTA FE
- SD 92126 1208-J6
5200 SD 92067 1188-D2
8100 SD 92121 1228-H1
8800 SD 92121 1208-H4
9400 SDCo 92127 1169-C1
CAMINO SAN THOMAS
- SDCo 92127 1169-E2
CAMINO SAUCITO
6600 SDCo 92067 1168-G6
CAMINO SCARPITTA
700 SDCo 91901 1233-G7
CAMINO SELVA
6100 SDCo 92067 1168-E3
CAMINO SERBAL
2800 CRLB 92009 1147-H2
CAMINO SERENO
7700 SDCo 92029 1148-H2
CAMINO SIERRA DEL SUR
16900 SDCo 92067 1168-G6
CAMINO SIN PUENTE
- SDCo 92067 1148-J5
CAMINO SUSANA
13700 SDCo 92021 1232-E6

CAMINO TABLERO
100 ESCN 92029 1150-A2
CAMINO TERESA
1300 SOLB 92075 1167-J6
CAMINO TERNURA
1100 SD 92154 1350-D1
CAMINO TICINO
4100 SD 92122 1228-C4
CAMINO TRANQUILO
7800 SD 92122 1228-C4
CAMINO TRES AVES
35300 SDCo 91962 (1299-A1 See Page 1298)
CAMINO VALENCIA
3400 CRLB 92009 1127-J6
3400 CRLB 92009 1128-A5
CAMINO VALLAREAL
3200 ESCN 92029 1150-A2
CAMINO VERDE
- SMCS 92078 1129-A1
2300 SDCo 92028 1028-B5
CAMINO VIDA ROBLE
1900 CRLB 92008 1127-C3
2000 CRLB 92011 1127-E4
CAMINO VINCENTE
6300 SD 92037 1247-F2
CAMINO VISTA
18700 SDCo 92065 1153-E3
CAMINO VISTA REAL
100 CHV 91910 1330-E1
100 CHV 91910 1310-F7
CAMINO VUELO
12500 SD 92128 1150-C7
CAMINO YNEZ
600 SOLB 92075 1167-H6
CAMINO ZALCE
1400 SD 92111 1268-J2
CAMINO ZARA
1300 SDCo 92028 1028-D4
CAMIONES WY
5500 SD 92173 1350-H5
CAMLAU DR
200 CHV 91911 1330-E1
CAMOMILE WY
- SD 92123 1249-D1
CAMP CT
- SDCo 91977 1291-A2
CAMPANIA AV
9600 SDCo 92127 1169-E2
CAMPANILE DR
4700 SD 92115 1270-C3
CAMPANILE WY
5600 SD 92115 1270-B3
CAMPBELL LN
4200 SDCo 92019 1272-F2
CAMPBELL PL
- CRLB 92009 1127-F2
- ESCN 92027 1110-D6
CAMPBELL RD
400 VSTA 92081 1107-J1
2000 ImCo 92243 430-L6
CAMPBELL WY
1100 SDCo 92065 1172-H1
CAMPBELL RANCH RD
- SDCo 91901 1235-H6
CAMP DE LUZ RD
- SDCo 92028 996-G7
- SDCo 92055 409-A6
- SDCo 92055 996-G7
CAMPESINO PL
1800 OCN 92054 1106-F1
CAMPHOR CT
2700 CHV 91914 1311-J4
CAMPHOR LN
- SDCo 92026 1089-B2
6800 SD 92139 1310-F1
CAMPHOR PL
- CRLB 92011 1127-B5
CAMPILLO CT
12300 SD 92128 1170-B1
CAMPILLO DR
17200 SD 92128 1170-B1
CAMPILLO ST
- CALX 92231 6620-F6
CAMPINA DR
9000 LMSA 91942 1251-A7
CAMPINA PL
6400 SD 92037 1247-H1
CAMP KETTLE DR
- SDCo 92004 1058-G7
200 SDCo 92004 (1078-G1 See Page 1058)
CAMP LOCKETT RD
- SDCo 91906 (1318-C5 See Page 1298)
CAMPO PL
2100 ESCN 92027 1110-B5
CAMPO RD
8700 SDCo 91941 1271-A4
8700 SDCo 91977 1271-C5
10400 SDCo 91978 1271-E5
CAMPO RD Rt#-94
11100 SDCo 91978 1272-A7
11100 SDCo 91978 1271-G5
11100 SDCo 91941 1271-G5
11100 SDCo 92019 1271-J6
12100 SDCo 91978 1292-C1
12700 SDCo 91935 1272-D7
13100 SDCo 91935 1292-F1
14100 SDCo 91935 1293-B6
14700 SDCo 91935 (1313-F2 See Page 1293)
16000 SDCo 91917 (1313-F2 See Page 1293)
21100 SDCo 91917 (1314-B5 See Page 1294)
22000 SDCo 91917 429-J10
22600 SDCo 91980 429-K10
CAMPO ST
- SDCo 91934 (1321-H5 See Page 1300)
3200 SDCo 91935 1272-J7
CAMPO TKTR
- SDCo 91906 1298-C7
- SDCo 91906 (1318-B2 See Page 1298)
CAMPOBELLO ST
4500 SD 92130 1188-C6
CAMPO LINDO RD
12900 SDCo 91935 1273-H4
CAMPUS AV
4100 SD 92103 1269-C5
4300 SD 92116 1269-C5
CAMPUS DR
3500 OCN 92056 1106-J1
3500 OCN 92056 1107-A1
E CAMPUS DR
6000 SD 92120 1270-C2
6000 SD 92182 1270-C2
CAMPUS WY
- SMCS 92096 1128-J1
CAMPUS POINT CT
4100 SD 92121 1208-B7

CAMPUS POINT DR
9400 SD 92037 1228-B1
9700 SD 92121 1208-B7
9700 SD 92121 1228-C1
CAMPUS VIEW CT
- SD 92130 1187-J7
CAMPUS VIEW DR
- SMCS 92096 1128-J2
CAMROSE AV
4400 SD 92122 1228-F5
CAMULOS ST
2500 SD 92107 1268-B6
3200 SD 92110 1268-C5
CANA LN
1300 SDCo 92028 1027-J5
CANADIAN HONKER RD
29800 SDCo 91906 (1297-F6 See Page 1296)
CANAL RD
16600 SDCo 92082 1091-C2
CANAL ST
100 CALX 92231 6620-E7
1700 SD 92154 1329-J6
1700 SD 92154 1330-A6
W CANAL ST
- CALX 92231 6620-F7
CANALEJA WY
9700 SD 92129 1209-F1
CANANEA ST
200 VSTA 92084 1087-H4
CANARIO ST
4000 CRLB 92008 1106-F7
CANARIOS CT
800 CHV 91910 1310-J6
CANARY CT
1100 SMCS 92078 1128-E3
CANARY WY
7900 SD 92123 1249-B6
CANARYWOOD CT
10800 SD 92131 1210-A2
CANBERRA CT
- SDCo 92127 1169-F2
CANCHA DE GOLF
3700 SDCo 92091 1168-C7
CANCIONES DEL CIELO
- VSTA 92084 1088-C3
CANCUN CT
- IMP 92251 6499-H1
400 SDCo 92028 1027-E5
CANCUN DR
- IMP 92251 6499-G1
CANDELA DR
- CHV 91914 1311-D2
CANDELA PL
12900 SD 92130 1187-J5
CANDIA CT
4200 OCN 92056 1087-C6
4200 VSTA 92083 1087-C6
CANDICE CT
1900 SDCo 92028 1048-A4
CANDICE PL
100 VSTA 92083 1087-G3
CANDIDA ST
9500 SD 92126 1209-E6
CANDIL PL
2900 CRLB 92009 1127-H7
CANDLE LN
1800 ELCJ 92019 1252-C3
1800 SDCo 92019 1252-C3
CANDLE WY
13400 SDCo 92082 1090-D1
CANDLEBERRY CT
11200 SD 92128 1189-J2
CANDLELIGHT AV
1700 ESCN 92029 1129-G5
CANDLELIGHT DR
5300 SD 92037 1247-H3
5300 SD 92109 1247-H4
CANDLELIGHT GN
1300 ESCN 92029 1129-G6
CANDLELIGHT PL
800 SD 92037 1247-G4
CANDLELIGHT ST
5200 OCN 92056 1107-F4
CANDLELITE DR
900 SMCS 92069 1109-A5
CANDLEWOOD LN
1100 SDCo 92020 1251-J7
1100 SDCo 92020 1271-J1
CANDLEWOOD PL
2700 OCN 92056 1087-E5
CANDY LN
100 ENCT 92024 1167-J1
9600 SDCo 91941 1271-C1
CANDY ROSE CT
12200 SD 92131 1190-B7
12200 SD 92131 1210-B1
CANDY ROSE WY
11700 PWY 92064 1210-B1
11700 SD 92131 1210-B1
11700 SD 92131 1190-B7
CANDY TUFT PTH
- SD 92130 1188-F4
CANE RD
14200 SDCo 92082 1070-F4
CANEBRAKE RD
300 SDCo 92036 430-D3
2200 SDCo 91905 430-C5
CANEEL BAY CT
4600 OCN 92057 1066-H6
CANERIDGE PL
11900 SD 92128 1190-B7
CANERIDGE RD
11900 SD 92128 1190-A7
CANFIELD PL
18200 SD 92128 1150-C6
CANFIELD RD Rt#-S6
3400 SDCo 92060 1032-E7
3400 SDCo 92060 1052-E1
CANFORERO TER
5300 SD 92124 1249-F1
CANIS LN
8800 SD 92126 1209-D2
CANNA DR
- NATC 91950 1289-H7
- SD 92113 1289-H7
CANNAS CT
1700 CRLB 92011 1127-E6
CANNELI DR
13700 PWY 92064 1190-F4
CANNES PL
- CHV 91913 1311-E7
CANNING AV
3800 SD 92111 1248-G4
CANNING CT
5200 SD 92111 1248-G4
CANNING PL
5200 SD 92111 1248-G4
CANNINGTON DR
4200 SD 92117 1248-J2
CANNON RD
- CRLB 92008 1127-A1
100 CRLB 92008 1126-G2
1700 ImCo 92243 6500-D5

CANNON RD
1700 ImCo 92243 6560-E1
3500 CRLB 92010 1107-B6
3500 OCN 92056 1107-E4
4000 SDCo 92081 1107-E4
4600 CRLB 92008 1107-A7
CANNON GATE
- SDCo 92028 1027-G6
CANOE CREEK WY
1400 CHV 91915 (1312-A6 See Page 1293)
CANON DR
300 IMP 92251 6439-F3
CANON ST
900 SD 92106 1287-J3
2600 SD 92106 1288-A1
CANONITA DR
1900 SDCo 92028 1028-E5
CANOPUS DR
- SD 92126 1209-E6
CANOPY DR
- SMCS 92069 1108-G6
CANOSA AV
5000 SD 92117 1248-G2
CANRIGHT WY
9900 SD 92126 1209-A6
CANTABERRA CT
- SD 92129 1188-H4
CANTA LOMAS
1900 SDCo 92019 1252-C7
CANTALOUPE ST
- ImCo 92249 6560-B7
CANTAMAR PL
1900 SD 92154 1330-A7
CANTAMAR RD
1900 SD 92154 1330-A7
CANTARA LN
1700 VSTA 92081 1107-E2
CANTARA WY
24800 SDCo 92065 1173-G3
CANTARANAS
16900 SDCo 92067 1168-B3
CANTATA DR
- CHV 91914 1311-D2
CANTATA LN
- SD 92127 1168-J7
CANTEBURY PL
- ESCN 92025 1129-H4
CANTEGRA GN
2800 ESCN 92025 1130-B7
2800 ESCN 92025 1150-B1
CANTER RD
1200 SDCo 92027 1130-C3
CANTERBURY CT
4700 OCN 92056 1087-D4
CANTERBURY DR
4300 LMSA 91941 1270-H4
4800 SD 92116 1269-G2
E CANTERBURY DR
4100 SD 92116 1269-H3
CANTERBURY ST
2800 CRLB 92010 1107-A4
CANTER HEIGHTS DR
- SD 92130 1208-C2
CANTERO WY
3000 CRLB 92009 1147-H1
CANTIL ST
6700 CRLB 92009 1127-H5
CANTLE LN
3800 ENCT 92024 1148-C2
CANTON DR
7300 LMGR 91945 1290-G1
8000 SDCo 91977 1290-G1
CANTON RIDGE TER
- SD 92127 1169-B4
CANVAS DR
- CHV 91913 1311-F7
- CHV 91913 1331-F1
CANVAS ST
4700 OCN 92057 1087-B1
CANVASBACK CT
- CRLB 92011 1127-B6
CANVAS BACK DR
29900 SDCo 91906 (1297-G5 See Page 1296)
W CANYON AV
3000 SD 92123 1249-F5
CANYON CT
1400 CHV 91902 1311-B4
CANYON DR
400 SOLB 92075 1167-F6
500 CHV 91902 1311-B4
500 CHV 91913 1311-B4
1200 SDCo 92036 1136-C6
1500 SDCo 92036 1156-D1
10100 SDCo 92026 1109-E2
N CANYON DR
100 OCN 92054 1086-B5
S CANYON DR
100 OCN 92054 1086-C6
CANYON HTS
- SMCS 92078 1128-G3
CANYON LN
- ESCN 92025 1130-A6
CANYON PASS
- PWY 92064 1171-A6
CANYON PL
600 SOLB 92075 1167-F6
1800 CRLB 92008 1106-F4
CANYON RD
- SD 92102 1289-G4
- SDCo 92036 430-D4
100 SDCo 92036 1156-F7
1500 SDCo 91977 1291-B2
2300 ESCN 92025 1130-C7
2500 ESCN 92025 1150-C1
28500 SDCo 92082 1090-D1
CANYON ST
3100 CRLB 92008 1106-G4
W CANYON TER
- SD 92123 1249-F5
CANYON BACK LN
13300 PWY 92064 1190-E1
CANYON BLUFF CT
6200 SD 92121 1208-G3
CANYON BREEZE DR
7400 SD 92126 1208-J3
7400 SD 92126 1209-A3
CANYON BREEZE RD
7200 SD 92126 1208-J3
CANYON COUNTRY LN
9700 SDCo 92026 1089-D1
10100 SDCo 92026 1069-E7
CANYON CREEK AV
2000 CHV 91913 1311-E5
CANYON CREEK PL
1000 ESCN 92025 1130-D6
CANYON CREEK RD
1000 ESCN 92025 1130-D7
CANYON CREEK WY
- OCN 92057 1086-J3
2400 ESCN 92025 1130-D6
CANYON CREST DR
2500 ESCN 92027 1130-F2

CANYON CREST DR
2500 SDCo 92027 1130-F2
5700 SD 92182 1270-B1
CANYON DE ORO
3900 ENCT 92024 1148-E3
3900 SDCo 92024 1148-E3
4200 SDCo 92029 1148-E3
CANYON ESTATES RD
30300 SDCo 92084 1068-A4
CANYON GLEN CT
- SD 92129 1188-J4
CANYON HEIGHTS RD
1500 SDCo 92028 998-H5
CANYON HILL CT
7200 SD 92126 1208-J3
CANYON HILL LN
10800 SD 92126 1208-J3
CANYON HILL PL
7100 SD 92126 1208-J3
CANYON HILL WY
7100 SD 92126 1208-J3
CANYON LAKE DR
10500 SD 92131 1209-G4
CANYON LODGE PL
500 OCN 92054 1086-D7
CANYON MESA LN
10900 SD 92126 1209-A3
CANYON OAK PL
2700 ESCN 92029 1129-D4
CANYON PARK DR
11200 SNTE 92071 1231-H6
CANYON PARK TER
9100 SNTE 92071 1231-G5
CANYON PEAK LN
7300 SD 92126 1208-J3
CANYON POINT CT
11000 SD 92126 1209-A3
CANYON POINT LN
7600 SD 92126 1209-A3
CANYON RIDGE DR
300 CHV 91902 1311-B3
CANYON RIDGE LN
1200 SDCo 92025 1130-D6
CANYONRIDGE PL
10100 SDCo 91977 1271-E7
CANYON RIM DR
300 SDCo 92021 1253-A2
CANYON RIM RW
6600 SD 92111 1268-H3
CANYONSIDE CT
10000 SDCo 91977 1271-D6
CANYONSIDE WY
300 OCN 92054 1086-B6
CANYONSIDE PARK DR
- SD 92129 1189-C7
CANYON SLOPE PL
7900 SD 92120 1250-D3
CANYONTOP ST
10000 SDCo 91977 1271-D6
CANYONVIEW CT
10000 SDCo 91977 1271-E6
CANYON VIEW DR
- OCN 92054 1086-D3
100 SDCo 92021 1252-H2
CANYON VIEW GN
2300 ESCN 92026 1109-B3
CANYON VIEW LN
7300 LMGR 91945 1270-F7
CANYON VIEW RD
2200 SDCo 92028 996-H3
CANYON VIEW WY
- PWY 92064 1171-A6
CANYON VISTA CT
6400 SD 92111 1248-H6
CANYON VISTA DR
- OCN 92057 1086-J3
2300 SDCo 92028 1028-A1
CANYON VISTA WY
- OCN 92057 1086-J3
CANYON WASH CT
- SDCo 92026 1069-B4
CANYON WAY CT
- SDCo 92026 1069-B4
CANYONWOOD LN
10000 SDCo 91977 1271-E7
CAPALINA RD
3400 SMCS 92069 1108-D6
CAPAZO CT
2900 CRLB 92009 1127-H4
CAPCANO RD
8900 SD 92126 1189-D7
8900 SD 92126 1209-D1
CAPE AIRE LN
1100 CRLB 92008 1106-G7
CAPE BRETON
500 SDCo 92084 1088-D7
CAPE COD CIR
2900 CRLB 92010 1107-B5
CAPE COD CT
- SDCo 91977 1271-C6
CAPE COD BAY CT
2000 SD 92105 1290-C1
CAPEHART ST
5000 SD 92117 1228-E7
CAPE HORN AV
2300 SDCo 92036 1136-B7
CAPE JEWELS TR
- SD 92130 1188-E4
CAPELLA CT
3700 SDCo 91941 1271-A5
CAPE MAY AV
4300 SD 92107 1267-J6
4700 SD 92107 1267-J5
CAPE MAY PL
1700 CRLB 92008 1106-H6
2000 SD 92107 1267-J5
CAPE SEBASTIAN PL
2900 ENCT 92007 1167-F5
CAPEWOOD LN
13900 SD 92128 1189-J2
CAPILLA CT
17000 SD 92127 1169-J2
CAPILLA PL
17000 SD 92127 1169-H2
CAPILLA RD
11100 SD 92127 1169-H2
CAPISTRANO AV
1000 SDCo 91977 1291-C2
CAPISTRANO DR
500 OCN 92054 1085-J6
500 OCN 92054 1086-A5
CAPISTRANO GN
1700 ESCN 92026 1109-D5
CAPISTRANO LN
1200 VSTA 92081 1107-E1
CAPISTRANO PL
700 SD 92109 1267-H4
CAPISTRANO ST
1800 SD 92106 1288-B1
1900 SD 92106 1268-B7
CAPISTRANO WY
- SMCS 92078 1129-C1
CAPITAN AV
2400 SD 92104 1269-E7

CAPITAN AV
2400 SD 92104 1289-E1
CAPITOL ST
3800 LMSA 91941 1270-F5
CAPPS ST
2800 SD 92104 1269-D6
CAPRA WY
1000 SDCo 92028 1028-C1
CAPRI CT
2000 SDCo 92019 1272-C4
CAPRI DR
1000 VSTA 92084 1087-J5
6100 SD 92120 1250-C7
CAPRI RD
800 ENCT 92024 1147-C3
CAPRICE PL
11300 SDCo 92026 1089-H7
CAPRICHO WY
- OCN 92057 1086-G2
CAPRICORN WY
8400 SD 92126 1209-B2
CAPRIOLE CT
5300 SDCo 91902 1311-A2
CAPRISE DR
- SMCS 92078 1128-E6
CAPS WY
2500 SDCo 92028 998-B6
CAPSTAN DR
- CRLB 92011 1127-A7
CAPSTONE DR
13100 SD 92130 1188-B4
CAPTAINS CT
8600 SDCo 92026 1068-J4
CAR ST
1100 SD 92114 1290-H2
CARA CT
8800 SDCo 91977 1291-A5
CARA LN
16000 SDCo 92082 1071-B6
CARA ST
- ESCN 92025 1130-A6
CARA WY
11700 SD 92128 1189-F7
11700 SD 92131 1189-F7
CARACAS PL
31300 SDCo 92003 1067-J2
CARACOL CT
2000 CRLB 92009 1127-F6
CARAMAY PL
1500 SD 92154 1350-E2
CARANCHO RD
27300 RivC 92590 997-J1
CARANCHO ST
3800 LMSA 91941 1270-F5
CARAS CT
15900 SDCo 92065 1174-B4
CARAVELLE PL
10800 SD 92124 1249-J2
CARAWAY CT
12700 SDCo 92040 1232-B4
CARAWAY ST
2000 ESCN 92026 1109-F5
9600 SDCo 92040 1232-B4
CARBAJAL CT
600 CHV 91911 1330-H3
CARBET PL
10800 SD 92124 1249-H2
CARBINE WY
- SD 92154 1350-G2
CARBO CT
3800 LMSA 91941 1270-H5
CAR COUNTRY DR
5200 CRLB 92008 1126-H2
CARDAMOM CT
800 CHV 91910 1330-J1
CARDENO DR
5200 SD 92109 1247-J4
5400 SD 92037 1247-J2
CARDIFF DR
1100 ENCT 92024 1167-F2
CARDIFF ST
300 SD 92114 1290-H3
CARDIFF BAY DR
4800 OCN 92057 1066-J6
CARDIGAN WY
1900 SD 92111 1269-A1
CARDIN ST
4600 SD 92111 1249-A2
CARDINAL CT
1000 SMCS 92078 1128-H5
7600 SD 92123 1249-A6
CARDINAL DR
2000 SD 92123 1269-A1
2100 SD 92123 1249-A7
CARDINAL LN
2400 SD 92123 1249-A7
CARDINAL PL
1200 CHV 91911 1330-G2
7600 SD 92123 1249-A7
CARDINAL RD
2600 SD 92123 1249-A7
CARDINAL WY
- SDCo 92055 1023-E3
200 OCN 92057 1086-J6
CARDONA AV
700 CHV 91910 1310-J5
CARDOZA DR
9900 SNTE 92071 1231-D3
CAREFREE DR
700 SD 92114 1290-E5
10100 SNTE 92071 1231-D4
CAREN RD
1100 VSTA 92083 1087-E6
CARETTA WY
400 ENCT 92007 1167-D2
CAREY RD
- ImCo 92227 431-C3
100 OCN 92054 1086-C6
CAREYBROOK LN
7500 SD 92114 1290-G5
CARGILL AV
7700 SD 92122 1228-C4
CARIB CT
4400 SD 92117 1248-F1
CARIB DR
6900 SDCo 92029 1128-F7
6900 SDCo 92029 1148-F1
CARIBE CAY BLVD N
- CORD 92118 1329-E1
CARIBOU CT
- CRLB 92010 1127-G1
- SD 92129 1188-J4
CARIE WY
2300 SDCo 91901 1253-H2
CARILLO CIR
600 OCN 92057 1066-J5
CARILLO RD
3300 SDCo 92004 (1078-J6 See Page 1058)
3300 SDCo 92004 (1079-A7 See Page 1058)
CARILLO WY
- CRLB 92009 1127-J3

CARILLON CT
10600 SD 92131 1209-J2
10600 SD 92131 1210-A2
CARINGA WY
2300 CRLB 92009 1127-G7
CARINO WY
- OCN 92057 1086-G2
CARIOCA CT
10200 SD 92124 1249-G1
CARIOCA PL
- VSTA 92084 1088-D6
CARISSA AV
1400 CHV 91911 1330-H3
CARISSA CT
1400 CHV 91911 1330-H3
CARISSA DR
200 OCN 92057 1087-A1
CARISSA LN
10000 SDCo 91977 1291-D2
CARISSA WY
- CRLB 92011 1127-D4
CARITA CT
9700 SNTE 92071 1231-A4
CARITA RD
9200 SNTE 92071 1231-A4
CARIUTO CT
10700 SD 92124 1249-H2
CARL DR
18000 SDCo 91935 1274-D4
CARLA AV
500 CHV 91910 1310-D6
CARLA CT
- SDCo 92026 1089-G3
CARLA WY
400 SD 92037 1247-G4
CARLANN DR
100 SMCS 92069 1108-H6
CARLANN LN
600 ESCN 92027 1110-C6
CARLATA LN
27300 SDCo 92082 1091-G4
CARLETON SQ
1400 SD 92106 1288-A1
CARLETON ST
2700 SD 92106 1288-B1
CARLETTE ST
8000 LMSA 91942 1250-H7
CARLEY CIR
8900 SD 92126 1209-D1
CARLIN HTS
2500 SDCo 92025 1130-C7
CARLIN PL
4400 LMSA 91941 1271-A3
CARLIN ST
100 SDCo 92065 1152-D7
CARLINA ST
7400 CRLB 92009 1147-J1
CARLING DR
4400 SD 92115 1270-C4
CARLING WY
6100 SD 92115 1270-C4
CARLISLE DR
7800 LMGR 91945 1290-H2
7800 LMGR 92114 1290-H2
7800 SD 92114 1290-H2
CARLO ST
400 SMCS 92078 1108-C6
CARLOS ST
300 SD 92102 1289-H4
CARLOS CANYON CT
500 CHV 91910 1310-J4
CARLOS CANYON DR
1100 CHV 91910 1310-J4
1100 CHV 91910 1311-A4
CARLOTA ST
11000 SD 92129 1169-H7
CARLOTTA WY
200 OCN 92057 1086-H3
CARLOW CT
600 ELCJ 92020 1251-B4
CARLOW LN
- ELCJ 92020 1251-B4
CARLOW ST
2500 ELCJ 92020 1251-B4
CARLOW WY
700 ELCJ 92020 1251-B4
CARLSBAD BLVD Rt#-S21
200 CRLB 92011 1126-H6
2200 CRLB 92008 1106-D4
3900 CRLB 92008 1126-F1
7100 CRLB 92011 1146-J1
7300 CRLB 92024 1147-A2
7300 ENCT 92024 1147-A2
7400 CRLB 92024 1146-J1
CARLSBAD CT
1000 SD 92114 1290-H2
CARLSBAD ST
500 SDCo 91977 1290-J2
800 SD 92114 1290-J2
CARLSBAD VILLAGE DR
100 CRLB 92008 1106-E5
2300 CRLB 92010 1106-J3
2700 CRLB 92010 1107-A4
CARLSON CT
300 VSTA 92083 1087-C7
300 VSTA 92083 1107-C1
14400 PWY 92064 1190-H1
CARLSON ST
14600 PWY 92064 1190-H1
CARLTON PL
9900 SNTE 92071 1231-A3
CARLTON WY
2800 SDCo 92028 1048-E1
CARLTON HILLS BLVD
8900 SNTE 92071 1231-A4
CARLTON OAKS DR
8200 SD 92071 1230-H6
8200 SNTE 92071 1230-H6
8800 SNTE 92071 1231-A6
CARLY CT
1400 SD 92114 1290-F5
CARMACK WY
9500 SNTE 92071 1231-B3
CARMAR WY
2800 SD 92139 1310-F2
CARMEL AV
1500 CHV 91913 1311-C7
CARMEL CIR
700 VSTA 92084 1087-J3
CARMEL DR
2600 CRLB 92010 1106-J5
S CARMEL RD
200 SMCS 92078 1129-A1
CARMEL ST
100 SMCS 92078 1128-J1
400 SMCS 92078 1108-J7
400 SMCS 92078 1109-A7
CARMEL BROOKS WY
3900 SD 92130 1188-A7
CARMEL CANYON RD
4400 SD 92130 1188-C6
CARMEL CAPE
12400 SD 92130 1188-A7

SAN DIEGO CO.

STREET
Block City ZIP Pg-Grid

CARMEL CENTER RD
4200 SD 92130 1188-B6
CARMEL COUNTRY RD
- SD 92130 1208-D1
4000 SD 92130 1188-A5
CARMEL CREEK RD
11200 SD 92130 1208-B1
12700 SD 92130 1188-B5
CARMEL CREEPER PL
- ENCT 92024 1147-C5
CARMEL GROVE RD
3800 SD 92130 1188-A7
CARMELINA DR
1800 SD 92116 1269-C3
CARMELITA PL
200 SOLB 92075 1167-F7
CARMEL KNOLLS DR
5000 SD 92130 1188-D5
CARMEL MISSION RD
12600 SD 92130 1188-B6
CARMEL MOUNTAIN RD
3300 SD 92121 1208-A3
3500 SD 92130 1208-D2
8200 SD 92129 1189-J1
11200 SD 92128 1189-J1
11600 SD 92128 1190-A1
12000 SD 92128 1170-A7
CARMELO DR
400 OCN 92054 1085-J6
1500 SDCo 92055 1085-J6
CARMELO ST
4400 SD 92107 1287-H2
CARMEL PARK DR
11900 SD 92130 1188-A7
CARMEL POINTE
12400 SD 92130 1188-A7
CARMEL RIDGE RD
14500 SD 92128 1190-B1
CARMEL SPRINGS WY
3900 SD 92130 1188-A7
CARMEL VALLEY RD
- SD 92127 1169-D7
- SD 92129 1169-D7
- SD 92130 1189-A3
- SDCo 92127 1169-D7
100 DLMR 92014 1187-G7
100 SD 92014 1187-G7
1800 SD 92014 1207-G1
2100 SD 92121 1207-G1
3000 SD 92130 1207-G1
3800 SD 92130 1208-A1
6300 SD 92130 1188-E5
14400 SD 92127 1189-B2
14400 SD 92129 1189-B2
CARMEL VIEW RD
3600 SD 92130 1188-A7
4000 SD 92130 1187-J7
CARMEL VISTA RD
12200 SD 92130 1187-J7
12200 SD 92130 1188-A7
12200 SD 92130 1208-A1
CARMEN CT
900 SDCo 92069 1109-B5
CARMEN DR
4400 SDCo 91941 1271-F3
CARMEN ST
5500 SD 92105 1290-B1
CARMENA RD
23500 SDCo 92065 1173-D3
CARMENITA RD
7200 LMSA 91941 1270-F5
CARMICHAEL DR
9300 SDCo 91941 1271-B3
9300 LMSA 91941 1271-B3
CARMIR DR
8800 SNTE 92071 1251-A1
CARMONA CT
800 CHV 91910 1310-H5
CARNABY CT
4500 CRLB 92010 1106-J5
CARNABY WY
- SD 92123 1249-D1
CARNATION AV
100 CORD 91932 1329-E7
100 IMPB 91932 1329-F7
3300 SDCo 92065 1172-C3
CARNATION CT
- SMCS 92078 1128-H3
CARNATION DR
6600 CRLB 92011 1127-A6
CARNATION GN
3700 ESCN 92025 1150-C3
CARNATION LN
600 SDCo 92028 1027-G4
CARNATION ST
- SDCo 92055 1086-A4
CARNEGIE CT
3100 SD 92122 1228-C6
CARNEGIE DR
3700 OCN 92056 1086-J7
3700 OCN 92056 1087-A7
CARNEGIE PL
3100 SD 92122 1228-C6
CARNEGIE ST
5600 SD 92122 1228-C6
CARNEGIE WY
3200 SD 92122 1228-C6
CARNELIAN CT
- CRLB 92009 1127-F6
CARNELIAN LN
3400 OCN 92056 1107-D2
CARNELIAN ST
1100 ELCJ 92021 1252-A3
CARNELL AV
3200 SD 92154 1350-D1
CARNELL CT
1300 SD 92154 1350-D1
CARNERO PL
10200 SDCo 92040 1231-F3
CARNEROS VALLEY ST
1300 CHV 91913 1331-B1
CARNES RD
- SDCo 92055 1085-J2
- SDCo 92055 1086-A3
CARNEY LN
13000 SDCo 92082 1050-C4
CARNEY RD
36300 SDCo 92082 1050-C5
CARNITAS ST
14300 PWY 92064 1190-H1
CARNOUSTIE RD
6900 SD 92154 1352-A2
CARNTON WY
17400 SD 92128 1170-A1
CARNY ST
- SD 92152 1288-A5
CAROB LN
1700 SDCo 92004 (1099-F2
See Page 1098)
CAROB WY
100 CORD 92118 1288-G7
200 OCN 92057 1086-J5
CAROB TREE LN
1800 SDCo 92021 1252-C2

CAROL CT
700 SMCS 92069 1109-B6
CAROL LN
3700 SDCo 92065 1172-B3
CAROL PL
800 CRLB 92008 1106-F6
1300 NATC 91950 1290-C7
CAROL ST
1800 SD 92154 1329-J6
1800 SD 92154 1330-A6
6000 SD 92115 1270-C3
CAROL WY
3700 SDCo 91977 1271-A5
CAROL ANN LN
47400 RivC 92592 999-G1
CAROL ANNE RD
40000 SDCo 92028 997-A1
40000 SDCo 92028 409-A4
CAROLDALE RW
6000 SD 92037 1248-A1
CAROLEE AV
13200 SD 92129 1189-D4
CAROLINA LN
900 SD 92102 1290-A3
CAROLINA PL
4900 SD 92102 1290-A3
CAROLINA RD
400 DLMR 92014 1187-F5
CAROLINA ST
700 IMPB 91932 1329-G7
CAROLINE DR
4700 SD 92115 1269-J3
CAROLINE LN
4900 SDCo 92028 1047-E6
CAROLINE WY
100 ESCN 92025 1129-G4
CAROLITA
- SDCo 92040 1232-B7
CAROLTON LN
1900 SDCo 92028 1028-A6
CAROL VIEW DR
2200 ENCT 92007 1167-E3
CAROLWOOD DR
500 SD 92139 1290-H5
CAROLYN CIR
3200 OCN 92054 1086-E5
CAROLYN DR
1800 CHV 91913 1311-D5
CAROLYN PL
2300 ENCT 92024 1147-J7
CAROLYN VISTA LN
5300 SDCo 91902 1311-A3
CAROUSEL LN
13100 SD 92014 1187-J7
CAROWAY CT
3500 SDCo 92019 1272-C6
CAROWIND LN
- SD 92131 1210-G1
CARPA
7200 CRLB 92009 1128-A7
CARPENTER LN
4000 SDCo 91941 1271-G4
CARPENTER RD
2300 OCN 92054 1086-C5
CARR DR
3200 OCN 92056 1107-B1
CARRANZA DR
17000 SD 92127 1169-H1
CARRARA PL
5100 SD 92122 1228-D3
CARRERA CT
2400 SDCo 91977 1291-B1
CARRETA CT
10300 SNTE 92071 1231-E3
CARRETA DR
10000 SNTE 92071 1231-E3
CARRIAGE CIR
- VSTA 92081 1107-D1
2300 OCN 92056 1106-H1
CARRIAGE CT
- SD 92130 1188-D5
CARRIAGE DR
800 SMCS 92069 1109-A5
CARRIAGE LN
1700 SDCo 92028 1028-B5
CARRIAGE RD
12800 PWY 92064 1190-D3
CARRIAGEDALE RW
2500 SD 92037 1248-A1
CARRIAGE HEIGHTS CIR
13300 PWY 92064 1190-D4
CARRIAGE HEIGHTS WY
12700 PWY 92064 1190-D4
CARRIAGE HILLS CT
17000 PWY 92064 1170-D2
CARRIAGE RUN DR
- SD 92130 1208-C2
CARRIBEAN WY
8700 SNTE 92071 1230-H7
CARRIE CIR
500 SMCS 92069 1108-H6
CARRIE ELLEN CT
10100 SNTE 92071 1231-A3
CARRIE RIDGE WY
7400 SD 92139 1290-G6
CARRILLO WY
2800 CRLB 92009 1127-H4
CARRINGTON DR
10500 SD 92126 1208-J4
CARRIO DR
1300 SD 92084 1068-A6
CARRIZO DR
7200 SD 92037 1227-G7
CARRIZO PL
1500 ESCN 92027 1110-A5
CARRIZO ST
- SDCo 91934 (1321-H5
See Page 1300)
CARRIZO CREEK RD
- SDCo 91934 430-F9
CARRIZO GORGE RD
- SDCo 91934 (1301-G7
See Page 1300)
- SDCo 91934 (1321-H2
See Page 1300)
1100 SDCo 91934 430-F9
CARROLL LN
2300 SDCo 92027 1130-E2
CARROLL RD
6000 SD 92121 1208-G7
6700 SD 92121 1228-H1
7400 SD 92121 1209-A7
7500 SD 92121 1229-A1
7500 SD 92126 1229-A1
CARROLL WY
9000 SD 92121 1209-A7
CARROLL CANYON RD
4900 SD 92121 1208-E7
9400 SD 92126 1209-E5
9800 SD 92131 1209-E5
CARROLL CENTRE RD
9600 SD 92126 1209-E5

CARROLL PARK CT
9200 SD 92121 1208-H7
CARROLL PARK DR
9300 SD 92121 1208-H7
CARROLLTON SQ
12100 SD 92128 1190-B3
CARROTWOOD GN
1100 ESCN 92026 1129-F1
CARROZA CT
11200 SD 92124 1249-J2
11200 SD 92124 1250-A2
CARRYLL PARR CT
1000 SDCo 92028 1027-G3
CARSON PL
9800 SDCo 92029 1149-E4
CARSON ST
- CORD 92135 1288-F4
3800 SD 92117 1248-E4
CARSTENZ
500 SMCS 92078 1128-C1
CARTA LN
9700 SDCo 92021 1233-C1
CARTAGENA DR
4100 SD 92115 1270-D4
CARTEGENA WY
2300 OCN 92056 1106-J1
CARTER PL
7800 LMSA 91941 1270-G3
CARTER RD
600 ImCo 92227 431-B2
CARTER ST
200 ELCJ 92020 1251-G7
CARTHAGE ST
6300 SD 92120 1250-B5
CARTHAY CIR
9200 SDCo 91977 1271-B4
CARTULINA RD
4200 SD 92124 1249-J2
CARTWRIGHT ST
6500 SD 92120 1249-J5
CARVALLO CT
3200 CRLB 92009 1147-J1
CARVALOS DR
400 SDCo 91910 1310-D6
CARVEACRE RD
3300 SDCo 91901 1275-A1
CARVER ST
100 CHV 91911 1330-E4
CARY CT
1400 ELCJ 92019 1252-A7
CARY WY
1300 SD 92109 1247-J4
CARYL DR
10500 SNTE 92071 1231-E7
CARYN CT
25700 SDCo 92065 1173-J4
25700 SDCo 92065 1174-A4
CASA AVD
12700 PWY 92064 1170-C6
CASA CT
12800 PWY 92064 1190-D5
CASA DR
- OCN 92057 1066-J7
CASA LN
7000 LMGR 91945 1270-F6
CASA PL
1600 NATC 91950 1310-B1
CASA ALTA
2200 SDCo 91977 1271-D7
CASA BLANCA CT
3100 SDCo 91902 1310-H1
CASABLANCA CT
1900 VSTA 92081 1107-H4
CASA BLANCA PL
8100 SD 92126 1209-B4
CASABLANCA WY
2900 SDCo 92028 1028-D7
CASA BONITA CT
4800 SDCo 91902 1310-H1
CASA BONITA DR
3100 SDCo 91902 1310-H1
CASA BONITA WY
1100 VSTA 92081 1107-E1
1900 ESCN 92025 1129-J6
CASA BUENA WY
4200 OCN 92057 1086-J3
CASA CIELO
2200 SDCo 91977 1271-D7
CASA DE CAROL
22300 SDCo 92065 1173-A6
CASA DE LA TORRE CT
9600 SDCo 91977 1271-C3
CASA DEL SOL CT
- SD 92154 1350-G1
CASA DE MACHADO
4200 SDCo 91941 1271-C3
CASA DE ORO BLVD
10000 SDCo 91977 1271-E5
CASA DE ORO PL
800 ESCN 92025 1129-J6
CASA DE ROCA WY
1400 SDCo 91901 1234-J5
CASA DE VEREDA
2000 SDCo 92084 1088-D4
CASA GRANDE AV
13100 SDCo 92040 1232-C2
CASA GRANDE WY
5700 SDCo 91902 1290-J6
CASA HERMOSA CT
- ENCT 92024 1148-A5
CASA LINDA WY
2700 SMCS 92069 1108-C5
CASA LOMA CT
3100 SDCo 91902 1310-H1
CASALS PL
4800 SD 92124 1250-A1
CASA NOVA CT
- SD 92154 1350-H1
CASA NUEVA ST
10000 SDCo 91977 1271-E6
CASA REAL CT
700 VSTA 92083 1087-F5
CASA REAL LN
1500 ESCN 92026 1109-D6
1500 SMCS 92069 1109-D6
CASATA GN
- ESCN 92025 1130-D5
CASA VERDE CT
3200 SDCo 91902 1310-H1
CASA VISTA
13200 PWY 92064 1190-E5
CASA VISTA RD
12600 SDCo 92040 1232-B4
CASCA WY
3300 CRLB 92009 1148-A1
CASCADA WY
11200 SD 92124 1250-A3
CASCADE
500 SMCS 92078 1128-B1
CASCADE CRSG
- PWY 92064 1150-G7
CASCADE CT
3700 SD 92122 1228-D5

CASCADE PL
- CHV 91913 1331-A2
1400 SDCo 92021 1231-F7
1400 SDCo 92021 1251-F1
CASCADE RD
300 SDCo 92021 1251-F1
CASCADE ST
6300 SD 92122 1228-D5
CASCADIA LN
- ENCT 92024 1147-E5
CASCADITA CIR
4500 OCN 92057 1087-B1
CASCAJO CT
10800 SD 92124 1249-J2
CASCIO CT
8100 LMGR 91945 1270-H5
CASCO CT
8400 SD 92129 1189-B6
CASE ST
8300 LMSA 91942 1270-J1
CASEMAN AV
3900 SD 92154 1330-F7
CASEMENT ST
2300 SD 92123 1249-C7
CASERAS DR
3400 OCN 92056 1086-J7
CASERO CT
12200 SD 92128 1170-B3
CASERO PL
1700 ESCN 92029 1129-F6
12200 SD 92128 1170-B3
CASERO RD
16500 SD 92128 1170-B3
CASE SPRINGS RD
- SDCo 92055 408-L4
- SDCo 92055 409-A6
- SDCo 92055 996-A5
CASEY GN
- SD 92127 1169-B3
CASEY RD
3200 ImCo 92250 431-D3
CASEY ST
2500 SD 92139 1290-G7
2700 SD 92139 1310-G1
CASITA CT
100 VSTA 92083 1107-C1
CASITA LN
- SMCS 92069 1108-E5
CASITA WY
3900 SD 92115 1270-E5
CASITAS CT
- CHV 91910 1310-C7
CASITAS LN
- ESCN 92029 1129-F4
CASITAS ST
700 SD 92107 1287-H3
CASITAS DEL SOL
2200 SDCo 92028 1028-A2
CASMEG WY
3000 SDCo 92019 1272-C6
CASNER RD
19500 SDCo 92065 1154-A2
CASPER DR
7200 SD 92119 1250-F5
CASPER LN
200 VSTA 92084 1087-J6
CASPER ST
1300 OCN 92056 1087-D3
CASPIAN DR
5000 OCN 92057 1087-B1
5000 OCN 92057 1067-C7
CASPIAN PL
- SD 92131 1210-J2
CASPIAN WY
- CRLB 92011 1127-B5
300 IMPB 91932 1349-F1
CASPI GARDENS DR
9800 SNTE 92071 1231-D4
CASS ST
4100 SD 92109 1247-H4
CASSANDRA LN
5100 SD 92109 1248-A4
CASSANNA WY
4300 OCN 92057 1087-A4
CASSELBERRY WY
6300 SD 92119 1250-E6
CASSELMAN CT
- CHV 91910 1310-C4
CASSELMAN PL
500 CHV 91910 1310-C4
CASSELMAN ST
400 CHV 91910 1310-A5
500 CHV 91910 1309-J5
CASSIA PL
700 CHV 91910 1310-G7
17900 SD 92127 1149-J7
CASSIA RD
4000 CRLB 92011 1127-D5
CASSIA GLEN DR
- SDCo 92127 1169-E2
CASSIDY ST
100 OCN 92054 1106-D2
CASSINI CT
12000 SD 92131 1210-B1
CASSINS ST
1300 CRLB 92011 1127-B6
CASSIO CT
1200 VSTA 92081 1107-H4
CASSIOEPIA WY
8800 SD 92126 1209-D2
CASSIOPEIA LN
- SD 92154 1350-G1
CASSOU RD
100 SDCo 92069 1108-G2
100 SMCS 92069 1108-J2
CASSOWARY CT
10600 SD 92131 1209-H1
CASTAIC CT
9600 SNTE 92071 1231-C4
CASTAIC PL
- CHV 91913 1331-E2
CASTANA PZ
1000 CHV 91910 1311-C2
CASTANA ST
4700 SD 92102 1289-J4
5100 SD 92114 1290-A4
CASTANEDA DR
2800 ESCN 92025 1150-B1
CASTANO LN
8600 SDCo 92021 1232-F6
CASTAWAY CV
- SD 92154 1330-J7
CASTEEL CT
1500 SD 92114 1290-D6
CASTEEL LN
1600 SDCo 92065 1172-H2
CASTEJON DR
6100 SD 92037 1247-J1
CASTELAR ST
4400 SD 92107 1268-A5
CASTELLANA RD
1700 SD 92037 1227-G6
CASTELLANO DR
- OCN 92057 1067-A5

CASTELLANO WY
4900 OCN 92057 1067-A5
CASTELLO CIR
17000 SDCo 92127 1169-E2
CASTELLON TER
2500 SDCo 92019 1272-E2
CASTILE WY
- SD 92128 1190-A3
CASTILLA PL
2800 CRLB 92009 1147-H2
CASTILLA WY
2100 OCN 92056 1086-J7
2100 OCN 92056 1106-J1
CASTILLO GN
- SD 92130 1188-D4
CASTLE AV
4700 SD 92105 1269-J6
CASTLE CT
7200 LMGR 91945 1270-F7
CASTLE GN
1800 ESCN 92029 1129-F5
CASTLE HTS
- SDCo 92082 1069-F5
CASTLEBAY
- SDCo 92028 1027-G6
CASTLE BROOK CT
8800 SDCo 92040 1232-C6
CASTLE COURT DR
12500 SDCo 92040 1232-B4
CASTLE CREEK LN
29500 SDCo 92026 1069-A6
CASTLE CREEK WY
- SDCo 92026 1069-A6
CASTLECREST DR
30100 SDCo 92082 1069-F4
CASTLEGATE LN
2200 VSTA 92084 1088-C6
CASTLE GLEN DR
3400 SD 92123 1249-D4
CASTLEHILL RD
- CHV 91915 1311-J6
- CHV 91915 (1312-A7
See Page 1293)
CASTLE HILLS DR
5100 SD 92109 1247-J4
5500 SD 92037 1247-J4
CASTLE ISLAND CV
4700 SD 92154 1330-H6
CASTLE PEAK LN
15600 SDCo 91935 1273-D5
CASTLERIDGE RD
29600 SDCo 92082 1069-F6
CASTLETON DR
5400 SD 92117 1248-H2
CASTLETON WY
4500 SD 92117 1248-H2
CASTLE VIEW DR
29100 SDCo 92026 1069-D7
CASTLEWOOD CT
1300 CHV 91915 (1312-A6
See Page 1293)
1800 SDCo 92021 1251-H1
CASTLEWOOD DR
1100 SDCo 92021 1251-H1
CASTRO ST
700 SOLB 92075 1187-G1
CASTRO LANE RD
2000 ImCo 92243 6500-H4
CATALINA AV
2000 SDCo 92084 1088-C5
2000 VSTA 92084 1088-C5
CATALINA BLVD
200 SD 92152 1287-J4
300 SD 92106 1287-J3
1000 SD 92106 1288-A1
1000 SD 92107 1287-J3
1000 SD 92107 1288-A1
1600 SD 92107 1268-A7
CATALINA CIR
2300 OCN 92056 1087-E4
CATALINA CT
4200 SD 92107 1268-A6
CATALINA DR
3400 CRLB 92010 1106-H4
4500 OCN 92057 1066-H6
CATALINA PL
2500 VSTA 92084 1088-D5
2500 SDCo 92084 1088-D5
4100 SD 92107 1268-A7
CATALINA HEIGHTS WY
2400 SDCo 92084 1088-D5
2400 VSTA 92084 1088-D5
CATALPA CT
- CHV 91915 1311-J7
CATALPA LN
400 SDCo 92028 1027-G2
CATALPA RD
1700 CRLB 92011 1127-E6
CATALPA WY
700 ELCJ 92021 1251-G4
CATAMARAN DR
6800 CRLB 92011 1126-H6
CATAMARAN WY
1900 OCN 92054 1106-F1
CATAMARCA DR
3700 SD 92124 1249-J3
CATANIA ST
200 SD 92113 1289-H4
CATARACT PL
2800 ELCJ 92020 1251-A5
CATARINA DR
200 SDCo 92004 1058-G4
CATARINA LN
- SD 92128 1189-H6
CATAWBA DR
13600 PWY 92064 1190-E3
CATBIRD LN
- SDCo 91935 1274-C3
CATES ST
- SDCo 92055 1067-A1
300 SD 92114 1290-H4
CATFISH LN
3800 OCN 92054 1086-G2
CATHAN LN
1800 SDCo 92084 1108-C2
CATHEDRAL GN
1800 ESCN 92029 1129-F5
CATHEDRAL WY
- SDCo 92065 1174-B4
CATHER AV
4400 SD 92122 1228-E4
CATHER CT
7100 SD 92122 1228-E4
CATHERINE AV
700 SMCS 92069 1109-A6
4500 SD 92115 1270-D3
CATHERINE RD
- SDCo 92003 1067-E1
CATHY CT
600 ESCN 92026 1109-J7
CATHY DR
39700 SDCo 92028 997-B2
CATHY LN
700 ENCT 92007 1167-E1

CATHY ST
1800 SD 92154 1330-A6
CATHYWOOD DR
9400 SNTE 92071 1231-B4
CATOCTIN DR
4800 SD 92115 1270-D2
CATSPAW PL
1100 ESCN 92029 1129-F5
CATSPAW CAPE
- CORD 92118 1329-E1
CATTAIL CT
- ELCN 92243 6559-J3
CATTAIL PL
- CRLB 92011 1127-B6
CATTAIL RD
15700 SD 92127 1169-J5
CAUBY ST
3000 SD 92110 1268-E5
CAUDOR ST
1400 ENCT 92024 1147-B2
CAULFIELD DR
2500 SD 92154 1330-C7
CAURINA CT
- CRLB 92011 1127-C5
CAVALIER CT
28300 SDCo 92026 1089-F3
CAVALLO ST
12400 SD 92130 1188-C7
CAVALRY CT
13000 SD 92129 1189-C4
CAVE ST
1200 SD 92037 1227-F6
CAVERN PL
3700 CRLB 92010 1107-B4
CAVERN POINT CT
1500 CHV 91911 1330-J3
CAVIT ST
- SD 92140 1268-F6
CAVITE CT
6700 SD 92120 1250-E7
6700 SD 92120 1270-E1
CAY DR
3500 CRLB 92010 1107-B3
CAYENNE LN
6400 CRLB 92009 1127-G5
CAYENNE CREEK CT
- SDCo 92127 1169-F5
CAYENNE CREEK PL
- SDCo 92127 1169-F5
CAYENNE CREEK RD
- SDCo 92127 1169-F5
CAYENNE CREEK WY
- SDCo 92127 1169-F5
CAYENNE RIDGE RD
- SDCo 92127 1169-F4
CAYMAN WY
1800 VSTA 92081 1107-G6
CAYOTE AV
13000 SD 92129 1189-C4
CAYUCOS CT
13900 SD 92129 1189-C3
CAYUCOS WY
8700 SD 92129 1189-C3
CAYUGA DR
13400 PWY 92064 1190-D4
CAYWOOD ST
5000 SD 92117 1228-E7
CAZADERO DR
2600 CRLB 92009 1127-H5
CAZADOR LN
3600 SDCo 92028 1047-F3
3600 SDCo 92055 1047-F3
CAZORLA AV
600 CHV 91910 1310-H6
CEANOTHUS CT
1600 CRLB 92011 1127-D6
CEANOTHUS PL
4800 OCN 92057 1067-A7
CEBADA CT
11600 SD 92124 1250-A2
CEBU CT
2800 CRLB 92009 1127-H5
CEBU PL
2800 CRLB 92009 1127-H5
CECELIA TER
2000 SD 92110 1268-F1
2200 SD 92110 1248-F7
CECELIA JO RD
3400 SDCo 92065 1172-B3
CECIL RD
- CORD 92135 1288-F4
CECILIA WY
200 OCN 92057 1086-G6
CECILWOOD DR
9500 SNTE 92071 1231-C4
CEDAR AV
100 CHV 91910 1310-A5
200 ELCN 92243 6499-J7
600 CHV 91910 1330-B1
800 CHV 91911 1330-B2
CEDAR CT
- SDCo 92040 1232-D6
CEDAR DR
2400 SDCo 91906 (1297-E5
See Page 1296)
3900 SDCo 92036 1156-E2
CEDAR GN
- ESCN 92025 1130-A4
CEDAR LN
5000 LMSA 91941 1271-B1
5000 SDCo 91941 1271-B1
7600 SDCo 91962 1237-C7
20200 SDCo 92029 1149-E1
CEDAR RD
100 VSTA 92083 1107-C1
900 VSTA 92083 1087-C7
2000 OCN 92056 1087-C7
CEDAR ST
- SMCS 92078 1129-C2
100 ELCJ 92021 1251-G4
100 SD 92101 1289-A2
300 SD 92114 1290-D4
400 SDCo 92065 1152-D4
500 SMCS 92069 1108-J6
500 SMCS 92078 1128-C1
500 SD 92101 1288-J2
1800 SD 92154 1329-J6
1800 SD 92154 1330-A7
2800 SD 92102 1289-E2
3700 SD 92105 1289-G2
N CEDAR ST
100 ESCN 92025 1130-A1
900 ESCN 92026 1110-A7
900 ESCN 92026 1130-A1
S CEDAR ST
100 ESCN 92025 1130-A2
CEDAR WY
900 ESCN 92026 1110-A7
CEDARBEND WY
800 CHV 91910 1310-H7
CEDARBRAE LN
3600 SD 92106 1287-J4
CEDAR BRIDGE WY
3500 CRLB 92010 1107-A3

CEDAR BROOK
1000 ESCN 92025 1130-A1
CEDAR CREEK RD
- SDCo 92036 1174-H4
- SDCo 92036 1175-A5
CEDARCREST WY
11000 SD 92121 1208-G3
CEDAR GLEN WY
3600 SD 92154 1350-E1
CEDAR GROVE CT
2500 CHV 91915 1311-J6
CEDAR HILL CT
9500 SD 92129 1189-E4
CEDARHURST LN
11700 SD 92128 1190-A1
CEDARIDGE DR
200 SD 92114 1290-H4
CEDAR LAKE AV
7800 SD 92119 1250-G6
CEDAR RIDGE CT
14500 PWY 92064 1190-H3
CEDAR RIDGE PL
4600 OCN 92056 1087-D3
CEDAR RIDGE RD
9700 SDCo 92021 1233-C2
CEDARSPRING DR
1900 CHV 91913 1311-D4
CEDAR SPRINGS DR
10000 SNTE 92071 1231-D3
CEDAR SUMMIT DR
1100 SDCo 92065 1152-D4
CEDAR TRAILS LN
9200 SDCo 92082 1069-B6
CEDAR TRAILS RD
29500 SDCo 92082 1069-B6
CEDAR TREE WY
12600 PWY 92064 1170-D3
CEDARVALE LN
- SNTE 92071 1230-G5
CEDAR VALE WY
3700 SDCo 92028 1048-D3
CEDARWOOD CIR
2900 SDCo 91902 1290-H7
CEDARWOOD DR
3000 SDCo 91902 1290-H7
CEDARWOOD WY
2800 CRLB 92008 1106-F3
CEDILLA PL
12900 SD 92128 1150-D7
12900 SD 92128 1170-D1
CEDRAL PL
6800 LMGR 91945 1270-E7
CEDRO AV
- IMP 92251 6499-H2
N CEDROS AV
100 SOLB 92075 1167-E7
S CEDROS AV
100 SOLB 92075 1167-E7
100 SOLB 92075 1187-F2
800 DLMR 92014 1187-F2
CEDROS DESIGN DISTRICT
300 SOLB 92075 1187-F1
CELADON CT
1300 OCN 92056 1087-D2
CELATA CT
7500 SD 92129 1189-A7
CELATA LN
7300 SD 92129 1189-A7
7900 SD 92129 1188-J7
CELAYA CT
100 SOLB 92075 1167-D7
CELESTE DR
3800 OCN 92056 1107-B1
CELESTE WY
6200 SD 92111 1248-G7
CELESTIAL CT
12600 PWY 92064 1190-C4
CELESTIAL RD
13500 PWY 92064 1190-C4
CELESTIAL WY
- SD 92154 1350-G1
CELESTIAL WATERS DR
- SDCo 91977 1291-D2
CELESTINE AV
8600 SD 92123 1249-C6
CELIA VISTA DR
6300 SD 92115 1270-D5
CELINDA DR
3200 CRLB 92008 1106-H4
CELITA CT
9800 SNTE 92071 1231-A4
CELOME CT
7100 SD 92129 1188-J7
CELOME LN
12000 SD 92129 1188-J7
CELOME WY
7100 SD 92129 1188-J7
CELTIC CT
- SD 92129 1189-B2
24800 SDCo 92065 1173-G3
CENTAURUS WY
8800 SD 92126 1209-D2
CENTELLA ST
7800 CRLB 92009 1147-J2
CENTENNIAL DR
800 VSTA 92081 1107-F2
CENTENNIAL WY
1800 ESCN 92026 1110-A5
1800 ESCN 92026 1109-J5
CENTER AV
1000 OCN 92054 1086-B7
CENTER DR
700 SMCS 92069 1129-D1
8200 LMSA 91942 1270-J1
8800 LMSA 91942 1250-J7
8800 LMSA 91942 1251-A7
CENTER PL
2300 ELCJ 92020 1251-B5
CENTER ST
- CHV 91910 1310-A6
100 SD 92173 1350-G4
8100 LMSA 91942 1270-H2
CENTER WY
1700 SD 92110 1268-F2
CENTER OF THE WORLD DR
- ImCo - 432-A5
CENTERSTAGE GN
- ESCN 92025 1130-B4
CENTINELA AV
700 ELCN 92243 6559-H1
CENTINELLA DR
10200 SDCo 91941 1271-E4
CENTRAL AV
- SD 92102 1289-G4
- SDCo 91950 1310-C3
2100 SDCo 91977 1291-A1
2100 SDCo 91977 1271-A6
3000 SD 92105 1269-G4
4300 SD 92116 1269-G4
5000 CHV 91902 1310-J2
5000 SDCo 91902 1310-J2
5300 SDCo 91902 1311-A1

STREET
Block City ZIP Pg-Grid

CENTRAL AV
6700 LMGR 91945 1270-E6
24200 SDCo 91916 1235-J3
24300 SDCo 91916 1236-A3
CENTRAL CT
8700 SDCo 91977 1271-A7
8700 SDCo 91977 1291-A1
CENTRAL PZ
- SD 92123 1249-C2
CENTRAL WY
2400 SDCo 91977 1271-A7
CENTRAL CIRCLE LN
- SD 92123 1249-C1
CENTRALOMA DR
3700 SD 92107 1268-B7
CENTRAL WAYSIDE CT
2400 SDCo 91977 1271-A7
CENTRE LN
3900 SD 92103 1269-C5
CENTRE ST
3700 SD 92103 1269-C5
CENTRE CITY PKWY
- ESCN 92025 1129-G1
1800 ESCN 92026 1129-G1
2100 ESCN 92026 1109-F4
25700 SDCo 92026 1109-F4
N CENTRE CITY PKWY
1800 ESCN 92026 1109-E1
1800 SDCo 92026 1109-E1
25500 SDCo 92026 1089-D7
S CENTRE CITY PKWY
1800 ESCN 92025 1129-J4
2300 ESCN 92025 1130-A5
2600 ESCN 92025 1150-A1
2700 SDCo 92025 1150-A1
2900 ESCN 92029 1150-A2
2900 SDCo 92029 1150-A2
CENTURION PL
900 ESCN 92026 1129-F1
CENTURION ST
2000 SD 92154 1351-G3
CENTURY ST
6800 LMSA 91941 1270-E3
6800 SD 92115 1270-E3
CENTURY WY
1800 ESCN 92026 1110-A5
1900 ESCN 92026 1109-J4
CENTURY PARK CT
8300 SD 92123 1249-C2
CEPIN DR
28400 SDCo 92082 1089-J2
28400 SDCo 92082 1090-A2
CERAMIC LN
700 SDCo 92028 1027-F1
CERCA BLANCA PL
1600 SDCo 92019 1252-B5
CERCA DEL ARROYO
8200 SDCo 92067 1149-A4
CERCO ROSADO
100 SMCS 92069 1109-C7
CEREUS CT
1700 CRLB 92011 1127-E6
CEREUS ST
200 ENCT 92024 1147-B5
CEREZA ST
4700 SD 92102 1289-J4
CEREZO DR
100 CRLB 92008 1126-G2
CERRADA DEL COYOTE
32100 SDCo 92086 409-K8
CERRISSA CT
2000 SD 92154 1330-A7
CERRISSA ST
700 SD 92154 1330-A7
CERRITOS CT
1300 CHV 91910 1311-B6
CERRO AV
3600 OCN 92056 1107-C3
CERRO ST
100 ENCT 92024 1147-G7
300 ENCT 92024 1167-G1
1500 SDCo 92021 1251-G2
CERRO BONITA DR
700 SMCS 92069 1129-E1
CERRO DEL SOL
- SDCo 92067 1149-B6
CERRO DEL SUR
- SD 92127 1169-A5
CERRO DE ORO
2100 SDCo 92084 1088-C3
2100 VSTA 92084 1088-C3
CERRO DE PAUMA
31600 SDCo 92082 1050-J7
31600 SDCo 92082 1051-A7
CERRO DE PAZ
11500 SDCo 92040 1211-G5
CERRO GORDO AV
700 SD 92102 1289-D3
CERRO LARGO DR
1000 SOLB 92075 1167-H6
CERRO LINDO
800 VSTA 92084 1088-B5
CERRO PEDREGOSO
19900 SDCo 92029 1148-F3
CERRO SERENO
2100 ELCJ 92019 1252-E4
2100 SDCo 92019 1252-E4
CERROS REDONDOS
3100 SDCo 92067 1148-B7
CERRO VERDE DR
1000 SOLB 92075 1167-H6
CERRO VISTA WY
24200 SDCo 92065 1173-E2
CERULEAN WY
- OCN 92057 1067-A3
CERVANTES AV
5000 SD 92113 1290-A6
5100 SD 92114 1290-B5
CERVEZA CT
28400 SDCo 92026 1089-F2
CERVEZA DR
10300 SDCo 92026 1089-E2
CERVEZA BAJA
10200 SDCo 92026 1089-E3
CESAR E CHAVEZ PKWY
400 SD 92113 1289-C5
CESPED DR
11400 SD 92124 1250-A3
CESSNA LN
4200 SDCo 92004 1100-B4
CESSNA ST
4200 SD 92117 1248-E6
CETUS RD
8600 SD 92126 1209-C1
CEZANNE LN
5200 SDCo 91902 1290-G6
CHABAD WY
17000 PWY 92064 1170-D3
CHABAD CENTER DR
- SD 92131 1209-J5
CHABLIS CT
900 ESCN 92029 1129-E4
CHABLIS LN
800 VSTA 92083 1087-D6
CHABLIS RD
18200 SDCo 92065 1171-H3
CHABOLA RD
9400 SD 92129 1189-E7
CHACO CT
13400 SD 92129 1189-C4
CHAD CT
400 VSTA 92083 1087-G4
CHAD RD
15100 SDCo 92021 1233-A2
CHADWELL AV
2500 SD 92154 1330-B7
CHADWICK AV
6000 SD 92139 1310-D2
CHAFFEE ST
2700 SDCo 91950 1310-C2
CHAFFIN PL
9000 SDCo 91977 1291-B4
CHAFFINCH CT
- SD 92131 1209-G2
CHAILLY DR
- CHV 91913 1311-F7
CHAISSON DR
- SDCo 92672 1023-D2
CHALAR ST
2700 SD 92123 1249-C6
CHALCEDONY ST
700 SD 92109 1247-H5
1500 SD 92109 1248-B4
CHALET DR
4900 OCN 92057 1087-C1
CHALET PL
8000 SD 92126 1209-B4
CHALICE DR
8800 SDCo 92026 1089-A1
CHALK CT
4800 OCN 92057 1087-B2
CHALLENGE BLVD
10200 SDCo 91941 1271-E4
CHALLENGER CIR
- SDCo 91978 1291-F2
CHALLENGER CT
- SDCo 91978 1291-E2
CHALLIS PL
- CHV 91913 1311-F1
CHALMERS ST
1500 SD 92103 1268-H6
1900 SD 92101 1268-H6
CHALON LN
11900 SD 92128 1190-A3
CHALUPNIK RD
- ImCo 92227 411-D11
- ImCo 92233 411-C11
1100 ImCo 92227 431-C1
CHAMBERLAIN AV
100 ELCJ 92020 1251-F6
CHAMBERLAIN PL
800 ESCN 92025 1150-C1
CHAMBERLAIN ST
600 ELCJ 92020 1251-E6
CHAMBERS AV
1800 ESCN 92029 1129-F5
CHAMBERS ST
100 ELCJ 92020 1251-F4
1900 ESCN 92029 1129-F5
CHAMBERY PL
- CHV 91913 1311-F1
CHAMBORD CT
1200 OCN 92054 1106-D3
CHAMBORD WY
- SD 92130 1188-E5
CHAMISAL CT
- CRLB 92011 1127-D6
CHAMISAL PL
9500 SD 92121 1208-E4
CHAMISE CT
800 SMCS 92069 1108-H6
CHAMISE WY
2700 SDCo 91935 1293-B4
CHAMOUNE AV
2900 SD 92105 1269-J5
4200 SD 92115 1269-J4
CHAMPA ST
100 VSTA 92083 1087-G3
CHAMPAGNE BLVD
26900 SDCo 92026 1089-A1
28700 SDCo 92026 1069-A7
28800 SDCo 92026 1068-J6
CHAMPAGNE VILLAGE DR
- SDCo 92026 1089-B2
CHAMPION ST
1900 SD 92105 1290-B1
CHAMPIONSHIP RD
- OCN 92057 1067-B3
CHAMPIONS VALLEY CT
- SD 92130 1187-J7
CHAMPLAIN ST
2700 OCN 92056 1087-D1
CHAMPLAIN WY
4400 SD 92117 1228-E7
CHANCELLOR WY
13900 PWY 92064 1190-G4
CHANCE MOUNTAIN PL
1400 CHV 91913 1331-A2
CHANCERY CT
4500 CRLB 92010 1106-J5
4500 CRLB 92010 1107-A5
CHANDELLE LN
1500 SDCo 92028 997-H7
CHANDLER DR
5500 SD 92117 1248-J2
CHANDON CT
12700 SD 92130 1188-D6
CHANEY ST
1300 ELCJ 92020 1251-D4
CHANNEL LN
300 OCN 92054 1106-C3
CHANNEL RD
100 CRLB 92011 1126-H6
9700 SDCo 92040 1232-A3
CHANNEL WY
3300 SD 92110 1268-D4
CHANNING ST
5200 SD 92117 1248-H1
CHANTECLER AV
6500 SD 92114 1290-E5
CHANTEL CT
500 CHV 91910 1310-F5
CHANTILLY AV
8600 SD 92123 1249-C6
CHANTILLY CT
10900 SNTE 92071 1231-F6
CHANUTE ST
3500 SD 92154 1330-E6
CHAPALA CT
100 SOLB 92075 1167-D7
CHAPALA WY
100 SOLB 92075 1167-D7
CHAPALA CANYON CT
- SD 92129 1188-H4
CHAPALITA DR
100 ENCT 92024 1147-G7
300 ENCT 92024 1167-G1
CHAPARAJOS CT
5400 SD 92120 1250-B4
CHAPARRAL VALLEY CT
- SD 92131 1210-C3
CHAPARRAL DR
- ELCN 92243 6559-G2
- SNTE 92071 1231-D2
1500 CHV 91902 1311-B3
1500 SMCS 92069 1109-D7
1800 VSTA 92081 1108-A4
11400 SDCo 92040 1211-G7
11400 SDCo 92040 1231-G1
CHAPARRAL HTS
3200 SDCo 91935 1273-C7
CHAPARRAL LN
700 ESCN 92025 1130-C5
700 SDCo 92025 1130-C5
CHAPARRAL TER
- SD 92130 1188-G3
CHAPARRAL WY
13700 SDCo 92082 1090-E2
1400 OCN 92057 1067-F6
4900 SD 92115 1270-B2
16600 PWY 92064 1171-D6
CHAPARRAL HILLS RD
700 SDCo 91901 1253-G2
CHAPARRAL RIDGE RD
4600 SD 92130 1188-C5
CHAPARRAL SLOPE RD
3100 SDCo 91935 1293-B1
CHAPARRO WY
10800 SD 92121 1208-F3
CHAPARRO HILLS PL
12700 SD 92130 1188-D6
CHAPEL LN
3300 SDCo 92065 1172-B3
CHAPEL RD
3100 SD 92101 1289-C1
CHAPEL HILL DR
- CHV 91914 1311-H3
CHAPIN DR
900 SDCo 92036 1136-D7
CHAPMAN ST
3900 SD 92110 1268-C5
CHAPO CT
3000 SDCo 91977 1271-D6
CHAPULIN LN
1800 SDCo 92028 1028-A4
CHARAE ST
6000 SD 92122 1228-E5
CHARBONO PT
10800 SD 92131 1210-B2
CHARBONO ST
12100 SD 92131 1210-B3
CHARBONO TER
10700 SD 92131 1210-B3
CHARDON LN
2000 SDCo 92019 1272-C2
CHARDONNAY CT
- SMCS 92069 1108-J6
CHARDONNAY PL
10900 SD 92131 1210-B2
CHARDONNAY ST
12100 SD 92131 1210-B2
CHARDONNAY TER
2000 CHV 91913 1311-D3
CHARDONNEY WY
800 ESCN 92029 1129-D3
CHARGER BLVD
4200 SD 92117 1248-J2
CHARING PL
4300 SD 92117 1248-H2
CHARING ST
5900 SD 92117 1248-H2
CHARING CROSS RD
10800 SDCo 91978 1271-G6
CHARIOT CT
1300 SDCo 92003 1068-A4
1300 SDCo 92084 1068-A4
CHARISE CT
200 SDCo 91977 1290-J5
CHARISE ST
- ESCN 92025 1130-A6
CHARITY WY
15000 ESCN 92027 1130-J5
CHARLAN RD
13000 SDCo 92082 1090-D4
CHARLEEN CIR
2000 CRLB 92008 1106-G5
CHARLENE AV
6600 SD 92114 1270-E7
6600 SD 92114 1290-D1
CHARLES AV
2100 SD 92154 1330-A6
2200 CHV 91911 1330-A6
CHARLES DR
500 OCN 92057 1067-A6
CHARLES LN
1300 SDCo 92065 1172-G2
CHARLES ST
3400 SD 92106 1288-A3
3500 SD 92106 1287-J3
3900 LMSA 91941 1270-F5
CHARLES WY
2200 ELCJ 92020 1251-B5
CHARLES DEWITT WY
2100 SDCo 91901 1253-J1
CHARLES SWISHER CT
- SDCo 92028 1027-J2
CHARLESTON LN
1700 ENCT 92024 1147-H7
CHARLESTON PL
- CHV 91914 1311-H2
CHARLESTON BAY CT
10200 SDCo 92040 1231-J2
CHARLIE HORSE WY
1600 OCN 92057 1067-E7
CHARLOTTA WY
1300 ESCN 92026 1110-A5
CHARLOTTE DR
500 SMCS 92069 1108-H6
CHARLYN LN
1000 SDCo 92028 1027-H6
CHARMAINE WY
- SD 92131 1189-G7
- SD 92131 1209-G1
CHARMANT DR
7300 SD 92122 1228-B3
CHARMARIE CIR
7100 LMSA 91941 1270-F3
CHARRO CT
1500 CHV 91902 1311-B3
CHARRO ST
1600 ENCT 92024 1147-G7
CHARTER AV
5600 SD 92120 1250-B6
CHARTER OAK DR
3400 CRLB 92008 1106-G4
CHART HOUSE ST
9000 SD 92126 1209-D3
CHARTRES PL
- CHV 91913 1311-F1
CHARWOOD CT
3000 SDCo 91978 1271-G7
CHASE AV
1100 SDCo 92020 1251-H7
1100 SDCo 92020 1271-H1
1700 SDCo 92020 1272-A2
1900 SDCo 92019 1272-B2
E CHASE AV
100 ELCJ 92020 1251-G7
700 SDCo 92020 1251-G7
W CHASE AV
100 ELCJ 92020 1251-E7
CHASE CT
3200 OCN 92056 1107-B1
CHASE LN
1400 SDCo 92020 1271-J1
CHASE TER
1400 SDCo 92020 1271-J1
CHASE WY
- SD 92130 1188-G3
CHASE CREEK LN
- SDCo 92040 1231-H2
CHASEWOOD DR
3400 SD 92111 1248-J4
CHASIN ST
4100 OCN 92056 1087-C7
4200 VSTA 92083 1087-C7
CHATEAU CT
2000 CHV 91913 1311-E5
4600 SD 92117 1248-G1
CHATEAU DR
3800 SDCo 92036 1156-E2
4500 SD 92117 1248-F1
CHATEAU PL
600 ESCN 92025 1129-D3
4800 SD 92117 1248-G2
CHATEAU WY
3100 LMGR 91945 1270-E6
CHATEAU HAUT-BRION
- SDCo 92003 1068-B3
CHATEAU LAFITE
- SDCo 92003 1068-B3
CHATEAU MONTELENA
- SDCo 92003 1068-B3
CHATEAU ST JEAN
- SDCo 92003 1068-A3
CHATHAM RD
3500 CRLB 92010 1107-A4
CHATHAM ST
2200 ELCJ 92020 1251-A5
2200 SD 92119 1251-A5
CHATSBURY ST
1600 ELCJ 92021 1252-B2
CHATSWOOD DR
2200 LMGR 91945 1270-H7
CHATSWORTH BLVD
1500 SD 92107 1288-A1
1500 SD 92106 1288-A1
1800 SD 92106 1268-C7
1800 SD 92107 1268-C7
CHATSWORTH WY
2800 CRLB 92010 1107-A4
CHATTANOOGA ST
5500 SD 92139 1310-C2
CHAUCER AV
4900 SD 92120 1250-A6
CHAUMONT DR
5800 SD 92114 1290-C1
CHAUMONT PL
1900 SD 92114 1290-C1
CHAUNCEY DR
2600 SD 92123 1249-C5
CHAUNCEY RD
2200 SD 92106 1268-D7
3500 OCN 92056 1107-E3
CHAVACAN LN
10100 SDCo 91977 1271-E7
CHAVEZ RD
2900 SD 92154 1350-D3
CHAZ PL
8100 LMSA 91942 1250-H7
CHEAMES WY
6500 SD 92117 1248-J2
CHELAN CT
13400 SD 92129 1189-C3
CHELAUREN
17000 SDCo 92065 1171-E2
CHELFORD ST
4300 SD 92117 1248-J2
CHELLY CT
13400 SD 92129 1189-C4
CHELSEA AV
5500 SD 92037 1247-F3
CHELSEA CT
1000 VSTA 92084 1088-A7
1000 VSTA 92084 1108-A1
CHELSEA DR
4500 CRLB 92010 1107-A5
CHELSEA LN
800 ENCT 92024 1148-A5
CHELSEA PL
300 SD 92037 1247-F4
CHELSEA ST
5100 SD 92037 1247-G4
CHELSEA PARK CIR
3200 SDCo 91978 1271-G6
CHELTERHAM TER
5000 SD 92130 1188-D4
CHEMISAL LN
2200 SDCo 92021 1252-J4
CHEMISE CREEK RD
14700 SDCo 92065 1173-G7
14700 SDCo 92065 (1193-G1 See Page 1192)
CHENAULT ST
2300 SD 92123 1249-C7
CHENIN WY
200 SMCS 92069 1108-J6
CHERBOURG DR
1800 CHV 91913 1311-E7
CHERI LN
17500 PWY 92064 1150-G7
CHERI ST
1700 SD 92154 1329-J6
1700 SD 92154 1330-A6
CHERIMOYA DR
2200 SDCo 92084 1108-C4
2500 SMCS 92069 1108-C4
CHERIMOYA GN
3200 ESCN 92025 1150-C1
CHERIMOYA ST
3100 SDCo 91935 1272-H7
CHERISH WY
- SDCo 92065 1174-B4
CHERISSE LN
- SDCo 92021 1232-E5
CHEROKEE AV
3300 SD 92104 1269-G4
3300 SD 92105 1269-G4
4400 SD 92116 1269-G3
CHEROKEE LN
2000 ESCN 92026 1109-F5
4200 SDCo 92004 1100-B4
CHEROKEE ST
1500 SMCS 92078 1108-D7
CHERRY AV
- ImCo 92243 6560-A7
100 CRLB 92008 1106-E7
400 IMPB 91932 1329-F6
CHERRY CT
800 ESCN 92026 1109-D5
800 SMCS 92069 1109-D5
CHERRY LN
2900 SDCo 91977 1271-A6
CHERRY PL
1600 ESCN 92027 1130-C1
CHERRY RD
- SDCo 92055 1086-A4
8800 SDCo 92040 1231-H6
CHERRY BLOSSOM LN
- SDCo 92127 1169-G1
CHERRY BLOSSOM ST
3600 NATC 91950 1290-C6
CHERRYBROOK CT
3500 SDCo 92028 1048-E2
CHERRY HILL DR
- SD 92130 1208-D1
CHERRY HILLS LN
400 CHV 91902 1311-B3
CHERRY HILLS RD
8700 SNTE 92071 1230-J5
8800 SNTE 92071 1231-A5
CHERRYPOINT CT
3100 SDCo 92028 1048-E1
CHERRY POINT DR
600 CHV 91911 1330-J5
CHERRYSTONE ST
3700 OCN 92054 1086-G2
CHERRY TREE CT
1300 ENCT 92024 1147-F7
CHERRY TREE LN
- ESCN 92029 1129-E5
CHERRYWOOD DR
5000 OCN 92056 1087-C2
CHERRYWOOD ST
1900 VSTA 92081 1107-G5
12600 PWY 92064 1190-C1
CHERRYWOOD WY
800 ELCJ 92021 1251-G4
CHERUB CT
8500 SNTE 92071 1230-J7
CHERVIL CT
800 CHV 91910 1330-J1
CHERYL LN
1000 SMCS 92069 1109-B6
2000 VSTA 92083 1087-C7
CHERYL PL
200 CHV 91911 1330-F2
CHERYL CREEK DR
- SDCo 92021 1232-E5
CHERYL LEE CT
14000 SDCo 92040 1232-F5
CHERYL RIDGE CT
11600 SD 92126 1208-J1
CHESAPEAKE CT
- SMCS 92069 1108-H6
2700 CHV 91914 1311-J4
5700 SD 92123 1229-D7
CHESAPEAKE DR
9100 SD 92123 1229-D7
9400 SD 92123 1249-E1
CHESAPEAKE PL
800 CHV 91914 1311-J3
CHESHIRE AV
3600 CRLB 92010 1107-A3
CHESHIRE ST
4600 SD 92117 1248-G2
CHESHIRE WY
1700 ESCN 92026 1109-D5
CHESTER ST
500 SD 92114 1290-E3
CHESTER WY
700 ELCJ 92020 1251-E7
CHESTERFIELD CIR
- SMCS 92069 1108-J5
CHESTERFIELD DR
- ENCT 92007 1167-D3
CHESTERWOOD PL
- SD 92130 1208-B2
CHESTNUT AV
300 CRLB 92008 1106-F5
400 SMCS 92069 1108-J6
2400 CRLB 92010 1106-J4
CHESTNUT CT
900 CHV 91910 1310-J7
CHESTNUT DR
900 ESCN 92025 1130-A3
CHESTNUT LN
300 ESCN 92025 1130-A4
1400 VSTA 92084 1088-A7
CHESTNUT ST
500 ESCN 92025 1130-A3
9400 SDCo 91977 1291-C2
9700 SDCo 92040 1232-B3
CHESTNUT WY
200 OCN 92057 1086-J6
CHESTNUT HILL LN
14000 SD 92128 1190-B2
CHESTNUT ROAN DR
400 SDCo 91901 1233-F6
CHESTNUT ROAN WY
8800 SDCo 91901 1233-E6
CHETENHAM CT
18300 SD 92128 1150-B6
CHETENHAM LN
12500 SD 92128 1150-B6
CHEVALIER DR
1800 CHV 91913 1331-E1
CHEVIOT CT
10300 SD 92126 1208-J5
CHEVY LN
10400 SDCo 91941 1271-E1
S CHEVY CHASE
- SD 92127 1169-B4
CHEVY CHASE DR
8500 LMSA 91941 1270-J2
8500 LMSA 91941 1271-A2
CHEYENNE AV
3200 SD 92117 1248-E5
CHEYENNE CIR
1900 OCN 92056 1087-C5
CHEYENNE LN
200 ESCN 92026 1109-G5
CHEYENNE TR
- PWY 92064 1150-G6
CHEYENNE WY
1700 SDCo 92004 1058-G6
CHEYNE RD
- SDCo 92026 1109-F3
CHI ST
8400 LMSA 91942 1250-J7
CHIANTI CV
- SD 92123 1249-D1
CHICA RD
2500 SDCo 92028 998-J3
CHICADEE ST
1500 SD 92114 1290-D2
CHICAGO DR
- LMSA 91941 1270-G5
CHICAGO ST
1800 SD 92110 1268-E1
2200 SD 92110 1248-E7
2800 SD 92117 1248-E5
CHICARITA CREEK RD
13900 SD 92128 1189-J2
CHICK RD
400 ImCo 92243 6560-C2
CHICKADEE WY
4400 OCN 92057 1087-A3
CHICKASAW CT
4600 SD 92117 1248-F1
CHICO LN
- OCN 92054 1086-G3
CHICO ST
1700 SD 92109 1248-A6
CHICORY LN
200 SDCo 92021 1253-A1
CHIEFTAIN CT
18000 SD 92127 1149-J7
CHIHUAHUA VALLEY RD
- SDCo 92004 409-K6
27500 SDCo 92086 409-J6
CHILDRENS WY
3000 SD 92123 1249-B5
CHILDS AV
6100 SD 92139 1310-E2
CHILTREN CT
- OCN 92057 1067-A3
CHIMNEY FLATS LN
1100 CHV 91915 1311-H5
CHIMNEY ROCK DR
600 OCN 92054 1086-D3
CHIMNEY ROCK LN
9300 SDCo 92021 1232-H5
CHINA ST
- SD 92140 1268-F6
CHINABERRY LN
200 SMCS 92069 1108-G7
CHINON CIR
10600 SD 92126 1208-J4
CHINOOK CT
4500 SD 92117 1248-F1
CHINQUAPIN AV
200 CRLB 92008 1106-F7
CHIPMUNK LN
8300 SDCo 91962 1237-C5
CHIPPENHAM WY
11600 SD 92128 1190-A2
CHIPPEWA CT
3800 SD 92117 1248-E4
CHIPWOOD CT
3000 SDCo 91978 1271-G7
CHIQUITO RD
- SDCo 91916 1235-G1
CHIRIQUI LN
6400 CRLB 92009 1127-H5
CHISHOLM TR
1300 SMCS 92069 1109-C6
CHISOLM TR
300 IMP 92251 6439-F4
CHISWICK CT
1600 ELCJ 92020 1251-C5
CHLOE AV
8400 LMSA 91942 1250-J7
CHOC CLIFF DR
5100 SDCo 91902 1310-J3
5100 SDCo 91902 1311-A3
CHOCOLATE BELL TR
1600 SDCo 91901 1234-A7
CHOCOLATE CREEK RD
9700 SDCo 92021 1233-F3
CHOCOLATE SUMMIT DR
9600 SDCo 92021 1233-E3
CHOCTAW DR
4700 SD 92115 1270-D3
CHOCTAW RIDGE RD
12300 SDCo 92082 1090-B1
CHOISSER LN
13600 SDCo 92040 1232-D3
CHOLLA PL
1000 CHV 91910 1310-H7
1000 CHV 91910 1330-H1
CHOLLA RD
700 CHV 91910 1310-H7
700 CHV 91910 1330-H1
CHOLLAS PKWY
4600 SD 92105 1289-J1
4600 SD 92102 1289-J1
5000 SD 92105 1270-A6
5400 SD 92115 1270-B6
CHOLLAS PL
3200 SD 92105 1270-A6
CHOLLAS RD
2800 SD 92105 1270-A7
CHOLLAS STATION RD
5400 SD 92105 1270-B6
5500 SD 92115 1270-B6
CHOPIN WY
- ENCT 92007 1167-D2
- OCN 92054 1106-F2
CHORLITO ST
6300 CRLB 92009 1127-H4
CHOUFA CT
- SDCo 92082 1050-J7
- SDCo 92082 1051-A7
- SDCo 92082 1071-A1
CHOUKAIR DR
- SDCo 91935 1273-F4
CHOURREE ST
- CORD 92135 1288-G3
CHOYA CANYON RD
2100 ESCN 92025 1130-C6
CHRETIEN CT
18100 SD 92128 1150-A7
CHRIS LN
9000 SDCo 91931 1236-H3
CHRIS DEE DR
14200 SDCo 92082 1050-G6
CHRISMARK AV
6000 SD 92120 1250-C6
CHRISSY WY
13000 SDCo 92040 1232-C3
CHRISTA CT
5800 LMSA 91942 1251-B7
CHRISTATA WY
9000 SDCo 92040 1232-C6
CHRISTEN WY
100 SMCS 92069 1108-H6
CHRISTI DR
1800 VSTA 92084 1087-H3
CHRISTI WY
1000 SDCo 92028 1027-J4
CHRISTIANA ST
9000 SDCo 91977 1291-B3
CHRISTIANSEN WY
100 CRLB 92008 1106-D5
CHRISTIANSON CT
- SDCo 92055 1086-A3
CHRISTINA CT
- OCN 92054 1086-G1
CHRISTINA LN
9300 SDCo 92040 1231-H5
CHRISTINA WY
1400 SDCo 92065 1172-G2
CHRISTINE PL
- ENCT 92024 1147-B3
CHRISTINE ST
3600 SD 92117 1248-D1
CHRISTMAS CIR
Rt#-S22
600 SDCo 92004 (1078-H2 See Page 1058)
CHRISTMAS TREE LN
9600 SDCo 92040 1232-C4
CHRISTOPHER LN
16300 SDCo 91935 1293-J3
CHRISTOPHER ST
2600 SD 92109 1248-C4
CHRISTY LN
1900 DLMR 92014 1187-F3
CHRISTY WY
3100 SDCo 91977 1271-A6
CHROMA DR
4700 OCN 92057 1087-B3
CHUBB LN
10400 SNTE 92071 1231-E5
CHUCK WAGON RD
15400 SDCo 92065 1172-J5
15400 SDCo 92065 1173-A5
CHU LAI AV
- SD 92140 1268-F7
CHULA VISTA ST
200 CHV 91910 1310-B5
600 CHV 91910 1309-J5
CHUMASH TR
900 SDCo 92084 1067-J6
CHUPAROSA LN
1800 SDCo 92004 (1099-F4 See Page 1098)
CHUPAROSA WY
1300 CRLB 92008 1106-E4
CHURCH AV
200 CHV 91910 1310-B5
700 CHV 91910 1330-C1
CHURCH PL
100 SDCo 92028 1027-F2
CHURCH RD
- SDCo 91906 (1299-E3 See Page 1298)
N CHURCH SQ
14100 SD 92128 1190-B1
CHURCH ST
2200 SD 92136 1289-E6
7500 LMGR 91945 1270-G6
CHURCH WY
400 ELCJ 92020 1251-B5
CHURCHILL DR
8200 SDCo 92021 1251-G1
CHURCHILL LN
- SMCS 92078 1128-J3
CHURCHILL PL
1200 CORD 92118 1288-H7
1200 CORD 92118 1308-H1
CHURCHILL DOWNS
15400 SDCo 92067 1168-E7
CHURCHILL DOWNS RD
5800 OCN 92057 1067-G7
CHURCHWARD ST
5100 SD 92114 1290-B4
CHURRITUCK DR
700 SD 92154 1330-E7
CIARDI CT
- CRLB 92008 1107-A7
CIBOLA CT
8000 SD 92120 1250-D4
CIBOLA RD
6200 SD 92120 1250-D4
CICADA CT
7900 SD 92129 1189-B6
CICERO CT
13200 PWY 92064 1190-F4
CICERO WY
13800 PWY 92064 1190-F4
CICHLID WY
8100 SD 92129 1189-B6
CIELITA LINDA DR
900 VSTA 92083 1087-E5
CIELO AV
4200 OCN 92056 1107-C3
CIELO CT
17900 PWY 92064 1150-E7
CIELO DR
6500 SD 92114 1290-D4
CIELO PL
3000 CRLB 92009 1147-H1
CIELO VISTA
9800 SDCo 92026 1089-D2
CIENEGA DR
3600 SDCo 91902 1310-E3
CIERA CT
- PWY 92064 1150-G7
CIGNO CT
- CRLB 92011 1127-B7
CIJON ST
12600 SD 92129 1189-F5
CILANTRO GN
2400 ESCN 92029 1149-G1
CIMA CT
2000 CRLB 92009 1147-F2
CIMA DR
1000 SMCS 92078 1128-E3
CIMA DEL REY
1200 CHV 91910 1311-A5
CIMARRON TER
900 SDCo 92029 1129-J7
2500 SDCo 92029 1149-J1
CIMARRON WY
- SD 92154 1350-H2
CIMARRON CANYON DR
- SDCo 92127 1169-E4
CIMARRON CREST DR
- SDCo 92127 1169-E3
CIMARRON CREST WY
- SDCo 92127 1169-E4
CIMBRIA WY
- SDCo 92040 1232-A5
CIMMARON LN
7800 LMSA 91941 1270-G3
CINCHONA ST
1200 VSTA 92083 1087-E7
CINCHRING DR
14900 PWY 92064 1190-J4
CINCO ARROYOS
- SDCo 92028 998-A4
CINDERELLA PL
8100 LMGR 91945 1270-H7
CINDERELLA WY
2500 LMGR 91945 1270-H7
CINDY AV
4900 CRLB 92008 1107-A6
CINDY LN
400 VSTA 92083 1087-G5
CINDY ST
1800 SD 92154 1330-A6
4200 SD 92117 1248-E2

STREET
Block City ZIP Pg-Grid

CINDY JO LN
- SDCo 92026 1109-J3
CINDY LYNN LN
8000 SDCo 92021 1252-C1
CINNABAR DR
7800 LMSA 91941 1270-H4
CINNAMON CT
800 CHV 91910 1330-J1
CINNAMON DR
20400 SDCo 91935 (1295-A6 See Page 1294)
20500 SDCo 91935 1294-J7
CINNAMON WY
3800 OCN 92057 1086-H5
CINNAMON ROCK RD
17900 SDCo 92065 1153-G5
CINNAMON TEAL ST
- CRLB 92011 1127-B6
CINTA CT
4800 SD 92122 1228-F6
CINTHIA ST
7900 LMSA 91941 1270-H4
CIPRIANO LN
2300 CRLB 92008 1106-E4
CIRCA DE CERRO
- SDCo 92082 1070-G2
CIRCA DEL CIELO
- SDCo 92028 1047-G7
CIRCA DE LINDO
3800 SDCo 92091 1168-B7
CIRCA DEL LAGO
1500 SDCo 92078 1128-C3
CIRCA DEL NORTE
16300 SDCo 92067 1168-F5
CIRCA DE LOMA
- SDCo 92028 1047-G7
CIRCA DEL SUR
6600 SDCo 92067 1168-F6
CIRCA DE MEDIA
7100 SDCo 92029 1148-G2
CIRCA DE TIERRA
3100 ENCT 92024 1148-B6
CIRCA ORIENTE
17100 SDCo 92067 1168-G5
CIRCA VALLE VERDE
9800 SDCo 92021 1232-H2
CIRCLE DR
- SD 92109 1248-C6
200 OCN 92054 1085-H6
600 SOLB 92075 1167-E6
1000 ESCN 92025 1130-B3
1400 ELCJ 92020 1251-D7
2500 SDCo 92029 1149-H2
3600 SDCo 92036 1156-E2
4800 SD 92116 1269-G3
7600 LMGR 91945 1270-G7
7600 LMGR 91945 1290-G1
CIRCLE DR S
- SD 92109 1248-C6
CIRCLE HILL RD
9400 SDCo 92021 1232-J4
CIRCLE J DR
300 SDCo 92004 (1078-J1 See Page 1058)
700 SDCo 92004 (1079-A1 See Page 1058)
CIRCLE P LN
10100 SDCo 92026 1089-E5
CIRCLE PARK LN
1900 ENCT 92024 1147-H5
CIRCLE R CT
29600 SDCo 92026 1069-A5
CIRCLE R DR
8600 SDCo 92026 1068-J5
8600 SDCo 92026 1069-B4
9100 SDCo 92082 1069-B4
CIRCLE R LN
30000 SDCo 92082 1069-D4
CIRCLE R WY
29800 SDCo 92026 1069-A5
CIRCLE RANCH WY
- OCN 92057 1067-E7
CIRCLE R COURSE LN
8500 SDCo 92026 1068-J5
8500 SDCo 92026 1069-A5
CIRCLE R CREEK LN
29800 SDCo 92026 1068-J6
CIRCLE R GREENS DR
29500 SDCo 92026 1068-J6
29500 SDCo 92026 1069-A6
CIRCLE R OAKS LN
9000 SDCo 92026 1069-A6
CIRCLE R VALLEY LN
8700 SDCo 92026 1068-J6
8700 SDCo 92026 1069-A5
CIRCLE R VIEW LN
8900 SDCo 92026 1069-A6
CIRCLE VIEW DR
5600 SDCo 92003 1068-B1
CIRCO DEL CIELO DR
1700 ELCJ 92020 1271-F2
CIRCO DIEGUENO
9900 SDCo 92067 1168-F7
CIRCO DIEGUENO CT
6500 SDCo 92067 1188-F1
CIRCO DIEGUENO RD
6300 SDCo 92067 1168-F7
10000 SDCo 92067 1188-F1
CIRCULO ADORNO
3400 CRLB 92009 1147-J3
3400 CRLB 92009 1148-A3
CIRCULO BRINDISI
- CHV 91915 1311-G7
CIRCULO CORONADO
2100 CHV 91914 1311-E2
CIRCULO DARDO
12800 SD 92128 1150-D7
CIRCULO MARGEN
9100 SDCo 91977 1291-B5
CIRCULO PAPAYO
- CRLB 92009 1128-A7
- CRLB 92009 1148-A1
CIRCULO SANTIAGO
2300 CRLB 92008 1106-G3
CIRCULO SEQUOIA
- CRLB 92009 1148-B1
CIRCULO VERDE
1000 CHV 91910 1311-A7
CIRQUE CT
1600 ENCT 92024 1147-G5
CIRRO VISTA WY
3900 SDCo 92028 1047-J4
CIRRUS ST
5900 SD 92110 1268-G3
6000 SD 92111 1268-G3
CIRUELA CT
1500 CHV 91911 1330-E4
CITA AV
2700 SDCo 92029 1149-J1
CITADEL CIR
5900 SD 92037 1247-H2
CITADEL CT
1800 CHV 91913 1311-D5

CITRACADO CIR
6000 CRLB 92009 1127-H2
CITRACADO DR
34400 SDCo 92061 1030-J7
34400 SDCo 92061 1050-J1
34500 SDCo 92061 1051-A1
CITRACADO LN
- ESCN 92026 1129-G1
CITRACADO PKWY
300 ESCN 92025 1130-A7
500 ESCN 92025 1129-J7
800 ESCN 92029 1129-D4
1300 SDCo 92029 1129-D4
N CITRACADO PKWY
300 ESCN 92029 1129-D2
CITRADORA DR
4000 SDCo 91977 1271-B4
CITRINE DR
- CRLB 92009 1127-G5
- ESCN 92027 1110-F4
CITRINE WY
- SMCS 92078 1128-F6
CITRON PL
- ESCN 92027 1130-E1
CITRONELLA ST
2400 LMGR 91945 1270-G7
CITRUS AV
100 IMPB 91932 1329-E7
400 ESCN 92027 1110-C6
400 ESCN 92027 1130-E1
1100 SDCo 92027 1130-D3
2200 SD 92154 1330-B7
N CITRUS AV
100 ESCN 92027 1110-D6
100 VSTA 92084 1087-H4
S CITRUS AV
100 VSTA 92084 1087-H6
CITRUS DR
4000 SDCo 92028 1028-F6
CITRUS PL
800 CRLB 92008 1106-F6
CITRUS RDG
1400 SDCo 92027 1130-D4
CITRUS ST
3100 LMGR 91945 1270-F6
3600 LMSA 91941 1270-F5
CITRUS WY
500 OCN 92054 1086-F3
1500 CHV 91911 1330-E5
CITRUS CREST DR
- SDCo 92082 1070-J3
CITRUS GLEN CT
1800 SDCo 92027 1130-E3
CITRUS GLEN DR
1700 SDCo 92027 1130-E3
CITRUS HILLS LN
1600 SDCo 92027 1130-D3
CITRUS PARK LN
1400 SDCo 92027 1130-D3
CITRUS TREE LN
2100 SDCo 91977 1271-E7
CITRUS VIEW CT
9200 SD 92126 1209-D2
CITTA WY
- SD 92108 1249-D7
CITY VIEW LN
- SDCo 92026 1109-G4
CIUDAD LEON CT
5800 SD 92120 1250-E7
CIVIC CENTER DR
- SNTE 92071 1231-D6
- NATC 91950 1309-G2
- SMCS 92069 1108-J7
100 OCN 92054 1085-J7
100 OCN 92054 1086-A7
13200 PWY 92064 1190-E4
C K CLARKE ST
200 CALX 92231 6680-G1
CLAIBORNE SQ
9600 SD 92037 1227-J1
CLAIM JUMPER LN
1300 CHV 91913 1311-E6
CLAIMJUMPER WY
4100 SDCo 91977 1271-D4
CLAIRE AV
400 CHV 91910 1310-D6
CLAIRE DR
4700 OCN 92057 1066-J6
4700 OCN 92057 1067-A6
12600 PWY 92064 1190-G5
CLAIRE ST
600 SD 92154 1330-A7
CLAIREMONT CT
2800 SD 92117 1248-F7
CLAIREMONT DR
2300 SD 92109 1248-E5
2300 SD 92110 1248-E5
2500 SD 92117 1248-E2
CLAIREMONT MESA BLVD
3200 SD 92117 1248-F1
4800 SD 92111 1248-F1
4800 SD 92111 1249-A1
8500 SD 92123 1249-D1
9700 SD 92123 1229-F7
9800 SD 92124 1229-F7
10000 SD 92124 1249-G1
10900 SD 92124 1250-A1
CLAIRMONT AV
100 NATC 91950 1290-B6
N CLAIRMONT AV
- NATC 91950 1290-B6
200 SD 92114 1290-B6
CLAIRTON PL
2100 SD 92154 1350-A2
CLAMAGORO CIR
10200 SD 92124 1249-G5
CLAMATH ST
600 SDCo 91977 1291-C3
CLAMBAKE DR
- SDCo 92127 1168-J1
CLANTON PL
- SD 92154 1350-G2
CLARA LEE AV
6300 SD 92120 1249-J6
CLAREMORE AV
6500 SD 92120 1250-D5
CLAREMORE LN
6300 SD 92120 1250-D5
CLARENCE DR
1200 SDCo 92084 1108-B1
1200 VSTA 92084 1108-B1
CLARENCE LN
100 ESCN 92029 1150-A1
100 SDCo 92029 1150-A1
300 SDCo 92029 1149-J1
CLARENDON ST
1200 ELCJ 92021 1251-J3
CLARET CT
11900 SD 92131 1210-B4
CLARIDGE CT
10600 SD 92131 1209-H2
CLARISS ST
400 CHV 91911 1330-C3

CLARISSA CT
3000 LMGR 91945 1270-F6
CLARK AV
700 ENCT 92024 1147-C5
CLARK CT
1400 VSTA 92081 1107-J5
CLARK LN
- ImCo 92259 430-H7
CLARK RD
- ELCN 92243 6559-H4
- ImCo 92231 431-B7
- ImCo 92251 431-B4
- IMP 92243 6499-G1
- IMP 92251 431-B4
300 IMP 92251 6439-G4
300 ImCo 92251 6439-G2
700 IMP 92251 6499-G1
1100 ImCo 92243 6559-H4
1400 ELCN 92243 6499-G1
2300 ImCo 92251 6499-G1
2300 ImCo 92243 6499-G1
CLARK ST
100 ESCN 92025 1129-J2
300 SOLB 92075 1167-E7
1800 SD 92110 1268-G6
3000 SD 92103 1268-G6
CLARKE DR
1200 ELCJ 92021 1252-A3
CLARKVIEW LN
14200 SD 92130 1188-H3
14200 SDCo 92067 1188-H3
CLASICO CT
- SDCo 92127 1169-F3
CLASSIQUE WY
14100 SD 92129 1189-D2
CLATSOP LN
8500 SD 92129 1189-B3
CLAUDAN RD
2000 ESCN 92029 1129-E6
2000 SDCo 92029 1129-E6
CLAUDE LN
- CHV 91913 1311-F7
- CHV 91913 1331-F1
CLAUDIA AV
10300 SNTE 92071 1231-E5
CLAUDIA LN
10300 SNTE 92071 1231-B1
CLAUDIA WY
100 OCN 92057 1086-H3
CLAUSER ST
10100 SD 92126 1208-J5
CLAVELITA PL
1500 SD 92154 1350-E2
CLAVELITA ST
3200 SD 92154 1350-D1
CLAY AV
2700 SD 92113 1289-E4
5800 LMSA 91942 1250-J7
CLAYBURN CT
- SDCo 91901 1233-G7
CLAYDELLE AV
100 ELCJ 92020 1251-G5
CLAYFORD ST
4300 SD 92117 1248-J2
CLAYMONT CT
12900 SD 92130 1188-B5
CLAYMORE CT
- SD 92129 1189-B2
CLAYTON CT
500 ELCJ 92021 1252-A4
CLAYTON DR
9400 SD 92126 1209-D6
CLAYTON PL
2700 SDCo 92069 1089-A6
CLAYTON PARKINSON CT
- SDCo 92028 1027-J2
CLEARBROOK DR
1900 CHV 91913 1311-D4
CLEARBROOK LN
1000 VSTA 92084 1087-J5
1000 VSTA 92084 1088-A5
10000 SDCo 91977 1271-E7
CLEARCREEK PL
200 SNTE 92071 1231-C5
CLEAR CREST CIR
600 VSTA 92084 1087-H4
CLEARCREST LN
1100 SDCo 92028 1027-H7
CLEARFIELD AV
2500 SDCo 91977 1271-E7
CLEARLAKE WY
9100 SDCo 92040 1232-C5
CLEAR SKY RD
7500 SD 92120 1250-C5
CLEAR SKY TER
6700 SD 92120 1250-D4
CLEAR SPRING RD
11300 SD 92126 1209-C2
CLEAR VALLEY RD
1900 ENCT 92024 1147-H5
CLEARVIEW DR
4200 CRLB 92008 1106-H6
CLEAR VIEW GN
2100 ESCN 92026 1109-B3
CLEARVIEW LN
18700 SDCo 92082 1091-F3
CLEARVIEW RD
14900 PWY 92064 1171-B7
14900 PWY 92064 1191-B1
CLEARVIEW WY
- SMCS 92078 1128-D6
4800 LMSA 91941 1270-H2
CLEARWATER CT
8300 SDCo 91977 1290-J5
CLEAR WATER PL
1600 ENCT 92024 1147-G6
CLEARWATER PL
2000 CHV 91913 1311-E3
CLEARWATER RD
8800 SDCo 92028 998-J7
8800 SDCo 92028 999-A7
8800 SDCo 92028 1028-J1
8800 SDCo 92028 1029-A1
CLEARWATER RDG
1500 VSTA 92081 1107-H6
CLEARWATER ST
- CRLB 92011 1126-J5
CLEARWATER WY
- SD 92154 1350-D5
- SD 92173 1350-D5
CLEARWOOD CT
11700 SD 92131 1210-A2
CLEARY ST
9900 SNTE 92071 1231-F4
CLEBURN DR
8700 LMSA 91942 1251-A6
CLEECO PL
17300 PWY 92064 1170-D2
CLEEVE WY
6400 SD 92117 1248-J2
CLEGG CT
2700 SDCo 91977 1271-A7

CLEGHORN WY
1100 SDCo 91901 1233-H7
CLEMATIS ST
2100 SD 92105 1289-J1
CLEMENS CT
- CRLB 92008 1127-B1
CLEMENS ST
- SDCo 91905 1300-B1
CLEMENTE PL
5300 SD 92117 1228-D7
CLEMENTINE ST
300 OCN 92054 1106-B1
N CLEMENTINE ST
100 OCN 92054 1086-A7
S CLEMENTINE ST
100 OCN 92054 1086-A7
100 OCN 92054 1106-B1
CLEMMENS LN
200 SDCo 92028 1027-F4
E CLEMMENS LN
100 SDCo 92028 1027-G4
CLEMSON CIR
1600 SD 92037 1247-H3
CLEO CT
1000 ESCN 92027 1110-B6
CLEO ST
6300 SD 92115 1270-D1
CLEVELAND AV
- CALX 92231 6620-J5
- ImCo 92231 6620-J5
400 ESCN 92026 1109-J3
500 SDCo 92026 1109-J3
1200 SD 92103 1269-B5
1300 NATC 91950 1309-G2
1500 SD 92116 1269-C4
N CLEVELAND ST
100 OCN 92054 1106-A1
200 OCN 92054 1086-A7
500 OCN 92054 1085-J7
S CLEVELAND ST
100 OCN 92054 1106-A1
CLEVELAND TR
1500 SDCo 92084 1108-D1
CLEVELAND FOREST DR
29400 SDCo 91906 (1297-E6 See Page 1296)
CLIFF CIR
- CRLB 92010 1107-A4
N CLIFF DR
900 OCN 92054 1085-J6
CLIFF PL
5000 SD 92116 1269-E2
CLIFF ST
2200 SD 92116 1269-C3
E CLIFF ST
100 SOLB 92075 1167-E6
W CLIFF ST
100 SOLB 92075 1167-E6
CLIFF WY
3600 OCN 92056 1107-C3
CLIFFDALE RD
1500 ELCJ 92020 1251-C4
CLIFFORD AV
1000 ImCo 92249 6560-D7
1000 ImCo 92249 6620-D1
CLIFFORD ST
4700 SD 92105 1269-J7
CLIFFORD HEIGHTS RD
8500 SNTE 92071 1251-A1
8600 SNTE 92071 1231-A7
CLIFFRIDGE AV
8300 SD 92037 1227-J3
CLIFFRIDGE CT
2800 SD 92037 1227-J4
CLIFFRIDGE LN
8300 SD 92037 1227-J4
CLIFFRIDGE WY
2800 SD 92037 1227-J4
CLIFFROSE CIR
- SDCo 92065 1153-A3
CLIFFSIDE AV
2500 SDCo 91977 1271-E7
CLIFFSIDE PL
10100 SDCo 91977 1271-E7
CLIFFTOP AV
- SMCS 92078 1128-F6
CLIFFTOP LN
2600 SDCo 91977 1271-D7
CLIFFVIEW PL
9900 SDCo 91977 1271-D7
CLIFFWOOD DR
10100 SDCo 91941 1271-E4
CLIFTON ST
500 ELCJ 92020 1251-G4
CLIMAX CT
8600 SD 92119 1250-J4
CLINE RD
4900 SDCo 91941 1271-D2
CLINTON AV
- SD 92145 1229-G3
CLINTON ST
3700 SD 92113 1289-G4
CLIPPER CT
1000 SOLB 92014 1187-H1
CLIQUOT CT
17100 PWY 92064 1170-E2
CLIVIA ST
10900 SDCo 92040 1231-F3
10900 SNTE 92071 1231-F3
CLOS DUVAL
- SDCo 92003 1068-B3
CLOUD WY
5300 SD 92117 1228-G6
CLOUDCREST DR
11200 SD 92127 1169-J4
CLOUDCROFT CT
13500 PWY 92064 1170-E2
CLOUDCROFT DR
16900 PWY 92064 1170-E3
CLOUDESLY DR
12400 SD 92128 1150-B6
CLOUDVIEW LN
500 ENCT 92024 1147-G5
CLOUD VIEW PL
5900 SD 92120 1250-C4
CLOUDWALK CANYON DR
1100 CHV 91911 1330-H1
CLOUDY MOON DR
600 SDCo 92004 (1078-H2 See Page 1058)
15900 SDCo 92065 1171-F5
CLOVE ST
1200 SD 92106 1288-B1
1300 SDCo 92021 1251-H1
2100 SD 92106 1268-C7
CLOVE WY
3700 OCN 92057 1086-H5
CLOVER CIR
9000 SD 92126 1209-D3
CLOVER CT
6700 CRLB 92011 1126-J5
CLOVER TR
37800 SDCo 91905 (1299-H3 See Page 1298)

CLOVER WY
- ELCN 92243 6559-J3
1900 ESCN 92026 1109-C5
CLOVERDALE RD
1400 ESCN 92027 1130-G4
1400 SDCo 92027 1130-G4
1900 SD 92027 1130-G5
CLOVERFIELD PT
10800 SD 92131 1210-B2
CLOVER GLEN CT
9200 SD 92126 1209-E2
CLOVERHURST WY
10800 SD 92130 1208-D1
CLOVERIDGE RD
2300 SDCo 92027 1130-F4
CLOVERLEAF CT
1900 VSTA 92081 1107-J4
CLOVERLEAF DR
1100 ELCJ 92019 1252-B7
CLOVER TREE CT
1700 CHV 91913 1311-D6
CLOVIS CT
1500 CHV 91913 1311-C7
CLOVIS ST
2500 SD 92107 1268-B5
E CLUB CIR
3100 SDCo 92004 (1079-C5 See Page 1058)
W CLUB CIR
3100 SDCo 92004 (1079-B5 See Page 1058)
CLUB DR
1500 SDCo 92028 1028-F4
CLUB LN
200 OCN 92054 1106-C2
CLUB HEIGHTS LN
1700 VSTA 92081 1107-H5
CLUBHOUSE AV
3300 SD 92154 1350-D1
CLUB HOUSE DR
- SDCo 92028 998-G5
CLUBHOUSE DR
2300 CHV 91915 1311-G6
5300 SD 92067 1188-E2
5300 SDCo 92067 1188-E2
CLUBHOUSE LN
- SD 92108 1249-D7
CLUBHOUSE RD
200 SMCS 92069 1108-D5
CLUB VIEW TER
900 CHV 91911 1330-D1
CLUB VISTA LN
31300 SDCo 92003 1068-B2
CLYDE AV
6300 SD 92139 1310-E1
CLYDESDALE CT
1700 OCN 92057 1067-F7
CLYTIE LN
2100 SDCo 91977 1291-A1
COACH DR
2400 SDCo 91978 1271-G7
COACH LN
- SD 92130 1188-E5
COACH RD
- ESCN 92025 1150-D3
COACHELLA CANAL RD
- ImCo - 411-C7
12200 ImCo 92257 411-A5
18800 ImCo 92257 410-L4
COACH HORSE CT
- SD 92130 1208-C2
COACHMAN CT
3100 OCN 92056 1106-H1
12700 PWY 92064 1170-C5
COACHWOOD
300 ELCJ 92019 1252-E5
COALINGA PL
1300 CHV 91913 1331-C1
COAST AV
- SMCS 92078 1128-A3
COAST BLVD
100 SD 92037 1227-E6
1500 DLMR 92014 1187-F4
COAST BLVD S
300 SD 92037 1227-E6
N COAST HWY
1400 SDCo 92055 1085-J6
N COAST HWY Rt#-S21
100 OCN 92054 1086-A7
100 OCN 92054 1106-B2
1200 OCN 92054 1085-J6
1400 SDCo 92055 1085-J6
S COAST HWY Rt#-S21
2000 CRLB 92008 1106-D4
2000 OCN 92054 1106-D4
N COAST HWY 101 Rt#-S21
100 ENCT 92024 1147-A2
S COAST HWY 101 Rt#-S21
300 ENCT 92024 1147-C7
800 ENCT 92024 1167-D3
900 ENCT 92007 1167-D3
COAST WK
1500 SD 92037 1227-F6
COASTAL HILLS DR
- CHV 91914 1311-J2
COASTLINE AV
4400 CRLB 92008 1106-H7
COAST OAK TR
- SDCo 91906 (1318-B7 See Page 1298)
COASTVIEW CT
3500 CRLB 92010 1107-B3
COASTWOOD RD
10700 SDCo 92127 1169-G3
COATLINE PL
- SD 92110 1268-D6
COBALT DR
- CRLB 92009 1127-E5
4200 LMSA 91941 1270-H4
COBALT WY
- OCN 92057 1067-A3
COBAN ST
5200 SD 92114 1290-A5
COBB CT
5200 SD 92117 1228-F7
COBB DR
4600 SD 92117 1228-F7
COBB LN
27600 SDCo 92082 1091-A2
COBB PL
5200 SD 92117 1228-F7
COBBLECREEK LN
- SD 92131 1210-J1
COBBLECREEK ST
- CHV 91913 1331-E1
COBBLESTONE DR
- CRLB 92011 1127-B4
800 SD 92101 1289-B2
COBBLESTONE LN
2300 VSTA 92081 1108-A5
COBBLESTONE PL
300 SNTE 92071 1231-C5

COBBLESTONE RD
1400 CRLB 92011 1127-B4
COBBLESTONE CREEK RD
12600 PWY 92064 1190-B6
COBBLESTONE CREEK TR
11900 PWY 92064 1190-B6
COBB MEADOW PL
2200 CHV 91915 1311-G5
COBRA WY
6600 SD 92121 1208-H4
COBRIDGE WY
4100 SD 92117 1248-E6
COBURN ST
2800 SDCo 91950 1310-C2
COCAPAH ST
500 VSTA 92083 1087-F5
COCHABAMBA ST
1500 SD 92154 1349-J2
COCHERA RD
12800 SDCo 92040 1232-B5
COCHISE CT
- VSTA 92084 1087-H4
COCHISE WY
4500 SD 92117 1248-D2
COCHRAN AV
400 SD 92154 1330-E6
COCHRAN ST
3600 SD 92152 1287-J4
COCHRAN TR
800 SDCo 92019 1253-C2
COCKATOO CIR
500 VSTA 92083 1087-F4
COCKATOO CT
- OCN 92057 1067-B2
COCONINO CT
3700 SD 92117 1248-E1
COCONINO WY
4600 SD 92117 1248-E1
COCONUT LN
1600 SDCo 92021 1252-A2
COCONUT WY
3500 OCN 92054 1086-F2
COCONUT GROVE CT
- SDCo 92127 1168-J2
COCO PALMS DR
300 OCN 92054 1086-F2
1100 SDCo 92020 1271-J1
COCOS DR
800 SMCS 92078 1128-J3
800 SMCS 92078 1129-A3
CODORNIZ
5400 SDCo 92067 1168-C3
CODORNIZ LN
300 SDCo 92021 1252-H4
CODORNIZ WY
- OCN 92057 1067-C7
CODY LN
700 ESCN 92025 1150-C1
CODY ST
3800 SD 92117 1248-E4
COE PL
1900 CHV 91913 1311-D5
COEUR D ALENE CT
- SDCo 92082 1090-F5
COFAIR AV
100 SOLB 92075 1187-F1
COFAIR CT
800 SOLB 92075 1187-F2
COFFEE POT TR
700 SDCo 92036 1138-B6
COHANSEY RD
11500 SD 92131 1209-H1
COHASSET CT
700 SD 92109 1267-H4
COKELEY CT
2800 ESCN 92027 1110-E7
COKER WY
1300 ELCJ 92021 1251-J3
1300 ELCJ 92021 1252-A3
COLBERT DR
100 SDCo 91977 1291-A5
COLBY LN
31800 SDCo 92061 1051-C7
COLBY RD Rt#-S24
- ImCo 92283 432-D4
COLBY POINT PL
- CHV 91914 1311-H1
COLCHESTER RD
- SD 92154 1351-E2
COLDBROOK CT
800 CHV 91913 1311-E4
COLD SPRING TR
- SDCo 92060 1052-E2
COLD SPRINGS CT
10900 SD 92128 1189-H4
COLDSTREAM DR
600 ELCJ 92020 1251-G7
700 SDCo 92020 1251-G7
COLDWATER CT
12100 SD 92128 1190-B3
COLDWELL LN
3900 SD 92154 1330-F7
COLE CT
- ESCN 92026 1109-J7
4100 SD 92117 1228-E6
COLE DR
2800 SD 92110 1268-E6
COLE RD
- SD 92152 1287-J5
- ImCo 92231 6620-B6
100 CALX 92231 431-C7
100 CALX 92231 6620-B6
100 ImCo 92231 431-C7
COLE ST
4800 SD 92117 1248-E1
4900 SD 92117 1228-E6
COLE WY
- OCN 92054 1106-D1
4100 SD 92117 1228-E7
COLE BEECH CANAL RD
- ImCo 92231 6620-F5
100 CALX 92231 6620-F5
COLEEN CT
900 ELCJ 92021 1252-A3
COLE GRADE LN
13800 SDCo 92082 1070-E4
COLE GRADE RD
28200 SDCo 92082 1090-F1
28900 SDCo 92082 1070-F3
31800 SDCo 92082 1050-F7
32600 SDCo 92061 1050-G5
33200 SDCo 92061 1051-A3
COLEMAN AV
3700 SD 92154 1330-F7
COLEMAN CIR
2900 SDCo 92036 1136-A7
COLEMAN CT
700 SD 92154 1330-F7
COLE RANCH RD
100 ENCT 92024 1147-J7
100 ENCT 92024 1167-J1
400 ENCT 92024 1148-A6

COLERIDGE CT
- CRLB 92008 1107-B7
- CRLB 92008 1127-B1
COLESHILL DR
6900 SD 92119 1250-J3
COLEUS CT
4300 SD 92154 1330-G7
COLEVILLE CT
- SD 92154 1350-C1
COLFAX CT
1100 CHV 91913 1311-C7
COLFAX DR
1600 LMGR 91945 1290-H1
COLGATE CIR
1700 SD 92037 1247-H2
COLGATE DR
2800 OCN 92056 1087-A7
COLIBRI LN
2600 CRLB 92009 1127-G5
COLIMA CT
- IMP 92251 6499-G1
300 SD 92037 1247-F4
COLIMA ST
300 SD 92037 1247-G4
COLIN CT
2200 SDCo 92027 1109-J4
2200 SDCo 92027 1110-A4
COLINA CT
3900 OCN 92054 1086-G1
COLINA DR
4900 LMSA 91941 1270-J2
COLINA TER
200 VSTA 92084 1088-A5
COLINA CREEK TR
800 SDCo 92028 1028-B1
COLINA DE LA COSTA
- CRLB 92009 1127-F7
COLINA DORADA DR
3800 SD 92124 1250-A3
COLINA ENCANTADA WY
20100 SDCo 92029 1148-H2
COLINA FUERTE
18300 SDCo 92067 1148-C6
COLINA GRANDE
- SDCo 92019 1272-C1
COLINA LINDA
1100 SOLB 92014 1187-J2
COLINAS CTE
2400 SDCo 92019 1252-E6
COLINAS MIRA
600 SDCo 92019 1252-E5
COLINAS PASEO
2400 SDCo 92019 1252-E6
COLINA VERDE LN
3000 SDCo 91935 1292-F2
COLINA VISTA
1600 SDCo 92028 1028-D5
COLLADO CTE
2600 SDCo 91901 1253-J2
COLLADO LN
1000 SMCS 92069 1109-A4
COLLEGE AV
2900 LMGR 91945 1270-E6
3000 LMGR 92115 1270-E6
3100 SD 92115 1270-C2
5100 SD 92182 1270-C2
5300 SD 92120 1270-C2
5500 SD 92120 1250-C6
COLLEGE BLVD
3600 OCN 92056 1107-B1
3700 CRLB 92010 1107-B5
3800 OCN 92056 1087-B7
4400 OCN 92057 1087-B3
4700 OCN 92057 1067-B7
5600 CRLB 92008 1107-C6
5600 CRLB 92008 1127-C1
COLLEGE PL
3200 LMGR 91945 1270-E6
5000 SD 92115 1270-C2
COLLEGE ST
100 SDCo 92028 1027-E3
700 SDCo 92055 1027-E3
E COLLEGE ST
100 SDCo 92028 1027-F3
COLLEGE WY
4500 SD 92115 1270-C4
COLLEGE GARDENS CT
4900 SD 92115 1270-A2
COLLEGE GROVE DR
5400 SD 92105 1270-B7
5900 SD 92115 1270-B7
COLLEGE GROVE WY
2500 SD 92115 1270-D6
COLLEGIO DR
11100 SD 92124 1250-A1
COLLETT WY
10100 SD 92124 1249-G3
COLLEY LN
3000 SDCo 92025 1130-E7
3000 SDCo 92025 1150-E1
COLLIER AV
2500 SD 92116 1269-D3
4900 SD 92115 1270-A3
COLLIER WY
700 SDCo 92019 1253-C2
COLLING RD E
4300 SDCo 91902 1311-A3
COLLING RD W
4200 SDCo 91902 1311-A3
COLLINGWOOD DR
1700 SD 92109 1248-A4
2700 SD 92109 1247-J4
COLLINOS WY
4700 OCN 92056 1107-E5
COLLINS AV
5400 LMSA 91942 1270-F1
COLLINS RD
1200 ImCo 92283 432-D4
COLLINS TER
600 SDCo 92026 1109-H5
COLLINS RANCH CT
- SD 92130 1188-J3
COLLINS RANCH PL
- SD 92130 1188-J3
COLLINS RANCH TER
- SD 92130 1188-J2
COLLINSWOOD LN
1100 VSTA 92081 1107-G1
COLLINWOOD DR
10900 SNTE 92071 1231-F6
COLLOMIA CT
- SDCo 91901 1254-A3
COLLURA ST
2900 SD 92105 1270-A7
COLLWOOD BLVD
4400 SD 92115 1270-A2
COLLWOOD LN
4100 SD 92115 1270-A3
COLLWOOD WY
5000 SD 92115 1270-A2
COLLYN ST
500 VSTA 92083 1087-D7
COLO CT
11800 SD 92129 1189-F7

STREET
Block City ZIP Pg-Grid

COLONEL CT
500 SDCo 92065 1152-G4
COLONIAL AV
1800 SD 92105 1289-G1
COLONIAL WY
5100 OCN 92057 1066-J4
5100 OCN 92057 1067-A4
COLONNADES PL
18000 SD 92128 1150-A7
COLONY DR
7300 LMSA 91941 1270-F2
12200 PWY 92064 1190-B1
COLONY PL
2700 ESCN 92027 1130-F1
COLONY RD
7000 LMSA 91941 1270-F3
COLONY TER
4200 ENCT 92024 1167-J1
COLONY WY
14600 PWY 92064 1190-B1
COLORADO AV
400 CHV 91910 1309-J7
600 CHV 91910 1330-A2
700 CHV 91911 1330-A3
6800 LMSA 91942 1270-E1
COLORADO DR
- CALX 92231 6620-H7
COLORADO ST
- CORD 92135 1288-G5
COLORAMA WY
9200 SDCo 92040 1232-D5
COLT LN
9800 SDCo 92040 1232-D3
COLT PL
- CRLB 92009 1127-G2
COLT TER
- SD 92130 1188-E5
COLTER LAKE CT
1700 SDCo 92019 1272-C3
COLTON AV
3100 SD 92136 1289-E6
COLTON CT
1200 CHV 91913 1331-B1
COLTRANE PL
- ESCN 92027 1130-D2
COLTRIDGE LN
1700 CHV 91902 1311-C4
1700 CHV 91913 1311-C4
COLTRIDGE PL
1800 ESCN 92029 1129-F7
COLTS WY
4100 SD 92115 1270-B5
COLUCCI DR
2000 VSTA 92084 1087-J2
COLUMBA PL
11000 SD 92126 1209-C3
COLUMBIA DR
2800 OCN 92056 1087-A7
COLUMBIA ST
600 SD 92101 1289-A2
1600 CHV 91913 1311-C5
1800 SD 92101 1288-J1
2500 SD 92103 1288-J1
2700 SD 92103 1268-H7
21800 SDCo 92070 1135-B2
COLUMBINE DR
2300 SDCo 91901 1233-J4
2500 SDCo 91901 1234-A5
7000 CRLB 92011 1127-E7
COLUMBINE RD
2500 SDCo 91901 1234-A5
COLUMBINE ST
- SDCo 92055 1086-B2
2600 SD 92105 1269-H7
COLUMBUS PL
3500 LMGR 91945 1270-H5
COLUMBUS ST
8000 SD 92126 1209-B4
10900 SNTE 92071 1231-F4
COLUMBUS WY
1100 VSTA 92081 1107-J4
COLUSA DR
4900 OCN 92056 1107-F3
COLUSA ST
800 SD 92108 1268-G3
800 SD 92110 1268-G3
1600 CHV 91913 1311-D7
COLUSA WY
200 VSTA 92083 1087-E7
COLVER AV
25800 SDCo 92026 1109-E1
COLVIN DR
8300 SNTE 92071 1251-B1
COMALETTE LN
8500 SD 92126 1209-C2
COMANCHE DR
4900 LMSA 91941 1270-G2
COMANCHE ST
1800 OCN 92056 1087-C5
COMANCHERO DR
300 SDCo 92065 1152-J5
COMBE WY
4100 SD 92122 1228-E5
COMBS
1900 ELCN 92243 6559-J1
COMET CIR
- SMCS 92069 1108-E6
COMET CT
1400 ELCJ 92019 1252-A5
COMET LN
200 ELCJ 92019 1252-A5
COMET VIEW CT
7400 SD 92120 1250-C5
COMLY CT
6600 SD 92111 1248-H6
COMLY ST
6500 SD 92111 1248-H6
COMMERCE AV
8400 SD 92121 1228-J1
COMMERCE ST
900 SMCS 92078 1128-E1
1100 OCN 92054 1106-C1
COMMERCE TR
- IMP 92251 6499-E1
COMMERCE WY
- IMP 92251 6499-E1
2500 VSTA 92081 1108-A7
COMMERCIAL AV
- ELCN 92243 6500-A6
400 ELCN 92243 6499-F6
COMMERCIAL ST
1300 SD 92101 1289-C4
1300 SD 92113 1289-C4
1900 ESCN 92029 1129-E2
8100 LMSA 91942 1270-H1
COMMODORE DR
3800 SMCS 92078 1108-D7
COMMONWEALTH AV
2100 SD 92104 1289-F1
2400 SD 92104 1269-F7
COMMUNITY DR
100 SMCS 92069 1108-D5
COMMUNITY RD
12100 PWY 92064 1190-E4
COMMUNITY BUILDING RD
1200 SDCo 91917 (1314-C7 See Page 1294)
COMMUNITY CHURCH DR
- SDCo 92061 1051-B5
COMO
9400 SDCo 92040 1232-F4
COMO ESTA CT
25100 SDCo 92065 1173-G3
COMONDU CT
700 ELCJ 92020 1251-F6
COMPADRE WY
24200 SDCo 92065 1173-E2
COMPANERO AV
2600 SDCo 92084 1108-E3
N COMPASS CIR
- CHV 91914 1311-H3
S COMPASS CIR
- CHV 91914 1311-H3
COMPASS CT
600 CRLB 92011 1127-A7
COMPASS RD
300 OCN 92054 1086-F6
COMPASS WY
- SD 92154 1330-J7
COMPASS LAKE DR
7700 SD 92119 1250-G5
COMPASS POINT DR N
9400 SD 92126 1209-E1
COMPLEX DR
8700 SD 92123 1249-C1
COMPLEX ST
5300 SD 92123 1229-D7
5300 SD 92123 1249-D1
COMPOSITION CT
4900 OCN 92057 1087-B2
COMPTON ST
300 ELCJ 92020 1251-F4
COMSTOCK AV
300 SMCS 92069 1108-J6
COMSTOCK CT
6600 SD 92111 1248-H6
COMSTOCK ST
2100 SD 92111 1268-J1
2200 SD 92111 1248-H6
COMUNA DR
13500 PWY 92064 1190-E3
CONCANNON CT
4900 SD 92130 1188-C5
CONCEPCION AV
400 SDCo 91977 1291-B4
CONCERTO GN
600 ESCN 92025 1150-C4
CONCERTO LN
- SD 92127 1168-J7
CONCHA LN
400 SMCS 92069 1108-E6
CONCHITA RD
18800 SDCo 92082 1091-F4
CONCHITA WY
- SDCo 92082 1091-F4
CONCHO CIR
4800 OCN 92057 1067-A5
CONCHO CT
18200 SDCo 92082 1091-E4
CONCHO PL
4900 OCN 92057 1067-A5
CONCHOS DR
14900 PWY 92064 1170-C7
14900 PWY 92064 1190-C1
CONCORD CT
900 VSTA 92081 1108-A4
CONCORD PL
200 SMCS 92069 1108-J4
CONCORD ST
1000 SD 92106 1288-A2
3300 CRLB 92010 1106-J3
CONCORD WY
1500 CHV 91911 1330-H4
CONCORDE HILL RD
- SDCo 92065 1171-G4
CONCORDIA LN
4000 SDCo 92028 1047-F4
CONCORD RIDGE TER
- SD 92127 1169-B3
CONCORD WOODS WY
- SD 92130 1208-F2
CONCOURS CT
2100 SDCo 92019 1272-B4
CONCOURSE CT
- SD 92123 1249-C2
CONDADO WY
400 SDCo 92025 1130-B5
CONDE PL
4400 SD 92103 1268-G4
CONDE ST
3800 SD 92110 1268-F5
4400 SD 92103 1268-G4
CONDESA DR
13700 SD 92014 1187-G6
CONDESSA CT
200 OCN 92057 1087-A1
CONDON DR
6800 SD 92122 1228-D4
CONDOR AV
1400 ELCJ 92019 1252-A4
CONDOR CT
1300 ENCT 92024 1147-D2
CONDOR GN
1300 ESCN 92029 1129-G6
CONDOR LN
500 SMCS 92078 1129-A1
CONDUIT RD
3200 SDCo 91902 1291-A7
3200 SDCo 91902 1311-A1
CONEFLOWER DR
6300 CRLB 92011 1127-A4
CONEFLOWER ST
200 ENCT 92024 1147-E6
CONEJO CT
1300 ELCJ 92021 1252-C3
CONEJO LN
10100 SNTE 92071 1231-D4
CONEJO PL
10000 SNTE 92071 1231-D4
CONEJO RD
4900 SDCo 92028 1047-E6
9700 SNTE 92071 1231-D4
CONEJOS VALLEY RD
- SDCo 91901 429-J4
- SDCo 91901 1235-A1
- SDCo 91916 429-J4
- SDCo 91916 (1194-H5 See Page 1175)
CONEJO VISTA CT
1300 ELCJ 92021 1252-C3
CONESTOGA CIR
2800 SDCo 91901 1254-C3
CONESTOGA CT
2800 SDCo 91901 1254-D3
7300 SD 92120 1250-B4
CONESTOGA DR
5300 SD 92120 1250-B4
CONESTOGA LN
400 IMP 92251 6439-F4
CONESTOGA PL
7200 SD 92120 1250-B5
CONESTOGA WY
7100 SD 92120 1250-B5
CONFERENCE WY
11700 SD 92128 1170-A7
CONGRESS ST
2200 SD 92110 1268-F5
CONGRESSIONAL DR
2300 SDCo 92019 1272-B5
CONGRESSIONAL GN
1700 ESCN 92026 1109-C3
CONIFER AV
300 SD 92154 1330-B7
CONIFER DR
200 OCN 92057 1087-A1
CONIFER GN
300 ESCN 92026 1109-G6
CONIFER RD
- SDCo 92060 1052-H2
CONKLING RD
- ImCo 92243 431-A7
CONLEY ST
12900 PWY 92064 1190-D5
CONN PL
700 ELCJ 92021 1251-H4
CONNECTICUT AV
- ELCJ 92020 1251-A1
5400 LMSA 91942 1270-E1
E CONNECTICUT AV
100 VSTA 92084 1087-H5
W CONNECTICUT AV
100 VSTA 92083 1087-G6
CONNECTICUT ST
900 IMPB 91932 1329-G7
900 IMPB 91932 1349-G2
CONNELL RD
10000 SD 92131 1210-A4
CONNELLY RD
- ImCo 92250 431-E6
CONNEMARA DR
- SDCo 92029 1149-C5
- SDCo 92067 1149-C5
CONNER CT
4100 SD 92117 1248-C3
CONNER WY
3000 SD 92117 1248-C3
CONNIE DR
6300 SD 92115 1270-C2
CONNIE LN
4200 SDCo 92004 1100-B4
CONNOLEY AV
1500 CHV 91911 1330-E4
CONNOLEY CIR
- CHV 91911 1330-E5
CONO DR
1700 ELCJ 92020 1271-G1
CONOSA WY
- CRLB 92011 1127-D6
CONQUISTADOR
4100 OCN 92056 1087-B4
CONQUISTADOR RD
3100 SDCo 92028 997-D4
CONQUISTADOR WY
12400 SD 92128 1170-B2
CONRAD AV
3400 SD 92117 1228-F7
3400 SD 92117 1248-D1
CONRAD CT
- SNTE 92071 1231-A7
- SNTE 92071 1251-A1
4800 SD 92117 1248-D1
CONRAD DR
3800 SDCo 91977 1271-C4
4100 SDCo 91941 1271-C4
CONROCK RD
9000 SD 92126 1209-E5
CONSOLIDATED WY
6700 SD 92121 1228-J2
CONSTANCE DR
4600 SD 92115 1269-J3
CONSTANCIA WY
1500 ELCJ 92019 1252-A5
CONSTANT CREEK RD
700 SDCo 92028 1027-G4
CONSTELLATION DR
11200 SDCo 92020 1271-H1
CONSTITUTION RD
5100 SD 92117 1228-F6
CONSTRUCTION CT
7100 SD 92121 1228-J1
CONTINENTAL LN
1700 ESCN 92029 1129-F7
CONTINENTAL RD
1400 SD 92154 1351-E2
CONTINENTAL ST
- SD 92154 1351-D1
CONTOUR BLVD
4500 SD 92115 1270-A3
CONTOUR CT
4800 OCN 92057 1087-B2
CONTOUR PL
3600 CRLB 92010 1107-B4
CONTRERAS CT
700 CALX 92231 6680-D1
1500 SD 92114 1290-E5
CONTUT CT
3000 SDCo 91977 1271-D6
CONURE CT
- OCN 92057 1067-C2
CONVENTION WY
300 SD 92101 1289-A4
CONVERSE AV
8600 SD 92123 1249-C7
CONVERTIBLE LN
700 SDCo 92028 1027-H1
CONVOY CT
6600 SD 92111 1228-J7
6600 SD 92117 1228-J7
7000 SD 92111 1229-A7
CONVOY ST
- SD 92145 1229-B7
3800 SD 92111 1249-B2
4900 SD 92111 1229-B7
CONVOY TER
- SD 92111 1229-A7
CONWAY DR
1000 ESCN 92027 1110-A5
1400 ESCN 92027 1109-J6
1700 ESCN 92026 1109-H2
N CONWAY DR
1600 ESCN 92027 1109-J5
1600 ESCN 92027 1110-A5
CONWAY WY
1600 ESCN 92026 1109-J5
1600 ESCN 92027 1109-J5
COOGAN WY
100 ELCJ 92020 1251-F3
COOK CT
- CHV 91910 1310-D6
COOK PL
2100 SDCo 92065 1172-E2
COOK ST
1100 SDCo 92065 1172-E2
COOKE ST
- SMCS 92078 1128-D6
COOKIE LN
800 SDCo 92028 1027-G4
COOLEY RD
- ELCN 92243 6500-C5
- ImCo 92243 6500-C5
- ImCo 92251 431-C4
- ImCo 92251 6500-C1
COOLEY ST
400 ELCN 92243 6500-C6
1900 ImCo 92243 6500-C6
COOLIDGE AV
900 NATC 91950 1309-H2
COOLIDGE ST
1500 SD 92111 1268-J2
COOL LAKE TER
10900 SD 92128 1189-H4
COOL LAKE WY
13300 SD 92128 1189-H4
COOLNGREEN LN
2000 ENCT 92024 1147-H5
COOLNGREEN WY
2000 ENCT 92024 1147-J5
COOL RIDGE HTS
1500 SDCo 92027 1130-E5
COOLSPRINGS CT
1600 CHV 91913 1311-D6
COOL VALLEY LN
15500 SDCo 92082 1071-A3
COOL VALLEY RD
13900 SDCo 92082 1070-E3
15500 SDCo 92082 1071-A3
COOL VALLEY HIGHLANDS RD
30400 SDCo 92082 1070-H4
COOL VALLEY RANCH LN
14700 SDCo 92082 1070-G2
COOL VALLEY RANCH RD
14600 SDCo 92082 1070-F3
COOLWATER DR
100 SD 92114 1290-H4
COOL WATER RANCH LN
27400 SDCo 92082 1091-A4
COOL WATER RANCH RD
27000 SDCo 92082 1091-A4
27300 SDCo 92082 1090-H4
COOP CT
100 ENCT 92024 1147-A3
COOP ST
1400 ENCT 92024 1147-A3
COOPER RD
- ImCo 92227 431-D3
700 CHV 91911 1330-J3
COOPER ST
3400 SD 92104 1269-F7
COOPERAGE CT
13200 PWY 92064 1170-E2
COOPER CANYON RD
- SD 92129 1188-J4
COOPER CIENEGA TKTR
38100 SDCo 92086 409-J5
COOS BAY CT
5700 SD 92105 1290-B1
COPA DE ORO DR
1500 SD 92037 1247-H3
COPAL PL
- CRLB 92009 1127-F6
COPE RD
15800 SDCo 92065 1173-J4
COPELAND AV
4200 SD 92105 1269-H4
4400 SD 92116 1269-H4
COPELAND PL
4200 SD 92116 1269-G4
COPING PL
12000 SDCo 92040 1231-J2
12000 SDCo 92040 1232-A1
COPLEY AV
2700 SD 92116 1269-D3
COPLEY DR
- SD 92111 1228-J7
- SD 92111 1229-A7
COPLEY PL
200 ELCJ 92020 1251-G5
COPLEY PARK PL
7400 SD 92111 1229-A7
COPPER AV
100 VSTA 92083 1087-F7
COPPER CT
- SMCS 92078 1128-C6
COPPER DR
500 VSTA 92083 1087-F7
COPPER CREST RD
3500 ENCT 92024 1148-B3
COPPER PENNY DR
- CHV 91915 1331-H1
1500 CHV 91915 1311-H7
COPPERWIND LN
- SD 92129 1188-J4
COPPERWOOD WY
100 OCN 92054 1086-E4
CORAL DR
3100 OCN 92056 1107-A1
CORAL ST
1100 ELCJ 92021 1251-J4
2400 VSTA 92081 1108-A6
CORAL WY
- CRLB 92011 1127-B4
- SMCS 92078 1128-D6
CORAL BERRY LN
- ENCT 92024 1147-A3
CORAL CREST WY
3800 SD 92173 1350-F5
CORAL GATE LN
1300 SD 92173 1350-F5
CORAL GUM CT
- SD 92139 1290-D6
CORAL LAKE AV
6300 SD 92119 1250-G5
CORAL REEF AV
- CRLB 92011 1126-J6
5400 SD 92037 1248-A3
CORAL RIDGE RD
8700 SNTE 92071 1230-G7
CORAL SEA RD
1900 SD 92139 1290-D7
CORAL SHORES CT
3700 SD 92173 1350-F5
CORAL TREE LN
3000 SDCo 92028 1048-A1
CORALWOOD CIR
4600 CRLB 92008 1106-J6
CORALWOOD CT
200 CHV 91910 1310-C5
CORALWOOD DR
100 SD 92114 1290-G5
CORA MAE PL
8500 SNTE 92071 1231-E7
CORAZON PL
17600 SD 92127 1149-J7
CORBEL CT
17500 SD 92128 1170-D1
CORBEL WY
- SMCS 92024 1128-B6
- SMCS 92078 1128-B6
CORBETT CT
12800 SD 92130 1188-C5
CORBIE CIR
1300 VSTA 92083 1087-G4
CORBIN ST
1800 SD 92154 1350-B3
CORBINA AL
- SD 92136 1289-E6
CORD LN
8900 SD 92126 1209-D4
CORD PL
1800 SDCo 92019 1272-C3
CORDELIA CT
- SD 92131 1210-G2
CORDELIA ST
1500 CHV 91913 1311-C7
1500 CHV 91913 1331-C1
CORDELL CT
1500 ELCJ 92020 1251-C1
CORDELLE LN
4200 SDCo 91910 1310-E5
CORDERO RD
2000 DLMR 92014 1187-G6
2000 SD 92014 1187-G6
CORDGRASS CT
- CRLB 92011 1127-B6
CORDIAL RD
8400 SDCo 92021 1232-F7
CORDOBA CV
2700 SD 92014 1187-J6
CORDOBA PL
2000 CRLB 92008 1106-J7
N CORDOBA ST
3900 SDCo 91977 1271-D5
S CORDOBA ST
3400 SDCo 91977 1271-D6
CORDOBA WY
1000 VSTA 92081 1107-H4
4500 OCN 92056 1107-E4
CORDOBA BAY CT
- SD 92105 1290-B1
CORDOBES CV
4200 SD 92130 1188-B7
CORDOVA CT
1000 CHV 91910 1311-A7
CORDOVA DR
900 CHV 91910 1310-J7
900 CHV 91910 1311-A7
CORDOVA ST
700 SD 92107 1287-H2
CORDREY CT
1800 SD 92105 1289-H1
CORDREY DR
2800 SDCo 92029 1129-C7
CORDREY LN
3100 SDCo 92029 1129-C7
COREY CT
9500 SNTE 92071 1231-C5
CORFMAN RD
1000 ImCo 92249 431-B7
CORIANDER CT
800 CHV 91910 1330-J1
CORINE WY
2200 SDCo 91901 1253-G2
CORINIA CT
700 ENCT 92024 1147-J6
CORINNA CT
2400 SD 92105 1290-A1
CORINTH ST
4200 SD 92115 1270-C4
CORINTHIA WY
4900 OCN 92056 1107-F5
CORINTIA ST
3100 CRLB 92009 1128-A5
6500 CRLB 92009 1127-H5
CORK PL
4800 SD 92117 1228-G7
CORK TREE LN
1200 ESCN 92029 1129-E5
CORKWOOD AV
10000 SNTE 92071 1231-D2
CORLEY CT
11400 SD 92126 1209-B1
CORLISS ST
4800 SD 92105 1269-J7
4800 SD 92105 1270-A7
CORLITA CT
4900 SD 92122 1228-G5
CORMORANT AV
- CRLB 92011 1127-D6
CORMORANT DR
- CRLB 92011 1127-D6
CORNELIUS PL
2700 LMGR 91945 1270-F7
CORNELL AV
800 CHV 91913 1311-D5
7100 LMSA 91941 1270-F3
CORNELL DR
3800 OCN 92056 1087-A7
CORNER PL
500 SDCo 92021 1252-J4
CORNER CREEK LN
- SDCo 92028 1028-A3
CORNERSTONE CT
- ELCJ 92021 1252-C1
6000 SD 92121 1208-F6
CORNET PL
1300 SD 92154 1350-D1
CORNFLOWER TR
- SD 92130 1188-F4
CORNISH DR
400 SD 92106 1287-H3
500 ENCT 92024 1147-C7
500 SD 92107 1287-J2
900 ENCT 92024 1167-C1
1300 OCN 92054 1086-F7
1300 ENCT 92007 1167-C1
CORNWALL GN
- ESCN 92027 1110-D7
CORNWALL ST
1300 SDCo 91977 1290-J2
2500 OCN 92054 1106-E1
CORNWALLIS SQ
12200 SD 92128 1190-B1
CORNWELL CT
900 SMCS 92069 1109-C5
COROLYN DR
3900 LMSA 91941 1270-H5
CORONA CT
600 VSTA 92081 1107-H1
2400 SD 92037 1248-A3
CORONA DR
700 OCN 92057 1087-C1
CORONA ST
2500 LMGR 91945 1270-G7
3700 LMSA 91941 1270-G5
CORONA WY
- ENCT 92024 1147-D7
- ENCT 92024 1167-D1
13000 PWY 92064 1190-E5
CORONA BOREALIS
- SD 92154 1350-G1
CORONADO AV
600 CORD 92118 1288-G6
1000 SDCo 91977 1291-C2
1400 SD 91932 1349-J1
1400 SD 92154 1349-J1
1700 SD 92154 1350-A1
3700 SD 92107 1288-A1
4200 SD 92107 1268-A7
4400 SD 92107 1267-H7
CORONADO CIR
600 VSTA 92084 1087-J4
CORONADO CT
700 SD 92109 1267-H3
CORONADO DR
4500 OCN 92057 1066-H6
CORONADO PL
2500 VSTA 92081 1107-J5
CORONADO ST
10500 SNTE 92071 1231-F6
CORONADO VW
1800 SDCo 91901 1253-J2
1800 SDCo 91901 1254-A2
CORONADO WY
- SMCS 92078 1129-C1
CORONADO BAY RD
5000 CORD 92118 1309-E7
5000 CORD 92118 1329-D1
CORONADO CAYS BLVD
5000 CORD 92118 1329-D1
CORONADO HILLS DR
400 SMCS 92078 1129-A3
CORONADO TERRACE DR
16300 SDCo 91901 1253-G4
CORONADO VIEW RD
6000 SDCo 91901 1253-H4
CORONA ORIENTE RD
3500 SD 92109 1268-B1
3600 SD 92109 1248-B7
CORONA VISTA
1300 CHV 91902 1311-A4
1900 SDCo 92019 1272-C3
CORPORAL DR
3200 SD 92124 1249-H4
CORPORAL WY
10400 SD 92124 1249-H4
CORPORATE CT
3500 SD 92123 1249-D4
CORPORATE CTR
- OCN 92056 1087-A6
CORPORATE DR
400 ESCN 92029 1129-C2
CORPORATE VW
3200 VSTA 92081 1128-A1
CORPORATE CENTER DR
- SD 92154 1351-B1
CORRAL CT
300 CHV 91902 1310-G4
CORRAL GN
1100 ESCN 92026 1129-F1
CORRAL WY
5800 SD 92037 1247-G3
CORRAL CANYON RD
700 CHV 91902 1311-B3
700 CHV 91913 1311-B3
3600 SDCo 91902 1311-A2
CORRALES LN
1100 CHV 91910 1310-J5
1100 CHV 91910 1311-A5
CORRALES ST
- CALX 92231 6620-G6
CORRAL VIEW AV
- CHV 91913 1311-D7
CORREA LN
900 SDCo 91977 1291-D3
CORRE CAMINO
1900 SDCo 92084 1088-C1
CORRE CAMINO WY
1800 SDCo 92084 1088-B1
CORRELL RD
- ImCo 92243 6560-A7
- ImCo 92249 6560-B6
CORRIDOR ST
9900 SD 92131 1209-J5
CORRIGAN ST
14200 SD 92129 1189-G2
CORSAIR PL
9800 SD 92126 1209-F2
CORSICA ST
1500 SD 92111 1268-H2
CORSICA WY
3300 OCN 92056 1106-J1
6400 SD 92111 1268-H2
CORSO DI ITALIA
- CHV 91910 1310-A4
CORTA ST
100 OCN 92054 1086-G1
CORTA DEL SUR
1500 LMGR 91945 1290-F2
CORTA MADRE WY
24100 SDCo 92065 1173-E2
CORTE ACEBO
- CRLB 92009 1147-F3
CORTE ACIANO
- CRLB 92009 1148-A1
CORTE ACUARIO
- SD 92130 1208-B4
CORTE ADALINA
- CRLB 92009 1128-A5
CORTE ALACANTE
5000 OCN 92057 1066-J5
CORTE ALEJANDRO
- SDCo 91901 1254-E3
CORTE AL FRESCO
4300 SD 92130 1188-B6
CORTE ALISO
- CRLB 92009 1127-J5
CORTE ALMERIA
1300 OCN 92057 1066-J5
CORTE ALVEO
1300 OCN 92057 1066-J4
1300 OCN 92057 1067-A4
CORTE AMALIA
- SD 92173 1350-E3
CORTE AMARILLO
1800 OCN 92056 1087-C4
CORTE AMOR
- SDCo 91901 1234-A6
CORTE ANACAPA
- CHV 91914 1311-E1
- SDCo 91914 1311-E1
CORTE ANANAS
- CRLB 92009 1147-F2
CORTE ANDANTE
1600 OCN 92056 1087-C4
CORTE ARAUCO
12800 SD 92128 1150-D7
CORTE ARBOLES
1000 CRLB 92009 1147-F4
CORTE ASOLEADO
- SDCo 91901 1254-A3
CORTE AVISPON
1300 SMCS 92069 1108-E4
CORTE AZUL
4500 OCN 92056 1087-B4
CORTE BAGALSO
- SMCS 92069 1108-E4
CORTE BAHAMA
- CHV 91902 1311-C2
CORTE BALDRE
3000 CRLB 92009 1147-H3
CORTE BARQUERO
17700 SD 92128 1150-C7
CORTE BAUTISTA
- CHV 91914 1311-E2
CORTE BELLAGIO
800 SDCo 92026 1129-F1
CORTE BELLA VISTA
- SD 92129 1189-A4
CORTE BELLEZA
- SD 92130 1208-C3
CORTE BELLO
1200 SMCS 92069 1108-E6
CORTE BOCINA
1300 OCN 92057 1066-J5
CORTE BOSQUE
- CRLB 92009 1127-J6
CORTE BRAVO
1400 SMCS 92069 1108-E4
CORTE BREZO
- CRLB 92009 1148-A1
CORTE BRISA
- CRLB 92009 1148-B1
CORTE CADIZ
- CRLB 92009 1147-J4
1100 OCN 92057 1087-A3
CORTE CAFETAL
2800 SD 92173 1350-D2
CORTE CALANDRIA
10900 SD 92127 1169-H5
CORTE CALYPSO
300 CHV 91914 1311-E2
CORTE CANGREJO
- SD 92130 1208-B3
CORTE CAPRIANA
1500 SDCo 92026 1129-E1
CORTE CARDO
7900 CRLB 92009 1148-A2
CORTE CAROLINA
7900 CRLB 92009 1147-H3
CORTE CASITAS
2500 CRLB 92009 1127-G6
CORTE CASTILLO
- CHV 91914 1311-E2
- CRLB 92009 1148-A4
CORTE CELESTE
2900 CRLB 92009 1147-H4
CORTE CENTINELLA
4100 SDCo 91941 1271-E4
CORTE CERRADA
600 CHV 91910 1310-G7
CORTE CICUTA
- CRLB 92009 1147-F2
CORTE CIDRO
- CRLB 92009 1147-F3
CORTE CIELO
1200 SMCS 92069 1108-E5
CORTE CIERNA
12700 SD 92128 1150-D7
CORTE CISCO
6500 CRLB 92009 1127-J5
CORTE CLARITA
3400 CRLB 92009 1147-J4
CORTE CLASICA
1400 SMCS 92069 1108-E4
CORTE CODORNIZ
10900 SD 92127 1169-H5
CORTE CONDESA
- CHV 91914 1311-E2
CORTE CRESTA
1700 OCN 92056 1087-C4
CORTE CRISALIDA
10700 SD 92127 1169-G5
CORTE CRISTAL
- SMCS 92069 1108-F4
CORTE CURVA
3400 CRLB 92009 1147-J4
CORTE DANIEL
1500 OCN 92056 1087-B4
CORTE DE ACEITUNOS
18100 SD 92128 1150-D7
CORTE DE CANDILEJAS
13100 SD 92128 1150-D7
CORTE DE CASARES
18200 SD 92128 1150-D7
CORTE DE CERA
1100 CHV 91910 1311-A6
CORTE DE CHUCENA
13300 SD 92128 1150-D7
CORTE DE COMARES
13300 SD 92128 1150-D7
CORTE DE ESTEPONA
13300 SD 92128 1150-D7
CORTE DEL ABETO
6200 CRLB 92011 1127-D4
CORTE DE LA DONNA
- SNTE 92071 1251-C1
CORTE DE LA FONDA
4300 SD 92130 1188-B6
CORTE DE LA PINA
2200 CRLB 92011 1127-E3
CORTE DE LA SIENA
4100 SD 92130 1188-B6
CORTE DE LAS PIEDRAS
1300 SDCo 92019 1252-F7
1300 SDCo 92019 1272-G1
CORTE DE LA VISTA
2800 CRLB 92009 1127-H7
CORTE DEL CEDRO
6100 CRLB 92011 1127-E3
CORTE DEL CRUCE
- CRLB 92009 1147-J4
CORTE DELFINIO
- CRLB 92009 1148-A2
CORTE DEL NOGAL
2000 CRLB 92011 1127-D3
CORTE DEL SOL
8000 SNTE 92071 1251-A1
CORTE DE LUZ
- SD 92127 1169-B7
CORTE DE MARIN
- SD 92130 1208-B4
CORTE DE MIJA
1500 OCN 92056 1087-B4
CORTE DE POWELL
1500 SDCo 92065 1153-B5
CORTE DE SAUSALITO
- SD 92130 1208-B4
CORTE DESEO
1400 SMCS 92069 1108-E4
CORTE DE TIBURON
- SD 92130 1208-B4

STREET — Block City ZIP Pg-Grid

CORTE DE VELA
1200 CHV 91910 1311-A6
CORTE DE VERDAD
14400 SD 92129 1189-D1
CORTE DIANA
6600 CRLB 92009 1127-H5
CORTE DIEGO
- CRLB 92009 1128-A5
CORTE DOMINGO
- CRLB 92009 1148-A3
CORTE DORADO ESPUELA
- SDCo 91901 1254-B3
CORTE DOROTEA
12800 PWY 92064 1170-D4
CORTE DULCE
- CRLB 92009 1148-A4
1200 SMCS 92069 1108-E5
4500 OCN 92056 1087-B4
CORTE EDUARDO
- CRLB 92009 1128-A4
CORTE EMPARRADO
17800 SD 92128 1150-C7
CORTE ENCANTO
1200 SMCS 92069 1108-E5
CORTE ENTRADA
100 CHV 91910 1310-E7
100 CHV 91910 1330-E1
CORTE ERIZO
17700 SD 92128 1150-C7
CORTE ESPERANZA
3500 CRLB 92009 1148-A4
CORTE ESPLENDOR
3300 CRLB 92009 1147-J3
CORTE FACIL
4200 SD 92130 1188-B6
CORTE FAMOSA
1200 SMCS 92069 1108-E5
4200 SD 92130 1188-B6
CORTE FAVOR
4200 SD 92130 1188-B5
CORTE FELIPE
7900 CRLB 92009 1147-H3
CORTE FLABA
- SDCo 92091 1148-F5
CORTE FLORES
- CHV 91914 1311-F3
CORTE FRAGATA
8400 SD 92129 1189-B4
CORTE FRESA
- CRLB 92009 1148-A1
CORTE FRESCO
- CHV 91914 1311-F2
- SDCo 92091 1148-F5
CORTE FUERTE
- CHV 91914 1311-F3
CORTE GACELA
9400 SDCo 91977 1291-B4
CORTE GALANTE
600 SMCS 92069 1108-E5
CORTE GANSO
13800 SD 92129 1189-C3
CORTE GANZO
9300 SDCo 91977 1291-B4
CORTE GOLETA
300 CHV 91914 1311-E2
CORTE GOYA
1400 OCN 92056 1087-B3
CORTE GUERA
11600 SD 92128 1170-A5
CORTE HELENA AV
100 CHV 91910 1310-C5
CORTE HORTENSIA
- CRLB 92009 1148-B2
CORTE HUASCO
17800 SD 92128 1150-D7
CORTE ISABELINO
- SD 92130 1208-B3
CORTE ISLA
- CHV 91914 1311-F2
CORTE JARDIN
2900 CRLB 92009 1147-H3
CORTE JARDIN DEL MAR
4400 SD 92130 1208-C4
CORTE JUANA
12900 PWY 92064 1170-D3
CORTE LA BELLA
- ENCT 92024 1148-B3
CORTE LADERA
1100 SMCS 92069 1108-F5
1600 ESCN 92025 1130-B4
CORTE LAGARTO
15800 SD 92127 1169-H5
CORTE LA LUZ
- CRLB 92009 1127-J4
CORTE LA MANTUA
1400 SDCo 92026 1129-F2
CORTE LAMPARA
14400 SD 92129 1189-D1
CORTE LANGOSTA
- CRLB 92009 1127-J6
CORTE LANGOSTINO
4200 SD 92130 1208-B4
CORTE LA PAZ
6500 CRLB 92009 1127-J5
CORTE LARGO
6000 SDCo 92067 1168-D3
CORTE LAS LENAS
- SD 92129 1189-B6
CORTE LAS TONADAS
3400 SD 92173 1350-E3
CORTE LIMON
- CRLB 92009 1147-F3
CORTE LIRA ST
1300 SMCS 92069 1108-E4
CORTE LOMA
2700 SDCo 91901 1254-E3
6600 CRLB 92009 1127-J5
CORTE LOMAS VERDES
17500 PWY 92064 1170-E1
CORTE LOREN
600 SMCS 92069 1108-E5
CORTE LORO
3400 SD 92173 1350-E3
CORTE LUISA
3600 CRLB 92009 1148-B4
CORTE LUPE
- CRLB 92009 1128-A4
CORTE LUSSO
6900 SDCo 92091 1148-G5
CORTE LUZ DEL SOL
10900 SD 92130 1208-C3
CORTE MACIDO
- CRLB 92009 1147-J2
CORTE MADEIRA
2000 SDCo 91901 1254-B2
CORTE MADERA RD
5700 SDCo 91962 429-L6
7300 SDCo 91962 1237-B7
CORTE MADURO
- CHV 91914 1311-F3
CORTE MAGNA
1300 OCN 92057 1066-J5

CORTE MANGO
- CRLB 92009 1147-F3
CORTE MANOLITO
700 SMCS 92069 1108-F4
CORTE MANZANA
- CRLB 92009 1148-A1
CORTE MAR ASOMBROSA
- SD 92130 1208-C4
CORTE MAR DE BRISA
- SD 92130 1208-B3
CORTE MAR DE CRISTAL
- SD 92130 1208-B3
CORTE MAR DE DELFINAS
- SD 92130 1208-B3
CORTE MAR DE HIERBA
- SD 92130 1208-B3
CORTE MAR DEL CORAZON
- SD 92130 1208-C2
CORTE MARIA
- SDCo 91901 1254-A3
6600 CRLB 92009 1127-J5
CORTE MARIA AV
- CHV 91910 1310-C4
900 CHV 91911 1330-E2
CORTE MARIN
- CRLB 92009 1147-J2
CORTE MARIPOSA
4700 SDCo 91902 1310-G1
CORTE MAZATLAN
3200 CRLB 92009 1147-J4
CORTE MEJILLONES
10900 SD 92130 1208-B3
CORTE MERANO
800 SDCo 92026 1129-F1
CORTE MISTICO
- CHV 91914 1311-F2
CORTE MONTANOSO
15500 SD 92127 1169-H6
CORTE MONTECITO
3000 CRLB 92009 1127-J4
CORTE MORA
- CRLB 92009 1128-A5
CORTE MORAL
- CRLB 92009 1147-F3
CORTE MOREA
14400 SD 92129 1189-D1
CORTE MORERA
2800 CRLB 92009 1147-H2
CORTE MORITA
11600 SD 92128 1170-A5
CORTE NACION
300 CHV 91910 1310-F7
CORTE NAPOLI
- CHV 91914 1311-F2
CORTE NINA
12100 SD 92128 1190-B2
CORTE ORCHIDIA
- CRLB 92009 1127-H7
CORTE PACIFICA
- CRLB 92011 1127-C5
CORTE PAGUERA
- CRLB 92009 1127-J6
1300 OCN 92057 1066-J4
1300 OCN 92057 1067-A4
CORTE PALOMA
- CRLB 92009 1127-J6
CORTE PAPAYA
2800 CRLB 92009 1147-G3
CORTE PASTEL
4500 OCN 92056 1087-B4
CORTE PATIO
- CHV 91914 1311-F3
CORTE PATO
9300 SDCo 91977 1291-B4
CORTE PAULINA
16500 PWY 92064 1170-D4
CORTE PEDRO
2900 CRLB 92009 1147-H3
CORTE PELLEJO
8900 SDCo 91977 1291-A5
CORTE PENCA
- CRLB 92009 1148-A3
CORTE PESCADO
- CHV 91914 1311-F2
- SMCS 92069 1108-F4
CORTE PINO
- CRLB 92009 1148-A1
CORTE PINTURA
5200 OCN 92057 1067-A4
CORTE PLATA ESPUELA
- SDCo 91901 1254-B3
CORTE PLAYA AZTECA
11200 SD 92124 1229-J7
11200 SD 92124 1230-A7
CORTE PLAYA BARCELONA
10900 SD 92124 1229-J7
CORTE PLAYA CANCUN
13300 SD 92124 1230-A7
CORTE PLAYA CARTAGENA
5900 SD 92124 1229-J6
CORTE PLAYA CATALINA
5000 SD 92124 1230-A7
CORTE PLAYA CORONA
11200 SD 92124 1229-J7
CORTE PLAYA DE CASTILLA
4900 SD 92124 1229-J7
CORTE PLAYA DE CORTES
11300 SD 92124 1230-A7
CORTE PLAYA ENCINO
4900 SD 92124 1229-J7
CORTE PLAYA JACINTO
5300 SD 92124 1229-J7
CORTE PLAYA LAGUNA
11400 SD 92124 1230-A7
CORTE PLAYA LAS BRISAS
11500 SD 92124 1230-A7
CORTE PLAYA MADERA
11200 SD 92124 1229-J7
CORTE PLAYA MAJORCA
10800 SD 92124 1229-J7
CORTE PLAYA MAZATLAN
10900 SD 92124 1229-J7
CORTE PLAYA MERIDA
11000 SD 92124 1229-J7
CORTE PLAYA PACIFICA
5900 SD 92124 1229-J6
CORTE PLAYA PALMERA
4900 SD 92124 1229-H7
CORTE PLAYA SAN JUAN
5100 SD 92124 1230-A7
CORTE PLAYA SOLANA
10800 SD 92124 1229-J7

CORTE PLAYA TAMPICO
11000 SD 92124 1229-J7
CORTE PLAYA TOLUCA
10800 SD 92124 1229-J7
CORTE PLENO VERANO
- SD 92130 1208-B3
CORTE POCO
- CRLB 92009 1147-J2
CORTE POTOSI
12800 SD 92128 1150-D7
CORTE POZOS
8900 SDCo 91977 1291-B5
CORTE PRESIDO
- CRLB 92009 1147-J2
CORTE PRIMAVERA
1100 CHV 91910 1311-A7
1100 CHV 91910 1331-A1
CORTE PROMENADE
- CRLB 92009 1147-J2
CORTE PULSERA
1800 OCN 92056 1087-C4
CORTE QUEZADA
8900 SDCo 91977 1291-B5
CORTE QUINTA MAR
7300 CRLB 92009 1127-F7
CORTE RAMON
6800 CRLB 92009 1128-A5
CORTE RAPALLO
1400 SDCo 92026 1129-F2
CORTE RAPOSO
15500 SD 92127 1169-J6
CORTE RAQUEL
600 SMCS 92069 1108-E5
CORTE RAYITO
2800 SD 92173 1350-D2
12700 PWY 92064 1170-C6
CORTE REAL
6600 CRLB 92009 1128-A5
CORTE ROBERTO
1500 OCN 92056 1087-B4
CORTE ROCA
2700 SDCo 91901 1254-E3
CORTE ROMERO
- CRLB 92009 1148-B1
CORTE ROSADO
- CRLB 92009 1148-A4
CORTE SABIO
12200 SD 92128 1170-B5
CORTE SAN LUIS
- OCN 92057 1086-J3
CORTE SANO
4300 LMSA 91941 1271-A4
CORTE SAN RIO
- SMCS 92078 1128-G2
CORTE SAN SIMEON
- CHV 91914 1311-E2
CORTE SANTA FE
6900 SD 92121 1228-H1
CORTE SANTICO
4900 OCN 92056 1087-C3
CORTE SASAFRAS
8000 CRLB 92009 1147-H3
CORTE SEGUNDO
1800 OCN 92056 1087-C5
CORTE SELVA
- CRLB 92009 1148-A1
CORTE SIERRA
- SDCo 91901 1254-A3
CORTE SOBRADO
17600 SD 92128 1150-D7
CORTE SOL DEL DIOS
4600 SD 92130 1208-C3
CORTE SONRISA
3400 CRLB 92009 1147-J4
CORTE SOSEGADO
11700 SD 92128 1170-A4
CORTE STAGNA
6800 SDCo 92091 1148-F5
CORTE STELLINA
- SD 92129 1188-J4
CORTE SUAVE
4500 OCN 92056 1087-B3
CORTE SUSANA
13000 PWY 92064 1170-D4
CORTE TAMARINDO
- CRLB 92009 1127-J5
CORTE TEMPLANZA
11700 SD 92128 1170-A4
CORTE TERRAL
3300 CRLB 92009 1128-A5
CORTE TEZCUCO
11900 SD 92128 1150-A7
CORTE TIBURON
3300 CRLB 92009 1147-J3
CORTE TIERRA ALTA
4000 SDCo 91941 1271-E4
CORTE TIERRA BAJA
10200 SDCo 91941 1271-E4
CORTE TILO
3000 CRLB 92009 1147-H3
CORTE TOMILLO
- CRLB 92009 1148-B2
CORTE TORERO
1800 OCN 92056 1087-C4
CORTE TRABUCO
3000 CRLB 92009 1127-J6
CORTE TRADICION
- CRLB 92009 1147-J2
CORTE TROVA
300 CHV 91914 1311-F2
CORTE VALDEZ
3000 CRLB 92009 1127-J4
CORTE VENTANA
1700 OCN 92056 1087-C4
CORTE VENTURA
300 CHV 91914 1311-F1
CORTE VERA CRUZ
3200 CRLB 92009 1147-J4
CORTE VERANO
1600 OCN 92056 1087-C4
CORTE VERDE
- OCN 92057 1086-J3
2900 SDCo 91901 1254-F3
CORTE VERSO
3300 CRLB 92009 1147-J3
CORTE VICENZA
12100 SD 92128 1190-B2
CORTE VIEJO
- CHV 91914 1311-F3
1700 OCN 92056 1087-C4
3400 CRLB 92009 1127-J5
CORTE VILLANUEVA
- SD 92129 1188-J5
CORTE VIOLETA
7700 CRLB 92009 1147-J3
CORTE VISTA
- CHV 91915 1311-F7
CORTE YOLANDA
- CRLB 92009 1128-A4
CORTEZ
19200 SDCo 92029 1149-E4
CORTEZ AV
- SDCo 92026 1109-E5
- IMPB 91932 1349-E2

CORTEZ AV
600 VSTA 92084 1087-H4
1800 ESCN 92026 1109-E5
CORTEZ GN
1800 ESCN 92026 1109-E5
CORTEZ PL
200 SD 92037 1247-E3
CORTEZ WY
3700 OCN 92056 1107-A1
4000 SDCo 91977 1271-D4
CORTE ZAFIRO
- SMCS 92069 1108-G4
CORTILE BELLAZA
- SD 92129 1188-J5
CORTINA CIR
1400 ESCN 92029 1149-G1
1900 ESCN 92029 1129-G7
CORTINA CT
7600 CRLB 92009 1147-H1
CORTINA PL
- SD 92131 1209-F1
CORTINA ST
- CRLB 92009 1127-J5
CORTO LN
1300 SDCo 92020 1271-J1
CORTO ST
300 SOLB 92075 1167-F7
2800 OCN 92054 1086-E6
CORVALLA DR
1700 VSTA 92084 1087-J2
1700 VSTA 92084 1088-A2
CORVALLIS ST
3400 CRLB 92010 1106-J4
CORVIDAE ST
1300 CRLB 92011 1127-B7
CORVINA ST
600 IMPB 91932 1329-F7
CORVUS PL
8700 SD 92126 1209-C2
CORY CT
8800 SDCo 91977 1271-A7
COSALA ST
200 VSTA 92084 1087-H4
COSGROVE DR
2200 SDCo 91901 1234-A5
COSIRA CT
4200 SD 92124 1249-J2
COSMIT LN
- SDCo 92036 1175-J3
- SDCo 92036 1176-A2
COSMIT WY
- SDCo 92036 1175-J3
- SDCo 92036 1176-A2
COSMO AV
800 ELCJ 92019 1252-B7
1500 SDCo 92019 1252-B7
COSMO CT
7000 SD 92111 1248-J3
COSMO ST
4000 SD 92111 1248-J3
COSMOS CT
2200 CRLB 92011 1127-E3
COSOY WY
4200 SD 92103 1268-F4
COSTA AV
1300 CHV 91911 1330-C4
COSTA LN
14400 SDCo 92021 1232-H5
COSTA PL
300 SD 92037 1247-F3
COSTA ALTA DR
3000 CRLB 92009 1127-J5
COSTA BELLA DR
3800 LMSA 91941 1270-H5
COSTA BELLA ST
3600 LMGR 91945 1270-G5
3800 LMSA 91941 1270-G5
COSTA BELLA WY
3800 LMSA 91941 1270-G5
COSTADA CT
1700 LMGR 91945 1290-F1
COSTA DEL MAR RD
2000 CRLB 92009 1147-E1
2100 CRLB 92009 1127-E7
COSTA DEL REY
3700 OCN 92056 1107-B1
COSTA LAGO ST
9800 SDCo 91977 1291-D3
COSTALOT LN
11800 SDCo 92040 1211-J5
COSTALOTA RD
29300 SDCo 92082 1069-B7
COSTA VERDE BLVD
8500 SD 92122 1228-C3
COSTA VERDE LN
1700 SDCo 92084 1108-C2
COSTA VISTA WY
2000 OCN 92054 1106-F1
COSTEBELLE DR
2600 SD 92037 1227-J6
COSTEBELLE WY
7900 SD 92037 1227-J5
COTORRO RD
18000 SD 92128 1150-A7
COTORRO WY
12000 SD 92128 1150-B7
COTTAGE AV
5400 SD 92120 1250-B5
COTTAGE DR
- CRLB 92009 1127-G3
COTTAGE WY
- ENCT 92024 1147-F4
2000 VSTA 92081 1108-A5
COTTAGE GARDEN RD
- SDCo 92082 1071-A6
COTTAGE GLEN CT
1600 ENCT 92024 1147-G5
COTTAGE GROVE DR
1700 ENCT 92024 1147-H6
COTTAGE GROVE LN
200 ENCT 92024 1147-H6
COTTINGHAM CT
200 OCN 92054 1086-E5
COTTINGHAM ST
2900 OCN 92054 1086-D5
COTTINGTON LN
7100 SD 92139 1290-G7
COTTON ST
600 SD 92102 1289-J3
COTTONPATCH WY
100 ELCJ 92020 1251-C6
COTTONTAIL LN
1300 SD 92037 1247-G2
31300 SDCo 92003 1068-D2
COTTONTAIL RD
1000 VSTA 92081 1108-A5
COTTONWOOD AV
1700 CRLB 92011 1127-E6
8600 SNTE 92071 1231-E5
COTTONWOOD CIR
2000 ELCN 92243 6559-F1
COTTONWOOD CT
1400 SMCS 92069 1109-C6
3300 SD 92037 1228-B4

COTTONWOOD DR
- ImCo 92243 6559-F2
- VSTA 92081 1107-D2
1100 ELCN 92243 6499-F3
1100 ELCN 92243 6559-F1
1200 OCN 92056 1087-C2
COTTONWOOD PL
1800 ESCN 92026 1109-D5
COTTONWOOD RD
- SDCo 91906 1296-C6
- SDCo 91906 (1297-A7 See Page 1296)
- SDCo 91906 (1317-C1 See Page 1296)
100 SD 92173 1350-F4
COTTONWOOD ST
- SDCo 92055 1086-B2
3700 SD 92113 1289-G7
COTTONWOOD GROVE CT
- SD 92128 1190-A6
COTTONWOOD SPRINGS LN
3000 SDCo 91935 1272-D5
3000 SDCo 92019 1272-D5
COTTONWOOD VIEW DR
3000 SDCo 92019 1272-C5
COUGAR DR
2400 CRLB 92010 1127-D1
COUGAR PASS RD
26800 SDCo 92026 1089-G3
27200 ESCN 92026 1089-H4
COUGAR SUMMIT
3500 SDCo 91901 1275-B4
COULTER LN
2100 SDCo 92036 1156-A5
COULTER CREEK
29400 SDCo 92082 1069-G6
COULTER RIDGE RD
- SDCo 92036 1156-F5
COUNA WY
23900 SDCo 92065 1173-E2
COUNTRY LN
300 ESCN 92025 1130-B5
300 SDCo 92025 1130-B5
2300 SDCo 92028 1028-D6
S COUNTRY LN
1700 ESCN 92025 1130-B5
COUNTRY PL
2100 ESCN 92026 1109-G5
COUNTRY RD
2200 SDCo 92028 1028-E6
12500 SDCo 92082 1070-B4
COUNTRY TER
500 SDCo 92065 1152-G4
COUNTRY WY
2900 SDCo 92019 1272-D6
COUNTRY CLUB CIR
- CHV 91911 1330-E2
COUNTRY CLUB DR
- CHV 91911 1330-D1
400 ESCN 92029 1129-D3
400 SDCo 92029 1129-D3
3100 SDCo 92036 1156-E1
6800 SD 92037 1247-G1
6800 SD 92037 1227-G7
E COUNTRY CLUB DR
2500 SDCo 92029 1129-C6
COUNTRY CLUB LN
200 OCN 92054 1086-C7
300 ESCN 92026 1109-D5
400 CORD 92118 1288-G6
2900 SDCo 92028 1028-D7
12000 SDCo 92040 1231-J2
COUNTRY CLUB PL
8800 SDCo 91977 1271-A4
COUNTRY CLUB RD
2500 SDCo 92004 (1078-J3 See Page 1058)
4000 SDCo 92004 (1079-A7 See Page 1058)
COUNTRY CREEK RD
2200 SMCS 92069 1108-J1
13800 PWY 92064 1190-F1
COUNTRY CREST DR
1300 ELCJ 92021 1252-B2
COUNTRY DAY LN
- SD 92037 1228-C2
COUNTRY DAY RD
16000 PWY 92064 1170-G3
COUNTRY ESTATES DR
1200 VSTA 92084 1088-A2
COUNTRY GARDEN LN
500 SDCo 92069 1088-J6
600 SDCo 92069 1089-A6
COUNTRY GIRL LN
- SDCo 92127 1169-A1
COUNTRY GLEN RD
- SDCo 92028 1047-G6
COUNTRY GROVE LN
1900 ENCT 92024 1147-H6
COUNTRYHAVEN CT
2000 ENCT 92024 1147-H6
COUNTRYHAVEN RD
100 ENCT 92024 1147-H7
COUNTRY HEIGHTS RD
- SDCo 92026 1109-G4
COUNTRY HILL RD
15100 PWY 92064 1170-H7
COUNTRY MEADOW LN
3300 ESCN 92025 1150-D2
3300 SDCo 92025 1150-D2
COUNTRY MEADOWS RD
2600 SDCo 91901 1234-C5
COUNTRY OAKS LN
26900 SDCo 92082 1090-G5
COUNTRY RIDGE CT
- SDCo 92026 1109-G4
COUNTRY ROSE CIR
3200 ENCT 92024 1148-C4
COUNTRY SCENES CT
10100 SNTE 92071 1231-D4
COUNTRYSIDE DR
- ELCN 92243 6559-J3
- ELCN 92243 6560-A3
1600 VSTA 92081 1107-H5
5100 SD 92115 1270-A2
COUNTRYSIDE PL
1500 CHV 91913 1331-A2
1700 VSTA 92081 1107-H5
COUNTRY SQUIRE
1700 VSTA 92081 1107-H5
COUNTRY SQUIRE DR
15800 PWY 92064 1170-C5
COUNTRY TRAILS
3600 SDCo 91902 1311-B1
4300 CHV 91902 1311-B1
COUNTRY TRAILS LN
4300 CHV 91902 1311-C3
COUNTRY VIEW GN
2300 ESCN 92026 1109-B4
COUNTRYVIEW LN
1400 VSTA 92081 1107-H4
COUNTRY VIEW RD
10000 SDCo 91941 1271-D1

COUNTRY VILLA RD
15800 SDCo 92065 1173-D4
COUNTRY VISTAS LN
1500 CHV 91902 1311-A3
COUNTRYWOOD CT
2000 ENCT 92024 1147-H6
COUNTRYWOOD LN
100 ENCT 92024 1147-H6
1100 VSTA 92081 1107-J3
1100 VSTA 92081 1108-A4
COUNTRYWOOD WY
2000 ENCT 92024 1147-H6
COUNTY CENTER TWO RD
- ImCo 92243 6559-G6
COURAGE ST
- VSTA 92081 1107-G5
COURAGEOUS LN
4800 CRLB 92008 1106-H7
COURIER WY
13900 PWY 92064 1190-G4
COURSER AV
2900 SD 92117 1248-C2
COURSER CT
4300 SD 92117 1248-C2
COURT ST
2100 DLMR 92014 1187-F3
COURT WY
900 SD 92103 1268-J4
COURTLAND TER
13200 SD 92130 1187-J5
COURTNEY DR
7200 SD 92111 1268-J1
7200 SD 92111 1269-A1
COURTNEY LN
8300 SNTE 92071 1250-J1
COURTYARD DR
9900 SD 92131 1209-H5
COURTYARD VIEW DR
- SDCo 92026 1069-A5
COUSER WY
10400 SDCo 92059 1029-E7
10400 SDCo 92059 1049-E1
10400 SDCo 92082 1049-E1
COUSER CANYON RD
10600 SDCo 92026 1049-B1
10600 SDCo 92028 1049-B1
10600 SDCo 92059 1049-B1
10600 SDCo 92028 1029-B7
14600 SDCo 92082 1049-F4
COUSHATTA LN
1100 SDCo 91977 1291-A2
COUSINO WY
1700 SDCo 92019 1272-C2
COUSTEAU CT
2300 VSTA 92081 1107-H7
COUTS ST
3400 SD 92140 1268-G6
3500 SD 92110 1268-G6
4100 SD 92103 1268-G5
COVE CT
1500 SMCS 92069 1129-C1
2600 VSTA 92081 1107-H5
COVE DR
4500 CRLB 92008 1106-H7
COVENTRY RD
1200 VSTA 92084 1088-A6
2600 CRLB 92010 1106-J5
COVE VIEW PL
5000 SD 92154 1350-J1
COVE VIEW WY
1100 SD 92154 1350-J1
COVEY LN
8900 SDCo 92026 1069-B1
COVEY PL
1000 CHV 91913 1311-D6
COVINA CIR
8700 SD 92126 1209-C5
COVINA CT
10200 SD 92126 1209-C5
COVINA PL
10200 SD 92126 1209-C5
COVINA ST
8500 SD 92126 1209-C5
COVINGTON AV
- SMCS 92078 1128-J3
COVINGTON RD
2600 SD 92104 1269-F7
COW TR
9300 SNTE 92071 1231-E5
COWBOY CT
100 SDCo 92065 1152-J5
COWELL CT
10100 SD 92124 1249-G3
COWLES MOUNTAIN BLVD
5600 LMSA 91942 1250-G7
6100 SD 92119 1250-J2
7600 SNTE 92071 1250-J2
COWLES MOUNTAIN CT
7800 SD 92119 1250-G4
COWLES MOUNTAIN PL
7800 SD 92119 1250-G6
COWLEY WY
2100 SD 92110 1268-G1
2300 SD 92110 1248-G6
2800 SD 92111 1248-F5
2800 SD 92117 1248-F5
COWRIE AV
- SD 92037 1227-G6
COX RD
- ImCo 92233 411-A9
300 SMCS 92069 1108-J2
300 SMCS 92069 1109-A3
COY CT
1300 ELCJ 92021 1252-A2
COY RD
- ImCo 92251 6439-B2
COYOTE AV
- CALX 92231 6620-H6
- ImCo 92243 6560-A6
COYOTE CT
- CRLB 92010 1107-D7
1700 VSTA 92084 1087-J3
17000 PWY 92064 1170-D2
COYOTE RD
700 SDCo 91901 1234-C4
COYOTE RDG
1800 SDCo 92021 1252-D3
COYOTE RUN
30200 SDCo 92082 1070-G4
COYOTE RW
- SDCo 91935 1292-E3
COYOTE TR
- SDCo 92082 1069-F3
COYOTE WY
- SDCo 92004 410-B6
COYOTE #2 RD
- ImCo 92259 430-J8
COYOTE BUSH DR
9200 SD 92127 1169-D2
9200 SDCo 92127 1169-D2
COYOTE CANYON RD
2500 SDCo 92025 1150-D2

COYOTE CHASE DR
- SDCo 92004 (1099-H4 See Page 1098)
COYOTE CREEK TR
15900 PWY 92064 1171-C6
COYOTE CREST
1700 SDCo 92028 1028-A5
COYOTE HILL GN
10500 ESCN 92026 1109-F3
10500 SDCo 92026 1109-F3
COYOTE HOLLER RD
23200 SDCo 91963 (1315-H6 See Page 1294)
COYOTE NO 1 RD
- ImCo 92259 430-H8
COYOTE RIDGE LN
- CHV 91915 1311-H5
COYOTE RIDGE TER
- CHV 91915 1311-H5
COYOTERO DR
13100 PWY 92064 1190-E4
COYOTES WY
1100 SMCS 92078 1128-E3
COYOTE VISTA WY
13000 SDCo 91935 1272-H6
COZUMEL CT
100 SOLB 92075 1167-D7
COZUMEL DR
- IMP 92251 6499-G1
COZY CT
800 SDCo 92028 1027-E3
COZZENS CT
4300 SD 92122 1228-E6
COZZENS ST
5800 SD 92122 1228-E6
C QUIROZ ST
500 CALX 92231 6620-E7
CRABAPPLE CT
4300 SD 92154 1330-G7
CRABTREE ST
6400 SD 92114 1290-D6
CRADLE MOUNTAIN LN
12700 SDCo 92040 1212-B7
CRAFTSMAN WY
- SDCo 92127 1169-E3
CRAIG CT
2100 LMGR 91945 1290-J1
CRAIG RD
- SD 92152 1288-A5
CRAIGIE ST
4400 SD 92102 1289-J3
CRAIGMONT ST
1300 ELCJ 92019 1251-J7
1300 ELCJ 92019 1252-A7
CRAIGMORE AV
1700 ESCN 92027 1130-D2
CRAMPTON CT
6600 SD 92119 1250-F5
CRANBERRY CT
4300 SD 92154 1350-G1
CRANBERRY ST
5300 OCN 92057 1067-D6
CRANBROOK CT
3000 SD 92037 1228-A4
CRANDALL CT
2500 SD 92111 1248-J7
2500 SD 92111 1249-A7
CRANDALL DR
1800 SD 92111 1268-J1
1800 SD 92111 1269-A1
2100 SD 92111 1249-A7
2500 SD 92111 1248-J7
CRANE CT
- CRLB 92011 1127-C6
- ImCo 92249 6560-B7
CRANE PL
3700 SD 92103 1268-J6
CRANE ST
2800 LMGR 91945 1270-J6
CRANN AV
1300 CHV 91911 1330-C4
CRANSTON DR
2200 ESCN 92025 1130-A7
CRANSTON CREST
200 ESCN 92025 1130-A7
CRARY ST
7500 LMSA 91942 1250-G6
CRATER
14100 SDCo 92040 1232-F4
CRATER DR
11100 SD 92126 1209-D2
CRATER PL
11100 SD 92126 1209-C2
CRATER LAKE WY
4300 OCN 92054 1086-G1
CRATER RIM RD
- CRLB 92010 1107-B5
CRAVEN DR
- SMCS 92096 1128-H2
CRAVEN RD
100 SMCS 92078 1128-F2
4100 OCN 92057 1086-H3
CRAVEN ST
2300 NATC 92136 1309-G1
2300 SD 92136 1289-G7
2300 SD 92136 1309-G1
CRAVEN RIDGE WY
10800 SD 92130 1208-E1
CRAWFORD CT
- SD 92120 1249-J7
CRAWFORD ST
6000 SD 92120 1249-J7
CRAY CT
10600 SD 92121 1207-J6
CRAZY COLT CIR
800 VSTA 92081 1107-H2
CRAZY HORSE DR
11200 SDCo 92040 1211-F6
11300 SDCo 92040 1231-F1
11300 SNTE 92071 1231-F1
CRAZY HORSE TR
10500 SNTE 92071 1231-E6
CRECIENTE CT
11300 SD 92127 1149-J7
CRECIENTE WY
17700 SD 92127 1149-J7
CREE CT
12900 PWY 92064 1190-D4
CREE DR
13000 PWY 92064 1190-D4
CREEK RD
- SDCo 92036 1156-E7
400 OCN 92054 1086-G2
11800 PWY 92064 1210-D1
11800 SD 92131 1210-D1
11800 PWY 92064 1190-C7
E CREEK RD
- SDCo 92021 1233-C3
CREEK ST
1500 SMCS 92078 1108-D7
CREEK BLUFF DR
11700 PWY 92064 1210-C1
CREEKBRIDGE PL
10800 SD 92128 1189-H6

STREET Block City ZIP Pg-Grid

CREEKFORD DR
8900 SDCo 92040 1231-J6
CREEK HILLS RD
- SDCo 92021 1233-A1
15500 SDCo 92021 1213-B7
CREEK HOLLOW DR
25000 SDCo 92065 1153-H4
CREEK HOLLOW PL
2200 ESCN 92026 1109-J3
CREEKNETTLE RD
600 SMCS 92078 1128-G2
CREEK OAK DR
- SDCo 92028 1047-G7
CREEK PARK DR
12900 PWY 92064 1190-E5
CREEK PARK LN
13200 PWY 92064 1190-E5
CREEKSIDE AV
600 OCN 92057 1067-D6
CREEKSIDE CT
9300 SNTE 92071 1231-G5
12100 SD 92131 1210-A2
N CREEKSIDE DR
- CHV 91915 1311-H5
S CREEKSIDE DR
1300 CHV 91915 1311-J7
CREEKSIDE LN
- VSTA 92081 1107-D1
13200 PWY 92064 1190-E5
CREEKSIDE PL
- SMCS 92078 1128-G1
700 CHV 91914 1311-G3
2100 ESCN 92029 1129-E6
CREEKSTONE LN
11300 SD 92128 1189-J6
11300 SD 92128 1190-A6
CREEKVIEW DR
12300 SD 92128 1189-H6
CREEKVIEW LN
2100 SDCo 92028 1027-H7
CREEKWOOD CT
12600 SD 92129 1189-C5
CREEKWOOD LN
8600 SD 92129 1189-C5
CREEKWOOD WY
800 CHV 91913 1311-E4
CREELMAN LN
100 SDCo 92065 1173-A2
300 SDCo 92065 1172-G2
CREENCIA PL
1400 ESCN 92027 1110-A6
CREGAR ST
100 OCN 92054 1086-C6
CREIGHTON WY
5900 SD 92114 1290-C5
CRELA ST
3000 SDCo 91902 1310-D4
CRENSHAW ST
1800 SD 92105 1289-G1
CRESCENDO DR
26300 SDCo 92026 1109-H1
26400 SDCo 92026 1089-H7
CRESCENT BEND
900 SDCo 92028 1027-H4
CRESCENT CT
900 VSTA 92084 1088-A7
N CRESCENT CT
600 SD 92103 1268-J6
S CRESCENT CT
600 SD 92103 1268-J6
CRESCENT DR
500 VSTA 92084 1087-J7
600 CHV 91911 1330-H1
900 VSTA 92084 1088-A7
2300 SD 92103 1268-G5
3800 SDCo 92036 1156-E2
CRESCENT LN
600 VSTA 92084 1088-A7
CRESCENT PL
- SMCS 92078 1128-C6
CRESCENT BAY DR
- SD 92154 1350-J2
CRESCENT BEND PL
1100 SDCo 92028 1027-H4
CRESCENT HEIGHTS DR
4700 OCN 92056 1087-D4
CRESCENT HEIGHTS RD
22800 SDCo 92070 409-J10
CRESCENT HILL WY
28300 SDCo 92026 1089-E3
CRESCENT KNOLLS GN
1600 ESCN 92029 1129-F6
CRESCENT MOON DR
30300 SDCo 92082 1070-G1
CRESCENT POINT RD
4000 CRLB 92008 1106-H6
CRESCENT RIDGE RD
7500 SNTE 92071 1230-G7
N CRESCENT RIDGE RD
1100 SDCo 92028 1027-H4
CRESITA DR
5000 SD 92115 1270-C2
CRESPO DR
1500 SD 92037 1227-G6
CRESSA CT
1400 CRLB 92011 1127-C7
CRESSY CT
1500 ELCJ 92020 1251-B3
CREST DR
- ESCN 92025 1130-A6
400 VSTA 92084 1087-J7
500 ENCT 92024 1147-F7
500 CHV 91910 1310-G7
500 CHV 91910 1330-G1
600 SDCo 92019 1252-E6
900 ENCT 92024 1167-F1
2000 SDCo 92021 1252-H4
2100 ENCT 92007 1167-F2
2500 CRLB 92008 1106-F3
9300 SDCo 91977 1271-C7
CREST HTS
4000 SDCo 92028 1028-F4
CREST RD
700 DLMR 92014 1187-G4
700 SD 92014 1187-G5
12000 PWY 92064 1190-B5
N CREST RD
100 SDCo 92021 1252-J2
CREST ST
100 ESCN 92025 1129-H1
2000 ESCN 92029 1129-E6
CREST WY
13800 SD 92014 1187-G6
CRESTA CT
3600 OCN 92056 1107-D3
12500 SD 92128 1170-C2
CRESTA DR
16600 SD 92128 1170-C3
CRESTA PL
12500 SD 92128 1170-C3
CRESTA WY
- CHV 91910 1310-D5
12500 SD 92128 1170-C3

CRESTA BLANCA
- VSTA 92081 1107-C2
CRESTA BONITA DR
3700 SDCo 91902 1310-E3
CRESTA LOMA
2800 SDCo 92025 1130-E7
CRESTA LOMA DR
2700 SDCo 92028 1047-J1
CRESTA LOMA LN
2700 SDCo 92028 1047-J1
CRESTA VERDE LN
4400 SDCo 91902 1310-G2
CRESTBROOK PL
- SD 92128 1190-A6
CRESTCOURT LN
- SDCo 92028 1027-H1
CRESTED BUTTE ST
500 CHV 91911 1330-A3
CRESTGLEN LN
9900 SDCo 91977 1271-D6
CRESTHAVEN DR
1900 VSTA 92084 1087-H2
6200 LMSA 91942 1251-C6
CRESTHAVEN PL
1400 OCN 92056 1087-E3
CREST HILL LN
2200 SDCo 92028 1027-H6
CRESTHILL PL
1100 SDCo 92021 1251-J2
CRESTHILL RD
1200 SDCo 92021 1251-J2
CREST KNOLLS CT
12600 SD 92130 1188-C6
CRESTLAND DR
4800 SDCo 91941 1271-E2
CRESTLANE CT
9900 SDCo 91977 1271-D7
CRESTLINE DR
2100 OCN 92054 1086-C6
2400 LMGR 91945 1270-H7
14500 PWY 92064 1191-E3
CRESTLINE RD
32000 SDCo 92060 1052-G4
CRESTMAR PT
8900 SD 92121 1208-J7
8900 SD 92121 1228-J1
CRESTMONT PL
4700 OCN 92056 1087-E3
CRESTMORE AV
8800 SDCo 91977 1290-J3
CRESTON DR
5500 SD 92114 1290-B3
CRESTOP LN
2500 SDCo 91977 1271-D7
CRESTRIDGE CT
- SDCo 92026 1089-B1
CRESTRIDGE DR
1400 OCN 92054 1086-E7
CRESTSIDE PL
10100 SDCo 91977 1271-E7
CRESTSTONE PL
3800 SD 92130 1188-A4
CRESTVIEW CT
700 SMCS 92078 1128-E2
15200 PWY 92064 1170-G7
CRESTVIEW DR
- ENCT 92024 1167-F3
300 CHV 91902 1311-A3
1300 OCN 92056 1087-E3
4200 SDCo 91941 1271-E4
4700 CRLB 92008 1107-A7
CREST VIEW GN
2300 ESCN 92026 1109-C3
CRESTVIEW GN
200 ESCN 92026 1109-G4
CRESTVIEW HTS
10100 SDCo 91941 1271-D3
CRESTVIEW PL
300 VSTA 92081 1107-J1
CREST VIEW RD
700 VSTA 92081 1107-H1
CREST VIEW ESTATES PL
2300 SDCo 92027 1130-E2
CRESTWIND DR
21600 SDCo 92029 1129-A5
CRESTWOOD AV
12700 PWY 92064 1190-C2
CRESTWOOD DR
500 OCN 92054 1086-D3
CRESTWOOD PL
600 ESCN 92026 1109-H4
3600 SD 92103 1269-C6
CRESTWOOD RD
- SDCo 91906 (1299-E1 See Page 1298)
- SDCo 91962 (1299-E1 See Page 1298)
CRESWICK CT
12200 SD 92128 1190-B1
CRETE CT
- ENCT 92024 1147-C3
CRETE ST
3300 SD 92117 1248-E6
CRIBBAGE LN
400 SMCS 92078 1128-F1
CRICKET DR
- CHV 91915 1331-G1
CRICKET HILL ST
13400 PWY 92064 1170-E4
CRIMSON DR
800 SMCS 92069 1109-A4
CRIMSON FIRE CT
9700 SDCo 91941 1271-C4
CRISIE LN
2600 SDCo 92025 1130-C7
2600 ESCN 92025 1130-C7
CRISP CT
5300 SD 92117 1228-G6
CRISP WY
4700 SD 92117 1228-G7
CRISSCROSS LN
12200 SD 92129 1189-B7
CRISTALLO PL
12900 SD 92130 1188-B5
CRISTIANITOS RD
- SDCo 92055 408-J5
- SDCo 92672 1023-C1
CRISTOBAL DR
9900 SDCo 91977 1271-E6
CRISTOBAL WY
3200 SDCo 91977 1271-E6
CROCKER RD
14800 PWY 92064 1190-H1
14800 PWY 92064 1170-H7
CROCKETT ST
8700 LMSA 91942 1251-A6
CROCUS CT
300 ENCT 92024 1147-B4
CROFT ST
- SD 92105 1270-B6
E CROFTON LN
1700 ESCN 92027 1110-C7

CROFTON ST
2000 SDCo 91977 1291-A1
CROMWELL CT
5200 SD 92116 1269-F2
CROMWELL PL
3400 SD 92116 1269-F2
CROMWELL WY
700 VSTA 92084 1088-A7
CRONAN CIR
7900 SD 92126 1209-A3
CROOKED CREEK CT
4700 SD 92113 1289-J5
CROOKED OAK LN
28300 SDCo 92026 1089-E3
CROOKED PATH PL
- CHV 91914 1311-H3
CROOKED TRAIL RD
- CHV 91914 1311-F2
CROSBY RD
400 SD 92113 1289-C5
400 SD 92101 1289-C5
CROSBY ST
900 ELCJ 92021 1251-J3
1000 SDCo 92021 1251-J3
CROSBY TENNIS DR
- SDCo 92127 1168-J1
- SDCo 92127 1169-A1
CROSLEY TKTR
- SDCo 92060 409-F5
CROSS RD
- IMP 92251 6499-H2
- SDCo 91905 430-C7
2100 ELCN 92243 6499-H3
2100 ImCo 92243 6499-H3
2100 ImCo 92251 6499-H1
CROSS ST
1800 SD 92110 1268-G2
CROSSBILL CT
- CRLB 92011 1127-D4
CROSS CREEK LN
2400 ESCN 92025 1130-D6
CROSS CREEK PL
2500 ESCN 92025 1130-D7
CROSS CREEK RD
1600 SDCo 92084 1068-B6
CROSSCREEK RD
2000 CHV 91913 1311-E4
CROSS CREEK TER
10300 SD 92131 1209-H4
CROSS FOX CT
16000 PWY 92064 1170-G4
CROSSHAVEN LN
2500 SD 92139 1290-G7
CROSSLAND CT
10100 SNTE 92071 1231-A3
CROSSLE CT
2000 SDCo 92019 1272-C4
CROSSPOINT CT
800 SD 92114 1290-G3
CROSSROADS ST
- CHV 91915 1331-H1
CROSSROADS WY
- CHV 91915 1331-H1
CROSSROCK RD
14000 PWY 92064 1190-B3
CROSS STONE DR
- SDCo 92127 1169-E5
CROSS STONE PL
- SDCo 92127 1169-F5
CROSSWAY CT
8700 SNTE 92071 1230-H7
CROSSWINDS RD
14100 SDCo 92065 1152-F3
N CROSTHWAITE CIR
12200 PWY 92064 1190-F6
CROSWAITHE ST
100 OCN 92054 1106-B3
CROTON CT
5300 SD 92109 1248-B3
CROUCH ST
100 OCN 92054 1086-D7
800 OCN 92054 1106-D1
CROW CT
5900 SD 92120 1250-C5
CROWDER LN
4700 LMSA 91941 1270-F3
CROWELL ST
1500 SD 92103 1268-H6
CROWLEY CT
7100 SD 92119 1250-F4
CROWN CT
1600 SDCo 92028 1027-J5
CROWN ST
5100 SD 92110 1268-F2
CROWN CREST LN
2600 SD 92037 1227-J1
CROWN HILL LN
23600 SDCo 92027 1111-D4
CROWNHILL RD
2100 SD 92109 1248-A4
CROWN POINT CT
1500 CHV 91911 1330-H4
CROWNPOINT CT
3800 CRLB 92010 1107-B4
CROWN POINT DR
3300 SD 92109 1268-A1
3600 SD 92109 1248-A7
CROWNPOINT PL
2700 ESCN 92027 1130-F1
CROWNRIDGE LN
2700 SDCo 91977 1271-E7
CROWN RIDGE RD
- CHV 91915 1311-J6
- CHV 91915 (1312-A7 See Page 1293)
CROWN VALLEY RD
15900 PWY 92064 1170-D5
CROWNVIEW CT
- SMCS 92069 1108-J4
CROWN VIEW TER
3400 OCN 92056 1086-H7
CROWN VIEW WY
2100 OCN 92056 1086-J7
CROWS NEST CT
- OCN 92057 1067-B3
CROWS NEST LN
- SDCo 92019 1253-D1
7200 SD 92126 1208-J3
CROWTHORNE CT
- SDCo 92084 1108-D1
CROYDON LN
100 ELCJ 92020 1251-C5
CRUCES DR
37500 SDCo 92086 409-K5
CRUICKSHANK DR
- ELCN 92243 6499-E3
CRUICKSHANK RD
- ImCo 92243 6500-B3
CRUSADER AV
- ESCN 92027 1130-C1
CRYSTAL CT
- SMCS 92078 1128-D6
3100 SDCo 92025 1150-D1

CRYSTAL CV
- SD 92154 1330-J7
- SD 92154 1350-J1
CRYSTAL DR
4900 SD 92109 1247-G5
5100 SD 92037 1247-G5
CRYSTAL LN
1100 SDCo 92020 1251-J7
1100 SDCo 92020 1271-J1
CRYSTAL ST
4100 OCN 92056 1087-C6
CRYSTALAIRE DR
6400 SD 92120 1250-D6
CRYSTAL BLUFF CT
- SD 92154 1350-J2
CRYSTAL CLEAR DR
- SDCo 91978 1291-F2
CRYSTAL CLEAR LN
- SDCo 91978 1291-F2
CRYSTAL COVE WY
- SMCS 92078 1128-A3
CRYSTAL CREEK CT
800 CHV 91910 1311-B6
CRYSTAL DAWN LN
4000 SD 92122 1228-C3
CRYSTAL DOWNS DR
1100 CHV 91915 1311-G6
CRYSTAL DOWNS GN
- ESCN 92026 1109-H3
CRYSTAL GROVE CT
- SD 92130 1188-J3
CRYSTAL LAKE AV
6200 SD 92119 1250-H6
CRYSTALLINE DR
- CRLB 92011 1127-B5
CRYSTALLITE LN
13600 SDCo 92082 1070-D2
CRYSTAL OAKS WY
- SD 92131 1209-G2
CRYSTAL RIDGE CT
1600 VSTA 92081 1107-G4
9700 SDCo 92026 1089-C2
CRYSTAL RIDGE DR
9700 SDCo 92026 1089-C2
CRYSTAL RIDGE GN
2200 ESCN 92026 1109-B3
CRYSTAL RIDGE RD
2800 ENCT 92024 1148-A5
CRYSTAL RIDGE WY
1700 VSTA 92081 1107-G5
CRYSTAL SPRINGS DR
1200 CHV 91915 1311-G6
CRYSTAL SPRINGS PL
- ESCN 92026 1129-F1
CRYSTAL SPRINGS RD
10900 SNTE 92071 1231-F6
CRYSTAL VIEW LN
15500 PWY 92064 1191-B2
CRYSTAL VIEW RD
14800 SDCo 92021 1232-J4
CRYSTAL WOOD DR
3400 OCN 92054 1086-E3
CUADRO VISTA
- SDCo 92078 1128-B4
CUATRO LN
1700 SDCo 92028 1027-J4
CUBA AV
- SD 92140 1268-F6
CUBIST CT
4700 OCN 92057 1087-B1
CUCA ST
14100 SD 92129 1189-H2
CUCHARA DR
1100 DLMR 92014 1187-G5
CUCHILLO ST
700 OCN 92057 1067-C7
700 OCN 92057 1087-C1
CUDAHY PL
1000 SD 92110 1268-E3
CUERVO RD
1900 SDCo 92084 1088-C7
CUESTA PL
1100 SDCo 91977 1291-D2
CUESTA DEL SOL
11400 SDCo 92040 1232-E5
CUESTA NORTE
1300 SDCo 92028 1027-H5
CUFF RD
- ImCo - 411-C5
- ImCo 92257 411-C7
CUIN RD
- ImCo 92251 430-L5
CUISSE LN
1800 SDCo 92004 1058-G6
CULBERTSON AV
4400 LMSA 91941 1270-G3
CULEBRA AV
- SD 92140 1268-F6
CULEBRA ST
400 DLMR 92014 1187-F4
CULLEN ST
7500 SD 92111 1249-A5
CULLEN CREST TR
- SD 92130 1188-F4
CULLODEN CT
- SDCo 92028 1027-G5
CULLY CT
1700 SDCo 91901 1233-J6
1700 SDCo 91901 1234-A6
CULOWEE ST
7900 LMSA 91941 1270-H2
CULVER CT
- ESCN 92027 1110-E6
11200 SDCo 92020 1271-G3
CULVER RD
2300 SDCo 92028 996-J4
CULVER ST
4400 SD 92109 1248-B5
CULVER WY
5100 SD 92109 1248-B5
CUMANA TER
17600 SD 92128 1150-D7
17600 SD 92128 1170-D1
CUMBERLAND DR
15800 PWY 92064 1170-G5
CUMBERLAND ST
5500 SD 92139 1310-D1
CUMBRE CT
2000 CRLB 92009 1147-F2
CUMBRE PL
2100 ELCJ 92020 1251-C1
CUMBRE VW
600 CHV 91902 1311-B4
CUMBRES RD
12400 SDCo 92082 1070-B5
CUMBRES TER
12400 SDCo 92082 1070-B5
CUMMINGS RD
100 NATC 92136 1309-F1
100 SD 92136 1309-F1
3400 SD 92136 1289-F7
CUMMINS PL
9900 SD 92131 1209-H5

CUMULUS LN
6000 SD 92110 1268-G3
CUNARD ST
900 SD 92154 1330-B7
CUNNING LN
13600 SDCo 92040 1232-D3
CUNNINGHAM LN
600 SDCo 92019 1252-C6
CUPENO CT
2800 SDCo 91935 1293-A3
CURIE PL
2500 SD 92122 1228-B7
CURIE ST
2900 SD 92122 1228-C7
CURIE WY
5400 SD 92122 1228-C7
CURL RD
1700 SD 92101 1289-C1
CURLEW ST
2200 SD 92101 1288-J1
2200 SD 92101 1289-A1
2500 SD 92103 1268-J6
2500 SD 92103 1288-J1
CURLEW TER
6600 CRLB 92011 1127-B5
CURRAN CT
30900 SDCo 92082 1070-J1
CURRAN ST
- SD 92154 1351-D1
CURRANT CT
13000 SDCo 92040 1232-C4
CURRANT ST
3300 SD 92111 1249-A5
CURRANT WY
200 OCN 92057 1086-J6
CURRY DR
4800 SD 92115 1270-D2
CURRY WY
3700 OCN 92057 1086-H4
CURRY COMB DR
1600 SMCS 92069 1108-E5
CURTIS DR
1900 SDCo 92084 1087-H2
CURTIS LN
1400 SDCo 91901 1234-B3
CURTIS ST
- CORD 92135 1288-E4
3000 SD 92106 1268-C7
3700 SD 92110 1268-C6
CUSHING RD
1700 SD 92106 1288-D1
2100 SD 92106 1268-D7
CUSHMAN AV
1100 SD 92110 1268-F2
CUSHMAN PL
5200 SD 92110 1268-F3
CUSTER AV
- SMCS 92078 1128-J3
CUSTER RD
- SDCo 91906 (1318-B7 See Page 1298)
300 SDCo 91906 430-B10
CUSTER ST
5300 SD 92110 1268-F3
CUSTOMHOUSE CT
2600 SD 92154 1351-J4
CUSTOMHOUSE PZ
9200 SD 92154 1351-J4
9300 SD 92154 1352-A4
CUTTER CT
1800 SDCo 92019 1272-B3
CUVAISON
- SDCo 92003 1068-B3
CUVEE CT
17200 PWY 92064 1170-E2
CUVIER ST
7300 SD 92037 1247-E1
7300 SD 92037 1227-E7
CUYAMACA AV
400 SD 92113 1289-H5
800 CHV 91911 1330-E1
1100 SDCo 91977 1291-D2
7500 LMGR 91945 1270-G7
CUYAMACA CT
2100 SDCo 91977 1271-D7
2100 SDCo 91977 1291-D1
CUYAMACA HWY Rt#-79
3400 SDCo 92036 1136-B7
3700 SDCo 92036 1156-D1
8200 SDCo 91916 1236-C4
8500 SDCo 92036 1176-F4
9600 SDCo 91916 1216-E3
12500 SDCo 91916 (1196-F4 See Page 1176)
13900 SDCo 92036 (1196-F4 See Page 1176)
CUYAMACA ST
- SDCo 92055 1085-J4
- SDCo 92055 1086-A4
700 ELCJ 92020 1251-D1
1900 ELCJ 92020 1231-C6
8500 SNTE 92071 1231-D2
CUYAMACA WY
1400 CHV 91911 1330-F4
CUYAMACA COLLEGE DR E
- SDCo 92019 1271-J5
CUYAMACA COLLEGE DR W
- SDCo 92019 1271-J5
CUYAMACA FOREST RD
- SDCo 92036 1176-E3
CUYAMACA MEADOWS RD
- SDCo 92036 1156-G7
CYCAD DR
900 SMCS 92078 1129-A3
CYMBAL CT
2200 SDCo 92019 1252-D6
CYNTHIA CT
600 SMCS 92069 1109-B6
CYNTHIA LN
1200 CRLB 92008 1106-E4
1400 ELCJ 92019 1252-A5
13600 PWY 92064 1190-F4
CYNTHIA PL
4400 SD 92105 1289-J1
CYPRESS AV
- SD 92102 1289-G4
100 CRLB 92008 1106-D5
100 ELCJ 92020 1251-F5
400 IMPB 91932 1329-G6
1000 SD 92103 1269-B6
1800 SD 92104 1269-C6
2200 LMGR 91945 1270-G7
2200 LMGR 91945 1290-H1
CYPRESS CIR
1000 SMCS 92069 1109-B5
CYPRESS CT
1200 SD 92103 1269-B6
CYPRESS DR
- ImCo 92243 6559-G3
- SD 92102 1289-G4
200 SD 92173 1350-G4
800 VSTA 92084 1088-A7

CYPRESS DR
1100 VSTA 92084 1108-A1
1400 ELCN 92243 6559-G1
2400 SDCo 91906 (1297-E5 See Page 1296)
CYPRESS LN
100 ELCJ 92020 1251-E2
100 SDCo 92020 1251-E2
24700 SDCo 91916 1236-A2
28900 SDCo 91962 1237-C6
CYPRESS PT
- PWY 92064 1150-G6
CYPRESS RD
3600 OCN 92054 1086-F1
CYPRESS RDG
27000 SDCo 92082 1090-D5
CYPRESS ST
100 CHV 91910 1310-B6
1700 SD 92154 1329-J7
1700 SD 92154 1330-A7
3200 NATC 91950 1310-C3
3200 SDCo 91950 1310-C3
4800 LMSA 91941 1270-J2
9500 SDCo 92040 1232-C4
CYPRESS WY
1000 SD 92103 1269-B6
CYPRESS CANYON RD
11400 SD 92131 1210-A1
11800 SD 92131 1189-J7
11800 SD 92131 1209-J1
CYPRESS CANYON PARK DR
11000 SD 92131 1210-B1
11500 PWY 92064 1210-B1
CYPRESS CREEK CT
- VSTA 92084 1088-B3
CYPRESS CREST TER
300 ESCN 92025 1130-B5
CYPRESS DEL MAR
3900 SD 92130 1188-A7
CYPRESS GLEN PL
4600 SD 92130 1188-C6
CYPRESS HILL RD
2700 CRLB 92008 1106-F3
CYPRESS HILLS DR
- ENCT 92024 1147-E5
CYPRESS LAKES WY
8800 SNTE 92071 1230-J4
CYPRESS POINT CT
1300 CHV 91915 1311-H6
CYPRESS POINT GN
1700 ESCN 92026 1109-D4
CYPRESS POINT RD
6100 SD 92120 1250-D6
CYPRESS POINT TER
- SDCo 92082 1090-G5
CYPRESS POINT WY
800 OCN 92054 1066-F7
CYPRESS TERRACE PL
11400 SD 92131 1210-C1
CYPRESS VALLEY DR
11800 SD 92131 1210-A1
CYPRESS WOODS CT
12500 SD 92131 1210-C1
CYPRESS WOODS DR
11300 SD 92131 1210-C1
CYPRUS ISLAND CT
- SDCo 92028 1028-G5
CYRUS WY
4600 OCN 92056 1107-E5

D

D AV
- NATC 91950 1289-H7
100 CORD 92118 1288-H7
200 SDCo 92055 1066-C2
300 NATC 91950 1309-H1
3100 CHV 91950 1309-J3
D CT
200 CHV 91910 1310-F7
D ST
- CHV 91910 1310-A5
- SDCo 92059 1029-H4
100 IMP 92251 6439-E6
200 SDCo 92036 1136-B7
200 SDCo 92065 1152-H5
500 CHV 91910 1309-J5
1300 SD 92110 1268-F2
1600 SDCo 92084 1108-G2
2500 NATC 91950 1310-C3
E D ST
- ENCT 92024 1147-C7
W D ST
400 ENCT 92024 1147-B7
DABNEY DR
10400 SD 92126 1209-A4
10700 SD 92126 1208-J4
DAFFODIL
15300 SDCo 92021 1233-B3
DAFFODIL DR
- SD 92109 1248-C6
DAFFODIL LN
5700 SD 92120 1250-E7
DAFFODIL PL
7100 CRLB 92011 1127-B6
DAFFODIL ST
- SDCo 92055 1086-A4
3800 SD 92121 1208-B6
DAFNE LN
10100 SD 92124 1249-G1
DAFTER DR
4900 SD 92102 1290-A1
DAFTER PL
4900 SD 92102 1290-A1
DA GAMA CT
- SDCo 92026 1109-E6
DAGGET ST
7600 SD 92111 1249-A2
DAGGETT WY
5800 LMSA 91942 1251-C7
DAHLIA AV
- IMPB 91932 1329-E7
1600 SD 92154 1329-J7
1700 SD 92154 1330-A7
DAHLIA CT
800 SD 92154 1330-C7
DAHLIA DR
- NATC 91950 1289-H7
100 SOLB 92075 1187-E1
DAHLIA LN
100 IMP 92251 6439-E6
DAHLIA ST
- SDCo 92055 1086-B2
2900 SD 92105 1269-H7
DAHLIA WY
1000 CRLB 92011 1127-A6
DAILEY CT
5100 LMSA 91941 1271-A2
DAILEY RD
8900 LMSA 91941 1271-A1
DAILY DR
2300 SDCo 92028 996-J2
2300 SDCo 92028 997-A2

DAILY RD
- SDCo 92028 996-H2
2500 SDCo 92028 997-B1
48400 SDCo 92028 409-B4
DAIN CT
2200 LMGR 91945 1270-J7
2200 LMGR 91945 1290-J1
DAIN DR
1900 LMGR 91945 1290-J1
DAIRY RD
3100 SDCo 91902 1291-B7
DAIRY MART RD
1600 SD 92173 1350-E4
2100 SD 92154 1350-E4
DAISY AV
- IMPB 91932 1329-E7
900 CRLB 92011 1127-B6
6000 SD 92114 1290-C6
DAISY CT
1000 CRLB 92011 1127-B6
DAISY LN
400 SMCS 92078 1128-F1
2500 SDCo 92028 1028-G7
DAISY PL
3900 OCN 92056 1107-A1
6000 SD 92114 1290-C6
DAISY ST
1100 ESCN 92027 1110-B6
N DAISY ST
700 ESCN 92027 1110-A6
DAISY WY
1400 SD 92114 1290-D6
DAKOTA DR
4200 SD 92117 1248-E5
DAKOTA WY
400 OCN 92056 1087-A4
DAKOTA RANCH RD
- SNTE 92071 1231-D1
DALAI
9200 SDCo 92040 1232-F4
DALBERGIA CT
3800 SD 92113 1289-G7
DALBERGIA ST
3500 SD 92113 1289-G6
DALBY CV
- SD 92126 1209-D2
DALBY PL
11200 SD 92126 1209-D2
DALE AV
400 ESCN 92026 1109-H7
4300 LMSA 91941 1270-G3
9600 SDCo 91977 1271-C5
DALE CT
800 CHV 91910 1310-G7
900 SMCS 92069 1109-B5
DALE ST
1300 SD 92102 1289-E2
2000 SD 92104 1289-E2
2700 SD 92104 1269-E7
DALEA PL
4700 OCN 92057 1087-A1
DALECREST LN
2200 SDCo 91977 1271-D7
DALEGROVE LN
- SD 92114 1290-F5
DALEHAVEN PL
4900 SD 92102 1290-A1
DALEHURST RD
9200 SNTE 92071 1231-A3
DALEN AV
5400 SD 92122 1228-C6
DALEN PL
- SD 92122 1228-C6
DALERIDGE PL
2600 SDCo 91977 1271-E7
DALEWOOD AV
8700 SD 92123 1249-C7
DALEY ST
2400 SDCo 92065 1152-C7
DALEY TKTR
15700 SDCo 91935 1293-F2
DALEY CENTER DR
3300 SD 92123 1249-F4
DALEY FLAT RD
2500 SDCo 92070 1155-D1
3100 SDCo 92070 1135-E7
DALEY RANCH TKTR
15700 SDCo 91935 (1312-H4 See Page 1293)
15700 SDCo 91935 (1313-A3 See Page 1293)
15700 SDCo 91935 1292-J7
15700 SDCo 91935 1293-C5
DALHART AV
6100 LMSA 91942 1250-H6
DALHOUSIE RD
14200 SD 92129 1189-D2
DALIA LN
14100 SDCo 92067 1188-D2
14200 SDCo 92067 1188-D2
DALILA CT
- CALX 92231 6620-J7
DALISAY ST
2600 SD 92154 1350-C3
DALLAS RD
1100 SDCo 92028 1028-A4
DALLAS ST
8300 LMSA 91942 1250-J6
8600 LMSA 91942 1251-A6
DALLES AV
3900 SD 92117 1248-E3
DALLES CT
4300 SD 92117 1248-E3
DALTON CT
2100 CRLB 92008 1127-D1
DAMAS PL
500 CHV 91910 1311-A4
DAMASCO CT
12400 SD 92128 1150-B7
DAMATO ST
4500 SD 92124 1249-G3
DAM OAKS DR
24800 SDCo 92065 409-H11
DAMON AV
2900 SD 92109 1248-C4
DAMON LN
4400 SDCo 92020 1271-H3
DAMROCK CIR
8600 LMSA 91941 1271-A3
DAN WY
800 ESCN 92025 1129-G2
DANA CT
2300 CRLB 92008 1106-H4
DANA DR
700 VSTA 92083 1087-F5
4500 LMSA 91941 1270-F3
DANA PL
3700 SD 92103 1268-J6
DANA LANDING RD
1300 SD 92109 1268-A3
DANANCY CT
9500 SDCo 91977 1291-C4
DA NANG DR
- CORD 92118 1309-D6

STREET Block City ZIP Pg-Grid

DANA POINT CT
1600 CHV 91911 1330-J4
DANA POINT WY
800 OCN 92054 1066-G7
DANA VISTA
13000 PWY 92064 1190-E5
DANAWOODS CT
7100 SD 92114 1290-F4
DANAWOODS LN
- SD 92114 1290-F4
DANBURY WY
6200 SD 92120 1249-J7
6200 SD 92120 1250-A7
DANBY CT
9100 SD 92129 1189-D1
DANCER CT
- ESCN 92026 1109-C5
DANCER PL
- ESCN 92026 1109-C5
DANCOL TER
1800 SDCo 92021 1252-C3
DANCY CT
10500 SD 92126 1209-A4
DANCY PL
10400 SD 92126 1208-J5
DANCY RD
7200 SD 92126 1208-J5
7600 SD 92126 1209-A4
DANDELION WY
- SD 92130 1188-G3
- SMCS 92078 1128-D7
DANDRIDGE LN
5800 SD 92115 1270-C5
DANE DR
600 SMCS 92069 1108-J5
700 SMCS 92069 1109-A5
DANENBURG DR
100 ELCN 92243 6559-J3
100 ELCN 92243 6560-A3
100 ImCo 92243 6560-A3
DANERIN WY
2900 SDCo 91935 1272-E6
DANES RD
12400 PWY 92064 1190-C5
DANIA CT
8700 SNTE 92071 1231-A7
DANICA PL
600 ESCN 92025 1129-J6
DANICA MAE DR
8800 SD 92122 1228-C3
DANIEL AV
2600 SD 92111 1249-A6
DANIEL CT
7300 SD 92111 1249-A6
DANIEL GN
2600 ESCN 92027 1110-E7
DANIELLE DR
7700 LMGR 91945 1290-H2
DANIELS ST
200 CALX 92231 6620-G6
DANIELSON CT
12600 PWY 92064 1190-E6
DANIELSON ST
13000 PWY 92064 1190-E6
DANNAN CT
12700 SD 92130 1188-D6
DANNENBERG RD
- ELCN 92243 6559-G3
DANNER PL
100 ELCJ 92020 1251-F6
DANNY LN
1600 SDCo 92021 1251-G1
DANNY ST
300 SDCo 92021 1251-F2
DANNY WY
1600 SDCo 92021 1251-G1
DANNY BOY RD
- SDCo 92127 1169-A2
DANOBER DR
1100 SD 92154 1350-F1
DANTE ST
5200 SD 92117 1248-H1
DANTE TER
2200 SDCo 92084 1108-D2
DANUBE LN
9000 SD 92126 1209-D1
DANVERS CIR
11900 SD 92128 1190-A2
DANVILLE AV
6600 SD 92120 1250-D6
DANVILLE CT
6500 SD 92120 1250-D6
DANZA CIR
11500 SD 92127 1149-J7
DAPHNE CT
800 CRLB 92011 1127-A6
DAPHNE ST
100 ENCT 92024 1147-A5
DAPPER CT
8400 SD 92126 1209-C1
DAPPLE CT
11900 SD 92128 1190-B7
DAPPLE WY
11900 SD 92128 1190-B7
DAPPLE GRAY PL
- SDCo 92127 1169-F4
DARBY ST
1100 SDCo 91977 1290-J2
2100 ESCN 92025 1130-A6
DARCY CT
9300 SNTE 92071 1231-B5
DARCY LN
1300 SDCo 92065 1172-F2
DARDAINA DR
3000 SD 92139 1310-E2
DARDANELLE GN
2400 ESCN 92027 1110-D7
DARDEN CT
7500 SD 92126 1208-J5
7500 SD 92126 1209-A5
DARDEN RD
10300 SD 92126 1208-J5
DAREN GN
2000 ESCN 92026 1109-D4
DARIEN DR
100 ENCT 92024 1147-H7
100 ENCT 92024 1167-H1
DARKWOOD RD
12100 SD 92129 1189-B7
DARLA LN
700 SDCo 92028 1027-F1
DARLENE LN
3300 SDCo 91935 1273-A6
DARLING DR
1500 SDCo 92026 1089-D7
DARLINGTON CT
2000 SDCo 92019 1272-C4
DARLINGTON RW
2300 SD 92037 1247-J1
2400 SD 92037 1248-A1
DARROW GN
2100 ESCN 92027 1130-D2
DARRYL CT
13600 SDCo 92021 1232-E5
DARRYL ST
8000 LMGR 91945 1270-H6
DARTFORD WY
5600 SD 92120 1270-D1
DARTINGTON WY
- CRLB 92009 1127-F3
DARTMOOR CIR
1500 OCN 92057 1067-F7
DARTMOOR DR
1600 LMGR 91945 1290-E1
1600 LMGR 92114 1290-E1
DARTMOUTH DR
2800 OCN 92056 1087-A7
DARTMOUTH ST
1600 CHV 91913 1311-C5
DARTOLO RD
16100 SDCo 92065 1173-G3
DARVIEW LN
13300 SD 92129 1189-B4
DARWELL CT
10500 SD 92126 1208-J4
DARWIN AV
3800 SD 92154 1350-F1
DARWIN CT
5900 CRLB 92008 1127-C2
DARWIN DR
1400 OCN 92056 1087-E2
DARWIN PL
1000 SD 92154 1330-F7
1000 SD 92154 1350-F1
DARWIN WY
4200 SD 92154 1350-F1
DASH WY
14600 PWY 92064 1190-E1
DASHERO PL
1700 ESCN 92029 1129-F6
DASSCO CT
4900 SD 92102 1290-A3
DASSCO ST
700 SD 92102 1290-A3
DASSIA WY
5000 OCN 92056 1107-F5
DATCHO DR
4000 SD 92117 1248-E3
DATE AV
- CHV 91910 1310-A5
- IMPB 91932 1329-E7
200 CRLB 92008 1106-F7
600 CHV 91910 1330-B1
800 CHV 91911 1330-B1
1500 SD 92154 1329-J7
4300 LMSA 91941 1270-H2
DATE CT
400 CHV 91911 1330-F6
DATE LN
20000 SDCo 92029 1149-E1
DATE PL
4900 SD 92102 1290-A2
DATE ST
100 CHV 91911 1330-F5
200 SD 92101 1289-A2
300 SD 92114 1290-D4
500 SD 92101 1288-J2
1300 ESCN 92026 1109-J6
1500 VSTA 92083 1087-C7
2800 SD 92102 1289-E2
4800 SD 92102 1290-A2
9400 SDCo 91977 1291-C2
N DATE ST
100 ESCN 92025 1130-A2
S DATE ST
100 ESCN 92025 1130-A2
DATHE ST
200 SDCo 91977 1291-B4
DATSUN ST
6400 SD 92154 1351-C1
DAUCUS CT
200 SD 92129 1189-C6
DAUER AV
4500 LMSA 91941 1270-F3
DAUM RD
20800 SDCo 91935 (1315-A1 See Page 1294)
DAUNTLESS ST
9800 SD 92126 1209-E2
DAVENPORT AV
13800 SD 92129 1189-D2
DAVENPORT LN
500 CHV 91911 1330-H2
2600 LMGR 91945 1270-D7
DAVENRICH ST
9000 SDCo 91977 1291-A3
DAVENTRY ST
6900 LMGR 91945 1290-E1
6900 LMGR 92114 1290-E1
DAVES WY
3900 SD 92154 1330-F7
DAVEY WY
900 SMCS 92069 1109-B5
DAVID DR
800 CHV 91910 1310-G7
1500 ESCN 92026 1109-D5
DAVID GN
1900 ESCN 92026 1109-D4
DAVID PL
- CRLB 92008 1106-G3
DAVID ST
1800 SD 92111 1268-J1
DAVID WY
2100 DLMR 92014 1187-F3
DAVIDANN RD
10800 SNTE 92071 1231-F6
DAVID NAVARRO AV
800 CALX 92231 6680-D1
DAVIDSON AV
7500 LMGR 91945 1270-G7
DAVIDSON ST
200 CHV 91910 1310-C5
DAVIES DR
- CHV 91911 1330-J3
DA VINCI ST
4500 SD 92130 1188-C7
DAVIS AV
- SD 92126 1209-B7
2500 CRLB 92008 1106-E4
DAVIS CT
- SDCo 92055 1086-B2
900 VSTA 92081 1107-H2
DAVIS DR
200 SDCo 92028 1027-J1
DAVIS PL
2600 CRLB 92008 1106-E4
DAVIS RD
- ImCo 92233 411-B8
- ImCo 92257 411-B6
DAVIS ST
500 SDCo 92065 1152-E5
DAVIS CUP LN
15600 SDCo 92065 1173-H4
DAWES CT
1900 VSTA 92081 1107-J4
DAWES ST
4000 SD 92109 1247-H4
DAWN CT
500 CHV 91910 1310-G6
1400 SMCS 92069 1129-C1
DAWN LN
4200 OCN 92056 1107-C2
DAWN PL
1700 ESCN 92027 1110-C7
DAWNCREST CT
2500 SDCo 92036 1136-D7
DAWN CREST LN
- CHV 91915 1331-G1
DAWNE ST
4900 SD 92117 1228-G7
DAWNELL DR
1100 SD 92154 1350-F1
DAWN MARIE DR
3300 SDCo 91901 1234-D5
DAWNRIDGE AV
1100 SDCo 92021 1251-J2
1100 ELCJ 92021 1251-J2
DAWN VIEW GN
2000 ESCN 92026 1109-B3
DAWN VIEW WY
100 SDCo 92021 1252-J2
100 SDCo 92021 1253-A2
DAWSON AV
4300 SD 92115 1270-A4
DAWSON DR
1200 CHV 91911 1330-J1
1200 CHV 91911 1331-A1
1500 VSTA 92081 1107-H6
DAWSONIA ST
3600 SDCo 91902 1310-J2
3700 SDCo 91902 1311-A2
DAX CT
13200 SD 92129 1189-C4
DAXI LN
1100 SDCo 92029 1129-H6
DAY ST
100 SDCo 92065 1152-E7
3400 SD 92105 1270-B6
DAYBREAK CT
5500 OCN 92057 1067-D6
DAYBREAK PL
- VSTA 92084 1087-J3
1600 ESCN 92027 1109-J5
1600 ESCN 92027 1110-A5
DAYLIGHT PL
100 SDCo 92065 1173-D2
DAY LILY CT
800 SMCS 92078 1129-B1
DAYLILY DR
- CRLB 92011 1127-B4
2300 SDCo 92028 1028-E6
DAYMARK CT
12000 SD 92131 1190-B7
DAYSAILOR CT
4800 SD 92154 1330-J6
DAY STAR CT
- VSTA 92084 1087-J2
DAY STAR WY
20000 SDCo 92065 1152-D2
DAYTON DR
1700 LMGR 91945 1290-G1
DAYTON ST
4400 SD 92115 1270-B4
DAYTONA ST
7300 LMGR 91945 1270-F6
DAZA DR
16200 SDCo 92065 1173-G3
DEAD STICK RD
8700 SD 92154 1351-H1
DEADWOOD DR
500 SMCS 92029 1128-H6
DEAL CT
700 SD 92109 1267-J3
DEALWOOD AV
500 ELCN 92243 6560-B1
500 ImCo 92243 6560-C1
DEALWOOD RD
700 ImCo 92243 431-D6
700 ImCo 92243 6560-G1
DEAN DR
1100 ENCT 92007 1167-F3
DEANA PL
1000 ESCN 92025 1130-A3
DEANLY CT
13800 SDCo 92040 1232-E4
DEANLY ST
9400 SDCo 92040 1232-E5
DEANLY WY
9300 SDCo 92040 1232-E5
DE ANZA CT
400 OCN 92057 1086-J4
1100 CHV 91910 1331-A1
DE ANZA DR
1400 SDCo 92004 1058-G5
DE ANZA RD
2700 SD 92109 1248-D6
DE ANZA SPUR
400 SDCo 92004 1058-G5
DE ANZA TR
- SDCo 92004 410-B5
- SDCo 92004 1058-H1
DE ANZA BAY DR
- SD 92109 1248-D6
DEARBORN DR
1000 SD 92154 1330-C7
1000 SD 92154 1350-C1
DEARBORN PL
12100 PWY 92064 1190-F7
DEARBORN RD
- ImCo 92243 431-A7
DEARBORN ST
3600 OCN 92057 1086-G5
DEARFLOWER RD
3100 SD 92115 1270-D6
DEATON DR
4800 SD 92102 1290-A1
DEAUVILLE ST
2400 SD 92139 1310-E1
DEAVER LN
- SD 92173 1350-E4
DEAVERS DR
500 SMCS 92069 1109-D7
DEBANN RD
1600 ENCT 92007 1167-E2
DEBBIE CT
9400 SDCo 92021 1232-H4
DEBBY DR
5000 SD 92115 1270-B2
DEBBY PL
600 ESCN 92026 1109-J7
DEBBY ST
200 SDCo 92028 1027-H3
DEBBYANN PL
3000 SD 92154 1330-F7
DEBCO DR
2200 LMGR 91945 1270-J7
2200 LMGR 91945 1290-J1
DEBENMARK PL
1200 SD 92154 1350-D1
DEBI LN
14200 SDCo 92082 1070-E1
DEBORAH PL
7800 LMGR 91945 1270-H7
DEBRA CIR
4100 OCN 92056 1087-C7
DEBRA LN
1800 VSTA 92084 1087-H2
DEBRA PL
500 SMCS 92078 1128-D1
DEBRA ANN DR
400 SDCo 92028 1027-H2
DEBRECENI WY
- SDCo 92127 1169-G2
DE BURN DR
5100 SD 92105 1290-A1
DE CAMP DR
6200 LMSA 91942 1251-B5
DECANT DR
12900 PWY 92064 1170-D2
DECANTURE CT
6100 SD 92120 1250-D4
DECANTURE CV
7200 SD 92120 1250-D4
DECANTURE ST
6200 SD 92120 1250-D4
DECANTURE WY
7200 SD 92120 1250-D4
DECATUR CIR
9000 SD 92126 1209-D3
DECATUR CT
- SD 92106 1268-D6
DECATUR RD
1700 SD 92106 1288-C1
2000 SD 92106 1268-D7
10900 SD 92126 1209-D3
DECATUR WY
300 ESCN 92026 1129-G1
DECENA DR
6100 SD 92120 1249-J7
DECISION ST
500 VSTA 92081 1128-A1
DECKER ST
1000 ELCJ 92020 1251-H5
1000 ELCJ 92019 1251-H5
DECORA CIR
3500 SMCS 92078 1108-C7
DECORO ST
4100 SD 92122 1228-C4
DEDDIE TER
200 SDCo 92028 1027-F5
DEDO PL
11400 SD 92126 1209-B1
DEEB CT
100 SDCo 92084 1088-E5
DEEB DR
2800 SDCo 92084 1088-E6
DEELAN LN
13100 PWY 92064 1190-H4
DEEM PL
1100 ELCJ 92021 1251-H4
DEEP CANYON CT
10600 SDCo 92026 1089-F3
DEEP CANYON DR
10800 SDCo 92026 1089-G3
DEEP DELL CT
7600 SD 92114 1290-H5
DEEP DELL CV
7400 SD 92114 1290-G4
DEEP DELL RD
- SD 92114 1290-G4
500 SD 92139 1290-G4
S DEEP DELL RD
300 SD 92114 1290-G5
DEEP HAVEN LN
1800 SD 92154 1350-C3
DEEP VALLEY RD
6800 SD 92120 1250-D3
DEEP WELL TR
- SDCo 92004 (1099-E1 See Page 1098)
DEER PTH
400 ENCT 92024 1147-A2
DEERBEN RD
20100 SDCo 92065 1153-G1
DEERBROOK DR
- SMCS 92069 1108-H4
DEER CANYON CT
- SD 92131 1210-D2
DEER CANYON DR
26900 SDCo 92065 1154-E2
DEER CANYON PL
- SD 92129 1189-A4
DEER CREEK TR
28700 SDCo 91962 1237-C6
DEER CREEK WY
- OCN 92057 1086-J2
DEERFIELD CT
800 OCN 92054 1086-E2
DEERFIELD RD
1700 ENCT 92024 1147-H6
DEERFIELD ST
7800 SD 92120 1250-D3
DEERFOOT RD
11900 SD 92131 1210-B3
DEERFORD RW
6000 SD 92037 1248-A1
DEERGRASS CT
13800 PWY 92064 1170-F5
DEERGRASS WY
- CRLB 92024 1147-E3
DEERHAVEN
500 ELCJ 92019 1252-D4
DEERHAVEN DR
1000 VSTA 92084 1087-J5
1000 VSTA 92084 1088-A5
DEER HILL CT
1400 SD 92037 1247-G3
DEER HILL ESTATES
- SDCo 92040 1191-E5
- SDCo 92064 1191-E5
DEER HOLLOW CT
9700 SNTE 92071 1231-F4
DEER HOLLOW PL
6800 SD 92120 1250-D3
DEERHORN OAKS RD
- SDCo 91935 (1315-B3 See Page 1294)
DEERHORN SPRING LN
2300 SDCo 91935 1294-H7
DEERHORN VALLEY RD
18400 SDCo 91935 1294-F7
20500 SDCo 91935 (1314-J1 See Page 1294)
20500 SDCo 91935 (1315-A2 See Page 1294)
DEERHURST CT
7000 SD 92139 1290-G7
DEERHURST WY
2400 SD 92139 1290-G7
DEERING ST
10800 SD 92126 1209-B3
DEER LAKE PARK RD
3900 SDCo 92036 1155-J2
3900 SDCo 92036 1156-A2
DEEROCK PL
100 SD 92114 1290-G4
DEERPARK DR
2100 SD 92110 1268-G1
2300 SD 92110 1248-F6
DEER PARK RD
- SDCo 91962 (1217-D2 See Page 1216)
- SDCo 92036 (1177-C7 See Page 1176)
- SDCo 92036 (1197-C2 See Page 1176)
- SDCo 92036 (1217-D2 See Page 1216)
DEER PARK WY
- SD 92130 1188-E5
DEER PATH LN
- CHV 91915 1331-H2
DEER PEAK CT
1600 CHV 91913 1311-D7
DEER RIDGE CT
- SDCo 92127 1169-E4
DEER RIDGE PL
- SDCo 92127 1169-E4
DEER RIDGE RD
- SDCo 92127 1169-E4
DEERRUN PL
6800 SD 92120 1250-D3
DEER SPRINGS PL
2500 SDCo 92069 1089-A6
DEER SPRINGS RD
1400 SDCo 91901 1234-H6
DEER SPRINGS RD Rt#-S12
100 SMCS 92069 1108-J1
500 SDCo 92069 1088-J7
500 SDCo 92069 1089-A7
500 SDCo 92069 1108-J1
500 SDCo 92069 1109-A1
1000 SDCo 92026 1089-A7
DEER TRAIL CT
- SDCo 92127 1169-E5
DEER TRAIL DR
- SDCo 92127 1169-E5
DEER TRAIL PL
- SDCo 92127 1169-E5
DEER TRAIL WY
- SDCo 92127 1169-E5
DEER VALLEY TR
- SDCo 91916 429-K4
- SDCo 91916 1216-A7
DEER VALLEY WY
- OCN 92057 1086-J2
DEER VALLEY ESTATES
18300 PWY 92064 1150-H7
18500 PWY 92064 1151-A6
DEER VIEW DR
10100 SDCo 92026 1089-D5
DEER WALK CT
- SDCo 91917 (1315-G5 See Page 1294)
- SDCo 91963 (1315-G5 See Page 1294)
DEER WALK RD
- SDCo 91963 (1315-G5 See Page 1294)
DEERWOOD CT
6700 SD 92120 1250-C3
DEERWOOD ST
14600 PWY 92064 1190-C1
14800 PWY 92064 1170-C7
DEFENDER CT
1000 SOLB 92014 1187-H1
DEFIANCE WY
4900 SD 92115 1270-A2
DEFREITAS AV
9200 SD 92129 1189-D3
DEGEN DR
3000 SDCo 91902 1290-J7
DEHESA CT
7500 CRLB 92009 1147-J1
DEHESA RD
1700 ELCJ 92019 1252-C6
1700 SDCo 92019 1252-G3
3700 SDCo 92019 1253-G3
7000 SDCo 91901 1253-G3
7600 SDCo 91901 1254-A3
DEHESA WY
300 SDCo 92021 1252-J4
DEHESA MEADOW RD
3500 SDCo 92019 1252-H7
DEHESA MOUNTAIN LN
500 SDCo 92021 1252-J5
DEHESA RANCH RD
1200 SDCo 92019 1253-F3
DEHIA ST
14500 PWY 92064 1190-H3
DEIT LN
1200 SDCo 92028 1027-H5
DE LA FUENTE CT
- SDCo 92154 1352-C1
DE LA GARZA RD
- SD 92145 1228-J2
- SD 92145 1229-A2
DE LA GARZA ST
- SDCo 92055 1023-E2
DELAGE CT
400 ENCT 92024 1167-G1
DELAGE DR
300 ENCT 92024 1167-G1
DEL AMO CT
16300 SDCo 92065 1173-E3
DEL AMO PL
24000 SDCo 92065 1173-E2
DEL AMO RD
23900 SDCo 92065 1173-E3
24500 SDCo 92065 1153-F7
DE LAND CT
700 ELCJ 92020 1271-E1
DELAND DR
2400 SDCo 91901 1254-B1
DELANE ST
1700 SDCo 92065 1152-E6
DELANEY CT
- CRLB 92008 1127-A1
DELANO AV
5600 SD 92120 1250-B6
DELANO CT
- CHV 91913 1311-C7
DELANY DR
2200 SD 92173 1350-G3
DELAPORT CT
- CORD 92118 1329-D3
DELAPORT LN
- CORD 92118 1329-D3
DELAPORT PL
- CORD 92118 1329-D3
DELAPORT WY
- CORD 92118 1329-D3
DE LA RONDO
100 OCN 92057 1087-A2
DE LA ROSA LN
6000 OCN 92057 1067-D3
DE LAS FLORES ST
500 CALX 92231 6620-E7
DE LA TOBA RD
700 CHV 91911 1330-J3
700 CHV 91911 1331-A3
DE LA VALLE PL
14800 SD 92014 1188-A1
14800 SDCo 92014 1188-A1
DELAWARE AV
6800 LMSA 91942 1270-E1
DELAWARE ST
300 IMPB 91932 1329-G7
900 IMPB 91932 1349-G1
4500 SD 92116 1269-B4
DELBARTON ST
6300 SD 92120 1249-J6
DELCARDO AV
600 SD 92154 1330-G7
DEL CERO AV
3600 OCN 92056 1107-C3
DEL CERRO AV
5600 SD 92120 1270-D1
5600 SD 92120 1250-D7
DEL CERRO BLVD
5400 SD 92120 1250-A7
6500 SD 92120 1270-E1
DEL CERRO CT
6300 SD 92120 1270-D1
DEL CHARRO RD
3300 SDCo 91935 1272-D7
DEL CIELO ESTE
5300 SDCo 92003 1048-B7
DEL CIELO OESTE
5000 SDCo 92003 1048-B7
DEL CORONADO LN
10300 SNTE 92071 1231-D2
DEL CORRO CT
500 CHV 91910 1310-G5
DEL CORRO PL
700 CHV 91910 1310-G5
DEL DIABLO LN
14900 SD 92129 1169-H7
14900 SD 92129 1189-H1
DEL DIABLO ST
11000 SD 92129 1189-H1
11200 SD 92129 1169-J7
DEL DIABLO WY
11100 SD 92129 1169-J7
DEL DIOS HWY Rt#-S6
500 SDCo 92029 1149-D2
500 SDCo 92067 1149-D6
1100 ESCN 92029 1129-F6
9800 ESCN 92029 1149-D2
9900 SDCo 92029 1129-F6
DEL DIOS RD
900 ESCN 92029 1129-F5
DE LEON AV
- CALX 92231 6620-H7
DELEON DR
1100 CHV 91910 1311-B7
DE LEONE RD
3500 SMCS 92069 1108-D5
DEL ESTE DR
- ESCN 92029 1129-F4
DEL ESTE WY
3400 OCN 92056 1107-C2
DELEVAN DR
1100 SD 92102 1289-F3
DELFERN ST
6500 SD 92120 1250-B6
DELFINA
- SD 92127 1168-J7
- SD 92127 1188-J1
DELFINA PL
3000 CRLB 92009 1147-H2
DEL FLORA ST
300 OCN 92054 1086-F1
DELGADO PL
800 ESCN 92025 1129-J5
7500 CRLB 92009 1147-J1
DELIA LN
9900 SNTE 92071 1231-F3
DELICIAS CT
100 SOLB 92075 1167-D7
DELIGHT ST
1400 ELCJ 92021 1252-B2
DELIGHT WY
1100 ESCN 92026 1109-J7
DELL CT
400 SOLB 92075 1167-F6
DELL ST
600 SOLB 92075 1167-F6
DELLA LN
1600 OCN 92054 1106-D1
DELLA PL
4900 SD 92117 1228-C7
DEL LAGO BLVD
- ESCN 92025 1150-A2
3200 ESCN 92029 1150-A2
DELL ANNE PL
800 SD 92114 1290-H2
DELLCREST LN
1300 SD 92037 1227-F7
DELLCREST WY
700 ESCN 92027 1130-C2
DELL RIM CT
7900 SD 92126 1209-A1
DELLTOP LN
2100 SDCo 91977 1271-D7
2100 SDCo 91977 1291-D1
DELL VIEW RD
15600 SDCo 92021 1233-C3
DELLWOOD ST
4100 SD 92111 1249-A3
DEL MAR AV
- CHV 91910 1310-B4
600 CHV 91910 1330-C1
800 CHV 91911 1330-C1
3700 SD 92106 1288-A1
3900 SD 92107 1288-A1
4300 SD 92107 1267-J7
4300 SD 92107 1268-A7
N DEL MAR AV
- CHV 91910 1310-B4
DEL MAR CT
400 CHV 91910 1310-C6
DEL MAR GN
3900 SD 92130 1188-A7
DEL MAR RD
1500 OCN 92057 1067-G6
DEL MAR DOWNS RD
800 DLMR 92014 1187-F2
800 SOLB 92075 1187-F2
DEL MAR HEIGHTS PL
12900 SD 92130 1188-A5
DEL MAR HEIGHTS RD
300 DLMR 92014 1187-H6
300 SD 92014 1187-H6
2800 SD 92130 1187-H6
3000 SD 92130 1188-D4
DEL MAR HILLS DR
13800 SD 92130 1187-J6
DEL MARINO AV
13500 PWY 92064 1190-H3
DEL MAR MEADOWS
3900 SD 92130 1188-A7
DEL MAR MESA RD
5100 SD 92130 1188-D7
DEL MAR OAKS
12300 SD 92130 1188-A7
DEL MAR SCENIC PKWY
2100 SD 92014 1207-G1
2300 SD 92014 1187-H7
DEL MAR SHORES TER
100 SOLB 92075 1187-E1
DEL MAR TRAILS RD
3900 SD 92130 1188-B7
DEL MESA CT
200 OCN 92054 1086-G1
DEL MESA ST
200 OCN 92054 1086-G1
DEL MONTE AV
100 CHV 91911 1330-D5
4200 SD 92107 1268-A7
4500 SD 92107 1267-J6
DEL NORTE
16000 PWY 92064 1170-D4
DELOR CT
6000 SD 92120 1249-J7
DELORES CT
- SMCS 92069 1109-B7
DEL ORO CT
8300 SD 92037 1227-H4
DEL ORO LN
1900 SDCo 92025 1130-C5
DELOS DR
7000 SD 92139 1290-F7
DELOS ST
2200 SD 92139 1290-F7
DELOS WY
4700 OCN 92056 1107-E6
DEL PASO AV
6100 SD 92120 1250-D6
DEL PASO CT
3600 OCN 92056 1107-D3
DEL PASO DR
17700 PWY 92064 1150-F7
17700 PWY 92064 1170-F1
DEL PASO PL
6800 SD 92120 1250-D5
DEL PENA CT
11100 SD 92128 1189-J4
DELPHI ST
9900 SNTE 92071 1231-F4
DELPHINIUM ST
100 ENCT 92024 1147-E6
DELPHINUS WY
11000 SD 92126 1209-D2
DEL PONIENTE CT
15200 PWY 92064 1170-F7
DEL PONIENTE RD
13500 PWY 92064 1170-E6
DEL PRADO CT
1100 CHV 91910 1331-A1
DEL PRADO ST
4800 SDCo 91902 1310-H3
DEL RAY PL
600 CHV 91910 1310-G7
600 CHV 91910 1330-H1
DEL REY AV
3000 CRLB 92009 1147-H1
DEL REY BLVD
700 CHV 91910 1310-G6
DEL REY ST
3400 SD 92109 1248-D5
DELRIDGE LN
26900 SDCo 92082 1091-F5
DEL RIEGO AV
700 ENCT 92024 1147-C4
DEL RIO AV
700 ENCT 92024 1147-C4
DEL RIO CT
1100 CHV 91910 1311-A7
3300 CRLB 92009 1147-J1
DEL RIO RD
10000 SDCo 91977 1271-D5
10200 SDCo 91978 1271-E5
DEL RIO WY
300 VSTA 92083 1087-G5
3500 SDCo 91978 1271-F5
DEL ROSA LN
1300 SDCo 92078 1128-B3
DELROSE AV
8800 SDCo 91977 1290-J3
DEL ROY DR
100 SMCS 92069 1108-H4
DEL SOL BLVD
3000 SD 92154 1350-D1
DEL SOL CT
4200 SD 92154 1350-G1
DEL SOL LN
1200 SD 92154 1350-E1
DEL SOL RD
12500 SDCo 92040 1232-B5
DEL SOL WY
1200 SD 92154 1350-G1
DEL SUR BLVD
1200 SD 92154 1350-E2
1500 SD 92173 1350-E2
DEL SUR CT
- SD 92127 1169-B5
1100 CHV 91910 1331-A1
DEL SURENO
100 SDCo 92028 1027-H2
DELTA LN
300 VSTA 92083 1087-F7
DELTA RD
- SD 92126 1209-C7
DELTA ST
1700 NATC 91950 1289-J6
1700 NATC 91950 1290-A6
3800 SD 92113 1289-G6
4600 SD 91950 1289-J6
8700 LMSA 91942 1250-J7
8700 LMSA 91942 1251-A7
DELTA WY
- CRLB 92010 1107-B3
DE LUZ RD
700 SDCo 92028 1027-F1
800 SDCo 92028 997-A6
800 SDCo 92055 997-A6
25000 SDCo 92028 996-G3
38800 SDCo 92055 996-G3
DE LUZ HEIGHTS DR
2500 SDCo 92028 997-C2
DE LUZ HEIGHTS RD
- SDCo 92028 997-E3
DE LUZ MURRIETA RD
35900 SDCo 92028 996-G1
39800 SDCo 92028 409-B4
DEL VALLE DR
200 SDCo 92028 1047-F5
DEL VINO CT
- SD 92130 1188-G7
DEL VISTA WY
16300 SDCo 92021 1233-F3
DE MAYO RD
2000 DLMR 92014 1187-G6

STREET
Block City ZIP Pg-Grid

DE MAYO RD
2000 SD 92014 1187-G6
DEMETER WY
2900 SD 92139 1310-E2
4800 OCN 92056 1107-E6
DEMONA PL
100 SDCo 91977 1290-J5
DE MOTT LN
9000 SNTE 92071 1231-A7
DEMPSTER DR
9300 SNTE 92071 1230-H6
DEMUS ST
3800 SD 92115 1270-C5
DENARA RD
13200 SD 92130 1187-J5
DENBY ST
400 SD 92102 1289-H3
DENDIA WY
1300 SDCo 92020 1272-A1
DENDY SKY LN
- SDCo 92082 1069-D4
DENIA WY
4700 OCN 92056 1107-F4
DENISE CIR
1400 OCN 92054 1106-E1
DENISE CT
1000 SMCS 92078 1129-B4
DENISE LN
700 ELCJ 92020 1251-G7
DENISE CANYON CT
3800 SDCo 91902 1311-A3
DENISON WY
300 SDCo 92084 1087-G1
DENK LN
- ENCT 92024 1167-J1
DENNERY RD
600 SD 92154 1330-J6
600 SD 92154 1350-H1
DENNIG PL
11300 SD 92126 1208-J2
DENNING DR
- CRLB 92009 1128-B7
- CRLB 92009 1148-C1
- SDCo 92024 1128-C7
- SDCo 92024 1148-C1
- SMCS 92024 1128-C7
DENNIS AV
600 CHV 91910 1310-E7
DENNIS CT
- IMP 92251 6499-H2
DENNIS DR
2200 SDCo 92083 1108-B4
2200 VSTA 92083 1108-B4
DENNIS LN
2700 LMGR 91945 1270-J7
DENNISON PL
7100 SD 92122 1228-D4
DENNISON ST
6300 SD 92122 1228-D4
DENNSTEDT CT
1000 ELCJ 92020 1251-D7
DENNSTEDT PL
900 ELCJ 92020 1251-C7
DENNY WY
100 SDCo 92020 1251-F2
DENOVA DR
2300 SDCo 91901 1253-H2
DENSTONE PL
1700 LMGR 91945 1290-E1
DENT CT
8600 SD 92119 1250-J3
DENT DR
8600 SD 92119 1250-J3
8600 SD 92119 1251-A3
DENTON ST
8400 LMSA 91942 1250-J6
DENTRO DE LOMAS
2700 SDCo 92084 1068-E5
DENTRO DE LOMAS RD
1500 SDCo 92003 1067-J3
1500 SDCo 92003 1068-A3
DENVER DR
- LMSA 91941 1270-G5
DENVER LN
1100 ELCJ 92021 1251-H3
DENVER ST
1800 SD 92110 1268-E1
2200 SD 92110 1248-E7
2700 SD 92117 1248-E6
DENWOOD RD
4600 LMSA 91941 1270-G3
DEODAR DR
- ELCJ 92019 1251-J6
DEODAR RD
700 SMCS 92069 1129-F1
700 SDCo 92026 1129-F1
1100 ESCN 92026 1109-F7
1100 ESCN 92026 1129-F1
DEODAR TR
7600 SDCo 91962 1237-B7
DE PAOLI ST
- IMP 92251 6499-H2
DEPRISE CV
- SD 92131 1210-G2
- SD 92145 1210-G2
DERALD RD
9600 SNTE 92071 1231-A4
DERBY CT
5700 OCN 92057 1067-G7
DERBY ST
900 SD 92114 1290-B3
DERBY BLUFFS WY
3700 SD 92130 1188-A4
DERBY DOWNS CT
- SD 92130 1188-A4
DERBY DOWNS RD
3700 SD 92130 1188-A4
DERBY FARMS RD
4300 SD 92130 1188-D2
4600 SD 92130 1188-D2
DERBY HILL PT
- SD 92130 1208-D2
DEREK WY
1600 CHV 91911 1330-G5
DERK DR
5700 LMSA 91942 1250-J7
DERMID RD
29800 SDCo 92082 1070-C5
DERON AV
13100 SD 92129 1189-D4
DERRICK CT
5100 SD 92117 1248-G1
DERRICK DR
4300 SD 92117 1248-G2
DERRICK RD
1800 ImCo 92243 430-L6
DERRICK WY
2200 ESCN 92029 1129-H7
DERRINGER PL
2700 ESCN 92027 1110-D6
DERRINGER RD
14800 PWY 92064 1170-G7
14800 PWY 92064 1190-F1

DERRYDOWN WY
10900 SD 92130 1208-D1
DESCANSO AV
- IMPB 91932 1349-E2
1300 SMCS 92069 1108-E6
1600 SMCS 92078 1108-E6
DESCANSO LN
2400 SDCo 92021 1252-H4
DESCANSO TR
- SDCo 91916 429-K4
DESCANSO CREEK PL
1200 CHV 91915 1311-H6
DESERET RD
10200 SDCo 92065 1049-D2
DESERT DR
3800 SDCo 92004 (1099-F1 See Page 1098)
DESERT GN
1600 ESCN 92026 1109-D6
DESERT RD
- ImCo - 431-F6
- ImCo 92250 431-F6
DESERT GARDENS DR
400 ELCN 92243 6559-E1
DESERT INN WY
3500 CHV 91902 1310-G2
DESERT ORIOLE DR
4600 SDCo 92004 (1099-G5 See Page 1098)
DESERT ROSE CT
- IMP 92251 6499-E2
DESERT ROSE LN
1700 CHV 91915 1331-H2
DESERT ROSE WY
1000 CRLB 92009 1148-A5
1000 ENCT 92024 1148-A5
DESERT ROSE RANCH RD
- SDCo 91934 (1321-C3 See Page 1300)
DESERTVIEW AV
- ELCN 92243 6559-G4
DESERT VIEW DR
5600 SD 92037 1248-A2
DESERT VISTA DR
4400 SDCo 92004 (1099-F4 See Page 1098)
DESERT VISTA TER
- SDCo 92004 (1099-F4 See Page 1098)
DESIGN CT
700 CHV 91911 1330-J5
DESIREE LN
8400 ELCJ 92020 1251-C1
8400 SNTE 92071 1251-C1
DESMOND CIR
4600 OCN 92056 1107-F3
DE SOLA ST
- SDCo 92127 1169-F4
DESOTO CT
1100 CHV 91910 1311-B7
4200 SDCo 91941 1271-G4
DE SOTO PL
19200 SDCo 92029 1149-E4
DE SOTO ST
4600 SD 92109 1248-C4
DESPEJO PL
5800 SD 92124 1229-H7
DESTINY WY
1100 OCN 92056 1087-B4
DESTINY MOUNTAIN CT
- SDCo 91978 1291-F2
DESTREE RD
1100 ESCN 92027 1130-C3
1100 SDCo 92027 1130-C3
DESTY CT
2600 SD 92154 1330-C7
DESTY ST
700 SD 92154 1330-C7
DETRICH WY
- SDCo 92036 1155-H3
DETROIT PL
400 SD 92114 1290-D5
DETWILER RD
8800 SDCo 92029 1149-B4
DEVELBISS ST
400 NATC 92136 1309-F1
DEVEREUX RD
17500 SD 92128 1170-A1
17600 SD 92128 1150-A7
DEVERILL DR
14500 SDCo 92021 1232-H4
DE VIDA CT
10900 SD 92124 1249-J2
DEVILLE DR
7400 LMGR 91945 1290-G2
7500 SD 92114 1290-G2
DEVIN DR
- SDCo 92028 1027-J5
DEVINEY LN
1500 SDCo 92065 1172-G5
DEVON CT
- SDCo 91935 1272-F5
700 SD 92109 1267-H3
DEVON DR
- SDCo 91935 1272-E5
DEVON PL
- ESCN 92025 1129-J5
1600 SDCo 92084 1108-C3
DEVONSHIRE DR
900 ENCT 92024 1147-C7
900 ENCT 92024 1167-C1
1000 SD 92107 1287-H1
DEVONSHIRE GN
400 ESCN 92027 1110-D6
DEVONSHIRE RD
1000 ENCT 92024 1167-C1
DE VOS DR
8400 SNTE 92071 1230-J6
DEWANE DR
200 ELCJ 92020 1251-D4
DEWES WY
4100 SD 92117 1248-E6
DEWEY PL
1300 SDCo 91906 (1318-A5 See Page 1298)
DEWEY RD
- SD 92106 1268-D7
DEWEY ST
300 SD 92113 1289-C5
1200 NATC 92136 1309-F3
DEWITT AV
700 ENCT 92024 1147-C7
1000 ENCT 92024 1167-C1
DEWITT CT
100 ELCJ 92020 1271-G2
100 SDCo 91941 1271-G2
DEWITT ESTATES RD
1600 SDCo 91901 1253-J1
1700 SDCo 91901 1254-A1
DEW POINT AV
- CRLB 92011 1126-J7
DEWSBURY AV
8700 SD 92126 1209-C3

DEXTER DR
4000 LMSA 91941 1270-J4
8500 SDCo 91941 1270-J4
DEXTER PL
1100 ESCN 92029 1129-G7
1100 SDCo 92029 1129-G7
DIABLO PL
1200 VSTA 92081 1107-E1
DIABLO POINT CT
1500 CHV 91911 1330-J3
DIA DEL SOL
16200 SDCo 92082 1071-B7
DIAMANTE WY
- OCN 92056 1106-J2
DIAMOND
14100 SDCo 92040 1232-H5
DIAMOND CIR
4100 OCN 92056 1087-C6
DIAMOND CT
1100 CHV 91911 1330-H1
DIAMOND DR
600 CHV 91911 1330-H1
1100 SDCo 92065 1172-H1
DIAMOND GN
- ESCN 92027 1110-D7
DIAMOND LN
1300 SDCo 92021 1251-H2
1400 ELCJ 92021 1251-H2
DIAMOND ST
600 SD 92109 1247-H6
1500 SD 92109 1248-A5
1800 SMCS 92078 1128-B5
DIAMOND WY
600 VSTA 92083 1087-F7
DIAMONDBACK DR
- SNTE 92071 1231-G6
DIAMOND BAR RD
600 SDCo 92004 (1078-J3 See Page 1058)
700 SDCo 92004 (1079-A3 See Page 1058)
DIAMOND GEM LN
3200 SDCo 91935 1273-F7
3200 SDCo 91935 1293-F1
DIAMOND HEAD CT
10100 SDCo 91977 1291-D2
DIAMOND HEAD DR
1300 ENCT 92024 1167-F1
DIAMOND RANCH RD
- SDCo 92027 1130-F5
DIANA ST
100 ENCT 92024 1147-A4
DIANE AV
4600 SD 92117 1248-F1
4900 SD 92117 1228-G7
9400 SDCo 91977 1271-B6
DIANE CT
4900 SD 92117 1228-G7
DIANE DR
8700 SNTE 92071 1231-F7
DIANE PL
600 ESCN 92026 1109-J7
4900 SD 92117 1228-G6
DIANE WY
4500 SD 92117 1248-F1
DIAZ DR
16600 SD 92128 1170-C3
DIAZ GN
2700 ESCN 92027 1110-E7
DIAZ RD
30500 SDCo 92082 1069-E3
30600 SDCo 92026 1069-E3
DICENZA LN
8000 SD 92119 1250-E3
DICENZA WY
6700 SD 92119 1250-E3
DICHONDRA CT
9900 SD 92131 1209-J5
DICHONDRA PL
9900 SD 92131 1209-H4
DICHOSO DR
1600 ESCN 92025 1130-B4
DICHTER ST
300 ELCJ 92019 1252-B6
DICK ST
4900 SD 92115 1270-A3
DICKENS ST
2800 SD 92106 1288-B2
DICKERMAN RD
- ImCo 92227 431-D1
DICKEY DR
4500 SDCo 91941 1271-E3
DICKEY ST
1600 SDCo 92028 1028-A5
DICKINSON DR
- CRLB 92008 1107-A7
- CRLB 92008 1127-A1
DICKINSON ST
100 SD 92103 1269-A4
2600 SD 92103 1268-J4
DIEGO DR
16700 SD 92128 1170-A3
DIEGOS CT
4300 SDCo 92028 1028-H7
4300 SDCo 92028 1048-H1
DIEGUENO RD
- SDCo 92004 1058-H6
2000 SDCo 92004 (1078-H1 See Page 1058)
DIEHL RD
- ImCo 92243 431-A6
2100 ImCo 92243 430-L6
DIESEL DR
1800 SD 92019 1252-C4
DIETRICH RD
- ImCo 92227 431-C1
5300 ImCo 92227 411-C11
DI FOSS ST
2300 LMGR 91945 1270-H7
DI GIORGIO RD
- SDCo 92004 410-C6
- SDCo 92004 (1099-B1 See Page 1098)
800 SDCo 92004 (1059-A1 See Page 1058)
2300 SDCo 92004 (1079-A1 See Page 1058)
DILLARD ST
1500 SD 92114 1290-D6
DILLON DR
9100 LMSA 91941 1271-B2
9100 SDCo 91941 1271-B2
DILLON RD
15200 SDCo 92021 1233-B2
DILLON WY
4100 SD 92117 1248-E6
DILLONS TR
1100 SD 92154 1351-A3
DILMAN ST
300 SDCo 92019 1252-B6
400 ELCJ 92019 1252-B6
DIMAIO PL
- ESCN 92027 1110-D5

DI MARINO ST
900 SD 92114 1290-F2
DINAMICA WY
2400 VSTA 92081 1108-B6
DINARA DR
2300 SDCo 92029 1129-D3
DI NOVO ST
7100 SD 92114 1290-F2
DIPPER ST
6000 SD 92114 1290-C2
DIPPONS LN
2200 ESCN 92027 1110-C5
DIRAC ST
5800 SD 92122 1228-E6
DIRECTORS PL
- SD 92121 1208-D6
DISCOVERY RD
- CRLB 92009 1127-F2
DISCOVERY ST
300 SMCS 92078 1128-G1
DISCOVERY WY
8600 SD 92093 1227-J3
DISCOVERY BAY DR
1200 CHV 91915 1311-G6
DISCOVERY FALLS DR
- CHV 91915 1331-G1
DISNEY LN
29800 SDCo 92084 1068-E4
DISSINGER AV
6300 SD 92139 1310-E1
DISTRIBUTION AV
9500 SD 92121 1228-J1
9700 SD 92121 1208-J7
DISTRIBUTION ST
200 SMCS 92078 1129-A1
DISTRIBUTION WY
1400 VSTA 92081 1107-J6
N DITMAR ST
100 OCN 92054 1086-A7
S DITMAR ST
100 OCN 92054 1086-A7
200 OCN 92054 1106-B1
DIVELLOS DR
- SDCo 91901 1233-E4
DIVERSEY DR
13300 PWY 92064 1190-G4
DIVERSION DR
3400 SDCo 91977 1271-E6
DIVINE WY
4700 SDCo 91941 1271-D3
DIVISION ST
- SD 92113 1289-G7
- NATC 91950 1289-J7
200 OCN 92054 1086-B7
1700 NATC 91950 1290-A7
3700 NATC 92136 1289-G7
3700 SD 92136 1289-G7
5400 SD 92114 1290-C6
DI VITA DR
- CRLB 92009 1127-G3
DIXIE DR
4800 SD 92109 1247-H5
6100 LMSA 91942 1251-B6
DIXIE LN
- SDCo 92127 1168-J1
DIXIE ST
1700 OCN 92054 1086-C7
DIXON CT
1300 CHV 91911 1330-E3
DIXON DR
1100 CHV 91911 1330-E2
DIXON LN
- ESCN 92025 1130-A6
DIXON PL
3700 SD 92107 1288-A1
DIXON RD
5200 OCN 92056 1087-E1
DIXON WY
1200 CHV 91911 1330-E3
DIZA RD
100 SD 92173 1350-G2
D MERCADO ST
1000 CALX 92231 6680-E1
DOBYNS DR
8500 SNTE 92071 1231-A7
8500 SNTE 92071 1251-A1
DOCENA DR
8400 SDCo 91977 1290-J5
DOCENA RD
- CRLB 92011 1127-C5
DOCK CT
6900 SD 92139 1290-F7
DOCK ST
- SD 92152 1288-A5
DOCKSIDE ST
5900 SD 92139 1290-D7
DODD LN
- SDCo 91906 (1318-B7 See Page 1298)
DODDER CT
13800 PWY 92064 1170-F5
DODGE DR
700 SD 92037 1247-F3
DODIE ST
8100 SD 92114 1290-G2
DODSON ST
300 SD 92102 1289-E4
DOE PT
8100 SD 92120 1250-D3
DOGWOOD
9800 SDCo 92021 1233-B3
DOGWOOD CT
4500 OCN 92056 1087-D4
15800 PWY 92064 1170-G4
DOGWOOD GN
- SDCo 92026 1089-F4
DOGWOOD LN
9800 SDCo 92026 1089-D4
DOGWOOD PL
2100 ESCN 92026 1109-G4
DOGWOOD RD
- CRLB 92009 1127-F3
15800 PWY 92064 1170-G4
DOGWOOD RD Rt#-S31
- ImCo 92249 431-C7
- ImCo 92249 6560-B5
- ImCo 92249 6620-B1
- IMP 92251 6500-A2
200 BRW 92227 431-B3
400 ImCo 92231 431-C7
400 ImCo 92231 6620-B4
400 ImCo 92231 6680-B1
1300 ImCo 92243 6560-B5
1300 ELCN 92243 6560-B2
1700 ELCN 92243 6500-A5
2100 ELCN 92243 6500-A2
2100 ImCo 92243 6500-A2
2800 ImCo 92251 431-B3
3600 ImCo 92227 431-B3
DOGWOOD ST
6800 SD 92115 1270-E4
DOGWOOD TR
- SDCo 92060 1052-E2

DOGWOOD WY
- SD 92130 1188-G3
2400 VSTA 92081 1108-B6
DOHENY RD
9400 SNTE 92071 1231-B5
DOHENY BAY CT
4800 OCN 92057 1066-J6
DOLAN PL
3200 SDCo 91902 1310-H1
DOLE WY
- SMCS 92078 1128-H3
DOLIVA DR
4600 SD 92117 1248-H1
DOLLAR CT
10800 SDCo 92040 1232-B1
DOLLIMORE RD
300 ENCT 92024 1147-C6
DOLLY PL
9000 SD 92123 1249-D6
DOLO ST
200 SD 92114 1290-F4
DOLORE PL
1400 ESCN 92027 1110-A6
DOLORES CT
500 SDCo 92065 1152-G5
DOLORES DR
3200 SDCo 92036 1156-E1
DOLORES ST
9900 SDCo 91977 1271-D5
DOLPHIN AL
- SD 92136 1289-E6
DOLPHIN CIR
1200 VSTA 92084 1088-B4
DOLPHIN CT
- SMCS 92078 1128-D6
DOLPHIN CV
200 DLMR 92014 1187-G7
DOLPHIN DR
- ImCo 92274 410-H6
DOLPHIN LN
- OCN 92054 1086-E1
DOLPHIN PL
5600 SD 92037 1247-F4
DOLPHIN RD
- SDCo 92055 1085-H6
DOLSTRA LN
900 SDCo 92028 1027-G1
DOMER RD
9400 SNTE 92071 1231-B4
DOMINGO GN
2100 ESCN 92026 1109-E3
DOMINGUEZ WY
300 ELCJ 92021 1251-H5
DOMINICAN DR
16800 SD 92128 1170-B3
DOMINION ST
800 SD 92113 1289-H5
DOMINO DR
9600 SDCo 92040 1232-D4
DON CT
1100 SD 92154 1350-E1
DON WY
4200 SD 92117 1248-E2
DONAHOE ST
- CHV 91911 1330-E1
DONAHUE DR
1800 SDCo 92019 1272-C3
DONAHUE ST
1000 SD 92110 1268-G3
DONAKER ST
8600 SD 92129 1189-B2
DON ALBERTO DR
3400 CRLB 92010 1107-C6
DONALD AV
4300 SD 92117 1248-E2
DONALD CT
4100 SD 92117 1248-E3
N DONALD WY
1200 ESCN 92027 1110-B6
DONALDSON DR
4500 SD 92109 1248-B5
DONALOR DR
1600 SDCo 92027 1130-D2
1700 ESCN 92027 1130-D2
DON ALVAREZ DR
3200 CRLB 92010 1107-B6
DONART DR
14000 PWY 92064 1190-G2
DON ARTURO DR
3400 CRLB 92010 1107-B6
DONAX AV
100 IMPB 91932 1329-F7
1300 IMPB 92154 1329-J7
1300 SD 92154 1329-J7
1700 SD 92154 1330-A7
DONAX CT
1500 SD 92154 1329-J7
DON CARLOS CT
- CHV 91910 1311-B6
DON CARLOS DR
3400 CRLB 92010 1107-C6
DONCAROL AV
1500 ELCJ 92019 1252-B6
DON COTA DR
3400 CRLB 92010 1107-B6
DON DIABLO DR
3300 CRLB 92010 1107-C7
DONEE DIEGO
3100 SDCo 92025 1150-E1
DON FELIPE DR
5400 CRLB 92010 1107-C6
DONITA DR
1500 SDCo 92020 1271-H1
DON JOSE DR
3400 CRLB 92010 1107-B6
DON JUAN DR
2900 CRLB 92010 1107-C6
DON LEE PL
1800 ESCN 92029 1129-D2
DONLEY ST
3200 SD 92117 1248-E6
DON LORENZO DR
3400 CRLB 92010 1107-C6
3500 SD 92117 1248-D4
DON LUIS DR
5400 CRLB 92010 1107-C6
DON MATA DR
5100 CRLB 92010 1107-B6
DON MIGUEL DR
5100 CRLB 92010 1107-B7
DONNA AV
3900 SD 92115 1270-E5
DONNA CT
3700 CRLB 92008 1106-G5
DONNA DR
3200 CRLB 92008 1106-G4
DONNA ST
8700 SNTE 92071 1231-E7
DONNA WY
6800 SD 92115 1270-E4
DONNAJEAN LN
8800 SNTE 92071 1231-E6
DONNALEE LN
9000 SNTE 92071 1231-A7

DONNAN PL
900 VSTA 92084 1088-A5
DONNER ST
9900 SNTE 92071 1231-F4
DONNIL LN
2300 SDCo 92028 996-J4
2300 SDCo 92028 997-A4
DONNINGTON WY
2300 SD 92139 1290-G7
DON ORTEGA DR
3400 CRLB 92010 1107-C6
DONOVAN STATE PRISON RD
2200 SDCo 92154 1332-B7
DON PABLO DR
3300 CRLB 92010 1107-B7
DON PANCHO WY
3000 SD 92173 1350-D3
DON PICO CT
10300 SDCo 91978 1271-E6
DON PICO RD
10200 SDCo 91978 1271-E6
DON PORFIRIO DR
5100 CRLB 92010 1107-B6
DON QUIXOTE DR
3300 CRLB 92010 1107-B7
DONRAY DR
700 SDCo 92065 1172-H1
DON RICARDO DR
5200 CRLB 92010 1107-B6
DON RODOLFO DR
5100 CRLB 92010 1107-B6
DON ROLANDO
3000 SDCo 92025 1150-E1
DONS WY
2100 SDCo 92084 1088-C7
DON TOMASO DR
3300 CRLB 92010 1107-C7
DON VALDEZ DR
5200 CRLB 92010 1107-B7
DONZEE ST
3400 SD 92123 1249-B5
DOOL AV
300 CALX 92231 6680-H2
DOOLITTLE AV
500 SD 92154 1330-E6
DOOMEY DR
1100 SDCo 92065 1152-E4
DORA DR
1700 ENCT 92007 1167-F3
DORADO CT
1000 CHV 91910 1311-A7
7900 SD 92037 1227-H5
DORADO LN
200 ELCJ 92019 1252-A5
DORADO PL
3300 CRLB 92009 1147-J1
DORADO WY
1000 CHV 91910 1311-A7
DORAL CT
4600 OCN 92057 1086-J1
4600 OCN 92057 1087-A1
DORAL GN
1700 ESCN 92026 1109-D4
DORAL WY
4000 CHV 91902 1310-F3
DORAN CT
- CHV 91910 1310-C4
DORAN ST
1800 SD 92154 1350-B3
DORATHEA TER
12900 PWY 92064 1190-B5
DORA VISTA LN
3000 SDCo 91935 1292-J1
DORCAS ST
1100 SD 92110 1268-F2
DORCHESTER DR
3300 SD 92123 1249-E4
DORCHESTER PL
4400 CRLB 92010 1106-J5
DORCHESTER ST
8100 SDCo 91977 1290-H2
DOREEN LN
2100 SDCo 92069 1108-G1
DOREEN RD
8200 SD 92120 1250-D3
DOREET WY
2900 CRLB 92008 1106-G3
DORENA CT
4900 SD 92122 1228-G5
DORIA WY
2900 SD 92139 1310-E2
DORIANA ST
6700 SD 92139 1290-F7
DORINDA CT
1500 SD 92154 1350-D2
DORINDA DR
600 OCN 92057 1087-B1
DORIS DR
700 ENCT 92024 1147-F7
900 ENCT 92024 1167-F1
DORIS ST
1800 SD 92154 1330-A7
DORIS JEAN PL
1600 VSTA 92083 1087-D7
DORM WY
2500 SDCo 91977 1271-D7
DORMAE LN
100 SDCo 92021 1252-J2
DORMAN DR
5100 SD 92115 1270-A1
DORMOUSE CT
7900 SD 92129 1189-A6
DORMOUSE RD
12100 SD 92129 1189-A6
DORNOCH CT
1700 SD 92154 1352-A2
DOROTHEA AV
700 SMCS 92069 1109-B6
1500 SDCo 92028 1027-J5
1600 SDCo 92028 1028-A5
DOROTHY AV
- SDCo 91905 1300-C7
DOROTHY CT
200 ESCN 92027 1130-D1
DOROTHY DR
5400 SD 92115 1270-B2
DOROTHY LN
16000 SDCo 92082 1071-B5
DOROTHY ST
400 ELCJ 92019 1252-A6
700 CHV 91911 1330-A5
DOROTHY WY
5600 SD 92115 1270-B2
DORSAL DR
9600 SDCo 92040 1232-D3
DORSET WY
13000 PWY 92064 1170-E2
DORSEY WY
200 VSTA 92083 1087-G4
DORSIE LN
3900 SDCo 91941 1271-H4
DORTHA CT
8500 SNTE 92071 1230-J7

DORTMUND PL
2500 SDCo 91901 1253-G2
DORY DR
3500 SDCo 91902 1310-J1
DORY LN
- CRLB 92011 1126-J7
DOS AMIGOS TR
13800 PWY 92064 1190-J3
DOS AMIGOS WY
17000 PWY 92064 1190-J3
DOS ARRONS WY
2700 VSTA 92081 1108-A7
DOS CABAZOS PL
- ESCN 92029 1149-J2
- ESCN 92029 1150-A3
DOS CABEZA RD
- ImCo 92259 430-F7
- SDCo 92259 430-F7
DOS CAMEOS DR
38400 SDCo 92028 997-C5
DOS HERMANOS GN
1200 ESCN 92027 1110-B5
DOS HERMANOS RD
17100 PWY 92064 1191-D2
DOS LOMAS
2500 SDCo 92028 1048-C1
DOS LOMAS PL
2900 SDCo 92028 1048-C2
DOS NINAS
32100 SDCo 92003 1048-H7
DOS NINOS RD
3700 SDCo 92028 1028-E5
DOS PICOS PARK RD
17500 SDCo 92065 1171-H5
DOTI POINT DR
6700 SD 92139 1290-F7
DOUBLE BRIDLE TER
- SD 92130 1208-C2
DOUBLE CANYON RD
32700 SDCo 92082 1049-C2
33300 SDCo 92059 1049-C2
DOUBLE D DR
1800 ELCJ 92021 1252-C3
1800 SDCo 92021 1252-C3
DOUBLE EAGLE GN
- ESCN 92026 1109-H4
DOUBLE K RD
28400 SDCo 92082 1089-J1
28800 SDCo 92082 1069-J7
DOUBLE LL RANCH RD
2300 ENCT 92024 1148-B4
DOUBLE LYNN LN
- SDCo 91935 1274-B7
DOUBLE M RD
8600 SNTE 92071 1231-B7
DOUBLE O RD
2600 SDCo 92004 (1079-A3 See Page 1058)
DOUBLE PEAK DR
- SMCS 92078 1128-F5
DOUBLETREE RD
2200 SDCo 91978 1291-G1
2300 SDCo 91978 1271-G7
DOUGHERTY ST
100 SDCo 92028 1027-F2
W DOUGHERTY ST
200 SDCo 92028 1027-F2
DOUG HILL
- SD 92127 1168-J7
- SD 92127 1169-A7
- SD 92127 1189-A1
DOUG HILL CT
- SD 92127 1168-J7
- SD 92127 1169-A7
- SD 92127 1188-J1
DOUGLAS AV
600 SMCS 92069 1109-D6
E DOUGLAS AV
100 ELCJ 92020 1251-F5
W DOUGLAS AV
100 ELCJ 92020 1251-F5
DOUGLAS DR
100 OCN 92057 1086-G3
100 OCN 92054 1086-G3
300 OCN 92054 1066-G7
800 OCN 92057 1066-H6
1300 VSTA 92084 1088-A2
5000 OCN 92057 1067-A3
N DOUGLAS DR
100 OCN 92054 1086-G2
200 OCN 92057 1086-G2
600 OCN 92054 1066-G7
600 OCN 92057 1066-G7
DOUGLAS ST
500 CHV 91910 1310-G7
DOUGLASTON GN
- ESCN 92026 1109-H3
DOVARY RD
200 SDCo 91910 1310-D6
DOVE AV
29900 SDCo 91906 (1297-F6 See Page 1296)
DOVE CIR
500 VSTA 92083 1087-F5
DOVE CT
- ImCo 92249 6560-B7
3500 SD 92103 1268-J6
DOVE LN
1700 CRLB 92011 1127-E5
1800 CRLB 92009 1127-E5
DOVE ST
1300 ELCJ 92020 1251-D3
2600 SD 92103 1288-J1
2700 SD 92103 1268-J6
7700 SNTE 92071 1230-G7
DOVE CANYON RD
- SDCo 92127 1169-F4
DOVE CREEK RD
- SDCo 92127 1169-E5
DOVECREST CT
3100 SDCo 91977 1271-A6
DOVECREST PL
- CHV 91914 1311-H3
DOVE FLOWER WY
6000 SD 92115 1270-C6
DOVE HILL DR
8600 SNTE 92071 1231-A7
DOVE HOLLOW RD
3200 ENCT 92024 1148-C4
DOVER CT
700 SD 92109 1267-J3
800 CHV 91910 1310-G7
800 SMCS 92078 1128-F2
DOVER ST
1400 OCN 92057 1067-A3
DOVER WY
4500 CRLB 92010 1107-B5
DOVERHILL RD
11000 SD 92131 1209-J2
DOVE RUN RD
1100 ENCT 92024 1148-A5
DOVE SONG WY
- ENCT 92024 1148-A5

STREET	Block	City	ZIP	Pg-Grid
DOVE TAIL DR				
	-	SMCS	92024	1128-B7
	-	SMCS	92078	1128-B7
DOVE TAIL TER				
	11000	SD	92128	1189-H4
DOVEVIEW CT				
	3500	SDCo	91977	1271-C5
DOVEWOOD CT				
	15700	PWY	92064	1170-F5
DOW PL				
	3000	SD	92117	1248-C1
DOW ST				
	-	SD	92152	1287-J4
DOWDEN RD				
	600	ImCo	92233	411-C10
DOWDY DR				
	9300	SD	92126	1209-B7
DOWITCHER CT				
	1100	CRLB	92011	1127-A4
DOWITCHER WY				
	4200	OCN	92057	1087-A3
	4200	OCN	92057	1086-J3
DOWLING DR				
	6300	SD	92037	1247-F2
DOWLING LN				
	32100	SDCo	92082	1049-J7
	32100	SDCo	92082	1050-A6
DOWNER AV				
	500	ELCJ	92020	1251-E7
DOWNEY CT				
	900	CHV	91911	1330-J2
	900	CHV	91911	1331-A2
DOWNING LN				
	-	SD	92131	1210-D2
DOWNING ST				
	1100	IMPB	91932	1349-G1
DOWN MEMORY LN				
	-	SDCo	92127	1169-A2
DOWNS ST				
	1200	OCN	92054	1086-D7
	1300	OCN	92054	1106-E1
DOWNWIND WY				
	2300	SD	92093	1227-H3
DOYLE ST				
	400	NATC	92136	1289-G7
	400	NATC	92136	1309-G1
	400	SD	92136	1289-G7
DRACAENA CT				
	6100	SD	92114	1290-C6
DRACMA DR				
	1000	SD	92154	1330-C7
	1000	SD	92154	1350-C1
DRACO RD				
	10900	SD	92126	1209-D3
DRAGONFLY ST				
	-	CHV	91915	1331-H1
DRAGOYE DR				
	9700	SNTE	92071	1231-C4
DRAGT PL				
	1000	ESCN	92029	1129-F4
DRAKE BAY				
	300	OCN	92057	1066-H6
DRAKE CT				
	1500	CHV	91902	1311-C4
DRAKE ST				
	6700	SD	92114	1290-E3
DRAKEWOOD TER				
	4800	SD	92130	1188-C4
DR AMALIA ST				
	-	CALX	92231	6680-J2
DRAPER AV				
	6600	SD	92037	1247-F1
	7300	SD	92037	1227-E7
DRAYTON HALL WY				
	17400	SD	92128	1170-A1
	17500	SD	92128	1150-A7
DRAZIL RD				
	1100	SDCo	92028	1027-H5
DREAM ST				
	5500	SD	92114	1290-B4
DRELL CT				
	1500	ELCJ	92021	1251-H2
DRESCHER ST				
	1800	SD	92111	1268-J1
W DRESCHER ST				
	1700	SD	92111	1268-H1
DRESDEN PL				
	2400	SD	92037	1248-B3
DRESSAGE DR				
	5300	SDCo	91902	1311-A2
	5300	SDCo	91902	1310-J2
DRESSAGE LN				
	-	SD	92130	1188-E5
DREW LN				
	2700	LMGR	91945	1270-F7
DREW RD				
	2000	ESCN	92027	1110-B5
DREW RD Rt#-S29				
	-	ImCo	92273	431-A7
	400	ImCo	92231	431-A7
	400	ImCo	92243	431-A7
DREW VIEW LN				
	500	SD	92113	1290-A5
DREXEL AV				
	-	NATC	91950	1290-B6
N DREXEL AV				
	-	NATC	91950	1290-B6
	-	SD	92114	1290-B6
DREXEL CT				
	8000	LMGR	91945	1290-H1
DREXEL DR				
	1500	LMGR	91945	1290-H1
	1500	SDCo	91977	1290-H2
DREXEL LN				
	-	LMGR	91945	1290-H2
DRIFTING LN				
	-	CHV	91915	1331-H2
DRIFTING CIRCLE DR				
	1000	VSTA	92081	1107-G2
DRIFTWOOD CIR				
	1800	CRLB	92008	1106-J6
DRIFTWOOD CT				
	-	VSTA	92083	1087-D7
	3200	SD	92037	1228-B4
DRIFTWOOD DR				
	100	ELCN	92243	6559-F1
	10600	SD	92126	1209-E3
DRIFTWOOD LN				
	700	SDCo	92028	1027-G3
DRIFTWOOD PL				
	3500	OCN	92056	1107-C2
DRIFTWOOD WY				
	4700	OCN	92057	1087-B2
DRIFTWOOD CREEK RD				
	14900	SDCo	92021	1232-H3
DRISCOLL DR				
	3000	SD	92117	1248-C3
DRIVE E				
	-	ESCN	92029	1129-G5
DRIVE F				
	-	CRLB	92011	1127-B4
	-	ESCN	92029	1129-G5
DRIVE G				
	-	CRLB	92011	1127-B4
DRIVE H				
	-	CRLB	92011	1127-B4
	-	ESCN	92029	1129-G5
DRIVE I				
	-	CRLB	92011	1127-B4
DRIVE J				
	-	CRLB	92011	1127-B4
	-	ESCN	92029	1129-G5
DRIVE K				
	-	CRLB	92011	1127-B4
	-	ESCN	92029	1129-G5
DRIVE L				
	-	CRLB	92011	1127-B4
	-	ESCN	92029	1129-G5
DRIVER WY				
	3300	OCN	92056	1086-H7
D R KINCAD ST				
	-	CALX	92231	6620-F7
DROVER DR				
	5300	SD	92115	1270-A1
DRUCELLA ST				
	2300	SD	92154	1330-B7
DRUCKER LN				
	2500	SD	92154	1351-J4
DRUMCLIFF AV				
	10200	SD	92126	1209-C5
DRURY LN				
	1600	VSTA	92084	1088-B4
	7400	SD	92037	1227-F6
DRY BARK CT				
	11500	SD	92126	1209-A1
DRY CREEK DR				
	700	CHV	91914	1311-G3
DRY CREEK PL				
	7700	LMGR	91945	1290-G2
	7700	SD	92114	1290-G2
DRYDEN PL				
	5800	CRLB	92008	1127-B3
DRYDEN RD				
	2200	ELCJ	92020	1251-B5
DRY FLATS RD				
	-	SDCo	91962	430-B6
DUANE DR				
	8700	SNTE	92071	1231-C7
DUARTE PL				
	1500	SD	92114	1290-D6
DUBE CT				
	8300	SNTE	92071	1230-H6
DUBLIN DR				
	100	ENCT	92007	1167-D4
	2000	SD	92154	1351-F3
DUBLIN LN				
	1500	ESCN	92027	1110-B4
DUBOIS DR				
	4800	SD	92117	1248-F1
	4900	SD	92117	1228-E7
DU BOIS RD				
	-	ImCo	92243	6559-C1
DUBOIS TKTR				
	-	SDCo	91901	429-J4
	-	SDCo	91916	429-J4
	-	SDCo	91916	(1195-C7 See Page 1175)
DUBONNET ST				
	8500	SD	92123	1249-C4
DUBUQUE ST				
	1300	OCN	92054	1086-B6
DUCHESS ST				
	6800	SD	92115	1270-E5
DUCK POND LN				
	-	SD	92130	1188-G7
	-	SDCo	92065	1172-D5
DUCK POND TR				
	-	SD	92130	1188-G7
DUCKWALK RD				
	-	SMCS	92069	1108-H4
DUCKWEED TR				
	-	SDCo	91906	(1318-C6 See Page 1298)
DUCOMMUN AV				
	2900	SD	92122	1228-C5
DUCOS PL				
	4900	SD	92124	1249-H2
DUDLEY ST				
	700	SD	92106	1288-A3
	3600	SD	92106	1287-J3
DUENDA RD				
	11100	SD	92127	1149-J7
	11400	SD	92127	1169-J1
DUFF RD				
	100	ImCo	92243	6559-J4
DUFFER CT				
	3100	SDCo	92004	(1079-B5 See Page 1058)
DUFFWOOD LN				
	29100	SDCo	92082	1070-J6
DUFFY WY				
	3700	SDCo	91902	1310-E4
DUFRESNE PL				
	8300	SD	92129	1189-B4
DUGAN AV				
	5500	LMSA	91942	1270-J1
	5500	LMSA	91942	1250-H6
DUKE ST				
	1900	CHV	91913	1311-D5
	3200	SD	92110	1268-C5
DUKE MIGUEL CT				
	10600	SNTE	92071	1231-E2
DUKES PL				
	1200	SDCo	92065	1152-J6
DULCI PL				
	500	ELCJ	92019	1251-J6
DULENE DR				
	9100	SDCo	92040	1232-E6
DULIN PL				
	4400	OCN	92057	1087-A3
DULIN RD				
	3800	SDCo	92003	1048-G5
	3800	SDCo	92028	1048-H3
DULLES CT				
	-	IMP	92251	6499-C1
DULUTH AV				
	5800	SD	92114	1290-C5
DU LUZ RD				
	-	SDCo	92055	409-A6
DULZURA AV				
	2400	SD	92104	1289-E1
DUMAR AV				
	1400	ELCJ	92019	1252-A6
DUMAS ST				
	3000	SD	92106	1268-C6
DUNANT ST				
	6000	SD	92122	1228-C5
DUNAWAY DR				
	8600	SD	92037	1227-J4
DUNAWAY RD				
	-	ImCo	92259	430-K6
DUNBAR CT				
	700	CALX	92231	6620-G7
DUNBAR LN				
	9600	SDCo	92021	1233-D2
DUNBAR PL				
	16000	SDCo	92021	1233-D3
DUNBARTON RD				
	9200	SNTE	92071	1231-A5
DUNBROOK RD				
	7800	SD	92126	1209-B6
DUNCAN CT				
	11300	SD	92126	1209-D1
DUNCAN DR				
	10100	SDCo	92040	1232-C2
DUNCAN RD				
	8800	SD	92126	1209-C3
DUNCAN TER				
	32200	SDCo	92082	1050-F6
DUNCAN WY				
	-	SDCo	92082	1069-F1
DUNCANNON CT				
	8500	SD	92126	1209-C1
DUNCAN RANCH RD				
	800	CHV	91914	1311-H2
DUNDEE AV				
	5400	SD	92120	1250-B5
DUNDEE CT				
	-	SMCS	92069	1108-G6
	2700	CRLB	92010	1107-A5
DUNDEE GN				
	-	ESCN	92026	1109-H3
DUNDEE WY				
	2500	VSTA	92081	1107-J5
DUNE LN				
	7200	SD	92037	1247-E1
DUNEDIN CT				
	9700	SNTE	92071	1231-A4
DUNEMERE DR				
	300	SD	92037	1247-E1
DUNES PL				
	3400	OCN	92054	1086-F4
DUNHAM CT				
	-	SD	92130	1188-C5
DUNHAM PL				
	-	SMCS	92078	1128-J3
DUNHAM WY				
	4600	SD	92130	1188-C5
DUNHAVEN ST				
	2100	SD	92110	1268-F1
DUNHILL CT				
	4500	OCN	92056	1107-D2
DUNHILL ST				
	3500	SD	92121	1208-B5
DUNHOLME ST				
	8900	SD	92126	1209-D4
DUNLAP RD				
	-	SD	92140	1268-E7
DUNLIN PL				
	300	SD	92114	1290-D4
DUNLOP ST				
	2200	SD	92111	1248-J7
W DUNLOP ST				
	2200	SD	92111	1248-J7
DUNNING CIR				
	1900	SD	92154	1350-A1
DUNSMORE CT				
	400	ENCT	92024	1147-G6
DUNSMUIR CT				
	-	CHV	91913	1331-D1
DUNSMUIR ST				
	1300	ELCJ	92019	1251-J6
DUNSTAN ST				
	2200	OCN	92054	1086-E7
DUNWOOD WY				
	7500	SD	92114	1290-G5
DUNWOODIE RD				
	8500	SNTE	92071	1230-J6
DUO CT				
	800	VSTA	92084	1087-H5
DUORO DR				
	700	CHV	91910	1310-J6
DUPONT DR				
	1500	LMGR	91945	1290-H1
DUPONT ST				
	3500	SD	92106	1288-A3
	3600	SD	92106	1287-J3
DURANGO CIR				
	7200	CRLB	92011	1127-E7
DURANGO DR				
	13600	SD	92014	1187-H6
DURANT ST				
	3200	SD	92113	1289-F4
DURASNO LN				
	2200	SDCo	91977	1271-E7
DURAZNITOS PL				
	2400	SDCo	92065	1172-C4
DURAZNITOS RD				
	2200	SDCo	92065	1172-C4
DURGIN ST				
	100	SDCo	92065	1172-D1
	200	SDCo	92065	1152-D7
DURHAM CIR				
	3500	OCN	92056	1107-E3
DURHAM PL				
	-	CHV	91914	1311-H2
DURHAM ST				
	-	SD	92152	1288-A4
	500	ELCJ	92019	1252-A4
DURHULLEN DR				
	14100	PWY	92064	1170-G7
DURIAN CT				
	1300	VSTA	92083	1087-E6
DURIAN ST				
	100	VSTA	92083	1087-D7
	100	VSTA	92083	1107-D1
DURWARD ST				
	800	CHV	91910	1310-G7
DUSK DR				
	2100	SD	92139	1290-E7
	2100	SD	92139	1310-F1
DUSK LN				
	4200	OCN	92056	1107-C2
DUSK SKY LN				
	-	CHV	91915	1331-G1
DUSTY LN				
	3000	ENCT	92024	1148-A3
DUSTY RD				
	200	SMCS	92069	1108-G7
DUSTY TR				
	3000	ENCT	92024	1148-B3
DUSTY ACRES CT				
	500	ENCT	92024	1147-J7
DUSTY ROSE PL				
	6900	CRLB	92011	1127-E6
DUSTY TRAIL DR				
	-	IMP	92251	6439-F3
DUTTON DR				
	10700	SDCo	91941	1271-F3
DUVAL ST				
	600	SD	92102	1289-J2
	700	SD	92102	1290-A3
DUXBURY LN				
	-	SDCo	92127	1169-F3
DWANE AV				
	6300	SD	92120	1250-D7
DWIGHT ST				
	2100	SD	92104	1269-D6
	3600	SD	92105	1269-G6
	5400	SD	92105	1270-B6
	5900	SD	92115	1270-C6
DYANNA CT				
	1200	SDCo	92084	1108-A1
	1200	VSTA	92084	1108-A1
DYE RD				
	2000	SDCo	92065	1172-C3
DYE ST				
	200	SDCo	92065	1172-B4
DYER DR				
	2600	SD	92110	1268-E6
DYKES AV				
	6300	SD	92114	1290-D5
DYLAN ST				
	6900	SD	92139	1290-F7
DYLAN WY				
	-	ENCT	92024	1147-D2
E				
E AV				
	-	SDCo	92055	1066-D1
	100	CORD	92118	1288-H7
	200	NATC	91950	1289-H7
	300	NATC	91950	1309-H1
E ST				
	-	NATC	91950	1310-C3
	100	IMP	92251	6439-E6
	200	CHV	91910	1310-F7
	300	SDCo	92065	1152-F6
	300	SD	92101	1289-A3
	700	SD	92101	1288-J3
	1300	SD	92110	1268-F2
	1800	SDCo	92084	1108-G2
	1900	SD	92102	1289-C3
E ST Rt#-S17				
	-	CHV	91910	1310-B5
	200	CHV	91910	1309-J6
E E ST				
	-	ENCT	92024	1147-C7
W E ST				
	100	ENCT	92024	1147-B7
EADS AV				
	7100	SD	92037	1247-F1
	7200	SD	92037	1227-E6
EADY AV				
	600	CALX	92231	6620-E7
	800	CALX	92231	6680-E1
EADY LN				
	40500	SDCo	91905	1300-F7
EADY RD				
	-	ImCo	92231	431-C7
	-	ImCo	92231	6620-A4
EAGLE CRSG				
	400	OCN	92054	1086-B6
EAGLE DR				
	-	CRLB	92010	1127-J2
EAGLE GN				
	1300	ESCN	92029	1129-G6
EAGLE LN				
	1500	ELCJ	92020	1251-D2
EAGLE PASS				
	3600	SDCo	91901	1275-B3
EAGLE RDG				
	3600	SDCo	92036	1155-F4
EAGLE ST				
	600	SD	92103	1268-J5
EAGLE CANYON PL				
	-	SDCo	92127	1169-F1
EAGLE CANYON RD				
	-	SDCo	92127	1169-F1
EAGLE CANYON WY				
	-	SDCo	92127	1169-F1
EAGLE CREST LN				
	2400	VSTA	92081	1107-J5
EAGLE HILL LN				
	20200	SDCo	92065	1152-E1
EAGLEHILL RD				
	28000	SDCo	92082	1090-J3
	28000	SDCo	92082	1091-A2
EAGLE LAKE DR				
	10300	SDCo	92029	1129-F7
EAGLE MINE DR				
	14200	PWY	92064	1190-J3
EAGLE MOUNTAIN RD				
	6900	SDCo	92003	1068-E4
EAGLE PEAK CT				
	1400	CHV	91910	1311-B5
EAGLE PEAK RD				
	-	SDCo	92036	1154-H7
	-	SDCo	92036	1174-G3
	-	SDCo	92036	1175-A1
	-	SDCo	92036	(1194-C2 See Page 1175)
	4000	SDCo	92036	1155-G3
EAGLE RIDGE CT				
	7600	SD	92119	1250-G4
EAGLE RIDGE DR				
	7700	SD	92119	1250-G4
EAGLE RIDGE PL				
	1000	CHV	91913	1331-A1
EAGLE ROCK AV				
	10200	SD	92126	1209-C5
EAGLE ROCK DR				
	-	SDCo	92026	1109-E7
	-	SMCS	92069	1109-E7
EAGLE ROCK LN				
	1300	ESCN	92026	1129-F1
EAGLE ROCK WY				
	-	OCN	92054	1086-B6
EAGLES CREEK CT				
	11200	SD	92128	1189-J4
EAGLES CREST RD				
	-	SDCo	92025	1151-A5
	16400	SDCo	92065	1151-A5
EAGLES NEST WY				
	1700	OCN	92054	1086-B6
EAGLES NEST STATION				
	-	PWY	92064	1170-G1
EAGLES NOEL				
	30300	SDCo	92082	1070-G4
EAGLES PERCH LN				
	31200	SDCo	92003	1068-E2
EAGLE SUMMIT PL				
	1800	ESCN	92026	1109-F6
EAGLESVIEW CT				
	11500	SD	92127	1169-J5
EAGLES VIEW GN				
	1800	ESCN	92026	1109-B4
EAGLE VALLEY DR				
	2400	CHV	91914	1311-F3
EAGLE VIEW DR				
	9600	SDCo	92026	1089-D5
EAGLE VIEW LN				
	15800	SDCo	92082	1071-A6
EAMES ST				
	8500	SD	92123	1249-C4
EARHART AV				
	-	IMP	92251	6499-D1
EARHART CT				
	-	IMP	92251	6499-D2
EARHART ST				
	8900	SD	92123	1249-D5
EARIE LN				
	14000	PWY	92064	1190-G4
EARL GN				
	2000	ESCN	92026	1109-C4
EARL ST				
	2000	SD	92113	1289-H7
	9200	LMSA	91942	1251-B6
EARLE DR				
	1200	NATC	91950	1290-C7
	1200	NATC	91950	1310-C1
EARLGATE CT				
	13000	PWY	92064	1190-F5
EARLHAM ST				
	100	SDCo	92065	1152-H5
E EARLHAM ST				
	200	SDCo	92065	1152-J4
EARLING WY				
	700	SDCo	92021	1251-G1
EARLS ST				
	100	ELCN	92243	6500-B6
EARNSCLIFF PL				
	3600	SD	92111	1248-H4
EARTH DR				
	700	VSTA	92083	1087-D6
EARTHSTAR CT				
	11500	SD	92127	1169-J4
EAST DR				
	300	VSTA	92083	1087-G4
	3400	SD	92110	1268-E5
E EAST DR				
	100	VSTA	92084	1087-H4
EAST LN				
	100	SDCo	92021	1252-J3
	1100	IMPB	91932	1349-G2
EAST ST				
	-	SD	92102	1289-J4
	2700	OCN	92054	1086-D7
EASTBOURNE RD				
	11900	SD	92128	1190-B1
EASTBROOK RD				
	2200	VSTA	92081	1127-G1
	2200	VSTA	92081	1107-H7
EASTBURY DR				
	700	ESCN	92027	1130-C2
EASTCLIFF CT				
	4800	SD	92130	1188-C6
EAST COUNTY DR				
	8500	SDCo	92021	1232-D7
	8500	SDCo	92021	1252-E1
EASTER PL				
	1600	ESCN	92029	1129-F5
EASTER WY				
	9400	SD	92121	1228-D1
EASTERLEIGH RW				
	6300	SD	92037	1247-J1
EASTERN AV				
	13900	PWY	92064	1190-F3
EASTFIELD RD				
	11600	PWY	92064	1210-C1
EASTGATE CT				
	8400	SD	92121	1228-F1
EASTGATE DR				
	5700	SD	92121	1228-E1
EASTGATE MALL				
	4100	SD	92037	1228-D2
	4300	SD	92121	1228-E1
EASTGLEN ST				
	11900	SD	92131	1210-A3
EASTHAVEN CT				
	10800	SNTE	92071	1231-E1
EASTHAVEN DR				
	10200	SNTE	92071	1231-D1
EASTHILL DR				
	7500	SD	92114	1290-G3
EAST LAKE DR				
	6200	LMSA	91942	1251-A6
	6200	SD	92119	1251-A5
EASTLAKE DR				
	600	CHV	91913	1311-E4
EASTLAKE PKWY				
	-	CHV	91915	1331-G1
	700	CHV	91913	1311-F4
	700	CHV	91914	1311-F4
	1000	CHV	91915	1311-F7
EASTMAN ST				
	6900	SD	92111	1248-J7
EASTMONT PL				
	900	SDCo	92026	1109-H2
EASTMORE PL				
	1400	OCN	92056	1087-E3
EASTOM WY				
	2100	SDCo	92028	1028-A6
EASTON AV				
	5600	SD	92120	1250-B6
EASTON CT				
	6800	SD	92120	1250-B6
EAST POINTE AV				
	1700	CRLB	92008	1106-H6
EASTRIDGE CT				
	12700	SD	92131	1210-C1
EASTRIDGE DR				
	4100	LMSA	91941	1270-H4
EASTRIDGE LN				
	200	ESCN	92026	1109-G4
EASTRIDGE LP				
	2300	CHV	91915	1311-G5
EASTRIDGE PL				
	11400	SD	92131	1210-C1
EASTSHORE TER				
	700	CHV	91913	1311-E4
EASTSIDE RD				
	900	ELCJ	92020	1251-D3
EASTVALE RD				
	14800	PWY	92064	1170-J6
	15300	PWY	92064	1171-B6
EASTVIEW CT				
	1400	OCN	92056	1087-E3
	11400	SD	92131	1210-C1
EASTVIEW PT				
	11400	SD	92131	1210-C2
EASTVIEW TER				
	-	SDCo	92025	1130-E7
EASTWIND PT				
	11400	SD	92131	1209-J4
EASTWOOD LN				
	1800	ENCT	92024	1147-H6
EASY PL				
	200	CRLB	92011	1126-H4
EASY ST				
	1700	SDCo	92069	1108-G2
	3200	SD	92105	1270-B6
	6400	CRLB	92011	1126-H4
EASY STROLL LN				
	-	CHV	91915	1331-H1
EATON ST				
	100	OCN	92054	1106-C4
EATON WY				
	100	VSTA	92084	1087-H5
EBANO CT				
	100	SOLB	92075	1167-D7
EBBS PL				
	5600	SD	92114	1290-C6
EBBS ST				
	1400	SD	92114	1290-C6
EBB TIDE ST				
	-	CRLB	92011	1127-A4
EBBTIDE WY				
	-	SD	92154	1330-H7
EBERHART ST				
	6800	SD	92115	1270-E2
EBERLY CT				
	10800	SD	92126	1209-D3
EBERS ST				
	1300	SD	92107	1287-H1
	1300	SD	92107	1267-J7
	2000	SD	92107	1268-A6
EBERSOLE DR				
	4300	SD	92154	1330-G7
EBOE AV				
	1400	SD	92154	1349-J1
EBONY AV				
	-	IMPB	91932	1349-E1
EBONY RIDGE RD				
	-	SD	92102	1290-A4
ECCLESIA DR				
	100	OCN	92054	1086-C5
ECHO AV				
	-	CRLB	92009	1127-G3
ECHO CT				
	8600	LMSA	91941	1270-J4
ECHO DR				
	4000	SDCo	92036	1156-E3
	4200	LMSA	91941	1271-A4
	8500	LMSA	91941	1270-J4
ECHO LN				
	-	SD	92101	1288-C2
	-	SD	92147	1288-C2
	100	SMCS	92078	1128-G1
	100	SMCS	92069	1108-G7
ECHO PL				
	4000	OCN	92056	1107-B1
ECHO CANYON WY				
	-	OCN	92057	1086-J1
ECHO DELL RD				
	8200	SD	92119	1250-D3
ECHO HILL LN				
	4800	SDCo	92014	1168-A7
ECHO LN ACCESS RD				
	-	SMCS	92078	1128-G1
ECHO RIDGE CT				
	2800	CHV	91915	(1312-A5 See Page 1293)
ECHO RIDGE PL				
	2800	CHV	91915	(1312-A5 See Page 1293)
ECHO RIDGE TER				
	1300	CHV	91915	1311-J5
N ECHO RIDGE WY				
	1300	CHV	91915	1311-J5
	1300	CHV	91915	(1312-A5 See Page 1293)
S ECHO RIDGE WY				
	1300	CHV	91915	(1312-A6 See Page 1293)
ECHO VALLEY LN				
	1700	ESCN	92026	1109-F4
	1700	SDCo	92026	1109-F4
ECHO VALLEY RD				
	2800	SDCo	91935	1292-D3
ECKEN RD				
	600	ELCJ	92020	1251-E7
ECKE RANCH RD				
	-	ENCT	92024	1147-D5
ECKMAN AV				
	1300	CHV	91911	1330-F3
ECKMAN CT				
	100	CHV	91911	1330-F3
ECKSTROM AV				
	7000	SD	92111	1248-J3
	7300	SD	92111	1249-A2
ECLIPSE DR				
	-	SMCS	92078	1128-F6
ECLIPSE PL				
	12500	SD	92129	1189-B6
ECLIPSE RD				
	7900	SD	92129	1189-A6
ECLOGA CT				
	25100	SDCo	92065	1173-H3
ECOCHEE AV				
	3300	SD	92117	1248-D3
	3800	SD	92117	1248-E3
EDDIE DR				
	300	VSTA	92083	1087-H7
EDDIE JONES WY				
	-	OCN	92054	1086-D4
EDDING DR				
	2400	LMGR	91945	1270-G7
EDDINGTON RD				
	10900	SNTE	92071	1231-F6
EDDINS RD Rt#-S30				
	-	ImCo	92233	411-A10
EDDY LN				
	-	SMCS	92069	1108-H6
EDELL PL				
	2900	SD	92117	1228-C7
EDELWEISS				
	15200	SDCo	92021	1233-B3
EDELWEISS LN				
	700	ENCT	92024	1148-A6
EDEN CT				
	-	SMCS	92078	1128-C6
EDEN DR				
	1700	SD	92109	1268-A1
EDEN GRV				
	14200	PWY	92064	1170-G6
EDEN LN				
	900	ELCJ	92020	1251-H7
	900	SDCo	92020	1251-H7
EDEN PL				
	800	ESCN	92026	1129-G2
EDENBRIDGE LN				
	2300	SD	92139	1290-F7
EDENDALE ST				
	-	CRLB	92009	1127-F3
EDEN MILLS PL				
	-	SD	92131	1210-G2
EDENOAKS ST				
	10600	SD	92131	1210-C3
EDENVALE AV				
	4600	LMSA	91941	1270-J3
EDEN VALLEY LN				
	2600	SDCo	92029	1129-C3
EDGAR PL				
	9800	SDCo	91941	1271-D3
EDGAR RD				
	-	ImCo	92251	431-A3
EDGEBROOK PL				
	1700	ESCN	92026	1109-D5
EDGEBURT DR				
	100	ENCT	92024	1147-A3
EDGE CLIFF DR				
	1400	SD	92109	1268-A1
EDGEFIELD LN				
	1700	ENCT	92024	1147-G6
EDGEHILL DR				
	-	CHV	91913	1331-D1
EDGEHILL LN				
	300	OCN	92054	1086-E6
EDGEHILL RD				
	2000	SDCo	92084	1088-D4
	2000	VSTA	92084	1088-D4
EDGELAKE DR				
	9800	SDCo	91941	1271-D1
EDGELAND ST				
	700	ELCJ	92021	1251-G3
EDGEMERE AV				
	-	CHV	91910	1310-A3
	3000	NATC	91950	1310-A3
	3200	CHV	91950	1310-A3
	3200	NATC	91910	1310-A3
EDGEMONT PL				
	1000	SD	92102	1289-E3
EDGEMONT ST				
	1000	SD	92102	1289-E3
EDGEMOOR DR				
	8900	SNTE	92071	1231-E6
EDGEMOOR ST				
	13500	PWY	92064	1190-F3
EDGE PARK WY				
	4800	SD	92124	1249-G1
EDGER CT				
	-	SDCo	92055	1086-A2
EDGERTON DR				
	2300	LMGR	91945	1270-G7
EDGERTON WY				
	800	NATC	91950	1309-J1
EDGEVIEW DR				
	4800	SDCo	92020	1271-G2
EDGEVIEW ST				
	3300	SMCS	92078	1128-B1
EDGEWARE RD				
	4500	SD	92116	1269-H2
EDGEWARE WY				
	2900	CRLB	92010	1107-A4
EDGEWATER AV				
	500	OCN	92057	1067-D6
EDGEWATER DR				
	-	SMCS	92078	1129-A1
	700	CHV	91913	1311-E4
EDGEWATER ST				
	5900	SD	92139	1310-D1
EDGEWOOD CT				
	4300	SDCo	91941	1271-C3
EDGEWOOD DR				
	100	OCN	92054	1086-D6
	3600	SDCo	92036	1156-E2
	9100	LMSA	91941	1271-B3
	9100	SDCo	91941	1271-B3
EDGEWOOD PL				
	-	SD	92131	1210-G1
	1000	CHV	91913	1311-E6
	2200	OCN	92054	1086-C6
EDGEWOOD BEND CT				
	-	SD	92130	1188-E5
EDGEWORTH RD				
	5000	SD	92109	1248-A3
EDIE LN				
	9500	SDCo	92040	1231-J5
EDILEE DR				
	1600	ENCT	92007	1167-E2
EDINA CT				
	13100	PWY	92064	1170-D2
EDINA WY				
	13000	PWY	92064	1170-D2
EDINBURG AV				
	1800	ENCT	92007	1167-D3
EDINBURGH CT				
	6700	SD	92120	1250-E7
EDINBURGH DR				
	4700	CRLB	92010	1107-A5
EDISON PL				
	5800	CRLB	92008	1127-C3
EDISON ST				
	4100	SD	92117	1248-E6
EDITH DR				
	1900	ESCN	92026	1109-D4
EDITH LN				
	3100	SD	92106	1268-C7
EDITHA DR				
	200	SDCo	92019	1253-D1
EDIWHAR AV				
	3400	SD	92123	1249-D4
EDMONDS ST				
	6300	SD	92114	1290-D4
EDMONTON AV				
	6400	SD	92122	1228-E4
EDNA PL				
	3800	SD	92116	1269-G3
EDNA WY				
	500	VSTA	92081	1107-J3
	500	VSTA	92081	1108-A3
EDNABELLE CT				
	900	ELCJ	92021	1251-H4
EDSON RD				
	-	SD	92145	1229-C1
EDULIS CT				
	8700	SD	92129	1189-C6
EDWARD				
	9400	SDCo	92040	1232-F4
EDWARD ST				
	400	ELCJ	92020	1251-B5
EDWARD LLOYD LN				
	-	ENCT	92024	1148-B4
EDWIN LN				
	1900	SDCo	92069	1108-H2
EDWIN PL				
	4900	SD	92117	1228-C7
EDWINA WY				
	900	ENCT	92007	1167-E2
EDWORDS ACCESS RD				
	10200	SDCo	92026	1109-G3
EEL AL				
	-	SD	92136	1289-E6
EGAN ST				
	3400	SD	92115	1270-D6
EGLANTINE CT				
	10600	SD	92131	1209-H1
EGRET ST				
	-	CRLB	92011	1127-D7
	6000	SD	92114	1290-C1
EGRET WY				
	1400	ELCJ	92019	1252-A7
EICHENLAUB ST				
	3200	SD	92117	1248-D3
EIDER CT				
	-	CRLB	92011	1127-C6
EIDER ST				
	6400	SD	92114	1290-D2
EIDER WY				
	1000	OCN	92057	1087-A3
EILEEN DR				
	2400	SD	92123	1249-E7
EILEEN ST				
	8600	SDCo	91977	1291-A2
EISENHOWER AV				
	13800	PWY	92064	1190-C3
EISENHOWER CT				
	-	PWY	92064	1190-B3
EKLUND CT				
	1100	VSTA	92083	1107-J1
EL ACEBO				
	5000	SDCo	92067	1168-A4

STREET Block City ZIP Pg-Grid

EL ACEBO DEL NORTE
- SDCo 92067 1168-A4
EL AGUILA LN
2500 CRLB 92009 1127-G5
ELAINE AV
500 OCN 92057 1067-A6
ELAINE WY
6800 SD 92120 1250-E7
EL AIRE PL
1700 ESCN 92026 1109-E6
EL AMIGO RD
300 DLMR 92014 1187-G6
2100 SD 92014 1187-H6
EL AMO
400 OCN 92054 1086-F2
ELAN LN
1800 SDCo 92019 1272-D3
EL APAJO
5700 SDCo 92067 1168-D6
5700 SDCo 92091 1168-D6
EL ARBOL DR
5300 CRLB 92008 1126-G2
EL ARCO IRIS
4800 SDCo 92067 1168-A5
EL ASADO ST
14200 SD 92129 1189-C2
EL ASPECTO
4700 SDCo 92067 1168-A3
EL ASTILLERO PL
7900 CRLB 92009 1147-G3
EL BANQUERO CT
8100 SD 92119 1250-E3
EL BANQUERO PL
6700 SD 92119 1250-E3
EL BERRO
- CALX 92231 6620-H5
400 OCN 92054 1086-F2
ELBERT CT
11500 SD 92126 1209-D1
ELBERT TER
9000 SD 92126 1209-D1
ELBERT WY
11400 SD 92126 1209-D1
EL BOSQUE AV
2400 CRLB 92009 1147-G3
EL BOSQUE CT
4300 SD 92154 1330-G7
EL BRAZO
17900 SDCo 92067 1149-A5
ELBROOK DR
300 SDCo 92028 1027-G3
EL CABALLO AV
10600 SDCo 92127 1169-F4
EL CABALLO DR
700 OCN 92057 1067-A5
EL CABO CT
5700 SD 92124 1229-H7
EL CABRILLO
600 ENCT 92024 1147-F5
EL CAJON BLVD
- LMSA 91942 1270-E2
100 ELCJ 92020 1251-D7
1800 SD 92103 1269-C4
1900 SD 92104 1269-C4
3700 SD 92105 1269-G4
4300 SD 92115 1269-G4
4400 SD 92115 1270-E2
7300 LMSA 91941 1270-E2
EL CAJON LN
1800 SDCo 92065 1172-F1
EL CAJON MOUNTAIN TKTR
- SDCo 92040 (1193-G2 See Page 1192)
EL CALOR LN
1400 ESCN 92026 1109-E6
EL CAMINITO
1000 VSTA 92081 1107-G1
EL CAMINITO RD
700 SDCo 92028 1027-H4
EL CAMINO CT
1400 ENCT 92024 1167-G3
EL CAMINO DR
1200 SMCS 92078 1128-D2
5600 SD 92121 1208-F6
EL CAMINO DEL LA FLORES
- ESCN 92026 1109-F7
EL CAMINO DEL NORTE
2200 ENCT 92024 1147-J6
2300 ENCT 92024 1148-A6
2700 SDCo 92024 1148-A6
2800 SDCo 92067 1148-C7
6800 SDCo 92067 1168-F1
EL CAMINO DEL TEATRO
1500 SD 92037 1247-G1
EL CAMINO DE PINOS
8700 SDCo 92026 1068-J5
EL CAMINO ENTRADA
15400 PWY 92064 1170-F5
EL CAMINO PEQUENO
100 ELCJ 92019 1252-D5
EL CAMINO REAL
- SDCo 92055 408-K7
- SDCo 92055 1023-E3
- SDCo 92672 1023-E3
- SMCS 92078 1129-C2
11300 SD 92130 1207-J1
11300 SD 92130 1208-A1
12200 SD 92130 1187-J3
12700 SD 92130 1188-A2
14300 SD 92014 1188-B1
14800 SDCo 92014 1188-B1
15100 SDCo 92014 1168-A6
15100 SDCo 92067 1168-A6
15100 SDCo 92067 1188-B1
16000 SDCo 92014 1167-J5
16000 SDCo 92067 1167-J4
EL CAMINO REAL Rt#-S11
1000 CRLB 92024 1147-E1
1000 ENCT 92024 1147-E1
1000 CRLB 92009 1147-E1
1100 CRLB 92011 1147-E1
1200 CRLB 92011 1127-E4
1300 CRLB 92009 1127-D1
1600 CRLB 92010 1127-D1
1600 CRLB 92008 1127-D1
1800 CRLB 92010 1107-A6
1800 CRLB 92008 1107-A6
2100 CRLB 92010 1106-H5
2100 CRLB 92008 1106-H5
2300 OCN 92056 1106-H5
2300 OCN 92054 1106-H5
2400 CRLB 92054 1106-H5
N EL CAMINO REAL
- OCN 92054 1086-G2
100 OCN 92057 1086-G2
N EL CAMINO REAL Rt#-S11
100 ENCT 92024 1147-F4
1000 CRLB 92009 1147-F4
1000 CRLB 92024 1147-F4

STREET Block City ZIP Pg-Grid

N EL CAMINO REAL Rt#-S11
1000 ENCT 92009 1147-F4
S EL CAMINO REAL
100 ENCT 92024 1147-G7
100 OCN 92054 1086-F5
100 OCN 92057 1086-F5
400 ENCT 92024 1167-G3
1200 OCN 92056 1086-G7
1400 OCN 92054 1106-G1
1400 OCN 92056 1106-G1
3100 SCLE 92672 1023-B1
3900 SDCo 92672 1023-B1
EL CAMINO VERDE
2800 SDCo 91935 1293-J3
EL CAMINO VILLAS
2300 OCN 92056 1106-H2
EL CANTO DR
3600 SDCo 91977 1271-E4
3800 SDCo 91941 1271-E4
EL CAPITAN
- SMCS 92078 1129-C2
EL CAPITAN CT
4300 CRLB 92010 1106-J5
EL CAPITAN DR
- CHV 91911 1330-E1
7900 LMSA 91941 1270-H2
EL CAPITAN TKTR
- SDCo 91901 429-J4
- SDCo 91916 429-J4
- SDCo 91916 (1194-G7 See Page 1175)
14700 SDCo 92040 (1193-G1 See Page 1192)
14700 SDCo 92065 1173-H7
14700 SDCo 92065 (1193-G1 See Page 1192)
14900 SDCo 92036 (1194-A1 See Page 1175)
14900 SDCo 92040 (1194-A1 See Page 1175)
14900 SDCo 92065 (1194-A1 See Page 1175)
EL CAPITAN PEAK
15500 SDCo 92021 1233-C1
EL CAPITAN REAL LN
15400 SDCo 92021 1233-B2
EL CAPITAN REAL RD
10200 SDCo 92021 1233-B2
EL CAPORAL
17200 SDCo 92067 1168-H2
EL CARMEL PL
700 SD 92109 1267-H2
EL CEDRO CT
4300 SD 92154 1330-G7
EL CENTRO AV
- SDCo 91934 (1321-G5 See Page 1300)
400 ELCN 92243 6499-G5
EL CENTRO ST
1100 IMPB 91932 1349-F2
EL CENTRO TER
- SDCo 91948 1218-F7
EL CENTRO RAVINE RD
- SDCo 91948 1218-D7
EL CERISE
900 SDCo 92028 1028-B1
EL CERRITO DR
4500 SD 92115 1270-B4
EL CERRITO PL
4700 SD 92115 1270-B3
EL CERRO
400 OCN 92054 1086-F2
EL CERRO DR
9100 SDCo 92040 1232-D6
EL CHICO
1400 SDCo 92078 1128-C3
EL CHICO LN
200 CORD 92118 1288-J6
EL CIELITO
5400 SDCo 92067 1168-B4
EL CIELO
- SDCo 92067 1148-J5
- SDCo 92067 1149-A5
EL CIELO LN
1400 ESCN 92026 1109-E6
EL CIRCULO
5100 OCN 92056 1087-D2
6300 SDCo 92067 1168-E1
ELCO ST
3700 SD 92111 1248-J3
EL COMAL DR
10400 SD 92124 1229-H7
EL COPA LN
100 SDCo 92083 1108-C3
EL CORRAL LN
1300 SDCo 92078 1128-G5
EL CORTEZ CT
1200 CHV 91910 1311-B7
EL CORTO
2400 SDCo 92084 1108-D4
EL COYOTE RUN
2800 SDCo 92028 998-C4
ELDEAN LN
1300 OCN 92054 1086-F7
ELDEN AV
1300 CHV 91911 1330-C4
ELDEN ST
8700 LMSA 91942 1250-J7
8700 LMSA 91942 1251-A7
ELDER AV
- IMPB 91932 1349-E1
100 CHV 91910 1310-A5
600 CHV 91910 1330-B1
1300 SD 92154 1349-J1
1800 SD 92154 1350-A1
ELDER CT
800 CRLB 92011 1126-J5
6300 SD 92120 1250-B6
ELDER PL
700 ESCN 92025 1129-J1
700 ESCN 92025 1130-A1
6200 SD 92120 1250-B6
ELDER ST
200 SDCo 92028 1027-E3
500 SDCo 92055 1027-E3
E ELDER ST
100 SDCo 92028 1027-G2
ELDERBERRY CT
800 SMCS 92069 1109-A6
ELDERBERRY GN
3700 ESCN 92025 1150-C3
ELDERBERRY WY
- SD 92130 1188-G3
5400 OCN 92057 1067-D7
ELDERBURRY CT
10800 SD 92126 1209-D3
ELDERGARDENS ST
5800 SD 92120 1250-B6
ELDERWOOD CT
10900 SD 92131 1210-B2
ELDERWOOD LN
10700 SD 92131 1210-B2

STREET Block City ZIP Pg-Grid

ELDERWOOD RD
10900 SD 92131 1210-B2
EL DIABLO CT
400 ESCN 92026 1109-H5
EL DOLORA WY
14100 PWY 92064 1190-G1
ELDON CT
1700 ELCJ 92021 1252-B2
ELDORA ST
1700 LMGR 91945 1290-G1
EL DORADO AV
800 ELCN 92243 6499-F4
EL DORADO CT
1700 VSTA 92084 1108-B1
ELDORADO DR
300 ESCN 92025 1130-B5
300 SDCo 92025 1130-B5
EL DORADO PKWY
8900 SDCo 92021 1232-E6
EL DORADO TER
1700 SDCo 92025 1130-C5
ELDRED LN
1700 VSTA 92083 1087-D7
ELDRIDGE CT
5400 SD 92120 1250-B6
ELDRIDGE ST
6500 SD 92120 1250-B6
ELEANOR DR
6400 SD 92114 1290-D4
ELEANOR PL
3400 NATC 91950 1290-C7
ELEANOR ROOSEVELT LN
- SD 92093 1228-A2
ELECTRIC AV
6200 SD 92037 1247-E2
ELECTRON DR
3700 SD 92152 1287-J4
ELEGANS PL
- CRLB 92011 1127-B7
ELEGANT TERN PL
- CRLB 92011 1127-C5
ELENA DR
1700 CALX 92231 6620-G7
1700 SMCS 92069 1108-H3
ELENA LN
19300 SDCo 91935 1294-F7
ELENA WY
100 OCN 92057 1086-H3
ELEONORE CT
12100 SD 92131 1210-B1
EL ESCNDDO DEL DIOS HWY Rt#-S6
6900 SDCo 92067 1168-F1
7600 SDCo 92067 1149-A7
7800 SDCo 92067 1148-J7
EL ESCORIAL WY
5900 SD 92124 1229-J6
ELETA PL
2200 SDCo 91977 1271-D7
ELEVADA ST
2000 OCN 92054 1106-F2
ELEVADO RD
1600 SDCo 92084 1088-C1
1600 VSTA 92084 1088-B2
2200 SDCo 92084 1068-B7
ELEVADO HILLS DR
2000 SDCo 92084 1088-B2
ELEVATION RD
1300 SD 92110 1268-F2
EL EXTENSO CT
8000 SD 92119 1250-E3
EL-FARRA ST
9700 SDCo 92069 1088-G2
ELFIN GN
19600 SDCo 92029 1148-H3
ELFIN FOREST LN
19900 SDCo 92029 1148-G2
ELFIN FOREST RD
19900 SDCo 92029 1148-F1
20500 SMCS 92078 1128-D6
20500 SDCo 92029 1128-E7
ELFIN OAKS RD
6900 SDCo 92029 1148-F2
ELFINORA LN
9500 SDCo 92029 1148-J2
ELFORD CT
8700 SD 92129 1189-C1
EL FUEGO
16900 SDCo 92067 1168-D3
EL FUERTE ST
5900 CRLB 92010 1127-F1
6200 CRLB 92009 1127-G2
EL GAVILAN CT
2500 CRLB 92009 1127-G4
ELGIN AV
5400 SD 92120 1250-B5
EL GRANADA RD
2600 CHV 91914 1311-G2
EL GRANDE PL
9600 SDCo 92040 1232-C4
EL GRANITO AV
9400 SDCo 91941 1271-B1
EL HONCHO PL
10300 SD 92124 1229-G7
ELIASON DR
- SDCo 92055 1085-G1
ELIJAH CT
- SD 92130 1187-J6
- SD 92130 1188-A6
ELIJO WY
14800 SDCo 91935 1293-C4
ELIOT PL
5200 CRLB 92008 1127-B1
ELIOT ST
- OCN 92057 1067-A4
ELISA LN
100 SD 92128 1189-H6
ELISE ST
800 CHV 91911 1330-A5
800 SD 91911 1330-A5
ELISE WY
100 OCN 92057 1086-H3
ELIVO CT
100 SD 92173 1350-G2
ELIZABETH DR
19300 SDCo 92082 1091-H4
ELIZABETH LN
300 SDCo 92065 1153-B5
ELIZABETH ST
- ELCJ 92019 1252-A7
500 SD 92113 1289-J5
600 SMCS 92069 1109-B6
ELIZABETH WY
- ELCJ 92019 1252-B6
1300 SDCo 92028 1027-G5
EL JARDIN CT
1800 ELCJ 92020 1271-G2
ELK ST
5600 SD 92114 1290-B4
ELKELTON BLVD
400 SDCo 91977 1291-A4
600 SDCo 91977 1290-J2

STREET Block City ZIP Pg-Grid

ELKELTON PL
300 SDCo 91977 1291-A4
ELK GROVE LN
- SD 92131 1210-G2
ELKHART ST
5000 SD 92105 1270-A7
ELKHORN CT
500 CHV 91902 1311-B4
ELKHORN LN
400 ESCN 92026 1109-G5
ELKHORN ST
8300 LMGR 91945 1290-J1
ELKINS CV
11800 SD 92126 1209-C1
ELK LAKE DR
2000 SDCo 92029 1129-F7
ELK RUN PL
1000 CHV 91913 1311-D6
ELKS LN
900 CHV 91910 1330-G1
EL-KU AV
3000 ESCN 92025 1150-A2
ELKWOOD AV
- IMPB 91932 1349-F1
ELLA LN
- SD 92114 1290-E5
EL LANDO CT
3100 OCN 92056 1106-H1
ELLEN LN
- OCN 92054 1086-G3
600 ELCJ 92019 1252-B7
ELLEN RD
- IMP 92251 6439-E5
ELLENBEE RD
9200 SNTE 92071 1231-A5
ELLENTOWN RD
2400 SD 92037 1227-J3
ELLENWOOD CIR
8800 SDCo 91977 1290-J3
ELLERY ST
100 OCN 92054 1086-D6
ELLIE LN
16300 PWY 92064 1171-D7
ELLINGER PL
- SD 92173 1350-E4
ELLINGHAM ST
8800 SD 92129 1189-C3
ELLIOT LN
- SNTE 92071 1251-A1
ELLIOTT CIR
- SDCo 92055 1067-A2
ELLIOTT ST
- SDCo 92055 1067-A1
3000 SD 92106 1268-C6
ELLIS LN
100 SDCo 92028 1027-G2
ELLIS MOUNTAIN DR
2000 SDCo 92019 1252-C7
ELLISON PL
5000 SD 92116 1269-E2
EL LORO ST
300 CHV 91911 1330-D4
ELLSWORTH CIR
8700 SNTE 92071 1231-B7
ELLSWORTH LN
8500 SNTE 92071 1231-B7
8500 SNTE 92071 1251-B1
ELLSWORTH ST
5100 SD 92110 1268-F2
EL LUGAR ST
1300 CHV 91911 1330-D4
ELM
9700 SDCo 92021 1233-B3
ELM AV
- IMPB 91932 1329-E7
100 CRLB 92008 1106-E5
200 CHV 91910 1310-C5
700 CHV 91910 1330-C1
800 CHV 91911 1330-D2
1300 IMPB 92154 1329-J7
1300 SD 92154 1329-J7
1500 ELCN 92243 6499-E7
1700 SD 92154 1330-A7
2300 CRLB 92010 1106-J3
2700 CRLB 92010 1107-A4
ELM CIR
- ELCN 92243 6499-D7
ELM CT
- SDCo 92040 1232-D6
ELM DR
- NATC 91950 1289-H7
1500 VSTA 92084 1088-B4
9400 SDCo 91916 1236-A2
ELM LN
20100 SDCo 92029 1149-E2
ELM RD
28900 SDCo 91962 1237-C7
ELM ST
- SMCS 92078 1129-C2
100 OCN 92054 1106-A1
100 SD 92101 1289-A2
300 CHV 91910 1310-C6
300 SD 92114 1290-D4
300 SDCo 92065 1152-H1
500 VSTA 92083 1087-F6
600 ESCN 92025 1130-A1
1300 ESCN 92026 1109-J6
2800 SD 92102 1289-E2
3600 SMCS 92078 1128-C1
3600 SD 92104 1289-F2
4300 SD 92105 1289-H1
4900 SD 92102 1290-A1
N ELM ST
100 ESCN 92025 1130-A2
S ELM ST
100 ESCN 92025 1130-A2
ELMA LN
4300 LMSA 91941 1270-E4
EL MAC PL
900 SD 92106 1287-J2
N ELMAN ST
6700 SD 92111 1268-H1
S ELMAN ST
6700 SD 92111 1268-J1
EL MAR AV
13500 PWY 92064 1190-H3
EL MARBEA LN
10700 SDCo 91941 1271-F2
EL MATADOR LN
10300 SNTE 92071 1231-E7
ELMBRANCH DR
1200 ENCT 92024 1147-F7
ELMCREST DR
6300 SD 92119 1250-E6
ELMDALE DR
10300 SDCo 91977 1291-E2
EL MERCADO WY
1200 OCN 92057 1087-B3
ELMFIELD LN
12800 PWY 92064 1170-D3
ELMHURST DR
6300 SD 92120 1250-D7
ELMHURST ST
1600 CHV 91913 1311-C5

STREET Block City ZIP Pg-Grid

EL MIO DR
1200 ELCJ 92020 1251-D6
ELMIRA ST
300 ELCJ 92019 1251-J6
EL MIRADOR
- SMCS 92078 1129-C1
16800 SDCo 92067 1168-F2
EL MIRAR
4700 SDCo 92067 1168-A3
EL MIRASO
500 VSTA 92083 1087-H7
EL MIRLO
4500 SDCo 92067 1168-A1
EL MIRLO DR
4900 OCN 92057 1067-A5
EL MODENA RD
1800 CHV 91913 1311-E6
ELMOND DR
9500 SDCo 92026 1069-C3
EL MONTE DR
2100 OCN 92054 1086-C6
EL MONTE PL
300 SDCo 92021 1252-H4
400 ESCN 92027 1130-B1
EL MONTE RD
100 ELCJ 92020 1251-D4
13900 SDCo 92040 1232-G1
15400 SDCo 92040 1212-J7
15500 SDCo 92040 1213-B6
EL MONTEVIDEO
5500 SDCo 92067 1148-C7
5500 SDCo 92067 1168-D1
ELMORE ST
6700 SD 92111 1268-J2
EL MORRO LN
- OCN 92054 1086-G3
ELMPARK LN
12700 PWY 92064 1190-D4
ELMPORT LN
14400 PWY 92064 1190-H5
ELM RIDGE DR
1900 VSTA 92081 1107-G5
ELMSTONE CT
11400 SD 92131 1210-A2
ELM TREE CT
2900 SDCo 91978 1271-G7
ELM TREE DR
4700 OCN 92056 1087-E5
ELM TREE LN
500 SDCo 92028 1047-G1
1100 SMCS 92069 1109-A5
ELMVIEW DR
800 ENCT 92024 1167-G1
ELMWOOD CT
1400 CHV 91915 1311-G7
ELMWOOD DR
600 ESCN 92025 1130-A1
ELMWOOD LN
- OCN 92054 1106-C1
ELMWOOD ST
2800 CRLB 92008 1106-F4
ELMWOOD WY
3300 SMCS 92078 1128-B1
EL NIDO
4600 SDCo 92067 1168-A5
EL NIDO DR
1200 SDCo 92028 1047-J3
1600 SDCo 92028 1048-A4
EL NOCHE WY
5300 SD 92124 1249-H1
EL NOPAL
9900 SNTE 92071 1231-C3
10800 SDCo 92040 1231-G3
EL NORA PL
24800 SDCo 92065 1173-G3
EL NORTE
600 SDCo 92021 1251-G2
3600 OCN 92054 1086-F2
E EL NORTE PKWY
100 ESCN 92026 1109-H7
800 ESCN 92027 1109-H7
1000 ESCN 92027 1110-C5
W EL NORTE PKWY
100 ESCN 92026 1109-C5
1800 SDCo 92026 1109-F6
EL NORTE HILLS PL
500 ESCN 92027 1110-D5
EL NORTE VISTA
27600 SDCo 92082 1091-F3
ELON LN
1500 ENCT 92024 1147-G5
EL ONTONO WY
5400 SD 92121 1208-E4
EL ORIENTE
600 ENCT 92024 1147-F5
EL PAISANO DR
600 SDCo 92028 1028-B1
1000 SDCo 92028 998-B7
EL PAJODO PL
900 VSTA 92084 1088-A7
EL PASEO
500 SDCo 92084 1088-G1
700 SDCo 92084 1068-H7
EL PASEO DR
1500 SDCo 92078 1128-B3
EL PASEO GRANDE
7800 SD 92037 1227-H4
8500 SD 92093 1227-H4
EL PASILLO
2100 SDCo 91977 1291-A1
EL PASO ST
1700 SDCo 92065 1152-C5
7500 LMSA 91942 1250-G6
EL PASO ALTO
400 SDCo 92084 1088-F5
600 SDCo 92069 1088-G4
EL PASO ALTO NORTE
3700 SDCo 92084 1088-F5
EL PASO REAL
3000 SD 92037 1247-G1
EL PATO CT
6400 CRLB 92009 1127-G4
EL PEDREGAL DR
300 SOLB 92075 1167-H6
EL PENON WY
4600 SD 92117 1248-B1
EL PERICO LN
6400 CRLB 92009 1127-H5
EL PICO CT
900 VSTA 92083 1087-G5
EL PICO DR
1700 ELCJ 92020 1251-C4
EL POQUITO LN
10100 SNTE 92071 1231-F3
EL PORTAL DR
600 CHV 91914 1311-G2
EL PORTAL ST
100 ENCT 92024 1147-B5
N EL PORTAL ST
200 ENCT 92024 1147-B5
S EL PORTAL ST
100 ENCT 92024 1147-B6
EL PORVENIR WY
3000 SD 92173 1350-D3

STREET Block City ZIP Pg-Grid

EL PRADO
1200 SD 92101 1289-B1
EL PRADO AV
1400 LMGR 91945 1290-G1
2200 LMGR 91945 1270-G7
EL PRADO LN
- OCN 92054 1086-G3
EL PRADO PL
1400 ESCN 92027 1130-B1
EL PRADO ST
1500 SD 92101 1289-C1
EL PRESIDIO TR
- SD 92130 1188-D4
EL RANCHO DR
600 ELCJ 92019 1252-C4
600 SDCo 92019 1252-C4
EL RANCHO LN
400 ESCN 92027 1130-B1
1600 SDCo 92028 1027-J1
EL RANCHO GRANDE
3300 SDCo 91902 1291-C7
3300 SDCo 91902 1311-C1
EL RANCHO VERDE
1600 SDCo 92078 1128-G4
EL RANCHO VISTA
- CHV 91910 1310-D6
- SDCo 91910 1310-D6
N EL RANCHO VISTA
400 SDCo 91910 1310-D6
EL RASTRO LN
2800 CRLB 92009 1147-G4
EL RETIRO
28600 SDCo 92082 1089-J1
28700 SDCo 92082 1069-J7
EL REY AV
1100 ELCJ 92021 1251-J2
1100 SDCo 92021 1251-J2
EL REY CT
1300 ELCJ 92021 1251-J2
EL REY VISTA
12800 PWY 92064 1190-E5
EL ROCKO RD
2700 SDCo 92029 1129-D4
ELROD AV
- SD 92126 1209-D7
ELROD RD
- SD 92126 1209-E7
EL RODEO CT
14000 SDCo 92067 1188-H2
EL ROMERO
6100 SDCo 92067 1168-D3
EL ROSAL PL
1700 ESCN 92026 1109-E6
ELROSE CT
1100 SD 92154 1350-C1
ELROSE DR
2700 SD 92154 1350-C1
ELROY DR
1600 LMGR 91945 1290-G1
ELSA RD
4700 SD 92120 1249-J7
4800 SD 92120 1250-A7
ELSBERRY ST
6300 SD 92114 1290-D6
EL SEBO PL
24700 SDCo 92065 1173-G2
EL SECRETO
4700 SDCo 92067 1168-B3
EL SECRITO
5100 OCN 92056 1087-D2
EL SENDERO DR
34300 SDCo 92061 1050-H1
34400 SDCo 92061 1030-G7
34500 SDCo 92059 1030-G7
EL SENTIDO
14800 SDCo 92067 1188-H1
ELSER LN
1700 SDCo 92026 1109-D6
EL SERENO WY
2500 SDCo 92083 1108-C4
2600 SDCo 92069 1108-C4
2600 SMCS 92069 1108-C4
EL SICOMORO
6300 SDCo 92067 1168-E4
ELSIE WY
600 CHV 91910 1310-D7
ELSINORE PL
3400 SD 92117 1248-D3
ELSINORE ST
5300 OCN 92056 1087-E1
EL SOL RD
16900 SDCo 92065 1172-A2
ELSTON PL
8100 SD 92126 1209-B3
EL SUENO
- SOLB 92075 1167-F7
EL SUR
300 OCN 92054 1086-F3
EL TAE RD
32400 SDCo 92061 1051-A5
ELTANIN WY
11400 SD 92126 1209-D1
EL TEJADO RD
9300 SDCo 91941 1271-B2
9400 LMSA 91941 1271-B2
EL TEJON RD
3300 SDCo 92004 (1079-A6 See Page 1058)
EL TESORO RD
27100 SDCo 92066 410-A8
37000 SDCo 92066 409-L8
EL TIEMPO
- SDCo 92067 1149-B3
EL TIGRE CT
200 SMCS 92069 1108-C5
ELTINGE DR
2300 SDCo 91901 1234-B6
ELTINGE PL
2800 SDCo 91901 1234-B7
ELTON DR
9200 SNTE 92071 1231-B7
EL TOPO DR
14200 PWY 92064 1170-G7
EL TORDO
5900 SDCo 92067 1168-D3
EL TORO LN
800 SMCS 92069 1109-C5
10300 SNTE 92071 1231-E7
ELVA CT
1400 ENCT 92024 1167-G1
ELVA ST
1800 SDCo 92019 1272-C4
ELVA TER
1400 ENCT 92024 1167-G1
ELVADO WY
200 SD 92114 1290-E4
EL VALLE
- SDCo 92040 1232-D6
EL VALLECITO
1000 VSTA 92083 1087-G4
EL VALLE OPULENTO
100 SDCo 92083 1108-B3
EL VECINO DR
3300 SDCo 92028 1047-J2

STREET Block City ZIP Pg-Grid

EL VERDE CT
1900 LMGR 91945 1290-J1
EL VESTIDO ST
14300 SD 92129 1189-C2
EL VIENTO
300 SOLB 92075 1167-F7
ELVIS CT
1100 SD 92154 1350-E1
EL VUELO
17100 SDCo 92067 1168-F2
EL VUELO DEL ESTE
7000 SDCo 92067 1168-G2
ELWELL CT
11600 SD 92131 1210-A1
ELWOOD AV
900 SD 92114 1290-A3
ELY CIR
6900 SD 92114 1290-F4
ELY ST
100 OCN 92054 1086-F5
ELYSIAN DR
3800 SDCo 92036 1156-E2
ELYSSEE ST
2500 SD 92123 1249-C6
ELYSUM DR
- SD 92109 1248-C6
EL ZORRO VISTA
16500 SDCo 92067 1168-E3
EMBARCADERO LN
- CRLB 92011 1126-J5
EMBASSY WY
10100 SD 92126 1209-B5
EMBERWOOD WY
2100 ESCN 92029 1129-E6
EMBRY CT
7700 SD 92126 1209-A5
EMBRY PT
7700 SD 92126 1209-A5
EMBRY WY
10000 SD 92126 1209-A6
EMDEN RD
9100 SD 92129 1189-C1
E MEDINA ST
- CALX 92231 6620-J6
EMELENE ST
4900 SD 92109 1248-A4
EMELITA ST
1000 SDCo 92028 1027-H2
EMERALD AV
- CALX 92231 6620-H7
300 ELCJ 92020 1251-E6
1200 ELCJ 92020 1271-E1
EMERALD BAY
5700 SD 92105 1290-B1
EMERALD CT
700 SD 92109 1247-H6
EMERALD CV
- SD 92154 1330-J7
EMERALD DR
100 OCN 92056 1107-D2
100 VSTA 92081 1107-D1
100 VSTA 92083 1107-D1
400 OCN 92056 1087-D7
400 VSTA 92083 1087-D7
3500 SDCo 92081 1107-D2
3600 SDCo 92036 1156-E2
EMERALD LN
14400 SDCo 92067 1188-F2
EMERALD PL
- CRLB 92009 1127-H5
2600 ESCN 92027 1130-F1
EMERALD ST
600 SD 92109 1247-H6
1500 SD 92109 1248-A5
EMERALD BAY DR
- SD 92154 1350-J2
EMERALD CITY DR
16000 SDCo 92082 1071-B4
EMERALD GROVE AV
8900 SDCo 92040 1231-J6
EMERALD HEIGHTS RD
1200 ELCJ 92020 1271-F1
1200 SDCo 91941 1271-F1
EMERALD HILL LN
9700 SDCo 92040 1232-A4
EMERALD HILL RD
30500 OCN 92003 1067-H4
30500 SDCo 92003 1067-H4
EMERALD HOLLOW DR
- VSTA 92081 1107-D1
EMERALD LAKE AV
6200 SD 92119 1250-H6
EMERALD OAKS GN
- ESCN 92027 1130-F2
EMERALD POINT CT
1300 SDCo 92019 1272-B5
EMERALD POINT LN
1300 SDCo 92019 1272-B5
EMERALD RIDGE RD
700 SDCo 92028 1027-G5
EMERALD SEA WY
- SMCS 92078 1128-A2
EMERALD VISTA DR
9400 SDCo 92040 1231-J5
EMERAUDE GN
1300 ESCN 92029 1149-G1
1300 SDCo 92029 1149-G1
EMERSON AV
600 CALX 92231 6680-F2
1000 CALX 92231 6620-F7
EMERSON ST
- CHV 91911 1330-C3
2800 SD 92106 1288-A1
E EMERSON ST
- CHV 91911 1330-E2
EMERY RD
600 SDCo 91980 429-L10
EMERYVILLE CT
- CHV 91913 1311-E6
EMET CT
4200 SD 92117 1248-E3
EMILA DR
600 CALX 92231 6680-E1
EMIL HASHEM AV
- CALX 92231 6620-J7
N EMILIA LN
100 SDCo 92028 1028-A2
S EMILIA LN
100 SDCo 92028 1028-A2
EMILY CT
4300 SDCo 91935 1274-B4
EMILY DR
4300 SDCo 91935 1274-A4
EMMA DR
900 ENCT 92007 1167-E3
EMMA LN
500 SDCo 92084 1088-F7
EMMA RD
3600 SDCo 92084 1088-F7
3800 SDCo 92069 1088-F7
EMMANUEL WY
3300 SDCo 91901 1274-J4
3300 SDCo 91901 1275-A3

STREET
Block City ZIP Pg-Grid

EMMAUS RD
11900 SDCo 92040 1232-A7
EMOGENE PL
1700 ESCN 92026 1109-C5
EMORY ST
500 IMPB 91932 1329-G7
900 IMPB 91932 1349-G1
3200 SD 92101 1268-H6
EMPIRE ST
8900 SD 92126 1209-B7
EMPRESS AV
10100 SD 92126 1209-B5
ENBORNE LN
6900 SD 92139 1290-F7
ENCANTADA
1500 SDCo 92021 1251-G2
ENCANTADA CT
1400 CHV 91913 1311-B5
ENCANTO AV
\- IMPB 91932 1349-E2
ENCANTO DR
\- CRLB 92009 1127-G3
100 ESCN 92027 1110-E7
800 CALX 92231 6680-H1
ENCANTO TER
800 CALX 92231 6680-H1
ENCELA LN
1000 SDCo 91977 1291-D3
ENCELIA DR
7100 SD 92037 1227-G7
ENCENDIDO
\- SD 92127 1168-J6
\- SD 92127 1169-A6
ENCHANTE WY N
1300 OCN 92056 1087-B3
ENCHANTE WY S
1400 OCN 92056 1087-B4
ENCHANTED PL
2200 SD 92173 1350-G3
ENCHANTMENT AV
1500 VSTA 92081 1107-G4
ENCINA AV
800 IMPB 91932 1329-G7
ENCINA CTE
\- SDCo 92065 1173-D2
ENCINA DR
5300 SD 92114 1290-B5
ENCINAS AV
\- CALX 92231 6620-H7
200 CALX 92231 6680-H2
ENCINA VERDE
\- SDCo 91905 (1319-H3 See Page 1298)
ENCINITA ST
4500 SD 92173 1350-G5
ENCINITAS AV
200 SD 92114 1290-H3
ENCINITAS BLVD Rt#-S9
\- ENCT 92024 1147-D7
1900 ENCT 92024 1167-J1
ENCINITAS WY
8500 SD 92114 1290-H4
ENCINO AV
8400 SD 92123 1249-B7
ENCINO CT
400 ESCN 92025 1130-B5
400 SDCo 92025 1130-B5
ENCINO DR
300 VSTA 92083 1087-G3
500 ESCN 92025 1130-B5
500 SDCo 92025 1130-B5
ENCINO LN
800 CORD 92118 1288-H7
ENCINO RW
1000 CORD 92118 1288-H7
ENCLAVE LN
\- CHV 91913 1331-F2
ENDEAVOR LN
4700 CRLB 92008 1106-H7
ENDERS AV
6900 SD 92122 1228-G4
ENELRA PL
5100 SD 92117 1228-G7
ENERGY WY
700 CHV 91911 1331-A5
ENERO CT
3700 SD 92154 1350-F1
ENERO ST
4100 SD 92154 1350-F1
ENERO WY
3900 SD 92154 1350-F1
ENFIELD ST
1500 SDCo 91977 1290-H2
ENGEL ST
100 ESCN 92029 1129-F3
ENGELMAN CT
1500 CHV 91911 1330-J3
ENGELMANN RD
\- SDCo 92027 1090-F7
\- SDCo 92082 1090-F7
ENGELMANN OAK LN
2500 SDCo 91901 1234-C7
2500 SDCo 91901 1254-C1
ENGELMANN OAK TR
28200 SDCo 92026 1089-F3
ENGINEER RD
7100 SD 92111 1249-A1
ENGINEER ST
2000 VSTA 92081 1107-J6
ENGINEERING LN
\- SD 92093 1228-A1
ENGINEERS RD
6000 SDCo 92036 1175-H2
6900 SDCo 92036 1176-A2
ENGLAND PL
700 SDCo 91901 1234-B4
ENGLEWOOD DR
1700 LMGR 91945 1290-H1
ENGLEWOOD WY
2800 CRLB 92010 1107-A4
ENGLISH RD
\- ImCo 92233 411-B9
\- ImCo 92257 411-B6
ENGLISH HOLLY LN
700 SMCS 92078 1129-B1
ENID CT
11600 SD 92131 1210-A1
ENIWETOK RD
2300 CORD 92155 1309-B1
ENNAR RD
31000 SDCo 92003 1048-H7
31000 SDCo 92003 1068-J1
ENRICO FERMI DR
2000 SD 92154 1352-B3
ENRICO FERMI PL
\- SD 92154 1352-B3
\- SDCo 92154 1352-B3
ENRIGHT DR
2200 SD 92173 1350-G3
ENSENADA CT
700 SD 92109 1267-H3
ENSENADA DR
\- IMP 92251 6499-H1

ENSENADA ST
1700 LMGR 91945 1290-G1
ENSIGN ST
5000 SD 92117 1228-F7
ENTERPRISE CT
3000 VSTA 92081 1108-A7
ENTERPRISE DR
\- ELCJ 92021 1251-H5
ENTERPRISE ST
300 ESCN 92029 1129-E2
300 SMCS 92078 1128-J1
400 SMCS 92078 1129-A1
3500 SD 92110 1268-F6
ENTERPRISE WY
\- IMP 92251 6499-F2
ENTERTAINMENT CIR
\- CHV 91911 1331-B6
ENTRADA AV
2200 SDCo 92084 1108-D3
ENTRADA GN
1200 ESCN 92027 1110-B5
ENTRADA PL
800 CHV 91910 1310-H7
ENTRADA ANGELICA
\- SD 92127 1189-B1
ENTRADA DEL SOL
3900 SDCo 92003 1067-F2
ENTRADA DE LUZ E
\- SD 92127 1169-A7
ENTRADA DE LUZ W
\- SD 92127 1169-A7
ENTRADA LAZANJA
\- SD 92127 1188-J1
ENTRANCE DR
3700 ESCN 92025 1150-C2
ENTREKEN AV
13000 SD 92129 1189-C4
ENTREKEN PL
8400 SD 92129 1189-C4
ENTREKEN WY
8300 SD 92129 1189-B4
ENTRY ST
300 OCN 92057 1086-H2
ENZ RD
1000 ImCo 92250 431-E6
EOLUS AV
800 ENCT 92024 1147-B2
EPANOW AV
4000 SD 92117 1248-E3
EPAULETTE ST
2800 SD 92123 1249-D6
EPEI HILL RD
\- SDCo 92070 409-K10
EPICA CT
12600 SD 92128 1170-C3
EPINETTE AV
4700 SD 92117 1248-B1
EPPERSON WY
10000 SD 92124 1249-G3
EPPICK CT
8000 LMGR 91945 1290-H2
8000 SDCo 91977 1290-H2
EPSILON ST
3800 SD 92113 1289-G7
EQUALITY LN
\- SD 92093 1228-A1
EQUESTRIAN CT
100 SMCS 92069 1108-J1
EQUESTRIAN TR
2000 SDCo 92065 1172-D3
EQUINOX WY
1200 CHV 91911 1330-H2
EQUITATION LN
\- SDCo 91902 1310-D4
ERIC LN
\- SDCo 91977 1291-B2
ERIC PL
9400 SDCo 92021 1232-H4
ERIC RD
2400 SDCo 92028 409-A4
2400 SDCo 92028 996-J1
N ERICA ST
600 ESCN 92027 1110-B6
ERICAS WY
11900 SDCo 92040 1211-H5
ERIDANUS CT
11400 SD 92126 1209-C1
ERIE CT
5300 OCN 92056 1087-E1
ERIE ST
1800 SD 92110 1268-E1
2200 SD 92110 1248-E7
2700 SD 92117 1248-E7
ERIK RD
3400 SDCo 92025 1150-E2
ERIN DR
900 ELCJ 92020 1251-B3
ERIN GN
\- SDCo 92003 1067-E1
ERIN LN
14300 PWY 92064 1190-H5
ERIN WY
9700 SNTE 92071 1231-D4
ERINS PL
2000 ESCN 92027 1110-B5
ERITH ST
6700 SD 92111 1248-H4
ERLANGER ST
5700 SD 92122 1228-F6
ERMA RD
\- SD 92131 1209-F2
ERSKINE DR
\- SDCo 92672 1023-E2
ERSKINE RD
\- ImCo 92251 430-L4
\- ImCo 92251 431-A4
ERWIN LN
9700 SDCo 92040 1232-A4
ESCADERA DR
10200 SDCo 92040 1231-F2
ESCADERA PL
11000 SDCo 92040 1231-F2
ESCALA CIR
\- SD 92108 1269-D1
ESCALA CV
3900 OCN 92054 1086-G1
ESCALA DR
11800 SD 92128 1170-A1
11900 SD 92128 1150-B6
ESCALA LN
12400 SD 92128 1150-C7
12400 SD 92128 1170-C1
ESCALA WY
\- SD 92108 1249-D7
\- SD 92108 1269-D1
ESCALLONIA CT
7300 CRLB 92011 1126-J7
ESCALON PL
\- CHV 91913 1311-E7
ESCARCHOSA LN
5400 SD 92124 1249-G1
ESCENICO TER
2000 CRLB 92009 1147-F2

ESCHELMAN DR
\- ELCN 92243 6559-J1
ESCOBA PL
11400 SD 92127 1149-J7
11500 SD 92127 1169-J1
ESCOBAR DR
10600 SD 92124 1249-H2
ESCONDIDO AV
100 VSTA 92084 1087-J6
900 VSTA 92083 1087-J6
1100 VSTA 92081 1107-G2
1100 VSTA 92081 1107-H2
2500 SD 92123 1249-B6
ESCONDIDO BLVD
100 ESCN 92025 1129-H2
N ESCONDIDO BLVD
600 ESCN 92025 1129-H1
900 ESCN 92026 1129-H1
1200 ESCN 92026 1109-G7
S ESCONDIDO BLVD
100 ESCN 92025 1129-J3
1300 ESCN 92025 1130-A5
2400 ESCN 92025 1150-A1
ESCONDIDO FRWY I-15
\- ESCN - 1109-E3
\- ESCN - 1129-H5
\- ESCN - 1150-A1
\- RivC - 998-H5
\- SD - 1150-A1
\- SD - 1169-J6
\- SD - 1170-A3
\- SD - 1189-F6
\- SD - 1209-F4
\- SD - 1229-F5
\- SD - 1249-F3
\- SD - 1269-G2
\- SDCo - 998-H5
\- SDCo - 1028-G4
\- SDCo - 1048-J4
\- SDCo - 1068-J3
\- SDCo - 1088-J1
\- SDCo - 1089-A2
\- SDCo - 1109-E3
\- SDCo - 1129-H5
\- SDCo - 1130-A7
\- SDCo - 1150-A1
\- SDCo - 1209-F4
ESCONDIDO FRWY Rt#-15
\- SD - 1269-G6
\- SD - 1289-F2
ESCONDIDO LN
300 CORD 92118 1288-J6
300 CORD 92118 1289-A6
ESCUADRO DR
3800 SDCo 92004 (1099-D1 See Page 1098)
ESCUELA GN
100 ESCN 92026 1109-H6
ESCUELA ST
100 SD 92102 1289-J3
ESFERA ST
7200 CRLB 92009 1128-A7
7300 CRLB 92009 1148-A1
7300 CRLB 92009 1147-J1
ESHELMAN DR
\- ELCN 92243 6559-J1
ESKER WY
\- CRLB 92010 1107-B4
ESLA DR
700 CHV 91910 1310-J6
ESMERALDAS DR
10600 SD 92124 1249-H1
ESMOND CT
10800 SD 92126 1209-B3
ESPANA DR
3600 OCN 92054 1086-F3
ESPANAS GN
100 ESCN 92026 1109-H7
100 ESCN 92026 1129-H1
ESPARTA CT
9700 SNTE 92071 1231-B4
ESPERANZA PL
700 CHV 91914 1311-H3
ESPERANZA WY
4100 OCN 92056 1087-C6
E ESPERANZA WY
1400 ESCN 92027 1110-A6
ESPERAR DR
13400 SDCo 92021 1232-D7
ESPINOSA SQ
9900 SD 92131 1209-H5
ESPINOZA RD
\- SDCo 92021 1213-B7
\- SDCo 92021 1233-B1
ESPINOZA ST
200 CALX 92231 6620-G6
ESPLANADE CT
4200 SD 92122 1228-C3
ESPLANADE ST
3600 OCN 92056 1107-B3
ESPLANADE PARK LN
\- SD 92123 1249-C1
ESPLANADE SANTA MONICA
\- SD 92127 1168-H7
ESPLENDENTE BLVD
5100 SD 92124 1249-H2
ESPLENDIDO AV
1900 SDCo 92084 1108-E3
ESPOLA RD Rt#-S5
14100 PWY 92064 1190-G1
14800 PWY 92064 1170-D3
16900 SD 92128 1170-D3
ESPRIT AV
13500 SD 92128 1190-B3
ESPUELA LN
400 SDCo 92026 1109-G3
ESPUELAS CT
1000 CHV 91910 1310-J5
ESQUIER DR
\- SDCo 92026 1089-A2
ESQUIRE GN
1800 ESCN 92029 1129-F5
ESSENCE AV
800 OCN 92057 1087-B1
ESSENCE RD
13500 SD 92128 1190-B3
ESSEX CT
4500 CRLB 92010 1106-J5
ESSEX ST
1000 SD 92103 1269-B5
1200 IMPB 91932 1349-H1
6300 ELCJ 92020 1251-C5
6300 LMSA 91942 1251-C5
ESSINGTON CT
\- SD 92154 1330-H7
ESTABLO ST
\- CALX 92231 6620-H6
ESTADA CIR
300 OCN 92057 1087-A1
ESTADA DR
4400 OCN 92057 1087-A2

ESTANCIA DR
3900 OCN 92054 1086-G2
ESTANCIA ST
7800 CRLB 92009 1147-J2
ESTANCIA LA JOLLA
\- SD 92037 1227-J1
ESTATE DR
4300 SDCo 92028 1048-B5
ESTATES CT
4900 SDCo 92020 1271-G2
ESTATES WY
4900 SDCo 92020 1271-G1
ESTEE CT
\- SDCo 92028 1027-H1
ESTELA DR
1900 ELCJ 92020 1251-C1
ESTELLE ST
5800 SD 92115 1270-C4
ESTEREL DR
7700 SD 92037 1227-J5
ESTERLINA DR
3500 SDCo 92028 1048-B3
ESTERO DR
2000 OCN 92054 1106-F2
ESTERO ST
2000 OCN 92054 1106-F2
ESTERO WY
800 ESCN 92026 1129-G1
ESTES ST
900 ELCJ 92020 1251-F7
ESTE VISTA CT
1300 ENCT 92024 1167-F3
ESTHER ST
4500 SD 92115 1270-C3
ESTIVAL PL
\- SDCo 92040 1231-G3
ESTORIL PL
\- SDCo 92003 1067-H2
ESTORNINO LN
300 SDCo 92021 1252-H3
ESTRADA CT
14300 SD 92129 1189-H2
ESTRADA ST
\- SDCo 92055 1085-G1
ESTRADA WY
1900 SD 92037 1247-H1
ESTRELITA DR
100 SDCo 92084 1108-C3
ESTRELLA AV
3800 SD 92105 1269-J5
4600 SD 92115 1269-J4
6100 SD 92120 1249-J7
6400 SD 92120 1250-A6
ESTRELLA DR
9800 SDCo 91977 1271-D4
9900 SDCo 91941 1271-D4
ESTRELLA LN
\- OCN 92054 1086-G3
ESTRELLA ST
100 SOLB 92075 1167-E7
ESTRELLA DE MAR CT
1900 CRLB 92009 1127-F6
ESTRELLA DE MAR RD
\- CRLB 92009 1147-F1
7000 CRLB 92009 1127-F5
ESTRELLA VISTA
12800 PWY 92064 1190-E5
ESTREMOZ CT
500 OCN 92057 1086-H4
ESTUARY WY
3500 SD 92121 1208-A5
ESTUDILLO ST
3500 SD 92110 1268-G6
ESTURION CT
2800 CRLB 92009 1127-H4
ESTURION PL
2800 CRLB 92009 1127-H4
ESTURION ST
2800 CRLB 92009 1127-H4
ETA ST
800 NATC 91950 1289-H7
800 SD 92113 1289-G7
ETCHEVERRY ST
100 SDCo 92065 1172-D1
ETCHINGS WY
9100 SDCo 92040 1232-D5
ETHAN ALLEN AV
3500 SD 92117 1248-D5
ETHEL PL
800 NATC 91950 1290-C7
ETHEL ST
400 CALX 92231 6680-G1
ETHEL TR
800 SDCo 92019 1253-C2
ETHELDA PL
4200 SD 92116 1269-H4
ETHELWYN LN
\- SDCo 92036 1136-C6
ETIWANDA ST
2200 SD 92107 1268-A6
ETON AV
3300 SD 92122 1228-D6
ETON CT
900 CHV 91913 1311-D5
5900 SD 92122 1228-D6
ETON GREENS CT
3300 SDCo 91978 1271-G6
ETUDE RD
13600 SD 92128 1190-B2
EUBANK LN
9900 SDCo 91977 1291-D2
EUCALYPTUS AV
100 VSTA 92084 1087-H6
300 ELCN 92243 6499-H5
800 VSTA 92084 1088-A6
1700 ENCT 92024 1147-A2
2100 SDCo 92029 1129-G6
2100 ESCN 92029 1129-G7
2300 ESCN 92029 1149-F1
EUCALYPTUS CT
200 CHV 91910 1310-D5
9700 SNTE 92071 1231-E4
EUCALYPTUS DR
800 ELCJ 92020 1251-E7
1400 SDCo 92021 1252-H3
EUCALYPTUS LN
1200 VSTA 92084 1088-A7
3200 SD 92037 1228-A4
4900 CRLB 92008 1107-A6
EUCALYPTUS RD
\- SDCo 92082 1071-E1
EUCALYPTUS ST
200 OCN 92054 1106-B2
9400 SDCo 91977 1291-C1
EUCALYPTUS GROVE LN
\- SD 92093 1227-J2
\- SD 92093 1228-A2
EUCALYPTUS HEIGHTS RD
16000 PWY 92064 1191-B1
EUCALYPTUS HILL
7400 LMSA 91941 1270-G3
EUCALYPTUS HILLS DR
11300 SDCo 92040 1231-G1

EUCALYPTUS HILLS DR
11400 SDCo 92040 1211-H7
EUCALYPTUS WOODS RD
700 SDCo 92069 1109-B2
EUCLID AV
100 SD 92114 1290-A5
100 SD 92113 1290-A5
400 ELCN 92243 6499-F5
1300 SD 91950 1290-A5
1500 NATC 91950 1310-B2
1700 ImCo 92243 6499-F5
1800 ELCJ 92019 1252-C5
1800 SDCo 92019 1252-C5
2100 SDCo 91950 1310-B2
2500 SD 92105 1270-A7
2800 SD 92105 1269-J6
4100 SD 92115 1269-J4
N EUCLID AV
\- NATC 91950 1290-A6
1000 SD 92114 1290-A1
1100 SD 92102 1290-A4
1300 SD 92113 1290-A6
1300 SD 91950 1290-A6
1700 SD 92105 1290-A1
2300 SD 92105 1270-A7
2300 SD 92102 1270-A7
S EUCLID AV
\- NATC 91950 1290-B7
700 NATC 91950 1310-B1
EUCLID AVEX
2800 SDCo 91950 1310-B3
2900 NATC 91950 1310-B3
EUCLID CT
4900 SD 92102 1290-A1
4900 SD 92105 1290-A1
EUCLID LN
600 SDCo 92019 1252-D6
EUCLID PL
\- SD 92113 1290-A5
EUGENE PL
3500 SD 92116 1269-G2
EUGENIE AV
700 ENCT 92024 1147-D4
EULA LN
2000 ELCJ 92019 1252-D4
2000 SDCo 92019 1252-D4
EUREKA PL
\- CHV 91913 1311-D6
3200 CRLB 92008 1106-F5
EUREKA RD
10600 SDCo 91978 1271-F6
EUREKA ST
1000 SD 92110 1268-G3
EUROPA ST
100 ENCT 92024 1147-A4
EVA DR
15900 PWY 92064 1170-D5
EVA DE LUCA WY
15400 SDCo 92082 1070-J3
EVALYN CT
12900 PWY 92064 1190-B5
EVALYN PL
12900 PWY 92064 1190-B5
EVAN HEWES HWY I-8
\- ImCo - 431-F6
EVAN HEWES HWY Rt#-S80
\- ImCo 92250 431-A5
200 ImCo 92243 6500-F5
600 ImCo 92243 6499-B6
900 ELCN 92243 6500-C6
900 ImCo 92243 431-A5
1700 ImCo 92273 431-A5
1800 ImCo 92273 430-J6
1900 ImCo 92251 430-J6
2800 ImCo 92259 430-J6
EVAN HEWES HWY Rt#-115
400 HOLT 92250 431-E5
1500 ImCo 92250 431-D5
EVANS AV
900 CHV 91911 1330-E1
EVANS PL
500 SD 92103 1269-A6
9600 SDCo 91941 1271-C1
E EVANS RD
\- SD 92106 1288-D1
W EVANS RD
\- SD 92106 1288-C1
EVANS ST
\- SD 92113 1289-D4
100 SD 92102 1289-D4
EVANSTON DR
13200 PWY 92064 1190-G4
EVANS WOOD WY
\- SD 92130 1208-F2
EVE LN
9500 SNTE 92071 1231-B1
EVE WY
10300 SNTE 92071 1231-E5
EVELYN LN
1200 VSTA 92081 1087-E7
1200 VSTA 92081 1107-E1
EVELYN ST
1000 SD 91945 1290-E2
1000 SD 92114 1290-E2
EVENING WY
3100 SD 92037 1228-A3
EVENING CANYON RD
3500 OCN 92056 1107-E2
EVENING CREEK DR E
10900 SD 92128 1189-H4
EVENING CREEK DR N
13100 SD 92128 1189-H4
EVENING CREEK DR S
13100 SD 92128 1189-H5
EVENING PRIMROSE TR
32000 SDCo 91906 (1318-B6 See Page 1298)
EVENINGSIDE GN
200 ESCN 92026 1109-G4
EVENING SKY CT
\- SD 92130 1188-C5
EVENING STAR CIR
\- SDCo 92082 1070-H2
EVENING STAR DR
14600 PWY 92064 1190-G1
EVENING STAR ST
\- CHV 91915 1311-H7
2400 CHV 91915 1331-H1
EVENING VIEW DR
\- CHV 91914 1311-J1
EVENSON WY
\- SDCo 92065 1173-J7
EVENSTAR LN
\- SDCo 92036 1155-H4
EVERELL PL
10300 SNTE 92071 1231-F3
EVERETT PL
23400 SDCo 92065 1173-C3
EVERETT ST
2100 SD 92113 1289-D4
5200 OCN 92057 1067-A3

EVERETT WY
\- VSTA 92084 1088-A2
EVERGLADES AV
6900 SD 92119 1250-F5
EVERGOLD ST
11500 SD 92131 1210-B1
11800 SD 92131 1190-B7
EVERGREEN AV
100 IMPB 91932 1349-E1
1500 SD 92154 1349-E1
1500 SD 92154 1329-J7
EVERGREEN CIR
1700 CRLB 92008 1106-F5
EVERGREEN CT
3700 SDCo 92028 1048-E1
EVERGREEN DR
900 ENCT 92024 1167-E1
1200 ENCT 92007 1167-E1
3400 SDCo 92084 1067-J6
29400 SDCo 91906 (1297-E4 See Page 1296)
EVERGREEN LN
800 SDCo 92084 1067-H6
1400 SMCS 92069 1109-D7
14100 PWY 92064 1170-G7
EVERGREEN PKWY
100 OCN 92054 1106-C2
EVERGREEN RD
3300 SDCo 91902 1310-G2
EVERGREEN ST
1000 SD 92106 1288-B2
2000 SD 92106 1268-C7
2900 SD 92110 1268-D6
N EVERGREEN ST
2900 SD 92110 1268-D6
EVERGREEN TR
\- SDCo 92060 1052-E2
EVERGREEN VILLAGE LN
\- SD 92102 1290-A4
EVERGREEN VILLAGE RD
\- SD 92102 1290-A4
EVERSTON RD
12600 SD 92128 1189-J6
EVERTS ST
4000 SD 92109 1247-J5
EVERVIEW RD
1400 SD 92110 1268-F2
EVILO ST
1100 ELCJ 92021 1251-H4
EVLOUISE DR
25200 ESCN 92026 1109-H2
25200 SDCo 92026 1109-H2
EVREN CT
\- IMP 92251 6499-H2
EVVIA CT
100 SDCo 92083 1108-B3
100 VSTA 92083 1108-B3
EWALD CIR
9100 SNTE 92071 1231-B7
EWELL CT
1100 SD 92154 1350-E1
EWING DR
1400 CHV 91911 1330-H3
EWING ST
5100 SD 92115 1270-D2
EXBURY CT
4400 SD 92130 1188-C5
EXCALIBUR WY
4500 SD 92122 1228-D3
EXCELLANTE ST
2000 SD 92154 1351-F3
EXCEPTION PL
3800 ESCN 92025 1150-D3
EXCHANGE PL
7600 SD 92037 1227-F6
EXCITATION GN
4000 ESCN 92025 1150-C4
EXECUTIVE DR
4100 SD 92037 1228-D2
4300 SD 92121 1228-D2
EXECUTIVE PL
2800 ESCN 92029 1129-C2
EXECUTIVE RDG
3200 VSTA 92081 1128-A1
EXECUTIVE SQ
4200 SD 92037 1228-C2
EXECUTIVE WY
9000 SD 92121 1228-D2
EXECUTIVE CENTER CT
\- SD 92154 1351-B1
EXETER ST
1200 ELCJ 92019 1251-J6
EXPEDITION WY
8700 SD 92093 1227-H3
EXPLORATION FALLS DR
\- CHV 91915 1311-G7
\- CHV 91915 1331-G1
EXPLORER CT
4200 SDCo 91941 1271-H4
EXPLORER PL
10900 SDCo 91941 1271-G3
EXPLORER RD
10800 SDCo 91941 1271-G3
EXPOSITION DR
18000 SDCo 91935 1274-D4
EXPOSITION WY
\- SD 92154 1351-B1
EYRIE RD
4900 SD 92116 1269-E3
EZEE ST
600 ENCT 92024 1147-C5
EZRA LN
14100 PWY 92064 1190-G1

F

F AV
\- SDCo 92055 1066-E1
100 NATC 91950 1289-H7
100 CORD 92118 1288-H7
400 NATC 91950 1309-H1
3000 NATC 91950 1310-A4
F CT
800 CHV 91910 1310-F7
F ST
\- CHV 91910 1310-A6
100 IMP 92251 6439-F6
200 SDCo 92065 1152-H5
500 CHV 91910 1309-J7
700 SD 92101 1288-J3
1600 SDCo 92055 409-A7
2400 SD 92105 1270-B7
2400 SD 92105 1290-B1
2500 NATC 91950 1310-C3
4500 SD 92102 1289-J3
E F ST
\- ENCT 92024 1147-C7
W F ST
100 ENCT 92024 1147-B7
FABER WY
5000 SD 92115 1270-A2

FABIENNE WY
8800 LMSA 91941 1271-A3
FABLED WATERS CT
\- SDCo 91977 1291-E1
FABLED WATERS DR
\- SDCo 91977 1271-E7
\- SDCo 91977 1291-E1
FAIR LN
1500 VSTA 92084 1108-B1
1600 ESCN 92029 1129-F5
8900 SDCo 92040 1231-J6
9000 SDCo 92040 1232-A6
FAIR ACRES LN
3100 SDCo 91978 1292-C1
3100 SDCo 91978 1272-C7
FAIRBANKS AV
9400 SD 92123 1249-E5
FAIRBROOK RD
12500 SD 92131 1210-B4
FAIRBURN ST
14600 PWY 92064 1190-J4
FAIRCHILD WY
\- SD 92154 1351-C2
FAIR COUNTRY RD
1500 SDCo 92019 1272-A2
FAIRCREST WY
28200 SDCo 92026 1089-G2
FAIRCROSS PL
3900 SD 92115 1270-C5
FAIRDALE AV
1700 ESCN 92027 1130-C1
FAIREN LN
9200 SNTE 92071 1231-B7
FAIRFAX DR
1600 LMGR 91945 1290-H1
FAIRFIELD AV
2800 CRLB 92010 1107-A4
FAIRFIELD DR
100 ELCN 92243 6500-A6
1500 ELCN 92243 6560-A1
FAIRFIELD ST
1200 CHV 91913 1311-C7
2100 SD 92110 1268-F1
2600 SD 92110 1248-F7
FAIRFIELD WY
\- ImCo 92249 6560-D7
FAIRFORD RD
12600 SD 92128 1190-A6
FAIRGATE DR
13600 PWY 92064 1190-F4
FAIR GLEN RD
1500 SDCo 92019 1272-A2
FAIRGREEN WY
5400 SDCo 92003 1068-B1
FAIRGROVE LN
9400 SD 92129 1189-E4
FAIRHAVEN ST
1900 LMGR 91945 1290-G1
FAIR HILL
\- SD 92127 1169-C3
FAIRHILL CT
600 OCN 92057 1087-C1
FAIRHILL DR
10100 SDCo 91977 1291-E2
FAIRHILL TER
1000 SDCo 91977 1291-E2
FAIRHOPE CT
17400 SD 92128 1170-A1
FAIRHOPE LP
2100 VSTA 92081 1107-G5
FAIRHOPE RD
11900 SD 92128 1170-A1
FAIRHURST PL
2400 SDCo 91977 1271-H7
FAIRLANE AV
900 SMCS 92069 1109-B7
FAIRLANE RD
26800 SDCo 92082 1090-E6
FAIRLAWN ST
9200 SNTE 92071 1231-G5
FAIRLEE DR
1900 ENCT 92024 1147-H7
1900 ENCT 92024 1167-H1
FAIRLEE LN
200 ENCT 92024 1167-H1
FAIRLIE RD
17400 SD 92128 1170-A1
FAIRLINDO WY
3600 NATC 91950 1310-D3
FAIRLOMAS RD
3200 NATC 91950 1310-D3
FAIRMONT PL
1500 ESCN 92027 1110-A5
FAIRMOUNT AV
1800 SD 92105 1289-J1
2400 SD 92105 1269-H6
4200 SD 92115 1269-H1
4300 SD 92116 1269-H1
4600 SD 92108 1269-H1
4700 SD 92120 1269-H1
5800 SD 92108 1249-H7
6000 SD 92120 1249-H7
FAIR OAK CT
2200 ESCN 92026 1109-H3
FAIR OAKS DR
3100 SDCo 91978 1292-C1
3100 SDCo 91978 1272-C7
FAIR OAKS LN
3100 SDCo 91978 1292-C1
3200 SDCo 91978 1272-C7
FAIRPORT WY
\- SD 92130 1208-C2
FAIRTREE TER
14700 PWY 92064 1190-D1
FAIR VALLEY RD
1500 SDCo 92019 1272-A2
FAIRVIEW AV
8000 LMSA 91941 1270-H3
9000 SDCo 91977 1291-A5
FAIRVIEW CIR
3600 SDCo 92084 1067-J5
3600 SDCo 92084 1068-A5
FAIRVIEW DR
2900 SDCo 92084 1068-A5
FAIRVIEW LN
3300 SDCo 92084 1068-A5
FAIRWATER PL
6400 CRLB 92011 1127-C4
FAIRWAY CT
\- SDCo 92004 1058-H4
800 CHV 91911 1330-D1
3000 OCN 92056 1106-G2
FAIRWAY DR
3200 SDCo 91941 1270-J5
3200 SDCo 91941 1271-A6
3200 SDCo 91977 1271-A6
3500 SDCo 92028 1028-F4
FAIRWAY LN
1500 SDCo 92004 1058-H5
FAIRWAY PK
1800 ESCN 92026 1109-D5
FAIRWAY PL
5900 SDCo 92067 1188-E2

STREET
Block City ZIP Pg-Grid

FAIRWAY RD
6800 SD 92037 1247-G1
6900 SD 92037 1227-G7
FAIRWAY CIRCLE DR
1800 SDCo 92078 1128-D2
FAIRWAY HEIGHTS RW
16200 SD 92128 1170-A4
FAIRWAY HILL CIR
- SDCo 92026 1089-A1
FAIRWAY OAKS DR
2300 CHV 91915 1311-G5
FAIRWAY PINE PL
- SDCo 92026 1089-B1
FAIRWAY POINTE RW
12200 SD 92128 1170-B4
FAIRWAY VISTA
- ENCT 92024 1147-D3
FAIRWIND CT
- SD 92130 1208-B2
FAIRWIND WY
- SD 92130 1208-B2
FAISAN WY
11400 SD 92124 1250-A3
FAISEL DR
2700 SDCo 91901 1254-A2
FAITH AV
500 ENCT 92007 1167-D1
FAITH CIR
1400 OCN 92054 1106-E1
FAITH RD
1800 ESCN 92029 1129-F5
FAIVRE ST
2300 CHV 91911 1330-B6
FALCHION DR
1800 SDCo 92004 1058-G7
FALCON DR
3100 CRLB 92008 1106-G4
FALCON GN
1300 ESCN 92029 1129-G6
FALCON LN
1400 ELCJ 92020 1251-D2
FALCON PL
400 SMCS 92069 1108-J7
700 SD 92103 1268-J6
FALCON ST
3000 SD 92103 1268-J4
FALCON BLUFF CT
- SDCo 92127 1169-E3
FALCON BLUFF ST
- SDCo 92127 1169-E3
FALCON CREST CT
- SDCo 92127 1169-G5
FALCON CREST DR
- SDCo 92127 1169-F5
FALCONER CT
1800 VSTA 92081 1107-J3
FALCONER RD
100 ESCN 92027 1110-E6
900 ESCN 92027 1130-F1
FALCONFIRE WY
300 SD 92114 1290-F3
FALCON HEIGHTS RD
16200 SDCo 92065 1151-B6
FALCON HILL CT
1600 ENCT 92007 1167-E2
FALCONHURST TER
4700 SD 92154 1330-H7
FALCON PEAK ST
1600 CHV 91913 1311-D7
FALCON RIDGE CT
4500 SD 92130 1188-C6
FALCON RIM PT
10600 SD 92131 1209-J3
FALCON VALLEY DR
2400 CHV 91914 1311-F3
FALDA PL
7700 CRLB 92009 1147-F2
FALDA DEL CERRO
- SDCo 92019 1272-A1
FALKIRK RW
2300 SD 92037 1247-J1
FALL PL
2400 OCN 92056 1087-D6
2400 VSTA 92083 1087-D6
FALLBROOK CT
1200 CHV 91902 1310-J3
1200 CHV 91902 1311-A4
1200 SDCo 91902 1311-A4
FALLBROOK LN
2800 SD 92117 1248-E7
FALLBROOK PL
- ESCN 92027 1130-H3
- SD 92027 1130-H3
FALLBROOK ST
1100 SDCo 92028 1028-A4
E FALLBROOK ST
1700 SDCo 92028 1027-J3
E FALLBROOK ST Rt#-S15
100 SDCo 92028 1027-G3
W FALLBROOK ST
100 SDCo 92028 1027-F3
100 SDCo 92055 1027-F3
FALLEN LEAF LN
2100 SDCo 92028 1028-A1
FALLEN LEAF RD
13300 PWY 92064 1170-E4
FALLEN OAK RD
800 SDCo 92028 1047-E4
FALLEN TREE LN
28400 SDCo 92026 1089-D3
FALLEN WOOD LN
5700 SD 92121 1208-F4
FALL GLEN CT
10200 SD 92126 1209-D5
FALLING LEAF CT
1900 SMCS 92078 1128-B2
FALLINGLEAF RD
2200 OCN 92056 1087-D5
FALLING STAR CIR
- SDCo 92082 1070-G2
FALLING STAR DR
1500 CHV 91915 1311-H7
1500 CHV 91915 1331-H1
FALLING WATERS CT
- CHV 91915 (1312-A5 See Page 1293)
FALLON CIR
3700 SD 92130 1188-A5
FALL RIVER WY
9200 SD 92129 1189-D4
FALLRIVER WY
1200 SMCS 92078 1128-A3
FALLS WY
6300 SD 92115 1270-C1
FALLSBRAE RD
4100 SDCo 92028 1048-A5
E FALLS VIEW DR
5100 SD 92115 1270-C1
W FALLS VIEW DR
5300 SD 92115 1270-C1
FALLSVIEW LN
100 OCN 92056 1107-D2
FALLSVIEW PL
1400 ESCN 92027 1109-J6
FALLSVIEW RD
- SMCS 92024 1128-B6
FALLWOOD AV
8900 SD 92126 1209-D5
FALMOUTH DR
1900 ELCJ 92020 1251-C5
2100 LMSA 91942 1251-C5
FALSE PT CT
600 CHV 91911 1330-J4
FALVY AV
2700 SD 92111 1249-A6
FAMILY CIR
7600 SD 92111 1249-A5
FAMILY PL
- SDCo 91977 1271-B5
FAMOSA BLVD
2200 SD 92107 1268-B6
2400 SD 92110 1268-B5
FANITA DR
600 ELCJ 92020 1251-B3
6900 SNTE 92071 1251-B1
8400 SNTE 92071 1231-B6
FANITA PKWY
9300 SNTE 92071 1231-A3
FANITA RANCHO RD
9000 SNTE 92071 1251-B1
9200 ELCJ 92020 1251-B1
FANITA RIO WY
8700 SNTE 92071 1231-B7
FANTASIA CT
11700 SD 92131 1210-B1
FANTASIA WY
11700 SD 92131 1210-B1
FANTASY LN
2200 SD 92173 1350-G3
FANTERO AV
1900 ESCN 92029 1129-F6
FANUEL ST
4000 SD 92109 1247-J4
FANWOOD CT
1900 OCN 92054 1106-E2
FARADAY AV
- CRLB 92008 1126-J1
1400 VSTA 92081 1127-G1
1400 CRLB 92010 1127-E1
1600 CRLB 92008 1127-B1
FARAWAY LN
7900 SDCo 92029 1148-J2
FARAWAY PL
14200 SDCo 92082 1070-F4
FAREL ST
2600 OCN 92054 1106-G1
FARENHOLT AV
1800 SD 92134 1289-C2
FARGATE TER
7200 SD 92126 1208-J4
FARGO AV
1500 ELCJ 92019 1252-A5
4600 SD 92117 1248-B1
FARGO GN
100 ESCN 92027 1110-E7
FARGO LN
1800 CHV 91913 1311-E7
FARINA PL
600 VSTA 92084 1088-A7
FARLAND PL
100 ESCN 92027 1130-C1
FARLEY CT
4200 SD 92122 1228-E5
FARLEY DR
6300 SD 92122 1228-E5
FARLEY LN
4200 SD 92122 1228-E5
FARLEY RD
2400 SDCo 92036 1135-F6
FARLEY FLAT RD
- SDCo 91916 1216-F6
- SDCo 91916 1236-G2
- SDCo 91931 1236-G2
FARLIN RD
1600 SDCo 91901 1235-B5
FARMDALE ST
7200 SD 92114 1290-G6
FARMER DR
- ELCN 92243 6559-F2
FARMER RD
700 SDCo 92036 1136-B3
FARMERVILLE ST
1200 CHV 91913 1311-C7
FARMINGDALE ST
- SD 92131 1209-G2
FARMINGTON DR
9500 SDCo 92040 1232-A4
FARMINGTON PL
2000 SMCS 92078 1128-B3
FARMS VIEW CT
6800 SDCo 92067 1188-H2
FARNHAM ST
9300 SD 92123 1249-D1
FARNSWORTH CT
5900 CRLB 92008 1127-C2
FARNSWORTH LN
1400 ImCo 92243 6560-A3
1400 ELCN 92243 6560-A3
FAROL CT
7700 CRLB 92009 1147-H2
FAROL PL
7700 CRLB 92009 1147-H2
FARR AV
900 ESCN 92026 1109-J7
1000 ESCN 92026 1110-A7
FARRA ST
- SDCo 92028 999-E6
FARRADAY RIDGE DR
3400 SDCo 91935 1272-F5
FARRAGUT CIR
400 ELCJ 92020 1251-F6
FARRAGUT RD
2500 SD 92106 1288-D1
2900 SD 92106 1268-C7
FARRAND CT
1000 SDCo 92028 1027-H5
FARRAND RD
1300 SDCo 92028 1027-H5
FARREL ST
600 CHV 91911 1330-H3
FARRINGTON CT
- SNTE 92071 1251-A1
FARRINGTON DR
2000 ELCJ 92020 1251-B1
6800 SNTE 92071 1251-A1
FAR VALLEY RD
1200 SDCo 91906 (1318-F5 See Page 1298)
FARVIEW CT
- ELCJ 92021 1251-G3
FAR VIEW PL
2400 SDCo 92084 1108-D4
FARVIEW ST
600 ELCJ 92021 1251-G3
FASANO DR
10300 SDCo 92040 1231-F3
FASHION HILLS BLVD
6800 SD 92111 1268-J2
FASHION VALLEY RD
1100 SD 92108 1268-J3
FATHER JUNIPERO SERRA TR
- SD 92119 1230-E7
- SD 92119 1250-D2
7300 SD 92071 1230-F6
7300 SD 92124 1230-F6
7500 SNTE 92071 1230-F6
FATHOM CT
500 SD 92154 1330-J6
FAULCONER ST
5400 SD 92105 1290-B1
FAUNA CT
6100 SD 92115 1270-D6
FAUNA DR
6000 SD 92115 1270-C6
FAUNTLEROY RD
- SDCo 91905 1300-C5
FAWCETT RD
- ImCo 92249 431-C7
- ImCo 92249 6620-B1
FAWLEY DR
1600 SDCo 92083 1108-A2
FAWN AV
3000 SD 92117 1248-C1
FAWN RDG
- SD 92130 1208-B2
FAWN CREEK LN
2400 SDCo 92026 1109-J3
FAWNTAIL CT
1700 CHV 91913 1311-D6
FAWNTAIL ST
- SMCS 92078 1128-J3
FAWNWOOD LN
7900 LMGR 91945 1270-J7
FAXON ST
100 SDCo 91977 1291-B4
FAY AV
7000 SD 92037 1247-F1
7300 SD 92037 1227-F7
FAYETTE ST
1300 ELCJ 92020 1251-D2
FAZIO RD
- SDCo 91901 1234-E5
FEATHER AV
4200 SD 92117 1248-E3
FEATHER DR
- SMCS 92069 1108-F5
FEATHER BLUFF DR
- SDCo 92127 1169-E3
FEATHERHILL LN
11200 SD 92126 1209-E2
FEATHER RIVER PL
1400 CHV 91915 1311-H7
FEATHER RIVER RD
2300 CHV 91915 1311-H7
FEATHER ROCK CT
3900 SDCo 91902 1311-B2
FEATHERSTONE CANYON RD
22100 SDCo 92040 (1193-C4 See Page 1192)
FEBO CT
3300 CRLB 92009 1127-J7
FEBRUARY CT
2100 SD 92110 1268-G1
FEBRUARY ST
4900 SD 92110 1268-G1
FECANIN WY
15800 SDCo 92065 1174-A4
FEDERAL BLVD
3900 SD 92105 1289-H2
4000 SD 92102 1289-H2
4800 SD 92102 1290-A2
5100 SD 92105 1290-A2
6000 SD 92114 1290-C1
6300 SD 92114 1270-D7
6400 LMGR 91945 1270-D7
FEDERAL BLVD W
3700 SD 92102 1289-G3
FEDERMAN LN
4100 SD 92130 1188-B5
FEENEY GN
- ESCN 92025 1129-J7
- ESCN 92025 1130-A7
FEGAN DR
- SDCo 92672 1023-E2
FEGHALI LN
500 SDCo 92065 1153-A5
FEGHALI RD
200 SDCo 92065 1153-A5
FEILER PL
3000 SD 92123 1249-F5
FELDSPAR AV
- CALX 92231 6620-J7
FELDSPAR CT
16600 SDCo 92065 1171-F2
FELICE DR
1900 ESCN 92026 1109-C4
16300 SD 92128 1170-B4
FELICIA LN
500 SMCS 92069 1109-B6
9900 SDCo 91977 1291-D3
FELICITA WY
2800 SDCo 92084 1068-E5
FELICIDAD DR
900 SDCo 92028 1027-G3
FELICITA AV
500 SDCo 91977 1291-B4
W FELICITA AV
500 ESCN 92025 1129-J6
500 ESCN 92025 1130-A5
FELICITA CT
1600 ESCN 92025 1129-J5
FELICITA LN
1200 SDCo 92029 1149-G1
1600 ESCN 92025 1129-J5
1700 VSTA 92083 1087-G3
FELICITA PL
600 ESCN 92025 1129-J5
FELICITA RD
1900 ESCN 92025 1129-J7
2100 ESCN 92029 1129-J7
2200 SDCo 92029 1129-J7
2500 SDCo 92029 1149-J1
FELINDA WY
2500 OCN 92056 1087-C6
FELINO WY
600 CHV 91910 1311-A5
FELIPE RD
17200 SDCo 92065 1173-F1
FELIX DR
10600 SNTE 92071 1231-D2
FELLER CV
10500 SD 92126 1209-A4
FELLOWS LN
- SDCo 92040 1231-H2
FELSON RD
9000 SD 92129 1189-C1
FELSPAR CT
4500 SD 92109 1248-B5
FELSPAR ST
700 SD 92109 1247-H6
1500 SD 92109 1248-A5
FELTON ST
1300 SD 92102 1289-F2
1800 SD 92104 1289-F1
2500 SD 92104 1269-F4
4400 SD 92116 1269-F4
FENDER RD
- SDCo 92036 1156-E7
FENELON ST
2900 SD 92106 1288-B1
FENIMORE WY
6000 SD 92120 1249-J7
FENNELL AV
5900 SD 92114 1290-C4
FENNELL CT
200 SD 92114 1290-C4
FENOVAL DR
1800 SDCo 92004 1058-G7
FENSMUIR ST
8500 SD 92123 1249-C4
FENTON PKWY
- SD 92108 1249-D7
2100 SD 92108 1269-E1
FENTON PL
2500 SDCo 91950 1310-C2
FENTON RD
5700 SD 92121 1208-G7
FENTON ST
2300 CHV 91914 1311-G4
2400 CHV 91915 1311-G4
FENWAY CIR
1400 OCN 92057 1067-A4
FENWAY RD
9200 SNTE 92071 1231-A3
FENWICK DR
3700 SDCo 91941 1271-A5
3700 SDCo 91977 1271-A5
FENWICK RD
10700 SD 92126 1209-B4
FERBER ST
5700 SD 92122 1228-F6
FERDINAND RD
2500 ELCJ 92020 1251-B5
FERGUS ST
700 SD 92114 1290-C3
FERGUSON RD
- ImCo 432-E1
- ImCo 92283 432-E1
FERGUSON WY
8900 SD 92119 1251-A4
FERMI AV
9100 SD 92123 1249-E5
FERMI CT
5600 CRLB 92008 1127-D1
FERN AV
400 IMPB 91932 1349-F1
1500 SD 92154 1349-J1
FERN GN
200 SD 92037 1247-E1
FERN PL
1300 SDCo 92081 1107-G3
7000 CRLB 92011 1127-E6
FERN ST
400 CHV 91910 1310-A5
1300 SD 92102 1289-E2
2000 SD 92104 1289-E2
2900 SD 92154 1350-C1
N FERN ST
600 ESCN 92027 1110-B6
FERN TR
- SDCo 92060 1052-E2
FERNANDO CT
12200 SD 92128 1150-B7
FERNANDO DR
12300 SD 92128 1150-B6
FERNANDO WY
18200 SD 92128 1150-B6
FERNBROOK CT
- ELCJ 92019 1252-C5
FERNBROOK DR
14000 SDCo 92065 1192-B2
FERN CANYON RD
3400 SDCo 91935 1272-H5
FERNCREEK LN
- ESCN 92027 1130-J3
FERNCREST PL
12000 SD 92128 1190-B2
FERNDALE LN
4100 SDCo 92028 1047-E4
FERNDALE ST
- CHV 91913 1311-C7
8600 SD 92126 1209-C5
FERN FLAT FIRE RD
- SDCo 91916 (1196-C3 See Page 1176)
- SDCo 92036 (1196-C3 See Page 1176)
FERN FOREST RD
1600 SDCo 92084 1068-B6
FERNGLEN RD
2700 CRLB 92008 1106-F3
FERNHILL WY
1100 ELCJ 92020 1251-H7
FERN MEADOW RD
- SDCo 92060 1052-D3
FERN RIDGE CT
500 OCN 92054 1086-D3
FERNRIDGE RD
7500 SNTE 92071 1230-G7
FERNTREE LN
2100 SDCo 91977 1291-D1
FERNVALE LN
- SNTE 92071 1230-G5
FERN VALLEY RD
2500 CHV 91915 1311-J6
FERNVIEW ST
1000 ELCJ 92020 1251-H7
FERNWOOD AV
- ESCN 92027 1130-C1
FERNWOOD DR
6200 LMSA 91942 1251-C6
FERNWOOD RD
1700 CHV 91913 1311-D6
FERRARA CT
- ESCN 92025 1129-H5
FERRARA WY
300 VSTA 92083 1087-G6
FERRELL LN
15000 SDCo 92021 1233-B7
FERRELL RD
400 ImCo 92231 431-B7
FERRIS SQ
6200 SD 92121 1208-G7
FERRY LN
- SMCS 92069 1108-H6
FESLER ST
500 ELCJ 92020 1251-D3
FESTIVAL CT
3700 CHV 91911 1330-E5
FESTIVAL DR
100 OCN 92057 1066-H7
FEZ ST
4300 SD 92121 1228-C2
F HERRERA ST
- CALX 92231 6620-H5
FIAT CT
2000 SDCo 92019 1272-C3
FICUS LN
1000 SMCS 92069 1109-B7
FICUS PL
- CRLB 92011 1127-D5
FIDDLETOWN RD
14000 PWY 92064 1190-G1
FIDELIO CT
11700 SD 92131 1210-B1
FIDELIO WY
12100 SD 92131 1210-B1
FIEGER ST
2100 SD 92105 1290-B1
FIELD CT
2900 SD 92110 1248-F7
FIELD ST
4400 SD 92117 1248-E6
4800 SD 92110 1248-F6
FIELDBROOK ST
1300 CHV 91913 1331-B1
FIELDBROOK WY
500 ESCN 92027 1110-D5
FIELDCREST PL
2500 ESCN 92027 1110-E7
2500 SDCo 91977 1271-E7
FIELDCREST ST
10000 SDCo 91977 1271-D7
FIELDGATE RD
4500 OCN 92056 1107-E2
FIELDLANE PL
2400 SDCo 91977 1271-D7
FIELDRIDGE PL
2400 SDCo 91977 1271-H7
FIELDS CT
- OCN 92057 1067-A4
FIELDSTONE DR
12400 SD 92128 1150-B5
FIELDSTONE LN
700 ENCT 92024 1147-G5
FIELDTHORN ST
- SDCo 92127 1169-E4
FIELDVIEW AV
- ELCN 92243 6559-G3
FIELDVIEW CT
- ELCN 92243 6559-G3
FIELDVIEW WY
14700 PWY 92064 1190-D1
FIERPOINT PL
- CRLB 92008 1106-H7
FIESTA AV
- CALX 92231 6620-H7
FIESTA BLVD
- CALX 92231 6620-F5
FIESTA DR
12800 PWY 92064 1190-E5
FIESTA GN
2000 ESCN 92027 1110-B5
FIESTA LN
200 ELCJ 92019 1252-A5
FIESTA WY
4200 OCN 92057 1086-J3
FIESTA ISLAND RD
- SD 92109 1248-C7
1700 SD 92109 1268-C1
FIFIELD RD
4300 ImCo 92227 431-D2
FIFIELD ST
500 CHV 91910 1310-G7
FIG AV
200 CHV 91910 1310-A6
500 CHV 91910 1330-B1
FIG CT
600 ESCN 92025 1129-J1
1200 NATC 91950 1289-J7
FIG ST
100 SDCo 92028 1027-F2
3900 SMCS 92078 1128-C1
E FIG ST
100 SDCo 92028 1027-F2
N FIG ST
100 ESCN 92025 1130-A2
700 ESCN 92025 1129-J1
800 ESCN 92026 1109-J7
800 ESCN 92026 1129-J1
S FIG ST
100 ESCN 92025 1130-A2
W FIG ST
- SDCo 92028 1027-E2
FIGTREE CT
- SD 92131 1210-C3
FIGTREE ST
12400 SD 92131 1210-B3
FIGUEROA BLVD
2600 SD 92109 1248-C5
FILAGO CT
9400 SD 92129 1189-E6
FILAREE CT
1600 CRLB 92011 1127-D6
FILBERT ST
300 ELCJ 92020 1251-G6
3600 SD 92136 1289-G7
FILERA RD
12300 SD 92128 1170-B4
FILIPO ST
4700 SD 92115 1270-D3
FILLBROOK DR
10900 SDCo 92040 1232-B1
FILLMONT GN
2600 ESCN 92029 1149-H1
FILLMORE LN
- SD 92123 1249-D1
FILLY LN
3600 SDCo 91902 1311-A1
FILMORE PL
1400 CHV 91913 1331-C1
FILOI AV
4500 SD 92173 1350-G3
FINANCIAL CT
2600 SD 92117 1248-B2
FINCH LN
2000 SD 92123 1269-A1
2000 SD 92123 1249-A7
FINCH PL
1200 CHV 91911 1330-G2
FINCH ST
900 ELCJ 92020 1251-D3
FINCHLEY TER
4700 SD 92130 1188-C4
FINE LN
1800 ESCN 92029 1129-F5
FINK RD
- SDCo 92070 409-J7
- SDCo 92070 (1053-J4 See Page 1052)
FINLEY AV
8200 LMSA 91941 1270-J3
FINNEY RD
- ImCo 92227 431-D3
FINNILA PL
- CRLB 92009 1127-G2
FINO DR
5100 SD 92124 1249-H2
FINO GN
700 ESCN 92025 1150-C4
FINSEN AV
4600 SD 92122 1228-F4
FIONA PL
6600 CRLB 92011 1127-D5
FIONA WY
8600 SNTE 92071 1231-D7
FIORE TER
5200 SD 92122 1228-E3
FIORENZA LN
- SD 92128 1189-H6
FIORI DR
2200 SDCo 92084 1108-D2
FIR LN
9700 SDCo 92029 1149-E2
FIR RD
- SDCo 91962 1237-C7
FIR ST
100 OCN 92054 1106-A1
100 SD 92101 1289-A2
300 SD 92114 1290-D4
500 SD 92101 1288-J2
600 VSTA 92083 1087-F6
2800 SD 92102 1289-E1
3400 SD 92104 1289-F1
3800 SMCS 92078 1128-C1
4800 SD 92102 1290-A1
FIRBROOK LN
12800 PWY 92064 1170-D3
FIRE RD
3700 SDCo 92028 1048-E3
FIREBAUGH PL
- CHV 91913 1311-D6
FIREBIRD ST
300 SMCS 92069 1108-H7
FIREBRAND DR
2800 SDCo 91901 1254-C2
FIREBRAND PL
2600 SDCo 91901 1254-D2
FIREBRAND WY
2800 SDCo 91901 1254-D2
FIRECREST WY
- SDCo 92028 1027-H7
FIRE MOUNTAIN DR
1700 OCN 92054 1106-F1
FIRE MOUNTAIN PL
300 ESCN 92026 1109-H5
FIRE OPAL CT
- SDCo 92127 1169-F5
FIRESIDE AV
8400 SD 92123 1249-C6
FIRESIDE CT
2800 SD 92123 1249-C6
FIRESIDE LN
700 VSTA 92084 1088-B7
FIRESIDE ST
100 OCN 92054 1086-F3
FIRESTONE DR
1700 ESCN 92026 1109-D5
FIRESTONE ST
4600 SD 92117 1228-F7
FIRETHORN GN
1900 ESCN 92027 1110-A4
FIRETHORN LN
4500 SDCo 92004 (1099-F4 See Page 1098)
FIRETHORN ST
700 SD 92154 1330-G7
900 SD 92154 1350-G1
FIREWATER TR
7500 SDCo 92036 1138-C7
7500 SDCo 92036 (1158-C1 See Page 1138)
FIREWAY DR
3400 SD 92111 1248-H4
FIRNPINE DR
3100 SD 92115 1270-D6
FIRST AMERICAN WY
- PWY 92064 1190-G6
FIRST LIGHT RD
- SMCS 92078 1128-F6
FIRST STAR DR
- CHV 91915 1331-H2
FIRTREE CT
300 ENCT 92024 1147-G7
FIR TREE PL
900 CRLB 92011 1127-A5
FIRWOOD RW
6000 SD 92037 1248-A1
FISHER CV
14800 SDCo 92014 1188-A1
FISHER LN
2900 LMGR 91945 1270-F6
FISHER RD
- SDCo 91905 1300-E7
1200 ImCo 92283 432-D4
1300 ImCo 92231 431-A7
1300 ImCo 92243 431-A7
FISHERMAN DR
- CRLB 92011 1127-C5
FISHERMAN LN
- OCN 92054 1086-E1
FISK AV
6600 SD 92122 1228-D4
FITCH CT
6900 SD 92111 1268-J2
FITCH LP
- SD 92152 1288-A6
FITZGERALD WY
9000 SDCo 91977 1271-A6
FITZPATRICK RD
300 SMCS 92069 1108-H6
FIVE CROWNS WY
100 ENCT 92024 1147-H7
FIVE D DR
1300 SDCo 92021 1251-H2
FIVE DIAMONDS RD
2300 SDCo 92004 (1078-G2 See Page 1058)
FIVE POINT LN
9100 SNTE 92071 1231-A7
FIX CT
- SD 92173 1350-F5
FLAG LN
1300 SDCo 92021 1251-H2
FLAG PZ
8300 SDCo 91977 1290-J6
FLAG LAKE ST
7600 SD 92119 1250-G5
FLAGSHIP CT
- SMCS 92078 1128-D5
FLAGSTAFF CT
2500 CHV 91914 1311-G3
FLAGSTONE CT
700 SMCS 92069 1109-C6
FLAGSTONE RW
6100 SD 92037 1248-A1
FLAIR LN
15700 SDCo 92065 1174-A4
FLAIR ENCINITAS DR
1400 ENCT 92024 1147-G6
FLAMBEAU PL
10700 SD 91941 1271-F4
FLAMENCO ST
6400 CRLB 92009 1127-H5
FLAME TREE LN
1400 CRLB 92011 1127-A4
FLAME TREE PL
200 OCN 92057 1087-A1
FLAMETREE RD
2300 SDCo 92084 1068-C7
FLAMINGO AV
1100 ELCJ 92021 1251-J2
1100 SDCo 92021 1251-J2
FLAMINGO DR
100 OCN 92054 1086-F4
FLAMINGO PL
1300 ELCJ 92021 1251-J2
FLANDERS CT
10200 SD 92121 1208-H5
FLANDERS CV
10400 SD 92126 1209-A4
FLANDERS DR
6400 SD 92121 1208-H5
7500 SD 92126 1208-H5
7600 SD 92126 1209-C4
FLANDERS PL
10400 SD 92126 1209-A4
FLAT ROCK ST
- CRLB 92010 1107-B3
FLAVEN LN
8100 SDCo 92021 1252-C1
FLAX CT
1000 SD 92154 1350-C1
FLAX DR
2800 SD 92154 1350-C1
FLAXTON TER
4900 SD 92130 1188-C4
FLEET ST
- CRLB 92008 1126-H2
FLEETRIDGE DR
1100 SD 92106 1288-A2
FLEETWOOD ST
1800 ESCN 92029 1129-F5
2300 SD 92111 1248-J7
FLEISCHMANN CT
- SDCo 92055 1086-A2
FLEISHBEIN ST
- CHV 91913 1331-E2
FLEMING CT
- SD 92145 1229-C2
FLEMING DR
3000 SD 92139 1310-E2
FLEMING RD
- SD 92152 1287-J5
FLEMISH PL
800 OCN 92057 1086-G5
FLETCHER DR
9100 LMSA 91941 1271-B2
FLETCHER PKWY
1000 ELCJ 92020 1251-C4
1000 ELCJ 92021 1251-C4
2900 LMSA 91942 1251-A7
7700 LMSA 91941 1270-H1
7700 LMSA 91942 1270-H1
8500 LMSA 91942 1250-J7
FLETCHER PT
- SDCo 92036 1155-G4
FLETCHER RD
4200 SDCo 92004 1100-B5
FLETCHER VALLEY DR
8900 SNTE 92071 1251-A1
FLICKER LN
100 OCN 92057 1086-H2
FLICKER ST
600 SD 92114 1290-F3
FLIGHTPATH WY
8500 SD 92154 1351-G1
FLINN CREST ST
9300 SDCo 92021 1232-H4
FLINN SPRINGS LN
9400 SDCo 92021 1232-J4
FLINN SPRINGS RD
- CHV 91915 1311-H6
9500 SDCo 92021 1232-J3
9500 SDCo 92021 1233-A4
FLINT AV
2100 ESCN 92027 1130-D1
FLINT PL
12100 PWY 92064 1190-E7
FLINT ST
900 ELCJ 92021 1251-H2
FLINTKOTE AV
11000 SD 92121 1208-A5
FLINTRIDGE DR
2100 SD 92139 1310-C1
FLINTRIDGE PL
600 ESCN 92026 1109-F4
FLINTWOOD WY
- SD 92130 1188-E5
FLIPPER DR
5900 SD 92114 1290-C4
FLO DR
1400 SDCo 91901 1234-A6
FLO BOB LN
- SDCo 91901 1234-H5
FLOOD RD
1300 ImCo 92283 432-D4
FLORA AV
1000 CORD 92118 1288-H7
1100 CORD 92118 1308-H1
FLORA DR
600 OCN 92057 1067-A6
FLORA AZALEA CT
10500 SNTE 92071 1231-E2
FLORA CAMELLIA CT
10500 SNTE 92071 1231-E2
FLORAL AV
13300 PWY 92064 1190-J4
FLORAL CT
800 SMCS 92069 1108-J5
800 SMCS 92069 1109-A5
FLORA MAGNOLIA CT
10400 SNTE 92071 1231-E2
FLORA VERDA CT
10500 SNTE 92071 1231-E2
FLORA VISTA
1400 SDCo 92027 1130-E5
12800 PWY 92064 1190-E5
FLORENCE LN
3400 SD 92113 1289-F5
FLORENCE ST
500 IMPB 91932 1329-H7
900 IMPB 91932 1349-H1
3400 SD 92113 1289-F5
FLORENCE TER
3100 SDCo 91978 1292-C1
FLORENCIA LN
400 VSTA 92083 1087-G6
FLORES LN
- LMGR 91945 1270-E7
FLORES DE ORO
300 SDCo 92067 1148-A7

STREET / Block City ZIP Pg-Grid

FLORES DE ORO
500 SDCo 92024 1148-A7
FLORESTA CT
12400 SD 92128 1170-B1
FLORESTA WY
12400 SD 92128 1170-B1
FLOREY CT
7300 SD 92122 1228-F4
FLOREY ST
6800 SD 92122 1228-F4
FLORIDA CT
1900 SD 92103 1269-C6
1900 SD 92104 1269-C6
FLORIDA DR
1700 SD 92101 1289-C1
1700 SD 92134 1289-C1
2600 SD 92101 1269-C7
FLORIDA ST
400 IMPB 91932 1329-H7
900 IMPB 91932 1349-H1
3400 SD 92104 1269-C5
4300 SD 92116 1269-C5
FLORIDO PZ
1000 CHV 91910 1311-A7
FLORINDO RD
11100 SD 92127 1169-H2
FLORINE DR
3100 LMGR 91945 1270-F6
FLORISSANT CT
8400 SD 92129 1189-B3
FLORITA ST
100 ENCT 92024 1147-B6
FLOWER AV
- CORD 92135 1288-F4
2200 SD 92154 1350-B1
FLOWER DR
- NATC 91950 1289-H7
FLOWER LN
300 VSTA 92083 1087-D7
FLOWER ST
- CHV 91910 1310-C5
500 CHV 91910 1309-J6
1700 ESCN 92027 1130-C1
E FLOWER ST
- CHV 91910 1310-C5
FLOWERDALE LN
200 SD 92114 1290-H4
FLOWER FIELDS WY
2600 CRLB 92010 1106-H3
FLOWER HILL DR
2500 SD 92014 1187-H1
FLOWER HILL WY
- SMCS 92078 1129-B1
FLOWER MEADOW CT
11500 SD 92126 1209-A2
FLOWER MEADOW DR
7500 SD 92126 1209-A2
FLOWERPOT LN
- CHV 91915 1331-H2
FLOWERS LN
24700 SDCo 91916 1236-A2
FLOWERWOOD LN
- SDCo 92028 1048-C3
FLOWING WELLS
- ImCo - 411-C8
FLOYD AV
600 CHV 91910 1310-F6
FLOYD SMITH DR
300 ELCJ 92020 1251-E2
FLUME DR
1700 SDCo 92021 1252-C2
1700 ELCJ 92021 1252-C2
FLUME RD
- SDCo 92020 1271-G1
8300 LMSA 91942 1250-J6
8300 SD 92119 1250-J6
8700 SD 92119 1251-A6
FLUSHING DR
2200 SD 92111 1248-J7
2200 SD 92111 1249-A7
2200 SD 92111 1268-J1
FLYING CLOUD CT
- IMP 92251 6499-C1
FLYING CLOUD WY
4700 CRLB 92008 1106-H7
FLYING H RD
3100 SDCo 92004 (1078-J5 See Page 1058)
FLYING HILLS CT
2000 ELCJ 92020 1251-B3
FLYING HILLS LN
1900 ELCJ 92020 1251-B3
FLYING LC LN
- CRLB 92009 1127-J3
FLYING U RD
2400 SDCo 92004 (1078-J2 See Page 1058)
2400 SDCo 92004 (1079-A2 See Page 1058)
FLYNN GN
- ESCN 92025 1130-B5
FLYNN HEIGHTS DR
700 SDCo 92069 1109-B2
F NECOCHEA ST
500 CALX 92231 6620-E7
FOG RDG
21000 SDCo 91901 1275-A3
FOGG CT
4400 SD 92109 1248-C5
FOGG ST
2400 SD 92109 1248-B5
FOGGY POINT DR
- CHV 91914 1311-J1
FOLEX WY
- SDCo 91978 1291-F1
FOLKESTONE ST
1500 LMGR 91945 1290-J1
1500 SDCo 91977 1290-J1
FOLLETT DR
9600 SNTE 92071 1231-F4
FOLLETTE ST
- CRLB 92011 1127-D5
FOLSOM DR
5800 SD 92037 1247-F3
FONDALE CT
600 ESCN 92027 1130-D2
FOND DU LAC AV
4000 SD 92117 1248-E1
FOND DU LAC CT
4000 SD 92117 1248-E1
FONDO RD
10000 SDCo 91977 1271-E5
FONTAINE PL
7100 SD 92120 1250-B5
FONTAINE ST
5100 SD 92120 1250-A5
FONTANA AV
3200 SD 92117 1248-E5
FONTANELLE CT
- SD 92128 1190-A3
FONTANELLE PL
- SD 92128 1190-A3
FONTEYN CT
9100 SNTE 92071 1231-H5

FONTICELLO WY
17600 SD 92128 1150-D7
17600 SD 92128 1170-D1
FONTS POINT DR
2800 SDCo 92004 (1099-G4 See Page 1098)
FONZIE AV
- ImCo 92251 6499-H1
- IMP 92251 6499-H1
FOOLS GOLD WY
1200 CHV 91913 1311-E6
FOOTBRIDGE WY
600 ESCN 92027 1110-D6
FOOTE PATH WY
1200 SDCo 91941 1251-D7
1200 ELCJ 92020 1251-D7
FOOTHILL AV
3900 CRLB 92010 1107-C3
FOOTHILL BLVD
4900 SD 92109 1247-J4
8000 SDCo 91962 1237-C4
FOOTHILL CT
- SDCo 91977 1291-E1
FOOTHILL DR
1100 VSTA 92084 1088-A4
2000 SDCo 92084 1088-C6
2800 SDCo 92084 1108-C1
FOOTHILL RD
200 SD 92173 1350-F3
FOOTHILL ST
3200 ESCN 92025 1150-C1
FOOTHILL RANCH LN
2200 SDCo 92084 1088-C6
2200 VSTA 92084 1088-C6
FOOTHILLS RIVER LN
9700 SDCo 92040 1231-J4
FOOTHILL TRANS CORR Rt#-241
- SDCo 92672 1023-C2
FOOTHILL VIEW PL
2000 ESCN 92026 1109-C4
2100 SDCo 92069 1109-C4
FOOTMAN CT
12700 PWY 92064 1170-C5
FOOTMAN LN
12600 PWY 92064 1170-C5
FORBELL PL
3800 SDCo 92028 1047-J4
FORBES AV
5400 SD 92120 1250-B5
FORD AV
500 SOLB 92075 1167-F6
FORD DR
- ELCN 92243 6499-F3
FORDHAM AV
800 CHV 91913 1311-C5
FORDHAM CT
3600 OCN 92056 1087-B7
FORDHAM ST
3200 SD 92110 1268-D5
FORDYCE ST
300 ELCJ 92019 1251-H6
FORECASTLE CT
5300 CRLB 92008 1107-C7
FOREST AV
1200 CRLB 92008 1106-F3
FOREST DR
11400 SDCo 92026 1109-J1
FOREST GN
1500 ESCN 92026 1109-G6
FOREST PL
300 VSTA 92083 1087-D7
FOREST RD
3600 OCN 92054 1086-F2
FOREST WY
500 DLMR 92014 1187-G4
FORESTDALE DR
1600 ENCT 92024 1147-H7
FORESTER LN
600 CHV 91902 1311-C4
FORESTER CREEK RD
1900 SDCo 92021 1252-D3
FOREST GLEN RD
3600 SD 92154 1350-E1
FOREST HILL DR
- SDCo 92065 1173-D2
FOREST HILL PL
1000 CHV 91913 1311-F5
FOREST LAKE DR
1000 CHV 91915 1311-G5
FOREST MEADOW CT
2300 CHV 91915 1311-H7
FOREST MEADOW RD
- SDCo 92036 1175-J2
FOREST OAKS DR
2300 CHV 91915 1311-G5
FOREST PARK LN
2000 CRLB 92008 1106-F3
FOREST PARK RD
2500 SDCo 91935 1274-F4
FOREST RANCH WY
- OCN 92057 1086-J2
FORESTVIEW LN
11000 SD 92131 1209-H4
FOREST VIEW WY
2700 CRLB 92008 1106-G3
FORGE LN
1100 SDCo 92028 1027-G4
W FORK RD
14100 SDCo 92059 1030-E7
FORMAL CT
7300 SD 92120 1250-C5
FORMULA PL
7600 SD 92121 1209-A7
FORNEY AV
3900 SD 92117 1248-E3
FORRESTAL CT
6900 SD 92120 1250-E4
FORRESTAL RD
7600 SD 92120 1250-E4
FORREST BLUFF
500 ENCT 92024 1147-E6
FORRESTER CT
3000 SD 92123 1249-E5
FORRESTER RD
1100 ImCo 92243 6559-A6
FORRESTER RD Rt#-S30
- ImCo 92227 411-A11
- WEST 92281 411-A11
1100 ImCo 92243 6559-A3
1800 ImCo 92243 431-A4
2200 ImCo 92251 431-A4
3900 ImCo 92227 431-A4
3900 ImCo 92259 431-A4
5000 ImCo 92281 431-A4
5200 WEST 92281 431-A4
5300 ImCo 92281 411-A11
FORREST GATE RD
400 SDCo 91906 430-B10
FORSBERG CT
1600 SD 92114 1290-D6
FORSTER ST
100 OCN 92054 1106-A2

FORSTERS TERN DR
- CRLB 92011 1127-B5
FORTINO PT
- SD 92131 1210-D2
FORTON WY
7400 SD 92111 1249-A7
FORT STOCKTON DR
400 SD 92103 1268-G5
FORTUNA AV
1400 SD 92109 1248-A6
FORTUNA ST
1700 CHV 91911 1330-E1
FORTUNADA ST
200 OCN 92057 1066-J7
FORTUNA DEL ESTE
19400 SDCo 92029 1148-F3
FORTUNA DEL NORTE
20700 SDCo 92029 1148-F1
20700 SDCo 92029 1128-F7
FORTUNA DEL SUR
20300 SDCo 92029 1148-F1
20300 SDCo 92024 1148-F1
FORTUNA RANCH RD
3200 ENCT 92024 1148-C4
3600 SDCo 92024 1148-E4
FORTUNA VISTA CT
7400 SNTE 92071 1230-F7
FORTUNE LN
9300 LMSA 91941 1271-B2
FORTUNE RD
- SMCS 92078 1128-H3
FORTUNE WY
2400 VSTA 92081 1108-A6
FORTUNELLA CT
- ESCN 92027 1110-D6
FORTY ROD TR
7400 SDCo 92036 1138-C7
FORUM ST
6500 SD 92111 1248-J3
FORWARD ST
300 SD 92037 1247-F4
FOSCA ST
3200 CRLB 92009 1127-J7
3300 CRLB 92009 1147-J1
3300 CRLB 92009 1148-A1
FOSS LN
1300 SDCo 91901 1233-H7
FOSS RD
1300 SDCo 91901 1233-H7
FOSS ST
3400 SD 92154 1330-E6
FOSTER LN
- SD 92126 1209-D7
FOSTER ST
2100 OCN 92054 1086-C7
7000 SD 92114 1290-F3
FOSTER TKTR
12900 SDCo 92040 1191-G3
12900 SDCo 92065 1191-H5
13800 SDCo 92065 1192-A1
FOSTORIA CT
9200 SDCo 92127 1169-D2
FOUCAUD WY
8500 SD 92129 1189-C7
FOULDS RD
- ImCo 92227 411-A10
FOUNTAIN PL
1000 ESCN 92026 1109-F5
FOUNTAIN ST
4200 SD 92109 1248-B5
FOUNTAIN GROVE PL
1400 CHV 91915 1311-H7
FOUR CORNERS RD
24900 SDCo 92065 1173-G7
24900 SDCo 92065 (1193-F1 See Page 1192)
FOUR CORNERS ST
- CHV 91914 1311-J1
FOUR CORNERS TR
- SDCo 92065 1173-H7
- SDCo 92065 (1193-H1 See Page 1192)
FOUR CS RANCH RD
39800 SDCo 91905 1300-D4
FOUR GEE RD
- SD 92127 1169-E2
9800 SDCo 92127 1169-E2
FOUR HUNDRED RD
27500 SDCo 92082 1090-B3
FOUR SEASONS PT
7100 CRLB 92011 1127-C6
FOURSOME DR
3500 SDCo 91941 1270-J5
3500 SDCo 91977 1270-J5
3500 SDCo 91977 1271-A5
FOURSOME DR E
2700 SDCo 92004 (1079-C3 See Page 1058)
FOURSOME DR W
- SDCo 92004 (1079-B4 See Page 1058)
FOUSSAT RD
100 OCN 92054 1086-E4
N FOUSSAT RD
100 OCN 92054 1086-E4
FOUTZ AV
2200 SD 92109 1248-B6
FOWLER DR
2100 SD 92139 1290-F7
FOWLER WY
9800 SNTE 92071 1231-B4
FOWLER CANYON RD
3400 SDCo 91935 1272-F6
FOWLES ST
200 OCN 92054 1086-E6
FOX AV
3400 SD 92117 1248-D3
FOX GN
1200 ESCN 92029 1129-F5
FOX LN
10300 SDCo 92026 1089-D6
FOX PL
3300 SD 92117 1248-D3
FOXBORO AV
1100 CHV 91911 1330-H1
FOXBOROUGH CT
8700 SDCo 92040 1232-C6
FOXBOROUGH LN
8800 SDCo 92040 1232-C7
FOXBOROUGH PT
- SD 92130 1208-D2
FOX BRIDGE CT
1800 SDCo 92028 1028-G5
FOXBURY GN
1700 ESCN 92026 1109-D2
FOXCROFT CT
12500 SD 92129 1189-C6
FOXCROFT PL
8500 SD 92129 1189-C5
FOXDALE PL
100 ESCN 92027 1130-C1
FOXFIRE CT
- ESCN 92026 1109-D6

FOXFIRE LN
200 SDCo 92028 1027-F5
FOXFIRE PL
1600 ESCN 92026 1109-D5
FOXFIRE RD
1700 SDCo 92028 1027-F5
FOXGLOVE LN
3800 SDCo 92028 1048-F1
FOXGLOVE ST
700 ENCT 92024 1147-E6
FOXGLOVE VW
1000 CRLB 92011 1127-B6
FOXGLOVE WY
- SD 92130 1188-G3
FOXGROVE PL
3600 SD 92130 1187-J5
3600 SD 92130 1188-A5
FOXHALL CT
- SMCS 92078 1128-G2
FOXHALL DR
700 SMCS 92078 1128-G2
FOXHALL GN
3000 ESCN 92029 1150-A2
FOXHILLS TER
1800 VSTA 92081 1108-E2
FOXHOLLOW CT
4400 SD 92130 1188-B6
FOXHOUND WY
- SD 92130 1208-D2
FOX HUNT LN
14800 SD 92128 1170-B7
FOXLEY DR
3600 ESCN 92027 1110-F4
FOX MEADOW RD
- SDCo 92127 1169-E4
FOX POINT LN
- SDCo 92004 (1099-H4 See Page 1098)
FOX RUN LN
29100 SDCo 92082 1070-J7
N FOX RUN PL
- CHV 91914 1311-H3
S FOX RUN PL
- CHV 91914 1311-H3
FOX RUN RW
14200 SD 92130 1188-D2
E FOX RUN WY
3000 SD 92111 1248-H5
W FOX RUN WY
3000 SD 92111 1248-H5
FOXTAIL CT
4500 OCN 92056 1087-D4
FOXTAIL LP
- CRLB 92010 1107-D7
FOXTAIL ST
1900 VSTA 92081 1107-J4
FOXTAIL WY
- SD 92130 1188-G3
FOXTAIL CANYON DR
1400 CHV 91913 1331-A2
FOXTAIL PINE DR
- CHV 91915 (1312-A7 See Page 1293)
FOXTRAIL DR
- ELCN 92243 6559-J3
FOX VALLEY CT
- SDCo 92127 1169-E4
FOX VALLEY DR
- SDCo 92127 1169-E4
FOX VALLEY LN
- SDCo 92127 1169-E4
FOX VALLEY WY
- SDCo 92127 1169-E4
FOXWOOD DR
600 OCN 92057 1066-H7
FOXWOOD RD
10700 SD 92126 1209-B4
FOY LN
600 ESCN 92025 1129-J6
600 ESCN 92025 1130-A6
FOYLE WY
6500 SD 92117 1248-J2
FOYT CT
1900 SDCo 92019 1272-C3
F PEDROZA CT
- CALX 92231 6620-J6
FRACE LN
27500 SDCo 92082 1090-B3
FRAKES ST
7100 SD 92111 1248-J4
FRAME CT
13200 PWY 92064 1190-C4
FRAME RD
13300 PWY 92064 1190-C4
FRAMES PORT PL
11600 SD 92126 1208-J1
FRANCES DR
100 SDCo 92019 1253-C1
1900 VSTA 92084 1087-J5
FRANCESCA DR
200 OCN 92057 1087-A2
FRANCINE CT
12800 PWY 92064 1190-A5
FRANCINE PL
12800 PWY 92064 1190-B5
FRANCINE TER
12800 PWY 92064 1190-A5
FRANCIS DR
8700 SNTE 92071 1231-E7
9400 SDCo 91977 1271-B6
FRANCIS ST
200 SD 92102 1289-F4
5100 OCN 92057 1067-B5
S FRANCIS ST
- SD 92113 1289-F4
FRANCIS WY
4200 LMSA 91941 1270-F4
FRANCISCAN RD
- CRLB 92011 1126-H5
FRANCISCAN WY
- OCN 92057 1086-G2
1100 SD 92116 1269-B3
FRANCISCO DR
17300 SD 92128 1170-B1
FRANK LN
10300 SNTE 92071 1231-B1
FRANK WY
9500 SNTE 92071 1231-E5
FRANK DANIELS WY
10600 SD 92131 1210-A2
FRANKEL WY
2900 SD 92111 1248-H6
FRANKFORT ST
1300 SD 92110 1268-E1
2200 SD 92110 1248-E7
2700 SD 92117 1248-E6
FRANKIE CT
9000 SDCo 92040 1231-J6
9000 SDCo 92040 1232-A6
FRANKLIN
14100 SDCo 92040 1232-H5
FRANKLIN AV
800 ELCJ 92020 1251-E6
2000 SD 92113 1289-D4

FRANKLIN AV
4800 SD 92113 1290-A4
FRANKLIN LN
500 VSTA 92084 1087-H5
1300 SDCo 92065 1172-G2
FRANKLIN RD
- IMP 92251 6439-F5
FRASCATI WY
9500 SNTE 92071 1231-B4
FRAULINE DR
1300 SD 92154 1350-A2
FRAXINELLA ST
200 ENCT 92024 1147-E6
FRAZEE RD
1300 SD 92108 1269-A2
5000 OCN 92057 1086-J1
5000 OCN 92057 1087-A1
FRAZIER DR
8600 SD 92119 1250-J3
FRED DR
13200 PWY 92064 1190-C4
FREDA LN
1600 ENCT 92007 1167-F2
FREDAS HILL RD
3300 SDCo 92084 1108-E1
FRED CANYON RD
- SDCo 91962 430-B6
FREDCURT LN
11300 SDCo 92040 1231-G1
FREDERICK ST
8900 SDCo 91977 1291-A3
FREDERICKA PKWY
200 CHV 91910 1310-B5
FRED MARTIN LN
- SDCo 92040 1231-J2
FREDONIA ST
5500 SD 92105 1290-B1
FREDRICKS AV
200 OCN 92054 1086-F3
FREDRICKS RD
500 ImCo 92227 431-B1
FREEBORN WY
2800 ELCJ 92020 1251-A5
FREED MANOR LN
6800 SD 92114 1290-E6
FREEDOM CT
3000 ESCN 92029 1150-A2
FREEDOM LN
1000 SOLB 92014 1187-H1
FREEDOM WY
- VSTA 92081 1107-G5
FREEDOM HILL
- SDCo 92040 1232-F4
FREEMAN ST
100 OCN 92054 1086-A7
100 OCN 92054 1106-A1
3000 SD 92106 1268-C6
N FREEMAN ST
100 OCN 92054 1086-A7
FREEPORT CT
10100 SD 92129 1189-F4
FREEPORT RD
13500 SD 92129 1189-F3
FRWY I-8
- ELCJ - 1251-F4
- ELCJ - 1252-B3
- ELCN - 1271-C1
- ELCN - 6559-J2
- ELCN - 6560-C1
- ImCo - 430-K6
- ImCo - 431-D6
- ImCo - 432-A5
- ImCo - 6559-F2
- ImCo - 6560-J1
- LMSA - 1251-B7
- LMSA - 1270-E1
- LMSA - 1271-C1
- SD - 1269-H1
- SD - 1270-A1
- SDCo - 430-A6
- SDCo - 1232-J4
- SDCo - 1233-E3
- SDCo - 1234-A5
- SDCo - 1235-F5
- SDCo - 1236-A7
- SDCo - 1237-A7
- SDCo - 1252-B3
- SDCo - (1299-C1 See Page 1298)
- SDCo - 1300-A2
- SDCo - (1301-A6 See Page 1300)
- SDCo - (1321-F1 See Page 1300)
FRWY Rt#-52
- SD - 1228-H6
- SD - 1229-D6
- SD - 1230-C4
- SD - 1231-A7
- SNTE - 1230-H6
- SNTE - 1231-A7
FRWY Rt#-94
- LMGR - 1270-J5
- LMSA - 1271-A4
- SD - 1270-J4
- SDCo - 1271-A4
FRWY Rt#-111
- ImCo - 431-C2
- ImCo - 6500-E1
- ImCo - 6560-E1
FRWY Rt#-125
- ELCJ - 1251-A2
- LMGR - 1270-J5
- LMGR - 1290-J1
- LMSA - 1251-A5
- LMSA - 1270-J5
- LMSA - 1271-A1
- SD - 1251-A6
- SD - 1270-J4
- SDCo - 1271-A4
- SDCo - 1290-J1
- SDCo - 1291-A6
- SNTE - 1231-A7
- SNTE - 1251-A1
FRWY Rt#-163
- SD - 1249-A6
FRWY Rt#-905
- SD - 1350-G2
- SD - 1351-A2
FREEWAY LN
- OCN 92054 1106-C1
FREEZER RD
- SDCo 91917 (1314-C6 See Page 1294)
FREMONT PL
19200 SDCo 92029 1149-E4
FREMONT ST
1400 VSTA 92084 1087-J4
3500 SD 92103 1268-H6
FREMONTIA LN
5400 SD 92115 1269-J1
FRENATA PL
- CRLB 92011 1127-C5
FRENCH CT
1400 OCN 92054 1106-E1

FRENZEL CIR
3600 OCN 92056 1106-J1
3600 OCN 92056 1107-A1
FRESCA CT
700 SOLB 92075 1187-F1
FRESCA ST
600 SOLB 92075 1187-F1
FRESCO LN
- SD 92129 1188-J4
FRESH WATERS CT
- SDCo 91978 1291-E2
FRESHWIND CT
11500 SD 92127 1169-J5
FRESNILLO CT
100 SOLB 92075 1167-D7
FRESNILLO WY
100 SOLB 92075 1167-D7
FRESNO AV
1600 CHV 91911 1330-D5
8300 LMSA 91941 1270-J3
FRESNO ST
1000 SD 92110 1268-G3
FREY CT
13400 PWY 92064 1190-J4
FRIANT ST
8600 SD 92126 1209-C4
FRIAR PL
1400 CHV 91911 1330-E4
FRIARS RD
4500 SD 92109 1268-E3
4700 SD 92110 1268-F3
5500 SD 92108 1269-D1
5800 SD 92108 1268-F3
5900 SD 92111 1268-F3
7100 SD 92111 1269-B2
9200 SD 92108 1249-F7
9900 SD 92124 1249-G7
10100 SD 92120 1249-G7
FRIED AV
2900 SD 92122 1228-C6
FRIEDELL DR
2600 SD 92110 1268-E6
FRIEDRICK DR
1700 SD 92104 1289-F2
FRIENDLY CIR
800 ELCJ 92021 1251-G4
FRIENDLY CT
500 ELCJ 92021 1251-G4
FRIENDLY DR
1900 SDCo 92084 1088-C4
1900 VSTA 92084 1088-C4
FRIENDLY PL
6500 CRLB 92011 1126-H4
FRIENDS WY
1300 SDCo 92028 1027-J5
FRIENDSHIP DR
1900 ELCJ 92020 1251-D1
FRIENDSHIP LN
1600 SDCo 92026 1109-E6
FRINK AV
4800 SD 92117 1248-F1
4900 SD 92117 1228-F7
FRINK RD
- ImCo 92257 411-A5
FRISBIE ST
3500 SDCo 91902 1310-J1
FRISIUS DR
1600 SDCo 92036 1156-A5
2300 SDCo 92036 1155-J4
FROBISHER CIR
10500 SD 92126 1209-C4
FROBISHER ST
8600 SD 92126 1209-C4
FROEBEL DR
200 ESCN 92025 1130-A6
FROG HOLLOW
11500 SDCo 92082 1069-H2
FROLIC WY
1800 SDCo 92028 1028-A2
N FROLIC WY
100 SDCo 92028 1028-A2
FROME
9300 SDCo 92040 1232-H5
FRONDOSO DR
17300 SD 92128 1170-C1
17600 SD 92128 1150-C7
FRONSAC ST
12300 SD 92131 1210-B2
FRONT ST
- SD 92152 1288-A5
100 ELCJ 92020 1251-D6
200 SD 92101 1289-A1
500 SD 92173 1350-G5
FRONTAGE RD
- SMCS 92069 1108-H4
1200 ELCN 92243 6499-F4
1200 SD 92154 1350-C1
1200 CHV 91911 1330-A4
1900 SD 91911 1330-A5
8100 SD 92123 1249-B4
8100 SD 92037 1228-A6
47000 RivC 92592 999-A1
FRONTERA DR
- CALX 92231 6620-H7
FRONTERA RD
12200 SD 92128 1170-B2
FRONTIER DR
100 OCN 92054 1086-F4
FROST AV
- CRLB 92008 1107-A7
FROST ST
7900 SD 92123 1249-B5
FROSTMAR PL
8300 SD 92121 1228-H2
FROUDE ST
1000 SD 92107 1287-H1
1400 SD 92107 1267-J7
1800 SD 92107 1268-A6
FRUCHT ST
2200 SD 92136 1289-G7
FRUITLAND DR
2900 SDCo 92084 1068-A7
2900 SDCo 92084 1067-J6
FRUIT TREE WY
500 OCN 92054 1086-F2
FRUITVALE HTS
29100 SDCo 92082 1071-A7
FRUITVALE LN
29000 SDCo 92082 1070-H7
FRUITVALE RD
14200 SDCo 92082 1070-H7
15600 SDCo 92082 1071-A7
FRY LN
12100 SDCo 92082 1070-A5
FRYDEN CT
3100 SD 92117 1248-D3
FRYING PAN RD
2600 SDCo 92004 (1078-J3 See Page 1058)
2900 SDCo 92004 (1079-A4 See Page 1058)
F TORRES ST
- CALX 92231 6620-H5

FUCHSIA CT
1800 OCN 92054 1106-E2
FUCHSIA DR
- SD 92109 1248-C6
FUCHSIA LN
800 SD 92154 1330-G7
900 CRLB 92011 1126-J5
900 CRLB 92011 1127-A5
1000 SD 92154 1350-G1
FUERTE DR
1800 SDCo 92020 1272-A2
3400 SDCo 92020 1271-J2
9100 LMSA 91941 1271-B1
9300 SDCo 91941 1271-B1
FUERTE LN
2000 ESCN 92026 1109-D4
FUERTE ST
1700 SDCo 92028 1028-A5
2200 OCN 92054 1106-E1
FUERTE BLUFF DR
1600 SDCo 92019 1272-A2
FUERTE ESTATES DR
1700 SDCo 92019 1271-J3
FUERTE FARMS RD
11300 SDCo 92020 1271-H3
FUERTE HEIGHTS LN
1400 SDCo 92019 1272-A3
FUERTE HILLS DR
1600 SDCo 92020 1271-J2
FUERTE KNOLLS LN
1600 SDCo 92020 1271-J2
FUERTE RANCH RD
1600 SDCo 92019 1272-A2
FUERTE VALLEY DR
1700 SDCo 92019 1271-J3
1700 SDCo 92019 1272-A3
FUERTE VISTA LN
1700 SDCo 92020 1271-J3
FUJI ST
6800 SD 92139 1290-F7
FULHAM WY
2300 SD 92139 1290-G7
FULLER ST
- SDCo 92055 1067-A2
FULLERTON AV
9200 SD 92123 1249-E6
FULMAR ST
6000 SD 92114 1290-C1
FULTON RD
800 SMCS 92069 1109-A6
1400 ESCN 92026 1109-B6
FULTON ST
6700 SD 92111 1248-J7
7200 SD 92111 1249-A7
FULVIA ST
300 ENCT 92024 1147-B4
FULWOOD LN
7300 SD 92111 1249-A7
FUN LN
1600 ESCN 92029 1129-F5
FUNQUEST DR
900 SDCo 92028 1027-G3
FURLONG PL
- SD 92130 1208-D2
FURNACE CREEK RD
15200 SDCo 92021 1232-J1
FURNER ST
2100 ELCJ 92020 1251-B1
FURY LN
10800 SDCo 91941 1271-G4
11300 SDCo 92019 1271-G4
11900 SDCo 92019 1272-A5
FUSCO LN
22100 SDCo 91901 1275-C1
FUTURA ST
12600 SD 92130 1188-B6
FUTURITY LN
200 SDCo 92028 1047-G3

G

G AV
100 CORD 92118 1288-H6
200 NATC 91950 1289-H7
400 NATC 91950 1309-J1
G CT
800 CHV 91910 1310-F7
G RD E
- CORD 92135 1288-F6
G ST
- NATC 91950 1310-C3
- CHV 91910 1310-C6
200 SD 92101 1289-A3
200 IMP 92251 6439-F6
300 SDCo 92065 1152-H6
500 SD 92101 1288-J3
700 CHV 91910 1309-H7
900 CHV 91910 1329-H1
1500 SDCo 92055 1047-A5
1900 SD 92102 1289-C3
E G ST
- ENCT 92024 1147-C7
W G ST
100 ENCT 92024 1147-B7
GABACHO DR
10600 SD 92124 1249-H1
GABACHO ST
7800 CRLB 92009 1147-H2
GABARDA RD
16200 SD 92128 1170-C3
GABBIANO LN
7400 CRLB 92011 1127-A7
GABELWOOD WY
- SD 92130 1208-F2
GABILAN RD
13200 SD 92128 1189-J4
GABLE WY
700 ELCJ 92020 1251-E3
GABLER DR
29900 SDCo 92082 1069-H6
GABLE RIDGE RD
14800 SD 92128 1170-B7
14800 SD 92128 1190-B4
GABLES ST
5500 SD 92139 1310-C1
GABRIEL WY
4700 SDCo 91941 1271-D3
GABRIELIENO AV
4900 OCN 92057 1067-B7
GABRIELLE GN
2000 ESCN 92029 1129-E5
GABRIELSON AV
2800 SD 92111 1249-A6
GADWALL CT
7400 CRLB 92011 1127-D4
GAEBRAIL CT
- IMP 92251 6499-H2
GAELYN CT
14200 PWY 92064 1190-E2
GAETANO ALTIERI DR
30600 SDCo 92082 1070-J3
GAFFNEY CT
3900 SD 92130 1188-A4

STREET
Block City ZIP Pg-Grid

GAGE DR
- SDCo 92055 1086-A2
500 SD 92106 1288-A3
GAGE LN
3400 SD 92106 1288-A3
GAGE PL
3400 SD 92106 1288-A3
GAI CT
900 SD 92154 1330-G7
GAI DR
1000 SD 92154 1330-G7
1000 SD 92154 1350-G1
GAIL DR
200 VSTA 92084 1087-H3
3700 OCN 92056 1107-A2
GAIL PL
13200 SDCo 92040 1232-C5
GAILES BLVD
1600 SD 92154 1351-F2
GAILLON CT
- SD 92128 1150-C6
GAIL PARK LN
14700 PWY 92064 1190-F1
GAIN DR
7000 SD 92119 1250-J3
GAINARD WY
4500 SD 92124 1249-F2
GAINES ST
3200 SD 92110 1268-F3
5400 SD 92110 1268-F3
GAINSBOROUGH AV
8800 SD 92129 1189-C2
GALA AV
5400 SD 92120 1250-B5
GALAHAD RD
2200 SD 92123 1249-C7
GALANTE WY
- OCN 92057 1086-G2
GALATEA LN
9600 SDCo 92026 1089-D4
GALAXY CT
7500 SD 92120 1250-C4
GALAXY DR
500 VSTA 92083 1087-D6
800 SDCo 92083 1087-D6
GALBAR PL
4100 OCN 92056 1087-C7
GALBAR ST
4000 OCN 92056 1087-C7
GALDAR PL
1000 CHV 91910 1310-J5
GALE ST
1000 ESCN 92027 1110-B6
GALENA AV
- CRLB 92009 1127-G6
4900 SD 92110 1268-F1
GALENA ST
500 ELCJ 92019 1252-B4
GALENA CANYON RD
- SDCo 92127 1149-E7
GALEON CT
500 SDCo 91977 1291-C3
GALERIA CIR
- SDCo 92065 1173-D2
GALEWOOD ST
6900 SD 92120 1250-C6
GALICIA WY
2600 CRLB 92009 1147-G1
4700 OCN 92056 1107-E5
GALLATIN WY
4700 SD 92117 1248-C1
4800 SD 92117 1228-C7
GALLEGOS TER
6300 SD 92114 1290-D6
GALLEON WY
7600 CRLB 92009 1147-H1
GALLERY CT
900 SD 92114 1290-C5
GALLERY DR
800 OCN 92057 1087-B2
GALLINETA WY
24700 SDCo 92065 1173-G2
GALLINULE CT
8800 SD 92129 1189-C6
GALLOP PL
13200 SDCo 92040 1232-C5
GALLOPING WY
5600 SDCo 91902 1311-B2
GALLOWAY DR
3100 SD 92122 1228-C5
GALLOWAY PL
5700 SDCo 92003 1048-B7
GALLOWAY VALLEY CT
300 SDCo 91901 1233-E7
GALLOWAY VALLEY LN
400 SDCo 91901 1233-E7
GALLOWAY VALLEY RD
300 SDCo 91901 1233-E7
GALOPAGO ST
600 SDCo 91977 1291-C3
GALSTON DR
9200 SNTE 92071 1231-A4
GALT DR
800 ELCJ 92019 1252-B6
800 SDCo 92019 1252-B6
GALT ST
4100 SD 92117 1228-E7
GALT WY
5100 SD 92117 1228-E7
GALVANI LN
2200 SDCo 92084 1108-D2
GALVESTON ST
1400 SD 92110 1268-E1
2200 SD 92110 1248-E7
GALVESTON WY
500 CHV 91902 1311-C3
GALVEZ CT
1900 SD 92154 1350-D3
GALVIN AV
9300 SD 92126 1209-E2
GALWAY CT
1600 ELCJ 92020 1251-C4
GALWAY PL
- SD 92129 1189-B2
1600 ELCJ 92020 1251-C4
GAM LN
1600 SDCo 92065 1152-F7
GAMAN ST
9100 SDCo 92040 1232-D6
GAMAY TER
1800 CHV 91913 1311-D3
GAMAY WY
- SD 92130 1188-E5
GAMBLE LN
- ESCN 92029 1129-F6
900 SDCo 92029 1129-G6
GAMBLE PL
- SDCo 92029 1129-H6
GAMBLE ST
800 ESCN 92025 1129-J1
800 ESCN 92026 1129-J1
1000 ESCN 92026 1109-H7
GAMBUSA PL
9100 SD 92129 1189-D5
GAMBUSA WY
12800 SD 92129 1189-D5
GAMMA ST
1700 NATC 91950 1289-J6
1700 NATC 91950 1290-A6
3800 SD 92113 1289-G6
G ANAYA ST
- CALX 92231 6680-J2
GANDY AV
9800 SNTE 92071 1231-B4
GANESTA RD
11100 SD 92126 1209-C2
GANLEY RD
9000 SNTE 92071 1231-A2
GANNET DR
200 VSTA 92083 1087-G4
GANNET ST
- SD 92114 1290-C4
GANNON DR
2500 SD 92110 1268-E6
GANNON PL
500 ESCN 92025 1129-H3
GANTHER SQ
9900 SD 92131 1209-H5
GANTRY WY
15900 SDCo 92065 1174-A4
GARBER AV
6400 SD 92139 1310-F2
GARBONI RD
- SDCo 91962 1236-E6
GARBOSO PL
7700 CRLB 92009 1147-J2
GARBOSO ST
3000 CRLB 92009 1147-H2
GARDE CT
8600 SD 92126 1209-C3
GARDE ST
10900 SD 92126 1209-C3
GARDE WY
8600 SD 92126 1209-C3
GARDEN CT
- SD 92127 1188-J1
GARDEN DR
14900 PWY 92064 1190-J4
GARDEN LN
3700 SD 92106 1287-J3
24700 SDCo 91916 1236-A2
GARDEN PL
400 CHV 91911 1330-B1
GARDEN RD
14200 PWY 92064 1190-H4
14900 PWY 92064 1191-A4
GARDEN TER
- SD 92127 1188-J1
GARDEN WY
8200 SNTE 92071 1230-J7
10600 SDCo 91978 1271-F6
GARDENA AV
4500 SD 92110 1268-E1
GARDENA CT
500 ENCT 92024 1147-D7
GARDENA LN
11800 SDCo 92040 1231-J7
GARDENA PL
1800 SD 92110 1268-F2
GARDENA RD
700 ENCT 92024 1147-D7
700 ENCT 92024 1167-D1
8500 SDCo 92040 1231-J6
GARDENA WY
8800 SDCo 92040 1231-J6
GARDENDALE RD
200 ENCT 92024 1147-H5
GARDEN GATE LN
- SDCo 92127 1169-F4
GARDEN GLEN LN
1000 ELCJ 92019 1252-B7
GARDEN GROVE LN
200 ELCJ 92020 1251-A5
GARDEN HOUSE RD
- CRLB 92009 1127-F3
GARDENIA AV
14000 PWY 92064 1190-F3
GARDENIA CT
1000 SMCS 92078 1128-E2
7000 CRLB 92011 1127-A6
GARDENIA DR
- SD 92109 1248-C6
GARDENIA GN
600 ESCN 92025 1150-C3
GARDENIA ST
4700 OCN 92057 1087-A1
4700 OCN 92057 1067-A7
GARDEN KNOLL WY
9400 SDCo 92040 1232-A5
GARDEN PARK CT
1900 SD 92114 1290-F6
GARDEN PATH DR
- SDCo 92127 1169-F2
GARDENSIDE CT
- SDCo 92028 1027-H2
GARDEN TRAILS
- SD 92127 1188-J1
GARDEN VIEW CT
700 ENCT 92024 1147-F5
GARDEN VIEW RD
1200 ENCT 92024 1147-E4
GARDEN WALK CT
- SDCo 92127 1169-G1
GARDEN WALK WY
- SDCo 92127 1169-F2
GARDNER DR
32100 RivC 92592 999-F1
GARDNER ST
400 ELCJ 92020 1251-E5
GARDNER WY
500 SMCS 92069 1108-J6
GAREY DR
400 VSTA 92084 1087-H3
GARFIELD AV
800 ELCJ 92020 1251-B4
GARFIELD LN
4700 LMSA 91941 1271-A3
GARFIELD RD
2000 SD 92110 1268-F1
2200 SD 92110 1248-F7
GARFIELD ST
- CALX 92231 6620-J6
300 OCN 92054 1086-F7
400 OCN 92054 1106-B1
2400 CRLB 92008 1106-D5
4500 LMSA 91941 1271-A2
GARIBALDI PL
3300 CRLB 92010 1106-H4
GARJAN LN
16900 SDCo 92065 1171-H3
GARLAND AV
- SMCS 92078 1128-J3
GARLAND DR
900 SD 92154 1330-C7
1000 SD 92154 1350-C1
GARNER PL
3600 ENCT 92024 1167-H2
GARNET AV
700 SD 92109 1247-H6
1500 SD 92109 1248-A5
GARNET CT
8300 LMSA 91941 1270-J4
GARNET LN
4400 OCN 92056 1107-D2
GARNET PL
- CRLB 92009 1127-H5
GARNET ST
- CALX 92231 6620-J7
GARNET FALLS DR
- CHV 91915 1331-G1
GARNET MINE TR
24400 SDCo 92065 1173-F7
GARNET PEAK RD
- SDCo 91948 430-B3
- SDCo 91948 1218-A1
2500 CHV 91915 1311-H6
GARRETT AV
100 CHV 91910 1310-B5
600 CHV 91910 1330-B1
1200 CHV 91911 1330-C3
GARRISON PL
1500 SD 92106 1288-A1
GARRISON ST
400 OCN 92054 1086-F6
2900 SD 92106 1288-B1
GARRISON WY
1700 SDCo 92019 1252-B6
GARST RD
7500 ImCo 92233 411-B9
GARSTON ST
2100 SD 92111 1248-J7
2100 SD 92111 1268-J1
2100 SD 92111 1269-A1
GARWOOD CT
8400 SDCo 91977 1290-J2
GARWOOD RD
9500 SDCo 91916 1235-H2
GARY CIR
2400 CRLB 92010 1106-H5
GARY CT
6400 SD 92115 1270-D2
GARY LN
1100 ESCN 92026 1109-E4
GARY ST
4900 SD 92115 1270-D1
GARYWOOD ST
1600 SDCo 92021 1251-G1
GASCONADE AV
5000 SD 92110 1268-F2
GASCONY RD
1500 ENCT 92024 1147-C2
GASKILL PEAK RD
3700 SDCo 91901 1275-A3
GASLIGHT CT
14400 PWY 92064 1190-F2
GASTON DR
7700 SD 92126 1209-A4
GATCHELL RD
- SD 92152 1287-J7
- SD 92152 1308-A2
GATE DR
12900 PWY 92064 1190-F5
GATE RD
- SD 92152 1288-A5
GATE EIGHT PL
2800 CHV 91914 1311-J4
GATE ELEVEN PL
2800 CHV 91914 1311-J3
GATE FIFTEEN PL
2800 CHV 91914 1311-J3
GATE FIVE PL
2900 CHV 91914 1311-J4
2900 CHV 91914 (1312-A4
See Page 1293)
GATE FOUR PL
2800 CHV 91914 1311-J4
GATE FOURTEEN PL
2900 CHV 91914 1311-J3
GATEMOORE WY
11100 SD 92131 1209-J2
GATE NINE PL
2800 CHV 91914 1311-J4
GATE ONE PL
2800 CHV 91914 1311-J4
GATEPOST RD
1800 ENCT 92024 1147-H6
GATE SEVEN PL
2800 CHV 91914 1311-J4
GATESHEAD RD
4700 CRLB 92010 1107-A5
GATESHEAD ST
7400 SD 92111 1249-A7
7500 SD 92111 1269-A1
GATESIDE RD
3800 LMSA 91941 1270-J4
GATE SIX PL
2800 CHV 91914 1311-J4
GATE TEN PL
2800 CHV 91914 1311-J3
GATE THIRTEEN PL
2900 CHV 91914 1311-J3
GATE THREE PL
2800 CHV 91914 1311-J4
GATE TWELVE PL
2800 CHV 91914 1311-J3
GATE TWO PL
2800 CHV 91914 1311-J4
GATEVIEW DR
- SDCo 92028 1047-H6
GATEWAY DR
1700 SD 92105 1289-G1
1800 VSTA 92081 1107-J4
GATEWAY PL
- PWY 92064 1190-H6
GATEWAY RD
- CRLB 92009 1127-F2
GATEWAY CENTER AV
3600 SD 92102 1289-G3
GATEWAY CENTER DR
600 SD 92102 1289-G3
GATEWAY CENTER WY
600 SD 92102 1289-G3
GATEWAY PARK DR
6500 SD 92154 1351-C2
GATEWAY PARK RD
12600 PWY 92064 1170-C5
GATEWAY VIEW CT
- SDCo 92021 1232-E6
GATEWAY VIEW DR
- SDCo 92021 1232-E6
GATEWAY VIEW PL
- SDCo 92021 1232-E6
GATEWOOD AV
10100 SDCo 92040 1232-B3
GATEWOOD LN
7200 SD 92114 1290-G6
GATITO CT
11600 SD 92127 1150-A7
GATLIN ST
1100 IMPB 91932 1349-H2
GATLING CT
1200 VSTA 92083 1087-E6
2300 SD 92111 1248-J7
2300 SD 92111 1249-A7
GATTY CT
500 SD 92154 1330-F6
GATTY ST
3600 SD 92154 1330-E6
GATUN ST
2000 DLMR 92014 1187-G4
GAUCHO LN
9000 SDCo 92021 1232-F6
GAUCHO PL
1100 ESCN 92029 1129-F5
GAUL WY
10200 SDCo 91977 1271-E5
GAVAN VISTA RD
14800 PWY 92064 1170-J5
GAVILAN WY
- OCN 92057 1067-C7
GAVILAN MOUNTAIN RD
40300 SDCo 92028 997-H4
GAVIN ST
300 SD 92102 1289-H4
GAVIOTA CIR
2900 CRLB 92009 1147-H2
GAVIOTA CT
4600 SDCo 91902 1310-G1
GAVIOTA PL
7800 CRLB 92009 1147-H2
GAVIOTO CT
4600 OCN 92057 1066-J7
GAYLA CT
3000 SDCo 91978 1271-F6
GAY LAKE AV
6400 SD 92119 1250-G5
GAYLAND ST
100 ESCN 92027 1130-C1
GAYLE ST
3500 SD 92115 1270-C5
GAYLE WY
2000 CRLB 92008 1106-G4
GAYLEMONT LN
- SD 92130 1208-D2
GAYLEN RD
7900 SD 92126 1209-B3
GAYLORD CT
3500 SD 92117 1228-D7
GAYLORD DR
4900 SD 92117 1248-D1
5000 SD 92117 1228-D7
GAYLORD PL
5200 SD 92117 1228-D7
GAYNESWOOD WY
7400 SD 92139 1290-G6
GAYO CT
1600 SD 92154 1350-B3
GAYOLA LN
10900 SDCo 92040 1231-F3
GAY RIO CT
- SDCo 92040 1232-A6
GAY RIO DR
12000 SDCo 92040 1231-J6
12000 SDCo 92040 1232-A6
12400 SDCo 92021 1232-A6
GAY RIO LN
- SDCo 92040 1232-A6
GAY RIO TER
12100 SDCo 92040 1232-A6
GAY RIO WY
12000 SDCo 92040 1232-A7
GAYUBA LN
10100 SD 92124 1249-G1
GAYWOOD ST
1100 SD 92154 1349-J1
GAZANIA CT
1100 SMCS 92078 1129-B2
G BURT AV
- CALX 92231 6620-E7
GEARALD WY
1000 SDCo 92028 1027-H3
GEARING DR
2600 SD 92110 1268-E6
4700 SD 92106 1288-C2
GEDDES DR
3200 SD 92117 1248-C2
GEHRING CT
11800 SD 92126 1209-A1
GEIGER CT
5900 CRLB 92008 1127-D2
GEIGER CREEK CT
2600 CHV 91915 1311-J6
GEISE CT
2800 ESCN 92027 1110-E6
GELBOURNE PL
13300 SD 92130 1188-A4
GEM CT
13300 PWY 92064 1190-H4
GEM LN
500 SDCo 92065 1172-H3
2000 ESCN 92026 1109-E4
GEM HILL LN
11200 SDCo 92040 1211-G6
GEMINI AV
9000 SD 92126 1209-D3
GEM LAKE AV
6400 SD 92119 1250-G5
GEM TREE WY
10000 SNTE 92071 1231-D3
GEM VIEW DR
2300 OCN 92056 1087-C6
GENAI RD
- SDCo 92028 998-C4
GENERAL ATOMICS CT
3300 SD 92121 1207-J7
3300 SD 92121 1208-A7
GENESEE AV
2400 SD 92123 1249-A6
2400 SD 92111 1249-A6
2700 SD 92111 1248-H5
4200 SD 92117 1248-G2
5200 SD 92117 1228-E6
5800 SD 92122 1228-D4
8300 SD 92121 1228-B1
8300 SD 92037 1228-B1
9900 SD 92121 1208-B7
10300 SD 92037 1208-B7
GENESEE AV Rt#-S21
10400 SD 92037 1208-A7
10400 SD 92121 1208-A7
10400 SD 92093 1208-A7
10700 SD 92121 1207-J7
GENESEE CT E
5500 SD 92111 1248-H3
GENESEE CV
5200 SD 92122 1228-E5
GENESIS WY
12900 SDCo 92040 1212-D4
GENESTA ST
1900 SD 92102 1290-A1
GENETIC CENTER DR
10200 SD 92121 1208-G5
GENEVA
9400 SDCo 92040 1232-F4
GENEVA AV
5000 SD 92114 1290-B2
GENEVA CIR
1800 SMCS 92078 1128-B2
GENEVA PL
2100 ESCN 92027 1130-E2
GENEVA ST
2000 OCN 92054 1106-G1
GENEVIEVE AV
800 CHV 91913 1311-E5
GENEVIEVE ST
700 SOLB 92075 1167-G7
900 SOLB 92014 1167-G7
GENIE LN
1000 ENCT 92007 1167-E3
GENINE DR
3900 OCN 92056 1107-B1
GENISTA PL
3600 SDCo 92028 1048-C3
GENOA DR
1400 VSTA 92081 1107-H3
5600 SD 92120 1270-C1
5600 SD 92120 1250-C7
GENOA WY
- SMCS 92078 1128-E6
3300 OCN 92056 1106-J1
GENTER ST
500 SD 92037 1247-E1
900 SD 92037 1227-F7
GENTIAN WY
2000 SDCo 91901 1234-A5
GENTLE BREEZE LN
400 ENCT 92024 1147-G6
GENTLE KNOLL ST
- CRLB 92010 1107-B5
GENTLE OAKS TR
- SDCo 92082 1050-A7
- SDCo 92082 1069-J1
- SDCo 92082 1070-A1
GENTRY LN
- CHV 91911 1330-E3
GENTRY RD
6500 ImCo 92233 411-A10
GENTRY RD Rt#-S30
5800 ImCo 92227 411-A11
5800 ImCo 92233 411-A11
GENTRY WY
- CHV 91911 1330-E3
GEODE LN
- CRLB 92009 1127-F4
GEORGE
14100 SDCo 92040 1232-H5
GEORGE AV
900 CALX 92231 6680-F1
1000 CALX 92231 6620-F7
GEORGE CT
1100 SD 92154 1350-D1
GEORGE RD
600 ImCo 92231 431-B7
600 ImCo 92243 431-B7
GEORGE WY
1100 ELCJ 92019 1251-J6
GEORGETOWN AV
5000 SD 92110 1268-F2
GEORGETOWN PL
500 CHV 91911 1330-H4
GEORGIA CT
1900 SD 92103 1269-C6
1900 SD 92104 1269-C6
GEORGIA LN
1000 VSTA 92083 1087-G5
GEORGIA ST
700 IMPB 91932 1329-H7
900 IMPB 91932 1349-H1
3500 SD 92103 1269-C5
3700 SD 92104 1269-C5
4300 SD 92116 1269-C5
GEORGINA ST
- CHV 91910 1310-D7
GEORGINE RD
500 SDCo 92028 1047-E5
GEORGIOS WY
16700 SDCo 92065 1173-G2
GERALD CT
2600 SD 92105 1270-A7
GERALDINE AV
8800 SD 92123 1249-C6
GERALDINE PL
9000 SD 92123 1249-D5
GERANA ST
10800 SD 92129 1189-H2
GERANIUM ST
1700 CRLB 92011 1127-E7
2300 SD 92109 1248-B4
GERLAR LN
1400 SDCo 92065 1152-G7
GERMAINE LN
5900 SD 92037 1247-G3
GERONA CT
14200 SD 92129 1189-H2
GERONIMO AV
3100 SD 92117 1248-F6
GERONIMO PL
- VSTA 92084 1087-H4
GERSHWIN ST
- ENCT 92007 1167-D2
GERTRUDE ST
1200 SD 92110 1268-E2
GESNER PL
2600 SD 92110 1248-F7
4600 SD 92117 1248-E6
GESNER ST
4000 SD 92117 1248-E7
4800 SD 92110 1248-F7
GETTYSBURG DR
- SDCo 92127 1169-E4
GEYER LN
2400 SDCo 91901 1253-J2
GEYSERVILLE ST
- CHV 91913 1311-E7
G FIGUEROA AV
- CALX 92231 6620-H5
GIANELLI LN
2600 ESCN 92025 1130-C7
GIANT ROCK LN
- SDCo 92026 1089-C3
GIBBONS ST
2400 ELCJ 92020 1251-B2
GIBBS DR
8500 SD 92123 1249-C4
GIBBS RD
- ImCo 92227 431-E2
GIBRALTAR CT
17400 SD 92128 1170-C2
GIBRALTAR DR
12600 SD 92128 1170-C2
GIBRALTAR ST
7500 CRLB 92009 1147-H1
GIBRALTER GN
2100 ESCN 92029 1129-D6
GIBSON PT
- SOLB 92075 1167-E6
GIBSON ST
1400 SD 92114 1290-E2
1600 LMGR 92114 1290-E2
GIBSON HIGHLANDS
1300 SDCo 92021 1233-A7
GIDDINGS RANCH RD
1000 SDCo 92084 1088-C7
1000 SDCo 92084 1108-C1
GIDEON CIR N
9100 SDCo 92040 1232-D6
GIDEON CIR S
9100 SDCo 92040 1232-D6
GIDEON CT
13300 SDCo 92040 1232-D6
GIENKE LN
10300 SNTE 92071 1231-E7
GIFFIN WY
10500 SD 92126 1209-A4
GIFFORD WY
6700 SD 92111 1248-H7
6700 SD 92111 1268-H1
GIGANTIC ST
8100 SD 92154 1351-F2
GI GI CT
3300 SDCo 92028 1048-D2
GIL WY
1600 SDCo 92084 1088-B7
GILA AV
4200 SD 92117 1248-E2
GILA CT
3800 SD 92117 1248-E3
GILBERT DR
5400 SD 92115 1270-B3
GILBERT LN
- NATC 91950 1289-J7
GILBERT PL
600 CHV 91910 1310-G6
GILDRED SQ
9200 SD 92037 1228-C2
GILEAD WY
100 SDCo 92028 1027-H2
GILES AV
200 CALX 92231 6680-H2
GILES WY
11700 SD 92126 1209-C1
GILFORD CT
1200 SDCo 91977 1290-J2
GILLESPIE RD
- ImCo 92257 411-B7
GILLESPIE WY
1700 ELCJ 92020 1251-C1
GILLETT RD
200 ImCo 92243 6500-E6
E GILLETT RD
900 ELCN 92243 6500-C6
1200 ImCo 92243 6500-D6
GILLETTE ST
3200 SD 92102 1289-F4
GILLISPIE DR
600 SDCo 91977 1291-A3
GILL VILLAGE WY
2200 SD 92108 1269-C2
GILMAN CT
- SD 92037 1228-A5
GILMAN DR
4200 SD 92093 1228-A2
8100 SD 92037 1228-A4
8100 SD 92122 1228-A4
9400 SD 92161 1228-A2
GILMARTIN DR
1500 SD 92114 1290-E6
GILMORE PL
1300 ESCN 92026 1110-A5
GILMORE ST
3600 SD 92113 1289-G4
GINA AV
100 ELCJ 92019 1252-A5
GINA LN
800 SMCS 92069 1109-B5
GINA WY
200 VSTA 92083 1087-G5
GINGER AV
800 CRLB 92011 1127-A5
GINGER GN
1000 SMCS 92078 1128-E2
GINGER WY
2600 SDCo 92029 1129-D2
3700 OCN 92057 1086-H5
GINGER GLEN RD
- SD 92130 1188-E4
GINGER GLEN TR
- SD 92130 1188-F4
GINGER SNAP CT
12500 SD 92129 1189-C5
GINGER SNAP LN
8700 SD 92129 1189-C6
GINGERTREE LN
- CORD 92118 1329-D1
GINGERWOOD CV
- SD 92130 1208-E2
GINNA PL
800 SD 92114 1290-B5
GINNY LN
2000 ESCN 92025 1130-B5
2000 SDCo 92025 1130-B5
GINSBERG CT
1600 SD 92114 1290-D6
GINSTAR CT
12200 SD 92131 1190-B7
12200 SD 92131 1210-B1
GIRARD AV
7400 SD 92037 1227-F6
GIRARD CT
1200 VSTA 92084 1088-A6
GIRARD WY
300 VSTA 92084 1088-A6
GIRD RD
1700 SDCo 92028 1028-C6
2700 SDCo 92028 1048-D3
GIST RD
2600 SDCo 92069 1088-J4
2900 SDCo 92069 1089-A4
GITANO ST
1600 ENCT 92024 1147-G7
GIVENS ST
800 SD 92154 1330-F7
900 CHV 91911 1330-J2
GIVERNY WY
- CHV 91913 1311-F7
GLACIER AV
4400 SD 92120 1249-H7
4800 SD 92120 1250-A7
GLACIER RD
1500 OCN 92056 1087-E1
GLADE PL
1600 ESCN 92029 1129-G7
GLADE ST
3300 SD 92115 1270-D5
GLADEHOLLOW CT
12200 SD 92128 1190-B7
GLADING DR
4000 SD 92154 1330-F7
GLADIOLA DR
- NATC 91950 1289-H7
2400 SDCo 91906 (1297-E5
See Page 1296)
GLADIOLA LN
100 SDCo 92019 1253-C1
GLADSTONE CT
4400 CRLB 92010 1106-J5
28500 SDCo 92026 1089-D3
GLADYS ST
900 ELCJ 92021 1251-H2
GLANCY DR
3100 SD 92173 1350-E5
GLASER DR
3400 OCN 92056 1106-J1
3400 OCN 92056 1107-A1
GLASGOW AV
1700 ENCT 92007 1167-D2
GLASGOW CT
- SMCS 92069 1108-G6
GLASGOW DR
2600 CRLB 92010 1107-A5
4800 SD 92117 1248-D1
4900 SD 92117 1228-D7
GLASGOW LN
1500 ESCN 92027 1110-C5
GLASOE LN
4800 SD 92108 1269-B3
4800 SD 92116 1269-B3
GLASS CT
1900 SD 92154 1350-A1
E GLAUCUS ST
100 ENCT 92024 1147-B3
W GLAUCUS ST
100 ENCT 92024 1147-A4
GLEASON RD
900 SD 92109 1267-J2
GLEBE RD
2400 LMGR 91945 1270-F7
GLEE LN
1600 ESCN 92029 1129-F5
GLEN DR
3400 SDCo 91977 1271-D5
GLEN LN
13500 SDCo 92082 1050-D7
GLEN RD
900 SD 92114 1290-B3
GLEN ST
4400 LMSA 91941 1271-A2
GLEN ABBEY BLVD
3100 SDCo 91910 1310-E5
GLEN ABBEY DR
3600 SDCo 91902 1310-F4
GLENAIR WY
15800 SDCo 92082 1071-C1
GLEN ARBOR DR
100 ENCT 92024 1147-G5
GLEN ARVEN LN
17000 PWY 92064 1170-F1
GLEN ASPEN CT
- SDCo 92127 1169-F2
GLEN ASPEN DR
- SDCo 92127 1169-F2
GLEN AVON DR
1400 SMCS 92069 1109-C7
GLENBROOK ST
2900 CRLB 92010 1107-A3
GLENBROOK WY
2800 SD 92037 1227-J3
GLEN CANYON CIR
2800 SDCo 91977 1271-D7
GLEN CIRCLE RD
12800 PWY 92064 1170-D5
GLENCLIFF WY
13200 SD 92130 1188-C4
GLENCO LN
- SDCo 92036 1156-C5
GLENCOE DR
800 SD 92114 1290-H3
1000 LMGR 91945 1290-G1
1400 LMGR 92114 1290-G2
GLENCOLUM DR
3300 SD 92123 1249-D5
GLENCREEK CIR
10900 SD 92131 1210-A3
GLEN CREEK DR
300 CHV 91902 1311-B3
GLENCREST DR
- SMCS 92078 1128-D5
300 SOLB 92075 1167-F6
500 SD 92139 1290-G6
GLENCREST PL
600 SOLB 92075 1167-F6
GLENDA CT
10900 SD 92126 1209-B3
GLENDA WY
7900 SD 92126 1209-B3
GLENDALE AV
300 SMCS 92069 1108-G6
800 SD 92102 1289-D3
GLENDALE WY
- SMCS 92069 1108-G6
E GLENDON CIR
10000 SNTE 92071 1231-E3
W GLENDON CIR
10000 SNTE 92071 1231-E3
GLENDORA DR
- CHV 91913 1331-E1
- OCN 92057 1067-A4
GLENDORA ST
2900 SD 92109 1248-C5
GLENDOVER LN
10600 SD 92126 1208-H4
GLEN DREW RD
1900 ESCN 92027 1110-B5
GLENEAGLES PL
1000 VSTA 92081 1108-E2
GLENELLEN AV
10400 SD 92126 1209-D4
GLENELLEN LN
10300 SD 92126 1209-D4
GLEN ELLEN PIKE
- SMCS 92078 1128-E6
GLEN ELLEN ST
- CHV 91913 1311-B7
- CHV 91913 1331-B1
GLENFIELD ST
3100 SD 92105 1269-H6
GLENFLORA AV
6900 SD 92119 1250-F5
GLENGARRY LN
28100 SDCo 92026 1089-D4
GLENGATE PL
13600 PWY 92064 1190-F5
GLENHART PL
- SDCo 92028 1027-G6
GLENHAVEN DR
4800 OCN 92056 1087-E4
GLENHAVEN ST
8600 SD 92123 1249-C4
GLENHAVEN WY
100 CHV 91911 1330-D3
GLEN H CURTISS RD
3600 SD 92123 1249-C4

STREET Block City ZIP Pg-Grid

GLENHEATHER DR
500 SMCS 92069 1109-B6
GLENHILL RD
1000 ELCJ 92020 1251-H7
GLENHOLLOW CIR
4800 OCN 92057 1087-B3
GLEN HOLLOW CT
1600 ENCT 92024 1147-H5
GLENHOPE RD
11800 SD 92128 1190-A6
GLENHURST WY
11300 SD 92128 1189-J2
GLENIRA AV
8700 LMSA 91941 1271-A2
GLENIRA WY
4300 LMSA 91941 1271-A3
GLENLEA LN
5900 SD 92120 1250-E7
GLENMEADE WY
9800 SDCo 92026 1089-D3
GLEN MEADOW LN
2300 ESCN 92027 1110-D6
GLENMERE RD
1000 VSTA 92084 1088-A5
1000 VSTA 92084 1087-J5
GLENMONT DR
300 SOLB 92075 1167-F6
GLENMONT ST
6300 SD 92120 1270-D1
GLENN RD
2300 SDCo 92028 996-J2
3100 OCN 92056 1107-B1
GLENNA DR
1500 SDCo 92025 1130-B4
GLENNAIRE DR
1900 ESCN 92025 1130-B5
1900 SDCo 92025 1130-B5
GLENNCHESTER RW
6100 SD 92037 1247-J1
GLENN CRAWFORD ST
- SDCo 92028 1027-J2
GLENN ELLEN CT
23800 SDCo 92065 1173-D2
GLENN ELLEN WY
23300 SDCo 92065 1173-C4
GLENNON ST
10000 SD 92124 1249-G2
GLENOAK RD
12300 PWY 92064 1190-C2
GLEN OAKS DR N
500 SDCo 91901 1233-G5
GLEN OAKS DR S
500 SDCo 91901 1233-G6
GLEN OAKS PL
600 SDCo 91901 1233-G6
GLEN OAKS WY
- SNTE 92071 1231-A7
GLENRIDGE RD
1800 ESCN 92027 1130-E1
GLENROY ST
6400 SD 92120 1250-B5
GLENSIDE PL
10000 SDCo 91977 1271-D7
GLENSIDE RD
4800 SDCo 92070 1135-D5
GLENSIDE ST
300 SDCo 91977 1271-D7
GLENSTONE WY
5600 SD 92121 1208-E4
GLEN TREE RD
15400 SDCo 92082 1090-J2
GLEN VERDE CT
3700 SDCo 91902 1310-J2
GLEN VERDE DR
5000 SDCo 91902 1310-J2
GLENVIEW DR
4500 OCN 92057 1066-H7
GLENVIEW LN
500 SD 92037 1247-E1
2200 SDCo 92084 1087-F1
GLEN VIEW PL
5100 SDCo 91902 1310-J2
GLENVIEW WY
- SDCo 92025 1130-D7
GLENVILLE ST
14500 PWY 92064 1190-H5
GLEN VISTA CT
8300 SD 92114 1290-H5
GLEN VISTA ST
200 SD 92114 1290-H5
300 SDCo 91977 1290-H5
GLEN VISTA WY
- SNTE 92071 1231-A7
GLENWAY DR
1000 ELCJ 92020 1251-H7
GLENWICK LN
8600 SD 92037 1227-J4
GLENWICK PL
2700 SD 92037 1227-J4
GLENWOOD DR
- ELCN 92243 6559-D1
800 OCN 92057 1087-C1
1400 SD 92103 1268-H6
GLENWOOD RD
1800 ImCo 92243 6499-D6
GLENWOOD WY
800 ESCN 92026 1109-H3
GLENWOOD SPRINGS AV
- CHV 91913 1331-E1
GLIDDEN CT
1700 SD 92111 1268-H1
GLIDDEN LN
6500 SD 92111 1268-H1
GLIDDEN ST
6300 SD 92111 1268-H2
GLOAMING AV
7400 SD 92114 1290-G3
GLORIA LN
3900 CRLB 92008 1106-G6
GLORIA ST
300 SD 92113 1290-A5
GLORIA LAKE AV
7700 SD 92119 1250-G6
GLORIETTA BLVD
200 CORD 92118 1289-A6
400 CORD 92118 1288-J7
900 CORD 92118 1308-J1
900 CORD 92118 1309-A1
GLORIETTA PL
300 CORD 92118 1288-J5
300 CORD 92118 1289-A6
GLOVER AV
100 CHV 91910 1310-B5
700 CHV 91910 1330-B1
N GLOVER AV
- CHV 91910 1310-A4
GLOVER CT
- CHV 91910 1310-A5
GLOVER PL
600 CHV 91910 1330-B1
GLOXINA ST
200 ENCT 92024 1147-E6
G LUNA ST
- CALX 92231 6680-D1

GOBAT AV
2600 SD 92122 1228-B6
GODDARD WY
2400 SD 92101 1288-G1
GODFREY ST
100 OCN 92054 1106-B2
GODS WY
- SDCo 91935 1294-F7
GODSAL LN
300 SD 92103 1268-J6
GODWIT DR
4400 OCN 92057 1087-A3
GOEN PL
- SD 92120 1250-A4
GOESNO PL
3200 NATC 91950 1309-G5
GOETSCHL ST
600 SD 92114 1290-D5
GOETTING WY
200 VSTA 92083 1087-G6
GOETZE ST
2500 SD 92139 1310-E1
GOFF CT
1400 SD 92114 1290-F5
GOING MY WY
- SDCo 92127 1169-A2
GOLD DR
500 OCN 92057 1067-A6
GOLD ST
11100 SNTE 92071 1231-G6
GOLDA ODESSA LN
15200 SDCo 92040 1212-H6
GOLD BAR LN
- SDCo 92040 1212-A7
GOLD BAR WY
- SDCo 92040 1212-A7
- SDCo 92040 1232-A1
GOLDBORO ST
1800 SD 92110 1268-F2
GOLD CANYON LN
- SDCo 92020 1271-J2
GOLD COAST CT
10300 SD 92126 1209-D5
GOLD COAST DR
7900 SD 92126 1209-A5
GOLD COAST PL
10300 SD 92126 1209-D5
GOLD COAST WY
10300 SD 92126 1209-D5
GOLD CREST LN
7600 SD 92114 1290-G5
GOLD DUST LN
- SDCo 92036 1136-D7
- SDCo 92036 1175-J3
GOLDEN AV
2200 LMGR 91945 1270-H6
GOLDEN CIR
11700 SDCo 92040 1231-J7
GOLDEN LN
- SDCo 92036 1135-J7
- SDCo 92036 1136-A7
700 SDCo 92028 1027-G3
3200 LMGR 91945 1270-J6
GOLDEN RD
400 SDCo 92028 1027-G3
1000 ENCT 92024 1167-D1
GOLDEN TR
1000 VSTA 92081 1107-H2
GOLDEN WY
13200 PWY 92064 1190-G4
GOLDEN ACORN WY
- SDCo 91906 (1299-E2 See Page 1298)
GOLDEN BIRCH WY
5000 SD 92131 1209-G2
GOLDENBUSH DR
6400 CRLB 92011 1127-B4
GOLDEN CIRCLE DR
1800 ESCN 92026 1109-C5
GOLDEN CREST DR
1400 SDCo 92029 1129-G6
GOLDEN EAGLE RD
12100 SDCo 92040 1212-C4
GOLDEN EAGLE TR
- SDCo 92078 1128-G6
- SMCS 92078 1128-G6
GOLDEN EYE LN
12400 PWY 92064 1190-B6
GOLDENEYE VW
- CRLB 92011 1126-J4
- CRLB 92011 1127-A4
GOLDEN GATE AV
- CHV 91913 1331-E1
GOLDEN GATE DR
900 SD 92116 1269-A4
GOLDEN GROVE PL
2800 LMGR 91945 1270-J7
GOLDEN HARVEST LN
1400 SDCo 92019 1272-F1
GOLDEN HAVEN DR
4600 SD 92122 1228-D3
GOLDEN HILL DR
- SD 92101 1289-D2
1900 VSTA 92084 1087-H2
GOLDENLEAF PL
- SDCo 92026 1089-F4
GOLDEN MEADOW LN
- SDCo 92028 1047-H5
GOLDEN OAK PL
- ESCN 92027 1130-H2
GOLDEN OAK WY
3000 SDCo 91978 1271-G7
GOLDEN PARK AV
700 SD 92106 1288-A3
GOLDEN RIDGE DR
4500 OCN 92056 1087-C4
GOLDEN RIDGE RD
8400 SDCo 92040 1231-H7
GOLDENROD LN
1800 VSTA 92081 1108-A3
N GOLDENROD ST
600 ESCN 92027 1110-B6
GOLDENROD WY
7000 CRLB 92011 1127-E6
GOLDEN SANDS PL
- SD 92154 1330-H7
GOLDEN STAR CT
4100 SDCo 91941 1271-F4
GOLDEN STAR LN
7300 CRLB 92011 1127-C7
GOLDEN SUNSET CT
14800 PWY 92064 1170-H7
14800 PWY 92064 1190-H1
GOLDEN SUNSET DR
- SMCS 92078 1128-D6
GOLDEN SUNSET LN
14300 PWY 92064 1170-G7
GOLDENTOP DR
- SDCo 92040 1232-C5
GOLDENTOP RD
16900 SDCo 92127 1169-F3
GOLDEN TRAIL WY
5600 OCN 92057 1067-F7

GOLDEN VIEW TER
3400 LMGR 91945 1270-H6
GOLDEN WAGON CT
- SDCo 92127 1169-F1
GOLDEN WEST LN
9900 SNTE 92071 1231-D3
GOLDFIELD ST
1500 SD 92110 1268-E1
GOLDFIELD WY
- ImCo 92249 6560-D7
GOLDFINCH PL
700 SD 92103 1268-J6
7100 CRLB 92011 1127-C6
GOLDFINCH ST
3100 SD 92103 1268-J5
GOLDFINCH WY
900 SMCS 92078 1128-H5
4400 OCN 92057 1086-J1
GOLDFISH CT
12300 SD 92129 1189-A6
GOLDFISH WY
7700 SD 92129 1189-A6
GOLD FLOWER RD
- CRLB 92011 1127-A5
GOLD GULCH
- SD 92101 1289-B1
GOLD LAKE RD
2300 LMGR 91945 1270-E7
GOLD NUGGET LP
- SDCo 92040 1232-F4
GOLD OAK CT
800 CHV 91910 1310-J7
GOLD PAN AL
- SDCo 92040 1212-A7
- SDCo 92040 1232-A1
GOLD ROCK RANCH RD
- ImCo - 431-L3
GOLD RUN DR
1200 CHV 91913 1311-D7
GOLD RUN RD
1500 CHV 91913 1331-D1
1500 CHV 91913 1311-D7
GOLD RUSH CIR
600 CHV 91902 1311-C4
GOLD RUSH CT
- SDCo 92065 1172-D3
GOLD RUSH WY
1400 OCN 92057 1067-E6
GOLDSMITH ST
3000 SD 92106 1268-D6
GOLDSTONE RD
- CRLB 92009 1127-F6
GOLDSTONE ST
1600 ELCJ 92019 1252-B7
GOLETA RD
7900 SD 92126 1209-B3
GOLETA ST
900 OCN 92057 1066-H6
GOLF DR
3300 SDCo 91941 1270-J5
5200 SDCo 91977 1270-J5
5200 SDCo 91977 1271-A5
8700 SDCo 91941 1271-A5
GOLF CLUB DR
31300 SDCo 92003 1068-B2
GOLF COURSE DR
1400 SD 92101 1289-D2
1400 SD 92102 1289-D2
GOLF COURSE RD
- SDCo 92055 1066-G2
GOLFCREST CT
2100 OCN 92056 1106-H1
GOLF CREST DR
4600 SDCo 92004 (1099-G4 See Page 1098)
GOLFCREST DR
3300 OCN 92056 1086-H7
3300 OCN 92056 1106-H1
6400 SD 92119 1250-E3
GOLFCREST LP
2400 CHV 91915 1311-G5
GOLFCREST PL
1400 VSTA 92081 1107-H4
7300 SD 92119 1250-F5
GOLF CREST RIDGE RD
3800 SDCo 92028 1047-J3
3000 SDCo 92019 1272-C6
GOLFERS DR
3300 OCN 92056 1106-J1
GOLF GLEN DR
- SMCS 92069 1108-J5
GOLFGLEN RD
4900 SDCo 91902 1310-J2
GOLF GREEN DR
31700 SDCo 92061 1051-C7
31700 SDCo 92082 1051-C7
GOLF POINTE DR
10400 SDCo 91978 1291-E2
GOLFVIEW DR
2800 SDCo 92028 1048-E1
GOLONDRIA WY
- OCN 92057 1067-C7
GOLONDRINA DR
9100 LMSA 91941 1271-B3
9200 SDCo 91941 1271-B3
GOLSH RD
- SDCo 92082 1071-D2
GOMEZ CREEK RD
400 SDCo 92028 999-D7
1300 SDCo 92028 1029-C1
GONDER RD
1100 ImCo 92227 431-D2
GONDER RD Rt#-S32
- ImCo 92227 431-E2
GONDER RD Rt#-S33
- ImCo 92227 431-E2
GONSALVES AV
- SD 92126 1209-E7
- SD 92126 1229-E1
- SD 92145 1229-E1
GONZALES ST
800 SOLB 92075 1187-G1
GONZALES WY
1200 CHV 91910 1311-B7
GONZALEZ CT
700 CALX 92231 6620-G7
GOODARD ST
- SMCS 92078 1128-D6
GOODBODY ST
3700 SD 92154 1330-E7
GOODE ST
3300 SD 92139 1290-H6
S GOODE ST
2300 SD 92139 1290-G7
GOODING DR
1500 ELCJ 92021 1251-H2
1500 SDCo 92021 1251-H2
GOOD KARMA LN
5700 SDCo 91902 1311-B2
GOOD LAND DR
400 OCN 92054 1085-J6
GOODMAN LN
7300 LMGR 91945 1270-F6
GOODSTONE CT
7200 SD 92111 1249-A7

GOODSTONE ST
2400 SD 92111 1249-A7
GOODWICK CT
9400 SD 92123 1249-F7
GOODWIN DR
1500 VSTA 92084 1087-H3
GOODWIN ST
6500 SD 92111 1268-H1
GOODYEAR ST
1000 SD 92113 1289-G6
GOOSEBERRY WY
5300 OCN 92057 1067-D6
GOOSE VALLEY LN
1200 SDCo 92065 1153-A2
GOPHER CANYON CT
2600 SDCo 92084 1068-A7
GOPHER CANYON RD
600 SDCo 92084 1067-J7
600 SDCo 92084 1068-A6
6700 SDCo 92026 1068-F6
GORDON CT
100 ESCN 92025 1129-G4
6900 LMSA 91941 1270-E4
GORDON WY
4200 LMSA 91941 1270-E4
GORDON HILL RD
28400 SDCo 92082 1069-A7
GORGE AV
9000 SNTE 92071 1231-A6
GORGE CT
8900 SNTE 92071 1231-B6
GORGE PL
3500 CRLB 92010 1107-C3
8900 SNTE 92071 1231-B6
GORGE RUN WY
1200 CHV 91913 1311-E7
GORGE VIEW TER
7400 SD 92120 1250-C5
GORRION CT
13800 SDCo 92021 1232-F6
GORSLINE DR
1000 ELCJ 92021 1252-A3
GOSHAWK ST
2000 SD 92123 1269-A1
GOSHEN ST
1000 SD 92110 1268-G3
GOSNELL WY
100 SMCS 92069 1108-H7
GOTHAM ST
1600 CHV 91913 1311-C5
GOTTA PL
9100 SDCo 92040 1232-D6
GOUDIE TKTR
- SDCo 91901 429-K4
- SDCo 91916 429-K4
GOULBURN CT
400 ELCJ 92020 1251-C5
GOULD AV
- CHV 91911 1330-H2
GOULD LN
2600 SD 92154 1330-C7
2400 VSTA 92081 1108-A5
GOVERNOR DR
2800 SD 92122 1228-E5
5200 SD 92145 1228-E5
GOWAN ST
- CORD 92135 1288-F4
GOWDY AV
8800 SD 92123 1249-C6
GOWER TKTR
- SDCo 92065 1173-J6
- SDCo 92065 1174-A6
18400 SDCo 92065 1154-B5
GOWIN ST
1400 SDCo 91977 1291-A2
1500 SDCo 91977 1290-J2
GOWLING RD
2300 ImCo 92250 431-D5
GOYA PL
- SMCS 92078 1128-A3
GOYETTE PL
9300 SNTE 92071 1230-J6
GRABLE ST
7100 LMSA 91942 1270-F1
GRACE CT
3800 SDCo 92028 1047-J3
6400 SD 92111 1248-J3
GRACE LN
2200 SDCo 91901 1253-J2
GRACE RD
4300 SDCo 91902 1310-G2
GRACE ST
100 OCN 92054 1086-C7
GRACE WY
1200 SDCo 92026 1109-E7
GRACE LAMAY TER
1600 SMCS 92078 1128-C1
GRACELAND WY
9600 SD 92129 1189-E5
GRACEWOOD PL
10600 SD 92130 1208-D2
GRACEY LN
2100 SDCo 92028 1028-B7
GRACIA PASEO
3500 SDCo 91977 1271-A5
GRACILIOR CT
9000 SDCo 92026 1069-A6
GRACILIOR DR
8900 SDCo 92026 1069-A6
GRACILIOR PL
8900 SDCo 92026 1069-A6
GRACIOSA CT
17300 SD 92128 1170-A2
GRACIOSA RD
17300 SD 92128 1170-A1
GRADE PL
2700 SDCo 91977 1271-E7
E GRADE RD Rt#-S7
21500 SDCo 92060 1052-H5
23200 SDCo 92060 (1053-A5 See Page 1052)
23500 SDCo 92060 (1073-G1 See Page 1052)
23500 SDCo 92070 (1073-J5 See Page 1052)
24100 SDCo 92070 409-J8
S GRADE RD
20400 SDCo 92060 1052-B6
S GRADE RD Rt#-S6
31600 SDCo 92060 1052-D5
31600 SDCo 92082 1052-D5
31600 SDCo 92061 1052-D5
GRADO CIPRESO
- CRLB 92009 1147-G2
GRADO EL TUPELO
- CRLB 92009 1147-F3
GRADO MARBELLA
7000 CRLB 92009 1127-G6
GRADY PL
1500 CRLB 92008 1106-G6
GRAESER RD
- ImCo 92250 431-F5
GRAFTON RD
200 ImCo 92243 6560-D2

GRAFTON ST
2100 ELCJ 92020 1251-B3
GRAHAM AV
- SD 92126 1209-D7
GRAHAM PL
1300 ESCN 92026 1109-J5
GRAHAM RD
1700 ImCo 92243 431-A6
GRAHAM ST
1300 SD 92109 1248-A7
GRAHAM TER
8500 SNTE 92071 1230-J7
GRAIN LN
13500 SD 92129 1189-E4
GRAIN MILL RD
- SMCS 92078 1128-F6
GRAINWOOD WY
12400 SD 92131 1210-B4
GRAMERCY DR
8800 SD 92123 1249-D5
GRAMMER RD
3600 SDCo 92084 1068-G6
GRANADA AV
1300 SD 92102 1289-E2
2000 SD 92104 1289-E2
2700 SD 92104 1269-E6
N GRANADA AV
3900 SDCo 91977 1271-D5
S GRANADA AV
2500 SDCo 91977 1271-D5
GRANADA CIR
2500 SDCo 91977 1271-D7
GRANADA DR
700 OCN 92056 1087-E5
700 VSTA 92083 1087-E5
12800 PWY 92064 1190-E5
GRANADA LN
- SDCo 92028 997-H3
GRANADA ST
10500 SNTE 92071 1231-E6
GRANADA WY
1000 CHV 91910 1311-A7
1200 SMCS 92078 1128-E2
2400 CRLB 92010 1106-H4
N GRANADOS AV
100 SOLB 92075 1167-F6
S GRANADOS AV
100 SOLB 92075 1167-F7
300 SOLB 92075 1187-F1
GRANBY WY
10600 SD 92126 1208-H4
GRAND AV
600 SMCS 92078 1128-F1
600 SMCS 92078 1108-C6
700 SD 92109 1247-H6
1000 CRLB 92008 1106-D5
1100 ImCo 92249 6560-B7
1300 ESCN 92027 1130-D1
1500 SD 92109 1248-A6
1700 DLMR 92014 1187-F4
2400 VSTA 92081 1108-A5
E GRAND AV
100 ESCN 92025 1129-J2
400 ESCN 92025 1130-A2
1200 ESCN 92027 1130-A2
W GRAND AV
100 ESCN 92025 1129-H3
W GRAND AV Rt#-S6
800 ESCN 92025 1129-G3
GRAND CT
900 ESCN 92025 1129-H4
GRANDA DR
400 SDCo 92004 1058-G7
GRAND CARIBE CSWY
500 CORD 92118 1329-E2
GRAND DEL MAR WY
- SD 92130 1188-D7
GRANDEE CT
12300 SD 92128 1170-B2
GRANDEE PL
17200 SD 92128 1170-C1
GRANDEE RD
12300 SD 92128 1170-B2
GRANDEE WY
17000 SD 92128 1170-B2
GRANDE VISTA
- SMCS 92078 1129-C2
GRANDFATHERS LN
29200 SDCo 92082 1071-A6
GRAND FORK DR
10700 SNTE 92071 1231-F4
GRAND FORKS RD
2300 CHV 91915 1311-H7
GRANDON AV
1600 ESCN 92025 1130-B6
GRANDRIDGE RD
5200 SDCo 92020 1271-G1
GRAND TETON CT
1500 CHV 91911 1330-F4
GRAND TETON WY
10600 SNTE 92071 1231-E4
GRANDVIA PT
13300 SD 92130 1187-J5
GRANDVIEW
2900 SDCo 92029 1129-C6
GRANDVIEW DR
9500 SDCo 91941 1271-C3
GRAND VIEW GN
2000 ESCN 92026 1109-C3
GRANDVIEW HTS
30100 SDCo 92082 1069-J5
GRANDVIEW PL
3800 SDCo 91902 1310-D4
GRANDVIEW RD
- SDCo 92036 1156-A7
- SDCo 92036 1176-A1
1300 VSTA 92084 1088-C4
1700 SDCo 92084 1088-B2
GRANDVIEW ST
100 ENCT 92024 1147-A3
1500 OCN 92054 1106-D1
2300 SD 92110 1248-F6
2300 SD 92110 1268-G1
GRANDVIEW TER
4600 SDCo 91941 1271-D3
GRANDVIEW WY
- SDCo 92036 1176-A1
GRAND VISTA LN
- SDCo 92028 1028-D2
GRANERO DR
- CALX 92231 6620-G6
GRANERO PL
1800 ESCN 92029 1129-F6
GRANGE PL
- PWY 92064 1210-C1
GRANGE ST
2500 LMGR 91945 1270-G7
GRANGE HALL RD
900 ENCT 92007 1167-E1
GRANGER AV
1400 ESCN 92027 1110-A7
1800 NATC 91950 1310-C2
2400 SDCo 91950 1310-C2

GRANGER ST
700 SD 92154 1329-J7
900 SD 92154 1349-J1
1200 IMPB 91932 1349-J1
1400 IMPB 92154 1349-J1
4400 SD 92107 1287-J1
GRANITE CT
- CRLB 92010 1107-B3
GRANITE CV
500 ELCJ 92021 1252-A4
GRANITE DR
16600 SDCo 92065 1171-D2
GRANITE PL
- OCN 92057 1067-A4
GRANITE RD
300 SMCS 92069 1108-E6
GRANITE ST
800 SMCS 92078 1129-C2
GRANITE CREEK RD
13300 SD 92128 1189-J4
GRANITE HILLS CIR
700 ELCJ 92019 1252-A6
GRANITE HILLS CT
1400 ELCJ 92019 1252-A6
GRANITE HILLS DR
1200 ELCJ 92019 1251-J7
1200 ELCJ 92019 1252-B5
1200 SDCo 92019 1251-J7
1500 SDCo 92019 1252-B5
GRANITE HOUSE LN
8700 SNTE 92071 1231-B7
GRANITE MOUNTAIN TKTR
1100 SDCo 92036 410-A11
GRANITE MOUNTAIN VIEW RD
1200 SDCo 92036 410-A11
1200 SDCo 92036 1138-A5
GRANITE OAKS RD
- SDCo 91935 1294-C2
GRANITE RIDGE DR
9600 SD 92123 1249-F4
GRANITE RIDGE RD
27800 SDCo 92026 1089-G4
GRANITE ROCK RD
1700 SDCo 92028 998-H7
GRANITE SPRINGS DR
1300 CHV 91915 1311-H6
GRANITE VIEW LN
500 SDCo 91977 1290-J5
GRANITE VISTA WY
- SDCo 91901 1235-J7
GRANJAS RD
1000 CHV 91911 1330-B3
GRANT AV
400 ELCJ 92020 1251-E6
8400 LMSA 91941 1270-J2
GRANT ST
100 CALX 92231 6680-D1
300 OCN 92054 1086-B7
400 OCN 92054 1106-B1
5300 SD 92110 1268-F3
GRANT WY
2600 SD 92102 1289-D4
GRANT LINE RD
1900 VSTA 92081 1107-H6
GRANTO CT
8000 SD 92122 1228-C4
GRANTWOOD LN
1100 SDCo 92021 1251-H1
GRANVILLE DR
13800 PWY 92064 1190-F4
GRAPE LN
9700 SDCo 92029 1149-E2
GRAPE ST
100 SD 92101 1289-A1
200 ESCN 92025 1130-A2
300 ESCN 92025 1129-J1
400 OCN 92054 1086-G2
500 ELCJ 92021 1252-A4
500 SD 92101 1288-J2
1000 ESCN 92026 1129-J1
1000 SMCS 92069 1109-C7
1000 ESCN 92026 1109-J7
1300 SD 92102 1289-E1
1300 SD 92104 1289-E1
5400 SD 92105 1290-B1
7800 LMSA 91941 1270-H3
S GRAPE ST
100 ESCN 92025 1130-A2
GRAPE ARBOR CT
17100 PWY 92064 1170-D2
GRAPE ARBOR WY
13100 PWY 92064 1170-D2
GRAPE FERN CT
11100 SD 92131 1209-J1
GRAPEFRUIT DR
500 SDCo 92065 1153-B7
GRAPEVINE CT
1400 VSTA 92083 1087-D7
GRAPEVINE LN
- VSTA 92083 1087-D7
GRAPEVINE RD
100 VSTA 92083 1107-D1
100 VSTA 92083 1087-D7
800 OCN 92056 1087-D7
GRAPEVINE CANYON RD
- SDCo 92036 (1118-A3 See Page 1098)
- SDCo 92066 410-A10
- SDCo 92066 (1118-A3 See Page 1098)
29200 SDCo 92066 409-L9
GRAPEVINE RANCH RD
200 SDCo 91963 (1315-H4 See Page 1294)
GRASSHOPPER LN
- CHV 91915 1331-H1
GRASS VALLEY LN
8700 SNTE 92071 1230-J3
GRASS VALLEY RD
1000 CHV 91913 1311-E5
GRASSY WY
28000 SDCo 92026 1089-F3
GRASSY MEADOW RD
- SDCo 92061 1050-H3
GRASSY TRAIL DR
11200 SD 92127 1169-J5
GRAVES AV
400 ELCJ 92020 1251-F3
600 ELCJ 92021 1251-F3
1200 SDCo 92021 1251-F2
2700 SNTE 92021 1251-F1
3200 SNTE 92071 1231-F7
8600 SNTE 92071 1231-F7
GRAVES CT
300 SDCo 92021 1251-F1
GRAVES LN
1200 SDCo 92021 1251-F2
GRAVILLA PL
500 SD 92037 1247-F2
GRAVILLA ST
200 SD 92037 1247-E2

GRAVITY WY
1400 SD 92114 1290-C2
GRAY DR
900 ELCJ 92020 1251-H7
GRAYBAR CT
3300 OCN 92056 1086-J7
GRAYDON RD
4100 SD 92130 1188-B5
GRAYFISH LN
500 OCN 92054 1086-G2
GRAYFOX DR
10200 SD 92131 1209-H4
GRAY MARE CT
- SDCo 91901 1254-G3
GRAY MARE WY
- SDCo 91901 1254-G3
GRAY RABBIT HOLLOW LN
- SDCo 92028 1028-A6
GRAYSON CT
- CHV 91913 1331-D1
GRAYSON DR
4000 SD 92130 1188-A4
GRAYSTONE PL
2500 SDCo 91977 1271-E7
GREAT BLUE HERON WY
- SDCo 91962 (1299-B1 See Page 1298)
GREAT EAGLE WY
- SDCo 91962 (1299-B2 See Page 1298)
GREAT MEADOW DR
- SD 92130 1208-D2
GREAT OAK LN
- SDCo 91901 1254-G7
GREAT PLAINS RD
14000 PWY 92064 1170-G4
GREAT ROCK RD
10300 SNTE 92071 1231-E3
GREAT SANDY TR
600 SDCo 92036 1138-B7
GRT STHN OVLD STG RT OF 1849
- SDCo 92036 410-A11
- SDCo 92036 430-B2
- SDCo 92036 1138-A5
- SDCo 92036 (1158-C7 See Page 1138)
GREBE DR
7300 CRLB 92011 1127-B7
GRECOURT WY
3700 CRLB 92008 1106-F6
GREDOS PL
700 CHV 91910 1310-J5
GREELY AV
3000 SD 92113 1289-E5
GREEN AV
100 ESCN 92025 1130-A5
GREEN LN
11500 SDCo 92040 1231-J7
GREEN RD Rt#-S33
4200 ImCo 92227 431-E2
GREEN ST
- SDCo 92028 1028-G5
700 SD 92154 1330-A7
800 SD 92154 1350-A1
GREENACRES DR
1800 SDCo 91901 1254-A1
GREENACRES RD
2100 SDCo 92028 1027-J6
GREEN BAY ST
1100 SD 92154 1350-A1
GREENBELT RD
17200 SDCo 92065 1171-H1
GREENBERG LN
8800 SD 92129 1189-C3
GREENBERG WY
8800 SD 92129 1189-C3
GREEN BRIAR CT
1600 SDCo 92028 1028-A5
GREEN BRIAR DR
1600 SDCo 92028 1028-B5
GREENBRIAR DR
2300 CHV 91915 1311-G5
GREEN BRIAR LN
1600 SDCo 92028 1028-B5
GREENBRIER AV
4700 SD 92120 1249-J6
4900 SD 92120 1250-A6
GREENBRIER CT
6700 SD 92120 1250-A6
GREENBRIER DR
500 OCN 92054 1086-C7
500 OCN 92054 1106-D1
GREENBROOK ST
5100 OCN 92057 1067-B5
GREENBROOK WY
8800 SNTE 92071 1230-J4
GREENBUSH LN
1100 SDCo 92084 1108-D1
GREEN CANYON LN
2100 SDCo 92028 1028-A5
GREEN CANYON RD
1300 SDCo 92028 1028-A7
1400 SDCo 92028 1047-H2
2300 SDCo 92028 1027-J7
GREENCASTLE ST
10700 SNTE 92071 1231-F4
GREENCRAIG LN
4800 SD 92123 1249-E1
GREENCRAIG WY
5000 SD 92123 1249-E1
GREENCREST CT
1500 SDCo 92019 1272-B4
GREENCREST DR
2100 SDCo 92019 1272-B4
GREENE ST
4300 SD 92107 1268-A5
GREENERY CIR
700 OCN 92057 1067-B5
GREENE VIEW PL
2600 SDCo 91905 1300-B4
GREENFIELD CT
- CHV 91913 1331-D1
1700 ELCJ 92021 1252-B3
GREENFIELD DR
200 SDCo 92020 1251-F3
200 SDCo 92021 1251-H3
500 ELCJ 92021 1251-H3
1300 ELCJ 92021 1252-B2
1700 ELCJ 92019 1252-D4
1800 SDCo 92019 1252-C3
1800 SDCo 92021 1252-C3
GREENFIELD WY
- SDCo 92060 1052-J3
GREENFORD DR
10300 SD 92126 1209-D3
GREEN GABLES AV
6500 SD 92119 1250-F5
GREEN GABLES CT
6500 SD 92119 1250-F6
GREEN GARDEN DR
1200 SDCo 92021 1251-J1

STREET
Block City ZIP Pg-Grid

GREEN GLEN RD
- SDCo 92065 1173-D2
GREEN GROVE AV
1500 ELCJ 92021 1252-B2
GREENHAVEN DR
- CRLB 92009 1127-G3
GREEN HAVEN LN
15800 SDCo 92065 1173-E4
GREEN HEATHER LN
3000 SDCo 92028 1048-A1
GREENHEDGE RW
6000 SD 92037 1248-A1
GREEN HILL CT
800 SMCS 92069 1108-J5
GREEN HILLS DR
2800 SDCo 92028 1048-A1
GREEN HILLS PL
2100 SDCo 92028 1048-B1
GREEN HILLS RD
6200 OCN 92057 1067-F3
GREEN HILLS WY
2200 SDCo 92084 1088-B1
GREEN HOUSE LN
- SD 92093 1228-B1
GREEN LAKE CT
6900 LMGR 91945 1270-E7
GREENLAKE CT
900 ENCT 92007 1167-E2
GREENLAKE DR
1200 ENCT 92007 1167-E1
GREENLAWN DR
8100 SD 92114 1290-H4
GREENLEAF RD
10100 SDCo 91977 1291-E2
GREEN LINKS DR
- SDCo 92004 (1079-C3 See Page 1058)
GREEN MEADOW DR
2400 SDCo 92083 1108-C4
GREEN MOUNTAIN LN
2800 SDCo 92025 1130-E7
GREEN MOUNTAIN RD
2800 SDCo 92025 1130-E7
GREEN OAK RD
700 VSTA 92081 1108-A5
1100 VSTA 92081 1107-H6
GREEN OAKS DR
26700 SDCo 92070 409-J10
GREEN OAKS RD
11100 SDCo 92040 1211-F7
GREENOCK CT
2700 CRLB 92010 1107-A5
GREEN ORCHARD PL
1200 ENCT 92024 1147-G4
GREENRIDGE AV
8800 SDCo 91977 1290-J3
GREENRIDGE DR
1500 VSTA 92081 1107-H5
GREEN RIVER DR
2200 CHV 91915 1311-G6
GREENS EAST RD
12200 SD 92128 1170-B1
GREENSGATE DR
2200 CHV 91915 1311-F5
GREENSHADE RD
5600 SD 92121 1208-E4
GREENSTONE CT
- SD 92131 1210-E2
GREENSVIEW CT
5900 SDCo 92067 1188-E2
N GREENSVIEW DR
1100 CHV 91915 1311-G5
S GREENSVIEW DR
1200 CHV 91915 1311-G7
GREEN TERRACE RD
13400 PWY 92064 1170-E3
GREEN TOP LN
1600 SDCo 92020 1271-J2
GREENTREE LN
2600 SD 92037 1227-J2
GREEN TREE RD
- ESCN 92029 1129-E5
GREENTREE RD
1700 ENCT 92024 1147-H6
12200 PWY 92064 1170-B7
GREEN TURTLE RD
- CORD 92118 1329-E1
GREENVALE DR
8400 SNTE 92071 1230-J7
GREEN VALLEY CT
- SD 92131 1210-F1
GREEN VALLEY RD
2300 SDCo 92028 996-J4
2500 CHV 91915 1311-H6
GREEN VALLEY TKTR
14200 PWY 92064 1170-H3
14200 PWY 92064 1171-A2
15900 SDCo 92065 1151-A7
15900 SDCo 92065 1171-A2
GREEN VALLEY HEIGHTS RD
15800 SDCo 92065 1151-B6
GREENVIEW DR
- CRLB 92009 1127-F7
GREEN VIEW LN
200 SDCo 92028 1028-A1
GREENVIEW PL
8800 SDCo 91977 1271-A4
GREENVIEW RD
800 ESCN 92026 1109-F6
1800 SDCo 92026 1109-F6
GREENVIEW ST
1900 ESCN 92027 1130-C1
GREEN VISTA LN
1900 SDCo 92028 1028-A7
GREENWAY RD
- OCN 92057 1067-A3
GREENWAY RISE
1300 ESCN 92027 1110-B5
GREENWICH DR
6200 SD 92122 1228-G5
GREENWICH ST
2900 CRLB 92010 1107-A3
GREENWICK PL
1600 SDCo 92019 1272-B4
GREENWICK RD
2100 SDCo 92019 1272-B4
GREENWILLOW LN
- SD 92130 1208-D1
GREENWING DR
2300 SD 92123 1249-B7
GREENWOOD LN
100 OCN 92054 1106-C1
GREENWOOD PL
- ESCN 92029 1129-G6
300 CHV 91902 1310-J3
GREENWOOD ST
3700 SD 92110 1268-E5
GREENWOOD TR
- SDCo 92060 1052-D2
GREGG CT
5800 LMSA 91942 1251-C7
12900 PWY 92064 1190-E7
GREGG ST
13000 PWY 92064 1190-E7
GREGORY DR
2500 CRLB 92008 1106-E4
GREGORY LN
700 OCN 92057 1066-H7
GREGORY ST
100 SD 92113 1289-F4
1300 SD 92102 1289-F2
2000 SD 92104 1289-E2
2700 SD 92104 1269-F7
9300 LMSA 91942 1251-B6
GREMLIN WY
1600 SDCo 91977 1291-D2
GRENACHE ROSE WY
18300 SDCo 92065 1171-H2
GRENADINE GN
2500 ESCN 92029 1149-G1
GRESHAM RD
- ImCo 92243 6500-H7
- ImCo 92243 6560-H1
GRESHAM ST
3900 SD 92109 1248-A7
4000 SD 92109 1247-J5
GRETA ST
1000 ELCJ 92021 1251-H2
1000 SDCo 92021 1251-H2
GRETCHEN RD
600 CHV 91910 1310-E7
GRETLER PL
10400 SDCo 91941 1271-E3
GRETNA GREEN WY
700 ESCN 92025 1130-C7
700 ESCN 92025 1150-C1
700 SDCo 92025 1130-C7
GREVILLA AV
- SD 92102 1289-G4
GREVILLEA PL
- SD 92130 1188-G7
GREVILLEA WY
700 SDCo 91902 1310-G3
GREWIA CT
1500 SD 92114 1290-C6
GREWIA ST
5800 SD 92114 1290-C6
GREYCOURT AV
5700 SD 92114 1290-C6
GREYCOURT WY
1400 SD 92114 1290-C6
GREYFIELD CT
- SDCo 92028 1027-G6
GREY HAWK CT
- CRLB 92010 1127-J2
700 OCN 92057 1067-C7
700 OCN 92057 1087-C1
GREYLING DR
2400 SD 92123 1249-C6
GREYLING PL
8800 SD 92123 1249-C7
GREY OAKS CT
1400 OCN 92056 1087-E3
GREYSTONE AV
10300 SDCo 92026 1109-F1
GREYSTONE CT
2900 SDCo 91935 1272-E6
GREYSTONE DR
3400 SDCo 91935 1272-D6
3400 SDCo 92019 1272-D6
GREY STONE RD
15900 PWY 92064 1170-G4
GRIBBLE ST
7300 SD 92114 1290-G4
GRIFFIN DR
- ELCJ 92020 1251-A2
GRIFFIN RD
- ImCo 92227 431-D2
GRIFFIN ST
1600 OCN 92054 1106-D2
GRIFFITH RD
- SDCo 92040 1211-G4
1400 SDCo 92065 1153-B7
1600 SDCo 92065 1173-B1
GRIFFITH PARK WY
8800 SNTE 92071 1230-J5
8800 SNTE 92071 1231-A5
GRILLO CT
11400 SD 92127 1149-J7
GRIM AV
3100 SD 92104 1269-E6
GRIMSLEY AV
12700 PWY 92064 1190-H5
GRISSOM ST
700 SD 92154 1330-E7
GRIVETTA CT
900 CRLB 92011 1127-A7
GROGAN CIR
3400 SD 92154 1330-E7
GROGAN CT
700 SD 92154 1330-E7
GROSALIA AV
9800 SDCo 91941 1271-C1
GROSS CT
2600 SD 92139 1310-E1
GROSS ST
6300 SD 92139 1310-E1
GROSSE POINTE
- SD 92128 1190-A3
GROSSMONT AV
700 ELCJ 92020 1251-D7
GROSSMONT BLVD
8700 LMSA 91941 1271-A1
9000 SDCo 91941 1271-A1
9500 LMSA 91942 1251-C7
9500 LMSA 91942 1271-B1
GROSSMONT CT
900 CHV 91913 1311-D6
GROSSMONT CENTER DR
5400 LMSA 91942 1271-A1
5500 LMSA 91942 1251-A7
5600 LMSA 91942 1250-J7
GROSSMONT COLLEGE DR
2400 ELCJ 92020 1251-A3
GROSSMONT SUMMIT DR
9400 LMSA 91941 1271-B1
GROSSMONT VIEW DR
1600 ELCJ 92020 1251-C6
GROS VENTRE AV
4000 SD 92117 1248-E3
GROTON PL
2500 SDCo 92025 1130-D7
GROTON ST
3800 SD 92110 1268-C5
GROTON WY
3100 SD 92110 1268-C5
GROUSE ST
900 ELCJ 92020 1251-D3
GROUTER ST
- SD 92136 1289-E6
GROVE AV
400 IMPB 91932 1349-F1
700 SD 92154 1350-A1
1500 SD 92154 1349-J1
2700 CRLB 92008 1106-F3
GROVE CT
3600 LMGR 91945 1270-H5
GROVE PL
1900 ESCN 92027 1130-D2
GROVE RD
1200 SDCo 92020 1271-J1
1700 SDCo 92020 1272-A1
GROVE ST
1200 NATC 91950 1310-B1
1300 SD 92102 1289-E2
2200 SDCo 91950 1310-B3
3400 LMGR 91945 1270-H6
3700 LMGR 91941 1270-H6
3700 LMSA 91941 1270-H6
GROVE WY
2700 NATC 91950 1310-B3
2700 SDCo 91950 1310-B3
GROVE CANYON RD
3500 SDCo 92025 1150-D1
GROVE HILL DR
600 SDCo 92026 1109-D6
600 SMCS 92069 1109-D6
GROVE KNOLL LN
12800 SDCo 92082 1090-C2
GROVELAND DR
5100 SD 92114 1290-A4
GROVELAND TER
1300 ELCJ 92021 1252-A3
GROVE PARK PL
- CHV 91915 1311-G7
GROVE VIEW RD
700 OCN 92057 1067-E4
2200 SD 92139 1290-G6
GRUBSTAKE TR
7500 SDCo 92036 1138-C7
7500 SDCo 92036 (1158-C1 See Page 1138)
GRULLA ST
6600 CRLB 92009 1127-G5
GRUMBLE RD
800 ImCo 92251 431-D4
GRUMMAN ST
- SD 92154 1351-D2
GRUTLY ST
30200 SDCo 92070 1135-B3
GUACAMAYO CT
12900 SD 92128 1150-C6
GUACAMOLE FARM RD
- SDCo 92028 996-J1
GUADALAJARA DR
1000 ENCT 92024 1147-E7
GUADALCANAL AV
- SD 92140 1268-E7
GUADALCANAL RD
2900 CORD 92155 1309-A2
GUADALIMAR WY
10900 SD 92129 1189-H1
GUADALUPE AV
600 CORD 92118 1288-J7
GUADALUPE DR
3600 OCN 92054 1086-F2
GUAJOME ST
- VSTA 92083 1087-H7
GUAJOME LAKE RD
500 OCN 92057 1067-D6
1700 OCN 92056 1067-D7
2200 SDCo 92084 1087-F1
2200 VSTA 92084 1087-F1
2800 OCN 92056 1087-F1
2800 OCN 92057 1087-F1
GUANAJUATO CT
100 SOLB 92075 1167-D7
GUANTANAMO ST
- SD 92101 1268-F7
- SD 92140 1268-F7
GUATAY AV
900 CHV 91911 1330-E2
GUATAY RD
24800 SDCo 91916 1236-C2
GUATAY ST
8100 SD 92114 1290-G3
GUATAY VIEW LN
9000 SDCo 91931 1236-H3
GUAVA AV
100 CHV 91910 1310-A5
600 CHV 91910 1330-B1
4900 LMSA 91941 1270-G2
GUAVA GN
1700 ESCN 92026 1109-D6
GUAVA LN
1600 SDCo 92020 1271-J2
GUAVA WY
- SD 92130 1188-G3
3500 OCN 92054 1086-F2
GUAYMAS BAY CT
2100 SD 92105 1290-C1
GUEJITO RD
15700 SDCo 92027 1111-C1
GUEJITO TKTR
- SDCo 92027 409-G10
GUERRO CT
100 SOLB 92075 1167-D6
GUESSMAN AV
5200 LMSA 91942 1270-F1
GUEVARA RD
1700 CRLB 92008 1106-F3
GUIDERO WY
500 ENCT 92024 1147-C5
GUIJAROS RD
- SD 92106 1288-B7
- SD 92106 1308-B1
GUILD AV
9200 SD 92123 1249-E4
GUILD ST
5100 LMSA 91942 1270-H2
GUILDER GN
1800 ESCN 92029 1129-F5
GUILDFORD CT
1000 ENCT 92024 1147-D4
GUILITOY AV
3000 SD 92117 1248-C1
GUILITOY CT
4600 SD 92117 1248-C1
GUINCHO CT
5600 SD 92124 1229-G7
GUINCHO PL
10400 SD 92124 1229-H7
GUINCHO RD
5600 SD 92124 1229-G7
GUINDA CT
5200 SD 92124 1249-F1
GUINEVERE ST
2600 OCN 92054 1086-E6
GUISANTE LN
5200 SD 92124 1249-F1
GUISANTE TER
9700 SD 92124 1249-F1
GUIZOT ST
1000 SD 92107 1287-J1
1500 SD 92107 1267-J7
1700 SD 92107 1268-A7
GULL CT
1300 CRLB 92011 1127-B5
GULL PL
200 ELCJ 92019 1252-A5
GULLETT RD
2500 ImCo 92251 431-A5
GULLSTRAND ST
5800 SD 92122 1228-F6
GUMBARK PL
10200 SD 92131 1209-H4
GUM TREE GN
3700 ESCN 92025 1150-C3
GUMTREE LN
1600 SDCo 92028 1027-J1
1900 SDCo 92028 1028-B1
GUNN ST
2800 SD 92104 1269-D6
GUNNER AV
13200 SD 92129 1189-C4
GUNNISON CT
13900 SD 92129 1189-C3
GUNN STAGE PL
16900 SDCo 92065 1173-D3
GUNN STAGE RD
15900 SDCo 92065 1173-D3
GUNPOWDER POINT DR
1000 CHV 91910 1309-H6
GUNSLINGER TR
7500 SDCo 92036 1138-C7
7500 SDCo 92036 (1158-C1 See Page 1138)
GUNSTON CT
4900 SD 92130 1188-C4
GUNZAN ST
7000 SD 92139 1290-G7
GUPPY CT
8200 SD 92129 1189-B7
GURKE ST
4700 SD 92124 1249-G2
GURNARD CT
3400 SD 92124 1249-H4
GURNARD ST
10100 SD 92124 1249-G4
GURUJAN WY
1400 SDCo 91901 1234-A6
GUSTAVO ST
1400 ELCJ 92019 1252-A7
GUSTINE ST
1100 CHV 91913 1311-C6
GUTHRIE RD
- ImCo 92251 431-A4
GUTHRIE WY
7400 SD 92114 1290-G3
GUY ST
1200 SD 92110 1268-H6
1500 SD 92103 1268-G5
GUYMON ST
4700 SD 92102 1289-J3
4800 SD 92105 1290-A3
GWEN ST
- SD 92114 1290-B5
G WOO AV
- CALX 92231 6620-J5
GWYNNE AV
2600 SDCo 91950 1310-C2
GYMKHANA RD
23800 SDCo 92065 1173-D1
GYPSY LN
1200 SDCo 92065 1172-G1

H

H AV
- SD 92145 1229-J2
- SD 92145 1230-A1
100 CORD 92118 1288-H6
H CT
- CHV 91910 1310-F7
H RD E
- CORD 92135 1288-F6
H ST
- ImCo 92281 431-A1
- SMCS 92078 1128-H3
- CHV 91910 1310-A7
200 SDCo 92065 1152-J5
300 IMP 92251 6439-F6
700 CHV 91910 1329-J1
700 CHV 91910 1330-A1
700 SDCo 92065 1172-F1
E H ST
- ENCT 92024 1147-C7
200 CHV 91910 1310-D6
300 SDCo 91910 1310-F6
1000 CHV 91910 1311-A6
1300 CHV 91913 1311-D4
1400 CHV 91902 1311-D4
1500 CHV 91914 1311-D4
W H ST
100 ENCT 92024 1147-C7
100 ENCT 92024 1167-B1
HAALAND GN
- SD 92127 1169-B4
HAAS ST
2400 SDCo 92025 1150-D1
6100 LMSA 91942 1250-G6
HABER ST
5800 SD 92122 1228-B6
HABERO DR
2000 ESCN 92029 1129-F6
HACIENDA CIR
1900 ELCJ 92020 1251-C2
HACIENDA CT
200 VSTA 92081 1087-G7
HACIENDA DR
- CALX 92231 6620-F7
100 VSTA 92081 1087-E7
200 VSTA 92081 1107-D1
600 ELCJ 92020 1251-B2
800 SDCo 92036 1156-D1
3400 OCN 92054 1086-F4
HACIENDA GN
2400 ESCN 92026 1109-B4
HACIENDA LN
14200 PWY 92064 1170-G7
HACIENDA PL
1700 ELCJ 92020 1251-C2
HACIENDA RD
8500 SNTE 92071 1231-D7
HACKAMORE RD
1000 VSTA 92083 1087-E7
1600 OCN 92057 1067-G6
HACKBERRY PL
- CHV 91915 1311-H1
700 SDCo 92028 1027-G3
HACKLEMAN RD
1000 ImCo 92243 431-A5
1000 ImCo 92251 431-A5
HADA DR
17400 SD 92127 1169-J1
HADAR DR
11400 SD 92126 1209-C1
HADDEN HALL CT
18200 SD 92128 1150-B6
HADLEY PL
9000 SD 92126 1209-D1
HAFFLY AV
1900 NATC 91950 1309-G3
HAGANS CIR
8000 SD 92126 1209-A1
HAGBERG RD
1400 ImCo 92283 432-D4
HAGEN OAKES CT
- ESCN 92026 1129-F1
- SDCo 92026 1129-F1
HAGERSWOOD CT
12700 SD 92129 1189-C5
HAGLAR WY
1200 CHV 91913 1311-E7
HAGMANN CT
900 SD 92114 1290-F2
HAGMANN ST
7200 SD 92114 1290-F2
HA-HANA RD
12900 SDCo 92040 1232-C6
HAIDAS AV
3000 SD 92117 1248-C1
HAINES ST
3700 SD 92109 1248-A6
4400 SD 92109 1247-J5
HAITI AV
- SD 92140 1268-F6
HAKONE
9300 SDCo 92040 1232-F4
HAL ST
800 SD 92102 1290-A3
HALBERNS BLVD
9400 SNTE 92071 1231-B4
HALCON CT
- CALX 92231 6620-G7
HALCYON RD
100 ENCT 92024 1147-B5
HALE AV
100 ESCN 92025 1129-F3
100 ESCN 92029 1129-F3
HALE CT
800 ELCJ 92020 1251-F7
HALE DR
700 SDCo 91901 1234-B4
HALE PL
100 ESCN 92029 1129-F4
900 CHV 91914 1311-G4
HALE ST
400 CHV 91910 1310-F7
HALECREST DR
800 CHV 91910 1310-G7
900 ESCN 92025 1130-A3
HALES PL
- SDCo 92036 1156-E7
HALEY LN
9400 SDCo 91941 1271-C4
HALEY RD
- ImCo - 411-D9
HALEY ST
200 SDCo 92065 1152-D7
HALFBEAK WY
3700 SD 92124 1249-G3
HALF DOME PL
2600 CRLB 92010 1106-J5
HALF MILE DR
3700 SD 92130 1187-J4
3700 SD 92130 1188-A4
HALF MOON BEND
- CORD 92118 1329-D1
HALF MOON TR
- SDCo 91962 1237-D7
HALF MOON BAY DR
1200 CHV 91915 1311-G6
14100 SD 92014 1187-H5
HALF MOON BAY WY
4200 OCN 92054 1066-E6
HALFOAK TER
11900 SD 92128 1190-B7
HALFPENNY LN
- CORD 92118 1329-E2
HALFWAY TKTR
- SDCo 92060 409-J6
- SDCo 92086 409-J6
HALIFAX ST
6800 SD 92120 1250-A5
HALITE PL
- CRLB 92009 1127-F4
HALL AV
100 SD 92173 1350-F4
HALLER ST
2400 SD 92104 1269-F6
2400 SD 92104 1289-G1
HALLEY CT
1200 CHV 91911 1330-H1
1300 SD 92154 1350-A1
HALLEY ST
1600 SD 92154 1349-J1
1700 SD 92154 1350-A2
HALLMARK PL
- ESCN 92029 1129-F7
HALLMARK WY
600 SD 92102 1290-A3
HALL MEADOW RD
10600 SD 92131 1209-G1
HALLYEYAAW LN
100 SDCo 92070 409-H10
HALO CIR
9900 SDCo 91941 1271-D2
HALO ST
1500 IMPB 91932 1349-J1
1500 SD 92154 1349-J1
1700 SD 92154 1350-A1
HALPER RD
14000 PWY 92064 1190-C3
HALSEY RD
4400 SD 92101 1288-D1
4600 SD 92106 1288-D1
HALSEY ST
100 CHV 91910 1310-C7
400 CHV 91910 1330-A1
HALSING CT
- CRLB 92011 1126-J7
- CRLB 92011 1127-B5
HALSTED ST
8800 SD 92123 1249-D4
HALTER PL
1500 SMCS 92069 1108-E6
HAMBAUGH WY
400 VSTA 92081 1107-H1
HAMBURG SQ
3100 SD 92037 1227-J1
HAMDEN DR
2100 CHV 91913 1311-E3
HAMDEN LN
28100 SDCo 92026 1089-E3
HAMDEN WY
3100 CRLB 92010 1107-A3
HAMILL AV
5500 SD 92120 1250-C5
HAMILTON AV
100 ELCN 92243 6499-D7
100 ELCN 92243 6500-A7
HAMILTON LN
- SDCo 91931 1236-H3
700 SDCo 92028 1028-A1
700 SDCo 92029 1129-H7
800 ESCN 92029 1129-F7
HAMILTON ST
3900 SD 92104 1269-D5
4300 SD 92116 1269-D3
HAMLET AV
7200 SD 92120 1250-C5
HAMLET CT
7200 SD 92120 1250-C5
HAMLET DR
1100 SDCo 92021 1252-J2
HAMLIN CT
- ESCN 92027 1110-D5
- SDCo 92065 1171-D3
HAMMERBERG CV
10300 SD 92124 1249-G4
HAMMOND DR
8800 SD 92123 1249-D5
HAMPE CT
8800 SD 92129 1189-C2
HAMPSHIRE LN
600 CHV 91911 1330-H2
18300 SD 92128 1150-B6
HAMPSON PL
16100 SDCo 92065 1173-D3
HAMPSTEAD WY
2300 SD 92139 1290-G7
HAMPTON CT
- ENCT 92024 1147-D4
800 VSTA 92081 1107-H2
1700 CHV 91902 1311-C5
5800 SD 92120 1250-B7
HAMPTON GN
2400 ESCN 92026 1109-D3
HAMPTON RD
1100 SMCS 92078 1128-B3
34100 SDCo 92061 1050-H1
HANA CT
- ENCT 92024 1147-A2
HANCOCK CIR
- CRLB 92009 1127-F2
4500 OCN 92056 1107-D2
HANCOCK RD
3500 SDCo 92028 1047-H3
HANCOCK ST
1600 SD 92110 1268-G6
1600 SD 92110 1268-H6
2000 SD 92110 1268-G4
HANDEL CT
7900 SD 92126 1209-A4
HANDEL WY
7800 SD 92126 1209-A4
HANDLEBAR RD
16900 SDCo 92065 1171-J2
HANDRICH CT
11900 SD 92131 1210-A4
HANDRICH DR
11700 SD 92131 1210-A4
HANES PL
100 VSTA 92084 1087-H6
HANEY ST
1100 ELCJ 92020 1251-G7
HANFORD CT
- CHV 91913 1311-C7
HANFORD DR
1800 SD 92111 1269-A1
2100 SD 92111 1249-A7
HANFORD GN
400 ESCN 92027 1110-D7
HANFORD PL
7400 SD 92111 1249-A7
HANIMAN DR
2000 SD 92105 1290-A1
HANNA ST
5400 SD 92105 1290-B1
HANNAH CT
- IMP 92251 6499-H2
HANNALEI DR
100 SDCo 92083 1108-A2
HANNALEI LN
400 SDCo 92083 1108-A2
HANNALEI PL
300 SDCo 92083 1108-A3
HANNIBAL PL
3900 SD 92115 1270-E5
HANNIGANS WY
500 SMCS 92069 1109-C7
HANNON CT
6200 SD 92117 1248-J1
HANOVER PL
1100 SDCo 91901 1253-H2
HANOVER ST
900 SD 92114 1290-B3
HANSEL DR
1900 SD 92154 1350-A2
HANSOM LN
10800 SDCo 91978 1271-G7
HANSON LN
- ELCJ 92021 1252-C2
100 SDCo 92065 1173-A1
400 SDCo 92065 1172-F1
HANSON WY
1200 SDCo 92065 1172-F1
HAPPINESS WY
800 CRLB 92011 1126-H4
HAPPY LN
10300 SNTE 92071 1231-E6
HAPPY WY N
8500 SDCo 92021 1232-D7
HAPPY WY S
8400 SDCo 92021 1232-D7
HAPPY HILL DR
1100 SDCo 92084 1108-C1
HAPPY HOLLOW
- SDCo 92061 1050-H3
HAPPY LILAC TR
28400 SDCo 92026 1089-D2
HARBIN PL
10300 SNTE 92071 1231-F3
HARBINSON AV
4200 LMSA 91941 1270-F4
4800 SD 92115 1270-F4
HARBISON AV
- NATC 91950 1290-B6
- SD 92114 1290-B6
1200 NATC 91950 1310-C1
HARBISON PL
800 NATC 91950 1290-C7
HARBISON WY
3100 NATC 91950 1290-C7
HARBISON CANYON RD
100 SDCo 91901 1233-D7
100 SDCo 92019 1233-D7
100 SDCo 92019 1253-B5
HARBOR DR
- ImCo 92274 410-H7
300 SD 92101 1289-A4
500 SD 92101 1288-J4
800 SMCS 92078 1128-F2
1100 SD 92113 1289-C6
1200 OCN 92054 1085-J6
1200 SDCo 92055 1085-J6
1500 VSTA 92081 1107-H5
1600 NATC 91950 1309-G1
2200 NATC 92136 1309-G1
2700 SD 92136 1289-C6
3500 SD 92136 1309-G1
4000 CRLB 92008 1106-F7
N HARBOR DR
500 SD 92101 1288-E1
4100 SD 92106 1288-E1
4500 SD 92147 1288-E1
HARBOR DR N
400 OCN 92054 1085-H5
HARBOR DR S
1200 OCN 92054 1085-J6
HARBOR LN
500 SD 92101 1288-J4
HARBOR RD
- SDCo 92055 1085-H4
HARBOR WY
- OCN 92056 1087-A4
HARBOR CLIFF WY
- OCN 92054 1086-A6
HARBOR CREST WY
3600 OCN 92056 1107-C3
HARBOR ISLAND DR
800 SD 92101 1288-E2
HARBOR POINT RD
800 CRLB 92011 1126-J5
800 CRLB 92011 1127-A5
HARBOR VIEW DR
900 SD 92106 1288-A3
HARBOR VIEW LN
1100 CRLB 92008 1106-G6
HARBOR VIEW PL
800 SD 92106 1288-A3
HARBOR VIEW WY
3600 OCN 92056 1107-C3
HARBOUR HEIGHTS CT
5200 SD 92109 1248-A4
HARBOUR HEIGHTS RD
2100 SD 92109 1248-A4
HARBOUR TOWN PL
- CHV 91915 1311-G7
HARCOURT DR
2300 SD 92123 1249-F6
HARDELL LN
400 SDCo 92084 1088-E5
HARDIN DR
1100 ELCJ 92020 1251-E7
1200 ELCJ 92020 1271-E1
HARDING AV
1100 NATC 91950 1309-H2
3700 SD 92113 1289-G4
HARDING ST
100 OCN 92057 1067-B6
600 ESCN 92027 1130-A1
700 ESCN 92027 1110-A7
800 CRLB 92008 1106-E5
HARDING WY
2800 NATC 91950 1309-H4
HARD MAPLE RD
- CHV 91915 1311-H1
HARD SCRAMBLE TR
7200 SDCo 92036 1138-B6
HARDSHIP DR
15700 SDCo 92065 1171-H4
HARDY AV
5500 SD 92115 1270-B2
HARDY DR
2400 LMGR 91945 1270-H7
HARDY RD
2500 ImCo 92243 430-L6
HARE KRISHNA GN
- ESCN 92026 1109-J3
HARJOAN AV
8600 SD 92123 1249-C6
HARLAN CIR
900 SD 92114 1290-G2
HARLAN CT
- CHV 91911 1330-H2
700 CALX 92231 6620-G7
HARLAN PL
7500 SD 92114 1290-G2
HARLINGTON DR
8700 SD 92126 1209-C4
HARLOW TER
8400 SD 92126 1209-B1
HARMARSH ST
7900 SD 92123 1249-B5
HARMONY LN
3400 SDCo 91977 1271-E6
5000 LMSA 91941 1271-B1
HARMONY PL
11300 SDCo 92026 1089-H7
HARMONY WY
- VSTA 92081 1107-G5
HARMONY GROVE RD
1800 ESCN 92029 1129-E4
2000 SDCo 92029 1129-D6
7800 SDCo 92029 1149-B1
9100 SDCo 92029 1148-J2
HARMONY HILL
- SDCo 92028 1047-G3
HARNESS PT
11800 SD 92128 1190-B7
HARNESS ST
8500 SDCo 91977 1290-J2
8600 SDCo 91977 1291-A2
HARNEY ST
3800 SD 92110 1268-F5
4400 SD 92103 1268-G4
HAROL ST
1300 ELCJ 92020 1271-E1
HAROLD AV
700 CALX 92231 6680-F1
1000 CALX 92231 6620-F7
HAROLD PL
- CHV 91914 1311-G4
HAROLD RD
1700 ESCN 92026 1109-D5
HARPER RD
- ImCo 92283 432-D5
1200 SDCo 92065 1152-G3
HARPER FIRE RD
- SDCo 91916 (1196-H6 See Page 1176)
- SDCo 91916 (1197-B5 See Page 1176)
- SDCo 92036 (1196-H6 See Page 1176)
- SDCo 92036 (1197-B5 See Page 1176)
HARPER RANCH RD
2800 SDCo 91935 1293-G3
HARPS CT
6000 SD 92114 1290-C5
HARRIER CT
1600 CRLB 92011 1127-D6
HARRIET ST
2700 OCN 92056 1087-D7
HARRIGAN RD
1000 ImCo 92243 431-A7
HARRILS MILL AV
- CHV 91913 1311-D6

SAN DIEGO CO.

STREET Block City ZIP Pg-Grid

HARRINGTON ST
700 CALX 92231 6620-H6
HARRIS AV
700 SD 92154 1330-B7
HARRIS DR
- SDCo 92055 1067-A1
100 SDCo 92028 1028-A2
2900 SDCo 92084 1067-H7
HARRIS RD
500 ImCo 92251 6439-D1
600 ImCo 92251 431-B3
1000 ImCo 92250 431-D3
HARRIS ST
3200 LMGR 91945 1270-F6
3600 LMSA 91941 1270-F5
HARRIS TR
38300 SDCo 92028 997-D3
HARRISBURG DR
300 ENCT 92024 1147-G7
HARRISON AV
1700 NATC 91950 1309-G3
1800 SD 92113 1289-D4
HARRISON ST
100 OCN 92057 1067-B6
4000 CRLB 92008 1106-F7
HARRISON PARK RD
16800 SDCo 92036 1156-F6
HARRIS PLANT RD
8900 SD 92145 1229-E4
HARRIS RANCH RD
600 SDCo 91963 429-L10
600 SDCo 91963 (1316-H7 See Page 1296)
HARRITT RD
9300 SDCo 92040 1232-F4
HARROW LN
15300 PWY 92064 1170-G5
HARROW PL
14200 PWY 92064 1170-G5
HARRY ST
900 ELCJ 92020 1251-H7
HART DR
100 ELCJ 92021 1251-F3
100 SDCo 92021 1251-F3
4800 SD 92116 1269-H3
HART RD
- ImCo 92227 431-D2
HARTFELL RD
30000 SDCo 91906 (1297-G5 See Page 1296)
HARTFIELD AV
13000 SD 92130 1188-A4
HARTFORD CT
- LMSA 91941 1270-G5
2800 SD 92117 1248-F7
HARTFORD PL
4500 CRLB 92010 1107-B4
HARTFORD ST
600 CHV 91913 1311-E3
2100 SD 92110 1268-E1
2200 SD 92110 1248-F7
HARTLAND CIR
9600 SNTE 92071 1231-B4
HARTLEY DR
6300 SD 92037 1247-G2
HARTLEY RD
10800 SNTE 92071 1231-F5
HARTLEY ST
4500 SD 92102 1289-J3
HARTLEY HILL RD
24100 SDCo 91963 (1315-J5 See Page 1294)
25200 SDCo 91963 (1316-A5 See Page 1296)
HARTMAN DR
1300 ELCJ 92020 1251-D4
HARTMAN WY
3000 SD 92117 1248-C3
HARTON PL
8200 SD 92123 1269-B1
HARTON RD
1900 SD 92123 1269-B1
HARTSHORN RD
- ImCo 92250 431-D4
HARTWELL CT
1600 SD 92114 1290-D6
HART WRIGHT RD
1700 SDCo 92084 1108-C3
HARTZEL DR
3400 SDCo 91977 1271-A5
8700 SDCo 91941 1271-A5
HARTZEL CREST DR
3500 SDCo 91977 1271-A5
HARVALA ST
6800 SD 92115 1270-E4
HARVARD AV
4300 LMSA 91941 1270-F4
HARVARD DR
3600 OCN 92056 1107-A2
HARVARD ST
1600 CHV 91913 1311-C5
HARVESON PL
- ESCN 92029 1129-E3
HARVEST CRES
14200 PWY 92064 1170-H6
HARVEST CT
5200 OCN 92057 1067-A4
14300 PWY 92064 1170-H6
HARVEST LN
1100 VSTA 92081 1108-A5
HARVEST RD
600 SDCo 92154 1331-J7
600 SDCo 92154 1351-J1
1600 SD 92154 1351-J3
HARVEST DANCE WY
11000 SD 92127 1169-H1
HARVEST MOON CIR
- SDCo 92082 1070-G1
HARVEST POINT WY
- SDCo 92065 1173-D1
HARVEST RUN DR
- SD 92130 1208-D2
HARVEST VIEW WY
- SD 92128 1189-G6
HARVEST VISTA LN
- SDCo 92028 1027-H7
HARVEY RD
4600 SD 92116 1269-B3
HARVEY HOMESTEAD RD
- SDCo 91935 (1314-G3 See Page 1294)
HARWELL DR
8400 SD 92119 1250-J4
HARWICH DR
1000 SMCS 92069 1109-C6
3400 CRLB 92010 1107-A3
HARWICK LN
12800 SD 92130 1188-C5
HARWICK PL
4900 SD 92130 1188-C5
HARWOOD ST
800 SD 92154 1329-J7
900 SD 92154 1349-J1

HASBROOK RD
10800 SD 92131 1209-H1
HASKELL DR
- ELCN 92243 6559-D1
1800 ELCN 92243 6499-D6
HASKELL RD
1900 ImCo 92273 431-A5
HASKELL ST
2600 SD 92109 1248-C4
HASTAIN RD
- ImCo 92227 411-D11
HASTINGS CT
700 SMCS 92069 1109-C6
HASTINGS DR
3500 CRLB 92010 1107-A3
HASTINGS RD
5000 SD 92116 1269-H2
HASTY ST
3300 SD 92115 1270-D6
HATACA RD
3100 CRLB 92009 1147-H1
HATCHER LN
9000 SD 92126 1209-D2
HATCREEK CT
1200 VSTA 92081 1107-J4
HAT CREEK RD
15000 PWY 92064 1170-G7
HATFIELD CIR
3500 OCN 92056 1107-E2
HATFIELD DR
- SMCS 92078 1128-H3
HATFIELD LN
500 SDCo 92065 1153-A5
HATFIELD RD
- ImCo 92233 411-B10
- SDCo 91917 (1314-C7 See Page 1294)
HATFIELD CREEK DR
- SDCo 92065 1153-B6
HATHAWAY ST
4000 SD 92111 1248-J3
HATHERLY ST
500 VSTA 92083 1087-D7
HATTERAS AV
3500 SD 92117 1248-D2
HATTON ST
3700 SD 92111 1248-J3
3900 SD 92111 1249-A3
HAUBERK CT
300 SDCo 92004 1058-G7
HAUBERK DR
1800 SDCo 92004 1058-G7
HAUSER ST
6400 SD 92114 1290-D6
HAVASUPAI AV
2600 SD 92117 1248-B1
2900 SD 92117 1228-C7
HAVEN DR
8000 LMGR 91945 1270-H7
HAVEN PL
1200 ESCN 92027 1130-E1
HAVEN BROOK PL
10600 SD 92130 1208-E2
HAVENCREST DR
2500 SDCo 92028 1027-J7
2600 SDCo 92028 1047-J1
HAVENHURST DR
900 SD 92037 1247-F2
HAVENHURST PL
6100 SD 92037 1247-F3
HAVENHURST PT
800 SD 92037 1247-F2
HAVENRIDGE WY
5500 SD 92130 1208-E2
HAVENS RD
- ImCo 92243 431-A5
- ImCo 92273 431-A5
HAVENS POINT PL
1700 CRLB 92008 1106-H6
HAVENVIEW LN
- OCN 92056 1107-D2
HAVENWOOD AV
4800 SD 92120 1250-A5
HAVENWOOD DR
1500 OCN 92056 1087-D4
HAVERFIELD WY
11200 SD 92126 1209-D2
HAVERFORD RD
300 SDCo 92065 1152-F3
HAVERFORD RD Rt#-78
1200 SDCo 92065 1152-F3
HAVERHILL RD
700 ELCJ 92020 1251-B4
HAVERHILL ST
3600 CRLB 92010 1106-J4
HAVETEUR WY
8700 SD 92123 1249-D4
HAWAII AV
700 SD 92154 1330-D7
1000 SD 92154 1350-D1
HAWAII PL
900 ESCN 92025 1109-F4
HAWICK DR
13900 SDCo 92021 1232-E7
HAWICK TER
13900 SDCo 92021 1232-F7
HAWK LN
1300 ELCJ 92020 1251-D2
HAWK ST
- ImCo 92243 6560-A7
- ImCo 92249 6560-B7
3100 SD 92103 1268-J4
HAWKE BAY CT
2000 SD 92105 1290-C1
HAWKEN DR
1400 SD 92154 1350-H2
HAWKEYE WY
11500 SD 92126 1209-E1
HAWKEYE DOWNS WY
19600 SDCo 92065 1151-J2
19600 SDCo 92065 1152-A2
HAWKHILL RD
29900 SDCo 92084 1068-F5
HAWKINS PL
- LMGR 91945 1290-H1
HAWKINS WY
2000 SDCo 91977 1291-A1
HAWK RIDGE PL
1600 ESCN 92027 1130-C1
HAWKS BLUFF CT
- CHV 91915 (1312-A5 See Page 1293)
HAWKSBURY LN
15400 SDCo 92082 1070-J6
HAWKS PEAK WY
7500 SD 92126 1209-A3
HAWKSVIEW PL
- CHV 91914 1311-J3
HAWKS VIEW WY
- SDCo 92028 1028-D3
HAWKS VISTA LN
- SDCo 91901 1253-J3
HAWK VIEW DR
1600 ENCT 92024 1147-D2

HAWLEY AV
9000 LMSA 91941 1271-A1
HAWLEY BLVD
4500 SD 92116 1269-F3
HAWLEY CT
15600 SDCo 92021 1233-C3
HAWLEY DR
2000 VSTA 92084 1087-J2
HAWLEY PL
15500 SDCo 92021 1233-B3
HAWLEY RD
9700 SDCo 92021 1233-C1
10500 SDCo 92021 1213-C7
HAWLEY CREEK
- SDCo 92021 1233-C3
HAWORTH ST
6900 SD 92122 1228-F5
HAWTHORN GN
2400 ESCN 92027 1110-D7
HAWTHORN ST
100 SD 92101 1288-J1
500 SD 92101 1289-A1
2800 SD 92104 1289-D1
HAWTHORNE AV
400 ELCJ 92020 1251-E6
900 CRLB 92011 1127-A5
HAWTHORNE CIR
200 VSTA 92083 1108-A2
HAWTHORNE CT
900 SMCS 92078 1128-B2
HAWTHORNE DR
500 SDCo 92036 1156-E2
HAWTHORNE ST
100 SDCo 92028 1027-F2
W HAWTHORNE ST
100 SDCo 92028 1027-F2
HAWTHORNE CREEK DR
900 CHV 91914 1311-H4
HAXTON PL
13200 SD 92130 1188-B4
HAY CT
12500 SDCo 92021 1232-B7
HAYA ST
100 SD 92102 1289-J4
HAYDEN DR
100 ESCN 92027 1110-E7
HAYDEN LN
1200 ELCJ 92021 1252-B3
HAYDEN WY
2100 SD 92110 1268-G5
HAYDEN LAKE PL
- SD 92127 1169-A3
HAYDEN RANCH RD
- VSTA 92084 1087-H2
HAYDN DR
1600 ENCT 92007 1167-C2
HAYES AV
900 SD 92103 1269-B5
HAYES ST
100 OCN 92054 1106-A2
8600 LMSA 91941 1270-J2
8600 LMSA 91941 1271-A2
HAYFORD RD
1500 CHV 91913 1311-D7
HAYFORD WY
- SD 92130 1188-D4
HAYFORK PL
1400 CHV 91913 1331-B2
HAYMAR DR
2700 CRLB 92010 1106-H2
3500 OCN 92010 1106-H2
3500 OCN 92010 1107-A2
3500 OCN 92056 1107-A2
HAYMARKET RD
1800 ENCT 92024 1147-A2
HAYUCO PZ
1000 CHV 91910 1311-C2
HAYVIN RD
31700 SDCo 92082 1050-J7
HAYWARD CT
2100 SD 92139 1290-E7
HAYWARD PL
500 ESCN 92027 1110-D6
HAYWARD WY
6400 SD 92139 1290-E7
HAZARD WY
9300 SD 92123 1229-E7
HAZARD CENTER DR
7600 SD 92108 1269-A2
HAZEL WY
200 OCN 92057 1086-J5
HAZELDON DR
8800 SNTE 92071 1231-B7
HAZELHURST CT
3600 SDCo 91902 1310-J2
HAZELHURST PL
3600 SDCo 91902 1310-J1
HAZELNUT CT
- CHV 91915 1311-H1
1900 SMCS 92078 1128-B2
HAZELTINE RD
- SDCo 92082 1090-H5
HAZELWOOD PL
1900 SD 92105 1289-J1
HAZEN DR
900 SMCS 92069 1109-B6
HAZY GLEN CT
800 CHV 91910 1311-B5
HAZY MEADOW LN
15600 SDCo 92040 1212-J6
H DE LA VEGA ST
- CALX 92231 6620-G6
HEADQUARTERS PT
5100 SD 92121 1208-D5
HEALD LN
300 SDCo 92028 1027-H3
HEALIS PL
- SD 92129 1188-J4
- SD 92129 1189-A4
HEALTHCARE DR
8800 LMSA 91942 1251-A7
8900 LMSA 91942 1271-A1
HEALTH CTR DR
2700 SD 92123 1249-B6
HEALTH SCIENCES DR
- SD 92037 1228-C2
HEALY CT
10600 SNTE 92071 1231-E2
HEALY ST
10400 SNTE 92071 1231-E2
HEALY WY
10600 SNTE 92071 1231-E2
E HEANEY CIR
9300 SNTE 92071 1231-B5
W HEANEY CIR
9300 SNTE 92071 1231-A5
HEARD LN
700 SDCo 92065 1152-H6
HEARTLAND LN
1700 SDCo 92019 1252-B6
HEARTWOOD CT
- SD 92131 1209-G2
HEARTWOOD WY
- SD 92131 1209-G2

HEATER CT
10500 SD 92121 1208-H4
HEATH CT
6700 CRLB 92011 1126-J5
HEATH DR
14900 PWY 92064 1170-C7
HEATHBROOK CT
- SD 92154 1330-H7
HEATH CLIFF CT
8500 SDCo 92021 1252-E1
HEATHER CT
500 CHV 91911 1330-H3
HEATHER DR
1000 VSTA 92084 1087-J5
1000 VSTA 92084 1088-A5
HEATHER LN
2100 DLMR 92014 1187-F3
3100 SDCo 91901 1234-D4
3300 OCN 92056 1107-B1
HEATHER PL
2500 ESCN 92027 1110-E7
HEATHER ST
3000 SD 92105 1269-H6
HEATHER WY
800 CRLB 92011 1127-A6
10600 SD 92126 1209-E3
HEATHER CANYON CT
3800 SDCo 91902 1311-A3
HEATHERDALE ST
9100 SNTE 92071 1231-G5
HEATHER FIELD LN
12500 SD 92128 1150-B6
HEATHER GLEN WY
14800 SD 92128 1170-B7
14800 SD 92128 1190-B1
HEATHERLY DR
- SD 92130 1188-J3
HEATHERMIST CT
- SDCo 92019 1272-B2
HEATHERRIDGE CT
3300 SMCS 92078 1108-C6
HEATHER RIDGE DR
- SD 92130 1208-D1
HEATHERRIDGE RD
500 SMCS 92078 1108-C6
HEATHERS COUNTRY LN
- SDCo 91962 (1299-C2 See Page 1298)
HEATHER STONE CT
- SDCo 92127 1169-F5
HEATHERTON CT
12500 SD 92128 1189-J6
HEATHERWOOD AV
- CHV 91913 1311-E7
- CHV 91913 1331-E1
HEATHERWOOD CT
2400 ESCN 92026 1109-H3
HEATHERWOOD DR
3400 SDCo 92019 1272-C6
5200 OCN 92056 1087-D2
HEATHERWOOD LN
800 VSTA 92081 1108-A4
HEATHERWOOD HOLLOW CT
- SD 92128 1190-A7
HEAVEN DR
- SDCo 92028 998-G5
HEAVENLY PL
31600 SDCo 92003 1067-H2
HEAVENLY WY
9900 SDCo 91941 1271-D2
HEBER AV
100 CALX 92231 6680-G2
1000 CALX 92231 6620-G7
HEBER RD
200 ImCo 92243 431-B7
300 ImCo 92249 6560-B6
900 ImCo 92249 431-D6
900 ImCo 92250 431-D6
HEBER RD Rt#-86
- ImCo 92243 431-C7
- ImCo 92243 6620-A1
- ImCo 92249 431-C7
- ImCo 92249 6620-A1
- ImCo 92249 6560-D7
HEBER ST
- SDCo 91934 (1321-G5 See Page 1300)
1000 ImCo 92249 6560-B7
1000 ImCo 92249 6620-B1
HEBRIDES CIR
10400 SD 92126 1209-C4
HEBRIDES DR
8500 SD 92126 1209-C4
HECTOR AV
9100 SD 92123 1249-E6
HECTOR PL
3200 SDCo 91935 1273-B7
HEDERA HILLS RD
- SDCo 92127 1149-F7
- SDCo 92127 1169-F1
HEDGE WY
300 CHV 91910 1310-A6
HEDGEROW LN
- SD 92126 1209-E3
HEDGES WY
6600 SD 92139 1310-F2
HEDGETREE CT
12600 PWY 92064 1190-C1
HEDGEWOOD RW
5900 SD 92037 1248-A1
HEDIONDA AV
1300 VSTA 92081 1107-F3
1400 SDCo 92081 1107-F3
HEDIONDA CT
4400 SD 92117 1248-D2
HEDY DR
16100 SDCo 92065 1171-F4
HEFFERNAN AV
100 CALX 92231 6680-G2
1000 ImCo 92249 6620-C1
1000 ImCo 92249 431-C7
1100 ImCo 92249 6560-C7
HEFFNER LN
9900 SD 92126 1209-A6
HEGG ST
4000 SD 92115 1270-C5
HEIDE LN
3200 SDCo 91935 1273-A7
3200 SDCo 91935 1293-A1
HEIDEN CT
500 SMCS 92069 1109-A3
HEIDI CIR
1400 VSTA 92084 1087-H4
HEIDI ST
5400 LMSA 91942 1270-H1
5500 LMSA 91942 1250-H7
HEIGHTS CT
- SDCo 92027 1130-D4
HEIGHTS LN
2600 SDCo 91977 1271-E7
HEIL AV
100 ELCN 92243 6499-E7
100 ELCN 92243 6500-A7

HEIL CIR
- ELCN 92243 6499-D7
HEIL CT
100 ELCN 92243 6499-J7
HEINRICH HERTZ DR
9400 SD 92154 1352-A3
HEISE PARK RD
- SDCo 92036 1156-C5
HEITING CT
9300 SNTE 92071 1230-J6
HELEN CIR
1000 NATC 91950 1310-B1
HELEN DR
600 OCN 92057 1067-B5
39700 SDCo 92028 997-A2
HELEN RD
2300 SDCo 92028 996-J2
2300 SDCo 92028 997-A1
HELEN WY
100 ESCN 92025 1130-B5
100 SDCo 92025 1130-B5
HELENA PL
5600 SD 92120 1250-C7
5600 SD 92120 1270-C1
HELENA ST
4000 SDCo 92028 1028-F4
HELENITE PL
- CRLB 92009 1127-F5
HELENJAMES AV
8800 SD 92126 1209-D5
HELEN PARK LN
14700 PWY 92064 1190-E1
HELIOTROPE DR
- SDCo 92036 1136-E7
- SDCo 92036 1156-E1
HELIX AV
800 CHV 91911 1330-E2
N HELIX AV
100 SOLB 92075 1167-E7
S HELIX AV
200 SOLB 92075 1187-E1
HELIX CT
8700 SDCo 91977 1291-A2
HELIX LN
3900 SDCo 91977 1271-B5
HELIX PL
1800 SDCo 91977 1291-A1
HELIX ST
1200 SDCo 91977 1291-B1
2500 SDCo 91977 1271-B5
HELIX TER
5000 SDCo 91941 1271-D1
HELIX WY
400 OCN 92057 1086-J4
1400 CHV 91911 1330-F4
HELIX CANYON DR
- SDCo 91941 1271-C3
HELIX DEL SUR
4200 SDCo 91941 1271-E4
HELIX GLEN DR
4700 LMSA 91941 1271-B3
HELIX HILLS TER
4900 LMSA 91941 1271-C2
HELIX MONT CIR
9900 SDCo 91941 1271-D4
HELIX MONT DR
9900 SDCo 91941 1271-D4
HELIX VIEW DR
1200 ELCJ 92020 1251-D7
HELIX VILLAGE CT
1200 ELCJ 92020 1251-D7
HELIX VILLAGE DR
1000 ELCJ 92020 1251-D7
HELIX VISTA DR
8700 SDCo 91977 1291-A2
HELL CREEK RD
27800 SDCo 92082 1091-H3
HELLERS BEND
3800 SDCo 92028 1047-H4
HELM ST
8000 SD 92114 1290-G2
HELMER LN
11800 SD 92131 1210-A3
HELMSDALE RD
- SMCS 92069 1108-G6
HELVETIA DR
2600 SDCo 92036 1136-D7
HELVETIA ST
30200 SDCo 92070 1135-B3
HEMINGWAY AV
7800 SD 92120 1250-D3
HEMINGWAY CT
1800 ESCN 92027 1130-D2
6900 SD 92120 1250-E4
HEMINGWAY DR
- CRLB 92008 1107-A7
- CRLB 92008 1127-A1
6600 SD 92120 1250-D3
HEMLOCK AV
100 CRLB 92008 1106-E7
300 ESCN 92026 1129-H1
700 IMPB 91932 1349-G2
2100 SD 92154 1350-B2
HEMLOCK ST
3600 SD 92113 1289-G5
HEMLOCK WY
200 OCN 92057 1086-J2
HEMPDEN CT
1300 ELCJ 92020 1251-D5
HEMPHILL CT
10300 SD 92126 1209-B5
HEMPHILL DR
500 SMCS 92069 1108-J6
7700 SD 92126 1209-A5
HEMPHILL PL
10300 SD 92126 1209-B5
HEMPHILL WY
10300 SD 92126 1209-A5
N HEMPSTEAD CIR
4000 SD 92116 1269-G2
S HEMPSTEAD CIR
4000 SD 92116 1269-G2
HENDERSON AV
1200 SD 92140 1268-E7
HENDERSON CT
1700 VSTA 92083 1087-G3
HENDERSON DR
- SDCo 92055 1067-A1
6000 LMSA 91942 1251-C6
6300 ELCJ 92020 1251-C6
HENDERSON RD
- SDCo 92059 1029-J4
- SDCo 92059 1030-A3
HENDERSON CANYON RD
400 SDCo 92004 1058-H3
400 SDCo 92004 (1059-D3 See Page 1058)
HENDRICKS CT
10100 SD 92126 1209-A5
HENDRICKS DR
7800 SD 92126 1209-A5
HENDRIX PL
1500 CHV 91911 1330-J3

HENIE HILLS DR
1900 OCN 92056 1086-G7
HENLEY DR
5800 SD 92120 1250-B7
HENNA PL
1800 SDCo 92019 1272-D2
HENRIETTA CT
200 SD 92114 1290-E4
HENRY LN
100 CHV 91911 1330-D3
HENRY ST
3900 SD 92103 1268-G6
3900 SD 92110 1268-G6
HENRY SILVERS PL
2400 SDCo 92036 1136-B6
HENSHAW CT
- SDCo 92055 1086-A2
HENSHAW RD
- SDCo 92070 409-J7
- SDCo 92070 (1073-J5 See Page 1052)
1300 OCN 92056 1087-D1
HENSLEY ST
100 SD 92113 1289-D4
100 SD 92102 1289-D4
HENSON
500 SMCS 92069 1108-G6
HENSON ST
100 SD 92114 1290-D4
HENSON HEIGHTS DR
400 SMCS 92069 1108-G6
HEPBURN CT
3200 SD 92124 1249-G4
HERALDRY ST
8800 SD 92123 1249-D4
HERALDS WY
1500 SDCo 92065 1172-J1
HERBERT CT
- CALX 92231 6680-H2
HERBERT PL
1600 SD 92103 1269-C6
HERBERT ST
500 ELCJ 92020 1251-G7
700 OCN 92057 1067-B5
3400 SD 92103 1269-C6
HERBERT YORK LN
- SD 92093 1228-A3
HERBY WY
1200 OCN 92054 1106-C2
HERCULES ST
8300 LMSA 91942 1270-J1
HERDER LN
700 ENCT 92024 1147-E7
HERDFIELD WY
10200 SDCo 91977 1271-E5
HEREFORD DR
25100 SDCo 92065 1173-H4
HERENCIA DR
12800 PWY 92064 1190-D5
HERITAGE CT
1300 ESCN 92027 1130-B2
HERITAGE DR
- CRLB 92009 1127-G3
- PWY 92064 1150-F5
HERITAGE LN
- ENCT 92024 1147-E6
900 VSTA 92081 1108-A5
HERITAGE RD
900 CHV 91913 1331-B1
900 CHV 92154 1331-C7
900 SD 92154 1331-C7
900 SD 92154 1351-C1
4300 CHV 91911 1331-B6
HERITAGE ST
100 OCN 92054 1086-F3
HERITAGE WY
14600 PWY 92064 1190-B1
HERITAGE GLEN CT
12700 SD 92130 1188-C6
HERITAGE GLEN LN
4400 SD 92130 1188-B6
HERITAGE PARK RW
2400 SD 92110 1268-F5
HERITAGE RANCH RD
- SDCo 92065 1152-F2
HERMAN AV
3100 SD 92104 1269-E6
HERMANA CT
1300 VSTA 92084 1088-A3
HERMANOS CT
10500 SD 92124 1229-H7
HERMANOS RD
10400 SD 92124 1229-H7
HERMES AV
500 ENCT 92024 1147-A3
HERMES CT
1300 SD 92154 1349-J2
HERMES LN
1400 SD 92154 1349-J2
HERMES ST
1500 SD 92154 1349-J2
1700 SD 92154 1350-A2
HERMOSA PL
20600 SDCo 92029 1149-E4
HERMOSA WY
4100 SD 92103 1268-H4
10100 SDCo 91941 1271-D2
HERMOSILLO GN
1100 ESCN 92026 1109-E5
HERMOSILLO WY
14000 PWY 92064 1190-E2
HERMOSITA DR
1200 SDCo 92078 1128-B4
HERNANDEZ CT
400 CALX 92231 6620-G6
HERNANDEZ ST
200 CALX 92231 6620-G6
800 SOLB 92075 1187-G1
HERON AV
1300 ELCJ 92020 1251-D3
HERON CIR
- CRLB 92011 1127-B5
HERON DR
1000 VSTA 92081 1108-A6
HERRERA CT
1500 SD 92114 1290-E5
HERRICK ST
6500 SD 92114 1290-D3
HERRING CV
11300 SD 92126 1209-B2
HERSCHEL AV
7400 SD 92037 1227-F6
HERSHEY ST
3400 SD 92115 1270-D6
HESBY CT
8700 SD 92129 1189-C1
HESMAY DR
100 SDCo 92083 1108-B3
HESS DR
10700 SDCo 91941 1271-F2
HESTA ST
15000 PWY 92064 1170-C7
HESTIA WY
- ENCT 92024 1147-B5

HESTON PL
13300 SD 92130 1188-A4
HETZEL RD
2200 ImCo 92251 430-L5
HEWES SQ
12100 SD 92128 1190-B4
HEWLETT DR
5200 SD 92115 1270-A1
HEYNEMAN HOLLOW
2400 SDCo 92028 1028-B3
HEYWOOD CIR
- SDCo 92055 1067-A1
H FRITSCH ST
- CALX 92231 6680-D1
HIALEAH LN
2400 SDCo 91901 1234-C6
HIAWATHA CT
3800 SD 92117 1248-D3
HIAWATHA GN
1300 ESCN 92027 1130-B2
HIAWATHA WY
3800 SD 92117 1248-E3
HIBERT ST
9900 SD 92131 1209-F3
HIBISCUS AV
2300 VSTA 92081 1108-B5
2400 SDCo 92081 1108-B5
13900 PWY 92064 1190-F3
HIBISCUS CIR
3700 CRLB 92008 1106-F6
HIBISCUS CT
500 CHV 91911 1330-H3
HIBISCUS DR
- SD 92109 1248-C6
6700 LMGR 91945 1270-E7
HIBISCUS GN
600 ESCN 92025 1150-C3
HICKMAN PL
3200 SDCo 92036 1156-D1
HICKMAN FIELD DR
- SD 92111 1228-J7
HICKOK PT
- SD 92154 1350-G2
HICKORY CT
700 IMPB 91932 1349-G1
900 CRLB 92011 1127-A5
12600 PWY 92064 1190-D3
HICKORY RD
200 SMCS 92069 1108-H5
HICKORY ST
100 ESCN 92025 1129-J1
1900 SD 92103 1268-G4
13900 PWY 92064 1190-D3
S HICKORY ST
100 ESCN 92025 1130-A2
HICKORY TER
400 CHV 91902 1311-B4
HICKORY WY
3700 OCN 92057 1086-H4
HICKORYHILL DR
200 ENCT 92024 1147-F7
300 ENCT 92024 1167-F1
HICKORY NUT PL
- CHV 91915 1311-J7
HICKS ST
1600 OCN 92054 1106-D2
HICOCK ST
3900 SD 92110 1268-E4
HIDALGO AV
4500 SD 92117 1248-C1
HIDDEN LN
800 SDCo 92036 1138-B6
HIDDEN BAY CT
2100 SD 92105 1290-C1
HIDDEN CANYON RD
- SDCo 92024 1128-D7
- SDCo 92024 1148-D1
- SDCo 92078 1148-D1
- SMCS 92024 1128-D7
- SMCS 92024 1148-D1
- SMCS 92078 1148-D1
HIDDEN CANYON WY
500 OCN 92054 1086-D7
HIDDEN CREEK LN
3000 SDCo 92026 1109-J2
HIDDEN CREST DR
1900 SDCo 92019 1272-C1
HIDDEN DUNE CT
4900 SD 92130 1188-C5
HIDDEN ESTATES LN
- ESCN 92027 1110-F7
- ESCN 92027 1130-F1
HIDDEN GLEN DR
- SDCo 91901 1254-F7
HIDDEN GLEN RD
19500 SDCo 91901 1254-G7
HIDDEN GROVE WY
4400 SDCo 92003 1067-H2
HIDDEN HAVEN
3100 SDCo 92084 1068-A6
HIDDEN HILLS LN
400 SDCo 92029 1149-J1
400 SDCo 92029 1150-A1
HIDDEN HOLLOW CT
1300 SDCo 92019 1272-C1
HIDDEN KNOLL CT
1300 SDCo 92019 1272-C1
HIDDEN KNOLL RD
14600 PWY 92064 1190-H3
HIDDEN LAKE LN
300 SDCo 92084 1087-H1
HIDDEN MEADOWS LN
10100 SDCo 92026 1089-E4
HIDDEN MEADOWS RD
10200 SDCo 92026 1089-F4
HIDDEN MESA CT
1400 SDCo 92019 1272-B1
HIDDEN MESA RD
1500 SDCo 92019 1272-A1
HIDDEN MESA TR
1400 SDCo 92019 1272-C1
HIDDEN MESA VIEW DR
1400 SDCo 92019 1272-B1
HIDDEN MOUNTAIN DR
1200 SDCo 92019 1272-C1
HIDDEN OAKS CT
1800 SDCo 92019 1272-B1
HIDDEN OAKS LN
- ESCN 92027 1130-H3
HIDDEN OAKS RD
- SDCo 92059 999-J5
HIDDEN OAKS TR
1200 SDCo 92084 1108-D2
HIDDEN PALM CT
1800 SDCo 92019 1272-B1
HIDDEN PATH DR
- CHV 91915 1331-H1
HIDDEN PINES LN
400 DLMR 92014 1187-G7
HIDDEN PINES RD
300 DLMR 92014 1187-G7
HIDDEN PLATEAU CT
1300 SDCo 92019 1272-C1

STREET Block City ZIP Pg-Grid

HIDDEN RIDGE CT
- ENCT 92024 1147-E6
HIDDEN RIDGE RD
3600 SDCo 91935 1272-J6
3700 SDCo 91935 1273-A5
HIDDEN ROCK CT
1800 SDCo 92019 1272-B1
HIDDEN SKY CT
- VSTA 92081 1107-G1
HIDDEN SPRINGS CT
- SDCo 92019 1272-C1
HIDDEN SPRINGS DR
1800 SDCo 92019 1272-C1
HIDDEN SPRINGS PL
1300 CHV 91915 1311-H6
HIDDEN SPRINGS TR
1100 SDCo 92026 1109-J2
HIDDEN TRAIL DR
3400 SDCo 91935 1273-A5
3800 SDCo 91935 1272-J5
HIDDEN TRAIL WY
14700 SDCo 91935 1273-A6
HIDDEN TRAILS RD
- ESCN 92027 1110-E6
- SD 92154 1351-A1
HIDDEN VALE DR
1000 VSTA 92081 1107-H1
HIDDEN VALLEY AV
1400 CHV 91915 1311-H7
HIDDEN VALLEY CT
- SDCo 91977 1291-D1
7700 SD 92037 1227-J6
HIDDEN VALLEY DR
15300 PWY 92064 1191-A4
HIDDEN VALLEY PL
2500 SD 92037 1227-J6
HIDDEN VALLEY RD
- CRLB 92011 1127-A3
2500 SD 92037 1227-H6
5800 CRLB 92008 1126-J1
5800 CRLB 92008 1127-A2
6100 OCN 92028 1067-D1
HIDDEN VIEW LN
- ESCN 92027 1110-F7
- ESCN 92027 1130-F1
800 SDCo 92065 1152-G6
HIDDEN VISTA DR
400 CHV 91910 1310-F6
HIDDEN WALK LN
1400 SDCo 92028 1027-J5
HIDDEN WOOD RD
14500 SDCo 91935 1272-J5
14500 SDCo 91935 1273-A5
HIDEAWAY LN
- SD 92131 1210-D2
28800 SDCo 92082 1090-C1
HIDEAWAY PL
4400 SDCo 91941 1271-D3
HIDEAWAY TER
700 VSTA 92081 1107-H1
HIDEAWAY LAKE RD
12600 SDCo 92082 1090-C1
HIDEWAY RD
- SDCo 92036 1156-E4
HIEL ST
8700 SDCo 91977 1291-A3
HIERBA DR
16900 SD 92128 1170-B2
HIERBA PL
12000 SD 92128 1170-B2
HIGA PL
12600 SD 92128 1170-C4
HIGGINS ST
900 CHV 91911 1330-J2
1300 OCN 92054 1086-B6
HIGGINS TER
12200 SDCo 92040 1232-A6
HIGH AV
7300 SD 92037 1227-F7
HIGH CT
7700 LMSA 91941 1270-G5
HIGH ST
1100 SDCo 92026 1129-F2
7500 LMGR 91941 1270-G5
7500 LMSA 91941 1270-J4
HIGHBLUFF AV
- SMCS 92078 1128-E6
HIGH BLUFF DR
12300 SD 92130 1187-J5
HIGHBRIDGE RD
- SDCo 92127 1169-E4
HIGH COUNTRY CT
6700 SD 92120 1250-D4
HIGH COUNTRY RD
- SDCo 92065 1173-G5
HIGHCREST PL
1600 ESCN 92025 1130-B4
HIGHDALE RD
9700 SNTE 92071 1231-A4
HIGHFIELD AV
8900 LMSA 91941 1271-A2
HIGHGATE CT
5900 LMSA 91942 1250-G7
HIGHGATE LN
7700 LMSA 91942 1250-G7
HIGH GLEN RD
- SDCo 91901 1254-H7
- SDCo 91901 1274-H1
HIGHGROVE DR
1500 SDCo 92027 1130-E5
HIGH HILL RD
- SDCo 92036 1176-A2
HIGH KNOLL RD
6400 SD 92111 1248-H6
HIGHLAND AV
- NATC 91950 1289-H7
300 ELCJ 92020 1251-F6
500 NATC 91950 1309-J1
800 DLMR 92014 1187-G5
2400 SD 92105 1269-H5
2400 SD 92105 1289-J1
2400 NATC 91950 1310-A3
3200 NATC 91910 1310-A3
4100 SD 92115 1269-H4
7800 LMSA 91941 1270-G3
HIGHLAND CT
900 SOLB 92075 1187-G1
3500 SD 92075 1187-G1
HIGHLAND CV
1600 SDCo 92014 1167-J7
1600 SOLB 92014 1167-J7
HIGHLAND DR
700 VSTA 92083 1087-F5
900 SOLB 92075 1187-G1
1000 SOLB 92014 1187-H1
1100 SOLB 92014 1167-J6
1200 SOLB 92075 1167-J6
1700 SDCo 92014 1167-J6
1800 SDCo 92067 1167-J6
1800 SDCo 92075 1167-J6
2200 CRLB 92008 1106-F3
3600 SDCo 92036 1156-D2
HIGHLAND PK
- SDCo 92028 1027-G6

HIGHLAND PL
300 ESCN 92027 1130-C1
HIGHLAND ST
600 ESCN 92027 1130-C2
HIGHLAND WY
2900 SDCo 91977 1271-D7
HIGHLANDER DR
- SDCo 92065 1151-G7
- SDCo 92065 1171-F1
HIGHLAND GLEN WY
4200 SDCo 91941 1271-C3
HIGHLAND HEIGHTS CT
3400 SDCo 91935 1273-C7
HIGHLAND HEIGHTS LN
1100 SDCo 92026 1109-E7
HIGHLAND HEIGHTS RD
14800 SDCo 91935 1273-B7
HIGHLAND HILLS DR
19300 SDCo 92065 1151-J2
HIGHLAND MEADOW CT
17100 SDCo 92065 1171-F1
HIGHLAND MESA DR
16000 SDCo 92025 1151-B4
HIGHLAND OAKS CT
300 SDCo 92028 1047-F5
HIGHLAND OAKS LN
- SDCo 92028 1047-F5
HIGHLAND OAKS ST
200 SDCo 92028 1047-F5
HIGHLAND RANCH RD
14100 SD 92128 1190-A1
HIGHLANDS BLVD
2600 SDCo 91977 1271-D6
HIGHLANDS TER
13700 PWY 92064 1170-F5
HIGHLANDS CREST WY
- SDCo 92025 1151-A3
HIGHLANDS RANCH CIR
17800 PWY 92064 1150-D7
HIGHLANDS RANCH PL
17900 PWY 92064 1150-E7
HIGHLANDS RANCH RD
13200 PWY 92064 1150-E7
HIGHLANDS RANCH TER
17900 PWY 92064 1150-E7
HIGHLANDS VIEW RD
1600 SDCo 91901 1234-D6
HIGHLANDS WEST DR
2000 SDCo 92029 1129-F7
HIGHLAND TRAILS DR
16500 SDCo 92065 1151-D4
HIGHLAND VALLEY CT
- SDCo 92065 1172-B3
HIGHLAND VALLEY RD
3300 SDCo 92065 1151-D3
11000 SD 92128 1150-B5
13000 SD 92025 1150-F4
13400 SDCo 92025 1150-J3
15300 SDCo 92025 1151-A3
16300 SDCo 92065 1171-D1
18500 SDCo 92065 1172-A2
HIGHLAND VIEW GN
2000 ESCN 92026 1109-B3
HIGHLAND VILLAGE CTR
- SDCo 92129 1189-A4
HIGHLINE RD Rt#-S33
- ImCo 92227 431-E4
2200 ImCo 92250 431-E4
HIGHLINE TR
100 SDCo 92021 1252-J3
HIGH MEAD CIR
2700 SDCo 92084 1067-J7
HIGH MEADOW CT
8000 SD 92119 1250-E3
HIGH MEADOW RD
12400 SDCo 92040 1212-C5
HIGH MEADOW RANCH LN
5800 SDCo 92036 1175-G1
HIGH MEADOW RANCH SPUR
6000 SDCo 92036 1175-H1
HIGH MESA CT
18200 SD 92127 1149-H7
HIGH MOUNTAIN DR
10200 SDCo 92026 1089-E5
HIGH MOUNTAIN LN
27800 SDCo 92026 1089-D5
HIGH PARK LN
9500 SD 92129 1189-E4
HIGH PINE ST
14300 PWY 92064 1190-H5
HIGHPLACE DR
5800 SD 92120 1250-C4
HIGH POINT DR
29300 SDCo 92082 1070-G7
HIGH POINT TKTR
- SDCo 92060 409-G5
- SDCo 92086 409-G5
HIGH RANCH RD
11300 SDCo 92040 1211-G6
HIGH RIDGE AV
1800 CRLB 92008 1106-H6
HIGHRIDGE DR
1400 OCN 92056 1087-D4
HIGHRIDGE RD
1500 SDCo 91977 1291-E2
7400 SNTE 92071 1230-F7
HIGH RISE WY
9200 SNTE 92071 1231-H5
HIGH ROSE TER
- SD 92129 1169-B4
HIGH SIERRA RD
14000 PWY 92064 1170-G3
HIGHSMITH LN
8800 SD 92119 1251-A4
HIGH SOCIETY WY
- SDCo 92127 1149-A7
- SDCo 92127 1169-A1
HIGH TIME RDG
- SDCo 92127 1169-A2
HIGHTOP TER
9200 SDCo 92040 1231-H5
HIGH TRAIL CT
- CHV 91914 1311-G2
HIGHTREE LN
7300 SD 92114 1290-G5
HIGHTREE PL
400 SD 92114 1290-G5
HIGH VALLEY RD
14200 PWY 92064 1170-G7
HIGH VIEW DR
3200 SD 92104 1289-E1
HIGHVIEW LN
2300 SDCo 91977 1291-B1
HIGH VIEW PT
2500 SDCo 91905 (1299-H4 See Page 1298)
HIGHVIEW TR
2200 SDCo 92084 1108-D2
HIGH VISTA DR
27500 SDCo 92026 1089-D5

HIGHWAY Rt#-7
- ImCo 92231 431-E7
HIGHWAY Rt#-67
10200 SDCo 92040 1232-A1
11200 SDCo 92040 1212-A7
11300 SDCo 92040 1211-G1
13000 SDCo 92040 1191-D3
13800 SDCo 92071 1191-E5
13900 SDCo 92064 1191-E3
14400 PWY 92064 1191-D1
15000 PWY 92064 1171-E5
15400 SDCo 92065 1171-F3
17600 SDCo 92065 1172-A3
HIGHWAY Rt#-75
- CORD 92113 1289-B7
1500 CORD 92118 1288-J6
1500 CORD 92118 1289-A6
1900 SD 92113 1289-C5
HIGHWAY Rt#-76
- SDCo 92027 (1072-H1 See Page 1052)
- SDCo 92060 (1072-F1 See Page 1052)
- SDCo 92082 (1072-F1 See Page 1052)
300 OCN 92057 1086-J2
3400 OCN 92054 1086-G3
4700 OCN 92057 1087-A1
14800 SDCo 92061 1051-H5
19900 SDCo 92061 1052-A5
20400 SDCo 92060 1052-B6
20400 SDCo 92082 1052-B6
23500 SDCo 92060 (1073-A1 See Page 1052)
23500 SDCo 92070 (1073-C3 See Page 1052)
23500 SDCo 92027 (1073-A1 See Page 1052)
28500 SDCo 92070 409-J8
HIGHWAY Rt#-78
- ImCo - 411-L7
- ImCo - 412-A3
- ImCo - 431-J1
- ImCo 92227 410-K10
- ImCo 92227 430-L1
- ImCo 92227 431-A1
- ImCo 92259 410-J10
- ImCo 92259 430-L1
- ImCo 92281 431-A1
- SDCo 92004 410-F10
- SDCo 92036 1138-C1
- WEST 92281 431-A1
1700 SDCo 92004 (1118-J5 See Page 1098)
1700 SDCo 92004 (1119-D5 See Page 1098)
1700 SDCo 92036 (1118-J5 See Page 1098)
3000 SDCo 92004 (1120-J1 See Page 1100)
4400 SDCo 92004 (1121-A1 See Page 1100)
35600 SDCo 92036 410-A11
35800 SDCo 92036 1136-J7
35800 SDCo 92036 1156-H1
HIGHWAY Rt#-79
- SDCo 92086 1033-J1
21900 SDCo 92070 409-K8
21900 SDCo 92070 1135-B1
23400 SDCo 92086 409-G5
HIGHWAY Rt#-86
- BRW 92227 431-B2
- ImCo 92227 431-B2
- ImCo 92243 431-B7
- ImCo 92249 6560-F7
- ImCo 92251 431-B3
- ImCo 92251 6439-F1
- ImCo 92259 410-H7
- ImCo 92274 410-H4
- IMP 92251 431-B4
- IMP 92251 6439-F3
- IMP 92251 6499-F1
1300 ImCo 92243 6559-J3
1500 ELCN 92243 6559-J2
HIGHWAY Rt#-94
- SDCo 91906 430-B10
- SDCo 91963 429-L10
- SDCo 91963 430-A10
- SDCo 91980 429-K10
28500 SDCo 91906 (1318-J2 See Page 1298)
32100 SDCo 91906 (1319-G1 See Page 1298)
36700 SDCo 91906 (1299-H7 See Page 1298)
37100 SDCo 91905 (1299-J6 See Page 1298)
37700 SDCo 91905 1300-C6
HIGHWAY Rt#-98
- CALX 92231 431-D7
- CALX 92231 6620-J7
- CALX 92231 6680-D1
- ImCo - 431-H6
- ImCo 92231 6620-J7
- ImCo 92231 6680-D1
- ImCo 92249 431-D7
- ImCo 92250 431-F7
- ImCo 92259 430-G7
- ImCo 92259 431-A8
900 ImCo 92231 431-E7
HIGHWAY Rt#-111
- BRW 92227 431-C1
- CALX 92231 431-C7
- CALX 92231 6620-F4
- CALX 92231 6680-F1
- CALX 92249 431-C7
- CALX 92249 6620-F3
- CLPT 92233 411-C10
- ImCo - 410-J4
- ImCo 92227 411-C11
- ImCo 92227 431-C1
- ImCo 92233 411-B8
- ImCo 92243 6560-E2
- ImCo 92249 431-C7
- ImCo 92249 6560-F4
- ImCo 92249 6620-F1
- ImCo 92257 410-L5
- ImCo 92257 411-A5
- ImCo 92259 410-K5
HIGHWAY Rt#-115
- HOLT 92250 431-E5
- ImCo 92227 411-D11
- ImCo 92227 431-D1
- ImCo 92233 411-C10
2900 ImCo 92250 431-D3
HIGHWAY Rt#-186
- ImCo - 432-B6
HIGHWAY Rt#-905
1300 SD 92154 1351-J2
2100 SD 92154 1352-A3
HIGHWAY 76 Rt#-76
4900 OCN 92057 1086-H3
4900 OCN 92057 1087-A1

N HWY 101 Rt#-S21
100 SOLB 92075 1167-E7
S HWY 101 Rt#-S21
100 SOLB 92075 1167-E7
100 SOLB 92075 1187-F1
200 DLMR 92014 1187-F1
200 DLMR 92075 1187-F1
1700 ENCT 92007 1167-E7
HIGHWAY TO THE STARS Rt#-S6
3400 SDCo 92060 1032-E6
HIGH WINDS WY
8300 SD 92120 1250-D4
HIGHWOOD AV
7800 LMSA 91941 1270-G4
HIGHWOOD DR
8400 SD 92119 1250-J4
8600 SD 92119 1251-A3
8900 ELCJ 92020 1251-A3
HIGUERA AV
800 CALX 92231 6680-E1
HIHILL WY
300 ELCJ 92020 1251-C6
HI HOPES DR
11800 SDCo 92040 1211-H5
HIJOS WY
10900 SD 92124 1249-H1
HIKE LN
13500 SD 92129 1189-E4
HIKER HILL RD
9400 SD 92129 1189-E4
HIKERS TRAIL DR
1500 CHV 91915 1311-H7
HIKERS TRAIL WY
2400 CHV 91915 1311-H7
HILARY DR
4100 SDCo 91935 1274-A4
HILBERT DR
500 SDCo 92028 1027-G7
600 SDCo 92028 1027-F1
HILCORTE DR
1500 SDCo 92026 1109-D6
1500 SMCS 92069 1109-D6
HILDA RD
5000 SD 92110 1268-F2
HILDALE CIR
- VSTA 92083 1087-H7
HILE LN
1900 SDCo 92028 1028-A4
HILGER ST
1200 SD 92114 1290-E2
HILL AV
400 SDCo 92028 1027-F2
HILL CT
300 SDCo 92028 1027-F5
HILL DR
100 VSTA 92083 1087-D7
100 VSTA 92083 1107-E1
500 SMCS 92078 1109-A7
500 SMCS 92078 1129-A1
2500 NATC 91950 1290-B7
HILL LN
9400 SDCo 91916 1236-A2
HILL ST
200 SOLB 92075 1167-E7
300 SD 92173 1350-G4
1300 ELCJ 92020 1251-D7
1400 VSTA 92083 1087-D7
1500 ESCN 92025 1129-J5
3200 SD 92106 1288-A2
4100 SD 92107 1287-J2
4100 SD 92106 1287-J2
HILL ST Rt#-S21
100 OCN 92054 1086-A7
100 OCN 92054 1106-C3
HILLANDALE CT
6000 SD 92120 1250-C4
HILLANDALE DR
7700 SD 92120 1250-C3
HILLBRAE CT
10800 SD 92121 1208-F3
HILL COUNTRY DR
12300 PWY 92064 1190-C6
HILLCREEK LN
9600 SNTE 92071 1231-F4
HILLCREEK RD
10800 SNTE 92071 1231-F4
HILLCREEK WY
9500 SNTE 92071 1231-F4
HILLCREST
600 SDCo 92081 1107-H3
HILLCREST AV
4700 LMSA 91941 1270-J2
25700 SDCo 92026 1109-F2
HILLCREST CIR
3400 CRLB 92008 1106-G4
HILLCREST DR
100 ENCT 92024 1147-A3
1200 SDCo 91901 1234-G6
13300 SDCo 92082 1070-D2
HILLCREST LN
100 SDCo 92065 1152-J6
200 SDCo 92028 1027-G1
HILLCREST PL
800 SDCo 92028 1027-J1
900 OCN 92054 1086-C5
HILLCREST TER
- SDCo 92028 1027-H1
HILLCREST SCENIC LN
1700 ENCT 92024 1147-A2
HILLDALE RD
4000 SD 92116 1269-G2
13500 SDCo 92082 1070-E3
HILLDALE ST
2100 OCN 92054 1086-C6
HILLEARY PL
13500 PWY 92064 1190-E4
HILLEARY PARK DR
13400 PWY 92064 1190-E4
HILLERO CT
17300 SD 92128 1170-B1
HILLERY DR
8600 SD 92126 1209-D4
HILLFIELD CT
900 OCN 92054 1086-E2
HILLGREEN WY
1000 SMCS 92069 1109-B6
HILLGROVE DR
6400 SD 92120 1250-D7
HILLHAVEN DR
600 SMCS 92078 1128-B1
HILLHAVEN RD
900 SDCo 92027 1130-C4
HILLMAN WY
9100 SDCo 92040 1231-H6
HILLNDALE WY
14400 PWY 92064 1190-E1
HILLOCK PL
500 ENCT 92024 1147-H5
HILLPARK LN
800 SDCo 92028 1027-H1
HILLPOINT CT
- SDCo 92082 1090-B2

HILLPOINTE RW
6000 SD 92037 1248-A1
HILL RANCH DR
- SDCo 92028 1047-F7
HILLRIDGE LN
2500 SDCo 91977 1271-D7
HILLRISE RD
1900 SDCo 92028 1048-A5
S HILLS DR
- CHV 91915 1311-G7
HILLSBORO CT
2800 CRLB 92010 1107-A5
HILLSBORO ST
7000 SD 92120 1250-B5
HILLSBORO WY
- SMCS 92069 1129-E1
HILLSBOROUGH ST
- CHV 91913 1331-D1
HILLSDALE LN
1700 SDCo 92019 1272-B3
HILLSDALE RD
1500 SDCo 92019 1272-A3
HILLSIDE CT
300 VSTA 92084 1087-H5
HILLSIDE DR
800 SDCo 92036 1156-D1
1200 SDCo 92028 1047-J2
1600 SDCo 92028 1048-A2
1900 CHV 91913 1311-E7
4100 CRLB 92008 1106-H6
7000 SD 92037 1227-G6
7800 LMSA 91941 1270-H2
9200 SDCo 91977 1271-E7
9400 SDCo 92029 1129-C6
14000 SDCo 91935 1292-H2
HILLSIDE LN
1000 OCN 92054 1106-C2
3300 SDCo 92028 1047-J2
HILLSIDE PL
200 SDCo 92021 1252-H4
HILLSIDE TER
100 VSTA 92084 1087-H5
HILLSIDE WY
- SMCS 92078 1129-B1
1300 ELCJ 92020 1251-D6
HILLSIDE ESTATES DR
- SDCo 91935 1292-J2
- SDCo 91935 1293-A2
HILLSIDE VIEW CT
- SDCo 92026 1069-B4
HILLSLAKE DR
2000 ELCJ 92020 1251-B2
HILLS LANE CIR
400 ELCJ 92020 1251-D5
HILLS LANE DR
400 ELCJ 92020 1251-D5
HILLSLOPE AV
8800 SDCo 91977 1290-J3
HILLSMONT DR
1400 ELCJ 92020 1251-C5
HILLSMONT PL
400 ELCJ 92020 1251-D5
HILLSTAR LN
13200 SDCo 92082 1070-C2
HILLSTONE AV
1500 ESCN 92029 1129-G7
HILLSVIEW RD
600 ELCJ 92020 1251-D4
HILLTOP CIR
15200 PWY 92064 1170-B6
HILLTOP CT
- CHV 91911 1330-E2
HILLTOP DR
- CHV 91910 1310-C4
600 CHV 91910 1330-E1
700 CHV 91911 1330-E2
800 SD 92102 1289-H3
800 SD 92102 1290-A3
1500 SDCo 92020 1271-J1
3700 LMGR 91945 1270-H5
5000 SD 92114 1290-A3
31000 SDCo 92082 1070-D2
HILL TOP LN
1600 ENCT 92024 1147-G5
HILLTOP PL
13400 SDCo 92082 1070-D2
HILLTOP TER
13400 SDCo 92082 1070-D2
HILLTOP WY
5700 SD 92182 1270-B1
HILLVALE AV
9300 SDCo 92040 1231-H5
HILLVALE LN
9300 SDCo 92040 1231-H5
HILL VALLEY DR
2800 ESCN 92029 1129-C2
2800 SDCo 92029 1129-C2
HILLVIEW CT
1300 CRLB 92008 1106-F6
HILLVIEW DR
4400 SDCo 91941 1271-E3
30800 SDCo 92082 1070-D3
HILLVIEW LN
- OCN 92056 1107-D2
HILLVIEW WY
3700 OCN 92056 1107-E3
HILLWARD ST
600 ESCN 92027 1110-C6
HILLWAY DR
400 VSTA 92084 1088-A6
HILLYER ST
- CRLB 92008 1107-B7
HILMEN DR
300 SOLB 92075 1167-F6
HILMEN PL
400 SOLB 92075 1167-F7
HILMER DR
9300 LMSA 91942 1251-B7
HILO DR
1700 VSTA 92081 1107-J3
HILO GN
1100 ESCN 92026 1109-E6
HILO WY
500 VSTA 92081 1107-J2
500 VSTA 92081 1108-A2
600 SDCo 92081 1107-J2
HILO W WY
400 SDCo 92083 1108-A2
HILTON PL
7000 SD 92111 1248-J4
HILTON HEAD CT
1600 SDCo 92019 1272-B5
HILTON HEAD GN
2200 ESCN 92026 1109-D4
HILTON HEAD PL
2400 SDCo 92019 1272-B5
HILTON HEAD RD
1800 SDCo 92019 1272-B4
2200 CHV 91915 1311-G5
HIMALAYA DR
3500 SMCS 92078 1128-B1
HIME RD
1100 ImCo 92243 431-B7
1100 ImCo 92243 6559-A7

HIMMER CT
- CHV 91913 1331-F2
HIMMER ST
- SDCo 92055 1085-G1
HINES ST
- SD 92152 1288-A4
HINRICHS WY
1300 ESCN 92027 1130-D2
HINSDALE ST
9700 SNTE 92071 1231-F4
HINSON PL
4600 SD 92115 1270-B3
HINTON DR
9500 SNTE 92071 1231-E4
HI PASS RD
37900 SDCo 91905 (1299-J4 See Page 1298)
37900 SDCo 91905 1300-A4
HIRAM DR
- SD 92102 1289-G4
HIRAM WY
10000 SDCo 92040 1232-C3
HIRES WY
2200 SD 92173 1350-E4
HI RIDGE RD
11500 SDCo 92040 1211-H6
HIRSCH RD
9700 SNTE 92071 1231-B4
HISER LN
8700 SNTE 92071 1230-G7
HISPANO DR
16400 SD 92128 1170-B4
HITACHI WY
900 CHV 91914 1311-G4
HITCHING POST DR
1000 OCN 92057 1067-D7
HITCHING POST LN
1100 CHV 91915 1311-H5
HITCHING POST RD
800 VSTA 92081 1107-H2
HITCHING POST WY
- SNTE 92071 1231-C2
HITO CT
9300 SD 92129 1189-E7
HIXSON AV
1800 SD 92105 1289-H1
H J GOFF CT
- CALX 92231 6620-J6
H NAJERA AV
- CALX 92231 6620-H5
HOBART ST
6200 SD 92115 1270-C3
HOBBIT LN
2400 SDCo 92028 1028-B2
HOBBLE LN
10800 SDCo 91978 1271-G7
HOBBS RD
300 ImCo 92257 411-B6
HOBBS ST
- CHV 91911 1330-J3
HOBERG RD
2100 SDCo 92004 1058-F7
2100 SDCo 92004 (1078-F2 See Page 1058)
HOCHMUTH AV
- SD 92140 1268-F6
HODGES RD
1300 OCN 92056 1087-E2
HODSON ST
6000 SD 92120 1249-J7
HOFER DR
2000 SD 92154 1350-A1
HOFFING AV
8800 SD 92123 1249-C6
HOFFMAN AV
6900 LMSA 91941 1270-E5
6900 SD 92115 1270-E5
HOFFMAN ST
900 SD 92116 1269-B4
HOGAN WY
2300 OCN 92056 1106-H2
HOGAN RIDGE LN
- SDCo 92082 1070-G7
HOHOKUM WY
11300 SD 92127 1149-J7
HOITT ST
300 SD 92102 1289-E4
HOLABIRD ST
6200 SD 92120 1249-J7
HOLBORN CT
10600 SNTE 92071 1231-E3
HOLBORN ST
10000 SNTE 92071 1231-E3
HOLCOMBE RD
- SD 92152 1288-A5
HOLDEN RD
8500 SNTE 92071 1231-A7
8500 SNTE 92071 1251-A1
HOLDEN TRAILS RD
10200 SDCo 92040 1231-G3
HOLDER WY
10200 SD 92124 1249-G2
HOLDERNESS LN
2600 SD 92154 1330-C7
HOLDRIDGE RD
- ImCo - 431-F7
HOLDRIDGE ST
700 CALX 92231 6620-G7
HOLIDAY CT
3200 SD 92037 1228-A3
3700 CHV 91911 1330-E5
HOLIDAY WY
200 OCN 92057 1066-H7
HOLLAND PL
12500 PWY 92064 1190-C2
HOLLAND RD
12100 PWY 92064 1190-B2
HOLLENBECK RD
200 SMCS 92069 1108-D5
HOLLENCREST RD
3400 SMCS 92069 1108-D5
HOLLIDAY LN
- LMGR 91945 1270-F7
HOLLINGSWORTH WY
- SDCo 92127 1169-F3
HOLLINS RD
300 OCN 92056 1087-D1
HOLLISTER ST
100 CHV 91911 1330-B6
100 SD 92154 1330-B6
800 SD 92154 1350-B2
HOLLOW CT
1500 SDCo 92019 1272-A2
HOLLOW PL
1600 SDCo 92019 1272-B2
HOLLOWBROOK CT
- SMCS 92078 1128-F6
HOLLOWGLEN CT
600 OCN 92057 1067-B5
HOLLOW GLEN RD
3500 SDCo 92036 1136-C7
HOLLOWGLEN RD
600 OCN 92057 1067-B5

HOLLOW MESA CT
7900 SD 92126 1209-A2
HOLLOW TREE DR
3300 OCN 92054 1086-D3
HOLLY AV
700 IMPB 91932 1349-G2
2100 ESCN 92027 1110-C6
25800 SDCo 92026 1109-F1
HOLLY DR
4900 SD 92113 1290-A4
HOLLY LN
500 SDCo 92084 1108-D3
4100 OCN 92057 1067-G5
4100 SDCo 92003 1067-G5
HOLLY RD
100 SDCo 92021 1252-H3
2800 SDCo 91901 1234-D4
HOLLY ST
200 OCN 92054 1086-B6
HOLLY WY
3200 SDCo 91910 1310-E5
HOLLYBERRY DR
1200 SDCo 92084 1108-E1
HOLLYBERRY TR
3700 SDCo 92084 1088-F7
3700 SDCo 92084 1108-F1
HOLLY BRAE LN
3900 CRLB 92008 1106-H5
HOLLYBROOK AV
1100 CHV 91913 1311-D6
HOLLYCREST CT
6600 SD 92121 1208-G3
HOLLY FERN CT
11400 SD 92131 1209-J2
11400 SD 92131 1210-A2
HOLLY FERN WY
11300 SD 92131 1209-J2
HOLLYFIELD CT
- SD 92130 1188-A5
HOLLYHILL RD
4300 SDCo 92084 1068-H6
HOLLYHOCK AV
1300 ESCN 92027 1110-A6
HOLLYHOCK CT
800 CRLB 92011 1127-A5
HOLLYHOCK DR
9300 SDCo 91977 1271-B5
HOLLYHOCK LN
- NATC 91950 1290-C6
HOLLY LEAF CT
17200 SDCo 92127 1169-D2
HOLLY MEADOWS
10700 SNTE 92071 1231-E6
HOLLY OAK LN
- ESCN 92027 1130-H2
HOLLY OAK WY
- PWY 92064 1190-F2
HOLLYRIDGE DR
600 ENCT 92024 1167-G1
HOLLY TREE LN
13200 PWY 92064 1190-E4
HOLLY VALLEY DR
2300 SDCo 92084 1068-E7
HOLLYWOOD DR
2500 SDCo 91906 (1297-E5 See Page 1296)
HOLLYWOOD LN
400 SD 92114 1290-C3
HOLMBY WY
9200 SNTE 92071 1231-A3
HOLMWOOD LN
300 SOLB 92075 1167-F6
HOLSOFAR RD
8400 SDCo 92021 1232-D7
HOLSTROM PL
2300 SD 92114 1290-D1
HOLT AV
100 ELCN 92243 6499-E7
100 ELCN 92243 6500-A7
HOLT AV Rt#-S32
400 HOLT 92250 431-E5
1500 ImCo 92250 431-E5
HOLT CIR
- ELCN 92243 6499-D7
HOLT RD Rt#-S32
2300 ImCo 92250 431-E3
3900 ImCo 92227 431-E3
HOLT ST
8200 SDCo 91977 1290-J5
HOLTON RD
300 ImCo 92243 6500-H4
HOLTVILLE ST
- SDCo 91934 (1321-G5 See Page 1300)
HOLZAPPLE LN
600 SMCS 92069 1108-J6
HOME AV
800 CRLB 92008 1106-E5
3600 SD 92102 1289-G2
3700 SD 92105 1289-H2
4500 SD 92105 1269-J7
10700 SDCo 92020 1251-F1
HOMEDALE ST
2600 SD 92139 1310-E2
HOMER ST
3000 SD 92106 1268-D6
HOMESITE DR
2400 SD 92139 1310-E1
HOMESTEAD DR
2700 SDCo 92069 1088-J6
HOMESTEAD LN
47300 RivC 92592 999-F1
HOMESTEAD PL
900 ESCN 92026 1109-F7
HOMEWARD WY
700 SDCo 91901 1234-C4
HOMEWOOD PL
7600 LMSA 91941 1270-G3
HONDO LN
20700 SDCo 91901 1275-A2
HONDO ST
3600 SD 92105 1270-A6
HONESTIDAD RD
1700 SD 92154 1350-B3
HONEY DR
2100 SD 92139 1290-F6
HONEY LN
9100 SNTE 92071 1231-B7
HONEY RDG
- SD 92130 1208-B2
HONEY BEE LN
- SDCo 91962 (1299-B2 See Page 1298)
- VSTA 92081 1107-F2
HONEYBEE ST
- CHV 91915 1331-G1
HONEYBELL LN
- ESCN 92027 1110-C5
HONEYCOMB CT
100 ENCT 92024 1147-H7
HONEYCUTT ST
3900 SD 92109 1248-B6
HONEYDEW LN
700 VSTA 92084 1087-J3

STREET / Block City ZIP Pg-Grid

HONEYGLEN DR
1100 SMCS 92078 1128-F2
HONEY HILL RD
1400 ELCJ 92020 1251-D2
HONEY HILL TER
1500 ELCJ 92020 1251-C3
HONEY HILL RANCH RD
- SDCo 91901 1234-D6
HONEY LAKE RD
- CHV 91913 1311-E5
HONEY OAK LN
2200 SDCo 91901 1253-J1
HONEY SPRINGS RD
1800 SDCo 91935 (1313-E1 See Page 1293)
1900 SDCo 91935 1293-F7
2000 SDCo 91935 1294-D2
2000 SDCo 91935 (1314-A1 See Page 1294)
HONEYSUCKLE CT
1600 ENCT 92024 1147-G5
HONEYSUCKLE DR
900 SMCS 92078 1128-E2
HONEYSUCKLE LN
500 NATC 91950 1290-C6
900 CRLB 92011 1127-A7
1100 SD 92114 1290-C6
1800 SDCo 92019 1252-C3
HONEYSUCKLE TR
- SDCo 92060 1052-D2
HONEYSUCKLE WY
1000 ESCN 92026 1109-J4
HONEY WAGON RD
- ImCo 92259 410-L5
HONNELL WY
3000 SDCo 91935 1292-G1
HONOR CT
3100 SDCo 92004 (1079-C5 See Page 1058)
HONORS CT
2900 SD 92122 1228-C6
HONORS DR
5400 SD 92122 1228-B6
HOOK CT
3100 SDCo 92004 (1079-C6 See Page 1058)
HOOP ST
- SD 92152 1288-A5
HOOPER BLVD
- CORD 91932 1329-E4
HOOPER CT
10100 SD 92124 1249-G4
HOOPER ST
10100 SD 92124 1249-G4
HOOSIER LN
5000 SDCo 91901 1234-J5
5000 SDCo 91901 1235-A5
HOOVER AV
100 NATC 92136 1289-G7
100 NATC 92136 1309-G1
100 SD 92136 1289-G7
800 NATC 91950 1309-H2
HOOVER ST
200 OCN 92054 1086-D7
1000 CRLB 92008 1106-G7
N HOOVER ST
600 ESCN 92027 1110-A6
600 ESCN 92027 1130-A1
HOPE AV
- SD 92102 1289-G4
2700 CRLB 92008 1106-E5
HOPE LN
1800 ESCN 92029 1129-F5
HOPE ST
- SMCS 92078 1128-E6
100 ELCN 92243 6500-A6
800 ELCN 92243 6560-A1
2600 OCN 92056 1087-C6
3900 SD 92115 1270-E5
N HOPE ST
100 SDCo 92065 1172-D1
200 SDCo 92065 1152-D7
S HOPE ST
- SDCo 92065 1172-D1
HOPEDALE CT
6500 SD 92120 1250-D6
HOPI PL
3300 SD 92117 1248-C2
HOPI PTH
3800 SDCo 92004 (1099-E2 See Page 1098)
HOPKINS DR
- SD 92093 1208-A7
9700 SD 92093 1228-A1
HOPKINS ST
2300 SD 92139 1310-C1
HOPLAND CT
1200 CHV 91913 1311-B7
HOPPER AV
900 SMCS 92069 1109-B5
HOPSCOTCH DR
1500 CHV 91915 1311-H7
1500 CHV 91915 1331-H1
HOPSEED LN
8400 SD 92129 1189-C6
HORADO CT
16400 SD 92128 1170-C4
HORADO RD
12200 SD 92128 1170-B4
HORIZON CT
- SMCS 92078 1128-F6
14300 PWY 92064 1170-G4
HORIZON DR
200 ENCT 92024 1147-G7
4200 CRLB 92008 1106-H7
HORIZON LN
100 OCN 92056 1107-D2
400 ELCJ 92020 1271-G1
HORIZON RDG
1100 ELCJ 92020 1251-H7
1100 SDCo 92020 1251-H7
1200 SDCo 92020 1271-H1
HORIZON WY
2400 SD 92037 1227-H2
2400 SD 92037 1228-A2
HORIZON HEIGHTS CIR
- ELCJ 92019 1252-B3
HORIZON HILLS DR
200 ELCJ 92020 1271-F2
400 SDCo 92020 1271-F2
HORIZON POINTE
1400 SDCo 92020 1271-H1
HORIZON VIEW DR
400 CHV 91910 1310-E5
19100 SDCo 92065 1152-B2
23100 SDCo 91963 (1315-G4 See Page 1294)
HORIZON VIEW GN
2100 ESCN 92026 1109-C3
HORIZON VIEW RD
22900 SDCo 91963 (1315-H4 See Page 1294)
HORNBEAM GN
- ESCN 92025 1130-A4

HORNBILL AV
7600 SD 92123 1269-A1
HORNBLEND ST
700 SD 92109 1247-H6
1500 SD 92109 1248-C5
HORNBUCKLE DR
9400 SNTE 92071 1231-B4
HORN CANYON AV
1400 CHV 91915 1311-J6
1400 CHV 91915 (1312-A6 See Page 1293)
HORNE PL
900 OCN 92054 1106-C2
HORNE RD
- ImCo 92283 432-C5
200 ImCo 92243 6559-H3
N HORNE ST
100 OCN 92054 1086-A7
S HORNE ST
100 OCN 92054 1086-B7
200 OCN 92054 1106-B1
HORNED OWL RD
11600 SDCo 92040 1212-C5
HORNER ST
7100 SD 92120 1250-C6
HORSEBACK LN
9300 SDCo 92040 1232-C5
HORSE CREEK TR
13900 SDCo 92082 1070-F7
HORSEMANS LN
- SDCo 92067 1167-J5
HORSEMILL RD
200 SDCo 92021 1232-J7
200 SDCo 92021 1233-A7
200 SDCo 92021 1253-A1
HORSE RIDGE WY
5400 SDCo 91902 1311-A2
HORSESHOE CIR
700 VSTA 92081 1107-G2
HORSESHOE CT
- IMP 92251 6439-F3
1700 CHV 91902 1311-C4
HORSESHOE LN
9300 SNTE 92071 1231-E5
HORSESHOE RD
- SDCo 92004 410-B6
- SDCo 92004 1058-G1
HORSE SHOE WY
1600 OCN 92057 1067-E7
HORSETHIEF RD
- SDCo 91901 1236-D6
- SDCo 91916 1236-D6
- SDCo 91962 1236-D6
HORSETHIEF CANYON RD
- SDCo 91901 1255-H1
HORTENSIA ST
3800 SD 92110 1268-G6
4200 SD 92103 1268-G4
HORTON AV
- SD 92102 1289-G4
2400 SD 92101 1288-J1
3100 SD 92103 1268-J7
HORTON CIR
700 SDCo 91902 1310-G4
HORTON DR
6000 LMSA 91942 1251-B6
HORTON RD
4100 SDCo 91902 1310-G4
4100 CHV 91902 1310-G4
HOSEA CT
- CALX 92231 6620-H7
HOSKA DR
- DLMR 92014 1187-G5
HOSKA LN
- DLMR 92014 1187-G5
HOSKINGS RANCH RD
2700 SDCo 92070 1135-D6
HOSMER ST
300 ELCJ 92020 1251-B5
HOSP WY
- CRLB 92008 1106-G3
HOSPITAL LP
- ImCo 92243 6559-H5
HOTEL CIR N
500 SD 92108 1268-H4
HOTEL CIR S
- SD 92108 1268-G4
200 SD 92108 1269-A4
HOTEL CIRCLE CT
4400 SD 92108 1268-J4
HOTEL CIRCLE PL
2400 SD 92108 1268-G4
HOT MINERAL SPA RD
1700 ImCo 92257 410-L5
HOT SPRINGS WY
- VSTA 92081 1107-J7
HOTZ ST
400 SDCo 91977 1290-J4
HOUSE RD
2900 ImCo 92259 430-L4
HOUSTON ST
3800 SD 92110 1268-D4
HOVANEC ST
1600 SD 92114 1290-E6
HOVENWEEP CT
8400 SD 92129 1189-B3
HOVLAND SQ
9900 SD 92131 1209-H5
HOVLEY RD
- BRW 92227 431-B1
4800 ImCo 92227 431-B1
HOWARD AV
300 ESCN 92029 1129-E4
1500 SD 92173 1350-D3
1800 SD 92103 1269-C5
1900 SD 92104 1269-C5
HOWARD LN
- SDCo 92672 1023-E1
HOWARD RD
4300 SDCo 92004 1100-B4
HOWE CT
6900 SD 92111 1268-J2
HOWE PL
400 ESCN 92025 1129-J6
400 ESCN 92025 1130-A6
HOWE RD
- SD 92126 1209-D7
HOWELL DR
5900 LMSA 91942 1251-B6
HOWELL RD
- ImCo 92257 411-A6
HOWELL ST
2500 SDCo 92065 1152-C7
2500 SDCo 92065 1172-D1
HOWELL HEIGHTS DR
- ESCN 92025 1129-G4
HOXIE RANCH PL
2700 SDCo 92084 1068-D6
HOXIE RANCH RD
29600 SDCo 92084 1068-D6
HOYDALE RW
11300 SD 92128 1189-J3

HOYT ST
- CHV 91913 1331-E2
HOYT PARK DR
10000 SD 92131 1209-G4
HUARACHA CT
5300 SD 92124 1249-H1
HUB CT
1100 ELCJ 92020 1251-D7
1100 SDCo 91941 1251-D7
HUBBARD AV
700 ESCN 92026 1109-H6
700 SDCo 92026 1109-H6
1000 ESCN 92027 1109-H6
HUBBARD PL
- ESCN 92027 1109-J5
HUBBARD RD
600 SDCo 91905 (1319-J1 See Page 1298)
HUBBERT ST
5200 OCN 92056 1087-E1
HUBBLES LN
8500 ELCJ 92020 1231-D7
8500 ELCJ 92020 1251-D1
8500 SNTE 92071 1231-D7
HUBER CT
9700 SNTE 92071 1231-B4
HUBNER RD
5500 SD 92105 1270-B6
HUCKLEBERRY LN
800 ESCN 92025 1150-C3
3700 SDCo 92069 1088-F2
21000 SDCo 92084 1088-F2
HUDSON DR
8000 SD 92119 1250-H4
HUDSON LN
100 SDCo 92019 1253-C1
HUDSON PL
6600 SD 92119 1250-H4
HUDSON BAY TER
5600 SD 92105 1290-B1
HUE CITY AV
- SD 92140 1268-F7
HUELVA CT
300 OCN 92057 1086-J4
HUENEME ST
1200 SD 92110 1268-G3
HUENNEKENS ST
9900 SD 92121 1208-G5
HUERFANO AV
4000 SD 92117 1248-C2
HUERFANO CT
3200 SD 92117 1248-C2
HUERTO PL
500 CHV 91910 1310-H5
HUEY LN
1500 SDCo 91901 1253-J1
1500 SDCo 91901 1254-A1
HUFF RD
2000 ImCo 92251 430-L4
HUFF ST
100 VSTA 92083 1087-D7
100 VSTA 92083 1107-D1
HUFFSTATLER ST
1900 SDCo 92028 998-H4
HUGGINS ST
4300 SD 92122 1228-E4
HUGGINS WY
4600 SD 92122 1228-F4
HUGHES CT
3900 SD 92115 1270-C5
HUGHES LN
800 SDCo 92028 1047-H1
HUGHES ST
500 SDCo 92065 1152-C6
5700 SD 92115 1270-C5
7500 LMGR 91945 1290-G2
7500 SD 92114 1290-G2
HUGO ST
3000 SD 92106 1288-B1
HULBURD GROVE DR
9900 SDCo 91916 1235-J1
HULL ST
200 SD 92152 1287-J4
HUMBOLDT BAY WY
4200 OCN 92056 1066-E6
HUME RD
9600 SNTE 92071 1231-C4
HUMISTON WY
23800 SDCo 92065 1173-D2
HUMMINGBIRD CT
700 SDCo 92019 1252-E6
HUMMINGBIRD LN
- OCN 92057 1086-H2
1700 VSTA 92084 1088-B3
7800 SD 92123 1249-B6
HUMMINGBIRD RD
1900 CRLB 92011 1127-D7
HUMMINGBIRD ST
- CHV 91915 1331-G1
HUMMINGBIRD WY
- CHV 91915 1331-G1
HUMMINGBIRD HILL
100 ENCT 92024 1167-J1
HUMMINGBIRD HILL LN
2400 SDCo 92028 1027-H7
HUMMOCK DR
3500 CRLB 92010 1107-C3
HUMMOCK LN
1800 ENCT 92024 1147-H5
HUMO DR
13900 PWY 92064 1190-G3
HUMPHREY PL
800 CHV 91911 1330-J2
1600 SDCo 92025 1130-B4
HUMPHREYS RD
- SD 92152 1308-A2
HUMPHRIES RD
24100 SDCo 91980 429-L10
HUNECK DR
5700 LMSA 91942 1251-B7
HUNRICHS WY
- SD 92117 1248-C3
HUNSAKER ST
1400 OCN 92054 1106-D2
HUNT RD
1600 SDCo 92021 1251-J1
2100 ImCo 92250 431-E6
HUNTALAS LN
2400 SDCo 92084 1088-D6
HUNTE PKWY
- CHV 91915 1331-J1
- SDCo 91914 1311-H2
800 CHV 91914 1311-H3
1100 CHV 91915 1311-H5
HUNTER CT
- SDCo 91901 1233-E6
HUNTER DR
1800 SDCo 92004 (1099-F4 See Page 1098)
HUNTER LN
300 SDCo 91901 1233-F5
HUNTER PASS
8800 SDCo 91901 1233-E6

HUNTER ST
100 SDCo 92065 1152-E7
400 SDCo 92065 1172-E1
600 OCN 92054 1086-F2
1000 SD 92103 1268-H5
N HUNTER ST
100 SDCo 92065 1152-D6
HUNTER GREEN CT
11200 SD 92126 1209-E2
HUNTER RIDGE PL
- CHV 91914 1311-H3
HUNTERS RD
9200 SDCo 91941 1271-C1
HUNTERS GLEN AV
- CHV 91913 1331-E1
HUNTERS GLEN DR
10600 SD 92130 1208-E2
HUNTERS POINTE AV
- CHV 91913 1331-F1
HUNTERS RIDGE PL
- SDCo 92127 1149-E7
HUNTERS RIDGE RD
- SDCo 92127 1149-E7
HUNTHAVEN RD
7700 SD 92114 1290-G4
HUNTINGRIDE CIR
11200 SNTE 92071 1231-G5
HUNTINGTON AV
9100 SD 92123 1249-D6
HUNTINGTON CT
- PWY 92064 1170-G7
HUNTINGTON DR
- CRLB 92009 1127-G3
HUNTINGTON RD
1100 SMCS 92078 1128-B3
HUNTINGTON GATE DR
15000 PWY 92064 1170-F7
15000 PWY 92064 1190-F1
HUNTINGTON POINT RD
- CHV 91914 1311-F3
HUNTLEY RD
9100 SDCo 92028 1029-B4
HUNZA HILL CT
13100 SDCo 92082 1090-D2
HUNZA HILL TER
- SDCo 92082 1090-D2
HURD CT
6200 SD 92122 1228-D5
HURD PL
4100 SD 92103 1269-A5
HURLBUT PL
3300 SD 92123 1249-C5
HURLBUT ST
8200 SD 92123 1249-B5
HURLEY DR
4100 LMSA 91941 1270-H4
HURON AV
4600 SD 92117 1248-F6
HURON CT
5300 OCN 92056 1087-E1
HURON ST
9700 SDCo 91977 1291-D3
HURSLEY ST
400 ELCJ 92019 1251-J6
HURSTDALE AV
1000 ENCT 92007 1167-E3
HUSTED PL
28700 SDCo 92082 1070-H7
HUSTON RD
100 ImCo 92251 431-B4
100 ImCo 92251 6439-J6
HUTCHISON ST
2000 SDCo 92084 1087-H1
2600 SDCo 92084 1067-H7
HUTTON AV
6400 SD 92139 1310-F1
HUULA DR
- OCN 92054 1086-D3
HUXLEY ST
4600 SD 92110 1248-F7
HYACINTH CIR
6700 CRLB 92011 1126-J5
HYACINTH DR
3600 SD 92106 1268-C6
HYACINTH RD
2300 SDCo 91901 1233-J5
2300 SDCo 91901 1234-A5
HYACINTH WY
200 OCN 92057 1086-J5
HYADES WY
10900 SD 92126 1209-D3
HYANOAK CT
- SDCo 91901 1255-D7
HYATT AV
3500 OCN 92054 1086-F3
HYATT ST
7100 SD 92111 1248-J7
7200 SD 92111 1249-A7
E HYATT ST
7100 SD 92111 1248-J7
HYBETH DR
7000 LMSA 91941 1270-F4
HYDE RD
1300 ImCo 92243 430-L6
HYDE PARK DR
6800 SD 92119 1250-E5
HYDE PARK LN
2200 SDCo 91906 (1297-J7 See Page 1296)
2200 SDCo 91906 (1317-H1 See Page 1296)
HYDRA CT
- SMCS 92069 1108-D5
HYDRA LN
- SMCS 92069 1108-D5
8100 SD 92126 1209-B3
HYDRANGEA CT
4300 SD 92154 1350-G1
HYGEIA AV
500 ENCT 92024 1147-A2
HYGEIA CT
200 ENCT 92024 1147-B4
HYMAN PL
6500 SD 92139 1310-F1
HYMETTUS AV
700 ENCT 92024 1147-B3
HYPATIA WY
1900 SD 92037 1227-G6
HYPOINT AV
2800 ESCN 92027 1110-E6
HYPOINT PL
200 ESCN 92027 1110-F6

I

I AV
100 CORD 92118 1288-H7
400 NATC 91950 1289-J7
500 NATC 91950 1309-J1
2200 NATC 91950 1310-A3
I RD E
- CORD 92135 1288-F6
I ST
- CHV 91910 1310-C7
400 CHV 91910 1330-A1
600 SDCo 92065 1152-H6
700 CHV 91910 1329-J1
E I ST
- CHV 91910 1310-D7
- ENCT 92024 1167-C1
W I ST
100 ENCT 92024 1167-B1
I 3RD ST N
- CORD 92135 1288-F4
I 4TH ST N
- CORD 92135 1288-F3
- SD 92135 1288-F3
I 5TH ST N
- CORD 92135 1288-F4
IAN WY
8600 SNTE 92071 1231-D7
IAVELLI WY
12200 PWY 92064 1190-D6
IBERIA PL
11600 SD 92128 1170-A3
IBEX CT
14600 SD 92129 1189-C1
IBIS CT
3900 SD 92103 1268-J5
IBIS LN
- SD 92103 1268-J7
IBIS PL
7000 CRLB 92011 1127-E6
IBIS ST
1100 SD 92103 1268-J5
IBIS WY
4400 OCN 92057 1087-A3
IBIZA PL
- SDCo 92003 1067-H1
IBSEN ST
3000 SD 92106 1268-D6
ICARIA WY
4900 OCN 92056 1107-F5
ICARUS LN
12300 PWY 92064 1190-C1
ICE SKATE PL
11000 SD 92126 1209-E2
IDA AV
500 SOLB 92075 1167-G7
600 SOLB 92075 1187-G1
IDA ST
7400 LMGR 91945 1270-G7
IDAHO AV
300 ESCN 92025 1130-B4
600 SDCo 92025 1130-C3
800 SDCo 92027 1130-C3
IDAHO LN
1500 SDCo 92027 1130-C3
IDAHO ST
3900 SD 92104 1269-D5
4400 SD 92116 1269-D3
IDAHO TER
1700 SDCo 92027 1130-D4
IDERDELL LN
8200 LMGR 91945 1270-H6
IDLE HOUR LN
2600 SD 92037 1227-J1
IDLEWILD LN
300 OCN 92054 1106-C2
IDLEWILD WY
3000 SD 92117 1248-C1
IDYL DR
13200 SDCo 92040 1232-C5
IDYL PL
9200 SDCo 92040 1232-C5
IDYLLWILD LN
8900 SD 92119 1251-A3
I ESPLANADE
600 CHV 91910 1330-A1
IGUALA CT
100 SOLB 92075 1167-D6
ILDICA CT
2100 SDCo 91977 1291-A1
ILDICA ST
8100 LMGR 91945 1290-J1
8600 SDCo 91977 1290-J1
8700 SDCo 91977 1291-A1
9000 SDCo 91977 1271-A7
ILDICA WY
2000 SDCo 91977 1291-A1
ILENE ST
12900 PWY 92064 1190-D4
ILEX AV
1900 SD 92154 1350-A2
ILEXEY AV
1100 SD 92154 1350-G1
ILLAHEE DR
- SDCo 91901 1255-E5
ILLERONGIS RD
3000 SDCo 91935 1292-G3
ILLINOIS ST
3900 SD 92104 1269-E5
4400 SD 92116 1269-E5
ILLION ST
1800 SD 92110 1268-F1
2200 SD 92110 1248-F7
ILUMINADO
- SD 92127 1168-J6
IMHOFF RD
- SDCo 92055 1085-G4
IMLER RD
- ImCo 92251 430-L3
- ImCo 92251 431-A3
- ImCo 92259 430-L3
IMOGENE AV
2100 SD 92154 1350-A1
IMOGENE WY
- SDCo 92065 1152-J4
IMPALA DR
2400 CRLB 92010 1127-E1
IMPERIAL AV
- ImCo 92251 6439-F7
100 IMP 92251 6439-F6
200 ELCN 92243 6499-F6
1100 ELCN 92243 6559-G1
1100 SD 92101 1289-C4
1200 SD 92113 1289-C4
1500 LMGR 91945 1290-D3
2500 SD 92102 1289-E4
3900 SD 92102 1289-H4
4800 SD 92113 1290-A4
4800 SD 92102 1290-A4
5000 SD 92114 1290-D3
N IMPERIAL AV Rt#-86
600 ELCN 92243 6499-F4
1800 ImCo 92243 6499-F4
1800 ImCo 92251 6499-F4
1800 IMP 92251 6499-F4
IMPERIAL AV E
1300 CALX 92231 6620-F7
IMPERIAL AV W
1700 CALX 92231 6620-F7
IMPERIAL DR
500 ESCN 92026 1109-F5
3800 SDCo 92036 1156-E3

IMPERIAL HWY Rt#-S2
- ImCo 92259 430-G6
IMPERIAL RD Rt#-S24
- ImCo 92283 432-E4
IMPERIAL BEACH BLVD
1000 IMPB 91932 1349-F1
IMPERIAL BUSINESS PARK DR
- IMP 92251 6499-E2
IMPERIAL DAM RD
- ImCo 92283 432-F3
IMPERIAL DAM RD Rt#-S24
1900 ImCo 92283 432-E4
IMPERIAL GABLES RD
- ImCo - 411-K9
IMPERVIOUS PL
2300 SDCo 91901 1253-F2
IMPINK PL
3100 SDCo 91935 1292-H1
IMPRESSIONIST DR
- CHV 91913 1311-E7
- CHV 91913 1331-E1
INCAPA RD
15400 SDCo 92036 1176-D4
W INCENSE CEDAR LN
4200 SDCo 92036 1156-E4
E INCENSE CEDAR RD
700 SDCo 92036 1156-E5
W INCENSE CEDAR RD
900 SDCo 92036 1156-D5
INCHON CT
- CORD 92118 1309-D6
INCHON RD
2300 CORD 92155 1309-B1
INCLINADO DR
1800 ELCJ 92020 1251-C2
INCREDIBLE LN
12100 SDCo 92082 1070-A7
INDEPENDENCE WY
1200 VSTA 92084 1088-B4
INDIA LN
500 SDCo 92028 1028-G4
INDIA ST
500 SD 92101 1288-J1
1000 SD 92103 1288-J1
1700 SD 92103 1268-H6
INDIAN
14100 SDCo 92040 1232-F4
INDIAN CT
5100 OCN 92057 1066-J4
INDIAN PL
2000 ESCN 92027 1110-C7
INDIAN WY
3600 SD 92117 1248-D3
INDIANA AV
100 ELCJ 92020 1251-A2
100 VSTA 92084 1087-H6
S INDIANA AV
100 VSTA 92084 1087-H6
INDIANA ST
3500 SD 92103 1269-C6
INDIANAPOLIS AV
2500 SD 92105 1270-A7
INDIAN BEND DR
32400 SDCo 92061 1050-H6
32400 SDCo 92082 1050-H6
INDIAN CANYON LN
13900 PWY 92064 1170-F1
INDIAN CREEK DR
1200 CHV 91915 1311-H6
INDIAN CREEK LN
9900 SDCo 92021 1232-G3
INDIAN CREEK PL
1300 CHV 91915 1311-H6
INDIAN CREEK RD
28200 SDCo 92082 1090-F1
INDIAN CREEK WY
9600 SDCo 92026 1089-D4
INDIAN FIG DR
3100 SD 92115 1270-C6
INDIAN FLATS TKTR
- SDCo 92086 409-K7
INDIAN HEAD CT
15500 SDCo 92065 1173-E5
INDIAN HEAD RANCH RD
500 SDCo 92004 410-B6
500 SDCo 92004 1058-G1
INDIAN HILL PL
- SDCo 92026 1069-A6
INDIAN HILL RD
8700 SDCo 92026 1068-J7
8700 SDCo 92026 1069-A6
INDIAN HILL WY
6500 OCN 92028 1047-E7
INDIAN HILLS DR
3100 SDCo 91935 1293-F1
INDIAN LORE CT
11000 SD 92127 1149-H7
INDIAN MILLS LN
3100 SDCo 91935 1272-D5
INDIAN OAK TR
- SDCo 92061 1051-G3
INDIAN OAKS RD
19800 SDCo 92065 1152-C2
INDIAN PALMS CT
900 CHV 91915 1311-G4
INDIAN PASS RD
- ImCo - 412-A11
- ImCo - 431-L2
- ImCo - 432-A1
INDIAN PEAK LN
14800 PWY 92064 1170-F7
14800 PWY 92064 1190-F1
INDIAN PEAK TR
13700 PWY 92064 1190-F1
INDIAN RIDGE RD
- SDCo 92029 1128-J4
21800 SDCo 92029 1129-A4
INDIAN ROCK RD
- ImCo 92283 432-C5
- SDCo 92036 1156-E7
E INDIAN ROCK RD
100 VSTA 92084 1087-H4
W INDIAN ROCK RD
100 VSTA 92083 1087-G4
INDIAN SPRINGS DR
13600 SDCo 91935 1292-G1
INDIAN SPRINGS RD
14500 PWY 92064 1190-H1
INDIAN SUMMER CT
1500 SMCS 92069 1109-D6
INDIAN SUMMER PL
700 SMCS 92069 1109-D6
INDIAN SUMMER RD
1500 SDCo 92026 1109-D6
1500 SMCS 92069 1109-D6
INDIAN TRAIL RD
12800 PWY 92064 1170-C4
INDIAN TRAIL WY
6500 OCN 92028 1047-E7
INDIAN VALLEY RD
- SDCo 91935 1293-G1

INDIAN VIEW DR
1500 OCN 92028 1047-D7
1500 OCN 92028 1067-D1
INDIAN WELLS CT
8800 SNTE 92071 1230-J5
8800 SNTE 92071 1231-A5
INDIGO DR
2200 SDCo 92019 1272-D2
INDIGO LN
1700 SDCo 92004 (1099-F2 See Page 1098)
INDIGO ST
3800 OCN 92056 1107-F4
INDIGO WY
10600 SDCo 92127 1169-F2
INDIGO BLOSSOM LN
10600 SD 92121 1208-E4
INDIGO CANYON RD
600 CHV 91911 1330-H1
INDIO
- SDCo 92040 1232-D7
INDUSTRIAL AV
1100 ESCN 92029 1129-E3
INDUSTRIAL BLVD
900 CHV 91911 1330-A3
1600 SD 92154 1330-A3
INDUSTRIAL CT
2100 VSTA 92081 1108-A4
3300 SD 92121 1208-A4
INDUSTRIAL LN
8300 LMSA 91942 1270-H2
INDUSTRIAL PL
1000 ELCJ 92020 1251-E5
INDUSTRIAL ST
100 SMCS 92078 1128-J1
INDUSTRIAL WY
500 SDCo 92028 1027-G2
INDUSTRY RD
12100 SDCo 92040 1231-J3
12100 SDCo 92040 1232-A3
INDUSTRY ST
2300 OCN 92054 1086-E7
INDUSTRY WY
- ELCN 92243 6500-B7
- IMP 92251 6499-D1
INEZ LN
3500 SD 92106 1288-A2
INEZ ST
3500 SD 92106 1288-A2
INEZ WY
200 OCN 92057 1086-H3
INGALLS ST
4000 SD 92103 1268-J5
INGELOW ST
2900 SD 92106 1288-B1
E INGERSOLL ST
2400 SD 92111 1249-A7
W INGERSOLL ST
2400 SD 92111 1249-A7
INGLESIDE AV
4200 SD 92103 1268-G5
INGLESIDE PL
600 ESCN 92026 1109-H6
INGLETON AV
- CRLB 92009 1127-F3
INGLEWOOD CT
800 VSTA 92084 1087-H5
INGRAHAM ST
3400 SD 92109 1268-A2
3600 SD 92109 1248-A6
4700 SD 92109 1247-J5
INGRAM AV
- ImCo 92249 6560-B7
- ImCo 92249 6620-B1
INGRAM ST
- CHV 91911 1330-H3
INGRID AV
2100 SD 92154 1350-A1
INGULF ST
2500 SD 92110 1248-F7
INKOPAH ST
100 CHV 91911 1330-F1
IN-KO-PAH PARK RD
48600 SDCo 91934 430-F8
INLET DR
- CRLB 92010 1107-B4
INMAN CT
2500 SD 92111 1248-H7
INMAN ST
6200 SD 92111 1248-H7
INNIS PT
11800 SD 92126 1209-C1
NW INNIS ARDEN WY Rt#-94
36700 SDCo 91906 (1299-G7 See Page 1298)
36700 SDCo 91906 (1319-G1 See Page 1298)
37100 SDCo 91905 (1299-G7 See Page 1298)
37700 SDCo 91905 1300-A6
INNOVATION DR
15000 SD 92128 1170-A6
INNOVATION WY
- CRLB 92009 1127-F2
INNOVATIVE DR
- SD 92154 1351-C2
INNSDALE AV
8700 SD 92114 1290-J3
8700 SDCo 91977 1290-J3
8900 SDCo 91977 1291-A3
INNSDALE LN
8400 SD 92114 1290-J4
INNUIT AV
3200 SD 92117 1248-C2
INSPIRATION DR
1100 SD 92037 1247-G2
INSPIRATION LN
600 ESCN 92025 1150-C3
INSPIRATION WY
6100 SD 92037 1247-G2
INSPIRATION POINT RD
400 SDCo 92036 1156-F3
INTEGRITY CT
- SDCo 92084 1068-E7
INTEGRITY WY
3200 SDCo 92028 1048-B2
INTERLACHEN TER
- SDCo 92082 1090-H4
INTERMEZZO WY
12600 SD 92130 1188-C6
INTERNATIONAL RD
1800 SD 92154 1350-C4
7800 ImCo 92233 411-C8
7800 ImCo 92257 411-C8
INTREPID CT
900 SOLB 92014 1187-H1
INTREPID WY
- VSTA 92081 1107-G5
INVERARY DR
1700 SDCo 92019 1272-B5
INVERLOCHY DR
- SDCo 92028 1027-G6

STREET Block City ZIP Pg-Grid

INVERNESS AV
- CHV 91915 1311-H6
- SDCo 92082 1090-H5
INVERNESS CT
2700 SD 92037 1227-J4
4700 CRLB 92010 1107-A5
INVERNESS DR
2700 CRLB 92010 1107-A5
2700 SD 92037 1227-J4
4400 OCN 92057 1066-H7
INVERNESS RD
9000 SNTE 92071 1230-H6
INVERNESS WY
3200 SDCo 91935 1273-E5
INVIERNO DR
11600 SD 92124 1250-A2
INWOOD DR
9200 SNTE 92071 1230-J6
9200 SNTE 92071 1231-A6
INYAHA LN
2600 SD 92037 1227-J2
INYO LN
6400 SD 92139 1290-E7
IOLA WY
12800 PWY 92064 1190-A5
IONA CT
500 ESCN 92027 1110-D6
IONA DR
400 SD 92114 1290-C3
IONIAN ST
1500 IMPB 91932 1349-J2
1500 IMPB 92154 1349-J2
1500 SD 92154 1349-J2
1700 SD 92154 1350-A2
IOTA PL
5600 LMSA 91942 1250-J7
IOWA AV
700 SDCo 92028 1027-F1
IOWA ST
300 SDCo 92028 1027-F2
600 SD 92154 1330-A6
3900 SD 92104 1269-E5
4400 SD 92116 1269-E4
IOWA HILL CT
1300 CHV 91913 1311-D7
IPAI CT
11000 SD 92127 1169-H1
IPANEMA LN
- VSTA 92084 1088-D5
IPAVA DR
13900 PWY 92064 1190-G3
IRELAND LN
13100 SD 92129 1189-B4
IRENE CT
8000 SDCo 92021 1252-A1
IRENE RD
600 OCN 92057 1067-B5
IRIS AV
- CALX 92231 6620-J7
600 IMPB 91932 1349-F2
2100 SD 92154 1350-B2
2400 SD 92173 1350-C2
IRIS CT
1000 CRLB 92011 1127-B6
IRIS DR
- SD 92109 1248-C6
IRIS LN
14000 PWY 92064 1190-G2
N IRIS LN
1800 ESCN 92026 1109-G4
1900 SDCo 92026 1109-G5
S IRIS LN
1600 ESCN 92026 1109-G6
IRIS WY
1700 ESCN 92027 1110-B6
IRISDALE CT
1900 ENCT 92024 1147-H7
IRISH EYES LN
- SDCo 92127 1169-A2
IRISH OAKS RD
28100 SDCo 92082 1090-H2
IRON DR
200 VSTA 92083 1087-F6
IRONBARK WY
13200 PWY 92064 1190-E2
IRON GATE LN
- CHV 91914 1311-J1
IRONGATE LN
9200 SD 92126 1209-E2
IRON HORSE CT
800 SMCS 92078 1128-G2
IRON HORSE DR
800 SMCS 92078 1128-G2
IRON HORSE PL
- CHV 91914 1311-J3
IRON MOUNTAIN DR
16800 PWY 92064 1191-D3
17300 SDCo 92040 1191-D3
IRON SPRINGS PL
35100 SDCo 92036 1156-E7
IRON SPRINGS RD
16900 SDCo 92036 1156-E7
35200 SDCo 92036 1176-D1
IRON SPRINGS WY
35100 SDCo 92036 1156-E7
IRONSTONE CT
16600 SDCo 92065 1171-D3
IRON VIEW RW
12100 SD 92128 1170-A4
IRONWOOD AV
10400 SNTE 92071 1231-D2
IRON WOOD CT
- CHV 91915 1311-H2
IRONWOOD CT
9900 SD 92131 1209-J4
IRONWOOD LN
4500 SDCo 92004 (1099-F4 See Page 1098)
IRONWOOD PL
3300 OCN 92056 1086-H7
9900 SD 92131 1209-J4
IRONWOOD RD
10800 SD 92131 1209-H5
IRON WOOD VW
- SDCo 92026 1089-B3
IROQUOIS AV
4600 SD 92117 1248-F6
IROQUOIS WY
3000 SD 92117 1248-E6
IRVINE RD
- ImCo 92227 411-E11
- ImCo 92227 431-E1
IRVING AV
1800 SD 92113 1289-C4
IRVINGTON AV
9100 SD 92123 1249-E6
IRWIN AV
5200 SD 92120 1250-B5
IRWIN ST
- CHV 91913 1331-E2
ISAAC ST
9200 SNTE 92071 1231-F6
ISABEL ST
2200 SD 92105 1289-J1

ISABELLA AV
1000 CORD 92118 1288-H7
ISABELLA DR
3100 OCN 92056 1106-J1
3100 OCN 92056 1107-A2
ISHAM SPRINGS CT
2700 SDCo 91977 1291-E1
ISHIHARA
700 VSTA 92084 1087-J3
ISIDORE ST
700 OCN 92057 1067-B5
ISLA DE LA GAITA
1800 SD 92173 1350-E3
ISLA DEL CAMPANERO
1700 SD 92173 1350-E3
ISLA DEL CARMEN WY
1700 SD 92173 1350-D3
ISLA DEL REY
- SDCo 92065 1173-D2
ISLAND AV
100 SD 92101 1289-A4
400 SD 92102 1289-E3
ISLAND CT
700 SD 92109 1267-H2
ISLAND DR
- SDCo 92078 1128-B3
- SMCS 92078 1128-B3
ISLAND WY
- OCN 92054 1086-G2
1800 CRLB 92011 1126-H5
ISLAND BREEZE LN
400 SD 92154 1330-H6
ISLANDER ST
300 OCN 92054 1086-E6
ISLAND KETCH CT
- SD 92154 1351-A1
ISLAND PINE WY
- SDCo 92127 1169-D2
ISLAND SHORE WY
- SMCS 92078 1128-A2
ISLAND VIEW LN
1100 ENCT 92024 1147-F7
ISLAND VIEW WY
3100 VSTA 92081 1128-A1
ISLA VISTA DR
3200 SD 92105 1269-J6
ISLA VISTA RD
15200 SDCo 91935 1293-D1
ISLE DR
4000 CRLB 92008 1106-G6
ISLE WY
1100 CHV 91910 1311-B7
ISLE ROYALE CT
5000 OCN 92057 1087-C1
ISLETA AV
4600 SD 92117 1248-C1
ISLEWORTH AV
10400 SD 92126 1209-D4
ISOCOMA ST
12900 SD 92129 1189-D5
ISOM CT
900 CHV 91911 1331-A1
ISRAEL CT
- CHV 91911 1331-A3
ISTHMUS CT
700 SD 92109 1267-H2
ISTHMUS DR
- CRLB 92011 1126-H6
ISTHMUS WY
300 OCN 92054 1086-B6
ITHACA CT
900 CHV 91913 1311-D5
ITHACA DR
1700 VSTA 92081 1107-G5
ITHACA PL
5800 SD 92122 1228-D6
ITHACA ST
1600 CHV 91913 1311-D5
3400 SD 92122 1228-D6
ITO CT
6300 SD 92114 1290-D4
ITURRALDE CT
- CALX 92231 6620-H7
ITZAMNA RD
10600 SDCo 91941 1271-F3
IVANHO ST
9700 SDCo 91977 1291-D3
IVANHOE AV
7600 SD 92037 1227-F6
IVANHOE AV E
7600 SD 92037 1227-F6
IVANHOE RANCH RD
3000 SDCo 92019 1272-D5
IVERSON ST
8500 SD 92123 1249-C5
IVERSON POINT WY
700 OCN 92054 1066-E6
IVES CT
6800 SD 92111 1268-J2
IVEY RANCH RD
1200 OCN 92057 1086-J4
IVEY VISTA WY
4000 OCN 92057 1086-J4
IVORY AV
100 ELCJ 92019 1252-A5
IVORY CT
1300 ELCJ 92019 1252-A5
IVORY PL
- CRLB 92009 1127-F5
IVORY COAST DR
8300 SD 92126 1209-C4
IVORY GULL WY
200 SMCS 92078 1129-A1
IVY CT
500 CHV 91911 1330-G1
IVY LN
100 VSTA 92084 1087-H6
300 SDCo 92028 1027-F2
500 SD 92103 1269-A6
1100 IMPB 91932 1349-H1
2300 ESCN 92027 1110-D6
9200 SDCo 91977 1271-B7
IVY RD
1700 OCN 92054 1106-E2
IVY ST
100 SDCo 92028 1027-F2
100 SD 92101 1289-A1
200 ESCN 92025 1129-J3
300 ESCN 92025 1130-A3
500 SD 92101 1288-J1
1000 ESCN 92026 1129-J1
1000 ESCN 92026 1109-H7
2800 SD 92104 1289-D1
2800 SD 92104 1289-E1
7000 CRLB 92011 1127-A6
9300 SDCo 91977 1271-C7
N IVY ST
100 ESCN 92025 1129-J2
S IVY ST
100 ESCN 92025 1129-J2
W IVY ST
100 SDCo 92028 1027-E2
IVY TER
300 SDCo 92028 1027-F2

IVY TR
- SDCo 92060 1052-D2
IVY WY
2200 SDCo 91977 1271-D7
IVY DELL LN
2700 SDCo 92026 1109-F3
IVYGLEN DR
1400 ENCT 92024 1167-G1
IVY HILL DR
10800 SD 92131 1189-H7
IVY HILL RD
- SMCS 92024 1128-B6
IVY PASS CIR
- SDCo 92065 1173-D1
IVYWOOD CT
700 SMCS 92069 1109-A5
IWO AV
- SD 92140 1268-F7
I YTURRALDE ST
- CALX 92231 6620-J6
- ImCo 92231 6620-J6

J

J AV
- NATC 91950 1289-J7
100 CORD 92118 1288-H6
500 NATC 91950 1309-J1
2000 NATC 91950 1310-A3
J PL
700 CHV 91910 1310-D7
J RD E
- CORD 92135 1288-F6
J ST
- CHV 91910 1310-D7
100 CHV 91910 1330-B1
200 IMP 92251 6439-F6
1000 SD 92101 1289-B4
1700 SDCo 92084 1108-F2
1900 SD 92102 1289-C4
E J ST
- CHV 91910 1310-E7
- ENCT 92024 1167-C1
900 CHV 91910 1311-B7
W J ST
100 ENCT 92024 1167-C1
JACALA DR
12400 PWY 92064 1170-C7
12400 PWY 92064 1190-C1
JACARANDA AV
2500 CRLB 92009 1147-G4
JACARANDA CT
2700 OCN 92056 1087-E5
JACARANDA DR
- ELCN 92243 6559-G3
- ImCo 92243 6559-G3
400 CHV 91910 1310-D6
400 SDCo 91910 1310-D6
3000 SD 92101 1269-D7
JACARANDA PL
800 ESCN 92026 1109-J6
2500 SD 92101 1269-D6
JACARANDA BLOSSOM DR
- SDCo 92082 1090-D4
JACARTE CT
13200 SD 92130 1187-J5
JACINTO PL
700 CORD 92118 1288-J7
JACINTO RD
- SDCo 92055 1085-J3
JACKAL TR
7500 SDCo 92036 1138-B7
JACKASS TR
800 SDCo 92036 1138-B7
JACKDAW ST
3400 SD 92103 1268-J5
JACKIE DR
8400 SD 92119 1250-J4
JACKIE ST
17300 SDCo 92065 1171-F4
JACKMAN ST
700 ELCJ 92020 1251-E4
JACK N JILL LN
- SDCo 92065 1152-F1
JACK OAK LN
13800 SDCo 92040 1232-E5
JACK OAK RD
9400 SDCo 92040 1232-E5
JACK PINE CT
5200 OCN 92056 1087-E2
JACKRABBIT DR
- ELCN 92243 6559-J3
- ELCN 92243 6560-A3
JACK RABBIT RD
13600 PWY 92064 1170-F3
JACK RABBIT ACRES
25000 SDCo 92026 1109-G4
25100 ESCN 92026 1109-G4
JACKS CREEK PL
- ESCN 92027 1110-E5
JACKS CREEK RD
- ESCN 92027 1110-E5
JACKSON DR
4900 LMSA 91941 1271-A1
5200 LMSA 91942 1270-J1
5200 LMSA 91942 1271-A1
5600 LMSA 91942 1250-F5
6100 SD 92119 1250-E3
7400 SD 92120 1250-E3
JACKSON PL
1100 SDCo 92026 1109-E7
JACKSON RD
- ImCo 92233 411-C11
1500 SDCo 92028 1047-J1
JACKSON ST
- CHV 91913 1331-E2
2500 SD 92103 1268-F4
2500 SD 92110 1268-F4
JACKSON HEIGHTS CT
8300 SDCo 92021 1252-B1
JACKSON HEIGHTS DR
12500 SDCo 92021 1252-B1
JACKSON HILL CT
1600 SDCo 92021 1252-B1
JACKSON HILL DR
12500 SDCo 92021 1252-B1
12700 SDCo 92021 1232-B7
JACKSON HILL LN
12500 SDCo 92021 1252-B1
12500 SDCo 92021 1232-B7
JACKSON HILL WY
12700 SDCo 92021 1232-B7
12700 SDCo 92021 1252-B1
JACKSPAR DR
- CRLB 92008 1107-B7
JACMAR AV
7100 SD 92114 1290-F3
JACOB LN
800 ENCT 92024 1147-B4
JACOB ST
- SMCS 92078 1128-H3

JACOB DEKEMA FRWY I-805
- CHV - 1310-B3
- CHV - 1330-G2
- NATC - 1289-H1
- NATC - 1290-A7
- NATC - 1310-B3
- SD - 1208-C6
- SD - 1228-E1
- SD - 1248-J1
- SD - 1249-A3
- SD - 1269-C1
- SD - 1289-H1
- SD - 1330-G2
- SD - 1350-G3
- SDCo - 1310-B3
JACOBY RD
9900 SDCo 91977 1291-D2
JACOT LN
2100 SD 92104 1289-F1
JACQUA ST
100 CHV 91911 1330-B5
JACQUELENE CT
700 ENCT 92024 1147-J6
JACQUELINE CT
900 SDCo 92021 1251-H3
JACQUELINE LN
3000 OCN 92056 1107-C1
JACQUELINE WY
1000 CHV 91911 1330-D2
JACUMBA LN
- SDCo 92055 1086-A3
JACUMBA ST
- SDCo 91934 (1321-G5 See Page 1300)
700 SD 92114 1290-H3
JADAM WY
8300 LMGR 91945 1270-J7
8300 LMGR 91945 1290-J1
JADE AV
1500 ELCJ 92019 1252-B4
1500 CHV 91911 1330-F5
JADE CT
1400 CHV 91911 1330-F4
JADE LN
- CRLB 92009 1127-G5
4400 OCN 92056 1107-D2
JADE PL
1200 SMCS 92069 1109-C5
JADE COAST DR
8300 SD 92126 1209-C5
JADE COAST LN
8900 SD 92126 1209-D5
JADE COAST RD
7600 SD 92126 1209-A5
JADE COVE CT
- SD 92154 1350-J1
- SD 92154 1351-A1
JADERO PL
1900 ESCN 92029 1129-F6
JADESTONE WY
13500 SD 92130 1188-A4
JAEGER RD
900 SDCo 91977 1291-D2
JAFFA CT
- ESCN 92027 1110-C5
JAFFE CT
6500 SD 92119 1251-A4
JAG CT
1900 SDCo 92019 1272-C3
JAGROSS CT
- SDCo 92019 1272-C3
JAGUAR CT
11500 SD 92131 1210-B1
JAIME CT
1000 SD 92154 1350-E1
JAIME LYNN LN
1700 SDCo 92019 1272-C3
JAKE RD
13800 SDCo 92082 1090-E1
JAKE MILLS CT
1800 SD 92114 1290-E6
JAKE VIEW LN
9300 SD 92129 1189-A3
JAKIRK LN
1000 SDCo 92065 1172-H1
JALAL ST
8400 SDCo 92040 1232-A7
JALAPA CT
100 SOLB 92075 1167-D6
JALISCO RD
1800 SDCo 92019 1272-B3
JALNA LN
2600 SDCo 92028 998-B7
JAMACHA BLVD
9300 SDCo 91977 1291-E1
JAMACHA BLVD Rt#-S17
8700 SDCo 91977 1291-A4
10200 SDCo 91978 1291-E2
10600 SDCo 91978 1271-F7
JAMACHA LN
1100 SDCo 91977 1291-A2
JAMACHA RD
6800 SD 92114 1290-F3
8500 LMGR 92114 1290-G3
8500 SDCo 91977 1290-G3
8600 SDCo 91977 1291-B2
JAMACHA RD Rt#-54
100 ELCJ 92019 1251-J5
100 ELCJ 92019 1252-A6
1000 SDCo 92019 1252-A6
1100 ELCJ 92019 1272-A5
1100 SDCo 92019 1272-A5
1100 SDCo 92020 1272-A5
2700 SDCo 92019 1271-J6
E JAMACHA RD
8000 SDCo 91977 1290-J2
8500 SDCo 91977 1291-A2
JAMACHA WY
1500 SDCo 92019 1272-B3
JAMACHA HILLS RD
14000 SDCo 91935 1272-G6
JAMACHA VIEW DR
3000 SDCo 92019 1272-C6
3100 SDCo 91978 1272-C6
JAMAICA CT
700 SD 92109 1267-H2
JAMAICA LN
- ESCN 92025 1129-J5
JAMAICA WY
1800 VSTA 92081 1107-G5
JAMAICA VILLAGE RD
- CORD 92118 1329-D1
JAMAR CT
4700 SD 92117 1248-J1
JAMAR DR
5900 SD 92117 1248-J1
JAMBOREE ST
4500 OCN 92057 1066-H7
JAMES CIR
3500 SDCo 91977 1271-B5
JAMES CT
- SDCo 92024 1148-D2

JAMES CT
400 CHV 91910 1330-B1
E JAMES CT
300 CHV 91910 1310-F7
JAMES DR
1600 CRLB 92008 1106-F4
JAMES RD
2000 ImCo 92243 6500-J4
2300 ImCo 92251 6500-J1
JAMES ST
200 ESCN 92027 1110-E6
500 CHV 91910 1330-B1
800 SDCo 92065 1152-D5
3000 SD 92106 1268-C6
3000 SD 92106 1268-D6
3100 SD 92106 1268-D6
3200 SD 92106 1268-D6
3700 SD 92106 1268-C5
3700 SD 92106 1268-C6
E JAMES ST
200 CHV 91910 1310-E7
JAMES GAYNOR ST
- SDCo 92028 1027-J2
JAMES HILL DR
10900 SDCo 92040 1211-F7
JAMESTOWN CT
4500 SD 92117 1228-F7
JAMESTOWN DR
- CHV 91913 1311-E7
JAMESTOWN PL
- ENCT 92024 1147-A2
JAMESTOWN RD
5100 SD 92117 1228-F6
JAMESTOWN WY
4500 SD 92117 1228-F7
JAMIE AV
2100 SD 92139 1290-F7
JAMIE CT
8900 SDCo 91977 1291-A5
JAMIES LN
- SDCo 92059 1029-D7
JAMIES WY
2900 SD 92105 1269-H7
JAMISON CT
1400 SD 92114 1290-F5
JAMUL AV
100 CHV 91911 1330-E2
4100 SD 92113 1289-H5
JAMUL CT
400 CHV 91911 1330-G1
JAMUL DR
3200 SDCo 91935 1272-D5
14200 SDCo 91935 1292-H1
JAMUL LN
- SDCo 92055 1085-J4
- SDCo 92055 1086-A3
JAMUL HEIGHTS DR
2800 SDCo 92019 1272-C6
JAMUL HIGHLANDS RD
2800 SDCo 91935 1293-B1
3100 SDCo 91935 1273-B7
JAN DR
5800 LMSA 91942 1251-C7
JANA CT
8900 SDCo 91977 1291-B5
JANA LN
28800 SDCo 92082 1070-G7
28800 SDCo 92082 1090-H1
JANA PL
900 ESCN 92026 1109-F5
JANAE GN
- ESCN 92025 1129-J1
JANAL WY
14300 SD 92129 1189-H2
JANAN WY
4300 SD 92122 1228-E5
JANE CT
13100 SD 92129 1189-B4
JANE ST
8300 SD 92129 1189-B4
JANEEN PL
13600 PWY 92064 1190-F4
JANES LN
9300 SNTE 92071 1231-B7
JANET CIR
2000 OCN 92054 1106-E1
JANET LN
9400 SDCo 92040 1232-A5
JANET PL
1000 SMCS 92069 1109-B6
4600 SD 92115 1269-J2
JANET KAY WY
12400 SDCo 92021 1232-A7
12400 SDCo 92021 1252-A1
JANETTA PL
13100 SD 92130 1187-J5
JANETTE LN
13700 PWY 92064 1190-F3
JANFRED WY
9400 LMSA 91942 1251-C7
JANICE CT
10900 SD 92126 1209-E3
JANICE ST
1400 SDCo 91977 1290-J2
1400 SDCo 91977 1291-A2
JANICH RANCH CT
1900 ELCJ 92019 1252-C4
JANIS WY
2000 CRLB 92008 1106-G5
JANIS LYNN LN
1400 VSTA 92083 1087-D7
JANITA TER
3900 SDCo 92069 1108-G1
JANNEY CT
6800 SD 92111 1268-J2
JANSE WY
- SD 92173 1350-E5
JANSEN CT
1400 SD 92114 1290-F5
JANS OAK VW
22300 SDCo 92065 1173-A6
JANUARY PL
8900 SD 92122 1228-D3
JAPATUL LN
- SDCo 91901 1255-C5
JAPATUL RD
- SDCo 91901 1255-G4
6200 SDCo 91901 1254-B3
18900 SDCo 91901 1274-J1
18900 SDCo 91901 1275-A1
JAPATUL SPUR
- SDCo 91901 1275-B1
JAPATUL HIGHLANDS RD
- SDCo 91901 1255-D4
JAPATUL VALLEY RD
19900 SDCo 91901 1275-D1
21800 SDCo 91901 1255-H2
23200 SDCo 91901 1235-J7
JAPATUL VALLEY RD Rt#-79
8100 SDCo 91901 1236-A6
8100 SDCo 91916 1236-A6
23400 SDCo 91901 1235-J6

JAPATUL VISTA LN
- SDCo 91901 1255-E4
JAPPA AV
3200 SD 92117 1248-C2
JARAMA CT
2100 SDCo 92019 1272-C4
JARDIN CT
8200 SD 92122 1228-C3
JARDIN RD
12700 SD 92128 1170-C3
JARDIN DEL SOL
- SDCo 92065 1173-D2
JARDINE CT
1800 VSTA 92081 1107-J3
JARED PL
1000 ESCN 92025 1130-A3
JARMAN PL
13300 SD 92130 1188-A4
J A RODNEY CT
- CALX 92231 6620-J6
JARRETT CT
4800 SD 92113 1290-A5
JARRETT LN
100 SDCo 92021 1252-H3
JARRITO CT
11600 SD 92127 1150-A7
JARRON PZ
1000 CHV 91910 1311-A7
JARVIS ST
2800 SD 92106 1288-B1
JASMINE AV
14000 PWY 92064 1190-F3
JASMINE CT
900 CRLB 92011 1127-B6
1000 VSTA 92081 1108-A3
JASMINE DR
- SD 92109 1248-C6
JASMINE PL
3300 ESCN 92025 1150-C2
JASMINE ST
- CALX 92231 6620-J7
500 CHV 91911 1330-H3
1600 ELCJ 92021 1252-B2
4700 OCN 92056 1087-D4
JASMINE WY
100 CHV 91910 1310-B5
JASMINE CREST
3300 ENCT 92024 1148-C5
JASMINE CREST LN
10900 SD 92121 1208-F3
JASMINE VALLEY WY
- SD 92102 1290-A4
JASON CT
2500 OCN 92056 1087-E4
9800 SDCo 92082 1069-D4
JASON GN
2000 ESCN 92026 1109-D4
JASON LN
400 SMCS 92078 1129-A3
JASON PL
300 CHV 91910 1330-B1
JASON RD
3000 SDCo 92028 1047-J1
JASON ST
1500 IMPB 91932 1349-J2
1500 IMPB 92154 1349-J2
1500 SD 92154 1349-J2
1700 SD 92154 1350-A2
2500 OCN 92056 1087-E4
E JASON ST
100 ENCT 92024 1147-A3
W JASON ST
100 ENCT 92024 1147-A3
JASPER AV
1500 CHV 91911 1330-F5
JASPER CT
1400 CHV 91911 1330-F4
JASPER GN
2400 ESCN 92029 1129-E6
JASPER LN
4400 OCN 92056 1107-D2
JASPER RD
200 CALX 92249 6620-E3
200 ImCo 92249 6620-C3
500 CALX 92249 431-C7
500 ImCo 92249 431-C7
JASPER ST
100 ENCT 92024 1147-A4
JAVA LN
1800 LMGR 91945 1290-H1
JAVA HILLS DR
1400 SDCo 92028 998-B7
JAVELIN WY
9900 SDCo 91977 1291-D2
JAVIER ST
5200 SD 92117 1248-H1
JAY CT
- SMCS 92069 1108-F5
- SNTE 92071 1231-D2
JAY BIRD LN
1100 SDCo 92065 1172-G2
JAY JAY WY
- SDCo 92026 1069-D2
JAYKEN WY
1400 CHV 91911 1330-B4
JAYLEE AV
8800 SDCo 91977 1290-J3
JAYNIA PL
2700 LMGR 91945 1270-E7
JAYTON LN
1900 ENCT 92024 1147-H7
S JAYTON LN
2100 ENCT 92024 1167-H1
JAZMIN CT
5300 SD 92124 1249-J1
J B RODRIQUEZ ST
- CALX 92231 6620-J6
JEAN AV
100 ESCN 92027 1130-D1
JEAN DR
4700 SD 92115 1269-J3
8700 SNTE 92071 1231-E7
JEAN ANN LN
2000 SDCo 92065 1172-H2
JEANETTE AV
5700 LMSA 91942 1250-H7
JEANNE PL
1500 CRLB 92008 1106-G6
JEANNE RD
7000 LMGR 91945 1270-E7
JEANNE TER
10700 SNTE 92071 1231-F6
JEANNINE LN
1200 SDCo 92021 1251-H3
JEAN-O-RENO RD
14000 PWY 92064 1190-G4
JED RD
2700 ESCN 92027 1110-E7
JEFF ST
6300 SD 92115 1270-D5
JEFFER LN
4700 SDCo 91941 1271-C3
JEFFERS PL
- CRLB 92008 1107-B7

JEFFERSON AV
100 CHV 91910 1309-J6
500 CHV 91910 1310-A7
500 CHV 91910 1330-A1
500 ELCJ 92020 1251-F6
800 CHV 91911 1330-B3
1200 ESCN 92027 1130-A1
1400 ESCN 92027 1110-C6
8700 LMSA 91941 1271-A2
JEFFERSON RD
3000 SDCo 91935 1292-H2
JEFFERSON ST
- CALX 92231 6620-J6
2300 SD 92110 1268-E4
3800 CRLB 92008 1106-F3
8100 LMGR 91945 1270-H6
JEFFERY LN
28800 SDCo 91962 1237-C6
JEFF PARK LN
14600 PWY 92064 1190-E1
JEFFREE ST
500 ELCJ 92020 1251-G4
JEFFREY AV
1500 ESCN 92027 1130-C2
JEFFREY CT
10900 SD 92126 1209-D3
JEFFREY PL
1400 ESCN 92027 1130-C2
JEFFREY RD
900 SOLB 92014 1187-H1
1800 ImCo 92243 430-L6
JEFFREY HEIGHTS RD
31800 SDCo 92082 1070-D1
31800 SDCo 92082 1050-D7
JEFFRIES RANCH RD
5700 OCN 92057 1067-F6
JELLETT ST
4100 SD 92110 1248-E7
JEMA WY
8200 SDCo 92040 1252-A1
JEMEZ DR
3000 SD 92117 1248-C1
JENDAY CT
- OCN 92057 1067-C2
JENELL ST
15000 PWY 92064 1170-C7
JENKINS ST
3100 SD 92106 1288-A4
JENNA CT
200 SD 92114 1290-D4
JENNA PL
2000 ESCN 92029 1129-F7
JENNER ST
7900 SD 92037 1227-E6
JENNIFER CIR
1000 VSTA 92083 1087-G4
JENNIFER CT
1100 ESCN 92026 1109-J7
1900 SDCo 92028 1048-B4
4800 SD 92117 1248-D1
JENNIFER DR
- IMP 92251 6499-H2
9900 SNTE 92071 1231-D4
JENNIFER LN
2300 ENCT 92024 1147-J7
JENNIFER ST
3600 SD 92117 1248-D1
JENNILEAH LN
400 SMCS 92069 1109-A2
JENNINGS PL
800 SD 92106 1288-A3
JENNINGS ST
800 SD 92106 1287-J3
3400 SD 92106 1288-A3
JENNINGS VISTA CIR
9100 SDCo 92040 1232-F5
JENNINGS VISTA CT
14200 SDCo 92040 1232-F4
JENNINGS VISTA DR
14100 SDCo 92040 1232-F5
JENNINGS VISTA TR
14200 SDCo 92040 1232-F4
JENNINGS VISTA WY
14200 SDCo 92040 1232-F4
JENNITE DR
7500 SD 92119 1250-F3
JENNY AV
8600 SD 92123 1249-C6
JENNY LN
29700 SDCo 92084 1068-E6
JENNY JAY CT
28600 SDCo 92082 1090-E1
JENSEN CT
- ENCT 92024 1147-E4
JEPSON LN
- SD 92131 1189-G7
JERABACK DR
10200 SD 92131 1209-H4
JEREMY LN
2000 ESCN 92027 1110-B5
JEREMY PL
2100 ESCN 92027 1110-B5
JEREMY ST
9500 SNTE 92071 1231-F5
JEREMY WY
36000 SDCo 92028 999-D7
36100 SDCo 92028 1029-E1
JEREMY POINT CT
1600 CHV 91911 1330-J5
JEREZ CT
7500 CRLB 92009 1147-H1
JERGENS CT
9000 SD 92126 1209-D2
JERI WY
4600 SDCo 92020 1271-H2
JERICHO DR
700 SDCo 92028 1028-A1
JERICHO RD
9400 LMSA 91942 1251-B6
JERICHO CIRCLE GN
200 ESCN 92027 1110-E7
JEROME DR
14200 PWY 92064 1170-G7
JERRILYNN PL
1600 ENCT 92024 1167-G1
JERSEY CT
700 SD 92109 1267-H2
JESMOND DR
10100 SDCo 92026 1109-E2
JESMOND DENE RD
2800 ESCN 92026 1109-E1
2800 SDCo 92026 1109-E1
2900 SDCo 92026 1089-D7
JESMOND DENE HEIGHTS PL
2900 SDCo 92026 1109-F2
JESMOND DENE HEIGHTS RD
2800 SDCo 92026 1109-F3
J ESPLANADE
600 CHV 91910 1330-A1
JESSICA LN
- ESCN 92027 1130-E1
11500 SDCo 92040 1231-H6

STREET Block City ZIP Pg-Grid

JESSICA LYNN LN
1500 SDCo 92065 1172-J1
JESSIE AV
4600 LMSA 91941 1270-G3
JESSIE LN
200 VSTA 92083 1107-J1
JESSIE JAMES LN
- SDCo 92065 1171-G2
JESSOP LN
2300 SD 92110 1268-F6
JESTER ST
1700 SD 92114 1290-D6
JETHROW WY
1400 ELCJ 92019 1252-A7
JETS PL
- ESCN 92026 1109-J7
JETTY PT
- CRLB 92010 1107-B4
JEWELL DR
500 SD 92113 1289-G5
JEWELL RDG
2000 VSTA 92081 1107-H6
JEWELL ST
3300 SD 92109 1268-A1
3600 SD 92109 1248-A4
JEWEL VALLEY CT
39500 SDCo 91905 1300-C7
JEWEL VALLEY LN
2000 SDCo 91905 1300-C7
JEWEL VALLEY RD
1400 SDCo 91905 (1320-D1 See Page 1300)
1500 SDCo 91905 1300-D7
JEWEL VALLEY WY
39500 SDCo 91905 1300-C7
E JEWETT ST
2200 SD 92111 1248-J7
W JEWETT ST
2300 SD 92111 1248-J7
JIBSAIL ST
3300 OCN 92054 1086-F5
JICAMA WY
- CHV 91911 1330-E4
JICARILLO AV
4500 SD 92117 1248-C2
JILL LN
3700 LMSA 91941 1270-F5
JILL ST
4400 OCN 92057 1066-H7
9900 SNTE 92071 1231-D4
JILLIAN DR
- IMP 92251 6499-H2
JILLIANS WY
- VSTA 92084 1088-A2
JIM LN
9500 SNTE 92071 1231-E5
JIMDORA WY
2300 SDCo 92003 1048-D7
JIMENEZ CT
- SD 92126 1209-D7
JIMMY DURANTE BLVD
1900 DLMR 92014 1187-F3
JIMMY DURANTE WY
2200 DLMR 92014 1187-G3
JIMZEL RD
9600 LMSA 91942 1251-C5
JIOLA WY
9500 LMSA 91941 1271-C2
J M GRIJALVA AV
- CALX 92231 6620-J6
J M OSTREY ST
500 CALX 92231 6620-E7
JOAN CT
5200 SD 92115 1270-A2
JOAN LN
2700 SDCo 92028 997-B2
JOAN ST
9000 SDCo 91977 1291-A4
JOANN CIR
400 VSTA 92084 1087-H4
JOANN DR
2500 OCN 92056 1087-C6
JOANNA DR
700 SD 92114 1290-G3
JOANNE WY
800 ELCJ 92020 1251-D7
JOANNIE WY
200 SDCo 92083 1108-A3
JOBE HILL DR
500 VSTA 92081 1107-E1
JOCATAL PL
11600 SD 92127 1150-A7
JOCELYN ST
4400 SD 92105 1289-H1
JOCKEY WY
5600 SDCo 91902 1311-A2
JOCKEY CLUB
2300 SDCo 92003 1048-B7
JODI ST
3800 SD 92115 1270-C5
JODI ANN CT
- SDCo 92026 1069-B4
JODY LN
2900 OCN 92056 1087-B7
JODY PL
2700 ESCN 92027 1110-E7
JOE PL
200 ESCN 92027 1130-D1
JOE ACUNA CT
- CALX 92231 6620-H6
JOE CROSSON DR
1600 ELCJ 92020 1251-E2
JOEL LN
6000 LMSA 91942 1251-C7
JOEVE CT
8700 SD 92119 1251-A3
JOEY AV
400 ELCJ 92020 1251-G4
JOEY PL
400 ESCN 92026 1109-J7
JOHANNESBERG DR
13200 PWY 92064 1190-F4
JOHANNESBERG WY
13200 PWY 92064 1190-F4
JOHN CT
1100 SD 92154 1350-D1
JOHN ST
3400 SD 92106 1287-J2
3400 SD 92106 1288-A3
JOHN DEWITT PL
2100 SDCo 91901 1253-J1
JOHN HENRY LN
16600 SDCo 92065 1171-H3
JOHN HOPKINS CT
3300 SD 92121 1207-J7
3300 SD 92121 1208-A7
JOHN JAY HOPKINS DR
3500 SD 92121 1207-J6
10900 SD 92121 1208-A7
JOHN J MONTGOMERY DR
3700 SD 92123 1249-C3
JOHN KENNEDY ST
100 CALX 92231 6620-F6

STREET Block City ZIP Pg-Grid

JOHNSON AV
800 SD 92103 1269-B5
N JOHNSON AV
1000 ELCJ 92020 1251-E3
S JOHNSON AV
200 ELCJ 92020 1251-E6
JOHNSON CT
- SDCo 92055 1086-A3
JOHNSON DR
1100 ESCN 92025 1130-A3
3000 OCN 92056 1087-A7
3000 OCN 92056 1107-A1
8900 LMSA 91941 1271-A2
JOHNSON LN
900 SDCo 92065 1152-G4
1900 ImCo 92243 6499-A6
1900 ImCo 92243 6559-B1
JOHNSON RD
- SD 92145 1228-H3
- SD 92145 1229-A3
JOHNSON ST
- CORD 91932 1329-E4
JOHNSON LAKE RD
11500 SDCo 92040 1211-H5
JOHNSTON GN
- ESCN 92029 1129-D6
- SDCo 92029 1129-D6
JOHNSTON LN
100 SMCS 92069 1108-H7
100 SMCS 92069 1128-H1
JOHNSTON RD
2100 ESCN 92029 1129-D6
2100 SDCo 92029 1129-D6
JOHNS VIEW WY
2200 SDCo 91977 1291-A1
JOHN TOWERS AV
1800 ELCJ 92020 1251-D1
JOHN WAYNE LN
18600 SDCo 92082 1071-B7
18600 SDCo 92082 1091-B1
JOJO CT
200 SD 92114 1290-D4
JOLIET CT
100 ELCJ 92019 1252-A5
JOLIET ST
1300 ELCJ 92019 1252-A5
JOLINA WY
400 ENCT 92024 1147-G6
JOLLEY LN
14300 PWY 92064 1190-H5
JON LN
- OCN 92054 1086-G2
JONAH RD
300 ESCN 92027 1110-F7
JONAS CT
8800 SD 92123 1249-C6
JONATHAN PARK LN
13300 PWY 92064 1190-E1
JONATHON PL
600 ESCN 92027 1110-C6
4200 OCN 92056 1087-C7
4200 VSTA 92083 1087-C7
JONATHON ST
1500 VSTA 92083 1087-D7
4000 OCN 92056 1087-C7
JONBELL PL
10000 SNTE 92071 1231-D4
JONEL WY
6400 SDCo 91902 1311-C1
JONELL CT
9100 LMSA 91942 1251-B6
JONES CT
- SDCo 92055 1086-A2
JONES RD
500 OCN 92054 1086-D5
39500 SDCo 92028 996-H1
JONES ST
- CHV 91913 1331-E2
JONES WY
- SDCo 92026 1049-A5
JONI LN
3000 SDCo 92069 1088-J6
JONNY LN
11700 SD 92126 1209-B1
JONQUIL DR
2600 SD 92106 1268-C6
JOPLIN AV
3600 SD 92117 1248-D2
JOPLIN DR
900 ELCJ 92021 1251-H2
JORDAN ST
600 ESCN 92027 1130-D1
8200 SD 92123 1249-B5
JORDAN RIDGE CT
12700 SD 92130 1188-D6
JORIS WY
8800 LMSA 91941 1271-A3
JOSE LN
1600 ESCN 92026 1109-H6
JOSEFINA PL
600 CHV 91910 1311-A5
JOSEPHINE ST
1300 SD 92110 1268-G3
JOSH CT
- IMP 92251 6499-H2
JOSH WY
500 SDCo 91901 1234-C4
JOSHUA AV
300 SMCS 92069 1108-J6
JOSHUA PL
800 SD 92154 1330-F7
JOSHUA ST
1000 ESCN 92026 1129-H1
1100 ESCN 92026 1109-H7
JOSHUA WY
1100 VSTA 92081 1107-J7
1100 VSTA 92081 1108-A7
JOSHUA CREEK PL
1100 CHV 91914 1311-J4
JOSHUA CREEK RD
2700 CHV 91914 1311-J4
JOSHUA TREE CT
14400 PWY 92064 1190-F2
JOSHUA TREE LN
1600 SDCo 92028 1027-J5
JOSHUA TREE ST
- IMP 92251 6499-E2
JOSIE JO LN
10100 SNTE 92071 1231-E3
JOSSELYN AV
1200 CHV 91911 1330-E3
JOSTEN WY
400 SDCo 92028 1027-E5
JOUGLARD ST
6300 SD 92114 1290-D6
JOURNEY ST
- CHV 91915 1331-H2
JOURNEY WY
- CHV 91915 1331-H2
JOVIC RD
9200 SDCo 92040 1232-A5
JOY CT
- SMCS 92078 1128-F2

STREET Block City ZIP Pg-Grid

JOY LN
1600 ESCN 92029 1129-F5
JOY RD
1200 SDCo 92028 1027-J5
JOYAS CT
11600 SD 92124 1250-B3
17800 PWY 92064 1170-E1
JOYCE PL
5100 SD 92105 1270-A6
JOYCE ST
200 ELCJ 92020 1251-G7
JR VILLA CT
- CALX 92231 6680-J1
JUAN ST
2200 SD 92103 1268-G5
2300 SD 92110 1268-F5
JUANENO AV
200 OCN 92057 1067-B7
JUANITA LN
100 SDCo 92021 1252-H4
1800 SDCo 92028 1027-J3
JUANITA ST
800 SOLB 92075 1187-G1
3200 SD 92105 1270-C6
JUANITA WY
30500 SDCo 92082 1070-G1
JUAREZ DR
16600 SD 92128 1170-B3
JUBA RD
29200 SDCo 92082 1090-F1
JUBE WRIGHT
- SD 92127 1169-A3
JUBILEE DR
5600 SDCo 92028 999-A5
JUBILEE WY
38900 SDCo 92028 999-B4
JUD ST
1100 SD 92114 1290-H2
JUDIANN LN
2800 SDCo 92084 1088-D7
JUDICIAL DR
- SD 92122 1228-E2
9200 SD 92121 1228-D1
JUDILYN DR
900 VSTA 92083 1087-F5
JUDITH AV
2000 SD 92154 1350-B2
JUDITH PL
1700 ESCN 92026 1109-C5
JUDSON CT
7500 SD 92111 1249-A7
JUDSON ST
600 ESCN 92027 1130-D1
2000 SD 92111 1269-A1
2200 SD 92111 1249-A7
N JUDSON ST
7400 SD 92111 1249-A7
JUDSON WY
1100 CHV 91911 1330-F3
4500 LMSA 91941 1270-E3
4500 SD 92115 1270-E1
JUDY DR
9900 SNTE 92071 1231-D4
JUDY LN
1100 ENCT 92007 1167-F2
JUDY LEE PL
6500 SD 92115 1270-D4
JUERGENS VISTA
- SDCo 91901 1255-D6
JUGADOR CT
1100 SDCo 92078 1128-E3
1100 SMCS 92078 1128-E3
JULA CT
300 SDCo 91977 1290-J4
JULIAN AV
100 ELCJ 92020 1251-F5
1700 SD 92113 1289-D5
12300 SDCo 92040 1232-B4
JULIAN LN
- SDCo 92036 1136-A7
JULIAN RD Rt#-67
2500 SDCo 92065 1172-B3
JULIAN RD Rt#-78
100 SDCo 92065 1152-J4
300 SDCo 92065 1153-J1
1700 SDCo 92065 409-J11
2000 SDCo 92065 1154-D2
18600 SDCo 92070 409-J11
18600 SDCo 92070 1135-B3
JULIAN RD Rt#-79
2200 SDCo 92036 1136-A7
2800 SDCo 92036 1135-D3
2800 SDCo 92070 1135-D3
E JULIAN RD
100 SDCo 92065 1152-J5
JULIAN ST
100 SDCo 92065 1152-E7
400 SDCo 92065 1172-E1
JULIAN ESTATES RD
700 SDCo 92036 1156-E5
JULIANNA ST
1800 SDCo 92019 1272-B2
JULIAN ORCHARDS DR
1000 SDCo 92036 1135-J3
1000 SDCo 92036 1136-A3
JULIE CT
800 SMCS 92069 1109-B6
JULIE LN
3900 SDCo 91941 1271-H4
JULIE PL
2200 CRLB 92008 1107-A6
JULIE ST
6400 SD 92115 1270-D1
JULIELYNN WY
- LMGR 91945 1270-H6
JULIETTE PL
1100 SDCo 92028 1027-H3
7200 LMSA 91941 1270-F2
JULINDA WY
2800 SDCo 92029 1150-A2
JULIO PL
10200 SNTE 92071 1231-E3
JULY ST
5000 SD 92110 1268-G1
JUMANO AV
4700 SD 92117 1248-F6
JUMILLA ST
5100 SD 92124 1230-A7
JUNCO PL
8700 SD 92129 1189-C6
JUNCUS CT
7300 SD 92129 1188-J7
JUNE ST
1300 SDCo 92028 1027-J3
JUNE WY
500 ELCJ 92021 1251-H4
JUNEBERRY CT
- SD 92123 1249-D1
JUNE LAKE DR
7900 SD 92119 1250-H5
JUNGLE OAKS DR
3600 SDCo 92028 1047-H4
JUNIOR HIGH DR
7600 LMSA 91941 1270-G4

STREET Block City ZIP Pg-Grid

JUNIPER AV
100 CRLB 92008 1106-E7
JUNIPER LN
900 SDCo 92081 1108-B6
9700 SDCo 92029 1149-E2
JUNIPER RD
600 SD 92101 1289-A1
JUNIPER ST
100 SD 92101 1289-A1
500 SD 92101 1288-J1
500 CHV 91911 1330-H3
2800 SD 92104 1289-E1
3800 SD 92105 1289-G1
N JUNIPER ST
300 ESCN 92025 1129-J2
S JUNIPER ST
100 ESCN 92025 1129-J3
500 ESCN 92025 1130-A4
2000 SDCo 92025 1130-A4
JUNIPER WY
200 OCN 92057 1086-J5
12200 PWY 92064 1190-C7
JUNIPER FIELD TR
- SDCo 92065 1173-D2
JUNIPERHILL DR
1500 ENCT 92024 1167-G1
JUNIPER PARK LN
10700 SD 92121 1208-E3
JUNIPER RIDGE LN
- SDCo 92028 1028-E5
JUNO AV
100 ENCT 92024 1147-A3
JUPITER GN
- ESCN 92025 1129-H2
JUPITER ST
100 ENCT 92024 1147-A3
3900 SD 92110 1268-C4
JUST CT
1100 SD 92154 1350-F1
JUST ST
3700 SD 92154 1350-F1
JUSTA LN
8800 SNTE 92071 1231-B7
JUSTICE LN
- SD 92093 1228-A1
JUSTIN PL
31300 SDCo 92082 1070-G1
JUSTIN RD
1300 ENCT 92007 1167-E2
JUSTIN WY
500 ESCN 92027 1110-D6
JUSTINA DR
300 OCN 92057 1086-J4
JUSTO CT
11800 SD 92129 1189-F7
JUTLAND CT
3000 SD 92117 1248-C2
JUTLAND DR
4200 SD 92117 1248-C1
JUTLAND PL
4500 SD 92117 1248-C2

K

K AV
400 NATC 91950 1289-J7
700 NATC 91950 1309-J1
1800 NATC 91950 1310-A2
K ST
- CHV 91910 1330-C1
- CHV 91911 1330-C1
200 IMP 92251 6439-F6
300 SD 92101 1289-B4
1900 SD 92102 1289-C4
W K ST
100 ENCT 92024 1167-C1
KAANAPALI WY
2900 SD 92154 1330-C6
KACHINA CT
17800 SD 92127 1169-H1
KADIN DR
- IMP 92251 6499-H2
KADWELL WY
1700 ELCJ 92021 1252-B2
KAE CREST
3100 SDCo 91935 1273-B7
KAHLUA CT
9300 SDCo 91941 1271-B4
9300 SDCo 91977 1271-B4
KAHLUA WY
4000 SDCo 91941 1271-B4
4000 SDCo 91977 1271-B4
KAIBAB CT
3000 SD 92117 1248-F6
KAILE LN
500 ESCN 92027 1110-E6
KAIMALINO LN
1300 SD 92109 1247-H4
KAISER PL
10200 SD 92126 1209-A5
KAISER RD
6000 ImCo 92233 411-D10
KAITZ ST
12600 PWY 92064 1170-C7
KAL GN
1700 ESCN 92029 1129-G5
KALAMATH DR
700 DLMR 92014 1187-G5
KALAMIS WY
4700 OCN 92056 1107-E6
KALAPANA ST
14600 PWY 92064 1190-G1
KALBAUGH ST
100 SDCo 92065 1152-D6
200 SDCo 92065 1172-D1
KALBFUS ST
3100 SD 92136 1289-E7
3400 SD 92136 1309-F1
KALIN RD
- ImCo 92233 411-B10
- ImCo 92281 411-B11
KALIN RD Rt#-S26
- ImCo 92281 411-B11
KALMIA CIR
- CRLB 92011 1127-D5
KALMIA LN
9700 SDCo 92029 1149-E2
KALMIA PL
2800 SD 92104 1289-E1
KALMIA ST
100 SD 92101 1289-A1
400 SD 92101 1288-J1
1300 ESCN 92025 1130-A4
2300 SD 92104 1289-E1
5000 SD 92105 1290-A1
E KALMIA ST
100 SDCo 92028 1027-F2
N KALMIA ST
100 ESCN 92025 1129-J2
S KALMIA ST
100 ESCN 92025 1129-J3
800 ESCN 92025 1130-A3
W KALMIA ST
100 SDCo 92028 1027-F2

STREET Block City ZIP Pg-Grid

KALPATI CIR
800 CRLB 92008 1106-F7
KAMLOOP AV
4300 SD 92117 1248-C2
KAMM RD
1500 ImCo 92250 431-D4
KAMWOOD CT
10200 SD 92126 1208-J5
KAMWOOD PL
10200 SD 92126 1208-J5
KAMWOOD ST
7200 SD 92126 1208-J5
KANDACE CT
5100 SD 92105 1270-A7
KANDACE WY
2700 SD 92105 1270-A7
KANE DR
8200 LMSA 91941 1270-J5
KANE ST
4100 SD 92110 1248-E7
KANEKO CT
- SD 92173 1350-F5
KANSAS ST
3900 SD 92104 1269-E5
4300 SD 92116 1269-E3
KANTOR CT
5800 SD 92122 1228-F6
KANTOR ST
5800 SD 92122 1228-F6
KAPALUA CT
3000 SD 92154 1330-D7
KAPLAN DR
8200 SD 92123 1269-B1
KAPLAN WY
3900 NATC 91950 1310-E3
KAPPA ST
5800 LMSA 91942 1250-J7
KARDEELIN CT
12500 SDCo 92021 1252-B1
KAREN CT
900 SMCS 92069 1109-C5
KAREN LN
9900 SNTE 92071 1231-D4
KAREN WY
1000 CHV 91911 1330-D2
4600 SDCo 92020 1271-G3
KARENA CT
700 VSTA 92083 1087-F4
KAREN SUE AV
4200 SD 92122 1228-E6
KAREN SUE LN
5900 SD 92122 1228-E6
KARERLLYN DR
9200 SNTE 92071 1231-G5
KARI CT
2600 SDCo 91977 1271-A7
KARI LN
4100 OCN 92057 1067-G4
4100 SDCo 92003 1067-G4
KARIBU LN
27000 SDCo 92082 1090-J5
KARMA DR
- SD 92126 1209-E3
KARNES WY
3000 SD 92117 1248-C3
KAROK AV
3200 SD 92117 1248-C2
KARRA CT
400 CHV 91910 1310-F6
KARREN LN
2000 CRLB 92008 1106-G5
KARST RD
- CRLB 92010 1107-B4
KARWARREN CT
500 SDCo 92026 1109-H5
KASCHUBE WY
9300 SNTE 92071 1230-H6
KASHMERE LN
10300 SDCo 92029 1129-E7
KATELLA CT
1400 ESCN 92027 1130-B2
KATELLA ST
1800 SD 92154 1350-B3
KATELLA WY
1400 ESCN 92027 1130-C2
KATELYN CT
- SD 92120 1250-A4
KATERRI DR
2000 SDCo 92084 1088-C7
KATE SESSIONS WY
5000 SD 92109 1248-A4
KATHERINE CT
1200 SD 92154 1350-D1
2500 ELCJ 92020 1251-B4
KATHERINE PL
4600 LMSA 91941 1270-F3
KATHERINE ST
2300 ELCJ 92020 1251-A3
KATHERINE CLAIRE CT
- SD 92127 1169-B3
KATHERINE CLAIRE LN
- SD 92127 1169-B3
KATHERINES VIEW WY
900 SDCo 92065 1152-F1
KATHLEEN PL
2400 SD 92105 1270-B7
KATHRINER PL
1200 SDCo 92065 1172-G2
KATHRYN CROSBY CT
- SDCo 92127 1169-A2
KATHY ST
9500 LMSA 91942 1251-C6
KATIE CT
1900 SDCo 92028 1048-B3
KATIE LN
- SDCo 92040 1231-J6
KATIE KING LN
- SDCo 91901 1254-E1
KATIE LENDRE DR
3600 SDCo 92028 1048-D3
KATIE VIEW LN
- SDCo 91977 1271-B6
KATKAT CT
32300 SDCo 92061 1051-A6
KATO ST
8100 LMSA 91942 1270-H1
8100 LMSA 91942 1250-H7
KATY CT
4600 SDCo 91941 1271-C3
KATY PL
1700 ESCN 92026 1109-D5
KATYDID CIR
12200 SD 92129 1189-A7
KAUANA LOA DR
2600 ESCN 92029 1129-D4
2600 SDCo 92029 1129-D4
KAUFMAN WY
9900 SD 92126 1208-J5
9900 SD 92126 1209-A6
KAUSMAN ST
2700 SD 92139 1310-E1
KAVA CT
- ENCT 92024 1167-E1

STREET Block City ZIP Pg-Grid

KAVANAUGH RD
- ImCo 92250 431-E5
KAVANAUGH RD Rt#-S33
- ImCo 92250 431-E5
KAY DEE LN
16000 SDCo 92065 1171-H4
KAY JAY CT
13600 SDCo 92040 1232-E6
KAY JAY LN
9000 SDCo 92040 1232-E6
KAYLYN WY
600 SMCS 92069 1129-E2
KAYMAR DR
300 SD 92114 1290-F3
KAYWOOD CIR
11400 SDCo 92026 1109-H1
KAYWOOD CT
25900 SDCo 92026 1109-J1
KAYWOOD DR
3000 SDCo 92026 1109-H1
25900 SDCo 92026 1089-H7
KAYWOOD LN
11500 SDCo 92026 1109-J2
KAYWOOD PL
11500 SDCo 92026 1109-J1
KAYWOOD TER
26000 SDCo 92026 1109-H1
KAYWOOD WY
25900 SDCo 92026 1109-J1
KEA ST
1300 OCN 92054 1086-E7
KEAR PL
12100 PWY 92064 1190-F7
KEARNEY AV
1700 SD 92113 1289-C5
KEARNEY CT
200 CHV 91910 1310-E7
KEARNEY ST
100 CHV 91910 1330-B1
KEARNY MESA RD
4100 SD 92111 1249-C2
5400 SD 92111 1229-C7
9200 SD 92126 1209-F6
KEARNY VILLA CT
9100 SD 92123 1229-D7
KEARNY VILLA LN
3200 SD 92123 1249-B5
KEARNY VILLA RD
- SD 92124 1229-E6
- SD 92126 1229-F1
- SD 92145 1229-F1
3300 SD 92123 1249-C2
5400 SD 92123 1229-E6
9400 SD 92126 1209-E6
KEARNY VILLA WY
5200 SD 92123 1249-C1
KEARSARGE RD
1600 SD 92037 1227-G6
KEATING ST
1600 SD 92103 1268-H6
3500 SD 92110 1268-H6
KEATS PL
- CRLB 92008 1107-B7
KEATS ST
2800 SD 92106 1288-B1
KECK CT
9400 SD 92129 1189-E6
KEDZIE AV
700 SD 92154 1330-G7
KEEGAN PL
13300 SD 92130 1188-A4
KEELER AV
4200 SD 92113 1289-H6
KEELER CT
1200 SD 92113 1289-H6
KEEMO CT
8800 SDCo 92040 1232-B6
KEEMO TER
12400 SDCo 92040 1232-B6
KEEN DR
2500 SD 92139 1310-E1
KEENAN ST
9000 SD 92126 1209-B7
KEENELAND DR
- CRLB 92009 1127-F3
KEENELAND RW
9700 SD 92037 1227-J1
KEENEY ST
4900 LMSA 91941 1270-F2
4900 SD 92115 1270-F2
KEIGHLEY CT
7000 SD 92120 1250-A5
KEIGHLEY ST
7000 SD 92120 1250-A5
KEIR ST
9000 SD 92123 1249-D6
KEISHA CV
11400 SD 92126 1208-J2
KEISHA TER
7400 SD 92126 1208-J2
KEITH ST
10600 SNTE 92071 1231-D2
KELBURN AV
8800 SDCo 91977 1290-J4
KELD CT
12200 SD 92129 1188-J7
KELGLEN LN
1300 SDCo 92084 1108-A1
1300 VSTA 92084 1108-A1
KELLAM CT
13100 SD 92130 1188-A5
KELLBARA CT
14100 SD 92129 1189-E2
KELLEEN DR
100 VSTA 92083 1087-G4
KELLI LN
14100 SDCo 92021 1232-G5
KELLIE CT
3700 NATC 91950 1310-D3
KELLINGTON CT
3500 OCN 92056 1107-E3
KELLINGTON PL
1700 ENCT 92024 1147-H7
KELLOGG AV
1900 CRLB 92008 1127-C3
KELLOGG DR
3300 SD 92106 1287-J4
3300 SD 92106 1288-A4
KELLOGG ST
- SMCS 92078 1128-H3
2800 SD 92106 1288-A4
KELLOGG WY
3300 SD 92106 1288-A4
KELLRAE LN
400 ESCN 92026 1109-G2
KELLY AV
1900 SDCo 92065 1152-E7
2100 SDCo 92065 1172-D1
KELLY CT
400 ESCN 92027 1130-D1
KELLY DR
900 SDCo 92019 1253-B1
1200 ENCT 92024 1167-F1

STREET Block City ZIP Pg-Grid

KELLY DR
4800 CRLB 92008 1106-J7
KELLY PL
6500 SD 92111 1268-H1
KELLY ST
100 OCN 92054 1106-C3
6500 SD 92111 1268-H1
KELLYN LN
4200 SDCo 92084 1068-E4
KELLY WILLIAM LN
1400 SDCo 91901 1234-A6
1400 SDCo 91901 1233-J6
KELOWNA LN
14000 SDCo 92082 1070-E1
KELOWNA RD
11100 SD 92126 1209-C2
KELSEY ST
3300 SD 92124 1249-G4
KELSFORD PL
3300 SD 92130 1188-A6
KELSO CT
- CHV 91911 1330-H2
KELSO RD
- SD 92126 1209-C7
KELSO ST
8700 SDCo 91977 1291-A3
KELSON PL
1800 ESCN 92029 1129-F6
KELTON AV
5700 LMSA 91942 1250-J7
KELTON CT
5600 SD 92114 1290-B3
KELTON DR
3700 OCN 92056 1086-J6
3700 OCN 92056 1087-A7
KELTON PL
5600 SD 92114 1290-B2
KELTON RD
800 SD 92114 1290-B2
KEMAH LN
10800 SD 92131 1209-H4
KEMBERLY LN
3100 SDCo 91935 1293-A1
KEMERTON RD
10500 SD 92126 1208-J4
KEMP CT
- CALX 92231 6620-H7
KEMP RD
- ImCo 92231 6680-C1
KEMPER CT
3600 SD 92110 1268-C5
KEMPER ST
3100 SD 92110 1268-D5
4300 LMSA 91941 1270-F4
KEMPF ST
3000 LMGR 91945 1270-H6
KEMPTON ST
100 SDCo 91977 1291-B3
KEN LN
10400 SNTE 92071 1231-E3
KENALAN DR
1100 SD 92154 1350-F1
KENAMAR CT
7700 SD 92121 1209-A7
KENAMAR DR
8900 SD 92121 1229-A1
9000 SD 92121 1209-A7
KENDA WY
2400 SDCo 91901 1234-C6
KENDALL ST
3700 SD 92109 1248-A4
KENDI LN
1200 SDCo 92028 1028-D4
KENDLE RD
- ImCo 92227 431-E2
KENDRA CT
14300 PWY 92064 1190-E2
KENDRA WY
14100 PWY 92064 1190-E2
KENDRICK WY
1400 ELCJ 92019 1252-A7
KENESAW CT
9700 SNTE 92071 1231-F4
KENISON DR
900 SDCo 92036 1136-D7
900 SDCo 92036 1156-D1
KENMORE TER
4700 SD 92116 1269-E3
KENNEBECK CT
700 SD 92109 1267-H2
KENNEBUNK ST
14400 PWY 92064 1190-H5
KENNEDY LN
300 OCN 92054 1086-D6
KENNEDY ST
200 CHV 91911 1330-D3
KENNEDY WY
- SMCS 92078 1128-H3
KENNELWORTH LN
3200 SDCo 91902 1310-H1
KENNESTER ST
3000 LMGR 91945 1270-E7
KENNEY ST
10300 ELCJ 92020 1231-E7
10600 SNTE 92020 1231-E7
KENNINGTON RD
1700 ENCT 92024 1147-A2
KENORA DR
1600 ESCN 92027 1130-C2
3200 SDCo 91977 1271-C5
KENORA LN
9600 SDCo 91977 1271-C6
KENORA PL
1300 ESCN 92027 1130-B2
KENORA ST
1400 ESCN 92027 1130-C2
KENORA VW
9600 SDCo 91977 1271-D6
KENORA WOODS LN
9700 SDCo 91977 1271-C6
KENOSHA AV
3900 SD 92117 1248-D4
KENOVA ST
8000 SD 92126 1209-B4
KENS RD
100 SDCo 92021 1252-J3
KENSAL CT
15000 SDCo 92082 1070-H6
KENSETT PL
9100 SD 92126 1209-D2
KENSINGTON DR
100 SMCS 92078 1108-D7
4500 SD 92116 1269-G3
KENSINGTON GN
1700 ESCN 92026 1109-D3
KENSINGTON PL
5700 SDCo 92003 1048-B7
KENSLEY WY
6900 SD 92126 1208-H4
KENT AV
1200 ESCN 92026 1110-A7
1200 ESCN 92027 1110-A7
KENT DR
700 SDCo 92021 1252-H1

STREET Block City ZIP Pg-Grid
KENT PL
1700 SDCo 92084 1108-C1
5800 SD 92120 1250-B7
KENT ST
1900 CHV 91913 1311-D5
KENTFIELD CT
- PWY 92064 1190-F2
KENTFIELD DR
- PWY 92064 1190-F1
- SMCS 92069 1108-J5
KENTFIELD PL
- PWY 92064 1190-E1
KENT HILL WY
- PWY 92064 1190-F1
KENTMERE TER
700 SD 92154 1330-H7
N KENTON AV
- NATC 91950 1290-B6
- SD 92114 1290-B6
S KENTON AV
- NATC 91950 1290-B6
KENTUCKY AV
- ELCJ 92020 1251-A1
KENTUCKY ST
400 SDCo 92028 1027-F1
KENTWOOD DR
700 SDCo 92036 1156-D1
KENWELL ST
5900 SD 92139 1290-D7
KENWOOD CT
3700 SDCo 91977 1271-B5
KENWOOD DR
4000 SDCo 91977 1271-B5
4000 SDCo 91941 1271-A5
KENWOOD PL
- SMCS 92078 1128-E6
KENWOOD ST
5600 SD 92114 1290-B3
KENWYN ST
2300 OCN 92054 1106-E1
KENYATTA CT
100 SD 92114 1290-C4
KENYATTA DR
100 SD 92114 1290-C4
KENYON ST
3700 SD 92110 1268-D5
KEOKI CT
7200 SD 92126 1208-J5
KEOKI ST
10200 SD 92126 1208-J5
KEOKUK CT
3200 SD 92117 1248-C2
KEOS WY
4900 OCN 92056 1107-F5
KEPHART RD
- SD 92106 1288-A7
KEPPLER DR
10000 SD 92124 1249-G2
KEPPLER PL
10200 SD 92124 1249-G2
KERCH ST
6100 SD 92115 1270-D5
KEREMEOS WY
8800 SD 92126 1209-D1
KERI WY
3700 SDCo 92028 1048-A4
KERISIANO WY
1700 OCN 92054 1106-E2
KERN CRES
- SD 92127 1169-B3
KERN CT
- OCN 92057 1086-H1
KERN PL
1100 ESCN 92027 1109-J6
KERNEL PL
900 CHV 91910 1310-G6
KERNS ST
- SD 92154 1351-G4
KERR WY
1300 OCN 92054 1106-D2
KERRAN ST
12300 PWY 92064 1190-D7
KERRI LN
25100 SDCo 92065 1173-H3
KERRIA DR
- SD 92109 1248-C6
KERRICK RD
- SD 92106 1288-B7
KERRIGAN CT
10500 SNTE 92071 1231-E2
KERRIGAN ST
10100 SNTE 92071 1231-E2
KERRY LN
- SD 92130 1188-J3
KERSEY PL
11900 SD 92128 1190-A2
KERSHAW RD
- ImCo 92227 411-C11
- ImCo 92233 411-C11
KERSHAWN PL
1000 SDCo 92029 1149-H2
KERWOOD CT
4100 SD 92130 1188-B5
KESLING CT
4800 SD 92117 1248-G1
KESLING PL
4800 SD 92117 1248-H1
KESLING ST
5000 SD 92117 1248-G1
KESTON CT
3400 SD 92111 1248-J4
KESTRAL DR
300 SMCS 92078 1128-G2
KESTREL DR
7000 CRLB 92011 1127-B7
KESTREL PL
9300 SD 92129 1189-E6
KESTREL ST
12400 SD 92129 1189-E5
KESTREL WY
9400 SD 92129 1189-E6
KESTREL FALLS RD
- CHV 91915 1331-G1
KESWICK CT
4700 SD 92130 1188-C4
KETCH WY
6700 CRLB 92011 1127-A5
KETRON AV
13400 PWY 92064 1190-E3
KETTERING LN
28300 SDCo 92026 1089-D4
KETTNER BLVD
500 SD 92101 1288-J1
2700 SD 92103 1288-J1
2700 SD 92101 1268-H7
2700 SD 92103 1268-H7
3000 SD 92110 1268-H6
KEVIN DR
1800 VSTA 92084 1087-H3
KEW ST
10200 SDCo 92026 1109-E1
KEW TER
2600 SD 92104 1269-F7

KEY LN
1700 ELCJ 92021 1252-A2
1700 SDCo 92021 1252-A2
KEYES RD
1100 SDCo 92065 1152-J7
1500 SDCo 92065 1172-J1
KEY LARGO DR
1800 VSTA 92081 1107-H5
KEY LARGO PL
300 ELCJ 92021 1251-G5
KEYPORT ST
300 OCN 92057 1066-H6
KEYS PL
1400 SDCo 92081 1107-G3
KEYS CREEK RD
11900 SDCo 92082 1049-H7
12100 SDCo 92082 1050-A7
KEYSER CT
1500 SDCo 92065 1172-G1
KEYSER RD
1300 SDCo 92065 1172-G2
KEYSTONE CIR
3500 OCN 92056 1107-E3
KEYSTONE CT
8600 SD 92126 1209-C2
KEYSTONE RD Rt#-S27
- ImCo 92227 431-C3
- ImCo 92251 431-C3
KEYSTONE WY
1200 VSTA 92081 1127-J1
1200 VSTA 92081 1128-A1
KHAYYAM RD
100 ESCN 92025 1129-J4
100 ESCN 92025 1130-A3
KHE SANH ST
- SD 92140 1268-F7
KHISH LN
1000 SDCo 91901 1233-H7
KHURAM ST
13400 SDCo 92040 1232-D4
KHURTZ RD
4800 SDCo 92004 (1099-G3
See Page 1098)
KIAVO DR
19300 SDCo 92082 1091-H4
KIBBINGS RD
13200 SD 92130 1188-A4
KIBLER DR
10000 SD 92126 1209-A5
KICA CT
32300 SDCo 92061 1050-J5
KICKAPOO CT
4500 SD 92117 1248-D2
KICKIN HORSE TR
7300 SDCo 92036 1138-C6
KIDD ST
900 NATC 92136 1309-G2
1200 NATC 91950 1309-G2
KIDD WY
500 ELCJ 92020 1251-F7
KIEFER RD
900 ImCo 92250 431-E7
KIEFFER LN
3600 OCN 92057 1086-G5
KIEL RD
1000 SDCo 92028 1027-G4
S KIHRIDGE LN
100 ENCT 92024 1167-H1
KIKA CT
9700 SD 92129 1189-F7
KILBIRNIE LN
- SDCo 92084 1068-C6
KILBOURN DR
8600 SD 92037 1228-A4
KILBY LN
1300 VSTA 92083 1108-A1
KILDARE WY
1100 ELCJ 92020 1251-A3
KILDEER CT
1100 ENCT 92024 1147-D3
KILEY RD
500 CHV 91910 1310-F6
KILGORE RD
1600 ImCo 92243 6559-H3
KILKEE ST
- SD 92117 1228-H7
KILKENNY DR
100 ENCT 92007 1167-D4
KILLARNEY TER
400 SMCS 92069 1108-J4
KILLDEER LN
- OCN 92057 1086-H2
KILLIAN RD
- SDCo 92028 1028-E2
KILLIAN WY
- SDCo 92028 1028-E2
KILT CT
7600 SD 92111 1249-A3
KIM PL
1400 CHV 91911 1330-E4
2600 SD 92123 1249-F6
KIMBALL ST
600 ESCN 92027 1130-C2
KIMBALL TER
300 CHV 91910 1310-A5
KIMBALL WY
400 NATC 91950 1309-J2
KIMBALL VALLEY RD
19300 SDCo 92065 1192-C3
KIMBER LN
9000 SDCo 92040 1232-D6
KIMBERLY CT
2300 CRLB 92008 1106-G4
KIMBERLY DR
6100 LMSA 91942 1250-H6
KIMBERLY LN
4100 OCN 92056 1087-C6
KIMBERLY PL
2400 ESCN 92027 1110-D6
KIMBERLY WY
1400 SDCo 91906 (1318-G4
See Page 1298)
KIMBERLY WOODS DR
1500 ELCJ 92020 1271-E1
KIMBLE VW
- SDCo 92028 1027-G3
KIMDA CT
14400 SDCo 91935 1292-J1
14400 SDCo 91935 1293-A1
KIMI LN
6300 ELCJ 92020 1251-C5
6300 LMSA 91942 1251-C5
KIMMY CT
6300 SD 92114 1290-D4
KIMSUE WY
3800 SD 92154 1350-F1
KINCAID AV
- CHV 91913 1331-D2
KINCAID RD
1900 SD 92101 1288-E1
2100 SD 92101 1268-E7
KINCAID ST
9900 SNTE 92071 1231-F4

KING CT
- SDCo 92055 1086-A2
KING LN
100 SDCo 92028 1027-J2
KING RD
- ImCo 92250 431-E6
KING ST
- CHV 91910 1310-D7
3600 LMSA 91941 1270-E5
3600 SD 91941 1270-E5
3600 SD 92115 1270-E5
KING ARTHUR CT
2300 SD 92037 1247-H1
KING ARTHURS CT
3100 SDCo 91977 1271-A6
KINGBIRD AV
8600 SNTE 92071 1230-G7
KINGBIRD LN
- CRLB 92011 1127-D4
KING CREEK CIR
- CHV 91915 1311-H5
KING CREEK DR
- CHV 91915 1311-H5
KING CREEK WY
- CHV 91915 1311-H5
KINGFISHER LN
7100 CRLB 92011 1127-C7
KINGFISHER CREEK RD
10700 SDCo 92021 1232-J1
10700 SDCo 92021 1233-A1
KING KELLY CT
8000 SDCo 92021 1252-A1
KING KELLY DR
7900 SDCo 92021 1252-A1
KINGLET RD
1700 SDCo 92078 1128-A4
KINGLET WY
- CRLB 92011 1127-D4
KINGMAN RD
15600 PWY 92064 1170-J6
KING PHILLIP CT
10600 SNTE 92071 1231-E2
KINGRIDGE DR
2400 SDCo 92028 1028-C7
KINGS AV
3600 OCN 92056 1107-D3
KINGS RD
1000 ESCN 92027 1110-B6
1700 VSTA 92084 1088-B3
KINGS TR
8500 SNTE 92071 1231-D7
KINGS WY
1500 ESCN 92027 1110-A5
1700 VSTA 92084 1088-B3
4800 SD 92117 1248-G1
KING SANDAY LN
10400 SDCo 92082 1069-E3
KINGS CROSS CT
700 ENCT 92007 1167-E2
KINGS CROSS DR
1400 ENCT 92007 1167-E2
KINGSFIELD CT
- SD 92130 1188-A5
KINGSFORD CT
12200 SDCo 92021 1252-A1
KINGSGATE SQ
12200 SD 92128 1170-B4
KINGSLAND RD
8400 SD 92123 1249-B7
KINGSLEY ST
3000 SD 92106 1268-C5
3000 SD 92106 1268-D6
3100 SD 92106 1268-D6
3200 SD 92106 1268-D6
3200 SD 92106 1268-D6
3600 SD 92106 1268-C6
3600 SD 92106 1268-D6
3700 SD 92106 1268-C5
3700 SD 92106 1268-C6
KING SOLOMON AV
- SD 92102 1289-G4
KINGSPINE AV
12300 SD 92131 1210-B4
KINGSPORT WY
- SMCS 92078 1128-D5
KINGSTON CT
700 SD 92109 1267-H2
KINGSTON CT E
9900 SNTE 92071 1231-B4
KINGSTON CT N
- CORD 92118 1329-E2
KINGSTON CT S
- CORD 92118 1329-E2
KINGSTON CT W
- CORD 92118 1329-E2
KINGSTON DR
1400 ESCN 92027 1130-C2
KINGSTON ST
3600 CRLB 92010 1106-J4
3600 CRLB 92010 1107-A4
KINGS VIEW CIR
2100 SDCo 91977 1271-A7
KINGS VIEW CT
5800 SD 92114 1290-C4
KINGS VILLA RD
1400 SDCo 92065 1152-E2
KINGSWOOD CT
5200 OCN 92056 1087-D1
KINGSWOOD DR
- CHV 91911 1330-E4
KINGSWOOD ST
300 SD 92114 1290-F6
KINROSS CT
1900 SDCo 92027 1130-D4
KINSELLA PT
13000 SD 92130 1187-J5
13000 SD 92130 1188-A5
KIOWA DR
5300 LMSA 91942 1270-F1
5500 SD 91942 1270-F1
5500 SD 91942 1250-F7
KIPLING LN
5400 CRLB 92008 1107-C7
KIRA PL
31300 SDCo 92082 1070-F2
KIRBY CT
9000 SD 92126 1209-D1
KIRBY PL
11500 SD 92126 1209-D1
KIRK PL
1700 CRLB 92008 1106-H6
KIRKCALDY DR
4100 SD 92111 1249-A3
KIRKCALDY RD
900 SDCo 92028 1027-G6
KIRKHAM CT
12400 PWY 92064 1190-D6
KIRKHAM RD
12100 PWY 92064 1190-D6
KIRKHAM WY
13000 PWY 92064 1190-E7
KIRKLAND AV
2500 SDCo 92029 1129-H7
2500 SDCo 92029 1149-H1
KIRKS WY
500 SDCo 92065 1152-J7

KIRKWALL AV
2700 CRLB 92010 1107-A5
KIRKWALL DR
- SMCS 92069 1108-G6
KIRKWOOD PL
600 SD 92037 1247-G4
KIRMAR PL
1200 OCN 92054 1106-D3
KIRSTEN LN
29800 SDCo 92084 1068-D6
KIRSTEN PL
2800 SDCo 91977 1271-B7
KIRSTIE LN
1400 ENCT 92024 1148-D4
KIRTRIGHT ST
500 SD 92114 1290-C5
KISMET RD
11700 SD 92128 1189-J6
11700 SD 92128 1190-A6
KISO GN
1300 ESCN 92025 1129-H5
KISO LN
1800 SDCo 92069 1109-A2
1800 SMCS 92069 1109-A2
KIT CARSON PL
10200 SNTE 92071 1231-F3
KITCHEN CREEK RD
3100 SDCo 91962 430-B7
KITE LN
1000 VSTA 92081 1108-A6
KITE PL
- CRLB 92011 1127-A4
KITE ST
3400 SD 92103 1268-J6
KITE HILL LN
11000 SD 92126 1209-E2
KIT FOX LN
- SDCo 92004 (1099-G4
See Page 1098)
KITTERY ST
14500 PWY 92064 1190-H4
KITTIWAKE LN
900 CHV 91911 1330-C2
KITTIWAKE WY
4400 OCN 92057 1087-A3
KITTY LN
8600 SNTE 92071 1231-F7
KITTY HAWK CT
1400 IMP 92251 6499-C2
KIVA LN
1500 VSTA 92084 1087-H3
KIWI GN
1700 ESCN 92026 1109-D6
KIWI PL
- CRLB 92011 1127-D4
KIWI ST
7600 SD 92123 1249-A7
KIWI MEADOW LN
9600 SDCo 92026 1069-D7
9600 SDCo 92026 1089-D1
KLAMATH
14100 SDCo 92040 1232-H5
KLAMATH DR
1400 CHV 91913 1331-B2
KLAMATH ST
- OCN 92057 1086-H1
KLAUBER AV
1000 SD 92114 1290-D2
1900 LMGR 92114 1290-E2
KLEAVELAND PL
500 VSTA 92084 1087-H4
KLEEFELD AV
4500 SD 92117 1248-E1
KLINE ST
700 SD 92037 1227-E7
KLISH WY
800 DLMR 92014 1187-G5
KLOKE AV
- ImCo 92231 6680-E1
900 CALX 92231 6680-E1
KLOKE RD
- CALX 92231 6620-E7
600 ImCo 92231 431-C7
600 ImCo 92231 6620-D4
KLUCEWICH RD
2900 SDCo 91901 1234-B4
KNABE LN
9900 SNTE 92071 1231-B4
KNAPP DR
1700 VSTA 92084 1087-G3
W KNAPP DR
300 VSTA 92083 1087-G3
KNAPP ST
4600 SD 92117 1248-F5
KNAUL CT
8900 SD 92129 1189-C4
KNIGHT DR
10000 SD 92126 1209-A5
KNIGHTSBRIDGE CT
700 ENCT 92007 1167-E2
KNIGHTS FERRY DR
- CHV 91913 1311-D6
KNIGHTS REALM
1500 SMCS 92078 1128-D2
KNOB HILL DR
800 SDCo 92036 1156-D2
1900 SDCo 91977 1291-A1
KNOB HILL RD
1100 SMCS 92069 1109-C7
KNOLL CT
5000 LMSA 91941 1271-B2
KNOLL DR
1300 OCN 92054 1086-F7
KNOLL RD
- SMCS 92069 1128-G1
- VSTA 92083 1087-G6
500 SMCS 92069 1108-G7
KNOLL VW
2200 ESCN 92029 1129-E6
KNOLL CREST PL
12100 SDCo 92040 1232-A5
KNOLL EDGE CT
- SDCo 92065 1173-D2
KNOLLFIELD WY
1700 ENCT 92024 1147-G6
KNOLL PARK GN
- ESCN 92029 1129-H5
KNOLL PARK LN
800 SDCo 92028 997-H7
800 SDCo 92028 1027-H1
KNOLLVIEW DR
9900 SDCo 91977 1291-D1
9900 SDCo 91977 1271-H7
KNOLLVIEW LN
2200 SDCo 91977 1271-H7
2200 SDCo 91977 1291-D1
KNOLL VISTA DR
900 SDCo 92078 1128-D2
KNOLLWOOD AV
2100 SDCo 92028 1027-H6
KNOLL WOOD CT
4700 OCN 92056 1087-D3
KNOLLWOOD DR
3500 CRLB 92010 1107-C3

KNOLLWOOD PL
1400 CHV 91915 1311-G7
KNOLLWOOD RD
7900 SD 92114 1290-G3
KNOLLWOOD WY
9300 SNTE 92071 1231-A6
KNOTS LN
- CRLB 92011 1146-J1
KNOTT ST
2100 SD 92139 1290-F7
KNOTTWOOD WY
2600 SDCo 92028 1048-B3
KNOWLES AV
900 CRLB 92008 1106-E4
KNOWLTON CT
9400 SNTE 92071 1231-A5
KNOWLTON WILLIAMS RD
100 NATC 92136 1309-F1
100 SD 92136 1309-F1
3600 SD 92136 1289-F7
KNOX ST
4900 SD 92110 1268-F2
KNOXIE ST
3600 SD 92105 1270-A6
KNOXVILLE ST
1200 SD 92110 1268-E2
KOALA WY
1400 ELCJ 92019 1252-A7
KOBE DR
2600 SD 92123 1249-D6
KOBE PL
8900 SD 92123 1249-D6
KOBE WY
8900 SD 92123 1249-D5
KOE ST
1100 SD 92114 1290-G2
1500 LMGR 91945 1290-G2
KOELPER ST
- SDCo 92055 1085-H5
KOESTER ST
- CHV 91913 1331-E2
KOLMAR ST
200 SD 92037 1247-E2
KONA WY
3000 SD 92106 1288-A3
KONA KAI LN
1400 ESCN 92029 1129-D4
KOONCE DR
9000 SDCo 91977 1271-B5
KOONCE RD
8900 SNTE 92071 1231-H6
KOREA ST
- SD 92140 1268-E6
KORINK AV
2600 SD 92111 1249-A6
2600 SD 92111 1248-J6
KORITE PL
- CRLB 92009 1127-G5
KORNBLUM DR
26000 SDCo 92026 1089-E7
26000 SDCo 92026 1109-E1
KORREY DR
14100 SD 92129 1189-G2
KORY LN
1400 SDCo 92065 1152-J7
KOSTNER DR
700 SD 92154 1330-G7
900 SD 92154 1350-G1
KOZY CREST LN
12200 PWY 92064 1190-B1
KQ RANCH RD
- SDCo 92036 1156-G6
KRAFT ST
1600 OCN 92054 1086-B5
KRAMAR RD
- ImCo 92243 431-A6
1000 ImCo 92243 6559-A3
KRAMER ST
6700 SD 92111 1268-J1
KREINER WY
8400 SNTE 92071 1230-H6
KREMEYER CIR
2600 CRLB 92008 1106-E4
KRENNING ST
5100 SD 92105 1270-A7
KRENZ ST
8300 SD 92123 1249-B5
KRIM PL
1500 OCN 92054 1106-D2
KRIS RD
4100 SDCo 91935 1273-J4
4100 SDCo 91935 1274-A5
KRIS WY
9500 SNTE 92071 1231-B1
KRISHEN HEIGHTS RD
300 SDCo 92019 1253-D1
KRISTA CT
400 CHV 91910 1310-F6
KRISTEN CT
200 ENCT 92024 1147-D6
KRISTEN GN
- SD 92127 1169-C3
KRISTEN WY
9800 SDCo 92082 1069-D5
KRISTEN VILLA CT
100 SDCo 92065 1153-A6
KRISTI CT
2000 SDCo 92028 1048-B4
KRISTIE LN
1300 ELCJ 92019 1252-A5
KRISTIN CT
200 SD 92114 1290-D4
KRISTY LN
200 OCN 92054 1106-C3
KRUG CT
1300 VSTA 92081 1107-J3
KRYSTAL PL
- ESCN 92026 1109-D6
KUBLER RD
- ImCo 92231 431-A7
KUEBLER RANCH RD
- SDCo 92154 1332-C7
KUGEL CT
- CHV 91913 1331-D2
KUHN DR
800 CHV 91914 1311-F4
KUHNER WY
12100 SDCo 92040 1232-A1
KUMBERG MESA RD
- ImCo 92250 431-E7
KUMBERG MESA RD Rt#-S33
- ImCo 92250 431-F7
KUMEYAAY WY
- SDCo 92082 1091-B4
KUMEYAI TR
17300 SDCo 91901 1233-J2
17300 SDCo 91901 1234-A2
KUMQUAT DR
9600 SDCo 92040 1232-A4
KUMQUAT WY
600 OCN 92054 1086-F2

KUNDE CT
- SD 92130 1188-J3
KUNKLER LN
- SDCo 92004 (1121-J3
See Page 1100)
KUNYAAN PATH RD
- SDCo 92082 1091-B4
KUNYAAW PL
- SDCo 92082 1091-C3
KUPA DR
16200 SDCo 92061 1051-B6
KURDSON WY
400 SDCo 91977 1291-B4
KURENDA WY
1800 SDCo 92083 1108-A3
KURLEY CT
2000 SDCo 91977 1290-J1
2300 SDCo 91977 1271-A7
KURTZ CT
- CORD 91932 1329-E4
KURTZ ST
1400 OCN 92054 1106-D1
1600 SD 92101 1268-E6
1700 SD 92110 1268-D4
KUTZ RD
- ImCo 92251 430-L4
KWAAYMII PT
- SDCo 92036 (1197-G5
See Page 1176)
KWAJALEIN RD
2300 CORD 92155 1309-B1
KYANITE PL
- CRLB 92009 1127-F4
KYLE LN
1100 VSTA 92084 1087-J4
KYLE PL
- SDCo 92021 1251-H2
KYRSTEN TER
1400 SDCo 91901 1233-J6
KYRSTEN TRCT
1400 SDCo 91901 1233-J6

L

L AV
100 NATC 91950 1289-J7
800 NATC 91950 1309-J1
1400 NATC 91950 1310-A2
L AVEX
1200 NATC 91950 1309-J1
1200 NATC 91950 1310-A1
L ST
- CHV 91911 1330-B2
100 IMP 92251 6439-F6
500 SD 92101 1289-B4
1900 SD 92102 1289-C4
E L ST
- CHV 91911 1330-E1
LA ALAMEDA
- ESCN 92026 1109-G7
600 ENCT 92024 1147-F5
12400 SDCo 92021 1252-A1
LA ALBERCA AV
- SDCo 92127 1169-F4
LA AMAPOLA
17800 SDCo 92067 1148-J7
LA AMATISTA RD
300 DLMR 92014 1187-G6
300 SD 92014 1187-G6
LA BAJADA Rt#-S9
17400 SDCo 92067 1168-A2
17600 SDCo 92067 1167-J2
LA BARCA ST
500 SDCo 91977 1291-C3
LA BARRANCA DR
200 SOLB 92075 1167-H6
LA BELLA CIR
1800 OCN 92054 1106-D1
LABON WY
500 SD 92113 1289-F5
LA BONITA
- VSTA 92081 1107-D2
LA BONITA CT
1600 SDCo 92078 1128-C2
1600 SMCS 92078 1128-C2
LA BONITA DR
800 SDCo 92078 1128-C3
800 SMCS 92078 1128-C3
LA BONITA WY
1600 SDCo 92078 1128-C2
1600 SMCS 92078 1128-C2
LABRADOR LN
3500 SMCS 92078 1108-D6
9500 SDCo 92021 1232-J4
LA BREA CT
100 SDCo 92065 1152-F6
LA BREA ST
1600 SDCo 92065 1152-E7
1900 ESCN 92026 1109-E5
2200 SDCo 92065 1172-D1
LA BRISA
17200 SDCo 92067 1168-H2
LA BRUCHERIE RD
500 ImCo 92251 6439-E5
500 IMP 92251 6439-E5
800 ImCo 92243 431-B7
1300 ImCo 92243 6559-F4
1600 ELCN 92243 6559-E1
1800 ELCN 92243 6499-E2
2000 ImCo 92243 6499-E5
2000 ImCo 92251 6499-E2
2000 IMP 92251 6499-E2
2700 IMP 92251 431-B4
LA BRUSCA WY
7900 CRLB 92009 1147-G4
LA BUENA VIDA
- SDCo 92028 1027-H7
LA BUTTE LN
8600 SNTE 92071 1231-A7
LA CALLECITA
2200 SD 92103 1268-G5
LA CALMA
500 ESCN 92029 1149-J3
LA CAMESA ST
8800 SD 92129 1189-C2
LA CAMPANA CT
3800 SMCS 92078 1128-C1
LA CANADA RD
3600 SDCo 92028 1048-A4
4600 SDCo 92028 1047-J5
LA CANADA ST
300 SD 92037 1247-F3
LA CAPELA PL
7900 CRLB 92009 1147-G3
LA CARTERA ST
8800 SD 92129 1189-C2
LA CASA DR
1100 SDCo 92078 1128-B3
LA CASA LN
1100 SDCo 92078 1128-C3
LA CASITA DR
1500 SDCo 92078 1128-C2
LA CASITA WY
4200 OCN 92057 1086-J3

LA CATRINA
17600 SDCo 92067 1149-A6
LACAVA PL
2000 SDCo 92019 1272-C4
LA CAZADORA
18300 SDCo 92067 1148-D7
LACE PL
4900 SD 92102 1290-A2
LACEBARK ST
800 SMCS 92069 1109-B5
LA CHICA DR
1400 CHV 91911 1330-J3
LACIE LN
12000 SDCo 92040 1231-J7
12000 SDCo 92040 1232-A7
LA CIENAGA RD
1200 SMCS 92069 1109-C5
LA CIENEGA RD
100 SMCS 92069 1108-J3
400 SMCS 92069 1109-A3
W LA CIENEGA RD
100 SMCS 92069 1108-H3
LA CIMA DR
1500 SD 92109 1268-A1
LA CINTURA CT
8800 SD 92129 1189-C2
LACK RD
- ImCo 92227 431-A1
- ImCo 92259 431-A2
5600 ImCo 92227 411-A11
LACKAWANNA WY
3000 SD 92117 1248-F6
LACO DR
4500 SD 92115 1270-D4
LA COLINA DR
900 ESCN 92027 1130-F1
LA COLINA RD
11600 SD 92131 1210-A4
LA COLUSA DR
3700 SMCS 92078 1108-C7
3700 SMCS 92078 1128-D1
LACONIA ST
2200 SD 92114 1270-E7
2200 SD 92114 1290-E1
LA CORTA CIR
1400 LMGR 91945 1290-E2
LA CORTA ST
1400 LMGR 91945 1290-F1
LA CORUNA PL
7600 CRLB 92009 1147-G1
LA COSTA
- SMCS 92078 1129-C1
LA COSTA AV
100 ENCT 92024 1147-D1
200 CRLB 92024 1147-A2
2200 CRLB 92009 1147-F1
2500 CHV 91915 1311-G4
3400 CRLB 92009 1148-A2
LA COSTA MEADOWS DR
1600 SMCS 92078 1128-A5
1800 CRLB 92078 1128-A5
LA CRESCENTA
5500 SDCo 92067 1148-B7
5500 SDCo 92067 1168-C1
LA CRESCENTIA DR
400 SD 92106 1288-A4
1200 CHV 91910 1311-A5
LA CRESTA BLVD
100 SDCo 92021 1232-J7
100 SDCo 92021 1252-J1
LA CRESTA DR
400 OCN 92054 1086-F6
3600 SD 92107 1268-B7
3700 SD 92107 1288-B1
LA CRESTA RD
9800 SDCo 91977 1271-D7
E LA CRESTA RD
1900 SDCo 92021 1252-C3
W LA CRESTA RD
100 SDCo 92021 1252-F3
LA CRESTA TR
100 SDCo 92019 1253-C1
LA CRESTA WY
3900 SDCo 91902 1310-J3
LA CRESTA HEIGHTS CT
800 SDCo 92021 1252-H2
LA CRESTA HEIGHTS RD
100 SDCo 92021 1252-H2
LA CROSSE AV
4400 SD 92117 1248-D2
LACROSSE PL
600 ESCN 92025 1130-B4
LA CRUZ DR
4700 LMSA 91941 1271-C2
4700 SDCo 91941 1271-C2
LA CRUZ PL
4800 SDCo 91941 1271-C2
LA CUENTA CT
10700 SD 92124 1249-H3
LA CUENTA DR
4400 SD 92124 1249-H1
LA CUESTA DR
9300 SDCo 91941 1271-B3
LA CUMBRE DR
1500 SD 92037 1247-G2
LACY AV
800 CALX 92231 6680-E1
900 CALX 92231 6620-E7
LADD ST
4100 SD 92109 1248-B6
LADDECK CT
7200 SD 92114 1290-F2
LADDIE LN
8800 SD 92123 1249-D5
LADERA CT
2000 CRLB 92009 1147-F2
LADERA ST
4400 SD 92107 1287-H3
LADERA WY
200 OCN 92054 1086-E6
LADERA LINDA
1200 SOLB 92014 1167-H7
1200 SOLB 92014 1187-J2
LADERA LINDA WY
1200 SOLB 92014 1187-J2
LADERA PIEDRA WY
16100 PWY 92064 1170-C5
LADERA SARINA
4800 SDCo 92014 1168-A7
LADERA VISTA RD
3800 SDCo 92028 1047-G4
LADERO PL
1900 ESCN 92029 1129-F6
LADIOSA CT
900 CHV 91910 1310-H4
LADLEHILL DR
2300 SD 92139 1290-G7
LADNER ST
4700 SD 92113 1289-J5
LADO DE LOMA DR
100 VSTA 92083 1087-G7
600 VSTA 92083 1107-H1

STREET
Block City ZIP Pg-Grid

LADOGA LN
1700 SDCo 92083 1108-A2
LA DONNA LN
12200 SDCo 92040 1232-A7
LA DORNA ST
5000 SD 92115 1270-D2
LADRIDO LN
23600 SDCo 92065 409-H11
LADRILLO ST
7000 SD 92111 1248-J6
LA DUELA LN
2600 CRLB 92009 1147-G3
LA DUENA WY
10300 SD 92124 1229-G7
LADY LN
10800 SDCo 92040 1232-B1
LADY BESS PL
8000 SD 92126 1209-B5
LADY BESS WY
10100 SD 92126 1209-B5
LADYBIRD LN
5500 SD 92037 1247-G4
LADYBUG LN
600 SDCo 92069 1088-G6
LADYBUG PL
- CHV 91915 1331-H1
LADY FERN CT
11200 SD 92131 1209-J2
LADY HILL RD
3400 SD 92130 1187-J5
LADYSMITH DR
700 ELCJ 92020 1251-G7
700 SDCo 92020 1251-G7
LADYS SECRET CT
5900 SDCo 92067 1188-E1
LADYS SECRET DR
15200 SDCo 92067 1188-F1
LAE RD
2200 CORD 92155 1309-A2
LA ENTRADA
400 ENCT 92024 1147-F5
1100 SDCo 92028 1027-H2
3000 SDCo 92026 1109-G2
17400 SDCo 92067 1168-A2
LA ENTRADITA
3200 SDCo 92026 1109-G2
LA ESPADA
6500 SDCo 92067 1168-E4
LA FAMILIA CT
13600 SDCo 92040 1232-E5
LAFAYETTE CT
2300 CRLB 92010 1106-H4
LAFAYETTE PL
800 CHV 91913 1311-E5
LAFE DR
10000 SNTE 92071 1231-D2
LA FELICE LN
900 SDCo 92028 1027-H6
LAFFEY CT
10100 SD 92124 1249-G3
LA FIESTA CT
1500 SDCo 92078 1128-C2
LA FIESTA DR
1500 SDCo 92078 1128-C2
LA FIESTA LN
900 SDCo 92078 1128-C2
LA FIESTA PL
900 SDCo 92078 1128-C2
LA FIESTA WY
900 SDCo 92078 1128-C2
LA FLECHA
5900 SDCo 92067 1168-D3
LA FLORA DR
1600 SDCo 92078 1128-C2
LA FLORESTA
4800 SDCo 92014 1168-A6
LA FORCE RD
400 SDCo 91901 1233-F7
LA FRANCE ST
2400 SD 92109 1248-B4
LA FREMONTIA
6100 SDCo 92067 1168-D2
LA GACHA LN
7900 CRLB 92009 1147-G4
LAGAN AV
1200 VSTA 92083 1087-G4
LA GARZA CT
6400 CRLB 92009 1127-G5
LAGASCA PL
800 CHV 91910 1310-H5
LAGEWAART RD
2200 SDCo 92065 1172-E4
LA GLORIETA
5200 SDCo 92067 1168-B4
LAGO CTE
6600 SDCo 92067 1188-G2
LAGO DI GRATA CIR
- SD 92130 1208-B2
LAGO GRANDE DR
6400 OCN 92003 1067-G3
LAGO LINDO
5600 SDCo 92067 1168-E1
6400 SDCo 92067 1148-F7
LA GOLONDRINA ST
2500 CRLB 92009 1127-G4
LAGO MADERO
2100 CHV 91914 1311-F3
LAGO MARCOS
- SMCS 92078 1129-C1
LAGOON DR
700 CHV 91910 1309-H7
LAGOON VIEW CT
1100 ENCT 92007 1167-F4
LAGOON VIEW DR
1800 CRLB 92008 1106-E2
1800 OCN 92054 1106-E2
2200 ENCT 92007 1167-F4
LAGO SERENO
3600 ESCN 92029 1150-A4
LAGO VENTANA
2100 CHV 91914 1311-F3
LAGO VISTA
18000 SDCo 92067 1148-E6
LA GRACIA
600 ENCT 92024 1147-F5
15800 SDCo 92067 1168-D3
LA GRAN AVD
1200 ENCT 92024 1147-F5
LA GRAN VIA
2500 CRLB 92009 1147-G1
LA GRANADA
6000 SDCo 92067 1168-D3
LA GRANADA Rt#-S9
4800 SDCo 92067 1168-A3
LA GRANADA CT
- SDCo 92067 1168-D3
LA GRANADA DR
1100 SDCo 92078 1128-E3
LA GRAN AVENIDA NORTE
1100 ENCT 92024 1147-F5
LAGRANGE RD
- CHV 91913 1311-D6

LAGUARDIA AV
- IMP 92251 6499-D1
LAGUARDIA CT
- IMP 92251 6499-D2
LAGUNA AV
600 ELCJ 92020 1251-E7
LAGUNA DR
500 CRLB 92008 1106-E4
500 SMCS 92069 1109-A6
LAGUNA LN
- SDCo 91962 1237-D7
1700 VSTA 92084 1088-A3
LAGUNA PL
19200 SDCo 92029 1149-D4
LAGUNA ST
200 SDCo 91934 (1321-H5 See Page 1300)
500 CHV 91910 1310-C7
1100 OCN 92054 1106-C2
LAGUNA TR
7400 SDCo 91962 1237-C7
LAGUNA MEADOW RD
- SDCo 91948 (1217-F4 See Page 1216)
- SDCo 91948 1218-A4
- SDCo 91962 (1217-F4 See Page 1216)
LAGUNA POINT CT
600 CHV 91911 1330-J4
LAGUNA SECA LP
1000 CHV 91915 1311-F5
LAGUNA VISTA
13500 SDCo 92021 1232-E7
LAGUNA VISTA CT
13500 SDCo 92021 1232-E7
LAGUNITA LN
900 SDCo 92084 1067-J6
LAGUNITA WY
- OCN 92057 1087-A1
LA HABRA DR
1400 SDCo 92078 1128-C3
LA HABRA GN
2000 ESCN 92026 1109-E5
LA HABRA ST
2000 ESCN 92026 1109-E5
LA HAINA PL
500 SDCo 92065 1152-F7
LA HAINA ST
1300 SDCo 92065 1152-F7
LA HARINA CT
14300 SD 92129 1189-C2
LAHINCH DR
1900 SD 92154 1351-E3
LAHITTE CT
3200 SD 92122 1228-C5
LA HONDA DR
1100 ESCN 92027 1110-B4
1300 SDCo 92027 1110-B4
LAHOUD DR
1700 ENCT 92007 1167-F3
LA HUERTA WY
700 SD 92154 1330-G7
LAIRD ST
8000 LMSA 91942 1250-H7
LAIRWOOD DR
10200 SNTE 92071 1231-D3
LAJA DR
12400 PWY 92064 1170-C7
LA JACARANDA
4800 SDCo 92067 1168-A2
LA JOLLA BLVD
5000 SD 92109 1247-F4
5100 SD 92037 1247-E1
7300 SD 92037 1227-E7
LA JOLLA PKWY
2400 SD 92037 1227-H6
2700 SD 92037 1228-A7
LA JOLLA PL
- SMCS 92078 1129-C1
LA JOLLA COLONY DR
6000 SD 92122 1228-A5
LA JOLLA CORONA CT
800 SD 92037 1247-G3
LA JOLLA CORONA DR
5700 SD 92037 1247-G3
LA JOLLA FARMS RD
9300 SD 92037 1227-H1
LA JOLLA HERMOSA AV
5200 SD 92037 1247-F3
LA JOLLA KNOLL
1400 SD 92037 1227-G7
LA JOLLA MESA DR
5200 SD 92109 1247-G2
5300 SD 92037 1247-G2
LA JOLLA PALMS BLVD
- CALX 92231 6620-H5
LA JOLLA RANCHO RD
800 SD 92037 1247-H2
LA JOLLA SCENIC DR N
7600 SD 92037 1227-J3
7800 SD 92037 1228-A4
LA JOLLA SCENIC DR S
5900 SD 92037 1247-H2
6600 SD 92037 1227-J6
LA JOLLA SHORES DR
7900 SD 92037 1227-H5
8500 SD 92093 1227-H3
LA JOLLA SHORES LN
9000 SD 92037 1227-H3
9000 SD 92093 1227-H3
LA JOLLA VILLAGE DR
2800 SD 92093 1227-J3
2800 SD 92037 1227-J3
2900 SD 92037 1228-D2
2900 SD 92093 1228-A3
3200 SD 92161 1228-A3
3400 SD 92122 1228-D2
4300 SD 92121 1228-D2
LA JOLLA VISTA DR
7700 SD 92037 1227-J6
7700 SD 92037 1228-A6
LAJOS LN
15800 SDCo 92082 1071-A7
15800 SDCo 92082 1091-A1
LA JOTA WY
7900 SD 92037 1227-G6
LA JUNTA AV
3300 SD 92117 1248-C2
LAKE BLVD
3500 OCN 92056 1107-B2
LAKE CT
6800 SD 92111 1268-J1
LAKE DR
1200 ENCT 92007 1167-F3
1200 ENCT 92024 1167-F2
8300 SDCo 91977 1290-J6
19000 SD 92029 1149-D6
19000 SD 92067 1149-D6
19000 SDCo 92067 1149-D6
19500 SDCo 92029 1149-E1
20100 SDCo 92029 1129-E7

LAKE ADLON CT
6400 SD 92119 1250-G5
LAKE ADLON DR
7600 SD 92119 1250-G5
LAKE ALAMOR AV
6200 SD 92119 1250-J6
LAKE ALBANO AV
6200 SD 92119 1250-J5
LAKE ALTURAS AV
6200 SD 92119 1250-J5
LAKE ANDRITA AV
7700 SD 92119 1250-G5
LAKE ANGELA DR
8600 SD 92119 1250-J6
8600 SD 92119 1251-A5
LAKE APOPKA PL
6200 SD 92119 1251-A5
LAKE ARAGO AV
6200 SD 92119 1250-J5
LAKE ARAL DR
6200 SD 92119 1250-J5
LAKE ARIANA AV
6200 SD 92119 1250-J5
LAKE ARROWHEAD DR
6200 SD 92119 1251-A5
6400 SD 92119 1250-J5
LAKE ARTEMUS AV
8300 SD 92119 1250-J5
LAKE ASHMERE CT
6500 SD 92119 1251-A4
LAKE ASHMERE DR
8600 SD 92119 1250-J5
8700 SD 92119 1251-A5
LAKE ASHWOOD AV
8300 SD 92119 1250-J5
LAKE ATHABASKA PL
6200 SD 92119 1251-A6
LAKE ATHABASKA WY
8700 SD 92119 1251-A5
LAKE ATLIN AV
6200 SD 92119 1250-J5
LAKE BACA DR
8300 SD 92119 1250-J5
LAKE BADIN AV
6200 LMSA 91942 1250-H6
6200 SD 92119 1250-H6
LAKE BEN AV
8300 SD 92119 1250-J4
LAKE BLUFF CIR
8500 SDCo 91977 1290-J5
8500 SDCo 91977 1291-A5
LAKE BREEZE CT
- SDCo 91977 1291-D2
LAKE BREEZE DR
- SDCo 91977 1291-D2
LAKE CANYON CT
9900 SNTE 92071 1231-A4
LAKE CANYON RD
9200 SNTE 92071 1231-A4
LAKE CAYUGA DR
7900 SD 92119 1250-H5
LAKE CIRCLE AV
4900 SDCo 92028 1048-J3
LAKE CIRCLE CT
3300 SDCo 92028 1048-J3
LAKE CIRCLE DR
3300 SDCo 92028 1048-H3
LAKE CIRCLE LN
4800 SDCo 92028 1048-J3
LAKE CIRCLE PL
3300 SDCo 92028 1048-H3
LAKE CIRCLE RD
4900 SDCo 92028 1048-J3
LAKE CIRCLE ST
4200 SDCo 92028 1048-J4
LAKE COMO AV
6300 SD 92119 1250-H5
LAKE COUNTRY DR
9200 SNTE 92071 1231-A5
LAKE CREST CT
2800 CHV 91915 (1312-A6 See Page 1293)
LAKE CREST DR
1200 CHV 91915 1311-J5
1200 CHV 91915 (1312-A6 See Page 1293)
LAKECREST PT
10600 SD 92131 1209-J3
LAKEDALE RD
1300 SDCo 92070 1135-D3
LAKE DECATUR AV
6300 SD 92119 1250-H5
LAKE DORA AV
6300 SD 92119 1250-H5
LAKE DRIVE CIR
- SDCo 92082 1090-B1
LAKE FOREST AV
4700 SD 92117 1248-D1
LAKE FOREST ST
2300 ESCN 92026 1109-J4
LAKE GABY AV
8300 SD 92119 1250-J4
LAKE GARDEN DR
3100 SDCo 92028 1048-E1
LAKE GROVE CT
11700 SD 92131 1210-A4
LAKE HELIX DR
- LMSA 91941 1271-D1
LAKE HELIX TER
9700 LMSA 91941 1271-C2
LAKE HILL PL
- CHV 91914 1311-J2
LAKE HILL RD
9200 SNTE 92071 1231-A5
LAKEHOUSE PL
- CHV 91914 1311-J3
LAKEHURST AV
3600 SD 92117 1248-D1
LAKE JENNINGS PARK RD
9200 SDCo 92021 1232-D3
9200 SDCo 92040 1232-D3
LAKE KATHLEEN AV
6300 SD 92119 1250-H5
LAKELAND DR
10100 SNTE 92071 1231-A3
LAKE LEVEN DR
6200 SD 92119 1250-G6
LAKE LOMOND DR
6200 SD 92119 1250-G6
LAKE LUCERNE DR
6200 SD 92119 1250-G6
LAKE MADERA CT
9200 SDCo 92040 1232-C5
LAKE MARCIA DR
6300 SD 92119 1250-J5
LAKEMEADOW DR
27900 SDCo 92026 1089-E4
LAKEMEADOW LN
10100 SDCo 92026 1089-E4
LAKE MERE CT
6400 SD 92119 1251-A5
LAKEMONT DR
2800 SDCo 92028 1048-E1

LAKE MORENA DR
1700 SDCo 91906 (1297-F6 See Page 1296)
1700 SDCo 91906 (1317-G1 See Page 1296)
LAKE MURRAY BLVD
5200 LMSA 91941 1270-F1
5200 LMSA 91942 1270-F1
5500 LMSA 91942 1250-G7
8300 SD 92119 1250-G7
8800 SD 92119 1251-A4
LAKE PARK AV
3500 SDCo 92028 1048-J3
LAKE PARK CT
4900 SDCo 92028 1048-J3
LAKE PARK LN
3900 SDCo 92028 1048-J3
LAKE PARK PL
4800 SDCo 92028 1048-J3
LAKE PARK RD
3500 SDCo 92028 1048-J3
LAKE PARK ST
3800 SDCo 92028 1048-J3
LAKE PARK WY
5500 LMSA 91942 1250-G7
5500 LMSA 91942 1270-G1
LAKEPORT RD
7900 SD 92126 1209-B4
LAKE POWAY RD
13400 PWY 92064 1170-G4
LAKE REE AV
7500 SD 92119 1250-G6
LAKE RIDGE CIR
100 SDCo 92028 1047-F3
LAKERIDGE CIR
2000 CHV 91913 1311-E4
LAKE RIDGE CT
10300 SDCo 91977 1291-E2
LAKE RIDGE DR
900 SMCS 92078 1128-B2
LAKERIDGE LN
1400 ELCJ 92020 1251-C2
LAKE RIDGE RD
3600 SDCo 92028 1047-G3
LAKE RIM RD
11200 SD 92131 1209-J3
LAKE SAN MARCOS DR
1500 SDCo 92078 1128-C2
1600 SMCS 92078 1128-C2
LAKE SHORE AV
3500 SDCo 92028 1048-J3
LAKE SHORE CT
4900 SDCo 92028 1048-J3
LAKE SHORE DR
2400 SDCo 91906 (1297-E5 See Page 1296)
6100 SD 92119 1250-G5
LAKESHORE DR
800 SMCS 92078 1128-F2
2000 CHV 91913 1311-E3
12200 SDCo 92040 1232-A3
LAKE SHORE LN
3900 SDCo 92028 1048-J3
LAKE SHORE PL
4800 SDCo 92028 1048-J3
LAKE SHORE RD
3500 SDCo 92028 1048-J3
LAKE SHORE ST
3800 SDCo 92028 1048-J3
LAKESIDE AV
11300 SDCo 92040 1231-G1
12000 SDCo 92040 1232-A2
LAKESIDE CT
11900 SDCo 92040 1231-J2
LAKESIDE DR
700 SMCS 92078 1128-F1
LAKESIDE LN
100 OCN 92056 1107-D2
LAKESIDE RD
2000 SDCo 92084 1108-C2
LAKE SYCAMORE DR
4500 SDCo 92028 1048-A6
LAKE TAHOE AV
7700 SD 92119 1250-G5
LAKE TAHOE CIR
6400 SD 92119 1250-G5
LAKE TAHOE CT
6400 SD 92119 1250-G5
LAKETREE DR
2900 SDCo 92028 1048-D1
3500 SDCo 92028 1028-E7
LAKE VALLEY RD
9100 SDCo 92021 1232-E6
LAKE VICENTE DR
11400 SDCo 92040 1212-C3
LAKEVIEW AV
100 SDCo 91977 1291-A5
LAKE VIEW CT
- CHV 91915 (1312-A5 See Page 1293)
LAKEVIEW CT
13700 SDCo 92040 1232-E5
LAKE VIEW DR
29800 SDCo 91906 (1297-F5 See Page 1296)
LAKEVIEW DR
2700 SDCo 92036 1136-D7
3000 SDCo 92036 1156-D1
3300 SDCo 91977 1270-J6
3300 SDCo 91977 1271-A6
9400 LMSA 91942 1251-C7
40000 SDCo 92028 997-B2
LAKE VIEW LN
100 SDCo 92021 1232-J7
100 SDCo 92021 1252-J1
LAKEVIEW RD
2100 SDCo 92084 1108-D2
8800 SDCo 92040 1232-D3
16100 PWY 92064 1170-F4
E LAKEVIEW RD
13300 SDCo 92040 1232-D5
W LAKEVIEW RD
13200 SDCo 92040 1232-D5
LAKEVIEW ST
25700 SDCo 92026 1109-E2
LAKE VIEW TER
- SDCo 92028 998-G5
3300 SDCo 92029 1149-G3
LAKEVIEW TER
9200 SDCo 92040 1232-E5
LAKEVIEW WY
13300 SDCo 92040 1232-C3
LAKEVIEW GRANADA DR
13000 SDCo 92040 1232-C5
LAKE VISTA CIR
5600 SDCo 92003 1068-B2
LAKE VISTA DR
5600 SDCo 92003 1068-B2
LAKE VISTA TER
30900 SDCo 92003 1068-B3
LAKEWIND ST
1600 ELCJ 92020 1251-B2
LAKE WOHLFORD CT
24800 ESCN 92027 1110-F4

LAKE WOHLFORD LN
16600 SDCo 92082 1091-C3
LAKE WOHLFORD RD
3600 ESCN 92027 1110-F3
24800 SDCo 92027 1110-J2
25500 SDCo 92027 1111-A1
N LAKE WOHLFORD RD
25900 SDCo 92027 1091-C6
25900 SDCo 92027 1111-C1
25900 SDCo 92082 1091-C4
LAKEWOOD AV
- ESCN 92027 1130-C1
LAKEWOOD CT
4900 SD 92122 1228-G5
LAKEWOOD DR
- LMSA 91942 1251-A7
LAKEWOOD LN
200 OCN 92054 1106-C2
LAKEWOOD ST
3400 CRLB 92010 1106-J4
6100 SD 92122 1228-G5
LAKY LN
900 SDCo 92065 1152-C5
LALANI DR
- SDCo 91941 1271-G4
LA LARGA VISTA
9100 SDCo 91977 1291-B1
LAL BAGH LN
10300 SDCo 92026 1069-E3
LA LINDA DR
1400 SDCo 92078 1128-C3
LALLEY LN
6900 SD 92119 1250-J3
LA LOMA DR
1400 SDCo 92078 1128-C3
LA LOMA SERENA
2100 SDCo 92084 1088-C1
LA LOMITA DR
100 ESCN 92026 1109-H6
LA MAC LN
29100 SDCo 92082 1070-F7
LA MACARENA AV
2400 CRLB 92009 1147-G4
LA MADERA
1600 SDCo 92078 1128-C2
LA MADRESELVA
15500 SDCo 92067 1168-B7
LA MANCHA DR
1400 SD 92109 1268-A1
LA MANCHA PL
1300 CHV 91910 1311-B7
LA MANDA DR
15000 PWY 92064 1170-C7
LA MANTANZA
- SD 92127 1168-H7
- SD 92127 1188-H1
LA MANZANA LN
1700 ESCN 92026 1109-E6
LAMAR CT
- SDCo 91977 1271-A6
LAMAR ST
900 SDCo 92065 1152-D5
8600 SDCo 91977 1270-J6
8600 SDCo 91977 1271-A6
LA MARIQUITA SENDA
1600 SD 92173 1350-G2
LA MARQUE ST
2400 SD 92109 1248-B4
LAMAR SPRINGS CT
3100 SDCo 91977 1271-B6
LAMAS ST
5600 SD 92122 1228-B6
LAMBAR ST
1200 ESCN 92029 1129-G4
LAMBDA DR
6100 SD 92120 1250-C7
LAMBDA LN
5600 LMSA 91942 1250-J7
LAMBERT LN
5000 SD 92115 1270-E2
LAMBERT WY
6700 SD 92115 1270-E2
LAMBETH CT
2600 CRLB 92010 1106-J5
LA MEDIA RD
- CHV 91913 1311-D6
- CHV 91913 1331-D1
1200 SD 92154 1331-G7
1200 SD 92154 1351-G1
LAMENTIN CT
10800 SD 92124 1249-H1
LA MESA
- SMCS 92078 1129-C1
LA MESA AV
100 ENCT 92024 1147-B5
1000 SDCo 91977 1291-D2
LA MESA BLVD
7800 LMSA 91941 1270-H2
8600 LMSA 91941 1271-A2
8900 LMSA 91942 1271-A2
LA MESA CT
2100 SDCo 91977 1271-C7
2100 SDCo 91977 1291-D1
LA MESA CV
1400 SDCo 91977 1291-C2
LA MESITA PL
7300 LMSA 91941 1270-F2
LAMIA WY
4900 OCN 92056 1107-E5
LA MILLA
8000 SDCo 92067 1148-J5
LAMINACK LN
18900 SDCo 91935 (1314-G1 See Page 1294)
LA MIRADA AV
700 ENCT 92024 1147-C4
1100 ESCN 92026 1109-E5
LA MIRADA CT
- VSTA 92081 1108-A6
LA MIRADA DR
1400 SMCS 92078 1108-C7
2100 VSTA 92081 1107-J6
2400 VSTA 92081 1108-A6
4600 OCN 92057 1066-J7
LA MIRADA WY
1300 ESCN 92026 1109-E5
LAMONT ST
3800 SD 92109 1248-A5
LA MORADA CT
5800 SD 92124 1229-G7
LA MORADA DR
10300 SD 92124 1229-G7
LA MOREE RD
100 SMCS 92078 1128-J1
100 SMCS 92096 1128-J1
100 SMCS 92096 1129-A1
100 SMCS 92078 1129-A1
LAMOUR LN
- SDCo 92127 1169-A1
LAMPASAS WY
3900 SMCS 92078 1128-C1
LAMPLIGHT DR
800 SD 92037 1247-G4

LAMPLIGHTER RD
700 SMCS 92069 1109-A5
LAMPLITE LN
13200 SDCo 92040 1232-C7
LAN LN
9900 SDCo 92026 1089-D2
LANA DR
5900 SD 92117 1248-J1
LANA LN
4700 SD 92117 1248-J1
LANAI DR
1700 SDCo 92019 1252-B4
LANAI WY
- OCN 92057 1087-B1
LANAKAI LN
- CRLB 92011 1126-H5
LANAO LN
2300 SD 92154 1330-C7
LANCASHIRE PL
- SMCS 92069 1108-J4
LANCASHIRE WY
18500 SD 92128 1150-B5
LANCASTER DR
5500 SD 92120 1250-B7
LANCASTER RD
200 ImCo 92243 6559-H3
2800 CRLB 92010 1107-B5
LANCASTER CREEK RD
4300 SDCo 92026 1049-A4
4300 SDCo 92028 1048-J3
4300 SDCo 92028 1049-A4
LANCASTER MOUNTAIN RD
31800 SDCo 92026 1049-B6
LANCE AV
8800 SDCo 91977 1290-J4
LANCE CT
6400 SD 92120 1250-B6
LANCE DR
9900 SDCo 92040 1232-C3
LANCE PL
6200 SD 92120 1250-C6
LANCE ST
5700 SD 92120 1250-C6
LANCE WY
6400 SD 92120 1250-B6
LANCELOT DR
2600 OCN 92054 1086-E6
LANCER AV
100 OCN 92054 1086-F3
LANCER GN
1200 ESCN 92029 1129-F5
LANCER WY
3300 CRLB 92008 1106-G5
LANCER PARK AV
600 SMCS 92069 1109-C6
LANCEWOOD LN
- CRLB 92024 1147-E2
LANCEWOOD WY
2800 SDCo 92028 1048-C3
LANCHA ST
2700 SD 92111 1248-J6
LANDALE LN
100 SDCo 92019 1252-C5
LANDAU CT
5900 CRLB 92008 1127-D2
LANDAVO DR
900 SDCo 92027 1130-C4
LANDAVO RANCHO RD
1000 SDCo 92027 1130-C3
LANDBREEZE WY
11800 SD 92126 1209-A1
LANDFAIR CT
3600 SD 92130 1187-J4
LANDFAIR RD
13300 SD 92130 1187-J5
13500 SD 92130 1188-A4
LANDING DR
1700 VSTA 92081 1107-G4
LANDIS AV
100 CHV 91910 1310-B5
600 CHV 91910 1330-C1
LANDIS ST
2100 SD 92104 1269-C6
3600 SD 92105 1269-J5
5100 SD 92105 1270-A5
LANDMARK CT
- SMCS 92069 1108-J5
LANDMARK LN
37500 SDCo 92066 410-A9
LANDMARK PL
400 SMCS 92069 1108-J5
LANDON PL
7900 SD 92126 1209-B4
LANDQUIST DR
1600 ENCT 92024 1167-G1
LANDSCAPE DR
2700 SD 92139 1310-E2
LANDS END CT
1000 CRLB 92011 1127-A5
LANDS END WY
- OCN 92054 1086-B6
LANDSFORD WY
3500 CRLB 92010 1107-A3
LANE AV
900 CHV 91914 1311-G4
LA NEVASCA LN
2800 CRLB 92009 1147-H3
LANEWOOD CT
6800 SD 92111 1248-J4
LANEWOOD PL
800 ESCN 92026 1109-H3
LANG AV
2100 SDCo 91977 1291-A1
LANGDON LN
9000 SDCo 91977 1291-A1
LANGE AV
2600 SD 92122 1228-B6
LANGFORD
2600 SDCo 92084 1087-G1
LANGFORD ST
800 OCN 92054 1086-B6
LANGHOLM RD
8600 SDCo 92021 1232-F6
LANGLEY CT
10100 SDCo 92026 1109-E1
LANGLEY ST
300 SD 92102 1289-D4
LANGMUIR ST
2200 SD 92111 1248-H7
LANING RD
2600 SD 92101 1288-D1
2700 SD 92106 1288-C1
LA NOCHE DR
900 SMCS 92078 1128-D2
1100 SDCo 92078 1128-D2
LANOITAN AV
1300 NATC 91950 1310-B1
N LANOITAN AV
- NATC 91950 1290-B6
LA NORIA
600 ENCT 92024 1147-F5
4300 SDCo 92067 1167-J3
4700 SDCo 92067 1168-A2

LA NORIA DR
3600 OCN 92054 1086-F2
LANPHIER LN
2700 SDCo 92070 1135-E7
LANSDALE DR
4600 SD 92130 1188-C4
LANSDOWN LN
3200 SDCo 92065 1172-C3
LANSFORD LN
10500 SD 92126 1208-H4
LANSING CIR
300 ESCN 92025 1129-J2
LANSING DR
7600 LMGR 91945 1290-H2
LANSLEY WY
100 CHV 91910 1310-B5
LANSTON ST
6400 SD 92111 1248-H7
LANTANA AV
1400 CHV 91911 1330-H3
LANTANA CT
- SMCS 92069 1109-A5
LANTANA DR
- NATC 91950 1309-H1
4700 SD 92105 1269-J5
4900 SD 92105 1270-A6
LANTANA TER
7000 CRLB 92011 1127-A6
LANTANA WY
800 VSTA 92081 1108-A4
LANYARD PL
2300 CRLB 92008 1107-C7
LANZA CT
1000 SDCo 92078 1128-G4
LA ORILLA
4400 SDCo 92067 1167-J4
4400 SDCo 92067 1168-A4
LA ORQUIDA
7600 SDCo 92067 1148-H6
LA PALMA
7000 SDCo 92067 1168-F1
LA PALMA DR
700 SDCo 92028 1027-H3
LA PALMA ST
1300 SD 92109 1247-J7
1300 SD 92109 1248-A7
LA PALOMA
6300 OCN 92057 1067-E3
LA PALOMA AV
1200 ESCN 92026 1109-E5
LA PALOMA GN
1200 ESCN 92026 1109-E5
LA PALOMA ST
4100 SD 92107 1288-A1
4100 SD 92107 1287-J1
6400 CRLB 92009 1127-G5
LA PAZ DR
- IMP 92251 6499-G1
5000 SD 92113 1290-A5
5000 SD 92114 1290-A5
LA PAZ ST
2300 OCN 92054 1106-F2
LAPEER CT
9200 SNTE 92071 1231-A3
LA PERLA WY
4800 SDCo 91941 1271-C2
LA PINATA WY N
4200 OCN 92057 1086-J3
LA PINATA WY S
4200 OCN 92057 1086-J3
LA PINTURA DR
6100 SD 92037 1247-H1
LAPIS RD
- CRLB 92009 1127-G4
LAPIZ DR
8200 SD 92126 1209-B2
LA PLACE CT
5900 CRLB 92008 1127-E2
LA PLANCHA LN
2400 CRLB 92009 1147-G3
LA PLATA
- SD 92127 1168-H7
LA PLATA CT
15200 SDCo 92065 1173-E5
LA PLAYA AV
1400 SD 92109 1248-A7
LA PLAZA DR
1400 SDCo 92078 1128-C3
LA PLUMA CT
1000 SDCo 92078 1128-G4
LA PLUMA LN
2400 CRLB 92009 1147-G3
LAPORT ST
6100 LMSA 91942 1250-F6
LA PORTALADA DR
4100 CRLB 92010 1106-J5
LA POSADA DR
- SDCo 92004 (1099-F3 See Page 1098)
LA POSADA ST
1800 NATC 91950 1289-J6
1800 NATC 91950 1290-A6
LA POSADA WY
- SDCo 92036 1155-H4
LA POSTA CIR
2900 SDCo 91906 430-B7
2900 SDCo 91962 430-B7
LA POSTA RD
1800 SDCo 91906 1298-E3
1800 SDCo 91906 (1318-F1 See Page 1298)
2400 SDCo 91906 430-B7
LA POSTA TKTR
- SDCo 91906 1298-A5
3400 SDCo 91962 430-B7
LAPPED CIRCLE DR
3300 SDCo 92004 (1078-J6 See Page 1058)
LA PRADERA LN
500 ESCN 92026 1109-G2
500 SDCo 92026 1109-G2
LA PRESA AV
400 SDCo 91977 1291-C2
LA PRIMAVERA DR
30400 SDCo 92084 1068-A4
LA PUERTA PL
1800 LMGR 91945 1290-F1
LA PUERTE
- ESCN 92029 1129-F4
LA PURISMA WY
300 OCN 92057 1087-A2
LA QUEBRADA
700 ENCT 92024 1148-A6
LA QUINTA PL
4400 OCN 92057 1066-G7
LA RAMADA LN
2400 ESCN 92027 1130-E1
LARAMIE CT
7700 SD 92120 1250-C4
LARAMIE ST
300 SDCo 92004 1058-G6
LARAMIE WY
5500 SD 92120 1250-B4

STREET
Block City ZIP Pg-Grid

LARCH ST
4500 SD 92105 1289-J1
LARCHMONT ST
12700 PWY 92064 1170-D7
LARCHWOOD AV
5900 SD 92120 1250-C4
LARCHWOOD DR
500 SMCS 92069 1109-B6
1200 OCN 92056 1087-D2
LARCHWOOD WY
7700 SD 92120 1250-C4
LAREDO CT
1400 CHV 91902 1311-B3
LAREDO LN
3400 SDCo 92025 1150-E2
LAREDO ST
3600 CRLB 92010 1106-J4
LA REINA DR
1000 SDCo 92078 1128-D3
LARGA CIR
3400 SD 92110 1268-D5
LARGA CT
3100 SD 92110 1268-D6
LARGA VISTA
31400 SDCo 92082 1069-J2
LARGA VISTA CT
9100 SDCo 91977 1291-B1
LARGO LN
3100 SDCo 92026 1109-H2
LARIAT DR
- SNTE 92071 1231-C3
LARIAT LN
300 IMP 92251 6439-F5
10300 SDCo 91941 1271-E4
LARIAT WY
5400 OCN 92057 1067-D7
LARIO LN
9600 SDCo 92127 1169-E2
LARK GN
2100 ESCN 92026 1109-E5
LARK ST
900 ELCJ 92021 1251-H5
3400 SD 92103 1268-H5
7700 SNTE 92071 1230-G7
LARK WY
200 OCN 92057 1086-J6
LARKDALE AV
8200 SD 92123 1249-C5
LARKDALE PL
3200 SD 92123 1249-C5
LARK FIELD CT
- SD 92130 1188-A5
LARKHAVEN DR
1500 CHV 91911 1330-F4
LARKHAVEN GN
1700 ESCN 92026 1109-D4
LARK HILL DR
1100 VSTA 92084 1088-A2
LARKIN PL
2600 SD 92123 1249-D6
LARKRIDGE ST
9000 SNTE 92071 1231-G6
LARK SONG LN
1000 ENCT 92024 1147-J5
1100 ENCT 92024 1148-A5
LARKSPUR CT
800 SMCS 92078 1128-F3
1500 CHV 91913 1311-C7
LARKSPUR DR
1900 SDCo 91901 1233-J4
LARKSPUR LN
1100 CRLB 92008 1106-F6
1500 SDCo 92028 1028-E4
LARKSPUR ST
4600 SD 92107 1268-A5
LARK VISTA DR
- SDCo 92127 1169-F3
LARKWOOD CT
3100 SDCo 92028 1048-D3
LARMAR AV
- CRLB 92009 1127-G5
LARMIER CIR
11400 SD 92131 1209-J2
11400 SD 92131 1210-A2
LA ROCA GRANDE
10100 SDCo 92026 1069-D1
LA ROCHELLE AV
- CHV 91913 1311-E7
LA ROCHI WY
700 SDCo 92019 1252-C6
LA ROSA DR
3800 SMCS 92078 1108-D7
LA ROUCHE DR
8400 SD 92119 1250-J4
LARRABEE AV
9400 SD 92123 1249-F6
LARRABEE PL
2400 SD 92123 1249-F6
LARRY LN
- SDCo 91901 1255-F5
- ESCN 92025 1130-A6
LARRY ST
15100 PWY 92064 1170-D7
LARSEN RD
300 ImCo 92251 6439-A2
500 ImCo 92251 431-B4
LARSEN WY
8600 LMSA 91941 1271-A2
LARSON LN
1500 SDCo 92028 1027-J4
LA RUE AV
900 SDCo 92028 1027-G3
LA RUE WY
500 ELCJ 92021 1251-H4
LA RUEDA DR
4600 SDCo 91941 1271-F3
LA RUEDA RD
900 SDCo 92084 1088-D7
1000 SDCo 92084 1108-D1
LARWOOD RD
1000 SD 92114 1290-F2
1100 LMGR 91945 1290-F2
1100 LMGR 92114 1290-F2
LA SALINA PL
1400 OCN 92054 1106-C2
LA SALINA ST
300 OCN 92054 1106-C2
LA SALLE CT
1300 VSTA 92081 1107-J4
2000 CHV 91913 1311-E5
LA SALLE ST
3900 SD 92110 1268-C4
LAS ALTURAS TER
5500 SD 92114 1290-B4
LAS ANIMAS
5200 SD 92114 1290-B4
LAS ARBOLEDAS
6600 SDCo 92067 1148-F6
LAS ARDILLAS
- SDCo 92026 1109-G4
LAS BANCAS CT
1000 CHV 91911 1330-F2
LAS BANDERAS DR
100 SOLB 92075 1167-H7

LAS BRISAS CT
7300 CRLB 92009 1147-J1
LAS BRISAS DR
400 ESCN 92027 1110-E6
LAS BRISAS TR
3000 SDCo 91935 1292-G2
LAS BRISAS WY
900 ENCT 92007 1167-E3
LAS BUJIAS CT
1600 SD 92173 1350-G2
LAS CANAS CT
100 SOLB 92075 1167-D6
LAS CANAS WY
100 SOLB 92075 1167-D7
LAS CASITAS DR
- SDCo 92004 (1099-F4 See Page 1098)
LAS COLINAS
6300 SDCo 92067 1168-E3
LAS COLINAS DR
- SDCo 92029 1129-J7
LAS CONICAS
9900 SD 92129 1189-F5
LAS CRUCES AV
3900 SMCS 92078 1128-C1
LAS CUESTAS
16500 SDCo 92067 1168-F4
LA SELVA RD
4700 SDCo 91935 1274-A3
LA SELVA WY
7900 CRLB 92009 1147-G3
LA SENA AV
7000 SD 92114 1290-F4
LA SENCILLA
5300 SDCo 92067 1168-C4
LAS ENCINAS DR
19100 SDCo 92065 1172-A5
LA SENDA WY
800 CHV 91910 1310-H7
LA SENDITA
5900 SDCo 92067 1168-D3
LASER LN
9300 SDCo 91941 1271-B4
LA SERENA
2500 SDCo 92025 1130-D7
LAS ESTANCIAS DR
500 CHV 91910 1310-J4
LAS ESTRELLAS
- SMCS 92078 1129-C1
LAS FLORES
- SMCS 92078 1129-C1
LAS FLORES DR
- CHV 91910 1310-B4
1000 CRLB 92008 1106-E4
3800 SDCo 92008 1047-J3
N LAS FLORES DR
- SMCS 92078 1108-D6
100 SMCS 92069 1108-D6
S LAS FLORES DR
300 SMCS 92078 1108-C7
700 SMCS 92078 1128-C1
LAS FLORES RD
- CALX 92231 6620-F7
LAS FLORES ST
100 SD 92114 1290-B4
LAS FLORES TER
100 SD 92114 1290-B5
LAS HACIENDAS
- SD 92127 1168-J7
- SD 92127 1169-A7
LASHLEE LN
1800 SD 92173 1350-F3
LA SIERRA DR
600 SMCS 92078 1108-C7
600 SMCS 92078 1128-C1
LA SIESTA WY
1800 NATC 91950 1310-B1
LASKEY LN
9700 SDCo 91941 1271-D4
LAS LIDIA CT
6700 SD 92114 1290-E5
LASLO DR
1600 SDCo 92025 1130-C4
LAS LOMAS
2000 VSTA 92084 1088-C3
LAS LOMAS DR
9300 SNTE 92071 1231-A3
LAS LOMAS RD
15600 SDCo 92021 1233-C2
LAS LOMAS ST
2100 SD 92107 1268-B7
LAS LUNAS
- SD 92127 1168-H7
LAS MANANAS
14800 SDCo 92067 1188-H1
LAS MANZANITAS RD
15400 SDCo 92065 1172-A4
LAS MIENTES LN
7900 CRLB 92009 1147-G3
LAS MILPAS
- SDCo 92040 1232-D7
LAS MONTANAS
- SDCo 91906 (1318-G6 See Page 1298)
18200 SDCo 92067 1148-C7
LAS NUBES CT
1200 SDCo 92078 1128-E3
LAS NUECES PL
7900 CRLB 92009 1147-G3
LAS NUEVAS
1000 SDCo 92028 1027-H4
LA SOBRINA CT
1300 SOLB 92014 1167-H7
1300 SOLB 92075 1167-H7
LA SOLANA DR
1000 SDCo 92028 1027-H2
LAS OLAS CT
- CRLB 92009 1147-H4
LA SOLDADERA
7200 SDCo 92067 1168-G2
LA SOLEDAD
- SDCo 92040 1232-B7
LA SOLEDAD WY
300 OCN 92057 1087-A2
LA SOMBRA CT
1200 ELCJ 92020 1251-D6
LA SOMBRA DR
400 ELCJ 92020 1251-D6
900 SMCS 92078 1128-E2
1100 SDCo 92078 1128-E2
LAS PALMAS AV
2600 ESCN 92025 1130-A7
3000 ESCN 92025 1150-B1
3100 SDCo 92025 1130-B7
LAS PALMAS CV
2700 SD 92014 1187-J7
LAS PALMAS DR
700 VSTA 92081 1107-G1
2000 CRLB 92011 1127-D4
LAS PALMAS LN
1400 ESCN 92026 1109-E6
LAS PALMAS RD
14000 SDCo 91935 1292-H3

LAS PALMAS SQ
4100 SD 92122 1228-C3
LAS PALOMAS
5400 SDCo 92067 1168-C7
LA SPAZIA WY
- SD 92108 1249-D7
LAS PESETAS
- SDCo 92067 1149-A3
LAS PLANIDERAS
15100 SDCo 92067 1168-B6
15100 SDCo 92067 1188-B1
N LAS POSAS RD
- SMCS 92078 1108-E7
100 SMCS 92069 1108-E5
S LAS POSAS RD
200 SMCS 92078 1108-E7
300 SMCS 92078 1128-E1
LAS POTRAS WY
13500 SDCo 92040 1232-D5
LAS PULGAS RD
- SDCo 92055 408-L7
LAS QUINTAS
14700 SDCo 92067 1188-F2
LAS RAMBLAS
700 SDCo 92028 1027-H3
LAS REPOLAS
17600 SDCo 92067 1148-J6
LAS ROSAS CT
1000 CHV 91910 1311-B7
LASSEN DR
4900 OCN 92056 1107-F3
LASSEN LN
4300 CRLB 92010 1106-J4
LASSEN ST
1800 SD 92139 1290-E6
LASSEN PEAK PL
1100 CHV 91913 1311-E6
LASSIE LN
8800 SD 92123 1249-D5
LASSING RD
- SD 92152 1288-A5
LASSO WY
9200 SNTE 92071 1231-A2
LAST CHANCE TR
7500 SDCo 92036 (1158-C1 See Page 1138)
LAST DOLLAR TR
7400 SDCo 92036 1138-C7
LAS TIENDAS WY
- OCN 92056 1106-J2
LA STRADA DR
700 SDCo 92028 1027-H3
LAS TUNAS DR
5900 OCN 92057 1067-D4
LA SUBIDA WY
1900 SDCo 92078 1128-E3
LA SUVIDA DR
9300 LMSA 91942 1251-B7
LAS VEGAS DR
3300 OCN 92054 1086-E5
LASVEN CT
3000 SDCo 92019 1272-C5
LAS VENTANAS
6700 SDCo 92067 1188-H1
LAS VERAS PL
500 ESCN 92026 1109-G2
500 SDCo 92026 1109-G2
LAS VILLAS WY
1300 ESCN 92026 1109-G7
LAS VISTAS RD
900 SDCo 92028 998-C7
900 SDCo 92028 1028-D1
LAS VISTILLAS LN
1200 SDCo 92078 1128-E3
LA TARA LN
2300 SDCo 92028 1047-G2
LA TEMPRA CTE
1300 CHV 91911 1330-D4
LA TENAJA TR
4000 SDCo 92036 1156-B3
LA TENISTA
6100 SDCo 92067 1168-F7
LA TERRAZA BLVD
- ESCN 92025 1129-G4
LATHROP LN
100 SDCo 92021 1252-J3
LATHROP RD
- ImCo 92251 6439-J5
LA TIERA DR
4200 OCN 92056 1107-C3
LA TIERRA CT
1700 SDCo 92078 1128-C2
LA TIERRA DR
800 SDCo 92078 1128-C2
800 SMCS 92078 1128-C2
LA TIERRA LN
1600 SDCo 92078 1128-C2
LATIGO CV
1100 CHV 91915 1311-F6
LATIGO RD
27100 SDCo 92082 1091-F4
LATIGO RW
3400 ENCT 92024 1148-D3
LATIGO CANYON PL
- SD 92129 1188-J4
LATIMER CT
5900 SD 92114 1290-C4
LATIMER ST
100 SD 92114 1290-C4
LA TINADA CT
2400 CRLB 92009 1147-G3
LATISHA PL
700 ELCJ 92021 1251-H4
LA TORTOLA
12500 SD 92129 1189-F6
LA TORTOLA CT
9800 SD 92129 1189-F5
LA TORTOLA PL
9800 SD 92129 1189-F6
LA TORTUGA DR
800 VSTA 92081 1087-F7
800 VSTA 92081 1107-E1
LA TRIESTE PL
2900 ESCN 92025 1150-A1
LATROBE CIR
7100 SD 92139 1290-G7
LA TRUCHA ST
14200 SD 92129 1189-C2
LATTICE LN
- CHV 91915 1331-H2
LAUDER ST
5900 SD 92139 1310-D1
LAUGHTON WY
700 VSTA 92081 1107-F2
LAU HALA CANYON RD
1000 SDCo 92081 1107-G3
1000 VSTA 92081 1107-G3
LAURA CT
7200 SD 92120 1250-B5
LAURA DR
2000 ESCN 92027 1110-B5
LAURA LN
1000 ESCN 92025 1130-D6

LAURA ST
5300 SD 92120 1250-B5
LAURALYNN PL
1500 OCN 92054 1106-D2
LAURASHAWN LN
2900 ESCN 92026 1109-H1
2900 SDCo 92026 1109-H1
LAUREE ST
700 ELCJ 92020 1251-F7
LAUREL AV
- NATC 91950 1289-J7
1300 CHV 91911 1330-H3
LAUREL CIR
- VSTA 92081 1107-E1
LAUREL DR
100 SMCS 92069 1108-H5
29400 SDCo 91906 (1297-E5 See Page 1296)
LAUREL LN
- ELCJ 92019 1251-J6
9700 SDCo 92029 1149-E2
19200 SDCo 92065 1192-B2
LAUREL PTH
- SDCo 92026 1089-F4
LAUREL RD
1500 OCN 92054 1086-F7
1500 OCN 92054 1106-E1
LAUREL ST
100 SD 92101 1289-A1
200 SD 92101 1288-H1
1400 OCN 92054 1086-B6
2900 SD 92104 1289-E1
3000 SD 92104 1269-E7
4300 SD 92105 1269-H7
5000 SD 92105 1270-A7
5200 SD 92105 1290-A1
12200 SDCo 92040 1232-B3
LAUREL CHASE DR
- SD 92130 1208-E1
LAUREL GROVE DR
- CHV 91915 (1312-A7 See Page 1293)
LAURELHURST CT
9200 SD 92126 1209-D2
LAUREL LEE LN
11900 SDCo 92040 1231-J6
LAURELRIDGE CT
6700 SD 92120 1250-D4
LAUREL RIDGE DR
31500 SDCo 92082 1069-J1
31500 SDCo 92082 1070-A1
LAURELRIDGE RD
7700 SD 92120 1250-D4
LAUREL TREE LN
- CRLB 92011 1127-A3
LAUREL VALLEY DR
2200 SDCo 92084 1068-E7
LAURELWOOD CT
800 SMCS 92069 1109-A6
LAURELWOOD ST
900 CRLB 92011 1127-A5
14700 PWY 92064 1190-D1
LAURELWOOD WY
700 ELCJ 92021 1251-G4
LAUREN CT
- ENCT 92024 1147-D3
LAUREN LN
- SDCo 91901 1253-G2
LAUREN WY
- SNTE 92071 1231-E3
LAURENTIAN DR
9300 SD 92129 1189-D2
LAURETTA ST
5400 SD 92110 1268-F3
LAURIE CIR
2000 CRLB 92008 1106-G4
LAURIE LN
2400 SD 92105 1269-H7
2400 SD 92105 1289-H1
5400 SDCo 92067 1168-D4
LAURINDA PL
2000 SD 92105 1289-J1
LAURINE LN
100 SDCo 92028 1027-F5
E LAURINE LN
100 SDCo 92028 1027-G5
LAURISTON DR
1100 SD 92154 1350-C1
LAUSANNE DR
4000 SD 92114 1290-F3
S LAUSANNE DR
100 SD 92114 1290-F4
LAVA CT
7900 LMSA 91941 1270-H4
LAVADE LN
5300 SDCo 91902 1311-A2
LAVALA LN
1700 ELCJ 92021 1252-C1
LA VALHALLA PL
1700 SDCo 92019 1272-B3
LA VALLE PLATEADA
6300 SDCo 92067 1168-E2
LA VANCO CT
6400 CRLB 92009 1127-G5
LAVANDULA CT
- SD 92130 1188-G6
LA VARONA PL
100 ESCN 92025 1150-A1
LAVELL ST
9100 SDCo 91941 1271-B3
9200 LMSA 91941 1271-B3
LAVENDER CT
- SMCS 92069 1109-A5
LAVENDER LN
200 SDCo 92083 1108-C4
LAVENDER WY
5800 SD 92130 1188-G3
7000 CRLB 92011 1127-A6
LAVENDER POINT LN
- SDCo 92026 1069-D2
LAVENDER STAR DR
9500 SDCo 92127 1169-D2
LA VENTA DR
13200 PWY 92064 1190-D4
LA VENTANA CT
1000 SDCo 92078 1128-G4
LA VERDE DR
1600 SDCo 92078 1128-B3
LA VERDE LN
1200 SDCo 92078 1128-B3
LA VEREDA
8100 SD 92037 1227-G5
LAVERNE PL
4000 SD 92104 1269-F5
LA VETA AV
100 ENCT 92024 1147-B5
LA VIA FELIZ
16400 SDCo 92067 1168-E4
LA VIDA CIR
700 VSTA 92083 1087-G5
LA VIDA CT
1100 CHV 91915 1311-H5
LAVIGNE RD
- CALX 92231 6620-J7

LAVIGNE RD
- ImCo 92231 6620-J7
LA VINE LN
1500 SDCo 92084 1108-B1
LA VISTA
- ESCN 92026 1109-F7
600 ENCT 92024 1147-F5
LA VISTA AV
1400 ELCJ 92020 1251-D6
9700 SDCo 91941 1271-C1
LA VISTA WY
12700 PWY 92064 1190-D5
LA VITA CT
10400 SD 92131 1210-A3
LA VONNE AV
900 SDCo 92028 1027-G3
LA VUELTA
100 SMCS 92069 1108-H3
LAW ST
600 SD 92109 1247-H5
1100 SMCS 92078 1128-E1
1600 SD 92109 1248-A5
LAWANA ST
1300 VSTA 92083 1087-E7
LAWFORD CT
7600 LMGR 91945 1290-G1
LAWFORD PL
7300 SD 92114 1290-F4
7600 LMGR 91945 1290-G1
LAWLER CT
4600 SDCo 91941 1271-C3
LAWNDALE RD
- SDCo 92019 1272-B2
LAWNDALE ST
1900 SD 92154 1350-C3
LAWNSDALE PL
- SMCS 92069 1108-J5
LAWNVIEW DR
400 CHV 91910 1310-F6
LAWRENCE LN
1800 SDCo 92065 1172-F1
2900 SDCo 92025 1130-E7
2900 SDCo 92025 1150-E1
LAWRENCE ST
2800 SD 92106 1288-A4
3400 CRLB 92010 1106-J4
LAWRENCE WELK CT
28300 SDCo 92026 1088-J2
LAWRENCE WELK DR
8800 SDCo 92026 1089-A1
28800 SDCo 92026 1088-J1
LAWRENCE WELK LN
29100 SDCo 92026 1088-J1
29200 SDCo 92026 1068-H7
LAWSON HILLS RD
18100 SDCo 91935 1274-C2
LAWSON VALLEY RD
15200 SDCo 91935 1273-H4
15200 SDCo 91935 1274-A3
LAWTON DR
2200 LMGR 91945 1270-J7
2200 LMGR 91945 1290-J1
LAYANG LAYANG CIR
4000 CRLB 92008 1106-F7
LAYLA CT
4200 SD 92154 1350-G1
LAYLA WY
4200 SD 92154 1350-G1
LAYNE PL
1700 SDCo 92019 1272-C3
LAYTON ST
900 ELCJ 92021 1251-G2
LAYTONVILLE PL
1400 CHV 91913 1331-C1
LAZANJA DR
- SD 92127 1168-J7
- SD 92127 1188-J1
LAZANJA PASS
- SD 92127 1188-J1
LAZAROFF LN
- SDCo 91935 1274-A2
LAZO CT
800 CHV 91910 1310-H6
LAZY ACRES DR
- SDCo 92040 1191-E5
- SDCo 92064 1191-E5
LAZY CIRCLE DR
700 VSTA 92081 1107-G2
LAZY CLOUDS PT
6800 SD 92120 1250-D4
LAZY CREEK RD
15100 SDCo 92021 1232-H2
LAZY DOG WY
- SDCo 92021 1232-H4
LAZY H DR
- SDCo 92082 1071-B1
15600 SDCo 92061 1051-B7
15600 SDCo 92082 1051-B7
LAZY JAYS WY
3800 SDCo 92036 1155-H3
LAZY LADDER DR
200 SDCo 92004 (1078-F2 See Page 1058)
LAZY S DR
1600 SDCo 92004 1058-G5
2100 SDCo 92004 (1078-H1 See Page 1058)
LAZY TRAIL CT
5900 SDCo 91902 1311-C3
L DOWE CT
- CALX 92231 6620-H6
LEA ST
5200 SD 92105 1270-B5
LEADA WY
24700 SDCo 92065 1173-G3
LEADROPE WY
5800 SDCo 91902 1311-B2
LEAF CT
6200 SD 92114 1290-D5
LEAF LN
1100 SDCo 92026 1109-E7
LEAF TER
1200 SD 92114 1290-D5
LEAF PINE CT
- SDCo 92026 1089-B2
LEAFWOOD PL
2000 ENCT 92024 1147-H6
10300 SD 92131 1209-G4
LEAH LN
800 SDCo 92029 1149-H1
LEAILA LN
13100 PWY 92064 1190-H5
LEANING TREE LN
13300 PWY 92064 1190-H4
E LEANNA CT
200 CHV 91911 1330-F2
LEANNA ST
- CHV 91911 1330-E2
LEAR LN
3500 CRLB 92008 1106-G5
LEARY ST
10300 SD 92124 1249-G2
LEASE RD
- SDCo 92066 410-A8

LEAST TERN CT
12000 SD 92129 1188-J7
LEATA TER
1500 SDCo 91901 1233-J7
LEA TERRACE DR
11000 SNTE 92071 1231-G6
LEATHERS RD
1100 ImCo 92283 432-D4
LEATHERS ST
4500 SD 92117 1248-B1
LEATHERWOOD ST
1900 SD 92154 1350-C3
LEBANON RD
28600 SDCo 91962 1237-B6
LE BARRON RD
5200 SD 92115 1269-J2
LEBAUN DR
1800 LMGR 91945 1290-H1
LEBON DR
3300 SD 92122 1228-B3
LECHUZA LN
100 SDCo 91977 1290-J5
LE CLAIR LN
400 SDCo 92026 1109-G3
LE CONTE ST
700 OCN 92057 1086-G5
7300 SD 92114 1290-F4
LEDESMA LN
1200 SDCo 92065 1172-F1
LEDGE AV
2100 SDCo 91977 1291-D1
LEDGE ST
- SMCS 92078 1128-G5
LEDGESIDE LN
2100 SDCo 91977 1271-D7
2100 SDCo 91977 1291-D1
LEDGESIDE ST
9900 SDCo 91977 1291-D1
9900 SDCo 91977 1271-D7
LEDGETOP PL
2600 SDCo 91977 1271-D7
LEDGEVIEW AV
2100 SDCo 91977 1271-E7
LEDGEVIEW LN
2500 SDCo 91977 1271-D7
LEDGEVIEW PL
2500 SDCo 91977 1271-D7
LEDGEWOOD LN
200 SD 92114 1290-G5
LEDGEWOOD PL
7400 SD 92114 1290-G5
LEE AV
800 CALX 92231 6680-E1
900 CALX 92231 6620-E7
2100 ESCN 92027 1110-C6
4400 LMSA 91941 1270-G3
LEE CIR
500 CHV 91911 1330-H2
LEE CT
- SD 92101 1288-D1
- SDCo 92026 1109-F2
2000 CRLB 92008 1106-G5
LEE DR
1300 OCN 92056 1087-E4
2000 ESCN 92027 1110-C6
LEE RD
500 ImCo 92251 6439-D5
500 IMP 92251 6439-D5
LEE ST
4300 SD 92109 1248-C6
LEEANN LN
300 ENCT 92024 1147-B4
LEEDS LN
- PWY 92064 1190-C4
LEEDS ST
4000 SD 92121 1228-C1
LEEPISH DR
- OCN 92054 1086-E3
LEEWARD AV
- SMCS 92078 1128-F6
LEEWARD CT
300 OCN 92054 1086-F6
LEEWARD ST
7000 CRLB 92011 1126-J6
LEGACY CT
14200 SDCo 92021 1232-G6
LEGACY DR
1400 SMCS 92069 1108-H5
LEGACY LN
14200 SDCo 92021 1232-G6
LEGACY PL
12700 SD 92131 1210-C2
LEGACY RD
12600 SD 92131 1210-C1
LEGACY TER
11300 SD 92131 1210-C2
LEGACY CANYON PL
11300 SD 92131 1210-C2
LEGACY CANYON WY
12700 SD 92131 1210-C2
LEGATE CT
500 CHV 91910 1310-F5
LEGAYE DR
1500 ENCT 92007 1167-E2
LEGEND WY
- SDCo 92026 1109-G1
LEGENDALE DR
11500 SDCo 92040 1211-G6
LEGEND ROCK RD
10200 SDCo 92026 1089-E5
LEGHORN AV
400 SD 92114 1290-E5
LEGOLAND DR
- CRLB 92008 1126-H2
LEHARDY ST
2800 SD 92136 1289-E6
LEHIGH AV
700 CHV 91913 1311-E5
LEHIGH CT
2800 OCN 92056 1087-A7
LEHIGH ST
1300 SD 92110 1268-E2
LEHNER AV
500 SDCo 92026 1109-H5
800 ESCN 92026 1109-H5
1100 SDCo 92027 1109-H5
1100 SDCo 92027 1110-A4
LEHRER DR
4500 SD 92117 1228-G7
LEICESTER ST
7000 SD 92120 1250-A5
LEICESTER WY
5100 SD 92120 1250-A5
LEIGH AV
8700 SDCo 91977 1291-A5
LEIGHTON CIR
- CRLB 92009 1127-G2
LEIGHTON CT
2100 SD 92139 1290-F7
LEILA LN
10300 SNTE 92071 1231-B1
LEILA WY
9500 SNTE 92071 1231-E5

LEILANI WY
2900 SD 92154 1330-C7
LEISURE LN
8600 SDCo 92026 1068-J6
LEISURE VILLAGE DR
4600 OCN 92056 1107-E4
LEISURE VILLAGE WY
4600 OCN 92056 1107-F4
LE JEUNE ST
- SDCo 92055 1067-A2
LEJOS DR
1900 SDCo 92025 1130-B5
LELAND PL
700 ELCJ 92019 1251-J6
700 SDCo 92019 1251-J6
LELAND ST
800 SDCo 91977 1291-A3
3600 SD 92106 1268-C5
3600 SD 92110 1268-C5
LELAND WY
1300 SDCo 92026 1109-E6
LEMA WY
6700 SD 92119 1250-F5
LEMAIRE DR
- RivC 92590 998-G2
LEMARAND AV
6500 SD 92115 1270-D6
LEMAT PL
- SD 92154 1350-H2
LE MAY AV
500 SD 92154 1330-E6
LEMIRE CT
300 CHV 91910 1310-F7
LEMIRE DR
300 CHV 91910 1310-F7
LEMNOS WY
4000 OCN 92056 1107-E5
LEMON AV
600 VSTA 92084 1087-H5
600 ELCJ 92020 1251-E7
1200 ELCJ 92020 1271-E1
2000 ESCN 92029 1129-H6
2000 SDCo 92029 1129-H6
3400 SD 92123 1249-E4
7400 LMGR 91945 1270-F6
8000 LMSA 91941 1270-J2
8600 LMSA 91941 1271-A2
9100 SDCo 91941 1271-B2
LEMON CIR
7900 LMSA 91941 1270-H3
LEMON LN
3200 LMGR 91945 1270-J6
LEMON PL
1200 SDCo 92027 1130-D4
LEMON ST
1300 OCN 92054 1086-B6
9000 SDCo 91977 1271-A7
LEMONA AV
3500 SD 92105 1270-A6
LEMONBERRY LN
- CRLB 92024 1147-E2
LEMON BLOSSOM LN
- SDCo 92028 1027-J6
- SDCo 92028 1028-A6
LEMON BLOSSOM RD
- SDCo 92082 1071-A6
LEMONCREST DR
9500 SDCo 92040 1231-J5
9500 SDCo 92040 1232-A4
LEMON DROP LN
400 VSTA 92081 1107-H1
LEMON GROVE AV
900 LMGR 91945 1290-F2
900 SD 91945 1290-F2
900 SD 92114 1290-F2
2200 LMGR 91945 1270-G7
3700 LMGR 91941 1270-G5
3700 LMSA 91941 1270-G5
LEMON GROVE DR
100 SDCo 92028 1047-F4
LEMON GROVE RD
- SDCo 92055 1085-H3
LEMON GROVE WY
7800 LMGR 91945 1270-H5
LEMON HEIGHTS DR
1700 OCN 92056 1087-D4
LEMON HILL RD
- SDCo 92061 1030-J7
LEMON LEAF DR
- CRLB 92011 1127-B5
LEMON PINE CT
13000 SD 92129 1189-C5
LEMONSEED DR
4100 SD 92154 1330-G7
LEMON TREE CT
- SMCS 92078 1128-F6
3900 SD 92130 1208-A3
LEMONWOOD CT
500 OCN 92054 1086-F2
LEMONWOOD DR
- SDCo 92028 1047-F7
LEMONWOOD LN
1900 VSTA 92081 1107-J4
7000 LMGR 91945 1270-F6
9900 SD 92124 1249-G1
LEMORA LN
3200 SDCo 92025 1130-F6
LEN CT
10400 SNTE 92071 1231-E2
LEN ST
10400 SNTE 92071 1231-E2
LEN WY
10400 SNTE 92071 1231-E2
LENDEE DR
1700 ESCN 92025 1130-C4
1700 SDCo 92025 1130-C4
LENINE DR
30300 SDCo 92082 1070-A4
LENNIE DR
30300 SDCo 92082 1069-J4
LENNON LN
29000 SDCo 92026 1089-C1
LENNY LN
300 SDCo 92021 1252-H4
LENORE DR
4600 SD 92115 1270-D1
4600 SD 92115 1270-E3
4700 SD 92115 1270-E3
5000 SD 92115 1270-D1
5000 SD 92115 1270-D2
5000 SD 92115 1270-D1
5100 SD 92115 1270-D1
LENORE ST
5100 OCN 92057 1067-A5
LENOX CT
3700 CRLB 92010 1107-A4
LENOX DR
5100 SD 92114 1290-B2
LENREY AV
400 ELCN 92243 6499-F7
1800 ELCN 92243 6559-E1
LENREY CT
- ELCN 92243 6559-D1

STREET Block City ZIP Pg-Grid

LENSER WY
700 ESCN 92025 1129-G2
LENTEJA LN
13600 SDCo 92040 1232-D3
LENTO LN
300 SDCo 92021 1252-H3
LEO CT
2000 ESCN 92026 1109-F5
LEO ST
5000 SD 92115 1270-D2
LEOMA LN
100 CHV 91911 1330-E3
LEON AV
1500 SD 92154 1349-J2
1700 SD 92154 1350-A2
LEON LN
1400 SDCo 92036 1156-D2
LEON ST
4400 SD 92107 1287-H1
5100 OCN 92057 1067-B5
LEON WY
3400 SDCo 92028 1028-D1
LEONA LN
12200 PWY 92064 1190-B4
LEONARD AV
300 OCN 92054 1106-B1
LEONARD ST
2800 NATC 91950 1310-C2
LEONE AV
- SDCo 91905 1300-C7
LEONE WY
- PWY 92064 1190-B2
LEONEY CT
15500 SDCo 91935 1293-E1
LEONEY LN
15500 SDCo 91935 1293-E1
LEORA LN
600 SMCS 92069 1129-E1
1600 ENCT 92024 1147-B2
LEPPERT CT
800 SD 92114 1290-F3
LEPPERT ST
800 SD 92114 1290-F3
LEPRECHAUN LN
32200 SDCo 92003 1048-G6
LEPUS RD
8500 SD 92126 1209-C1
LERIDA DR
4200 SD 92115 1270-D4
LERKAS WY
4900 OCN 92056 1107-E5
LERMAS CT
- LMGR 91945 1290-F1
LEROY ST
1000 SD 92106 1288-B2
LES RD
9000 SNTE 92071 1231-A5
LESA RD
5400 LMSA 91942 1270-G1
LES ARBRES PL
10400 SD 92131 1210-A3
LES FLEURS TER
10400 SD 92131 1210-A3
LESLIE CT
1400 SMCS 92069 1109-D7
1400 SMCS 92069 1129-D1
LESLIE LN
100 ESCN 92026 1109-H6
400 SDCo 92026 1109-H6
LESLIE RD
900 ELCJ 92020 1251-F7
LESTER AV
7800 LMGR 91945 1270-H6
LETHBRIDGE WY
9200 SD 92129 1189-D2
LETICIA DR
9300 SNTE 92071 1230-H6
LETTON ST
100 SDCo 92065 1152-E7
LETTUCE ST
- ImCo 92249 6560-B7
LEUCADIA AV
8200 SD 92114 1290-H3
LEUCADIA BLVD
100 ENCT 92024 1147-B4
W LEUCADIA BLVD
100 ENCT 92024 1147-A4
LEUCADIA SCENIC CT
1900 ENCT 92024 1147-B2
LEUCADIA VILLAGE CT
1600 ENCT 92024 1147-B2
LEUCITE PL
- CRLB 92009 1127-G5
LEVANT LN
- CHV 91913 1311-F7
- CHV 91913 1331-F1
LEVANT ST
6900 SD 92111 1248-J6
LEVANT WY
200 OCN 92057 1087-A1
LEVANTE ST
- CRLB 92024 1147-E3
2100 CRLB 92009 1147-F1
LEVEE DR
3500 CRLB 92010 1107-B3
LEVEE RD
1500 ImCo 92283 432-E5
LEVITA CT
15000 PWY 92064 1170-C7
LEW LN
- CHV 91913 1331-F2
LEWIS
14100 SDCo 92040 1232-H5
LEWIS CT
1400 VSTA 92081 1107-J5
LEWIS LN
2600 CRLB 92008 1106-E4
13900 ESCN 92027 1110-F4
LEWIS ST
100 SD 92103 1268-H5
4000 OCN 92056 1087-B7
4200 VSTA 92083 1087-B7
E LEWIS ST
100 SD 92103 1269-A5
W LEWIS ST
200 SD 92103 1269-A5
300 SD 92103 1268-J5
LEWISON AV
5200 SD 92120 1250-B5
LEWISON CT
5200 SD 92120 1250-A5
LEWISON DR
7000 SD 92120 1250-B5
LEWISON PL
5200 SD 92120 1250-A5
LEWISTON ST
13800 SD 92128 1190-A2
LEXINE LN
700 ESCN 92025 1130-C5
700 SDCo 92025 1130-C5
LEXINGTON AV
1300 ELCJ 92019 1252-A5
1600 SDCo 92019 1252-B5
E LEXINGTON AV
1000 ELCJ 92020 1251-H5
1200 ELCJ 92019 1251-H5
1200 ELCJ 92019 1252-A5
W LEXINGTON AV
600 ELCJ 92020 1251-E6
LEXINGTON CIR
400 OCN 92057 1086-J3
2900 CRLB 92010 1107-B5
LEXINGTON CT
- OCN 92057 1086-J4
LEXINGTON DR
1200 VSTA 92084 1088-A6
LEXINGTON ST
1500 IMPB 91932 1349-H2
LEYENDEKKER CT
9500 SDCo 92040 1232-B4
LEYENDEKKER RD
12500 SDCo 92040 1232-B4
LEYTE RD
1100 CORD 92118 1309-C5
LEYTE POINT DR
6700 SD 92139 1290-F7
LIBBY ST
100 OCN 92054 1086-C6
LIBELLE CT
12100 SD 92131 1210-B1
LIBERTAD DR
17100 SD 92127 1169-H2
LIBERTY DR
300 SMCS 92069 1108-G7
LIBERTY PL
- CRLB 92009 1127-G2
1500 ESCN 92025 1129-J5
LIBERTY WY
1200 VSTA 92081 1127-J1
1200 VSTA 92081 1128-A1
LIBERTY CREEK PL
1400 CHV 91913 1331-B2
LIBRA DR
8700 SD 92126 1209-D2
LIBRA LN
- SD 92126 1209-E7
LIBRE GN
100 ESCN 92025 1130-A5
LICIA WY
12100 SD 92129 1189-A7
LIDDIARD ST
2500 ELCJ 92020 1251-B2
LIDO CT
700 SD 92109 1267-H2
LIEBEL CT
4800 SD 92117 1248-J1
LIEBERT RD
1100 ImCo 92243 430-L7
LIEDER DR
1900 SD 92154 1350-A1
LIETA ST
1400 SD 92110 1268-E2
LIGGETT DR
3500 SD 92106 1288-A1
LIGGETT WY
1400 SD 92106 1288-A1
LIGHTHOUSE RD
- SMCS 92078 1128-D5
1000 CRLB 92011 1127-A5
LIGHTHOUSE WY
13400 SD 92130 1188-D4
LIGHTHOUSE RIDGE LN
- SD 92110 1268-D6
LIGHTHOUSE VIEW PL
300 SD 92154 1330-J7
LIGHTNING DR
3300 SDCo 92004 (1078-H6 See Page 1058)
LIGHTNING TRAIL LN
2600 CHV 91915 1311-H5
LIGHTWAVE AV
9000 SD 92123 1249-D1
LIGIA PL
5000 SDCo 92020 1271-H1
LILA DR
4700 SD 92115 1269-J2
4700 SD 92115 1270-A3
LILA LN
300 SDCo 92021 1252-H4
LILAC AV
1300 CHV 91911 1330-H3
LILAC CT
800 SMCS 92078 1128-E2
1800 CRLB 92011 1127-E6
LILAC DR
- SD 92109 1248-C6
200 SDCo 92021 1252-H3
2700 SDCo 92036 1136-D7
29400 SDCo 91906 (1297-E5 See Page 1296)
LILAC LN
- SDCo 91916 1235-J1
- SDCo 91916 1236-A1
- SDCo 92036 1156-F7
1800 SDCo 91901 1233-G7
1800 SDCo 91901 1253-G1
8000 SDCo 91962 1237-C6
38400 SDCo 91905 (1299-J5 See Page 1298)
LILAC PL
- SDCo 92026 1069-B1
LILAC RD
- SDCo 92059 1030-A5
1300 SDCo 92065 1152-G1
28200 SDCo 92082 1090-C1
28900 SDCo 92082 1070-A5
29900 SDCo 92082 1069-H2
32400 SDCo 92082 1049-G2
33200 SDCo 92082 1029-H7
33600 SDCo 92059 1029-H7
W LILAC RD
5500 SDCo 92003 1048-H6
5500 SDCo 92003 1068-B1
8500 SDCo 92026 1048-H6
8500 SDCo 92026 1049-A6
9300 SDCo 92026 1069-D2
10200 SDCo 92026 1069-F3
LILAC TR
2500 SDCo 91905 (1299-H3 See Page 1298)
LILAC WK
9500 SDCo 92026 1049-B7
9500 SDCo 92026 1069-B1
LILAC CREST
- SDCo 92082 1069-J4
- SDCo 92082 1070-A4
LILAC HEIGHTS CT
- SDCo 92082 1070-A5
30000 SDCo 92082 1069-J5
LILAC HILL
12000 SDCo 92082 1069-H3
LILAC HILL DR
26500 SDCo 92026 1089-H7
26500 ESCN 92026 1089-H7
LILAC HILLS LN
12100 SDCo 92082 1069-E3
LILAC KNOLLS RD
12000 SDCo 92082 1069-J4
12000 SDCo 92082 1070-A4
LILAC RIDGE RD
10100 SDCo 92026 1069-D2
LILAC SUMMIT
3400 ENCT 92024 1148-C5
LILAC VISTA DR
11200 SDCo 92082 1069-G2
LILAC WOOD LN
16000 SDCo 91935 1273-G5
LILAC WOOD RD
3200 SDCo 91935 1273-G6
LILA HILL LN
11900 SDCo 92040 1232-A7
LILAS
14200 SD 92129 1189-H2
LILE ST
3400 OCN 92056 1107-A2
LILIUM LN
- CRLB 92011 1127-D4
LILLIAN LN
1000 ELCJ 92020 1251-G7
LILLIAN ST
4900 SD 92110 1268-E2
LILLIAN WY
100 SDCo 92028 1027-G2
LILLIE LN
- SDCo 91905 1300-C6
LILY AV
1400 ELCJ 92021 1252-A2
1400 SDCo 92021 1252-A2
LILY PL
7300 CRLB 92011 1127-B6
LIMA CT
1500 ELCJ 92019 1252-A5
LIMAR WY
9600 SD 92129 1189-E5
LIMBER PINE RD
- SDCo 92028 1048-C4
LIME PL
1000 VSTA 92081 1107-G2
LIME ST
7300 LMSA 91941 1270-F5
LIME GROVE RD
15800 PWY 92064 1170-E5
LIMERICK AV
4500 SD 92117 1248-H1
4900 SD 92117 1228-H7
LIMERICK CT
5400 SD 92117 1228-G6
LIMERICK WY
4400 SD 92117 1248-H2
LIME ROCK CT
2100 SDCo 92019 1272-C4
LIMESTONE LN
- SDCo 92127 1169-E3
LIMETREE LN
10300 SDCo 91977 1291-E2
LIME TREE WY
500 OCN 92054 1086-E2
LIMON LN
8200 SDCo 92021 1251-H1
LIMONITE CT
- CRLB 92009 1127-E5
LINALDA DR
1200 SDCo 92021 1251-H3
LINARES CT
100 SOLB 92075 1167-D6
LINARES ST
11100 SD 92129 1169-H6
LINAZA LN
- SDCo 91977 1290-J5
LINBROOK DR
1500 SD 92111 1268-J1
1500 SD 92111 1269-A2
LINBROOK PL
7300 SD 92111 1269-A1
LINCOLN AV
200 ELCJ 92020 1251-G6
600 ELCN 92243 6499-E4
1000 SD 92103 1269-B5
1900 SD 92104 1269-C5
E LINCOLN AV
100 ESCN 92026 1129-H1
700 ESCN 92026 1109-J7
900 ESCN 92026 1110-A7
1200 SDCo 92027 1110-A7
W LINCOLN AV
300 ESCN 92026 1129-H1
LINCOLN CT
2700 NATC 91950 1310-B3
2700 SDCo 91950 1310-B3
LINCOLN DR
- SD 92102 1289-G4
LINCOLN PKWY
100 ESCN 92025 1129-H1
100 ESCN 92026 1129-H1
LINCOLN PL
- CALX 92231 6680-F1
900 LMGR 91945 1290-G2
900 SD 92114 1290-G2
LINCOLN ST
100 CALX 92231 6680-E1
1900 OCN 92054 1106-D3
3000 CRLB 92008 1106-E6
7800 LMGR 91945 1270-H6
LINCOLN HIGH SCHOOL PL
- SD 92113 1290-A4
LINCOLNSHIRE ST
12400 SD 92128 1150-B6
LINDA CT
- ESCN 92027 1110-D6
LINDA DR
2900 OCN 92056 1087-B7
3000 OCN 92056 1107-B1
LINDA LN
500 CHV 91910 1310-C7
800 SMCS 92069 1109-B6
2000 CRLB 92008 1106-G4
3700 SDCo 91977 1271-C5
6500 SD 92120 1250-E7
LINDA ST
700 CALX 92231 6680-G1
1500 SDCo 92028 1028-A4
LINDA WY
300 ELCJ 92020 1251-E5
5300 SD 92037 1247-G4
LINDA MAR DR
200 SOLB 92075 1187-E1
LINDAMERE LN
13500 SD 92128 1190-B3
LINDA ROSA AV
5400 SD 92037 1247-G3
LINDA SUE LN
1400 ENCT 92024 1147-G6
LINDA VISTA
- SMCS 92078 1129-C1
- VSTA 92081 1107-C2
LINDA VISTA CT
- SDCo 92081 1128-B1
- SMCS 92078 1128-B1
- SMCS 92081 1128-B1
2700 SD 92111 1249-A6
LINDA VISTA DR
900 SMCS 92078 1108-B7
900 SMCS 92078 1128-B1
3200 SDCo 92081 1128-B1
3200 VSTA 92081 1128-B1
3300 SDCo 92078 1128-B1
3600 SDCo 92028 1048-B3
LINDA VISTA RD
5100 SD 92110 1268-G2
6000 SD 92111 1268-G2
6900 SD 92111 1248-J6
7300 SD 92111 1249-A5
LINDA VISTA TER
3400 SDCo 92028 1048-A3
LINDBERGH ST
3400 SD 92154 1330-E6
LINDBERGH WY
500 SD 92154 1330-F6
LINDELL AV
100 ELCJ 92020 1251-F6
LINDEN DR
900 VSTA 92083 1087-F6
LINDEN LN
8900 LMSA 91941 1271-A2
LINDEN RD
7500 SDCo 91962 1237-C7
8200 SDCo 92040 1252-A1
8200 SDCo 92040 1251-J1
LINDEN TER
7100 CRLB 92011 1127-A6
LINDEN WY
4900 LMSA 91941 1271-A2
LINDENWOOD DR
1300 SDCo 92021 1251-G1
LINDERO PL
1100 SDCo 92028 1027-H4
LINDHOLM LN
2600 LMGR 91945 1270-E7
LINDLY CT
11600 SD 92131 1209-H1
LINDO LN
12700 SDCo 92040 1232-C3
LINDO LAKE PL
9900 SDCo 92040 1232-B3
LINDO PASEO
5500 SD 92115 1270-B2
LINDOS WY
4200 OCN 92056 1107-F6
LINDSAY DR
2200 CRLB 92008 1127-C1
2200 CRLB 92008 1107-C7
LINDSAY LN
10300 SDCo 92028 1027-J5
LINDSAY ST
- CHV 91913 1331-B1
500 ELCJ 92020 1251-G4
LINDSAY MICHELLE DR
2100 SDCo 91901 1234-A4
LINDSEY CT
- SDCo 92028 1028-B4
LINDSEY LN
- ENCT 92024 1147-D6
LINDSEY RD
- CLPT 92233 411-B9
- ImCo 92233 411-A9
LINDSLEY PARK DR
1100 SMCS 92069 1109-D7
1900 SDCo 92026 1109-D7
LIND VERN CT
8700 SNTE 92071 1231-D7
LINDY LN
1000 VSTA 92084 1108-A1
LINDY WY
- SDCo 92069 1108-G2
LINEA DEL CIELO
Rt#-S8
4800 SDCo 92014 1168-A6
4900 SDCo 92067 1168-C4
LINEN DR
7900 SNTE 92071 1230-H7
7900 SNTE 92071 1250-H1
LINFIELD AV
5600 SD 92120 1270-D1
LINGEL DR
600 SDCo 92019 1253-C2
LINGRE AV
13200 PWY 92064 1190-E2
LINK DR
3300 SDCo 91941 1270-J5
LINKS WY
2400 VSTA 92081 1107-J4
LINMAR LN
3900 CRLB 92008 1106-F6
LINNA PL
7300 SD 92120 1250-B5
LINNET ST
5900 SD 92114 1290-C4
LINNIE LN
13000 PWY 92064 1190-F5
LINO CT
8200 SD 92129 1189-B6
LINROE DR
12200 SDCo 92040 1232-A7
LINSAY PL
1300 ESCN 92026 1109-J5
1800 SDCo 92026 1109-J5
LINTHICUM DR
1500 ESCN 92026 1109-H6
LINTON RD
27200 SDCo 92086 409-J7
LINVIEW AV
900 ESCN 92026 1109-J6
900 ESCN 92027 1109-J6
LINWOOD PL
1100 ESCN 92027 1130-D2
LINWOOD ST
300 ESCN 92027 1130-C1
900 SD 92103 1268-H6
1700 SD 92110 1268-F5
LION CIR
- CHV 91910 1310-D6
LIONEL ST
2600 SD 92123 1249-C6
LIONS GATE
- VSTA 92084 1088-C6
LIONSHEAD AV
- CRLB 92010 1127-H2
- CRLB 92010 1128-A1
- VSTA 92081 1128-A1
LION VALLEY RD
100 ESCN 92027 1110-D7
100 ESCN 92027 1130-D1
LIPIZZAN WY
600 SDCo 92019 1252-C6
LIPMANN ST
6200 SD 92122 1228-E5
LIPSCOMB DR
10100 SD 92126 1209-D5
LIQUID CT
8800 SD 92121 1228-H1
LIQUID AMBER LN
- SDCo 92082 1090-D4
LIQUID AMBER WY
- SMCS 92078 1128-F6
LIRIO CTE
1100 CHV 91910 1311-A7
LIRIO ST
300 SOLB 92075 1187-F1
LIRIOS
10800 SD 92129 1189-H2
LIROPE ST
6000 SD 92114 1290-C6
LISA AV
1600 VSTA 92084 1087-H3
LISA LN
1800 SDCo 92021 1252-C3
LISA ST
2200 CRLB 92008 1107-A6
LISA TER
1800 SDCo 92021 1252-C3
LISA WY
1400 ESCN 92027 1110-B5
LISA MEADOWS
10700 SNTE 92071 1231-E6
LISANN ST
4500 SD 92117 1248-B1
LISBON LN
1600 SDCo 92019 1252-B7
LISBON PL
1600 ESCN 92029 1129-F5
LISBON ST
6900 SD 92114 1290-F3
LISE AV
4900 SD 92102 1290-A3
LISIEUX TER
6100 SD 92120 1250-C6
LISMORE PL
- CRLB 92009 1127-F3
LISTER ST
4100 SD 92110 1248-E7
LISZT AV
100 ENCT 92007 1167-D2
LITA LN
1100 SDCo 92084 1108-B1
1100 VSTA 92084 1108-B1
LITCHFIELD RD
5000 SD 92116 1269-E2
LITHROP PL
4700 SD 92117 1248-G1
LITTEN WY
15900 SDCo 92065 1174-B4
LITTLE DR
- SD 92140 1268-E6
LITTLE LN
2900 LMGR 91945 1270-H6
9300 SDCo 92040 1232-B5
LITTLE ST
1900 SD 92037 1227-G6
LITTLE BROOK LN
13400 SDCo 92040 1232-D5
LITTLE CANYON LN
9700 SDCo 92026 1089-C2
LITTLE CREEK LN
13800 SDCo 92082 1070-E7
LITTLE CREEK RD
7600 SDCo 92029 1128-H7
LITTLE DAWN LN
13400 PWY 92064 1190-E3
LITTLE DIPPER WY
1600 SD 92173 1350-E2
LITTLE FIELD LN
18900 SDCo 92082 1091-G5
LITTLEFIELD ST
100 SD 92110 1268-E1
LITTLEFIELD WY
- ImCo 92249 6560-C7
LITTLE FLOWER ST
3400 SD 92104 1269-F7
LITTLE GOPHER CANYON RD
1000 SDCo 92084 1067-J4
1000 SDCo 92084 1068-A5
LITTLE KLONDIKE RD
22200 SDCo 92065 1172-J5
22200 SDCo 92065 1173-A5
LITTLE LAKE ST
1300 CHV 91913 1311-E7
LITTLE MCGONIGLE RANCH RD
- SD 92130 1188-G7
LITTLE OAKS LN
1100 SDCo 91901 1253-H1
LITTLE OAKS RD
100 ENCT 92024 1147-H7
LITTLE ORPHAN AL
100 DLMR 92014 1187-F6
LITTLEPAGE LN
18400 SDCo 92065 1154-B4
LITTLEPAGE RD
18400 SDCo 92065 1154-C4
LITTLE POND RD
13600 SDCo 92082 1070-D6
LITTLE QUAIL RUN
15300 SDCo 92082 1070-J3
LITTLER DR
6600 SD 92119 1250-F5
LITTLER LN
2300 OCN 92056 1106-J2
LITTLE ROCK RD
4000 SDCo 92028 997-G4
8100 SNTE 92071 1230-H7
LITTLE ROSS RD
40300 SDCo 92028 997-B1
LITTLE SIERRA
15500 SDCo 92082 1071-A5
LITTLE SILVER CT
12000 SD 92131 1210-B1
LITTLETON CT
- SDCo 92055 1086-A3
LITTLETON RD
2400 ELCJ 92020 1251-B4
LIVE OAK CT
4700 OCN 92056 1087-D4
LIVE OAK DR
400 ELCJ 92020 1251-D6
LIVE OAK LN
- SDCo 92026 1089-A2
LIVE OAK PL
2900 SDCo 92029 1129-B6
LIVE OAK RD
900 VSTA 92081 1107-H4
2300 ESCN 92029 1129-D3
LIVE OAK ST
1500 CHV 91913 1311-C7
LIVE OAK TR
2400 SDCo 91905 (1299-H2 See Page 1298)
LIVE OAK PARK RD
2500 SDCo 92028 1028-B2
S LIVE OAK PARK RD
100 SDCo 92028 1028-B3
LIVE OAK RANCH RD
46900 RivC 92592 999-E2
LIVE OAKS DR
- CRLB 92009 1127-G3
LIVE OAK SPRINGS RD
- SDCo 91906 (1299-G6 See Page 1298)
- SDCo 91905 (1299-G6 See Page 1298)
LIVERING LN
5200 SD 92117 1248-H1
LIVERPOOL CT
700 SD 92109 1267-H2
LIVERPOOL DR
100 ENCT 92007 1167-D3
LIVEWOOD WY
10400 SD 92131 1210-B4
LIVINGSTON ST
1300 CHV 91913 1311-D7
6800 SD 92115 1270-E6
6800 LMGR 92115 1270-E6
LIZA LN
1400 SDCo 91901 1233-J6
LIZARD ROCKS RD
28400 SDCo 92082 1090-F1
LLAMA CT
2700 CRLB 92009 1127-H6
LLAMA ST
2700 CRLB 92009 1127-H6
LLANOS CT
- CALX 92231 6620-H5
LLOYD PL
- SDCo 92027 1130-D3
3600 SD 92117 1248-E5
LLOYD ST
200 ELCJ 92021 1251-F4
2800 SD 92117 1248-E6
LLOYD TER
3600 SD 92117 1248-E6
LOBELIA CT
1700 CRLB 92011 1127-E6
LOBELIA DR
200 VSTA 92083 1108-B3
200 SDCo 92083 1108-C3
LOBELIA PTH
6700 SD 92037 1247-G1
LOBELIA RD
2600 SDCo 91901 1234-A5
LOBO LN
8700 SDCo 91977 1291-A2
LOBRANO ST
9100 LMSA 91941 1271-B3
LOBRICO CT
- SD 92114 1290-F3
LO CASCIO WY
2700 ESCN 92027 1110-E7
LOCDEL CT
400 CHV 91911 1330-C4
LOCH LOMOND DR
1300 ENCT 92007 1167-D1
LOCHLOMOND ST
4200 SD 92111 1249-A2
LOCH LOMOND HIGHLANDS
2000 SDCo 92084 1088-C7
LOCHMOOR DR
6300 SD 92120 1250-E6
LOCH NESS DR
- SDCo 92028 1027-G5
LOCHRIDGE PL
2300 ESCN 92026 1109-G4
LOCHWOOD PL
700 ESCN 92026 1109-H3
LOCKE PL
2100 LMGR 91945 1290-G1
LOCKFORD AV
6400 SD 92139 1310-F2
LOCK HORN RD
- SDCo 91935 (1314-J3 See Page 1294)
- SDCo 91935 (1315-A3 See Page 1294)
LOCKLAND CT
8400 SDCo 91977 1290-J2
LOCKRIDGE ST
3900 SD 92102 1289-G4
LOCKSLEY ST
18300 SD 92128 1150-B5
LOCKWOOD DR
3300 SD 92123 1249-E4
LOCKWOOD PL
700 OCN 92057 1087-C1
LOCUST AV
1000 CRLB 92008 1106-G7
LOCUST ST
1100 SD 92106 1288-B2
2100 SD 92106 1268-C7
3000 SD 92110 1268-C7
LODGEPOLE RD
1700 SDCo 92078 1128-B2
1700 SMCS 92078 1128-B2
LODI CT
4300 SD 92117 1228-E6
LODI GN
1800 ESCN 92026 1109-F6
LODI PL
5400 SD 92117 1228-E6
LODI ST
5200 SD 92117 1228-D6
LODI WY
4100 SD 92117 1228-E7
LOFBERG ST
3500 SD 92124 1249-G3
LOFTY GROVE DR
4600 OCN 92056 1087-E5
LOFTY TRAIL CT
15500 SD 92127 1169-J5
LOFTY TRAIL DR
15700 SD 92127 1169-J5
LOFTY VIEW PT
6700 SD 92120 1250-C4
LOGAN AV
1600 SD 92113 1289-C5
4700 SD 92113 1290-A5
5000 SD 92114 1290-A5
LOGAN CT
- ESCN 92027 1130-D2
LOGANBERRY CT
800 SMCS 92069 1109-A5
LOGANBERRY DR
7100 CRLB 92011 1126-J6
LOGANBERRY WY
5400 OCN 92057 1067-D6
LOGGIA WY
- SD 92108 1249-D7
LOGRONO DR
4300 SD 92115 1270-D4
LOGWOOD PL
3600 SDCo 92028 1048-D2
LOIRE AV
10600 SD 92131 1210-B3
LOIRE CIR
12100 SD 92131 1210-B3
LOIRE CT
12100 SD 92131 1210-B3
LOIS LN
- SDCo 92036 1156-E7
100 DLMR 92014 1187-F5
LOIS ST
4000 LMSA 91941 1270-E4
4000 SD 92115 1270-E4
LOIS CANYON RD
3500 SDCo 91935 1272-H5
LOKER AV E
2800 CRLB 92010 1127-G2
LOKER AV W
2700 CRLB 92010 1127-F2
LOKOYA DR
- CHV 91913 1331-E1
LOLA LN
1800 SDCo 92019 1272-D3
LOLALI LN
1100 SDCo 92084 1108-C1
LOLIN LN
14200 PWY 92064 1190-H5
LOLITA ST
200 ENCT 92024 1147-B6
LOLLY LN
6200 SD 92114 1290-D4
LOMA AV
1000 CORD 92118 1288-H7
LOMA CT
900 ELCJ 92020 1251-A4
1500 CHV 91911 1330-H3
4900 CRLB 92008 1106-J7
LOMA DR
2300 LMGR 91945 1270-G7
2300 LMGR 91945 1290-G1
LOMA LN
100 ESCN 92026 1109-F6
1100 CORD 92118 1288-H7
1100 CORD 92118 1308-H1
1400 CHV 91911 1330-F4
10300 SDCo 91978 1271-E6
LOMA PASS
4100 SD 92103 1268-G5
LOMA VW
900 CHV 91910 1310-H7
LOMA WY
3600 SD 92106 1288-A2
4900 CRLB 92008 1106-J7
LOMA ALEGRE
- SDCo 92067 1148-C6
LOMA ALTA DR
- SMCS 92069 1108-E5
100 OCN 92054 1086-D6
3800 SD 92115 1270-E4
LOMA ALTA TER
700 VSTA 92083 1087-F5
LOMACITA TER
1600 ELCJ 92021 1252-C2
LOMACITAS LN
3500 NATC 91902 1310-E3
3500 SDCo 91902 1310-E3
LOMA CORTA DR
200 SOLB 92075 1167-H6
LOMA DEL SOL DR
3200 SDCo 91902 1311-A1
LOMA DE NARANJAS
1300 SDCo 92027 1130-D3
LOMA DE PAZ
1300 ESCN 92027 1130-C3
1300 SDCo 92027 1130-C3
LOMA ESTATES CT
3100 SDCo 91935 1273-D7
LOMA HELIX CT
4300 SDCo 91941 1271-D3
LOMA LAGUNA DR
4900 CRLB 92008 1106-J7
LOMA LA LUNA
31400 SDCo 92026 1069-E1
LOMALAND DR
3800 SD 92106 1287-J3
3900 SD 92107 1287-J3
LOMA LARGA DR
300 SOLB 92075 1167-J6
LOMA LINDA DR
17600 SDCo 92067 1168-C1
LOMA PASEO
4300 SDCo 91902 1310-G3
LOMA PORTAL DR
900 ELCJ 92020 1251-C3
LOMA RANCHO DR
10200 SDCo 91978 1271-E6
LOMA RIVIERA CIR
4000 SD 92110 1268-C5
LOMA RIVIERA CT
4300 SD 92110 1268-B5
LOMA RIVIERA DR
3000 SD 92110 1268-C5
LOMA RIVIERA LN
4100 SD 92110 1268-C5
LOMAS DE ORO CT
600 ENCT 92024 1147-J6
LOMAS SANTA FE DR
Rt#-S8
100 SOLB 92075 1167-F7
1500 SOLB 92014 1167-F7
1500 SOLB 92075 1167-F7
1600 SDCo 92014 1168-A6
LOMAS SERENAS DR
3300 ESCN 92029 1150-A3
LOMAS VERDES DR
13000 PWY 92064 1170-D1
LOMA VALLEY PL
800 SD 92106 1288-A3
LOMA VALLEY RD
700 SD 92106 1288-A3
LOMA VERDE
- ESCN 92026 1109-F7
600 ENCT 92024 1147-F5
5100 OCN 92056 1087-D2
LOMA VERDE DR
5500 SDCo 92067 1168-C2
LOMA VIEW CT
8200 SDCo 91977 1290-J5
LOMA VISTA
- SMCS 92078 1129-C2
LOMA VISTA AV
2600 ESCN 92025 1130-B7
LOMA VISTA DR
3200 SDCo 91935 1272-J7
7600 LMSA 91941 1270-G2
LOMA VISTA PL
200 SDCo 92021 1252-H3
LOMA VISTA WY
1100 SDCo 92084 1108-C1
LOMAX ST
12700 PWY 92064 1190-D4
LOMBARD PL
8900 SD 92122 1228-D3
LOMBARD ST
1400 VSTA 92084 1087-J4
LOMICA DR
11800 SD 92128 1170-A3
LOMICA PL
2200 ESCN 92029 1129-G7
2300 ESCN 92029 1149-H1
LOMITA RD
1100 SDCo 92020 1271-H1
LOMITA ST
2600 OCN 92054 1086-D6

SAN DIEGO CO.

STREET Block City ZIP Pg-Grid

LOMITA WY
3900 SMCS 92078 1128-C1
LOMITA DEL SOL
800 VSTA 92083 1087-G5
LOMITAS DR
4700 SD 92116 1269-C3
LOMKER CT
9200 SNTE 92071 1230-J6
LOMKER WY
8400 SNTE 92071 1230-H6
LOMO DEL SUR
4200 SDCo 91941 1271-D3
LOMOND DR
5800 SD 92120 1250-B7
LONDONDERRY AV
10300 SD 92126 1209-D5
LONE BLUFF CT
- SDCo 92127 1169-E4
LONE BLUFF DR
- SDCo 92127 1169-E4
LONE BLUFF WY
- SDCo 92127 1169-F4
LONE CYPRESS PL
12600 SD 92130 1188-B6
LONE DOVE LN
3600 ENCT 92024 1148-D3
LONE DOVE ST
- SDCo 92127 1169-E4
LONE HAWK DR
- SDCo 92127 1169-F4
LONE HILL LN
3200 ENCT 92024 1148-C3
LONE JACK RD
2400 ENCT 92024 1148-B4
LONE OAK LN
- SDCo 92028 998-G4
2200 SDCo 92084 1108-D2
LONE OAK PL
- CHV 91914 1311-H2
LONE OAK RD
1500 SDCo 92084 1108-D2
LONE OAK TR
14900 SDCo 92065 1173-G7
LONE PINE CT
2500 CHV 91915 1311-H6
LONE PINE TR
28700 SDCo 91962 1237-B5
LONE QUAIL RD
- SD 92127 1169-E3
- SDCo 92127 1169-E3
LONE RAY LN
1900 SDCo 92084 1088-B2
1900 VSTA 92084 1088-B2
LONESOME OAK WY
12600 SDCo 92082 1090-C1
LONESPUR CT
4600 OCN 92056 1087-D3
LONE STAR DR
5500 SD 92120 1250-B4
LONE STAR RD
- SDCo 92154 1332-A7
- SDCo 92154 1352-A1
6300 SD 92154 1331-H7
6300 SDCo 92154 1331-H7
LONE STAR ST
7600 SD 92120 1250-B4
LONE TREE RD
1700 CHV 91913 1311-D6
LONE VALLEY RD
- CHV 91913 1311-E6
LONG PL
3900 CRLB 92008 1106-F7
LONG BOAT CV
2600 SD 92014 1207-H1
LONG BOAT WY
12900 SD 92014 1207-J1
LONG BRANCH AV
4300 SD 92107 1268-A6
4700 SD 92107 1267-J5
LONG CANYON DR
3900 SDCo 91902 1311-A3
LONG CREST DR
500 OCN 92054 1086-D3
LONGDALE DR
7800 LMGR 91945 1270-H7
LONGDALE PL
- SD 92131 1209-F2
LONGDEN LN
300 SOLB 92075 1187-F2
LONGFELLOW CT
- OCN 92057 1067-A4
LONGFELLOW LN
13500 SD 92129 1189-E4
LONGFELLOW RD
- CRLB 92008 1107-B7
1300 VSTA 92081 1107-J4
LONGFORD CT
4900 SD 92117 1248-G1
LONGFORD PL
4900 SD 92117 1248-G1
LONGFORD ST
4800 SD 92117 1248-G1
4900 SD 92117 1228-G7
LONGHORN DR
1600 VSTA 92081 1107-G5
LONG LAKE CT
6900 LMGR 91945 1270-E7
LONGMONT RD
- SDCo 92084 1088-D6
- VSTA 92084 1088-D6
LONG PALM ST
300 OCN 92054 1106-C2
LONG POINT CT
1500 CHV 91911 1330-J4
LONG RIDGE ST
1700 CHV 91913 1311-D6
LONGRIDGE WY
9200 SD 92126 1209-D2
LONG RUN DR
3500 SD 92130 1187-J5
3500 SD 92130 1188-A5
LONG SHADOW CT
1000 ELCJ 92019 1252-A7
LONGS HILL RD
1900 SDCo 92021 1252-D3
LONGSHORE CT
- SD 92130 1208-C2
LONGSHORE WY
- SD 92130 1208-B2
LONGSPUR DR
- SDCo 92055 1023-E3
LONGSTAFF CT
- SMCS 92078 1128-C6
LONG TRAIL CT
- ImCo 92243 6560-A6
LONG VIEW DR
1200 CHV 91915 1311-J6
LONGVIEW DR
3700 CRLB 92010 1106-H4
LONG VIEW WY
4900 SDCo 92020 1271-G1
LONGWOOD ST
8600 SD 92126 1209-C5

LONI LN
1200 VSTA 92084 1108-A1
LONICERA ST
- CRLB 92011 1127-A5
LONJA WY
1700 SD 92173 1350-D3
LONNIE ST
4000 OCN 92056 1087-B7
LONNY LN
7000 LMGR 91945 1270-F7
LONSDALE DR
1000 VSTA 92084 1087-J5
LONSDALE LN
700 VSTA 92084 1087-J4
LOOKOUT CT
3500 OCN 92056 1107-G4
LOOKOUT DR
7700 SD 92037 1227-G6
LOOKOUT LN
20200 SDCo 92029 1149-E1
LOOKOUT LP
7500 SDCo 91962 1237-D7
LOOKOUT PL
3300 SMCS 92078 1128-B1
LOOKOUT RD
- SDCo 92036 (1196-B3 See Page 1176)
LOOKOUT TR
800 SDCo 92019 1253-C2
LOOKOUT MOUNTAIN RD
2400 SDCo 92028 998-F4
LOOKOUT POINT PL
1800 ESCN 92026 1109-F5
LOOSE CREEK RD
2800 SDCo 91935 1293-G3
LOPELIA MEADOWS PL
- SD 92130 1188-G3
LOPEZ CT
200 CALX 92231 6620-G6
E LOPEZ DR
- SD 92102 1289-G3
W LOPEZ DR
- SD 92102 1289-G3
LOPEZ ST
1600 OCN 92054 1106-D2
LOPEZ RIDGE WY
11000 SD 92121 1208-G3
LOPEZ RIDGE PARK DRIVEWAY
- SD 92126 1208-J3
LOPING LN
5600 SDCo 91902 1311-A2
LOQUAT CT
800 ELCJ 92020 1251-E6
LOQUAT PL
2100 OCN 92054 1106-E1
LORCA DR
6100 SD 92115 1270-C4
LORCA WY
4700 OCN 92056 1107-F4
LORD ST
3500 SD 92123 1249-C4
LORD CECIL ST
5600 SD 92122 1228-B6
LORELEI LN
2000 SDCo 92028 998-A7
2000 SDCo 92028 1028-A1
LOREN DR
9200 LMSA 91942 1251-B7
LORENA LN
11200 SDCo 92020 1271-G2
LORENA PL
4700 SDCo 92020 1271-H2
LORENE LN
800 SDCo 92028 1028-A1
LORENZ AV
1400 SD 92114 1290-B6
LORENZO DR
1300 SDCo 92028 1027-J7
1300 SDCo 92028 1047-H1
LORETO CT
- IMP 92251 6499-H1
LORETO GN
1800 ESCN 92027 1110-A5
1800 ESCN 92026 1110-A5
2000 ESCN 92026 1109-J4
2000 SDCo 92026 1109-J4
LORETTA ST
700 OCN 92054 1086-A5
LORI CT
800 SMCS 92069 1109-B6
LORI LN
700 CHV 91910 1310-G7
LORI PL
- SDCo 92021 1232-D7
LORI ST
1200 CHV 91913 1331-B1
LORIENT CT
- SD 92130 1188-E7
LORIENT PL
- CHV 91913 1311-F1
LORIKEET ST
- OCN 92057 1067-B3
LORI MAR CT
9300 SDCo 91977 1271-B6
LORIMER LN
3600 ENCT 92024 1167-G2
LORING ST
600 SD 92109 1247-J4
1900 SD 92109 1248-A4
LORIRAE PL
11500 SD 92126 1209-B1
LORIS ST
4900 SD 92105 1270-A6
LORITA LN
3900 SDCo 92028 1028-G6
LOR-LAR LN
400 SDCo 92065 1152-G5
LORNA AV
1100 ELCJ 92020 1251-G7
1100 ELCJ 92020 1271-G1
LORNA LN
2400 CRLB 92008 1106-F3
LORNSTEAN LN
- SDCo 91977 1271-B5
LORRAINE CT
13700 SDCo 92040 1191-F6
LORRAINE DR
1500 ENCT 92024 1147-A3
4700 SD 92115 1269-J2
4700 SD 92115 1270-A3
LORRAINE LN
- ELCJ 92019 1252-A6
LORRAINE PL
1700 ESCN 92026 1109-D5
LORRAINE WY
9700 SNTE 92071 1231-C4
LORRAINE ANN DR
4000 SDCo 91941 1271-G4
LORREL PL
3400 SDCo 91935 1272-E7
LORRI WY
1900 ESCN 92026 1109-D5

LORRY LN
1700 ESCN 92029 1129-F6
LOS ALAMOS DR
100 SD 92114 1290-C5
LOS ALAMOS WY
4600 OCN 92057 1087-B3
LOS ALISOS N
700 SDCo 92028 1028-B4
LOS ALISOS S
2500 SDCo 92028 1028-C4
LOS ALISOS DR
2400 SDCo 92028 1028-B4
LOS ALISOS N LN
2700 SDCo 92028 1028-B3
LOS ALTOS CT
5100 SD 92109 1247-J4
LOS ALTOS DR
500 CHV 91914 1311-G2
LOS ALTOS RD
1600 SD 92109 1248-A4
1600 SD 92109 1247-J4
LOS ALTOS WY
1700 SD 92109 1248-A4
LOS ALTOS DE CERRO
2200 SDCo 92065 1152-F1
LOS AMIGOS
- SMCS 92078 1129-C2
1300 SDCo 92028 1028-A4
LOS AMIGOS WY
12000 SDCo 92040 1232-A6
W LOS ANGELES DR
100 VSTA 92083 1087-G5
LOS ANGELES PL
300 SD 92114 1290-B4
LOS ARBOLES
16100 SDCo 92067 1168-C5
LOS ARBOLES RANCH RD
26000 SDCo 92026 1109-G1
LOS ARBOLITOS BLVD
700 OCN 92054 1086-F2
LOS ARCHOS
- SDCo 92040 1232-D6
LOS ARCOS PL
1200 CHV 91910 1311-B7
LOS BANDITOS DR
100 SDCo 92065 1152-J5
LOS BARBOS
16500 SDCo 92067 1168-F4
LOS BRAZOS
- SD 92127 1168-H7
LOS CABALLITOS
1000 SOLB 92014 1167-G7
LOS CAMPANEROS
1100 SDCo 92078 1128-G4
LOS CAMPOS DR
2900 SDCo 92028 1048-E1
LOS CEDROS LN
1400 ESCN 92026 1109-E6
LOS CERRITOS LN
2500 SDCo 92028 1028-B3
LOS CIELOS
14000 SDCo 92025 1130-F7
LOS COCHES CT
1300 CHV 91910 1311-B6
12700 SDCo 92040 1232-B6
LOS COCHES RD
8300 SDCo 92021 1252-D1
9400 SDCo 92021 1232-D7
9600 SDCo 92040 1232-B4
LOS COCHES RD E
13300 SDCo 92021 1232-D7
LOS COLINAS
400 OCN 92054 1086-F3
600 ENCT 92024 1147-F5
LOS CONEJOS
- SDCo 91916 (1195-D6 See Page 1175)
1300 SDCo 92028 1028-A4
LOS CORDEROS
1100 SDCo 92078 1128-C3
LOS COYOTES CT
- IMP 92251 6439-F4
LOS COYOTES RD
- SDCo 92086 409-K8
LOS ENCINOS DR
32600 RivC 92592 999-G1
LOS EUCALIPTOS
17500 SDCo 92067 1168-E1
LOS HERMANOS RD
3500 SDCo 92028 1028-E2
LOS HERMANOS RANCH RD
18500 SDCo 92082 1091-F4
LOS HUECOS RD
- SDCo 91948 1218-C6
LOS INDIOS CT
1100 CHV 91910 1310-J5
LOS MIRLITOS
5300 SDCo 92067 1168-B1
LOS MOCHIS WY
3400 OCN 92056 1107-C2
LOS MORROS
10800 SDCo 92067 1167-J4
10800 SDCo 92067 1168-A2
LOS MORROS Rt#-S9
17200 SDCo 92067 1168-A2
LOS MORROS WY
100 OCN 92057 1067-A6
LOS NARANJOS CT
6200 SDCo 92067 1168-E4
LOS NIDOS LN
- SDCo 92026 1089-E2
LOS NIETOS AV
14100 PWY 92064 1190-G1
LOS NOPALITOS
10200 SDCo 92040 1231-F3
LOS OLIVAS DR
400 SMCS 92069 1108-G6
LOS OLIVOS AV
13400 PWY 92064 1190-H4
LOS PADRES DR
4100 SDCo 92028 1028-G7
LOS PINOS
4500 SDCo 92067 1167-J3
LOS PINOS AV
4200 SD 92113 1289-H5
LOS PINOS CIR
7800 CRLB 92009 1147-G3
7800 ENCT 92024 1147-G3
LOS PINOS CT
1000 CHV 91910 1311-B7
LOS PINOS DR
7900 CRLB 92009 1147-G3
LOS PINOS RD
- SDCo 91962 429-L7
LOS PLATEROS
8300 SDCo 92067 1149-A3
LOS RANCHITOS RD
9900 SNTE 92071 1231-F4
9900 SDCo 92040 1231-F4
LOS REYES DR
300 SD 92114 1290-F4

LOS ROBLES DR
5100 CRLB 92008 1126-G2
LOS ROBLES RD
40500 SDCo 92028 997-G3
LOS ROSALES ST
16300 SDCo 92127 1169-F4
LOS SABALOS ST
8100 SD 92126 1209-B2
LOS SANTOS
- SDCo 92040 1232-B7
LOS SICOMOROS LN
3400 SDCo 92028 1028-D7
LOS SONETO CT
7100 SD 92114 1290-F4
LOS SONETO DR
200 SD 92114 1290-F4
LOST TR
20400 SDCo 91901 1274-J3
20400 SDCo 91901 1275-A3
LOST ARROW PL
1200 CHV 91913 1331-A1
LOST CREEK RD
1400 CHV 91915 1311-J6
LOST DUTCHMAN DR
14200 PWY 92064 1190-J3
LOS TERRINITOS
- SDCo 91901 1235-J5
- SDCo 91901 1236-A5
LOST HORIZON DR
- SDCo 92059 409-E5
- SDCo 92059 999-J5
LOSTINDA ST
1100 ELCJ 92019 1252-A7
LOST OAK LN
400 ESCN 92025 1150-A1
400 SDCo 92025 1130-A7
400 SDCo 92025 1150-A1
LOST VALLEY CT
- CHV 91913 1311-E6
LOST VALLEY RD
- SDCo 92086 409-K6
LOST VALLEY TKTR
- SDCo 92004 409-K6
- SDCo 92086 409-K6
LOS VALLECITOS BLVD
500 SMCS 92069 1108-E7
500 SMCS 92069 1128-G1
LOS VECINOS
4200 SDCo 92028 1047-G5
LOS VERDES DR
3100 SDCo 92028 1048-A2
LOS VIENTOS SERRENO
6900 SDCo 92029 1148-F2
LOT A RD
2600 SDCo 92036 1135-J7
2600 SDCo 92036 1136-A7
LOTT PT
11300 SD 92126 1209-B1
LOTUS AV
100 ELCN 92243 6499-E6
1700 ImCo 92243 6559-E1
1700 ELCN 92243 6559-E1
LOTUS CT
1800 CRLB 92011 1127-E7
LOTUS DR
100 CHV 91911 1330-F5
3600 SD 92106 1268-C6
LOTUS GN
1600 ESCN 92026 1109-D6
LOTUS LN
1200 SDCo 92021 1252-D3
LOTUS ST
100 OCN 92054 1086-D6
4600 SD 92107 1268-A5
4800 SD 92107 1267-J5
LOTUS BLOSSOM ST
700 ENCT 92024 1147-F5
LOTUS POND LN
10500 SDCo 92026 1089-F4
LOU ST
3300 NATC 91950 1290-C6
LOUALTA WY
- CHV 91910 1310-D6
LOUDEN LN
1100 IMPB 91932 1349-G2
LOUETTA LN
14300 PWY 92064 1190-H5
LOUIE PL
1000 VSTA 92084 1087-H4
LOUIS DR
1900 ESCN 92026 1109-D4
LOUIS LN
8600 SNTE 92071 1231-D7
LOUISA DR
10500 SDCo 91941 1271-F4
LOUISANA AV
100 SD 92173 1350-G4
LOUISE CT
2300 ELCJ 92020 1251-B5
LOUISE DR
1400 SDCo 91901 1234-C5
4800 SD 92115 1269-J3
LOUISE LN
1000 SDCo 92025 1130-D6
LOUISE ST
2800 OCN 92056 1087-C7
LOUISIANA ST
3400 SD 92104 1269-D5
4300 SD 92116 1269-D5
LOUKELTON CIR
6100 SD 92120 1249-J7
LOUKELTON WY
4800 SD 92120 1249-J7
LOURDES TER
6100 SD 92120 1250-C6
LOURET AV
1700 SD 92154 1329-J6
1700 SD 92154 1330-A6
LOVAJO RD
- SD 92109 1247-J4
LOVE LN
- SDCo 92065 1174-B4
1600 ESCN 92029 1129-G5
LOVEENY DR
2000 SDCo 92084 1108-C3
LOVELAND LN
17400 SDCo 91935 1254-A7
17400 SDCo 91935 1274-A1
LOVELAND RD
4500 ImCo 92227 431-B2
LOVELL LN
9200 LMSA 91941 1271-B1
9200 SDCo 91941 1271-B1
LOVELOCK ST
5200 SD 92110 1268-E3
LOVELY LN
1500 SDCo 92083 1108-A2
LOVETT LN
2100 SDCo 92020 1271-D4
LOW RD
- ImCo 92243 431-A5
LOW CHAPARRAL DR
1800 SMCS 92069 1109-B2
1900 SDCo 92069 1109-B2

LOWE RD
- ImCo - 411-K9
LOWELL CT
7400 LMSA 91941 1270-F3
LOWELL ST
3100 SD 92106 1288-B1
4000 LMSA 91941 1270-G4
LOWELL WY
3500 SD 92106 1288-B1
LOWER LN
900 SDCo 92069 1108-G2
900 SDCo 92084 1108-G2
LOWER LAKE CT
1500 ENCT 92007 1167-F2
LOWER NORTH PEAK WY
- SDCo 92036 1176-C3
LOWER RIDGE RD
3100 SD 92130 1187-J5
LOWER SCARBOROUGH CT
- SD 92127 1169-B4
LOWER SCARBOROUGH LN
- SD 92127 1169-B4
LOWER SCARBOROUGH PL
- SD 92127 1169-B4
LOWER SPRINGS RD
- SDCo 92028 1047-E6
LOWERY LN
- SMCS 92069 1108-H7
LOWEWOOD PL
500 CHV 91910 1310-F5
LOWRY PL
2000 SD 92037 1227-H6
LOWRY TER
7900 SD 92037 1227-H5
LOYOLA CT
1800 CHV 91913 1311-D5
LOZANA RD
2300 SD 92014 1187-H5
LOZITA WY
10300 SDCo 92040 1231-F3
LUANA DR
2900 OCN 92056 1107-B1
LUBBOCK AV
5900 LMSA 91942 1251-A6
LUBER ST
5600 SD 92114 1290-B2
LUCAS LN
- SDCo 92082 1070-G3
LUCAYA CT
- VSTA 92081 1107-H5
LUCERA CT
17000 SD 92127 1169-J2
LUCERA PL
11400 SD 92127 1169-J2
LUCERNE CIR
1800 SMCS 92078 1128-B2
LUCERNE DR
2200 SD 92106 1268-B7
LUCERO CT
1300 CHV 91911 1331-A2
LUCIA CT
7700 CRLB 92009 1147-G1
LUCIA WY
200 OCN 92057 1086-H3
6200 SD 92111 1248-G7
LUCIDI FARMS WY
15000 PWY 92064 1191-D1
LUCIERNAGA CT
6800 CRLB 92009 1127-G6
LUCIERNAGA PL
6700 CRLB 92009 1127-G5
LUCIERNAGA ST
2500 CRLB 92009 1127-H5
LUCILLA ST
3700 SMCS 92078 1128-C1
LUCILLE DR
4500 SD 92115 1269-J2
4800 SD 92115 1270-A3
LUCILLE PL
4800 SD 92115 1270-A2
LUCINDA ST
3200 SD 92106 1288-A3
LUCITA RD
- SDCo 91935 1274-D3
LUCKETT CT
13200 SD 92130 1188-D4
LUCKY ST
1400 OCN 92054 1106-C2
LUCKY DEVIL TR
600 SDCo 92036 (1158-C1 See Page 1138)
LUCY LN
300 SDCo 92021 1251-G2
500 ESCN 92027 1130-D1
LUCYLLE LN
600 ENCT 92024 1148-A6
LUDINGTON LN
1600 SD 92037 1227-G6
LUDINGTON PL
7700 SD 92037 1227-G6
LUELF CT
2400 SDCo 92065 1172-D4
LUELF ST
2700 SDCo 92065 1172-D5
LUGANO LN
1600 SDCo 92014 1167-J7
1600 SOLB 92014 1167-J7
LUGAR PLAYA CATALINA
11600 SD 92124 1230-A7
LUGO DR
- SDCo 92004 (1099-G5 See Page 1098)
LUIGI TER
5100 SD 92122 1228-D4
LUIS ST
15000 PWY 92064 1170-C7
LUISENO
12800 PWY 92064 1170-D5
LUISENO AV
200 OCN 92057 1067-B7
LUISENO CIRCLE DR
32400 SDCo 92061 1051-A5
LUIS REY HEIGHTS RD
7500 SDCo 92003 1068-G4
LUKE LN
1500 ELCJ 92021 1252-A3
LUMINARIA WY
- OCN 92057 1086-G2
LUNA AV
2600 SD 92117 1248-B1
LUNA CT
1000 VSTA 92083 1087-G4
LUNA DR
500 OCN 92057 1067-A6
3700 OCN 92057 1066-J7
LUNADA PL
12700 SD 92128 1150-C5
LUNADA PT
18700 SD 92128 1150-C6

LUNA DE MIEL
17400 SDCo 92067 1168-H1
LUNA DE ORO
7400 SDCo 92067 1168-H1
LUNA MEDIA
- SD 92127 1168-J7
- SD 92127 1188-J1
LUNAR LN
10300 SNTE 92071 1231-E7
LUNA VISTA DR
700 ESCN 92025 1130-A3
LUNA VISTA PL
700 ESCN 92025 1130-A3
LUND ST
2500 ELCJ 92020 1251-B1
2500 SNTE 92071 1251-B1
LUNDY WY
1400 SDCo 92028 1027-J2
LUNDY LAKE DR
2000 SDCo 92029 1129-F7
2200 SDCo 92029 1149-F1
LUNETA DR
- SDCo 92036 1155-H4
1100 DLMR 92014 1187-F4
LUNETA LN
3500 SDCo 92028 1047-E3
3500 SDCo 92055 1047-E3
LUNETA VW
- SDCo 92036 1155-H5
LUNGOS CT
2700 SD 92154 1330-C7
LUPIN WY
10700 SDCo 91941 1271-F4
LUPINE DR
700 SMCS 92078 1128-F2
2400 SDCo 91906 (1297-E6 See Page 1296)
LUPINE LN
3600 SDCo 92028 1028-F6
LUPINE RD
1600 CRLB 92011 1127-E7
LUPINE WY
400 OCN 92057 1086-J4
LUPINE HILLS DR
900 VSTA 92081 1108-A3
1200 VSTA 92081 1107-H3
LUPITA CT
12600 SD 92130 1188-B6
LURA AV
800 ELCJ 92020 1251-F7
LUSARDI TKTR
- SDCo 92027 (1073-B2 See Page 1052)
19500 SDCo 92065 409-G10
LUSK BLVD
6000 SD 92121 1208-C5
LUSTROSOS ST
200 OCN 92057 1066-J6
LUTHER DR
700 SDCo 91977 1291-C3
LUTHER ST
2400 SD 92139 1290-E7
LUTHERAN CT
9700 SNTE 92071 1231-B4
LUTHERAN WY
9500 SNTE 92071 1231-B4
LUX DR
1300 SDCo 92027 1130-C3
LUX CANYON DR
1300 ENCT 92024 1167-G3
LUXEMBOURG WY
- SD 92131 1209-G2
LUZ PL
11400 SD 92127 1169-J1
LUZ RD
11400 SD 92127 1169-J1
LUZ WY
2100 OCN 92056 1086-J7
2100 OCN 92056 1106-J1
LUZEIRO DR
100 SDCo 92084 1088-D5
100 VSTA 92084 1088-D5
LUZON AV
300 DLMR 92014 1187-F4
LYALL PL
13700 SDCo 92021 1232-E5
13700 SDCo 92040 1232-E5
LYCOMING ST
- SD 92154 1351-D2
LYDEN WY
5700 SD 92120 1250-B7
LYDIA LN
1100 SDCo 92028 1027-H1
LYDIA ST
5500 SD 92139 1310-D2
LYERLY RD
- ImCo 92233 411-B10
LYLE DR
5000 SD 92105 1290-A1
LYMAN LN
3100 SD 92093 1228-A2
LYMER DR
4100 SD 92116 1269-H3
LYNCAROL DR
9800 SDCo 91941 1271-D3
LYNCH CT
- CRLB 92008 1107-B7
LYNCH LN
3500 SD 92173 1350-E5
LYNDA PL
3700 NATC 91950 1310-D3
LYNDA RD
2500 SDCo 92028 997-C1
LYNDA PARK LN
14700 PWY 92064 1190-E1
LYNDEN LN
500 SDCo 92028 1027-G2
LYNDHURST TER
- SD 92154 1330-H7
LYNDINE ST
2200 LMGR 91945 1270-H7
2200 LMGR 91945 1290-H1
LYNDON RD
1800 SD 92103 1268-H5
LYNDSIE LN
1000 SDCo 92065 1152-G6
LYNDY LN
1800 SDCo 92028 1048-A4
LYNMAR LN
100 VSTA 92084 1088-B6
1600 SDCo 92028 1027-J3
LYNN CT
3100 OCN 92056 1086-G7
LYNN LN
- OCN 92054 1086-G2
3000 SDCo 92069 1088-J6
LYNN PL
- ELCJ 92020 1251-G6
LYNN ST
5800 SD 92105 1270-C6
LYNN WY
2500 VSTA 92081 1108-B5
LYNNDALE LN
4300 SDCo 91910 1310-E5

LYNNDALE PL
3100 SDCo 91910 1310-E5
LYNNE ANNE LN
9600 SD 92129 1189-E2
LYNNETTE CIR
500 VSTA 92084 1087-H4
4100 OCN 92056 1087-C7
LYNNHAVEN LN
6500 SD 92119 1250-J5
6500 SD 92119 1251-A5
LYNN OAK DR
1400 SDCo 91901 1234-J5
LYNNWOOD DR
3300 SDCo 91910 1310-E5
3300 CHV 91910 1310-E5
LYNRIDGE CT
7100 SD 92120 1250-E5
LYNRIDGE RD
7200 SD 92120 1250-E5
LYNWOOD AV
300 SOLB 92075 1167-F6
LYNWOOD DR
- ENCT 92024 1147-E4
LYNWOOD LN
400 SMCS 92069 1109-B6
LYNX GN
1800 ESCN 92026 1109-F6
LYNX RD
8600 SD 92126 1209-C2
LYNX WY
- CRLB 92010 1107-D7
LYON CIR
200 VSTA 92083 1087-H7
LYON ST
4800 SD 92102 1289-J2
4800 SD 92102 1290-A2
LYONS CT
2700 CRLB 92010 1106-J4
LYONS DR
4500 SDCo 91941 1271-F3
LYONS LN
1200 SDCo 92021 1251-H3
LYONS RD
- ImCo 92243 431-A7
LYONS CREEK LN
2900 SDCo 91935 1294-B1
LYONS CREEK RD
17200 SDCo 91935 1294-A1
LYONS PEAK LN
18300 SDCo 91935 1294-D4
LYONS PEAK RD
- SDCo 91935 1294-B2
LYONS VALLEY RD
13800 SDCo 91935 1292-G1
14000 SDCo 91935 1272-J7
14300 SDCo 91935 1273-A7
15700 SDCo 91935 1293-G2
16500 SDCo 91935 1294-A2
19200 SDCo 91901 1294-H3
21000 SDCo 91901 1274-J7
21000 SDCo 91901 1275-D2
21000 SDCo 91901 (1295-A1 See Page 1294)
LYRA CT
10900 SD 92126 1209-D3
LYRIC LN
4500 SD 92117 1248-H2
LYTHAM GN
- ESCN 92026 1109-H4
LYTTON ST
2900 SD 92110 1268-D6
3000 SD 92106 1268-D6
3000 SD 92140 1268-D6
LYTTON CREEK CT
2800 CHV 91915 (1312-A6 See Page 1293)

M

M AV
400 NATC 91950 1289-J7
600 NATC 91950 1309-J1
1700 NATC 91950 1310-A1
2800 CHV 91950 1310-A3
N M AV
300 CORD 92135 1288-H5
S M AV
400 CORD 92135 1288-G5
M ST
100 ENCT 92007 1167-C1
200 IMP 92251 6439-G6
M & R RANCH RD
2200 SDCo 92028 998-A7
M 1ST ST W
- CORD 92135 1288-C7
- SD 92135 1288-C7
M 2ND ST W
- SD 92135 1288-C7
M 3RD ST S
- CORD 92135 1288-C7
- SD 92135 1288-C7
MABLE WY
4900 SD 92117 1228-H7
MABON PL
3600 SD 92117 1248-D2
MABUHAY WY
2200 SD 92154 1330-D6
MAC LN
9000 SDCo 91977 1271-A6
MACADAMIA CT
4700 SDCo 92057 1067-B7
4700 OCN 92057 1087-A1
MACADAMIA DR
700 CRLB 92011 1126-J6
1300 SDCo 92028 998-B6
MACAMBO DR
- ELCJ 92021 1251-H5
MACARIO DR
4900 OCN 92057 1067-A6
MACARTHUR AV
2000 CRLB 92008 1106-H6
MACARTHUR DR
6400 LMGR 91945 1270-D7
6400 SD 92114 1270-D7
MACAULAY ST
3000 SD 92106 1288-B1
MACAW LN
7600 SD 92123 1269-A1
MACAWA AV
8300 SD 92123 1249-C5
MACCOOL LN
9600 SNTE 92071 1231-C7
MACDONALD ST
2700 OCN 92054 1086-D6
MACE ST
100 CHV 91911 1330-E5
MACERO ST
1700 ESCN 92029 1129-F6
MACHADO ST
1400 OCN 92054 1106-C2
MACHUM PL
- ELCJ 92021 1251-H5
MACKENZIE DR
300 SMCS 92078 1128-G2

STREET
Block City ZIP Pg-Grid

MACKENZIE CREEK RD
2300 CHV 91914 1311-F3
MACKEY DR
2900 SDCo 92028 1047-G1
MACKEY LN
800 SDCo 92028 1047-G1
MACKINNON AV
600 ENCT 92007 1167-E2
MACKINNON CT
700 ENCT 92007 1167-E1
MACKINNON RANCH RD
- ENCT 92007 1167-E4
MACKINZIE WY
16200 SDCo 92082 1071-B7
MACLAY ST
600 SDCo 91977 1291-B3
MACLEAN RD
1500 SDCo 92004 (1099-E2 See Page 1098)
MACLURA ST
4700 OCN 92057 1087-A1
MACNAUGHTON LN
2100 ESCN 92027 1110-C4
MACON ST
500 ELCJ 92019 1252-A4
MACOUBA PL
10800 SD 92124 1249-J2
MACQUARIE ST
7100 LMSA 91942 1270-F1
MACRONALD DR
4300 SDCo 91941 1271-C3
MACS RD
- SDCo 92055 408-L8
MAC TAN LN
15600 SDCo 92082 1071-A6
MAC TAN RD
28400 SDCo 92082 1091-A1
28700 SDCo 92082 1071-A4
28900 SDCo 92082 1070-J7
MACTIBBY ST
3700 SD 92117 1248-E5
MADDEN AV
800 SD 92154 1330-C7
900 SD 92154 1350-C1
MADDEN CT
2800 SD 92154 1330-C7
MADDIE LN
- SD 92154 1330-C7
- SD 92154 1350-C1
MADDOX DR
10000 SD 92124 1249-F2
MADDOX RD
500 ImCo 92231 6620-D6
MADELINE ST
6100 SD 92115 1270-C3
MADERA CT
3100 CRLB 92009 1147-H1
MADERA LN
1100 VSTA 92084 1088-A3
MADERA ST
800 SD 92114 1290-E2
1300 LMGR 92114 1290-E2
1400 LMGR 91945 1290-E2
MADERA ROSA WY
11400 SD 92124 1250-A3
MADERA VERDE PL
1800 SDCo 92021 1252-H3
MADIERA DR
2100 OCN 92056 1086-J7
MADISON AV
- CHV 91910 1309-J5
500 CHV 91910 1330-A1
500 CHV 91910 1310-A7
600 SD 92116 1269-E3
800 ESCN 92026 1109-J6
800 CHV 91911 1330-B2
900 ESCN 92027 1109-J6
4500 SD 92115 1269-J3
4800 SD 92115 1270-A3
7400 LMGR 91945 1270-G6
8700 LMSA 91941 1271-A2
9200 SDCo 91941 1271-B2
E MADISON AV
100 ELCJ 92020 1251-H5
400 ELCJ 92021 1251-H5
1000 ELCJ 92021 1252-B4
1100 ELCJ 92019 1252-B4
1800 SDCo 92019 1252-D4
W MADISON AV
100 ELCJ 92020 1251-E4
MADISON CT
- CALX 92231 6620-J6
MADISON ST
100 OCN 92057 1067-B7
2600 CRLB 92008 1106-E5
MADRA AV
5700 SD 92120 1250-D7
5700 SD 92120 1270-D1
MADRA LN
- OCN 92054 1086-G3
MADRESELVA WY
2100 SD 92154 1350-B3
MADRID DR
1500 VSTA 92081 1107-H3
MADRID ST
3100 SD 92110 1268-D6
MADRID WY
10100 SDCo 91977 1271-E5
MADRIGAL CT
1200 CHV 91910 1311-B7
MADRIGAL ST
10900 SD 92129 1169-H6
MADRILENA WY
7600 CRLB 92009 1147-G2
MADRONA ST
100 CHV 91910 1310-A6
MADRONCILLO ST
2300 SD 92114 1270-E7
2300 SD 92114 1290-E1
MADRONE AV
6300 SD 92114 1290-D3
MADRONE CIR
- IMP 92251 6499-H2
MADRONE GN
1600 ESCN 92027 1110-A5
MADRUGADA CT
11700 SD 92124 1250-B2
MAELEE DR
2200 SDCo 92084 1087-H1
MAEMAR DR
16600 SDCo 92082 1091-C5
MAESTRIA CT
10800 SD 92124 1249-J2
MAESTRO CT
12500 SD 92130 1188-B7
MAEZEL LN
3200 CRLB 92008 1106-G4
MAGARIAN RD
700 SDCo 92028 1027-H3
MAGDALENA AV
- CHV 91913 1311-E7
- CHV 91913 1331-E1
MAGDALENA DR
100 OCN 92057 1087-A2
300 OCN 92057 1086-J1
MAGDALENE WY
1900 SD 92110 1268-E1
MAGEE RD
35900 SDCo 92059 999-H2
37300 SDCo 92059 1030-C1
MAGEE HEIGHTS RD
- SDCo 92059 999-J2
MAGELLAN CIR
3700 OCN 92056 1107-A2
MAGELLAN LN
2500 VSTA 92081 1107-J4
MAGELLAN ST
- CRLB 92011 1127-A7
- CRLB 92011 1147-A1
3100 SD 92154 1330-D7
MAGELLAN WY
1100 CHV 91910 1311-B7
MAGENS BAY
4600 OCN 92057 1066-H6
MAGENTA ST
900 SD 92113 1289-J5
MAGGIO DR
9300 SDCo 91916 1236-C2
MAGICAL WATERS CT
- SDCo 91978 1291-F1
MAGNA LN
10900 SDCo 92040 1231-F3
MAGNATRON BLVD
5500 SD 92111 1229-C7
MAGNOLIA AV
100 SDCo 92065 1153-A3
300 ELCN 92243 6499-H5
600 CRLB 92008 1106-E6
900 ELCJ 92020 1251-F3
1000 SDCo 92020 1251-F3
1100 ELCJ 92020 1271-F1
1200 ESCN 92027 1110-A7
1600 SNTE 92020 1251-F3
1700 SNTE 92020 1231-E6
2600 SD 92109 1248-C5
8500 SNTE 92071 1231-E1
13900 PWY 92064 1190-F3
N MAGNOLIA AV
- ELCJ 92021 1251-F5
100 ELCJ 92020 1251-F5
S MAGNOLIA AV
100 ELCJ 92020 1251-F6
MAGNOLIA CIR
- VSTA 92081 1107-E1
MAGNOLIA CT
400 SMCS 92069 1108-H5
1800 OCN 92054 1106-E2
MAGNOLIA HTS
- SDCo 92065 1153-A4
MAGNOLIA PL
1500 ESCN 92027 1110-B7
MAGNOLIA RD
3800 OCN 92054 1086-F2
MAGNOLIA PARK DR
9700 SNTE 92071 1231-D4
MAGNOLIA POINT CT
- CHV 91914 1311-H2
MAGNUS WY
4700 SD 92113 1289-J6
4700 SD 92113 1290-A6
4900 NATC 91950 1290-A6
MAGRUDER ST
7100 LMSA 91942 1270-F1
MAGUAY RD
- SDCo 91935 1274-E3
MAGUIRE RD
- SD 92173 1350-E4
MAHAILA AV
3900 SD 92122 1228-C3
MAHOGANY CV
- SD 92131 1210-E2
MAHOGANY DR
600 ELCJ 92019 1252-B6
4700 OCN 92056 1087-E5
MAHOGANY GN
300 ESCN 92026 1109-G6
MAHOGANY ST
- SMCS 92078 1128-J3
MAHOGANY RANCH RD
- SDCo 92065 1171-J6
- SDCo 92065 1172-A6
MAHOGANY VISTA LN
- SD 92102 1290-A4
MAIDEN LN
- CALX 92231 6680-F1
1200 DLMR 92014 1187-F5
4900 LMSA 91941 1270-H2
MAIN AV
- SDCo 91950 1310-C3
200 SDCo 92028 1027-F2
N MAIN AV Rt#-S13
100 SDCo 92028 1027-F2
S MAIN AV Rt#-S13
100 SDCo 92028 1027-F3
MAIN ST
- SDCo 92036 1156-H1
100 SD 92173 1350-G4
100 VSTA 92083 1087-H6
100 VSTA 92084 1087-H6
100 CHV 91911 1330-B5
400 ELCN 92243 6499-F6
700 CHV 91911 1331-A5
1500 LMGR 91945 1290-G1
1600 SD 92113 1289-C5
1600 SD 92113 1330-B5
2000 SD 92154 1330-B5
2200 SDCo 92036 1136-B7
2200 LMGR 91945 1270-G7
2700 SD 92136 1289-E6
3800 NATC 91950 1289-E6
MAIN ST Rt#-S30
300 CLPT 92233 411-C10
MAIN ST Rt#-S80
100 ELCN 92243 6499-J6
100 ELCN 92243 6500-A6
MAIN ST Rt#-67
900 SDCo 92065 1152-E7
1900 SDCo 92065 1172-D1
MAIN ST Rt#-78
100 BRW 92227 431-C2
200 ImCo 92227 431-C2
200 SDCo 92065 1152-G6
MAIN ST Rt#-79
1800 SDCo 92036 1136-B7
MAIN ST Rt#-115
100 ImCo 92233 411-C10
500 CLPT 92233 411-C10
E MAIN ST
100 ELCJ 92020 1251-H5
500 ELCJ 92021 1251-H5
800 ELCJ 92019 1251-H5
1200 ELCJ 92019 1252-A4
1200 ELCJ 92021 1252-B2
1900 SDCo 92021 1252-B2
W MAIN ST
- SDCo 92004 (1121-G2 See Page 1100)
1000 ELCJ 92020 1251-E5
2500 ELCN 92243 6499-C6
2500 ImCo 92243 6499-C6
MAINE AV
9700 SDCo 92040 1232-B3
MAINSAIL RD
300 OCN 92054 1086-F6
MAISEL WY
5400 SD 92115 1270-B3
MAITLAND AV
500 SD 92154 1330-E6
MAJANO PL
2400 CRLB 92009 1147-G3
MAJELLA DR
24100 SDCo 92065 1173-E2
MAJELLA RD
2500 SDCo 92084 1087-F1
2500 SDCo 92084 1067-F7
MAJESTAD LN
1100 CHV 91910 1310-J5
MAJESTIC DR
3500 SD 92154 1350-E1
MAJORCA WY
4600 OCN 92056 1107-E4
MAKAHA WY
2900 SD 92154 1330-C6
MAKENNA LN
- SDCo 91901 1253-F1
MAKIN RD
2300 CORD 92155 1309-A1
MALABAR DR
12200 PWY 92064 1170-B7
MALACHITE PL
- CRLB 92009 1127-F4
MALAGA DR
4900 OCN 92057 1067-A6
MALAGA ST
3000 SD 92110 1268-D6
MALAGA WY
1500 SDCo 92028 1027-F5
MALCOLM DR
6000 SD 92115 1270-C4
MALCOLM ST
5300 OCN 92056 1087-E1
MALDEN ST
1600 SD 92109 1247-J4
1600 SD 92109 1248-A4
MALEA WY
6000 OCN 92056 1107-F5
MALEK LN
12100 SDCo 92082 1070-C4
MALENE LN
1000 SDCo 92021 1251-H2
MALER RD
9100 SD 92129 1189-D1
MALEY ST
7100 SD 92111 1248-J6
7100 SD 92111 1249-A6
MALIBU PL
2700 ESCN 92027 1110-D6
MALIBU WY
2400 SD 92014 1187-H5
MALIBU POINT CT
1500 CHV 91911 1330-J3
MALIBU POINT WY
800 OCN 92054 1066-G7
MALITO CT
200 CHV 91911 1330-G5
MALITO DR
3400 SDCo 91902 1310-F2
MALLARD CT
- CRLB 92011 1127-B7
- ImCo 92249 6560-B7
MALLARD DR
29800 SDCo 91906 (1297-F5 See Page 1296)
MALLARD ST
- ImCo 92243 6560-A7
- ImCo 92249 6560-A7
6300 SD 92114 1290-D1
6800 LMGR 91945 1290-D1
6800 SD 91945 1290-D1
MALLEE ST
- CRLB 92011 1127-D5
MALLORCA DR
1500 VSTA 92081 1107-H3
MALLORCA PL
2600 CRLB 92009 1147-G1
MALLOW CT
1700 CRLB 92011 1127-E6
MALONEY ST
1300 SMCS 92069 1108-H3
MALOREY ST
7500 LMSA 91942 1250-G6
MA LOU DR
3000 SDCo 91935 1292-J1
3000 SDCo 91935 1293-A1
3100 SDCo 91935 1272-J7
MALPAZO CT
3400 SDCo 91902 1310-G2
MALTA AV
1500 CHV 91911 1330-G4
MALTA ST
- SD 92111 1248-J4
MALTA WY
3300 OCN 92056 1106-J1
MALVERN CT
5700 SD 92120 1250-B7
MAMMOTH DR
2500 SD 92123 1249-E6
N MAMMOTH PL
2100 ESCN 92029 1129-E6
S MAMMOTH PL
1700 ESCN 92029 1129-F6
MANACOR CT
10800 SD 92124 1249-H2
MANAGUA PL
2900 CRLB 92009 1127-H7
MANAJO RD
9100 SDCo 92040 1232-C6
MANAJO WY
13000 SDCo 92040 1232-C5
MANANA PL
6500 SD 92037 1247-F2
MANASSAS ST
- SDCo 92127 1169-E4
MANCHESTER AV
1900 ENCT 92007 1167-D3
2000 ESCN 92027 1110-D3
3200 ENCT 92024 1167-H3
3400 ENCT 92067 1167-F4
MANCHESTER DR
- OCN 92056 1087-D1
MANCHESTER PL
1700 ESCN 92027 1130-C1
MANCHESTER RD
5100 SD 92115 1270-E2
MANCHESTER ST
900 NATC 91950 1290-C7
MANCILLA CT
4200 SD 92130 1188-B6
MANDA PL
1200 ELCJ 92021 1251-G3
1200 SDCo 92021 1251-G3
MANDALAY PL
5200 SD 92115 1270-E2
MANDALAY RD
6900 SD 92115 1270-E2
MANDAN WY
3100 SD 92117 1248-C1
MANDARIN CV
- SD 92105 1270-B5
- SD 92115 1270-B5
MANDARIN DR
800 SDCo 92028 1027-G3
5100 OCN 92056 1087-D2
MANDARIN TER
- SD 92115 1270-B5
MANDARIN WY
500 SDCo 92028 1027-G3
MANDELL WEISS LN
- SD 92093 1227-J3
MANDEVILLA CT
- SMCS 92069 1109-A6
MANDEVILLE CT
9400 SNTE 92071 1231-B5
MANDEVILLE DR
1200 CHV 91910 1330-J2
1400 ESCN 92029 1149-G1
1400 ESCN 92029 1129-G7
MANDEVILLE PL
1400 ESCN 92029 1129-G7
MANDEVILLE RD
9400 SD 92093 1228-A2
9400 SNTE 92071 1231-B5
MANDEZ DR
2000 SDCo 92065 1172-E3
MANDI LN
- SNTE 92071 1231-C3
100 SDCo 92065 1152-J3
MANDRAKE CT
11700 SD 92131 1210-A2
MANDRAKE PT
11300 SD 92131 1210-A2
MANDY LN
3300 SDCo 91977 1271-D6
MANFRED CT
1700 ELCJ 92021 1252-B2
MANGANO CIR
100 ENCT 92024 1147-C6
MANGO CT
700 SMCS 92069 1109-C6
MANGO CV
14300 SD 92014 1187-H5
MANGO DR
13200 SD 92014 1187-H5
MANGO GN
900 SDCo 92084 1088-D5
MANGO WY
2400 SD 92014 1187-H5
MANGONEL DR
2000 SDCo 92004 1058-G7
MANGO VIEW DR
200 ENCT 92024 1147-E7
MANGRUM PL
2300 OCN 92056 1106-H1
MANHASSET DR
5100 SD 92115 1270-A2
MANHATTAN CT
700 SD 92109 1267-H2
MANIFESTO PL
12500 SD 92130 1188-B7
MANILA AV
10400 SD 92126 1209-B4
MANILA CIR
7900 SD 92126 1209-B4
MANILA TR
7500 SDCo 91962 1237-C7
MANION ST
2300 ELCJ 92020 1251-B1
MANITOU WY
4400 SD 92117 1248-F1
MANKATO ST
100 CHV 91910 1310-B7
600 CHV 91910 1330-A1
E MANKATO ST
- CHV 91910 1310-D6
MANLEY ST
4700 SD 92124 1249-G2
MANN AV
100 NATC 91950 1290-A6
MANNEN WY
13200 SDCo 92040 1232-C7
MANNING ST
6600 SD 92111 1248-H7
MANNING WY
- SD 92102 1289-G3
800 SD 92154 1330-B7
MANNIS AV
- CHV 91913 1311-C7
- CHV 91913 1331-C1
MANNIX CT
7300 SD 92129 1188-J7
MANNIX RD
- SD 92129 1188-J7
MANOCK CV
13000 SD 92130 1188-D5
MANOMET ST
4900 SD 92113 1290-A5
MANON ST
5800 LMSA 91942 1250-G6
MANOR DR
500 ELCJ 92020 1251-E1
500 SDCo 92021 1251-J2
1600 VSTA 92084 1087-G3
9100 LMSA 91942 1251-B6
E MANOR DR
600 CHV 91910 1330-A1
W MANOR DR
600 CHV 91910 1330-A1
6100 LMSA 91942 1251-B6
MANOR WY
900 SD 92106 1288-A2
MANOR RIDGE LN
4900 SD 92130 1208-D1
MANOS DR
2700 SD 92139 1310-D2
MANRESA CT
16900 SD 92128 1170-C2
MANSFIELD ST
4600 SD 92116 1269-F3
MANSIONES LN
1100 CHV 91910 1310-J5
MANSON ST
7200 SD 92111 1248-J6
MANTECA DR
- OCN 92057 1067-A4
MANTILLA RD
12300 SD 92128 1170-C4
MANTON WY
100 VSTA 92084 1087-G2
MANTUA CT
5400 SD 92124 1249-H1
MANUEL ORTIZ AV
- ELCN 92243 6559-G3
MANYA CIR
7000 SD 92154 1330-B5
MANYA ST
2200 SD 92154 1330-B5
MANZANA WY
2300 SD 92139 1290-H5
MANZANARES WY
5100 SD 92114 1290-A4
MANZANILLA WY
- OCN 92057 1087-A2
MANZANILLO CT
100 SOLB 92075 1167-D6
MANZANITA AV
1400 ESCN 92027 1110-A7
MANZANITA CT
1800 VSTA 92083 1108-B3
MANZANITA DR
- ELCN 92243 6559-G2
- ImCo 92243 6559-G2
- SDCo 92036 1155-G4
200 OCN 92057 1067-A7
600 SDCo 92036 1156-E1
800 SDCo 92036 1136-C7
3800 SD 92105 1269-G7
24300 SDCo 91916 1236-A2
29400 SDCo 91906 (1297-E5 See Page 1296)
MANZANITA LN
800 SMCS 92069 1108-J6
11500 SDCo 92040 1211-G7
25000 SDCo 91916 1236-B2
MANZANITA PL
300 ESCN 92026 1129-H1
3200 SD 92105 1269-H6
MANZANITA RD
- SDCo 91905 430-D7
- SDCo 91905 (1299-J1 See Page 1298)
- SDCo 91905 1300-A1
11200 SDCo 92040 1211-H6
MANZANITA ST
500 CHV 91911 1330-G1
7000 CRLB 92011 1127-E7
MANZANITA TR
2400 SDCo 91905 (1299-H4 See Page 1298)
28900 SDCo 91962 1237-B7
MANZANITA WY
- SDCo 91905 1300-D6
4300 OCN 92057 1086-J2
20500 SDCo 91935 (1315-A1 See Page 1294)
MANZANITA CREST RD
31100 SDCo 92082 1070-A3
MANZANITA DULCE
39500 SDCo 91905 1300-C5
MANZANITA RANCH RD
- SDCo 92065 1173-H6
MANZANITA VIEW RD
2800 SDCo 91901 1234-C7
MANZANO DR
100 CRLB 92008 1126-G3
MANZANO PL
400 CHV 91910 1310-H4
MANZELLA DR
14200 SD 92129 1189-G2
MAPLE
9700 SDCo 92021 1233-B3
MAPLE AV
- ImCo 92243 6560-A6
- ImCo 92249 6560-B7
100 CRLB 92008 1106-E6
200 ELCN 92243 6499-J7
500 SMCS 92069 1108-H5
500 SMCS 92069 1109-A5
4200 LMSA 91941 1270-G2
MAPLE CT
300 CHV 91911 1330-G3
2900 SD 92104 1269-E7
MAPLE DR
1600 CHV 91911 1330-G5
4400 OCN 92056 1087-D5
MAPLE LN
9700 SDCo 92029 1149-E2
MAPLE RDG
- SD 92130 1208-B2
MAPLE ST
- SMCS 92078 1129-C2
100 SD 92101 1289-A1
100 SDCo 92065 1152-F4
100 SD 92103 1289-A1
100 SD 92101 1288-J1
500 SD 92103 1288-J1
2500 SD 92104 1269-D7
4300 SD 92105 1269-H7
5200 SD 92105 1270-A7
N MAPLE ST
100 ESCN 92025 1129-J3
S MAPLE ST
100 ESCN 92025 1129-J3
1000 ESCN 92025 1130-A4
MAPLEBROOK CT
1900 ELCJ 92019 1252-C5
MAPLE GROVE LN
- SD 92131 1210-H2
- SD 92145 1210-H2
MAPLE LEAF CT
- SD 92131 1210-G2
MAPLELEAF CT
1600 ENCT 92024 1167-G1
MAPLELEAF DR
2300 VSTA 92081 1108-A5
6800 CRLB 92011 1127-A5
MAPLETON CT
- SD 92127 1169-A3
MAPLE TREE RD
10100 SNTE 92071 1231-D3
MAPLEVIEW ST
12300 SDCo 92040 1232-C2
MAPLEWOOD CIR
5100 OCN 92056 1087-D2
MAPLEWOOD CT
12700 PWY 92064 1190-C2
MAPLEWOOD LN
11900 SDCo 92040 1231-J3
MAPLEWOOD PL
- ESCN 92027 1130-J3
MAPLEWOOD ST
14300 PWY 92064 1190-C2
MAPLEWOOD WY
700 ELCJ 92021 1251-G4
MAR AV
7300 SD 92037 1227-F7
MARA LN
15800 SDCo 92065 1172-A4
MARABOU LN
1300 VSTA 92083 1087-F4
MARANDA DR
9100 SNTE 92071 1231-A5
MARATHON DR
2500 SD 92123 1249-E5
MARATHON WY
4800 OCN 92056 1107-E6
MARAVILLA LN
600 SDCo 92028 1047-E3
MARAVILLA WY
2400 OCN 92056 1087-C5
MARAZON LN
700 VSTA 92081 1107-E1
MAR AZUL WY
2000 CRLB 92009 1127-F7
MARBELLA CIR
700 CHV 91910 1311-A5
MARBELLA CT
1200 CHV 91910 1311-A5
MARBELLA DR
1600 VSTA 92081 1107-G4
MARBELLA PL
1200 CHV 91910 1311-A5
MARBLE CT
1500 CHV 91911 1330-G4
MARBLE LN
- SMCS 92078 1128-B5
MARBLE ST
500 ELCJ 92020 1251-G4
MARBLE WY
1500 CHV 91911 1330-G4
MARBLE CANYON WY
1400 CHV 91915 1311-J6
1500 CHV 91915 (1312-A6 See Page 1293)
MARBLEHEAD BAY DR
4600 OCN 92057 1066-J6
MARBO TER
1000 VSTA 92084 1087-J4
MARBOK WY
3000 SDCo 91935 1292-G1
MARBROOK WY
13700 SDCo 92021 1232-E7
MARBURY AV
10600 SD 92126 1209-D3
MARC TR
1700 SDCo 91906 (1318-E3 See Page 1298)
MARCA PL
2300 CRLB 92009 1147-G2
MARCASEL PL
13400 SD 92130 1188-B4
MARCASITE PL
- CRLB 92009 1127-F5
MARCELLA CT
10100 SNTE 92071 1231-A3
MARCELLA ST
4100 OCN 92056 1087-B6
MARCELLENA RD
4400 SD 92115 1270-A4
MARCH PL
2100 SD 92110 1268-F1
MARCHETA ST
100 ENCT 92024 1147-B6
MARCI WY
- SDCo 92028 1048-A4
MARCIA CT
4300 SD 92154 1350-G1
MARCIA LN
4600 SDCo 92020 1271-H2
MARCILLA WY
600 CHV 91910 1310-H6
MARCONI CT
2300 SD 92154 1352-B3
MARCONI DR
9700 SD 92154 1352-A3
MARCONI PL
2300 SD 92154 1352-B3
MARCOS ST
300 SMCS 92069 1108-G7
MARCOS VISTA LN
700 SMCS 92078 1108-C6
MARCWADE CT
3800 SD 92154 1350-F1
MARCWADE DR
3900 SD 92154 1350-F1
MARCY AV
2600 SD 92113 1289-D5
MARCYN LN
1600 ESCN 92026 1109-H6
MARDAVIDO LN
2100 SDCo 92028 1028-B6
MARDAVIDO PL
2100 SDCo 92028 1028-B6
MARDI GRAS CT
- CORD 92118 1329-D3
MARDI GRAS RD
- CORD 92118 1329-E2
MARDI GRAS ST
4600 OCN 92057 1066-H7
MARE RD
5300 OCN 92057 1067-B5
MARENGO AV
5200 LMSA 91942 1270-H1
5500 LMSA 91942 1250-H7
MARGALE LN
29800 SDCo 92084 1068-F6
MARGARET CT
9000 SDCo 91977 1291-A2
MARGARET ST
5200 SDCo 91902 1310-J1
MARGARET WY
3800 CRLB 92008 1106-G6
MARGARITA AV
500 CORD 92118 1288-J7
1000 CORD 92118 1289-A7
MARGARITA GN
1300 SDCo 92028 998-C6
MARGARITA LN
14100 SDCo 92082 1070-F2
MARGARITA ST
- CALX 92231 6620-J7
12600 SD 92130 1208-A2
MARGARITA VISTA
3000 SDCo 92028 998-C7
MARGARITTA RD
6600 SD 92114 1290-E4
MARGATE AV
12800 PWY 92064 1190-H5
MARGE WY
4200 SD 92154 1350-G1
MARGERUM AV
6200 SD 92120 1250-C4
MARGIE PL
500 SMCS 92078 1128-D1
MARGIE WY
- VSTA 92084 1088-D6
MARGINATA CT
11900 SD 92131 1210-A1
MARGO CT
300 CHV 91910 1310-F7
MARGO PL
1100 VSTA 92081 1107-E1
MARGUERITA LN
4800 LMSA 91941 1271-B2
4800 SDCo 91941 1271-B2
MARGUERITE LN
900 CRLB 92011 1127-A6
MARGUERITE WY
200 OCN 92057 1086-H3
MARGUERITE CANYON RD
11100 SDCo 92040 1212-H6
MARIA AV
400 SDCo 91977 1291-C2
MARIA CT
2100 LMGR 91945 1290-J1
MARIA LN
3600 CRLB 92008 1106-H5
MARIA PL
1500 CORD 92118 1288-J7
MARIA WY
800 CHV 91911 1330-F1
MARIAN AV
2100 SD 92154 1330-A6
MARIAN ST
3900 LMSA 91941 1270-E5
MARIAN WY
5400 SD 92110 1268-F3
MARIANA DR
14200 PWY 92064 1190-B2
MARIANA WY
- OCN 92057 1086-G6
MARIANNE LN
2600 SDCo 92028 1028-B4
MARIANOPOLIS WY
14200 SD 92129 1189-D2
MARICOTTE PL
13200 SD 92130 1187-J5
MARIE AV
7600 LMSA 91941 1270-G3
MARIE CT
700 ENCT 92024 1147-G5
MARIE LN
1600 SDCo 91977 1291-A2
MARIELLE PL
- CHV 91913 1311-F1
MARIETTA ST
400 CHV 91910 1310-A5
MARIGOLD
9600 SDCo 92021 1233-B3
MARIGOLD CIR
300 OCN 92057 1066-H6
MARIGOLD CT
800 CRLB 92011 1127-A5
MARIGOLD DR
- SD 92109 1248-C6
600 VSTA 92083 1087-F5
13600 PWY 92064 1190-F2
MARIGOLD PL
100 CHV 91910 1310-C5
2200 SD 92105 1289-G1
MARIGOLD ST
2300 SD 92105 1289-G1
MARIGOLD WY
800 SMCS 92078 1128-F2
MARIGOT PL
5200 SD 92124 1249-J1
MARILLA DR
9200 SDCo 92040 1231-H5
MARILOU RD
4800 SD 92102 1289-J2
4800 SD 92102 1290-A2
MARILOUISE WY
2400 SD 92103 1268-G4
MARILYN LN
1600 SMCS 92069 1109-A1
1900 SDCo 92069 1109-A1
MARIN DR
- SMCS 92069 1108-H5
4900 OCN 92056 1107-F3
MARINA AV
500 CORD 92118 1288-G7
MARINA CT
- IMP 92251 6499-H2
MARINA DR
- ImCo 92274 410-H6
4700 CRLB 92008 1106-H7
MARINA PKWY
300 CHV 91910 1309-H7
400 CHV 91910 1329-J1
700 CHV 91910 1330-A1
MARINA WY
- NATC 91950 1309-G4
900 CHV 91910 1329-H2
MARINA DEL REY AV
100 OCN 92054 1066-E6
MARINA PARK WY
200 SD 92101 1289-A5
MARINA SPRINGS LN
9300 SDCo 92021 1232-J4
MARINDUSTRY DR
6200 SD 92121 1228-G1
MARINE PL
- CRLB 92011 1127-A7
MARINE RD
- SDCo 92055 1047-A4
MARINE ST
200 SD 92037 1247-E1
400 SD 92037 1227-E7
MARINE WY
- SD 92109 1248-C6
1400 CORD 92118 1288-J5
MARINER ST
900 CRLB 92011 1126-J4
MARINERS BAY
4500 OCN 92057 1066-H6
MARINERS WY
1000 SD 92109 1267-J3
MARINE VIEW AV
100 SOLB 92075 1167-G7
400 SOLB 92014 1167-G7
600 SOLB 92014 1187-G1
3900 SD 92113 1289-G7
MARINE VIEW DR
1000 SDCo 92084 1107-H3
MARING PL
5200 SD 92105 1290-A1
MARIO PL
3700 SD 92111 1248-H4
MARION CT
1500 CHV 91913 1311-C7
MARION LN
2200 SDCo 92025 1130-D6
MARIPOSA
5400 SDCo 92067 1168-C3
MARIPOSA CIR
600 CHV 91911 1330-G1
MARIPOSA CT
1200 VSTA 92084 1088-A3
MARIPOSA DR
1500 SDCo 92004 1058-F5
MARIPOSA LN
8500 LMSA 91941 1271-A3
MARIPOSA PL
900 ESCN 92026 1109-F5
5600 SD 92114 1290-C6
MARIPOSA RD
1100 CRLB 92011 1127-A4
MARIPOSA ST
500 CHV 91911 1330-G1
1400 SD 92114 1290-B6
8600 LMSA 91941 1270-J3
8600 LMSA 91941 1271-A3

STREET
Block City ZIP Pg-Grid

MARISA CT
2300 ENCT 92024 1147-J6
2300 ENCT 92024 1148-A5
MARISA LN
800 ENCT 92024 1147-J5
800 ENCT 92024 1148-A6
MARISCO PT
12300 SD 92130 1188-B7
MARISMA WY
1600 SD 92037 1247-G1
MARITA LN
1700 SDCo 92028 1027-J3
MARITIME DR
1500 CRLB 92011 1127-C4
MARITIME PL
12900 SD 92130 1187-J5
MARJAY DR
13300 SDCo 92040 1232-D6
MARJEAN LN
10200 SDCo 92040 1231-G3
MARJO CT
2500 OCN 92056 1087-D6
MARJORIE AV
1400 ESCN 92027 1110-A6
MARJORIE DR
700 SD 92114 1290-G3
MARJORIE LN
3600 CRLB 92008 1106-G5
MARJORIE PL
1200 ESCN 92027 1110-A7
MARJORIE ST
1500 OCN 92056 1087-E2
MARK AV
2000 ESCN 92027 1110-B6
MARK CIR
2400 CRLB 92010 1106-H4
MARK PL
2200 ESCN 92027 1110-C6
MARK TER
4000 SD 92117 1248-E5
MARK TR
- SDCo 91935 1274-A4
16700 SDCo 91935 1273-J5
MARKAB DR
11300 SD 92126 1209-C1
MARKAR RD
15000 PWY 92064 1170-J6
MARKELL LN
300 SDCo 92028 1027-F4
MARKER LN
3100 SDCo 92004 (1079-B5 See Page 1058)
MARKER RD
- SD 92130 1188-J3
- SD 92130 1189-A3
MARKERRY AV
1500 ELCJ 92019 1252-B5
MARKET PL
- SD 92101 1288-J4
- ESCN 92029 1129-E3
MARKET ST
100 SD 92101 1289-A3
500 SD 92101 1288-J4
1400 VSTA 92084 1087-J4
1700 SD 92102 1289-C3
4700 SD 92102 1290-A3
5000 SD 92114 1290-B3
MARKETPLACE AV
- SD 92113 1289-H5
MARKHAM ST
7600 SD 92111 1249-A5
MARK LEE DR
17900 SDCo 91935 1274-C4
MARK STEVENS RD
13700 PWY 92064 1190-G3
MARKWOOD DR
9500 SNTE 92071 1231-B4
MARKY WY
9700 SDCo 91941 1271-C3
MARL AV
1500 CHV 91911 1330-G4
MARL CT
1400 CHV 91911 1330-G3
MARLBOROUGH AV
3100 SD 92105 1269-H6
4400 SD 92116 1269-G4
MARLBOROUGH DR
4700 SD 92116 1269-G3
MARLEN WY
5100 LMSA 91941 1271-A1
MARLENA WY
3100 SDCo 91978 1292-D1
3100 SDCo 91978 1272-C7
MARLESTA DR
3200 SD 92111 1248-J4
3900 SD 92111 1249-A3
MARLIN DR
900 VSTA 92084 1087-J6
900 VSTA 92084 1088-A6
MARLIN LN
- CRLB 92011 1127-A7
MARLIN RD
- SDCo 92055 1085-H6
MARLINDA WY
1800 SDCo 92021 1251-G1
MARLINE AV
1100 ELCJ 92021 1251-J4
1300 ELCJ 92021 1252-A4
MARLOWE DR
6600 SD 92115 1270-E5
MARLTON DR
3200 SD 92102 1289-F1
3200 SD 92104 1289-F1
MARLYNN CT
- ESCN 92025 1130-B5
MARMAC DR
15600 SDCo 92065 1172-A4
MAR MARY CIR
- SDCo 92003 1068-G1
MARMIL AV
3000 SD 92139 1310-D2
MARMIL PL
7300 SD 92114 1290-F3
MARMIL WY
5900 SD 92139 1310-D2
MARMOL CT
2600 CRLB 92009 1127-G6
MARNE AV
5600 SD 92120 1250-D7
5600 SD 92120 1270-C1
MAROON PEAK CT
11600 SD 92131 1190-A7
MARQUAND CT
- SDCo 91901 1234-B6
MARQUETTE AV
- SMCS 92078 1128-H3
MARQUETTE PL
3800 SD 92106 1268-C5
MARQUETTE RD
2000 CHV 91913 1311-E5
MARQUETTE ST
1200 OCN 92054 1086-A6
2900 SD 92106 1268-C5

STREET
Block City ZIP Pg-Grid

MARQUEZ CT
2300 SDCo 92084 1087-H1
MARQUIS CT
1900 CHV 91913 1311-E5
MARQUITA PL
2600 CRLB 92009 1147-G2
MARRACO DR
4300 SD 92115 1270-D4
MARRACO WY
4400 SD 92115 1270-D4
MARROKAL LN
8600 SNTE 92071 1230-J7
MARRON RD
- CRLB 92010 1107-A3
- OCN 92056 1107-A3
1700 CRLB 92008 1106-F3
2500 CRLB 92010 1106-G3
MARRON ST
100 OCN 92054 1106-A2
3800 SD 92115 1270-C5
MARRON VALLEY RD
500 SDCo 91917 429-J10
500 SDCo 91917 (1314-B7 See Page 1294)
MARS GN
- ESCN 92025 1129-H2
MARS WY
4000 SDCo 91941 1271-G4
MARSALA TER
- SD 92123 1249-D1
MARSAT CT
600 CHV 91911 1330-B4
MAR SCENIC DR
13600 SD 92014 1187-H7
MARSDEN CT
100 ELCJ 92020 1251-D5
MARSEILLES ST
4400 SD 92107 1287-H2
MARSHA CT
2600 SD 92105 1270-A7
MARSHALL AV
100 ELCJ 92020 1251-E5
N MARSHALL AV
400 ELCJ 92020 1251-D1
MARSHALL CT
2300 SDCo 91901 1234-B6
MARSHALL LN
2800 SD 92093 1227-J1
3000 SDCo 91977 1271-A6
MARSHALL RD
1400 SDCo 91901 1234-B6
N MARSHALL RD
1300 SDCo 91901 1234-B6
MARSHALL ST
1400 OCN 92054 1106-C2
MARSHALL WY
2300 SDCo 91901 1234-B6
19400 SDCo 92082 1091-H3
MARSH HARBOR DR
400 SD 92154 1330-H6
MARSH WREN ST
- CRLB 92011 1127-B6
MARSOLAN AV
600 SOLB 92075 1187-F1
MARSON ST
1700 OCN 92054 1086-B5
MARSOPA
3000 CRLB 92009 1127-J5
MARSOPA DR
700 VSTA 92081 1107-F1
MARTA PL
- VSTA 92084 1087-H6
MARTEE LN
9400 SNTE 92071 1231-C7
MARTELL ST
300 ELCJ 92019 1252-B5
MARTHA ST
3600 SD 92117 1248-D1
MARTIN AV
3000 SD 92113 1289-E5
MARTIN DR
900 ESCN 92026 1109-J7
900 ESCN 92026 1129-J1
MARTIN PL
1300 CHV 91911 1330-H2
MARTIN ST
5000 OCN 92057 1067-A6
MARTIN WY
- SDCo 91901 1255-J1
MARTINA CT
1000 SDCo 92078 1128-G4
MARTIN CANYON CT
4000 SDCo 91902 1311-A3
MARTINCOIT RD
16000 PWY 92064 1170-E3
MARTINDALE CT
3000 SD 92123 1249-E5
MARTINEZ ST
900 SD 92106 1288-A2
MARTINEZ RANCH RD
2600 SD 92154 1351-E4
MARTINGALE CT
1500 CRLB 92011 1127-C4
MARTINGALE LN
- SDCo 91901 1234-A3
500 SMCS 92069 1108-E5
MARTINIQUE DR
900 CHV 91913 1311-E5
MARTINIQUE WY
10900 SD 92126 1209-A3
MARTIN LUTHER KING AV
- CALX 92231 6620-G6
MARTIN L KING JR FRWY Rt#-94
- LMGR - 1270-D7
- SD - 1270-D7
- SD - 1289-F3
- SD - 1290-A2
MARTIN RIDGE RD
16000 SDCo 92036 1176-D2
MARTINVIEW DR
2000 SD 92105 1289-H1
MARTOS PL
700 CHV 91910 1310-J5
MARVEJO
- SDCo 92040 1232-D6
MARVEL TER
1100 SDCo 92065 1153-B1
MARVIEW DR
400 SOLB 92075 1167-F6
MARVIEW LN
500 SOLB 92075 1167-F6
MARVIN ST
3800 OCN 92056 1087-B7
5400 SD 92105 1270-B6
MARVINGA LN
- SDCo 92028 996-J2
2700 SDCo 92028 997-A2
MAR VISTA DR
100 VSTA 92083 1108-A2
400 VSTA 92083 1107-H2
400 VSTA 92081 1107-H2
500 SOLB 92075 1167-F6

STREET
Block City ZIP Pg-Grid

MAR VISTA DR
700 SDCo 92028 1027-G1
MARWOOD LN
100 OCN 92054 1106-C2
MARY AV
100 CALX 92231 6680-G2
1000 ImCo 92249 6560-C7
1000 ImCo 92249 6620-C1
MARY CT
800 NATC 91950 1290-C7
MARY LN
1000 SDCo 92025 1130-E5
1100 NATC 91950 1290-C7
2600 ESCN 92025 1130-D5
2600 SDCo 92025 1150-D1
3500 ESCN 92025 1150-C2
11300 SDCo 92040 1212-B7
11300 SDCo 92040 1232-B1
MARY LN S
3300 SDCo 92025 1150-C2
MARY ST
1000 ELCJ 92021 1251-H4
MARY ANN ST
1500 SDCo 91977 1291-B2
MARYANN WY
1900 SDCo 92019 1272-A1
MARY DEAN LN
- SDCo 92040 1231-J7
MARYEARL CT
13500 PWY 92064 1190-F1
MARYEARL LN
13400 PWY 92064 1190-E1
MARY FELLOWS AV
5200 LMSA 91942 1270-F1
MARYFORD DR
8600 SD 92119 1250-J3
MARYGOLD DR
2500 SDCo 91906 (1297-E5 See Page 1296)
MARY JOE LN
1600 SDCo 91905 (1320-A2 See Page 1300)
MARYLAND AV
5200 LMSA 91942 1270-F1
5500 LMSA 91942 1250-F7
MARYLAND CT
700 VSTA 92083 1087-F6
4500 SD 92116 1269-B4
MARYLAND DR
700 VSTA 92083 1087-F6
MARYLAND PL
1200 SD 92103 1269-B4
MARYLAND ST
4100 SD 92103 1269-B4
4400 SD 92116 1269-B4
MARY LANE CT
1100 SDCo 92025 1130-D7
MARY LANE DR
5400 SD 92115 1270-B2
MARY LANE PL
2600 SDCo 92025 1130-D7
MARY LEWIS DR
2900 SDCo 92028 1048-D3
MARY LOU ST
1400 SD 92102 1290-A2
MARYMAC PL
1800 SDCo 92028 1028-A6
MARYMONT PL
17600 SD 92128 1170-A1
MARY PAT LN
- LMGR 91945 1290-H1
MARYSVILLE AV
- CHV 91913 1331-B1
MARZO ST
3500 SD 92154 1350-E2
MASCARI CT
1100 SDCo 92021 1251-H3
MASCARI PL
3900 SDCo 91941 1271-C4
3900 SDCo 91977 1271-C4
MASON CIR
600 SDCo 92084 1067-J7
600 SDCo 92084 1087-J1
MASON DR
3700 LMGR 91945 1270-J5
MASON RD
100 SDCo 92084 1067-H7
100 SDCo 92084 1087-H1
900 SDCo 92084 1088-A1
MASON ST
3900 SD 92110 1268-F4
MASON WY
2700 SDCo 92084 1067-H7
MASON HEIGHTS LN
7400 SD 92126 1208-J2
MASONRY PL
1100 ESCN 92029 1129-F5
MASON VALLEY TKTR
- SDCo 92036 1176-G1
- SDCo 92036 (1177-H1 See Page 1176)
MASSACHUSETTS AV
400 VSTA 92084 1087-H6
1800 LMGR 91945 1290-F1
2200 LMGR 91945 1270-F7
3700 LMGR 91941 1270-F7
3700 LMSA 91941 1270-F7
MASSACHUSETTS ST
4500 SD 92116 1269-B4
MASSASOIT AV
2900 SD 92117 1248-C1
MASSENA ST
1300 SD 92037 1227-F7
MASSERY LN
8500 SNTE 92071 1231-B7
8500 SNTE 92071 1251-B1
MASSOT AV
9200 SNTE 92071 1230-J6
MAST BLVD
- SD 92124 1230-H6
- SDCo 92040 1231-G4
8200 SD 92145 1230-H5
8200 SD 92071 1230-H5
8200 SNTE 92071 1230-H5
8900 SNTE 92071 1231-E4
MASTERPIECE DR
1100 SDCo 92057 1087-B2
MASTERS DR
700 OCN 92057 1087-B1
MASTERS PL
3000 SD 92123 1249-E5
MASTERS RD
- CRLB 92008 1107-B7
- CRLB 92008 1127-B1
MASTERSON LN
- SD 92154 1350-G2
MASTERS RIDGE RD
1000 CHV 91915 1311-G4
MATA WY
100 SMCS 92069 1109-A7
MATADOR CT
10200 SD 92124 1229-G7
10200 SD 92124 1249-G1

STREET
Block City ZIP Pg-Grid

MATAGUAL DR
500 VSTA 92081 1087-G7
500 VSTA 92081 1107-G1
MATAMO PL
1000 SDCo 92019 1252-G6
MATAMOROS CT
100 SOLB 92075 1167-D7
MATANZA RD
12700 SD 92128 1170-C3
MATARO DR
4400 SD 92115 1270-D3
MATCH POINT DR
14200 PWY 92064 1190-G4
MATEO PL
2700 CRLB 92009 1147-G2
MATERA LN
- SD 92108 1249-D7
MATER DEI DR
- CHV 91913 1331-E1
MATHER AV
500 SD 92154 1330-E6
MATHEW RD
15600 SDCo 92082 1091-A4
MATHEWS DR
2700 SD 92110 1268-E6
MATHIESON ST
10500 SD 92129 1189-G2
MATILDE GOMEZ
700 CALX 92231 6680-D1
MATIN CIR
200 SMCS 92069 1109-E7
1800 SMCS 92069 1129-D1
MATINAL CIR
10500 SD 92127 1149-J7
10700 SD 92127 1169-J1
MATINAL DR
17400 SD 92127 1169-J1
MATINAL RD
17000 SD 92127 1169-H1
MATISSE LN
5200 SDCo 91902 1290-G6
MATLIN RD
25900 SDCo 92065 1174-A4
MATOR AV
- SD 92126 1209-D7
MATOR DR
- SD 92126 1209-D6
MATOR WY
- SD 92126 1209-D6
MATSON PL
7600 SD 92126 1208-J4
7600 SD 92126 1209-A4
MATSON WY
10500 SD 92126 1209-A4
MATTE LN
- SDCo 92081 1108-B5
MATTERHORN DR
8500 SNTE 92071 1230-H7
8500 SNTE 92071 1250-H1
MATTHEW CT
500 SDCo 92065 1152-D6
900 VSTA 92081 1107-H2
MATTHEW LN
600 SMCS 92069 1109-D6
MATTHEW PL
2000 ESCN 92027 1110-C6
MATTHEWS AV
- SD 92126 1209-E7
MATTHEWS LN
- SD 92093 1228-A1
MATTOLE ST
- OCN 92057 1066-H7
- OCN 92057 1086-H1
MATTY CT
4700 SDCo 91941 1271-C3
MATURIN DR
15200 SD 92127 1169-J5
MAUDE RD
13800 SDCo 92082 1070-E5
MAUDEY BELL CT
2500 SDCo 92019 1272-E2
MAUKA DR
11700 SDCo 92082 1069-J5
MAUREEN CT
9500 SNTE 92071 1231-B5
MAURY CT
8600 SD 92119 1250-J4
MAURY DR
6600 SD 92119 1250-J4
MAVERICK CT
16600 PWY 92064 1170-E3
MAVERICK GN
1900 ESCN 92027 1110-A4
MAVERICK LN
16600 PWY 92064 1170-E3
MAVERICK PL
300 CHV 91902 1310-H4
MAVERICK WY
- CRLB 92009 1148-A3
MAVIN DR
9500 SNTE 92071 1231-E4
MAX AV
1300 CHV 91911 1330-F3
MAX DR
4500 SD 92115 1269-J4
MAXAM AV
- SD 92126 1209-E7
- SD 92126 1229-F1
MAXFIELD BLVD
- CORD 92135 1288-F4
MAXFIELD RD
13900 SDCo 91935 1292-H2
MAXIE PL
- ESCN 92027 1130-E1
MAXIM ST
300 SD 92102 1289-J4
MAXSON ST
1600 OCN 92054 1086-C7
MAXWELL AV
1000 ELCJ 92020 1251-G7
MAXWELL LN
1500 VSTA 92084 1088-B3
MAXWELL RD
1700 CHV 91911 1330-J5
1800 CHV 91911 1331-A5
MAY AV
- CHV 91913 1331-E2
MAY CT
200 ENCT 92007 1167-D2
3900 CRLB 92008 1106-H5
6900 SD 92139 1290-F7
MAYA CT
1800 VSTA 92081 1107-J3
MAYA ST
900 SDCo 91977 1291-C2
MAYA ST Rt#-S17
9600 SDCo 91977 1291-E2
10000 SDCo 91978 1291-E2
MAYA LINDA RD
9900 SD 92126 1209-E5
MAYAN CT
11200 SD 92127 1149-H7
MAYAPAN DR
4300 SDCo 91941 1271-G3

STREET
Block City ZIP Pg-Grid

MAYAPAN DR
4700 SDCo 92020 1271-G2
MAYAPAN LN
- SDCo 91941 1271-G3
MAYAPPLE CT
- SD 92131 1209-G2
MAYAPPLE WY
- SD 92131 1209-G2
MAYBERRY LN
- ELCJ 92021 1251-F4
1100 VSTA 92083 1087-G4
MAYBERRY ST
4300 SD 92113 1289-J6
MAYBRITT CIR
600 SMCS 92069 1108-J5
MAYCREST LN
6600 SD 92121 1208-G3
MAYE PL
1400 SDCo 92027 1130-D3
MAYFAIR CT
4400 CRLB 92010 1106-J5
MAYFAIR ST
100 OCN 92054 1086-F4
MAYFIELD CT
1500 CHV 91913 1311-C7
MAYFIELD DR
- OCN 92057 1086-J4
7600 SD 92111 1249-A6
MAYFLOWER AV
- ESCN 92027 1130-C1
MAYFLOWER WY
4300 SD 92117 1228-E7
4600 OCN 92057 1087-A1
MAYITA WY
4700 SD 92124 1250-A1
MAYNARD ST
4900 SD 92122 1228-G4
9100 SDCo 91977 1291-B3
MAYO ST
4200 SD 92110 1268-E1
MAYOR CIR
10200 SD 92126 1209-B5
MAYS HOLLOW LN
700 ENCT 92024 1147-D6
MAYTEN CT
4700 OCN 92057 1067-A7
4700 OCN 92057 1087-A1
MAYWIND CT
11700 SD 92131 1210-A4
MAYWOOD CT
- CHV 91913 1331-D1
MAYWOOD LN
- OCN 92054 1106-C1
MAYWOOD ST
600 ESCN 92027 1110-C6
MAZAGON LN
800 CHV 91910 1310-H6
MAZATLAN CT
14100 PWY 92064 1190-E2
MAZATLAN DR
- ImCo 92251 6499-H1
- IMP 92251 6499-H1
MAZATLAN WY
14000 PWY 92064 1190-E3
MAZE GN
600 ESCN 92025 1150-C4
MAZER ST
8000 LMGR 91945 1270-H7
MAZZETTI LN
- SDCo 92082 1071-E2
MAZZOLA
1000 SDCo 92021 1251-H3
M B MARTINEZ ST
500 CALX 92231 6620-E7
MCBURNEY CT
2600 SD 92154 1330-C7
MCBURNEY RIDGE LN
- SD 92131 1209-G2
MCCABE RD
- ImCo 92243 6560-F4
100 ImCo 92243 6559-B5
100 ImCo 92249 6560-F4
MCCABE RD Rt#-S30
- ImCo 92243 6559-A5
1100 ImCo 92243 431-A6
MCCAIN BLVD
100 CORD 92135 1288-G5
MCCAIN LN
- SDCo 91905 1300-F7
MCCAIN RD
1900 SD 92101 1288-E1
2100 SD 92101 1268-E7
MCCAIN VALLEY CT
- CHV 91913 1331-A2
MCCAIN VALLEY RD
2100 SDCo 91934 1300-H6
2100 SDCo 91905 1300-H3
2300 SDCo 91905 430-C5
MCCALL ST
2800 SD 92106 1288-A4
MCCANDLESS BLVD
100 NATC 92136 1309-G1
3300 SD 92136 1289-F7
3700 SD 92136 1309-G1
MCCARDLE WY
9700 SNTE 92071 1231-B4
MCCARRAN CT
- IMP 92251 6499-C1
MCCAULEY LN
1800 CRLB 92008 1106-F4
MCCAWLEY DR
- SDCo 92055 1067-A1
MCCLELLAN AV
- SD 92104 1289-G2
MCCLELLAN RD
- SD 92106 1288-A6
- SD 92152 1287-J5
- SD 92152 1288-A6
MCCLELLAND ST
1200 SMCS 92069 1109-C6
MCCLINTOCK ST
4300 SD 92105 1269-G4
4400 SD 92116 1269-G4
MCCLOUD RIVER RD
1900 CHV 91913 1311-E6
MCCLOY WY
3200 SD 92124 1249-G4
MCCLURE ST
700 ELCJ 92021 1251-H4
MCCONNELL RD
- ImCo 92227 431-C3
- ImCo 92251 431-C4
1700 SD 92101 1288-D2
1700 SD 92147 1288-D2
1800 SD 92106 1288-D2
2100 ImCo 92243 6500-G2
2200 ImCo 92251 6500-G2
MCCONNELL RD Rt#-S27
- ImCo 92227 431-C3
- ImCo 92251 431-C3
MCCORMICK LN
- SDCo 92082 1071-E3

STREET
Block City ZIP Pg-Grid

MCCULLOM ST
- ELCN 92243 6560-A1
300 ELCN 92243 6500-A6
MCCUNE RD
- SD 92106 1288-A7
MCDANIEL RD
1100 ImCo 92283 432-D5
MCDONALD LN
600 ESCN 92025 1129-J6
600 ESCN 92025 1130-A6
MCDONALD RD
200 ImCo 92233 411-B8
700 SDCo 92028 1027-H5
MCDONALD ST
2100 ELCN 92243 6499-G4
MCDONALD MEADOWS
- SDCo 92028 1027-H4
MCDONOUGH LN
- SD 92106 1288-C1
MCDONOUGH RD
2400 SD 92101 1288-C1
2400 SD 92147 1288-C1
2500 SD 92106 1288-C1
MCDOUGAL PL
2400 SDCo 91901 1234-B4
MCDOUGAL TER
- ELCJ 92021 1252-C2
MCDOWELL CT
- SD 92131 1209-G2
MCENTEE ST
9700 SD 92129 1189-E2
MCFERON RD
12400 PWY 92064 1190-C4
MCGANN DR
5300 SD 92105 1290-A1
M C GARCIA ST
- CALX 92231 6620-E7
MCGAVRAN DR
700 VSTA 92081 1107-F1
MCGAVRAN TER
1200 VSTA 92081 1107-F1
MCGILL WY
4900 SD 92130 1188-D6
MCGONIGLE RD
1900 SD 92014 1207-G1
1900 SD 92121 1207-G1
MCGONIGLE TER
- SD 92130 1188-J3
MCGRAW ST
2900 SD 92117 1248-D5
MCGREGORY LN
1700 VSTA 92084 1088-B6
MCGUIRE DR
4000 SD 92130 1188-A5
MCHANEY CT
6100 SD 92114 1290-D6
MCHUGH ST
5600 SD 92114 1290-B3
MCINNEY RD
- SD 92152 1288-A5
MCINTIRE CIR
3500 OCN 92056 1106-J1
MCINTIRE DR
1900 SD 92101 1289-C2
1900 SD 92134 1289-C2
MCINTIRE LN
2100 SDCo 92069 1109-A1
MCINTOSH ST
500 CHV 91910 1309-J5
500 CHV 91910 1310-A5
MCIVERS CT
12300 PWY 92064 1190-E6
MCKEAN ST
2200 SD 92136 1289-F7
MCKEE ST
1900 SD 92110 1268-H6
MCKELLAR CT
10100 SD 92121 1208-E5
MCKENNA HEIGHTS CT
- SDCo 92082 1071-A5
MCKENZIE AV
13700 PWY 92064 1190-E3
MCKENZIE ST
- SDCo 92055 1023-F2
MCKIM RD
- ImCo 92251 431-C4
MCKINLEY AV
800 NATC 92136 1309-G2
1200 NATC 91950 1309-G2
1200 ESCN 92027 1130-B1
1300 ESCN 92027 1110-B7
MCKINLEY ST
- CALX 92231 6680-E1
100 OCN 92057 1067-B6
3000 SD 92104 1269-F7
3200 CRLB 92008 1106-F5
MCKINNEY CT
- SD 92131 1209-G1
MCKNIGHT DR
2200 LMGR 91945 1290-F1
2200 LMGR 91945 1270-F7
MCLAIN ST
500 ESCN 92027 1130-C2
MCLANANAN ST
3100 SD 92136 1289-E7
MCLANE LN
1300 SDCo 92026 1109-E6
MCLARENS LN
3200 SD 92102 1289-F4
MCLEES CT
1900 SDCo 92026 1109-E6
MCMAHER LN
5800 SD 92120 1249-H7
MCMAHR RD
900 SMCS 92078 1128-E2
MCNALLY RD
12100 SDCo 92082 1049-J4
12100 SDCo 92082 1050-A4
MCNEIL ST
500 OCN 92054 1086-B6
MCNEILL AV
- ENCT 92024 1147-C7
MCNERNEY RD
- ImCo 92233 411-A9
MCRAE AV
5400 LMSA 91942 1270-F1
MCWAY CT
500 ELCJ 92021 1251-H4
MCWEST LN
12000 SDCo 92040 1232-A7
MEAD RD
100 ImCo 92227 431-C2
MEAD ST
5300 OCN 92056 1087-E1
MEADE AV
1000 SD 92116 1269-B4
1200 SD 92103 1269-B4
1900 SD 92104 1269-F4
3600 SD 92105 1269-F4
4300 SD 92115 1269-J4
4400 SD 92115 1270-A4
MEADOW DR
- CALX 92231 6620-G6
- CRLB 92010 1107-B5

STREET
Block City ZIP Pg-Grid

MEADOW DR
1400 NATC 91950 1310-B1
8300 SDCo 91977 1290-J6
MEADOW LN
200 SMCS 92069 1108-D5
2500 ESCN 92027 1130-E1
2600 ESCN 92027 1110-E7
3200 LMGR 91945 1270-J6
3600 OCN 92056 1107-A1
9800 SDCo 91916 1236-A1
MEADOW RD
1400 ELCJ 92021 1252-B2
MEADOW VW
- SDCo 92028 998-G5
MEADOWBROOK CT
800 CHV 91913 1311-E4
7600 SD 92114 1290-G3
MEADOWBROOK DR
200 SD 92114 1290-G3
4700 OCN 92056 1087-E4
MEADOWBROOK LN
12100 PWY 92064 1190-B3
MEADOWBROOK PL
2500 ESCN 92027 1130-E1
MEADOW CREEK LN
- ESCN 92027 1110-F6
12900 PWY 92064 1190-G5
MEADOW CREEK RD
11400 SDCo 92020 1271-H3
MEADOW CREST DR
100 ELCJ 92020 1251-A5
6200 LMSA 91942 1251-A5
MEADOW CREST PL
- ESCN 92027 1110-F6
MEADOWDALE LN
12800 SD 92131 1210-C4
MEADOW FLOWER PL
11300 SD 92127 1169-J5
MEADOWGATE ST
3700 SD 92111 1248-J4
MEADOWGLEN LN
1600 ENCT 92024 1147-G4
MEADOW GLEN WY
12900 PWY 92064 1190-D5
MEADOW GLEN WY E
9900 SDCo 92026 1089-G3
MEADOW GLEN WY W
28300 SDCo 92026 1089-C2
MEADOW GLEN WAY EAST NORTH EXT
11100 SDCo 92026 1089-G3
MEADOW GRASS CT
- SD 92128 1190-A6
MEADOW GRASS LN
- ESCN 92027 1110-F6
- SD 92128 1189-J6
- SD 92128 1190-A6
MEADOW GRASS PL
- ESCN 92027 1110-G6
MEADOWGREEN CT
2100 ENCT 92024 1147-J5
MEADOW GROVE DR
3000 SD 92110 1268-D5
MEADOW GROVE PL
500 ESCN 92027 1110-E7
MEADOWHAVEN CT
1800 ENCT 92024 1147-H4
MEADOW LAKE DR
900 VSTA 92084 1087-J5
900 VSTA 92084 1088-A5
MEADOW LAKE RD
26500 SDCo 92070 409-J10
MEADOWLARK AV
100 CHV 91911 1330-F4
MEADOW LARK DR
2200 SD 92123 1249-B6
MEADOWLARK DR
- SDCo 92055 1023-E3
MEADOWLARK LN
2500 ESCN 92027 1110-E7
3200 CRLB 92008 1106-G4
MEADOWLARK WY
1100 SDCo 92065 1152-F3
MEADOWLARK RANCH CIR
2000 SDCo 92078 1128-A5
MEADOWLARK RANCH LN
2000 SDCo 92078 1128-A5
2000 CRLB 92078 1128-A5
MEADOWLARK RANCH RD
1800 CRLB 92078 1128-A5
1800 SDCo 92078 1128-A5
1800 SMCS 92078 1128-A5
MEADOWLARK RIDGE RD
- SDCo 92127 1169-F3
MEADOW MESA DR
9600 SDCo 92026 1089-D1
MEADOW MESA LN
28300 SDCo 92026 1089-D2
MEADOWMIST CT
500 ENCT 92024 1148-A7
MEADOWMIST LN
2500 ENCT 92024 1148-A7
MEADOW OAK LN
28200 SDCo 92026 1089-E3
MEADOW OAKS LN
15500 SDCo 92021 1213-C7
15500 SDCo 92021 1233-C1
MEADOWOOD CT
1700 SD 92173 1350-D2
MEADOWPOINTE RW
6000 SD 92037 1248-A1
MEADOWRIDGE LN
9800 SDCo 91977 1271-C7
MEADOWRIDGE PL
2300 SDCo 91977 1271-H7
MEADOWRIDGE RD
4700 SDCo 92070 1135-D4
MEADOWRUN CT
9000 SD 92129 1189-C2
MEADOWRUN DR
4500 OCN 92057 1066-H7
MEADOWRUN PL
9000 SD 92129 1189-C2
MEADOWRUN ST
14200 SD 92129 1189-D2
MEADOWRUN WY
9000 SD 92129 1189-C2
MEADOWS RD
- CALX 92231 431-C7
- ImCo 92231 431-C7
- ImCo 92231 6620-H2
1000 ImCo 92249 6560-H6
1000 ImCo 92249 6620-H2
1000 CALX 92231 6620-H6
MEADOWS DEL MAR
- SD 92130 1188-F7
- SD 92130 1208-F1
MEADOWSIDE PL
- ESCN 92027 1110-F6
2300 SDCo 91977 1271-H7
MEADOW SPRING WY
- OCN 92057 1086-J2

STREET
Block City ZIP Pg-Grid

MEADOWS TRAIL LN
2600 CHV 91915 1311-H5
MEADOW TERRACE DR
11000 SNTE 92071 1231-G5
MEADOWVIEW AV
- ELCN 92243 6559-G3
MEADOW VIEW DR
3400 OCN 92054 1086-D2
MEADOWVIEW DR
10200 SD 92131 1209-H4
MEADOW VIEW LN
- SDCo 91901 1274-G1
MEADOWVIEW LN
600 SMCS 92069 1109-A6
MEADOW VIEW RD
11300 SDCo 92020 1271-G3
MEADOW VISTA WY
200 ENCT 92024 1147-J7
MEADOW WOOD PL
1200 ENCT 92024 1147-G4
MEAJEAN PL
11800 SD 92129 1189-E7
MEALEY RD
- ImCo 92251 430-L4
MEANDER RD
- CHV 91915 1331-G1
MEANDRO CT
16700 SD 92128 1170-B3
MEANDRO DR
16700 SD 92128 1170-B3
MEANDRO RD
12300 SD 92128 1170-B3
MEANLEY DR
10000 SD 92131 1209-G4
MEANWHILE RANCH RD
1000 SDCo 91906 (1318-E6 See Page 1298)
MECCA DR
1600 SD 92037 1227-G7
MEDALIST CT
- OCN 92057 1067-C3
MEDALLION LN
13200 SDCo 92040 1232-C6
MEDFORD AV
2100 ESCN 92027 1110-C6
MEDFORD CT
2600 CRLB 92010 1106-J4
MEDFORD PL
2200 ESCN 92027 1110-C6
MEDFORD ST
600 ELCJ 92020 1251-A4
1400 OCN 92057 1067-A3
MEDIATRICE LN
14200 SD 92129 1189-D2
MEDICAL CENTER CT
700 CHV 91911 1330-J2
MEDICAL CENTER DR
- SD 92037 1228-B2
900 CHV 91911 1330-H1
MEDILL AV
8100 SDCo 92021 1252-C1
8200 SDCo 92021 1232-C7
MEDINA DR
9400 SNTE 92071 1230-J5
MEDINA GN
2200 ESCN 92026 1109-D4
MEDINAH DR
2400 SDCo 92019 1272-B5
MEDINAH RD
1600 SMCS 92069 1108-J3
MEDINAH WY
- SDCo 92082 1090-F5
MEDIO ST
6300 SD 92114 1290-D4
MEDIO TER
900 SDCo 92028 1027-G1
MEDOC CT
10500 SD 92131 1210-B3
MEDOC LN
12000 SD 92131 1210-B3
MEEKS BAY DR
- CHV 91913 1311-D6
MEGAN CT
2400 SD 92102 1290-A1
MEGAN LN
3800 ENCT 92024 1148-B2
MEGAN TER
9700 SDCo 92026 1069-C3
MEGAN WY
4900 SD 92102 1290-A1
4900 SD 92105 1289-J1
4900 SD 92105 1290-A1
MEGHAN CT
9000 SDCo 91977 1271-B6
MEKNES ST
15400 SD 92129 1169-J6
MEKNES WY
11400 SD 92129 1169-H6
MEL CT
1100 SD 92154 1350-D1
MELALEUCA AV
6800 CRLB 92011 1127-A5
MELALEUCA LN
2700 SDCo 92028 998-B6
MELANIE CT
10800 SNTE 92071 1231-F3
MELANIE WY
- DLMR 92014 1187-F5
MELBA RD
100 ENCT 92024 1147-F7
200 ENCT 92024 1167-C1
MELBOURNE DR
2400 SD 92123 1249-E5
MELBOURNE GN
- ESCN 92026 1109-H3
MELIC CT
12900 SD 92129 1189-E5
MELINDA AV
800 SMCS 92069 1109-B6
MELINDA WY
200 OCN 92057 1086-H3
MELINDA DE ORO
- SDCo 91905 (1319-H7 See Page 1298)
MELISANDE PL
- CHV 91913 1311-E7
MELISSA CT
2400 VSTA 92081 1108-B5
MELISSA LN
13500 PWY 92064 1190-F4
MELISSA WY
4400 SD 92117 1248-C2
MELISSA PARK TER
900 SDCo 92021 1252-J2
MELKSEE ST
- SD 92154 1351-H4
MELLMANOR DR
8500 LMSA 91942 1250-J7
8500 LMSA 91942 1251-A7
MELODIA TER
- CRLB 92011 1127-B7
MELODIE LN
14100 PWY 92064 1190-G3

MELODY LN
- OCN 92054 1086-C5
1300 ELCJ 92019 1251-J5
1300 ELCJ 92019 1252-A5
1400 SDCo 92019 1252-A5
7000 LMSA 91942 1270-F1
35000 SDCo 92036 1156-E7
MELODY RD
13800 SDCo 91935 1292-G3
MELOJO LN
10200 SD 92124 1249-G1
MELOLAND RD
1900 ImCo 92243 431-D5
1900 ImCo 92250 431-D5
MELORA CT
13400 SDCo 91935 1272-E7
MELOTTE ST
7300 SD 92119 1250-E3
MELROSE AV
100 ENCT 92024 1147-B6
200 CHV 91911 1310-E7
200 CHV 91911 1330-F1
600 CHV 91910 1310-E7
MELROSE CIR
1600 CHV 91911 1330-G5
MELROSE CT
1600 CHV 91911 1330-G5
MELROSE DR
- CRLB 92010 1127-H2
- VSTA 92010 1127-H2
- VSTA 92081 1127-H2
500 OCN 92057 1067-D6
1500 OCN 92056 1087-F3
1500 VSTA 92083 1087-F3
6700 CRLB 92009 1128-A5
6900 SMCS 92078 1128-A5
N MELROSE DR
100 VSTA 92083 1087-F4
S MELROSE DR
- CRLB 92009 1127-H2
- CRLB 92010 1127-H2
100 VSTA 92081 1087-G7
300 VSTA 92081 1107-G1
1000 VSTA 92083 1087-G7
1200 OCN 92056 1107-G1
1500 SDCo 92081 1107-G1
1800 VSTA 92081 1127-H1
6600 CRLB 92009 1128-A5
MELROSE LN
8100 SDCo 92021 1252-A1
8200 SDCo 92021 1232-B7
8400 SDCo 92040 1232-B7
MELROSE PL
600 VSTA 92083 1087-F5
700 SD 92114 1290-B3
12500 SDCo 92021 1232-B7
MELROSE ST
800 NATC 91950 1289-H7
2200 NATC 91950 1290-A6
MELROSE WY
300 CHV 91911 1330-G5
1000 VSTA 92081 1107-E2
1500 SDCo 92081 1107-E2
MELRU LN
2400 SDCo 92026 1109-J2
MELTON CT
11100 SD 92131 1209-H1
MELVA RD
10700 SDCo 91941 1271-F2
MELVIN LN
1500 SDCo 92021 1252-A2
MELWIER WY
12900 SDCo 92040 1232-C4
MEMIKE PL
8900 SD 92119 1251-A3
MEMORIAL DR
4800 LMSA 91941 1270-J2
MEMORIAL WY
400 CHV 91910 1310-A6
MEMORY LN
1000 ESCN 92026 1109-F5
1200 VSTA 92084 1088-A4
9000 SDCo 91977 1271-B5
MENARD ST
3200 NATC 91950 1310-D3
MENDE CT
2200 SD 92103 1268-G5
MENDECK AV
9900 SNTE 92071 1231-B3
MENDEL RIVERS RD
- SDCo 92055 1067-A1
MENDENARO CT
- SDCo 92028 1048-C4
MENDIOLA PT
11800 SD 92129 1189-E7
MENDIP ST
- OCN 92057 1067-A3
MENDOCINO BLVD
1900 SD 92107 1268-A7
MENDOCINO CT
800 SMCS 92078 1128-G2
MENDOCINO DR
900 SMCS 92078 1128-G3
1500 CHV 91911 1330-H4
MENDOTA ST
1700 CHV 91913 1311-D6
1800 SD 92106 1287-J6
1800 SD 92106 1288-B1
MENDOZA
- SDCo 92082 1071-E2
MENENDEZ CT
1900 SD 92154 1350-D3
MENGIBAR AV
12700 SD 92129 1189-F6
MENKAR PL
11400 SD 92126 1209-B1
MENKAR RD
8300 SD 92126 1209-C1
MENLO AV
- SD 92105 1269-J5
4100 SD 92115 1269-J4
MENNONITE PT
13900 SD 92129 1189-D2
MENORCA DR
5600 SD 92124 1229-H7
MENORCA WY
10500 SD 92124 1229-H7
MENSHA PL
4400 SD 92130 1188-B5
MENTA CTE
1100 CHV 91910 1311-C2
MENTONE ST
4200 SD 92107 1268-B5
MERCADO DR
13600 SD 92014 1187-H6
MERCADO GN
1400 ESCN 92026 1109-E4
MERCANTILE ST
500 VSTA 92083 1087-H7
MERCED DR
3600 OCN 92056 1107-E4
MERCED PL
2600 SDCo 91935 1293-C4

MERCEDES RD
100 SDCo 92028 1027-H2
MERCED LAKE AV
6200 SD 92119 1250-H6
MERCED RIVER RD
900 CHV 91913 1331-A2
MERCER CT
3500 SD 92122 1228-D5
MERCER LN
3000 SD 92122 1228-C5
MERCER ST
6100 SD 92122 1228-D5
MERCURIO ST
4500 SD 92130 1188-C6
MERCURY CT
8100 SD 92111 1229-B7
MERCURY DR
2500 LMGR 91945 1270-F7
MERCURY GN
- ESCN 92025 1129-H2
MERCURY PT
- SD 92111 1229-B7
MERCURY ST
4400 SD 92111 1249-B2
5000 SD 92111 1229-B7
MERCY PL
- ESCN 92026 1109-J4
MERCY RD
9300 SD 92129 1189-F6
MEREDITH AV
5600 SD 92120 1250-D7
5600 SD 92120 1270-D1
MEREDITH RD
- SDCo 92028 1028-B4
MERGANSER LN
7400 CRLB 92011 1127-B7
MERGHO IMPASSE
2100 SD 92110 1268-G6
MERIDA CT
2100 SD 92037 1247-H1
MERIDA DR
300 SDCo 92028 1027-F5
MERIDEN LN
11800 SD 92128 1190-A2
MERIDIAN AV
3400 SD 92115 1270-D6
MERIDIAN CT
- OCN 92057 1067-B3
MERIDIAN LN
1100 CHV 91911 1330-H1
MERIDIAN ST
- ImCo 92249 6560-C7
MERIDIAN WY
- CRLB 92011 1126-J7
- CRLB 92011 1127-B5
MERIDIAN RIDGE TR
- SDCo 91962 (1299-C2 See Page 1298)
MERILL DR
8200 SDCo 92040 1252-A1
8300 SDCo 92040 1232-A7
MERILL PL
12000 SDCo 92040 1252-A1
MERION CIR
- SDCo 92082 1090-F4
MERION GN
- ESCN 92026 1109-H3
MERIVALE AV
3800 SD 92116 1269-G3
MERL RD Rt#-78
- ImCo 92281 431-A1
- WEST 92281 431-A1
MERLIN CT
900 SMCS 92069 1109-C5
MERLIN DR
- CRLB 92011 1127-A4
400 SD 92114 1290-C3
MERLIN PL
2700 OCN 92054 1086-E6
MERLO CT
900 CRLB 92011 1127-A7
MERLOT AV
- SMCS 92069 1108-J6
MERLOT CT
1500 VSTA 92083 1087-D6
MERLOT PL
500 CHV 91913 1311-E3
17200 PWY 92064 1170-E2
MERLYN CT
1700 SDCo 92019 1272-B4
MERLYN PL
2100 SDCo 92019 1272-B4
MERMAID LN
7400 CRLB 92011 1127-A7
MERRIAM RD
1700 SDCo 92078 1128-B2
MERRICK CT
4600 OCN 92056 1107-E3
MERRIMAC AV
3400 SD 92117 1228-D7
3700 SD 92117 1248-E1
MERRIMAC CT
5000 SD 92117 1228-D7
MERRING RD Rt#-S24
800 ImCo 92283 432-E4
MERRINGTON PL
7900 SD 92126 1209-B3
MERRITAGE CT
- SD 92131 1210-D2
MERRITT BLVD
4100 LMSA 91977 1271-A4
4100 SDCo 91977 1271-A4
4100 LMSA 91941 1271-A3
MERRITT CT
1000 SDCo 92020 1251-H7
MERRITT DR
800 ELCJ 92020 1251-H7
1000 SDCo 92020 1251-H7
1400 SDCo 92020 1271-J1
MERRITT LN
1000 SDCo 92020 1251-J7
1000 SDCo 92020 1271-J1
MERRITT TER
1300 SDCo 92020 1251-J7
1300 SDCo 92020 1252-A7
MERRITT PARK LN
14600 PWY 92064 1190-E1
MERRIWEATHER WY
1400 ELCJ 92019 1252-A7
MERRY LN
1600 ESCN 92029 1129-G5
MERRYFIELD RW
3100 SD 92121 1207-J5
3100 SD 92121 1208-A6
MERRYMOUNT CT
5700 OCN 92057 1067-F7
MERRYWOOD LN
300 SDCo 92025 1130-B7
MERTENSIA ST
5100 OCN 92056 1107-F4
MERTON AV
2700 SD 92111 1248-J6
2700 SD 92111 1249-A6

MERTON CT
7100 SD 92111 1248-J6
MERWELL ST
6600 SD 92122 1228-D5
MERWIN DR
- CRLB 92008 1107-B7
C MESA
- SD 92037 1228-C2
N MESA
- SD 92037 1228-C2
MESA AV
- NATC 91950 1290-A6
200 SD 92173 1350-G3
9800 SNTE 92071 1231-D5
MESA CT
900 CHV 91910 1310-H7
MESA DR
2200 OCN 92054 1086-F5
3100 OCN 92056 1086-F5
3100 OCN 92057 1086-H5
4000 OCN 92057 1087-B3
4000 OCN 92056 1087-B3
MESA DR N
16300 SDCo 92061 1051-C3
MESA DR S
17600 SDCo 92061 1051-D4
MESA PL
800 CHV 91910 1310-H7
MESA RD
8100 SNTE 92071 1250-J1
8200 SNTE 92071 1230-J7
MESA TER
5000 SDCo 91941 1271-B1
8400 SNTE 92071 1250-J1
W MESA TKTR
- SDCo 91916 1216-A1
MESA WY
300 SD 92037 1247-E2
MESA BREEZE WY
500 OCN 92054 1086-B6
MESA BROOK ST
800 SD 92114 1290-F6
MESA COLLEGE DR
3200 SD 92111 1249-A4
7300 SD 92111 1248-J4
7700 SD 92123 1249-A5
MESA CREST PL
- SD 92129 1188-J4
MESA CREST RD
- SDCo 92082 1070-B4
12300 PWY 92064 1190-B5
MESA ESTATES CT
15200 SDCo 92065 1173-H6
MESA ESTATES RD
25000 SDCo 92065 1173-H5
E MESA FIRE RD
- SDCo 91916 1216-F4
MESA GRANDE PL
1300 CHV 91910 1311-B7
MESA GRANDE RD
1700 ESCN 92029 1129-F6
24000 SDCo 92070 409-H9
MESA GROVE RD
- SDCo 92028 1028-G7
- SDCo 92028 1048-H1
MESA HEIGHTS RD
8400 SNTE 92071 1250-J1
MESA HILLS CT
1900 SD 92114 1290-F6
MESA LILAC RD
32500 SDCo 92026 1049-A5
MESA MADERA CT
11500 SD 92131 1209-J4
MESA MADERA DR
9900 SD 92131 1209-J4
MESAMINT ST
16900 SDCo 92127 1169-G3
MESA OAK CT
2700 SDCo 92065 1172-D4
MESA OAK PL
- ESCN 92027 1130-H2
MESA PARK LN
1900 SD 92114 1290-F6
MESA RANCH DR
- ESCN 92026 1109-D2
- SDCo 92026 1109-D2
MESA RIDGE CT
10000 SD 92121 1208-H5
MESA RIDGE RD
6600 SD 92121 1208-H5
8400 SNTE 92071 1250-J1
MESA RIM RD
9900 SD 92121 1208-H5
MESA ROCK RD
1200 SDCo 92026 1089-C7
25900 SDCo 92026 1109-D1
MESA SPRINGS WY
9700 SD 92126 1209-F5
MESA TOP PL
11000 SD 92121 1208-G3
MESA VERDE DR
1500 VSTA 92084 1088-B5
11500 SDCo 92082 1069-H2
12000 SDCo 92082 1070-A2
MESA VERDE RD
3200 SDCo 91902 1310-E4
MESA VIEW RD
8400 SNTE 92071 1250-J1
MESA VIEW WY
8300 SDCo 91977 1290-J5
MESA VISTA AV
9200 LMSA 91941 1271-B1
9200 SDCo 91941 1271-B1
MESA VISTA LN
3300 SDCo 91902 1310-E4
MESA VISTA PL
- SD 92131 1210-C2
MESA VISTA WY
3600 SDCo 91902 1310-E4
MESA WOODS AV
9000 SD 92126 1209-D3
MESCALITA CT
200 OCN 92054 1086-G1
MESETA LN
12800 SDCo 92040 1232-B5
MESITA DR
6000 SD 92115 1270-C2
MESQUITE LN
4600 SDCo 92004 (1099-G5 See Page 1098)
MESQUITE RD
5000 SD 92115 1270-A2
MESQUITE ST
- IMP 92251 6499-E2
MESQUITE TREE TR
15400 PWY 92064 1170-G6
MESSIAH DR
300 ELCN 92243 6499-H4
MESSINA DR
4000 SD 92113 1289-G5
MESSINA WY
100 SD 92113 1289-H4

MESTO CT
16200 SD 92128 1170-B4
MESTO DR
16100 SD 92128 1170-B4
METATE LN
12400 PWY 92064 1190-E5
METCALF GN
1000 ESCN 92026 1129-F1
1000 SDCo 92026 1129-F1
METCALF PL
1000 ESCN 92026 1129-F2
METCALF ST
600 ESCN 92025 1129-F2
900 ESCN 92026 1129-F1
1000 SDCo 92026 1129-F1
METRO ST
5300 SD 92110 1268-F3
METROPOLITAN DR
7500 SD 92108 1269-A1
METROPOLITAN ST
- CRLB 92009 1127-F3
MEWALL DR
6700 SD 92119 1251-A3
MEXICALI CT
100 SOLB 92075 1167-D7
MEXICAN CANYON RD
14100 SDCo 91935 1272-H7
MEYERS AV
2100 ESCN 92029 1129-C2
MEYERS RD
- SD 92152 1288-A6
MEYNCKE WY
7900 SD 92126 1209-A1
MEZIN WY
6700 SD 92114 1290-E4
MIAMI CT
4300 SD 92117 1248-E2
MIAMI DR
- LMSA 91941 1270-G5
MIAMI WY
4500 SD 92117 1248-E2
MICA RD
- CRLB 92009 1127-F4
MICAELA CT
- SDCo 92040 1232-E5
MICHAEL CT
2100 SDCo 91901 1253-G1
MICHAEL GN
1700 ESCN 92026 1109-D4
MICHAEL ST
600 OCN 92057 1067-A5
5500 SD 92105 1270-B6
MICHAEL FARADAY DR
2100 SD 92154 1352-B3
MICHAEL JOHN DR
6600 SD 92037 1247-F1
MICHAELMAS TER
3200 SD 92110 1268-E6
MICHALA PL
10200 SNTE 92071 1231-D2
MICHELE DR
300 VSTA 92084 1087-H3
MICHELLE CT
2600 NATC 91950 1310-A3
9400 SDCo 91977 1271-B6
MICHELLE DR
7800 LMSA 91942 1250-G6
MICHELLE RENE WY
- SDCo 91901 1253-E2
- SDCo 92019 1253-E2
MICHIGAN AV
100 VSTA 92084 1087-H6
300 OCN 92054 1106-A1
900 OCN 92054 1086-B7
MICRO PL
2200 ESCN 92029 1129-C2
MIDBLUFF AV
13100 SD 92128 1189-H4
MIDBURY CT
7300 SD 92126 1209-D2
MIDDLE ST
900 ELCJ 92020 1251-C7
MIDDLEBROOK SQ
12100 SD 92128 1190-B1
MIDDLEBUSH DR
200 SD 92114 1290-H4
MIDDLE FORK PL
- CHV 91914 1311-H3
MIDDLE PEAK LOOP FIRE RD
- SDCo 92036 1176-C6
MIDDLE RIDGE TER
11300 SD 92128 1189-J4
MIDDLESEX DR
4100 SD 92116 1269-H2
MIDDLETON DR
4500 CRLB 92010 1107-A4
MIDDLETON RD
5100 SD 92109 1248-A3
MIDDLETON WY
2200 SD 92109 1248-A3
MIDGROVE CT
13800 PWY 92064 1190-F3
MIDLAND RD
13300 PWY 92064 1190-F2
15200 PWY 92064 1170-F6
MIDLAND ST
8400 LMSA 91942 1250-J7
MIDNIGHT WY
- OCN 92057 1067-A3
MIDORI CT
- SOLB 92075 1167-E6
MIDORI LN
700 SOLB 92075 1167-E6
MIDRANCH LN
12300 SDCo 92040 1212-A7
MIDVALE DR
1700 SD 92105 1289-G1
MIDWAY AV
- SD 92101 1268-F7
- SD 92140 1268-F7
MIDWAY CT
1300 SDCo 91901 1233-J6
MIDWAY DR
800 SDCo 91901 1233-H5
1100 ELCJ 92020 1251-D7
2300 SD 92110 1268-D5
N MIDWAY DR
100 ESCN 92027 1130-C1
200 ESCN 92027 1110-B6
S MIDWAY DR
100 ESCN 92027 1130-C1
MIDWAY LN
800 SDCo 91901 1233-G5
MIDWAY PL
1300 SDCo 91901 1233-H6
MIDWAY ST
300 SD 92037 1247-F4
MIDWICK ST
5700 SD 92139 1310-C1
MIGUEL AV
1600 CORD 92118 1288-J7
1700 CORD 92118 1289-A7

MIGUEL LN
14500 SDCo 92021 1232-H4
MIGUEL RD
- ImCo 92283 432-D5
MIGUEL GARDEN WY
13300 PWY 92064 1190-H4
MIGUEL TRAIL PL
- CHV 91914 1311-G2
MIGUEL VIEW RD
4200 SDCo 91941 1271-G4
MIGUEL VISTA PL
8400 SD 92114 1290-J4
MIJO LN
13500 SDCo 92040 1232-D5
MIKE CT
1100 SD 92154 1350-E1
MILAGROS ST
3400 SD 92123 1249-C4
MILAGROSA CIR
400 CHV 91910 1310-H4
MILAGROSA CT
400 CHV 91910 1310-G5
MILAGROSA PL
800 CHV 91910 1310-H5
MILAGROSA WY
500 CHV 91910 1310-H5
MILAN GN
1400 ESCN 92026 1110-A5
1400 ESCN 92027 1110-A5
MILAN ST
1200 OCN 92056 1087-C3
3700 SD 92107 1288-B1
3800 SD 92107 1268-A7
MILAN WY
- SMCS 92078 1128-E6
MILANE LN
- ESCN 92026 1110-A7
N MILANE LN
800 ESCN 92026 1110-A7
800 ESCN 92026 1130-A1
MILANO DR
4200 CRLB 92010 1106-J6
MILANO WY
4200 OCN 92057 1087-A3
MIL ARBOLES
14400 SDCo 92067 1188-G2
MILBANK RD
1700 ENCT 92024 1147-A2
MILBRAE ST
300 SD 92113 1289-G5
MILBURN AV
8800 SDCo 91977 1290-J4
8800 SDCo 91977 1291-A4
MILBURY RD
8500 SD 92129 1189-C2
MILCH RD
9400 SD 92121 1228-J2
MILDEN ST
9500 LMSA 91942 1251-C7
MILDRED AV
100 SDCo 91905 1300-C6
MILDRED ST
5400 SD 92110 1268-F3
MILDRED WY
100 SDCo 92019 1253-C1
8200 LMGR 91945 1270-H7
MILE HIGH RD
- SDCo 92036 1156-F7
MILE-OF-CARS WY
- NATC 91950 1309-H3
MILES CT
3700 SDCo 91977 1271-C5
MILES RANCH RD
100 SDCo 92028 1047-G7
200 SDCo 92028 1067-G1
MILETUS WY
4700 OCN 92056 1107-E5
MILFORD PL
1900 ELCJ 92020 1251-C4
3600 CRLB 92010 1107-A3
MILISSI WY
5000 OCN 92056 1107-E4
MILK RANCH RD
- SDCo 92036 1176-D7
- SDCo 92036 (1196-D1 See Page 1176)
MILKY WAY PT
7500 SD 92120 1250-C4
MILLAGRA DR
1400 SDCo 92028 1028-F5
MILLAN CT
- CHV 91910 1330-D1
E MILLAN CT
300 CHV 91910 1310-F7
MILLAN ST
100 CHV 91910 1330-C1
E MILLAN ST
100 CHV 91910 1310-E7
MILLAR AV
100 ELCJ 92020 1251-E5
MILLAR ANITA LN
2900 SDCo 91978 1292-A2
MILLARDS RD
13700 PWY 92064 1190-J2
MILLARDS RANCH LN
13500 PWY 92064 1190-H3
MILLARDS RANCH WY
13600 PWY 92064 1190-J2
MILLAR RANCH RD
2100 SDCo 91978 1292-A1
3100 SDCo 91978 1271-J7
3100 SDCo 91978 1272-A7
MILLAY CT
- CRLB 92008 1107-A7
MILLBRAE CT
1500 CHV 91913 1311-C7
MILLBROOK PL
800 ESCN 92026 1109-J7
MILLBROOK ST
6800 SD 92120 1249-J5
MILLCO LN
14000 SDCo 92082 1070-E6
MILLCO WY
29500 SDCo 92082 1070-F6
MILL CREEK RD
- SD 92130 1188-E5
- SDCo 92061 1050-H3
MILLCROFT CT
13100 SD 92130 1187-J5
MILLEGAR LN
2400 SDCo 92084 1108-D3
MILLENNIUM CT
1000 SDCo 92065 1152-J6
MILLER AV
1900 ESCN 92025 1129-J7
2300 SDCo 92029 1129-J7
2300 SDCo 92029 1149-J1
MILLER AV Rt#-S26
- ImCo 92281 431-A1
- WEST 92281 431-A1
MILLER DR
800 CHV 91914 1311-F4
MILLER LN
29800 SDCo 92082 1070-F5

MILLER RD
28600 SDCo 92082 1090-E1
28900 SDCo 92082 1070-F5
MILLER RD Rt#-S33
1000 ImCo 92250 431-F6
MILLER ST
4000 SD 92103 1268-G5
MILLER WY
13600 SDCo 92082 1070-E5
MILLER VALLEY RD
2900 SDCo 91962 (1299-A1 See Page 1298)
MILLIKIN AV
3200 SD 92122 1228-D5
MILL PEAK RD
5500 SD 92120 1270-C1
5500 SD 92120 1250-C7
MILLPOND WY
13500 SD 92129 1189-G3
MILLS CT
1400 SMCS 92069 1109-D7
MILLS PL
1500 ESCN 92027 1110-B7
MILLS RD
700 SDCo 92028 1047-E5
MILLS ST
600 ESCN 92027 1110-A7
600 ESCN 92027 1130-B1
1600 CHV 91913 1311-C5
3600 SD 92152 1287-J4
4900 LMSA 91941 1270-H2
MILLSTONE CT
- SDCo 92028 1027-G5
MILL VALLEY CT
4100 SDCo 91941 1271-H4
MILL VALLEY RD
- CHV 91913 1311-E7
MILLWOOD RD
- SDCo 92036 1175-J2
- SDCo 92036 1176-A2
4900 SD 92117 1228-F7
MILOS WY
5000 OCN 92056 1107-F5
MILPAS DR
2700 SDCo 92029 1129-C3
MILPITAS DR
- CALX 92231 6680-J2
MILPITAS WASH RD
- ImCo - 411-K4
- ImCo - 412-A6
MIL PITRERO RD
11900 SD 92128 1190-A7
MIL SORPRESAS DR
1900 SDCo 92028 998-A7
MILTON CT
2200 SD 92110 1268-F1
MILTON RD
- CRLB 92008 1127-B1
3700 LMGR 91945 1270-J5
MILTON ST
2200 SD 92110 1268-F1
MILTON MANOR DR
1700 SDCo 92021 1252-A2
MILWAUKEE CT
- LMSA 91941 1270-G5
MIMIKA PL
2700 SD 92111 1248-J6
MIMOSA
16900 SDCo 92067 1168-C3
MIMOSA AV
100 SDCo 92081 1108-B5
MIMOSA CT
1300 ESCN 92027 1110-B5
4800 OCN 92057 1067-A7
MIMOSA DR
6800 CRLB 92011 1127-E5
MIMOSA CREEK LN
- SDCo 92065 1152-G7
MIMULUS
5700 SDCo 92067 1168-D2
MIMULUS WY
1600 SD 92037 1227-G7
MINA ST
3400 SD 92105 1270-A6
MINA DE ORO RD
14800 PWY 92064 1191-B1
14900 PWY 92064 1171-C7
MINDANAO WY
2300 SD 92154 1330-C7
MINDEN DR
1300 SD 92111 1269-A2
MINEO AV
200 ELCN 92243 6560-A1
MINER CT
9400 SDCo 91977 1271-C7
MINERAL DR
6700 SD 92119 1250-H4
MINER CREEK LN
1800 CHV 91913 1311-E7
MINERS CT
- SDCo 92036 1136-D7
MINERS PL
- SDCo 92040 1232-F5
MINERS TR
- SDCo 91916 1235-G2
MINERVA DR
7300 SD 92114 1290-F3
MINESHAFT DR
- SDCo 92040 1212-A7
- SDCo 92040 1232-C2
MING CT
11400 SDCo 92021 1251-H1
MINNEOLA CIR
11500 SDCo 92082 1069-H5
MINNEOLA DR
- SDCo 92028 1047-G1
MINNEOLA LN
- ESCN 92027 1110-D5
MINNESOTA AV
100 ELCJ 92020 1251-F7
200 OCN 92054 1106-A1
MINNESOTA ST
400 SDCo 92028 1027-G2
MINNEWAWA TKTR
- SDCo 91935 (1313-B6 See Page 1293)
- SDCo 91917 (1333-C2 See Page 1332)
- SDCo 91935 (1333-C2 See Page 1332)
MINOA WY
3000 SD 92139 1310-E2
MINOR DR
800 SDCo 92025 1130-C4
MINORCA CV
14200 SD 92014 1187-H5
MINORCA WY
2600 SD 92014 1187-H5
MINOT AV
- CHV 91910 1310-C5
MINT AV
1500 ELCJ 92019 1252-A4
MINT PL
3500 OCN 92054 1086-F4

STREET
Block City ZIP Pg-Grid

MINT CANYON PTH
1400 SD 92037 1227-G7
1400 SD 92037 1247-G1
MINUTEMAN ST
3000 SD 92124 1249-G5
MINYA LN
14300 PWY 92064 1190-H5
MIO METATE LN
9800 SDCo 91916 1235-G1
MIRA PZ
- VSTA 92081 1107-C2
MIRABEL LN
10200 SD 92124 1249-G1
MIRACIELO CT
1300 SDCo 92078 1128-E3
MIRACLE DR
4700 SD 92115 1269-J3
MIRACLE WATERS CT
10400 SDCo 91977 1291-E1
MIRACOSTA CIR
1600 CHV 91913 1311-D6
MIRA COSTA ST
4000 OCN 92056 1107-B2
MIRA COSTA COLLEGE RD
2300 ENCT 92024 1167-G4
MIRACREST PL
8400 SD 92121 1228-J1
MIRADOR
2300 SDCo 92084 1088-C1
MIRA ESTE CT
9200 SD 92126 1209-B7
MIRA FLORES CT
1300 OCN 92056 1107-D3
MIRA FLORES DR
5500 SD 92114 1290-B5
MIRAFLORES GN
3600 ESCN 92026 1109-E5
MIRAGE CT
1600 SDCo 92019 1272-B4
MIRAGE LN
4200 OCN 92056 1107-D3
MIRAGE PL
2100 SDCo 92019 1272-B4
MIRA GRANDE LN
- SDCo 92082 1070-A3
MIRA LAGO TER
10600 SD 92131 1209-J3
10600 SD 92131 1210-A3
MIRA LAGO WY
- SMCS 92078 1129-B1
- SMCS 92096 1128-J1
11700 SD 92131 1209-J3
MIRALANI DR
8100 SD 92126 1209-C6
MIRA LOMA CT
13300 PWY 92064 1150-E7
MIRA LOMA LN
300 ESCN 92025 1130-B4
MIRAMAR AV
7500 SD 92037 1227-F7
MIRAMAR CT
- SD 92126 1229-F1
MIRAMAR DR
800 SDCo 92081 1107-H2
2000 VSTA 92081 1107-J3
MIRAMAR MALL
8200 SD 92121 1228-G1
MIRA MAR PL
900 OCN 92054 1085-J7
MIRAMAR PL
8300 SD 92121 1228-G1
MIRAMAR RD
- SD 92145 1229-A1
5000 SD 92121 1228-F2
5000 SD 92122 1228-F2
5000 SD 92145 1228-F2
7000 SD 92121 1229-A1
7000 SD 92126 1229-A1
7800 SD 92126 1209-D6
9900 SDCo 92126 1209-D6
9900 SDCo 92131 1209-D6
MIRAMAR ST
- SD 92037 1228-B2
MIRAMAR WY
- SD 92126 1229-B1
- SD 92145 1229-E1
MIRAMAR GUN CLUB RD
- SD 92145 1229-E4
MIRA MESA AV
3100 OCN 92056 1107-B1
MIRA MESA BLVD
5300 SD 92121 1208-G5
7000 SD 92126 1208-G5
7600 SD 92126 1209-E3
9800 SD 92131 1209-E3
MIRA MONTANA DR
13500 SD 92014 1187-H6
MIRA MONTANA PL
2600 SD 92014 1187-H7
MIRA MONTE
300 SD 92037 1247-F3
MIRA MONTE DR
- CRLB 92010 1107-C3
3500 OCN 92056 1107-C2
MIRA MONTE GN
1100 ESCN 92026 1109-E5
MIRA MONTE PZ
6000 SD 92037 1247-F3
MIRA MONTE RD
4100 SDCo 92028 997-G3
MIRAMONTE ST
4600 LMSA 91941 1270-J3
4600 LMSA 91941 1271-A3
MIRAMONTES RD
3000 SDCo 91935 1293-A1
MIRANDO ST
14400 PWY 92064 1190-H4
MIRA PACIFIC DR
3500 OCN 92056 1106-J2
3500 OCN 92056 1107-A1
MIRAR CT
5400 SDCo 91902 1311-A2
MIRAR DE VALLE RD
12200 SDCo 92082 1090-A4
MIRA SOL
2200 SDCo 92084 1108-D3
MIRASOL CT
12200 SD 92128 1150-B7
MIRASOL DR
17800 SD 92128 1150-B7
MIRASOL PL
12200 SD 92128 1150-B7
MIRASOL WY
12100 SD 92128 1150-B7
MIRA SORRENTO PL
5300 SD 92121 1208-D7
MIRATECH DR
- SD 92121 1208-H6
- SD 92126 1208-H6
MIRA VERDE ST
4000 OCN 92056 1107-B3
MIRA VISTA LN
6400 SD 92120 1250-E6

STREET
Block City ZIP Pg-Grid

MIRA ZANJA
7100 SD 92130 1188-H2
MIRA ZANJA CTE
14100 SD 92130 1188-H2
MIRIAM PL
4300 SDCo 91941 1271-D3
MIRO CIR
- SD 92131 1209-G3
MIRROR LAKE PL
2000 CHV 91913 1311-E5
MISS ELLE WY
1400 SDCo 91901 1234-C6
MISS ELLIE LN
15700 SDCo 92040 1232-G1
MISSION AV
- OCN 92054 1106-A1
300 OCN 92054 1086-C6
700 CHV 91910 1310-F7
900 CHV 91911 1330-F1
1800 SD 92103 1269-C4
1800 SD 92116 1269-C4
MISSION AV Rt#-76
3400 OCN 92054 1086-H2
3900 OCN 92057 1086-H2
4500 OCN 92057 1087-A1
4900 OCN 92057 1067-G6
5300 OCN 92056 1067-D7
5600 SDCo 92084 1067-G6
5600 SDCo 92003 1067-G6
E MISSION AV
100 ESCN 92025 1129-J1
800 ESCN 92026 1129-J1
800 ESCN 92026 1130-A1
800 ESCN 92025 1130-A1
1100 ESCN 92027 1130-A1
1200 ESCN 92027 1110-A7
W MISSION AV Rt#-S14
300 ESCN 92025 1129-G2
1200 ESCN 92029 1129-G2
MISSION BLVD
2600 SD 92109 1267-J3
3800 SD 92109 1247-H5
MISSION CT
- SDCo 91905 (1299-H3 See Page 1298)
600 CHV 91910 1310-E7
1000 CHV 91911 1330-F1
MISSION RD
- SDCo 92028 998-F7
- SDCo 92028 1028-F1
MISSION RD Rt#-76
5900 SDCo 92003 1067-H3
5900 SDCo 92084 1067-H3
31200 SDCo 92003 1068-A1
31800 SDCo 92003 1048-A7
E MISSION RD
2100 ESCN 92029 1149-J4
2100 ESCN 92029 1150-A3
2100 SD 92029 1149-J4
2100 SD 92029 1150-A4
2100 SDCo 92029 1149-J4
3800 SDCo 92028 1028-E1
E MISSION RD Rt#-S13
100 SDCo 92028 1027-H1
2000 SDCo 92028 1028-A1
2500 SDCo 92028 998-B7
E MISSION RD Rt#-S14
100 SMCS 92069 1108-J7
500 SMCS 92069 1109-B7
1000 SMCS 92069 1129-C1
1400 SMCS 92078 1129-C1
N MISSION RD
100 SDCo 92028 1027-F2
S MISSION RD
100 SDCo 92028 1027-F3
S MISSION RD Rt#-S13
1100 SDCo 92028 1027-G6
2600 SDCo 92028 1047-H1
4900 SDCo 92028 1048-A7
5000 SDCo 92003 1048-A7
W MISSION RD
100 SDCo 92028 1027-F2
W MISSION RD Rt#-S14
1000 SMCS 92069 1108-F7
1300 ESCN 92029 1129-E2
2000 SMCS 92078 1129-E2
MISSION VW
2300 SDCo 92003 1048-B7
MISSION WY
- SMCS 92078 1129-C1
MISSION BAY DR
4200 SD 92109 1248-C4
E MISSION BAY DR
1700 SD 92109 1268-D2
2300 SD 92109 1248-D7
N MISSION BAY DR
2200 SD 92109 1248-C6
W MISSION BAY DR
800 SD 92109 1267-J2
1200 SD 92109 1268-A3
3900 SD 92110 1268-C4
MISSION BAY PKWY
- SD 92109 1268-C3
MISSION BAY PL
800 SD 92109 1267-J2
MISSION BELL LN
4600 LMSA 91941 1271-A3
MISSION BONITA DR
7900 SD 92120 1250-C3
MISSION CARMEL CV
2400 SD 92014 1187-H5
MISSION CENTER CT
7800 SD 92108 1269-B2
MISSION CENTER RD
5100 SD 92108 1269-B2
5400 SD 92123 1269-B2
5500 SD 92123 1249-B7
MISSION CITY CT
9000 SD 92108 1249-E7
MISSION CITY PKWY
5000 SD 92108 1269-E1
MISSION CLIFF DR
1600 SD 92116 1269-C3
MISSION CREEK DR
9500 SNTE 92071 1231-C5
MISSION CREEK RD
1000 SDCo 92028 1047-H2
MISSION DAM TER
7300 SNTE 92071 1230-F7
MISSION GATE DR
4200 OCN 92057 1086-J3
MISSION GORGE PL
4500 SD 92120 1249-H7
4500 SD 92120 1269-J1
MISSION GORGE RD
5900 SD 92120 1249-J5
5900 SD 92120 1269-H1
7100 SD 92120 1250-E2
7100 SD 92124 1249-J5

STREET
Block City ZIP Pg-Grid

MISSION GORGE RD
7100 SD 92124 1250-A4
7300 SNTE 92071 1230-G7
8100 SD 92119 1250-E2
8600 SNTE 92071 1231-A6
9000 SD 92119 1230-G7
MISSION GREENS CT
8800 SNTE 92071 1231-D7
MISSION GREENS RD
8800 SNTE 92071 1231-D7
MISSION HEIGHTS RD
7700 SD 92108 1269-B2
MISSION HILLS CT
- SMCS 92069 1109-A6
MISSION MANZANA PL
7900 SD 92120 1250-C3
MISSION MEADOWS DR
1500 OCN 92057 1067-F7
MISSION MESA WY
3400 SD 92120 1250-C3
MISSION MONTANA DR
3600 SD 92120 1250-C3
MISSION MONTANA PL
7800 SD 92120 1250-C3
MISSION OAKS RD
- SDCo 92028 1027-F5
MISSION PARK CT
11000 SNTE 92071 1231-F5
MISSION PARK PL
9400 SNTE 92071 1231-G5
MISSION PRESERVE PL
- SD 92131 1210-H2
MISSION RIDGE RD
200 SDCo 92028 998-F7
200 SDCo 92028 1028-G1
MISSION SAN CARLOS DR
8600 SNTE 92071 1230-F7
MISSION TRAILS DR
7300 SNTE 92071 1230-F7
MISSION VALLEY CT
7600 SD 92108 1269-A1
MISSION VALLEY FRWY I-8
- SD - 1268-F4
- SD - 1269-B3
MISSION VALLEY RD
7500 SD 92108 1269-A1
MISSION VEGA CT
8800 SNTE 92071 1231-D7
MISSION VEGA RD
8800 SNTE 92071 1231-D6
MISSION VIEJO CT
9800 SNTE 92071 1231-D7
MISSION VIEW WY
- OCN 92057 1087-A2
MISSION VILLAGE DR
2100 SD 92108 1249-E5
2100 SD 92123 1249-E5
MISSION VISTA DR
7800 SD 92120 1250-C3
MISSISSIPPI ST
3400 SD 92104 1269-C5
4400 SD 92116 1269-C5
MISSOURI AV
200 OCN 92054 1106-A1
MISSOURI ST
600 SD 92109 1247-H5
1600 SD 92109 1248-A5
MISSY CT
6800 SD 92115 1270-E4
MISTER B PL
- SDCo 92082 1070-F6
MISTLETOE LN
800 CRLB 92011 1127-A5
MISTLETOE ST
400 VSTA 92083 1087-E6
MISTRAL PL
4300 SD 92130 1188-B6
MISTY CIR
1900 ENCT 92024 1147-H6
MISTY LN
4200 OCN 92056 1107-C2
MISTY RDG
- SD 92130 1208-B2
MISTY BLUE CT
12200 SD 92131 1210-B1
MISTY CREEK CT
1100 CHV 91913 1331-B1
MISTY CREEK ST
1000 CHV 91913 1331-A1
MISTY MEADOW CT
800 CHV 91910 1311-B6
MISTY MEADOW LN
9600 SDCo 92026 1089-C2
MISTY OAK RD
13700 SDCo 92082 1070-E7
MISTY RIDGE PL
1300 CHV 91913 1311-D7
1300 CHV 91913 1331-D1
MISTY SEA WY
- SMCS 92078 1128-D5
MITCHELL ST
1200 OCN 92054 1106-B2
MITCHELLS CAMP RD
- ImCo - 412-A6
MITRA CT
500 SDCo 91977 1291-D3
MITSCHER LN
- SD 92106 1288-C1
MITSCHER ST
- CHV 91910 1310-C7
300 CHV 91910 1330-B1
MITSCHER WY
- SD 92126 1209-D7
- SD 92126 1229-D1
- SD 92145 1229-D1
MITTEN LN
2500 SDCo 92065 1152-D7
MITZI LN
9100 SDCo 92021 1232-E6
MIZPAH LN
9500 SDCo 91916 1236-B1
MIZPAH SPUR
9700 SDCo 91916 1236-B1
M KNECHEL AV
1600 CALX 92231 6620-E7
MOA DR
400 VSTA 92083 1087-F4
MOANA DR
800 SD 92106 1287-J2
1000 SD 92107 1287-J2
MOANA KIA LN
8700 SNTE 92071 1230-J4
MOBLEY ST
2500 SD 92123 1249-D5
MOCCASIN AV
3200 SD 92117 1248-D1
MOCCASIN PL
4700 SD 92117 1248-D1
MOCHA CT
5100 OCN 92056 1107-F4
MOCKINGBIRD CIR
700 ESCN 92025 1130-C7

STREET
Block City ZIP Pg-Grid

MOCKINGBIRD DR
7600 SD 92123 1249-A7
MOCKINGBIRD LN
100 OCN 92057 1086-H2
1000 SMCS 92078 1128-E2
9400 SDCo 91941 1271-B2
MODE DR
3100 SDCo 92026 1109-H2
MODEL A FORD LN
4400 SDCo 92019 1273-A2
MODENA PL
- SD 92130 1188-A3
MODESTO ST
2300 SD 92105 1269-H7
2300 SD 92105 1289-H1
MODOC ST
3800 SD 92117 1248-E4
MOFFETT RD
- CORD 92135 1288-C5
- SD 92135 1288-C5
MOHAWK ST
6600 SD 92115 1270-E2
7300 LMSA 91941 1270-F2
MOHICAN AV
3200 SD 92117 1248-E5
MOHLER ST
6100 SD 92120 1249-J7
MOIOLA AV
2300 ELCN 92243 6499-E7
MOISAN WY
8900 LMSA 91941 1271-A2
MOLA VISTA WY
800 SOLB 92075 1167-G7
MOLCHAN RD
2300 SDCo 91906 (1297-F6 See Page 1296)
MOLE RD
1100 NATC 92136 1309-F2
MOLINO RD
10200 SNTE 92071 1231-D3
MOLLENDO BLVD
5200 SD 92124 1249-H2
MOLLIE LN
- SNTE 92071 1231-C2
MOLLIE ST
1200 SD 92110 1268-F3
N MOLLISON AV
300 ELCJ 92020 1251-G3
300 ELCJ 92021 1251-G3
1700 SDCo 92021 1251-G3
S MOLLISON AV
100 ELCJ 92020 1251-H6
100 ELCJ 92021 1251-H6
MOLLY CIR
1500 OCN 92054 1106-E1
MOLLYWOODS AV
9100 LMSA 91941 1271-B1
9300 SDCo 91941 1271-B1
MOLOKAI WY
2200 SD 92154 1330-C6
MOLUCCAN ST
- OCN 92057 1067-B2
MOMA LN
19500 SDCo 92065 1153-E2
MOMAR LN
500 ESCN 92027 1130-D1
MONA LN
- SD 92130 1188-J3
MONA PL
1100 ELCJ 92020 1251-E7
1100 ELCJ 92020 1271-E1
MONACO CT
2000 SDCo 92019 1272-C3
MONACO DR
1800 CHV 91913 1331-E1
1800 CHV 91913 1311-E7
MONACO ST
4300 SD 92107 1287-H2
MONAGHAN CT
2200 SDCo 91977 1291-B1
MONAHAN RD
4400 SDCo 91941 1271-E3
MONAIR DR
3300 SD 92117 1248-D4
MONA LISA ST
12300 SD 92130 1188-C7
MONARCH ST
2700 SD 92123 1249-E5
MONARCH WY
200 OCN 92057 1087-A1
MONARCHE DR
- CHV 91913 1331-C1
MONARCH RIDGE CIR
1700 SDCo 92019 1272-D2
MONARCH RIDGE LN
1900 SDCo 92019 1272-D3
MONDAVI CIR
1200 VSTA 92081 1107-J3
MONEL AV
8900 SD 92123 1229-D7
8900 SD 92123 1249-D1
MONET LN
5200 SDCo 91902 1290-H7
MONETTE DR
2400 SD 92123 1249-E6
MONICA CIR
500 OCN 92057 1067-A5
600 OCN 92057 1066-J5
MONIQUE CT
1200 VSTA 92084 1088-A3
9400 SDCo 91977 1271-C5
MONIQUE LN
3300 SDCo 91977 1271-B6
MONIQUE WY
400 SDCo 92026 1109-G3
MONITOR RD
1300 SD 92110 1268-F2
MONMOUTH DR
1600 SD 92109 1247-J5
1600 SD 92109 1248-A5
MONO LAKE DR
8300 SD 92119 1250-J5
MONONA DR
9200 LMSA 91942 1251-B7
MONONGAHELA ST
4600 SD 92117 1248-B1
4900 SD 92117 1228-B7
MONROE AV
1200 SD 92116 1269-B4
4400 SD 92115 1269-J4
4800 SD 92115 1270-A4
MONROE ST
100 OCN 92057 1067-A7
2100 CRLB 92008 1106-F3
MONSANTO CT
10800 SD 92129 1189-H2
MONSERATE AV
700 CHV 91910 1310-E7
800 CHV 91911 1330-E1
MONSERATE PL
3600 SDCo 92028 1048-E4
MONSERATE TER
3000 SDCo 92028 1048-A3

STREET
Block City ZIP Pg-Grid

MONSERATE WY
1600 SDCo 92028 1047-J4
1600 SDCo 92028 1048-A4
MONSERATE HILL CT
3600 SDCo 92028 1048-E4
MONSERATE HILL RD
3400 SDCo 92028 1048-E3
MONSERRAT WY
1800 VSTA 92081 1107-H5
MONSERRATE ST
- SDCo 92055 1086-A4
MONTAGE GN
- ESCN 92029 1129-G5
MONTAGE RD
600 OCN 92057 1087-C1
MONTALVO ST
4200 SD 92107 1268-B5
MONTANA RD
1600 CHV 91913 1311-D6
MONTANA ST
7800 LMGR 91945 1270-G7
MONTANA LUNA CT
- ESCN 92025 1130-B5
MONTANA SERENA
1400 SDCo 92021 1233-B6
MONTANA SERENA CT
1400 SDCo 92021 1233-B6
MONTANES LN
7000 CRLB 92009 1127-G7
MONTANYA DR
12300 SDCo 92082 1070-A4
MONTANYA LN
13400 SDCo 92082 1070-D4
MONTARA AV
7900 SD 92126 1209-B2
MONTARA CT
11100 SD 92126 1209-B2
MONTAUBON CIR
11000 SD 92131 1209-J2
MONTAUBON WY
11000 SD 92131 1209-J2
MONTAUK ST
12700 PWY 92064 1190-C5
MONTBURY PL
- SD 92131 1210-J2
MONTCALM ST
300 CHV 91911 1330-F2
MONTCLAIR ST
200 CHV 91911 1330-F1
2000 SD 92104 1289-G1
2400 SD 92104 1269-F7
MONTCLIFF RD
2000 SD 92139 1290-G6
MONTE DR
- LMSA 91941 1270-G5
MONTE RD
1100 ImCo 92227 431-A1
5900 SDCo 92003 1048-C7
MONTE ALTO TER
- SD 92127 1169-C3
MONTE AZUL LN
1000 SDCo 92036 1138-A6
MONTEBELLO ST
- CHV 91910 1310-C5
MONTECITO AV
- IMP 92251 6499-J2
MONTECITO DR
- CRLB 92009 1127-G3
- SDCo 92028 1047-J1
MONTECITO GN
- SD 92130 1188-E4
300 ESCN 92025 1150-B1
MONTECITO LN
- SDCo 92028 1047-J1
MONTECITO RD
- CHV 91914 1311-G2
- SDCo 91901 1235-A5
- SDCo 92065 1151-H6
1400 SDCo 92065 1152-A6
E MONTECITO RD
100 SDCo 92065 1152-F6
MONTECITO WY
600 SD 92103 1268-H5
800 SDCo 92065 1152-B5
E MONTECITO WY
200 SD 92103 1269-A5
W MONTECITO WY
1000 SD 92103 1269-A5
MONTE DE JOSUE
16900 SDCo 92065 1151-E6
MONTEFRIO CT
3900 SD 92130 1188-B7
MONTE FUEGO
6500 SDCo 92067 1188-G2
MONTEGO AV
700 ESCN 92026 1109-F5
MONTEGO CT
- CORD 92118 1329-D1
1300 VSTA 92081 1107-H4
MONTEGO CV
2700 SD 92014 1187-J6
MONTEGO DR
10500 SD 92124 1249-H1
13300 PWY 92064 1190-H4
MONTEGO PL
5300 SD 92124 1249-H1
MONTEGO BAY CT
300 OCN 92057 1066-H6
MONTELEONE AV
- CHV 91913 1311-F1
MONTELLANO TER
12500 SD 92130 1188-B6
MONTEMAR AV
2100 ESCN 92027 1110-C6
MONTEMAR DR
9300 SDCo 91977 1271-C7
MONTE MAR RD
1100 VSTA 92084 1088-A4
MONTE MIRA DR
1800 ENCT 92024 1147-C1
MONTE MIRA LN
800 ENCT 92024 1147-C1
MONTERA CT
500 CHV 91910 1310-G5
MONTERA ST
1300 CHV 91913 1331-B1
MONTE REAL
3500 ESCN 92029 1150-A4
MONTEREY AV
700 CHV 91910 1310-E7
1000 CHV 91911 1330-F2
1700 CORD 92118 1288-J7
1700 CORD 92118 1308-J1
1800 CORD 92118 1289-A7
MONTEREY CIR
500 SMCS 92069 1109-A6
MONTEREY CT
700 SD 92109 1267-H1
800 CHV 91911 1330-F1
MONTEREY DR
500 OCN 92054 1085-J6
600 OCN 92054 1086-A5
1300 SDCo 92020 1251-J7
2400 ESCN 92029 1149-G1

STREET
Block City ZIP Pg-Grid

MONTEREY GN
2400 ESCN 92029 1149-G1
MONTEREY LN
600 VSTA 92084 1087-J3
MONTEREY PL
- ENCT 92024 1147-F5
1300 SDCo 91901 1233-H5
MONTEREY RD
1100 SDCo 92019 1251-H7
1100 SDCo 92020 1251-H7
MONTEREY CREST DR
3200 SDCo 91935 1273-B7
MONTEREY CYPRESS WY
12600 SD 92130 1188-B6
MONTEREY PARK DR
1500 SD 92173 1350-D2
MONTEREY PINE DR
1500 SD 92173 1350-C2
MONTEREY RIDGE CT
- SDCo 92127 1169-F2
MONTEREY RIDGE DR
- SDCo 92127 1169-F2
MONTEREY RIDGE WY
- SDCo 92127 1169-F2
MONTEREY VISTA PL
1100 ENCT 92024 1167-F1
MONTEREY VISTA WY
1000 ENCT 92024 1167-F1
MONTE RICO DR
1400 ELCJ 92021 1252-A2
1400 SDCo 92021 1252-A2
MONTERO CT
12500 SD 92128 1170-C2
MONTERO PL
1900 ESCN 92029 1129-F6
12500 SD 92128 1170-C2
MONTERO RD
17200 SD 92128 1170-C2
17700 PWY 92064 1170-C2
MONTERO WY
12500 SD 92128 1170-C2
MONTESANO RD
3100 SDCo 92029 1149-J2
MONTE SERENO AV
1200 CHV 91913 1311-B7
1200 CHV 91913 1331-B1
MONTESSA ST
4900 SD 92124 1250-A1
5000 SD 92124 1230-A7
MONTE VERDE DR
6800 SD 92119 1250-E3
MONTEVIDEO PL
31400 SDCo 92003 1067-J1
MONTE VIEW CT
11700 SDCo 92019 1272-A4
MONTE VISTA
- SMCS 92078 1129-C1
MONTE VISTA AV
- CHV 91910 1310-A5
7000 SD 92037 1247-E1
7400 SD 92037 1227-E7
MONTE VISTA CT
12700 PWY 92064 1170-D6
MONTE VISTA DR
1100 VSTA 92084 1108-A1
1500 VSTA 92084 1088-B7
1700 SDCo 92084 1108-D1
MONTE VISTA RD
1700 SDCo 92020 1271-J3
12600 PWY 92064 1170-C6
MONTE VISTA WY
- OCN 92057 1086-J2
MONTEZUMA
- SD 92140 1268-F6
MONTEZUMA CT
1600 SDCo 92004 1058-F5
MONTEZUMA PL
5000 SD 92115 1270-C2
MONTEZUMA RD
- SD 92116 1269-J2
100 SDCo 92004 1058-F5
4500 SD 92115 1269-J2
4900 SD 92115 1270-B2
5400 SD 92182 1270-B2
MONTEZUMA VALLEY RD Rt#-S22
31300 SDCo 92066 410-A9
33400 SDCo 92066 409-L9
33900 SDCo 92066 1098-A2
34400 SDCo 92004 (1078-D7 See Page 1058)
34400 SDCo 92066 (1078-D7 See Page 1058)
35500 SDCo 92086 409-L9
MONTFORT CT
14000 SD 92128 1190-A2
MONTGOMERY AV
1800 ENCT 92007 1167-D2
MONTGOMERY DR
1400 SDCo 92084 1108-B2
MONTGOMERY RD
- ImCo 92233 411-B9
MONTGOMERY ST
100 CHV 91911 1330-D5
MONTIA CT
6700 CRLB 92011 1126-J5
MONTIA PL
2200 ESCN 92029 1129-H7
MONTICELLO DR
800 SDCo 92029 1129-J7
MONTICOOK CT
11200 SD 92127 1149-H7
MONTIEL RD
1100 ESCN 92026 1129-E1
1100 SDCo 92026 1129-F2
1400 SMCS 92069 1129-C1
MONTIEL TKTR
3800 SDCo 91935 1254-A7
3800 SDCo 91935 1274-B1
MONTIEN
- SD 92127 1168-J5
MONTIEN PASS
- SD 92127 1168-J5
MONTIJO RD
- SDCo 92055 996-C5
MONTONGO CIR
7900 SD 92126 1209-A3
MONTONGO ST
10700 SD 92126 1209-A2
MONTRACHET ST
- SDCo 92003 1067-J5
- SDCo 92084 1067-J5
- SDCo 92084 1068-A5
MONTROS PL
1200 ESCN 92027 1110-A7
MONTROSE CT
500 ELCJ 92020 1251-F4
MONTROSE WY
100 OCN 92057 1087-A1
8900 SD 92122 1228-D3
MONTURA AV
10100 SNTE 92071 1231-E3
MONTURA CT
10600 SNTE 92071 1231-E3

STREET
Block City ZIP Pg-Grid

MONTURA DR
17000 SD 92128 1170-C2
MONTURA RD
1100 SDCo 92078 1128-B2
MONTVIEW DR
500 ESCN 92025 1130-A6
600 ESCN 92025 1129-J6
MONTVIEW GN
1100 ESCN 92025 1129-H6
MONUMENT PL
3900 ESCN 92025 1150-D3
MONUMENT RD
400 IMPB 91932 1349-G5
400 SD 91932 1349-G5
400 SD 92154 1349-G5
1800 SD 92154 1350-A5
MONUMENT HILL
1300 SDCo 92020 1272-A1
MONUMENT PEAK RD
- SDCo 91948 1218-F4
- SDCo 92036 1218-F4
MONUMENT TRAIL DR
1300 CHV 91915 1311-H6
MOODY DR
900 ESCN 92027 1130-E1
MOON RD
1400 VSTA 92083 1087-D6
MOONBEAM LN
- CHV 91915 1331-G1
MOONCREST CT
3100 SMCS 92078 1108-B6
3100 VSTA 92081 1108-B6
MOONCREST RD
27300 SDCo 92065 1154-C2
MOONEY ST
3100 SD 92117 1248-E6
MOON FIELD DR
- CRLB 92010 1107-B5
MOONFLOWER MEADOWS TR
- SD 92130 1188-E4
MOONGLOW CT
1900 VSTA 92081 1107-J4
23700 SDCo 92065 1173-D5
MOONGLOW DR
15000 SDCo 92065 1173-D5
MOONLIGHT GN
2300 ESCN 92026 1109-B4
MOONLIGHT LN
400 ENCT 92024 1147-B7
4200 OCN 92056 1107-C2
5400 SD 92037 1247-H3
MOONLIGHT PL
31000 SDCo 92082 1070-E2
MOONLIGHT WY
600 SDCo 92065 1152-E5
MOONLIGHT TRAIL LN
2600 CHV 91915 1311-H5
MOONLIT TR
- SDCo 91905 1300-D4
MOONLITE HILL RD
- SDCo 92028 1027-J7
- SDCo 92028 1028-A7
MOONRIDGE DR
2800 SD 92037 1227-J6
MOONRIDGE PL
7700 SD 92037 1227-J6
MOON RIDGE RD
9100 SDCo 92028 1029-A2
MOONRISE TR
2000 SDCo 91905 1300-E7
MOON ROCK RD
1600 SDCo 92028 997-G7
MOON SHADOW DR
- OCN 92054 1086-D3
MOONSHADOW RDG
1700 SDCo 92028 1027-J6
1700 SDCo 92028 1028-A6
MOON SONG CT
18100 SD 92127 1149-H6
MOONSTONE DR
2400 SD 92123 1249-E6
MOONSTONE PL
- CRLB 92009 1127-H5
1000 CHV 91913 1331-A1
MOONSTONE BAY DR
300 OCN 92057 1066-J6
MOON VALLEY RD
37500 SDCo 91905 (1319-G6 See Page 1298)
38000 SDCo 91905 (1320-A6 See Page 1300)
MOON VIEW DR
300 CHV 91910 1310-F5
MOON VIEW WY
10300 SDCo 92026 1089-F3
MOONWIND CIR
- SDCo 92026 1089-A1
MOORE AV
- SD 92126 1209-E7
MOORE ST
2200 SD 92110 1268-E5
MOOREFIELD DR
5700 SDCo 92019 1253-D3
MOORGATE RD
100 ENCT 92024 1147-A2
100 ENCT 92024 1146-J2
MOORHEN PL
6800 CRLB 92011 1127-E5
MOORLAND DR
1400 SD 92109 1248-A7
MOORLAND HEIGHTS WY
10500 SD 92121 1208-E4
MOORPARK CT
2900 SDCo 91978 1271-F7
MOORPARK ST
10200 SDCo 91978 1271-F7
MORA CIR
13500 PWY 92064 1190-H4
MORADA ST
7700 CRLB 92009 1147-H2
MORAEA ST
1300 SD 92114 1290-D5
MORAGA AV
3700 SD 92117 1248-D2
MORAGA CT
3300 SD 92117 1248-D3
MORAGA PL
3300 SD 92117 1248-D3
MORAGA WY
400 OCN 92054 1086-G2
MORALES LN
- SDCo 92082 1071-E3
MORAN CT
100 VSTA 92081 1107-D1
MORAN WY
12700 SD 92129 1189-D6
MORANDA CT
11200 SD 92128 1189-J4
MORATALLA TER
4000 SD 92130 1188-B6
MORAVA PL
2700 SD 92110 1248-F7

STREET Block City ZIP Pg-Grid

MORCADO CIR
9400 SDCo 91941 1271-C4
MOREHOUSE DR
5400 SD 92121 1208-E6
MOREHOUSE PL
300 CHV 91911 1330-D4
MORELIA CT
100 SOLB 92075 1167-D7
MORELLA WY
2100 OCN 92056 1086-J7
2100 OCN 92056 1106-J1
MORENA BLVD
400 SD 92110 1268-E1
2200 SD 92110 1248-D5
2700 SD 92117 1248-B3
W MORENA BLVD
1100 SD 92110 1268-E3
MORENA PL
5100 SD 92110 1268-F3
MORENA RESERVOIR RD
- SD 91906 (1297-A5 See Page 1296)
2500 SDCo 91906 (1297-A5 See Page 1296)
MORENA STOKES VALLEY RD
- SDCo 91906 430-A7
- SDCo 91906 (1297-D1 See Page 1296)
MORENA VIEW DR
29800 SDCo 91906 (1297-F5 See Page 1296)
MORENCI ST
1400 SD 92110 1268-E2
MORENE ST
12900 PWY 92064 1190-D5
MORENO AV
11000 SDCo 92040 1232-B1
11100 SDCo 92040 1212-A5
11900 SDCo 92040 1211-J3
MORENO ST
1400 OCN 92054 1106-C2
MORENO WY
1300 OCN 92054 1106-C2
MORETON GN
- SD 92130 1188-E4
MORGAN CT
- SDCo 92004 (1079-C6 See Page 1058)
MORGAN PL
300 SDCo 92083 1108-C4
MORGAN RD
2200 CRLB 92008 1107-C7
2200 CRLB 92008 1127-C1
MORGAN ST
- SDCo 92055 1023-F2
MORGAN WY
500 ELCJ 92020 1251-F7
MORGAN CREEK WY
- OCN 92057 1086-J2
MORGANDALE CT
2900 SDCo 91977 1271-B6
MORGAN HILL DR
1000 CHV 91913 1311-B7
1200 CHV 91913 1331-B1
MORGANS AV
- SMCS 92078 1128-D6
MORLAN ST
3600 SD 92117 1228-D7
MORLEY DR
- SD 92102 1289-G4
MORLEY ST
2200 SD 92111 1248-J7
2200 SD 92111 1268-J1
MORLEY FIELD DR
1700 SD 92101 1269-C6
1700 SD 92103 1269-C6
MORNING WY
3100 SD 92037 1228-A3
MORNING AIR RD
14200 PWY 92064 1170-G4
MORNING BREEZE LN
1600 NATC 91950 1310-B1
MORNING BREEZE WY
9300 SD 92126 1209-E2
MORNING CANYON RD
4700 OCN 92056 1107-E2
MORNING CREEK CT
- CHV 91914 1311-J3
MORNING CREEK DR
10900 SD 92128 1189-H5
MORNING CREEK DR N
10900 SD 92128 1189-H4
MORNING CREEK RD
- CHV 91914 1311-J2
MORNING DEW CT
- CHV 91915 1331-G1
MORNING DOVE RD
11000 SDCo 92040 1211-F7
MORNING DOVE WY
4400 OCN 92057 1086-J1
MORNING GLORY DR
9300 SDCo 92040 1232-C5
MORNING GLORY LN
2700 CRLB 92008 1106-E4
MORNING GLORY TR
- IMP 92251 6499-D2
MORNING GLORY WY
- SD 92130 1188-G4
MORNINGLORY LN
1400 VSTA 92084 1108-A1
MORNINGLORY PL
1300 VSTA 92084 1108-A1
MORNINGLORY TER
1400 VSTA 92084 1108-A1
MORNING MIST CT
- VSTA 92084 1087-J2
8300 SD 92119 1250-J2
MORNING MIST GN
1900 ESCN 92026 1109-B3
MORNINGSIDE CT
12200 PWY 92064 1170-B7
MORNINGSIDE DR
500 VSTA 92084 1087-H6
3100 OCN 92056 1107-C1
14800 PWY 92064 1170-B7
14800 PWY 92064 1190-B1
MORNINGSIDE GN
1600 ESCN 92026 1109-G6
MORNINGSIDE PL
500 VSTA 92084 1087-J7
MORNINGSIDE ST
2200 SD 92139 1310-C1
MORNINGSIDE TER
2800 SDCo 92029 1149-G2
MORNINGSIDE TR
200 VSTA 92084 1087-J6
2200 SDCo 92065 1172-D4
MORNING STAR CIR
- SDCo 92082 1070-H2
MORNING STAR CT
4100 SDCo 91941 1271-G4
MORNING STAR DR
1600 CHV 91915 1331-H1
10800 SDCo 91941 1271-G4
MORNINGSTAR LN
1300 SDCo 92028 1027-F4
MORNING SUN CT
2200 ENCT 92024 1147-J5
MORNING SUN DR
800 ENCT 92024 1147-J5
MORNING TERRACE GN
- ESCN 92027 1130-J4
MORNING VIEW CT
4300 SDCo 91941 1271-D3
MORNING VIEW DR
- VSTA 92084 1087-J3
1000 ESCN 92026 1109-G7
1000 ESCN 92026 1129-G1
3300 OCN 92054 1086-D2
MOROCCO DR
8000 LMSA 91942 1270-H1
MORONGO DR
- IMP 92251 6439-F3
MOROSE ST
2200 LMGR 91945 1270-H7
2200 LMGR 91945 1290-H1
MORRELL ST
3900 SD 92109 1248-A5
MORRIS ST
2200 SD 92136 1289-F7
MORRISON PL
19300 SDCo 92065 1192-B2
MORRISON ST
400 SD 92102 1289-H3
MORRIS RANCH RD
- SDCo 91948 430-B5
- SDCo 91962 430-B5
MORRO RD
100 SDCo 92028 1027-G4
MORRO WY
5600 LMSA 91942 1270-H1
MORRO BAY ST
4500 OCN 92057 1066-H6
MORRO HEIGHTS RD
6600 OCN 92057 1067-D2
MORRO HILLS PL
5100 SDCo 92028 1047-G7
MORRO HILLS RD
100 SDCo 92028 1047-F6
MORRO POINT DR
600 CHV 91911 1330-J4
MORROW WY
1400 SD 92103 1269-B5
MORSA WY
3200 CRLB 92009 1127-J5
MORSE CT
6900 SD 92111 1268-J1
MORSE ST
100 OCN 92054 1106-D2
1400 OCN 92054 1106-D2
MORTON GN
1900 ESCN 92025 1129-H5
MORTON WY
2900 SD 92139 1310-F2
MOSAIC CIR
600 OCN 92057 1087-B1
MOSAIC GN
- ESCN 92029 1129-G5
MOSELLE ST
10300 SD 92131 1210-A3
MOSELLE WY
12000 SD 92131 1210-B3
MOSS ST
- CHV 91911 1330-D2
E MOSS ST
300 CHV 91911 1330-F1
MOSSBERG CT
1200 VSTA 92083 1087-E5
MOSS LANDING AV
1900 CHV 91913 1311-E6
MOSS TREE LN
9700 SDCo 92026 1089-D4
MOSSWOOD CV
- SD 92130 1208-E2
MOSSY ROCK DR
1700 SDCo 92084 1068-B6
MOTHER GRUNDY DR
1800 SDCo 91935 (1314-G2 See Page 1294)
MOTHER GRUNDY TKTR
- SDCo 91917 (1314-D6 See Page 1294)
300 SDCo 91935 (1314-H1 See Page 1294)
1500 SDCo 91935 1294-H7
MOTHER LODE WY
1300 CHV 91913 1311-E6
MOTIF ST
4800 OCN 92057 1087-B2
MOTT ST
5700 SD 92122 1228-B6
MOTTINO DR
2500 OCN 92056 1087-C6
MOULTRIE AV
3500 SD 92117 1248-D5
MOUND AV
5400 SD 92120 1250-B5
MOUNDGLEN LN
2600 SDCo 91977 1271-C7
MOUNDTOP LN
2600 SDCo 91977 1271-D7
MOUNDVIEW PL
2600 SDCo 91977 1271-D7
MOUNT WY
1700 VSTA 92081 1107-G4
MOUNT AACHEN AV
3200 SD 92111 1248-H5
MOUNT ABBEY AV
3500 SD 92111 1248-H4
MOUNT ABERNATHY AV
4200 SD 92117 1248-J1
MOUNT ABRAHAM AV
3600 SD 92111 1248-H3
MOUNT ACADIA BLVD
2800 SD 92110 1248-G5
2800 SD 92111 1248-G5
MOUNT ACARA DR
5500 SD 92111 1248-H5
MOUNT ACKERLY DR
5600 SD 92111 1248-H4
MOUNT ACKERMAN DR
6200 SD 92111 1248-H3
MOUNT ACLARE AV
3400 SD 92111 1248-H4
MOUNT ACMAR CT
3100 SD 92111 1248-H5
MOUNT ACOMITA AV
3400 SD 92111 1248-H4
MOUNT ACONIA DR
5500 SD 92111 1248-G5
MOUNT ACONIA WY
5500 SD 92111 1248-H5
MOUNT ACRE WY
6300 SD 92111 1248-H3
MOUNT ADA RD
6300 SD 92111 1248-J3
MOUNT ADELBERT DR
6300 SD 92111 1248-H3
MOUNT AGUILAR DR
5900 SD 92111 1248-H3
S MOUNTAIN DR
13000 SDCo 92040 1232-C3
MOUNTAIN LN
2200 SDCo 92065 1172-E2
MOUNTAIN RD
14200 PWY 92064 1190-G1
E MOUNTAIN VW
100 CHV 91910 1310-B5
N MOUNTAIN VW
100 CHV 91910 1310-B5
S MOUNTAIN VW
200 CHV 91910 1310-B5
MOUNTAIN WY
31500 SDCo 92003 1068-G1
MOUNTAIN ASH AV
900 CHV 91914 1311-H4
MOUNTAIN BLUEBIRD CT
11300 SDCo 92040 1212-C6
MOUNTAINBROOK RD
4700 SDCo 92070 1135-D4
MOUNTAIN CIRCLE DR
35700 SDCo 92036 1176-D1
MOUNTAIN CREST GN
- ESCN 92027 1130-F2
MOUNTAIN GLEN TER
10400 SD 92131 1209-J4
MOUNTAIN HEIGHTS DR
1000 ESCN 92029 1149-H1
1000 SDCo 92029 1149-H1
MOUNTAIN HILLS PL
1700 ESCN 92029 1129-F6
MOUNTAIN LILAC RD
28600 SDCo 92026 1089-E2
MOUNTAIN LION RD
11400 SDCo 92040 1212-D4
MOUNTAIN MEADOW DR
1400 OCN 92056 1087-D4
MOUNTAIN MEADOW RD
- SDCo 92036 1175-J2
15700 SDCo 92026 1089-D1
28800 SDCo 92026 1069-D7
MOUNTAIN MEADOW TR
4400 SDCo 92036 1155-J4
MOUNTAIN PARK PL
1200 ESCN 92027 1130-E2
MOUNTAIN PASS CIR
1600 VSTA 92081 1107-H7
MOUNTAIN PASS RD
11900 SD 92128 1190-B7
MOUNTAIN PEAK PL
- SDCo 92065 1173-D2
MOUNTAIN QUAIL CT
11400 SDCo 92040 1212-C5
MOUNTAIN RANCHES RD
11800 SDCo 92040 1212-C5
MOUNTAIN RIDGE RD
2200 CHV 91914 1311-E2
31000 SDCo 92026 1069-C2
31000 SDCo 92082 1069-C2
MOUNTAIN RIM RD
- SDCo 92028 1029-B2
MOUNTAIN SHADOW DR
9200 SDCo 92040 1232-D5
MOUNTAIN SHADOW LN
16400 SDCo 92065 1171-F3
MOUNTAINSIDE DR
13400 PWY 92064 1190-C4
MOUNTAIN SPRING RD
- ImCo 92259 430-F8
MOUNTAIN SPRINGS RD
- ImCo 92259 430-F8
MOUNT AINSWORTH AV
3700 SD 92111 1248-H3
MOUNT AINSWORTH CT
6300 SD 92111 1248-H3
MOUNT AINSWORTH WY
6300 SD 92111 1248-H3
MOUNTAIN TOP CT
6700 SD 92120 1250-D4
MOUNTAIN TOP DR
1100 SDCo 92021 1233-A7
MOUNTAIN VALLEY LN
1900 ESCN 92029 1129-F6
MOUNTAIN VALLEY PL
15600 SDCo 92040 1212-J6
15600 SDCo 92040 1213-A6
MOUNTAIN VIEW AV
1600 OCN 92054 1106-C1
MOUNTAINVIEW AV
- ELCN 92243 6559-G3
MOUNTAIN VIEW CT
600 VSTA 92083 1087-F4
14100 PWY 92064 1190-G2
MOUNTAIN VIEW DR
500 SDCo 92036 1156-E1
2000 ESCN 92027 1130-D2
2400 CRLB 92008 1106-D4
2500 SDCo 92027 1130-F2
E MOUNTAIN VIEW DR
4600 SD 92116 1269-F2
N MOUNTAIN VIEW DR
3100 SD 92116 1269-F2
W MOUNTAIN VIEW DR
3200 SD 92116 1269-E3
MOUNTAIN VIEW LN
1300 CHV 91911 1330-G3
10300 SDCo 92040 1231-G3
24800 SDCo 92065 1173-G5
MOUNTAIN VIEW PL
- SDCo 92021 1252-J1
- SDCo 92021 1253-A1
MOUNTAIN VIEW RD
100 SDCo 92021 1252-J2
400 SDCo 92021 1253-A2
1200 SDCo 92021 1233-B7
1300 SDCo 92019 1233-B7
1300 SDCo 92019 1253-A2
9500 SDCo 91916 1235-G2
32200 SDCo 92003 1048-H5
MOUNTAIN VIEW WY
3800 SDCo 91902 1310-E4
MOUNTAIN VISTA DR
400 ENCT 92024 1147-G6
MOUNTAIN VISTA WY
2000 OCN 92054 1106-F1
MOUNT ALADIN AV
3700 SD 92111 1248-G4
MOUNT ALBERTINE AV
3800 SD 92111 1248-H3
MOUNT ALBERTINE CT
6500 SD 92111 1248-J3
MOUNT ALBERTINE WY
3900 SD 92111 1248-J3
MOUNT ALIFAN CT
4000 SD 92111 1248-F4
MOUNT ALIFAN DR
4400 SD 92111 1248-G3
MOUNT ALIFAN PL
4100 SD 92111 1248-H3
MOUNT ALIFAN WY
4000 SD 92111 1248-F4
MOUNT ALMAGOSA DR
4700 SD 92111 1248-G4
MOUNT ALMAGOSA PL
3700 SD 92111 1248-F4
MOUNT ALVAREZ AV
3400 SD 92111 1248-H4
MOUNT ANTERO DR
4900 SD 92111 1248-G4
MOUNT ARARAT DR
4800 SD 92111 1248-G4
MOUNT ARARAT WY
7700 SDCo 92003 1068-G1
MOUNT ARIANE CT
5200 SD 92111 1248-G5
MOUNT ARIANE DR
3300 SD 92111 1248-G5
MOUNT ARIANE TER
5200 SD 92111 1248-F5
MOUNT ARMET DR
4600 SD 92117 1248-F3
MOUNT ARMOUR CT
3400 SD 92111 1248-F5
MOUNT ARMOUR DR
4800 SD 92111 1248-G5
MOUNT ARMOUR PL
3400 SD 92111 1248-G5
MOUNT ASHMUN CT
3600 SD 92111 1248-G4
MOUNT ASHMUN DR
4700 SD 92111 1248-G4
MOUNT ASHMUN PL
3700 SD 92111 1248-F4
MOUNT AUGUSTUS AV
3700 SD 92111 1248-G4
MOUNT BAGOT AV
4100 SD 92117 1248-F3
MOUNT BARNARD AV
4000 SD 92111 1248-G3
MOUNT BIGELOW CT
4100 SD 92111 1248-F4
MOUNT BIGELOW DR
4400 SD 92111 1248-F3
MOUNT BIGELOW WY
4100 SD 92111 1248-F3
MOUNT BLACKBURN AV
3600 SD 92111 1248-G4
MOUNT BLANCA DR
5000 SD 92111 1248-G3
MOUNT BOLANAS CT
4000 SD 92111 1248-G3
MOUNT BROSS AV
4000 SD 92111 1248-G3
MOUNT BRUNDAGE AV
3800 SD 92111 1248-G4
MOUNT BULLION DR
1900 CHV 91913 1311-E7
MOUNT BURNHAM CT
3400 SD 92111 1248-G5
MOUNT BURNHAM DR
5200 SD 92111 1248-G5
MOUNT BURNHAM PL
3500 SD 92111 1248-G5
MOUNT CARMEL DR
100 SD 92173 1350-G3
MOUNT CAROL DR
3000 SD 92111 1248-H5
MOUNT CASAS CT
4200 SD 92117 1248-F3
MOUNT CASAS DR
4700 SD 92117 1248-G3
MOUNT CASTLE AV
4300 SD 92117 1248-G2
MOUNT CERVIN DR
4700 SD 92117 1248-G1
MOUNT CRESTI DR
4700 SD 92117 1248-G1
MOUNT CULEBRA AV
4100 SD 92111 1248-G3
4200 SD 92117 1248-G3
MOUNT DANA DR
1000 CHV 91913 1331-B2
MOUNT DAVIS AV
4200 SD 92117 1248-G3
MOUNT DURBAN DR
4700 SD 92117 1248-F3
MOUNT ELBRUS CT
4300 SD 92117 1248-F3
MOUNT ELBRUS DR
4800 SD 92117 1248-G2
MOUNT ELENA WY
2300 SDCo 91935 1294-G6
MOUNT ETNA DR
4600 SD 92117 1248-G2
MOUNT EVEREST BLVD
3400 SD 92111 1248-G4
4200 SD 92117 1248-G3
MOUNT FORAKER AV
4300 SD 92117 1248-G2
MOUNT FORDE AV
4600 SD 92117 1248-F3
MOUNT FOSTER AV
4200 SD 92117 1248-F3
MOUNT FRISSELL DR
4500 SD 92117 1248-F2
MOUNT GAYWAS DR
4500 SD 92117 1248-F2
MOUNT HARRIS DR
4700 SD 92117 1248-G2
MOUNT HAY DR
4700 SD 92117 1248-G2
MOUNT HELIX DR
4700 SDCo 91941 1271-D2
MOUNT HELIX HIGHLANDS DR
4200 SDCo 91941 1271-C3
MOUNT HENRY AV
4200 SD 92117 1248-F2
MOUNT HENRY PL
4500 SD 92117 1248-F3
MOUNT HENRY WY
4500 SD 92117 1248-F3
MOUNT HERBERT AV
4100 SD 92117 1248-F2
MOUNT HIGHPINE PL
4500 SD 92117 1248-F2
MOUNT HILLS PL
300 ELCJ 92020 1251-C5
MOUNT HORTON DR
4600 SD 92117 1248-F3
MOUNT HUBBARD AV
4500 SD 92117 1248-F3
MOUNT HUKEE AV
4100 SD 92117 1248-F3
MOUNT ISRAEL PL
8900 SDCo 92029 1149-C4
MOUNT ISRAEL RD
8700 SDCo 92029 1149-C4
MOUNT JEFFERS AV
4300 SD 92117 1248-F3
MOUNT KING DR
4500 SD 92117 1248-F2
MOUNT LANGLEY DR
- CHV 91913 1311-E6
MOUNT LA PALMA DR
4700 SD 92117 1248-G2
MOUNT LA PLATTA CT
4500 SD 92117 1248-G2
MOUNT LA PLATTA DR
4600 SD 92117 1248-G2
MOUNT LA PLATTA PL
4500 SD 92117 1248-G1
MOUNT LAUDO DR
4600 SD 92117 1248-F2
MOUNT LAURENCE DR
3300 SD 92117 1248-D4
MOUNT LINDSEY AV
4400 SD 92117 1248-F2
MOUNT LINDSEY PL
4500 SD 92117 1248-F2
MOUNT LONGS DR
4600 SD 92117 1248-G2
MOUNT MACCLURE ST
1400 CHV 91913 1331-B2
MOUNT MIGUEL DR
3000 SD 92139 1310-D3
MOUNT MIGUEL RD
- CHV 91902 1311-E2
2100 CHV 91914 1311-E2
MOUNT OLYMPUS DR
6900 SDCo 92028 999-E5
MOUNT OLYMPUS VALLEY RD
9900 SDCo 92028 999-D4
MOUNT OWEN CT
- CHV 91913 1331-A1
MOUNT PUTMAN AV
4100 SD 92117 1248-F3
MOUNT PUTMAN CT
4600 SD 92117 1248-F3
MOUNT RIAS PL
4100 SD 92111 1248-H3
MOUNT ROYAL AV
4700 SD 92117 1248-G1
MOUNT ROYAL CT
4800 SD 92117 1248-G1
MOUNT ROYAL PL
4800 SD 92117 1248-G1
MOUNT SAINT HELENS CT
4700 SD 92117 1248-G1
MOUNT SAINT HELENS DR
4700 SD 92117 1248-G1
MOUNT SAINT HELENS WY
4700 SD 92117 1248-G1
MOUNT SANDY DR
3700 SD 92117 1248-D5
MOUNT SHASTA
3500 SMCS 92078 1128-B1
MOUNT TAMALPAIS AV
- CHV 91913 1331-E2
MOUNT TAMI DR
3100 SD 92111 1248-H5
MOUNT TAMI LN
3300 SD 92111 1248-H5
MOUNT TERMINUS DR
4000 SD 92111 1248-F4
MOUNT VERNON AV
800 OCN 92057 1086-G5
MOUNT VERNON ST
6900 LMGR 91945 1270-F7
MOUNT VIEW RD
- SDCo 92029 1129-C6
MOUNT VOSS DR
4200 SD 92117 1248-F3
MOUNT WHITNEY CT
900 CHV 91913 1331-A2
MOUNT WHITNEY RD
1000 CHV 91913 1331-A2
2800 SDCo 92029 1129-C4
MOUNT WOODSON RD
17100 SDCo 92065 1171-E4
MOUNT WOODSON WY
17300 SDCo 92065 1171-F3
MOWER PL
- SD 92130 1188-G7
MOYA PL
500 CHV 91910 1310-H5
MOYLA CT
- OCN 92054 1086-D3
MOYLA DR
16200 SDCo 92061 1051-B5
MOZART AV
100 ENCT 92007 1167-D3
MOZELLE LN
9800 SDCo 91941 1271-D4
M STUART ST
- CALX 92231 6620-J5
MUCHACHA WY
10300 SD 92124 1229-G7
MUDDY LN
300 VSTA 92084 1088-A6
MUDGE LN
1700 ESCN 92026 1109-F5
MUFFIN CT
9900 SD 92129 1189-F3
MUIR AV
4300 SD 92107 1268-A6
4800 SD 92107 1267-J5
MUIR LN
9500 SD 92093 1227-J2
MUIRA LN
2000 SDCo 92019 1272-C3
MUIR COLLEGE DR
2700 SD 92093 1227-J1
MUIRFIELD AV
- SDCo 92082 1090-G4
MUIRFIELD DR
800 OCN 92054 1086-D2
2500 SDCo 92019 1272-B5
MUIRFIELD GN
1700 ESCN 92026 1109-D4
MUIRFIELD WY
200 SMCS 92069 1108-J3
17000 SDCo 92067 1168-G7
MUIRFIELDS DR
- CRLB 92009 1127-F4
MUIRLANDS DR
800 SD 92037 1247-G1
W MUIRLANDS DR
900 SD 92037 1247-F1
MUIRLANDS LN
6300 SD 92037 1247-G2
MUIRLANDS VISTA WY
700 SD 92037 1247-F2
MUIR TRAIL PL
1300 CHV 91913 1331-B1
MUIRWOOD DR
700 OCN 92057 1087-C2
MULBERRY CT
1100 CRLB 92011 1127-A5
MULBERRY DR
300 SMCS 92069 1109-A3
1800 SDCo 92069 1109-A1
MULBERRY LN
- SDCo 92026 1089-B3
700 ELCN 92243 6559-H1
MULBERRY ST
3700 OCN 92054 1086-F2
6500 SD 92114 1290-D1
MULBERRY WY
2700 CHV 91914 1311-J4
MULBERRY TREE CT
13600 PWY 92064 1190-E4
MULBERRY TREE LN
13100 PWY 92064 1190-E4
MULDER ST
2400 LMGR 91945 1270-H7
MULGRAVE RD
11000 SD 92131 1209-H1
MULGREW ST
400 ELCJ 92019 1252-A6
MULHOLLAND CT
12200 SD 92128 1190-B3
MULLEN WY
1000 VSTA 92083 1107-J1
MULLINIX DR
1700 CORD 92118 1289-A6
MULVANEY DR
8600 SD 92119 1250-J4
8600 SD 92119 1251-A3
MUNCIE CT
1800 SDCo 92019 1272-D3
MUNDA RD
1500 SD 92139 1290-D6
2300 CORD 92155 1309-A2
MUNDIAL ST
11500 SD 92131 1210-B1
MUNDY TER
600 ELCJ 92020 1251-D4
MUNEVAR CT
700 ENCT 92007 1167-E1
MUNEVAR RD
700 ENCT 92007 1167-E1
MUNROE ST
4600 LMSA 91941 1270-G3
MUNSTER PLATZ WY
31100 SDCo 92082 1069-G3
MURAL ST
600 OCN 92057 1087-C1
MURANO LN
9500 SDCo 92127 1169-E2
MURAT CT
4600 SD 92117 1248-C1
MURAT PL
4700 SD 92117 1248-C1
MURAT ST
2800 SD 92117 1248-B1
MURCIA CT
2100 SD 92037 1247-H1
MUREL TRAILS
14000 PWY 92064 1190-J3
14000 PWY 92064 1191-A2
MURIEL LN
- ESCN 92025 1130-A7
MURIEL PL
7400 LMSA 91941 1270-G4
MURILLO LN
7000 CRLB 92009 1127-G7
MURPHY AV
4500 SD 92122 1228-F5
MURPHY RD
- CORD 91932 1329-F5
- ImCo 92251 431-B4
500 ImCo 92251 6439-A5
MURPHY CANYON RD
2400 SD 92123 1249-F1
5500 SD 92123 1229-E7
MURRAY AV
400 ELCJ 92020 1251-D6
MURRAY CT
100 ESCN 92025 1129-G4
MURRAY DR
200 ELCJ 92020 1251-D6
200 LMSA 91942 1271-A1
5200 LMSA 91942 1270-J1
8900 LMSA 91942 1251-C6
MURRAY ST
- CORD 92135 1288-F3
- CHV 91910 1310-C7
MURRAY CANYON RD
1600 SD 92108 1269-A2
MURRAY HILL RD
3800 LMSA 91941 1270-F5
MURRAY PARK CT
6300 SD 92119 1250-E6
MURRAY PARK DR
6600 SD 92120 1250-E6
6700 SD 92119 1250-E6
MURRAY RANCHO RD
1900 SDCo 92020 1272-A1
MURRAY RIDGE RD
3300 SD 92123 1249-C5
MURRIETA CIR
4400 SD 92154 1330-G6
MUSCAT ST
2000 SD 92105 1290-B1
MUSEUM CT
1000 OCN 92057 1087-B2
MUSEUM WY
- VSTA 92083 1087-G2
MUSIC LN
500 SDCo 92026 1109-H2
MUSLO LN
7300 CRLB 92009 1148-A1
MUSSEY GRADE RD
13700 SDCo 92065 1192-A1
15000 SDCo 92065 1172-A5
15200 SDCo 92065 1171-J5
MUSTANG CT
- IMP 92251 6439-F4
MUSTANG DR
12500 PWY 92064 1190-C6
MUSTANG GN
600 ESCN 92027 1130-B2
MUSTANG LN
300 IMP 92251 6439-F4
MUSTANG PL
300 CHV 91902 1310-G4
MUSTANG RD
- ImCo 92243 6560-A5
MUSTANG ST
4100 SD 92111 1249-A3
MUSTANG WY
1600 OCN 92057 1067-E7
3200 SMCS 92078 1108-C6
MUSTANG RIDGE DR
- SD 92130 1208-C2
MUSTANG RIDGE PT
- SD 92130 1208-C2
MUSTARD SEED LN
1300 ELCN 92243 6559-J3
MUTH VALLEY RD
11800 SDCo 92040 1212-B3
MUUTAMA LN
13500 SDCo 92082 1050-D3
MUUTAMA RD
36200 SDCo 92082 1050-B4
MY WY
700 SD 92154 1330-B7
MYCENAE WY
5000 OCN 92056 1107-F5
MYCORTE DR
700 SDCo 92026 1109-D6
MYERS DR
9400 SD 92093 1228-A2
MYERS ST
100 OCN 92054 1106-A1
300 OCN 92054 1086-A7
400 OCN 92054 1085-J7
S MYERS ST
100 OCN 92054 1106-A1
MYERS COUNTRY LN
- SDCo 92082 1069-H7
- SDCo 92082 1089-H1
MYKONOS LN
3800 SD 92130 1188-A6
MYKRANTZ TKTR
- SDCo 92065 1173-H6
MYNAH PL
500 VSTA 92083 1087-F4
MYRA AV
600 CHV 91910 1310-E7
800 CHV 91911 1330-F1
1100 CHV 91911 1330-F2
MYRA CT
1300 CHV 91911 1330-F3
1600 CHV 91911 1330-G4
1600 CHV 91911 1330-G5
MYRA ST
2700 LMGR 91945 1270-H7
MYRICA LN
17900 SD 92127 1149-J7
MYRICKS CT
1000 SDCo 92065 1152-G6
MYRTLE AV
1200 SD 92103 1269-B6
1900 SD 92104 1269-C6
3300 SD 92105 1269-G6
MYRTLE CT
- SDCo 92026 1089-B2
900 CRLB 92011 1127-A7
MYRTLE LN
4800 LMSA 91941 1271-B2
MYRTLE RD
2300 IMP 92251 6499-F2
MYRTLE ST
- OCN 92054 1066-G7
14100 SDCo 91935 1272-H7
MYRTLE WY
1000 SD 92103 1269-B6
MYRTLE BEACH WY
2400 CHV 91915 1311-H7
MYRTLEWOOD CT
500 ESCN 92027 1110-D6
600 OCN 92054 1086-F2
MYSTERY MOUNTAIN RD
11000 SDCo 92082 1069-F7
MYSTIC HILL RD
1500 SDCo 92084 1068-B6
MYSTIK RD
4600 OCN 92056 1087-D4
MYSTRA DR
4000 OCN 92056 1107-E4

N

N AV
800 NATC 91950 1309-J1
800 NATC 91950 1310-A1
2800 CHV 91950 1310-A3
N ST
100 ENCT 92007 1167-C1
400 IMP 92251 6439-G6
NABAL DR
4000 SDCo 91941 1271-F3
NABAL ST
700 ESCN 92025 1150-C1
700 SDCo 92025 1150-C1
NACIDO CT
16200 SD 92128 1170-C4
NACIDO DR
12300 SD 92128 1170-C4
NACION AV
700 CHV 91910 1310-F7
900 CHV 91911 1330-F1
NADEEN WY
500 ELCJ 92021 1251-H4
NAGA WY
8700 SD 92093 1227-H3
NAGEL ST
5600 LMSA 91942 1250-J7
NAGORSKI LN
29900 SDCo 92082 1070-E5
NAHAMA LN
- SD 92130 1208-D3
NAHANT CT
700 SD 92109 1267-H1
NAIAD ST
400 ENCT 92024 1147-B4
NALCO ST
11100 SD 92126 1209-B2
NALINI CT
9300 SNTE 92071 1230-H6
NANCE RD
2600 ImCo 92251 6439-D5
NANCITA CT
6000 SD 92114 1290-C4
NANCY DR
6000 LMSA 91942 1251-B6
NANCY ST
500 ESCN 92027 1130-C1
NANCY WY
1100 VSTA 92083 1107-J1
NANCY LEE LN
1300 SDCo 91901 1233-H6
NANCY RIDGE DR
6300 SD 92121 1208-F7
6300 SD 92121 1228-H1
NANDAY CT
- OCN 92057 1067-B2
NANDINA CT
9000 SDCo 92026 1069-A6
NANDINA DR
29700 SDCo 92026 1069-A5
NANETTE LN
6100 SD 92122 1228-G5
NANETTE ST
400 CHV 91911 1330-G1
NANNETTE ST
5100 SDCo 91902 1290-H7
NANSEN AV
2600 SD 92122 1228-B6
NANTASKET CT
700 SD 92109 1267-H1
NANTES PL
- CHV 91913 1311-F1
NANTUCKET CT
500 ENCT 92024 1147-B2
NANTUCKET DR
500 CHV 91911 1330-H2

STREET
Block City ZIP Pg-Grid

NANTUCKET GN
4400 ESCN 92027 1110-D6
NANTUCKET LN
2800 CRLB 92010 1107-A5
NANTUCKET PARK WY
- SD 92130 1208-C2
NAOMI DR
1000 VSTA 92083 1087-G4
NAPA AV
1100 CHV 91911 1330-F2
NAPA CT
1400 CHV 91911 1330-G3
3600 OCN 92056 1107-F3
NAPA DR
200 SMCS 92069 1108-H5
NAPA ST
5300 SD 92110 1268-F3
NAPIER ST
4100 SD 92110 1268-E1
NAPLES CT
600 OCN 92057 1067-C7
600 OCN 92057 1087-C1
2700 CRLB 92010 1106-J4
E NAPLES CT
200 CHV 91911 1330-H1
NAPLES PL
4900 SD 92110 1268-E3
NAPLES ST
- CHV 91911 1330-C3
1100 SD 92110 1268-E2
E NAPLES ST
- CHV 91911 1330-G1
NAPOLI ST
1300 OCN 92056 1087-C3
NARANCA AV
700 ELCJ 92021 1251-H4
1300 ELCJ 92021 1252-A4
1600 SDCo 92019 1252-B4
NARANJA ST
1800 ESCN 92025 1130-A5
5100 SD 92114 1290-A4
NARCISSA CT
- SDCo 92026 1089-E4
NARCISSUS DR
- SD 92109 1248-D6
2600 SD 92106 1268-C6
NARCISSUS SUMMIT
- ENCT 92024 1148-C5
NARDITO LN
600 SOLB 92075 1187-F1
N NARDO AV
100 SOLB 92075 1167-F7
S NARDO AV
100 SOLB 92075 1167-F7
300 SOLB 92075 1187-F1
NARDO RD
600 ENCT 92024 1147-D7
900 ENCT 92024 1167-D1
NARRAGANSETT AV
3600 SD 92106 1288-B1
3700 SD 92107 1268-A7
3700 SD 92107 1288-B1
4500 SD 92107 1267-H6
NARRAGANSETT CT
1800 SD 92107 1268-A7
NARRAGANSETT BAY DR
1900 SD 92105 1290-B1
NARWHAL ST
800 SD 92154 1330-E7
NASH LN
1100 VSTA 92083 1087-E7
NASHVILLE ST
1300 SD 92110 1268-E2
NASSAU DR
3600 SD 92115 1270-E5
NATAL WY
100 VSTA 92083 1087-J7
NATALIE DR
4500 SD 92115 1269-J3
NATALIE WY
- SDCo 92028 1027-G4
NATCHEZ AV
3100 SD 92117 1248-F6
NATCHEZ TR
34500 SDCo 92036 1176-E4
NATE WY
10400 SNTE 92071 1231-E3
NATE HARRISON GRADE
- SDCo 92060 1031-G7
- SDCo 92060 1051-D1
- SDCo 92060 1052-A1
16000 SDCo 92061 1051-D1
NATHAN ST
3000 LMGR 91945 1270-H6
NATHANIEL CT
- SDCo 92127 1169-A3
NATHANIEL LN
- SDCo 91901 1253-H1
NATIONAL AV
- SD 92113 1289-C5
NATIONAL GN
1700 ESCN 92026 1109-D4
NATIONAL CITY BLVD
- NATC 91950 1289-H7
200 NATC 91950 1309-H1
NATOMA WY
1200 OCN 92057 1087-B3
NATURES WY
- SDCo 91962 (1299-C2 See Page 1298)
NAUGATUCK AV
2900 SD 92117 1248-C1
NAUTICAL DR
3700 CRLB 92008 1106-F6
NAUTILUS ST
- SDCo 92055 1085-H5
200 SD 92037 1247-E1
NAUTILUS WY
- OCN 92056 1087-A4
NAVA CT
100 SOLB 92075 1167-D7
NAVA WY
100 SOLB 92075 1167-D7
NAVAJA LN
11900 SDCo 92020 1271-J2
NAVAJA RD
1600 SDCo 92020 1271-J2
NAVAJO AV
4300 OCN 92056 1087-C5
NAVAJO PL
1800 ESCN 92029 1129-F5
NAVAJO RD
2600 ELCJ 92020 1251-A4
5800 SD 92120 1250-D5
6800 SD 92119 1250-G4
8600 SD 92119 1251-A4
34600 SDCo 92036 1176-D4
NAVAJO ST
100 SMCS 92078 1108-D7
NAVARRA DR
2500 CRLB 92009 1147-G1
NAVARRO ST
4400 OCN 92057 1086-H1
NAVEL PL
1200 SDCo 92081 1107-G3
1200 VSTA 92081 1107-G3
1400 SDCo 92027 1130-D4
NAVELLO ST
1100 ELCJ 92021 1252-A3
NAVELLO TER
1300 ELCJ 92021 1251-J3
1300 ELCJ 92021 1252-A2
NAVIGATOR CIR
3200 OCN 92056 1107-A2
7500 CRLB 92011 1127-A7
7500 CRLB 92011 1147-A1
NAVIGATOR CT
600 CRLB 92011 1127-A7
NAWA CT
15400 SD 92129 1169-H6
NAWA WY
11300 SD 92129 1169-H6
NAYLOR RD
2700 SD 92173 1350-F4
NAZARETH DR
- SD 92108 1249-G7
NAZAS DR
12400 PWY 92064 1170-C7
NEALE ST
1600 SD 92103 1268-H6
NEBLINA DR
4900 CRLB 92008 1106-H7
NEBO DR
4400 LMSA 91941 1270-H2
NEBRASKA AV
7200 SD 92139 1290-G6
NECHES CT
3800 SDCo 92004 (1099-D2 See Page 1098)
NECKEL RD
- ImCo 92251 6439-D4
100 ImCo 92251 431-B4
300 IMP 92251 6439-H4
NECTAR WY
23900 SDCo 92065 1173-E5
NECTARINE CIR
3700 OCN 92054 1086-G2
NECTARINE DR
9600 SDCo 92040 1232-A4
NEDDICK AV
12700 PWY 92064 1190-H4
NEDRA LN
800 ELCJ 92019 1252-B7
NEEDHAM RD
2300 ELCJ 92020 1251-B4
NEEDLEGRASS DR
3300 SD 92115 1270-D6
NEEDLEROCK PL
800 ESCN 92025 1150-C1
800 SDCo 92025 1150-C1
NEGLEY AV
10900 SD 92131 1209-H5
NEGLEY DR
11600 SD 92131 1210-A4
NEIGHBORLY LN
900 SDCo 92065 1153-A6
NEIL TER
200 SDCo 92084 1067-H7
NEILL RD
200 ImCo 92243 6500-D6
NEILSON LN
1700 SDCo 92026 1109-F4
NELLA LN
29700 SDCo 92084 1068-E6
NELMS ST
1200 OCN 92054 1086-B6
NELSON LN
13100 PWY 92064 1190-H4
NELSON RD
8600 SDCo 92026 1068-J4
NELSON ST
6100 SD 92115 1270-C5
NELSON WY
8600 SDCo 92026 1068-J3
8600 SDCo 92026 1069-A3
NELSON PIT RD
2500 ImCo 92250 431-F5
NEMAHA DR
4100 SD 92117 1248-D3
NEMO ST
12700 PWY 92064 1190-D4
NENTRA ST
8400 LMSA 91942 1250-J6
NEOMA ST
2400 SD 92109 1248-B5
NEOSHO PL
3200 SD 92117 1248-D1
NEPETA WY
6700 CRLB 92011 1126-J5
NEPTUNE AV
1000 CHV 91911 1330-F1
1000 ENCT 92024 1147-A3
NEPTUNE CT
700 CHV 91910 1310-F7
NEPTUNE DR
1000 CHV 91911 1330-G2
7400 CRLB 92011 1127-A7
NEPTUNE PL
100 ESCN 92026 1109-H6
200 SD 92037 1247-E1
NEPTUNE WY
200 OCN 92054 1085-J7
500 OCN 92054 1086-A7
NERAK CT
5500 SDCo 91902 1290-J7
NEREIS DR
3600 SDCo 91941 1271-A5
3600 SDCo 91977 1271-A5
NEREUS ST
10400 SD 92124 1249-G3
NERI DR
7000 LMSA 91941 1270-E4
NERINE WY
- CRLB 92011 1127-D4
NESMITH DR
11000 SDCo 92026 1089-G7
NESMITH PL
26500 SDCo 92026 1089-H7
NESTOR WY
1100 SD 92154 1350-B1
NETTLE PL
3500 SDCo 92028 1048-C3
NETTLE CREEK CT
2800 CHV 91915 (1312-A6 See Page 1293)
NETTLE CREEK WY
1400 CHV 91915 (1312-A6 See Page 1293)
NETTLETON RD
100 VSTA 92083 1107-C1
200 VSTA 92083 1087-C7
NEUROCRINE PL
- SD 92130 1188-A6
NEVA AV
8300 SD 92123 1249-C5
NEVADA AV
100 VSTA 92084 1087-H5
NEVADA GN
2200 ESCN 92029 1129-E6
NEVADA ST
100 OCN 92054 1086-A7
100 OCN 92054 1106-B1
N NEVADA ST
100 OCN 92054 1086-A7
NEVILLE CIR
- SDCo 92055 1066-J1
- SDCo 92055 1067-A1
NEVILLE RD
- SD 92101 1268-E7
- SD 92140 1268-E7
NEVIN ST
1100 SD 92154 1350-G1
NEVOSO WY
11500 SD 92127 1149-J7
11500 SD 92127 1150-A6
NEW ST
100 ELCN 92243 6499-J6
NEW TRWY
- CHV 91914 1311-G2
NEW BEDFORD CT
10200 SDCo 92040 1231-J3
NEWBERRY ST
3200 NATC 91950 1310-D3
6800 SD 92120 1249-J5
NEWBOLD CT
6800 SD 92111 1268-J1
NEW BRANCH CT
3300 OCN 92054 1086-D2
NEWCASTLE AV
2000 ENCT 92007 1167-D3
NEWCASTLE CT
- OCN 92056 1087-D1
1200 CHV 91913 1311-C7
6000 SD 92114 1290-C5
NEWCASTLE PL
6100 SD 92114 1290-C5
NEWCASTLE ST
5900 SD 92114 1290-C5
NEWCASTLE WY
2800 CRLB 92010 1107-A3
NEW CHATEL DR
1300 SD 92154 1350-A2
NEW COLT CT
9400 SDCo 92021 1232-G4
NEWCREST PT
3600 SD 92130 1187-J4
3600 SD 92130 1188-A4
NEWELL ST
1800 NATC 91950 1310-B2
2500 SDCo 91950 1310-B2
3000 SD 92106 1288-B1
NEW HAMPSHIRE ST
4400 SD 92116 1269-A4
NEW HAVEN DR
2100 CHV 91913 1311-E3
NEW HAVEN PL
4400 SD 92117 1228-F7
4500 CRLB 92010 1107-B4
NEW HAVEN RD
1900 SMCS 92078 1128-A3
4900 SD 92117 1228-F7
NEWHOPE CT
1400 SD 92114 1290-F5
NEW JERSEY AV
2400 LMGR 91945 1270-G7
NEW JERSEY ST
4300 SD 92116 1269-B4
NEWKIRK DR
900 SD 92037 1247-F2
NEWLAND RD
3500 OCN 92056 1107-E3
NEWLIN LN
- SD 92126 1209-E7
NEWMAN WY
- SDCo 92036 1135-G7
NEW MILLS RD
5400 SD 92115 1270-B3
NEWMONT DR
8900 SD 92129 1189-C2
NEW MORNING RD
11200 SDCo 91941 1271-G4
NEW ORLEANS AV
200 SD 92173 1350-G5
NEW PARK LN
- SD 92127 1169-B3
NEW PARK TER
- SD 92127 1169-B3
NEWPORT AV
2200 ENCT 92007 1167-D4
4200 SD 92107 1268-A7
4600 SD 92107 1267-J6
NEWPORT CT
900 CHV 91911 1330-J2
NEWPORT DR
100 SMCS 92069 1108-E7
600 VSTA 92084 1087-J5
NEWPORT ST
900 OCN 92057 1066-H6
NEWPORT TER
700 VSTA 92084 1087-J5
NEWPORT WY
3700 CRLB 92010 1107-A4
NEWPORTER WY
14000 SD 92128 1190-A2
NEW RANCH CT
- CHV 91914 1311-J2
NEW RANCH RD
4900 SDCo 92020 1271-H2
NEW ROCHELLE WY
- SDCo 92127 1169-F3
NEW SALEM CIR
10900 SD 92126 1209-A3
NEW SALEM CT
10900 SD 92126 1209-A3
NEW SALEM CV
10800 SD 92126 1209-A3
NEW SALEM PL
10800 SD 92126 1209-A3
NEW SALEM PT
10800 SD 92126 1209-B3
NEW SALEM ST
7300 SD 92126 1208-J3
7500 SD 92126 1209-A3
NEW SALEM TER
10800 SD 92126 1209-B3
NEW SALEM WY
10800 SD 92126 1208-J3
NEW SEABURY DR
8900 SNTE 92071 1230-J4
8900 SNTE 92071 1231-A4
NEW SEABURY WY
2400 CHV 91915 1311-H7
NEWSHIRE ST
3000 CRLB 92010 1107-A3
NEWSOME DR
6300 SD 92115 1270-D5
NEWTON AV
1300 SD 92101 1289-B4
1300 SD 92113 1289-B4
1300 SD 92113 1289-B5
1300 SD 92113 1289-C5
NEWTON AV
2800 SD 92113 1289-E6
3700 SD 92113 1289-G4
3800 SD 92113 1289-G6
NEWTON DR
5800 CRLB 92008 1127-C1
NEWTON HILL
- SD 92127 1169-B3
NEW YORK ST
4500 SD 92116 1269-B4
NEXUS CENTER DR
4700 SD 92121 1228-E2
NIAGARA AV
4200 SD 92107 1268-A7
4500 SD 92107 1267-J6
NIANTIC CT
700 SD 92109 1267-H1
NIBLICK DR
3300 SDCo 91941 1270-J5
NIBLICK TER
2100 OCN 92056 1086-H7
NICARAGUA CIR
- SD 92140 1268-F6
NICHALS ST
7800 LMGR 91945 1290-G1
NICHOLAS LN
700 ELCJ 92019 1252-B7
NICHOLAS PL
1500 ELCJ 92019 1252-B6
NICHOLAS ST
- SDCo 92055 1067-A1
700 ELCJ 92019 1252-B6
NICHOLAS WY
1600 ELCJ 92019 1252-B6
NICHOLS RD
- ImCo 92251 6439-B7
- ImCo 92251 6499-B2
900 ImCo 92243 6559-C1
1900 ImCo 92243 6499-B6
NICHOLS ST
2900 SD 92106 1288-A4
NICKLAUS DR
2300 OCN 92056 1106-H2
NICKMAN ST
400 CHV 91911 1330-C3
NICOLA RANCH RD
2100 SDCo 92028 998-A7
NICOLA TESLA CT
9400 SD 92154 1352-A3
NICOLE DR
300 VSTA 92084 1087-H4
NICOLE ST
1900 SDCo 92065 1153-A1
1900 SDCo 92065 1152-J1
NICOLE WY
9500 SNTE 92071 1231-C5
NICOLES VISTA
- SDCo 92082 1050-E7
NICOLETTE AV
- CHV 91913 1311-F1
NICOLIA DR
1800 CRLB 92011 1127-D4
NICOLINA DR
1300 SDCo 92028 997-H7
NICOLO CT
- ESCN 92025 1130-A6
NICOSIA LN
10900 SDCo 92040 1231-F3
NIDA PL
2600 LMGR 91945 1270-H7
NIDER RD
- ImCo - 411-D8
NIDO LN
4500 SD 92117 1248-D2
NIDO AGUILA
2300 SDCo 91901 1254-C1
NIDRAH ST
1000 ELCJ 92020 1251-E7
NIEGO LN
12500 SD 92128 1170-C4
NIELS BOHR CT
2200 SD 92154 1352-A3
NIELSEN CT
2300 ELCJ 92020 1251-B1
NIELSEN ST
2200 ELCJ 92020 1251-B1
NIEMANN RANCH RD
6600 SDCo 92067 1188-G2
NIGHTFALL LN
- CHV 91915 1311-G7
- CHV 91915 1331-G1
NIGHTFALL TER
13000 SD 92128 1189-H5
NIGHTHAWK CT
5000 OCN 92056 1107-E4
7000 CRLB 92011 1127-E6
NIGHTHAWK LN
4900 OCN 92056 1107-E3
NIGHTINGALE PL
1000 ESCN 92027 1110-C5
NIGHTINGALE WY
7700 SD 92123 1249-B6
NIGHTSHADE RD
1300 CRLB 92011 1127-B5
NIGHTSKY RD
- SDCo 92065 1173-D2
NIGHT STAR CT
2400 SDCo 91901 1234-B5
NIGHT STAR PL
2400 SDCo 91901 1234-B5
NIGHTWATCH WY
- SDCo 91901 1254-A3
NIGUEL ST
- OCN 92057 1067-A5
NIKI ST
- ImCo 92249 6560-B7
NIKI LYNN PL
1100 CRLB 92008 1106-E4
NIKITA CT
12100 SD 92131 1210-B1
NIKKI LN
13400 SDCo 92082 1070-D1
NILA LN
400 ELCJ 92020 1271-G1
NILAND AV
- ImCo 92233 411-B8
- ImCo 92257 411-B8
NILAND MARINA RD
- ImCo 92257 411-A6
NILE AV
1100 CHV 91911 1330-G2
NILE CT
1200 CHV 91911 1330-G2
NILE ST
2700 SD 92104 1269-F6
NILES AV
- ImCo 92274 410-H6
NILO WY
1700 SD 92139 1290-H6
NIMBUS LN
1100 SD 92110 1268-G3
NIMITZ BLVD
2700 SD 92106 1288-C1
3500 SD 92106 1268-B6
NIMITZ BLVD
3700 SD 92107 1268-B6
NINA CT
1900 SDCo 91977 1291-A1
NINA PL
1900 ESCN 92026 1109-H5
NINA RD
- ImCo 92249 6560-C7
2600 LMGR 91945 1270-F7
NINA ST
3500 OCN 92056 1106-J1
NIPOMA PL
3800 SD 92106 1268-C5
NIPOMA ST
2700 SD 92106 1268-C6
NIRA LN
31700 SDCo 92003 1068-G1
NIRVANA AV
1800 CHV 91911 1331-A5
NITA CT
900 CHV 91911 1330-F1
8700 SNTE 92071 1231-E7
NITA LN
1000 VSTA 92083 1087-G4
8700 SNTE 92071 1231-E7
NIVEL CT
12000 SD 92128 1170-B4
NIXON CIR
100 OCN 92057 1067-B6
NIXON PL
200 CHV 91910 1310-B4
NOAH WY
5200 SD 92117 1228-F6
NOAKES RD
10500 SDCo 91941 1271-F1
E NOAKES ST
100 SDCo 92019 1253-D1
W NOAKES ST
100 SDCo 92019 1253-C1
NOB AV
100 DLMR 92014 1187-G6
100 SD 92014 1187-G6
NOB CIR
700 VSTA 92084 1087-J4
NOBEL CT
- ENCT 92024 1147-D7
NOBEL DR
- SD 92145 1228-D4
3300 SD 92037 1228-A3
3400 SD 92122 1228-D4
NOB HILL DR
1500 ESCN 92026 1109-H6
1500 SDCo 92026 1109-H6
2200 CRLB 92008 1106-G4
NOBLE ST
1800 LMGR 91945 1290-G1
NOBLE CANYON RD
2500 CHV 91915 1311-H5
NOCHE TAPATIA
7300 SDCo 92067 1168-G2
NOCTURNE CT
300 CHV 91911 1330-F2
NODEN ST
200 ELCJ 92020 1251-G7
NOELINE AV
8300 SD 92114 1290-J4
8500 SDCo 91977 1290-J4
8800 SDCo 91977 1291-A4
NOELINE CT
100 SD 92114 1290-H4
NOELINE LN
8300 SD 92114 1290-H4
NOELINE PL
8400 SD 92114 1290-H4
NOELINE WY
100 SD 92114 1290-J4
NOELL ST
3400 SD 92110 1268-G6
NOFFSINGER RD
- ImCo - 411-C8
- ImCo 92233 411-C8
- ImCo 92257 411-B8
NOGAL ST
200 SD 92102 1289-J4
4800 SD 92102 1290-A4
NOGALES DR
13600 SD 92014 1187-G6
NOKOMIS ST
5500 LMSA 91942 1251-B7
NOKONI DR
13300 PWY 92064 1190-E4
NOLAN AV
700 CHV 91910 1310-F7
1100 CHV 91911 1330-F2
NOLAN CT
1400 CHV 91911 1330-G3
NOLAN LN
1000 CHV 91911 1330-F1
NOLAN PL
4700 SDCo 92020 1271-H2
NOLAN RD
- ImCo 92227 431-D2
NOLAN WY
300 CHV 91911 1330-F1
NOLBEY ST
800 ENCT 92007 1167-E2
NOLINA CT
- CRLB 92011 1127-D4
NOLINA WY
- SD 92130 1188-G4
NOMA LN
1600 ENCT 92024 1147-B2
NOMAD PL
4000 ESCN 92025 1150-D4
NOMEL LN
2700 LMGR 91945 1270-H7
NON RD
16300 SDCo 92082 1091-B1
NONIE TER
12400 SD 92129 1189-C6
NORAAK CT
5900 LMSA 91942 1250-G6
NORCANYON WY
7600 SD 92126 1209-A1
NORCROFT RD
13200 SD 92130 1188-B4
NORDAHL RD
500 ESCN 92029 1129-D1
500 SMCS 92029 1129-D1
600 SMCS 92069 1129-D1
900 SMCS 92069 1109-E7
900 ImCo 92283 432-D4
1000 SDCo 92026 1109-E7
1300 ESCN 92026 1109-E7
NORDICA AV
4000 SD 92113 1289-H7
NOREEN CT
900 SMCS 92069 1109-C5
NOREEN PL
100 OCN 92054 1086-E5
NOREEN WY
100 OCN 92054 1086-E5
N NOREEN WY
1100 ESCN 92027 1110-A6
N NOREEN WY
1100 ESCN 92027 1109-J6
NORELLA ST
900 CHV 91910 1310-J6
NOREN PL
2800 SD 92106 1288-B3
NORFOLK DR
100 ENCT 92007 1167-E3
NORFOLK ST
2400 NATC 91950 1290-A6
NORFOLK TER
4000 SD 92116 1269-G2
NORLAK AV
700 ESCN 92025 1129-H3
NORM ST
600 SD 92114 1290-H3
NORMA CT
1000 CHV 91911 1330-F1
NORMA DR
4500 SD 92115 1269-J3
NORMA ST
2600 OCN 92056 1087-C7
NORMA GARDENS DR
10200 SNTE 92071 1231-D4
NORMAL AV
7500 LMSA 91941 1270-H3
NORMAL ST
3900 SD 92103 1269-C5
NORMAN LN
5900 SD 92120 1250-D7
NORMANDIE CT
2700 SDCo 92025 1130-E7
NORMANDIE PL
4500 LMSA 91941 1270-F3
4800 SD 92115 1270-F3
NORMANDY CIR
3500 OCN 92056 1107-E2
NORMANDY DR
1300 CHV 91913 1311-E7
1400 CHV 91913 1331-E1
NORMANDY GN
1800 ESCN 92027 1110-A5
NORMANDY LN
200 CRLB 92008 1106-D5
NORMANDY RD
600 ENCT 92024 1147-C4
NORMANDY WY
700 SDCo 92019 1253-C2
NORMANDY HILL LN
1000 ENCT 92024 1147-C4
NORMAN SCOTT RD
2800 SD 92136 1289-E7
3700 NATC 92136 1289-F7
NORMAN SMITH ST
2700 SD 92110 1268-E6
NORMAN STRASSE RD
2900 SMCS 92069 1108-D5
NORMANTON CT
11200 SD 92131 1209-H2
NORMANTON WY
11100 SD 92131 1209-G2
NORMARK TER
800 VSTA 92084 1087-J6
NORMOUNT RD
3500 OCN 92056 1107-F3
NORRAN AV
1500 ELCJ 92019 1252-B6
NORRIS RD
5100 SD 92115 1270-A2
NORRISH RD
1700 ImCo 92250 431-D4
NORSE LN
800 SDCo 92025 1130-C4
NORS RANCH RD
1400 SDCo 92003 1068-B4
NORSTAD AV
500 SD 92154 1330-E6
NORSTAD ST
600 SD 92154 1330-E7
NORSTAR LN
1500 SDCo 92028 1047-J2
1600 SDCo 92028 1048-A2
NORTE DR
23800 SDCo 92065 1173-D2
NORTE MESA DR
9900 SDCo 91977 1271-D5
NORTE VILLA WY
2700 ESCN 92027 1110-D5
NORTE VISTA
- SDCo 92078 1128-B4
NORTH AV
500 SDCo 92026 1109-H2
600 ESCN 92026 1109-H2
700 OCN 92056 1087-E5
700 VSTA 92083 1087-E5
1700 SD 92103 1269-C4
1700 SD 92116 1269-C4
6800 LMGR 91945 1270-E6
NORTH CT
100 ENCT 92024 1147-B5
4700 SD 92116 1269-C3
NORTH DR
1000 VSTA 92083 1087-G4
NORTH LN
100 SDCo 92021 1252-H3
200 SD 92037 1247-E1
400 SD 92173 1350-F3
4200 SDCo 92014 1167-J7
4200 SOLB 92014 1167-J7
4400 SDCo 92014 1168-A7
11400 SDCo 92040 1231-H6
NORTH WY
3500 OCN 92056 1106-J2
3600 OCN 92056 1107-A2
NORTHAVEN AV
4900 SD 92110 1248-F7
4900 SD 92110 1268-F1
NORTHBROOK AV
- CHV 91914 1311-H2
NORTHBROOK CT
1900 SDCo 92083 1108-C3
NORTHCLIFF DR
3500 SDCo 92028 1048-E1
NORTHCOTE RD
9000 SNTE 92071 1231-G5
NORTHCREST CT
8500 SNTE 92071 1231-B7
NORTHCREST LN
1500 VSTA 92083 1087-G3
13800 PWY 92064 1170-G6
NORTHERLY ST
4800 OCN 92056 1087-D3
NORTHERN LIGHTS
- SD 92127 1168-J6
- SD 92127 1169-A6
NORTHERN MOON WY
- SD 92154 1350-G1
NORTH FORK DR
- SDCo 92084 1068-D5
NORTHGATE ST
300 SD 92114 1290-F5
NORTHHILL TER
11800 SDCo 92040 1231-J5
NORTHMORE PL
4700 OCN 92056 1087-E3
NORTH PARK DR
100 SDCo 92021 1252-H3
NORTH PARK WY
2800 SD 92104 1269-E5
NORTH PEAK RD
15400 SDCo 92036 1176-C3
NORTH POINT DR
- SD 92093 1207-J7
- SD 92093 1208-A7
NORTH POINT LN
10000 SD 92093 1207-J7
NORTHRIDGE AV
5200 SD 92117 1228-H7
NORTHRIDGE CT
5400 SD 92117 1228-H6
NORTHRIDGE PL
9300 SNTE 92071 1251-B1
NORTHRIM CT
1400 SD 92111 1268-H2
NORTH RIVER RD
600 OCN 92057 1067-F5
1300 OCN 92003 1067-F5
1300 SDCo 92003 1067-F5
2400 OCN 92057 1066-H7
3400 OCN 92054 1066-H7
NORTHROP RD
- ImCo 92243 431-A6
- ImCo 92243 6559-A4
NORTHRUP DR
7400 SD 92126 1208-J5
7400 SD 92126 1209-A5
NORTHRUP PL
7600 SD 92126 1209-A5
NORTHRUP PT
10000 SD 92126 1209-A5
NORTH SHORE DR
100 SOLB 92075 1187-E2
NORTHSHORE DR
2000 CHV 91913 1311-E3
NORTHSIDE DR
- SD 92108 1249-E7
- SD 92108 1269-E1
NORTH SLOPE TER
8900 SDCo 91977 1291-A1
NORTH STAR DR
3200 SD 92117 1248-D3
NORTH STAR WY
- SDCo 92082 1070-H2
NORTHSTAR WY
- SMCS 92078 1128-B6
NORTHVIEW CIR
9300 SNTE 92071 1231-B7
NORTH VIEW CT
9800 SDCo 92026 1069-D7
NORTHVIEW DR
1300 SDCo 92019 1251-J7
NORTH VIEW LN
29100 SDCo 92026 1069-D7
NORTHVIEW LN
8500 SNTE 92071 1231-B7
8500 SNTE 92071 1251-B1
NORTHVIEW RD
- ESCN 92029 1149-G1
NORTHVIEW TER
9300 SNTE 92071 1231-B7
NORTHWEST
- SD 92109 1248-C6
NORTHWICK WY
- SD 92131 1209-G2
NORTHWOOD CIR
9100 SD 92126 1209-D3
NORTHWOOD DR
3300 OCN 92054 1086-E2
18000 SDCo 91935 1274-C3
NORTHWOODS DR
800 CHV 91914 1311-J3
NORTHWOODS WY
900 CHV 91914 1311-J3
NORTON AV
100 NATC 91950 1289-J7
NORWALK AV
4700 SD 92117 1248-D1
NORWALK LN
14400 PWY 92064 1190-E2
NORWALK ST
13400 PWY 92064 1190-E2
NORWAY CT
600 ESCN 92025 1129-J2
NORWICH PL
4500 CRLB 92010 1107-B4
NORWICH ST
5500 SD 92117 1228-H7
NORWOOD ST
4500 SD 92115 1269-J4
NORWOOD WY
800 ESCN 92025 1129-G4
NORWYNN LN
600 SDCo 92028 1027-J4
NORZEL DR
3100 SD 92111 1248-G5
NOSOTROS ST
800 CALX 92231 6680-D1
NOSTALGIA PL
1000 VSTA 92084 1108-A1
NOTHOMB ST
300 ELCJ 92019 1252-A6
NOTNIL CT
9700 SNTE 92071 1231-F4
NOTRE DAME AV
3700 SD 92122 1228-D6
NOTTINGHAM GN
2400 ESCN 92027 1110-D7
NOTTINGHAM PL
8500 SD 92037 1227-J3
NOTTINGHILL CT
- SMCS 92069 1108-H5
NOUGHT ST
3500 SD 92115 1270-D6
NOVA GN
1800 ESCN 92026 1109-F6
NOVA PL
300 CHV 91911 1330-F1
NOVA WY
300 CHV 91911 1330-F1
NOVARA ST
1000 SD 92107 1287-H2
NOVATO PL
24400 SDCo 92065 1173-F2
NOVELETA ST
- SD 92140 1268-F7
NOYA WY
3200 OCN 92056 1086-J7
NOYES ST
4100 SD 92109 1248-B5
NUBBIN CT
10400 SNTE 92071 1231-E3
NUECES LN
2300 SDCo 91977 1271-E7
NUERTO LN
10000 SDCo 91977 1271-E7
NUESTRA LN
2800 SDCo 92028 1028-D6

STREET
Block City ZIP Pg-Grid

NUEVA CASTILLA WY
7600 CRLB 92009 1147-G1
NUEVO MUNDO RD
- SDCo 92065 1173-C1
NUEVO VALLARTA DR
- IMP 92251 6499-G1
NUFFER RD
600 ImCo 92243 6559-E3
NUGENT CT
1000 ELCJ 92020 1251-A3
NUGGET CT
- SDCo 92040 1232-A1
NUMBERS AV
3400 OCN 92054 1086-E3
NURSERY RD
1500 SD 92101 1289-C2
1500 SD 92134 1289-C2
NUTBY LN
9700 SDCo 92026 1049-C7
NUTE WY
3000 SD 92117 1248-C3
NUTMEG CIR
1800 ESCN 92026 1109-F6
NUTMEG LN
9700 SDCo 92029 1149-E2
NUTMEG PL
2700 SD 92104 1269-E7
NUTMEG ST
100 SD 92103 1269-A7
800 SD 92103 1288-J1
1800 ESCN 92026 1109-F3
1800 SDCo 92026 1109-F3
2800 SD 92104 1269-D7
4700 SD 92105 1269-J7
5200 SD 92105 1270-A7
W NUTMEG ST
400 SD 92103 1268-J7
400 SD 92103 1269-A7
NUTMEG WY
3800 OCN 92057 1086-H4
7000 CRLB 92011 1127-A6
NYE ST
2500 SD 92111 1248-H6
NYEMII PASS RD
16300 SDCo 92082 1091-C3
NYLER CT
9500 SNTE 92071 1231-C4

O

O AV
1200 NATC 91950 1310-A1
O ST
100 IMP 92251 6439-G6
OAK
- SDCo 92040 1232-D6
9800 SDCo 92021 1233-B3
OAK AV
- ImCo 92243 6560-A7
300 CRLB 92008 1106-F5
OAK CT
300 CHV 91911 1330-G2
OAK DR
- SDCo 92019 1272-E3
1000 VSTA 92084 1087-J4
1000 VSTA 92084 1088-A4
29400 SDCo 91906 (1297-E5 See Page 1296)
OAK GN
100 SDCo 92025 1130-B6
OAK LN
- SDCo 92036 1156-F6
900 SDCo 92029 1149-E1
900 SDCo 92029 1129-H7
25100 SDCo 91916 1236-A2
28800 SDCo 91962 1237-B7
OAK PL
400 CHV 91911 1330-G2
37700 SDCo 91905 (1299-H3 See Page 1298)
OAK ST
- SDCo 92082 1090-B1
100 OCN 92054 1106-A2
300 SDCo 92065 1152-G4
600 VSTA 92083 1087-F6
900 ELCN 92243 6499-H4
3800 SMCS 92078 1128-C1
OAK TER
4600 OCN 92056 1087-D4
OAK WY
35000 SDCo 92036 1156-D7
OAKANA RD
24800 SDCo 92065 1153-F1
OAKBEND DR
10500 SD 92131 1210-A3
OAK BLUFF PL
- ESCN 92027 1110-G6
OAKBOURNE RD
9300 SNTE 92071 1230-J5
OAKBRANCH DR
300 ENCT 92024 1147-G7
300 ENCT 92024 1167-G1
OAK BRIDGE DR
- SDCo 92084 1068-C6
OAK BRIDGE TR
- SDCo 92003 1068-C4
OAKBROOK CT
1900 ELCJ 92019 1252-C4
12600 PWY 92064 1170-D3
OAK BURL LN
700 ENCT 92024 1147-G5
OAK CANYON PL
2400 ESCN 92025 1130-D6
OAK CANYON RD
15300 PWY 92064 1170-J5
15300 PWY 92064 1171-A5
OAK CLIFF DR
3100 SDCo 92028 1048-E1
OAK CREEK
14200 SDCo 92021 1232-G5
14800 SDCo 92082 1070-H3
OAKCREEK CT
2000 VSTA 92081 1107-H6
OAK CREEK DR
10600 SDCo 92040 1231-G1
11000 SDCo 92040 1211-F6
OAKCREEK LN
1400 VSTA 92081 1107-J5
OAK CREEK RD
14800 SDCo 92021 1232-J3
14800 SDCo 92021 1233-A2
OAK CREEK TR
16200 PWY 92064 1170-F4
OAKCREST DR
4000 SD 92105 1270-A5
OAK CREST RD
- SDCo 92028 998-G5
OAKCREST PARK DR
1100 ENCT 92024 1147-F7
OAKDALE AV
1200 ELCJ 92021 1251-J4
1300 ELCJ 92021 1252-A4
1500 ELCJ 92019 1252-A4

OAKDALE LN
500 ELCJ 92021 1251-J4
OAKDEN DR
1500 SD 92154 1350-B2
OAK FERN CT
11100 SD 92131 1209-J1
OAKFIELD CT
9500 SDCo 91977 1271-C6
OAKFIELD WY
12800 PWY 92064 1170-D3
OAK FOREST PL
- ESCN 92027 1110-G6
OAKFOREST RD
1500 SDCo 92070 1135-D4
OAKFORT CT
12400 SD 92131 1210-C4
OAKFORT PL
12400 SD 92131 1210-C4
OAKGATE RW
6000 SD 92037 1248-A1
OAK GLADE CT
- SDCo 92028 1028-A4
OAK GLADE DR
- SDCo 92028 1028-A3
OAK GLEN CIR
1000 SDCo 92019 1252-G6
OAK GLEN CT
7000 LMGR 91945 1290-F1
OAK GLEN DR
2000 VSTA 92081 1107-H3
OAK GLEN LN
3400 SD 92117 1248-D2
31000 SDCo 92082 1070-E1
OAK GLEN RD
13800 SDCo 92082 1070-E1
23400 SDCo 92082 1050-E7
W OAK GLEN RD
13600 SDCo 92082 1070-E1
OAK GLEN WY
3300 SDCo 92019 1252-G6
OAK GROVE DR
- SDCo 92019 1155-G4
9400 SDCo 91916 1236-A2
9700 SDCo 91916 1235-J1
OAK GROVE RD
17000 SDCo 92065 1151-H3
OAK GROVE TKTR
37100 SDCo 92086 1033-F1
OAKHAM WY
7200 SD 92139 1290-G7
OAK HAVEN RD
1800 SDCo 91901 1234-A7
OAK HILL DR
1000 CHV 91915 1311-G5
1200 ESCN 92025 1130-D1
1300 ESCN 92027 1130-D1
2700 ESCN 92027 1110-E7
OAK HILL LN
2700 SDCo 92070 1135-F7
OAK HILLS LN
- SDCo 92028 999-G5
OAK HOLLOW RD
17200 SDCo 92065 1153-G6
OAKHURST DR
700 SD 92114 1290-C5
OAK ISLAND LN
4200 SDCo 92028 1028-G5
OAK KNOLL CT
2500 CHV 91914 1311-G3
OAK KNOLL DR
1200 VSTA 92084 1088-A4
13000 PWY 92064 1190-B5
OAK KNOLL LN
14600 SDCo 92082 1070-G3
OAK KNOLL RD
12200 PWY 92064 1190-B5
OAK LAKE LN
17800 SDCo 92036 1156-F7
OAK LAND RD
1600 SDCo 92036 1156-D2
OAKLAND RD
5300 LMSA 91942 1270-F1
OAKLAWN AV
- CHV 91910 1309-J5
400 CHV 91910 1310-A7
500 CHV 91910 1330-A1
800 CHV 91911 1330-B3
OAK LEAF CT
2000 VSTA 92081 1107-H3
OAKLEAF CT
3500 SDCo 91977 1271-C6
OAKLEAF DR
600 OCN 92054 1086-F2
OAKLEAF LN
1300 SDCo 92065 1172-G2
OAKLEAF PT
5300 SD 92124 1249-G1
OAK LEE LN
700 SDCo 91901 1234-C4
OAKLEY CT
23400 SDCo 92065 1173-C3
OAKLEY PL
23400 SDCo 92065 1173-C3
OAKLEY RD
16000 SDCo 92065 1173-C3
OAKLINE CT
13100 PWY 92064 1190-E1
OAKLINE RD
14700 PWY 92064 1190-E1
OAK MEADOW DR
23800 SDCo 92065 1173-D2
OAK MEADOW RD
14200 SDCo 92082 1070-F2
OAKMONT RD
26800 SDCo 92082 1090-F6
OAKMONT TER
9800 SDCo 92021 1233-A3
OAK MOUNTAIN RD
19400 SDCo 92065 1153-G2
OAK PARK DR
5200 SD 92105 1270-A7
OAKPOINT AV
- CHV 91913 1311-E7
- CHV 91913 1331-E1
OAK RANCH LN
10300 SDCo 92026 1089-E4
OAK RANCH PL
28000 SDCo 92026 1089-E3
OAK RANCH RD
27700 SDCo 92026 1089-E4
OAK RANCH WY
10300 SDCo 92026 1089-E3
OAKRIDGE CV
2400 SD 92014 1187-H5
OAK RIDGE LN
18500 SDCo 92065 1153-C6
OAKRIDGE PL
2300 ESCN 92026 1109-G4
OAK RIDGE RD
9800 SDCo 92026 1089-D1
OAKRIDGE RD
6200 SD 92120 1250-D4
7500 SNTE 92071 1230-G7

OAK RIDGE WY
2500 VSTA 92081 1107-H7
2500 VSTA 92081 1127-H1
OAKS CT
1400 SMCS 92069 1109-D6
37700 SDCo 91905 (1299-H3 See Page 1298)
W OAKS WY
1700 CRLB 92011 1127-B3
OAK SHADE LN
- SDCo 92065 1172-D5
OAK SHADOWS DR
- SDCo 92026 1089-B2
OAKS HEIGHTS RD
900 SDCo 92036 1156-D1
OAKSHIRE CT
1800 SD 92102 1290-A1
OAKS NORTH DR
12500 SD 92128 1170-C1
OAK SPRINGS RD
2500 CHV 91915 1311-H6
16100 SDCo 92065 1173-C3
OAK SPUR WY
- SDCo 92026 1089-E4
OAKSTAND CT
15500 PWY 92064 1170-F6
OAKSTAND RD
13800 PWY 92064 1170-F6
OAKSTONE CT
9900 SNTE 92071 1231-C3
OAKSTONE CREEK PL
- ESCN 92027 1110-E5
OAK TRAIL CT
14800 PWY 92064 1150-J6
OAK TRAIL RD
26000 SDCo 92082 1091-G6
OAK TREE LN
12800 PWY 92064 1190-C5
OAKTREE LN
700 SMCS 92069 1108-J6
OAK TREE PL
500 ESCN 92027 1110-E6
OAKTREE WY
2800 SDCo 92028 1048-E1
OAKVALE LN
- SNTE 92071 1230-G5
OAKVALE RD
14900 SDCo 92027 1110-H3
14900 SDCo 92027 1111-A2
OAK VALLEY LN
- ESCN 92027 1110-G6
2800 SDCo 92084 1068-E7
OAK VALLEY RD
2000 SDCo 92065 1172-B4
OAK VALLEY TR
2400 SDCo 91935 1274-G6
OAKVIEW CT
3700 SDCo 92028 1048-E1
OAK VIEW PL
1900 SDCo 91901 1234-C7
OAK VIEW TER
1600 CHV 91902 1311-C3
OAK VIEW WY
1100 ESCN 92029 1129-D4
OAKVIEW WY
11900 SD 92128 1190-B6
OAK VILLAGE DR
- SDCo 92065 1152-G7
OAK VILLAGE PL
- SDCo 92065 1152-G7
OAKWOOD AV
- SD 92102 1289-G4
- SDCo 92102 1289-G4
OAKWOOD DR
3200 SDCo 92036 1156-E1
OAK WOOD LN
- ESCN 92027 1110-G7
OAKWOOD LN
- OCN 92054 1106-C1
11800 SDCo 92040 1231-J3
OAKWOOD WY
600 ELCJ 92021 1251-G4
OAKWOOD CREEK PL
- ESCN 92027 1110-D5
OAKWOOD CREEK WY
- ESCN 92027 1110-D5
OAKWOOD GLEN PL
13800 SDCo 92082 1070-E7
OASIS AV
1100 CHV 91911 1330-G1
OASIS DR
1200 ESCN 92026 1129-F1
1200 SDCo 92026 1129-F1
OASIS LN
1500 VSTA 92083 1087-D6
OASIS RD
- SDCo 91948 1218-B2
OAT HILL RD
9800 SDCo 92026 1089-D1
O B DR
2100 SDCo 91901 1254-B1
OBELISCO CIR
7100 CRLB 92009 1127-H6
OBELISCO CT
2700 CRLB 92009 1127-H6
OBELISCO PL
2600 CRLB 92009 1127-H6
OBELISCOS ST
- CALX 92231 6620-H7
OBERLIN DR
5500 SD 92121 1208-E7
OBISPO LN
16700 SD 92128 1170-B3
OBISPO RD
11900 SD 92128 1170-B3
OBREGON AV
- SD 92126 1229-C1
- SD 92145 1229-C1
OBRIEN PL
2600 ESCN 92027 1110-D6
10100 SD 92124 1249-G2
OBSERVATION PL
3800 ESCN 92025 1150-D3
OBSERVATION POINT DR
- SDCo 92060 1052-H3
OBSIDIAN DR
16800 SDCo 92065 1171-D3
OBSIDIAN GN
- ESCN 92027 1110-C7
OBSIDIAN PL
- CRLB 92009 1127-F4
OCALA AV
1100 CHV 91911 1330-G1
1500 CHV 91911 1330-H4
1600 CHV 91911 1330-H5
OCALA CT
1400 CHV 91911 1330-G3
OCANA PL
4700 SD 92124 1250-A1
OCASO DR
12600 SD 92128 1170-C4
OCASO WY
4100 OCN 92056 1087-D5

OCCIDENTAL ST
3100 SD 92122 1228-C6
OCEAN AV
1200 SD 92154 1350-D1
1400 DLMR 92014 1187-F5
OCEAN BLVD
200 CORD 92118 1288-G7
1000 CORD 92118 1308-H1
4100 SD 92109 1247-G5
OCEAN CT
- CORD 92118 1288-G7
OCEAN DR
- CORD 92118 1288-G7
OCEAN LN
700 IMPB 91932 1329-E7
900 IMPB 91932 1349-E1
8000 SD 92037 1227-E6
OCEAN ST
100 SOLB 92075 1167-E6
2300 CRLB 92008 1106-D5
E OCEAN AIR DR
10600 SD 92130 1208-C2
W OCEAN AIR DR
10500 SD 92130 1208-B4
OCEAN BEACH FRWY I-8
- SD - 1268-B5
OCEAN BLUFF AV
- SD 92130 1208-A3
OCEAN BLUFF WY
- ENCT 92024 1147-D7
OCEAN BREEZE CT
5200 SD 92109 1247-J4
OCEAN BREEZE ST
2000 SMCS 92078 1128-B3
OCEAN BREEZE WY
500 CHV 91914 1311-E3
3300 SDCo 91935 1273-B6
OCEAN COVE DR
2500 ENCT 92007 1167-F4
OCEAN CREST AV
- CRLB 92011 1127-C5
OCEANCREST DR
4200 OCN 92056 1107-C3
OCEAN CREST RD
700 ENCT 92007 1167-E1
OCEAN FRONT
1700 DLMR 92014 1187-F3
OCEAN FRONT ST
1400 SD 92107 1267-H6
OCEAN FRONT WK
2500 SD 92109 1267-H1
3800 SD 92109 1247-H7
OCEAN HEIGHTS WY
10700 SD 92121 1208-E4
OCEAN HILLS DR
4800 OCN 92056 1107-F5
OCEANIC DR
1000 ENCT 92024 1167-F1
3900 OCN 92056 1087-A6
OCEANIC WY
- OCN 92056 1086-J6
6900 OCN 92056 1087-A6
OCEAN RANCH BLVD
- OCN 92056 1086-J5
- OCN 92056 1087-A5
OCEAN RIDGE CT
- OCN 92056 1087-E2
OCEAN RIDGE WY
- SD 92130 1208-C2
OCEANSIDE BLVD
100 OCN 92054 1106-C1
1800 OCN 92054 1086-D7
3000 OCN 92056 1086-H6
3600 OCN 92056 1087-E4
OCEANSIDE BLVD S
1700 OCN 92054 1106-C1
OCEANSIDE DR
- OCN 92054 1085-J6
OCEAN SURF DR
700 SOLB 92075 1187-E2
OCEAN VALLEY LN
4400 SD 92130 1188-C6
OCEAN VIEW AV
100 DLMR 92014 1187-G7
900 ENCT 92024 1147-C4
OCEAN VIEW BLVD
300 SD 92113 1289-D4
4800 SD 92113 1290-A5
OCEAN VIEW CT
100 VSTA 92084 1087-H7
300 ENCT 92024 1147-C6
OCEAN VIEW DR
- SDCo 92029 1128-J4
- SDCo 92029 1129-A4
- SMCS 92078 1128-J4
100 VSTA 92084 1087-H6
6400 CRLB 92011 1126-H4
OCEAN VIEW LN
500 CHV 91914 1311-E3
OCEAN VIEW PL
100 VSTA 92084 1087-J7
OCEANVIEW PL
2400 SDCo 92021 1252-H4
OCEANVIEW RD
2000 OCN 92056 1086-H7
2000 OCN 92056 1106-H1
OCEAN VIEW TER
- ENCT 92024 1147-C6
- VSTA 92084 1087-J7
OCEAN VIEW HILLS PKWY
- SD 92154 1351-A1
4900 SD 92154 1330-H7
5000 SD 92154 1350-J1
OCEANVIEW RIDGE LN
5800 SD 92121 1208-F4
OCEAN VILLAGE WY
2800 OCN 92054 1106-G1
OCEAN VISTA RD
13200 SD 92130 1187-J5
OCELOT AV
1100 CHV 91911 1330-G1
OCHRE CT
11000 SD 92128 1189-H4
OCONNELL RD
8300 SDCo 92021 1251-H1
OCONNOR AV
- CHV 91913 1331-E2
OCONNOR ST
700 ELCJ 92020 1251-E2
OCOTILLO CIR
200 SDCo 92004 (1078-G1 See Page 1058)
OCOTILLO DR
- ImCo 92243 6559-E1
200 ELCN 92243 6559-E1
2000 VSTA 92083 1087-G5
OCOTILLO PL
200 OCN 92057 1067-B7
OCTANS ST
8600 SD 92126 1209-C1
OCULTO CT
17000 SD 92127 1169-J2

OCULTO PL
17000 SD 92127 1169-J2
OCULTO RD
11400 SD 92127 1169-J2
OCULTO WY
17000 SD 92127 1169-J2
ODELL CIR
1800 VSTA 92084 1088-C4
ODELL PL
7900 SD 92126 1209-A4
ODELL RD
10400 SD 92126 1209-A4
ODESSA AV
5800 LMSA 91942 1250-J7
5800 LMSA 91942 1251-A6
ODESSA CT
2100 LMGR 91945 1290-G1
ODOM ST
3700 SD 92115 1270-D5
ODYSSEY DR
2000 VSTA 92081 1107-J2
OFELIA LN
900 SDCo 92019 1252-E7
OFFBROOK RD
2100 SDCo 92028 1027-J6
OFFSHORE PT
500 SD 92154 1330-H7
OFFY CT
2000 SDCo 92019 1272-C3
OFRIA AV
6800 SD 92120 1250-E4
OFRIA CT
6900 SD 92120 1250-D4
OFTEDAHL WY
13500 SD 92129 1189-E4
OGALALA AV
3100 SD 92117 1248-D1
OGARD RANCH RD
1200 SDCo 92019 1253-E3
OGDEN ST
5200 SD 92105 1270-A5
OGIER RD
- ImCo 92250 431-E5
OGILBY RD Rt#-S34
- ImCo - 411-K11
- ImCo - 431-L1
- ImCo - 432-A3
OGRAM DR
9800 SDCo 91941 1271-C3
OGUNQUIT AV
13400 PWY 92064 1190-H4
OHANA WY
- SDCo 92040 1211-F6
OHARA CT
- SD 92114 1290-F5
O HARE AV
- IMP 92251 6499-D1
O HARE CT
- IMP 92251 6499-D2
OHEARN RD
- SDCo 92028 1027-F5
OHIO AV
6900 LMSA 91942 1270-E1
E OHIO AV
700 ESCN 92025 1130-A2
1100 ESCN 92027 1130-A2
OHIO PL
7400 LMSA 91941 1270-G3
OHIO ST
3900 SD 92104 1269-E5
4300 SD 92116 1269-E5
OHM CT
6200 SD 92122 1228-D5
OJEDA RD
1600 SDCo 92084 1088-B1
OKEEFE ST
3100 SD 92173 1350-F5
OKINAWA RD
- CORD 92118 1309-C5
OKRA CT
800 CRLB 92011 1127-A6
OLA CT
4300 SDCo 91910 1310-D5
OLAMAR WY
1600 SD 92139 1290-H6
OLD RD
13400 SDCo 92082 1090-D3
OLD BARN LN
- CHV 91915 1331-G1
OLD BARN RD
3300 SDCo 92084 1068-B5
OLD BARONA RD
12900 SDCo 92040 1212-F2
12900 SDCo 92040 1192-F7
OLD BATTLEFIELD RD
15400 ESCN 92027 1130-J4
17400 SD 92027 1130-J4
OLD BEND RD
2000 SDCo 92021 1252-F3
OLD BRIDGE RD
700 SDCo 92028 1027-H3
OLD BRIDGEPORT WY
3000 SD 92111 1248-H5
OLD BUCKMAN SPRINGS RD
4000 SDCo 91962 430-A6
OLD CALIFORNIA WY
2800 SDCo 92019 1272-D6
OLD CAMPO RD
12500 SDCo 91978 1272-B7
12600 SDCo 91978 1292-C1
OLD CARMEL VALLEY RD
4100 SD 92130 1188-E6
OLD CAROUSEL RANCH RD
18300 SDCo 92065 1171-J3
OLD CASTLE PL
- SDCo 92026 1069-A6
OLD CASTLE RD
8700 SDCo 92026 1068-J6
8700 SDCo 92026 1069-A6
8700 SDCo 92082 1069-F6
11900 SDCo 92082 1070-A5
OLD CASTLE WY
- SDCo 92082 1069-H5
OLD CEDAR RD
1400 SDCo 92025 1130-B3
OLD CHASE AV
1000 ELCJ 92020 1251-H7
1000 SDCo 92020 1251-H7
1000 SDCo 92020 1271-H1
OLD CLIFFS RD
4700 SD 92120 1249-J5
4700 SD 92120 1250-A5
OLD COACH DR
18200 PWY 92064 1150-G6
OLD COACH RD
16900 PWY 92064 1170-F2
17600 PWY 92064 1150-G7
OLD COACH WY
18500 PWY 92064 1150-H3
19900 SDCo 92025 1150-H3

OLD COBBLE CT
3400 SD 92111 1248-H5
OLD COBBLE RD
3500 SD 92111 1248-H5
OLD COLE GRADE RD
- SDCo 92061 1050-F5
- SDCo 92082 1050-F5
OLD COLONY RD
2300 OCN 92056 1087-E1
2300 SDCo 92084 1087-E1
OLD COMMUNITY RD
14200 PWY 92064 1190-E2
OLD COURSE RD
- SDCo 92127 1169-A1
OLD CREEK CT
1500 ENCT 92007 1167-F2
OLD CREEK RD
- SD 92131 1210-H2
OLD CUYAMACA RD
3200 SDCo 92036 1156-C1
OLD DAIRY CT
5300 SDCo 91902 1310-J2
5300 SDCo 91902 1311-A2
OLD DAIRY LN
3800 SDCo 91902 1310-J2
3800 SDCo 91902 1311-A2
OLD DAIRY WY
5300 SDCo 91902 1310-J2
8500 SDCo 91902 1311-A2
OLD DAIRY MART RD
2500 SD 92154 1350-E6
2900 SD 92173 1350-E6
OLD DESERT CLUB RD
3100 SDCo 92004 (1078-H5 See Page 1058)
OLDE GROVE LN
4900 SDCo 91941 1271-F2
OLDE HIGHWAY 80
14100 SDCo 92021 1232-G5
14900 SDCo 92021 1233-A4
OLD EL CAMINO REAL
12600 SD 92130 1207-J1
13600 SD 92130 1188-A3
OLD ESPOLA RD
16900 PWY 92064 1170-D3
OLDFIELD CT
1800 SDCo 92019 1272-C3
OLD GLEN ST
- SMCS 92078 1128-F7
OLD GLOBE WY
1200 SD 92101 1269-C7
1200 SD 92101 1289-B1
OLD GROVE RD
200 OCN 92057 1087-A4
4000 OCN 92056 1087-B4
9900 SD 92131 1209-F5
N OLD GROVE RD
100 OCN 92057 1086-J1
S OLD GROVE RD
100 OCN 92057 1086-J3
100 OCN 92057 1087-A3
OLD GUEJITO RD
15500 ESCN 92027 1110-E6
15600 SDCo 92027 1110-H7
16200 SDCo 92027 1111-A6
OLD GUEJITO GRADE RD
16600 SDCo 92027 1111-C4
OLDHAM CT
900 ENCT 92024 1147-D4
OLDHAM WY
1000 ENCT 92024 1147-C4
OLD HEATHER RD
3100 SD 92111 1248-H5
OLD HIGHWAY 80
26000 SDCo 91916 1236-D3
26400 SDCo 91931 1236-D3
28600 SDCo 91931 1237-A4
29500 SDCo 91962 1237-B7
29700 SDCo 91962 430-A7
34000 SDCo 91906 430-A7
34400 SDCo 91962 (1299-B1 See Page 1298)
36100 SDCo 91906 (1299-G3 See Page 1298)
36700 SDCo 91905 1300-A6
36700 SDCo 91905 (1299-G3 See Page 1298)
37300 SDCo 91934 1300-H7
37600 SDCo 91934 (1320-J1 See Page 1300)
37600 SDCo 91934 (1321-B2 See Page 1300)
38700 SDCo 91934 430-A7
OLD HIGHWAY 80 Rt#-S1
29800 SDCo 91962 430-A6
OLD HIGHWAY 80 Rt#-94
36800 SDCo 91905 1300-C6
OLD HWY 101
- SDCo 92055 408-K6
- SDCo 92055 1023-H5
- SDCo 92672 1023-D3
OLD HWY 395
- SDCo 92028 998-H5
700 SDCo 92028 1028-F1
1900 SDCo 92028 1048-H2
29700 SDCo 92026 1068-J3
31700 SDCo 92003 1068-J1
31800 SDCo 92003 1048-J6
47900 RivC 92592 999-A2
47900 SDCo 92028 999-A2
OLD HILL RD
200 SDCo 92028 1027-J2
200 SDCo 92028 1028-A2
OLD HORSE TR
- SDCo 91901 1233-F7
OLD JANAL RANCH RD
1100 CHV 91915 1311-J5
OLD JAPATUL RD
20900 SDCo 91901 1274-J1
20900 SDCo 91901 1275-A1
OLD JULIAN HWY
200 SDCo 92065 1152-J6
300 SDCo 92065 1153-E4
19400 SDCo 92065 1154-A3
OLD JULIAN TR
23000 SDCo 92065 1153-H4
OLD KANE SPRING RD
5900 SDCo 92004 (1120-E3 See Page 1100)
5900 SDCo 92004 (1121-B5 See Page 1100)
OLD KETTLE RD
3000 SD 92111 1248-H5
OLD LANTERN LN
9800 SDCo 92026 1089-D3
OLD LILAC RD
31500 SDCo 92082 1069-H1
31500 SDCo 92082 1049-H7
OLD MAN RIVER RD
- SDCo 92127 1168-J1

OLD MANZANITA RD
23500 SDCo 92027 1111-C7
OLD MEADOW RD
3300 SD 92111 1248-H5
OLD MELROSE RANCH RD
24200 SDCo 92027 1111-C4
OLD MEMORY LN
1300 SD 92114 1290-C2
OLD MILKY WY
3200 SD 92025 1130-H7
3200 SD 92025 1131-A7
3200 SD 92027 1131-A7
14200 SD 92027 1130-H7
OLD MILL CT
1700 ENCT 92024 1147-H6
OLD MILL RD
1700 ENCT 92024 1147-H6
OLD MINE RD
- SDCo 91905 430-C7
OLD MINERS TR
2300 SDCo 92036 1136-B6
OLD MISSION CT
7300 SNTE 92071 1230-F7
OLD MOUNTAIN VIEW RD
1000 SDCo 92021 1233-A7
1000 SDCo 92021 1253-A1
OLD NANTUCKET CT
5600 SD 92111 1248-H5
OLD OAK DR
100 SD 92114 1290-G4
OLD OAK RDG
700 SDCo 92069 1109-B2
OLD OAK TR
21200 SDCo 91901 1275-B4
OLD OAK HOLLER
10900 SDCo 92082 1049-C3
OLD OAK TREE LN
1100 SDCo 92026 1109-H2
OLD ORCHARD LN
100 CHV 91902 1310-G3
100 SDCo 91902 1310-G3
OLD PALO VERDE RD
- ImCo - 412-A4
OLD POMERADO RD
11800 PWY 92064 1190-B6
OLD POST RD
3000 SDCo 92028 1048-D1
OLD QUARRY RD
- SD 92108 1249-E7
OLD RANCH DR
12600 SDCo 92082 1090-C2
OLD RANCH RD
- ESCN 92027 1130-H2
- SDCo 91901 1235-G7
100 SDCo 91910 1310-D6
5400 OCN 92057 1067-E7
OLD RIDGE RD
- SDCo 91977 1271-D7
OLD RIVER RD
3500 SDCo 92003 1067-J5
3500 SDCo 92084 1067-J5
6000 SDCo 92003 1068-A2
OLD RIVER ST
600 OCN 92057 1086-H1
OLD SAN PASQUAL RD
2500 SDCo 92027 1130-F5
4100 SDCo 92025 1130-F5
OLD SAYBROOK DR
10700 SD 92129 1189-H2
OLD SCHOOLHOUSE RD
3100 SDCo 92019 1272-C5
OLD SPANISH TR
2400 SDCo 92025 1130-B7
OLD SPRING CT
3400 SD 92111 1248-H5
OLD SPRINGS RD
- SDCo 92004 (1079-J2 See Page 1058)
OLD SPUR CT
- SDCo 91901 1254-G3
OLD SPUR DR
- SDCo 91901 1254-F3
OLD STAGE CT
300 SDCo 92028 1027-F3
OLD STAGE RD
100 SDCo 92028 1027-F4
OLD STAGECOACH RUN
300 SDCo 91901 1234-A3
OLD STAGECOACH TR
- SDCo 91901 1234-A4
OLD STATION RD
14000 PWY 92064 1170-G7
OLD STONE RD
12300 PWY 92064 1190-B7
12300 PWY 92128 1190-B7
12300 SD 92128 1190-B7
OLD STONE HILL RD
30600 SDCo 92086 409-J5
OLD SURVEY RD
16500 SD 92025 1151-D2
16500 SDCo 92025 1151-D2
OLD SYCAMORE DR
13000 SD 92128 1189-H5
OLD TAYLOR ST
900 VSTA 92084 1087-J2
900 VSTA 92084 1088-A2
OLD TELGRAPH CANYON RD
- CHV 91910 1330-H1
OLD THAMES WY
5500 SD 92111 1248-H5
OLD TOWN AV
3800 SD 92110 1268-F5
OLD TRAIL DR
2000 CHV 91914 1311-G2
OLD VIA RANCHO DR
300 ESCN 92029 1149-J2
300 ESCN 92029 1150-A2
OLD WAGON RD
23200 SDCo 92027 1111-C4
23800 SDCo 92027 1131-C1
OLD WATNEY WY
5500 SD 92111 1248-H5
OLD WEST AV
13000 SD 92129 1189-C5
OLD WEST WY
13000 SD 92129 1189-D5
OLD WINEMASTER CT
13300 PWY 92064 1170-D1
OLD WINEMASTER WY
17800 PWY 92064 1170-E1
OLD WINERY CT
13100 PWY 92064 1170-D1
OLD WINERY RD
13100 PWY 92064 1170-D1
13300 PWY 92064 1150-E7
OLD WINERY WY
17700 PWY 92064 1170-E1
OLD YUCCA TR
16400 SDCo 92027 1111-D6
OLEA LN
6400 CRLB 92011 1127-E4

STREET
Block City ZIP Pg-Grid

OLEANDER
15300 SDCo 92021 1233-B3
OLEANDER AV
700 VSTA 92081 1108-A5
700 SDCo 92081 1108-B5
900 CHV 91911 1330-G1
1000 ELCN 92243 6499-G5
2900 SMCS 92078 1108-C6
OLEANDER DR
100 CHV 91910 1310-B5
200 OCN 92057 1087-A1
3600 SD 92106 1268-C6
13600 PWY 92064 1190-F3
OLEANDER LN
1700 SDCo 92004 (1099-F2
See Page 1098)
OLEANDER PL
700 SDCo 92081 1108-B6
700 VSTA 92081 1108-B6
800 ESCN 92027 1110-B7
3700 SD 92106 1268-C6
OLEANDER ST
3300 SD 92121 1207-J4
3300 SD 92121 1208-A3
OLEANDER WY
- SD 92130 1188-G4
6700 CRLB 92011 1126-J5
OLE BURN WY
16000 SDCo 91935 1293-F2
OLGA AV
3400 SD 92123 1249-B4
OLINDA ST
600 ESCN 92027 1110-B7
OLIPHANT ST
3000 SD 92106 1288-B1
3600 SD 92106 1268-B7
OLITE CT
2000 SD 92037 1247-H1
OLIVA RD
12300 SD 92128 1170-B4
OLIVE AV
100 ELCN 92243 6499-E6
100 VSTA 92083 1087-E6
200 CRLB 92008 1106-F7
200 ELCN 92243 6500-A6
400 SDCo 92028 1027-F1
700 CORD 92118 1288-H7
800 SDCo 92065 1152-J3
800 NATC 91950 1290-C7
1000 SD 92139 1290-C7
1200 SDCo 92083 1087-D6
1400 OCN 92056 1087-D6
1500 CHV 91911 1330-H4
1900 SD 92139 1310-C1
4100 LMSA 91941 1270-G3
7300 SDCo 91902 1291-D7
OLIVE CT
1500 CHV 91911 1330-H4
OLIVE DR
1000 SD 92173 1350-G4
4000 OCN 92056 1087-C6
8800 SDCo 91977 1271-A6
OLIVE LN
1000 CORD 92118 1288-G7
8800 SNTE 92071 1231-C7
9700 SDCo 92029 1149-D3
28900 SDCo 92082 1070-G7
OLIVE PL
4600 LMSA 91941 1270-G3
OLIVE RD
500 ELCN 92243 6499-E7
OLIVE ST
100 SDCo 92069 1108-J2
100 SMCS 92069 1108-J2
200 SMCS 92069 1109-A2
300 SD 92103 1269-A7
700 SDCo 92065 1152-D5
1000 SD 92103 1268-J7
1000 SD 92103 1288-J1
1200 SD 92101 1288-J1
1400 OCN 92054 1086-B7
2700 LMGR 91945 1270-G6
3000 SD 92104 1269-E7
3200 SDCo 91950 1310-C3
4300 SD 92105 1269-H7
5100 SD 92105 1270-A7
W OLIVE ST
300 SD 92103 1269-A7
OLIVE TER
1000 SDCo 92065 1152-D5
14100 SDCo 92021 1232-G5
OLIVEBROOK CT
1900 ELCJ 92019 1252-C5
OLIVE CREST DR
900 ENCT 92024 1147-J5
OLIVE CREST WY
13900 PWY 92064 1190-E3
OLIVE GROVE DR
13200 PWY 92064 1190-E3
OLIVE GROVE LN
- SMCS 92078 1128-C6
OLIVE GROVE PL
13800 PWY 92064 1190-E3
OLIVE HILL LN
2400 SDCo 92028 1047-G1
OLIVE HILL RD
- SNTE 92071 1230-G7
2500 SDCo 92028 1027-G7
2600 SDCo 92028 1047-G3
5100 SDCo 92003 1047-H2
5300 SDCo 92003 1067-H1
OLIVE HILL TR
- SDCo 92003 1047-H7
- SDCo 92028 1047-H7
OLIVE HILL WY
200 SDCo 92028 1047-G2
OLIVE HILLS AV
1300 ELCJ 92021 1252-B2
OLIVE KNOLL CT
- SD 92131 1210-G2
OLIVE KNOLL PL
- ESCN 92027 1130-H3
OLIVE MEADOWS DR
13200 PWY 92064 1190-E3
OLIVE MEADOWS PL
14000 PWY 92064 1190-E3
OLIVE MESA CT
13900 PWY 92064 1190-E3
OLIVE MILL WY
13800 PWY 92064 1190-E3
OLIVENHAIN RD
Rt#-S10
1600 ENCT 92024 1147-F4
1600 CRLB 92009 1147-F4
OLIVENHAIN FARMS RD
1600 ENCT 92024 1148-B5
OLIVE PARK PL
13800 PWY 92064 1190-E3
OLIVER AV
700 SD 92109 1247-H7
1400 SD 92109 1248-A6
OLIVER CT
4200 SD 92109 1247-H7

OLIVER LN
4700 LMSA 91941 1270-J3
OLIVER PL
700 SD 92109 1247-H7
OLIVERA AV
- SDCo 92127 1169-F4
OLIVET LN
1400 SD 92037 1227-F6
OLIVET ST
1300 SD 92037 1227-F7
OLIVETAS AV
7100 SD 92037 1247-E1
7300 SD 92037 1227-E7
OLIVE TREE LN
13200 PWY 92064 1190-G4
OLIVE VIEW RD
2800 SDCo 91901 1234-C7
OLIVE VISTA DR
13900 SDCo 91935 1292-H1
14400 SDCo 91935 1293-A1
OLIVEWOOD LN
1400 SDCo 91901 1234-B7
OLIVEWOOD TER
300 SD 92113 1289-G5
OLIVIA GN
- ESCN 92025 1130-A5
OLIVINE CT
- CRLB 92009 1127-F5
OLIVOS CT
4200 SDCo 92028 1028-G7
4200 SDCo 92028 1048-H1
OLLIE AV
- ImCo 92231 6620-F7
900 CALX 92231 6680-F1
1000 CALX 92231 6620-F7
OLLIE ST
3200 SD 92110 1268-C5
OLLY CT
1000 VSTA 92083 1107-J1
OLMEDA CT
13000 SD 92128 1150-C6
OLMEDA PL
18700 SD 92128 1150-D6
OLMEDA ST
1600 ENCT 92024 1147-H7
OLMEDA WY
17000 SD 92127 1169-H2
OLNEY ST
4100 SD 92109 1248-B5
OLSON DR
9700 SD 92121 1228-F1
OLSON WY
- OCN 92054 1106-F2
OLVERA AV
5100 SD 92114 1290-B5
OLVERA RD
10600 SDCo 91977 1271-F5
OLVIDA DR
200 SMCS 92078 1129-A1
E OLYMPIA CT
- CHV 91911 1330-E3
OLYMPIA DR
2600 CRLB 92010 1106-J3
E OLYMPIA ST
100 CHV 91911 1330-F2
OLYMPIA FIELDS RW
11300 SD 92128 1189-J3
OLYMPIC PKWY
- CHV 91913 1311-E7
- CHV 91913 1331-D1
- CHV 91915 1331-D1
700 CHV 91911 1330-J3
700 CHV 91911 1331-A3
2700 CHV 91915 1311-E7
2700 CHV 91915 (1312-A7
See Page 1293)
OLYMPIC PL
5700 SD 92115 1270-C5
OLYMPIC PT
- PWY 92064 1150-G5
OLYMPIC ST
4000 SD 92115 1270-C5
OLYMPIC WY
500 OCN 92054 1086-G1
OLYMPIC VISTA RD
2700 CHV 91915 1311-J7
2700 CHV 91915 (1312-A6
See Page 1293)
OLYMPUS CT
- SD 92126 1209-D2
OLYMPUS ST
600 ENCT 92024 1147-B3
OLYMPUS LOOP DR
1600 VSTA 92081 1107-G4
OMA RD
30700 SDCo 92082 1069-F3
OMAHA CT
400 ELCJ 92020 1251-G7
OMAR CT
5100 OCN 92057 1067-B5
OMAR DR
800 ESCN 92025 1129-J3
800 ESCN 92025 1130-A3
OMEARA ST
400 SD 92114 1290-D5
OMEGA DR
6500 SD 92139 1310-F1
OMEGA ST
600 SDCo 91977 1291-D3
OMEGA WY
- SMCS 92078 1128-H4
ONAGER DR
300 SDCo 92004 1058-G7
ONALASKA AV
8300 SD 92123 1249-C5
ONATE AV
4800 SD 92117 1248-H1
ONDA PL
6500 CRLB 92009 1127-G5
E ONEIDA CT
- CHV 91911 1330-E3
ONEIDA PL
3700 SD 92103 1269-B6
E ONEIDA ST
- CHV 91911 1330-F3
ONEIDA WY
900 SD 92103 1269-B6
ONEONTA AV
400 IMPB 91932 1349-G2
ONLEY DR
600 VSTA 92083 1087-F5
ONLEY WY
600 VSTA 92083 1087-F5
ONONDAGA AV
4300 SD 92117 1248-E2
ONSTAD ST
5000 SD 92110 1268-F2
ONTARIO AV
3600 SD 92105 1270-A6
ONTARIO CT
200 SDCo 92019 1272-C3
ONTARIO ST
900 ESCN 92025 1129-H5
5300 OCN 92056 1087-D1

ONYX AV
1600 ELCJ 92019 1252-B4
ONYX CT
- SDCo 92019 1272-B3
ONYX DR
2200 SDCo 92019 1272-C2
ONYX GN
- ESCN 92027 1110-D7
ONYX PL
- CRLB 92009 1127-G4
OOS RD
- SDCo 92082 1091-D3
OPAL CT
- CALX 92231 6620-J7
OPAL CV
- SD 92154 1330-J7
OPAL DR
500 SDCo 92036 1156-E1
OPAL GN
- ESCN 92027 1110-D7
OPAL LN
4400 OCN 92056 1107-D2
OPAL RDG
2100 VSTA 92081 1107-H6
OPAL ST
700 SD 92109 1247-H5
1600 SMCS 92078 1128-B5
OPAL WY
- CRLB 92011 1127-B4
OPALINE PL
- CHV 91913 1311-F1
OPALO WY
2300 SD 92111 1248-G7
OPALOCKA RD
39200 SDCo 91905 1300-C2
OPEN VIEW RD
- SDCo 92065 1173-D2
OPIMO CT
16400 SD 92128 1170-C4
OPIMO DR
12600 SD 92128 1170-C4
OPORTO CT
4700 SD 92124 1250-A1
OPORTO PL
4700 SD 92124 1250-A1
OPOSSUM CT
12100 SDCo 92040 1212-C5
OPPER ST
500 ESCN 92029 1129-D2
OPPORTUNITY RD
7100 SD 92111 1249-A2
OPTIMIST WY
2200 VSTA 92081 1108-A4
ORA ST
- SD 92105 1270-B5
ORA AVO DR
600 SDCo 92084 1088-E7
1000 SDCo 92084 1108-E1
ORA AVO LN
3100 SDCo 92084 1088-E7
ORA AVO TER
1100 SDCo 92084 1088-E7
ORA BELLE LN
8300 SDCo 92021 1232-D7
ORALANE DR
11400 SDCo 92020 1271-H3
ORANADO LN
- SDCo 92014 1167-J7
- SOLB 92014 1167-J7
ORANGE AV
100 ELCJ 92020 1251-F5
100 ELCN 92243 6499-E7
200 SDCo 92028 1027-F1
200 ELCN 92243 6500-A7
1300 ELCJ 92020 1271-F1
1800 SDCo 92065 1153-A2
2100 SDCo 92029 1129-G7
2100 SDCo 92065 409-H11
2200 ESCN 92029 1129-F7
3200 SD 92104 1269-F5
3600 SD 92105 1269-H3
4300 SD 92115 1269-H3
4800 SD 92105 1270-A4
4800 SD 92115 1270-A4
8000 LMSA 91941 1270-H3
ORANGE AV Rt#-75
100 CORD 92118 1288-H7
1300 CORD 92118 1308-J1
E ORANGE AV
- CHV 91911 1330-G4
S ORANGE AV
200 SDCo 92028 1027-F3
W ORANGE AV
- CHV 91911 1330-D4
ORANGE CT
1400 ELCJ 92020 1271-F1
ORANGE DR
100 CHV 91911 1330-F5
ORANGE LN
9800 SDCo 92029 1149-E1
ORANGE PL
1500 ESCN 92025 1129-J4
1500 ESCN 92025 1130-A5
2800 LMGR 91945 1270-H6
ORANGE ST
1300 NATC 91950 1310-B1
3100 SDCo 91935 1272-H7
3200 SDCo 91950 1310-C3
E ORANGE ST
100 VSTA 92084 1087-H6
N ORANGE ST
100 ESCN 92025 1129-H3
S ORANGE ST
100 ESCN 92025 1129-J3
W ORANGE ST
100 VSTA 92083 1087-G6
ORANGE TER
28100 SDCo 92082 1090-E2
ORANGE WY
3800 OCN 92057 1086-H4
ORANGE BLOSSOM CT
- SDCo 92082 1051-A7
- SDCo 92082 1071-A1
ORANGE BLOSSOM DR
- SDCo 92082 1090-D6
ORANGE BLOSSOM LN
13400 PWY 92064 1190-E1
ORANGE BLOSSOM WY
1000 ESCN 92026 1109-J4
1700 ENCT 92024 1147-G5
ORANGEBURG AV
12800 SD 92129 1189-E5
ORANGEBURG CT
9600 SD 92129 1189-E5
ORANGECREST CT
12100 SDCo 92040 1232-A4
ORANGECREST DR
9500 SDCo 92040 1232-A4
ORANGE GROVE AV
400 VSTA 92084 1087-J6
ORANGE GROVE PL
- ESCN 92027 1130-H2
ORANGEGROVE RD
1300 SDCo 92021 1251-G1

ORANGE HILL
4300 SDCo 92028 1048-B5
ORANGETREE CT
1400 ENCT 92024 1147-G7
ORANGE TREE LN
- SDCo 92003 1068-D5
- SDCo 92084 1068-D5
ORANGEVIEW DR
1500 ENCT 92024 1167-G1
ORANGE VISTA LN
1800 SDCo 92021 1252-A1
ORANGEWOOD DR
1000 SDCo 92025 1130-D6
ORCAS WY
10000 SDCo 92040 1232-C3
ORCHARD AV
- SDCo 92021 1252-D5
2200 ELCJ 92019 1252-D5
2200 SDCo 92019 1252-D5
3800 SD 92107 1288-A1
4300 SD 92107 1287-J1
4400 SD 92107 1267-J7
8200 LMSA 91941 1270-H2
ORCHARD DR
4200 SDCo 91977 1271-C4
ORCHARD LN
900 SDCo 92036 1135-E4
ORCHARD RD
1400 ImCo 92250 431-E6
11900 SDCo 92040 1251-J1
ORCHARD RD Rt#-S32
- HOLT 92250 431-E5
1600 ImCo 92250 431-E5
ORCHARD WY
3400 OCN 92054 1086-F2
ORCHARD BEND RD
16200 PWY 92064 1170-F3
ORCHARD GATE RD
13400 PWY 92064 1170-E5
ORCHARD GLEN CIR
1200 ENCT 92024 1147-G4
ORCHARD HILL RD
3200 SDCo 91902 1310-G2
ORCHARD VIEW LN
- ESCN 92027 1130-H2
14900 PWY 92064 1170-H7
ORCHARD VISTA RD
13000 SDCo 92082 1090-B5
ORCHARD WOOD RD
1600 ENCT 92024 1147-G4
ORCHID AV
700 SMCS 92078 1128-A3
14100 PWY 92064 1190-F3
ORCHID CT
- VSTA 92081 1108-B5
ORCHID GN
3700 ESCN 92025 1150-C3
ORCHID LN
500 DLMR 92014 1187-G5
2800 SD 92154 1350-C1
ORCHID WY
800 SD 92154 1330-D7
900 CRLB 92011 1127-A6
ORCUTT AV
4500 SD 92120 1249-H6
4800 SD 92120 1250-A6
ORD WY
1800 OCN 92056 1087-D5
ORDE CT
1200 CHV 91911 1330-C4
ORDVIEW CT
1200 CHV 91911 1330-C4
ORDWAY RD
600 SDCo 92028 1028-H2
OREGANO WY
3800 OCN 92057 1086-H4
OREGON AV
6900 LMSA 91942 1270-F1
OREGON ST
3900 SD 92104 1269-D5
4300 SD 92116 1269-D3
OREO LN
2100 SD 92154 1350-A1
ORGANDY LN
8500 SNTE 92071 1230-H7
8500 SNTE 92071 1250-H1
ORIBIA RD
1200 DLMR 92014 1187-G4
ORIEN AV
7300 LMSA 91941 1270-G4
ORIENTE DR
700 SDCo 92084 1067-H6
ORIENTE PL
700 SDCo 92084 1067-H6
ORIENTE WY
23500 SDCo 92065 1173-D3
ORILLA DR
16600 SD 92128 1170-B3
ORINDA CT
- CHV 91913 1331-D2
ORINDA DR
2100 ENCT 92007 1167-D3
ORINDA PL
1300 ESCN 92029 1129-G7
ORINOCO DR
2800 SDCo 92070 1135-F2
2800 SDCo 92070 1155-F1
ORIOLE CT
400 CHV 91911 1330-H2
1700 CRLB 92011 1127-E5
ORIOLE LN
- OCN 92057 1086-H2
ORIOLE PL
1300 CHV 91911 1330-G3
ORIOLE ST
1700 SD 92114 1290-D1
ORIOLE WY
1000 SMCS 92078 1128-E2
ORION CT
- SD 92126 1209-D6
ORION DR
3600 SDCo 91941 1271-A5
8900 SD 92126 1209-D6
ORION PL
400 ESCN 92026 1109-J7
400 ESCN 92026 1129-J1
ORION ST
5700 CRLB 92010 1127-E1
ORION WY
- SMCS 92078 1128-F6
2500 CRLB 92010 1127-E1
11100 SD 92126 1209-C2
ORISKANY RD
1800 SD 92139 1290-D7
ORIZABA ST
2000 SD 92103 1268-G5
ORKNEY LN
1200 ENCT 92007 1167-D1
ORLA ST
800 SMCS 92069 1108-J5
ORLANDO CT
- CHV 91911 1330-E3

E ORLANDO CT
- CHV 91911 1330-E3
ORLANDO ST
400 ELCJ 92021 1251-J5
1200 SMCS 92069 1109-C6
E ORLANDO ST
100 CHV 91911 1330-F3
ORLEANS E
3000 SD 92110 1268-C5
ORLEANS AV
100 ESCN 92027 1110-E7
400 ESCN 92027 1130-E1
ORLEAVO DR
900 VSTA 92084 1087-J7
ORLECK CT
4800 SD 92124 1249-G2
ORLECK PL
4900 SD 92124 1249-G2
ORLECK ST
10100 SD 92124 1249-G2
ORMA DR
900 SD 92106 1287-J2
ORMOND CT
700 SD 92109 1267-H1
ORMSBY ST
800 SDCo 92084 1067-J7
ORMSBY WY
2700 SDCo 92084 1068-A7
OR NO WY
10800 SDCo 92040 1232-A1
ORO CT
- CHV 91915 1311-H6
ORO GN
1500 ESCN 92026 1109-H6
ORO ST
700 ELCJ 92021 1251-J3
900 SDCo 92021 1251-J3
ORO GRANDE
3400 VSTA 92081 1107-C2
ORO GRANDE ST
800 OCN 92057 1087-C1
OROHAVEN LN
12600 PWY 92064 1190-C4
OROLA LN
6800 LMSA 91941 1270-E3
OROSCO TKTR
- SDCo 92065 409-G11
OROSCO GUEJITO TKTR
- SD 92027 409-G11
- SDCo 92027 409-G11
- SDCo 92065 409-G11
ORO VERDE RD
2000 SDCo 92027 1130-E4
ORO VISTA RD
1300 SD 92154 1350-B1
OROZCO RD
10300 SD 92124 1229-G7
ORPHA CT
12800 PWY 92064 1190-D5
ORPHEUS AV
300 ENCT 92024 1147-B3
ORR ST
3500 OCN 92054 1086-E2
6600 SD 92111 1248-H6
ORRELL DR
400 NATC 91950 1309-J3
ORSETT ST
400 CHV 91911 1330-C4
ORTEN ST
4500 SD 92110 1268-E1
ORTEZ PL
14400 PWY 92064 1190-H1
ORVIL WY
100 SDCo 92028 1028-A2
ORVILLE ST
8600 SDCo 91977 1291-A3
ORWELL LN
300 ENCT 92024 1147-G7
ORWELL RD
300 ENCT 92024 1147-H7
OSAGE AV
1000 CHV 91911 1330-G1
OSAGE DR
1000 SDCo 91977 1290-H2
OSAGE ST
700 SDCo 91977 1290-J4
900 SD 92114 1290-J4
1500 SMCS 92078 1108-D6
9600 SDCo 91977 1291-C3
OSAGE TR
11500 SDCo 92040 1231-H7
OSBORN ST
2000 SD 92113 1289-G7
OSBORNE ST
100 SDCo 92084 1087-G1
100 VSTA 92084 1087-G1
1000 SDCo 92084 1088-A1
OSBORNE TER
2400 SDCo 92084 1087-J1
OSCEOLA AV
3000 SD 92117 1248-C1
OSGOOD WY
10000 SD 92126 1209-A5
10000 SD 92126 1209-A6
OSHIA LN
11300 SDCo 92082 1069-G1
OSLER LN
3000 SD 92093 1228-A2
OSLER ST
6200 SD 92111 1248-H6
OSO RD
9100 SDCo 91977 1291-B1
OSOYOOS PL
11400 SD 92126 1209-C1
OSPREY ST
4200 SD 92107 1287-H1
OSPREY WY
300 OCN 92057 1087-A3
OSSA AV
10000 CHV 91911 1330-G1
OSTEND CT
700 SD 92109 1267-H1
OSTERLING CT
6800 SD 92114 1290-E6
OSTROW ST
7700 SD 92111 1249-A3
OTAY PL
700 SD 92114 1290-D3
OTAY ST
700 SD 92114 1290-D3
OTAY CENTER CT
2200 SD 92154 1351-J3
OTAY CENTER DR
2400 SD 92154 1351-J3
2400 SD 92154 1352-A3
OTAY HEIGHTS CT
1600 SD 92154 1351-D2
OTAY LAKES RD
2300 CHV 91915 1311-E5
2300 CHV 91914 1311-E5
2600 CHV 91915 (1312-B5
See Page 1293)
2600 SDCo 91915 (1312-B5
See Page 1293)

OTAY LAKES RD
2600 CHV 91914 (1312-B5
See Page 1293)
2600 SDCo 91914 (1312-B5
See Page 1293)
2800 CHV 91913 1311-E5
3200 CHV 91910 1311-A4
3500 CHV 91902 1311-A4
3700 CHV 91902 1310-H3
3700 CHV 91910 1310-H3
3800 SDCo 91902 1310-H3
13500 SDCo 91935 (1312-B5
See Page 1293)
13500 SDCo 91935 (1313-B3
See Page 1293)
14600 SDCo 91917 (1313-B3
See Page 1293)
OTAY MESA PL
4300 SD 92173 1350-G3
OTAY MESA RD
4200 SD 92173 1350-H2
4500 SD 92154 1350-H2
5100 SD 92154 1351-J2
9300 SDCo 92154 1351-J2
9300 SDCo 92154 1352-A2
OTAY MESA RD
Rt#-905
5100 SD 92154 1351-A2
8800 SDCo 92154 1351-F2
OTAY MESA CENTER RD
1600 SD 92154 1351-G2
OTAY MOUNTAIN TKTR
200 SDCo 91917 429-J10
400 SDCo 91917 (1333-D4
See Page 1332)
1300 SDCo 92154 1332-D6
1300 SDCo 92154 (1333-A7
See Page 1332)
1300 SDCo 92154 1352-H1
1300 SDCo 92154 (1353-A1
See Page 1332)
OTAY VALLEY CIR
300 CHV 91911 1330-G5
OTAY VALLEY RD
200 CHV 91911 1330-F5
1000 CHV 92154 1331-C7
1000 SD 92154 1331-C7
1000 SD 92154 1351-C1
OTERO WY
23900 SDCo 92065 1173-E2
OTESGO DR
800 SD 92103 1268-J6
OTHELLO AV
7500 SD 92111 1249-A3
OTIS CT
6900 SD 92111 1268-J1
OTIS PL
13800 PWY 92064 1190-F4
OTIS ST
100 CHV 91910 1310-C6
OTIS POST RD
13200 PWY 92064 1190-G4
OTOMI AV
4600 SD 92117 1248-D1
OTONO ST
1200 SD 92154 1350-F1
OTSEGO DR
500 SD 92103 1268-J6
OTTAWA AV
3400 SD 92117 1248-E5
OTTILIE PL
5100 SD 92105 1270-A5
OTTO AV
2300 SDCo 91901 1234-D5
OTTO DR
3000 SDCo 91901 1234-D6
OUR WY
8700 SNTE 92071 1231-A7
OUR COUNTRY RD
2400 SDCo 92029 1129-H7
OURO PL
7300 LMSA 91941 1270-F4
OUTBACK PL
2900 SDCo 92065 1172-C3
OUTER DR
1700 SDCo 92021 1251-G1
OUTER RD
1000 SD 92154 1350-B1
OUTINDA ST
9000 SDCo 91977 1291-B4
OUTLOOK CT
- CRLB 92010 1106-H4
OUTLOOK PT
5300 SD 92124 1249-G1
OUTLOOK RD
13600 PWY 92064 1190-F1
OUTRIGGER LN
1800 CRLB 92008 1106-H7
OUTRIGGER WY
1900 OCN 92054 1106-F1
OVAL DR
3000 SD 92139 1310-F2
OVERBROOK LN
1000 SDCo 92028 1027-J5
OVERHILL DR
2900 SDCo 92084 1088-D7
OVERLAKE AV
5800 SD 92120 1250-E7
OVERLAND AV
4600 SD 92123 1249-D1
5000 SD 92123 1229-D7
OVERLAND CT
500 CHV 91902 1311-B4
OVERLAND PASG
2800 SDCo 91901 1234-D5
OVERLAND PASS
13600 PWY 92064 1170-F1
OVERLAND RD
400 ENCT 92024 1147-G6
OVERLAND SPUR
3400 SDCo 91901 1234-D5
OVERLAND TR
2800 SDCo 92028 1047-G1
OVERLOOK CIR
800 SMCS 92078 1128-F2
OVERLOOK DR
4900 OCN 92057 1087-C2
E OVERLOOK DR
600 SD 92115 1270-C4
W OVERLOOK DR
4200 SD 92115 1270-C4
OVERLOOK LN
800 SDCo 92019 1251-H6
OVERLOOK PL
2400 CHV 91914 1311-J2
OVERLOOK ST
600 ESCN 92027 1130-C2
OVERPARK RD
3400 SD 92130 1187-J5
11600 SD 92130 1188-A5
OVERTON AV
9200 SD 92123 1249-E6
OVERVIEW RD
15900 PWY 92064 1170-E5

OVID PL
5000 SD 92117 1228-E7
OVIEDO PL
2400 CRLB 92009 1147-G1
OVIEDO ST
8900 SD 92129 1189-E2
OVIEDO WY
9300 SD 92129 1189-E3
OWEGA CT
3900 SDCo 92004 (1099-D2
See Page 1098)
OWEN DR
1300 CHV 91911 1330-H2
OWEN ST
2800 SD 92106 1288-A4
OWENS AV
1900 CRLB 92008 1127-C3
OWL CT
9400 SD 92129 1189-E6
OWL GN
1300 ESCN 92029 1129-G5
OXBOW CIR
100 ENCT 92024 1147-H7
OXBOW LN
100 ENCT 92024 1147-H7
OXFORD AV
1700 ENCT 92007 1167-D2
OXFORD CT
- VSTA 92081 1107-H5
1100 CHV 91911 1330-C3
OXFORD PL
3800 OCN 92056 1087-A7
OXFORD ST
- CHV 91911 1330-D3
3600 CRLB 92010 1106-J4
4300 LMSA 91941 1270-F4
E OXFORD ST
- CHV 91911 1330-F2
OXFORD HILL
- SD 92127 1169-C3
OZARK RD
1400 OCN 92056 1087-D1
OZLAND AV
15900 SDCo 92082 1071-A3
OZZIE WY
400 SD 92114 1290-C5

P

PAAUWE DR
32200 SDCo 92061 1051-B6
PABELLON CIR
11200 SD 92124 1250-A2
PABELLON CT
11200 SD 92124 1250-A2
PABLO DR
16200 SD 92128 1170-C4
PABLO PL
1200 ESCN 92027 1109-J7
PACATO CIR N
12500 SD 92128 1170-C2
PACATO CIR S
12500 SD 92128 1170-C2
PACATO CT
17100 SD 92128 1170-C2
PACATO PL
17200 SD 92128 1170-C2
PACATO WY
17100 SD 92128 1170-C2
PACEMONT LN
11100 SD 92126 1209-E2
PACER LN
13300 PWY 92064 1170-E4
PACESETTER ST
500 OCN 92057 1067-E6
PACIFIC AV
100 CRLB 92008 1106-D5
100 SOLB 92075 1167-E6
1500 CHV 91911 1330-A4
1500 SD 91911 1330-A4
7200 LMGR 91945 1270-G6
PACIFIC HWY
600 SD 92101 1288-J1
1700 SD 92109 1268-E3
1900 SD 92110 1268-E3
3000 SD 92101 1268-H7
4800 SD 92140 1268-F6
PACIFIC LN
1200 DLMR 92014 1187-F5
PACIFIC ST
300 ENCT 92024 1147-B2
300 SMCS 92069 1108-E6
N PACIFIC ST
100 SMCS 92069 1108-E6
200 OCN 92054 1106-A1
300 OCN 92054 1085-J7
300 OCN 92054 1105-J1
S PACIFIC ST
100 SMCS 92078 1108-D7
200 SMCS 92078 1128-D1
300 OCN 92054 1106-A1
PACIFICA AV
1100 CHV 91913 1311-C6
PACIFICA DR
4800 SD 92109 1248-B3
5300 SD 92037 1248-B3
PACIFICA PL
- ENCT 92024 1147-F5
PACIFICA WY
- ENCT 92024 1147-F5
- OCN 92056 1087-A4
PACIFIC BEACH DR
700 SD 92109 1247-H7
1700 SD 92109 1248-A6
PACIFIC CANYON WY
10700 SD 92121 1208-F4
PACIFIC CENTER BLVD
5700 SD 92121 1208-E5
PACIFIC CENTER CT
10400 SD 92121 1208-F5
PACIFIC CREST DR
- SDCo 91901 1254-B2
PACIFIC CREST WY
29400 SDCo 91906 (1297-E4
See Page 1296)
PACIFIC GROVE LP
1100 CHV 91915 1311-F6
PACIFIC GROVE PL
5200 SD 92130 1188-D6
PACIFIC HAVEN CT
5800 SD 92121 1208-F3
PACIFIC HEIGHTS
BLVD
9500 SD 92121 1208-F5
PACIFIC HIGHLANDS
RANCH PKWY
- SD 92130 1188-F3
PACIFIC HILL ST
1000 CHV 91911 1330-H1
PACIFIC MESA BLVD
10000 SD 92121 1208-F6
PACIFIC MESA CT
5900 SD 92121 1208-F5

STREET
Block City ZIP Pg-Grid

PACIFIC MIST CT
1900 SD 92139 1290-D7
PACIFIC MIST RD
1900 SD 92139 1290-D7
PACIFICO RD
7100 CRLB 92009 1127-F6
PACIFIC OAKS PL
- ESCN 92029 1129-E5
PACIFIC PLAZA DR
3900 SD 92130 1208-B4
PACIFIC RANCH DR
1500 ENCT 92024 1167-H2
PACIFIC RIM CT
800 SD 92154 1351-D2
PACIFIC RIVIERA WY
- SD 92154 1350-G2
PACIFIC SHORES WY
- SD 92130 1208-C2
PACIFIC SUNSET TR
3000 SDCo 91901 1234-D4
PACIFIC SURF DR
700 SOLB 92075 1187-E2
PACIFIC VIEW CT
- VSTA 92084 1088-D5
PACIFIC VIEW DR
600 SD 92109 1247-G5
PACIFIC VIEW LN
- ENCT 92024 1147-D6
PACIFIC VISTA WY
800 SDCo 92069 1088-G7
PACKARD LN
3900 CRLB 92008 1106-H6
PACKARD PL
2100 SDCo 92019 1272-C3
PADDING RIVER RD
1900 CHV 91913 1311-E6
PADDOCK RD
5600 OCN 92057 1067-F7
PADDY PL
2000 ESCN 92027 1110-B6
PADEN DR
200 SDCo 91977 1291-B4
PADERA CT
800 CHV 91910 1310-H5
PADERA WY
500 CHV 91910 1310-H5
PADGETT ST
9500 SD 92126 1209-E6
PADILLA
900 CALX 92231 6680-D1
PADRE LN
9200 SNTE 92071 1231-B7
PADRE TULLIO DR
100 SD 92173 1350-G3
PADRONE PL
500 CHV 91910 1310-J5
PADUA HILLS PL
200 SD 92173 1350-F3
PADUCAH DR
3900 SD 92117 1248-D4
PAGE RD
- SD 92106 1288-A7
PAGE ST
3400 SD 92115 1270-C6
PAGEANT AV
13200 SD 92129 1189-D4
PAGEL PL
100 SD 92114 1290-E4
PAGODA WY
8500 SD 92126 1209-C5
PAGODA TREE LN
- SDCo 92127 1169-D2
PAGOSA LN
12100 SDCo 92040 1231-J1
PAGUERA CT
4900 SD 92124 1249-H2
PAHLS WY
900 SDCo 92065 1153-B1
PAHVANT ST
2500 OCN 92054 1086-D6
PAIGE CIR
- SDCo 92028 1028-A1
PAINE PL
12100 PWY 92064 1190-F7
PAINE ST
12100 PWY 92064 1190-F7
PAINT BRUSH CIR
- SDCo 91906 (1318-B7 See Page 1298)
PAINTBRUSH DR
- CHV 91913 1311-F7
PAINTED CANYON RD
- SDCo 92127 1169-F5
PAINTED COLT DR
- ImCo 92243 6560-B6
PAINTED DESERT RD
14000 PWY 92064 1170-G3
PAINTED GORGE RD
- ImCo 92259 430-H5
PAINTED NETTLES GN
- SD 92130 1188-E4
PAINTED PONY CIR
1000 VSTA 92081 1107-G2
PAINTED ROCK RD
23400 SDCo 92065 1173-D7
23400 SDCo 92065 (1193-F1 See Page 1192)
PAINT MOUNTAIN RD
1400 SDCo 92024 1148-F4
1400 SDCo 92029 1148-F4
PAISLEY CT
100 CHV 91911 1330-E3
E PAISLEY ST
- CHV 91911 1330-E3
PAIUTE PL
13000 PWY 92064 1190-D3
PAIZAY PL
- CHV 91913 1311-F1
PAJAMA DR
100 OCN 92054 1086-D6
PAJARO WY
11300 SD 92127 1149-J7
PAKAMA LN
6800 SDCo 92084 1068-E5
PALA CT
- CHV 91911 1330-E4
PALA RD
3400 OCN 92054 1086-G1
3900 OCN 92057 1086-G1
4400 OCN 92057 1087-A1
PALA RD Rt#-S16
47000 RivC 92592 999-G1
47800 SDCo 92028 999-G1
47800 SDCo 92059 999-G1
PALA RD Rt#-76
2200 SDCo 92003 1048-H2
2200 SDCo 92028 1048-H2
5600 SDCo 92059 1030-A4
5600 SDCo 92061 1030-E5
7500 SDCo 92059 1029-F4
8500 SDCo 92028 1029-C7
8600 SDCo 92028 1049-A1
16800 SDCo 92061 1051-B5
16800 SDCo 92082 1051-B5
33100 SDCo 92061 1050-H1
PALA ST
100 SDCo 92065 1152-E7
7900 SD 92114 1290-G3
PALABRA CIR
11400 SD 92124 1250-A2
PALABRA CT
11400 SD 92124 1250-A2
PALACE DR
2400 SD 92123 1249-F6
PALACIO CT
17000 SD 92127 1169-H2
PALACIO DR
7700 CRLB 92009 1147-F2
PALACIO PL
17000 SD 92127 1169-H2
PALACIO NORTE
100 SDCo 92028 1027-H2
PALA DEL NORTE RD
36300 SDCo 92059 1029-C4
PALAIE RD
7900 SDCo 92021 1252-A1
PALAKWAI CT
- SDCo 92028 1048-A4
PALA LAKE DR
- SDCo 92028 1028-G5
PALA LOMA DR
10800 SDCo 92082 1049-F3
PALA MESA CT
2700 SDCo 92028 1048-F1
PALA MESA DR
3600 SDCo 92028 1048-F1
4000 SDCo 92028 1028-G7
PALA MESA LN
3100 SDCo 92028 1048-F1
PALA MESA HEIGHTS DR
1200 SDCo 92028 1028-H5
1200 SDCo 92028 1029-A5
PALA MESA OAKS DR
4000 SDCo 92028 1028-G5
PALA MISSION RD
12100 SDCo 92059 1030-B4
12100 SDCo 92059 1029-G4
PALA MOUNTAIN DR
900 SDCo 92028 1028-J4
900 SDCo 92028 1029-A5
PALARO DR
800 ENCT 92024 1147-C2
PALA TEMECULA RD Rt#-S16
37100 SDCo 92028 999-G3
37100 SDCo 92059 999-G3
41800 SDCo 92059 1029-G2
PALAU CIR
1200 CORD 92118 1309-C5
PALAU RD
1100 CORD 92118 1309-C5
PALA VISTA DR
100 VSTA 92083 1087-J7
100 VSTA 92083 1107-J1
PALAWAN WY
100 SD 92114 1290-F5
PALE MOON RD
- SDCo 92127 1169-A1
PALENCIA CT
900 CHV 91910 1310-H5
PALENCIA PL
900 CHV 91910 1310-H5
PALENQUE ST
7700 CRLB 92009 1147-F2
PALEO DR
- SDCo 91935 1293-C1
14800 SDCo 91935 1273-B7
PALERMI PL
- CRLB 92011 1127-C5
PALERMO CT
1900 VSTA 92081 1107-H3
5000 OCN 92057 1087-C1
PALERMO DR
2200 SD 92106 1268-B7
2400 SD 92107 1268-B7
5000 OCN 92057 1087-B1
PALERO RD
12500 SD 92128 1170-C4
PALETTE CT
700 OCN 92057 1087-C1
PALIMO DR
31200 SDCo 92026 1068-J2
31200 SDCo 92026 1069-A2
PALIN ST
4900 SD 92113 1290-A5
5100 SD 92114 1290-A5
PALISADES CT
12800 PWY 92064 1190-D2
PALISADES DR
1800 CRLB 92008 1106-H6
13900 PWY 92064 1190-D2
PALISADES RD
4100 SD 92116 1269-G2
PALITO CT
11400 SD 92127 1149-J7
PALLETTE ST
200 ELCJ 92020 1251-G7
PALLON CT
4100 SD 92124 1249-J2
PALLON WY
10900 SD 92124 1249-J2
10900 SD 92124 1250-A2
PALLUX WY
8400 SD 92126 1209-C2
PALLUX STAR CT
15500 SDCo 91935 1293-E1
PALM AV
- ImCo 92243 6560-A7
- ImCo 92249 6560-A7
- SD 92102 1289-G4
- SD 92123 1249-C5
- NATC 91950 1289-J7
- IMPB 91932 1329-F7
100 CHV 91911 1330-F5
100 CORD 92118 1288-H5
300 NATC 91950 1290-A7
700 CRLB 92008 1106-F6
900 NATC 91950 1310-A1
2200 SD 92154 1330-B7
4200 LMSA 91941 1270-J2
PALM AV Rt#-75
900 IMPB 91932 1329-G7
1300 SD 92154 1329-G7
1300 IMPB 92154 1329-G7
1700 SD 92154 1330-A7
W PALM AV
100 ELCJ 92020 1251-E6
PALM DR
- DLMR 92014 1187-G3
- CALX 92231 6620-F7
200 VSTA 92084 1087-H5
3700 SDCo 91902 1310-J3
3800 CHV 91902 1310-J3
PALM LN
- SDCo 92040 1232-D6
2700 LMGR 91945 1270-J7
9700 SDCo 92029 1149-E3
PALM PL
- ELCJ 92019 1251-J6
PALM RD
400 SMCS 92069 1108-E6
1600 CHV 91911 1330-F5
PALM ST
100 SD 92103 1269-A7
400 SD 92103 1268-J7
700 VSTA 92083 1087-F6
1300 SD 92101 1268-J7
1300 SD 92101 1288-J1
2600 LMGR 91945 1270-H7
2800 SD 92104 1269-E7
3700 SMCS 92078 1128-C1
4700 SD 92105 1269-J7
5100 SD 92105 1270-A7
8500 LMGR 91977 1270-J7
8500 SDCo 91977 1270-J7
W PALM ST
600 CALX 92231 6620-E7
PALM TER
800 ESCN 92025 1129-J6
PALMAC ST
300 SMCS 92069 1108-E6
PALMAS CT
3600 OCN 92056 1107-D3
PALMAS DR
31500 SDCo 92086 409-K5
PALMAS HEIGHTS RD
- SDCo 92086 409-K5
PALMAS NORTE
100 SDCo 92028 1028-A2
PALMA VISTA CT
1200 SDCo 92025 1130-E6
PALMBARK ST
300 VSTA 92083 1087-E6
PALM BEACH LN
9600 SD 92129 1189-E5
PALM BEACH ST
1400 CHV 91915 1311-H7
PALM CANYON DR
- SDCo 92004 (1078-E2 See Page 1058)
- SMCS 92096 1128-J2
200 VSTA 92083 1087-E7
2600 SD 92037 1248-A2
PALM CANYON DR Rt#-S22
200 SDCo 92004 (1078-F2 See Page 1058)
700 SDCo 92004 (1079-D2 See Page 1058)
PALM CREST TER
3100 SMCS 92078 1108-C6
3100 VSTA 92081 1108-C6
PALMER DR
1900 OCN 92056 1106-G1
PALMER ST
2900 NATC 91950 1310-B1
PALMER WY
1200 NATC 91950 1290-B7
1200 NATC 91950 1310-C1
5600 CRLB 92010 1127-D1
PALMERA DR
5000 OCN 92056 1087-D3
PALMERO DR
16700 SD 92128 1170-C3
PALMETTO DR
- CRLB 92009 1127-G3
4800 OCN 92057 1067-B7
PALMETTO WY
4000 SD 92103 1268-H5
PALMETTO POINT CT
- CHV 91915 (1312-A5 See Page 1293)
PALM GLEN DR
10100 SNTE 92071 1231-E4
PALM HILL DR
3000 SDCo 92084 1088-E6
PALMILLA DR
7100 SD 92122 1228-B4
PALMITAS ST
400 SOLB 92075 1187-F1
PALM ROW DR
10100 SDCo 92040 1231-H2
PALM TREE CT
4100 SDCo 91941 1271-G4
PALM VALLEY CIR
900 CHV 91915 1311-G5
PALMVIEW AV
- ELCN 92243 6559-G4
PALM VIEW CT
1500 NATC 91950 1310-A1
PALM VIEW DR
1400 NATC 91950 1310-A1
PALM VIEW WY
900 NATC 91950 1310-A1
PALM VISTA CT
3000 SDCo 92019 1272-C5
PALMWOOD CT
500 SD 92139 1290-G6
PALMWOOD DR
500 SD 92139 1290-G6
PALMYRA AV
5200 SD 92117 1228-H7
PALMYRA DR
100 SDCo 92083 1108-C3
100 SDCo 92084 1108-C3
PALO CT
3700 SDCo 91902 1310-E4
PALO DR
3800 SDCo 91902 1310-E4
PALO GN
1800 ESCN 92026 1109-F6
PALO ALTO CT
800 SMCS 92069 1108-H6
PALO ALTO DR
- CHV 91914 1311-D2
PALO ALTO LN
6700 SD 92114 1290-E4
PALO DANZANTE
2300 SDCo 91901 1254-C1
PALOMA CT
- ENCT 92024 1147-E5
PALOMA LN
300 SDCo 92021 1252-H4
PALOMA ST
10700 SNTE 92071 1231-F6
PALOMA WY
1600 SDCo 91905 (1319-J2 See Page 1298)
PALOMA BAY CT
300 OCN 92057 1066-J6
PALOMAR AV
200 SD 92037 1247-E2
600 ELCJ 92020 1271-E1
PALOMAR DR
- CHV 91911 1330-D1
300 SMCS 92069 1109-D7
300 SMCS 92069 1129-D1
1500 SDCo 92028 1047-J3
3700 SDCo 92028 1048-A3
E PALOMAR DR
- CHV 91911 1330-E1
PALOMAR PL
1100 VSTA 92084 1088-A3
PALOMAR ST
- CHV 91911 1330-B4
E PALOMAR ST
- CHV 91911 1331-A2
- CHV 91913 1311-D7
- CHV 91911 1330-H2
1900 CHV 91913 1331-B1
PALOMAR TER
1200 ESCN 92027 1130-B2
PALOMAR VW
- SDCo 92082 1070-G1
PALOMAR WY
- CRLB 92008 1127-C2
- OCN 92056 1087-A4
PALOMAR AIRPORT RD Rt#-S12
- CRLB 92008 1126-H3
- CRLB 92011 1126-H3
1200 CRLB 92011 1127-F2
1200 CRLB 92008 1127-B3
2600 CRLB 92009 1127-F2
2600 CRLB 92010 1127-F2
3100 CRLB 92010 1128-A2
3100 SMCS 92078 1128-A2
3100 CRLB 92009 1128-A2
PALOMARCOS AV
1400 SMCS 92069 1108-E6
PALOMAR DIVIDE RD
- SDCo 92060 1032-F4
PALOMAR DIVIDE TKTR
- SDCo 92060 409-F5
- SDCo 92060 1031-E1
- SDCo 92060 1032-C3
PALOMARES CT
1200 SDCo 92028 1027-H6
PALOMARES RD
1800 SDCo 92028 1027-H6
PALOMAR OAKS CT
6300 CRLB 92011 1127-D4
PALOMAR OAKS WY
1700 CRLB 92011 1127-C4
1800 CRLB 92008 1127-C3
PALOMAR POINT WY
- CRLB 92008 1127-C2
PALOMAR VISTA DR
1500 OCN 92056 1087-D2
30300 SDCo 92082 1070-F1
PALOMAR VISTA RD
3400 SDCo 92060 1052-C2
PALOMINO CIR
2600 SD 92037 1248-A2
PALOMINO CT
900 SMCS 92069 1109-C5
1700 OCN 92057 1067-F7
PALOMINO DR
- ENCT 92024 1148-D4
800 SMCS 92069 1109-C5
PALOMINO LN
1600 SDCo 92025 1130-C4
PALOMINO RD
200 SDCo 92028 1027-G5
PALOMINO MESA CT
- SDCo 92127 1169-E5
PALOMINO MESA PL
- SDCo 92127 1169-F4
PALOMINO MESA RD
- SDCo 92127 1169-E5
PALOMINO MESA WY
- SDCo 92127 1169-F4
PALOMINO RIDGE DR
9000 SDCo 92040 1232-G4
9400 SDCo 92021 1232-G4
PALOMINO VALLEY CT
- SDCo 92127 1169-F5
PALOMINO VALLEY PL
- SDCo 92127 1169-F5
PALOMINO VALLEY RD
- SDCo 92127 1169-F5
PALOMIRA CT
2200 CHV 91915 1311-G6
PALOS TIERRA RD
12400 SDCo 92082 1070-B7
PALOS VERDES DR
31400 SDCo 92026 1069-A2
31700 SDCo 92026 1049-A7
31900 SDCo 92026 1068-J2
PALO VERDE AV
- IMP 92251 6499-D3
PALO VERDE DR
- SDCo 92055 1085-J4
PALO VERDE LN
- SDCo 92036 430-D3
4600 SDCo 92004 (1099-F4 See Page 1098)
PALO VERDE TER
4300 SD 92120 1269-H1
4400 SD 92115 1269-H1
PALO VERDE WY
3700 OCN 92056 1107-B1
PALO VISTA RD
2300 SDCo 92028 1028-C7
PALSERO AV
1900 ESCN 92029 1129-F6
P ALVARADO DR
- CALX 92231 6620-J5
PAM LN
13100 SDCo 92040 1232-C3
PAMBARA CIR
1400 OCN 92054 1106-E1
PAMELA CT
4100 SD 92117 1248-E2
PAMELA DR
100 SDCo 92028 1028-E1
PAMELA LN
800 ELCJ 92020 1271-E1
1800 ESCN 92026 1109-D4
PAMJOY LN
3400 SDCo 91977 1271-A5
PAMO AV
2400 SD 92104 1289-E1
2500 SD 92104 1269-E7
PAMO RD
1300 SDCo 92065 1152-H1
6500 SDCo 92065 409-G11
PAMOOSA LN
29300 SDCo 92082 1069-E6
PAMO VALLEY VW
22400 SDCo 92065 409-H11
PAMO WINTERCAMP RD
18700 SDCo 92065 1171-J5
PAMPA ST
8700 LMSA 91942 1251-A6
PAMPAS LN
1700 SDCo 92004 (1099-F2 See Page 1098)
PAMPLONA CT
- ESCN 92025 1130-B6
PAMPLONA WY
2200 CRLB 92009 1127-F7
PANA DR
- SDCo 92040 1232-D6
PANAMA PL
4900 SD 92116 1269-F2
PAN AMERICAN PZ
1900 SD 92101 1289-B1
PAN AMERICAN RD E
2100 SD 92101 1289-B1
PAN AMERICAN RD W
2300 SD 92101 1289-B1
PANAMINT RW
2400 SD 92139 1290-F7
PANASONIC WY
7500 SD 92154 1351-E2
PANAY CT
1900 SD 92105 1289-H1
PANCHOY DR
4600 SDCo 91941 1271-F3
PANCHOY LN
8200 LMGR 91945 1290-H1
PANDORA DR
9900 SDCo 91941 1271-D1
PANEL CT
6400 SD 92122 1228-F5
PANELLA CT
- OCN 92057 1067-A5
PANETTAH DR
1700 SDCo 91901 1233-G7
PANGEA DR
2700 SD 92093 1227-J1
PANHANDLE TR
7300 SDCo 92036 1138-B7
PANKEY RD
- SDCo 92028 1028-H4
2600 SDCo 92028 1048-H1
PANNONIA RD
4600 CRLB 92008 1106-H7
PANOCHA CT
6800 SD 92114 1270-E7
PANORAMA DR
1400 SDCo 92078 1128-C4
3200 SDCo 92036 1156-E1
4200 LMSA 91941 1271-A4
4200 LMSA 91977 1271-A4
4700 SD 92116 1269-C3
PANORAMA RD
1700 VSTA 92083 1087-G3
PANORAMA TR
- SDCo 92060 (1073-G1 See Page 1052)
- SDCo 92070 (1053-H7 See Page 1052)
- SDCo 92070 (1073-G1 See Page 1052)
PANORAMA VW
- SDCo 92082 1051-A6
PANORAMA CREST
2800 SDCo 92029 1150-A2
PANORAMA RIDGE CT
8300 SDCo 91977 1290-J5
PANORAMA RIDGE RD
1300 OCN 92056 1087-D4
PANORAMA RIDGE WY
- OCN 92056 1087-D3
PANORAMIC DR
- SDCo 92084 1068-C7
- SDCo 92084 1088-C1
PANORAMIC LN
5400 SD 92121 1208-E4
PANORAMIC PL
- SDCo 92084 1068-D7
PANORAMIC WY
- SDCo 92084 1068-D7
- SDCo 92084 1088-D1
PANSY WY
1000 SDCo 92019 1252-E7
PANTERA RD
13200 SD 92130 1187-J5
PANTERA WY
3500 SD 92130 1187-J5
PANTHER WY
- VSTA 92084 1087-H3
PAOLA PL
4600 SD 92117 1248-H1
PAOLA WY
4400 SD 92117 1248-H2
PAPAGALLO CT
11600 SD 92124 1250-B3
PAPAGALLO DR
- OCN 92057 1067-B2
PAPAGO DR
12700 PWY 92064 1190-D4
PAPAGO TR
15300 SDCo 92036 1176-E4
PAPAYA ST
400 VSTA 92083 1087-E6
PAPAYA WY
3500 OCN 92054 1086-F2
PAPIN ST
1400 OCN 92054 1086-B5
PAPOOSE CT
11100 SD 92127 1149-H7
PAPPAS CT
- CHV 91911 1331-A2
PAPPAS RD
24500 SDCo 92065 1173-F4
PAPRIKA RD
30100 SDCo 91906 (1297-F4 See Page 1296)
PAPRIKA WY
3800 OCN 92057 1086-H4
PAPYRUS CT
- OCN 92054 1106-F2
PAQUITA ST
900 ELCJ 92019 1252-B7
PAR DR
3200 SDCo 91941 1270-J5
3200 SDCo 91941 1271-A6
3200 SDCo 91977 1271-A6
3300 OCN 92056 1106-J1
PARADISE DR
800 NATC 91950 1290-A7
900 NATC 91950 1310-A1
14000 PWY 92064 1190-G2
PARADISE RD
- CRLB 92009 1127-G3
1400 SD 92114 1290-B6
PARADISE ST
400 NATC 92136 1309-F1
1700 ESCN 92026 1109-H5
1800 SD 92114 1290-D1
PARADISE WY
- VSTA 92083 1087-C7
PARADISE COVE WY
700 OCN 92054 1066-E6
PARADISE CREST VIEW WY
6600 SD 92114 1290-E6
PARADISE GLEN WY
1700 SDCo 92078 1128-A4
1700 SMCS 92078 1128-A4
PARADISE HILLS RD
1400 SD 92114 1290-F6
PARADISE KNOLL CT
- NATC 91950 1290-A7
PARADISE MEADOW LN
26900 SDCo 92082 1091-E4
PARADISE MESA RD
1700 SD 92114 1290-D6
PARADISE MOUNTAIN LN
17400 SDCo 92082 1091-E5
PARADISE MOUNTAIN RD
17200 SDCo 92082 1091-H4
PARADISE PARK DR
9000 SDCo 92040 1231-J6
PARADISE RIDGE CT
- CHV 91915 (1312-A5 See Page 1293)
PARADISE RIDGE RD
6400 SD 92114 1290-D6
N PARADISE RIDGE WY
- CHV 91915 1311-J5
- CHV 91915 (1312-A5 See Page 1293)
S PARADISE RIDGE WY
- CHV 91915 (1312-A6 See Page 1293)
PARADISE TRAIL RD
1100 CHV 91915 1311-H5
PARADISE VALLEY CT
8100 SDCo 91977 1290-H5
PARADISE VALLEY RD
3400 NATC 91950 1290-D6
6400 SD 92139 1290-H5
6400 SD 92114 1290-H5
8000 SDCo 91977 1290-H5
8300 SDCo 91977 1291-A4
26400 SDCo 92086 1033-J3
26400 SDCo 92086 409-J6
PARADISIO PL
- SDCo 92127 1169-G1
PARADOX LN
200 SDCo 92021 1252-J2
PARAGON MESA RD
16000 SDCo 92064 1191-C5
PARAISO AV
300 SDCo 91977 1291-C2
2100 SDCo 91977 1271-C7
PARAISO RD
3500 SDCo 92028 1047-E3
PARAKEET PL
1100 VSTA 92083 1087-G4
PARAMOUNT AV
- ESCN 92027 1130-C1
PARAMOUNT DR
4600 SD 92123 1249-D2
PARA SIEMPRE VISTA
20100 SDCo 92065 1152-E1
PARASIO CT
1400 NATC 91950 1289-J7
PARDEE PL
3500 SD 92113 1289-F5
PARDEE ST
- SD 92102 1289-F4
S PARDEE ST
- SD 92113 1289-F4
PAR FOUR DR
3400 SDCo 92019 1272-C6
PARIANOS DR
- CHV 91911 1330-D3
PARIS WY
6700 SD 92139 1310-F1
6800 SD 92139 1290-F7
PARISH RD
12500 SD 92128 1170-C3
PARIVA DR
1800 ENCT 92007 1167-E3
PARK AV
- ImCo 92233 411-C11
100 VSTA 92084 1087-H6
200 ESCN 92025 1129-J2
400 ELCN 92243 6499-G6
10300 SNTE 92071 1231-E6
E PARK AV
100 ELCJ 92020 1251-F5
200 SD 92173 1350-G4
600 ELCJ 92021 1251-G5
W PARK AV
100 ELCJ 92020 1251-F5
100 SD 92173 1350-G4
PARK BLVD
- SD 92101 1289-B2
100 SDCo 92021 1252-H3
1700 SD 92134 1289-B2
2800 SD 92101 1269-C6
2900 SD 92103 1269-C6
4300 SD 92116 1269-C4
PARK CT
4900 CRLB 92008 1106-J7
PARK DR
300 VSTA 92084 1087-H6
800 SDCo 92029 1149-H1
900 SDCo 92029 1129-H7
1300 CHV 91911 1330-G3
1800 SD 92109 1248-A4
3700 CRLB 92008 1106-G6
3800 SDCo 92036 1156-E2
4900 CRLB 92008 1107-A7
5400 SDCo 91977 1290-J6
9300 SDCo 91916 1235-J3
PARK LN
- ENCT 92024 1147-D7
- SDCo 91901 1254-G7
- SDCo 91901 1274-G1
200 OCN 92054 1085-J7
7900 LMSA 91941 1270-J4
E PARK LN
200 CHV 91910 1310-A6
600 CHV 91910 1330-A1
800 CHV 91911 1330-A1
PARK PL
300 SMCS 92078 1128-F1
500 ESCN 92025 1129-J1
800 SDCo 92025 1130-C6
1000 CORD 92118 1288-H7
4100 SD 92116 1269-G3
32200 RivC 92592 999-F1
PARK RD
2900 ESCN 92025 1150-B1
PARK RW
1200 SD 92037 1227-F6
PARK ST
25800 SDCo 92026 1109-F2
PARK TR
- SDCo 92036 1156-D7
PARK VW
2000 ESCN 92029 1129-E6
PARK WY
300 CHV 91910 1310-A7
PARKBROOK LN
8400 SD 92114 1290-J4
PARKBROOK PL
200 SD 92114 1290-H4
PARKBROOK ST
200 SDCo 91977 1290-J3
400 SDCo 91977 1291-A3
8300 SD 92114 1290-J4
PARKBROOK WY
100 SD 92114 1290-J4
PARK CENTER AV
1300 VSTA 92081 1127-H1
PARK CENTER DR
- SNTE 92071 1231-D5
900 VSTA 92081 1108-A7
900 VSTA 92081 1107-J7
1000 VSTA 92081 1127-J1
PARK CREEK CT
- SMCS 92078 1129-A1
PARKCREEK CT
100 SD 92114 1290-H4
PARK CREST DR
1900 ENCT 92007 1167-F3
10400 SNTE 92071 1231-E1
PARKCREST LN
9800 SD 92124 1249-F1
PARKCREST WY
5200 SD 92124 1249-F1
PARKDALE AV
9800 SD 92126 1209-A4
PARKDALE CIR
7600 SD 92126 1209-A4
PARKDALE CT
7700 SD 92126 1209-A3
PARKDALE CV
7700 SD 92126 1209-A4
PARK DALE LN
1800 ENCT 92024 1147-H6
PARKDALE PL
7700 SD 92126 1209-A4
PARKER LN
1600 SDCo 92065 1152-F7
PARKER PL
1000 VSTA 92084 1087-J6
1000 VSTA 92084 1088-A6
1200 SD 92109 1247-J7
PARKER RD
- ImCo 92243 6560-G1
- SDCo 92055 1085-G1
200 SDCo 91906 430-B10
200 SDCo 91906 (1318-A7 See Page 1298)
1800 ImCo 92243 6500-F5
PARKER ST
600 OCN 92057 1067-A5
E PARKER ST
5100 OCN 92057 1067-A5
PARKER MOUNTAIN RD
- CHV 91913 1311-E7
PARKETT LN
300 ELCJ 92020 1251-G5
PARK GROVE CT
7000 LMGR 91945 1290-F1
PARK HAVEN CT
4000 SD 92113 1289-H4
PARK HILL DR
900 ESCN 92025 1130-A3
PARK HILL LN
1000 ESCN 92025 1130-B4
1000 SDCo 92025 1130-B4
PARK HILL PL
- SDCo 92081 1107-H3
PARK HILL RD
- SDCo 92081 1107-H3
2000 VSTA 92081 1107-H3
PARK HILL TER
1000 ESCN 92025 1130-B3
PARKHURST SQ
- SD 92130 1208-B2
PARKLAND WY
1500 SD 92114 1290-E5
PARKLAWN DR
1600 SDCo 92021 1251-G1
PARK LILAC LN
11600 SDCo 92082 1049-H7
PARKMEAD CT
5800 SD 92114 1290-C5
PARK MEADOWS RD
1000 CHV 91915 1311-H5
PARK MESA WY
6900 SD 92111 1248-J6
PARKPLACE CT
- SD 92123 1249-C2
PARK PLAZA DR
9000 LMSA 91942 1251-A6
PARK RANCH PL
300 ESCN 92025 1150-B1
PARK RIDGE BLVD
6300 SD 91942 1250-E6
6300 SD 92120 1250-E6
6400 SD 92119 1250-E6
PARK RIDGE DR
- SDCo 92025 1130-D7
PARK RIM CT
3300 SD 92117 1228-D7
PARK RIM DR
4900 SD 92117 1228-D7
PARK RUN RD
8500 SD 92129 1189-C5
PARKS AV
4200 LMSA 91941 1270-G3
PARKSIDE AV
6000 SD 92139 1310-F1
PARKSIDE CRES
- SD 92127 1169-B3
PARKSIDE CT
400 CHV 91910 1310-G5
7000 SD 92139 1310-F1
PARKSIDE DR
400 OCN 92054 1086-E3
500 CHV 91910 1310-G5
PARKSIDE GN
200 ESCN 92026 1109-G5
PARKSIDE PL
200 SNTE 92071 1231-C5
3000 SD 92139 1310-E2
4100 CRLB 92008 1106-G6
PARKSIDE ST
12300 SDCo 92040 1232-A3
PARK TERRACE DR
9700 SNTE 92071 1231-D4
PARKTREE LN
2100 ESCN 92026 1109-H4
PARK VALLEY LN
1900 SD 92114 1290-F6
PARK VIEW CT
7300 SNTE 92071 1230-F7
PARKVIEW DR
- OCN 92057 1067-B4
1500 VSTA 92081 1107-H5
5400 SD 92037 1248-A3
PARK VIEW PL
1500 CORD 92118 1288-J7
PARKVIEW TER
1900 SD 92037 1248-A3
PARK VILLA DR
3500 SD 92104 1269-D6
PARK VILLA PL
900 ESCN 92025 1130-A3

STREET
Block City ZIP Pg-Grid

PARK VILLAGE RD
7100 SD 92129 1188-J7
7300 SD 92129 1189-B6
PARK VISTA CT
6900 SD 92114 1290-F6
PARKWAY DR
6800 LMSA 91942 1250-J7
7000 LMSA 91942 1270-H1
PARKWAY PZ
600 ELCJ 92020 1251-E4
PARKWAY CENTRE DR
12200 PWY 92064 1190-F7
PARK WEST AV
5000 SD 92117 1228-D7
PARK WEST LN
3400 SD 92117 1228-D7
PARKWOOD AV
- SDCo 92081 1108-B6
- VSTA 92081 1108-B6
PARKWOOD DR
500 SD 92139 1290-G6
10600 SD 92126 1209-E3
PARKWOOD LN
- OCN 92054 1106-C1
400 ENCT 92024 1147-B2
PARKYNS AV
1000 ImCo 92249 6560-B7
1000 ImCo 92249 6620-C1
PARLANGE PL
17600 SD 92128 1170-B1
PARLIAMENT RD
1800 ENCT 92024 1146-J2
PARMA CT
12500 SD 92128 1170-C2
PARMA LN
7600 SD 92126 1209-A3
PARNASSUS CIR
100 OCN 92054 1086-E6
PARRISH LN
300 DLMR 92014 1187-F5
PARROLETTE CT
- OCN 92057 1067-B3
PARROT ST
1500 SD 92105 1289-G1
PARROT MOUNTAIN RD
36700 SDCo 92066 409-L9
PARSLEY WY
800 OCN 92057 1086-H5
PARSONS LN
400 SMCS 92069 1109-A2
PARSONS LNDG
- SD 92154 1330-J7
PARTHENON DR
2600 SD 92139 1310-F1
PARTOW WY
4600 OCN 92056 1087-B4
PARTRIDGE AV
1300 ELCJ 92020 1251-D3
PARTRIDGE CIR
400 VSTA 92083 1087-G5
PARTRIDGE CT
1000 SMCS 92078 1128-H5
PARTRIDGE GN
1300 ESCN 92029 1129-G5
PARTRIDGE LN
1300 OCN 92054 1086-E7
PARTRIDGE PL
7000 CRLB 92011 1127-D6
PARUS PT
9300 SD 92129 1189-D6
PAR VALLEY DR
28500 SDCo 92069 1088-E1
28500 SDCo 92084 1088-E1
PARVENU LN
1500 SDCo 92028 1027-H5
PAR VIEW CT
28100 SDCo 92026 1089-F3
PARVO CT
18100 SD 92128 1150-B7
PASADENA AV
4200 LMSA 91941 1270-H3
N PASADENA AV
100 SDCo 92028 1027-F2
S PASADENA AV
100 SDCo 92028 1027-F2
PASADERO DR
1100 ESCN 92029 1129-F5
PASATIEMPO AV
6100 SD 92120 1250-D6
PASATIEMPO DR
100 SDCo 92065 1152-J5
PASATIEMPO GN
2500 ESCN 92025 1130-B7
2700 ESCN 92025 1150-B1
PASCAL CT
5900 CRLB 92008 1127-D2
PASCAL DR
1400 CHV 91913 1311-E7
PASCALI CT
- SMCS 92069 1109-A5
PASCOE ST
1000 SD 92103 1269-B5
PASEO DR
8500 ELCJ 92020 1231-D7
8500 SNTE 92071 1231-D7
PASEO PKWY
11500 SDCo 92040 1231-G3
PASEO ABRAZO
- CRLB 92009 1127-J5
PASEO ACAMPO
2900 CRLB 92009 1127-H2
PASEO ADELANTE
6500 CRLB 92009 1127-J4
PASEO AIROSO
- CRLB 92009 1127-J2
PASEO AJANTA
15300 SD 92129 1169-J6
PASEO ALAMEDA
6000 CRLB 92009 1127-J2
PASEO ALBACETE
11300 SD 92129 1169-J6
PASEO ALDABRA
13800 SD 92129 1189-D3
PASEO ALEGRE
400 SMCS 92069 1109-D7
PASEO ALISO
- CRLB 92009 1147-F3
- ENCT 92024 1147-F3
PASEO ALLEGRIA AV
10600 SDCo 92127 1169-F4
PASEO ALMENDRO
7800 CRLB 92009 1147-H3
PASEO ALMIAR
6100 CRLB 92009 1127-H3
PASEO AL MONTE
7700 SDCo 91962 1237-C6
PASEO ALTA RICO
- CRLB 92009 1127-H3
PASEO ANCHO
3400 CRLB 92009 1147-J4
3400 CRLB 92009 1148-A4
PASEO ARBOLADO
6100 SDCo 92067 1168-D3

PASEO ARRAYAN
8000 CRLB 92009 1147-H3
PASEO ASPADA
6300 CRLB 92009 1127-J4
PASEO AURORA
- SD 92154 1350-G1
PASEO AUSTIN
- IMP 92251 6499-E2
PASEO AVELLANO
8000 CRLB 92009 1147-G3
PASEO BELLO
8700 SNTE 92071 1230-H7
PASEO BONITA
1600 SD 92037 1247-H3
13700 PWY 92064 1190-G6
PASEO BURGA
500 CHV 91910 1310-J5
PASEO CALLADO
6200 CRLB 92009 1127-J3
PASEO CAMAS
6100 CRLB 92009 1127-H3
PASEO CAMINO REAL
- CALX 92231 6680-J1
PASEO CANADA
- SMCS 92078 1129-A2
PASEO CANDELERO
2300 CRLB 92009 1127-G6
PASEO CAPUCHINA
- CRLB 92009 1128-A7
- CRLB 92009 1148-A1
PASEO CARDIEL
13500 SD 92129 1189-F4
PASEO CARRETA
6000 CRLB 92009 1127-J2
PASEO CASTANADA
11000 SDCo 91941 1271-G5
PASEO CAZADOR
2900 CRLB 92009 1127-J4
PASEO CERRO
6300 CRLB 92009 1127-J4
6300 CRLB 92009 1128-A4
PASEO CEVERA
13700 SD 92129 1189-E3
PASEO CIELO
3000 SDCo 92067 1148-A7
PASEO COLINA
- CRLB 92009 1127-H3
12300 PWY 92064 1190-B6
PASEO CORONO
6300 CRLB 92009 1127-J4
PASEO CORTO
- CRLB 92009 1127-J3
PASEO CRESTA
2000 VSTA 92084 1087-G2
9100 SNTE 92071 1231-B7
PASEO CRISTAL
3000 ESCN 92029 1150-A2
PASEO CULZADA
3100 ESCN 92029 1150-A2
PASEO DE ALICIA
3400 OCN 92056 1106-B4
PASEO DE ALTEZA
- CALX 92231 6680-J1
PASEO DE ANZA
2000 VSTA 92084 1087-G2
PASEO DE BRISAS
3400 OCN 92056 1106-B4
PASEO DE CABALLO
- SDCo 92065 1173-H5
PASEO DE COLOMBO
3500 OCN 92056 1106-B4
PASEO DE COLORES
3400 OCN 92056 1106-B4
PASEO DE CONCHO
- SMCS 92078 1129-A2
PASEO DE ELENITA
3500 OCN 92056 1106-B4
PASEO DE FRANCISCO
3500 OCN 92056 1106-B4
PASEO DE LA FRONTERA
- SD 92154 1352-A4
PASEO DE LA FUENTE
- SD 92154 1351-J3
- SDCo 92154 1352-D1
PASEO DE LA FUENTE NORTE
- SD 92154 1351-H3
PASEO DE LA HUERTA
13600 PWY 92064 1170-F6
PASEO DEL ARQUERO
200 VSTA 92084 1088-A5
PASEO DEL ARROYO
1800 SDCo 92028 1028-A4
15500 PWY 92064 1170-F6
PASEO DE LAS AMERICAS
2100 SD 92154 1352-A3
PASEO DE LAS BRISAS
16600 SDCo 92065 1171-F2
PASEO DE LAS CUMBRES
13700 PWY 92064 1170-F6
PASEO DE LAS FLORES
- DLMR 92014 1187-F4
- ENCT 92024 1147-E4
PASEO DE LAS VERDES
- ENCT 92024 1147-E6
PASEO DE LAURA
2300 OCN 92056 1106-H2
PASEO DE LA VISTA
4000 SDCo 91902 1310-G1
PASEO DEL BIANCO
- SDCo 92025 1130-E7
PASEO DEL BOSQUE
500 VSTA 92081 1107-J2
PASEO DEL CAMPO
3200 SDCo 91978 1272-C7
PASEO DEL CERRO
1100 CHV 91910 1311-A7
PASEO DEL CONQUISTADOR
- CALX 92231 6680-J1
PASEO DEL EMPERADOR
- CALX 92231 6680-J1
PASEO DELICIAS
7000 SDCo 92067 1168-F1
PASEO DELICIAS Rt#-S6
6200 SDCo 92067 1168-F2
PASEO DELICIAS Rt#-S8
6100 SDCo 92067 1168-E2
PASEO DE LINDA
- SDCo 92127 1169-F2
PASEO DEL LAGO
1100 SDCo 92028 1047-H3
6300 CRLB 92011 1127-C4
PASEO DEL LAGO DR
1800 VSTA 92081 1107-G5
PASEO DEL MAR
13500 SDCo 92021 1232-E7
PASEO DEL NORTE
1000 CHV 91910 1311-A7

PASEO DEL NORTE
5400 CRLB 92008 1126-H4
6000 CRLB 92011 1126-H4
6600 CRLB 92011 1127-A6
PASEO DEL OCASO
7900 SD 92037 1227-H5
PASEO DE LOS AMERICANOS
3500 OCN 92056 1106-B4
PASEO DE LOS ARBOLES
1800 SDCo 92028 1028-A4
PASEO DE LOS CALIFORNIANOS
3500 OCN 92056 1106-B4
PASEO DE LOS CASTILLOS
- SNTE 92071 1251-C1
PASEO DE LOS PEREGRINOS
- SDCo 92082 1089-J2
PASEO DE LOS PEREGRINOS DR
- SDCo 92082 1089-J1
PASEO DE LOS REYES
- CALX 92231 6680-J1
PASEO DE LOS SUENOS
- SDCo 92067 1149-B3
PASEO DE LOS VIRREYES
- CALX 92231 6680-H1
PASEO DEL PASO
900 CHV 91910 1311-A7
900 CHV 91910 1330-J1
900 CHV 91910 1331-A1
PASEO DEL REY
600 CHV 91910 1310-H6
600 CHV 91910 1330-H1
1900 VSTA 92084 1087-G2
8600 SNTE 92071 1231-B7
PASEO DEL SOL
1900 VSTA 92084 1087-G2
2900 SDCo 92025 1130-E7
2900 SDCo 92025 1150-E1
8500 SNTE 92071 1231-B7
PASEO DEL SUR
- SD 92127 1169-B3
PASEO DEL TORRENO
29300 SDCo 91962 1237-D6
PASEO DEL VERANO
12500 SD 92128 1170-D1
PASEO DEL VERANO NORTE
12000 SD 92128 1150-C7
13000 SD 92128 1170-D1
PASEO DEL VISTA
6700 CRLB 92009 1128-A5
PASEO DE MAJESTAD
- CALX 92231 6680-J1
PASEO DE MARGUERITA
9100 SNTE 92071 1231-B7
PASEO DE OCHO MINOS
12600 SDCo 92064 1191-D6
12600 SDCo 92071 1191-D6
PASEO DE OLIVOS
3600 SDCo 92028 1047-H4
PASEO DE PIEDRAS
17300 SDCo 92127 1169-D1
PASEO DE SANTOS
9900 SDCo 92026 1089-E2
PASEO DESCANSO
6300 CRLB 92009 1127-J3
6300 CRLB 92009 1128-A4
PASEO DOMINGUEZ
6500 CRLB 92009 1127-J5
PASEO DONITO
2100 SDCo 91901 1234-D7
PASEO DORADO
- SMCS 92078 1129-A2
1900 SD 92037 1227-G5
PASEO ELEGANCIA
- CRLB 92009 1127-H3
PASEO ENCANTADA
7700 SDCo 91962 1237-D6
PASEO ENSILLAR
6100 CRLB 92009 1127-H3
PASEO ENTRADA
900 CHV 91910 1330-J1
900 CHV 91910 1331-A1
1000 CHV 91910 1311-A7
PASEO ESCUELA
- CRLB 92009 1127-H3
PASEO ESMERADO
- CRLB 92009 1148-A4
PASEO ESPLANADA
- SDCo 92067 1148-J4
- SDCo 92067 1149-A3
PASEO ESTABLO
6300 CRLB 92009 1127-H4
PASEO ESTRIBO
- CRLB 92009 1127-H3
PASEO FRATERNIDAD
1800 SD 92173 1350-F3
PASEO FRONTERA
6500 CRLB 92009 1127-J5
PASEO FUERTE
11900 SDCo 92020 1271-J3
PASEO GRANDE
2100 SDCo 92019 1272-C1
PASEO GRANDE RD
- SDCo 92003 1068-C5
- SDCo 92084 1068-C5
PASEO GRANITO
6100 CRLB 92009 1127-H3
PASEO HERMOSA
- CRLB 92009 1127-H2
1200 OCN 92056 1087-D2
17100 SDCo 92067 1168-G5
PASEO HERMOSO
15700 PWY 92064 1170-E5
PASEO IGLESIA
8400 SDCo 91977 1290-J5
PASEO JAQUITA
- CRLB 92009 1127-H3
PASEO JENGHIZ
15500 SD 92129 1169-J6
PASEO LA CRESTA
900 CHV 91910 1330-J1
900 CHV 91910 1331-A1
PASEO LADERA
900 CHV 91910 1310-J7
900 CHV 91910 1330-J1
1200 CHV 91911 1330-J2
2000 VSTA 92084 1087-G2
8600 SNTE 92071 1231-B7
8600 SNTE 92071 1251-B1
PASEO LADERA S
- CHV 91911 1330-J2
- CHV 91911 1331-A2
PASEO LAGO
11500 SDCo 92040 1231-H3
PASEO LA JOLLA
- CRLB 92009 1147-J2

PASEO LAREDO
6800 SD 92037 1247-H1
PASEO LAZO
6400 CRLB 92009 1127-H4
PASEO LINDO
31800 SDCo 92003 1067-G1
PASEO LOS GATOS
2300 CHV 91914 1311-F1
PASEO LOUISIANA
- SD 92173 1350-H5
PASEO LUCIDO
11800 SD 92128 1170-B4
PASEO LUNADA
- CRLB 92009 1127-H4
PASEO LUPINO
- CRLB 92009 1148-A1
PASEO MAGDA
1200 CHV 91910 1311-A6
PASEO MARGUERITA
- VSTA 92084 1087-G2
1100 CHV 91910 1310-J7
1100 CHV 91910 1330-J1
PASEO MEMBRILLO
7900 CRLB 92009 1147-H3
PASEO MIRADA
2600 SD 92037 1248-A2
PASEO MONONA
6000 CRLB 92009 1127-J2
PASEO MONTALBAN
9300 SD 92129 1189-E4
PASEO MONTANAS
4100 SD 92130 1188-B6
PASEO MONTANOSO
11200 SD 92127 1169-H6
PASEO MONTE
2400 SDCo 92028 1047-H3
PASEO MONTE BATALLA
12200 SD 92128 1150-B5
PASEO MONTENERO
- SD 92127 1169-C3
PASEO MONTRIL
9500 SD 92129 1189-F5
PASEO ORION
- SD 92154 1350-G1
PASEO OROZCO
3700 SDCo 91941 1271-G5
PASEO PACIFICA
300 ENCT 92024 1147-C7
PASEO PALERO
6100 CRLB 92009 1127-J3
PASEO PALMAS DR
10100 SDCo 92040 1231-H3
PASEO PALMAS WY
10300 SDCo 92040 1231-H3
PASEO PANTERA
200 SDCo 92065 1153-C5
PASEO PARK DR
10200 SDCo 92040 1231-H3
PASEO PENASCO
15300 SDCo 92025 1151-A2
PASEO PICADOR
6100 CRLB 92009 1127-H3
PASEO PIEDRAS
19200 SDCo 92067 1149-A3
PASEO PORTRERO
6300 CRLB 92009 1127-J4
PASEO POTRIL
2700 SDCo 91902 1290-J7
PASEO PRADERA
6000 CRLB 92009 1127-J2
PASEO PRIMAVERA
1100 CHV 91910 1311-A7
1100 CHV 91910 1331-A1
PASEO PRIVADO
6100 CRLB 92009 1127-J3
6100 CRLB 92009 1128-A3
PASEO RANCHERO
800 CHV 91910 1311-A6
1100 CHV 91910 1331-A1
PASEO RIO
600 VSTA 92081 1107-E1
PASEO ROBLES RD
29400 SDCo 92082 1070-J5
PASEO ROSAL
500 CHV 91910 1310-J5
PASEO SALAMONER
3500 SDCo 91941 1271-G5
PASEO SALIDA GN
1500 ESCN 92025 1130-A4
PASEO SALINERO
6000 CRLB 92009 1127-H3
PASEO SARINA
1100 CHV 91910 1311-A7
1100 CHV 91910 1331-A1
PASEO SAUCEDAL
- CRLB 92009 1147-G2
PASEO SEQUIEROS
3900 SDCo 91941 1271-G4
PASEO SIEMBRA
- SDCo 92003 1067-G1
PASEO SIERRA
1100 CHV 91910 1311-A7
PASEO SONORA GN
1500 ESCN 92025 1130-A4
PASEO TAMARINDO
- CRLB 92009 1148-A2
PASEO TAMAYO
3900 SDCo 91941 1271-H4
PASEO TAPAJOS
- CRLB 92009 1127-J3
PASEO TAXCO
8100 CRLB 92009 1147-J4
PASEO TEMPORADA
9500 SD 92129 1189-E4
PASEO TENIS
16100 SDCo 92067 1168-G7
PASEO TESORO
6100 CRLB 92009 1127-J2
PASEO TIEMPO GN
1500 ESCN 92025 1130-A4
PASEO TIENDA
6100 CRLB 92009 1127-J3
PASEO TIERRA
- SMCS 92078 1129-A2
PASEO TULIPERO
- CRLB 92009 1147-F3
PASEO VALENCIA
16000 SDCo 92067 1168-F7
16100 SDCo 92067 1188-G1
PASEO VALIENTE
6100 CRLB 92009 1127-J2
PASEO VALINDO
- CRLB 92009 1127-J2
PASEO VALLA
6100 CRLB 92009 1127-H3
PASEO VALLE ALTO
15500 PWY 92064 1170-F6
PASEO VERACRUZ
2300 CHV 91914 1311-E2
PASEO VERDE
- SD 92129 1189-A3
1100 CHV 91910 1331-A1
7300 CRLB 92009 1127-J7

PASEO VICTORIA
18200 SDCo 92067 1148-D7
PASEO VISTA
11500 SDCo 92040 1231-H3
PASEO VISTA FAMOSA
3700 SDCo 92091 1168-C7
PASEO VOLANTE
- CRLB 92009 1127-J2
PASEO VUELO
6400 CRLB 92009 1127-J4
PASEO ZALDIVAR
13800 SD 92129 1189-E3
PASEO ZUNIGA
3900 SDCo 91941 1271-G4
PASITA DE KRISTY
10900 SDCo 92040 1231-F3
PASO ALTO CT
2600 SDCo 91905 (1299-J3 See Page 1298)
PASO DE FLORA
- SDCo 92026 1069-D3
PASO DEL LAGOS
4000 SDCo 92003 1067-F2
PASO DEL NORTE
300 SDCo 92026 1109-G2
PASO DEL SOL
15000 SDCo 92014 1168-A7
PASO ORO VERDE
3900 SDCo 92028 997-G4
PASO ROBLES CT
2400 CHV 91914 1311-F3
29300 SDCo 92082 1070-J6
PASO ROBLES LN
- SDCo 92082 1070-J5
PASO ROBLES PL
15400 SDCo 92082 1070-J5
PASO ROBLES RD
29100 SDCo 92082 1070-J5
29100 SDCo 92082 1071-A6
PASO VERDE
3900 SDCo 92028 997-G4
PASQUAL HIGHLANDS RD
19900 SDCo 92065 1152-D2
PASSERINE WY
10600 SD 92121 1208-E4
PASSIFLORA AV
700 ENCT 92024 1147-D4
PASSIFLORA PL
800 ENCT 92024 1147-D4
PASSING LN
200 SDCo 92065 1153-C5
PASSION PL
- SDCo 92065 1152-G6
PASSY AV
2800 SD 92122 1228-B6
PASTEL CT
4800 OCN 92057 1087-C1
PASTEL GN
- ESCN 92029 1129-G5
PASTERNACK PL
3200 SD 92123 1249-D5
PASTEUR CT
2000 CRLB 92008 1127-C2
PASTORAL RD
12000 SD 92128 1170-B3
PASTORAL WY
1700 SDCo 92078 1128-B2
PAT ST
7900 LMSA 91942 1250-H6
PATA RANCH RD
13700 SDCo 92040 1212-F3
PATA VIEW DR
15300 SDCo 92040 1212-H6
PATE DR
- SDCo 92672 1023-D2
PATERO CT
1400 LMGR 91945 1290-F2
PATHFINDER WY
5900 SDCo 91902 1311-B2
PATHOS CT
8400 SD 92129 1189-C6
PATHOS LN
12300 SD 92129 1189-C6
PATHWAY ST
9500 SNTE 92071 1231-C7
PATIENCES PL
3200 OCN 92056 1067-D7
PATINA CT
4800 OCN 92057 1087-B1
10900 SD 92131 1210-A2
PATINA ST
- SDCo 92127 1169-F3
PATMOS WY
6000 OCN 92056 1107-F5
PATOS PL
500 CHV 91910 1311-B4
PATRA WY
5000 OCN 92056 1107-E4
PATRIA DR
4500 SD 92115 1270-D3
PATRICIA AV
300 CHV 91910 1310-C6
PATRICIA CIR
1100 VSTA 92084 1088-A7
PATRICIA CT
8700 SNTE 92071 1231-E7
PATRICIA LN
300 ELCJ 92020 1251-E6
600 VSTA 92084 1088-A7
PATRICIA PL
4600 SD 92115 1269-J3
PATRICIA RD
36400 SDCo 92082 1050-D5
PATRICK DR
200 SDCo 92019 1253-D1
PATRICK WY
- SDCo 92082 1049-F7
- SDCo 92082 1069-F1
PATRIOT ST
10200 SD 92124 1249-G5
PATTEN ST
300 SD 92114 1290-D4
PATTERSON RD
- SD 92152 1287-J5
2300 ESCN 92027 1130-D1
PATTI DR
300 VSTA 92084 1087-H3
PATTON OAK RD
200 SDCo 92028 997-F7
200 SDCo 92028 1027-F1
PATTY LN
300 ENCT 92024 1147-B3
PATTY HILL DR
200 SOLB 92075 1167-E6
PATTY LOU DR
10100 SDCo 92040 1232-B3
PAUL ST
600 ESCN 92027 1130-C2
PAUL WY
1000 ESCN 92027 1130-C2
PAULA DR
- ESCN 92026 1109-G6
- SDCo 92026 1109-G6

PAULA ST
800 ESCN 92027 1110-C6
3800 LMSA 91941 1270-F5
PAULA WY
1000 ESCN 92027 1110-B5
PAULANN CT
- SDCo 92028 1027-G4
PAUL BARWICK CT
11200 SD 92126 1208-J2
PAULIN AV
- ImCo 92249 6560-B7
- ImCo 92249 6620-G7
100 CALX 92231 6620-G7
200 CALX 92231 6680-G1
PAULINA TER
16500 PWY 92064 1170-D4
PAULINE AV
400 ELCJ 92020 1251-G6
PAULINE WY
2700 OCN 92056 1087-B7
PAULING AV
4500 SD 92122 1228-F4
PAUL JONES AV
3500 SD 92117 1248-D5
PAULSEN AV
700 ELCJ 92020 1251-E7
E PAULY DR
- SD 92102 1289-G3
W PAULY DR
- SD 92102 1289-G3
PAUMA PL
300 ESCN 92029 1129-F3
PAUMA ST
- SDCo 92055 1085-J4
- SDCo 92055 1086-A4
PAUMA ALTO DR
14200 SDCo 92082 1050-G7
14200 SDCo 92082 1070-G1
PAUMA HEIGHTS LN
31600 SDCo 92082 1070-J1
PAUMA HEIGHTS RD
30200 SDCo 92082 1070-F1
31100 SDCo 92082 1071-A1
31300 SDCo 92082 1051-A7
32100 SDCo 92061 1050-J5
32100 SDCo 92082 1050-J5
PAUMA RANCH RD
31600 SDCo 92061 1051-H7
PAUMA RESERVATION RD
- SDCo 92061 1031-B7
- SDCo 92061 1051-A1
14600 SDCo 92061 1050-H2
PAUMA RIDGE CIR
- SDCo 92059 1050-F1
PAUMA RIDGE RD
- SDCo 92059 1050-E1
34400 SDCo 92059 1030-F7
PAUMA VALLEY DR
32300 SDCo 92061 1051-A6
32500 SDCo 92061 1050-H5
PAUMA VIEW DR
- SDCo 92082 1070-J1
14400 SDCo 92082 1050-H6
31100 SDCo 92061 1050-H6
PAUMA VISTA DR
13700 SDCo 92082 1050-E6
PAUNACK ST
300 NATC 92136 1289-G7
300 NATC 92136 1309-G1
PAVLOV AV
4200 SD 92122 1228-E5
PAVO REAL DR
3900 SD 92124 1250-A3
PAWNEE DR
5800 LMSA 91942 1250-G7
PAWNEE GN
500 ESCN 92025 1130-A6
PAWNEE ST
100 SMCS 92078 1108-D7
PAXTON CT
2800 SD 92154 1350-C1
PAXTON DR
1100 SD 92154 1350-C1
PAXTON WY
- ENCT 92024 1147-A2
PAYMASTER RD
10200 SDCo 92082 1069-E4
PAYMOGO CT
11300 SD 92129 1169-H6
PAYMOGO ST
15500 SD 92129 1169-H6
PAYNE RD
- ImCo 92251 430-L4
- ImCo 92259 430-L4
PAYNE ST
100 SD 92113 1289-F4
PAYSON DR
2700 SDCo 92036 1136-A7
2800 SDCo 92036 1135-J6
PAYSON RD
4000 LMSA 91941 1270-J4
PEABODY WY
- CHV 91913 1331-E3
PEACEFUL CT
- SD 92173 1350-E3
10100 SNTE 92071 1231-D4
PEACEFUL DR
9800 SNTE 92071 1231-D4
PEACEFUL LN
400 VSTA 92083 1087-D7
700 ESCN 92026 1109-J7
PEACEFUL PL
1300 SDCo 91901 1233-J6
PEACEFUL VALLEY RANCH RD
14000 SDCo 91935 1292-J3
PEACE VALLEY LN
16600 SDCo 92065 1171-H3
PEACH AV
900 ELCJ 92021 1251-H4
1300 ELCJ 92021 1252-A4
PEACH CT
900 ELCJ 92021 1251-H4
PEACH WY
- SD 92130 1188-G4
500 SMCS 92069 1108-J5
900 ESCN 92026 1109-H6
PEACH BLOSSOM ST
3600 NATC 91950 1290-C6
PEACH GROVE LN
1200 VSTA 92084 1088-A6
PEACH POINT AV
7900 SD 92126 1209-B3
PEACHTREE CIR
2200 CHV 91915 1311-F5
PEACHTREE CT
- SMCS 92078 1128-G2
PEACH TREE LN
2200 SDCo 91977 1271-E7
PEACHTREE LN
14100 PWY 92064 1190-F2
PEACH TREE RD
6900 CRLB 92011 1127-A6

PEACH TREE WY
3400 OCN 92054 1086-F2
PEACHWOOD CT
12600 PWY 92064 1190-C1
PEACHWOOD DR
1300 ENCT 92024 1167-F1
PEACOCK BLVD
1300 OCN 92056 1087-D4
PEACOCK DR
7700 SD 92123 1249-B7
PEACOCK VALLEY RD
2300 CHV 91915 1311-H7
PEAK CT
4500 SDCo 91941 1271-E3
PEAR LN
- SDCo 92026 1089-B2
PEAR ST
900 ELCJ 92021 1251-H2
PEAR BLOSSOM AV
800 OCN 92057 1086-F5
PEAR BLOSSOM CIR
600 OCN 92057 1086-F5
PEAR BLOSSOM CT
- CHV 91915 1331-G1
PEAR BLOSSOM DR
600 OCN 92057 1086-F5
PEAR BLOSSOM PL
400 ESCN 92026 1109-H7
PEARCE GROVE DR
300 ENCT 92024 1147-B3
PEARL AV
1200 ESCN 92027 1110-A7
PEARL LN
500 SD 92173 1350-E3
3200 OCN 92056 1107-A2
PEARL PL
800 ELCJ 92020 1251-F7
1400 ESCN 92027 1110-A7
2900 CRLB 92009 1127-H5
PEARL ST
400 SD 92037 1227-E7
PEARLBUSH CT
1200 SDCo 92019 1252-E7
PEARLEAF CT
- SMCS 92078 1128-H3
PEARL HEIGHTS RD
1500 VSTA 92081 1107-H6
PEARL LAKE AV
6200 SD 92119 1250-H6
PEARLMAN WY
4900 SD 92130 1188-D5
PEARLWOOD RD
9400 SNTE 92071 1231-B4
PEARLWOOD ST
300 CHV 91911 1330-G3
PEARMAN LN
1000 SDCo 92065 1172-H1
PEARSON DR
4900 SD 92115 1270-D2
PEARSON ST
7100 LMSA 91941 1270-F5
PEARSON SPRINGS CT
1300 CHV 91913 1331-B2
PEARTREE CT
400 ENCT 92024 1147-G7
PEAR TREE DR
6800 CRLB 92011 1127-A5
PEAR TREE LN
700 OCN 92057 1086-G5
PEAR TREE PL
400 ESCN 92026 1109-J7
PEARTREE TER
12700 PWY 92064 1190-C1
PEARWOOD DR
700 OCN 92057 1086-G5
800 OCN 92056 1086-G5
PEBBLE CT
800 ELCJ 92019 1252-B7
PEBBLE PL
800 ELCJ 92019 1252-B7
PEBBLE ST
- CRLB 92010 1107-B4
PEBBLE BEACH CT
8900 SNTE 92071 1230-J4
PEBBLE BEACH DR
700 SMCS 92069 1108-J4
4400 OCN 92057 1066-H7
9300 SNTE 92071 1231-A6
9700 SNTE 92071 1230-J3
PEBBLE BEACH WY
- SDCo 92082 1090-F5
PEBBLEBROOK LN
14000 SD 92128 1189-J2
PEBBLEBROOK PL
1900 CHV 91913 1311-D4
PEBBLEBROOK WY
14100 SD 92128 1189-J2
PEBBLE CANYON DR
14400 PWY 92064 1190-H1
PEBBLE CREEK LN
10000 SDCo 92021 1232-G1
PEBBLE SPRINGS LN
1100 SDCo 92026 1109-E7
PEBBLESTONE LN
9200 SD 92126 1209-D2
PEBBLESTONE PL
400 SNTE 92071 1231-C5
PECAN CT
1800 VSTA 92083 1108-B3
PECAN PL
1200 CHV 91911 1330-G2
3000 ESCN 92027 1110-E6
PECAN TER
14100 SDCo 92021 1232-G6
PECAN PARK LN
13900 SDCo 92021 1232-G5
PECAN PEAK
14200 SDCo 92021 1232-G5
PECAN VALLEY DR
8700 SNTE 92071 1230-J4
PECK
- SDCo 92672 1023-E2
PECKHAM PL
1200 ENCT 92024 1147-H7
1200 ENCT 92024 1167-H1
PECOS DR
3800 SDCo 92004 (1099-D2 See Page 1098)
PECOS ST
600 SDCo 91977 1291-C3
PEDRAGAL DR
500 OCN 92054 1086-G1
PEDREGAL DR
1500 ESCN 92025 1130-B4
PEDRIZA RD
12600 PWY 92064 1170-C5
PEERLESS DR
1200 ELCJ 92021 1252-A2
1200 SDCo 92021 1252-A2
PEET LN
2300 ESCN 92025 1130-C7
2300 SDCo 92025 1130-C7
2700 ESCN 92025 1150-C1

SAN DIEGO CO.

STREET Block City ZIP Pg-Grid

PEET PL
- ESCN 92025 1130-C7
PEG CT
4200 SD 92154 1350-G1
PEGASO ST
1400 ENCT 92024 1167-G1
PEGASUS AV
10900 SD 92126 1209-D1
PEGASUS WY
- SMCS 92069 1108-D5
PEGEEN PL
11300 SDCo 92021 1251-G1
PEGGY DR
700 SD 92114 1290-G3
PEG LEG RD Rt#-S22
1300 SDCo 92004 (1059-J5 See Page 1058)
1300 SDCo 92004 (1079-J1 See Page 1058)
PEG LEG MINE RD
3100 SDCo 91935 1272-J7
PEINADO WY
6400 SD 92121 1208-G3
PELICAN ST
- CRLB 92011 1127-B7
PELICAN WY
700 ELCJ 92020 1251-E7
PELICAN HILL RD
1900 SD 92139 1290-D7
PELICAN POINT CT
1600 CHV 91911 1330-J4
PELL PL
3300 SD 92130 1188-A6
PELLET RD
- ImCo 92227 411-A11
- ImCo 92227 431-A1
PELTON CT
8900 SD 92126 1209-D2
PELUSA ST
5000 SD 92113 1290-A6
PEMBER AV
- CHV 91913 1331-E2
PEMBRIDGE LN
7000 SD 92139 1290-F7
PEMBROKE DR
6100 SD 92115 1270-C2
PENANOVA ST
11300 SD 92129 1169-H6
PENARA CT
7100 SD 92126 1208-J4
PENARA PL
7300 SD 92126 1208-J4
PENARA ST
10600 SD 92126 1208-J4
PENASCO RD
1500 SDCo 92019 1272-A1
PENASQUITOS CT
14700 SD 92129 1189-H1
PENASQUITOS DR
14300 SD 92129 1189-H1
14800 SD 92129 1169-H7
PENCE DR
2200 SDCo 92019 1252-D7
PENDIENTE CT
3800 SD 92124 1250-A3
PENDLETON DR
- SD 92140 1268-E6
PENDLETON RD
1500 CORD 92118 1288-J6
PENDLETON ST
4500 SD 92109 1248-B3
PENDON CT
7700 CRLB 92009 1147-F2
PENDRAGON RD
15400 SDCo 92064 1191-C5
PENELOPE DR
600 CHV 91910 1310-D7
PENFIELD PT
13500 SD 92130 1188-D4
PENFORD CT
14400 SD 92129 1189-C1
PENGUIN CIR
900 VSTA 92083 1087-G5
PENINA ST
13600 PWY 92064 1170-E1
PENINSULA DR
- CRLB 92010 1107-B4
PENKEA DR
2700 OCN 92054 1086-D6
PENMAR RD
9200 SNTE 92071 1231-A3
PENN ST
100 SDCo 92065 1152-J3
400 SDCo 92065 1153-A3
PENNACOOK CT
17700 SD 92127 1169-H1
PENNANT WY
2900 SD 92122 1228-C6
PENNINGTON LN
2500 SD 92139 1290-F7
PENNSYLVANIA AV
- ELCJ 92020 1251-A1
100 ESCN 92025 1129-J2
100 SD 92103 1269-B6
E PENNSYLVANIA AV
500 ESCN 92025 1130-A2
1200 ESCN 92027 1130-A2
W PENNSYLVANIA AV
100 SD 92103 1269-A6
300 SD 92103 1268-J6
PENNSYLVANIA LN
5300 LMSA 91942 1270-E1
5300 LMSA 92120 1270-E1
PENNY LN
- SD 92127 1169-B3
PENNY PL
5300 SD 92115 1270-A2
PENNYROYAL WY
300 OCN 92057 1086-J2
PENNYWOOD RD
9200 SNTE 92071 1231-A4
PENRIDGE ST
10500 SD 92126 1208-J4
PENROD CT
300 VSTA 92083 1087-G4
PENROD LN
10300 SD 92126 1208-J5
PENROSE CT
4800 SD 92110 1248-F7
PENROSE ST
2100 SD 92110 1268-F1
2300 SD 92110 1248-F7
PENSTEMON CT
- SDCo 92036 1175-H4
PENSTEMON LN
- SDCo 92036 1175-H3
PENSTEMON RD
- SDCo 92036 1175-H4
PENTAS CT
1800 CRLB 92011 1127-E6
PENTECOST WY
1600 SD 92105 1290-A2
PENTICTON WY
9000 SD 92126 1209-D2

PENTUCKETT AV
1700 SD 92104 1289-F2
PENVIEW DR
3100 SDCo 92084 1067-J6
PEONY DR
3800 SDCo 92028 1028-F5
PEPITA WY
7500 SD 92037 1227-F7
PEPPER CT
- ELCN 92243 6559-E1
PEPPER DR
100 SD 92173 1350-G4
300 SDCo 92021 1251-F1
300 SNTE 92021 1251-F1
900 ELCJ 92021 1251-F1
1200 ELCN 92243 6559-F1
1300 SDCo 92021 1252-A2
1400 SDCo 92082 1090-B1
1600 ELCJ 92021 1252-A2
4000 SD 92105 1289-G1
4000 SD 92105 1269-H7
PEPPER LN
- SDCo 92672 1023-E2
PEPPER WY
3800 OCN 92057 1086-H4
PEPPERBROOK LN
10500 SD 92131 1210-A3
PEPPERDINE AV
4100 OCN 92056 1087-B5
PEPPERDINE CT
900 CHV 91913 1311-D6
PEPPER GLEN WY
700 CHV 91914 1311-G3
PEPPERGRASS DR
3200 SD 92115 1270-D6
PEPPER HILL DR
1600 ELCJ 92021 1252-B2
1600 SDCo 92021 1252-B2
PEPPERMINT LN
2300 LMGR 91945 1270-E7
2300 LMGR 91945 1290-E1
PEPPERMINT PL
1900 ESCN 92029 1129-E4
PEPPER TREE CT
500 SMCS 92069 1109-D7
PEPPERTREE DR
2700 OCN 92056 1087-E5
PEPPER TREE LN
- SD 92106 1287-J3
100 SDCo 92028 1027-F5
12100 PWY 92064 1190-C6
PEPPERTREE LN
- ENCT 92024 1147-J7
100 ENCT 92024 1167-J1
500 SOLB 92075 1187-F1
1100 SDCo 92084 1108-B2
1100 VSTA 92084 1108-B2
PEPPER TREE PL
1500 SDCo 92028 1027-H5
2100 ESCN 92026 1109-G5
PEPPER TREE RD
- CHV 91910 1310-D6
- SD 91910 1310-D6
PEPPERTREE WY
- CRLB 92009 1127-F3
PEPPER VALLEY LN
1800 SDCo 92021 1252-A1
PEPPERVIEW TER
11200 SD 92131 1210-A2
PEPPER VILLA CT
900 ELCJ 92021 1251-H1
PEPPER VILLA DR
1300 SDCo 92021 1251-H2
1700 ELCJ 92021 1251-H2
PEPPERWOOD CT
500 CHV 91902 1311-C4
PEPPERWOOD DR
1600 SDCo 92021 1251-G1
PEPSI DR
4200 SD 92111 1249-B3
PEQUENA ST
1300 SD 92154 1350-F1
PEQUENITO CT
9300 SDCo 92040 1232-B5
PEQUENO PL
1200 ESCN 92027 1110-A6
PEQUOT DR
13400 PWY 92064 1190-E2
PERA ALTA DR
30000 SDCo 92036 1155-G4
PERALTA DR
35300 SDCo 92086 409-J6
PERCH LN
500 OCN 92054 1086-G2
PERCUSSION CT
2300 SDCo 92019 1252-D6
PERCY CT
12900 SD 92130 1188-B5
PERDIDO PL
3600 SMCS 92078 1108-C7
PERDIZ ST
7300 CRLB 92009 1127-J7
PEREGRINE RD
100 SDCo 92061 1051-C6
PEREZ CT
10200 SD 92124 1229-G7
PEREZ RD
- ImCo 92283 432-D5
PEREZ COVE WY
2200 SD 92109 1268-B3
PERGL ST
2500 LMGR 91945 1270-F7
PERIDOT CT
- CALX 92231 6620-J7
- CRLB 92009 1127-F5
PERIQUE ST
6200 SD 92115 1270-D5
PERIQUITO CT
1800 VSTA 92081 1107-H5
PERIWINKLE ST
700 ENCT 92024 1147-E6
PERIWINKLE WY
4000 OCN 92057 1086-J4
PERKINS DR
1400 CHV 91911 1330-J2
PERKON CT
2500 SD 92105 1270-A7
PERKON PL
4900 SD 92105 1270-A7
PERLA CT
12500 SD 92128 1170-C2
PERLAS CT
1300 CHV 91910 1311-A4
PERRIN PL
- CHV 91913 1331-E2
PERRY AV
- CALX 92231 6680-G1
2000 CALX 92231 6620-G6
PERRY RD
- CALX 92231 6620-G7
- SD 92106 1268-D7
PERRY ST
2800 SD 92106 1288-A3

PERSA ST
6500 CRLB 92009 1127-G5
PERSEUS RD
8600 SD 92126 1209-C2
PERSHING AV
3400 SD 92104 1269-D6
PERSHING DR
- SD 92102 1289-C2
1200 SD 92101 1289-C2
1900 SD 92101 1269-D7
PERSIMMON AV
1100 SDCo 92021 1251-H3
1200 ELCJ 92021 1251-H3
PERSIMMON CT
- CHV 91915 1311-H1
1100 SDCo 92021 1251-J3
PERSIMMON LN
30600 SDCo 92082 1070-H4
PERSIMMON WY
600 OCN 92054 1086-F2
1200 SDCo 92021 1251-J3
PERTH PL
6500 SD 92139 1310-E1
PERU PL
5500 SD 92105 1290-B1
PESCA CT
400 SDCo 91977 1291-C4
PESCADERO AV
4300 SD 92107 1287-J1
4500 SD 92107 1267-J7
PESCADERO DR
1400 SD 92107 1267-H7
PESCADERO POINT CT
1600 CHV 91911 1330-J4
PESCADO PL
400 ENCT 92024 1147-C7
PESOS PL
10800 SD 92124 1249-H1
PETAL DR
1500 SD 92114 1290-D6
PETALO PZ
1000 CHV 91910 1311-C2
PETALUMA DR
- CHV 91913 1311-E6
PETENWELL RD
11500 SD 92131 1209-H1
PETEO CT
400 CHV 91911 1330-B2
PETERLYNN CT
4000 SD 92154 1350-F1
PETERLYNN DR
1000 SD 92154 1330-F7
1000 SD 92154 1350-F1
PETERLYNN WY
4000 SD 92154 1350-F1
PETER PAN AV
7100 SD 92114 1290-F4
PETERS CT
- SD 92126 1209-D7
- SD 92126 1229-D1
PETERS DR
300 VSTA 92083 1087-H7
PETERS WY
3000 SD 92117 1248-C3
PETERSON RD
- ImCo 92233 411-B9
PETERSON WY
5300 SD 92182 1270-B1
PETERS STONE CT
- SD 92127 1169-B4
PETIRROJO CT
11600 SD 92124 1250-A3
PETIT CT
6900 SD 92111 1248-J3
PETIT ST
6800 SD 92111 1248-J3
PETITE LN
9500 SDCo 92040 1232-C3
PETRA DR
1700 SD 92104 1289-F2
PETRA PL
3400 SD 92104 1289-F1
PETRA WY
1100 SDCo 91901 1233-F5
PETREE ST
1000 ELCJ 92020 1251-D4
PETROLIA CT
- SDCo 92065 1171-F1
PETTIGO DR
2900 SD 92139 1310-E2
PETUNIA CT
- SMCS 92069 1108-H6
3200 SD 92117 1248-D4
PETUNIA PL
6400 CRLB 92011 1127-B4
PETUNIA WY
- SD 92130 1188-G4
PEUTZ VALLEY RD
200 SDCo 91901 1233-F4
900 SDCo 91901 1234-A3
PEWTER CT
1700 SDCo 92019 1272-D2
PEYRI DR
100 OCN 92057 1086-G2
PEYTON PL
5200 SD 92117 1228-H7
PFEIFER LN
1200 ELCJ 92020 1251-C3
PHANTOM LN
11500 SD 92126 1209-E1
PHEASANT CT
- ImCo 92249 6560-B7
1000 SMCS 92078 1128-E3
PHEASANT DR
2500 SD 92123 1249-B7
2900 SDCo 92036 1136-E7
2900 SDCo 92036 1156-E1
PHEASANT LN
- OCN 92057 1086-H2
PHEASANT PL
1900 ESCN 92026 1109-H5
PHEASANT RUN
2000 SDCo 92028 1028-A4
PHEASANT ST
- ImCo 92243 6560-A7
- ImCo 92249 6560-A7
PHEASANT HILL
1300 SDCo 92026 1109-E6
PHEASANT VALLEY CT
500 SDCo 92028 1027-G1
PHELPS RD
2000 SDCo 91906 (1317-H3 See Page 1296)
PHIDEL ST
3900 SD 92130 1188-A4
PHILBROOK SQ
3000 SD 92130 1208-B2
PHILLAR WY
8700 SNTE 92071 1231-C7
PHILLIPS CIR
1400 VSTA 92083 1108-A2
PHILLIPS CT
400 VSTA 92083 1107-H1
6800 SD 92111 1268-J1

PHILLIPS ST
600 VSTA 92083 1107-H1
1000 VSTA 92083 1108-A1
PHILLIPS WY
400 VSTA 92083 1107-J1
PHIL MAR LN
200 VSTA 92083 1108-A2
PHILTON DR
600 SDCo 92065 1153-B6
PHIPPS AV
- SD 92126 1209-E7
PHIRE PL
400 SDCo 91977 1291-B4
PHLOX CT
- CRLB 92011 1127-B4
PHOEBE PL
- CRLB 92011 1127-B5
PHOEBE ST
100 ENCT 92024 1147-A4
PHOENIX DR
7500 LMSA 91941 1270-G4
PHOENIX WY
700 SMCS 92078 1129-A3
PHYLLIS PL
8200 SD 92123 1249-B7
PIANTINO CIR
- SD 92108 1249-E7
PIANTINO WY
- SD 92108 1249-D7
PIATTO LN
- SD 92108 1249-E7
PIATTO WY
- SD 92108 1249-E7
PICACHO CT
600 OCN 92057 1067-C7
PICACHO RD
- ImCo 412-C11
- ImCo 432-C2
1100 ImCo 92283 432-C2
PICACHO RD Rt#-S24
300 ImCo 92283 432-D5
PICADILLY CT
4500 CRLB 92010 1107-A5
PICADOR BLVD
700 SD 92154 1330-E7
900 SD 92154 1350-E1
PICARTE PL
12600 SD 92128 1190-A5
PICASSO DR
2900 SDCo 91902 1290-H7
PICAZA PL
11000 SD 92127 1169-H1
PICCADILLY RD
1700 ENCT 92024 1147-A2
PICCARD AV
500 SD 92154 1330-F6
1000 SD 92154 1350-F1
PICKET FENCE DR
- CHV 91915 1331-J1
1500 CHV 91915 1311-J7
PICKETT GN
500 ESCN 92027 1110-D6
PICKETT RD
- ImCo 92233 411-C11
1700 ImCo 92227 411-D11
PICKETT ST
3400 SD 92110 1268-E4
PICKFORD RD
11700 SD 92131 1209-G1
PICKWICK ST
3300 SD 92102 1289-F3
PICNIC CT
2300 CHV 91915 1331-H1
PICNIC VIEW LN
200 OCN 92056 1107-D2
PICO AV
100 SDCo 92028 1027-F2
100 SMCS 92069 1108-H7
600 ELCN 92243 6499-F4
S PICO AV
200 SDCo 92028 1027-F2
PICO CT
- CHV 91911 1330-E3
PICO PL
800 ESCN 92026 1109-J6
2500 SD 92109 1248-C5
PICO RD
3500 SDCo 92084 1068-F4
PICO ST
4600 SD 92109 1248-C5
PICO WY
200 ESCN 92026 1109-H7
2500 SD 92109 1248-C4
PICO DE LA LOMA
300 ESCN 92029 1150-A3
PICRUS ST
12200 SD 92129 1189-B7
PICTOR LN
200 ELCJ 92019 1252-A5
PICTURESQUE PT
15100 SDCo 92021 1233-B7
PIDGEON ST
500 SD 92114 1290-F3
PIEDMONT DR
4300 SD 92107 1287-J2
PIEDMONT RD
900 SDCo 92065 1152-J3
PIEDMONT ST
1500 CHV 91913 1331-D1
1600 CHV 91913 1311-D7
9200 SDCo 91977 1291-B2
PIEDRA ST
1300 SD 92154 1350-E1
PIEDRAS ORO CALLE
700 ENCT 92024 1147-D7
PIEDRA TRACT
- SDCo 91948 1218-E5
PIEL PL
9100 SDCo 91977 1291-B4
PIENZA PL
9500 SDCo 92127 1169-E2
PIERCE AV
900 CALX 92231 6680-F1
PIERCE CT
2000 SDCo 92019 1272-C3
PIERCE LN
1300 SDCo 92065 1172-G4
PIERCE PL
4900 OCN 92057 1067-A7
PIERCE ST
700 ELCJ 92020 1251-D4
S PIERCE ST
300 ELCJ 92020 1251-D6
PIERINO DR
2000 SD 92114 1290-E1
PIERLE RD
- ImCo 92251 431-A4
PIERRE WY
1100 ELCJ 92021 1251-G3
1100 SDCo 92021 1251-G3
PIER VIEW WY
- OCN 92054 1105-J1
- OCN 92054 1106-A1

PIER VIEW WY
100 OCN 92054 1086-A7
PIKAKE ST
2600 SD 92154 1350-C3
PIKE LN
500 OCN 92054 1086-G2
PIKE RD
9300 SNTE 92071 1231-B5
PILAWEE WEE LN
9500 SDCo 91916 1236-A2
PILE ST
100 SDCo 92065 1152-H2
700 SDCo 92065 1153-A2
PILGRIM WY
1400 OCN 92057 1067-A3
PILLAR POINT WY
800 OCN 92054 1066-F7
PILLSBURY LN
1200 ELCJ 92020 1251-B3
PILON PT
4100 SD 92130 1188-B7
PILOT WY
6700 SD 92114 1270-E7
6700 SD 92114 1290-E1
PILOTS LN
9500 SNTE 92071 1251-C1
PIMA TR
34600 SDCo 92036 1176-D4
PIMLICO CTE
15400 SDCo 92067 1168-E7
PIMLICO PL
2400 SDCo 91901 1234-C6
PIMPERNEL DR
9000 SD 92129 1189-D5
PIMPERNEL WY
12800 SD 92129 1189-D5
PINA LN
300 VSTA 92083 1087-H7
PINAR PL
2100 SD 92014 1187-G6
PINATA DR
16700 SD 92128 1170-B3
PINDAR WY
4100 OCN 92056 1107-E6
PINE AV
200 CRLB 92008 1106-F5
PINE BLVD
7400 SDCo 91962 1237-C5
PINE CT
- CORD 92118 1288-G7
- SDCo 91962 1237-C5
300 CHV 91911 1330-G7
8300 LMSA 91941 1270-J2
PINE DR
1000 ELCJ 92020 1251-D7
1100 SDCo 91941 1271-D2
2400 SDCo 91906 (1297-E5 See Page 1296)
PINE HTS
800 SDCo 92065 1152-F1
PINE LN
3100 SDCo 91978 1272-C7
3100 SDCo 91978 1292-C1
PINE ST
- SMCS 92078 1129-C2
100 OCN 92054 1106-A1
1000 CORD 92118 1288-G7
1400 VSTA 92083 1087-F6
1400 SDCo 92082 1090-B1
1500 SDCo 92065 1152-F1
1700 ESCN 92025 1130-A5
2100 SD 92103 1268-G4
3700 SMCS 92078 1128-C1
4800 LMSA 91941 1270-J2
PINE ST Rt#-78
100 SDCo 92065 1152-G3
N PINE ST
100 ESCN 92025 1129-H3
S PINE ST
100 ESCN 92025 1129-H3
S PINE ST Rt#-78
100 SDCo 92065 1152-G6
PINE TER
14100 SDCo 92021 1232-G6
PINE WY
700 SDCo 92065 1152-F2
PINEAPPLE PL
9600 SDCo 92040 1232-A4
PINEAPPLE WY
1200 ESCN 92029 1129-E5
PINE BLOSSOM RD
- SDCo 92021 1232-H3
PINE BLUFF LN
6100 SD 92139 1290-D6
PINE BRANCH DR
1600 ENCT 92024 1167-G1
PINEBROOK CT
12600 PWY 92064 1170-D3
PINECASTLE ST
10100 SD 92131 1210-C4
PINECLIFFS CT
10400 SD 92131 1210-A3
PINE CONE DR
700 SDCo 92036 1156-D1
PINECONE LN
6500 SD 92139 1310-F1
PINE CREEK CRSG
8400 SDCo 91962 1237-C4
PINE CREEK RD
8300 SDCo 91931 1237-B5
8300 SDCo 91962 1237-C3
8400 SDCo 91962 (1217-D7 See Page 1216)
PINECREST AV
900 ESCN 92025 1129-H5
1100 SDCo 92025 1129-H5
8500 SD 92123 1249-C5
PINE CREST DR
2500 SDCo 92036 1136-D7
PINE CREST LN
47200 RivC 92592 999-F1
PINECREST ST
800 ESCN 92025 1129-H4
32200 RivC 92592 999-F1
PINECREST WY
2100 CRLB 92008 1106-G3
PINEFALLS CT
10100 SD 92131 1209-J3
PINEFIELD RD
12800 PWY 92064 1170-D3
PINE GLEN CT
- SDCo 92019 1272-E3
PINE GLEN LN
- SDCo 92019 1272-D3
PINE GLEN WY
1100 SD 92154 1350-E1
PINE GROVE CT
2900 SDCo 91978 1271-F7
PINE GROVE ST
10300 SDCo 91978 1271-F7
PINE HEIGHTS WY
1400 SDCo 92069 1129-E1
1400 SMCS 92069 1129-E1

PINE HILL PT
- SD 92130 1208-D2
PINE HILLS RD
3000 SDCo 92036 1155-J2
3200 SDCo 92036 1135-J7
PINEHILLS CREST DR
- SDCo 92036 1155-H4
PINEHURST AV
1600 ESCN 92026 1109-D5
PINEHURST CT
1700 SDCo 92028 1028-G5
PINEHURST DR
11100 SDCo 92040 1211-H6
11100 SDCo 92040 1231-H1
PINEHURST PL
- SD 92131 1210-H1
PINEHURST RD
1200 CHV 91915 1311-G6
PINE ISLAND DR
1000 CHV 91915 1311-G5
PINE KNOLL LN
9900 SD 92124 1249-F1
PINE MANOR CT
12900 SD 92129 1189-F5
PINE MEADOW CT
12800 SD 92130 1188-B5
PINE NEEDLES DR
300 DLMR 92014 1187-G7
13600 SD 92014 1187-G7
PINEOAK RIDGE RD
700 SDCo 92036 1156-D3
PINE OAKS RD
17100 SDCo 92036 1156-F7
PINE PATCH WY
- SDCo 92028 998-G5
PINE RIDGE AV
4700 SDCo 92036 1155-G4
PINERIDGE CT
500 CHV 91902 1311-B4
PINE RIDGE RD
1400 OCN 92056 1087-C3
PINERIDGE RD
7500 SNTE 92071 1230-G7
PINE RIDGE WY
- SDCo 92036 1155-H5
PINERY GRV
- SDCo 92040 1231-G3
PINESTONE CT
11200 SD 92128 1189-J2
PINETREE DR
10100 SD 92131 1209-G4
PINE TREE LN
17400 SDCo 92036 1156-F7
PINETREE LN
600 VSTA 92081 1107-H1
PINE TREE PL
400 ESCN 92025 1130-A4
PINEVALE LN
- SNTE 92071 1230-G5
PINE VALLEY DR
9200 SNTE 92071 1230-J6
PINE VALLEY GN
- ESCN 92026 1109-H4
PINE VALLEY RD
7400 SDCo 91962 1237-B7
PINE VALLEY LAS BANCAS RD
- SDCo 91916 1236-C5
- SDCo 91931 1236-F6
- SDCo 91931 1237-A5
- SDCo 91962 1236-F6
PINE VIEW RD
1700 SDCo 91901 1234-D7
PINE VISTA RD
1400 SDCo 92027 1130-E2
PINEWOOD CT
3200 SD 92037 1228-B4
PINEWOOD DR
800 OCN 92057 1087-C1
14200 SD 92014 1187-H5
PINEWOOD RD
1900 VSTA 92081 1107-F5
PINEWOOD ST
2500 SD 92014 1187-H5
PINEWOOD VW
10000 SNTE 92071 1231-D3
PINEZANITA LN
2900 SDCo 92036 1136-A7
PINION TR
6300 SDCo 92026 1089-F4
PINION PINE TR
38600 SDCo 91905 (1320-A3 See Page 1300)
PINKARD LN
- SD 92021 1232-F5
PINKARD WY
13800 SDCo 92021 1232-F5
PINNACLE CT
1700 VSTA 92081 1107-G4
PINNACLE LN
10100 SDCo 91941 1271-D2
PINNACLE PL
3800 ESCN 92025 1150-D3
PINNACLE WY
1600 VSTA 92081 1107-G4
PINNACLE PEAK DR
1200 CHV 91915 1311-H6
PINO CT
13100 SDCo 92040 1232-C2
PINO DR
10200 SDCo 92040 1232-C3
PINON PL
- SDCo 92040 1231-G3
PINON ST
900 SMCS 92069 1109-B5
PINON HILLS RD
1900 CHV 91913 1311-E6
PINOT PL
17200 PWY 92064 1170-D2
PINOT NOIR CIR
10800 SD 92131 1210-B2
PINTAIL CT
12400 PWY 92064 1190-B6
PINTAIL DR
6800 CRLB 92011 1127-D6
PINTO CT
1000 SMCS 92069 1109-C5
PINTO PL
3800 SDCo 91977 1271-F5
PINTO CANYON LN
1100 CHV 91915 1311-H5
PINTORESCO CT
2000 CRLB 92009 1147-F1
PINTO RIDGE CT
- SDCo 92127 1169-E4
PINTO RIDGE DR
- SDCo 92127 1169-E5
PINYON DR
- SDCo 92055 1085-J3
PINYON RIDGE DR
- CHV 91915 1311-H6
PINZOLO PT
- SDCo 92040 1231-H6

PINZON WY
10900 SD 92127 1169-H1
PIONEER AV
2500 VSTA 92081 1108-A6
PIONEER CIR
1400 OCN 92057 1066-J3
1400 OCN 92057 1067-A3
PIONEER PL
3100 ESCN 92025 1150-C1
3700 SD 92103 1268-J6
PIONEER TER
- SDCo 92040 1232-F4
PIONEER WY
1000 ELCJ 92020 1251-E2
2800 SDCo 91935 1292-F3
PIO PICO DR
2300 CRLB 92008 1106-E4
PIO PICO ST
3600 SD 92106 1287-J3
3600 SD 92106 1288-A3
PIOVANA CT
800 CRLB 92011 1127-A7
PIPER LN
4200 SDCo 92004 1100-C4
PIPER ST
4200 SD 92117 1248-E6
PIPER RANCH RD
1200 SD 92154 1351-H2
PIPES LN
- ENCT 92024 1147-D7
PIPESTONE WY
8800 SD 92129 1189-C3
PIPILO CT
12900 SD 92129 1189-D5
PIPILO ST
9200 SD 92129 1189-D6
PIPING ROCK LN
13500 SDCo 92021 1252-E1
13500 SDCo 92021 1232-E7
PIPIT CT
- CRLB 92011 1127-D4
12200 SD 92129 1189-A7
PIPIT PL
7600 SD 92129 1189-A7
PIPIT WY
12200 SD 92129 1189-A7
PIPO RD
12400 SD 92128 1170-C4
PIPPIN CT
- SMCS 92078 1128-E3
PIPPIN DR
200 SDCo 92028 1027-F4
PIRAEUS ST
900 ENCT 92024 1147-B3
1800 CRLB 92024 1147-B3
PIRAGUA ST
3300 CRLB 92009 1147-J1
5100 CRLB 92009 1127-J7
PIRATES COVE WY
- OCN 92054 1086-B7
PIRE AV
5400 SD 92122 1228-C7
PIRGOS WY
3400 OCN 92056 1107-E4
PIRINEOS WY
2600 CRLB 92009 1147-G1
PIROS WY
6000 OCN 92056 1107-F5
PIROTTE DR
5000 SD 92105 1290-A1
PISCES WY
11000 SD 92126 1209-C2
PISMO CT
700 SD 92109 1267-H1
PISMO BAY CT
300 OCN 92057 1066-J5
PISTOL RANGE RD
4300 SD 92173 1350-G2
PITA CT
13700 SDCo 91935 1292-G2
PITCAIRN ST
3100 SD 92154 1330-D7
PITMAN PL
900 ESCN 92027 1110-C6
PITMAN ST
600 ESCN 92027 1110-C6
PITTA ST
400 SD 92114 1290-C3
PITTSBURGH AV
6300 SD 92114 1290-D5
PITTZER RD
1000 ImCo 92249 6560-D5
1000 ImCo 92249 6620-D2
1500 ImCo 92243 6560-D2
PIUTE PL
4400 SD 92117 1248-E2
PIUTE TR
34800 SDCo 92036 1176-E5
PIZARRO LN
- SDCo 92026 1109-E6
PIZZO LN
700 SDCo 92028 1027-G4
PLACE MONACO
2200 SD 92014 1187-F6
PLACENTIA ST
7300 LMGR 91945 1290-F2
PLACER AV
400 SMCS 92069 1108-J6
PLACER TR
800 SDCo 92019 1253-B2
PLACERITA ST
1500 ENCT 92024 1147-G7
PLACER MINE LN
1200 CHV 91913 1311-E6
PLACE SAINT TROPEZ
2200 SD 92014 1187-F6
PLACID CT
1600 ELCJ 92021 1252-B2
PLACIDO CT
2100 CRLB 92009 1147-F2
PLACID VIEW DR
8500 SNTE 92071 1231-A7
8500 SNTE 92071 1251-A1
PLACITA SUENOS
- VSTA 92083 1087-D7
S PLAINS CT
15800 SDCo 92021 1233-D3
PLAINS WY
- CRLB 92010 1107-B5
PLAINVIEW RD
5000 SD 92110 1268-F2
PLANET RD
1400 VSTA 92083 1087-D6
PLANE TREE VW
- SDCo 92026 1089-B2
PLANICIE WY
1600 SD 92154 1350-A3
PLANK RD
- ELCN 92243 6499-D7
- ELCN 92243 6559-D1
PLANTANO ST
400 SD 92102 1289-J3
PLANTATION WY
1500 SDCo 92019 1272-A1

STREET Block City ZIP Pg-Grid

PLANTEL WY
3100 SD 92173 1350-D2
PLATA CT
1600 LMGR 91945 1290-F2
PLATANO CT
1400 CHV 91911 1330-E4
PLATANUS DR
29600 SDCo 92026 1069-A5
PLATANUS PL
9100 SDCo 92026 1069-A5
PLATEAU AV
- SMCS 92078 1128-H3
PLATEAU DR
6200 SD 92139 1310-E2
PLATEAU PL
3900 CRLB 92010 1107-C3
3900 ESCN 92025 1150-C3
PLATINUM PL
- CRLB 92009 1127-H5
16900 SDCo 92040 1191-D3
16900 SDCo 92064 1191-D3
PLATO DR
- CALX 92231 6620-H7
3000 SD 92139 1310-F2
PLATO PL
700 ENCT 92024 1147-B2
PLATTE RIVER LN
1800 CHV 91913 1311-E7
PLAYA RD
2000 CRLB 92009 1127-F7
PLAYA BLANCA
300 ENCT 92024 1147-C6
PLAYA CATALINA
5000 SD 92124 1230-A7
PLAYA DE CONCORD
- ESCN 92029 1129-C4
PLAYA DEL ALICANTE
- ESCN 92029 1129-C4
PLAYA DEL CARMEN DR
- IMP 92251 6499-G1
PLAYA DEL NORTE
200 SD 92037 1247-E2
PLAYA DEL REY
- OCN 92054 1066-E6
PLAYA DEL REY AV
100 OCN 92054 1086-G1
100 OCN 92054 1066-G7
PLAYA DEL SOL
- ESCN 92026 1109-F7
600 SDCo 92021 1251-G2
PLAYA DEL SUR
200 SD 92037 1247-E2
PLAYA DEL TOKAY
- ESCN 92029 1129-E4
PLAYA RIVIERA DR
1800 ENCT 92007 1167-E3
PLAYA VISTA
- SDCo 92078 1128-B4
PLAYER DR
7300 SD 92119 1250-F5
PLAYMOR TER
7900 SD 92122 1228-C4
PLAZA BLVD
1200 NATC 91950 1310-A1
2400 NATC 91950 1290-B7
4000 SD 92114 1290-D5
E PLAZA BLVD
- NATC 91950 1309-J1
1200 NATC 91950 1310-A1
W PLAZA BLVD
- NATC 91950 1309-H1
PLAZA CT
700 CHV 91910 1310-H6
PLAZA DR
- CALX 92231 6620-H7
2300 CRLB 92008 1106-G2
2500 CRLB 92010 1106-G2
3300 OCN 92056 1107-B2
3700 VSTA 92081 1107-B2
PLAZA SQ
- SD 92123 1249-C2
PLAZA ST
100 SOLB 92075 1167-E7
PLAZA ABIERTO
17400 SD 92128 1170-C1
PLAZA ACOSTA
17600 SD 92128 1150-D7
PLAZA AHORA
17800 SD 92128 1150-C7
PLAZA ALONZO
3000 SDCo 91902 1310-H1
PLAZA AMADA
12500 SD 92128 1170-C1
PLAZA AMISTAD
900 CHV 91910 1310-J7
900 CHV 91910 1311-A7
PLAZA AMPARADA
1100 CHV 91910 1311-B7
PLAZA ANIMADO
17400 SD 92128 1170-D1
PLAZA ANITA
3000 SDCo 91902 1290-H7
3000 SDCo 91902 1310-H1
PLAZA ARICA
17600 SD 92128 1150-C7
PLAZA ASCOPE
17600 SD 92128 1150-C7
PLAZA BONITA
2300 CRLB 92009 1127-F7
PLAZA BONITA RD
2900 SDCo 91902 1310-C4
2900 SDCo 91910 1310-D5
2900 CHV 91902 1310-D5
2900 CHV 91910 1310-D5
3000 NATC 91950 1310-C4
PLAZA BONITA CENTER WY
3000 NATC 91950 1310-E3
PLAZA CALIMAR
300 CHV 91914 1311-F2
PLAZA CAMBRIA
400 CHV 91914 1311-F2
PLAZA CAPOTE
1000 CHV 91910 1311-A7
PLAZA CARLOS
2900 SDCo 91902 1290-G6
PLAZA CATALONIA
800 CHV 91910 1311-A6
PLAZA CENTRADA
12500 SD 92128 1170-C2
PLAZA CERADO
17400 SD 92128 1170-C1
PLAZA CREST RIDGE RD
1600 SD 92114 1290-E6
PLAZA CUERNAVACA
6300 SD 92114 1290-D5
PLAZA CUERNAVACA WY
800 SD 92114 1290-E5
PLAZA DE BENITO JUAREZ
300 VSTA 92083 1087-G5
PLAZA DE LA COSTA
7200 CRLB 92009 1127-F7

PLAZA DE LA ROSA
17400 SD 92128 1170-F2
PLAZA DE LAS FLORES
2300 CRLB 92009 1127-F7
PLAZA DE LA SIENA
12600 SD 92130 1188-B6
PLAZA DEL CID
500 CHV 91910 1310-G5
PLAZA DEL CURTIDOR
17400 SD 92128 1170-C1
PLAZA DEL MAR
2400 SDCo 92025 1150-D1
PLAZA DE PALMAS
4000 SD 92122 1228-C3
PLAZA DE PANAMA
2300 SD 92101 1289-C1
PLAZA DESTACADO
17400 SD 92128 1170-F2
PLAZA DOLORES
17400 SD 92128 1170-D1
PLAZA ELENA
1000 CHV 91910 1311-A7
PLAZA ENTRADA
- NATC 91950 1290-C6
PLAZA ESCALANTE
1000 CHV 91910 1311-B6
PLAZA EVA
2300 CHV 91914 1311-F1
PLAZA FIEL
17400 SD 92128 1170-C2
PLAZA FLORA
800 CHV 91910 1310-F7
PLAZA GARDENIA
1000 CHV 91910 1311-B6
PLAZA GITANA
17500 SD 92128 1170-D1
PLAZA GUATA
12500 SD 92128 1170-C1
PLAZA GUILLERMO
17400 SD 92128 1170-C1
PLAZA KADIE
- CHV 91914 1311-E2
PLAZA KARENA
17500 SD 92128 1170-D1
PLAZA LA PAZ
- CHV 91910 1310-J7
PLAZA LEONARDO
3000 SDCo 91902 1310-H1
3000 SDCo 91902 1290-H7
PLAZA LORENZO
4600 SDCo 91902 1290-H7
4600 SDCo 91902 1310-H1
PLAZA LOS OSOS
300 CHV 91914 1311-E2
PLAZA MANZANA
- SDCo 91901 1234-A6
PLAZA MAR
800 CHV 91910 1310-F7
PLAZA MARIA
17300 SD 92128 1170-D2
PLAZA MARLENA
17500 SD 92128 1170-D1
PLAZA MENTA
12600 SD 92128 1150-C7
PLAZA MERCIA
3000 SDCo 91902 1290-H7
PLAZA MIGUEL
2900 SDCo 91902 1290-H7
PLAZA MIRALESTE
1100 CHV 91910 1311-A7
PLAZA MIRODA
700 CHV 91910 1311-A5
PLAZA NARISCO
1000 CHV 91910 1310-J7
1000 CHV 91910 1311-A7
PLAZA NATALIA
3000 SDCo 91902 1310-H1
PLAZA OTONAL
17200 SD 92128 1170-D1
PLAZA PALMERA
- CHV 91914 1311-E1
PLAZA PAOLO
3000 SDCo 91902 1290-G7
PLAZA PARAISO
- CHV 91914 1311-E2
PLAZA PARK LN
- SD 92123 1249-C1
PLAZA PASEO DR
10300 SDCo 92040 1231-H3
PLAZA REAL
1900 OCN 92056 1087-B5
PLAZA RIDGE RD
6400 SD 92114 1290-E6
PLAZA SEVILLE
700 CHV 91910 1311-A5
PLAZA SIERRA
800 CHV 91910 1310-F7
PLAZA SINUOSO
1000 CHV 91910 1311-A7
PLAZA SONADA
17400 SD 92128 1170-C2
PLAZA SONRISADA
17400 SD 92128 1170-C1
PLAZA TAXCO
800 SD 92114 1290-D5
PLAZA TOLUCA
300 CHV 91914 1311-F2
800 SD 92114 1290-E5
PLAZA TORREON
800 SD 92114 1290-E5
PLAZA ULTIMA
1000 CHV 91910 1311-B7
PLAZA VALDIVIA
17800 SD 92128 1150-C7
PLAZA VIEJAS
- SDCo 91901 1234-A6
PLAZA VISTA
1300 SD 92114 1290-D5
PLAZA VISTA MAR
1000 CHV 91910 1311-B7
PLAZUELA ST
2200 CRLB 92009 1147-F1
PLEASANT LN
700 NATC 91950 1290-B7
PLEASANT PL
1600 ENCT 92024 1147-G6
PLEASANT RDG
- SD 92130 1208-B2
PLEASANT WY
300 SMCS 92069 1108-H7
PLEASANTDALE DR
1700 ENCT 92024 1147-H7
PLEASANTDALE LN
200 ENCT 92024 1147-H7
PLEASANT GROVE RD
2100 ENCT 92024 1147-H7
PLEASANT HEIGHTS DR
1700 SDCo 92084 1088-B2
PLEASANT HILL ST
1100 ESCN 92026 1129-F1
1200 ESCN 92026 1109-F7
PLEASANT KNOLL LN
28700 SDCo 92082 1070-G7
28700 SDCo 92082 1090-G1

PLEASANTON RD
1500 CHV 91913 1311-D7
PLEASANT VALE DR
- CRLB 92010 1107-B5
PLEASANT VALLEY PL
- CHV 91915 1311-G7
PLEASANT VIEW DR
500 SDCo 92036 1156-E2
PLEASANT VIEW LN
3200 SDCo 91935 1273-A7
3200 SDCo 91935 1293-A1
PLEASANT WATERS CT
- SDCo 91977 1271-E7
- SDCo 91977 1291-E1
PLEASANTWOOD LN
2100 ESCN 92026 1109-H4
PLEIADES DR
1200 SDCo 92084 1108-D1
PLEIN AIRE
- SD 92127 1168-H6
PLEIN AIRE CT
- SD 92127 1168-J6
PLESS RD
- SD 92126 1229-A1
- SD 92145 1229-A1
PLIMPTON RD
9600 LMSA 91941 1271-C1
9600 SDCo 91941 1271-C1
PLONE WY
3000 SD 92117 1248-C3
PLOVER CT
- CRLB 92011 1127-D6
PLOVER ST
1500 SD 92114 1290-E1
PLOVER WY
1000 OCN 92057 1087-A3
PLUM CT
- ESCN 92027 1130-H2
29100 SDCo 92082 1071-A6
PLUM ST
1200 SD 92106 1288-B2
1900 SD 92106 1268-C7
PLUM WY
- SD 92130 1188-G4
PLUMAS ST
5600 SD 92139 1290-C7
PLUMAS PINES PL
1400 CHV 91915 1311-H7
PLUMBAGO LN
3500 SD 92154 1330-E7
PLUMB BROQUE CIR
1700 SDCo 92019 1252-B5
PLUMCREST LN
- SD 92130 1208-E2
PLUMERIA DR
- CRLB 92009 1127-G4
- SMCS 92069 1108-H6
1600 SDCo 92021 1251-G1
PLUMERIA LN
- SDCo 92127 1169-G1
PLUM HOLLOW PL
1700 VSTA 92081 1107-D2
PLUMMER CT
4700 SD 92130 1188-C4
PLUMOSA AV
100 SDCo 92083 1108-B4
500 SDCo 92081 1108-B5
500 VSTA 92081 1108-B4
500 VSTA 92083 1108-B4
PLUMOSA CT
2400 SDCo 92081 1108-B5
PLUMOSA DR
3600 SD 92106 1268-C6
PLUMOSA ST
100 OCN 92054 1086-F1
100 OCN 92054 1066-G7
PLUMOSA WY
1400 SD 92103 1268-H5
PLUMTREE DR
1500 ENCT 92024 1167-G1
PLUM TREE LN
- ESCN 92027 1130-J3
11000 SDCo 91977 1271-E7
PLUM TREE RD
1300 CRLB 92011 1127-A4
PLUM TREE WY
500 OCN 92054 1086-F2
PLUMWOOD ST
14600 PWY 92064 1190-D1
PLUTO CT
3400 SDCo 91902 1310-G1
PLUTO RD
1400 VSTA 92083 1087-D6
PLYMOUTH CT
- CHV 91911 1330-E3
PLYMOUTH DR
100 VSTA 92083 1087-G6
PLYMOUTH ST
5200 OCN 92057 1067-A3
POBLADO CT
17100 SD 92127 1169-J2
POBLADO RD
10000 SD 92127 1149-H7
10500 SD 92127 1169-H1
POBLADO WY
17100 SD 92127 1169-J2
POCAHONTAS AV
4300 SD 92117 1248-D1
POCAHONTAS CT
3600 SD 92117 1248-D1
POCAHONTAS PL
3600 SD 92117 1248-D1
POCANO WY
13300 SD 92128 1189-J4
POCATELLO ST
100 SD 92114 1290-D4
POCHARD WY
- SD 92131 1209-G2
POCHE PT
11200 SD 92131 1209-J2
POCITOS WY
3100 SD 92173 1350-D2
POCO PZ
- SMCS 92078 1129-C2
POCO WY
24300 SDCo 92065 1173-F2
POCO LAGO
6500 SDCo 92067 1188-G2
POCO MONTANA
- SDCo 92036 1175-H1
POD DR
2300 SDCo 92084 1108-D1
PODELL AV
9400 SD 92123 1249-F7
PODERIO CT
16100 SDCo 92065 1173-H3
PODERIO DR
25000 SDCo 92065 1173-H3
POE RD
5900 ImCo 92227 410-L11
5900 ImCo 92259 410-L11
POE ST
3000 SD 92106 1288-B1
3400 SD 92106 1268-B7

POE ST
3600 SD 92107 1268-B7
10300 SDCo 92026 1109-F2
POESIA CT
1600 SD 92154 1350-B2
POETS CT
1400 SDCo 92028 1027-F4
POETS SQ
300 SDCo 92028 1027-F4
POGO RW
- SD 92154 1331-E7
- SD 92154 1351-C1
POHL PL
800 VSTA 92083 1087-F5
POINCIANA DR
1600 SDCo 92021 1251-G1
POINSETIA CT
100 CHV 91910 1310-B5
POINSETT RD
11000 SD 92131 1209-H1
POINSETTIA AV
100 SDCo 92083 1108-C4
100 SDCo 92084 1108-C4
500 SDCo 92081 1108-C5
800 VSTA 92081 1108-B7
2100 VSTA 92081 1128-A1
POINSETTIA CT
200 SDCo 92083 1108-C4
POINSETTIA DR
2100 SD 92107 1268-B7
2200 SD 92106 1268-C6
13600 PWY 92064 1190-F3
POINSETTIA LN
- CRLB 92009 1127-G4
- CRLB 92011 1126-J6
800 CRLB 92011 1127-C4
POINSETTIA PK
700 ENCT 92024 1147-C5
POINSETTIA PK N
600 ENCT 92024 1147-C5
POINSETTIA PK S
600 ENCT 92024 1147-C5
POINSETTIA ST
500 CHV 91911 1330-H3
POINSETTIA PARK CT
600 ENCT 92024 1147-C5
W POINT DR
1500 CHV 91911 1330-J4
POINT RD
900 ESCN 92026 1129-J1
POINT ST
900 SD 92106 1288-A2
POINT ALTO
4800 SDCo 91941 1271-C2
POINT ARENA CT
500 CHV 91911 1330-H4
POINT ARGUELLO
700 OCN 92054 1066-G7
POINT ARGUELLO DR
1600 CHV 91911 1330-J3
POINT BARROW DR
600 CHV 91911 1330-J4
POINT BUCHON
800 OCN 92054 1066-G7
POINT BUCHON CT
600 CHV 91911 1330-J4
POINT CABRILLO
700 OCN 92054 1066-G7
POINT CABRILLO CT
1600 CHV 91911 1330-H4
POINT CAIMAN CT
600 CHV 91911 1330-H4
POINT CONCEPCION CT
1600 CHV 91911 1330-J4
POINT DEFIANCE CT
600 CHV 91911 1330-H4
POINT DEGADA
4400 OCN 92054 1066-G7
4400 OCN 92057 1066-G7
POINT DELGADA CT
1500 CHV 91911 1330-H4
POINT DUME CT
1500 CHV 91911 1330-J4
POINTE PKWY
- SDCo 91978 1291-F1
2700 SDCo 91977 1291-D1
POINTE DEL MAR WY
12800 SD 92014 1207-J1
POINTED OAK LN
10700 SD 92131 1210-A3
POINTER GN
2000 ESCN 92029 1129-E6
POINTER LN
100 VSTA 92084 1088-B5
POINT ESTERO DR
1600 CHV 91911 1330-J5
POINT FERMINE CT
600 CHV 91911 1330-J3
POINT HUENEME CT
1500 CHV 91911 1330-J4
POINTILLIST CT
4800 OCN 92057 1087-B2
POINTING ROCK DR
200 SDCo 92004 1058-F6
POINT LA JOLLA DR
1500 CHV 91911 1330-H4
POINT LOBAS CIR
700 OCN 92054 1066-G7
POINT LOMA AV
3800 SD 92106 1288-A1
4000 SD 92107 1288-A1
4100 SD 92107 1287-J1
4700 SD 92107 1267-H7
W POINT LOMA BLVD
3900 SD 92110 1268-A5
4300 SD 92107 1268-A5
4800 SD 92107 1267-J5
POINT LOMA CT
1600 CHV 91911 1330-J4
POINT LOMA PL
4800 OCN 92057 1066-J6
POINT LOMA WY
1400 SD 92106 1288-A1
POINT MALAGA PL
4700 OCN 92057 1066-J6
POINT MEDANAS CT
600 CHV 91911 1330-J3
POINT MUGU CT
1600 CHV 91911 1330-J4
POINT PACIFIC CT
1500 CHV 91911 1330-H4
POINT REYES
700 OCN 92054 1066-G7
POINT REYES CT
1600 CHV 91911 1330-H4
4300 CRLB 92010 1106-J4
POINT SAL CT
1600 CHV 91911 1330-H4
POINT SAN LUIS CT
500 CHV 91911 1330-J3
POINTSETTIA LN
- CRLB 92009 1127-E5
- CRLB 92011 1127-E5

POINT SUR
700 OCN 92054 1066-G7
POINT SUR CT
1600 CHV 91911 1330-J4
POINT VICENTE
4400 OCN 92054 1066-G7
POINT VICENTE CT
600 CHV 91911 1330-H4
POINTVIEW CT
4300 SDCo 91941 1271-D3
POINT WINDEMERE PL
300 OCN 92057 1066-J6
POIPU WY
2200 SD 92154 1330-D7
POLA CT
4900 SD 92110 1248-F7
POLACK ST
3900 SD 92110 1268-C6
POLANCO ST
8800 SD 92129 1189-C2
POLARIS DR
3800 SDCo 91941 1271-A5
10900 SD 92126 1209-D1
POLIZZI PL
8200 SD 92123 1269-B1
POLK AV
1600 SD 92103 1269-C5
1900 SD 92104 1269-C5
3600 SD 92105 1269-J5
4000 SD 92105 1270-A5
POLK RD
2800 SDCo 91901 1234-C4
POLK ST
100 OCN 92057 1067-B6
POLLAND AV
8700 SD 92123 1249-C6
POLLEY DR
3400 SMCS 92069 1108-D5
POLLY LN
3800 CRLB 92008 1106-G6
POLLYANNA TER
400 VSTA 92083 1087-G5
POLO CT
1700 OCN 92057 1067-F7
POLO PT
- SD 92014 1188-B1
- SDCo 92014 1188-B1
POLO CLUB DR
- SDCo 92084 1068-D6
POLO PEAK DR
1300 CHV 91913 1311-F7
POLVERA AV
12900 SD 92128 1150-C5
POLVERA CT
12900 SD 92128 1150-C6
POLVERA DR
18500 SD 92128 1150-C6
POLVERA WY
18000 SD 92128 1150-C6
POLVO DR
28700 SDCo 92082 1071-C7
28700 SDCo 92082 1091-C1
POMANI CT
1200 OCN 92056 1087-C3
POMARD CT
17100 PWY 92064 1170-D2
POMARD WY
12900 PWY 92064 1170-D2
POMEGRANATE AV
14000 PWY 92064 1190-F3
POMEGRANATE LN
1900 SDCo 92028 1027-H6
POMEGRANITE CT
- ESCN 92027 1130-H2
POMELO DR
300 VSTA 92081 1087-E7
300 VSTA 92081 1107-E1
700 SDCo 92081 1107-E2
POMELO WY
600 VSTA 92081 1107-E1
POMERADO CT
12400 SD 92128 1170-B2
POMERADO PL
12400 SD 92128 1170-C2
POMERADO RD
9900 SD 92131 1209-G6
9900 SD 92145 1209-G6
9900 SDCo 92131 1209-G6
9900 SDCo 92145 1209-G6
10800 SD 92131 1210-C2
11500 PWY 92064 1210-C2
11700 PWY 92064 1190-C2
14800 PWY 92064 1170-C7
15800 SD 92128 1170-C7
POMERADO RD Rt#-S5
- SD 92127 1150-B5
16900 SD 92128 1170-C3
17700 SD 92128 1150-B5
POMERADO WY
17100 SD 92128 1170-B2
POMEROY ST
3400 SD 92123 1249-D4
POMMEL WY
400 SMCS 92069 1108-E6
POMONA AV
900 CORD 92118 1288-J7
1500 CORD 92118 1308-J1
4300 LMSA 91941 1270-F4
POMONA AV Rt#-282
1200 CORD 92118 1288-J6
POMONA WY
7300 LMSA 91941 1270-F3
POMPEI LN
- SD 92108 1249-D7
PONCA CT
6000 SD 92120 1250-D5
PONCE DE LEON DR
4100 SDCo 91941 1271-H3
POND PL
100 VSTA 92083 1087-G3
PONDER WY
10500 SD 92126 1209-A4
PONDEROSA AV
1000 SMCS 92069 1109-B5
4100 SD 92123 1249-D3
PONDEROSA CT
- ESCN 92027 1110-C5
PONDEROSA DR
900 VSTA 92084 1088-A5
3500 OCN 92054 1086-F2
PONDEROSA LN
8600 SDCo 91962 1237-C4
PONDEROSA PINE LN
7600 SDCo 91962 1237-C7
PONS ST
600 SD 92114 1290-F3
PONTE AV
400 SMCS 92078 1108-C6
PONTE VEDRA WY
2400 CHV 91915 1311-H6
PONTIAC DR
3400 CRLB 92010 1106-J4
4500 CRLB 92010 1107-A5

PONTIAC ST
6000 SD 92115 1270-C2
PONTO DR
1800 CRLB 92011 1126-H5
6200 CRLB 92011 1146-J1
PONY CT
5600 OCN 92057 1067-F7
PONY LN
5500 SDCo 91902 1311-A2
PONY EXPRESS CIR
- SDCo 92040 1232-F4
POOLE ST
9400 SD 92037 1227-J2
POORE RD
- ImCo 92227 431-E2
POPLAR AV
400 SMCS 92069 1108-J6
POPLAR DR
1200 ELCN 92243 6559-G1
POPLAR RD
2000 OCN 92054 1086-C5
POPLAR ST
300 SD 92173 1350-F3
500 SDCo 92065 1152-F5
4000 SD 92105 1269-G7
POPLAR WY
300 ESCN 92026 1129-H1
POPLAR MEADOW LN
2800 SDCo 91935 1292-G3
POPLAR SPRING RD
- CHV 91915 1311-H5
POPLIN DR
7900 SNTE 92071 1250-H1
POPPY CIR
300 OCN 92057 1066-H6
POPPY DR
29500 SDCo 91906 (1297-E5 See Page 1296)
POPPY LN
900 CRLB 92011 1127-A6
3700 SDCo 92028 1028-E4
POPPY PL
4000 SD 92105 1269-G7
POPPY RD
800 SMCS 92078 1128-F2
POPPY ST
5900 LMSA 91942 1251-C6
POPPYFIELD GN
300 ESCN 92026 1109-H5
POPPYFIELD PL
2100 ENCT 92024 1147-J7
POPPY HILLS DR
2200 CHV 91915 1311-H7
POPPY HILLS LN
- ENCT 92024 1148-C6
POPPY HILLS WY
- SD 92128 1190-A3
POPPY PEAR HILL
- SDCo 92028 998-G5
POQUITO ST
12400 PWY 92064 1190-C6
POQUITO WY
4200 OCN 92057 1086-H3
PORCELINA CT
12200 SD 92131 1210-B1
PORCH SWING ST
2300 CHV 91915 1311-H7
PORRECA PT
11300 SD 92126 1208-J2
PORT CIR
3300 OCN 92056 1107-A2
PORTA PL
2400 CRLB 92010 1106-H5
PORTADA PL
12500 SD 92130 1188-B6
PORTAGE WY
- CRLB 92011 1126-J7
- CRLB 92011 1127-A7
PORTAL TER
11500 SD 92128 1190-A7
PORT ALBANS
1800 CHV 91913 1311-D4
PORT ASHLEY
600 CHV 91913 1311-E3
PORT CARDIFF
2000 CHV 91913 1311-E3
PORT CARNEY
1900 CHV 91913 1311-D3
PORT CHELSEA
600 CHV 91913 1311-D4
PORT CLARIDGE
600 CHV 91913 1311-D4
PORT DUNBAR
600 CHV 91913 1311-D4
POR TECHO CT
5400 SD 92124 1249-H1
PORTE DE MERANO
4100 SD 92122 1228-B4
PORTE DE PALMAS
4000 SD 92122 1228-B4
PORTE LA PAZ
4000 SD 92122 1228-B5
PORTENO CT
1000 SDCo 92078 1128-G4
PORTER LN
1800 SDCo 92036 1136-B7
PORTER RD
1700 SD 92106 1288-C1
4200 LMSA 91941 1271-A4
E PORTER RD
- SD 92106 1288-C1
W PORTER RD
- SD 92106 1288-C1
PORTER ST
300 SDCo 92028 1027-G1
600 SD 92114 1290-F3
PORTER WY
800 SDCo 92028 1027-G1
PORTER CREEK RD
- SD 92130 1188-E5
PORTERFIELD PL
1700 SDCo 92019 1272-B4
PORTER HILL RD
4900 LMSA 91941 1270-J2
PORTER HILL TER
8400 LMSA 91941 1270-J2
PORTERVILLE PL
1000 CHV 91913 1311-E5
PORTFOLIO ST
4800 OCN 92057 1087-B2
PORT HARWICK
500 CHV 91913 1311-D4
PORTIA AV
200 VSTA 92084 1087-H3
PORTICO BLVD
- CALX 92231 6620-F5
PORTICO DR
500 OCN 92054 1086-G1
PORTILLA PL
4100 SD 92130 1188-B7
PORTLAND CT
3700 CRLB 92010 1107-A4
PORTLAND ST
800 ELCJ 92020 1251-G7

PORT MARNOCK DR
17400 PWY 92064 1170-E1
PORT MARNOCK WY
13400 PWY 92064 1170-E1
PORTO CT
10500 SD 92124 1249-H1
PORTOBELO CT
5800 SD 92124 1229-H6
PORTOBELO DR
10500 SD 92124 1229-H7
10900 SD 92124 1230-A6
PORTOFINO CIR
12900 SD 92014 1207-J1
13100 SD 92014 1187-J7
PORTOFINO DR
1400 VSTA 92081 1107-H3
1800 OCN 92054 1106-F1
12700 SD 92014 1207-H1
13100 SD 92014 1187-J6
PORT-OF-SPAIN RD
- CORD 92118 1329-E2
PORTOLA AV
1000 SDCo 91977 1291-C2
1100 ESCN 92026 1109-E5
PORTOLA PL
3900 SD 92103 1268-H5
PORTOLA ST
1000 VSTA 92084 1087-J4
PORTON CT
- CALX 92231 6620-H7
PORT RENWICK
1800 CHV 91902 1311-D4
1800 CHV 91913 1311-D4
PORT ROYALE CV
10200 SD 92126 1209-A5
PORT ROYALE DR
7800 SD 92126 1209-A5
PORT ROYALE RD
- CORD 92118 1329-E2
PORT RUSH RW
11400 SD 92128 1189-J3
PORTSIDE PL
- SD 92154 1330-J7
- SMCS 92078 1128-D6
PORTSMOUTH CT
700 SD 92109 1267-H1
PORTSMOUTH DR
500 CHV 91911 1330-H3
PORTSMOUTH BAY CT
4800 OCN 92057 1066-J6
PORT STIRLING
600 CHV 91913 1311-E3
PORT TRINITY
600 CHV 91913 1311-D4
POSADA CT
- CALX 92231 6620-H7
3900 OCN 92054 1086-G1
POSEIDON WY
4800 OCN 92056 1107-E5
POSEY PL
4200 SD 92105 1289-H1
POSITAS RD
1200 CHV 91910 1311-A5
POSITIVE PL
- SMCS 92069 1108-H7
POSSUM PASS
18800 SDCo 92082 1091-F3
POSSUM CREEK LN
9900 SDCo 92021 1232-G2
POST RD
4300 SD 92117 1228-E7
POST TR
700 SDCo 92019 1253-C2
POSTAL WY
900 VSTA 92083 1087-J7
1000 VSTA 92083 1107-J1
POSTHILL PL
11400 SDCo 92040 1211-J7
POSTHILL RD
11100 SDCo 92040 1211-J7
POST OAK LN
- SDCo 92021 1233-A1
POTOMAC ST
5500 SD 92139 1310-C1
6000 SD 92139 1290-D7
POTRERO CIR
1400 SDCo 91963 (1316-C6 See Page 1296)
POTRERO CT
900 CHV 91911 1330-E1
POTRERO ST
8600 SD 92114 1290-H3
8600 SDCo 91977 1290-H3
POTRERO PARK DR
25600 SDCo 91963 429-L10
POTRERO VALLEY RD
600 SDCo 91963 (1316-F5 See Page 1296)
POTTER ST
100 SDCo 92028 1027-G3
POTTER VALLEY DR
- CHV 91913 1311-E6
POUMELE WY
1800 OCN 92054 1106-E2
POUND RD
300 ImCo 92233 411-B8
300 ImCo 92257 411-B8
POVERTY RDG
25100 SDCo 91916 1236-B3
POWAY RD Rt#-S4
11600 PWY 92064 1190-H2
11600 SD 92128 1190-B5
12000 SD 92128 1189-G6
15500 PWY 92064 1191-A1
POWAY CREEK RD
13000 PWY 92064 1190-E5
POWAY HILLS DR
13100 PWY 92064 1190-D1
POWAY MESA CT
14500 PWY 92064 1190-E1
POWAY MESA DR
14500 PWY 92064 1190-E1
POWAY OAKS DR
12800 PWY 92064 1190-C5
POWAY SPRINGS CT
15300 PWY 92064 1170-F6
POWAY SPRINGS RD
13600 PWY 92064 1170-F6
POWAY VALLEY RD
13800 PWY 92064 1190-G1
POWDERHORN DR
4100 SD 92154 1330-G6
POWELL DR
1900 ELCJ 92020 1251-C4
POWELL RD
1500 OCN 92056 1087-E1
POWERS CT
13200 PWY 92064 1190-C4
POWERS RD
13300 PWY 92064 1190-C4
POWHATAN AV
2700 SD 92117 1248-B1
POYNTELL CIR
10800 SD 92131 1210-A3

STREET Block City ZIP Pg-Grid

RAINBOW PEAKS TR
38700 SDCo 92028 999-C4
RAINBOW RIDGE LN
1200 ENCT 92024 1147-C3
RAINBOW VALLEY BLVD
900 SDCo 92028 998-J5
3000 SDCo 92028 999-A3
3100 RivC 92592 999-A3
RAINBOW VALLEY BLVD W
1500 SDCo 92028 998-J2
1500 SDCo 92028 999-A3
RAINBOW VALLEY CT
1000 SDCo 92028 998-G6
RAINBOW VISTA DR
4300 SDCo 92028 998-G6
RAINBROOK DR
100 SDCo 92028 1029-C3
RAINEY CT
- ENCT 92024 1147-D3
RAINEY ST
7900 LMSA 91942 1250-H6
RAIN FOREST RD
1300 CHV 91910 1311-B6
RAINIER AV
4400 SD 92120 1249-H6
RAINIER CT
100 CHV 91911 1330-F4
RAINIER WY
- OCN 92054 1086-G1
- OCN 92057 1086-G1
RAIN PATTER LN
- CHV 91915 1331-H2
RAINSWEPT CT
8500 SD 92119 1250-J2
8500 SNTE 92071 1250-J2
RAINSWEPT LN
7400 SD 92119 1250-J3
7600 SNTE 92071 1250-J3
RAINSWEPT PL
8500 SD 92119 1250-J3
RAINSWEPT WY
8400 SD 92119 1250-J2
RAINTREE DR
- ENCT 92024 1147-A3
500 VSTA 92084 1087-H5
2500 CRLB 92011 1126-J6
RAINTREE PL
800 VSTA 92084 1087-H5
2200 ESCN 92026 1109-F4
RAINTREE WY
5600 OCN 92057 1067-E6
RAINWOOD CT
600 OCN 92054 1086-D3
RAISSA PL
- CHV 91913 1311-F1
RAJU ST
11100 SD 92129 1169-H7
RALEIGH AV
300 ELCJ 92020 1251-E5
RALENE ST
2200 SD 92105 1289-G1
RALPH RD
- IMP 92251 6439-E3
- ImCo 92251 6439-E3
- ImCo 92251 431-B4
RALPH WY
700 SD 92154 1330-F7
RALPHS RANCH RD
- SDCo 92127 1149-F7
- SDCo 92127 1169-E1
RALSTON CIR
12800 SD 92130 1188-B5
RAM LN
1300 SDCo 92028 1047-H1
RAMADA DR
2100 OCN 92056 1086-J7
16400 SD 92128 1170-B4
RAMA DE LAS PALMAS
3700 SDCo 92091 1168-B7
RAMBLA BRISA
1400 SMCS 92069 1109-D7
RAMBLA DE LAS FLORES
16000 SDCo 92067 1168-A4
RAMBLA PUESTA
1400 SMCS 92069 1109-D7
RAMBLA SERENA
1400 SMCS 92069 1109-D7
RAMBLEWOOD RD
1500 SDCo 91901 1233-H6
RAMBLING RD
400 ENCT 92024 1147-G5
RAMBLING WY
500 SDCo 92065 1152-D6
RAMBLING VISTA RD
2700 CHV 91915 1311-J6
2700 CHV 91915 (1312-A6 See Page 1293)
RAMBUR ST
700 CHV 91911 1330-J3
RAMFOS CIR
6800 SD 92139 1310-G1
RAMFOS LN
6900 SD 92139 1290-F7
RAMFOS PL
2500 SD 92139 1290-F7
2600 SD 92139 1310-F1
RAMHAVEN LN
8200 SNTE 92071 1250-J1
RAMO CT
9700 SNTE 92071 1231-C4
RAMO RD
9700 SNTE 92071 1231-C5
RAMON ST
1700 LMGR 91945 1290-F1
RAMONA AV
400 SDCo 91977 1291-C1
2000 SDCo 91977 1271-C7
RAMONA CT
- IMP 92251 6439-F4
9200 SDCo 92021 1232-E5
RAMONA DR
700 SDCo 92036 1136-D7
2400 SDCo 92084 1087-F1
4300 SDCo 92028 1048-B6
10100 SDCo 91977 1271-E5
RAMONA LN
2100 SDCo 92084 1108-D2
RAMONA PL
700 SOLB 92014 1187-G1
RAMONA ST
100 SDCo 92065 1152-F6
500 SDCo 92065 1172-F1
N RAMONA ST
- SDCo 92065 1152-F6
RAMONA WY
- SMCS 92078 1129-C1
100 OCN 92057 1086-G6
RAMONA AIRPORT RD
2300 SDCo 92065 1152-B7
RAMONA HIGHLANDS DR
19700 SDCo 92065 1152-B1

RAMONA HIGHLANDS RD
19500 SDCo 92065 1152-B1
RAMONA OAKS RD
24500 SDCo 92065 1173-F4
26000 SDCo 92065 1174-A4
RAMONA REAL
100 SDCo 92065 1152-J1
1600 SDCo 92065 1153-A1
RAMONA TRAILS DR
19300 SDCo 92065 1153-D2
RAMONA VIEW CT
- SDCo 92065 1153-B5
RAMONA VIEW DR
18400 SDCo 92065 1153-B4
RAMSAY AV
4600 SD 92122 1228-F4
RAMSDELL CT
11600 SD 92131 1209-H1
11800 SD 92131 1189-H7
RAMSEY LN
1800 SDCo 92065 1172-F1
RAMSEY RD
1400 SDCo 91901 1234-B6
RAMSGATE DR
10700 SNTE 92071 1231-F4
RAMSGATE WY
9600 SNTE 92071 1231-F4
RAMS HILL DR
1900 SDCo 92004 (1099-F4 See Page 1098)
RAMS HILL RD
1700 SDCo 92004 (1099-F3 See Page 1098)
RANA CT
3000 CRLB 92009 1147-H1
RANCH RD
- ENCT 92024 1147-D3
W RANCH RD
900 SDCo 92078 1128-C2
RANCH BROOK RD
4000 SDCo 92028 998-E5
RANCH CREEK LN
13500 PWY 92064 1170-E6
14900 SDCo 92082 1070-H2
RANCH CREEK RD
30600 SDCo 92082 1070-G3
RANCHERO DR
1500 OCN 92057 1067-F6
RANCHEROS
1500 SDCo 92021 1251-G2
RANCHEROS DR
100 SMCS 92069 1108-H7
300 SMCS 92069 1128-J1
400 SMCS 92069 1109-B7
1100 SMCS 92069 1129-B1
RANCHETTE PL
1300 CHV 91913 1311-D7
RANCH GATE RD
- CHV 91914 1311-H1
700 SDCo 92021 1252-G1
RANCH HOLLOW RD
15900 PWY 92064 1170-E5
RANCH HOUSE RD
12200 SD 92128 1150-B7
RANCHITO CT
- SDCo 91901 1253-H1
RANCHITO DR
500 ESCN 92025 1130-C6
RANCHITO LN
1900 SDCo 91901 1253-H1
2100 SDCo 91901 1233-H7
RANCHITO DEL RIO
- SDCo 92067 1167-J2
RANCHITOS CT
10100 SDCo 92040 1231-F3
RANCHITOS PL
10100 SDCo 92040 1231-F3
RANCHITOS ST
11000 SDCo 92040 1231-F3
RANCHITO VISTA
- SDCo 91901 1253-H1
RANCHO CT
200 CHV 91911 1330-G5
5200 OCN 92056 1087-E2
RANCHO CTE
2000 VSTA 92084 1087-H2
RANCHO DR
200 CHV 91911 1330-G6
2100 SD 92139 1310-D1
9600 SDCo 92029 1149-D4
RANCHO RD
10300 SDCo 91941 1271-E4
RANCHO TER
500 SDCo 92026 1109-G3
RANCHO ADARME LN
3000 SDCo 92003 1067-F1
- SDCo 92028 1067-F1
RANCHO AGUA HADIONDA DR
3500 OCN 92056 1106-B4
RANCHO ALLEN LN
100 SDCo 92065 1153-A5
RANCHO AMIGOS RD
31200 SDCo 92003 1068-F2
RANCHO AMIGOS RD N
7600 SDCo 92003 1068-G2
RANCHO ANDREW
1900 SDCo 91901 1233-J7
1900 SDCo 91901 1253-J1
RANCHO ANTIGUO
14900 SDCo 92014 1188-A1
RANCHO ARROBA
3200 CRLB 92009 1127-J3
RANCHO BALLENA LN
19300 SDCo 92065 1154-B1
RANCHO BALLENA RD
19500 SDCo 92065 409-J11
RANCHO BARONA RD
25400 SDCo 92065 1173-H5
RANCHO BERNARDO RD
10200 SDCo 92127 1169-F3
10400 SD 92127 1169-F3
11700 SD 92127 1170-A2
11700 SD 92128 1170-A2
RANCHO BERNARDO RD Rt#-S5
12500 SD 92128 1170-D3
RANCHO BERNARDO TOWN CENTER DR
11900 SD 92128 1170-A3
RANCHO BONITO RD
3800 SDCo 92028 1047-F4
RANCHO BRASADO
2900 CRLB 92009 1127-J4
RANCHO BRAVADO
6000 CRLB 92009 1127-H2
RANCHO BRAYDON LN
800 SDCo 91901 1234-D5
RANCHO BRIDA
6100 CRLB 92009 1127-H3
RANCHO BULLARD LN
800 SDCo 92065 1152-G7
RANCHO CABALLO
- CRLB 92009 1127-J4

RANCHO CABALLO RD
12600 PWY 92064 1190-C6
RANCHO CABRILLO TR
- SD 92127 1188-J1
RANCHO CAJON PL
1700 SDCo 92019 1252-B4
RANCHO CAMINO
100 SDCo 92028 1047-G5
RANCHO CAMINO NORTE
4300 SDCo 92028 1047-H5
RANCHO CANADA RD
- SDCo 92021 1232-E7
- SDCo 92021 1252-D1
RANCHO CAPISTRANO BEND
- SD 92130 1188-D3
RANCHO CAPITAN
10000 SDCo 92040 1232-C2
RANCHO CARLSBAD DR
3300 CRLB 92010 1107-C7
RANCHO CARMEL DR
10100 SD 92128 1189-J1
11300 SD 92128 1169-J7
11300 SD 92128 1170-A7
RANCHO CARRIZO
3200 CRLB 92009 1127-J2
RANCHO CATALINA TR
- SD 92127 1188-H1
RANCHO CHARRO
- CRLB 92009 1127-H2
RANCHO CHIMNEY ROCK RD
28200 SDCo 92066 410-A8
RANCHO CIELO
6900 SDCo 92067 1148-F7
RANCHO COMPANERO
3200 CRLB 92009 1127-J3
RANCHO COPA
14500 SDCo 92082 1070-G7
RANCHO CORTES
2800 CRLB 92009 1127-J4
RANCHO COSTERO
- CRLB 92009 1127-H3
RANCHO DE CAROLE RD
17500 SDCo 92065 1171-G2
RANCHO DE KEVIN RD
16400 SDCo 92065 1171-G3
RANCHO DEL CTE
9300 SDCo 92040 1232-F5
RANCHO DE LA ANGEL RD
17400 SDCo 92065 1171-G3
RANCHO DEL ACACIA WY
- SD 92130 1188-G3
RANCHO DEL AZALEAS WY
- SD 92130 1188-G4
RANCHO DEL CANON
- CRLB 92009 1127-H2
RANCHO DEL CERRO
500 SDCo 92003 1067-F1
500 SDCo 92028 1067-F1
RANCHO DEL LADERA DR
200 SDCo 92065 1153-A4
RANCHO DEL MADISON
5000 SDCo 92014 1188-A1
RANCHO DEL MAR TR
- SD 92130 1188-B3
RANCHO DE LOMA RD
100 SDCo 92028 1028-E1
RANCHO DEL ORO DR
- OCN 92057 1086-H3
600 OCN 92056 1086-H5
RANCHO DEL ORO RD
1300 OCN 92056 1086-J6
2000 OCN 92056 1106-J1
RANCHO DEL PRADO TR
- SD 92127 1188-H1
RANCHO DEL RAY
100 SDCo 92025 1130-E7
RANCHO DEL REY PKWY
- CHV 91910 1310-H5
- CHV 91910 1311-A5
RANCHO DEL RIO
17400 SDCo 92067 1168-H1
RANCHO DEL SOL
2800 SDCo 92025 1130-E7
17800 SDCo 92065 1151-D6
RANCHO DEL SOL WY
- SD 92130 1188-G4
RANCHO DEL VERDE
400 SDCo 92025 1130-E7
RANCHO DEL VERDE PL
3000 SDCo 92025 1130-F7
RANCHO DEL VILLA
14000 SDCo 92040 1232-F5
RANCHO DE ORO RD
500 ESCN 92026 1109-G6
500 SDCo 92026 1109-G6
17400 SDCo 92065 1171-J4
17400 SDCo 92065 1172-A4
RANCHO DIAMONTE
- CRLB 92009 1127-H3
RANCHO DIEGO CIR
3400 SDCo 92019 1272-C6
RANCHO DIEGO CT
2300 SDCo 92029 1129-H7
RANCHO DIEGUENO RD
5700 SDCo 92067 1168-E7
5800 SDCo 92067 1188-F1
RANCHO DORADO BEND
- SD 92130 1188-C3
RANCHO DULZURA
- CRLB 92009 1127-H3
RANCHO EAST
7300 SDCo 92067 1148-G6
RANCHO ELEGANTE DR
- CALX 92231 6680-H2
RANCHO ENCINITAS DR
1100 ENCT 92024 1148-B5
RANCHO FALLBROOK
47200 RivC 92590 997-G1
RANCHO FAMOSA
3200 CRLB 92009 1127-J2
RANCHO FANITA DR
7800 SNTE 92071 1230-H7
7900 SNTE 92071 1250-H1
RANCHO FRONTERA AV
- CALX 92231 6620-H5
RANCHO GANADERO
2800 CRLB 92009 1127-H4
RANCHO GRANDE
4800 SDCo 92014 1168-A7
RANCHO GUADALUPE RD
13200 SDCo 92059 409-E5
RANCHO HEIGHTS RD
11400 SDCo 92059 999-G3
13000 SDCo 92059 409-E5
RANCHO HILLS DR
5700 SD 92139 1310-D1
RANCHO JAMUL DR
14400 SDCo 91935 1293-A4

RANCHO JANET
1800 SDCo 91901 1233-J7
1800 SDCo 91901 1253-J1
RANCHO JORIE
1800 SDCo 91901 1233-H7
RANCHO JUDITH
1800 SDCo 91901 1233-J7
RANCHO LA CIMA CTE
18000 SDCo 92067 1148-F6
RANCHO LA CIMA DR
6800 SDCo 92067 1148-F7
RANCHO LAGUNA BEND
- SD 92130 1188-B3
RANCHO LAKES CT
6700 SDCo 92067 1188-G3
RANCHO LA MIRADA LN
400 SDCo 92025 1129-J7
400 SDCo 92025 1130-A7
RANCHO LA NORIA
- SDCo 92067 1167-J2
RANCHO LA PRESA
- CRLB 92009 1127-H2
RANCHO LAS BRISAS TR
- SD 92130 1188-A3
RANCHO LAS PALMAS DR
2000 SDCo 92028 1048-A1
RANCHO LATIGO
- CRLB 92009 1127-H3
RANCHO LUISENO RD
1200 SDCo 92026 1109-C1
RANCHO MADERA BEND
- SD 92130 1188-D3
RANCHO MANZANITA DR
700 SDCo 91905 (1299-H7 See Page 1298)
RANCHO MARIA LN
2900 SDCo 92065 1172-C2
RANCHO MEADOWCREST RD
2100 SDCo 92021 1252-G4
RANCHO MIA
1400 SDCo 92028 1027-J6
RANCHO MIEL
- CRLB 92009 1127-J4
RANCHO MIGUEL RD
3200 SDCo 91935 1272-D7
RANCHO MILAGRO
3200 CRLB 92009 1127-J3
RANCHO MIRAGE LN
9600 SDCo 92040 1232-C4
RANCHO MISSION RD
5800 SD 92108 1269-G1
5900 SD 92108 1249-G7
RANCHO MONTANA
3100 CRLB 92009 1128-A4
3100 SDCo 92078 1128-A4
RANCHO NUEVO
14900 SDCo 92014 1168-A7
RANCHO OAKS LN
- SDCo 91978 1292-C1
RANCHO PACIFICA PL
900 VSTA 92084 1087-J7
900 VSTA 92084 1088-A7
RANCHO PANCHO
2800 CRLB 92009 1127-H4
RANCHO PARK CT
- VSTA 92084 1087-H3
RANCHO PARK DR
6400 SD 92120 1250-D6
RANCHO PENASQUITOS BLVD
12600 SD 92128 1189-F4
12600 SD 92129 1189-F4
RANCHO POSTA
2900 CRLB 92009 1127-H3
RANCHO QUARTILLO
3200 CRLB 92009 1127-J3
RANCHO QUINTA BEND
- SD 92130 1188-C3
RANCHO REAL
15100 SDCo 92014 1188-B1
RANCHO REATA
3200 CRLB 92009 1127-J2
RANCHO REPOSO
4600 SDCo 92014 1188-A1
RANCHO RIO CHICO
- CRLB 92009 1127-H3
RANCHO RIVER RD
14400 SDCo 92059 1030-F7
RANCHO ROBLE RD
10100 SDCo 92026 1089-E5
RANCHO ROSE WY
- OCN 92057 1067-E6
RANCHO RYAN RD
1100 SDCo 92028 1027-H1
RANCHO SAN DIEGO PKWY
- SDCo 92019 1271-J5
RANCHO SAN MARTIN DR
17800 SDCo 92065 1171-G1
RANCHO SANTA FE CT
1100 SDCo 92065 1153-E2
RANCHO SANTA FE RD
100 ENCT 92024 1147-J7
100 ENCT 92024 1167-J1
600 ENCT 92024 1148-A6
7000 CRLB 92009 1147-H4
RANCHO SANTA FE RD Rt#-S10
- CRLB 92009 1128-A7
- CRLB 92009 1148-A1
2900 CRLB 92009 1147-H3
RANCHO SANTA FE RD Rt#-S9
100 ENCT 92024 1167-J1
100 SDCo 92067 1167-J1
2600 SDCo 92067 1168-A1
N RANCHO SANTA FE RD Rt#-S10
100 SMCS 92078 1108-D6
100 SMCS 92069 1108-D6
S RANCHO SANTA FE RD Rt#-S10
100 SMCS 92078 1108-D7
400 SMCS 92078 1128-A3
2200 CRLB 92009 1128-A3
2200 CRLB 92078 1128-A3
RANCHO SANTA FE FARMS DR
6400 SDCo 92067 1188-G1
6900 SD 92127 1188-G1
RANCHO SANTA FE FARMS RD
13400 SD 92130 1188-G2
14100 SDCo 92130 1188-G2
RANCHO SANTA FE LAKES DR
14200 SDCo 92067 1188-G3
14200 SD 92130 1188-G3

RANCHO SANTA FE VIEW DR
- SDCo 92067 1148-H7
- SDCo 92067 1168-H1
RANCHO SANTA TERESA DR
24600 SDCo 92065 1153-F1
RANCHO SERENA RD
1400 SDCo 92067 1167-J5
RANCHO SIERRA
- SDCo 91901 1234-C7
RANCHO SIERRA BEND
- SD 92130 1188-B3
RANCHOS LADERA RD
32500 SDCo 92003 1048-H6
RANCHO SOL CT
4800 SDCo 92014 1188-A1
RANCHO SOLANA TR
- SD 92130 1188-D3
RANCHO SUENOS DR
17100 SDCo 92065 1171-F2
RANCHO SUMMIT
- SDCo 91901 1254-B2
RANCHO SUMMIT DR
1600 ENCT 92024 1148-D2
1600 SDCo 92024 1148-D2
1600 SMCS 92024 1148-D2
RANCHO TAZA RD
8300 SDCo 92028 998-J7
8300 SDCo 92028 1028-H1
RANCHO TIERRA TR
- SD 92130 1188-D3
RANCHO TOYON PL
- SD 92130 1188-G7
RANCHO TRAILS
500 SDCo 92065 1152-G1
RANCHO VACADA
- CRLB 92009 1127-J3
RANCHO VALENCIA DR
16000 SDCo 92067 1168-F7
RANCHO VALENCIA RD
5800 SDCo 92067 1168-E7
RANCHO VALENCIA ST
- SDCo 92082 1071-A7
RANCHO VALENCIA WY
- SDCo 92082 1071-A7
RANCHO VALENCIA VISTA
- SDCo 92067 1188-F1
RANCHO VALLE CT
1000 ELCJ 92020 1251-H7
RANCHO VENTANA TR
- SD 92127 1188-H1
RANCHO VERDE DR
2100 ESCN 92025 1130-B6
2100 SDCo 92025 1130-B6
RANCHO VERDE TR
- SD 92130 1188-C3
RANCHO VICENTE DR
15000 SDCo 92065 1172-J6
15000 SDCo 92065 1173-A6
RANCHO VIEJO DR
4800 SDCo 92014 1188-A1
RANCHO VIEW DR
47100 RivC 92592 999-F1
RANCHO VILLA RD
1700 SDCo 92065 1152-D1
RANCHO VISTA BEND
- SD 92130 1188-C3
RANCHO VISTA CT
12900 SDCo 92082 1090-C4
13800 SDCo 91935 1292-G1
RANCHO VISTA DR
18500 SDCo 92065 1153-C4
RANCHO VISTA PL
300 VSTA 92083 1087-H7
RANCHO VISTA RD
400 VSTA 92083 1087-H7
600 VSTA 92083 1107-H1
RANCHO VISTA WY
1600 SDCo 92028 1027-J1
RANCHO WILLITS
- SDCo 91901 1253-G2
RANCHO WINCHESTER LN
1900 SDCo 92019 1272-A1
RANCH TRAIL DR
14400 SDCo 92021 1232-G4
RANCH VIEW CT
- CHV 91914 1311-J2
RANCH VIEW DR
10600 SD 92131 1209-G4
RANCHVIEW PL
- ESCN 92027 1130-J2
RANCH VIEW RD
5800 OCN 92057 1067-F6
RANCH VIEW TER
2100 ENCT 92024 1147-J7
RANCHWOOD DR
10600 SDCo 91978 1271-G7
RANCHWOOD GN
300 ESCN 92026 1109-G4
RANCHWOOD LN
1500 SDCo 92028 1027-J5
RANDALL ST
4800 SD 92109 1248-B4
RANDLETT DR
4900 LMSA 91941 1270-J2
RANDOLPH ST
4000 SD 92103 1268-H5
RANDOM CT
1200 ELCJ 92020 1251-G7
RANDOM RD
1000 ELCJ 92020 1251-G7
1000 SDCo 92020 1251-G7
1100 ELCJ 92020 1271-G1
1100 SDCo 92020 1271-G1
RANDY CT
3300 SDCo 91910 1310-F4
RANDY LN
3400 SDCo 91910 1310-F4
RANETA LN
5400 SD 92124 1249-G1
N RANGE RD
- SDCo 92055 408-J5
RANGE ST
100 ENCT 92024 1147-A3
RANGELAND RD
18400 SDCo 92065 1151-J2
RANGE PARK PL
14500 PWY 92064 1190-H1
RANGE PARK RD
14300 PWY 92064 1190-H2
RANGER RD
200 SDCo 92028 1028-E1
5900 SD 92139 1290-D7
RANGE VIEW RD
1100 VSTA 92084 1108-C1
RANGEVIEW ST
800 SDCo 91977 1290-J3
RANGO WY
700 SDCo 92004 (1078-J7 See Page 1058)

RANGO WY
700 SDCo 92004 (1079-A7 See Page 1058)
RANLEIGH CT
3100 SD 92110 1268-D6
RANRIDO DR
800 SDCo 92025 1130-B3
RANRIDOS CT
1200 ESCN 92027 1110-C5
RANSOM ST
900 SD 92154 1330-G7
900 SD 92154 1350-G1
RANSOM HILL LN
100 SDCo 92065 1153-A4
RANZA RD
8700 SDCo 91977 1291-A5
RAPATEE CT
10900 SDCo 91941 1271-G4
RAPATEE DR
4000 SDCo 91941 1271-G4
RAPHAEL CT
400 ENCT 92024 1147-G6
RAPPAHANNOCK AV
4100 SD 92117 1248-E5
RAPPAPORT PL
10400 SNTE 92071 1231-E3
RAPTOR RD
15400 SDCo 92064 1191-B6
RAPTURE LN
9300 SNTE 92071 1231-B7
RAQUEL DR
4200 OCN 92056 1107-C2
RASCON CT
11600 SD 92131 1190-A7
RASHA ST
8600 SD 92121 1228-H1
RASMUSSEN WY
14100 SD 92129 1189-E2
RASPBERRY WY
500 OCN 92057 1067-D7
RASPBERRY ICE LN
9700 SDCo 91941 1271-C4
RATCLIFF RD
1700 CRLB 92008 1106-F3
RATHMOOR ST
1200 ELCJ 92020 1251-G7
RAULSTON TER
800 ESCN 92027 1130-C2
RAV CT
- SDCo 91935 1274-B2
RAVEAN CT
- ENCT 92024 1147-D2
RAVEN AV
1200 CHV 91911 1330-G2
RAVEN PL
1200 CHV 91911 1330-G2
RAVEN ST
500 SD 92102 1289-H3
RAVEN HILL PT
- SD 92130 1208-D2
RAVEN HILL RD
- SDCo 91935 1272-J7
RAVEN RIDGE PT
7500 SD 92126 1208-J2
RAVENROCK CT
1700 CHV 91913 1311-D6
RAVENSCROFT ST
100 NATC 92136 1309-G1
RAVENSTHORPE WY
- SD 92131 1209-G2
RAVENSWOOD RD
5800 SD 92037 1247-G3
RAVENWOOD DR
2200 LMGR 91945 1270-H7
2300 LMGR 91945 1290-H1
RAVINA DR
- CHV 91913 1331-E1
RAVINA ST
100 SD 92037 1227-E7
RAVINE CT
700 VSTA 92083 1087-D6
RAVINE DR
- CRLB 92010 1107-B5
RAVINE RD
1400 VSTA 92083 1087-D6
RAWHIDE CT
900 CHV 91902 1310-H4
RAWHIDE WY
- OCN 92057 1086-J2
RAWL PL
700 SOLB 92075 1167-F6
RAWLINS WY
9500 SNTE 92071 1231-C4
RAY ST
600 ESCN 92026 1109-J7
3400 SD 92104 1269-E6
RAYA WY
4100 SD 92122 1228-E5
RAYDEL CT
6300 SD 92120 1250-D7
RAYFORD DR
10000 SDCo 92026 1109-E1
10100 SDCo 92026 1089-E7
RAYLEY DR
10600 SDCo 91978 1271-F7
RAYLINE WY
10100 SDCo 91977 1271-E4
RAYMAR AV
5600 SD 92120 1250-D7
5600 SD 92120 1270-D1
RAYMELL DR
2500 SD 92123 1249-E7
RAYMOND AV
1800 SDCo 92065 1152-E7
2000 SDCo 92065 1172-D1
RAYMOND LN
1900 OCN 92054 1086-C7
RAYMOND PL
5000 SD 92116 1269-F2
RAYMOND ST
400 ELCJ 92020 1251-G7
RAYNELL WY
1600 ELCJ 92019 1252-B7
RAYS WY
13000 SDCo 92082 1050-C5
RAYTHEON RD
7400 SD 92111 1249-A1
RAZUKI LN
- SDCo 91935 1273-B6
R CARRILLO CT
- CALX 92231 6620-J6
REA AV
100 ELCJ 92020 1251-F5
READ RD
- CORD 92135 1288-F4
REAGAN CIR
8600 SD 92126 1209-C4
REAGAN CT
8600 SD 92126 1209-C4
REAGAN GN
8600 SD 92126 1209-C4
REAGAN LN
8600 SD 92127 1169-B3
REAGAN PL
8600 SD 92126 1209-C4

REAGAN RD
9100 SD 92126 1209-B3
REAL ST
- SMCS 92078 1128-H3
REALTY RD
1400 SDCo 92065 1152-F7
REAL WAY LN
1500 SDCo 91901 1253-J3
REASER LN
1000 SDCo 92065 1152-F3
REATA CT
12300 SD 92128 1150-B6
REATA WY
18200 SD 92128 1150-B6
REBECCA AV
200 VSTA 92084 1087-H3
9200 SD 92123 1249-E6
REBECCA LN
- ELCJ 92019 1252-B7
30900 SDCo 92082 1070-F3
REBECCA ST
- ELCJ 92019 1252-B6
- ELCN 92243 6559-J3
REBECCA WY
- ELCJ 92019 1252-A6
2100 LMGR 91945 1290-J1
2100 LMGR 91945 1270-J7
REBECCAS GREEN TR
1900 SDCo 92065 1172-F1
REBEL RD
4900 SD 92117 1228-F7
REBEL WIND DR
- SDCo 91916 1216-A2
REBOLLA LN
5300 SD 92124 1249-G1
RECHE RD
1300 SDCo 92028 1027-H4
RECHE RD Rt#-S15
1500 SDCo 92028 1027-J4
1700 SDCo 92028 1028-A4
RECHE WY
700 SDCo 92028 1027-J4
RECLUSE LN
400 ENCT 92024 1147-G6
RECODO CT
2200 CRLB 92009 1147-F2
RECREATION DR
100 VSTA 92083 1087-G6
1500 SDCo 92028 1028-F4
RECUERDO CV
2300 SD 92014 1187-H5
RECUERDO DR
13600 SD 92014 1187-H6
RED ALDER PL
700 ESCN 92027 1110-D5
RED BARK RD
1400 ESCN 92029 1129-F5
REDBARK WY
600 SD 92139 1310-F1
RED BARN RD
1700 ENCT 92024 1147-H6
REDBERRY CT
800 SMCS 92069 1109-A5
REDBIRD DR
2000 SD 92123 1269-B1
2100 SD 92123 1249-A7
RED BLUSH RD
- ESCN 92027 1110-C6
REDBROOK CT
4700 SD 92117 1248-J1
REDBROOK RD
5900 SD 92117 1248-J1
REDBUD CT
11200 SD 92127 1169-J5
REDBUD PL
800 CHV 91910 1310-H7
REDBUD RD
900 CHV 91910 1310-H7
RED CANYON DR
29800 SDCo 92082 1069-J6
RED CEDAR CT
10200 SD 92131 1209-H4
RED CEDAR DR
10600 SD 92131 1209-H4
RED CEDAR LN
11300 SD 92131 1209-J4
RED CEDAR PL
10300 SD 92131 1209-H4
RED CEDAR WY
11300 SD 92131 1209-J4
REDCLIFF CT
12000 SD 92131 1210-B3
RED CLOUD LN
13300 PWY 92064 1190-H4
RED COACH LN
2000 ENCT 92024 1147-H6
RED CORAL AV
- CRLB 92011 1126-J6
RED CORAL LN
400 SD 92154 1330-H6
REDCREST CT
8200 SD 92114 1290-H4
REDCREST DR
200 SD 92114 1290-H3
REDCREST PL
8200 SD 92114 1290-H4
RED DEER ST
6600 SD 92122 1228-E4
RED DIAMOND DR
9500 SDCo 92040 1232-C4
REDDING RD
5300 SD 92115 1270-A1
REDEL RD
100 SMCS 92078 1128-J1
REDEN LN
30600 SDCo 92082 1069-D4
RED FERN CIR
10800 SD 92131 1210-A3
REDFERN LN
12900 SDCo 92082 1070-C5
REDFIELD ST
9000 SDCo 91977 1291-A3
REDFORD PL
3000 SD 92139 1310-E2
RED FOX LN
- SMCS 92069 1108-H4
REDGAP CT
2100 ENCT 92024 1147-H7
RED GRANITE RD
900 CHV 91911 1331-A2
900 CHV 91913 1331-A2
RED GUM RD
1200 SDCo 92019 1253-E3
RED HAWK LN
- PWY 92064 1190-H1
RED HAWK RD
30600 SDCo 92082 1069-C4
RED HAWK RDG
- SDCo 91901 1255-E6
RED HAWK WY
100 SMCS 92078 1128-H5
RED HILL LN
1600 CHV 91902 1311-B4

STREET
Block City ZIP Pg-Grid

REDHILL LN
800 SMCS 92069 1109-B5
RED HILL RD
- ImCo 92233 411-A8
- ImCo 92259 411-A8
RED HILLS CT
9300 SNTE 92071 1230-J6
RED IRONBARK DR
- SDCo 92027 1090-D6
- SDCo 92082 1090-C4
RED KNOT ST
6500 CRLB 92011 1127-A4
REDLAND DR
5400 SD 92115 1270-B3
REDLAND PL
5400 SD 92115 1270-B3
REDLANDER WY
10800 SDCo 92040 1232-B1
REDLANDS PL
600 CHV 91902 1311-C4
REDLANDS ST
400 VSTA 92083 1087-G5
RED LEAF LN
- CHV 91915 1331-G1
REDMAN ST
- CORD 91932 1329-E5
RED MAPLE DR
1000 CHV 91910 1310-J7
1000 CHV 91910 1330-J1
RED MAPLE WY
4400 OCN 92057 1086-J2
RED MOUNTAIN CT
1300 CHV 91910 1311-B6
RED MOUNTAIN DR
29700 SDCo 92082 1069-J5
RED MOUNTAIN LN
100 SDCo 92028 1028-E1
RED MOUNTAIN TKTR
- RivC 92590 998-G1
- SDCo 92028 998-E2
RED MOUNTAIN DAM DR
3300 SDCo 92028 998-D7
3300 SDCo 92028 1028-D1
RED MOUNTAIN HEIGHTS DR
2800 SDCo 92028 998-C6
RED OAK CT
- SMCS 92078 1128-D6
RED OAK PL
1000 CHV 91910 1310-J7
RED OAK RD
- SDCo 91901 1235-B3
REDONDO CT
700 SD 92109 1267-H1
REDONDO DR
- OCN 92057 1066-J6
300 OCN 92057 1067-A7
4800 SDCo 91941 1271-F2
5700 SDCo 92003 1048-C7
N REDONDO DR
500 OCN 92057 1066-J6
500 OCN 92057 1067-A6
W REDONDO DR
400 OCN 92057 1066-J6
REDONDO ST
1700 SD 92107 1268-A7
1700 SD 92107 1288-A1
RED PINE CT
900 SD 92154 1330-B7
RED PINE DR
2400 SD 92154 1330-B7
2400 SD 92154 1350-B1
RED PLUM LN
- SDCo 92081 1107-J3
RED PONY LN
9600 SDCo 92021 1232-H3
RED RIVER DR
5500 SD 92120 1250-B4
RED ROBIN PL
11000 SD 92126 1208-J2
RED ROCK CT
9900 SD 92131 1209-H5
RED ROCK DR
10800 SD 92131 1209-H5
RED ROCK CANYON RD
2700 CHV 91915 1311-J6
2700 CHV 91915 (1312-A6 See Page 1293)
RED ROSE LN
- SDCo 92127 1169-G1
RED SAILS WY
4700 SD 92154 1330-H7
RED SHANK LN
2200 SDCo 91905 (1299-J4 See Page 1298)
2300 SDCo 91905 1300-A4
RED STONE LN
28200 SDCo 92026 1089-E3
RED TAIL HAWK CT
11500 SDCo 92040 1212-C5
RED TOP LN
3500 SDCo 92028 1048-B4
RED WAGON LN
- CHV 91915 1331-G1
RED WILLOW PL
- CHV 91915 1311-H1
REDWING DR
3300 OCN 92054 1086-D2
REDWING RD
400 CHV 91911 1330-G2
REDWING ST
1700 SDCo 92078 1128-A4
1700 SMCS 92078 1128-A4
REDWING WY
1700 SDCo 92078 1128-A4
REDWOOD AV
100 CRLB 92008 1106-E7
1000 ELCJ 92020 1251-J6
1100 ELCJ 92019 1251-J6
REDWOOD DR
100 SMCS 92069 1108-J5
8700 SNTE 92071 1231-B7
9100 SD 92093 1227-J3
REDWOOD LN
9700 SDCo 92029 1149-E3
REDWOOD PL
700 ESCN 92025 1129-J5
REDWOOD RD
- ELCJ 92019 1251-J6
REDWOOD ST
- SMCS 92078 1129-C2
100 SD 92103 1269-A7
600 SD 92103 1268-J7
1500 SD 92101 1268-H7
1700 ESCN 92025 1129-J5
1800 ESCN 92025 1130-A6
2700 SD 92101 1269-E7
2800 SD 92104 1269-E7
3000 SD 92105 1269-G7
3500 OCN 92054 1086-F1
5200 SD 92105 1270-B6
S REDWOOD ST
400 ESCN 92025 1129-J4

REDWOOD CREST
2000 VSTA 92081 1107-F5
REED AV
700 SD 92109 1247-H7
1400 SD 92109 1248-A6
REED CT
100 CHV 91911 1330-E5
REED RD
2500 ESCN 92027 1130-E1
REED TER
900 ESCN 92027 1130-F1
REEDLEY TER
4700 SD 92130 1188-C4
REEF DR
700 SD 92154 1330-D7
REEFPOINT WY
- OCN 92054 1086-G2
REES RD
1000 SMCS 92069 1109-D7
1000 SDCo 92026 1109-E6
1200 ESCN 92026 1109-E6
REESE LN
17000 SDCo 92065 1171-H3
REESE ST
800 OCN 92054 1106-B2
REEVE RD
- CRLB 92011 1146-J1
REEVES ST
400 NATC 92136 1309-F1
REFLECTION CIR
2200 VSTA 92081 1107-H7
REFLECTION DR
6500 SD 92124 1249-G6
REFLECTION ST
- SMCS 92078 1128-F6
REFUGIO AV
4800 CRLB 92008 1106-J6
REGAL RD
700 ENCT 92024 1147-D7
900 ENCT 92024 1167-D1
REGALO LN
17200 SD 92128 1170-A2
REGAL RIDGE RD
1000 ENCT 92024 1148-A5
REGATTA LN
4700 SD 92154 1330-H6
REGATTA RD
1500 CRLB 92011 1127-B4
REGENCY CIR
4500 OCN 92056 1107-E2
REGENCY CT
200 CHV 91911 1330-G5
REGENCY RD
8700 SD 92123 1249-C7
REGENCY WY
1700 CHV 91911 1330-F5
REGENT RD
2600 CRLB 92010 1106-J5
2600 CRLB 92010 1107-A6
REGENTS RD
4200 SD 92037 1228-B2
4900 SD 92117 1228-C6
4900 SD 92117 1248-C1
5300 SD 92122 1228-C3
REGENTS PARK RW
4100 SD 92037 1228-C2
REGINA AV
5600 SD 92117 1228-H6
REGINA GN
31300 SDCo 92082 1070-E1
REGINA LN
1100 VSTA 92083 1087-G4
REGINAS CT
10400 SNTE 92071 1231-E4
REGIS AV
5600 SD 92120 1270-D1
REGIS CT
900 VSTA 92084 1087-J5
REGLA CT
4900 SD 92122 1228-G5
REGNER CT
8600 SD 92119 1250-J4
REGNER RD
6900 SD 92119 1250-J3
REGULO PL
700 CHV 91910 1311-A6
REGULUS ST
1500 SD 92111 1269-A2
REHCO RD
8800 SD 92121 1228-H1
8800 SD 92121 1208-H7
REICHERT WY
- CHV 91913 1331-E2
REIDY CANYON PL
11200 SDCo 92026 1089-H6
REIDY CANYON RD
7800 SDCo 92026 1109-G1
10400 SDCo 92026 1089-F5
REIDY CANYON TR
10800 SDCo 92026 1089-G7
REILLVIEW DR
2400 SDCo 92025 1130-B7
REINEMAN RD
2100 SDCo 92028 1027-H6
REISLING TER
500 CHV 91913 1311-D3
REKLOW DR
1500 SD 92154 1350-B2
RELIANCE WY
1000 SOLB 92014 1187-G1
RELINDO CT
16300 SD 92128 1170-C4
RELINDO DR
12600 SD 92128 1170-C4
REMBRANDT GN
1200 ESCN 92026 1109-J7
REMEDIOS CT
100 SOLB 92075 1167-D7
REMINGTON CT
1200 VSTA 92083 1087-E5
REMINGTON RD
5100 SD 92115 1270-A1
5300 SD 92182 1270-A1
REMINGTON HILLS DR
- SD 92154 1350-G2
REMLEY PL
7300 SD 92037 1227-G7
REMORA ST
10500 SD 92124 1249-H1
REMSEN CT
6600 CRLB 92011 1127-B5
REMUDA CT
9300 SNTE 92071 1231-A3
RENA DR
700 OCN 92057 1067-B5
RENAISSANCE AV
5100 SD 92122 1228-D3
RENATO ST
8900 SD 92129 1189-C3
RENAUD CT
700 CALX 92231 6680-H2
RENAULT PL
2900 SD 92122 1228-C6

RENAULT ST
2900 SD 92122 1228-C6
RENAULT WY
5800 SD 92122 1228-C6
RENDON VALLEY RD
16700 SDCo 92065 1171-E2
RENDOVA CIR
2300 CORD 92155 1309-A2
RENDOVA RD
2000 CORD 92155 1309-A2
RENE CT
700 SD 92154 1330-G7
RENE DR
3900 SD 92154 1330-F7
E RENETTE AV
600 ELCJ 92020 1251-G7
W RENETTE AV
1000 ELCJ 92020 1251-E7
RENEX PL
4700 SD 92117 1248-G1
RENFRO WY
800 SDCo 92019 1253-C2
RENKRIB AV
6600 SD 92119 1250-H4
RENNES PL
- CHV 91913 1311-F1
RENO DR
4700 SD 92105 1269-J5
RENOIR LN
5200 SDCo 91902 1290-G6
RENOVO WY
4800 SD 92124 1250-B1
RENOWN DR
8500 SD 92119 1250-J4
8500 SD 92119 1251-A4
RENSHAW CT
2000 ELCJ 92020 1251-B1
RENWICK LN
1500 SDCo 92084 1108-B1
REO CT
1800 SD 92139 1290-C7
REO DR
- SD 91950 1310-E2
1800 SD 92139 1290-C7
2000 SD 92139 1310-D1
3300 NATC 91950 1310-E2
REO PL
6000 SD 92139 1310-D2
REO TER
5800 SD 92139 1310-D3
REOLA DR
10000 SDCo 92040 1232-C3
REO REAL DR
12800 PWY 92064 1190-D5
REPECHO DR
5300 SD 92124 1249-G1
REPOSA ALTA
16900 SDCo 92067 1167-J3
16900 SDCo 92067 1168-A4
REPOSADO DR
7600 CRLB 92009 1147-F1
REPRESA CIR
7900 CRLB 92009 1147-G3
REPUBLIC ST
1500 SD 92114 1290-D1
REPUBLICAN WY
16700 SDCo 92065 1173-F2
REQUEZA ST
100 ENCT 92024 1147-C7
RESAVA LN
14200 SDCo 92082 1070-F4
RESEARCH CT
- CHV 91911 1330-J5
RESERVATION DR
24500 SDCo 91916 1236-A2
RESERVE DR
- SDCo 92127 1169-E3
RESERVOIR CT
6600 SD 92115 1270-D2
RESERVOIR DR
5000 SDCo 91978 1291-E2
5200 SD 92115 1270-D1
5200 SD 92120 1270-D1
RESERVOIR LN
6600 SD 92115 1270-D2
RESERVOIR ST
3100 SDCo 91935 1292-H1
3100 SDCo 91935 1272-H7
RESMAR CT
10000 SDCo 91941 1271-E4
RESMAR PL
10000 SDCo 91941 1271-D3
RESMAR RD
4300 SDCo 91941 1271-E2
RESTFUL CT
10300 SNTE 92071 1231-E4
RETAHEIM WY
400 SD 92037 1247-F2
RETRATO CT
11000 SD 92124 1249-J2
11000 SD 92124 1250-A2
RETREAT CT
300 SDCo 92028 1027-G3
REUBEN FLEET DR
1300 ELCJ 92020 1251-C2
REVELLE DR
7700 SD 92037 1227-J6
7800 SD 92037 1228-A6
REVELLE COLLEGE DR
9200 SD 92093 1227-J3
REVELSTOKE TER
8900 SD 92126 1209-D1
REVELSTOKE WY
8800 SD 92126 1209-D1
REVENA ST
1800 SD 92154 1350-B3
REVERE AV
3500 SD 92109 1248-D5
REVERE CT
1900 VSTA 92081 1107-J4
REVILLO DR
4300 SD 92115 1270-D4
REVILLO WY
4500 SD 92115 1270-D3
REX AV
5100 SD 92105 1270-A5
REX LN
1300 SDCo 92021 1251-H1
REXFORD DR
1900 SD 92105 1289-G1
REX HALL ST
700 ELCJ 92021 1251-F4
REXVIEW DR
300 SD 92114 1290-E4
REYNARD WY
2600 SD 92101 1288-J1
2600 SD 92103 1288-J1
2700 SD 92103 1268-J6
REYNOLDS ST
4900 SD 92113 1290-A6
5100 SD 92114 1290-A6
REYNOSA CT
100 SOLB 92075 1167-D7

REZKO WY
- CHV 91902 1310-J4
R H DANA PL
1200 CORD 92118 1308-H1
RHEA GN
1000 ESCN 92026 1109-F6
RHEA LN
400 SMCS 92069 1108-J4
400 SMCS 92069 1109-A4
RHEA PL
1000 VSTA 92084 1087-H4
RHESA LN
200 SDCo 92028 1027-F5
RHINE ST
1100 SD 92154 1350-A1
RHOADES CT
6300 SD 92139 1310-E1
RHOADES RD
2600 SD 92139 1310-E2
RHODA DR
1200 SD 92037 1227-F7
RHODA LN
500 VSTA 92083 1087-H7
RHODE ISLAND ST
4500 SD 92116 1269-B4
RHODES CT
8700 SNTE 92071 1231-D7
RHODES WY
4100 OCN 92056 1107-E5
RHONDA LN
34200 SDCo 92061 1050-H1
RHONE RD
8500 SNTE 92071 1251-C1
8500 ELCJ 92020 1251-C1
8500 SNTE 92071 1231-C7
RIALTO GN
200 ESCN 92025 1150-B1
RIALTO ST
4300 SD 92107 1268-B5
RIATA DR
600 SDCo 92004 (1078-J5 See Page 1058)
RIBBON BEACH WY
400 OCN 92054 1086-B6
RIBBONWOOD RD
2400 SDCo 91905 1300-D3
3500 SDCo 91905 430-D7
RIBBONWOOD RD Rt#-94
2400 SDCo 91905 1300-D5
RICARD CT
2100 SDCo 92019 1272-D3
RICARDO DR
1100 CHV 91910 1311-B7
RICARDO PL
300 SD 92037 1247-F4
RICARDO RANCH RD
19100 SDCo 92082 1091-G4
RICE CT
8400 SD 92129 1189-B6
RICEBIRD DR
500 VSTA 92083 1087-F4
RICE CANYON RD
100 SDCo 92028 1029-A1
1200 SDCo 92028 998-J6
1200 SDCo 92028 999-A7
RICEWOOD DR
3200 OCN 92054 1086-D3
RICHANDAVE AV
1500 ELCJ 92019 1252-B6
1500 SDCo 92019 1252-B6
RICHARD CT
- OCN 92056 1087-F2
RICHARD LN
- VSTA 92081 1107-H2
RICHARD RD
- SDCo 92127 1169-F1
RICHARD ST
6400 SD 92115 1270-E1
RICHARDSON AV
100 ELCJ 92020 1251-E5
RICHETH RD
100 SD 92114 1290-C4
RICHFIELD AV
100 ELCJ 92020 1251-E5
RICH FIELD DR
- CRLB 92010 1107-B4
RICHLAND RD
200 SMCS 92069 1109-A3
800 SDCo 92069 1109-A4
RICHLAND ST
2600 SD 92111 1249-A7
RICHLAND VIEW CT
600 SDCo 92069 1109-A3
RICHLYNN RIDGE RD
2700 SDCo 92025 1150-E1
RICHMAR AV
100 SMCS 92069 1108-G7
RICHMOND ST
1300 SD 92103 1269-B6
2900 SD 92101 1269-B7
RICHMOND PARK CT
- CHV 91910 1310-D5
RICHMOND PARK PL
200 CHV 91910 1310-C5
RICHVALE DR
8300 SNTE 92071 1230-J7
RICK ST
12800 PWY 92064 1190-D5
RICKENBAKER AV
600 SD 92154 1330-F6
RICKERT RD
10600 SD 92126 1209-D3
RICKS RANCH CT
31600 SDCo 92082 1070-E1
RICKS RANCH RD
13400 SDCo 92082 1070-D1
RICKY LN
10300 SNTE 92071 1231-E7
RICKY PL
200 ESCN 92027 1110-E6
RICO CT
6800 SD 92111 1268-J1
RIDEABOUT CT
12500 SD 92129 1189-C5
RIDEABOUT LN
8600 SD 92129 1189-C5
RIDER PL
- SD 92130 1188-D5
RIDERWOOD TER
8900 SNTE 92071 1231-F6
RIDGE CT
2800 SDCo 92028 1028-C2
3700 CRLB 92010 1107-B3
RIDGE DR
200 SDCo 92028 1028-C2
N RIDGE DR
100 SDCo 92028 1028-C2
RIDGE LN
100 SDCo 92019 1253-C1
RIDGE PL
400 SDCo 92028 1028-C2
RIDGE RD
1200 SDCo 92081 1107-E2

RIDGE RD
1200 VSTA 92081 1107-E2
1600 OCN 92056 1107-E2
E RIDGE RD
9700 SDCo 92021 1233-C2
RIDGE TER
- ENCT 92024 1147-J7
RIDGE TR
500 SDCo 92019 1253-C2
1200 SDCo 92036 1136-C6
RIDGE VW
2200 ESCN 92029 1129-E6
RIDGE WY
500 SDCo 92028 1028-C3
RIDGEBACK RD
1400 CHV 91910 1311-A5
RIDGE CANYON RD
14100 SDCo 92082 1090-F6
RIDGECLIFF LN
3000 SDCo 91977 1271-D6
RIDGE CREEK DR
1700 CHV 91902 1311-C4
3000 SDCo 92028 1028-C2
RIDGE CREEK RD
30000 SDCo 92082 1069-B5
RIDGECREST DR
200 SD 92114 1290-G5
3200 CRLB 92008 1106-H4
9700 SDCo 91941 1271-C1
RIDGECREST PL
2000 ESCN 92029 1129-F7
RIDGECREST RD
7500 SNTE 92071 1230-G7
15300 PWY 92064 1171-A7
RIDGECREST TER
1800 SDCo 92021 1252-B1
RIDGEDALE DR
13100 PWY 92064 1190-C5
RIDGEFIELD AV
2900 CRLB 92010 1107-B4
RIDGEFIELD PL
8500 SD 92129 1189-B5
RIDGEGATE RW
2300 SD 92037 1247-J1
2600 SD 92037 1248-A1
RIDGEGROVE LN
1700 ESCN 92029 1129-G5
RIDGEHAVEN CT
9400 SD 92123 1249-E2
RIDGE HAVEN WY
- OCN 92057 1086-J3
RIDGE HEIGHTS DR
900 SDCo 92028 1027-H4
RIDGE HILL RD
13700 SDCo 92021 1232-F6
RIDGELINE AV
1900 VSTA 92081 1107-J7
RIDGELINE CT
- SD 92154 1350-H2
RIDGELINE PL
- ESCN 92027 1110-F7
600 SOLB 92075 1167-G6
RIDGE MANOR AV
6300 SD 92120 1250-D5
RIDGEMONT CIR
- ESCN 92027 1110-F7
RIDGEMONT CT
1300 OCN 92056 1087-E3
RIDGEMOOR DR
5800 SD 92120 1250-D7
RIDGEMOORE PL
1000 VSTA 92083 1087-G4
RIDGE OAK LN
- SDCo 92027 1090-F7
RIDGE POINT CT
1200 CHV 91913 1331-C1
RIDGE RANCH CT
14000 SDCo 92082 1090-G6
RIDGE RANCH RD
13900 SDCo 92082 1090-F6
14700 SDCo 92082 1091-A6
RIDGE ROCK CT
1600 CHV 91913 1311-D7
RIDGE ROUTE RD
8300 SD 92120 1250-D4
RIDGE RUN WY
- SD 92131 1209-G1
RIDGESIDE PL
2500 SDCo 91977 1271-D7
RIDGETON CT
8800 SDCo 92040 1232-C6
RIDGETON DR
12400 SDCo 92040 1232-C6
RIDGETON LN
8900 SDCo 92040 1232-C6
RIDGEVIEW CT
400 CHV 91902 1311-A4
RIDGE VIEW DR
1700 SD 92105 1289-H1
2400 SD 92105 1269-J7
2900 SD 92105 1270-A7
RIDGEVIEW LN
17700 SDCo 92065 1171-G3
RIDGEVIEW PL
2100 ESCN 92026 1109-G5
2500 SDCo 91977 1271-E7
15200 PWY 92064 1170-F6
RIDGEVIEW RD
16400 SDCo 92065 1171-G3
RIDGE VIEW WY
- OCN 92057 1086-J3
RIDGEVIEW WY
1200 CHV 91902 1311-A4
RIDGEWATER DR
800 CHV 91913 1311-E4
RIDGEWATER LN
10300 SD 92131 1209-H4
RIDGEWAY
4100 SD 92116 1269-H2
RIDGEWAY CT
400 SDCo 91977 1290-J5
RIDGEWAY DR
2300 SDCo 91950 1310-C2
2900 NATC 91950 1310-B3
RIDGE WAY GN
- ESCN 92029 1129-H6
RIDGEWAY ST
1400 OCN 92054 1106-D1
RIDGEWOOD DR
700 SDCo 92036 1156-E1
1800 SD 92139 1290-C7
RIDGEWOOD WY
3500 CRLB 92010 1107-A4
RIDING HIGH WY
- SDCo 92127 1168-J2
RIDING RIDGE RD
4800 SD 92130 1188-C6
RIDLEY RD
13500 SD 92129 1189-E4
RIENSTRA CT
400 CHV 91911 1330-G3
E RIENSTRA ST
- CHV 91911 1330-F4

RIENZI PL
17600 SD 92128 1150-A7
17600 SD 92128 1170-A1
RIESLING CT
12200 SD 92131 1210-B3
RIESLING DR
10600 SD 92131 1210-B3
RIFE WY
12700 SD 92129 1189-C4
RIFLE RD
- ELCJ 92021 1251-H5
RIFLE WY
13000 SD 92129 1189-D5
RIFT RD
- CRLB 92010 1107-B5
RIGEL ST
1300 SD 92113 1289-F6
RIGGS RD
5400 SDCo 92019 1253-D5
RIGLEY ST
900 CHV 91911 1330-J2
900 CHV 91911 1331-A2
RIGSBY DR
9300 ELCJ 92020 1251-B1
9300 SNTE 92071 1251-B1
RIHELY PL
- ENCT 92024 1147-E5
RILEY PL
200 ESCN 92027 1110-E6
RILEY ST
3200 SD 92110 1268-F3
3700 SD 92110 1268-E5
3800 SD 92110 1268-E4
3800 SD 92110 1268-E5
3900 SD 92110 1268-E4
5500 SD 92110 1268-F3
5500 SD 92110 1268-G3
RILL CT
3900 CRLB 92010 1107-C3
W RIM CT
9400 SDCo 92040 1232-B4
RIM RD
10900 SDCo 92026 1089-F3
W RIM RD
12600 SDCo 92040 1232-B4
RIMBACH RD
12200 PWY 92064 1190-B4
RIMBEY AV
2000 SD 92154 1350-A2
RIMCREST CT
1400 CHV 91902 1311-A3
RIMGATE CT
14400 SD 92129 1189-C1
RIMHURST CT
300 OCN 92054 1086-D2
RIMINI RD
500 DLMR 92014 1187-G5
RIM OF THE VALLEY
- SDCo 92082 1070-J1
- SDCo 92082 1071-A1
RIMPARK LN
5200 SD 92124 1249-F1
RIMPARK WY
9700 SD 92124 1249-F1
RIMRIDGE LN
8100 SD 92126 1209-B1
RIM ROCK CIR
3200 ENCT 92024 1148-C4
RIMROCK DR
1300 ESCN 92027 1110-A6
RIM ROCK RD
4700 OCN 92056 1087-D4
RIMROCK RD
500 ELCJ 92020 1251-C4
RIMROCK SUMMIT LN
9800 SDCo 92026 1089-C1
RIMSTONE LN
16100 SD 92127 1169-J4
RIMVIEW WY
5300 SD 92124 1249-G1
RINCADO RD
32000 SDCo 92061 1051-F5
RINCON AV
100 ESCN 92026 1109-J3
1600 SDCo 92026 1109-J3
1700 SDCo 92026 1110-A3
RINCON CT
3600 OCN 92056 1107-F4
RINCON PT
- CHV 91913 1331-C1
1200 CHV 91913 1311-C7
RINCON RD
300 ESCN 92025 1130-A4
RINCON ST
700 VSTA 92083 1087-H7
5100 SD 92115 1270-D2
RINCON DEL MUNDO
1100 SDCo 92029 1149-H2
RINCON RANCH RD
17400 SDCo 91935 1274-A2
RINCON RANCHO RD
32200 SDCo 92061 1051-E4
RINCON SPRINGS RD
16800 SDCo 92061 1051-D7
16800 SDCo 92082 1051-D7
RINCON VILLA DR
1300 ESCN 92027 1109-J6
RINCON VILLA PL
1000 ESCN 92027 1109-J6
RINDA LN
8600 SDCo 91977 1290-J2
8600 SDCo 91977 1291-A2
RINEHART LN
13800 SDCo 92082 1090-E5
RING RD
- NATC 91950 1310-C4
13500 PWY 92064 1190-C4
RINGDOVE CT
11400 SD 92131 1210-A1
RINGNECK CT
13200 SDCo 92040 1232-C4
RINGWOOD DR
300 SD 92114 1290-G4
RIO CT
14100 PWY 92064 1190-G1
RIO DR
- SMCS 92078 1128-E2
RIO WY
1200 VSTA 92081 1107-E1
3100 SDCo 91977 1271-B6
RIO BONITO WY
2200 SD 92108 1269-D1
RIO BRAVA CT
13100 SDCo 91935 1272-D7
RIO CAMINO
10200 SDCo 92040 1231-H3
RIO CLARO CT
800 OCN 92057 1087-C1
RIO CORTO DR
11700 SDCo 92040 1231-H2
RIO FONDO
11600 SDCo 92040 1231-H3
RIO GRANDE
3200 SDCo 91935 1272-J7

RIO HONDO AV
- CALX 92231 6680-J2
RIO IVANHOE WY
13400 SDCo 91935 1272-F6
RIO LARGO
- VSTA 92081 1107-D2
RIO LINDO DR
200 SD 92114 1290-E4
RIO MADRE LN
3100 SDCo 91935 1272-J7
RIO MARIA RD
16800 SDCo 92040 1191-E4
RIO PLATA DR
5200 OCN 92057 1087-C1
RIO PLATO CT
6700 SD 92114 1290-E5
RIO RANCHO
- SD 92127 1168-H7
RIOS AV
1700 CHV 91911 1330-F6
1700 SD 92154 1330-F6
N RIOS AV
100 SOLB 92075 1167-E6
S RIOS AV
100 SOLB 92075 1167-F7
100 SOLB 92075 1187-F1
RIOS CT
100 SOLB 92075 1167-E6
RIOS RD
12200 SD 92128 1170-C3
12700 PWY 92064 1170-D3
RIO SAN DIEGO DR
8300 SD 92108 1269-D1
RIOS CANYON LN
14300 SDCo 92021 1232-G6
RIOS CANYON RD
14100 SDCo 92021 1232-G6
15000 SDCo 92021 1233-A6
RIO SECO CT
2600 CHV 91915 1311-J6
RIOSECO ST
- CALX 92231 6620-H6
RIO SENDA
7800 SDCo 92067 1168-J1
RIO VALLE DR
5900 SDCo 92003 1047-J7
5900 SDCo 92003 1067-J1
RIO VERDE DR
24700 SDCo 92065 1173-G4
RIO VIENTO CT
800 OCN 92057 1087-C1
RIO VISTA
- VSTA 92081 1107-C2
RIO VISTA DR
- ESCN 92029 1129-F4
400 OCN 92054 1086-G2
700 SDCo 92028 1027-H1
2000 SDCo 92028 1048-B5
3200 SDCo 91902 1310-E4
RIO VISTA PL
3800 SDCo 91902 1310-E4
RIO VISTA RD
4500 SDCo 92028 1048-B5
16500 SDCo 92127 1168-J4
RIPARIAN RD
15500 PWY 92064 1170-F5
RIPPEY CT
2300 ELCJ 92020 1251-B3
RIPPEY ST
1100 ELCJ 92020 1251-B3
RIPPLE LN
13400 SDCo 92040 1232-D6
RIPPLE WY
16800 SDCo 92065 1171-J3
RISA CIR
4000 SD 92124 1249-J3
RISA CT
4000 SD 92124 1249-J3
RISA LN
6600 LMGR 91945 1270-E7
RISING DALE WY
23000 SDCo 92065 1153-C7
23000 SDCo 92065 1173-C1
RISING GLEN DR
4700 OCN 92056 1087-D4
RISING GLEN WY
2100 SD 92139 1290-E7
2300 CRLB 92008 1106-G3
RISING HILL
1100 SDCo 92029 1149-H1
RISING RIVER PL N
- SD 92127 1169-B3
RISING RIVER PL S
- SD 92127 1169-A3
RISING STAR CT
4100 SDCo 91941 1271-G4
RISING SUN LN
- LMSA 91941 1270-J4
RISUENO CT
1700 SD 92154 1350-B3
RITA ST
4500 SDCo 91941 1271-E3
RITCHEY ST
200 SD 92114 1290-E4
RITCHIE RD
3000 SDCo 92070 1135-E5
RITIDIAN WY
11800 SD 92128 1170-A1
RITSON RD
31600 SDCo 92026 1069-A2
RITTER CT
9900 SD 92131 1209-H5
RITTER PL
2200 ESCN 92029 1129-H7
RITTER RD
- CALX 92231 6620-G6
- ImCo 92231 6620-G6
RITVA PL
2300 SD 92139 1290-F7
RIVA LN
1500 ESCN 92027 1110-B7
RIVENDELL LN
- SDCo 92065 1152-D6
N RIVER CIR
400 OCN 92057 1067-A6
RIVER DR
9700 SDCo 91916 1236-A1
9800 SDCo 91916 1235-J1
N RIVER RD
800 OCN 92057 1067-D5
3700 OCN 92054 1066-G7
RIVER ST
9800 SDCo 92040 1232-A3
RIVERA CT
100 CHV 91911 1330-H3
400 CHV 91911 1330-H3
RIVERA PL
- CHV 91911 1330-F4
RIVERA ST
500 CHV 91911 1330-H3
RIVER ASH DR
1000 CHV 91910 1310-J7
RIVERBEND CT
15700 PWY 92064 1170-G5

STREET	Block	City	ZIP	Pg-Grid
RIVERBEND RD				
	14000	PWY	92064	1170-G4
RIVERBEND WY				
	500	CHV	91914	1311-E3
RIVERCREEK CT				
	400	CHV	91914	1311-E2
RIVER CREST RD				
	-	SMCS	92078	1128-C6
RIVERDALE ST				
	6200	SD	92120	1249-H7
RIVER DANCE CT				
	-	SDCo	91901	1234-C6
RIVER DANCE WY				
	-	SDCo	91901	1234-C6
RIVERFORD RD				
	9800	SDCo	92040	1231-H3
RIVER GLEN RW				
	1200	SD	92111	1268-H2
RIVERHEAD CT				
	13800	SD	92129	1189-F3
RIVERHEAD DR				
	9900	SD	92129	1189-F3
RIVERLAWN AV				
	700	CHV	91910	1330-A2
	800	CHV	91911	1330-A2
RIVER OAKS CT				
	900	CHV	91915	1311-G4
RIVER OAKS LN				
	-	SDCo	92028	997-G7
RIVER PARK DR				
	100	SNTE	92071	1231-C5
RIVER RANCH WY				
	-	OCN	92057	1086-J2
RIVER RIM RD				
	11600	SD	92126	1209-A1
RIVER ROCK CT				
	100	SNTE	92071	1231-C5
RIVER ROCK RD				
	700	CHV	91914	1311-G3
RIVER RUN CIR				
	-	SMCS	92069	1109-A5
RIVER RUN DR				
	2100	SD	92108	1269-D1
RIVER SHADOW CT				
	-	SDCo	91901	1234-C6
RIVERSIDE DR				
	8600	SDCo	91916	1236-A3
	11400	SDCo	92040	1231-H3
RIVERTON PL				
	13200	SD	92130	1188-B4
RIVER TRAIL PL				
	300	SNTE	92071	1231-C5
RIVERTREE DR				
	600	OCN	92054	1086-D2
RIVER VALLEY CT				
	8900	SNTE	92071	1230-J4
	8900	SNTE	92071	1231-A4
RIVERVIEW AV				
	-	ELCN	92243	6559-G3
	9200	SDCo	92040	1231-J5
RIVER VIEW CT				
	5100	SDCo	92028	1048-J2
RIVERVIEW DR				
	900	SDCo	92028	1028-A1
	1000	SDCo	92028	998-A6
RIVERVIEW LN				
	11900	SDCo	92040	1231-J5
RIVERVIEW PL				
	2400	SDCo	92028	998-A7
RIVERVIEW RD				
	2200	SDCo	92028	996-G4
RIVERVIEW ST				
	2300	SD	92108	1269-D3
	2300	SD	92116	1269-D3
RIVERVIEW WY				
	200	OCN	92057	1066-J7
RIVER VISTA RW				
	1200	SD	92111	1268-H3
RIVERWALK DR				
	9800	SNTE	92071	1231-C4
RIVERWOOD RD				
	1100	SDCo	92070	1135-D3
RIVIERA CT				
	600	SDCo	92084	1087-H2
RIVIERA DR				
	-	LMGR	91941	1270-H5
	100	OCN	92054	1086-F4
	1900	SDCo	92084	1087-J2
	1900	VSTA	92084	1087-J2
	2400	CHV	91915	1311-H6
	3300	SD	92109	1268-A1
	3600	SD	92109	1248-A7
	3700	LMSA	91941	1270-H5
RIVIERA WY				
	-	SDCo	92082	1090-G5
	1300	CHV	91915	1311-H6
RIVIERA POINTE ST				
	-	SD	92154	1350-H2
RIVIERA SHORES ST				
	-	SD	92154	1350-G1
RIVIERA SUMMIT RD				
	-	SD	92154	1350-H1
RIVOLI RD				
	-	SDCo	92082	1070-E2
ROACH DR				
	8400	LMSA	91941	1270-J2
ROAD B				
	2700	SD	92105	1270-C7
ROAD C				
	5600	SD	92105	1270-C7
ROAD D				
	2500	SD	92105	1270-B7
ROADLINER AV				
	-	ESCN	92027	1130-C1
ROADRUNNER DR N				
	-	SDCo	92004	(1099-G3 See Page 1098)
ROADRUNNER DR S				
	3200	SDCo	92004	(1099-G5 See Page 1098)
ROADRUNNER GN				
	1300	ESCN	92029	1129-G6
ROADRUNNER LN				
	100	OCN	92057	1086-H2
	300	IMP	92251	6439-F4
	39900	SDCo	91905	1300-D4
ROADRUNNER RD				
	3000	SDCo	92081	1108-C6
	3000	SMCS	92078	1108-C6
ROADRUNNER RDG				
	30400	SDCo	92082	1069-F3
ROADRUNNER RDG S				
	30400	SDCo	92082	1069-F4
ROADSIDE PL				
	10100	SDCo	91977	1271-E7
ROAD TO BALI				
	-	SDCo	92127	1169-A3
ROAD TO MOROCCO				
	-	SDCo	92127	1168-J3
	-	SDCo	92127	1169-A2
ROAD TO RIO				
	-	SDCo	92127	1168-J2
ROAD TO SINGAPORE				
	-	SDCo	92127	1168-J2
ROAD TO THE CURE				
	10800	SD	92121	1208-A5
ROAD TO UTOPIA				
	-	SDCo	92127	1168-H2
ROAD TO ZANZIBAR				
	-	SDCo	92127	1168-J2
ROAN RD				
	7700	SD	92129	1189-A6
ROAN WY				
	12200	SD	92129	1189-A6
ROANE DR				
	5600	OCN	92057	1067-F6
ROANOKE RD				
	100	ELCJ	92020	1251-G5
ROANOKE ST				
	5500	SD	92139	1310-E1
ROARING CAMP RD				
	14100	PWY	92064	1170-G7
ROBBIE LN				
	29700	SDCo	92084	1068-D6
ROBBIE WY				
	2300	LMGR	91945	1270-H7
ROBBIEJEAN PL				
	1500	ELCJ	92019	1252-A5
ROBBINS CT				
	6800	SD	92122	1228-F5
ROBBINS ST				
	4300	SD	92122	1228-E4
ROBBINS WY				
	6700	SD	92122	1228-F5
ROBB ROY CT				
	3300	SD	92154	1330-E7
ROBB ROY PL				
	3400	SD	92154	1330-E7
ROBBY LN				
	100	OCN	92054	1086-G2
ROBBY WY				
	600	SDCo	92028	1027-G2
ROBELINI DR				
	100	SDCo	92083	1108-C3
	100	VSTA	92083	1108-C3
ROBERT AV				
	600	CHV	91910	1310-E7
ROBERT LN				
	800	ENCT	92024	1147-G4
ROBERT ST				
	500	VSTA	92083	1087-F6
ROBERTA AV				
	500	ELCJ	92021	1251-J4
ROBERTA LN				
	3200	OCN	92054	1086-E5
ROBERT KENNEDY ST				
	200	CALX	92231	6620-G6
ROBERTO WY				
	12600	PWY	92064	1170-C7
ROBERTO RIO RD				
	14600	PWY	92064	1190-G1
ROBERTS AL				
	4300	SD	92103	1269-C4
ROBERTS DR				
	6100	SD	92139	1290-D7
ROBERTS PL				
	2000	ESCN	92029	1129-G7
ROBERTS ST				
	-	SD	92152	1288-A5
ROBERTS WY				
	12200	SDCo	92040	1232-A3
ROBERTSON DR				
	1000	ESCN	92025	1130-A3
ROBERTSON ST				
	1900	SDCo	92065	1152-E7
	2300	SDCo	92065	1172-C1
ROBIN CT				
	900	SMCS	92078	1128-E3
ROBIN LN				
	200	OCN	92057	1086-H2
	1400	ELCJ	92020	1251-D2
ROBIN PL				
	1100	SDCo	92084	1108-C1
	1200	CHV	91911	1330-G2
	1600	CRLB	92011	1127-D7
ROBIN ST				
	-	ImCo	92243	6560-A7
	-	ImCo	92249	6560-A7
	3400	SD	92115	1270-C6
	8500	LMGR	91945	1290-J1
ROBINEA DR				
	6400	CRLB	92011	1127-A4
ROBIN HILL DR				
	1100	SMCS	92069	1109-A5
ROBIN HILL LN				
	400	ESCN	92026	1109-G5
	400	SDCo	92026	1109-G5
ROBIN HOOD LN				
	8700	SD	92037	1227-J4
ROBINHOOD LN				
	3700	SDCo	92084	1108-F3
ROBINHOOD RD				
	1600	SDCo	92084	1108-G2
ROBIN HOOD WY				
	10600	SDCo	91941	1271-E2
ROBINIA CT				
	17700	SD	92127	1169-J1
ROBINRIDGE WY				
	9000	SNTE	92071	1231-G6
ROBINS NEST WY				
	-	SDCo	92127	1169-F4
ROBINSON AV				
	-	CALX	92231	6620-F5
	100	SD	92103	1269-B6
	1900	SD	92104	1269-B6
W ROBINSON AV				
	100	SD	92103	1269-A6
	300	SD	92103	1268-J6
ROBINSON MEWS				
	3400	SD	92103	1269-A6
ROBINSON PL				
	3600	SD	92103	1269-B6
ROBINSON RD				
	-	ImCo	92251	431-D4
ROBINSON WY				
	-	SD	92145	1229-E1
ROBINWOOD DR				
	900	OCN	92056	1087-D1
	5200	OCN	92057	1087-D1
ROBINWOOD RD				
	5100	SDCo	91902	1290-H7
ROBISON BLVD				
	12400	PWY	92064	1190-C4
ROBLE PL				
	7900	CRLB	92009	1147-G3
ROBLE WY				
	17000	SD	92128	1170-C2
ROBLEDA CT				
	18600	SD	92128	1150-C6
ROBLEDA CV				
	12900	SD	92128	1150-C6
ROBLEDO REAL RD				
	15000	SDCo	92021	1233-B3
ROBLE GRANDE LN				
	1500	SDCo	91901	1233-J7
ROBLE GRANDE RD				
	1600	SDCo	91901	1233-J7
	1700	SDCo	91901	1234-A7
ROBLE GRANDE TR				
	1700	SDCo	91901	1234-A7
ROBLES DR				
	1400	CHV	91911	1330-J3
	8600	SD	92119	1251-A3
	8700	SD	92119	1250-J3
ROBLES LN				
	29700	SDCo	92082	1070-A6
ROBLES WY				
	8700	SD	92119	1251-A3
ROBLE VERDE				
	29600	SDCo	92082	1070-B6
ROBLEY PL				
	900	ENCT	92007	1167-E2
ROBLEY RANCH RD				
	13400	PWY	92064	1190-F5
ROBUSTO RD				
	5600	SD	92124	1229-G7
ROBYN RD				
	1500	ESCN	92025	1130-B4
ROCA DR				
	16300	SD	92128	1170-C3
ROCA PL				
	600	SDCo	92084	1067-H6
	900	CHV	91910	1310-H7
ROCA RD				
	700	CHV	91910	1310-H7
ROCA GRANDE DR				
	12700	PWY	92064	1190-C5
ROCA VERDE				
	2600	SDCo	91977	1271-B7
ROCHDALE LN				
	1500	SD	92154	1350-B2
ROCHELLE AV				
	10300	SNTE	92071	1231-E4
ROCHELLE LN				
	10300	SNTE	92071	1231-B1
ROCHESTER RD				
	4000	SD	92116	1269-G2
ROCIO ST				
	7700	CRLB	92009	1147-G2
ROCK GN				
	2100	ESCN	92026	1109-C3
ROCK PL				
	6000	SD	92115	1270-C5
ROCK RD				
	17000	PWY	92064	1170-D2
ROCK ST				
	6000	SD	92115	1270-C5
ROCK ACRE DR				
	9200	SDCo	92040	1232-D5
ROCKAWAY CT				
	700	SD	92109	1267-H1
ROCKBROOK ST				
	9200	SDCo	91977	1271-B7
ROCK CANYON CT				
	11000	SD	92126	1209-A2
ROCK CANYON DR				
	7200	SD	92126	1208-J3
	7400	SD	92126	1209-A2
ROCKCLIFF LN				
	3000	SDCo	91977	1271-D6
ROCK CREEK DR				
	10400	SD	92131	1209-J4
	10500	SD	92131	1210-A3
ROCK CREEK LN				
	15300	SDCo	92021	1232-G2
ROCK CREEK PL				
	1200	CHV	91915	1311-H6
ROCK CREEK RD				
	13900	PWY	92064	1170-G5
ROCK CREST GN				
	2200	ESCN	92026	1109-B3
ROCKCREST LN				
	9400	SDCo	92040	1232-A5
ROCKCREST RD				
	11900	SDCo	92040	1231-J5
	11900	SDCo	92040	1232-A5
ROCKDALE LN				
	3000	SDCo	91977	1271-D6
ROCKDALE PL				
	-	SMCS	92078	1128-B6
ROCK DOVE ST				
	7000	CRLB	92011	1127-E7
ROCKET RIDGE RD				
	8900	SDCo	92040	1232-A6
ROCKEY				
	-	SDCo	92672	1023-E2
ROCKFIELD CT				
	3800	CRLB	92010	1107-B3
ROCKFIELD WY				
	9200	SD	92126	1209-E2
ROCKFORD DR				
	4900	SD	92115	1270-C2
ROCKGATE WY				
	9900	SDCo	91977	1271-D7
ROCKGLEN AV				
	6600	SD	92111	1248-J4
ROCK GLEN WY				
	100	SNTE	92071	1231-C5
ROCK HILL PL				
	1300	ESCN	92026	1109-F7
ROCKHILL RD				
	100	SDCo	92084	1088-B6
	100	VSTA	92084	1088-B6
ROCK HILL RANCH RD				
	15100	SDCo	92082	1090-H2
ROCKHOFF LN				
	1900	SDCo	92026	1109-E4
ROCKHOFF RD				
	1800	SDCo	92026	1109-E4
	1900	ESCN	92026	1109-E4
ROCK HOUSE RD				
	17100	SDCo	92036	1156-F7
ROCKHOUSE RD				
	17200	SDCo	92065	1171-F5
ROCKHOUSE TKTR				
	-	SDCo	92004	410-D6
ROCKHOUSE TR				
	-	SDCo	92004	410-B5
ROCKHOUSE TRAIL LN				
	2600	CHV	91915	1311-H5
ROCKHURST CT				
	5800	SD	92120	1250-D7
ROCKHURST DR				
	6100	SD	92120	1250-C7
ROCKING CHAIR DR				
	400	SDCo	92004	(1078-H4 See Page 1058)
ROCKING HORSE CIR				
	3300	ENCT	92024	1148-C4
ROCKING HORSE DR				
	-	ImCo	92243	6560-A6
	600	CHV	91914	1311-F2
ROCKING HORSE LN				
	5400	OCN	92057	1067-E7
ROCKING HORSE RD				
	31600	SDCo	92026	1049-A7
	31600	SDCo	92026	1069-A1
ROCKINGHORSE RD				
	700	VSTA	92081	1107-G2
ROCKIN OAKS WY				
	16600	SDCo	92065	1171-H3
ROCK ISLAND RD				
	-	SD	92139	1290-D7
ROCKLAND CT				
	1200	CHV	91913	1311-B7
ROCKLAND ST				
	6800	SD	92115	1270-E5
ROCKLEDGE RD				
	8500	LMSA	91941	1270-J4
ROCKLEDGE ST				
	500	SDCo	92054	1106-B1
ROCK MANOR DR				
	6900	SD	92119	1250-E6
ROCKMINT DR				
	800	SMCS	92078	1128-G2
ROCK MOUNTAIN DR				
	-	RivC	92590	997-G3
	40000	SDCo	92028	997-G3
ROCK MOUNTAIN RD				
	-	CHV	91913	1331-F3
	-	RivC	92590	997-G1
ROCKNE ST				
	2800	SD	92139	1310-F2
ROCK PILE RD				
	32200	SDCo	92003	1048-H6
ROCK POINT WY				
	10200	SDCo	91977	1291-D2
ROCKPORT CT				
	500	ENCT	92024	1147-B2
ROCKPORT BAY WY				
	4200	OCN	92054	1066-E6
ROCK RIDGE LN				
	12800	SDCo	92082	1090-C2
ROCK RIDGE PL				
	300	ESCN	92027	1130-C1
ROCK RIDGE RD				
	-	CRLB	92010	1107-B4
	-	SDCo	92028	1029-B1
ROCKRIDGE RD				
	5100	SDCo	91941	1271-D2
ROCK RIVER LN				
	3900	SDCo	91902	1311-B2
ROCK ROSE				
	-	SD	92127	1188-J1
ROCKROSE CT				
	12600	PWY	92064	1190-D3
ROCK ROSE LN				
	30500	SDCo	92082	1070-J3
ROCKROSE TER				
	7000	CRLB	92011	1127-B6
ROCKSIDE CT				
	11000	SD	92126	1208-J2
ROCK SPRINGS PL				
	4600	OCN	92056	1087-D3
ROCK SPRINGS RD				
	600	ESCN	92025	1129-G2
	800	SMCS	92069	1109-B6
	800	ESCN	92026	1129-F1
	1000	SDCo	92026	1109-E7
	1100	SDCo	92026	1129-F1
ROCK SPRINGS HOLLOW				
	1100	SDCo	92026	1109-D6
ROCK STONE RD				
	30100	SDCo	92082	1071-A3
ROCKSTREAM RD				
	12200	SDCo	92040	1231-J2
	12200	SDCo	92040	1232-A2
ROCK TERRACE PL				
	-	CHV	91914	1311-F3
ROCK TERRACE RD				
	1400	SDCo	91901	1234-C6
ROCK VALLEY CT				
	7100	SD	92122	1228-F4
ROCK VIEW CT				
	-	SD	92127	1168-H5
ROCKVIEW DR				
	8200	SDCo	92021	1251-G1
ROCK VIEW GN				
	2100	ESCN	92026	1109-B3
ROCKVILL ST				
	10700	SNTE	92071	1231-F6
ROCKWALL LN				
	500	SMCS	92069	1108-G6
ROCKWELL CT				
	12800	PWY	92064	1190-D3
ROCKWELL SPRING CT				
	900	ESCN	92025	1129-J6
ROCKWOOD AV				
	-	ImCo	92249	6560-C7
	100	CALX	92231	6680-G2
	1000	CALX	92231	6620-G5
ROCKWOOD PL				
	11000	SDCo	92020	1271-G2
ROCKWOOD RD				
	-	ImCo	92231	431-B8
	4800	SDCo	92020	1271-G2
	16300	SDCo	92027	1131-D2
	16400	SDCo	92027	1111-D7
	17100	SD	92027	1131-A5
	17100	SD	92027	1130-G3
	17500	ESCN	92027	1130-J4
	17500	SDCo	92027	1130-G3
ROCKY LN				
	11300	SDCo	92040	1212-B6
ROCKY PASS				
	28900	SDCo	91962	1237-C6
ROCKY RD				
	-	SDCo	92082	1071-D1
	19900	SDCo	92029	1148-F2
ROCKY CREEK RD				
	1600	SDCo	92021	1232-H7
	1600	SDCo	92021	1252-H1
ROCKYCREST RD				
	100	SDCo	92028	1027-F5
ROCKYHILL RD				
	700	ELCJ	92019	1251-H6
	700	SDCo	92019	1251-H6
ROCKY HILLS RD				
	25700	RivC	92590	997-H1
ROCKY HOME DR				
	11900	SDCo	92040	1231-J4
ROCKY KNOLL RD				
	-	SDCo	91905	1300-F5
ROCKY MOUNTAIN RD				
	15300	SDCo	91935	1273-C7
	15300	SDCo	91935	1293-C1
ROCKY MOUNTAIN TR				
	7200	SDCo	92036	1138-B7
ROCKY PASS WY				
	7800	SDCo	91962	1237-C6
ROCKY POINT CT				
	1600	CHV	91911	1330-J4
ROCKY POINT RD				
	7500	SNTE	92071	1230-G7
ROCKY POINT WY				
	-	SDCo	92026	1089-D2
	-	SMCS	92078	1128-A3
	1100	ESCN	92026	1109-J4
ROCKY RIDGE RD				
	9800	SDCo	92026	1089-D2
ROCKY SAGE RD				
	3200	SDCo	91935	1272-J6
	3200	SDCo	91935	1273-A7
ROCKY SHORE RD				
	1700	SD	92139	1290-D7
ROCKY VIEW CT				
	5900	SDCo	91902	1311-B1
ROCOSO LN				
	7900	CRLB	92009	1147-G3
ROCOSO RD				
	11300	SDCo	92040	1211-G5
ROCREST RD				
	1700	SDCo	91901	1233-G7
ROD ST				
	900	SDCo	92028	1027-H5
RODADA DR				
	16200	SD	92128	1170-C4
RODADO PL				
	2100	ELCJ	92020	1251-C1
RODEAL WY				
	12000	SDCo	92040	1232-A6
RODEAR RD				
	1600	SD	92154	1350-A3
RODELANE ST				
	2000	SD	92103	1268-G6
RODEO DR				
	-	IMP	92251	6439-F3
	-	SDCo	92040	1232-B5
	1300	SD	92037	1247-G2
RODEO RD				
	1000	IMP	92251	6439-F4
RODEO QUEEN DR				
	900	SDCo	92028	1027-G3
RODMAN AV				
	4900	SD	92120	1250-A6
RODNEY AV				
	-	CALX	92231	6680-J2
	100	ENCT	92024	1147-G6
RODRIGO DR				
	4300	SD	92115	1270-D4
RODRIGUEZ RD				
	-	SDCo	92082	1071-E2
	8900	SDCo	92026	1069-D1
ROE DR				
	9700	SNTE	92071	1231-B4
ROE ST				
	-	CORD	92135	1288-F3
ROEBLIN CT				
	6700	SD	92111	1248-H7
ROECREST DR				
	9700	SNTE	92071	1231-C4
ROGAN RD				
	200	CHV	91910	1310-C5
ROGERS CT				
	-	SDCo	92069	1109-A3
	-	SMCS	92069	1109-A3
ROGERS LN				
	-	SDCo	91977	1271-C4
ROGERS RD				
	-	CORD	92135	1288-C7
	-	SD	92135	1288-E7
	3800	SDCo	91977	1271-C5
N ROGERS RD				
	3900	SDCo	91977	1271-C4
ROGERS ST				
	2900	SD	92106	1288-A3
ROGUE RD				
	500	ELCJ	92020	1251-G4
ROGUE ISLE CT				
	1700	CRLB	92008	1106-H6
ROHN RD				
	1900	ESCN	92025	1129-H6
ROHR PL				
	9000	SD	92123	1249-D5
ROI RD				
	2300	CORD	92155	1309-B1
ROI WY				
	2300	CORD	92155	1309-B1
ROJA DR				
	500	OCN	92057	1067-A6
ROJA ST				
	500	OCN	92057	1067-A5
ROJO TIERRA RD				
	3700	LMSA	91941	1270-H5
ROLAND ACRES DR				
	8500	SNTE	92071	1231-E7
ROLANDO BLVD				
	4100	SD	92115	1270-D3
ROLANDO CT				
	4800	SD	92115	1270-D2
ROLANDO KNOLLS DR				
	6700	LMSA	91941	1270-E4
ROLFE RD				
	4300	SD	92117	1248-E2
ROLL DR				
	2200	SD	92154	1352-A3
ROLLIE PL				
	4500	SDCo	91941	1271-G3
	4500	SDCo	92020	1271-G3
ROLLING HILLS DR				
	1400	OCN	92056	1087-D4
	11000	SDCo	92020	1271-H2
	30100	SDCo	92082	1069-G4
ROLLING HILLS LN				
	300	SMCS	92069	1108-J6
	3500	SDCo	91902	1311-C1
ROLLING HILLS PL				
	5000	SDCo	92020	1271-J2
ROLLING HILLS RD				
	400	SDCo	92083	1108-A3
	400	VSTA	92083	1108-A3
	600	VSTA	92081	1107-J3
	600	VSTA	92081	1108-A3
ROLLING HILLS WY				
	11200	SDCo	92082	1069-G4
ROLLIN GLEN RD				
	13300	PWY	92064	1190-H4
ROLLING MEADOWS CT				
	12100	SD	92128	1190-A7
ROLLING OAK RD				
	7500	SNTE	92071	1230-G7
ROLLING RIDGE RD				
	2200	CHV	91914	1311-E2
ROLLING ROCK RD				
	28600	SDCo	92026	1089-E2
ROLLINGVIEW LN				
	-	SDCo	92028	1047-H5
ROLLINGWOOD LN				
	-	SDCo	92028	1047-H6
ROLLINS WY				
	100	VSTA	92083	1087-G7
ROLLSREACH DR				
	3300	SD	92111	1248-H4
ROMA AV				
	200	SMCS	92069	1108-H7
ROMA DR				
	1500	VSTA	92081	1107-H3
ROMAN WY				
	300	CHV	91911	1330-F1
ROMANCE RD				
	1400	SDCo	92029	1129-C4
ROMANY DR				
	6000	SD	92120	1250-C7
ROMBOUGH PL				
	5200	SD	92105	1270-A7
ROMEGA CT				
	5400	SDCo	91902	1290-J7
ROMERIA ST				
	7500	CRLB	92009	1147-H1
ROMERO CT				
	7300	SD	92037	1227-G7
ROMERO DR				
	7200	SD	92037	1227-G7
ROMFORD CT				
	7100	SD	92120	1250-A5
ROMINE RD				
	24800	SDCo	92065	1173-G5
ROMNEY RD				
	2300	SD	92109	1248-B3
ROMNEYA DR				
	200	OCN	92057	1067-B7
ROMO RD				
	-	SDCo	91917	(1314-E7 See Page 1294)
	-	SDCo	91917	429-J10
ROMO ST				
	6200	SD	92115	1270-D5
RON				
	10700	SD	92129	1189-H2
RON CT				
	8200	SD	92123	1249-B7
RON WY				
	2200	SD	92123	1249-B7
RONALD CT				
	3100	SDCo	91977	1271-A6
RONALD LN				
	1400	VSTA	92083	1108-A2
RONALD PACKARD PKWY Rt#-78				
	-	ESCN	-	1129-D2
	-	OCN	-	1106-E3
	-	OCN	-	1107-A2
	-	SDCo	-	1108-A3
	-	SDCo	-	1129-D2
	-	SMCS	-	1108-A3
	-	SMCS	-	1109-A7
	-	SMCS	-	1128-H1
	-	SMCS	-	1129-D2
	-	VSTA	-	1087-E7
	-	VSTA	-	1107-J1
	-	VSTA	-	1108-A3
RONAN DR				
	19300	SDCo	92065	1192-B2
RONDA AV				
	1200	ESCN	92027	1110-A7
	9000	SD	92123	1249-F6
RONDA PL				
	1400	ESCN	92027	1110-B7
RONDEL CT				
	7200	SD	92119	1250-E4
RONDEVOO RD				
	3000	LMGR	91945	1270-H6
RONICA WY				
	700	SDCo	92028	1027-J4
RONNA PL				
	300	CHV	91910	1310-E6
RONNIE CT				
	9400	SNTE	92071	1231-B4
RONSON CT				
	4800	SD	92111	1249-C1
RONSON RD				
	7100	SD	92111	1249-A1
ROOD RD				
	-	ImCo	92231	431-E7
ROOKWOOD DR				
	10200	SD	92131	1209-G5
ROOSEVELT AV				
	100	NATC	91950	1309-H1
	100	NATC	91950	1289-G7
	1400	SD	92109	1248-A7
	2900	LMGR	91945	1270-G6
ROOSEVELT LN				
	-	SDCo	92040	(1193-B5 See Page 1192)
ROOSEVELT RD				
	-	SD	92106	1268-D7
ROOSEVELT ST				
	-	CALX	92231	6680-F1
	100	CHV	91910	1310-C6
	500	CRLB	92008	1106-D5
	1100	ESCN	92027	1110-A7
	1200	ESCN	92027	1109-J6
N ROOSEVELT ST				
	600	ESCN	92027	1130-A1
ROOT ST				
	2400	SD	92123	1249-C6
ROPALT ST				
	7700	LMSA	91942	1250-G7
ROPER CT				
	100	ENCT	92024	1147-G7
ROREX DR				
	2000	ESCN	92025	1130-A7
ROSA CT				
	-	ESCN	92027	1110-E6
ROSA ST				
	400	SOLB	92075	1187-F1
ROSA WY				
	3500	SDCo	92028	1028-D1
ROSADA CT				
	8600	SDCo	92021	1232-E6
ROSADA GN				
	1400	ESCN	92027	1110-A5
ROSADA WY				
	8500	SDCo	92021	1232-E6
ROSAL CT				
	900	CHV	91910	1310-J5
ROSAL LN				
	2300	SDCo	91977	1271-E7
ROSALIE WY				
	500	SDCo	92019	1253-C1
ROSA LINDA ST				
	3400	SD	92154	1350-E1
ROSA RANCHO LN				
	4200	SDCo	92028	998-F4
ROSARIO LN				
	1000	VSTA	92084	1088-A5
ROSARITA DR				
	4000	LMSA	91941	1270-H4
ROSARITO DR				
	-	ImCo	92251	6499-G1
	-	IMP	92251	6499-G1
ROSAS				
	10900	SD	92129	1189-H2
ROSAS ST				
	-	CALX	92231	6620-H7
ROSCOE CT				
	5700	SD	92123	1229-E7
ROSCREA AV				
	4900	SD	92117	1228-H7
ROSE AV				
	1000	ELCN	92243	6499-G5
ROSE CT				
	600	SMCS	92069	1108-J5
	13900	PWY	92064	1190-F3
ROSE DR				
	-	SD	92109	1248-C6
	400	NATC	91950	1309-J3
	800	VSTA	92083	1087-E5
	4600	OCN	92056	1087-E5
	7100	CRLB	92011	1127-B6
ROSE LN				
	2900	SD	92154	1350-D2
	4200	OCN	92057	1067-G3
	4200	SDCo	92003	1067-G3
ROSE PL				
	100	OCN	92054	1086-D6
	4700	SD	92115	1270-C3
ROSE RD				
	2300	SDCo	92028	997-A1
ROSE ST				
	-	SD	92115	1270-C3
N ROSE ST				
	700	ESCN	92027	1110-A6
	800	ESCN	92027	1130-B1
S ROSE ST				
	100	ESCN	92027	1130-C2
ROSE WY				
	1500	ESCN	92027	1110-B7
ROSEANN AV				
	2800	ESCN	92027	1110-E6
ROSE ARBOR DR				
	900	SMCS	92078	1129-B2
ROSEBAY DR				
	100	ENCT	92024	1147-E6
ROSEBUD LN				
	300	SD	92114	1290-G5
	4300	LMSA	91941	1270-G3
ROSEBUSH LN				
	-	SDCo	92082	1091-B2
ROSECLIFF PL				
	-	SD	92130	1208-B1
ROSECRANS BLVD				
	-	SD	92106	1288-A7
	-	SD	92106	1308-B1
ROSECRANS PL				
	3000	SD	92110	1268-D6
ROSECRANS ST				
	200	SD	92106	1288-B2
	200	SD	92152	1288-A4
	2100	SD	92106	1268-D7
	3000	SD	92110	1268-E5
ROSE CREEK SHORE DR				
	-	SD	92109	1248-C6
ROSECREST DR				
	27700	SDCo	92026	1089-H4
ROSECROFT CT				
	-	SD	92130	1187-J3
	-	SD	92130	1188-A3
ROSECROFT LN				
	3600	SD	92106	1287-J4
	3600	SD	92106	1288-A4
	3600	SD	92152	1287-J4
ROSECROFT WY				
	-	SD	92130	1187-J3
	-	SD	92130	1188-A3
ROSEDALE CT				
	2900	SDCo	91977	1271-B6
ROSEDALE DR				
	3600	SDCo	91902	1310-F4
	9000	SDCo	91977	1271-B7
ROSEDALE PL				
	2800	SDCo	91977	1271-A7
ROSEDALE WY				
	2800	SDCo	91977	1271-A7
ROSEDOWN PL				
	17700	SD	92128	1150-A7
ROSEDUST GLEN DR				
	-	SD	92127	1169-F1
ROSE FERN LN				
	2100	SDCo	92065	1172-E2
ROSEFIELD DR				
	6700	SD	92115	1270-E3
	6800	LMSA	91941	1270-E3
ROSE GARDEN CT				
	-	SD	92131	1210-D2
ROSE GARDEN LN				
	-	CHV	91915	1331-H2
ROSEGLEN PL				
	9400	SDCo	91977	1271-B5
ROSE HEDGE DR				
	4900	LMSA	91941	1270-J2
ROSEHILL CT				
	1100	SDCo	92025	1130-D7
ROSEHILL RD				
	2600	SDCo	92025	1130-D7
ROSE LAKE AV				
	6200	SD	92119	1250-H6
ROSELAND DR				
	7800	SD	92037	1227-G5
E ROSELAND DR				
	-	SD	92037	1227-H6
ROSELAND PL				
	7700	SD	92037	1227-H6
ROSELAWN AV				
	3600	SD	92105	1269-J6
ROSELAWN ST				
	1200	NATC	91950	1310-A2
ROSELLE AV				
	500	ELCJ	92021	1251-J4
	3700	OCN	92056	1107-B1
ROSELLE CT				
	1100	ELCJ	92021	1251-J4
ROSELLE ST				
	3500	OCN	92056	1087-A7
	3600	OCN	92056	1107-B1
	10300	SD	92121	1208-A5
ROSELLE MEADOWS TR				
	-	SD	92130	1188-F4
ROSEMARIE LN				
	3000	SDCo	92028	1048-B1
ROSEMARY AV				
	900	CRLB	92011	1127-A6
ROSEMARY CT				
	300	ENCT	92024	1148-A7
	1700	ESCN	92026	1109-C5
ROSEMARY LN				
	300	ENCT	92024	1148-A7
	1000	VSTA	92081	1107-H1
	7000	LMGR	91945	1270-F7
ROSEMARY PL				
	100	CHV	91910	1310-C5
ROSEMARY WY				
	200	OCN	92057	1086-H4
ROSEMERE LN				
	-	SDCo	92028	1027-G3
ROSEMONT LN				
	2200	ENCT	92024	1167-J1
	15700	SDCo	92065	1172-A5
ROSEMONT ST				
	200	SD	92037	1247-E2
	200	CALX	92231	6680-G1
ROSE MOUNTAIN RD				
	-	SDCo	92069	1088-G7
	-	SDCo	92069	1108-G1
ROSENDA CT				
	4000	SD	92122	1228-B5
ROSE OF TRALEE LN				
	-	SDCo	92127	1168-J2
ROSE RANCH RD				
	600	SMCS	92069	1109-A5
ROSETA ST				
	200	ENCT	92024	1147-B6
ROSETTA CT				
	3800	SD	92111	1249-A3
ROSETTE RUN				
	15300	SDCo	92082	1070-J3

STREET Block City ZIP Pg-Grid

ROSEVIEW PL
300 CHV 91910 1310-C5
2500 SD 92105 1269-J7
ROSEWOOD CIR
2700 OCN 92056 1087-E5
ROSEWOOD DR
5100 OCN 92056 1087-D2
ROSEWOOD LN
- ESCN 92027 1130-J2
4600 SDCo 92004 (1099-G4 See Page 1098)
7900 LMGR 91945 1270-H7
ROSEWOOD PL
3600 SDCo 92028 1048-D2
ROSEWOOD ST
1900 VSTA 92081 1107-G5
3000 SD 92109 1248-D5
ROSEY RD
12400 SDCo 92021 1252-A1
ROSIE LN
10300 SNTE 92071 1231-B1
ROSIE WY
9600 SNTE 92071 1231-B1
ROSITA CT
600 CHV 91910 1311-A5
ROSLYN LN
1200 SD 92037 1227-F6
ROSS AV
- ELCN 92243 6500-A7
- ELCN 92243 6560-A1
200 ELCN 92243 6559-G1
2000 SDCo 91905 1300-E7
ROSS DR
500 ESCN 92029 1129-D2
500 SDCo 92029 1129-D2
ROSS LN
2700 ESCN 92025 1130-A7
2700 ESCN 92025 1150-A1
ROSS RD
200 ImCo 92243 6500-C7
500 ELCN 92243 6500-C7
700 ImCo 92243 6559-B1
1000 ImCo 92243 431-D5
1500 ImCo 92283 432-E5
2000 ELCN 92243 6559-B1
2600 SDCo 92028 997-A1
ROSS RD Rt#-S24
1400 ImCo 92283 432-D5
ROSSIN CT
1600 CHV 91913 1311-D7
ROSSINI DR
1800 ENCT 92007 1167-D2
ROSSITER LN
700 SDCo 92028 1027-G2
ROSSO CT
9400 SDCo 92021 1232-H4
ROSTRATA LN
13700 PWY 92064 1170-F4
ROSTRATA RD
13500 PWY 92064 1170-E4
ROSTRATA HILL RD
16200 PWY 92064 1170-F4
ROSVALL DR
600 SDCo 92028 1027-F2
ROSWELL ST
5100 SD 92114 1290-A3
ROSY AV
13600 SD 92129 1189-D3
ROTANZI ST
100 SDCo 92065 1152-D7
100 SDCo 92065 1172-E1
ROTELLA CT
11100 SD 92128 1189-J4
ROTH CT
200 SD 92114 1290-D4
ROTHERHAM AV
8900 SD 92129 1189-C2
ROTHGARD RD
10100 SDCo 91977 1271-E6
ROUGE DR
1800 CHV 91913 1311-E7
ROUGEMONT PL
12500 SD 92131 1210-C5
ROUND MEADOW CT
- SDCo 92028 1027-H7
ROUND POTRERO RD
1300 SDCo 91963 (1316-A3 See Page 1296)
1300 SDCo 91963 (1315-J4 See Page 1294)
ROUNDTREE DR
1700 OCN 92056 1087-D4
ROUNDTREE GN
300 ESCN 92026 1109-G5
ROUND TREE RD
15300 SDCo 92082 1090-J2
15300 SDCo 92082 1091-A2
ROUNDUP AV
- SD 92129 1189-C5
E ROUNDUP CIR
9200 SNTE 92071 1231-F5
N ROUNDUP CIR
10500 SNTE 92071 1231-E5
W ROUNDUP CIR
9200 SNTE 92071 1231-E5
S ROUNDUP TR
10500 SNTE 92071 1231-E6
ROUNDUP WY
1100 OCN 92057 1067-E7
ROUS ST
4200 SD 92122 1228-E4
ROUSH CT
900 CHV 91911 1331-A2
ROUSH DR
1200 CHV 91911 1330-J2
1200 CHV 91911 1331-A2
ROUSILLON CT
- SD 92128 1150-C6
ROUTE 7 Rt#-7
- ImCo 92231 431-E7
1600 ImCo 92250 431-E6
ROVER ST
8900 SDCo 91977 1291-A1
ROWAN GN
- ESCN 92025 1130-A4
ROWAN ST
1600 SD 92105 1289-G2
ROWCLIFF BLVD
- CORD 91932 1329-E4
ROWDY CT
9400 SDCo 91977 1271-C6
ROWE ST
3400 SD 92115 1270-D6
ROWEL CT
27300 SDCo 92082 1091-F4
ROWENA AV
1200 SMCS 92069 1108-H4
ROWENA ST
7300 SD 92119 1250-E3
ROWLETT AV
9000 SD 92129 1189-D4
ROWLEY AV
1700 SDCo 92065 1172-E1
ROWLEY WY
- SDCo 92065 1172-E1
ROXANNE DR
1300 SDCo 92021 1251-G1
1400 SDCo 92021 1231-G7
ROXBORO CT
11400 SD 92131 1209-J1
ROXBORO RD
11000 SD 92131 1209-H1
ROXBURY RD
5100 SD 92116 1269-H2
ROXBURY TER
14000 SDCo 92067 1188-H1
ROXTON CIR
13300 SD 92130 1187-J4
13300 SD 92130 1188-A4
ROXY LN
6500 SD 92115 1270-D2
ROY LN
- SDCo 92028 1028-D2
ROY ST
8000 LMGR 91945 1270-H6
ROYAL CIR
8100 SDCo 92021 1252-A1
ROYAL DR
3500 SDCo 92036 1156-E2
4000 CRLB 92008 1106-G6
37700 SDCo 91905 (1299-H3 See Page 1298)
ROYAL PL
3700 SDCo 91902 1310-D4
37700 SDCo 91905 (1299-G3 See Page 1298)
ROYAL RD
3300 SDCo 92084 1088-E7
11800 SDCo 92021 1251-J1
11900 SDCo 92021 1252-A1
ROYAL ANN AV
10100 SD 92126 1209-B5
ROYAL BIRKDALE PL
6900 SDCo 92067 1188-H1
ROYAL BIRKDALE RW
12000 SD 92128 1170-A5
ROYAL CREST CT
200 SDCo 92025 1130-B7
ROYAL CREST DR
2300 SDCo 92025 1130-B6
ROYAL CROWN RW
15600 SD 92128 1170-B5
ROYAL DORNOCH SQ
13800 SD 92128 1189-J3
ROYALE CRESCENT CT
2200 SD 92123 1249-C7
ROYAL GARDENS CT
8000 SDCo 92021 1252-A1
ROYAL GARDENS PL
8000 SDCo 92021 1252-A1
ROYAL GLEN DR
200 SDCo 92028 1027-F1
ROYAL GORGE CT
6500 SD 92119 1250-D3
ROYAL GORGE DR
6700 SD 92119 1250-D3
ROYAL GREENS PL
4800 SD 92117 1248-G1
ROYAL ISLAND WY
4800 SD 92154 1330-J6
ROYALITO LN
8000 SDCo 92021 1252-A1
ROYAL LYTHAM GN
2100 ESCN 92026 1109-D4
ROYAL LYTHAM RW
12100 SD 92128 1170-A5
ROYAL LYTHAM SQ
15600 SD 92128 1170-B5
ROYAL MELBOURNE SQ
13700 SD 92128 1189-J3
ROYAL OAK CT
7900 SD 92114 1290-H5
ROYAL OAK DR
100 SD 92114 1290-H4
2300 SDCo 92027 1130-F2
2400 ESCN 92027 1130-F2
4500 OCN 92056 1087-D5
S ROYAL OAK DR
100 SD 92114 1290-H4
ROYAL OAKS LN
17200 SDCo 92065 1171-G1
ROYAL PARK LN
8100 SDCo 92021 1252-A1
8100 SDCo 92040 1252-A1
ROYAL RIM DR
9600 SDCo 92026 1089-D2
ROYAL SAINT JAMES DR
2400 SDCo 92019 1272-A5
ROYAL TERN WY
900 OCN 92057 1087-A3
ROYAL TROON GN
- ESCN 92026 1109-H3
ROYAL VIEW RD
- SDCo 92027 1130-F4
ROYAL VISTA DR
1300 SDCo 92065 1172-E3
ROYAL WILLIE RD
33400 SDCo 91906 (1318-F3 See Page 1298)
ROYCE CT
8400 SD 92123 1249-B7
ROYCE LN
1400 SDCo 92028 1027-J7
1400 SDCo 92028 1047-J1
ROYMAR RD
100 OCN 92054 1086-D4
ROYSTON DR
1700 SD 92154 1349-J2
1700 SD 92154 1350-A2
R SANTOS ST
- CALX 92231 6620-J5
R TAMAYO ST
- CALX 92231 6620-J6
RUA ALTA VISTA
29300 SDCo 91962 1237-D6
RUA MICHELLE
25500 SDCo 92026 1109-F2
RUANE ST
7000 SD 92119 1250-E3
RUBENSTEIN AV
1200 ENCT 92007 1167-D1
RUBENSTEIN DR
1600 ENCT 92007 1167-D2
RUBENSTEIN PL
200 ENCT 92007 1167-C1
RUBY AV
- SDCo 91905 1300-C7
RUBY CT
- CALX 92231 6620-H7
RUBY DR
600 VSTA 92083 1087-D6
RUBY LN
4400 OCN 92056 1107-D2
6900 LMGR 91945 1290-E1
6900 LMGR 92114 1290-E1
RUBY RD
1900 ESCN 92026 1109-D5
RUBY ST
600 ELCJ 92020 1251-G7
5600 SD 92110 1268-F3
RUBY WY
- CRLB 92011 1127-B4
RUBY LAKE AV
6200 SD 92119 1250-H6
RUDD RD
400 VSTA 92084 1088-B6
RUDDER AV
- CRLB 92011 1126-J7
- CRLB 92011 1127-B5
- CRLB 92011 1146-J1
RUDDER RD
2400 OCN 92054 1106-F1
RUDDER WY
- OCN 92054 1106-F1
RUDDY DR
29800 SDCo 91906 (1297-F5 See Page 1296)
RUDDY DUCK CT
2200 ENCT 92007 1167-F4
RUDNICK DR
3100 SDCo 91935 1274-C4
RUDY RD
1400 SDCo 91977 1291-A2
RUE ADRIANE
2300 SD 92037 1227-H7
RUE AVALLON
600 CHV 91913 1311-D4
RUE BAYONNE
600 CHV 91913 1311-D4
RUE BIARRITZ
9900 SD 92131 1210-B5
RUE BIENVILLE PL
- CHV 91913 1311-F1
RUE CANNES
10200 SD 92131 1210-C5
RUE CAP FERRAT
1200 SDCo 92078 1128-B3
RUE CHAMBERRY
10200 SD 92131 1210-B5
RUE CHAMOND
600 CHV 91913 1311-D4
RUE CHAMONIX
10200 SD 92131 1210-C5
RUE CHANTEMAR
9900 SD 92131 1210-B5
RUE CHATEAU
1900 CHV 91913 1311-D4
RUE CHEAUMONT
12200 SD 92131 1210-B5
RUEDA CT
10800 SD 92124 1249-J2
RUEDA DR
3900 SD 92124 1249-J2
4300 SD 92124 1250-A2
RUEDA ACAYAN
12700 SD 92128 1150-D7
12700 SD 92128 1170-C1
RUEDA ALCALDE
7700 SDCo 91962 1237-C6
RUEDA MARGARITA
300 SMCS 92069 1109-C7
RUEDA MELILLA
12800 SD 92128 1150-C7
12800 SD 92128 1170-C1
RUE DE ANNE
2300 SD 92037 1227-H7
RUE DE ANTIBES
14000 SD 92014 1187-G6
RUE DE AZUR
14000 SD 92014 1187-G6
RUE DE FLEUR
- SDCo 92026 1109-G2
RUE DE LAC
- SDCo 92026 1109-F2
RUE DE LA MER
1700 OCN 92054 1106-D2
RUE DE LA MONTAGNE
2000 OCN 92054 1106-D1
RUE DENISE
2400 SD 92037 1227-H7
RUE DE ROARK
7200 SD 92037 1227-J7
RUE DES AMIS
11900 SD 92131 1210-A3
RUE DES CHATEAUX
2300 CRLB 92008 1106-D5
RUE DE VALLE
1600 SMCS 92078 1128-D1
RUE DORLEANS
3000 SD 92110 1268-B5
RUE DU NUAGE
10400 SD 92131 1210-A3
RUE FINISTERRE
10200 SD 92131 1210-B5
RUE FONTENAY
10300 SD 92131 1210-B4
RUE FOUNTAINEBLEAU
12300 SD 92131 1210-B4
RUEGGER RD
- ImCo 92233 411-A10
RUE LAUSANNE
- SDCo 92026 1109-F2
RUE LEBLANC
600 CHV 91913 1311-D4
RUELLE CT
8300 SNTE 92071 1230-H6
RUE MARRABELLE
12600 SD 92131 1210-C4
RUE MARSEILLES
600 CHV 91913 1311-D3
RUE MICHAEL
7200 SD 92037 1227-H7
RUE MICHELLE
1900 CHV 91913 1311-D3
RUE MONACO
14000 SD 92014 1187-G6
RUE MONTEREAU
12000 SD 92131 1210-B5
RUE MONT GRENOBLE
12100 SD 92131 1210-B4
RUE MONTREUX
- SDCo 92026 1109-F2
RUE PARC
600 CHV 91913 1311-D4
12600 SD 92131 1210-C5
RUE RIVIERE VERTE
10300 SD 92131 1210-C4
RUE SAINT JACQUES
10200 SD 92131 1210-B5
RUE SAINT JEAN
1200 SDCo 92078 1128-G4
RUE SAINT LAZARE
12400 SD 92131 1210-B5
RUE SAINT MARTIN
1200 SDCo 92078 1128-C3
RUE SAINT MORITZ
1200 SDCo 92078 1128-G4
RUE SAINT RAPHAEL
14000 SD 92014 1187-G6
RUE SAINT TROPEZ
14000 SD 92014 1187-G6
RUE SAN REMO
14000 SD 92014 1187-G6
RUE SIENNE NORD
12600 SD 92131 1210-C4
RUE TOURAINE
10200 SD 92131 1210-C5
RUETTE ABETO
17300 SD 92127 1169-J1
RUETTE ALLIANTE
12400 SD 92130 1188-A7
RUETTE CAMPANA
17100 SD 92128 1170-B2
RUETTE DE MER
4800 SD 92130 1188-D6
RUETTE DE VILLE
3900 SD 92130 1187-J7
3900 SD 92130 1188-A7
RUETTE LE PARC
13600 SD 92014 1187-J6
RUETTE MONTE CARLO
8500 SD 92037 1227-H4
RUETTE NICE
2500 SD 92037 1227-H4
RUETTE NICOLE
2500 SD 92037 1227-H4
RUETTE PARC LIDO
3400 SD 92154 1350-E1
RUETTE SAN RAPHAEL
- SD 92130 1208-A2
RUE VALBONNE
600 CHV 91913 1311-D3
RUE VINCENNES
12600 SD 92131 1210-C5
RUFFIN CT
9300 SD 92123 1249-E1
RUFFIN RD
3100 SD 92123 1249-E1
3100 SD 92123 1249-E5
5400 SD 92123 1229-E7
9200 SNTE 92071 1231-A5
RUFFNER ST
4300 SD 92111 1249-A1
5100 SD 92111 1229-A7
RUFUS CT
7900 SD 92129 1189-A6
RUGBY CT
9300 SD 92123 1249-E5
RUGER WY
- SDCo 92084 1068-C7
RUIS RD
14300 SDCo 92021 1232-G6
RUJEAN LN
700 SDCo 92028 1027-H7
RUMEX LN
8400 SD 92129 1189-B6
RUMSON DR
8300 SNTE 92071 1230-H5
8300 SNTE 92071 1230-H5
8800 SNTE 92071 1231-A5
RUNABOUT PL
2100 SDCo 92019 1272-D3
RUNNER RD
2500 SDCo 91906 (1297-G4 See Page 1296)
RUNNING CREEK LN
9700 SDCo 92026 1049-D7
RUNNING CREEK RD
9700 SDCo 92026 1049-D7
RUNNING CREEK TR
9600 SDCo 92026 1049-D7
RUNNING DEER TR
15300 PWY 92064 1171-C6
RUNNING M RD
3300 SDCo 92004 (1079-A6 See Page 1058)
RUNNING MARE LN
- SDCo 91901 1234-A4
RUNNING SPRING PL
2200 ENCT 92024 1147-J6
RUNNING STREAM RD
1800 SDCo 92084 1068-B5
RUNNYMEAD LN
9700 SD 92106 1288-A2
RUN OF THE KNOLLS
- SD 92127 1169-A6
RUN OF THE KNOLLS CT
- SD 92127 1169-B5
RUNWAY DR
31900 SDCo 92061 1051-C7
RUNYUN LN
14500 PWY 92064 1190-F1
RUPERTUS DR
- SDCo 92672 1023-D2
RUPP CT
9000 SNTE 92071 1231-A5
RUSH AV
1600 VSTA 92084 1087-H3
E RUSH AV
1600 VSTA 92084 1087-H3
RUSH DR
- SMCS 92078 1128-H2
RUSHDEN AV
4800 SD 92117 1248-G1
RUSHINGS TRC
- SDCo 91901 1234-C4
RUSH ROSE DR
- CRLB 92024 1147-E2
RUSHVILLE LN
4800 SDCo 91941 1271-E2
RUSHVILLE ST
500 SD 92037 1247-E1
RUSK CV
11500 SD 92126 1209-B1
RUSKIN PL
- SMCS 92069 1109-B5
RUSS BLVD
1100 SD 92101 1289-B2
1300 SD 92102 1289-D2
RUSSAN LN
7000 LMGR 91945 1290-F1
RUSSELIA CT
6700 CRLB 92011 1126-J5
RUSSELL AV
- SD 92140 1268-E7
RUSSELL DR
- ImCo 92251 6439-D7
- IMP 92251 6439-D7
9400 SD 92093 1228-A2
RUSSELL PL
1500 ESCN 92025 1129-H5
RUSSELL RD
1200 ELCJ 92020 1251-D5
10300 SDCo 91941 1271-E2
RUSSELL SQ
- SDCo 91941 1271-E1
RUSSELL ST
- SDCo 92055 1067-A2
3000 SD 92106 1288-C1
3400 SD 92106 1268-C7
RUSSET CT
900 SMCS 92078 1128-F2
RUSSET ST
17200 SDCo 92127 1169-F2
RUSSET LEAF CT
- SDCo 92019 1272-B2
RUSSET LEAF LN
13200 SD 92129 1189-B4
RUSSETT GN
2400 ESCN 92029 1149-G1
RUSSMAR DR
2600 SD 92123 1249-D6
RUSTIC DR
6300 SD 92139 1290-E7
RUSTIC RD
1000 ESCN 92025 1130-A1
RUSTIC CANYON RD
1600 SDCo 92084 1068-B6
RUSTICO DR
7600 CRLB 92009 1147-F1
RUSTIC RANCH RD
20000 SDCo 92065 1152-D1
RUSTIC VILLA RD
20200 SDCo 92065 1152-D1
RUSTIC WOOD ST
2600 CHV 91914 1311-H4
RUSTING LN
- CHV 91915 1331-G1
RUSTYS HACIENDA LN
18400 SDCo 92065 1151-E7
RUTGERS AV
800 CHV 91913 1311-D5
RUTGERS PL
2800 OCN 92056 1087-A7
RUTGERS RD
5400 SD 92037 1247-H3
RUTH AV
- SDCo 91905 1300-C6
RUTH CT
100 ELCJ 92019 1252-A5
RUTHERFORD RD
2200 CRLB 92008 1127-C1
24200 SDCo 92065 1173-E1
24200 SDCo 92065 1153-E7
RUTHERFORD RD Rt#-S26
- ImCo 92227 411-D11
- ImCo 92281 411-C11
900 ImCo 92233 411-C11
RUTHERFORD ST
1300 CHV 91913 1331-B1
RUTHIE WY
1900 SD 92139 1290-E7
RUTHLOR RD
1600 ENCT 92007 1167-E2
RUTHUPHAM AV
700 SD 92154 1330-E7
RUTLEDGE CT
5200 SD 92122 1228-G5
RUTLEDGE SQ
14400 SD 92128 1190-B1
RUTTLES CT
3000 SDCo 91978 1271-F6
RUXTON AV
400 SDCo 91977 1291-A4
RYAN CT
2000 SDCo 92019 1272-C4
RYAN DR
300 SMCS 92078 1128-E1
3100 SDCo 92025 1150-D2
3600 ESCN 92025 1150-D2
RYAN RD
- SD 92152 1288-A6
RYAN WY
- OCN 92054 1106-F1
- SDCo 92026 1109-H2
RYAN RIDGE RD
1300 SDCo 92021 1233-A7
RYANS WY
13200 SDCo 92040 1232-C6
RYDELL PL
- ELCJ 92021 1251-F4
RYDER CT
9600 SNTE 92071 1231-C4
RYDER RD
9600 SNTE 92071 1231-C4
RYDER ST
- SD 92152 1288-A5
RYKER RIDGE RD
500 SDCo 92065 1153-A5
RYNE RD
- SD 92152 1287-J5
RYTKO ST
600 SD 92114 1290-G3

S

S AV
- NATC 91950 1290-A6
SABADELL DR
400 OCN 92057 1086-H4
SABINA DR
3000 SD 92139 1310-E2
SABINAS CT
100 SOLB 92075 1167-D7
SABINAS WY
100 SOLB 92075 1167-D7
SABLE CT
5200 OCN 92056 1087-D1
SABOBA CT
- IMP 92251 6439-F4
SABRE ST
700 SD 92114 1290-H3
SABRE HILL DR
10700 SD 92128 1189-G5
SABRE SPRINGS PKWY
10100 SD 92128 1189-H5
11400 SD 92128 1190-A6
SABRE VIEW CV
- SD 92128 1189-G5
SABRINA TER
600 SDCo 92065 1152-H6
SABRINA WY
600 VSTA 92084 1087-J7
SACADA CIR
2400 CRLB 92009 1147-G1
SACO ST
14500 PWY 92064 1190-H4
SACRAMENTO AV
200 SDCo 91977 1291-B4
SACRAMENTO DR
- LMSA 91941 1270-G5
SADDLE DR
3400 SDCo 91977 1271-A5
3700 CRLB 92010 1107-B4
SADDLE RD
500 SDCo 92004 (1078-H2 See Page 1058)
SADDLE WY
1400 OCN 92057 1067-E6
SADDLEBACK DR
9900 SDCo 92040 1232-D3
SADDLEBACK LN
30800 SDCo 92082 1070-J2
SADDLEBACK RD
30400 SDCo 92082 1070-J2
N SADDLEBACK RD
31000 SDCo 92082 1070-J2
SADDLEBACK ST
2500 CHV 91914 1311-G3
SADDLE BACK WY
- SMCS 92078 1129-B1
SADDLEBACK MOUNTAIN RD
17400 SDCo 92065 1171-F2
SADDLEBROOK CT
- ELCJ 92019 1252-B5
15000 PWY 92064 1170-F7
SADDLEBROOK LN
15000 PWY 92064 1170-F7
SADDLEBROOK WY
- ELCJ 92019 1252-C5
- SDCo 92019 1252-C5
SADDLE COVE LN
- SD 92130 1208-D3
SADDLE CREEK DR
15000 SDCo 92082 1070-H2
SADDLE CREEK RD
- SDCo 92028 1047-G5
SADDLE HILL RD
9400 SDCo 92021 1232-J4
SADDLEHORN DR
- CHV 91914 1311-G3
1600 SMCS 92069 1108-E5
SADDLEHORN WY
- OCN 92057 1086-J1
SADDLE MOUNTAIN CT
4500 SD 92130 1188-C5
SADDLE RIDGE CT
13200 SDCo 92040 1232-C5
SADDLE RIDGE RD
- OCN 92057 1067-F6
13200 SDCo 92040 1232-C5
SADDLE ROCK RD
9100 SDCo 92040 1232-A6
SADDLERY SQ
5100 SD 92130 1188-D2
SADDLE SORE TR
600 SDCo 92036 1138-C7
SADDLE SUMMIT RD
16000 SDCo 92065 1171-G4
SADDLE VIEW CT
1300 ELCJ 92019 1251-J7
1300 ELCJ 92019 1252-A7
SADDLEWOOD DR
2900 SDCo 91902 1310-H1
3000 SDCo 91902 1290-H7
13900 PWY 92064 1190-D3
SADIE ST
9900 SNTE 92071 1231-F4
SADLERS CREEK RD
2700 CHV 91914 1311-J4
SADLERS CREEK WY
1100 CHV 91914 1311-J4
SAFARI DR
100 ELCJ 92021 1251-H5
SAFARI SQ
- ELCJ 92021 1251-H5
SAFFORD AV
700 SDCo 91977 1291-A3
SAFFRON GN
2400 ESCN 92029 1149-G1
SAFFRON RD
2900 SDCo 92028 1048-B1
SAFFRON WY
2100 SDCo 92028 1048-B1
SAGAMORE WY
- SD 92130 1208-D1
SAGASTI AV
4800 SD 92117 1248-H1
SAGE CT
800 IMP 92251 6439-G4
6900 CRLB 92011 1127-A6
SAGE DR
2400 SDCo 91906 (1297-E5 See Page 1296)
SAGE GN
3100 ESCN 92029 1149-J2
3100 SDCo 92029 1149-J2
SAGE RD
- SDCo 91948 (1217-J3 See Page 1216)
- SDCo 91948 1218-A2
100 SDCo 92021 1252-J2
3200 SDCo 92028 1048-E3
SAGE VW
2800 CHV 91910 1330-J1
SAGE WY
600 SD 92114 1290-D3
3700 OCN 92057 1086-H4
SAGEBRUSH CT
2400 SD 92037 1247-J2
9400 SDCo 92040 1232-C5
SAGEBRUSH RD
- CRLB 92011 1127-B6
5800 SD 92037 1247-J2
5800 SD 92037 1248-A2
SAGEBRUSH ST
- IMP 92251 6499-E2
SAGEBRUSH TER
- SDCo 92082 1051-A7
SAGE BRUSH TR
- SDCo 92082 1090-C4
SAGEBRUSH WY
1400 OCN 92057 1067-E6
SAGE CANYON DR
- ENCT 92024 1167-G2
SAGE CREEK RD
3600 SDCo 92028 1028-E6
SAGECREST DR
12700 PWY 92064 1170-D7
12700 PWY 92064 1190-C1
SAGEFLOWER DR
3200 SD 92115 1270-D6
SAGE GLEN TR
28400 SDCo 92026 1089-D3
SAGE HILL DR
25300 SDCo 92065 1173-G4
SAGE HILL WY
9500 SDCo 92026 1089-D3
SAGELAND DR
23200 SDCo 92065 1153-D7
SAGE MEADOW CT
- SDCo 92082 1070-D5
SAGE MEADOW LN
- SDCo 92082 1070-D6
SAGE MOUNTAIN LN
13600 SDCo 91935 1292-F2
SAGE SPARROW WY
400 SMCS 92078 1129-B1
SAGE TREE CT
1700 CHV 91913 1311-D6
SAGE VIEW DR
2800 SDCo 91901 1234-C6
SAGE VIEW RD
12100 PWY 92064 1190-B5
SAGEWOD DR
- OCN 92056 1087-E2
SAGEWOD DR
800 OCN 92057 1087-C2
SAGEWOOD DR
900 OCN 92056 1087-E2
13400 PWY 92064 1170-E3
SAGEWOOD LN
13700 PWY 92064 1170-F3
SAGEWOOD RD
1900 SDCo 92003 1068-B4
1900 SDCo 92084 1068-B4
SAGEWOOD WY
- SMCS 92078 1128-C6
SAGINA CT
4800 OCN 92057 1067-A7
SAGINAW AV
4200 SD 92117 1248-E2
SAGITTARIUS RD
11000 SD 92126 1209-C2
SAGUARO PL
200 OCN 92057 1067-A7
SAGUARO RD
9400 SDCo 92040 1231-J5
9400 SDCo 92040 1232-A5
SAGUARO WY
7600 SD 92120 1250-C4
SAHARA PL
3400 OCN 92054 1086-F4
SAILFISH LN
- SDCo 92055 1085-H5
SAILFISH PL
900 CRLB 92011 1126-J4
SAINT AGNES CT
12100 SD 92130 1188-B7
SAINT ALBANS DR
900 ENCT 92024 1147-D4
SAINT ALBANS PL
1000 ENCT 92024 1147-D4
SAINT ANDREWS AV
7700 SD 92154 1351-E2
SAINT ANDREWS CT
16900 PWY 92064 1170-E2
SAINT ANDREWS CV
1600 SD 92154 1351-E2
SAINT ANDREWS DR
9300 SNTE 92071 1230-J6
16800 PWY 92064 1170-E1
SAINT ANDREWS GN
- ESCN 92026 1109-H3
SAINT ANDREWS LN
- SDCo 92082 1090-F4
SAINT ANDREWS PL
4400 OCN 92057 1066-H7
13400 PWY 92064 1170-E1
SAINT ANDREWS RD
6600 SDCo 92067 1168-G7
6600 SDCo 92067 1188-G1
SAINT ANDREWS TER
1600 SD 92154 1351-F2
SAINT ANNE DR
2400 SDCo 92019 1272-B5
SAINT ANNE GN
1800 ESCN 92026 1109-D4
SAINT CHARLES ST
3000 SD 92110 1268-D6
SAINT CHRISTOPHERS LN
- CORD 92118 1329-E2
SAINT CLAIRE DR
1900 CHV 91913 1311-E5
SAINT CLOUD WY
- OCN 92056 1087-A4
SAINT CROIX CT
2100 LMGR 91945 1270-F7
2100 LMGR 91945 1290-F1
SAINT CROIX DR
2000 SDCo 92004 1058-H7
SAINT DENIS TER
5900 SD 92120 1250-C7
SAINT ETIENNE LN
- SD 92128 1150-B6
SAINT GEORGE CT
900 SDCo 91977 1291-A3
4200 CRLB 92010 1106-J5
SAINT GEORGE DR
500 SDCo 92019 1253-C2
SAINT GEORGE PL
800 SDCo 91977 1291-A3
SAINT GEORGE ST
8600 SDCo 91977 1291-A3
SAINT GEORGES LN
14200 SDCo 92082 1070-F7
SAINT GERMAIN RD
900 CHV 91913 1311-E5
SAINT HELENA AV
1200 CHV 91913 1331-B1
SAINT HELENA CT
17200 SDCo 92065 1173-E1
SAINT HELENA DR
17200 SDCo 92065 1173-E1
SAINT HELENE CT
1100 OCN 92054 1106-D2
SAINT JAMES CT
1600 CRLB 92008 1106-F5
SAINT JAMES DR
16800 PWY 92064 1170-D2
SAINT JAMES PL
3900 SD 92103 1268-H5
SAINT JOHN PL
8100 LMSA 91942 1250-H7
SAINT JOHNS CRSG
1500 OCN 92028 1067-E1
1500 SDCo 92003 1067-E1
1500 SDCo 92028 1067-E1
SAINT KITTS WY
- CORD 92118 1329-E2
SAINT LAURENT PL
2700 SD 92037 1227-J6
SAINT LOUIS TER
7900 SD 92037 1227-G6
SAINT LUCIA WY
1800 VSTA 92081 1107-G6
SAINT LUCY LN
15400 SDCo 92021 1233-B2
SAINT MALO BEACH
2100 OCN 92054 1106-C4
SAINT MARYS CT
- SDCo 92127 1169-A2
SAINT MORITZ TER
11800 SD 92131 1210-A3
SAINT NIKOLA CT
- SDCo 92069 1129-E1
SAINT ONGE DR
8100 LMSA 91942 1270-H1
SAINT PAUL DR
700 SDCo 92069 1129-E1
700 SMCS 92069 1129-E1
SAINT PETERS DR
1700 SDCo 92028 1027-J3
SAINT PETERS WY
1700 SDCo 92028 1027-J3
1700 SDCo 92028 1028-A3
SAINT PIERRE WY
11900 SD 92131 1210-A3
SAINT RITA CT
300 SD 92113 1290-A5

SAN DIEGO CO.

STREET
Block City ZIP Pg-Grid

SAINT RITA PL
5000 SD 92113 1290-A4
SAINT SAVA PL
- SDCo 92069 1129-E1
SAINTSBURY GN
- SD 92127 1169-E3
- SDCo 92127 1169-E3
SAINT STEFAN TER
- SDCo 92069 1129-E1
SAINT THERESE WY
5900 SD 92120 1250-C6
SAINT THOMAS DR
2000 SDCo 92004 1058-G7
SAINT THOMAS RD
1800 VSTA 92081 1107-G5
SAINT TROPEZ DR
2000 VSTA 92081 1107-H4
SAINT TROPEZ PL
2600 SD 92037 1227-J6
SAINT VINCENT DR
1900 SDCo 92004 1058-G7
SAIPAN DR
2100 SD 92139 1290-E7
2400 SD 92139 1310-E1
SAIPAN RD
1300 CORD 92118 1309-D5
SAKINA ST
1900 SDCo 92019 1272-C1
SAL GN
1700 ESCN 92029 1129-G5
SAL LN
1100 VSTA 92084 1088-C4
SALACOT CT
5800 SD 92124 1229-H7
SALAMANCA CT
100 SOLB 92075 1167-D7
SALEM CT
700 SD 92109 1267-H1
1400 OCN 92057 1066-J4
1400 OCN 92057 1067-A4
SALEM PL
4500 CRLB 92010 1107-B4
SALEM ST
800 SDCo 92084 1088-F7
800 SDCo 92084 1108-F1
SALERNO CT
1200 OCN 92056 1087-C3
SALERNO ST
6600 SD 92111 1248-J3
7400 SD 92111 1249-A3
SALET PL
- SMCS 92069 1109-A5
SALIDA DEL LUNA
16400 SDCo 92065 1171-C2
SALIDA DEL SOL
- SD 92127 1189-A1
15800 SDCo 92065 1171-B2
SALIENTE WY
2100 CRLB 92009 1147-F1
SALINA CT
300 VSTA 92083 1087-E7
SALINA ST
800 ELCJ 92020 1251-G7
SALINA CRUZ CT
100 SOLB 92075 1167-D6
SALINAS DR
- CHV 91914 1311-D1
SALINAS ST
- OCN 92057 1066-H7
- OCN 92057 1086-H1
SALINAS WY
10900 SD 92126 1209-A3
SALISBURY DR
2200 SD 92123 1249-B7
2600 CRLB 92010 1106-J5
SALIX CT
12100 SD 92129 1189-A7
SALIX PL
7600 SD 92129 1189-A7
SALIX WY
12100 SD 92129 1189-A7
SALIZAR CT
6400 SD 92111 1248-H3
SALIZAR ST
6500 SD 92111 1248-H3
7400 SD 92111 1249-A3
SALK AV
1900 CRLB 92008 1127-C1
SALK INSTITUTE RD
2700 SD 92037 1227-J1
SALLISAW CT
5900 SD 92120 1250-C5
SALLY PL
1700 ESCN 92026 1109-D5
SALMON LN
400 OCN 92054 1086-G2
SALMON RD
200 SDCo 92065 1153-B5
SALMON ST
3000 SD 92124 1249-G5
SALMON RIVER RD
12400 SD 92129 1189-E4
SALOT ST
700 NATC 91950 1290-C7
SALTA PL
3300 SD 92105 1270-A6
SALT AIR LN
900 SDCo 92028 1027-G1
SALTAIRE WY
- CRLB 92011 1127-A4
SALTBUSH LN
1200 SDCo 92019 1252-F7
1300 SDCo 92019 1272-F1
SALT CREEK RD
1500 CHV 91915 1311-J6
1800 CHV 91915 1331-J1
SALTGRASS AV
- CRLB 92011 1126-J6
SALTILLO CT
100 SOLB 92075 1167-D6
SALT MINE RD
17100 SDCo 92065 1171-F2
SALTON DR
- ImCo 92274 410-H7
SALTON BAY DR
- ImCo 92259 410-H6
- ImCo 92274 410-H6
SALTON VIEW DR
2100 SDCo 92036 1136-C6
SALTON VISTA DR
700 SDCo 92036 1156-E1
2500 SDCo 92036 1136-D7
SALUDA AV
10200 SD 92126 1209-C5
SALUTO CT
4500 SD 92130 1188-C7
SALVADOR GUILIN ST
800 CALX 92231 6680-D1
SALVIA WY
12200 SD 92129 1189-A7
SAM LN
17100 SDCo 92065 1171-G2

SAMAGATUMA VALLEY RD
- SDCo 91916 1236-G3
SAMANTHA AV
13300 SD 92129 1189-D3
SAMANTHA CT
- IMP 92251 6499-H2
9200 SD 92129 1189-D4
SAMANTHA LN
8600 SDCo 91977 1270-J7
SAMAR ST
- SD 92140 1268-E6
SAMARA WY
800 CRLB 92011 1127-A6
SAMBROSO PL
16500 SD 92128 1170-C3
SAM ELLIS ST
500 CALX 92231 6620-E7
SAMOA ST
- SD 92140 1268-F6
SAMOA WY
1800 OCN 92054 1106-E1
SAM-O-RENO RD
13900 PWY 92064 1190-G4
SAMOSET AV
4200 SD 92117 1248-E2
SAMPLE ST
10200 SD 92124 1249-G5
SAMPSON RD
1700 SD 92106 1288-C2
SAMPSON ST
- IMP 92251 6499-H2
200 SD 92113 1289-D6
SAMS HILL RD
1300 SDCo 92021 1251-G2
SAMS MOUNTAIN RD
32200 SDCo 92061 1051-C6
SAMUEL CT
- ENCT 92024 1147-E5
SAMUEL ST
5800 LMSA 91942 1250-H7
SAN ABELLA DR
1000 ENCT 92024 1147-E7
SAN ALBERTO WY
300 SD 92114 1290-A5
SAN ALTOS PL
1300 LMGR 91945 1290-F2
1300 LMGR 92114 1290-F2
1300 SD 92114 1290-F2
SAN ANDRADE DR
1000 ENCT 92024 1147-E7
SAN ANDRES DR
500 SOLB 92075 1167-G7
6100 SOLB 92014 1167-G7
13100 SOLB 92014 1187-H1
15700 SD 92014 1187-H1
SAN ANDRES ST
9100 SDCo 91977 1291-B4
SAN ANGELO AV
6100 LMSA 91942 1251-A6
6100 SD 92119 1251-A6
SAN ANGELO PL
700 CHV 91914 1311-G3
SAN ANSELMO ST
- CHV 91913 1331-D1
2500 SD 92109 1248-C4
SAN ANTONIO AV
300 SD 92106 1288-A4
SAN ANTONIO PL
800 SD 92106 1288-B3
SAN ANTONIO WY
10900 SDCo 92082 1049-F2
SAN ANTONIO ROSE CT
- SDCo 92127 1149-A7
- SDCo 92127 1169-A1
SAN AQUARIO DR
5000 SD 92109 1248-B3
SAN ARDO CV
4000 SD 92130 1188-B7
SAN AUGUSTINE WY
3900 SD 92130 1188-B7
SAN BARTOLO
7000 CRLB 92011 1126-J6
7300 CRLB 92011 1127-A6
SAN BENITO
7200 CRLB 92011 1126-J7
7300 CRLB 92011 1127-A7
SAN BENITO CT
1400 SOLB 92014 1167-H7
SAN BENITO RD
700 SDCo 92004 (1079-A7 See Page 1058)
SAN BERNARDINO AV
1000 SDCo 91977 1291-D2
SAN BERNARDO TER
5200 SD 92114 1290-B5
SAN BLAS CIR
10900 SD 92126 1209-D3
SANBORN RD
- ImCo 92227 411-D11
SAN BRILLO DR
500 OCN 92054 1086-F2
SAN BRISTO WY
2900 CRLB 92009 1147-H2
SAN BRUNO CV
4000 SD 92130 1188-B6
SAN BRUNO PL
- CHV 91914 1311-G3
SANCADO TER
500 SDCo 92028 1027-E3
SAN CARLOS
7000 CRLB 92011 1126-J6
SAN CARLOS CT
10300 SDCo 91978 1271-E6
SAN CARLOS DR
500 OCN 92054 1086-F2
3200 SDCo 91978 1271-F6
7900 SD 92119 1250-H5
SAN CARLOS PL
1400 ESCN 92026 1109-E5
SAN CARLOS RD
700 SDCo 92004 (1079-A7 See Page 1058)
SAN CARLOS ST
9200 SDCo 91977 1291-B4
SAN CLEMENTE AV
2200 VSTA 92084 1088-C6
SAN CLEMENTE ST
2100 SD 92107 1268-B7
SAN CLEMENTE TER
2500 SD 92122 1228-B7
SAN CLEMENTE WY
200 VSTA 92084 1088-D6
300 SDCo 92084 1088-D6
SAN COLLA ST
300 SD 92037 1247-F4
SAN CRISTOBAL RD
9800 SDCo 91941 1271-D4
9800 SDCo 91977 1271-D4
SAND CT
- CRLB 92010 1107-B4
SANDAL LN
1400 SD 92109 1247-J3

SANDALWOOD CT
- ELCN 92243 6559-D1
- ENCT 92024 1147-E5
SANDALWOOD DR
- CHV 91910 1310-C5
400 ELCJ 92021 1251-G4
1200 ELCN 92243 6559-D1
SANDALWOOD LN
1500 CRLB 92008 1106-F5
SANDAL WOOD PL
500 ESCN 92027 1110-D6
SANDALWOOD PL
5200 OCN 92056 1087-D1
SANDALWOOD WY
4700 OCN 92057 1087-B3
SANDALWOOD GLEN AV
- IMP 92251 6499-D2
SAND ASTER CIR
32000 SDCo 91906 (1318-B6 See Page 1298)
SAND ASTER CT
- CRLB 92011 1127-D6
SANDBAR DR
- SMCS 92078 1128-D5
SANDBAR WY
800 CRLB 92011 1126-J5
SANDBAR COVE WY
- SD 92154 1350-J2
SANDBURG AV
5400 SD 92122 1228-C6
SANDBURG CT
3000 SD 92122 1228-C6
SANDBURG WY
3000 SD 92122 1228-C6
SANDCASTLE DR
800 ENCT 92007 1167-E2
6700 CRLB 92011 1126-J6
6700 CRLB 92011 1127-A6
SANDCASTLE LN
- SD 92106 1268-D5
- SD 92110 1268-D5
SANDCASTLE WY
1900 OCN 92054 1106-F1
SAND CRAB PL
- SD 92130 1208-B4
SAND CREST DR
- ImCo 92274 410-H7
SAND CREST WY
- SMCS 92078 1128-A2
SANDDOLLAR CT
5200 SD 92130 1188-D6
SAND DOLLAR WY
- SMCS 92078 1128-A3
SAND DRIFT PT
- SD 92154 1350-J1
SAND DUNE WY
- SMCS 92078 1128-D5
SANDEL DR
300 VSTA 92083 1087-G5
SANDER CT
1100 ESCN 92026 1110-A7
SANDERLING CT
1600 CRLB 92011 1127-E7
SANDERS CT
6600 SD 92119 1250-F5
SANDHILL CT
5200 SD 92130 1188-D5
SAND HILL RD
14200 PWY 92064 1170-G5
SANDHILL TER
5200 SD 92130 1188-D5
SANDHURST WY
28400 SDCo 92026 1089-D4
SANDIA PL
5500 SD 92124 1249-H1
SANDIA CREEK DR
38200 SDCo 92028 997-F2
40300 SDCo 92028 409-B4
E SANDIA CREEK TER
4000 RivC 92590 997-G1
4000 SDCo 92028 997-G1
W SANDIA CREEK TER
3600 SDCo 92028 997-F1
SAN DIEGO AV
300 ELCN 92243 6499-H5
1700 SD 92103 1268-G6
1700 SD 92110 1268-F5
1900 SDCo 92065 1172-E1
SAN DIEGO FRWY I-5
- CHV - 1309-H4
- CHV - 1329-J1
- CHV - 1330-A3
- CRLB - 1106-F6
- CRLB - 1126-G2
- CRLB - 1127-A6
- CRLB - 1147-A1
- ENCT - 1147-C5
- ENCT - 1167-D2
- NATC - 1289-C2
- NATC - 1309-G1
- OCN - 1085-G2
- OCN - 1086-A6
- OCN - 1106-C1
- SCLE - 1023-E3
- SD - 1187-H2
- SD - 1207-J1
- SD - 1208-A4
- SD - 1228-B4
- SD - 1248-B2
- SD - 1268-E3
- SD - 1288-J1
- SD - 1289-C2
- SD - 1330-A6
- SD - 1350-D3
- SDCo - 408-H5
- SDCo - 1023-E3
- SDCo - 1085-G2
- SOLB - 1167-D2
- SOLB - 1187-H2
SAN DIEGO PL
1000 SD 92109 1267-J4
SAN DIEGO ST
100 OCN 92054 1086-B6
9200 SDCo 91977 1291-B4
SAN DIEGO CORONADO FERRY
- SD - 1288-H4
SAN DIEGO MISSION RD
9400 SD 92108 1249-F7
SAN DIEGUITO DR
500 ENCT 92024 1147-C7
600 ENCT 92024 1167-C1
1400 DLMR 92014 1187-G3
SAN DIEGUITO RD
- SD 92127 1169-A6
3700 SD 92130 1188-B2
3900 SD 92067 1188-D1
7200 SDCo 92067 1168-E7
10100 SDCo 92067 1188-D1
16000 SD 92127 1168-H5
16000 SDCo 92127 1168-H5
SAN DIMAS AV
200 OCN 92057 1086-G3
6000 SD 92111 1268-G2
SAN DIMAS CT
1100 CHV 91913 1311-C7
SAN DIONICIO ST
600 SD 92106 1288-A3
SANDLEFORD WY
6900 SD 92139 1290-F7
SANDLER CT
- SDCo 91901 1234-B3
SANDLEWOOD CT
3300 SD 92037 1228-B4
SANDLEWOOD DR
400 ELCN 92243 6559-H1
SANDMARK AV
8800 SD 92123 1249-C7
SAN DOMINGO
- VSTA 92081 1107-C2
SANDOR WY
3500 SDCo 92084 1088-F7
SANDOS ST
1600 ELCJ 92019 1252-B7
SANDOVAL CIR
2000 ImCo 92243 6500-H4
SANDOVAL LN
600 ImCo 92243 6500-H4
SANDOVER CT
2800 SDCo 91902 1290-J7
SANDOWN CT
14300 PWY 92064 1190-E2
SANDOWN WY
- SD 92130 1188-E5
SANDPIPER AV
- SDCo 92055 1023-E3
SAND PIPER PL
6900 CRLB 92009 1127-E5
SANDPIPER PL
900 SD 92037 1247-G3
3500 OCN 92056 1107-C2
SANDPIPER WY
400 CHV 91910 1309-H7
400 CHV 91910 1329-H1
SANDPIPER STRAND
- CORD 92118 1329-E1
SANDPOINT CT
3700 CRLB 92010 1107-B3
SANDRA CIR
1200 VSTA 92083 1108-A1
SANDRA LN
- ELCJ 92019 1252-D4
SANDRA ANN LN
- SDCo 92082 1069-H3
SANDROCK RD
3100 SD 92123 1249-C4
SANDS PL
100 OCN 92054 1086-F5
SAND SHELL AV
- CRLB 92011 1126-J6
SANDSHORE CT
4900 SD 92130 1188-D6
SANDSIDE CT
- CRLB 92011 1126-J5
SANDSTONE CIR
1500 SDCo 92004 1058-H5
SANDSTONE CT
300 CHV 91911 1330-G4
SANDSTONE DR
8500 SNTE 92071 1230-H7
8500 SNTE 92071 1250-H1
SANDSTONE ST
200 CHV 91911 1330-G4
SANDSTONE WY
- CRLB 92010 1107-B3
SANDSTONE VISTA LN
1900 ENCT 92024 1147-H7
SAND TRAP CT
2300 OCN 92056 1106-J2
SANDTRAP RW
12100 SD 92128 1170-A4
SANDY AV
600 ELCN 92243 6499-H4
SANDY CT
200 OCN 92054 1085-J6
SANDY LN
600 SMCS 92078 1129-A2
1100 VSTA 92081 1108-A5
2900 DLMR 92014 1187-F2
SANDY PL
3100 CRLB 92008 1106-G4
SANDY ST
300 ELCJ 92020 1251-F6
SANDY BEV LN
8600 SDCo 91945 1270-J6
8600 SDCo 91977 1270-J6
8600 SDCo 91977 1271-A6
SANDY CAPE CT
- SD 92154 1351-A1
SANDY CREEK
- SDCo 92036 1175-J2
SANDY CREEK DR
400 CHV 91902 1311-A3
SANDY CREST CT
12600 SD 92130 1188-D6
SANDY HILL DR
29300 SDCo 92026 1069-A7
SANDY HOOK RD
10800 SD 92126 1209-A3
SANDY POINTE
2900 DLMR 92014 1187-F3
SANDY SHORE CT
- SD 92139 1290-D7
SANDY SHORE ST
1700 SD 92139 1290-D6
SAN ELIJO
4800 SDCo 92067 1168-D1
SAN ELIJO AV
1300 ENCT 92007 1167-C2
SAN ELIJO RD
- CRLB 92009 1128-B6
- CRLB 92078 1128-B6
- SDCo 92024 1128-D7
9400 SMCS 92024 1128-D7
9400 SMCS 92078 1128-B6
SAN ELIJO ST
300 SD 92106 1288-A4
SAN FELIPE DR
- ImCo 92251 6499-H1
- IMP 92251 6499-H1
SAN FELIPE PL
300 SD 92114 1290-H3
SAN FELIPE RD Rt#-S2
21300 SDCo 92036 410-A10
22300 SDCo 92086 410-A10
25600 SDCo 92086 409-K9
29000 SDCo 92070 409-K9
SAN FELIPE ST
8000 SD 92114 1290-H4
SAN FELIPE WY
27500 SDCo 92086 409-K9
SAN FERNANDO PL
700 SD 92109 1267-H3
SAN FERNANDO ST
200 SD 92106 1288-A4

SANFORD DR
7800 LMGR 91945 1290-H2
SANFORD LN
300 ENCT 92024 1147-B3
2800 CRLB 92010 1107-A4
SANFORD ST
100 ENCT 92024 1147-A3
SAN FRANCISCO ST
8800 SDCo 91977 1291-A3
SANFRED CT
10600 SNTE 92071 1231-D2
SAN GABRIEL DR
3600 OCN 92054 1086-F2
SAN GABRIEL PL
700 CHV 91914 1311-F3
700 SD 92109 1267-H3
SAN GABRIEL WY
10800 SDCo 92082 1049-F4
SANGALLO LN
9500 SDCo 92127 1169-E2
SANGAMON AV
1000 SDCo 91977 1291-D2
SANGER PL
- SD 92173 1350-F4
SAN GERONIMO DR
32700 SDCo 92082 1049-J5
SAN GORGONIO ST
300 SD 92106 1288-A4
SAN GREGORIO WY
3900 SD 92130 1188-B7
SAN HELENA DR
3100 OCN 92056 1086-J7
SANIBELLE CIR
400 CHV 91910 1310-F6
SAN IGNACIO
1400 SOLB 92075 1167-H7
SAN JACINTO CIR
5200 SDCo 92028 1047-E6
SAN JACINTO CIR E
4900 SDCo 92028 1047-F6
SAN JACINTO CIR W
4800 SDCo 92028 1047-E6
N SAN JACINTO DR
100 SD 92114 1290-B4
SAN JACINTO GN
1100 ESCN 92026 1109-E5
SAN JACINTO PL
600 CHV 91914 1311-F3
5200 SD 92114 1290-B4
SAN JACINTO RD
- SDCo 92055 1085-J4
- SDCo 92055 1086-A5
SAN JACINTO TER
4700 SDCo 92028 1047-F6
SAN JOAQUIN CT
2500 SD 92109 1248-C4
SAN JOAQUIN DR
4800 SD 92109 1248-B4
SAN JOAQUIN ST
600 OCN 92057 1086-G1
4400 OCN 92057 1066-H7
SAN JOSE CT
600 CHV 91914 1311-G3
SAN JOSE PL
700 SD 92109 1267-H1
SAN JOSE ST
1500 OCN 92054 1086-A5
SAN JUAN DR
- SMCS 92078 1128-E2
SAN JUAN PL
700 CHV 91914 1311-G3
700 SD 92109 1267-H1
900 OCN 92054 1086-A5
9100 LMSA 91941 1271-B3
9100 SDCo 91941 1271-B3
SAN JUAN RD
- SDCo 92055 408-K6
2200 SD 92103 1268-G5
2200 SD 92110 1268-G5
SAN JUAN ST
1000 OCN 92054 1086-B5
9700 SDCo 91977 1271-D5
SAN JUAN WY
- SMCS 92078 1129-C1
SAN JUHN ST
600 SDCo 91977 1291-C3
SAN JULIAN DR
1000 SDCo 92078 1128-D3
SAN JULIAN LN
1300 SDCo 92078 1128-D3
SAN JULIAN PL
1200 SDCo 92078 1128-D3
SAN JULIO RD
600 SOLB 92014 1167-H7
600 SOLB 92075 1167-H7
SAN LEANDRO WY
3900 SD 92130 1188-B7
SAN LEON CT
1100 SOLB 92075 1167-H5
3500 SDCo 92004 (1079-A7 See Page 1058)
SAN LEON RD
700 SDCo 92004 (1079-A7 See Page 1058)
SANLIN DR
1500 SDCo 92019 1272-A1
SAN LORENZO CT
900 SOLB 92075 1167-H5
3900 OCN 92057 1086-H4
SAN LORI LN
1100 SDCo 92019 1252-B7
1100 SDCo 92019 1272-A1
SAN LUCAS
7200 CRLB 92011 1126-J7
SAN LUCAS CT
1300 SOLB 92075 1167-H7
SAN LUCAS DR
300 SOLB 92075 1167-J7
500 SOLB 92014 1167-J7
500 SOLB 92014 1187-J1
SAN LUCAS PL
500 CHV 91914 1311-F3
SAN LUIS
7200 CRLB 92011 1126-J6
7300 CRLB 92011 1127-A7
SAN LUIS AV
100 OCN 92057 1086-G2
SAN LUIS ST
700 SD 92102 1289-D3
SAN LUIS OBISPO DR
3600 OCN 92054 1086-F3
SAN LUIS OBISPO PL
700 SD 92109 1267-H2
SAN LUIS REY AV
800 CORD 92118 1288-J7
1500 VSTA 92084 1087-H3
SAN LUIS REY DR
500 OCN 92054 1085-J6
700 OCN 92054 1086-A5
11100 SDCo 92082 1049-F3
SAN LUIS REY PL
700 SD 92109 1267-H4
SAN LUIS REY RD
2900 OCN 92054 1086-D5

SAN LUIS REY MSN EXWY Rt#-76
800 OCN 92054 1085-J6
800 OCN 92054 1086-A5
SAN MARCOS AV
2400 SD 92104 1289-E1
2500 SD 92104 1269-E7
E SAN MARCOS BLVD
100 SMCS 92069 1108-H7
W SAN MARCOS BLVD Rt#-S12
200 SMCS 92069 1108-H7
300 SMCS 92069 1128-D2
700 SMCS 92078 1128-A2
SAN MARCOS PL
100 CHV 91911 1330-F2
SAN MARINO DR
900 SDCo 92078 1128-C3
SAN MARINO PL
- CHV 91914 1311-G3
SAN MARIO DR
500 SOLB 92075 1167-J5
SAN MARTIN
- SDCo 92040 1232-B7
SAN MARTINE WY
3900 SD 92130 1188-B7
SAN MATEO DR
5400 SD 92114 1290-B5
SAN MATEO RD
- SDCo 92055 408-J5
SAN MATEO ST
1500 OCN 92054 1086-A5
SAN MATEO POINT CT
1500 CHV 91911 1330-J4
SAN MIGUEL
7200 CRLB 92011 1126-J7
SAN MIGUEL AV
1000 SDCo 91977 1291-C2
4100 SD 92113 1289-H5
6600 LMGR 91945 1270-E7
6800 SDCo 91902 1291-D7
S SAN MIGUEL AV
500 SD 92113 1289-H5
SAN MIGUEL CT
100 CHV 91911 1330-D1
3500 NATC 91902 1310-E3
3900 OCN 92057 1086-H3
SAN MIGUEL DR
- CHV 91911 1330-C1
1100 SMCS 92078 1128-E2
E SAN MIGUEL DR
- CHV 91911 1330-D1
SAN MIGUEL RD
5400 SDCo 91902 1310-J1
5400 SDCo 91902 1311-A1
5900 SDCo 91902 1291-B7
SAN MIGUEL ST
600 SDCo 91977 1291-C3
SAN MIGUEL WY
3300 SDCo 91902 1311-A1
SAN MIGUEL RANCH RD
- CHV 91902 1311-C1
SAN MORITZ
15300 PWY 92064 1170-D6
SAN ONOFRE TER
5300 SD 92114 1290-B5
SAN PABLO AV
3800 OCN 92057 1086-G4
SAN PABLO CT
1300 SDCo 92004 (1079-A7 See Page 1058)
1300 SDCo 92078 1128-D2
SAN PABLO DR
800 SDCo 92078 1128-D2
800 SMCS 92078 1128-D2
SAN PABLO PL
- CHV 91914 1311-F3
SAN PABLO RD
700 SDCo 92004 (1079-A7 See Page 1058)
700 SDCo 92004 (1099-A1 See Page 1098)
SAN PABLO WY
900 SDCo 92078 1128-D2
SAN PASCUAL SCHOOL RD
- ImCo 92283 432-C5
SAN PASQUAL CT
2000 LMGR 91945 1290-F1
SAN PASQUAL RD
- SD 92027 1130-G7
700 ESCN 92025 1150-C2
2900 SD 92025 1130-G7
2900 SD 92025 1150-E2
2900 SDCo 92025 1130-G7
5500 SDCo 92025 1150-E2
14400 SDCo 92027 1130-G7
S SAN PASQUAL RD
- SDCo 92082 1091-C3
SAN PASQUAL ST
- CHV 91913 1331-D1
500 SD 92113 1289-H5
7200 LMGR 91945 1290-F1
SAN PASQUAL TR
14200 SDCo 92025 1130-F6
SAN PASQUAL WY
14300 SDCo 92025 1130-F6
SAN PASQUAL VALLEY RD Rt#-78
500 ESCN 92025 1130-B2
500 ESCN 92027 1130-B2
800 SDCo 92025 1130-B2
800 SDCo 92027 1130-B2
1400 SDCo 92065 1152-C1
2100 SD 92065 409-G11
2100 SDCo 92027 409-G11
2100 SDCo 92065 409-G11
2100 SD 92027 409-G11
2500 SD 92027 1130-G6
3500 SD 92025 1131-A6
3500 SD 92065 1131-F6
3500 SD 92027 1131-A6
16100 SDCo 92027 1131-F6
16100 SDCo 92025 1131-F6
SAN PATRICIO DR
1000 SOLB 92075 1167-H6
SAN PEDRO ST
6000 SD 92111 1268-G2
SAN PEDRO POINT CT
1500 CHV 91911 1330-J3
SAN PLACIDO CT
400 ESCN 92029 1150-A4
SAN RAFAEL DR
1300 OCN 92054 1085-J5
1600 SDCo 92055 1085-J5
SAN RAFAEL PL
700 CHV 91914 1311-G3
700 SD 92109 1247-H7
SAN RAFAEL RD
3300 SDCo 92004 (1079-A6 See Page 1058)
SAN RAMON
7200 CRLB 92011 1126-J7

SAN RAMON DR
3700 OCN 92057 1086-G3
10100 SD 92126 1209-C5
E SAN RAPHAEL DR
- SD 92130 1208-A2
W SAN RAPHAEL DR
- SD 92130 1208-A2
SAN REMO CIR
2200 SDCo 92084 1108-C2
SAN REMO CT
9700 SNTE 92071 1231-D4
SAN REMO DR
2000 OCN 92056 1086-J7
SAN REMO RD
9700 SNTE 92071 1231-D4
SAN REMO WY
400 SD 92106 1288-A4
SAN REY CT
4700 SDCo 92028 1048-H4
SAN REY LN
3300 SDCo 92028 1048-H3
SAN REY PL
4700 SDCo 92028 1048-H4
SAN RICARDO CT
1100 SOLB 92075 1167-H5
SAN RODOLFO DR
600 SOLB 92075 1167-F7
SAN ROQUE DR
300 SDCo 92025 1130-B6
SAN RUFO CT
- SDCo 92127 1169-F4
SAN SALVADOR CT
16600 SD 92128 1170-B3
SAN SALVADOR RD
16500 SD 92128 1170-B3
SAN SEBASTIAN AV
- CHV 91913 1311-E6
SAN SEBASTIAN WY
13900 PWY 92064 1170-F7
SANSHEY LN
- SDCo 92127 1169-G2
SAN SIMEON ST
1400 OCN 92054 1086-B4
SANS SOUCI DR
3100 ESCN 92029 1149-F1
3100 SDCo 92029 1149-F1
SANTA ALICIA
400 SOLB 92075 1167-G6
SANTA ALICIA AV
- CHV 91913 1331-C1
SANTA ANA DR
1500 SD 92110 1268-G2
1500 SD 92111 1268-G2
SANTA ANA ST
- CALX 92231 6620-G6
SANTA ANDREA ST
- CHV 91913 1331-C1
SANTA ANGELA CT
2600 CHV 91914 1311-G2
SANTA ANITA CT
600 CHV 91914 1311-G2
SANTA ANITA DR
100 VSTA 92084 1087-J7
1600 SD 92111 1268-G2
SANTA ANITA ST
1000 OCN 92054 1086-A5
SANTA ANTONIO DR
3600 OCN 92054 1086-F2
SANTA ARMINTA AV
7900 SD 92126 1209-B2
SANTA ASIS DR
3600 OCN 92054 1086-F3
SANTA BARBARA
7100 CRLB 92011 1126-J6
7300 CRLB 92011 1127-A7
SANTA BARBARA CT
2600 CHV 91914 1311-G2
SANTA BARBARA DR
- SMCS 92078 1128-G3
SANTA BARBARA PL
700 SD 92109 1267-H2
SANTA BARBARA ST
200 OCN 92054 1086-B6
1000 SD 92107 1287-J1
1500 SD 92107 1267-J7
1600 SD 92107 1268-A7
SANTA BARBARA WY
100 VSTA 92083 1087-E7
SANTA BARTOLA
400 SOLB 92075 1167-G6
SANTA CAMELIA DR
600 SOLB 92075 1167-J5
SANTA CARINA
500 SOLB 92075 1167-H5
700 ENCT 92007 1167-H5
SANTA CARINA RD
1400 CHV 91913 1331-A2
SANTA CATALINA RD
12300 SDCo 92082 1049-H5
SANTA CATERINA TR
- SDCo 92004 410-B6
- SDCo 92004 1058-H1
SANTA CECELIA
400 SOLB 92075 1167-G6
SANTA CHRISTINA CT
2400 SD 92154 1330-B7
SANTA CLARA
400 OCN 92054 1086-F2
SANTA CLARA CT
600 CHV 91914 1311-G2
SANTA CLARA DR
100 VSTA 92083 1087-E7
SANTA CLARA PL
700 SD 92109 1267-H1
SANTA CLARA WY
3400 CRLB 92010 1106-H4
SANTA CORA AV
1200 CHV 91913 1311-D6
SANTA CORINA CT
- SDCo 92127 1169-F4
SANTA CRISTOBAL ST
16400 SDCo 92127 1169-F4
SANTA CRUZ
7100 CRLB 92011 1126-J6
SANTA CRUZ AV
3800 SD 92107 1288-A1
4000 SD 92107 1268-A7
4400 SD 92107 1267-H6
SANTA CRUZ CT
1300 CHV 91910 1311-B7
SANTA CRUZ DR
3600 OCN 92054 1086-F2
SANTA DELORES DR
3600 OCN 92054 1086-F3
SANTA DELPHINA AV
1100 CHV 91913 1311-D6
SANTA DOMINGA
400 SOLB 92075 1167-G6
SANTA ELENA CT
1500 SOLB 92075 1167-J6
SANTA ELISABETH AV
- CHV 91913 1311-F7
SANTA ESTELLA
900 SOLB 92075 1167-G5

STREET Block City ZIP Pg-Grid

SANTA FE AV
100 SDCo 92055 1085-H5
1000 ESCN 92025 1129-G3
1800 DLMR 92014 1187-F4
N SANTA FE AV
800 SDCo 92057 1067-C7
N SANTA FE AV Rt#-S14
300 VSTA 92083 1087-G2
300 VSTA 92084 1087-G2
800 OCN 92057 1067-C7
800 OCN 92056 1087-D1
800 OCN 92057 1087-D1
2200 SDCo 92083 1087-G2
2200 SDCo 92084 1087-G2
2200 OCN 92084 1087-G2
2200 VSTA 92056 1087-G2
S SANTA FE AV Rt#-S14
100 VSTA 92083 1087-H7
100 VSTA 92084 1087-H7
1000 VSTA 92084 1088-A7
1000 VSTA 92084 1108-B2
1000 VSTA 92083 1088-A7
1000 VSTA 92083 1108-B2
1400 SDCo 92084 1108-B2
1400 SDCo 92083 1108-B2
2600 SMCS 92069 1108-C4
SANTA FE DR
- CALX 92231 6680-H1
- ENCT 92007 1167-E1
- ENCT 92024 1167-E1
SANTA FE PL
100 VSTA 92083 1087-J7
SANTA FE ST
4700 SD 92109 1248-C3
4700 SD 92117 1248-B1
SANTA FE TR
300 SDCo 92004 1058-G6
SANTA FE CANYON PL
- SD 92129 1188-H4
SANTA FE DOWNS SQ
2600 SD 92014 1187-J2
SANTA FE HIGHLANDS DR
- SDCo 92065 1153-A3
SANTA FE VISTA CT
2800 ENCT 92024 1148-A6
SANTA FLORA CT
3500 ESCN 92029 1150-A3
SANTA FLORA RD
1600 CHV 91913 1311-C7
SANTA FLORENCIA
700 SOLB 92075 1167-G5
1000 ENCT 92007 1167-G5
SANTA GABRIELLA
1000 SOLB 92075 1167-H5
SANTA HELENA
200 SOLB 92075 1167-G6
SANTA HELENA PARK CT
900 SOLB 92075 1167-G6
SANTA HIDALGA
800 SOLB 92075 1167-G5
SANTA INES WY
300 OCN 92057 1087-A2
SANTA INEZ
800 SOLB 92075 1167-G5
SANTA ISABEL DR
700 SD 92114 1290-B5
SANTA ISABEL ST
6600 CRLB 92009 1127-H5
SANTA LUCIA
13500 SDCo 92021 1232-E7
SANTA LUCIA RD
- CHV 91913 1331-C1
1200 CHV 91913 1311-C7
SANTA LUISA DR
1100 SOLB 92075 1167-H5
SANTA LUNA CT
3600 SMCS 92078 1108-D7
SANTA LUNA ST
- CHV 91913 1331-E3
SANTALUZ INLET
- SD 92127 1169-A7
SANTALUZ POINTE
- SD 92127 1169-B6
SANTALUZ VILLAGE GRN E
- SD 92127 1169-B6
SANTALUZ VILLAGE GRN N
- SD 92127 1169-A6
SANTALUZ VILLAGE GRN S
- SD 92127 1169-A6
SANTA MADERA AV
1100 CHV 91913 1311-C7
SANTA MADERA CT
1100 SOLB 92075 1167-H6
SANTA MARGARITA DR
900 SDCo 92028 1027-G1
1100 SDCo 92028 997-G6
SANTA MARGARITA ST
5200 SD 92114 1290-B4
SANTA MARGARITA TKTR
- SDCo 92028 996-G3
SANTA MARIA
1200 CHV 91913 1331-B1
SANTA MARIA AV
11300 SDCo 92040 1212-A7
SANTA MARIA CT
100 VSTA 92083 1087-G6
2600 CHV 91914 1311-G2
SANTA MARIA DR
- SMCS 92078 1128-E2
7300 LMSA 91941 1270-F3
SANTA MARIA ST
3500 OCN 92056 1106-J2
3500 OCN 92056 1107-A2
SANTA MARIA TER
5200 SD 92114 1290-B5
SANTA MARIANA CT
- SDCo 92127 1169-F4
SANTA MARINA CT
400 ESCN 92029 1150-A3
SANTA MARTA CT
1400 SOLB 92075 1167-J5
SANTA MONICA AV
4300 SD 92107 1268-A6
4600 SD 92107 1267-J6
SANTANA ST
10200 SNTE 92071 1231-E2
SANTANA RANCH DR
10300 SNTE 92071 1231-E3
SANTANA RANCH LN
10000 SNTE 92071 1231-E3
SANTA NELLA PL
3900 SD 92130 1188-B7
SANTANELLA ST
- SDCo 92127 1169-F4
SANTA OLIVIA
700 SOLB 92075 1167-G5

SANTA OLIVIA RD
1100 CHV 91913 1331-A1
SANTA PAULA
700 SOLB 92075 1167-G5
SANTA PAULA DR
- CHV 91913 1311-E6
1600 SD 92111 1268-G2
SANTA PAULA ST
800 OCN 92054 1086-A5
SANTA PETRA DR
1400 SOLB 92075 1167-J5
SANTA QUETA
900 SOLB 92075 1167-G5
SANTAR AV
7100 SD 92119 1250-F3
SANTAR PL
100 SMCS 92069 1109-A7
SANTA REGINA
800 SOLB 92075 1167-G6
SANTA RITA
1300 CHV 91913 1331-C1
SANTA RITA E
1400 CHV 91913 1331-C1
SANTA RITA W
1400 CHV 91913 1331-C1
SANTA RITA PL
700 SD 92109 1247-H7
SANTA ROSA
1800 ImCo 92243 6499-D6
7200 CRLB 92011 1126-J6
SANTA ROSA DR
- CHV 91913 1311-E6
- IMP 92251 6439-F3
100 SDCo 92055 1086-A4
SANTA ROSA RD
1300 SDCo 92004 1058-H4
SANTA ROSA ST
1400 OCN 92054 1086-B4
SANTA ROSALIA DR
- IMP 92251 6499-G2
200 SD 92114 1290-A5
SANTA ROSALINA CT
400 ESCN 92029 1149-J3
SANTA ROSITA
600 SOLB 92075 1167-G5
SANTA RUFINA CT
1100 SOLB 92075 1167-H5
SANTA RUFINA DR
700 SOLB 92075 1167-H5
SANTA SABA CT
800 SDCo 92004 (1079-A7 See Page 1058)
SANTA SABA RD
3400 SDCo 92004 (1079-A7 See Page 1058)
SANTA SABINA CT
1500 SOLB 92075 1167-J5
SANTA SIERRA CT
1500 CHV 91913 1331-A2
SANTA SIERRA DR
1400 CHV 91913 1331-B2
SANTA TERESITA CT
500 ESCN 92029 1149-J3
SANTA THERESA
600 SOLB 92075 1167-H6
SANTA THERESA PL
500 CHV 91914 1311-G2
SANTA TOMASA AV
- SDCo 92127 1169-F4
SANTA VALERA CT
- SDCo 92127 1169-F4
SANTA VELA DR
400 OCN 92054 1086-F3
SANTA VENETIA ST
- CHV 91913 1331-D1
SANTA VICTORIA
400 SOLB 92075 1167-H5
SANTA VIRGINIA DR
- SDCo 92082 1049-J5
13100 SDCo 92082 1050-A5
SANTA YNEZ AV
- CHV 91913 1331-B1
SANTA YNEZ WY
3700 OCN 92056 1107-B1
SANTA YSABEL GN
2000 ESCN 92026 1109-E5
SANTA YSABEL TKTR
- SDCo 92065 409-H10
SANTEE LN
18600 SDCo 92082 1091-F3
SANTEE LAKES BLVD
10400 SNTE 92071 1231-A2
SANTIAGO AV
- SD 92140 1268-G7
SANTIAGO DR
- CALX 92231 6620-H7
SANTIAGO RD E
12300 SD 92128 1170-B3
SANTIAGO RD W
12100 SD 92128 1170-B3
SANTO RD
2300 SD 92124 1249-G3
2300 SD 92120 1249-G6
5400 SD 92124 1229-H7
SANTO DOMINGO AV
- SD 92140 1268-F6
SANTOLINA CT
- SD 92130 1188-G6
SANTOLINA ST
- SDCo 92082 1090-D6
SAN TOMAS CT
12200 SD 92128 1170-B3
SAN TOMAS DR
3200 OCN 92056 1086-J7
16500 SD 92128 1170-B3
SAN TOMAS PL
12100 SD 92128 1170-B3
SANTORINI WY
- OCN 92056 1107-F5
SANTORO WY
13400 SD 92130 1187-J5
SANTO THOMAS DR
1300 SOLB 92075 1167-H6
SAN VICENTE AV
12200 SDCo 92040 1211-J6
12200 SDCo 92040 1212-A6
SAN VICENTE BLVD
10300 SDCo 91977 1271-F5
SAN VICENTE CT
600 SD 92114 1290-G3
SAN VICENTE FRWY Rt#-67
- ELCJ - 1251-F2
- SDCo - 1231-H4
- SDCo - 1232-A3
- SDCo - 1251-F2
- SNTE - 1231-F7
- SNTE - 1251-F2
SAN VICENTE RD
800 SDCo 92065 1152-G7
1100 SDCo 92065 1172-G1
22300 SDCo 92065 1173-B4
SAN VICENTE ST
7400 SD 92114 1290-G3

SAN VICENTE TER
1200 SDCo 92065 1172-G1
SAN VICENTE WY
600 SD 92114 1290-G3
SAN VICENTE OAKS RD
24300 SDCo 92065 1173-F7
SANYO AV
1900 SD 92154 1352-A2
2000 SDCo 92154 1352-A2
E SAN YSIDRO BLVD
100 SD 92173 1350-G4
W SAN YSIDRO BLVD
- SD 92173 1350-D3
SAN YSIDRO DR
300 SDCo 92004 1058-H4
SAO PAULO WY
24900 SDCo 92065 1173-G3
SAPONI CT
17900 SD 92127 1149-H7
SAPOTA DR
11800 SDCo 92040 1231-J7
SAPOTE CT
1000 VSTA 92084 1088-A5
SAPPHIRE DR
- CRLB 92011 1127-B3
SAPPHIRE GN
- ESCN 92027 1110-D7
SAPPHIRE LN
1500 VSTA 92081 1107-H6
4400 OCN 92056 1107-D2
SAPPHIRE PT
2000 VSTA 92084 1088-C5
SAPPHIRE ST
- CALX 92231 6620-J7
700 SD 92109 1247-H4
SAPPINGTON CT
9900 SNTE 92071 1231-D4
SARA WY
2200 CRLB 92008 1106-H4
SARAH AV
5800 LMSA 91942 1250-H7
SARAH CT
300 ELCJ 92019 1252-A6
SARAH DR
13700 SDCo 92021 1232-E5
SARAH ANN DR
3500 SDCo 92028 1048-D3
SARAHFAYE CT
1200 SDCo 92026 1109-E6
SARAJAYNE LN
7300 LMGR 91945 1270-F7
SARA MARIE PL
- SDCo 92065 1152-F7
SARAN CT
1500 OCN 92056 1087-E1
SARANAC AV
7700 LMSA 91941 1270-G2
SARANAC PL
7700 LMSA 91941 1270-G2
SARANAC ST
6500 SD 92115 1270-D2
6900 LMSA 92115 1270-E2
7000 LMSA 91941 1270-E2
SARAPE DR
16300 SD 92128 1170-C4
SARASONA WY
3700 SDCo 91902 1310-D4
SARASOTO DR
1400 SDCo 92004 (1099-D2 See Page 1098)
SARATOGA AV
4300 SD 92107 1268-A6
4600 SD 92107 1267-J6
SARATOGA CT
- CHV 91913 1311-C7
SARATOGA CTE
5800 SDCo 92067 1168-E7
SARATOGA GN
300 ESCN 92025 1130-B7
SARATOGA ST
600 OCN 92054 1086-C7
600 OCN 92054 1106-D1
1500 IMPB 91932 1349-H2
SARAWAK DR
8000 LMGR 91945 1290-H1
SARBONNE DR
2400 OCN 92054 1086-E7
SARDA CT
24700 SDCo 92065 1173-G2
SARDINA CV
12300 SD 92130 1188-B7
SARDIS PL
11600 SD 92131 1210-A1
SARDONYX ST
- CRLB 92009 1127-G4
SARGEANT RD
24000 SDCo 92065 1173-E1
SARITA ST
5900 LMSA 91942 1250-J6
SARNEN ST
- SD 92154 1351-H4
SARNO PL
400 ESCN 92026 1109-G2
SARSAPARILLA ST
12600 SD 92129 1189-C5
SARTORI WY
200 SDCo 92083 1108-C4
SARVER LN
2600 SDCo 92069 1088-J7
2600 SDCo 92069 1089-A6
SASKATCHEWAN AV
9600 SD 92129 1189-E5
SASS WY
16000 SDCo 92065 1173-H3
SASSAFRAS ST
1200 SD 92103 1268-J7
1500 SD 92101 1268-J7
SATANAS ST
14800 SD 92129 1169-J7
14800 SD 92129 1189-H1
SATELLITE BLVD
1500 IMPB 91932 1349-J2
1500 SD 92154 1349-J2
1700 SD 92154 1350-A2
SATIN DOLL LN
2700 SDCo 92069 1088-F3
SATINWOOD CT
1500 CHV 91911 1330-H4
SATINWOOD WY
200 SD 92114 1290-G5
400 CHV 91911 1330-G4
SATURN BLVD
200 SD 92154 1330-A6
900 SD 92154 1350-A1
SATURN GN
- ESCN 92025 1129-H2
SATUSUMA CT
24900 SDCo 92065 1173-G3
SAUFLEY ST
- CORD 92135 1288-F4
- SD 92135 1288-E3
SAUGERTIES AV
700 SD 92154 1330-E7

SAUK AV
4500 SD 92117 1248-F1
SAUL ST
- SDCo 92028 1028-D2
SAUNDERS CT
11100 SD 92131 1209-H4
SAUNDERS DR
10200 SD 92131 1209-H4
SAUSALITO AV
2600 CRLB 92010 1106-J5
SAUTERNE PL
500 CHV 91913 1311-D3
10600 SD 92131 1210-B3
SAVAGE CT
6800 SD 92111 1248-J7
SAVAGE WY
13800 PWY 92064 1190-G3
SAVANNAH CT
- CHV 91914 1311-H3
SAVANNAH LN
1300 CRLB 92011 1127-B7
SAVANNAH PL
5000 SD 92110 1268-E3
SAVANNAH ST
4800 SD 92110 1268-E2
SAVANNAH WY
- SMCS 92069 1108-J3
- SMCS 92069 1109-A3
SAVANNAH CREEK DR
- SD 92128 1189-H5
SAVIN DR
1500 ELCJ 92021 1252-A3
SAVONA CT
2100 SDCo 92084 1108-C2
SAVONA LN
- SMCS 92078 1128-J3
SAVONA PL
4600 SD 92130 1188-C4
SAVORY WY
3700 OCN 92057 1086-H4
SAVOY CIR
1400 SD 92107 1287-J1
1400 SD 92107 1288-A1
SAVOY ST
900 SD 92106 1287-J3
1000 SD 92107 1287-J2
1000 SD 92107 1288-A1
SAWDAY ST
300 SDCo 92065 1152-C7
N SAWDAY ST
100 SDCo 92065 1152-C7
100 SDCo 92065 1172-C1
S SAWDAY ST
300 SDCo 92065 1172-C1
SAWDAY TKTR
27100 SDCo 92065 1154-B3
SAWGRASS CIR
- SDCo 92082 1090-F5
SAWGRASS GN
1700 ESCN 92026 1109-D3
SAWGRASS PL
1400 CHV 91915 1311-H7
SAWGRASS ST
2300 SDCo 92019 1272-B4
SAW LEAF LN
- SDCo 92127 1169-D2
SAWTELLE AV
300 SD 92114 1290-H3
SAWTOOTH CT
9300 SD 92129 1189-D4
SAWTOOTH RD
13400 SD 92129 1189-D4
SAWTOOTH WY
9300 SD 92129 1189-D4
SAWYER LN
2200 CRLB 92008 1107-C7
SAXON PL
1500 ELCJ 92021 1251-J2
SAXON RD
- SDCo 91963 429-L10
SAXON ST
5300 SD 92115 1270-A2
SAXONY LN
300 ENCT 92024 1147-C6
SAXONY PL
- ENCT 92024 1147-C6
SAXONY RD
700 ENCT 92024 1147-C1
1400 CRLB 92024 1147-C1
SAYERS CT
10700 SNTE 92071 1231-E3
SAYLES CT
1100 SMCS 92069 1109-E7
SAYLOR DR
200 CHV 91910 1310-B5
SCABARD PL
13100 SD 92128 1189-H5
SCAMP ST
3500 SD 92124 1249-H4
SCANDIA CT
900 SDCo 92025 1130-A2
SCANNELL CT
11100 SD 92126 1209-B2
SCARBERY RD
16100 SDCo 92065 1173-D2
SCARBERY WY
23600 SDCo 92065 1173-D3
SCARBORO ST
14500 PWY 92064 1190-H5
SCARF PL
8400 SD 92119 1250-J4
SCARLATI PL
1000 SD 92037 1247-F1
SCARLET WY
100 SD 92114 1290-G4
SCARLET OAK WY
4400 OCN 92057 1086-J2
SCARLET SAGE TR
- SD 92130 1188-F4
SCARONI RD
- CALX 92249 6620-F2
- ImCo 92249 6560-F7
- ImCo 92249 6620-F2
500 CALX 92231 6620-F5
SCARSDALE WY
13500 SD 92128 1190-A3
SCAUP ST
6500 CRLB 92011 1127-A4
SCENIC DR
- SDCo 92028 998-G5
100 SDCo 92021 1252-H3
1300 ESCN 92029 1129-G6
SCENIC LN
4400 LMSA 91941 1271-A3
SCENIC PL
2800 SD 92037 1227-J4
2800 SD 92037 1228-A4
SCENIC TER
3400 SDCo 91978 1271-E6
SCENIC WY
3700 OCN 92056 1107-E3
SCENIC MOUNTAIN RD
- SDCo 91906 (1318-G2 See Page 1298)

SCENICO DR
500 OCN 92054 1086-F2
SCENIC TERRACE PL
- CHV 91914 1311-J3
SCENIC TRAIL PL
- CHV 91914 1311-F2
SCENIC TRAIL WY
1700 ESCN 92029 1129-F6
SCENIC VALLEY PL
1800 ESCN 92029 1129-F6
SCENIC VALLEY RD
26800 SDCo 92065 1154-D2
SCENIC VIEW PL
1800 SDCo 91901 1234-D7
SCENIC VIEW RD
2800 SDCo 91901 1234-C7
SCHAFER PL
500 ESCN 92025 1129-H4
SCHALER DR
12400 PWY 92064 1190-C4
SCHANIEL RD
- ImCo 92243 431-A7
SCHARTZ RD
- ImCo 92227 431-C2
SCHAUMBERG PL
4600 SDCo 91902 1310-G2
SCHEIDLER WY
5300 SD 92108 1269-F1
SCHENLEY TER
2700 SD 92122 1228-B7
SCHEYER LN
- SDCo 92672 1023-D2
SCHILLING AV
6900 SD 92126 1208-H4
SCHILT AV
- SD 92126 1209-C7
- SD 92126 1229-D1
- SD 92145 1229-D1
SCHIRRA ST
500 SD 92154 1330-E7
SCHLEE CANYON RD
3000 SDCo 91935 1292-G2
SCHLEY ST
1200 SD 92113 1289-D6
SCHMIDT CT
- SDCo 92672 1023-E1
SCHMIDT DR
- SDCo 92672 1023-E2
SCHNEPLE DR
8500 SD 92126 1209-C2
SCHOLARS DR
- SD 92093 1207-J7
2800 SD 92093 1227-J1
2900 SD 92093 1228-A2
SCHOLARS LN
- SD 92093 1227-J2
SCHOOL LN
3100 LMGR 91945 1270-H6
SCHOOL ST
3400 SD 92116 1269-F3
SCHOOL BUS LN
- SDCo 92082 1090-F1
SCHOOL DAZE LN
1200 SDCo 92065 1172-F1
SCHOOL HOUSE RD
- CHV 91915 1311-H6
900 SDCo 92065 1153-A4
SCHOOLHOUSE WY
- SMCS 92078 1128-D5
SCHOOL HOUSE CANYON RD
- SDCo 92070 409-K10
SCHOOLRIDGE LN
4200 LMSA 91941 1270-G4
SCHOONER WY
1700 CRLB 92008 1106-H6
SCHRIMPF RD
- ImCo 92233 411-B8
SCHUBERT PTH
100 ENCT 92007 1167-D2
SCHULLER LN
1000 SDCo 92028 1028-C3
SCHUYLER AV
4800 LMSA 91941 1270-J2
SCHUYLER ST
5800 SD 92139 1310-D1
SCIENCE CENTER DR
10300 SD 92121 1208-A7
SCIENCE PARK RD
3000 SD 92121 1207-J5
SCIMITAR DR
6300 SD 92114 1290-D2
SCOOTER LN
1600 SDCo 92028 1028-D5
SCORPIUS WY
8900 SD 92126 1209-D2
SCOTER PL
- CRLB 92011 1127-C6
SCOTS WY
13400 PWY 92064 1190-E3
SCOTSMAN RD
13300 SDCo 92040 1232-D5
SCOTT AV
800 ELCN 92243 6499-F5
SCOTT DR
1200 NATC 91950 1289-J6
3900 CRLB 92008 1106-G6
3900 OCN 92056 1107-C1
SCOTT LN
- SDCo 92084 1088-F1
SCOTT PL
1600 ENCT 92024 1147-F4
SCOTT ST
- SD 92152 1288-B3
900 SD 92106 1288-B2
3100 VSTA 92081 1127-J1
3100 VSTA 92081 1128-A1
SCOTT WY
2300 ESCN 92027 1110-C6
SCOTTFORD DR
200 SDCo 92021 1252-J1
SCOTTSBLUFF CT
9800 SNTE 92071 1231-F4
SCRANTON RD
9200 SD 92121 1208-E6
SCRANTON ST
700 ELCJ 92020 1251-G6
SCRIPPS AV
900 CHV 91913 1311-D5
SCRIPPS LN
- SD 92037 1227-E7
SCRIPPS ST
5600 SD 92122 1228-C6
SCRIPPS TER
5600 SD 92182 1270-B1
SCRIPPS TR
10200 SD 92131 1210-A4
SCRIPPS WY
3200 SD 92122 1228-C6
SCRIPPS CAPE VISTA POINTE
11700 SD 92131 1209-J3
SCRIPPS CREEK DR
11400 SD 92131 1209-J1

SCRIPPS CREEK DR
11800 SD 92131 1189-J7
SCRIPPS GATEWAY CT
- SD 92131 1189-G7
- SD 92131 1209-F1
SCRIPPS HIGHLANDS DR
- SD 92131 1189-G7
- SD 92131 1209-G1
SCRIPPS LAKE DR
9800 SD 92131 1209-F4
11600 SD 92131 1210-A3
SCRIPPS POWAY PKWY
9900 SD 92131 1189-G7
11300 SD 92131 1190-A7
11900 PWY 92064 1190-H6
15600 PWY 92064 1191-B5
15600 SDCo 92064 1191-B5
16700 SDCo 92040 1191-B5
SCRIPPS RANCH BLVD
9900 SD 92131 1209-F2
SCRIPPS RANCH CT
10200 SD 92131 1209-F5
SCRIPPS RANCH RW
10700 SD 92131 1209-H5
SCRIPPS SUMMIT CT
10300 SD 92131 1189-G7
SCRIPPS SUMMIT DR
11200 SD 92131 1189-G7
SCRIPPS VISTA WY
- SD 92131 1209-F2
SCRIPPS WESTVIEW CIR
- SD 92131 1209-F2
SCRIPPS WESTVIEW WY
- SD 92131 1209-F2
SCRUB JAY CT
1100 CRLB 92011 1127-A5
SCRUB JAY LN
7800 SDCo 91962 1237-C6
SCRUB OAKS LN
16700 SDCo 92065 1171-H3
SCULPIN ST
10200 SD 92124 1249-G4
SCULPTURE CT
4500 OCN 92057 1087-A2
SEA LN
- SD 92037 1247-E1
SEA BIRD WY
- SD 92154 1350-H1
SEA BLUFF CIR
4500 CRLB 92008 1106-H7
SEA BLUFFE
100 ENCT 92024 1147-A2
SEA BREEZE CT
1900 ENCT 92024 1147-B2
2100 CHV 91914 1311-E3
SEA BREEZE DR
200 CRLB 92011 1126-H4
1000 OCN 92054 1085-H6
SEABREEZE DR
2000 SD 92139 1290-D7
2100 SD 92139 1310-D1
SEA BREEZE WK
3400 OCN 92056 1107-C2
SEABREEZE FARMS DR
- SD 92130 1188-D6
SEABRIDGE LN
14200 SD 92128 1190-A2
SEA BRIGHT DR
4300 CRLB 92008 1106-H7
SEABRIGHT LN
400 SOLB 92075 1167-E6
SEA BRIGHT PL
4300 CRLB 92008 1106-H7
SEABROOK LN
1500 SD 92139 1290-H6
SEABURY ST
3100 CRLB 92010 1107-A3
SEACHASE ST
- SD 92130 1188-D4
SEACHASE WY
- SD 92130 1188-D5
SEA CLIFF DR
900 CRLB 92011 1126-J4
SEACLIFF LN
200 SOLB 92075 1187-E1
SEA CLIFF WY
100 OCN 92056 1086-J7
SEACLIFF WY
800 SMCS 92078 1128-F2
SEACOAST DR
600 CORD 91932 1329-E7
600 IMPB 91932 1329-E7
900 IMPB 91932 1349-E1
SEA COLONY CT
2200 SD 92107 1268-B6
SEA CORAL DR
- SD 92154 1350-H1
SEA COTTAGE WY
- OCN 92054 1085-J7
SEA COUNTRY LN
- SD 92130 1187-J3
SEA COVE PT
- SD 92154 1331-A6
SEACREST CT
2600 VSTA 92081 1107-H5
SEACREST DR
700 SMCS 92078 1128-F2
3300 CRLB 92008 1106-G4
SEA CREST WY
3600 OCN 92056 1107-C3
SEACREST WY
300 ENCT 92024 1147-C6
SEACREST VIEW RD
5900 SD 92121 1208-F3
SEA DRIFT WY
5000 SD 92154 1350-J1
SEAFARER DR
3500 OCN 92054 1086-E5
SEAFARER PL
- CRLB 92011 1126-J7
SEAFIELD PL
5000 SD 92154 1330-J7
SEA FIRE PT
- SD 92154 1351-A1
SEAFLOWER LN
3600 OCN 92056 1107-A2
SEAFOAM CT
1600 SD 92139 1290-D7
SEAFORD PL
4700 SD 92117 1248-H1
SEA FOREST CT
200 DLMR 92014 1187-G6
SEA GATE RD
900 CRLB 92011 1126-J4
SEAGAZE DR
- OCN 92054 1106-A1
400 OCN 92054 1086-A7
SEAGIRT CT
700 SD 92109 1267-H1
SEAGLASS CT
11800 SD 92128 1190-A1

SEAGLEN WY
- SD 92154 1350-J1
- SD 92154 1351-A1
SEAGREEN PL
- SD 92154 1351-A1
SEAGROVE CT
5100 SD 92130 1188-D5
SEAGROVE CV
5000 SD 92130 1188-D4
SEAGROVE PL
5100 SD 92130 1188-D4
SEAGROVE ST
13000 SD 92130 1188-D4
SEAGROVE WY
- OCN 92056 1087-A4
SEAGULL CT
7600 SD 92123 1269-A1
SEAGULL LN
- OCN 92057 1086-H2
2000 SD 92123 1269-A1
SEAHILL CT
- SD 92154 1351-A1
SEA HOLLY CT
- SD 92154 1330-J6
SEAHORN CIR
3500 SD 92130 1187-J5
SEAHORSE CT
1000 CRLB 92011 1127-A5
SEAHORSE LN
- SDCo 92055 1085-H6
SEA ISLAND PL
- SMCS 92078 1128-A3
2300 CHV 91915 1311-G5
SEA ISLE DR
500 SD 92154 1330-H6
SEA KNOLL CT
13100 SD 92130 1188-D5
SEALANE DR
900 ENCT 92024 1167-B1
SEA LARKE DR
1100 SDCo 92028 1027-H5
SEA LAVENDER WY
4800 SD 92154 1330-J6
SEAL BEACH PL
- SD 92139 1290-D7
SEA LILY CT
- SD 92154 1350-H1
SEA LION PL
5900 CRLB 92010 1127-G2
SEAL POINT CT
1500 CHV 91911 1330-H4
SEA MAID CT
- SD 92154 1350-H1
SEAMAN ST
6200 SD 92120 1249-J6
SEA MIST CT
5000 SD 92121 1208-E4
SEA MIST WY
10500 SD 92121 1208-D4
SEAN TAYLOR LN
7300 SD 92126 1208-J2
SEA ORBIT LN
100 DLMR 92014 1187-F5
SEA OTTER PL
5900 CRLB 92010 1127-G1
SEA PARK DR
900 IMPB 91932 1349-G2
SEA PINES RD
1700 SDCo 92019 1272-B5
SEAPOINT WY
10800 SD 92121 1208-F3
SEAPORT PL
6400 CRLB 92011 1127-C4
SEAQUEST TR
1800 SDCo 92024 1148-E3
SEA REEF DR
1600 SD 92154 1330-J7
1000 SD 92154 1350-J1
SEA REEF PL
- SD 92154 1350-J1
SEA RIDGE DR
300 SD 92037 1247-F5
SEA RIDGE RD
3500 OCN 92054 1086-F5
SEA ROBIN CT
- SD 92154 1350-H1
SEA ROSE PL
5700 SD 92037 1247-F3
SEARS AV
100 SD 92114 1290-H3
SEASCAPE DR
4800 OCN 92057 1087-B1
6100 SD 92139 1310-E1
6900 CRLB 92011 1127-A5
SEA SCAPE GN
2500 ESCN 92026 1109-B4
SEASHELL CT
7400 CRLB 92011 1127-A7
SEASHELL PL
5000 SD 92130 1188-D5
SEASIDE ST
2200 SD 92107 1268-A6
SEASIDE WY
2800 CRLB 92010 1107-A4
SEASONS RD
2300 OCN 92056 1087-D6
SEASPRAY LN
6800 CRLB 92011 1126-J5
SEA STAR LN
1900 SD 92139 1290-E7
SEA STAR WY
1900 SD 92139 1290-E7
SEA STRAND LN
- SD 92154 1351-A1
SEA TERN CT
4700 SD 92154 1330-H6
SEATTLE DR
- LMSA 91941 1270-G5
2500 ELCJ 92020 1251-A4
SEATTLE SLEW WY
1600 OCN 92057 1067-E7
SEA TURF CIR
800 SOLB 92075 1187-F2
SEA URCHIN DR
- SD 92154 1350-H1
SEA VALE CT
500 CHV 91910 1309-J5
500 CHV 91910 1310-A5
SEA VALE ST
- CHV 91910 1310-B5
600 CHV 91910 1309-J5
SEAVIEW AV
1300 OCN 92054 1106-D1
1700 DLMR 92014 1187-F4
SEA VIEW CT
- ENCT 92024 1147-D6
SEA VIEW DR
- ImCo 92274 410-H6
900 IMPB 91932 1349-G2
SEAVIEW PL
500 VSTA 92081 1107-H1
SEA VIEW WY
3900 SDCo 92024 1148-E3

STREET Block City ZIP Pg-Grid

SEAVIEW WY
3600 CRLB 92008 1106-H5
SEA VILLAGE CIR
2000 ENCT 92007 1167-F3
SEA VILLAGE DR
700 IMPB 91932 1329-F7
1000 ENCT 92007 1167-E3
SEA VILLAGE PL
1900 ENCT 92007 1167-F3
SEA VILLAGE WY
2000 ENCT 92007 1167-F3
SEA VISTA PL
2000 SMCS 92078 1128-B2
SEAWARD AV
- CRLB 92011 1126-H5
E SEAWARD AV
100 SD 92173 1350-G3
W SEAWARD AV
- SD 92173 1350-F3
SEAWARD CIR
3500 OCN 92056 1107-G4
SEAWATCH LN
800 CRLB 92011 1126-J6
800 CRLB 92011 1127-A6
SEA WATER LN
- SD 92154 1350-H1
SEA WIND CT
900 CRLB 92011 1126-J4
SEAWIND CV
11200 SD 92126 1209-A2
SEAWIND DR
2400 NATC 91950 1310-B1
SEAWIND LN
7900 SD 92126 1209-A2
SEAWIND WY
1900 OCN 92054 1106-F2
SEA WORLD DR
100 SD 92109 1268-C4
SEA WORLD WY
- SD 92109 1268-C3
SEBAGO AV
13400 PWY 92064 1190-H4
SEBASTOPOL ST
- CHV 91913 1311-E7
SEBRING CT
9800 SNTE 92071 1231-F4
SECA ST
2000 SDCo 92019 1272-C4
SECKEL PEAR
700 OCN 92057 1086-G5
SECLUDED LN
3500 SDCo 92028 1047-J2
SECO GN
1800 ESCN 92026 1109-F6
SECRET PL
3000 LMGR 91945 1270-J6
SECRET CANYON PL
2500 CHV 91915 1311-H5
SECRET LAKE LN
2600 SDCo 92028 1028-E7
2600 SDCo 92028 1048-E1
SECTION ST
300 OCN 92054 1086-B7
SECURIDAD ST
200 OCN 92057 1066-H7
SECURITY PL
1500 SMCS 92078 1128-C1
SECURITY WY
9200 SNTE 92071 1231-G4
SEDA CV
4600 SD 92124 1250-A2
SEDA DR
4600 SD 92124 1250-A1
SEDA PL
11300 SD 92124 1250-A2
SEDERO CT
11500 SD 92127 1149-J7
SEDGE CT
12900 SD 92129 1189-E5
SEDGEWICK ST
5700 SD 92139 1310-D2
SEDONA DR
2400 SDCo 92065 1172-H3
SEDONA GN
1500 ESCN 92027 1110-A5
SEDORUS ST
8300 SD 92129 1189-B4
SEEFOREVER DR
500 SMCS 92078 1129-B4
SEELEY AV
- SDCo 91934 (1321-G5 See Page 1300)
SEELY CT
1700 SMCS 92069 1109-B3
SEEMAN DR
100 ENCT 92024 1147-E6
SEFTON PL
1800 SD 92107 1268-A7
SEGO PL
2900 SD 92123 1249-D6
SEGOVIA CT
3000 CRLB 92009 1147-H2
15100 SD 92129 1169-J7
SEGOVIA WY
2800 CRLB 92009 1147-G2
SEGUNDO CT
14100 PWY 92064 1190-G1
SEIFERT DR
- SD 92152 1288-A5
SEIFERT ST
5500 SD 92105 1270-B7
SEILER ST
12900 PWY 92064 1190-D5
SELBY CT
10100 SNTE 92071 1231-A3
SELDEN WY
- SDCo 92672 1023-E2
SELECT WY
- SDCo 92028 999-A5
SELENA DR
- SMCS 92069 1109-A4
SELKIRK RW
2600 SD 92037 1247-J1
2600 SD 92037 1248-A1
SELLERS DR
2900 SD 92110 1268-E6
SELLO LN
3100 CRLB 92009 1127-J5
SELLSWAY ST
100 SD 92173 1350-F4
SELMA CT
12800 PWY 92064 1190-B5
SELMA DR
1300 OCN 92054 1106-C1
SELMA PL
700 SD 92114 1290-B3
SELMALITA TER
300 VSTA 92083 1087-G5
SELSEY ST
14600 PWY 92064 1190-H5
SELTZER CT
9400 SD 92123 1249-E5
SELVA DR
16100 SD 92128 1170-C5

SEMILLON BLVD
11700 SD 92131 1210-A2
SEMINOLE DR
4500 SD 92115 1270-D3
SEMINOLE ST
- SD 92140 1268-E6
1500 SMCS 92078 1108-D7
SEMPLE ST
- CHV 91913 1331-F2
SENATOR WASH RD
- ImCo 92283 432-E2
SENCILLO CT
17900 SD 92128 1150-B7
SENCILLO DR
17900 SD 92128 1150-B7
SENCILLO LN
17900 SD 92128 1150-B7
SENDA LN
2300 SDCo 92021 1252-J4
SENDA PL
16400 SD 92128 1170-C4
SENDA RD
12400 SD 92128 1170-C4
SENDA ACANTILADA
12600 SD 92128 1150-C7
SENDA ACUARIO
- SD 92130 1208-B4
SENDA ANGOSTA
5100 SDCo 91902 1290-H7
SENDA DE LA LUNA
16900 SDCo 92067 1168-D3
SENDA LUNA LLENA
11200 SD 92130 1208-B3
SENDA MAR DE PONDEROSA
11200 SD 92130 1208-C3
SENDA PANACEA
- SD 92129 1189-B6
SENDERO AV
800 ESCN 92026 1109-J7
1000 ESCN 92027 1109-J7
SENDERO ST
- CALX 92231 6620-J5
SENDERO WY
2400 SD 92111 1248-G7
SENDERO ANGELICA
- SD 92127 1169-B7
- SD 92127 1189-A1
SENDERO DE ALBA
- SD 92127 1169-B6
SENDERO DE LA PRADERA
- SD 92127 1169-C7
SENDERO DE ORO
- SD 92127 1169-A7
SENECA PL
7400 LMSA 91941 1270-G3
SENECIO PL
- SD 92130 1188-G7
SENEGAL ST
- OCN 92057 1067-B3
SENN RD
2200 SD 92136 1289-E7
SENN WY
7700 SD 92037 1227-J7
SENTENAC CREEK RD
2600 SDCo 92070 1135-F7
2600 SDCo 92070 1155-F1
SENTINEL
- SD 92127 1169-B7
SENWOOD WY
1100 SDCo 92028 1027-G4
SEPH WY
900 SDCo 92027 1130-B3
SEPIA CT
700 OCN 92057 1087-B1
12000 SD 92128 1189-H5
SEPTEMBER ST
4900 SD 92110 1268-G1
SEQUAN LN
28800 SDCo 91962 1237-C5
SEQUAN TKTR
- SDCo 91901 1253-H4
- SDCo 91901 1254-A4
- SDCo 91935 1253-F5
- SDCo 92019 1253-E7
SEQUENCE DR
6100 SD 92121 1208-G4
SEQUOIA AV
100 CRLB 92008 1106-E7
SEQUOIA CIR
- ELCJ 92019 1251-J6
SEQUOIA CT
400 CHV 91911 1330-G4
SEQUOIA LN
1500 SDCo 92081 1107-E2
SEQUOIA PL
4700 OCN 92057 1067-A7
4700 OCN 92057 1087-A1
SEQUOIA RD
28900 SDCo 91962 1237-C6
SEQUOIA ST
- SDCo 91962 1237-C7
500 CHV 91911 1330-H4
2000 SMCS 92078 1128-A2
3800 SD 92109 1248-A6
SEQUOIA CREST
2000 VSTA 92081 1107-G6
SERAFINA LN
- SD 92128 1189-H6
SERBIAN PL
3000 SD 92117 1248-E6
SERENA AV
4200 OCN 92056 1107-C3
SERENA CIR
1300 CHV 91910 1311-B5
SERENA LN
12100 SDCo 92040 1231-J1
12100 SDCo 92040 1232-A1
SERENA PL
10900 SDCo 92040 1232-A1
SERENA RD
12000 SDCo 92040 1231-J1
12100 SDCo 92040 1232-A1
SERENA WY
1000 SMCS 92078 1128-E3
SERENA HILLS DR
2200 SDCo 92065 1172-C4
SERENATA PL
4600 SD 92130 1188-C6
SERENDIPITY LN
1000 SDCo 92069 1089-C6
SERENE RD
1400 OCN 92057 1067-G7
SERENE WY
- SDCo 91935 1293-G1
SERENIDAD PL
4000 OCN 92056 1107-C2
SERENITY CT
8200 SDCo 92021 1232-C7
8200 SDCo 92021 1252-C1
SERENITY PTH
28300 SDCo 92082 1090-E2

SERENO CT
2100 CRLB 92009 1147-F2
SERENO VIEW LN
2200 ENCT 92024 1147-J6
SERENO VIEW RD
600 ENCT 92024 1147-J6
SERI ST
4100 SD 92117 1248-E2
SERIGRAPH CT
4600 OCN 92057 1087-B2
SERPENTINE DR
300 DLMR 92014 1187-F4
SERRA WY
15900 SDCo 92065 1173-C4
SERRANO DR
3100 CRLB 92009 1147-J2
SERRANO LN
500 CHV 91910 1310-J5
SERRANO PL
6500 SD 92115 1270-D3
SERRANO ST
1700 OCN 92054 1106-C3
SERRANOS CT
4000 SDCo 92028 1028-G7
SERRENA LN
600 SD 92154 1330-G6
SERRES DR
9500 SNTE 92071 1230-H5
SERVANDO AV
2300 SD 92154 1350-D4
SERVICE PL
1000 VSTA 92084 1108-A1
SERVICE RD
- SD 92103 1268-J5
- SD 92103 1269-A5
- SD 92106 1288-A7
- SD 92106 1308-A1
SESAME ST
700 CHV 91910 1330-H1
SESAME WY
3700 OCN 92057 1086-H5
SESI LN
14200 SDCo 92040 1232-G5
SESPE PL
14400 PWY 92064 1190-H2
SETH LN
9600 SNTE 92071 1231-E4
SETH WY
10300 SNTE 92071 1231-B1
SETON HALL ST
7500 LMSA 91942 1270-G1
SETTINERI LN
3800 SDCo 91977 1271-A5
SETTING SUN WY
5200 SD 92121 1208-E4
SETTLE CT
9800 SNTE 92071 1231-A4
SETTLE RD
9700 SNTE 92071 1231-A3
SETTLERS CT
- SMCS 92069 1109-A6
SETTLERS PL
14400 PWY 92064 1190-H2
SETTLERS RD
13800 SDCo 92040 1232-E4
SEVAN CT
7900 SD 92123 1249-B7
7900 SD 92123 1269-B1
SEVEN BRIDGES RD
18300 SDCo 92091 1148-F5
SEVEN OAKES RD
1200 ESCN 92026 1109-F7
1200 ESCN 92026 1129-F1
1200 SDCo 92026 1129-F1
SEVERE RD
- ImCo 92233 411-A10
SEVERIN DR
5300 LMSA 91941 1271-B1
5500 LMSA 91942 1251-B5
5500 LMSA 91942 1271-B1
6300 ELCJ 92020 1251-B5
SEVERINO LN
15800 SDCo 92082 1071-A6
SEVILLA WY
4800 CRLB 92008 1106-J7
SEVILLE ST
3000 SD 92110 1268-D6
SEWANEE DR
1400 SDCo 92004 (1099-D2 See Page 1098)
SEWELL AV
2800 SD 92154 1350-C1
SEYBERT RD
4400 ImCo 92227 431-C1
SEYMOUR ST
9900 SNTE 92071 1231-F4
SHACKLEFORD CT
9300 SD 92126 1209-E2
SHADE RD
4400 SDCo 91941 1271-E3
SHADETREE CT
- SD 92131 1210-E2
SHADETREE DR
- SMCS 92024 1128-C6
- SMCS 92078 1128-C6
SHADE TREE LN
700 SDCo 92028 1027-H3
SHADETREE LN
2000 ESCN 92029 1129-E7
SHADEWOOD LN
1700 SD 92139 1290-H6
SHADOW GN
1700 ESCN 92029 1129-E5
SHADOW LN
400 VSTA 92084 1087-J6
4200 OCN 92056 1107-C2
SHADOW RD
9400 LMSA 91941 1271-C1
9400 SDCo 91941 1271-C1
9700 ELCJ 92020 1271-C1
SHADOWBROOK CT
14700 PWY 92064 1190-D1
SHADOWBROOK LN
100 ELCJ 92019 1252-D5
SHADOWBROOK WY
- SMCS 92024 1128-C7
SHADOW CANYON WY
5800 SDCo 91902 1311-B3
SHADOW CREEK LN
11800 SDCo 92020 1271-J2
SHADOWCREST LN
1100 SDCo 92028 1027-H7
SHADOW CREST TER
2700 CHV 91915 1311-J5
SHADOW GLEN CT
100 ELCJ 92019 1252-D5
SHADOWGLEN RD
11600 SDCo 92020 1271-H2
SHADOW GROVE WY
2000 ENCT 92024 1147-H7
SHADOW HILL DR
7900 LMSA 91941 1270-H5
SHADOW HILL RD
9200 SNTE 92071 1231-F6

SHADOW HILL WY
11000 SNTE 92071 1231-G6
SHADOW HILLS CT
1300 SMCS 92069 1109-C7
SHADOW HILLS DR
500 SMCS 92069 1109-C6
SHADOW KNOLLS
1500 SDCo 92020 1272-A2
SHADOW KNOLLS CT
1500 SDCo 92020 1272-A2
SHADOW KNOLLS DR
1500 SDCo 92020 1272-A2
SHADOW KNOLLS PL
1800 SDCo 92020 1271-J2
1800 SDCo 92020 1272-A2
SHADOW LAKE RD
- SDCo 92026 1069-A3
SHADOWLAWN ST
3100 SD 92110 1268-D6
SHADOWLINE ST
12700 PWY 92064 1190-D1
SHADOW MOUNTAIN DR
1400 ENCT 92024 1147-G6
SHADOW MOUNTAIN RD
1900 SDCo 92021 1252-E3
SHADOW MOUNTAIN TER
1100 VSTA 92084 1088-A4
SHADOW OAK CT
- SDCo 92065 1172-D5
SHADOWOOD CIR
1800 VSTA 92081 1107-G5
SHADOWOOD LN
13700 SDCo 92082 1090-E6
SHADOW RANCH RD
11300 SDCo 91941 1271-H4
SHADOWRIDGE DR
700 VSTA 92083 1108-A4
700 VSTA 92081 1108-A4
1000 VSTA 92081 1107-F4
1900 OCN 92056 1107-F4
SHADOW RIDGE PL
- CHV 91914 1311-H3
SHADOW ROCK CT
4000 SDCo 91902 1311-B2
SHADOWSIDE LN
1300 SDCo 92019 1272-A2
SHADOW TREE DR
300 OCN 92054 1086-D2
SHADOW VALLEY
2800 SDCo 91935 1292-E4
SHADOW VALLEY RD
11700 SDCo 92020 1271-H2
SHADOW VISTA WY
1500 ELCJ 92019 1252-A7
1500 SDCo 92019 1252-A7
SHADWELL PL
4700 SD 92130 1188-C4
SHADY BEND
16300 SDCo 92065 1171-G3
SHADY LN
400 ELCJ 92021 1251-J5
700 SDCo 92028 1027-F1
4300 OCN 92056 1107-D2
SHADY ACRE CIR
1900 ENCT 92024 1147-H6
SHADY ACRE LN
2300 LMGR 91945 1270-F7
SHADY ACRES LN
- SDCo 92036 1175-J1
- SDCo 92036 1176-A1
SHADYBROOK PL
400 ESCN 92026 1109-G5
SHADY CREEK LN
30500 SDCo 92082 1070-E3
SHADY CREEK RD
13800 SDCo 92082 1070-E6
SHADYCREST CT
1700 ELCJ 92020 1251-C2
SHADYCREST PL
1600 ELCJ 92020 1251-C2
SHADY CREST RD
700 SMCS 92069 1109-A5
SHADY ELM PL
900 SD 92154 1330-B7
SHADYGLADE LN
7600 SD 92114 1290-G5
SHADY GLEN DR
300 SDCo 92028 1027-G3
SHADY HILL LN
- SDCo 92028 1047-H6
SHADY HOLLOW LN
3200 SDCo 91935 1273-E5
SHADY KNOLL RD
28300 SDCo 92082 1090-D3
SHADY OAK CT
12800 PWY 92064 1190-C5
SHADY OAK RD
100 SD 92114 1290-F5
SHADY OAKS DR
16300 SDCo 92065 1171-G3
SHADY OAKS LN
16300 SDCo 92065 1171-G3
47200 RivC 92592 999-F1
SHADY OAKS WY
15700 SDCo 92082 1071-A5
SHADYPINE ST
2900 SDCo 91978 1271-F7
SHADYRIDGE AV
2200 ESCN 92029 1129-E6
SHADY SANDS RD
8000 SD 92119 1250-E3
SHADY SPRINGS LN
600 SDCo 92065 1152-E6
SHADYTREE LN
2000 ENCT 92024 1147-H6
SHADYWOOD DR
500 ESCN 92026 1109-H4
SHAFER ST
1000 OCN 92054 1106-B1
SHAFTER ST
- SD 92106 1288-B2
SHAGGYBARK DR
10000 SNTE 92071 1231-D2
SHAHRAM WY
9100 SDCo 92026 1049-B7
SHALAMAR DR
7900 SDCo 92021 1252-B1
SHALE CT
3800 CRLB 92010 1107-B4
SHALE ROCK RD
3000 SDCo 92084 1088-D7
SHALIMAR CV
2600 SD 92014 1207-J2
SHALIMAR PL
1500 ESCN 92029 1129-G7
13000 SD 92014 1207-J2
13100 SD 92014 1187-J7
SHALLMAN ST
12400 PWY 92064 1190-C3
SHALOM RD
15900 SDCo 92065 1174-B4
SHALYN DR
- SDCo 92021 1232-E5

SHAMROCK CT
- IMP 92251 6499-E2
- SDCo 92003 1047-H7
SHAMROCK LN
9700 SDCo 92040 1232-A4
SHAMROCK PL
- CRLB 92009 1127-G2
SHAMROCK RD
32000 SDCo 92003 1047-H7
32000 SDCo 92003 1067-J1
SHAMROCK ST
2200 SD 92105 1289-H1
SHAMROCK WY
2500 ESCN 92025 1130-C7
SHANAS LN
500 ENCT 92024 1147-G5
SHANDRENIA
- SDCo 91935 1274-C7
SHANDY LN
100 SDCo 92065 1153-A6
SHANE PL
6400 SD 92115 1270-D2
SHANESSEY RD
1300 ELCJ 92019 1251-J7
1300 ELCJ 92019 1252-A7
SHANK RD
- ImCo 92227 431-D1
SHANKARA RD
- SDCo 92082 1091-B1
SHANNON AV
6600 SD 92115 1270-D3
SHANNONBROOK CT
8600 LMGR 91945 1270-J6
8600 SDCo 91945 1270-J6
SHANNON RIDGE LN
5400 SD 92130 1208-E1
SHANTEAU DR
14800 SDCo 92021 1232-J3
14900 SDCo 92021 1233-A3
SHANTUNG DR
7900 SNTE 92071 1250-H1
SHAPLEY WY
- SDCo 92672 1023-D2
SHARE CT
10500 SNTE 92071 1231-E4
SHARI WY
400 OCN 92054 1086-G2
1200 ELCJ 92019 1251-J6
SHARLENE LN
10500 SNTE 92071 1231-E7
SHARON WY
500 ELCJ 92020 1251-B4
SHARP PL
200 ENCT 92024 1147-G6
SHARRON PL
4200 SD 92115 1270-B4
SHASTA CT
- OCN 92057 1086-H1
SHASTA DR
- ENCT 92024 1147-E5
SHASTA LN
5500 LMSA 91942 1270-G1
SHASTA PL
2700 CRLB 92010 1106-J5
SHASTA ST
100 CHV 91910 1310-B7
3700 SD 92109 1248-A7
E SHASTA ST
200 CHV 91910 1310-D6
SHASTA TR
1600 SDCo 91905 (1319-J2 See Page 1298)
SHASTA WY
700 SDCo 91905 (1319-G2 See Page 1298)
700 SDCo 91906 (1319-G2 See Page 1298)
700 SDCo 91905 (1320-A2 See Page 1300)
SHASTA DAISY TR
- SD 92130 1188-E4
SHAULA WY
8800 SD 92126 1209-C2
SHAULES AV
6300 SD 92114 1290-D4
SHAUNA WY
26200 SDCo 92082 1091-F6
SHAW ST
5500 SD 92139 1310-C2
SHAWLINE ST
4800 SD 92111 1249-A1
5000 SD 92111 1229-A7
SHAW LOPEZ RD
10700 SD 92121 1208-F4
SHAW LOPEZ RW
10700 SD 92121 1208-F4
SHAWN AV
9200 SD 92123 1249-E6
SHAWN CT
2300 CRLB 92008 1106-H4
SHAWN WY
1100 VSTA 92081 1107-E1
SHAWNEE RD
3400 SD 92117 1248-E5
SHAWN ELISE WY
300 ENCT 92024 1147-G6
SHAW RIDGE RD
11400 SD 92130 1188-D7
SHAW VALLEY RD
11900 SD 92130 1188-C7
11900 SD 92130 1208-C1
SHAY PL
1100 ESCN 92026 1109-J4
SHAY RD
200 SDCo 92028 1027-F4
SHAYANN LN
12600 SDCo 92040 1232-B5
SHAYLENE WY
2300 SDCo 91901 1254-A1
SHAYS WY
500 SDCo 92065 1152-G4
SHEARER CRSG
3000 SDCo 92028 1048-J2
SHEARWATER DR
6700 CRLB 92011 1126-J5
SHEAR WATER WY
4400 OCN 92057 1087-A3
SHEBA WY
10000 SD 92129 1189-F3
SHEENA WY
1500 LMGR 91945 1290-E2
1500 LMGR 92114 1290-E2
SHEEPHEAD MOUNTAIN RD
- SDCo 91962 430-A6
- SDCo 91962 1237-H3
SHEEP RANCH LP
- CHV 91913 1311-E6
SHEFFIELD AV
- IMP 92251 6499-D2
400 ENCT 92007 1167-D2
SHEFFIELD CT
600 CHV 91910 1310-E6

SHEFFIELD DR
900 VSTA 92081 1108-A4
SHEILA LN
300 SDCo 92028 1028-D2
SHEILA ST
- SDCo 92021 1231-G7
8300 SDCo 92021 1251-G1
SHELBORNE ST
- SDCo 92127 1169-F3
SHELBY DR
2900 NATC 91950 1310-B3
2900 SDCo 91950 1310-B3
SHELBY LN
100 SDCo 92028 1027-H2
SHELBY ST
5200 SD 92105 1270-A6
SHELBY VIEW CT
- SDCo 92040 1231-J6
SHELDON AV
300 SD 92103 1268-J6
300 SD 92103 1269-A6
SHELDON DR
4300 LMSA 91941 1270-H4
SHELL AV
400 NATC 91950 1290-C6
400 SD 92114 1290-C6
SHELLBACK WY
8800 SD 92093 1227-H3
SHELL CANYON RD
- ImCo 92259 430-G6
SHELLEY PL
- CRLB 92008 1107-B7
SHELLY DR
- SMCS 92078 1109-A7
- SMCS 92078 1129-A1
4100 SD 92105 1270-B5
SHELSTEVE TER
800 VSTA 92084 1087-J6
SHELTER COVE WY
800 OCN 92054 1066-E6
SHELTER ISLAND DR
1400 SD 92106 1288-B2
SHENANDOAH CT
600 SMCS 92078 1128-F2
SHENANDOAH DR
2800 CHV 91914 1311-J4
3800 OCN 92056 1087-B7
10000 SNTE 92071 1231-C3
13000 SDCo 92040 1232-C3
SHEP ST
8900 SD 92123 1249-D6
SHEPHERD LN
600 SD 92154 1330-F7
SHEPHERD HILL RD
1300 SDCo 92084 1068-A6
SHEPHERDS KNOLL PL
1000 CHV 91910 1311-C1
SHERANN DR
12300 SDCo 92040 1232-A6
SHERBOURNE DR
3800 OCN 92056 1087-B7
SHERBOURNE LN
- SD 92129 1188-J4
SHERBROOKE ST
1500 SD 92139 1290-H6
SHERI LN
2600 LMGR 91945 1270-G7
SHERIDAN AV
100 ESCN 92026 1109-J6
800 ESCN 92027 1109-J6
1400 ESCN 92027 1110-A6
1800 SD 92103 1268-G5
SHERIDAN GN
- ESCN 92025 1130-C7
SHERIDAN LN
4300 SD 92120 1249-H7
SHERIDAN PL
- CRLB 92008 1106-F6
1500 ESCN 92027 1110-A5
SHERIDAN RD
1100 SDCo 91906 (1318-B7 See Page 1298)
1800 ENCT 92024 1147-A1
4500 OCN 92056 1107-E2
SHERIDAN ST
100 CALX 92231 6680-E1
SHERIDAN WY
- SMCS 92024 1128-B7
SHERILTON VALLEY RD
- SDCo 91916 1216-A1
SHERLOCK CT
4500 SD 92122 1228-D3
SHERM CIR
9700 SDCo 92040 1232-D3
SHERMAN DR
1500 CHV 91911 1330-H3
SHERMAN PL
100 ESCN 92025 1129-J2
SHERMAN RD
- CORD 92135 1288-F6
SHERMAN ST
100 CALX 92231 6680-E1
800 SD 92110 1268-F3
SHERMAN WY
1500 VSTA 92084 1088-B3
SHERRARD WY
11200 SD 92131 1209-J2
SHERRI LN
300 OCN 92054 1106-C3
SHERRIE LN
100 DLMR 92014 1187-F6
SHERWIN PL
4100 SDCo 91941 1271-E4
SHERWOOD DR
700 OCN 92054 1086-F2
2200 LMGR 91945 1270-H7
2200 LMGR 91945 1290-H1
SHERWOOD GN
1200 ESCN 92029 1129-F5
SHERWOOD LN
3300 SMCS 92078 1128-A2
SHERWOOD ST
- CHV 91911 1330-E4
SHERWOOD FOREST CT
8700 SDCo 92026 1069-A6
SHERYL AV
1300 CHV 91911 1330-C4
SHERYL LN
1400 NATC 91950 1310-A1
SHETLAND CT
5700 OCN 92057 1067-F7
SHETLAND WY
- SDCo 92028 1027-F4
SHIELD DR
- SD 92126 1209-E7
SHIELDS AV
1400 ENCT 92024 1147-G6
SHIELDS CT
10400 SD 92124 1249-H3
SHIELDS PL
4200 SD 92124 1249-H3
SHIELDS ST
3900 SD 92124 1249-G3

SHILOH LN
18800 SDCo 92082 1091-G5
SHILOH RD
3700 SD 92105 1270-A5
SHINEY STONE LN
- CHV 91915 1331-G1
SHINING LIGHT WY
11100 SDCo 92020 1271-H2
SHINLEY PL
1300 ESCN 92026 1110-A5
SHINOHARA LN
500 CHV 91911 1330-H5
SHIPLEY CT
1400 SD 92114 1290-G2
SHIPPEY LN
100 DLMR 92014 1187-F6
SHIRCLIFFE ST
- CHV 91913 1331-E2
SHIRE AV
1600 OCN 92057 1067-F7
SHIRE DR
1900 SDCo 92019 1252-C5
SHIREHALL DR
6400 SD 92111 1248-H4
SHIRLE LN
- OCN 92054 1086-G3
SHIRLENE PL
3800 LMSA 91941 1270-E5
SHIRLEY CT
9200 LMSA 91941 1271-B2
SHIRLEY DR
300 SMCS 92069 1108-J5
9100 LMSA 91941 1271-B2
SHIRLEY LN
1900 LMGR 91945 1290-F1
8700 SNTE 92071 1231-E7
SHIRLEY RD
32200 SDCo 92026 1049-B7
32200 SDCo 92026 1069-A1
SHIRLEY ST
200 CHV 91910 1310-B4
SHIRLEY ANN PL
4500 SD 92116 1269-D4
SHIRLEY GARDENS DR
9800 SNTE 92071 1231-E4
SHIR-MAR PL
7900 SDCo 92021 1251-J1
SHIRRA AV
12600 PWY 92064 1190-H6
SHOAL CREEK DR
11300 SD 92128 1189-J2
11600 SD 92128 1190-A3
SHOAL SUMMIT DR
- SD 92128 1190-A3
SHOCKEY TKTR
33300 SDCo 91906 (1318-F5 See Page 1298)
33500 SDCo 91906 430-C10
33500 SDCo 91906 (1319-A7 See Page 1298)
SHOEMAKER CT
300 SOLB 92075 1187-F2
SHOEMAKER LN
300 SOLB 92075 1187-F1
SHOEN LN
14800 SDCo 92065 1173-J7
SHOGO MOUNTAIN RD
- SDCo 92028 997-D5
SHONA WY
- SD 92110 1268-D5
SHOOTING IRON TR
700 SDCo 92036 1138-B6
SHOOTING STAR CT
1600 SD 92173 1350-E2
SHOOTING STAR DR
3600 SD 92173 1350-E2
SHOOTING STAR PL
2400 SDCo 91901 1234-B5
SHORE DR
- SD 92109 1248-C6
5200 CRLB 92008 1126-F2
SHOREACRES DR
1400 CHV 91915 1311-H7
SHOREBIRD LN
- CRLB 92011 1127-B7
SHORE CREST RD
900 CRLB 92011 1126-J4
SHOREDALE DR
9900 SNTE 92071 1231-D3
SHOREHAM PL
5000 SD 92122 1228-G5
SHOREHANG LN
200 ENCT 92024 1167-H1
SHORELINE DR
- CRLB 92011 1126-J5
7100 SD 92122 1228-E3
SHORELINE WY
- OCN 92056 1087-A4
SHORELINE BLUFF LN
- SD 92110 1268-D5
SHOREPOINTE CT
- SD 92130 1208-B2
SHOREPOINTE WY
- SD 92130 1208-C2
SHORE VIEW LN
300 ENCT 92024 1147-B3
SHOREVIEW PL
2100 CHV 91913 1311-E4
SHOREWOOD DR
7600 SD 92114 1290-G4
SHORT CT
3900 SDCo 91935 1292-H2
SHORT RD
- ImCo 92251 6439-H4
SHORT ST
4300 SD 92116 1269-H3
8100 SDCo 92040 1252-A1
12000 SDCo 92040 1251-J1
SHORT WY
- SDCo 92021 1252-H3
SHORTHILL DR
2300 OCN 92056 1106-H2
SHORT NINE DR E
- SDCo 92004 (1079-B3 See Page 1058)
SHOSHONE ST
1400 OCN 92054 1086-A6
SHOSHONEAN DR
- IMP 92251 6439-F3
SHOSHONI AV
4600 SD 92117 1248-F1
SHOWPLACE DR
9400 SDCo 91941 1271-C4
SHOWROOM PL
800 CHV 91914 1311-H4
SHRINER RD
- SDCo 91948 1218-B3
SHROPSHIRE LN
12400 SD 92128 1150-B6
SHUBIN LN
- SMCS 92078 1128-H1
SHUBORO ST
600 VSTA 92083 1087-F5

STREET
Block City ZIP Pg-Grid

SHUTTER CT
- CHV 91915 1331-H2
SHY LN
400 CHV 91911 1330-C4
SHYA WY
4000 SDCo 91901 1234-F7
SHY BIRD LN
10900 SD 92128 1189-H4
SICARD ST
400 SD 92113 1289-D5
SICILY WY
3300 OCN 92056 1106-J1
SIDDALL DR
1500 SDCo 92084 1108-F2
SIDEWINDER RD
- ImCo - 432-A4
- SD 92145 1229-A3
SIDEWINDER WY
13000 SD 92129 1189-C4
SIDNEY CT
- IMP 92251 6499-H2
SIDONIA CT
1100 ENCT 92024 1147-D4
SIDONIA ST
800 ENCT 92024 1147-D4
SIEFORT PL
400 NATC 92136 1309-F1
SIEGLE CT
2100 LMGR 91945 1290-J1
SIEGLE DR
1900 LMGR 91945 1290-J1
SIEMBRE ST
3500 SDCo 91902 1310-J1
SIEMPRE VIVA RD
- SDCo 92154 1352-A3
6900 SD 92154 1351-D4
9200 SD 92154 1352-A3
SIENA ST
100 SD 92114 1290-F5
N SIENA ST
100 SD 92114 1290-G4
SIENNA CT
- SD 92129 1189-B4
SIENNA ST
3600 OCN 92056 1107-F4
SIENNA CANYON CT
3800 ENCT 92024 1167-H2
SIENNA CANYON DR
1700 ENCT 92024 1167-H2
SIENNA HILLS DR
- SDCo 92127 1169-E1
SIENNA RIDGE DR
- SDCo 92127 1169-E2
SIENNA RIDGE PL
- SDCo 92127 1169-E2
N SIERRA AV
100 SOLB 92075 1167-E7
S SIERRA AV
100 SOLB 92075 1167-E7
100 SOLB 92075 1187-E1
800 DLMR 92014 1187-E1
800 DLMR 92075 1187-E1
SIERRA CIR
1300 ELCJ 92020 1271-E1
SIERRA CT
- IMP 92251 6499-H2
900 VSTA 92081 1107-H2
SIERRA DR
- ESCN 92026 1109-F7
SIERRA LN
14000 SDCo 92061 1050-G3
SIERRA ST
100 ESCN 92025 1150-B2
8900 SNTE 92071 1231-E6
SIERRA WY
- CHV 91911 1330-D1
E SIERRA WY
- CHV 91911 1330-E1
SIERRA ALTA WY
9000 SDCo 92021 1232-F6
SIERRA BONITA
2900 SDCo 92028 1028-D3
SIERRA BONITA ST
10000 SDCo 91977 1271-D6
SIERRA CIELO LN
17600 SDCo 91935 1294-C5
SIERRA CREST CT
11600 SD 92131 1209-J4
SIERRA GRANDE RD
15500 SDCo 92082 1070-J5
15500 SDCo 92082 1071-A5
SIERRA LINDA DR
1100 ESCN 92025 1150-D3
SIERRA MADRE DR
- SDCo 92055 1086-A3
SIERRA MADRE RD
9800 SDCo 91977 1271-C4
10100 SDCo 91941 1271-D4
SIERRA MAR DR
7700 SD 92037 1227-G6
SIERRA MESA CT
- SD 92129 1188-J4
SIERRA MORENA AV
2400 CRLB 92010 1106-H4
SIERRA RIDGE DR
200 ENCT 92024 1147-J6
SIERRA ROJO LN
29300 SDCo 92082 1069-J6
SIERRA ROJO RD
11400 SDCo 92082 1069-H7
12000 SDCo 92082 1070-A7
SIERRA ROSA TR
- SD 92130 1188-F4
SIERRA VERDE DR
700 VSTA 92084 1087-J7
SIERRA VERDE RD
1600 CHV 91913 1311-D7
19200 SDCo 92082 1091-H5
SIERRA VIEW WY
6000 SD 92120 1250-D6
SIERRA VISTA
1300 SMCS 92078 1129-B1
SIERRA VISTA AV
9300 SDCo 91941 1271-B1
9500 LMSA 91941 1271-C1
SIERRA VISTA DR
100 SDCo 92021 1252-J3
SIERRA VISTA LN
10400 SDCo 91941 1271-B1
SIERRA VISTA ST
4200 SD 92103 1268-H5
SIESTA DR
4800 OCN 92057 1066-J7
4800 OCN 92057 1067-A6
5400 SD 92115 1270-B3
SIESTA LN
19300 SDCo 92082 1091-H4
SIESTA PL
4800 OCN 92057 1066-J7
SIESTA RD
8600 SNTE 92071 1231-E7
SIESTA CALLE
1900 SDCo 92019 1252-D4

SIETE LEGUAS
7200 SDCo 92067 1168-G1
SIGGSON AV
1200 ESCN 92027 1109-J6
1200 ESCN 92027 1110-A6
SIGGSON CT
600 ESCN 92026 1109-J7
SIGLO CT
10900 SD 92124 1249-J2
SIGMA ST
5600 LMSA 91942 1250-J7
SIGNAL AV
1300 SD 92154 1350-A1
SIGNAL RD
- ImCo 92259 431-A8
SIGSBEE ST
800 SD 92113 1289-C5
SIKOKIS PL
2000 ESCN 92025 1130-A7
SIKORSKY ST
- SD 92154 1351-C1
SIKORSKY WY
- SD 92154 1351-D1
SILK PL
5100 SD 92105 1290-A1
SILK MILL PL
- SMCS 92069 1108-J7
SILKTREE LN
4600 SDCo 92004 (1099-F4 See Page 1098)
SILKTREE TER
- SD 92113 1289-F6
SILKWOOD DR
5200 OCN 92056 1087-D1
SILL ST
1700 NATC 91950 1289-J6
SILLA ST
14500 PWY 92064 1190-H3
SILSBEE RD
1200 ImCo 92243 431-A6
SILVA RD
- SD 92145 1229-D1
9700 SDCo 92021 1233-D2
SILVANA WY
500 VSTA 92084 1087-H3
SILVAS ST
1500 CHV 91911 1330-C5
SILVER CT
8900 SNTE 92071 1231-G6
SILVER DR
300 VSTA 92083 1087-F6
SILVER ST
700 SD 92037 1227-E7
SILVER ACACIA PL
- SD 92130 1188-G6
SILVERADO CT
10000 SNTE 92071 1231-C3
SILVERADO DR
1200 CHV 91915 1311-G6
1400 OCN 92057 1067-F6
SILVERADO PL
- ESCN 92027 1110-F7
- ESCN 92027 1130-F1
SILVERADO ST
- SMCS 92078 1128-B5
700 SD 92037 1227-E6
SILVERBERRY CT
1200 SDCo 92019 1252-F7
1300 SDCo 92019 1272-F1
SILVER BERRY PL
- ENCT 92024 1147-C5
SILVER BERRY WY
- SDCo 92082 1090-D5
SILVER BIRCH LN
1500 SDCo 92028 1047-J2
SILVER BIRCH WY
200 OCN 92057 1086-J2
SILVER BLUFF DR
4700 OCN 92057 1087-B1
5200 OCN 92057 1067-C7
SILVERBROOK DR
300 SDCo 92019 1253-B2
SILVER BUCKLE WY
11200 SD 92127 1169-J5
SILVER CLOUD PASS
- SDCo 92036 1155-G3
SILVERCREEK DR
100 SNTE 92071 1231-C5
SILVERCREEK GN
200 ESCN 92029 1150-A2
SILVER CREEK LN
10000 SDCo 92021 1232-G2
SILVER CREST DR
- SDCo 92127 1169-E2
SILVER CREST LN
- SDCo 92127 1169-E2
SILVER FOX LN
1700 VSTA 92083 1087-D6
SILVERFOX LN
1700 SDCo 92028 1027-F5
SILVER GATE AV
- SD 92152 1287-J4
100 SD 92106 1287-J4
400 SD 92106 1288-A3
SILVER GATE CT
300 SD 92106 1287-J4
300 SD 92152 1287-J4
SILVERGATE PL
3500 SD 92106 1287-J4
3500 SD 92106 1288-A4
SILVER GUM WY
17100 SDCo 92127 1169-D2
SILVER HAWK WY
1200 CHV 91915 1311-J5
SILVER HEIGHTS RD
14400 PWY 92064 1190-G4
SILVER LAKE DR
13100 PWY 92064 1190-D4
SILVERLEAF CIR
- CRLB 92024 1147-E3
SILVERLEAF LN
3500 SDCo 92084 1068-G7
3500 SDCo 92084 1088-F1
SILVER OAK CT
2700 CHV 91914 1311-J4
SILVER OAK LN
3300 SDCo 92084 1088-E7
SILVER OAK PL
900 CHV 91914 1311-J4
2700 ESCN 92029 1129-D3
SILVER OAKS WY
2600 SDCo 91977 1271-D7
SILVER PEAK PL
2200 ENCT 92024 1147-J6
SILVER PINE CT
- SDCo 92127 1169-E2
SILVER PINE PL
- SDCo 92127 1169-E2
SILVER PINE RD
- SDCo 92127 1169-E2
SILVER PINE WY
- SDCo 92127 1169-E2

SILVER RIDGE CT
3200 OCN 92054 1086-D3
SILVER RIDGE PT
11600 SD 92131 1209-J4
SILVER RIDGE RD
14200 PWY 92064 1190-G4
SILVER SADDLE CT
16400 PWY 92064 1170-E4
SILVER SADDLE LN
13100 PWY 92064 1170-D4
SILVER SAGE RD
- CHV 91915 1311-H5
SILVERSET ST
14300 PWY 92064 1190-D1
SILVER SHADOW DR
500 SMCS 92078 1129-A1
SILVER SHOALS PT
- SD 92154 1330-H7
SILVER SPRING WY
- OCN 92057 1086-J2
SILVER SPRINGS DR
1300 CHV 91915 1311-H6
SILVER SPRINGS LN
1000 SDCo 92028 1047-H1
SILVER SPRINGS PL
1000 ESCN 92026 1129-F1
SILVER SPUR CT
- IMP 92251 6439-F3
15900 SDCo 92021 1233-D2
SILVER SPUR RD
9700 SDCo 92021 1233-D3
SILVER SPUR WY
400 SMCS 92069 1108-E6
SILVER STALLION DR
1000 VSTA 92081 1107-G2
SILVERSTONE DR
1700 ELCJ 92021 1252-B2
SILVER STRAND
- CORD 91932 1329-F7
500 IMPB 91932 1329-F7
SILVER STRAND BLVD
Rt#-75
500 CORD 91932 1329-D2
500 IMPB 91932 1329-D2
1700 CORD 92118 1308-J1
1900 CORD 92118 1309-A3
1900 CORD 92155 1309-A3
2100 CORD 92118 1329-D2
SILVERTON AV
7800 SD 92126 1209-B7
SILVER TREE LN
1500 SDCo 92026 1089-D7
SILVERWOOD ST
600 OCN 92054 1086-F2
7000 SD 92114 1290-F5
SILVERY LN
400 ELCJ 92020 1251-C5
SIMA CT
10700 SNTE 92071 1231-E1
SIMBAR RD
3100 SDCo 91902 1290-J7
3100 SDCo 91902 1310-J1
SIMEON DR
7400 SNTE 92071 1230-F7
SIMEON PL
1200 ESCN 92029 1129-H7
SIMI CT
2600 SD 92139 1310-F1
SIMI PL
6700 SD 92139 1310-F1
6900 SD 92139 1290-F7
SIMI WY
6900 SD 92139 1310-G1
SIMMS CT
9300 SDCo 91977 1271-B5
SIMPATICO CT
1700 SD 92154 1350-B3
SIMPLE MELODY LN
- SDCo 92127 1168-J1
SIMPSON RD
- ImCo 92233 411-B8
SIMPSON WY
1300 ESCN 92029 1129-F3
SIMS RD
- SD 92106 1268-D7
SIMSBURY CT
3500 CRLB 92010 1107-A3
SINALOA CT
100 SOLB 92075 1167-D6
SINCLAIR LN
3700 SDCo 91977 1271-B5
SINCLAIR RD
- CLPT 92233 411-C9
- ImCo 92233 411-A9
SINGER LN
11900 SDCo 91978 1271-H6
SINGH RD
- ImCo 92243 6500-E7
200 ImCo 92243 6560-E1
SINGING HEIGHTS DR
700 SDCo 92019 1252-D7
SINGING RIDGE RD
900 SDCo 92019 1252-E7
SINGING TRAILS CT
700 SDCo 92019 1252-E6
SINGING TRAILS DR
700 SDCo 92019 1252-E7
SINGING VISTA CT
600 SDCo 92019 1252-E6
SINGING VISTA DR
600 SDCo 92019 1252-E6
SINGING VISTA WY
2500 SDCo 92019 1252-E6
SINGINGWOOD PL
2100 ESCN 92029 1129-E7
SINGING WOOD WY
8900 SNTE 92071 1231-B6
SINGLE OAK DR
9100 SDCo 92040 1232-A4
SINGLE OAK PL
12300 SDCo 92040 1232-A5
SINGLETREE LN
10800 SDCo 91978 1271-G7
SINGLETREE PL
1300 SDCo 92028 1047-J4
SINJON CIR
6000 LMSA 91942 1251-B6
SINKLER WY
800 VSTA 92083 1107-J1
SINSONTE LN
9100 SDCo 92040 1232-B5
SINTON PL
6000 LMSA 91942 1251-A6
SINTONTE CT
12200 SD 92128 1170-B1
SINTONTE DR
17700 SD 92128 1170-B1
17800 SD 92128 1150-B7
SIOUX AV
3700 SD 92117 1248-E5
SIPES CIR
- CHV 91911 1330-H2

SIPES LN
3600 SD 92173 1350-F5
SIRENA VISTA
- CRLB 92009 1127-J5
SIR FRANCIS DRAKE DR
11300 SDCo 91941 1271-H3
SIRGINSON ST
500 SMCS 92069 1108-J6
SIRGINSON WY
600 SMCS 92069 1108-J6
SIRIAS RD
11200 SD 92126 1209-C2
SIR LANCELOT DR
10100 SNTE 92071 1231-D1
SIROS WY
5000 OCN 92056 1107-F5
SIRRAH ST
800 SD 92154 1330-B7
SISSI LN
10200 SDCo 92040 1231-F3
SISSON ST
9300 LMSA 91942 1251-B6
SITIO ABETO
7800 CRLB 92009 1147-H2
SITIO ABRIDOR
7900 CRLB 92009 1147-H3
SITIO ALGODON
- CRLB 92009 1148-A2
SITIO ANDULCIA
- CRLB 92009 1147-J4
SITIO AVELLANA
- CRLB 92009 1128-A6
SITIO BANIANO
7900 CRLB 92009 1147-H3
SITIO BAYA
3400 CRLB 92009 1148-A2
SITIO BORDE
3400 CRLB 92009 1148-A2
SITIO CABALLERO
- CRLB 92009 1127-J5
- CRLB 92009 1128-A5
SITIO CALMAR
7800 CRLB 92009 1147-J3
SITIO CATANA
7900 CRLB 92009 1147-J3
SITIO CAUCHO
8000 CRLB 92009 1147-G3
SITIO CEDRELA
- CRLB 92011 1127-C5
SITIO COCO
- CRLB 92009 1147-G2
SITIO CORDERO
- CRLB 92009 1147-J6
SITIO DAMASCO
- CRLB 92009 1148-B2
SITIO ESPINO
- CRLB 92009 1148-A1
SITIO FRESCA
7900 CRLB 92009 1148-A4
SITIO FRESNO
7800 CRLB 92009 1147-H2
SITIO GRANADO
7900 CRLB 92009 1147-H2
SITIO ISADORA
- CRLB 92009 1127-H7
- CRLB 92009 1147-H1
SITIO LIMA
- CRLB 92009 1148-A2
SITIO LIRIO
- CRLB 92009 1148-A1
SITIO MANANA
- CRLB 92009 1148-A2
SITIO MIRTO
7900 CRLB 92009 1147-H2
SITIO MONTECILLO
- CRLB 92009 1127-J6
SITIO MUSICA
7700 CRLB 92009 1147-J3
SITIO NISPERO
7900 CRLB 92009 1147-H3
SITIO OCEANO
- CRLB 92009 1127-J5
SITIO OLMO
7800 CRLB 92009 1147-H2
SITIO PALMAS
6700 CRLB 92009 1127-H5
SITIO PERAL
7900 CRLB 92009 1147-H2
SITIO REDONDA
7900 CRLB 92009 1148-A3
SITIO ROSALIA
7300 CRLB 92009 1127-G7
SITIO SAGO
- CRLB 92011 1127-C5
SITIO SALVIA
- CRLB 92009 1148-A1
SITIO SENDERO
- CRLB 92009 1127-J6
SITIO SOLANA
- CRLB 92009 1148-A3
SITIO TEJO
- CRLB 92009 1147-F2
SITIO TOLEDO
- CRLB 92009 1147-H4
SITIO TORTUGA
- CRLB 92009 1128-A6
SITIO VAQUERO
- CRLB 92009 1148-A3
SIVA ST
1600 SD 92113 1289-F6
SIWANOY CT
8800 SNTE 92071 1230-J5
8800 SNTE 92071 1231-A5
SIXES CT
1800 SDCo 92065 1172-J2
SIXPENCE WY
- CORD 92118 1329-E1
SIXTH ST
- ImCo 92249 6560-C7
SKI WY
100 CHV 91911 1330-D3
SKIMMER CT
1700 CRLB 92011 1127-E5
SKIMMER WY
4400 OCN 92057 1087-A3
SKIPJACK LN
- SDCo 92055 1085-H5
SKIPPER ST
3000 SD 92123 1249-D5
SKUNK HOLLOW RD
- SDCo 91935 (1314-E3 See Page 1294)
SKY DR
26200 SDCo 92026 1089-H7
26200 SDCo 92026 1109-H1
SKY ST
4900 SD 92110 1268-F1
SKYBROOK PL
1900 CHV 91913 1311-E4
SKY COUNTRY CT
- SDCo 92028 1027-F5
SKYCREST DR
3100 SDCo 92028 1048-D1

SKY CREST GN
- ESCN 92029 1129-H5
SKYE VALLEY RD
- SDCo 91901 1275-B7
- SDCo 91901 (1295-A3 See Page 1294)
- SDCo 91935 1294-H3
- SDCo 91935 (1295-A3 See Page 1294)
SKY HARBOR RD
1700 SD 92139 1290-D7
SKY HAVEN LN
3400 OCN 92056 1107-D2
SKYHAWK RD
1600 SDCo 92029 1149-F2
SKYHAWK WY
4900 OCN 92056 1107-E3
SKYHIGH CT
12400 SDCo 92021 1232-B7
SKY HIGH RD
15300 SDCo 92025 1150-J2
SKYHILL CT
400 CHV 91910 1310-F7
SKYHILL PL
1800 ESCN 92026 1109-E6
SKYKNOLL WY
1900 ENCT 92024 1147-H5
SKYLARK DR
900 SD 92037 1247-G3
2200 OCN 92054 1086-E7
SKYLARK PL
5600 SD 92037 1247-G3
SKYLARK WY
1500 CHV 91911 1330-F5
SKYLINE AV
- ESCN 92027 1130-C1
SKYLINE CIR
300 SDCo 92028 1028-H4
SKYLINE DR
- SDCo 91948 (1197-G7 See Page 1176)
- SDCo 91948 (1217-F3 See Page 1216)
- SDCo 91962 (1217-F3 See Page 1216)
7900 SDCo 91977 1290-H1
300 SDCo 92084 1088-B6
300 VSTA 92084 1088-B6
1300 LMGR 91945 1290-H1
1300 LMGR 92114 1290-H1
1300 SD 92114 1290-D4
1700 SDCo 92027 1130-E4
2000 LMGR 91945 1270-H6
3000 OCN 92056 1086-G7
3000 OCN 92056 1106-G1
SKYLINE LN
1500 ELCJ 92019 1252-A7
1500 SDCo 92019 1252-A7
4600 LMSA 91941 1271-A3
SKYLINE PL
- SMCS 92078 1128-F4
SKYLINE RD
3700 CRLB 92008 1106-H5
SKYLINE SPUR
14500 SDCo 91935 1294-C1
SKYLINE TER
1900 SDCo 92027 1130-E4
SKYLINE TKTR
14500 SDCo 91935 1273-E6
16900 SDCo 91935 1274-B7
18000 SDCo 91935 1294-D1
SKYLINE VIEW GN
- ESCN 92027 1130-J4
SKY LOFT LN
1700 ENCT 92024 1147-C2
SKY LOFT RD
600 ENCT 92024 1147-B2
SKY MESA RD
- SDCo 91901 1233-F7
SKY MOUNTAIN LN
700 SDCo 91901 1234-B4
SKY PARK CT
9200 SD 92123 1249-E3
SKY PILOT WY
28500 SDCo 92082 1090-B1
SKY RANCH RD
40000 SDCo 92028 409-A4
SKY RIDGE CT
- SMCS 92078 1128-E6
SKYRIDGE LN
200 ESCN 92026 1109-G4
SKY RIDGE RD
3400 SDCo 91901 1275-B4
SKYRIDGE RD
15200 PWY 92064 1170-J5
15200 PWY 92064 1171-A6
SKY RIM DR
8500 SDCo 92021 1232-B7
8500 SDCo 92040 1232-B7
SKYROS WY
- ENCT 92024 1147-B3
SKYSAIL AV
800 CRLB 92011 1126-J5
SKYTRAIL RANCH RD
3100 SDCo 91935 1273-J6
SKY VALLEY DR
16500 SDCo 92065 1151-D6
SKYVIEW AV
- ELCN 92243 6559-G3
SKY VIEW CT
- IMP 92251 6499-C2
SKY VIEW DR
- ImCo 92259 410-H7
11900 SDCo 92082 1090-A2
SKYVIEW GN
1900 ESCN 92027 1110-A5
SKYVIEW LN
100 OCN 92056 1107-D2
SKYVIEW ST
500 ELCJ 92020 1271-E1
SKY VISTA WY
300 SDCo 92028 1027-H2
SKYWAY DR
28600 SDCo 92066 410-A8
SKYWOOD DR
10900 ELCJ 92020 1271-G1
10900 SDCo 92020 1271-G1
SLACK ST
12900 PWY 92064 1190-D5
SLADON CT
14300 PWY 92064 1190-E2
SLANT ROCK RD
3400 SDCo 91901 1275-B4
SLASH M RD
300 SDCo 92004 (1078-G6 See Page 1058)
SLATE CT
300 CHV 91911 1330-G4
SLATE ST
200 CHV 91911 1330-G4
SLATE TER
- SDCo 92019 1272-B2
SLATER PL
- CRLB 92009 1127-F2

SLAUGHTERHOUSE RD
- SDCo 92070 409-J11
27400 SDCo 92065 409-J11
27400 SDCo 92065 1154-C1
SLAUGHTERHOUSE CANYON RD
- SDCo 92040 1211-G4
SLAYEN WY
3000 SD 92117 1248-C3
SLAYTON RD
- ImCo 92250 431-E4
SLEEPING CIRCLE DR
2100 SDCo 92004 (1099-F5 See Page 1098)
SLEEPING INDIAN RD
500 OCN 92057 1067-D2
1400 OCN 92028 1067-D2
1500 OCN 92028 1047-E6
1500 SDCo 92028 1047-E6
SLEEPY WY
8400 SDCo 92021 1232-D7
SLEEPY CREEK RD
10100 SDCo 92021 1232-F2
SLEEPY HILL LN
2300 SDCo 92026 1109-D4
SLEEPY HOLLOW
2200 SDCo 92036 1136-C6
28700 SDCo 91962 1237-B5
SLEEPY HOLLOW LN
4200 SDCo 91902 1310-F4
SLEEPY HOLLOW RD
2000 SDCo 92026 1109-E4
SLEEPY HOLLOW WY
- VSTA 92081 1107-D1
SLICE CT
3100 SDCo 92004 (1079-B6 See Page 1058)
SLIPPERY ELM CT
- CHV 91915 1311-J7
SLIVKOFF DR
2900 ESCN 92027 1110-F7
SLOAN DR
1900 SDCo 92028 1028-A6
SLOANE ST
400 SD 92103 1268-J6
400 SD 92103 1269-A6
SLOANE TKTR
- SDCo 91935 1273-J3
SLOANE CANYON RD
1100 SDCo 91935 1273-D1
1100 SDCo 91935 1253-F7
1200 SDCo 92019 1273-A2
4500 SDCo 92019 1253-A7
S SLOPE DR
8500 SNTE 92071 1230-G5
8500 SNTE 92071 1250-J1
SLOPE ST
8500 SNTE 92071 1251-C1
SLUMBERING OAKS TR
3200 SDCo 92036 1156-C2
SMALLINS ST
400 NATC 92136 1309-G1
SMART CT
100 ENCT 92024 1147-G7
SMEDLEY AV
- SD 92126 1209-F7
SMELIK LN
8400 LMGR 91945 1270-J6
SMILAX RD
100 SDCo 92069 1108-C5
100 SDCo 92084 1108-C5
100 SDCo 92083 1108-C5
100 SDCo 92081 1108-C5
200 SMCS 92069 1108-C5
200 SMCS 92078 1108-C5
SMILIANA LN
400 SDCo 92083 1108-A2
SMITH AV
- CHV 91910 1309-J5
- CHV 91910 1310-A5
SMITH DR
700 VSTA 92084 1087-J5
1100 VSTA 92083 1087-G4
SMITH LN
- SDCo 92672 1023-D2
800 ImCo 92243 6499-B6
SMITH RD
- SD 92145 1229-C2
SMITH ST
3700 SD 92110 1268-F5
SMITH CANYON CT
4900 SD 92130 1188-C5
SMITHERS CT
11400 SD 92126 1209-D1
SMOKEBUSH CT
1200 SDCo 92019 1252-F7
1200 SDCo 92019 1272-F1
SMOKE SIGNAL DR
18100 SD 92127 1149-J7
SMOKETREE CIR
2100 ELCN 92243 6559-G2
SMOKETREE CT
800 SMCS 92078 1128-F2
2100 ELCN 92243 6559-G2
SMOKETREE DR
100 ELCN 92243 6559-H1
SMOKETREE GN
500 ESCN 92026 1109-G5
SMOKE TREE LN
1700 SDCo 92004 (1099-F3 See Page 1098)
SMOKE TREE PL
200 OCN 92057 1087-A1
SMOKEWOOD DR
8800 SNTE 92071 1230-H7
SMOKEWOOD PL
2400 ESCN 92026 1109-J3
SMOKEY LN
- SDCo 92036 1175-J2
1700 SDCo 91977 1291-B1
SMOKY CIR
400 CHV 91910 1310-F5
SMYTHE AV
1600 SD 92173 1350-F2
SNAFFLE BIT PL
5900 SDCo 91902 1311-B2
SNAPDRAGON
15200 SDCo 92021 1233-B3
SNAPDRAGON DR
7000 CRLB 92011 1127-A6
SNAPDRAGON LN
2000 SDCo 91901 1234-A5
SNAPDRAGON ST
700 ENCT 92024 1147-E6
SNEAD AV
2700 SD 92111 1248-G6
SNEAD DR
2300 OCN 92056 1106-H2
SNEATH WY
300 SDCo 91901 1234-B3
SNEEZY CT
13300 SDCo 92021 1232-E7
SNELSON WY
9400 SNTE 92071 1231-B3

SNIPE CT
- CRLB 92011 1127-A4
SNIPES CT
1100 SD 92154 1350-E1
SNOOK ST
9800 SD 92124 1249-G3
SNOWBELLS LN
- SDCo 92127 1169-F4
SNOWBERRY CT
- CRLB 92024 1147-E3
800 SMCS 92069 1109-A5
SNOWBOND CT
5800 SD 92120 1250-C6
SNOWBOND ST
6200 SD 92120 1250-C6
SNOWCREEK
1000 SDCo 92028 1027-H4
SNOWDEN PL
400 SDCo 92019 1253-C2
SNOWDROP ST
2500 SD 92105 1269-H7
SNOWDROP WY
- CRLB 92011 1127-B4
SNOWFALL CIR
4500 OCN 92056 1087-D5
SNOWS RD
3000 SDCo 92028 1047-J1
SNOW VIEW DR
9600 SDCo 92021 1233-A3
SNOW WHITE DR
8400 SDCo 92021 1232-D7
SNUG HARBOR
- SDCo 92065 1171-J2
SNUZ MOUNTAIN RD
15800 SDCo 92065 1171-H5
SNYDER RD
1900 ImCo 92250 431-E5
10600 SDCo 91941 1271-F2
SOARING DR
6600 SD 92119 1250-G4
SOARING BIRD PT
13000 SD 92128 1189-H5
SOBKE CT
1200 CALX 92231 6620-H7
SOBRE LOS CERROS
16900 SDCo 92067 1168-C3
SOCIN CT
- ESCN 92027 1110-E6
SOCORRO CT
11100 SD 92129 1169-J6
SOCORRO LN
2700 CRLB 92009 1127-H5
SOCORRO PL
15200 SD 92129 1169-J6
SOCORRO ST
11100 SD 92129 1169-J6
SOCORRO WY
15200 SD 92129 1169-J7
SODERBLOM AV
2400 SD 92122 1228-B6
SODERBLOM CT
5500 SD 92122 1228-A6
SOFIA CT
- IMP 92251 6499-H2
SOFTWIND LN
2100 ENCT 92024 1147-H5
SOFTWIND RD
800 VSTA 92081 1087-F7
800 VSTA 92081 1107-F1
SOHAIL ST
13400 SDCo 92040 1232-D4
SOL DR
500 OCN 92057 1067-A6
SOLACE CT
100 ENCT 92024 1147-G7
SOLAMAR DR
6300 CRLB 92011 1126-G4
SOLANA CIR E
600 SOLB 92075 1187-F1
SOLANA CIR W
600 SOLB 92075 1187-F1
800 DLMR 92014 1187-F1
SOLANA DR
1000 SOLB 92014 1167-H7
SOLANA GN
1700 ESCN 92026 1109-D5
SOLANA ST
8000 SD 92114 1290-G2
SOLANA GLEN CT
600 SOLB 92075 1167-G6
SOLANA HILLS CT
600 SOLB 92075 1167-G6
N SOLANA HILLS DR
500 SOLB 92075 1167-G6
S SOLANA HILLS DR
100 SOLB 92075 1167-G7
SOLANA POINT CIR
100 SOLB 92075 1167-E6
SOLANA REAL
400 SDCo 92028 1047-E7
SOLANA VISTA DR
100 SOLB 92075 1167-E6
SOLANDRA DR
- CRLB 92011 1127-A5
SOLANDRA LN
900 SDCo 91977 1291-D3
SOLANO DR
- CHV 91913 1331-E1
SOLANO RD
1800 ELCN 92243 6499-E6
SOLANO ST
7400 CRLB 92009 1147-H1
SOLANO BAY PL
300 OCN 92057 1066-J6
SOLANO ESTE DR
3600 OCN 92054 1086-F2
SOLAR LN
2700 SDCo 92069 1088-H6
SOLAR ST
5100 SD 92110 1268-F2
SOLAR CIR DR
3300 DLMR 92014 1187-F2
SOLAR VIEW DR
200 SDCo 92069 1088-H6
SOLAZAR WY
2400 OCN 92056 1087-C6
SOLDAU DR
3300 SD 92154 1350-D1
SOLDIER OAKS LN
12800 SDCo 92082 1090-C2
SOLDIN LN
9200 SDCo 92021 1232-H5
SOLE GN
- ESCN 92029 1129-E5
SOLEDAD AV
2000 SD 92037 1227-G6
SOLEDAD CT
2400 SD 92037 1248-A2
SOLEDAD FRWY Rt#-52
- SD - 1228-B7
- SD - 1248-A1
SOLEDAD PL
200 CORD 92118 1288-J5
200 CORD 92118 1289-A6

STREET
Block City ZIP Pg-Grid

SOLEDAD PL
3000 ESCN 92027 1110-E6
SOLEDAD RD
4900 SD 92109 1248-A4
5300 SD 92037 1247-J3
5300 SD 92037 1248-A2
5300 SD 92109 1247-J3
7000 SD 92037 1227-J7
SOLEDAD WY
1700 SD 92109 1247-J3
1700 SD 92109 1248-A3
SOLEDAD MOUNTAIN RD
4600 SD 92109 1248-A2
5300 SD 92037 1248-A2
5900 SD 92037 1247-J1
SOLEDAD RANCHO CT
5200 SD 92109 1248-A3
SOLEDAD RANCHO RD
2200 SD 92109 1248-A3
SOLERA WY
12900 PWY 92064 1170-D2
SOLITA AV
6400 SD 92115 1270-D3
SOLITARY LN
1000 SDCo 92028 1027-J6
SOLOLA AV
4700 SD 92113 1289-J6
4700 SD 92113 1290-A6
5000 SD 92114 1290-A6
SOLOMON AV
8300 SDCo 92021 1231-G7
8300 SDCo 92021 1251-G1
SOLO ROBLE
100 SMCS 92078 1129-A3
SOL SITIO
4800 OCN 92057 1066-J7
4800 OCN 92057 1067-A7
SOL VISTA
3300 SDCo 92028 1028-D1
SOL VISTA GN
800 ESCN 92025 1130-B3
SOL WOOD
1600 SDCo 91905 (1319-J3 See Page 1298)
1600 SDCo 91905 (1320-A3 See Page 1300)
SOLYMAR DR
900 SD 92037 1247-G2
SOMA PL
1500 ELCJ 92021 1252-A3
SOMAM AV
2200 SD 92110 1268-G1
4900 SD 92110 1248-F7
SOMBRA CT
10900 SD 92124 1249-J2
SOMBRA DEL MONTE
16400 SDCo 92065 1171-F3
SOMBRERO WY
1600 SD 92154 1349-J2
SOMBRIA RD
9200 SDCo 92040 1232-B5
SOMBROSA PL
2500 CRLB 92009 1147-G3
SOMBROSA ST
2600 CRLB 92009 1147-G3
SOMERLANE ST
1700 SDCo 92021 1251-J2
SOMERMONT DR
1300 SDCo 92021 1251-H1
SOMERSET AV
1400 ENCT 92007 1167-D2
8600 SD 92123 1249-C6
SOMERSET CT
\- SDCo 92065 1152-G7
900 CHV 91915 1311-G4
SOMERSET RD
13600 PWY 92064 1190-F3
SOMERSET WY
3500 CRLB 92010 1107-A4
SOMERSET HILLS GN
\- ESCN 92026 1109-H3
SOMMER PL
6400 LMSA 91942 1251-B5
SONATA
1600 SDCo 92078 1128-C2
SONATA LN
\- SD 92127 1168-J7
SONDRA CT
2900 CRLB 92009 1127-H7
SONETT ST
1800 SDCo 92019 1272-C4
SONGBIRD AV
\- CRLB 92011 1127-C5
SONGBIRD LN
900 CHV 91902 1310-H3
SONG SPARROW CIR
\- SDCo 91902 1291-B7
SONIA CT
1300 VSTA 92084 1088-C4
SONIA LN
300 CHV 91911 1330-F6
SONIA PL
900 ESCN 92026 1109-F5
SONJA CT
3000 OCN 92056 1086-G7
3000 OCN 92056 1106-G1
SONO PL
7300 LMSA 91941 1270-F4
SONOMA CT
1200 CHV 91911 1330-G2
SONOMA DR
3600 OCN 92054 1086-F2
SONOMA LN
1800 LMGR 91945 1290-F1
SONOMA PL
\- SD 92130 1188-E5
SONOMA ST
\- SMCS 92078 1128-G2
SONORA CT
2000 VSTA 92081 1107-J4
2400 CRLB 92010 1106-H4
SONORA DR
1500 CHV 91911 1330-H4
SONORA RD
12600 SD 92128 1170-C3
SONORA ST
10600 SNTE 92071 1231-E6
SONORA WY
2200 SDCo 92065 1152-C5
SONRISA GN
\- ESCN 92029 1129-G6
SONRISA ST
600 SOLB 92075 1187-F1
SONRISA WY
2400 OCN 92056 1087-C6
SOPER LN
7900 LMSA 91942 1270-H1
SOPHIA DR
12300 PWY 92064 1190-C2
SOPHIA WY
200 OCN 92057 1086-H3
SORA WY
\- CRLB 92011 1127-B5
12500 SD 92129 1189-C6

SORBONNE CT
\- SD 92128 1190-A3
SORIA DR
4600 SD 92115 1270-C3
SORIA GN
1200 ESCN 92026 1109-G7
1200 ESCN 92026 1129-G1
SORREL AV
9900 SDCo 92040 1232-C3
SORREL CT
1700 CRLB 92011 1127-E7
SORREL TREE PL
200 OCN 92057 1087-A1
SORRENTINO DR
1900 SDCo 92025 1130-D5
SORRENTO DR
1000 SD 92107 1287-J2
2100 OCN 92056 1086-J7
SORRENTO PKWY
\- SD 92121 1208-E7
SORRENTO PL
1200 ESCN 92027 1110-A6
SORRENTO VALLEY BLVD
3700 SD 92121 1208-F3
6800 SD 92126 1208-F3
SORRENTO VALLEY RD
9900 SD 92121 1208-A4
11800 SD 92121 1207-J2
SOTO ST
1500 OCN 92054 1106-D2
2200 SD 92107 1268-A6
SOULE ST
12600 PWY 92064 1190-C5
SOURWOOD PL
\- CHV 91915 1311-J7
SOUTH LN
100 SDCo 92021 1252-H4
200 SD 92037 1247-E1
4400 SDCo 92014 1167-J7
4400 SDCo 92014 1187-J1
4400 SDCo 92014 1188-A1
SOUTH ST
7500 LMSA 91941 1270-G3
SOUTHALL ST
800 NATC 92136 1309-F2
SOUTHAMPTON RD
2700 CRLB 92010 1106-J5
2900 CRLB 92010 1107-A5
SOUTHAMPTON ST
1200 SMCS 92078 1128-B3
4500 SD 92117 1248-G2
SOUTH BAY FRWY Rt#-54
\- CHV - 1309-J4
\- CHV - 1310-A4
\- NATC - 1309-J4
\- NATC - 1310-A4
\- NATC - 1310-F2
\- SDCo - 1290-H7
\- SDCo - 1291-A6
\- SDCo - 1310-A4
\- SDCo - 1310-F2
SOUTH BAY EXWY Rt#-125
\- CHV - 1311-D1
\- CHV - 1331-F1
\- SD - 1331-G6
\- SD - 1351-H1
\- SDCo - 1291-A6
\- SDCo - 1311-D1
\- SDCo - 1331-G6
\- SDCo - 1351-H1
SOUTHBRIDGE CT
500 ENCT 92024 1147-B2
SOUTHBROOK CT
11400 SD 92128 1190-A6
SOUTH CAYS CT
\- CORD 92118 1329-D3
SOUTHCREST AV
2100 SD 92110 1268-F1
SOUTHERN RD
6300 ELCJ 92020 1251-B5
6300 LMSA 91942 1251-B5
SOUTHERN HILLS LN
\- PWY 92064 1190-G2
SOUTHERN OAK RD
2300 SDCo 92065 1172-D5
SOUTHERN PINE PL
10400 SD 92131 1209-J4
SOUTHERNWOOD WY
3700 SD 92106 1288-A2
3700 SD 92106 1287-J2
SOUTH FORTY RD
\- SDCo 91901 1235-G7
\- SDCo 91901 1255-G1
SOUTHGATE CT
700 OCN 92057 1087-C1
SOUTHGATE DR
600 OCN 92057 1087-C1
6900 SD 92119 1251-A3
SOUTH GRADE RD
400 SDCo 91901 1233-G6
1100 SDCo 91901 1253-H1
1800 SDCo 91901 1254-A2
2700 SDCo 91901 1234-C7
SOUTHHAMPTON CV
5200 SD 92130 1188-D6
SOUTH LAKE CT
6200 SD 92119 1251-A6
SOUTHLOOK AV
200 SD 92113 1289-G5
SOUTH PARK PL
600 SDCo 92021 1252-J4
SOUTH POINT DR
1700 CHV 91902 1311-C4
SOUTHPORT WY
2600 NATC 91950 1309-H4
SOUTHRIDGE RD
3700 OCN 92056 1107-E3
SOUTHRIDGE WY
3700 OCN 92056 1107-E3
11100 SD 92131 1209-H4
SOUTH SHORE DR
100 SOLB 92075 1187-E2
SOUTHSHORE DR
800 CHV 91913 1311-E4
SOUTH SHORE RD
40000 SDCo 92028 997-B2
SOUTH SHORES RD
\- SD 92109 1268-B3
SOUTHVIEW CIR
1000 CHV 91910 1311-C6
SOUTHVIEW CT
1400 CHV 91910 1311-C7
SOUTH VIEW DR
1800 CRLB 92008 1106-H7
SOUTHVIEW DR
3700 SD 92117 1248-D4
SOUTH VISTA AV
200 SD 92173 1350-E3
SOUTHWIND DR
100 ELCN 92243 6559-F2
100 ELCN 92243 6560-A2

SOUTHWIND LN
3100 SDCo 92084 1068-E6
SOUTHWOOD CIR
9200 SD 92126 1209-E3
SOUTHWOOD DR
3300 OCN 92054 1086-E2
SOUVENIR DR
1400 ELCJ 92021 1252-A2
SOVEREIGN RD
8800 SD 92123 1249-D4
SOYLA DR
\- OCN 92054 1086-E3
SPA RD
\- ImCo 92257 410-L4
\- ImCo 92257 411-A5
SPA ST
3300 SD 92105 1270-B6
SPACE THEATER WY
\- SD 92101 1289-C1
\- SD 92134 1289-C1
SPALDING PL
1800 SD 92116 1269-C3
SPANGLER PEAK RD
16000 SDCo 92065 1173-C2
SPANISH SPUR
100 SDCo 92028 1047-G4
SPANISH WY
3400 CRLB 92008 1106-F5
SPANISH BAY CT
\- ENCT 92024 1147-E5
SPANISH BAY RD
2300 CHV 91915 1311-G6
SPANISH BIT DR
\- SDCo 91901 1254-E2
SPANISH BIT PL
3900 SDCo 91901 1254-E3
SPANISH OAK AV
500 SMCS 92069 1109-D7
SPANISH OAK CT
3800 OCN 92054 1086-F2
SPANISH OAK PL
1600 ELCJ 92019 1252-B6
SPANISH OAK WY
1900 VSTA 92081 1107-F5
SPAR CT
\- CRLB 92011 1127-A4
SPARKLING CREEK WY
\- ESCN 92026 1129-F1
SPARKLING OAKS TR
28200 SDCo 92026 1089-F3
SPARKS AV
4800 SD 92110 1268-F1
SPARKS CT
1800 SD 92110 1268-F2
SPARKS PL
1800 SD 92110 1268-F1
SPARLING ST
3400 SD 92115 1270-D6
SPARREN AV
13200 SD 92129 1189-C3
SPARREN CT
13400 SD 92129 1189-C4
SPARREN WY
8700 SD 92129 1189-C3
SPARROW CT
1000 SMCS 92078 1128-E2
SPARROW LN
\- SMCS 92078 1128-B5
SPARROW RD
1300 CRLB 92011 1127-C5
SPARROW ST
\- ImCo 92243 6560-A7
\- ImCo 92249 6560-A7
400 CHV 91911 1330-G3
1200 SD 92114 1290-D2
SPARROW WY
200 OCN 92057 1086-J1
SPARROW HAWK CT
11300 SDCo 92040 1212-B6
SPARROW LAKE RD
1100 CHV 91913 1331-B2
SPARRS RD
\- SD 92152 1288-A5
SPARTA DR
600 ENCT 92024 1147-C3
SPARTAN CIR
4200 SD 92115 1270-B4
SPARTAN DR
5600 SD 92115 1270-B4
SPEAR DR
1800 SD 92101 1289-C2
SPEAR ST
6400 SD 92120 1250-B6
SPEARFISH LN
3900 SD 92124 1249-G3
SPEARHEAD TR
30000 SDCo 92082 1069-E4
SPEARMAN LN
3000 SDCo 91978 1271-F7
SPECIALTY DR
1300 VSTA 92081 1108-A7
1300 VSTA 92081 1128-A1
SPECKELS LN
\- SD 92127 1169-B4
SPECKELS PL
\- SD 92127 1169-B4
SPECTRUM CT
4800 OCN 92057 1087-B3
SPECTRUM LN
8500 SD 92121 1228-J1
SPECTRUM CENTER BLVD
9000 SD 92123 1249-C2
SPENCER CT
\- OCN 92057 1067-A4
9300 SDCo 92040 1232-B5
SPENCER LN
5400 CRLB 92008 1107-C7
SPENCER MOUNTAIN RD
9600 SDCo 91977 1271-C7
SPENCERPORT WY
11200 SD 92131 1209-H2
SPERBER RD
\- ImCo 92243 6559-G5
SPERRY CT
6900 SD 92111 1268-J1
SPEYERS WY
3500 SDCo 91902 1311-C1
SPICA DR
11200 SD 92126 1209-C1
SPICE ST
9100 LMSA 91941 1271-B2
SPICE WY
\- SDCo 91935 1294-J6
\- SDCo 91935 (1295-A6 See Page 1294)
SPICEWOOD CT
10900 SD 92130 1208-D1
SPILLMAN DR
4100 SD 92105 1289-H2
SPINDLETOP RD
12500 SD 92129 1189-C5
SPINDLEWOOD CT
500 OCN 92054 1086-D2

SPINDRIFT CT
3400 OCN 92054 1086-E3
SPINDRIFT DR
700 SOLB 92014 1187-H1
700 SD 92014 1187-H1
1800 SD 92037 1227-G6
SPINDRIFT LN
800 CRLB 92011 1126-J5
SPINEFLOWER CT
3300 SD 92115 1270-D6
SPINEL AV
900 ELCJ 92021 1251-G2
SPINNAKER CT
100 DLMR 92014 1187-F6
SPINNAKER ST
\- CRLB 92011 1126-J7
SPINNAKER WY
\- CORD 92118 1329-E2
SPINNAKER BAY CT
4600 OCN 92057 1066-J6
SPINNAKER POINT TER
\- SD 92154 1330-J7
SPIRES ST
500 VSTA 92083 1087-F5
SPIRIT TR
4500 SDCo 91901 1275-A2
SPITFIRE RD
11200 SD 92126 1209-F1
SPLENDORWOOD PL
2100 ESCN 92026 1109-H4
SPLIT MOUNTAIN RD
5600 SDCo 92004 410-F10
E SPLITRAIL DR
500 ENCT 92024 1147-G5
SPLIT ROCK RD
19200 SDCo 92065 1172-B4
SPOKANE AV
3200 SD 92105 1269-G6
SPOKANE WY
600 ELCJ 92020 1251-G4
2700 CRLB 92010 1106-J4
SPOONBILL LN
7200 CRLB 92011 1127-D7
SPOON BILL WY
4200 OCN 92057 1086-J3
4200 OCN 92057 1087-A3
SPOONER CT
11100 SD 92131 1209-J1
SPORTFISHER DR
100 OCN 92054 1085-J7
200 OCN 92054 1086-A7
SPORTS ARENA BLVD
2300 SD 92110 1268-D5
SPOT DR
1500 SDCo 92021 1252-A2
SPRAY ST
2100 SD 92107 1267-J5
SPRIG PL
2400 SDCo 91906 (1297-F5 See Page 1296)
2600 SD 92123 1249-B7
SPRING AV
100 OCN 92057 1086-H2
SPRING CT
4200 SDCo 91941 1271-B4
SPRING DR
3800 SDCo 91977 1271-B5
SPRING LN
9100 SDCo 91941 1271-B4
SPRING PL
3900 SDCo 91977 1271-A5
SPRING RD
29000 SDCo 91962 1237-C7
SPRING ST
4200 LMSA 91941 1270-H2
4200 SDCo 91941 1270-J3
5000 LMSA 91942 1270-H2
5700 SDCo 91941 1271-A4
SPRING BROOK CT
3200 OCN 92054 1086-D3
SPRINGBROOK DR
12200 SD 92128 1190-A7
12200 SD 92131 1190-A7
12400 SD 92128 1189-J6
SPRING CANYON DR
8700 SDCo 91977 1291-A5
SPRING CANYON RD
\- SD 92145 1210-A2
9400 SD 92124 1230-F4
9400 SD 92145 1230-F4
10300 SD 92131 1189-H7
10500 SD 92131 1209-H1
11100 SD 92131 1210-A2
SPRING CANYON WY
\- OCN 92057 1086-J2
SPRING CREEK LN
1500 OCN 92057 1067-E7
SPRING CREEK RD
300 SMCS 92069 1108-H1
SPRINGDALE LN
1900 ENCT 92024 1147-H7
SPRINGER RD
1900 SD 92105 1289-H1
SPRINGFIELD AV
500 OCN 92057 1067-D6
8600 LMSA 91941 1271-A3
SPRINGFIELD CT
1200 VSTA 92083 1087-E6
SPRINGFIELD RD
\- SMCS 92078 1128-E6
SPRINGFIELD ST
6300 SD 92114 1290-D2
SPRING FLOWER DR
\- SDCo 92028 1028-A4
SPRINGFORD AV
7000 SD 92114 1290-F4
SPRING GARDEN PL
3300 SD 92102 1289-F4
SPRING GARDENS RD
4200 LMSA 91941 1270-J4
4200 LMSA 91941 1271-A4
SPRING GLEN LN
\- SDCo 91978 1291-E1
1300 SDCo 91977 1291-E1
SPRING GROVE LN
2300 SDCo 91977 1271-A7
SPRINGHURST DR
11900 SD 92128 1190-A6
SPRINGLAKE PL
700 ESCN 92027 1110-D5
SPRING MANOR CT
10100 SD 92126 1209-D5
SPRING MEADOW LN
11300 SD 92128 1189-J6
SPRING OAK WY
2200 SD 92139 1290-G6
SPRING OAKS PL
9700 SDCo 92021 1233-D3
SPRING OAKS RD
15900 SDCo 92021 1233-D2
SPRINGSIDE RD
11600 SD 92128 1189-J6
11600 SD 92128 1190-A6

SPRING SKY ST
\- CHV 91915 1331-G1
SPRINGS OF LIFE CT
\- SDCo 91977 1291-E1
SPRING STRAW LN
1800 CHV 91913 1311-E6
SPRING TIDE TER
\- SD 92110 1268-D6
SPRINGTIME DR
4400 OCN 92056 1087-D6
SPRINGTIME LN
2200 SDCo 92019 1252-D6
SPRINGTIME WY
700 SDCo 92019 1252-D6
SPRINGTREE PL
300 ESCN 92026 1109-H4
SPRINGVALE DR
8400 SNTE 92071 1230-J7
SPRINGVALE ST
14400 PWY 92064 1190-H4
SPRING VALLEY RD
\- SDCo 92061 1050-H4
SPRING VIEW CT
\- SDCo 92021 1232-H5
SPRINGVIEW LN
8700 LMSA 91941 1271-A3
SPRINGVIEW RD
1400 SDCo 92070 1135-E5
SPRING VIEW ST
9400 SDCo 91977 1271-C6
SPRING VISTA WY
8600 SDCo 91977 1290-J2
8600 SDCo 91977 1291-A2
SPRING WAGON RD
18300 SDCo 92065 1173-B2
18400 SDCo 92065 1153-C7
SPRINGWATER PT
12300 SD 92128 1189-H6
SPRINGWOOD DR
23600 SDCo 92065 1173-D3
SPRINGWOOD LN
900 ENCT 92024 1147-J5
SPRINT WY
\- SDCo 91935 1292-H2
SPRINTER LN
5600 SDCo 91902 1311-A2
SPRUANCE RD
4400 SD 92101 1288-D1
SPRUCE
9700 SDCo 92021 1233-B3
SPRUCE CT
200 CHV 91911 1330-G3
3500 OCN 92054 1086-F2
SPRUCE DR
\- SD 92102 1289-G4
100 SMCS 92069 1108-H5
SPRUCE LN
\- SD 92103 1268-J7
9700 SDCo 92029 1149-D3
13500 PWY 92064 1191-A3
SPRUCE RD
100 CHV 91911 1330-F5
28800 SDCo 91962 1237-C6
SPRUCE ST
300 CHV 91911 1330-G3
500 IMPB 91932 1329-F7
500 SD 92103 1269-A7
1400 SDCo 92082 1090-B1
2200 CRLB 92008 1106-E3
2800 SD 92104 1269-E7
5200 SD 92105 1270-A6
N SPRUCE ST
400 ESCN 92025 1129-G3
S SPRUCE ST
100 ESCN 92025 1129-H3
W SPRUCE ST
100 SD 92103 1269-A7
500 SD 92103 1268-J7
SPRUCE GROVE AV
10300 SD 92131 1210-B4
SPRUCE GROVE PL
12200 SD 92131 1210-B3
SPRUCE LAKE AV
6200 SD 92119 1250-G6
SPRUCE RUN DR
11300 SD 92131 1210-A1
11600 SD 92131 1209-J1
SPRUCEWOOD DR
200 ENCT 92024 1147-G7
SPRUCEWOOD LN
\- ESCN 92027 1130-H4
SPRUCE WOODLAND WY
\- SDCo 92026 1089-E4
SPUD MORENO ST
\- CALX 92231 6620-G5
SPUR AV
5600 OCN 92057 1067-F7
29700 SDCo 92084 1067-G7
SPUR CT
10300 SDCo 91941 1271-E4
SPUR LN
10500 SNTE 92071 1231-E5
SPUR POINT CT
\- SD 92130 1208-D2
SPYGLASS CIR
1700 VSTA 92081 1108-A4
1700 VSTA 92081 1107-J4
SPYGLASS CT
\- ENCT 92024 1147-E5
1800 CRLB 92008 1106-H6
SPYGLASS LN
17200 SDCo 92067 1168-H7
SPYGLASS PL
3600 OCN 92056 1107-C3
SPYGLASS TER
\- PWY 92064 1190-C1
SPYGLASS TR
28600 SDCo 92082 1090-B1
SQUAMISH RD
11200 SD 92126 1209-C2
SQUIRE PL
300 OCN 92054 1086-E6
SQUIRES PL
800 SDCo 92081 1107-F2
SQUIRREL RD
11300 SDCo 92040 1212-B5
STABLE RDG
400 ELCJ 92019 1252-D4
STABLE GLEN PL
\- SD 92130 1208-C2
STACEY AV
700 ELCN 92243 6499-G5
STACEY CT
1700 ELCN 92243 6499-F5
STACY AV
3800 SD 92117 1248-E4
STACY LN
1600 SDCo 92065 1172-J1
STACY PL
4300 SD 92117 1248-E4
STADDEN WY
\- VSTA 92084 1087-H6
STADIUM CT
3300 SD 92122 1228-D5

STADIUM PL
3400 SD 92122 1228-D6
STADIUM ST
5700 SD 92122 1228-D5
STADLER ST
8000 LMSA 91942 1250-H7
STAFFORD AV
300 ENCT 92007 1167-D3
STAFFORD PL
700 SD 92107 1287-J3
STAGE TER
800 SDCo 92028 1027-J1
STAGE COACH LN
\- PWY 92064 1170-F1
1600 SDCo 92028 997-J6
2000 SDCo 92028 998-D2
N STAGE COACH LN
100 SDCo 92028 1027-J1
1100 SDCo 92028 997-J7
S STAGE COACH LN
100 SDCo 92028 1027-H6
S STAGE COACH LN Rt#-S15
400 SDCo 92028 1027-J4
STAGECOACH PASS
\- SDCo 92127 1168-J1
\- SDCo 92127 1169-A1
STAGE COACH PL
\- SD 92129 1189-B4
STAGE COACH RD
300 OCN 92057 1086-G3
14200 PWY 92064 1150-J5
15000 PWY 92064 1151-A5
24400 SDCo 91963 429-L10
24400 SDCo 91963 (1316-B7 See Page 1296)
STAGECOACH RD
\- SDCo 92055 409-A7
\- SDCo 92055 1066-B1
STAGE COACH TR
900 SDCo 92036 1138-A5
13800 SDCo 92040 1232-E4
STAGECOACH TR
9300 SNTE 92071 1231-F5
STAGECOACH WY
500 SDCo 92004 1058-F2
STAGECOACH SPRINGS RD
\- SDCo 91962 (1299-B2 See Page 1298)
STAGECOACH TRAIL LP
1100 CHV 91915 1311-H6
STAGE STOP DR
12300 PWY 92064 1190-C7
STAGHORN CT
\- SDCo 92028 1048-C3
STAHL RD
\- ImCo 92227 431-C2
STALKER CT
1500 ELCJ 92020 1251-B3
STALLARD RD
\- ImCo - 412-A4
STALLION DR
200 OCN 92057 1067-B6
STALLION PL
300 CHV 91902 1310-H4
STALLION OAKS LN
\- SDCo 92019 1253-E5
STALLION OAKS RD
5800 SDCo 92019 1253-D5
STALLIONS LN
\- SD 92130 1208-D2
STALMER ST
7700 SD 92111 1249-A4
STAMEN CT
6300 SD 92114 1290-D5
STAMEN ST
1200 SD 92114 1290-D5
STAMNES RD
37600 SDCo 92086 409-K5
STAMPEDE AV
\- ImCo 92243 6560-A6
STAMPEDE WY
1200 CHV 91913 1311-E7
STANCREST LN
1400 NATC 91950 1310-B1
STANDEL LN
32400 SDCo 92026 1049-A6
STANDING ROCK RD
17400 SDCo 91935 1274-A3
STANDISH DR
12900 PWY 92064 1190-H4
STANDLAKE ST
1500 SD 92154 1350-A2
STANFIELD CIR
10400 SD 92126 1209-D4
STANFORD AV
800 CHV 91913 1311-D5
7000 LMSA 91941 1270-F3
STANFORD CT
31500 SDCo 92082 1070-F1
STANFORD DR
3700 OCN 92056 1087-A7
STANFORD ST
4300 CRLB 92010 1107-A4
STANISLAUS DR
1300 CHV 91913 1311-C7
1300 CHV 91913 1331-B1
STANLEY AV
200 ESCN 92026 1109-H4
500 SDCo 92026 1109-H4
6200 SD 92115 1270-D3
STANLEY CT
600 ELCJ 92019 1251-J6
600 ESCN 92026 1109-J7
10000 SNTE 92071 1231-D4
STANLEY DR
6100 LMSA 91942 1251-B6
STANLEY RD
\- ImCo - 411-D8
STANLEY ST
500 OCN 92054 1106-B1
E STANLEY WY
1200 ESCN 92027 1110-A6
STANSBURY ST
8400 SDCo 91977 1290-J2
STANTON RD
1800 ENCT 92024 1147-H7
4200 SD 92105 1289-H2
STANWELL CIR
10600 SD 92126 1209-C4
STANWELL CT
10600 SD 92126 1209-C4
STANWELL PL
10600 SD 92126 1209-C4
STANWELL ST
8600 SD 92126 1209-C4
STANWIX SQ
12100 SD 92128 1190-B3
STAPLES RD
15800 SDCo 92065 1174-A4
STAPLETON AV
\- IMP 92251 6499-D1

STAPLETON CT
\- IMP 92251 6499-D2
STAR AV
\- SDCo 91905 1300-C6
STAR LN
2000 SDCo 91901 1253-G1
STAR PL
\- SDCo 91901 1253-G1
E STAR RD
3200 SDCo 92004 (1078-J6 See Page 1058)
W STAR RD
3200 SDCo 92004 (1078-J6 See Page 1058)
STAR ACRES DR
3200 SDCo 91978 1272-B7
STAR ACRES LN
3200 SDCo 91978 1272-B7
3200 SDCo 92019 1272-B7
STARBEAM LN
17900 SDCo 92061 1051-F4
STARBOARD CIR
3500 OCN 92054 1086-F5
STARBOARD ST
\- CRLB 92011 1127-A7
STARBRIGHT LN
600 SDCo 91901 1234-B4
STARBURST LN
2100 SD 92154 1350-A1
STARCREST DR
9300 SNTE 92071 1251-B1
STAR CREST PL
\- SMCS 92078 1128-C6
STAR CREST RD
\- SDCo 91935 (1314-G2 See Page 1294)
STARDUST LN
13400 SDCo 92082 1070-D2
31500 SDCo 92082 1050-D7
STARFISH WY
5000 SD 92154 1330-H7
STARFLOWER RD
800 ENCT 92024 1147-F4
STARGAZE AV
8800 SD 92129 1189-C2
STARGAZE CT
\- SMCS 92078 1128-C5
STARGAZE DR
1500 CHV 91915 1311-H7
STARGAZE LN
29100 SDCo 92082 1070-H7
STARGAZE WY
2400 CHV 91915 1311-H7
STAR HAVEN DR
\- SDCo 92082 1070-G1
STARHAVEN LN
2500 SDCo 92084 1088-C6
STAR JASMINE LN
\- ENCT 92024 1147-A3
STARK LN
600 SDCo 92065 1153-A1
STARKEY WY
2500 SDCo 91901 1234-B3
STARLAND DR
8200 SDCo 92021 1252-C1
STARLIGHT AV
5500 OCN 92057 1067-D6
STARLIGHT CT
\- CHV 91915 1331-H1
STARLIGHT DR
1300 ENCT 92007 1167-D2
7700 SD 92037 1227-J5
STARLIGHT GN
2400 ESCN 92026 1109-B4
STARLIGHT LN
\- SMCS 92078 1128-E3
9500 SDCo 91941 1271-C1
STARLIGHT WY
\- SDCo 92036 1156-A7
\- SDCo 92036 1175-J1
\- SDCo 92036 1176-A1
STARLIGHT MOUNTAIN RD
1100 SDCo 92065 1153-E5
STARLING CT
1800 CRLB 92011 1127-D7
STARLING DR
500 VSTA 92083 1087-F4
7600 SD 92123 1249-B6
STARLING LN
200 OCN 92057 1086-H2
STARLING SIGHT RD
\- SDCo 92127 1169-G4
STARMOUNT WY
13300 PWY 92064 1170-E1
STAR PARK CIR
1100 CORD 92118 1288-H7
STAR PATH WY
\- OCN 92056 1087-A4
STAR PINE DR
\- LMGR 91945 1270-D7
\- SD 92114 1270-D7
STARPINE DR
8700 SNTE 92071 1230-G7
STARR RD
\- ImCo 92250 431-F4
STARRIDGE ST
13400 PWY 92064 1190-D3
STAR RUBY CT
\- ESCN 92027 1110-D6
STARRY WY
\- SD 92154 1350-G1
STARSHIP ST
\- SDCo 91934 (1320-J4 See Page 1300)
\- SDCo 91934 (1321-A2 See Page 1300)
STAR SHOWER LN
\- CHV 91915 1331-G1
STARSIDE LN
200 OCN 92056 1107-D3
STARSTONE DR
400 SMCS 92078 1108-C7
STARSTONE PL
600 SMCS 92078 1108-D7
STAR THISTLE LN
2400 SDCo 91901 1233-J5
STAR TRACK WY
3900 SDCo 92028 1048-F4
STARVALE LN
19300 SDCo 92065 1153-H2
STAR VALLEY RD
1400 SDCo 91901 1234-G6
STARVATION MOUNTAIN RD
18600 SDCo 92025 1151-A4
STARVIEW DR
1100 SDCo 92084 1088-D7
1100 SDCo 92084 1108-D1
8100 SDCo 92021 1252-B1
STARWOOD CIR
400 CHV 91910 1310-F5
STARWOOD LN
\- SD 92131 1210-D2

STREET / Block City ZIP Pg-Grid

STATE PL
100 ESCN 92029 1129-E3
STATE ST
- SD 92103 1268-H6
100 ELCN 92243 6499-E6
200 ELCN 92243 6500-A6
600 SD 92101 1289-A2
2000 SD 92101 1288-J1
2400 CRLB 92008 1106-D5
2600 SD 92103 1288-J1
STATE PARK RD
- SDCo 92060 1052-A1
STATE TREE DR
600 OCN 92054 1106-C1
STATICE CT
- CRLB 92011 1127-B4
STATION RD
- SDCo 92082 1091-C2
STATION VILLAGE LN
8200 SD 92108 1269-B2
STATION VILLAGE WY
- SD 92108 1269-C2
STATTON CT
1500 SD 92114 1290-F6
STEADMAN ST
10100 SD 92121 1208-G5
STEAMBOAT SPRINGS CT
2400 CHV 91915 1311-H7
STEBICK CT
12800 SD 92130 1188-C6
STEEL ST
3200 SD 92113 1289-F4
STEELE ST
600 ELCJ 92020 1251-E3
STEELE CANYON RD
2500 SDCo 92019 1272-C6
3200 SDCo 91978 1272-C6
STEELFISH LN
3700 OCN 92054 1086-G2
STEEL RANCH RD
- SDCo 91935 1274-F5
STEEN CIR
1400 VSTA 92083 1108-A2
STEEPLE GN
1200 ESCN 92029 1129-F5
STEEPLECHASE LN
- VSTA 92083 1087-D6
STEEPLECHASE RD
5900 SDCo 91902 1311-B2
STEEPLE CHASE RW
14200 SD 92130 1188-D2
STEEPLEGATE SQ
12700 SD 92130 1188-A6
STEFAS CT
900 CHV 91911 1330-J2
900 CHV 91911 1331-A2
STEFFY RD
200 SDCo 92065 1153-A7
300 SDCo 92065 1152-J7
STEIGER LN
2100 OCN 92056 1086-H7
2100 OCN 92056 1106-H1
STEINBECK AV
7200 SD 92122 1228-G4
STEINBECK CT
- CRLB 92008 1107-A7
- CRLB 92008 1127-A1
STEINER DR
1200 CHV 91911 1330-J2
STELLA CT
8000 SNTE 92071 1230-H7
STELLA ST
800 CHV 91911 1330-A4
800 SD 91911 1330-A4
STELLA MARIS LN
3900 CRLB 92010 1106-G6
STELLAR DR
3300 SD 92123 1249-E4
STEPHANIE LN
100 ELCJ 92019 1252-A5
100 VSTA 92084 1088-B5
STEPHANIE PL
4700 OCN 92057 1066-J6
4700 OCN 92057 1067-A6
STEPHANIE ST
- SMCS 92078 1128-E6
STEPHENS ST
4000 SD 92103 1268-H5
STEPHENS PORT
400 SDCo 92028 1047-F3
STEPPLING AV
- CALX 92231 6680-J2
STERLING AV
1200 CALX 92231 6620-G7
STERLING BRDG
700 SDCo 92028 1027-G6
STERLING CT
1500 ESCN 92029 1129-E2
4900 SD 92105 1270-A6
STERLING DR
7900 ELCJ 92021 1252-B1
7900 SDCo 92021 1252-B1
STERLING GROVE LN
4900 SD 92130 1208-D1
STERLING HILL LN
- SDCo 92040 1231-J6
STERLING RIDGE PL
2800 CHV 91915 1311-J6
2800 CHV 91915 (1312-A5 See Page 1293)
STERLING VIEW DR
900 SDCo 92028 1028-F1
STERN WY
- CRLB 92011 1146-J1
- CRLB 92011 1147-A1
STERNE ST
3000 SD 92106 1288-C1
3300 SD 92106 1268-C7
STETSON AV
3400 SD 92122 1228-D5
STETSON PL
1500 OCN 92057 1067-F7
6100 SD 92122 1228-D5
STETTLER WY
4100 SD 92122 1228-E5
STEUER WY
11700 SD 92131 1209-J2
STEVEMARK LN
3800 SDCo 91977 1271-E4
STEVEN CIR
2400 CRLB 92010 1106-H4
STEVEN LN
- OCN 92054 1086-G2
STEVENS AV
100 SOLB 92075 1167-F7
500 SOLB 92075 1187-G1
STEVENS AV W
- SOLB 92075 1167-F7
STEVENS PL
2100 ESCN 92027 1110-C4
STEVENS RD
- ImCo 92243 430-L6
9300 SNTE 92071 1231-F5

STEVENS WY
- SD 92114 1290-B4
- SDCo 92066 410-A9
STEVENSON CT
1500 SDCo 92069 1109-A3
1500 SMCS 92069 1109-A3
STEVENSON WY
7600 SD 92120 1250-E4
STEVENSON RANCH CT
- CHV 91914 1311-J2
STEVENS VISTA
15000 SDCo 92065 1172-J6
15000 SDCo 92065 1173-A6
STEWART CT
900 CHV 91911 1331-A2
1000 SD 92113 1289-G6
STEWART DR
500 VSTA 92083 1087-D7
STEWART PL
2300 ESCN 92027 1110-C6
STEWART ST
1300 OCN 92054 1106-C2
6200 SD 92115 1270-C3
STEWART CANYON RD
100 SDCo 92028 1028-G2
STEWART CREST RD
600 SDCo 92028 1028-H3
STICKLEY RANCH
10100 SDCo 92026 1089-E5
STILES CT
900 VSTA 92083 1087-F5
STILL BROOK LN
15400 SDCo 92061 1050-H3
STILLMAN PL
2000 SD 92139 1290-G6
STILLWATER CT
3300 CRLB 92010 1106-J3
STILL WATER GN
1700 ESCN 92026 1109-D4
STILLWATER RD
2300 SD 92101 1288-G1
STILLWATER COVE WY
800 OCN 92054 1066-E6
STILLWELL AV
900 SD 92114 1290-C5
STILSON LN
39900 SDCo 91905 1300-E6
STIMSON CT
8900 SD 92129 1189-C4
STINSON RD
2600 SDCo 92004 1100-A4
2700 SDCo 92004 (1099-H4 See Page 1098)
STIPA CT
8700 SD 92129 1189-C6
STIRLING AV
2700 CRLB 92010 1107-A5
STIRLING CT
2700 CRLB 92010 1107-A5
STIRRUP RD
2300 SDCo 92004 (1079-A2 See Page 1058)
STIRRUP WY
5400 OCN 92057 1067-D7
STITT AV
1800 SD 92101 1289-C2
STOCKALPER LN
400 SDCo 92065 1152-G5
STOCKETT WY
3000 SD 92117 1248-C3
STOCKMAN ST
3000 NATC 91950 1310-D3
STOCKTON LN
2400 SDCo 92084 1087-J1
STOCKTON PL
3500 CRLB 92010 1107-A3
STOCKWOOD CV
- SD 92131 1210-F1
STONE CT
5200 SD 92115 1270-A2
STONE DR
1200 SMCS 92078 1128-E1
STONE ST
- CORD 91932 1329-E5
STONEBRIDGE CT
3900 SDCo 92067 1167-H4
STONEBRIDGE LN
3900 SDCo 92067 1167-H4
STONEBRIDGE PKWY
- SD 92131 1191-A7
- SD 92131 1210-H1
- SD 92131 1211-A1
STONEBRIDGE RD
14800 SDCo 92027 1110-H7
15200 ESCN 92027 1110-H7
15200 ESCN 92027 1130-H1
15300 SDCo 92027 1111-A7
STONEBROOK LN
1800 ENCT 92024 1147-H6
STONE CALF CT
- ImCo 92243 6560-A6
STONE CANYON RD
700 CHV 91914 1311-G3
12500 SD 92128 1170-C5
12600 PWY 92064 1170-D4
STONE CASTLE
1900 SDCo 92028 1027-G6
STONECIPHER LN
2500 SDCo 91977 1271-C7
STONECREEK PL
2100 CHV 91913 1311-E3
STONECREST BLVD
9800 SD 92123 1249-F5
STONECREST CT
1900 VSTA 92081 1107-J4
STONECREST LN
1000 SDCo 92027 1130-B3
STONECROFT TER
- SD 92131 1210-E2
STONEDALE CT
11800 SD 92131 1210-A2
STONE EDGE CIR
1500 SDCo 92021 1251-G2
STONE EDGE CT
300 SDCo 92021 1251-G2
STONE EDGE DR
300 SDCo 92021 1251-G2
STONEFIELD CT
3500 SDCo 91935 1272-E5
STONEFIELD DR
3000 SDCo 91935 1272-E5
STONEGATE CT
900 CHV 91913 1331-A2
STONEGATE DR
28700 SDCo 92082 1090-B1
29000 SDCo 92082 1070-B7
STONEGATE PL
3500 SDCo 92028 1028-E2
STONE GATE ST
2600 CHV 91914 1311-H4
STONEHAVEN CT
- SDCo 92019 1272-B2
STONE HAVEN WY
10800 SD 92130 1208-E2

STONEHEDGE PL
1000 SMCS 92069 1109-B7
STONEHURST DR
10100 SDCo 92026 1109-E1
STONEMILL DR
- PWY 92064 1210-C1
STONEMONT PT
- SD 92131 1210-H2
STONEPINE LN
6600 SD 92139 1310-F1
STONE POINT LN
10200 SDCo 91977 1291-E2
STONEPOINTE DR
- ESCN 92025 1150-D3
STONE POST WY
700 SDCo 92028 997-G7
STONERIDGE CIR
1300 ESCN 92029 1129-G7
STONERIDGE CT
400 CHV 91902 1311-A4
1300 OCN 92056 1087-D3
STONERIDGE DR
1100 SDCo 91977 1290-J2
STONERIDGE RD
500 SDCo 92021 1253-A1
3800 CRLB 92010 1107-B3
STONERIDGE TER
200 VSTA 92083 1108-A2
STONERIDGE WY
- SMCS 92078 1128-G3
STONERIDGE COUNTRY CLUB LN
17100 PWY 92064 1170-E3
STONE VALLEY PL
2200 ESCN 92026 1109-J4
STONEVIEW CT
7400 SD 92119 1250-F3
STONEVIEW LN
2500 SDCo 91977 1271-D7
STONEWALL LN
1900 SDCo 92084 1088-C4
STONEWOOD WY
1200 SD 92154 1350-B1
STONEY LN
- SDCo 92036 1175-J2
STONEY WY
10600 SD 92131 1209-G2
STONEY ACRES RD
16000 PWY 92064 1170-E5
STONEYBRAE PL
500 ESCN 92027 1110-D5
STONEYBROOK LN
13200 SDCo 92021 1232-E7
STONEY CREEK CT
10700 SNTE 92071 1231-E2
STONEY CREEK RD
13500 SD 92129 1189-G3
STONEY GATE PL
13900 SD 92128 1189-J3
13900 SD 92128 1190-A2
STONEY OAK DR
3100 SDCo 91978 1292-C1
3100 SDCo 91978 1272-C7
STONEY PEAK DR
11700 SD 92128 1190-A1
STONEY POINT WY
400 OCN 92054 1086-B6
STONEYS LN
- ELCJ 92021 1251-G3
STONEY SPRING CT
1300 CHV 91913 1331-B1
STONINGTON WY
28200 SDCo 92026 1089-D3
STONYHURST CT
100 VSTA 92084 1087-H5
STONY KNOLL RD
100 SDCo 92019 1252-B5
100 ELCJ 92019 1252-B5
STONY RIDGE CT
- SD 92131 1209-G1
STONY RIDGE WY
- SD 92131 1209-G1
STORK ST
600 SD 92114 1290-D3
STORMY LN
1700 VSTA 92084 1088-B3
STOTLER CT
12500 PWY 92064 1190-D7
STOUTWOOD ST
12500 PWY 92064 1190-C1
STOWE DR
12300 PWY 92064 1190-C6
STOYER DR
9200 SNTE 92071 1231-B5
STRADA FRAGANTE
- SDCo 92091 1148-D6
STRADA RANCH RD
3900 SDCo 92070 1135-E6
STRAIGHTAWAY LN
- OCN 92057 1067-B3
STRAND ST
- CRLB 92011 1126-J5
STRAND WY
1600 CORD 92118 1308-J1
1700 CORD 92118 1309-A2
1700 CORD 92155 1309-A2
2600 SD 92109 1267-H1
3800 SD 92109 1247-H7
STRANSBURG CT
4600 OCN 92056 1107-F3
STRATA DR
3600 CRLB 92010 1107-B3
STRATFORD CIR
4500 OCN 92056 1107-D3
STRATFORD CT
100 DLMR 92014 1187-F5
1200 SMCS 92078 1128-B3
STRATFORD DR
500 ENCT 92024 1147-C7
600 ENCT 92024 1167-C1
STRATFORD LN
1100 CRLB 92008 1106-E4
STRATFORD PL
- VSTA 92081 1107-H5
STRATFORD WY
300 DLMR 92014 1187-F4
STRATFORD KNOLL
800 ENCT 92024 1148-A6
STRATFORD PARK CIR
200 DLMR 92014 1187-G7
STRATHMORE DR
10100 SNTE 92071 1231-A2
STRATTON AV
1000 SD 92113 1289-J5
STRATUS CT
7200 SD 92120 1250-D5
STRAWBERRY GN
800 ESCN 92025 1150-C1
STRAWBERRY LN
10300 SDCo 91977 1291-E2
STRAWBERRY PL
3500 OCN 92056 1107-A1
STRAWBERRY RD
14400 SDCo 92067 1188-E2

STRAWBERRY CREEK ST
- CHV 91913 1331-A2
STRAWBERRY HILL LN
900 SDCo 92084 1067-J7
STRAWBERRY VALLEY DR
1000 CHV 91913 1311-D6
STREAMVIEW DR
5000 SD 92105 1270-A6
5900 SD 92115 1270-C6
STREAMVIEW PL
3400 SD 92105 1270-A6
STREET A
100 VSTA 92083 1087-H7
STREIBY RD
1000 ImCo 92227 431-D2
STRESEMANN ST
5500 SD 92122 1228-B6
STROMBERG CIR
2400 CRLB 92010 1106-H5
STROMESA CT
7900 SD 92126 1209-B6
STRONG DR
3800 SD 92111 1248-J3
STROTHE RD
- SD 92152 1288-A4
STRUEDLE CT
1300 SD 92154 1350-A2
STU CT
4200 SD 92154 1350-F1
STUART AV
6900 LMSA 91941 1270-F4
STUART MESA RD
- SDCo 92055 408-L8
- SDCo 92055 1085-H1
STUDER RD
- ImCo 92251 431-C4
STUDIO LN
4600 OCN 92057 1087-B2
STURGEON CT
4100 SD 92130 1188-B5
STURGESS AV
7500 LMSA 91941 1270-G4
STURNELLA WY
14600 SDCo 92082 1070-G4
STURTEVANT ST
3100 SD 92136 1289-E7
SUBIDA TER
2100 CRLB 92009 1147-F1
SUBIDA AL CIELO
2100 SDCo 92084 1088-C1
SUBOL CT
2600 SD 92154 1330-C6
SUBURBAN HILLS DR
1100 SDCo 92027 1130-C4
SUCCESS AV
9300 SD 92123 1249-E4
SUDAN RD
12900 PWY 92064 1190-G4
SUDY ST
9100 LMSA 91942 1251-B6
SUE ST
3300 SD 92105 1270-B6
SUEMARK TER
1800 SDCo 92084 1088-C4
1800 VSTA 92084 1088-C4
SUERICH LN
7100 LMGR 91945 1270-F7
SUERTE DEL ESTE
18700 SDCo 92029 1148-F4
18700 SDCo 92091 1148-F4
SUFFOLK DR
3600 SD 92115 1270-E5
SUGAR BUSH CT
- CHV 91915 1331-G1
SUGARBUSH DR
900 SDCo 92084 1088-E7
1000 SDCo 92084 1108-E1
SUGARBUSH TER
3200 SDCo 92084 1088-E7
SUGAR BUSH WY
- SDCo 92082 1090-E4
SUGARLOAF DR
900 ESCN 92026 1109-F7
SUGARMAN CT
2800 SD 92037 1227-J4
SUGARMAN DR
8200 SD 92037 1228-A4
8500 SD 92037 1227-J4
SUGARMAN WY
2800 SD 92037 1227-J4
SUGAR MAPLE PL
- CHV 91915 1311-H2
SUGARPINE LN
2500 SDCo 92028 1028-D7
2500 SDCo 92028 1048-D1
SUGAR PINE PL
1400 CHV 91915 1311-J6
SUGAR PINE RD
1700 CRLB 92011 1127-E6
SUGAR PINE ST
700 OCN 92054 1086-F1
SUGAR PINE WY
- SDCo 92026 1089-F4
SUGARPLUM WY
- SDCo 92065 1174-B5
SUKAT CT
32300 SDCo 92061 1051-A6
SUKAT TR
32300 SDCo 92061 1051-A6
SULA WY
- SD 92139 1310-F1
SULLIVAN AV
6300 SD 92114 1290-D4
SULLIVAN CT
900 CHV 91911 1331-A1
SULLY WY
10200 SD 92126 1209-D5
SULTANA ST
200 SD 92105 1290-B1
SULZFELD WY
- ELCJ 92020 1251-F5
SUMAC CT
3200 SDCo 92028 1048-F2
SUMAC DR
2300 SD 92105 1289-H1
2400 SD 92105 1269-H7
SUMAC LN
800 CRLB 92011 1127-A6
SUMAC PL
- CHV 91915 1311-H1
800 ESCN 92027 1110-B7
4800 OCN 92057 1067-A7
SUMAC RD
3100 SDCo 92028 1048-F2
SUMAC TER
- SDCo 92082 1051-A7
SUMAC VW
- SDCo 92026 1089-B3
SUMAC SUMMIT
3800 SDCo 92028 998-F3
SUMATRA LN
100 SD 92114 1290-F5

SUMMER CT
- VSTA 92084 1088-A2
1000 ELCJ 92021 1251-H2
1000 SDCo 92021 1251-H2
SUMMER DR
2300 OCN 92056 1087-D6
SUMMER WY
3900 ESCN 92025 1150-C3
SUMMER BLOOM LN
- SDCo 92028 1028-A4
SUMMERBREEZE LN
12200 SD 92128 1170-B7
SUMMERBREEZE WY
14800 SD 92128 1170-B7
14800 SD 92128 1190-B1
SUMMER CREEK CT
- VSTA 92084 1088-B4
SUMMERCREEK WY
2300 ESCN 92029 1129-E6
SUMMERCREST LN
8700 SNTE 92071 1231-D7
SUMMERDALE RD
8400 SD 92126 1209-C3
SUMMERDALE WY
10900 SD 92126 1209-C3
SUMMERDAWN PL
1500 ENCT 92024 1147-G4
SUMMERFIELD CT
3600 SDCo 91977 1271-C5
SUMMERFIELD DR
3300 SDCo 91977 1271-C5
SUMMERFIELD LN
12600 PWY 92064 1170-D3
SUMMERFIELD PL
800 ESCN 92027 1130-E1
SUMMERFIELD ST
9500 SDCo 91977 1271-C5
SUMMER GLEN DR
1000 SDCo 92065 1152-C4
SUMMER GLEN VISTA
- SDCo 92021 1232-E5
SUMMERHILL AV
1100 CHV 91915 1311-G5
SUMMERHILL CT
400 SDCo 91901 1233-F6
800 ENCT 92024 1147-H5
SUMMERHILL DR
2100 ENCT 92024 1147-H5
5000 OCN 92057 1087-C2
SUMMER HILL LN
2400 SDCo 92028 1027-G7
SUMMERHILL PT
8800 SDCo 91901 1233-F6
SUMMERHILL TER
400 SDCo 91901 1233-F6
SUMMERHILL VW
400 SDCo 91901 1233-F6
SUMMERHOLLY DR
500 SMCS 92078 1128-G2
SUMMER HOLLY LN
900 ENCT 92024 1147-J5
SUMMER LAND RD
- SDCo 92003 1068-C4
SUMMER MOON RD
- SMCS 92078 1128-F6
SUMMER OAK RD
- SDCo 92066 409-L9
SUMMER PLACE DR
1700 SDCo 92021 1251-H2
SUMMER SAGE RD
15600 PWY 92064 1170-G4
SUMMERSET WY
3400 OCN 92056 1086-H7
SUMMERSHADE LN
11300 SD 92126 1209-E2
SUMMERSIDE LN
200 ENCT 92024 1147-H7
SUMMER SKY ST
- CHV 91915 1331-H1
SUMMERSONG CT
800 ENCT 92024 1147-H5
SUMMERSONG LN
700 ENCT 92024 1147-H5
SUMMERS RIDGE RD
- SD 92121 1208-H6
- SD 92126 1208-H6
SUMMERSUN LN
9800 SDCo 92040 1231-J4
SUMMERSUN PL
9800 SDCo 92040 1231-J4
SUMMERTIME DR
1600 SDCo 92021 1251-F1
SUMMERTREE LN
9900 SNTE 92071 1231-D7
SUMMER VIEW CIR
400 ENCT 92024 1147-D7
SUMMERVIEW CT
10100 SD 92126 1209-D5
SUMMERVIEW WY
- OCN 92056 1087-C6
SUMMERWIND PL
2300 CRLB 92008 1107-A7
SUMMERWOOD CT
10400 SD 92131 1210-A3
SUMMERWOOD LN
8000 LMGR 91945 1270-J7
SUMMIT AV
100 SDCo 92028 1027-E3
1200 ENCT 92007 1167-C2
10900 SNTE 92071 1211-D7
10900 SNTE 92071 1231-D1
SUMMIT CIR
9600 SDCo 91941 1271-C1
13500 PWY 92064 1170-E6
SUMMIT DR
1400 CHV 91910 1311-B5
1700 SDCo 92027 1130-D4
2000 SDCo 92025 1130-D5
4200 LMSA 91941 1270-H4
9800 SDCo 91941 1271-C1
SUMMIT GN
2500 ESCN 92026 1109-B3
SUMMIT LN
100 SDCo 92019 1253-D1
1600 SDCo 92025 1130-F6
24500 SDCo 92065 1236-A3
SUMMIT PL
1200 ENCT 92007 1167-C1
1600 SDCo 92025 1130-D5
4300 SD 92103 1268-J4
SUMMIT RD
100 SDCo 91917 429-J10
SUMMIT ST
400 OCN 92054 1086-A7
6200 SD 92114 1290-D3
SUMMIT TR
1000 SDCo 92025 1130-D5
1000 VSTA 92083 1108-A1
N SUMMIT CIRCLE GN
2200 ESCN 92026 1109-B4
S SUMMIT CIRCLE GN
2200 ESCN 92026 1109-B4
SUMMIT COVE LN
200 ENCT 92007 1167-C1

SUMMIT CREST
14000 SDCo 92025 1130-F6
SUMMIT CREST DR
10200 SNTE 92071 1231-D1
SUMMIT HILL DR
1800 SDCo 92027 1130-E4
SUMMIT MEADOW RD
3200 SDCo 91902 1291-B7
SUMMIT POINT WY
- SMCS 92078 1128-A3
SUMMIT RIDGE DR
1900 SDCo 92027 1130-E4
SUMMIT RIDGE WY
6800 SD 92120 1250-D4
SUMMITSIDE LN
10000 SDCo 91977 1271-D7
SUMMITVIEW LN
2600 SDCo 91977 1271-D7
SUMMIT VISTA DR
- SDCo 92127 1169-E3
SUMNER AV
1000 SDCo 92021 1251-H3
1000 ELCJ 92021 1251-H3
SUMNER PL
1000 SDCo 92021 1251-J3
SUMNER WY
- OCN 92054 1066-G7
- OCN 92054 1086-G1
SUMTER ST
3300 SD 92117 1248-E5
SUN CIR
- VSTA 92081 1107-J3
SUN CT
300 SDCo 92021 1251-F1
SUN ST
6900 SD 92111 1248-J6
SUN AND SHADOWS DR
400 SDCo 92004 (1078-H2 See Page 1058)
SUN AND SHADOWS LN
2500 SDCo 92004 (1078-H3 See Page 1058)
SUNBEAM RD
300 SDCo 92028 1027-F4
SUNBIRD CT
300 SMCS 92069 1108-J7
SUNBIRD WY
3500 SD 92124 1249-G4
SUNBRIGHT CT
5000 OCN 92056 1087-E2
SUNBRIGHT DR
1100 OCN 92056 1087-E2
SUNBRITE LN
9500 SDCo 92040 1232-A4
SUNBURST DR
1600 SDCo 92021 1252-A2
4400 OCN 92056 1087-D5
SUNBURST LN
500 CHV 91911 1330-H1
SUNBURST RD
4600 CRLB 92008 1106-H7
SUNBURY CT
1500 SDCo 92084 1108-B2
SUNBURY ST
1800 ESCN 92026 1109-D5
SUNCREEK DR
700 CHV 91913 1311-D4
SUNCREST AV
1900 OCN 92056 1087-E2
SUNCREST BLVD
1900 SDCo 92021 1252-G4
SUNCREST CT
5000 OCN 92056 1087-E2
SUNCREST DR
2900 SD 92116 1269-E3
7800 LMSA 91941 1270-H3
SUNCREST VISTA LN
- SDCo 91901 1234-D6
SUNCUP WY
- CRLB 92024 1147-E2
SUNDALE RD
1100 SDCo 92019 1271-J2
1100 SDCo 92019 1272-A2
SUNDANCE AV
- SMCS 92078 1128-D6
12500 SD 92129 1189-D4
SUNDANCE CIR
2300 OCN 92056 1087-D5
SUNDANCE CT
700 CHV 91911 1330-H1
9000 SD 92129 1189-D4
SUNDANCE DR
200 SDCo 92028 1028-A6
17200 SDCo 92065 1171-G2
SUNDANCE RD
13400 SDCo 92082 1070-D1
SUNDANCE WY
1400 OCN 92057 1067-E6
SUNDANCE VIEW LN
- SDCo 91916 1235-H1
SUNDAY DR
13800 SDCo 92082 1090-E4
SUNDERLAND ST
12900 PWY 92064 1190-H5
SUNDEVIL WY
9500 SD 92129 1189-E3
SUNDIAL CT
- OCN 92057 1067-A4
SUNDIAL PL
- CRLB 92011 1127-A7
SUNDIAL TER
1400 SDCo 92021 1252-A2
SUNDOWN DR
16600 SDCo 92082 1051-C7
SUNDOWN GN
1200 ESCN 92026 1129-G1
1200 ESCN 92026 1109-G7
SUNDOWN LN
1100 CHV 91911 1330-H1
4000 SDCo 91941 1271-G4
N SUNDOWN LN
10900 OCN 92056 1107-C2
S SUNDOWN LN
3400 OCN 92056 1107-C2
SUNDOWNER CT
- SD 92126 1209-D6
SUNDRIFT CT
5000 OCN 92056 1087-E2
SUNDROP CT
1200 CHV 91911 1330-H2
SUN ENERGY RD
16700 SDCo 92082 1091-C3
SUNFISH LN
300 OCN 92054 1086-G2
SUNFISH WY
- SDCo 91906 (1297-G4 See Page 1296)
SUNFLOWER CT
- ELCN 92243 6559-J3
SUNFLOWER GN
300 ESCN 92026 1109-H5
SUNFLOWER LN
9400 SDCo 92029 1129-C7

SUNFLOWER ST
700 ENCT 92024 1147-E6
SUNFLOWER TER
2400 SDCo 92083 1108-C4
SUNFLOWER WY
800 CRLB 92011 1127-A5
SUNFLOWER GLEN CT
3100 SDCo 91935 1272-D5
SUNGLOW CT
1200 OCN 92056 1087-E2
5300 SD 92117 1228-H7
SUNGLOW DR
1100 OCN 92056 1087-E2
8200 SDCo 92021 1232-B7
8200 SDCo 92021 1252-B1
SUNGOLD WY
- ESCN 92027 1110-D5
SUNGROVE CT
- SDCo 92019 1272-B2
SUNHAVEN CT
- SDCo 91901 1234-C6
SUNHAVEN RD
- SDCo 91901 1234-C6
SUN KING RD
- SD 92126 1209-D6
SUNKIST DR
2700 SDCo 92084 1088-D7
2700 SDCo 92084 1108-D1
SUNLIGHT CT
1900 OCN 92056 1087-F2
SUNLINE AV
4700 SD 92117 1248-C1
4900 SD 92117 1228-C7
SUNLIT WY
- SDCo 92065 1152-J5
SUN MAIDEN CT
18200 SD 92127 1149-H7
SUN MEADOW DR
600 ELCJ 92020 1271-E1
SUNMEADOW RD
5000 OCN 92056 1087-F3
SUNNINGDALE DR
600 OCN 92057 1066-G7
SUNNINGDALE WY
- SDCo 92082 1090-G4
SUNNY DR
- ENCT 92024 1147-C6
SUNNY LN
13400 SDCo 92040 1232-D4
SUNNY PT
- SDCo 92070 1135-D4
SUNNY ACRES AV
1300 SDCo 91901 1234-G5
SUNNY BRAE DR
6300 SD 92119 1250-F6
SUNNY BRAE PL
7100 SD 92119 1250-F6
SUNNYBROOK LN
700 SDCo 92021 1232-J7
700 SDCo 92021 1252-J1
SUNNY CREEK RD
2700 CRLB 92010 1107-C7
SUNNY CREST CIR
1200 VSTA 92084 1087-J4
SUNNY CREST LN
1700 CHV 91902 1311-C4
SUNNYCREST LN
2000 SDCo 92028 1028-A7
SUNNYDALE CT
11200 SD 92127 1169-J4
SUNNYFIELD PL
15800 SD 92127 1169-H5
SUNNY HEIGHTS RD
1300 SDCo 92028 998-C7
SUNNY HILL CT
900 SDCo 92028 1027-H1
SUNNYHILL DR
4000 CRLB 92008 1106-H6
SUNNY HILLS CT
700 SDCo 92065 1152-E5
SUNNY HILLS RD
4700 OCN 92056 1087-D4
SUNNYLAND AV
1400 ELCJ 92019 1252-A6
SUNNY MEADOW CT
10900 SD 92126 1208-J3
SUNNY MEADOW ST
10800 SD 92126 1208-J3
SUNNY MESA RD
10900 SD 92121 1208-G3
SUNNYRIDGE DR
- SDCo 92026 1089-B2
SUNNYRIDGE RD
7400 SNTE 92071 1230-F7
SUNNYSIDE AV
- SMCS 92078 1128-E6
300 SD 92114 1290-H3
1900 SDCo 92019 1252-C5
SUNNYSIDE CT
- ImCo 92249 6560-C7
SUNNYSIDE DR
5100 SDCo 91902 1310-H1
SUNNYSIDE LN
11300 SDCo 92026 1089-H6
SUNNY SLOPE DR
1900 SDCo 92027 1130-D4
SUNNYSLOPE LN
9700 SDCo 92029 1149-D4
SUNNY SLOPE TER
1800 SDCo 92027 1130-D4
SUNNY VIEW DR
5700 SDCo 91902 1311-A1
SUNNY VISTA LN
1900 SDCo 92069 1108-H2
1900 SMCS 92069 1108-H2
SUN RAY CT
11500 SD 92131 1210-B1
SUNRAY LN
4200 SDCo 91941 1271-G4
SUNRAY PL
10900 SDCo 91941 1271-G4
SUNRICH LN
800 ENCT 92024 1147-C3
SUNRIDGE DR
400 OCN 92056 1087-E2
8500 SNTE 92071 1230-H7
SUNRIDGE PL
400 ESCN 92026 1109-G4
SUNRISE AV
8400 LMSA 91941 1271-A3
8400 LMSA 91941 1270-J3
SUNRISE CIR
200 SDCo 92084 1088-C6
1500 CRLB 92008 1106-G6
SUNRISE CT
12200 PWY 92064 1190-B1
SUNRISE DR
- ImCo 92274 410-H7
300 SD 92173 1350-G5
400 SDCo 92084 1088-C6
400 VSTA 92084 1088-B7
1200 SDCo 92036 1136-D6
14800 PWY 92064 1170-B7
14800 PWY 92064 1190-B1

STREET Block City ZIP Pg-Grid

SUNRISE DR E
400 SDCo 92084 1088-C7
SUNRISE HWY Rt#-S1
6800 SDCo 91962 430-A6
6800 SDCo 91962 1237-G3
6800 SDCo 91948 1237-G3
9500 SDCo 91948 430-B5
10500 SDCo 91948 1218-A1
12200 SDCo 91948 (1217-J1 See Page 1216)
12300 SDCo 91948 (1197-F4 See Page 1176)
14100 SDCo 92036 1176-G2
14300 SDCo 92036 (1177-B6 See Page 1176)
14700 SDCo 92036 (1197-F4 See Page 1176)
SUNRISE LN
8700 LMSA 91941 1270-J3
8700 LMSA 91941 1271-A3
SUNRISE PL
300 SDCo 92084 1088-B6
SUNRISE RDG
4500 OCN 92056 1087-D4
SUNRISE ST
3300 SD 92102 1289-F3
SUNRISE WY
- ESCN 92029 1149-G1
- SDCo 92029 1149-H1
1100 SMCS 92078 1128-E3
SUNRISE BLUFF DR
- SD 92154 1350-J2
SUNRISE CANYON RD
14600 PWY 92064 1190-G3
SUNRISE CREST CT
- CHV 91915 (1312-A5 See Page 1293)
SUNRISE HILLS DR
4800 SDCo 92020 1271-H2
SUNRISE MOUNTAIN DR
1200 SDCo 92026 1109-J3
SUNRISE MOUNTAIN RD
1200 SDCo 92021 1252-J3
SUNRISE RANCH LN
- SDCo 91906 (1297-H6 See Page 1296)
SUNRISE RANCH RD
14100 PWY 92064 1190-H3
SUNRISE SHADOW CT
1500 ELCJ 92019 1252-A7
SUNRISE SUMMIT
11600 SDCo 92040 1231-H6
SUNRISE TRAIL PL
- CHV 91914 1311-G2
SUNRISE VALLEY DR
4800 SDCo 92020 1271-H2
SUNRISE VIEW DR
2100 SDCo 92028 1048-B1
SUNRISE VISTA
16900 SDCo 92065 1151-E6
SUNROAD BLVD
- SDCo 92154 1352-A1
SUNROSE CT
5000 OCN 92056 1087-E2
SUNSET AV
900 IMPB 91932 1349-H3
900 SD 92154 1349-H3
1600 SD 92154 1350-A3
9400 SDCo 91941 1271-C1
SUNSET BLVD
1700 SD 92103 1268-H5
SUNSET CT
600 SMCS 92069 1108-J5
700 SD 92109 1267-H1
SUNSET DR
- ESCN 92025 1130-A5
- IMP 92251 6439-F3
100 ENCT 92024 1147-B6
500 OCN 92054 1085-J5
500 VSTA 92081 1107-H2
600 OCN 92054 1086-A5
1300 SDCo 92081 1107-D2
1800 ELCN 92243 6499-D6
1900 OCN 92056 1107-D2
2000 SDCo 92025 1130-B6
2200 SDCo 92036 1136-C6
3100 ESCN 92025 1150-B3
3200 SDCo 92028 1047-H2
3400 SDCo 92036 1156-E1
7700 LMSA 91941 1270-G2
15700 PWY 92064 1170-H5
SUNSET LN
2200 SDCo 92036 1156-F7
3500 SD 92173 1350-E3
11800 SDCo 92040 1251-J1
SUNSET PT
- SDCo 91901 1234-A6
SUNSET RD
500 SDCo 92004 (1078-J3 See Page 1058)
4000 SD 92103 1268-G5
8100 SDCo 92021 1251-J1
8100 SDCo 92040 1251-J1
8300 SDCo 92040 1231-J7
28300 SDCo 92082 1091-B1
28600 SDCo 92082 1071-B7
SUNSET ST
2600 SD 92110 1268-F4
SUNSET TER
7900 LMGR 91945 1290-H2
16200 SDCo 92082 1091-B1
SUNSET TR
10900 SNTE 92071 1231-F7
SUNSET WY
- ImCo - 412-A3
- OCN 92054 1086-E1
16100 SDCo 92082 1071-B7
SUNSET BLUFFS WY
4400 SD 92130 1188-C6
SUNSET CLIFFS BLVD
- SD 92109 1268-A5
700 SD 92107 1287-H1
1400 SD 92107 1267-H7
2100 SD 92107 1268-A5
SUNSET CREST WY
- SD 92121 1208-F3
SUNSET CROSSING PT
- SD 92154 1330-J7
SUNSET GROVE RD
1200 SDCo 92028 1047-J3
1300 SDCo 92028 1048-A2
SUNSET HEIGHTS CT
- SD 92130 1188-C5
SUNSET HEIGHTS RD
- SDCo 92026 1109-E6
1000 ESCN 92026 1109-E6
SUNSET HILL DR
1800 CRLB 92008 1106-H7
SUNSET HILLS
2600 SDCo 92025 1150-E1
21200 SD 92025 1150-E1
SUNSET KNOLLS RD
11600 SDCo 92040 1231-H4

SUNSET MOUNTAIN WY
15700 PWY 92064 1170-H5
SUNSET OAKS
19400 SDCo 92065 1153-D2
SUNSET PEAK
- SDCo 92059 409-E5
SUNSET POINT CT
1600 CHV 91911 1330-J4
SUNSET POINT PL
- SD 92130 1188-C5
SUNSET POINT WY
- SD 92130 1188-C4
SUNSET RIDGE DR
10500 SD 92131 1210-A2
10600 SD 92131 1209-J2
SUNSET RIDGE PL
800 CHV 91914 1311-J3
SUNSET ROSE CT
- SDCo 92019 1272-B2
SUNSET VALLEY RD
- SDCo 91901 1233-J3
SUNSET VIEW DR
- SDCo 92036 1136-A7
SUNSET VIEW RD
13500 PWY 92064 1190-H3
SUNSET VISTA LN
27500 SDCo 92082 1091-E3
SUNSHINE AV
100 ELCJ 92020 1251-F6
SUNSHINE LN
100 SMCS 92069 1108-H6
SUNSHINE TR
1200 SDCo 92036 1136-C5
SUNSHINE MOUNTAIN RD
2100 SDCo 92069 1108-H1
SUNSHINE PEAK CT
11800 SD 92131 1190-A7
11800 SD 92131 1210-A1
SUNSHINE VALLEY LN
19300 SDCo 92065 1153-G3
SUNSHINE VALLEY RD
19000 SDCo 92065 1153-F2
SUNSTONE DR
- SDCo 92127 1169-F4
SUNSTONE PT
- SD 92130 1188-E4
SUN SUMMIT PT
16000 SD 92127 1169-J5
SUNSWEPT ST
200 SD 92114 1290-F5
SUNTREE PL
8400 SD 92119 1250-J2
SUN UP CT
3100 SDCo 91902 1311-B1
SUN VALLEY LN
15100 SDCo 92014 1168-A7
SUN VALLEY RD
- CHV 91915 1311-G6
- SMCS 92078 1128-A2
1200 SOLB 92075 1167-H6
4700 SDCo 92014 1168-A7
4800 SDCo 92014 1167-J7
SUNVIEW DR
8300 SDCo 92021 1252-B1
8300 SDCo 92021 1232-B7
SUNVIEW PL
- OCN 92057 1067-B3
SUN VILLA CT
- VSTA 92084 1088-C5
SUN WALK CT
17800 SD 92127 1149-H7
17800 SD 92127 1169-H1
SUNWEST GN
- ESCN 92025 1130-A6
SUNWOOD DR
8900 SNTE 92071 1231-A6
SUNWOOD TR
12200 PWY 92064 1190-B6
SUPALE RANCH RD
38600 SDCo 92028 997-B4
SUPERBA ST
3800 SD 92113 1289-G4
SUPERIOR ST
600 ESCN 92029 1129-F3
3800 SD 92113 1289-G4
SUPERIOR HOLLOW RD
30100 SDCo 92082 1070-B4
SUPREME CT
300 SMCS 92078 1129-B2
SURCO DR
11300 SD 92126 1209-B2
SURF PL
3500 OCN 92056 1107-C2
SURF RD
200 ENCT 92024 1147-A3
SURFBIRD CIR
- CRLB 92011 1127-C6
SURFBIRD WY
900 OCN 92057 1087-A3
SURFBREAKER PT
5000 SD 92154 1350-J1
SURFCLIFF PT
4900 SD 92154 1350-J1
SURF CREST DR
1200 SD 92154 1350-H1
SURF CREST ST
- CRLB 92011 1127-C5
SURFLINE WY
3600 OCN 92056 1107-C3
SURFPOINT WY
- SD 92154 1350-J1
SURFRIDER WY
100 OCN 92054 1085-J7
300 OCN 92054 1086-A7
SURF SHOAL PT
5000 SD 92154 1350-J1
SURFSIDE DR
5000 SD 92154 1350-J1
SURFSIDE LN
6400 CRLB 92011 1126-H5
SURFTIDE LN
1300 SD 92154 1350-J1
SURFVIEW CT
300 DLMR 92014 1187-F6
SURFWOOD LN
1100 SD 92154 1350-J1
SURREALIST CT
4800 OCN 92057 1087-B2
SURREY CT
5700 OCN 92057 1067-F6
SURREY DR
200 CHV 91902 1310-G4
14500 PWY 92064 1190-F1
SURREY HTS
1400 SDCo 92028 1027-J4
SURREY LN
2700 SDCo 92029 1129-C3
SURREY PL
200 CHV 91902 1310-G4
SURREY TR
700 SDCo 92036 1138-B7
SURREY HILLS CT
17000 PWY 92064 1170-D2

SURVEY PT
13000 SD 92130 1187-J5
SUSAN CIR
3000 OCN 92056 1107-B1
SUSAN CT
1100 SD 92154 1350-E1
2000 SDCo 92026 1109-E6
SUSAN LN
1000 SDCo 92065 1152-D5
SUSAN PL
2200 SD 92105 1290-A1
SUSANA CT
1000 SDCo 92078 1128-G4
SUSIE LN
10800 SNTE 92071 1231-E3
SUSIE PL
10400 SNTE 92071 1231-E3
SUSIE WY
19300 SDCo 92065 1172-C2
SU SIEMPRE PL
2900 ESCN 92025 1150-B1
SUSITA CT
11100 SD 92129 1169-J7
SUSITA ST
15100 SD 92129 1169-J7
SUSITA TER
11100 SD 92129 1169-J7
SUSQUEHANNA PL
4300 SD 92117 1248-E1
SUSSEX DR
4800 SD 92116 1269-G3
SUTHERLAND DR
20600 SDCo 92065 409-H11
SUTHERLAND ST
3400 SD 92110 1268-G6
SUTHERLAND DAM RD
20600 SDCo 92065 409-H11
SUTTER CT
400 SMCS 92069 1109-C7
3600 OCN 92056 1107-F4
SUTTER LN
1200 SMCS 92069 1109-C7
SUTTER ST
600 SD 92103 1268-H6
2600 CRLB 92010 1106-J5
SUTTER BUTTES ST
- CHV 91913 1311-E7
SUTTER MILL RD
13200 PWY 92064 1190-G4
SUTTER MILL WY
14200 PWY 92064 1190-G4
SUTTER RIDGE CT
1000 CHV 91914 1311-J4
SUTTER RIDGE DR
2700 CHV 91914 1311-J4
SUTTER RIDGE WY
- CHV 91914 1311-J4
SUTTON CT
9700 SNTE 92071 1231-B4
SUTTON HILL PL
700 SDCo 92028 1027-H3
SUZANNE LN
- CHV 91911 1330-E4
700 SDCo 92026 1129-E2
SVEA CT
1600 LMGR 91945 1290-G2
SWALERO RD
- ELCJ 92020 1251-A6
6200 LMSA 91942 1251-A6
SWALLOW DR
900 VSTA 92083 1087-F4
1300 ELCJ 92020 1251-C2
SWALLOW LN
100 OCN 92057 1086-H2
1900 CRLB 92009 1127-E5
1900 CRLB 92011 1127-E5
SWALLOWTAIL CT
1200 ENCT 92024 1147-D2
SWALLOWTAIL RD
1700 ENCT 92024 1147-D2
SWAMIS LN
- ENCT 92024 1147-D7
SWAN DR
30000 SDCo 91906 (1297-G5 See Page 1296)
SWAN RD
18600 SDCo 92065 1153-E5
SWAN ST
1800 SD 92114 1290-D1
SWAN CANYON CT
12500 SD 92131 1210-C2
SWAN CANYON PL
12500 SD 92131 1210-C2
SWAN CANYON RD
11300 SD 92131 1210-C2
SWANER ST
1000 SD 92114 1290-C2
SWAN LAKE DR
- SD 92131 1209-G1
SWANSEA GN
- ESCN 92027 1110-D7
SWANSEA PL
10900 SD 92126 1209-A3
SWANSON CT
11100 SD 92131 1209-J1
SWANTON DR
10100 SNTE 92071 1231-A3
SWARTHMORE ST
5300 LMSA 91942 1270-G1
SWARTZ CANYON RD
16200 SDCo 92065 1173-E3
SWATH CT
9900 SD 92129 1189-F5
SWATH PL
12900 SD 92129 1189-F5
SWEENEY CT
1500 SDCo 92019 1272-E2
SWEENEY PASS RD Rt#-S2
- SDCo 92036 430-E4
- SDCo 92259 430-E4
SWEET LN
22000 SDCo 92065 1153-G6
SWEET RD
- ImCo 92251 431-A3
SWEET ALICE LN
100 ENCT 92024 1147-E7
SWEETBRIAR CIR
1400 CRLB 92011 1127-A4
SWEETBRIAR LN
11800 SD 92131 1210-A2
SWEET FENNEL RD
600 SMCS 92078 1128-G2
SWEETGRASS CT
2500 SDCo 92003 1048-A6
SWEETGRASS LN
4800 SDCo 92003 1048-A6
SWEET GUM PL
- CHV 91915 1311-H2
SWEET LIME RD
1100 SDCo 92084 1068-A5
SWEET PEA LN
- CHV 91915 1331-G1

SWEET PEA PL
- ENCT 92024 1147-C5
SWEET SAGE ST
- CHV 91915 1331-H1
SWEETSHADE ST
100 OCN 92054 1066-G7
SWEET TREE LN
- SDCo 92084 1068-D5
SWEETWATER DR
- LMGR 91945 1290-J1
SWEETWATER GN
1300 ESCN 92026 1129-G1
1300 ESCN 92026 1109-G7
SWEETWATER LN
1100 SDCo 91977 1291-B2
SWEETWATER RD
500 SDCo 91977 1291-A3
1100 SDCo 91977 1290-J1
1400 CHV 91950 1310-B3
1400 NATC 91950 1310-B3
2100 SDCo 91950 1310-B3
2100 SDCo 91977 1270-J6
2800 LMGR 91945 1270-J6
2800 LMGR 91977 1270-J6
2800 SDCo 91945 1270-J6
3400 SDCo 91902 1310-G2
3900 CHV 91902 1310-G2
SWEETWATER RD Rt#-S17
5300 SDCo 91902 1290-J6
5300 SDCo 91902 1310-H1
5600 SDCo 91902 1291-A7
SWEETWATER ST
- CRLB 92011 1126-J6
SWEETWATER WY
3100 LMGR 91945 1270-J5
SWEETWATER SPRINGS BLVD
2500 SDCo 91978 1291-F1
2800 SDCo 91977 1271-E6
2800 SDCo 91977 1291-F1
2800 SDCo 91978 1271-E6
SWEETWAY CT
8300 SDCo 91977 1290-J5
SWEET WILLOW WY
- SD 92131 1210-H1
SWEETWOOD ST
200 SD 92114 1290-E4
SWIFT AV
3600 SD 92104 1269-F4
4400 SD 92116 1269-F4
SWIFT LN
1400 ELCJ 92020 1251-D2
SWIFT PL
- CRLB 92008 1127-C2
SWINGING V RD
3300 SDCo 92004 (1079-A6 See Page 1058)
SWITZER DR
8900 SDCo 91977 1271-A6
SWITZER ST
400 SD 92101 1289-B5
SWITZERLAND DR
1400 SD 92154 1350-A2
SWORD WY
13300 SD 92130 1188-C4
SYBIL CT
1200 SDCo 92026 1109-E6
SYCAMORE AV
100 CRLB 92008 1106-E6
300 VSTA 92083 1108-B4
500 SDCo 92083 1108-B4
500 VSTA 92081 1108-A6
1300 VSTA 92081 1107-H7
14000 PWY 92064 1190-F2
SYCAMORE CT
1000 IMP 92251 6439-G4
3300 SD 92037 1228-B4
SYCAMORE DR
1100 SDCo 92028 1047-J2
1600 CHV 91911 1330-F5
1700 SMCS 92069 1108-J3
1800 SDCo 92069 1109-A2
1800 SMCS 92069 1109-A2
2000 SDCo 92069 1108-J3
2600 OCN 92056 1087-F5
3900 SD 92105 1289-G1
4100 SD 92105 1269-H7
24600 SDCo 91916 1236-A2
SYCAMORE HTS
1300 SDCo 92028 1047-J2
SYCAMORE LN
- SDCo 92026 1089-A2
800 ELCJ 92019 1252-C4
800 SDCo 92019 1252-C4
3000 ESCN 92025 1130-C7
3500 SDCo 92028 1028-F4
SYCAMORE PL
1500 SDCo 92028 1047-J2
SYCAMORE RD
200 SD 92173 1350-G5
SYCAMORE WY
1600 SDCo 92028 1047-J2
SYCAMORE CANYON RD
- SD 92145 1211-C2
- SDCo 92145 1211-C2
13200 PWY 92064 1190-J4
13400 PWY 92064 1191-A6
15000 SD 92131 1191-A6
15000 SDCo 92071 1191-C7
15200 SDCo 92064 1191-A6
15400 SD 92071 1191-C7
15400 SDCo 92131 1191-C7
16300 SDCo 92071 1211-C2
SYCAMORE CREEK RD
17900 PWY 92064 1150-E6
18300 SD 92025 1150-E6
18300 SD 92128 1150-E6
SYCAMORE CREST PL
- ESCN 92027 1110-G7
SYCAMORE HEIGHTS PL
- ESCN 92027 1110-F7
SYCAMORE PARK DR
- SDCo 92071 1191-E7
SYCAMORE RIDGE CT
- SD 92131 1210-C3
SYCAMORE SPRINGS RD
20500 SDCo 91935 (1314-J1 See Page 1294)
20500 SDCo 91935 (1315-A1 See Page 1294)
SYCAMORE TRAIL RD
- SD 92131 1210-H2
SYCAMORE TREE LN
13600 PWY 92064 1190-E3
SYCAMORE VALLEY RD
13300 PWY 92064 1191-A4
SYCAMOREVIEW DR
1100 ENCT 92024 1167-F2
SYCHAR RD
100 SD 92114 1290-F4
S SYCHAR RD
100 SD 92114 1290-F4

SYCUAN RD
2000 SDCo 92019 1253-C6
SYCUAN SUMMIT DR
1000 SDCo 92019 1252-H6
SYDNEY CT
- SD 92122 1228-E2
SYDNEY PL
3500 SD 92116 1269-F2
SYDNEY TER
1700 ELCJ 92021 1252-C2
1700 SDCo 92021 1252-C2
SYDNEY RAE PL
- SD 92129 1189-A3
SYDNEY VIEW WY
- SDCo 92028 1028-D1
SYLVAN LN
3000 SDCo 92026 1109-H2
SYLVESTER RD
- SD 92106 1288-A7
- SD 92106 1308-A1
- SD 92152 1308-B3
SYLVIA CT
- IMP 92251 6499-H2
SYLVIA ST
300 ENCT 92024 1147-B6
2800 SDCo 91902 1290-J7
3000 SDCo 91902 1310-J1
SYLVIE CT
3600 SDCo 92084 1088-F7
SYLVIS WY
- SMCS 92078 1108-C6
SYLVY WY
2700 SD 92139 1310-F1
SYME DR
3900 CRLB 92008 1106-G6
SYMPHONY PL
1100 ESCN 92029 1129-E5
SYRACUSE AV
3400 SD 92122 1228-D6
SYRACUSE CT
3600 SD 92122 1228-D6
SYRACUSE LN
6100 SD 92122 1228-D6
SYRACUSE WY
6100 SD 92122 1228-D6
SZALAY WY
3300 SMCS 92069 1108-D5

T

T AV
- NATC 91950 1290-A6
T ST
3600 SD 92113 1289-G5
4700 SD 92113 1290-A5
TABBY LN
1100 ESCN 92026 1109-J7
1100 ESCN 92026 1110-A7
TABER CT
900 CHV 91911 1331-A2
TABER DR
900 CHV 91911 1331-A2
TABERNA VISTA WY
1800 SDCo 91901 1233-H4
TABLERO CT
17300 SD 92127 1169-J1
TABLERO PL
17300 SD 92127 1169-H1
TABLE ROCK AV
2500 CHV 91914 1311-H4
TABLE ROCK WY
2600 CHV 91914 1311-H4
TACAYME DR
4800 OCN 92057 1066-J7
4800 OCN 92057 1067-A7
TACAYME PL
4900 OCN 92057 1067-A7
TACOMA LN
1700 VSTA 92084 1088-B4
TACOMA ST
4200 SD 92117 1248-D3
TAECKER RD
- ImCo 92227 431-D1
TAEGAN LN
1600 ENCT 92024 1167-G1
TAFT AV
200 ELCJ 92020 1251-G5
800 NATC 92136 1309-G2
900 NATC 91950 1309-G2
4500 SDCo 91941 1271-F3
5400 SD 92037 1247-G3
TAFT CIR
100 OCN 92057 1067-B6
TAFT ST
1300 LMGR 91945 1290-G2
1300 ESCN 92026 1109-H7
TAG LN
500 SDCo 92065 1152-G6
TAGOTA CT
9100 SDCo 92040 1232-E6
TAHITI DR
- ESCN 92025 1129-J5
TAHOE ST
2900 ELCJ 92020 1251-A5
TAIA LN
11800 SDCo 92040 1251-J1
TAIL CREEK DR
- IMP 92251 6439-F3
TAIT ST
800 OCN 92054 1106-B2
6500 SD 92111 1268-H1
7200 SD 92111 1269-A1
TAKISHLA PL
32200 SDCo 92061 1051-A6
TALBOT AV
- SD 92145 1229-C2
TALBOT CT
- CHV 91913 1331-F2
TALBOT ST
2800 SD 92106 1288-A2
3700 SD 92106 1287-J2
TALCA AV
13800 SD 92129 1189-C3
TALCA CT
8900 SD 92129 1189-C3
TALIESIN WY
5200 SDCo 92003 1048-D7
TALISMAN CT
6900 SD 92119 1250-H4
TALL OAK DR
- SDCo 92026 1089-D4
TALL OAK LN
- SDCo 92026 1089-D4
TALLOW CT
500 CHV 91911 1330-H4
TALLOW TREE LN
- SDCo 92127 1169-D2
TALL PINE RD
- SDCo 92036 1156-G6
TALLUS GN
- SD 92127 1169-E3
E TALMADGE DR
4500 SD 92116 1269-H3

N TALMADGE DR
4300 SD 92116 1269-H3
W TALMADGE DR
4500 SD 92116 1269-H3
TALMADGE CANYON RW
4600 SD 92115 1269-J2
TALMADGE PARK RW
4700 SD 92115 1269-J2
TALON WY
2000 SD 92123 1269-B1
TALON RIDGE WY
300 OCN 92054 1086-B6
TALTEC DR
4800 LMSA 91941 1271-C2
4800 SDCo 91941 1271-C2
TALUS ST
200 CHV 91911 1330-G4
TALUS WY
- CRLB 92010 1107-B3
TAMAR TER
10700 SNTE 92071 1231-F6
TAMARA DR
600 SDCo 92026 1109-H2
TAMARA LN
2400 SDCo 92069 1088-G7
2400 SDCo 92069 1108-G1
TAMARACK AV
1000 CRLB 92008 1106-G6
2100 CRLB 92010 1106-J6
2200 CRLB 92010 1107-A3
TAMARACK CT
500 CHV 91911 1330-H4
TAMARACK LN
9700 SDCo 92029 1149-D4
TAMARACK ST
400 CHV 91911 1330-G5
TAMARACK TER
700 ELCJ 92019 1251-J6
TAMARAK AV
200 ESCN 92026 1109-H7
TAMARAND WY
1700 SD 92154 1349-J2
1700 SD 92154 1350-A2
TAMARINDO WY
- CHV 91911 1330-E5
TAMARISK CIR
4400 OCN 92057 1066-H6
TAMARISK LN
500 SMCS 92078 1128-E2
TAMARISK ST
- IMP 92251 6499-D2
TAMARISK WY
500 ELCJ 92020 1251-G4
TAMARISK GROVE DR
1300 CHV 91915 1311-H6
TAMARME TER
1700 ESCN 92025 1130-A5
TAMAYO DR
800 CHV 91910 1310-F7
TAMBERLY CT
8800 SNTE 92071 1231-D7
TAMBERLY LN
8800 SNTE 92071 1231-D7
TAMBERLY WY
8800 SNTE 92071 1231-D6
TAMBOR CT
4200 SD 92124 1249-J2
4200 SD 92124 1250-A2
TAMBOR RD
3900 SD 92124 1249-J3
TAMBOURINE LN
2300 SDCo 92019 1252-D6
TAMIL RD
10000 SDCo 92040 1232-B3
TAMILYNN CT
4100 SD 92122 1228-E6
TAMILYNN ST
6000 SD 92122 1228-E6
TAMMADGE HEIGHTS RD
200 SDCo 91901 1233-E7
200 SDCo 91901 1253-E1
200 SDCo 92019 1253-E1
TAM O SHANTER CT
13800 PWY 92064 1170-F2
TAM O SHANTER DR
500 SMCS 92069 1109-D7
17000 PWY 92064 1170-F1
TAMPA AV
2200 ELCJ 92020 1251-B4
TAMPA CT
1500 CHV 91902 1311-B4
TAMPERE CT
11100 SD 92131 1209-J1
TAMPICO CT
100 SOLB 92075 1167-D6
7800 SD 92126 1209-A3
TAMPICO DR
- IMP 92251 6499-G1
TAMPICO GN
200 ESCN 92025 1130-B7
TAMPICO WY
100 SOLB 92075 1167-D6
TAMRA CT
3500 SDCo 91935 1272-E5
TAMRES DR
5500 SD 92111 1248-G6
TANA WY
25000 SDCo 92065 1173-G4
TANAGER DR
7100 CRLB 92011 1127-D6
TANAGER LN
1300 ELCJ 92020 1251-D2
TANBARK CT
1600 CHV 91911 1330-H5
TANBARK ST
400 CHV 91911 1330-H5
TAN BOB LN
300 ESCN 92029 1150-A2
300 SDCo 92029 1150-A2
T ANCHOR DR
600 SDCo 92004 (1078-J3 See Page 1058)
700 SDCo 92004 (1079-A3 See Page 1058)
TANG DR
- SD 92130 1208-B1
TANGELO DR
12100 SDCo 92040 1232-A4
TANGELO WY
- SDCo 92082 1071-A7
TANGERINE DR
200 ELCN 92243 6559-H1
TANGERINE LN
- SDCo 92028 1047-G7
TANGERINE ST
1100 ELCJ 92021 1252-A3
TANGERINE WY
1200 ESCN 92029 1129-E5
TANGERINE COVE DR
500 VSTA 92083 1087-G7
TANGIER CT
600 OCN 92057 1087-B1
TANGIERS CT
700 SD 92109 1247-H7

TANGIERS CT
700 SD 92109 1267-H1
TANGLEFOOT TR
7400 SDCo 92036 1138-B7
TANGLEROD LN
7700 LMSA 91942 1250-G7
TANGLEWOOD DR
- SMCS 92029 1128-G6
- SMCS 92078 1128-G6
TANGLEWOOD LN
1500 ESCN 92029 1129-G5
9300 SD 92126 1209-E3
10400 SDCo 91916 1216-A7
10400 SDCo 91916 1235-J1
10400 SDCo 91916 1236-A1
TANGLEWOOD RD
6500 SD 92111 1248-J4
TANGLEWOOD WY
3700 SD 92111 1248-J4
TANGOR WY
9900 SDCo 91977 1271-D6
TANNER CT
7100 SD 92111 1248-J4
TANNER LN
3700 SD 92111 1248-J4
3700 SD 92111 1249-A4
TANNIN DR
17200 PWY 92064 1170-D2
TANOAK CT
500 CHV 91911 1330-H5
TANSY ST
3700 SD 92121 1208-C6
TAN TAM DR
2800 SDCo 92029 1149-G1
TANYA LN
1000 SDCo 92028 1027-H1
TANZANITE DR
- CRLB 92009 1127-F5
TAOS DR
4000 SD 92117 1248-D3
TAOS PL
3400 SD 92117 1248-D3
TARA CT
- CRLB 92008 1106-G6
1100 CHV 91911 1330-F2
TARA PL
5200 SD 92117 1248-H1
TARA WY
- SMCS 92078 1128-F7
3500 SDCo 91935 1272-E6
TARAKIM LN
1600 VSTA 92081 1107-J2
TARANGO PL
200 SDCo 91977 1290-J5
TARANTELLA LN
4500 SD 92130 1188-C6
TARASCAN DR
13200 PWY 92064 1190-E4
TARATA CT
400 CHV 91911 1330-H5
TARAWA RD
2900 CORD 92155 1309-A2
TARAY CT
9800 SD 92129 1209-F1
TARBOX ST
1300 LMGR 92114 1290-E2
1300 SD 92114 1290-E2
TAREK TER
1000 SDCo 92084 1068-G7
TARENTO DR
500 SD 92106 1287-J3
1000 SD 92107 1287-J2
TARGA PL
1800 SDCo 92019 1272-C4
TARLETON ST
1500 SDCo 91977 1290-H2
1600 LMGR 91945 1290-H2
TARLO CT
1000 ELCJ 92019 1252-A7
TARO CT
100 SD 92114 1290-G4
TARRAGON DR
4800 OCN 92057 1067-B7
TARRAGONA DR
4200 SD 92115 1270-C4
TARTAN TER
- SDCo 92065 1171-G1
TARUP CREEK RD
1100 CHV 91913 1311-E6
TARZANA RD
14100 PWY 92064 1190-B2
E TASHA VIEW WY
100 SDCo 92021 1252-J1
W TASHA VIEW WY
100 SDCo 92021 1252-J1
TASMAN PL
100 SD 92114 1290-F5
TASPA CT
- SDCo 92061 1050-J5
TASSEL RD
12400 PWY 92064 1190-C4
TATAS PL
10400 SDCo 92026 1109-F1
TATIA CT
17600 SD 92128 1170-A1
TATLER RD
- CRLB 92011 1127-C6
TATTENHAM RD
1700 ENCT 92024 1147-A2
1700 ENCT 92024 1146-J2
TATTERSALL SQ
5100 SD 92130 1188-D2
TATUM ST
500 VSTA 92083 1087-F5
TAU ST
5600 LMSA 91942 1250-J7
TAULBEES LN
1300 SMCS 92078 1108-E7
TAUNT PL
12500 PWY 92064 1190-C2
TAUNT RD
12500 PWY 92064 1190-C2
TAUPA WY
- SDCo 92061 1051-B6
TAURUS PL
8700 SD 92126 1209-C2
TAUSSIG CT
10200 SD 92124 1249-G4
TAUSSIG ST
3000 SD 92124 1249-G4
TAVARA PL
400 SD 92106 1288-A4
TAVERN CT
1800 SDCo 91901 1234-A6
TAVERN RD
800 SDCo 91901 1233-H5
1300 SDCo 91901 1234-A6
1900 SDCo 91901 1254-A1
2600 SDCo 91901 1253-J3
TAWANKA DR
13300 PWY 92064 1190-D4
TAWNY CT
700 OCN 92057 1087-C1

STREET Block City ZIP Pg-Grid

TAWNY PL
1800 ESCN 92026 1109-D5
TAWNY WY
13100 PWY 92064 1170-E2
TAXCO CT
1100 CHV 91910 1311-A7
1100 CHV 91910 1331-A1
TAXCO PL
- SDCo 92003 1067-H1
TAYLOR AV
1400 ESCN 92027 1110-B7
TAYLOR DR
- IMP 92251 6499-H2
TAYLOR PL
500 CALX 92231 6680-H1
1300 ESCN 92027 1110-C6
1300 ESCN 92027 1130-B1
TAYLOR RD
- SD 92106 1288-B7
TAYLOR ST
100 VSTA 92084 1087-H2
4000 SD 92110 1268-F4
4400 SD 92108 1268-F4
E TAYLOR ST
1100 VSTA 92084 1088-A2
W TAYLOR ST
900 VSTA 92084 1087-J3
900 VSTA 92084 1088-A3
TAYLOR WY
1000 SDCo 92019 1253-B2
TAZA RD
1300 SDCo 92028 1028-H1
1500 SDCo 92028 998-H7
TEABERRY GN
2400 ESCN 92027 1110-D7
TEABERRY ST
700 ENCT 92024 1147-E6
TEAK CT
500 CHV 91911 1330-H4
TEAK ST
3700 SD 92113 1289-G5
TEAKWOOD CT
700 SMCS 92069 1109-A5
TEAKWOOD GN
400 ESCN 92026 1109-G6
TEAKWOOD LN
1800 SDCo 92021 1251-H1
TEAKWOOD WY
1800 VSTA 92081 1107-G5
TEAL GN
2100 ESCN 92026 1109-H5
TEAL PL
2600 SD 92123 1249-A7
TEAL RD
29800 SDCo 91906 (1297-F5 See Page 1296)
TEAL ST
100 CHV 91911 1330-F5
TEAL WY
- OCN 92057 1067-A3
TEALE CHRISTINE CT
- SDCo 92040 1232-D6
TEAL STONE CT
- SDCo 92127 1169-F1
TEAL STONE ST
- SDCo 92127 1169-F1
TEALWOOD CT
8000 LMGR 91945 1270-J7
TEA MOUNTAIN LN
1900 SDCo 92021 1252-G4
TEA PARTY LN
3100 SD 92124 1249-G4
TEAROSE LN
- SDCo 91934 (1321-A3 See Page 1300)
TEASDALE AV
7000 SD 92122 1228-G4
TEA TREE DR
- CRLB 92011 1127-A5
TEA TREE LN
- SDCo 92127 1169-D2
TEATRO CIR
- ELCJ 92021 1252-A3
TEBO CT
3400 SD 92154 1330-E7
TECALOTE DR
1600 SDCo 92028 1028-F4
TECALOTE LN
4000 SDCo 92028 1028-H5
TECATE GN
1900 ESCN 92029 1129-E6
TECATE RD Rt#-188
400 SDCo 91980 429-K10
TECATE CYPRESS TR
- SDCo 91916 1236-E2
TECATE DIVIDE RD
2500 SDCo 91905 (1299-J4 See Page 1298)
TECATE MISSION RD
300 SDCo 91980 429-K10
TECH WY
8500 SD 92123 1249-C2
TECH CENTER CT
- PWY 92064 1190-E7
TECH CENTER DR
12100 PWY 92064 1190-F7
TECHNOLOGY DR
16200 SD 92127 1169-H4
TECHNOLOGY PL
10900 SD 92127 1169-H4
TECOLOTE CT
1300 NATC 91950 1310-B1
TECOLOTE RD
1200 SD 92109 1268-F2
1300 SD 92110 1268-F2
TECOMA PL
6400 CRLB 92011 1127-E4
TECUMSEH WY
4300 SD 92117 1248-E2
TED KIPF RD
- ImCo - 411-D8
- ImCo - 411-E8
- ImCo - 432-A4
TEDS PL
500 SDCo 92065 1152-D7
TED WILLIAMS FRWY Rt#-56
- SD - 1188-F5
- SD - 1189-A4
- SD - 1207-J2
- SD - 1208-A1
TED WILLIAMS PKWY
- SD 92128 1189-H3
- SD 92129 1189-H3
11600 SD 92128 1190-A2
12100 PWY 92064 1190-A2
TEE SQ
29000 SDCo 91962 1237-C7
TEE-A-WAY PL
6800 SD 92119 1250-F5
TEEBIRD LN
7600 SD 92123 1269-A1
TEELIN AV
1200 VSTA 92083 1087-G4

TEENA DR
100 CHV 91911 1330-D5
TEEPEE DR
1300 SDCo 92027 1130-E5
TEHACHAPI DR
500 SMCS 92078 1128-C1
TEHAMA DR
300 SMCS 92069 1108-H5
TEHNSEN
14100 SDCo 92040 1232-H5
TELEGRAPH CANYON RD
- CHV 91910 1330-E1
- CHV 91911 1330-E1
200 CHV 91910 1310-F7
200 CHV 91911 1310-F7
800 CHV 91913 1330-H1
800 CHV 91913 1331-A1
800 CHV 91910 1331-A1
1000 CHV 91910 1311-B7
1000 CHV 91913 1311-B7
TELESCOPE AV
4600 CRLB 92008 1106-H6
TELESIS CT
10100 SD 92121 1208-D5
TELFORD LN
300 SDCo 92065 1152-H6
300 SDCo 92065 1153-A6
TELKAIF ST
9300 SDCo 92040 1232-F4
TEMA ST
6700 SD 92120 1250-E7
TEMECULA ST
- SDCo 92055 1086-A4
4200 SD 92107 1268-B5
TEMECULA VALLEY FRWY I-15
- RivC - 998-J2
- RivC - 999-A1
TEMEPA RD
11500 SDCo 92059 999-G4
TEMET DR
32800 SDCo 92061 1050-J5
TEMPALA RD
- SDCo 92059 1029-G4
TEMPAS CT
6000 SD 92114 1290-C4
TEMPERA CT
900 OCN 92057 1087-B2
TEMPLE ST
- CALX 92231 6680-F1
700 SD 92106 1287-J2
13500 PWY 92064 1190-F2
TEMPLE TER
2000 SDCo 91935 (1314-H2 See Page 1294)
6900 SD 92119 1250-E5
TEMPLE TR
19600 SDCo 91935 (1314-H1 See Page 1294)
TEMPLE WY
13800 PWY 92064 1190-F2
TEMPLE HEIGHTS DR
1200 OCN 92056 1087-D3
TEMPRA PL
1300 CHV 91911 1330-D4
TEMPRANO CT
4500 SD 92124 1250-A2
TENAJA TKTR
- SDCo 92028 409-A4
TENAYA LAKE RD
1100 CHV 91913 1331-B2
TENBURY CT
7000 SD 92139 1290-G7
TENDERFOOT LN
1100 OCN 92057 1067-E7
TENNIE ST
100 SD 92173 1350-F4
TENNIS CT
- SDCo 91916 1236-A2
TENNIS PL
1800 ENCT 92024 1167-H3
TENNIS CLUB DR
1200 ENCT 92024 1167-G2
TENNIS COURT LN
3500 SDCo 91902 1310-H2
TENNIS MATCH WY
1500 ENCT 92024 1147-G6
TENNYSON ST
3000 SD 92106 1288-C1
3100 SD 92106 1268-B7
3700 SD 92107 1268-B7
TENSHAW PL
3200 SD 92117 1248-C2
TEQUILA WY
3000 SD 92173 1350-D2
TERALTA PL
4400 SD 92103 1268-H4
TERAN DR
500 SDCo 92028 1027-F3
TERCER VERDE
3000 SD 92014 1187-H1
3000 SOLB 92014 1187-H1
TERCER VERDE WY
15800 SD 92014 1187-H1
TERESA DR
8200 SD 92126 1209-B2
TERESA ST
4100 OCN 92056 1087-C7
TERESITA ST
2600 SD 92104 1269-F7
TERI DR
12300 PWY 92064 1190-C2
TERMAN CT
8900 SD 92121 1208-J7
TERMINAL AV
2400 NATC 91950 1309-G4
TERMINAL ST
800 SD 92101 1289-B5
TERN DR
2600 SD 92123 1249-B7
TERN PL
7100 CRLB 92011 1127-D7
TEROL CT
200 SD 92114 1290-D4
TERRA LN
500 ELCJ 92019 1252-B4
500 SDCo 92019 1252-B4
TERRACE AV
400 ESCN 92026 1109-H7
TERRACE CT
4000 SD 92116 1269-G3
TERRACE DR
- SDCo 92065 1089-B2
100 VSTA 92084 1087-H7
3300 SDCo 92036 1156-E3
4000 SD 92116 1269-G3
8900 LMSA 91941 1271-B4
8900 LMSA 91977 1271-B4
TERRACE LN
100 SMCS 92069 1108-J7
3300 OCN 92056 1106-H1
TERRACE PL
3600 CRLB 92010 1107-B4

TERRACE VW
2000 ESCN 92029 1129-E6
TERRACE CREST
800 ELCJ 92019 1252-A7
TERRACE HILL DR
1700 SDCo 92021 1252-B2
TERRACE KNOLL
1400 SDCo 91901 1234-B6
TERRACE PINE DR
2700 SD 92173 1350-C2
TERRACE PINE LN
1500 SD 92173 1350-C2
TERRACE VIEW LN
30400 SDCo 92082 1070-G4
TERRACEVIEW PL
2100 ESCN 92026 1109-G5
TERRACEWOOD LN
2100 ESCN 92026 1109-H4
TERRACINA CIR
1900 SDCo 91977 1291-A1
TERRACINA LN
- SD 92103 1268-J7
TERRACINA ST
4800 OCN 92056 1087-B3
TERRACINA WY
100 VSTA 92083 1087-G6
TERRACITA LN
1400 SDCo 91901 1233-J7
TERRA COTTA RD
6900 SD 92114 1290-F5
TERRAKAPPA AV
1900 SDCo 91977 1291-A1
TERRA NOVA DR
400 CHV 91910 1310-G5
TERRARAMA AV
8800 SDCo 91977 1291-A1
TERRA SECA TR
3100 SDCo 91935 1273-B7
TERRASPIRO AV
2000 SDCo 91977 1291-A1
TERRAZA CIR
4600 SD 92124 1250-A2
TERRAZA CT
4500 SD 92124 1250-A1
TERRAZA ST
1700 OCN 92054 1106-E1
TERRAZA DISOMA
7900 CRLB 92009 1148-A2
TERRAZA FLORACION
10800 SD 92127 1169-H5
TERRAZA GOYA
2300 CRLB 92009 1127-G7
TERRAZA GUITARA
2300 CRLB 92009 1127-G6
TERRAZA MAR MARVELOSA
- SD 92130 1208-C4
TERRAZA PANGA
2300 CRLB 92009 1127-G6
TERRAZA PLAYA CANCUN
13300 SD 92124 1230-A7
TERRAZA PLAYA CATALINA
5000 SD 92124 1230-A7
TERRAZA PORTICO
- CRLB 92009 1127-J4
- CRLB 92009 1128-A4
TERRAZA QUINTANA
5100 SD 92124 1230-A7
TERRAZA RIBERA
2300 CRLB 92009 1127-G6
TERRAZA SALVO
2300 CRLB 92009 1127-G6
TERREBONNE CT
- SD 92131 1210-H1
TERRELLA PL
2500 SDCo 92025 1150-D2
TERRENO CT
4400 SD 92124 1249-J1
TERRIER WY
- SMCS 92078 1128-H1
TERRILEE DR
13800 PWY 92064 1190-G3
TERRILEE LN
14100 PWY 92064 1190-G3
TERRY LN
1900 NATC 91950 1290-A7
1900 NATC 91950 1310-A1
4500 LMSA 91941 1270-E3
TERRY ST
4100 OCN 92056 1087-C6
TERRYHILL DR
6100 SD 92037 1247-F2
TERRYWOOD RD
9400 SNTE 92071 1231-B4
TESLA LN
1100 SDCo 92028 998-A7
TESLA ST
3000 SD 92117 1248-F6
TESORO AV
- SMCS 92069 1108-F5
TESORO CT
12300 SD 92128 1170-B2
TESORO DR
16900 SD 92128 1170-B3
TESORO GN
- ESCN 92025 1130-D5
TESORO WY
24500 SDCo 92065 1173-F3
TESORO GROVE WY
- SD 92154 1350-B1
TESOTA CT
400 CHV 91911 1330-H5
TESTIGO TR
- SDCo 91901 1255-C4
TETEN WY
2400 ENCT 92024 1147-J7
2400 ENCT 92024 1148-A7
TETILLAS CT
15300 SD 92128 1170-A6
TETON DR
1300 SDCo 92021 1251-F1
1300 SNTE 92021 1251-F1
1400 SDCo 92021 1231-F7
1400 SNTE 92021 1231-F7
TETON PASS ST
1800 SDCo 92019 1272-C3
TEWA ST
500 DLMR 92014 1187-G5
TEX ST
5700 LMSA 91942 1250-H7
TEXANA ST
12700 SD 92129 1189-C6
TEXAS ST
2000 SD 92108 1269-D3
3300 SD 92104 1269-D6
3400 SD 92104 1269-D5
4300 SD 92116 1269-D3
THALIA ST
1100 SD 92154 1349-J1
THAMES CT
2300 SD 92123 1249-B7

THAMES WY
3600 CRLB 92010 1107-A3
THANKSGIVING LN
10200 SD 92126 1209-D5
THATCHER CT
12200 PWY 92064 1190-E7
THAYER DR
500 SDCo 91977 1291-B3
TH BAR RANCH TR
8000 SDCo 91901 1233-E7
THEBES ST
14600 SD 92129 1189-H1
THEBES WY
4800 OCN 92056 1107-F6
THE CIRCLE
100 VSTA 92084 1087-H6
THE DEPOT RD
- OCN 92057 1067-E7
THE HILL RD
3800 SDCo 91902 1310-F4
THE INLET
- CORD 92118 1329-D1
THELBORN WY
1700 SD 92154 1349-J2
1700 SD 92154 1350-A2
THELMA WY
400 NATC 91950 1290-C6
400 SD 92114 1290-C6
THE NARROWS RD
- SDCo 92004 (1099-H3 See Page 1098)
- SDCo 92004 1100-A5
- SDCo 92004 (1120-A3 See Page 1100)
THEODORE DR
1200 SD 92114 1290-D5
THE POINT
- CORD 92118 1329-E1
THE PRESERVE CT
- SD 92130 1188-H6
THE PRESERVE TER
- SD 92129 1188-H6
- SD 92130 1188-H6
THE PRESERVE WY
- SD 92130 1188-H7
THERESA LN
9900 SNTE 92071 1231-D4
THERESA WY
100 CHV 91911 1330-F2
1300 CHV 91911 1330-F3
THE RIVER RD
- SDCo 92067 1168-D6
THE RIVER TR
- SDCo 92067 1168-D6
THERMAL AV
600 SD 92154 1349-J2
700 SD 92154 1329-J7
THE SQUARE
13400 PWY 92064 1170-E2
THE STRAND
200 OCN 92054 1105-J1
200 OCN 92054 1106-A1
300 OCN 92054 1085-J7
S THE STRAND
100 OCN 92054 1106-A1
THETA PL
5700 SD 92120 1250-C7
THE WOODS DR
1700 SDCo 92019 1272-B1
THE YELLOW BRICK RD
28900 SDCo 92082 1071-B6
THIBODO CT
2000 VSTA 92081 1108-B4
THIBODO RD
1500 VSTA 92081 1107-J2
1500 VSTA 92081 1108-A3
THIMBLE CT
8200 SD 92129 1189-B6
THING RD
- SDCo 91980 429-L10
THING VALLEY RD
- SDCo 91948 430-B5
- SDCo 91962 430-C6
THISTLE CT
8100 SD 92120 1250-D3
THISTLE BRAES TER
12000 SDCo 92040 1232-A6
THISTLE HILL PL
- SD 92130 1208-B1
THISTLEWOOD AV
1100 CHV 91913 1311-D6
THOMAS AV
- SD 92140 1268-G6
700 SD 92109 1247-H6
1400 SD 92109 1248-A6
1900 SD 92134 1289-C2
THOMAS PL
- VSTA 92084 1088-C5
1500 CHV 91911 1330-J3
THOMAS ST
4000 OCN 92056 1087-B7
N THOMAS WY
1000 ESCN 92027 1110-B6
THOMAS HAYES LN
11600 SD 92126 1209-A1
THOMAS PAINE DR
15600 SDCo 92065 1171-J5
THOMAS PAINE LN
18500 SDCo 92065 1171-J4
THOMPSON AV
- CHV 91913 1331-E2
THOMPSON RD
- ImCo 92251 431-A4
THOMSEN WY
400 SDCo 92065 1152-H4
THOMSON CT
6700 SD 92111 1248-H7
THO NINH PL
- ESCN 92027 1110-B7
THOR ST
1600 SD 92113 1289-G6
THORLEY WY
- SMCS 92078 1128-F7
THORN LN
9700 SDCo 92029 1149-E3
THORN ST
200 SD 92103 1269-E7
600 IMPB 91932 1329-F7
800 SD 92103 1268-J7
2800 SD 92104 1269-F6
3000 SD 92105 1269-G6
5700 SD 92105 1270-B6
5900 SD 92115 1270-C6
N THORN ST
5200 SD 92105 1270-A6
S THORN ST
5200 SD 92105 1270-A6
W THORN ST
300 SD 92103 1269-A7
400 SD 92103 1268-J7
THORNBUSH CT
12400 SD 92131 1210-C4
THORNBUSH RD
- SDCo 92065 1174-B5

THORN DALE RD
- SDCo 92003 1068-D5
- SDCo 92084 1068-D5
THORNE DR
5000 LMSA 91941 1270-G2
THORNMINT CT
17000 SDCo 92127 1169-G3
THORNMINT RD
10700 SDCo 92127 1169-F3
THORNTON DR
200 SDCo 92021 1252-H2
THORNTON PL
3000 SD 92105 1270-B7
THORNWOOD ST
6300 SD 92111 1248-H4
THORNY LOCUST PL
- CHV 91915 1311-H2
THOROUGHBRED AV
1700 OCN 92057 1067-F7
THOROUGHBRED LN
5900 SDCo 92003 1067-J1
THOROUGHBRED PL
- SD 92130 1188-D5
THORTON RD
1700 CHV 91902 1311-C4
THRASHER PL
- CRLB 92011 1127-C5
THRASHER WY
100 ELCJ 92020 1251-A5
THREE CANYONS CT
- SD 92130 1188-G6
THREE CANYONS PT
- SD 92130 1188-G6
THREE OAKS WY
10000 SNTE 92071 1231-D3
THREE PEAKS LN
- SDCo 92036 1155-J4
THREE SEASONS RD
9000 SD 92126 1209-D5
THREE SLASHES RD
- ImCo - 412-A6
THRUSH PL
7100 CRLB 92011 1127-C6
THRUSH ST
300 SD 92114 1290-C4
400 CHV 91911 1330-G2
THUMBKIN LN
2200 SDCo 92084 1087-H2
THUNDER DR
100 OCN 92056 1107-C1
2700 OCN 92056 1087-B7
3400 VSTA 92081 1107-C2
THUNDER GN
600 ESCN 92027 1130-B2
THUNDERBIRD DR
600 OCN 92057 1066-H7
THUNDERBIRD LN
5400 SD 92037 1248-A3
THUNDERBIRD PL
1300 CHV 91915 1311-H6
THUNDERHEAD ST
13100 SD 92129 1189-C5
THUNDER MOUNTAIN RD
24900 SDCo 92065 (1193-F1 See Page 1192)
THUNDERNUT LN
28300 SDCo 92082 1091-C1
THUNDER SPRING DR
1300 CHV 91915 1311-H6
THURSTON PL
4700 SD 92130 1188-C4
THYME WY
- SDCo 91935 (1295-A6 See Page 1294)
TIA MARIA WY
8400 LMSA 91941 1270-J2
TIARA ST
3800 SD 92111 1249-A3
TIBBETT ST
600 SD 92114 1290-F3
TIBER CT
100 SDCo 92083 1108-B3
TIBERON DR
4000 OCN 92056 1107-C2
TIBIDABO DR
1500 ESCN 92027 1110-A6
TIBURON AV
2700 CRLB 92010 1106-J5
2700 CRLB 92010 1107-A5
TIBURON DR
- CHV 91914 1311-D1
TIBURON ST
- SMCS 92078 1128-G2
TICANU DR
2100 SDCo 92036 1156-B3
TICINO ST
- SD 92070 1135-B3
TICKET ST
9000 SD 92126 1209-D3
TICKNOR CT
6000 SD 92114 1290-C4
TICO CT
1100 SD 92154 1350-G1
TICONDEROGA ST
3200 SD 92117 1248-D5
TIDE CT
900 CRLB 92011 1126-J4
TIDE WY
- SDCo 92069 1109-A4
- SMCS 92069 1109-A4
TIDELANDS
- CHV 91910 1310-C6
TIDELANDS AV
1300 NATC 91950 1309-G3
TIDE POOL PL
- SD 92139 1290-E7
TIE ST
3400 SD 92105 1270-C6
TIENTSE
- SD 92140 1268-F6
TIERNEY GN
- SD 92127 1169-B3
TIERRA ALTA
15000 SOLB 92014 1187-H1
15000 SOLB 92014 1167-H7
TIERRA BAJA WY
4900 SD 92115 1270-C2
TIERRA BLANCA AV
- SDCo 92055 1085-J3
TIERRA BONITA CT
14000 PWY 92064 1190-G1
TIERRA BONITA PL
1300 CHV 91910 1311-B7
TIERRA BONITA RD
13500 PWY 92064 1190-G2
TIERRA DE DIOS
3600 SDCo 92025 1150-D2
TIERRA DEL CIELO
1500 SDCo 92084 1088-C3
1500 VSTA 92084 1088-C3
TIERRA DEL ORO ST
5000 CRLB 92008 1126-F2
TIERRA DEL REY
1000 CHV 91910 1310-J7

TIERRA DEL SOL RD
500 SDCo 91905 430-C10
500 SDCo 91905 (1320-A1 See Page 1300)
500 SDCo 91906 430-C10
600 SDCo 91905 (1319-J5 See Page 1298)
1700 SDCo 91905 1300-A4
TIERRA DEL SUR
11500 SD 92130 1208-A2
TIERRA DE LUNA RD
900 SDCo 91905 (1319-H7 See Page 1298)
TIERRA DE MELANIE
37600 SDCo 91905 (1319-G7 See Page 1298)
TIERRA DURA RD
900 SMCS 92069 1109-C5
TIERRA ESTRELLA RD
900 SDCo 91905 (1319-G7 See Page 1298)
TIERRA GRANDE ST
9600 SD 92126 1209-E6
TIERRA HEIGHTS RD
2200 SDCo 91905 1300-A4
TIERRA LIBERTIA RD
1500 SDCo 92026 1089-D7
TIERRA LINDA LN
3500 SDCo 92028 1048-B4
TIERRA MONTANOSA
1600 SDCo 91901 1233-H7
TIERRA NUEVO
2400 SDCo 92028 998-D3
TIERRA REAL LN
1100 SDCo 91905 (1319-H6 See Page 1298)
TIERRA REAL RD
38100 SDCo 91905 (1319-F5 See Page 1298)
38100 SDCo 91906 (1319-F5 See Page 1298)
TIERRA ROJA DR
900 SDCo 92028 1028-D1
900 SDCo 92028 998-D7
TIERRASANTA BLVD
9800 SD 92124 1249-G2
11200 SD 92124 1250-A3
TIERRA TESORO
- SD 92127 1188-J1
TIERRA VERDE RD
2000 SDCo 92084 1088-C7
TIERRA VISTA
4100 SDCo 92003 1067-G1
TIERRA VISTA PL
3900 ESCN 92025 1150-D3
TIFFANY CT
600 CHV 91910 1310-G7
TIFFANY DR
2000 OCN 92056 1086-J7
TIFFANY LN
1400 SDCo 92084 1108-B1
TIFFANY WY
500 CHV 91910 1310-G7
TIFFANY PARK PL
- SDCo 92021 1232-F5
TIFFIN AV
6600 SD 92114 1270-E7
6600 SD 92114 1290-E1
TIGER WY
11000 SDCo 92065 1152-J6
TIGEREYE PL
- CRLB 92009 1127-G5
TIGER RUN CT
- CRLB 92010 1127-H2
TIGER TAIL LN
900 VSTA 92084 1088-A6
TIGER TAIL RD
800 VSTA 92084 1087-J6
800 VSTA 92084 1088-A6
TIKI DR E
700 VSTA 92083 1087-E6
TIKI DR N
- VSTA 92083 1087-E5
TIKI DR S
700 VSTA 92083 1087-E6
TIKI DR W
- VSTA 92083 1087-E6
TIKI LN
1200 VSTA 92083 1087-E6
TILDEN ST
1800 SD 92102 1289-J1
TILIA CT
400 CHV 91911 1330-G4
TILIA PL
6400 CRLB 92011 1127-E4
TILLAMOOK BAY
5700 SD 92105 1290-B1
TILLEY LN
600 SMCS 92078 1108-C7
TILLING WY
500 ELCJ 92020 1271-F1
TILOS WY
4900 OCN 92056 1107-E6
TILTING T DR
400 SDCo 92004 (1078-H5 See Page 1058)
700 SDCo 92004 (1079-B5 See Page 1058)
TILTON ST
10100 SD 92126 1208-J5
TIM ST
3900 SDCo 91902 1310-J3
3900 SDCo 91902 1311-A3
TIMARU WY
11800 SD 92128 1170-A1
TIMBER CT
400 CHV 91911 1330-H5
TIMBER GN
1300 ESCN 92027 1110-A5
TIMBER PASG
- SDCo 92065 1153-C7
TIMBER ST
500 CHV 91911 1330-H5
TIMBER TR
1800 VSTA 92081 1107-F5
TIMBER BRANCH WY
5200 SD 92130 1208-D1
TIMBER BROOK LN
- SD 92130 1208-F2
TIMBER COVE WY
700 OCN 92054 1066-E6
TIMBER CREEK LN
- SD 92127 1130-J3
TIMBER FEATHER LN
500 SDCo 92028 1027-G3
TIMBERGATE CIR
11200 SD 92128 1189-J2
TIMBERLAKE DR
11500 SD 92131 1209-J3
11600 SD 92131 1210-A3
TIMBERLANE WY
10000 SNTE 92071 1231-D3
TIMBERLINE CT
10000 SD 92131 1210-A4

TIMBERLINE LN
600 SMCS 92069 1108-J5
TIMBERLINE RD
2100 CRLB 92008 1106-G3
TIMBERPOND DR
1100 SDCo 92019 1272-B1
TIMBER RIDGE RD
4500 SD 92130 1188-C5
TIMBERWOOD PL
800 ESCN 92026 1109-H3
7400 SD 92139 1290-H6
TIMBOLL CT
5400 SDCo 91902 1290-J7
TIMELY TER
100 SD 92114 1290-E4
TIMINGO GATE WY
- OCN 92054 1106-E2
TIMKEN ST
5200 LMSA 91942 1270-J1
TIMNEH CT
- OCN 92057 1067-C2
TIMOTHY DR
5400 SD 92105 1290-B1
TIMOTHY PL
1700 VSTA 92083 1087-D7
TIMRICK LN
3900 SDCo 91902 1311-A3
TIMSFORD RD
11500 SD 92131 1209-H1
TINA CT
- SDCo 92019 1272-D1
TINA PL
1600 SDCo 92021 1251-G2
TINA ST
2200 SDCo 92019 1272-D1
TINAJA LN
4700 SDCo 92004 (1099-F5 See Page 1098)
7900 SD 92139 1290-H5
TINAMOU PL
1100 VSTA 92083 1087-G4
TINASA WY
4800 SD 92124 1250-A1
TIN CUP DR
25500 SDCo 92065 1173-J7
TINGLEY LN
900 SD 92106 1288-A2
TINING DR
13200 PWY 92064 1170-E2
TINING WY
13200 PWY 92064 1170-E2
TINY LN
300 ELCJ 92019 1252-A5
TIO DIEGO PL
8400 LMSA 91941 1270-J1
TIOGA TR
1500 SDCo 92028 1047-J1
TIOGA LAKE DR
10300 SDCo 92029 1129-F7
TIPPERARY WY
10600 SD 92131 1209-H1
TIPTON ST
5100 SD 92115 1270-D2
TISELLE WY
5000 SD 92105 1290-A1
TISH CT
2700 SDCo 91977 1270-J7
TISHA CIR
10200 SD 92126 1209-B5
TISHA ST
8100 SD 92126 1209-B5
TISHMAL CT
- OCN 92054 1086-D4
TITAN CT
1200 SDCo 92026 1109-E6
TITAN WY
13900 PWY 92064 1170-G6
TITANITE PL
- CRLB 92009 1127-F4
TITSWORTH RD
- ImCo 92233 411-C11
TITUS ST
1700 SD 92110 1268-H6
1900 SD 92103 1268-H6
TIVERTON RD
3600 SD 92130 1188-A4
TIVOLI ST
4400 SD 92107 1287-J1
TIVOLI PARK RW
11900 SD 92128 1190-A2
TOBACCO RD
1700 ESCN 92026 1109-F6
1700 SDCo 92026 1109-F6
TOBAGO RD
10900 SD 92126 1209-A3
TOBAGO WY
- CORD 92118 1329-E2
TOBEY ST
4700 SD 92120 1249-J7
TOBIAS DR
1100 CHV 91911 1330-E2
TOBIASSON RD
13100 PWY 92064 1190-C2
TOBIRA DR
9000 SDCo 92026 1069-A6
TOBOGGAN WY
1900 SD 92154 1350-A1
TOBRIA TER
6400 CRLB 92009 1127-E4
6400 CRLB 92011 1127-E4
TOCA LN
- SDCo 92065 1172-C3
TOCAYO AV
- SD 92154 1350-A3
TOCH ST
4200 SD 92117 1248-E2
TODD CT
200 OCN 92054 1086-E5
TODD ST
200 OCN 92054 1086-D6
TODOS SANTOS DR
9100 SNTE 92071 1251-B1
TODOS SANTOS PL
1500 SDCo 92028 1027-F5
TOGAN AV
- SD 92129 1189-D4
TOKAJ CT
9100 SDCo 91977 1291-B1
TOKAJ LN
9100 SDCo 91977 1291-B1
TOKAJ RD
2200 SDCo 91977 1291-B1
TOKAJ WY
9100 SDCo 91977 1291-B1
TOKALON CT
2500 SD 92110 1248-F7
TOKALON ST
2000 SD 92110 1268-F1
2200 SD 92110 1248-F7
TOKAY ST
2000 SD 92105 1290-B1
TOLAS CT
3400 NATC 91950 1290-C7

STREET
Block City ZIP Pg-Grid

TOLEDO DR
4500 SD 92115 1270-E3
TOLEDO RD
10100 SDCo 91977 1271-E5
TOLITA AV
700 CORD 92118 1288-H7
TOLKIEN WY
- CRLB 92008 1127-A1
TOLO WY
4900 OCN 92056 1107-E4
TOLOWA ST
4100 SD 92117 1248-E2
TOLTEC CT
17900 SD 92127 1149-H7
17900 SD 92127 1169-H1
TOLUCA CT
100 SOLB 92075 1167-D6
TOMAHAWK LN
3500 SD 92117 1248-F4
TOMBILL RD
22500 SDCo 92065 1173-A5
TOMBSTONE CREEK RD
15100 SDCo 92021 1233-A1
TOMCAT PL
9800 SD 92126 1209-F2
TOMEL CT
10400 SNTE 92071 1231-E3
TOMIKO CT
9300 SDCo 91941 1271-B4
TOMMIE LN
17300 SDCo 92065 1171-F4
TOMMY CT
8800 SD 92119 1251-A4
TOMMY DR
7800 SD 92119 1250-H4
8600 SD 92119 1251-A4
TOMMY ST
7700 SD 92119 1250-G4
TOMORRO LN
900 SDCo 92028 1027-G4
TOMPAU PL
2200 SDCo 91901 1253-H2
TOMPKINS ST
3400 SD 92102 1289-F4
TONALITE WY
30100 SDCo 91906 (1297-F5 See Page 1296)
TONAPAH ST
3300 OCN 92054 1086-E5
TONAWANDA DR
3000 SD 92139 1310-E2
TONDINO CT
11700 SD 92131 1210-A2
TONDINO RD
11000 SD 92131 1210-A2
TONE LN
8000 SDCo 92021 1252-A1
TONER CT
1300 SDCo 92021 1233-A7
TONI LN
4400 LMSA 91941 1270-E3
TONI RIDGE PL
6600 SD 92121 1228-H1
TONOPAH ST
4200 SD 92110 1268-E2
TONTO WY
2600 SD 92117 1248-B1
2700 SD 92117 1228-B7
TONY DR
3400 SD 92122 1228-D4
TONYA LN
9100 SNTE 92071 1231-B7
TONY GWYNN DR
100 SD 92101 1289-B4
TOOLEY CIR
1700 SD 92114 1290-C1
TOOLEY ST
5700 SD 92114 1290-C2
TOOMA ST
6900 SD 92139 1290-G7
TOOPAL DR
- OCN 92054 1086-D4
TOOTA CT
- OCN 92054 1086-C3
TOOTH ROCK RD
14800 PWY 92064 1170-J7
TOPA RD
15200 SDCo 92061 1030-H7
TOPA HILL CIR
12300 SDCo 92040 1232-A4
TOPATOPA DR
4400 SDCo 91941 1271-G3
TOPAZ CT
- CALX 92231 6620-J7
300 CHV 91911 1330-G5
500 ESCN 92027 1110-E7
4300 LMSA 91941 1270-J4
TOPAZ DR
500 SDCo 92036 1156-E2
TOPAZ LN
4400 OCN 92056 1107-D2
TOPAZ PL
1200 SMCS 92069 1109-C5
TOPAZ TER
1700 SDCo 92019 1272-C2
TOPAZ WY
- CRLB 92011 1127-B4
9100 SD 92123 1229-D7
TOPAZ LAKE AV
7500 SD 92119 1250-G5
TOPEKA ST
200 OCN 92054 1106-A1
600 OCN 92054 1086-B7
3400 CRLB 92010 1106-J4
TOPGUN AV
- SD 92126 1209-D6
TOP GUN ST
6600 SD 92121 1208-H4
TOPIARY ST
- CRLB 92009 1127-F3
TOPMAST DR
- CRLB 92011 1127-A3
TOPO LN
11000 SDCo 92040 1212-A6
TOP OF CROSBY
- SDCo 92127 1168-J3
TOP OF THE MORNING WY
- SDCo 92127 1168-J3
- SDCo 92127 1169-A2
TOP OF THE PINES LN
- SDCo 91962 1237-B7
TOPPER LN
1200 SDCo 92021 1251-J2
TOP RAIL LN
1300 SDCo 92027 1130-C3
TOPSAIL DR
- SD 92154 1330-J6
- SD 92154 1331-A6
TOPSHAM ST
14500 PWY 92064 1190-H4
TOPSIDE LN
- SD 92154 1330-J6
- SD 92154 1331-A6

STREET
Block City ZIP Pg-Grid

TORANO DR
200 VSTA 92084 1087-H3
TORBETT LN
- SDCo 92127 1169-G2
TORCA CT
5800 SD 92124 1229-H7
TORERO PL
8200 SD 92126 1209-B2
TORI CT
- IMP 92251 6499-H2
TORINO CT
29800 SDCo 92082 1070-E5
TOROLE CIR
1000 VSTA 92084 1087-J7
TORONGA WY
30400 SDCo 92082 1070-J3
TORRANCE ST
400 SD 92103 1268-H6
TORREJON PL
2400 CRLB 92009 1147-F1
TORRELL WY
8100 SD 92126 1209-B1
TORREM ST
7600 LMSA 91942 1250-G7
TORREON DR
3100 SDCo 91901 1234-D4
TORREY CIR
- SD 92130 1208-C3
TORREY DR
1200 ENCT 92024 1167-F2
TORREY GN
2100 ESCN 92026 1109-D4
TORREY LN
- SDCo 92672 1023-E1
7800 SD 92037 1227-G6
TORREYANA RD
10900 SD 92121 1207-J5
10900 SD 92121 1208-A5
TORREYANA CIR
6300 CRLB 92011 1127-A4
TORREY ARBOR LN
- SD 92129 1189-A4
TORREY BELLA CT
- SD 92129 1189-B3
TORREY BLUFF DR
13500 SD 92130 1188-B5
TORREY CREST CT
- SD 92129 1189-B4
TORREY DEL MAR DR
- SD 92130 1188-J3
TORREY GARDENS PL
- SD 92129 1189-A4
TORREY GLENN RD
- SD 92129 1189-B3
TORREY HILL CT
13600 SD 92130 1188-A4
TORREY HILL LN
3700 SD 92130 1188-A4
TORREY MEADOWS DR
- SD 92129 1188-J4
- SD 92129 1189-A4
TORREY MESA CT
- SD 92129 1188-J4
TORREY PARK TER
- SD 92129 1189-B4
N TORREY PINES CT
3300 SD 92037 1207-J7
TORREY PINES LN
2400 SD 92037 1227-H6
TORREY PINES PL
700 OCN 92054 1086-F1
N TORREY PINES PL
11100 SD 92037 1207-J5
TORREY PINES RD
1000 SD 92037 1227-J5
1000 CHV 91915 1311-H5
7900 SD 92093 1227-J5
N TORREY PINES RD
9000 SD 92093 1227-J2
9200 SD 92037 1227-J2
10000 SD 92037 1207-J7
10000 SD 92093 1207-J7
10200 SD 92121 1207-J7
N TORREY PINES RD Rt#-S21
10300 SD 92121 1207-G2
10500 SD 92037 1207-G2
12100 SD 92014 1207-G2
12600 SD 92014 1187-G7
12800 DLMR 92014 1187-G7
TORREY PINES TER
200 DLMR 92014 1187-G7
TORREY PINES PARK RD
10700 SD 92037 1207-G2
12000 SD 92121 1207-G2
TORREY PINES SCENIC DR
2800 SD 92037 1207-H7
2800 SD 92093 1207-H7
TORREY PINES SCIENCE PK S
- SD 92121 1207-J5
TORREY POINT RD
400 DLMR 92014 1187-G7
TORREY RANCH CT
- SD 92129 1189-A3
TORREY RIDGE DR
12900 SD 92130 1188-B5
TORREY SANTA FE CT
- SD 92129 1188-J4
TORREY SANTA FE RD
- SD 92129 1188-H4
- SD 92129 1189-A4
TORREY VIEW CT
- SD 92130 1208-A3
TORRINGTON ST
3900 SD 92130 1188-A5
TORRY CT
2900 CRLB 92009 1127-G7
TORTILLA CIR
4400 OCN 92057 1087-A1
TORTUGA CT
10300 SD 92124 1229-H7
10300 SD 92124 1249-G1
TORTUGA CV
3900 OCN 92054 1086-G2
TORTUGA RD
5700 SD 92124 1229-H7
TORTUGA POINT DR
500 CHV 91911 1330-H4
TOSCA WY
2400 SD 92111 1248-H7
TOSCANA DR
7500 SD 92122 1228-E3
TOSCANA WY
5200 SD 92122 1228-E3
TOSCANO CT
- ENCT 92024 1148-B3
TOUB ST
2200 SDCo 92065 1152-D7
TOUCAN DR
500 VSTA 92083 1087-F4

STREET
Block City ZIP Pg-Grid

TOUCANET CT
- OCN 92057 1067-A3
TOULON CT
700 SD 92109 1247-H7
TOULON ST
1300 OCN 92056 1087-B3
TOULOUSE DR
1800 CHV 91913 1311-E7
1800 CHV 91913 1331-E1
TOULOUSE LN
2700 SDCo 92028 1048-C1
TOURMALINE CT
300 CHV 91911 1330-G5
TOURMALINE LN
2100 SDCo 92028 1028-A6
TOURMALINE ST
- CHV 91911 1330-F5
600 SD 92109 1247-H5
TOURNAMENT DR
3300 OCN 92056 1106-J1
TOUSSACHS WY
- SDCo 92028 1027-G6
TOWELL LN
1600 ESCN 92029 1129-G5
TOWER DR
1100 VSTA 92083 1107-J1
1200 VSTA 92083 1108-A2
TOWER LN
1200 ESCN 92026 1109-J7
TOWER PL
700 ESCN 92026 1109-J7
1100 VSTA 92083 1107-J1
TOWER RD
- SD 92121 1208-A6
400 IMPB 91932 1349-G2
TOWER ST
6800 LMSA 91941 1270-E3
6800 SD 92115 1270-E3
TOWHEE LN
6600 CRLB 92011 1127-C5
TOWHEE ST
1800 SDCo 92078 1128-A4
TOWKISH DR
- OCN 92054 1086-D3
TOWLE CT
5100 SD 92105 1270-A5
TOWN CENTER DR
1000 ENCT 92024 1147-F4
TOWN CENTER PKWY
200 SNTE 92071 1231-C6
TOWN CENTER PL
- ENCT 92024 1147-F4
TOWNE CTR N
- OCN 92057 1087-B1
TOWNE LN
9700 SDCo 92021 1233-A3
TOWNE CENTRE CT
4500 SD 92121 1228-C1
TOWNE CENTRE DR
8800 SD 92122 1228-D3
9100 SD 92121 1228-C1
TOWNE CENTRE PL
4500 SD 92121 1228-D1
TOWNES TER
- SDCo 92040 1231-J2
TOWN GARDEN RD
- CRLB 92009 1127-F3
TOWNSEND PL
1900 SDCo 92019 1272-C2
TOWNSEND RD
1500 ImCo 92250 431-D3
TOWNSGATE DR
3300 SD 92130 1188-A6
TOWNSITE DR
3400 VSTA 92084 1087-H5
TOWN SQUARE PKWY
- SDCo 92127 1169-F3
TOWN VIEW CT
6700 SD 92120 1250-C3
TOWN VIEW LN
6800 SD 92120 1250-C3
TOWN VIEW TER
6700 SD 92120 1250-C3
TOWNWOOD CT
3400 OCN 92054 1086-E3
TOWNWOOD WY
100 ENCT 92024 1147-J7
TOWSER ST
3200 SD 92123 1249-D5
TOW WAY RD
- CORD 92135 1288-G5
TOYA LN
15100 SDCo 92021 1233-A2
TOYNE ST
400 SD 92102 1289-H3
TOYOFF WY
4900 SD 92115 1269-J1
TOYON CT
300 SMCS 92069 1108-H5
TOYON DR
1600 SDCo 92028 1028-F4
TOYON GN
1600 ESCN 92026 1109-D6
TOYON LN
- CHV 91910 1310-C5
TOYON RD
5400 SD 92115 1269-J1
TOYON TER
- SMCS 92069 1108-G5
TOYON CANYON RD
9500 SDCo 92029 1149-D4
TOYON HEIGHTS CT
- SDCo 92028 998-D7
TOYON HEIGHTS DR
3100 SDCo 92028 998-C7
TOYON HILLS DR
11000 SDCo 92040 1211-F7
11000 SDCo 92040 1231-F1
TOYON MESA CT
- SD 92130 1188-G7
TOYON MOUNTAIN LN
900 SDCo 92036 1156-D5
TOYON MOUNTAIN RD
4300 SDCo 92036 1156-E5
TOYON RIDGE TR
- SDCo 92082 1090-E5
TRABERT RANCH RD
1400 ENCT 92024 1167-H1
TRACE RD
2400 SDCo 91978 1271-G7
TRACEY LN
1300 SDCo 92021 1233-A7
TRACI LN
600 VSTA 92084 1088-A7
TRACY CT
1900 SDCo 92028 1048-B4
TRACY ST
7400 LMGR 91945 1270-G7
TRACY LYN DR
31700 SDCo 92082 1051-A7
TRADE PL
9100 SD 92121 1209-A7
9100 SD 92126 1209-A7

STREET
Block City ZIP Pg-Grid

TRADE ST
100 SMCS 92078 1128-J1
7500 SD 92121 1208-J7
7500 SD 92121 1209-A7
TRADEWIND AV
1300 SD 92154 1349-J2
TRADE WINDS DR
- SDCo 92127 1168-J2
TRADEWINDS DR
6800 CRLB 92011 1126-H6
TRADITION ST
13500 SD 92128 1190-B3
TRAFALGAR LN
2700 CRLB 92010 1107-A5
TRAFALGAR RD
5600 SDCo 92019 1253-C4
N TRAIL CT
- CHV 91914 1311-G2
S TRAIL CT
- CHV 91914 1311-G2
TRAIL DR
3000 SDCo 91935 1292-G2
TRAIL BLAZE CT
4000 SDCo 91902 1311-B2
TRAILBROOK LN
11400 SD 92128 1190-A6
11400 SD 92128 1189-J6
TRAILBRUSH PT
11500 SD 92126 1209-A1
TRAILBRUSH TER
7600 SD 92126 1209-A1
TRAIL CREST CT
- SD 92131 1189-G7
TRAIL CREST DR
- SD 92131 1189-G7
- SD 92131 1209-G1
TRAIL CREST PL
- SD 92131 1189-G7
TRAIL DUST AV
13000 SD 92129 1189-C5
TRAILHEAD PL
- CHV 91914 1311-H3
- SD 92129 1189-B4
TRAILING DR
4100 SD 92105 1289-H1
TRAIL MARKER PL
- CHV 91914 1311-G2
TRAILRIDGE DR
500 CHV 91902 1311-C4
TRAILS END
2300 SDCo 92028 1047-G2
TRAILS END CIR
10200 SD 92126 1209-A5
TRAILS END DR
13900 SDCo 91935 1292-F2
TRAIL SHRINE LN
2100 SDCo 92004 (1099-F5 See Page 1098)
TRAILSIDE CT
11200 SD 92127 1169-J4
TRAILSIDE PL
- SMCS 92078 1128-F3
TRAILSIDE RD
8900 SD 92127 1169-A4
8900 SDCo 92127 1169-A4
TRAILSIDE WY
11300 SD 92127 1169-J4
TRAILVIEW RD
300 ENCT 92024 1147-J6
TRAILWIND RD
14200 PWY 92064 1170-H4
TRAILWOOD AV
- CHV 91913 1331-E1
TRALEE TER
3400 SDCo 91977 1271-C5
TRAM PL
400 CHV 91910 1310-F5
TRANQUIL CT
500 ENCT 92024 1147-J5
TRANQUILITY GN
600 ESCN 92027 1130-B2
TRANQUILITY LN
26500 SDCo 92065 1174-B4
TRANQUILLO LN
- CHV 91911 1330-E3
TRANSIT ST
100 OCN 92054 1106-A1
TRANSITE AV
1300 SD 92154 1349-J2
1400 SD 92154 1350-A2
TRANSMITTER DR
3200 SD 92115 1270-D6
TRANSPORTATION AV
2400 NATC 91950 1309-H3
TRAPANI CV
1200 CHV 91915 1311-F6
TRAPPERS HOLLOW RD
- SDCo 91901 1255-G1
TRASKE RD
1500 ENCT 92024 1147-G6
TRAVELD WY
1500 ENCT 92024 1147-G6
TRAVELERS WY
- SMCS 92069 1128-G1
TRAVELODGE DR
200 ELCJ 92020 1251-D5
TRAVER CT
- CHV 91913 1331-B1
TRAVERS WY
6100 SD 92122 1228-B5
TRAVERTINE CT
12100 PWY 92064 1190-C7
12100 PWY 92064 1210-B1
TRAVERTINE PL
- SDCo 92019 1272-B2
TRAVIS CT
8400 SD 92126 1209-C1
TRAVIS PL
11300 SD 92126 1209-C1
TRAYLOR RD
17900 SDCo 92065 1171-H1
TREADWELL BLVD
200 ImCo 92274 410-G6
TREADWELL DR
11700 PWY 92064 1210-C1
11700 PWY 92064 1190-C7
TREASURE DR
4900 LMSA 91941 1271-B2
TREASURE VIEW LN
1000 ENCT 92024 1167-E1
TREAT ST
2700 SD 92102 1289-D3
TREBOL ST
11300 SD 92126 1209-B2
TREBUCHET DR
1900 SDCo 92004 1058-G7
TREE ST
9100 SNTE 92071 1231-A4
TREECREST ST
13100 PWY 92064 1190-D1
TREEHAVEN CT
10000 SD 92131 1210-A4
TREEHILL PL
12600 PWY 92064 1190-C2

STREET
Block City ZIP Pg-Grid

TREE HOLLOW LN
11400 SD 92128 1189-J7
11400 SD 92128 1190-A7
TREEHOUSE ST
2300 CHV 91915 1331-H1
2300 CHV 91915 1311-H7
TREENA ST
10400 SD 92131 1209-F4
TREERIDGE TER
12700 PWY 92064 1190-D1
TREESIDE LN
10900 SDCo 92026 1089-G3
TREE SONG LN
- CHV 91915 1331-H1
TREETOP LN
- CHV 91915 1331-H1
700 ELCJ 92021 1251-J4
TREEVIEW PL
11700 SD 92131 1210-A4
TREEWIND CT
11800 SD 92128 1190-A7
TREEWIND LN
- CHV 91915 1331-G1
TREEWOOD ST
100 SD 92114 1290-D4
TRELAWNEY LN
1300 SDCo 92028 1028-C4
TRELLIS LN
100 ESCN 92026 1109-H6
TRELLIS ST
- CHV 91915 1331-H2
TRELLIS WY
- CHV 91915 1331-H1
TREMAINE WY
1700 SD 92154 1349-J2
1700 SD 92154 1350-A2
TREMONT ST
100 CHV 91911 1330-C5
1600 OCN 92054 1106-C3
4300 SD 92102 1289-H3
N TREMONT ST
200 OCN 92054 1086-A7
600 OCN 92054 1085-J7
S TREMONT ST
100 OCN 92054 1106-A1
TRENCHARD ST
10000 SNTE 92071 1231-D2
TRENT WY
10800 SDCo 91941 1271-F4
TRENTHAM RD
2700 ImCo 92251 431-C4
TRENTO PL
14500 SD 92130 1188-A3
TRENTON AV
1100 CHV 91911 1330-A4
3400 SD 92117 1248-D5
TRENTON ST
500 ELCJ 92019 1252-B4
TRENTON WY
- SMCS 92078 1128-E6
TRESEDER CIR
1700 SDCo 92019 1272-B2
TRES ENCINOS
2600 SDCo 92069 1088-H6
TRES HERMANAS WY
1400 ENCT 92024 1147-G5
TRESHILL RD
- IMP 92251 6499-E3
TRES LAGOS CT
10100 SDCo 91977 1271-E7
10100 SDCo 91977 1291-E1
TRES LOMAS
2900 SDCo 92028 1048-C1
TRES LOMAS CT
2900 SDCo 92028 1048-C1
TRES LOMAS DR
1000 ELCJ 92021 1252-B3
TRES NINOS CTE
1100 VSTA 92084 1108-C1
TRES RANCHO LN
500 SDCo 92069 1109-A4
500 SMCS 92069 1109-A4
TRES VISTA CT
13700 SD 92129 1189-E3
TRETAGNIER CIR
12000 SD 92128 1150-A7
TREVINO AV
2100 OCN 92056 1106-G1
TREVISO CT
- SD 92130 1188-A4
TREVOR PL
2600 ELCJ 92020 1251-A3
TREVOR HOLLOW CT
- SD 92130 1188-D6
TREVORS CT
9500 SDCo 92040 1232-D4
TREYBURN WY
- SD 92131 1209-G2
TRIANA ST
4900 SD 92117 1248-G1
TRIAS ST
4100 SD 92103 1268-G5
TRIBUL LN
- CRLB 92011 1126-J7
TRIBUNA AV
11200 SD 92131 1209-J5
TRICIA PL
28300 SDCo 92026 1089-E3
TRICIA ST
14100 PWY 92064 1190-E2
TRICIA ANN CT
- SDCo 92026 1069-B4
TRIDLE PL
1400 CHV 91911 1330-J3
TRIDLE WY
3500 SD 92173 1350-E5
TRIESTE DR
1200 SD 92107 1287-J1
3400 CRLB 92010 1106-H4
TRIESTE WY
3000 OCN 92056 1106-J1
TRIGAL WY
10600 SNTE 92071 1231-E3
TRIGGER ST
13000 SD 92129 1189-C5
TRIGO LN
7400 CRLB 92009 1147-J1
7400 CRLB 92009 1148-A1
TRILLIUM CT
- CRLB 92024 1147-J2
- SD 92131 1209-G1
TRILLIUM WY
- SD 92131 1209-G1
TRILOGY ST
- SMCS 92078 1128-H3
TRILY RD
- ImCo 92257 410-L4
TRINAS WY
3500 SDCo 91935 1272-G5
TRINIDAD BEND
- CORD 92118 1329-E2
TRINIDAD CV
1200 CHV 91915 1311-F6

STREET
Block City ZIP Pg-Grid

TRINIDAD WY
5100 SD 92114 1290-B5
TRINITY PL
5700 SD 92120 1250-B7
TRINITY ST
- OCN 92057 1086-H1
- OCN 92057 1066-H7
TRINITY WY
5500 SD 92120 1250-A7
TRINITY BAY PL
- SD 92110 1268-D5
TRIPLE LN
11900 SDCo 92040 1231-J5
TRIPLE C RANCH RD
2400 ENCT 92024 1148-A7
TRIPLE CROWN DR
5200 SDCo 92003 1047-J7
5200 SDCo 92003 1067-J1
TRIPLE CROWN RW
4900 SD 92130 1188-D2
TRIPOLI
- SD 92140 1268-F6
TRIPOLI DR
- ELCJ 92021 1251-J5
TRIPOLI RD
7700 SD 92126 1209-A3
TRIPOLI WY
3300 OCN 92056 1106-J1
TRIPP CT
3400 SD 92121 1208-A4
TRISTANIA PL
17700 SD 92127 1169-J1
TRISTAN RIVER RD
1100 CHV 91913 1331-B2
TRITON AV
1300 SD 92154 1349-J2
TRITON CIR
100 ENCT 92024 1147-C7
TRITON PL
1500 SD 92154 1349-J1
TRITON ST
- CRLB 92011 1127-C5
TRIUMPH DR
12700 PWY 92064 1190-D1
TRIUMPH ST
- VSTA 92081 1107-G5
TROCHA DE PENNI
10100 SDCo 92040 1231-F3
TROJAN AV
4700 SD 92115 1269-J4
4800 SD 92115 1270-A4
TROLLEY CT
5400 LMSA 91942 1250-J7
TROON WY
4000 CHV 91902 1310-F3
TROPEA ST
- OCN 92057 1067-A5
TROPHY DR
3400 SDCo 91941 1270-J5
3500 SDCo 91941 1271-A5
TROPHY WY
- SDCo 92004 (1079-C4 See Page 1058)
TROPICANA DR
100 OCN 92054 1086-E5
TROPICO DR
9100 LMSA 91941 1271-B3
9100 SDCo 91941 1271-B3
9200 SDCo 91977 1271-B3
S TROPICO DR
4000 SDCo 91941 1271-B4
TROTTER DR
- SD 92130 1208-E2
TROTTING HORSE RD
1600 SDCo 92057 1067-G6
TROUSDALE DR
200 CHV 91910 1310-A4
TROUSDALE PL
1900 ESCN 92029 1129-F7
TROUT LN
- OCN 92054 1086-G2
TROUTMAN RD
- SD 92152 1288-A5
TROUVILLE LN
- CHV 91913 1311-F7
- CHV 91913 1331-F1
TROVITA CT
- ESCN 92027 1110-D6
TROY LN
1700 OCN 92054 1106-E2
4500 LMSA 91941 1270-G3
TROY PL
2000 VSTA 92084 1088-C5
TROY ST
8400 LMGR 91945 1270-J7
8600 LMGR 91977 1270-J7
8600 SDCo 91977 1270-J7
8600 SDCo 91977 1271-A6
TROY TER
7600 LMSA 91941 1270-G2
TRUCKEE AV
2200 SD 92123 1249-C7
TRUCKHAVEN TR
- ImCo 92004 410-G7
- ImCo 92274 410-G7
TRUDEAU WY
17600 SDCo 91935 1294-B6
TRUDY LN
3700 SD 92106 1287-J4
3700 SD 92152 1287-J4
TRUESDELL LN
2000 CRLB 92008 1106-G4
TRUETT LN
10100 SD 92124 1249-G5
TRUJILLO TER
2100 ESCN 92027 1110-B5
TRULY TER
600 VSTA 92084 1087-J5
TRUMAN ST
9000 SD 92129 1189-D6
TRUMBULL ST
3000 SD 92106 1288-A2
TRUNKS BAY
300 OCN 92057 1066-H6
TRUST DR
1800 ESCN 92029 1129-F4
TRUXTON RD
- SD 92106 1288-C1
TRUXTUN RD
1600 SD 92106 1288-C1
2200 SD 92106 1268-D7
TUBB CANYON RD
- SDCo 92004 1098-F1
- SDCo 92004 (1099-A1 See Page 1098)
- SDCo 92066 1098-F1
TUBEROSE ST
2400 SD 92105 1269-H7
TUCKAWAY ST
6900 SD 92119 1250-E5
TUCKER LN
1500 ENCT 92024 1147-G6
TUCKER TR
2800 SDCo 91935 1293-G2

STREET
Block City ZIP Pg-Grid

TUCSON CT
1100 ELCJ 92021 1252-A3
TUCUMAN ST
- OCN 92057 1067-B2
TUDOR LN
1700 SDCo 92028 1028-A3
TUDOR ST
9900 SD 92131 1209-H5
TUFTS ST
5200 LMSA 91942 1270-G1
TUK-A-WILE
3300 SDCo 91935 1272-G6
TUKMAL DR
- OCN 92054 1086-D3
TUKWUT CT
100 SDCo 92061 1051-A6
TULA CT
4800 SD 92122 1228-F5
TULAGI RD
- CORD 92155 1309-B2
TULANE AV
900 CHV 91913 1311-D5
TULANE CT
1900 OCN 92056 1087-C5
3300 SD 92122 1228-C6
TULANE ST
5600 SD 92122 1228-C6
TULANE WY
3300 SD 92122 1228-C6
TULARE CT
3600 OCN 92056 1107-F3
TULARE ST
8600 LMSA 91941 1270-J3
8600 LMSA 91941 1271-A3
TULAROSA LN
- SMCS 92078 1128-F7
TULE CT
1800 CRLB 92011 1127-E6
TULE JIM LN
2100 SDCo 91905 1300-F7
TULE SPRINGS RD
- SDCo 91916 (1194-H4 See Page 1175)
- SDCo 91916 (1195-A2 See Page 1175)
- SDCo 92036 (1195-A2 See Page 1175)
TULE SPRINGS TKTR
- SDCo 91901 (1194-B4 See Page 1175)
- SDCo 91916 (1194-D4 See Page 1175)
- SDCo 92036 (1194-B4 See Page 1175)
TULIP DR
- SD 92109 1248-C6
TULIP LN
4000 SD 92105 1289-H1
TULIP ST
500 ESCN 92025 1129-G3
1800 SD 92105 1289-H1
S TULIP ST
100 ESCN 92025 1129-H4
TULIP WY
1000 CRLB 92011 1127-B6
TULIPAN WY
2400 SD 92111 1248-H7
TULSA ST
1100 ELCJ 92019 1251-H6
TUMBLE CREEK LN
400 SDCo 92028 1028-A3
TUMBLE CREEK TER
700 SDCo 92028 1028-A3
TUMBLEWEED AV
- IMP 92251 6499-E2
TUMBLEWEED LN
500 SDCo 92028 1047-E4
TUMBLEWEED TER
8500 ELCJ 92020 1231-E7
8500 SNTE 92071 1231-E7
TUMBLEWEED TR
- SDCo 92082 1090-C5
TUMBLEWEED WY
5600 OCN 92057 1067-E6
TUMERIC WY
- SDCo 91935 1294-J7
- SDCo 91935 (1295-A7 See Page 1294)
TUNA LN
- SD 92101 1288-J3
TUNAPUNA LN
- CORD 92118 1329-E3
TUNGSTEN DR
4100 LMSA 91941 1270-H4
TUNICA CIR
2400 SD 92111 1248-G7
TUNIS DR
- ELCJ 92021 1251-H5
TUNRIF CT
2500 SDCo 92084 1068-D6
TUOLUMNE PL
4300 CRLB 92010 1107-A5
TUPELO CV
7500 SD 92126 1209-A2
TUPPER ST
1600 SD 92103 1268-H5
TURA LN
12300 PWY 92064 1190-C2
TURF LN
3400 SDCo 91941 1270-J5
TURF RD
15500 DLMR 92014 1187-G2
15500 SD 92014 1187-G2
TURF VIEW DR
200 SOLB 92075 1187-F2
TURFWOOD LN
700 SOLB 92075 1187-G1
TURLOCK CT
13400 SD 92129 1189-C3
TURMERIC TER
800 CHV 91910 1330-J1
TURNBERRY CT
17100 SDCo 92067 1168-G7
TURNBERRY DR
1600 SMCS 92069 1108-J3
1800 VSTA 92081 1108-E2
3500 SDCo 91935 1272-E6
TURNBERRY GN
- ESCN 92026 1109-H2
TURNBERRY WY
3100 SDCo 91935 1272-E5
TURNBRIDGE GN
2400 ESCN 92027 1110-D6
TURNBRIDGE WY
6700 SD 92119 1251-A4
TURNBULL ST
2800 OCN 92054 1086-D6
TURNER AV
100 ENCT 92024 1147-G6
TURNER LN
11100 SDCo 92026 1089-G1
TURNER HEIGHTS DR
11500 SDCo 92026 1089-H3

STREET	Block	City	ZIP	Pg-Grid
TURNER HEIGHTS LN				
	27900	SDCo	92026	1089-H3
TURNFORD DR				
	7300	SD	92119	1250-J3
TURNING TRAIL RD				
	-	CHV	91914	1311-G2
TURNSTONE RD				
	-	CRLB	92011	1126-J4
	-	CRLB	92011	1127-A4
TURNSTONE WY				
	1000	OCN	92057	1087-A3
TURQUOISE CT				
	300	CHV	91911	1330-G5
TURQUOISE DR				
	-	CRLB	92011	1127-B4
TURQUOISE LN				
	3400	OCN	92056	1107-D2
TURQUOISE ST				
	-	CALX	92231	6620-H6
	1100	SD	92109	1247-H4
	4400	SD	92037	1247-H4
TURRET DR				
	11000	SD	92131	1209-H4
TURTLEBACK CT				
	11200	SD	92127	1169-J4
TURTLEBACK LN				
	11300	SD	92127	1169-J4
TURTLEBACK RD				
	15800	SD	92127	1169-J5
TURTLE CAY PL				
	1200	CHV	91915	1311-G6
TURTLE CAY WY				
	1200	CHV	91915	1311-G6
TURTLE DOVE LN				
	1000	ESCN	92026	1109-F5
TURTLE POINT WY				
	-	SMCS	92069	1108-J4
	-	SMCS	92069	1109-A5
TURTLE ROCK RD				
	28200	SDCo	92082	1090-F2
TUSCAN SPRINGS AV				
	-	CHV	91913	1331-E2
TUSCANY AV				
	1200	SDCo	92069	1109-A5
	1200	SMCS	92069	1109-A5
TUSCANY CT				
	10600	SDCo	92127	1169-F2
TUSCANY LN				
	7500	SD	92126	1208-J4
TUSCANY WY				
	300	OCN	92057	1087-A4
TUSCARORA DR				
	13000	PWY	92064	1190-D4
TUSHAK RANCH RD				
	800	SDCo	92084	1067-H6
TUSK CT				
	10400	SD	92124	1249-G3
TUSTIN ST				
	1800	SD	92106	1288-B1
	12600	PWY	92064	1190-C5
TUTELA HTS				
	1500	ESCN	92026	1109-H6
TUTHER WY				
	7000	SD	92114	1290-F4
TUTHILL WY				
	9500	SNTE	92071	1231-B4
TUTTLE LN				
	1200	SDCo	92021	1251-G1
TUTTLE ST				
	2400	CRLB	92008	1106-E4
TUXEDO RD				
	6600	SD	92119	1250-E3
TUXFORD DR				
	7300	SD	92119	1250-J3
TWAIN AV				
	-	CRLB	92008	1107-B7
	-	CRLB	92008	1127-B1
	4300	SD	92108	1249-H7
	4300	SD	92120	1249-H7
	4900	SD	92120	1250-A7
TWAIN CT				
	1300	SDCo	92069	1109-A3
	1300	SMCS	92069	1109-A3
TWAIN WY				
	29300	SDCo	92082	1070-H6
TWEED LN				
	-	SD	92102	1289-G4
TWEED ST				
	7400	LMGR	91945	1270-G7
TWELVE OAKS TR				
	-	SDCo	92021	1232-H7
	5100	SDCo	92021	1252-G2
TWIGGS ST				
	3900	SD	92110	1268-F5
TWILA LN				
	6300	SD	92115	1270-D5
TWILIGHT CT				
	9100	SNTE	92071	1231-B7
TWILIGHT GN				
	1900	ESCN	92026	1109-B3
TWILIGHT LN				
	3500	OCN	92056	1107-C2
TWILIGHT RDG				
	-	SD	92130	1208-B2
TWILIGHT ST				
	-	CHV	91915	1331-H1
TWIN CIRCLE CT				
	13200	PWY	92064	1190-E2
TWIN CIRCLE WY				
	14400	PWY	92064	1190-E2
TWIN COUNTRY LN				
	-	SDCo	92028	1047-G1
TWINFORD CT				
	9300	SD	92126	1209-E2
TWIN GABLES CT				
	-	PWY	92064	1190-F2
TWINING AV				
	600	SD	92154	1330-F7
	1000	SD	92154	1350-F1
TWIN LAKE DR				
	6200	LMSA	91942	1250-G6
	6200	SD	92119	1250-G6
TWIN LAKES CT				
	14300	SDCo	92067	1188-G2
TWINLEAF CT				
	10900	SD	92131	1209-H2
TWINLEAF WY				
	11000	SD	92131	1209-H2
TWIN MOUNTAIN CIR				
	9300	SD	92126	1209-E3
TWIN OAK				
	14100	SDCo	92021	1232-G5
TWIN OAK LN				
	35100	SDCo	92036	1156-E7
TWIN OAKS AV				
	200	CHV	91910	1310-B5
	700	CHV	91910	1330-C1
	1100	CHV	91911	1330-D3
TWIN OAKS CIR				
	100	CHV	91910	1310-B5
TWIN OAKS CREST DR				
	3700	SDCo	92069	1088-G4
TWIN OAKS VALLEY RD				
	1400	SMCS	92078	1128-H3
TWIN OAKS VALLEY RD				
	2400	SDCo	92069	1088-F2
	2400	SDCo	92069	1108-J1
	2400	SMCS	92069	1108-J1
	28500	SDCo	92084	1068-F6
	28800	SDCo	92084	1088-F1
N TWIN OAKS VALLEY RD				
	100	SMCS	92069	1128-H1
	100	SMCS	92069	1108-H7
N TWIN OAKS VALLEY RD Rt#-S12				
	200	SMCS	92069	1108-H5
S TWIN OAKS VALLEY RD				
	-	SMCS	92069	1128-H2
	100	SMCS	92078	1128-H2
	200	SMCS	92096	1128-H2
TWIN PALM CIR				
	500	SDCo	92028	1027-G3
TWIN PEAKS PL				
	14600	PWY	92064	1190-H1
TWIN PEAKS RD				
	-	SDCo	92036	1155-J4
	12200	PWY	92064	1190-C1
	14500	PWY	92064	1191-A1
TWIN POND TER				
	11000	SD	92128	1189-H4
TWINS HAVEN RD				
	4600	OCN	92057	1087-A3
TWIN TRAILS CT				
	9000	SD	92129	1189-D4
TWIN TRAILS DR				
	8700	SD	92129	1189-C4
TWISTED BRANCH RD				
	14300	PWY	92064	1170-G3
TWISTED OAK				
	-	SDCo	91935	1294-C1
TWISTED OAK LN				
	2100	SDCo	91901	1253-J1
TWO MILE COULEE				
	-	SDCo	91935	1292-G2
TYAHA ST				
	-	SDCo	92028	999-D7
TYLEE ST				
	1000	VSTA	92083	1087-E7
TYLER AV				
	1400	SD	92103	1269-B5
TYLER CT				
	-	CALX	92231	6620-J5
	-	SDCo	92082	1050-F6
	2200	SDCo	91977	1270-J7
	2200	SDCo	91977	1271-A7
TYLER HTS				
	30400	SDCo	92082	1070-F1
TYLER LN				
	14500	SDCo	92082	1050-F7
	14500	SDCo	92082	1070-G1
TYLER RD				
	14200	SDCo	92082	1070-F1
	14400	SDCo	92082	1050-F7
TYLER ST				
	2300	SDCo	91977	1271-A7
	2800	CRLB	92008	1106-E5
	4900	OCN	92057	1067-B7
	8500	SNTE	92071	1250-J1
	8600	SDCo	91977	1270-J7
TYLER WY				
	2200	SDCo	92065	1153-B1
TYNEBOURNE CIR				
	3900	SD	92130	1188-A5
TYRIAN ST				
	6500	SD	92037	1247-F2
	7400	SD	92037	1227-E7
TYROLEAN RD				
	7700	SD	92126	1209-A2
TYROLEAN WY				
	11200	SD	92126	1209-A2
TYRONE ST				
	300	ELCJ	92020	1251-C4
TYSON ST				
	100	OCN	92054	1106-A1
TZENA WY				
	1400	ENCT	92024	1147-G6
U				
U AV				
	-	NATC	91950	1290-A7
N U AV				
	-	NATC	91950	1290-A6
UDALL ST				
	3000	SD	92106	1268-C7
	3000	SD	92106	1288-C1
	3700	SD	92107	1268-B6
UFANO DR				
	2700	SDCo	91935	1293-C3
UHL ST				
	5800	SD	92105	1270-C6
UKIAH ST				
	-	CHV	91913	1311-E6
ULLMAN ST				
	3300	SD	92106	1288-A2
ULRIC CT				
	3000	SD	92111	1248-H6
ULRIC ST				
	1400	SD	92111	1269-A2
	1400	SD	92111	1268-J1
	2100	SD	92111	1248-J6
ULTIMO AV				
	200	ESCN	92025	1130-A7
ULTRAMARINE LN				
	100	SD	92114	1290-F5
UMATILLA DR				
	1200	DLMR	92014	1187-G5
UMBER CT				
	200	SD	92114	1290-G5
UMBRIA WY				
	13900	PWY	92064	1170-F6
UNA ST				
	1600	SD	92113	1289-G6
UNICORNIO ST				
	2400	CRLB	92009	1127-H5
UNIDA PL				
	3400	SD	92123	1249-D4
UNION PL				
	1200	SD	92037	1227-F6
UNION ST				
	100	ENCT	92024	1147-B5
	500	SD	92101	1289-A1
	2300	SD	92101	1288-J1
	2500	SD	92103	1288-J1
	2900	SD	92103	1268-H6
UNION PLAZA CT				
	1300	OCN	92054	1106-D1
UNIONTOWN RD				
	5100	SD	92117	1228-F7
UNITY WY				
	100	VSTA	92083	1087-H7
UNIVERSITY AV				
	1200	SD	92103	1269-A5
	2100	SD	92104	1269-D5
	3600	SD	92105	1269-J5
	4800	SD	92105	1270-A5
UNIVERSITY AV				
	5400	SD	92115	1270-C5
	6900	LMSA	91941	1270-F4
W UNIVERSITY AV				
	700	SD	92103	1268-J5
	1000	SD	92103	1269-A5
UNIVERSITY DR				
	1800	VSTA	92083	1108-B3
UNIVERSITY PL				
	300	SD	92103	1268-J5
	8000	LMSA	91941	1270-H2
UNIVERSITY CENTER LN				
	8900	SD	92122	1228-B3
UNO CT				
	800	VSTA	92084	1087-H5
UNO VERDE CT				
	1500	SOLB	92075	1167-J7
UPAS LN				
	9700	SDCo	92029	1149-D3
UPAS ST				
	-	ESCN	92025	1129-G3
	500	SD	92103	1269-A6
	700	SD	92103	1268-J6
	1700	SD	92104	1269-E6
	1700	SD	92101	1269-D6
W UPAS ST				
	300	SD	92103	1269-A6
UPLAND DR				
	100	VSTA	92084	1088-B5
UPLAND ST				
	4400	LMSA	91941	1270-J3
	6000	SD	92114	1290-C2
	9500	SDCo	91977	1271-C6
UPPER HILLSIDE DR				
	1900	SD	92037	1227-H7
UPPER MEADOW RD				
	33300	SDCo	92060	1052-E3
UPPER NORTH PEAK WY				
	-	SDCo	92036	1176-C3
UPS CIR				
	2000	OCN	92054	1106-E1
UPSHUR DR				
	2600	SD	92110	1268-E6
UPSHUR ST				
	2800	SD	92106	1288-B2
UPTON CT				
	6800	SD	92111	1248-J7
URANIA AV				
	900	ENCT	92024	1147-C3
URBAN DR				
	5600	LMSA	91942	1251-B7
URBANA GN				
	-	ESCN	92025	1130-A7
URIBE PL				
	-	SDCo	92014	1168-A7
URSINA PL				
	1900	ENCT	92024	1147-H7
URUBU ST				
	6800	CRLB	92009	1127-H5
US ELEVATOR RD				
	10700	SDCo	91978	1291-F1
USHER PL				
	-	SD	92173	1350-F3
USHLA WY				
	32100	SDCo	92061	1051-B6
UTAH ST				
	3400	SD	92104	1269-D5
	4400	SD	92116	1269-D3
UTAH WY				
	600	ESCN	92025	1129-J6
	600	ESCN	92025	1130-A5
UTE DR				
	4100	SD	92117	1248-E4
UTGOFF AV				
	-	CORD	92135	1288-F4
UTICA CT				
	6500	SD	92139	1310-F1
UTICA DR				
	2700	SD	92139	1310-F1
	3800	SDCo	92004	(1099-D1 See Page 1098)
UTICA PL				
	6500	SD	92139	1310-F1
UTOPIA RD				
	13400	PWY	92064	1190-D4
	17300	SD	92128	1170-C2
UTOPIA WY				
	12500	SD	92128	1170-C2
UVADA PL				
	4900	SD	92116	1269-D3
UVALDE CT				
	10800	SD	92124	1249-H1
UVAS ST				
	4700	SD	92102	1289-J3
V				
V AV				
	400	NATC	91950	1290-A7
VACA PL				
	11600	SD	92124	1250-B2
VACATION RD				
	1400	SD	92109	1268-A2
VACHELL LN				
	15500	SDCo	92021	1233-B1
VADO WY				
	1300	SD	92114	1290-D5
VAIL CT				
	11600	SD	92131	1210-A1
VAIL RD				
	900	ImCo	92233	411-A10
VAIL CREEK CT				
	5100	SD	92130	1188-D6
VAKAS DR				
	1700	SDCo	92019	1272-C3
VALANCE ST				
	1900	SD	92154	1350-C3
VALBORG DR				
	-	SMCS	92029	1128-H5
VALBROOK DR				
	-	SDCo	92028	1028-B4
VAL DALE DR				
	-	SDCo	92025	1130-D7
VALDES DR				
	1700	SD	92037	1227-G6
VALDINA DR				
	11400	SD	92124	1250-A1
VALDINA WY				
	4700	SD	92124	1250-A1
VALDIVIA CT				
	1100	CHV	91910	1311-B7
VALDOSTA AV				
	7900	SD	92126	1209-B3
VALE WY				
	5400	SD	92115	1270-B4
VALECREST LN				
	2100	SDCo	91977	1291-D1
VALEMONT ST				
	3400	SD	92106	1288-A2
VALENCIA AV				
	900	SMCS	92078	1128-E3
	1800	CRLB	92008	1106-H7
VALENCIA CIR				
	5900	SDCo	92067	1168-F7
VALENCIA CT				
	900	CHV	91910	1311-B6
	1600	OCN	92054	1106-D2
VALENCIA DR				
	100	VSTA	92083	1087-G6
	1100	SDCo	92025	1130-D5
	4500	SD	92115	1270-D3
VALENCIA LN				
	9200	SDCo	91977	1271-B7
VALENCIA LP				
	1300	CHV	91910	1311-B6
VALENCIA PKWY				
	100	SD	92114	1290-C5
N VALENCIA PKWY				
	100	SD	92114	1290-C4
VALENCIA PL				
	2600	SDCo	91977	1271-A7
VALENCIA ST				
	1500	OCN	92054	1106-D2
	8600	SDCo	91977	1270-J7
	8600	SDCo	91977	1271-A7
VALENCIA VW				
	-	PWY	92064	1190-C7
VALENCIA WY				
	29000	SDCo	92082	1070-J7
VALENCIA CANYON				
	2600	SDCo	91977	1271-A7
VALENCIA GLEN CT				
	1800	SDCo	92027	1130-E3
VALENCIA VALLEY VISTA				
	-	SDCo	92082	1050-J7
VALENCIA VILLAS DR				
	-	SDCo	92067	1168-F7
VALENTINE LN				
	1200	SDCo	92028	1028-C1
VALENTINO ST				
	1900	SD	92154	1350-D3
VALERA WY				
	100	OCN	92057	1086-H3
VALERIE DR				
	400	VSTA	92084	1087-H4
	2400	SDCo	92028	1028-C7
VALERIO TR				
	-	SD	92130	1188-D4
VALERIO GATE				
	-	SD	92130	1188-E4
VALETA ST				
	3900	SD	92110	1268-B5
	4000	SD	92107	1268-B5
VALE TERRACE DR				
	900	VSTA	92084	1087-J5
	1000	VSTA	92084	1088-A5
VALE TERRACE PL				
	1400	VSTA	92084	1088-B6
VALETTA LN				
	2500	SDCo	91901	1234-A5
VALE VIEW CT				
	600	VSTA	92081	1107-H1
VALE VIEW DR				
	400	VSTA	92081	1087-G7
	400	VSTA	92081	1107-G1
VALEWOOD AV				
	2600	CRLB	92010	1106-J5
VALEWOOD CT				
	12300	PWY	92064	1190-C5
VALEWOOD RD				
	13100	PWY	92064	1190-C5
VALHALLA DR				
	12100	SDCo	92040	1232-A5
VALHALLA VIEW DR				
	2400	SDCo	92019	1272-D1
VALIENTE CT				
	10800	SD	92124	1249-J2
VALI HAI RD				
	15000	PWY	92064	1170-J6
	15100	PWY	92064	1171-A6
VALINDA PT				
	4600	SD	92130	1188-C4
VALINDO WY				
	1900	SDCo	92084	1108-C3
VALJEAN CT				
	6600	SD	92111	1248-H7
VALKYRIA LN				
	1700	SDCo	92019	1272-B3
VALLADARES DR				
	17600	SD	92127	1170-A1
	17600	SD	92127	1150-A7
VALLARTA CT				
	100	SOLB	92075	1167-D6
VALLATA CT				
	10000	SDCo	91977	1291-D3
VALLATA LN				
	900	SDCo	91977	1291-D3
VALLDEMOSA LN				
	10900	SD	92124	1249-H2
VALLE AV				
	3000	SD	92113	1289-E5
VALLE DR				
	4300	LMSA	91941	1270-H3
VALLEA ST				
	1600	ELCJ	92019	1252-B7
VALLE CABALLO LN				
	9900	SDCo	92021	1232-J2
VALLECITO CT				
	-	IMP	92251	6499-H2
VALLECITO DR				
	-	SMCS	92078	1128-E2
VALLECITO LN				
	-	SDCo	92055	1085-J4
VALLECITO WY				
	-	CHV	91910	1310-D7
	-	CHV	91910	1330-D1
VALLECITOS				
	2100	SD	92037	1227-G5
VALLECITOS CT				
	2400	SD	92037	1227-H5
VALLECITOS DR				
	3600	SMCS	92078	1108-B7
	3600	SMCS	92078	1128-C1
VALLECITOS DE ORO				
	100	SMCS	92069	1108-F7
VALLEDA LN				
	1400	ENCT	92024	1147-G5
VALLE DE LAS SOMBRAS				
	1100	SDCo	91901	1233-F6
VALLE DE LOBO DR				
	17700	PWY	92064	1170-E1
VALLE DE LOBO WY				
	13600	PWY	92064	1170-F1
VALLE DEL SOL				
	3700	SDCo	92003	1067-F1
	4500	OCN	92003	1067-G2
VALLE DE ORO				
	16100	SDCo	92067	1168-D5
VALLE DE PAZ RD				
	10000	SDCo	92021	1233-C2
VALLE GRANDE				
	1400	ESCN	92025	1150-E3
VALLEJO AV				
	4300	SD	92117	1248-E2
VALLEJO CT				
	4300	SD	92117	1248-F2
VALLEJO ST				
	10500	SNTE	92071	1231-E6
VALLEJO MILLS ST				
	-	CHV	91913	1311-E7
VALLE LINDO RD				
	13900	ESCN	92027	1110-F5
VALLE PASO				
	100	SDCo	92084	1088-F5
VALLERY CT				
	5200	SD	92130	1188-D5
VALLE VERDE RD				
	13200	PWY	92064	1170-E2
VALLE VERDE ST				
	3800	SDCo	91902	1310-H3
VALLE VERDE TER				
	13200	PWY	92064	1170-E3
VALLE VISTA				
	-	SMCS	92078	1129-C1
	5300	SDCo	91941	1271-B1
VALLE VISTA AV				
	1900	NATC	91950	1310-B1
VALLE VISTA BYPS				
	-	SDCo	92040	1231-J2
VALLE VISTA RD				
	10400	SDCo	92040	1231-J1
	11100	SDCo	92040	1211-G6
VALLE VISTA ST				
	4300	SD	92103	1268-H5
VALLEY AV				
	600	SOLB	92075	1167-G7
	600	SOLB	92075	1187-G1
	600	DLMR	92014	1187-G1
	3800	CHV	91911	1330-F6
VALLEY BLVD				
	1100	ImCo	92249	6560-B7
N VALLEY BLVD Rt#-S6				
	100	ESCN	92025	1129-J2
S VALLEY BLVD Rt#-S6				
	100	ESCN	92025	1129-J2
VALLEY DR				
	400	SDCo	92084	1088-B7
	700	VSTA	92084	1088-B7
	900	VSTA	92084	1108-B1
	8300	SDCo	91977	1290-J6
VALLEY PKWY Rt#-S6				
	900	ESCN	92025	1129-F4
	1100	ESCN	92029	1129-F4
E VALLEY PKWY				
	500	ESCN	92025	1129-J2
E VALLEY PKWY Rt#-S6				
	100	ESCN	92025	1129-J2
	500	ESCN	92025	1130-A2
	1100	ESCN	92027	1130-A2
	1800	ESCN	92027	1110-E6
W VALLEY PKWY				
	800	ESCN	92025	1129-G3
W VALLEY PKWY Rt#-S6				
	200	ESCN	92025	1129-H3
VALLEY PL				
	1700	CRLB	92008	1106-G5
	2800	SD	92113	1289-E4
VALLEY RD				
	-	SD	92139	1310-E3
	1900	OCN	92056	1086-H7
	2000	OCN	92056	1106-H1
	2500	NATC	91950	1310-C3
	3500	NATC	91902	1310-E3
	3600	SDCo	91902	1310-E3
VALLEY ST				
	2900	CRLB	92008	1106-F4
VALLEY VW				
	2200	ESCN	92029	1129-E6
VALLEY BEND ST				
	1700	CHV	91913	1311-D7
VALLEY CENTER RD Rt#-S6				
	3100	ESCN	92027	1110-E5
	24800	SDCo	92027	1090-E4
	24800	SDCo	92027	1110-E5
	24800	SDCo	92082	1090-E1
	30300	SDCo	92082	1091-A2
	31700	SDCo	92082	1071-E1
	33600	SDCo	92061	1051-D7
	33600	SDCo	92061	1071-E1
VALLEY CENTER SCHOOL RD				
	14200	SDCo	92082	1090-F1
VALLEY CENTRE DR				
	3500	SD	92130	1207-J1
	3500	SD	92130	1208-A1
	3700	SD	92130	1188-A7
VALLEYCREEK CIR				
	-	CHV	91914	1311-H2
VALLEY CREEK DR				
	-	CHV	91914	1311-H2
VALLEY CREST DR				
	700	OCN	92054	1086-D3
	800	SDCo	92084	1088-E7
	1000	SDCo	92084	1108-F1
VALLEYDALE LN				
	100	ENCT	92024	1147-H7
	100	ENCT	92024	1167-H1
VALLEY GARDENS DR				
	2300	CHV	91915	1311-H7
VALLEY GLEN DR				
	3100	OCN	92056	1106-H2
VALLEY GROVE LN				
	500	ESCN	92025	1130-C6
VALLEY HEIGHTS DR				
	400	OCN	92057	1087-A2
VALLEY HEIGHTS RD				
	-	OCN	92057	1087-A2
VALLEY HIGH RD				
	4800	SDCo	92040	1231-H7
	4800	SNTE	92040	1231-H7
	5700	SNTE	92040	1251-H1
VALLEY KNOLLS RD				
	2700	SDCo	91935	1292-G3
VALLEY LAKE DR				
	2000	ELCJ	92020	1251-B2
VALLEY LIGHTS DR				
	10900	SDCo	92020	1271-G2
VALLEY MEADOW PL				
	500	ESCN	92027	1110-E7
VALLEY MILL RD				
	2300	ELCJ	92020	1251-B2
VALLEY OAK LN				
	38100	SDCo	92086	409-K5
VALLEY OAKS BLVD E				
	1600	SDCo	92028	1028-F4
VALLEY OAKS BLVD W				
	1500	SDCo	92028	1028-F4
VALLEY OF THE KING RD				
	29600	SDCo	92084	1068-F6
VALLEY RANCH RD				
	-	SDCo	92021	1232-H3
VALLEY RIDGE ST				
	2100	CHV	91914	1311-E2
VALLEY RIM GN				
	2100	ESCN	92026	1109-C4
VALLEY RIM RD				
	1900	SDCo	92021	1252-D3
	2000	SDCo	92019	1252-D3
	2000	ELCJ	92019	1252-D4
VALLEYSIDE LN				
	-	ENCT	92024	1148-A5
VALLEY SPRINGS RD				
	14000	PWY	92064	1170-G3
VALLEY STREAM RD				
	-	SDCo	92082	1070-C6
VALLEYTREE PL				
	300	ESCN	92026	1109-H4
VALLEYVIEW AV				
	-	ELCN	92243	6559-G3
	-	ImCo	92243	6559-G3
VALLEY VIEW BLVD				
	1900	SDCo	92019	1252-C5
	1900	ELCJ	92019	1252-C5
VALLEY VIEW CIR				
	7900	LMSA	91941	1270-J4
VALLEY VIEW DR				
	900	SDCo	92036	1156-C1
	1000	SDCo	92036	1136-C7
N VALLEY VIEW DR				
	700	CHV	91914	1311-G3
S VALLEY VIEW DR				
	800	CHV	91914	1311-G3
VALLEY VIEW GN				
	2500	ESCN	92026	1109-B3
VALLEY VIEW LN				
	100	OCN	92054	1086-E6
	3400	SDCo	91977	1271-A6
VALLEY VIEW PL				
	200	VSTA	92083	1107-J1
	2300	ESCN	92026	1109-G4
VALLEY VIEW RD				
	12100	SDCo	92082	1090-A2
VALLEYVIEW RD				
	14600	PWY	92064	1150-H7
VALLEY VIEW TKTR				
	-	SDCo	92021	1252-D1
VALLEY VIEW TR				
	7800	SDCo	91962	1237-C5
VALLEY VILLAGE DR				
	600	ELCJ	92021	1251-G3
VALLEY VISTA DR				
	27000	SDCo	92082	1090-J5
VALLEY VISTA RD				
	3300	SDCo	91902	1310-F3
VALLEY VISTA WY				
	2800	OCN	92054	1106-F1
	3600	SDCo	91902	1310-F3
VALLEY VISTA FORK				
	3700	SDCo	91902	1310-E3
VALLEY WATERS CT				
	-	SDCo	91978	1291-E2
VALLEY WATERS DR				
	-	SDCo	91978	1291-F2
VALMONTE GN				
	2500	ESCN	92029	1149-G1
VALNER CT				
	2100	SD	92139	1290-D7
VALNER WY				
	6200	SD	92139	1290-D7
VALOMA PL				
	4300	SD	92122	1228-E6
VALOR PL				
	10700	SNTE	92071	1231-E3
VALPREDA RD				
	100	SMCS	92069	1108-J7
VAL SERENO DR				
	700	ENCT	92024	1148-B6
VALVA AV				
	-	NATC	91950	1290-A6
VAL VERDE CT				
	14400	SD	92129	1189-H2
VAL VISTA DR				
	8500	SNTE	92071	1250-J1
VAN ALLEN WY				
	5800	CRLB	92008	1127-C1
VAN ANDEL WY				
	9300	SNTE	92071	1230-J6
VAN BUREN AV				
	1400	SD	92103	1269-B4
VANCE ST				
	100	CHV	91910	1310-C6
VANCOUVER AV				
	2200	SD	92104	1289-G1
	2400	SD	92104	1269-F6
VANCOUVER ST				
	2600	CRLB	92010	1106-J3
VANDEGRIFT BLVD				
	-	SDCo	92055	409-A7
	-	SDCo	92055	1085-H3
	-	SDCo	92055	1086-A2
	400	OCN	92057	1067-A2
	900	SDCo	92055	1067-A2
	1200	SDCo	92055	1066-J1
VANDEMEN WY				
	-	SD	92131	1209-G2
VANDERBILT PL				
	700	SD	92103	1268-J6
VAN DER LINDEN RD				
	-	ImCo	92250	431-F6
VAN DER POEL RD				
	500	ImCo	92243	6559-B7
VANDEVER AV				
	4300	SD	92120	1249-H7
	4800	SD	92120	1250-A7
VAN DUESEN RD				
	-	SDCo	92036	1155-J1
	-	SDCo	92036	1156-A1
VAN DYKE AV				
	400	DLMR	92014	1187-G5
	3100	SD	92105	1269-H4
	4400	SD	92116	1269-H4
VAN DYKE PL				
	4200	SD	92116	1269-H4
VANESSA CIR				
	1400	ENCT	92024	1147-G5
VAN GOGH LN				
	5200	SDCo	91902	1290-H7
VANGUARD PL				
	8700	SDCo	92021	1232-C7
	8700	SDCo	92040	1232-C7
VANGUARD WY				
	13200	SDCo	92040	1232-C7
VAN HORN RD				
	600	SDCo	92019	1252-C7
VAN HORN ST				
	8700	LMSA	91942	1251-A7
VAN HORN WY				
	800	SDCo	92019	1252-C7
VAN HOUTEN AV				
	100	ELCJ	92020	1251-F5
VANILLA WY				
	600	OCN	92057	1086-H5
VANITA ST				
	800	SDCo	92028	1027-G1
VANITIE CT				
	700	SD	92109	1247-H7
VANN CT				
	1600	ELCJ	92020	1251-C4
VAN NESS AV				
	2000	NATC	91950	1310-C1
	2400	SDCo	91950	1310-C1
VAN NUYS CT				
	5300	SD	92109	1247-H4
VAN NUYS PL				
	5300	SD	92109	1247-H4
VAN NUYS ST				
	700	SD	92037	1247-G4
	700	SD	92109	1247-G4
VAN NUYS WY				
	5300	SD	92109	1247-H4
VAN ROY WY				
	2400	OCN	92054	1086-D6
VANTAGE CT				
	1300	VSTA	92081	1128-A1
VANTAGE PL				
	-	SDCo	92028	1027-H7
VANTAGE WY				
	2400	SD	92014	1187-H5
VAN VECHTEN RD				
	1300	ELCJ	92019	1252-A7
	1300	SDCo	92019	1252-A7
	1300	SDCo	92020	1252-A7
	1300	SDCo	92020	1272-A1
E VAQUERO CT				
	1300	CHV	91910	1311-B7
W VAQUERO CT				
	1200	CHV	91910	1311-B7
VAQUERO GN				
	1400	ESCN	92026	1109-D4
VARNEY DR				
	6100	SD	92114	1290-D5
VARONA ST				
	4000	SD	92106	1288-A2
	4100	SD	92107	1287-J2
	4100	SD	92107	1288-A2
VARS WY				
	-	SDCo	91901	1234-B4
VASQUEZ WY				
	-	SDCo	92127	1169-G2
VASSAR AV				
	800	CHV	91913	1311-D5
	7200	LMSA	91941	1270-F3
VAUGHAN RD				
	12400	PWY	92064	1190-C3
VECINIO DEL ESTE PL				
	13600	SDCo	92040	1232-E5
VECINO CT				
	300	SDCo	91977	1291-A4
VEEMAC AV				
	6000	LMSA	91942	1251-B6
VEGA ST				
	-	CALX	92231	6620-F7
	1100	SD	92110	1268-E2
VELA DR				
	11300	SD	92126	1209-C1
VELASCO CT				
	4300	SDCo	91941	1271-G3
VELITE DR				
	300	SDCo	92004	1058-G7
VELLA LAVELLA RD				
	2300	CORD	92155	1309-A2
VELMA TER				
	5200	SD	92114	1290-B5
VENADITO				
	3000	SDCo	91901	1254-D1
VENADO ST				
	3100	CRLB	92009	1127-H7
	3200	CRLB	92009	1147-J1
VENCILL RD				
	-	ImCo	92250	431-E6
VENDIMIA CT				
	-	VSTA	92084	1088-D6
VENDOLA DR				
	-	CHV	91913	1331-E1
VENDOR PL				
	17200	PWY	92064	1170-D2
VENETIA WY				
	100	OCN	92057	1087-A3
VENICE AV				
	-	SMCS	92078	1128-E6
VENICE CT				
	700	SD	92109	1247-H7
VENICE GN				
	800	ESCN	92026	1109-J7
VENICE ST				
	1500	SD	92107	1288-A1
	1600	SD	92107	1268-A7
VENTANA DR				
	1500	ESCN	92029	1149-G1
VENTANA WY				
	-	OCN	92057	1087-A1
	1900	ELCJ	92020	1251-B1
VENTERS DR				
	1400	CHV	91911	1330-J3
VENTURA PL				
	700	SD	92109	1267-H2
VENTURE ST				
	100	SMCS	92078	1128-J1
	100	SMCS	92078	1129-A1
	400	ESCN	92029	1129-E3
VENTURE VALLEY RD				
	1000	SDCo	92036	1138-A6
VENUS GN				
	-	ESCN	92025	1129-H2
VENUS ST				
	4100	SD	92110	1268-C5
VENUS VIEW DR				
	700	VSTA	92081	1107-G1
VERA CIR				
	100	VSTA	92084	1087-J5
VERA LN				
	2000	ESCN	92026	1109-D5
VERA ST				
	800	SOLB	92075	1187-G1
VERA CRUZ				
	1200	OCN	92056	1087-B4
VERA CRUZ AV				
	-	SD	92140	1268-G7
VERACRUZ CT				
	-	IMP	92251	6499-H1
	10300	SD	92124	1249-G1
VERALEE DR				
	3200	SD	92154	1350-D2
VERANDA CT				
	12400	SD	92128	1190-A6
VERANO CT				
	12000	SD	92128	1150-B7
VERANO DR				
	900	CHV	91910	1310-J7
	18000	SD	92128	1150-B7
VERANO PL				
	2500	ESCN	92025	1130-C7
	18300	SD	92128	1150-B6
VERANO BRISA DR				
	4300	SDCo	92024	1148-E3
VERANO VISTA				
	-	SDCo	92078	1128-C4

STREET
Block City ZIP Pg-Grid

VERBENA CT
- CRLB 92011 1127-B4
- ENCT 92024 1147-E5
VERBENA DR
100 SDCo 92004 (1078-G1
See Page 1058)
VERBENA LN
10000 SDCo 91977 1291-D2
VERBENA TER
1900 SDCo 91901 1233-J5
1900 SDCo 91901 1234-A5
VERDA AV
2700 ESCN 92025 1130-A7
2700 ESCN 92025 1150-A1
VERDANT PL
600 VSTA 92084 1087-J5
VERDANT WY
2600 SDCo 91950 1310-C3
VERDE AV
500 SDCo 92028 1047-E5
3100 CRLB 92009 1147-J1
VERDE CT
3200 SDCo 91902 1310-E4
VERDE DR
4900 OCN 92057 1067-A6
VERDE VIA
1900 SDCo 92027 1130-E4
VERDE GLENN
1900 SDCo 92019 1272-C2
VERDE ORO
300 SDCo 92028 1047-F3
VERDE RIDGE CT
400 SDCo 91977 1290-J5
VERDE RIDGE RD
8300 SDCo 91977 1290-J5
VERDE SCHOOL RD
- ImCo 92250 431-E6
VERDE VIEW RD
2800 SDCo 91901 1234-C7
VERDI AV
100 ENCT 92007 1167-C2
VERDIGRIS VALLEY RD
17100 SDCo 92065 1171-E1
VERDIN CT
- CRLB 92011 1127-D4
VERDIN ST
500 ELCJ 92019 1252-B4
VEREDA CT
1900 SDCo 92019 1272-C1
VEREDA DR
- CALX 92231 6620-H7
VEREDA RD
- SMCS 92069 1109-A6
VEREDA BARRANCA
1200 SDCo 92084 1088-C4
VEREDA CALLADA
900 SDCo 92029 1149-H1
VEREDA LUNA LLENA
4400 SD 92130 1208-B3
VEREDA LUZ DEL SOL
1700 SD 92130 1208-C3
VEREDA MAR DEL CORAZON
- SD 92130 1208-C2
VEREDA MAR DEL SOL
- SD 92130 1208-C3
VEREDA MAR DE PONDEROSA
4400 SD 92130 1208-C3
VEREDA SOL DEL DIOS
10800 SD 92130 1208-C4
VERGARA ST
5300 SD 92117 1248-H1
VERIN LN
800 CHV 91910 1310-H6
VERLA LN
1600 SDCo 92027 1130-C4
VERLANE DR
8600 SD 92119 1250-J4
8600 SD 92119 1251-A4
VERLEY CT
4400 SD 92117 1248-G2
VERMARINE CT
- CRLB 92009 1127-G4
VERMEL AV
1900 ESCN 92029 1129-F5
VERMILLION WY
100 SD 92114 1290-F5
E VERMONT AV
100 ESCN 92025 1130-B5
W VERMONT AV
200 ESCN 92025 1130-A6
VERMONT CT
- ELCJ 92020 1251-A2
VERMONT PL
600 ESCN 92025 1129-J6
600 ESCN 92025 1130-A6
VERMONT ST
1700 SDCo 92065 1152-E7
2200 SDCo 92065 1172-D1
3400 SD 92103 1269-B5
VERN DR
3800 SDCo 92028 1028-F6
VERNA DR
9000 SDCo 92026 1069-A6
VERNA WY
5100 SDCo 91941 1271-F1
VERNAL LN
4000 SDCo 91916 1236-A3
VERNARDO DR
100 CALX 92231 6620-F7
VERNAZZA CT
- SD 92130 1188-A4
VERNER WY
100 VSTA 92083 1087-F7
VERNETTE CT
11500 SDCo 92020 1271-H2
VERNETTE DR
4600 SDCo 92020 1271-H3
VERNIER DR
8200 LMGR 91945 1290-H1
VERNIE VISTA LN
32400 SDCo 92082 1050-F6
VERNON CT
- CHV 91913 1331-B1
VERNON WY
300 ELCJ 92020 1251-E3
300 SDCo 92020 1251-F3
VERONA CT
700 SD 92109 1247-H7
VERONA ST
4900 OCN 92056 1087-C3
VERONA HILLS CT
2100 SDCo 92084 1108-D3
VERONA HILLS PKWY
2000 SDCo 92084 1108-D2
VERONICA AV
6800 SD 92115 1270-E5
VERONICA CT
- CRLB 92011 1127-B5
400 CHV 91911 1330-G3
VERONICA PL
500 ESCN 92027 1110-D6

VERSAILLES CT
12000 SD 92128 1150-A7
VERSAILLES RD
1900 CHV 91913 1311-E5
VERUS ST
2200 SD 92154 1330-A5
VERVAIN ST
9300 SD 92129 1189-E5
VESPER LN
- CRLB 92011 1127-D4
VESPER RD
14400 SDCo 92082 1090-G1
15400 SDCo 92082 1091-A1
VESTA ST
900 NATC 92136 1309-F1
900 SD 92136 1309-F1
1700 SD 92113 1289-F7
2100 SD 92136 1289-F7
VESUVIA WY
3000 SD 92139 1310-E2
VETTER PL
4300 LMSA 91941 1270-F4
VEZELAY LN
- SD 92128 1150-B6
VIA ABACA
10900 SD 92126 1209-C3
VIA ABAJO
11100 SD 92129 1169-H7
VIA ABERTURA
13800 SD 92130 1188-H3
VIA ACANTILADA
17800 SD 92128 1150-C7
VIA ACAPULCO
7900 SD 92122 1228-E4
VIA ACOSTA
12800 SD 92128 1150-D7
VIA ACQUAVIVA
4300 SDCo 92028 1047-G5
VIA ADELFA
- CRLB 92009 1147-F2
VIA ADELIA
- SCLE 92672 1023-B2
VIA ADRIANA
1800 OCN 92056 1087-B5
VIA AFABLE
1600 SD 92154 1349-J1
VIA A LA CASA
16400 SDCo 92067 1168-E4
VIA ALBERTO
10700 SD 92129 1189-G2
VIA ALCAZAR
5300 SD 92111 1248-G6
6500 CRLB 92009 1127-J4
VIA ALDEA
4000 OCN 92057 1086-H2
VIA ALEGRE
800 SDCo 92028 1027-H1
1700 SDCo 92027 1130-D3
VIA ALEGRE DR
1000 SDCo 92065 1152-J6
VIA ALESSANDRO
3200 SD 92111 1248-G5
VIA ALEXANDRA
900 ESCN 92026 1109-F5
900 SDCo 92026 1109-F5
VIA ALFALFA
11900 SDCo 92019 1271-J3
VIA ALICANTE
3100 SD 92037 1228-A4
VIA ALICIA
- SDCo 92028 1048-C2
3600 OCN 92056 1107-G4
VIA ALISAL
14100 SD 92128 1190-B1
VIA ALLEGRA
- VSTA 92081 1107-H2
VIA ALLENA
1700 OCN 92056 1087-C4
VIA ALLONDRA
1500 SDCo 92078 1128-B4
1500 SMCS 92078 1128-B4
VIA ALMANSA
300 ENCT 92024 1147-F6
VIA ALMONTE
3200 SDCo 92028 1048-H2
VIA ALTA
1300 DLMR 92014 1187-G5
VIA ALTAMIRA
3200 SDCo 92028 1048-G2
VIA ALTA MIRASOL
17800 SD 92128 1150-B7
17800 SD 92128 1170-B1
VIA ALTA VISTA
3600 SMCS 92078 1108-B7
3600 SMCS 92078 1128-C1
32000 SDCo 92003 1048-C7
32000 SDCo 92003 1068-C1
VIA ALTIVA
17800 SD 92128 1150-B7
VIA AMABLE
4400 SD 92122 1228-D3
VIA AMADOR
3000 CRLB 92010 1106-H3
VIA AMALIA
3100 SD 92111 1248-G6
VIA AMATA
3100 SD 92111 1248-G6
VIA AMBIENTE
- SDCo 92029 1148-J3
8000 SDCo 92067 1148-J3
8000 SDCo 92067 1149-A4
VIA AMBROSA
- SD 92129 1188-J4
VIA AMISTOSA
3800 SDCo 92091 1168-C7
VIA ANACAPA
- SMCS 92069 1108-D4
VIA ANDALUSIA
300 ENCT 92024 1147-F6
VIA ANDAR
8800 SD 92122 1228-D3
VIA ANGELICA
1200 VSTA 92081 1107-E1
VIA ANGELINA
1100 SD 92037 1247-F2
VIA ANITA
2200 SD 92037 1247-J2
9100 SNTE 92071 1231-G5
VIA ANNA
10700 SDCo 91978 1271-F6
VIA ANTIGUA
12100 SDCo 92019 1272-A4
VIA ANTOINETTE
12900 SDCo 92082 1070-C5
VIA APRILIA
2200 SD 92014 1207-H1
VIA APUESTO
1200 SDCo 92078 1128-G4
VIA AQUARIO
5300 SD 92111 1248-G5
VIA ARANGO
10700 SD 92129 1189-H3
VIA ARARAT DR
31700 SDCo 92003 1048-G7

VIA ARARAT DR
31700 SDCo 92003 1068-G1
VIA ARBOLEDA
1200 SDCo 92029 1149-G2
VIA ARBOLES
400 SMCS 92069 1109-D7
VIA ARCE
8000 CRLB 92009 1147-G3
VIA ARCILLA
3100 SD 92111 1248-G5
VIA AREQUIPA
4900 CRLB 92008 1107-A7
VIA AREZZO
- SD 92127 1168-J7
- SD 92127 1188-J1
VIA ARGENTINA
1100 VSTA 92081 1107-E1
VIA ARMADO
600 CHV 91910 1311-A5
VIA ARROYO
2700 SDCo 92028 1028-B7
2800 SDCo 92028 1048-B1
VIA ARTISTA
- SMCS 92069 1108-E4
VIA ARTURO RD
- SDCo 91916 1235-E2
VIA ASCENSO
18100 SDCo 92067 1148-D6
VIA ASOLEADO
2700 SDCo 91901 1254-B3
VIA ASTI
11000 SD 92129 1189-H3
VIA ASTUTO
2500 CRLB 92010 1106-H3
VIA ASUNCION
5700 SDCo 92003 1067-J2
VIA AVANTE
4900 SD 92130 1188-D3
VIA AVOLA
7500 SD 92037 1227-H6
VIA AZUL
3000 SD 92014 1187-J1
11800 SDCo 92082 1069-J6
VIA BAHIA
700 SMCS 92069 1108-F4
VIA BALDONA
3600 OCN 92056 1107-F4
VIA BANCO
10900 SD 92126 1209-C3
VIA BANDITA
200 OCN 92057 1087-A2
VIA BARBERINI
- CHV 91910 1310-A4
VIA BARLETTA
2500 SD 92037 1227-H6
VIA BARLOVENTO
1600 SDCo 92078 1128-G4
VIA BARODA
14200 SD 92130 1188-D2
VIA BARONA
3000 CRLB 92009 1127-J4
VIA BARQUERO
- SMCS 92069 1108-F4
VIA BARRANCA
1200 SD 92037 1247-G1
VIA BARRANCA DEL ZORRO
6100 SDCo 92067 1168-F4
VIA BARTOLO
3200 SD 92111 1248-G5
VIA BEATRAIZ
10700 SD 92129 1189-H2
VIA BELFIORE
- SD 92129 1189-A4
VIA BELLA DONNA
800 SMCS 92078 1128-G3
VIA BELLA MARIA
800 SMCS 92078 1128-G3
VIA BELLA MONICA
800 SMCS 92078 1128-G3
VIA BELLARADO
- SD 92129 1189-A4
VIA BELLCANTO
- SD 92129 1188-J5
VIA BELLEZA
1200 SMCS 92069 1109-C7
1200 SMCS 92069 1129-C1
VIA BELLINI
- SD 92127 1168-J7
VIA BELLO
5300 SD 92111 1248-G5
VIA BELMONTE
4700 SDCo 92028 1048-G2
VIA BELOTA
2900 SDCo 91901 1254-D1
VIA BELTRAN
3400 SD 92117 1248-E5
VIA BENITO
3300 SD 92111 1248-G5
VIA BERGAMO
- SD 92127 1168-J7
VIA BERNARDO
3600 OCN 92056 1107-G4
VIA BETTONA
- SD 92127 1168-J7
VIA BISSOLOTTI
300 CHV 91910 1310-A4
VIA BLANCA
2100 OCN 92054 1106-G2
VIA BOCAS
2600 CRLB 92010 1106-C6
VIA BOGOTA
600 VSTA 92081 1107-F1
VIA BOLIVIA
600 VSTA 92081 1107-E1
VIA BOLSA
11600 SDCo 92019 1271-J3
VIA BOLTANA
13800 SD 92129 1189-E3
VIA BORGIA
12700 SD 92014 1207-H1
VIA BORREGOS
6800 CRLB 92009 1128-A6
VIA BOTERO
1500 OCN 92056 1087-C3
VIA BRILLANTE
4400 SD 92122 1228-D3
VIA BRISA DEL LAGO
1500 SDCo 92078 1128-C3
VIA BRITTNEY
10700 SDCo 92040 1231-H5
VIA BROMA
15900 SDCo 92091 1168-C7
VIA BUENA VISTA
1500 SDCo 92078 1128-B4
VIA CABALLO ROJO
12800 SD 92129 1189-F5
VIA CABANA
7000 CRLB 92009 1127-G6
VIA CABERNET
- ESCN 92029 1129-E4
VIA CABEZON
12400 SD 92129 1189-F6
VIA CABO VERDE
3300 ESCN 92029 1150-A3

VIA CABRERA
6300 SD 92037 1247-J1
VIA CABRILLO
3700 OCN 92056 1107-F4
VIA CACERES
9800 SD 92129 1189-E3
VIA CAFETAL
900 SMCS 92069 1108-E4
VIA CAJITA
3200 CRLB 92010 1106-C6
VIA CALABRIA
3600 ESCN 92025 1150-D3
VIA CALAFIA
7000 CRLB 92009 1127-G6
VIA CALANDRIA
- SCLE 92672 1023-B2
VIA CALANOVA
15700 SD 92128 1170-B5
VIA CALDRON
6500 CRLB 92009 1127-J6
VIA CALENDO
7900 CRLB 92009 1148-A2
VIA CALIENTE
- SMCS 92069 1108-F4
VIA CALIENTE DEL SOL
3100 SDCo 91935 1272-D7
VIA CALLADO
- OCN 92057 1067-B5
5500 SD 92037 1247-H3
VIA CALVILLO
5400 SDCo 92003 1067-G2
VIA CAMELLIA
1100 SMCS 92069 1109-C7
VIA CAMINAR
1600 SDCo 92078 1128-C3
VIA CAMINO VERDE
2100 OCN 92054 1106-F1
VIA CAMPESTRE
- SDCo 92082 1070-A6
3000 SD 92014 1187-J1
VIA CAMPO VERDE
6200 SDCo 92067 1168-F5
VIA CANADA DEL OSITO
5800 SDCo 92067 1168-E6
VIA CANCION
1600 SDCo 92078 1128-A3
1600 SMCS 92078 1128-A3
VIA CANDELA
18400 SDCo 92091 1148-E5
VIA CANDIDIZ
4100 SD 92130 1188-B6
VIA CANDREJO
7000 CRLB 92009 1127-G6
VIA CANGREJO
3900 SD 92130 1208-B3
VIA CANTAMAR
30500 SDCo 92026 1068-J4
30500 SDCo 92026 1069-A4
VIA CANTEBRIA
100 ENCT 92024 1147-F4
VIA CANYON DR
- SD 92129 1188-H5
VIA CAPRA DORADO
- SD 92122 1228-E4
VIA CAPRI
1700 CHV 91913 1311-D7
7000 SD 92037 1227-H6
VIA CAPRI CT
2300 SD 92037 1227-H6
VIA CARACAS
8900 SD 92126 1209-D3
VIA CARA LOMA
3700 ENCT 92024 1148-B3
VIA CARANCHO
5300 SD 92111 1248-G5
VIA CARDEL
2700 CRLB 92010 1106-C6
VIA CARINA
- VSTA 92081 1107-H2
VIA CARLOTTA
11600 SDCo 92019 1271-J4
VIA CAROLINA
1100 SD 92037 1247-F2
VIA CARRILLO
1300 SDCo 92078 1128-B4
VIA CARRIO
2800 CRLB 92010 1106-H3
VIA CARROZA
11200 SD 92124 1250-A2
VIA CASA ALTA
2100 SD 92037 1227-H7
VIA CASA DEL SOL
- CRLB 92009 1127-J5
VIA CASCABEL
2100 SDCo 92027 1130-F4
10800 SD 92124 1249-J2
VIA CASCADA
2800 CRLB 92010 1106-H3
VIA CASCADITA
4500 OCN 92057 1087-B1
VIA CASILINA
11600 SDCo 92019 1272-A5
VIA CASITAS
- SDCo 92003 1048-B7
- SDCo 92003 1068-C1
VIA CASSANDRA
200 SDCo 92028 1027-F4
VIA CASTANET
1200 SDCo 92078 1128-B4
VIA CASTILLA
5100 OCN 92057 1067-A4
VIA CATANIA
- SDCo 92091 1148-F5
VIA CAVOUR
300 CHV 91910 1310-A4
VIA CAZADERO
16200 SDCo 92067 1168-F7
VIA CEDRO
- CHV 91910 1311-A6
VIA CENOTE
- SDCo 92036 1156-B3
VIA CENTRE
1900 VSTA 92081 1107-C2
VIACHA CT
10900 SD 92124 1249-J3
VIACHA DR
10300 SD 92124 1249-J3
VIACHA WY
10500 SD 92124 1249-H3
VIA CHAPARRAL
1500 SDCo 92028 1028-E5
VIA CHARDONNAY
- ESCN 92029 1129-E4
VIA CHICA
- CRLB 92009 1147-J4
VIA CHICA CT
300 SOLB 92075 1167-H6
VIA CHINARROS
2700 SDCo 91901 1254-A2

VIA CHONA
11700 SD 92128 1170-A5
VIA CHRISTINA
1200 VSTA 92084 1088-A4
VIA CIBOLA
1300 OCN 92057 1067-A5
1300 OCN 92057 1066-J4
VIA CIELITO
- SDCo 92067 1149-A4
VIA CIELO AZUL
3700 SDCo 91901 1254-F2
VIA CIELO VISTA
1100 SDCo 92029 1149-H3
VIA CIMA BELLA
13500 SD 92129 1189-E4
VIA CIMBORIO CIR
10700 SD 92131 1210-A2
VIA CINERIA
- ESCN 92029 1129-E4
VIA CINTA
5100 SD 92122 1228-G6
VIA CLAREZ
2800 CRLB 92010 1106-H3
VIA CLEMENTE
400 OCN 92057 1087-A4
2300 CRLB 92008 1106-G3
VIA COELLO
7000 CRLB 92009 1127-G6
VIA COLIMA
2700 CRLB 92010 1106-H3
VIA COLINA
3600 OCN 92056 1107-F4
9200 SDCo 91941 1271-B4
VIA COLMENAR
- SD 92129 1189-B6
VIA COLONIA
8600 SD 92126 1209-C3
VIA COLORADO
4700 OCN 92056 1087-B4
VIA COLORSO
- SCLE 92672 1023-B2
VIA COLUMBIA
600 VSTA 92081 1107-E1
VIA CONCA DORO
700 SDCo 92084 1088-F7
VIA CONCEPCION
- SDCo 92067 1168-C6
VIA CONEJO
1100 SDCo 92029 1149-H3
VIA CONQUISTADOR
2800 CRLB 92009 1127-H4
VIA CONRAD
9800 SNTE 92071 1231-C3
VIA CONSTANZA
- SD 92129 1189-A4
VIA CONSUELO
8500 SDCo 92021 1232-E6
VIA CONTENTA
1000 SDCo 92029 1149-H2
VIA CONTESSA
- SMCS 92069 1108-F4
VIA CORDOBA
6700 SDCo 92067 1168-H6
VIA CORDONIZ
2500 SDCo 92028 997-C4
VIA CORDOVA
2200 SDCo 91978 1271-G7
2200 SDCo 91978 1291-G1
VIA CORINA
1800 SDCo 91901 1233-F7
1800 SDCo 91901 1253-G1
VIA CORONA
1500 SD 92037 1247-H3
VIA CORONADO
3700 SDCo 92091 1168-C7
VIA CORSINI
14000 SD 92128 1190-B2
VIA CORTA
- VSTA 92081 1107-C2
4900 CRLB 92008 1107-A6
VIA CORTA RD
2200 SDCo 92028 1048-B4
VIA CORTE
2100 SDCo 92029 1129-H6
VIA CORTINA
12700 SD 92014 1207-H1
VIA CORTONA
- SD 92127 1168-J7
- SNTE 92071 1230-H7
VIA COSCOJA
- CRLB 92009 1147-G2
VIA COSTA RICA
600 VSTA 92081 1107-F1
VIA COSTINA
1600 SD 92173 1350-D2
VIA CRESTA RD
- SD 92129 1188-J4
VIA CRISTAL
- SD 92129 1188-J4
- SD 92129 1189-A4
VIA CRISTOBAL
2800 CRLB 92010 1106-H3
VIA CRUZ
400 OCN 92057 1087-A4
400 OCN 92057 1086-J4
VIA CUARTO
1800 OCN 92056 1087-C5
VIA CUATRO CAMINOS
17200 SDCo 92067 1168-G1
VIA CUENCA
9900 SD 92129 1189-F3
VIA CUESTA
19300 SDCo 92065 1151-H2
VIA CUESTA ARRIBA
30300 SDCo 92003 1068-E4
VIA CUESTA MANSA
6800 SDCo 92067 1168-G7
VIA CUESTA VERDE
17000 SDCo 92067 1168-G6
VIA CUMBRES
2700 SDCo 92028 1028-C3
VIA CUMBRES LN
2800 SDCo 92028 1028-C3
VIA CUPENO
5100 OCN 92057 1067-B7
VIA CURVADA
600 CHV 91910 1310-G7
VIA CUYAMACA
9800 SNTE 92071 1231-C4
VIA DARDO
17600 SD 92128 1150-D7
VIA DAROCA
9900 SD 92129 1189-F3
VIA DE AGUACATE
2300 SDCo 92028 1028-B7
VIA DE AMO
200 SDCo 92028 1028-B3
VIA DE AMOR
9100 SNTE 92071 1231-B7
VIA DE ANZA
3700 SMCS 92078 1108-C7
VIA DEBBIE
9900 SNTE 92071 1231-D4

VIA DE CABALLO
3000 ENCT 92024 1148-B6
VIA DE CANTO
3100 CRLB 92010 1106-H3
VIA DE CASA
100 SDCo 92028 1028-B2
VIA DE CRISTINA
9100 SNTE 92071 1231-B7
VIA DE ENCANTO
1200 SDCo 92029 1149-H3
VIA DE FORTUNA
2300 CRLB 92009 1127-G7
17400 SDCo 92067 1168-C1
17800 SDCo 92067 1148-C7
VIA DE JAMUL
13800 SDCo 91935 1292-J2
VIA DE JUAN
9100 SNTE 92071 1231-B7
VIA DE LA AMISTAD
9700 SD 92154 1352-B4
VIA DE LA BANDOLA
3700 SD 92173 1350-F2
VIA DE LA CUESTA
1700 SDCo 92027 1130-D3
VIA DE LA CUMBRE
5500 SDCo 92067 1168-D2
VIA DE LA FLOR
6200 SDCo 92003 1068-D3
VIA DEL ALBA
15800 SDCo 92067 1168-C4
VIA DEL ALLAZON
2800 SDCo 91902 1290-H7
VIA DE LA MELODIA
1600 SD 92173 1350-F2
VIA DE LA MONTANA
- SDCo 91901 1233-F6
VIA DE LA NOLA
7300 SDCo 92067 1168-H2
VIA DE LA PAZ
4000 OCN 92057 1086-H4
VIA DE LA REINA
6700 SDCo 92003 1068-E3
VIA DE LA ROCA
40600 SDCo 92028 997-J3
VIA DE LAS FLORES
18300 SDCo 92091 1148-G5
18300 SDCo 92067 1148-G5
VIA DE LAS PALMAS
15900 SDCo 92091 1168-C7
15900 SDCo 92091 1188-C1
VIA DEL ASTRO
300 OCN 92057 1086-H4
VIA DE LAURENCIO
- CHV 91910 1310-D6
- SDCo 91910 1310-D6
VIA DE LA VALLE
3300 OCN 92054 1086-E4
VIA DE LA VALLE Rt#-S6
100 DLMR 92014 1187-G2
600 SD 92014 1187-J2
3200 SD 92014 1188-B1
4000 SD 92014 1188-B1
14900 SDCo 92067 1188-B1
14900 SDCo 92091 1188-B1
15000 SDCo 92067 1168-E3
15000 SDCo 92091 1168-D6
15100 SD 92075 1187-G2
VIA DEL BARDO
3900 SD 92173 1350-F2
VIA DEL BRAVO
17300 SDCo 92067 1168-G2
VIA DEL CABALLO
- SMCS 92078 1129-A2
VIA DEL CABALLO BLANCO
2800 SDCo 91902 1290-H7
VIA DEL CAMPO
600 SMCS 92078 1129-A2
16500 SD 92127 1169-H2
VIA DEL CAMPO CT
16800 SD 92127 1169-H3
VIA DEL CANON
14700 SD 92014 1188-A1
14700 SDCo 92014 1188-A1
VIA DEL CERRITO
100 ENCT 92024 1147-J7
100 ENCT 92024 1167-J1
VIA DEL CERRO
1200 SDCo 92084 1068-A6
VIA DEL CHARRO
6800 SDCo 92067 1148-G6
VIA DEL CIELO
2900 SDCo 92028 1028-E6
VIA DEL CONQUISTADOR
3600 SD 92117 1248-E5
VIA DEL CORVO
1400 SDCo 92078 1128-B4
VIA DEL COSIRA
10800 SD 92124 1249-J2
VIA DEL GAVILAN
41700 SDCo 92028 997-J3
41900 SDCo 92028 998-A4
VIA DEL LAGO
1700 SDCo 92028 997-J5
VIA DEL LOBO
- SDCo 92003 1068-D4
VIA DEL LUZ
8600 SDCo 92021 1232-D7
VIA DEL MAR
- SD 92130 1208-A2
600 VSTA 92081 1107-E1
VIA DEL MESONERO
1600 SD 92173 1350-F2
VIA DEL MONTE
200 OCN 92054 1086-D5
VIA DEL MONTE LIBANO
3100 SDCo 92084 1088-E6
VIA DEL NORTE
200 SD 92037 1247-F2
200 OCN 92054 1086-D5
VIA DEL ORO
1300 SDCo 92028 1028-A4
5200 OCN 92056 1107-F4
VIA DE LOS CEPILLOS
4400 SDCo 92003 1067-H2
VIA DE LOS ROSALES
16600 SDCo 92067 1168-F6
VIA DEL PARQUE
10500 SDCo 91978 1271-F7
VIA DEL PRADO
2100 SDCo 92084 1088-C1
2600 OCN 92054 1106-G1
VIA DEL RANCHO
3700 OCN 92056 1107-F4
VIA DEL REY
1700 SMCS 92078 1108-B7
VIA DEL RIO
43200 SDCo 92028 998-A4
VIA DEL ROBLES
2300 SDCo 92028 1028-B6

VIA DEL SANTO
29600 SDCo 92084 1068-E6
VIA DEL SAUCE
30000 SDCo 92082 1070-A5
VIA DEL SOL
1400 VSTA 92084 1088-A4
10700 SDCo 91978 1271-F6
VIA DEL SUD
10100 SD 92129 1189-G5
VIA DEL SUR
5200 OCN 92056 1107-F4
VIA DEL TANIDO
1700 SD 92173 1350-E3
VIA DEL TORO
12800 PWY 92064 1170-D4
VIA DEL TORRIE
1800 SDCo 91901 1254-A1
VIA DE LUNA
13200 SDCo 92082 1070-C7
VIA DEL VALEDOR
12900 SD 92129 1189-F5
VIA DEL VENADO
32700 SDCo 92082 1049-E5
VIA DEL VERDE
2500 SDCo 92028 1028-C7
VIA DE MARANATHA
1100 SDCo 92028 1028-A4
VIA DE MAYA
7000 SDCo 92067 1168-F1
VIA DENA LOMA
15800 SDCo 92065 1171-B2
VIA DENISE
3000 CRLB 92010 1106-C6
VIA DE ORO
9900 SDCo 91977 1271-D6
VIA DE PAZ
2900 CRLB 92010 1106-H3
30500 SDCo 92084 1068-E4
VIA DE PLATA
- SMCS 92069 1108-F4
VIA DE SANTA FE
15500 SDCo 92067 1168-D3
VIA DE SAN YSIDRO
100 SD 92173 1350-F5
VIA DE SUENO
17900 SDCo 92067 1148-C7
VIA DE TODOS SANTOS
3200 SDCo 92028 1048-H2
VIA DE VICTORIA
8700 SNTE 92071 1231-B7
VIA DE VISTA
300 SOLB 92075 1167-F7
300 SOLB 92075 1187-F1
VIA DIANA
11600 SDCo 92019 1271-J4
VIA DIANZA
3000 CRLB 92009 1127-J5
VIA DICHA
16300 SDCo 92091 1168-C7
VIA DIEGO
2800 CRLB 92010 1106-C6
12400 SDCo 92040 1232-C6
VIA DIEGO CT
8700 SDCo 92040 1232-B7
VIA DIEGO LN
8800 SDCo 92040 1232-B6
VIA DIEGO TER
8700 SDCo 92040 1232-B6
VIA DIEGUENOS
2000 SDCo 91901 1254-D1
VIA DI FELICITA
1000 ENCT 92024 1148-A5
VIA DOMINIQUE
11100 SD 92124 1250-A1
VIA DONADA
12700 SD 92014 1207-H1
VIA DON BENITO
2000 SD 92037 1247-H1
VIA DONITO
3000 SDCo 91901 1234-E7
3000 SDCo 91901 1254-E1
VIA DORA
8200 SDCo 92067 1148-J6
8200 SDCo 92067 1149-A6
VIA DORADO AV
1200 SMCS 92069 1109-D7
VIA DOS VALLES
6200 SDCo 92067 1168-F5
VIA DULCEA
2200 SDCo 92028 1048-B4
VIA DWIGHT
1300 SDCo 92065 1152-H7
VIA ECO
2600 CRLB 92010 1106-H3
VIA EL CENTRO
400 OCN 92054 1086-D5
VIA EL DORADO
4200 SDCo 92028 997-H3
VIA ELENA
12100 SDCo 92019 1271-J4
VIA ELISA
1500 ELCJ 92021 1252-A2
1600 SDCo 92021 1252-A2
VIA EMBELESO
16200 SD 92128 1170-A4
VIA EMERADO
2900 CRLB 92009 1147-H3
VIA EMILY
400 OCN 92057 1086-H1
VIA EMPRESA
1200 OCN 92056 1087-B3
VIA ENCANTADA
600 CHV 91913 1311-B5
VIA ENCANTADO
13700 SDCo 92082 1070-E6
VIA ENCANTADORAS
1700 SD 92173 1350-E3
VIA ENCATADORAS
1700 SD 92173 1350-E2
VIA ENCINOS DR
1200 SDCo 92028 1047-H3
VIA ENSENADA
7900 CRLB 92009 1147-J3
VIA ENTRADA
1700 SDCo 92028 1027-J3
VIA ENTRADA DEL LAGO
1500 SDCo 92078 1128-C3
VIA ESCALA
4700 OCN 92056 1087-B4
VIA ESCALADA
- SD 92129 1189-B6
VIA ESCALANTE
1100 CHV 91910 1311-A7
VIA ESCUDA
3800 SDCo 91941 1271-H4
VIA ESMARCA
1800 OCN 92054 1106-G1
VIA ESPANA
1100 SD 92037 1247-G3
VIA ESPARTO
2500 CRLB 92010 1106-H3
VIA ESPERIA
12700 SD 92014 1207-H1

STREET	Block	City	ZIP	Pg-Grid
VIA ESPRILLO				
	16400	SD	92127	1169-H3
VIA ESTRADA				
	3000	CRLB	92009	1127-J6
	6600	SD	92037	1247-H1
VIA ESTRELLADA				
	1000	SDCo	92028	997-H7
	1000	SDCo	92028	1027-J1
VIA EUCALIPTO				
	12000	SDCo	92019	1272-A3
VIA EXCELENCIA				
	9600	SD	92126	1209-E6
VIA FELICIA				
	11900	SDCo	92019	1271-J4
	12000	SDCo	92019	1272-A4
VIA FELICIDAD				
	800	VSTA	92084	1087-J3
	1100	SDCo	92029	1149-G2
VIA FELICITA				
	4400	OCN	92057	1086-J2
	4400	OCN	92057	1087-A2
VIA FELINO				
	12700	SD	92014	1207-H1
VIA FELIZ				
	1300	SDCo	92028	1027-J3
	3400	CRLB	92009	1147-J4
VIA FESTIVO				
	2700	CRLB	92010	1106-H3
VIA FIESTA				
	-	SD	92127	1168-J7
VIA FIRENZE				
	1200	SDCo	92078	1128-G4
VIA FIRUL				
	11600	SD	92128	1170-A6
VIA FLORA				
	700	SMCS	92078	1108-C7
	700	SMCS	92078	1128-C1
VIA FLORA RD				
	700	SMCS	92069	1129-E1
VIA FLORES				
	3500	SD	92106	1288-A4
VIA FLORESTA				
	900	SDCo	92028	1027-F1
VIA FORTE				
	8600	SD	92126	1209-C3
VIA FORTEZZA				
	-	SD	92129	1189-A4
VIA FORTUNA MARFIL				
	9400	SDCo	91941	1271-C4
VIA FRANCESCO				
	-	SD	92129	1189-A4
VIA FRANCIS				
	9800	SNTE	92071	1231-C4
VIA FRANCISCA				
	2300	CRLB	92008	1106-G3
VIA FRESA				
	2200	SD	92037	1247-J2
VIA FRONTERA				
	10900	SD	92127	1169-H4
VIA GALACIA				
	12600	SD	92128	1170-C6
VIA GALAN				
	15900	SDCo	92091	1168-C7
VIA GATO				
	900	SMCS	92069	1108-E4
VIA GAVIOTA				
	4500	SDCo	92067	1167-J5
VIA GERMO				
	11800	SDCo	92019	1271-J4
VIA GIANNELLI				
	4300	SDCo	92003	1048-E7
	4300	SDCo	92003	1068-E1
VIA GIANNITURCO				
	1700	SDCo	92028	1028-B5
VIA GOLD PAN				
	-	SDCo	92040	1212-A7
VIA GORDO				
	-	SDCo	92026	1129-F2
VIA GOYA				
	1100	CHV	91910	1311-A6
VIA GRACIA				
	17800	SD	92128	1150-B7
	17800	SD	92128	1170-B1
VIA GRANDA				
	2200	SDCo	91978	1291-G1
	2300	SDCo	91978	1271-G7
VIA GRANDAR				
	14200	SD	92130	1188-D2
VIA GRANERO				
	11800	SDCo	92019	1271-J4
VIA GREEN CANYON NORTE				
	-	SDCo	92028	1028-A4
VIA GRENACHE				
	-	ESCN	92029	1129-E4
VIA GRENADA				
	31400	SDCo	92003	1067-J1
VIA GRIMALDI				
	12700	SD	92014	1207-H1
VIA GUADALMINA				
	18200	SD	92128	1150-D7
VIA GUADALUPE				
	7000	SDCo	92067	1168-G2
VIA GUSTAVO				
	10700	SD	92129	1189-H2
VIA HACIENDA				
	-	SMCS	92069	1108-D5
	1400	CHV	91913	1311-B4
	1500	CHV	91902	1311-B4
	11800	SDCo	92019	1271-J5
	12000	SDCo	92019	1272-A4
VIA HACIENDA CT				
	-	SMCS	92069	1108-D5
VIA HELENA				
	8600	SDCo	92021	1232-E6
VIA HERMOSA				
	3000	SDCo	92029	1149-H2
VIA HINTON				
	4900	CRLB	92008	1107-A7
VIA HOJA				
	-	CRLB	92009	1147-F3
VIA HOLGURA				
	3900	SD	92130	1188-B6
VIA HONDITA				
	2200	ESCN	92027	1110-C5
VIA HONDONADA				
	15000	SD	92129	1169-H7
VIA HUELVA				
	13700	SD	92129	1189-F4
VIA INCA				
	4700	SDCo	92028	1048-H1
VIA INEZ				
	-	SD	92127	1168-J7
VIA INSPIRAR				
	1600	SDCo	92078	1128-C4
VIA IPANEMA				
	2900	CRLB	92009	1147-H3
VIA IRIS				
	-	CRLB	92009	1147-J2
VIA ISABEL				
	11600	SDCo	92019	1271-J4
VIA ISIDRO				
	1300	OCN	92056	1087-B4
VIA JACQUELINA				
	11600	SDCo	92019	1271-J4
VIA JAZMIN				
	-	SCLE	92672	1023-B2
VIA JUANITA				
	800	SMCS	92078	1128-C1
	2700	CRLB	92010	1106-H3
VIA JUDY				
	2600	CRLB	92010	1106-C6
VIA JULITA				
	300	ENCT	92024	1147-C6
VIA KENORA				
	9600	SDCo	91977	1271-C6
VIA KINO				
	8100	SD	92122	1228-E4
VIA LA CANTERA				
	10000	SD	92129	1189-F5
VIA LA CRESTA				
	800	SDCo	92021	1252-H2
VIA LACTEA				
	13800	SD	92129	1189-E3
VIA LA CUESTA				
	600	CHV	91913	1311-B4
	1100	SDCo	92029	1149-H2
VIA LADERA				
	700	SDCo	92029	1149-H1
	1700	SMCS	92078	1108-B7
VIA LADERA RD				
	1400	SDCo	92028	999-B6
VIA LADETA				
	2000	SD	92037	1247-H2
VIA LA GARDENIA				
	12600	PWY	92064	1170-C6
VIA LA GITANO				
	15300	PWY	92064	1170-C6
VIA LAGO AZUL				
	16500	SDCo	92067	1168-F6
VIA LA IZQUIERDA				
	15400	SDCo	92064	1191-B5
VIA LA JOLLA				
	4400	OCN	92057	1087-B1
VIA LA MANCHA				
	1500	SDCo	91901	1234-F6
VIA LA MIRADA				
	12600	SDCo	92082	1070-B4
VIA LAMPARA				
	2200	SDCo	91978	1271-G7
	2300	SDCo	91978	1291-G1
VIA LANDINI				
	-	SD	92127	1168-J7
VIA LA ORILLA				
	2300	SDCo	92028	1028-B7
VIA LA PALOMA				
	500	CHV	91910	1311-A4
VIA LA PAZ				
	100	SMCS	92069	1109-C7
	100	SMCS	92069	1129-C1
VIA LAPIZ				
	4900	SD	92122	1228-F5
VIA LA PLAZA				
	1600	SDCo	92078	1128-C4
VIA LA RANCHITA				
	1200	SMCS	92069	1109-C7
VIA LARGA VISTA				
	-	SDCo	92003	1048-C7
	-	SDCo	92003	1068-C1
VIA LARGO				
	3600	OCN	92056	1107-G4
VIA LAS BRISAS				
	100	SMCS	92069	1108-H3
VIA LAS CUMBRES				
	1000	SD	92111	1268-H2
VIA LA SENDA				
	14900	SOLB	92014	1167-J7
	14900	SOLB	92014	1187-J1
VIA LAS FALDAS				
	3200	SDCo	91935	1272-D7
VIA LAS LENAS				
	-	SD	92129	1189-B5
VIA LAS MAYAS				
	10800	SD	92129	1189-H2
VIA LAS PALMAS				
	1900	NATC	91950	1310-B2
	1900	SDCo	91950	1310-B2
VIA LAS POSADAS				
	10700	SD	92129	1189-G2
VIA LAS RAMBLAS				
	4400	SD	92122	1228-D3
VIA LAS ROSAS				
	2800	OCN	92054	1106-G2
	3000	OCN	92056	1106-G2
VIA LAS TONADAS				
	1800	SD	92173	1350-E3
VIA LAS VILLAS				
	3700	OCN	92056	1107-F4
VIA LATINA				
	12800	SD	92014	1207-H1
VIA LAURA				
	2000	SDCo	91935	(1314-F1 See Page 1294)
VIA LA VENTA				
	-	SMCS	92069	1108-D5
VIA LA VENTANA				
	-	SD	92131	1210-J2
VIA LECHUSA				
	4600	SDCo	92067	1167-J5
VIA LESLIE				
	9800	SNTE	92071	1231-D3
VIA LIBERTAD				
	2900	CRLB	92010	1106-H3
VIA LIDO				
	1700	SMCS	92078	1108-B7
VIA LIMA				
	1400	SDCo	92028	1027-J3
VIA LINDA				
	900	SDCo	92029	1129-H7
VIA LINDA DEL SUR				
	300	ENCT	92024	1147-C5
VIA LINDA VISTA				
	10700	SDCo	91978	1271-F5
VIA LISA				
	14000	PWY	92064	1190-G4
VIA LLANO				
	11100	SD	92129	1169-H7
VIA LOBO				
	1700	SDCo	92078	1128-G4
VIA LOMA				
	2600	SDCo	92028	1048-D2
VIA LOMA DR				
	17500	PWY	92064	1170-D1
VIA LOMA VISTA				
	1100	ELCJ	92019	1252-B3
	2900	SDCo	92029	1149-H2
VIA LOMITA				
	1000	ESCN	92027	1110-B6
VIA LOPEZ CT				
	24900	SDCo	92065	1173-G3
VIA LOS ARCOS				
	300	SMCS	92069	1109-C7
VIA LOS FAROLITOS				
	16800	SDCo	92067	1168-G6
VIA LOS NARCISOS				
	10800	SD	92129	1189-G2
VIA LOS NOPALES				
	-	SDCo	92067	1168-D6
VIA LOS PADRES				
	4000	OCN	92057	1086-H2
VIA LOS SANTOS				
	2300	CRLB	92008	1106-G3
VIA LUCIA				
	2200	SD	92037	1247-J2
VIA LUISENO				
	3100	SDCo	91901	1254-D1
VIA LUJOSA				
	3600	ESCN	92025	1150-D3
VIA LUNA				
	-	CHV	91910	1311-A7
	-	SDCo	92067	1148-J6
VIA MADEIRA				
	-	ESCN	92029	1129-F4
VIA MADERA CIR W				
	16100	SDCo	92091	1168-C7
VIA MADONNA				
	11200	SNTE	92071	1231-G5
VIA MADRID				
	5100	OCN	92057	1066-J4
	5100	OCN	92057	1067-A4
VIA MADRINA ST				
	1500	SD	92111	1268-H2
VIA MAGDALENA				
	-	SD	92129	1188-J4
	-	SD	92129	1189-A3
VIA MAGGIORE				
	-	CHV	91914	1311-J2
	-	CHV	91914	(1312-A2 See Page 1293)
VIA MAGIA				
	2800	CRLB	92010	1106-H3
VIA MAJELLA				
	2400	SDCo	92065	1172-C4
VIA MALAGA				
	400	ENCT	92024	1147-F6
VIA MALAGUENA				
	5100	OCN	92057	1067-A4
VIA MALLORCA				
	8000	SD	92037	1228-A4
VIA MANDRIL				
	3400	SDCo	91902	1310-G2
VIA MANOS				
	5000	OCN	92057	1067-C7
VIA MANTOVA				
	-	SD	92127	1168-J7
VIA MAR AZUL				
	-	CHV	91910	1311-A6
VIA MARBELLA				
	3100	SDCo	91978	1292-B1
	3100	SDCo	91978	1272-B7
VIA MARBRISA				
	1000	ENCT	92024	1147-E6
VIA MARCALA				
	14000	SD	92130	1188-D3
VIA MARCHENA				
	15600	SD	92128	1170-B5
VIA MARCO				
	-	SDCo	92084	1087-J2
	-	VSTA	92084	1087-J2
VIA MAR DE BALLENAS				
	-	SD	92130	1208-B3
VIA MAR DE DELFINAS				
	4100	SD	92130	1208-B3
VIA MARGARITA				
	31200	SDCo	92003	1068-E2
VIA MARGUERITA				
	1400	OCN	92056	1087-C3
VIA MARIA				
	100	SMCS	92069	1109-C7
	400	OCN	92057	1086-H1
	6300	SD	92037	1247-E2
VIA MARIA ELENA				
	30000	SDCo	92003	1068-C2
VIA MARIANA				
	-	CHV	91910	1311-A6
VIA MARIN				
	3200	SD	92037	1228-A5
VIA MARINERO				
	6800	CRLB	92009	1128-A5
VIA MARIPOSA				
	3000	CRLB	92009	1128-A5
	6800	SDCo	92003	1068-E2
VIA MARIPOSA CT				
	31200	SDCo	92003	1068-E2
VIA MARIPOSA NORTE				
	6800	SDCo	92003	1068-F2
VIA MARIPOSA SUR				
	6900	SDCo	92003	1068-E2
VIA MARK				
	13300	PWY	92064	1190-G4
VIA MARMOL				
	10000	SDCo	92026	1109-E1
VIA MARTA				
	4900	CRLB	92008	1107-A7
VIA MAR VALLE				
	2100	SD	92014	1187-G7
VIA MASADA				
	2600	CRLB	92010	1106-H4
VIA MATARO				
	-	ESCN	92029	1129-E4
VIA MAVIS				
	9900	SNTE	92071	1231-D4
VIA MAXIMO				
	-	CRLB	92009	1127-J4
	-	CRLB	92009	1128-A4
VIA MEDALLA				
	4500	SD	92122	1228-D3
VIA MEDANOS				
	11700	SD	92128	1170-A5
VIA MEDIA				
	2200	SD	92037	1247-J2
VIA MERANO				
	2500	SD	92014	1207-H1
VIA MERCADO				
	3600	SDCo	91941	1271-G5
VIA MERDE				
	2700	CRLB	92010	1106-C6
VIA MERIDA				
	11000	SDCo	91941	1271-G5
VIA MESA DR				
	-	SD	92129	1188-J4
VIA METATES				
	300	OCN	92057	1067-B7
VIA MICA				
	10700	SDCo	91978	1271-F6
VIA MICHELANGELO				
	-	SD	92129	1189-C2
VIA MILANO				
	12100	SD	92128	1190-B1
VIA MILAZZO				
	-	SD	92129	1189-A4
VIA MIL CUMBRES				
	900	SOLB	92075	1167-H6
VIA MILPAS				
	2500	SDCo	92028	998-B6
VIA MINDANAO				
	5100	OCN	92057	1066-J4
	5100	OCN	92057	1067-A4
VIA MIRADOR				
	-	CRLB	92009	1147-J3
VIA MIRALESTE				
	1000	CHV	91910	1311-A7
VIA MOLENA				
	1000	ENCT	92024	1147-F6
VIA MOLINERO				
	15200	PWY	92064	1170-G7
VIA MONADA				
	1100	CHV	91910	1311-B7
VIA MONALEX				
	14200	SDCo	92067	1168-G2
VIA MONCLOVA				
	4300	SD	92122	1228-E4
VIA MONSERATE				
	1500	SDCo	92028	1047-J5
	1600	SDCo	92028	1048-B5
VIA MONTALVO				
	400	ENCT	92024	1147-F6
VIA MONTANETA				
	3100	ESCN	92029	1150-A2
VIA MONTANOSA				
	300	ENCT	92024	1147-F6
VIA MONTE				
	-	SDCo	92067	1167-J5
VIA MONTE ALEGRE				
	400	SDCo	92003	1067-F1
VIA MONTEBELLO				
	-	SD	92129	1189-A4
VIA MONTECILLO				
	-	SMCS	92069	1108-H3
VIA MONTECITO				
	1100	ENCT	92024	1147-F6
VIA MONTE CLARO				
	12600	PWY	92064	1170-C6
VIA MONTECRISTO				
	-	SD	92127	1169-B3
VIA MONTELLANO				
	5700	SDCo	92003	1067-H2
VIA MONTENERO				
	-	SD	92127	1169-C3
VIA MONTEREY				
	16200	SDCo	92091	1168-D6
VIA MONTEVERDE				
	-	SD	92127	1168-J7
VIA MONTISI				
	-	SNTE	92071	1230-H7
VIA MONTORO				
	1100	ENCT	92024	1147-F6
VIA MONZON				
	9800	SD	92129	1189-F3
VIA MORELLA				
	100	ENCT	92024	1147-F6
VIA MOURA				
	12800	SD	92128	1150-D7
VIA MUNERA				
	2200	SD	92037	1247-J1
VIAN RD				
	13600	PWY	92064	1190-F2
VIA NANCITA				
	300	ENCT	92024	1147-C6
VIA NAPOLI				
	1500	SDCo	92028	997-H4
VIA NARANJA				
	2500	CRLB	92010	1106-H3
VIA NARANJAL				
	6200	SDCo	92067	1148-D6
VIA NASCA				
	12700	SD	92128	1150-D6
VIA NATIONAL				
	-	SD	92173	1350-G5
VIA NAVAJO				
	1200	SDCo	92078	1128-B4
VIANDA CT				
	6800	CRLB	92009	1127-G6
VIANE WY				
	4800	SD	92110	1268-F1
VIA NESTORE				
	12800	SD	92014	1207-H1
VIA NEW YORK				
	-	SD	92173	1350-G5
VIA NICOLE				
	11600	SDCo	92019	1271-J4
VIA NIEVE				
	12700	SD	92130	1188-B6
VIA NINA				
	2100	SD	92037	1247-J2
	9900	SNTE	92071	1231-D4
VIA NOMENTANA				
	-	CHV	91910	1310-A4
VIA NORTE				
	1100	SDCo	92029	1149-H2
VIA OAK GROVE LN				
	27900	SDCo	92066	410-A8
VIA OCIOSO				
	1600	SDCo	92078	1128-C3
VIA OESTE DR				
	2600	SDCo	92028	1028-E7
VIA OPUNTIA				
	-	CRLB	92009	1147-G2
VIA ORANGE WY				
	2700	SDCo	91978	1271-F7
VIA ORDAZ				
	10900	SD	92129	1189-H2
VIA ORILLIA				
	-	CRLB	92009	1148-A4
VIA ORO VERDE				
	200	SDCo	92028	1027-G4
VIA OSTIONES				
	7000	CRLB	92009	1127-G6
VIA OSTRA				
	6500	CRLB	92009	1127-J4
VIA OSUNA				
	3800	SDCo	92091	1168-C7
VIA OTANO				
	1500	OCN	92056	1087-B4
VIA PACIFICA				
	16200	SDCo	92091	1168-D7
VIA PADILLA				
	7000	CRLB	92009	1127-G6
VIA PAJARO				
	2800	CRLB	92010	1106-H3
VIA PALABRA				
	4500	SD	92124	1250-A2
VIA PALACIO				
	200	ENCT	92024	1147-F6
VIA PALMA				
	3700	SDCo	91941	1271-G5
VIA PALOMA				
	1500	SDCo	92026	1109-E7
	11600	SDCo	92019	1272-A4
VIA PALOMAR				
	700	SMCS	92078	1108-B7
	700	SMCS	92078	1128-C1
VIA PALO VERDE LAGO				
	-	SDCo	91901	1254-F2
VIA PAMELA				
	18900	SDCo	91935	(1314-F2 See Page 1294)
VIA PANACEA				
	-	SD	92129	1189-B5
VIA PANORAMA				
	40500	SDCo	92028	997-J3
	40500	SDCo	92028	998-A3
VIA PAPEETE				
	3000	SD	92154	1330-D7
VIA PAPEL				
	4900	SD	92122	1228-G6
VIA PARADISO				
	3700	SDCo	92084	1088-F7
VIA PARANZA				
	6500	CRLB	92009	1127-J4
VIA PARMA				
	11000	SD	92129	1189-H3
VIA PASAR				
	9800	SD	92126	1209-E5
VIA PASATIEMPO				
	3800	SDCo	92091	1168-C7
VIA PASEAR				
	4300	SD	92122	1228-D3
VIA PATO				
	15900	SDCo	92067	1168-A5
VIA PATRICIO				
	10800	SDCo	92082	1049-F3
VIA PATRON				
	-	CRLB	92009	1127-J4
VIA PAUMA				
	5200	OCN	92057	1067-C7
VIA PAVON				
	-	SMCS	92069	1108-F4
VIA PEDRERA				
	2200	SD	92037	1247-J1
VIA PEDRO				
	1500	VSTA	92084	1088-B5
VIA PELICANO				
	200	OCN	92057	1086-J3
	2300	CRLB	92009	1127-G6
VIA PENASCO				
	16400	SDCo	92065	1171-H3
VIA PENOLES				
	15400	SD	92128	1170-A6
VIA PEPITA				
	2900	CRLB	92009	1147-H4
VIA PEQUINITO				
	10800	SD	92129	1189-G2
VIA PEREZA				
	9500	SD	92129	1189-E4
VIA PERLITA				
	3300	SMCS	92078	1108-D6
VIA PESCADO				
	3200	CRLB	92010	1106-H4
VIA PICANTE				
	3500	SDCo	91941	1271-G5
VIA PIEDRA				
	28800	SDCo	92082	1070-C7
	28800	SDCo	92082	1090-C1
VIA PISA				
	2500	SD	92014	1207-H1
VIA PLATILLO				
	2300	CRLB	92009	1127-G7
VIA PLATO				
	2700	CRLB	92010	1106-H3
VIA PLAYA DE CORTES				
	11300	SD	92124	1230-A7
VIA PLAYA LOS SANTOS				
	5000	SD	92124	1230-A7
VIA PLAZA				
	-	VSTA	92081	1107-C2
VIA POCO				
	2500	ENCT	92007	1167-F4
VIA PORTOFINO				
	1200	SDCo	92078	1128-G4
VIA PORTOLA				
	700	SMCS	92078	1108-C7
	700	SMCS	92078	1128-C1
	5100	OCN	92057	1067-B7
VIA PORTOVECCHIO				
	1200	SDCo	92078	1128-B3
VIA POSADA				
	2800	SD	92037	1227-J5
	2900	SD	92037	1228-A5
VIA POSADA DEL NORTE				
	6000	SDCo	92067	1168-G4
VIA PRADO				
	1000	SDCo	92028	1027-J4
VIA PRAVIA				
	2200	SD	92037	1247-J1
VIA PRECIPICIO				
	4400	SD	92122	1228-D3
VIA PREMIO				
	3100	CRLB	92010	1106-H3
VIA PRIMERO				
	1800	OCN	92056	1087-C5
VIA PRIVADA				
	1100	SDCo	92029	1149-H3
VIA PROMESA				
	11400	SD	92124	1250-A2
VIA PUERTA				
	-	CRLB	92009	1127-J3
VIA PUERTA DEL SOL				
	5400	SDCo	92003	1047-H7
	5400	SDCo	92003	1067-G1
	30000	OCN	92003	1067-G4
	30000	OCN	92057	1067-G4
VIA QUINCELEAGUAS				
	39100	SDCo	92028	999-D3
VIA QUINTO				
	1800	OCN	92056	1087-C5
VIAR AV				
	7200	SD	92120	1250-C5
VIA RAFAEL				
	1200	SDCo	92078	1128-B4
VIA RAMON				
	1200	SDCo	92029	1149-G2
VIA RANCHEROS				
	2500	SDCo	92028	1048-C1
	2600	SDCo	92028	1028-B7
VIA RANCHEROS WY				
	2600	SDCo	92028	1048-C1
VIA RANCHITOS				
	39900	SDCo	92028	997-H3
VIA RANCHO				
	200	SCLE	92672	1023-B1
VIA RANCHO LN				
	10100	SDCo	92029	1129-F7
	10100	SDCo	92029	1149-F1
VIA RANCHO PKWY				
	-	SD	92027	1130-G7
	100	ESCN	92029	1150-A3
	100	ESCN	92025	1150-C2
	200	ESCN	92029	1149-G1
	500	SDCo	92029	1149-G1
	1900	SDCo	92029	1129-E7
	2900	SD	92025	1130-G7
	2900	SD	92025	1150-F1
	2900	SDCo	92025	1130-G7
	5500	SDCo	92025	1150-F1
	14400	SDCo	92027	1130-G7
VIA RANCHO RD				
	4000	OCN	92057	1086-J4
	4300	OCN	92057	1087-A4
VIA RANCHO CIELO				
	-	SDCo	92067	1149-B5
VIA RANCHO CUCA				
	-	SDCo	92060	1052-A6
	-	SDCo	92061	1052-A6
	-	SDCo	92082	1052-A6
VIA RANCHO DEL LAGO				
	100	SDCo	92003	1067-G2
VIA RANCHO DOS NINAS				
	2100	SDCo	92065	1172-E3
VIA RANCHO PACIFICA				
	900	SDCo	92084	1088-G7
VIA RANCHO SAN DIEGO				
	11300	SDCo	92019	1272-A5
VIA RAVELLO				
	-	SDCo	92091	1148-F4
VIA REALZAR				
	4400	SD	92122	1228-D3
VIA REATA				
	-	VSTA	92081	1107-H2
VIA RECANTO				
	17400	SDCo	92067	1168-B2
VIA REGLA				
	6000	SD	92122	1228-G6
VIA REPOSO				
	3800	SDCo	92091	1168-C7
VIA RIALTO				
	2300	SD	92037	1227-H6
VIA RIBERA				
	3200	ESCN	92029	1150-A2
VIA RICARDO				
	2800	CRLB	92010	1106-H3
VIA RICO				
	-	CRLB	92009	1147-J2
VIA RIMINI				
	13700	SD	92129	1189-H3
VIA RIO				
	400	OCN	92057	1086-H1
VIA RISA				
	1500	SDCo	92078	1128-C4
VIA RITA				
	9800	SNTE	92071	1231-D3
VIA RIVERA				
	-	SD	92129	1188-J4
VIA ROBERTO				
	2700	CRLB	92010	1106-C6
VIA ROBLAR CT				
	2900	SDCo	92019	1272-D6
VIA ROBLES				
	2100	OCN	92054	1106-G1
VIA ROJO				
	2500	CRLB	92010	1106-H3
VIA ROMAYA				
	3800	NATC	91950	1310-E3
VIA ROMAZA				
	3000	CRLB	92009	1147-H3
VIA RONDA				
	1400	SMCS	92069	1109-D7
VIA ROSA				
	3900	SMCS	92078	1128-C1
VIA ROSARITA				
	3000	CRLB	92010	1106-H3
VIA ROSE MARIE LN				
	900	SDCo	92028	1027-H4
VIA ROSSI				
	-	SD	92129	1189-A3
VIA ROSWITHA				
	18200	SDCo	92067	1148-D6
VIA ROTA				
	18000	SD	92128	1150-D7
VIA ROVELLO CT				
	-	SD	92129	1188-J5
VIA SABBIA				
	-	SD	92129	1189-A4
VIA SABINAS				
	3000	CRLB	92010	1106-C6
VIA SALARIA				
	300	CHV	91910	1310-A4
VIA SALERNO				
	-	SMCS	92069	1129-F1
	1400	SDCo	92026	1129-F1
VIA SALVADOR				
	15600	SDCo	92082	1071-A7
VIA SAN ALBERTO				
	4100	SDCo	92028	1048-H4
VIA SAN ARRONO				
	4100	SDCo	92028	1048-H4
VIA SAN ARTURO				
	4100	SDCo	92028	1048-H4
VIA SAN BLAS				
	10700	SD	92126	1209-D3
VIA SAN CLEMENTE				
	7900	CRLB	92009	1147-J3
VIA SAN JACINTO				
	1200	SDCo	92078	1128-B4
VIA SAN JUAN				
	4100	SDCo	92028	1048-H4
VIA SAN LORENO				
	12100	SD	92128	1190-B2
VIA SAN LORENZA				
	-	SD	92129	1188-J5
VIA SAN MANZANIA				
	4100	SDCo	92028	1048-H4
VIA SAN MARCO				
	10800	SD	92129	1189-H3
VIA SAN ROSARITO				
	4000	SDCo	92028	1048-G4
VIA SAN SABA				
	8000	SD	92122	1228-E4
VIA SANSAL				
	15300	PWY	92064	1170-C6
VIA SANTA BEATRICE				
	4000	SDCo	92028	1048-G4
VIA SANTA BRISA				
	-	SD	92131	1210-H1
VIA SANTA CALIFORNIA				
	4000	SDCo	92028	1048-G4
VIA SANTA CRUZ				
	600	VSTA	92081	1107-E1
VIA SANTA DOLORES				
	4000	SDCo	92028	1048-H4
VIA SANTA FELICE				
	4000	SDCo	92028	1048-H4
VIA SANTALINA				
	-	SMCS	92069	1108-D4
VIA SANTA PAULO				
	600	VSTA	92081	1107-E1
VIA SANTA VIENTA				
	-	SD	92131	1210-H2
VIA SAN THOMAS				
	4100	SDCo	92028	1048-H4
VIA SANTIAGO				
	600	VSTA	92081	1107-E1
	3000	CRLB	92009	1127-J6
VIA SANTILLANA				
	-	SD	92129	1188-J5
VIA SARASAN				
	200	ENCT	92024	1147-F6
VIA SASSARI				
	-	SDCo	92091	1148-F4
VIA SAUCE VEREDA				
	30000	SDCo	92082	1070-A5
VIA SAVOY				
	400	ENCT	92024	1147-F6
VIA SCOTT				
	1900	ESCN	92026	1109-F6
	1900	SDCo	92026	1109-F6
VIA SEFTON				
	11700	SDCo	92019	1271-J4
VIA SEGOVIA				
	1900	SD	92037	1247-H1
VIA SEGUNDO				
	2300	SD	92173	1350-F4
VIA SELMA				
	11900	SDCo	92019	1271-J4
VIA SENDERO				
	1200	SDCo	92029	1149-G2
VIA SENDERO VISTA				
	1200	SDCo	92029	1149-G2
VIA SEPULVEDA				
	4400	SD	92122	1228-E4
VIA SERENA				
	4300	SDCo	92003	1067-H2
	13600	PWY	92064	1170-E5
VIA SERENIDAD				
	-	SDCo	92065	1171-F1
VIA SERRA				
	300	OCN	92057	1086-H2
	4700	SDCo	92028	1048-G2
VIA SERRANO				
	12100	SDCo	92019	1272-A4
VIA SEVILLE				
	400	SMCS	92078	1108-C7
	400	SMCS	92078	1128-C1
	5100	OCN	92056	1107-F4
VIA SHAWNTY				
	19600	SDCo	91935	(1314-H2 See Page 1294)
VIA SIENA				
	2300	SD	92037	1227-H6
VIA SILVA				
	3600	OCN	92056	1107-G4
VIA SIMPATIA				
	-	CRLB	92009	1127-J3
VIA SIMPATICO				
	16100	SDCo	92091	1168-C7
VIA SINALDA				
	2000	SD	92037	1247-H2
VIA SINSONTE				
	1800	SDCo	92027	1130-F3
VIA SINUOSO				
	1000	CHV	91910	1311-A7
VIA SISTINA				
	300	CHV	91910	1310-A4
VIA SOBRADO				
	12800	SD	92128	1150-C7
VIA SOBRETTE				
	3000	CRLB	92010	1106-H3
VIA SOLANA				
	2900	SDCo	92029	1149-G2
VIA SOLARE				
	-	SD	92129	1189-A4
VIA SOLARO				
	100	ENCT	92024	1147-F6
VIA SOL ARRIBA				
	3400	SDCo	92025	1150-E2
VIA SOLEDAD				
	800	VSTA	92084	1087-J3
VIA SOMBRA				
	3100	CRLB	92010	1106-H3
VIA SOMBRAS				
	12700	PWY	92064	1170-C6
VIA SONOMA				
	8300	SD	92037	1228-B4
VIA SONORA				
	2100	OCN	92054	1106-G1
VIA SOPLADOR				
	300	SDCo	92028	1027-J3
VIA SORPRESA				
	4300	SD	92124	1249-J2
VIA SOVANA				
	-	SNTE	92071	1230-H7
VIA STEPHEN				
	13300	PWY	92064	1190-G4
VIA SUBRIA				
	2200	SDCo	92084	1088-D1
VIA SUENA				
	13000	SDCo	92082	1070-C7
VIA SUSPIRO				
	2800	SD	92173	1350-D2
VIA TABARA				
	2200	SD	92037	1247-J1
VIA TALA				
	4700	SDCo	92028	1048-G2
VIA TALAVERA				
	5200	SD	92130	1188-D3
VIA TAPIA				
	100	SDCo	91977	1291-B5
VIA TAQUITA				
	200	SDCo	92065	1152-J5
VIA TARIFA				
	18000	SD	92128	1150-D7
VIA TAVIRA				
	200	ENCT	92024	1147-F6
VIA TAVITO				
	11600	SD	92128	1170-A6
VIA TAZON				
	16900	SD	92127	1169-J2
VIA TECA				
	7800	CRLB	92009	1147-H2
VIA TEMPRANO				
	11000	SD	92124	1250-A2
VIA TERAMO				
	700	SDCo	92026	1129-F2
VIA TERCERO				
	2300	SD	92173	1350-E4
	4200	OCN	92056	1087-C5
VIA TERCETO				
	12700	SD	92130	1188-B6
VIA TERECINA				
	-	CHV	91910	1311-A6
VIA TERESA				
	1100	SMCS	92069	1109-C7
VIA TERRASSA				
	1300	ENCT	92024	1147-F7
VIA TESORO				
	2200	SDCo	91901	1254-C2
VIA THERESA				
	11200	SNTE	92071	1231-G5
VIA TIEMPO				
	2000	ENCT	92007	1167-F3
N VIA TIERRA				
	200	ENCT	92024	1147-E6
VIA TIMOTEO				
	10800	SDCo	91978	1271-G5
VIA TIZON				
	5200	OCN	92057	1067-C7
VIA TOMAS				
	10700	SD	92129	1189-H3
VIA TONALA				
	3200	CRLB	92010	1106-C6
VIA TONGA				
	3100	SD	92154	1330-E7
VIA TONGA CT				
	800	SD	92154	1330-D7
VIA TOPACIO				
	2800	CRLB	92010	1106-H3
VIA TORE				
	200	SDCo	92083	1108-A3
VIA TORINA				
	2500	SD	92014	1207-H1

STREET
Block City ZIP Pg-Grid

VIA TORTOLA
2200 SDCo 91978 1271-G7
2200 SDCo 91978 1291-G1
VIA TOSCANA
- CHV 91910 1311-A6
- SD 92129 1189-A4
VIA TRANQUILO
3900 SD 92122 1228-C4
VIA TRATO
- CRLB 92009 1127-J3
VIA TRESCA
- SD 92129 1189-A4
VIA TRES VISTA
13600 SD 92129 1189-E3
VIA TRIESTE
1100 CHV 91910 1330-F2
VIA TRUENO
2000 SDCo 91901 1254-B2
VIA TULIPAN
2700 CRLB 92010 1106-H3
VIA ULTIMO
400 ENCT 92024 1147-F6
VIA UNIDOS
1000 SDCo 92028 1027-H4
VIA URNER WY
8000 SDCo 92003 1068-H1
8100 SDCo 92003 1048-J7
VIA VALARTA
5100 SD 92124 1230-A7
5200 SD 92124 1250-A1
VIA VALENCIA
30200 SDCo 92082 1070-G5
VIA VALENTE
1400 SDCo 92029 1149-G2
VIA VALESCO
3100 ESCN 92029 1150-A2
VIA VALLE VERDE
3700 SDCo 92091 1168-C7
VIA VALLE VISTA
1100 SDCo 92029 1149-H3
VIA VALVERDE
6800 SD 92037 1247-G1
VIA VARESE
- SDCo 92091 1148-F5
VIA VASTAGO
1000 VSTA 92083 1087-E6
VIA VELASQUEZ
7000 CRLB 92009 1127-G6
VIA VELTRI
- SDCo 92082 1070-F6
VIA VENETO
- CHV 91910 1310-A4
2000 ESCN 92027 1110-C7
VIA VENTADA
3500 SDCo 92029 1149-H3
VIA VENUSTO
1400 OCN 92056 1087-C3
VIA VERA
2600 CRLB 92010 1106-C6
32000 SDCo 92003 1048-E7
VIA VERA CRUZ
100 SMCS 92078 1108-E7
100 SMCS 92078 1128-E1
VIA VERANO
6800 CRLB 92009 1128-A5
VIA VERDE
- CHV 91910 1311-A6
2200 SDCo 92019 1252-D5
VIA VERRAZZANO
- SD 92127 1168-J7
VIA VIAJERA
16000 SDCo 92091 1168-C7
VIA VIDA NUEVA
1300 SDCo 92026 1109-E6
VIA VIEJAS
2600 SDCo 91901 1254-C1
VIA VIEJAS OESTE
2500 SDCo 91901 1254-B2
VIA VIEJO
13600 SD 92130 1188-A4
VIA VIENTO
3800 SDCo 92028 1028-F7
VIA VIENTO SUAVE
1200 SDCo 92078 1128-G4
VIA VIESTA
2400 SD 92037 1227-H6
VIA VILLEGAS
2300 CRLB 92009 1127-G7
VIA VILLENA
200 ENCT 92024 1147-F6
VIA VISO
28000 SDCo 92082 1091-C3
VIA VISTA
1200 SDCo 92028 1028-C4
VIA VISTA CANADA
6500 SDCo 92067 1168-F6
VIA VISTA DEL RIO
3000 SDCo 92084 1067-H7
VIA VISTA GRANDE
19600 SDCo 92065 1151-G2
VIA VISTA MEJOR
31400 SDCo 92082 1070-A2
VIA VISTA ORIENTE
6000 SDCo 92067 1168-D3
VIA VIVALDI
- SD 92127 1168-J7
VIA VONNIE
2400 SDCo 92028 1048-C2
VIA VUELTA
3700 SDCo 92091 1168-C7
VIA WAKEFIELD
9900 SNTE 92071 1231-D4
VIA YUHA
5100 OCN 92057 1067-C7
VIA ZAFIRO
7700 SDCo 92067 1148-H7
VIA ZAMIA
- ENCT 92024 1147-D5
VIA ZAMORA
3200 ESCN 92029 1150-A2
VIA ZANCAS
1000 SDCo 92028 998-B7
1000 SDCo 92028 1028-B1
VIA ZAPADOR
8700 SNTE 92071 1231-C7
VIA ZAPATA
11900 SDCo 92019 1271-J4
11900 SDCo 92019 1272-A4
VIA ZARA
1100 SDCo 92028 1028-E4
VIA ZARA CT
3300 SDCo 92028 1028-D4
VIA ZURITA
5900 SD 92037 1247-H2
VICENTE MEADOW DR
15500 SDCo 92065 1173-A5
VICENTE VIEW DR
12700 SDCo 92040 1212-B3
VICEROY DR
18100 SD 92128 1150-B7
VICKERS RD
2400 SDCo 92028 997-A1
VICKERS ST
7700 SD 92111 1249-B1
VICKI PL
500 ESCN 92026 1109-J7
500 ESCN 92026 1129-J1
VICKIE DR
5100 SD 92109 1247-J4
VICKSBURG DR
1400 ELCJ 92021 1252-A3
VICTOR AV
1000 ELCJ 92021 1251-G3
1100 SDCo 92021 1251-G3
VICTORIA AV
2700 CRLB 92010 1106-J4
2700 CRLB 92010 1107-A4
VICTORIA CIR
2300 SDCo 91901 1234-B5
VICTORIA CT
- IMP 92251 6499-H2
7500 SD 92114 1290-G2
VICTORIA DR
- CALX 92231 6620-H6
- ELCJ 92021 1251-H5
E VICTORIA DR
3100 SDCo 91901 1234-D5
N VICTORIA DR
2700 SDCo 91901 1234-C4
W VICTORIA DR
1900 SDCo 91901 1234-B5
VICTORIA GN
1400 ESCN 92025 1150-E3
VICTORIA LN
3000 SDCo 91901 1234-D6
4200 SDCo 92028 998-F7
4200 SDCo 92028 1028-G1
VICTORIA PL
400 VSTA 92084 1087-H4
2800 SDCo 91901 1234-C5
VICTORIA WY
- OCN 92057 1086-H3
- SMCS 92069 1108-J3
- SMCS 92069 1109-A3
30800 SDCo 92026 1069-C2
VICTORIA BAY CT
5600 SD 92105 1290-B1
VICTORIA ESTATES LN
14400 PWY 92064 1190-E1
VICTORIA HEIGHTS PL
3500 SDCo 91901 1234-C5
VICTORIA KNOLLS CT
500 SDCo 91901 1234-C4
VICTORIA KNOLLS DR
500 SDCo 91901 1234-C4
VICTORIA MEADOWS DR
2300 SDCo 91901 1234-B5
VICTORIA PARK TER
1800 SDCo 91901 1233-J5
1900 SDCo 91901 1234-A5
VICTORY CT
- OCN 92057 1067-B3
VICTORY DR
1900 SDCo 92084 1108-D3
VICTORY RD
8400 LMSA 91941 1270-J2
VIDAS CIR
1100 SDCo 92026 1109-E7
VIEJAS BLVD
24600 SDCo 91916 1236-A3
VIEJAS RD
- SDCo 91901 1234-J2
- SDCo 91901 1235-A2
VIEJAS CREEK LN
4000 SDCo 91901 1234-F7
VIEJAS CREEK TR
1400 SDCo 91901 1234-F7
VIEJAS GRADE
- SDCo 91901 1235-A2
10300 SDCo 91916 1235-G1
VIEJAS GRADE RD
- SDCo 91901 1234-H4
- SDCo 91901 1235-A3
23100 SDCo 91916 1235-A3
23300 SDCo 91916 1236-A3
VIEJAS VIEW LN
1300 SDCo 91901 1235-A5
VIEJAS VIEW PL
2800 SDCo 91901 1234-C7
VIEJO CASTILLA WY
7500 CRLB 92009 1147-G1
VIENNA ST
3400 SD 92104 1289-F1
VIENTO FUERTE WY
9300 SDCo 91941 1271-B4
VIENTO VALLE
20700 SDCo 92025 1130-F7
VIETTA TER
11600 SD 92126 1208-J1
VIEW PL
4200 SD 92115 1270-C4
VIEW ST
1700 ESCN 92027 1130-C1
2200 OCN 92054 1106-E1
E VIEW ST
100 SDCo 92028 1027-F2
W VIEW ST
100 SDCo 92028 1027-F2
VIEW WY
1600 ELCJ 92020 1251-C5
VIEWCREST CT
10000 SDCo 91977 1271-E6
VIEWCREST DR
7100 SD 92114 1290-F2
VIEW CREST GN
2100 ESCN 92026 1109-C4
VIEWMONT DR
1100 SDCo 92027 1130-C4
VIEW PARK WY
- CHV 91913 1311-E7
- CHV 91913 1331-D1
VIEWPOINT CT
6300 SD 92139 1290-E7
6300 SD 92139 1310-E1
VIEWPOINT DR
700 SMCS 92078 1128-B2
6200 SD 92139 1310-E1
VIEWPOINT WY
3400 OCN 92056 1106-H1
VIEW POINTE AV
1300 ESCN 92027 1110-A7
VIEW POINTE RW
6300 SD 92128 1170-A5
VIEWRIDGE AV
4300 SD 92123 1249-E2
VIEWRIDGE CT
5200 SD 92123 1249-E1
VIEWRIDGE PL
2300 ESCN 92026 1109-F4
VIEWRIDGE WY
5000 OCN 92056 1107-E3
VIEWSIDE LN
9600 SDCo 92021 1233-C3
VIEW TRAIL CT
- CHV 91914 1311-G2
VIEW VERDE
3700 SDCo 91902 1310-J2
VIGILANT WY
4800 CRLB 92008 1106-H7
VIGILANTE RD
12400 SDCo 92040 1211-H4
VIGO DR
6600 LMSA 91941 1270-E4
6600 SD 92115 1270-E4
VIKING LN
900 SMCS 92069 1109-A5
VIKING PL
1100 ESCN 92027 1130-E2
VIKING WY
- CRLB 92008 1106-G5
800 SMCS 92069 1109-A5
1800 SD 92037 1227-G6
VIKING GROVE LN
15600 SDCo 92082 1071-A6
VILETTA DR
900 SDCo 92027 1130-C4
VILLA AV
- ELCN 92243 6499-E5
- ELCN 92243 6500-A4
- ImCo 92243 6500-A4
VILLA LN
- ImCo 92243 6500-B4
1600 ELCN 92243 6499-F5
VILLA TER
3400 SD 92104 1269-D6
VILLA ADOLEE
3000 SDCo 91978 1271-F7
VILLA ALEGRE DR
- CALX 92231 6620-H6
VILLA BLANCA CT
400 ENCT 92024 1147-D7
VILLA BONITA
10500 SDCo 91978 1271-F6
VILLA BONITA CT
- CALX 92231 6620-H6
VILLA CARDIFF DR
1400 ENCT 92007 1167-E2
VILLA COLINA
3100 SDCo 91978 1271-F6
VILLA CREST DR
1500 ELCJ 92021 1252-B2
VILLA DEL CIELO DR
- SDCo 92003 1067-F1
3500 SDCo 92028 1067-F1
VILLA DEL DIOS GN
1800 ESCN 92029 1129-F6
VILLA ESPANA
3100 SDCo 91978 1271-F6
VILLA FLORA CT
- SDCo 92003 1068-C3
VILLA FLORES
2100 ESCN 92029 1129-E6
VILLAGE CIR
- SDCo 91901 1234-A6
2000 CRLB 92008 1106-E6
VILLAGE CT
- OCN 92057 1067-B3
VILLAGE DR
- OCN 92057 1067-B3
- SMCS 92078 1128-H3
400 CHV 91911 1330-C3
400 CRLB 92008 1106-E6
VILLAGE PL
1700 SD 92101 1269-C7
2500 SD 92101 1289-C1
VILLAGE RD
100 ESCN 92026 1109-G4
VILLAGE RUN N
200 ENCT 92024 1147-G6
VILLAGE WY
2400 OCN 92054 1086-D7
VILLAGE CENTER DR
400 ENCT 92024 1147-H5
VILLAGE CENTER LOOP RD
- SD 92130 1188-F4
VILLAGE GLEN DR
9000 SD 92123 1249-D4
VILLAGE GREEN DR
- CRLB 92009 1127-F3
VILLAGE GREEN RD
100 ENCT 92024 1147-H6
VILLAGE PARK WY
1700 ENCT 92024 1147-H7
VILLAGE PINE DR
2800 SD 92173 1350-D2
VILLAGE PINE WY
1500 SD 92173 1350-C2
VILLAGE RIDGE RD
11300 SD 92131 1189-J7
VILLAGE SQUARE DR
100 ENCT 92024 1147-G7
VILLAGE VIEW PL
500 SDCo 92028 1027-G3
VILLAGE VIEW RD
1200 ENCT 92024 1147-H4
VILLAGE WOOD RD
1900 ENCT 92024 1147-H7
VILLA GLEN LN
1300 ELCJ 92021 1252-A3
VILLA HERMOSA CT
100 SDCo 92075 1167-D6
VILLA LA JOLLA DR
8500 SD 92037 1228-A4
9000 SD 92093 1228-A4
9000 SD 92161 1228-A4
VILLA MEDICI WY
- SDCo 92003 1068-C4
VILLA MONTE
13200 SDCo 92040 1232-C2
VILLAMOURA DR
17700 PWY 92064 1170-E1
VILLAMOURA WY
13600 PWY 92064 1170-F1
VILLANITAS RD
2100 ENCT 92024 1147-J6
VILLA NORTE
3100 SD 92037 1228-A3
VILLANOVA AV
3500 SD 92122 1228-D5
VILLA PAVRONE CT
- SDCo 92003 1068-C4
VILLARICA WY
5700 SD 92124 1229-J7
VILLA ROMA CT
- SDCo 92003 1068-D4
VILLAS
- SD 92127 1169-A7
VILLAS CT
4600 CHV 91902 1310-H3
VILLAS DR
4500 CHV 91902 1310-H3
5400 SDCo 92003 1068-B1
VILLAS WY
- SD 92108 1249-D7
- SD 92108 1269-D1
VILLA SANTINI CT
- SDCo 92003 1068-C3
VILLA SIERRA LN
15500 SD 92082 1070-J4
15500 SDCo 92082 1071-A4
VILLA SIERRA RD
15100 SDCo 92082 1070-J4
15500 SDCo 92082 1071-A5
VILLA SONOMA
2100 ESCN 92029 1129-F6
VILLA TEMPRA DR
1300 CHV 91911 1330-D3
VILLA TOSCANA RD
- SDCo 92003 1068-C4
VILLA VERDE RD
1900 ESCN 92029 1129-G7
VILLA VIEW LN
1300 ELCJ 92021 1252-A2
VILLA ZAPATA
2300 SDCo 91901 1253-J2
VINARUZ PL
16900 SD 92128 1170-C3
VINCA WY
1300 SD 92114 1290-C5
VINCENTE WY
400 SD 92037 1247-F2
VINCETTA CT
5400 LMSA 91942 1270-H1
VINCETTA DR
8100 LMSA 91942 1270-H1
VINE CIR
1900 ELCN 92243 6499-F7
2000 VSTA 92084 1088-C5
VINE DR
29300 SDCo 91906 (1297-E5 See Page 1296)
VINE LN
9700 SDCo 92029 1149-D3
VINE ST
100 SDCo 92028 1027-F2
400 ELCN 92243 6499-E7
500 OCN 92054 1106-C1
600 ESCN 92025 1129-H4
1400 SD 92103 1268-H7
1700 SD 92101 1268-H7
9600 SDCo 92040 1232-B2
S VINE ST
100 SDCo 92028 1027-F3
VINEWOOD DR
3500 SDCo 92036 1156-E2
VINEWOOD ST
100 ESCN 92029 1129-E3
S VINEWOOD ST
200 ESCN 92029 1129-E3
VINEYARD AV
300 ESCN 92029 1129-D2
1300 VSTA 92081 1107-H3
VINEYARD LN
17700 PWY 92064 1170-E1
VINEYARD RD
300 SMCS 92069 1108-J6
700 SMCS 92069 1109-A5
VINEYARD WY
- CHV 91914 1311-J1
- SDCo 91901 1234-A6
VINLEY PL
5700 SD 92120 1250-D7
VINTAGE DR
14600 SD 92129 1189-C1
VINTAGE PL
2100 ESCN 92027 1110-B4
VINTAGE POINT DR
800 SMCS 92078 1129-A3
VINTER WY
13200 PWY 92064 1170-E2
VINWOOD CT
- SD 92130 1188-E5
VINYARD ST
4500 OCN 92057 1066-H7
VIOLA ST
1200 SD 92110 1268-E2
VIOLET AV
- SMCS 92078 1128-H3
VIOLET CT
800 CRLB 92011 1127-A6
VIOLET DR
13600 PWY 92064 1190-F3
VIOLET GN
3800 ESCN 92025 1150-C3
VIOLET RDG
3200 ENCT 92024 1148-C5
VIOLET ST
2500 SD 92105 1269-H7
2500 SD 92105 1289-H1
3800 LMSA 91941 1270-F5
VIPER WY
- VSTA 92081 1108-B6
10500 SD 92121 1208-H4
VIREO CT
6600 CRLB 92011 1127-B5
VIRGINIA AV
- SD 92173 1350-H5
4500 SD 92115 1270-D3
VIRGINIA CT
2100 ELCJ 92020 1251-B5
VIRGINIA DR
2600 NATC 91950 1310-A3
VIRGINIA LN
900 ESCN 92027 1110-C6
1600 ImCo 92243 6559-H3
VIRGINIA PL
700 SMCS 92078 1108-C7
VIRGINIA WY
1000 SD 92037 1227-F6
VIRGINIAN LN
9200 SDCo 91941 1271-B1
VIRGIN ISLANDS RD
6800 SDCo 92003 1068-E2
VIRGO PL
11000 SD 92126 1209-C2
E VIRGO RD
3200 SD 92105 1270-B6
W VIRGO RD
3100 SD 92105 1270-B6
VISALIA CT
1200 CHV 91913 1331-B1
VISALIA RW
1700 CORD 92118 1288-J7
2000 CORD 92118 1289-A7
VISION DR
4300 SD 92121 1228-D1
VISPERA PL
6500 CRLB 92009 1127-G5
VISTA AV
300 ESCN 92026 1109-H5
400 SDCo 92026 1109-H5
3100 LMGR 91945 1270-F6
3600 LMSA 91941 1270-F5
VISTA DR
- SD 92102 1289-G4
- SDCo 92036 1136-D7
- SDCo 91910 1310-D6
8000 LMSA 91941 1270-H3
9200 SDCo 91977 1271-B6
VISTA LN
3200 SD 92173 1350-E3
4700 SD 92116 1269-H3
VISTA PL
400 CHV 91910 1310-D6
900 CORD 92118 1308-J1
4900 SD 92116 1269-D3
VISTA RDG
- SD 92130 1208-B2
VISTA ST
4500 SD 92116 1269-H3
VISTA TER
10900 SDCo 91941 1271-G4
VISTA WY
- ESCN 92026 1109-G7
- CHV 91910 1310-C4
100 SDCo 92021 1252-H4
100 OCN 92054 1106-F2
800 CHV 91911 1330-D1
1700 ELCJ 92019 1252-C7
1700 SDCo 92019 1252-C7
2700 SDCo 91950 1310-B3
3000 OCN 92056 1106-H2
3600 OCN 92056 1107-B2
4200 SDCo 91941 1271-E3
E VISTA WY Rt#-S13
600 VSTA 92084 1087-J4
1100 VSTA 92084 1088-A2
2100 SDCo 92084 1088-A2
2600 SDCo 92084 1067-J6
2600 SDCo 92084 1068-A7
S VISTA WY
2200 CRLB 92054 1106-G2
2200 OCN 92054 1106-G2
W VISTA WY
100 VSTA 92083 1107-C2
100 VSTA 92083 1087-F7
1300 OCN 92056 1107-C2
2100 OCN 92054 1106-F2
W VISTA WY Rt#-S13
300 VSTA 92083 1087-G7
VISTA ABIERTA
300 SDCo 92019 1252-E4
VISTA ACEDERA
2800 CRLB 92009 1147-G3
VISTA ALEGRIA
300 OCN 92057 1086-H4
VISTA ALETA
9400 SDCo 92082 1069-C7
VISTA ARROYO
300 SDCo 92028 1027-H3
4900 SDCo 91941 1271-D2
VISTA AZUL
3800 SCLE 92672 1023-B1
VISTA BELLA
500 OCN 92057 1086-G4
VISTA BLANCA
3800 SCLE 92672 1023-B1
VISTA BONITA
1100 VSTA 92083 1107-J1
3100 CRLB 92009 1127-H7
VISTA BONITA LN
4100 ESCN 92025 1150-E3
VISTA CALAVERAS
4000 OCN 92056 1107-C3
VISTA CAMINO
10200 SDCo 92040 1231-J2
VISTA CAMPANA N
3600 OCN 92057 1086-G4
VISTA CAMPANA S
500 OCN 92057 1086-G5
VISTA CANELA
7900 CRLB 92009 1147-G2
VISTA CANON CT
- SD 92130 1188-J3
VISTA CANYON CIR
- SDCo 92084 1088-F7
VISTA CAPITAN DR
1200 ELCJ 92020 1251-C3
VISTA CAPRI
4100 OCN 92057 1086-J4
4100 OCN 92057 1087-A4
VISTA CATALINA
15600 SDCo 92082 1071-A4
VISTA CHAPARRAL
- CRLB 92009 1147-F3
VISTA CIELO DR
12800 SDCo 91978 1272-C7
VISTA CIELO LN
3200 SDCo 91978 1272-C7
VISTA CLARIDAD
1400 SD 92037 1247-H3
VISTA COLINA DR
1200 SMCS 92078 1128-E3
VISTA CORONA
- SDCo 92028 1048-B3
VISTA CORONADO DR
4200 SDCo 91910 1310-E5
VISTA COYOTE
- SDCo 92040 1231-J2
VISTA DE BONITA CANADA
4000 SDCo 91941 1271-H4
VISTA DE CHAPARROS DR
3000 SDCo 91935 1273-B7
3000 SDCo 91935 1293-A1
VISTA DE FORTUNA
- SDCo 92067 1168-C1
VISTA DE GOLF
16000 SDCo 92091 1168-C7
VISTA DE LA BAHIA
3600 SD 92117 1248-E5
VISTA DE LA CANADA
3600 ESCN 92029 1150-A4
VISTA DE LA CRESTA
3300 SDCo 92029 1149-G2
VISTA DE LA CRUZ
10100 SDCo 91941 1271-E2
VISTA DEL AGUA WY
10600 SD 92121 1208-E4
VISTA DE LA MESA
6000 SD 92037 1247-F3
VISTA DE LA MONTANA
1900 SDCo 92019 1253-B5
VISTA DE LA ORILLA
3500 SD 92117 1248-E5
VISTA DE LA PATRIA
4500 SDCo 92014 1187-J1
4500 SDCo 92014 1188-A1
VISTA DE LA PLAYA
300 SD 92037 1247-E1
VISTA DE LA ROSA
2900 SDCo 91935 1292-F1
VISTA DE LA TIERRA
4300 SOLB 92014 1187-J1
4400 SD 92014 1187-J1
4600 SD 92014 1188-A1
4600 SDCo 92014 1168-A7
VISTA DEL CAJON PL
8400 SDCo 92021 1252-A1
8400 SDCo 92040 1232-A7
8400 SDCo 92040 1252-A1
VISTA DEL CAJON RD
12100 SDCo 92040 1232-A7
12100 SDCo 92040 1252-A1
12100 SDCo 92021 1252-A1
VISTA DEL CANON
1200 SOLB 92014 1187-H1
VISTA DEL CAPITAN
10200 SDCo 92040 1232-C2
VISTA DEL CERRO DR
10300 SNTE 92071 1231-E7
VISTA DEL CIELO
- SDCo 91905 (1319-H4 See Page 1298)
VISTA DEL CONQUISTADOR
2600 SDCo 91935 1293-B4
VISTA DEL CORONADOS
2100 SDCo 92021 1252-H4
VISTA DEL DIOS
5200 SD 92130 1188-D2
VISTA DEL ESCUELA
200 ELCJ 92019 1252-E4
VISTA DEL ESTERO
3000 SD 92154 1350-A5
3000 SD 92154 1349-J6
VISTA DEL INDIO
200 SDCo 92028 1028-A3
VISTA DEL LAGO DR
1500 SDCo 92028 997-J6
VISTA DEL MAR
1600 SDCo 92003 1068-C5
1600 SDCo 92084 1068-C5
7300 SD 92037 1247-E1
VISTA DEL MAR AV
6500 SD 92037 1247-E1
VISTA DEL MAR CT
- CHV 91910 1310-B4
VISTA DEL MONTE DR
900 SDCo 92020 1251-J7
VISTA DEL MONTE WY
900 SDCo 92020 1251-J7
VISTA DEL NORTE
1900 SDCo 92028 1048-A2
VISTA DEL OCEANO
100 SCLE 92672 1023-B1
14800 SDCo 92014 1187-J1
VISTA DE LOMAS
30600 SDCo 92003 1068-B3
VISTA DEL ORO
2700 CRLB 92009 1127-H5
3300 OCN 92056 1086-J7
VISTA DEL ORO WY
8700 SDCo 91977 1291-A1
VISTA DE LOS PINOS
13700 SDCo 91935 1292-G2
VISTA DEL OTERO
- SDCo 92065 1151-H2
VISTA DEL PACIFICO
4300 SDCo 92028 1028-F5
VISTA DEL PIEDRA
2700 SDCo 91935 1293-A4
VISTA DEL RANCHO
400 CHV 91910 1310-D6
400 SDCo 91910 1310-D6
VISTA DEL REY DR
300 ENCT 92024 1147-C7
VISTA DEL RIO
- SD 92154 1330-E6
2900 SDCo 92028 998-C4
VISTA DEL RIO WY
4200 OCN 92057 1086-J3
VISTA DEL SAGE
13000 SDCo 92082 1050-D5
VISTA DEL SEMBRADO
2700 SDCo 92025 1130-F7
2700 SDCo 92025 1150-F1
VISTA DEL SOL
9600 SDCo 91977 1271-C4
VISTA DEL SUR
10700 SDCo 91978 1271-G6
VISTA DEL VALLE BLVD
1200 SDCo 92019 1272-B1
1500 ELCJ 92019 1252-B7
1500 SDCo 92019 1252-B7
VISTA DEL VERDE
8400 SDCo 92021 1232-E7
VISTA DE MONTEMAR
1500 SDCo 92021 1252-E3
VISTA DE ORO
1000 SDCo 92029 1149-H3
VISTA DE PALOMAR
2600 SDCo 92028 1048-C1
VISTA DE PAUMA
14900 SDCo 92082 1050-G5
VISTA DIEGO RD
3100 SDCo 91935 1292-G1
3200 SDCo 91935 1272-G7
VISTA ELEVADA
- SD 92131 1210-C2
VISTA ENSUENO
700 SDCo 91901 1233-G7
VISTA ENTRADA
300 OCN 92057 1086-H4
9100 SDCo 92040 1232-G5
VISTA ESPERANZA LN
- SDCo 91901 1255-E5
VISTA FLUME
- ESCN 92026 1109-G3
- SDCo 92026 1109-G3
VISTA GLEN LN
100 VSTA 92084 1087-J6
VISTA GRANDE
3100 CRLB 92009 1127-H7
VISTA GRANDE CT
1800 SDCo 92019 1272-C2
VISTA GRANDE DR
1600 SDCo 92084 1088-A1
1600 VSTA 92084 1088-A1
3700 SD 92115 1270-E5
VISTA GRANDE GN
200 ESCN 92025 1130-A6
VISTA GRANDE PL
2000 VSTA 92084 1088-A2
VISTA GRANDE RD
700 SDCo 92019 1252-D6
1100 SDCo 92019 1272-C1
VISTA GRANDE TER
2100 SDCo 92084 1088-B1
VISTA GRANDE WY
700 OCN 92057 1086-J3
1900 SDCo 92019 1272-C2
VISTA GUYABA
7900 CRLB 92009 1147-H3
VISTA HERMOSA WY
2000 SDCo 92019 1272-C2
VISTA HIGUERA
7800 CRLB 92009 1147-J3
VISTA HILL AV
7800 SD 92123 1249-B6
VISTA HILLS DR
14200 SDCo 92040 1232-F4
VISTA HILLS PL
9500 SDCo 92040 1232-F4
VISTA HORIZON ST
200 SD 92113 1289-H5
VISTA JAMUL
13800 SDCo 91935 1293-D2
VISTA JUANITA CT
2600 LMGR 91945 1270-D7
VISTA LA CUESTA CT
10000 SD 92131 1209-J4
VISTA LA CUESTA DR
11200 SD 92131 1209-J4
VISTA LADERO
13200 SDCo 92040 1232-C5
VISTA LAGO PL
10500 SD 92131 1209-G4
VISTA LAGO TER
2400 SDCo 92029 1129-F7
2400 ESCN 92029 1129-F7
VISTA LAGUNA RD
- SDCo 92028 1048-B3
VISTA LA NISA
- CRLB 92009 1147-F2
VISTA LA QUEBRADA
14700 SDCo 91935 1293-C2
VISTA LAZANJA
- SD 92127 1188-J1
VISTA LOMA CIR
3300 OCN 92056 1107-B1
VISTA LOMAS DR
17900 PWY 92064 1150-E7
VISTA MADERA LN
1000 SDCo 92019 1252-E7
VISTA MADERA WY
2400 SDCo 92019 1252-E7
VISTA MAR
3100 CRLB 92009 1127-H7
VISTA MARAZUL
300 OCN 92057 1086-H4
VISTA MARGUERITE
- SDCo 92021 1251-J1
VISTA MARIANA
2700 CRLB 92009 1127-G7
VISTA MATAMO
3200 SDCo 92019 1272-G1
VISTA MEADOWS WY
100 SMCS 92069 1108-D5
VISTA MERRIAM
100 SDCo 92069 1088-J7
VISTA MINE RD
- ImCo - 411-K11
- ImCo - 431-K1
VISTA MIRANDA
500 CHV 91910 1311-A5
VISTA MONTANA WY
200 OCN 92054 1086-E6
VISTA MONTANOSO
10000 SDCo 92026 1089-E2
VISTAMONTE AV
- ESCN 92027 1130-J4
VISTAMONTE GN
- ESCN 92027 1130-J4
VISTA MOUNTAIN DR
- VSTA 92084 1088-D6
VISTA NACION DR
4400 SDCo 91910 1310-E5
VISTA NORTE
14300 SDCo 92025 1130-G6
VISTA NUEZ
7900 CRLB 92009 1147-H3
VISTA OAK PL
- CHV 91910 1310-J7
VISTA OCEANA
4200 OCN 92057 1086-J3
VISTA OCEANO
3600 OCN 92057 1086-F5
VISTA OLAS
7000 CRLB 92009 1127-G6
VISTA PACIFIC DR
2600 OCN 92056 1087-E5
VISTA PACIFICA
3200 SDCo 92084 1088-F6
VISTA PALMA
7900 CRLB 92009 1147-G2
VISTA PANORAMA
14300 SDCo 92040 1232-G5
VISTA PANORAMA WY
4200 OCN 92057 1086-J3
VISTA PARQUE
10000 SDCo 92040 1232-C3
VISTA PARQUE CT
13200 SDCo 92040 1232-D3
VISTA POINT CIR
- SDCo 92084 1088-G7
VISTA POINTE
3700 SDCo 91902 1310-E3
VISTA POINTE BLVD
- OCN 92057 1067-B4
VISTA PONIENTE DR
13700 PWY 92064 1170-F6
VISTA RAMONA RD
22600 SDCo 92065 1153-C7
23400 SDCo 92065 1173-D1
VISTA RANCHO
17600 SDCo 92067 1168-G1
VISTA RANCHO CT
7300 SDCo 92067 1168-H1
VISTA REAL DR
14100 SDCo 92082 1050-F6
VISTA REY
3600 OCN 92057 1086-F4
VISTA RICA
3100 CRLB 92009 1127-H7
VISTA RICARDO
13800 SDCo 92021 1232-E6
VISTA RIM PL
- SDCo 92084 1088-F6
VISTA ROBLES
3100 SDCo 92019 1272-G1
VISTA ROCOSA
3300 ESCN 92029 1149-J3
VISTA RODEO DR
2200 SDCo 92019 1252-E7
VISTA ROYAL
2300 SDCo 92084 1108-D1
VISTA SAGE LN
13400 SDCo 91935 1292-F2
VISTA SAGE PL
13900 SDCo 91935 1292-F2
VISTA SAN BENITO
- SD 92154 1331-A7
VISTA SAN CARLOS
- SD 92154 1331-B7
VISTA SAN FRANCISQUITO
- SD 92154 1331-B7
VISTA SAN GUADALUPE
- SD 92154 1331-B7
VISTA SAN IGNACIO
- SD 92154 1331-B7
VISTA SAN ISIDRO
- SD 92154 1331-B7
VISTA SAN JAVIER
- SD 92154 1331-A7
VISTA SAN JOSE
- SD 92154 1331-A6
VISTA SAN JUANICO
- SD 92154 1331-A7
VISTA SAN LUCAS
- CHV 91911 1331-A6
- SD 92154 1331-A6

STREET
Block City ZIP Pg-Grid

VISTA SAN MATIAS
- SD 92154 1331-B7
VISTA SAN MIGUEL
3900 SDCo 91902 1310-G4
VISTA SAN PABLO
- SD 92154 1331-B7
VISTA SAN PEDRO MARTIR
- SD 92154 1331-B7
VISTA SAN RAFAEL
- SD 92154 1331-A7
VISTA SAN RUFO
- SD 92154 1331-B7
VISTA SAN SIMEON
- SD 92154 1331-A7
VISTA SANTA CATARINA
- SD 92154 1331-B7
VISTA SANTA CLARA
- SD 92154 1331-B7
VISTA SANTA INES
- SD 92154 1331-B7
VISTA SANTA MARGARITA
- CHV 91911 1331-A6
- SD 92154 1331-A6
VISTA SANTA RITA
- SD 92154 1331-A6
VISTA SANTA ROSALIA
- SD 92154 1331-B7
VISTA SANTO DOMINGO
- SD 92154 1331-B7
VISTA SANTO TOMAS
- SD 92154 1331-B7
VISTA SECUNDA
9500 SD 92129 1189-E3
VISTA SERENA
12000 SDCo 92040 1232-A1
VISTA SIERRA DR
1000 SDCo 92019 1252-D7
1000 SDCo 92019 1272-E1
VISTA SONRISA AV
1300 CHV 91913 1311-D7
VISTA SORRENTO PKWY
- SD 92130 1208-B4
10500 SD 92121 1208-C6
VISTA SUMMIT DR
16700 SDCo 92065 1171-D2
VISTA TERCERA
9500 SD 92129 1189-E4
VISTA TERRAZA CT
12100 SDCo 92082 1070-A6
VISTA VALLE CT
10200 SD 92131 1209-G4
VISTA VALLE DR
10500 SD 92131 1209-H4
VISTA VALLE CAMINO
1000 SDCo 92028 1028-F4
VISTA VALLE VERDE
2200 SDCo 92028 1048-B2
VISTA VALLEY DR
28700 SDCo 92084 1088-E1
28800 SDCo 92084 1068-D7
VISTA VALLEY LN
2200 SDCo 92084 1088-E1
VISTA VALLEY RIM PL
2000 SDCo 92019 1252-D3
VISTA VERDE
700 SMCS 92069 1109-B5
VISTA VERDE DR
1500 ESCN 92027 1110-A5
1500 SD 92037 1247-G1
VISTA VERDE WY
- OCN 92057 1086-J1
1300 ESCN 92027 1110-B5
VISTA VEREDA
1500 SDCo 92019 1272-C1
VISTA VICENTE CT
24000 SDCo 92065 1173-E4
VISTA VICENTE DR
15400 SDCo 92065 1173-E4
VISTA VICENTE WY
22800 SDCo 92065 1173-C4
VISTA VIEJAS RD
9600 SDCo 91901 1234-A2
VISTA VIEW CT
13200 PWY 92064 1190-F4
VISTA VIEW DR
13100 PWY 92064 1190-F4
VISTA VILLAGE DR
100 VSTA 92083 1087-G6
200 VSTA 92081 1087-G6
VISTA VILLAGE DR Rt#-S13
100 VSTA 92084 1087-H6
100 VSTA 92083 1087-H6
E VISTA VILLAGE DR Rt#-S13
100 VSTA 92084 1087-H6
VISTA WAY VILLAGE DR
3400 OCN 92056 1106-B4
VISTOSA PL
2600 CRLB 92009 1147-G2
VITA RD
4800 SDCo 91941 1271-F2
VIVA CT
800 SOLB 92075 1187-G1
VIVALDI ST
- ENCT 92007 1167-D2
VIVARACHO CT
4300 SD 92124 1249-J1
VIVARACHO WY
10900 SD 92124 1249-J1
11000 SD 92124 1250-A2
VIVERA DR
5000 SDCo 91941 1271-D2
VIVIAN ST
4000 SD 92115 1270-D4
VIVIENDA CIR
3300 CRLB 92009 1147-J1
VIXEN DR
1300 SDCo 92065 1172-F2
VIZCAINO CT
- SDCo 92026 1109-E5
VIZCAYA WY
3200 OCN 92056 1106-J1
VLADIC LN
1600 SDCo 92027 1130-C4
VOGE ST
10100 SD 92124 1249-G4
VOGEL RD
1100 ImCo 92243 431-A7
VOIGT DR
3000 SD 92093 1228-A1
3600 SD 92037 1228-B1
VOIGT LN
2900 SD 92093 1227-J1
2900 SD 92093 1228-A1
VOISIN CT
11900 SD 92128 1150-A7
VOLANS ST
11300 SD 92126 1209-C1

VOLCAN RD
- SDCo 92055 1085-J3
- SDCo 92055 1086-A3
200 SDCo 92036 409-L10
200 SDCo 92036 1136-D1
VOLCAN MOUNTAIN RANCH RD
- SDCo 92036 409-K10
- SDCo 92036 1136-A1
VOLCANO CREEK RD
1900 CHV 91913 1311-E6
VOLCAN VIEW DR
1200 SDCo 92036 1136-C6
VOLCAN VIEW WY
3500 SDCo 92066 409-L9
3500 SDCo 92066 410-A9
VOLCLAY DR
7200 SD 92119 1250-F3
VOLMER PEAK CT
1100 CHV 91913 1311-C7
VOLNEY LN
300 ENCT 92024 1147-H7
VOLNEY RD
300 ENCT 92024 1147-H7
VOLTA CT
7100 SD 92111 1268-J2
7200 SD 92111 1269-A1
VOLTAIRE ST
3000 SD 92106 1268-B7
3600 SD 92107 1268-A6
4800 SD 92107 1267-J5
VOLUNTARY RD
1800 VSTA 92084 1087-J3
VOMAC RD
9400 SNTE 92071 1231-B4
VOORHES LN
17400 SDCo 92065 1171-J2
VORTEX PL
4000 ESCN 92025 1150-D4
VOUGHT ST
- CORD 92135 1288-E4
VOYAGE DR
- CHV 91915 1331-G1
VOYAGER CIR
3400 SD 92130 1187-J6
VOYAGER CT
3500 OCN 92054 1086-F6
VUE DE VILLE CT
1300 SD 92109 1247-J4
VUE DU BAY CT
1400 SD 92109 1247-J4
VUELTA CT
2100 CRLB 92009 1147-F2
N VULCAN AV
100 ENCT 92024 1147-A2
S VULCAN AV
100 ENCT 92024 1147-C7
900 ENCT 92024 1167-C1
1100 ENCT 92007 1167-C1
VULCAN PL
1100 ESCN 92027 1130-E1
VULCAN ST
1300 SDCo 92021 1251-F1

W

WABASH AV
3700 SD 92104 1269-F5
WABASH BLVD
1500 SD 92113 1289-F6
1600 SD 92136 1289-F6
WABASH ST
600 ESCN 92027 1110-B7
WABASKA CT
2100 SD 92107 1268-B7
WABASKA DR
3800 SD 92107 1268-B7
WACHE DR
3000 SDCo 91978 1292-A1
WACO ST
- SD 92111 1248-F5
3300 SD 92117 1248-F5
WADDELL CIR
10200 SD 92124 1249-G2
WADE DR
500 SMCS 92078 1128-C1
WADE ST
8500 SD 92114 1290-H2
WADE WY
12300 SDCo 92021 1252-A1
WAGNER AV
9300 SD 92123 1249-E4
WAGNER DR
1100 ELCJ 92020 1251-D4
WAGNER PL
3600 SD 92123 1249-E4
WAGON GN
1300 ESCN 92027 1130-B2
WAGON RD
3100 SDCo 92004 (1078-H7 See Page 1058)
WAGON TR
100 SDCo 92028 1027-J2
WAGON TONGUE CT
- SDCo 91901 1254-F3
WAGON WHEEL CT
2400 SDCo 91978 1271-G7
WAGON WHEEL DR
1500 OCN 92057 1067-F6
9300 SNTE 92071 1231-E5
10800 SDCo 91978 1271-G7
WAGONWHEEL WY
300 CHV 91902 1310-H4
WAHL RD
500 ImCo 92243 431-A7
WAHL ST
8600 SNTE 92071 1230-F7
WAHUPA RANCH RD
2900 SDCo 92029 1149-J2
WAILEA WY
2200 SD 92154 1330-D7
WAIMEA DR
700 SDCo 92019 1252-C4
WAITE DR
- LMGR 91945 1270-G5
6700 SD 92115 1270-E5
6900 LMSA 91941 1270-E5
6900 SD 91941 1270-E5
7400 LMGR 91941 1270-G5
WAKARUSA ST
8900 LMSA 91942 1251-A7
WAKE AV
- ImCo 92243 6559-F2
200 ELCN 92243 6559-F2
500 ELCN 92243 6560-B2
WAKE RD
- CORD 92118 1309-C5
WAKE ST
5500 LMSA 91942 1270-H1
WAKEFIELD CT
700 ELCJ 92020 1251-B4
WALA DR
- OCN 92054 1086-D3

WALBOLLEN ST
1300 SDCo 91977 1290-J1
1600 LMGR 91945 1290-J1
WALDEN CT
10300 SNTE 92071 1231-A3
WALDEN GN
- ESCN 92027 1130-J4
WALDGROVE PL
9900 SD 92131 1209-H5
WALDO CT
10500 SNTE 92071 1231-E5
WALDORF WY
11100 SD 92131 1209-J2
WALDRON CT
10200 SD 92124 1249-G4
WALDRON WY
10200 SD 92124 1249-G4
WALES DR
2000 ENCT 92007 1167-F4
WALES PL
2300 ENCT 92007 1167-F4
WALINCA WY
2500 SDCo 92084 1088-D5
WALKDEN LN
8700 SD 92119 1250-J4
8700 SD 92119 1251-A4
WALKER CT
9000 SD 92123 1249-D6
WALKER DR
2800 SD 92123 1249-D6
WALKER LN
- SDCo 92672 1023-E2
WALKER RD
- ImCo 92227 410-L11
- ImCo 92227 411-A11
WALKER RD Rt#-S30
- ImCo 92227 411-A11
WALKER WY
- ImCo - 431-L2
100 VSTA 92083 1087-G6
WALKING FERN CV
11200 SD 92131 1209-J1
WALKING H DR
700 SDCo 92004 (1078-J5 See Page 1058)
700 SDCo 92004 (1079-A5 See Page 1058)
WALKING PATH PL
13000 SD 92130 1187-J5
WALKING STICK CT
2500 CHV 91915 1311-H6
WALL PL
100 SDCo 92021 1252-H4
WALL RD
400 IMP 92251 6499-E2
WALL ST
1000 SD 92037 1227-F6
WALLABY CT
11200 SD 92128 1189-J4
WALLACE CT
900 SD 92113 1289-G5
WALLACE DR
3400 SDCo 91902 1310-G2
WALLACE LN
100 VSTA 92083 1108-A1
WALLACE ST
4000 SD 92110 1268-F5
WALLINGFORD CT
7500 SD 92126 1208-J4
WALLINGFORD RD
10600 SD 92126 1208-J4
WALLSEY DR
6800 SD 92119 1250-J3
6900 SD 92119 1251-A4
WALLY WY
- ELCJ 92021 1252-C2
WALMAR LN
2300 SD 92109 1248-B4
WALNUT AV
100 CRLB 92008 1106-E6
300 SD 92103 1269-A6
600 SD 92103 1268-H6
1100 CHV 91911 1330-A4
1900 SD 92101 1268-H6
W WALNUT AV
300 SD 92103 1269-A6
WALNUT CT
2600 OCN 92056 1087-E5
WALNUT DR
- CHV 91911 1330-F5
WALNUT GN
200 ESCN 92027 1110-E6
WALNUT LN
2000 SDCo 92084 1108-C2
WALNUT RD
11700 SDCo 92040 1231-J7
WALNUT RDG
- SD 92130 1208-B2
WALNUT ST
1100 SDCo 92065 1152-E6
WALNUT CREEK DR
1300 ENCT 92024 1167-F1
WALNUTDALE ST
10200 SD 92131 1210-C4
WALNUT GROVE AV
1100 CHV 91913 1311-E6
WALNUT HILLS DR
100 SMCS 92078 1129-A1
WALNUT TREE LN
1200 SDCo 92021 1251-G1
WALNUTVIEW DR
1300 ENCT 92024 1147-F7
WALPEN DR
1100 SD 92154 1350-A1
WALSALL RD
600 SDCo 92019 1252-D6
WALSH ST
200 OCN 92054 1086-D6
WALSH WY
5100 SD 92115 1270-A1
WALSING DR
700 SMCS 92069 1129-E1
WALTER AV
4900 SD 92120 1250-A6
WALTER WY
200 ELCJ 92021 1251-J5
WALTERS CAMP RD
- ImCo - 412-A6
WALTHAM AV
13200 PWY 92064 1190-H4
WALTON PL
3000 SD 92116 1269-E4
WALTON ST
- CHV 91913 1331-E2
1500 OCN 92054 1086-B5
WALTON WY
700 SDCo 92081 1107-D2
2300 ESCN 92027 1110-C6
WALTON HEATH RW
15500 SD 92128 1170-B5
WALTON HOMESTEAD
- SDCo 92021 1232-H4
WALZ CT
11500 SD 92126 1209-B1

WANDA CT
600 ESCN 92026 1109-J7
600 ESCN 92026 1129-J1
6000 SD 92120 1249-J7
WANDA DR
8700 SNTE 92071 1231-E7
WANDA WY
13900 SDCo 91935 1292-H2
WANDER ST
- CHV 91915 1331-H2
WANDERING RD
800 VSTA 92081 1087-F7
800 VSTA 92081 1107-F1
1400 ENCT 92024 1147-G5
WANDERING WY
- SMCS 92078 1128-H3
WANDERMERE CT
6600 SD 92120 1250-E5
WANDERMERE DR
6300 SD 92120 1250-D6
6700 SD 92119 1250-D6
WANEK RD
2400 ESCN 92027 1110-D6
WANESTA DR
13000 PWY 92064 1190-D4
WANNACUT PL
11500 SD 92131 1209-J1
WAPLES CT
10000 SD 92121 1208-G5
WAPLES ST
9400 SD 92121 1208-G5
WARBLER CT
1600 CRLB 92011 1127-D6
WARBLER WY
5500 SD 92037 1247-G4
WAR BONNET ST
13000 SD 92129 1189-C5
WARD CT
800 CALX 92231 6620-H7
WARD LN
10000 SDCo 91941 1271-D1
WARD PL
1300 ESCN 92026 1109-J5
WARD RD
100 NATC 92136 1309-F1
100 SD 92136 1309-F1
3100 SD 92136 1289-E7
3700 SD 92116 1269-G3
3800 SD 92108 1269-G1
WARDEN LN
- SD 92127 1169-B4
WARDLOW AV
2600 SD 92154 1350-C3
WARDLOW CT
1900 SD 92154 1350-C3
WARE CT
8900 SD 92121 1208-J7
WARE RD
- ImCo 92231 6620-C3
- ImCo 92249 431-C7
- ImCo 92249 6620-C3
WARFIELD WY
600 SDCo 92019 1253-C2
WARHEAD RD
- SD 92152 1288-A5
WAR HORSE ST
12700 SD 92129 1189-C5
WARING CT
3200 OCN 92056 1107-B1
WARING RD
3200 OCN 92056 1107-B1
5500 SD 92115 1270-A1
5500 SD 92120 1270-A1
5500 SD 92120 1250-B6
WARM HEARTH WY
- CHV 91914 1311-J1
WARMLANDS AV
800 VSTA 92084 1088-B3
1900 SDCo 92084 1088-B3
E WARMLANDS AV
2200 SDCo 92084 1088-A2
2200 VSTA 92084 1088-A2
WARM SPRINGS DR
1400 CHV 91913 1331-B2
WARMWELL DR
8600 SD 92119 1250-J3
WARMWOOD AV
8200 SD 92139 1290-H5
8200 SDCo 91977 1290-H5
WARNER ST
100 OCN 92054 1086-F3
3600 SD 92106 1287-J3
3600 SD 92106 1288-A3
WARNERS DR
900 SDCo 92004 (1079-A6 See Page 1058)
WARNERS RD
32100 SDCo 92086 409-K7
WARNOCK DR
1300 SDCo 92065 1172-F3
WARPAINT DR
700 SDCo 92065 1152-F7
WARPAINT PL
1700 ESCN 92029 1129-G5
WARREN PL
5900 LMSA 91942 1250-H7
WARRINGTON ST
1600 SD 92107 1288-A1
2300 SD 92107 1268-B6
WARWICK AV
500 ENCT 92007 1167-D2
WARWICK CIR
4500 OCN 92056 1107-E2
WARWOOD CT
2100 SDCo 92019 1272-B4
WASATCH PL
900 SMCS 92069 1109-B5
WASHINGTON AV
300 OCN 92054 1106-B1
2000 ESCN 92027 1110-C7
8600 LMSA 91941 1271-A2
E WASHINGTON AV
100 ELCJ 92020 1251-G6
700 ELCJ 92019 1251-G6
700 ELCJ 92019 1252-A6
1200 ESCN 92027 1130-A1
1500 ESCN 92027 1110-D5
E WASHINGTON AV Rt#-78
100 ESCN 92025 1129-J2
400 ESCN 92025 1130-A1
W WASHINGTON AV
- ESCN 92029 1129-F2
- ESCN 92025 1129-G2
900 ELCJ 92020 1251-E6
WASHINGTON CIR
2900 SDCo 92029 1129-C6
WASHINGTON PL
1000 SD 92103 1268-H5
WASHINGTON ST
100 VSTA 92084 1087-H6
200 SDCo 92065 1152-G1
400 CALX 92231 6680-G1
800 SD 92103 1269-A5

WASHINGTON ST
1700 LMGR 91945 1290-H1
1700 SDCo 91977 1290-H1
2200 LMGR 91945 1270-H7
2500 SDCo 92036 1136-A7
2700 CRLB 92008 1106-D5
21800 SDCo 92070 1135-B3
WASHINGTON ST Rt#-79
2200 SDCo 92036 1136-B7
W WASHINGTON ST
200 SD 92103 1269-A5
300 SD 92103 1268-H6
1500 SD 92110 1268-H6
1600 SD 92101 1268-H6
2200 SD 92140 1268-H6
WASHINGTON HEIGHTS PL
1000 SDCo 92019 1251-H6
WASHINGTON HEIGHTS RD
700 ELCJ 92019 1251-J6
700 SDCo 92019 1251-J6
WASHINGTONIA DR
100 SDCo 92029 1129-A4
100 SMCS 92078 1129-A4
2900 SDCo 92029 1128-J4
WATER ST
- SD 92140 1268-F6
900 SD 92101 1289-B5
1800 SD 92113 1289-B5
5500 ELCJ 92020 1251-C7
5500 LMSA 91942 1251-C7
WATER WY
3600 OCN 92056 1107-C3
WATERBURY
2000 CHV 91913 1311-E4
WATERBURY CT
1300 SMCS 92078 1128-B3
WATERBURY WY
2600 CRLB 92010 1106-J3
WATERCOURSE DR
6800 CRLB 92011 1126-J5
WATERCREST CT
3300 SDCo 91902 1311-A1
WATERCREST DR
5600 SDCo 91902 1311-A1
WATERFALL PL
6200 SD 92120 1249-J7
WATERFORD DR
3300 OCN 92056 1086-J7
WATERFORD LN
- SD 92129 1189-B2
WATERHILL RD
11700 SDCo 92040 1231-H4
WATERHOUSE GN
800 ESCN 92026 1109-J7
WATERIDGE CIR
10300 SD 92121 1208-D6
WATERIDGE VISTA DR
10600 SD 92121 1208-D6
WATER LILY DR
- CHV 91913 1311-F7
WATER LILY WY
- CHV 91913 1311-E7
WATERLOO AV
600 ELCJ 92019 1252-B7
WATERLOO WY
- SMCS 92078 1128-H3
WATERMAN AV
- ImCo 92243 6499-F3
200 ELCN 92243 6499-F3
1400 ELCN 92243 6559-F1
WATERMAN CT
900 ELCN 92243 6499-F5
6700 SD 92111 1248-J7
WATERS END DR
- CRLB 92011 1126-J5
WATERSIDE DR
2100 CHV 91913 1311-E4
WATERTON RD
10800 SD 92131 1209-H1
WATERTOWN LN
600 CHV 91913 1311-E3
WATER VIEW CT
8200 SDCo 91977 1290-J6
WATER VIEW LN
600 SDCo 91977 1290-J5
WATERVILLE RD
7800 SD 92154 1351-F2
WATERVILLE LAKE RD
1000 CHV 91915 1311-G5
WATERWOOD CT
2200 CHV 91915 1311-G7
WATKINS CT
11000 SD 92131 1209-H1
WATSON PL
8900 SNTE 92071 1251-A1
WATSON WY
1600 SDCo 92083 1108-A3
1800 VSTA 92081 1108-A4
2000 VSTA 92083 1108-A4
7200 LMSA 91941 1270-F2
WATSONIA ST
10300 SD 92121 1208-C7
WATSON RANCH RD
- SD 92129 1189-B3
WATT RD
24100 SDCo 92065 1173-E3
WATT WY
16100 SDCo 92065 1173-E3
WATTLE DR
7000 SD 92139 1290-G7
WATWOOD RD
1100 LMGR 91945 1290-F2
1100 SD 91945 1290-F2
1100 SD 92114 1290-F2
WAVE CT
6000 SD 92139 1290-D7
WAVE CREST CT
4000 SD 92109 1247-H7
WAVERLY AV
5300 SD 92037 1247-F2
WAVERLY CT
3400 SDCo 91935 1272-E6
WAVERLY LN
- SMCS 92078 1128-F6
WAVERLY PL
300 ESCN 92025 1129-J2
WAVERLY RD
4600 OCN 92056 1107-E3
WAVERLY DOWNS LN
12100 SD 92128 1170-B7
WAVERLY DOWNS WY
14800 SD 92128 1170-A7
14800 SD 92128 1190-B1
WAWONA DR
3500 SD 92106 1288-B1
3500 SD 92106 1268-B7
3700 SD 92107 1268-B7
WAXFLOWER LN
400 SDCo 92028 1027-J3
WAXIE WY
- SD 92123 1229-E7

WAXWING DR
1100 VSTA 92083 1087-F4
WAXWING LN
1200 CHV 91911 1330-G2
WAYFARER DR
9600 LMSA 91942 1251-C5
WAYFINDERS CT
- CRLB 92011 1127-B4
WAYLAND GROVE CT
13700 PWY 92064 1190-F3
WAYNE AV
500 ELCJ 92021 1251-J4
900 CHV 91913 1311-C5
WAYNE LN
3100 SD 92117 1248-C3
WAYNECREST LN
10000 SNTE 92071 1231-D3
WAYNE HILL
- SD 92127 1169-B3
WAYNES WY
900 SDCo 92065 1152-C5
WAYSIDE AV
1000 ELCJ 92021 1251-G3
W D HALL DR
100 ELCJ 92020 1251-G5
WEATHERBY AV
2100 ESCN 92027 1110-C7
WEATHERHILL CT
10600 SD 92131 1209-H2
WEATHERHILL WY
11400 SD 92131 1209-G1
WEATHERLY RD
1500 CRLB 92011 1127-C4
WEATHERS PL
6400 SD 92121 1208-G5
WEATHERSTONE CT
- SD 92130 1208-E2
WEATHERSTONE WY
- SMCS 92078 1128-F6
WEATHERVANE AV
2000 ESCN 92027 1130-D1
WEATHER VANE DR
600 SDCo 92004 (1078-J4 See Page 1058)
700 SDCo 92004 (1079-A4 See Page 1058)
WEATHERVANE PL
1700 ESCN 92027 1130-C1
WEATHERWOOD CT
- SMCS 92024 1128-C6
- SMCS 92078 1128-C6
WEATHERWOOD PL
11600 SD 92131 1210-A2
WEATHERWOOD TER
11000 SD 92131 1210-A2
WEAVER RD
400 ImCo 92227 431-B3
WEAVER ST
1200 SD 92114 1290-C2
WEAVERVILLE ST
1300 CHV 91913 1331-B1
WEAVING LN
17800 SD 92127 1169-H1
WEBB RD
- SD 92152 1288-A5
1700 SD 92101 1289-C2
1700 SD 92134 1289-C2
2600 ImCo 92250 431-E4
WEBBER WY
- CHV 91913 1331-E2
WEBER CT
9300 SDCo 91977 1271-B6
WEBER CREEK RD
- CHV 91913 1311-E6
WEBSTER AV
2800 SD 92113 1289-E4
WEDGEMERE CT
2700 ESCN 92027 1110-E7
WEDGEMERE RD
1800 ELCJ 92020 1251-C5
WEDGEWOOD AV
2500 ESCN 92027 1130-E1
WEDGEWOOD DR
100 SD 92114 1290-H4
2000 OCN 92056 1086-J7
WEED RD
500 ImCo 92231 431-B7
WEEKEND VILLA RD
1500 SDCo 92065 1152-D2
WEEPING WILLOW RD
- CHV 91915 (1312-A6 See Page 1293)
3600 OCN 92054 1086-F1
WEEPING WILLOW WY
2100 SDCo 92028 1027-H6
WEERS ST
1300 ELCJ 92020 1251-D4
WEISER AV
7500 SD 92111 1249-A6
WEISS WY
2100 SDCo 92026 1109-H4
WEISSER WY
400 CHV 91911 1330-C3
WEITZEL ST
200 OCN 92054 1086-A7
200 OCN 92054 1106-B1
WELCH PL
- CHV 91911 1331-A3
WELCH RD
1800 SD 92101 1289-C2
WELCOME VW
28900 SDCo 92026 1089-C3
WELCOME WY
15900 SDCo 92065 1173-J4
WELD BLVD
1700 ELCJ 92020 1251-B1
WELDON WY
2500 SDCo 92028 1028-B7
WELK HIGHLAND CT
- SDCo 92026 1069-C7
WELK HIGHLAND DR
28500 SDCo 92026 1089-C1
29300 SDCo 92026 1069-C7
WELK HIGHLAND LN
29500 SDCo 92026 1069-B7
WELK VIEW CT
- SDCo 92026 1089-C1
WELK VIEW DR
8800 SDCo 92026 1089-A1
9000 SDCo 92026 1069-B7
WELLBORN ST
3700 SD 92103 1268-H6
WELLBROOK ST
- CHV 91913 1331-E1
WELLER ST
6800 SD 92122 1228-F4
WELLES ST
3100 SD 92136 1289-E7
WELLESLEY ST
5200 LMSA 91942 1270-G1
WELLESLEY ST E
5400 LMSA 91942 1270-G1
WELLESLEY ST W
5400 LMSA 91942 1270-G1

WELLESLY AV
3300 SD 92122 1228-D5
WELLESLY CT
6300 SD 92122 1228-D5
WELLESLY PL
6500 SD 92122 1228-D5
WELLING WY
100 SD 92114 1290-F4
WELLINGTON LN
1900 VSTA 92081 1108-A4
WELLINGTON ST
2800 SD 92111 1249-A6
WELLINGTON WY
7400 SD 92111 1249-A5
WELLINGTON HILL DR
13100 SDCo 92040 1232-C7
WELLPOTT PL
900 VSTA 92084 1087-H4
WELLS AV
100 ELCJ 92020 1251-F5
WELLS ST
1900 SD 92107 1268-B7
WELLS FARGO TR
700 SDCo 92036 1138-B5
WELLSONA CT
- SD 92131 1209-G1
WELLSTON PT
4600 SD 92130 1188-B4
WELLWORTH PT
5000 SD 92130 1188-D4
WELMER PL
3200 SD 92122 1228-C4
WELMER ST
6600 SD 92122 1228-D4
WELSH RD
10900 SD 92126 1209-D3
WELSH WY
- SDCo 92065 1172-G1
WELTON LN
12800 PWY 92064 1190-G5
WELTON ST
400 CHV 91911 1330-B3
WELTY ST
2200 SDCo 92028 998-J5
WEMBLEY ST
7200 SD 92120 1250-A5
WENATCHEE AV
8000 SDCo 92021 1251-G1
8200 SDCo 92021 1231-G7
WENDELA ST
5200 OCN 92056 1087-E2
WENDELL ST
4600 SD 92105 1289-J1
WENDI CT
3800 SDCo 92028 1048-B4
WENDI ST
5600 LMSA 91942 1250-H7
5600 LMSA 91942 1270-H1
WENDOVER TER
- SD 92130 1188-D4
WENDY LN
1100 ESCN 92026 1109-J7
WENRICH DR
5900 SD 92120 1250-C6
WENRICH PL
5900 SD 92120 1250-C6
WENSLEY AV
- ELCN 92243 6500-A7
400 ELCN 92243 6499-D7
WENTWORTH CIR
900 VSTA 92081 1108-E2
WENTWORTH CT
3000 SDCo 91935 1272-D5
WENTWORTH DR
3300 SDCo 91935 1272-E5
WENTWORTH PL
- SMCS 92069 1108-J4
WENTWORTH WY
3300 SDCo 91935 1272-D5
WERNER ST
7100 SD 92122 1228-F4
WERNES ST
2000 SDCo 92065 1152-D7
WERRIS CREEK LN
14800 SD 92128 1170-B7
14800 SD 92128 1190-B4
WESCOTT CT
8700 SD 92129 1189-C1
WESLEY DR E
5000 SD 92109 1248-B4
WESLEY DR W
5000 SD 92109 1248-B4
WESLEY PL
6600 SD 92120 1270-D1
WESLEY WY
300 DLMR 92014 1187-G6
1600 VSTA 92081 1107-G4
WESLEYAN PL
4000 SD 92116 1269-G2
WESLEY DRIVE CIR
2300 SD 92109 1248-B3
WESMEAD ST
5800 SD 92114 1290-C5
WESSEX ST
18500 SD 92128 1150-B5
WEST AV
1600 NATC 91950 1309-H2
WEST DR
300 SDCo 92021 1252-H3
1800 VSTA 92083 1107-C1
WEST LN
400 SDCo 92021 1252-H3
1500 SDCo 92014 1187-J1
WEST ST
200 OCN 92054 1106-B2
200 SD 92113 1289-J5
3200 LMGR 91945 1270-F6
3600 LMSA 91941 1270-G5
WEST BLUFF CT
- ENCT 92024 1147-E6
WEST BLUFF DR
900 ENCT 92024 1147-E6
WEST BOUNDRY TKTR
500 SDCo 91901 1234-D2
WESTBOURNE ST
200 SD 92037 1247-E1
WESTBRIDGE GN
3000 ESCN 92029 1150-A2
WESTBROOK AV
7300 SD 92139 1290-H7
WESTBURY AV
7900 SD 92126 1209-A2
WESTBURY RD
3100 SDCo 92084 1088-E7
WESTBY ST
400 CHV 91911 1330-B2
WESTCHESTER AV
10300 SD 92126 1209-E5
WEST CLIFF CT
1800 CRLB 92008 1106-H6
WESTCLIFF DR
700 SMCS 92078 1128-F2
WESTCLIFF PL
3200 SD 92106 1268-C7

STREET Block City ZIP Pg-Grid

WESTDALE CT
100 ELCJ 92020 1251-C5
WESTER AV Rt#-86
300 BRW 92227 431-B2
WESTERLY CT
4700 OCN 92056 1087-D4
WESTERN ST
3900 SD 92110 1268-C4
WESTERN GAILES RW
11200 SD 92128 1189-J3
WESTERN SPRINGS RD
3400 ENCT 92024 1148-C4
WESTERN TRAILS DR
7900 SDCo 92021 1252-A1
WESTERRA CT
4300 SD 92121 1228-C1
WESTFORD WY
- SDCo 92127 1169-G2
WESTGATE PL
3800 SD 92105 1289-G1
WESTGROVE RD
- SDCo 92019 1272-B3
WESTHAVEN DR
3700 CRLB 92008 1106-H5
WESTHILL LN
9300 SDCo 92040 1231-H5
WESTHILL RD
8900 SDCo 92040 1231-H5
WESTHILL TER
11500 SDCo 92040 1231-H6
11500 SNTE 92071 1231-H6
WEST HILLS PKWY
8700 SD 92071 1230-H7
8700 SNTE 92071 1230-H7
8700 SD 92124 1230-H7
WESTHILL VISTA
11600 SDCo 92040 1231-H5
WESTIN WY
- SMCS 92078 1128-E6
WESTINGHOUSE ST
1700 SD 92111 1268-J1
2100 SD 92111 1248-J7
E WESTINGHOUSE ST
1700 SD 92111 1268-J1
WESTKNOLL DR
5300 SD 92109 1247-J4
5300 SD 92037 1247-J4
WESTKNOLL LN
5300 SD 92109 1247-J3
WESTLAKE DR
200 SMCS 92069 1108-G7
WESTLAKE ST
500 ENCT 92024 1147-D7
WESTLAND AV
2200 SD 92104 1289-F1
WESTLEIGH PL
6900 SD 92126 1208-H4
WESTLING CT
16900 PWY 92064 1170-F3
WESTLY LN
- SD 92131 1210-C2
WESTMARK WY
13200 PWY 92064 1190-F4
WESTMINSTER DR
200 ENCT 92007 1167-D2
WESTMINSTER PL
1300 ESCN 92027 1130-D2
WESTMINSTER TER
4900 SD 92116 1269-G2
WESTMONT CT
400 CHV 91902 1311-A4
WESTMONT DR
3100 SDCo 92028 1048-D1
WESTMORE CIR
10900 SD 92126 1209-B3
WESTMORE CT
10900 SD 92126 1209-B3
WESTMORE LN
10900 SD 92126 1209-B3
WESTMORE PL
1400 OCN 92056 1087-E3
10900 SD 92126 1209-B3
WESTMORE RD
7900 SD 92126 1209-B3
WESTMORELAND RD
2000 ImCo 92251 430-L5
WESTMORLAND ST
1500 CHV 91913 1331-C1
1500 CHV 91913 1311-D7
WESTON CIR
300 VSTA 92083 1087-G3
WESTON RD
4600 SDCo 91941 1271-E3
WESTON ST
2300 SD 92114 1270-E7
WESTONHILL DR
10100 SD 92126 1209-C2
WESTOVER PL
4900 SD 92102 1290-A1
5100 SD 92105 1290-A1
WEST POINT AV
7200 LMSA 91941 1270-F3
WEST POINT DR
1800 CRLB 92008 1106-H6
WESTPORT DR
4400 OCN 92054 1066-G7
4400 OCN 92057 1066-G7
WESTPORT LN
- VSTA 92084 1087-J7
WESTPORT RD
1200 SMCS 92078 1128-B3
WESTPORT ST
2200 SD 92139 1310-D1
3900 SD 92139 1290-D7
WESTPORT VIEW DR
- SD 92154 1330-J7
- SD 92154 1350-J1
- SD 92154 1351-A1
WESTRIDGE DR
4500 OCN 92056 1087-D5
WESTRIDGE LN
2100 SDCo 92084 1088-A2
WESTRIDGE PL
11600 SDCo 92040 1231-H5
WESTROSE LN
- SDCo 92082 1090-D6
WEST SIDE RD
- SDCo 92065 1154-F4
- SDCo 92065 1174-D2
WESTSIDE RD
- ImCo 92243 430-L6
WESTVALE RD
9000 SD 92129 1189-C2
WESTVIEW CT
600 CHV 91910 1310-G5
1900 SDCo 92028 1028-A6
WESTVIEW DR
- ENCT 92024 1167-F3
400 CHV 91910 1310-F5
4500 LMSA 91941 1270-H3
WESTVIEW PKWY
10600 SD 92126 1209-E1
WESTVIEW PL
600 CHV 91910 1310-G5
7000 LMGR 91945 1270-F6
WESTVIEW RD
1800 SDCo 92028 1028-A6
15000 PWY 92064 1171-B6
WEST VILLAGE DR
1300 SDCo 92019 1252-F7
1300 SDCo 92019 1272-F1
WESTWARD CT
- SD 92131 1209-F2
WESTWARD HO CIR
1800 SDCo 92021 1252-C3
WESTWAY DR
8400 SD 92037 1227-H4
WESTWIND DR
100 ELCJ 92020 1251-B5
200 ELCN 92243 6559-G1
WESTWOOD CIR
10600 SD 92126 1209-D3
WESTWOOD DR
2000 CRLB 92008 1106-G4
WESTWOOD PL
1400 ESCN 92026 1109-E5
1400 OCN 92056 1087-E3
WESTWOOD RD
2000 VSTA 92083 1107-C1
2100 OCN 92056 1107-C1
WESTWOOD ST
2300 SD 92139 1310-C1
WETHERLY ST
7900 LMSA 91941 1270-H4
WETHERSFIELD RD
9200 SNTE 92071 1230-J6
WEXFORD ST
10500 SD 92131 1189-G7
WEYMOUTH WY
5100 OCN 92057 1066-J4
5100 OCN 92057 1067-A3
WHALERS CT
- SD 92154 1331-A6
WHALE WATCH WY
8400 SD 92037 1227-H4
WHALEY AV
1700 SD 92104 1289-F1
WHALEY RD
- SD 92102 1289-G4
WHALEY ST
100 OCN 92054 1106-D2
WHARTON RD
- SD 92140 1268-E6
9400 SNTE 92071 1231-B5
WHARTON ST
- SDCo 92055 1067-A1
WHEAT DR
- SD 92126 1209-D6
- SD 92126 1229-A1
WHEAT ST
3200 SD 92117 1248-D3
WHEATLAND PL
- SD 92131 1210-G2
WHEATLAND ST
- CHV 91913 1331-B1
WHEATLANDS AV
10700 SNTE 92071 1231-F5
WHEATLANDS CT
9400 SNTE 92071 1231-F5
WHEATLANDS RD
9300 SNTE 92071 1231-F5
WHEATLEY ST
6900 SD 92111 1248-J6
7100 SD 92111 1249-A6
WHEATON ST
5300 LMSA 91942 1270-G1
WHEATSTALK LN
5900 SDCo 91902 1311-B1
WHEATSTONE ST
2700 SD 92111 1248-G6
WHEATVILLE ST
1900 CHV 91913 1311-E6
WHEELER RD
- ImCo 92251 431-A4
- ImCo 92259 430-K3
WHEELER ST
1300 SDCo 91901 1234-B6
WHEELHOUSE DR
4800 SD 92154 1330-J6
WHEEL HUB PL
300 SDCo 92004 1058-G6
WHEELING LN
3100 SDCo 91902 1310-H1
WHELAN DR
7800 SD 92119 1250-H4
WHELAN LAKE RD
3500 OCN 92054 1066-F7
3500 OCN 92054 1086-F1
WHELLOCK WY
9400 SD 92129 1189-E4
WHIGHAM PL
1600 SDCo 92019 1252-B4
WHIMBREL CT
1000 CRLB 92011 1127-B7
WHINCHAT ST
1900 SD 92123 1269-A1
WHIP DR
200 SDCo 92004 (1078-F1 See Page 1058)
WHIPPLE AV
7000 SD 92122 1228-G4
WHIPPLE WY
4900 SD 92122 1228-F4
WHIPPLETREE LN
10800 SDCo 91978 1271-G7
WHIPPOORWILL LN
4800 SDCo 91902 1310-H1
WHIPPORWILL GN
300 ESCN 92026 1109-H5
WHIPTAIL CT
12100 SDCo 92040 1212-C4
WHIPTAIL LP
- CRLB 92010 1107-G7
- CRLB 92010 1127-G1
WHIRLWIND LN
16800 SDCo 92065 1171-J2
WHIRLYBIRD WY
5800 SDCo 91902 1311-B1
WHISPER DR
- CHV 91915 1331-G1
WHISPERING TR
9600 SDCo 91901 1234-A3
WHISPERING BROOK DR
300 VSTA 92083 1087-G3
WHISPERING HEIGHTS LN
- SD 92121 1208-G3
WHISPERING HIGHLANDS DR
1100 ESCN 92027 1130-E1
WHISPERING HIGHLANDS PL
1200 ESCN 92027 1130-F2
WHISPERING HILLS LN
- SD 92130 1208-D2
WHISPERING LEAVES LN
9300 SNTE 92071 1230-H6
WHISPERING MEADOWS LN
13700 SDCo 91935 1292-G3
WHISPERING OAKS DR
16300 SDCo 92065 1171-G3
WHISPERING OAKS LN
16800 SDCo 92065 1171-G3
WHISPERING PALM DR
1500 OCN 92056 1087-E2
WHISPERING PALMS LP
2500 CHV 91915 1311-H5
WHISPERING PINES DR
1500 SDCo 92036 1136-C5
WHISPERING RIDGE RD
- SD 92131 1210-F2
WHISPERING SAGE LN
- SDCo 92065 1152-F1
WHISPERING TRAILS DR
700 CHV 91914 1311-G3
WHISPERING TREE LN
12400 PWY 92064 1190-C5
WHISPERING WATER DR
1100 SMCS 92078 1129-B2
WHISPERING WILLOW DR
300 SNTE 92071 1231-C5
WHISPERING WOODS CT
4600 SD 92130 1188-C5
WHISPER TRACE RD
- SDCo 92084 1068-C5
WHISPER WIND DR
500 ENCT 92024 1147-J7
WHISPER WIND LN
2100 ENCT 92024 1147-J6
WHISPER WIND RD
- SDCo 92084 1068-D5
WHISTLER RD
- SD 92152 1287-J5
WHISTLING LN
- CHV 91915 1331-G1
WHISTLING STRAITS GN
- ESCN 92026 1109-H3
WHITAKER AV
- CHV 91911 1330-H2
WHITBY GN
- ESCN 92027 1110-D7
WHITE PL
9500 LMSA 91942 1251-B6
WHITE RD
2900 SD 92106 1288-A7
2900 SD 92106 1308-A1
WHITE ALDER AV
900 CHV 91914 1311-J4
WHITE ALDER CT
- SDCo 92127 1169-C2
WHITE BIRCH DR
400 CHV 91902 1311-B3
1800 VSTA 92081 1107-G5
10400 SD 92131 1209-J3
WHITE BUTTE DR
14900 PWY 92064 1190-J4
WHITECAP DR
6700 CRLB 92011 1126-J5
WHITE CAP LN
- OCN 92054 1085-H6
WHITE CHRISTMAS CT
- SDCo 92127 1168-J2
WHITECLIFF DR
2500 SD 92037 1227-H2
WHITE EMERALD DR
5100 SD 92130 1188-D4
WHITEFIELD PL
7700 SD 92037 1227-G6
WHITEFISH LN
3700 OCN 92054 1086-G2
WHITE FOX RUN
100 SDCo 92028 1028-B2
WHITE GOOSE RD
2400 SDCo 91906 (1297-G6 See Page 1296)
WHITEHALL CIR
10900 SD 92126 1209-A3
WHITEHALL RD
1700 ENCT 92024 1147-A2
10800 SD 92126 1209-A4
WHITEHAVEN WY
4900 SD 92110 1268-F1
WHITE HAWK RD
3200 ESCN 92027 1110-F7
3300 ESCN 92027 1130-F1
WHITEHEAD PL
8100 LMSA 91942 1250-H7
WHITE HICKORY PL
- CHV 91915 1311-H2
WHITEHILLS RD
9900 SDCo 92040 1232-C3
WHITEHORN
9700 SDCo 92021 1233-B3
WHITE HORSE CT
1500 CHV 91902 1311-B3
WHITE HORSE LN
200 SDCo 92028 1047-F3
WHITE LILAC RD
4200 SDCo 92028 998-G7
4200 SDCo 92028 1028-G1
WHITE OAK CT
1900 SMCS 92078 1128-B2
5200 OCN 92056 1087-E2
WHITE OAK DR
1800 SDCo 91901 1254-A1
WHITE OAK LN
- SD 92130 1188-E5
WHITE OAK PL
2500 ESCN 92027 1110-D6
WHITE OAK WY
12400 PWY 92064 1190-C5
WHITE OWL DR
2500 ENCT 92024 1148-A7
WHITE PINE CT
- CHV 91915 1311-J7
- CHV 91915 (1312-A7 See Page 1293)
WHITE PINE LN
10000 SNTE 92071 1231-D2
WHITE PINE WY
4400 OCN 92057 1086-J2
WHITEPORT LN
8800 SD 92119 1251-A4
WHITE ROCK STATION RD
13200 PWY 92064 1170-F2
WHITE ROSE LN
- SDCo 92127 1169-G1
WHITE SAGE LN
3600 SD 92105 1289-G2
WHITE SAGE PT
- SDCo 91906 (1318-B6 See Page 1298)
WHITESAGE RD
500 SMCS 92078 1128-G2
WHITESAIL ST
6700 CRLB 92011 1127-A5
WHITESANDS CT
3700 CRLB 92010 1107-B3
WHITE SANDS DR
- SMCS 92078 1128-A2
WHITE STAR LN
14200 SDCo 92082 1070-F2
WHITESTONE RD
1300 SDCo 91977 1291-E2
WHITE VALE LN
15400 PWY 92064 1170-J6
WHITEWATER DR
13200 PWY 92064 1190-J4
WHITEWATER ST
- CRLB 92011 1126-J6
WHITE WING DR
2300 SDCo 91935 1294-E6
WHITEWING PL
1200 CHV 91913 1331-A1
WHITEWOOD PL
200 ENCT 92024 1147-J6
WHITE WOOD CANYON
13600 PWY 92064 1170-F1
WHITEY DR
1700 CRLB 92008 1106-G7
WHITING CT
700 SD 92109 1247-H7
WHITING WOODS DR
1500 SDCo 92026 1109-D1
WHITLOCK RD
- ImCo 92227 431-F2
WHITMAN ST
2200 SD 92103 1268-G5
2800 SD 92110 1268-F4
WHITMAN WY
- CRLB 92008 1127-A1
WHITMORE RD
1200 ImCo 92283 432-D4
WHITMORE ST
400 SD 92102 1289-G3
WHITNEY CT
6900 SD 92111 1248-J6
WHITNEY PL
- CRLB 92009 1127-G2
WHITNEY ST
- CHV 91910 1310-C7
600 CHV 91910 1330-A1
2700 SD 92111 1248-J6
E WHITNEY ST
- CHV 91910 1310-D6
WHITNEY WY
- ELCN 92243 6559-F2
WHITSETT DR
1100 ELCJ 92020 1251-B3
WHITTAKER LN
12200 SDCo 92040 1232-A5
WHITTIER ST
3000 SD 92106 1268-C7
4100 SD 92107 1268-B6
WICHITA AV
600 ELCJ 92019 1252-B6
WICKER PL
1300 ESCN 92027 1110-A6
WICKERBAY CV
12300 SD 92128 1190-A6
WICKHAM WY
2800 CRLB 92008 1106-F3
WICKLEY PL
4600 OCN 92056 1107-E3
WICOPEE PL
3300 SD 92117 1248-D3
WIDDECKE LN
- SDCo 92672 1023-D2
WIDE OAK RD
1700 SDCo 91935 (1315-A3 See Page 1294)
WIDE VALLEY LN
11400 SD 92131 1209-J4
WIDGEON LN
900 CHV 91911 1330-C2
WIDGEON RD
29800 SDCo 91906 (1297-F5 See Page 1296)
WIEBER AV
1800 SD 92101 1289-C2
1800 SD 92134 1289-C2
WIEGAND ST
1000 ENCT 92024 1148-B4
WIEGHORST WY
11500 SDCo 92019 1271-J4
WIENERT RD
- ImCo 92251 431-A4
- ImCo 92251 6439-A2
WIEST RD
- ImCo 92233 411-C9
3800 ImCo 92227 431-D3
WIGEON PL
6800 CRLB 92011 1127-D6
WIGGINS WY
900 ELCJ 92020 1251-E7
WIGHT WY
1800 SDCo 92021 1252-A1
WIGHTMAN ST
2400 SD 92104 1269-C5
3600 SD 92105 1269-H5
4700 SD 92105 1270-A5
WIGWAM CT
8800 SNTE 92071 1230-J5
WIKIUP RD
16200 SDCo 92065 1173-E2
WILAJOBI WY
- SDCo 92040 1191-F6
WILBEE CT
2800 SD 92123 1249-D6
WILBUR AV
700 SD 92109 1247-H5
1900 SD 92109 1248-A4
WILCOX ST
300 OCN 92054 1086-E5
3500 SD 92106 1288-A3
3600 SD 92106 1287-J3
WILD ACRES RD
1500 SDCo 92084 1068-G5
WILDAUR ST
- CHV 91911 1330-H2
WILD BLOSSOM TER
5300 SD 92121 1208-E4
WILDBROOK PL
1900 CHV 91913 1311-E4
WILD CANARY LN
1100 ENCT 92024 1147-J5
WILD CANYON DR
- SMCS 92078 1128-F5
WILDCAT CANYON RD
1000 SDCo 92040 1212-F4
1000 SDCo 92040 1192-G7
1100 SDCo 92040 (1193-A5 See Page 1192)
11600 SDCo 92040 1232-C1
15000 SDCo 92065 1173-A6
WILDCAT CANYON RD
15000 SDCo 92065 (1193-A5 See Page 1192)
15000 SDCo 92040 1173-A6
WILD CHERRY CT
- CHV 91915 1311-H2
WILD COLT PL
14700 SDCo 91935 1273-A5
WILDER WY
- SDCo 92040 1231-H5
WILDERNESS RD
16500 PWY 92064 1170-F3
WILDERNESS WY
- ELCJ 92021 1251-J5
WILDERTHORN LN
8000 SDCo 92021 1251-J1
WILDFLOWER DR
- VSTA 92083 1087-D7
3000 ENCT 92024 1148-C5
WILD FLOWER LN
13100 PWY 92064 1170-D4
WILDFLOWER LN
3500 SDCo 92028 1028-E5
WILDFLOWER PL
600 ESCN 92026 1109-F4
WILD FLOWER WY
8000 SD 92120 1250-D3
WILDFLOWER WY
- SDCo 92082 1090-C5
WILDFLOWER VALLEY DR
- ENCT 92024 1148-B5
WILD GRAPE DR
9800 SD 92131 1209-G5
WILDGROVE RD
14500 PWY 92064 1170-H5
WILD HOLLY LN
15900 PWY 92064 1170-E5
WILD HORSE DR
- ImCo 92243 6560-B6
WILD HORSE GN
- SD 92127 1169-E2
WILDHORSE LN
500 SMCS 92078 1108-C6
WILD HORSE TR
10500 SNTE 92071 1231-E5
WILD HORSE CREEK
18500 PWY 92064 1150-H6
WILDHORSE TRAIL WY
2600 CHV 91915 1311-J6
WILD IRIS PL
1200 CHV 91913 1331-A1
WILD IRIS RD
2300 SDCo 91901 1234-A5
WILDLIFE RD
10000 SD 92131 1210-A4
WILD LILAC CIR
- SMCS 92078 1128-G2
WILD LILAC TR
1800 SDCo 92036 1136-D5
WILD MEADOW PL
- SD 92131 1210-D2
WILDMEADOW PL
1700 ENCT 92024 1147-G4
WILD MUSTANG PL
14700 SDCo 91935 1273-A6
WILD OAK LN
- ESCN 92027 1130-H2
WILD OAK RD
900 CHV 91910 1310-J7
28900 SDCo 91962 1237-C5
WILD OATS LN
3600 SDCo 91902 1311-B1
WILD ORCHID WY
- SDCo 92127 1169-F2
WILDROSE GN
3800 ESCN 92025 1150-C3
WILDROSE LN
9300 SD 92126 1209-E3
WILD ROSE RD
900 SDCo 92036 1156-D5
WILDROSE TER
6900 CRLB 92011 1127-B6
WILD STALLION PL
14700 SDCo 91935 1273-A6
WILD WEST PL
14400 SDCo 91935 1272-J5
WILDWIND DR
2800 SDCo 92019 1272-B6
WILDWOOD CT
1100 CHV 91913 1331-B1
WILDWOOD DR
600 SDCo 92036 1156-E1
4900 OCN 92057 1087-C1
WILDWOOD LN
- SDCo 91901 1254-F7
WILDWOOD RD
1700 SD 92107 1288-A1
3800 SD 92107 1268-A7
WILDWOOD GLEN LN
- SDCo 91901 1235-F4
- SDCo 91901 1236-A5
WILER DR
800 CHV 91910 1310-G7
WIL EV DR
400 SMCS 92069 1108-J6
WILFRED ST
900 ELCJ 92021 1251-H2
WILGEN RD
21400 SDCo 92029 1129-B5
WILHITE LN
29600 SDCo 92082 1070-G5
WILKERSON CT
7800 SD 92111 1249-A3
WILKES RD
11100 SDCo 92082 1069-G5
28300 SDCo 92082 1089-H1
28400 SDCo 92026 1089-H2
WILKIE WY
100 SDCo 92021 1252-J3
WILKINS RD
- ImCo 92283 432-D5
8200 ImCo 92257 411-C7
WILKINSON DR
200 SMCS 92078 1129-A1
WILKINSON RD
200 ImCo 92233 411-B9
WILLA WY
7900 SD 92119 1250-H4
WILLAMAN DR
- SDCo 92084 1068-D5
WILLAMETTE AV
3900 SD 92117 1248-E2
WILLAPA CV
11400 SD 92131 1209-J1
WILLARD ST
3200 SD 92122 1228-C5
WILLET CIR
- CRLB 92011 1127-D7
WILLET ST
500 ELCJ 92020 1251-G4
WILLIAM AV
1300 CHV 91911 1330-C4
WILLIAMS AV
4900 LMSA 91941 1270-G2
WILLIAMS CT
8700 SNTE 92071 1230-J3
WILLIAMS LN
1800 OCN 92054 1106-F1
WILLIAMS RD
- ImCo 92227 411-D11
- SDCo 91905 430-C7
- SDCo 91905 (1299-G2 See Page 1298)
400 ImCo 92233 411-C11
WILLIAMS TER
- SDCo 92024 1148-D3
WILLIAMS WY
- SD 92145 1229-B2
WILLIAMSBURG LN
4700 LMSA 91941 1270-G3
WILLIAMS RANCH RD
2700 SDCo 92070 1135-E7
WILLIAMSTON ST
800 VSTA 92084 1087-J5
WILLIAMS VALLEY CT
- SDCo 92026 1069-B4
WILLIAM TELL ST
21800 SDCo 92070 1135-B2
WILLIE BAKER WY
- SDCo 91978 1291-F1
WILLIE JAMES JONES AV
300 SD 92102 1290-A5
300 SD 92113 1290-A5
S WILLIE JAMES JONES AV
1100 SD 92113 1290-A5
WILLIS CT
400 ELCJ 92020 1251-C5
WILLIS RD
1900 ELCJ 92020 1251-C5
WILLITS RD
2200 SDCo 91901 1253-G2
WILLMAN WY
5200 SDCo 92028 1047-G7
5200 SDCo 92028 1067-G1
WILLOUGHBY RD
- ImCo 92231 431-B7
- ImCo 92231 6620-B4
- ImCo 92243 431-B7
- ImCo 92243 6620-B4
WILLOW AV
2100 OCN 92054 1086-C5
WILLOW CT
10800 SDCo 92127 1169-G3
WILLOW DR
- SDCo 92040 1232-D6
400 SMCS 92069 1108-H5
1900 ELCN 92243 6559-H1
WILLOW GN
700 ESCN 92025 1130-C7
WILLOW LN
- SDCo 92026 1089-B3
1900 SD 92106 1288-C1
9700 SDCo 92029 1149-D4
25700 SDCo 92026 1109-E2
WILLOW PL
6400 CRLB 92011 1127-B4
WILLOW RD
200 SD 92173 1350-G4
12400 SDCo 92040 1232-A1
14200 SDCo 92040 1212-J6
WILLOW ST
100 CHV 91902 1310-F3
100 SDCo 91902 1310-F3
1100 SD 92106 1288-B1
2000 SD 92106 1268-C7
WILLOW TER
8600 SNTE 92071 1231-C7
WILLOW TR
- SDCo 92026 1089-F4
WILLOW WY
- ELCJ 92019 1251-J6
1800 VSTA 92081 1107-G5
WILLOW BEND DR
- ELCN 92243 6559-J3
1500 SDCo 92019 1272-F1
WILLOW BEND PL
2600 SDCo 92019 1272-F1
WILLOWBROOK CT
800 CHV 91913 1311-E4
1900 ELCJ 92019 1252-C4
WILLOWBROOK DR
1900 OCN 92056 1087-F2
WILLOWBROOK ST
2100 ESCN 92029 1129-E7
2100 SDCo 92029 1129-E7
WILLOWBROOK WY
100 SNTE 92071 1231-B5
WILLOW CREEK CIR
2200 CHV 91915 1311-F5
WILLOW CREEK DR
- VSTA 92084 1088-B3
WILLOWCREEK LN
- SDCo 92028 998-A7
WILLOW CREEK PL
- ESCN 92027 1130-H2
WILLOW CREEK RD
9800 SD 92131 1209-F5
WILLOWCREST WY
400 CHV 91910 1310-F7
WILLOW GLEN DR
800 SDCo 92019 1252-F7
1300 SDCo 92019 1272-D3
WILLOW GLEN LN
- SDCo 92019 1272-E3
WILLOW GLEN RD
1500 SDCo 92028 998-B5
WILLOWGREEN CT
1400 ENCT 92024 1147-G4
WILLOWGROVE AV
8900 SNTE 92071 1231-B6
WILLOWGROVE CIR
9000 SNTE 92071 1231-B6
WILLOWGROVE CT
9000 SNTE 92071 1231-B6
WILLOW GROVE PL
- ESCN 92027 1110-F6
WILLOWGROVE PL
9000 SNTE 92071 1231-C6
WILLOWHAVEN RD
1600 ENCT 92024 1147-G4
WILLOW HEIGHTS RD
- SDCo 92028 998-C7
WILLOW MEADOW PL
- ESCN 92027 1110-F6
WILLOWMERE LN
5500 SD 92130 1208-E1
WILLOW OAK DR
- SDCo 92065 1172-D5
WILLOWOOD LN
2000 ENCT 92024 1147-H6
WILLOW PARK RD
28600 SDCo 92026 1089-E2
WILLOW POND RD
100 SNTE 92071 1231-B5
WILLOW RANCH RD
14000 PWY 92064 1170-G6
WILLOW RANCH TR
15400 PWY 92064 1170-G6
WILLOW RIDGE DR
1900 VSTA 92081 1107-G5
WILLOW RUN RD
13500 PWY 92064 1170-F3
WILLOWS RD
4000 SDCo 91901 1234-F6
5100 SDCo 91901 1235-A5
WILLOWS WY
3800 NATC 91950 1310-D3
WILLOWSIDE LN
3800 SDCo 91977 1271-B4
WILLOWSIDE TER
1200 SDCo 91901 1234-G5
WILLOWSPRING CT
2100 ENCT 92024 1147-J6
WILLOWSPRING DR N
200 ENCT 92024 1147-G5
WILLOWSPRING DR S
500 ENCT 92024 1147-G7
WILLOWSPRING PL
2100 ENCT 92024 1147-J6
WILLOW TREE CT
3400 OCN 92054 1086-E2
WILLOW TREE LN
- ESCN 92027 1110-F6
800 SDCo 92028 1027-H3
WILLOWVIEW CT
1400 ENCT 92024 1167-G1
WILLOW VIEW LN
31000 SDCo 92082 1070-E2
WILLOW WALK RD
- OCN 92057 1067-A3
WILLOWWOOD DR
11200 SD 92127 1169-J5
WILLS CREEK RD
11300 SD 92131 1210-A2
11300 SD 92131 1209-J1
WILLSON RD
1000 SDCo 92019 1253-D3
WILL VALLEY RD
- SDCo 92060 (1053-F6 See Page 1052)
WILMA PL
1500 ESCN 92025 1130-B4
WILMA ST
2700 SDCo 91950 1310-C3
WILMINGTON AV
12100 SDCo 92082 1070-A7
12100 SDCo 92082 1090-A1
WILMINGTON DR
- CHV 91914 1311-H2
WILMINGTON RD
11800 SD 92128 1190-A2
WILSEY WY
12100 PWY 92064 1190-B2
WILSHIRE AV
3600 CRLB 92010 1107-A4
WILSHIRE DR
5300 SD 92116 1269-F2
WILSHIRE RD
200 OCN 92057 1067-C4
1400 OCN 92028 1067-D2
6500 OCN 92028 1047-D7
WILSHIRE TER
3500 SD 92104 1269-C6
WILSON AV
700 ELCJ 92020 1251-E7
1200 NATC 91950 1309-G2
1400 ESCN 92027 1110-B7
3500 SD 92104 1269-F6
4400 SD 92116 1269-F4
WILSON CT
- CALX 92231 6620-J5
WILSON PL
1300 ESCN 92027 1110-C6
WILSON RD
- ImCo 92283 432-D5
1300 SDCo 92065 1153-A7
1500 SDCo 92065 1173-A1
WILSON ST
300 ELCN 92243 6499-G6
2500 CRLB 92008 1106-F3
5100 LMSA 91941 1271-A1
WILSTONE AV
1700 ENCT 92024 1147-A2
WILT RD
1400 SDCo 92028 1028-E5
2600 SDCo 92028 1048-F1
WILTON RD
1800 ENCT 92024 1147-A2
WILTS PL
5100 SD 92117 1248-G1
WILTSIE WY
4800 SD 92124 1249-G2
WILVINN DR
8000 SNTE 92071 1251-B1
WIMBELTON LN
28400 SDCo 92026 1089-D3
WIMBERLY SQ
13000 SD 92128 1189-H5
WINAMAR AV
200 SD 92037 1247-E2
WINAMAR PL
2000 ESCN 92029 1129-G7
WINANS CV
7900 SD 92126 1209-A1
WINCHECK RD
10500 SD 92131 1209-G1
WINCHESTER CT
1200 VSTA 92083 1087-E6
WINCHESTER DR
- ELCJ 92021 1251-H5
WINCHESTER LN
300 IMP 92251 6439-F4
WINCHESTER ST
2000 OCN 92054 1086-C7
5500 SD 92139 1310-C2
WINCHESTER WY
9900 SDCo 92040 1232-D3
WIND PL
4000 ESCN 92025 1150-D4
WINDBREAK CT
3300 SD 92130 1187-J5
WINDBREAK RD
13100 SD 92130 1187-J5
WINDBROOK WY
- SD 92131 1209-G2
WIND CAVE PL
900 CHV 91914 1311-H4
WINDCHIME AV
- CHV 91913 1331-D1
WINDCHIME DR
- CHV 91913 1331-E1
WIND CREEK RD
- SDCo 91901 1253-J3
- SDCo 91901 1254-A3
WINDCREST DR
800 CRLB 92011 1126-J5
WINDCREST LN
11500 SD 92128 1189-J2

STREET
Block City ZIP Pg-Grid

WINDCREST LN
11500 SD 92128 1190-A2
WIND DRIFT DR
900 CRLB 92011 1126-J4
WINDEMERE CT
700 SD 92109 1247-H7
WINDEMERE DR
- SMCS 92078 1128-C6
WINDER ST
1600 SD 92103 1268-H6
WINDERMERE ST
10300 SDCo 92026 1109-F2
WINDERMERE POINT WY
700 OCN 92054 1066-E6
WINDFALL TR
700 SDCo 92036 1138-B6
4600 OCN 92056 1087-D3
WINDFLOWER DR
6400 CRLB 92011 1127-A4
WIND FLOWER WY
300 OCN 92057 1086-J2
WINDFLOWER WY
900 SD 92106 1288-A2
WINDHAM CT
8900 SDCo 91977 1271-A7
WINDING WY
700 ENCT 92024 1147-G5
WINDING CREEK DR
6600 SD 92119 1250-D3
WINDING FENCE WY
- CHV 91914 1311-J2
WINDING OAK DR
1000 CHV 91910 1310-J7
1000 CHV 91910 1330-J1
WINDING RIDGE DR
11000 SD 92131 1209-G2
WINDINGWALK ST
1500 CHV 91915 1311-H7
1500 CHV 91915 1331-G1
WINDINGWALK WY
2400 CHV 91915 1311-J7
WINDJAMMER CIR
300 CHV 91910 1310-F6
WINDJAMMER WY
4800 CRLB 92008 1106-H7
WINDMILL PL
1500 CHV 91913 1331-A2
WINDMILL RD
1300 ELCJ 92019 1251-J7
1300 SDCo 92019 1251-J7
WINDMILL ST
5100 OCN 92056 1087-D2
WINDMILL RANCH RD
600 ENCT 92024 1148-A6
31400 SDCo 92026 1069-E2
WINDMILL VIEW RD
1900 ELCJ 92020 1251-B2
WINDOM PEAK WY
11900 SD 92131 1190-A7
WINDPIPER RD
16200 PWY 92064 1170-G3
WINDRIDGE CIR
900 SMCS 92078 1128-F2
WINDRIDGE DR
1300 SDCo 92020 1251-J7
1400 ELCJ 92020 1252-A7
1400 SDCo 92020 1252-A7
WINDRIFT WY
3500 OCN 92056 1107-G4
WIND RIVER RD
1100 CHV 91913 1331-B2
1700 SDCo 92019 1272-B4
WINDRIVER ST
- SMCS 92078 1128-F6
WIND RIVER WY
- OCN 92057 1086-J2
WINDROSE CIR
200 CRLB 92011 1127-A7
WINDROSE CT
15800 SD 92127 1169-H5
WINDROSE WY
400 CHV 91910 1310-F5
15800 SD 92127 1169-H5
W WINDS RDG
1600 SDCo 91901 1234-B6
WINDSOCK ST
8400 SD 92154 1351-G1
WIND SOCK WY
- CRLB 92011 1126-J7
WINDSONG LN
1200 SDCo 92026 1109-D1
1300 SDCo 92026 1089-C7
WINDSONG RD
7500 SD 92126 1209-A3
WINDSOR CIR
600 CHV 91910 1310-E6
WINDSOR CT
700 VSTA 92084 1087-J6
2700 CRLB 92010 1107-A5
WINDSOR DR
5000 SD 92109 1247-J4
7900 LMSA 91941 1270-H3
WINDSOR PL
700 ESCN 92029 1129-F4
WINDSOR RD
1200 ENCT 92007 1167-E2
3500 OCN 92056 1107-F3
WINDSOR CREEK CT
900 ENCT 92007 1167-E2
WIND STAR WY
- CRLB 92011 1127-A4
WINDSTONE GN
- ESCN 92027 1110-E7
WINDSWEPT TER
3600 SD 92130 1188-A4
WINDVANE LN
100 CRLB 92011 1126-J6
WINDWARD DR
800 SDCo 92036 1156-E1
WINDWARD LN
800 CRLB 92011 1126-J5
WINDWARD ST
6700 SD 92114 1290-F5
WINDWARD WY
- OCN 92054 1085-J7
400 OCN 92054 1086-A7
WINDWARD RIDGE WY
6500 SD 92121 1208-G3
WINDWOOD WY
2800 SDCo 92019 1272-C6
WINDY LN
300 VSTA 92083 1087-F6
3000 SDCo 91902 1310-D4
WINDY WY
100 SMCS 92069 1108-H6
500 CHV 91914 1311-E3
WINDY BLUFF LN
10700 SD 92121 1208-E4
WINDY HEIGHTS WY
12600 SD 92130 1188-D6
WINDY HILL TER
900 ENCT 92024 1167-E1
WINDY MOUNTAIN LN
13200 SDCo 92082 1050-C7
WINDYRIDGE GN
300 ESCN 92026 1109-G6
WINDY RIDGE RD
7500 SD 92126 1208-J1
7500 SD 92126 1209-A1
WINDY RIDGE WY
11500 SD 92126 1209-A2
WINDY SUMMIT PL
11400 SD 92127 1169-J5
WINECREEK CT
- SDCo 92127 1169-E5
WINECREEK RD
- SDCo 92127 1169-E5
WINECREST RD
- SDCo 92127 1169-E5
WINEN WY
9000 SD 92123 1249-D6
WINERIDGE PL
800 ESCN 92029 1129-E3
WINESPRING CT
- SDCo 92127 1169-F6
WINESPRING DR
- SDCo 92127 1169-F5
WINEWOOD ST
200 SD 92114 1290-F3
WINFIELD AV
6000 LMSA 91942 1251-A6
WING AV
1800 SDCo 92020 1251-F1
WING ST
2900 SD 92110 1268-D5
WINGATE
4600 OCN 92056 1107-E3
WINGED FOOT CIR
- SDCo 92082 1090-F4
WINGED FOOT GN
2100 ESCN 92026 1109-D4
WING FLIGHT CT
7800 SD 92119 1250-G4
WINGFOOT PL
1700 SDCo 92019 1272-B5
WING SPAN DR
7700 SD 92119 1250-G4
WINLAND HILLS DR
14500 SD 92067 1188-E1
14500 SDCo 92067 1188-E1
WINLOW ST
3100 SD 92105 1270-B6
WINNEBAGO AV
4600 SD 92117 1248-F1
WINNERS CIR
1000 SDCo 92065 1172-H1
5700 SDCo 91902 1311-B2
WINNETKA DR
3000 SDCo 91902 1310-G1
WINNETT ST
1400 SD 92114 1290-D1
WINN RANCH RD
- SDCo 92036 1156-G7
WINONA AV
3700 SD 92105 1270-A5
4100 SD 92115 1270-A2
6200 SD 92120 1250-A6
WINONA CT
5100 OCN 92057 1087-C1
WINROW RD
1800 SDCo 92021 1252-C3
WINSHIP LN
2300 SD 92101 1288-G1
WINSLOW RD
300 ImCo 92257 411-B6
3500 OCN 92056 1107-E2
3500 SDCo 92081 1107-E2
WINSOME DR
1500 ESCN 92029 1149-G1
WINSOME PL
300 ENCT 92024 1147-H6
2200 ESCN 92029 1129-G7
2200 ESCN 92029 1149-G1
WINSOME WY
2000 ENCT 92024 1147-H6
WINSTANLEY WY
13300 SD 92130 1188-C4
WINSTON DR
700 SD 92114 1290-A3
WINTER LN
1300 SDCo 92021 1252-A1
WINTER RD
2400 OCN 92056 1087-D6
WINTER CREEK LN
14600 SDCo 92082 1070-G2
WINTERCREEK PL
100 SNTE 92071 1231-B5
WINTERCREST DR
12000 SDCo 92040 1231-J4
12000 SDCo 92040 1232-A4
WINTER GARDENS BLVD
1300 SDCo 92021 1251-J2
5400 SDCo 92040 1251-J2
8300 SDCo 92040 1231-J3
9100 SDCo 92040 1232-A4
WINTER GARDENS DR
12000 SDCo 92040 1251-J1
12000 SDCo 92040 1231-J7
12000 SDCo 92040 1232-A7
12300 SDCo 92021 1232-A7
WINTERGREEN DR
2700 CRLB 92008 1106-G3
12100 SDCo 92040 1232-A4
WINTERGREEN GN
1700 ESCN 92026 1109-G6
WINTER GREEN LN
2400 SDCo 92028 1028-B6
WINTERGREEN PL
400 SMCS 92069 1109-B7
WINTERHAVEN CT
2300 SDCo 92028 1028-C7
WINTERHAVEN DR
2100 ImCo 92283 432-C6
WINTERHAVEN LN
2300 SDCo 92028 1028-B7
WINTER HAVEN RD
1100 SDCo 92028 1027-G7
WINTERHAVEN RD
1300 SDCo 92028 1027-J7
1600 SDCo 92028 1028-A7
W WINTER HAVEN RD
700 SDCo 92028 1027-G7
WINTERHAWK LN
100 ENCT 92024 1148-A7
100 ENCT 92024 1167-J1
100 ENCT 92024 1168-A1
WINTER HUNT LN
5300 SD 92130 1208-D2
WINTERS CT
300 SMCS 92069 1108-J7
WINTERS HILL
3000 SDCo 92084 1088-E7
WINTERSWEET ST
1900 SD 92154 1350-D3
WINTER VIEW CT
- SDCo 92021 1251-J1
WINTER VIEW PL
- SDCo 92021 1251-J1
WINTERWARM DR
1600 SDCo 92028 1047-J1
1600 SDCo 92028 1048-A1
1800 SDCo 92028 1028-A7
WINTERWOOD LN
7500 SD 92126 1209-A4
WINTHROP AV
2800 CRLB 92010 1107-A4
WINTHROP ST
5100 SD 92117 1228-H7
WIRELESS WY
- SD 92121 1208-E5
WIRE MOUNTAIN RD
- SDCo 92055 1085-H4
- SDCo 92055 1086-A4
WIRT RD
1200 ImCo 92233 411-D10
WISCONSIN AV
- OCN 92054 1106-B2
300 ELCJ 92020 1251-F5
700 SDCo 92028 1027-F3
6900 LMSA 91942 1270-E1
S WISCONSIN AV
100 SDCo 92028 1027-F2
WISE ST
- CHV 91911 1330-J2
1000 CHV 91911 1331-A2
WISECARVER LN
3100 SDCo 91935 1274-C6
WISECARVER TKTR
3100 SDCo 91935 1274-C7
WISHBONE WY
3000 ENCT 92024 1148-B3
WISHING STAR DR
1500 CHV 91915 1311-H7
WISHING STAR WY
2400 CHV 91915 1311-H7
WISKON WY
32000 SDCo 92061 1051-B6
WISTER DR
9100 SDCo 91941 1271-B1
9200 LMSA 91941 1271-B1
WISTERIA
15300 SDCo 92021 1233-B3
WISTERIA AV
13900 PWY 92064 1190-F3
WISTERIA CT
- IMP 92251 6499-D2
1900 SDCo 92019 1272-D3
WISTERIA DR
300 SMCS 92078 1128-G2
3300 SD 92106 1268-D6
5100 OCN 92056 1107-F4
WISTERIA GN
1600 ESCN 92026 1109-D6
WISTERIA ST
500 CHV 91911 1330-H3
WISTERIA WY
7100 CRLB 92011 1127-B6
WISTFUL VISTA
7900 SNTE 92071 1230-H7
WITCH CREEK MOUNTAIN RD
27500 SDCo 92065 1154-C1
WITHAM RD
100 ENCT 92024 1147-F7
WITHERBY ST
100 OCN 92054 1106-B3
3600 SD 92140 1268-F6
3600 SD 92110 1268-G5
3900 SD 92103 1268-G5
WITHERSPOON WY
200 ELCJ 92020 1251-B5
WITT PL
12400 PWY 92064 1190-C3
WITT RD
12200 PWY 92064 1190-B3
WITTMAN WY
3100 SD 92173 1350-F4
WIXOM RD
- ImCo 92243 430-L6
- ImCo 92243 431-A6
WIZARD WY
16000 SDCo 92082 1071-B5
W L MORENO
900 CALX 92231 6680-D1
WODEN ST
700 NATC 92136 1309-F1
1800 SD 92113 1289-G7
2300 SD 92136 1289-G7
WOHLFORD ST
5200 OCN 92056 1087-D1
WOLAHI RD
- SDCo 92036 1176-C5
WOLBERT PL
200 SD 92113 1289-F4
WOLF CANYON LP
- CHV 91913 1331-E2
WOLFF CT
5800 LMSA 91942 1251-C7
WOLFORD DR
400 SDCo 91977 1290-J4
WOLF POINT CT
600 OCN 92057 1067-C7
WOLFSDORF WY
- CHV 91913 1331-E2
WOLFS HILL RD
- CHV 91913 1311-E6
WOLFSTAR CT
6100 SD 92122 1228-G5
WOLVERINE TER
1500 CRLB 92010 1107-D7
WOLVERINE WY
- SD 92129 1189-B3
1700 VSTA 92083 1088-B5
WOLVISTON WY
1700 SD 92154 1349-J2
1700 SD 92154 1350-A2
WOMACK LN
400 SDCo 92028 1027-F3
WOMBLE RD
2700 SD 92106 1268-D7
2700 SD 92106 1288-D1
WOMBLE ST
- NATC 92136 1309-F3
WOMSI LN
15400 SDCo 92061 1050-J5
WOMSI RD
32400 SDCo 92061 1050-J5
WONDER LN
8000 SDCo 92021 1252-A1
WONDER VIEW DR
2000 SDCo 92084 1088-B2
WONJU CIR
- SDCo 92055 409-A7
WOOD DR
700 ENCT 92024 1147-C3
WOOD LN
15600 SDCo 92082 1071-A3
WOOD ST
4900 LMSA 91941 1271-A2
WOODACRE DR
2300 OCN 92056 1106-H1
WOODBINE PL
1700 OCN 92054 1106-D2
WOODBINE WY
7500 SD 92114 1290-G4
WOODBRIDGE RD
1700 ESCN 92026 1109-D5
WOODBROOK LN
1700 SDCo 92028 1027-G5
WOODBURN ST
1700 ELCJ 92021 1251-H2
WOODBURY CT
2900 CRLB 92010 1107-B4
WOODBURY PL
2100 ESCN 92026 1109-G5
WOODCHUCK PT
10400 SD 92131 1209-J4
WOODCRAFT WY
- SD 92131 1209-H2
WOODCREEK PL
13200 PWY 92064 1190-E2
WOODCREEK RD
900 SDCo 92028 1027-H3
14100 PWY 92064 1190-E2
WOODCREST DR
200 SDCo 92028 1027-F3
WOODCREST ST
1400 CHV 91910 1311-C6
WOODDALE RW
6000 SD 92037 1248-A1
WOOD DUCK DR
- SDCo 92127 1149-F7
WOODED HILL RD
- SDCo 91948 430-B5
WOODED VISTA LN
12000 SD 92128 1190-A7
WOOD ENERGY RD
200 SDCo 92065 1152-B7
200 SDCo 92065 1172-B1
WOODEN VALLEY ST
- CHV 91913 1311-E7
WOODFERN LN
- CRLB 92024 1147-F3
WOODFORD DR
2900 SD 92037 1227-J6
2900 SD 92037 1228-A6
WOODFORDS PL
1300 CHV 91913 1331-C1
WOODGATE PL
13700 PWY 92064 1190-F5
WOODGLEN PL
2100 ESCN 92026 1109-G5
WOODGLEN TER
1400 CHV 91902 1311-A2
WOODGLEN WY
1900 ELCJ 92020 1251-C3
WOODGLEN VISTA DR
9900 SNTE 92071 1231-C3
WOODGROVE DR
900 ENCT 92007 1167-E2
WOODHAVEN DR
1000 SDCo 91977 1290-J3
1200 OCN 92056 1087-C2
WOODHILL ST
1400 ELCJ 92019 1252-A6
WOODHOLLOW LN
14100 PWY 92064 1190-E2
WOODHOUSE AV
500 CHV 91910 1310-F6
WOODHUE LN
14600 PWY 92064 1190-E1
WOODLAKE DR
900 ENCT 92007 1167-E2
WOODLAND CT
1300 SMCS 92069 1109-C6
4100 LMSA 91941 1271-B4
WOODLAND DR
100 SDCo 92083 1108-B2
100 VSTA 92083 1108-B2
4100 LMSA 91941 1271-B4
WOODLAND GN
1900 ESCN 92027 1110-B5
WOODLAND LN
300 SDCo 92021 1252-J4
WOODLAND PKWY
100 SMCS 92078 1129-B1
100 SMCS 92069 1109-B7
100 SMCS 92078 1109-B7
1000 ESCN 92026 1109-B7
1400 SDCo 92026 1109-B7
14000 PWY 92064 1170-G4
WOODLAND RD
2500 SDCo 92036 1136-C7
WOODLAND WY
2500 OCN 92054 1106-F2
3400 CRLB 92008 1106-F5
WOODLAND HEIGHTS GN
1900 ESCN 92026 1109-B3
3100 SDCo 92026 1109-B3
WOODLAND HILLS DR
300 SDCo 92029 1149-J1
400 SDCo 92029 1150-A1
WOODLANDS LN
8500 SD 92037 1228-B4
WOODLANDS GLENN
6900 LMSA 91941 1270-E5
WOODLAND VALLEY GN
2000 ESCN 92026 1109-C4
WOODLAND VISTA DR
9600 SDCo 92040 1232-D3
WOODLARK CT
1500 CHV 91911 1330-F5
WOODLARK LN
- CHV 91911 1330-F5
1700 SDCo 92028 1027-G5
WOODLAWN AV
- CHV 91910 1309-J5
- CHV 91910 1310-A7
400 CHV 91910 1330-A1
800 CHV 91911 1330-A3
WOODLAWN DR
800 SDCo 92036 1156-D1
9000 SD 92126 1209-D4
WOODLEY PL
800 ENCT 92024 1147-D4
WOODMAN ST
200 SD 92114 1290-F6
1300 SD 92139 1290-F6
1300 SD 92139 1310-G1
1300 SDCo 91902 1310-G1
N WOODMAN ST
300 SD 92114 1290-E4
WOODMEADOW LN
300 SDCo 92065 1153-B5
WOODMONT PL
13100 PWY 92064 1190-D2
WOODMONT ST
13100 PWY 92064 1190-D2
WOODMOSS CT
2000 ENCT 92024 1147-H5
WOODPARK DR
9900 SNTE 92071 1231-E3
WOODPARK WY
200 OCN 92054 1086-F3
WOODPECKER WY
7900 SNTE 92071 1230-H7
WOODPINE DR
1500 SDCo 92019 1272-B4
WOODRAIL DR
1100 VSTA 92083 1087-G4
WOODRIDGE CIR
2800 CRLB 92008 1106-F3
WOODRIDGE LN
- SDCo 92086 409-H5
WOODRIDGE WY
7300 SD 92114 1290-G6
WOOD ROCK LN
15900 SDCo 92065 1172-A4
WOODROSE AV
10000 SNTE 92071 1231-D3
WOODROW AV
700 SD 92114 1290-F3
1400 LMGR 91945 1290-F3
WOODRUFF WY
9300 SNTE 92071 1231-A5
WOODRUN PL
1600 SDCo 92019 1272-B4
WOODRUSH CT
11200 SD 92128 1189-J2
WOODRUSH LN
11200 SD 92128 1189-J2
WOODS DR
500 SMCS 92069 1109-C6
800 CHV 91914 1311-J3
WOODSHADOW LN
100 ENCT 92024 1147-H7
WOODSHAWN DR
7100 SD 92114 1290-F5
WOODS HILL LN
18300 SDCo 92065 1153-C7
WOODSIDE AV
10500 SNTE 92071 1231-F5
11400 SDCo 92040 1231-H4
12100 SDCo 92040 1232-A4
WOODSIDE AV N
10800 SNTE 92071 1231-F5
11000 SDCo 92040 1231-F5
WOODSIDE CT
- CHV 91914 1311-F3
WOODSIDE DR
1900 ELCN 92243 6559-H1
WOODSIDE LN
800 ENCT 92024 1147-J5
WOODSIDE PL
600 ESCN 92026 1109-F4
WOODSIDE WY
1000 SOLB 92014 1187-G1
WOODSON CT
18900 SDCo 92065 1172-A2
N WOODSON CT
17200 SDCo 92065 1171-F3
N WOODSON DR
16400 SDCo 92065 1171-F3
S WOODSON DR
15900 SDCo 92065 1171-E3
WOODSON CREST RD
16100 SDCo 92065 1171-B3
WOODSON RIDGE RD
16100 SDCo 92065 1171-B3
WOODSON VIEW LN
17100 SDCo 92065 1171-E3
WOODSON VIEW RD
16300 PWY 92064 1170-F4
WOODSPRING DR
800 CHV 91913 1311-E4
WOODSTOCK PL
13700 SDCo 92082 1090-E6
WOODSTOCK ST
4500 CRLB 92010 1107-B5
WOODSTORK LN
100 SDCo 92028 1027-G5
WOODSTREAM PT
10800 SD 92131 1210-A2
WOODS VALLEY CT
27100 SDCo 92082 1090-E5
WOODS VALLEY RD
13800 SDCo 92082 1090-F5
15200 SDCo 92082 1091-A5
WOODTHRUSH LN
100 SDCo 92028 1027-G5
WOODVALE DR
3800 CRLB 92008 1106-H5
8400 SNTE 92071 1230-J7
WOOD VALLEY TR
16000 SDCo 91935 1273-G5
WOODVIEW CT
1300 OCN 92056 1087-D3
WOODVIEW DR
1200 OCN 92056 1087-C2
WOODVIEW PL
9500 SD 92123 1249-E4
WOODVILLE AV
1300 CHV 91913 1331-D1
WOODWARD AV
200 ESCN 92025 1129-H2
500 ELCN 92243 6499-F5
WOODWARD RD
- SD 92152 1287-J5
WOODWARD ST
500 SMCS 92069 1108-J5
600 SMCS 92069 1109-A4
WOODWAY CT
200 SD 92114 1290-G5
WOODWAYNE DR
10300 SNTE 92071 1231-D3
WOODWIND DR
2100 ENCT 92024 1147-J7
WOODWIND RD
2700 CRLB 92008 1106-F3
WOODWIND ST
- CHV 91913 1331-D1
WOODY LN
13000 PWY 92064 1190-G5
WOODYARD AV
5000 LMSA 91941 1270-G2
WOODY HILLS DR
1500 SDCo 92019 1272-B1
WOOSTER DR
3800 OCN 92056 1087-B6
WORCESTER GN
2500 ESCN 92027 1110-D7
WORCHESTER PL
6900 SD 92126 1208-H4
WORDEN ST
2100 SD 92107 1268-B6
2400 SD 92106 1268-C5
2800 SD 92106 1268-C5
WORKS PL
4700 SD 92116 1269-E3
WORLD TRADE DR
12000 SD 92128 1190-A1
12100 SD 92128 1170-A7
WORMWOOD RD
700 ImCo 92243 431-A7
WORSCH DR
12100 SD 92130 1188-B7
WORSCH WY
4100 SD 92130 1188-B7
WORTHING AV
10800 SD 92126 1209-B3
WORTHINGTON RD
- SDCo 91905 (1320-A3 See Page 1300)
WORTHINGTON RD Rt#-S28
- ImCo 92251 431-A4
500 ImCo 92251 6439-C6
500 IMP 92251 431-A4
500 IMP 92251 6439-C6
1000 ImCo 92250 431-A4
1900 ImCo 92251 430-L4
WORTHINGTON ST
100 SDCo 91977 1290-J3
100 SD 92114 1290-J3
S WORTHINGTON ST
100 SDCo 91977 1290-J5
100 SDCo 91902 1290-J5
WOTAN DR
1000 ENCT 92024 1167-F1
WRANGLER CT
900 CHV 91902 1310-H4
WRANGLERS DR
300 SDCo 92004 1058-G6
WRELTON DR
600 SD 92037 1247-G5
600 SD 92109 1247-G5
WREN GN
1100 ESCN 92026 1109-E5
WREN ST
1100 SD 92114 1290-D2
7700 SNTE 92071 1230-G7
WREN WY
900 SMCS 92078 1128-E2
WREN BLUFF DR
- SDCo 92127 1169-E4
WREN HAVEN WY
- SDCo 92127 1169-G4
WRIGHT AV
- CORD 92135 1288-G3
WRIGHT PL
1900 CRLB 92008 1127-C3
WRIGHT RD
- ImCo 92250 431-D4
WRIGHT ST
3400 SD 92140 1268-G6
3500 SD 92110 1268-G6
WRIGHT CANYON RD
- SDCo 92040 (1193-E4 See Page 1192)
WRIGHTWOOD RD
31600 SDCo 92003 1068-D1
31800 SDCo 92003 1048-D7
WUESTE RD
1700 CHV 91915 (1312-A5 See Page 1293)
1800 CHV 91915 1332-A1
2200 SD 91915 1332-A1
WULFF ST
800 SMCS 92069 1109-B5
WUNDERLIN AV
6000 SD 92114 1290-C3
WYANDOTTE AV
2700 SD 92117 1228-B7
2700 SD 92117 1248-B1
WYATT CT
- SD 92154 1350-H2
WYATT PL
- SD 92154 1350-H2
1500 ELCJ 92020 1251-D4
WYCLIFFE ST
10000 SNTE 92071 1231-D2
WYCONDA LN
4800 SD 92113 1290-A6
WYCONDA WY
1300 SD 92113 1290-A6
WYE ST
14600 SD 92129 1189-H1
WYEPORT RD
15400 SDCo 92065 1172-A5
WYETH RD
13700 SDCo 92021 1232-E5
WYKES ST
400 CHV 91911 1330-B3
WYMAN WY
9600 SDCo 91977 1271-C7
WYNDEMERE CT
- SDCo 92026 1109-G1
WYNDEMERE LN
- SDCo 92026 1109-G1
WYNDHAVEN DR
13300 SD 92130 1188-A4
13600 SD 92130 1187-J4
WYNELAND RD
15600 SDCo 92025 1151-B3
WYNELL LN
3000 LMGR 91945 1270-J6
WYNGATE PT
13300 SD 92130 1188-C4
WYNN ST
1200 OCN 92054 1086-A5
WYNOLA RD
3700 SDCo 92036 1136-A3
3800 SDCo 92036 1135-G5
WYNOLA ST
100 SDCo 92065 1172-D1
WYNWOOD CT
- ESCN 92027 1130-J3
WYOMING AV
6900 LMSA 91942 1270-E1
WYSTONE DR
1300 SD 92113 1290-A6

X

XANA WY
6700 CRLB 92009 1127-J4
6700 CRLB 92009 1128-A5
XAVIER AV
800 CHV 91913 1311-C5
XENOPHON ST
3000 SD 92106 1268-C7
3800 SD 92107 1268-B6

Y

YACON CIR
200 VSTA 92083 1087-E7
YACON ST
200 VSTA 92083 1087-E7
YACOO CT
- SDCo 91935 1292-G2
YAH WY
3600 SDCo 91902 1310-J1
YALE AV
4000 LMSA 91941 1270-F4
YALE DR
3700 OCN 92056 1107-A2
YALE ST
1600 CHV 91913 1311-C5
YAMA ST
2100 SD 92113 1289-G7
YANKEE CT
2100 ESCN 92029 1129-E6
YANKEE POINT WY
800 OCN 92054 1066-E6
YANKTON DR
12900 PWY 92064 1190-D4
YAQUI DR
14000 SDCo 92036 1176-E5
YAQUI RD
1400 SDCo 92004 1058-G5
YAQUI PASS RD
3400 SDCo 92004 (1079-F6 See Page 1058)
3700 SDCo 92004 (1099-F1 See Page 1098)
YAQUI PASS RD Rt#-S3
3700 SDCo 92004 (1099-E6 See Page 1098)
3700 SDCo 92004 (1118-J5 See Page 1098)
3700 SDCo 92004 (1119-A4 See Page 1098)
5600 SDCo 92036 (1118-J5 See Page 1098)
YAQUI WELLS RD
- SDCo 92004 (1118-E5 See Page 1098)
- SDCo 92036 (1118-E5 See Page 1098)
YARMOUTH CT
700 SD 92109 1247-H7
YARROW DR
6100 CRLB 92011 1127-D3
YARROW WY
- SMCS 92078 1128-H3
YAWEH LN
- SDCo 91906 (1317-G3 See Page 1296)
YAZOO ST
14400 SD 92129 1189-H2
YBARRA RD
3300 SDCo 91978 1271-F6
YEARLING CT
5700 SDCo 91902 1311-B2
YEARLING GLEN RD
- SD 92130 1208-C2
YELLOW PINE CT
- SDCo 92026 1089-B2
YELLOW PINE PL
- CHV 91915 1311-H2
YELLOW ROSE LN
- SDCo 92127 1169-G1
YELLOWSTONE AV
1400 CHV 91915 1311-J6
YELLOWSTONE PL
9700 SNTE 92071 1231-E4
YELLOWTAIL WY
2000 SD 92139 1290-D7
YELLOWTHROAT RD
13800 PWY 92064 1170-F5
YERBA LN
3500 CHV 91902 1310-G3
YERBA ANITA DR
5200 SD 92115 1270-A1
5400 SD 92115 1269-J1
YERBA ANITA WY
4900 SD 92115 1270-A2
YERBA BUENA DR
3200 SDCo 92028 1028-D1
YERBA SANTA DR
4400 SD 92115 1269-J1
4700 SD 92115 1270-A2
YERBA SANTA RD
23900 SDCo 91963 (1315-J5 See Page 1294)
23900 SDCo 91963 (1316-A5 See Page 1296)
YERBA VALLEY RD
12400 SDCo 92040 1212-D4
YERBA VALLEY WY
12400 SDCo 92040 1212-D3
YERBA VERDE DR
1100 ELCJ 92020 1251-D3
YERMO CT
16500 SDCo 92127 1169-F4
YESTERYEAR LN
2500 SDCo 92028 1028-B2
YETTFORD RD
1700 VSTA 92083 1108-A3
1800 SDCo 92083 1108-A3
YEW LN
9600 SDCo 92029 1149-D4
YMCA WY
100 SD 92102 1289-J4
YNEZ PL
1300 CORD 92118 1288-J7
1400 CORD 92118 1308-J1
YNEZ PTH
3800 SDCo 92004 (1099-E1 See Page 1098)
YOCUM RD
- ImCo 92233 411-C10
YODEL LN
1900 SD 92154 1350-A1
YOKOHAMA CT
5800 SD 92120 1250-E7
YOKUM CT
100 SDCo 92028 1027-E2
YOLANDA AV
9400 SD 92123 1249-F6
YOLANDA PL
2400 SD 92123 1249-F6
YOLO CT
8300 SD 92129 1189-B6
YONGE ST
3000 SD 92106 1268-C7
4000 SD 92107 1268-B6
YORBA CT
1300 CHV 91910 1311-B6
YORBA LINDA CT
24200 SDCo 92065 1173-E2
YORK AV
1200 ESCN 92027 1110-A7
13800 PWY 92064 1190-E2
YORK CT
700 SD 92109 1247-H7
YORK DR
1100 VSTA 92083 1108-B1
1200 SDCo 92084 1108-B2
YORK PL
1500 ESCN 92027 1110-B7
YORK RD
2700 CRLB 92010 1106-J4
YORK RD Rt#-S24
1400 ImCo 92283 432-D4
YORKSHIRE AV
5600 LMSA 91942 1250-J7
YORKTOWN DR
3700 SD 92124 1249-G5
YORKTOWN ST
1500 IMPB 91932 1349-J2
YORK VIEW CIR
1700 SDCo 92084 1108-C2

STREET
Block City ZIP Pg-Grid

YOSEMITE DR
800 CHV 91914 1311-H4
YOSEMITE ST
3400 SD 92109 1268-A1
3600 SD 92109 1248-A7
4300 CRLB 92010 1106-J5
YOSEMITE WY
2600 CHV 91914 1311-H4
YOST CIR
5200 SD 92109 1247-J4
YOST DR
1400 SD 92109 1247-J4
YOST PL
5200 SD 92109 1247-J4
YOUNG RD
- ImCo 92233 411-C10
YOUNG ST
1300 ELCJ 92020 1251-D4
YOUNGSTOWN WY
9200 SD 92121 1208-F7
YOURELL AV
1200 CRLB 92008 1106-E3
YOURMAN RD
- ImCo 92243 6560-F3
700 CALX 92231 6620-F4
700 CALX 92249 6620-F4
1000 ImCo 92249 6560-F6
1000 ImCo 92249 6620-F2
YSABEL CREEK RD
15800 SD 92025 1131-B7
15800 SD 92025 1151-B1
YSIDRO DR
24300 SDCo 92065 1173-E1
YUBA DR
700 CHV 91902 1311-D5
YUCATAN WY
1600 SDCo 92028 1027-F5
YUCCA AV
3300 SD 92117 1248-D3
YUCCA DR
200 ELCN 92243 6559-F1
2500 SDCo 91906 (1297-E5
See Page 1296)
3200 SDCo 92036 1156-E1
YUCCA RD
400 SDCo 92028 1028-D1
1700 OCN 92054 1106-F1
YUCCA ST
- IMP 92251 6499-D3
14000 SDCo 91935 1272-H7
14000 SDCo 91935 1292-H1
YUCCA TER
900 SDCo 92028 1028-D3
YUCCA TR
10400 SDCo 92026 1089-F2
YUCCA WY
3500 SDCo 92028 1028-D2
YUCCA HILL RD
2200 SDCo 91901 1253-J1
YUCCA RIDGE LN
700 SDCo 92069 1109-B2
YUKI LN
4300 CRLB 92008 1106-G7
YUKON ST
14500 SD 92129 1189-H1
YUMA AV
4700 OCN 92057 1087-B1
4800 OCN 92057 1067-B7
YUMA GN
1000 ESCN 92026 1109-F6
YUMA RD
34600 SDCo 92036 1176-D4
YUMA ST
5700 SD 92110 1268-G3
YVETTE WY
3700 CRLB 92008 1106-G6
YVONNE ST
2800 OCN 92056 1087-C7

Z

Z ST
3500 SD 92113 1289-F6
25800 SDCo 92026 1109-E1
ZABEL CT
8800 SDCo 91977 1271-A5
ZABYN ST
2200 OCN 92054 1106-E1
ZAC CANYON PL
1400 CHV 91913 1331-B2
ZACHARY GN
1500 ESCN 92027 1110-B5
ZADA LN
200 VSTA 92084 1088-A6
ZAGALA CT
11000 SD 92124 1250-A2
ZAMORA CT
- CHV 91913 1331-E2
ZAMORA WY
4600 OCN 92056 1107-F4
7200 CRLB 92009 1127-F7
ZANE CT
6700 SD 92111 1248-J6
ZANJA PL
24700 SDCo 92065 1173-G2
ZANZIBAR CT
700 SD 92109 1247-H7
ZANZIBAR RD
- ELCJ 92021 1251-J5
ZAPATA AV
10000 SD 92126 1209-B2
E ZAPATA ST
- CALX 92231 6620-H6
ZAPO ST
1700 DLMR 92014 1187-F4
ZAPPONE RD
- ImCo - 411-J11
ZARINA LN
400 ENCT 92024 1147-G5
ZARINA LAKE DR
- SDCo 91905 (1320-A4
See Page 1300)
ZARZA CTE
1100 CHV 91910 1311-A7
ZEALAND WY
8100 LMGR 91945 1270-H7
ZEBRINA PL
6900 CRLB 92011 1127-E6
ZED ST
3900 SD 92117 1248-E4
ZEIGLER CT
15700 SDCo 92065 1173-J4
ZEIJL LN
8500 SDCo 92040 1232-A7
ZEILIN ST
- SDCo 92055 1067-A1
ZEISS ST
1400 OCN 92054 1086-B5
ZELDA AV
4600 LMSA 91941 1270-F3
ZELLER ST
1700 SD 92114 1290-E1
ZEMBER CT
200 VSTA 92083 1108-A2
ZEMCO DR
7500 LMGR 91945 1290-G2
ZEMKE AV
13700 SD 92129 1189-D3
ZENA DR
6400 SD 92115 1270-D5
ZENAKO CT
6000 SD 92122 1228-E6
ZENAKO ST
3900 SD 92122 1228-E6
ZENCARO AV
8800 SD 92123 1249-C6
ZENITH LN
4200 OCN 92056 1107-C2
ZENITH ST
100 CHV 91911 1330-C5
ZENOR LN
- SDCo 92127 1169-G2
ZENOS RD
1200 ImCo 92250 431-D5
ZENOS WY
4800 OCN 92056 1107-F6
ZEPHYR AV
1500 ELCJ 92021 1252-B2
ZERMATT LN
3600 SDCo 92025 1150-D2
ZEST CT
500 SD 92139 1290-G6
ZEST ST
7200 SD 92139 1290-G6
ZETA ST
8200 LMSA 91942 1250-J7
ZEZERE DR
400 OCN 92057 1086-J4
ZIGA DR
28800 SDCo 92082 1071-A7
ZILLIOX LN
500 SMCS 92069 1108-J6
ZIMMER CV
5000 SD 92130 1188-D5
ZINFANDEL TER
500 CHV 91913 1311-D4
ZINNIA CT
4300 SD 92154 1330-G7
6800 CRLB 92011 1127-A5
ZINNIA HILLS PL
- SD 92130 1188-F3
ZION AV
4400 SD 92120 1249-J6
4800 SD 92120 1250-A6
ZION CT
300 SDCo 92065 1153-A7
ZIPS WY
- SDCo 92082 1049-F7
- SDCo 92082 1069-F1
ZIRBEL CT
11900 SD 92131 1210-B1
ZIRBEL WY
- SD 92131 1210-B1
ZIRCON PL
- CRLB 92009 1127-H5
ZIRCON ST
5500 SD 92114 1290-B2
ZLATIBOR RANCH RD
600 ESCN 92025 1130-C5
1900 SDCo 92025 1130-C5
ZLATIBOR RANCH TER
600 SDCo 92025 1130-C5
ZODIAC ST
6700 CRLB 92009 1127-G6
ZOE ST
3800 SD 92117 1248-E5
ZOLA GN
1800 ESCN 92026 1109-F6
ZOLA ST
3000 SD 92106 1268-C6
ZOLDER CT
2000 SDCo 92019 1272-C4
ZOLDERO RD
11400 SDCo 91941 1271-H4
11400 SDCo 92020 1271-H4
ZONA GALE RD
900 ENCT 92024 1147-F6
ZOO DR
2900 SD 92101 1269-C7
3000 SD 92103 1269-C7
ZOO PL
1800 SD 92101 1269-C7
2000 SD 92101 1289-C1
ZOO RD
- SD 92027 1130-J6
ZORA ST
6000 LMSA 91942 1250-G6
ZORITA CT
11200 SD 92124 1250-A2
ZORO WY
1600 SD 92154 1349-J2
ZUBARON LN
7000 CRLB 92009 1127-G7
ZUKOR GN
- ESCN 92025 1129-H2
ZULU WY
2600 SD 92139 1310-F1
ZUMAQUE ST
6900 SDCo 92067 1168-G3
ZUMBROTA RD
3200 SDCo 91901 1234-D4
ZUNI DR
400 DLMR 92014 1187-F4
ZUNI TR
1600 SDCo 92004 (1099-E1
See Page 1098)
ZURA WY
- SD 92115 1270-C2
- SD 92182 1270-C2
ZURICH DR
1100 SD 92154 1350-A1
ZUTANO LN
1500 SDCo 92028 998-B6

#

1ST AV
- CHV 91910 1310-C4
300 SD 92101 1289-A1
600 ImCo 92283 432-C5
600 CHV 91910 1330-D1
700 CHV 91911 1330-E3
2600 SD 92103 1269-A5
2600 SD 92103 1289-A1
1ST LN
1400 SD 92154 1350-D2
1ST PL
800 SDCo 92029 1149-E2
1ST ST
- CORD 92135 1288-F4
- ImCo 92251 6439-E7
- SDCo 92004 (1121-G2
See Page 1100)
- NATC 91950 1289-H7
- SDCo 92059 1029-J4
100 SDCo 92065 1152-J6
100 CALX 92231 6680-G2
100 IMP 92251 6439-E7
200 ELCN 92243 6499-J6
300 CORD 92118 1288-J5
800 ELCN 92243 6559-J1
1000 ELCJ 92021 1251-H2
1000 SDCo 92021 1251-H2
1100 ENCT 92024 1167-C1
1200 SDCo 92036 1136-B7
1400 CORD 92118 1289-A5
1400 OCN 92054 1086-B7
2100 NATC 91950 1290-A6
3800 SMCS 92078 1128-C1
5100 SDCo 92028 998-J4
9000 SNTE 92071 1231-E6
10600 SDCo 91978 1271-F7
10600 SDCo 91978 1291-F1
N 1ST ST
500 ELCJ 92021 1251-H4
800 SDCo 92021 1251-H4
S 1ST ST
100 ELCJ 92019 1251-H6
100 ELCJ 92020 1251-H6
2ND AV
- CHV 91910 1310-B5
300 SD 92101 1289-A1
600 CHV 91910 1330-C1
700 CHV 91911 1330-D3
2600 SD 92103 1269-A7
2600 SD 92103 1289-A1
E 2ND AV
400 ESCN 92025 1129-J2
400 ESCN 92025 1130-A2
E 2ND AV Rt#-S6
100 ESCN 92025 1129-J3
N 2ND AV
- CHV 91910 1310-B4
3000 NATC 91950 1310-B3
3200 CHV 91950 1310-B3
3200 NATC 91910 1310-B3
W 2ND AV
500 ESCN 92025 1129-H3
W 2ND AV Rt#-S6
200 ESCN 92025 1129-J3
2ND LN
1400 SD 92154 1350-D2
2ND PL
19800 SDCo 92029 1149-E2
2ND ST
- CORD 92135 1288-F4
- ImCo 92243 6560-A7
- ImCo 92249 6560-B7
- SD 92152 1308-A1
- SDCo 92004 (1121-G2
See Page 1100)
- SDCo 92055 1066-B2
- NATC 91950 1289-H7
- SDCo 92059 1029-J4
- CALX 92231 6680-G2
100 ENCT 92024 1147-B6
100 IMP 92251 6439-E6
200 SDCo 92065 1152-H5
200 ELCN 92243 6499-J6
300 CORD 92118 1288-J5
700 IMPB 91932 1329-F7
800 ENCT 92024 1167-C1
900 IMPB 91932 1349-F1
1400 CORD 92118 1289-A6
1600 ELCN 92243 6559-J1
1800 SDCo 92036 1136-B7
2000 NATC 91950 1290-B6
4900 SDCo 92028 998-H4
10400 SNTE 92071 1231-E3
10700 SDCo 91978 1291-F1
10700 SDCo 91978 1271-F7
10800 SDCo 92040 1231-E3
N 2ND ST
700 ELCJ 92021 1251-J3
1500 SDCo 92021 1251-J3
N 2ND ST Rt#-54
300 ELCJ 92021 1251-J5
S 2ND ST
- ELCN 92243 6559-J2
200 ELCJ 92019 1251-J6
300 SDCo 92019 1251-J7
W 2ND ST
- NATC 91950 1289-H7
- NATC 91950 1309-G1
100 CALX 92231 6680-F2
3RD AV
- CHV 91910 1310-A4
300 SD 92101 1289-A1
800 CHV 91910 1330-C1
1000 CHV 91911 1330-C1
2600 SD 92103 1269-A4
2600 SD 92103 1289-A1
E 3RD AV
100 ESCN 92025 1129-J3
500 ESCN 92025 1130-A2
W 3RD AV
100 ESCN 92025 1129-J3
3RD LN
1400 SD 92154 1350-D2
3RD PL
19400 SDCo 92029 1149-E2
3RD ST
- CORD 92135 1288-F4
- ImCo 92249 6560-B7
- SD 92152 1308-A1
- SDCo 92004 (1121-G2
See Page 1100)
- CALX 92231 6680-G2
100 ENCT 92024 1147-B6
100 IMP 92251 6439-E6
200 SDCo 92065 1152-H5
200 NATC 91950 1289-H7
200 NATC 91950 1309-H1
200 SDCo 92055 1066-B2
200 SDCo 92036 1136-B7
300 CORD 92118 1289-A6
500 ELCN 92243 6499-J5
500 IMPB 91932 1329-F7
700 ELCJ 92021 1252-A4
800 ENCT 92024 1167-B1
800 CORD 92118 1288-J6
900 IMPB 91932 1349-F1
1700 ELCN 92243 6559-J1
2000 NATC 91950 1290-A7
4500 LMSA 91941 1270-J3
10700 SDCo 91978 1291-F1
10700 SDCo 91978 1271-F7
3RD ST Rt#-S16
- SDCo 92059 1029-H4
3RD ST Rt#-282
300 CORD 92118 1288-H5
E 3RD ST
- NATC 91950 1309-H1
N 3RD ST
100 ELCJ 92019 1252-A5
600 ELCJ 92021 1252-A5
S 3RD ST
100 ELCJ 92019 1252-A5
W 3RD ST
- NATC 91950 1309-G1
4TH AV
- CHV 91910 1310-A5
200 SD 92101 1289-A2
600 CHV 91910 1330-C2
800 CHV 91911 1330-C2
2600 SD 92103 1269-A5
2600 SD 92103 1289-A2
E 4TH AV
100 ESCN 92025 1129-J3
300 ESCN 92025 1130-A2
N 4TH AV
- CHV 91910 1310-A4
2200 NATC 91910 1310-A4
W 4TH AV
100 ESCN 92025 1129-J3
4TH LN
1300 SD 92154 1350-C2
4TH PL
19300 SDCo 92029 1149-E2
4TH ST
- CORD 92135 1288-F5
- SDCo 92055 1066-C1
- CALX 92231 6680-G2
100 ENCT 92024 1147-B6
100 IMP 92251 6439-E6
100 DLMR 92014 1187-F6
200 ELCJ 92019 1252-B4
200 SDCo 92065 1152-H5
500 IMPB 91932 1329-F7
500 NATC 91950 1289-J7
500 NATC 91950 1309-H1
600 SDCo 92019 1252-B4
800 ENCT 92024 1167-B1
900 ELCN 92243 6499-H5
900 IMPB 91932 1349-F1
1500 NATC 91950 1290-A7
1900 SDCo 92036 1136-B7
3100 SD 92114 1290-A7
4400 LMSA 91941 1270-J3
8900 SNTE 92071 1231-E6
10700 SDCo 91978 1291-F1
4TH ST Rt#-S32
200 HOLT 92250 431-E5
4TH ST Rt#-75
300 CORD 92118 1288-H5
4TH ST Rt#-86
400 ELCN 92243 6499-H6
1700 ELCN 92243 6559-J1
4TH ST Rt#-282
300 CORD 92118 1288-H5
E 4TH ST
- NATC 91950 1309-H1
W 4TH ST
- NATC 91950 1309-G1
200 NATC 92136 1309-F1
4S COMMONS DR
- SDCo 92127 1169-F3
4S RANCH PKWY
- SDCo 92127 1169-F1
5TH AV
- CHV 91910 1310-A5
100 SD 92101 1289-A2
500 CHV 91910 1330-B1
800 CHV 91911 1330-C3
2600 SD 92103 1269-A5
2600 SD 92103 1289-A2
E 5TH AV
200 ESCN 92025 1129-J3
300 ESCN 92025 1130-A3
N 5TH AV
- CHV 91910 1310-A5
W 5TH AV
800 ESCN 92025 1129-J3
5TH PL
9700 SDCo 92029 1149-E2
5TH ST
- SDCo 92055 1066-C1
- SDCo 92059 1029-H4
100 CALX 92231 6680-F2
100 IMP 92251 6439-E6
100 SDCo 92065 1152-H5
100 ENCT 92024 1147-B6
200 SDCo 92036 1136-B7
300 CORD 92118 1288-H6
400 ELCN 92243 6499-H5
500 IMPB 91932 1329-F6
800 NATC 91950 1289-J7
1100 ELCN 92243 6559-H1
1100 IMPB 91932 1349-F2
1300 SDCo 92055 1085-H5
1300 NATC 91950 1290-C6
2300 ENCT 92024 1167-J1
2600 ENCT 92024 1168-A1
3100 NATC 91950 1309-J1
4900 SDCo 92028 998-H5
5300 SDCo 92028 999-A5
10700 SDCo 91978 1291-F1
5TH ST Rt#-115
100 HOLT 92250 431-E5
E 5TH ST
- CALX 92231 6680-J2
- ImCo 92231 6680-J2
- NATC 91950 1309-H1
N 5TH ST
100 SDCo 92065 1152-H5
W 5TH ST
2900 NATC 91950 1309-H1
6TH AV
300 SD 92101 1289-B2
2500 SD 92103 1289-B2
2600 SD 92103 1269-A5
E 6TH AV
100 ESCN 92025 1129-J3
200 ESCN 92025 1130-A3
W 6TH AV
100 ESCN 92025 1129-J3
6TH PL
19400 SDCo 92029 1149-D3
6TH ST
- SDCo 92036 1136-B7
- SDCo 92055 1066-C1
- CALX 92231 6680-H1
- NATC 91950 1309-H1
- ImCo 92249 6560-B7
100 DLMR 92014 1187-F6
100 SDCo 92055 1085-H4
100 SDCo 92065 1152-H5
100 CORD 92118 1288-H6
200 SDCo 92059 1029-H4
200 ELCN 92243 6499-H4
200 IMP 92251 6439-E6
1000 NATC 91950 1289-J7
1100 ELCN 92243 6559-H1
1300 NATC 91950 1290-A7
2200 SDCo 91978 1271-F7
2200 SDCo 91978 1291-F1
7TH AV
300 SD 92101 1289-B2
2600 SD 92103 1269-A6
E 7TH AV
100 ESCN 92025 1129-J3
200 ESCN 92025 1130-A3
W 7TH AV
100 ESCN 92025 1129-J3
7TH PL
12400 SDCo 92029 1149-D3
7TH ST
- ImCo 92231 6680-H1
- ImCo 92281 411-A11
- SDCo 92055 1066-C1
- WEST 92281 411-A11
- CALX 92231 6680-F1
- ImCo 92249 6560-B7
100 CHV 91911 1330-C5
100 SDCo 92055 1085-H4
100 SDCo 92065 1152-H6
100 DLMR 92014 1187-F6
100 IMP 92251 6439-E6
300 CORD 92118 1288-H6
300 IMPB 91932 1329-G7
300 ELCN 92243 6499-H4
900 IMPB 91932 1349-G1
1100 ELCN 92243 6559-H1
1400 SMCS 92078 1108-C7
1500 NATC 91950 1289-J7
1500 NATC 91950 1290-C6
2200 ENCT 92024 1147-J7
2300 SDCo 91978 1291-F1
2300 ENCT 92024 1148-A7
3000 VSTA 92081 1108-C7
E 7TH ST
- NATC 91950 1309-H1
N 7TH ST
100 SDCo 92065 1152-G5
W 7TH ST
- NATC 91950 1309-H1
800 NATC 92136 1309-G2
8TH AV
400 SD 92101 1289-B1
3600 SD 92103 1269-B5
E 8TH AV
300 ESCN 92025 1130-A3
W 8TH AV
100 ESCN 92025 1129-H4
8TH PL
1200 SDCo 92029 1149-D4
8TH ST
- SDCo 92055 1066-D1
- CALX 92231 6680-G1
100 SDCo 92055 1085-H4
100 CORD 92118 1288-H6
100 DLMR 92014 1187-F6
100 SDCo 92065 1152-G6
400 SD 92014 1187-F6
500 ELCN 92243 6499-G3
600 IMPB 91932 1329-G7
900 IMPB 91932 1349-G1
1000 ELCN 92243 6559-G1
1100 OCN 92054 1086-A6
1400 ImCo 92243 6559-G1
1500 SMCS 92078 1108-D7
1500 NATC 91950 1290-B7
1700 ImCo 92243 6499-G3
1700 ImCo 92251 6499-G3
2000 SDCo 92028 998-J5
2200 SDCo 91978 1291-F1
2400 ENCT 92024 1147-J7
2400 ENCT 92024 1148-A7
5400 SDCo 92028 999-A5
E 8TH ST
- NATC 91950 1309-H1
1400 NATC 91950 1310-A1
1900 NATC 91950 1290-C7
N 8TH ST
100 SDCo 92065 1152-G5
W 8TH ST
100 NATC 91950 1309-G1
100 NATC 92136 1309-G1
2100 ENCT 92024 1147-J7
9TH AV
400 SD 92101 1289-B2
3900 SD 92103 1269-B4
E 9TH AV
100 ESCN 92025 1129-J4
100 ESCN 92025 1130-A3
W 9TH AV
200 ESCN 92025 1129-J4
1200 ESCN 92029 1129-F4
9TH ST
- SDCo 92055 1066-D1
- CALX 92231 6680-F1
- ImCo 92249 6620-B1
100 SDCo 92055 1085-G4
100 DLMR 92014 1187-F5
100 SDCo 92065 1152-G6
100 IMP 92251 6439-E5
300 CORD 92118 1288-G6
500 IMPB 91932 1329-G7
900 IMPB 91932 1349-G1
1000 ELCN 92243 6499-G6
1500 SMCS 92078 1108-C7
1600 NATC 91950 1310-A1
1800 ELCN 92243 6559-G1
2100 NATC 91950 1290-A7
2200 ENCT 92024 1147-J6
2200 SDCo 91978 1291-F1
2400 ENCT 92024 1148-A6
12300 PWY 92064 1190-C4
E 9TH ST
- NATC 91950 1309-H1
1000 NATC 91950 1310-A1
N 9TH ST
100 SDCo 92065 1152-G5
W 9TH ST
- NATC 91950 1309-H1
600 NATC 92136 1309-G2
10TH AV
1100 SD 92101 1289-B2
3700 SD 92103 1269-B5
E 10TH AV
100 ESCN 92025 1130-A4
W 10TH AV
100 ESCN 92025 1129-J4
100 ESCN 92025 1130-A4
10TH ST
- ImCo 92249 6620-B1
- CALX 92231 6680-F1
100 DLMR 92014 1187-F5
100 IMP 92251 6439-F5
200 CORD 92118 1288-G7
300 ELCN 92243 6499-G5
300 SDCo 92065 1152-G6
400 IMPB 91932 1329-H7
900 SDCo 92055 1066-D1
900 IMPB 91932 1349-H1
1000 ELCN 92243 6559-G1
1000 SDCo 92055 1085-H4
1600 NATC 91950 1310-A1
2100 NATC 91950 1290-B7
2200 SDCo 91978 1291-F1
W 10TH ST
1200 NATC 92136 1309-F2
11TH AV
- SD 92101 1289-B3
E 11TH AV
300 ESCN 92025 1130-A4
W 11TH AV
400 ESCN 92025 1129-J4
900 ESCN 92025 1130-A4
1400 ESCN 92029 1129-F5
11TH ST
- ELCN 92243 6499-G6
- SDCo 92055 409-A7
- SDCo 92055 1066-E1
- ImCo 92249 6620-B1
100 SDCo 92055 1085-H4
100 DLMR 92014 1187-F5
100 SDCo 92065 1152-G6
200 IMP 92251 6439-E5
500 IMPB 91932 1329-H7
900 IMPB 91932 1349-H1
1700 ELCN 92243 6559-G1
1700 NATC 91950 1310-A1
2200 ENCT 92024 1147-J6
2300 ENCT 92024 1148-A6
2800 NATC 91950 1290-B7
E 11TH ST
- NATC 91950 1309-H1
N 11TH ST
100 SDCo 92065 1152-G6
W 11TH ST
- NATC 91950 1309-G2
1200 NATC 92136 1309-F3
W 12TH AV
500 ESCN 92025 1129-J5
12TH PL
20200 SDCo 92029 1149-E2
12TH ST
- ImCo 92251 6439-E5
100 SDCo 92055 1085-G3
100 IMP 92251 6439-E5
100 SDCo 92065 1152-F6
100 DLMR 92014 1187-F5
200 ELCN 92243 6499-G4
500 IMPB 91932 1329-H7
900 IMPB 91932 1349-H1
1100 ELCN 92243 6559-G1
1600 NATC 91950 1310-A1
2200 ENCT 92024 1147-J5
2200 ENCT 92024 1148-A5
E 12TH ST
- NATC 91950 1309-J1
W 12TH ST
- NATC 91950 1309-G2
800 NATC 92136 1309-G3
E 13TH AV
200 ESCN 92025 1130-A4
W 13TH AV
500 ESCN 92025 1129-J4
800 ESCN 92025 1130-A4
13TH ST
100 SDCo 92055 1085-G3
100 DLMR 92014 1187-F5
100 SDCo 92065 1152-F6
100 IMP 92251 6439-E5
400 IMPB 91932 1329-H7
800 NATC 91950 1309-J1
900 IMPB 91932 1349-H1
1000 SD 92101 1289-B4
2100 ENCT 92024 1147-J5
2200 ENCT 92024 1148-A5
2200 NATC 91950 1310-B1
N 13TH ST
100 SDCo 92065 1152-F6
S 13TH ST
- SD 92101 1289-B4
W 14TH PL
900 ESCN 92025 1129-J5
14TH ST
- ImCo 92249 6620-B1
- ImCo 92251 6439-E5
- NATC 91950 1309-H2
- SD 92101 1289-B4
100 SDCo 92055 1085-G3
100 ESCN 92025 1130-A4
100 IMP 92251 6439-E5
100 SDCo 92065 1152-F6
200 ELCN 92243 6499-G6
300 DLMR 92014 1187-F5
800 SD 92154 1329-J7
900 SD 92154 1349-J2
1100 ELCN 92243 6559-G1
1100 IMPB 91932 1349-J2
1100 SD 91932 1349-J2
1100 NATC 91950 1310-A1
2100 ENCT 92024 1147-J5
2100 ENCT 92024 1148-A5
E 14TH ST
500 NATC 91950 1309-J2
N 14TH ST
100 SDCo 92065 1152-F6
S 14TH ST
- SD 92113 1289-B4
W 14TH ST
700 NATC 91950 1309-G2
E 15TH AV
100 ESCN 92025 1130-A4
W 15TH AV
400 ESCN 92025 1129-J5
500 ESCN 92025 1130-A4
15TH ST
100 DLMR 92014 1187-F5
100 IMP 92251 6439-E5
300 SD 92101 1289-C4
800 SD 92154 1329-J7
900 SD 92154 1349-J2
1100 IMPB 91932 1349-J2
1100 IMPB 92154 1349-J2
1100 SD 91932 1349-J2
1400 NATC 91950 1310-A1
1500 SDCo 92055 1047-A5
E 15TH ST
- NATC 91950 1309-H2
S 15TH ST
- SD 92113 1289-C4
W 15TH ST
- NATC 91950 1309-H2
W 16TH AV
700 ESCN 92025 1129-J5
16TH ST
- ELCN 92243 6559-F2
100 SDCo 92065 1152-F7
200 SD 92101 1289-C4
400 SDCo 92055 1047-A5
800 SD 92154 1329-J7
900 SD 92154 1349-J1
1000 SD 92113 1289-C4
1600 NATC 91950 1310-B1
3000 SD 92139 1310-B1
E 16TH ST
- NATC 91950 1309-H2
1100 NATC 91950 1310-A2
S 16TH ST
300 SD 92113 1289-C4
W 16TH ST
- NATC 91950 1309-G2
17TH AV
300 ESCN 92025 1130-B5
700 ESCN 92025 1130-C4
900 SDCo 92027 1130-C4
1200 SD 92101 1289-C2
17TH ST
100 SD 92113 1289-C4
100 NATC 91950 1309-H2
300 SD 92101 1289-C4
900 ELCN 92243 6499-F4
1000 NATC 91950 1310-B1
2700 SD 92139 1310-B1
S 17TH ST
200 SD 92113 1289-C4
18TH AV
500 ESCN 92025 1130-A5
18TH ST
- ImCo 92243 6559-F2
100 DLMR 92014 1187-F4
600 SD 92154 1330-A7
900 ELCN 92243 6499-F4
900 SD 92154 1350-A1
1100 ELCN 92243 6559-F1
1100 NATC 91950 1310-C1
2800 SD 92139 1310-C1
E 18TH ST
- NATC 91950 1309-J2
1000 NATC 91950 1310-A2
W 18TH ST
- NATC 91950 1309-G3
19TH ST
100 DLMR 92014 1187-F4
100 SD 92102 1289-C3
100 SD 92113 1289-C3
200 SD 92154 1330-A6
300 NATC 91950 1309-G3
800 ELCN 92243 6499-E5
900 SD 92154 1350-A1
1000 ELCN 92243 6559-F1
1100 SD 92101 1289-C3
1300 NATC 92136 1309-G3
2400 NATC 91950 1310-B1
2900 SD 92139 1310-C1
E 19TH ST
600 NATC 91950 1309-J2
S 19TH ST
- SD 92113 1289-C4
20TH ST
100 DLMR 92014 1187-F4
100 SD 92113 1289-C3
100 SD 92102 1289-C3
1000 NATC 91950 1310-B1
3100 SD 92139 1310-B1
E 20TH ST
- NATC 91950 1309-J2
1000 NATC 91950 1310-A2
S 20TH ST
- SD 92113 1289-C4
W 20TH ST
400 NATC 91950 1309-G3
21ST ST
100 DLMR 92014 1187-F4
100 ELCN 92243 6499-E6
100 SD 92113 1289-C3
100 SD 92102 1289-C3
E 21ST ST
100 NATC 91950 1309-J2
900 NATC 91950 1310-A2
S 21ST ST
- SD 92113 1289-C4
W 21ST ST
400 NATC 91950 1309-H3
22ND ST
100 DLMR 92014 1187-F4
100 ELCN 92243 6499-E6
300 SD 92102 1289-C3
900 NATC 91950 1310-A2
1000 SD 92113 1289-C3
1500 ELCN 92243 6559-E1
E 22ND ST
- NATC 91950 1309-J3
900 NATC 91950 1310-A2
S 22ND ST
- SD 92113 1289-C4
W 22ND ST
- NATC 91950 1309-G3
23RD ST
100 DLMR 92014 1187-F3
100 ELCN 92243 6499-E6
800 SD 92102 1289-C3
900 NATC 91950 1310-A2
1600 ELCN 92243 6559-E1
E 23RD ST
800 NATC 91950 1309-J3
1000 NATC 91950 1310-A3
W 23RD ST
700 NATC 91950 1309-G3
24TH ST
- SD 92113 1289-D4
100 DLMR 92014 1187-F3
100 SD 92102 1289-D3
700 SD 92154 1330-B7
900 NATC 91950 1310-A2
1500 ELCN 92243 6559-E1
1900 SDCo 91950 1310-B2
E 24TH ST
- NATC 91950 1309-J3
800 NATC 91950 1310-A3
S 24TH ST
- SD 92113 1289-D4
W 24TH ST
1500 NATC 91950 1309-G4
25TH ST
- NATC 91950 1309-H3
100 DLMR 92014 1187-F3
100 SD 92102 1289-D4
1100 SD 92154 1350-B1
1300 SD 92101 1289-D4
S 25TH ST
- SD 92113 1289-D4
26TH ST
100 DLMR 92014 1187-F3
600 SD 92102 1289-D3
900 NATC 91950 1310-A3
2500 SD 92104 1269-D7
E 26TH ST
- NATC 91950 1309-J3
S 26TH ST
900 SD 92113 1289-D4
W 26TH ST
- NATC 91950 1309-H3
26TH STREET RD
1300 SD 92101 1289-D2
27TH ST
100 CHV 91911 1330-C5
100 DLMR 92014 1187-F3
100 NATC 91950 1309-J3
100 SD 92102 1289-D3
800 SD 92154 1330-C7
900 SD 92154 1350-C2
S 27TH ST
200 SD 92113 1289-D4
28TH ST
100 SD 92102 1289-D2
200 DLMR 92014 1187-F3
800 NATC 91950 1310-A3
2000 SD 92101 1289-D2
2600 SD 92104 1269-D6
2600 SD 92101 1269-D7

STREET Block	City	ZIP	Pg-Grid
E 28TH ST			
-	NATC	91950	1309-J3
700	NATC	91950	1310-A3
S 28TH ST			
-	SD	92113	1289-E5
1200	SD	92136	1289-E5
W 28TH ST			
-	NATC	91950	1309-G4
29TH ST			
100	DLMR	92014	1187-F3
100	SD	92102	1289-E2
200	NATC	91950	1309-J4
2000	SD	92104	1289-E2
2700	SD	92104	1269-E6
S 29TH ST			
-	SD	92113	1289-E5
30TH PL			
600	SD	92102	1289-E3
30TH ST			
100	SD	92102	1289-E2
600	NATC	91950	1310-A3
1100	SD	92154	1350-D1
1200	CHV	91950	1310-A3
2000	SD	92104	1289-E2
2500	SD	92104	1269-E5
4400	SD	92116	1269-E5
E 30TH ST			
-	NATC	91950	1309-J4
600	NATC	91950	1310-A3
S 30TH ST			
-	SD	92113	1289-E5
1300	SD	92136	1289-E6
W 30TH ST			
-	NATC	91950	1309-H4
31ST ST			
-	NATC	91950	1309-J4
100	SD	92102	1289-E2
2000	SD	92104	1289-E2
3000	SD	92104	1269-E6
S 31ST ST			
-	SD	92113	1289-E5
32ND ST			
-	SD	92113	1289-F3
100	SD	92102	1289-E2
200	CHV	91950	1309-J4
400	NATC	91950	1309-G5
400	NATC	91950	1310-C3
2000	SD	92104	1289-E2
2300	SDCo	91950	1310-C3
2500	SD	92104	1269-E5
4400	SD	92116	1269-E3
S 32ND ST			
-	SD	92113	1289-F5
-	SD	92102	1289-F5
1400	SD	92136	1289-F6
33RD PL			
4300	SD	92104	1269-F4
4400	SD	92116	1269-F4
33RD ST			
-	NATC	91950	1309-J4
100	SD	92102	1289-F1
2600	SD	92104	1269-F4
2700	SD	92104	1289-F1
4400	SD	92116	1269-F4
S 33RD ST			
-	SD	92102	1289-F5
-	SD	92113	1289-F5
34TH ST			
300	SD	92102	1289-F3
2400	SD	92104	1269-F4
2400	SD	92104	1289-F1
4100	SD	92116	1269-F4
35TH PL			
4500	SD	92116	1269-F4
35TH ST			
-	NATC	91950	1309-J5
3600	SD	92104	1269-F4
4300	SD	92116	1269-F2
N 35TH ST			
-	SD	92102	1289-F3
S 35TH ST			
-	SD	92113	1289-F5
36TH ST			
300	SD	92102	1289-G4
1400	SD	92113	1289-G4
3500	SD	92104	1269-F4
4400	SD	92116	1269-F4
N 36TH ST			
100	SD	92102	1289-F4
S 36TH ST			
100	SD	92113	1289-G5
37TH ST			
3400	SD	92105	1269-G6
4200	SD	92104	1269-G4
4400	SD	92116	1269-G4
S 37TH ST			
200	SD	92113	1289-G5
38TH ST			
3000	SD	92105	1269-G4
4400	SD	92116	1269-G3
N 38TH ST			
1000	SD	92102	1289-G3
1300	SD	92105	1289-G2
S 38TH ST			
200	SD	92113	1289-G6
39TH ST			
2800	SD	92105	1269-G4
3800	SD	92116	1269-G3
N 39TH ST			
800	SD	92102	1289-G3
1700	SD	92105	1289-G1
S 39TH ST			
700	SD	92113	1289-G5
40TH ST			
2500	SD	92105	1269-G5
4500	SD	92116	1269-G4
N 40TH ST			
600	SD	92102	1289-G3
S 40TH ST			
200	SD	92113	1289-H5
41ST ST			
3100	SD	92105	1269-G4
4400	SD	92116	1269-G4
N 41ST ST			
300	SD	92102	1289-H3
S 41ST ST			
700	SD	92113	1289-H6
42ND ST			
3400	SD	92105	1269-H4
4400	SD	92116	1269-H3
N 42ND ST			
800	SD	92102	1289-H3
1600	SD	92105	1289-H2
S 42ND ST			
600	SD	92113	1289-H5
43RD ST			
3100	SD	92105	1269-H6
N 43RD ST			
-	SDCo	92102	1289-H4
300	SD	92102	1289-H4
S 43RD ST			
900	SD	92113	1289-H6
1700	NATC	91950	1289-H6
44TH ST			
100	SD	92102	1289-H3
100	SDCo	92102	1289-J4
2400	SD	92105	1289-H1
2500	SD	92105	1269-H5
4100	SD	92115	1269-H4
S 44TH ST			
700	SD	92113	1289-H5
45TH ST			
3000	SD	92105	1269-J5
4100	SD	92115	1269-H4
N 45TH ST			
400	SD	92102	1289-J3
S 45TH ST			
200	SD	92113	1289-J5
46TH ST			
900	SD	92102	1289-J3
2500	SD	92105	1269-J5
4200	SD	92115	1269-J4
N 46TH ST			
400	SD	92102	1289-J4
S 46TH ST			
200	SD	92113	1289-J5
47TH ST			
500	SD	92102	1289-J3
1400	SD	92105	1289-J2
2800	SD	92105	1269-J5
4200	SD	92115	1269-J4
S 47TH ST			
100	SD	92113	1289-J4
100	SD	92113	1289-J5
48TH ST			
600	SD	92102	1289-J1
1200	SD	92113	1290-A6
4000	SD	92113	1289-J5
4000	SD	92105	1269-J5
4200	SD	92115	1269-J4
6000	SD	92120	1249-J7
49TH ST			
100	SD	92102	1290-A2
1600	SD	92102	1289-J2
3800	SD	92105	1270-A5
4100	SD	92115	1270-A3
6300	SD	92120	1250-A6
S 49TH ST			
1000	SD	92113	1290-A5
50TH ST			
100	SD	92102	1290-A1
1300	SD	92113	1290-A6
1300	NATC	91950	1290-A6
3600	SD	92105	1270-A5
4100	SD	92115	1270-A4
5000	SD	92120	1250-A5
51ST ST			
500	SD	92114	1290-A3
2600	SD	92105	1270-A6
4200	SD	92115	1270-A3
6500	SD	92120	1250-A5
52ND PL			
5200	SD	92105	1270-A5
52ND ST			
2100	SD	92105	1290-A1
2400	SD	92105	1270-A5
4100	SD	92115	1270-A5
53RD ST			
200	SD	92114	1290-B4
2800	SD	92105	1270-B7
4300	SD	92115	1270-A4
54TH PL			
4100	SD	92105	1270-B4
4200	SD	92115	1270-B4
54TH ST			
400	SD	92114	1290-B3
1800	SD	92105	1290-A1
2400	SD	92105	1270-B5
4200	SD	92115	1270-A2
55TH PL			
5000	SD	92115	1270-B2
55TH ST			
2100	SD	92105	1290-B1
2100	SD	92114	1290-B4
2400	SD	92105	1270-B6
4500	SD	92115	1270-B1
5100	SD	92182	1270-B1
56TH PL			
5500	SD	92114	1290-B3
56TH ST			
600	SD	92114	1290-B3
2300	SD	92105	1270-B7
4300	SD	92115	1270-B4
57TH ST			
900	SD	92114	1290-B2
58TH PL			
5700	SD	92115	1270-B4
58TH ST			
100	SD	92114	1290-C5
3800	SD	92105	1270-B6
3800	SD	92115	1270-B4
59TH ST			
300	SD	92114	1290-C3
4400	SD	92115	1270-C3
S 59TH ST			
400	SD	92114	1290-C5
60TH ST			
500	SD	92114	1290-C2
3200	SD	92105	1270-C6
3900	SD	92115	1270-C3
61ST ST			
100	SD	92114	1290-C3
62ND ST			
500	SD	92114	1290-D3
4500	SD	92115	1270-C3
63RD ST			
300	SD	92114	1290-D3
4500	SD	92115	1270-C2
64TH ST			
500	SD	92114	1290-D3
4900	SD	92115	1270-D2
65TH ST			
100	SD	92114	1290-D3
66TH ST			
200	SD	92114	1290-E3
67TH ST			
600	SD	92114	1290-E3
4500	SD	92115	1270-E2
68TH ST			
200	SD	92114	1290-E3
4200	LMSA	91941	1270-E3
4200	SD	92115	1270-E2
69TH PL			
4800	SD	92115	1270-E2
69TH ST			
100	SD	92114	1290-E3
1300	LMGR	91945	1290-E2
1300	LMGR	92114	1290-E2
1300	SD	91945	1290-E2
2300	LMGR	91945	1270-E7
3600	SD	92115	1270-E2
70TH ST			
4200	LMSA	91941	1270-E4
4800	SD	92115	1270-E4
5000	LMSA	92115	1270-E4
5100	SD	91941	1270-E4
71ST ST			
600	SD	92114	1290-F3
4300	LMSA	91941	1270-F3
4800	SD	92115	1270-F2
5000	LMSA	92115	1270-F2
72ND ST			
4900	SD	92115	1270-F2
73RD ST			
4500	LMSA	91941	1270-F3
4800	SD	92115	1270-F3
NW 191ST PL			
9600	SNTE	92071	1231-A4
NW 204TH ST			
1400	SD	92037	1227-G7
I-5 SAN DIEGO FRWY			
-	CHV	-	1309-H4
-	CHV	-	1329-J1
-	CHV	-	1330-A3
-	CRLB	-	1106-F6
-	CRLB	-	1126-G2
-	CRLB	-	1127-A6
-	CRLB	-	1147-A1
-	ENCT	-	1147-C5
-	ENCT	-	1167-D2
-	NATC	-	1289-C2
-	NATC	-	1309-G1
-	OCN	-	1085-G2
-	OCN	-	1086-A6
-	OCN	-	1106-C1
-	SCLE	-	1023-E3
-	SD	-	1187-H2
-	SD	-	1207-J1
-	SD	-	1208-A4
-	SD	-	1228-B4
-	SD	-	1248-B2
-	SD	-	1268-E3
-	SD	-	1288-J1
-	SD	-	1289-C2
-	SD	-	1330-A6
-	SD	-	1350-D3
-	SDCo	-	408-H5
-	SDCo	-	1023-E3
-	SDCo	-	1085-G2
-	SOLB	-	1167-D2
-	SOLB	-	1187-H2
I-8 Bus HIGHWAY 8 BUSINESS			
2000	ELCJ	-	1252-C1
9700	SDCo	-	1252-C1
13000	SDCo	-	1232-E6
13100	SDCo	-	1232-E6
I-8 EVAN HEWES HWY			
-	ImCo	-	431-F6
I-8 FRWY			
-	ELCJ	-	1251-F4
-	ELCJ	-	1252-B3
-	ELCJ	-	1271-C1
-	ELCN	-	6559-J2
-	ELCN	-	6560-C1
-	ImCo	-	430-K6
-	ImCo	-	431-D6
-	ImCo	-	432-A5
-	ImCo	-	6559-F2
-	ImCo	-	6560-J1
-	LMSA	-	1251-B7
-	LMSA	-	1270-E1
-	LMSA	-	1271-C1
-	SD	-	1269-H1
-	SD	-	1270-A1
-	SDCo	-	430-A6
-	SDCo	-	1232-J4
-	SDCo	-	1233-E3
-	SDCo	-	1234-A5
-	SDCo	-	1235-F5
-	SDCo	-	1236-A7
-	SDCo	-	1237-A7
-	SDCo	-	1252-B3
-	SDCo	-	(1299-C1
			See Page 1298)
-	SDCo	-	1300-A2
-	SDCo	-	(1301-A6
			See Page 1300)
-	SDCo	-	(1321-F1
			See Page 1300)
I-8 MISSION VALLEY FRWY			
-	SD	-	1268-F4
-	SD	-	1269-B3
I-8 OCEAN BEACH FRWY			
-	SD	-	1268-B5
I-15 AVOCADO HWY			
-	ESCN	-	1109-E3
-	ESCN	-	1129-F1
-	RivC	-	998-H3
-	RivC	-	999-A2
-	SDCo	-	998-H3
-	SDCo	-	1028-G4
-	SDCo	-	1048-H4
-	SDCo	-	1068-H4
-	SDCo	-	1088-J1
-	SDCo	-	1089-B4
-	SDCo	-	1109-E3
-	SDCo	-	1129-F1
I-15 ESCONDIDO FRWY			
-	ESCN	-	1109-E3
-	ESCN	-	1129-H5
-	ESCN	-	1150-A1
-	RivC	-	998-H5
-	SD	-	1150-A1
-	SD	-	1169-J6
-	SD	-	1170-A3
-	SD	-	1189-F6
-	SD	-	1209-F4
-	SD	-	1229-F5
-	SD	-	1249-F3
-	SD	-	1269-G2
-	SDCo	-	998-H5
-	SDCo	-	1028-G4
-	SDCo	-	1048-J4
-	SDCo	-	1068-J3
-	SDCo	-	1088-J1
-	SDCo	-	1089-A2
-	SDCo	-	1109-E3
-	SDCo	-	1129-H5
-	SDCo	-	1130-A7
-	SDCo	-	1150-A1
-	SDCo	-	1209-F4
I-15 TEMECULA VALLEY FRWY			
-	RivC	-	998-J2
-	RivC	-	999-A1
I-805 JACOB DEKEMA FRWY			
-	CHV	-	1310-B3
-	CHV	-	1330-G2
-	NATC	-	1289-H1
-	NATC	-	1290-A7
-	NATC	-	1310-B3
-	SD	-	1208-C6
-	SD	-	1228-E1
-	SD	-	1248-J1
-	SD	-	1249-A3
-	SD	-	1269-C1
I-805 JACOB DEKEMA FRWY			
-	SD	-	1289-H1
-	SD	-	1330-G2
-	SD	-	1350-G3
-	SDCo	-	1310-B3
Rt#-S1 BUCKMAN SPRINGS RD			
1300	SDCo	91906	(1318-A4
			See Page 1298)
1300	SDCo	91906	(1317-H1
			See Page 1296)
2100	SDCo	91906	(1297-G1
			See Page 1296)
2600	SDCo	91906	430-A7
2600	SDCo	91962	430-A7
Rt#-S1 OLD HIGHWAY 80			
29800	SDCo	91962	430-A6
Rt#-S1 SUNRISE HWY			
6800	SDCo	91962	430-A6
6800	SDCo	91962	1237-G3
6800	SDCo	91948	1237-G3
9500	SDCo	91948	430-B5
10500	SDCo	91948	1218-A1
12200	SDCo	91948	(1217-J1
			See Page 1216)
12300	SDCo	91948	(1197-F4
			See Page 1176)
14100	SDCo	92036	1176-G2
14300	SDCo	92036	(1177-B6
			See Page 1176)
14700	SDCo	92036	(1197-F4
			See Page 1176)
Rt#-S2 GRT STHN OVLD STG RT			
-	SDCo	92036	410-A11
-	SDCo	92036	430-B2
-	SDCo	92036	1138-A5
-	SDCo	92036	(1158-C7
			See Page 1138)
Rt#-S2 IMPERIAL HWY			
-	ImCo	92259	430-G6
Rt#-S2 SAN FELIPE RD			
21300	SDCo	92036	410-A10
22300	SDCo	92086	410-A10
25600	SDCo	92086	409-K9
29000	SDCo	92070	409-K9
Rt#-S2 SWEENEY PASS RD			
-	SDCo	92036	430-E4
-	SDCo	92259	430-E4
Rt#-S3 BORREGO SPRINGS RD			
2500	SDCo	92004	(1078-J3
			See Page 1058)
3500	SDCo	92004	(1079-A7
			See Page 1058)
3500	SDCo	92004	(1099-A1
			See Page 1098)
Rt#-S3 YAQUI PASS RD			
3700	SDCo	92004	(1099-E6
			See Page 1098)
3700	SDCo	92004	(1118-J5
			See Page 1098)
3700	SDCo	92004	(1119-A4
			See Page 1098)
5600	SDCo	92036	(1118-J5
			See Page 1098)
Rt#-S4 POWAY RD			
11600	PWY	92064	1190-H2
11600	SD	92128	1190-B5
12000	SD	92128	1189-G6
15500	PWY	92064	1191-A1
Rt#-S5 ESPOLA RD			
14100	PWY	92064	1190-G1
14800	PWY	92064	1170-D3
16900	SD	92128	1170-D3
Rt#-S5 POMERADO RD			
-	SD	92127	1150-B5
16900	SD	92128	1170-C3
17700	SD	92128	1150-B5
Rt#-S5 RANCHO BERNARDO RD			
12500	SD	92128	1170-D3
Rt#-S6 W 2ND AV			
200	ESCN	92025	1129-J3
Rt#-S6 E 2ND AV			
100	ESCN	92025	1129-J3
Rt#-S6 CANFIELD RD			
3400	SDCo	92060	1032-E7
3400	SDCo	92060	1052-E1
Rt#-S6 DEL DIOS HWY			
500	SDCo	92029	1149-D2
500	SDCo	92067	1149-D6
1100	ESCN	92029	1129-F6
9800	ESCN	92029	1149-D2
9900	SDCo	92029	1129-F6
Rt#-S6 EL ESCONDIDO DEL DIOS			
6900	SDCo	92067	1168-F1
7600	SDCo	92067	1149-A7
7800	SDCo	92067	1148-J7
Rt#-S6 S GRADE RD			
31600	SDCo	92060	1052-D5
31600	SDCo	92082	1052-D5
31600	SDCo	92061	1052-D5
Rt#-S6 W GRAND AV			
800	ESCN	92025	1129-G3
Rt#-S6 HIGHWAY TO THE STARS			
3400	SDCo	92060	1032-E6
Rt#-S6 PASEO DELICIAS			
6200	SDCo	92067	1168-F2
Rt#-S6 N VALLEY BLVD			
100	ESCN	92025	1129-J2
Rt#-S6 S VALLEY BLVD			
100	ESCN	92025	1129-J2
Rt#-S6 VALLEY PKWY			
900	ESCN	92025	1129-F4
1100	ESCN	92029	1129-F4
Rt#-S6 E VALLEY PKWY			
100	ESCN	92025	1129-J2
500	ESCN	92025	1130-A2
1100	ESCN	92027	1130-A2
1800	ESCN	92027	1110-E6
Rt#-S6 W VALLEY PKWY			
200	ESCN	92025	1129-H3
Rt#-S6 VALLEY CENTER RD			
3100	ESCN	92027	1110-E5
24800	SDCo	92027	1090-E4
24800	SDCo	92027	1110-E5
24800	SDCo	92082	1090-E1
30300	SDCo	92082	1091-A2
31700	SDCo	92082	1071-E1
33600	SDCo	92061	1051-D7
Rt#-S6 VALLEY CENTER RD			
33600	SDCo	92061	1071-E1
Rt#-S6 VIA DE LA VALLE			
100	DLMR	92014	1187-G2
600	SD	92014	1187-J2
3200	SD	92014	1188-B1
4000	SDCo	92014	1188-B1
14900	SDCo	92067	1188-B1
14900	SDCo	92091	1188-B1
15000	SDCo	92067	1168-E3
15000	SDCo	92091	1168-D6
15100	SD	92075	1187-G2
Rt#-S7 E GRADE RD			
21500	SDCo	92060	1052-H5
23200	SDCo	92060	(1053-A5
			See Page 1052)
23500	SDCo	92060	(1073-G1
			See Page 1052)
23500	SDCo	92070	(1073-J5
			See Page 1052)
24100	SDCo	92070	409-J8
Rt#-S8 LINEA DEL CIELO			
4800	SDCo	92014	1168-A6
4900	SDCo	92067	1168-C4
Rt#-S8 LOMAS SANTA FE DR			
100	SOLB	92075	1167-F7
1500	SDCo	92014	1167-F7
1500	SOLB	92014	1167-F7
1600	SDCo	92014	1168-A6
Rt#-S8 PASEO DELICIAS			
6100	SDCo	92067	1168-E2
Rt#-S9 ENCINITAS BLVD			
-	ENCT	92024	1147-D7
1900	ENCT	92024	1167-J1
Rt#-S9 LA BAJADA			
17400	SDCo	92067	1168-A2
17600	SDCo	92067	1167-J2
Rt#-S9 LA GRANADA			
4800	SDCo	92067	1168-A3
Rt#-S9 LOS MORROS			
17200	SDCo	92067	1168-A2
Rt#-S9 RANCHO SANTA FE RD			
100	ENCT	92024	1167-J1
100	SDCo	92067	1167-J1
2600	SDCo	92067	1168-A1
Rt#-S10 OLIVENHAIN RD			
1600	ENCT	92024	1147-F4
1600	CRLB	92009	1147-F4
Rt#-S10 RANCHO SANTA FE RD			
-	CRLB	92009	1128-A7
-	CRLB	92009	1148-A1
2900	CRLB	92009	1147-H3
Rt#-S10 N RANCHO SANTA FE RD			
100	SMCS	92078	1108-D6
100	SMCS	92069	1108-D6
Rt#-S10 S RANCHO SANTA FE RD			
100	SMCS	92078	1108-D7
400	SMCS	92078	1128-A3
2200	CRLB	92009	1128-A3
2200	CRLB	92078	1128-A3
Rt#-S11 EL CAMINO REAL			
1000	CRLB	92024	1147-E1
1000	ENCT	92024	1147-E1
1000	CRLB	92009	1147-E1
1100	CRLB	92011	1147-E1
1200	CRLB	92011	1127-E4
1300	CRLB	92009	1127-D1
1600	CRLB	92010	1127-D1
1600	CRLB	92008	1127-D1
1800	CRLB	92010	1107-A6
1800	CRLB	92008	1107-A6
2100	CRLB	92010	1106-H5
2100	CRLB	92008	1106-H5
2300	OCN	92056	1106-H5
2300	OCN	92054	1106-H5
2400	CRLB	92054	1106-H5
Rt#-S11 N EL CAMINO REAL			
100	ENCT	92024	1147-F4
1000	CRLB	92009	1147-F4
1000	CRLB	92024	1147-F4
1000	ENCT	92009	1147-F4
Rt#-S12 DEER SPRINGS RD			
100	SMCS	92069	1108-J1
500	SDCo	92069	1088-J7
500	SDCo	92069	1089-A7
500	SDCo	92069	1108-J1
500	SDCo	92069	1109-A1
1000	SDCo	92026	1089-A7
Rt#-S12 PALOMAR AIRPORT RD			
-	CRLB	92008	1126-H3
-	CRLB	92011	1126-H3
1200	CRLB	92011	1127-F2
1200	CRLB	92008	1127-B3
2600	CRLB	92009	1127-F2
2600	CRLB	92010	1127-F2
3100	CRLB	92010	1128-A2
3100	SMCS	92078	1128-A2
3100	CRLB	92009	1128-A2
Rt#-S12 W SAN MARCOS BLVD			
200	SMCS	92069	1108-H7
300	SMCS	92069	1128-D2
700	SMCS	92078	1128-A2
Rt#-S12 N TWIN OAKS VALLEY RD			
200	SMCS	92069	1108-H5
Rt#-S13 N MAIN AV			
100	SDCo	92028	1027-F2
Rt#-S13 S MAIN AV			
100	SDCo	92028	1027-F3
Rt#-S13 E MISSION RD			
100	SDCo	92028	1027-H1
2000	SDCo	92028	1028-A1
2500	SDCo	92028	998-B7
Rt#-S13 S MISSION RD			
1100	SDCo	92028	1027-G6
2600	SDCo	92028	1047-H1
4900	SDCo	92028	1048-A7
5000	SDCo	92003	1048-A7
Rt#-S13 VISTA VILLAGE DR			
100	VSTA	92084	1087-H6
100	VSTA	92083	1087-H6
Rt#-S13 E VISTA VILLAGE DR			
100	VSTA	92084	1087-H6
Rt#-S13 E VISTA WY			
600	VSTA	92084	1087-J4
1100	VSTA	92084	1088-A2
2100	SDCo	92084	1088-A2
2600	SDCo	92084	1067-J6
2600	SDCo	92084	1068-A7
Rt#-S13 W VISTA WY			
300	VSTA	92083	1087-G7
Rt#-S14 E MISSION RD			
100	SMCS	92069	1108-J7
500	SMCS	92069	1109-B7
1000	SMCS	92069	1129-C1
1400	SMCS	92078	1129-C1
Rt#-S14 W MISSION AV			
300	ESCN	92025	1129-G2
1200	ESCN	92029	1129-G2
Rt#-S14 W MISSION RD			
1000	SMCS	92069	1108-F7
1300	ESCN	92029	1129-E2
2000	SMCS	92078	1129-E2
Rt#-S14 N SANTA FE AV			
300	VSTA	92083	1087-G2
300	VSTA	92084	1087-G2
800	OCN	92057	1067-C7
800	OCN	92056	1087-D1
800	OCN	92057	1087-D1
2200	SDCo	92083	1087-G2
2200	SDCo	92084	1087-G2
2200	OCN	92084	1087-G2
2200	VSTA	92056	1087-G2
Rt#-S14 S SANTA FE AV			
100	VSTA	92083	1087-H7
100	VSTA	92084	1087-H7
1000	VSTA	92084	1088-A7
1000	VSTA	92084	1108-B2
1000	VSTA	92083	1088-A7
1000	VSTA	92083	1108-B2
1400	SDCo	92084	1108-B2
1400	SDCo	92083	1108-B2
2600	SMCS	92069	1108-C4
Rt#-S15 E FALLBROOK ST			
100	SDCo	92028	1027-G3
Rt#-S15 RECHE RD			
1500	SDCo	92028	1027-J4
1700	SDCo	92028	1028-A4
Rt#-S15 S STAGE COACH LN			
400	SDCo	92028	1027-J4
Rt#-S16 3RD ST			
-	SDCo	92059	1029-H4
Rt#-S16 PALA RD			
47000	RivC	92592	999-G1
47800	SDCo	92028	999-G1
47800	SDCo	92059	999-G1
Rt#-S16 PALA TEMECULA RD			
37100	SDCo	92028	999-G3
37100	SDCo	92059	999-G3
41800	SDCo	92059	1029-G2
Rt#-S17 BONITA RD			
-	CHV	91910	1310-D5
2800	SDCo	91910	1310-E4
3000	SDCo	91902	1310-J1
3600	CHV	91902	1310-H3
Rt#-S17 E ST			
-	CHV	91910	1310-B5
200	CHV	91910	1309-J6
Rt#-S17 JAMACHA BLVD			
8700	SDCo	91977	1291-A4
10200	SDCo	91978	1291-E2
10600	SDCo	91978	1271-F7
Rt#-S17 MAYA ST			
9600	SDCo	91977	1291-E2
10000	SDCo	91978	1291-E2
Rt#-S17 SWEETWATER RD			
5300	SDCo	91902	1290-J6
5300	SDCo	91902	1310-H1
5600	SDCo	91902	1291-A7
Rt#-S21 CAMINO DEL MAR			
400	DLMR	92014	1187-F4
Rt#-S21 S CAMINO DEL MAR			
100	DLMR	92014	1187-G7
Rt#-S21 CARLSBAD BLVD			
200	CRLB	92011	1126-H6
2200	CRLB	92008	1106-D4
3900	CRLB	92008	1126-F1
7100	CRLB	92011	1146-J1
7300	CRLB	92024	1147-A2
7300	ENCT	92024	1147-A2
7400	CRLB	92024	1146-J1
Rt#-S21 N COAST HWY			
100	OCN	92054	1086-A7
100	OCN	92054	1106-B2
1200	OCN	92054	1085-J6
1400	SDCo	92055	1085-J6
Rt#-S21 S COAST HWY			
2000	CRLB	92008	1106-D4
2000	OCN	92054	1106-D4
Rt#-S21 N COAST HWY 101			
100	ENCT	92024	1147-A2
Rt#-S21 S COAST HWY 101			
300	ENCT	92024	1147-C7
800	ENCT	92024	1167-D3
900	ENCT	92007	1167-D3
Rt#-S21 GENESEE AV			
10400	SD	92037	1208-A7
10400	SD	92121	1208-A7
10400	SD	92093	1208-A7
10700	SD	92121	1207-J7
Rt#-S21 N HWY 101			
100	SOLB	92075	1167-E7
Rt#-S21 S HWY 101			
100	SOLB	92075	1167-E7
100	SOLB	92075	1187-F1
200	DLMR	92014	1187-F1
200	DLMR	92075	1187-F1
1700	ENCT	92007	1167-E7
Rt#-S21 HILL ST			
100	OCN	92054	1086-A7
100	OCN	92054	1106-C3
Rt#-S21 N TORREY PINES RD			
10300	SD	92121	1207-G2
10500	SD	92037	1207-G2
12100	SD	92014	1207-G2
12600	SD	92014	1187-G7
12800	DLMR	92014	1187-G7
Rt#-S22 BORREGO SALTON SEAWAY			
-	ImCo	92004	410-F7
-	ImCo	92259	410-F7
Rt#-S22 BORREGO SALTON SEAWAY			
-	ImCo	92274	410-F7
-	SDCo	92004	410-D7
-	SDCo	92004	(1059-J4
			See Page 1058)
Rt#-S22 CHRISTMAS CIR			
600	SDCo	92004	(1078-H2
			See Page 1058)
Rt#-S22 MONTEZUMA VALLEY RD			
31300	SDCo	92066	410-A9
33400	SDCo	92066	409-L9
33900	SDCo	92066	1098-A2
34400	SDCo	92004	(1078-D7
			See Page 1058)
34400	SDCo	92066	(1078-D7
			See Page 1058)
35500	SDCo	92086	409-L9
Rt#-S22 PALM CANYON DR			
200	SDCo	92004	(1078-F2
			See Page 1058)
700	SDCo	92004	(1079-D2
			See Page 1058)
Rt#-S22 PEG LEG RD			
1300	SDCo	92004	(1059-J5
			See Page 1058)
1300	SDCo	92004	(1079-J1
			See Page 1058)
Rt#-S24 BARD RD			
1100	ImCo	92283	432-D5
Rt#-S24 COLBY RD			
-	ImCo	92283	432-D4
Rt#-S24 IMPERIAL DAM RD			
1900	ImCo	92283	432-E4
Rt#-S24 MERRING RD			
800	ImCo	92283	432-E4
Rt#-S24 PICACHO RD			
300	ImCo	92283	432-D5
Rt#-S24 ROSS RD			
1400	ImCo	92283	432-D5
Rt#-S24 YORK RD			
1400	ImCo	92283	432-D4
Rt#-S26 BOARTS RD			
400	ImCo	92281	411-B11
400	ImCo	92281	431-B1
Rt#-S26 KALIN RD			
-	ImCo	92281	411-B11
Rt#-S26 MILLER AV			
-	ImCo	92281	431-A1
-	WEST	92281	431-A1
Rt#-S26 RUTHERFORD RD			
-	ImCo	92227	411-D11
-	ImCo	92281	411-C11
900	ImCo	92233	411-C11
Rt#-S27 KEYSTONE RD			
-	ImCo	92227	431-C3
-	ImCo	92251	431-C3
Rt#-S27 MCCONNELL RD			
-	ImCo	92227	431-C3
-	ImCo	92251	431-C3
Rt#-S28 BARIONI ST			
100	IMP	92251	431-B4
100	IMP	92251	6439-E6
Rt#-S28 WORTHINGTON RD			
-	ImCo	92251	431-A4
500	ImCo	92251	6439-C6
500	IMP	92251	431-A4
500	IMP	92251	6439-C6
1000	ImCo	92250	431-A4
1900	ImCo	92251	430-L4
Rt#-S29 DREW RD			
-	ImCo	92273	431-A7
400	ImCo	92231	431-A7
400	ImCo	92243	431-A7
Rt#-S30 BROCKMAN RD			
500	ImCo	92231	431-A7
600	ImCo	92243	431-A7
Rt#-S30 EDDINS RD			
-	ImCo	92233	411-A10
Rt#-S30 FORRESTER RD			
-	ImCo	92227	411-A11
-	WEST	92281	411-A11
1100	ImCo	92243	6559-A3
1800	ImCo	92243	431-A4
2200	ImCo	92251	431-A4
3900	ImCo	92227	431-A4
3900	ImCo	92259	431-A4
5000	ImCo	92281	431-A4
5200	WEST	92281	431-A4
5300	ImCo	92281	411-A11
Rt#-S30 GENTRY RD			
5800	ImCo	92227	411-A11
5800	ImCo	92233	411-A11
Rt#-S30 MAIN ST			
300	CLPT	92233	411-C10
Rt#-S30 MCCABE RD			
-	ImCo	92243	6559-A5
1100	ImCo	92243	431-A6
Rt#-S30 WALKER RD			
-	ImCo	92227	411-A11
Rt#-S31 DOGWOOD RD			
-	ImCo	92249	431-C7
-	ImCo	92249	6560-B5
-	ImCo	92249	6620-B1
-	IMP	92251	6500-A2
200	BRW	92227	431-B3
400	ImCo	92231	431-C7
400	ImCo	92231	6620-B4
400	ImCo	92231	6680-B1
1300	ImCo	92243	6560-B5
1300	ELCN	92243	6560-B2
1700	ELCN	92243	6500-A5
2100	ImCo	92243	6500-A2
2100	ImCo	92251	6500-A2
2800	ImCo	92251	431-B3
3600	ImCo	92227	431-B3
Rt#-S32 4TH ST			
200	HOLT	92250	431-E5
Rt#-S32 BUTTERS RD			
4300	ImCo	92227	431-E1
5300	ImCo	92227	411-E11
Rt#-S32 GONDER RD			
-	ImCo	92227	431-E2
Rt#-S32 HOLT AV			
400	HOLT	92250	431-E5
1500	ImCo	92250	431-E5
Rt#-S32 HOLT RD			
2300	ImCo	92250	431-E3
3900	ImCo	92227	431-E3
Rt#-S32 ORCHARD RD			
-	HOLT	92250	431-E5
1600	ImCo	92250	431-E5
Rt#-S33 BONESTEELE RD			
700	ImCo	92250	431-F7

Block	City	ZIP	Pg-Grid
Rt#-S33 GONDER RD			
-	ImCo	92227	431-E2
Rt#-S33 GREEN RD			
4200	ImCo	92227	431-E2
Rt#-S33 HIGHLINE RD			
-	ImCo	92227	431-E4
2200	ImCo	92250	431-E4
Rt#-S33 KAVANAUGH RD			
-	ImCo	92250	431-E5
Rt#-S33 KUMBERG MESA RD			
-	ImCo	92250	431-F7
Rt#-S33 MILLER RD			
1000	ImCo	92250	431-F6
Rt#-S34 OGILBY RD			
-	ImCo	-	411-K11
-	ImCo	-	431-L1
-	ImCo	-	432-A3
Rt#-S80 ADAMS AV			
600	ELCN	92243	6499-E6
600	ImCo	92243	6499-E6
Rt#-S80 EVAN HEWES HWY			
-	ImCo	92250	431-A5
200	ImCo	92243	6500-F5
600	ImCo	92243	6499-B6
900	ELCN	92243	6500-C6
900	ImCo	92243	431-A5
1700	ImCo	92273	431-A5
1800	ImCo	92273	430-J6
1900	ImCo	92251	430-J6
2800	ImCo	92259	430-J6
Rt#-S80 MAIN ST			
100	ELCN	92243	6499-J6
100	ELCN	92243	6500-A6
Rt#-7 HIGHWAY			
-	ImCo	92231	431-E7
Rt#-15 ESCONDIDO FRWY			
-	SD	-	1269-G6
-	SD	-	1289-F2
Rt#-52 FRWY			
-	SD	-	1228-H6
-	SD	-	1229-D6
-	SD	-	1230-C4
-	SD	-	1231-A7
-	SNTE	-	1230-H6
-	SNTE	-	1231-A7
Rt#-52 SOLEDAD FRWY			
-	SD	-	1228-B7
-	SD	-	1248-A1
Rt#-54 N 2ND ST			
300	ELCJ	92021	1251-J5
Rt#-54 JAMACHA RD			
100	ELCJ	92019	1251-J5
100	ELCJ	92019	1252-A6
1000	SDCo	92019	1252-A6
1100	ELCJ	92019	1272-A5
1100	SDCo	92019	1272-A5
1100	SDCo	92020	1272-A5
2700	SDCo	92019	1271-J6
Rt#-54 SOUTH BAY FRWY			
-	CHV	-	1309-J4
-	CHV	-	1310-A4
-	NATC	-	1309-J4
-	NATC	-	1310-A4
-	SDCo	-	1290-H7
-	SDCo	-	1291-A6
-	SDCo	-	1310-A4
Rt#-56 TED WILLIAMS FRWY			
-	SD	-	1188-F5
-	SD	-	1189-A4
-	SD	-	1207-J2
-	SD	-	1208-A1
Rt#-67 HIGHWAY			
10200	SDCo	92040	1232-A1
11200	SDCo	92040	1212-A7
11300	SDCo	92040	1211-G1
13000	SDCo	92040	1191-D3
13800	SDCo	92071	1191-E5
13900	SDCo	92064	1191-D3
14400	PWY	92064	1191-D1
15000	PWY	92064	1171-E5
15400	SDCo	92065	1171-F3
17600	SDCo	92065	1172-A3
Rt#-67 JULIAN RD			
2500	SDCo	92065	1172-B3
Rt#-67 MAIN ST			
900	SDCo	92065	1152-E7
1900	SDCo	92065	1172-D1
Rt#-67 SAN VICENTE FRWY			
-	ELCJ	-	1251-F2
-	SDCo	-	1231-H4
-	SDCo	-	1232-A3
-	SDCo	-	1251-F2
-	SNTE	-	1231-F7
-	SNTE	-	1251-F2
Rt#-75 4TH ST			
300	CORD	92118	1288-H5
Rt#-75 HIGHWAY			
-	CORD	92113	1289-B7
1500	CORD	92118	1288-J6
1500	CORD	92118	1289-A6
1900	SD	92113	1289-C5
Rt#-75 ORANGE AV			
100	CORD	92118	1288-H7
1300	CORD	92118	1308-J1
Rt#-75 PALM AV			
900	IMPB	91932	1329-G7
1300	SD	92154	1329-G7
1300	IMPB	92154	1329-G7
1700	SD	92154	1330-A7
Rt#-75 SILVER STRAND BLVD			
500	CORD	91932	1329-D2
500	IMPB	91932	1329-D2
1700	CORD	92118	1308-J1
1900	CORD	92118	1309-A3
1900	CORD	92155	1309-A3
2100	CORD	92118	1329-D2
Rt#-76 HIGHWAY			
-	SDCo	92027	(1072-H1 See Page 1052)
-	SDCo	92060	(1072-F1 See Page 1052)
-	SDCo	92082	(1072-F1 See Page 1052)
300	OCN	92057	1086-J2
3400	OCN	92054	1086-G3
4700	OCN	92057	1087-A1
14800	SDCo	92061	1051-H5
19900	SDCo	92061	1052-A5
20400	SDCo	92060	1052-B6
20400	SDCo	92082	1052-B6
23500	SDCo	92060	(1073-A1 See Page 1052)
23500	SDCo	92070	(1073-C3 See Page 1052)
23500	SDCo	92027	(1073-A1 See Page 1052)
28500	SDCo	92070	409-J8
Rt#-76 HIGHWAY 76			
4900	OCN	92057	1086-H3
4900	OCN	92057	1087-A1
Rt#-76 MISSION AV			
3400	OCN	92054	1086-H2
3900	OCN	92057	1086-H2
4500	OCN	92057	1087-A1
4900	OCN	92057	1067-G6
5300	OCN	92056	1067-D7
5600	SDCo	92084	1067-G6
5600	SDCo	92003	1067-G6
Rt#-76 MISSION RD			
5900	SDCo	92003	1067-H3
5900	SDCo	92084	1067-H3
31200	SDCo	92003	1068-A1
31800	SDCo	92003	1048-A7
Rt#-76 PALA RD			
2200	SDCo	92003	1048-H2
2200	SDCo	92028	1048-H2
5600	SDCo	92059	1030-A4
5600	SDCo	92061	1030-E5
7500	SDCo	92059	1029-F4
8500	SDCo	92028	1029-C7
8600	SDCo	92028	1049-A1
16800	SDCo	92061	1051-B5
16800	SDCo	92082	1051-B5
33100	SDCo	92061	1050-H1
Rt#-76 SAN LUIS REY MSN EXWY			
800	OCN	92054	1085-J6
800	OCN	92054	1086-A5
Rt#-78 N ASH ST			
100	ESCN	92025	1130-A1
100	ESCN	92027	1130-A1
Rt#-78 S ASH ST			
100	ESCN	92027	1130-B2
100	ESCN	92025	1130-B2
Rt#-78 BANNER RD			
1200	SDCo	92036	1136-B5
36100	SDCo	92036	1156-H1
Rt#-78 N BROADWAY			
600	ESCN	92025	1129-H2
Rt#-78 HAVERFORD RD			
1200	SDCo	92065	1152-F3
Rt#-78 HIGHWAY			
-	ImCo	-	411-L7
-	ImCo	-	412-A3
-	ImCo	-	431-J1
-	ImCo	92227	410-K10
-	ImCo	92227	430-L1
-	ImCo	92227	431-A1
-	ImCo	92259	410-J10
-	ImCo	92259	430-L1
-	ImCo	92281	431-A1
-	SDCo	92004	410-F10
-	SDCo	92036	1138-C1
-	WEST	92281	431-A1
1700	SDCo	92004	(1118-J5 See Page 1098)
1700	SDCo	92004	(1119-D5 See Page 1098)
1700	SDCo	92036	(1118-J5 See Page 1098)
3000	SDCo	92004	(1120-J1 See Page 1100)
4400	SDCo	92004	(1121-A1 See Page 1100)
35600	SDCo	92036	410-A11
35800	SDCo	92036	1136-J7
35800	SDCo	92036	1156-H1
Rt#-78 JULIAN RD			
100	SDCo	92065	1152-J4
300	SDCo	92065	1153-J1
1700	SDCo	92065	409-J11
2000	SDCo	92065	1154-D2
18600	SDCo	92070	409-J11
18600	SDCo	92070	1135-B3
Rt#-78 MAIN ST			
100	BRW	92227	431-C2
200	ImCo	92227	431-C2
200	SDCo	92065	1152-G6
Rt#-78 MERL RD			
-	ImCo	92281	431-A1
-	WEST	92281	431-A1
Rt#-78 PINE ST			
100	SDCo	92065	1152-G3
Rt#-78 S PINE ST			
100	SDCo	92065	1152-G6
Rt#-78 RONALD PACKARD PKWY			
-	ESCN	-	1129-D2
-	OCN	-	1106-E3
-	OCN	-	1107-A2
-	SDCo	-	1108-A3
-	SDCo	-	1129-D2
-	SMCS	-	1108-A3
-	SMCS	-	1109-A7
-	SMCS	-	1128-H1
-	SMCS	-	1129-D2
-	VSTA	-	1087-E7
-	VSTA	-	1107-J1
-	VSTA	-	1108-A3
Rt#-78 SAN PASQUAL VALLEY RD			
500	ESCN	92025	1130-B2
500	ESCN	92027	1130-B2
800	SDCo	92025	1130-B2
800	SDCo	92027	1130-B2
1400	SDCo	92065	1152-C1
2100	SD	92065	409-G11
2100	SDCo	92027	409-G11
2100	SDCo	92065	409-G11
2100	SD	92027	409-G11
2500	SD	92027	1130-G6
3500	SD	92025	1131-A6
3500	SD	92065	1131-F6
3500	SD	92027	1131-A6
16100	SDCo	92027	1131-F6
16100	SDCo	92025	1131-F6
Rt#-78 E WASHINGTON AV			
100	ESCN	92025	1129-J2
400	ESCN	92025	1130-A1
Rt#-79 CUYAMACA HWY			
3400	SDCo	92036	1136-B7
3700	SDCo	92036	1156-D1
8200	SDCo	91916	1236-C4
8500	SDCo	92036	1176-F4
9600	SDCo	91916	1216-E3
12500	SDCo	91916	(1196-F4 See Page 1176)
13900	SDCo	92036	(1196-F4 See Page 1176)
Rt#-79 HIGHWAY			
-	SDCo	92086	1033-J1
21900	SDCo	92070	409-K8
21900	SDCo	92070	1135-B1
23400	SDCo	92086	409-G5
Rt#-79 JAPATUL VALLEY RD			
8100	SDCo	91901	1236-A6
8100	SDCo	91916	1236-A6
23400	SDCo	91901	1235-J6
Rt#-79 JULIAN RD			
2200	SDCo	92036	1136-A7
2800	SDCo	92036	1135-D3
2800	SDCo	92070	1135-D3
Rt#-79 MAIN ST			
1800	SDCo	92036	1136-B7
Rt#-79 WASHINGTON ST			
2200	SDCo	92036	1136-B7
Rt#-86 4TH ST			
400	ELCN	92243	6499-H6
1700	ELCN	92243	6559-J1
Rt#-86 ADAMS AV			
400	ELCN	92243	6499-F6
Rt#-86 HEBER RD			
-	ImCo	92243	431-C7
-	ImCo	92243	6620-A1
-	ImCo	92249	431-C7
-	ImCo	92249	6620-A1
-	ImCo	92249	6560-D7
Rt#-86 HIGHWAY			
-	BRW	92227	431-B2
-	ImCo	92227	431-B2
-	ImCo	92243	431-B7
-	ImCo	92249	6560-F7
-	ImCo	92251	431-B3
-	ImCo	92251	6439-F1
-	ImCo	92259	410-H7
-	ImCo	92274	410-F4
-	IMP	92251	431-B4
-	IMP	92251	6439-F3
-	IMP	92251	6499-F1
1300	ImCo	92243	6559-J3
1500	ELCN	92243	6559-J2
Rt#-86 N IMPERIAL AV			
600	ELCN	92243	6499-F4
1800	ImCo	92243	6499-F4
1800	ImCo	92251	6499-F4
1800	IMP	92251	6499-F4
Rt#-86 WESTER AV			
300	BRW	92227	431-B2
Rt#-94 CAMPO RD			
11100	SDCo	91978	1272-A7
11100	SDCo	91978	1271-G5
11100	SDCo	91941	1271-G5
11100	SDCo	92019	1271-J6
12100	SDCo	91978	1292-C1
12700	SDCo	91935	1272-D7
13100	SDCo	91935	1292-F1
14100	SDCo	91935	1293-B6
14700	SDCo	91935	(1313-F2 See Page 1293)
16000	SDCo	91917	(1313-F2 See Page 1293)
21100	SDCo	91917	(1314-B5 See Page 1294)
22000	SDCo	91917	429-J10
22600	SDCo	91980	429-K10
Rt#-94 FRWY			
-	LMGR	-	1270-J5
-	LMSA	-	1270-J4
-	LMSA	-	1271-A4
-	SDCo	-	1270-J4
-	SDCo	-	1271-A4
Rt#-94 HIGHWAY			
-	SDCo	91906	430-B10
-	SDCo	91963	429-L10
-	SDCo	91963	430-A10
-	SDCo	91980	429-K10
28500	SDCo	91906	(1318-J2 See Page 1298)
32100	SDCo	91906	(1319-G1 See Page 1298)
36700	SDCo	91906	(1299-H7 See Page 1298)
37100	SDCo	91905	(1299-J6 See Page 1298)
37700	SDCo	91905	1300-C6
Rt#-94 NW INNIS ARDEN WY			
36700	SDCo	91906	(1299-G7 See Page 1298)
36700	SDCo	91906	(1319-G1 See Page 1298)
37100	SDCo	91905	(1299-G7 See Page 1298)
37700	SDCo	91905	1300-A6
Rt#-94 MARTIN L KING JR FRWY			
-	LMGR	-	1270-D7
-	SD	-	1270-D7
-	SD	-	1289-F3
-	SD	-	1290-A2
Rt#-94 OLD HIGHWAY 80			
36800	SDCo	91905	1300-C6
Rt#-94 RIBBONWOOD RD			
2400	SDCo	91905	1300-D5
Rt#-98 HIGHWAY			
-	CALX	92231	431-D7
-	CALX	92231	6620-J7
-	CALX	92231	6680-D1
-	ImCo	-	431-H6
-	ImCo	92231	6620-J7
-	ImCo	92231	6680-D1
-	ImCo	92249	431-D7
-	ImCo	92250	431-F7
-	ImCo	92259	430-G7
-	ImCo	92259	431-A8
900	ImCo	92231	431-E7
Rt#-111 FRWY			
-	ImCo	-	431-C2
-	ImCo	-	6500-E1
-	ImCo	-	6560-E1
Rt#-111 HIGHWAY			
-	BRW	92227	431-C1
-	CALX	92231	431-C7
-	CALX	92231	6620-F4
-	CALX	92231	6680-F1
-	CALX	92249	431-C7
-	CALX	92249	6620-F3
-	CLPT	92233	411-C10
-	ImCo	-	410-J4
-	ImCo	92227	411-C11
-	ImCo	92227	431-C1
-	ImCo	92233	411-B8
-	ImCo	92243	6560-E2
-	ImCo	92249	431-C7
-	ImCo	92249	6560-F4
-	ImCo	92249	6620-F1
-	ImCo	92257	410-L5
-	ImCo	92257	411-A5
-	ImCo	92259	410-K5
Rt#-115 5TH ST			
100	HOLT	92250	431-E5
Rt#-115 EVAN HEWES HWY			
400	HOLT	92250	431-E5
1500	ImCo	92250	431-D5
Rt#-115 HIGHWAY			
-	HOLT	92250	431-E5
-	ImCo	92227	411-D11
-	ImCo	92227	431-D1
-	ImCo	92233	411-C10
2900	ImCo	92250	431-D3
Rt#-115 MAIN ST			
-	ImCo	92233	411-C10
500	CLPT	92233	411-C10
Rt#-125 FRWY			
-	ELCJ	-	1251-A2
-	LMGR	-	1270-J5
-	LMGR	-	1290-J1
-	LMSA	-	1251-A5
-	LMSA	-	1270-J5
-	LMSA	-	1271-A1
-	SD	-	1251-A6
-	SDCo	-	1270-J4
-	SDCo	-	1271-A4
-	SDCo	-	1290-J1
-	SDCo	-	1291-A6
-	SNTE	-	1231-A7
-	SNTE	-	1251-A1
Rt#-125 SOUTH BAY EXWY			
-	CHV	-	1311-D1
-	CHV	-	1331-F1
-	SD	-	1331-G6
-	SD	-	1351-H1
-	SDCo	-	1291-A6
-	SDCo	-	1311-D1
-	SDCo	-	1331-G6
-	SDCo	-	1351-H1
Rt#-163 CABRILLO FRWY			
-	SD	-	1229-D6
-	SD	-	1249-B4
-	SD	-	1269-A1
-	SD	-	1289-B1
Rt#-163 FRWY			
-	SD	-	1249-A6
Rt#-186 HIGHWAY			
-	ImCo	-	432-B6
Rt#-188 TECATE RD			
400	SDCo	91980	429-K10
Rt#-241 FOOTHILL TRANS CORR			
-	SDCo	92672	1023-C2
Rt#-274 BALBOA AV			
9800	SD	92123	1249-F2
Rt#-282 3RD ST			
300	CORD	92118	1288-H5
Rt#-282 4TH ST			
300	CORD	92118	1288-H5
Rt#-282 ALAMEDA BLVD			
300	CORD	92135	1288-G6
300	CORD	92118	1288-G6
Rt#-282 POMONA AV			
1200	CORD	92118	1288-J6
Rt#-905 FRWY			
-	SD	-	1350-G2
-	SD	-	1351-A2
Rt#-905 HIGHWAY			
1300	SD	92154	1351-J2
2100	SD	92154	1352-A3
Rt#-905 OTAY MESA RD			
5100	SD	92154	1351-A2
8800	SDCo	92154	1351-F2

AIRPORTS

FEATURE NAME / Address City, ZIP Code	PAGE-GRID
BLACKINTON AIRSTRIP AIRFLIGHT DR, SDCo, 92082	1069 - G5
BORREGO VALLEY (SEE PAGE 1058) 1820 PALM CANYON DR, SDCo, 92004	1079 - G1
BRAWLEY MUNICIPAL 948 KEN BEMIS DR, BRW, 92227	431 - C1
BROWN FIELD MUNICIPAL 1424 CONTINENTAL ST, SD, 92154	1331 - F7
CALEXICO 801 W 2ND ST, CALX, 92231	6680 - D2
DOUTHITT STRIP 751 MAIN ST, ELCN, 92243	6500 - B6
FALLBROOK COMM AIRPARK 2141 S MISSION RD, SDCo, 92028	1027 - F6
GILLESPIE FIELD 1960 JOE CROSSON DR, ELCJ, 92020	1251 - D1
IMPERIAL COUNTY 1099 AIRPORT RD, IMP, 92251	6499 - E1
JACUMBA (SEE PAGE 1300) OLD HWY 80, SDCo, 91934	1321 - J6
LAKE WOHLFORD RESORT AIRSTRIP LAKE WOHLFORD RD, SDCo, 92027	1110 - H2
LANDING FIELD VANDERGRIFT BLVD, SDCo, 92055	1066 - B1
LYALL ROBERTS AIRSTRIP HWY 76 & COLE GRADE RD, SDCo, 92061	1050 - J3
MCCLELLAN PALOMAR 2198 PALOMAR AIRPORT RD, CRLB, 92008	1127 - E2
MONTGOMERY FIELD 3750 JOHN J MONTGOMERY DR, SD, 92123	1249 - C3
OCEANSIDE MUNICIPAL 480 AIRPORT RD, OCN, 92054	1086 - D4
RAMONA 2450 MONTECITO RD, SDCo, 92065	1152 - B6
SAN DIEGO INTL 3707 N HARBOR DR, SD, 92101	1288 - H1

BEACHES, HARBORS & WATER REC

FEATURE NAME / Address City, ZIP Code	PAGE-GRID
CARDIFF ST BCH SOUTH COAST HWY 101, ENCT, 92007	1167 - D5
CARLSBAD ST BCH CARLSBAD BLVD, CRLB, 92008	1106 - D6
CHILDRENS POOL BEACH COAST BLVD & JENNER ST, SD, 92037	1227 - E6
CORONADO MUNICIPAL BEACH OCEAN BLVD & MARINA AV, CORD, 92118	1288 - G7
CUYAMACA RESERVOIR CUYAMACA HWY & SUNRISE HWY, SDCo, 92036	1176 - G4
DEL MAR CITY BEACH 18TH ST, DLMR, 92014	1187 - E3
DEL MAR SHORES BEACH PK 180 DEL MAR SHORES TER, SOLB, 92075	1187 - E2
DOG BEACH W POINT LOMA BL & VOLTAIRE ST, SD, 92109	1267 - J5
ECOLOGICAL RESERVE LA JOLLA BAY, SD, 92037	1227 - F5
EL CAPITAN RESERVOIR END OF EL MONTE RD, SDCo, 92040	1213 - H6
LA JOLLA SHORES BEACH LA VEREDA, SD, 92037	1227 - G4
LA JOLLA STRAND PK NEPTUNE PL & PALOMAR AV, SD, 92037	1247 - E2
LAKE HODGES ROUTE S6, SD, 92029	1149 - E3
LAKE JENNINGS JENNINGS PK RD & AMERICAN WY, SDCo, 92040	1232 - E3
LEUCADIA ST BCH NEPTUNE AV & JUPITER ST, ENCT, 92024	1146 - J3
MARINE STREET BEACH MARINE ST, SD, 92037	1247 - E1
MISSION BEACH PK OCEAN FRONT WK & VENTURA PL, SD, 92109	1247 - H7
MOONLIGHT BEACH 400 B ST, ENCT, 92024	1147 - B7
MORENA RESERVOIR (SEE PAGE 1296) OAK DR & BUCKMAN SPRINGS RD, SDCo, 91906	1297 - D3
NEWBREAK BEACH LOMALAND DR, SD, 92107	1287 - H3
NORTH SEASCAPE SURF BEACH PK 501 S SIERRA AV, SOLB, 92075	1187 - E1
OCEAN BEACH PK 5121 SARATOGA AV, SD, 92107	1267 - H5
OCEANSIDE CITY BEACH OCEANSIDE BLVD & PACIFIC ST, OCN, 92054	1106 - A2
OTAY RESERVOIR (SEE PAGE 1293) WUESTE RD, SDCo, 91915	1312 - B7
PACIFIC BEACH PK OCEAN BLVD & GRAND AV, SD, 92109	1247 - G6
PESCADERO ST BCH PESCADERO AV & CABLE ST, SD, 92107	1267 - H7
SAN CLEMENTE ST BCH 3030 AVD DEL PRESIDENTE, SCLE, 92672	1023 - A1
SAN DIEGO LA JOLLA UNDERWATER PK LA JOLLA COVE, SD, 92037	1227 - F1
SAN ELIJO ST BCH S COAST HWY 101 & CHESTERFIELD, ENCT, 92007	1167 - C2
SAN ONOFRE ST BCH OLD HWY 101, SDCo, 92672	1023 - E4
SAN VICENTE RESERVOIR MORENO AV, SDCo, 92065	1212 - A2
SCRIPPS INSTITUTE SUBMERGED LAND AREA NW OF SCRIPPS PIER, SD, 92037	1227 - G3
SHELL BEACH COAST BLVD & GIRARD AV, SD, 92037	1227 - E6
SHORELINE PK BEACH SHELTER ISLAND DR, SD, 92106	1288 - C3
SILVER STRAND ST BCH SILVER STRAND BLVD, CORD, 92118	1309 - C7
SOUTH BEACH AVD DEL SOL, CORD, 92118	1308 - H1
SOUTH CARLSBAD ST BCH 7201 CARLSBAD BLVD, CRLB, 92011	1126 - H5
SOUTH CASA BEACH COAST BLVD, SD, 92037	1227 - E6
SWAMIS BEACH 1298 S COAST HWY 101, ENCT, 92024	1167 - B1
TORREY PINES CITY BEACH TORREY PINES SCENIC DR, SD, 92037	1207 - G7
TORREY PINES ST BCH 12000 N TORREY PINES RD, SD, 92037	1207 - G6
TOURMALINE SURFING PK CHELSEA ST & CRYSTAL DR, SD, 92037	1247 - G5
WHISPERING SANDS BEACH COAST BLVD, SD, 92037	1227 - E7
WINDANSEA BEACH 6800 NEPTUNE PL, SD, 92037	1247 - E1
WIPEOUT BEACH COAST BLVD, SD, 92037	1227 - E6

BUILDINGS

FEATURE NAME / Address City, ZIP Code	PAGE-GRID
FOR DOWNTOWN BLDGS SEE PAGE H	-
1 AMERICA PLAZA 600 W BROADWAY, SD, 92101	1288 - J3
BOTANICAL BLDG OLD GLOBE WY, SD, 92101	1289 - C1
BURNHAM, JOHN BLDG 1420 INDIA ST, SD, 92101	1288 - J2
CABOT, CABOT & FORBES BLDG COLUMBIA ST & C ST, SD, 92101	1289 - A3
CASA DEL PRADO 1800 EL PRADO, SD, 92101	1289 - C1
CENTERSIDE BLDG CAMINO DEL RIO N, SD, 92108	1269 - E2
CLAIREMONT TOWER BALBOA AV & MOUNT EVEREST BLVD, SD, 92117	1248 - G3
COMMERCIAL VEHICLE GATE CUSTOMHOUSE PZ, SD, 92154	1352 - A4
EMERALD PLAZA 402 W BROADWAY, SD, 92101	1289 - A3
FIRST NATL BANK BLDG 401 A ST W, SD, 92101	1289 - A3
GENERAL ATOMICS FACILITY 3550 GENERAL ATOMICS CT, SD, 92121	1208 - A6
HALL OF NATIONS PAN AMERICAN RD W, SD, 92101	1289 - B1
HOUSE OF HOSPITALITY 1549 EL PRADO, SD, 92101	1289 - C1
KIMMEL, SIDNEY CANCER CTR 3099 SCIENCE PARK RD, SD, 92121	1207 - J6
KOLL BLDG 501 W BROADWAY, SD, 92101	1289 - A3
LA JOLLA CANCER RESEARCH FND N TORREY PINES RD, SD, 92121	1207 - J6
LA JOLLA GATEWAY 9191 TOWNE CENTRE DR, SD, 92122	1228 - D2
MOORES UCSD CANCER CTR 3855 HEALTH SCIENCES DR, SD, 92037	1228 - C2
MUNICIPAL GYMNASIUM PAN AMERICAN PZ, SD, 92101	1289 - B1
NAVY EXCHANGE 32ND ST, SD, 92136	1289 - F6
NEUROSCIENCES INSTITUTE, THE 10640 JOHN JAY HOPKINS DR, SD, 92121	1207 - J7
NORTH COUNTY ANIMAL SHELTER 2481 PALOMAR AIRPORT RD, CRLB, 92011	1127 - E2
PERLMAN AMBULATORY CARE CTR 9350 CAMPUS POINT DR, SD, 92037	1228 - B2
PUBLIC SERVICE BLDG 1300 1ST ST, CORD, 92118	1288 - J5
SAN DIEGO CALIFORNIA TEMPLE 7474 CHARMANT DR, SD, 92122	1228 - B3
SAN DIEGO CRUISE SHIP TERMINAL B ST PIER, SD, 92101	1288 - H3
SAN DIEGO TECH CTR 9605 SCRANTON RD, SD, 92121	1208 - E6
SCRIPPS CORP PLAZA 10650 TREENA ST, SD, 92131	1209 - F4
SCRIPPS RESEARCH INSTITUTE 10550 N TORREY PINES RD, SD, 92037	1207 - J6
SEMPRA BLDG 101 ASH ST, SD, 92101	1289 - A2
SHILEY EYE CTR 9415 CAMPUS POINT DR, SD, 92037	1228 - B2
SOUTH COUNTY ANIMAL SHELTER 5821 SWEETWATER RD, SDCo, 91902	1290 - J6
UNION BANK OF CALIFORNIA BLDG 530 B ST, SD, 92101	1289 - A3
UNITED NATIONS BLDG PAN AMERICAN RD W, SD, 92101	1289 - B1
WESTMINSTER MANOR 1730 3RD AV, SD, 92101	1289 - A2
YMCA C ST & 12TH AV, SD, 92101	1289 - B3
ZOO RESEARCH BLDG SAN DIEGO ZOO, SD, 92101	1269 - B7

BUILDINGS - GOVERNMENTAL

FEATURE NAME / Address City, ZIP Code	PAGE-GRID
BAILEY, GEORGE F DETENTION FACILITY 446 ALTA RD, SDCo, 92154	1332 - B6
CALTRANS DIST 11 HEADQUARTERS TAYLOR ST, SD, 92110	1268 - F4
COUNTY ADMIN CTR 1600 PACIFIC HWY, SD, 92101	1288 - H2
COUNTY BLDG S GRAPE ST & E VALLEY PKWY, ESCN, 92025	1130 - A2
COUNTY OPERATIONS CTR 5555 OVERLAND AV, SD, 92123	1229 - D7
DEPARTMENT OF PUBLIC WORKS 5555 OVERLAND AV, SD, 92123	1229 - E7
DESCANSO DETENTION FACILITY 7878 CAMPBELL RANCH RD, SDCo, 91901	1235 - H6
DONOVAN, RJ CORRECTIONAL FACILITY DONOVAN STATE PRISON RD, SDCo, 92154	1332 - A6
EAST MESA DETENTION FACILITY 446 ALTA RD, SDCo, 92154	1332 - C5
EDUCATION CTR NORMAL ST & TYLER AV, SD, 92103	1269 - C4
EL CAJON MUNICIPAL COURT 250 E MAIN ST, ELCJ, 92020	1251 - G5
FEDERAL COURTHOUSE 940 FRONT ST, SD, 92101	1289 - A3
FEDERAL JAIL 808 UNION ST, SD, 92101	1289 - A3
FEDERAL OFFICE BLDG 880 FRONT ST, SD, 92101	1289 - A3
IMPERIAL COUNTY COURTHOUSE 939 MAIN ST, ELCN, 92243	6499 - G6
IMPERIAL COUNTY CRIMINAL COURTS 415 E 4TH ST, CALX, 92231	6680 - G2
JUVENILE HALL 2851 MEADOW LARK DR, SD, 92123	1249 - B6
OTAY MESA INSPECTION FACILITY 2335 ENRICO FERMI DR DR, SDCo, 92154	1352 - B3
RAMONA BRANCH MUNICIPAL COURT 1428 MONTECITO RD, SDCo, 92065	1152 - F6
SAN DIEGO CITY ADMIN BLDG 202 C ST, SD, 92101	1289 - A3
SAN DIEGO CITY OPERATIONS BLDG 1222 1ST AV, SD, 92101	1289 - A3
SAN DIEGO COUNTY COURTHOUSE 220 W BROADWAY, SD, 92101	1289 - A3
SAN DIEGO CO OFFICE OF EDUCATION 6401 LINDA VISTA RD, SD, 92111	1268 - H2
SAN DIEGO DEPARTMENT OF FISH & GAME 4949 VIEWRIDGE AV, SD, 92123	1249 - E1
SAN DIEGO MUNICIPAL COURT 1409 4TH AV, SD, 92101	1289 - A2
SAN DIEGO MUNICIPAL COURTS 325 S MELROSE DR, VSTA, 92081	1107 - F1
SAN DIEGO UNIFIED PORT DIST 3165 PACIFIC HWY, SD, 92101	1268 - H7
SELLERS US POSTAL CTR 11251 RANCHO CARMEL DR, SD, 92128	1190 - A1
SOUTHBAY MUNICIPAL COURT 500 3RD AV, CHV, 91910	1310 - B7
STATE HIGHWAY BLDG JUAN ST & WALLACE ST, SD, 92110	1268 - F4
STATE OFFICE BLDG 1350 FRONT ST, SD, 92101	1289 - A2
UNITED STATES CUSTOMS 200 1ST ST, CALX, 92231	6680 - G2
UNITED STATES CUSTOMS HIGHWAY 905, SD, 92154	1352 - A4
UNITED STATES CUSTOMS I-5 AT US BORDER, SD, 92173	1350 - H5
UNITED STATES FEDERAL COURTS 321 S WATERMAN AV, ELCN, 92243	6499 - F6
WOMENS DETENTION FACILITY LAS COLINAS 9000 COTTONWOOD AV, SNTE, 92071	1231 - D6

CASINOS

FEATURE NAME / Address City, ZIP Code	PAGE-GRID
BARONA VALLEY RANCH RESORT & CASINO 1000 WILDCAT CANYON RD, SDCo, 92040	1192 - G7
GOLDEN ACORN CASINO (SEE PAGE 1298) 1800 GOLDEN ACORN WY, SDCo, 91906	1299 - F2
HARRAHS RINCON CASINO 33750 VALLEY CENTER RD, SDCo, 92082	1071 - E3
PALA CASINO 11154 HIGHWAY SR 76, SDCo, 92059	1029 - G4
PAUMA CASINO 777 PAUMA RESERVATION RD, SDCo, 92061	1050 - J1
SYCUAN CASINO 5469 DEHESA RD, SDCo, 92019	1253 - D6
VALLEY VIEW CASINO 16300 NYEMMI PASS RD, SDCo, 92082	1091 - C3
VIEJAS CASINO AND TURF CLUB 5000 WILLOW RD, SDCo, 91901	1234 - J5

CEMETERIES

FEATURE NAME / Address City, ZIP Code	PAGE-GRID
ALL SAINTS CEM 200 PEYRI DR, OCN, 92057	1086 - H2
ALPINE CEM 2495 W VICTORIA DR, SDCo, 91901	1234 - B5
CYPRESS VIEW MAUSOLEUM 3953 IMPERIAL AV, SD, 92113	1289 - G4
DEARBORN MEM PK 14361 TIERRA BONITA RD, PWY, 92064	1190 - G2
EL CAJON CEM 2080 DEHESA RD, SDCo, 92019	1252 - C6
EL CAMINO MEM PK CEM 5600 CARROLL CANYON RD, SD, 92121	1208 - H6
ETERNAL HILLS CEM 1999 EL CAMINO REAL, OCN, 92054	1086 - G7
EVERGREEN CEM MARKET ST, SD, 92102	1289 - G4
FORT ROSECRANS NATL CEM CABRILLO MEMORIAL DR, SD, 92106	1288 - A7
GLEN ABBEY MEM PK CEM 3838 BONITA RD, SDCo, 91902	1310 - F4
GREENWOOD CEM IMPERIAL AV & I-805 FRWY, SDCo, 92102	1289 - H4
HOLY CROSS CEM 4470 HILLTOP DR, SD, 92102	1289 - J2
HOME OF PEACE CEM 3668 IMPERIAL AV, SD, 92102	1289 - G4
JULIAN CEM FARMER RD & A ST, SDCo, 92036	1136 - A7
LA VISTA MEM PK 3191 ORANGE ST, SDCo, 91950	1310 - C3
MASONIC CEM 1177 SANTA MARGARITA DR, SDCo, 92028	1027 - G1
MISSION SAN LUIS REY DE FRANCIA CEM 4050 MISSION, OCN, 92057	1086 - H2
MOUNT HOPE CEM 3751 MARKET ST, SD, 92102	1289 - G4
OAK HILL MEM PK 2640 GLENRIDGE RD, ESCN, 92027	1130 - F1
OCEANVIEW MEM PK CEM GODFREY ST & S COAST HWY, OCN, 92054	1106 - B2
ODD FELLOWS COMM CEM ALTURAS RD & CLEMMENS LN, SDCo, 92028	1027 - E4
RAMONA CEM 532 ASH ST, SDCo, 92065	1152 - G4
SAN MARCOS CEM 1021 MULBERRY DR, SMCS, 92069	1109 - A4
SAN PASQUAL CEM SAN PASQ VLY RD & BANDY CYN RD, SDCo, 92027	1131 - F6
SINGING HILLS MEM PK 2800 DEHESA RD, SDCo, 92019	1252 - F6
VALLEY CENTER CEM 28953 MILLER RD, SDCo, 92082	1070 - E7

CHAMBERS OF COMMERCE

FEATURE NAME / Address City, ZIP Code	PAGE-GRID
ALPINE 2157 ALPINE BLVD, SDCo, 91901	1234 - B6
BORREGO SPRINGS (SEE PAGE 1058) 786 PALM CANYON DR, SDCo, 92004	1078 - J2
CALEXICO 1100 IMPERIAL AV E, CALX, 92231	6620 - F7
CARDIFF BY THE SEA 2051 SAN ELIJO AV, ENCT, 92007	1167 - D3
CARLSBAD 5934 PRIESTLY DR, CRLB, 92008	1127 - E2
CARLSBAD CONV & VISITORS BUREAU 400 CARLSBAD VILLAGE DR, CRLB, 92008	1106 - E5
CHULA VISTA 233 4TH AV, CHV, 91910	1310 - B6
CORONADO 1224 10TH ST, CORD, 92118	1288 - H7
EAST COUNTY REGL 201 S MAGNOLIA AV, ELCJ, 92020	1251 - F5
EL CENTRO 1095 4TH ST, ELCN, 92243	6499 - J7
ENCINITAS 138 ENCINITAS BLVD, ENCT, 92024	1147 - C6
ESCONDIDO 720 N BROADWAY, ESCN, 92025	1129 - H1
FALLBROOK 233 E MISSION RD, SDCo, 92028	1027 - F2
GREATER DEL MAR 1104 CM DEL MAR, DLMR, 92014	1187 - F5
I-15 DIAMOND GATEWAY 12778 RANCHO PENSAQUITOS BLVD, SD, 92129	1189 - G5
IMPERIAL 101 E 4TH ST, IMP, 92251	6439 - F6
IMPERIAL BEACH 600 PALM AV, IMPB, 91932	1329 - G7
INTL VISITORS INFORMATION CTR 1ST AV & F ST, SD, 92101	1289 - A3
JULIAN 2129 MAIN ST, SDCo, 92036	1136 - B7
LAKESIDE 12418 PARKSIDE ST, SDCo, 92040	1232 - B3
LEMON GROVE 3443 MAIN ST, LMGR, 91945	1270 - G6
NATIONAL CITY 901 NATIONAL CITY BLVD, NATC, 91950	1309 - H1
OCEANSIDE C OF C & TOURISM CTR 928 N COAST HWY, OCN, 92054	1085 - J6
OTAY MESA 9163 SIEMPRE VIVA RD, SD, 92154	1352 - A3
POWAY 13381 POWAY RD, PWY, 92064	1190 - E4
RAMONA 960 MAIN ST, SDCo, 92065	1152 - G6
RANCHO BERNARDO 11650 IBERIA PL, SD, 92128	1170 - A3
SAN DIEGO N CO VISITORS BUREAU 360 N ESCONDIDO BLVD, ESCN, 92025	1129 - H2
SAN DIEGO REGL 402 W BROADWAY, SD, 92101	1289 - A3
SAN DIEGO VISITORS AND CONV CTR 401 B ST, SD, 92101	1289 - A3
SAN MARCOS 939 GRAND AV, SMCS, 92078	1108 - F7
SANTEE 10315 MISSION GORGE RD, SNTE, 92071	1231 - E6
SAN YSIDRO INTL 663 E SAN YSIDRO BLVD, SD, 92173	1350 - H5
SOLANA BEACH 210 W PLAZA ST, SOLB, 92075	1167 - E7

FEATURE NAME	Address City, ZIP Code	PAGE-GRID
SPRING VALLEY	3322 SWEETWATER SPRINGS BLVD, SDCo, 91977	1271 - E6
VISITORS INFORMATION CTR	E MISSION BAY DR & CLAIREMONT, SD, 92109	1248 - D7
VISTA	201 E WASHINGTON ST, VSTA, 92084	1087 - H6

CITY HALLS

FEATURE NAME	Address City, ZIP Code	PAGE-GRID
CALEXICO	408 HERBER AV, CALX, 92231	6680 - G2
CARLSBAD	1200 CARLSBAD VILLAGE DR, CRLB, 92008	1106 - F5
CHULA VISTA	276 4TH AV, CHV, 91910	1310 - A6
CORONADO	1825 STRAND WY, CORD, 92118	1308 - J1
DEL MAR	1050 CM DEL MAR, DLMR, 92014	1187 - F5
EL CAJON	200 E MAIN ST, ELCJ, 92020	1251 - F5
EL CENTRO	1275 MAIN ST, ELCN, 92243	6499 - G6
ENCINITAS	505 S VULCAN AV, ENCT, 92024	1147 - C7
ESCONDIDO	201 N BROADWAY, ESCN, 92025	1129 - J2
IMPERIAL	420 IMPERIAL AV, IMP, 92251	6439 - F6
IMPERIAL BEACH	825 IMPERIAL BEACH BLVD, IMPB, 91932	1349 - G1
JULIAN	2129 MAIN ST, SDCo, 92036	1136 - B7
LA MESA	8130 ALLISON AV, LMSA, 91941	1270 - H2
LEMON GROVE	3232 MAIN ST, LMGR, 91945	1270 - G6
NATIONAL CITY	1243 NATIONAL CITY BLVD, NATC, 91950	1309 - H2
OCEANSIDE	300 N COAST HWY, OCN, 92054	1086 - A7
POWAY	13325 CIVIC CENTER DR, PWY, 92064	1190 - E5
SAN DIEGO	202 C ST, SD, 92101	1289 - A3
SAN MARCOS	1 CIVIC CENTER DR, SMCS, 92069	1108 - J7
SANTEE	10601 MAGNOLIA AV, SNTE, 92071	1231 - E2
SOLANA BEACH	635 S HWY 101, SOLB, 92075	1187 - E1
VISTA	600 EUCALYPTUS AV, VSTA, 92084	1087 - J6

COLLEGES & UNIVERSITIES

FEATURE NAME	Address City, ZIP Code	PAGE-GRID
ALLIANT INTL UNIV	10455 POMERADO RD, SD, 92131	1209 - J5
BAPTIST COLLEGE	ULRIC ST & EASTMAN ST, SD, 92111	1248 - J7
CALIFORNIA STATE UNIV SAN MARCOS	333 S TWIN OAKS VALLEY RD, SMCS, 92096	1128 - J2
CHRISTIAN HERITAGE COLLEGE	2100 GREENFIELD DR, ELCJ, 92019	1252 - D4
CUYAMACA COLLEGE	900 RANCHO SAN DIEGO PKWY, SDCo, 92019	1271 - J5
FASHION INST OF DESIGN &-MERCHANDISING	1010 2ND AV, SD, 92101	1289 - A3
GROSSMONT COLLEGE	8800 GROSSMONT COLLEGE DR, ELCJ, 92020	1251 - A2
IMPERIAL VALLEY COLLEGE	380 E ATEN RD, ImCo, 92251	6500 - E1
MIRACOSTA COLLEGE	1 BARNARD DR, OCN, 92056	1087 - A7
MIRA COSTA COLLEGE SAN ELIJO CAMPUS	3333 MANCHESTER AV, ENCT, 92024	1167 - F3
NATIONAL UNIV	4141 CM DL RIO S, SD, 92116	1269 - G1
NATIONAL UNIV NORTH CO CAMPUS	2022 UNIVERSITY DR, VSTA, 92083	1108 - A3
PALOMAR COLLEGE	1140 W MISSION RD, SMCS, 92069	1108 - F5
PALOMAR COMM COLLEGE	1951 E VALLEY PKWY, ESCN, 92027	1110 - C7
POINT LOMA NAZARENE UNIV	3900 LOMALAND DR, SD, 92106	1287 - J3
SAN DIEGO CITY COLLEGE	1313 PARK BLVD, SD, 92101	1289 - B2
SAN DIEGO MESA COLLEGE	7250 MESA COLLEGE DR, SD, 92111	1248 - J4
SAN DIEGO MIRAMAR COLLEGE	10440 BLACK MOUNTAIN RD, SD, 92126	1209 - E4
SAN DIEGO STATE UNIV	5500 CAMPANILE DR, SD, 92182	1270 - B1
SCRIPPS INSTITUTION OF OCEANOGRAPHY	8602 LA JOLLA SHORES DR, SD, 92037	1227 - H4
SIXTH COLLEGE	UC SAN DIEGO CAMPUS, SD, 92093	1228 - A2
SOUTHWESTERN COLLEGE	900 OTAY LAKES RD, CHV, 91910	1311 - C6
UNIV OF CALIFORNIA SAN DIEGO	9500 GILMAN DR, SD, 92093	1228 - B1
UCSD-ELEANOR ROOSEVELT COLLEGE	UC SAN DIEGO CAMPUS, SD, 92093	1227 - J1
UCSD-JOHN MUIR COLLEGE	UC SAN DIEGO CAMPUS, SD, 92093	1227 - J2
UCSD OF MEDICINE	UC SAN DIEGO CAMPUS, SD, 92093	1228 - A2
UCSD-REVELLE COLLEGE	UC SAN DIEGO CAMPUS, SD, 92093	1227 - J2
UCSD-THURGOOD MARSHALL COLLEGE	UC SAN DIEGO CAMPUS, SD, 92093	1227 - J1
UCSD-WARREN COLLEGE	UC SAN DIEGO CAMPUS, SD, 92093	1228 - A1
UNIV OF SAN DIEGO	5998 ALCALA PARK, SD, 92110	1268 - G2
WEST COAST UNIV	9682 VIA EXCELENCIA, SD, 92126	1209 - E5
WESTMINSTER THEOLOGICAL SEMINARY	1725 BEAR VALLEY PKWY, ESCN, 92027	1130 - D3

DEPARTMENT OF MOTOR VEHICLES

FEATURE NAME	Address City, ZIP Code	PAGE-GRID
CHULA VISTA	30 N GLOVER AV, CHV, 91910	1310 - A5
EL CAJON	1450 GRAVES AV, SDCo, 92021	1251 - F2
EL CENTRO	233 N IMPERIAL AV, ELCN, 92243	6499 - F6
ESCONDIDO	725 N ESCONDIDO BLVD, ESCN, 92025	1129 - H2
OCEANSIDE	4005 PLAZA DR, OCN, 92056	1107 - C2
POWAY	13301 POWAY RD, PWY, 92064	1190 - E4
SAN DIEGO	3960 NORMAL ST, SD, 92103	1269 - C5
SAN DIEGO CLAIREMONT	4375 DERRICK DR, SD, 92117	1248 - G2
SAN YSIDRO	3702 DEL SOL BLVD, SD, 92154	1350 - E1

ENTERTAINMENT & SPORTS

FEATURE NAME	Address City, ZIP Code	PAGE-GRID
BELMONT PARK	3146 MISSION BLVD, SD, 92109	1267 - J3
CAJON SPEEDWAY	1875 JOE CROSSON DR, ELCJ, 92020	1251 - E2
COX ARENA	5500 CANYON CREST DR, SD, 92182	1270 - B1
DEL MAR FAIRGROUNDS	2260 JIMMY DURANTE BLVD, DLMR, 92014	1187 - F2
DEL MAR RACE TRACK	2260 JIMMY DURANTE BLVD, DLMR, 92014	1187 - G2
DEVORE STADIUM	900 OTAY LAKES RD, CHV, 91910	1311 - C5
IPAYONE CENTER	3500 SPORTS ARENA BLVD, SD, 92110	1268 - D4
KNOTTS SOAK CITY USA	2052 ENTERTAINMENT CIR, CHV, 91911	1331 - A6
LEGOLAND CALIFORNIA	1 LEGOLAND DR, CRLB, 92008	1126 - J2
PETCO PARK	100 PARK BLVD, SD, 92101	1289 - B4
POWAY SKATE PARK	13094 CIVIC CENTER WY, PWY, 92064	1190 - E4
QUALCOMM STADIUM	9449 FRIARS RD, SD, 92108	1249 - F7
SAN DIEGO CONV CTR	111 W HARBOR DR, SD, 92101	1289 - A4
SAN DIEGO VELODROME	2221 MORLEY FIELD DR, SD, 92101	1269 - D7
SAN LUIS REY DOWNS	VIA CASITAS, SDCo, 92003	1048 - B7
SEA WORLD	500 SEA WORLD DR, SD, 92109	1268 - B3
SKATE PARK	ORION WY, CRLB, 92010	1127 - F1

GOLF COURSES

FEATURE NAME	Address City, ZIP Code	PAGE-GRID
ADMIRAL BAKER GC	ADMIRAL BAKER RD & FRIARS RD, SD, 92124	1249 - H6
ARROWOOD GC	5201 VILLAGE DR, OCN, 92057	1067 - B3
AULD GC	525 HUNTE PKWY, SDCo, 91914	1291 - H7
AVIARA GC	7447 BATIQUITOS DR, CRLB, 92011	1127 - C6
BALBOA PK MUNICIPAL GC	2600 GOLF COURSE DR, SD, 92101	1269 - D7
BARONA CREEK GC	1932 WILDCAT CANYON RD, SDCo, 92040	1192 - G5
BERNARDO HEIGHTS CC	16066 BERNARDO HEIGHTS PKWY, SD, 92128	1169 - J5
BONITA GC	5540 SWEETWATER RD, SDCo, 91902	1291 - A7
BORREGO SPRINGS RESORT & CC- (SEE PAGE 1058)	1112 TILTING T DR, SDCo, 92004	1079 - B4
BRIDGES CLUB, THE	18550 SEVEN BRIDGES RD, SDCo, 92091	1148 - F5
BROKEN SPOKE CC	225 WAKE AV, ELCN, 92243	6559 - J2
CARLTON OAKS CC	9200 INWOOD DR, SD, 92071	1230 - J6
CARMEL HGHLND DBLETREE GOLF & TENNIS	14455 PENASQUITOS DR, SD, 92129	1169 - J7
CARMEL MTN RANCH CC	14050 CARMEL RIDGE RD, SD, 92128	1189 - J2
CASTLE CREEK CC	8797 CIRCLE R DR, SDCo, 92026	1068 - J6
CENTER CITY GC	2323 GREENBRIER DR, OCN, 92054	1106 - C1
CHULA VISTA MUNICIPAL GC	4475 BONITA RD, CHV, 91902	1310 - G3
COLINA PARK GC	4085 52ND ST, SD, 92105	1270 - A5
CORONADO GC	2000 VISALIA RW, CORD, 92118	1289 - A7
COTTONWOOD AT RANCHO SAN DIEGO GC	3121 WILLOW GLEN DR, SDCo, 92019	1272 - C5
CC OF RANCHO BERNARDO	12280 GREENS EAST RD, SD, 92128	1150 - B7
DE ANZA CC	509 CATARINA DR, SDCo, 92004	1058 - G4
DEL MAR CC	6001 COUNTRY CLUB RD, SDCo, 92067	1188 - E2
EAGLE CREST GC	2492 OLD RANCH RD, ESCN, 92027	1130 - H2
EASTLAKE CC	2375 CLUBHOUSE DR, CHV, 91915	1311 - G6
EL CAMINO CC	3202 VISTA WY, OCN, 92056	1086 - G7
EMERALD ISLE GC	660 EL CAMINO REAL, OCN, 92057	1086 - F5
ENCINITAS RANCH GC	1275 QUAIL GARDENS DR, ENCT, 92024	1147 - E3
ESCONDIDO CC	1800 COUNTRY CLUB LN, ESCN, 92026	1109 - D4
FAIRBANKS RANCH CC	15150 SAN DIEGUITO RD, SD, 92067	1188 - C1
FALLBROOK GC	2757 GIRD RD, SDCo, 92028	1028 - D7
GOLF COURSE OF CALIFORNIA, THE	3742 FLOWERWOOD LN, SDCo, 92028	1048 - C3
LA COSTA RESORT & SPA	2100 COSTA DEL MAR RD, CRLB, 92009	1127 - F5
LA JOLLA CC	7301 HIGH AV, SD, 92037	1227 - F7
LAKE SAN MARCOS CC	1750 SAN PABLO DR, SDCo, 92078	1128 - D2
LAKE SAN MARCOS EXECUTIVE GC	1556 CM DL ARROYO, SDCo, 92078	1128 - B3
LOMAS SANTA FE CC	1505 LOMAS SANTA FE DR, SOLB, 92014	1187 - H1
LOMAS SANTA FE EXECUTIVE GC	1580 SUN VALLEY RD, SOLB, 92075	1167 - H5
MADERAS GC	17750 OLD COACH RD, PWY, 92064	1150 - G7
MEADOW LAKE CC	10333 MEADOW GLEN WY E, SDCo, 92026	1089 - E4
MEADOWS DEL MAR GC	5300 MEADOWS DEL MAR, SD, 92130	1188 - F7
MIRAMAR MEM GC	MIRAMAR WY & MIRAMAR RD, SD, 92126	1209 - C7
MISSION BAY GC	2702 N MISSION BAY DR, SD, 92109	1248 - C5
MISSION TRAILS GC	7380 GOLFCREST PL, SD, 92119	1250 - G5
MORGAN RUN RESORT AND CLUB	5690 CANCHA DE GOLF, SDCo, 92091	1168 - D7
MOUNT WOODSON CC	16422 N WOODSON DR, SDCo, 92065	1171 - E3
NATIONAL CITY GC	1439 SWEETWATER RD, NATC, 91950	1310 - A2
NAVAL STATION GC	WABASH BL & NORMAN SCOTT RD, SD, 92136	1289 - F6
OAKS NORTH GC	12602 OAKS NORTH DR, SD, 92128	1150 - D7
OCEAN HILLS CC	4701 LEISURE VILLAGE WY, OCN, 92056	1107 - E5
OCEANSIDE MUNICIPAL GC	825 DOUGLAS DR, OCN, 92057	1066 - H6
PALA MESA RESORT	2001 OLD HWY 395, SDCo, 92028	1028 - G5
PAUMA VALLEY CC	HWY 76 & PAUMA VALLEY DR, SDCo, 92061	1050 - J5
PENDLETON MARINE MEM GC	GOLF COURSE RD, SDCo, 92055	1066 - F5
PRESIDIO HILLS GC	4136 WALLACE ST, SD, 92110	1268 - F4
RAMS HILL CC (SEE PAGE 1098)	1881 RAMS HILL RD, SDCo, 92004	1099 - G4
RANCHO BERNARDO INN GC	17550 BERNARDO OAKS DR, SD, 92128	1150 - B7
RANCHO CARLSBAD GC	5200 EL CAMINO REAL, CRLB, 92010	1107 - C6
RANCHO MONSERATE CC	4650 DULIN RD, SDCo, 92028	1048 - H4
RANCHO SANTA FE GC	5827 VIA D LA CUMBRE, SDCo, 92067	1168 - C2
RANCHO SANTA FE FARMS GC	8500 SAINT ANDREWS RD, SDCo, 92067	1168 - G7
REIDY CREEK GC	2300 N BROADWAY, ESCN, 92026	1109 - H3
RIVERWALK GC	1150 FASHION VALLEY RD, SD, 92108	1268 - H3
ROADRUNNER GOLF & CC (SEE PAGE 1058)	1010 PALM CANYON DR, SDCo, 92004	1079 - B1
SAIL HO GC	10 SELLERS PZ, SD, 92106	1268 - D6
SAN DIEGO CC	88 L ST, CHV, 91911	1330 - D2
SAN LUIS REY DOWNS CC	31474 GOLF CLUB DR, SDCo, 92003	1048 - A7
SAN VICENTE CC	24157 SAN VICENTE RD, SDCo, 92065	1173 - E4
SEA N AIR GC	CORONADO AV, CORD, 92135	1288 - G6
SHADOWRIDGE CC	1980 GATEWAY DR, VSTA, 92081	1107 - J4
SINGING HILLS CC	3007 DEHESA RD, SDCo, 92019	1252 - F6
SKYLINE RANCH CC	18218 PARADISE MOUNTAIN RD, SDCo, 92082	1091 - F4
SPINDRIFT GC	2000 SPINDRIFT DR, SD, 92037	1227 - G5
STEELE CANYON GC	3199 STONEFIELD DR, SDCo, 91935	1272 - E4
STONERIDGE CC	17166 STONERIDGE COUNTRY CLUB, PWY, 92064	1170 - E2
SUN VALLEY GC	5080 MEMORIAL DR, LMSA, 91941	1270 - J2
TECOLOTE CANYON GC	2755 SNEAD AV, SD, 92111	1248 - G6
TORREY PINES MUNICIPAL GC	11480 N TORREY PINES RD, SD, 92037	1207 - H5
TWIN OAKS GC	1425 N TWIN OAKS VALLEY RD, SMCS, 92069	1108 - J4
VINEYARD AT ESCONDIDO GC, THE	925 SAN PASQUAL RD, ESCN, 92025	1150 - C2
VISTA VALLEY CC	29354 VISTA VALLEY DR, SDCo, 92084	1068 - D7
WELK, LAWRENCE RESORT GC	8860 LAWRENCE WELK DR, SDCo, 92026	1089 - A2
WILLOWBROOK CC	11905 RIVERSIDE DR, SDCo, 92040	1231 - J3
WOODS VALLEY GC	14616 WOODS VALLEY RD, SDCo, 92082	1090 - F4

HOSPITALS

FEATURE NAME	Address City, ZIP Code	PAGE-GRID
ALVARADO HOSP MED CTR	6655 ALVARADO RD, SD, 92120	1270 - D1
BAYVIEW HOPSITAL	330 MOSS ST, CHV, 91911	1330 - C2
CHILDRENS HOSP & HEALTH CTR	3020 CHILDRENS WY, SD, 92123	1249 - B5
EL CENTRO REGL MED CTR	1415 ROSS AV, ELCN, 92243	6559 - G1
FALLBROOK HOSP DIST	624 E ELDER ST, SDCo, 92028	1027 - G3
GROSSMONT HOSP ANNEX	WAKARUSA ST, LMSA, 91942	1251 - A7
KAISER FOUNDATION HOSP	4647 ZION AV, SD, 92120	1249 - J6
KINDRED HOSP SAN DIEGO	1940 EL CAJON BLVD, SD, 92104	1269 - C4
NAVAL MED CTR	34800 BOB WILSON DR, SD, 92134	1289 - C2
PALOMAR MED CTR	555 E VALLEY PKWY, ESCN, 92025	1130 - A2
PARADISE VALLEY HOSP	2400 E 4TH ST, NATC, 91950	1290 - B7
POMERADO HOSP	15615 POMERADO RD, PWY, 92064	1170 - C6
SCRIPPS GREEN HOSP	10666 N TORREY PINES RD, SD, 92037	1207 - J6
SCRIPPS MEM HOSP CHULA VISTA	435 H ST, CHV, 91910	1310 - B7
SCRIPPS MEM HOSP ENCINITAS	354 SANTA FE DR, ENCT, 92024	1167 - D1
SCRIPPS MEM HOSP LA JOLLA	9888 GENESEE AV, SD, 92037	1228 - B1
SCRIPPS MERCY HOSP	4077 5TH AV, SD, 92103	1269 - A5
SHARP CHULA VISTA MED CTR	751 MEDICAL CENTER CT, CHV, 91911	1330 - J2
SHARP CORONADO HOSP	250 PROSPECT PL, CORD, 92118	1289 - A6
SHARP GROSSMONT HOSP	5555 GROSSMONT CENTER DR, LMSA, 91942	1251 - A7
SHARP MEM HOSP	7901 FROST ST, SD, 92123	1249 - B5
TRI-CITY MED CTR	4002 VISTA WY, OCN, 92056	1107 - B1
UCSD MED CTR HILLCREST	200 W ARBOR DR, SD, 92103	1268 - J4
UCSD MED CENTER-THORNTON HOSP	9300 CAMPUS POINT DR, SD, 92037	1228 - B2
UNIV COMM MED CTR	5550 UNIVERSITY AV, SD, 92105	1270 - B5
VETERANS AFFAIRS MED CTR	3350 LA JOLLA VILLAGE DR, SD, 92161	1228 - A2

HOTELS

FEATURE NAME	Address City, ZIP Code	PAGE-GRID
ALL SEASONS INNS	699 E ST, CHV, 91910	1309 - J6
AMERICANA INN & SUITES	815 W SAN YSIDRO BLVD, SD, 92173	1350 - E3
BAHIA RESORT HOTEL	998 W MISSION BAY DR, SD, 92109	1267 - J2
BARONA VALLEY RANCH RESORT & CASINO	1000 WILDCAT CANYON RD, SDCo, 92040	1192 - G6
BAY CLUB HOTEL	2131 SHELTER ISLAND DR, SD, 92106	1288 - C3
BEST WESTERN BAYSIDE INN	555 W ASH ST, SD, 92101	1289 - A2
BEST WESTERN BEACH TERRACE INN	2775 OCEAN ST, CRLB, 92008	1106 - D5
BEST WESTERN BEACH VIEW LODGE	3180 CARLSBAD BLVD, CRLB, 92008	1106 - E6
BEST WESTERN BLUE SEA LODGE	707 PACIFIC BEACH DR, SD, 92109	1247 - H7
BEST WESTERN CAVALIER MOTOR HOTEL	710 E ST, CHV, 91910	1309 - J6
BEST WESTERN CONTINENTAL INN	650 N MOLLISON AV, ELCJ, 92021	1251 - G4

FEATURE NAME / Address City, ZIP Code	PAGE-GRID
BEST WESTERN COURTESY INN 1355 E MAIN ST, ELCJ, 92019	1251 - J5
BEST WESTERN ESCONDIDO 1700 SEVEN OAKS RD, ESCN, 92026	1109 - F6
BEST WESTERN FRANCISCAN INN 1635 S MISSION RD, SDCo, 92028	1027 - F5
BEST WESTERN HACIENDA 4041 HARNEY ST, SD, 92110	1268 - F5
BEST WESTERN HANALEI HOTEL 2270 HOTEL CIR N, SD, 92108	1268 - G4
BEST WESTERN INN BY THE SEA 7830 FAY AV, SD, 92037	1227 - E6
BEST WESTERN ISLAND PALMS HTL &-MARINA 2051 SHELTER ISLAND DR, SD, 92106	1288 - B4
BEST WESTERN MARTYS VALLEY INN 3240 E MISSION AV, OCN, 92054	1086 - E5
BEST WESTERN MIRAMAR 9310 KEARNY MESA RD, SD, 92126	1209 - F6
BEST WESTERN OCEANSIDE INN 1680 OCEANSIDE BLVD, OCN, 92054	1106 - C1
BEST WESTERN POSADA INN 5005 N HARBOR DR, SD, 92147	1288 - C2
BEST WESTERN SEVEN SEAS 411 S HOTEL CIR, SD, 92108	1268 - J4
BEST WESTERN STRATFORD INN 710 CM DEL MAR, DLMR, 92014	1187 - G6
BEST WESTERN SUITES CORONADO 275 ORANGE AV, CORD, 92118	1288 - J6
CATAMARAN RESORT HOTEL 3999 MISSION BLVD, SD, 92109	1247 - H7
CLARION CARRIAGE HOUSE DEL MAR 720 CM DEL MAR, DLMR, 92014	1187 - G6
CLARION HOTEL BAY VIEW 660 K ST, SD, 92101	1289 - A4
COMFORT INN & SUITES-ZOO/SEA WORLD 2485 HOTEL CIRCLE PL, SD, 92108	1268 - G4
COMFORT INN AT OLD TOWN 1955 SAN DIEGO AV, SD, 92110	1268 - G6
COMFORT INN LA MESA 8000 PARKWAY DR, LMSA, 91942	1270 - G1
COMFORT SUITES MISSION VALLEY 631 CM DL RIO S, SD, 92108	1269 - A4
COUNTRY INN CARDIFF-BY-THE-SEA 1661 VILLA CARDIFF DR, ENCT, 92007	1167 - E2
COURTYARD BY MARRIOTT 717 S HWY 101, SOLB, 92075	1187 - E1
COURTYARD BY MARRIOTT 9650 SCRANTON RD, SD, 92121	1208 - E7
COURTYARD DOWNTOWN 530 BROADWAY, SD, 92101	1289 - A3
DANA INN & MARINA 1710 W MISSION BAY DR, SD, 92109	1268 - A3
DAYS INN HOTEL CIRCLE 543 HOTEL CIR S, SD, 92108	1268 - J4
DAYS INN LA MESA 1250 EL CAJON BLVD, ELCJ, 92020	1251 - D7
DAYS INN MISSION BAY 2575 CLAIREMONT DR, SD, 92110	1248 - E7
DAYS INN SUITES SEA WORLD 3350 ROSECRANS ST, SD, 92110	1268 - E6
DOUBLETREE CARMEL HIGHLANDS RESORT 14455 PENASQUITOS DR, SD, 92129	1189 - H1
DOUBLETREE CLUB HOTEL 11611 BERNARDO PLAZA CT, SD, 92128	1170 - A3
DOUBLETREE CLUB HOTEL 1515 HOTEL CIR S, SD, 92108	1268 - H4
DOUBLETREE HOTEL 7450 HAZARD CENTER DR, SD, 92108	1269 - A2
DOUBLETREE HOTEL DEL MAR 11915 EL CAMINO REAL, SD, 92130	1208 - A1
EMBASSY SUITES 4550 LA JOLLA VILLAGE DR, SD, 92121	1228 - D2
EMBASSY SUITES SAN DIEGO BAY 601 PACIFIC HWY, SD, 92101	1288 - J4
EMPRESS HOTEL OF LA JOLLA, THE 7766 FAY AV, SD, 92037	1227 - E7
ESTANCIA LA JOLLA HOTEL 9700 N TORREY PINES RD, SD, 92037	1227 - J1
FOUR POINTS HOTEL SAN DIEGO 8110 AERO DR, SD, 92123	1249 - B4
FOUR SEASONS RESORT AVIARA 1500 FOUR SEASONS PT, CRLB, 92011	1127 - C6
GOOD NITE INN SEA WORLD 3880 GREENWOOD ST, SD, 92110	1268 - E5
GOOD NITE INN SOUTH BAY 225 BAY BLVD W, CHV, 91910	1309 - J7
HALF MOON INN & SUITES 2303 SHELTER ISLAND DR, SD, 92106	1288 - C3
HAMPTON INN 11920 EL CAMINO REAL, SD, 92130	1207 - J1
HAMPTON INN 5434 KEARNY MESA RD, SD, 92111	1229 - C7
HAMPTON INN 3888 GREENWOOD ST, SD, 92110	1268 - E5
HANDLERY HOTEL & RESORT 950 HOTEL CIR N, SD, 92108	1268 - H4
HILTON-HARBOR ISLAND 1960 HARBOR ISLAND DR, SD, 92101	1288 - E2
HILTON GARDEN INN CARLSBAD BEACH 6450 CARLSBAD BLVD, CRLB, 92011	1126 - G3
HILTON LA JOLLA TORREY PINES 10950 N TORREY PINES RD, SD, 92037	1207 - J5
HILTON SAN DIEGO 1775 E MISSION BAY DR, SD, 92109	1268 - D1
HILTON SAN DIEGO/DEL MAR 15575 JIMMY DURANTE BLVD, SD, 92014	1187 - G2
HOLIDAY INN CARLSBAD BY THE SEA 850 PALOMAR AIRPORT RD, CRLB, 92008	1126 - H3
HOLIDAY INN EXPRESS 3950 JUPITER ST, SD, 92110	1268 - C5
HOLIDAY INN HARBOR VIEW 1617 1ST AV, SD, 92101	1289 - A2
HOLIDAY INN HOTEL & SUITES - OLD TOWN 2435 JEFFERSON ST, SD, 92110	1268 - F5
HOLIDAY INN MISSION BAY/SEA WORLD 3737 SPORTS ARENA BLVD, SD, 92110	1268 - D5
HOLIDAY INN MISSION VALLEY 3805 MURPHY CANYON RD, SD, 92123	1249 - F4
HOLIDAY INN ON THE BAY 1355 N HARBOR DR, SD, 92101	1288 - J2
HOLIDAY INN RANCHO BERNARDO 17065 W BERNARDO DR, SD, 92127	1169 - J2
HOLIDAY INN SAN DIEGO BAYSIDE 4875 N HARBOR DR, SD, 92147	1288 - C2
HOLIDAY INN SELECT HOTEL CIRCLE 595 HOTEL CIR S, SD, 92108	1268 - J4
HOLIDAY INN SELECT MIRAMAR 9335 KEARNY MESA RD, SD, 92126	1209 - E6
HOLIDAY INN SOUTH BAY 700 NATIONAL CITY BLVD, NATC, 91950	1309 - H1
HORTON GRAND HOTEL 311 ISLAND AV, SD, 92101	1289 - A4
HOTEL CIRCLE INN & SUITES 2201 HOTEL CIR S, SD, 92108	1268 - G4
HOTEL DEL CORONADO 1500 ORANGE AV, CORD, 92118	1308 - H1
HUMPHREYS HALF MOON INN 2303 SHELTER ISLAND DR, SD, 92106	1288 - C3
HYATT ISLANDIA 1441 QUIVIRA RD, SD, 92109	1268 - A3
HYATT REGENCY LA JOLLA 3777 LA JOLLA VILLAGE DR, SD, 92122	1228 - B3
INNS OF AMERICA 751 RAINTREE DR, CRLB, 92011	1126 - J6
KINGS INN 1333 HOTEL CIR S, SD, 92108	1268 - J4
LA CASA DEL ZORRO DESERT RESORT- (SEE PAGE 1098) BORREGO SPRINGS & YAQUI PASS, SDCo, 92004	1099 - F1
LA COSTA RESORT & SPA 2100 COSTA DEL MAR RD, CRLB, 92009	1147 - E1
LA JOLLA COVE SUITES 1155 COAST BLVD, SD, 92037	1227 - F6
LA QUINTA INN 10185 PAS MONTRIL, SD, 92129	1189 - G5
LA QUINTA INN 150 BONITA RD, CHV, 91910	1310 - D5
LA QUINTA INN 630 SYCAMORE AV, VSTA, 92081	1108 - B4
L AUBERGE DEL MAR RESORT & SPA 1540 CM DEL MAR, DLMR, 92014	1187 - F4
LA VALENCIA HOTEL 1132 PROSPECT ST, SD, 92037	1227 - F6
LOEWS CORONADO BAY RESORT 4000 CORONADO BAY RD, CORD, 92118	1309 - E7
MANCHESTER GRAND HYATT 1 MARKET PL, SD, 92101	1289 - A4
MARRIOTT DOWNTOWN 701 A ST, SD, 92101	1289 - B2
MARRIOTT MISSION VALLEY 8757 RIO SAN DIEGO DR, SD, 92108	1269 - D2
MARRIOTT RESIDENCE INN LA JOLLA 8901 GILMAN DR, SD, 92037	1228 - A3
MARRIOTT RESIDENCE INN SORRENTO MESA 5995 PACIFIC MESA CT, SD, 92121	1208 - F5
MARRIOTT RESORT CORONADO ISLAND 2000 2ND ST, CORD, 92118	1289 - A6
MARRIOTT SAN DIEGO MARINA 333 W HARBOR DR, SD, 92101	1289 - A4
OMNI SAN DIEGO HOTEL 675 L ST, SD, 92101	1289 - B4
PALA MESA RESORT 2001 OLD HWY 395, SDCo, 92028	1028 - H6
PRIME HOTEL 5975 LUSK BLVD, SD, 92121	1208 - F6
QUAILS INN 1025 LA BONITA DR, SDCo, 92078	1128 - C3
QUALITY INN & SUITES 1430 7TH AV, SD, 92101	1289 - B2
QUALITY INN & SUITES 760 MACADAMIA DR, CRLB, 92011	1126 - J5
QUALITY INN 2901 NIMITZ BLVD, SD, 92106	1288 - C1
QUALITY SUITES 9880 MIRA MESA BLVD, SD, 92131	1209 - F3
RADISSON HARBOR VIEW 1646 FRONT ST, SD, 92101	1289 - A2
RADISSON HOTEL LA JOLLA 3299 HOLIDAY CT, SD, 92037	1228 - A3
RADISSON HOTEL - SAN DIEGO 1433 CM DL RIO S, SD, 92116	1269 - B3
RADISSON INN 801 NATIONAL CITY BLVD, NATC, 91950	1309 - H1
RADISSON INN ENCINITAS 85 ENCINITAS BLVD, ENCT, 92024	1147 - C6
RADISSON RANCHO BERNARDO 11520 W BERNARDO CT, SD, 92127	1169 - J3
RAMADA INN 1455 OCOTILLO DR, ELCN, 92243	6559 - G1
RAMADA INN NORTH 5550 KEARNY MESA RD, SD, 92111	1229 - C7
RAMADA INN - OLD TOWN 3900 OLD TOWN AV, SD, 92110	1268 - F5
RAMADA INN SOUTH 91 BONITA RD, CHV, 91910	1310 - D5
RAMADA LIMITED SUITES 12979 RANCHO PENASQUITOS BLVD, SD, 92129	1189 - F5
RAMADA LIMITED SUITES MISSION VALLEY 641 CM DL RIO S, SD, 92108	1269 - A3
RAMADA PLAZA HOTEL CIRCLE 2151 HOTEL CIR S, SD, 92108	1268 - H4
RAMS HILL RESORT (SEE PAGE 1098) 4343 YAQUI PASS RD, SDCo, 92004	1099 - F3
RANCHO BERNARDO INN 17550 BERNARDO OAKS DR, SD, 92128	1170 - B1
RESIDENCE INN 11002 RANCHO CARMEL DR, SD, 92128	1189 - J1
RESIDENCE INN 5400 KEARNY MESA RD, SD, 92111	1229 - C7
SAN DIEGO MARRIOTT LA JOLLA 4240 LA JOLLA VILLAGE DR, SD, 92037	1228 - C2
SAN DIEGO MISSION VALLEY HILTON 901 CM DL RIO S, SD, 92108	1269 - B3
SAN DIEGO PARADISE POINT RESORT 1404 W VACATION RD, SD, 92109	1268 - A2
SEA LODGE 8110 CM DL ORO, SD, 92037	1227 - G5
SHELTER POINT HOTEL 1551 SHELTER ISLAND DR, SD, 92106	1288 - B4
SHERATON SAN DIEGO HOTEL & MARINA-EAST 1380 HARBOR ISLAND DR, SD, 92101	1288 - F1
SHERATON SAN DIEGO HOTEL & MARINA-WEST 1590 HARBOR ISLAND DR, SD, 92101	1288 - E2
SINGING HILLS LODGE 3007 DEHESA RD, SDCo, 92019	1252 - F6
TAMARACK BEACH RESORT 3200 CARLSBAD BLVD, CRLB, 92008	1106 - E6
TOWN & COUNTRY HOTEL 500 HOTEL CIR N, SD, 92108	1268 - J3
US GRANT HOTEL 326 BROADWAY, SD, 92101	1289 - A3
VACATION INN 2015 COTTONWOOD CIR, ELCN, 92243	6559 - F1
WELK RESORT CTR 8860 LAWRENCE WELK DR, SDCo, 92026	1089 - B2
WESTGATE HOTEL 1055 2ND AV, SD, 92101	1289 - A3
WESTIN HOTEL HORTON PLAZA 910 BROADWAY CIR, SD, 92101	1289 - A3
WOODFIN SUITE HOTEL 10044 PACIFIC MESA BLVD, SD, 92121	1208 - F6
WYNDHAM EMERALD PLAZA HOTEL 400 W BROADWAY, SD, 92101	1289 - A3

LIBRARIES

FEATURE NAME / Address City, ZIP Code	PAGE-GRID
ALPINE BRANCH 2130 ARNOLD WY, SDCo, 91901	1234 - B6
BALBOA BRANCH 4255 MT ABERNATHY AV, SD, 92117	1248 - H2
BECKWOURTH BRANCH 721 SAN PASQUAL ST, SD, 92113	1289 - H5
BENJAMIN BRANCH 5188 ZION AV, SD, 92120	1250 - A6
BONITA-SUNNYSIDE BRANCH 5047 CENTRAL AV, SDCo, 91902	1310 - J2
BORREGO SPRINGS BRANCH- (SEE PAGE 1058) 652 PALM CANYON DR, SDCo, 92004	1078 - J2
CALEXICO 850 ENCINAS AV, CALX, 92231	6680 - H1
CAMPO-MORENA VILLAGE BRANCH- (SEE PAGE 1298) 31466 HWY 94, SDCo, 91906	1318 - A5
CARDIFF BY THE SEA BRANCH 2027 SAN ELIJO AV, ENCT, 92007	1167 - D3
CARLSBAD CITY 1775 DOVE LN, CRLB, 92011	1127 - E5
CARLSBAD-GEORGINA COLE 1250 CARLSBAD VILLAGE DR, CRLB, 92008	1106 - F4
CARMEL MOUNTAIN RANCH BRANCH 12095 WORLD TRADE DR, SD, 92128	1190 - A1
CARMEL VALLEY BRANCH 3919 TOWNSGATE DR, SD, 92130	1188 - A5
CASA DE ORO BRANCH 9628 CAMPO RD, SDCo, 91977	1271 - C5
CHULA VISTA CIVIC CTR 365 F ST, CHV, 91910	1310 - B6
CITY HEIGHTS WEINGART BRANCH 3795 FAIRMOUNT AV, SD, 92105	1269 - H5
CLAIREMONT BRANCH 2920 BURGENER BLVD, SD, 92110	1248 - F6
COLLEGE ROLANDO BRANCH 6600 MONTEZUMA RD, SD, 92115	1270 - E2
CORONADO 640 ORANGE AV, CORD, 92118	1288 - J6
CREST BRANCH 105 JUANITA LN, SDCo, 92021	1252 - H4
DEL MAR BRANCH 1309 CM DL MAR, DLMR, 92014	1187 - F5
DESCANSO BRANCH 9545 RIVER DR, SDCo, 91916	1236 - A2
EASTLAKE 1120 EASTLAKE PKWY, CHV, 91915	1311 - F6
EL CAJON BRANCH 201 E DOUGLAS AV, ELCJ, 92020	1251 - F5
EL CENTRO 539 STATE ST, ELCN, 92243	6499 - H6
EL CENTRO BRANCH 375 S 1ST ST, ELCN, 92243	6499 - J6
ENCINITAS BRANCH 540 CORNISH DR, ENCT, 92024	1147 - C7
ESCONDIDO 239 S KALMIA ST, ESCN, 92025	1129 - J3
ESCONDIDO EAST VALLEY BRANCH 2245 E VALLEY PKWY, ESCN, 92027	1110 - D7
ESCONDIDO PIONEER ROOM 247 S KALMIA ST, ESCN, 92025	1129 - J3
FALLBROOK BRANCH 124 S MISSION RD, SDCo, 92028	1027 - F2
FLETCHER HILLS BRANCH 576 GARFIELD AV, ELCJ, 92020	1251 - B4
GEISEL UC SAN DIEGO CAMPUS, SD, 92093	1228 - A1
IMPERIAL 200 W 9TH ST, IMP, 92251	6439 - F6
IMPERIAL BEACH BRANCH 810 IMPERIAL BEACH BLVD, IMPB, 91932	1349 - G1
JACUMBA BRANCH (SEE PAGE 1300) 44605 OLD HWY 80, SDCo, 91934	1321 - G5
JULIAN BRANCH 2133 4TH ST, SDCo, 92036	1136 - B7
KENSINGTON-NORMAL HEIGHTS BRANCH 4121 ADAMS AV, SD, 92116	1269 - G3
LA JOLLA RIFORD BRANCH 7555 DRAPER AV, SD, 92037	1227 - E7
LAKESIDE BRANCH 9839 VINE ST, SDCo, 92040	1232 - B3
LA MESA BRANCH 8055 UNIVERSITY AV, LMSA, 91941	1270 - H2
LEMON GROVE BRANCH 8073 BROADWAY, LMGR, 91945	1270 - H6
LINCOLN ACRES BRANCH 2725 GRANGER AV, SDCo, 91950	1310 - C2
LINDA VISTA BRANCH 2160 ULRIC ST, SD, 92111	1268 - J1
LOGAN HEIGHTS BRANCH 811 S 28TH ST, SD, 92113	1289 - E5
MALCOLM X-VALENCIA PARK BRANCH 5148 MARKET ST, SD, 92114	1290 - A3
MIRA MESA BRANCH 8405 NEW SALEM ST, SD, 92126	1209 - C3
MISSION BRANCH 3861 MISSION AV, OCN, 92054	1086 - G3
MISSION HILLS BRANCH 925 W WASHINGTON ST, SD, 92103	1268 - J5
MISSION VALLEY BRANCH FELTON PKWY, SD, 92108	1269 - E1
NATIONAL CITY 200 E 12TH ST, NATC, 91950	1309 - H2
NATIONAL CITY PUBLIC 2020 VAN NESS AV, NATC, 91950	1310 - C1
NORTH CLAIREMONT BRANCH 4616 CLAIREMONT DR, SD, 92117	1248 - E2
NORTH PARK BRANCH 3795 31ST ST, SD, 92104	1269 - E5
OAK PARK BRANCH 2802 54TH ST, SD, 92105	1270 - B7
OCEAN BEACH BRANCH 4801 SANTA MONICA AV, SD, 92107	1267 - J6
OCEANSIDE 330 N COAST HWY, OCN, 92054	1086 - A7
OTAY MESA BRANCH 3003 CORONADO AV, SD, 92154	1350 - D1
PACIFIC BEACH TAYLOR BRANCH 4275 CASS ST, SD, 92109	1247 - J6
PARADISE HILLS BRANCH 5922 RANCHO HILLS DR, SD, 92139	1310 - D1
PINE VALLEY BRANCH 28804 OLD HWY 80, SDCo, 91962	1237 - B7
POINT LOMA BRANCH 2130 POINSETTIA DR, SD, 92107	1268 - B7
POWAY BRANCH 13137 POWAY RD, PWY, 92064	1190 - E4
RAMONA BRANCH 1406 MONTECITO RD, SDCo, 92065	1152 - F6
RANCHO BERNARDO BRANCH 17110 BERNARDO CENTER DR, SD, 92128	1170 - A2
RANCHO DEL REY 870 PAS RANCHERO, CHV, 91910	1311 - A6
RANCHO PENASQUITOS BRANCH 13330 SALMON RIVER RD, SD, 92129	1189 - E4
RANCHO SANTA FE BRANCH 17040 AVD DE ACACIAS, SDCo, 92067	1168 - D3
SAN CARLOS BRANCH 7265 JACKSON DR, SD, 92119	1250 - F5
SAN DIEGO CENTRAL 820 E ST, SD, 92101	1289 - B3
SAN MARCOS BRANCH 2 CIVIC CENTER DR, SMCS, 92069	1108 - J7
SANTEE BRANCH 9225 CARLTON HILLS BLVD, SNTE, 92071	1231 - B5
SAN YSIDRO BRANCH 101 W SAN YSIDRO BLVD, SD, 92173	1350 - G4
SCRIPPS INSTITUTE 8602 LA JOLLA SHORES DR, SD, 92093	1227 - H3
SCRIPPS RANCH BRANCH 10301 SCRIPPS LAKE DR, SD, 92131	1209 - G4
SERRA MESA BRANCH 3440 SANDROCK RD, SD, 92123	1249 - C4
SKYLINE HILLS BRANCH 480 S MEADOWBROOK DR, SD, 92114	1290 - H5
SOLANA BEACH BRANCH 981 LOMAS SANTA FE DR, SOLB, 92075	1167 - G7
SOUTH CHULA VISTA 389 ORANGE AV, CHV, 91911	1330 - D4
SPRING VALLEY BRANCH 1043 ELKELTON BLVD, SDCo, 91977	1290 - J3
TIERRASANTA BRANCH 4985 LA CUENTA DR, SD, 92124	1249 - H2

FEATURE NAME Address City, ZIP Code	PAGE-GRID
UNIV COMM BRANCH 4155 GOVERNOR DR, SD, 92122	1228 - E5
UNIVERSITY HEIGHTS BRANCH 4193 PARK BLVD, SD, 92103	1269 - C5
VALLEY CENTER BRANCH 29200 COLE GRADE RD, SDCo, 92082	1070 - F7
VISTA BRANCH 700 EUCALYPTUS AV, VSTA, 92084	1087 - J6

MILITARY INSTALLATIONS

FEATURE NAME Address City, ZIP Code	PAGE-GRID
ARMORY 4TH ST & PALM AV, NATC, 91950	1290 - A7
CARRIZO IMPACT AREA (CLOSED) ImCo, 92259	430 - G3
CHOCOLATE MTN NAVAL RES AERIAL-GUNNERY THE BRADSHAW TR, ImCo	411 - D6
EL CENTRO NAVAL AUXILIARY AIR STA HAVENS RD, ImCo, 92243	431 - A5
FLEET ANTI-SUB WARFARE 32444 ECHO LN, SD, 92147	1288 - C2
FORT ROSECRANS MILITARY RESV POINT LOMA, SD, 92106	1288 - A6
IMPERIAL BEACH NAVAL AUXILIARY-LANDING TOWER RD, IMPB, 91932	1349 - G2
LA POSTA MICROWAVE STA LA POSTA RD, SDCo, 91906	1298 - D7
NATIONAL GUARD ARMORY ARMSTRONG ST & MESA COLLEGE DR, SD, 92111	1249 - A5
NAVAL MED CTR 34800 BOB WILSON DR, SD, 92134	1289 - C1
NORTH ISLAND NAVAL AIR STA MCCAIN BLVD & ALAMEDA BLVD, CORD, 92135	1288 - D5
SALTON SEA MILITARY RESV ImCo, 92259	410 - J7
U S COAST GUARD STA HUMPHREYS RD, SD, 92152	1308 - A3
U S COAST GUARD STA N HARBOR DR, SD, 92101	1288 - H1
U S MARINE CORP AIR STA MIRAMAR I-15 FRWY & MIRAMAR WY, SD, 92145	1229 - E4
USMC BASE CAMP JOSEPH H PENDLETON SAN DIEGO FRWY & BASILONE RD, SDCo, 92055	1023 - H3
U S MARINE CORPS RECRUIT DEPOT BARNETT AV & PACIFIC HWY, SD, 92140	1268 - F6
U S NAVAL AIR FACILITY WHEELER RD, ImCo, 92259	430 - K4
U S NAVAL AMPHIBIOUS BASE SILVER STRAND BLVD, CORD, 92118	1289 - B7
U S NAVAL RADIO STA SILVER STRAND BLVD, CORD, 91932	1329 - E5
U S NAVAL RESV HARBOR DR, NATC, 92136	1309 - F1
U S NAVAL RESV HARBOR DR, SD, 92136	1289 - F7
U S NAVAL RESV HIGHWAY 78, ImCo	431 - G2
U S NAVAL RESV OFF IMPERIAL HWY, ImCo, 92259	430 - H3
U S NAVAL RESV POINT LOMA, SD, 92152	1287 - J5
U S NAVAL RESV POINT LOMA, SD, 92152	1288 - A5
US NAVAL WEAPONS STA FALLBROOK FALLBROOK RD, SDCo, 92055	1027 - C2

MUSEUMS

FEATURE NAME Address City, ZIP Code	PAGE-GRID
ANTIQUE GAS & STEAM ENGINE MUS 2040 N SANTA FE AV, VSTA, 92083	1087 - F2
ANZA-BORREGO DESERT STATE PK MUS-(SEE PAGE 1058) 200 PALM CANYON DR, SDCo, 92004	1078 - F2
BANCROFT RANCH HOUSE MUS 9050 MEMORY LN, SDCo, 91977	1271 - B5
BOEHM GALLERY 1140 W MISSION RD, SMCS, 92069	1108 - F6
BONITA HIST MUS 4035 BONITA RD, CHV, 91902	1310 - G3
CALIFORNIA SURF MUS 223 N COAST HWY, OCN, 92054	1086 - A7
CALIFORNIA SURF MUS 308 N PACIFIC ST, OCN, 92054	1106 - A1
CAMPO MOTOR TRANSPORT MUS-(SEE PAGE 1298) 31949 HWY 94, SDCo, 91906	1318 - B5
CAMPO RAILROAD MUSUEM (SEE PAGE 1298) FOREST GATE RD, SDCo, 91906	1318 - A7
CENTRO CULTURAL DE LA RAZA 2004 PARK BLVD, SD, 92101	1289 - C1
CHILDRENS DISCOVERY MUS OF N COUNTY 300 CARLSBAD VILLAGE DR, CRLB, 92008	1106 - D5
CHILDRENS MUS OF SAN DIEGO 200 ISLAND AV, SD, 92101	1289 - A4
CHULA VISTA HERITAGE MUS 360 3RD AV, CHV, 91910	1310 - B6
CHULA VISTA NATURE CTR 1000 GUNPOWDER POINT DR, CHV, 91910	1309 - H6
DAVIS, WILLIAM HEATH HOUSE MUS 410 ISLAND AV, SD, 92101	1289 - A4
DEER PARK ESCONDIDO & AUTO MUS 29013 CHAMPAGNE BLVD, SDCo, 92026	1089 - A1
FIREHOUSE MUS 1572 COLUMBIA ST, SD, 92101	1288 - J2
FLYING LEATHERNECK AVIATION MUS USMCAS MIRAMAR, SD, 92126	1209 - C7
GROSSMONT COLLEGE HYDE ART GALLERY 8800 GROSSMONT COLLEGE DR, ELCJ, 92020	1251 - A3
HERITAGE OF THE AMERICAS MUS 12110 CUYAMACA COLLEGE DR W, SDCo, 92019	1271 - J6
HERITAGE PARK VILLAGE MUS 220 PEYRIE DR, OCN, 92057	1086 - G2
HERITAGE WALK MUS 321 N BROADWAY, ESCN, 92025	1129 - H2
HOUSE OF PACIFIC RELATIONS PAN AMERICAN RD W, SD, 92101	1289 - B1
JAPANESE FRIENDSHIP GARDEN 2215 PAN AMERICAN RD, SD, 92101	1289 - C1
JULIAN PIONEER MUS 2811 WASHINGTON ST, SDCo, 92036	1136 - A7
LA MESA DEPOT MUS LA MESA BLVD & NEBO DR, LMSA, 91941	1270 - H3
MARINE CORPS RECRUIT DEPOT COM MUS 1600 HENDERSON AV, SD, 92140	1268 - E6
MINGEI INTL MUS 1439 EL PRADO, SD, 92101	1289 - B1
MINGEI INTL MUS N COUNTY 155 W GRAND AV, ESCN, 92025	1129 - J3
MISSION SAN LUIS REY MUS 4050 MISSION AV, OCN, 92057	1086 - H2
MUS OF CONTEMPORARY ART SAN DIEGO 1001 KETTNER BLVD, SD, 92101	1288 - J3
MUS OF CONTEMPORARY ART SD-LA JOLLA 700 PROSPECT ST, SD, 92037	1227 - E6
MUS OF MAKING MUSIC 5790 ARMADA DR, CRLB, 92008	1126 - H3
MUS OF PHOTOGRAPHIC ARTS 1649 EL PRADO, SD, 92101	1289 - C1
OCEANSIDE MUS OF ART 704 PIER VIEW WY, OCN, 92054	1086 - A7
SAN DIEGO AEROSPACE MUS 2001 PAN AMERICAN PZ, SD, 92101	1289 - B1
SAN DIEGO ARCHAEOLOGICAL CTR 16666 SAN PASQUAL VALLEY RD, SD, 92027	1131 - C7
SAN DIEGO AUTOMOTIVE MUS 2080 PAN AMERICAN PZ, SD, 92101	1289 - B1
SAN DIEGO HALL OF CHAMPIONS SPORTS-MUS 2131 PAN AMERICAN PZ, SD, 92101	1289 - B1
SAN DIEGO HIST SOC MUS & RESRCH-ARCHVS 1649 EL PRADO, SD, 92101	1289 - C1
SAN DIEGO MARITIME MUS 1492 N HARBOR DR, SD, 92101	1288 - J2
SAN DIEGO MODEL RAILROAD MUS 1649 EL PRADO, SD, 92101	1289 - C1
SAN DIEGO MUS OF ART 1450 EL PRADO, SD, 92101	1289 - B1
SAN DIEGO MUS OF MAN 1350 EL PRADO, SD, 92101	1289 - B1
SAN DIEGO NATURAL HIST MUS 1788 EL PRADO, SD, 92101	1289 - C1
SAN DIEGUITO HERITAGE MUS 561 S VULCAN AV, ENCT, 92024	1147 - C7
SAN MARCOS HIST SOCIETY 270 W SAN MARCOS BLVD, SMCS, 92069	1108 - H7
SERRA MUS 2727 PRESIDIO DR, SD, 92103	1268 - F4
TIMKEN MUS OF ART 1500 EL PRADO, SD, 92101	1289 - C1
UNIV ART GALLERY SDSU AZTEC CIRCLE DR & AV OF ARTS, SD, 92182	1270 - C1
UNIV ART GALLERY UCSD 9500 GILMAN DR, SD, 92093	1228 - A2
VETERANS MUS AND MEM CTR 2115 PARK BLVD, SD, 92101	1289 - C1
VILLA MONTEZUMA MUS 1925 K ST, SD, 92102	1289 - C4
VISTA HIST MUS 651 E VISTA WY, VSTA, 92084	1087 - J5
WELLS FARGO HIST MUS 2733 SAN DIEGO AV, SD, 92110	1268 - F5
WHALEY, THOMAS HOUSE MUS 2482 SAN DIEGO AV, SD, 92110	1268 - F5
WORLD WAR II FLYING MUS 1850 JOE CROSSON DR, ELCJ, 92020	1251 - E1

OPEN SPACE PRESERVES

FEATURE NAME Address City, ZIP Code	PAGE-GRID
AGUA TIBIA WILDERNESS AREA SDCo, 92060	409 - E5
BEAR, MARIAN MEM NATURAL PK REGENTS RD, SD, 92117	1228 - D7
BLACK MOUNTAIN PK BLACK MOUNTAIN RD, SD, 92129	1169 - F7
BLUE SKY CANYON ECOLOGICAL RESERVE ESPOLA RD & GREEN VALLEY TKTR, PWY, 92064	1170 - J3
BONSALL PRESERVE S MISSION RD, SDCo, 92003	1048 - A7
CHULA VISTA WILDLIFE REFUGE SAN DIEGO BAY, CHV, 91910	1329 - H2
CIBOLA NATL WILDLIFE REFUGE HIGHWAY 78, ImCo	412 - B6
CREST CANYON OPEN SPACE PK DEL MAR HTS RD & DURANGO DR, SD, 92014	1187 - G4
DALEY RANCH LA HONDA DR, ESCN, 92026	1089 - J5
DINWIDDIE PRESERVE S STAGE COACH LN & BROOKE RD, SDCo, 92028	1027 - J6
EL CAPITAN COUNTY OPEN SPACE PRESERVE-(SEE PAGE 1192) WILDCAT CANYON RD, SDCo, 92040	1193 - C7
HELLHOLE CYN CO OPEN SPACE PRESERVE KIAVO DR & SANTEE LN, SDCo, 92082	1071 - H6
IMPERIAL NATL WILDLIFE REFUGE FISHERS LANDING, ImCo	412 - D11
IMPERIAL WATERFOWL MANAGEMENT AREA HIGHWAY 111 & DOWDEN RD, ImCo, 92233	411 - B10
JACUMBA NAT COOP LND & WLDLF MGMT-(SEE PAGE 1300) SDCo, 91934	1301 - J3
LA JOLLA NATURAL PK COUNTRY CLUB DR, SD, 92037	1227 - G6
LARWIN PK CARLSBAD VILLAGE DR, CRLB, 92010	1106 - H3
LOPEZ CANYON OPEN SPACE CAMINO SANTA FE, SD, 92121	1208 - F4
LOS JILGUEROS PRESERVE S MISSION RD & PEPPER TREE LN, SDCo, 92028	1027 - G5
LOS PENASQUITOS CANYON PRESERVE 12020 BLACK MOUNTAIN RD, SD, 92130	1208 - E2
MISSION TRAILS REGL PK 7300 FATHER JUNIPERO SERRA TR, SD, 92119	1250 - C1
MOUNT GOWER COUNTY OPEN SPACE-PRESERVE GUNN STAGE RD, SDCo, 92065	1153 - H6
MOUNT GOWER COUNTY OPEN SPACE-PRESERVE GUNN STAGE RD, SDCo, 92065	1173 - H1
NORTHERN WILDLIFE PRESERVE PACIFIC BEACH DR & NOYES ST, SD, 92109	1248 - B6
OAK OASIS COUNTY OPEN SPACE PRESERVE 12620 WILDCAT CANYON RD, SDCo, 92040	1212 - D2
OPEN SPACE LAUREL ST & N HARBOR DR, SD, 92101	1288 - H1
OTAY COUNTY OPEN SPACE PRESERVE WUESTE RD, SDCo, 91915	1332 - B3
OVERLOOK PK HIGH BLUFF DR, SD, 92130	1187 - J4
ROSE CANYON OPEN SPACE GENESEE AV, SD, 92122	1228 - A6
SAN ELIJO LAGOON CO PK & ECOLOGIC RES MANCHESTER AV OFF S D FRWY, ENCT, 92067	1167 - G5
SAN MATEO CANYON WILDERNESS ORTEGA HWY, SDCo, 92055	408 - L4
SANTA MARGARITA ECOLOGICAL RESERVE RED MOUNTAIN TKTR, SDCo, 92028	998 - D3
SCRIPPS, JAMES BLUFF PRESERVE CM DL MAR, DLMR, 92014	1187 - E2
SEAL ROCK RESERVE COAST BLVD, SD, 92037	1227 - E6
SILVERWOOD WILDLIFE SANCTUARY BARONA RD, SDCo, 92040	1212 - G2
SOLEDAD NATURAL PK LA JOLLA PKWY & I-5, SD, 92037	1227 - J7
SOUTH BAY STUDY AREA SILVER STRAND BLVD, CORD, 91932	1329 - F4
SOUTH SAN DIEGO BAY NATL WLDLF REFUGE SAN DIEGO BAY, SD, 91950	1329 - F4
SWEETWATER MARSH NATL WLDLF REGUGE 1000 GUNPOWDER POINT DR, CHV, 91910	1309 - G5
SYCAMORE CANYON CO OPEN SPACE-PRESERVE 13920 HIGHWAY 67, SDCo, 92071	1191 - C7
TECOLOTE CANYON NATURAL PK TECOLOTE CANYON, SD, 92111	1248 - F4
TIJUANA RIV NAT ESTUARINE SANCTUARY SUNSET AV, SD, 92154	1349 - H4
TIJUANA SLOUGH NATL WILDLIFE REFUGE 301 CASPIAN WY, IMPB, 91932	1349 - F2
TORREY HIGHLANDS PK LANSDALE DR & DEL MAR HEIGHTS, SD, 92130	1188 - B4
TORREY PINES STATE RESERVE N TORREY PINES RD, SD, 92014	1187 - H7
VOLCAN MTN WILDERNESS PRESERVE VOLCAN RD, SDCo, 92036	1136 - D2
WISTER WATERFOWL MANAGEMENT AREA HIGHWAY 111 & HOWELL RD, ImCo, 92257	411 - A6

PARK & RIDE

FEATURE NAME Address City, ZIP Code	PAGE-GRID
PARK & RIDE 195 S TREMONT ST, OCN, 92054	1106 - A1
PARK & RIDE 47TH ST & CASTANA ST, SD, 92102	1289 - J4
PARK & RIDE 62ND ST & AKINS AV, SD, 92114	1290 - D3
PARK & RIDE AMAYA DR & AMAYA CT, LMSA, 91942	1251 - B7
PARK & RIDE FLETCHER PKY & GROSSMONT CTR, LMSA, 91942	1250 - J7
PARK & RIDE HOLLISTER ST & PALM AV, SD, 92154	1330 - B7
PARK & RIDE INTERSTATE 5 & E ST, CHV, 91910	1309 - J6
PARK & RIDE IRIS AV & 30TH ST, SD, 92154	1350 - D2
PARK & RIDE MASSACHUSETTS AV, LMGR, 91945	1290 - F1
PARK & RIDE N EUCLID AV & MARKET ST, SD, 92102	1290 - A3
PARK & RIDE PALOMAR ST & INDUSTRIAL BLVD, CHV, 91911	1330 - B4
PARK & RIDE SPRING ST, LMSA, 91941	1270 - J4
PARK & RIDE W 8TH ST & HARBOR DR, NATC, 92136	1309 - G1
PARK & RIDE WILSON AV & MILES-OF-CARS WY, NATC, 91950	1309 - H3
PARK & RIDE W SEAWARD AV, SD, 92173	1350 - F3
PARK & RIDE W VALLEY PKWY & N QUINCE ST, ESCN, 92025	1129 - H3
PARK & RIDE LOT 1 3642 AGUA DULCE BLVD, SDCo, 91977	1271 - E5
PARK & RIDE LOT 2 11575 WOODSIDE AV, SDCo, 92040	1231 - H4
PARK & RIDE LOT 3 1785 ESCONDIDO BLVD, ESCN, 92025	1130 - A5
PARK & RIDE LOT 4 CARMEL MTN RD & FREEPORT RD, SD, 92129	1189 - F4
PARK & RIDE LOT 5 1667 MAXSON ST, OCN, 92054	1086 - B7
PARK & RIDE LOT 6 4929 MIRA MESA BLVD, SD, 92126	1209 - E3
PARK & RIDE LOT 7 12791 SORRENTO VALLEY RD, SD, 92121	1207 - J2
PARK & RIDE LOT 8 7675 HIGH ST, LMSA, 91941	1270 - G5
PARK & RIDE LOT 9 2300 SWEETWATER RD, SDCo, 91950	1310 - C3
PARK & RIDE LOT 10 12522 MAPLEVIEW ST, SDCo, 92040	1232 - B3
PARK & RIDE LOT 11 871 N BROADWAY, ESCN, 92025	1129 - H1
PARK & RIDE LOT 12 2885 LEMON GROVE AV, LMGR, 91945	1270 - G6
PARK & RIDE LOT 16 12668 SABRE SPRINGS PKWY, SD, 92128	1189 - H6
PARK & RIDE LOT 17 4300 TAYLOR ST, SD, 92110	1268 - G4
PARK & RIDE LOT 18 TED WILLIAMS PKWY & SABRE SPGS, SD, 92128	1189 - J3
PARK & RIDE LOT 19 PALA RD & OLD HWY 395, SDCo, 92028	1048 - H2
PARK & RIDE LOT 20 5196 GOVERNOR RD, SD, 92122	1228 - G4
PARK & RIDE LOT 21 501 SEAVIEW PL, VSTA, 92081	1107 - H1
PARK & RIDE LOT 22 8725 MURRAY DR, LMSA, 91942	1271 - A1
PARK & RIDE LOT 24 I-805 & VISTA SORRENTO PKWY, SD, 92121	1208 - D7
PARK & RIDE LOT 25 1441 E WASHINGTON AV, ELCJ, 92019	1252 - A6
PARK & RIDE LOT 26 CARMEL MTN RD & RANCHO CARMEL, SD, 92128	1189 - J1
PARK & RIDE LOT 29 7838 JAPATUL VALLEY RD, SDCo, 91901	1235 - J6
PARK & RIDE LOTS 30 & 38 1699 SEVEN OAKES RD, ESCN, 92026	1109 - F6
PARK & RIDE LOT 31 10155 RANCHO CARMEL DR, SD, 92128	1189 - J3
PARK & RIDE LOT 32 710 LA COSTA AV, CRLB, 92024	1147 - B1
PARK & RIDE LOT 33 INTERSTATE 15 & DEER SPGS RD, SDCo, 92026	1089 - C6
PARK & RIDE LOT 34 INTERSTATE 15 & MTN MEADOW RD, SDCo, 92026	1089 - D6
PARK & RIDE LOT 35 INTERSTATE 15 & GOPHER CANYON, SDCo, 92026	1068 - J6
PARK & RIDE LOT 37 3601 AVOCADO BLVD, SDCo, 91941	1271 - F5
PARK & RIDE LOT 39 3700 HAYNER DR, OCN, 92056	1107 - B2
PARK & RIDE LOT 40 8627 JAMACHA BLVD, SDCo, 91977	1291 - A4
PARK & RIDE LOT 41 13702 CM CANADA, SDCo, 92021	1252 - D1
PARK & RIDE LOT 42 9001 BLOSSOM VALLEY RD, SDCo, 92021	1232 - F5
PARK & RIDE LOT 43 8002 GILMAN DR, SD, 92037	1228 - A6
PARK & RIDE LOT 44 1928 MORENO ST, OCN, 92054	1106 - D3
PARK & RIDE LOT 45 COLLEGE BLVD & VISTA WY, OCN, 92056	1107 - B2
PARK & RIDE LOT 46 4980 SWEETGRASS LN, SDCo, 92003	1048 - A6
PARK & RIDE LOT 47 1600 VILLA CARDIFF DR, ENCT, 92007	1167 - E2
PARK & RIDE LOT 48 13734 TWIN PEAKS RD, PWY, 92064	1190 - F1
PARK & RIDE LOT 49 7850 NAVAJO RD, SD, 92119	1250 - H4
PARK & RIDE LOT 50 610 PAS DL REY, CHV, 91910	1330 - H1
PARK & RIDE LOT 51 12862 RANCHO PENASQUITOS BLVD, SD, 92129	1189 - F5
PARK & RIDE LOT 52 14350 COMMUNITY RD, PWY, 92064	1190 - E2
PARK & RIDE LOT 53 10060 CARMEL MOUNTAIN RD, SD, 92129	1189 - F4
PARK & RIDE LOT 54 VIA RANCHO PKWY & DEL LAGO BL, ESCN, 92029	1150 - A2
PARK & RIDE LOT 56 BUENA VISTA WY & EAST H ST, CHV, 91910	1311 - B5
PARK & RIDE LOT 57 10330 CARMEL MOUNTAIN RD, SD, 92129	1189 - G3
PARK & RIDE LOT 58 10440 BLACK MOUNTAIN RD, SD, 92126	1209 - E4
PARK & RIDE LOT 59 5230 BANCROFT DR, LMSA, 91941	1271 - B1
PARK & RIDE LOT 60 5480 BANCROFT DR, LMSA, 91941	1271 - B1
PARK & RIDE LOT 61 9307 MURRAY DR, LMSA, 91942	1251 - B7
PARK & RIDE LOT 62 170 CL MAGDALENA, ENCT, 92024	1147 - C7
PARK & RIDE LOT 63 1855 MAIN ST, SDCo, 92065	1152 - E7

FEATURE NAME Address City, ZIP Code	PAGE-GRID
PARK & RIDE LOT 64 2245 E VALLEY PKWY, ESCN, 92027	1110 - D7
PARK & RIDE LOT 65 RCHO BERNARDO RD & I-15, SD, 92127	1169 - J2
PARK & RIDE LOT 66 CENTRE CITY PKWY & DECATUR WY, ESCN, 92026	1129 - G1
PARK & RIDE LOT 69 855 E BARNHAM RD, SMCS, 92078	1129 - B1
PARK & RIDE LOT 70 MISSION GORGE RD & BIG ROCK RD, SNTE, 92071	1230 - H7
PARK & RIDE LOT 71 2782 SWEETWATER SPRINGS BLVD, SDCo, 91977	1271 - E7
PARK & RIDE LOT 72 8805 MAGNOLIA AV, SNTE, 92071	1231 - F7
PARK & RIDE LOT 73 MISSION AV & FRONTIER DR, OCN, 92054	1086 - F4
PARK & RIDE LOT 74 COLLEGE GROVE DR, SD, 92115	1270 - D6
PARK & RIDE LOT 75 3394 CHAPEL LN, SDCo, 92065	1172 - B3

PARKS & RECREATION

FEATURE NAME Address City, ZIP Code	PAGE-GRID
39TH STREET PK, SD	1269 - G3
ADAMS AVENUE PK, SD	1269 - F3
ADAMS PK, ELCN	6499 - H6
ADAMS, ROBERT COMM PK, SDCo	1070 - G7
ADOBE BLUFFS PK, SD	1189 - C2
ADOBE RIDGE MINI PK, PWY	1190 - C1
AGUA CALIENTE COUNTY PK, SDCo	430 - C3
AGUILAR PK, ELCN	6499 - F4
ALAMOSA PK, OCN	1087 - C1
ALLEN, DENNIS V PK, SD	1289 - G3
ALLIED GARDENS COMM PK, SD	1250 - A5
ANZA-BORREGO DESERT STATE PK, SDCo- (SEE PAGE 1300)	1301 - H5
ARBOLITOS SPORT FIELDS, PWY	1190 - C1
ASHLEY FALLS PK, SD	1188 - D5
AUGUSTA PK, CHV	1311 - G5
AVIARA COMM PK, CRLB	1127 - D4
AZALEA PK, SD	1269 - G7
AZTEC PK, LMSA	1270 - H1
BALBOA PK, SD	1269 - D7
BALDERAMA, JOE PK, OCN	1086 - B6
BANCROFT COUNTY PK, SDCo	1271 - B5
BANDEL, L C PK, CORD	1288 - G7
BAY BOULEVARD PK, CHV	1309 - J7
BAY CIRCLE PK, CORD	1308 - J1
BAYSIDE PK, CHV	1329 - H1
BAY TERRACES COMM PK, SD	1290 - G7
BAYVIEW PK, CORD	1288 - H5
BEL ESPRIT PK, SMCS	1108 - G5
BENDIXEN, BETTE PK, PWY	1190 - B6
BERRY PK, SD	1350 - A2
BERRY STREET PK, LMGR	1270 - F7
BIG ROCK PK, SNTE	1230 - H7
BILL BECK PK, ELCJ	1251 - D4
BIRD PK, SD	1269 - D6
BIRD ROCK PK, SD	1247 - G4
BISHOP, MELBA PK, OCN	1067 - B6
BLACK MTN RANCH COMM PK, SD	1169 - D7
BONITA LONG CANYON PK, CHV	1311 - C3
BONITAS HACIENDAS MINI PK, CHV	1311 - B4
BOONE PK, SD	1290 - G5
BORDER FIELD STATE PK, IMPB	1349 - G6
BOSTONIA PK, ELCJ	1251 - J3
BOUGHER, HELEN PK, SMCS	1109 - C5
BRADLEY PK, SMCS	1108 - D7
BREEZE HILL PK, VSTA	1107 - F1
BREEZEWOOD PK, CHV	1311 - D6
BRENGLE TERRACE PK, VSTA	1088 - A5
BREWER, DEPUTY LONNIE G COUNTY PK, SDCo	1271 - G4
BRIERCREST PK, LMSA	1251 - A7
BRIERLY FIELD, CRLB	1106 - E6
BROWN, MAXTON PK, CRLB	1106 - D4
BUCCANEER BEACH PK, OCN	1106 - B3
BUCKLIN PK, ELCN	6559 - G1
BUENA VISTA PK, VSTA	1107 - H6
CABRILLO HEIGHTS PK, SD	1249 - B4
CACTUS COUNTY PK, SDCo	1232 - C2
CADENCIA PK, CRLB	1127 - J7
CADMAN COMM PK, SD	1248 - C3
CAJON VALLEY PK, ELCJ	1251 - G5
CALAVERA PK, CRLB	1107 - A4
CALUMET PK, SD	1247 - F4
CANNON PK, CRLB	1126 - F2
CANYONSIDE COMM PK, SD	1189 - C7
CAPISTRANO PK, OCN	1086 - A5
CARDIFF PK, ENCT	1167 - D3
CARDIFF SPORTS PK, ENCT	1167 - F2
CARMEL CREEK PK, SD	1188 - B5
CARMEL DEL MAR PK, SD	1188 - B7
CARMEL GROVE PK, SD	1188 - A7
CARMEL MISSION PK, SD	1188 - B6
CARMEL MTN RANCH COMM PK, SD	1189 - H3
CARMEL VALLEY COMM PK, SD	1188 - A6
CARRASCO, JOSEPH PK, OCN	1086 - E7
CARRILLO, LEO RANCH HIST PK, CRLB	1127 - J3
CARSON, KIT PK, ESCN	1130 - B7
CEDAR LANE PK, VSTA	1087 - G6
CENTENNIAL PK, CORD	1288 - J5
CERRO DE LAS POSAS PK, SMCS	1108 - E5
CHASE FIELD, CRLB	1106 - F6
CHAVEZ, CESAR E PK, SD	1289 - C6
CHAVEZ, CESAR PK, OCN	1086 - B7
CHICANO PK, SD	1289 - C5
CHOLLAS COMM PK, SD	1270 - C7
CHULA VISTA BAYFRONT PK, CHV	1329 - H2
CHULA VISTA COMM PK, CHV	1311 - F5
CIRCLE PK, CHV	1311 - H5
CITY HEIGHTS COMM PK, SD	1269 - H5
CITY PK, ELCN	6499 - H6
CITY PK, SD	1289 - A3
CIVIC CENTER PK, VSTA	1087 - J6
CLAIREMONT COMM PK, SD	1248 - E5
CLAY PK, SD	1270 - D3
CLEATOR COMM PK, SD	1268 - B6
CLEVELAND NATL FOREST, SDCo	1218 - C3
CLIFFRIDGE PK, SD	1227 - J5
COAST BLVD PK, SD	1227 - E7
COBBLESTONE PK, CHV	1311 - E3
COLINA DEL SOL COMM PK, SD	1270 - A5
COLLIER COUNTY PK, SDCo	1152 - H6
COLLIER PK, LMSA	1270 - J3
COLLIER PK WEST, SD	1268 - A6
CONNOLEY PK, CHV	1330 - E5
CORAL GATE PK, SD	1350 - F5
CORONADO CAYS SPORTS PK, CORD	1329 - D2
COTTONWOOD 3 COUNTY PK, SDCo	1272 - B5
COTTONWOOD CREEK PK, ENCT	1147 - C6
COTTONWOOD PK, CHV	1311 - D7
COUNTRYSIDE PK, CHV	1311 - E6
CREEKWALK PK, VSTA	1087 - G7
CRONAN PK, CORD	1288 - J7
CRUMMERT PK, CALX	6680 - H1
CUVIER PK (THE WEDDING BOWL), SD	1227 - E7
CUYAMACA PK, ELCJ	1251 - E7
CUYAMACA RANCHO STATE PK, SDCo- (SEE PAGE 1176)	1196 - F2
CYPRESS CANYON PK, SD	1210 - B1
DAILARD PK, SD	1250 - D4
DAMON LANE COUNTY PK, SDCo	1271 - H3
DEL MAR TRAILS PK, SD	1188 - C7
DENE, JESMOND PK, ESCN	1109 - G3
DISCOVERY LAKE PK, SMCS	1128 - G3

FEATURE NAME Address City, ZIP Code	PAGE-GRID
DISCOVERY PK, CHV	1311 - A5
DIXON LAKE REC AREA, ESCN	1110 - D4
DOLPHIN BEACH CLUB, CHV	1311 - H6
DOS PICOS COUNTY PK, SDCo	1171 - H5
DOYLE COMM PK, SD	1228 - C3
DUNES PK, IMPB	1329 - E7
DUSSAULT, DAN PK, SDCo	1027 - E3
DUSTY RHODES PK, SD	1268 - A5
EAST CLAIREMONT ATHLETIC AREA, SD	1248 - G5
EASTLAKE BEACH CLUB, CHV	1311 - E4
EASTLAKE III PK, CHV	1332 - A2
ECKE, PAUL SPORTS PK, ENCT	1147 - C6
ELFIN FOREST RECREATIONAL RESERVE, SDCo	1149 - B2
EL MONTE COUNTY PK, SDCo	1212 - J5
ELMWOOD PK, ESCN	1130 - A1
EL NORTE PK, ESCN	1110 - A6
EL TOYON PK, NATC	1290 - A7
EMBARCADERO MARINA PK NORTH, SD	1288 - J4
EMBARCADERO MARINA PK SOUTH, SD	1289 - A4
EMERALD HILLS PK, SD	1290 - B2
EMERSON PK, CALX	6680 - G1
ENCANTO COMM PK, SD	1290 - D2
ESTRELLA COUNTY PK, SDCo	1271 - D4
EUCALYPTUS COUNTY PK, SDCo	1271 - B3
EUCALYPTUS PK, CHV	1310 - A5
EXPLORER PK, CHV	1310 - H6
FALLBROOK PK, SDCo	1027 - H3
FANUEL STREET PK, SD	1247 - J7
FELICITA COUNTY PK, SDCo	1149 - H1
FIRE MOUNTAIN PK, OCN	1086 - F7
FIRESIDE PK, OCN	1086 - E3
FIRE STATION PK, ELCJ	1251 - C4
FLETCHER COVE BEACH PK, SOLB	1167 - E7
FLETCHER HILLS PK, ELCJ	1251 - B5
FLINN SPRINGS COUNTY PK, SDCo	1232 - J5
FRAZIER FIELD, ELCN	6499 - H5
FRIENDSHIP PK, CHV	1310 - B6
FUERTE PK, CRLB	1127 - H6
GARDEN ROAD PK, PWY	1190 - J4
GERSHWIN PK, SD	1248 - D1
GLEN PK, ENCT	1167 - D4
GLORIETTA BAY PK, CORD	1308 - J1
GOLDEN HILL COMM CTR, SD	1289 - D2
GOMEZ PK, ELCN	6500 - A7
GOMPERS PK, SD	1290 - A3
GOODAN RANCH COUNTY PK, SDCo	1191 - C7
GOODLAND ACRES COUNTY PK, SDCo	1271 - A6
GRAND CARIBE SHORELINE PK, CORD	1329 - E1
GRANT HILL PK, SD	1289 - D4
GRANTVILLE PK, SD	1249 - J7
GRAPE DAY PK, ESCN	1129 - J2
GRIFFEN, HARRY PK, LMSA	1251 - C7
GROVE PK, ESCN	1130 - A1
GUAJOME REGL PK, OCN	1067 - D7
HALECREST PK, CHV	1310 - F6
HARBOR ISLAND DR PK, SD	1288 - F2
HARBORSIDE PK, CHV	1330 - B4
HARBORVIEW PK, CORD	1288 - J5
HARRIS, ADA PK, ENCT	1167 - E2
HARVEST PK, CHV	1311 - D7
HAWK VIEW PK, ENCT	1147 - D2
HEISE, WILLIAM COUNTY PK, SDCo	1156 - D5
HENDERSON, WILLIE SPORTS COMPLEX, SD	1289 - J6
HERITAGE PK, OCN	1086 - H2
HERITAGE PK, CHV	1331 - C1
HERITAGE PK, SD	1268 - G5
HERMOSA TERRACE PK, SD	1247 - E2
HIGHLAND RANCH PK, SD	1190 - A1
HIGHWOOD PK, LMSA	1270 - H4
HILLEARY PK, PWY	1190 - E4
HILLSIDE PK, ELCJ	1251 - C4
HILLTOP PK, CHV	1310 - D7
HILLTOP COMM PK, SD	1189 - E2
HOLIDAY PK, CRLB	1106 - F5
HOLLYWOOD PK, SD	1269 - H7
HORIZON PK, CHV	1331 - A2
HOSP GROVE PK, CRLB	1106 - E3
HOURGLASS FIELD COMM PK, SD	1209 - E4
HOWARD LANE PK, SD	1350 - D2
H STREET VIEWPOINT PK, ENCT	1147 - B7
IMPERIAL SAND DUNES REC AREA, ImCo	411 - E10
INAJA MEM PK, SDCo	1135 - C4
INDEPENDENCE PK, CHV	1311 - B6
I STREET VIEWPOINT PK, ENCT	1167 - B1
IVEY RANCH PK, OCN	1086 - H3
JACKSON PK, LMSA	1250 - H7
JACKS POND PK, SMCS	1129 - B1
JACUMBA COMM PK, SDCo- (SEE PAGE 1300)	1321 - H6
JANE, NANCY COUNTY PK, SDCo	1252 - H3
JERABEK PK, SD	1209 - J4
J STREET VIEWPOINT PK, ENCT	1167 - B1
JUDSON, C S PK, ELCJ	1251 - F5
KEARNY MESA COMM PK, SD	1248 - J5
KEILLER PK, SD	1290 - F3
KELLOGG PK, SD	1227 - G5
KELLY STREET PK, SD	1268 - H1
KENNEDY, JOHN F PK, ELCJ	1252 - B5
KENNEDY, JOHN F PK, SD	1289 - J5
KENSINGTON MINI PK, SD	1269 - H3
KENSINGTON RD PK, CHV	1311 - G3
KIMBALL PK, NATC	1309 - H2
KING, MARTIN L JR MEM COMM PK, SD	1290 - D5
KING, MARTIN LUTHER JR PK, OCN	1086 - J4
KING, MARTIN LUTHER JR PROMENADE, SD	1289 - A4
KNOB HILL PK, SMCS	1109 - D7
KUNKEL PK, LMGR	1270 - H5
LA COLONIA PK, SOLB	1187 - G1
LA COSTA CANYON PK, CRLB	1147 - H1
LAGUNA RIVIERA PK, CRLB	1106 - J7
LA JOLLA ATHLETIC AREA, SD	1227 - J3
LA JOLLA COMM PK, SD	1227 - E7
LA JOLLA HERMOSA PK, SD	1247 - F3
LAKE JENNINGS COUNTY PK, SDCo	1232 - E3
LAKE MORENA COUNTY PK, SDCo- (SEE PAGE 1296)	1297 - D5
LAKE MURRAY COMM PK, SD	1250 - E6
LAKE PK, OCN	1107 - F3
LAKE POWAY REC AREA, PWY	1170 - H4
LAKE VIEW PK, SD	1209 - J3
LAMAR COUNTY PK, SDCo	1271 - A6
LA MESITA PK, LMSA	1251 - A6
LANDES, JOHN PK, OCN	1087 - C7
LANE, FRANK PK, SDCo	1136 - A6
LAS PALMAS PK, NATC	1310 - B2
LAUDERBACH PK, CHV	1330 - C3
LEGION PK, CALX	6680 - F2
LEMON GROVE PK, LMGR	1270 - H7
LEUCADIA OAKS PK, ENCT	1147 - A2
LEUCADIA ROADSIDE PK, ENCT	1147 - A4
LEVANTE PK, CRLB	1147 - H2
LIBBY LAKE PK, OCN	1066 - J7
LINCOLN ACRES COUNTY PK, SDCo	1310 - C2
LINDA VISTA COMM PK, SD	1248 - J6
LINDBERGH PK, SD	1249 - A3
LINDO LAKE COUNTY PK, SDCo	1232 - B3
LIONS CLUB PK, OCN	1106 - C3
LITTLE OAKS PK, ENCT	1148 - B5
LIVE OAK COUNTY PK, SDCo	1028 - C5
LOMA VERDE PK, CHV	1330 - F4
LOMITA PK, SD	1290 - H3
LOPEZ RIDGE PK, SD	1208 - J3
LOS NINOS PK, CHV	1330 - F4
LOTUS PK, ELCN	6499 - J6
LOWER OTAY COUNTY PK, SDCo	1332 - B3

FEATURE NAME Address City, ZIP Code	PAGE-GRID
LUISENO PK, OCN	1067 - A4
MACARTHUR PK, LMSA	1270 - J2
MACDOWELL PK, SD	1228 - H7
MACKENZIE CREEK PK, CHV	1311 - F3
MACPHERSON, MILDRED PK, ENCT	1167 - C1
MADDOX PK, SD	1209 - A5
MADISON LN PK, CHV	1311 - G3
MAGEE PK, CRLB	1106 - D5
MARCY PK, SD	1228 - B6
MARINA VIEW PK, CHV	1329 - J2
MARISOL PK, CHV	1310 - H5
MARLADO HIGHLANDS PK, OCN	1086 - E2
MARSHALL PK, OCN	1106 - C2
MARTIN, JESS PK, SDCo	1136 - C7
MASON WILDLIFE COUNTY PK, SDCo- (SEE PAGE 1296)	1316 - G7
MAST PK, SNTE	1231 - B5
MATHEWSON PK, CORD	1288 - J7
MAYFLOWER DOG PK, ESCN	1110 - E5
MCGEE PK, ELCN	6499 - J6
MCLEOD, ROD PK, ESCN	1109 - G6
MEMORIAL COMM PK, SD	1289 - E5
MEMORIAL PK, CHV	1310 - B6
MESA VERDE PK, SD	1209 - B5
MESA VIKING PK, SD	1209 - C2
MINI PK, CHV	1311 - E4
MIRA MESA COMM PK, SD	1209 - C3
MISSION BAY ATHLETIC AREA, SD	1248 - C5
MISSION BAY PK, SD	1247 - J7
MISSION HEIGHTS PK, SD	1268 - J2
MISSION HILLS PK, SD	1268 - H5
MISSION SPORTS PK, SMCS	1108 - F7
MISSION TRAILS REGL PK, SD	1250 - E6
MONTCLAIR PK, SD	1269 - F7
MONTEREY HEIGHTS PK, LMGR	1290 - G1
MONTEVALLE PK, CHV	1311 - H3
MONTEZUMA PK, SD	1270 - D2
MONTGOMERY WALLER COMM PK, SD	1330 - D7
MONTIEL PK, SMCS	1129 - E1
MOUNT ACADIA PK, SD	1248 - H4
MOUNTAIN HAWK PK, CHV- (SEE PAGE 1293)	1312 - A6
MOUNTAIN VIEW PK, SD	1289 - H5
MOUNTAIN VIEW PK, ESCN	1130 - E1
MOUNT ETNA PK, SD	1248 - F2
MOUNT HELIX PK, SDCo	1271 - D2
MULBERRY PK, SMCS	1109 - A6
MULLEN, LEO SPORTS PK, ENCT	1147 - F4
MURRAY RIDGE PK, SD	1249 - C7
NESTOR PK, SD	1350 - B1
NOBEL ATHLETIC AREA, SD	1228 - E3
NORMAN PK, CHV	1310 - B6
NORTH CLAIREMONT COMM PK, SD	1248 - F1
NORTHMONT PK, LMSA	1251 - B6
NORTH PARK COMM PARK, SD	1269 - D5
OAKCREST PK, ENCT	1147 - F7
OAK CREST PK, CHV	1311 - C7
OAK PK, SD	1270 - A7
OAK RIPARIAN PK, OCN	1107 - E3
OCEAN BEACH ATHLETIC AREA (ROBB FLD), SD	1267 - J5
OCEAN BEACH COMM PK, SD	1267 - J6
OCOTILLO WELLS ST VEHICULAR REC AREA, - SDCo (SEE PAGE 1100)	1121 - H1
OLD IRONSIDES COUNTY PK, SDCo	1253 - D1
OLD POWAY PK, PWY	1190 - F2
OLD TROLLEY BARN PK, SD	1269 - C3
OLIVE GROVE COMM PK, SD	1248 - J2
ORANGE AVENUE FIELDS, CHV	1330 - F4
ORCHARD PK, CHV	1331 - B1
ORPHEUS PK, ENCT	1147 - B5
ORTEGA, RON RECREATION PK, OCN	1086 - B7
OTAY PK, CHV	1330 - E5
OTAY VALLEY REGIONAL PK, SD	1330 - G6
OUTFIELD PK, SD	1289 - B4
PACIFIC BEACH COMM PK, SD	1247 - J5
PACIFIC STREET LINEAR PK, OCN	1106 - A1
PALISADES PK, OCN	1086 - J7
PALISADES PK (LAW ST PARK), SD	1247 - G5
PALM PK, CORD	1288 - H5
PALM RIDGE PK, SD	1330 - G7
PALOMARES PK, SDCo	1027 - H6
PALOMAR MOUNTAIN STATE PK, SDCo	1051 - H1
PALOMAR PK, CHV	1330 - G3
PANTOJA PK, SD	1288 - J3
PARADISE HILLS COMM PK, SD	1290 - E6
PARK DE LA CRUZ, SD	1269 - G6
PARK LAND, CHV	1311 - A6
PARKSIDE PARK, SD	1310 - E2
PASEO DEL REY PK, CHV	1310 - H7
PENASQUITOS CREEK PK, SD	1189 - A7
PENN ATHLETIC AREA, SD	1310 - F1
PEPPER PK, NATC	1309 - G5
PICACHO STATE REC AREA, ImCo	412 - C11
PICNIC GROUNDS, SDCo	1218 - G7
PINE VALLEY COUNTY PK, SDCo	1237 - B6
PITTMAN, DEBBIE PK, ELCN	6499 - E7
PLUMOSA PK, SD	1268 - C6
POINSETTIA PK, CRLB	1126 - J4
POINT LOMA COMM PK, SD	1288 - A2
PORTER PK, LMSA	1270 - J2
PORTWOOD PIER PLAZA, IMPB	1349 - E1
POTRERO COUNTY PK, SDCo- (SEE PAGE 1296)	1316 - E7
POWAY COMM PK, PWY	1190 - D5
POWAY SPORTS PK, PWY	1190 - E6
POWERHOUSE PK, DLMR	1187 - F4
PRESIDIO COMM PK, SD	1268 - F4
PRINCESS DEL CERRO PK, SD	1250 - C6
RAINBOW PK, SDCo	998 - J5
RAINTREE PK, VSTA	1087 - H5
RAMONA COMM PK, SDCo	1152 - H4
RANCHO BERNARDO COMM PK, SD	1150 - A6
RANCHO DEL ORO COMM PK, OCN	1087 - B3
RANCHO DEL REY PK, CHV	1311 - B6
RANCHO MISSION CANYON PK, SD	1250 - C4
REAMA PK, IMPB	1349 - E1
REINSTRA BALL FIELDS, CHV	1330 - F4
RENETTE PK, ELCJ	1251 - E7
RIDGEWOOD PK, SD	1189 - F6
RIVER VIEW PK, SDCo	1231 - J5
ROADRUNNER PK, SD	1249 - H3
ROCKWOOD PLAZA, CALX	6680 - G2
ROGERS, GREG PK, CHV	1330 - H2
ROHR PK, CHV	1310 - G3
ROLANDO PK, LMSA	1270 - E4
ROLLING HILLS PK, SD	1169 - H7
ROSE TEMPLE MEM PK, IMPB	1329 - H7
ROTARY PK, OCN	1105 - J1
ROTARY PK, CORD	1288 - H7
ROTARY PK, CRLB	1106 - E5
RYAN PK, ESCN	1110 - F5
SABRE SPRINGS PK, SD	1189 - H5
SALT CREEK PK, CHV	1311 - J5
SALTON SEA STATE REC AREA, ImCo	410 - L5
SAN CARLOS COMM PK, SD	1250 - H5
SANDBURG PK, SD	1209 - B2
SAN DIEGO GAS & ELECTRIC PK, CHV	1330 - F4
SAN DIEGUITO COUNTY PK, SDCo	1167 - J6
SAN ELIJO PK, SMCS	1128 - D6
SAN ONOFRE ST BCH, SDCo	1023 - C2
SANTA CLARA POINT COMM PK, SD	1267 - J1
SANTEE LAKES REGL PK, SNTE	1211 - B7
SAN YSIDRO ATHLETIC AREA, SD	1350 - F5
SAN YSIDRO COMM ACTIVITY CTR, SD	1350 - F2
SAN YSIDRO COMM PK, SD	1350 - G4

FEATURE NAME Address City, ZIP Code	PAGE-GRID
SCOBEE PK, CHV	1311 - F4
SCOTT VALLEY PK, ENCT	1147 - F4
SCRIPPS ELLEN BROWNING PK, SD	1227 - E6
SCRIPPS RANCH COMM PK, SD	1210 - A1
SEAGROVE PK, DLMR	1187 - F5
SEPULVEDA, JOSEPH PK, OCN	1087 - A7
SERRA MESA COMM PK, SD	1249 - D4
SESSIONS, KATE O MEM PK, SD	1247 - J3
SHADOW HILL PK, SNTE	1231 - G6
SHADOWRIDGE PK, VSTA	1108 - A4
SHOREBIRD PK, CHV	1311 - E4
SHORELINE PK, SD	1288 - B4
SILVERSET PK, PWY	1190 - D1
SILVERWING PK, SD	1330 - E7
SIMMONS FAMILY PK, SMCS	1128 - A3
SKYLINE COMM PK, SD	1290 - H4
SKYVIEW PK, SD	1290 - F4
SMITH, CORKY GYM PK, SMCS	1108 - H7
SOLANA HIGHLANDS PK, SD	1187 - J5
SOUTH BAY COMM PK, SD	1350 - A1
SOUTH CREEK NEIGHBORHOOD PK, SD	1190 - A6
SOUTHCREST COMM PK, SD	1289 - H6
SOUTH LANE PK, SDCo	1252 - H4
SOUTH OCEANSIDE PK, OCN	1106 - D3
SPANISH LANDING PK, SD	1288 - D1
SPORTS PK, IMPB	1349 - F1
SPRECKELS PK, CORD	1288 - J6
SPRING CANYON PK, SD	1189 - H7
SPRING CREEK PK, OCN	1067 - E7
SPRING VALLEY COUNTY PK, SDCo	1291 - A4
STAGECOACH PK, CRLB	1147 - J2
STANDLEY COMM PK, SD	1228 - D6
STARKEY PK, SD	1247 - F1
STARK FIELD PK, ELCN	6499 - J7
STAR PK, CORD	1288 - H7
STARRIDGE PK, PWY	1190 - D3
STEELE CANYON COUNTY PK, SDCo	1272 - C6
STELZER, LOUIS A COUNTY PK, SDCo	1212 - D7
SUNBOW PK, CHV	1330 - H1
SUNFLOWER PK, ELCN	6499 - E6
SUNNYSLOPE PK, SD	1330 - B7
SUNRIDGE PK, CHV	1310 - J7
SUNSET CLIFFS PK, SD	1267 - H7
SUNSET PK, LMSA	1250 - F7
SUNSET PK, CORD	1288 - G7
SUNSHINE PK, LMSA	1270 - E3
SURF AND TURF RECREATION PK, SD	1187 - H2
SWAMIS PK, ENCT	1167 - B1
SWARTHOUT PK, ELCN	6499 - H5
SWEETWATER COUNTY PK, SDCo	1310 - J1
SWEETWATER HEIGHTS PK, NATC	1310 - D3
SWEETWATER LANE COUNTY PK, SDCo	1291 - A2
SWEETWATER REGL PK, SDCo	1291 - A6
TECOLOTE COMM PK, SD	1268 - F2
TERALTA NEIGHBORHOOD PK, SD	1269 - G5
TERRA NOVA PK, CHV	1310 - F5
THIBODO PK, VSTA	1107 - J3
TIDE BEACH PK, SOLB	1167 - E6
TIDELANDS PK, CORD	1289 - A6
TIERRASANTA COMM PK, SD	1249 - J1
TIFFANY PK, CHV	1311 - D5
TIJUANA RIVER VALLEY REGL PK, SD	1349 - J4
TODD, BUDDY PK, OCN	1086 - E6
TORREY HILLS NEIGHBORHOOD PK, SD	1208 - B3
TORREY PINES CITY PK, SD	1207 - H7
TOWN CENTER COMM PK, SNTE	1231 - D5
TOWNSITE PK, VSTA	1087 - H5
TRIANGLE PK, CORD	1288 - H6
TUTTLE PK, ELCJ	1251 - F7
TUXEDO PK, SD	1250 - E3
TWIN TRAILS PK, SD	1189 - C4
TYSON STREET PK, OCN	1106 - A1
UCSD PK, SD	1228 - A1
UNIV GARDENS PK, SD	1228 - F5
UNIV VILLAGE PK, SD	1228 - F4
VALLECITO COUNTY PK, SDCo	430 - C2
VALLE LINDO PK, CHV	1330 - H4
VALLE VERDE PK, PWY	1170 - D3
VAN ZANTEN PK, ELCJ	1252 - A3
VETERANS PK, IMPB	1329 - G7
VETTER PK, CORD	1288 - J7
VIA DEL PARQUE PK, SDCo	1271 - F7
VIEWPOINT PK, ENCT	1147 - C7
VIEWS WEST PK, SD	1189 - F5
VILLA LA JOLLA PK, SD	1228 - A5
VILLA MONTSERATE PK, SD	1229 - G7
VILLA NORTE PK, SD	1229 - J7
VISTA LA MESA PK, LMSA	1270 - E5
VISTA TERRACE PK, SD	1350 - F2
VOYAGER PK, CHV	1311 - B7
WALKER-WANGENHEIM PK, SD	1209 - E4
WALNUT GROVE PK, SMCS	1108 - J1
WASHINGTON PK, ESCN	1110 - B7
WAVE WATER PK, VSTA	1087 - G6
WEISS, MANDELL EASTGATE CITY PK, SD	1228 - C2
WELLS PK, ELCJ	1251 - H4
WESTERN HILLS PK, SD	1248 - F7
WEST HILLS PK, SNTE	1230 - H5
WESTSIDE PK, ESCN	1129 - H4
WESTVIEW PK, SD	1209 - E2
WIDEMAN MEM PK, SD	1290 - E3
WILDERNESS GARDENS COUNTY PK, SDCo	1030 - C6
WILDWOOD PK, VSTA	1087 - J6
WILLIAMSON, BUB PK, VSTA	1087 - D7
WINDRIVER COUNTY PK, SDCo	1272 - C4
WINDWOOD PK, SD	1188 - B6
WINTERWOOD COMM PK, SD	1208 - J4
WIRO PK, ENCT	1147 - J6
WISTERIA PK, CHV	1331 - C1
WOODGLEN VISTA PK, SNTE	1231 - D2
WOODHAVEN COUNTY PK, SDCo	1272 - C3
WOODLAND PK, SMCS	1109 - C6

PERFORMING ARTS

FEATURE NAME Address City, ZIP Code	PAGE-GRID
CALIFORNIA CTR FOR THE ARTS 340 N ESCONDIDO BLVD, ESCN, 92025	1129 - H2
CASA DEL PRADO THEATRE 1800 EL PRADO, SD, 92101	1289 - C1
COORS AMPHITHEATER 2050 ENTERTAINMENT CIR, CHV, 91911	1331 - B6
COPLEY SYMPHONY HALL 750 B ST, SD, 92101	1289 - B2
EAST COUNTY PERF ARTS CTR 210 E MAIN ST, ELCJ, 92020	1251 - F5
FLEET, REUBEN H SPACE THEATER & SCI-CTR 1875 EL PRADO, SD, 92101	1289 - C1
LAMBS PLAYERS THEATRE 1142 ORANGE AV, CORD, 92118	1288 - H7
MOONLIGHT STAGE PRODUCTIONS 1200 VALE TERRACE DR, VSTA, 92084	1088 - A5
OLD GLOBE THEATER 1363 OLD GLOBE WY, SD, 92101	1289 - B1
OPEN AIR THEATER 5500 CAMPANILE DR, SD, 92182	1270 - C1
PALISADES BLDG PAN AMERICAN RD W, SD, 92101	1289 - B1
POWAY CTR FOR THE PERF ARTS 15498 ESPOLA RD, PWY, 92064	1170 - G6
POWAY PERF ARTS COMPANY 13250 POWAY RD, PWY, 92064	1190 - E4
SAN DIEGO REPERTORY THEATRE 79 HORTON PZ, SD, 92101	1289 - A3
SPRECKELS ORGAN PAVILION 1549 EL PRADO, SD, 92101	1289 - B1
SPRECKELS THEATRE 121 BROADWAY, SD, 92101	1289 - A3
STARLIGHT BOWL 2005 PAN AMERICAN PZ, SD, 92101	1289 - B1
SUSHI PERFORMANCE AND VISUAL ART 320 11TH AV, SD, 92101	1289 - B4
WEISS, MANDELL FORUM MANDELL WEISS LN, SD, 92093	1227 - J3
WEISS, MANDELL THEATRE MANDELL WEISS LN, SD, 92093	1227 - J3

POINTS OF INTEREST

FEATURE NAME Address City, ZIP Code	PAGE-GRID
ANZA-BORREGO VISITORS CTR- (SEE PAGE 1058) 200 PALM CANYON DR, SDCo, 92004	1078 - E2
ARCO TRNING CTR(US OLYMPIC TRNING-CTR) 1750 WUESTE RD, CHV, 91915	1311 - J7
BALLAST POINT LIGHTHOUSE GUIJAROS RD, SD, 92106	1288 - B7
BIRCH AQUARIUM AT SCRIPPS 2300 EXPEDITION WY, SD, 92093	1227 - H4
BOAT HOUSE SANTA CLARA PL, SD, 92109	1267 - J1
BRAILLE INSTITUTE 4555 EXECUTIVE DR, SD, 92121	1228 - D2
DE LUZ ECOLOGY CTR DE LUZ MURRIETA RD, SDCo, 92028	996 - G1
FAA RADAR STA SUNRISE HWY & MONUMENT PEAK RD, SDCo, 91948	1218 - F5
FLOWER FIELDS OF CARLSBAD 5704 PAS DL NORTE, CRLB, 92008	1126 - H3
MISSION BAY YACHT CLUB 1215 EL CARMEL PL, SD, 92109	1267 - J2
MISSION BEACH PLUNGE 3115 OCEAN FRONT WK, SD, 92109	1267 - H3
OPERATIONAL LIGHTHOUSE CABRILLO RD, SD, 92152	1308 - A3
PALOMAR OBSERVATORY 35899 CANFIELD RD, SDCo, 92060	1032 - G4
PHOTOGRAPHIC ARTS BLDG 1790 VILLAGE PL, SD, 92101	1269 - C7
POINT LOMA CABRILLO RD & GATCHELL RD, SD, 92152	1308 - A3
PRINCE OF PEACE ABBEY-BENEDICTNE-MNSTRY 605 BENET HILL RD, OCN, 92054	1086 - B4
QUAIL BOTANICAL GARDENS 230 QUAIL GARDENS DR, ENCT, 92024	1147 - D6
QUEEN CALAFIAS MAGIC CIRCLE KIT CARSON PARK, ESCN, 92025	1150 - B1
SAN DIEGO WILD ANIMAL PK 15500 SAN PASQUAL VALLEY RD, SD, 92027	1130 - J6
SAN DIEGO ZOO 2920 ZOO DR, SD, 92101	1269 - B7
SAN ONOFRE NUCLEAR POWER PLANT OLD HWY 101, SDCo, 92055	1023 - G5
SCRIPPS RANCH SWIM & RACQUET CLUB 9875 AVIARY DR, SD, 92131	1209 - H5
SPANISH VILLAGE ART CTR 1770 VILLAGE PL, SD, 92101	1269 - C7
TIJUANA ESTUARY NATURAL PRES VIS CTR 301 CASPIAN WY, IMPB, 91932	1349 - F1
TORREY PINES GLIDERPORT 2800 TORREY PINES SCENIC DR, SD, 92037	1207 - H7
TORREY PINES PARK VISITORS CTR 12201 TORREY PINES PARK RD, SD, 92037	1207 - H3
USS MIDWAY 1355 N HARBOR DR, SD, 92101	1288 - H3

POINTS OF INTEREST - HISTORIC

FEATURE NAME Address City, ZIP Code	PAGE-GRID
BALBOA PARK CLUB PAN AMERICAN RD W, SD, 92101	1289 - B1
CABRILLO NATL MONUMENT END OF CABRILLO MEMORIAL DR, SD, 92152	1308 - A2
CAMP SALVATION 5TH ST & HEBER AV, CALX, 92231	6680 - G2
CAROUSEL PARK BLVD & ZOO PL, SD, 92101	1269 - C7
CASA DE BALBOA BLDG 1649 EL PRADO, SD, 92101	1289 - C1
EAGLE AND HIGH PEAK MINES OLD MINERS TR, SDCo, 92036	1136 - B6
GASLAMP QUARTER J ST & 5TH AV, SD, 92101	1289 - A4
GIANT DIPPER ROLLER COASTER BELMONT PARK, SD, 92109	1267 - H3
HIST FEDERAL BLDG 2131 PAN AMERICAN PZ, SD, 92101	1289 - B1
HIST LIGHTHOUSE HUMPHREYS RD, SD, 92152	1308 - A2
LOS COCHES MONUMENT 13472 BUSINESS ROUTE I-8, SDCo, 92040	1232 - D6
LOS PENASQUITOS ADOBE RANCH HOUSE CANYONSIDE PARK DR, SD, 92129	1189 - C7
MARSTON HOUSE 3525 7TH AV, SD, 92103	1269 - B6
MISSION SAN ANTONIO DE PALA PALA MISSION RD, SDCo, 92059	1029 - J4
MISSION SAN DIEGO DE ALCALA 10818 SAN DIEGO MISSION RD, SD, 92108	1249 - G7
MISSION SAN LUIS REY DE FRANCIA 4050 MISSION AV, OCN, 92057	1086 - H2
OLD MISSION DAM HIST SITE FATHER JUNIPERO SERRA TR, SD, 92124	1230 - F6
OLD TOWN SAN DIEGO STATE HIST PK TWIGGS ST & JUAN ST, SD, 92110	1268 - F5
PAUMA MISSION PAUMA RESERVATION RD, SDCo, 92061	1051 - A1
RANCHO BUENA VISTA ADOBE 651 E VISTA WY, VSTA, 92084	1087 - J6
RANCHO GUAJOME ADOBE 2210 N SANTA FE AV, VSTA, 92083	1087 - G2
SAN PASQUAL BATTLEFIELD STATE HIST SAN PASQUAL VALLEY RD, SD, 92027	1131 - B7
SANTA YSABEL INDIAN MISSION HWY 79, SDCo, 92070	1135 - B2
SERRA CROSS PRESIDIO DR, SD, 92110	1268 - F4
VETERANS WAR MEM BALBOA PARK, SD, 92101	1269 - C7

SCHOOLS - PRIVATE ELEMENTARY

FEATURE NAME Address City, ZIP Code	PAGE-GRID
ALL HALLOWS ACADEMY 2390 NAUTILUS ST, SD, 92037	1247 - H1
ALL SAINTS EPISCOPAL 3674 7TH AV, SD, 92103	1269 - B6
BEAUTIFUL SAVIOUR LUTHERAN 3030 VALLEY ST, CRLB, 92008	1106 - F4
BETH ISRAEL DAY JEWISH 2512 3RD AV, SD, 92101	1289 - A1
BLESSED SACRAMENT 4551 56TH ST, SD, 92115	1270 - B3
BONITA COUNTRY DAY 625 OTAY LAKES RD, CHV, 91913	1311 - B4
BOSTONIA CHRISTIAN 211 S 3RD ST, ELCJ, 92019	1252 - A6
CALEXICO MISSION ACADEMY 601 1ST ST, CALX, 92231	6680 - H2
CALVARY CHAPEL OF LA MESA CHRISTIAN 7525 EL CAJON BLVD, LMSA, 91941	1270 - G2
CALVARY CHRISTIAN 6866 LINDA VISTA RD, SD, 92111	1268 - J1
CALVARY CHRISTIAN 885 E VISTA WY, VSTA, 92084	1087 - J5
CALVIN CHRISTIAN OF ESCONDIDO 1868 N BROADWAY, ESCN, 92026	1109 - H5
CARLTON HILLS CHRISTIAN 9735 HALBERNS BLVD, SNTE, 92071	1231 - B4
CHABAD HEBREW ACADEMY 10785 POMERADO RD, SD, 92131	1209 - J5
CHILDRENS CREATIVE & PERF ARTS 4431 MT HERBERT AV, SD, 92117	1248 - F2
CHILDRENS MONTESSORI 2950 S BEAR VALLEY PKWY, ESCN, 92025	1150 - C1
CHILDS PRIMARY, THE 3811 MT ACADIA BLVD, SD, 92111	1248 - H4
CHRIST CHURCH DAY 926 C AV, CORD, 92118	1288 - H7
CHRISTIAN ACADEMY OF CHULA VISTA 494 E ST, CHV, 91910	1310 - A6
CHRISTIAN 6747 AMHERST ST, SD, 92115	1270 - E2
CHRIST LUTHERAN 7929 LA MESA BLVD, LMSA, 91941	1270 - H2
CHRIST THE CORNERSTONE ACADEMY 9028 WESTMORE RD, SD, 92126	1209 - D3
CHULA VISTA CHRISTIAN 960 5TH ST, CHV, 91911	1330 - B2
CHURCH OF NATIVITY 6309 EL APAJO, SDCo, 92067	1168 - E6
CITY TREE CHRISTIAN 320 DATE ST, SD, 92101	1289 - A2
COLEMAN PREP 7380 PARKWAY DR, LMSA, 91942	1270 - F1
CORNERSTONE CHRISTIAN 13617 MIDLAND RD, PWY, 92064	1190 - F3
COVENANT CHRISTIAN 505 E NAPLES ST, CHV, 91911	1330 - G1
DEL MAR PINES 3975 TORRINGTON ST, SD, 92130	1188 - A5
DIEGUENO COUNTRY 14963 CIRCO DIEGUENO, SDCo, 92067	1168 - F7
ESCONDIDO ADVENTIST ACADEMY 1233 W 9TH AV, ESCN, 92029	1129 - G5
ESCONDIDO CHRISTIAN 923 IDAHO AV, SDCo, 92025	1130 - B3
EVANS 6510 LA JOLLA SCENIC DR S, SD, 92037	1247 - J1
FAITH COMM 2285 MURRAY RIDGE RD, SD, 92123	1249 - C7
FAITH LUTHERAN 700 E BOBIER DR, VSTA, 92084	1087 - J4
GILLISPIE 7380 GIRARD AV, SD, 92037	1227 - F7
GOOD SHEPHERD 8180 GOLD COAST DR, SD, 92126	1209 - B5
GRACE LUTHERAN 3993 PARK BLVD, SD, 92103	1269 - C5
GRACE LUTHERAN 643 W 13TH AV, ESCN, 92025	1129 - J5
HARBORSIDE 1329 KETTNER BLVD, SD, 92101	1288 - J2
HEARTLAND CHRISTIAN HOME 3327 KENORA DR, SDCo, 91977	1271 - C6
HOLY FAMILY 1945 COOLIDGE ST, SD, 92111	1268 - J1
HOLY SPIRIT 2755 55TH ST, SD, 92105	1270 - B7
HOLY TRINITY 509 BALLARD ST, ELCJ, 92019	1251 - J6
HORIZON CHRISTIAN 4520 POCAHONTAS AV, SD, 92117	1248 - D2
ISLAMIC OF SAN DIEGO 7050 ECKSTROM AV, SD, 92111	1248 - J2
LA JOLLA COUNTRY DAY 9490 GENESEE AV, SD, 92037	1228 - C1
LA MESA CHRISTIAN 9407 JERICHO RD, LMSA, 91942	1251 - B6
LIGHT AND LIFE CHRISTIAN 120 N ASH ST, ESCN, 92027	1130 - B2
MARANATHA CHRISTIAN 12855 BLACK MOUNTAIN RD, SD, 92129	1189 - D5
MARIS, STELLA ACADEMY 7654 HERSCHEL AV, SD, 92037	1227 - F7
MERIDIAN CHRISTIAN 2100 GREENFIELD DR, ELCJ, 92019	1252 - D4
MIDWAY BAPTIST 2460 PALM AV, SD, 92154	1330 - B7
MIRA MESA CHRISTIAN 9696 CANDIDA ST, SD, 92126	1209 - E6
MISSION BAY MONTESSORI ACADEMY 2640 SODERBLOM AV, SD, 92122	1228 - B6
MISSION SAN ANTONIO DE PALA PALA MISSION RD, SDCo, 92059	1029 - J4
MONTESSORI, MARIA HOUSE 4544 POCAHONTAS AV, SD, 92117	1248 - D2
MONTESSORI OF SAN DIEGO 1323 W SPRUCE ST, SD, 92103	1268 - J7
MOUNT ERIE CHRISTIAN-BAPTIST ACADEMY 504 S 47TH ST, SD, 92113	1289 - J5
NAZARETH 10728 SAN DIEGO MISSION RD, SD, 92108	1249 - H7
NEW SONG CHRISTIAN 3985 MISSION AV, OCN, 92057	1086 - G3
NORTH COAST CHRISTIAN 1106 WHALEY ST, OCN, 92054	1106 - C2
OLD MISSION MONTESSORI 4070 MISSION AV, OCN, 92057	1086 - H2
OUR LADY 650 24TH ST, SD, 92102	1289 - C3
OUR LADY OF GRACE 2766 NAVAJO RD, ELCJ, 92020	1251 - A4
OUR LADY OF GUADALUPE 536 ROCKWOOD AV, CALX, 92231	6680 - G1
OUR LADY OF MOUNT CARMEL 4141 BEYER BLVD, SD, 92173	1350 - F3
OUR LADY OF PERPETUAL HELP 9825 PINO DR, SDCo, 92040	1232 - C3
OUR LADY OF THE SACRED HEART 4106 42ND ST, SD, 92105	1269 - H5
PARKER, FRANCIS W 4201 RANDOLPH ST, SD, 92103	1268 - H5
PILGRIM LUTHERAN 497 E ST, CHV, 91910	1310 - A6
RAMONA LUTHERAN 520 16TH ST, SDCo, 92065	1152 - F7
REFORMATION LUTHERAN 4670 MT ABERNATHY AV, SD, 92117	1248 - J1
RHOADES FOR THE GIFTED 141 RANCHO SANTA FE RD, ENCT, 92024	1167 - J1
SACRED HEART ACADEMY 4895 SARATOGA AV, SD, 92107	1267 - J6
SACRED HEART PARISH 706 C AV, CORD, 92118	1288 - J7
SAINT CHARLES BORROMEO ACADEMY 2808 CADIZ ST, SD, 92110	1268 - E6
SAINT CHARLES 929 18TH ST, SD, 92154	1350 - A1
SAINT COLUMBA 3327 GLENCOLUM DR, SD, 92123	1249 - D5
SAINT DIDACUS 4630 34TH ST, SD, 92116	1269 - F3

FEATURE NAME Address City, ZIP Code	PAGE-GRID
SAINT FRANCIS OF ASSISI 525 W VISTA WY, VSTA, 92083	1087 - G7
SAINT JAMES ACADEMY 623 S NARDO AV, SOLB, 92075	1187 - F1
SAINT JOHN 1003 ENCINITAS BLVD, ENCT, 92024	1147 - E7
SAINT JOHN OF THE CROSS 8175 LEMON GROVE WY, LMGR, 91945	1270 - H5
SAINT JOHNS EPISCOPAL 760 1ST AV, CHV, 91910	1330 - D1
SAINT JUDE ACADEMY 1228 S 38TH ST, SD, 92113	1289 - G6
SAINT KIERAN 1347 CAMILLO WY, ELCJ, 92021	1252 - A3
SAINT LUKES LUTHERAN CHRISTIAN DAY 5150 WILSON ST, LMSA, 91941	1271 - A1
SAINT MARTIN OF TOURS ACADEMY 7708 EL CAJON BLVD, LMSA, 91941	1270 - G2
SAINT MARYS CATHOLIC 700 S WATERMAN AV, ELCN, 92243	6499 - F7
SAINT MARYS 130 E 13TH AV, ESCN, 92025	1130 - A4
SAINT MARY STAR OF THE SEA 515 WISCONSIN AV, OCN, 92054	1106 - B1
SAINT MICHAEL ACADEMY 2637 HOMEDALE ST, SD, 92139	1310 - E1
SAINT MICHAEL 15542 POMERADO RD, PWY, 92064	1170 - C6
SAINT PATRICK 3583 30TH ST, SD, 92104	1269 - E6
SAINT PATRICK 3820 PIO PICO DR, CRLB, 92008	1106 - F6
SAINT PAULS LUTHERAN 1376 FELSPAR ST, SD, 92109	1247 - J6
SAINT PETERS CATHOLIC 450 S STAGE COACH LN, SDCo, 92028	1027 - J3
SAINT PIUS X 37 E EMERSON ST, CHV, 91911	1330 - E2
SAINT RITAS 5165 IMPERIAL AV, SD, 92114	1290 - A4
SAINT ROSE OF LIMA 473 3RD AV, CHV, 91910	1310 - B7
SAINT THERESE ACADEMY 6046 CM RICO, SD, 92120	1250 - C6
SAINT VINCENT DE PAUL 4061 IBIS ST, SD, 92103	1268 - J5
SAN DIEGO ACADEMY 2700 E 4TH ST, NATC, 91950	1290 - B7
SAN DIEGO JEWISH ACADEMY 8660 GILMAN DR, SD, 92037	1228 - A4
SANTA FE CHRISTIAN COMM 838 ACADEMY DR, SOLB, 92075	1167 - G7
SANTA SOPHIA ACADEMY 9806 SAN JUAN ST, SDCo, 91977	1271 - D5
SCHOOL OF THE MADELEINE 1875 ILLION ST, SD, 92110	1268 - F1
SOILLE SAN DIEGO HEBREW DAY 3630 AFTON RD, SD, 92123	1249 - C4
SOUTHPORT CHRISTIAN ACADEMY 142 E 16TH ST, NATC, 91950	1309 - H2
SOUTHWESTERN CHRISTIAN 482 L ST, CHV, 91911	1330 - B2
TABERNACLE CHRISTIAN ACADEMY 1765 PENTECOST WY, SD, 92105	1290 - A2
TIERRASANTA CHRISTIAN 10725 ESMERALDAS DR, SD, 92124	1249 - H1
TRI-CITY CHRISTIAN 302 N EMERALD DR, VSTA, 92083	1087 - C7
TRINITY CHRISTIAN 3902 KENWOOD DR, SDCo, 91941	1271 - A5
TRINITY LUTHERAN 7210 LISBON ST, SD, 92114	1290 - F3
VALLEY CHRISTIAN 1350 DISCOVERY ST, SMCS, 92078	1128 - D2
VISTA CHRISTIAN 290 N MELROSE DR, VSTA, 92083	1087 - F6
WALDORF OF SAN DIEGO 3547 ALTADENA AV, SD, 92105	1270 - A6
WALKER, WARREN 4605 POINT LOMA AV, SD, 92107	1287 - J1
WONDER WORLD 1375 E WASHINGTON AV, ELCJ, 92019	1252 - A6

SCHOOLS - PRIVATE HIGH

FEATURE NAME Address City, ZIP Code	PAGE-GRID
ACADEMY OF OUR LADY OF PEACE 4860 OREGON ST, SD, 92116	1269 - D3
ARMY & NAVY ACADEMY 2605 CARLSBAD BLVD, CRLB, 92008	1106 - D5
BISHOPS EPIS 7607 LA JOLLA BLVD, SD, 92037	1227 - E7
CALEXICO MISSION ACADEMY 601 1ST ST, CALX, 92231	6680 - H2
CALVARY CHRISTIAN 885 E VISTA WY, VSTA, 92084	1087 - J5
CALVIN CHRISTIAN 2000 N BROADWAY, ESCN, 92026	1109 - H5
CHRISTIAN 2100 GREENFIELD DR, ELCJ, 92019	1252 - D4
COLEMAN PREP 7380 PARKWAY DR, LMSA, 91942	1270 - F1
COVENANT CHRISTIAN 505 E NAPLES ST, CHV, 91911	1330 - G1
ESCONDIDO ADVENTIST ACADEMY 1233 W 9TH AV, ESCN, 92029	1129 - G5
FUTURES 2204 S EL CAMINO REAL, OCN, 92056	1106 - G2
HORIZON CHRISTIAN 5331 MT ALIFAN DR, SD, 92111	1248 - H3
HORIZON PREP 6233 EL APAJO, SDCo, 92067	1168 - E6
LA JOLLA COUNTRY DAY 9490 GENESEE AV, SD, 92037	1228 - C2
MARIAN CATHOLIC 1002 18TH ST, SD, 92154	1350 - A1
MATER DEI 1615 MATER DEI DR, CHV, 91913	1331 - E1
MIDWAY BAPTIST 2460 PALM AV, SD, 92154	1330 - B7
NORTH COAST CHRISTIAN 1106 WHALEY ST, OCN, 92054	1106 - C2
PARKER, FRANCIS W 6501 LINDA VISTA RD, SD, 92111	1268 - H2
PREUSS UCSD CHARTER 9500 GILMAN DR, SD, 92037	1228 - B1
SAINT AUGUSTINE 3266 NUTMEG ST, SD, 92104	1269 - F7
SAN DIEGO ACADEMY 2700 E 4TH ST, NATC, 91950	1290 - B7
SANTA FE CHRISTIAN COMM 838 ACADEMY DR, SOLB, 92075	1167 - G7
SOUTHPORT CHRISTIAN ACADEMY 142 E 16TH ST, NATC, 91950	1309 - H2
TABERNACLE CHRISTIAN ACADEMY 1765 PENTECOST WY, SD, 92105	1290 - A2
TRI-CITY CHRISTIAN 302 N EMERALD DR, VSTA, 92083	1087 - C7
UNIVERSITY OF SAN DIEGO 5961 LINDA VISTA RD, SD, 92110	1268 - G2
VINCENT MEM 525 SHERIDAN AV, CALX, 92231	6680 - F1

SCHOOLS - PRIVATE JUNIOR HIGH

FEATURE NAME Address City, ZIP Code	PAGE-GRID
ARMY & NAVY ACADEMY 2605 CARLSBAD BLVD, CRLB, 92008	1106 - D5

SCHOOLS - PRIVATE MIDDLE

FEATURE NAME Address City, ZIP Code	PAGE-GRID
PARKER, FRANCIS W 6501 LINDA VISTA RD, SD, 92111	1268 - H2

SCHOOLS - PUBLIC ELEMENTARY

FEATURE NAME Address City, ZIP Code	PAGE-GRID
ADAMS, JOHN 4672 35TH ST, SD, 92116	1269 - F3
ADOBE BLUFFS 8707 ADOBE BLUFFS DR, SD, 92129	1189 - C2
ALAMOSA PARK 5130 ALAMOSA PARK DR, OCN, 92057	1087 - C1
ALCOTT, LOUISA M 4680 HIDALGO AV, SD, 92117	1248 - C1
ALLEN-ANN DALY 4300 ALLEN SCHOOL RD, CHV, 91902	1310 - G4
ALPINE 1850 ALPINE BLVD, SDCo, 91901	1234 - A5
ANGIER, WILL 8450 HURLBUT ST, SD, 92123	1249 - C4
ANZA 1005 S ANZA ST, ELCJ, 92020	1251 - H7
ARROWOOD 5050 EL MIRLO DR, OCN, 92057	1067 - B5
ARROYO VISTA 2491 SCHOOL HOUSE RD, CHV, 91915	1311 - H6
ASHLEY FALLS 13030 ASHLEY FALLS DR, SD, 92130	1188 - D5
AUDUBON, JOHN J 8111 SAN VICENTE ST, SD, 92114	1290 - H3
AVIARA OAKS 6900 AMBROSIA LN, CRLB, 92011	1127 - D6
AVOCADO 3845 AVOCADO SCHOOL RD, SDCo, 91941	1271 - G4
AVONDALE 8401 STANSBURY ST, SDCo, 91977	1290 - J2
BAKER 4041 T ST, SD, 92113	1289 - H5
BALBOA, VASCO NUNEZ DE 1844 S 40TH ST, SD, 92113	1289 - H7
BALLANTYNE, JOHN 165 ROANOKE RD, ELCJ, 92020	1251 - G5
BANCROFT 8805 TYLER ST, SDCo, 91977	1271 - A7
BANDINI, EMERSON 3510 NEWTON AV, SD, 92113	1289 - F6
BARNARD 2930 BARNARD ST, SD, 92110	1268 - C5
BARNETT 23925 COUNA WY, SDCo, 92065	1173 - E2
BAY PARK 2433 DENVER ST, SD, 92110	1248 - E7
BAYSIDE 490 EMORY ST, IMPB, 91932	1329 - G6
BAYVIEW TERRACE 2445 FOGG ST, SD, 92109	1248 - C5
BEAUMONT 550 BEAUMONT DR, VSTA, 92084	1088 - A7
BENCHLEY/WEINBERGER 6269 TWIN LAKE DR, SD, 92119	1250 - G6
BERNARDO 1122 MOUNTAIN HEIGHTS DR, ESCN, 92029	1149 - H1
BERRY, GODFREY G 2001 RIMBEY AV, SD, 92154	1350 - A2
BETHUNE 6835 BENJAMIN HOLT RD, SD, 92114	1290 - E6
BEYER 2312 E BEYER BLVD, SD, 92173	1350 - G4
BIRD ROCK 5371 LA JOLLA HERMOSA AV, SD, 92037	1247 - G4
BIRNEY, ALICE 4345 CAMPUS AV, SD, 92103	1269 - C4
BLOSSOM VALLEY 9863 OAKMONT TER, SDCo, 92021	1233 - A3
BOBIER 220 W BOBIER DR, VSTA, 92083	1087 - G4
BONSALL 31505 OLD RIVER RD, SDCo, 92003	1068 - A1
BOONE, DANIEL 7330 BROOKHAVEN RD, SD, 92114	1290 - G5
BORREGO SPRINGS (SEE PAGE 1058) 1315 PALM CANYON DR, SDCo, 92004	1079 - C2
BOSTONIA 1390 BROADWAY, ELCJ, 92021	1252 - A3
BOULDER OAKS 2320 TAVERN RD, SDCo, 91901	1254 - A1
BREEZE HILL 1111 MELROSE WY, VSTA, 92081	1107 - G1
BROOKLYN 3035 ASH ST, SD, 92102	1289 - E2
BUENA VISTA 1330 BUENA VISTA WY, CRLB, 92008	1106 - E4
BURBANK, LUTHER 2146 JULIAN AV, SD, 92113	1289 - D5
CABRILLO, JUAN R 3120 TALBOT ST, SD, 92106	1288 - B2
CADMAN, CHARLES W 4370 KAMLOOP AV, SD, 92117	1248 - D2
CAJON PARK 10300 N MAGNOLIA AV, SNTE, 92071	1231 - E3
CALAVERA HILLS 4100 TAMARACK AV, CRLB, 92010	1107 - B3
CAMPO (SEE PAGE 1296) 1654 BUCKMAN SPRINGS RD, SDCo, 91906	1317 - H3
CANYON VIEW 9225 ADOLPHIA ST, SD, 92129	1189 - D6
CAPRI 941 CAPRI RD, ENCT, 92024	1147 - C3
CARDIFF 1888 MONTGOMERY AV, ENCT, 92007	1167 - D3
CARLTON HILLS 9353 PIKE RD, SNTE, 92071	1231 - B5
CARLTON OAKS 9353 WETHERSFIELD RD, SNTE, 92071	1230 - J6
CARMEL CREEK 4210 CARMEL CENTER RD, SD, 92130	1188 - B6
CARMEL DEL MAR 12345 CARMEL PARK DR, SD, 92130	1188 - A7
CARRILLO 2875 POINSETTIA LN, CRLB, 92009	1127 - J3
CARSON, KIT 6905 KRAMER ST, SD, 92111	1268 - J2
CARVER, GEORGE W 3251 JUANITA ST, SD, 92105	1270 - C6
CASA DE ORO 10235 RAMONA DR, SDCo, 91977	1271 - E5
CASILLAS, JOSEPH 1130 EAST J ST, CHV, 91910	1311 - A7
CASITA CTR FOR TECH-SCI-MATH 260 CEDAR RD, VSTA, 92083	1107 - C1
CASTLE PARK 25 EMERSON ST, CHV, 91911	1330 - E2
CENTRAL 122 W 4TH AV, ESCN, 92025	1129 - J3
CENTRAL 1290 EBONY AV, IMPB, 91932	1349 - H1
CENTRAL 4063 POLK AV, SD, 92105	1269 - G5
CENTRAL 933 E AV, NATC, 91950	1309 - J1
CHAPARRAL 17250 TANNIN DR, PWY, 92064	1170 - D2
CHASE AVENUE 195 E CHASE AV, ELCJ, 92020	1251 - F7
CHAVEZ, CESAR 1404 S 40TH ST, SD, 92113	1289 - G6
CHESTERTON 7335 WHEATLEY ST, SD, 92111	1249 - A6
CHOLLAS 545 45TH ST, SD, 92102	1289 - J3
CHULA VISTA HILLS 980 BUENA VISTA WY, CHV, 91910	1311 - B6
CLAY, HENRY 6506 SOLITA AV, SD, 92115	1270 - D3
CLEAR VIEW 455 WINDROSE WY, CHV, 91910	1310 - F5
CLOVER FLAT 39639 OLD HWY 80, SDCo, 91905	1300 - C6
CONCORDIA 3120 AVD DEL PRESIDENTE, SCLE, 92672	1023 - B1
CONWAY 1325 CONWAY DR, ESCN, 92027	1110 - A6
COOK, HAZEL G 875 CUYAMACA AV, CHV, 91911	1330 - E1
CORONADO VILLAGE 600 6TH ST, CORD, 92118	1288 - H6
CREEKSIDE 12362 SPRINGHURST DR, SD, 92128	1190 - A6
CREST 2000 SUNCREST BLVD, SDCo, 92021	1252 - H3
CRESTVIEW 510 SUNSET DR, VSTA, 92081	1107 - H1
CROWN POINT 4033 INGRAHAM ST, SD, 92109	1248 - A6
CUBBERLEY, ELLWOOD P 3201 MARATHON DR, SD, 92123	1249 - E5
CURIE, MARIE 4080 GOVERNOR DR, SD, 92122	1228 - E5
CUYAMACA 851 S JOHNSON AV, ELCJ, 92020	1251 - E7
DAILARD, RALPH 6425 CIBOLA RD, SD, 92120	1250 - E4
DE ANZA 1530 S WATERMAN AV, ELCN, 92243	6559 - F1
DEER CANYON 13455 RUSSET LEAF LN, SD, 92129	1189 - B4
DEHESA 4612 DEHESA RD, SDCo, 92019	1253 - A7
DEL MAR HEIGHTS 13555 BOQUITA DR, SD, 92014	1187 - H7
DEL MAR HILLS 14085 MANGO DR, SD, 92014	1187 - H5
DEL RIO 5207 E PARKER ST, OCN, 92057	1067 - B6
DESCANSO 24842 VIEJAS BLVD, SDCo, 91916	1236 - A2
DESERT GARDEN 1900 S 6TH ST, ELCN, 92243	6559 - H1
DEWEY, GEORGE 3251 ROSECRANS ST, SD, 92110	1268 - E6
DINGEMAN 11840 SCRIPPS CREEK DR, SD, 92131	1209 - J1
DISCOVERY 1100 CM BISCAY, CHV, 91910	1310 - J6
DISCOVERY 730 APPLEWILDE DR, SMCS, 92078	1128 - E2
DITMAR 1125 S DITMAR ST, OCN, 92054	1106 - B2
DOOL 800 ENCINAS AV, CALX, 92231	6680 - H1
DOYLE, ZETA O 3950 BERINO CT, SD, 92122	1228 - C4
DUKES, JAMES 24908 ABALAR WY, SDCo, 92065	1173 - G3
DUNN, ALVIN M 3697 LA MIRADA DR, SMCS, 92078	1108 - D7
EASTLAKE 1955 HILLSIDE DR, CHV, 91913	1311 - D4
ECKE, PAUL CENTRAL 185 UNION ST, ENCT, 92024	1147 - B5
EDISON, THOMAS 4077 35TH ST, SD, 92104	1269 - F5
EL CAMINO CREEK 7885 PAS ALISO, CRLB, 92009	1147 - F3
ELLIS, MAIE 400 W ELDER ST, SDCo, 92028	1027 - F3
EL TOYON 2000 E DIVISION ST, NATC, 91950	1290 - A7
EMORY 1915 CORONADO AV, SD, 92154	1350 - A1
EMPRESA 4850 AVD EMPRESA, OCN, 92056	1087 - C3
ENCANTO 822 65TH ST, SD, 92114	1290 - D3
ERICSON, LEIF 11174 WESTONHILL DR, SD, 92126	1209 - C2
EUCALYPTUS HILLS 11838 VALLE VISTA RD, SDCo, 92040	1211 - G6
EUCLID 4166 EUCLID AV, SD, 92105	1269 - J5
EXPLORER 8660 GILMAN DR, SD, 92037	1228 - A3
FALLBROOK STREET 405 W FALLBROOK ST, SDCo, 92028	1027 - F3
FEASTER EDISON CHARTER 670 FLOWER ST, CHV, 91910	1309 - J6
FELICITA 737 W 13TH AV, ESCN, 92025	1129 - J5
FIELD, EUGENE 4375 BANNOCK AV, SD, 92117	1248 - E1
FINNEY, MYRTLE S 3950 BYRD ST, SD, 92154	1330 - F6
FLETCHER, COL ED 7666 BOBOLINK WY, SD, 92123	1249 - A7
FLETCHER HILLS 2330 CENTER PL, ELCJ, 92020	1251 - B5
FLORA VISTA 1690 WANDERING RD, ENCT, 92024	1147 - G5
FLORENCE 3914 1ST AV, SD, 92103	1269 - A5
FLYING HILLS 1251 FINCH ST, ELCJ, 92020	1251 - D3
FOSTER, STEPHEN C 6550 51ST ST, SD, 92120	1250 - A6
FRANKLIN, BENJAMIN 4481 COPELAND AV, SD, 92116	1269 - H4
FRAZIER, WILLIAM H 1835 GUMTREE LN, SDCo, 92028	1027 - J2
FREESE, ELIZABETH 8140 GREENLAWN DR, SD, 92114	1290 - H4
FREMONT, JOHN C 2375 CONGRESS ST, SD, 92110	1268 - F5
FUERTE 11625 FUERTE DR, SDCo, 92020	1271 - H3
FULTON, ROBERT 7055 SKYLINE DR, SD, 92114	1290 - F4
GAGE, LYMAN J 6811 BISBY LAKE AV, SD, 92119	1250 - J4
GARDEN ROAD 14614 GARDEN RD, PWY, 92064	1190 - J4
GARFIELD 4487 OREGON ST, SD, 92116	1269 - D4

FEATURE NAME / Address City, ZIP Code	PAGE-GRID
GARRISON, E G 333 GARRISON ST, OCN, 92054	1086 - F6
GLEN VIEW 2201 E MISSION AV, ESCN, 92027	1110 - C6
GOLDEN AVENUE 7885 GOLDEN AV, LMGR, 91945	1270 - H6
GRANT, ULYSSES S 1425 WASHINGTON PL, SD, 92103	1268 - H5
GRAPEVINE 630 GRAPEVINE RD, VSTA, 92083	1087 - D6
GREEN, L R 3115 LAS PALMAS AV, ESCN, 92025	1150 - B1
GREEN, MYRON B. 7030 WANDERMERE DR, SD, 92119	1250 - E5
HAGE, WILLARD B 9750 GALVIN AV, SD, 92126	1209 - E2
HALECREST 475 E J ST, CHV, 91910	1310 - F7
HALL, W.D. 1376 PEPPER DR, SDCo, 92021	1252 - A1
HAMILTON, ALEXANDER 2807 FAIRMOUNT AV, SD, 92105	1269 - H7
HANCOCK, JOY B 3303 TAUSSIG ST, SD, 92124	1249 - G4
HANSON LANE 1825 HANSON LN, SDCo, 92065	1172 - F1
HARBISON, IRA 3235 E 8TH ST, NATC, 91950	1290 - C7
HARBORSIDE 681 NAPLES ST, CHV, 91911	1330 - B3
HARDING 950 S 7TH ST, ELCN, 92243	6499 - H7
HARDY, EDWARD L 5420 MONTEZUMA RD, SD, 92115	1270 - B2
HARRIS, ADA 1508 WINDSOR RD, ENCT, 92007	1167 - E2
HARRITT, CHET F 8120 ARLETTE ST, SNTE, 92071	1230 - J7
HAWTHORNE, NATHANIEL 4750 LEHRER DR, SD, 92117	1228 - G7
HEARST, PHOEBE A. 6230 DEL CERRO BLVD, SD, 92120	1250 - C7
HEDENKAMP 930 E PALOMAR MOUNTAIN ST, CHV, 91913	1331 - A2
HEDRICK 550 S WATERMAN AV, ELCN, 92243	6499 - F7
HERITAGE 1450 SANTA LUCIA RD, CHV, 91913	1331 - C1
HICKMAN, ALBERT JOE 10850 MONTONGO ST, SD, 92126	1209 - A3
HIGHLAND RANCH 14840 WAVERLEY DOWNS WY, SD, 92128	1190 - B1
HIGHLANDS 3131 S BARCELONA ST, SDCo, 91977	1271 - D6
HILL CREEK 9665 JEREMY ST, SNTE, 92071	1231 - F4
HILLTOP DRIVE 30 MURRAY ST, CHV, 91910	1310 - D7
HOLMES, OLIVER W 4902 MT ARARAT DR, SD, 92111	1248 - G4
HOOVER 5TH GRADE CLUSTER 3838 ORANGE AV, SD, 92105	1269 - G4
HOPE 3010 TAMARACK AV, CRLB, 92010	1107 - A4
HORTON, ALONZO E 5050 GUYMON ST, SD, 92102	1290 - A3
HULSE 303 S D ST, IMP, 92251	6439 - E6
IMPERIAL BEACH 650 IMPERIAL BEACH BLVD, IMPB, 91932	1349 - G1
IVEY RANCH 4275 VIA RANCHO RD, OCN, 92057	1087 - A4
JACKSON, ANDREW 5465 EL CAJON BLVD, SD, 92115	1270 - B4
JACUMBA (SEE PAGE 1300) 44343 OLD HWY 80, SDCo, 91934	1321 - G6
JAMACHA 2962 JAMUL DR, SDCo, 92019	1272 - C6
JAMUL PRIMARY 14567 LYONS VALLEY RD, SDCo, 91935	1273 - A7
JEFFERSON 1120 E 7TH ST, CALX, 92231	6680 - J1
JEFFERSON 3743 JEFFERSON ST, CRLB, 92008	1106 - F6
JEFFERSON, THOMAS 3770 UTAH ST, SD, 92104	1269 - D5
JERABEK, CHAUNCY I 10050 AVD MAGNIFICA, SD, 92131	1210 - A4
JOHNSON 500 W MADISON AV, ELCJ, 92020	1251 - E4
JOHNSON, HENRY C 1355 KELTON RD, SD, 92114	1290 - B2
JONES, JOHN P 2751 GREYLING DR, SD, 92123	1249 - C6
JUAREZ, BENITO 2633 MELBOURNE DR, SD, 92123	1249 - E6
JUAREZ-LINCOLN 849 TWINING AV, SD, 92154	1330 - F7
JULIAN 1704 HWY 78, SDCo, 92036	1136 - C7
JUNIPER 1809 S JUNIPER ST, ESCN, 92025	1130 - B5
KELLOGG, DR KARL H 229 E NAPLES ST, CHV, 91911	1330 - F2
KELLY 4885 KELLY DR, CRLB, 92008	1106 - J7
KEMPTON STREET 740 KEMPTON ST, SDCo, 91977	1291 - B3
KENNEDY GARDEN 2300 ROCKWOOD AV, CALX, 92231	6620 - G6
KENNEDY, JOHN F 445 S 47TH ST, SD, 92113	1289 - J5
KIMBALL 302 W 18TH ST, NATC, 91950	1309 - H3
KIMBROUGH 321 HOITT ST, SD, 92102	1289 - E4
KING, MARTIN L 415 31ST ST, SD, 92102	1289 - E4
KING, MARTIN LUTHER JR 1950 VILLA AV, ELCN, 92243	6499 - F5
KNOB HILL 1825 KNOB HILL RD, SMCS, 92069	1109 - D7
KNOX, HARLEY E 1098 S 49TH ST, SD, 92113	1290 - A5
KUMEYAAY 6475 ANTIGUA BLVD, SD, 92124	1229 - J7
KWACHIIYOA CHARTER 6365 LAKE ATLIN AV, SD, 92119	1250 - J5
LA COSTA HEIGHTS 3035 LEVANTE ST, CRLB, 92009	1147 - H2
LA COSTA MEADOWS 6889 EL FUERTE ST, CRLB, 92009	1127 - H6
LAFAYETTE, MARQUIS DE 6125 PRINTWOOD WY, SD, 92117	1248 - J2
LA JOLLA 1111 MARINE ST, SD, 92037	1227 - F7
LAKE 4950 LAKE BLVD, OCN, 92056	1107 - F3
LAKESIDE FARMS 11915 LAKESIDE AV, SDCo, 92040	1231 - J2
LAKEVIEW 9205 LAKEVIEW RD, SDCo, 92040	1232 - D5
LA MESA DALE 4370 PARKS AV, LMSA, 91941	1270 - G4
LA MIRADA 222 AVD D LA MADRID, SD, 92173	1350 - F2
LANGUAGE ACADEMY 4961 64TH ST, SD, 92115	1270 - D2
LA PALOMA 300 HEALD LN, SDCo, 92028	1027 - H3
LA PRESA 519 LA PRESA AV, SDCo, 91977	1291 - C4
LAS PALMAS 1900 E 18TH ST, NATC, 91950	1310 - B2
LAUDERBACH, CALVIN J 390 PALOMAR ST, CHV, 91911	1330 - C4
LAUREL 1410 LAUREL ST, OCN, 92054	1086 - B6
LEE, ROBERT E 6196 CHILDS AV, SD, 92139	1310 - E2
LEMON AVENUE 8787 LEMON AV, LMSA, 91941	1271 - A2
LEMON CREST 12463 LEMON CREST DR, SDCo, 92040	1232 - B4
LEXINGTON 533 S 1ST ST, ELCJ, 92019	1251 - H6
LIBBY 423 W REDONDO DR, OCN, 92057	1066 - J6
LIBERTY 2175 PROCTOR VALLEY RD, CHV, 91914	1311 - E2
LINCOLN ACRES 2200 LANOITAN AV, NATC, 91950	1310 - C2
LINCOLN 1029 N BROADWAY, ESCN, 92026	1129 - H1
LINCOLN 200 N 12TH ST, ELCN, 92243	6499 - G6
LINDA VISTA 2772 ULRIC ST, SD, 92111	1248 - J6
LINDBERGH, CHARLES A 4133 MT ALBERTINE AV, SD, 92111	1248 - J3
LINDO PARK 12824 LAKESHORE DR, SDCo, 92040	1232 - B3
LIVE OAK 1978 RECHE RD, SDCo, 92028	1028 - A4
LOGAN 2875 OCEAN VIEW BLVD, SD, 92113	1289 - E5
LOMA 10355 LOMA LN, SDCo, 91978	1271 - F6
LOMA PORTAL 3341 BROWNING ST, SD, 92106	1268 - C7
LOMA VERDE 1450 LOMA LN, CHV, 91911	1330 - F4
LONGFELLOW, HENRY W 5055 JULY ST, SD, 92110	1268 - G1
LOS ALTOS 1332 KENALAN DR, SD, 92154	1350 - F1
LOS PENASQUITOS 14125 CUCA ST, SD, 92129	1189 - H3
MACDOWELL 5095 ARVINELS AV, SD, 92117	1228 - H7
MADISON AVENUE 1615 E MADISON AV, ELCJ, 92019	1252 - B5
MAGNOLIA 1905 MAGNOLIA AV, CRLB, 92008	1106 - G5
MAGNOLIA 650 GREENFIELD DR, ELCJ, 92021	1251 - G3
MAINS 655 SHERIDAN AV, CALX, 92231	6680 - E1
MARSHALL 2295 MACKENZIE CREEK RD, CHV, 91914	1311 - F3
MARSHALL, JOHN 3550 ALTADENA AV, SD, 92105	1270 - A6
MARVIN, JOHN G. 5720 BRUNSWICK AV, SD, 92120	1250 - C5
MARYLAND AVENUE 5400 MARYLAND AV, LMSA, 91942	1270 - F1
MASON, LOWELL 10340 SAN RAMON DR, SD, 92126	1209 - C4
MCAULIFFE, CHRISTA 3701 KELTON DR, OCN, 92056	1086 - J6
MCCABE 701 W MCCABE RD, ImCo, 92243	6559 - D5
MCKINLEY 1177 N 8TH ST, ELCN, 92243	6499 - G5
MCKINLEY, WILLIAM 3045 FELTON ST, SD, 92104	1269 - F7
MCMILLIN 1450 SANTA CORA AV, CHV, 91913	1311 - D7
MEAD, FRANCIS 730 45TH ST, SD, 92102	1289 - J3
MEADOWS 2059 BOWKER RD, ImCo, 92243	6500 - H4
MENDOZA 2050 CORONADO AV, SD, 92154	1350 - A1
MERIDIAN 651 S 3RD ST, ELCJ, 92019	1252 - A6
MIDLAND 13910 MIDLAND RD, PWY, 92064	1190 - F3
MILLER, DORIS 4343 SHIELDS ST, SD, 92124	1249 - G3
MILLER 1975 MILLER AV, ESCN, 92025	1129 - J6
MIRAMAR RANCH 10770 RED CEDAR DR, SD, 92131	1209 - H4
MISSION 2100 MISSION AV, OCN, 92054	1086 - C6
MISSION ESTANCIA 3330 CL BARCELONA, CRLB, 92009	1147 - J3
MISSION MEADOWS 5657 SPUR AV, OCN, 92057	1067 - F7
MONTEREY HEIGHTS 7550 CANTON DR, LMGR, 91945	1290 - G1
MONTE VISTA 1720 MONTE VISTA DR, VSTA, 92084	1108 - B1
MONTGOMERY, JOHN J 1601 4TH AV, CHV, 91911	1330 - D5
MORNING CREEK 10925 MORNING CREEK DR S, SD, 92128	1189 - H5
MOUNT VERNON 8350 MOUNT VERNON ST, LMGR, 91945	1270 - J7
MOUNT WOODSON 17427 ARCHIE MOORE RD, SDCo, 92065	1151 - F7
MUELLER, ROBERT L 715 I ST, CHV, 91910	1330 - A1
MUIR ALTERNATIVE 3390 ARMSTRONG ST, SD, 92111	1249 - A5
MURDOCK, GLENN E. 4354 CONRAD DR, SDCo, 91941	1271 - D3
MURRAY MANOR 8305 EL PASO ST, LMSA, 91942	1250 - H6
NARANCA 1030 NARANCA AV, ELCJ, 92021	1251 - H4
NESTOR 1455 HOLLISTER ST, SD, 92154	1350 - B2
NEW HORIZONS 1830 E DIVISION ST, NATC, 91950	1290 - A7
NICHOLS 4250 OLD GROVE RD, OCN, 92057	1086 - H1
NICOLOFF 1777 HOWARD AV, SD, 92173	1350 - D2
NORTH BROADWAY 2301 N BROADWAY, ESCN, 92026	1109 - G4
NORTHMONT 9405 GREGORY ST, LMSA, 91942	1251 - B6
NORTH PARK 4041 OREGON ST, SD, 92104	1269 - D5
NORTH TERRACE 940 CAPISTRANO DR, OCN, 92054	1086 - A5
NUBIA LEADERSHIP ACADEMY 6126 BENSON AV, SD, 92114	1290 - C4
NYE 981 VALENCIA PKWY, SD, 92114	1290 - C5
OAK HILL 1820 OAK HILL DR, ESCN, 92027	1130 - C1
OAK PARK 2606 54TH ST, SD, 92105	1270 - B7
OCEAN BEACH 4741 SANTA MONICA AV, SD, 92107	1267 - J6
OCEAN KNOLL 910 MELBA RD, ENCT, 92024	1147 - E7
OCEAN VIEW HILLS 4919 DEL SOL BLVD, SD, 92154	1350 - J1
OLIVE 836 OLIVE AV, VSTA, 92083	1087 - F6
OLIVENHAIN PIONEER 8000 CL ACERVO, CRLB, 92009	1147 - J4
OLIVEWOOD 2505 F AV, NATC, 91950	1309 - J3
OLYMPIC VIEW 1220 S GREENSVIEW DR, CHV, 91915	1311 - G6
ONEONTA 1311 10TH ST, IMPB, 91932	1349 - H1
ORANGE GLEN 2861 E VALLEY PKWY, ESCN, 92027	1110 - E6
OTAY 1651 ALBANY AV, CHV, 91911	1330 - E5
OTIS, JOHN A 621 E 18TH ST, NATC, 91950	1309 - J2
PACIFICA 4991 MACARIO DR, OCN, 92057	1067 - A6
PACIFIC BEACH 1234 TOURMALINE ST, SD, 92109	1247 - J4
PACIFIC RIM 1100 CM D LAS ONDAS, CRLB, 92011	1127 - A5
PACIFIC VIEW 608 3RD ST, ENCT, 92024	1147 - B7
PAINTED ROCK 16711 MARTINCOIT RD, PWY, 92064	1170 - E3
PALMER WAY 2900 PALMER ST, NATC, 91950	1310 - B1
PALMQUIST 1999 CALIFORNIA ST, OCN, 92054	1106 - D1
PALOMA 660 CM MAGNIFICO, SMCS, 92069	1108 - F5
PALOMAR 300 E PALOMAR ST, CHV, 91911	1330 - G3
PARADISE HILLS 5816 ALLEGHANY ST, SD, 92139	1290 - C7
PARK DALE LANE 2050 PARK DALE LN, ENCT, 92024	1147 - H6
PARKS, ROSA 4510 LANDIS ST, SD, 92105	1269 - J5
PARKVIEW 575 JUNIPER ST, CHV, 91911	1330 - H2
PARK VILLAGE 7930 PARK VILLAGE RD, SD, 92129	1189 - B7
PAUMA 33158 COLE GRADE RD, SDCo, 92061	1050 - H4
PENCE, HOWARD 877 VIA TONGA CT, SD, 92154	1330 - E7
PENN, WILLIAM 2797 UTICA DR, SD, 92139	1310 - F1
PEPPER DRIVE 1935 MARLINDA WY, SDCo, 92021	1251 - G1
PERKINS, GRACE W 1110 BEARDSLEY ST, SD, 92113	1289 - C5
PERRY, OLIVER H 6290 ORISKANY RD, SD, 92139	1290 - D7
PINE VALLEY 7454 PINE BLVD, SDCo, 91962	1237 - C7
PIONEER 980 N ASH ST, ESCN, 92027	1110 - A7
POMERADO 12321 9TH ST, PWY, 92064	1190 - B4
PROSPECT AVENUE 9303 PROSPECT AV, SNTE, 92071	1231 - B7
RAMONA 415 8TH ST, SDCo, 92065	1152 - G6
RANCHO 8845 NOELINE AV, SDCo, 91977	1290 - J4
RANCHO SAN DIEGO 12151 CL ALBARA, SDCo, 92019	1272 - A4
RANCHO SANTA FE 5927 LA GRANADA, SDCo, 92067	1168 - D3
REIDY CREEK 2869 N BROADWAY, ESCN, 92026	1109 - H3
REYNOLDS 4575 DOUGLAS DR, OCN, 92057	1066 - H6
RICE, LILIAN J 915 4TH AV, CHV, 91911	1330 - C2
RICHLAND 910 BORDEN RD, SMCS, 92069	1109 - B5
RILEY 5650 MT ACKERLY DR, SD, 92111	1248 - H4
RIO SECO 9545 CUYAMACA ST, SNTE, 92071	1231 - D4
RIOS 14314 RIOS CANYON RD, SDCo, 92021	1232 - G6
RIVERVIEW 9308 WINTER GARDENS BLVD, SDCo, 92040	1231 - J5
ROCK SPRINGS 1155 DEODAR RD, ESCN, 92026	1109 - F7
ROCKWOOD 1000 ROCKWOOD AV, CALX, 92231	6680 - G1
ROGERS, GREG 510 E NAPLES ST, CHV, 91911	1330 - G1
ROHR, FRED H 1540 MALTA AV, CHV, 91911	1330 - G4
ROLANDO 6925 TOWER ST, LMSA, 91941	1270 - E3
ROLANDO PARK 6620 MARLOWE DR, SD, 92115	1270 - E5
ROLLING HILLS 15255 PENASQUITOS DR, SD, 92129	1169 - H7
ROSEBANK 80 FLOWER ST, CHV, 91910	1310 - C5
ROSE 906 N ROSE ST, ESCN, 92027	1110 - B7
ROSS, PETE W 7470 BAGDAD ST, SD, 92111	1249 - A4
ROWAN, STEPHEN 1755 ROWAN ST, SD, 92105	1289 - G2
SAGE CANYON 5290 HARVEST RUN DR, SD, 92130	1208 - D2
SALT CREEK 1055 HUNTE PKWY, CHV, 91914	1311 - H5
SAN ALTOS 1750 MADERA ST, LMGR, 91945	1290 - F1
SANDBURG, CARL 11230 AVD DEL GATO, SD, 92126	1209 - B2
SAN ELIJO 1215 SAN ELIJO RD, SMCS, 92078	1128 - E6
SAN LUIS REY 3535 HACIENDA DR, OCN, 92054	1086 - F4
SAN MARCOS 300 W SAN MARCOS BLVD, SMCS, 92069	1108 - H7
SAN MIGUEL 7059 SAN MIGUEL AV, LMGR, 91945	1270 - F7
SAN ONOFRE 200 PATE DR, SDCo, 92672	1023 - E2
SAN PASQUAL UNION 15305 ROCKWOOD RD, SD, 92027	1130 - H4

FEATURE NAME Address City, ZIP Code	PAGE-GRID
SAN RAFAEL 1616 SAN RAFAEL DR, SDCo, 92055	1085 - J5
SANTA MARGARITA 1 CARNES RD, SDCo, 92055	1086 - A2
SANTEE 10445 MISSION GORGE RD, SNTE, 92071	1231 - E6
SCRIPPS, ELLEN BROWNING 10380 SPRING CANYON RD, SD, 92131	1189 - H7
SEQUOIA 4690 LIMERICK AV, SD, 92117	1248 - H1
SESSIONS, KATE 2150 BERYL ST, SD, 92109	1248 - B4
SHADOW HILLS 8770 HARBISON CANYON RD, SDCo, 91901	1233 - E6
SHERMAN, MATTHEW 450 24TH ST, SD, 92102	1289 - C4
SHOAL CREEK 11775 SHOAL CREEK DR, SD, 92128	1190 - A3
SILVER GATE 1499 VENICE ST, SD, 92107	1288 - A1
SILVER STRAND 1350 LEYTE RD, CORD, 92118	1309 - D6
SILVER WING 3730 AREY DR, SD, 92154	1330 - E7
SKYLINE 606 LOMAS SANTA FE DR, SOLB, 92075	1167 - F6
SMYTHE 1880 SMYTHE AV, SD, 92173	1350 - F2
SOJOURNER TRUTH LEARNING ACADEMY 5825 IMPERIAL AV, SD, 92114	1290 - B4
SOLANA HIGHLANDS 3520 LONG RUN DR, SD, 92130	1187 - J5
SOLANA SANTE FE 6570 EL APAJO, SDCo, 92067	1168 - F6
SOLANA VISTA 780 SANTA VICTORIA, SOLB, 92075	1167 - H5
SOUTH OCEANSIDE 1806 S HORNE ST, OCN, 92054	1106 - D3
SPRECKELS, JOHN D 6033 STADIUM ST, SD, 92122	1228 - D6
SPRING VALLEY 3845 SPRING DR, SDCo, 91977	1271 - B5
SUNDANCE 8944 TWIN TRAILS DR, SD, 92129	1189 - C4
SUNFLOWER 2450 MAIN ST, ELCN, 92243	6499 - E6
SUNNYSIDE 5430 SAN MIGUEL RD, SDCo, 91902	1311 - A1
SUNNYSLOPE 2500 ELM AV, SD, 92154	1330 - B7
SUNSET 3825 SUNSET LN, SD, 92173	1350 - F3
SUNSET HILLS 9291 OVIEDO ST, SD, 92129	1189 - D3
SUNSET VIEW 4365 HILL ST, SD, 92106	1287 - J2
SWEETWATER SPRINGS COMM 10129 AUSTIN DR, SDCo, 91977	1271 - E7
SYCAMORE CANYON 10201 SETTLE RD, SNTE, 92071	1231 - A3
TIERRA BONITA 14678 TIERRA BONITA RD, PWY, 92064	1190 - G1
TIERRASANTA 5450 LA CUENTA DR, SD, 92124	1249 - H1
TIFFANY, BURTON C 1691 ELMHUSRT ST, CHV, 91913	1311 - C5
TOLER, WILLIAM P 3350 BAKER ST, SD, 92117	1248 - D5
TORREY HILLS 10830 CL MAR DE MARIPOSA, SD, 92130	1208 - B4
TORREY PINES 8350 CLIFFRIDGE AV, SD, 92037	1227 - J4
TUBMAN VILLAGE 6880 MOHAWK ST, SD, 92115	1270 - E2
TURTLEBACK 15855 TURTLEBACK RD, SD, 92127	1169 - J5
TWIN OAKS 1 CASSOU RD, SMCS, 92069	1108 - J2
VALENCIA PARK 5880 SKYLINE DR, SD, 92114	1290 - C4
VALLECITOS 5211 5TH ST, SDCo, 92028	998 - J5
VALLE LINDO 1515 OLEANDER AV, CHV, 91911	1330 - H4
VALLEY 13000 BOWRON RD, PWY, 92064	1190 - E5
VALLEY CENTER 28751 COLE GRADE RD, SDCo, 92082	1090 - F1
VALLEY CENTER PRIMARY 14249 FRUITVALE RD, SDCo, 92082	1070 - F7
VALLEY VISTA 3724 VALLEY VISTA WY, SDCo, 91902	1310 - F3
VISTA ACADEMY 600 N SANTA FE AV, VSTA, 92083	1087 - G5
VISTA GRANDE 1908 VIS GRANDE RD, SDCo, 92019	1272 - C2
VISTA GRANDE 5606 ANTIGUA BLVD, SD, 92124	1229 - G7
VISTA LA MESA 3900 VIOLET ST, LMSA, 91941	1270 - F5
VISTA SQUARE 540 G ST, CHV, 91910	1310 - A7
WALKER, MARY CHASE 9225 HILLERY DR, SD, 92126	1209 - E4
WASHINGTON 223 S 1ST ST, ELCN, 92243	6499 - J6
WASHINGTON, GEORGE 1789 STATE ST, SD, 92101	1289 - A2
WEBESTER, NOAH 4801 ELM ST, SD, 92102	1289 - J2
WEGEFORTH, HARRY M 3443 EDIWHAR AV, SD, 92123	1249 - D4
WEST VIEW 525 3RD ST, IMPB, 91932	1329 - F6
WESTWOOD 17449 MATINAL RD, SD, 92127	1169 - J1
WHITMAN, WALT 4050 APPLETON ST, SD, 92117	1228 - E7
WILLOW 226 WILLOW RD, SD, 92173	1350 - G5
WINTER GARDENS 8501 PUEBLO RD, SDCo, 92040	1232 - A7
ZAMORANO 2655 CASEY ST, SD, 92139	1290 - G7

SCHOOLS - PUBLIC HIGH

FEATURE NAME Address City, ZIP Code	PAGE-GRID
ABRAXAS 12450 GLENOAK RD, PWY, 92064	1190 - C2
ALBA SECONDARY 3760 4TH AV, SD, 92103	1269 - A6
ALTA VISTA 1575 BONAIR RD, VSTA, 92084	1088 - B3
ANTHONY, SARAH SIERRA VISTA 2801 MEADOW LARK DR, SD, 92123	1249 - B6
AURORA 641 ROCKWOOD AV, CALX, 92231	6680 - G1
BONITA VISTA 751 OTAY LAKES RD, CHV, 91913	1311 - B5
BORREGO SPRINGS (SEE PAGE 1058) 2281 DIEGUENO RD, SDCo, 92004	1078 - H1
CALEXICO 1030 ENCINAS AV, CALX, 92231	6680 - H1
CARLSBAD 3557 MONROE ST, CRLB, 92008	1106 - G5
CARLSBAD VILLAGE ACADEMY 1640 MAGNOLIA AV, CRLB, 92008	1106 - G5
CASTLE PARK 1395 HILLTOP DR, CHV, 91911	1330 - F3
CENTRAL UNION 1001 BRIGHTON AV, ELCN, 92243	6499 - G7
CHAPPARALL 1600 CUYAMACA ST, ELCJ, 92020	1251 - D2
CHARTER OF SAN DIEGO 2245 SAN DIEGO AV, SD, 92110	1268 - G5
CHULA VISTA 820 4TH AV, CHV, 91911	1330 - B2
CLAIREMONT 4150 UTE DR, SD, 92117	1248 - E4
CORONADO 650 D AV, CORD, 92118	1288 - H6
CRAWFORD, WILL C 4191 COLTS WY, SD, 92115	1270 - B5
EASTLAKE 1120 EASTLAKE PKWY, CHV, 91915	1311 - F6
EL CAJON VALLEY 1035 E MADISON AV, ELCJ, 92021	1251 - H5
EL CAMINO 400 RANCHO DEL ORO DR, OCN, 92057	1086 - H4
EL CAPITAN 10410 ASHWOOD ST, SDCo, 92040	1232 - B2
ESCONDIDO 1535 N BROADWAY, ESCN, 92026	1109 - G6
FALLBROOK 2400 S STAGE COACH LN, SDCo, 92028	1027 - G7
GARFIELD 1255 16TH ST, SD, 92101	1289 - C2
GOMPERS 1005 47TH ST, SD, 92102	1289 - J2
GRANITE HILLS 1719 E MADISON AV, ELCJ, 92019	1252 - C4
GROSSMONT 1100 MURRAY DR, ELCJ, 92020	1251 - C7
GUAJOME PARK ACADEMY 2000 N SANTA FE AV, VSTA, 92083	1087 - G2
HELIX 7323 UNIVERSITY AV, LMSA, 91941	1270 - F4
HENRY, PATRICK 6702 WANDERMERE DR, SD, 92120	1250 - E5
HIGH TECH 2861 WOMBLE RD, SD, 92106	1268 - D7
HILLTOP 555 CLAIRE AV, CHV, 91910	1310 - E6
HOOVER, HERBERT 4474 EL CAJON BLVD, SD, 92115	1269 - H4
IMPERIAL 517 W BARIONI BLVD, IMP, 92251	6439 - E6
IVY 1056 WINTER HAVEN RD, SDCo, 92028	1027 - H7
JULIAN UNION 1656 HWY 78, SDCo, 92036	1136 - C7
KEARNY, STEPHEN W 7651 WELLINGTON ST, SD, 92111	1249 - A5
LA COSTA CANYON 3451 CM D LOS COCHES, CRLB, 92009	1148 - A3
LA JOLLA 750 NAUTILUS ST, SD, 92037	1247 - F1
LINCOLN, ABRAHAM PREP 150 S 49TH ST, SD, 92113	1290 - A4
MADISON, JAMES 4833 DOLIVA DR, SD, 92117	1248 - H1
MAR VISTA 505 ELM AV, IMPB, 91932	1349 - F1
MIRA MESA 10510 REAGAN RD, SD, 92126	1209 - C4
MISSION BAY 2475 GRAND AV, SD, 92109	1248 - C5
MISSION HILLS 1 MISSION HILLS CT, SMCS, 92069	1109 - A7
MONTECITO 720 9TH ST, SDCo, 92065	1152 - G6
MONTE VISTA 3230 SWEETWATER SPRINGS BLVD, SDCo, 91977	1271 - E6
MONTGOMERY 3250 PALM AV, SD, 92154	1330 - D6
MORSE, SAMUEL F B 6905 SKYLINE DR, SD, 92114	1290 - E4
MOUNT CARMEL 9550 CARMEL MOUNTAIN RD, SD, 92129	1189 - E3
MOUNT MIGUEL 1800 SWEETWATER RD, SDCo, 91977	1290 - J1
OASIS 237 E MISSION RD, SDCo, 92028	1027 - F2
OCEAN SHORES 3131 OCEANSIDE BLVD, OCN, 92056	1086 - G6
OCEANSIDE SEAGAZE DR & HORNE ST, OCN, 92054	1086 - B7
ORANGE GLEN 2200 GLENRIDGE RD, ESCN, 92027	1130 - D1
OTAY RANCH 1250 OLYMPIC PKWY, CHV, 91913	1331 - D1
PALOMAR 480 PALOMAR ST, CHV, 91911	1330 - C4
POINT LOMA 2335 CHATSWORTH BLVD, SD, 92106	1268 - C7
POWAY 15500 ESPOLA RD, PWY, 92064	1170 - G5
RAMONA COMM 1710 MONTECITO RD, SDCo, 92065	1152 - E6
RAMONA 1401 HANSON LN, SDCo, 92065	1172 - G1
RANCHO BERNARDO 13010 PAS LUCIDO, SD, 92128	1170 - B6
RANCHO BUENA VISTA 1601 LONGHORN DR, VSTA, 92081	1107 - H4
SAN DIEGO 1405 PARK BLVD, SD, 92101	1289 - B2
SAN DIEGO OF CREATIVE & PERF ARTS 2425 DUSK DR, SD, 92139	1290 - E7
SAN DIEGUITO 800 SANTA FE DR, ENCT, 92024	1167 - E1
SAN MARCOS 1615 W SAN MARCOS BLVD, SMCS, 92078	1128 - C2
SAN PASQUAL 3300 BEAR VALLEY PKWY, ESCN, 92025	1150 - C2
SANTANA 9915 MAGNOLIA AV, SNTE, 92071	1231 - E4
SAN YSIDRO 5353 AIRWAY RD, SD, 92154	1351 - A2
SCRIPPS RANCH 10410 TREENA ST, SD, 92131	1209 - F4
SERRA, JUNIPERO 5156 SANTO RD, SD, 92124	1249 - G2
SOUTHWEST 1685 HOLLISTER ST, SD, 92154	1350 - B2
SOUTHWEST 2001 OCOTILLO DR, ELCN, 92243	6559 - E2
STEELE CANYON 12440 CAMPO RD, SDCo, 91978	1272 - A7
SUNSET 684 REQUEZA ST, ENCT, 92024	1147 - D7
SWEETWATER 2900 HIGHLAND AV, NATC, 91950	1310 - A4
TARGETED OPPORTUNITIES PROGRAM 3596 5TH AV, SD, 92103	1269 - A6
TORREY PINES 3710 DEL MAR HEIGHTS RD, SD, 92130	1188 - B5
TWAIN CONT EAST CAMPUS 5510 TROJAN AV, SD, 92115	1270 - B4
TWAIN CONT MESA CAMPUS 10440 REAGAN RD, SD, 92126	1209 - C4
TWAIN 6402 LINDA VISTA RD, SD, 92111	1268 - H2
TWIN OAKS 158 CASSOU RD, SMCS, 92069	1108 - J2
UNIV CITY 6949 GENESEE AV, SD, 92122	1228 - D4
VALHALLA 1725 HILLSDALE RD, SDCo, 92019	1272 - B3
VALLEY VALLEY CTR RD & HIDDEN TRAILS, ESCN, 92027	1110 - E5
VALLEY CENTER 31322 COLE GRADE RD, SDCo, 92082	1070 - F1
VISTA 1 PANTHER WY, VSTA, 92084	1087 - H3
VISTA VILLAGE LEARNING PLAZA 115 MAIN ST, VSTA, 92084	1087 - H6
WEST HILLS 8756 MAST BLVD, SNTE, 92071	1230 - J5
WESTVIEW CAMINO DEL SUR, SD, 92129	1189 - B3

SCHOOLS - PUBLIC INTERMEDIATE

FEATURE NAME Address City, ZIP Code	PAGE-GRID
JAMUL 14545 LYONS VALLEY RD, SDCo, 91935	1273 - A7
LINCOLN 1029 N BROADWAY, ESCN, 92026	1129 - H1
WRIGHT 515 W 10TH ST, IMP, 92251	6439 - E5

SCHOOLS - PUBLIC JUNIOR HIGH

FEATURE NAME Address City, ZIP Code	PAGE-GRID
BELL, A G 620 BRIARWOOD RD, SD, 92139	1290 - G6
BURGENER, CLAIR ACADEMY 707 CAREY RD, OCN, 92054	1086 - C6
CORREIA, STEVEN B 4302 VALETA ST, SD, 92107	1268 - B6
DARNALL, ORTON E 6020 HUGHES ST, SD, 92115	1270 - C5
DE ANZA 824 BLAIR AV, CALX, 92231	6680 - G1
DIEGUENO 2150 VILLAGE PARK WY, ENCT, 92024	1147 - J5
GOMPERS 1005 47TH ST, SD, 92102	1289 - J3
GRANGER 2101 GRANGER AV, NATC, 91950	1310 - C1
JULIAN 1704 HWY 78, SDCo, 92036	1136 - C7
MEMORIAL 2850 LOGAN AV, SD, 92113	1289 - E5
MONTGOMERY, JOHN J 2470 ULRIC ST, SD, 92111	1248 - J7
OAK CREST 675 BALOUR DR, ENCT, 92024	1147 - F7
OFARRELL COMM 6130 SKYLINE DR, SD, 92114	1290 - C4
POTTER, JAMES E 1743 RECHE RD, SDCo, 92028	1028 - A4
ROOSEVELT, THEODORE 3366 PARK BLVD, SD, 92103	1269 - C6
SOUTHWEST 2710 IRIS AV, SD, 92154	1350 - C2
TWAIN CAMPUS 4455 UTE DR, SD, 92117	1248 - F4
VALLEY 1645 MAGNOLIA AV, CRLB, 92008	1106 - G5
WARREN, EARL 155 STEVENS AV, SOLB, 92075	1167 - F7
WILSON 600 S WILSON ST, ELCN, 92243	6499 - G7

SCHOOLS - PUBLIC MIDDLE

FEATURE NAME Address City, ZIP Code	PAGE-GRID
AVIARA OAKS 6880 AMBROSIA LN, CRLB, 92011	1127 - D6
BERNARDO HEIGHTS 12990 PAS LUCIDO, SD, 92128	1170 - B6
BLACK MOUNTAIN 9353 OVIEDO ST, SD, 92129	1189 - D3
BONITA VISTA 650 OTAY LAKES RD, CHV, 91910	1311 - B5
BORREGO SPRINGS (SEE PAGE 1058) 2281 DIEGUENO RD, SDCo, 92004	1078 - H1
CAJON VALLEY 395 BALLANTYNE ST, ELCJ, 92020	1251 - G5
CARMEL VALLEY 3800 MYKONOS LN, SD, 92130	1188 - A6
CASTLE PARK 160 QUINTARD ST, CHV, 91911	1330 - E4
CHALLENGER 10810 PARKDALE AV, SD, 92126	1209 - A4
CHULA VISTA 415 5TH AV, CHV, 91910	1310 - A7
CLARK 4388 THORN ST, SD, 92105	1269 - H6
CORONADO 550 F AV, CORD, 92118	1288 - H6
DANA 1775 CHATSWORTH BLVD, SD, 92106	1288 - B1
DEL DIOS 1400 W 9TH AV, ESCN, 92029	1129 - G4
DE PORTOLA 11010 CLAIREMONT MESA BLVD, SD, 92124	1249 - J1
EASTLAKE 900 DUNCAN RANCH RD, CHV, 91914	1311 - H4
EMERALD 1221 EMERALD AV, ELCJ, 92020	1251 - F7
FARB 4880 LA CUENTA DR, SD, 92124	1249 - H2
GRANT 939 E MISSION AV, ESCN, 92025	1130 - A1
GREENFIELD 1495 GREENFIELD DR, ELCJ, 92021	1252 - A3
GUAJOME PARK ACADEMY 2000 N SANTA FE AV, VSTA, 92083	1087 - G2
HIDDEN VALLEY 2700 REED RD, ESCN, 92027	1130 - F1
HILLSDALE 1301 BRABHAM ST, SDCo, 92019	1272 - A5
HILLTOP 44 E J ST, CHV, 91910	1310 - D7
JEFFERSON 823 ACACIA AV, OCN, 92054	1086 - C5
KEILLER, ANNIE B 7270 LISBON ST, SD, 92114	1290 - F3
KENNEDY 900 N 6TH ST, ELCN, 92243	6499 - H5
KING 1290 IVEY RANCH RD, OCN, 92057	1086 - J5
KROC, RAY 5050 CONRAD AV, SD, 92117	1228 - G7
LAKESIDE 11833 WOODSIDE AV, SDCo, 92040	1231 - J4
LA MESA 4200 PARKS AV, LMSA, 91941	1270 - G4
LA PRESA 1001 LELAND ST, SDCo, 91977	1291 - B3
LEMON GROVE 7866 LINCOLN ST, LMGR, 91945	1270 - H6
LEWIS, HARVEY L 5170 GREENBRIER AV, SD, 92120	1250 - B5

FEATURE NAME	Address City, ZIP Code	PAGE-GRID
LINCOLN	151 ESCONDIDO AV, VSTA, 92084	1087 - H6
LINCOLN	2000 CALIFORNIA ST, OCN, 92054	1106 - D1
MACQUEEN, JOAN	2001 TAVERN RD, SDCo, 91901	1234 - A7
MADISON	4930 LAKE BLVD, OCN, 92056	1107 - F3
MANN, HORACE	4345 54TH ST, SD, 92115	1270 - B4
MARSHALL	11778 CYPRESS CANYON RD, SD, 92131	1210 - A1
MARSTON, GEORGE W	3799 CLAIREMONT DR, SD, 92117	1248 - E4
MAR VISTA	1267 THERMAL AV, SD, 92154	1349 - J1
MEADOWBROOK	12320 MEADOWBROOK LN, PWY, 92064	1190 - C3
MESA VERDE	8375 ENTREKEN WY, SD, 92129	1189 - B4
MONTGOMERY	1051 PICADOR BLVD, SD, 92154	1350 - E1
MONTGOMERY	1570 MELODY LN, ELCJ, 92019	1252 - B5
MUIRLANDS	1056 NAUTILUS ST, SD, 92037	1247 - F1
NATIONAL CITY	1701 D AV, NATC, 91950	1309 - J2
OAK GROVE	14344 OLIVE VISTA DR, SDCo, 91935	1292 - J1
OAK VALLEY	16055 WINECREEK RD, SDCo, 92127	1169 - F5
PACIFIC BEACH	4676 INGRAHAM ST, SD, 92109	1247 - J5
PALM	8425 PALM ST, LMGR, 91945	1270 - J7
PARKWAY	9009 PARK PLAZA DR, LMSA, 91942	1251 - A6
PEIRCE, OLIVE E. MIDDLE	1521 HANSON LN, SDCo, 92065	1172 - G1
PERSHING, JOHN J.	8204 SAN CARLOS DR, SD, 92119	1250 - H5
RANCHO DEL REY	1174 E J ST, CHV, 91910	1311 - A7
RANCHO SANTA FE	5927 LA GRANADA, SDCo, 92067	1168 - D3
RINCON	925 LEHNER AV, ESCN, 92026	1109 - J5
ROOSEVELT	850 SAGEWOOD DR, OCN, 92057	1087 - C2
SAN ELIJO	1215 SAN ELIJO RD, SMCS, 92078	1128 - E6
SAN MARCOS	650 W MISSION RD, SMCS, 92069	1108 - G6
SAN YSIDRO	4345 OTAY MESA RD, SD, 92173	1350 - G3
SPRING VALLEY	3900 CONRAD DR, SDCo, 91977	1271 - C4
STANDLEY	6298 RADCLIFFE DR, SD, 92122	1228 - D5
SULLIVAN, NORMAN	7350 W LILAC RD, SDCo, 92003	1048 - F7
TAFT, WILLIAM H	9191 GRAMERCY DR, SD, 92123	1249 - D5
TIERRA DEL SOL	9611 PETITE LN, SDCo, 92040	1232 - C4
TWIN PEAKS	14640 TIERRA BONITA RD, PWY, 92064	1190 - G1
VALLEY CENTER	28102 N LAKE WOHLFORD RD, SDCo, 92082	1091 - C2
WANGENHEIM, JULIUS	9230 GOLD COAST DR, SD, 92126	1209 - E4
WASHINGTON	740 OLIVE AV, VSTA, 92083	1087 - F6
WILSON, WOODROW	3838 ORANGE AV, SD, 92105	1269 - G4
WOODLAND PARK	1270 ROCK SPRINGS RD, SMCS, 92069	1109 - C6

SHOPPING - COMMUNITY

FEATURE NAME	Address City, ZIP Code	PAGE-GRID
ALLIED GARDENS CTR	5105 WARING RD, SD, 92120	1250 - A6
ALPINE CREEK	TAVERN RD & ALPINE BLVD, SDCo, 91901	1234 - A6
BALBOA MESA	5667 BALBOA AV, SD, 92111	1248 - H3
BALTIMORE WEST	PARKWAY DR & BALTIMORE DR, LMSA, 91942	1270 - H1
BAY PLAZA	1430 E PLAZA BLVD, NATC, 91950	1310 - A1
BAZAAR DEL MUNDO	2754 CALHOUN ST, SD, 92110	1268 - F5
BEACH WALK	437 S HWY 101, SOLB, 92075	1187 - E1
BERNARDO HEIGHTS SHOPPING CTR	BERNARDO HEIGHTS PKWY & POMERA, SD, 92128	1170 - C5
BEST PLAZA	OCEANSIDE BL & STATE TREE DR, OCN, 92054	1106 - C1
BLACK MOUNTAIN VILLAGE	BLACK MTN RD & MIRA MESA BL, SD, 92126	1209 - D3
BONITA CENTER	4240 BONITA RD, SDCo, 91902	1310 - G3
BONITA CENTER EAST	4500 BONITA RD, CHV, 91902	1310 - G3
BONITA POINT PLAZA	700 OTAY LAKES RD, CHV, 91910	1311 - B5
BROADWAY PLAZA	550 BROADWAY, ELCJ, 92021	1251 - G4
CAMINO TOWN & CC	2213 S EL CAMINO REAL, OCN, 92054	1106 - G2
CAMINO VILLAGE	11295 CM RUIZ, SD, 92126	1209 - C2
CAMINO VILLAGE PLAZA	256 N EL CAMINO REAL, ENCT, 92024	1147 - F6
CAMPUS MARKETPLACE	306 S TWIN OAKS VALLEY RD, SMCS, 92078	1128 - H2
CAMPUS PLAZA	6083 EL CAJON BLVD, SD, 92115	1270 - C3
CANYON PLAZA	505 TELEGRAPH CANYON RD, CHV, 91910	1310 - G7
CARDIFF TOWNE CENTRE	2005 SAN ELIJO AV, ENCT, 92007	1167 - D3
CARLSBAD PLAZA	2502 EL CAMINO REAL, CRLB, 92010	1106 - G2
CARLSBAD PREMIUM OUTLETS	5620 PAS DL NORTE, CRLB, 92008	1126 - H3
CARMEL COUNTRY PLAZA	12750 CARMEL COUNTRY RD, SD, 92130	1188 - A5
CARMEL MOUNTAIN RANCH TOWN CTR	11845 CARMEL MTN RD, SD, 92128	1190 - A1
CARRIAGE CTR WEST	12845 POWAY RD, PWY, 92064	1190 - D4
CASA DE ORO PLAZA	9716 CAMPO RD, SDCo, 91977	1271 - C5
CENTER OF EL CENTRO	1150 N IMPERIAL AV, ELCN, 92243	6499 - F5
CIVIC CTR PLAZA	311 N ESCONDIDO BLVD, ESCN, 92025	1129 - H3
CLAIREMONT SQUARE	3962 CLAIREMONT MESA BLVD, SD, 92117	1248 - E1
CLAIREMONT VILLAGE	CLAIREMONT DR & BURGENER BLVD, SD, 92110	1248 - F6
COAST WALK CTR	1298 PROSPECT ST, SD, 92037	1227 - F6
COLLEGE CENTER, THE	6331 EL CAJON BLVD, SD, 92115	1270 - D3
COLLEGE PLAZA	3514 COLLEGE BLVD, OCN, 92056	1107 - B2
COLONY PLAZA	1309 S MAIN ST, SDCo, 92028	1027 - F4
COLONY PLAZA	7708 REGENTS RD, SD, 92122	1228 - B4
CONVOY VILLAGE	CONVOY ST & BALBOA AV, SD, 92111	1249 - A2
COPPERWOOD CTR	110 COPPERWOOD WY, OCN, 92054	1086 - E4
CORNER MARKET	MAST BLVD & CUYAMACA ST, SNTE, 92071	1231 - C4
CORONADO PLAZA	1300 ORANGE AV, ELCJ, 92020	1271 - F1
COSTA VERDE	8610 GENESEE AV, SD, 92122	1228 - C3
COSTCO PLAZA	1140 BROADWAY, CHV, 91911	1330 - B3
COUNTRY CORNER	601 N BROADWAY, ESCN, 92025	1129 - H2
COURTYARD AT CARMEL MTN RANCH, THE	11160 RANCHO CARMEL DR, SD, 92128	1189 - J1
CREEKSIDE MARKETPLACE	SAN MARCOS BLVD & GRAND AV, SMCS, 92078	1128 - G1
CREEKSIDE PLAZA	13409 POWAY RD, PWY, 92064	1190 - F4
DE LA PLAZA ENCINITAS	201 S EL CAMINO REAL, ENCT, 92024	1147 - G7
DEL MAR CTR	2651 VIA DE LA VALLE, SD, 92014	1187 - H2
DEL MAR HEIGHTS VILLAGE	DEL MAR HEIGHTS RD & MANGO DR, SD, 92014	1187 - H5
DEL MAR HIGHLANDS TOWN CTR	3455 DEL MAR HEIGHTS RD, SD, 92130	1188 - A6
DEL MAR PLAZA	1555 CAMINO DEL MAR, DLMR, 92014	1187 - F4
DEL NORTE PLAZA	330 W EL NORTE PKWY, ESCN, 92026	1109 - G7
DIANE CTR	CLAIREMONT MESA BL & DIANE AV, SD, 92117	1248 - G1
EAST COUNTY SQUARE	LOS COCHES RD & CAMINO CANADA, SDCo, 92021	1252 - D1
EASTLAKE VILLAGE CTR	EASTLAKE PKWY & OTAY LAKES RD, CHV, 91915	1311 - F5
EL CAJON TOWNE CTR	301 N MAGNOLIA AV, ELCJ, 92020	1251 - F5
EL CAMINO PROMENADE	204 N EL CAMINO REAL, ENCT, 92024	1147 - F6
EL NORTE PARKWAY PLAZA	I-15 & EL NORTE PKWY, ESCN, 92026	1109 - F6
ENCINITAS MARKETPLACE	ENCINITAS BL & EL CAMINO REAL, ENCT, 92024	1147 - F6
ENCINITAS RANCH TOWN CTR	1044 N EL CAMINO REAL, ENCT, 92024	1147 - F4
ENCINITAS TOWN & CC	407 ENCINITAS BLVD, ENCT, 92024	1147 - D7
ENCINITAS VILLAGE	111 N EL CAMINO REAL, ENCT, 92024	1147 - G6
ESCONDIDO HILLS PLAZA	2345 E VALLEY PKWY, ESCN, 92027	1110 - D7
ESCONDIDO MISSION VILLAGE	E VALLEY PKWY & MIDWAY DR, ESCN, 92027	1110 - C7
ESCONDIDO SQUARE	640 N ESCONDIDO BLVD, ESCN, 92025	1129 - H2
ESCONDIDO TOWN & CC	1171 E VALLEY PKWY, ESCN, 92027	1130 - B1
ESCONDIDO VILLAGE MALL	1261 E VALLEY PKWY, ESCN, 92027	1130 - B1
FALLBROOK MERCANTILE	845 S MAIN AV, SDCo, 92028	1027 - F3
FALLBROOK TOWNE CTR	1133 S MISSION RD, SDCo, 92028	1027 - F4
FELICITA JUNCTION	CENTRE CITY PKWY & FELICITA AV, ESCN, 92025	1130 - A5
FELICITA PLAZA	325 W FELICITA AV, ESCN, 92025	1130 - A5
FELICITA TOWN CTR	1855 S CENTRE CITY PKWY, ESCN, 92025	1130 - A5
FELICITA VILLAGE	330 W FELICITA AV, ESCN, 92025	1130 - A5
FENTON MARKETPLACE	2149 FENTON PKWY, SD, 92108	1269 - E1
FERRARA PLAZA	VALLEY PKWY & CITRUS AV, ESCN, 92027	1110 - D7
FERRY LANDING MARKETPLACE	1201 1ST ST, CORD, 92118	1288 - J5
FIRE MOUNTAIN	2500 VISTA WY, OCN, 92054	1106 - F2
FLETCHER HILLS CTR	2320 FLETCHER PKWY, ELCJ, 92020	1251 - B4
FLOWER HILL	2720 VIA DE LA VALLE, SD, 92014	1187 - H2
FORUM, THE	CL BARCELONA & EL CAMINO REAL, CRLB, 92024	1147 - F3
FRIARS MISSION CTR	5680 MISSION CENTER RD, SD, 92108	1269 - A2
FRIARS VILLAGE	FRIARS RD & ZION AV, SD, 92120	1249 - H6
GATEWAY	1929 W SAN MARCOS BLVD, SMCS, 92078	1128 - C2
GATEWAY CTR	VALLEY PKWY & TULIP ST, ESCN, 92025	1129 - G3
GENESEE PLAZA	5454 BALBOA AV, SD, 92117	1248 - H2
HAZARD CTR	7510 HAZARD CENTER DR, SD, 92108	1269 - B2
HILLCREST COLONNADE	1240 UNIVERSITY AV, SD, 92103	1269 - B5
HOME DEPOT CTR	VALLEY PKWY & W 9TH AV, ESCN, 92029	1129 - F4
HOMESTAR	MAIN ST & 14TH ST, SDCo, 92065	1152 - F6
IMPERIAL CTR	9TH ST & PALM AV, IMPB, 91932	1329 - G7
INDEPENDENCE SQUARE	7305 CLAIREMONT MESA BLVD, SD, 92111	1249 - A1
JAMACHA VILLAGE CTR	JAMACHA RD & E MAIN ST, ELCJ, 92019	1251 - J5
KEARNY MESA	ULRIC ST & COMSTOCK ST, SD, 92111	1268 - J1
KEARNY VILLAGE	CLAIREMONT MESA BLVD, SD, 92111	1249 - C1
LA COSTA PLAZA	EL CAMINO REAL & LA COSTA AV, CRLB, 92009	1147 - F1
LA COSTA TOWN CTR	LA COSTA AV & EL CAMINO REAL, CRLB, 92009	1147 - E1
LA JOLLA MARKET PLACE	GIRARD AV & PEARL ST, SD, 92037	1227 - F7
LA JOLLA VILLAGE CTR	8813 VILLA LA JOLLA DR, SD, 92037	1228 - A3
LA JOLLA VILLAGE PLAZA	737 PEARL ST, SD, 92037	1227 - F7
LA JOLLA VILLAGE SQUARE	8657 VILLA LA JOLLA DR, SD, 92037	1228 - A3
LAKE MURRAY SQUARE	6055 LAKE MURRAY BLVD, LMSA, 91942	1250 - G7
LAKE MURRAY VILLAGE	5550 LAKE MURRAY BLVD, LMSA, 91942	1250 - G7
LAKE SAN MARCOS CTR	1145 SAN MARINO DR, SDCo, 92078	1128 - C3
LA MESA CROSSROADS	5020 BALTIMORE DR, LMSA, 91941	1270 - H2
LA MESA SPRINGS SHOPPING CTR	8011 UNIVERSITY AV, LMSA, 91941	1270 - H3
LA MESA SQUARE	CENTER DR & JACKSON DR, LMSA, 91942	1270 - J1
LA MESA VILLAGE	5901 SEVERIN DR, LMSA, 91942	1251 - B6
LEMON GROVE PLAZA	7090 BROADWAY, LMGR, 91945	1270 - F6
LINDA VISTA PLAZA	LINDA VISTA RD & ULRIC ST, SD, 92111	1248 - J7
LOMA SQUARE	3337 ROSECRANS ST, SD, 92110	1268 - E6
LOMAS SANTA FE PLAZA	931 LOMAS SANTA FE DR, SOLB, 92075	1167 - G7
MADISON SQUARE	5487 CLAIREMONT MESA BLVD, SD, 92117	1248 - H1
MAGNOLIA SHOPPING CTR	HWY 67 & BRADLEY AV, SDCo, 92020	1251 - F2
MALL, THE (SEE PAGE 1058)	PALM CANYON DR & COUNTY CLUB, SDCo, 92004	1078 - H2
MELROSE VILLAGE PLAZA	1601 S MELROSE DR, VSTA, 92081	1107 - G4
MERCADO DE OCEANA	EL CAMINO REAL & VISTA OCEANA, OCN, 92057	1086 - F4
MESA	8901 MIRA MESA BLVD, SD, 92126	1209 - D3
METROPOLITAN CTR	1755 EUCLID AV, SD, 92105	1290 - A1
MIDLAND-POWAY	13644 POWAY RD, PWY, 92064	1190 - F4
MIDWAY TOWNE	3944 W POINT LOMA BLVD, SD, 92110	1268 - C5
MIRAMAR VILLAGE	7160 MIRAMAR RD, SD, 92121	1229 - A1
MIRA MESA MARKETCENTER	MIRA MESA BLVD & I-15, SD, 92126	1209 - E3
MIRA MESA SQUARE	9326 MIRA MESA BLVD, SD, 92126	1209 - E3
MISSION CTR	N RANCHO SANTA FE RD, SMCS, 92069	1108 - D6
MISSION DOUGLAS PLAZA	3925 MISSION AV, OCN, 92057	1086 - G3
MISSION GORGE SHOPPING CTR	6501 MISSION GORGE RD, SD, 92120	1249 - H6
MISSION GORGE SQUARE	9740 MISSION GORGE RD, SNTE, 92071	1231 - C6
MISSION MARKETPLACE	443 COLLEGE BLVD, OCN, 92057	1067 - B7
MISSION PLAZA REAL CTR	3875 MISSION AV, OCN, 92054	1086 - G3
MISSION SQUARE	1002 MISSION AV, OCN, 92054	1086 - A7
MISSION VILLAGE	4180 RUFFIN RD, SD, 92123	1249 - D5
MONTGOMERY PLAZA	PALM AV & PICADOR BL, SD, 92154	1330 - E7
MOONLIGHT PLAZA	ENCINITAS BL & S COAST HWY 101, ENCT, 92024	1147 - B6
MORENA PLAZA	W MORENA BL & BUENOS AV, SD, 92110	1268 - E3
NATIONAL CITY PLAZA	DIVISION ST & N EUCLID AV, NATC, 91950	1290 - A6
NAVAJO VILLAGE	8634 LAKE MURRAY BLVD, SD, 92119	1251 - A4
NEW MERCADO, THE	11844 RANCHO BERNARDO RD, SD, 92128	1170 - A2
NORTH COUNTY PLAZA	1824 MARRON RD, CRLB, 92008	1106 - F3
NORTH COUNTY SQUARE	1841 UNIVERSITY DR, VSTA, 92083	1108 - B3
OCEANSIDE 5	I-5 & OCEANSIDE BLVD, OCN, 92054	1106 - C1
OCEANSIDE PLAZA	2007 MISSION AV, OCN, 92054	1086 - C6
OCEANSIDE SHOPPING CTR	3744 MISSION AV, OCN, 92054	1086 - F3
OCEANSIDE VILLAGE SQUARE	1906 OCEANSIDE BLVD, OCN, 92054	1106 - D1
OLD GROVE MARKETPLACE	HWY 76 & N OLD GROVE RD, OCN, 92057	1086 - J2
OLD POWAY VILLAGE	13029 MIDLAND RD, PWY, 92064	1190 - F3
OTTO SQUARE	NATIONAL AV & 35TH ST, SD, 92113	1289 - F5
PACIFIC COAST PLAZA	2170 W VISTA WY, OCN, 92054	1106 - E2
PACIFIC PLAZA I	1702 GARNET AV, SD, 92109	1248 - A5
PACIFIC PLAZA II	4640 GARNET AV & JEWEL ST, SD, 92109	1248 - A5
PALADION	G ST & 1ST AV, SD, 92101	1289 - A3
PALM PLAZA CTR	3500 PALM AV, SD, 92154	1330 - D7
PALM PROMENADE	710 DENNERY RD, SD, 92154	1330 - G7
PALM RIDGE	4360 PALM AV, SD, 92154	1330 - G7
PALOMAR PLAZA	762 S RANCHO SANTA FE, SMCS, 92078	1128 - C1
PALOMAR TROLLEY CTR	660 PALOMAR ST, CHV, 91911	1330 - B4
PARK PLAZA AT THE VILLAGE	300 3RD AV, CHV, 91910	1310 - B6
PARKWAY WEST CTR	825 ARNELE AV, ELCJ, 92020	1251 - E4
PIAZZA CARMEL	3810 VALLEY CENTRE DR, SD, 92130	1188 - A7
PLAZA DE CUYAMACA	9711 MISSION GORGE RD, SNTE, 92071	1231 - C7
PLAZA DE LAS PALMAS	AVOCADO BL & E CHASE AV, ELCJ, 92020	1251 - G7
PLAZA DEL LAGO	VIA RANCHO PKWY & DEL LAGO BL, ESCN, 92029	1150 - A3
PLAZA DEL SOL	4688 CONVOY ST, SD, 92111	1249 - A2
PLAZA LAS PALMAS	1000 W VALLEY PKWY, ESCN, 92025	1129 - G3
PLAZA PASEO REAL	6949 EL CAMINO REAL, CRLB, 92011	1127 - E6
PLAZA RANCH DEL ORO	4120 OCEANSIDE BLVD, OCN, 92056	1087 - B5
PLAZA RANCHO	2990 JAMACHA RD, SDCo, 92019	1271 - J6
PLAZA RANCHO PENASQUITOS & PRADO	9869 CARMEL MOUNTAIN RD, SD, 92129	1189 - F4
PLAZA SORRENTO	6755 MIRA MESA BLVD, SD, 92121	1208 - H5
PLAZA SOUTH	MARRON RD & EL CAMINO REAL, CRLB, 92010	1106 - G3
PLAZA TOWNE	1001 E PLAZA BLVD, NATC, 91950	1309 - J1
PLAZA VILLAGE	3100 E PLAZA BLVD, NATC, 91950	1290 - C7
POINSETTIA VILLAGE	7130 POINSETTIA LN, CRLB, 92011	1126 - J6
POINT LOMA PLAZA	3683 MIDWAY DR, SD, 92110	1268 - D5
POWAY PLAZA	12622 POWAY RD, PWY, 92064	1190 - C4
POWAY TOWN & CC	POWAY RD & COMMUNITY RD, PWY, 92064	1190 - F4
POWAY VALLEY CTR	13315 POWAY RD, PWY, 92064	1190 - E4

FEATURE NAME Address City, ZIP Code	PAGE-GRID
PRICE CLUB PLAZA 12350 CARMEL MOUNTAIN RD, SD, 92128	1170 - A7
PROMENADE AT PACIFIC BEACH MISSION BL & PACIFIC BEACH DR, SD, 92109	1247 - H7
PROSPECT PLAZA 8504 MAGNOLIA AV, SNTE, 92071	1231 - F7
QUARRY CREEK COLLEGE BL & RONALD PACKARD PK, OCN, 92056	1107 - A2
RANCHO BERNARDO TOWN CTR BERNARDO PLAZA DR, SD, 92128	1170 - A2
RANCHO BERNARDO VILLAGE 12425 RANCHO BERNARDO RD, SD, 92128	1170 - C3
RANCHO DEL ORO GATEWAY 4201 OCEANSIDE BLVD, OCN, 92056	1087 - C5
RANCHO DEL REY CTR 1040 TIERRA DEL REY, CHV, 91910	1310 - J6
RANCHO PENASQUITOS TOWN CTR 13289 BLACK MOUNTAIN RD, SD, 92129	1189 - D4
RANCHO SAN DIEGO TOWN & COUNTRY CTR 2652 JAMACHA RD, SDCo, 92019	1272 - A5
RANCHO SAN DIEGO TOWNE CTR JAMACHA RD & CAMPO RD, SDCo, 92019	1271 - J6
RANCHO SAN DIEGO VILLAGE 3605 AVOCADO BLVD, SDCo, 91941	1271 - G5
RANCHO SAN MARCOS VILLAGE SAN MARCOS BL & RCHO SANTA FE, SMCS, 92078	1128 - C1
REGENTS MARKETPLACE 4150 REGENTS PARK RW, SD, 92037	1228 - C2
RENAISSANCE TOWNE CTR 8935 TOWNE CENTER DR, SD, 92122	1228 - D3
RIO VISTA SHOPPING CTR 8440 RIO SAN DIEGO DR, SD, 92108	1269 - C2
RIVER VILLAGE SAN LUIS REY 5256 S MISSION RD, SDCo, 92003	1048 - A7
ROCKY HOME PLAZA 9530 WINTERCREST DR, SDCo, 92040	1231 - J4
ROLANDO CTR 6415 UNIVERSITY AV, SD, 92115	1270 - D4
RUFFIN VILLAGE 9353 CLAIRMONT MESA BLVD, SD, 92123	1249 - E1
SAN CARLOS CTR 7393 JACKSON DR, SD, 92119	1250 - F4
SAN CARLOS VILLAGE CTR 8788 NAVAJO RD, SD, 92119	1250 - J4
SAN MARCOS PLAZA 1921 W SAN MARCOS BLVD, SMCS, 92078	1128 - C2
SAN MARCOS VILLAGE S RANCHO SANTA FE RD, SMCS, 92078	1108 - D6
SANTANA VILLAGE 9802 MAGNOLIA AV, SNTE, 92071	1231 - E4
SANTEE CTR 9300 MISSION GORGE RD, SNTE, 92071	1231 - B6
SANTEE PLAZA TOWN CTR PKWY & CUYAMACA ST, SNTE, 92071	1231 - C6
SANTEE TROLLEY SQUARE MISSION GORGE RD & CUYAMACA ST, SNTE, 92071	1231 - D6
SANTEE VILLAGE SQUARE 9621 MISSION GORGE RD, SNTE, 92071	1231 - C6
SAN YSIDRO VILLAGE 4498 CAM DE LA PLAZA, SD, 92173	1350 - H5
SCRIPPS RANCH MARKETPLACE SCRIPPS POWAY PKWY, SD, 92131	1189 - G7
SCRIPPS RANCH VILLAGE 10006 SCRIPPS RANCH BLVD, SD, 92131	1209 - H5
SEAPORT VILLAGE 849 W HARBOR DR, SD, 92101	1288 - J4
SERRA MESA 3332 SANDROCK RD, SD, 92123	1249 - C5
SHADOWRIDGE PLAZA SYCAMORE AV & SHADOWRIDGE DR, VSTA, 92083	1108 - A4
SHOPPING ARENA, THE HWY 67 & WYNOLA ST, SDCo, 92065	1172 - D1
SILVER STRAND PLAZA PALM AV & RAINBOW DR, IMPB, 91932	1329 - G7
SOLANA BEACH TOWNE CENTRE 622 SAN RODOLFO DR, SOLB, 92075	1167 - F7
SOUTH BAY MARKET PLACE NATIONAL CITY BLVD & C ST, CHV, 91910	1309 - J5
SOUTH BAY PLAZA NORTH 1130 E PLAZA BLVD, NATC, 91950	1309 - J1
SOUTH BAY PLAZA SOUTH 1121 E HIGHLAND AV, NATC, 91950	1309 - J1
SOUTHLAND PLAZA 655 SATURN BLVD, SD, 92154	1330 - A7
SOUTHWESTERN COLLEGE ESTATES CTR 903 OTAY LAKES RD, CHV, 91913	1311 - C6
SPORTS ARENA PLAZA 3245 SPORTS ARENA BLVD, SD, 92110	1268 - D5
SPORTS ARENA SQUARE 3350 SPORTS ARENA BLVD, SD, 92110	1268 - E5
SPRING VALLEY CTR 543 SWEETWATER RD, SDCo, 91977	1291 - A3
STONECREST PLAZA 3382 MURPHY CANYON RD, SD, 92123	1249 - F4
SWEETWATER PLAZA 1625 SWEETWATER RD, NATC, 91950	1310 - B3
SWEETWATER TOWN & CC 1502 SWEETWATER RD, NATC, 91950	1310 - B3
SWEETWATER VILLAGE SWEETWATER SPGS BL & AUSTIN DR, SDCo, 91977	1271 - E7
TERRA NOVA PLAZA 394 E H ST, CHV, 91910	1310 - E6
TIERRASANTA GATEWAY SHOPPING CTR SANTO RD & SR52, SD, 92124	1229 - H6
TIERRASANTA TOWN CTR 10601 TIERRASANTA BLVD, SD, 92124	1249 - H2
TOWN & CC E VALLEY PKWY & N ROSE ST, ESCN, 92027	1130 - C1
TOWN & COUNTRY CTR 2646 FLETCHER PKWY, ELCJ, 92020	1251 - A5
TOWN & COUNTRY VILLAGE 328 N 2ND ST, ELCJ, 92021	1251 - J4
TOWN CTR NORTH 705 COLLEGE BLVD, OCN, 92057	1087 - B1
TRI-CITY CROSSROADS 3817 PLAZA DR, OCN, 92056	1107 - B2
TWIN PEAKS PLAZA 14721 POMERADO RD, PWY, 92064	1190 - C1
UNIV CITY SHOPPING CTR 3202 GOVERNOR DR, SD, 92122	1228 - C5
UNIV SQUARE 5931 UNIVERSITY AV, SD, 92115	1270 - C5
VALLECITOS TOWN CTR 707 CENTER DR, SMCS, 92069	1129 - D1
VIEJAS OUTLET CTR 5005 WILLOWS RD, SDCo, 91901	1234 - J5
VINEYARD, THE 1528 E VALLEY PKWY, ESCN, 92027	1130 - B1
VISTA PLACE 1830 HACIENDA DR, VSTA, 92081	1107 - D1
VISTA VILLAGE MAIN ST & S SANTA FE AV, VSTA, 92083	1087 - H6
VONS CTR 3883 GOVERNOR DR, SD, 92122	1228 - E5
WEST BLUFF PLAZA EL CAMINO REAL & ALGA RD, CRLB, 92009	1127 - F6
WESTWOOD CTR BERNARDO CTR DR & DUENDA RD, SD, 92127	1170 - A1
WILD WEST VILLAGE 802 JACKMAN ST, ELCJ, 92020	1251 - E4

SHOPPING - REGIONAL

FEATURE NAME Address City, ZIP Code	PAGE-GRID
CARMEL MOUNTAIN PLAZA 11640 CARMEL MOUNTAIN RD, SD, 92128	1189 - J1
CHULA VISTA CTR 555 BROADWAY, CHV, 91910	1310 - A7
EL CAMINO NORTH CTR HWY 78 & EL CAMINO REAL, OCN, 92054	1106 - G2
ESCONDIDO PROMENADE 1272 AUTO PARK WY, ESCN, 92029	1129 - G4
FASHION VALLEY 352 FASHION VALLEY RD, SD, 92108	1269 - A3
GROSSMONT CTR 5500 GROSSMONT CENTER DR, LMSA, 91942	1271 - A1
LAS AMERICAS MALL 4345 CAMINO DE LA PLAZA, SD, 92173	1350 - G5
MARKETPLACE AT THE GROVE 3490 COLLEGE GROVE DR, SD, 92115	1270 - E6
MIRA MESA MALL 8232 MIRA MESA BLVD, SD, 92126	1209 - B4
VALLEY PLAZA 1501 W MAIN ST, ELCN, 92243	6499 - F6
WESTFIELD SHOPPINGTOWN HORTON PLAZA BROADWAY CIR & 4TH AV, SD, 92101	1289 - A3
WESTFIELD SHOPPINGTOWN MISSION VALLEY 1640 CM DL RIO N, SD, 92108	1269 - B3
WESTFIELD SHOPPINGTOWN NORTH COUNTY 272 VIA RANCHO PKWY, ESCN, 92025	1150 - B3
WESTFIELD SHOPPINGTOWN PARKWAY 415 PARKWAY PZ, ELCJ, 92020	1251 - E4
WESTFIELD SHOPPINGTOWN PLAZA BONITA 3030 PLZ BONITA RD, NATC, 91950	1310 - D3
WESTFIELD SHOPPINGTOWN PLZ CAMINO-REAL 2525 EL CAMINO REAL, CRLB, 92008	1106 - F3
WESTFIELD SHOPPINGTOWN UTC 4545 LA JOLLA VILLAGE DR, SD, 92122	1228 - D2

TRANSPORTATION

FEATURE NAME Address City, ZIP Code	PAGE-GRID
AMTRAK OCEANSIDE STA 235 S TREMONT ST, OCN, 92054	1106 - A1
AMTRAK SAN DIEGO STA 1050 KETTNER BLVD, SD, 92101	1288 - J3
AMTRAK SOLANA BEACH STA 105 CEDROS AV, SOLB, 92075	1167 - E7
COASTER 235 S TREMONT ST, OCN, 92054	1106 - A1
GREYHOUND BUS STA 460 STATE ST, ELCN, 92243	6499 - J6
GREYHOUND BUS STA 120 W BROADWAY, SD, 92101	1289 - A3
METROLINK 235 S TREMONT ST, OCN, 92054	1106 - A1
TRANSIT CTR BIRMINGHAM DR & NEWCASTLE AV, ENCT, 92007	1167 - D3
TRANSIT CTR - 12TH & IMPERIAL IMPERIAL AV & 12TH AV, SD, 92101	1289 - B4
TRANSIT CTR - 70TH ST 7225 ALVARADO RD, LMSA, 91941	1270 - F2
TRANSIT CTR - AMERICA PLAZA BROADWAY & KETTNER BL, SD, 92101	1288 - J3
TRANSIT CTR - BAYFRONT/E ST INTERSTATE 5 & E ST, CHV, 91910	1309 - J6
TRANSIT CTR - CARLSBAD POINSETTIA AVENIDA ENCINAS, CRLB, 92011	1126 - H5
TRANSIT CTR - CARLSBAD VILLAGE GRAND AV & STATE ST, CRLB, 92008	1106 - E5
TRANSIT CTR - COLLEGE GROVE COLLEGE GROVE DR, SD, 92115	1270 - E6
TRANSIT CTR - N COUNTY FAIR BEAR VLY PKWY & BEETHOVEN DR, ESCN, 92025	1150 - B3
TRANSIT CTR - EL CAJON MARSHALL AV & W PALM AV, ELCJ, 92020	1251 - E6
TRANSIT CTR - ENCINITAS ENCINITAS BL & S VULCAN AV, ENCT, 92024	1147 - C7
TRANSIT CTR - ESCONDIDO WASHINGTON AV & QUINCE ST, ESCN, 92025	1129 - H3
TRANSIT CTR - EUCLID N EUCLID AV & MARKET ST, SD, 92102	1290 - A3
TRANSIT CTR - FASHION VALLEY FASHION VALLEY RD, SD, 92108	1268 - J3
TRANSIT CTR - GRANTVILLE STA 4464 ALVARADO CANYON RD, SD, 92120	1269 - H1
TRANSIT CTR - GROSSMONT GROSSMONT CENTER DR, LMSA, 91942	1251 - A7
TRANSIT CTR - H ST H ST & SAN DIEGO FRWY, CHV, 91910	1309 - J7
TRANSIT CTR - IRIS AV IRIS AV & HOWARD AV, SD, 92154	1350 - D2
TRANSIT CTR - KEARNY MESA CLAIREMONT MESA BLVD & COMPLEX, SD, 92123	1249 - D1
TRANSIT CTR - OCEANSIDE 195 S TREMONT ST, OCN, 92054	1106 - A1
TRANSIT CTR - OLD TOWN TAYLOR ST & PACIFIC HWY, SD, 92110	1268 - F4
TRANSIT CTR - PALOMAR COLLEGE PALOMAR COLLEGE, SMCS, 92069	1108 - E6
TRANSIT CTR - PALOMAR CLG/ESCONDIDO GRAND AV & MIDWAY DR, ESCN, 92027	1130 - D1
TRANSIT CTR - PARKWAY PLAZA FLETCHER PKWY & MAGNOLIA AV, ELCJ, 92020	1251 - F3
TRANSIT CTR - PLAZA BONITA RING RD, NATC, 91950	1310 - D4
TRANSIT CTR - RANCHO SD TOWN CTR JAMACHA RD & CAMO RD, SDCo, 92019	1271 - J6
TRANSIT CTR - SAN YSIDRO E SAN YSIDRO BLVD, SD, 92173	1350 - H5
TRANSIT CTR - SDSU AZTEC WK & MONTEZUMA PL, SD, 92182	1270 - B2
TRANSIT CTR - SORRENTO VALLEY SORRENTO VALLEY RD, SD, 92121	1208 - B5
TRANSIT CTR - SOUTHWESTERN COLLEGE OTAY LAKES RD, CHV, 91910	1311 - C5
TRANSIT CTR - TOWN CTR NORTH TOWNE CENTER DR & COLLEGE BLVD, OCN, 92057	1087 - B1
TRANSIT CTR - US BORDER E SAN YSIDRO BLVD, SD, 92173	1350 - H5
TRANSIT CTR - UTC GENESEE AV & LA JOLLA VLG DR, SD, 92122	1228 - D3
TRANSIT CTR - VA HOSP LA JOLLA DR & GILMAN DR, SD, 92161	1228 - A2
TRANSIT CTR - VISTA W BROADWAY & S SANTE FE AV, VSTA, 92083	1087 - G6
TROLLEY STA - 5TH AV 5TH AV & C ST, SD, 92101	1289 - A3
TROLLEY STA - 8TH ST W 8TH ST & HARBOR DR, NATC, 92136	1309 - G1
TROLLEY STA - 24TH ST WILSON AV & MILES-OF-CARS WY, NATC, 91950	1309 - H3
TROLLEY STA - 25TH & COMMERCIAL COMMERCIAL ST & 25TH ST, SD, 92113	1289 - D4
TROLLEY STA - 32ND & COMMERCIAL COMMERCIAL ST & 32ND ST, SD, 92113	1289 - F4
TROLLEY STA - 47TH ST 47TH ST & MARKET ST, SD, 92102	1289 - J4
TROLLEY STA - ALVARADO MED CTR 6658 ALVARADO RD, SD, 92120	1270 - D1
TROLLEY STA - AMAYA DR AMAYA DR & FLETCHER PKWY, LMSA, 91942	1251 - B7
TROLLEY STA - ARNELE AV MARSHALL AV & ARNELE AV, ELCJ, 92020	1251 - E4
TROLLEY STA - BARRIO LOGAN CROSBY ST & HARBOR DR, SD, 92113	1289 - C5
TROLLEY STA - BAYFRONT/E ST WOODLAWN AV & E ST, CHV, 91910	1309 - J6
TROLLEY STA - BEYER BLVD BEYER BLVD & COTTONWOOD RD, SD, 92173	1350 - F3
TROLLEY STA - CITY COLLEGE C ST & 12TH AV, SD, 92101	1289 - B3
TROLLEY STA - CIVIC CTR 2ND AV & C ST, SD, 92101	1289 - A3
TROLLEY STA - CONV CTR WEST HARBOR DR & J ST, SD, 92101	1289 - A4
TROLLEY STA - CO CTR LITTLE ITALY CEDAR ST & CALIFORNIA ST, SD, 92101	1288 - J2
TROLLEY STA - EL CAJON FRONT ST & W PALM AV, ELCJ, 92020	1251 - E6
TROLLEY STA - ENCANTO/62ND ST IMPERIAL AV & 62ND ST, SD, 92114	1290 - D3
TROLLEY STA - EUCLID AV N EUCLID AV & MARKET ST, SD, 92102	1290 - A3
TROLLEY STA - FASHION VALLEY FRIARS RD & FASHION VALLEY RD, SD, 92108	1268 - J3
TROLLEY STA - FENTON END OF FENTON PKWY, SD, 92108	1269 - E1
TROLLEY STA - GASLAMP/CONV CTR HARBOR DR & L ST, SD, 92101	1289 - B4
TROLLEY STA - GILLESPIE FIELD N MARSHALL AV & CUYAMACA ST, ELCJ, 92020	1251 - D1
TROLLEY STA - HARBORSIDE 28TH ST & HARBOR DR, SD, 92136	1289 - E6
TROLLEY STA - HAZARD CTR HAZARD CENTER DR & FRAZEE RD, SD, 92108	1269 - A2
TROLLEY STA - H ST H ST & SAN DIEGO FRWY, CHV, 91910	1309 - J7
TROLLEY STA - IMPERIAL & 12TH IMPERIAL AV & 12TH AV, SD, 92101	1289 - B4
TROLLEY STA - LA MESA BLVD LA MESA BLVD & NEBO DR, LMSA, 91941	1270 - H3
TROLLEY STA - LEMON GROVE DEPOT BROADWAY & MAIN ST, LMGR, 91945	1270 - G6
TROLLEY STA - MARKET & 12TH MARKET ST & 12TH AV, SD, 92101	1289 - B3
TROLLEY STA - MASSACHUSETTS AV LEMON GROVE AV & MASSACHUSETTS, LMGR, 91945	1290 - F1
TROLLEY STA - MIDDLETOWN PALM ST & KETTNER BLVD, SD, 92101	1268 - J7
TROLLEY STA - MISSION SAN DIEGO RANCHO MISSION RD & WARD RD, SD, 92108	1269 - G1
TROLLEY STA - MISSION VALLEY CTR MISSION VALLEY CENTER, SD, 92108	1269 - B2
TROLLEY STA - MORENA / LINDA VISTA NAPA ST & FRIARS RD, SD, 92110	1268 - F3
TROLLEY STA - PACIFIC FLEET 32ND ST & HARBOR DR, SD, 92136	1289 - F7
TROLLEY STA - PALM AV HOLLISTER ST & PALM AV, SD, 92154	1330 - B7
TROLLEY STA - PALOMAR ST PALOMAR ST & INDUSTRIAL BLVD, CHV, 91911	1330 - B4
TROLLEY STA - QUALCOMM STADIUM QUALCOMM STADIUM, SD, 92108	1269 - F1
TROLLEY STA - RIO VISTA QUALCOMM WY & RIO SAN DIEGO DR, SD, 92108	1269 - C2
TROLLEY STA - SANTA FE DEPOT KETTNER BLVD & C ST, SD, 92101	1288 - J3
TROLLEY STA - SANTEE TOWN CTR MISSION GORGE RD & CUYAMACA ST, SNTE, 92071	1231 - D6
TROLLEY STA - SEAPORT VILLAGE HARBOR DR & MARKET ST, SD, 92101	1288 - J3
TROLLEY STA - SPRING ST SPRING ST, LMSA, 91941	1270 - J4
TROLLEY STA - WASHINGTON ST I-5 & WASHINGTON ST, SD, 92110	1268 - H6

WINERIES

FEATURE NAME Address City, ZIP Code	PAGE-GRID
BELLE MARIE 26312 MESA ROCK RD, SDCo, 92026	1109 - D1
BERNARDO 13330 PAS DL VERANO N, PWY, 92064	1170 - D1
DEER PARK ESCONDIDO & AUTO MUS 29013 CHAMPAGNE BLVD, SDCo, 92026	1089 - A1
FERRARA 1120 W 15TH AV, ESCN, 92025	1129 - H5
MENGHINI 1150 JULIAN ORCHARDS DR, SDCo, 92036	1136 - A3
ORFILA VINEYARDS 13455 SAN PASQUAL RD, SD, 92025	1150 - D2
SCHWAESDALL 17677 RANCHO DE ORO RD, SDCo, 92065	1171 - J4
WITCH CREEK 2906 CARLSBAD BLVD, CRLB, 92008	1106 - D5

CUT ALONG DOTTED LINE

The Thomas Guide®

Thank you for purchasing this Rand McNally Thomas Guide!
We value your comments and suggestions.

Please help us serve you better by completing this postage-paid reply card.
This information is for internal use ONLY and will not be distributed or sold to any external third party.

Missing pages? Maybe not... Please refer to the "Using Your Street Guide" page for further explanation.

Thomas Guide Title: San Diego County **ISBN# 0-528-85933-1** **Edition: 2007** **MKT: SDO**

Today's Date: ____________ Gender: ☐M ☐F Age Group: ☐18-24 ☐25-31 ☐32-40 ☐41-50 ☐51-64 ☐65+

1. What type of industry do you work in?
   ☐Real Estate ☐Trucking ☐Delivery ☐Construction ☐Utilities ☐Government
   ☐Retail ☐Sales ☐Transportation ☐Landscape ☐Service & Repair
   ☐Courier ☐Automotive ☐Insurance ☐Medical ☐Police/Fire/First Response
   ☐Other, please specify: ____________
2. What type of job do you have in this industry? ____________
3. Where did you purchase this Thomas Guide? (store name & city) ____________
4. Why did you purchase this Thomas Guide? ____________
5. How often do you purchase an updated Thomas Guide? ☐Annually ☐2 yrs. ☐3-5 yrs. ☐Other: ____________
6. Where do you use it? ☐Primarily in the car ☐Primarily in the office ☐Primarily at home ☐Other: ____________
7. How do you use it? ☐Exclusively for business ☐Primarily for business but also for personal or leisure use
   ☐Both work and personal evenly ☐Primarily for personal use ☐Exclusively for personal use
8. What do you use your Thomas Guide for?
   ☐Find Addresses ☐In-route navigation ☐Planning routes ☐Other: ____________
   Find points of interest: ☐Schools ☐Parks ☐Buildings ☐Shopping Centers ☐Other: ____________
9. How often do you use it? ☐Daily ☐Weekly ☐Monthly ☐Other: ____________
10. Do you use the internet for maps and/or directions? ☐Yes ☐No
11. How often do you use the internet for directions? ☐Daily ☐Weekly ☐Monthly ☐Other: ____________
12. Do you use any of the following mapping products in addition to your Thomas Guide?
    ☐Folded paper maps ☐Folded laminated maps ☐Wall maps ☐GPS ☐PDA ☐In-car navigation ☐Phone maps
13. What features, if any, would you like to see added to your Thomas Guide? ____________
14. What features or information do you find most useful in your Rand McNally Thomas Guide? (please specify)
15. Please provide any additional comments or suggestions you have. ____________

We strive to provide you with the most current updated information available if you know of a map correction, please notify us here.

Where is the correction? Map Page #: ________ Grid #: ________ Index Page #: ________

Nature of the correction: ☐Street name missing ☐Street name misspelled ☐Street information incorrect
☐Incorrect location for point of interest ☐Index error ☐Other: ____________

Detail: ____________

CUT ALONG DOTTED LINE

I would like to receive information about updated editions and special offers from Rand McNally
☐via e-mail E-mail address: ____________
☐via postal mail
Your Name: ____________ Company (if used for work): ____________
Address: ____________ City/State/ZIP: ____________

Thank you for your time and help. We are working to serve you better.
This information is for internal use ONLY and will not be distributed or sold to any external third party.

TG-noCD.06

TAPE SHUT

TAPE SHUT

get directions at

randmcnally.com

CUT ALONG DOTTED LINE

2ND FOLD LINE

NO POSTAGE
NECESSARY
IF MAILED
IN THE
UNITED STATES

BUSINESS REPLY MAIL

FIRST-CLASS MAIL PERMIT NO. 388 CHICAGO IL

POSTAGE WILL BE PAID BY ADDRESSEE

RAND MCNALLY
CONSUMER AFFAIRS
PO BOX 7600
CHICAGO IL 60680-9915

1ST FOLD LINE

RAND McNALLY

The most trusted name on the map.

You'll never need to ask for directions again with these Rand McNally products!

- EasyFinder® Laminated Maps
- Folded Maps
- Street Guides
- Wall Maps
- CustomView Wall Maps
- Road Atlases
- Motor Carriers' Road Atlases

CUT ALONG DOTTED LINE